Collins

FRENCH

DICTIONARY

HarperCollins Publishers
Westerhill Road
Bishopbriggs
Glasgow
G64 2QT

Seventh Edition 2018

10 9 8 7 6 5 4 3 2 1

© HarperCollins Publishers 1997, 2000,
2004, 2006, 2007, 2010, 2014, 2017

HarperCollins Publishers
195 Broadway
New York
NY 10007

ISBN 978-0-06-284490-3

Collins® is a registered trademark of
HarperCollins Publishers Limited

www.collinsdictionary.com
www.collins.co.uk

A catalogue record for this book is
available from the British Library

Typeset by Davidson Publishing Solutions

Printed and bound in the United State of
America by LSC Communications

Acknowledgements

We would like to thank those authors
and publishers who kindly gave
permission for copyright material to be
used in the Collins Corpus. We would also
like to thank Times Newspapers Ltd for
providing valuable data.

HarperCollins does not warrant
that www.collinsdictionary.com,
www.collins.co.uk or any other website
mentioned in this title will be provided
uninterrupted, that any website will be
error free, that defects will be corrected,
or that the website or the server that
makes it available are free of viruses
or bugs. For full terms and conditions
please refer to the site terms provided
on the website.

EDITOR
Susie Beattie

CONTRIBUTORS
Phyllis Buchanan
Laurent Jouet
Joyce Littlejohn
Helen Newstead
Maggie Seaton

TECHNICAL SUPPORT
Thomas Callan
Agnieszka Urbanowicz
Dave Wark

FOR THE PUBLISHER
Gerry Breslin
Catherine Love
Evelyn Sword

Contributors to the previous edition
Jean-François Allain, Gaëlle Amiot-Cadey,
Cécile Aubinière-Robb, Harry Campbell,
Pierre-Henri Cousin, Keith Foley,
Genevieve Gerrard, Janet Gough,
Lorna Sinclair Knight, Jean-Benoît
Ormal-Grenon, Megan Thomson

Table des matières

Contents

Introduction

You may be starting French for the first time, or you may wish to extend your knowledge of the language. Perhaps you want to read and study French books, newspapers and magazines, or perhaps simply have a conversation with French speakers. Whatever the reason, whether you're a student, a tourist or want to use French for business, this is the ideal book to help you understand and communicate. This modern, user-friendly dictionary gives priority to everyday vocabulary and the language of current affairs, business, computing and tourism, and, as in all Collins dictionaries, the emphasis is firmly placed on contemporary language and expressions.

How to use the dictionary

Below you will find an outline of how information is presented in your dictionary. Our aim is to give you the maximum amount of detail in the clearest and most helpful way.

Entries

A typical entry in your dictionary will be made up of the following elements:

Phonetic transcription

Phonetics appear in square brackets immediately after the headword. They are shown using the International Phonetic Alphabet (IPA), and a complete list of the symbols used in this system can be found on pages x and xi.

Grammatical information

All words belong to one of the following parts of speech: noun, verb, adjective, adverb, pronoun, article, conjunction, preposition.

Nouns can be singular or plural and, in French, masculine or feminine. Verbs can be transitive, intransitive, reflexive or impersonal : on the French side, each verb is followed by a bold number, which corresponds to verb tables on pages xii-xiii. Parts of speech appear in SMALL CAPS immediately after the phonetic spelling of the headword. The gender of the translation appears in *italics* immediately following the key element of the translation.

Often a word can have more than one part of speech. Just as the English word **chemical** can be an adjective or a noun, the French word **rose** can be an adjective ("pink") or a feminine noun ("rose"). In the same way the verb **to walk** is sometimes transitive, ie it takes an object ("to walk the dog") and sometimes intransitive, ie it doesn't take an object ("to walk to school"). To help you find the meaning you are looking for quickly and for clarity of presentation, the different part of speech categories are separated by a solid black triangle ▶.

Meaning divisions

Most words have more than one meaning. Take, for example, **punch** which can be, amongst other things, a blow with the fist or an object used for making holes. Other words are translated differently depending on the context in which they are used. The transitive verb **to roll up**, for example, can be translated by "rouler" or "retrousser" depending on what it is you are rolling up. To help you select the most appropriate translation in every context, entries are divided according to meaning. Different meanings are introduced by an "indicator" in *italics* and in brackets. Thus, the examples given above will be shown as follows:

> **punch** [pʌntʃ] N (*blow*) coup *m* de poing; (*fig:*
> *force*) vivacité *f*, mordant *m*; (*tool*) poinçon *m*;

> ▶ **roll up** VI (*inf: arrive*) arriver, s'amener ▶ VT
> (*carpet, cloth, map*) rouler; (*sleeves*) retrousser

Likewise, some words can have a different meaning when used to talk about a specific subject area or field. For example, **bishop**, which we generally use to mean a high-ranking clergyman, is also the name of a chess piece. To show English speakers which translation to use, we have added "subject field labels" in *italics*, starting with a capital letter, and in brackets, in this case (*Chess*):

> **bishop** ['bɪʃəp] N évêque *m*; (*Chess*) fou *m*

Field labels are often shortened to save space. You will find a complete list of abbreviations used in the dictionary on pages viii and ix.

Translations

Most English words have a direct translation in French and vice versa, as shown in the examples given above. Sometimes, however, no exact equivalent exists in the target language. In such cases we have given an approximate equivalent, indicated by the sign ≈. An example is **National Insurance**, the French equivalent of which is "Sécurité Sociale". There is no exact equivalent since the systems of the two countries are quite different:

> **National Insurance** N (*Brit*) ≈ Sécurité Sociale

On occasion it is impossible to find even an approximate equivalent. This may be the case, for example, with the names of types of food:

> **mince pie** N *sorte de tarte aux fruits secs*

Here the translation (which doesn't exist) is replaced by an explanation. For increased clarity the explanation, or "gloss", is shown in *italics*.

It is often the case that a word, or a particular meaning of a word, cannot be translated in isolation. The translation of **Dutch**, for example, is "hollandais(e), neérlandais(e)". However, the phrase **to go Dutch** is rendered by "partager les frais".

Even an expression as simple as **washing powder** needs a separate translation since it translates as "lessive (en poudre)", not "poudre à laver". This is where your dictionary will prove to be particularly informative and useful since it contains an abundance of compounds, phrases and idiomatic expressions.

Levels of formality and familiarity

In English you instinctively know when to say "I don't have any money" and when to say "I'm broke" or "I'm a bit short of cash". When you are trying to understand someone who is speaking French, however, or when you yourself try to speak French, it is important to know what is polite and what is less so, and what you can say in a relaxed situation but not in a formal context. To help you with this, on the French–English side we have added the label (*fam*) to show that a French meaning or expression is colloquial, while those meanings or expressions which are vulgar are followed by an exclamation mark in brackets (*!*), warning you they can cause serious offence. Note also that on the English–French side, colloquial English words are labelled as (*inf*), vulgar English words as (*inf!*) and vulgar French translations as (*!*).

Keywords

Words labelled in the text as KEYWORDS, such as **be** and **do** or their French equivalents **être** and **faire**, have been given special treatment because they form the basic elements of the language. This extra help will ensure that you know how to use these complex words with confidence.

Cultural information

Entries which appear next to a fading vertical bar explain aspects of culture in French and English-speaking countries. Subject areas covered include politics, education, media and national festivals, for example **Assemblée nationale, baccalauréat, BBC** and **Hallowe'en**.

Abréviations

Abbreviations

abréviation	AB(B)R	abbreviation
adjectif, locution adjectivale	ADJ	adjective, adjectival phrase
administration	Admin	administration
adverbe, locution adverbiale	ADV	adverb, adverbial phrase
agriculture	Agr	agriculture
anatomie	Anat	anatomy
architecture	Archit	architecture
article défini	ART DÉF	definite article
article indéfini	ART INDÉF	indefinite article
automobile	Aut(o)	the motor car and motoring
aviation, transports aériens	Aviat	flying, air travel
biologie	Bio(l)	biology
botanique	Bot	botany
anglais britannique	BRIT	British English
chimie	Chem	chemistry
cinéma	Ciné, Cine	cinema
commerce, finance, banque	Comm	commerce, finance, banking
informatique	Comput	computing
conjonction	CONJ	conjunction
construction	Constr	building
nom utilisé comme adjectif	CPD	compound element
cuisine	Culin	cookery
article défini	DEF ART	definite article
déterminant: article; adjectif démonstratif ou indéfini etc	DÉT	determiner: article, demonstrative etc
économie	Écon, Econ	economics
électricité, électronique	Élec, Elec	electricity, electronics
en particulier	esp	especially
exclamation, interjection	EXCL	exclamation, interjection
féminin	f	feminine
langue familière (! emploi vulgaire)	fam(!)	colloquial usage (! particularly offensive)
emploi figuré	fig	figurative use
(verbe anglais) dont la particule est inséparable	FUS	(phrasal verb) where the particle is inseparable
généralement	gén, gen	generally
géographie, géologie	Géo, Geo	geography, geology
géométrie	Géom, Geom	geometry
langue familière (! emploi vulgaire)	inf(!)	colloquial usage (! particularly offensive)
infinitif	infin	infinitive
informatique	Inform	computing
invariable	inv	invariable
irrégulier	irrég, irreg	irregular
domaine juridique	Jur	law

Abréviations

Abbreviations

grammaire, linguistique	*Ling*	grammar, linguistics
masculin	*m*	masculine
mathématiques, algèbre	*Math*	mathematics, calculus
médecine	*Méd, Med*	medical term, medicine
masculin *ou* féminin	*m/f*	masculine *or* feminine
domaine militaire	*Mil*	military matters
musique	*Mus*	music
nom	N	noun
navigation, nautisme	*Navig, Naut*	sailing, navigation
nom *ou* adjectif numéral	NUM	numeral noun *or* adjective
	o.s.	oneself
péjoratif	*péj, pej*	derogatory, pejorative
photographie	*Phot(o)*	photography
physiologie	*Physiol*	physiology
pluriel	*pl*	plural
politique	*Pol*	politics
participe passé	*pp*	past participle
préposition	PRÉP, PREP	preposition
pronom	PRON	pronoun
psychologie, psychiatrie	*Psych*	psychology, psychiatry
temps du passé	*pt*	past tense
quelque chose	*qch*	
quelqu'un	*qn*	
religion, domaine ecclésiastique	*Rel*	religion
	sb	somebody
enseignement, système scolaire et universitaire	*Scol*	schooling, schools and universities
singulier	*sg*	singular
	sth	something
subjonctif	*sub*	subjunctive
sujet (grammatical)	*su(b)j*	(grammatical) subject
superlatif	*superl*	superlative
techniques, technologie	*Tech*	technical term, technology
télécommunications	*Tél, Tel*	telecommunications
télévision	*TV*	television
typographie	*Typ(o)*	typography, printing
anglais des USA	US	American English
verbe auxiliaire	VB (AUX)	(auxiliary) verb
verbe intransitif	VI	intransitive verb
verbe transitif	VT	transitive verb
zoologie	*Zool*	zoology
marque déposée	®	registered trademark
indique une équivalence culturelle	≈	introduces a cultural equivalent

Transcription phonétique

Consonnes		Consonants
poupée	p	puppy
bombe	b	baby
tente thermal	t	tent
dinde	d	daddy
coq qui képi	k	cork kiss chord
gag bague	g	gag guess
sale ce nation	s	so rice kiss
zéro rose	z	cousin buzz
tache chat	ʃ	sheep sugar
gilet juge	ʒ	pleasure beige
	tʃ	church
	dʒ	judge general
fer phare	f	farm raffle
valve	v	very rev
	θ	thin maths
	ð	that other
lent salle	l	little ball
rare rentrer	ʀ	
	r	rat rare
maman femme	m	mummy comb
non nonne	n	no ran
agneau vigne	ɲ	
	ŋ	singing bank
hop!	h	hat reheat
yeux paille pied	j	yet
nouer oui	w	wall bewail
huile lui	ɥ	
	x	loch

Divers / Miscellaneous

pour l'anglais: le "r" final se prononce en liaison devant une voyelle	ʳ	in English transcription: final "r" can be pronounced before a vowel
pour l'anglais: précède la syllabe accentuée	'	in French wordlist: no liaison before aspirate "h"

NB: p, b, t, d, k, g sont suivis d'une aspiration en anglais.
p, b, t, d, k, g are not aspirated in French.

En règle générale, la prononciation est donnée entre crochets après chaque entrée. Toutefois, du côté anglais-français et dans le cas des expressions composées de deux ou plusieurs mots non réunis par un trait d'union et faisant l'objet d'une entrée séparée, la prononciation doit être cherchée sous chacun des mots constitutifs de l'expression en question.

Phonetic transcription

Voyelles

ici vie lyrique	i i:
	ɪ
jouer été	e
lait jouet merci	ɛ
plat amour	a æ
bas pâte	ɑ ɑ:
	ʌ
le premier	ə
beurre peur	œ
peu deux	ø ə:
or homme	ɔ
mot eau gauche	o ɔ:
genou roue	u
	u:
rue urne	y

Vowels

i i:	heel bead
ɪ	hit pity
e	
ɛ	set tent
a æ	bat apple
ɑ ɑ:	after car calm
ʌ	fun cousin
ə	over above
œ	
ø ə:	urgent fern work
ɔ	wash pot
o ɔ:	born cork
u	full hook
u:	boom shoe
y	

Diphtongues

ɪə	beer tier
ɛə	tear fair there
eɪ	date plaice day
aɪ	life buy cry
au	owl foul now
əu	low no
ɔɪ	boil boy oily
uə	poor tour

Diphthongs

ɪə	beer tier
ɛə	tear fair there
eɪ	date plaice day
aɪ	life buy cry
au	owl foul now
əu	low no
ɔɪ	boil boy oily
uə	poor tour

Nasales

matin plein	ɛ̃
brun	œ̃
sang an dans	ɑ̃
non pont	ɔ̃

Nasal vowels

NB: La mise en équivalence de certains sons n'indique qu'une ressemblance
approximative.
The pairing of some vowel sounds only indicates approximate equivalence.

In general, we give the pronunciation of each entry in square brackets after
the word in question. However, on the English-French side, where the entry is
composed of two or more unhyphenated words, each of which is given elsewhere
in this dictionary, you will find the pronunciation of each word in its alphabetical
position.

French verb tables

a Present participle b Past participle c Present d Imperfect e Future f Conditional
g Present subjunctive

1 ARRIVER a arrivant b arrivé
c arrive, arrives, arrive, arrivons,
arrivez, arrivent d arrivais e arriverai
f arriverais g arrive

2 FINIR a finissant b fini c finis, finis,
finit, finissons, finissez, finissent
d finissais e finirai f finirais g finisse

3 PLACER a plaçant b placé c place,
places, place, plaçons, placez, placent
d plaçais, plaçais, plaçait, placions,
placiez, plaçaient e placerai, placeras,
placera, placerons, placerez, placeront
f placerais, placerais, placerait,
placerions, placeriez, placeraient
g place

3 BOUGER a bougeant b bougé c bouge,
bougeons d bougeais, bougions
e bougerai f bougerais g bouge

4 appeler a appelant b appelé c appelle,
appelons d appelais e appellerai
f appellerais g appelle

4 jeter a jetant b jeté c jette, jetons
d jetais e jetterai f jetterais g jette

5 geler a gelant b gelé c gèle, gelons
d gelais e gèlerai f gèlerais g gèle

6 CÉDER a cédant b cédé c cède, cèdes,
cède, cédons, cédez, cèdent d cédais,
cédais, cédait, cédions, cédiez,
cédaient e céderai, céderas, cédera,
céderons, céderez, céderont f céderais,
céderais, céderait, céderions, céderiez,
céderaient g cède

7 épier a épiant b épié c épie, épions
d épiais e épierai f épierais g épie

8 noyer a noyant b noyé c noie, noyons
d noyais e noierai f noierais g noie

9 ALLER a allant b allé c vais, vas, va,
allons, allez, vont d allais e irai f irais
g aille

10 HAÏR a haïssant b haï c hais, hais, hait,
haïssons, haïssez, haïssent d haïssais,
haïssais, haïssait, haïssions, haïssiez,
haïssaient e haïrai, haïras, haïra,
haïrons, haïrez, haïront f haïrais,
haïrais, haïrait, haïrions, haïriez,
haïraient g haïsse

11 courir a courant b couru c cours,
courons d courais e courrai g coure

12 cueillir a cueillant b cueilli c cueille,
cueillons d cueillais e cueillerai
g cueille

13 assaillir – a assaillant b assailli
c assaille, assaillons d assaillais
e assaillirai g assaille

14 servir a servant b servi c sers, servons
d servais g serve

15 bouillir a bouillant b bouilli c bous,
bouillons d bouillais g bouille

16 partir a partant b parti c pars, partons
d partais g parte

17 fuir a fuyant b fui c fuis, fuyons, fuient
d fuyais g fuie

18 couvrir a couvrant b couvert c couvre,
couvrons d couvrais g couvre

19 mourir a mourant b mort c meurs,
mourons, meurent d mourais
e mourrai g meure

20 vêtir a vêtant b vêtu c vêts, vêtons
d vêtais e vêtirai g vête

21 acquérir a acquérant b acquis
c acquiers, acquérons, acquièrent
d acquérais e acquerrai g acquière

22 venir a venant b venu c viens, venons,
viennent d venais e viendrai g vienne

23 pleuvoir a pleuvant b plu c pleut,
pleuvent d pleuvait e pleuvra g pleuve

24 prévoir like voir e prévoirai

25 pourvoir a pourvoyant b pourvu
c pourvois, pourvoyons, pourvoient
d pourvoyais g pourvoie

26 asseoir a asseyant b assis c assieds,
asseyons, asseyez, asseyent d asseyais
e assiérai g asseye

28 RECEVOIR a recevant b reçu c reçois,
reçois, reçoit, recevons, recevez,
reçoivent d recevais e recevrai
f recevrais g reçoive

29 valoir a valant b valu c vaux, vaut,
valons d valais e vaudrai g vaille

30 voir a voyant b vu c vois, voyons,
voient d voyais e verrai g voie

31 vouloir a voulant **b** voulu **c** veux, veut, voulons, veulent **e** voulais **g** veuille; *impératif* veuillez!

32 savoir a sachant **b** su **c** sais, savons, savent **d** savais **e** saurai **g** sache *impératif* sache! sachons! sachez!

33 pouvoir a pouvant **b** pu **c** peux, peut, pouvons, peuvent **d** pouvais **e** pourrai **g** puisse

34 AVOIR a ayant **b** eu **c** ai, as, a, avons, avez, ont **d** avais **e** aurai **f** aurais **g** aie, aies, ait, ayons, ayez, aient

35 conclure a concluant **b** conclu **c** conclus, concluons **d** concluais **g** conclue

36 rire a riant bri cris, rions driais grie

37 dire a disant **b** dit **c** dis, disons, dites, disent **d** disais **g** dise

38 nuire a nuisant **b** nui **c** nuis, nuisons **d** nuisais **e** nuirai **f** nuirais **g** nuise

39 écrire a écrivant **b** écrit **c** écris, écrivons **d** écrivais **g** écrive

40 suivre a suivant **b** suivi **c** suis, suivons **d** suivais **g** suive

41 RENDRE a rendant **b** rendu **c** rends, rends, rend, rendons, rendez, rendent **d** rendais **e** rendrai **f** rendrais **g** rende

42 vaincre a vainquant **b** vaincu **c** vaincs, vainc, vainquons **d** vainquais **g** vainque

43 lire a lisant **b** lu **c** lis, lisons **d** lisais **g** lise

44 croire a croyant **b** cru **c** crois, croyons, croient **d** croyais **g** croie

45 CLORE a closant **b** clos **c** clos, clos, clôt, closent **e** clorai, cloras, clora, clorons, clorez, cloront **f** clorais, clorais, clorait, clorions, cloriez, cloraient

46 vivre a vivant **b** vécu **c** vis, vivons **d** vivais **g** vive

47 MOUDRE a moulant **b** moulu **c** mouds, mouds, moud, moulons, moulez, moulent **d** moulais, moulais, moulait, moulions, mouliez, moulaient **e** moudrai, moudras, moudra, moudrons, moudrez, moudront **f** moudrais, moudrais, moudrait, moudrions, moudriez, moudriaent **g** moule

48 coudre a cousant **b** cousu **c** couds, cousons, cousez, cousent **d** cousais **g** couse

49 joindre a joignant **b** joint **c** joins, joignons **d** joignais **g** joigne

50 TRAIRE a trayant **b** trait **c** trais, trais, trait, trayons, trayez, traient **d** trayais, trayais, trayait, trayions, trayiez, trayaient **e** trai rai, trairas, traira, trairons, trairez, trairont **f** trairais, trairais, trairait, trairions, trairiez, trairiaent **g** traie

51 ABSOUDRE a absolvant **b** absous **c** absous, absous, absout, absolvons, absolvez, absolvent **d** absolvais, absolvais, absolvait, absolvions, absolviez, absolvaient **e** absoudrai, absoudras, absoudra, absoudrons, absoudrez, absoudront **f** absoudrais, absoudrais, absoudrait, absoudrions, absoudriez, absoudraient **g** absolve

52 craindre a craignant **b** craint **c** crains, craignons **d** craignais **g** craigne

53 boire a buvant **b** bu **c** bois, buvons, boivent **d** buvais **g** boive

54 plaire a plaisant **b** plu **c** plais, plaît, plaisons **d** plaisais **g** plaise

55 croître a croissant **b** crû, crue, crus, crues **c** croîs, croissons **d** croissais **g** croisse

56 mettre a mettant **b** mis **c** mets, mettons **d** mettais **g** mette

57 connaître a connaissant **b** connu **c** connais, connaît, connaissons **d** connaissais **g** connaisse

58 prendre a prenant **b** pris **c** prends, prenons, prennent **d** prenais **g** prenne

59 naître a naissant **b** né **c** nais, naît, naissons **d** naissais **g** naisse

60 FAIRE a faisant **b** fait **c** fais, fais, fait, faisons, faites, font **d** faisais **e** ferai **f** ferais **g** fasse

61 ÊTRE a étant **b** été **c** suis, es, est, sommes, êtes, sont **d** étais **e** serai **f** serais **g** sois, sois, soit, soyons, soyez, soient

Les nombres

un (une)	1
deux	2
trois	3
quatre	4
cinq	5
six	6
sept	7
huit	8
neuf	9
dix	10
onze	11
douze	12
treize	13
quatorze	14
quinze	15
seize	16
dix-sept	17
dix-huit	18
dix-neuf	19
vingt	20
vingt et un (une)	21
vingt-deux	22
trente	30
quarante	40
cinquante	50
soixante	60
soixante-dix	70
soixante et onze	71
soixante-douze	72
quatre-vingts	80
quatre-vingt-un (-une)	81
quatre-vingt-dix	90
cent	100
cent un (une)	101
deux cents	200
deux cent un (une)	201
quatre cents	400
mille	1000
cinq mille	5000
un million	1000 000

Numbers

one
two
three
four
five
six
seven
eight
nine
ten
eleven
twelve
thirteen
fourteen
fifteen
sixteen
seventeen
eighteen
nineteen
twenty
twenty-one
twenty-two
thirty
forty
fifty
sixty
seventy
seventy-one
seventy-two
eighty
eighty-one
ninety
a hundred, one hundred
a hundred and one
two hundred
two hundred and one
four hundred
a thousand
five thousand
a million

Les nombres

premier (première), 1er (1ère)
deuxième, 2e *or* 2ème
troisième, 3e *or* 3ème
quatrième, 4e *or* 4ème
cinquième, 5e *or* 5ème
sixième, 6e *or* 6ème
septième
huitième
neuvième
dixième
onzième
douzième
treizième
quatorzième
quinzième
seizième
dix-septième
dix-huitième
dix-neuvième
vingtième
vingt et unième
vingt-deuxième
trentième
centième
cent unième
millième

Numbers

first, 1st
second, 2nd
third, 3rd
fourth, 4th
fifth, 5th
sixth, 6th
seventh
eighth
ninth
tenth
eleventh
twelfth
thirteenth
fourteenth
fifteenth
sixteenth
seventeenth
eighteenth
nineteenth
twentieth
twenty-first
twenty-second
thirtieth
hundredth
hundred-and-first
thousandth

L'heure

quelle heure est-il?
   il est ...

minuit
une heure (du matin)
une heure cinq
une heure dix
une heure et quart
une heure vingt-cinq
une heure et demie,
   une heure trente
deux heures moins vingt-cinq,
   une heure trente-cinq
deux heures moins vingt,
   une heure quarante
deux heures moins le quart,
   une heure quarante-cinq
deux heures moins dix,
   une heure cinquante
midi
deux heures (de l'après-midi),
   quatorze heures
sept heures (du soir),
   dix-neuf heures

à quelle heure?
à minuit
à sept heures

dans vingt minutes
il y a un quart d'heure

The time

what time is it?
   it's ...

midnight, twelve a.m.
one o'clock (in the morning), one (a.m.)
five past one
ten past one
a quarter past one, one fifteen
twenty-five past one, one twenty-five
half past one,
   one thirty
twenty-five to two,
   one thirty-five
twenty to two,
   one forty
a quarter to two,
   one forty-five
ten to two,
   one fifty
twelve o'clock, midday, noon
two o'clock (in the afternoon),
   two (p.m.)
seven o'clock (in the evening),
   seven (p.m.)

(at) what time?
at midnight
at seven o'clock

in twenty minutes
fifteen minutes ago

La date

aujourd'hui
demain
après-demain
hier
avant-hier
la veille
le lendemain

le matin
le soir
ce matin
ce soir
cet après-midi
hier matin
hier soir
demain matin
demain soir
dans la nuit du samedi au
   dimanche
il viendra samedi
le samedi
tous les samedis
samedi passé *ou* dernier
samedi prochain
samedi en huit
samedi en quinze
du lundi au samedi
tous les jours
une fois par semaine
une fois par mois
deux fois par semaine
il y a une semaine *ou* huit jours
il y a quinze jours
l'année passée *ou* dernière
dans deux jours
dans huit jours *ou* une semaine
dans quinze jours
le mois prochain
l'année prochaine

quel jour sommes-nous?
le 1ᵉʳ/24 octobre 2013

en 2013
mille neuf cent quatre-vingt seize
44 av. J.-C.
14 apr. J.-C.
au XIXᵉ (siècle)
dans les années trente
il était une fois ...

The date

today
tomorrow
the day after tomorrow
yesterday
the day before yesterday
the day before, the previous day
the next *or* following day

morning
evening
this morning
this evening
this afternoon
yesterday morning
yesterday evening
tomorrow morning
tomorrow evening
during Saturday night, during the
   night of Saturday to Sunday
he's coming on Saturday
on Saturdays
every Saturday
last Saturday
next Saturday
a week on Saturday
a fortnight *or* two weeks on Saturday
from Monday to Saturday
every day
once a week
once a month
twice a week
a week ago
a fortnight *or* two weeks ago
last year
in two days
in a week
in a fortnight *or* two weeks
next month
next year

what day is it?
the 1st/24th of October 2013,
   October 1st/24th 2013

in 2013
nineteen ninety-six
44 BC
14 AD
in the nineteenth century
in the thirties
once upon a time ...

Aa

A, a [ɑ] NM INV A, a ▶ ABR = **anticyclone**; **are**; (*ampère*) amp; (*autoroute*) ≈ M (BRIT); **A comme Anatole** A for Andrew (BRIT) ou Able (US); **de a à z** from a to z; **prouver qch par a + b** to prove sth conclusively

a [a] VB *voir* **avoir**

MOT-CLÉ

à [a] (*à + le* = **au**, *à + les* = **aux**) PRÉP **1** (*endroit, situation*) at, in; **être à Paris/au Portugal** to be in Paris/Portugal; **être à la maison/à l'école** to be at home/at school; **à la campagne** in the country; **c'est à 10 m/km/à 20 minutes (d'ici)** it's 10 m/km/20 minutes away

2 (*direction*) to; **aller à Paris/au Portugal** to go to Paris/Portugal; **aller à la maison/à l'école** to go home/to school; **à la campagne** to the country

3 (*temps*): **à 3 heures/minuit** at 3 o'clock/ midnight; **au printemps** in the spring; **au mois de juin** in June; **à Noël/Pâques** at Christmas/Easter; **au départ** at the start, at the outset; **à demain/la semaine prochaine!** see you tomorrow/next week!; **visites de 5 heures à 6 heures** visiting from 5 to ou till 6 o'clock

4 (*attribution, appartenance*) to; **le livre est à Paul/à lui/à nous** this book is Paul's/his/ours; **donner qch à qn** to give sth to sb; **un ami à moi** a friend of mine; **c'est à moi de le faire** it's up to me to do it

5 (*moyen*) with; **se chauffer au gaz** to have gas heating; **à bicyclette** on a ou by bicycle; **à pied** on foot; **à la main/machine** by hand/ machine; **à la télévision/la radio** on television/the radio

6 (*provenance*) from; **boire à la bouteille** to drink from the bottle

7 (*caractérisation: manière*): **l'homme aux yeux bleus** the man with the blue eyes; **à la russe** the Russian way; **glace à la framboise** raspberry ice cream

8 (*but: destination*): **tasse à café** coffee cup; **maison à vendre** house for sale; **je n'ai rien à lire** I don't have anything to read; **à bien réfléchir ...** thinking about it ..., on reflection ...; **problème à régler** problem to sort out

9 (*rapport: évaluation: distribution*): **100 km/unités**

à l'heure 100 km/units per ou an hour; **payé à l'heure** paid by the hour; **cinq à six** five to six **10** (*conséquence: résultat*): **à ce qu'il prétend** according to him; **à leur grande surprise** much to their surprise; **à nous trois nous n'avons pas su le faire** we couldn't do it even between the three of us; **ils sont arrivés à quatre** four of them arrived (together)

Å ABR (= *Ångstrom*) Å ou A

AB ABR = **assez bien**

abaissement [abɛsmɑ̃] NM lowering; pulling down

abaisser [abese] /1/ VT to lower, bring down; (*manette*) to pull down; (*fig*) to debase; to humiliate; **s'abaisser** VI to go down; (*fig*) to demean o.s.; **s'abaisser à faire/à qch** to stoop ou descend to doing/to sth

abandon [abɑ̃dɔ̃] NM abandoning; deserting; giving up; withdrawal; surrender; relinquishing; (*fig*) lack of constraint; relaxed pose ou mood; **être à l'~** to be in a state of neglect; **laisser à l'~** to abandon

abandonné, e [abɑ̃dɔne] ADJ (*solitaire*) deserted; (*route, usine*) disused; (*jardin*) abandoned

abandonner [abɑ̃dɔne] /1/ VT (*personne*) to leave, abandon, desert; (*projet, activité*) to abandon, give up; (*Sport*) to retire ou withdraw from; (*Inform*) to abort; (*céder*) to surrender, relinquish; **s'abandonner** VI to let o.s. go; **s'abandonner à** (*paresse, plaisirs*) to give o.s. up to; **~ qch à qn** to give sth up to sb

abasourdir [abazurdir] /2/ VT to stun, stagger

abat *etc* [aba] VB *voir* **abattre**

abat-jour [abaʒur] NM INV lampshade

abats [aba] VB *voir* **abattre** ▶ NMPL (*de bœuf, porc*) offal *sg* (BRIT), entrails (US); (*de volaille*) giblets

abattage [abataʒ] NM cutting down, felling

abattant [abatɑ̃] VB *voir* **abattre** ▶ NM leaf, flap

abattement [abatmɑ̃] NM (*physique*) enfeeblement; (*moral*) dejection, despondency; (*déduction*) reduction; **~ fiscal** ≈ tax allowance

abattis [abati] VB *voir* **abattre** ▶ NMPL giblets

abattoir [abatwar] NM abattoir (BRIT), slaughterhouse

abattre [abatr] /41/ VT (*arbre*) to cut down, fell; (*mur, maison*) to pull down; (*avion, personne*) to shoot down; (*animal*) to shoot, kill; (*fig: physiquement*) to wear out, tire out; (: *moralement*) to demoralize; **s'abattre** VI to crash down; **ne pas se laisser abattre** to keep one's spirits up, not to let things get one down; **s'abattre sur** (*pluie*) to beat down on; (*coups, injures*) to rain down on; **~ ses cartes** (*aussi fig*) to lay one's cards on the table; **~ du travail** *ou* **de la besogne** to get through a lot of work

abattu, e [abaty] PP *de* **abattre** ▶ ADJ (*déprimé*) downcast

abbatiale [abasjal] NF abbey (*church*)

abbaye [abei] NF abbey

abbé [abe] NM priest; (*d'une abbaye*) abbot; **M l'~** Father

abbesse [abɛs] NF abbess

abc, ABC [abese] NM alphabet primer; (*fig*) rudiments *pl*

abcès [apsɛ] NM abscess

abdication [abdikasjɔ̃] NF abdication

abdiquer [abdike] /**1**/ VI to abdicate ▶ VT to renounce, give up

abdomen [abdɔmɛn] NM abdomen

abdominal, e, -aux [abdɔminal, -o] ADJ abdominal; **abdominaux** NMPL: **faire des abdominaux** to do sit-ups

abécédaire [abesedɛʀ] NM alphabet primer

abeille [abɛj] NF bee

aberrant, e [abeʀɑ̃, -ɑ̃t] ADJ absurd

aberration [abeʀasjɔ̃] NF aberration

abêtir [abetiʀ] /**2**/ VT to make morons (*ou* a moron) of (*péj*)

abêtissant, e [abetisɑ̃, -ɑ̃t] ADJ stultifying

abhorrer [abɔʀe] /**1**/ VT to abhor, loathe

abîme [abim] NM abyss, gulf

abîmer [abime] /**1**/ VT to spoil, damage; **s'abîmer** VI to get spoilt *ou* damaged; (*fruits*) to spoil; (*tomber*) to sink, founder; **s'abîmer les yeux** to ruin one's eyes *ou* eyesight

abject, e [abʒɛkt] ADJ abject, despicable

abjurer [abʒyʀe] /**1**/ VT to abjure, renounce

ablatif [ablatif] NM ablative

ablation [ablasjɔ̃] NF removal

ablutions [ablysjɔ̃] NFPL: **faire ses ~** to perform one's ablutions

abnégation [abnegasjɔ̃] NF (self-)abnegation

aboie *etc* [abwa] VB *voir* **aboyer**

aboiement [abwamɑ̃] NM bark, barking *no pl*

aboierai *etc* [abwajəʀe] VB *voir* **aboyer**

abois [abwa] NMPL: **aux ~** at bay

abolir [abɔliʀ] /**2**/ VT to abolish

abolition [abɔlisjɔ̃] NF abolition

abolitionniste [abɔlisjɔnist] ADJ, NMF abolitionist

abominable [abɔminabl] ADJ abominable

abomination [abɔminasjɔ̃] NF abomination

abondamment [abɔ̃damɑ̃] ADV abundantly

abondance [abɔ̃dɑ̃s] NF abundance; (*richesse*) affluence; **en ~** in abundance

abondant, e [abɔ̃dɑ̃, -ɑ̃t] ADJ plentiful, abundant, copious

abonder [abɔ̃de] /**1**/ VI to abound, be plentiful; **~ en** to be full of, abound in; **~ dans le sens de qn** to concur with sb

abonné, e [abɔne] NM/F subscriber; season ticket holder ▶ ADJ: **être ~ à un journal** to subscribe to *ou* have a subscription to a periodical; **être ~ au téléphone** to be on the (tele)phone

abonnement [abɔnmɑ̃] NM subscription; (*pour transports en commun, concerts*) season ticket

abonner [abɔne] /**1**/: **s'abonner à** VT to subscribe to, take out a subscription to

abord [abɔʀ] NM: **être d'un ~ facile** to be approachable; **être d'un ~ difficile** (*personne*) to be unapproachable; (*lieu*) to be hard to reach *ou* difficult to get to; **abords** NMPL (*environs*) surroundings; **d'~** *adv* first; **de prime ~, au premier ~** at first sight, initially; **tout d'~** first of all

abordable [abɔʀdabl] ADJ (*personne*) approachable; (*marchandise*) reasonably priced; (*prix*) affordable, reasonable

abordage [abɔʀdaʒ] NM boarding

aborder [abɔʀde] /**1**/ VI to land ▶ VT (*sujet, difficulté*) to tackle; (*personne*) to approach; (*rivage etc*) to reach; (*Navig: attaquer*) to board; (: *heurter*) to collide with

abords [abɔʀ] NMPL surroundings

aborigène [abɔʀiʒɛn] NM aborigine, native

Abou Dhabî, Abu Dhabî [abudabi] NM Abu Dhabi

aboulique [abulik] ADJ totally lacking in willpower

aboutir [abutiʀ] /**2**/ VI (*négociations etc*) to succeed; (*abcès*) to come to a head; **~ à/dans/sur** to end up at/in/on; **n'~ à rien** to come to nothing

aboutissants [abutisɑ̃] NMPL *voir* **tenant**

aboutissement [abutismɑ̃] NM success; (*de concept, projet*) successful realization; (*d'années de travail*) successful conclusion

aboyer [abwaje] /**8**/ VI to bark

abracadabrant, e [abʀakadabʀɑ̃, -ɑ̃t] ADJ incredible, preposterous

abrasif, -ive [abʀazif, -iv] ADJ, NM abrasive

abrégé [abʀeʒe] NM summary; **en ~** in a shortened *ou* abbreviated form

abréger [abʀeʒe] /**3, 6**/ VT (*texte*) to shorten, abridge; (*mot*) to shorten, abbreviate; (*réunion, voyage*) to cut short, shorten

abreuver [abʀœve] /**1**/ VT to water; (*fig*): **~ qn de** to shower *ou* swamp sb with; (*injures etc*) to shower sb with; **s'abreuver** VI to drink

abreuvoir [abʀœvwaʀ] NM watering place

abréviation [abʀevjasjɔ̃] NF abbreviation

abri [abʀi] NM shelter; **être à l'~** to be under cover; **se mettre à l'~** to shelter; **à l'~ de** sheltered from; (*danger*) safe from

Abribus® [abʀibys] NM bus shelter

abricot [abʀiko] NM apricot

abricotier [abʀikɔtje] NM apricot tree

abrité, e [abʀite] ADJ sheltered

abriter [abʀite] /**1**/ VT to shelter; (*loger*) to accommodate; **s'abriter** VI to shelter, take cover

abrogation [abʀɔgasjɔ̃] NF (*Jur*) repeal, abrogation

abroger [abʀɔʒe] /**3**/ VT to repeal, abrogate

abrupt, e [abʀypt] ADJ sheer, steep; (*ton*) abrupt

abruti, e [abʀyti] ADJ stunned, dazed ▸ NM/F (fam) idiot; **~ de travail** overworked

abrutir [abʀytiʀ] /2/ VT to daze; (fatiguer) to exhaust; (abêtir) to stupefy

abrutissant, e [abʀytisɑ̃, -ɑ̃t] ADJ (bruit, travail) stupefying

abscisse [apsis] NF X axis, abscissa

absence [apsɑ̃s] NF absence; (Méd) blackout; **en l'~ de** in the absence of; **avoir des absences** to have mental blanks

absent, e [apsɑ̃, -ɑ̃t] ADJ absent; (chose) missing, lacking; (distrait: air) vacant, faraway ▸ NM/F absentee

absentéisme [apsɑ̃teism] NM absenteeism

absenter [apsɑ̃te] /1/: **s'absenter** VI to take time off work; (sortir) to leave, go out

abside [apsid] NF (Archit) apse

absinthe [apsɛ̃t] NF (boisson) absinth(e); (Bot) wormwood, absinth(e)

absolu, e [apsɔly] ADJ absolute; (caractère) rigid, uncompromising ▸ NM (Philosophie): **l'~** the Absolute; **dans l'~** in the absolute, in a vacuum

absolument [apsɔlymɑ̃] ADV absolutely

absolution [apsɔlysjɔ̃] NF absolution; (Jur) dismissal (of case)

absolutisme [apsɔlytism] NM absolutism

absolvais etc [apsɔlvɛ] VB voir **absoudre**

absorbant, e [apsɔʀbɑ̃, -ɑ̃t] ADJ absorbent; (tâche) absorbing, engrossing

absorbé, e [apsɔʀbe] ADJ absorbed, engrossed

absorber [apsɔʀbe] /1/ VT to absorb; (gén, Méd: manger, boire) to take; (Écon: firme) to take over, absorb

absorption [apsɔʀpsjɔ̃] NF absorption

absoudre [apsudʀ] /51/ VT to absolve; (Jur) to dismiss

absous, -oute [apsu, -ut] PP de absoudre

abstenir [apstəniʀ] /22/: **s'abstenir** VI (Pol) to abstain; **s'abstenir de qch/de faire** to refrain from sth/from doing

abstention [apstɑ̃sjɔ̃] NF abstention

abstentionnisme [apstɑ̃sjɔnism] NM abstaining

abstentionniste [apstɑ̃sjɔnist] NM abstentionist

abstenu, e [apstəny] PP de abstenir

abstiendrai [apstjɛ̃dʀe], **abstiens** etc [apstjɛ̃] VB voir **abstenir**

abstinence [apstinɑ̃s] NF abstinence; **faire ~** to abstain (from meat on Fridays)

abstint etc [apstɛ̃] VB voir **abstenir**

abstraction [apstʀaksjɔ̃] NF abstraction; **faire ~ de** to set ou leave aside; **~ faite de ...** leaving aside ...

abstraire [apstʀɛʀ] /50/ VT to abstract; **s'abstraire** VI: **s'abstraire (de)** (s'isoler) to cut o.s. off (from)

abstrait, e [apstʀɛ, -ɛt] PP de abstraire ▸ ADJ abstract ▸ NM: **dans l'~** in the abstract

abstraitement [apstʀɛtmɑ̃] ADV abstractly

abstrayais etc [apstʀeje] VB voir abstraire

absurde [apsyʀd] ADJ absurd ▸ NM absurdity; (Philosophie): **l'~** absurd; **par l'~** ad absurdum

absurdité [apsyʀdite] NF absurdity

abus [aby] NM (excès) abuse, misuse; (injustice) abuse; **~ de confiance** breach of trust; (détournement de fonds) embezzlement; **il y a de l'~!** (fam) that's a bit much!

abuser [abyze] /1/ VI to go too far, overstep the mark ▸ VT to deceive, mislead; **s'abuser** VI (se méprendre) to be mistaken; **~ de** vt (force, droit) to misuse; (alcool) to take to excess; (violer, duper) to take advantage of

abusif, -ive [abyzif, -iv] ADJ exorbitant; (punition) excessive; (pratique) improper

abusivement [abyzivmɑ̃] ADV exorbitantly; excessively; improperly

AC SIGLE F = **appellation contrôlée**

acabit [akabi] NM: **du même ~** of the same type

acacia [akasja] NM (Bot) acacia

académicien, ne [akademisjɛ̃, -ɛn] NM/F academician

académie [akademi] NF (société) learned society; (école: d'art, de danse) academy; (Art: nu) nude; (Scol: circonscription) ≈ regional education authority; **l'A~ (française)** the French Academy; see note

> The Académie française was founded by Cardinal Richelieu in 1635, during the reign of Louis XIII. It is made up of forty elected scholars and writers who are known as les Quarante or les Immortels. One of the Académie's functions is to keep an eye on the development of the French language, and its recommendations are frequently the subject of lively public debate. It has produced several editions of its famous dictionary and also awards various literary prizes.

académique [akademik] ADJ academic

Acadie [akadi] NF: **l'~** the Maritime Provinces

acadien, ne [akadjɛ̃, -ɛn] ADJ Acadian, of ou from the Maritime Provinces

acajou [akaʒu] NM mahogany

acariâtre [akaʀjatʀ] ADJ sour(-tempered) (BRIT), cantankerous

accablant, e [akablɑ̃, -ɑ̃t] ADJ (chaleur) oppressive; (témoignage, preuve) overwhelming

accablement [akabləmɑ̃] NM deep despondency

accabler [akable] /1/ VT to overwhelm, overcome; (témoignage) to condemn, damn; **~ qn d'injures** to heap ou shower abuse on sb; **~ qn de travail** to overwork sb; **accablé de dettes/soucis** weighed down with debts/cares

accalmie [akalmi] NF lull

accaparant, e [akapaʀɑ̃, -ɑ̃t] ADJ that takes up all one's time ou attention

accaparer [akapaʀe] /1/ VT to monopolize; (travail etc) to take up (all) the time ou attention of

accéder [aksede] /6/: **~ à** vt (lieu) to reach; (fig: pouvoir) to accede to (: poste) to attain; (accorder: requête) to grant, accede to

accélérateur [akseleʀatœʀ] NM accelerator

accélération [akseleʀasjɔ̃] NF speeding up; acceleration

accéléré [akseleʀe] NM: **en ~** (Ciné) speeded up

accélérer [akselere] /6/ vt (*mouvement, travaux*) to speed up ▶ vi (*Auto*) to accelerate

accent [aksɑ̃] nm accent; (*inflexions expressives*) tone (of voice); (*Phonétique, fig*) stress; **aux accents de** (*musique*) to the strains of; **mettre l'~ sur** (*fig*) to stress; **~ aigu/grave/circonflexe** acute/grave/circumflex accent

accentuation [aksɑ̃tɥasjɔ̃] nf accenting; stressing

accentué, e [aksɑ̃tɥe] adj marked, pronounced

accentuer [aksɑ̃tɥe] /1/ vt (*Ling: orthographe*) to accent; (: *phonétique*) to stress, accent; (*fig*) to accentuate, emphasize; (*effort, pression*) to increase; **s'accentuer** vi to become more marked ou pronounced

acceptable [akseptabl] adj satisfactory, acceptable

acceptation [akseptasjɔ̃] nf acceptance

accepter [aksepte] /1/ vt to accept; (*tolérer*): **~ que qn fasse** to agree to sb doing; **~ de faire** to agree to do

acception [aksepsjɔ̃] nf meaning, sense; **dans toute l'~ du terme** in the full sense ou meaning of the word

accès [aksɛ] nm (*à un lieu, Inform*) access; (*Méd*) attack; (: *de toux*) fit; (: *de fièvre*) bout ▶ nmpl (*routes etc*) means of access, approaches; **d'~ facile/malaisé** easily/not easily accessible; **facile d'~** easy to get to; **donner ~ à** (*lieu*) to give access to; (*carrière*) to open the door to; **avoir ~ auprès de qn** to have access to sb; **l'~ aux quais est interdit aux personnes non munies d'un billet** ticket-holders only on platforms, no access to platforms without a ticket; **~ de colère** fit of anger; **~ de joie** burst of joy

accessible [aksesibl] adj accessible; (*personne*) approachable; (*livre, sujet*): **~ à qn** within the reach of sb; (*sensible*): **~ à la pitié/l'amour** open to pity/love

accession [aksesjɔ̃] nf: **~ à** accession to; (*à un poste*) attainment of; **~ à la propriété** home-ownership

accessit [aksesit] nm (*Scol*) ≈ certificate of merit

accessoire [akseswar] adj secondary, of secondary importance; (*frais*) incidental ▶ nm accessory; (*Théât*) prop

accessoirement [akseswarmɑ̃] adv secondarily; incidentally

accessoiriste [akseswarist] nmf (*TV, Ciné*) property man/woman

accident [aksidɑ̃] nm accident; **par ~** by chance; **~ de parcours** mishap; **~ de la route** road accident; **~ du travail** accident at work; industrial injury ou accident; **accidents de terrain** unevenness of the ground

accidenté, e [aksidɑ̃te] adj damaged ou injured (in an accident); (*relief, terrain*) uneven; hilly

accidentel, le [aksidɑ̃tɛl] adj accidental

accidentellement [aksidɑ̃tɛlmɑ̃] adv (*par hasard*) accidentally; (*mourir*) in an accident

accise [aksiz] nf: **droit d'~(-s)** excise duty

acclamation [aklamasjɔ̃] nf: **par ~** (*vote*) by acclamation; **acclamations** nfpl cheers, cheering *sg*

acclamer [aklame] /1/ vt to cheer, acclaim

acclimatation [aklimatasjɔ̃] nf acclimatization

acclimater [aklimate] /1/ vt to acclimatize; **s'acclimater** vi to become acclimatized

accointances [akwɛ̃tɑ̃s] nfpl: **avoir des ~ avec** to have contacts with

accolade [akɔlad] nf (*amicale*) embrace; (*signe*) brace; **donner l'~ à qn** to embrace sb

accoler [akɔle] /1/ vt to place side by side

accommodant, e [akɔmɔdɑ̃, -ɑ̃t] adj accommodating, easy-going

accommodement [akɔmɔdmɑ̃] nm compromise

accommoder [akɔmɔde] /1/ vt (*Culin*) to prepare; (*points de vue*) to reconcile; **~ qch à** (*adapter*) to adapt sth to; **s'accommoder de** to put up with; (*se contenter de*) to make do with; **s'accommoder à** (*s'adapter*) to adapt to

accompagnateur, -trice [akɔ̃paɲatœr, -tris] nm/f (*Mus*) accompanist; (*de voyage*) guide; (*de voyage organisé*) courier; (*d'enfants*) accompanying adult

accompagnement [akɔ̃paɲmɑ̃] nm (*Mus*) accompaniment; (*Mil*) support

accompagner [akɔ̃paɲe] /1/ vt to accompany, be ou go ou come with; (*Mus*) to accompany; **s'accompagner de** to bring, be accompanied by

accompli, e [akɔ̃pli] adj accomplished

accomplir [akɔ̃plir] /2/ vt (*tâche, projet*) to carry out; (*souhait*) to fulfil; **s'accomplir** vi to be fulfilled

accomplissement [akɔ̃plismɑ̃] nm carrying out; fulfilment (BRIT), fulfillment (US)

accord [akɔr] nm (*entente, convention, Ling*) agreement; (*entre des styles, tons etc*) harmony; (*consentement*) agreement, consent; (*Mus*) chord; **donner son ~** to give one's agreement; **mettre deux personnes d'~** to make two people come to an agreement, reconcile two people; **se mettre d'~** to come to an agreement (with each other); **être d'~** to agree; **être d'~ avec qn** to agree with sb; **d'~!** OK!, right!; **d'un commun ~** of one accord; **~ parfait** (*Mus*) tonic chord

accord-cadre [akɔrkadr] (*pl* **accords-cadres**) nm framework ou outline agreement

accordéon [akɔrdeɔ̃] nm (*Mus*) accordion

accordéoniste [akɔrdeɔnist] nmf accordionist

accorder [akɔrde] /1/ vt (*faveur, délai*) to grant; (*attribuer*): **~ de l'importance/de la valeur à qch** to attach importance/value to sth; (*harmoniser*) to match; (*Mus*) to tune; **s'accorder** vi to get on together; (*être d'accord*) to agree; (*couleurs, caractères*) to go together, match; (*Ling*) to agree; **je vous accorde que ...** I grant you that ...

accordeur [akɔrdœr] nm (*Mus*) tuner

accoster [akɔste] /1/ vt (*Navig*) to draw alongside; (*personne*) to accost ▶ vi (*Navig*) to berth

accotement [akɔtmɑ̃] nm (*de route*) verge (BRIT),

shoulder; **~ stabilisé/non stabilisé** hard shoulder/soft verge *ou* shoulder

accoter [akɔte] /**1**/ VT: **~ qch contre/à** to lean *ou* rest sth against/on; **s'~ contre/à** to lean against/on

accouchement [akuʃmɑ̃] NM delivery, (child)birth; (*travail*) labour (BRIT), labor (US); **~ à terme** delivery at (full) term; **~ sans douleur** natural childbirth

accoucher [akuʃe] /**1**/ VI to give birth, have a baby; (*être en travail*) to be in labour (BRIT) *ou* labor (US) ▶ VT to deliver; **~ d'un garçon** to give birth to a boy

accoucheur [akuʃœR] NM: **(médecin) ~** obstetrician

accoucheuse [akuʃøz] NF midwife

accouder [akude] /**1**/: **s'accouder** VI: **s'accouder à/contre/sur** to rest one's elbows on/against/on; **accoudé à la fenêtre** leaning on the windowsill

accoudoir [akudwaR] NM armrest

accouplement [akupləmɑ̃] NM coupling; mating

accoupler [akuple] /**1**/ VT to couple; (*pour la reproduction*) to mate; **s'accoupler** VI to mate

accourir [akuRiR] /**11**/ VI to rush *ou* run up

accoutrement [akutRəmɑ̃] NM (*péj*) getup (BRIT), outfit

accoutrer [akutRe] /**1**/ (*péj*) VT to do *ou* get up; **s'accoutrer** to do *ou* get o.s. up

accoutumance [akutymɑ̃s] NF (*gén*) adaptation; (*Méd*) addiction

accoutumé, e [akutyme] ADJ (*habituel*) customary, usual; **comme à l'~** as is customary *ou* usual

accoutumer [akutyme] /**1**/ VT: **~ qn à qch/faire** to accustom sb to sth/to doing; **s'accoutumer à** to get accustomed *ou* used to

accréditer [akRedite] /**1**/ VT (*nouvelle*) to substantiate; **~ qn (auprès de)** to accredit sb (to)

accro [akRo] NMF (*fam*: = *accroché(e)*) addict

accroc [akRo] NM (*déchirure*) tear; (*fig*) hitch, snag; **sans ~** without a hitch; **faire un ~ à** (*vêtement*) to make a tear in, tear; (*fig: règle etc*) to infringe

accrochage [akRɔʃaʒ] NM hanging (up); hitching (up); (*Auto*) (minor) collision; (*Mil*) encounter, engagement; (*dispute*) clash, brush

accroche-cœur [akRɔʃkœR] NM kiss-curl

accrocher [akRɔʃe] /**1**/ VT (*suspendre*) to hang; (*fig*) to catch, attract ▶ VI to stick, get stuck; (*fig: pourparlers etc*) to hit a snag; (*plaire: disque etc*) to catch on; **s'accrocher** VI (*se disputer*) to have a clash *ou* brush; (*ne pas céder*) to hold one's own, hang on in (*fam*); **~ qch à** (*suspendre*) to hang sth (up) on; (*attacher: remorque*) to hitch sth (up) to; (*déchirer*) to catch sth (on); **il a accroché ma voiture** he bumped into my car; **s'accrocher à** (*rester pris à*) to catch on; (*agripper, fig*) to hang on *ou* cling to

accrocheur, -euse [akRɔʃœR, -øz] ADJ (*vendeur, concurrent*) tenacious; (*publicité*) eye-catching; (*titre*) catchy, eye-catching

accroire [akRwaR] /**44**/ VT: **faire** *ou* **laisser ~ à qn qch/que** to give sb to believe sth/that

accrois [akRwa], **accroissais** *etc* [akRwasɛ] VB *voir* **accroître**

accroissement [akRwasmɑ̃] NM increase

accroître [akRwatR] /**55**/ VT, **s'accroître** VI to increase

accroupi, e [akRupi] ADJ squatting, crouching (down)

accroupir [akRupiR] /**2**/: **s'accroupir** VI to squat, crouch (down)

accru, e [akRy] PP *de* **accroître**

accu [aky] NM (*fam*: = *accumulateur*) accumulator, battery

accueil [akœj] NM welcome; (*endroit*) reception (desk); (*dans une gare*) information kiosk; **comité/centre d'~** reception committee/centre

accueillant, e [akœjɑ̃, -ɑ̃t] ADJ welcoming, friendly

accueillir [akœjiR] /**12**/ VT to welcome; (*aller chercher*) to meet, collect; (*loger*) to accommodate

acculer [akyle] /**1**/ VT: **~ qn à** *ou* **contre** to drive sb back against; **~ qn dans** to corner sb in; **~ qn à** (*faillite*) to drive sb to the brink of

accumulateur [akymylatœR] NM accumulator, battery

accumulation [akymylasjɔ̃] NF accumulation; **chauffage/radiateur à ~** (night-)storage heating/heater

accumuler [akymyle] /**1**/ VT to accumulate, amass; **s'accumuler** VI to accumulate; to pile up

accusateur, -trice [akyzatœR, -tRis] NM/F accuser ▶ ADJ accusing; (*document, preuve*) incriminating

accusatif [akyzatif] NM (*Ling*) accusative

accusation [akyzasjɔ̃] NF (*gén*) accusation; (*Jur*) charge; (*partie*): **l'~** the prosecution; **mettre en ~** to indict; **acte d'~** bill of indictment

accusé, e [akyze] NM/F accused; (*prévenu(e)*) defendant ▶ NM: **~ de réception** acknowledgement of receipt

accuser [akyze] /**1**/ VT to accuse; (*fig*) to emphasize, bring out; (*: montrer*) to show; **s'accuser** VI (*s'accentuer*) to become more marked; **~ qn de** to accuse sb of; (*Jur*) to charge sb with; **~ qn/qch de qch** (*rendre responsable*) to blame sb/sth for sth; **s'accuser de qch/d'avoir fait qch** to admit sth/having done sth; to blame o.s. for sth/for having done sth; **~ réception de** to acknowledge receipt of; **~ le coup** (*aussi fig*) to be visibly affected

acerbe [asɛRb] ADJ caustic, acid

acéré, e [aseRe] ADJ sharp

acétate [asetat] NM acetate

acétique [asetik] ADJ: **acide ~** acetic acid

acétone [asetɔn] NF acetone

acétylène [asetilɛn] NM acetylene

ach. ABR = **achète**

acharné, e [aʃaRne] ADJ (*lutte, adversaire*) fierce, bitter; (*travail*) relentless, unremitting

acharnement [aʃaRnəma] NM fierceness; relentlessness

acharner [aʃaʀne] /1/: **s'acharner** VI: **s'acharner sur** to go at fiercely, hound; **s'acharner contre** to set o.s. against; to dog, pursue; (*malchance*) to hound; **s'acharner à faire** to try doggedly to do; to persist in doing

achat [aʃa] NM buying *no pl*; (*article acheté*) purchase; **faire l'~ de** to buy, purchase; **faire des achats** to do some shopping, buy a few things

acheminement [aʃminmã] NM conveyance

acheminer [aʃmine] /1/ VT (*courrier*) to forward, dispatch; (*troupes*) to convey, transport; (*train*) to route; **s'~ vers** to head for

acheter [aʃte] /5/ VT to buy, purchase; (*soudoyer*) to buy, bribe; **~ qch à** (*marchand*) to buy *ou* purchase sth from; (*ami etc: offrir*) to buy sth for; **~ à crédit** to buy on credit

acheteur, -euse [aʃtœʀ, -øz] NM/F buyer; shopper; (*Comm*) buyer; (*Jur*) vendee, purchaser

achevé, e [aʃve] ADJ: **d'un ridicule ~** thoroughly *ou* absolutely ridiculous; **d'un comique ~** absolutely hilarious

achèvement [aʃɛvmã] NM completion, finishing

achever [aʃ(ə)ve] /5/ VT to complete, finish; (*blessé*) to finish off; **s'achever** VI to end

achoppement [aʃɔpmã] NM: **pierre d'~** stumbling block

acide [asid] ADJ sour, sharp; (*ton*) acid, biting; (*Chimie*) acid(ic) ▶ NM acid

acidifier [asidifje] /7/ VT to acidify

acidité [asidite] NF sharpness; acidity

acidulé, e [asidyle] ADJ slightly acid; **bonbons acidulés** acid drops (BRIT), ≈ lemon drops (US)

acier [asje] NM steel; **~ inoxydable** stainless steel

aciérie [asjeʀi] NF steelworks *sg*

acné [akne] NF acne

acolyte [akɔlit] NM (*péj*) associate

acompte [akɔ̃t] NM deposit; (*versement régulier*) instalment; (*sur somme due*) payment on account; (*sur salaire*) advance; **un ~ de 10 euros** 10 euros on account

acoquiner [akɔkine] /1/: **s'acoquiner avec** VT (*péj*) to team up with

Açores [asɔʀ] NFPL: **les ~** the Azores

à-côté [akote] NM side-issue; (*argent*) extra

à-coup [aku] NM (*du moteur*) (hic)cough; (*fig*) jolt; **sans à-coups** smoothly; **par à-coups** by fits and starts

acoustique [akustik] NF (*d'une salle*) acoustics *pl*; (*science*) acoustics *sg* ▶ ADJ acoustic

acquéreur [akeʀœʀ] NM buyer, purchaser; **se porter/se rendre ~ de qch** to announce one's intention to purchase/to purchase sth

acquérir [akeʀiʀ] /21/ VT to acquire; (*par achat*) to purchase, acquire; (*valeur*) to gain; (*résultats*) to achieve; **ce que ses efforts lui ont acquis** what his efforts have won *ou* gained (for) him

acquiers *etc* [akjɛʀ] VB *voir* **acquérir**

acquiescement [akjɛsmã] NM acquiescence, agreement

acquiescer [akjese] /3/ VI (*opiner*) to agree; (*consentir*): **~ (à qch)** to acquiesce *ou* assent (to sth)

acquis, e [aki, -iz] PP *de* **acquérir** ▶ NM (accumulated) experience; (*avantage*) gain ▶ ADJ (*achat*) acquired; (*valeur*) gained; (*résultats*) achieved; **être ~ à** (*plan, idée*) to be in full agreement with; **son aide nous est ~** we can count on *ou* be sure of his help; **tenir qch pour ~** to take sth for granted

acquisition [akizisjɔ̃] NF acquisition; (*achat*) purchase; **faire l'~ de** to acquire; to purchase

acquit [aki] VB *voir* **acquérir** ▶ NM (*quittance*) receipt; **pour ~** received; **par ~ de conscience** to set one's mind at rest

acquittement [akitmã] NM acquittal; payment, settlement

acquitter [akite] /1/ VT (*Jur*) to acquit; (*facture*) to pay, settle; **s'~ de** to discharge; (*promesse, tâche*) to fulfil (BRIT), fulfill (US), carry out

âcre [akʀ] ADJ acrid, pungent

âcreté [akʀəte] NF acridness, pungency

acrimonie [akʀimɔni] NF acrimony

acrobate [akʀɔbat] NMF acrobat

acrobatie [akʀɔbasi] NF (*art*) acrobatics *sg*; (*exercice*) acrobatic feat; **~ aérienne** aerobatics *sg*

acrobatique [akʀɔbatik] ADJ acrobatic

acronyme [akʀɔnim] NM acronym

Acropole [akʀɔpɔl] NF: **l'~** the Acropolis

acrylique [akʀilik] ADJ, NM acrylic

acte [akt] NM act, action; (*Théât*) act; **actes** NMPL (*compte-rendu*) proceedings; **prendre ~** to note, take note of; **faire ~ de présence** to put in an appearance; **faire ~ de candidature** to submit an application; **~ d'accusation** charge (BRIT), bill of indictment; **~ de baptême** baptismal certificate; **~ de mariage/naissance** marriage/birth certificate; **~ de vente** bill of sale

acteur [aktœʀ] NM actor

actif, -ive [aktif, -iv] ADJ active ▶ NM (*Comm*) assets *pl*; (*Ling*) active (voice); (*fig*): **avoir à son ~** to have to one's credit; **actifs** NMPL people in employment; **mettre à son ~** to add to one's list of achievements; **~ toxique** toxic asset; **l'~ et le passif** assets and liabilities; **prendre une part active à qch** to take an active part in sth; **population active** working population

action [aksjɔ̃] NF (*gén*) action; (*Comm*) share; **une bonne/mauvaise ~** a good/an unkind deed; **mettre en ~** to put into action; **passer à l'~** to take action; **sous l'~ de** under the effect of; **l'~ syndicale** (the) union action; **un film d'~** an action film *ou* movie; **~ en diffamation** libel action; **~ de grâce(s)** (*Rel*) thanksgiving

actionnaire [aksjɔnɛʀ] NMF shareholder

actionner [aksjɔne] /1/ VT to work; (*mécanisme*) to activate; (*machine*) to operate

active [aktiv] ADJ F *voir* **actif**

activement [aktivmã] ADV actively

activer [aktive] /1/ VT to speed up; (*Chimie*) to activate; **s'activer** VI (*s'affairer*) to bustle about; (*se hâter*) to hurry up

activisme [aktivism] NM activism

activiste [aktivist] NMF activist

activité [aktivite] NF activity; **en ~** (*volcan*) active; (*fonctionnaire*) in active life; (*militaire*) on active service

actrice [aktris] NF actress
actualiser [aktyalize] /1/ VT to actualize; (*mettre à jour*) to bring up to date
actualité [aktyalite] NF (*d'un problème*) topicality; (*événements*): **l'~** current events; **les actualités** (*Ciné, TV*) the news; **l'~ politique/ sportive** the political/sports ou sporting news; **les actualités télévisées** the television news; **d'~** topical
actuel, le [aktyɛl] ADJ (*présent*) present; (*d'actualité*) topical; (*non virtuel*) actual; **à l'heure ~** at this moment in time, at the moment
actuellement [aktyɛlmɑ̃] ADV at present, at the present time
acuité [akyite] NF acuteness
acuponcteur, acupuncteur [akypɔ̃ktœr] NM acupuncturist
acuponcture, acupuncture [akypɔ̃ktyr] NF acupuncture
adage [adaʒ] NM adage
adagio [ada(d)ʒjo] ADV, NM adagio
adaptable [adaptabl] ADJ adaptable
adaptateur, -trice [adaptatœr, -tris] NM/F adapter
adaptation [adaptasjɔ̃] NF adaptation
adapter [adapte] /1/ VT to adapt; **s'~ (à)** (*personne*) to adapt (to); (*objet, prise etc*) to apply (to); **~ qch à** (*approprier*) to adapt sth to (fit); **~ qch sur/dans/à** (*fixer*) to fit sth on/into/to
addenda [adɛ̃da] NM INV addenda
Addis-Ababa [adisababa], **Addis-Abeba** [adisabəba] N Addis Ababa
additif [aditif] NM additional clause; (*substance*) additive; **~ alimentaire** food additive
addition [adisjɔ̃] NF addition; (*au café*) bill
additionnel, le [adisjɔnɛl] ADJ additional
additionner [adisjɔne] /1/ VT to add (up); **s'additionner** VI to add up; **~ un produit d'eau** to add water to a product
adduction [adyksjɔ̃] NF (*de gaz, d'eau*) conveyance
adepte [adɛpt] NMF follower
adéquat, e [adekwa(t), -at] ADJ appropriate, suitable
adéquation [adekwasjɔ̃] NF appropriateness; (*Ling*) adequacy
adhérence [aderɑ̃s] NF adhesion
adhérent, e [aderɑ̃, -ɑ̃t] NM/F (*de club*) member
adhérer [adere] /6/ VI (*coller*) to adhere, stick; **~ à** (*coller*) to adhere ou stick to; (*se rallier à: parti, club*) to join, to be a member of; (*opinion, mouvement*) to support
adhésif, -ive [adezif, -iv] ADJ adhesive, sticky ▶ NM adhesive; **ruban ~** sticky ou adhesive tape
adhésion [adezjɔ̃] NF (*à un club*) joining; membership; (*à une opinion*) support
ad hoc [adɔk] ADJ INV ad hoc
adieu, x [adjø] EXCL goodbye ▶ NM farewell; **dire ~ à qn** to say goodbye ou farewell to sb; **dire ~ à qch** (*renoncer*) to say ou wave goodbye to sth
adipeux, -euse [adipø, -øz] ADJ bloated, fat; (*Anat*) adipose
adjacent, e [adʒasɑ̃, -ɑ̃t] ADJ: **~ (à)** adjacent (to)

adjectif [adʒɛktif] NM adjective; **~ attribut** adjectival complement; **~ épithète** attributive adjective
adjectival, e, -aux [adʒɛktival, -o] ADJ adjectival
adjoignais *etc* [adʒwaɲɛ] VB *voir* **adjoindre**
adjoindre [adʒwɛ̃dr] /49/ VT: **~ qch à** to attach sth to; (*ajouter*) to add sth to; **~ qn à** (*personne*) to appoint sb as an assistant to; (*comité*) to appoint sb to, attach sb to; **s'adjoindre** VT (*collaborateur etc*) to take on, appoint
adjoint, e [adʒwɛ̃, -wɛ̃t] PP *de* **adjoindre** ▶ NM/F assistant; **~ au maire** deputy mayor; **directeur ~** assistant manager
adjonction [adʒɔ̃ksjɔ̃] NF (*voir adjoindre*) attaching; addition; appointment
adjudant [adʒydɑ̃] NM (*Mil*) warrant officer; **~-chef** ≈ warrant officer 1st class (BRIT), ≈ chief warrant officer (US)
adjudicataire [adʒydikatɛr] NMF successful bidder, purchaser; (*pour travaux*) successful tenderer (BRIT) ou bidder (US)
adjudicateur, -trice [adʒydikatœr, -tris] NM/F (*aux enchères*) seller
adjudication [adʒydikasjɔ̃] NF sale by auction; (*pour travaux*) invitation to tender (BRIT) ou bid (US)
adjuger [adʒyʒe] /3/ VT (*prix, récompense*) to award; (*lors d'une vente*) to auction (off); **s'adjuger** VT to take for o.s.; **adjugé!** (*vendu*) gone!, sold!
adjurer [adʒyre] /1/ VT: **~ qn de faire** to implore ou beg sb to do
adjuvant [adʒyvɑ̃] NM (*médicament*) adjuvant; (*additif*) additive; (*stimulant*) stimulant
admettre [admɛtr] /56/ VT (*visiteur, nouveau-venu*) to admit, let in; (*candidat: Scol*) to pass; (*Tech: gaz, eau, air*) to admit; (*tolérer*) to allow, accept; (*reconnaître*) to admit, acknowledge; (*supposer*) to suppose; **j'admets que ...** I admit that ...; **je n'admets pas que tu fasses cela** I won't allow you to do that; **admettons que ...** let's suppose that ...; **admettons** let's suppose so
administrateur, -trice [administratœr, -tris] NM/F (*Comm*) director; (*Admin*) administrator; **~ délégué** managing director; **~ judiciaire** receiver
administratif, -ive [administratif, -iv] ADJ administrative ▶ NM person in administration
administration [administrasjɔ̃] NF administration; **l'A~** ≈ the Civil Service
administré, e [administre] NM/F ≈ citizen
administrer [administre] /1/ VT (*firme*) to manage, run; (*biens, remède, sacrement etc*) to administer
admirable [admirabl] ADJ admirable, wonderful
admirablement [admirabləmɑ̃] ADV admirably
admirateur, -trice [admiratœr, -tris] NM/F admirer
admiratif, -ive [admiratif, -iv] ADJ admiring
admiration [admirasjɔ̃] NF admiration; **être en ~ devant** to be lost in admiration before

7

admirativement [admiʀativmɑ̃] ADV admiringly

admirer [admiʀe] /1/ VT to admire

admis, e [admi, -iz] PP *de* **admettre**

admissibilité [admisibilite] NF eligibility; admissibility, acceptability

admissible [admisibl] ADJ (*candidat*) eligible; (*comportement*) admissible, acceptable; (*Jur*) receivable

admission [admisjɔ̃] NF admission; **tuyau d'~** intake pipe; **demande d'~** application for membership; **service des admissions** admissions

admonester [admɔneste] /1/ VT to admonish

ADN SIGLE M (= *acide désoxyribonucléique*) DNA

ado [ado] NMF (*fam*: = *adolescent(e)*) adolescent, teenager

adolescence [adɔlesɑ̃s] NF adolescence

adolescent, e [adɔlesɑ̃, -ɑ̃t] NM/F adolescent, teenager

adonner [adɔne] /1/: **s'adonner à** VT (*sport*) to devote o.s. to; (*boisson*) to give o.s. over to

adopter [adɔpte] /1/ VT to adopt; (*projet de loi etc*) to pass

adoptif, -ive [adɔptif, -iv] ADJ (*parents*) adoptive; (*fils, patrie*) adopted

adoption [adɔpsjɔ̃] NF adoption; **son pays/sa ville d'~** his adopted country/town

adorable [adɔʀabl] ADJ adorable

adoration [adɔʀasjɔ̃] NF adoration; (*Rel*) worship; **être en ~ devant** to be lost in adoration before

adorer [adɔʀe] /1/ VT to adore; (*Rel*) to worship

adosser [adose] /1/ VT: **~ qch à** *ou* **contre** to stand sth against; **s'~ à** *ou* **contre** to lean with one's back against; **être adossé à** *ou* **contre** to be leaning with one's back against

adoucir [adusiʀ] /2/ VT (*goût, température*) to make milder; (*avec du sucre*) to sweeten; (*peau, voix, eau*) to soften; (*caractère, personne*) to mellow; (*peine*) to soothe, allay; **s'adoucir** VI to become milder; to soften; (*caractère*) to mellow

adoucissement [adusismɑ̃] NM becoming milder; sweetening; softening; mellowing; soothing

adoucisseur [adusisœʀ] NM: **~ (d'eau)** water softener

adr. ABR = **adresse**; **adresser**

adrénaline [adʀenalin] NF adrenaline

adresse [adʀɛs] NF (*voir adroit*) skill, dexterity; (*domicile, Inform*) address; **à l'~ de** (*pour*) for the benefit of; **~ électronique** email address; **~ Web** web address

adresser [adʀese] /1/ VT (*lettre: expédier*) to send; (: *écrire l'adresse sur*) to address; (*injure, compliments*) to address; **s'adresser à** (*parler à*) to speak to, address; (*s'informer auprès de*) to go and see, go and speak to; (: *bureau*) to enquire at; (*livre, conseil*) to be aimed at; **~ qn à un docteur/bureau** to refer *ou* send sb to a doctor/an office; **~ la parole à qn** to speak to *ou* address sb

Adriatique [adʀijatik] NF: **l'~** the Adriatic

adroit, e [adʀwa, -wat] ADJ (*joueur, mécanicien*) skilful (*BRIT*), skillful (*US*), dext(e)rous; (*politicien etc*) shrewd, skilled

adroitement [adʀwatmɑ̃] ADV skilfully (*BRIT*), skillfully (*US*), dext(e)rously; shrewdly

AdS SIGLE F = **Académie des Sciences**

ADSL SIGLE M (= *asymmetrical digital subscriber line*) ADSL, broadband; **avoir l'~** to have broadband

aduler [adyle] /1/ VT to adulate

adulte [adylt] NMF adult, grown-up ▸ ADJ (*personne, attitude*) adult, grown-up; (*chien, arbre*) fully-grown, mature; **l'âge ~** adulthood; **formation/film pour adultes** adult training/film

adultère [adyltɛʀ] ADJ adulterous ▸ NMF adulterer/adulteress ▸ NM (*acte*) adultery

adultérin, e [adylteʀɛ̃, -in] ADJ born of adultery

advenir [advəniʀ] /22/ VI to happen; **qu'est-il advenu de …?** what has become of …?; **quoi qu'il advienne** whatever befalls *ou* happens

adventiste [advɑ̃tist] NMF (*Rel*) Adventist

adverbe [advɛʀb] NM adverb; **~ de manière** adverb of manner

adverbial, e, -aux [advɛʀbjal, -o] ADJ adverbial

adversaire [advɛʀsɛʀ] NMF (*Sport, gén*) opponent, adversary; (*Mil*) adversary, enemy

adverse [advɛʀs] ADJ opposing

adversité [advɛʀsite] NF adversity

AELE SIGLE F (= *Association européenne de libre-échange*) EFTA (= *European Free Trade Association*)

AEN SIGLE F (= *Agence pour l'énergie nucléaire*) ≈ AEA (= *Atomic Energy Authority*)

aérateur [aeʀatœʀ] NM ventilator

aération [aeʀasjɔ̃] NF airing; (*circulation de l'air*) ventilation; **conduit d'~** ventilation shaft; **bouche d'~** air vent

aéré, e [aeʀe] ADJ (*pièce, local*) airy, well-ventilated; (*tissu*) loose-woven; **centre ~** outdoor centre

aérer [aeʀe] /6/ VT to air; (*fig*) to lighten; **s'aérer** VI to get some (fresh) air

aérien, ne [aeʀjɛ̃, -ɛn] ADJ (*Aviat*) air cpd, aerial; (*câble, métro*) overhead; (*fig*) light; **compagnie ~** airline (company); **ligne ~** airline

aérobic [aeʀɔbik] NF aerobics sg

aérobie [aeʀɔbi] ADJ aerobic

aéro-club [aeʀɔklœb] NM flying club

aérodrome [aeʀɔdʀom] NM airfield, aerodrome

aérodynamique [aeʀɔdinamik] ADJ aerodynamic, streamlined ▸ NF aerodynamics sg

aérofrein [aeʀɔfʀɛ̃] NM air brake

aérogare [aeʀɔɡaʀ] NF airport (buildings); (*en ville*) air terminal

aéroglisseur [aeʀɔɡlisœʀ] NM hovercraft

aérogramme [aeʀɔɡʀam] NM air letter, aerogram(me)

aéromodélisme [aeʀɔmɔdelism] NM model aircraft making

aéronaute [aeʀɔnot] NMF aeronaut

aéronautique [aeʀɔnotik] ADJ aeronautical ▸ NF aeronautics sg

aéronaval, e [aeʀɔnaval] ADJ air and sea cpd

Aéronavale [aeʀɔnaval] NF ≈ Fleet Air Arm (*BRIT*), ≈ Naval Air Force (*US*)

aéronef [aeʀɔnɛf] NM aircraft
aérophagie [aeʀɔfaʒi] NF wind, (*Méd*) aerophagia; **il fait de l'~** he suffers from abdominal wind
aéroport [aeʀɔpɔʀ] NM airport; **~ d'embarquement** departure airport
aéroporté, e [aeʀɔpɔʀte] ADJ airborne, airlifted
aéroportuaire [aeʀɔpɔʀtɥɛʀ] ADJ of an *ou* the airport, airport *cpd*
aéropostal, e, -aux [aeʀɔpɔstal, -o] ADJ airmail *cpd*
aérosol [aeʀɔsɔl] NM aerosol
aérospatial, e, -aux [aeʀɔspasjal, -o] ADJ aerospace ▶ NF the aerospace industry
aérostat [aeʀɔsta] NM aerostat
aérotrain [aeʀɔtʀɛ̃] NM hovertrain
AF SIGLE FPL = **allocations familiales** ▶ SIGLE F (*Suisse*) = **Assemblée fédérale**
AFAT [afat] SIGLE M (= *Auxiliaire féminin de l'armée de terre*) member of the women's army
affabilité [afabilite] NF affability
affable [afabl] ADJ affable
affabulateur, -trice [afabylatœr, -tʀis] NM/F storyteller
affabulation [afabylasjɔ̃] NF invention, fantasy
affabuler [afabyle] /1/ VI to make up stories
affacturage [afaktyʀaʒ] NM factoring
affadir [afadiʀ] /2/ VT to make insipid *ou* tasteless
affaiblir [afeblir] /2/ VT to weaken; **s'affaiblir** VI to weaken, grow weaker; (*vue*) to grow dim
affaiblissement [afeblismɑ̃] NM weakening
affaire [afɛʀ] NF (*problème, question*) matter; (*criminelle, judiciaire*) case; (*scandaleuse etc*) affair; (*entreprise*) business; (*marché, transaction*) deal, (piece of) business *no pl*; (*occasion intéressante*) good deal; **affaires** NFPL affairs; (*activité commerciale*) business *sg*; (*effets personnels*) things, belongings; **affaires de sport** sports gear; **tirer qn/se tirer d'~** to get sb/o.s. out of trouble; **ceci fera l'~** this will do (nicely); **avoir ~** (*comme adversaire*) to be faced with; (*en contact*) to be dealing with; **tu auras ~ à moi!** (*menace*) you'll have me to contend with!; **c'est une ~ de goût/d'argent** it's a question *ou* matter of taste/money; **c'est l'~ d'une minute/heure** it'll only take a minute/an hour; **ce sont mes affaires** (*cela me concerne*) that's my business; **occupe-toi de tes affaires!** mind your own business!; **toutes affaires cessantes** forthwith; **les affaires étrangères** (*Pol*) foreign affairs
affairé, e [afeʀe] ADJ busy
affairer [afeʀe] /1/: **s'affairer** VI to busy o.s., bustle about
affairisme [afeʀism] NM (political) racketeering
affaissement [afɛsmɑ̃] NM subsidence; collapse
affaisser [afese] /1/: **s'affaisser** VI (*terrain, immeuble*) to subside, sink; (*personne*) to collapse
affaler [afale] /1/: **s'affaler** VI: **s'affaler dans/sur** to collapse *ou* slump into/onto

affamé, e [afame] ADJ starving, famished
affamer [afame] /1/ VT to starve
affectation [afɛktasjɔ̃] NF (*voir affecter*) allotment; appointment; posting; (*voir affecté*) affectedness
affecté, e [afɛkte] ADJ affected
affecter [afɛkte] /1/ VT (*émouvoir*) to affect, move; (*feindre*) to affect, feign; (*telle ou telle forme etc*) to take on, assume; **~ qch à** to allocate *ou* allot sth to; **~ qn à** to appoint sb to; (*diplomate*) to post sb to; **~ qch de** (*de coefficient*) to modify sth by
affectif, -ive [afɛktif, -iv] ADJ emotional, affective
affection [afɛksjɔ̃] NF affection; (*mal*) ailment; **avoir de l'~ pour** to feel affection for; **prendre en ~** to become fond of
affectionner [afɛksjɔne] /1/ VT to be fond of
affectueusement [afɛktɥøzmɑ̃] ADV affectionately
affectueux, -euse [afɛktɥø, -øz] ADJ affectionate
afférent, e [afeʀɑ̃, -ɑ̃t] ADJ: **~ à** pertaining *ou* relating to
affermir [afɛʀmiʀ] /2/ VT to consolidate, strengthen
affichage [afiʃaʒ] NM billposting, billsticking; (*électronique*) display; "**~ interdit**" "stick no bills", "billsticking prohibited"; **~ à cristaux liquides** liquid crystal display, LCD; **~ numérique** *ou* **digital** digital display
affiche [afiʃ] NF poster; (*officielle*) (public) notice; (*Théât*) bill; **être à l'~** (*Théât*) to be on; **tenir l'~** to run
afficher [afiʃe] /1/ VT (*affiche*) to put up, post up; (*réunion*) to put up a notice about; (*électroniquement*) to display; (*fig*) to exhibit, display; **s'afficher** VI (*péj*) to flaunt o.s.; (*électroniquement*) to be displayed; "**défense d'~**" "no bill posters"
affichette [afiʃɛt] NF small poster *ou* notice
affilé, e [afile] ADJ sharp
affilée [afile]: **d'~** *adv* at a stretch
affiler [afile] /1/ VT to sharpen
affiliation [afiljasjɔ̃] NF affiliation
affilié, e [afilje] ADJ: **être ~ à** to be affiliated to ▶ NM/F affiliated party *ou* member
affilier [afilje] /7/: **s'affilier à** VT to become affiliated to
affiner [afine] /1/ VT to refine; **s'affiner** VI to become (more) refined
affinité [afinite] NF affinity
affirmatif, -ive [afiʀmatif, -iv] ADJ affirmative ▶ NF: **répondre par l'affirmative** to reply in the affirmative; **dans l'affirmative** (*si oui*) if (the answer is) yes …, if he does (*ou* you do *etc*) …
affirmation [afiʀmasjɔ̃] NF assertion
affirmativement [afiʀmativmɑ̃] ADV affirmatively, in the affirmative
affirmer [afiʀme] /1/ VT (*prétendre*) to maintain, assert; (*autorité etc*) to assert; **s'affirmer** VI to assert o.s.; to assert itself
affleurer [aflœʀe] /1/ VI to show on the surface
affliction [afliksjɔ̃] NF affliction
affligé, e [afliʒe] ADJ distressed, grieved; **~ de** (*maladie, tare*) afflicted with
affligeant, e [afliʒɑ̃, -ɑ̃t] ADJ distressing

affliger [aflíʒe] /**3**/ vт (*peiner*) to distress, grieve

affluence [aflyɑ̃s] NF crowds *pl*; **heures d'~** rush hour *sg*; **jours d'~** busiest days

affluent [aflyɑ̃] NM tributary

affluer [aflye] /**1**/ vɪ (*secours, biens*) to flood in, pour in; (*sang*) to rush, flow

afflux [afly] NM flood, influx; rush

affolant, e [afɔlɑ̃, -ɑ̃t] ADJ terrifying

affolé, e [afɔle] ADJ panic-stricken, panicky

affolement [afɔlmɑ̃] NM panic

affoler [afɔle] /**1**/ vт to throw into a panic; **s'affoler** vɪ to panic

affranchir [afʀɑ̃ʃiʀ] /**2**/ vт to put a stamp *ou* stamps on; (*à la machine*) to frank (BRIT), meter (US); (*esclave*) to enfranchise, emancipate; (*fig*) to free, liberate; **s'affranchir de** to free o.s. from; **machine à ~** franking machine, postage meter

affranchissement [afʀɑ̃ʃismɑ̃] NM franking (BRIT), metering (US); freeing; (*Postes: prix payé*) postage; **tarifs d'~** postage rates

affres [afʀ] NFPL: **dans les ~ de** in the throes of

affréter [afʀete] /**6**/ vт to charter

affreusement [afʀøzmɑ̃] ADV dreadfully, awfully

affreux, -euse [afʀø, -øz] ADJ dreadful, awful

affriolant, e [afʀijɔlɑ̃, -ɑ̃t] ADJ tempting, enticing

affront [afʀɔ̃] NM affront

affrontement [afʀɔ̃tmɑ̃] NM (*Mil, Pol*) clash, confrontation

affronter [afʀɔ̃te] /**1**/ vт to confront, face; **s'affronter** to confront each other

affubler [afyble] /**1**/ vт (*péj*): **~ qn de** to rig *ou* deck sb out in; (*surnom*) to attach to sb

affût [afy] NM (*de canon*) gun carriage; **à l'~ (de)** (*gibier*) lying in wait (for); (*fig*) on the look-out (for)

affûter [afyte] /**1**/ vт to sharpen, grind

afghan, e [afgɑ̃, -an] ADJ Afghan

Afghanistan [afganistɑ̃] NM: **l'~** Afghanistan

afin [afɛ̃]: **~ que** *conj* so that, in order that; **~ de faire** in order to do, so as to do

AFNOR [afnɔʀ] SIGLE F (= *Association française de normalisation*) industrial standards authority

a fortiori [afɔʀsjɔʀi] ADV all the more, a fortiori

AFP SIGLE F = **Agence France-Presse**

AFPA SIGLE F = **Association pour la formation professionnelle des adultes**

africain, e [afʀikɛ̃, -ɛn] ADJ African ▶ NM/F: **A~, e** African

afrikaans [afʀikɑ̃] NM, ADJ INV Afrikaans

Afrique [afʀik] NF: **l'~** Africa; **l'~ australe/du Nord/du Sud** southern/North/South Africa

afro [afʀo] ADJ INV: **coupe ~** afro hairstyle ▶ NMF: **A~** Afro

afro-américain, e [afʀoameʀikɛ̃, -ɛn] ADJ Afro-American

AG SIGLE F = **assemblée générale**

ag. ABR = **agence**

agaçant, e [agasɑ̃, -ɑ̃t] ADJ irritating, aggravating

agacement [agasmɑ̃] NM irritation, aggravation

agacer [agase] /**3**/ vт to pester, tease; (*involontairement*) to irritate, aggravate; (*aguicher*) to excite, lead on

agapes [agap] NFPL (*humoristique: festin*) feast

agate [agat] NF agate

AGE SIGLE F = **assemblée générale extraordinaire**

âge [ɑʒ] NM age; **quel ~ as-tu?** how old are you? **une femme d'un certain ~** a middle-aged woman, a woman who is getting on (in years); **bien porter son ~** to wear well; **prendre de l'~** to be getting on (in years), grow older; **limite d'~** age limit; **dispense d'~** special exemption from age limit; **le troisième ~** (*personnes âgées*) senior citizens; (*période*) retirement; **l'~ ingrat** the awkward *ou* difficult age; **~ légal** legal age; **~ mental** mental age; **l'~ mûr** maturity, middle age; **~ de raison** age of reason

âgé, e [ɑʒe] ADJ old, elderly; **~ de 10 ans** 10 years old

agence [aʒɑ̃s] NF agency, office; (*succursale*) branch; **~ immobilière** estate agent's (office) (BRIT), real estate office (US); **~ matrimoniale** marriage bureau; **~ de placement** employment agency; **~ de publicité** advertising agency; **~ de voyages** travel agency

agencé, e [aʒɑ̃se] ADJ: **bien/mal ~** well/badly put together; well/badly laid out *ou* arranged

agencement [aʒɑ̃smɑ̃] NM putting together; arrangement, laying out

agencer [aʒɑ̃se] /**3**/ vт to put together; (*local*) to arrange, lay out

agenda [aʒɛ̃da] NM diary; **~ électronique** PDA

agenouiller [aʒ(ə)nuje] /**1**/: **s'agenouiller** vɪ to kneel (down)

agent, e [aʒɑ̃, -ɑ̃t] NM/F (*aussi:* **agent(e) de police**) policeman (policewoman); (*Admin*) official, officer; (*fig: élément, facteur*) agent; **~ d'assurances** insurance broker; **~ de change** stockbroker; **~ commercial** sales representative; **~ immobilier** estate agent (BRIT), realtor (US); **~ (secret)** (secret) agent

agglo [aglo] NM (*fam*) = **aggloméré**

agglomérat [aglɔmeʀa] NM (*Géo*) agglomerate

agglomération [aglɔmeʀasjɔ̃] NF town; (*Auto*) built-up area; **l'~ parisienne** the urban area of Paris

aggloméré [aglɔmeʀe] NM (*bois*) chipboard; (*pierre*) conglomerate

agglomérer [aglɔmeʀe] /**6**/ vт to pile up; (*Tech: bois, pierre*) to compress; **s'agglomérer** vɪ to pile up

agglutiner [aglytine] /**1**/ vт to stick together; **s'agglutiner** vɪ to congregate

aggravant, e [agʀavɑ̃, -ɑ̃t] ADJ: **circonstances aggravantes** aggravating circumstances

aggravation [agʀavasjɔ̃] NF worsening, aggravation; increase

aggraver [agʀave] /**1**/ vт to worsen, aggravate; (*Jur: peine*) to increase; **s'aggraver** vɪ to worsen; **~ son cas** to make one's case worse

agile [aʒil] ADJ agile, nimble

agilement [aʒilmɑ̃] ADV nimbly

agilité [aʒilite] NF agility, nimbleness

agio [aʒjo] NM (bank) charges *pl*

agir [aʒiʀ] /**2**/ VI (*se comporter*) to behave, act; (*faire quelque chose*) to act, take action; (*avoir de l'effet*) to act; **il s'agit de** it's a matter ou question of; (*ça traite de*) it is about; (*il importe que*): **il s'agit de faire** we (*ou* you *etc*) must do; **de quoi s'agit-il?** what is it about?

agissements [aʒismã] NMPL (*péj*) schemes, intrigues

agitateur, -trice [aʒitatœʀ, -tʀis] NM/F agitator

agitation [aʒitasjɔ̃] NF (*hustle and*) bustle; (*trouble*) agitation, excitement; (*politique*) unrest, agitation

agité, e [aʒite] ADJ (*remuant*) fidgety, restless; (*trouble*) agitated, perturbed; (*journée*) hectic; (*mer*) rough; (*sommeil*) disturbed, broken

agiter [aʒite] /**1**/ VT (*bouteille, chiffon*) to shake; (*bras, mains*) to wave; (*préoccuper, exciter*) to trouble, perturb; **s'agiter** VI to bustle about; (*dormeur*) to toss and turn; (*enfant*) to fidget; (*Pol*) to grow restless; "**~ avant l'emploi**" "shake before use"

agneau, x [aɲo] NM lamb; (*toison*) lambswool

agnelet [aɲlɛ] NM little lamb

agnostique [agnɔstik] ADJ, NMF agnostic

agonie [agɔni] NF mortal agony, death pangs *pl*; (*fig*) death throes *pl*

agonir [agɔniʀ] /**2**/ VT: **~ qn d'injures** to hurl abuse at sb

agoniser [agɔnize] /**1**/ VI to be dying; (*fig*) to be in its death throes

agrafe [agʀaf] NF (*de vêtement*) hook, fastener; (*de bureau*) staple; (*Méd*) clip

agrafer [agʀafe] /**1**/ VT to fasten; to staple

agrafeuse [agʀaføz] NF stapler

agraire [agʀɛʀ] ADJ agrarian; (*mesure, surface*) land *cpd*

agrandir [agʀãdiʀ] /**2**/ VT (*magasin, domaine*) to extend, enlarge; (*trou*) to enlarge, make bigger; (*Photo*) to enlarge, blow up; **s'agrandir** VI (*ville, famille*) to grow, expand; (*trou, écart*) to get bigger

agrandissement [agʀãdismã] NM extension; enlargement; (*photographie*) enlargement

agrandisseur [agʀãdisœʀ] NM (*Photo*) enlarger

agréable [agʀeabl] ADJ pleasant, nice

agréablement [agʀeabləmã] ADV pleasantly

agréé, e [agʀee] ADJ: **concessionnaire ~** registered dealer; **magasin ~** registered dealer('s)

agréer [agʀee] /**1**/ VT (*requête*) to accept; **~ à** VT to please, suit; **veuillez ~, Monsieur/Madame, mes salutations distinguées** (*personne nommée*) yours sincerely; (*personne non nommée*) yours faithfully

agrég [agʀeg] NF (*fam*) = **agrégation**

agrégat [agʀega] NM aggregate

agrégation [agʀegasjɔ̃] NF *highest teaching diploma in France*; *see note*

> The *agrégation*, informally known as the *agrég*, is a prestigious competitive examination for the recruitment of secondary school teachers in France. The number of candidates always far exceeds the number of vacant posts. Most teachers of *classes préparatoires* and most university lecturers have passed the *agrégation*.

agrégé, e [agʀeʒe] NM/F holder of the *agrégation*

agréger [agʀeʒe] /**3**/: **s'agréger** VI to aggregate

agrément [agʀemã] NM (*accord*) consent, approval; (*attraits*) charm, attractiveness; (*plaisir*) pleasure; **voyage d'~** pleasure trip

agrémenter [agʀemãte] /**1**/ VT: **~ (de)** to embellish (with), adorn (with)

agrès [agʀɛ] NMPL (gymnastics) apparatus *sg*

agresser [agʀese] /**1**/ VT to attack

agresseur [agʀesœʀ] NM aggressor, attacker; (*Pol, Mil*) aggressor

agressif, -ive [agʀesif, -iv] ADJ aggressive

agression [agʀesjɔ̃] NF attack; (*Pol, Mil, Psych*) aggression

agressivement [agʀesivmã] ADV aggressively

agressivité [agʀesivite] NF aggressiveness

agreste [agʀɛst] ADJ rustic

agricole [agʀikɔl] ADJ agricultural, farm *cpd*

agriculteur, -trice [agʀikyltœʀ, -tʀis] NM/F farmer

agriculture [agʀikyltyʀ] NF agriculture; farming

agripper [agʀipe] /**1**/ VT to grab, clutch; (*pour arracher*) to snatch, grab; **s'~ à** to cling (on) to, clutch, grip

agroalimentaire [agʀɔalimãtɛʀ] ADJ farming *cpd* ▶ NM farm-produce industry; **l'~** agribusiness

agronome [agʀɔnɔm] NMF agronomist

agronomie [agʀɔnɔmi] NF agronomy

agronomique [agʀɔnɔmik] ADJ agronomic(al)

agrumes [agʀym] NMPL citrus fruit(s)

aguerrir [ageʀiʀ] /**2**/ VT to harden; **s'~ (contre)** to become hardened (to)

aguets [agɛ]: **aux ~** *adv*: **être aux ~** to be on the look-out

aguichant, e [agiʃã, -ãt] ADJ enticing

aguicher [agiʃe] /**1**/ VT to entice

aguicheur, -euse [agiʃœʀ, -øz] ADJ enticing

ah [a] EXCL ah!; **ah bon?** really?, is that so?; **ah mais …** yes, but …; **ah non!** oh no!

ahuri, e [ayʀi] ADJ (*stupéfait*) flabbergasted; (*idiot*) dim-witted

ahurir [ayʀiʀ] /**2**/ VT to stupefy, stagger

ahurissant, e [ayʀisã, -ãt] ADJ stupefying, staggering, mind-boggling

ai [ɛ] VB *voir* **avoir**

aide [ɛd] NMF assistant ▶ NF assistance, help; (*secours financier*) aid; **à l'~ de** with the help *ou* aid of; **aller à l'~ de qn** to go to sb's aid, go to help sb; **venir en ~ à qn** to help sb, come to sb's assistance; **appeler (qn) à l'~** to call for help (from sb); **à l'~!** help!; **~ de camp** *nm* aide-de-camp; **~ comptable** *nm* accountant's assistant; **~ électricien** *nm* electrician's mate; **~ familiale** *nf* mother's help, ≈ home help; **~ judiciaire** *nf* legal aid; **~ de laboratoire** *nmf* laboratory assistant; **~ ménagère** *nf* ≈ home help (BRIT) *ou* helper (US); **~ sociale** *nf* (*assistance*) state aid; **~ soignant, e** *nmf* auxiliary nurse; **~ technique** *nf* ≈ VSO (BRIT), ≈ Peace Corps (US)

aide-éducateur, -trice [ɛdmedykatœʀ, -tʀis] NM/F classroom assistant

aide-mémoire [ɛdmemwaʀ] NM INV

memoranda pages *pl*; (*key facts*) handbook

aider [ede] /**1**/ VT to help; **~ à qch** to help
(towards) sth; **~ qn à faire qch** to help sb to do
sth; **s'~ de** (*se servir de*) to use, make use of

aide-soignant, e [ɛdswaɲɑ̃, -ɑ̃t] NM/F
auxiliary nurse

aie *etc* [ɛ] VB *voir* **avoir**

aïe [aj] EXCL ouch!

AIEA SIGLE F (= *Agence internationale de l'énergie
atomique*) IAEA (= *International Atomic Energy
Agency*)

aïeul, e [ajœl] NM/F grandparent, grandfather/
grandmother; (*ancêtre*) forebear

aïeux [ajø] NMPL grandparents; forebears,
forefathers

aigle [ɛgl] NM eagle

aiglefin [ɛgləfɛ̃] NM = **églefin**

aigre [ɛgʀ] ADJ sour, sharp; (*fig*) sharp, cutting;
tourner à l'~ to turn sour

aigre-doux, -douce [ɛgʀədu, -dus] ADJ (*fruit*)
bitter-sweet; (*sauce*) sweet and sour

aigrefin [ɛgʀəfɛ̃] NM swindler

aigrelet, te [ɛgʀəlɛ, -ɛt] ADJ (*goût*) sourish; (*voix,
son*) sharpish

aigrette [ɛgʀɛt] NF (*plume*) feather

aigreur [ɛgʀœʀ] NF sourness; sharpness;
aigreurs d'estomac heartburn *sg*

aigri, e [egʀi] ADJ embittered

aigrir [egʀiʀ] /**2**/ VT (*personne*) to embitter;
(*caractère*) to sour; **s'aigrir** VI to become
embittered; to sour; (*lait etc*) to turn sour

aigu, ë [egy] ADJ (*objet, arête*) sharp, pointed; (*son,
voix*) high-pitched, shrill; (*note*) high(-pitched);
(*douleur, intelligence*) acute, sharp

aigue-marine [ɛgmaʀin] (*pl* **aigues-marines**)
NF aquamarine

aiguillage [egɥijaʒ] NM (*Rail*) points *pl*

aiguille [egɥij] NF needle; (*de montre*) hand; **~ à
tricoter** knitting needle

aiguiller [egɥije] /**1**/ VT (*orienter*) to direct; (*Rail*)
to shunt

aiguillette [egɥijɛt] NF (*Culin*) aiguillette

aiguilleur [egɥijœʀ] NM: **~ du ciel** air traffic
controller

aiguillon [egɥijɔ̃] NM (*d'abeille*) sting; (*fig*) spur,
stimulus

aiguillonner [egɥijɔne] /**1**/ VT to spur *ou* goad on

aiguiser [egize] /**1**/ VT to sharpen, grind; (*fig*) to
stimulate; (: *esprit*) to sharpen; (: *sens*) to excite

aiguisoir [egizwaʀ] NM sharpener

aïkido [ajkido] NM aikido

ail [aj] NM garlic

aile [ɛl] NF wing; (*de voiture*) wing (BRIT), fender
(US); **battre de l'~** (*fig*) to be in a sorry state;
voler de ses propres ailes to stand on one's
own two feet; **~ libre** hang-glider

ailé, e [ele] ADJ winged

aileron [ɛlʀɔ̃] NM (*de requin*) fin; (*d'avion*) aileron

ailette [ɛlɛt] NF (*Tech*) fin; (: *de turbine*) blade

ailier [elje] NM (*Sport*) winger

aille *etc* [aj] VB *voir* **aller**

ailleurs [ajœʀ] ADV elsewhere, somewhere else;
partout/nulle part ~ everywhere/nowhere
else; **d'~** *adv* (*du reste*) moreover, besides; **par ~**

adv (*d'autre part*) moreover, furthermore

ailloli [ajɔli] NM garlic mayonnaise

aimable [ɛmabl] ADJ kind, nice; **vous êtes bien
~** that's very nice *ou* kind of you, how kind (of
you)!

aimablement [ɛmabləmɑ̃] ADV kindly

aimant¹ [ɛmɑ̃] NM magnet

aimant², e [ɛmɑ̃, -ɑ̃t] ADJ loving, affectionate

aimanté, e [ɛmɑ̃te] ADJ magnetic

aimanter [ɛmɑ̃te] /**1**/ VT to magnetize

aimer [eme] /**1**/ VT to love; (*d'amitié, affection, par
goût*) to like; (*souhait*): **j'aimerais ...** I would like
...; **s'aimer** to love each other; to like each
other; **je n'aime pas beaucoup Paul** I don't
like Paul much, I don't care much for Paul;
~ faire qch to like doing sth, like to do sth;
j'aime faire du ski I like skiing; **je t'aime** I
love you; **aimeriez-vous que je vous
accompagne?** would you like me to come with
you?; **j'aimerais (bien) m'en aller** I should
(really) like to go; **bien ~ qn/qch** to like sb/sth;
j'aime mieux Paul (que Pierre) I prefer Paul
(to Pierre); **j'aime mieux** *ou* **autant vous dire
que** I may as well tell you that; **j'aimerais
autant** *ou* **mieux y aller maintenant** I'd
sooner *ou* rather go now; **j'aime assez aller au
cinéma** I quite like going to the cinema

aine [ɛn] NF groin

aîné, e [ene] ADJ elder, older; (*le plus âgé*) eldest,
oldest ▶ NM/F oldest child *ou* one, oldest boy *ou*
son/girl *ou* daughter; **aînés** NMPL (*fig: anciens*)
elders; **il est mon ~ de 2 ans** he's (2 years)
older than me, he's (2 years) my senior

aînesse [enes] NF: **droit d'~** birthright

ainsi [ɛ̃si] ADV (*de cette façon*) like this, in this
way, thus; (*ce faisant*) thus ▶ CONJ thus, so;
~ que (*comme*) (just) as; (*et aussi*) as well as; **pour
~ dire** so to speak, as it were; **~ donc** and so;
~ soit-il (*Rel*) so be it; **et ~ de suite** and so on
(and so forth)

aïoli [ajɔli] NM = **ailloli**

air [ɛʀ] NM air; (*mélodie*) tune; (*expression*) look,
(*atmosphère, ambiance*): **dans l'~** in the air
(*fig*); **prendre de grands airs (avec qn)** to give
o.s. airs (with sb); **en l'~** (up) into the air; **tirer
en l'~** to fire shots in the air; **paroles/menaces
en l'~** empty words/threats; **prendre l'~** to get
some (fresh) air; (*avion*) to take off; **avoir l'~
(sembler)** to look, appear; **avoir l'~ triste** to look
ou seem sad; **avoir l'~ de qch** to look like sth;
avoir l'~ de faire to look as though one is
doing, appear to be doing; **courant d'~**
draught (BRIT), draft (US); **le grand ~** the open
air; **mal de l'~** air-sickness; **tête en l'~**
scatterbrain; **~ comprimé** compressed air;
~ conditionné air-conditioning

airbag [ɛʀbag] NM airbag

aire [ɛʀ] NF (*zone, fig, Math*) area; (*nid*) eyrie
(BRIT), aerie (US); **~ d'atterrissage** landing
strip; landing patch; **~ de jeu** play area; **~ de
lancement** launching site; **~ de
stationnement** parking area

airelle [ɛʀɛl] NF bilberry

aisance [ɛzɑ̃s] NF ease; (*Couture*) easing,

freedom of movement; (*richesse*) affluence;
être dans l'~ to be well-off *ou* affluent
aise [ɛz] NF comfort ▸ ADJ: **être bien ~ de/que** to
be delighted to/that; **aises** NFPL: **aimer ses
aises** to like one's (creature) comforts;
prendre ses aises to make o.s. comfortable;
frémir d'~ to shudder with pleasure; **être à l'~
ou à son ~** to be comfortable; (*pas embarrassé*) to
be at ease; (*financièrement*) to be comfortably off;
se mettre à l'~ to make o.s. comfortable; **être
mal à l'~** *ou* **à son ~** to be uncomfortable; (*gêné*)
to be ill at ease; **mettre qn à l'~** to put sb at his
(*ou* her) ease; **mettre qn mal à l'~** to make sb
feel ill at ease; **à votre ~** please yourself, just as
you like; **en faire à son ~** to do as one likes; **en
prendre à son ~ avec qch** to be free and easy
with sth, do as one likes with sth
aisé, e [eze] ADJ easy; (*assez riche*) well-to-do,
well-off
aisément [ezemɑ̃] ADV easily
aisselle [ɛsɛl] NF armpit
ait [ɛ] VB *voir* **avoir**
ajonc [aʒɔ̃] NM gorse *no pl*
ajouré, e [aʒuʀe] ADJ openwork *cpd*
ajournement [aʒuʀnəmɑ̃] NM adjournment;
deferment, postponement
ajourner [aʒuʀne] /1/ VT (*réunion*) to adjourn;
(*décision*) to defer, postpone; (*candidat*) to refer;
(*conscrit*) to defer
ajout [aʒu] NM addition; **merci pour l'~** thanks
for the add
ajouter [aʒute] /1/ VT to add; **~ à** (*accroître*) to add
to; **s'~ à** to add to; **~ que** to add that; **~ foi à** to
lend *ou* give credence to
ajustage [aʒystaʒ] NM fitting
ajusté, e [aʒyste] ADJ: **bien ~** (*robe etc*) close-
fitting
ajustement [aʒystəmɑ̃] NM adjustment
ajuster [aʒyste] /1/ VT (*régler*) to adjust; (*vêtement*)
to alter; (*coup de fusil*) to aim; (*cible*) to aim at;
(*adapter*): **~ qch à** to fit sth to; **~ sa cravate** to
adjust one's tie
ajusteur [aʒystœʀ] NM metal worker
alaise [alɛz] NF = **alèse**
alambic [alɑ̃bik] NM still
alambiqué, e [alɑ̃bike] ADJ convoluted,
overcomplicated
alangui, e [alɑ̃gi] ADJ languid
alanguir [alɑ̃giʀ] /2/: **s'alanguir** VI to grow
languid
alarmant, e [alaʀmɑ̃, -ɑ̃t] ADJ alarming
alarme [alaʀm] NF alarm; **donner l'~** to give *ou*
raise the alarm; **jeter l'~** to cause alarm
alarmer [alaʀme] /1/ VT to alarm; **s'alarmer** VI
to become alarmed
alarmiste [alaʀmist] ADJ alarmist
Alaska [alaska] NM: **l'~** Alaska
albanais, e [albanɛ, -ɛz] ADJ Albanian ▸ NM
(*Ling*) Albanian ▸ NM/F: **A~, e** Albanian
Albanie [albani] NF: **l'~** Albania
albâtre [albɑtʀ] NM alabaster
albatros [albatʀos] NM albatross
albigeois, e [albiʒwa, -waz] ADJ of *ou* from Albi
albinos [albinos] NMF albino

album [albɔm] NM album; **~ à colorier**
colouring book; **~ de timbres** stamp album
albumen [albymɛn] NM albumen
albumine [albymin] NF albumin; **avoir** *ou*
faire de l'~ to suffer from albuminuria
alcalin, e [alkalɛ̃, -in] ADJ alkaline
alchimie [alʃimi] NF alchemy
alchimiste [alʃimist] NM alchemist
alcool [alkɔl] NM: **l'~** alcohol; **un ~** a spirit, a
brandy; **bière sans ~** non-alcoholic *ou*
alcohol-free beer; **~ à brûler** methylated
spirits (BRIT), wood alcohol (US); **~ à 90°**
surgical spirit; **~ camphré** camphorated
alcohol; **~ de prune** *etc* plum *etc* brandy
alcoolémie [alkɔlemi] NF blood alcohol level
alcoolique [alkɔlik] ADJ, NMF alcoholic
alcoolisé, e [alkɔlize] ADJ alcoholic; **une
boisson non ~** a soft drink
alcoolisme [alkɔlism] NM alcoholism
alco(o)test® [alkɔtɛst] NM (*objet*)
Breathalyser®; (*test*) breath-test; **faire subir
l'alco(o)test à qn** to Breathalyse® sb
alcôve [alkov] NF alcove, recess
aléas [alea] NMPL hazards
aléatoire [aleatwaʀ] ADJ uncertain; (*Inform,
Statistique*) random
alémanique [alemanik] ADJ: **la Suisse ~**
German-speaking Switzerland
ALENA [alena] SIGLE M (= *Accord de libre-échange
nord-américain*) NAFTA (= *North American Free Trade
Agreement*)
alentour [alɑ̃tuʀ] ADV around (about);
alentours NMPL surroundings; **aux alentours
de** in the vicinity *ou* neighbourhood of, around
about; (*temps*) around about
alerte [alɛʀt] ADJ agile, nimble; (*style*) brisk,
lively ▸ NF alert; warning; **donner l'~** to give
the alert; **à la première ~** at the first sign of
trouble *ou* danger; **~ à la bombe** bomb scare
alerter [alɛʀte] /1/ VT to alert
alèse [alɛz] NF (*drap*) undersheet, draw-sheet
aléser [aleze] /6/ VT to ream
alevin [alvɛ̃] NM alevin, young fish
alevinage [alvinaʒ] NM fish farming
Alexandrie [alɛksɑ̃dʀi] N Alexandria
alexandrin [alɛksɑ̃dʀɛ̃] NM alexandrine
alezan, e [alzɑ̃, -an] ADJ chestnut
algarade [algaʀad] NF row, dispute
algèbre [alʒɛbʀ] NF algebra
algébrique [alʒebʀik] ADJ algebraic
Alger [alʒe] N Algiers
Algérie [alʒeʀi] NF: **l'~** Algeria
algérien, ne [alʒeʀjɛ̃, -ɛn] ADJ Algerian ▸ NM/F:
A~, ne Algerian
algérois, e [alʒeʀwa, -waz] ADJ of *ou* from Algiers
▸ NM: **l'A~** (*région*) the Algiers region
algorithme [algɔʀitm] NM algorithm
algue [alg] NF seaweed *no pl*; (*Bot*) alga
alias [aljas] ADV alias
alibi [alibi] NM alibi
aliénation [aljenasjɔ̃] NF alienation
aliéné, e [aljene] NM/F insane person, lunatic (*péj*)
aliéner [aljene] /6/ VT to alienate; (*bien, liberté*) to
give up; **s'aliéner** VT to alienate

alignement [aliɲmɑ̃] NM alignment, lining up; **à l'~** in line

aligner [aliɲe] /**1**/ VT to align, line up; (idées, chiffres) to string together; (adapter): **~ qch sur** to bring sth into alignment with; **s'aligner** VI (soldats etc) to line up; **s'aligner sur** (Pol) to align o.s. with

aliment [alimɑ̃] NM food; **~ complet** whole food

alimentaire [alimɑ̃tɛʀ] ADJ food cpd; (péj: besogne) done merely to earn a living; **produits alimentaires** foodstuffs, foods

alimentation [alimɑ̃tasjɔ̃] NF feeding; (en eau etc, de moteur) supplying, supply; (commerce) food trade; (produits) groceries pl; (régime) diet; (Inform) feed; **~ (générale)** (general) grocer's; **~ de base** staple diet; **~ en feuilles/en continu/en papier** form/stream/sheet feed

alimenter [alimɑ̃te] /**1**/ VT to feed; (Tech): **~ (en)** to supply (with), feed (with); (fig) to sustain, keep going

alinéa [alinea] NM paragraph; **"nouvel ~"** "new line"

aliter [alite] /**1**/: **s'aliter** VI to take to one's bed; **infirme alité** bedridden person ou invalid

alizé [alize] ADJ, NM: **(vent) ~** trade wind

allaitement [alɛtmɑ̃] NM feeding; **~ maternel/au biberon** breast-/bottle-feeding; **~ mixte** mixed feeding

allaiter [alete] /**1**/ VT (femme) to (breast-)feed, nurse; (animal) to suckle; **~ au biberon** to bottle-feed

allant [alɑ̃] NM drive, go

alléchant, e [aleʃɑ̃, -ɑ̃t] ADJ tempting, enticing

allécher [aleʃe] /**6**/ VT: **~ qn** to make sb's mouth water; to tempt sb, entice sb

allée [ale] NF (de jardin) path; (en ville) avenue, drive; **allées et venues** comings and goings

allégation [alegasjɔ̃] NF allegation

allégé, e [aleʒe] ADJ (yaourt etc) low-fat

alléger [aleʒe] /**6, 3**/ VT (voiture) to make lighter; (chargement) to lighten; (souffrance) to alleviate, soothe

allégorie [alegɔʀi] NF allegory

allégorique [alegɔʀik] ADJ allegorical

allègre [alɛɡʀ] ADJ lively, jaunty (BRIT); (personne) gay, cheerful

allégresse [alegʀɛs] NF elation, gaiety

allegretto [al(l)egʀɛt(t)o] ADV, NM allegretto

allegro [al(l)egʀo] ADV, NM allegro

alléguer [alege] /**6**/ VT to put forward (as proof ou an excuse)

Allemagne [almaɲ] NF: **l'~** Germany; **l'~ de l'Est/Ouest** East/West Germany; **l'~ fédérale (RFA)** the Federal Republic of Germany (FRG)

allemand, e [almɑ̃, -ɑ̃d] ADJ German ▶ NM (Ling) German ▶ NM/F: **A~, e** German; **A~ de l'Est/l'Ouest** East/West German

aller [ale] /**9**/ NM (trajet) outward journey; (billet) single (BRIT) ou one-way ticket (US) ▶ VI (gén) to go; **~ simple** (billet) single (BRIT) ou one-way ticket; **~ (et) retour** (trajet) return trip ou journey (BRIT), round trip (US); (billet) return (BRIT) ou round-trip (US) ticket; **~ à** (convenir) to suit; (forme, pointure etc) to fit; **cela me va** (couleur) that suits me; (vêtement) that suits me; that fits me; (projet, disposition) that suits me, that's fine ou OK by me; **~ à la chasse/pêche** to go hunting/fishing; **~ avec** (couleurs, style etc) to go (well) with; **je vais le faire/me fâcher** I'm going to do it/to get angry; **~ voir/chercher qn** to go and see/look for sb; **comment allez-vous?** how are you?; **comment ça va?** how are you?; (affaires etc) how are things?; **ça va? — oui (ça va)!** how are things? — fine!; **pour ~ à** how do I get to; **ça va (comme ça)** that's fine (as it is); **il va bien/mal** he's well/ not well, he's fine/ill; **ça va bien/mal** (affaires etc) it's going well/not going well; **tout va bien** everything's fine; **ça ne va pas!** (mauvaise humeur etc) that's not on!, hey, come on!; **ça ne va pas sans difficultés** it's not without difficulties; **~ mieux** to be better; **il y va de leur vie** their lives are at stake; **se laisser ~** to let o.s. go; **~ jusqu'à** to go as far as; **ça va de soi, ça va sans dire** that goes without saying; **tu y vas un peu fort** you're going a bit (too) far; **allez!** go on!; come on!; **allons!** come now!; **allons-y!** let's go!; **allez, au revoir!** right ou OK then, bye-bye!

allergène [alɛʀʒɛn] NM allergen

allergie [alɛʀʒi] NF allergy

allergique [alɛʀʒik] ADJ allergic; **~ à** allergic to

allez [ale] VB voir **aller**

alliage [aljaʒ] NM alloy

alliance [aljɑ̃s] NF (Mil, Pol) alliance; (mariage) marriage; (bague) wedding ring; **neveu par ~** nephew by marriage

allié, e [alje] NM/F ally; **parents et alliés** relatives and relatives by marriage

allier [alje] /**7**/ VT (métaux) to alloy; (Pol, gén) to ally; (fig) to combine; **s'allier** VI to become allies; (éléments, caractéristiques) to combine; **s'allier à** to become allied to ou with

alligator [aligatɔʀ] NM alligator

allitération [aliteʀasjɔ̃] NF alliteration

allô [alo] EXCL hullo, hallo

allocataire [alɔkatɛʀ] NM/F beneficiary

allocation [alɔkasjɔ̃] NF allowance; **~ (de) chômage** unemployment benefit; **~ (de) logement** rent allowance; **allocations familiales** ≈ child benefit no pl; **allocations de maternité** maternity allowance

allocution [alɔkysjɔ̃] NF short speech

allongé, e [alɔ̃ʒe] ADJ (étendu): **être ~** to be stretched out ou lying down; (long) long; (étiré) elongated; (oblong) oblong; **rester ~** to be lying down; **mine ~** long face

allonger [alɔ̃ʒe] /**3**/ VT to lengthen, make longer; (étendre: bras, jambe) to stretch (out); (: sauce) to spin out, make go further; **s'allonger** VI to get longer; (se coucher) to lie down, stretch out; **~ le pas** to hasten one's step(s)

allouer [alwe] /**1**/ VT: **~ qch à** to allocate sth to, allot sth to

allumage [alymaʒ] NM (Auto) ignition

allume-cigare [alymsigaʀ] NM INV cigar lighter

allume-gaz [alymgɑz] NM INV gas lighter

allumer [alyme] /**1**/ vt (*lampe, phare, radio*) to put *ou* switch on; (*pièce*) to put *ou* switch the light(s) on in; (*feu, bougie, cigare, pipe, gaz*) to light; (*chauffage*) to put on; **s'allumer** vi (*lumière, lampe*) to come *ou* go on; **~ (la lumière** *ou* **l'électricité)** to put on the light

allumette [alymɛt] NF match; (*morceau de bois*) matchstick; (*Culin*): **~ au fromage** cheese straw; **~ de sûreté** safety match

allumeuse [alymøz] NF (*péj*) tease (*woman*)

allure [alyʀ] NF (*vitesse*) speed; (: *à pied*) pace; (*démarche*) walk; (*maintien*) bearing; (*aspect, air*) look; **avoir de l'~** to have style; **à toute ~** at full speed

allusion [a(l)lyzjɔ̃] NF allusion; (*sous-entendu*) hint; **faire ~ à** to allude *ou* refer to; to hint at

alluvions [alyvjɔ̃] NFPL alluvial deposits, alluvium *sg*

almanach [almana] NM almanac

aloès [alɔɛs] NM (*Bot*) aloe

aloi [alwa] NM: **de bon/mauvais ~** of genuine/ doubtful worth *ou* quality

(MOT-CLÉ)

alors [alɔʀ] ADV **1** (*à ce moment-là*) then, at that time; **il habitait alors à Paris** he lived in Paris at that time; **jusqu'alors** up till *ou* until then

2 (*par conséquent*) then; **tu as fini? alors je m'en vais** have you finished? I'm going then

3 (*expressions*): **alors? quoi de neuf?** well *ou* so? what's new?; **et alors?** so (what)?; **ça alors!** (well) really!

▶ CONJ: **alors que** (*au moment où*) when, as; **il est arrivé alors que je partais** he arrived as I was leaving; (*tandis que*) whereas, while; **alors que son frère travaillait dur, lui se reposait** while his brother was working hard, HE would rest; (*bien que*) even though; **il a été puni alors qu'il n'a rien fait** he was punished, even though he had done nothing; (*pendant que*) while, when; **alors qu'il était à Paris, il a visité ...** while *ou* when he was in Paris, he visited ...

alouette [alwɛt] NF (sky)lark

alourdir [aluʀdiʀ] /**2**/ vt to weigh down, make heavy; **s'alourdir** vi to grow heavy *ou* heavier

aloyau [alwajo] NM sirloin

alpaga [alpaga] NM (*tissu*) alpaca

alpage [alpaʒ] NM high mountain pasture

Alpes [alp] NFPL: **les ~** the Alps

alpestre [alpɛstʀ] ADJ alpine

alphabet [alfabɛ] NM alphabet; (*livre*) ABC (book), primer

alphabétique [alfabetik] ADJ alphabetic(al); **par ordre ~** in alphabetical order

alphabétisation [alfabetizasjɔ̃] NF literacy teaching

alphabétiser [alfabetize] /**1**/ vt to teach to read and write; (*pays*) to eliminate illiteracy in

alphanumérique [alfanymeʀik] ADJ alphanumeric

alpin, e [alpɛ̃, -in] ADJ (*plante etc*) alpine; (*club*) climbing

alpinisme [alpinism] NM mountaineering, climbing

alpiniste [alpinist] NMF mountaineer, climber

Alsace [alzas] NF Alsace; **l'~** Alsace

alsacien, ne [alzasjɛ̃, -ɛn] ADJ Alsatian ▶ NM/F: **A~, ne** Alsatian

altercation [altɛʀkasjɔ̃] NF altercation

alter ego [altɛʀego] NM alter ego

altérer [alteʀe] /**6**/ vt (*faits, vérité*) to falsify, distort; (*qualité*) to debase, impair; (*données*) to corrupt; (*donner soif à*) to make thirsty; **s'altérer** vi to deteriorate; to spoil

altermondialisme [altɛʀmɔ̃djalism] NM anti-globalism

altermondialiste [altɛʀmɔ̃djalist] ADJ, NMF anti-globalist

alternance [altɛʀnɑ̃s] NF alternation; **en ~** alternately; **formation en ~** sandwich course

alternateur [altɛʀnatœʀ] NM alternator

alternatif, -ive [altɛʀnatif, -iv] ADJ alternating ▶ NF alternative

alternative NF (*choix*) alternative

alternativement [altɛʀnativmɑ̃] ADV alternately

alterner [altɛʀne] /**1**/ vt to alternate ▶ vi: **~ (avec)** to alternate (with); **(faire) ~ qch avec qch** to alternate sth with sth

Altesse [altɛs] NF Highness

altier, -ière [altje, -jɛʀ] ADJ haughty

altimètre [altimɛtʀ] NM altimeter

altiport [altipɔʀ] NM mountain airfield

altiste [altist] NM/F viola player, violist

altitude [altityd] NF altitude, height; **à 1000 m d'~** at a height *ou* an altitude of 1000 m; **en ~** at high altitudes; **perdre/prendre de l'~** to lose/ gain height; **voler à haute/basse ~** to fly at a high/low altitude

alto [alto] NM (*instrument*) viola ▶ NF (*contr*)alto

altruisme [altʀɥism] NM altruism

altruiste [altʀɥist] ADJ altruistic

aluminium [alyminjɔm] NM aluminium (BRIT), aluminum (US)

alun [alœ̃] NM alum

alunir [alyniʀ] /**2**/ vi to land on the moon

alunissage [alynisaʒ] NM (moon) landing

alvéole [alveɔl] NM OU F (*de ruche*) alveolus

alvéolé, e [alveɔle] ADJ honeycombed

AM SIGLE F = **assurance maladie**

amabilité [amabilite] NF kindness; **il a eu l'~ de** he was kind *ou* good enough to

amadou [amadu] NM touchwood, amadou

amadouer [amadwe] /**1**/ vt to coax, cajole; (*adoucir*) to mollify, soothe

amaigrir [amegʀiʀ] /**2**/ vt to make thin *ou* thinner

amaigrissant, e [amegʀisɑ̃, -ɑ̃t] ADJ: **régime ~** slimming (BRIT) *ou* weight-reduction (US) diet

amalgame [amalgam] NM amalgam; (*fig: de gens, d'idées*) hotch-potch, mixture

amalgamer [amalgame] /**1**/ vt to amalgamate

amande [amɑ̃d] NF (*de l'amandier*) almond; (*de noyau de fruit*) kernel; **en ~** (*yeux*) almond *cpd*, almond-shaped

amandier [amɑ̃dje] NM almond (tree)

amanite [amanit] NF (*Bot*) *mushroom of the genus Amanita*; ~ **tue-mouches** *fly agaric*

amant [amã] NM *lover*

amarre [amaʀ] NF (*Navig*) (*mooring*) *rope ou line*; **amarres** NFPL *moorings*

amarrer [amaʀe] /1/ VT (*Navig*) *to moor*; (*gén*) *to make fast*

amaryllis [amaʀilis] NF *amaryllis*

amas [amɑ] NM *heap, pile*

amasser [amɑse] /1/ VT *to amass*; **s'amasser** VI *to pile up, accumulate*; (*foule*) *to gather*

amateur [amatœʀ] NM *amateur*; **en ~** (*péj*) *amateurishly*; **musicien/sportif ~** *amateur musician/sportsman*; **~ de musique/sport** *etc music/sport etc lover*

amateurisme [amatœʀism] NM *amateurism*; (*péj*) *amateurishness*

Amazone [amazon] NF: **l'~** *the Amazon*

amazone [amazon] NF *horsewoman*; **en ~** *side-saddle*

Amazonie [amazɔni] NF: **l'~** *Amazonia*

ambages [ābaʒ]: **sans ~** *adv without beating about the bush, plainly*

ambassade [ābasad] NF *embassy*; (*mission*): **en ~** *on a mission*; **l'~ de France** *the French Embassy*

ambassadeur, -drice [ābasadœʀ, -dʀis] NM/F *ambassador/ambassadress*

ambiance [ābjãs] NF *atmosphere*; **il y a de l'~** *everyone's having a good time*

ambiant, e [ābjã, -ãt] ADJ (*air, milieu*) *surrounding*; (*température*) *ambient*

ambidextre [ābidɛkstʀ] ADJ *ambidextrous*

ambigu, ë [ābigy] ADJ *ambiguous*

ambiguïté [ābigɥite] NF *ambiguousness no pl, ambiguity*

ambitieux, -euse [ābisjø, -jøz] ADJ *ambitious*

ambition [ābisjɔ̃] NF *ambition*

ambitionner [ābisjɔne] /1/ VT *to have as one's aim ou ambition*

ambivalent, e [ābivalã, -ãt] ADJ *ambivalent*

amble [ābl] NM: **aller l'~** *to amble*

ambre [ābʀ] NM: **~ (jaune)** *amber*; **~ gris** *ambergris*

ambré, e [ābʀe] ADJ (*couleur*) *amber*; (*parfum*) *ambergris-scented*

ambulance [ābylãs] NF *ambulance*

ambulancier, -ière [ābylãsje, -jɛʀ] NM/F *ambulanceman/woman* (*BRIT*), *paramedic* (*US*)

ambulant, e [ābylã, -ãt] ADJ *travelling, itinerant*

âme [ɑm] NF *soul*; **rendre l'~** *to give up the ghost*; **bonne ~** (*aussi ironique*) *kind soul*; **un joueur/tricheur dans l'~** *a gambler/cheat through and through*; **~ sœur** *kindred spirit*

amélioration [ameljɔʀasjɔ̃] NF *improvement*

améliorer [ameljɔʀe] /1/ VT *to improve*; **s'améliorer** VI *to improve, get better*

aménagement [amenaʒmã] NM *fitting out; laying out; development*; **aménagements** NMPL *developments*; **l'~ du territoire** ≈ *town and country planning*; **aménagements fiscaux** *tax adjustments*

aménager [amenaʒe] /3/ VT (*agencer: espace, local*) *to fit out*; (: *terrain*) *to lay out*; (: *quartier, territoire*) *to develop*; (*installer*) *to fix up, put in*; **ferme aménagée** *converted farmhouse*

amende [amãd] NF *fine*; **mettre à l'~** *to penalize*; **faire ~ honorable** *to make amends*

amendement [amãdmã] NM (*Jur*) *amendment*

amender [amãde] /1/ VT (*loi*) *to amend*; (*terre*) *to enrich*; **s'amender** VI *to mend one's ways*

amène [amɛn] ADJ *affable*; **peu ~** *unkind*

amener [am(ə)ne] /5/ VT *to bring*; (*causer*) *to bring about*; (*baisser: drapeau, voiles*) *to strike*; **s'amener** VI (*fam*) *to show up, turn up*; **~ qn à qch/à faire** *to lead sb to sth/to do*

amenuiser [amənɥize] /1/: **s'amenuiser** VI *to dwindle*; (*chances*) *to grow slimmer, lessen*

amer, amère [amɛʀ] ADJ *bitter*

amèrement [amɛʀmã] ADV *bitterly*

américain, e [ameʀikɛ̃, -ɛn] ADJ *American* ▶ NM (*Ling*) *American (English)* ▶ NM/F: **A~, e** *American*; **en vedette ~** *as a special guest (star)*

américaniser [ameʀikanize] /1/ VT *to Americanize*

américanisme [ameʀikanism] NM *Americanism*

amérindien, ne [ameʀɛ̃djɛ̃, -ɛn] ADJ *Amerindian, American Indian*

Amérique [ameʀik] NF *America*; **l'~ centrale** *Central America*; **l'~ latine** *Latin America*; **l'~ du Nord** *North America*; **l'~ du Sud** *South America*

Amerloque [amɛʀlɔk] NM/F (*fam*) *Yank, Yankee*

amerrir [ameʀiʀ] /2/ VI *to land (on the sea)*; (*capsule spatiale*) *to splash down*

amerrissage [ameʀisaʒ] NM *landing (on the sea); splash-down*

amertume [amɛʀtym] NF *bitterness*

améthyste [ametist] NF *amethyst*

ameublement [amœblǝmã] NM *furnishing*; (*meubles*) *furniture*; **articles d'~** *furnishings*; **tissus d'~** *soft furnishings, furnishing fabrics*

ameuter [amøte] /1/ VT (*badauds*) *to draw a crowd of*; (*peuple*) *to rouse, stir up*

ami, e [ami] NM/F *friend*; (*amant/maîtresse*) *boyfriend/girlfriend* ▶ ADJ: **pays/groupe ~** *friendly country/group*; **être (très) ~ avec qn** *to be (very) friendly with sb*; **être ~ de l'ordre** *to be a lover of order*; **un ~ des arts** *a patron of the arts*; **un ~ des chiens** *a dog lover*; **petit ~/petite ~** (*fam*) *boyfriend/girlfriend*

amiable [amjabl]: **à l'~** *adv* (*Jur*) *out of court*; (*gén*) *amicably*

amiante [amjãt] NM *asbestos*

amibe [amib] NF *amoeba*

amical, e, -aux [amikal, -o] ADJ *friendly* ▶ NF (*club*) *association*

amicalement [amikalmã] ADV *in a friendly way*; (*formule épistolaire*) *regards*

amidon [amidɔ̃] NM *starch*

amidonner [amidɔne] /1/ VT *to starch*

amincir [amɛ̃siʀ] /2/ VT (*objet*) *to thin (down)*; **s'amincir** VI *to get thinner ou slimmer*; **~ qn** *to make sb thinner ou slimmer*; (*vêtement*) *to make sb look slimmer*

amincissant, e [amɛ̃sisɑ̃, -ɑ̃t] ADJ slimming; **régime ~** diet; **crème ~** slimming cream
aminé, e [amine] ADJ: **acide ~** amino acid
amiral, -aux [amiral, -o] NM admiral
amirauté [amirote] NF admiralty
amitié [amitje] NF friendship; **prendre en ~** to take a liking to; **faire** *ou* **présenter ses amitiés à qn** to send sb one's best wishes; **amitiés** (*formule épistolaire*) (with) best wishes
ammoniac [amɔnjak] NM: **(gaz) ~** ammonia
ammoniaque [amɔnjak] NF ammonia (water)
amnésie [amnezi] NF amnesia
amnésique [amnezik] ADJ amnesic
Amnesty International [amnɛsti-] N Amnesty International
amniocentèse [amnjosɛ̃tɛz] NF amniocentesis
amnistie [amnisti] NF amnesty
amnistier [amnistje] /7/ VT to amnesty
amocher [amɔʃe] /1/ VT (*fam*) to mess up
amoindrir [amwɛ̃driʀ] /2/ VT to reduce
amollir [amɔliʀ] /2/ VT to soften
amonceler [amɔ̃s(ə)le] /4/ VT to pile *ou* heap up; **s'amonceler** to pile *ou* heap up; (*fig*) to accumulate
amoncellement [amɔ̃sɛlmɑ̃] NM piling *ou* heaping up; accumulation; (*tas*) pile, heap, accumulation
amont [amɔ̃]: **en ~** *adv* upstream; (*sur une pente*) uphill; **en ~ de** *prép* upstream from; uphill from, above
amoral, e, -aux [amɔral, -o] ADJ amoral
amorce [amɔʀs] NF (*sur un hameçon*) bait; (*explosif*) cap; (*tube*) primer; (: *contenu*) priming; (*fig*: *début*) beginning(s), start
amorcer [amɔʀse] /3/ VT to bait; to prime; (*commencer*) to begin, start
amorphe [amɔʀf] ADJ passive, lifeless
amortir [amɔʀtiʀ] /2/ VT (*atténuer*: *choc*) to absorb, cushion; (: *bruit, douleur*) to deaden; (*Comm*: *dette*) to pay off, amortize; (: *mise de fonds, matériel*) to write off; **~ un abonnement** to make a season ticket pay (for itself)
amortissable [amɔʀtisabl] ADJ (*Comm*) that can be paid off
amortissement [amɔʀtismɑ̃] NM (*de matériel*) writing off; (*d'une dette*) paying off
amortisseur [amɔʀtisœʀ] NM shock absorber
amour [amuʀ] NM love; (*liaison*) love affair, love; (*statuette etc*) cupid; **un ~ de** a lovely little; **faire l'~ to** to make love
amouracher [amuʀaʃe] /1/: **s'amouracher de** VT (*péj*) to become infatuated with
amourette [amuʀɛt] NF passing fancy
amoureusement [amuʀøzmɑ̃] ADV lovingly
amoureux, -euse [amuʀø, -øz] ADJ (*regard, tempérament*) amorous; (*vie, problèmes*) love *cpd*; (*personne*) **être ~ (de qn)** to be in love (with sb) ▶ NM/F lover ▶ NMPL courting couple(s); **tomber ~ de qn** to fall in love with sb; **être ~ de qch** to be passionately fond of sth; **un ~ de la nature** a nature lover
amour-propre [amuʀpʀɔpʀ] (*pl* **amours-propres**) NM self-esteem, pride
amovible [amɔvibl] ADJ removable, detachable

ampère [ɑ̃pɛʀ] NM amp(ere)
ampèremètre [ɑ̃pɛʀmɛtʀ] NM ammeter
amphétamine [ɑ̃fetamin] NF amphetamine
amphi [ɑ̃fi] NM (*Scol*: *fam*: = *amphithéâtre*) lecture hall *ou* theatre
amphibie [ɑ̃fibi] ADJ amphibious
amphibien [ɑ̃fibjɛ̃] NM (*Zool*) amphibian
amphithéâtre [ɑ̃fiteɑtʀ] NM amphitheatre; (*d'université*) lecture hall *ou* theatre
amphore [ɑ̃fɔʀ] NF amphora
ample [ɑ̃pl] ADJ (*vêtement*) roomy, ample; (*gestes, mouvement*) broad; (*ressources*) ample; **jusqu'à plus ~ informé** (*Admin*) until further details are available
amplement [ɑ̃pləmɑ̃] ADV amply; **~ suffisant** ample, more than enough
ampleur [ɑ̃plœʀ] NF scale, size; (*de dégâts, problème*) extent, magnitude
ampli [ɑ̃pli] NM (*fam*: = *amplificateur*) amplifier, amp
amplificateur [ɑ̃plifikatœʀ] NM amplifier
amplification [ɑ̃plifikasjɔ̃] NF amplification; expansion, increase
amplifier [ɑ̃plifje] /7/ VT (*son, oscillation*) to amplify; (*fig*) to expand, increase
amplitude [ɑ̃plityd] NF amplitude; (*des températures*) range
ampoule [ɑ̃pul] NF (*électrique*) bulb; (*de médicament*) phial; (*aux mains, pieds*) blister
ampoulé, e [ɑ̃pule] ADJ (*péj*) pompous, bombastic
amputation [ɑ̃pytasjɔ̃] NF amputation
amputer [ɑ̃pyte] /1/ VT (*Méd*) to amputate; (*fig*) to cut *ou* reduce drastically; **~ qn d'un bras/ pied** to amputate sb's arm/foot
Amsterdam [amstɛʀdam] N Amsterdam
amulette [amylɛt] NF amulet
amusant, e [amyzɑ̃, -ɑ̃t] ADJ (*divertissant, spirituel*) entertaining, amusing; (*comique*) funny, amusing
amusé, e [amyze] ADJ amused
amuse-gueule [amyzgœl] NM INV appetizer, snack
amusement [amyzmɑ̃] NM (*voir amusé*) amusement; (*voir amuser*) entertaining, amusing; (*jeu etc*) pastime, diversion
amuser [amyze] /1/ VT (*divertir*) to entertain, amuse; (*égayer, faire rire*) to amuse; (*détourner l'attention de*) to distract; **s'amuser** VI (*jouer*) to amuse o.s., play; (*se divertir*) to enjoy o.s., have fun; (*fig*) to mess around; **s'amuser de qch** (*trouver comique*) to find sth amusing; **s'amuser avec** *ou* **de qn** (*duper*) to make a fool of sb
amusette [amyzɛt] NF idle pleasure, trivial pastime
amuseur [amyzœʀ] NM entertainer; (*péj*) clown
amygdale [amidal] NF tonsil; **opérer qn des amygdales** to take sb's tonsils out
amygdalite [amidalit] NF tonsillitis
AN SIGLE F = **Assemblée nationale**
an [ɑ̃] NM year; **être âgé de** *ou* **avoir 3 ans** to be 3 (years old); **en l'an 1980** in the year 1980; **le jour de l'an, le premier de l'an, le nouvel an** New Year's Day

anabolisant [anabɔlizɑ̃] NM anabolic steroid
anachronique [anakrɔnik] ADJ anachronistic
anachronisme [anakrɔnism] NM
anachronism
anaconda [anakɔ̃da] NM (Zool) anaconda
anaérobie [anaerɔbi] ADJ anaerobic
anagramme [anagram] NF anagram
ANAH SIGLE F = **Agence nationale pour
l'amélioration de l'habitat**
anal, e, -aux [anal, -o] ADJ anal
analgésique [analʒezik] NM analgesic
anallergique [analɛrʒik] ADJ hypoallergenic
analogie [analɔʒi] NF analogy
analogique [analɔʒik] ADJ (Logique: raisonnement)
analogical; (: calculateur, montre etc) analogue;
(Inform) analog
analogue [analɔg] ADJ: **~ (à)** analogous (to),
similar (to)
analphabète [analfabɛt] NMF illiterate
analphabétisme [analfabetism] NM illiteracy
analyse [analiz] NF analysis; (Méd) test; **faire
l'~ de** to analyse; **une ~ approfondie** an
in-depth analysis; **en dernière ~** in the last
analysis; **avoir l'esprit d'~** to have an
analytical turn of mind; **~ grammaticale**
grammatical analysis, parsing (Scol)
analyser [analize] /1/ VT to analyse; (Méd) to
test
analyste [analist] NMF analyst; (psychanalyste)
(psycho)analyst
analyste-programmeur, -euse [analist-]
(pl **analystes-programmeurs, analystes-
programmeuses**) NM/F systems analyst
analytique [analitik] ADJ analytical
analytiquement [analitikmɑ̃] ADV analytically
ananas [anana(s)] NM pineapple
anarchie [anarʃi] NF anarchy
anarchique [anarʃik] ADJ anarchic
anarchisme [anarʃism] NM anarchism
anarchiste [anarʃist] ADJ anarchistic ▶ NMF
anarchist
anathème [anatɛm] NM: **jeter l'~ sur, lancer
l'~ contre** to anathematize, curse
anatomie [anatɔmi] NF anatomy
anatomique [anatɔmik] ADJ anatomical
ancestral, e, -aux [ɑ̃sɛstral, -o] ADJ ancestral
ancêtre [ɑ̃sɛtr] NMF ancestor; (fig): **l'~ de** the
forerunner of
anche [ɑ̃ʃ] NF reed
anchois [ɑ̃ʃwa] NM anchovy
ancien, ne [ɑ̃sjɛ̃, -jɛn] ADJ old; (de jadis, de
l'antiquité) ancient; (précédent, ex-) former, old;
(par l'expérience) senior ▶ NM (mobilier ancien): **l'~**
antiques pl ▶ NM/F (dans une tribu etc) elder; **un ~
ministre** a former minister; **mon ~ voiture**
my previous car; **être plus ~ que qn dans une
maison** to have been in a firm longer than sb;
(dans la hiérarchie) to be senior to sb in a firm;
~ combattant ex-serviceman; **~ (élève)** (Scol)
ex-pupil (BRIT), alumnus (US)
anciennement [ɑ̃sjɛnmɑ̃] ADV formerly
ancienneté [ɑ̃sjɛnte] NF oldness; antiquity;
(Admin) (length of) service; (privilèges obtenus)
seniority

ancrage [ɑ̃kraʒ] NM anchoring; (Navig)
anchorage; (Constr) anchor
ancre [ɑ̃kr] NF anchor; **jeter/lever l'~** to cast/
weigh anchor; **à l'~** at anchor
ancrer [ɑ̃kre] /1/ VT (Constr: câble etc) to anchor;
(fig) to fix firmly; **s'ancrer** VI (Navig) to (cast)
anchor
andalou, -ouse [ɑ̃dalu, -uz] ADJ Andalusian
Andalousie [ɑ̃daluzi] NF: **l'~** Andalusia
andante [ɑ̃dɑ̃t] ADV, NM andante
Andes [ɑ̃d] NFPL: **les ~** the Andes
Andorre [ɑ̃dɔr] NF Andorra
andouille [ɑ̃duj] NF (Culin) sausage made of
chitterlings; (fam) clot, nit
andouillette [ɑ̃dujɛt] NF small andouille
âne [ɑn] NM donkey, ass; (péj) dunce, fool
anéantir [aneɑ̃tir] /2/ VT to annihilate, wipe
out; (fig) to obliterate, destroy; (déprimer) to
overwhelm
anecdote [anɛkdɔt] NF anecdote
anecdotique [anɛkdɔtik] ADJ anecdotal
anémie [anemi] NF anaemia
anémié, e [anemje] ADJ anaemic; (fig) enfeebled
anémique [anemik] ADJ anaemic
anémone [anemɔn] NF anemone; **~ de mer** sea
anemone
ânerie [ɑnri] NF stupidity; (parole etc) stupid ou
idiotic comment etc
anéroïde [anerɔid] ADJ voir **baromètre**
ânesse [ɑnɛs] NF she-ass
anesthésie [anɛstezi] NF anaesthesia; **sous ~**
under anaesthetic; **~ générale/locale** general/
local anaesthetic; **faire une ~ locale à qn** to
give sb a local anaesthetic
anesthésier [anɛstezje] /7/ VT to anaesthetize
anesthésique [anɛstezik] ADJ anaesthetic
anesthésiste [anɛstezist] NMF anaesthetist
anfractuosité [ɑ̃fraktɥozite] NF crevice
ange [ɑ̃ʒ] NM angel; **être aux anges** to be over
the moon; **~ gardien** guardian angel
angélique [ɑ̃ʒelik] ADJ angelic(al) ▶ NF angelica
angelot [ɑ̃ʒlo] NM cherub
angélus [ɑ̃ʒelys] NM angelus; (cloches) evening
bells pl
angevin, e [ɑ̃ʒvɛ̃, -in] ADJ of ou from Anjou; of ou
from Angers
angine [ɑ̃ʒin] NF sore throat, throat infection;
~ de poitrine angina (pectoris)
angiome [ɑ̃ʒjom] NM angioma
anglais, e [ɑ̃glɛ, -ɛz] ADJ English ▶ NM (Ling)
English ▶ NM/F: **A~, e** Englishman/woman;
les A~ the English; **filer à l'~** to take French
leave; **à l'~** (Culin) boiled
anglaises [ɑ̃glɛz] NFPL (cheveux) ringlets
angle [ɑ̃gl] NM angle; (coin) corner; **~ droit/
obtus/aigu/mort** right/obtuse/acute/dead
angle
Angleterre [ɑ̃glətɛr] NF: **l'~** England
anglican, e [ɑ̃glikɑ̃, -an] ADJ, NM/F Anglican
anglicanisme [ɑ̃glikanism] NM Anglicanism
anglicisme [ɑ̃glisism] NM anglicism
angliciste [ɑ̃glisist] NMF English scholar;
(étudiant) student of English
anglo... [ɑ̃glɔ] PRÉFIXE Anglo-, Anglo(-)

anglo-américain, e [ɑ̃glɔameʀikɛ̃, -ɛn] ADJ
Anglo-American ▸ NM (*Ling*) American English
anglo-arabe [ɑ̃glɔaʀab] ADJ Anglo-Arab
anglo-canadien, ne [ɑ̃glɔkanadjɛ̃, -ɛn] ADJ
Anglo-Canadian ▸ NM (*Ling*) Canadian English
anglo-normand, e [ɑ̃glɔnɔʀmɑ̃, -ɑ̃d] ADJ
Anglo-Norman; **les îles anglo-normandes**
the Channel Islands
anglophile [ɑ̃glɔfil] ADJ Anglophilic
anglophobe [ɑ̃glɔfɔb] ADJ Anglophobic
anglophone [ɑ̃glɔfɔn] ADJ English-speaking
anglo-saxon, ne [ɑ̃glɔsaksɔ̃, -ɔn] ADJ
Anglo-Saxon
angoissant, e [ɑ̃gwasɑ̃, -ɑ̃t] ADJ harrowing
angoisse [ɑ̃gwas] NF: **l'~** anguish *no pl*
angoissé, e [ɑ̃gwase] ADJ anguished; (*personne*)
distressed
angoisser [ɑ̃gwase] /**1**/ VT to harrow, cause
anguish to ▸ VI to worry, fret
Angola [ɑ̃gɔla] NM: **l'~** Angola
angolais, e [ɑ̃gɔlɛ, -ɛz] ADJ Angolan
angora [ɑ̃gɔʀa] ADJ, NM angora
anguille [ɑ̃gij] NF eel; **~ de mer** conger (eel); **il y
a ~ sous roche** (*fig*) there's something going
on, there's something beneath all this
angulaire [ɑ̃gylɛʀ] ADJ angular
anguleux, -euse [ɑ̃gylø, -øz] ADJ angular
anhydride [anidʀid] NM anhydride
anicroche [anikʀɔʃ] NF hitch, snag
animal, e, -aux [animal, -o] ADJ, NM animal;
~ domestique/sauvage domestic/wild animal
animalier, -ière [animalje, -jɛʀ] ADJ: **peintre ~**
animal painter
animateur, -trice [animatœʀ, -tʀis] NM/F (*de
télévision*) host; (*de music-hall*) compère; (*de
groupe*) leader, organizer; (*Ciné: technicien*)
animator
animation [animasjɔ̃] NF (*voir animé*) busyness,
liveliness; (*Ciné: technique*) animation;
animations NFPL (*activité*) activities; **centre d'~**
≈ community centre
animé, e [anime] ADJ (*rue, lieu*) busy, lively;
(*conversation, réunion*) lively, animated; (*opposé à
inanimé, aussi Ling*) animate
animer [anime] /**1**/ VT (*ville, soirée*) to liven up,
enliven; (*mettre en mouvement*) to drive; (*stimuler*)
to drive, impel; **s'animer** VI to liven up, come to
life
animosité [animozite] NF animosity
anis [ani(s)] NM (*Culin*) aniseed; (*Bot*) anise
anisette [anizɛt] NF anisette
Ankara [ɑ̃kaʀa] N Ankara
ankyloser [ɑ̃kiloze] /**1**/: **s'ankyloser** VI to get stiff
annales [anal] NFPL annals
anneau, x [ano] NM (*de rideau, bague*) ring; (*de
chaîne*) link; (*Sport*): **exercices aux ~** ring
exercises; **~ gastrique** (*Méd*) gastric band
année [ane] NF year; **souhaiter la bonne ~ à
qn** to wish sb a Happy New Year; **tout au long
de l'~** all year long; **d'une ~ à l'autre** from one
year to the next; **d'~ en ~** from year to year; **l'~
scolaire/fiscale** the school/tax year
année-lumière [anelymjɛʀ] (*pl* **années-
lumières**) NF light year

annexe [anɛks] ADJ (*problème*) related; (*document*)
appended; (*salle*) adjoining ▸ NF (*bâtiment*)
annex(e); (*de document, ouvrage*) annex,
appendix; (*jointe à une lettre, un dossier*) enclosure
annexer [anɛkse] /**1**/ VT to annex; **s'annexer**
(*pays*) to annex; **~ qch à** (*joindre*) to append
sth to
annexion [anɛksjɔ̃] NF annexation
annihiler [aniile] /**1**/ VT to annihilate
anniversaire [anivɛʀsɛʀ] NM birthday; (*d'un
événement, bâtiment*) anniversary ▸ ADJ: **jour ~**
anniversary
annonce [anɔ̃s] NF announcement; (*signe,
indice*) sign; (*aussi*: **annonce publicitaire**)
advertisement; (*Cartes*) declaration;
~ personnelle personal message; **les petites
annonces** the small *ou* classified ads
annoncer [anɔ̃se] /**3**/ VT to announce; (*être le
signe de*) to herald; (*Cartes*) to declare; **je vous
annonce que …** I wish to tell you that …;
s'annoncer bien/difficile VI to look promising/
difficult; **~ la couleur** (*fig*) to lay one's cards on
the table
annonceur, -euse [anɔ̃sœʀ, -øz] NM/F (*TV,
Radio: speaker*) announcer; (*publicitaire*) advertiser
annonciateur, -trice [anɔ̃sjatœʀ, -tʀis] ADJ:
~ d'un événement presaging an event
Annonciation [anɔ̃sjasjɔ̃] NF: **l'~** (*Rel*) the
Annunciation; (*jour*) Annunciation Day
annotation [anɔtasjɔ̃] NF annotation
annoter [anɔte] /**1**/ VT to annotate
annuaire [anɥɛʀ] NM yearbook, annual;
~ téléphonique (telephone) directory, phone
book
annuel, le [anɥɛl] ADJ annual, yearly
annuellement [anɥɛlmɑ̃] ADV annually, yearly
annuité [anɥite] NF annual instalment
annulaire [anɥlɛʀ] NM ring *ou* third finger
annulation [anylasjɔ̃] NF cancellation;
annulment; quashing, repeal
annuler [anyle] /**1**/ VT (*rendez-vous, voyage*) to
cancel, call off; (*mariage*) to annul; (*jugement*) to
quash (BRIT), repeal (US); (*résultats*) to declare
void; (*Math, Physique*) to cancel out; **s'annuler** to
cancel each other out
anoblir [anɔbliʀ] /**2**/ VT to ennoble
anode [anɔd] NF anode
anodin, e [anɔdɛ̃, -in] ADJ harmless; (*sans
importance*) insignificant, trivial
anomalie [anɔmali] NF anomaly
ânon [ɑnɔ̃] NM baby donkey; (*petit âne*) little
donkey
ânonner [ɑnɔne] /**1**/ VI, VT to read in a drone;
(*hésiter*) to read in a fumbling manner
anonymat [anɔnima] NM anonymity; **garder
l'~** to remain anonymous
anonyme [anɔnim] ADJ anonymous; (*fig*)
impersonal
anonymement [anɔnimmɑ̃] ADV anonymously
anorak [anɔʀak] NM anorak
anorexie [anɔʀɛksi] NF anorexia
anorexique [anɔʀɛksik] ADJ, NMF anorexic
anormal, e, -aux [anɔʀmal, -o] ADJ abnormal;
(*insolite*) unusual, abnormal

anormalement [anɔʀmalmɑ̃] ADV abnormally; unusually

ANPE SIGLE F (= *Agence nationale pour l'emploi*) national employment agency (functions include job creation)

anse [ɑ̃s] NF handle; (*Géo*) cove

antagonisme [ɑ̃tagɔnism] NM antagonism

antagoniste [ɑ̃tagɔnist] ADJ antagonistic ▶ NM antagonist

antan [ɑ̃tɑ̃]: **d'~** *adj* of yesteryear, of long ago

antarctique [ɑ̃taʀktik] ADJ Antarctic ▶ NM: **l'A~** the Antarctic; **le cercle A~** the Antarctic Circle; **l'océan A~** the Antarctic Ocean

antécédent [ɑ̃tesedɑ̃] NM (*Ling*) antecedent; **antécédents** NMPL (*Méd etc*) past history *sg*; **antécédents professionnels** record, career to date

antédiluvien, ne [ɑ̃tedilyvjɛ̃, -ɛn] ADJ (*fig*) ancient, antediluvian

antenne [ɑ̃tɛn] NF (*de radio, télévision*) aerial; (*d'insecte*) antenna, feeler; (*poste avancé*) outpost; (*petite succursale*) sub-branch; **sur l'~** on the air; **passer à/avoir l'~** to go/be on the air; **deux heures d'~** two hours' broadcasting time; **hors ~** off the air; **~ chirurgicale** (*Mil*) advance surgical unit; **~ parabolique** satellite dish; **~-relais** mobile phone mast (BRIT), cell tower (US)

antépénultième [ɑ̃tepenyltjɛm] ADJ antepenultimate

antérieur, e [ɑ̃teʀjœʀ] ADJ (*d'avant*) previous, earlier; (*de devant*) front; **~ à** prior *ou* previous to; **passé/futur ~** (*Ling*) past/future anterior

antérieurement [ɑ̃teʀjœʀmɑ̃] ADV earlier; (*précédemment*) previously; **~ à** prior *ou* previous to

antériorité [ɑ̃teʀjɔʀite] NF precedence (*in time*)

anthologie [ɑ̃tɔlɔʒi] NF anthology

anthracite [ɑ̃tʀasit] NM anthracite ▶ ADJ: **(gris) ~** charcoal (grey)

anthropologie [ɑ̃tʀɔpɔlɔʒi] NF anthropology

anthropologue [ɑ̃tʀɔpɔlɔg] NMF anthropologist

anthropomorphisme [ɑ̃tʀɔpɔmɔʀfism] NM anthropomorphism

anthropophage [ɑ̃tʀɔpɔfaʒ] ADJ cannibalistic

anthropophagie [ɑ̃tʀɔpɔfaʒi] NF cannibalism, anthropophagy

anti... [ɑ̃ti] PRÉFIXE anti...

antiaérien, ne [ɑ̃tiaeʀjɛ̃, -ɛn] ADJ anti-aircraft; **abri ~** air-raid shelter

antialcoolique [ɑ̃tialkɔlik] ADJ anti-alcohol; **ligue ~** temperance league

antiatomique [ɑ̃tiatɔmik] ADJ: **abri ~** fallout shelter

antibiotique [ɑ̃tibjɔtik] NM antibiotic

antibrouillard [ɑ̃tibʀujaʀ] ADJ: **phare ~** fog lamp

antibruit [ɑ̃tibʀɥi] ADJ INV: **mur ~** (*sur autoroute*) sound-muffling wall

antibuée [ɑ̃tibɥe] ADJ INV: **dispositif ~** demister; **bombe ~** demister spray

anticancéreux, -euse [ɑ̃tikɑ̃seʀø, -øz] ADJ cancer *cpd*

anticasseur, anticasseurs [ɑ̃tikɑsœʀ] ADJ: **loi/mesure ~(s)** law/measure against damage done by demonstrators

antichambre [ɑ̃tiʃɑ̃bʀ] NF antechamber, anteroom; **faire ~** to wait (for an audience)

antichar [ɑ̃tiʃaʀ] ADJ antitank

antichoc [ɑ̃tiʃɔk] ADJ shockproof

anticipation [ɑ̃tisipasjɔ̃] NF anticipation; (*Comm*) payment in advance; **par ~** in anticipation, in advance; **livre/film d'~** science fiction book/film

anticipé, e [ɑ̃tisipe] ADJ (*règlement, paiement*) early, in advance; (*joie etc*) anticipated, early; **avec mes remerciements anticipés** thanking you in advance *ou* anticipation

anticiper [ɑ̃tisipe] /1/ VT (*événement, coup*) to anticipate, foresee; (*paiement*) to pay *ou* make in advance ▶ VI to look *ou* think ahead; (*en racontant*) to jump ahead; (*prévoir*) to anticipate; **~ sur** to anticipate

anticlérical, e, -aux [ɑ̃tikleʀikal, -o] ADJ anticlerical

anticoagulant, e [ɑ̃tikɔagylɑ̃, -ɑ̃t] ADJ, NM anticoagulant

anticolonialisme [ɑ̃tikɔlɔnjalism] NM anticolonialism

anticonceptionnel, le [ɑ̃tikɔ̃sɛpsjɔnɛl] ADJ contraceptive

anticonformisme [ɑ̃tikɔ̃fɔrmism] NM nonconformism

anticonstitutionnel, le [ɑ̃tikɔ̃stitysjɔnɛl] ADJ unconstitutional

anticorps [ɑ̃tikɔʀ] NM antibody

anticyclone [ɑ̃tisiklon] NM anticyclone

antidater [ɑ̃tidate] /1/ VT to backdate, predate

antidémocratique [ɑ̃tidemɔkʀatik] ADJ antidemocratic; (*peu démocratique*) undemocratic

antidépresseur [ɑ̃tidepʀesœʀ] NM antidepressant

antidérapant, e [ɑ̃tideʀapɑ̃, -ɑ̃t] ADJ nonskid

antidopage [ɑ̃tidɔpaʒ], **antidoping** [ɑ̃tidɔpiŋ] ADJ (*lutte*) antidoping; (*contrôle*) dope *cpd*

antidote [ɑ̃tidɔt] NM antidote

antienne [ɑ̃tjɛn] NF (*fig*) chant, refrain

antigang [ɑ̃tigɑ̃g] ADJ INV: **brigade ~** commando unit

antigel [ɑ̃tiʒɛl] NM antifreeze

antigène [ɑ̃tiʒɛn] NM antigen

antigouvernemental, e, -aux [ɑ̃tiguvɛʀnəmɑ̃tal, -o] ADJ antigovernment

Antigua et Barbude [ɑ̃tigaebaʀbyd] NF Antigua and Barbuda

antihistaminique [ɑ̃tiistaminik] NM antihistamine

anti-inflammatoire [ɑ̃tiɛ̃flamatwaʀ] ADJ anti-inflammatory

anti-inflationniste [ɑ̃tiɛ̃flasjɔnist] ADJ anti-inflationary

antillais, e [ɑ̃tijɛ, -ɛz] ADJ West Indian, Caribbean ▶ NM/F: **A~, e** West Indian, Caribbean

Antilles [ɑ̃tij] NFPL: **les ~** the West Indies; **les Grandes/Petites ~** the Greater/Lesser Antilles

antilope [ãtilɔp] NF antelope

antimilitarisme [ãtimilitaRism] NM antimilitarism

antimilitariste [ãtimilitaRist] ADJ antimilitarist

antimissile [ãtimisil] ADJ antimissile

antimite(s) [ãtimit] ADJ, NM: **(produit)** **antimite(s)** moth proofer, moth repellent

antimondialisation [ãtimõdjalizasjõ] NF anti-globalization

antinucléaire [ãtinykleɛR] ADJ antinuclear

antioxydant [ãtiɔksidã] NM antioxidant

antiparasite [ãtipaRazit] ADJ (Radio, TV) anti-interference; **dispositif ~** suppressor

antipathie [ãtipati] NF antipathy

antipathique [ãtipatik] ADJ unpleasant, disagreeable

antipelliculaire [ãtipelikylɛR] ADJ anti-dandruff

antiphrase [ãtifRaz] NF: **par ~** ironically

antipodes [ãtipɔd] NMPL (Géo): **les ~** the antipodes; (fig): **être aux ~ de** to be the opposite extreme of

antipoison [ãtipwazõ] ADJ INV: **centre ~** poison centre

antipoliomyélitique [ãtipɔljɔmjelitik] ADJ polio cpd

antiquaire [ãtikɛR] NMF antique dealer

antique [ãtik] ADJ antique; (très vieux) ancient, antiquated

antiquité [ãtikite] NF (objet) antique; **l'A~** Antiquity; **magasin/marchand d'antiquités** antique shop/dealer

antirabique [ãtiRabik] ADJ rabies cpd

antiraciste [ãtiRasist] ADJ antiracist, anti racialist

antireflet [ãtiRəflɛ] ADJ INV (verres) antireflective

antirépublicain, e [ãtiRepyblikɛ̃, -ɛn] ADJ antirepublican

antirides [ãtiRid] ADJ INV (crème) anti wrinkle

antirouille [ãtiRuj] ADJ INV anti-rust cpd; **peinture ~** antirust paint; **traitement ~** rustproofing

antisémite [ãtisemit] ADJ anti-Semitic

antisémitisme [ãtisemitism] NM anti-Semitism

antiseptique [ãtisɛptik] ADJ, NM antiseptic

antisocial, e, -aux [ãtisɔsjal, -o] ADJ antisocial

antispasmodique [ãtispasmɔdik] ADJ, NM antispasmodic

antisportif, -ive [ãtispɔRtif, -iv] ADJ unsporting; (hostile au sport) antisport

antitétanique [ãtitetanik] ADJ tetanus cpd

antithèse [ãtitɛz] NF antithesis

antitrust [ãtitRœst] ADJ INV (loi, mesures) antimonopoly

antituberculeux, -euse [ãtitybɛRkylø, -øz] ADJ tuberculosis cpd

antitussif, -ive [ãtitysif, -iv] ADJ antitussive, cough cpd

antivariolique [ãtivaRjɔlik] ADJ smallpox cpd

antiviral, e, -aux [ãtiviral, -o] ADJ (Méd) antiviral

antivirus [ãtiviRys] NM (Inform) antivirus (program)

antivol [ãtivɔl] ADJ, NM: **(dispositif) ~** antitheft device; (pour vélo) padlock

antonyme [ãtɔnim] NM antonym

antre [ãtR] NM den, lair

anus [anys] NM anus

Anvers [ãvɛR] N Antwerp

anxiété [ãksjete] NF anxiety

anxieusement [ãksjøzmã] ADV anxiously

anxieux, -euse [ãksjø, -jøz] ADJ anxious, worried; **être ~ de faire** to be anxious to do

AOC SIGLE F (= Appellation d'origine contrôlée) guarantee of quality of wine; see note

> AOC (appellation d'origine contrôlée) is the highest French wine classification. It indicates that the wine meets strict requirements concerning vineyard of origin, type of grape, method of production and alcoholic strength.

aorte [aɔRt] NF aorta

août [u(t)] NM August; voir aussi **Assomption**; **juillet**

aoûtien, ne [ausjɛ̃, -ɛn] NM/F August holiday-maker

AP SIGLE F = **Assistance publique**

apaisant, e [apɛzã, -ãt] ADJ soothing

apaisement [apɛzmã] NM calming; soothing; (aussi Pol) appeasement; **apaisements** NMPL soothing reassurances; (pour calmer) pacifying words

apaiser [apeze] /1/ VT (colère) to calm, quell, soothe; (faim) to appease, assuage; (douleur) to soothe; (personne) to calm (down), pacify; **s'apaiser** VI (tempête, bruit) to die down, subside; (personne) to calm down

apanage [apanaʒ] NM: **être l'~ de** to be the privilege ou prerogative of

aparté [apaRte] NM (Théât) aside; (entretien) private conversation; **en ~** adv in an aside (BRIT); (entretien) in private

apartheid [apaRtɛd] NM apartheid

apathie [apati] NF apathy

apathique [apatik] ADJ apathetic

apatride [apatRid] NMF stateless person

APCE SIGLE F (= Agence pour la création d'entreprises) business start-up agency

apercevoir [apɛRsəvwaR] /28/ VT to see; **s'apercevoir de** VT to notice; **s'apercevoir que** to notice that; **sans s'en apercevoir** without realizing ou noticing

aperçu, e [apɛRsy] PP de **apercevoir** ▸ NM (vue d'ensemble) general survey; (intuition) insight

apéritif, -ive [apeRitif, -iv] ADJ which stimulates the appetite ▸ NM (boisson) aperitif; (réunion) (pre-lunch ou -dinner) drinks pl; **prendre l'~** to have drinks (before lunch ou dinner) ou an aperitif

apesanteur [apəzãtœR] NF weightlessness

à-peu-près [apøpRɛ] NM INV (péj) vague approximation

apeuré, e [apœRe] ADJ frightened, scared

aphasie [afazi] NF aphasia

aphone [afɔn] ADJ voiceless

aphorisme [afɔʀism] NM aphorism

aphrodisiaque [afʀɔdizjak] ADJ, NM aphrodisiac

aphte [aft] NM mouth ulcer

aphteuse [aftøz] ADJ F: **fièvre ~** foot-and-mouth disease

à-pic [apik] NM cliff, drop

apicole [apikɔl] ADJ beekeeping *cpd*

apiculteur, -trice [apikyltœʀ, -tʀis] NM/F beekeeper

apiculture [apikyltyʀ] NF beekeeping, apiculture

apitoiement [apitwamɑ̃] NM pity, compassion

apitoyer [apitwaje] /8/ VT to move to pity; **~ qn sur qn/qch** to move sb to pity for sb/over sth; **s'~ (sur qn/qch)** to feel pity *ou* compassion (for sb/over sth)

ap. J.-C. ABR (= *après Jésus-Christ*) AD

APL SIGLE F (= *aide personnalisée au logement*) *housing benefit*

aplanir [aplaniʀ] /2/ VT to level; (*fig*) to smooth away, iron out

aplati, e [aplati] ADJ flat, flattened

aplatir [aplatiʀ] /2/ VT to flatten; **s'aplatir** VI to become flatter; (*écrasé*) to be flattened; (*fig*) to lie flat on the ground; (: *fam*) to fall flat on one's face; (: *péj*) to grovel

aplomb [aplɔ̃] NM (*équilibre*) balance, equilibrium; (*fig*) self-assurance; (: *péj*) nerve; **d'~** *adv* steady; (*Constr*) plumb

APN SIGLE M (= *appareil photo(graphique) numérique*) digital camera

apocalypse [apɔkalips] NF apocalypse

apocalyptique [apɔkaliptik] ADJ (*fig*) apocalyptic

apocryphe [apɔkʀif] ADJ apocryphal

apogée [apɔʒe] NM (*fig*) peak, apogee

apolitique [apɔlitik] ADJ (*indifférent*) apolitical; (*indépendant*) unpolitical, non-political

apologie [apɔlɔʒi] NF praise; (*Jur*) vindication

apoplexie [apɔplɛksi] NF apoplexy

a posteriori [apɔsteʀjɔʀi] ADV after the event, with hindsight, a posteriori

apostolat [apɔstɔla] NM (*Rel*) apostolate, discipleship; (*gén*) evangelism

apostolique [apɔstɔlik] ADJ apostolic

apostrophe [apɔstʀɔf] NF (*signe*) apostrophe; (*appel*) interpellation

apostropher [apɔstʀɔfe] /1/ VT (*interpeller*) to shout at, address sharply

apothéose [apɔteoz] NF pinnacle (of achievement); (*Mus etc*) grand finale

apothicaire [apɔtikɛʀ] NM apothecary

apôtre [apotʀ] NM apostle, disciple

apparaître [apaʀɛtʀ] /57/ VI to appear ▸ VB COPULE to appear, seem

apparat [apaʀa] NM: **tenue/dîner d'~** ceremonial dress/dinner

appareil [apaʀɛj] NM (*outil, machine*) piece of apparatus, device; (*électrique etc*) appliance; (*politique, syndical*) machinery; (*avion*) (aero)plane (BRIT), (air)plane (US), aircraft *inv*; (*téléphonique*) telephone; (*dentier*) brace (BRIT), braces (US); **~ digestif/reproducteur**

digestive/reproductive system *ou* apparatus; **l'~ productif** the means of production; **qui est à l'~?** who's speaking?; **dans le plus simple ~** in one's birthday suit; **~ (photo)** camera; **~ numérique** digital camera

appareillage [apaʀɛjaʒ] NM (*appareils*) equipment; (*Navig*) casting off, getting under way

appareiller [apaʀeje] /1/ VI (*Navig*) to cast off, get under way ▸ VT (*assortir*) to match up

appareil photo [apaʀɛjfɔto] (*pl* **appareils photos**) NM camera

apparemment [apaʀamɑ̃] ADV apparently

apparence [apaʀɑ̃s] NF appearance; **malgré les apparences** despite appearances; **en ~** apparently, seemingly

apparent, e [apaʀɑ̃, -ɑ̃t] ADJ visible; (*évident*) obvious; (*superficiel*) apparent; **coutures apparentes** topstitched seams; **poutres apparentes** exposed beams

apparenté, e [apaʀɑ̃te] ADJ: **~ à** related to; (*fig*) similar to

apparenter [apaʀɑ̃te] /1/: **s'apparenter à** VT to be similar to

apparier [apaʀje] /7/ VT (*gants*) to pair, match

appariteur [apaʀitœʀ] NM attendant, porter (*in French universities*)

apparition [apaʀisjɔ̃] NF appearance; (*surnaturelle*) apparition; **faire son ~** to appear

appartement [apaʀtəmɑ̃] NM flat (BRIT), apartment (US)

appartenance [apaʀtənɑ̃s] NF: **~ à** belonging to, membership of

appartenir [apaʀtəniʀ] /22/: **~ à** vt to belong to; (*faire partie de*) to belong to, be a member of; **il lui appartient de** it is up to him to

appartiendrai [apaʀtjɛ̃dʀe], **appartiens** *etc* [apaʀtjɛ̃] VB *voir* **appartenir**

apparu, e [apaʀy] PP *de* **apparaître**

appas [apɑ] NMPL (*d'une femme*) charms

appât [apɑ] NM (*Pêche*) bait; (*fig*) lure, bait

appâter [apate] /1/ VT (*hameçon*) to bait; (*poisson, fig*) to lure, entice

appauvrir [apovʀiʀ] /2/ VT to impoverish; **s'appauvrir** VI to grow poorer, become impoverished

appauvrissement [apovʀismɑ̃] NM impoverishment

appel [apɛl] NM call; (*nominal*) roll call; (: *Scol*) register; (*Mil: recrutement*) call-up; (*Jur*) appeal; **faire ~ à** (*invoquer*) to appeal to; (*avoir recours à*) to call on; (*nécessiter*) to call for, require; **faire** *ou* **interjeter ~** (*Jur*) to appeal, lodge an appeal; **faire l'~** to call the roll; (*Scol*) to call the register; **indicatif d'~** call sign; **numéro d'~** (*Tél*) number; **produit d'~** (*Comm*) loss leader; **sans ~** (*fig*) final, irrevocable; **~ d'air** in-draught; **~ d'offres** (*Comm*) invitation to tender; **faire un ~ de phares** to flash one's headlights; **~ (téléphonique)** (tele)phone call

appelé [ap(ə)le] NM (*Mil*) conscript

appeler [ap(ə)le] /4/ VT (*gén*) to call; (*Tél*) to call, ring; (*faire venir: médecin etc*) to call, send for; (*fig: nécessiter*) to call for, demand; **s'appeler** VI: **elle**

s'appelle Gabrielle her name is Gabrielle, she's called Gabrielle; **comment vous appelez-vous?** what's your name?; **comment ça s'appelle?** what is it *ou* that called?; **~ au secours** to call for help; **~ qn à l'aide** *ou* **secours** to call to sb for help; **~ qn à un poste/des fonctions** to appoint sb to a post/assign duties to sb; **être appelé à** (*fig*) to be destined to; **~ qn à comparaître** (*Jur*) to summon sb to appear; **en ~ à** to appeal to

appellation [apelasjɔ̃] NF designation, appellation; **vin d'~ contrôlée** "appellation contrôlée" wine, *wine guaranteed of a certain quality*

appelle *etc* [apɛl] VB *voir* **appeler**

appendice [apɛ̃dis] NM appendix

appendicite [apɑ̃disit] NF appendicitis

appentis [apɑ̃ti] NM lean-to

appert [apɛʀ] VB: **il ~ que** it appears that, it is evident that

appesantir [apəzɑ̃tiʀ] /2/: **s'appesantir** VI to grow heavier; **s'appesantir sur** (*fig*) to dwell at length on

appétissant, e [apetisɑ̃, -ɑ̃t] ADJ appetizing, mouth-watering

appétit [apeti] NM appetite; **couper l'~ à qn** to take away sb's appetite; **bon ~!** enjoy your meal!

applaudimètre [aplodimɛtʀ] NM applause meter

applaudir [aplodiʀ] /2/ VT to applaud ▸ VI to applaud, clap; **~ à** *vt* (*décision*) to applaud, commend

applaudissements [aplodismɑ̃] NMPL applause *sg*, clapping *sg*

appli [apli] NF app

applicable [aplikabl] ADJ applicable

applicateur [aplikatœʀ] NM applicator

application [aplikasjɔ̃] NF application; (*d'une loi*) enforcement; **mettre en ~ to** implement

applique [aplik] NF wall lamp

appliqué, e [aplike] ADJ (*élève etc*) industrious, assiduous; (*science*) applied

appliquer [aplike] /1/ VT to apply; (*loi*) to enforce; (*donner: gifle, châtiment*) to give; **s'appliquer** VI (*élève etc*) to apply o.s.; **s'appliquer à** (*loi, remarque*) to apply to; **s'appliquer à faire qch** to apply o.s. to doing sth, take pains in doing sth; **s'appliquer sur** (*coïncider avec*) to fit over

appoint [apwɛ̃] NM (extra) contribution *ou* help; **avoir/faire l'~** (*en payant*) to have/give the right change *ou* money; **chauffage d'~** extra heating

appointements [apwɛ̃tmɑ̃] NMPL salary *sg*, stipend

appointer [apwɛ̃te] /1/ VT: **être appointé à l'année/au mois** to be paid yearly/monthly

appontage [apɔ̃taʒ] NM landing (*on an aircraft carrier*)

appontement [apɔ̃tmɑ̃] NM landing stage, wharf

apponter [apɔ̃te] /1/ VI (*avion, hélicoptère*) to land

apport [apɔʀ] NM supply; (*argent, biens etc*) contribution

apporter [apɔʀte] /1/ VT to bring; (*preuve*) to give, provide; (*modification*) to make; (*remarque*) to contribute, add

apposer [apoze] /1/ VT to append; (*sceau etc*) to affix

apposition [apozisjɔ̃] NF appending; affixing; (*Ling*): **en ~** in apposition

appréciable [apʀesjabl] ADJ (*important*) appreciable, significant

appréciation [apʀesjasjɔ̃] NF appreciation; estimation, assessment; **appréciations** NFPL (*avis*) assessment *sg*, appraisal *sg*

apprécier [apʀesje] /7/ VT to appreciate; (*évaluer*) to estimate, assess; **j'apprécierais que tu ...** I should appreciate (it) if you ...

appréhender [apʀeɑ̃de] /1/ VT (*craindre*) to dread; (*arrêter*) to apprehend; **~ que** to fear that; **~ de faire** to dread doing

appréhensif, -ive [apʀeɑ̃sif, -iv] ADJ apprehensive

appréhension [apʀeɑ̃sjɔ̃] NF apprehension

apprendre [apʀɑ̃dʀ] /58/ VT to learn; (*événement, résultats*) to learn of, hear of; **~ qch à qn** (*informer*) to tell sb (of) sth; (*enseigner*) to teach sb sth; **tu me l'apprends!** that's news to me!; **~ à faire qch** to learn to do sth; **~ à qn à faire qch** to teach sb to do sth

apprenti, e [apʀɑ̃ti] NM/F apprentice; (*fig*) novice, beginner

apprentissage [apʀɑ̃tisaʒ] NM learning; (*Comm, Scol: période*) apprenticeship; **école** *ou* **centre d'~** training school *ou* centre; **faire l'~ de qch** (*fig*) to be initiated into sth

apprêt [apʀɛ] NM (*sur un cuir, une étoffe*) dressing; (*sur un mur*) size; (*sur un papier*) finish; **sans ~** (*fig*) without artifice, unaffectedly

apprêté, e [apʀete] ADJ (*fig*) affected

apprêter [apʀete] /1/ VT to dress, finish; **s'apprêter** VI: **s'apprêter à qch/à faire qch** to prepare for sth/for doing sth

appris, e [apʀi, -iz] PP *de* **apprendre**

apprivoisé, e [apʀivwaze] ADJ tame, tamed

apprivoiser [apʀivwaze] /1/ VT to tame

approbateur, -trice [apʀɔbatœʀ, -tʀis] ADJ approving

approbatif, -ive [apʀɔbatif, -iv] ADJ approving

approbation [apʀɔbasjɔ̃] NF approval; **digne d'~** (*conduite, travail*) praiseworthy, commendable

approchant, e [apʀɔʃɑ̃, -ɑ̃t] ADJ similar, close; **quelque chose d'~** something similar

approche [apʀɔʃ] NF approaching; (*arrivée, attitude*) approach; **approches** NFPL (*abords*) surroundings; **à l'~ du bateau/de l'ennemi** as the ship/enemy approached *ou* drew near; **l'~ d'un problème** the approach to a problem; **travaux d'~** (*fig*) manoeuvrings

approché, e [apʀɔʃe] ADJ approximate

approcher [apʀɔʃe] /1/ VI to approach, come near ▸ VT (*vedette, artiste*) to approach, come close to; (*rapprocher*): **~ qch (de qch)** to bring *ou* put *ou* move sth near (to sth); **s'approcher de** VT

23

to approach, go *ou* come *ou* move near to; **~ de** vt (*lieu, but*) to draw near to; (*quantité, moment*) to approach; **approchez-vous** come *ou* go nearer
approfondi, e [apʀɔfɔ̃di] ADJ thorough, detailed
approfondir [apʀɔfɔ̃diʀ] /2/ VT to deepen; (*question*) to go further into; **sans ~** without going too deeply into it
appropriation [apʀɔpʀijasjɔ̃] NF appropriation
approprié, e [apʀɔpʀije] ADJ: **~ (à)** appropriate (to), suited (to)
approprier [apʀɔpʀije] /7/ VT (*adapter*) adapt; **s'approprier** VT to appropriate, take over; **s'approprier en** to stock up with
approuver [apʀuve] /1/ VT to agree with; (*autoriser: loi, projet*) to approve, pass; (*trouver louable*) to approve of; **je vous approuve entièrement/ne vous approuve pas** I agree with you entirely/don't agree with you; **lu et approuvé** (read and) approved
approvisionnement [apʀɔvizjɔnmɑ̃] NM supplying; (*provisions*) supply, stock
approvisionner [apʀɔvizjɔne] /1/ VT to supply; (*compte bancaire*) to pay funds into; **~ qn en** to supply sb with; **s'approvisionner** VI: **s'approvisionner dans un certain magasin/au marché** to shop in a certain shop/at the market; **s'approvisionner en** to stock up with
approximatif, -ive [apʀɔksimatif, -iv] ADJ approximate, rough; (*imprécis*) vague
approximation [apʀɔksimasjɔ̃] NF approximation
approximativement [apʀɔksimativmɑ̃] ADV approximately, roughly; vaguely
appt ABR = **appartement**
appui [apɥi] NM support; **prendre ~ sur** to lean on; (*objet*) to rest on; **point d'~** fulcrum; (*fig*) something to lean on; **à l'~ de** (*pour prouver*) in support of; **à l'~** adv to support one's argument; **l'~ de la fenêtre** the windowsill, the window ledge
appuie etc [apɥi] VB voir **appuyer**
appui-tête, appuie-tête [apɥitɛt] NM INV headrest
appuyé, e [apɥije] ADJ (*regard*) meaningful; (: *insistant*) intent, insistent; (*excessif: politesse, compliment*) exaggerated, overdone
appuyer [apɥije] /8/ VT (*poser, soutenir: personne, demande*) to support, back (up) ▶ VI: **~ sur** (*bouton*) to press, push; (*mot, détail*) to stress, emphasize; **s'appuyer sur** VT (*chose: peser sur*) to rest (heavily) on, press against, to lean on; (*compter sur*) to rely on; **~ qch sur/contre/à** to lean *ou* rest sth on/against/on; **~ sur le frein** to brake, to apply the brakes; **~ sur le champignon** to put one's foot down; **~ contre** (*toucher: mur, porte*) to lean *ou* rest against; **~ à droite** *ou* **sur sa droite** to bear (to the) right; **s'appuyer sur qn** to lean on sb
apr. ABR = **après**
âpre [ɑpʀ] ADJ acrid, pungent; (*fig*) harsh; (*lutte*) bitter; **~ au gain** grasping, greedy
après [apʀɛ] PRÉP after ▶ ADV afterwards; **deux heures ~** two hours later; **~ qu'il est parti/avoir fait** after he left/having done; **courir ~**

qn to run after sb; **crier ~ qn** to shout at sb; **être toujours ~ qn** (*critiquer etc*) to be always on at sb; **~ quoi** after which; **d'~** prép (*selon*) according to; **d'~ lui** according to him; **d'~ moi** in my opinion; **~ coup** adv after the event, afterwards; **~ tout** (*au fond*) after all; **et (puis) ~?** so what?
après-demain [apʀɛdmɛ̃] ADV the day after tomorrow
après-guerre [apʀɛgɛʀ] NM post-war years pl; **d'~** adj post-war
après-midi [apʀɛmidi] NM OU F INV afternoon
après-rasage [apʀɛʀazaʒ] NM INV after-shave
après-shampooing [apʀɛʃɑ̃pwɛ̃] NM INV conditioner
après-ski [apʀɛski] NM INV (*chaussure*) snow boot; (*moment*) après-ski
après-soleil [apʀɛsɔlɛj] ADJ INV after-sun cpd ▶ NM after-sun cream *ou* lotion
après-vente [apʀɛvɑ̃t] ADJ INV after-sales cpd
âpreté [ɑpʀəte] NF (*voir âpre*) pungency; harshness; bitterness
à-propos [apʀopo] NM (*d'une remarque*) aptness; **faire preuve d'~** to show presence of mind, do the right thing; **avec ~** suitably, aptly
apte [apt] ADJ: **~ à qch/faire qch** capable of sth/ doing sth; **~ (au service)** (*Mil*) fit (for service)
aptitude [aptityd] NF ability, aptitude
apurer [apyʀe] /1/ VT (*Comm*) to clear
aquaculture [akwakyltyʀ] NF fish farming
aquaplanage [akwaplanaʒ] NM (*Auto*) aquaplaning
aquaplane [akwaplan] NM (*planche*) aquaplane; (*sport*) aquaplaning
aquaplaning [akwaplaniŋ] NM aquaplaning
aquarelle [akwaʀɛl] NF (*tableau*) watercolour (BRIT), watercolor (US); (*genre*) watercolo(u)rs pl, aquarelle
aquarelliste [akwaʀelist] NMF painter in watercolo(u)rs
aquarium [akwaʀjɔm] NM aquarium
aquatique [akwatik] ADJ aquatic, water cpd
aqueduc [akdyk] NM aqueduct
aqueux, -euse [akø, -øz] ADJ aqueous
aquilin [akilɛ̃] ADJ M: **nez ~** aquiline nose
AR SIGLE M = **accusé de réception**; (*Aviat, Rail etc*) = **aller (et) retour** ▶ ABR (*Auto*) = **arrière**; **lettre/paquet avec AR** recorded delivery letter/parcel
arabe [aʀab] ADJ Arabic; (*désert, cheval*) Arabian; (*nation, peuple*) Arab ▶ NM (*Ling*) Arabic ▶ NMF: **A~** Arab
arabesque [aʀabɛsk] NF arabesque
Arabie [aʀabi] NF: **l'~** Arabia; **l'~ Saoudite** *ou* **Séoudite** Saudi Arabia
arable [aʀabl] ADJ arable
arachide [aʀaʃid] NF groundnut (plant); (*graine*) peanut, groundnut
araignée [aʀeɲe] NF spider; **~ de mer** spider crab
araser [aʀaze] /1/ VT to level; (*en rabotant*) to plane (down)
aratoire [aʀatwaʀ] ADJ: **instrument ~** ploughing implement
arbalète [aʀbalɛt] NF crossbow

arbitrage [aʀbitʀaʒ] NM refereeing; umpiring; arbitration

arbitraire [aʀbitʀɛʀ] ADJ arbitrary

arbitre [aʀbitʀ] NM (*Sport*) referee; (: *Tennis*, *Cricket*) umpire; (*fig*) arbiter, judge; (*Jur*) arbitrator

arbitrer [aʀbitʀe] /1/ VT to referee; to umpire; to arbitrate

arborer [aʀbɔʀe] /1/ VT to bear, display; (*avec ostentation*) to sport

arborescence [aʀbɔʀesɑ̃s] NF tree structure

arboricole [aʀbɔʀikɔl] ADJ (*animal*) arboreal; (*technique*) arboricultural

arboriculture [aʀbɔʀikyltyʀ] NF arboriculture; ~ **fruitière** fruit (tree) growing

arbre [aʀbʀ] NM tree; (*Tech*) shaft; ~ **à cames** (*Auto*) camshaft; ~ **fruitier** fruit tree; ~ **généalogique** family tree; ~ **de Noël** Christmas tree; ~ **de transmission** (*Auto*) drive shaft

arbrisseau, x [aʀbʀiso] NM shrub

arbuste [aʀbyst] NM small shrub, bush

arc [aʀk] NM (*arme*) bow; (*Géom*) arc; (*Archit*) arch; ~ **de cercle** arc of a circle; **en ~ de cercle** *adj* semi-circular

arcade [aʀkad] NF arch(way); **arcades** arcade *sg*, arches; ~ **sourcilière** arch of the eyebrows

arcanes [aʀkan] NMPL mysteries

arc-boutant [aʀkbutɑ̃] (*pl* **arcs-boutants**) NM flying buttress

arc-bouter [aʀkbute] /1/: **s'arc-bouter** VI: **s'arc-bouter contre** to lean *ou* press against

arceau, x [aʀso] NM (*métallique etc*) hoop

arc-en-ciel [aʀkɑ̃sjɛl] (*pl* **arcs-en-ciel**) NM rainbow

archaïque [aʀkaik] ADJ archaic

archaïsme [aʀkaism] NM archaism

archange [aʀkɑ̃ʒ] NM archangel

arche [aʀʃ] NF arch; ~ **de Noé** Noah's Ark

archéologie [aʀkeɔlɔʒi] NF arch(a)eology

archéologique [aʀkeɔlɔʒik] ADJ arch(a)eological

archéologue [aʀkeɔlɔg] NMF arch(a)eologist

archer [aʀʃe] NM archer

archet [aʀʃɛ] NM bow

archevêché [aʀʃəveʃe] NM archbishopric; (*palais*) archbishop's palace

archevêque [aʀʃəvɛk] NM archbishop

archi… [aʀʃi] PRÉFIXE (*très*) dead, extra

archibondé, e [aʀʃibɔ̃de] ADJ chock-a-block (*BRIT*), packed solid

archiduc [aʀʃidyk] NM archduke

archiduchesse [aʀʃidyʃɛs] NF archduchess

archipel [aʀʃipɛl] NM archipelago

archisimple [aʀʃisɛ̃pl] ADJ dead easy *ou* simple

architecte [aʀʃitɛkt] NM architect

architectural, e, -aux [aʀʃitɛktyʀal, -o] ADJ architectural

architecture [aʀʃitɛktyʀ] NF architecture

archive [aʀʃiv] NF file

archiver [aʀʃive] /1/ VT to file

archives [aʀʃiv] NFPL (*collection*) archives

archiviste [aʀʃivist] NMF archivist

arçon [aʀsɔ̃] NM *voir* **cheval**

arctique [aʀktik] ADJ Arctic ▶ NM: **l'A~** the Arctic; **le cercle A~** the Arctic Circle; **l'océan A~** the Arctic Ocean

ardemment [aʀdamɑ̃] ADV ardently, fervently

ardent, e [aʀdɑ̃, -ɑ̃t] ADJ (*soleil*) blazing; (*fièvre*) raging; (*amour*) ardent, passionate; (*prière*) fervent

ardeur [aʀdœʀ] NF blazing heat; (*fig*) fervour, ardour

ardoise [aʀdwaz] NF slate

ardu, e [aʀdy] ADJ (*travail*) arduous; (*problème*) difficult; (*pente*) steep, abrupt

are [aʀ] NM are, 100 square metres

arène [aʀɛn] NF arena; (*fig*): **l'~ politique** the political arena; **arènes** NFPL bull-ring *sg*

arête [aʀɛt] NF (*de poisson*) bone; (*d'une montagne*) ridge; (*Géom etc*) edge (*where two faces meet*)

arg. ABR = **argus**

argent [aʀʒɑ̃] NM (*métal*) silver; (*monnaie*) money; (*couleur*) silver; **en avoir pour son ~** to get value for money; **gagner beaucoup d'~** to earn a lot of money; ~ **comptant** (hard) cash; ~ **de poche** pocket money; ~ **liquide** ready money, (ready) cash

argenté, e [aʀʒɑ̃te] ADJ silver(y); (*métal*) silver-plated

argenter [aʀʒɑ̃te] /1/ VT to silver(-plate)

argenterie [aʀʒɑ̃tʀi] NF silverware; (*en métal argenté*) silver plate

argentin, e [aʀʒɑ̃tɛ̃, -in] ADJ Argentinian, Argentine ▶ NM/F: **A~, e** Argentinian, Argentine

Argentine [aʀʒɑ̃tin] NF: **l'~** Argentina, the Argentine

argentique [aʀʒɑ̃tik] ADJ (*appareil photo*) film *cpd*

argile [aʀʒil] NF clay

argileux, -euse [aʀʒilø, -øz] ADJ clayey

argot [aʀgo] NM slang; *see note*

> Argot was the term originally used to describe the jargon of the criminal underworld, characterized by colourful images and distinctive intonation and designed to confuse the outsider. Some French authors write in *argot* and so have helped it spread and grow. More generally, the special vocabulary used by any social or professional group is also known as *argot*.

argotique [aʀgɔtik] ADJ slang *cpd*; (*très familier*) slangy

arguer [aʀgɥe] /1/: ~ **de** vt to put forward as a pretext *ou* reason; ~ **que** to argue that

argument [aʀgymɑ̃] NM argument

argumentaire [aʀgymɑ̃tɛʀ] NM list of sales points; (*brochure*) sales leaflet

argumentation [aʀgymɑ̃tasjɔ̃] NF (*fait d'argumenter*) arguing; (*ensemble des arguments*) argument

argumenter [aʀgymɑ̃te] /1/ VI to argue

argus [aʀgys] NM guide to second-hand car etc prices

arguties [aʀgysi] NFPL pettifoggery *sg* (*BRIT*), quibbles

aride [aʀid] ADJ arid

aridité [aʀidite] NF aridity

arien, ne [aʀjɛ̃, -ɛn] ADJ Arian

25

aristocrate [aristɔkrat] NMF aristocrat

aristocratie [aristɔkrasi] NF aristocracy

aristocratique [aristɔkratik] ADJ aristocratic

arithmétique [aritmetik] ADJ arithmetic(al)
▶ NF arithmetic

armada [armada] NF (fig) army

armagnac [armaɲak] NM Armagnac

armateur [armatœr] NM shipowner

armature [armatyr] NF framework; (de tente etc) frame; (de corset) bone; (de soutien-gorge) wiring

arme [arm] NF weapon; (section de l'armée) arm; **armes** NFPL weapons, arms; (blason) (coat of) arms; **les armes** (profession) soldiering sg; **à armes égales** on equal terms; **en armes** up in arms; **passer par les armes** to execute (by firing squad); **prendre/présenter les armes** to take up/present arms; **se battre à l'~ blanche** to fight with blades; **~ à feu** firearm; **armes de destruction massive** weapons of mass destruction

armé, e [arme] ADJ armed; **~ de** armed with

armée [arme] NF army; **~ de l'air** Air Force; **l'~ du Salut** the Salvation Army; **~ de terre** Army

armement [arməmɑ̃] NM (matériel) arms pl, weapons pl; (: d'un pays) arms pl, armament; (action d'équiper: d'un navire) fitting out; **armements nucléaires** nuclear armaments; **course aux armements** arms race

Arménie [armeni] NF: **l'~** Armenia

arménien, ne [armenjɛ̃, -ɛn] ADJ Armenian ▶ NM (Ling) Armenian ▶ NM/F: **A~, ne** Armenian

armer [arme] /1/ VT to arm; (arme à feu) to cock; (appareil photo) to wind on; **s'armer** VI: **s'armer de** to arm o.s. with; **~ qch de** to fit sth with; (renforcer) to reinforce sth with; **~ qn de** to arm ou equip sb with

armistice [armistis] NM armistice; **l'A~** ≈ Remembrance (BRIT) ou Veterans (US) Day

armoire [armwar] NF (tall) cupboard; (penderie) wardrobe (BRIT), closet (US); **~ à pharmacie** medicine chest

armoiries [armwari] NFPL coat of arms sg

armure [armyr] NF armour no pl, suit of armour

armurerie [armyrri] NF arms factory; (magasin) gunsmith's (shop)

armurier [armyrje] NM gunsmith; (Mil, d'armes blanches) armourer

ARN SIGLE M (= acide ribonucléique) RNA

arnaque [arnak] (fam) NF swindling; **c'est de l'~** it's daylight robbery

arnaquer [arnake] /1/ (fam) VT to do (fam), swindle; **se faire ~** to be had (fam) ou done

arnaqueur [arnakœr] NM swindler

arnica [arnika] NM: **(teinture d')~** arnica

arobase [arɔbaz] NF (Inform) 'at' symbol, @; **"paul ~ société point fr"** "paul at société dot fr"

aromates [arɔmat] NMPL seasoning sg, herbs (and spices)

aromathérapie [arɔmaterapi] NF aromatherapy

aromatique [arɔmatik] ADJ aromatic

aromatisé, e [arɔmatize] ADJ flavoured

arôme [arom] NM aroma; (d'une fleur etc) fragrance

arpège [arpɛʒ] NM arpeggio

arpentage [arpɑ̃taʒ] NM (land) surveying

arpenter [arpɑ̃te] /1/ VT to pace up and down

arpenteur [arpɑ̃tœr] NM land surveyor

arqué, e [arke] ADJ arched; (jambes) bow cpd, bandy

arr. ABR = **arrondissement**

arrachage [araʃaʒ] NM: **~ des mauvaises herbes** weeding

arraché [araʃe] NM (Sport) snatch; **obtenir à l'~** (fig) to snatch

arrache-pied [araʃpje]: **d'~** adv relentlessly

arracher [araʃe] /1/ VT to pull out; (page etc) to tear off, tear out; (déplanter: légume, herbe, souche) to pull up; (: bras etc: par explosion) to blow off; (: par accident) to tear off; **s'arracher** VT (article très recherché) to fight over; **~ qch à qn** to snatch sth from sb; (fig) to wring sth out of sb, wrest sth from sb; **~ qn à** (solitude, rêverie) to drag sb out of; (famille etc) to tear ou wrench sb away from; **se faire arracher une dent** to have a tooth out ou pulled (US); **s'arracher de** (lieu) to tear o.s. away from; (habitude) to force o.s. out of

arraisonner [arɛzɔne] /1/ VT to board and search

arrangeant, e [arɑ̃ʒɑ̃, -ɑ̃t] ADJ accommodating, obliging

arrangement [arɑ̃ʒmɑ̃] NM arrangement

arranger [arɑ̃ʒe] /3/ VT to arrange; (réparer) to fix, put right; (régler) to settle, sort out; (convenir à) to suit, be convenient for; **cela m'arrange** that suits me (fine); **s'arranger** VI (se mettre d'accord) to come to an agreement ou arrangement; (s'améliorer: querelle, situation) to be sorted out; (se débrouiller) **s'arranger pour que …** to arrange things so that …; **je vais m'~** I'll manage; **ça va s'arranger** it'll sort itself out; **s'arranger pour faire** to make sure that ou see to it that one can do

arrangeur [arɑ̃ʒœr] NM (Mus) arranger

arrestation [arɛstasjɔ̃] NF arrest

arrêt [arɛ] NM stopping; (de bus etc) stop; (Jur) judgment, decision; (Football) save; **arrêts** NMPL (Mil) arrest sg; **être à l'~** to be stopped, have come to a halt; **rester ou tomber en ~ devant** to stop short in front of; **sans ~** without stopping, non-stop; (fréquemment) continually; **~ d'autobus** bus stop; **~ facultatif** request stop; **~ de mort** capital sentence; **~ de travail** stoppage (of work)

arrêté, e [arete] ADJ (idées) firm, fixed ▶ NM order, decree; **~ municipal** ≈ bylaw, bye-law

arrêter [arete] /1/ VT to stop; (chauffage etc) to turn off, switch off; (Comm: compte) to settle; (Couture: point) to fasten off; (fixer: date etc) to appoint, decide on; (criminel, suspect) to arrest; **s'arrêter** VI to stop; (s'interrompre) to stop o.s.; **~ de faire** to stop doing; **arrête de te plaindre** stop complaining; **ne pas ~ de faire** to keep on doing; **s'arrêter de faire** to stop doing; **s'arrêter sur** (choix, regard) to fall on

arrhes [aR] NFPL deposit *sg*
arrière [aRjɛR] NM back; (*Sport*) fullback ▸ ADJ
INV: **siège/roue ~** back *ou* rear seat/wheel;
arrières (*fig*) NMPL: **protéger ses arrières** to
protect the rear; **à l' ~** *adv* behind, at the back;
en ~ *adv* behind; (*regarder*) back, behind; (*tomber,
aller*) backwards; **en ~ de** *prép* behind
arriéré, e [aRjeRe] ADJ (*péj*) backward ▸ NM
(*d'argent*) arrears *pl*
arrière-boutique [aRjɛRbutik] NF back shop
arrière-cour [aRjɛRkuR] NF backyard
arrière-cuisine [aRjɛRkɥizin] NF scullery
arrière-garde [aRjɛRgaRd] NF rearguard
arrière-goût [aRjɛRgu] NM aftertaste
arrière-grand-mère [aRjɛRgRɑ̃mɛR] (*pl*
arrière-grands-mères) NF great-grandmother
arrière-grand-père [aRjɛRgRɑ̃pɛR] (*pl*
arrière-grands-pères) NM great-grandfather
arrière-grands-parents [aRjɛRgRɑ̃paRɑ̃] NMPL
great-grandparents
arrière-pays [aRjɛRpei] NM INV hinterland
arrière-pensée [aRjɛRpɑ̃se] NF ulterior motive;
(*doute*) mental reservation
arrière-petite-fille [aRjɛRpətitfij] (*pl*
arrière-petites-filles) NF great-granddaughter
arrière-petit-fils [aRjɛRpətifis] (*pl* **arrière-
petits-fils**) NM great-grandson
arrière-petits-enfants [aRjɛRpətizɑ̃fɑ̃] NMPL
great-grandchildren
arrière-plan [aRjɛRplɑ̃] NM background; **à l' ~**
in the background; **d' ~** *adj* (*Inform*) background
cpd
arriérer [aRjeRe] /6/: **s'arriérer** VI (*Comm*) to fall
into arrears
arrière-saison [aRjɛRsezɔ̃] NF late autumn
arrière-salle [aRjɛRsal] NF back room
arrière-train [aRjɛRtRɛ̃] NM hindquarters *pl*
arrimer [aRime] /1/ VT (*cargaison*) to stow; (*fixer*)
to secure, fasten securely
arrivage [aRivaʒ] NM consignment
arrivant, e [aRivɑ̃, -ɑ̃t] NM/F newcomer
arrivée [aRive] NF arrival; (*ligne d'arrivée*) finish;
~ d'air/de gaz air/gas inlet; **courrier à l' ~**
incoming mail; **à mon ~** when I arrived
arriver [aRive] /1/ VI to arrive; (*survenir*) to
happen, occur; **j'arrive!** (I'm just coming!); **il
arrive à Paris à 8 h** he gets to *ou* arrives in Paris
at 8; **~ à destination** to arrive at one's
destination; **~ à** (*atteindre*) to reach; **~ à (faire)
qch** (*réussir*) to manage (to do) sth; **~ à échéance**
to fall due; **en ~ à faire ...** to end up doing ...,
get to the point of doing ...; **il arrive que ...** it
happens that ...; **il lui arrive de faire ...** he
sometimes does ...
arrivisme [aRivism] NM ambition,
ambitiousness
arriviste [aRivist] NMF go-getter
arrobase [aRɔbaz] NF (*Inform*) 'at' symbol, @
arrogance [aRɔgɑ̃s] NF arrogance
arrogant, e [aRɔgɑ̃, -ɑ̃t] ADJ arrogant
arroger [aRɔʒe] /3/: **s'arroger** VT to assume
(*without right*); **s'arroger le droit de ...** to
assume the right to ...
arrondi, e [aRɔ̃di] ADJ round ▸ NM roundness

arrondir [aRɔ̃diR] /2/ VT (*forme, objet*) to round;
(*somme*) to round off; **s'arrondir** VI to become
round(ed); **~ ses fins de mois** to supplement
one's pay
arrondissement [aRɔ̃dismɑ̃] NM (*Admin*)
≈ district
arrosage [aRozaʒ] NM watering; **tuyau d' ~**
hose(pipe)
arroser [aRoze] /1/ VT to water; (*victoire etc*) to
celebrate (over a drink); (*Culin*) to baste
arroseur [aRozœR] NM (*tourniquet*) sprinkler
arroseuse [aRozøz] NF water cart
arrosoir [aRozwaR] NM watering can
arrt ABR = **arrondissement**
arsenal, -aux [aRsənal, -o] NM (*Navig*) naval
dockyard; (*Mil*) arsenal; (*fig*) gear,
paraphernalia
art [aR] NM art; **avoir l' ~ de faire** (*fig: personne*) to
have a talent for doing; **les arts** the arts; **livre/
critique d' ~** art book/ critic; **objet d' ~** objet
d'art; **~ dramatique** dramatic art; **arts
martiaux** martial arts; **arts et métiers**
applied arts and crafts; **arts ménagers** home
economics *sg*; **arts plastiques** plastic arts
art. ABR = **article**
artère [aRtɛR] NF (*Anat*) artery; (*rue*) main road
artériel, le [aRteRjɛl] ADJ arterial
artériosclérose [aRteRjoskleRoz] NF
arteriosclerosis
arthrite [aRtRit] NF arthritis
arthrose [aRtRoz] NF (degenerative)
osteoarthritis
artichaut [aRtiʃo] NM artichoke
article [aRtikl] NM article; (*Comm*) item, article;
faire l' ~ (*Comm*) to do one's sales spiel; **faire l' ~
de** (*fig*) to sing the praises of; **à l' ~ de la mort** at
the point of death; **~ défini/indéfini** definite/
indefinite article; **~ de fond** (*Presse*) feature
article; **articles de bureau** office equipment;
articles de voyage travel goods *ou* items
articulaire [aRtikylɛR] ADJ of the joints,
articular
articulation [aRtikylasjɔ̃] NF articulation;
(*Anat*) joint
articulé, e [aRtikyle] ADJ (*membre*) jointed;
(*poupée*) with moving joints
articuler [aRtikyle] /1/ VT to articulate;
s'articuler (sur) VI (*Anat, Tech*) to articulate
(with); **s'articuler autour de** (*fig*) to centre
around *ou* on, turn on
artifice [aRtifis] NM device, trick
artificiel, le [aRtifisjɛl] ADJ artificial
artificiellement [aRtifisjɛlmɑ̃] ADV artificially
artificier [aRtifisje] NM pyrotechnist
artificieux, -euse [aRtifisjø, -øz] ADJ guileful,
deceitful
artillerie [aRtijRi] NF artillery, ordnance
artilleur [aRtijœR] NM artilleryman, gunner
artisan [aRtizɑ̃] NM artisan, (self-employed)
craftsman; **l' ~ de la victoire/du malheur** the
architect of victory/of the disaster
artisanal, e, -aux [aRtizanal, -o] ADJ of *ou* made
by craftsmen; (*péj*) cottage industry *cpd*,
unsophisticated; **de fabrication ~** home-made

27

artisanalement [aʀtizanalmɑ̃] ADV by craftsmen

artisanat [aʀtizana] NM arts and crafts pl

artiste [aʀtist] NMF artist; (Théât, Mus) artist, performer; (de variétés) entertainer

artistique [aʀtistik] ADJ artistic

artistiquement [aʀtistikmɑ̃] ADV artistically

aryen, ne [aʀjɛ̃, -ɛn] ADJ Aryan

AS SIGLE FPL (Admin) = **assurances sociales** ▸ SIGLE F (Sport: = Association sportive) ≈ FC (= Football Club)

as VB [a] voir **avoir** ▸ NM [ɑs] ace

a/s ABR (= aux soins de) c/o

ASBL SIGLE F (= association sans but lucratif) non-profit-making organization

asc. ABR = **ascenseur**

ascendance [asɑ̃dɑ̃s] NF (origine) ancestry; (Astrologie) ascendant

ascendant, e [asɑ̃dɑ̃, -ɑ̃t] ADJ upward ▸ NM influence; **ascendants** NMPL ascendants

ascenseur [asɑ̃sœʀ] NM lift (BRIT), elevator (US)

ascension [asɑ̃sjɔ̃] NF ascent; (de montagne) climb; **l'A~** (Rel) the Ascension (: jour férié) Ascension (Day); see note; **(île de) l'A~** Ascension Island

> The *fête de l'Ascension* is a public holiday in France. It always falls on a Thursday, usually in May. Many French people take the following Friday off work too and enjoy a long weekend.

ascète [asɛt] NMF ascetic

ascétique [asetik] ADJ ascetic

ascétisme [asetism] NM asceticism

ascorbique [askɔʀbik] ADJ: **acide ~** ascorbic acid

ASE SIGLE F (= Agence spatiale européenne) ESA (= European Space Agency)

asepsie [asɛpsi] NF asepsis

aseptique [asɛptik] ADJ aseptic

aseptisé, e [asɛptize] (péj) ADJ sanitized

asexué, e [asɛksɥe] ADJ asexual

asiatique [azjatik] ADJ Asian, Asiatic ▸ NMF: **A~** Asian

Asie [azi] NF: **l'~** Asia

asile [azil] NM (refuge) refuge, sanctuary; (pour malades, vieillards etc) home; **droit d'~** (Pol) (political) asylum; **accorder l'~ politique à qn** to grant ou give sb political asylum; **chercher/ trouver ~ quelque part** to seek/find refuge somewhere

asocial, e, -aux [asɔsjal, -o] ADJ antisocial

aspect [aspɛ] NM appearance, look; (fig) aspect, side; (Ling) aspect; **à l'~ de** at the sight of

asperge [aspɛʀʒ] NF asparagus no pl

asperger [aspɛʀʒe] /3/ VT to spray, sprinkle

aspérité [asperite] NF excrescence, protruding bit (of rock etc)

aspersion [aspɛʀsjɔ̃] NF spraying, sprinkling

asphalte [asfalt] NM asphalt

asphyxiant, e [asfiksjɑ̃, -ɑ̃t] ADJ suffocating; **gaz ~** poison gas

asphyxie [asfiksi] NF suffocation, asphyxia, asphyxiation

asphyxier [asfiksje] /7/ VT to suffocate, asphyxiate; (fig) to stifle; **mourir asphyxié** to die of suffocation ou asphyxiation

aspic [aspik] NM (Zool) asp; (Culin) aspic

aspirant, e [aspiʀɑ̃, -ɑ̃t] ADJ: **pompe ~** suction pump ▸ NM (Navig) midshipman

aspirateur [aspiʀatœʀ] NM vacuum cleaner, hoover®; **passer l'~** to vacuum

aspiration [aspiʀasjɔ̃] NF inhalation, sucking (up); drawing up; **aspirations** NFPL (ambitions) aspirations

aspirer [aspiʀe] /1/ VT (air) to inhale; (liquide) to suck (up); (appareil) to suck ou draw up; **~ à** VT to aspire to

aspirine [aspiʀin] NF aspirin

assagir [asaʒiʀ] /2/ VT, **s'assagir** VI to quieten down, settle down

assaillant, e [asajɑ̃, -ɑ̃t] NM/F assailant, attacker

assaillir [asajiʀ] /13/ VT to assail, attack; **~ qn de** (questions) to assail ou bombard sb with

assainir [aseniʀ] /2/ VT to clean up; (eau, air) to purify

assainissement [asenismɑ̃] NM cleaning up; purifying

assaisonnement [asɛzɔnmɑ̃] NM seasoning

assaisonner [asɛzɔne] /1/ VT to season; **bien assaisonné** highly seasoned

assassin [asasɛ̃] NM murderer; assassin

assassinat [asasina] NM murder; assassination

assassiner [asasine] /1/ VT to murder; (Pol) to assassinate

assaut [aso] NM assault, attack; **prendre d'~** (take by) storm, assault; **donner l'~ (à)** to attack; **faire ~ de** (rivaliser) to vie with ou rival each other in

assèchement [asɛʃmɑ̃] NM draining, drainage

assécher [aseʃe] /6/ VT to drain

ASSEDIC [asedik] SIGLE F (= Association pour l'emploi dans l'industrie et le commerce) unemployment insurance scheme

assemblage [asɑ̃blaʒ] NM (action) assembling; (Menuiserie) joint; **un ~ de** (fig) a collection of; **langage d'~** (Inform) assembly language

assemblée [asɑ̃ble] NF (réunion) meeting; (public, assistance) gathering; assembled people; (Pol) assembly; (Rel): **l'~ des fidèles** the congregation; **l'A~ nationale (AN)** the (French) National Assembly; see note

> The *Assemblée nationale* is the lower house of the French Parliament, the upper house being the *Sénat*. It is housed in the Palais Bourbon in Paris. Its members, or *députés*, are elected every five years.

assembler [asɑ̃ble] /1/ VT (joindre, monter) to assemble, put together; (amasser) to gather (together), collect (together); **s'assembler** VI to gather, collect

assembleur [asɑ̃blœʀ] NM assembler, fitter; (Inform) assembler

assener /5/, **asséner** [asene] VT: **~ un coup à qn** to deal sb a blow

assentiment [asɑ̃timɑ̃] NM assent, consent; (approbation) approval

asseoir [aswaʀ] /**26**/ vt (*malade, bébé*) to sit up; (*personne debout*) to sit down; (*autorité, réputation*) to establish; **s'asseoir** vi to sit (o.s.) up; to sit (o.s.) down; **faire ~ qn** to ask sb to sit down; **asseyez-vous!, assieds-toi!** sit down!; **~ qch sur** to build sth on; (*appuyer*) to base sth on

assermenté, e [asɛʀmɑ̃te] ADJ sworn, on oath

assertion [asɛʀsjɔ̃] NF assertion

asservir [asɛʀviʀ] /**2**/ vt to subjugate, enslave

asservissement [asɛʀvismɑ̃] NM (*action*) enslavement; (*état*) slavery

assesseur [asesœʀ] NM (*Jur*) assessor

asseyais *etc* [asɛjɛ] VB *voir* **asseoir**

assez [ase] ADV (*suffisamment*) enough, sufficiently; (*passablement*) rather, quite, fairly; **~!** enough!, that'll do!; **~/pas ~ cuit** well enough done/underdone; **est-il ~ fort/rapide?** is he strong/fast enough?; **il est passé ~ vite** he went past rather ou quite ou fairly fast; **~ de pain/livres** enough ou sufficient bread/books; **vous en avez ~?** have you got enough?; **en avoir ~ de qch** (*en être fatigué*) to have had enough of sth; **j'en ai ~!** I've had enough!; **travailler ~** to work (hard) enough

assidu, e [asidy] ADJ assiduous, painstaking; (*régulier*) regular; **~ auprès de qn** attentive towards sb

assiduité [asidɥite] NF assiduousness, painstaking regularity; attentiveness; **assiduités** NFPL assiduous attentions

assidûment [asidymɑ̃] ADV assiduously, painstakingly; attentively

assied *etc* [asje] VB *voir* **asseoir**

assiégé, e [asjeʒe] ADJ under siege, besieged

assiéger [asjeʒe] /**3, 6**/ vt to besiege, lay siege to; (*foule, touristes*) to mob, besiege

assiérai *etc* [asjeʀe] VB *voir* **asseoir**

assiette [asjɛt] NF plate; (*contenu*) plate(ful); (*équilibre*) seat; (*de colonne*) seating; (*de navire*) trim; **il n'est pas dans son ~** he's not feeling quite himself; **~ à dessert** dessert ou side plate; **~ anglaise** assorted cold meats; **~ creuse** (soup) dish, soup plate; **~ de l'impôt** basis of (tax) assessment; **~ plate** (dinner) plate

assiettée [asjete] NF plateful

assignation [asiɲasjɔ̃] NF assignation; (*Jur*) summons; (*: de témoin*) subpoena; **~ à résidence** compulsory order of residence

assigner [asiɲe] /**1**/ vt: **~ qch à** to assign ou allot sth to; (*valeur, importance*) to attach sth to; (*somme*) to allocate sth to; (*limites*) to set ou fix sth to; (*cause, effet*) to ascribe ou attribute sth to; **~ qn à** (*affecter*) to assign sb to; **~ qn à résidence** (*Jur*) to give sb a compulsory order of residence

assimilable [asimilabl] ADJ easily assimilated ou absorbed

assimilation [asimilasjɔ̃] NF assimilation, absorption

assimiler [asimile] /**1**/ vt to assimilate, absorb; (*comparer*): **~ qch/qn à** to liken ou compare sth/sb to; **s'assimiler** vi (*s'intégrer*) to be assimilated ou absorbed; **ils sont assimilés aux infirmières** (*Admin*) they are classed as nurses

assis, e [asi, -iz] PP *de* **asseoir** ▸ ADJ sitting

(down), seated ▸ NF (*Constr*) course; (*Géo*) stratum (*pl* -a); (*fig*) basis (*pl* bases), foundation; **~ en tailleur** sitting cross-legged

assises [asiz] NFPL (*Jur*) assizes; (*congrès*) (annual) conference

assistanat [asistana] NM assistantship; (*à l'université*) probationary lectureship

assistance [asistɑ̃s] NF (*public*) audience; (*aide*) assistance; **porter** ou **prêter ~ à qn** to give sb assistance; **A~ publique** public health service; **enfant de l'A~ (publique)** child in care; **~ technique** technical aid

assistant, e [asistɑ̃, -ɑ̃t] NM/F assistant; (*d'université*) probationary lecturer; **les assistants** NMPL (*auditeurs etc*) those present; **~ sociale** social worker

assisté, e [asiste] ADJ (*Auto*) power-assisted ▸ NM/F person receiving aid from the State; **~ par ordinateur** computer-assisted; **direction ~** power steering

assister [asiste] /**1**/ vt to assist; **~ à** vt (*scène, événement*) to witness; (*conférence*) to attend, be (present) at; (*spectacle, match*) to be at, see

association [asɔsjasjɔ̃] NF association; (*Comm*) partnership; **~ d'idées/images** association of ideas/images

associé, e [asɔsje] NM/F associate; (*Comm*) partner

associer [asɔsje] /**7**/ vt to associate; **~ qn à** (*profits*) to give sb a share of; (*affaire*) to make sb a partner in; (*joie, triomphe*) to include sb in; **~ qch à** (*joindre, allier*) to combine sth with; **s'associer** vi, vt to join together; (*Comm*) to form a partnership; (*collaborateur*) to take on (as a partner); **s'associer à** (*couleurs, qualités*) to be combined with; (*opinions, joie de qn*) to share in; **s'associer à** ou **avec qn pour faire** to join (forces) ou join together with sb to do

assoie *etc* [aswa] VB *voir* **asseoir**

assoiffé, e [aswafe] ADJ thirsty; **~ de** (*sang*) thirsting for; (*gloire*) thirsting after

assoirai [aswaʀe], **assois** *etc* [aswa] VB *voir* **asseoir**

assolement [asɔlmɑ̃] NM (*systematic*) rotation of crops

assombrir [asɔ̃bʀiʀ] /**2**/ vt to darken; (*fig*) to fill with gloom; **s'assombrir** vi to darken; (*devenir nuageux, fig: visage*) to cloud over; (*fig*) to become gloomy

assommer [asɔme] /**1**/ vt (*étourdir, abrutir*) to knock out, stun; (*fam: ennuyer*) to bore stiff

Assomption [asɔ̃psjɔ̃] NF: **l'~** the Assumption; *see note*

> The *fête de l'Assomption*, more commonly known as *le 15 août* is a national holiday in France. Traditionally, large numbers of holidaymakers leave home on 15 August, frequently causing chaos on the roads.

assorti, e [asɔʀti] ADJ matched, matching; **fromages/légumes assortis** assorted cheeses/vegetables; **~ à** matching; **~ de** accompanied with; (*conditions, conseils*) coupled with; **bien/mal ~** well/ill-matched

assortiment [asɔʀtimɑ̃] NM (*choix*) assortment,

selection; (*harmonie de couleurs, formes*) arrangement; (*Comm: lot, stock*) selection

assortir [asɔʀtiʀ] /**2**/ VT to match; **s'assortir** VI to go well together, match; ~ **qch à** to match sth with; ~ **qch** to accompany sth with; **s'assortir de** to be accompanied by

assoupi, e [asupi] ADJ dozing, sleeping; (*fig*) (be)numbed; (*sens*) dulled

assoupir [asupiʀ] /**2**/: **s'assoupir** VI (*personne*) to doze off; (*sens*) to go numb

assoupissement [asupismɑ̃] NM (*sommeil*) dozing; (*fig: somnolence*) drowsiness

assouplir [asupliʀ] /**2**/ VT to make supple, soften; (*membres, corps*) to limber up, make supple; (*fig*) to relax; (*: caractère*) to soften, make more flexible; **s'assouplir** VI to soften; to limber up; to relax; to become more flexible

assouplissant [asuplisɑ̃] NM (fabric) softener

assouplissement [asuplismɑ̃] NM softening; limbering up; relaxation; **exercices d'~** limbering up exercises

assourdir [asuʀdiʀ] /**2**/ VT (*bruit*) to deaden, muffle; (*bruit*) to deafen

assourdissant, e [asuʀdisɑ̃, -ɑ̃t] ADJ (*bruit*) deafening

assouvir [asuviʀ] /**2**/ VT to satisfy, appease

assoyais *etc* [aswaje] VB *voir* **asseoir**

assujetti, e [asyʒeti] ADJ: ~ **(à)** subject (to); (*Admin*) ~ **à l'impôt** subject to tax(ation)

assujettir [asyʒetiʀ] /**2**/ VT to subject, subjugate; (*fixer: planches, tableau*) to fix securely; ~ **qn à** (*règle, impôt*) to subject sb to

assujettissement [asyʒetismɑ̃] NM subjection, subjugation

assumer [asyme] /**1**/ VT (*fonction, emploi*) to assume, take on; (*accepter: conséquence, situation*) to accept

assurance [asyʀɑ̃s] NF (*certitude*) assurance; (*confiance en soi*) (self-)confidence; (*contrat*) insurance (policy); (*secteur commercial*) insurance; **prendre une ~ contre** to take out insurance *ou* an insurance policy against; ~ **contre l'incendie** fire insurance; ~ **contre le vol** insurance against theft; **société d'~**, **compagnie d'assurances** insurance company; ~ **au tiers** third party insurance; ~ **maladie** health insurance; ~ **tous risques** (*Auto*) comprehensive insurance; **assurances sociales** ≈ National Insurance (BRIT), ≈ Social Security (US)

assurance-vie [asyʀɑ̃svi] (*pl* **assurances-vie**) NF life assurance *ou* insurance

assurance-vol [asyʀɑ̃svɔl] (*pl* **assurances-vol**) NF insurance against theft

assuré, e [asyʀe] ADJ (*réussite, échec, victoire etc*) certain, sure; (*démarche, voix*) assured; (*pas*) steady, (self-)confident; (*certain*): ~ **de** confident of; (*Assurances*) insured ▶ NM/F insured (person); ~ **social** ≈ member of the National Insurance (BRIT) *ou* Social Security (US) scheme

assurément [asyʀemɑ̃] ADV assuredly, most certainly

assurer [asyʀe] /**1**/ VT (*Comm*) to insure; (*stabiliser*) to steady, stabilize; (*victoire etc*) to

ensure, make certain; (*frontières, pouvoir*) to make secure; (*service, garde*) to provide, operate; **s'assurer (contre)** VI (*Comm*) to insure o.s. (against); ~ **qch à qn** (*garantir*) to secure *ou* guarantee sth for sb; (*certifier*) to assure sb of sth; ~ **à qn que** to assure sb that; **je vous assure que non/si** I assure you that that is not the case/is the case; ~ **qn de** to assure sb of; ~ **ses arrières** (*fig*) to be sure one has something to fall back on; **s'assurer de/que** (*vérifier*) to make sure of/that; **s'assurer (de)** (*aide de qn*) to secure; **s'assurer sur la vie** to take out life insurance; **s'assurer le concours/la collaboration de qn** to secure sb's aid/collaboration

assureur [asyʀœʀ] NM insurance agent; (*société*) insurers *pl*

Assyrie [asiʀi] NF: **l'~** Assyria

astérisque [asteʀisk] NM asterisk

astéroïde [asteʀɔid] NM asteroid

asthmatique [asmatik] ADJ, NMF asthmatic

asthme [asm] NM asthma

asticot [astiko] NM maggot

asticoter [astikɔte] /**1**/ VT (*fam*) to needle, get at

astigmate [astigmat] ADJ (*Méd: personne*) astigmatic, having an astigmatism

astiquer [astike] /**1**/ VT to polish, shine

astrakan [astʀakɑ̃] NM astrakhan

astral, e, -aux [astʀal, -o] ADJ astral

astre [astʀ] NM star

astreignant, e [astʀɛɲɑ̃, -ɑ̃t] ADJ demanding

astreindre [astʀɛ̃dʀ] /**49**/ VT: ~ **qn à qch** to force sth upon sb; ~ **qn à faire** to compel *ou* force sb to do; **s'~ à** to compel *ou* force o.s. to

astringent, e [astʀɛ̃ʒɑ̃, -ɑ̃t] ADJ astringent

astrologie [astʀɔlɔʒi] NF astrology

astrologique [astʀɔlɔʒik] ADJ astrological

astrologue [astʀɔlɔg] NMF astrologer

astronaute [astʀonot] NMF astronaut

astronautique [astʀonotik] NF astronautics *sg*

astronome [astʀonɔm] NMF astronomer

astronomie [astʀonɔmi] NF astronomy

astronomique [astʀonɔmik] ADJ astronomic(al)

astrophysicien, ne [astʀofizisjɛ̃, -ɛn] NM/F astrophysicist

astrophysique [astʀofizik] NF astrophysics *sg*

astuce [astys] NF shrewdness, astuteness; (*truc*) trick, clever way; (*plaisanterie*) wisecrack

astucieusement [astysjøzmɑ̃] ADV shrewdly, cleverly, astutely

astucieux, -euse [astysjø, -øz] ADJ shrewd, clever, astute

asymétrique [asimetʀik] ADJ asymmetric(al)

AT SIGLE M (= *Ancien Testament*) OT

atavisme [atavism] NM atavism, heredity

atelier [atəlje] NM workshop; (*de peintre*) studio

atermoiements [atɛʀmwamɑ̃] NMPL procrastination *sg*

atermoyer [atɛʀmwaje] /**8**/ VI to temporize, procrastinate

athée [ate] ADJ atheistic ▶ NMF atheist

athéisme [ateism] NM atheism

Athènes [atɛn] N Athens

athénien, ne [atenjɛ̃, -ɛn] ADJ Athenian

athlète [atlɛt] NMF (*Sport*) athlete; (*costaud*) muscleman

athlétique [atletik] ADJ athletic

athlétisme [atletism] NM athletics *sg*; **faire de l'~** to do athletics; **tournoi d'~** athletics meeting

Atlantide [atlɑ̃tid] NF: **l'~** Atlantis

atlantique [atlɑ̃tik] ADJ Atlantic ▶ NM: **l'(océan) A~** the Atlantic (Ocean)

atlantiste [atlɑ̃tist] ADJ, NMF Atlanticist

Atlas [atlɑs] NM: **l'~** the Atlas Mountains

atlas [atlɑs] NM atlas

atmosphère [atmɔsfɛʀ] NF atmosphere

atmosphérique [atmɔsferik] ADJ atmospheric

atoll [atɔl] NM atoll

atome [atom] NM atom

atomique [atɔmik] ADJ atomic, nuclear; (*usine*) nuclear; (*nombre, masse*) atomic

atomiseur [atɔmizœʀ] NM atomizer

atomiste [atɔmist] NMF (*aussi:* **savant, ingénieur** *etc* **atomiste**) atomic scientist

atone [atɔn] ADJ lifeless; (*Ling*) unstressed, unaccented

atours [atuʀ] NMPL attire *sg*, finery *sg*

atout [atu] NM trump; (*fig*) asset; (: *plus fort*) trump card; "**~ pique/trèfle**" "spades/clubs are trumps"

ATP SIGLE F (= *Association des tennismen professionnels*) ATP (= *Association of Tennis Professionals*) ▶ SIGLE MPL = **arts et traditions populaires**; **musée des ~** ≈ folk museum

âtre [ɑtʀ] NM hearth

atroce [atʀɔs] ADJ atrocious, horrible

atrocement [atʀɔsmɑ̃] ADV atrociously, horribly

atrocité [atʀɔsite] NF atrocity

atrophie [atʀɔfi] NF atrophy

atrophier [atʀɔfje] /7/: **s'atrophier** VI to atrophy

attabler [atable] /1/: **s'attabler** VI to sit down at (the) table; **s'attabler à la terrasse** to sit down (at a table) on the terrace

ATTAC SIGLE F (= *Association pour la Taxation des Transactions pour l'Aide aux Citoyens*) ATTAC, organization critical of globalization originally set up to demand a tax on foreign currency speculation

attachant, e [ataʃɑ̃, -ɑ̃t] ADJ engaging, likeable

attache [ataʃ] NF clip, fastener; (*fig*) tie; **attaches** NFPL (*relations*) connections; **à l'~** (*chien*) tied up

attaché, e [ataʃe] ADJ: **être ~ à** (*aimer*) to be attached to ▶ NM (*Admin*) attaché; **~ de presse/d'ambassade** press/embassy attaché; **~ commercial** commercial attaché

attaché-case [ataʃekez] NM INV attaché case (BRIT), briefcase

attachement [ataʃmɑ̃] NM attachment

attacher [ataʃe] /1/ VT to tie up; (*étiquette*) to attach, tie on; (*ceinture*) to fasten; (*souliers*) to do up ▶ VI (*poêle, riz*) to stick; **s'attacher** VI (*robe etc*) to do up; **s'attacher à** (*par affection*) to become attached to; **s'attacher à faire qch** to endeavour to do sth; **~ qch à** to tie ou fasten ou attach sth to; **~ qn à** (*fig: lier*) to attach sb to;

~ du prix/de l'importance à to attach great value/attach importance to

attaquant [atakɑ̃] NM (*Mil*) attacker; (*Sport*) striker, forward

attaque [atak] NF attack; (*cérébrale*) stroke; (*d'épilepsie*) fit; **être/se sentir d'~** to be/feel on form; **~ à main armée** armed attack

attaquer [atake] /1/ VT to attack; (*en justice*) to sue, bring an action against; (*travail*) to tackle, set about ▶ VI to attack; **s'attaquer à** VT (*personne*) to attack; (*épidémie, misère*) to tackle, attack

attardé, e [ataʀde] ADJ (*passants*) late; (*enfant*) backward; (*conceptions*) old-fashioned

attarder [ataʀde] /1/: **s'attarder** VI (*sur qch, en chemin*) to linger; (*chez qn*) to stay on

atteignais *etc* [atɛɲɛ] VB *voir* **atteindre**

atteindre [atɛ̃dʀ] /49/ VT to reach; (*blesser*) to hit; (*contacter*) to reach, contact, get in touch with; (*émouvoir*) to affect

atteint, e [atɛ̃, -ɛ̃t] PP *de* **atteindre** ▶ ADJ (*Méd*): **être ~ de** to be suffering from ▶ NF attack; **hors d'~** out of reach; **porter ~ à** to strike a blow at, undermine

attelage [atlaʒ] NM (*de remorque etc*) coupling (BRIT), (*trailer*) hitch (US); (*animaux*) team; (*harnachement*) harness; (: *de bœufs*) yoke

atteler [atle] /4/ VT (*cheval, bœufs*) to hitch up; (*wagons*) to couple; **s'atteler à** (*travail*) to buckle down to

attelle [atɛl] NF splint

attenant, e [atnɑ̃, -ɑ̃t] ADJ: **~ (à)** adjoining

attendant, e [atɑ̃dɑ̃] : **en ~** adv (*dans l'intervalle*) meanwhile, in the meantime

attendre [atɑ̃dʀ] /41/ VT to wait for; (*être destiné ou réservé à*) to await, be in store for ▶ VI to wait; **je n'attends plus rien (de la vie)** I expect nothing more (from life); **attendez que je réfléchisse** wait while I think; **s'~ à (ce que)** (*escompter*) to expect (that); **je ne m'y attendais pas** I didn't expect that; **ce n'est pas ce à quoi je m'attendais** that's not what I expected; **attendez-moi, s'il vous plaît** wait for me, please; **~ un enfant** to be expecting a baby; **~ de pied ferme** to wait determinedly; **~ de faire/d'être** to wait until one does/is; **~ que** to wait until; **attendez qu'il vienne** wait until he comes; **~ qch de** to expect sth of; **faire ~ qn** to keep sb waiting; **se faire ~** to keep people (ou us *etc*) waiting; **en attendant** *adv voir* **attendant**

attendri, e [atɑ̃dʀi] ADJ tender

attendrir [atɑ̃dʀiʀ] /2/ VT to move (to pity); (*viande*) to tenderize; **s'~ (sur)** to be moved ou touched (by)

attendrissant, e [atɑ̃dʀisɑ̃, -ɑ̃t] ADJ moving, touching

attendrissement [atɑ̃dʀismɑ̃] NM (*tendre*) emotion; (*apitoyé*) pity

attendrisseur [atɑ̃dʀisœʀ] NM tenderizer

attendu, e [atɑ̃dy] PP *de* **attendre** ▶ ADJ (*événement*) long-awaited; (*prévu*) expected ▶ NM: **attendus** reasons adduced for a judgment; **~ que** *conj* considering that, since

a

31

attentat [atɑ̃ta] NM (*contre une personne*) assassination attempt; (*contre un bâtiment*) attack; ~ **à la bombe** bomb attack; ~ **à la pudeur** (*exhibitionnisme*) indecent exposure *no pl*; (*agression*) indecent assault *no pl*; ~ **suicide** suicide bombing

attente [atɑ̃t] NF wait; (*espérance*) expectation; **contre toute** ~ contrary to (all) expectations

attenter [atɑ̃te] /1/: ~ **à** vt (*liberté*) to violate; ~ **à la vie de qn** to make an attempt on sb's life; ~ **à ses jours** to make an attempt on one's life

attentif, -ive [atɑ̃tif, -iv] ADJ (*auditeur*) attentive; (*soin*) scrupulous; (*travail*) careful; ~ **à** paying attention to; (*devoir*) mindful of; ~ **à faire** careful to do

attention [atɑ̃sjɔ̃] NF attention; (*prévenance*) attention, thoughtfulness *no pl*; **mériter** ~ to be worthy of attention; **à l'~ de** for the attention of; **porter qch à l'~ de qn** to bring sth to sb's attention; **attirer l'~ de qn sur qch** to draw sb's attention to sth; **faire** ~ (**à**) to be careful (of); **faire** ~ (**à ce**) **que** to be ou make sure that; ~! careful!, watch!, watch out!; ~ **à la voiture!** watch out for that car!; ~, **si vous ouvrez cette lettre** (*sanction*) just watch out, if you open that letter; ~, **respectez les consignes de sécurité** be sure to observe the safety instructions

attentionné, e [atɑ̃sjɔne] ADJ thoughtful, considerate

attentisme [atɑ̃tism] NM wait-and-see policy

attentiste [atɑ̃tist] ADJ (*politique*) wait-and-see
  ▶ NMF believer in a wait-and-see policy

attentivement [atɑ̃tivmɑ̃] ADV attentively

atténuant, e [atenɥɑ̃, -ɑ̃t] ADJ: **circonstances atténuantes** extenuating circumstances

atténuer [atenɥe] /1/ VT (*douleur*) to alleviate, ease; (*couleurs*) to soften; (*diminuer*) to lessen; (*amoindrir*) to mitigate the effects of; **s'atténuer** VI to ease; (*violence etc*) to abate

atterrer [atere] /1/ VT to dismay, appal

atterrir [aterir] /2/ VI to land

atterrissage [aterisaʒ] NM landing; ~ **sur le ventre/sans visibilité/forcé** belly/blind/forced landing

attestation [atɛstasjɔ̃] NF certificate, testimonial; ~ **médicale** doctor's certificate

attester [atɛste] /1/ VT to testify to, vouch for; (*démontrer*) to attest, testify to; ~ **que** to testify that

attiédir [atjediʀ] /2/: **s'attiédir** VI to become lukewarm; (*fig*) to cool down

attifé, e [atife] ADJ (*fam*) got up (BRIT), decked out

attifer [atife] /1/ VT to get (BRIT) ou do up, deck out

attique [atik] NM: **appartement en** ~ penthouse (flat (BRIT) ou apartment (US))

attirail [atiraj] NM gear; (*péj*) paraphernalia

attirance [atirɑ̃s] NF attraction; (*séduction*) lure

attirant, e [atirɑ̃, -ɑ̃t] ADJ attractive, appealing

attirer [atire] /1/ VT to attract; (*appâter*) to lure, entice; ~ **qn dans un coin/vers soi** to draw sb into a corner/towards one; ~ **l'attention de qn** to attract sb's attention; ~ **l'attention de qn**

sur qch to draw sb's attention to sth; ~ **des ennuis à qn** to make trouble for sb; **s'~ des ennuis** to bring trouble upon o.s., get into trouble

attiser [atize] /1/ VT (*feu*) to poke (up), stir up; (*fig*) to fan the flame of, stir up

attitré, e [atitre] ADJ qualified; (*agréé*) accredited, appointed

attitude [atityd] NF attitude; (*position du corps*) bearing

attouchements [atuʃmɑ̃] NMPL touching *sg*; (*sexuels*) fondling *sg*, stroking *sg*

attractif, -ive [atraktif, -iv] ADJ attractive

attraction [atraksjɔ̃] NF attraction; (*de cabaret, cirque*) number

attrait [atrɛ] NM appeal, attraction; (*plus fort*) lure; **attraits** NMPL attractions; **éprouver de l'~ pour** to be attracted to

attrape [atrap] NF *voir* **farce**

attrape-nigaud [atrapnigo] NM con

attraper [atrape] /1/ VT to catch; (*habitude, amende*) to get, pick up; (*fam: duper*) to con, take in (BRIT); **se faire** ~ (*fam*) to be told off

attrayant, e [atrɛjɑ̃, -ɑ̃t] ADJ attractive

attribuer [atribɥe] /1/ VT (*prix*) to award; (*rôle, tâche*) to allocate, assign; (*imputer*): ~ **qch à** to attribute sth to, ascribe sth to, put sth down to; **s'attribuer** VT (*s'approprier*) to claim for o.s.

attribut [atriby] NM attribute; (*Ling*) complement

attribution [atribysjɔ̃] NF (*voir* attribuer) awarding; allocation, assignment; attribution; **attributions** NFPL (*compétence*) attributions; **complément d'~** (*Ling*) indirect object

attristant, e [atristɑ̃, -ɑ̃t] ADJ saddening

attrister [atriste] /1/ VT to sadden; **s'~ de qch** to be saddened by sth

attroupement [atrupmɑ̃] NM crowd, mob

attrouper [atrupe] /1/: **s'attrouper** VI to gather

au [o] PRÉP *voir* **à**

aubade [obad] NF dawn serenade

aubaine [obɛn] NF godsend; (*financière*) windfall; (*Comm*) bonanza

aube [ob] NF dawn, daybreak; (*Rel*) alb; **à l'~** at dawn *ou* daybreak; **à l'~ de** (*fig*) at the dawn of

aubépine [obepin] NF hawthorn

auberge [obɛrʒ] NF inn; ~ **de jeunesse** youth hostel

aubergine [obɛrʒin] NF aubergine (BRIT), eggplant (US)

aubergiste [obɛrʒist] NMF inn-keeper, hotel-keeper

auburn [obœrn] ADJ INV auburn

aucun, e [okœ̃, -yn] ADJ, PRON no; (*positif*) any
  ▶ PRON none; (*positif*) any(one); **il n'y a ~ livre** there isn't any book, there is no book; **je n'en vois ~ qui …** I can't see any which …, I (can) see none which …; ~ **homme** no man; **sans ~ doute** without any doubt; **sans ~ hésitation** without hesitation; **plus qu'~ autre** more than any other; **il le fera mieux qu'~ de nous** he'll do it better than any of us; **plus qu'~ de ceux qui …** more than any of those who …; **en**

~ façon in no way at all; **~ des deux** neither of the two; **~ d'entre eux** none of them; **d'aucuns** (*certains*) some

aucunement [okynmɑ̃] ADV in no way, not in the least

audace [odas] NF daring, boldness; (*péj*) audacity; **il a eu l'~ de ...** he had the audacity to ...; **vous ne manquez pas d'~!** you're not lacking in nerve *ou* cheek!

audacieux, -euse [odasjø, -øz] ADJ daring, bold

au-dedans [odədɑ̃] ADV, PRÉP inside

au-dehors [odəɔR] ADV, PRÉP outside

au-delà [od(ə)la] ADV beyond ▶ NM: **l'~** the hereafter; **~ de** *prép* beyond

au-dessous [odsu] ADV underneath; below; **~ de** *prép* under(neath), below; (*limite, somme etc*) below, under; (*dignité, condition*) below

au-dessus [odsy] ADV above; **~ de** *prép* above

au-devant [od(ə)vɑ̃]: **~ de** *prép*: **aller ~ de** (*personne, danger*) to go (out) and meet; (*souhaits de qn*) to anticipate

audible [odibl] ADJ audible

audience [odjɑ̃s] NF audience; (*Jur: séance*) hearing; **trouver ~ auprès de** to arouse much interest among, get the (interested) attention of

audimat® [odimat] NM (*taux d'écoute*) ratings *pl*

audio-visuel, le [odjovizɥɛl] ADJ audio-visual ▶ NM (*équipement*) audio-visual aids *pl*; (*méthodes*) audio-visual methods *pl*; **l'~** radio and television

auditeur, -trice [oditœR, -tRis] NM/F (*à la radio*) listener; (*à une conférence*) member of the audience, listener; **~ libre** unregistered student (*attending lectures*), auditor (US)

auditif, -ive [oditif, -iv] ADJ (*mémoire*) auditory; **appareil ~** hearing aid

audition [odisjɔ̃] NF (*ouïe, écoute*) hearing; (*Jur: de témoins*) examination; (*Mus, Théât: épreuve*) audition

auditionner [odisjone] /1/ VT, VI to audition

auditoire [oditwaR] NM audience

auditorium [oditɔRjɔm] NM (*public*) studio

auge [oʒ] NF trough

augmentation [ɔgmɑ̃tasjɔ̃] NF (*action*) increasing; raising; (*résultat*) increase; **~ (de salaire)** rise (in salary) (BRIT), (pay) raise (US)

augmenter [ɔgmɑ̃te] /1/ VT to increase; (*salaire, prix*) to increase, raise, put up; (*employé*) to increase the salary of, give a (salary) rise (BRIT) *ou* (pay) raise (US) ▶ VI to increase; **~ de poids/volume** to gain (in) weight/volume

augure [ogyR] NM soothsayer, oracle; **de bon/mauvais ~** of good/ill omen

augurer [ogyRe] /1/ VT: **~ qch de** to foresee sth (coming) from *ou* out of; **~ bien de** to augur well for

auguste [ogyst] ADJ august, noble, majestic

aujourd'hui [oʒuRdɥi] ADV today; **~ en huit/quinze** a week/two weeks today, a week/two weeks from now; **à dater** *ou* **partir d'~** from today('s date)

aumône [omon] NF alms *sg* (*pl inv*); **faire l'~ (à qn)** to give alms (to sb); **faire l'~ de qch à qn**

(*fig*) to favour sb with sth

aumônerie [omonRi] NF chaplaincy

aumônier [omonje] NM chaplain

auparavant [oparavɑ̃] ADV before(hand)

auprès [opRɛ]: **~ de** *prép* next to, close to; (*recourir, s'adresser*) to; (*en comparaison de*) compared with, next to; (*dans l'opinion de*) in the opinion of

auquel [okel] PRON *voir* **lequel**

aura *etc* [ɔRa] VB *voir* **avoir**

aurai *etc* [ɔRe] VB *voir* **avoir**

auréole [ɔReɔl] NF halo; (*tache*) ring

auréolé, e [ɔReɔle] ADJ (*fig*): **~ de gloire** crowned with *ou* in glory

auriculaire [ɔRikylɛR] NM little finger

aurons *etc* [ɔRɔ̃] VB *voir* **avoir**

aurore [ɔRɔR] NF dawn, daybreak; **~ boréale** northern lights *pl*

ausculter [ɔskylte] /1/ VT to sound

auspices [ɔspis] NMPL: **sous les ~ de** under the patronage *ou* auspices of; **sous de bons/mauvais ~** under favourable/unfavourable auspices

aussi [osi] ADV (*également*) also, too; (*de comparaison*) as ▶ CONJ therefore, consequently; **~ fort que** as strong as; **moi ~** me too; **lui ~** (*sujet*) he too; (*objet*) him too; **~ bien que** (*même que*) as well as

aussitôt [osito] ADV straight away, immediately; **~ que** as soon as; **~ envoyé** as soon as it is (*ou* was) sent; **~ fait** no sooner done

austère [ostɛR] ADJ austere; (*sévère*) stern

austérité [ostteRite] NF austerity; **plan/budget d'~** austerity plan/budget

austral, e [ɔstRal] ADJ southern; **l'océan A~** the Antarctic Ocean; **les Terres Australes** Antarctica

Australie [ɔstRali] NF: **l'~** Australia

australien, ne [ɔstRaljẽ, -ɛn] ADJ Australian ▶ NM/F: **A~, ne** Australian

autant [otɑ̃] ADV so much; **je ne savais pas que tu la détestais ~** I didn't know you hated her so much; (*comparatif*): **~ (que)** as much (as); (*nombre*) as many (as); **~ (de)** so much (*ou* many); as much (*ou* many); **n'importe qui aurait pu en faire ~** anyone could have done the same *ou* as much; **~ partir** we (*ou* you *etc*) may as well leave; **~ ne rien dire** best not say anything; **~ dire que ...** one might as well say that ...; **fort ~ que courageux** as strong as he is brave; **pour ~** for all that; **il n'est pas découragé pour ~** he isn't discouraged for all that; **pour ~ que** *conj* assuming, as long as; **d'~** *adv* accordingly, in proportion; **d'~ plus/mieux (que)** all the more/the better (since)

autarcie [otaRsi] NF autarky, self-sufficiency

autel [otɛl] NM altar

auteur [otœR] NM author; **l'~ de cette remarque** the person who said that; **droit d'~** copyright

auteur-compositeur [otœRkɔ̃pozitœR] NMF composer-songwriter

authenticité [otɑ̃tisite] NF authenticity

authentifier [otɑ̃tifje] /7/ VT to authenticate

authentique [otɑ̃tik] ADJ authentic, genuine

autiste [otist] ADJ autistic

auto [oto] NF car; **autos tamponneuses** bumper cars, Dodgems®

auto... [ɔto] PRÉFIXE auto..., self-

autobiographie [ɔtɔbjɔgrafi] NF autobiography

autobiographique [ɔtɔbjɔgrafik] ADJ autobiographical

autobronzant [ɔtɔbrɔ̃zɑ̃] NM self-tanning cream (ou lotion etc)

autobus [ɔtɔbys] NM bus

autocar [ɔtɔkar] NM coach

autochtone [ɔtɔktɔn] NMF native

autocollant, e [ɔtɔkɔlɑ̃, -ɑ̃t] ADJ self-adhesive; (enveloppe) self-seal ▶ NM sticker

auto-couchettes [ɔtɔkuʃɛt] ADJ INV: **train ~** car sleeper train, motorail® train (BRIT)

autocratique [ɔtɔkratik] ADJ autocratic

autocritique [ɔtɔkritik] NF self-criticism

autocuiseur [ɔtɔkwizœr] NM (Culin) pressure cooker

autodéfense [ɔtɔdefɑ̃s] NF self-defence; **groupe d'~** vigilante committee

autodétermination [ɔtɔdetɛrminasjɔ̃] NF self-determination

autodidacte [ɔtɔdidakt] NMF self-taught person

autodiscipline [ɔtɔdisiplin] NF self-discipline

autodrome [ɔtɔdrom] NM motor-racing stadium

auto-école [ɔtɔekɔl] NF driving school

autofinancement [ɔtɔfinɑ̃smɑ̃] NM self-financing

autogéré, e [ɔtɔʒere] ADJ self-managed, managed internally

autogestion [ɔtɔʒɛstjɔ̃] NF joint worker-management control

autographe [ɔtɔgraf] NM autograph

autoguidé, e [ɔtɔgide] ADJ self-guided

automate [ɔtɔmat] NM (robot) automaton; (machine) (automatic) machine

automatique [ɔtɔmatik] ADJ automatic ▶ NM: **l'~** (Tél) ≈ direct dialling

automatiquement [ɔtɔmatikmɑ̃] ADV automatically

automatisation [ɔtɔmatizasjɔ̃] NF automation

automatiser [ɔtɔmatize] /1/ VT to automate

automédication [ɔtɔmedikasjɔ̃] NF self-medication

automitrailleuse [ɔtɔmitrɑjøz] NF armoured car

automnal, e, -aux [ɔtɔnal, -o] ADJ autumnal

automne [ɔtɔn] NM autumn (BRIT), fall (US)

automobile [ɔtɔmɔbil] ADJ motor cpd ▶ NF (motor) car; **l'~** motoring; (industrie) the car ou automobile (US) industry

automobiliste [ɔtɔmɔbilist] NMF motorist

automutilation [ɔtɔmytilasjɔ̃] NF self-harm

autonettoyant, e [ɔtɔnɛtwajɑ̃, -ɑ̃t] ADJ: **four ~** self-cleaning oven

autonome [ɔtɔnɔm] ADJ autonomous

autonomie [ɔtɔnɔmi] NF autonomy; (Pol) self-government, autonomy; **~ de vol** range

autonomiste [ɔtɔnɔmist] NMF separatist

autoportrait [ɔtɔpɔrtrɛ] NM self-portrait

autopsie [ɔtɔpsi] NF post-mortem (examination), autopsy

autopsier [ɔtɔpsje] /7/ VT to carry out a post-mortem ou an autopsy on

autoradio [otoradjo] NF car radio

autorail [ɔtɔrɑj] NM railcar

autorisation [ɔtɔrizasjɔ̃] NF permission, authorization; (papiers) permit; **donner à qn l'~ de** to give sb permission to, authorize sb to; **avoir l'~ de faire** to be allowed ou have permission to do, be authorized to do

autorisé, e [ɔtɔrize] ADJ (opinion, sources) authoritative; (permis): **~ à faire** authorized ou permitted to do; **dans les milieux autorisés** in official circles

autoriser [ɔtɔrize] /1/ VT to give permission for, authorize; (fig) to allow (of), sanction; **~ qn à faire** to give permission to sb to do, authorize sb to do

autoritaire [ɔtɔritɛr] ADJ authoritarian

autoritarisme [ɔtɔritarism] NM authoritarianism

autorité [ɔtɔrite] NF authority; **faire ~** to be authoritative; **autorités constituées** constitutional authorities

autoroute [otorut] NF motorway (BRIT), expressway (US); **~ de l'information** (Inform) information superhighway

Motorways in France, indicated by blue road signs with the letter A followed by a number, are toll roads. The speed limit is 130 km/h (110 km/h when it is raining). At the tollgate, the lanes marked réservé and with an orange T are reserved for people who subscribe to télépéage, an electronic payment system.

autoroutier, -ière [ɔtɔrutje, -jɛr] ADJ motorway cpd (BRIT), expressway cpd (US)

autosatisfaction [ɔtɔsatisfaksjɔ̃] NF self-satisfaction

auto-stop [otostɔp] NM: **l'~** hitch-hiking; **faire de l'~** to hitch-hike; **prendre qn en ~** to give sb a lift

auto-stoppeur, -euse [ɔtɔstɔpœr, -øz] NM/F hitch-hiker, hitcher (BRIT)

autosuffisant, e [ɔtɔsyfizɑ̃, -ɑ̃t] ADJ self-sufficient

autosuggestion [ɔtɔsygʒɛstjɔ̃] NF autosuggestion

autour [otur] ADV around; **~ de** prép around; (environ) around, about; **tout ~** adv all around

$\boxed{\textbf{MOT-CLÉ}}$

autre [otr] ADJ **1** (différent) other, different; **je préférerais un autre verre** I'd prefer another ou a different glass; **d'autres verres** different glasses; **se sentir autre** to feel different; **la difficulté est autre** the difficulty is ou lies elsewhere

2 (supplémentaire) other; **je voudrais un autre verre d'eau** I'd like another glass of water

3: **autre chose** something else; **autre part** somewhere else; **d'autre part** on the other hand

▸ PRON **1: un autre** another (one); **nous/vous autres** us/you; **d'autres** others; **l'autre** the other (one); **les autres** the others; (*autrui*) others; **l'un et l'autre** both of them; **ni l'un ni l'autre** neither of them; **se détester l'un l'autre/les uns les autres** to hate each other *ou* one another; **d'une semaine/minute à l'autre** from one week/minute *ou* moment to the next; (*incessamment*) any week/minute *ou* moment now; **de temps à autre** from time to time; **entre autres** (*personnes*) among others; (*choses*) among other things
2 (*expressions*): **j'en ai vu d'autres** I've seen worse; **à d'autres!** pull the other one!

autrefois [otʀəfwa] ADV in the past
autrement [otʀəmɑ̃] ADV differently; (*d'une manière différente*) in another way; (*sinon*) otherwise; **je n'ai pas pu faire ~** I couldn't do anything else, I couldn't do otherwise; **~ dit** in other words; (*c'est-à-dire*) that is to say
Autriche [otʀiʃ] NF: **l'~** Austria
autrichien, ne [otʀiʃjɛ̃, -ɛn] ADJ Austrian ▸ NM/F: **A~, ne** Austrian
autruche [otʀyʃ] NF ostrich; **faire l'~** (*fig*) to bury one's head in the sand
autrui [otʀɥi] PRON others
auvent [ovɑ̃] NM canopy
auvergnat, e [ovɛʀɲa, -at] ADJ of *ou* from the Auvergne
Auvergne [ovɛʀɲ] NF: **l'~** the Auvergne
aux [o] PRÉP *voir* **à**
auxiliaire [ɔksiljɛʀ] ADJ, NM/F auxiliary
auxquels, auxquelles [okɛl] PRON *voir* **lequel**
AV SIGLE M (*Banque*: = *avis de virement*) advice of bank transfer ▸ ABR (*Auto*) = **avant**
av. ABR (= *avenue*) Av(e)
avachi, e [avaʃi] ADJ limp, flabby; (*chaussure, vêtement*) out-of-shape; (*personne*): **~ sur qch** slumped on *ou* across sth
avais *etc* [avɛ] VB *voir* **avoir**
aval [aval] NM (*accord*) endorsement, backing; (*Géo*): **en ~** downstream, downriver; (*sur une pente*) downhill; **en ~ de** downstream *ou* downriver from; downhill from
avalanche [avalɑ̃ʃ] NF avalanche; **~ poudreuse** powder snow avalanche
avaler [avale] /1/ VT to swallow
avaliser [avalize] /1/ VT (*plan, entreprise*) to back, support; (*Comm, Jur*) to guarantee
avance [avɑ̃s] NF (*de troupes etc*) advance; (*progrès*) progress; (*d'argent*) advance; (*opposé à retard*) lead; being ahead of schedule; **avances** NFPL overtures; (*amoureuses*) advances; **une ~ de 300 m/4 h** (*Sport*) a 300 m/4 hour lead; (**être**) **en ~** (to be) early; (*sur un programme*) (to be) ahead of schedule; **on n'est pas en ~!** we're kind of late!; **être en ~ sur qn** to be ahead of sb; **d'~, à l'~, par ~** in advance; **~ (du) papier** (*Inform*) paper advance
avancé, e [avɑ̃se] ADJ advanced; (*travail etc*) well on, well under way; (*fruit, fromage*) overripe ▸ NF projection; overhang; **il est ~ pour son âge** he is advanced for his age

avancement [avɑ̃smɑ̃] NM (*professionnel*) promotion; (*de travaux*) progress
avancer [avɑ̃se] /3/ VI to move forward, advance; (*projet, travail*) to make progress; (*être en saillie*) to overhang; to project; (*montre, réveil*) to be fast; (: *d'habitude*) to gain ▸ VT to move forward, advance; (*argent*) to advance; (*montre, pendule*) to put forward; (*faire progresser: travail etc*) to advance, move on; **s'avancer** VI to move forward, advance; (*fig*) to commit o.s.; (*faire saillie*) to overhang; to project; **j'avance (d'une heure)** I'm (an hour) fast
avanies [avani] NFPL snubs (BRIT), insults
avant [avɑ̃] PRÉP before ▸ ADV: **trop/plus ~** too far/further forward ▸ ADJ INV: **siège/roue ~** front seat/wheel ▸ NM (*d'un véhicule, bâtiment*) front; (*Sport: joueur*) forward; **~ qu'il parte/de partir** before he leaves/leaving; **~ qu'il (ne) pleuve** before it rains (*ou* rained); **~ tout** (*surtout*) above all; **à l'~** (*dans un véhicule*) in (the) front; **en ~** *adv* (*se pencher, tomber*) forward(s); **partir en ~** to go on ahead; **en ~ de** *prép* in front of; **aller de l'~** to steam ahead (*fig*), make good progress
avantage [avɑ̃taʒ] NM advantage; (*Tennis*): **~ service/dehors** advantage *ou* van (BRIT) *ou* ad (US) in/out; **tirer ~ de** to take advantage of; **vous auriez ~ à faire** you would be well-advised to do, it would be to your advantage to do; **à l'~ de qn** to sb's advantage; **être à son ~** to be at one's best; **avantages en nature** benefits in kind; **avantages sociaux** fringe benefits
avantager [avɑ̃taʒe] /3/ VT (*favoriser*) to favour; (*embellir*) to flatter
avantageux, -euse [avɑ̃taʒø, -øz] ADJ (*prix*) attractive; (*intéressant*) attractively priced; (*portrait, coiffure*) flattering; **conditions avantageuses** favourable terms
avant-bras [avɑ̃bʀa] NM INV forearm
avant-centre [avɑ̃sɑ̃tʀ] NM centre-forward
avant-coureur [avɑ̃kuʀœʀ] ADJ INV (*bruit etc*) precursory; **signe ~** advance indication *ou* sign
avant-dernier, -ière [avɑ̃dɛʀnje, -jɛʀ] ADJ, NM/F next to last, last but one
avant-garde [avɑ̃gaʀd] NF (*Mil*) vanguard; (*fig*) avant-garde; **d'~** avant-garde
avant-goût [avɑ̃gu] NM foretaste
avant-hier [avɑ̃tjɛʀ] ADV the day before yesterday
avant-poste [avɑ̃pɔst] NM outpost
avant-première [avɑ̃pʀəmjɛʀ] NF (*de film*) preview; **en ~** as a preview, in a preview showing
avant-projet [avɑ̃pʀɔʒɛ] NM preliminary draft
avant-propos [avɑ̃pʀɔpo] NM foreword
avant-veille [avɑ̃vɛj] NF: **l'~** two days before
avare [avaʀ] ADJ miserly, avaricious ▸ NM/F miser; **~ de compliments** stingy *ou* sparing with one's compliments
avarice [avaʀis] NF avarice, miserliness
avarié, e [avaʀje] ADJ (*viande, fruits*) rotting, going off (BRIT); (*Navig: navire*) damaged
avaries [avaʀi] NFPL (*Navig*) damage *sg*

avatar [avatar] NM misadventure; (*transformation*) metamorphosis

avec [avɛk] PRÉP with; (*à l'égard de*) to(wards), with ▸ ADV (*fam*) with it (*ou* him *etc*); **~ habileté/lenteur** skilfully/slowly; **~ eux/ces maladies** with them/these diseases; **~ ça** (*malgré ça*) for all that; **et ~ ça?** (*dans un magasin*) anything *ou* something else?

avenant, e [avnã, -ãt] ADJ pleasant ▸ NM (*Assurances*) additional clause; **à l'~** *adv* in keeping

avènement [avɛnmã] NM (*d'un roi*) accession, succession; (*d'un changement*) advent; (*d'une politique, idée*) coming

avenir [avniʀ] NM: **l'~** the future; **à l'~** in future; **sans ~** with no future, without a future; **carrière/politicien d'~** career/politician with prospects *ou* a future

Avent [avã] NM: **l'~** Advent

aventure [avãtyʀ] NF: **l'~** adventure; **une ~** an adventure; (*amoureuse*) an affair; **partir à l'~** to go off in search of adventure; (*au hasard*) to go where one's fancy takes one; **roman/film d'~** adventure story/film

aventurer [avãtyʀe] /1/ VT (*somme, réputation, vie*) to stake; (*remarque, opinion*) to venture; **s'aventurer** VI to venture; **s'aventurer à faire qch** to venture into sth

aventureux, -euse [avãtyʀø, -øz] ADJ adventurous, venturesome; (*projet*) risky, chancy

aventurier, -ière [avãtyʀje, -jɛʀ] NM/F adventurer ▸ NF (*péj*) adventuress

avenu, e [avny] ADJ: **nul et non ~** null and void

avenue [avny] NF avenue

avéré, e [aveʀe] ADJ recognized, acknowledged

avérer [aveʀe] /6/: **s'avérer** VR: **s'avérer faux/coûteux** to prove (to be) wrong/expensive

averse [avɛʀs] NF shower

aversion [avɛʀsjɔ̃] NF aversion, loathing

averti, e [avɛʀti] ADJ (well-)informed

avertir [avɛʀtiʀ] /2/ VT: **~ qn (de qch/que)** to warn sb (of sth/that); (*renseigner*) to inform sb (of sth/that); **~ qn de ne pas faire qch** to warn sb not to do sth

avertissement [avɛʀtismã] NM warning

avertisseur [avɛʀtisœʀ] NM horn, siren; **~ d'incendie** (fire) alarm

aveu, x [avø] NM confession; **passer aux ~** to make a confession; **de l'~ de** according to

aveuglant, e [avœglã, -ãt] ADJ blinding

aveugle [avœgl] ADJ blind ▸ NMF blind person; **les aveugles** blind people; **test en (double) ~** (double) blind test

aveuglement [avœgləmã] NM blindness

aveuglément [avœglemã] ADV blindly

aveugler [avœgle] /1/ VT to blind

aveuglette [avœglɛt] : **à l'~** *adv* groping one's way along; (*fig*) in the dark, blindly

avez [ave] VB *voir* **avoir**

aviateur, -trice [avjatœʀ, -tʀis] NM/F aviator, pilot

aviation [avjasjɔ̃] NF (*secteur commercial*) aviation; (*sport, métier de pilote*) flying; (*Mil*) air force; **terrain d'~** airfield; **~ de chasse** fighter force

aviculteur, -trice [avikyltœʀ, -tʀis] NM/F poultry farmer; bird breeder

aviculture [avikyltyʀ] NF (*de volailles*) poultry farming

avide [avid] ADJ eager; (*péj*) greedy, grasping; **~ de** (*sang etc*) thirsting for; **~ d'honneurs/d'argent** greedy for honours/money; **~ de connaître/d'apprendre** eager to know/learn

avidité [avidite] NF eagerness; greed

avilir [aviliʀ] /2/ VT to debase

avilissant, e [avilisã, -ãt] ADJ degrading

aviné, e [avine] ADJ drunken

avion [avjɔ̃] NM (aero)plane (BRIT), (air)plane (US); **aller (quelque part) en ~** to go (somewhere) by plane, fly (somewhere); **par ~** by airmail; **~ de chasse** fighter; **~ de ligne** airliner; **~ à réaction** jet (plane)

avion-cargo [avjɔ̃kaʀgo] NM air freighter

avion-citerne [avjɔ̃sitɛʀn] NM air tanker

aviron [aviʀɔ̃] NM oar; (*sport*): **l'~** rowing

avis [avi] NM opinion; (*notification*) notice; (*Comm*): **~ de crédit/débit** credit/debit advice; **à mon ~** in my opinion; **je suis de votre ~** I share your opinion, I am of your opinion; **être d'~ que** to be of the opinion that; **changer d'~** to change one's mind; **sauf ~ contraire** unless you hear to the contrary; **sans ~ préalable** without notice; **jusqu'à nouvel ~** until further notice; **~ de décès** death announcement

avisé, e [avize] ADJ sensible, wise; **être bien/mal ~ de faire** to be well-/ill-advised to do

aviser [avize] /1/ VT (*voir*) to notice, catch sight of; (*informer*): **~ qn de/que** to advise *ou* inform *ou* notify sb of/that ▸ VI to think about things, assess the situation; **nous aviserons sur place** we'll work something out once we're there; **s'~ de qch/que** to become suddenly aware of sth/that; **s'~ de faire** to take it into one's head to do

aviver [avive] /1/ VT (*douleur, chagrin*) to intensify; (*intérêt, désir*) to sharpen; (*colère, querelle*) to stir up; (*couleur*) to brighten up

av. J.-C. ABR (= *avant Jésus-Christ*) BC

avocat, e [avɔka, -at] NM/F (*Jur*) ≈ barrister (BRIT), lawyer; (*fig*) advocate, champion ▸ NM (*Culin*) avocado (pear); **se faire l'~ du diable** to be the devil's advocate; **l'~ de la défense/partie civile** the counsel for the defence/plaintiff; **~ d'affaires** business lawyer; **~ général** assistant public prosecutor

avocat-conseil [avɔkakɔ̃sɛj] (*pl* **avocats-conseils**) NM ≈ barrister (BRIT)

avocat-stagiaire [avɔkastaʒjɛʀ] (*pl* **avocats-stagiaires**) NM ≈ barrister doing his articles (BRIT)

avoine [avwan] NF oats *pl*

MOT-CLÉ

avoir [avwaʀ] /34/ VT **1** (*posséder*) to have; **elle a deux enfants/une belle maison** she has (got) two children/a lovely house; **il a les yeux**

bleus he has (got) blue eyes; **vous avez du sel?** do you have any salt?; **avoir du courage/de la patience** to be brave/patient

2 (*éprouver*): **qu'est-ce que tu as?, qu'as-tu?** what's wrong?, what's the matter?; **avoir de la peine** to be *ou* feel sad; *voir aussi* **faim; peur** *etc*

3 (*âge, dimensions*) to be; **il a 3 ans** he is 3 (years old); **le mur a 3 mètres de haut** the wall is 3 metres high

4 (*fam: duper*) to do, have; **on vous a eu!** you've been done *ou* had!; (*fait une plaisanterie*) we *ou* they had you there

5: en avoir contre qn to have a grudge against sb; **en avoir assez** to be fed up; **j'en ai pour une demi-heure** it'll take me half an hour; **n'avoir que faire de qch** to have no use for sth

6 (*obtenir, attraper*) to get; **j'ai réussi à avoir mon train** I managed to get *ou* catch my train; **j'ai réussi à avoir le renseignement qu'il me fallait** I managed to get (hold of) the information I needed

▶ VB AUX **1** to have; **avoir mangé/dormi** to have eaten/slept; **hier je n'ai pas mangé** I didn't eat yesterday

2 (*avoir +à +infinitif*): **avoir à faire qch** to have to do sth; **vous n'avez qu'à lui demander** you only have to ask him; **tu n'as pas à me poser des questions** it's not for you to ask me questions

▶ VB IMPERS **1: il y a** (+ *singulier*) there is; (+ *pluriel*) there are; **il y avait du café/des gâteaux** there was coffee/there were cakes; **qu'y a-t-il?, qu'est-ce qu'il y a?** what's the matter?, what is it?; **il doit y avoir une explication** there must be an explanation; **il n'y a qu'à ...** we (*ou* you *etc*) will just have to ...; **il ne peut y en avoir qu'un** there can only be one

2: il y a (*temporel*): **il y a 10 ans** 10 years ago; **il y a 10 ans/longtemps que je le connais** I've known him for 10 years/a long time; **il y a 10 ans qu'il est arrivé** it's 10 years since he arrived

▶ NM assets *pl*, resources *pl*; (*Comm*) credit; **avoir fiscal** tax credit

avoisinant, e [avwazinã, -ãt] ADJ neighbouring

avoisiner [avwazine] /1/ VT to be near *ou* close to; (*fig*) to border *ou* verge on

avons [avɔ̃] VB *voir* **avoir**

avortement [avɔʀtəmã] NM abortion

avorter [avɔʀte] /1/ VI (*Méd*) to have an abortion; (*fig*) to fail; **faire ~** to abort; **se faire ~** to have an abortion

avorton [avɔʀtɔ̃] NM (*péj*) little runt

avouable [avwabl] ADJ respectable; **des pensées non avouables** unrepeatable thoughts

avoué, e [avwe] ADJ avowed ▶ NM (*Jur*) ≈ solicitor (BRIT), lawyer

avouer [avwe] /1/ VT (*crime, défaut*) to confess (to) ▶ VI (*se confesser*) to confess; (*admettre*) to admit; **~ avoir fait/que** to admit *ou* confess to having done/that; **~ que oui/non** to admit that that is so/not so

avril [avʀil] NM April; *voir aussi* **juillet**

axe [aks] NM axis (*pl* axes); (*de roue etc*) axle; (*fig*) main line; **dans l'~ de** directly in line with; **~ routier** trunk road (BRIT), main road, highway (US)

axer [akse] /1/ VT: **~ qch sur** to centre sth on

axial, e, -aux [aksjal, -o] ADJ axial

axiome [aksjom] NM axiom

ayant [ɛjã] VB *voir* **avoir** ▶ NM: **~ droit** assignee; **~ droit à** (*pension etc*) person eligible for *ou* entitled to

ayons *etc* [ɛjɔ̃] VB *voir* **avoir**

azalée [azale] NF azalea

Azerbaïdjan [azɛʀbaidʒã] NM Azerbaijan

azimut [azimyt] NM azimuth; **tous azimuts** *adj* (*fig*) omnidirectional

azote [azɔt] NM nitrogen

azoté, e [azɔte] ADJ nitrogenous

AZT SIGLE M (= *azidothymidine*) AZT

aztèque [aztɛk] ADJ Aztec

azur [azyʀ] NM (*couleur*) azure, sky blue; (*ciel*) skies *pl*

azyme [azim] ADJ: **pain ~** unleavened bread

Bb

B, b [be] NM INV B, b ▶ ABR = **bien**; **B comme Bertha** B for Benjamin (BRIT) *ou* Baker (US)
BA SIGLE F (= *bonne action*) good deed
baba [baba] ADJ INV: **en être ~** (*fam*) to be flabbergasted ▶ NM: **~ au rhum** rum baba
babil [babi] NM prattle
babillage [babijaʒ] NM chatter
babiller [babije] /1/ VI to prattle, chatter; (*bébé*) to babble
babines [babin] NFPL chops
babiole [babjɔl] NF (*bibelot*) trinket; (*vétille*) trifle
bâbord [babɔR] NM: **à** *ou* **par ~** to port, on the port side
babouin [babwẽ] NM baboon
baby-foot [babifut] NM INV table football
Babylone [babilɔn] N Babylon
babylonien, ne [babilɔnjẽ, -ɛn] ADJ Babylonian
baby-sitter [babisitœR] NMF baby-sitter
baby-sitting [babisitiŋ] NM baby-sitting; **faire du ~** to baby-sit
bac [bak] NM (*Scol*) = **baccalauréat**; (*bateau*) ferry; (*récipient*) tub; (: *Photo etc*) tray; (: *Industrie*) tank; **~ à glace** ice-tray; **~ à légumes** vegetable compartment *ou* rack
baccalauréat [bakalɔRea] NM ≈ A-levels *pl* (BRIT), ≈ high school diploma (US); *see note*

> The *baccalauréat* or *bac* is the school-leaving examination taken at a French *lycée* at the age of 18; it marks the end of seven years' secondary education. Several subject combinations are available, although in all cases a broad range is studied. Successful candidates can go on to university, if they so wish.

bâche [baʃ] NF tarpaulin, canvas sheet
bachelier, -ière [baʃəlje, -jɛR] NM/F *holder of the baccalauréat*
bâcher [baʃe] /1/ VT to cover (with a canvas sheet *ou* a tarpaulin)
bachot [baʃo] NM = **baccalauréat**
bachotage [baʃɔtaʒ] NM (*Scol*) cramming
bachoter [baʃɔte] /1/ VI (*Scol*) to cram (for an exam)
bacille [basil] NM bacillus
bâcler [bakle] /1/ VT to botch (up)
bacon [bekɔn] NM bacon
bactéricide [bakteRisid] NM (*Méd*) bactericide
bactérie [bakteRi] NF bacterium

bactérien, ne [bakteRjẽ, -ɛn] ADJ bacterial
bactériologie [bakteRjɔlɔʒi] NF bacteriology
bactériologique [bakteRjɔlɔʒik] ADJ bacteriological
bactériologiste [bakteRjɔlɔʒist] NMF bacteriologist
badaud, e [bado, -od] NM/F idle onlooker
baderne [badɛRn] NF (*péj*): **(vieille) ~** old fossil
badge [badʒ] NM badge
badigeon [badiʒɔ̃] NM distemper; colourwash
badigeonner [badiʒɔne] /1/ VT to distemper; to colourwash; (*péj: barbouiller*) to daub; (*Méd*) to paint
badin, e [badẽ, -in] ADJ light-hearted, playful
badinage [badinaʒ] NM banter
badine [badin] NF switch (*stick*)
badiner [badine] /1/ VI: **~ avec qch** to treat sth lightly; **ne pas ~ avec qch** not to trifle with sth
badminton [badminton] NM badminton
BAFA [bafa] SIGLE M (= *Brevet d'aptitude aux fonctions d'animation*) *diploma for youth leaders and workers*
baffe [baf] NF (*fam*) slap, clout
Baffin [bafin] NF: **terre de ~** Baffin Island
baffle [bafl] NM baffle (board)
bafouer [bafwe] /1/ VT to deride, ridicule
bafouillage [bafujaʒ] NM (*fam: propos incohérents*) jumble of words
bafouiller [bafuje] /1/ VI, VT to stammer
bâfrer [bafRe] /1/ VI, VT (*fam*) to guzzle, gobble
bagage [bagaʒ] NM: **bagages** luggage *sg*, baggage *sg*; (*connaissances*) background, knowledge; **faire ses bagages** to pack (one's bags); **~ littéraire** (stock of) literary knowledge; **bagages à main** hand-luggage
bagarre [bagaR] NF fight, brawl; **il aime la ~** he loves a fight, he likes fighting
bagarrer [bagaRe] /1/: **se bagarrer** VI to (have a) fight
bagarreur, -euse [bagaRœR, -øz] ADJ pugnacious ▶ NM/F: **il est ~** he loves a fight
bagatelle [bagatɛl] NF trifle, trifling sum (*ou matter*)
Bagdad, Baghdâd [bagdad] N Baghdad
bagnard [baɲaR] NM convict
bagne [baɲ] NM penal colony; **c'est le ~** (*fig*) it's forced labour
bagnole [baɲɔl] NF (*fam*) car, wheels *pl* (BRIT)

bagout [bagu] NM glibness; **avoir du ~** to have the gift of the gab

bague [bag] NF ring; **~ de fiançailles** engagement ring; **~ de serrage** clip

baguenauder [bagnode] /1/: **se baguenauder** VI to trail around, loaf around

baguer [bage] /1/ VT to ring

baguette [baget] NF stick; (*cuisine chinoise*) chopstick; (*de chef d'orchestre*) baton; (*pain*) stick of (French) bread; (*Constr: moulure*) beading; **mener qn à la ~** to rule sb with a rod of iron; **~ magique** magic wand; **~ de sourcier** divining rod; **~ de tambour** drumstick

Bahamas [baamas] NFPL **les (îles) ~** the Bahamas

Bahreïn [baʀɛn] NM Bahrain *ou* Bahrein

bahut [bay] NM chest

bai, e [bɛ] ADJ (*cheval*) bay

baie [bɛ] NF (*Géo*) bay; (*fruit*) berry; **~ (vitrée)** picture window

baignade [bɛɲad] NF (*action*) bathing; (*bain*) bathe; (*endroit*) bathing place; **"~ interdite"** "no bathing"

baigné, e [bɛɲe] ADJ: **~ de** bathed in; (*trempé*) soaked with; (*inondé*) flooded with

baigner [bɛɲe] /1/ VT (*bébé*) to bath ▶ VI: **~ dans son sang** to lie in a pool of blood; **~ dans la brume** to be shrouded in mist; **se baigner** VI to go swimming *ou* bathing; (*dans une baignoire*) to have a bath; **ça baigne!** (*fam*) everything's great!

baigneur, -euse [bɛɲœʀ, -øz] NM/F bather ▶ NM (*poupée*) baby doll

baignoire [bɛɲwaʀ] NF bath(tub); (*Théât*) ground-floor box

bail [baj] (*pl* **baux** [bo]) NM lease; **donner** *ou* **prendre qch à ~** to lease sth

bâillement [bajmɑ̃] NM yawn

bâiller [baje] /1/ VI to yawn; (*être ouvert*) to gape

bailleur [bajœʀ] NM: **~ de fonds** sponsor, backer; (*Comm*) sleeping *ou* silent partner

bâillon [bajɔ̃] NM gag

bâillonner [bajɔne] /1/ VT to gag

bain [bɛ̃] NM (*dans une baignoire, Photo, Tech*) bath; (*dans la mer, une piscine*) swim; **costume de ~** bathing costume (BRIT), swimsuit; **prendre un ~** to have a bath; **se mettre dans le ~** (*fig*) to get into (the way of) it *ou* things; **~ de bouche** mouthwash; **~ de foule** walkabout; **~ moussant** bubble bath; **~ de pieds** footbath; (*au bord de la mer*) paddle; **~ de siège** hip bath; **~ de soleil** sunbathing *no pl*; **prendre un ~ de soleil** to sunbathe; **bains de mer** sea bathing *sg*; **bains(-douches) municipaux** public baths

bain-marie [bɛ̃maʀi] (*pl* **bains-marie**) NM double boiler; **faire chauffer au ~** (*boîte etc*) to immerse in boiling water

baïonnette [bajɔnɛt] NF bayonet; (*Élec*): **douille à ~** bayonet socket; **ampoule à ~** bulb with a bayonet fitting

baisemain [bɛzmɛ̃] NM kissing a lady's hand

baiser [beze] /1/ NM kiss ▶ VT (*main, front*) to kiss; (!) to screw (!)

baisse [bɛs] NF fall, drop; (*Comm*): **"~ sur la viande"** "meat prices down"; **en ~** (*cours, action*)

falling; **à la ~** downwards

baisser [bese] /1/ VT to lower; (*radio, chauffage*) to turn down; (*Auto: phares*) to dip (BRIT), lower (US) ▶ VI to fall, drop, go down; (*vue, santé*) to fail, dwindle; **se baisser** VI to bend down

bajoues [baʒu] NFPL chaps, chops

bal [bal] NM dance; (*grande soirée*) ball; **~ costumé/masqué** fancy-dress/masked ball; **~ musette** dance (*with accordion accompaniment*)

balade [balad] (*fam*) NF (*à pied*) walk, stroll; (*en voiture*) drive; **faire une ~** to go for a walk *ou* stroll; to go for a drive

balader [balade] /1/ (*fam*) VT (*traîner*) to trail around; **se balader** VI to go for a walk *ou* stroll; to go for a drive

baladeur [baladœʀ] NM personal stereo, Walkman®; **~ numérique** MP3 player

baladeuse [baladøz] NF inspection lamp

baladin [baladɛ̃] NM wandering entertainer

balafre [balafʀ] NF gash, slash; (*cicatrice*) scar

balafrer [balafʀe] /1/ VT to gash, slash

balai [balɛ] NM broom, brush; (*Auto: d'essuie-glace*) blade; (*Mus: de batterie etc*) brush; **donner un coup de ~** to give the floor a sweep; **~ mécanique** carpet sweeper

balai-brosse [balɛbʀɔs] (*pl* **balais-brosses**) NM (long-handled) scrubbing brush

balance [balɑ̃s] NF (*à plateaux*) scales *pl*; (*de précision*) balance; (*Comm, Pol*): **~ des comptes** *ou* **paiements** balance of payments; (*signe*): **la B~** Libra, the Scales; **être de la B~** to be Libra; **~ commerciale** balance of trade; **~ des forces** balance of power; **~ romaine** steelyard

balancelle [balɑ̃sɛl] NF garden hammock-seat

balancer [balɑ̃se] /3/ VT to swing; (*lancer*) to fling, chuck; (*renvoyer, jeter*) to chuck out ▶ VI to swing; **se balancer** VI to swing; (*bateau*) to rock; (*branche*) to sway; **se balancer de qch** (*fam*) not to give a toss about sth

balancier [balɑ̃sje] NM (*de pendule*) pendulum; (*de montre*) balance wheel; (*perche*) (balancing) pole

balançoire [balɑ̃swaʀ] NF swing; (*sur pivot*) seesaw

balayage [balɛjaʒ] NM sweeping; scanning

balayer [baleje] /8/ VT (*feuilles etc*) to sweep up, brush up; (*pièce, cour*) to sweep; (*chasser*) to sweep away *ou* aside; (*radar*) to scan; (: *phares*) to sweep across

balayette [balɛjɛt] NF small brush

balayeur, -euse [balɛjœʀ, -øz] NM/F road sweeper ▶ NF (*engin*) road sweeper

balayures [balɛjyʀ] NFPL sweepings

balbutiement [balbysimɑ̃] NM (*paroles*) stammering *no pl*; **balbutiements** NMPL (*fig: débuts*) first faltering steps

balbutier [balbysje] /7/ VI, VT to stammer

balcon [balkɔ̃] NM balcony; (*Théât*) dress circle

baldaquin [baldakɛ̃] NM canopy

Bâle [bal] N Basle *ou* Basel

Baléares [baleaʀ] NFPL: **les ~** the Balearic Islands, the Balearics

baleine [balɛn] NF whale; (*de parapluie*) rib; (*de corset*) bone

baleinier [balenje] NM (Navig) whaler
baleinière [balɛnjɛʀ] NF whaleboat
balisage [balizaʒ] NM (signaux) beacons pl; buoys pl; runway lights pl; signs pl, markers pl
balise [baliz] NF (Navig) beacon, (marker) buoy; (Aviat) runway light, beacon; (Auto, Ski) sign, marker
baliser [balize] /1/ VT to mark out (with beacons ou lights etc)
balistique [balistik] ADJ (engin) ballistic ▶ NF ballistics
balivernes [balivɛʀn] NFPL twaddle sg (BRIT), nonsense sg
balkanique [balkanik] ADJ Balkan
Balkans [balkɑ̃] NMPL: **les** ~ the Balkans
ballade [balad] NF ballad
ballant, e [balɑ̃, -ɑ̃t] ADJ dangling
ballast [balast] NM ballast
balle [bal] NF (de fusil) bullet; (de sport) ball; (du blé) chaff; (paquet) bale; (fam: franc) franc; ~ **perdue** stray bullet
ballerine [bal(ə)ʀin] NF (danseuse) ballet dancer; (chaussure) pump, ballet shoe
ballet [balɛ] NM ballet; (fig): ~ **diplomatique** diplomatic to-ings and fro-ings
ballon [balɔ̃] NM (de sport) ball; (jouet, Aviat, de bande dessinée) balloon; (de vin) glass; ~ **d'essai** (météorologique) pilot balloon; (fig) feeler(s); ~ **de football** football; ~ **d'oxygène** oxygen bottle
ballonner [balɔne] /1/ VT: **j'ai le ventre ballonné** I feel bloated
ballon-sonde [balɔ̃sɔ̃d] (pl **ballons-sondes**) NM sounding balloon
ballot [balo] NM bundle; (péj) nitwit
ballottage [balɔtaʒ] NM (Pol) second ballot
ballotter [balɔte] /1/ VI to roll around; (bateau etc) to toss ▶ VT to shake ou throw about; to toss; **être ballotté entre** (fig) to be shunted between; (: indécis) to be torn between
ballottine [balɔtin] NF (Culin): ~ **de volaille** meat loaf made with poultry
ball-trap [baltʀap] NM (appareil) trap; (tir) clay pigeon shooting
balluchon [balyʃɔ̃] NM bundle (of clothes)
balnéaire [balneɛʀ] ADJ seaside cpd; **station** ~ seaside resort
balnéothérapie [balneɔteʀapi] NF spa bath therapy
BALO SIGLE M (= Bulletin des annonces légales obligatoires) ≈ Public Notices (in newspapers etc)
balourd, e [baluʀ, -uʀd] ADJ clumsy ▶ NM/F clodhopper
balourdise [baluʀdiz] NF clumsiness; (gaffe) blunder
balte [balt] ADJ Baltic ▶ NMF: **B~** native of the Baltic States
baltique [baltik] ADJ Baltic ▶ NF: **la (mer) B~** the Baltic (Sea)
baluchon [balyʃɔ̃] NM = **balluchon**
balustrade [balystʀad] NF railings pl, handrail
bambin [bɑ̃bɛ̃] NM little child
bambou [bɑ̃bu] NM bamboo
ban [bɑ̃] NM round of applause, cheer; **être/ mettre au ~ de** to be outlawed/to outlaw from;

le ~ **et l'arrière-~ de sa famille** every last one of his relatives; **bans (de mariage)** banns, bans
banal, e [banal] ADJ banal, commonplace; (péj) trite; **four/moulin** ~ village oven/mill
banalisé, e [banalize] ADJ (voiture de police) unmarked
banalité [banalite] NF banality; (remarque) truism, trite remark
banane [banan] NF banana; (sac) waist-bag, bum-bag
bananeraie [banan ʀɛ] NF banana plantation
bananier [bananje] NM banana tree; (bateau) banana boat
banc [bɑ̃] NM seat, bench; (de poissons) shoal; ~ **des accusés** dock; ~ **d'essai** (fig) testing ground; ~ **de sable** sandbank; ~ **des témoins** witness box; ~ **de touche** dugout
bancaire [bɑ̃kɛʀ] ADJ banking; (chèque, carte) bank cpd
bancal, e [bɑ̃kal] ADJ wobbly; (personne) bow-legged; (fig: projet) shaky
bandage [bɑ̃daʒ] NM bandaging; (pansement) bandage; ~ **herniaire** truss
bande [bɑ̃d] NF (de tissu etc) strip; (Méd) bandage; (motif, dessin) stripe; (Ciné) film; (Radio, groupe) band; (péj): **une** ~ **de** a bunch ou crowd of; **par la** ~ in a roundabout way; **donner de la** ~ to list; **faire** ~ **à part** to keep to o.s.; ~ **dessinée** strip cartoon (BRIT), comic strip; ~ **magnétique** magnetic tape; ~ **passante** (Inform) bandwidth; ~ **perforée** punched tape; ~ **de roulement** (de pneu) tread; ~ **sonore** sound track; ~ **de terre** strip of land; ~ **Velpeau**® (Méd) crêpe bandage
bandé, e [bɑ̃de] ADJ bandaged; **les yeux bandés** blindfold
bande-annonce [bɑ̃danɔ̃s] (pl **bandes-annonces**) NF (Ciné) trailer
bandeau, x [bɑ̃do] NM headband; (sur les yeux) blindfold; (Méd) head bandage
bandelette [bɑ̃dlɛt] NF strip of cloth, bandage
bander [bɑ̃de] /1/ VT (blessure) to bandage; (muscle) to tense; (arc) to bend ▶ VI (!) to have a hard on (!); ~ **les yeux à qn** to blindfold sb
banderole [bɑ̃dʀɔl] NF banderole; (dans un défilé etc) streamer
bande-son [bɑ̃dsɔ̃] (pl **bandes-son**) NF (Ciné) soundtrack
bandit [bɑ̃di] NM bandit
banditisme [bɑ̃ditism] NM violent crime, armed robberies pl
bandoulière [bɑ̃duljɛʀ] NF: **en** ~ (slung ou worn) across the shoulder
Bangkok [bɑ̃kkɔk] N Bangkok
Bangladesh [bɑ̃gladɛʃ] NM: **le** ~ Bangladesh
banjo [bɑ̃(d)ʒo] NM banjo
banlieue [bɑ̃ljø] NF suburbs pl; **quartiers de** ~ suburban areas; **trains de** ~ commuter trains
banlieusard, e [bɑ̃ljøzaʀ, -aʀd] NM/F suburbanite
bannière [banjɛʀ] NF banner
bannir [baniʀ] /2/ VT to banish
banque [bɑ̃k] NF bank; (activités) banking; ~ **des yeux/du sang** eye/blood bank; ~ **d'affaires**

b

merchant bank; **~ de dépôt** deposit bank; **~ de données** (*Inform*) data bank; **~ d'émission** bank of issue

banqueroute [bɑ̃kʀut] NF bankruptcy

banquet [bɑ̃kɛ] NM (*de club*) dinner; (*de noces*) reception; (*d'apparat*) banquet

banquette [bɑ̃kɛt] NF seat

banquier [bɑ̃kje] NM banker

banquise [bɑ̃kiz] NF ice field

bantou, e [bɑ̃tu] ADJ Bantu

baptême [batɛm] NM (*sacrement*) baptism; (*cérémonie*) christening; baptism; (*d'un navire*) launching; (*d'une cloche*) consecration, dedication; **~ de l'air** first flight

baptiser [batize] /**1**/ VT to christen; to baptize; to launch; to consecrate, dedicate

baptiste [batist] ADJ, NMF Baptist

baquet [bakɛ] NM tub, bucket

bar [baʀ] NM bar; (*poisson*) bass

baragouin [baʀagwɛ̃] NM gibberish

baragouiner [baʀagwine] /**1**/ VI to gibber, jabber

baraque [baʀak] NF shed; (*fam*) house; **~ foraine** fairground stand

baraqué, e [baʀake] ADJ (*fam*) well-built, hefty

baraquements [baʀakmɑ̃] NMPL huts (*for refugees, workers etc*)

baratin [baʀatɛ̃] NM (*fam*) smooth talk, patter

baratiner [baʀatine] /**1**/ VT to chat up

baratte [baʀat] NF churn

Barbade [baʀbad] NF: **la ~** Barbados

barbant, e [baʀbɑ̃, -ɑ̃t] ADJ (*fam*) deadly (boring)

barbare [baʀbaʀ] ADJ barbaric ▸ NMF barbarian

Barbarie [baʀbaʀi] NF: **la ~** the Barbary Coast

barbarie [baʀbaʀi] NF barbarism; (*cruauté*) barbarity

barbarisme [baʀbaʀism] NM (*Ling*) barbarism

barbe [baʀb] NF beard; (**au nez et**) **à la ~ de qn** (*fig*) under sb's very nose; **la ~!** (*fam*) damn it!; **quelle ~!** (*fam*) what a drag ou bore!; **~ à papa** candy-floss (*BRIT*), cotton candy (*US*)

barbecue [baʀbəkju] NM barbecue

barbelé [baʀbəle] ADJ, NM: (**fil de fer**) **~** barbed wire *no pl*

barber [baʀbe] /**1**/ VT (*fam*) to bore stiff

barbiche [baʀbiʃ] NF goatee

barbichette [baʀbiʃɛt] NF small goatee

barbiturique [baʀbityʀik] NM barbiturate

barboter [baʀbɔte] /**1**/ VI to paddle, dabble ▸ VT (*fam*) to filch

barboteuse [baʀbɔtøz] NF rompers *pl*

barbouiller [baʀbuje] /**1**/ VT to daub; (*péj: écrire, dessiner*) to scribble; **avoir l'estomac barbouillé** to feel queasy ou sick

barbu, e [baʀby] ADJ bearded

barbue [baʀby] NF (*poisson*) brill

Barcelone [baʀsəlɔn] N Barcelona

barda [baʀda] NM (*fam*) kit, gear

barde [baʀd] NF (*Culin*) piece of fat bacon ▸ NM (*poète*) bard

bardé, e [baʀde] ADJ: **~ de médailles** *etc* bedecked with medals *etc*

bardeaux [baʀdo] NMPL shingle *no pl*

barder [baʀde] /**1**/ VT (*Culin: rôti, volaille*) to bard

▸ VI (*fam*): **ça va ~** sparks will fly

barème [baʀɛm] NM (*Scol*) scale; (*liste*) table; **~ des salaires** salary scale

barge [baʀʒ] NF barge

baril [baʀi(l)] NM (*tonneau*) barrel; (*de poudre*) keg

barillet [baʀijɛ] NM (*de revolver*) cylinder

bariolé, e [baʀjɔle] ADJ many-coloured, rainbow-coloured

barman [baʀman] NM barman

baromètre [baʀɔmɛtʀ] NM barometer; **~ anéroïde** aneroid barometer

baron [baʀɔ̃] NM baron

baronne [baʀɔn] NF baroness

baroque [baʀɔk] ADJ (*Art*) baroque; (*fig*) weird

baroud [baʀud] NM: **~ d'honneur** gallant last stand

baroudeur [baʀudœʀ] NM (*fam*) fighter

barque [baʀk] NF small boat

barquette [baʀkɛt] NF small boat-shaped tart; (*récipient: en aluminium*) tub; (: *en bois*) basket; (*pour repas*) tray; (*pour fruits*) punnet

barracuda [baʀakyda] NM barracuda

barrage [baʀaʒ] NM dam; (*sur route*) roadblock, barricade; **~ de police** police roadblock

barre [baʀ] NF (*de fer etc*) rod; (*Navig*) helm; (*écrite*) line, stroke; (*Danse*) barre; (*Jur*): **comparaître à la ~** to appear as a witness; (*niveau*): **la livre a franchi la ~ des 1,70 euros** the pound has broken the 1.70 euros barrier; **être à ou tenir la ~** (*Navig*) to be at the helm; **coup de ~** (*fig*): **c'est le coup de ~!** it's daylight robbery!; **j'ai le coup de ~!** I'm all in!; **~ fixe** (*Gym*) horizontal bar; **~ de mesure** (*Mus*) bar line; **~ à mine** crowbar; **barres parallèles/asymétriques** (*Gym*) parallel/asymmetric bars

barreau, x [baʀo] NM bar; (*Jur*): **le ~** the Bar

barrer [baʀe] /**1**/ VT (*route etc*) to block; (*mot*) to cross out; (*chèque*) to cross (*BRIT*); (*Navig*) to steer; **se barrer** VI (*fam*) to clear off

barrette [baʀɛt] NF (*pour cheveux*) (hair) slide (*BRIT*) ou clip (*US*); (*broche*) brooch

barreur [baʀœʀ] NM helmsman; (*aviron*) coxswain

barricade [baʀikad] NF barricade

barricader [baʀikade] /**1**/ VT to barricade; **se barricader** VI: **se barricader chez soi** (*fig*) to lock o.s. in

barrière [baʀjɛʀ] NF fence; (*obstacle*) barrier; (*porte*) gate; **la Grande B~** the Great Barrier Reef; **~ de dégel** (*Admin: on roadsigns*) no heavy vehicles — road liable to subsidence due to thaw; **barrières douanières** trade barriers

barrique [baʀik] NF barrel, cask

barrir [baʀiʀ] /**2**/ VI to trumpet

bar-tabac [baʀtaba] NM bar (*which sells tobacco and stamps*)

baryton [baʀitɔ̃] NM baritone

bas, basse [bɑ, bɑs] ADJ low; (*action*) low, ignoble ▸ NM (*vêtement*) stocking; (*partie inférieure*): **le ~ de** the lower part ou foot ou bottom of ▸ NF (*Mus*) bass ▸ ADV low; (*parler*) softly; **plus ~** lower down; more softly; (*dans un texte*) further on, below; **la tête basse** with lowered head; (*fig*) with head hung low; **avoir**

la vue basse to be short-sighted; **au ~ mot** at the lowest estimate; **enfant en ~ âge** infant, young child; **en ~** down below; (*d'une liste, d'un mur etc*) at (*ou* to) the bottom; (*dans une maison*) downstairs; **en ~ de** at the bottom of; **de ~ en haut** upwards; from the bottom to the top; **des hauts et des ~** ups and downs; **un ~ de laine** (*fam: économies*) money under the mattress (*fig*); **mettre ~** *vi* (*animal*) to give birth; **à ~ la dictature!** down with dictatorship!; **~ morceaux** (*viande*) cheap cuts

basalte [bazalt] NM basalt

basané, e [bazane] ADJ (*teint*) tanned, bronzed; (*foncé: péj*) swarthy

bas-côté [bakote] NM (*de route*) verge (BRIT), shoulder (US); (*d'église*) (side) aisle

bascule [baskyl] NF: **(jeu de) ~** seesaw; **(balance à) ~** scales *pl*; **fauteuil à ~** rocking chair; **système à ~** tip-over device; rocker device

basculer [baskyle] /**1**/ *vi* to fall over, topple (over); (*benne*) to tip up ▶ *vt* (*aussi:* **faire basculer**) to topple over; (*: contenu*) to tip out; (*: benne*) tip up

base [baz] NF base; (*fondement, principe*) basis (*pl* bases); **la ~** (*Pol*) the rank and file, the grass roots; **jeter les bases de** to lay the foundations of; **à la ~ de** (*fig*) at the root of; **sur la ~ de** (*fig*) on the basis of; **de ~** basic; **à ~ de café** *etc* coffee *etc* -based; **~ de données** (*Inform*) database; **~ de lancement** launching site

base-ball [bezbol] NM baseball

baser [baze] /**1**/ *vt*: **~ qch sur** to base sth on; **se ~ sur** (*données, preuves*) to base one's argument on; **être basé à/dans** (*Mil*) to be based at/in

bas-fond [bafɔ̃] NM (*Navig*) shallow; **bas-fonds** NMPL (*fig*) dregs

basilic [bazilik] NM (*Culin*) basil

basilique [bazilik] NF basilica

basket [basket], **basket-ball** [basketbol] NM basketball

baskets [basket] NFPL (*chaussures*) trainers (BRIT), sneakers (US)

basketteur, -euse [basketœr, -øz] NM/F basketball player

basquaise [baskez] ADJ F Basque ▶ NF: **B~** Basque

basque [bask] ADJ, NM (*Ling*) Basque ▶ NMF: **B~** Basque; **le Pays ~** the Basque country

basques [bask] NFPL skirts; **pendu aux ~ de qn** constantly pestering sb; (*mère etc*) hanging on sb's apron strings

bas-relief [baʀəljɛf] NM bas-relief

basse [bas] ADJ *voir* **bas** ▶ NF (*Mus*) bass

basse-cour [baskur] (*pl* **basses-cours**) NF farmyard; (*animaux*) farmyard animals

bassement [basmɑ̃] ADV basely

bassesse [bases] NF baseness; (*acte*) base act

basset [base] NM (*Zool*) basset (hound)

bassin [basɛ̃] NM (*cuvette*) bowl; (*pièce d'eau*) pond, pool; (*de fontaine, Géo*) basin; (*Anat*) pelvis; (*portuaire*) dock; **~ houiller** coalfield

bassine [basin] NF basin; (*contenu*) bowl, bowlful

bassiner [basine] /**1**/ *vt* (*plaie*) to bathe; (*lit*) to warm with a warming pan; (*fam: ennuyer*) to bore; (*: importuner*) to bug, pester

bassiste [basist] NMF (*double*) bass player

basson [basɔ̃] NM bassoon

bastide [bastid] NF (*maison*) country house (*in Provence*); (*ville*) walled town (*in SW France*)

bastion [bastjɔ̃] NM (*aussi fig, Pol*) bastion

bas-ventre [bavɑ̃tʀ] NM (lower part of the) stomach

bat [ba] VB *voir* **battre**

bât [ba] NM packsaddle

bataille [bataj] NF battle; (*rixe*) fight; **en ~** (*en travers*) at an angle; (*en désordre*) awry; **elle avait les cheveux en ~** her hair was a mess; **~ rangée** pitched battle

bataillon [batajɔ̃] NM battalion

bâtard, e [batar, -ard] ADJ (*enfant*) illegitimate; (*fig*) hybrid ▶ NM/F illegitimate child, bastard (*péj*) ▶ NM (*Boulangerie*) ≈ Vienna loaf; **chien ~** mongrel

batavia [batavja] NF ≈ Webb lettuce

bateau, x [bato] NM boat; (*grand*) ship ▶ ADJ INV (*banal, rebattu*) hackneyed; **~ de pêche/à moteur/à voiles** fishing/motor/sailing boat

bateau-citerne [batositɛʀn] NM tanker

bateau-mouche [batomuʃ] NM (passenger) pleasure boat (*on the Seine*)

bateau-pilote [batopilɔt] NM pilot ship

bateleur, -euse [batlœʀ, -øz] NM/F street performer

batelier, -ière [batəlje, -jɛʀ] NM/F ferryman/-woman

bâti, e [bati] ADJ (*terrain*) developed ▶ NM (*armature*) frame; (*Couture*) tacking; **bien ~** (*personne*) well-built

batifoler [batifole] /**1**/ *vi* to frolic *ou* lark about

batik [batik] NM batik

bâtiment [batimɑ̃] NM building; (*Navig*) ship, vessel; (*industrie*): **le ~** the building trade

bâtir [batir] /**2**/ *vt* to build; (*Couture: jupe, ourlet*) to tack; **fil à ~** (*Couture*) tacking thread

bâtisse [batis] NF building

bâtisseur, -euse [batisœʀ, -øz] NM/F builder

batiste [batist] NF (*Couture*) batiste, cambric

bâton [batɔ̃] NM stick; **mettre des bâtons dans les roues à qn** to put a spoke in sb's wheel; **à bâtons rompus** informally; **parler à bâtons rompus** to chat about this and that; **~ de rouge (à lèvres)** lipstick; **~ de ski** ski stick

bâtonnet [batɔnɛ] NM short stick *ou* rod

bâtonnier [batɔnje] NM (*Jur*) ≈ President of the Bar

batraciens [batʀasjɛ̃] NMPL amphibians

bats [ba] VB *voir* **battre**

battage [bataʒ] NM (*publicité*) (hard) plugging

battant, e [batɑ̃, -ɑ̃t] VB *voir* **battre** ▶ ADJ: **pluie ~** lashing rain ▶ NM (*de cloche*) clapper; (*de volets*) shutter, flap; (*de porte*) side; (*fig: personne*) fighter; **porte à double ~** double door; **tambour ~** briskly

batte [bat] NF (*Sport*) bat

battement [batmɑ̃] NM (*de cœur*) beat; (*intervalle*) interval (*between classes, trains etc*); **~ de**

paupières blinking *no pl* (of eyelids); **un ~ de 10 minutes**, **10 minutes de ~** 10 minutes to spare

batterie [batʀi] NF (*Mil*, *Élec*) battery; (*Mus*) drums *pl*, drum kit; **~ de cuisine** kitchen utensils *pl*; (*casseroles etc*) pots and pans *pl*; **une ~ de tests** a string of tests

batteur [batœʀ] NM (*Mus*) drummer; (*appareil*) whisk

batteuse [batøz] NF (*Agr*) threshing machine

battoir [batwaʀ] NM (*à linge*) beetle (*for laundry*); (*à tapis*) (carpet) beater

battre [batʀ] /41/ VT to beat; (*pluie*, *vagues*) to beat *ou* lash against; (*œufs etc*) to beat up, whisk; (*blé*) to thresh; (*cartes*) to shuffle; (*passer au peigne fin*) to scour ▶ VI (*cœur*) to beat; (*volets etc*) to bang, rattle; **se battre** VI to fight; **~ la mesure** to beat time; **~ en brèche** (*Mil*: *mur*) to batter; (*fig*: *théorie*) to demolish; (: *institution etc*) to attack; **~ son plein** to be at its height, be going full swing; **~ pavillon britannique** to fly the British flag; **~ des mains** to clap one's hands; **~ des ailes** to flap its wings; **~ de l'aile** (*fig*) to be in a bad way *ou* in bad shape; **~ la semelle** to stamp one's feet; **~ en retraite** to beat a retreat

battu, e [baty] PP *de* **battre** ▶ NF (*chasse*) beat; (*policière etc*) search, hunt

baud [bo(d)] NM baud

baudruche [bodʀyʃ] NF: **ballon en ~** (toy) balloon; (*fig*) windbag

baume [bom] NM balm

bauxite [boksit] NF bauxite

bavard, e [bavaʀ, -aʀd] ADJ (very) talkative; gossipy

bavardage [bavaʀdaʒ] NM chatter *no pl*; gossip *no pl*

bavarder [bavaʀde] /1/ VI to chatter; (*indiscrètement*) to gossip; (*révéler un secret*) to blab

bavarois, e [bavaʀwa, -waz] ADJ Bavarian ▶ NM *ou* F (*Culin*) bavarois

bave [bav] NF dribble; (*de chien etc*) slobber, slaver (*BRIT*), drool (*US*); (*d'escargot*) slime

baver [bave] /1/ VI to dribble; (*chien*) to slobber, slaver (*BRIT*), drool (*US*); (*encre*, *couleur*) to run; **en ~** (*fam*) to have a hard time (of it)

bavette [bavɛt] NF bib

baveux, -euse [bavø, -øz] ADJ dribbling; (*omelette*) runny

Bavière [bavjɛʀ] NF: **la ~** Bavaria

bavoir [bavwaʀ] NM (*de bébé*) bib

bavure [bavyʀ] NF smudge; (*fig*) hitch; (*policière etc*) blunder

bayer [baje] /1/ VI: **~ aux corneilles** to stand gaping

bazar [bazaʀ] NM general store; (*fam*) jumble

bazarder [bazaʀde] /1/ VT (*fam*) to chuck out

BCBG SIGLE ADJ (= *bon chic bon genre*) smart and trendy, ≈ preppy

BCG SIGLE M (= *bacille Calmette-Guérin*) BCG

bcp ABR = **beaucoup**

BD SIGLE F = **bande dessinée**; (= *base de données*) DB

bd ABR = **boulevard**

b.d.c. ABR (*Typo*: = *bas de casse*) l.c.

béant, e [beɑ̃, -ɑ̃t] ADJ gaping

béarnais, e [beaʀnɛ, -ɛz] ADJ of *ou* from the Béarn

béat, e [bea, -at] ADJ showing open-eyed wonder; (*sourire etc*) blissful

béatitude [beatityd] NF bliss

beau, bel, belle, beaux [bo, bɛl] ADJ beautiful, lovely; (*homme*) handsome ▶ NF (*Sport*) decider ▶ ADV: **il fait ~** the weather's fine ▶ NM: **avoir le sens du ~** to have an aesthetic sense; **le temps est au ~** the weather is set fair; **un ~ geste** (*fig*) a fine gesture; **un ~ salaire** a good salary; **un ~ gâchis/rhume** a fine mess/nasty cold; **en faire/dire de belles** to do/say (some) stupid things; **le ~ monde** high society; **~ parleur** smooth talker; **un ~ jour** one (fine) day; **de plus belle** more than ever, even more; **bel et bien** well and truly; (*vraiment*) really (and truly); **le plus ~ c'est que …** the best of it is that …; **c'est du ~!** that's great, that is!; **on a ~ essayer** however hard *ou* no matter how hard we try; **il a ~ jeu de protester** *etc* it's easy for him to protest *etc*; **faire le ~** (*chien*) to sit up and beg

$\boxed{\text{MOT-CLÉ}}$

beaucoup [boku] ADV **1** a lot; **il boit beaucoup** he drinks a lot; **il ne boit pas beaucoup** he doesn't drink much *ou* a lot

2 (*suivi de plus*, *trop etc*) much, a lot, far; **il est beaucoup plus grand** he is much *ou* a lot *ou* far taller; **c'est beaucoup plus cher** it's a lot *ou* much more expensive; **il a beaucoup plus de temps que moi** he has much *ou* a lot more time than me; **il y a beaucoup plus de touristes ici** there are a lot *ou* many more tourists here; **beaucoup trop vite** much too fast; **il fume beaucoup trop** he smokes far too much

3: **beaucoup de** (*nombre*) many, a lot of; (*quantité*) a lot of; **pas beaucoup de** (*nombre*) not many, not a lot of; (*quantité*) not much, not a lot of; **beaucoup d'étudiants/de touristes** a lot of *ou* many students/tourists; **beaucoup de courage** a lot of courage; **il n'a pas beaucoup d'argent** he hasn't got much *ou* a lot of money; **il n'y a pas beaucoup de touristes** there aren't many *ou* a lot of tourists

4: **de beaucoup** by far

▶ PRON: **beaucoup le savent** lots of people know that

beau-fils [bofis] (*pl* **beaux-fils**) NM son-in-law; (*remariage*) stepson

beau-frère [bofʀɛʀ] (*pl* **beaux-frères**) NM brother-in-law

beau-père [bopɛʀ] (*pl* **beaux-pères**) NM father-in-law; (*remariage*) stepfather

beauté [bote] NF beauty; **de toute ~** beautiful; **en ~** *adv* with a flourish, brilliantly; **finir qch en ~** to complete sth brilliantly

beaux-arts [bozaʀ] NMPL fine arts

beaux-parents [bopaʀɑ̃] NMPL wife's/husband's family, in-laws

bébé [bebe] NM baby

b

43

bébé-éprouvette [bebeepʀuvɛt] (*pl* **bébés-éprouvette**) NM test-tube baby

bec [bɛk] NM beak, bill; (*de plume*) nib; (*de cafetière etc*) spout; (*de casserole etc*) lip; (*d'une clarinette etc*) mouthpiece; (*fam*) mouth; **clouer le ~ à qn** (*fam*) to shut sb up; **ouvrir le ~** (*fam*) to open one's mouth; **~ de gaz** (street) gaslamp; **~ verseur** pouring lip

bécane [bekan] NF (*fam*) bike

bécarre [bekaʀ] NM (*Mus*) natural

bécasse [bekas] NF (*Zool*) woodcock; (*fam*) silly goose

bec-de-cane [bɛkdəkan] (*pl* **becs-de-cane**) NM (*poignée*) door handle

bec-de-lièvre [bɛkdəljɛvʀ] (*pl* **becs-de-lièvre**) NM harelip

béchamel [beʃamɛl] NF: (**sauce**) **~** white sauce, bechamel sauce

bêche [bɛʃ] NF spade

bêcher [beʃe] /1/ VT (*terre*) to dig; (*personne: critiquer*) to slate; (: *snober*) to look down on

bêcheur, -euse [beʃœʀ, -øz] ADJ (*fam*) stuck-up ► NM/F fault-finder; (*snob*) stuck-up person

bécoter [bekɔte] /1/: **se bécoter** VI to smooch

becquée [beke] NF: **donner la ~ à** to feed

becqueter [bɛkte] /4/ VT (*fam*) to eat

bedaine [bədɛn] NF paunch

bédé [bede] NF (*fam*) = **bande dessinée**

bedeau, x [bədo] NM beadle

bedonnant, e [bədɔnɑ̃, -ɑ̃t] ADJ paunchy, potbellied

bée [be] ADJ: **bouche ~** gaping

beffroi [befʀwa] NM belfry

bégaiement [begemɑ̃] NM stammering, stuttering

bégayer [begeje] /8/ VT, VI to stammer

bégonia [begɔnja] NM (*Bot*) begonia

bègue [bɛg] NMF: **être ~** to have a stammer

bégueule [begœl] ADJ prudish

beige [bɛʒ] ADJ beige

beignet [bɛɲɛ] NM fritter

bel [bɛl] ADJ M *voir* **beau**

bêler [bele] /1/ VI to bleat

belette [bəlɛt] NF weasel

belge [bɛlʒ] ADJ Belgian ► NMF: **B~** Belgian; *see note*

> The *fête nationale belge*, on 21 July, marks the day in 1831 when Leopold of Saxe-Coburg Gotha was crowned King Leopold I.

Belgique [bɛlʒik] NF: **la ~** Belgium

Belgrade [bɛlgʀad] N Belgrade

bélier [belje] NM ram; (*engin*) (battering) ram; (*signe*): **le B~** Aries, the Ram; **être du B~** to be Aries

Bélize [beliz] NM: **le ~** Belize

bellâtre [bɛlɑtʀ] NM dandy

belle [bɛl] ADJ *voir* **beau** ► NF (*Sport*): **la ~** the decider

belle-famille [bɛlfamij] (*pl* **belles-familles**) NF (*fam*) in-laws *pl*

belle-fille [bɛlfij] (*pl* **belles-filles**) NF daughter-in-law; (*remariage*) stepdaughter

belle-mère [bɛlmɛʀ] (*pl* **belles-mères**) NF mother-in-law; (*remariage*) stepmother

belle-sœur [bɛlsœʀ] (*pl* **belles-sœurs**) NF sister-in-law

belliciste [belisist] ADJ warmongering

belligérance [beliʒeʀɑ̃s] NF belligerence

belligérant, e [beliʒeʀɑ̃, -ɑ̃t] ADJ belligerent

belliqueux, -euse [belikø, -øz] ADJ aggressive, warlike

belote [bəlɔt] NF belote (*card game*)

belvédère [bɛlvedɛʀ] NM panoramic viewpoint (*or small building there*)

bémol [bemɔl] NM (*Mus*) flat

ben [bɛ̃] EXCL (*fam*) well

bénédiction [benediksjɔ̃] NF blessing

bénéfice [benefis] NM (*Comm*) profit; (*avantage*) benefit; **au ~ de** in aid of

bénéficiaire [benefisjɛʀ] NMF beneficiary

bénéficier [benefisje] /7/ VI: **~ de** to enjoy; (*profiter*) to benefit by *ou* from; (*obtenir*) to get, be given

bénéfique [benefik] ADJ beneficial

Benelux [benelyks] NM: **le ~** Benelux, the Benelux countries

benêt [bənɛ] NM simpleton

bénévolat [benevɔla] NM voluntary service *ou* work

bénévole [benevɔl] ADJ voluntary, unpaid

bénévolement [benevɔlmɑ̃] ADV voluntarily

Bengale [bɛ̃gal] NM: **le ~** Bengal; **le golfe du ~** the Bay of Bengal

bengali [bɛ̃gali] ADJ Bengali, Bengalese ► NM (*Ling*) Bengali

Bénin [benɛ̃] NM: **le ~** Benin

bénin, -igne [benɛ̃, -iɲ] ADJ minor, mild; (*tumeur*) benign

bénir [beniʀ] /2/ VT to bless

bénit, e [beni, -it] ADJ consecrated; **eau ~** holy water

bénitier [benitje] NM stoup, font (*for holy water*)

benjamin, e [bɛ̃ʒamɛ̃, -in] NM/F youngest child; (*Sport*) under-13

benne [bɛn] NF skip; (*de téléphérique*) (cable) car; **~ basculante** tipper (BRIT), dump *ou* dumper truck; **~ à ordures** (*amovible*) skip

benzine [bɛ̃zin] NF benzine

béotien, ne [beɔsjɛ̃, -ɛn] NM/F philistine

BEP SIGLE M (= *Brevet d'études professionnelles*) school-leaving diploma, taken at approx. 18 years

BEPC SIGLE M (= *Brevet d'études du premier cycle*) former school certificate (taken at approx. 16 years)

béquille [bekij] NF crutch; (*de bicyclette*) stand

berbère [bɛʀbɛʀ] ADJ Berber ► NM (*Ling*) Berber ► NMF: **B~** Berber

bercail [bɛʀkaj] NM fold

berceau, x [bɛʀso] NM cradle, crib

bercer [bɛʀse] /3/ VT to rock, cradle; (*musique etc*) to lull; **~ qn de** (*promesses etc*) to delude sb with

berceur, -euse [bɛʀsœʀ, -øz] ADJ soothing ► NF (*chanson*) lullaby

berceuse NF lullaby

BERD [bɛʀd] SIGLE F (= *Banque européenne pour la reconstruction et le développement*) EBRD

béret [beʀɛ] NM (*aussi*: **béret basque**) beret

bergamote [bɛʀgamɔt] NF (*Bot*) bergamot

berge [bɛʀʒ] NF bank

berger, -ère [bɛʀʒe, -ɛʀ] NM/F shepherd/ shepherdess; **~ allemand** (*chien*) alsatian (dog) (BRIT), German shepherd (dog) (US)

bergerie [bɛʀʒəʀi] NF sheep pen

bergeronnette [bɛʀʒəʀɔnɛt] NF wagtail

béribéri [beʀibeʀi] NM beriberi

Berlin [bɛʀlɛ̃] N Berlin; **~-Est/-Ouest** East/West Berlin

berline [bɛʀlin] NF (*Auto*) saloon (car) (BRIT), sedan (US)

berlingot [bɛʀlɛ̃go] NM (*emballage*) carton (*pyramid shaped*); (*bonbon*) lozenge

berlinois, e [bɛʀlinwa, -waz] ADJ of ou from Berlin ▶ NM/F: **B~, e** Berliner

berlue [bɛʀly] NF: **j'ai la ~** I must be seeing things

bermuda [bɛʀmyda] NM (*short*) Bermuda shorts

Bermudes [bɛʀmyd] NFPL: **les (îles) ~** Bermuda

Berne [bɛʀn] N Bern

berne [bɛʀn] NF: **en ~** at half-mast; **mettre en ~** to fly at half-mast

berner [bɛʀne] /1/ VT to fool

bernois, e [bɛʀnwa, -waz] ADJ Bernese

berrichon, ne [beʀiʃɔ̃, -ɔn] ADJ of ou from the Berry

besace [bəzas] NF beggar's bag

besogne [bəzɔɲ] NF work no pl, job

besogneux, -euse [bəzɔɲø, -øz] ADJ hard-working

besoin [bəzwɛ̃] NM need; (*pauvreté*): **le ~** need, want; **le ~ d'argent/de gloire** the need for money/glory; **besoins (naturels)** nature's needs; **faire ses besoins** to relieve o.s.; **avoir ~ de qch/faire qch** to need sth/to do sth; **il n'y a pas ~ de (faire)** there is no need to (do); **au ~, si ~ est** if need be; **pour les besoins de la cause** for the purpose in hand; **être dans le ~** to be in need ou want

bestial, e, -aux [bɛstjal, -o] ADJ bestial, brutish ▶ NMPL cattle

bestiole [bɛstjɔl] NF (tiny) creature

bétail [betaj] NM livestock, cattle pl

bétaillère [betajɛʀ] NF livestock truck

bête [bɛt] NF animal; (*bestiole*) insect, creature ▶ ADJ stupid, silly; **les bêtes** (the) animals; **chercher la petite ~** to nit-pick; **~ noire** pet hate, bugbear (BRIT); **~ sauvage** wild beast; **~ de somme** beast of burden

bêtement [bɛtmɑ̃] ADV stupidly; **tout ~** quite simply

Bethléem [bɛtleɛm] N Bethlehem

bêtifier [betifje] /7/ VI to talk nonsense

bêtise [betiz] NF stupidity; (*action, remarque*) stupid thing (to say ou do); (*bonbon*) type of mint sweet (BRIT) ou candy (US); **faire/dire une ~** to do/say something stupid

béton [betɔ̃] NM concrete; **(en) ~** (fig: alibi, argument) cast iron; **~ armé** reinforced concrete; **~ précontraint** prestressed concrete

bétonner [betɔne] /1/ VT to concrete (over)

bétonnière [betɔnjɛʀ] NF cement mixer

bette [bɛt] NF (Bot) (Swiss) chard

betterave [bɛtʀav] NF (*rouge*) beetroot (BRIT), beet (US); **~ fourragère** mangel-wurzel;

~ sucrière sugar beet

beugler [bøgle] /1/ VI to low; (*péj: radio etc*) to blare ▶ VT (*péj: chanson etc*) to bawl out

Beur [bœʀ] ADJ, NMF see note

> Beur is a term used to refer to a person born in France of North African immigrant parents. It is not racist and is often used by the media, anti-racist groups and second-generation North Africans themselves. The word itself comes from back slang or verlan.

beurre [bœʀ] NM butter; **mettre du ~ dans les épinards** (fig) to add a little to the kitty; **~ de cacao** cocoa butter; **~ noir** brown butter (sauce)

beurrer [bœʀe] /1/ VT to butter

beurrier [bœʀje] NM butter dish

beuverie [bœvʀi] NF drinking session

bévue [bevy] NF blunder

Beyrouth [beʀut] N Beirut

Bhoutan [butɑ̃] NM: **le ~** Bhutan

bi... [bi] PRÉFIXE bi...

Biafra [bjafʀa] NM: **le ~** Biafra

biafrais, e [bjafʀɛ, -ɛz] ADJ Biafran

biais [bjɛ] NM (*moyen*) device, expedient; (*aspect*) angle; (*bande de tissu*) piece of cloth cut on the bias; **en ~, de ~** (*obliquement*) at an angle; (fig) indirectly; **par le ~ de** by means of

biaiser [bjeze] /1/ VI (fig) to sidestep the issue

biathlon [biatlɔ̃] NM biathlon

bibelot [biblo] NM trinket, curio

biberon [bibʀɔ̃] NM (feeding) bottle; **nourrir au ~** to bottle-feed

bible [bibl] NF bible

bibliobus [biblijɔbys] NM mobile library van

bibliographie [biblijɔgʀafi] NF bibliography

bibliophile [biblijɔfil] NMF book-lover

bibliothécaire [biblijɔtekɛʀ] NMF librarian

bibliothèque [biblijɔtɛk] NF library; (*meuble*) bookcase; **~ municipale** public library

biblique [biblik] ADJ biblical

bic® [bik] NM Biro®

bicarbonate [bikaʀbɔnat] NM: **~ (de soude)** bicarbonate of soda

bicentenaire [bisɑ̃tnɛʀ] NM bicentenary

biceps [bisɛps] NM biceps

biche [biʃ] NF doe

bichonner [biʃɔne] /1/ VT to groom

bicolore [bikɔlɔʀ] ADJ two-coloured (BRIT), two-colored (US)

bicoque [bikɔk] NF (*péj*) shack, dump

bicorne [bikɔʀn] NM cocked hat

bicyclette [bisiklɛt] NF bicycle

bidasse [bidas] NM (fam) squaddie (BRIT)

bide [bid] NM (fam: ventre) belly; (Théât) flop

bidet [bidɛ] NM bidet

bidoche [bidɔʃ] NF (fam) meat

bidon [bidɔ̃] NM can ▶ ADJ INV (fam) phoney

bidonnant, e [bidɔnɑ̃, -ɑ̃t] ADJ (fam) hilarious

bidonville [bidɔ̃vil] NM shanty town

bidule [bidyl] NM (fam) thingamajig

bielle [bjɛl] NF connecting rod; (Auto) track rod

biélorusse [bjelɔʀys] ADJ Belarussian ▶ NMF: **B~** Belarussian

Biélorussie [bjelɔʀysi] NF Belorussia

MOT-CLÉ

bien [bjɛ̃] NM **1** (*avantage, profit*): **faire le bien** to do good; **faire du bien à qn** to do sb good; **ça fait du bien de faire** it does you good to do; **dire du bien de** to speak well of; **c'est pour son bien** it's for his own good; **changer en bien** to change for the better; **le bien public** the public good; **vouloir du bien à qn** (*vouloir aider*) to have sb's (best) interests at heart; **je te veux du bien** (*pour mettre en confiance*) I don't wish you any harm

2 (*possession, patrimoine*) possession, property; **son bien le plus précieux** his most treasured possession; **avoir du bien** to have property; **biens (de consommation** *etc*) (consumer *etc*) goods; **biens durables** (consumer) durables **3** (*moral*): **le bien** good; **distinguer le bien du mal** to tell good from evil

▶ ADV **1** (*de façon satisfaisante*) well; **elle travaille/ mange bien** she works/eats well; **je me porte bien** to be well; **croyant bien faire, je/ il …** thinking I/he was doing the right thing, I/ he …; **tiens-toi bien!** (*assieds-toi correctement*) sit up straight!; (*debout*) stand up straight!; (*sois sage*) behave yourself!; (*prépare-toi*) wait for it! **2** (*valeur intensive*) quite; **bien jeune** quite young; **bien assez** quite enough; **bien mieux** (very) much better; **bien du temps/des gens** quite a time/a number of people; **j'espère bien y aller** I do hope to go; **je veux bien le faire** (*concession*) I'm quite willing to do it; **il faut bien le faire** it has to be done; **il y a bien deux ans** at least two years ago; **cela fait bien deux ans que je ne l'ai pas vu** I haven't seen him for at least *ou* a good two years; **il semble bien que** it really seems that; **peut-être bien** it could well be; **aimer bien** to like; **Paul est bien venu, n'est-ce pas?** Paul HAS come, hasn't he?; **où peut-il bien être passé?** where on earth can he have got to?

3 (*conséquence, résultat*): **si bien que** with the result that; **on verra bien** we'll see; **faire bien de …** to be right to …

▶ EXCL right!, OK!, fine!; **eh bien!** well!; (*c'est*) **bien fait!** it serves you (*ou* him *etc*) right!; **bien sûr!, bien entendu!** certainly!, of course!

▶ ADJ INV **1** (*en bonne forme, à l'aise*): **je me sens bien, je suis bien** I feel fine; **je ne me sens pas bien, je ne suis pas bien** I don't feel well; **on est bien dans ce fauteuil** this chair is very comfortable

2 (*joli, beau*) good-looking; **tu es bien dans cette robe** you look good in that dress **3** (*satisfaisant*) good; **elle est bien, cette maison/secrétaire** it's a good house/she's a good secretary; **c'est très bien (comme ça)** it's fine (like that); **ce n'est pas si bien que ça** it's not as good *ou* great as all that; **c'est bien?** is that all right?

4 (*moralement*) right; (*: personne*) good, nice; (*respectable*) respectable; **ce n'est pas bien de …** it's not right to …; **elle est bien, cette femme** she's a nice woman, she's a good sort; **des gens bien** respectable people

5 (*en bons termes*): **être bien avec qn** to be on good terms with sb

bien-aimé, e [bjɛ̃neme] ADJ, NM/F beloved
bien-être [bjɛ̃nɛtʀ] NM well-being
bienfaisance [bjɛ̃fəzɑ̃s] NF charity
bienfaisant, e [bjɛ̃fəzɑ̃, -ɑ̃t] ADJ (*chose*) beneficial
bienfait [bjɛ̃fɛ] NM act of generosity, benefaction; (*de la science etc*) benefit
bienfaiteur, -trice [bjɛ̃fɛtœʀ, -tʀis] NM/F benefactor/benefactress
bien-fondé [bjɛ̃fɔ̃de] NM soundness
bien-fonds [bjɛ̃fɔ̃] NM property
bienheureux, -euse [bjɛ̃nœʀø, -øz] ADJ happy; (*Rel*) blessed, blest
biennal, e, -aux [bjenal, -o] ADJ biennial
bien-pensant, e [bjɛ̃pɑ̃sɑ̃, -ɑ̃t] ADJ right-thinking ▶ NM/F: **les bien-pensants** right-minded people
bien que [bjɛ̃k] CONJ although
bienséance [bjɛ̃seɑ̃s] NF propriety, decorum *no pl*; **les bienséances** (*convenances*) the proprieties
bienséant, e [bjɛ̃seɑ̃, -ɑ̃t] ADJ proper, seemly
bientôt [bjɛ̃to] ADV soon; **à** ~ see you soon
bienveillance [bjɛ̃vɛjɑ̃s] NF kindness
bienveillant, e [bjɛ̃vɛjɑ̃, -ɑ̃t] ADJ kindly
bienvenu, e [bjɛ̃vny] ADJ welcome ▶ NM/F: **être le ~/la ~** to be welcome ▶ NF: **souhaiter la ~ à** to welcome; ~ **à** welcome to
bière [bjɛʀ] NF (*boisson*) beer; (*cercueil*) bier; ~ **blonde** lager; ~ **brune** brown ale (*Brit*), dark beer (*US*); ~ **(à la) pression** draught beer
biffer [bife] /1/ VT to cross out
bifteck [biftɛk] NM steak
bifurcation [bifyʀkasjɔ̃] NF fork (*in road*); (*fig*) new direction
bifurquer [bifyʀke] /1/ VI (*route*) to fork; (*véhicule*) to turn off
bigame [bigam] ADJ bigamous
bigamie [bigami] NF bigamy
bigarré, e [bigaʀe] ADJ multicoloured (*Brit*), multicolored (*US*); (*disparate*) motley
bigarreau, x [bigaʀo] NM *type of cherry*
bigleux, -euse [biglø, -øz] ADJ (*fam: qui louche*) cross-eyed; (: *qui voit mal*) short-sighted; **il est complètement** ~ he's as blind as a bat
bigorneau, x [bigɔʀno] NM winkle
bigot, e [bigo, -ɔt] (*péj*) ADJ bigoted ▶ NM/F bigot
bigoterie [bigɔtʀi] NF bigotry
bigoudi [bigudi] NM curler
bigrement [bigʀəmɑ̃] ADV (*fam*) fantastically
bijou, x [biʒu] NM jewel
bijouterie [biʒutʀi] NF (*magasin*) jeweller's (shop) (*Brit*), jewelry store (*US*); (*bijoux*) jewellery, jewelry
bijoutier, -ière [biʒutje, -jɛʀ] NM/F jeweller (*Brit*), jeweler (*US*)
bikini [bikini] NM bikini
bilan [bilɑ̃] NM (*Comm*) balance sheet(s); (*annuel*) end of year statement; (*fig*) (*net*) outcome; (*: de victimes*) toll; **faire le** ~ **de** to assess; to review; **déposer son** ~ to file a bankruptcy statement;

~ **de santé** (*Méd*) check-up; ~ **social** *statement of a firm's policies towards its employees*

bilatéral, e, -aux [bilateral, -o] ADJ bilateral

bilboquet [bilbɔkɛ] NM (*jouet*) cup-and-ball game

bile [bil] NF bile; **se faire de la ~** (*fam*) to worry o.s. sick

biliaire [biljɛʀ] ADJ biliary

bilieux, -euse [biljø, -øz] ADJ bilious; (*fig: colérique*) testy

bilingue [bilɛ̃g] ADJ bilingual

bilinguisme [bilɛ̃gɥism] NM bilingualism

billard [bijaʀ] NM billiards *sg*; (*table*) billiard table; **c'est du ~** (*fam*) it's a cinch; **passer sur le ~** (*fam*) to have an (*ou* one's) operation; **~ électrique** pinball

bille [bij] NF ball; (*du jeu de billes*) marble; (*de bois*) log; **jouer aux billes** to play marbles

billet [bijɛ] NM (*aussi*: **billet de banque**) (bank)note; (*de cinéma, de bus etc*) ticket; (*courte lettre*) note; **~ à ordre** *ou* **de commerce** (*Comm*) promissory note, IOU; **~ d'avion/de train** plane/train ticket; **~ circulaire** round-trip ticket; **~ doux** love letter; **~ de faveur** complimentary ticket; **~ de loterie** lottery ticket; **~ de quai** platform ticket; **~ électronique** e-ticket

billetterie [bijɛtʀi] NF ticket office; (*distributeur*) ticket dispenser; (*Banque*) cash dispenser

billion [biljɔ̃] NM billion (Bʀɪᴛ), trillion (US)

billot [bijo] NM block

bimbeloterie [bɛ̃blɔtʀi] NF (*objets*) fancy goods

bimensuel, le [bimɑ̃sɥɛl] ADJ bimonthly, twice-monthly

bimestriel, le [bimɛstʀijɛl] ADJ bimonthly, two-monthly

bimoteur [bimɔtœʀ] ADJ twin-engined

binaire [binɛʀ] ADJ binary

biner [bine] /1/ VT to hoe

binette [binɛt] NF (*outil*) hoe

binoclard, e [binɔklaʀ, -aʀd] (*fam*) ADJ specky ▶ NM/F four-eyes

binocle [binɔkl] NM pince-nez

binoculaire [binɔkylɛʀ] ADJ binocular

binôme [binom] NM binomial

bio [bjo] ADJ (*fam*) = **biologique**; (*produits, aliments*) organic

bio... [bjɔ] PRÉFIXE bio...

biocarburant [bjokaʀbyʀɑ̃] NM biofuel

biochimie [bjɔʃimi] NF biochemistry

biochimique [bjɔʃimik] ADJ biochemical

biochimiste [bjɔʃimist] NMF biochemist

biodégradable [bjodegʀadabl] ADJ biodegradable

biodiesel [bjodjezɛl] NM biodiesel

biodiversité [bjodivɛʀsite] NF biodiversity

bioéthique [bjoetik] NF bioethics *sg*

biographe [bjɔgʀaf] NMF biographer

biographie [bjɔgʀafi] NF biography

biographique [bjɔgʀafik] ADJ biographical

biologie [bjɔlɔʒi] NF biology

biologique [bjɔlɔʒik] ADJ biological; (*produits*) organic

biologiste [bjɔlɔʒist] NMF biologist

biomasse [bjɔmas] NF biomass

biométrie NF biometrics

biopsie [bjɔpsi] NF (*Méd*) biopsy

biosphère [bjɔsfɛʀ] NF biosphere

biotechnologie [bjotɛknɔlɔʒi] NF biotechnology

bioterrorisme [bjotɛʀɔʀism] NM bioterrorism

bioterroriste [bjotɛʀɔʀist] NMF bioterrorist

biotope [bjɔtɔp] NM biotope

bipartisme [bipaʀtism] NM two-party system

bipartite [bipaʀtit] ADJ (*Pol*) two-party, bipartisan

bipède [bipɛd] NM biped, two-footed creature

biphasé, e [bifaze] ADJ (*Élec*) two-phase

biplace [biplas] ADJ, NM (*avion*) two-seater

biplan [biplɑ̃] NM biplane

bique [bik] NF nanny goat; (*péj*) old hag

biquet, te [bikɛ, -ɛt] NM/F: **mon ~** (*fam*) my lamb

BIRD [biʀd] SIGLE F (= *Banque internationale pour la reconstruction et le développement*) IBRD

biréacteur [biʀeaktœʀ] NM twin-engined jet

birman, e [biʀmɑ̃, -an] ADJ Burmese

Birmanie [biʀmani] NF Burma; **la ~** Burma

bis¹ [bi, biz] ADJ (*couleur*) greyish brown ▶ NF (*baiser*) kiss; (*vent*) North wind; **faire une** *ou* **la ~ à qn** to kiss sb; **grosses bises (de)** (*sur lettre*) love and kisses (from)

bis² [bis] ADV: **12 ~ 12a** *ou* A ▶ EXCL, NM encore

bisaïeul, e [bizajœl] NM/F great-grandfather/great-grandmother

bisannuel, le [bizanɥɛl] ADJ biennial

bisbille [bisbij] NF: **être en ~ avec qn** to be at loggerheads with sb

Biscaye [biske] NF: **le golfe de ~** the Bay of Biscay

biscornu, e [biskɔʀny] ADJ crooked; (*bizarre*) weird(-looking)

biscotte [biskɔt] NF toasted bread (*sold in packets*)

biscuit [biskɥi] NM biscuit (Bʀɪᴛ), cookie (US); (*gâteau*) sponge cake; **~ à la cuiller** sponge finger

biscuiterie [biskɥitʀi] NF biscuit manufacturing

bise [biz] ADJ F, NF *voir* **bis²**

biseau, x [bizo] NM bevelled edge; **en ~** bevelled

biseauter [bizote] /1/ VT to bevel

bisexué, e [bisɛksɥe] ADJ bisexual

bisexuel, le [bisɛksɥɛl] ADJ, NM/F bisexual

bismuth [bismyt] NM bismuth

bison [bizɔ̃] NM bison

bisou [bizu] NM (*fam*) kiss

bisque [bisk] NF: **~ d'écrevisses** shrimp bisque

bissectrice [bisɛktʀis] NF bisector

bisser [bise] /1/ VT (*faire rejouer: artiste, chanson*) to encore; (*rejouer: morceau*) to give an encore of

bissextile [bisɛkstil] ADJ: **année ~** leap year

bistouri [bisturi] NM lancet

bistre [bistʀ] ADJ (*couleur*) bistre; (*peau, teint*) tanned

bistro(t) [bistʀo] NM bistro, café

BIT SIGLE M (= *Bureau international du travail*) ILO

bit [bit] NM (*Inform*) bit

biterrois, e [bitɛʀwa, -waz] ADJ of *ou* from Béziers

bitte [bit] NF: ~ **d'amarrage** bollard (Navig)
bitume [bitym] NM asphalt
bitumer [bityme] /**1**/ VT to asphalt
bivalent, e [bivalɑ̃, -ɑ̃t] ADJ bivalent
bivouac [bivwak] NM bivouac
bizarre [bizaʀ] ADJ strange, odd
bizarrement [bizaʀmɑ̃] ADV strangely, oddly
bizarrerie [bizaʀʀi] NF strangeness, oddness
blackbouler [blakbule] /**1**/ VT (à une élection) to
blackball
blafard, e [blafaʀ, -aʀd] ADJ wan
blague [blag] NF (propos) joke; (farce) trick; **sans**
~**!** no kidding!; ~ **à tabac** tobacco pouch
blaguer [blage] /**1**/ VI to joke ▶ VT to tease
blagueur, -euse [blagœʀ, -øz] ADJ teasing
▶ NM/F joker
blair [blɛʀ] NM (fam) conk
blaireau, x [blɛʀo] NM (Zool) badger; (brosse)
shaving brush
blairer [blɛʀe] /**1**/ VT: **je ne peux pas le** ~ I can't
bear ou stand him
blâmable [blɑmabl] ADJ blameworthy
blâme [blɑm] NM blame; (sanction) reprimand
blâmer [blɑme] /**1**/ VT (réprouver) to blame;
(réprimander) to reprimand
blanc, blanche [blɑ̃, blɑ̃ʃ] ADJ white; (non
imprimé) blank; (innocent) pure ▶ NM/F white,
white man/woman ▶ NM (couleur) white; (linge):
le ~ whites pl; (espace non écrit) blank; (aussi:
blanc d'œuf) (egg-)white; (aussi: **blanc de
poulet**) breast, white meat; (aussi: **vin blanc**)
white wine ▶ NF (Mus) minim (BRIT), half-note
(US); (fam: drogue) smack; **d'une voix blanche**
in a toneless voice; **aux cheveux blancs**
white-haired; **le** ~ **de l'œil** the white of the
eye; **laisser en** ~ to leave blank; **chèque en** ~
blank cheque; **à** ~ adv (chauffer) white-hot; (tirer,
charger) with blanks; **saigner à** ~ to bleed
white; ~ **cassé** off-white
blanc-bec [blɑ̃bɛk] (pl **blancs-becs**) NM
greenhorn
blanchâtre [blɑ̃ʃɑtʀ] ADJ (teint, lumière) whitish
blancheur [blɑ̃ʃœʀ] NF whiteness
blanchir [blɑ̃ʃiʀ] /**2**/ VT (gén) to whiten; (linge, fig:
argent) to launder; (Culin) to blanch; (fig:
disculper) to clear ▶ VI to grow white; (cheveux) to
go white; **blanchi à la chaux** whitewashed
blanchissage [blɑ̃ʃisaʒ] NM (du linge) laundering
blanchisserie [blɑ̃ʃisʀi] NF laundry
blanchisseur, -euse [blɑ̃ʃisœʀ, -øz] NM/F
launderer
blanc-seing [blɑ̃sɛ̃] (pl **blancs-seings**) NM
signed blank paper
blanquette [blɑ̃kɛt] NF (Culin): ~ **de veau** veal in
a white sauce, blanquette de veau
blasé, e [blɑze] ADJ blasé
blaser [blaze] /**1**/ VT to make blasé
blason [blazɔ̃] NM coat of arms
blasphémateur, -trice [blasfematœʀ, -tʀis]
NM/F blasphemer
blasphématoire [blasfematwaʀ] ADJ
blasphemous
blasphème [blasfɛm] NM blasphemy
blasphémer [blasfeme] /**6**/ VI to blaspheme

▶ VT to blaspheme against
blatte [blat] NF cockroach
blazer [blazɛʀ] NM blazer
blé [ble] NM wheat; ~ **en herbe** wheat on the
ear; ~ **noir** buckwheat
bled [blɛd] NM (péj) hole; (en Afrique du Nord): **le** ~
the interior
blême [blɛm] ADJ pale
blêmir [blemiʀ] /**2**/ VI (personne) to (turn) pale;
(lueur) to grow pale
blennorragie [blenɔʀaʒi] NF blennorrhoea
blessant, e [blɛsɑ̃, -ɑ̃t] ADJ hurtful
blessé, e [blese] ADJ injured ▶ NM/F injured
person, casualty; **un** ~ **grave, un grand** ~ a
seriously injured ou wounded person
blesser [blese] /**1**/ VT to injure; (délibérément: Mil
etc) to wound; (souliers etc, offenser) to hurt; **se
blesser** to injure o.s.; **se blesser au pied** etc to
injure one's foot etc
blessure [blesyʀ] NF (accidentelle) injury;
(intentionnelle) wound
blet, te [blɛ, blɛt] ADJ overripe
blette [blɛt] NF = **bette**
bleu, e [blø] ADJ blue; (bifteck) very rare ▶ NM
(couleur) blue; (novice) greenhorn; (contusion)
bruise; (vêtement: aussi: **bleus**) overalls pl (BRIT),
coveralls pl (US); **avoir une peur** ~ to be scared
stiff; **zone** ~ ≈ restricted parking area;
fromage ~ blue cheese; **au** ~ (Culin) au bleu;
~ **(de lessive)** ≈ blue bag; ~ **de méthylène** (Méd)
methylene blue; ~ **marine/nuit/roi** navy/
midnight/royal blue
bleuâtre [bløɑtʀ] ADJ (fumée etc) bluish, blueish
bleuet [bløɛ] NM cornflower
bleuir [bløiʀ] /**2**/ VT, VI to turn blue
bleuté, e [bløte] ADJ blue-shaded
blindage [blɛ̃daʒ] NM armo(u)r-plating
blindé, e [blɛ̃de] ADJ armoured (BRIT), armored
(US); (fig) hardened ▶ NM armoured ou armored
car; (char) tank
blinder [blɛ̃de] /**1**/ VT to armour (BRIT), armor
(US); (fig) to harden
blizzard [blizaʀ] NM blizzard
bloc [blɔk] NM (de pierre etc, Inform) block; (de papier
à lettres) pad; (ensemble) group, block; **serré à** ~
tightened right down; **en** ~ as a whole;
wholesale; **faire** ~ to unite; ~ **opératoire**
operating ou theatre block; ~ **sanitaire** toilet
block; ~ **sténo** shorthand notebook
blocage [blɔkaʒ] NM (voir bloquer) blocking;
jamming; (des prix) freezing; (Psych) hang-up
bloc-cuisine [blɔkkɥizin] (pl **blocs-cuisines**)
NM kitchen unit
bloc-cylindres [blɔksilɛ̃dʀ] (pl **blocs-cylindres**)
NM cylinder block
bloc-évier [blɔkevje] (pl **blocs-éviers**) NM sink
unit
bloc-moteur [blɔkmɔtœʀ] (pl **blocs-moteurs**)
NM engine block
bloc-notes [blɔknɔt] (pl **blocs-notes**) NM note
pad
blocus [blɔkys] NM blockade
blog, blogue [blɔg] NM blog
blogging [blɔgiŋ] NM blogging

b

blogosphère [blɔgɔsfɛʀ] NF (*Inform*) blogosphere
bloguer [blɔge] /1/ VI to blog
blond, e [blɔ̃, -ɔ̃d] ADJ fair; (*plus clair*) blond; (*sable, blés*) golden ▶ NM/F fair-haired *ou* blond man/woman; ~ **cendré** ash blond
blondeur [blɔ̃dœʀ] NF fairness; blondness
blondin, e [blɔ̃dɛ̃, -in] NM/F fair-haired *ou* blond child *ou* young person
blondinet, te [blɔ̃dinɛ, -ɛt] NM/F blondy
blondir [blɔ̃diʀ] /2/ VI (*personne, cheveux*) to go fair *ou* blond
bloquer [blɔke] /1/ VT (*passage*) to block; (*pièce mobile*) to jam; (*crédits, compte*) to freeze; (*personne, négociations etc*) to hold up; (*regrouper*) to group; ~ **les freins** to jam on the brakes
blottir [blɔtiʀ] /2/: **se blottir** VI to huddle up
blousant, e [bluzɑ̃, -ɑ̃t] ADJ blousing out
blouse [bluz] NF overall
blouser [bluze] /1/ VI to blouse out
blouson [bluzɔ̃] NM blouson (jacket); ~ **noir** (*fig*) ≈ rocker
blue-jean [bludʒin], **blue-jeans** [bludʒins] NM jeans
blues [bluz] NM blues *pl*
bluet [blye] NM = **bleuet**
bluff [blœf] NM bluff
bluffer [blœfe] /1/ VI, VT to bluff
BNF SIGLE F = **Bibliothèque nationale de France**
boa [bɔa] NM (*Zool*): ~ **(constricteur)** boa (constrictor); (*tour de cou*) (feather *ou* fur) boa
bob [bɔb] NM = **bobsleigh**
bobard [bɔbaʀ] NM (*fam*) tall story
bobèche [bɔbɛʃ] NF candle-ring
bobine [bɔbin] NF (*de fil*) reel; (*de machine à coudre*) spool; (*de machine à écrire*) ribbon; (*Élec*) coil; ~ **(d'allumage)** (*Auto*) coil; ~ **de pellicule** (*Photo*) roll of film
bobo [bobo] SIGLE MF (= *bourgeois bohème*) boho ▶ NM (*fam*) sore spot
bobsleigh [bɔbslɛg] NM bob(sleigh)
bocage [bɔkaʒ] NM (*Géo*) bocage, farmland criss-crossed by hedges and trees; (*bois*) grove, copse (*BRIT*)
bocal, -aux [bɔkal, -o] NM jar
bock [bɔk] NM (*beer*) glass; (*contenu*) glass of beer
body [bɔdi] NM body(suit); (*Sport*) leotard
bœuf [bœf] (*pl* **bœufs** [bø]) NM ox, steer; (*Culin*) beef; (*Mus: fam*) jam session
bof [bɔf] EXCL (*fam: indifférence*) don't care!, meh; (: *pas terrible*) nothing special
Bogota [bɔgɔta] N Bogotá
bogue [bɔg] NF (*Bot*) husk ▶ NM (*Inform*) bug
Bohème [bɔɛm] NF: **la** ~ Bohemia
bohème [bɔɛm] ADJ happy-go-lucky, unconventional
bohémien, ne [bɔemjɛ̃, -ɛn] ADJ Bohemian ▶ NM/F gipsy
boire [bwaʀ] /53/ VT to drink; (*s'imprégner de*) to soak up; ~ **un coup** to have a drink
bois [bwa] VB *voir* **boire** ▶ NM wood; (*Zool*) antler; (*Mus*): **les** ~ the woodwind; **de** ~, **en** ~ wooden; ~ **vert** green wood; ~ **mort** deadwood; ~ **de lit** bedstead

boisé, e [bwaze] ADJ woody, wooded
boiser [bwaze] /1/ VT (*galerie de mine*) to timber; (*chambre*) to panel; (*terrain*) to plant with trees
boiseries [bwazʀi] NFPL panelling *sg*
boisson [bwasɔ̃] NF drink; **pris de** ~ drunk, intoxicated; **boissons alcoolisées** alcoholic beverages *ou* drinks; **boissons non alcoolisées** soft drinks
boit [bwa] VB *voir* **boire**
boîte [bwat] NF box; (*fam: entreprise*) firm, company; **aliments en** ~ canned *ou* tinned (*BRIT*) foods; ~ **à gants** glove compartment; ~ **à musique** musical box; ~ **à ordures** dustbin (*BRIT*), trash can (*US*); ~ **aux lettres** letter box, mailbox (*US*); (*Inform*) mailbox; ~ **crânienne** cranium; ~ **d'allumettes** box of matches; (*vide*) matchbox; ~ **de conserves** can *ou* tin (*BRIT*) (of food); ~ **de nuit** night club; ~ **de sardines/ petits pois** can *ou* tin (*BRIT*) of sardines/peas; **mettre qn en** ~ (*fam*) to have a laugh at sb's expense; ~ **de vitesses** gear box; ~ **noire** (*Aviat*) black box; ~ **postale** PO box; ~ **vocale** voice mail
boiter [bwate] /1/ VI to limp; (*fig*) to wobble; (: *raisonnement*) to be shaky
boiteux, -euse [bwatø, -øz] ADJ lame; wobbly; shaky
boîtier [bwatje] NM case; (*d'appareil photo*) body; ~ **de montre** watch case
boitiller [bwatije] /1/ VI to limp slightly, have a slight limp
boive etc [bwav] VB *voir* **boire**
bol [bɔl] NM bowl; (*contenu*): **un** ~ **de café** etc a bowl of coffee etc; **un** ~ **d'air** a breath of fresh air; **en avoir ras le** ~ (*fam*) to have had a bellyful; **avoir du** ~ (*fam*) to be lucky
bolée [bɔle] NF bowlful
boléro [bɔleʀo] NM bolero
bolet [bɔlɛ] NM boletus (mushroom)
bolide [bɔlid] NM racing car; **comme un** ~ like a rocket
Bolivie [bɔlivi] NF: **la** ~ Bolivia
bolivien, ne [bɔlivjɛ̃, -ɛn] ADJ Bolivian ▶ NM/F: **B~, ne** Bolivian
bolognais, e [bɔlɔɲɛ, -ɛz] ADJ Bolognese
Bologne [bɔlɔɲ] N Bologna
bombance [bɔ̃bɑ̃s] NF: **faire** ~ to have a feast, revel
bombardement [bɔ̃baʀdəmɑ̃] NM bombing
bombarder [bɔ̃baʀde] /1/ VT to bomb; ~ **qn de** (*cailloux, lettres*) to bombard sb with; ~ **qn directeur** to thrust sb into the director's seat
bombardier [bɔ̃baʀdje] NM (*avion*) bomber; (*aviateur*) bombardier
bombe [bɔ̃b] NF bomb; (*atomiseur*) (aerosol) spray; (*Équitation*) riding cap; **faire la** ~ (*fam*) to go on a binge; ~ **atomique** atomic bomb; ~ **à retardement** time bomb
bombé, e [bɔ̃be] ADJ rounded; (*mur*) bulging; (*front*) domed; (*route*) steeply cambered
bomber [bɔ̃be] /1/ VI to bulge; (*route*) to camber ▶ VT: ~ **le torse** to swell out one's chest

MOT-CLÉ

bon, bonne [bɔ̃, bɔn] ADJ **1** (*agréable, satisfaisant*) good; **un bon repas/restaurant** a good meal/restaurant; **être bon en maths** to be good at maths
2 (*charitable*): **être bon (envers)** to be good (to), to be kind (to); **vous êtes trop bon** you're too kind
3 (*correct*) right; **le bon numéro/moment** the right number/moment
4 (*souhaits*): **bon anniversaire!** happy birthday!; **bon courage!** good luck!; **bon séjour!** enjoy your stay!; **bon voyage!** have a good trip!; **bon week-end!** have a good weekend!; **bonne année!** happy New Year!; **bonne chance!** good luck!; **bonne fête!** happy holiday!; **bonne nuit!** good night!
5 (*approprié*): **bon à/pour** fit to/for; **bon à jeter** fit for the bin; **c'est bon à savoir** that's useful to know; **à quoi bon (...)?** what's the point *ou* use (of ...)?
6 (*intensif*): **ça m'a pris deux bonnes heures** it took me a good two hours; **un bon nombre de** a good number of
7: bon enfant *adj inv* accommodating, easy-going; **bonne femme** (*péj*) woman; **de bonne heure** early; **bon marché** cheap; **bon mot** witticism; **pour faire bon poids ...** to make up for it ...; **bon sens** common sense; **bon vivant** jovial chap; **bonnes œuvres** charitable works, charities; **bonne sœur** nun ▶ NM **1** (*billet*) voucher; (*aussi:* **bon cadeau**) gift voucher; **bon de caisse** cash voucher; **bon d'essence** petrol coupon; **bon à tirer** pass for press; **bon du Trésor** Treasury bond
2: avoir du bon to have its good points; **il y a du bon dans ce qu'il dit** there's some sense in what he says; **pour de bon** for good ▶ NM/F: **un bon à rien** a good-for-nothing ▶ ADV: **il fait bon** it's *ou* the weather is fine; **sentir bon** to smell good; **tenir bon** to stand firm; **juger bon de faire ...** to think fit to do ... ▶ EXCL right!, good!; **ah bon?** really?; **bon, je reste** right, I'll stay; *voir aussi* **bonne**

bonasse [bɔnas] ADJ soft, meek
bonbon [bɔ̃bɔ̃] NM (boiled) sweet
bonbonne [bɔ̃bɔn] NF demijohn; carboy
bonbonnière [bɔ̃bɔnjɛʀ] NF sweet (BRIT) *ou* candy (US) box
bond [bɔ̃] NM leap; (*d'une balle*) rebound, ricochet; **faire un ~** to leap in the air; **d'un seul ~** in one bound, with one leap; **~ en avant** (*fig: progrès*) leap forward
bonde [bɔ̃d] NF (*d'évier etc*) plug; (: *trou*) plughole; (*de tonneau*) bung; bunghole
bondé, e [bɔ̃de] ADJ packed (full)
bondieuserie [bɔ̃djøzʀi] NF (*péj: objet*) religious knick-knack
bondir [bɔ̃diʀ] /2/ VI to leap; **~ de joie** (*fig*) to jump for joy; **~ de colère** (*fig*) to be hopping mad
bonheur [bɔnœʀ] NM happiness; **avoir le ~ de** to have the good fortune to; **porter ~ (à qn)** to bring (sb) luck; **au petit ~** haphazardly; **par ~** fortunately
bonhomie [bɔnɔmi] NF good-naturedness
bonhomme [bɔnɔm] (*pl* **bonshommes** [bɔ̃zɔm]) NM fellow ▶ ADJ good-natured; **un vieux ~** an old chap; **aller son ~ de chemin** to carry on in one's own sweet way; **~ de neige** snowman
boni [bɔni] NM profit
bonification [bɔnifikasjɔ̃] NF bonus
bonifier [bɔnifje] /7/: **se bonifier** VI to improve
boniment [bɔnimɑ̃] NM patter *no pl*
bonjour [bɔ̃ʒuʀ] EXCL hello; (*selon l'heure*) good morning (*ou* afternoon); **donner** *ou* **souhaiter le ~ à qn** to bid sb good morning *ou* afternoon; **c'est simple comme ~!** it's easy as pie!
Bonn [bɔn] N Bonn
bonne [bɔn] ADJ F *voir* **bon** ▶ NF (*domestique*) maid; **~ à toute faire** general help; **~ d'enfant** nanny
bonne-maman [bɔnmamɑ̃] (*pl* **bonnes-mamans**) NF granny, grandma, gran
bonnement [bɔnmɑ̃] ADV: **tout ~** quite simply
bonnet [bɔnɛ] NM bonnet, hat; (*de soutien-gorge*) cup; **~ d'âne** dunce's cap; **~ de bain** bathing cap; **~ de nuit** nightcap
bonneterie [bɔnɛtʀi] NF hosiery
bon-papa [bɔ̃papa] (*pl* **bons-papas**) NM grandpa, grandad
bonsoir [bɔ̃swaʀ] EXCL good evening
bonté [bɔ̃te] NF kindness *no pl*; **avoir la ~ de** to be kind *ou* good enough to
bonus [bɔnys] NM (*Assurances*) no-claims bonus; (*de DVD*) extras *pl*
bonze [bɔ̃z] NM (*Rel*) bonze
boomerang [bumʀɑ̃g] NM boomerang
boots [buts] NFPL boots
borborygme [bɔʀbɔʀigm] NM rumbling noise
bord [bɔʀ] NM (*de table, verre, falaise*) edge; (*de rivière, lac*) bank; (*de route*) side; (*de vêtement*) edge, border; (*de chapeau*) brim; (**monter**) **à ~** (to go) on board; **jeter par-dessus ~** to throw overboard; **le commandant de ~/les hommes du ~** the ship's master/crew; **du même ~** (*fig*) of the same opinion; **au ~ de la mer/route** at the seaside/roadside; **être au ~ des larmes** to be on the verge of tears; **virer de ~** (*Navig*) to tack; **sur les bords** (*fig*) slightly; **de tous bords** on all sides; **~ du trottoir** kerb (BRIT), curb (US)
bordeaux [bɔʀdo] NM Bordeaux ▶ ADJ INV maroon
bordée [bɔʀde] NF broadside; **une ~ d'injures** a volley of abuse; **tirer une ~** to go on the town
bordel [bɔʀdɛl] NM brothel; (!) bloody (BRIT) *ou* goddamn (US) mess (!) ▶ EXCL hell!
bordelais, e [bɔʀdəlɛ, -ɛz] ADJ of *ou* from Bordeaux
border [bɔʀde] /1/ VT (*être le long de*) to line, border; (*qn dans son lit*) to tuck up; **~ qch** (*garnir*) to line sth with; to trim sth with
bordereau, x [bɔʀdəʀo] NM docket, slip
bordure [bɔʀdyʀ] NF border; (*sur un vêtement*) trim(ming), border; **en ~ de** on the edge of
boréal, e, -aux [bɔʀeal, -o] ADJ boreal, northern

borgne [bɔʀɲ] ADJ one-eyed; **hôtel** ~ shady hotel; **fenêtre** ~ obstructed window
bornage [bɔʀnaʒ] NM (*d'un terrain*) demarcation
borne [bɔʀn] NF boundary stone; (*aussi:* **borne kilométrique**) kilometre-marker, ≈ milestone; **bornes** NFPL (*fig*) limits; **dépasser les bornes** to go too far; **sans ~(s)** boundless
borné, e [bɔʀne] ADJ narrow; (*obtus: personne*) narrow-minded
Bornéo [bɔʀneo] NM: **le** ~ Borneo
borner [bɔʀne] **/1/** VT (*délimiter*) to limit; (*limiter*) to confine; **se** ~ **à faire** (*se contenter de*) to content o.s. with doing; (*se limiter à*) to limit o.s. to doing
bosniaque [bɔznjak] ADJ Bosnian ▶ NMF: **B~** Bosnian
Bosnie [bɔzni] NF Bosnia
Bosnie-Herzégovine [bɔzniɛʀzegɔvin] NF Bosnia-Herzegovina
bosnien, ne [bɔznjɛ̃, -ɛn] ADJ Bosnian ▶ NM/F: **B~, ne** Bosnian
Bosphore [bɔsfɔʀ] NM: **le** ~ the Bosphorus
bosquet [bɔskɛ] NM copse (BRIT), grove
bosse [bɔs] NF (*de terrain etc*) bump; (*enflure*) lump; (*du bossu, du chameau*) hump; **avoir la** ~ **des maths** *etc* (*fam*) to have a gift for maths *etc*; **il a roulé sa** ~ (*fam*) he's been around
bosseler [bɔsle] **/4/** VT (*ouvrer*) to emboss; (*abîmer*) to dent
bosser [bɔse] **/1/** VI (*fam*) to work; (: *dur*) to slave (away), slog (hard) (BRIT)
bosseur, -euse [bɔsœʀ, -øz] NM/F (hard) worker, slogger (BRIT)
bossu, e [bɔsy] NM/F hunchback
bot [bo] ADJ M: **pied** ~ club foot
botanique [bɔtanik] NF botany ▶ ADJ botanic(al)
botaniste [bɔtanist] NMF botanist
Botswana [bɔtswana] NM: **le** ~ Botswana
botte [bɔt] NF (*soulier*) (high) boot; (*Escrime*) thrust; (*gerbe*): ~ **de paille** bundle of straw; ~ **de radis/d'asperges** bunch of radishes/asparagus; **bottes de caoutchouc** wellington boots
botter [bɔte] **/1/** VT to put boots on; (*donner un coup de pied à*) to kick; (*fam*): **ça me botte** I fancy that
bottier [bɔtje] NM bootmaker
bottillon [bɔtijɔ̃] NM bootee
bottin® [bɔtɛ̃] NM directory
bottine [bɔtin] NF ankle boot
botulisme [bɔtylism] NM botulism
bouc [buk] NM goat; (*barbe*) goatee; ~ **émissaire** scapegoat
boucan [bukɑ̃] NM din, racket
bouche [buʃ] NF mouth; **une ~ à nourrir** a mouth to feed; **les bouches inutiles** the non-productive members of the population; **faire du ~ à ~ à qn** to give sb the kiss of life (BRIT), give sb mouth-to-mouth resuscitation; **de ~ à oreille** confidentially; **pour la bonne ~** (*pour la fin*) till last; **faire venir l'eau à la ~** to make one's mouth water; ~ **cousue!** mum's the word!; **rester ~ bée** to stand open-mouthed; ~ **d'aération** air vent; ~ **de chaleur**

hot air vent; ~ **d'égout** manhole; ~ **d'incendie** fire hydrant; ~ **de métro** métro entrance
bouché, e [buʃe] ADJ (*flacon etc*) stoppered; (*temps, ciel*) overcast; (*carrière*) blocked; (*péj: personne*) thick; (*trompette*) muted; **avoir le nez** ~ to have a blocked(-up) nose; **c'est un secteur** ~ there's no future in that area; **l'évier est** ~ the sink's blocked
bouchée [buʃe] NF mouthful; **ne faire qu'une ~ de** (*fig*) to make short work of; **pour une ~ de pain** (*fig*) for next to nothing; **bouchées à la reine** chicken vol-au-vents
boucher [buʃe] **/1/** NM butcher ▶ VT (*pour colmater*) to stop up; (*trou*) to fill up; (*obstruer*) to block (up); **se boucher** VI (*tuyau etc*) to block up, get blocked up; **j'ai le nez bouché** my nose is blocked; **se boucher le nez** to hold one's nose
bouchère [buʃɛʀ] NF butcher; (*femme du boucher*) butcher's wife
boucherie [buʃʀi] NF butcher's (shop); (*métier*) butchery; (*fig*) slaughter, butchery
bouche-trou [buʃtʀu] NM (*fig*) stop-gap
bouchon [buʃɔ̃] NM (*en liège*) cork; (*autre matière*) stopper; (*de tube*) top; (*fig: embouteillage*) holdup; (*Pêche*) float; ~ **doseur** measuring cap
bouchonner [buʃɔne] **/1/** VT to rub down ▶ VI to form a traffic jam
bouchot [buʃo] NM mussel bed
bouclage [buklaʒ] NM sealing off
boucle [bukl] NF (*forme, figure, aussi Inform*) loop; (*objet*) buckle; ~ **(de cheveux)** curl; ~ **d'oreille** earring
bouclé, e [bukle] ADJ (*cheveux*) curly; (*tapis*) uncut
boucler [bukle] **/1/** VT (*fermer: ceinture etc*) to fasten; (: *magasin*) to shut; (*terminer*) to finish off; (: *circuit*) to complete; (*budget*) to balance; (*enfermer*) to shut away; (: *condamné*) to lock up; (: *quartier*) to seal off ▶ VI to curl; **faire** ~ (*cheveux*) to curl; ~ **la boucle** (*Aviat*) to loop the loop
bouclette [buklɛt] NF small curl
bouclier [buklije] NM shield
bouddha [buda] NM Buddha
bouddhisme [budism] NM Buddhism
bouddhiste [budist] NMF Buddhist
bouder [bude] **/1/** VI to sulk ▶ VT (*chose*) to turn one's nose up at; (*personne*) to refuse to have anything to do with
bouderie [budʀi] NF sulking *no pl*
boudeur, -euse [budœʀ, -øz] ADJ sullen, sulky
boudin [budɛ̃] NM (*Culin*): ~ **(noir)** black pudding; (*Tech*) roll; ~ **blanc** white pudding
boudiné, e [budine] ADJ (*doigt*) podgy; (*serré*): ~ **dans** (*vêtement*) bulging out of
boudoir [budwaʀ] NM boudoir; (*biscuit*) sponge finger
boue [bu] NF mud
bouée [bwe] NF buoy; (*de baigneur*) rubber ring; ~ **(de sauvetage)** lifebuoy; (*fig*) lifeline
boueux, -euse [bwø, -øz] ADJ muddy ▶ NM (*fam*) refuse (BRIT) ou garbage (US) collector
bouffant, e [bufɑ̃, -ɑ̃t] ADJ puffed out
bouffe [buf] NF (*fam*) grub, food
bouffée [bufe] NF (*de cigarette*) puff; **une ~ d'air pur** a breath of fresh air; ~ **de chaleur** (*gén*)

b

blast of hot air; (*Méd*) hot flush (*BRIT*) *ou* flash (*US*); **~ de fièvre/de honte** flush of fever/shame; **~ d'orgueil** fit of pride

bouffer [bufe] /**1**/ VI (*fam*) to eat; (*Couture*) to puff out ▶ VT (*fam*) to eat

bouffi, e [bufi] ADJ swollen

bouffon, ne [bufɔ̃, -ɔn] ADJ farcical, comical ▶ NM jester

bouge [buʒ] NM (*bar louche*) (low) dive; (*taudis*) hovel

bougeoir [buʒwaʀ] NM candlestick

bougeotte [buʒɔt] NF: **avoir la ~** to have the fidgets

bouger [buʒe] /**3**/ VI to move; (*dent etc*) to be loose; (*changer*) to alter; (*agir*) to stir; (*s'activer*) to get moving ▶ VT to move; **les prix/les couleurs n'ont pas bougé** prices/colours haven't changed; **se bouger** VI (*fam*) to move (oneself)

bougie [buʒi] NF candle; (*Auto*) spark(ing) plug

bougon, ne [bugɔ̃, -ɔn] ADJ grumpy

bougonner [bugɔne] /**1**/ VI, VT to grumble

bougre [bugʀ] NM chap; (*fam*): **ce ~ de ...** that confounded ...

boui-boui [bwibwi] NM (*fam*) greasy spoon

bouillabaisse [bujabɛs] NF *type of fish soup*

bouillant, e [bujɑ̃, -ɑ̃t] ADJ (*qui bout*) boiling; (*très chaud*) boiling (hot); (*fig: ardent*) hot-headed; **~ de colère** *etc* seething with anger *etc*

bouille [buj] NF (*fam*) mug

bouilleur [bujœʀ] NM: **~ de cru** (*home*) distiller

bouillie [buji] NF gruel; (*de bébé*) cereal; **en ~** (*fig*) crushed

bouillir [bujiʀ] /**15**/ VI to boil ▶ VT (*Culin: aussi*: **faire bouillir**) to boil; **~ de colère** *etc* to seethe with anger *etc*

bouilloire [bujwaʀ] NF kettle

bouillon [bujɔ̃] NM (*Culin*) stock *no pl*; (*bulles, écume*) bubble; **~ de culture** culture medium

bouillonnement [bujɔnmɑ̃] NM (*d'un liquide*) bubbling; (*des idées*) ferment

bouillonner [bujɔne] /**1**/ VI to bubble; (*fig: idées*) to bubble up; (*torrent*) to foam

bouillotte [bujɔt] NF hot-water bottle

boulanger, -ère [bulɑ̃ʒe, -ɛʀ] NM/F baker ▶ NF (*femme du boulanger*) baker's wife

boulangerie [bulɑ̃ʒʀi] NF bakery, baker's (shop); (*commerce*) bakery; **~ industrielle** bakery

boulangerie-pâtisserie [bulɑ̃ʒʀipatisʀi] (*pl* **boulangeries-pâtisseries**) NF baker's and confectioner's (shop)

boule [bul] NF (*gén*) ball; (*de pétanque*) bowl; (*de machine à écrire*) golf ball; **roulé en ~** curled up in a ball; **se mettre en ~** (*fig*) to fly off the handle, blow one's top; **perdre la ~** (*fig: fam*) to go off one's rocker; **~ de gomme** (*bonbon*) gum(drop), pastille; **~ de neige** snowball; **faire ~ de neige** (*fig*) to snowball

bouleau, x [bulo] NM (*silver*) birch

bouledogue [buldɔg] NM bulldog

bouler [bule] /**1**/ VI (*fam*): **envoyer ~ qn** to send sb packing; **je me suis fait ~** (*à un examen*) they flunked me

boulet [bulɛ] NM (*aussi*: **boulet de canon**) cannonball; (*de bagnard*) ball and chain; (*charbon*) (coal) nut

boulette [bulɛt] NF (*de viande*) meatball

boulevard [bulvaʀ] NM boulevard

bouleversant, e [bulvɛʀsɑ̃, -ɑ̃t] ADJ (*récit*) deeply distressing; (*nouvelle*) shattering

bouleversé, e [bulvɛʀse] ADJ (*ému*) deeply distressed; (*nouvelle*) shattered

bouleversement [bulvɛʀsəmɑ̃] NM (*politique, social*) upheaval

bouleverser [bulvɛʀse] /**1**/ VT (*émouvoir*) to overwhelm; (*causer du chagrin à*) to distress; (*pays, vie*) to disrupt; (*papiers, objets*) to turn upside down, upset

boulier [bulje] NM abacus; (*de jeu*) scoring board

boulimie [bulimi] NF bulimia; compulsive eating

boulimique [bulimik] ADJ bulimic

boulingrin [bulɛ̃gʀɛ̃] NM lawn

bouliste [bulist] NMF bowler

boulocher [bulɔʃe] /**1**/ VI (*laine etc*) to develop little snarls

boulodrome [bulɔdʀɔm] NM bowling pitch

boulon [bulɔ̃] NM bolt

boulonner [bulɔne] /**1**/ VT to bolt

boulot[1] [bulo] NM (*fam: travail*) work

boulot[2], te [bulo, -ɔt] ADJ plump, tubby

boum [bum] NM bang ▶ NF (*fam*) party

bouquet [bukɛ] NM (*de fleurs*) bunch (of flowers), bouquet; (*de persil etc*) bunch; (*parfum*) bouquet; (*fig*) crowning piece; **c'est le ~!** that's the last straw!; **~ garni** (*Culin*) bouquet garni

bouquetin [buktɛ̃] NM ibex

bouquin [bukɛ̃] NM (*fam*) book

bouquiner [bukine] /**1**/ VI (*fam*) to read

bouquiniste [bukinist] NMF bookseller

bourbeux, -euse [buʀbø, -øz] ADJ muddy

bourbier [buʀbje] NM (quag)mire

bourde [buʀd] NF (*erreur*) howler; (*gaffe*) blunder

bourdon [buʀdɔ̃] NM bumblebee

bourdonnement [buʀdɔnmɑ̃] NM buzzing *no pl*, buzz; **avoir des bourdonnements d'oreilles** to have a buzzing (noise) in one's ears

bourdonner [buʀdɔne] /**1**/ VI to buzz; (*moteur*) to hum

bourg [buʀ] NM small market town (*ou* village)

bourgade [buʀgad] NF township

bourgeois, e [buʀʒwa, -waz] ADJ ≈ (upper) middle class; (*péj*) bourgeois; (*maison etc*) very comfortable ▶ NM/F (*autrefois*) burgher

bourgeoisie [buʀʒwazi] NF ≈ upper middle classes *pl*; bourgeoisie; **petite ~** middle classes

bourgeon [buʀʒɔ̃] NM bud

bourgeonner [buʀʒɔne] /**1**/ VI to bud

Bourgogne [buʀgɔɲ] NF: **la ~** Burgundy ▶ NM: **bourgogne** Burgundy (wine)

bourguignon, ne [buʀgiɲɔ̃, -ɔn] ADJ *ou* from Burgundy, Burgundian; **bœuf ~** bœuf bourguignon

bourlinguer [buʀlɛ̃ge] /**1**/ VI to knock about a lot, get around a lot

bourrade [buʀad] NF shove, thump

b

bourrage [buʀaʒ] NM (*papier*) jamming; ~ **de crâne** brainwashing; (*Scol*) cramming

bourrasque [buʀask] NF squall

bourratif, -ive [buʀatif, -iv] (*fam*) ADJ filling, stodgy

bourre [buʀ] NF (*de coussin, matelas etc*) stuffing

bourré, e [buʀe] ADJ (*rempli*): ~ **de** crammed full of; (*fam*: *ivre*) pickled, plastered

bourreau, x [buʀo] NM executioner; (*fig*) torturer; ~ **de travail** workaholic, glutton for work

bourrelé, e [buʀle] ADJ: **être ~ de remords** to be racked by remorse

bourrelet [buʀlɛ] NM draught (*Brit*) *ou* draft (*US*) excluder; (*de peau*) fold *ou* roll (of flesh)

bourrer [buʀe] /**1**/ VT (*pipe*) to fill; (*poêle*) to pack; (*valise*) to cram (full); ~ **de** to cram (full) with, stuff with; ~ **de coups** to hammer blows on, pummel; ~ **le crâne à qn** to pull the wool over sb's eyes; (*endoctriner*) to brainwash sb

bourricot [buʀiko] NM small donkey

bourrique [buʀik] NF (*âne*) ass

bourru, e [buʀy] ADJ surly, gruff

bourse [buʀs] NF (*subvention*) grant; (*porte-monnaie*) purse; **sans ~ délier** without spending a penny; **la B~** the Stock Exchange; ~ **du travail** ≈ trades union council (regional headquarters)

boursicoter [buʀsikɔte] /**1**/ VI (*Comm*) to dabble on the Stock Market

boursier, -ière [buʀsje, -jɛʀ] ADJ (*Comm*) Stock Market *cpd* ▸ NM/F (*Scol*) grant-holder

boursouflé, e [buʀsufle] ADJ swollen, puffy; (*fig*) bombastic, turgid

boursoufler [buʀsufle] /**1**/ VT to puff up, bloat; **se boursoufler** VI (*visage*) to swell *ou* puff up; (*peinture*) to blister

boursouflure [buʀsuflyʀ] NF (*du visage*) swelling, puffiness; (*de la peinture*) blister; (*fig*: *du style*) pomposity

bous [bu] VB *voir* **bouillir**

bousculade [buskylad] NF (*hâte*) rush; (*poussée*) crush

bousculer [buskyle] /**1**/ VT to knock over; (*heurter*) to knock into; (*fig*) to push, rush

bouse [buz] NF: ~ **(de vache)** (cow) dung *no pl* (*Brit*), manure *no pl*

bousiller [buzije] /**1**/ VT (*fam*) to wreck

boussole [busɔl] NF compass

bout [bu] VB *voir* **bouillir** ▸ NM bit; (*extrémité: d'un bâton etc*) tip; (: *d'une ficelle, table, rue, période*) end; **au ~ de** at the end of, after; **au ~ du compte** at the end of the day; **pousser qn à ~** to push sb to the limit (of his patience); **venir à ~ de** to manage to finish (off) *ou* overcome; ~ **à** ~ end to end; **à tout ~ de champ** at every turn; **d'un ~ à l'autre, de ~ en ~** from one end to the other; **à ~ portant** at point-blank range; **un ~ de chou** (*enfant*) a little tot; ~ **d'essai** (*Ciné etc*) screen test; ~ **filtre** filter tip

boutade [butad] NF quip, sally

boute-en-train [butɑ̃tʀɛ̃] NM INV live wire (*fig*)

bouteille [butɛj] NF bottle; (*de gaz butane*) cylinder

boutiquaire [butikɛʀ] ADJ: **niveau ~** shopping level

boutique [butik] NF shop (*Brit*), store (*US*); (*de grand couturier, de mode*) boutique

boutiquier, -ière [butikje, -jɛʀ] NM/F shopkeeper (*Brit*), storekeeper (*US*)

boutoir [butwaʀ] NM: **coup de ~** (*choc*) thrust; (*fig*: *propos*) barb

bouton [butɔ̃] NM (*de vêtement, électrique etc*) button; (*Bot*) bud; (*sur la peau*) spot; (*de porte*) knob; ~ **de manchette** cuff-link; ~ **d'or** buttercup

boutonnage [butɔnaʒ] NM (*action*) buttoning(-up); **un manteau à double ~** a coat with two rows of buttons

boutonner [butɔne] /**1**/ VT to button up, do up; **se boutonner** to button one's clothes up

boutonneux, -euse [butɔnø, -øz] ADJ spotty

boutonnière [butɔnjɛʀ] NF buttonhole

bouton-poussoir [butɔ̃puswaʀ] (*pl* **boutons-poussoirs**) NM pushbutton

bouton-pression [butɔ̃pʀesjɔ̃] (*pl* **boutons-pression**) NM press stud, snap fastener

bouture [butyʀ] NF cutting; **faire des boutures** to take cuttings

bouvreuil [buvʀœj] NM bullfinch

bovidé [bɔvide] NM bovine

bovin, e [bɔvɛ̃, -in] ADJ bovine ▸ NM: **bovins** cattle *pl*

bowling [boliŋ] NM (*tenpin*) bowling; (*salle*) bowling alley

box [bɔks] NM lock-up (garage); (*de salle, dortoir*) cubicle; (*d'écurie*) loose-box; (*aussi*: **box-calf**) box calf; **le ~ des accusés** the dock

boxe [bɔks] NF boxing

boxer [bɔkse] /**1**/ VI to box ▸ NM [bɔksɛʀ] (*chien*) boxer

boxeur [bɔksœʀ] NM boxer

boyau, x [bwajo] NM (*corde de raquette etc*) (cat) gut; (*galerie*) passage(way); (narrow) gallery; (*pneu de bicyclette*) tubeless tyre ▸ NMPL (*viscères*) entrails, guts

boyaux [bwajo] NMPL (*viscères*) entrails, guts

boycottage [bɔjkɔtaʒ] NM (*d'un produit*) boycotting

boycotter [bɔjkɔte] /**1**/ VT to boycott

BP SIGLE F = **boîte postale**

brabançon, ne [bʀabɑ̃sɔ̃, -ɔn] ADJ of *ou* from Brabant

Brabant [bʀabɑ̃] NM: **le ~** Brabant

bracelet [bʀaslɛ] NM bracelet

bracelet-montre [bʀaslemɔ̃tʀ] NM wristwatch

braconnage [bʀakɔnaʒ] NM poaching

braconner [bʀakɔne] /**1**/ VI to poach

braconnier [bʀakɔnje] NM poacher

brader [bʀade] /**1**/ VT to sell off, sell cheaply

braderie [bʀadʀi] NF clearance sale; (*par des particuliers*) ≈ car boot sale (*Brit*), ≈ garage sale (*US*); (*magasin*) discount store; (*sur marché*) cut-price (*Brit*) *ou* cut-rate (*US*) stall

braguette [bʀagɛt] NF fly, flies *pl* (*Brit*), zipper (*US*)

braillard, e [bʀajaʀ, -aʀd] ADJ (*fam*) bawling, yelling

braille [bʀɑj] NM Braille

braillement [bʀɑjmɑ̃] NM (*cri*) bawling *no pl*, yelling *no pl*

brailler [bʀɑje] /**1**/ VI to bawl, yell ▶ VT to bawl out, yell out

braire [bʀɛʀ] /**50**/ VI to bray

braise [bʀɛz] NF embers *pl*

braiser [bʀeze] /**1**/ VT to braise; **bœuf braisé** braised steak

bramer [bʀame] /**1**/ VI to bell; (*fig*) to wail

brancard [bʀɑ̃kaʀ] NM (*civière*) stretcher; (*bras, perche*) shaft

brancardier [bʀɑ̃kaʀdje] NM stretcher-bearer

branchages [bʀɑ̃ʃaʒ] NMPL branches, boughs

branche [bʀɑ̃ʃ] NF branch; (*de lunettes*) side(-piece)

branché, e [bʀɑ̃ʃe] ADJ (*fam*) switched-on, trendy ▶ NM/F (*fam*) trendy

branchement [bʀɑ̃ʃmɑ̃] NM connection

brancher [bʀɑ̃ʃe] /**1**/ VT to connect (up); (*en mettant la prise*) to plug in; ~ **qn/qch sur** (*fig*) to get sb/sth launched onto

branchies [bʀɑ̃ʃi] NFPL gills

brandade [bʀɑ̃dad] NF brandade (*cod dish*)

brandebourgeois, e [bʀɑ̃dəbuʀʒwa, -waz] ADJ of ou from Brandenburg

brandir [bʀɑ̃diʀ] /**2**/ VT (*arme*) to brandish, wield; (*document*) to flourish, wave

brandon [bʀɑ̃dɔ̃] NM firebrand

branlant, e [bʀɑ̃lɑ̃, -ɑ̃t] ADJ (*mur, meuble*) shaky

branle [bʀɑ̃l] NM: **mettre en ~** to set swinging; **donner le ~ à** to set in motion

branle-bas [bʀɑ̃lbɑ] NM INV commotion

branler [bʀɑ̃le] /**1**/ VI to be shaky, be loose ▶ VT: **~ la tête** to shake one's head

braquage [bʀakaʒ] NM (*fam*) stick-up, hold-up; (*Auto*): **rayon de ~** turning circle

braque [bʀak] NM (*Zool*) pointer

braquer [bʀake] /**1**/ VI (*Auto*) to turn (the wheel) ▶ VT (*revolver etc*): **~ qch sur** to aim sth at, point sth at; (*mettre en colère*): **~ qn** to antagonize sb, put sb's back up; **son regard sur** to fix one's gaze on; **se braquer** VI: **se braquer (contre)** to take a stand (against)

bras [bʀɑ] NM arm; (*de fleuve*) branch ▶ NMPL (*fig*: *travailleurs*) labour *sg* (BRIT), labor *sg* (US); hands; **~ dessus ~ dessous** arm in arm; **à ~ raccourcis** with fists flying; **à tour de ~** with all one's might; **baisser les ~** to give up; **se retrouver avec qch sur les ~** (*fam*) to be landed with sth; **~ droit** (*fig*) right hand man; **~ de fer** arm-wrestling; **une partie de ~ de fer** (*fig*) a trial of strength; **~ de levier** lever arm; **~ de mer** arm of the sea, sound

brasero [bʀazeʀo] NM brazier

brasier [bʀazje] NM blaze, (blazing) inferno; (*fig*) inferno

Brasilia [bʀazilja] N Brasilia

bras-le-corps [bʀalkɔʀ]: **à ~** adv (a)round the waist

brassage [bʀasaʒ] NM (*de la bière*) brewing; (*fig*) mixing

brassard [bʀasaʀ] NM armband

brasse [bʀas] NF (*nage*) breast-stroke; (*mesure*) fathom; **~ papillon** butterfly(-stroke)

brassée [bʀase] NF armful; **une ~ de** (*fig*) a number of

brasser [bʀase] /**1**/ VT (*bière*) to brew; (*remuer*: *salade*) to toss; (: *cartes*) to shuffle; (*fig*) to mix; **~ l'argent/les affaires** to handle a lot of money/ business

brasserie [bʀasʀi] NF (*restaurant*) bar (*selling food*), brasserie; (*usine*) brewery

brasseur [bʀasœʀ] NM (*de bière*) brewer; **~ d'affaires** big businessman

brassière [bʀasjɛʀ] NF (*baby's*) vest (BRIT) ou undershirt (US); (*de sauvetage*) life jacket

bravache [bʀavaʃ] NM blusterer, braggart

bravade [bʀavad] NF: **par ~** out of bravado

brave [bʀav] ADJ (*courageux*) brave; (*bon, gentil*) good, kind

bravement [bʀavmɑ̃] ADV bravely; (*résolument*) boldly

braver [bʀave] /**1**/ VT to defy

bravo [bʀavo] EXCL bravo! ▶ NM cheer

bravoure [bʀavuʀ] NF bravery

BRB SIGLE F (*Police*: = *Brigade de répression du banditisme*) ≈ serious crime squad

break [bʀɛk] NM (*Auto*) estate car (BRIT), station wagon (US)

brebis [bʀəbi] NF ewe; **~ galeuse** black sheep

brèche [bʀɛʃ] NF breach, gap; **être sur la ~** (*fig*) to be on the go

bredouille [bʀəduj] ADJ empty-handed

bredouiller [bʀəduje] /**1**/ VI, VT to mumble, stammer

bref, brève [bʀɛf, bʀɛv] ADJ short, brief ▶ ADV in short ▶ NF (*voyelle*) short vowel; (*information*) brief news item; **d'un ton ~** sharply, curtly; **en ~** in short, in brief; **à ~ délai** shortly

brelan [bʀəlɑ̃] NM: **un ~** three of a kind; **un ~ d'as** three aces

breloque [bʀəlɔk] NF charm

brème [bʀɛm] NF bream

Brésil [bʀezil] NM: **le ~** Brazil

brésilien, ne [bʀeziljɛ̃, -ɛn] ADJ Brazilian ▶ NM/F: **B~, ne** Brazilian

bressan, e [bʀesɑ̃, -an] ADJ of ou from Bresse

Bretagne [bʀətaɲ] NF: **la ~** Brittany

bretelle [bʀətɛl] NF (*de fusil etc*) sling; (*de vêtement*) strap; (*d'autoroute*) slip road (BRIT), entrance ou exit ramp (US); **bretelles** NFPL (*pour pantalon*) braces (BRIT), suspenders (US); **~ de contournement** (*Auto*) bypass; **~ de raccordement** (*Auto*) access road

breton, ne [bʀətɔ̃, -ɔn] ADJ Breton ▶ NM (*Ling*) Breton ▶ NM/F: **B~, ne** Breton

breuvage [bʀœvaʒ] NM beverage, drink

brève [bʀɛv] ADJ F, NF *voir* bref

brevet [bʀəvɛ] NM diploma, certificate; **~ d'apprentissage** certificate of apprenticeship; **~ (des collèges)** school certificate, taken at approx. 16 years; **~ (d'invention)** patent

breveté, e [bʀəvte] ADJ patented; (*diplômé*) qualified

breveter [bʀəvte] /**4**/ VT to patent

bréviaire [bʀevjɛʀ] NM breviary

BRGM SIGLE M = **Bureau de recherches géologiques et minières**

briard, e [bʀijaʀ, -aʀd] ADJ of ou from Brie ▶ NM (*chien*) briard

bribes [bʀib] NFPL bits, scraps; (*d'une conversation*) snatches; **par ~** piecemeal

bric [bʀik]: **de ~ et de broc** adv with any old thing

bric-à-brac [bʀikabʀak] NM INV bric-a-brac, jumble

bricolage [bʀikɔlaʒ] NM: **le ~** do-it-yourself (jobs); (*péj*) patched-up job

bricole [bʀikɔl] NF (*babiole, chose insignifiante*) trifle; (*petit travail*) small job

bricoler [bʀikɔle] /1/ VI to do odd jobs; (*en amateur*) to do DIY jobs; (*passe-temps*) to potter about ▶ VT (*réparer*) to fix up; (*mal réparer*) to tinker with; (*trafiquer: voiture etc*) to doctor, fix

bricoleur, -euse [bʀikɔlœʀ, -øz] NM/F handyman/woman, DIY enthusiast

bride [bʀid] NF bridle; (*d'un bonnet*) string, tie; **à ~ abattue** flat out, hell for leather; **tenir en ~** to keep in check; **lâcher la ~ à, laisser la ~ sur le cou à** to give free rein to

bridé, e [bʀide] ADJ: **yeux bridés** slit eyes

brider [bʀide] /1/ VT (*réprimer*) to keep in check; (*cheval: volaille*) to bridle; (*Culin: volaille*) to truss

bridge [bʀidʒ] NM (*Cartes*) bridge

brie [bʀi] NM Brie (*cheese*)

brièvement [bʀijɛvmɑ̃] ADV briefly

brièveté [bʀijɛvte] NF brevity

brigade [bʀigad] NF (*Police*) squad; (*Mil*) brigade

brigadier [bʀigadje] NM (*Police*) ≈ sergeant; (*Mil*) bombardier; corporal

brigadier-chef [bʀigadjeʃɛf] (*pl* **brigadiers-chefs**) NM ≈ lance-sergeant

brigand [bʀigɑ̃] NM brigand

brigandage [bʀigɑ̃daʒ] NM robbery

briguer [bʀige] /1/ VT to aspire to; (*suffrages*) to canvass

brillamment [bʀijamɑ̃] ADV brilliantly

brillant, e [bʀijɑ̃, -ɑ̃t] ADJ brilliant; (*remarquable*) bright; (*luisant*) shiny, shining ▶ NM (*diamant*) brilliant

briller [bʀije] /1/ VI to shine

brimade [bʀimad] NF vexation, harassment *no pl*; bullying *no pl*

brimbaler [bʀɛ̃bale] /1/ VB = **bringuebaler**

brimer [bʀime] /1/ VT to harass; to bully

brin [bʀɛ̃] NM (*de laine, ficelle etc*) strand; (*fig*): **un ~ de** a bit of; **un ~ mystérieux** *etc* (*fam*) a weeny bit mysterious *etc*; **~ d'herbe** blade of grass; **~ de muguet** sprig of lily of the valley; **~ de paille** wisp of straw

brindille [bʀɛ̃dij] NF twig

bringue [bʀɛ̃g] NF (*fam*): **faire la ~** to go on a binge

bringuebaler [bʀɛ̃gbale] /1/ VI to shake (about) ▶ VT to cart about

brio [bʀijo] NM brilliance; (*Mus*) brio; **avec ~** brilliantly, with panache

brioche [bʀijɔʃ] NF brioche (bun); (*fam: ventre*) paunch

brioché, e [bʀijɔʃe] ADJ brioche-style

brique [bʀik] NF brick; (*de lait*) carton; (*fam*) 10 000 francs ▶ ADJ INV brick red

briquer [bʀike] /1/ VT (*fam*) to polish up

briquet [bʀikɛ] NM (*cigarette*) lighter

briqueterie [bʀiktʀi] NF brickyard

bris [bʀi] NM: **~ de clôture** (*Jur*) breaking in; **~ de glaces** (*Auto*) breaking of windows

brisant [bʀizɑ̃] NM reef; (*vague*) breaker

brise [bʀiz] NF breeze

brisé, e [bʀize] ADJ broken; **~ (de fatigue)** exhausted; **d'une voix ~** in a voice broken with emotion; **pâte ~** shortcrust pastry

brisées [bʀize] NFPL: **aller** ou **marcher sur les ~ de qn** to compete with sb in his own province

brise-glace, brise-glaces [bʀizglas] NM INV (*navire*) icebreaker

brise-jet [bʀizʒɛ] NM INV tap swirl

brise-lames [bʀizlam] NM INV breakwater

briser [bʀize] /1/ VT to break; **se briser** VI to break

brise-tout [bʀiztu] NM INV wrecker

briseur, -euse [bʀizœʀ, -øz] NM/F: **~ de grève** strike-breaker

brise-vent [bʀizvɑ̃] NM INV windbreak

bristol [bʀistɔl] NM (*carte de visite*) visiting card

britannique [bʀitanik] ADJ British ▶ NMF: **B~** Briton, British person; **les Britanniques** the British

broc [bʀo] NM pitcher

brocante [bʀɔkɑ̃t] NF (*objets*) secondhand goods *pl*, junk; (*commerce*) secondhand trade; junk dealing

brocanteur, -euse [bʀɔkɑ̃tœʀ, -øz] NM/F junk shop owner; junk dealer

brocart [bʀɔkaʀ] NM brocade

broche [bʀɔʃ] NF brooch; (*Culin*) spit; (*fiche*) spike, peg; (*Méd*) pin; **à la ~** spit-roasted, roasted on a spit

broché, e [bʀɔʃe] ADJ (*livre*) paper-backed; (*tissu*) brocaded

brochet [bʀɔʃɛ] NM pike *inv*

brochette [bʀɔʃɛt] NF (*ustensile*) skewer; (*plat*) kebab; **~ de décorations** row of medals

brochure [bʀɔʃyʀ] NF pamphlet, brochure, booklet

brocoli [bʀɔkɔli] NM broccoli

brodequins [bʀɔdkɛ̃] NMPL (*de marche*) (lace-up) boots

broder [bʀɔde] /1/ VT to embroider ▶ VI: **~ (sur des faits** ou **une histoire)** to embroider the facts

broderie [bʀɔdʀi] NF embroidery

bromure [bʀɔmyʀ] NM bromide

broncher [bʀɔ̃ʃe] /1/ VI: **sans ~** without flinching, without turning a hair

bronches [bʀɔ̃ʃ] NFPL bronchial tubes

bronchite [bʀɔ̃ʃit] NF bronchitis

broncho-pneumonie [bʀɔ̃kɔpnømɔni] NF broncho-pneumonia *no pl*

bronzage [bʀɔ̃zaʒ] NM (*hâle*) (sun)tan

bronze [bʀɔ̃z] NM bronze

bronzé, e [bʀɔ̃ze] ADJ tanned

bronzer [bʀɔ̃ze] /1/ VT to tan ▶ VI to get a tan; **se bronzer** to sunbathe

b

55

brosse [bʀɔs] NF brush; **donner un coup de ~ à qch** to give sth a brush; **coiffé en ~** with a crewcut; **~ à cheveux** hairbrush; **~ à dents** toothbrush; **~ à habits** clothesbrush

brosser [bʀɔse] /**1**/ VT (*nettoyer*) to brush; (*fig: tableau etc*) to paint; to draw; **se brosser** VT, VI to brush one's clothes; **se brosser les dents** to brush one's teeth; **tu peux te ~!** (*fam*) you can sing for it!

brou [bʀu] NM: **~ de noix** (*pour bois*) walnut stain; (*liqueur*) walnut liqueur

brouette [bʀuɛt] NF wheelbarrow

brouhaha [bʀuaa] NM hubbub

brouillage [bʀujaʒ] NM (*d'une émission*) jamming

brouillard [bʀujaʀ] NM fog; **être dans le ~** (*fig*) to be all at sea

brouille [bʀuj] NF quarrel

brouillé, e [bʀuje] ADJ (*fâché*): **il est ~ avec ses parents** he has fallen out with his parents; (*teint*) muddy

brouiller [bʀuje] /**1**/ VT (*œufs, message*) to scramble; (*idées*) to mix up; to confuse; (*Radio*) to cause interference to; (: *délibérément*) to jam; (*rendre trouble*) to cloud; (*désunir: amis*) to set at odds; **se brouiller** VI (*ciel, vue*) to cloud over; (*détails*) to become confused; **se brouiller (avec)** to fall out (with); **~ les pistes** to cover one's tracks; (*fig*) to confuse the issue

brouillon, ne [bʀujɔ̃, -ɔn] ADJ (*sans soin*) untidy; (*qui manque d'organisation*) disorganized, unmethodical ▶ NM (*first*) draft; **cahier de ~** rough (work) book; (*papier*) ~ rough paper

broussailles [bʀusɑj] NFPL undergrowth *sg*

broussailleux, -euse [bʀusajø, -øz] ADJ bushy

brousse [bʀus] NF: **la ~** the bush

brouter [bʀute] /**1**/ VT to graze on ▶ VI to graze; (*Auto*) to judder

broutille [bʀutij] NF trifle

broyer [bʀwaje] /**8**/ VT to crush; **~ du noir** to be down in the dumps

bru [bʀy] NF daughter-in-law

brucelles [bʀysɛl] NFPL: **(pinces) ~** tweezers

brugnon [bʀyɲɔ̃] NM nectarine

bruine [bʀɥin] NF drizzle

bruiner [bʀɥine] /**1**/ VB IMPERS: **il bruine** it's drizzling, there's a drizzle

bruire [bʀɥiʀ] /**2**/ VI (*eau*) to murmur; (*feuilles, étoffe*) to rustle

bruissement [bʀɥismɑ̃] NM murmuring; rustling

bruit [bʀɥi] NM: **un ~** a noise, a sound; (*fig: rumeur*) a rumour (BRIT), a rumor (US); **le ~** noise; **pas/trop de ~** no/too much noise; **sans ~** without a sound, noiselessly; **faire du ~** to make a noise; **~ de fond** background noise

bruitage [bʀɥitaʒ] NM sound effects *pl*

bruiteur, -euse [bʀɥitœʀ, -øz] NM/F sound-effects engineer

brûlant, e [bʀylɑ̃, -ɑ̃t] ADJ burning (hot); (*liquide*) boiling (hot); (*regard*) fiery; (*sujet*) red-hot

brûlé, e [bʀyle] ADJ (*fig: démasqué*) blown; (: *homme politique etc*) discredited ▶ NM: **odeur de ~** smell of burning

brûle-pourpoint [bʀylpuʀpwɛ̃]: **à ~** adv point-blank

brûler [bʀyle] /**1**/ VT to burn; (*eau bouillante*) to scald; (*consommer: électricité, essence*) to use; (: *feu rouge, signal*) to go through (without stopping) ▶ VI to burn; **se brûler** to burn o.s.; (*s'ébouillanter*) to scald o.s.; **tu brûles** (*jeu*) you're getting warm *ou* hot; **se brûler la cervelle** to blow one's brains out; **~ les étapes** to make rapid progress; (*aller trop vite*) to cut corners; **~ (d'impatience) de faire qch** to burn with impatience to do sth, be dying to do sth

brûleur [bʀylœʀ] NM burner

brûlot [bʀylo] NM (*Culin*) flaming brandy; **un ~ de contestation** (*fig*) a hotbed of dissent

brûlure [bʀylyʀ] NF (*lésion*) burn; (*sensation*) burning *no pl*, burning sensation; **brûlures d'estomac** heartburn *sg*

brume [bʀym] NF mist

brumeux, -euse [bʀymø, -øz] ADJ misty; (*fig*) hazy

brumisateur [bʀymizatœʀ] NM atomizer

brun, e [bʀœ̃, -yn] ADJ (*gén, bière*) brown; (*cheveux, personne, tabac*) dark; **elle est ~** she's got dark hair ▶ NM (*couleur*) brown ▶ NF (*cigarette*) cigarette made of dark tobacco; (*bière*) ≈ brown ale, ≈ stout

brunâtre [bʀynɑtʀ] ADJ brownish

brunch [bʀœntʃ] NM brunch

Brunei [bʀynei] NM: **le ~** Brunei

brunir [bʀyniʀ] /**2**/ VI, **se brunir** VT to get a tan; to tan

brushing [bʀœʃiŋ] NM blow-dry

brusque [bʀysk] ADJ (*soudain*) abrupt, sudden; (*rude*) abrupt, brusque

brusquement [bʀyskəmɑ̃] ADV (*soudainement*) abruptly, suddenly

brusquer [bʀyske] /**1**/ VT to rush

brusquerie [bʀyskəʀi] NF abruptness, brusqueness

brut, e [bʀyt] ADJ raw, crude, rough; (*diamant*) uncut; (*soie, minéral, Inform: données*) raw; (*Comm*) gross ▶ NF brute; **(champagne) ~** brut champagne; **(pétrole) ~** crude (oil)

brutal, e, -aux [bʀytal, -o] ADJ brutal

brutalement [bʀytalmɑ̃] ADV brutally

brutaliser [bʀytalize] /**1**/ VT to handle roughly, manhandle

brutalité [bʀytalite] NF brutality *no pl*

brute [bʀyt] ADJ F, NF *voir* **brut**

Bruxelles [bʀysɛl] N Brussels

bruxellois, e [bʀysɛlwa, -waz] ADJ of *ou* from Brussels ▶ NM/F: **B~, e** inhabitant *ou* native of Brussels

bruyamment [bʀɥijamɑ̃] ADV noisily

bruyant, e [bʀɥijɑ̃, -ɑ̃t] ADJ noisy

bruyère [bʀyjɛʀ] NF heather

BT SIGLE M (= *Brevet de technicien*) *vocational training certificate, taken at approx. 18 years*

BTA SIGLE M (= *Brevet de technicien agricole*) *agricultural training certificate, taken at approx. 18 years*

BTP SIGLE MPL (= *Bâtiments et travaux publics*) *public buildings and works sector*

BTS SIGLE M (= *Brevet de technicien supérieur*)

b

vocational training certificate taken at end of two-year higher education course

BU SIGLE F = **Bibliothèque universitaire**

bu, e [by] PP *de* **boire**

buanderie [bɥɑ̃dri] NF laundry

Bucarest [bykaʀɛst] N Bucharest

buccal, e, -aux [bykal, -o] ADJ: **par voie ~** orally

bûche [byʃ] NF log; **prendre une ~** (*fig*) to come a cropper (BRIT), fall flat on one's face; **~ de Noël** Yule log

bûcher [byʃe] /1/ NM (*funéraire*) pyre; bonfire; (*supplice*) stake ▶ VI (*fam: étudier*) to swot (BRIT), grind (US), slave (away) ▶ VT to swot up (BRIT), cram, slave away at

bûcheron [byʃʀɔ̃] NM woodcutter

bûchette [byʃɛt] NF (*de bois*) stick, twig; (*pour compter*) rod

bûcheur, -euse [byʃœʀ, -øz] NM/F (*fam: étudiant*) swot (BRIT), grind (US)

bucolique [bykɔlik] ADJ bucolic, pastoral

Budapest [bydapɛst] N Budapest

budget [bydʒɛ] NM budget

budgétaire [bydʒetɛʀ] ADJ budgetary, budget *cpd*

budgétiser [bydʒetize] /1/ VT to budget (for)

buée [bɥe] NF (*sur une vitre*) mist; (*de l'haleine*) steam

Buenos Aires [bwenɔzɛʀ] N Buenos Aires

buffet [byfe] NM (*meuble*) sideboard; (*de réception*) buffet; **~ (de gare)** (station) buffet, snack bar

buffle [byfl] NM buffalo

buis [bɥi] NM box tree; (*bois*) box(wood)

buisson [bɥisɔ̃] NM bush

buissonnière [bɥisɔnjɛʀ] ADJ F: **faire l'école ~** to play truant (BRIT), skip school

bulbe [bylb] NM (*Bot, Anat*) bulb; (*coupole*) onion-shaped dome

bulgare [bylgaʀ] ADJ Bulgarian ▶ NM (*Ling*) Bulgarian ▶ NMF: **B~** Bulgarian, Bulgar

Bulgarie [bylgaʀi] NF: **la ~** Bulgaria

bulldozer [buldozœʀ] NM bulldozer

bulle [byl] ADJ, NM: **(papier) ~** manil(l)a paper ▶ NF bubble; (*de bande dessinée*) balloon; (*papale*) bull; **~ de savon** soap bubble

bulletin [byltɛ̃] NM (*communiqué, journal*) bulletin; (*papier*) form; (: *de bagages*) ticket; (*Scol*) report; **~ d'informations** news bulletin; **~ de naissance** birth certificate; **~ de salaire** pay slip; **~ de santé** medical bulletin; **~ (de vote)** ballot paper; **~ météorologique** weather report

buraliste [byʀalist] NMF (*de bureau de tabac*) tobacconist; (*de poste*) clerk

bure [byʀ] NF homespun; (*de moine*) frock

bureau, x [byʀo] NM (*meuble*) desk; (*pièce, service*) office; **~ de change** (foreign) exchange office *ou* bureau; **~ d'embauche** ≈ job centre; **~ d'études** design office; **~ de location** box office; **~ des objets trouvés** lost property office (BRIT), lost

and found (US); **~ de placement** employment agency; **~ de poste** post office; **~ de tabac** tobacconist's (shop), smoke shop (US); **~ de vote** polling station

bureaucrate [byʀokʀat] NM bureaucrat

bureaucratie [byʀokʀasi] NF bureaucracy

bureaucratique [byʀokʀatik] ADJ bureaucratic

bureautique [byʀotik] NF office automation

burette [byʀɛt] NF (*de mécanicien*) oilcan; (*de chimiste*) burette

burin [byʀɛ̃] NM cold chisel; (*Art*) burin

buriné, e [byʀine] ADJ (*fig: visage*) craggy, seamed

Burkina [byʀkina], **Burkina-Faso** [byʀkinafaso] NM: **le ~(-Faso)** Burkina Faso

burlesque [byʀlɛsk] ADJ ridiculous; (*Littérature*) burlesque

burnous [byʀnu(s)] NM burnous

Burundi [buʀundi] NM: **le ~** Burundi

bus¹ VB [by] *voir* **boire**

bus² NM [bys] (*véhicule: aussi Inform*) bus

busard [byzaʀ] NM harrier

buse [byz] NF buzzard

busqué, e [byske] ADJ: **nez ~** hook(ed) nose

buste [byst] NM (*Anat*) chest; (: *de femme*) bust; (*sculpture*) bust

bustier [bystje] NM (*soutien-gorge*) long-line bra

but [by] VB *voir* **boire** ▶ NM (*cible*) target; (*fig*) goal, aim; (*Football etc*) goal; **de ~ en blanc** point-blank; **avoir pour ~ de faire** to aim to do; **dans le ~ de** with the intention of

butane [bytan] NM butane; (*domestique*) Calor gas® (BRIT), butane

buté, e [byte] ADJ stubborn, obstinate ▶ NF (*Archit*) abutment; (*Tech*) stop

buter [byte] /1/ VI: **~ contre** *ou* **sur** to bump into; (*trébucher*) to stumble against ▶ VT to antagonize; **se buter** VI to get obstinate, dig in one's heels

buteur [bytœʀ] NM striker

butin [bytɛ̃] NM booty, spoils *pl*; (*d'un vol*) loot

butiner [bytine] /1/ VI (*abeilles*) to gather nectar

butor [bytɔʀ] NM (*fig*) lout

butte [byt] NF mound, hillock; **être en ~ à** to be exposed to

buvable [byvabl] ADJ (*eau, vin*) drinkable; (*Méd: ampoule etc*) to be taken orally; (*fig: roman etc*) reasonable

buvais *etc* [byvɛ] VB *voir* **boire**

buvard [byvaʀ] NM blotter

buvette [byvɛt] NF refreshment room *ou* stall; (*comptoir*) bar

buveur, -euse [byvœʀ, -øz] NM/F drinker

buvons *etc* [byvɔ̃] VB *voir* **boire**

BVP SIGLE M (= *Bureau de vérification de la publicité*) *advertising standards authority*

Byzance [bizɑ̃s] N Byzantium

byzantin, e [bizɑ̃tɛ̃, -in] ADJ Byzantine

BZH ABR (= *Breizh*) Brittany

Cc

C, c [se] NM INV C, c ▸ ABR (= *centime*) c; (= *Celsius*)
C; **C comme Célestin** C for Charlie

c' [s] PRON *voir* **ce**

CA SIGLE M = **chiffre d'affaires; conseil
d'administration; corps d'armée** ▸ SIGLE F
= **chambre d'agriculture**

ça [sa] PRON (*pour désigner*) this; (: *plus loin*) that;
(*comme sujet indéfini*) it; **ça m'étonne que** it
surprises me that; **ça va?** how are you?; how
are things?; (*d'accord?*) OK?, all right?; **où ça?**
where's that?; **pourquoi ça?** why's that?; **qui
ça?** who's that?; **ça alors!** (*désapprobation*) well!,
really!; (*étonnement*) heavens!; **c'est ça** that's
right; **ça y est** that's it

çà [sa] ADV: **çà et là** here and there

cabale [kabal] NF (*Théât, Pol*) cabal, clique

caban [kabɑ̃] NM reefer jacket, donkey jacket

cabane [kaban] NF hut, cabin

cabanon [kabanɔ̃] NM chalet, (country) cottage

cabaret [kabaʀɛ] NM night club

cabas [kabɑ] NM shopping bag

cabestan [kabɛstɑ̃] NM capstan

cabillaud [kabijo] NM cod *inv*

cabine [kabin] NF (*de bateau*) cabin; (*de plage*)
(beach) hut; (*de piscine etc*) cubicle; (*de camion,
train*) cab; (*d'avion*) cockpit; **~ (d'ascenseur)** lift
cage; **~ d'essayage** fitting room; **~ de
projection** projection room; **~ spatiale** space
capsule; **~ (téléphonique)** call *ou* (tele)phone
box, (tele)phone booth

cabinet [kabinɛ] NM (*petite pièce*) closet; (*de
médecin*) surgery (BRIT), office (US); (*de notaire etc*)
office; (: *clientèle*) practice; (*Pol*) cabinet; (*d'un
ministre*) advisers *pl*; **cabinets** NMPL (*w.-c.*) toilet
sg; **~ d'affaires** business consultants' (bureau),
business partnership; **~ de toilette** toilet; **~ de
travail** study

câble [kɑbl] NM cable; **le ~** (TV) cable television,
cablevision (US)

câblé, e [kɑble] ADJ (*fam*) switched on; (*Tech*)
linked to cable television

câbler [kɑble] /1/ VT to cable; **~ un quartier** (TV)
to put cable television into an area

cabosser [kabɔse] /1/ VT to dent

cabot [kabo] NM (*péj: chien*) mutt

cabotage [kabotaʒ] NM coastal navigation

caboteur [kabotœʀ] NM coaster

cabotin, e [kabotɛ̃, -in] NM/F (*péj: personne*
maniérée*) poseur; (: *acteur*) ham ▸ ADJ dramatic,
theatrical

cabotinage [kabotinaʒ] NM playacting;
third-rate acting, ham acting

cabrer [kabʀe] /1/: **se cabrer** VI (*cheval*) to rear up;
(*avion*) to nose up; (*fig*) to revolt, rebel; to jib

cabri [kabʀi] NM kid

cabriole [kabʀijɔl] NF caper; (*gymnastique etc*)
somersault

cabriolet [kabʀijɔlɛ] NM convertible

CAC [kak] SIGLE F = **Compagnie des agents de
change; indice ~** ≈ FT index (BRIT), ≈ Dow Jones
average (US)

caca [kaka] NM (*langage enfantin*) poo; (*couleur*):
~ d'oie greeny-yellow; **faire ~** (*fam*) to do a poo

cacahuète [kakaɥɛt] NF peanut

cacao [kakao] NM cocoa (powder); (*boisson*)
cocoa

cachalot [kaʃalo] NM sperm whale

cache [kaʃ] NM mask, card (*for masking*) ▸ NF
hiding place

cache-cache [kaʃkaʃ] NM: **jouer à ~** to play
hide-and-seek

cache-col [kaʃkɔl] NM scarf

cachemire [kaʃmiʀ] NM cashmere ▸ ADJ: **dessin
~** paisley pattern; **le C~** Kashmir

cache-nez [kaʃne] NM INV scarf, muffler

cache-pot [kaʃpo] NM INV flower-pot holder

cache-prise [kaʃpʀiz] NM INV socket cover

cacher [kaʃe] /1/ VT to hide, conceal; **~ qch à qn**
to hide *ou* conceal sth from sb; **se cacher** VI
(*volontairement*) to hide; (*être caché*) to be hidden
ou concealed; **il ne s'en cache pas** he makes no
secret of it

cache-sexe [kaʃsɛks] NM INV G-string

cachet [kaʃe] NM (*comprimé*) tablet; (*sceau: du roi*)
seal; (: *de la poste*) postmark; (*rétribution*) fee; (*fig*)
style, character

cacheter [kaʃte] /4/ VT to seal; **vin cacheté**
vintage wine

cachette [kaʃɛt] NF hiding place; **en ~** on the
sly, secretly

cachot [kaʃo] NM dungeon

cachotterie [kaʃɔtʀi] NF mystery; **faire des
cachotteries** to be secretive

cachottier, -ière [kaʃɔtje, -jɛʀ] ADJ secretive

cachou [kaʃu] NM: **pastille de ~** cachou (*sweet*)

cacophonie [kakɔfɔni] NF cacophony, din

cacophonique [kakɔfɔnik] ADJ cacophonous
cactus [kaktys] NM cactus
c.-à-d. ABR (= *c'est-à-dire*) i.e.
cadastre [kadastʀ] NM land register
cadavéreux, -euse [kadavɛʀø, -øz] ADJ (*teint, visage*) deathly pale
cadavérique [kadaveʀik] ADJ deathly (pale), deadly pale
cadavre [kadavʀ] NM corpse, (dead) body
Caddie® [kadi] NM (supermarket) trolley (BRIT), (grocery) cart (US)
cadeau, x [kado] NM present, gift; **faire un ~ à qn** to give sb a present *ou* gift; **faire ~ de qch à qn** to make a present of sth to sb, give sb sth as a present
cadenas [kadnɑ] NM padlock
cadenasser [kadnase] /1/ VT to padlock
cadence [kadɑ̃s] NF (*Mus*) cadence; (: *rythme*) rhythm; (*de travail etc*) rate; **cadences** NFPL (*en usine*) production rate *sg*; **en ~** rhythmically; in time
cadencé, e [kadɑ̃se] ADJ rhythmic(al); **au pas ~** (*Mil*) in quick time
cadet, te [kadɛ, -ɛt] ADJ younger; (*le plus jeune*) youngest ▶ NM/F youngest child *ou* one, youngest boy *ou* son/girl *ou* daughter; **il est mon ~ de deux ans** he's two years younger than me, he's two years my junior; **les cadets** (*Sport*) the minors (15–17 *years*); **le ~ de mes soucis** the least of my worries
cadrage [kadʀaʒ] NM framing (*of shot*)
cadran [kadʀɑ̃] NM dial; **~ solaire** sundial
cadre [kadʀ] NM frame; (*environnement*) surroundings *pl*; (*limites*) scope ▶ NMF (*Admin*) managerial employee, executive ▶ ADJ: **loi ~** outline *ou* blueprint law; **~ moyen/supérieur** (*Admin*) middle/senior management employee, junior/senior executive; **rayer qn des cadres** to discharge sb; to dismiss sb; **dans le ~ de** (*fig*) within the framework *ou* context of
cadrer [kadʀe] /1/ VI: **~ avec** to tally *ou* correspond with ▶ VT (*Ciné, Photo*) to frame
cadreur, -euse [kadʀœʀ, -øz] NM/F (*Ciné*) cameraman/woman
caduc, -uque [kadyk] ADJ obsolete; (*Bot*) deciduous
CAF SIGLE F (= *Caisse d'allocations familiales*) family allowance office
caf ABR (*coût, assurance, fret*) cif
cafard [kafaʀ] NM cockroach; **avoir le ~** to be down in the dumps, be feeling low
cafardeux, -euse [kafaʀdø, -øz] ADJ (*personne, ambiance*) depressing, melancholy
café [kafe] NM coffee; (*bistro*) café ▶ ADJ INV coffee *cpd*; **~ crème** coffee with cream; **~ au lait** white coffee; **~ noir** black coffee; **~ en grains** coffee beans; **~ en poudre** instant coffee; **~ liégeois** coffee ice cream with whipped cream
café-concert [kafekɔ̃sɛʀ] (*pl* **cafés-concerts**) NM (*aussi*: **caf'conc'**) café with a cabaret
caféine [kafein] NF caffeine
café-tabac [kafetaba] NM *tobacconist's or newsagent's also serving coffee and spirits*
cafétéria [kafeteʀja] NF cafeteria

café-théâtre [kafeteatʀ] (*pl* **cafés-théâtres**) NM *café used as a venue by (experimental) theatre groups*
cafetière [kaftjɛʀ] NF (*pot*) coffee-pot
cafouillage [kafujaʒ] NM shambles *sg*
cafouiller [kafuje] /1/ VI to get in a shambles; (*machine etc*) to work in fits and starts
cage [kaʒ] NF cage; (*des buts*) goal; **en ~** in a cage, caged up *ou* in; **~ d'ascenseur** lift shaft; **~ d'escalier** (stair)well; **~ thoracique** rib cage
cageot [kaʒo] NM crate
cagibi [kaʒibi] NM shed
cagneux, -euse [kaɲø, -øz] ADJ knock-kneed
cagnotte [kaɲɔt] NF kitty
cagoule [kagul] NF cowl; hood; (*Ski etc*) cagoule; (*passe-montagne*) balaclava
cahier [kaje] NM notebook; (*Typo*) signature; (*revue*): **cahiers** journal; **~ de revendications/doléances** list of claims/grievances; **~ de brouillons** rough book, jotter; **~ des charges** specification; **~ d'exercices** exercise book
cahin-caha [kaɛ̃kaa] ADV: **aller ~** to jog along; (*fig*) to be so-so
cahot [kao] NM jolt, bump
cahoter [kaɔte] /1/ VI to bump along, jog along
cahoteux, -euse [kaɔtø, -øz] ADJ bumpy
cahute [kayt] NF shack, hut
caïd [kaid] NM big chief, boss
caillasse [kajas] NF (*pierraille*) loose stones *pl*
caille [kaj] NF quail
caillé, e [kaje] ADJ: **lait ~** curdled milk, curds *pl*
caillebotis [kajbɔti] NM duckboard
cailler [kaje] /1/ VI (*lait*) to curdle; (*sang*) to clot; (*fam*) to be cold
caillot [kajo] NM (blood) clot
caillou, x [kaju] NM (little) stone
caillouter [kajute] /1/ VT (*chemin*) to metal
caillouteux, -euse [kajutø, -øz] ADJ stony; pebbly
cailloutis [kajuti] NM (*petits graviers*) gravel
caïman [kaimɑ̃] NM cayman
Caïmans [kaimɑ̃] NFPL: **les ~** the Cayman Islands
Caire [kɛʀ] NM: **le ~** Cairo
caisse [kɛs] NF box; (*où l'on met la recette*) cashbox; (: *machine*) till; (*où l'on paye*) cash desk (BRIT), checkout counter; (: *au supermarché*) checkout; (*de banque*) cashier's desk; (*Tech*) case, casing; **faire sa ~** (*Comm*) to count the takings; **~ claire** (*Mus*) side *ou* snare drum; **~ éclair** express checkout; **~ enregistreuse** cash register; **~ d'épargne** savings bank; **~ noire** slush fund; **~ de retraite** pension fund; **~ de sortie** checkout; *voir* **grosse**
caissier, -ière [kesje, -jɛʀ] NM/F cashier
caisson [kesɔ̃] NM box, case
cajoler [kaʒɔle] /1/ VT to wheedle, coax; to surround with love and care, make a fuss of
cajoleries [kaʒɔlʀi] NFPL coaxing *sg*, flattery *sg*
cajou [kaʒu] NM cashew nut
cake [kɛk] NM fruit cake
CAL SIGLE M (= *Comité d'action lycéen*) pupils' action group seeking to reform school system
cal [kal] NM callus

cal. ABR = **calorie**

calamar [kalamaʀ] NM = **calmar**

calaminé, e [kalamine] ADJ (*Auto*) coked up

calamité [kalamite] NF calamity, disaster

calandre [kalɑ̃dʀ] NF radiator grill; (*machine*) calender, mangle

calanque [kalɑ̃k] NF rocky inlet

calcaire [kalkɛʀ] NM limestone ▸ ADJ (*eau*) hard; (*Géo*) limestone *cpd*

calciné, e [kalsine] ADJ burnt to ashes

calcium [kalsjɔm] NM calcium

calcul [kalkyl] NM calculation; **le ~** (*Scol*) arithmetic; **~ différentiel/intégral** differential/integral calculus; **~ mental** mental arithmetic; **~ (biliaire)** (gall)stone; **~ (rénal)** (kidney) stone; **d'après mes calculs** by my reckoning

calculateur [kalkylatœʀ] NM, **calculatrice** [kalkylatʀis] NF calculator

calculé, e [kalkyle] ADJ: **risque ~** calculated risk

calculer [kalkyle] /**1**/ VT to calculate, work out, reckon; (*combiner*) to calculate; **~ qch de tête** to work sth out in one's head

calculette [kalkylɛt] NF (pocket) calculator

cale [kal] NF (*de bateau*) hold; (*en bois*) wedge, chock; **~ sèche ou de radoub** dry dock

calé, e [kale] ADJ (*fam*) clever, bright

calebasse [kalbɑs] NF calabash, gourd

calèche [kalɛʃ] NF horse-drawn carriage

caleçon [kalsɔ̃] NM (*d'homme*) boxer shorts; (*de femme*) leggings; **~ de bain** bathing trunks *pl*

calembour [kalɑ̃buʀ] NM pun

calendes [kalɑ̃d] NFPL: **renvoyer aux ~ grecques** to postpone indefinitely

calendrier [kalɑ̃dʀije] NM calendar; (*fig*) timetable

cale-pied [kalpje] NM INV toe clip

calepin [kalpɛ̃] NM notebook

caler [kale] /**1**/ VT to wedge, chock up; **~ (son moteur/véhicule)** to stall (one's engine/vehicle); **se ~ dans un fauteuil** to make o.s. comfortable in an armchair ▸ VI (*moteur, véhicule*) to stall

calfater [kalfate] /**1**/ VT to caulk

calfeutrage [kalføtʀaʒ] NM draughtproofing (*Brit*), draftproofing (*US*)

calfeutrer [kalføtʀe] /**1**/ VT to (make) draughtproof (*Brit*) ou draftproof (*US*); **se calfeutrer** VI to make o.s. snug and comfortable

calibre [kalibʀ] NM (*d'un fruit*) grade; (*d'une arme*) bore, calibre (*Brit*), caliber (*US*); (*fig*) calibre, caliber

calibrer [kalibʀe] /**1**/ VT to grade

calice [kalis] NM (*Rel*) chalice; (*Bot*) calyx

calicot [kaliko] NM (*tissu*) calico

calife [kalif] NM caliph

Californie [kalifɔʀni] NF: **la ~** California

californien, ne [kalifɔʀnjɛ̃, -ɛn] ADJ Californian

califourchon [kalifuʀʃɔ̃]: **à ~** adv astride; **à ~ sur** astride, straddling

câlin, e [kɑlɛ̃, -in] ADJ cuddly, cuddlesome; (*regard, voix*) tender

câliner [kɑline] /**1**/ VT to fondle, cuddle

câlineries [kɑlinʀi] NFPL cuddles

calisson [kalisɔ̃] NM diamond-shaped sweet or candy made with ground almonds

calleux, -euse [kalø, -øz] ADJ horny, callous

calligraphie [kaligʀafi] NF calligraphy

callosité [kalozite] NF callus

calmant [kalmɑ̃] NM tranquillizer, sedative; (*contre la douleur*) painkiller

calmar [kalmaʀ] NM squid

calme [kalm] ADJ calm, quiet ▸ NM calm(ness), quietness; **sans perdre son ~** without losing one's cool ou calmness; **~ plat** (*Navig*) dead calm

calmement [kalməmɑ̃] ADV calmly, quietly

calmer [kalme] /**1**/ VT to calm (down); (*douleur, inquiétude*) to ease, soothe; **se calmer** VI to calm down

calomniateur, -trice [kalɔmnjatœʀ, -tʀis] NM/F slanderer; libeller

calomnie [kalɔmni] NF slander; (*écrite*) libel

calomnier [kalɔmnje] /**7**/ VT to slander; to libel

calomnieux, -euse [kalɔmnjø, -øz] ADJ slanderous; libellous

calorie [kalɔʀi] NF calorie

calorifère [kalɔʀifɛʀ] NM stove

calorifique [kalɔʀifik] ADJ calorific

calorifuge [kalɔʀifyʒ] ADJ (heat-)insulating, heat-retaining

calot [kalo] NM forage cap

calotte [kalɔt] NF (*coiffure*) skullcap; (*gifle*) slap; **la ~** (*péj: clergé*) the cloth, the clergy; **~ glaciaire** icecap

calque [kalk] NM (*aussi*: **papier calque**) tracing paper; (*dessin*) tracing; (*fig*) carbon copy

calquer [kalke] /**1**/ VT to trace; (*fig*) to copy exactly

calvados [kalvados] NM Calvados (apple brandy)

calvaire [kalvɛʀ] NM (*croix*) wayside cross, calvary; (*souffrances*) suffering, martyrdom

calvitie [kalvisi] NF baldness

camaïeu [kamajø] NM: **(motif en) ~** monochrome motif

camarade [kamaʀad] NMF friend, pal; (*Pol*) comrade

camaraderie [kamaʀadʀi] NF friendship

camarguais, e [kamaʀgɛ, -ɛz] ADJ of ou from the Camargue

Camargue [kamaʀg] NF: **la ~** the Camargue

cambiste [kɑ̃bist] NM (*Comm*) foreign exchange dealer, exchange agent

Cambodge [kɑ̃bɔdʒ] NM: **le ~** Cambodia

cambodgien, ne [kɑ̃bɔdʒjɛ̃, -ɛn] ADJ Cambodian ▸ NM/F: **C~, ne** Cambodian

cambouis [kɑ̃bwi] NM dirty oil ou grease

cambré, e [kɑ̃bʀe] ADJ: **avoir les reins cambrés** to have an arched back; **avoir le pied très ~** to have very high arches ou insteps

cambrer [kɑ̃bʀe] /**1**/ VT to arch; **se cambrer** VI to arch one's back; **~ la taille** ou **les reins** to arch one's back

cambriolage [kɑ̃bʀijɔlaʒ] NM burglary

cambrioler [kɑ̃bʀijɔle] /**1**/ VT to burgle (*Brit*), burglarize (*US*)

cambrioleur, -euse [kɑ̃bʀijɔlœʀ, -øz] NM/F burglar

cambrure [kɑ̃bʀyʀ] NF (*du pied*) arch; (*de la route*)

camber; **~ des reins** small of the back
cambuse [kɑ̃byz] NF storeroom
came [kam] NF: **arbre à cames** camshaft;
arbre à cames en tête overhead camshaft
camée [kame] NM cameo
caméléon [kameleɔ̃] NM chameleon
camélia [kamelja] NM camellia
camelot [kamlo] NM street pedlar
camelote [kamlɔt] (fam) NF rubbish, trash,
junk
camembert [kamɑ̃bɛʀ] NM Camembert (cheese)
caméra [kameʀa] NF (Ciné, TV) camera;
(d'amateur) cine-camera; **~ de
vidéosurveillance** CCTV camera
caméraman [kameʀaman] NM
cameraman/-woman
Cameroun [kamʀun] NM: **le ~** Cameroon
camerounais, e [kamʀunɛ, -ɛz] ADJ
Cameroonian
caméscope® [kameskɔp] NM camcorder
camion [kamjɔ̃] NM lorry (BRIT), truck; (plus
petit, fermé) van; (charge): **~** lorry-load (BRIT) ou truck-load of sand/stones;
~ de dépannage breakdown (BRIT) ou tow (US)
truck
camion-citerne [kamjɔ̃sitɛʀn] (pl **camions-
citernes**) NM tanker
camionnage [kamjɔnaʒ] NM haulage (BRIT),
trucking (US); **frais/entreprise de ~** haulage
costs/business
camionnette [kamjɔnɛt] NF (small) van
camionneur [kamjɔnœʀ] NM (entrepreneur)
haulage contractor (BRIT) ou trucker (US);
(chauffeur) lorry (BRIT) ou truck driver; van driver
camisole [kamizɔl] NF: **~ (de force)** straitjacket
camomille [kamɔmij] NF camomile; (boisson)
camomile tea
camouflage [kamuflaʒ] NM camouflage
camoufler [kamufle] /1/ VT to camouflage; (fig)
to conceal, cover up
camouflet [kamuflɛ] NM (fam) snub
camp [kɑ̃] NM camp; (fig) side; **~ de nudistes/
vacances** nudist/holiday camp; **~ de
concentration** concentration camp
campagnard, e [kɑ̃paɲaʀ, -aʀd] ADJ country cpd
▶ NM/F countryman/woman
campagne [kɑ̃paɲ] NF country, countryside;
(Mil, Pol, Comm) campaign; **en ~** (Mil) in the
field; **à la ~** in/to the country; **faire ~ pour** to
campaign for; **~ électorale** election campaign;
~ de publicité advertising campaign
campanile [kɑ̃panil] NM (tour) bell tower
campé, e [kɑ̃pe] ADJ: **bien ~** (personnage, tableau)
well-drawn
campement [kɑ̃pmɑ̃] NM camp, encampment
camper [kɑ̃pe] /1/ VI to camp ▶ VT (chapeau etc) to
pull ou put on firmly; (dessin) to sketch; **se ~
devant** to plant o.s. in front of
campeur, -euse [kɑ̃pœʀ, -øz] NM/F camper
camphre [kɑ̃fʀ] NM camphor
camphré, e [kɑ̃fʀe] ADJ camphorated
camping [kɑ̃piŋ] NM camping; (terrain de) **~**
campsite, camping site; **faire du ~** to go
camping; **faire du ~ sauvage** to camp rough

camping-car [kɑ̃piŋkaʀ] NM camper,
motorhome (US)
camping-gaz® [kɑ̃piŋgaz] NM INV camp(ing)
stove
campus [kɑ̃pys] NM campus
camus, e [kamy, -yz] ADJ: **nez ~** pug nose
Canada [kanada] NM: **le ~** Canada
canadair® [kanadɛʀ] NM fire-fighting plane
canadien, ne [kanadjɛ̃, -ɛn] ADJ Canadian
▶ NM/F: **C~, ne** Canadian ▶ NF (veste) fur-lined
jacket
canaille [kanɑj] NF (péj) scoundrel; (populace)
riff-raff ▶ ADJ raffish, rakish
canal, -aux [kanal, -o] NM canal; (naturel, TV)
channel; (Admin): **par le ~ de** through (the
medium of), via; **~ de distribution/télévision**
distribution/television channel; **~ de
Panama/Suez** Panama/Suez Canal
canalisation [kanalizasjɔ̃] NF (tuyau) pipe
canaliser [kanalize] /1/ VT to canalize; (fig) to
channel
canapé [kanape] NM settee, sofa; (Culin)
canapé, open sandwich
canapé-lit [kanapeli] (pl **canapés-lits**) NM sofa
bed
canaque [kanak] ADJ of ou from New Caledonia
▶ NMF: **C~** native of New Caledonia
canard [kanaʀ] NM duck; (fam: journal) rag
canari [kanaʀi] NM canary
Canaries [kanaʀi] NFPL: **les (îles) ~** the Canary
Islands, the Canaries
cancaner [kɑ̃kane] /1/ VI to gossip (maliciously);
(canard) to quack
cancanier, -ière [kɑ̃kanje, -jɛʀ] ADJ gossiping
cancans [kɑ̃kɑ̃] NMPL (malicious) gossip sg
cancer [kɑ̃sɛʀ] NM cancer; (signe): **le C~** Cancer,
the Crab; **être du C~** to be Cancer; **il a un ~** he
has cancer
cancéreux, -euse [kɑ̃seʀø, -øz] ADJ cancerous;
(personne) suffering from cancer
cancérigène [kɑ̃seʀiʒɛn] ADJ carcinogenic
cancérologue [kɑ̃seʀɔlɔg] NMF cancer
specialist
cancre [kɑ̃kʀ] NM dunce
cancrelat [kɑ̃kʀəla] NM cockroach
candélabre [kɑ̃delɑbʀ] NM candelabrum;
(lampadaire) street lamp, lamppost
candeur [kɑ̃dœʀ] NF ingenuousness
candi [kɑ̃di] ADJ INV: **sucre ~** (sugar-)candy
candidat, e [kɑ̃dida, -at] NM/F candidate; (à un
poste) applicant, candidate
candidature [kɑ̃didatyʀ] NF (Pol) candidature;
(à poste) application; **poser sa ~** to submit an
application, apply; **poser sa ~ à un poste** to
apply for a job; **~ spontanée** unsolicited job
application
candide [kɑ̃did] ADJ ingenuous, guileless, naïve
cane [kan] NF (female) duck
caneton [kantɔ̃] NM duckling
canette [kanɛt] NF (de bière) (flip-top) bottle; (de
machine à coudre) spool
canevas [kanva] NM (Couture) canvas (for
tapestry work); (fig) framework, structure
caniche [kaniʃ] NM poodle

caniculaire [kanikylɛʀ] ADJ (*chaleur, jour*) scorching

canicule [kanikyl] NF scorching heat; midsummer heat, dog days *pl*

canif [kanif] NM penknife, pocket knife

canin, e [kanɛ̃, -in] ADJ canine ▶ NF canine (tooth), eye tooth; **exposition** ~ dog show

caniveau, x [kanivo] NM gutter

cannabis [kanabis] NM cannabis

canne [kan] NF (walking) stick; ~ **à pêche** fishing rod; ~ **à sucre** sugar cane; **les cannes blanches** (*les aveugles*) blind people

canné, e [kane] ADJ (*chaise*) cane *cpd*

cannelé, e [kanle] ADJ fluted

cannelle [kanɛl] NF cinnamon

cannelure [kanlyʀ] NF fluting *no pl*

canner [kane] /1/ VT (*chaise*) to make *ou* repair with cane

cannibale [kanibal] NMF cannibal

cannibalisme [kanibalism] NM cannibalism

canoë [kanɔe] NM canoe; (*sport*) canoeing; ~ **(kayak)** kayak

canon [kanɔ̃] NM (*arme*) gun; (*Hist*) cannon; (*d'une arme: tube*) barrel; (*fig*) model; (*Mus*) canon ▶ ADJ: **droit** ~ canon law; ~ **rayé** rifled barrel

cañon [kaɲɔ̃] NM canyon

canonique [kanɔnik] ADJ: **âge** ~ respectable age

canoniser [kanɔnize] /1/ VT to canonize

canonnade [kanɔnad] NF cannonade

canonnier [kanɔnje] NM gunner

canonnière [kanɔnjɛʀ] NF gunboat

canot [kano] NM boat, ding(h)y; ~ **pneumatique** rubber *ou* inflatable ding(h)y; ~ **de sauvetage** lifeboat

canotage [kanɔtaʒ] NM rowing

canoter [kanɔte] /1/ VI to go rowing

canoteur, -euse [kanɔtœʀ, -øz] NM/F rower

canotier [kanɔtje] NM boater

Cantal [kɑ̃tal] NM: **le** ~ Cantal

cantate [kɑ̃tat] NF cantata

cantatrice [kɑ̃tatʀis] NF (opera) singer

cantilène [kɑ̃tilɛn] NF (*Mus*) cantilena

cantine [kɑ̃tin] NF canteen; (*réfectoire d'école*) dining hall

cantique [kɑ̃tik] NM hymn

canton [kɑ̃tɔ̃] NM district (*consisting of several communes*); *see note*; (*en Suisse*) canton

> A French *canton* is the administrative division represented by a councillor in the *Conseil général*. It comprises a number of *communes* and is, in turn, a subdivision of an *arrondissement*. In Switzerland the *cantons* are the 23 autonomous political divisions which make up the Swiss confederation.

cantonade [kɑ̃tɔnad]: **à la** ~ *adv* to everyone in general; (*crier*) from the rooftops

cantonais, e [kɑ̃tɔnɛ, -ɛz] ADJ Cantonese ▶ NM (*Ling*) Cantonese

cantonal, e, -aux [kɑ̃tɔnal, -o] ADJ cantonal, ≈ district

cantonnement [kɑ̃tɔnmɑ̃] NM (*lieu*) billet; (*action*) billeting

cantonner [kɑ̃tɔne] /1/ VT (*Mil*) to billet (*BRIT*), quarter; to station; **se ~ dans** to confine o.s. to

cantonnier [kɑ̃tɔnje] NM roadmender

canular [kanylaʀ] NM hoax

CAO SIGLE F (= *conception assistée par ordinateur*) CAD

caoutchouc [kautʃu] NM rubber; ~ **mousse** foam rubber; **en** ~ rubber *cpd*

caoutchouté, e [kautʃute] ADJ rubberized

caoutchouteux, -euse [kautʃutø, -øz] ADJ rubbery

CAP SIGLE M (= *Certificat d'aptitude professionnelle*) vocational training certificate taken at secondary school

cap [kap] NM (*Géo*) cape; (*promontoire*) headland; (*fig*) hurdle; (: *tournant*) watershed; (*Navig*): **changer de** ~ to change course; **mettre le** ~ **sur** to head *ou* steer for; **doubler** *ou* **passer le** ~ (*fig*) to get over the worst; **Le C**~ Cape Town; **le** ~ **de Bonne Espérance** the Cape of Good Hope; **le** ~ **Horn** Cape Horn; **les îles du C**~ **Vert** (*aussi*: **le Cap-Vert**) the Cape Verde Islands

capable [kapabl] ADJ able, capable; ~ **de qch/faire** capable of sth/doing; **il est** ~ **d'oublier** he could easily forget; **spectacle** ~ **d'intéresser** show likely to be of interest

capacité [kapasite] NF (*compétence*) ability; (*Jur, Inform, d'un récipient*) capacity; ~ **(en droit)** basic legal qualification

caparaçonner [kapaʀasɔne] /1/ VT (*fig*) to clad

cape [kap] NF cape, cloak; **rire sous** ~ to laugh up one's sleeve

capeline [kaplin] NF wide-brimmed hat

CAPES [kapɛs] SIGLE M (= *Certificat d'aptitude au professorat de l'enseignement du second degré*) secondary teaching diploma; *see note*

> The French *CAPES* (*certificat d'aptitude au professorat de l'enseignement du second degré*) is a competitive examination sat by prospective secondary school teachers after the *licence*. Successful candidates become fully qualified teachers (*professeurs certifiés*).

capésien, ne [kapesjɛ̃, -ɛn] NM/F *person who holds the CAPES*

CAPET [kapɛt] SIGLE M (= *Certificat d'aptitude au professorat de l'enseignement technique*) technical teaching diploma

capharnaüm [kafaʀnaɔm] NM shambles *sg*

capillaire [kapilɛʀ] ADJ (*soins, lotion*) hair *cpd*; (*vaisseau etc*) capillary; **artiste** ~ hair artist *ou* designer

capillarité [kapilaʀite] NF capillary action

capilotade [kapilɔtad]: **en** ~ *adv* crushed to a pulp; smashed to pieces

capitaine [kapitɛn] NM captain; ~ **des pompiers** fire chief (*BRIT*), fire marshal (*US*); ~ **au long cours** master mariner

capitainerie [kapitɛnʀi] NF (*du port*) harbour (*BRIT*) *ou* harbor (*US*) master's (office)

capital, e, -aux [kapital, -o] ADJ (*œuvre*) major; (*question, rôle*) fundamental; (*Jur*) capital ▶ NM capital; (*fig*) stock; asset ▶ NF (*ville*) capital; (*lettre*) capital (letter); **d'une importance** ~ of capital importance; **capitaux** NMPL (*fonds*) capital *sg*, money *sg*; **les sept péchés capitaux** the seven deadly sins; **peine** ~ capital punishment; ~ **(social)** authorized capital;

~ **d'exploitation** working capital

capitaliser [kapitalize] /1/ VT to amass, build up; (*Comm*) to capitalize ▸ VI to save

capitalisme [kapitalism] NM capitalism

capitaliste [kapitalist] ADJ, NMF capitalist

capiteux, -euse [kapitø, -øz] ADJ (*vin, parfum*) heady; (*sensuel*) sensuous, alluring

capitonnage [kapitɔnaʒ] NM padding

capitonné, e [kapitɔne] ADJ padded

capitonner [kapitɔne] /1/ VT to pad

capitulation [kapitylasjɔ̃] NF capitulation

capituler [kapityle] /1/ VI to capitulate

caporal, -aux [kapɔral, -o] NM lance corporal

caporal-chef [kapɔralʃef] (*pl* **caporaux-chefs** [kapɔro-]) NM corporal

capot [kapo] NM (*Auto*) bonnet (BRIT), hood (US)

capote [kapɔt] NF (*de voiture*) hood (BRIT), top (US); (*de soldat*) greatcoat; ~ **(anglaise)** (*fam*) rubber, condom

capoter [kapɔte] /1/ VI to overturn; (*négociations*) to founder

câpre [kɑpr] NF caper

caprice [kapris] NM whim, caprice; passing fancy; **caprices** NMPL (*de la mode etc*) vagaries; **faire un** ~ to throw a tantrum; **faire des caprices** to be temperamental

capricieux, -euse [kaprisjø, -øz] ADJ (*fantasque*) capricious; whimsical; (*enfant*) temperamental

Capricorne [kaprikɔrn] NM: **le** ~ Capricorn, the Goat; **être du** ~ to be Capricorn

capsule [kapsyl] NF (*de bouteille*) cap; (*amorce*) primer; cap; (*Bot etc, spatiale*) capsule

captage [kaptaʒ] NM (*d'une émission de radio*) picking-up; (*d'énergie, d'eau*) harnessing

capter [kapte] /1/ VT (*ondes radio*) to pick up; (*eau*) to harness; (*fig*) to win, capture

capteur [kaptœr] NM: ~ **solaire** solar collector

captieux, -euse [kapsjø, -øz] ADJ specious

captif, -ive [kaptif, -iv] ADJ, NM/F captive

captivant, e [kaptivɑ̃, -ɑ̃t] ADJ captivating

captiver [kaptive] /1/ VT to captivate

captivité [kaptivite] NF captivity; **en** ~ in captivity

capture [kaptyr] NF capture, catching *no pl*; catch

capturer [kaptyre] /1/ VT to capture, catch

capuche [kapyʃ] NF hood

capuchon [kapyʃɔ̃] NM hood; (*de stylo*) cap, top

capucin [kapysɛ̃] NM Capuchin monk

capucine [kapysin] NF (*Bot*) nasturtium

Cap-Vert [kabvɛr] NM: **le** ~ Cape Verde

caquelon [kaklɔ̃] NM (*ustensile de cuisson*) fondue pot

caquet [kakɛ] NM: **rabattre le** ~ **à qn** to bring sb down a peg or two

caqueter [kakte] /4/ VI (*poule*) to cackle; (*fig*) to prattle

car [kar] NM coach (BRIT), bus ▸ CONJ because, for; ~ **de police** police van; ~ **de reportage** broadcasting *ou* radio van

carabine [karabin] NF carbine, rifle; ~ **à air comprimé** airgun

carabiné, e [karabine] ADJ violent; (*cocktail, amende*) stiff

Caracas [karakas] N Caracas

caracoler [karakɔle] /1/ VI to caracole, prance

caractère [karaktɛr] NM (*gén*) character; **en caractères gras** in bold type; **en petits caractères** in small print; **en caractères d'imprimerie** in block capitals; **avoir du** ~ to have character; **avoir bon/mauvais** ~ to be good-/ill-natured *ou* tempered; ~ **de remplacement** wild card (*Inform*); **caractères/ seconde (cps)** characters per second (cps)

caractériel, le [karakterjel] ADJ (*enfant*) (emotionally) disturbed ▸ NM/F problem child; **troubles caractériels** emotional problems

caractérisé, e [karakterize] ADJ: **c'est une grippe/de l'insubordination** ~ it is a clear(-cut) case of flu/insubordination

caractériser [karakterize] /1/ VT to characterize; **se** ~ **par** to be characterized *ou* distinguished by

caractéristique [karakteristik] ADJ, NF characteristic

carafe [karaf] NF decanter; (*pour eau, vin ordinaire*) carafe

carafon [karafɔ̃] NM small carafe

caraïbe [karaib] ADJ Caribbean; **les Caraïbes** NFPL the Caribbean (Islands); **la mer des Caraïbes** the Caribbean Sea

carambolage [karɑ̃bɔlaʒ] NM multiple crash, pileup

caramel [karamel] NM (*bonbon*) caramel, toffee; (*substance*) caramel

caraméliser [karamelize] /1/ VT to caramelize

carapace [karapas] NF shell

carapater [karapate] /1/: **se carapater** VI to take to one's heels, scram

carat [kara] NM carat; **or à 18 carats** 18-carat gold

caravane [karavan] NF caravan

caravanier [karavanje] NM caravanner

caravaning [karavaniŋ] NM caravanning; (*emplacement*) caravan site

caravelle [karavɛl] NF caravel

carbonate [karbɔnat] NM (*Chimie*): ~ **de soude** sodium carbonate

carbone [karbɔn] NM carbon; (*feuille*) carbon, sheet of carbon paper; (*double*) carbon (copy); **compensation** ~ carbon offset; **crédit de compensation** ~ carbon offset credit

carbonique [karbɔnik] ADJ: **gaz** ~ carbon dioxide; **neige** ~ dry ice

carbonisé, e [karbɔnize] ADJ charred; **mourir** ~ to be burned to death

carboniser [karbɔnize] /1/ VT to carbonize; (*brûler complètement*) to burn down, reduce to ashes

carburant [karbyrɑ̃] NM (*motor*) fuel

carburateur [karbyratœr] NM carburettor

carburation [karbyrasjɔ̃] NF carburation

carburer [karbyre] /1/ VI (*moteur*): **bien/mal** ~ to be well/badly tuned

carcan [karkɑ̃] NM (*fig*) yoke, shackles *pl*

carcasse [karkas] NF carcass; (*de véhicule etc*) shell

carcéral, e, -aux [karseral, -o] ADJ prison *cpd*

carcinogène [kaʀsinɔʒɛn] ADJ carcinogenic

cardan [kaʀdɑ̃] NM universal joint

carder [kaʀde] /**1**/ VT to card

cardiaque [kaʀdjak] ADJ cardiac, heart *cpd* ▶ NMF heart patient; **être** ~ to have a heart condition

cardigan [kaʀdigɑ̃] NM cardigan

cardinal, e, -aux [kaʀdinal, -o] ADJ cardinal ▶ NM *(Rel)* cardinal

cardiologie [kaʀdjɔlɔʒi] NF cardiology

cardiologue [kaʀdjɔlɔg] NMF cardiologist, heart specialist

cardio-vasculaire [kaʀdjɔvaskylɛʀ] ADJ cardiovascular

cardon [kaʀdɔ̃] NM cardoon

Carême [kaʀɛm] NM: **le** ~ Lent

carence [kaʀɑ̃s] NF incompetence, inadequacy; *(manque)* deficiency; ~ **vitaminique** vitamin deficiency

carène [kaʀɛn] NF hull

caréner [kaʀene] /**6**/ VT *(Navig)* to careen; *(carrosserie)* to streamline

caressant, e [kaʀɛsɑ̃, -ɑ̃t] ADJ affectionate, caressing, tender

caresse [kaʀɛs] NF caress

caresser [kaʀese] /**1**/ VT to caress; *(animal)* to stroke, fondle; *(fig: projet, espoir)* to toy with

cargaison [kaʀgɛzɔ̃] NF cargo, freight

cargo [kaʀgo] NM cargo boat, freighter; ~ **mixte** cargo and passenger ship

cari [kaʀi] NM = **curry**

caricatural, e, -aux [kaʀikatyʀal, -o] ADJ caricatural, caricature-like

caricature [kaʀikatyʀ] NF caricature; *(politique etc)* (satirical) cartoon

caricaturer [kaʀikatyʀe] /**1**/ VT *(personne)* to caricature; *(politique etc)* to satirize

caricaturiste [kaʀikatyʀist] NMF caricaturist, (satirical) cartoonist

carie [kaʀi] NF: **la** ~ **(dentaire)** tooth decay; **une** ~ a bad tooth

carié, e [kaʀje] ADJ: **dent** ~ bad *ou* decayed tooth

carillon [kaʀijɔ̃] NM *(d'église)* bells *pl*; *(de pendule)* chimes *pl*; *(de porte)*: ~ **(électrique)** (electric) door chime *ou* bell

carillonner [kaʀijɔne] /**1**/ VI to ring, chime, peal

caritatif, -ive [kaʀitatif, -iv] ADJ charitable

carlingue [kaʀlɛ̃g] NF cabin

carmélite [kaʀmelit] NF Carmelite nun

carmin [kaʀmɛ̃] ADJ INV crimson

carnage [kaʀnaʒ] NM carnage, slaughter

carnassier, -ière [kaʀnasje, -jɛʀ] ADJ carnivorous ▶ NM carnivore

carnation [kaʀnasjɔ̃] NF complexion; **carnations** NFPL *(Peinture)* flesh tones

carnaval [kaʀnaval] NM carnival

carné, e [kaʀne] ADJ meat *cpd*, meat-based

carnet [kaʀnɛ] NM *(calepin)* notebook; *(de tickets, timbres etc)* book; *(d'école)* school report; *(journal intime)* diary; ~ **d'adresses** address book; ~ **de chèques** cheque book (BRIT), checkbook (US); ~ **de commandes** order book; ~ **de notes** *(Scol)* (school) report; ~ **à souches** counterfoil book

carnier [kaʀnje] NM gamebag

carnivore [kaʀnivɔʀ] ADJ carnivorous ▶ NM carnivore

Carolines [kaʀɔlin] NFPL: **les** ~ the Caroline Islands

carotide [kaʀɔtid] NF carotid (artery)

carotte [kaʀɔt] NF *(aussi fig)* carrot

Carpates [kaʀpat] NFPL: **les** ~ the Carpathians, the Carpathian Mountains

carpe [kaʀp] NF carp

carpette [kaʀpɛt] NF rug

carquois [kaʀkwa] NM quiver

carre [kaʀ] NF *(de ski)* edge

carré, e [kaʀe] ADJ square; *(fig: franc)* straightforward ▶ NM *(de terrain, jardin)* patch, plot; *(Math)* square; *(Navig: salle)* wardroom; ~ **blanc** *(TV)* "adults only" symbol; ~ **d'as/de rois** *(Cartes)* four aces/kings; **élever un nombre au** ~ to square a number; **mètre/kilomètre** ~ square metre/kilometre; ~ **de soie** silk headsquare *ou* headscarf; ~ **d'agneau** loin of lamb

carreau, x [kaʀo] NM *(en faïence etc)* (floor) tile; *(au mur)* (wall) tile; *(de fenêtre)* (window) pane; *(motif)* check, square; *(Cartes: couleur)* diamonds *pl*; *(: carte)* diamond; **tissu à** ~ checked fabric; **papier à** ~ squared paper

carrefour [kaʀfuʀ] NM crossroads *sg*

carrelage [kaʀlaʒ] NM tiling; *(sol)* (tiled) floor

carreler [kaʀle] /**4**/ VT to tile

carrelet [kaʀlɛ] NM *(poisson)* plaice

carreleur [kaʀlœʀ] NM (floor) tiler

carrément [kaʀemɑ̃] ADV *(franchement)* straight out, bluntly; *(sans détours, sans hésiter)* straight; *(nettement)* definitely; *(intensif)* completely; **c'est** ~ **impossible** it's completely impossible; **il l'a** ~ **mis à la porte** he threw him straight out

carrer [kaʀe] /**1**/: **se carrer** VI: **se carrer dans un fauteuil** to settle o.s. comfortably *ou* ensconce o.s. in an armchair

carrier [kaʀje] NM: **(ouvrier)** ~ quarryman, quarrier

carrière [kaʀjɛʀ] NF *(de roches)* quarry; *(métier)* career; **militaire de** ~ professional soldier; **faire** ~ **dans** to make one's career in

carriériste [kaʀjeʀist] NMF careerist

carriole [kaʀjɔl] NF *(péj)* old cart

carrossable [kaʀɔsabl] ADJ suitable for (motor) vehicles

carrosse [kaʀɔs] NM (horse-drawn) coach

carrosserie [kaʀɔsʀi] NF body, bodywork *no pl* (BRIT); *(activité, commerce)* coachwork (BRIT), (car) body manufacturing; **atelier de** ~ *(pour réparations)* body shop, panel beaters' (yard) (BRIT)

carrossier [kaʀɔsje] NM coachbuilder (BRIT), (car) body repairer; *(dessinateur)* car designer

carrousel [kaʀuzɛl] NM *(Équitation)* carousel; *(fig)* merry-go-round

carrure [kaʀyʀ] NF build; *(fig)* stature, calibre

cartable [kaʀtabl] NM *(d'écolier)* satchel, (school)bag

carte [kaʀt] NF *(de géographie)* map; *(marine, du ciel)* chart; *(de fichier, d'abonnement etc, à jouer)* card;

(*au restaurant*) menu; (*aussi:* **carte postale**) (post)card; (*aussi:* **carte de visite**) (visiting) card; **avoir/donner ~ blanche** to give/have carte blanche *ou* a free hand; **tirer les cartes à qn** to read sb's cards; **jouer aux cartes** to play cards; **jouer cartes sur table** (*fig*) to put one's cards on the table; **à la ~** (*au restaurant*) à la carte; **~ à circuit imprimé** printed circuit; **~ à puce** smartcard, chip and PIN card; **~ bancaire** cash card; **C~ Bleue**® debit card; **~ de crédit** credit card; **~ de fidélité** loyalty card; **la ~ des vins** the wine list; **~ d'état-major** ≈ Ordnance (*BRIT*) *ou* Geological (*US*) Survey map; **~ d'identité** identity card; **la ~ grise** (*Auto*) ≈ the (car) registration document; **~ jeune** young person's railcard; **~ mémoire** (*d'appareil photo numérique*) memory card; **~ perforée** punch(ed) card; **~ routière** road map; **~ de séjour** residence permit; **~ SIM** SIM card; **~ téléphonique** phonecard; **la ~ verte** (*Auto*) the green card

cartel [kartɛl] NM cartel

carte-lettre [kartəlɛtr] (*pl* **cartes-lettres**) NF letter-card

carte-mère [kartəmɛr] (*pl* **cartes-mères**) NF (*Inform*) mother board

carter [karter] NM (*Auto: d'huile*) sump (*BRIT*), oil pan (*US*); (: *de la boîte de vitesses*) casing; (*de bicyclette*) chain guard

carte-réponse [kart(ə)repɔ̃s] (*pl* **cartes-réponses**) NF reply card

cartésien, ne [kartezjɛ̃, -ɛn] ADJ Cartesian

carte vitale N *see note*

> The French national health service issues everyone with a green chip card containing a photo. Doctors and other health care services have a card reader they use for submitting costs incurred to health insurance providers. Thus, the insured can be reimbursed later.

Carthage [karta3] N Carthage

carthaginois, e [kartaʒinwa, -waz] ADJ Carthaginian

cartilage [kartilaʒ] NM (*Anat*) cartilage

cartilagineux, -euse [kartilaʒinø, -øz] ADJ (*viande*) gristly

cartographe [kartɔgraf] NMF cartographer

cartographie [kartɔgrafi] NF cartography, map-making

cartomancie [kartɔmɑ̃si] NF fortune-telling, card-reading

cartomancien, ne [kartɔmɑ̃sjɛ̃, -ɛn] NM/F fortune-teller (*with cards*)

carton [kartɔ̃] NM (*matériau*) cardboard; (*boîte*) (cardboard) box; (*d'invitation*) invitation card; (*Art*) sketch; cartoon; **en ~** cardboard *cpd*; **faire un ~** (*au tir*) to have a go at the rifle range; to score a hit; **~ (à dessin)** portfolio

cartonnage [kartɔnaʒ] NM cardboard (packing)

cartonné, e [kartɔne] ADJ (*livre*) hardback, cased

carton-pâte [kartɔ̃pɑt] NM pasteboard; **de ~** (*fig*) cardboard *cpd*

cartouche [kartuʃ] NF cartridge; (*de cigarettes*) carton

cartouchière [kartuʃjɛr] NF cartridge belt

cas [kɑ] NM case; **faire peu de ~/grand ~ de** to attach little/great importance to; **ne faire aucun ~ de** to take no notice of; **le ~ échéant** if need be; **en aucun ~** on no account, under no circumstances (whatsoever); **au ~ où** in case; **dans ce ~** in that case; **en ~ de** in case of, in the event of; **en ~ de besoin** if need be; **en ~ d'urgence** in an emergency; **en ce ~** in that case; **en tout ~** in any case, at any rate; **~ de conscience** matter of conscience; **~ de force majeure** case of absolute necessity; (*Assurances*) act of God; **~ limite** borderline case; **~ social** social problem

Casablanca [kazablɑ̃ka] N Casablanca

casanier, -ière [kazanje, -jɛr] ADJ stay-at-home

casaque [kazak] NF (*de jockey*) blouse

cascade [kaskad] NF waterfall, cascade; (*fig*) stream, torrent

cascadeur, -euse [kaskadœr, -øz] NM/F stuntman/girl

case [kɑz] NF (*hutte*) hut; (*compartiment*) compartment; (*pour le courrier*) pigeonhole; (*d'échiquier*) square; (*sur un formulaire, de mots croisés*) box

casemate [kazmat] NF blockhouse

caser [kaze] /1/ (*fam*) VT (*mettre*) to put; (*loger*) to put up; (*péj*) to find a job for; to marry off; **se caser** VI (*se marier*) to settle down; (*trouver un emploi*) to find a (steady) job

caserne [kazern] NF barracks

casernement [kazernəmɑ̃] NM barrack buildings *pl*

cash [kaʃ] ADV: **payer ~** to pay cash down

casier [kazje] NM (*à journaux etc*) rack; (*de bureau*) filing cabinet; (: *à cases*) set of pigeonholes; (*case*) compartment; (*pour courrier*) pigeonhole; (: *à clef*) locker; (*Pêche*) lobster pot; **~ à bouteilles** bottle rack; **~ judiciaire** police record

casino [kazino] NM casino

casque [kask] NM helmet; (*chez le coiffeur*) (hair-)dryer; (*pour audition*) (head-)phones *pl*, headset; **les Casques bleus** the UN peacekeeping force

casquer [kaske] /1/ VI (*fam*) to cough up, stump up (*BRIT*)

casquette [kaskɛt] NF cap

cassable [kasabl] ADJ (*fragile*) breakable

cassant, e [kasɑ̃, -ɑ̃t] ADJ brittle; (*fig*) brusque, abrupt

cassate [kasat] NF: (*glace*) **~** cassata

cassation [kasasjɔ̃] NF: **se pourvoir en ~** to lodge an appeal; **recours en ~** appeal to the Supreme Court

casse [kas] NF (*pour voitures*): **mettre à la ~** to scrap, send to the breakers (*BRIT*); (*dégâts*): **il y a eu de la ~** there were a lot of breakages; (*Typo*): **haut/bas de ~** upper/lower case

cassé, e [kase] ADJ (*voix*) cracked; (*vieillard*) bent

casse-cou [kasku] ADJ INV daredevil, reckless; **crier ~ à qn** to warn sb (*against a risky undertaking*)

casse-croûte [kaskrut] NM INV snack

casse-noisettes [kasnwazɛt], **casse-noix** [kasnwa] NM INV nutcrackers *pl*

casse-pieds [kɑspje] NMF INV (*fam*): **il est ~, c'est un ~** he's a pain (in the neck)

casser [kɑse] /1/ VT to break; (*Admin: gradé*) to demote; (*Jur*) to quash; (*Comm*): **~ les prix** to slash prices; **se casser** VI, VT to break; (*fam*) to go, leave; **~ les pieds à qn** (*fam: irriter*) to get on sb's nerves; **se casser la jambe/une jambe** to break one's leg/a leg; **se casser la tête** (*fam*) to go to a lot of trouble; **à tout ~** fantastic, brilliant; **se casser net** to break clean off

casserole [kɑsʁɔl] NF saucepan; **à la ~** (*Culin*) braised

casse-tête [kɑstɛt] NM INV (*fig*) brain teaser; (*difficultés*) headache (*fig*)

cassette [kɑsɛt] NF (*bande magnétique*) cassette; (*coffret*) casket; **~ numérique** digital compact cassette; **~ vidéo** video

casseur [kɑsœʁ] NM hooligan; rioter

cassis [kɑsis] NM blackcurrant; (*de la route*) dip, bump

cassonade [kɑsɔnad] NF brown sugar

cassoulet [kɑsulɛ] NM *sausage and bean hotpot*

cassure [kɑsyʁ] NF break, crack

castagnettes [kɑstaɲɛt] NFPL castanets

caste [kɑst] NF caste

castillan, e [kɑstijɑ̃, -an] ADJ Castilian ▶ NM (*Ling*) Castilian

Castille [kɑstij] NF: **la ~** Castile

castor [kɑstɔʁ] NM beaver

castrer [kɑstʁe] /1/ VT (*mâle*) to castrate; (*femelle*) to spay; (*cheval*) to geld; (*chat, chien*) to doctor (*BRIT*), fix (*US*)

cataclysme [kataklism] NM cataclysm

catacombes [katakɔ̃b] NFPL catacombs

catadioptre [katadjɔptʁ] NM = **cataphote**

catafalque [katafalk] NM catafalque

catalan, e [katalɑ̃, -an] ADJ Catalan, Catalonian ▶ NM (*Ling*) Catalan

Catalogne [katalɔɲ] NF: **la ~** Catalonia

catalogue [katalɔg] NM catalogue

cataloguer [katalɔge] /1/ VT to catalogue, list; (*péj*) to put a label on

catalyse [kataliz] NF catalysis

catalyser [katalize] /1/ VT to catalyze

catalyseur [katalizœʁ] NM catalyst

catalytique [katalitik] ADJ catalytic; **pot ~** catalytic converter

catamaran [katamaʁɑ̃] NM (*voilier*) catamaran

cataphote [katafɔt] NM reflector

cataplasme [kataplasm] NM poultice

catapulte [katapylt] NF catapult

catapulter [katapylte] /1/ VT to catapult

cataracte [kataʁakt] NF cataract; **opérer qn de la ~** to operate on sb for a cataract

catarrhe [kataʁ] NM catarrh

catarrheux, -euse [kataʁø, -øz] ADJ catarrhal

catastrophe [katastʁɔf] NF catastrophe, disaster; **atterrir en ~** to make an emergency landing; **partir en ~** to rush away

catastropher [katastʁɔfe] /1/ VT (*personne*) to shatter

catastrophique [katastʁɔfik] ADJ catastrophic, disastrous

catch [katʃ] NM (all-in) wrestling

catcheur, -euse [katʃœʁ, -øz] NM/F (all-in) wrestler

catéchiser [kateʃize] /1/ VT to indoctrinate; to lecture

catéchisme [kateʃism] NM catechism

catéchumène [katekymɛn] NMF catechumen, *person attending religious instruction prior to baptism*

catégorie [kategɔʁi] NF category; (*Boucherie*): **morceaux de première/deuxième ~** prime/second cuts

catégorique [kategɔʁik] ADJ categorical

catégoriquement [kategɔʁikmɑ̃] ADV categorically

catégoriser [kategɔʁize] /1/ VT to categorize

caténaire [katenɛʁ] NF (*Rail*) catenary

cathédrale [katedʁal] NF cathedral

cathéter [katetɛʁ] NM (*Méd*) catheter

cathode [katɔd] NF cathode

cathodique [katɔdik] ADJ: **rayons cathodiques** cathode rays; **tube/écran ~** cathode-ray tube/screen

catholicisme [katɔlisism] NM (Roman) Catholicism

catholique [katɔlik] ADJ, NMF (Roman) Catholic; **pas très ~** a bit shady *ou* fishy

catimini [katimini]: **en ~** adv on the sly, on the quiet

catogan [katɔgɑ̃] NM bow (*tying hair on neck*)

Caucase [kɔkaz] NM: **le ~** the Caucasus (Mountains)

caucasien, ne [kɔkazjɛ̃, -ɛn] ADJ Caucasian

cauchemar [koʃmaʁ] NM nightmare

cauchemardesque [koʃmaʁdɛsk] ADJ nightmarish

causal, e [kozal] ADJ causal

causalité [kozalite] NF causality

causant, e [kozɑ̃, -ɑ̃t] ADJ chatty, talkative

cause [koz] NF cause; (*Jur*) lawsuit, case; brief; **faire ~ commune avec qn** to take sides with sb; **être ~ de** to be the cause of; **à ~ de** because of, owing to; **pour ~ de** on account of; owing to; **(et) pour ~** and for (a very) good reason; **être en ~** (*intérêts*) to be at stake; (*personne*) to be involved; (*qualité*) to be in question; **mettre en ~** to implicate; to call into question; **remettre en ~** to challenge, call into question; **c'est hors de ~** it's out of the question; **en tout état de ~** in any case

causer [koze] /1/ VT to cause ▶ VI to chat, talk

causerie [kozʁi] NF talk

causette [kozɛt] NF: **faire la** *ou* **un brin de ~** to have a chat

caustique [kostik] ADJ caustic

cauteleux, -euse [kotlø, -øz] ADJ wily

cautériser [koteʁize] /1/ VT to cauterize

caution [kosjɔ̃] NF guarantee, security; deposit; (*Jur*) bail (bond); (*fig*) backing, support; **payer la ~ de qn** to stand bail for sb; **se porter ~ pour qn** to stand security for sb; **libéré sous ~** released on bail; **sujet à ~** unconfirmed

cautionnement [kosjɔnmɑ̃] NM (*somme*) guarantee, security

cautionner [kosjɔne] /1/ VT to guarantee; (*soutenir*) to support

cavalcade [kavalkad] NF (*fig*) stampede
cavale [kaval] NF: **en ~** on the run
cavalerie [kavalʀi] NF cavalry
cavalier, -ière [kavalje, -jɛʀ] ADJ (*désinvolte*)
offhand ▶ NM/F rider; (*au bal*) partner ▶ NM
(*Échecs*) knight; **faire ~ seul** to go it alone; **allée**
ou piste cavalière riding path
cavalièrement [kavaljɛʀmɑ̃] ADV offhandedly
cave [kav] NF cellar; (*cabaret*) (cellar) nightclub
▶ ADJ: **yeux caves** sunken eyes; **joues caves**
hollow cheeks
caveau, x [kavo] NM vault
caverne [kavɛʀn] NF cave
caverneux, -euse [kavɛʀnø, -øz] ADJ cavernous
caviar [kavjaʀ] NM caviar(e)
cavité [kavite] NF cavity
Cayenne [kajɛn] N Cayenne
CB [sibi] SIGLE F (= *citizens' band; canaux banalisés*)
CB; = **carte bancaire**
CC SIGLE M = **le corps consulaire; compte**
courant
CCI SIGLE F = **chambre de commerce et**
d'industrie
CCP SIGLE M = **compte chèque postal**
CD SIGLE M (= *chemin départemental*) secondary
road, ≈ B road (*BRIT*); (*Pol*) = **le corps**
diplomatique; (= *compact disc*) CD; (= *comité*
directeur) steering committee
CDD SIGLE M (= *contrat à durée déterminée*)
fixed-term contract
CDI SIGLE M (= *Centre de documentation et*
d'information) school library; (= *contrat à durée*
indéterminée) permanent *ou* open-ended contract
CD-ROM [sedeʀɔm] NM INV (= *Compact Disc Read*
Only Memory) CD-Rom
CDS SIGLE M (= *Centre des démocrates sociaux*) political
party
CE SIGLE F (= *Communauté européenne*) EC; (*Comm*)
= **caisse d'épargne** ▶ SIGLE M (*Industrie*) = **comité**
d'entreprise; (*Scol*) = **cours élémentaire**

(MOT-CLÉ)

ce, cette [sə, sɛt] (*devant nm* **cet** + *voyelle ou h aspiré*)
(*pl* **ces**) ADJ DÉM (*proximité*) this; these *pl*;
(*non-proximité*) that; those *pl*; **cette maison(-ci/**
là) this/that house; **cette nuit** (*qui vient*)
tonight; (*passée*) last night
▶ PRON 1: **c'est** it's, it is; **c'est petit/grand/un**
livre it's *ou* it is small/big/a book; **c'est un**
peintre he's *ou* he is a painter; **ce sont des**
peintres they're *ou* they are painters; **c'est le**
facteur *etc* (*à la porte*) it's the postman *etc*; **qui**
est-ce? who is it?; (*en désignant*) who is he/she?;
qu'est-ce? what is it?; **c'est toi qui lui as**
parlé it was you who spoke to him
2: **c'est que: c'est qu'il est lent/qu'il n'a pas**
faim the fact is, he's slow/he's not hungry
3 (*expressions*): **c'est ça** (*correct*) that's it, that's
right; **c'est toi qui le dis!** that's what YOU say!
4: **ce qui, ce que** what; **ce qui me plaît, c'est**
sa franchise what I like about him *ou* her is his
ou her frankness; (*chose qui*): **il est bête, ce qui**
me chagrine he's stupid, which saddens me;
tout ce qui bouge everything that *ou* which

moves; **tout ce que je sais** all I know; **ce dont**
j'ai parlé what I talked about; **ce que c'est**
grand! it's so big!; *voir aussi* **c'est-à-dire**; *voir* **-ci**;
est-ce que; n'est-ce pas

CEA SIGLE M (= *Commissariat à l'énergie atomique*)
≈ AEA (= *Atomic Energy Authority* (*BRIT*)), ≈ AEC
(= *Atomic Energy Commission* (*US*))
CECA [seka] SIGLE F (= *Communauté européenne du*
charbon et de l'acier) ECSC (= *European Coal and Steel*
Community)
ceci [səsi] PRON this
cécité [sesite] NF blindness
céder [sede] /6/ VT to give up ▶ VI (*pont, barrage*)
to give way; (*personne*) to give in; **~ à** to yield to,
give in to
cédérom [sedeʀɔm] NM CD-ROM
CEDEX [sedɛks] SIGLE M (= *courrier d'entreprise à*
distribution exceptionnelle) accelerated postal service
for bulk users
cédille [sedij] NF cedilla
cèdre [sɛdʀ] NM cedar
CEE SIGLE F (= *Communauté économique européenne*)
EEC
CEI SIGLE F (= *Communauté des États indépendants*)
CIS
ceindre [sɛ̃dʀ] /52/ VT (*mettre*) to put on;
(*entourer*): **~ qch de qch** to put sth round sth
ceinture [sɛ̃tyʀ] NF belt; (*taille*) waist; (*fig*) ring;
belt; circle; **~ de sauvetage** lifebelt (*BRIT*), life
preserver (*US*); **~ de sécurité** safety *ou* seat belt;
~ (de sécurité) à enrouleur inertia reel seat
belt; **~ verte** green belt
ceinturer [sɛ̃tyʀe] /1/ VT (*saisir*) to grasp (round
the waist); (*entourer*) to surround
ceinturon [sɛ̃tyʀɔ̃] NM belt
cela [s(ə)la] PRON that; (*comme sujet indéfini*) it;
~ m'étonne que it surprises me that; **quand/**
où ~? when/where (was that?)
célébrant [selebʀɑ̃] NM (*Rel*) celebrant
célébration [selebʀasjɔ̃] NF celebration
célèbre [selɛbʀ] ADJ famous
célébrer [selebʀe] /6/ VT to celebrate; (*louer*) to
extol
célébrité [selebʀite] NF fame; (*star*) celebrity
céleri [sɛlʀi] NM: **~-(rave)** celeriac; **~ (en**
branche) celery
célérité [seleʀite] NF speed, swiftness
céleste [selɛst] ADJ celestial; heavenly
célibat [seliba] NM celibacy, bachelor/
spinsterhood
célibataire [selibatɛʀ] ADJ single, unmarried
▶ NMF bachelor/unmarried *ou* single woman;
mère ~ single *ou* unmarried mother
celle, celles [sɛl] PRON *voir* **celui**
cellier [selje] NM storeroom
cellophane® [selɔfan] NF cellophane
cellulaire [selylɛʀ] ADJ (*Bio*) cell *cpd*, cellular;
voiture *ou* **fourgon ~** prison *ou* police van;
régime ~ confinement
cellule [selyl] NF (*gén*) cell; **~ (photo-**
électrique) electronic eye; **~ souche** stem cell
cellulite [selylit] NF cellulite
celluloïd® [selylɔid] NM Celluloid

cellulose [selyloz] NF cellulose

celte [sɛlt], **celtique** [sɛltik] ADJ Celt, Celtic

[MOT-CLÉ]

celui, celle [səlɥi, sɛl] (*mpl* **ceux**, *fpl* **celles**) PRON
1: **celui-ci/là, celle-ci/là** this one/that one;
ceux-ci, celles-ci these (ones); **ceux-là,
celles-là** those (ones); **celui de mon frère** my
brother's; **celui du salon/du dessous** the one
in (*ou* from) the lounge/below
2 (+*relatif*): **celui qui bouge** the one which *ou*
that moves; (*personne*) the one who moves;
celui que je vois the one (which *ou* that) I see;
(*personne*) the one (whom) I see; **celui dont je
parle** the one I'm talking about
3 (*valeur indéfinie*): **celui qui veut** whoever wants

cénacle [senakl] NM (*literary*) coterie *ou* set

cendre [sɑ̃dʀ] NF ash; **cendres** (*d'un foyer*)
ash(es), cinders; (*volcaniques*) ash *sg*; (*d'un défunt*)
ashes; **sous la ~** (*Culin*) in (the) embers

cendré, e [sɑ̃dʀe] ADJ (*couleur*) ashen; (**piste**) ~
cinder track

cendreux, -euse [sɑ̃dʀø, -øz] ADJ (*terrain,
substance*) cindery; (*teint*) ashen

cendrier [sɑ̃dʀije] NM ashtray

cène [sɛn] NF: **la ~** (Holy) Communion; (*Art*) the
Last Supper

censé, e [sɑ̃se] ADJ: **être ~ faire** to be supposed
to do

censément [sɑ̃semɑ̃] ADV supposedly

censeur [sɑ̃sœʀ] NM (*Scol*) deputy head (BRIT),
vice-principal (US); (*Ciné, Pol*) censor

censure [sɑ̃syʀ] NF censorship

censurer [sɑ̃syʀe] /1/ VT (*Ciné, Presse*) to censor;
(*Pol*) to censure

cent [sɑ̃] NUM a hundred, one hundred ▶ NM
(US, Canada, partie de l'euro etc) cent; **pour ~** (%)
per cent (%); **faire les ~ pas** to pace up and
down

centaine [sɑ̃tɛn] NF: **une ~ (de)** about a
hundred, a hundred or so; (*Comm*) a hundred;
plusieurs centaines (de) several hundred;
des centaines (de) hundreds (of)

centenaire [sɑ̃tnɛʀ] ADJ hundred-year-old
▶ NMF centenarian ▶ NM (*anniversaire*)
centenary; (*monnaie*) cent

centième [sɑ̃tjɛm] NUM hundredth

centigrade [sɑ̃tigʀad] NM centigrade

centigramme [sɑ̃tigʀam] NM centigramme

centilitre [sɑ̃tilitʀ] NM centilitre (BRIT),
centiliter (US)

centime [sɑ̃tim] NM centime; **~ d'euro** euro
cent

centimètre [sɑ̃timɛtʀ] NM centimetre (BRIT),
centimeter (US); (*ruban*) tape measure,
measuring tape

centrafricain, e [sɑ̃tʀafʀikɛ̃, -ɛn] ADJ *ou* from
the Central African Republic

central, e, -aux [sɑ̃tʀal, -o] ADJ central ▶ NM:
~ (téléphonique) (telephone) exchange ▶ NF:
power station; **~ d'achat** (*Comm*) central buying
service; **~ électrique/nucléaire** electric/
nuclear power station; **~ syndicale** group of
affiliated trade unions

centralisation [sɑ̃tʀalizasjɔ̃] NF centralization

centraliser [sɑ̃tʀalize] /1/ VT to centralize

centralisme [sɑ̃tʀalism] NM centralism

centraméricain, e [sɑ̃tʀameʀikɛ̃, -ɛn] ADJ
Central American

centre [sɑ̃tʀ] NM centre (BRIT), center (US);
~ commercial/sportif/culturel shopping/
sports/arts centre; **~ aéré** outdoor centre;
~ d'appels call centre; **~ d'apprentissage**
training college; **~ d'attraction** centre of
attraction; **~ de gravité** centre of gravity; **~ de
loisirs** leisure centre; **~ d'enfouissement des
déchets** landfill site; **~ hospitalier** hospital
complex; **~ de tri** (*Postes*) sorting office;
centres nerveux (*Anat*) nerve centres

centrer [sɑ̃tʀe] /1/ VT to centre (BRIT), center (US)
▶ VI (*Football*) to centre the ball

centre-ville [sɑ̃tʀəvil] (*pl* **centres-villes**) NM
town centre (BRIT) *ou* center (US), downtown
(area) (US)

centrifuge [sɑ̃tʀifyʒ] ADJ: **force ~** centrifugal
force

centrifuger [sɑ̃tʀifyʒe] /3/ VT to centrifuge

centrifugeuse [sɑ̃tʀifyʒøz] NF (*pour fruits*) juice
extractor

centripète [sɑ̃tʀipɛt] ADJ: **force ~** centripetal
force

centrisme [sɑ̃tʀism] NM centrism

centriste [sɑ̃tʀist] ADJ, NMF centrist

centuple [sɑ̃typl] NM: **le ~ de qch** a hundred
times sth; **au ~** a hundredfold

centupler [sɑ̃typle] /1/ VI, VT to increase a
hundredfold

CEP SIGLE M = **Certificat d'études (primaires)**

cep [sɛp] NM (vine) stock

cépage [sepaʒ] NM (type of) vine

cèpe [sɛp] NM (edible) boletus

cependant [s(ə)pɑ̃dɑ̃] ADV however, nevertheless

céramique [seʀamik] ADJ ceramic ▶ NF
ceramic; (*art*) ceramics *sg*

céramiste [seʀamist] NMF ceramist

cerbère [sɛʀbɛʀ] NM (*fig: péj*) bad-tempered
doorkeeper

cerceau, x [sɛʀso] NM (*d'enfant, de tonnelle*) hoop

cercle [sɛʀkl] NM circle; (*objet*) band, hoop;
décrire un ~ (*avion*) to circle; (*projectile*) to
describe a circle; **~ d'amis** circle of friends;
~ de famille family circle; **~ vicieux** vicious
circle

cercler [sɛʀkle] /1/ VT: **lunettes cerclées d'or**
gold-rimmed glasses

cercueil [sɛʀkœj] NM coffin

céréale [seʀeal] NF cereal

céréalier, -ière [seʀealje, -jɛʀ] ADJ (*production,
cultures*) cereal *cpd*

cérébral, e, -aux [seʀebʀal, -o] ADJ (*Anat*)
cerebral, brain *cpd*; (*fig*) mental, cerebral

cérémonial [seʀemɔnjal] NM ceremonial

cérémonie [seʀemɔni] NF ceremony; **sans ~**
(*inviter, manger*) informally; **cérémonies** NFPL
(*péj*) fuss *sg*, to-do *sg*

cérémonieux, -euse [seʀemɔnjø, -øz] ADJ
ceremonious, formal

cerf [sɛʀ] NM stag

cerfeuil [sɛʀfœj] NM chervil

cerf-volant [sɛʀvɔlɑ̃] NM kite; **jouer au ~** to fly a kite

cerisaie [sǝʀizɛ] NF cherry orchard

cerise [sǝʀiz] NF cherry

cerisier [sǝʀizje] NM cherry (tree)

CERN [sɛʀn] SIGLE M (= *Centre européen de recherche nucléaire*) CERN

cerné, e [sɛʀne] ADJ: **les yeux cernés** with dark rings *ou* shadows under the eyes

cerner [sɛʀne] /**1**/ VT (*Mil etc*) to surround; (*fig: problème*) to delimit, define

cernes [sɛʀn] NFPL (dark) rings, shadows (under the eyes)

certain, e [sɛʀtɛ̃, -ɛn] ADJ certain; (*sûr*): **~ (de/ que)** certain *ou* sure (of/ that); **d'un ~ âge** past one's prime, not so young; **un ~ temps** (quite) some time; **sûr et ~** absolutely certain; **un ~ Georges** someone called Georges; **certains** *pron* some

certainement [sɛʀtɛnmɑ̃] ADV (*probablement*) most probably *ou* likely; (*bien sûr*) certainly, of course

certes [sɛʀt] ADV (*sans doute*) admittedly; (*bien sûr*) of course; indeed (yes)

certificat [sɛʀtifika] NM certificate; **C~ d'études (primaires)** former school leaving certificate (taken at the end of primary education); **C~ de fin d'études secondaires** school leaving certificate

certifié, e [sɛʀtifje] ADJ: **professeur ~** qualified teacher; (*Admin*) **copie ~ conforme (à l'original)** certified copy (of the original)

certifier [sɛʀtifje] /**7**/ VT to certify, guarantee; **~ à qn que** to assure sb that, guarantee to sb that; **~ qch à qn** to guarantee sth to sb

certitude [sɛʀtityd] NF certainty

cérumen [seʀymɛn] NM (ear)wax

cerveau, x [sɛʀvo] NM brain; **~ électronique** electronic brain

cervelas [sɛʀvǝla] NM saveloy

cervelle [sɛʀvɛl] NF (*Anat*) brain; (*Culin*) brain(s); **se creuser la ~** to rack one's brains

cervical, e, -aux [sɛʀvikal, -o] ADJ cervical

cervidés [sɛʀvide] NMPL cervidae

CES SIGLE M (= *Collège d'enseignement secondaire*) ≈ (junior) secondary school (BRIT), ≈ junior high school (US)

ces [se] ADJ DÉM *voir* **ce**

césarienne [sezaʀjɛn] NF caesarean (BRIT) *ou* cesarean (US) (section)

cessantes [sɛsɑ̃t] ADJ FPL: **toutes affaires ~** forthwith

cessation [sɛsasjɔ̃] NF: **~ des hostilités** cessation of hostilities; **~ de paiements/ commerce** suspension of payments/trading

cesse [sɛs] NF: **sans ~** adv (*tout le temps*) continually, constantly; (*sans interruption*) continuously; **il n'avait de ~ que** he would not rest until

cesser [sese] /**1**/ VT to stop ▶ VI to stop, cease; **~ de faire** to stop doing; **faire ~** (*bruit, scandale*) to put a stop to

cessez-le-feu [seselfø] NM INV ceasefire

cession [sɛsjɔ̃] NF transfer

c'est [sɛ] = **ce**

c'est-à-dire [setadiʀ] ADV that is (to say); (*demander de préciser*): **~?** what does that mean?; **~ que ...** (*en conséquence*) which means that ...; (*manière d'excuse*) well, in fact ...

CET SIGLE M (= *Collège d'enseignement technique*) (*formerly*) technical school

cet [sɛt] ADJ DÉM *voir* **ce**

cétacé [setase] NM cetacean

cette [sɛt] ADJ DÉM *voir* **ce**

ceux [sø] PRON *voir* **celui**

cévenol, e [sevnɔl] ADJ of *ou* from the Cévennes region

cf. ABR (= *confer*) cf, cp

CFAO SIGLE F (= *conception de fabrication assistée par ordinateur*) CAM

CFC SIGLE MPL (= *chlorofluorocarbures*) CFC

CFDT SIGLE F (= *Confédération française démocratique du travail*) trade union

CFF SIGLE M (= *Chemins de fer fédéraux*) Swiss railways

CFL SIGLE M (= *Chemins de fer luxembourgeois*) Luxembourg railways

CFP SIGLE M = **Centre de formation professionnelle** ▶ SIGLE F = **Compagnie française des pétroles**

CFTC SIGLE F (= *Confédération française des travailleurs chrétiens*) trade union

CGC SIGLE F (= *Confédération générale des cadres*) management union

CGPME SIGLE F = **Confédération générale des petites et moyennes entreprises**

CGT SIGLE F (= *Confédération générale du travail*) trade union

CH ABR (= *Confédération helvétique*) CH

ch. ABR = **charges**; **chauffage**; **cherche**

chacal [ʃakal] NM jackal

chacun, e [ʃakœ̃, -yn] PRON each; (*indéfini*) everyone, everybody

chagrin, e [ʃagʀɛ̃, -in] ADJ morose ▶ NM grief, sorrow; **avoir du ~** to be grieved *ou* sorrowful

chagriner [ʃagʀine] /**1**/ VT to grieve, distress; (*contrarier*) to bother, worry

chahut [ʃay] NM uproar

chahuter [ʃayte] /**1**/ VT to rag, bait ▶ VI to make an uproar

chahuteur, -euse [ʃaytœʀ, -øz] NM/F rowdy

chai [ʃɛ] NM wine and spirit store(house)

chaîne [ʃɛn] NF chain; (*Radio, TV: stations*) channel; (*Inform*) string; **chaînes** NFPL (*liens, asservissement*) fetters, bonds; **travail à la ~** production line work; **réactions en ~** chain reactions; **faire la ~** to form a (human) chain; **~ alimentaire** food chain; **~ compacte** music centre; **~ d'entraide** mutual aid association; **~ (haute-fidélité** *ou* **hi-fi)** hi-fi system; **~ (de montage** *ou* **de fabrication)** production *ou* assembly line; **~ (de montagnes)** (mountain) range; **~ de solidarité** solidarity network; **~ (stéréo** *ou* **audio)** stereo (system)

chaînette [ʃɛnɛt] NF (small) chain

chaînon [ʃɛnɔ̃] NM link

chair [ʃɛʀ] NF flesh ▶ ADJ INV: **(couleur) ~** flesh-coloured; **avoir la ~ de poule** to have

69

goose pimples *ou* goose flesh; **bien en** ~ plump, well-padded; **en** ~ **et en os** in the flesh; ~ **à saucisse** sausage meat

chaire [ʃɛʀ] NF (*d'église*) pulpit; (*d'université*) chair

chaise [ʃɛz] NF chair; ~ **de bébé** high chair; ~ **électrique** electric chair; ~ **longue** deckchair

chaland [ʃalɑ̃] NM (*bateau*) barge

châle [ʃɑl] NM shawl

chalet [ʃalɛ] NM chalet

chaleur [ʃalœʀ] NF heat; (*fig: d'accueil*) warmth; fire, fervour (*BRIT*), fervor (*US*); heat; **en** ~ (*Zool*) on heat

chaleureusement [ʃalœʀøzmɑ̃] ADV warmly

chaleureux, -euse [ʃalœʀø, -øz] ADJ warm

challenge [ʃalɑ̃ʒ] NM contest, tournament

challenger [ʃalɑ̃ʒɛʀ] NM (*Sport*) challenger

chaloupe [ʃalup] NF launch; (*de sauvetage*) lifeboat

chalumeau, x [ʃalymo] NM blowlamp (*BRIT*), blowtorch

chalut [ʃaly] NM trawl (net); **pêcher au** ~ to trawl

chalutier [ʃalytje] NM trawler; (*pêcheur*) trawlerman

chamade [ʃamad] NF: **battre la** ~ to beat wildly

chamailler [ʃamaje] /1/: **se chamailler** VI to squabble, bicker

chamarré, e [ʃamaʀe] ADJ richly brocaded

chambard [ʃɑ̃baʀ] NM rumpus

chambardement [ʃɑ̃baʀdəmɑ̃] NM: **c'est le grand** ~ everything has been (*ou* is being) turned upside down

chambarder [ʃɑ̃baʀde] /1/ VT to turn upside down

chamboulement [ʃɑ̃bulmɑ̃] NM disruption

chambouler [ʃɑ̃bule] /1/ VT to disrupt, turn upside down

chambranle [ʃɑ̃bʀɑl] NM (door) frame

chambre [ʃɑ̃bʀ] NF bedroom; (*Tech*) chamber; (*Pol*) chamber, house; (*Jur*) court; (*Comm*) chamber; federation; **faire** ~ **à part** to sleep in separate rooms; **stratège/alpiniste en** ~ armchair strategist/mountaineer; **à un lit/deux lits** single/twin-bedded room; ~ **pour une/deux personne(s)** single/double room; ~ **d'accusation** court of criminal appeal; ~ **d'agriculture** *body responsible for the agricultural interests of a département*; ~ **à air** (*de pneu*) (inner) tube; ~ **d'amis** spare *ou* guest room; ~ **de combustion** combustion chamber; ~ **de commerce et d'industrie** chamber of commerce and industry; ~ **à coucher** bedroom; **la C~ des députés** the Chamber of Deputies, ≈ the House of (Commons) (*BRIT*), ≈ the House of Representatives (*US*); ~ **forte** strongroom; ~ **froide** *ou* **frigorifique** cold room; ~ **à gaz** gas chamber; ~ **d'hôte** ≈ bed and breakfast (*in private home*); ~ **des machines** engine-room; ~ **des métiers** *chamber of commerce for trades*; ~ **meublée** bedsit(ter) (*BRIT*), furnished room; ~ **noire** (*Photo*) dark room

chambrée [ʃɑ̃bʀe] NF room

chambrer [ʃɑ̃bʀe] /1/ VT (*vin*) to bring to room temperature

chameau, x [ʃamo] NM camel

chamois [ʃamwa] NM chamois ▶ ADJ INV: (**couleur**~) ~ fawn, buff

champ [ʃɑ̃] NM (*aussi Inform*) field; (*Photo: aussi*: **dans le champ**) in the picture; **prendre du** ~ to draw back; **laisser le** ~ **libre à qn** to leave sb a clear field; ~ **d'action** sphere of operation(s); ~ **de bataille** battlefield; ~ **de courses** racecourse; ~ **d'honneur** field of honour; ~ **de manœuvre** (*Mil*) parade ground; ~ **de mines** minefield; ~ **de tir** shooting *ou* rifle range; ~ **visuel** field of vision

Champagne [ʃɑ̃paɲ] NF: **la** ~ Champagne, the Champagne region

champagne [ʃɑ̃paɲ] NM champagne

champenois, e [ʃɑ̃pənwa, -waz] ADJ of *ou* from Champagne; (*vin*): **méthode** ~ champagne-type

champêtre [ʃɑ̃pɛtʀ] ADJ country *cpd*, rural

champignon [ʃɑ̃piɲɔ̃] NM mushroom; (*terme générique*) fungus; (*fam: accélérateur*) accelerator, gas pedal (*US*); ~ **de couche** *ou* **de Paris** button mushroom; ~ **vénéneux** toadstool, poisonous mushroom

champion, ne [ʃɑ̃pjɔ̃, -ɔn] ADJ, NM/F champion

championnat [ʃɑ̃pjɔna] NM championship

chance [ʃɑ̃s] NF: **la** ~ luck; **chances** NFPL (*probabilités*) chances; **une** ~ a stroke *ou* piece of luck *ou* good fortune; (*occasion*) a lucky break; **avoir de la** ~ to be lucky; **il a des chances de gagner** he has a chance of winning; **il y a de fortes chances pour que Paul soit malade** it's highly probable that Paul is ill; **bonne** ~! good luck!; **encore une** ~ **que tu viennes!** it's lucky you're coming!; **je n'ai pas de** ~ I'm out of luck; (*toujours*) I never have any luck; **donner sa** ~ **à qn** to give sb a chance

chancelant, e [ʃɑ̃slɑ̃, -ɑ̃t] ADJ (*personne*) tottering; (*santé*) failing

chanceler [ʃɑ̃sle] /4/ VI to totter

chancelier [ʃɑ̃səlje] NM (*allemand*) chancellor; (*d'ambassade*) secretary

chancellerie [ʃɑ̃sɛlʀi] NF (*en France*) ministry of justice; (*en Allemagne*) chancellery; (*d'ambassade*) chancery

chanceux, -euse [ʃɑ̃sø, -øz] ADJ lucky, fortunate

chancre [ʃɑ̃kʀ] NM canker

chandail [ʃɑ̃daj] NM (thick) jumper *ou* sweater

Chandeleur [ʃɑ̃dlœʀ] NF: **la** ~ Candlemas

chandelier [ʃɑ̃dəlje] NM candlestick; (*à plusieurs branches*) candelabra

chandelle [ʃɑ̃dɛl] NF (tallow) candle; (*Tennis*): **faire une** ~ to lob; (*Aviat*): **monter en** ~ to climb vertically; **tenir la** ~ to play gooseberry; **dîner aux chandelles** candlelight dinner

change [ʃɑ̃ʒ] NM (*Comm*) exchange; **opérations de** ~ (foreign) exchange transactions; **contrôle des changes** exchange control; **gagner/perdre au** ~ to be better/worse off (for it); **donner le** ~ **à qn** (*fig*) to lead sb up the garden path

changeant, e [ʃɑ̃ʒɑ̃, -ɑ̃t] ADJ changeable, fickle

changement [ʃɑ̃ʒmɑ̃] NM change; ~ **climatique** climate change; ~ **de vitesse**

(*dispositif*) gears pl; (*action*) gear change

changer [ʃɑ̃ʒe] /**3**/ VT (*modifier*) to change, alter; (*remplacer, Comm, rhabiller*) to change ▶ VI to change, alter; **se changer** VI to change (o.s.); **~ de** (*remplacer: adresse, nom, voiture etc*) to change one's; **~ de train** to change trains; **~ d'air** to get a change of air; **~ de couleur/direction** to change colour/direction; **~ d'avis**, **~ d'idée** to change one's mind; **~ de place avec qn** to change places with sb; **~ de vitesse** (*Auto*) to change gear; **~ qn/qch de place** to move sb/sth to another place; **~ (de bus** *etc*) to change (buses *etc*); **~ qch en** to change sth into

changeur [ʃɑ̃ʒœR] NM (*personne*) moneychanger; **~ automatique** change machine; **~ de disques** record changer, autochange

chanoine [ʃanwan] NM canon

chanson [ʃɑ̃sɔ̃] NF song

chansonnette [ʃɑ̃sɔnɛt] NF ditty

chansonnier [ʃɑ̃sɔnje] NM cabaret artist (*specializing in political satire*); (*recueil*) song book

chant [ʃɑ̃] NM song; (*art vocal*) singing; (*d'église*) hymn; (*de poème*) canto; (*Tech*): **posé de** *ou* **sur ~** placed edgeways; **~ de Noël** Christmas carol

chantage [ʃɑ̃taʒ] NM blackmail; **faire du ~** to use blackmail; **soumettre qn à un ~** to blackmail sb

chantant, e [ʃɑ̃tɑ̃, -ɑ̃t] ADJ (*accent, voix*) sing-song

chanter [ʃɑ̃te] /**1**/ VT, VI to sing; **~ juste/faux** to sing in tune/out of tune; **si cela lui chante** (*fam*) if he feels like it *ou* fancies it

chanterelle [ʃɑ̃tRɛl] NF chanterelle (*edible mushroom*)

chanteur, -euse [ʃɑ̃tœR, -øz] NM/F singer; **~ de charme** crooner

chantier [ʃɑ̃tje] NM (building) site; (*sur une route*) roadworks pl; **mettre en ~** to start work on; **~ naval** shipyard

chantilly [ʃɑ̃tiji] NF *voir* **crème**

chantonner [ʃɑ̃tɔne] /**1**/ VI, VT to sing to oneself, hum

chantre [ʃɑ̃tR] NM (*fig*) eulogist

chanvre [ʃɑ̃vR] NM hemp

chaos [kao] NM chaos

chaotique [kaɔtik] ADJ chaotic

chap. ABR (= *chapitre*) ch

chapardage [ʃapaRdaʒ] NM pilfering

chaparder [ʃapaRde] /**1**/ VT to pinch

chapeau, x [ʃapo] NM hat; (*Presse*) introductory paragraph; **~!** well done!; **~ melon** bowler hat; **~ mou** trilby; **~ de roues** hub caps

chapeauter [ʃapote] /**1**/ VT (*Admin*) to head, oversee

chapelain [ʃaplɛ̃] NM (*Rel*) chaplain

chapelet [ʃaplɛ] NM (*Rel*) rosary; (*fig*): **un ~ de** a string of; **dire son ~** to tell one's beads

chapelier, -ière [ʃapəlje, -jɛR] NM/F hatter; milliner

chapelle [ʃapɛl] NF chapel; **~ ardente** chapel of rest

chapellerie [ʃapɛlRi] NF (*magasin*) hat shop; (*commerce*) hat trade

chapelure [ʃaplyR] NF (dried) breadcrumbs pl

chaperon [ʃapRɔ̃] NM chaperon

chaperonner [ʃapRɔne] /**1**/ VT to chaperon

chapiteau, x [ʃapito] NM (*Archit*) capital; (*de cirque*) marquee, big top

chapitre [ʃapitR] NM chapter; (*fig*) subject, matter; **avoir voix au ~** to have a say in the matter

chapitrer [ʃapitRe] /**1**/ VT to lecture, reprimand

chapon [ʃapɔ̃] NM capon

chaque [ʃak] ADJ each, every; (*indéfini*) every

char [ʃaR] NM (*à foin etc*) cart, waggon; (*de carnaval*) float; **~ (d'assaut)** tank; **~ à voile** sand yacht

charabia [ʃaRabja] NM (*péj*) gibberish, gobbledygook (BRIT)

charade [ʃaRad] NF riddle; (*mimée*) charade

charbon [ʃaRbɔ̃] NM coal; **~ de bois** charcoal

charbonnage [ʃaRbɔnaʒ] NM: **les charbonnages de France** the (French) Coal Board sg

charbonnier [ʃaRbɔnje] NM coalman

charcuterie [ʃaRkytRi] NF (*magasin*) pork butcher's shop and delicatessen; (*produits*) cooked pork meats pl

charcutier, -ière [ʃaRkytje, -jɛR] NM/F pork butcher

chardon [ʃaRdɔ̃] NM thistle

chardonneret [ʃaRdɔnRɛ] NM goldfinch

charentais, e [ʃaRɑ̃tɛ, -ɛz] ADJ of *ou* from Charente ▶ NF (*pantoufle*) slipper

charge [ʃaRʒ] NF (*fardeau*) load; (*explosif, Élec, Mil, Jur*) charge; (*rôle, mission*) responsibility; **charges** NFPL (*du loyer*) service charges; **à la ~ de** (*dépendant de*) dependent upon, supported by; (*aux frais de*) chargeable to, payable by; **j'accepte, à ~ de revanche** I accept, provided I can do the same for you (in return) one day; **prendre en ~** to take charge of; (*véhicule*) to take on; (*dépenses*) to take care of; **~ utile** (*Auto*) live load; (*Comm*) payload; **charges sociales** social security contributions

chargé [ʃaRʒe] ADJ (*voiture, animal, personne*) laden; (*fusil, batterie, caméra*) loaded; (*occupé: emploi du temps, journée*) busy, full; (: *estomac*) heavy, full; (: *langue*) furred; (: *décoration, style*) heavy, ornate ▶ NM: **~ d'affaires** chargé d'affaires; **~ de cours** ≈ lecturer; **~ de** (*responsable de*) responsible for

chargement [ʃaRʒəmɑ̃] NM (*action*) loading; charging; (*objets*) load

charger [ʃaRʒe] /**3**/ VT (*voiture, fusil, caméra*) to load; (*batterie*) to charge ▶ VI (*Mil etc*) to charge; **se ~ de** VT to see to, take care of; **~ qn de qch/faire qch** to give sb the responsibility for sth/of doing sth; to put sb in charge of sth/doing sth; **se ~ de faire qch** to take it upon o.s. to do sth

chargeur [ʃaRʒœR] NM (*dispositif: de batterie*) charger; (: *d'arme à feu*) magazine; (: *Photo*) cartridge

chariot [ʃaRjo] NM trolley; (*charrette*) waggon; (*de machine à écrire*) carriage; **~ élévateur** fork-lift truck

charisme [kaRism] NM charisma

charitable [ʃaRitabl] ADJ charitable; kind

charité [ʃaRite] NF charity; **faire la ~** to give to charity; to do charitable works; **faire la ~ à** to give (something) to; **fête/vente de ~** fête/sale in aid of charity

charivari [ʃaʀivaʀi] NM hullabaloo

charlatan [ʃaʀlatɑ̃] NM charlatan

charlotte [ʃaʀlɔt] NF (*Culin*) charlotte

charmant, e [ʃaʀmɑ̃, -ɑ̃t] ADJ charming

charme [ʃaʀm] NM charm; **charmes** NMPL (*appas*) charms; **c'est ce qui en fait le ~** that is its attraction; **faire du ~** to be charming, turn on the charm; **aller** *ou* **se porter comme un ~** to be in the pink

charmer [ʃaʀme] /1/ VT to charm; **je suis charmé de ...** I'm delighted to ...

charmeur, -euse [ʃaʀmœʀ, -øz] NM/F charmer; **~ de serpents** snake charmer

charnel, le [ʃaʀnɛl] ADJ carnal

charnier [ʃaʀnje] NM mass grave

charnière [ʃaʀnjɛʀ] NF hinge; (*fig*) turning-point

charnu, e [ʃaʀny] ADJ fleshy

charogne [ʃaʀɔɲ] NF carrion *no pl*; (!) bastard (!)

charolais, e [ʃaʀɔlɛ, -ɛz] ADJ of *ou* from the Charolais

charpente [ʃaʀpɑ̃t] NF frame(work); (*fig*) structure, framework; (*carrure*) build, frame

charpenté, e [ʃaʀpɑ̃te] ADJ: **bien** *ou* **solidement ~** (*personne*) well-built; (*texte*) well-constructed

charpenterie [ʃaʀpɑ̃tʀi] NF carpentry

charpentier [ʃaʀpɑ̃tje] NM carpenter

charpie [ʃaʀpi] NF: **en ~** (*fig*) in shreds *ou* ribbons

charretier [ʃaʀtje] NM carter; (*péj: langage, manières*): **de ~** uncouth

charrette [ʃaʀɛt] NF cart

charrier [ʃaʀje] /7/ VT to carry (along); to cart, carry ▸ VI (*fam*) to exaggerate

charrue [ʃaʀy] NF plough (BRIT), plow (US)

charte [ʃaʀt] NF charter

charter [tʃaʀtœʀ] NM (*vol*) charter flight; (*avion*) charter plane

chasse [ʃas] NF hunting; (*au fusil*) shooting; (*poursuite*) chase; (*aussi*: **chasse d'eau**) flush; **la ~ est ouverte** the hunting season is open; **la ~ est fermée** it is the close (BRIT) *ou* closed (US) season; **aller à la ~** to go hunting; **prendre en ~, donner la ~ à** to give chase to; **tirer la ~ (d'eau)** to flush the toilet, pull the chain; **~ aérienne** aerial pursuit; **~ à courre** hunting; **~ à l'homme** manhunt; **~ gardée** private hunting grounds *pl*; **~ sous-marine** underwater fishing

châsse [ʃɑs] NF reliquary, shrine

chassé-croisé [ʃasekʀwaze] (*pl* **chassés-croisés**) NM (*Danse*) chassé-croisé; (*fig*) mix-up (*where people miss each other in turn*)

chasse-neige [ʃasnɛʒ] NM INV snowplough (BRIT), snowplow (US)

chasser [ʃase] /1/ VT to hunt; (*expulser*) to chase away *ou* out, drive away *ou* out; (*dissiper*) to chase *ou* sweep away; to dispel, drive away

chasseur, -euse [ʃasœʀ, -øz] NM/F hunter ▸ NM (*avion*) fighter; (*domestique*) page (boy), messenger (boy); **~ d'images** roving photographer; **~ de têtes** (*fig*) headhunter; **chasseurs alpins** mountain infantry

chassieux, -euse [ʃasjø, -øz] ADJ sticky, gummy

châssis [ʃɑsi] NM (*Auto*) chassis; (*cadre*) frame; (*de jardin*) cold frame

chaste [ʃast] ADJ chaste

chasteté [ʃastəte] NF chastity

chasuble [ʃazybl] NF chasuble; **robe ~** pinafore dress (BRIT), jumper (US)

chat¹ [ʃa] NM cat; **~ sauvage** wildcat

chat² [tʃat] NM (*Internet: salon*) chat room; (: *conversation*) chat

châtaigne [ʃatɛɲ] NF chestnut

châtaignier [ʃatɛɲe] NM chestnut (tree)

châtain [ʃatɛ̃] ADJ INV chestnut (brown); (*personne*) chestnut-haired

château, x [ʃato] NM (*forteresse*) castle; (*résidence royale*) palace; (*manoir*) mansion; **~ d'eau** water tower; **~ fort** stronghold, fortified castle; **~ de sable** sand castle

châtelain, e [ʃatlɛ̃, -ɛn] NM/F lord/lady of the manor ▸ NF (*ceinture*) chatelaine

châtier [ʃatje] /7/ VT to punish, castigate; (*fig: style*) to polish, refine

chatière [ʃatjɛʀ] NF (*porte*) cat flap

châtiment [ʃatimɑ̃] NM punishment, castigation; **~ corporel** corporal punishment

chatoiement [ʃatwamɑ̃] NM shimmer(ing)

chaton [ʃatɔ̃] NM (*Zool*) kitten; (*Bot*) catkin; (*de bague*) bezel; stone

chatouillement [ʃatujmɑ̃] NM (*gén*) tickling; (*dans le nez, la gorge*) tickle

chatouiller [ʃatuje] /1/ VT to tickle; (*l'odorat, le palais*) to titillate

chatouilleux, -euse [ʃatujø, -øz] ADJ ticklish; (*fig*) touchy, over-sensitive

chatoyant, e [ʃatwajɑ̃, -ɑ̃t] ADJ (*reflet, étoffe*) shimmering; (*couleurs*) sparkling

chatoyer [ʃatwaje] /8/ VI to shimmer

châtrer [ʃatʀe] /1/ VT (*mâle*) to castrate; (*femelle*) to spay; (*cheval*) to geld; (*chat, chien*) to doctor (BRIT), fix (US); (*fig*) to mutilate

chatte [ʃat] NF (she-)cat

chatter [tʃate] /1/ VI (*Internet*) to chat

chatterton [ʃatɛʀtɔ̃] NM (*ruban isolant*: Élec) (adhesive) insulating tape

chaud, e [ʃo, -od] ADJ (*gén*) warm; (*très chaud*) hot; (*fig: félicitations*) hearty; (*discussion*) heated ▸ NM: **tenir au ~** to keep in a warm place; **il fait ~** it's warm; it's hot; **manger ~** to have something hot to eat; **avoir ~** to be warm; to be hot; **tenir ~** to keep hot; **ça me tient ~** it keeps me warm; **rester au ~** to stay in the warm

chaudement [ʃodmɑ̃] ADV warmly; (*fig*) hotly

chaudière [ʃodjɛʀ] NF boiler

chaudron [ʃodʀɔ̃] NM cauldron

chaudronnerie [ʃodʀɔnʀi] NF (*usine*) boilerworks; (*activité*) boilermaking; (*boutique*) coppersmith's workshop

chauffage [ʃofaʒ] NM heating; **~ au gaz/à l'électricité/au charbon** gas/electric/solid fuel heating; **~ central** central heating; **~ par le sol** underfloor heating

chauffagiste [ʃofaʒist] NM (*installateur*) heating engineer

chauffant, e [ʃofɑ̃, -ɑ̃t] ADJ: **couverture ~** electric blanket; **plaque ~** hotplate

chauffard [ʃofaʀ] NM (péj) reckless driver; road hog; (: après un accident) hit-and-run driver

chauffe-bain [ʃofbɛ̃] NM = **chauffe-eau**

chauffe-biberon [ʃofbibʀɔ̃] NM (baby's) bottle warmer

chauffe-eau [ʃofo] NM INV water heater

chauffe-plats [ʃofpla] NM INV dish warmer

chauffer [ʃofe] /1/ VT to heat ▸ VI to heat up, warm up; (trop chauffer: moteur) to overheat; **se chauffer** VI (se mettre en train) to warm up; (au soleil) to warm o.s.

chaufferie [ʃofʀi] NF boiler room

chauffeur [ʃofœʀ] NM driver; (privé) chauffeur; **voiture avec/sans ~** chauffeur-driven/ self-drive car; **~ de taxi** taxi driver

chauffeuse [ʃoføz] NF fireside chair

chauler [ʃole] /1/ VT (mur) to whitewash

chaume [ʃom] NM (du toit) thatch; (tiges) stubble

chaumière [ʃomjɛʀ] NF (thatched) cottage

chaussée [ʃose] NF road(way); (digue) causeway

chausse-pied [ʃospje] NM shoe-horn

chausser [ʃose] /1/ VT (bottes, skis) to put on; (enfant) to put shoes on; (soulier) to fit; **~ du 38/42** to take size 38/42; **~ grand/bien** to be big-/ well-fitting; **se chausser** to put one's shoes on

chausse-trappe [ʃostʀap] NF trap

chaussette [ʃosɛt] NF sock

chausseur [ʃosœʀ] NM (marchand) footwear specialist, shoemaker

chausson [ʃosɔ̃] NM slipper; (de bébé) bootee; **~ (aux pommes)** (apple) turnover

chaussure [ʃosyʀ] NF shoe; (commerce): **la ~** the shoe industry ou trade; **chaussures basses** flat shoes; **chaussures montantes** ankle boots; **chaussures de ski** ski boots

chaut [ʃo] VB: **peu me ~** it matters little to me

chauve [ʃov] ADJ bald

chauve-souris [ʃovsuʀi] (pl **chauves-souris**) NF bat

chauvin, e [ʃovɛ̃, -in] ADJ chauvinistic; jingoistic

chauvinisme [ʃovinism] NM chauvinism; jingoism

chaux [ʃo] NF lime; **blanchi à la ~** whitewashed

chavirer [ʃaviʀe] /1/ VI to capsize, overturn

chef [ʃɛf] NM head, leader; (patron) boss; (de cuisine) chef; **au premier ~** extremely, to the nth degree; **de son propre ~** on his ou her own initiative; **général/commandant en ~** general-/commander-in-chief; **~ d'accusation** (Jur) charge, count (of indictment); **~ d'atelier** (shop) foreman; **~ de bureau** head clerk; **~ de clinique** senior hospital lecturer; **~ d'entreprise** company head; **~ d'équipe** team leader; **~ d'état** head of state; **~ de famille** head of the family; **~ de file** (de parti etc) leader; **~ de gare** station master; **~ d'orchestre** conductor (BRIT), leader (US); **~ de rayon** department(al) supervisor; **~ de service** departmental head

chef-d'œuvre [ʃɛdœvʀ] (pl **chefs-d'œuvre**) NM masterpiece

chef-lieu [ʃɛfljø] (pl **chefs-lieux**) NM county town

cheftaine [ʃɛftɛn] NF (guide) captain

cheik, cheikh [ʃɛk] NM sheik

chemin [ʃəmɛ̃] NM path; (itinéraire, direction, trajet) way; **en ~, ~ faisant** on the way; **~ de fer** railway (BRIT), railroad (US); **par ~ de fer** by rail; **les chemins de fer** the railways (BRIT), the railroad (US); **~ de terre** dirt track

cheminée [ʃəmine] NF chimney; (à l'intérieur) chimney piece, fireplace; (de bateau) funnel

cheminement [ʃəminmā] NM progress; course

cheminer [ʃəmine] /1/ VI to walk (along)

cheminot [ʃəmino] NM railwayman (BRIT), railroad worker (US)

chemise [ʃəmiz] NF shirt; (dossier) folder; **~ de nuit** nightdress

chemiserie [ʃəmizʀi] NF (gentlemen's) outfitters'

chemisette [ʃəmizɛt] NF short-sleeved shirt

chemisier [ʃəmizje] NM blouse

chenal, -aux [ʃənal, -o] NM channel

chenapan [ʃənapā] NM (garnement) rascal; (péj: vaurien) rogue

chêne [ʃɛn] NM oak (tree); (bois) oak

chenet [ʃənɛ] NM fire-dog, andiron

chenil [ʃənil] NM kennels pl

chenille [ʃənij] NF (Zool) caterpillar; (Auto) caterpillar track; **véhicule à chenilles** tracked vehicle, caterpillar

chenillette [ʃənijɛt] NF tracked vehicle

cheptel [ʃɛptɛl] NM livestock

chèque [ʃɛk] NM cheque (BRIT), check (US); **faire/toucher un ~** to write/cash a cheque; **par ~** by cheque; **~ barré/sans provision** crossed (BRIT)/bad cheque; **~ en blanc** blank cheque; **~ au porteur** cheque to bearer; **~ postal** post office cheque, ≈ giro cheque (BRIT); **~ de voyage** traveller's cheque

chèque-cadeau [ʃɛkkado] (pl **chèques-cadeaux**) NM gift token

chèque-repas [ʃɛkʀəpɑ] (pl **chèques-repas**), **chèque-restaurant** [ʃɛkʀɛstɔʀɑ̃] (pl **chèques-restaurant**) NM ≈ luncheon voucher

chéquier [ʃekje] NM cheque book (BRIT), checkbook (US)

cher, -ère [ʃɛʀ] ADJ (aimé) dear; (coûteux) expensive, dear ▸ ADV: **coûter/payer ~** to cost/ pay a lot ▸ NF: **la bonne chère** good food; **cela coûte ~** it's expensive, it costs a lot of money; **mon ~, ma chère** my dear

chercher [ʃɛʀʃe] /1/ VT to look for; (gloire etc) to seek; **~ des ennuis/la bagarre** to be looking for trouble/a fight; **aller ~** to go for, go and fetch; **~ à faire** to try to do

chercheur, -euse [ʃɛʀʃœʀ, -øz] NM/F researcher, research worker; **~ de** seeker of; hunter of; **~ d'or** gold digger

chère [ʃɛʀ] ADJ F, NF voir **cher**

chèrement [ʃɛʀmā] ADV dearly

chéri, e [ʃeʀi] ADJ beloved, dear; **(mon) ~** darling

chérir [ʃeʀiʀ] /2/ VT to cherish

cherté [ʃɛʀte] NF: **la ~ de la vie** the high cost of living

chérubin [ʃeʀybɛ̃] NM cherub

chétif, -ive [ʃetif, -iv] ADJ puny, stunted

cheval, -aux [ʃəval, -o] NM horse; (*Auto*):
~ (**vapeur**) horsepower *no pl*; **50 chevaux (au
frein**) 50 brake horsepower, 50 b.h.p.; **10
chevaux (fiscaux**) 10 horsepower (*for tax
purposes*); **faire du ~** to ride; **à ~** on horseback; **à
~ sur** astride, straddling; (*fig*) overlapping;
~ **d'arçons** vaulting horse; ~ **à bascule** rocking
horse; ~ **de bataille** charger; (*fig*) hobby-horse;
~ **de course** race horse; **chevaux de bois** (*des
manèges*) wooden (fairground) horses; (*manège*)
merry-go-round

chevaleresque [ʃəvalʀɛsk] ADJ chivalrous
chevalerie [ʃəvalʀi] NF chivalry; knighthood
chevalet [ʃəvalɛ] NM easel
chevalier [ʃəvalje] NM knight; ~ **servant** escort
chevalière [ʃəvaljɛʀ] NF signet ring
chevalin, e [ʃəvalɛ̃, -in] ADJ of horses, equine;
(*péj*) horsy; **boucherie ~** horse-meat butcher's
cheval-vapeur [ʃəvalvapœʀ] (*pl* **chevaux-
vapeur** [ʃəvo-]) NM *voir* **cheval**
chevauchée [ʃəvoʃe] NF ride; cavalcade
chevauchement [ʃəvoʃmɑ̃] NM overlap
chevaucher [ʃəvoʃe] /1/ VI (*aussi*: **se chevaucher**)
to overlap (each other) ▶ VT to be astride,
straddle
chevaux [ʃəvo] NMPL *voir* **cheval**
chevelu, e [ʃəvly] ADJ with a good head of hair,
hairy (*péj*)
chevelure [ʃəvlyʀ] NF hair *no pl*
chevet [ʃəvɛ] NM: **au ~ de qn** at sb's bedside;
lampe de ~ bedside lamp
cheveu, x [ʃəvø] NM hair ▶ NMPL (*chevelure*) hair
sg; **avoir les ~ courts/en brosse** to have short
hair/a crew cut; **se faire couper les ~** to get *ou*
have one's hair cut; **tiré par les ~** (*histoire*)
far-fetched
cheville [ʃəvij] NF (*Anat*) ankle; (*de bois*) peg;
(*pour enfoncer une vis*) plug; **être en ~ avec qn** to
be in cahoots with sb; ~ **ouvrière** (*fig*) kingpin
chèvre [ʃɛvʀ] NF (she-)goat; **ménager la ~ et le
chou** to try to please everyone
chevreau, x [ʃəvʀo] NM kid
chèvrefeuille [ʃɛvʀəfœj] NM honeysuckle
chevreuil [ʃəvʀœj] NM roe deer *inv*; (*Culin*)
venison
chevron [ʃəvʀɔ̃] NM (*poutre*) rafter; (*motif*)
chevron, v(-shape); **à chevrons** chevron-
patterned; (*petits*) herringbone
chevronné, e [ʃəvʀɔne] ADJ seasoned,
experienced
chevrotant, e [ʃəvʀɔtɑ̃, -ɑ̃t] ADJ quavering
chevroter [ʃəvʀɔte] /1/ VI (*personne, voix*) to
quaver
chevrotine [ʃəvʀɔtin] NF buckshot *no pl*
chewing-gum [ʃwiŋgɔm] NM chewing gum

[MOT-CLÉ]

chez [ʃe] PRÉP **1** (*à la demeure de*) at; (*: direction*) to;
chez qn at/to sb's house *ou* place; **je suis chez
moi** I'm at home; **je rentre chez moi** I'm
going home; **allons chez Nathalie** let's go to
Nathalie's
2 (*+profession*) at; (*: direction*) to; **chez le boulanger/
dentiste** at *ou* to the baker's/dentist's

3 (*dans le caractère, l'œuvre de*) in; **chez les
renards/Racine** in foxes/Racine; **chez ce
poète** in this poet's work; **chez les Français**
among the French; **chez lui, c'est un devoir**
for him, it's a duty; **c'est ce que je préfère
chez lui** that's what I like best about him
4 (*à l'entreprise de*): **il travaille chez Renault** he
works for Renault, he works at Renault('s)
▶ NM INV: **mon chez moi/ton chez toi** *etc* my/
your *etc* home *ou* place

chez-soi [ʃeswa] NM INV home
Chf. cent. ABR (= *chauffage central*) c.h.
chiadé, e [ʃjade] ADJ (*fam: fignolé, soigné*) wicked
chialer [ʃjale] /1/ VI (*fam*) to blubber; **arrête de ~!**
stop blubbering!
chiant, e [ʃjɑ̃, -ɑ̃t] ADJ (!) bloody annoying (!;
BRIT), damn annoying; **qu'est-ce qu'il est ~!**
he's such a bloody pain! (!)
chic [ʃik] ADJ INV chic, smart; (*généreux*) nice,
decent ▶ NM stylishness; **avoir le ~ de** *ou* **pour**
to have the knack of *ou* for; **de ~** *adv* off the cuff;
~! great!, terrific!
chicane [ʃikan] NF (*obstacle*) zigzag; (*querelle*)
squabble
chicaner [ʃikane] /1/ VI (*ergoter*): ~ **sur** to quibble
about
chiche [ʃiʃ] ADJ (*mesquin*) niggardly, mean;
(*pauvre*) meagre (BRIT), meager (US) ▶ EXCL (*en
réponse à un défi*) you're on!; **tu n'es pas ~ de lui
parler!** you wouldn't (dare) speak to her!
chichement [ʃiʃmɑ̃] ADV (*pauvrement*) meagrely
(BRIT), meagerly (US); (*mesquinement*) meanly
chichi [ʃiʃi] NM (*fam*) fuss; **faire des chichis** to
make a fuss
chichis [ʃiʃi] NMPL (*fam*) fuss *sg*
chicorée [ʃikɔʀe] NF (*café*) chicory; (*salade*)
endive; ~ **frisée** curly endive
chicot [ʃiko] NM stump
chien [ʃjɛ̃] NM dog; (*de pistolet*) hammer; **temps
de ~** rotten weather; **vie de ~** dog's life; **couché
en ~ de fusil** curled up; ~ **d'aveugle** guide dog;
~ **de chasse** gun dog; ~ **de garde** guard dog;
~ **policier** police dog; ~ **de race** pedigree dog;
~ **de traîneau** husky
chiendent [ʃjɛ̃dɑ̃] NM couch grass
chien-loup [ʃjɛ̃lu] (*pl* **chiens-loups**) NM
wolfhound
chienne [ʃjɛn] NF (she-)dog, bitch
chier [ʃje] /7/ VI (!) to crap (!), shit (!); **faire ~ qn**
(*importuner*) to bug sb; (*causer des ennuis à*) to piss
sb around (!); **se faire ~** (*s'ennuyer*) to be bored
rigid
chiffe [ʃif] NF: **il est mou comme une ~, c'est
une ~ molle** he's spineless *ou* wet
chiffon [ʃifɔ̃] NM (*piece of*) rag
chiffonné, e [ʃifɔne] ADJ (*fatigué: visage*)
worn-looking
chiffonner [ʃifɔne] /1/ VT to crumple, crease;
(*tracasser*) to concern
chiffonnier [ʃifɔnje] NM ragman, rag-and-bone
man; (*meuble*) chiffonier
chiffrable [ʃifʀabl] ADJ numerable
chiffre [ʃifʀ] NM (*représentant un nombre*) figure;

numeral; *(montant, total)* total, sum; *(d'un code)* code, cipher; **chiffres romains/arabes** Roman/Arabic figures *ou* numerals; **en chiffres ronds** in round figures; **écrire un nombre en chiffres** to write a number in figures; ~ **d'affaires** turnover; ~ **de ventes** sales figures

chiffrer [ʃifʀe] **/1/** ᴠᴛ *(dépense)* to put a figure to, assess; *(message)* to (en)code, cipher ▸ ᴠɪ: ~ **à, se** ~ **à** to add up to

chignole [ʃiɲɔl] ɴꜰ drill

chignon [ʃiɲɔ̃] ɴᴍ chignon, bun

chiite [ʃiit] ᴀᴅᴊ Shiite ▸ ɴᴍꜰ: **C**~ Shiite

Chili [ʃili] ɴᴍ: **le** ~ Chile

chilien, ne [ʃiljɛ̃, -ɛn] ᴀᴅᴊ Chilean ▸ ɴᴍ/ꜰ: **C**~, **ne** Chilean

chimère [ʃimɛʀ] ɴꜰ *(wild)* dream, pipe dream, idle fancy

chimérique [ʃimeʀik] ᴀᴅᴊ *(utopique)* fanciful

chimie [ʃimi] ɴꜰ chemistry

chimio [ʃimjo], **chimiothérapie** [ʃimjɔteʀapi] ɴꜰ chemotherapy

chimiothérapie [ʃimjɔteʀapi] ɴꜰ chemotherapy

chimique [ʃimik] ᴀᴅᴊ chemical; **produits chimiques** chemicals

chimiste [ʃimist] ɴᴍꜰ chemist

chimpanzé [ʃɛ̃pɑ̃ze] ɴᴍ chimpanzee

chinchilla [ʃɛ̃ʃila] ɴᴍ chinchilla

Chine [ʃin] ɴꜰ: **la** ~ China; **la** ~ **libre, la république de** ~ the Republic of China, Nationalist China *(Taiwan)*

chine [ʃin] ɴᴍ rice paper; *(porcelaine)* china *(vase)*

chiné, e [ʃine] ᴀᴅᴊ flecked

chinois, e [ʃinwa, -waz] ᴀᴅᴊ Chinese; *(fig: péj)* pernickety, fussy ▸ ɴᴍ *(Ling)* Chinese ▸ ɴᴍ/ꜰ: **C**~, **e** Chinese

chinoiserie [ʃinwazʀi] ɴꜰ, **chinoiseries** ɴꜰᴘʟ *(péj)* red tape, fuss

chiot [ʃjo] ɴᴍ pup(py)

chiper [ʃipe] **/1/** ᴠᴛ *(fam)* to pinch

chipie [ʃipi] ɴꜰ shrew

chipolata [ʃipɔlata] ɴꜰ chipolata

chipoter [ʃipɔte] **/1/** ᴠɪ *(manger)* to nibble; *(ergoter)* to quibble, haggle

chips [ʃips] ɴꜰᴘʟ *(aussi:* **pommes chips**) crisps (ʙʀɪᴛ), (potato) chips (ᴜꜱ)

chique [ʃik] ɴꜰ quid, chew

chiquenaude [ʃiknod] ɴꜰ flick, flip

chiquer [ʃike] **/1/** ᴠɪ to chew tobacco

chiromancie [kiʀɔmɑ̃si] ɴꜰ palmistry

chiromancien, ne [kiʀɔmɑ̃sjɛ̃, -ɛn] ɴᴍ/ꜰ palmist

chiropracteur [kiʀɔpʀaktœʀ] ɴᴍ, **chiropraticien, ne** [kiʀɔpʀatisjɛ̃, -ɛn] ɴᴍ/ꜰ chiropractor

chirurgical, e, -aux [ʃiʀyʀʒikal, -o] ᴀᴅᴊ surgical

chirurgie [ʃiʀyʀʒi] ɴꜰ surgery; ~ **esthétique** cosmetic *ou* plastic surgery

chirurgien, ne [ʃiʀyʀʒjɛ̃] ɴᴍ/ꜰ surgeon; ~ **dentiste** dental surgeon

chiure [ʃjyʀ] ɴꜰ: **chiures de mouche** fly specks

ch.-l. ᴀʙʀ = **chef-lieu**

chlore [klɔʀ] ɴᴍ chlorine

chloroforme [klɔʀɔfɔʀm] ɴᴍ chloroform

chlorophylle [klɔʀɔfil] ɴꜰ chlorophyll

chlorure [klɔʀyʀ] ɴᴍ chloride

choc [ʃɔk] ɴᴍ *(heurt)* impact; shock; *(collision)* crash; *(moral)* shock; *(affrontement)* clash ▸ ᴀᴅᴊ: **prix** ~ amazing *ou* incredible price/prices; **de** ~ *(troupe, traitement)* shock *cpd*; *(patron etc)* high-powered; ~ **opératoire/nerveux** post-operative/nervous shock; ~ **en retour** return shock; *(fig)* backlash

chocolat [ʃɔkɔla] ɴᴍ chocolate; *(boisson)* (hot) chocolate; ~ **chaud** hot chocolate; ~ **à cuire** cooking chocolate; ~ **au lait** milk chocolate; ~ **en poudre** drinking chocolate

chocolaté, e [ʃɔkɔlate] ᴀᴅᴊ chocolate *cpd*, chocolate-flavoured

chocolaterie [ʃɔkɔlatʀi] ɴꜰ *(fabrique)* chocolate factory

chocolatier, -ière [ʃɔkɔlatje, -jɛʀ] ɴᴍ/ꜰ chocolate maker

chœur [kœʀ] ɴᴍ *(chorale)* choir; *(Opéra, Théât)* chorus; *(Archit)* choir, chancel; **en** ~ in chorus

choir [ʃwaʀ] ᴠɪ to fall

choisi, e [ʃwazi] ᴀᴅᴊ *(de premier choix)* carefully chosen; select; **textes choisis** selected writings

choisir [ʃwaziʀ] **/2/** ᴠᴛ to choose; *(entre plusieurs)* to choose, select; ~ **de faire qch** to choose *ou* opt to do sth

choix [ʃwa] ɴᴍ choice; selection; **avoir le** ~ to have the choice; **je n'avais pas le** ~ I had no choice; **de premier** ~ *(Comm)* class *ou* grade one; **de** ~ choice *cpd*, selected; **au** ~ as you wish *ou* prefer; **de mon/son** ~ of my/his *ou* her choosing

choléra [kɔleʀa] ɴᴍ cholera

cholestérol [kɔlesteʀɔl] ɴᴍ cholesterol

chômage [ʃomaʒ] ɴᴍ unemployment; **mettre au** ~ to make redundant, put out of work; **être au** ~ to be unemployed *ou* out of work; ~ **partiel** short-time working; ~ **structurel** structural unemployment; ~ **technique** lay-offs *pl*

chômer [ʃome] **/1/** ᴠɪ to be unemployed, be idle; **jour chômé** public holiday

chômeur, -euse [ʃomœʀ, -øz] ɴᴍ/ꜰ unemployed person, person out of work

chope [ʃɔp] ɴꜰ tankard

choper [ʃɔpe] **/1/** *(fam)* ᴠᴛ *(objet, maladie)* to catch

choquant, e [ʃɔkɑ̃, -ɑ̃t] ᴀᴅᴊ shocking

choquer [ʃɔke] **/1/** ᴠᴛ *(offenser)* to shock; *(commotionner)* to shake (up)

choral, e [kɔʀal] ᴀᴅᴊ choral ▸ ɴꜰ choral society, choir

chorale [kɔʀal] ɴꜰ choir

chorégraphe [kɔʀegʀaf] ɴᴍꜰ choreographer

chorégraphie [kɔʀegʀafi] ɴꜰ choreography

choriste [kɔʀist] ɴᴍꜰ choir member; *(Opéra)* chorus member

chorus [kɔʀys] ɴᴍ: **faire** ~ **(avec)** to voice one's agreement (with)

chose [ʃoz] ɴꜰ thing ▸ ɴᴍ *(fam: machin)* thingamajig ▸ ᴀᴅᴊ ɪɴᴠ: **être/se sentir tout** ~ *(bizarre)* to be/feel a bit odd; *(malade)* to be/feel out of sorts; **dire bien des choses à qn** to give sb's regards to sb; **parler de ~(s) et d'autre(s)** to talk about one thing and another; **c'est peu de ~** it's nothing much

chou, x [ʃu] NM cabbage ▸ ADJ INV cute; **mon petit ~** (my) sweetheart; **faire ~ blanc** to draw a blank; **feuille de ~** (fig: journal) rag; **~ à la crème** cream bun (made of choux pastry); **~ de Bruxelles** Brussels sprout

choucas [ʃuka] NM jackdaw

chouchou, te [ʃuʃu, -ut] NM/F (Scol) teacher's pet

chouchouter [ʃuʃute] /1/ VT to pet

choucroute [ʃukʀut] NF sauerkraut; **~ garnie** sauerkraut with cooked meats and potatoes

chouette [ʃwɛt] NF owl ▸ ADJ (fam) great, smashing

chou-fleur [ʃuflœʀ] (pl **choux-fleurs**) NM cauliflower

chou-rave [ʃuʀav] (pl **choux-raves**) NM kohlrabi

choyer [ʃwaje] /8/ VT to cherish; to pamper

CHR SIGLE M = **Centre hospitalier régional**

chrétien, ne [kʀetjɛ̃, -ɛn] ADJ, NM/F Christian

chrétiennement [kʀetjɛnmɑ̃] ADV in a Christian way ou spirit

chrétienté [kʀetjɛ̃te] NF Christendom

Christ [kʀist] NM: **le ~** Christ; **christ** (crucifix etc) figure of Christ; **Jésus ~** Jesus Christ

christianiser [kʀistjanize] /1/ VT to convert to Christianity

christianisme [kʀistjanism] NM Christianity

chromatique [kʀɔmatik] ADJ chromatic

chrome [kʀom] NM chromium; (revêtement) chrome, chromium

chromé, e [kʀome] ADJ chrome-plated, chromium-plated

chromosome [kʀɔmozom] NM chromosome

chronique [kʀɔnik] ADJ chronic ▸ NF (de journal) column, page; (historique) chronicle; (Radio, TV): **la ~ sportive/théâtrale** the sports/theatre review; **la ~ locale** local news and gossip

chroniqueur [kʀɔnikœʀ] NM columnist; chronicler

chrono [kʀɔno] NM (fam) = **chronomètre**

chronologie [kʀɔnɔlɔʒi] NF chronology

chronologique [kʀɔnɔlɔʒik] ADJ chronological

chronologiquement [kʀɔnɔlɔʒikmɑ̃] ADV chronologically

chronomètre [kʀɔnɔmɛtʀ] NM stopwatch

chronométrer [kʀɔnɔmetʀe] /6/ VT to time

chronométreur [kʀɔnɔmetʀœʀ] NM timekeeper

chrysalide [kʀizalid] NF chrysalis

chrysanthème [kʀizɑ̃tɛm] NM chrysanthemum

> Chrysanthemums are strongly associated with funerals in France, and therefore should not be given as gifts.

CHU SIGLE M (= Centre hospitalo-universitaire) ≈ (teaching) hospital

chu, e [ʃy] PP de **choir**

chuchotement [ʃyʃɔtmɑ̃] NM whisper

chuchoter [ʃyʃɔte] /1/ VT, VI to whisper

chuintement [ʃɥɛ̃tmɑ̃] NM hiss

chuinter [ʃɥɛ̃te] /1/ VI to hiss

chut [ʃyt] EXCL sh! ▸ VB [ʃy] voir **choir**

chute [ʃyt] NF fall; (de bois, papier: déchet) scrap; **la ~ des cheveux** hair loss; **faire une ~ (de 10 m)** to fall (10 m); **chutes de pluie/neige** rain/ snowfalls; **~ (d'eau)** waterfall; **~ du jour** nightfall; **~ libre** free fall; **~ des reins** small of the back

Chypre [ʃipʀ] NMF Cyprus

chypriote [ʃipʀiɔt] ADJ, NMF = **cypriote**

-ci, ci- [si] ADV voir **par**; **ci-contre**; **ci-joint** etc ▸ ADJ DÉM: **ce garçon~/-là** this/that boy; **ces femmes~/-là** these/those women

CIA SIGLE F CIA

cial ABR = **commercial**

ciao [tʃao] EXCL (fam) (bye-)bye

ci-après [siapʀɛ] ADV hereafter

cibiste [sibist] NM CB enthusiast

cible [sibl] NF target

cibler [sible] /1/ VT to target

ciboire [sibwaʀ] NM ciborium (vessel)

ciboule [sibul] NF (large) chive

ciboulette [sibulɛt] NF (small) chive

ciboulot [sibulo] NM (fam) head, nut; **il n'a rien dans le ~** he's got nothing between his ears

cicatrice [sikatʀis] NF scar

cicatriser [sikatʀize] /1/ VT to heal; **se cicatriser** to heal (up), form a scar

ci-contre [sikɔ̃tʀ] ADV opposite

CICR SIGLE M (= Comité international de la Croix-Rouge) ICRC

ci-dessous [sidəsu] ADV below

ci-dessus [sidəsy] ADV above

ci-devant [sidəvɑ̃] NMF INV aristocrat who lost his/ her title in the French Revolution

CIDJ SIGLE M (= Centre d'information et de documentation de la jeunesse) careers advisory service

cidre [sidʀ] NM cider

cidrerie [sidʀəʀi] NF cider factory

Cie ABR (= compagnie) Co

ciel [sjɛl] NM sky; (Rel) heaven; **ciels** NMPL (Peinture etc) skies; **cieux** NMPL sky sg, skies; (Rel) heaven sg; **à ~ ouvert** open-air; (mine) opencast; **tomber du ~** (arriver à l'improviste) to appear out of the blue; (être stupéfait) to be unable to believe one's eyes; **C~!** good heavens!; **~ de lit** canopy

cierge [sjɛʀʒ] NM candle; **~ pascal** Easter candle

cieux [sjø] NMPL voir **ciel**

cigale [sigal] NF cicada

cigare [sigaʀ] NM cigar

cigarette [sigaʀɛt] NF cigarette; **~ (à) bout filtre** filter cigarette

ci-gît [siʒi] ADV here lies

cigogne [sigɔɲ] NF stork

ciguë [sigy] NF hemlock

ci-inclus, e [siɛ̃kly, -yz] ADJ, ADV enclosed

ci-joint, e [siʒwɛ̃, -ɛ̃t] ADJ, ADV enclosed; (to email) attached; **veuillez trouver ~** please find enclosed ou attached

cil [sil] NM (eye)lash

ciller [sije] /1/ VI to blink

cimaise [simɛz] NF picture rail

cime [sim] NF top; (montagne) peak

ciment [simɑ̃] NM cement; ~ **armé** reinforced concrete

cimenter [simɑ̃te] /1/ VT to cement

cimenterie [simɑ̃tʀi] NF cement works sg

cimetière [simtjɛʀ] NM cemetery; (d'église) churchyard; ~ **de voitures** scrapyard

cinéaste [sineast] NMF film-maker

ciné-club [sineklœb] NM film club; film society

cinéma [sinema] NM cinema; **aller au** ~ to go to the cinema ou pictures ou movies; ~ **d'animation** cartoon (film)

cinémascope® [sinemaskɔp] NM Cinemascope®

cinémathèque [sinematɛk] NF film archives pl ou library

cinématographie [sinematɔgʀafi] NF cinematography

cinématographique [sinematɔgʀafik] ADJ film cpd, cinema cpd

cinéphile [sinefil] NMF film buff

cinérama® [sinerama] NM: **en** ~ in Cinerama®

cinétique [sinetik] ADJ kinetic

cingalais, cinghalais, e [sɛ̃galɛ, -ɛz] ADJ Sin(g)halese

cinglant, e [sɛ̃glɑ̃, -ɑ̃t] ADJ (propos, ironie) scathing, biting; (échec) crushing

cinglé, e [sɛ̃gle] ADJ (fam) crazy

cingler [sɛ̃gle] /1/ VT to lash; (fig) to sting ▶ VI (Navig): ~ **vers** to make ou head for

cinq [sɛ̃k] NUM five

cinquantaine [sɛ̃kɑ̃tɛn] NF: **une** ~ **(de)** about fifty; **avoir la** ~ (âge) to be around fifty

cinquante [sɛ̃kɑ̃t] NUM fifty

cinquantenaire [sɛ̃kɑ̃tnɛʀ] ADJ, NMF fifty-year-old

cinquantième [sɛ̃kɑ̃tjɛm] NUM fiftieth

cinquième [sɛ̃kjɛm] NUM fifth ▶ NF (Scol) year 8 (BRIT), seventh grade (US)

cinquièmement [sɛ̃kjɛmmɑ̃] ADV fifthly

cintre [sɛ̃tʀ] NM coat-hanger; (Archit) arch; **plein** ~ semicircular arch

cintré, e [sɛ̃tʀe] ADJ curved; (chemise) fitted, slim-fitting

CIO SIGLE M (= Comité international olympique) IOC (= International Olympic Committee); (= centre d'information et d'orientation) careers advisory centre

cirage [siʀaʒ] NM (shoe) polish

circoncis, e [siʀkɔ̃si, -iz] ADJ circumcised

circoncision [siʀkɔ̃sizjɔ̃] NF circumcision

circonférence [siʀkɔ̃feʀɑ̃s] NF circumference

circonflexe [siʀkɔ̃flɛks] ADJ: **accent** ~ circumflex accent

circonlocution [siʀkɔ̃lɔkysjɔ̃] NF circumlocution

circonscription [siʀkɔ̃skʀipsjɔ̃] NF district; ~ **électorale** (d'un député) constituency; ~ **militaire** military area

circonscrire [siʀkɔ̃skʀiʀ] /39/ VT to define, delimit; (incendie) to contain; (propriété) to mark out; (sujet) to define

circonspect, e [siʀkɔ̃spɛkt] ADJ circumspect, cautious

circonspection [siʀkɔ̃spɛksjɔ̃] NF circumspection, caution

circonstance [siʀkɔ̃stɑ̃s] NF circumstance; (occasion) occasion; **œuvre de** ~ occasional work; **air de** ~ fitting air; **tête de** ~ appropriate demeanour (BRIT) ou demeanor (US); **circonstances atténuantes** mitigating circumstances

circonstancié, e [siʀkɔ̃stɑ̃sje] ADJ detailed

circonstanciel, le [siʀkɔ̃stɑ̃sjɛl] ADJ: **complément/proposition ~(le)** adverbial phrase/clause

circonvenir [siʀkɔ̃vniʀ] /22/ VT to circumvent

circonvolutions [siʀkɔ̃vɔlysjɔ̃] NFPL twists, convolutions

circuit [siʀkɥi] NM (trajet) tour, (round) trip; (Élec, Tech) circuit; ~ **automobile** motor circuit; ~ **de distribution** distribution network; ~ **fermé** closed circuit; ~ **intégré** integrated circuit

circulaire [siʀkylɛʀ] ADJ, NF circular

circulation [siʀkylasjɔ̃] NF circulation; (Auto): **la** ~ (the) traffic; **bonne/mauvaise** ~ good/bad circulation; **mettre en** ~ to put into circulation

circulatoire [siʀkylatwaʀ] ADJ: **avoir des troubles circulatoires** to have problems with one's circulation

circuler [siʀkyle] /1/ VI (véhicules) to drive (along); (passants) to walk along; (train etc) to run; (sang, devises) to circulate; **faire** ~ (nouvelle) to spread (about), circulate; (badauds) to move on

cire [siʀ] NF wax; ~ **à cacheter** sealing wax

ciré [siʀe] NM oilskin

cirer [siʀe] /1/ VT to wax, polish

cireur [siʀœʀ] NM shoeshine boy

cireuse [siʀøz] NF floor polisher

cireux, -euse [siʀø, -øz] ADJ (fig: teint) sallow, waxen

cirque [siʀk] NM circus; (arène) amphitheatre (BRIT), amphitheater (US); (Géo) cirque; (fig: désordre) chaos, bedlam; (: chichis) carry-on; **quel** ~! what a carry-on!

cirrhose [siʀoz] NF: ~ **du foie** cirrhosis of the liver

cisaille [sizaj] NF, **cisailles** NFPL (gardening) shears pl

cisailler [sizaje] /1/ VT to clip

ciseau, x [sizo] NM: ~ **(à bois)** chisel ▶ NMPL (paire de ciseaux) (pair of) scissors; **sauter en** ~ to do a scissors jump; ~ **à froid** cold chisel

ciseler [sizle] /5/ VT to chisel, carve

ciselure [sizlyʀ] NF engraving; (bois) carving

Cisjordanie [sisʒɔʀdani] NF: **la** ~ the West Bank (of Jordan)

citadelle [sitadɛl] NF citadel

citadin, e [sitadɛ̃, -in] NM/F city dweller ▶ ADJ town cpd, city cpd, urban

citation [sitasjɔ̃] NF (d'auteur) quotation; (Jur) summons sg; (Mil: récompense) mention

cité [site] NF town; (plus grande) city; ~ **ouvrière** (workers') housing estate; ~ **universitaire** students' residences pl

cité-dortoir [sitedɔʀtwaʀ] NF (pl **cités-dortoirs**) NF dormitory town

cité-jardin [sitezaʀdɛ̃] (pl **cités-jardins**) NF garden city

citer [site] /1/ VT (un auteur) to quote (from); (nommer) to name; (Jur) to summon; **~ (en exemple)** (personne) to hold up (as an example); **je ne veux ~ personne** I don't want to name names

citerne [sitɛʀn] NF tank

cithare [sitaʀ] NF zither

citoyen, ne [sitwajɛ̃, -ɛn] NM/F citizen

citoyenneté [sitwajɛnte] NF citizenship

citrique [sitʀik] ADJ: **acide ~** citric acid

citron [sitʀɔ̃] NM lemon; **~ pressé** (fresh) lemon juice; **~ vert** lime

citronnade [sitʀɔnad] NF still lemonade

citronné, e [sitʀɔne] ADJ (boisson) lemon-flavoured (BRIT) ou -flavored (US); (eau de toilette) lemon-scented

citronnelle [sitʀɔnɛl] NF citronella

citronnier [sitʀɔnje] NM lemon tree

citrouille [sitʀuj] NF pumpkin

cive [siv] NF chive

civet [sivɛ] NM stew; **~ de lièvre** jugged hare; **~ de lapin** rabbit stew

civette [sivɛt] NF (Bot) chives pl; (Zool) civet (cat)

civière [sivjɛʀ] NF stretcher

civil, e [sivil] ADJ (Jur, Admin, poli) civil; (non militaire) civilian ▶ NM civilian; **en ~** in civilian clothes; **dans le ~** in civilian life

civilement [sivilmɑ̃] ADV (poliment) civilly; **se marier ~** to have a civil wedding

civilisation [sivilizasjɔ̃] NF civilization

civilisé, e [sivilize] ADJ civilized

civiliser [sivilize] /1/ VT to civilize

civilité [sivilite] NF civility; **présenter ses civilités** to present one's compliments

civique [sivik] ADJ civic; **instruction ~** (Scol) civics sg

civisme [sivism] NM public-spiritedness

cl. ABR (= centilitre) cl

clafoutis [klafuti] NM batter pudding (containing fruit)

claie [klɛ] NF grid, riddle

clair, e [klɛʀ] ADJ light; (chambre) light, bright; (eau, son, fig) clear ▶ ADV: **voir ~** to see clearly ▶ NM: **mettre au ~** (notes etc) to tidy up; **tirer qch au ~** to clear sth up, clarify sth; **bleu ~** light blue; **pour être ~** so as to make it plain; **y voir ~** (comprendre) to understand, see; **le plus ~ de son temps/argent** the better part of his time/money; **en ~** (non codé) in clear; **~ de lune** moonlight

claire [klɛʀ] NF: **(huître de) ~** fattened oyster

clairement [klɛʀmɑ̃] ADV clearly

claire-voie [klɛʀvwa]: **à ~** adj letting the light through; openwork cpd

clairière [klɛʀjɛʀ] NF clearing

clair-obscur [klɛʀɔpskyʀ] (pl **clairs-obscurs**) NM half-light; (fig) uncertainty

clairon [klɛʀɔ̃] NM bugle

claironner [klɛʀɔne] /1/ VT (fig) to trumpet, shout from the rooftops

clairsemé, e [klɛʀsəme] ADJ sparse

clairvoyance [klɛʀvwajɑ̃s] NF clear-sightedness

clairvoyant, e [klɛʀvwajɑ̃, -ɑ̃t] ADJ perceptive, clear-sighted

clam [klam] NM (Zool) clam

clamer [klame] /1/ VT to proclaim

clameur [klamœʀ] NF clamour (BRIT), clamor (US)

clan [klɑ̃] NM clan

clandestin, e [klɑ̃dɛstɛ̃, -in] ADJ clandestine, covert; (Pol) underground, clandestine; (travailleur, immigration) illegal; **passager ~** stowaway

clandestinement [klɑ̃dɛstinmɑ̃] ADV secretly; **s'embarquer ~** to stow away

clandestinité [klɑ̃dɛstinite] NF: **dans la ~** (en secret) under cover; (en se cachant: vivre) underground; (entrer dans la ~) to go underground

clapet [klapɛ] NM (Tech) valve

clapier [klapje] NM (rabbit) hutch

clapotement [klapɔtmɑ̃] NM lap(ping)

clapoter [klapɔte] /1/ VI to lap

clapotis [klapɔti] NM lap(ping)

claquage [klakaʒ] NM pulled ou strained muscle

claque [klak] NF (gifle) slap; (Théât) claque ▶ NM (chapeau) opera hat

claquement [klakmɑ̃] NM (de porte: bruit répété) banging; (: bruit isolé) slam

claquemurer [klakmyʀe] /1/: **se claquemurer** VI to shut o.s. away, closet o.s.

claquer [klake] /1/ VI (drapeau) to flap; (porte) to bang, slam; (fam: mourir) to snuff it; (coup de feu) to ring out ▶ VT (porte) to slam, bang; (doigts) to snap; (fam: dépenser) to blow; **elle claquait des dents** her teeth were chattering; **être claqué** (fam) to be dead tired; **se ~ un muscle** to pull ou strain a muscle

claquettes [klakɛt] NFPL tap-dancing sg; (chaussures) flip-flops

clarification [klaʀifikasjɔ̃] NF (fig) clarification

clarifier [klaʀifje] /7/ VT (fig) to clarify

clarinette [klaʀinɛt] NF clarinet

clarinettiste [klaʀinetist] NMF clarinettist

clarté [klaʀte] NF lightness; brightness; (d'un son, de l'eau) clearness; (d'une explication) clarity

classe [klas] NF class; (Scol: local) class(room); (: leçon, élèves) class, form; **1ère/2ème ~** 1st/2nd class; **un (soldat de) deuxième ~** (Mil: armée de terre) ≈ private (soldier); (: armée de l'air) ≈ aircraftman (BRIT), ≈ airman basic (US); **de ~** luxury cpd; **faire ses classes** (Mil) to do one's (recruit's) training; **faire la ~** (Scol) to be a ou the teacher; to teach; **aller en ~** to go to school; **aller en ~ verte/de neige/de mer** to go to the countryside/skiing/to the seaside with the school; **~ préparatoire** class which prepares students for the Grandes Écoles entry exams; see note; **~ sociale** social class; **~ touriste** economy class

> Classes préparatoires are the two years of intensive study which coach students for the competitive entry examinations to the grandes écoles. These extremely demanding courses follow the baccalauréat and are usually done at a lycée. Schools which provide such classes are more highly regarded than those which do not.

classement [klɑsmɑ̃] NM classifying; filing; grading; closing; (rang: Scol) place; (: Sport) placing; (liste: Scol) class list (in order of merit); (: Sport) placings pl; **premier au ~ général** (Sport) first overall

classer [klɑse] /1/ VT (idées, livres) to classify; (papiers) to file; (candidat, concurrent) to grade; (personne: juger: péj) to rate; (Jur: affaire) to close; **se ~ premier/dernier** to come first/last; (Sport) to finish first/last

classeur [klɑsœʀ] NM (cahier) file; (meuble) filing cabinet; **~ à feuillets mobiles** ring binder

classification [klɑsifikɑsjɔ̃] NF classification

classifier [klɑsifje] /7/ VT to classify

classique [klɑsik] ADJ (sobre: coupe etc) classic(al), classical; (habituel) standard, classic ▶ NM classic; classical author; **études classiques** classical studies, classics

claudication [klodikɑsjɔ̃] NF limp

clause [kloz] NF clause

claustrer [klostʀe] /1/ VT to confine

claustrophobie [klostʀɔfɔbi] NF claustrophobia

clavecin [klav(ə)sɛ̃] NM harpsichord

claveciniste [klavsinist] NMF harpsichordist

clavicule [klavikyl] NF clavicle, collarbone

clavier [klavje] NM keyboard

clé, clef [kle] NF key; (Mus) clef; (de mécanicien) spanner (BRIT), wrench (US) ▶ ADJ INV: **problème/position** ~ key problem/position; **mettre sous** ~ to place under lock and key; **prendre la ~ des champs** to run away, make off; **prix clés en main** (d'une voiture) on-the-road price; (d'un appartement) price with immediate entry; **~ de sol/de fa/d'ut** treble/bass/alto clef; **livre/film** etc **à** ~ book/film etc in which real people are depicted under fictitious names; **à la** ~ (à la fin) at the end of it all; **~ anglaise** = **clé à molette**; **~ de contact** ignition key; **~ à molette** adjustable spanner (BRIT) ou wrench, monkey wrench; **~ USB** (Inform) USB key, flash drive; **~ de voûte** keystone

clématite [klematit] NF clematis

clémence [klemɑ̃s] NF mildness; leniency

clément, e [klemɑ̃, -ɑ̃t] ADJ (temps) mild; (indulgent) lenient

clémentine [klemɑ̃tin] NF (Bot) clementine

clenche [klɑ̃ʃ] NF latch

cleptomane [klɛptɔman] NMF = **kleptomane**

clerc [klɛʀ] NM: **~ de notaire** ou **d'avoué** lawyer's clerk

clergé [klɛʀʒe] NM clergy

clérical, e, -aux [kleʀikal, -o] ADJ clerical

cliché [kliʃe] NM (fig) cliché; (Photo) negative; print; (Typo) (printing) plate; (Ling) cliché

client, e [klijɑ̃, -ɑ̃t] NM/F (acheteur) customer, client; (d'hôtel) guest, patron; (du docteur) patient; (de l'avocat) client

clientèle [klijɑ̃tɛl] NF (du magasin) customers pl, clientèle; (du docteur, de l'avocat) practice; **accorder sa** ~ **à** to give one's custom to; **retirer sa** ~ **à** to take one's business away from

cligner [kliɲe] /1/ VI: **~ des yeux** to blink (one's eyes); **~ de l'œil** to wink

clignotant [kliɲɔtɑ̃] NM (Auto) indicator

clignoter [kliɲɔte] /1/ VI (étoiles etc) to twinkle; (lumière: à intervalles réguliers) to flash; (: vaciller) to flicker; (yeux) to blink

climat [klima] NM climate

climatique [klimatik] ADJ climatic

climatisation [klimatizɑsjɔ̃] NF air conditioning

climatisé, e [klimatize] ADJ air-conditioned

climatiseur [klimatizœʀ] NM air conditioner

clin d'œil [klɛ̃dœj] NM wink; **en un** ~ in a flash

clinique [klinik] ADJ clinical ▶ NF nursing home, (private) clinic

clinquant, e [klɛ̃kɑ̃, -ɑ̃t] ADJ flashy

clip [klip] NM (pince) clip; (boucle d'oreille) clip-on; **(vidéo)** ~ pop (ou promotional) video

clique [klik] NF (péj: bande) clique, set; **prendre ses cliques et ses claques** to pack one's bags

cliquer [klike] /1/ VI (Inform) to click; **~ deux fois** to double-click ▶ VT to click; **~ sur** to click on

cliqueter [klikte] /4/ VI to clash; (ferraille, clefs, monnaie) to jangle, jingle; (verres) to chink

cliquetis [klikti] NM jangle; jingle; chink

clitoris [klitɔʀis] NM clitoris

clivage [klivaʒ] NM cleavage; (fig) rift, split

cloaque [klɔak] NM (fig) cesspit

clochard, e [klɔʃaʀ, -aʀd] NM/F tramp

cloche [klɔʃ] NF (d'église) bell; (fam) clot; (chapeau) cloche (hat); **~ à fromage** cheese-cover

cloche-pied [klɔʃpje]: **à** ~ adv on one leg, hopping (along)

clocher [klɔʃe] /1/ NM church tower; (en pointe) steeple ▶ VI (fam) to be ou go wrong; **de** ~ (péj) parochial

clocheton [klɔʃtɔ̃] NM pinnacle

clochette [klɔʃɛt] NF bell

clodo [klɔdo] NM (fam: = clochard) tramp

cloison [klwazɔ̃] NF partition (wall); **~ étanche** (fig) impenetrable barrier, brick wall (fig)

cloisonner [klwazɔne] /1/ VT to partition (off), to divide up; (fig) to compartmentalize

cloître [klwatʀ] NM cloister

cloîtrer [klwatʀe] /1/: **se cloîtrer** VT to shut o.s. away; (Rel) to enter a convent ou monastery

clonage [klɔnaʒ] NM cloning

clone [klɔn] NM clone

cloner [klɔne] /1/ VT to clone

clope [klɔp] (fam) NM ou F fag (BRIT), cigarette

clopin-clopant [klɔpɛ̃klɔpɑ̃] ADV hobbling along; (fig) so-so

clopiner [klɔpine] /1/ VI to hobble along

cloporte [klɔpɔʀt] NM woodlouse

cloque [klɔk] NF blister

cloqué, e [klɔke] ADJ: **étoffe** ~ seersucker

cloquer [klɔke] /1/ VI (peau, peinture) to blister

clore [klɔʀ] /45/ VT to close; **~ une session** (Inform) to log out

clos, e [klo, -oz] PP de **clore** ▶ ADJ voir **maison**; **huis**; **vase** ▶ NM (enclosed) field

clôt [klo] VB voir **clore**

clôture [klotyʀ] NF closure, closing; (barrière) enclosure, fence

clôturer [klotyʀe] /1/ VT (terrain) to enclose, close off; (festival, débats) to close

clou [klu] NM nail; (Méd) boil; **clous** NMPL
= **passage clouté**; **pneus à clous** studded tyres;
le ~ du spectacle the highlight of the show;
~ de girofle clove

cloud computing M cloud computing

clouer [klue] /1/ VT to nail down (ou up); (fig):
~ sur/contre to pin to/against

cloué, e [klue] ADJ studded

clown [klun] NM clown; **faire le ~** (fig) to clown
(about), play the fool

clownerie [klunri] NF clowning no pl; **faire des
clowneries** to clown around

club [klœb] NM club

CM SIGLE F = **chambre des métiers** ▶ SIGLE M
= **conseil municipal**; (Scol) = **cours moyen**

cm. ABR (= centimètre) cm

CMU SIGLE F (= couverture maladie universelle) system
of free health care for those on low incomes

CNAT SIGLE F (= Commission nationale d'aménagement
du territoire) national development agency

CNC SIGLE M (= Conseil national de la consommation)
national consumers' council

CNDP SIGLE M = **Centre national de
documentation pédagogique**

CNE SIGLE M (= Contrat nouvelles embauches) less
stringent type of employment contract for use by small
companies

CNED SIGLE M (= Centre national d'enseignement à
distance) ≈ Open University

CNIL SIGLE F (= Commission nationale de l'informatique
et des libertés) board which enforces law on data
protection

CNIT SIGLE M (= Centre national des industries et des
techniques) exhibition centre in Paris

CNJA SIGLE M (= Centre national des jeunes
agriculteurs) farmers' union

CNL SIGLE F (= Confédération nationale du logement)
consumer group for housing

CNRS SIGLE M (= Centre national de la recherche
scientifique) ≈ SERC (BRIT), ≈ NSF (US)

c/o ABR (= care of) c/o

coagulant [kɔagylɑ̃] NM (Méd) coagulant

coaguler [kɔagyle] /1/ VI, VT, **se coaguler** VI
(sang) to coagulate

coaliser [kɔalize] /1/: **se coaliser** VI to unite, join
forces

coalition [kɔalisjɔ̃] NF coalition

coasser [kɔase] /1/ VI to croak

coauteur [kɔotœʀ] NM co-author

coaxial, e, -aux [kɔaksjal, -o] ADJ coaxial

cobaye [kɔbaj] NM guinea-pig

cobra [kɔbʀa] NM cobra

coca® [kɔka] NM Coke®

cocagne [kɔkaɲ] NF: **pays de ~** land of plenty;
mât de ~ greasy pole (fig)

cocaïne [kɔkain] NF cocaine

cocarde [kɔkaʀd] NF rosette

cocardier, -ière [kɔkaʀdje, -jɛʀ] ADJ jingoistic,
chauvinistic; militaristic

cocasse [kɔkas] ADJ comical, funny

coccinelle [kɔksinɛl] NF ladybird (BRIT),
ladybug (US)

coccyx [kɔksis] NM coccyx

cocher [kɔʃe] /1/ NM coachman ▶ VT to tick off;

(entailler) to notch

cochère [kɔʃɛʀ] ADJ F voir **porte**

cochon, ne [kɔʃɔ̃, -ɔn] NM pig ▶ NM/F (péj: sale)
(filthy) pig; (: méchant) swine ▶ ADJ (fam) dirty,
smutty; **~ d'Inde** guinea-pig; **~ de lait** (Culin)
sucking pig

cochonnaille [kɔʃɔnaj] NF (péj: charcuterie) (cold)
pork

cochonnerie [kɔʃɔnʀi] NF (fam: saleté) filth;
(: marchandises) rubbish, trash

cochonnet [kɔʃɔnɛ] NM (Boules) jack

cocker [kɔkɛʀ] NM cocker spaniel

cocktail [kɔktɛl] NM cocktail; (réception) cocktail
party

coco [kɔko] NM voir **noix**; (fam) bloke (BRIT), dude
(US)

cocon [kɔkɔ̃] NM cocoon

cocorico [kɔkɔʀiko] EXCL, NM cock-a-doodle-do

cocotier [kɔkɔtje] NM coconut palm

cocotte [kɔkɔt] NF (en fonte) casserole; **ma ~**
(fam) sweetie (pie); **~ (minute)®** pressure
cooker; **~ en papier** paper shape

cocu [kɔky] NM cuckold

code [kɔd] NM code ▶ ADJ: **phares codes** dipped
lights; **se mettre en ~(s)** to dip (BRIT) ou dim
(US) one's (head)lights; **~ à barres** bar code;
~ de caractère (Inform) character code; **~ civil**
Common Law; **~ machine** machine code;
~ pénal penal code; **~ postal** (numéro) postcode
(BRIT), zip code (US); **~ de la route** highway
code; **~ secret** cipher

codéine [kɔdein] NF codeine

coder [kɔde] /1/ VT to (en)code

codétenu, e [kɔdetny] NM/F fellow prisoner ou
inmate

codicille [kɔdisil] NM codicil

codifier [kɔdifje] /7/ VT to codify

codirecteur, -trice [kɔdiʀɛktœʀ, -tʀis] NM/F
co-director

coéditeur, -trice [kɔeditœʀ, -tʀis] NM/F
co-publisher; (rédacteur) co-editor

coefficient [kɔefisjɑ̃] NM coefficient;
~ d'erreur margin of error

coéquipier, -ière [kɔekipje, -jɛʀ] NM/F
team-mate, partner

coercition [kɔɛʀsisjɔ̃] NF coercion

cœur [kœʀ] NM heart; (Cartes: couleur) hearts pl;
(: carte) heart; (Culin): **~ de laitue/d'artichaut**
lettuce/artichoke heart; (fig): **~ du débat** heart
of the debate; **~ de l'été** height of summer;
~ de la forêt depths pl of the forest; **affaire de
~** love affair; **avoir bon ~** to be kind-hearted;
avoir mal au ~ to feel sick; **contre** ou **sur son ~**
to one's breast; **opérer qn à ~ ouvert** to
perform open-heart surgery on sb; **recevoir qn
à ~ ouvert** to welcome sb with open arms;
parler à ~ ouvert to open one's heart; **de tout
son ~** with all one's heart; **avoir le ~ gros** ou
serré to have a heavy heart; **en avoir le ~ net**
to be clear in one's own mind (about it); **par ~**
by heart; **de bon ~** willingly; **avoir à ~ de faire**
to be very keen to do; **cela lui tient à ~** that's
(very) close to his heart; **prendre les choses à
~** to take things to heart; **à ~ joie** to one's

heart's content; **être de tout ~ avec qn** to be (completely) in accord with sb
coexistence [kɔɛgzistɑ̃s] NF coexistence
coexister [kɔɛgziste] /1/ VI to coexist
coffrage [kɔfʀaʒ] NM (*Constr: dispositif*) form(work)
coffre [kɔfʀ] NM (*meuble*) chest; (*coffre-fort*) safe; (*d'auto*) boot (BRIT), trunk (US); **avoir du ~** (*fam*) to have a lot of puff
coffre-fort [kɔfʀəfɔʀ] (*pl* **coffres-forts**) NM safe
coffrer [kɔfʀe] /1/ VT (*fam*) to put inside, lock up
coffret [kɔfʀɛ] NM casket; **~ à bijoux** jewel box
cogérant, e [kɔʒeʀɑ̃, -ɑ̃t] NM/F joint manager/ manageress
cogestion [kɔʒɛstjɔ̃] NF joint management
cogiter [kɔʒite] /1/ VI to cogitate
cognac [kɔɲak] NM brandy, cognac
cognement [kɔɲmɑ̃] NM knocking
cogner [kɔɲe] /1/ VI to knock, bang; **se cogner** VI to bump o.s.; **se cogner contre** to knock *ou* bump into; **se cogner la tête** to bang one's head
cohabitation [kɔabitasjɔ̃] NF living together; (*Pol, Jur*) cohabitation
cohabiter [kɔabite] /1/ VI to live together
cohérence [kɔeʀɑ̃s] NF coherence
cohérent, e [kɔeʀɑ̃, -ɑ̃t] ADJ coherent, consistent
cohésion [kɔezjɔ̃] NF cohesion
cohorte [kɔɔʀt] NF troop
cohue [kɔy] NF crowd
coi, coite [kwa, kwat] ADJ: **rester ~** to remain silent
coiffe [kwaf] NF headdress
coiffé, e [kwafe] ADJ: **bien/mal ~** with tidy/ untidy hair; **~ d'un béret** wearing a beret; **~ en arrière** with one's hair brushed *ou* combed back; **~ en brosse** with a crew cut
coiffer [kwafe] /1/ VT (*fig: surmonter*) to cover, top; **~ qn** to do sb's hair; **~ qn d'un béret** to put a beret on sb; **se coiffer** VI to do one's hair; to put on a *ou* one's hat
coiffeur, -euse [kwafœʀ, -øz] NM/F hairdresser ▶ NF (*table*) dressing table
coiffure [kwafyʀ] NF (*cheveux*) hairstyle, hairdo; (*chapeau*) hat, headgear *no pl*; (*art*): **la ~** hairdressing
coin [kwɛ̃] NM corner; (*pour graver*) die; (*pour coincer*) wedge; (*poinçon*) hallmark; **l'épicerie du ~** the local grocer; **dans le ~** (*aux alentours*) in the area, around about; (*habiter*) locally; **je ne suis pas du ~** I'm not from here; **au ~ du feu** by the fireside; **du ~ de l'œil** out of the corner of one's eye; **regard en ~** side(ways) glance; **sourire en ~** half-smile
coincé, e [kwɛ̃se] ADJ stuck, jammed; (*fig: inhibé*) inhibited, with hang-ups
coincer [kwɛ̃se] /3/ VT to jam; (*fam*) to catch (out); to nab; **se coincer** VI to get stuck *ou* jammed
coïncidence [kɔɛ̃sidɑ̃s] NF coincidence
coïncider [kɔɛ̃side] /1/ VI: **~ (avec)** to coincide (with); (*correspondre: témoignage etc*) to correspond *ou* tally (with)

coin-coin [kwɛ̃kwɛ̃] NM INV quack
coing [kwɛ̃] NM quince
coït [kɔit] NM coitus
coite [kwat] ADJ F *voir* **coi**
coke [kɔk] NM coke
col [kɔl] NM (*de chemise*) collar; (*encolure, cou*) neck; (*de montagne*) pass; **~ roulé** polo-neck; **~ de l'utérus** cervix
coléoptère [kɔleɔptɛʀ] NM beetle
colère [kɔlɛʀ] NF anger; **une ~** a fit of anger; **être en ~ (contre qn)** to be angry (with sb); **mettre qn en ~** to make sb angry; **se mettre en ~ contre qn** to get angry with sb; **se mettre en ~** to get angry
coléreux, -euse [kɔleʀø, -øz], **colérique** [kɔleʀik] ADJ quick-tempered, irascible
colibacille [kɔlibasil] NM colon bacillus
colibacillose [kɔlibasiloz] NF colibacillosis
colifichet [kɔlifiʃɛ] NM trinket
colimaçon [kɔlimasɔ̃] NM: **escalier en ~** spiral staircase
colin [kɔlɛ̃] NM hake
colin-maillard [kɔlɛ̃majaʀ] NM (*jeu*) blind man's buff
colique [kɔlik] NF diarrhoea (BRIT), diarrhea (US); (*douleurs*) colic (pains *pl*); (*fam: personne ou chose ennuyeuse*) pain
colis [kɔli] NM parcel; **par ~ postal** by parcel post
colistier, -ière [kɔlistje, -jɛʀ] NM/F fellow candidate
colite [kɔlit] NF colitis
coll. ABR = **collection**; **collaborateurs**; **et** ~ et al
collaborateur, -trice [kɔlabɔʀatœʀ, -tʀis] NM/F (*aussi Pol*) collaborator; (*d'une revue*) contributor
collaboration [kɔlabɔʀasjɔ̃] NF collaboration
collaborer [kɔ(l)labɔʀe] /1/ VI to collaborate; **~ à** to collaborate on; (*revue*) to contribute to
collage [kɔlaʒ] NM (*Art*) collage
collagène [kɔlaʒɛn] NM collagen
collant, e [kɔlɑ̃, -ɑ̃t] ADJ sticky; (*robe etc*) clinging, skintight; (*péj*) clinging ▶ NM (*bas*) tights *pl*; (*de danseur*) leotard
collatéral, e, -aux [kɔlateʀal, -o] NM/F collateral
collation [kɔlasjɔ̃] NF light meal
colle [kɔl] NF glue; (*à papiers peints*) (wallpaper) paste; (*devinette*) teaser, riddle; (*Scol: fam*) detention; **~ forte** superglue®
collecte [kɔlɛkt] NF collection; **faire une ~** to take up a collection
collecter [kɔlɛkte] /1/ VT to collect
collecteur [kɔlɛktœʀ] NM (*égout*) main sewer
collectif, -ive [kɔlɛktif, -iv] ADJ collective; (*visite, billet etc*) group *cpd* ▶ NM: **~ budgétaire** mini-budget (BRIT), mid-term budget; **immeuble ~** block of flats
collection [kɔlɛksjɔ̃] NF collection; (*Édition*) series; **pièce de ~** collector's item; **faire (la) ~ de** to collect; **(toute) une ~ de ...** (*fig*) a (complete) set of ...
collectionner [kɔlɛksjɔne] /1/ VT (*tableaux, timbres*) to collect

C

81

collectionneur, -euse [kɔlɛksjɔnœʀ, -øz] NM/F
collector

collectivement [kɔlɛktivmɑ̃] ADV collectively

collectiviser [kɔlɛktivize] /1/ VT to collectivize

collectivisme [kɔlɛktivism] NM collectivism

collectiviste [kɔlɛktivist] ADJ collectivist

collectivité [kɔlɛktivite] NF group; **la ~** the
community, the collectivity; **les collectivités
locales** local authorities

collège [kɔlɛʒ] NM (*école*) (secondary) school;
see note; (*assemblée*) body; **~ électoral** electoral
college

> A *collège* is a state secondary school for
> children between 11 and 15 years of age.
> Pupils follow a national curriculum which
> prescribes a common core along with
> several options. Schools are free to arrange
> their own timetable and choose their own
> teaching methods. Before leaving this
> phase of their education, students are
> assessed by examination and course work
> for their *brevet des collèges*.

collégial, e, -aux [kɔleʒjal, -o] ADJ collegiate

collégien, ne [kɔleʒjɛ̃, -ɛn] NM/F secondary
school pupil (BRIT), high school student (US)

collègue [kɔ(l)lɛg] NMF colleague

coller [kɔle] /1/ VT (*papier, timbre*) to stick (on);
(*affiche*) to stick up; (*appuyer, placer contre*) **~ son
front à la vitre** to press one's face to the
window; (*enveloppe*) to stick down; (*morceaux*) to
stick *ou* glue together; (*Inform*) to paste; (*fam:
mettre, fourrer*) to stick, shove; (*Scol: fam*) to keep
in, give detention to ▶ VI (*être collant*) to be
sticky; (*adhérer*) to stick; **~ qch sur** to stick (*ou*
paste *ou* glue) sth on(to); **~ à** to stick to; (*fig*) to
cling to; **être collé à un examen** (*fam*) to fail
an exam

collerette [kɔlʀɛt] NF ruff; (*Tech*) flange

collet [kɔlɛ] NM (*piège*) snare, noose; (*cou*):
prendre qn au ~ to grab sb by the throat;
~ monté *adj inv* straight-laced

colleter [kɔlte] /4/ VT (*adversaire*) to collar, grab
by the throat; **se ~ avec** to wrestle with

colleur [kɔlœʀ] NM: **~ d'affiches** bill-poster

collier [kɔlje] NM (*bijou*) necklace; (*de chien, Tech*)
collar; **~ (de barbe), barbe en ~** narrow beard
along the line of the jaw; **~ de serrage** choke
collar

collimateur [kɔlimatœʀ] NM: **être dans le ~**
(*fig*) to be in the firing line; **avoir qn/qch dans
le ~** (*fig*) to have sb/sth in one's sights

colline [kɔlin] NF hill

collision [kɔlizjɔ̃] NF collision, crash; **entrer en
~ (avec)** to collide (with)

colloque [kɔlɔk] NM colloquium, symposium

collusion [kɔlyzjɔ̃] NF collusion

collutoire [kɔlytwaʀ] NM (*Méd*) oral
medication; (*en bombe*) throat spray

collyre [kɔliʀ] NM (*Méd*) eye lotion

colmater [kɔlmate] /1/ VT (*fuite*) to seal off;
(*brèche*) to plug, fill in

Cologne [kɔlɔɲ] N Cologne

colombage [kɔlɔ̃baʒ] NM half-timbering; **une
maison à colombages** a half-timbered house

colombe [kɔlɔ̃b] NF dove

Colombie [kɔlɔ̃bi] NF: **la ~** Colombia

colombien, ne [kɔlɔ̃bjɛ̃, -ɛn] ADJ Colombian
▶ NM/F: **C~, ne** Colombian

colon [kɔlɔ̃] NM settler; (*enfant*) boarder (*in
children's holiday camp*)

côlon [kɔlɔ̃] NM colon (*Méd*)

colonel [kɔlɔnɛl] NM colonel; (*de l'armée de l'air*)
group captain

colonial, e, -aux [kɔlɔnjal, -o] ADJ colonial

colonialisme [kɔlɔnjalism] NM colonialism

colonialiste [kɔlɔnjalist] ADJ, NMF colonialist

colonie [kɔlɔni] NF colony; **~ (de vacances)**
holiday camp (*for children*)

colonisation [kɔlɔnizasjɔ̃] NF colonization

coloniser [kɔlɔnize] /1/ VT to colonize

colonnade [kɔlɔnad] NF colonnade

colonne [kɔlɔn] NF column; **se mettre en ~
par deux/quatre** to get into twos/fours; **en ~
par deux** in double file; **~ de secours** rescue
party; **~ (vertébrale)** spine, spinal column

colonnette [kɔlɔnɛt] NF small column

colophane [kɔlɔfan] NF rosin

colorant [kɔlɔʀɑ̃] NM colouring

coloration [kɔlɔʀasjɔ̃] NF colour(ing); **se faire
faire une ~** (*chez le coiffeur*) to have one's hair
dyed

coloré, e [kɔlɔʀe] ADJ (*fig*) colourful

colorer [kɔlɔʀe] /1/ VT to colour; **se colorer** VI to
turn red; to blush

coloriage [kɔlɔʀjaʒ] NM colouring

colorier [kɔlɔʀje] /7/ VT to colour (in); **album à
~** colouring book

coloris [kɔlɔʀi] NM colour, shade

coloriste [kɔlɔʀist] NMF colourist

colossal, e, -aux [kɔlɔsal, -o] ADJ colossal, huge

colosse [kɔlɔs] NM giant

colostrum [kɔlɔstʀɔm] NM colostrum

colporter [kɔlpɔʀte] /1/ VT to peddle

colporteur, -euse [kɔlpɔʀtœʀ, -øz] NM/F
hawker, pedlar

colt [kɔlt] NM revolver, Colt®

coltiner [kɔltine] /1/ VT to lug about

colza [kɔlza] NM rape(seed)

coma [kɔma] NM coma; **être dans le ~** to be in a
coma

comateux, -euse [kɔmatø, -øz] ADJ comatose

combat [kɔ̃ba] VB *voir* **combattre** ▶ NM fight;
fighting *no pl*; **~ de boxe** boxing match; **~ de
rues** street fighting *no pl*; **~ singulier** single
combat

combatif, -ive [kɔ̃batif, -iv] ADJ with a lot of
fight

combativité [kɔ̃bativite] NF fighting spirit

combattant [kɔ̃batɑ̃] VB *voir* **combattre** ▶ NM
combatant; (*d'une rixe*) brawler; **ancien ~** war
veteran

combattre [kɔ̃batʀ] /41/ VI to fight ▶ VT to
fight; (*épidémie, ignorance*) to combat, fight
against

combien [kɔ̃bjɛ̃] ADV (*quantité*) how much;
(*nombre*) how many; (*exclamatif*) how; **~ de** how
much; (*nombre*) how many; **~ de temps** how
long, how much time; **c'est ~?, ça fait ~?** how

much is it?; **~ coûte/pèse ceci?** how much does this cost/weigh?; **vous mesurez ~?** what size are you?; **ça fait ~ en largeur?** how wide is that?; **on est le ~ aujourd'hui?** *(fam)* what's the date today?

combinaison [kɔ̃binɛzɔ̃] NF combination; *(astuce)* device, scheme; *(de femme)* slip; *(d'aviateur)* flying suit; *(de plongée)* wetsuit; *(bleu de travail)* boilersuit *(BRIT)*, coveralls pl *(US)*

combine [kɔ̃bin] NF trick; *(péj)* scheme, fiddle *(BRIT)*

combiné [kɔ̃bine] NM *(aussi: combiné téléphonique)* receiver; *(Ski)* combination (event); *(vêtement de femme)* corselet

combiner [kɔ̃bine] /1/ VT to combine; *(plan, horaire)* to work out, devise

comble [kɔ̃bl] ADJ *(salle)* packed (full) ▶ NM *(du bonheur, plaisir)* height; **combles** NMPL *(Constr)* attic sg, loft sg; **de fond en ~** from top to bottom; **pour ~ de malchance** to cap it all; **c'est le ~!** that beats everything!, that takes the biscuit! *(BRIT)*; **sous les combles** in the attic

combler [kɔ̃ble] /1/ VT *(trou)* to fill in; *(besoin, lacune)* to fill; *(déficit)* to make good; *(satisfaire)* to gratify, fulfil *(BRIT)*, fulfill *(US)*; **~ qn de joie** to fill sb with joy; **~ qn d'honneurs** to shower sb with honours

combustible [kɔ̃bystibl] ADJ combustible ▶ NM fuel

combustion [kɔ̃bystjɔ̃] NF combustion

COMECON [kɔmekɔn] SIGLE M Comecon

comédie [kɔmedi] NF comedy; *(fig)* playacting no pl; **jouer la ~** *(fig)* to put on an act; **faire une ~** *(fig)* to make a fuss; **la C~ française** *see note*; **~ musicale** musical

> Founded in 1680 by Louis XIV, the *Comédie française* is the French national theatre. The company is subsidized by the state and mainly performs in the Palais Royal in Paris, tending to concentrate on classical French drama.

comédien, ne [kɔmedjɛ̃, -ɛn] NM/F actor/actress; *(comique)* comedy actor/actress, comedian/comedienne; *(fig)* sham

comestible [kɔmɛstibl] ADJ edible; **comestibles** NMPL foods

comète [kɔmɛt] NF comet

comice [kɔmis] NM: **~ agricole** agricultural show

comique [kɔmik] ADJ *(drôle)* comical; *(Théât)* comic ▶ NM *(artiste)* comic, comedian; **le ~ de qch** the funny ou comical side of sth

comité [kɔmite] NM committee; **petit ~** select group; **~ directeur** management committee; **~ d'entreprise** works council; **~ des fêtes** festival committee

commandant [kɔmɑ̃dɑ̃] NM *(gén)* commander, commandant; *(Mil: grade)* major; *(: armée de l'air)* squadron leader; *(Navig)* captain; **~ (de bord)** *(Aviat)* captain

commande [kɔmɑ̃d] NF *(Comm)* order; *(Inform)* command; **commandes** NFPL *(Aviat etc)* controls; **passer une ~ (de)** to put in an order (for); **sur ~** to order; **~ à distance** remote

control; **véhicule à double ~** vehicle with dual controls

commandement [kɔmɑ̃dmɑ̃] NM command; *(ordre)* command, order; *(Rel)* commandment

commander [kɔmɑ̃de] /1/ VT *(Comm)* to order; *(diriger, ordonner)* to command; **~ à** *(Mil)* to command; *(contrôler, maîtriser)* to have control over; **~ à qn de faire** to command ou order sb to do

commanditaire [kɔmɑ̃ditɛʀ] NM sleeping *(BRIT)* ou silent *(US)* partner

commandite [kɔmɑ̃dit] NF: **(société en) ~** limited partnership

commanditer [kɔmɑ̃dite] /1/ VT *(Comm)* to finance, back; to commission

commando [kɔmɑ̃do] NM commando (squad)

(MOT-CLÉ)

comme [kɔm] PRÉP **1** *(comparaison)* like; **tout comme son père** just like his father; **fort comme un bœuf** as strong as an ox; **joli comme tout** ever so pretty

2 *(manière)* like; **faites-le comme ça** do it like this, do it this way; **comme ça ou cela on n'aura pas d'ennuis** that way we won't have any problems; **comme ci, comme ça** so-so, middling; **comment ça va? — comme ça** how are things? — OK; **comme on dit** as they say

3 *(en tant que)* as a; **donner comme prix** to give as a prize; **travailler comme secrétaire** to work as a secretary

4: **comme quoi** *(d'où il s'ensuit que)* which shows that; **il a écrit une lettre comme quoi il …** he's written a letter saying that …

5: **comme il faut** *adv* properly; *adj (correct)* proper, correct

▶ CONJ **1** *(ainsi que)* as; **elle écrit comme elle parle** she writes as she talks; **il est malin comme c'est pas permis** he's as smart as anything; **comme si** as if

2 *(au moment où, alors que)* as; **il est parti comme j'arrivais** he left as I arrived

3 *(parce que, puisque)* as, since; **comme il était en retard, il …** as he was late, he …

▶ ADV: **comme il est fort/c'est bon!** he's so strong/it's so good!

commémoratif, -ive [kɔmemɔratif, -iv] ADJ commemorative; **un monument ~** a memorial

commémoration [kɔmemɔrasjɔ̃] NF commemoration

commémorer [kɔmemɔre] /1/ VT to commemorate

commencement [kɔmɑ̃smɑ̃] NM beginning, start, commencement; **commencements** NMPL *(débuts)* beginnings

commencer [kɔmɑ̃se] /3/ VT to begin, start, commence ▶ VI to begin, start, commence; **~ à** ou **de faire** to begin ou start doing; **~ par qch** to begin with sth; **~ par faire qch** to begin by doing sth

commensal, e, -aux [kɔmɑ̃sal, -o] NM/F companion at table

comment [kɔmɑ̃] ADV how; **~?** *(que dites-vous)* (I

beg your) pardon?; ~! what! ▶ NM: **le ~ et le pourquoi** the whys and wherefores; **et ~!** and how!; **~ donc!** of course!; **~ faire?** how will we do it?; **~ se fait-il que …?** how is it that …?

commentaire [kɔmɑ̃tɛʀ] NM comment; remark; **~ (de texte)** (Scol) commentary; **~ sur image** voice-over

commentateur, -trice [kɔmɑ̃tatœʀ, -tʀis] NM/F commentator

commenter [kɔmɑ̃te] /1/ VT (jugement, événement) to comment (up)on; (Radio, TV: match, manifestation) to cover, give a commentary on

commérages [kɔmeʀaʒ] NMPL gossip sg

commerçant, e [kɔmɛʀsɑ̃, -ɑ̃t] ADJ commercial; trading; (rue) shopping cpd; (personne) commercially shrewd ▶ NM/F shopkeeper, trader

commerce [kɔmɛʀs] NM (activité) trade, commerce; (boutique) business; **le petit ~** small shop owners pl, small traders pl; **faire ~ de** to trade in; (fig: péj) to trade on; **chambre de ~** Chamber of Commerce; **livres de ~** (account) books; **vendu dans le ~** sold in the shops; **vendu hors-~** sold directly to the public; **~ en** ou **de gros/détail** wholesale/retail trade; **~ électronique** e-commerce; **~ équitable** fair trade; **~ intérieur/extérieur** home/foreign trade

commercer [kɔmɛʀse] /3/ VI: **~ avec** to trade with

commercial, e, -aux [kɔmɛʀsjal, -o] ADJ commercial, trading; (péj) commercial ▶ NM: **les commerciaux** the commercial people

commercialisable [kɔmɛʀsjalizabl] ADJ marketable

commercialisation [kɔmɛʀsjalizasjɔ̃] NF marketing

commercialiser [kɔmɛʀsjalize] /1/ VT to market

commère [kɔmɛʀ] NF gossip

commettant [kɔmetɑ̃] VB voir **commettre** ▶ NM (Jur) principal

commettre [kɔmɛtʀ] /56/ VT to commit; **se commettre** VI to compromise one's good name

commis¹ [kɔmi] NM (de magasin) (shop) assistant (BRIT), sales clerk (US); (de banque) clerk; **~ voyageur** commercial traveller (BRIT) ou traveler (US)

commis², e [kɔmi, -iz] PP de **commettre**

commisération [kɔmizeʀasjɔ̃] NF commiseration

commissaire [kɔmisɛʀ] NM (de police) ≈ (police) superintendent (BRIT), ≈ (police) captain (US); (de rencontre sportive etc) steward; **~ du bord** (Navig) purser; **~ aux comptes** (Admin) auditor

commissaire-priseur [kɔmisɛʀpʀizœʀ] (pl **commissaires-priseurs**) NM (official) auctioneer

commissariat [kɔmisaʀja] NM (aussi: **commissariat de police**) police station; (Admin) commissionership

commission [kɔmisjɔ̃] NF (comité, pourcentage) commission; (message) message; (course) errand; **commissions** NFPL (achats) shopping sg; **~ d'examen** examining board

commissionnaire [kɔmisjɔnɛʀ] NM delivery boy (ou man); messenger; (Transports) (forwarding) agent

commissure [kɔmisyʀ] NF: **les commissures des lèvres** the corners of the mouth

commode [kɔmɔd] ADJ (pratique) convenient, handy; (facile) easy; (air, personne) easy-going; (personne): **pas ~** awkward (to deal with) ▶ NF chest of drawers

commodité [kɔmɔdite] NF convenience

commotion [kɔmɔsjɔ̃] NF: **~ (cérébrale)** concussion

commotionné, e [kɔmɔsjɔne] ADJ shocked, shaken

commuer [kɔmɥe] /1/ VT to commute

commun, e [kɔmœ̃, -yn] ADJ common; (pièce) communal, shared; (réunion, effort) joint ▶ NF (Admin) commune, ≈ district; (: urbaine) ≈ borough; **communs** NMPL (bâtiments) outbuildings; **cela sort du ~** it's out of the ordinary; **le ~ des mortels** the common run of people; **sans ~ mesure** incomparable; **être ~ à** (chose) to be shared by; **en ~ (faire)** jointly; **mettre en ~** to pool, share; **peu ~** unusual; **d'un ~ accord** of one accord; with one accord

communal, e, -aux [kɔmynal, -o] ADJ (Admin) of the commune, ≈ (district ou borough) council cpd

communard, e [kɔmynaʀ, -aʀd] NM/F (Hist) Communard; (péj: communiste) commie

communautaire [kɔmynotɛʀ] ADJ community cpd

communauté [kɔmynote] NF community; (Jur): **régime de la ~** communal estate settlement

commune [kɔmyn] ADJ F, NF voir **commun**

communément [kɔmynemɑ̃] ADV commonly

Communes [kɔmyn] NFPL (en Grande-Bretagne: parlement) Commons

communiant, e [kɔmynjɑ̃, -ɑ̃t] NM/F communicant; **premier ~** child taking his first communion

communicant, e [kɔmynikɑ̃, -ɑ̃t] ADJ communicating

communicatif, -ive [kɔmynikatif, -iv] ADJ (personne) communicative; (rire) infectious

communication [kɔmynikasjɔ̃] NF communication; **~ (téléphonique)** (telephone) call; **avoir la ~ (avec)** to get ou be through (to); **vous avez la ~** you're through; **donnez-moi la ~ avec** put me through to; **mettre qn en ~ avec qn** (en contact) to put sb in touch with sb; (au téléphone) to connect sb with sb; **~ interurbaine** long-distance call; **~ en PCV** reverse charge (BRIT) ou collect (US) call; **~ avec préavis** personal call

communier [kɔmynje] /7/ VI (Rel) to receive communion; (fig) to be united

communion [kɔmynjɔ̃] NF communion

communiqué [kɔmynike] NM communiqué; **~ de presse** press release

communiquer [kɔmynike] /1/ VT (nouvelle, dossier) to pass on, convey; (maladie) to pass on; (peur etc) to communicate; (chaleur, mouvement) to transmit ▶ vi to communicate; **~ avec** (*salle*) to communicate with; **se ~ à** (*se propager*) to spread to

communisme [kɔmynism] NM communism

communiste [kɔmynist] ADJ, NMF communist

commutateur [kɔmytatœR] NM (*Élec*) (change-over) switch, commutator

commutation [kɔmytasjɔ̃] NF (*Inform*): **~ de messages** message switching; **~ de paquets** packet switching

Comores [kɔmɔR] NFPL: **les (îles) ~** the Comoros (Islands)

comorien, ne [kɔmɔRjɛ̃, -ɛn] ADJ of *ou* from the Comoros

compact, e [kɔ̃pakt] ADJ (*dense*) dense; (*appareil*) compact

compagne [kɔ̃paɲ] NF companion

compagnie [kɔ̃paɲi] NF (*firme, Mil*) company; (*groupe*) gathering; (*présence*): **la ~ de qn** sb's company; **homme/femme de ~** escort; **tenir ~ à qn** to keep sb company; **fausser ~ à qn** to give sb the slip, slip *ou* sneak away from sb; **en ~ de** in the company of; **Dupont et ~, Dupont et Cie** Dupont and Company, Dupont and Co; **~ aérienne** airline (company)

compagnon [kɔ̃paɲɔ̃] NM companion; (*autrefois: ouvrier*) craftsman; journeyman

comparable [kɔ̃paRabl] ADJ: **~ (à)** comparable (to)

comparaison [kɔ̃paRɛzɔ̃] NF comparison; (*métaphore*) simile; **en ~ (de)** in comparison (with); **par ~ (à)** by comparison (with)

comparaître [kɔ̃paRɛtR] /**57**/ vi: **~ (devant)** to appear (before)

comparatif, -ive [kɔ̃paRatif, -iv] ADJ, NM comparative

comparativement [kɔ̃paRativmɑ̃] ADV comparatively; **~ à** by comparison with

comparé, e [kɔ̃paRe] ADJ: **littérature** *etc* **~** comparative literature *etc*

comparer [kɔ̃paRe] /**1**/ vT to compare; **~ qch/qn à** *ou* **et** (*pour choisir*) to compare sth/sb with *ou* and; (*pour établir une similitude*) to compare sth/sb to *ou* and

comparse [kɔ̃paRs] NMF (*péj*) associate, stooge

compartiment [kɔ̃paRtimɑ̃] NM compartment

compartimenté, e [kɔ̃paRtimɑ̃te] ADJ partitioned; (*fig*) compartmentalized

comparu, e [kɔ̃paRy] PP *de* **comparaître**

comparution [kɔ̃paRysjɔ̃] NF appearance

compas [kɔ̃pa] NM (*Géom*) (pair of) compasses *pl*; (*Navig*) compass

compassé, e [kɔ̃pase] ADJ starchy, formal

compassion [kɔ̃pasjɔ̃] NF compassion

compatibilité [kɔ̃patibilite] NF compatibility

compatible [kɔ̃patibl] ADJ compatible; **~ (avec)** compatible (with)

compatir [kɔ̃patiR] /**2**/ vi: **~ (à)** to sympathize (with)

compatissant, e [kɔ̃patisɑ̃, -ɑ̃t] ADJ sympathetic

compatriote [kɔ̃patRijɔt] NMF compatriot, fellow countryman/woman

compensateur, -trice [kɔ̃pɑ̃satœR, -tRis] ADJ compensatory

compensation [kɔ̃pɑ̃sasjɔ̃] NF compensation; (*Banque*) clearing; **en ~** in *ou* as compensation

compensé, e [kɔ̃pɑ̃se] ADJ: **semelle ~** platform sole

compenser [kɔ̃pɑ̃se] /**1**/ vT to compensate for, make up for

compère [kɔ̃pɛR] NM accomplice; fellow musician *ou* comedian *etc*

compétence [kɔ̃petɑ̃s] NF competence

compétent, e [kɔ̃petɑ̃, -ɑ̃t] ADJ (*apte*) competent, capable; (*Jur*) competent

compétitif, -ive [kɔ̃petitif, -iv] ADJ competitive

compétition [kɔ̃petisjɔ̃] NF (*gén*) competition; (*Sport: épreuve*) event; **la ~** competitive sport; **être en ~ avec** to be competing with; **la ~ automobile** motor racing

compétitivité [kɔ̃petitivite] NF competitiveness

compilateur [kɔ̃pilatœR] NM (*Inform*) compiler

compiler [kɔ̃pile] /**1**/ vT to compile

complainte [kɔ̃plɛ̃t] NF lament

complaire [kɔ̃plɛR] /**54**/: **se complaire** vi: **se complaire dans/parmi** to take pleasure in/in being among

complaisais *etc* [kɔ̃plɛzɛ] vB *voir* **complaire**

complaisamment [kɔ̃plɛzamɑ̃] ADV kindly; complacently

complaisance [kɔ̃plɛzɑ̃s] NF kindness; (*péj*) indulgence; (: *fatuité*) complacency; **attestation de ~** *certificate produced to oblige a patient etc*; **pavillon de ~** flag of convenience

complaisant, e [kɔ̃plɛzɑ̃, -ɑ̃t] vB *voir* **complaire** ▶ ADJ (*aimable*) kind; obliging; (*péj*) accommodating; (: *fat*) complacent

complaît [kɔ̃plɛ] vB *voir* **complaire**

complément [kɔ̃plemɑ̃] NM complement; (*reste*) remainder; (*Ling*) complement; **~ d'information** (*Admin*) supplementary *ou* further information; **~ d'agent** agent; **~ (d'objet) direct/indirect** direct/indirect object; **~ (circonstanciel) de lieu/temps** adverbial phrase of place/time; **~ de nom** possessive phrase

complémentaire [kɔ̃plemɑ̃tɛR] ADJ complementary; (*additionnel*) supplementary

complet, -ète [kɔ̃plɛ, -ɛt] ADJ complete; (*plein: hôtel etc*) full ▶ NM (*aussi:* **complet-veston**) suit; **pain ~** wholemeal bread; **au (grand) ~** all together

complètement [kɔ̃plɛtmɑ̃] ADV (*en entier*) completely; (*absolument: fou, faux etc*) absolutely; (*à fond: étudier etc*) fully, in depth

compléter [kɔ̃plete] /**6**/ vT (*porter à la quantité voulue*) to complete; (*augmenter: connaissances, études*) to complement, supplement; (: *garde-robe*) to add to; **se compléter** vi (*personnes*) to complement one another; (*collection etc*) to become complete

complexe [kɔ̃plɛks] ADJ complex ▶ NM (*Psych*) complex, hang-up; (*bâtiments*): **~ hospitalier/ industriel** hospital/industrial complex

complexé, e [kɔ̃plɛkse] ADJ mixed-up, hung-up

complexité [kɔ̃plɛksite] NF complexity

complication [kɔ̃plikasjɔ̃] NF complexity,

C

intricacy; *(difficulté, ennui)* complication; **complications** NFPL *(Méd)* complications

complice [kɔ̃plis] NM accomplice

complicité [kɔ̃plisite] NF complicity

compliment [kɔ̃plimɑ̃] NM *(louange)* compliment; **compliments** NMPL *(félicitations)* congratulations

complimenter [kɔ̃plimɑ̃te] /1/ VT: ~ **qn (sur** *ou* **de)** to congratulate *ou* compliment sb (on)

compliqué, e [kɔ̃plike] ADJ complicated, complex, intricate; *(personne)* complicated

compliquer [kɔ̃plike] /1/ VT to complicate; **se compliquer** VI *(situation)* to become complicated; **se compliquer la vie** to make life difficult *ou* complicated for o.s.

complot [kɔ̃plo] NM plot

comploter [kɔ̃plɔte] /1/ VI, VT to plot

complu, e [kɔ̃ply] PP *de* **complaire**

comportement [kɔ̃pɔrtəmɑ̃] NM behaviour (BRIT), behavior (US); *(Tech: d'une pièce, d'un véhicule)* behavio(u)r, performance

comporter [kɔ̃pɔrte] /1/ VT *(consister en)* to consist of, be composed of, comprise; *(être équipé de)* to have; *(impliquer)* to entail, involve; **se comporter** VI to behave; *(Tech)* to behave, perform

composant [kɔ̃pozɑ̃] NM component, constituent

composante [kɔ̃pozɑ̃t] NF component

composé, e [kɔ̃poze] ADJ *(visage, air)* studied; *(Bio, Chimie, Ling)* compound ▶ NM *(Chimie, Ling)* compound; ~ **de** made up of

composer [kɔ̃poze] /1/ VT *(musique, texte)* to compose; *(mélange, équipe)* to make up; *(faire partie de)* to make up, form; *(Typo)* to (type)set ▶ VI *(Scol)* to sit *ou* do a test; *(transiger)* to come to terms; **se ~ de** to be composed of, be made up of; ~ **un numéro** *(au téléphone)* to dial a number

composite [kɔ̃pozit] ADJ heterogeneous

compositeur, -trice [kɔ̃pozitœr, -tris] NM/F *(Mus)* composer; *(Typo)* compositor, typesetter

composition [kɔ̃pozisjɔ̃] NF composition; *(Scol)* test; *(Typo)* (type)setting, composition; **de bonne ~** *(accommodant)* easy to deal with; **amener qn à ~** to get sb to come to terms; **~ française** *(Scol)* French essay

compost [kɔ̃pɔst] NM compost

composter [kɔ̃pɔste] /1/ VT to date-stamp; *(billet)* to punch

> In France you have to punch your ticket on the platform to validate it before getting onto the train.

composteur [kɔ̃pɔstœr] NM date stamp; punch; *(Typo)* composing stick

compote [kɔ̃pɔt] NF stewed fruit *no pl*; ~ **de pommes** stewed apples

compotier [kɔ̃pɔtje] NM fruit dish *ou* bowl

compréhensible [kɔ̃preɑ̃sibl] ADJ comprehensible; *(attitude)* understandable

compréhensif, -ive [kɔ̃preɑ̃sif, -iv] ADJ understanding

compréhension [kɔ̃preɑ̃sjɔ̃] NF understanding; comprehension

comprendre [kɔ̃prɑ̃dr] /58/ VT to understand;

(se composer de) to comprise, consist of; *(inclure)* to include; **se faire ~** to make o.s. understood; to get one's ideas across; **mal ~** to misunderstand

compresse [kɔ̃prɛs] NF compress

compresser [kɔ̃prese] /1/ VT to squash in, crush together; *(Inform)* to zip

compresseur [kɔ̃presœr] ADJ M *voir* **rouleau**

compressible [kɔ̃presibl] ADJ *(Physique)* compressible; *(dépenses)* reducible

compression [kɔ̃presjɔ̃] NF compression; *(d'un crédit etc)* reduction

comprimé, e [kɔ̃prime] ADJ: **air ~** compressed air ▶ NM tablet

comprimer [kɔ̃prime] /1/ VT to compress; *(fig: crédit etc)* to reduce, cut down

compris, e [kɔ̃pri, -iz] PP *de* **comprendre** ▶ ADJ *(inclus)* included; ~? understood?, is that clear?; ~ **entre** *(situé)* contained between; **la maison ~/ non ~, y/non ~ la maison** including/excluding the house; **service ~** service (charge) included; **100 euros tout ~** 100 euros all inclusive *ou* all-in

compromettant, e [kɔ̃prɔmetɑ̃, -ɑ̃t] ADJ compromising

compromettre [kɔ̃prɔmetr] /56/ VT to compromise

compromis [kɔ̃prɔmi] VB *voir* **compromettre** ▶ NM compromise

compromission [kɔ̃prɔmisjɔ̃] NF compromise, deal

comptabiliser [kɔ̃tabilize] /1/ VT *(valeur)* to post; *(fig)* to evaluate

comptabilité [kɔ̃tabilite] NF *(activité, technique)* accounting, accountancy; *(d'une société: comptes)* accounts pl, books pl; *(: service)* accounts office *ou* department; ~ **à partie double** double-entry book-keeping

comptable [kɔ̃tabl] NMF accountant ▶ ADJ accounts cpd, accounting

comptant [kɔ̃tɑ̃] ADV: **payer ~** to pay cash; **acheter ~** to buy for cash

compte [kɔ̃t] NM count, counting; *(total, montant)* count, (right) number; *(bancaire, facture)* account; **comptes** NMPL accounts, books; *(fig)* explanation *sg*; **ouvrir un ~** to open an account; **rendre des comptes à qn** *(fig)* to be answerable to sb; **faire le ~ de** to count up, make a count of; **tout ~ fait** on the whole; **à ce ~-là** *(dans ce cas)* in that case; *(à ce train-là)* at that rate; **en fin de ~** *(fig)* all things considered, weighing it all up; **au bout du ~** in the final analysis; **à bon ~** at a favourable price; *(fig)* lightly; **avoir son ~** *(fig: fam)* to have had it; **s'en tirer à bon ~** to get off lightly; **pour le ~ de** on behalf of; **pour son propre ~** for one's own benefit; **sur le ~ de qn** *(à son sujet)* about sb; **travailler à son ~** to work for oneself; **mettre qch sur le ~ de qn** *(le rendre responsable)* to attribute sth to sb; **prendre qch à son ~** to take responsibility for sth; **trouver son ~ à qch** to do well out of sth; **régler un ~** *(s'acquitter de qch)* to settle an account; *(se venger)* to get one's own back; **rendre ~ (à qn) de qch** to give (sb) an account of sth; **rendre des comptes à qn** *(fig)*

to be answerable to sb; **tenir ~ de qch** to take
sth into account; **~ tenu de** taking into
account; **~ en banque** bank account;
~ chèque(s) current account; **~ chèque postal**
Post Office account; **~ client** (*sur bilan*) accounts
receivable; **~ courant** current account; **~ de
dépôt** deposit account; **~ d'exploitation**
operating account; **~ fournisseur** (*sur bilan*)
accounts payable; **~ à rebours** countdown;
~ rendu account, report; (*de film, livre*) review;
voir aussi **rendre**
compte-gouttes [kɔ̃tgut] NM INV dropper
compter [kɔ̃te] /1/ VT to count; (*facturer*) to
charge for; (*avoir à son actif, comporter*) to have;
(*prévoir*) to allow, reckon; (*tenir compte de, inclure*)
to include; (*penser, espérer*): **~ réussir/revenir** to
expect to succeed/return ▶ VI to count; (*être
économe*) to economize; (*être non négligeable*) to
count, matter; (*valoir*): **~ pour** to count for;
(*figurer*): **~ parmi** to be *ou* rank among; **~ sur** to
count (up)on; **~ avec qch/qn** to reckon with *ou*
take account of sth/sb; **~ sans qch/qn** to
reckon without sth/sb; **sans ~ que** besides
which; **à ~ du 10 janvier** (*Comm*) (as) from 10th
January
compte-tours [kɔ̃ttur] NM INV rev(olution)
counter
compteur [kɔ̃tœr] NM meter; **~ de vitesse**
speedometer
comptine [kɔ̃tin] NF nursery rhyme
comptoir [kɔ̃twar] NM (*de magasin*) counter;
(*de café*) counter, bar; (*colonial*) trading post
compulser [kɔ̃pylse] /1/ VT to consult
comte, comtesse [kɔ̃t, kɔ̃tɛs] NM/F
count/countess
con, ne [kɔ̃, kɔn] ADJ (!) bloody (*BRIT*) *ou* damned
stupid
concasser [kɔ̃kase] /1/ VT (*pierre, sucre*) to crush;
(*poivre*) to grind
concave [kɔ̃kav] ADJ concave
concéder [kɔ̃sede] /6/ VT to grant; (*défaite, point*)
to concede; **~ que** to concede that
concentration [kɔ̃sɑ̃trasjɔ̃] NF concentration
concentrationnaire [kɔ̃sɑ̃trasjɔnɛr] ADJ of *ou*
in concentration camps
concentré [kɔ̃sɑ̃tre] NM concentrate; **~ de
tomates** tomato purée
concentrer [kɔ̃sɑ̃tre] /1/ VT to concentrate;
se concentrer VI to concentrate
concentrique [kɔ̃sɑ̃trik] ADJ concentric
concept [kɔ̃sɛpt] NM concept
concepteur, -trice [kɔ̃sɛptœr, -tris] NM/F
designer
conception [kɔ̃sɛpsjɔ̃] NF conception; (*d'une
machine etc*) design
concernant [kɔ̃sɛrnɑ̃] PRÉP (*se rapportant à*)
concerning; (*en ce qui concerne*) as regards
concerner [kɔ̃sɛrne] /1/ VT to concern; **en ce
qui me concerne** as far as I am concerned; **en
ce qui concerne ceci** as far as this is
concerned, with regard to this
concert [kɔ̃sɛr] NM concert; **de ~** adv in unison;
together; (*décider*) unanimously
concertation [kɔ̃sɛrtasjɔ̃] NF (*échange de vues*)

dialogue; (*rencontre*) meeting
concerter [kɔ̃sɛrte] /1/ VT to devise; **se
concerter** VI (*collaborateurs etc*) to put our (*ou*
their *etc*) heads together, consult (each other)
concertiste [kɔ̃sɛrtist] NMF concert artist
concerto [kɔ̃sɛrto] NM concerto
concession [kɔ̃sesjɔ̃] NF concession
concessionnaire [kɔ̃sesjɔnɛr] NMF agent,
dealer
concevable [kɔ̃svabl] ADJ conceivable
concevoir [kɔ̃s(ə)vwar] /28/ VT (*idée, projet*)
to conceive (of); (*méthode, plan d'appartement,
décoration etc*) to plan, design; (*comprendre*) to
understand; (*enfant*) to conceive; **maison bien/
mal conçue** well-/badly-designed *ou* -planned
house
concierge [kɔ̃sjɛrʒ] NMF caretaker; (*d'hôtel*)
head porter
conciergerie [kɔ̃sjɛrʒəri] NF caretaker's lodge
concile [kɔ̃sil] NM council, synod
conciliable [kɔ̃siljabl] ADJ (*opinions etc*)
reconcilable
conciliabules [kɔ̃siljabyl] NMPL (private)
discussions, confabulations (*BRIT*)
conciliant, e [kɔ̃siljɑ̃, -ɑ̃t] ADJ conciliatory
conciliateur, -trice [kɔ̃siljatœr, -tris] NM/F
mediator, go-between
conciliation [kɔ̃siljasjɔ̃] NF conciliation
concilier [kɔ̃silje] /7/ VT to reconcile; **se ~
qn/l'appui de qn** to win sb over/sb's support
concis, e [kɔ̃si, -iz] ADJ concise
concision [kɔ̃sizjɔ̃] NF concision, conciseness
concitoyen, ne [kɔ̃sitwajɛ̃, -ɛn] NM/F fellow
citizen
conclave [kɔ̃klav] NM conclave
concluant, e [kɔ̃klyɑ̃, -ɑ̃t] VB *voir* **conclure** ▶ ADJ
conclusive
conclure [kɔ̃klyr] /35/ VT to conclude; (*signer:
accord, pacte*) to enter into; (*déduire*): **~ qch de qch**
to deduce sth from sth; **~ à l'acquittement** to
decide in favour of an acquittal; **~ au suicide** to
come to the conclusion (*ou* (*Jur*) to pronounce)
that it is a case of suicide; **~ un marché** to
clinch a deal; **j'en conclus que** from that I
conclude that
conclusion [kɔ̃klyzjɔ̃] NF conclusion;
conclusions NFPL (*Jur*) submissions; findings;
en ~ in conclusion
concocter [kɔ̃kɔkte] /1/ VT to concoct
conçois [kɔ̃swa], **conçoive** *etc* [kɔ̃swav] VB *voir*
concevoir
concombre [kɔ̃kɔ̃br] NM cucumber
concomitant, e [kɔ̃kɔmitɑ̃, -ɑ̃t] ADJ
concomitant
concordance [kɔ̃kɔrdɑ̃s] NF concordance; **la ~
des temps** (*Ling*) the sequence of tenses
concordant, e [kɔ̃kɔrdɑ̃, -ɑ̃t] ADJ (*témoignages,
versions*) corroborating
concorde [kɔ̃kɔrd] NF concord
concorder [kɔ̃kɔrde] /1/ VI to tally, agree
concourir [kɔ̃kurir] /11/ VI (*Sport*) to compete;
~ à vt (*effet etc*) to work towards
concours [kɔ̃kur] VB *voir* **concourir** ▶ NM
competition; (*Scol*) competitive examination;

(*assistance*) aid, help; **recrutement par voie de** ~ recruitment by (competitive) examination; **apporter son** ~ **à** to give one's support to; ~ **de circonstances** combination of circumstances; ~ **hippique** horse show; *voir* **'hors-concours**

concret, -ète [kɔ̃kʀɛ, -ɛt] ADJ concrete

concrètement [kɔ̃kʀɛtmã] ADV in concrete terms

concrétisation [kɔ̃kʀetizasjɔ̃] NF realization

concrétiser [kɔ̃kʀetize] /1/ VT to realize; **se concrétiser** VI to materialize

conçu, e [kɔ̃sy] PP *de* **concevoir**

concubin, e [kɔ̃kybɛ̃, -in] NM/F (*Jur*) cohabitant

concubinage [kɔ̃kybinaʒ] NM (*Jur*) cohabitation

concupiscence [kɔ̃kypisɑ̃s] NF concupiscence

concurremment [kɔ̃kyʀamã] ADV concurrently; jointly

concurrence [kɔ̃kyʀɑ̃s] NF competition; **jusqu'à** ~ **de** up to; **faire** ~ **à** to be in competition with; ~ **déloyale** unfair competition

concurrencer [kɔ̃kyʀɑ̃se] /3/ VT to compete with; **ils nous concurrencent dangereusement** they are a serious threat to us

concurrent, e [kɔ̃kyʀɑ̃, -ɑ̃t] ADJ competing ▶ NM/F (*Sport, Écon etc*) competitor; (*Scol*) candidate

concurrentiel, le [kɔ̃kyʀɑ̃sjɛl] ADJ competitive

conçus [kɔ̃sy] VB *voir* **concevoir**

condamnable [kɔ̃danabl] ADJ (*action, opinion*) reprehensible

condamnation [kɔ̃danasjɔ̃] NF (*action*) condemnation; sentencing; (*peine*) sentence; conviction; ~ **à mort** death sentence

condamné, e [kɔ̃dane] NM/F (*Jur*) convict

condamner [kɔ̃dane] /1/ VT (*blâmer*) to condemn; (*Jur*) to sentence; (*porte, ouverture*) to fill in, block up; (*malade*) to give up (hope for); (*obliger*): ~ **qn à qch/à faire** to condemn sb to sth/to do; ~ **qn à deux ans de prison** to sentence sb to two years' imprisonment; ~ **qn à une amende** to impose a fine on sb

condensateur [kɔ̃dɑ̃satœʀ] NM condenser

condensation [kɔ̃dɑ̃sasjɔ̃] NF condensation

condensé [kɔ̃dɑ̃se] NM digest

condenser [kɔ̃dɑ̃se] /1/: **se condenser** VI to condense

condescendance [kɔ̃desɑ̃dɑ̃s] NF condescension

condescendant, e [kɔ̃desɑ̃dɑ̃, -ɑ̃t] ADJ (*personne, attitude*) condescending

condescendre [kɔ̃desɑ̃dʀ] /41/ VI: ~ **à** to condescend to

condiment [kɔ̃dimã] NM condiment

condisciple [kɔ̃disipl] NMF school fellow, fellow student

condition [kɔ̃disjɔ̃] NF condition; **conditions** NFPL (*tarif, prix*) terms; (*circonstances*) conditions; **sans** ~ *adj* unconditional; *adv* unconditionally; **sous** ~ **que** on condition that; **à** ~ **de** *ou* **que** provided that; **en bonne** ~ in good condition; **mettre en** ~ (*Sport etc*) to get fit; (*Psych*) to condition (mentally); **conditions de vie** living conditions

conditionnel, le [kɔ̃disjɔnɛl] ADJ conditional ▶ NM conditional (tense)

conditionnement [kɔ̃disjɔnmã] NM (*emballage*) packaging; (*fig*) conditioning

conditionner [kɔ̃disjɔne] /1/ VT (*déterminer*) to determine; (*Comm: produit*) to package; (*fig: personne*) to condition; **air conditionné** air conditioning; **réflexe conditionné** conditioned reflex

condoléances [kɔ̃dɔleɑ̃s] NFPL condolences

conducteur, -trice [kɔ̃dyktœʀ, -tʀis] ADJ (*Élec*) conducting ▶ NM/F (*Auto etc*) driver; (*d'une machine*) operator ▶ NM (*Élec etc*) conductor

conduire [kɔ̃dɥiʀ] /38/ VT (*véhicule, passager*) to drive; (*délégation, troupeau*) to lead; **se conduire** VI to behave; ~ **vers/à** to lead towards/to; ~ **qn quelque part** to take sb somewhere; to drive sb somewhere

conduit, e [kɔ̃dɥi, -it] PP *de* **conduire** ▶ NM (*Tech*) conduit, pipe; (*Anat*) duct, canal

conduite [kɔ̃dɥit] NF (*en auto*) driving; (*comportement*) behaviour (*Brit*), behavior (*US*); (*d'eau, de gaz*) pipe; **sous la** ~ **de** led by; ~ **forcée** pressure pipe; ~ **à gauche** left-hand drive; ~ **intérieure** saloon (car); ~ **sous l'emprise de stupéfiants** drug-driving

cône [kon] NM cone; **en forme de** ~ cone-shaped

conf. ABR = **confort; tt conf.** all mod cons (*Brit*)

confection [kɔ̃fɛksjɔ̃] NF (*fabrication*) making; (*Couture*): **la** ~ the clothing industry, the rag trade (*fam*); **vêtement de** ~ ready-to-wear *ou* off-the-peg garment

confectionner [kɔ̃fɛksjɔne] /1/ VT to make

confédération [kɔ̃fedeʀasjɔ̃] NF confederation

conférence [kɔ̃feʀɑ̃s] NF (*exposé*) lecture; (*pourparlers*) conference; ~ **de presse** press conference; ~ **au sommet** summit (conference)

conférencier, -ière [kɔ̃feʀɑ̃sje, -jɛʀ] NM/F lecturer

conférer [kɔ̃feʀe] /6/ VT: ~ **à qn** (*titre, grade*) to confer on sb; ~ **à qch/qn** (*aspect etc*) to endow sth/sb with, give (to) sth/sb

confesser [kɔ̃fese] /1/ VT to confess; **se confesser** VI (*Rel*) to go to confession

confesseur [kɔ̃fesœʀ] NM confessor

confession [kɔ̃fesjɔ̃] NF confession; (*culte: catholique etc*) denomination

confessionnal, -aux [kɔ̃fesjɔnal, -o] NM confessional

confessionnel, le [kɔ̃fesjɔnɛl] ADJ denominational

confetti [kɔ̃feti] NM confetti *no pl*

confiance [kɔ̃fjɑ̃s] NF (*en l'honnêteté de qn*) confidence, trust; (*en la valeur de qch*) faith; **avoir** ~ **en** to have confidence *ou* faith in, trust; **faire** ~ **à** to trust; **en toute** ~ with complete confidence; **de** ~ trustworthy, reliable; **mettre qn en** ~ to win sb's trust; **vote de** ~ (*Pol*) vote of confidence; **inspirer** ~ **à** to inspire confidence in; ~ **en soi** self-confidence; *voir* **question**

confiant, e [kɔ̃fjɑ̃, -ɑ̃t] ADJ confident; trusting

confidence [kɔ̃fidɑ̃s] NF confidence

confident, e [kɔ̃fidɑ̃, -ɑ̃t] NM/F confidant/
confidante

confidentiel, le [kɔ̃fidɑ̃sjɛl] ADJ confidential

confidentiellement [kɔ̃fidɑ̃sjɛlmɑ̃] ADV in
confidence, confidentially

confier [kɔ̃fje] /**7**/ VT: **~ à qn** (objet en dépôt, travail
etc) to entrust to sb; (secret, pensée) to confide to
sb; **se ~ à qn** to confide in sb

configuration [kɔ̃figyʀasjɔ̃] NF configuration,
layout; (Inform) configuration

configurer [kɔ̃figyʀe] /**1**/ VT to configure

confiné, e [kɔ̃fine] ADJ enclosed; (air) stale

confiner [kɔ̃fine] /**1**/ VT: **~ à** to confine to;
(toucher) to border on; **se ~ dans** ou **à** to confine
o.s. to

confins [kɔ̃fɛ̃] NMPL: **aux ~ de** on the borders of

confirmation [kɔ̃fiʀmasjɔ̃] NF confirmation

confirmer [kɔ̃fiʀme] /**1**/ VT to confirm; **~ qn
dans une croyance/ses fonctions** to
strengthen sb in a belief/his duties

confiscation [kɔ̃fiskasjɔ̃] NF confiscation

confiserie [kɔ̃fizʀi] NF (magasin) confectioner's
ou sweet shop (BRIT), candy store (US);
confiseries NFPL (bonbons) confectionery sg,
sweets, candy no pl

confiseur, -euse [kɔ̃fizœʀ, -øz] NM/F
confectioner

confisquer [kɔ̃fiske] /**1**/ VT to confiscate

confit, e [kɔ̃fi, -it] ADJ: **fruits confits**
crystallized fruits ▶ NM: **~ d'oie** potted goose

confiture [kɔ̃fityʀ] NF jam; **~ d'oranges**
(orange) marmalade

conflagration [kɔ̃flagʀasjɔ̃] NF cataclysm

conflictuel, le [kɔ̃fliktɥɛl] ADJ full of clashes ou
conflicts

conflit [kɔ̃fli] NM conflict

confluent [kɔ̃flyɑ̃] NM confluence

confondre [kɔ̃fɔ̃dʀ] /**41**/ VT (jumeaux, faits) to
confuse, mix up; (témoin, menteur) to confound;
se confondre VI to merge; **se confondre en
excuses** to offer profuse apologies, apologize
profusely; **~ qch/qn avec qch/qn d'autre** to
mistake sth/sb for sth/sb else

confondu, e [kɔ̃fɔ̃dy] PP de **confondre** ▶ ADJ
(stupéfait) speechless, overcome; **toutes
catégories confondues** taking all categories
together

conformation [kɔ̃fɔʀmasjɔ̃] NF conformation

conforme [kɔ̃fɔʀm] ADJ: **~ à** (en accord avec: loi,
règle) in accordance with, in keeping with;
(identique à) true to; **copie certifiée ~** (Admin)
certified copy; **~ à la commande** as per order

conformé, e [kɔ̃fɔʀme] ADJ: **bien ~** well-formed

conformément [kɔ̃fɔʀmemɑ̃] ADV: **~ à** in
accordance with

conformer [kɔ̃fɔʀme] /**1**/ VT: **~ qch à** to model
sth on; **se ~ à** to conform to

conformisme [kɔ̃fɔʀmism] NM conformity

conformiste [kɔ̃fɔʀmist] ADJ, NMF conformist

conformité [kɔ̃fɔʀmite] NF conformity;
agreement; **en ~ avec** in accordance with

confort [kɔ̃fɔʀ] NM comfort; **tout ~** (Comm)
with all mod cons (BRIT) ou modern
conveniences

confortable [kɔ̃fɔʀtabl] ADJ comfortable

confortablement [kɔ̃fɔʀtabləmɑ̃] ADV
comfortably

conforter [kɔ̃fɔʀte] /**1**/ VT to reinforce,
strengthen

confrère [kɔ̃fʀɛʀ] NM colleague; fellow
member

confrérie [kɔ̃fʀeʀi] NF brotherhood

confrontation [kɔ̃fʀɔ̃tasjɔ̃] NF confrontation

confronté, e [kɔ̃fʀɔ̃te] ADJ: **~ à** confronted by,
facing

confronter [kɔ̃fʀɔ̃te] /**1**/ VT to confront; (textes)
to compare, collate

confus, e [kɔ̃fy, -yz] ADJ (vague) confused;
(embarrassé) embarrassed

confusément [kɔ̃fyzemɑ̃] ADV (distinguer,
ressentir) vaguely; (parler) confusedly

confusion [kɔ̃fyzjɔ̃] NF (voir confus) confusion;
embarrassment; (voir confondre) confusion;
mixing up; (erreur) confusion; **~ des peines** (Jur)
concurrency of sentences

congé [kɔ̃ʒe] NM (vacances) holiday; (arrêt de
travail) time off no pl, leave no pl; (Mil) leave no pl;
(avis de départ) notice; **en ~** on holiday; off
(work); on leave; **semaine/jour de ~** week/day
off; **prendre ~ de qn** to take one's leave of sb;
donner son ~ à to hand ou give in one's notice
to; **~ de maladie** sick leave; **~ de maternité**
maternity leave; **congés payés** paid holiday ou
leave

congédier [kɔ̃ʒedje] /**7**/ VT to dismiss

congélateur [kɔ̃ʒelatœʀ] NM freezer, deep
freeze

congélation [kɔ̃ʒelasjɔ̃] NF freezing; (de l'huile)
congealing

congeler [kɔ̃ʒ(ə)le] /**5**/ VT to freeze; **les
produits congelés** frozen foods; **se congeler** VI
to freeze

congénère [kɔ̃ʒenɛʀ] NMF fellow (bear ou lion
etc), fellow creature

congénital, e, -aux [kɔ̃ʒenital, -o] ADJ
congenital

congère [kɔ̃ʒɛʀ] NF snowdrift

congestion [kɔ̃ʒɛstjɔ̃] NF congestion; **~ cérébrale**
stroke; **~ pulmonaire** congestion of the lungs

congestionner [kɔ̃ʒɛstjɔne] /**1**/ VT to congest;
(Méd) to flush

conglomérat [kɔ̃glɔmeʀa] NM conglomerate

Congo [kɔ̃go] NM: **le ~** (pays, fleuve) the Congo

congolais, e [kɔ̃gɔlɛ, -ɛz] ADJ Congolese ▶ NM/F:
C~, e Congolese

congratuler [kɔ̃gʀatyle] /**1**/ VT to congratulate

congre [kɔ̃gʀ] NM conger (eel)

congrégation [kɔ̃gʀegasjɔ̃] NF (Rel)
congregation; (gén) assembly; gathering

congrès [kɔ̃gʀɛ] NM congress

congressiste [kɔ̃gʀesist] NMF delegate,
participant (at a congress)

congru, e [kɔ̃gʀy] ADJ: **la portion ~** the smallest
ou meanest share

conifère [kɔnifɛʀ] NM conifer

conique [kɔnik] ADJ conical

conjecture [kɔ̃ʒɛktyʀ] NF conjecture,
speculation no pl

conjecturer [kɔ̃ʒɛktyʀe] /1/ VT, VI to conjecture
conjoint, e [kɔ̃ʒwɛ̃, -wɛt] ADJ joint ▶ NM/F
spouse
conjointement [kɔ̃ʒwɛtmɑ̃] ADV jointly
conjonctif, -ive [kɔ̃ʒɔ̃ktif, -iv] ADJ: **tissu ~**
connective tissue
conjonction [kɔ̃ʒɔ̃ksjɔ̃] NF (Ling) conjunction
conjonctivite [kɔ̃ʒɔ̃ktivit] NF conjunctivitis
conjoncture [kɔ̃ʒɔ̃ktyʀ] NF circumstances pl; **la**
~ (économique) the economic climate ou
situation
conjoncturel, le [kɔ̃ʒɔ̃ktyʀɛl] ADJ: **variations/**
tendances conjoncturelles economic
fluctuations/trends
conjugaison [kɔ̃ʒygɛzɔ̃] NF (Ling) conjugation
conjugal, e, -aux [kɔ̃ʒygal, -o] ADJ conjugal;
married
conjugué, e [kɔ̃ʒyge] ADJ combined
conjuguer [kɔ̃ʒyge] /1/ VT (Ling) to conjugate;
(efforts etc) to combine
conjuration [kɔ̃ʒyʀasjɔ̃] NF conspiracy
conjuré, e [kɔ̃ʒyʀe] NM/F conspirator
conjurer [kɔ̃ʒyʀe] /1/ VT (sort, maladie) to avert;
(implorer): **~ qn de faire qch** to beseech ou
entreat sb to do sth
connais [kɔnɛ], **connaissais** etc [kɔnɛsɛ] VB
voir **connaître**
connaissance [kɔnɛsɑ̃s] NF (savoir) knowledge
no pl; (personne connue) acquaintance; (conscience)
consciousness; **connaissances** NFPL
knowledge no pl; **être sans ~** to be unconscious;
perdre/reprendre ~ to lose/regain
consciousness; **à ma/sa ~** to (the best of) my/
his knowledge; **faire ~ avec qn** ou **la ~ de qn**
(rencontrer) to meet sb; (apprendre à connaître) to get
to know sb; **avoir ~ de** to be aware of; **prendre**
~ de (document etc) to peruse; **en ~ de cause** with
full knowledge of the facts; **de ~** (personne,
visage) familiar
connaissant etc [kɔnɛsɑ̃] VB voir **connaître**
connaissement [kɔnɛsmɑ̃] NM bill of lading
connaisseur, -euse [kɔnɛsœʀ, -øz] NM/F
connoisseur ▶ ADJ expert
connaître [kɔnɛtʀ] /57/ VT to know; (éprouver) to
experience; (avoir: succès) to have; to enjoy; **~ de**
nom/vue to know by name/sight; **se connaître**
VI to know each other; (soi-même) to know o.s.;
ils se sont connus à Genève they (first) met in
Geneva; **s'y connaître en qch** to know about
sth
connasse [kɔnas] NF (!) stupid bitch (!) ou
cow (!)
connecté, e [kɔnɛkte] ADJ (Inform) on line
connecter [kɔnɛkte] /1/ VT to connect; **se ~ à**
Internet to log onto the Internet
connerie [kɔnʀi] NF (fam) (bloody) stupid (BRIT)
ou damn-fool (US) thing to do ou say
connexe [kɔnɛks] ADJ closely related
connexion [kɔnɛksjɔ̃] NF connection
connivence [kɔnivɑ̃s] NF connivance
connotation [kɔnɔtasjɔ̃] NF connotation
connu, e [kɔny] PP de **connaître** ▶ ADJ (célèbre)
well-known
conque [kɔ̃k] NF (coquille) conch (shell)

conquérant, e [kɔ̃keʀɑ̃, -ɑ̃t] NM/F conqueror
conquérir [kɔ̃keʀiʀ] /21/ VT to conquer, win
conquerrai etc [kɔ̃keʀʀe] VB voir **conquérir**
conquête [kɔ̃kɛt] NF conquest
conquière, conquiers etc [kɔ̃kjɛʀ] VB voir
conquérir
conquis, e [kɔ̃ki, -iz] PP de **conquérir**
consacrer [kɔ̃sakʀe] /1/ VT (Rel) to consecrate;
(fig: usage etc) to sanction, establish; **~ qch à**
(employer) to devote ou dedicate sth to; (Rel) to
consecrate sth to; **se ~ à qch/faire** to dedicate
ou devote o.s. to sth/to doing
consanguin, e [kɔ̃sɑ̃gɛ̃, -in] ADJ between blood
relations; **frère ~** half-brother (on father's side);
mariage ~ intermarriage
consciemment [kɔ̃sjamɑ̃] ADV consciously
conscience [kɔ̃sjɑ̃s] NF conscience; (perception)
consciousness; **avoir/prendre ~ de** to be/
become aware of; **perdre/reprendre ~** to lose/
regain consciousness; **avoir bonne/mauvaise**
~ to have a clear/guilty conscience; **en (toute)**
~ in all conscience
consciencieux, -euse [kɔ̃sjɑ̃sjø, -øz] ADJ
conscientious
conscient, e [kɔ̃sjɑ̃, -ɑ̃t] ADJ conscious; **~ de**
aware ou conscious of
conscription [kɔ̃skʀipsjɔ̃] NF conscription
conscrit [kɔ̃skʀi] NM conscript
consécration [kɔ̃sekʀasjɔ̃] NF consecration
consécutif, -ive [kɔ̃sekytif, -iv] ADJ consecutive;
~ à following upon
consécutivement [kɔ̃sekytivmɑ̃] ADV
consecutively; **~ à** following on
conseil [kɔ̃sɛj] NM (avis) piece of advice, advice
no pl; (assemblée) council; (expert): **~ en**
recrutement recruitment consultant ▶ ADJ:
ingénieur-~ engineering consultant; **tenir ~**
to hold a meeting; to deliberate; **donner un ~**
ou **des conseils à qn** to give sb (a piece of)
advice; **demander ~ à qn** to ask sb's advice;
prendre ~ (auprès de qn) to take advice (from
sb); **~ d'administration** board (of directors);
~ de classe (Scol) meeting of teachers, parents and
class representatives to discuss pupils' progress; **~ de**
discipline disciplinary committee; **~ général**
regional council; see note; **~ de guerre**
court-martial; **le ~ des ministres** ≈ the
Cabinet; **~ municipal** town council;
~ régional regional board of elected representatives;
~ de révision recruitment ou draft (US) board

> Each département of France is run by a Conseil
> général, whose remit covers personnel,
> transport infrastructure, housing, school
> grants and economic development. The
> council is made up of conseillers généraux, each
> of whom represents a canton and is elected
> for a six-year term. Half of the council's
> membership are elected every three years.

conseiller¹ [kɔ̃seje] VT (personne) to advise;
(méthode, action) to recommend, advise; **~ qch à**
qn to recommend sth to sb; **~ à qn de faire qch**
to advise sb to do sth
conseiller², -ière [kɔ̃seje, -ɛʀ] NM/F adviser;
~ général regional councillor; **~ matrimonial**

marriage guidance counsellor; **~ municipal** town councillor; **~ d'orientation** (Scol) careers adviser (Brit), (school) counselor (US)

consensuel, le [kɔ̃sãsɥɛl] ADJ consensual

consensus [kɔ̃sẽsys] NM consensus

consentement [kɔ̃sãtmã] NM consent

consentir [kɔ̃sãtiʀ] /16/ VT: **~ (à qch/faire)** to agree ou consent (to sth/to doing); **~ qch à qn** to grant sb sth

conséquence [kɔ̃sekãs] NF consequence, outcome; **conséquences** NFPL consequences, repercussions; **en ~** (donc) consequently; (de façon appropriée) accordingly; **ne pas tirer à ~** to be unlikely to have any repercussions; **sans ~** unimportant; **de ~** important

conséquent, e [kɔ̃sekã, -ãt] ADJ logical, rational; (fam: important) substantial; **par ~** consequently

conservateur, -trice [kɔ̃sɛʀvatœʀ, -tʀis] ADJ conservative ▶ NM/F (Pol) conservative; (de musée) curator ▶ NM (pour aliments) preservative

conservation [kɔ̃sɛʀvasjɔ̃] NF retention; keeping; preserving, preservation

conservatisme [kɔ̃sɛʀvatism] NM conservatism

conservatoire [kɔ̃sɛʀvatwaʀ] NM academy; (Écologie) conservation area

conserve [kɔ̃sɛʀv] NF (gén pl) canned ou tinned (Brit) food; **conserves de poisson** canned ou tinned (Brit) fish; **en ~** canned, tinned (Brit); **de ~** (ensemble) in concert; (naviguer) in convoy

conservé, e [kɔ̃sɛʀve] ADJ: **bien ~** (personne) well-preserved

conserver [kɔ̃sɛʀve] /1/ VT (faculté) to retain, keep; (habitude) to keep up; (amis, livres) to keep; (préserver, Culin) to preserve; **se conserver** VI (aliments) to keep; **"~ au frais"** "store in a cool place"

conserverie [kɔ̃sɛʀvʀi] NF canning factory

considérable [kɔ̃sideʀabl] ADJ considerable, significant, extensive

considération [kɔ̃sideʀasjɔ̃] NF consideration; (estime) esteem, respect; **considérations** NFPL (remarques) reflections; **prendre en ~** to take into consideration ou account; **ceci mérite ~** this is worth considering; **en ~ de** given, because of

considéré, e [kɔ̃sideʀe] ADJ respected; **tout bien ~** all things considered

considérer [kɔ̃sideʀe] /6/ VT to consider; (regarder) to consider, study; **~ qch comme** to regard sth as

consigne [kɔ̃siɲ] NF (Comm) deposit; (de gare) left luggage (office) (Brit), checkroom (US); (punition: Scol) detention; (: Mil) confinement to barracks; (ordre, instruction) instructions pl; **~ automatique** left-luggage locker; **consignes de sécurité** safety instructions

consigné, e [kɔ̃siɲe] ADJ (Comm: bouteille, emballage) returnable; **non ~** non-returnable

consigner [kɔ̃siɲe] /1/ VT (note, pensée) to record; (marchandises) to deposit; (punir: Mil) to confine to barracks; (: élève) to put in detention; (Comm) to put a deposit on

consistance [kɔ̃sistãs] NF consistency

consistant, e [kɔ̃sistã, -ãt] ADJ thick; solid

consister [kɔ̃siste] /1/ VI: **~ en/dans/à faire** to consist of/in/in doing

consœur [kɔ̃sœʀ] NF (lady) colleague; fellow member

consolation [kɔ̃sɔlasjɔ̃] NF consolation no pl, comfort no pl

console [kɔ̃sɔl] NF console; **~ graphique** ou **de visualisation** (Inform) visual display unit, VDU; **~ de jeux** games console

consoler [kɔ̃sɔle] /1/ VT to console; **se ~ (de qch)** to console o.s. (for sth)

consolider [kɔ̃sɔlide] /1/ VT to strengthen, reinforce; (fig) to consolidate; **bilan consolidé** consolidated balance sheet

consommateur, -trice [kɔ̃sɔmatœʀ, -tʀis] NM/F (Écon) consumer; (dans un café) customer

consommation [kɔ̃sɔmasjɔ̃] NF (Écon) consumption; (Jur) consummation; (boisson) drink; **~ aux 100 km** (Auto) (fuel) consumption per 100 km, ≈ miles per gallon (mpg), ≈ gas mileage (US); **de ~** (biens, société) consumer cpd

consommé, e [kɔ̃sɔme] ADJ consummate ▶ NM consommé

consommer [kɔ̃sɔme] /1/ VT (personne) to eat ou drink, consume; (voiture, usine, poêle) to use, consume; (Jur: mariage) to consummate ▶ VI (dans un café) to (have a) drink

consonance [kɔ̃sɔnãs] NF consonance; **nom à ~ étrangère** foreign-sounding name

consonne [kɔ̃sɔn] NF consonant

consortium [kɔ̃sɔʀsjɔm] NM consortium

consorts [kɔ̃sɔʀ] NMPL: **et ~** (péj) and company, and his bunch ou like

conspirateur, -trice [kɔ̃spiʀatœʀ, -tʀis] NM/F conspirator, plotter

conspiration [kɔ̃spiʀasjɔ̃] NF conspiracy

conspirer [kɔ̃spiʀe] /1/ VI to conspire, plot; **~ à** (tendre à) to conspire to

conspuer [kɔ̃spɥe] /1/ VT to boo, shout down

constamment [kɔ̃stamã] ADV constantly

constance [kɔ̃stãs] NF permanence, constancy; (d'une amitié) steadfastness; **travailler avec ~** to work steadily; **il faut de la ~ pour la supporter** (fam) you need a lot of patience to put up with her

constant, e [kɔ̃stã, -ãt] ADJ constant; (personne) steadfast ▶ NF constant

Constantinople [kɔ̃stãtinɔpl] N Constantinople

constat [kɔ̃sta] NM (d'huissier) certified report (by bailiff); (de police) report; (observation) (observed) fact, observation; (affirmation) statement; **(à l'amiable)** (jointly agreed) statement for insurance purposes; **~ d'échec** acknowledgement of failure

constatation [kɔ̃statasjɔ̃] NF noticing; certifying; (remarque) observation

constater [kɔ̃state] /1/ VT (remarquer) to note, notice; (Admin, Jur: attester) to certify; (dégâts) to note; **~ que** (dire) to state that

constellation [kɔ̃stelasjɔ̃] NF constellation

constellé, e [kɔ̃stele] ADJ: **~ de** (étoiles) studded ou spangled with (: *taches*) spotted with

consternant, e [kɔ̃stɛʁnɑ̃ -ɑ̃t] ADJ (*nouvelle*) dismaying; (*attristant, étonnant*: *bêtise*) appalling

consternation [kɔ̃stɛʁnasjɔ̃] NF consternation, dismay

consterner [kɔ̃stɛʁne] /1/ VT to dismay

constipation [kɔ̃stipasjɔ̃] NF constipation

constipé, e [kɔ̃stipe] ADJ constipated; (*fig*) stiff

constituant, e [kɔ̃stitɥɑ̃, -ɑ̃t] ADJ (*élément*) constituent; **assemblée ~** (*Pol*) constituent assembly

constitué, e [kɔ̃stitɥe] ADJ: **~ de** made up *ou* composed of; **bien ~** of sound constitution; well-formed

constituer [kɔ̃stitɥe] /1/ VT (*comité, équipe*) to set up, form; (*dossier, collection*) to put together, build up; (*éléments, parties*: *composer*) to make up, constitute; (: *représenter, être*) to constitute; **se ~ prisonnier** to give o.s. up; **se ~ partie civile** to bring an independent action for damages

constitution [kɔ̃stitysjɔ̃] NF setting up; building up; (*composition*) composition, make-up; (*santé, Pol*) constitution

constitutionnel, le [kɔ̃stitysjɔnɛl] ADJ constitutional

constructeur [kɔ̃stʁyktœʁ] NMF manufacturer, builder

constructif, -ive [kɔ̃stʁyktif, -iv] ADJ (*positif*) constructive

construction [kɔ̃stʁyksjɔ̃] NF construction, building

construire [kɔ̃stʁɥiʁ] /38/ VT to build, construct; **se construire** VI: **l'immeuble s'est construit très vite** the building went up *ou* was built very quickly

consul [kɔ̃syl] NM consul

consulaire [kɔ̃sylɛʁ] ADJ consular

consulat [kɔ̃syla] NM consulate

consultant, e [kɔ̃syltɑ̃, -ɑ̃t] ADJ, NM consultant

consultatif, -ive [kɔ̃syltatif, -iv] ADJ advisory

consultation [kɔ̃syltasjɔ̃] NF consultation; **consultations** NFPL (*Pol*) talks; **être en ~** (*délibération*) to be in consultation; (*médecin*) to be consulting; **aller à la ~** (*Méd*) to go to the surgery (BRIT) *ou* doctor's office (US); **heures de ~** (*Méd*) surgery (BRIT) *ou* office (US) hours

consulter [kɔ̃sylte] /1/ VT to consult ▶ VI (*médecin*) to hold surgery (BRIT), be in (the office) (US); **se consulter** VI to confer

consumer [kɔ̃syme] /1/ VT to consume; **se consumer** VI to burn; **se consumer de chagrin/douleur** to be consumed with sorrow/ grief

consumérisme [kɔ̃symeʁism] NM consumerism

contact [kɔ̃takt] NM contact; **au ~ de** (*air, peau*) on contact with; (*gens*) through contact with; **mettre/couper le ~** (*Auto*) to switch on/off the ignition; **entrer en ~** (*fils, objets*) to come into contact, make contact; **se mettre en ~ avec** (*Radio*) to make contact with; **prendre ~ avec** (*relation d'affaires, connaissance*) to get in touch *ou* contact with

contacter [kɔ̃takte] /1/ VT to contact,

get in touch with

contagieux, -euse [kɔ̃taʒjø, -øz] ADJ infectious; (*par le contact*) contagious

contagion [kɔ̃taʒjɔ̃] NF contagion

container [kɔ̃tenɛʁ] NM container

contamination [kɔ̃taminasjɔ̃] NF infection; contamination

contaminer [kɔ̃tamine] /1/ VT (*par un virus*) to infect; (*par des radiations*) to contaminate

conte [kɔ̃t] NM tale; **~ de fées** fairy tale

contemplatif, -ive [kɔ̃tɑ̃platif, -iv] ADJ contemplative

contemplation [kɔ̃tɑ̃plasjɔ̃] NF contemplation; (*Rel, Philosophie*) meditation

contempler [kɔ̃tɑ̃ple] /1/ VT to contemplate, gaze at

contemporain, e [kɔ̃tɑ̃pɔʁɛ̃, -ɛn] ADJ, NM/F contemporary

contenance [kɔ̃tnɑ̃s] NF (*d'un récipient*) capacity; (*attitude*) bearing, attitude; **perdre ~** to lose one's composure; **se donner une ~** to give the impression of composure; **faire bonne ~ (devant)** to put on a bold front (in the face of)

conteneur [kɔ̃tnœʁ] NM container; **~ (de bouteilles)** bottle bank

conteneurisation [kɔ̃tnœʁizasjɔ̃] NF containerization

contenir [kɔ̃t(ə)niʁ] /22/ VT to contain; (*avoir une capacité de*) to hold; **se contenir** VI (*se retenir*) to control o.s. *ou* one's emotions, contain o.s.

content, e [kɔ̃tɑ̃, -ɑ̃t] ADJ pleased, glad; **~ de** pleased with; **je serais ~ que tu …** I would be pleased if you …

contentement [kɔ̃tɑ̃tmɑ̃] NM contentment, satisfaction

contenter [kɔ̃tɑ̃te] /1/ VT to satisfy, please; (*envie*) to satisfy; **se ~ de** to content o.s. with

contentieux [kɔ̃tɑ̃sjø] NM (*Comm*) litigation; (: *service*) litigation department; (*Pol etc*) contentious issues *pl*

contenu, e [kɔ̃t(ə)ny] PP *de* **contenir** ▶ NM (*d'un bol*) contents *pl*; (*d'un texte*) content

conter [kɔ̃te] /1/ VT to recount, relate; **en ~ de belles à qn** to tell tall stories to sb

contestable [kɔ̃tɛstabl] ADJ questionable

contestataire [kɔ̃tɛstatɛʁ] ADJ (*journal, étudiant*) anti-establishment ▶ NMF (anti-establishment) protester

contestation [kɔ̃tɛstasjɔ̃] NF questioning, contesting; (*Pol*): **la ~** anti-establishment activity, protest

conteste [kɔ̃tɛst]: **sans ~** *adv* unquestionably, indisputably

contesté, e [kɔ̃tɛste] ADJ (*roman, écrivain*) controversial

contester [kɔ̃tɛste] /1/ VT to question, contest ▶ VI (*Pol*: *gén*) to rebel (against established authority), protest

conteur, -euse [kɔ̃tœʁ, -øz] NM/F story-teller

contexte [kɔ̃tɛkst] NM context

contiendrai [kɔ̃tjɛ̃dʁe], **contiens** *etc* [kɔ̃tjɛ̃] VB *voir* **contenir**

contigu, ë [kɔ̃tigy] ADJ: **~ (à)** adjacent (to)

continent [kɔ̃tinɑ̃] NM continent

continental – contrefaire

continental, e, -aux [kɔ̃tinɑ̃tal, -o] ADJ continental

contingences [kɔ̃tɛ̃ʒɑ̃s] NFPL contingencies

contingent [kɔ̃tɛ̃ʒɑ̃] NM (*Mil*) contingent; (*Comm*) quota

contingenter [kɔ̃tɛ̃ʒɑ̃te] /1/ VT (*Comm*) to fix a quota on

contins *etc* [kɔ̃tɛ̃] VB *voir* **contenir**

continu, e [kɔ̃tiny] ADJ continuous; **faire la journée ~** to work without taking a full lunch break; (**courant**) **~** direct current, DC

continuation [kɔ̃tinɥasjɔ̃] NF continuation

continuel, le [kɔ̃tinɥɛl] ADJ (*qui se répète*) constant, continual; (*continu*) continuous

continuellement [kɔ̃tinɥɛlmɑ̃] ADV continually; continuously

continuer [kɔ̃tinɥe] /1/ VT (*travail, voyage etc*) to continue (with), carry on (with), go on with; (*prolonger: alignement, rue*) to continue ▸ VI (*pluie, vie, bruit*) to continue, go on; (*voyageur*) to go on; **se continuer** VI to carry on; **~ à** *ou* **de faire** to go on *ou* continue doing

continuité [kɔ̃tinɥite] NF continuity; continuation

contondant, e [kɔ̃tɔ̃dɑ̃, -ɑ̃t] ADJ: **arme ~** blunt instrument

contorsion [kɔ̃tɔrsjɔ̃] NF contortion

contorsionner [kɔ̃tɔrsjɔne] /1/: **se contorsionner** VI to contort o.s., writhe about

contorsionniste [kɔ̃tɔrsjɔnist] NMF contortionist

contour [kɔ̃tur] NM outline, contour; **contours** NMPL (*d'une rivière etc*) windings

contourner [kɔ̃turne] /1/ VT to bypass, walk *ou* drive round; (*difficulté*) to get round

contraceptif, -ive [kɔ̃traseptif, -iv] ADJ, NM contraceptive

contraception [kɔ̃trasepsjɔ̃] NF contraception

contracté, e [kɔ̃trakte] ADJ (*muscle*) tense, contracted; (*personne: tendu*) tense, tensed up; **article ~** (*Ling*) contracted article

contracter [kɔ̃trakte] /1/ VT (*muscle etc*) to tense, contract; (*maladie, dette, obligation*) to contract; (*assurance*) to take out; **se contracter** VI (*métal, muscles*) to contract

contraction [kɔ̃traksjɔ̃] NF contraction

contractuel, le [kɔ̃traktɥɛl] ADJ contractual ▸ NM/F (*agent*) traffic warden; (*employé*) contract employee

contradiction [kɔ̃tradiksjɔ̃] NF contradiction

contradictoire [kɔ̃tradiktwar] ADJ contradictory, conflicting; **débat ~** (open) debate

contraignant, e [kɔ̃trɛɲɑ̃, -ɑ̃t] VB *voir* **contraindre** ▸ ADJ restricting

contraindre [kɔ̃trɛ̃dr] /52/ VT: **~ qn à faire** to force *ou* compel sb to do

contraint, e [kɔ̃trɛ̃, -ɛ̃t] PP *de* **contraindre** ▸ ADJ (*mine, air*) constrained, forced ▸ NF constraint; **sans ~** unrestrainedly, unconstrainedly

contraire [kɔ̃trɛr] ADJ, NM opposite; **~ à** contrary to; **au ~** adv on the contrary

contrairement [kɔ̃trɛrmɑ̃] ADV: **~ à** contrary to, unlike

contralto [kɔ̃tralto] NM contralto

contrariant, e [kɔ̃trarjɑ̃, -ɑ̃t] ADJ (*personne*) contrary, perverse; (*incident*) annoying

contrarier [kɔ̃trarje] /7/ VT (*personne*) to annoy, bother; (*fig*) to impede; (*projets*) to thwart, frustrate

contrariété [kɔ̃trarjete] NF annoyance

contraste [kɔ̃trast] NM contrast

contraster [kɔ̃traste] /1/ VT, VI to contrast

contrat [kɔ̃tra] NM contract; (*fig: accord, pacte*) agreement; **~ de travail** employment contract

contravention [kɔ̃travɑ̃sjɔ̃] NF (*infraction*): **~** contravention of; (*amende*) fine; (*PV pour stationnement interdit*) parking ticket; **dresser ~ à** (*automobiliste*) to book; to write out a parking ticket for

contre [kɔ̃tr] PRÉP against; (*en échange*) (in exchange) for; **par ~** on the other hand

contre-amiral, -aux [kɔ̃tramiral, -o] NM rear admiral

contre-attaque [kɔ̃tratak] NF counterattack

contre-attaquer [kɔ̃tratake] /1/ VI to counterattack

contre-balancer [kɔ̃trəbalɑ̃se] /3/ VT to counterbalance; (*fig*) to offset

contrebande [kɔ̃trəbɑ̃d] NF (*trafic*) contraband, smuggling; (*marchandise*) contraband, smuggled goods *pl*; **faire la ~ de** to smuggle

contrebandier, -ière [kɔ̃trəbɑ̃dje, -jɛr] NM/F smuggler

contrebas [kɔ̃trəbɑ] : **en ~** adv (down) below

contrebasse [kɔ̃trəbɑs] NF (double) bass

contrebassiste [kɔ̃trəbasist] NMF (double) bass player

contre-braquer [kɔ̃trəbrake] /1/ VI to steer into a skid

contrecarrer [kɔ̃trəkare] /1/ VT to thwart

contrechamp [kɔ̃trəʃɑ̃] NM (*Ciné*) reverse shot

contrecœur [kɔ̃trəkœr] : **à ~** adv (be)grudgingly, reluctantly

contrecoup [kɔ̃trəku] NM repercussions *pl*; **par ~** as an indirect consequence

contre-courant [kɔ̃trəkurɑ̃] : **à ~** adv against the current

contredire [kɔ̃trədir] /37/ VT (*personne*) to contradict; (*témoignage, assertion, faits*) to refute; **se contredire** VI to contradict o.s.

contredit, e [kɔ̃trədi, -it] PP *de* **contredire** ▸ NM: **sans ~** without question

contrée [kɔ̃tre] NF region; land

contre-écrou [kɔ̃trekru] NM lock nut

contre-enquête [kɔ̃trɑ̃kɛt] NF counter-inquiry

contre-espionnage [kɔ̃trɛspjɔnaʒ] NM counter-espionage

contre-exemple [kɔ̃trɛgzɑ̃pl] NF counter-example

contre-expertise [kɔ̃trɛkspɛrtiz] NF second (expert) assessment

contrefaçon [kɔ̃trəfasɔ̃] NF forgery; **~ de brevet** patent infringement

contrefaire [kɔ̃trəfɛr] /60/ VT (*document, signature*) to forge, counterfeit; (*personne, démarche*) to mimic; (*dénaturer: sa voix etc*) to disguise

93

contrefait, e [kɔ̃trəfɛ, -ɛt] PP *de* **contrefaire**
▸ ADJ misshapen, deformed

contrefasse [kɔ̃trəfas], **contreferai** *etc*
[kɔ̃trəfʀe] VB *voir* **contrefaire**

contre-filet [kɔ̃trəfilɛ] NM (*Culin*) sirloin

contreforts [kɔ̃trəfɔʀ] NMPL foothills

contre-haut [kɔ̃trəo]: **en ~** (up) above

contre-indication [kɔ̃trɛ̃dikasjɔ̃] (*pl*
contre-indications) NF (*Méd*) contra-
indication; "**~ en cas d'eczéma**" "should not
be used by people with eczema"

contre-indiqué, e [kɔ̃trɛ̃dike] ADJ (*Méd*)
contraindicated; (*déconseillé*) unadvisable,
ill-advised

contre-interrogatoire [kɔ̃trɛ̃tɛrɔgatwaʀ] NM:
faire subir un ~ à qn to cross-examine sb

contre-jour [kɔ̃trəʒuʀ]: **à ~** *adv* against the light

contremaître [kɔ̃trəmɛtr] NM foreman

contre-manifestant, e [kɔ̃trəmanifɛstɑ̃, -ɑ̃t]
NM/F counter-demonstrator

contre-manifestation [kɔ̃trəmanifɛstasjɔ̃] NF
counter-demonstration

contremarque [kɔ̃trəmark] NF (*ticket*) pass-out
ticket

contre-offensive [kɔ̃trɔfɑ̃siv] NF
counteroffensive

contre-ordre [kɔ̃trɔrdr] NM = **contrordre**

contrepartie [kɔ̃trəparti] NF compensation;
en ~ in compensation; in return

contre-performance [kɔ̃trəpɛrfɔrmɑ̃s] NF
below-average performance

contrepèterie [kɔ̃trəpetri] NF spoonerism

contre-pied [kɔ̃trəpje] NM (*inverse, opposé*):
le ~ de ... the exact opposite of ...; **prendre le ~
de** to take the opposing view of; to take the
opposite course to; **prendre qn à ~** (*Sport*) to
wrong-foot sb

contre-plaqué [kɔ̃trəplake] NM plywood

contre-plongée [kɔ̃trəplɔ̃ʒe] NF low-angle
shot

contrepoids [kɔ̃trəpwa] NM counterweight,
counterbalance; **faire ~** to act as a
counterbalance

contre-poil [kɔ̃trəpwal]: **à ~** *adv* the wrong
way

contrepoint [kɔ̃trəpwɛ̃] NM counterpoint

contrepoison [kɔ̃trəpwazɔ̃] NM antidote

contrer [kɔ̃tre] /1/ VT to counter

contre-révolution [kɔ̃trərevɔlysjɔ̃] NF
counter-revolution

contre-révolutionnaire [kɔ̃trərevɔlysjɔnɛr]
NMF counter-revolutionary

contresens [kɔ̃trəsɑ̃s] NM (*erreur*)
misinterpretation; (*mauvaise traduction*)
mistranslation; (*absurdité*) nonsense *no pl*; **à ~**
adv the wrong way

contresigner [kɔ̃trəsiɲe] /1/ VT to countersign

contretemps [kɔ̃trətɑ̃] NM hitch, contretemps;
à ~ *adv* (*Mus*) out of time; (*fig*) at an inopportune
moment

contre-terrorisme [kɔ̃trətɛrɔrism] NM
counter-terrorism

contre-terroriste [kɔ̃trətɛrɔrist] NMF
counter-terrorist

contre-torpilleur [kɔ̃trətɔrpijœr] NM
destroyer

contrevenant, e [kɔ̃trəvnɑ̃, -ɑ̃t] VB *voir*
contrevenir ▸ NM/F offender

contrevenir [kɔ̃trəvnir] /22/: **~ à** vt to
contravene

contre-voie [kɔ̃trəvwa]: **à ~** *adv* (*en sens inverse*)
on the wrong track; (*du mauvais côté*) on the
wrong side

contribuable [kɔ̃tribɥabl] NMF taxpayer

contribuer [kɔ̃tribɥe] /1/: **~ à** vt to contribute
towards

contribution [kɔ̃tribysjɔ̃] NF contribution; **les
contributions** (*bureaux*) the tax office; **mettre
à ~** to call upon; **contributions directes/
indirectes** direct/indirect taxation

contrit, e [kɔ̃tri, -it] ADJ contrite

contrôlable [kɔ̃trolabl] ADJ (*maîtrisable: situation,
débit*) controllable; (: *alibi, déclarations*) verifiable

contrôle [kɔ̃trol] NM checking *no pl*, check;
supervision; monitoring; (*test*) test,
examination; **perdre le ~ de son véhicule** to
lose control of one's vehicle; **des changes**
(*Comm*) exchange controls; **~ continu** (*Scol*)
continuous assessment; **~ d'identité** identity
check; **~ des naissances** birth control; **~ des
prix** price control

contrôler [kɔ̃trole] /1/ VT (*vérifier*) to check;
(*surveiller: opérations*) to supervise; (: *prix*) to
monitor, control; (*maîtriser, Comm: firme*) to
control; **se contrôler** VI to control o.s.

contrôleur, -euse [kɔ̃trolœr, -øz] NM/F (*de train*)
(ticket) inspector; (*de bus*) (bus) conductor/
tress; **~ de la navigation aérienne, ~ aérien**
air traffic controller; **~ financier** financial
controller

contrordre [kɔ̃trɔrdr] NM counter-order,
countermand; **sauf ~** unless otherwise
directed

controverse [kɔ̃trɔvɛrs] NF controversy

controversé, e [kɔ̃trɔvɛrse] ADJ (*personnage,
question*) controversial

contumace [kɔ̃tymas]: **par ~** *adv* in absentia

contusion [kɔ̃tyzjɔ̃] NF bruise, contusion

contusionné, e [kɔ̃tyzjɔne] ADJ bruised

conurbation [kɔnyrbasjɔ̃] NF conurbation

convaincant, e [kɔ̃vɛ̃kɑ̃, -ɑ̃t] VB *voir* **convaincre**
▸ ADJ convincing

convaincre [kɔ̃vɛ̃kr] /42/ VT: **~ qn (de qch)** to
convince sb (of sth); **~ qn (de faire)** to persuade
sb (to do); **~ qn de** (*Jur: délit*) to convict sb of

convaincu, e [kɔ̃vɛ̃ky] PP *de* **convaincre** ▸ ADJ:
d'un ton ~ with conviction

convainquais *etc* [kɔ̃vɛ̃kɛ] VB *voir* **convaincre**

convalescence [kɔ̃valesɑ̃s] NF convalescence;
maison de ~ convalescent home

convalescent, e [kɔ̃valesɑ̃, -ɑ̃t] ADJ, NM/F
convalescent

convenable [kɔ̃vnabl] ADJ suitable; (*décent*)
acceptable, proper; (*assez bon*) decent,
acceptable; adequate, passable

convenablement [kɔ̃vnabləmɑ̃] ADV (*placé,
choisi*) suitably; (*s'habiller, s'exprimer*) properly;
(*payé, logé*) decently

convenance [kɔ̃vnɑ̃s] NF: **à ma/votre** ~ to my/ your liking; **convenances** NFPL proprieties

convenir [kɔ̃vniʀ] /**22**/ VI to be suitable; ~ **à** to suit; **il convient de** it is advisable to; (bienséant) it is right ou proper to; ~ **de** (bien-fondé de qch) to admit (to), acknowledge; (date, somme etc) to agree upon; ~ **que** (admettre) to admit that, acknowledge the fact that; ~ **de faire qch** to agree to do sth; **il a été convenu que** it has been agreed that; **comme convenu** as agreed

convention [kɔ̃vɑ̃sjɔ̃] NF convention; **conventions** NFPL (convenances) convention sg, social conventions; **de** ~ conventional; ~ **collective** (Écon) collective agreement

conventionnalisme [kɔ̃vɑ̃sjɔnalism] NM (des idées) conventionality

conventionné, e [kɔ̃vɑ̃sjɔne] ADJ (Admin) applying charges laid down by the state

conventionnel, le [kɔ̃vɑ̃sjɔnɛl] ADJ conventional

conventionnellement [kɔ̃vɑ̃sjɔnɛlmɑ̃] ADV conventionally

conventuel, le [kɔ̃vɑ̃tɥɛl] ADJ monastic; monastery cpd, conventual, convent cpd

convenu, e [kɔ̃vny] PP de **convenir** ▶ ADJ agreed

convergent, e [kɔ̃vɛʀʒɑ̃, -ɑ̃t] ADJ convergent

converger [kɔ̃vɛʀʒe] /**3**/ VI to converge; ~ **vers** ou **sur** to converge on

conversation [kɔ̃vɛʀsasjɔ̃] NF conversation; **avoir de la** ~ to be a good conversationalist

converser [kɔ̃vɛʀse] /**1**/ VI to converse

conversion [kɔ̃vɛʀsjɔ̃] NF conversion; (Ski) kick turn

convertible [kɔ̃vɛʀtibl] ADJ (Écon) convertible; **(canapé)** ~ sofa bed

convertir [kɔ̃vɛʀtiʀ] /**2**/ VT: ~ **qn (à)** to convert sb (to); ~ **qch en** to convert sth into; **se** ~ **(à)** to be converted (to)

convertisseur [kɔ̃vɛʀtisœʀ] NM (Élec) converter

convexe [kɔ̃vɛks] ADJ convex

conviction [kɔ̃viksjɔ̃] NF conviction

conviendrai [kɔ̃vjɛ̃dʀe], **conviens** etc [kɔ̃vjɛ̃] VB voir **convenir**

convienne etc [kɔ̃vjɛn] VB voir **convenir**

convier [kɔ̃vje] /**7**/ VT: ~ **qn à** (dîner etc) to (cordially) invite sb to; ~ **qn à faire** to urge sb to do

convint etc [kɔ̃vɛ̃] VB voir **convenir**

convive [kɔ̃viv] NMF guest (at table)

convivial, e [kɔ̃vivjal] ADJ (Inform) user-friendly

convocation [kɔ̃vɔkasjɔ̃] NF (voir convoquer) convening, convoking; summoning; invitation; (document) notification to attend; (Jur) summons sg

convoi [kɔ̃vwa] NM (de voitures, prisonniers) convoy; (train) train; ~ **(funèbre)** funeral procession

convoiter [kɔ̃vwate] /**1**/ VT to covet

convoitise [kɔ̃vwatiz] NF covetousness; (sexuelle) lust, desire

convoler [kɔ̃vɔle] /**1**/ VI: ~ **(en justes noces)** to be wed

convoquer [kɔ̃vɔke] /**1**/ VT (assemblée) to convene, convoke; (subordonné, témoin) to

summon; (candidat) to ask to attend; ~ **qn (à)** (réunion) to invite sb (to attend)

convoyer [kɔ̃vwaje] /**8**/ VT to escort

convoyeur [kɔ̃vwajœʀ] NM (Navig) escort ship; ~ **de fonds** security guard

convulsé, e [kɔ̃vylse] ADJ (visage) distorted

convulsif, -ive [kɔ̃vylsif, -iv] ADJ convulsive

convulsions [kɔ̃vylsjɔ̃] NFPL convulsions

cookie [kuki] NM (Inform) cookie

coopérant [kɔɔperɑ̃] NM ≈ person doing Voluntary Service Overseas (BRIT), ≈ member of the Peace Corps (US)

coopératif, -ive [kɔɔperatif, -iv] ADJ, NF co-operative

coopération [kɔɔperasjɔ̃] NF co-operation; (Admin): **la C~** ≈ Voluntary Service Overseas (BRIT) ou the Peace Corps (US: done as alternative to military service)

coopérer [kɔɔpere] /**6**/ VI: ~ **(à)** to co-operate (in)

coordination [kɔɔʀdinasjɔ̃] NF coordination

coordonnateur, -trice [kɔɔʀdɔnatœʀ, -tʀis] ADJ coordinating ▶ NM/F coordinator

coordonné, e [kɔɔʀdɔne] ADJ coordinated ▶ NF (Ling) coordinate clause; **coordonnés** NMPL (vêtements) coordinates; **coordonnées** NFPL (Math) coordinates; (détails personnels) address, phone number, schedule etc; whereabouts; **donnez-moi vos coordonnées** (fam) can I have your details please?

coordonner [kɔɔʀdɔne] /**1**/ VT to coordinate

copain, copine [kɔpɛ̃, kɔpin] NM/F mate (BRIT), pal; (petit ami) boyfriend; (petite amie) girlfriend ▶ ADJ: **être ~ avec** to be pally with

copeau, x [kɔpo] NM shaving; (de métal) turning

Copenhague [kɔpənag] N Copenhagen

copie [kɔpi] NF copy; (Scol) script, paper; exercise; ~ **certifiée conforme** certified copy; ~ **papier** (Inform) hard copy

copier [kɔpje] /**7**/ VT, VI to copy; ~ **coller** (Inform) copy and paste; ~ **sur** to copy from

copieur [kɔpjœʀ] NM (photo)copier

copieusement [kɔpjøzmɑ̃] ADV copiously

copieux, -euse [kɔpjø, -øz] ADJ copious, hearty

copilote [kɔpilɔt] NM (Aviat) co-pilot; (Auto) co-driver, navigator

copinage [kɔpinaʒ] NM: **obtenir qch par** ~ to get sth through contacts

copine [kɔpin] NF voir **copain**

copiste [kɔpist] NMF copyist, transcriber

coproduction [kɔpʀɔdyksjɔ̃] NF coproduction, joint production

copropriétaire [kɔpʀɔpʀijetɛʀ] NMF co-owner

copropriété [kɔpʀɔpʀijete] NF co-ownership, joint ownership; **acheter en** ~ to buy on a co-ownership basis

copulation [kɔpylasjɔ̃] NF copulation

copyright [kɔpiʀajt] NM copyright

coq [kɔk] NM cockerel, rooster ▶ ADJ INV (Boxe): **poids** ~ bantamweight; ~ **de bruyère** grouse; ~ **du village** (fig: péj) ladykiller; ~ **au vin** coq au vin

coq-à-l'âne [kɔkalɑn] NM INV abrupt change of subject

coque [kɔk] NF (*de noix, mollusque*) shell; (*de bateau*) hull; **à la ~** (*Culin*) (soft-)boiled

coquelet [kɔklɛ] NM (*Culin*) cockerel

coquelicot [kɔkliko] NM poppy

coqueluche [kɔklyʃ] NF whooping-cough; (*fig*): **être la ~ de qn** to be sb's flavour of the month

coquet, te [kɔkɛ, -ɛt] ADJ appearance-conscious; (*joli*) pretty; (*logement*) smart, charming

coquetier [kɔk(ə)tje] NM egg-cup

coquettement [kɔkɛtmɑ̃] ADV (*s'habiller*) attractively; (*meubler*) prettily

coquetterie [kɔkɛtRi] NF appearance-consciousness

coquillage [kɔkijaʒ] NM (*mollusque*) shellfish *inv*; (*coquille*) shell

coquille [kɔkij] NF shell; (*Typo*) misprint; **~ de beurre** shell of butter; **~ d'œuf** *adj* (*couleur*) eggshell; **~ de noix** nutshell; **~ St Jacques** scallop

coquillettes [kɔkijɛt] NFPL pasta shells

coquin, e [kɔkɛ̃, -in] ADJ mischievous, roguish; (*polisson*) naughty ▶ NM/F (*péj*) rascal

cor [kɔR] NM (*Mus*) horn; (*Méd*): **~ (au pied)** corn; **réclamer à ~ et à cri** to clamour for; **~ anglais** cor anglais; **~ de chasse** hunting horn

corail, -aux [kɔRaj, -o] NM coral *no pl*

Coran [kɔRɑ̃] NM: **le ~** the Koran

coraux [kɔRo] NMPL *de* **corail**

corbeau, x [kɔRbo] NM crow

corbeille [kɔRbɛj] NF basket; (*Inform*) recycle bin; (*Bourse*): **la ~** ≈ the floor (of the Stock Exchange); **~ de mariage** (*fig*) wedding presents *pl*; **~ à ouvrage** work-basket; **~ à pain** breadbasket; **~ à papier** waste paper basket *ou* bin

corbillard [kɔRbijaR] NM hearse

cordage [kɔRdaʒ] NM rope; **cordages** NMPL (*de voilure*) rigging *sg*

corde [kɔRd] NF rope; (*de violon, raquette, d'arc*) string; (*trame*) la ~ the thread; (*Athlétisme*): (*Auto*) **la ~** the rails *pl*; **les cordes** (*Boxe*) the ropes; **les (instruments à) cordes** (*Mus*) the strings, the stringed instruments; **semelles de ~** rope soles; **tenir la ~** (*Athlétisme, Auto*) to be in the inside lane; **tomber des cordes** to rain cats and dogs; **tirer sur la ~** to go too far; **la ~ sensible** the right chord; **usé jusqu'à la ~** threadbare; **~ à linge** washing *ou* clothes line; **~ lisse** (climbing) rope; **~ à nœuds** knotted climbing rope; **~ raide** tightrope; **~ à sauter** skipping rope; **cordes vocales** vocal cords

cordeau, x [kɔRdo] NM string, line; **tracé au ~** as straight as a die

cordée [kɔRde] NF (*d'alpinistes*) rope, roped party

cordelière [kɔRdəljɛR] NF cord (belt)

cordial, e, -aux [kɔRdjal, -o] ADJ warm, cordial ▶ NM cordial, pick-me-up

cordialement [kɔRdjalmɑ̃] ADV cordially, heartily; (*formule épistolaire*) (kind) regards

cordialité [kɔRdjalite] NF warmth, cordiality

cordillère [kɔRdijɛR] NF: **la ~ des Andes** the Andes cordillera *ou* range

cordon [kɔRdɔ̃] NM cord, string; **~ sanitaire/de police** sanitary/police cordon; **~ littoral** sandbank, sandbar; **~ ombilical** umbilical cord

cordon-bleu [kɔRdɔ̃blø] ADJ, NMF cordon bleu

cordonnerie [kɔRdɔnRi] NF shoe repairer's *ou* mender's (shop)

cordonnier [kɔRdɔnje] NM shoe repairer *ou* mender, cobbler

cordouan, e [kɔRduɑ̃, -an] ADJ Cordovan

Cordoue [kɔRdu] N Cordoba

Corée [kɔRe] NF: **la ~** Korea; **la ~ du Sud/du Nord** South/North Korea; **la République (démocratique populaire) de ~** the (Democratic People's) Republic of Korea

coréen, ne [kɔReɛ̃, -ɛn] ADJ Korean ▶ NM (*Ling*) Korean ▶ NM/F: **C~, ne** Korean

coreligionnaire [kɔReliʒjɔnɛR] NMF fellow Christian/Muslim/Jew *etc*

Corfou [kɔRfu] N Corfu

coriace [kɔRjas] ADJ tough

coriandre [kɔRjɑ̃dR] NF coriander

Corinthe [kɔRɛ̃t] N Corinth

cormoran [kɔRmɔRɑ̃] NM cormorant

cornac [kɔRnak] NM elephant driver

corne [kɔRn] NF horn; (*de cerf*) antler; (*de la peau*) callus; **~ d'abondance** horn of plenty; **~ de brume** (*Navig*) foghorn

cornée [kɔRne] NF cornea

corneille [kɔRnɛj] NF crow

cornélien, ne [kɔRneljɛ̃, -ɛn] ADJ (*débat etc*) where love and duty conflict

cornemuse [kɔRnəmyz] NF bagpipes *pl*; **joueur de ~** piper

corner¹ [kɔRnɛR] NM (*Football*) corner (kick)

corner² [kɔRne] VT (*pages*) to make dog-eared ▶ VI (*klaxonner*) to blare out

cornet [kɔRnɛ] NM (paper) cone; (*de glace*) cornet, cone; **~ à pistons** cornet

cornette [kɔRnɛt] NF cornet (*headgear*)

corniaud [kɔRnjo] NM (*chien*) mongrel; (*péj*) twit, clot

corniche [kɔRniʃ] NF (*de meuble, neigeuse*) cornice; (*route*) coast road

cornichon [kɔRniʃɔ̃] NM gherkin

Cornouailles [kɔRnwaj] FPL Cornwall

cornue [kɔRny] NF retort

corollaire [kɔRɔlɛR] NM corollary

corolle [kɔRɔl] NF corolla

coron [kɔRɔ̃] NM mining cottage; mining village

coronaire [kɔRɔnɛR] ADJ coronary

corporation [kɔRpɔRasjɔ̃] NF corporate body; (*au Moyen-Âge*) guild

corporel, le [kɔRpɔRɛl] ADJ bodily; (*punition*) corporal; **soins corporels** care *sg* of the body

corps [kɔR] NM (*gén*) body; (*cadavre*) (dead) body; **à son ~ défendant** against one's will; **à ~ perdu** headlong; **perdu ~ et biens** lost with all hands; **prendre ~** to take shape; **faire ~ avec** to be joined to; to form one body with; **~ d'armée** army corps; **~ de ballet** corps de ballet; **~ constitués** (*Pol*) constitutional bodies; **le ~ consulaire** the consular corps; **~ à ~** *adv* hand-to-hand; *nm* clinch; **le ~ du délit** (*Jur*) corpus delicti; **le ~ diplomatique** the diplomatic corps; **le ~ électoral** the electorate;

le ~ **enseignant** the teaching profession;
~ **étranger** (*Méd*) foreign body;
~ **expéditionnaire** task force; ~ **de garde**
guardroom; ~ **législatif** legislative body;
le ~ **médical** the medical profession

corpulence [kɔrpylɑ̃s] NF build; (*embonpoint*)
stoutness (*Brit*), corpulence; **de forte** ~ of large
build

corpulent, e [kɔrpylɑ̃, -ɑ̃t] ADJ stout (*Brit*),
corpulent

corpus [kɔrpys] NM (*Ling*) corpus

correct, e [kɔrɛkt] ADJ (*exact*) accurate, correct;
(*bienséant, honnête*) correct; (*passable*) adequate

correctement [kɔrɛktəmɑ̃] ADV accurately;
correctly; adequately

correcteur, -trice [kɔrɛktœr, -tris] NM/F (*Scol*)
examiner, marker; (*Typo*) proofreader

correctif, -ive [kɔrɛktif, -iv] ADJ corrective
▶ NM (*mise au point*) rider, qualification

correction [kɔrɛksjɔ̃] NF (*voir corriger*) correction;
marking; (*voir correct*) correctness; (*rature,
surcharge*) correction, emendation; (*coups*)
thrashing; ~ **sur écran** (*Inform*) screen editing;
~ **(des épreuves)** proofreading

correctionnel, le [kɔrɛksjɔnɛl] ADJ (*Jur*):
tribunal ~ ≈ criminal court

corrélation [kɔrelasjɔ̃] NF correlation

correspondance [kɔrɛspɔ̃dɑ̃s] NF
correspondence; (*de train, d'avion*) connection;
ce train assure la ~ avec l'avion de 10 heures
this train connects with the 10 o'clock plane;
cours par ~ correspondence course; **vente par
~** mail-order business

correspondancier, -ière [kɔrɛspɔ̃dɑ̃sje, -jɛr]
NM/F correspondence clerk

correspondant, e [kɔrɛspɔ̃dɑ̃, -ɑ̃t] NM/F
correspondent; (*Tél*) person phoning (*ou* being
phoned)

correspondre [kɔrɛspɔ̃dr] /41/ VI (*données,
témoignages*) to correspond, tally; (*chambres*) to
communicate; ~ **à** to correspond to; ~ **avec qn**
to correspond with sb

Corrèze [kɔrɛz] NF: **la** ~ the Corrèze

corrézien, ne [kɔrezjɛ̃, -ɛn] ADJ of *ou* from the
Corrèze

corrida [kɔrida] NF bullfight

corridor [kɔridɔr] NM corridor, passage

corrigé [kɔriʒe] NM (*Scol: d'exercice*) correct
version; fair copy

corriger [kɔriʒe] /3/ VT (*devoir*) to correct, mark;
(*texte*) to correct, emend; (*erreur, défaut*) to
correct, put right; (*punir*) to thrash; ~ **qn de**
(*défaut*) to cure sb of; **se ~ de** to cure o.s. of

corroborer [kɔrɔbɔre] /1/ VT to corroborate

corroder [kɔrɔde] /1/ VT to corrode

corrompre [kɔrɔ̃pr] /41/ VT (*dépraver*) to corrupt;
(*acheter: témoin etc*) to bribe

corrompu, e [kɔrɔ̃py] ADJ corrupt

corrosif, -ive [kɔrozif, -iv] ADJ corrosive

corrosion [kɔrozjɔ̃] NF corrosion

corruption [kɔrypsjɔ̃] NF corruption; (*de
témoins*) bribery

corsage [kɔrsaʒ] NM (*d'une robe*) bodice;
(*chemisier*) blouse

corsaire [kɔrsɛr] NM pirate, corsair; privateer

corse [kɔrs] ADJ Corsican ▶ NMF: **C~** Corsican
▶ NF: **la C~** Corsica

corsé, e [kɔrse] ADJ vigorous; (*café etc*)
full-flavoured (*Brit*) *ou* -flavored (*US*); (*goût*) full;
(*sauce*) spicy; (*problème*) tough, tricky

corselet [kɔrsəlɛ] NM corselet

corser [kɔrse] /1/ VT (*difficulté*) to aggravate;
(*intrigue*) to liven up; (*sauce*) to add spice to

corset [kɔrsɛ] NM corset; (*d'une robe*) bodice;
~ **orthopédique** surgical corset

corso [kɔrso] NM: ~ **fleuri** procession of floral
floats

cortège [kɔrtɛʒ] NM procession

cortisone [kɔrtizon] NF (*Méd*) cortisone

corvée [kɔrve] NF chore, drudgery *no pl*; (*Mil*)
fatigue (duty)

cosaque [kɔzak] NM cossack

cosignataire [kɔsiɲatɛr] ADJ, NMF co-signatory

cosinus [kɔsinys] NM (*Math*) cosine

cosmétique [kɔsmetik] NM (*pour les cheveux*)
hair-oil; (*produit de beauté*) beauty care product

cosmétologie [kɔsmetɔlɔʒi] NF beauty care

cosmique [kɔsmik] ADJ cosmic

cosmonaute [kɔsmɔnot] NMF cosmonaut,
astronaut

cosmopolite [kɔsmɔpɔlit] ADJ cosmopolitan

cosmos [kɔsmɔs] NM outer space; cosmos

cosse [kɔs] NF (*Bot*) pod, hull

cossu, e [kɔsy] ADJ opulent-looking, well-to-do

Costa Rica [kɔstarika] NM: **le** ~ Costa Rica

costaricien, ne [kɔstarisjɛ̃, -ɛn] ADJ Costa Rican
▶ NM/F: **C~, ne** Costa Rican

costaud, e [kɔsto, -od] ADJ strong, sturdy

costume [kɔstym] NM (*d'homme*) suit; (*de théâtre*)
costume

costumé, e [kɔstyme] ADJ dressed up

costumier, -ière [kɔstymje, -jɛr] NM/F
(*fabricant, loueur*) costumier; (*Théât*) wardrobe
master/mistress

cotangente [kɔtɑ̃ʒɑ̃t] NF (*Math*) cotangent

cotation [kɔtasjɔ̃] NF quoted value

cote [kɔt] NF (*en Bourse etc*) quotation; quoted
value; (*d'un candidat etc*) rating; (*mesure: sur une
carte*) spot height; (*: sur un croquis*) dimension; (*de
classement*) (classification) mark; reference
number; **la ~ de** (*d'un cheval*) the odds *pl* on;
avoir la ~ to be very popular; **inscrit à la ~**
quoted on the Stock Exchange; ~ **d'alerte**
danger *ou* flood level; ~ **mal taillée** (*fig*)
compromise; ~ **de popularité** popularity
rating

coté, e [kɔte] ADJ: **être** ~ to be listed *ou* quoted;
être ~ en Bourse to be quoted on the Stock
Exchange; **être bien/mal** ~ to be highly/poorly
rated

côte [kot] NF (*rivage*) coast(line); (*pente*) slope;
(*: sur une route*) hill; (*Anat*) rib; (*d'un tricot, tissu*)
rib, ribbing *no pl*; ~ **à** ~ *adv* side by side; **la C~
(d'Azur)** the (French) Riviera; **la C~ d'Ivoire**
the Ivory Coast; ~ **de porc** pork chop

côté [kote] NM (*gén*) side; (*direction*) way,
direction; **de chaque ~ (de)** on each side of; **de
tous les côtés** from all directions; **de quel ~**

est-il parti? which way ou in which direction did he go?; **de ce/de l'autre ~** this/the other way; **d'un ~ ... de l'autre ~ ...** (alternative) on (the) one hand ... on the other (hand) ...; **du ~ de** (provenance) from; (direction) towards; **du ~ de Lyon** (proximité) near Lyons; **du ~ gauche** on the left-hand side; **de ~** adv (regarder) sideways; on one side; to one side; aside; **laisser de ~** to leave on one side; **mettre de ~** to put aside, put on one side; **mettre de l'argent de ~** to save some money; **de mon ~** (quant à moi) for my part; **à ~** adv (right) nearby; (voisins) next door; (d'autre part) besides; **à ~ de** beside; next to; (fig) in comparison to; **à ~ (de la cible)** off target, wide (of the mark); **être aux côtés de** to be by the side of

coteau, x [kɔto] NM hill

Côte d'Ivoire [kotdivwaʀ] NF: **la ~** Côte d'Ivoire, the Ivory Coast

côtelé, e [kotle] ADJ ribbed; **pantalon en velours ~** corduroy trousers pl

côtelette [kotlɛt] NF chop

coter [kɔte] /1/ VT (Bourse) to quote

coterie [kɔtʀi] NF set

côtier, -ière [kotje, -jɛʀ] ADJ coastal

cotisation [kɔtizasjɔ̃] NF subscription, dues pl; (pour une pension) contributions pl

cotiser [kɔtize] /1/ VI: **~ (à)** to pay contributions (to); (à une association) to subscribe (to); **se cotiser** VI to club together

coton [kɔtɔ̃] NM cotton; **~ hydrophile** cotton wool (Brit), absorbent cotton (US)

cotonnade [kɔtɔnad] NF cotton (fabric)

Coton-Tige® [kɔtɔ̃tiʒ] NM cotton bud

côtoyer [kotwaje] /8/ VT to be close to; (rencontrer) to rub shoulders with; (longer) to run alongside; (fig: friser) to be bordering ou verging on

cotte [kɔt] NF: **~ de mailles** coat of mail

cou [ku] NM neck

couac [kwak] NM (fam) bum note

couard, e [kwaʀ, -aʀd] ADJ cowardly

couchage [kuʃaʒ] NM voir **sac**

couchant, e [kuʃɑ̃, ɑ̃t] ADJ: **soleil ~** setting sun

couche [kuʃ] NF (strate: gén, Géo) layer, stratum (pl -a); (de peinture, vernis) coat; (de poussière, crème) layer; (de bébé) nappy (Brit), diaper (US); **~ d'ozone** ozone layer; **couches** NFPL (Méd) confinement sg; **couches sociales** social levels ou strata

couché, e [kuʃe] ADJ (étendu) lying down; (au lit) in bed

couche-culotte [kuʃkylɔt] NF (pl **couches-culottes**) NF (plastic-coated) disposable nappy (Brit) ou diaper (US)

coucher [kuʃe] /1/ NM (du soleil) setting ▶ VT (personne) to put to bed; (: loger) to put up; (objet) to lay on its side; (écrire) to inscribe, couch ▶ VI (dormir) to sleep, spend the night; **~ avec qn** to sleep with sb, to go to bed with sb; **se coucher** VI (pour dormir) to go to bed; (pour se reposer) to lie down; (soleil) to set, go down; **à prendre avant le ~** (Méd) take at night ou before going to bed; **~ de soleil** sunset

couchette [kuʃɛt] NF couchette; (de marin) bunk; (pour voyageur, sur bateau) berth

coucheur [kuʃœʀ] NM: **mauvais ~** awkward customer

couci-couça [kusikusa] ADV (fam) so-so

coucou [kuku] NM cuckoo ▶ EXCL peek-a-boo

coude [kud] NM (Anat) elbow; (de tuyau, de la route) bend; **~ à ~** adv shoulder to shoulder, side by side

coudée [kude] NF: **avoir ses coudées franches** (fig) to have a free rein

cou-de-pied [kudpje] (pl **cous-de-pied**) NM instep

coudoyer [kudwaje] /8/ VT to brush past ou against; (fig) to rub shoulders with

coudre [kudʀ] /48/ VT (bouton) to sew on; (robe) to sew (up) ▶ VI to sew

couenne [kwan] NF (de lard) rind

couette [kwɛt] NF duvet; **couettes** NFPL (cheveux) bunches

couffin [kufɛ̃] NM Moses basket; (straw) basket

couilles [kuj] NFPL (!) balls (!)

couiner [kwine] /1/ VI to squeal

coulage [kulaʒ] NM (Comm) loss of stock (due to theft or negligence)

coulant, e [kulɑ̃, -ɑ̃t] ADJ (indulgent) easy-going; (fromage etc) runny

coulée [kule] NF (de lave, métal en fusion) flow; **~ de neige** snowslide

couler [kule] /1/ VI to flow, run; (fuir: stylo, récipient) to leak; (: nez) to run; (sombrer: bateau) to sink ▶ VT (cloche, sculpture) to cast; (bateau) to sink; (faire échouer: personne) to bring down, ruin; (passer): **~ une vie heureuse** to enjoy a happy life; **se ~ dans** (interstice etc) to slip into; **faire ~** (eau) to run; **faire ~ un bain** to run a bath; **il a coulé une bielle** (Auto) his big end went; **~ de source** to follow on naturally; **~ à pic** to sink ou go straight to the bottom

couleur [kulœʀ] NF colour (Brit), color (US); (Cartes) suit; **couleurs** NFPL (du teint) colo(u)r sg; **les couleurs** (Mil) the colo(u)rs; **en couleurs** (film) in colo(u)r; **télévision en couleurs** colo(u)r television; **de ~** (homme, femme: vieilli) colo(u)red; **sous ~ de** on the pretext of; **de quelle ~** of what colo(u)r

couleuvre [kulœvʀ] NF grass snake

coulisse [kulis] NF (Tech) runner; **coulisses** NFPL (Théât) wings; (fig): **dans les coulisses** behind the scenes; **porte à ~** sliding door

coulisser [kulise] /1/ VI to slide, run

couloir [kulwaʀ] NM corridor, passage; (d'avion) aisle; (de bus) gangway; (: sur la route) bus lane; (Sport: de piste) lane; (Géo) gully; **~ aérien** air corridor ou lane; **~ de navigation** shipping lane

coulpe [kulp] NF: **battre sa ~** to repent openly

coup [ku] NM (heurt, choc) knock; (affectif) blow, shock; (agressif) blow; (avec arme à feu) shot; (de l'horloge) chime, stroke; (Sport: golf) stroke; (: tennis) shot; (Échecs) move; (fam: fois) time; **~ de coude/genou** nudge (with the elbow)/ with the knee; **à coups de hache/marteau** (hitting) with an axe/a hammer; **~ de tonnerre** clap of thunder; **~ de sonnette** ring of the bell; **~ de crayon/pinceau** stroke of the pencil/brush; **donner un ~ de balai** to give the floor a sweep, sweep up; **donner un ~ de chiffon** to go round with the duster; **avoir le ~** (fig) to have the knack; **être dans le/hors du ~** to be in/not to be in on it; (à la page) to be hip ou trendy; **du ~** as a result; **boire un ~** to have a drink; **d'un seul ~** (subitement) suddenly; (à la fois) at one go, in one blow; **du ~** so (you see); **du premier ~** first time ou go, at the first attempt; **du même ~** at the same time; **à ~ sûr** definitely, without fail; **après ~** afterwards; **~ sur ~** in quick succession; **être sur un ~** to be on to something; **sur le ~** outright; **sous le ~ de** (surprise etc) under the influence of; **tomber sous le ~ de la loi** to constitute a statutory offence; **à tous les coups** every time; **tenir le ~** to hold out; **il a raté son ~** he missed his turn; **pour le ~** for once; **~ bas** (fig): **donner un ~ bas à qn** to hit sb below the belt; **~ de chance** stroke of luck; **~ de chapeau** (fig) pat on the back; **~ de couteau** stab (of a knife); **~ dur** hard blow; **~ d'éclat** (great) feat; **~ d'envoi** kick-off; **~ d'essai** first attempt; **~ d'état** coup d'état; **~ de feu** shot; **~ de filet** (Police) haul; **~ de foudre** (fig) love at first sight; **~ fourré** stab in the back; **~ franc** free kick; **~ de frein** (sharp) braking no pl; **~ de fusil** rifle shot; **~ de grâce** coup de grâce; **~ du lapin** (Auto) whiplash; **~ de main**: **donner un ~ de main à qn** to give sb a (helping) hand; **~ de maître** master stroke; **~ d'œil** glance; **~ de pied** kick; **~ de poing** punch; **~ de soleil** sunburn no pl; **~ de sonnette** ring of the bell; **~ de téléphone** phone call; **~ de tête** (fig) (sudden) impulse; **~ de théâtre** (fig) dramatic turn of events; **~ de tonnerre** clap of thunder; **~ de vent** gust of wind; **en ~ de vent** (rapidement) in a tearing hurry

coupable [kupabl] ADJ guilty; (pensée) guilty, culpable ▸ NMF (gén) culprit; (Jur) guilty party; **~ de** guilty of

coupant, e [kupɑ̃, -ɑ̃t] ADJ (lame) sharp; (fig: voix, ton) cutting

coupe [kup] NF (verre) goblet; (à fruits) dish; (Sport) cup; (de cheveux, de vêtement) cut; (graphique, plan) (cross) section; **être sous la ~ de** to be under the control of; **faire des coupes sombres dans** to make drastic cuts in

coupé, e [kupe] ADJ (communications) cut, blocked; (vêtement): **bien/mal ~** well/badly cut ▸ NM (Auto) coupé ▸ NF (Navig) gangway

coupe-circuit [kupsirkɥi] NM INV cutout, circuit breaker

coupe-feu [kupfø] NM INV firebreak

coupe-gorge [kupgɔrʒ] NM INV cut-throats' den

coupe-ongles [kupɔ̃gl] NM INV (pince) nail clippers; (ciseaux) nail scissors

coupe-papier [kuppapje] NM INV paper knife

couper [kupe] /1/ VT to cut; (retrancher) to cut (out), take out; (route, courant) to cut off; (appétit) to take away; (fièvre) to take down, reduce; (vin, cidre) to blend; (: à table) to dilute (with water) ▸ VI to cut; (prendre un raccourci) to take a short-cut; (Cartes: diviser le paquet) to cut; (: avec l'atout) to trump; **se couper** VI (se blesser) to cut o.s.; (en témoignant etc) to give o.s. away; **~ l'appétit à qn** to spoil sb's appetite; **~ la parole à qn** to cut sb short; **~ les vivres à qn** to cut off sb's vital supplies; **~ le contact** ou **l'allumage** (Auto) to turn off the ignition; **~ les ponts avec qn** to break with sb; **se faire couper les cheveux** to have ou get one's hair cut; **nous avons été coupés** we've been cut off

couperet [kupRε] NM cleaver, chopper

couperosé, e [kupRoze] ADJ blotchy

couple [kupl] NM couple; **~ de torsion** torque

coupler [kuple] /1/ VT to couple (together)

couplet [kuplε] NM verse

coupleur [kuplœr] NM: **~ acoustique** acoustic coupler

coupole [kupɔl] NF dome; cupola

coupon [kupɔ̃] NM (ticket) coupon; (de tissu) remnant; roll

coupon-réponse [kupɔ̃repɔ̃s] (pl **coupons-réponses**) NM reply coupon

coupure [kupyr] NF cut; (billet de banque) note; (de journal) cutting; (: de courant) power cut

cour [kur] NF (de ferme, jardin) (court)yard; (d'immeuble) back yard; (Jur, royale) court; **faire la ~ à qn** to court sb; **~ d'appel** appeal court (BRIT), appellate court (US); **~ d'assises** court of assizes, ≈ Crown Court (BRIT); **~ de cassation** final court of appeal; **~ des comptes** (Admin) revenue court; **~ martiale** court-martial; **~ de récréation** (Scol) playground, schoolyard

courage [kuraʒ] NM courage, bravery

courageusement [kuraʒøzmɑ̃] ADV bravely, courageously

courageux, -euse [kuraʒø, -øz] ADJ brave, courageous

couramment [kuramɑ̃] ADV commonly; (parler) fluently

courant, e [kurɑ̃, -ɑ̃t] ADJ (fréquent) common; (Comm, gén: normal) standard; (en cours) current ▸ NM current; (fig) movement; (: d'opinion) trend; **être au ~ (de)** (fait, nouvelle) to know (about); **mettre qn au ~ (de)** (fait, nouvelle) to tell sb (about); (nouveau travail etc) to teach sb the basics (of), brief sb (about); **se tenir au ~ (de)** (techniques etc) to keep o.s. up-to-date (on); **dans le ~ de** (pendant) in the course of; **~ octobre** etc in the course of October etc; **le 10 ~** (Comm) the 10th inst.; **~ d'air** draught (BRIT), draft (US); **~ électrique** (electric) current, power

courbature [kurbatyr] NF ache

courbaturé, e [kurbatyre] ADJ aching

courbe [kurb] ADJ curved ▸ NF curve; **~ de niveau** contour line

courber [kurbe] /1/ VT to bend; **~ la tête** to bow one's head; **se courber** VI (branche etc) to bend, curve; (personne) to bend (down)

courbette [kurbεt] NF low bow

coure etc [kur] VB voir **courir**

coureur, -euse [kurœr, -øz] NM/F (Sport) runner (ou driver); (péj) womanizer/manhunter; **~ cycliste/automobile** racing cyclist/driver

courge [kuʀʒ] NF (*Bot*) gourd; (*Culin*) marrow
courgette [kuʀʒɛt] NF courgette (*BRIT*),
zucchini (*US*)
courir [kuʀiʀ] /**11**/ VI (*gén*) to run; (*se dépêcher*) to
rush; (*fig*: *rumeurs*) to go round; (*Comm*: *intérêt*) to
accrue ▸ VT (*Sport*: *épreuve*) to compete in; (: *risque*)
to run; (: *danger*) to face; **~ les cafés/bals** to do
the rounds of the cafés/ dances; **le bruit court
que** the rumour is going round that; **par les
temps qui courent** at the present time;
~ après qn to run after sb, chase (after) sb;
laisser ~ to let things alone; **faire ~ qn** to make
sb run around (all over the place); **tu peux
(toujours) ~!** you've got a hope!
couronne [kuʀɔn] NF crown; (*de fleurs*) wreath,
circlet; **~ (funéraire** ou **mortuaire)** (funeral)
wreath
couronnement [kuʀɔnmɑ̃] NM coronation,
crowning; (*fig*) crowning achievement
couronner [kuʀɔne] /**1**/ VT to crown
courons [kuʀɔ̃], **courrai** etc [kuʀe] VB *voir*
courir
courre [kuʀ] VB *voir* **chasse**
courriel [kuʀjɛl] NM email; **envoyer qch par ~**
to email sth
courrier [kuʀje] NM mail, post; (*lettres à écrire*)
letters pl; (*rubrique*) column; **qualité ~** letter
quality; **long/moyen ~** adj (*Aviat*) long-/
medium-haul; **~ du cœur** problem page;
est-ce que j'ai du ~? are there any letters for
me?; **~ électronique** electronic mail, email
courroie [kuʀwa] NF strap; (*Tech*) belt; **~ de
transmission/de ventilateur** driving/fan belt
courrons etc [kuʀɔ̃] VB *voir* **courir**
courroucé, e [kuʀuse] ADJ wrathful
cours [kuʀ] VB *voir* **courir** ▸ NM (*leçon*) class;
(: *particulier*) lesson; (*série de leçons*) course;
(*cheminement*) course; (*écoulement*) flow; (*avenue*)
walk; (*Comm*: *de devises*) rate; (: *de denrées*) price;
(*Bourse*) quotation; **donner libre ~ à** to give free
expression to; **avoir ~** (*monnaie*) to be legal
tender; (*fig*) to be current; (*Scol*) to have a class ou
lecture; **en ~** (*année*) current; (*travaux*) in
progress; **en ~ de route** on the way; **au ~ de** in
the course of, during; **le ~ du change** the
exchange rate; **~ d'eau** waterway;
~ élémentaire 2nd and 3rd years of primary school;
~ moyen 4th and 5th years of primary school;
~ préparatoire ≈ infants' class (*BRIT*), ≈ 1st
grade (*US*); **~ du soir** night school
course [kuʀs] NF running; (*Sport*: *épreuve*) race;
(: *trajet*: *du soleil*) course; (: *d'un projectile*) flight;
(: *d'une pièce mécanique*) travel; (*excursion*) outing;
climb; (*d'un taxi, autocar*) journey, trip; (*petite
mission*) errand; **courses** NFPL (*achats*) shopping
sg; (*Hippisme*) races; **faire les** ou **ses courses** to
go shopping; **jouer aux courses** to bet on the
races; **à bout de ~** (*épuisé*) exhausted;
~ automobile car race; **~ de côte** (*Auto*) hill
climb; **~ par étapes** ou **d'étapes** race in stages;
~ d'obstacles obstacle race; **~ à pied** walking
race; **~ de vitesse** sprint; **courses de chevaux**
horse racing
coursier, -ière [kuʀsje, -jɛʀ] NM/F courier

court, e [kuʀ, kuʀt] ADJ short ▸ ADV short ▸ NM:
~ (de tennis) (tennis) court; **tourner ~** to come
to a sudden end; **couper ~ à** to cut short; **à ~ de**
short of; **prendre qn de ~** to catch sb
unawares; **pour faire ~** briefly, to cut a long
story short; **ça fait ~** that's not very long; **tirer
à la ~ paille** to draw lots; **faire la ~ échelle à
qn** to give sb a leg up; **~ métrage** (*Ciné*) short
(film)
court-bouillon [kuʀbujɔ̃] (*pl* **courts-bouillons**)
NM court-bouillon
court-circuit [kuʀsiʀkɥi] (*pl* **courts-circuits**)
NM short-circuit
court-circuiter [kuʀsiʀkɥite] /**1**/ VT (*fig*) to
bypass
courtier, -ière [kuʀtje, -jɛʀ] NM/F broker
courtisan [kuʀtizɑ̃] NM courtier
courtisane [kuʀtizan] NF courtesan
courtiser [kuʀtize] /**1**/ VT to court, woo
courtois, e [kuʀtwa, -waz] ADJ courteous
courtoisement [kuʀtwazmɑ̃] ADV courteously
courtoisie [kuʀtwazi] NF courtesy
couru, e [kuʀy] PP *de* **courir** ▸ ADJ (*spectacle etc*)
popular; **c'est ~ (d'avance)!** (*fam*) it's a safe bet!
cousais etc [kuzɛ] VB *voir* **coudre**
couscous [kuskus] NM couscous
cousin, e [kuzɛ̃, -in] NM/F cousin ▸ NM (*Zool*)
mosquito; **~ germain** first cousin
cousons etc [kuzɔ̃] VB *voir* **coudre**
coussin [kusɛ̃] NM cushion; **~ d'air** (*Tech*) air
cushion
cousu, e [kuzy] PP *de* **coudre** ▸ ADJ: **~ d'or** rolling
in riches
coût [ku] NM cost; **le ~ de la vie** the cost of
living
coûtant [kutɑ̃] ADJ M: **au prix ~** at cost price
couteau, x [kuto] NM knife; **à cran d'arrêt**
flick-knife; **~ de cuisine** kitchen knife; **~ à
pain** bread knife; **~ de poche** pocket knife
couteau-scie [kutosi] (*pl* **couteaux-scies**) NM
serrated(-edged) knife
coutelier, -ière [kutəlje, -jɛʀ] ADJ: **l'industrie
coutelière** the cutlery industry ▸ NM/F cutler
coutellerie [kutɛlʀi] NF cutlery shop; cutlery
coûter [kute] /**1**/ VT to cost ▸ VI to cost; **~ à qn**
to cost sb a lot; **~ cher** to be expensive; **~ cher à
qn** (*fig*) to cost sb dear ou dearly; **combien ça
coûte?** how much is it?, what does it cost?;
coûte que coûte at all costs
coûteux, -euse [kutø, -øz] ADJ costly, expensive
coutume [kutym] NF custom; **de ~** usual,
customary
coutumier, -ière [kutymje, -jɛʀ] ADJ customary;
elle est coutumière du fait that's her usual
trick
couture [kutyʀ] NF sewing; (*profession*)
dress-making; (*points*) seam
couturier [kutyʀje] NM fashion designer,
couturier
couturière [kutyʀjɛʀ] NF dressmaker
couvée [kuve] NF brood, clutch
couvent [kuvɑ̃] NM (*de sœurs*) convent; (*de frères*)
monastery; (*établissement scolaire*) convent
(school)

couver [kuve] /**1**/ VT to hatch; (*maladie*) to be sickening for ▶ VI (*feu*) to smoulder (BRIT), smolder (US); (*révolte*) to be brewing; **~ qn/qch des yeux** to look lovingly at sb/sth; (*convoiter*) to look longingly at sb/sth

couvercle [kuvɛrkl] NM lid; (*de bombe aérosol etc, qui se visse*) cap, top

couvert, e [kuvɛr, -ɛrt] PP *de* **couvrir** ▶ ADJ (*ciel*) overcast; (*coiffé d'un chapeau*) wearing a hat ▶ NM place setting; (*place à table*) place; (*au restaurant*) cover charge; **couverts** NMPL place settings; (*ustensiles*) cutlery *sg*; **~ de** covered with *ou* in; **bien ~** (*habillé*) well wrapped up; **mettre le ~** to lay the table; **à ~** under cover; **sous le ~ de** under the shelter of; (*fig*) under cover of

couverture [kuvɛrtyr] NF (*de lit*) blanket; (*de bâtiment*) roofing; (*de livre, fig: d'un espion etc, Assurances*) cover; (*Presse*) coverage; **de ~** (*lettre etc*) covering; **~ chauffante** electric blanket

couveuse [kuvøz] NF (*à poules*) sitter, brooder; (*de maternité*) incubator

couvre *etc* [kuvr] VB *voir* **couvrir**

couvre-chef [kuvrəʃef] NM hat

couvre-feu, x [kuvrəfø] NM curfew

couvre-lit [kuvrəli] NM bedspread

couvre-pieds [kuvrəpje] NM INV quilt

couvreur [kuvrœr] NM roofer

couvrir [kuvrir] /**18**/ VT to cover; (*dominer, étouffer: voix, pas*) to drown out; (*erreur*) to cover up; (*Zool: s'accoupler à*) to cover; **se couvrir** VI (*ciel*) to cloud over; (*s'habiller*) to cover up, wrap up; (*se coiffer*) to put one's hat on; (*par une assurance*) to cover o.s.; **se couvrir de** (*fleurs, boutons*) to become covered in

cover-girl [kɔvœrgœrl] NF model

cow-boy [kɔbɔj] NM cowboy

coyote [kɔjɔt] NM coyote

CP SIGLE M = **cours préparatoire**

CPAM SIGLE F (= *Caisse primaire d'assurances maladie*) health insurance office

cps ABR (= *caractères par seconde*) cps

cpt ABR = **comptant**

CQFD ABR (= *ce qu'il fallait démontrer*) QED (= *quod erat demonstrandum*)

CR SIGLE M = **compte rendu**

crabe [krab] NM crab

crachat [kraʃa] NM spittle *no pl*, spit *no pl*

craché, e [kraʃe] ADJ: **son père tout ~** the spitting image of his (*ou* her) father

cracher [kraʃe] /**1**/ VI to spit ▶ VT to spit out; (*fig: lave etc*) to belch (out); **~ du sang** to spit blood

crachin [kraʃɛ̃] NM drizzle

crachiner [kraʃine] /**1**/ VI to drizzle

crachoir [kraʃwar] NM spittoon; (*de dentiste*) bowl

crachotement [kraʃɔtmɑ̃] NM crackling *no pl*

crachoter [kraʃɔte] /**1**/ VI (*haut-parleur, radio*) to crackle

crack [krak] NM (*intellectuel*) whiz kid; (*sportif*) ace; (*poulain*) hot favourite (BRIT) *ou* favorite (US)

Cracovie [krakɔvi] N Cracow

cradingue [kradɛ̃g] ADJ (*fam*) disgustingly dirty, filthy-dirty

craie [krɛ] NF chalk

craignais *etc* [krɛɲɛ] VB *voir* **craindre**

craindre [krɛ̃dr] /**52**/ VT to fear, be afraid of; (*être sensible à: chaleur, froid*) to be easily damaged by; **~ de/que** to be afraid of/that; **je crains qu'il (ne) vienne** I am afraid he may come

crainte [krɛ̃t] NF fear; **de ~ de/que** for fear of/that

craintif, -ive [krɛ̃tif, -iv] ADJ timid

craintivement [krɛ̃tivmɑ̃] ADV timidly

cramer [krame] /**1**/ VI (*fam*) to burn

cramoisi, e [kramwazi]·ADJ crimson

crampe [krɑ̃p] NF cramp; **j'ai une ~ à la jambe** I've got cramp in my leg

crampon [krɑ̃pɔ̃] NM (*de semelle*) stud; (*Alpinisme*) crampon

cramponner [krɑ̃pɔne] /**1**/: **se cramponner** VI: **se cramponner (à)** to hang *ou* cling on (to)

cran [krɑ̃] NM (*entaille*) notch; (*de courroie*) hole; (*courage*) guts *pl*; **~ d'arrêt/de sûreté** safety catch; **~ de mire** bead

crâne [krɑn] NM skull

crâner [krɑne] /**1**/ VI (*fam*) to swank, show off

crânien, ne [krɑnjɛ̃, -ɛn] ADJ cranial, skull *cpd*, brain *cpd*

crapaud [krapo] NM toad

crapule [krapyl] NF villain

crapuleux, -euse [krapylø, -øz] ADJ: **crime ~** villainous crime

craquelure [kraklyr] NF crack; crackle *no pl*

craquement [krakmɑ̃] NM crack, snap; (*du plancher*) creak, creaking *no pl*

craquer [krake] /**1**/ VI (*bois, plancher*) to creak; (*fil, branche*) to snap; (*couture*) to come apart, burst; (*fig: accusé*) to break down, fall apart; (: *être enthousiasmé*) to go wild ▶ VT: **~ une allumette** to strike a match; **j'ai craqué** (*fam*) I couldn't resist it

crasse [kras] NF grime, filth ▶ ADJ (*fig: ignorance*) crass

crasseux, -euse [krasø, -øz] ADJ filthy

crassier [krasje] NM slag heap

cratère [kratɛr] NM crater

cravache [kravaʃ] NF (riding) crop

cravacher [kravaʃe] /**1**/ VT to use the crop on

cravate [kravat] NF tie

cravater [kravate] /**1**/ VT to put a tie on; (*fig*) to grab round the neck

crawl [krol] NM crawl; **dos crawlé** backstroke

crawlé, e [krole] ADJ: **dos ~** backstroke

crayeux, -euse [krɛjø, -øz] ADJ chalky

crayon [krɛjɔ̃] NM pencil; (*de rouge à lèvres etc*) stick, pencil; **écrire au ~** to write in pencil; **~ à bille** ball-point pen; **~ de couleur** crayon; **~ optique** light pen

crayon-feutre [krɛjɔ̃føtr] (*pl* **crayons-feutres**) NM felt(-tip) pen

crayonner [krɛjone] /**1**/ VT to scribble, sketch

CRDP SIGLE M (= *Centre régional de documentation pédagogique*) teachers' resource centre

créance [kreɑ̃s] NF (*Comm*) (financial) claim, (recoverable) debt; **donner ~ à qch** to lend credence to sth

créancier, -ière [kreɑ̃sje, -jɛr] NM/F creditor

créateur, -trice [kreatœr, -tris] ADJ creative
▶ NM/F creator; **le C~** (*Rel*) the Creator
créatif, -ive [kreatif, -iv] ADJ creative
création [kreasjɔ̃] NF creation
créativité [kreativite] NF creativity
créature [kreatyr] NF creature
crécelle [kresɛl] NF rattle
crèche [krɛʃ] NF (*de Noël*) crib; *see note*; (*garderie*)
crèche, day nursery

> In France the Christmas crib (*crèche*) usually
> contains figurines representing a miller, a
> wood-cutter and other villagers as well as
> the Holy Family and the traditional cow,
> donkey and shepherds. The Three Wise Men
> are added to the nativity scene at Epiphany
> (6 January, Twelfth Night).

crédence [kredãs] NF (small) sideboard
crédibilité [kredibilite] NF credibility
crédible [kredibl] ADJ credible
crédit [kredi] NM (*gén*) credit; **crédits** NMPL
funds; **acheter à ~** to buy on credit *ou* on easy
terms; **faire ~ à qn** to give sb credit;
~ municipal pawnshop; **~ relais** bridging
loan; **~ carbone** carbon credit
crédit-bail [kredibaj] (*pl* **crédits-bails**) NM
(*Écon*) leasing
créditer [kredite] /**1**/ VT: **~ un compte (de)** to
credit an account (with)
créditeur, -trice [kreditœr, -tris] ADJ in credit,
credit *cpd* ▶ NM/F customer in credit
credo [kredo] NM credo, creed
crédule [kredyl] ADJ credulous, gullible
crédulité [kredylite] NF credulity, gullibility
créer [kree] /**1**/ VT to create; (*Théât: pièce*) to
produce (for the first time); (: *rôle*) to create
crémaillère [kremajɛr] NF (*Rail*) rack; (*tige
crantée*) trammel; **direction à ~** (*Auto*) rack and
pinion steering; **pendre la ~** to have a
house-warming party
crémation [kremasjɔ̃] NF cremation
crématoire [krematwar] ADJ: **four ~**
crematorium
crématorium [krematɔrjɔm] NM
crematorium
crème [krɛm] NF cream; (*entremets*) cream
dessert ▶ ADJ INV cream; **un (café) ~** ≈ a white
coffee; **~ anglaise** (egg) custard; **~ chantilly**
whipped cream, crème Chantilly; **~ fouettée**
whipped cream; **~ glacée** ice cream; **~ à raser**
shaving cream; **~ solaire** sun cream
crémerie [kremri] NF dairy; (*tearoom*) teashop
crémeux, -euse [kremø, -øz] ADJ creamy
crémier, -ière [kremje, -jɛr] NM/F
dairyman/-woman
créneau, x [kreno] NM (*de fortification*) crenel(le);
(*fig, aussi Comm*) gap, slot; (*Auto*): **faire un ~** to
reverse into a parking space (*between cars
alongside the kerb*)
créole [kreɔl] ADJ, NMF Creole
crêpe [krɛp] NF (*galette*) pancake ▶ NM (*tissu*)
crêpe; (*de deuil*) black mourning crêpe; (*ruban*)
black armband (*ou* hatband *ou* ribbon); **semelle
(de) ~** crêpe sole; **~ de Chine** crêpe de Chine
crêpé, e [krepe] ADJ (*cheveux*) backcombed

crêperie [krɛpri] NF pancake shop *ou*
restaurant
crépi [krepi] NM roughcast
crépir [krepir] /**2**/ VT to roughcast
crépitement [krepitmã] NM (*du feu*) crackling
no pl; (*d'une arme automatique*) rattle *no pl*
crépiter [krepite] /**1**/ VI to sputter, splutter,
crackle
crépon [krepɔ̃] NM seersucker
CREPS [krɛps] SIGLE M (= *Centre régional d'éducation
physique et sportive*) ≈ sports *ou* leisure centre
crépu, e [krepy] ADJ frizzy, fuzzy
crépuscule [krepyskyl] NM twilight, dusk
crescendo [kreʃɛndo] NM, ADV (*Mus*) crescendo;
aller ~ (*fig*) to rise higher and higher, grow ever
greater
cresson [kresɔ̃] NM watercress
Crète [krɛt] NF: **la ~** Crete
crête [krɛt] NF (*de coq*) comb; (*de vague, montagne*)
crest
crétin, e [kretɛ̃, -in] NM/F cretin
crétois, e [kretwa, -waz] ADJ Cretan
cretonne [krǝtɔn] NF cretonne
creuser [krøze] /**1**/ VT (*trou, tunnel*) to dig; (*sol*) to
dig a hole in; (*bois*) to hollow out; (*fig*) to go
(deeply) into; **ça creuse** that gives you a real
appetite; **se ~ (la cervelle)** to rack one's brains
creuset [krøze] NM crucible; (*fig*) melting pot,
(*severe*) test
creux, -euse [krø, -øz] ADJ hollow ▶ NM hollow;
(*fig: sur graphique etc*) trough; **heures creuses**
slack periods; (*électricité, téléphone*) off-peak
periods; **le ~ de l'estomac** the pit of the
stomach; **avoir un ~** (*fam*) to be hungry
crevaison [krǝvɛzɔ̃] NF puncture, flat
crevant, e [krǝvã, -ãt] ADJ (*fam: fatigant*)
knackering; (: *très drôle*) priceless
crevasse [krǝvas] NF (*dans le sol*) crack, fissure;
(*de glacier*) crevasse; (*de la peau*) crack
crevé, e [krǝve] ADJ (*fam: fatigué*) shattered (*BRIT*),
exhausted
crève-cœur [krɛvkœr] NM INV heartbreak
crever [krǝve] /**5**/ VT (*papier*) to tear, break;
(*tambour, ballon*) to burst ▶ VI (*pneu*) to burst;
(*automobiliste*) to have a puncture (*BRIT*) *ou* a flat
(tire) (*US*); (*abcès, outre, nuage*) to burst (open);
(*fam*) to die; **cela lui a crevé un œil** it blinded
him in one eye; **~ l'écran** to have real screen
presence
crevette [krǝvɛt] NF: **~ (rose)** prawn; **~ grise**
shrimp
CRF SIGLE F (= *Croix-Rouge française*) French Red
Cross
cri [kri] NM cry, shout; (*d'animal: spécifique*) cry,
call; **à grands cris** at the top of one's voice;
c'est le dernier ~ it's the latest fashion
criant, e [krijã, -ãt] ADJ (*injustice*) glaring
criard, e [krijar, -ard] ADJ (*couleur*) garish, loud;
(*voix*) yelling
crible [kribl] NM riddle; (*mécanique*) screen, jig;
passer qch au ~ to put sth through a riddle;
(*fig*) to go over sth with a fine-tooth comb
criblé, e [krible] ADJ: **~ de** riddled with
cric [krik] NM (*Auto*) jack

cricket [kʀikɛt] NM cricket
criée [kʀije] NF: (**vente à la**) ~ (sale by) auction
crier [kʀije] **/7/** VI (pour appeler) to shout, cry (out); (de peur, de douleur etc) to scream, yell; (fig: grincer) to squeal, screech ▶ VT (ordre, injure) to shout (out), yell (out); **sans ~ gare** without warning; **~ grâce** to cry for mercy; **~ au secours** to shout for help
crieur, -euse [kʀijœʀ, -øz] NM/F: **~ de journaux** newspaper seller
crime [kʀim] NM crime; (meurtre) murder
Crimée [kʀime] NF: **la ~** the Crimea
criminalité [kʀiminalite] NF criminality, crime
criminel, le [kʀiminɛl] ADJ criminal ▶ NM/F criminal; murderer; **~ de guerre** war criminal
criminologie [kʀiminɔlɔʒi] NF criminology
criminologiste [kʀiminɔlɔʒist] NMF criminologist
criminologue [kʀiminɔlɔg] NMF criminologist
crin [kʀɛ̃] NM (de cheval) hair no pl; (fibre) horsehair; **à tous crins**, **à tout ~** diehard, out-and-out
crinière [kʀinjɛʀ] NF mane
crique [kʀik] NF creek, inlet
criquet [kʀikɛ] NM grasshopper
crise [kʀiz] NF crisis (pl crises); (Méd) attack; (: d'épilepsie) fit; **~ cardiaque** heart attack; **~ de foi** crisis of belief; **avoir une ~ de foie** to have really bad indigestion; **~ de nerfs** attack of nerves; **piquer une ~ de nerfs** to go hysterical
crispant, e [kʀispɑ̃, -ɑ̃t] ADJ annoying, irritating
crispation [kʀispasjɔ̃] NF (spasme) twitch; (contraction) contraction; tenseness
crispé, e [kʀispe] ADJ tense, nervous
crisper [kʀispe] **/1/** VT to tense; (poings) to clench; **se crisper** to tense; to clench; (personne) to get tense
crissement [kʀismɑ̃] NM crunch; rustle; screech
crisser [kʀise] **/1/** VI (neige) to crunch; (tissu) to rustle; (pneu) to screech
cristal, -aux [kʀistal, -o] NM crystal; **crystaux** NMPL (objets) crystal(ware) sg; **~ de plomb** (lead) crystal; **~ de roche** rock-crystal; **cristaux de soude** washing soda sg
cristallin, e [kʀistalɛ̃, -in] ADJ crystal-clear ▶ NM (Anat) crystalline lens
cristalliser [kʀistalize] **/1/** VI, VT, **se cristalliser** VI to crystallize
critère [kʀitɛʀ] NM criterion (pl criteria)
critiquable [kʀitikabl] ADJ open to criticism
critique [kʀitik] ADJ critical ▶ NMF (de théâtre, musique) critic ▶ NF criticism; (Théât etc: article) review; **la ~** (activité) criticism; (personnes) the critics pl
critiquer [kʀitike] **/1/** VT (dénigrer) to criticize; (évaluer, juger) to assess, examine (critically)
croasser [kʀɔase] **/1/** VI to caw
croate [kʀɔat] ADJ Croatian ▶ NM (Ling) Croat, Croatian ▶ NMF: **C~** Croat, Croatian
Croatie [kʀɔasi] NF: **la ~** Croatia
croc [kʀo] NM (dent) fang; (de boucher) hook
croc-en-jambe [kʀɔkɑ̃ʒɑ̃b] (pl **crocs-en-jambe**) NM: **faire un ~ à qn** to trip sb up

croche [kʀɔʃ] NF (Mus) quaver (BRIT), eighth note (US); **double ~** semiquaver (BRIT), sixteenth note (US)
croche-pied [kʀɔʃpje] NM = **croc-en-jambe**
crochet [kʀɔʃɛ] NM hook; (clef) picklock; (détour) detour; (Boxe): **~ du gauche** left hook; (Tricot: aiguille) crochet hook; (: technique) crochet; **crochets** NMPL (Typo) square brackets; **vivre aux crochets de qn** to live ou sponge off sb
crocheter [kʀɔʃte] **/5/** VT (serrure) to pick
crochu, e [kʀɔʃy] ADJ hooked; claw-like
crocodile [kʀɔkɔdil] NM crocodile
crocus [kʀɔkys] NM crocus
croire [kʀwaʀ] **/44/** VT to believe; **~ qn honnête** to believe sb (to be) honest; **se ~ fort** to think one is strong; **~ que** to believe ou think that; **vous croyez?** do you think so?; **~ être/faire** to think one is/does; **~ à**, **~ en** to believe in
croîs etc [kʀwa] VB voir **croître**
croisade [kʀwazad] NF crusade
croisé, e [kʀwaze] ADJ (veston) double-breasted ▶ NM (guerrier) crusader ▶ NF (fenêtre) window, casement; **~ d'ogives** intersecting ribs; **à la ~ des chemins** at the crossroads
croisement [kʀwazmɑ̃] NM (carrefour) crossroads sg; (Bio) crossing; (: résultat) crossbreed
croiser [kʀwaze] **/1/** VT (personne, voiture) to pass; (route) to cross, cut across; (Bio) to cross ▶ VI (Navig) to cruise; **~ les jambes/bras** to cross one's legs/fold one's arms; **se croiser** VI (personnes, véhicules) to pass each other; (routes) to cross, intersect; (lettres) to cross (in the post); (regards) to meet; **se croiser les bras** (fig) to fold one's arms, to twiddle one's thumbs
croiseur [kʀwazœʀ] NM cruiser (warship)
croisière [kʀwazjɛʀ] NF cruise; **vitesse de ~** (Auto etc) cruising speed
croisillon [kʀwazijɔ̃] NM: **motif/fenêtre à croisillons** lattice pattern/window
croissais etc [kʀwasɛ] VB voir **croître**
croissance [kʀwasɑ̃s] NF growing, growth; **troubles de la ~** growing pains; **maladie de ~** growth disease; **~ économique** economic growth
croissant, e [kʀwasɑ̃, -ɑ̃t] VB voir **croître** ▶ ADJ growing; rising ▶ NM (à manger) croissant; (motif) crescent; **~ de lune** crescent moon
croître [kʀwatʀ] **/55/** VI to grow; (lune) to wax
croix [kʀwa] NF cross; **en ~** adj, adv in the form of a cross; **la C~ Rouge** the Red Cross
croquant, e [kʀɔkɑ̃, -ɑ̃t] ADJ crisp, crunchy ▶ NM/F (péj) yokel, (country) bumpkin
croque-madame [kʀɔkmadam] NM INV toasted cheese sandwich with a fried egg on top
croque-mitaine [kʀɔkmitɛn] NM bog(e)y-man (pl-men)
croque-monsieur [kʀɔkməsjø] NM INV toasted ham and cheese sandwich
croque-mort [kʀɔkmɔʀ] NM (péj) pallbearer
croquer [kʀɔke] **/1/** VT (manger) to crunch; (: fruit) to munch; (dessiner) to sketch ▶ VI to be crisp ou crunchy; **chocolat à ~** plain dessert chocolate
croquet [kʀɔkɛ] NM croquet

croquette [kʀɔkɛt] NF croquette
croquis [kʀɔki] NM sketch
cross [kʀɔs], **cross-country** [kʀɔskuntri] (pl **~(-countries)**) NM cross-country race ou run; cross-country racing ou running
crosse [kʀɔs] NF (de fusil) butt; (de revolver) grip; (d'évêque) crook, crosier; (de hockey) hockey stick
crotale [kʀɔtal] NM rattlesnake
crotte [kʀɔt] NF droppings pl; ~! (fam) damn!
crotté, e [kʀɔte] ADJ muddy, mucky
crottin [kʀɔtɛ̃] NM dung, manure; (fromage) (small round) cheese (made of goat's milk)
croulant, e [kʀulɑ̃, -ɑ̃t] NM/F (fam) old fogey
crouler [kʀule] /1/ VI (s'effondrer) to collapse; (être délabré) to be crumbling
croupe [kʀup] NF croup, rump; **en ~** pillion
croupier [kʀupje] NM croupier
croupion [kʀupjɔ̃] NM (d'un oiseau) rump; (Culin) parson's nose
croupir [kʀupiʀ] /2/ VI to stagnate
CROUS [kʀus] SIGLE M (= Centre régional des œuvres universitaires et scolaires) students' representative body
croustade [kʀustad] NF (Culin) croustade
croustillant, e [kʀustijɑ̃, -ɑ̃t] ADJ crisp; (fig) spicy
croustiller [kʀustije] /1/ VI to be crisp ou crusty
croûte [kʀut] NF crust; (du fromage) rind; (de vol-au-vent) case; (Méd) scab; **en ~** (Culin) in pastry, in a pie; **~ aux champignons** mushrooms on toast; **~ au fromage** cheese on toast no pl; **~ de pain** (morceau) crust (of bread); **~ terrestre** earth's crust
croûton [kʀutɔ̃] NM (Culin) crouton; (bout du pain) crust, heel
croyable [kʀwajabl] ADJ believable, credible
croyais etc [kʀwaje] VB voir **croire**
croyance [kʀwajɑ̃s] NF belief
croyant, e [kʀwajɑ̃, -ɑ̃t] VB voir **croire** ▶ ADJ: **être/ne pas être ~** to be/not to be a believer ▶ NM/F believer
Crozet [kʀɔzɛ] N: **les îles ~** the Crozet Islands
CRS SIGLE FPL (= Compagnies républicaines de sécurité) state security police force ▶ SIGLE M member of the CRS
cru, e [kʀy] PP de **croire** ▶ ADJ (non cuit) raw; (lumière, couleur) harsh; (description) crude; (paroles, langage: franc) blunt; (: grossier) crude ▶ NM (vignoble) vineyard; (vin) wine ▶ NF (d'un cours d'eau) swelling, rising; **de son (propre) ~** (fig) of his own devising; **monter à ~** to ride bareback; **du ~** local; **en ~** in spate; **un grand ~** a great vintage; **jambon ~** Parma ham
crû [kʀy] PP de **croître**
cruauté [kʀyote] NF cruelty
cruche [kʀyʃ] NF pitcher, (earthenware) jug
crucial, e, -aux [kʀysjal, -o] ADJ crucial
crucifier [kʀysifje] /7/ VT to crucify
crucifix [kʀysifi] NM crucifix
crucifixion [kʀysifiksjɔ̃] NF crucifixion
cruciforme [kʀysifɔʀm] ADJ cruciform, cross-shaped
cruciverbiste [kʀysivɛʀbist] NMF crossword puzzle enthusiast
crudité [kʀydite] NF crudeness no pl; harshness

no pl; **crudités** NFPL (Culin) selection of raw vegetables
crue [kʀy] NF (inondation) flood; voir aussi **cru**
cruel, le [kʀyɛl] ADJ cruel
cruellement [kʀyɛlmɑ̃] ADV cruelly
crûment [kʀymɑ̃] ADV (voir cru) harshly; bluntly; crudely
crus, crûs etc [kʀy] VB voir **croire**; **croître**
crustacés [kʀystase] NMPL shellfish
crypte [kʀipt] NF crypt
crypter [kʀipte] VT (Inform, Tél) encrypt
CSA SIGLE F (= Conseil supérieur de l'audiovisuel) French broadcasting regulatory body, ≈ IBA (BRIT), ≈ FCC (US)
cse ABR = **cause**
CSEN SIGLE F (= Confédération syndicale de l'éducation nationale) group of teachers' unions
CSG SIGLE F (= contribution sociale généralisée) supplementary social security contribution in aid of the underprivileged
CSM SIGLE M (= Conseil supérieur de la magistrature) French magistrates' council
Cte ABR = **Comtesse**
CU SIGLE F = **communauté urbaine**
Cuba [kyba] NM Cuba; **le ~** Cuba
cubage [kybaʒ] NM cubage, cubic content
cubain, e [kybɛ̃, -ɛn] ADJ Cuban ▶ NM/F: **C~, e** Cuban
cube [kyb] NM cube; (jouet) brick, building block; **gros ~** powerful motorbike; **mètre ~** cubic metre; **2 au ~ = 8** 2 cubed is 8; **élever au ~** to cube
cubique [kybik] ADJ cubic
cubisme [kybism] NM cubism
cubiste [kybist] ADJ, NMF cubist
cubitus [kybitys] NM ulna
cueillette [kœjɛt] NF picking; (quantité) crop, harvest
cueillir [kœjiʀ] /12/ VT (fruits, fleurs) to pick, gather; (fig) to catch
cuiller, cuillère [kɥijɛʀ] NF spoon; **~ à café** coffee spoon; (Culin) ≈ teaspoonful; **~ à soupe** soup spoon; (Culin) ≈ tablespoonful
cuillerée [kɥijʀe] NF spoonful; (Culin): **~ à soupe/café** tablespoonful/teaspoonful
cuir [kɥiʀ] NM leather; (avant tannage) hide; **~ chevelu** scalp
cuirasse [kɥiʀas] NF breastplate
cuirassé [kɥiʀase] NM (Navig) battleship
cuire [kɥiʀ] /38/ VT: **(faire) ~** (aliments) to cook; (au four) to bake; (poterie) to fire ▶ VI to cook; (picoter) to smart, sting, burn; **bien cuit** (viande) well done; **trop cuit** overdone; **pas assez cuit** underdone; **cuit à point** medium done; done to a turn
cuisant, e [kɥizɑ̃, -ɑ̃t] VB voir **cuire** ▶ ADJ (douleur) smarting, burning; (fig: souvenir, échec) bitter
cuisine [kɥizin] NF (pièce) kitchen; (art culinaire) cookery, cooking; (nourriture) cooking, food; **faire la ~** to cook
cuisiné, e [kɥizine] ADJ: **plat ~** ready-made meal ou dish
cuisiner [kɥizine] /1/ VT to cook; (fam) to grill ▶ VI to cook

cuisinette [kɥizinɛt] NF kitchenette
cuisinier, -ière [kɥizinje, -jɛʀ] NM/F cook ▶ NF (poêle) cooker; **cuisinière électrique/à gaz** electric/gas cooker
cuisis etc [kɥizi] VB voir **cuire**
cuissardes [kɥisaʀd] NFPL (de pêcheur) waders; (de femme) thigh boots
cuisse [kɥis] NF (Anat) thigh; (Culin) leg
cuisson [kɥisɔ̃] NF cooking; (de poterie) firing
cuissot [kɥiso] NM haunch
cuistre [kɥistʀ] NM prig
cuit, e [kɥi, -it] PP de **cuire** ▶ NF (fam): **prendre une ~** to get plastered ou smashed
cuivre [kɥivʀ] NM copper; **les cuivres** (Mus) the brass; **~ rouge** copper; **~ jaune** brass
cuivré, e [kɥivʀe] ADJ coppery; (peau) bronzed
cul [ky] NM (!) arse (BRIT!), ass (US!), bum (BRIT); **~ de bouteille** bottom of a bottle
culasse [kylas] NF (Auto) cylinder-head; (de fusil) breech
culbute [kylbyt] NF somersault; (accidentelle) tumble, fall
culbuter [kylbyte] /1/ VI to (take a) tumble, fall (head over heels)
culbuteur [kylbytœʀ] NM (Auto) rocker arm
cul-de-jatte [kydʒat] (pl **culs-de-jatte**) NM/F legless cripple (péj)
cul-de-sac [kydsak] (pl **culs-de-sac**) NM cul-de-sac
culinaire [kylinɛʀ] ADJ culinary
culminant, e [kylminɑ̃, -ɑ̃t] ADJ: **point ~** highest point; (fig) height, climax
culminer [kylmine] /1/ VI to reach its highest point; to tower
culot [kylo] (fam) NM (d'ampoule) cap; (effronterie) cheek, nerve
culotte [kylɔt] NF (de femme) panties pl, knickers pl (BRIT); (d'homme) underpants pl; (pantalon) trousers pl (BRIT), pants pl (US); **~ de cheval** riding breeches pl
culotté, e [kylɔte] ADJ (pipe) seasoned; (cuir) mellowed; (effronté) cheeky
culpabiliser [kylpabilize] /1/ VT: **~ qn** to make sb feel guilty
culpabilité [kylpabilite] NF guilt
culte [kylt] ADJ: **livre/film ~** cult film/book ▶ NM (religion) religion; (hommage, vénération) worship; (protestant) service
cultivable [kyltivabl] ADJ cultivable
cultivateur, -trice [kyltivatœʀ, -tʀis] NM/F farmer
cultivé, e [kyltive] ADJ (personne) cultured, cultivated
cultiver [kyltive] /1/ VT to cultivate; (légumes) to grow, cultivate
culture [kyltyʀ] NF cultivation; growing; (connaissances etc) culture; **(champs de) cultures** land(s) under cultivation; **les cultures intensives** intensive farming; **~ physique** physical training
culturel, le [kyltyʀɛl] ADJ cultural
culturisme [kyltyʀism] NM body-building
culturiste [kyltyʀist] NMF body-builder
cumin [kymɛ̃] NM (Culin) cumin

cumul [kymyl] NM (voir **cumuler**) holding (ou drawing) concurrently; **~ de peines** sentences to run consecutively
cumulable [kymylabl] ADJ (fonctions) which may be held concurrently
cumuler [kymyle] /1/ VT (emplois, honneurs) to hold concurrently; (salaires) to draw concurrently; (Jur: droits) to accumulate
cupide [kypid] ADJ greedy, grasping
cupidité [kypidite] NF greed
curable [kyʀabl] ADJ curable
Curaçao [kyʀaso] N Curaçao ▶ NM: **curaçao** curaçao
curare [kyʀaʀ] NM curare
curatif, -ive [kyʀatif, -iv] ADJ curative
cure [kyʀ] NF (Méd) course of treatment; (Rel) cure, ≈ living; presbytery, ≈ vicarage; **faire une ~ de fruits** to go on a fruit cure ou diet; **faire une ~ thermale** to take the waters; **n'avoir ~ de** to pay no attention to; **~ d'amaigrissement** slimming course; **~ de repos** rest cure; **~ de sommeil** sleep therapy no pl
curé [kyʀe] NM parish priest; **M le ~** ≈ Vicar
cure-dent [kyʀdɑ̃] NM toothpick
curée [kyʀe] NF (fig) scramble for the pickings
cure-ongles [kyʀɔ̃gl] NM INV nail cleaner
cure-pipe [kyʀpip] NM pipe cleaner
curer [kyʀe] /1/ VT to clean out; **se ~ les dents** to pick one's teeth
curetage [kyʀtaʒ] NM (Méd) curettage
curieusement [kyʀjøzmɑ̃] ADV oddly
curieux, -euse [kyʀjø, -øz] ADJ (étrange) strange, curious; (indiscret) curious, inquisitive; (intéressé) inquiring, curious ▶ NMPL (badauds) onlookers, bystanders
curiosité [kyʀjozite] NF curiosity, inquisitiveness; (objet) curio(sity); (site) unusual feature ou sight
curiste [kyʀist] NMF person taking the waters at a spa
curriculum vitae [kyʀikylɔmvite] NM INV curriculum vitae
curry [kyʀi] NM curry; **poulet au ~** curried chicken, chicken curry
curseur [kyʀsœʀ] NM (Inform) cursor; (de règle) slide; (de fermeture-éclair) slider
cursif, -ive [kyʀsif, -iv] ADJ: **écriture cursive** cursive script
cursus [kyʀsys] NM degree course
curviligne [kyʀvilin] ADJ curvilinear
cutané, e [kytane] ADJ cutaneous, skin cpd
cuti-réaction [kytiʀeaksjɔ̃] NF (Méd) skin-test
cuve [kyv] NF vat; (à mazout etc) tank
cuvée [kyve] NF vintage
cuvette [kyvɛt] NF (récipient) bowl, basin; (du lavabo) (wash)basin; (des w.-c.) pan; (Géo) basin
CV SIGLE M (Auto) = **cheval (vapeur)**; (Admin) = **curriculum vitae**
CVS SIGLE ADJ (= corrigées des variations saisonnières) seasonally adjusted
cx ABR (= coefficient de pénétration dans l'air) drag coefficient
cyanure [sjanyʀ] NM cyanide
cybercafé [sibɛʀkafe] NM Internet café

105

cyberculture [sibɛʁkyltyʁ] NF cyberculture
cyberespace [sibɛʁɛspas] NM cyberspace
cybernaute [sibɛʁnot] NMF Internet user
cybernétique [sibɛʁnetik] NF cybernetics sg
cyclable [siklabl] ADJ: **piste ~** cycle track
cyclamen [siklamɛn] NM cyclamen
cycle [sikl] NM cycle; (Scol): **premier/second ~**
≈ middle/upper school (BRIT), ≈ junior/senior
high school (US)
cyclique [siklik] ADJ cyclic(al)
cyclisme [siklism] NM cycling
cycliste [siklist] NMF cyclist ▸ ADJ cycle cpd;
coureur ~ racing cyclist
cyclo-cross [siklɔkʁɔs] NM (Sport) cyclo-cross;
(épreuve) cyclo-cross race
cyclomoteur [siklɔmɔtœʁ] NM moped
cyclomotoriste [siklɔmɔtɔʁist] NMF moped
rider
cyclone [siklon] NM hurricane

cyclotourisme [siklɔtuʁism] NM (bi)cycle
touring
cygne [siɲ] NM swan
cylindre [silɛ̃dʁ] NM cylinder; **moteur à 4
cylindres en ligne** straight-4 engine
cylindrée [silɛ̃dʁe] NF (Auto) (cubic) capacity;
une (voiture de) grosse ~ a big-engined car
cylindrique [silɛ̃dʁik] ADJ cylindrical
cymbale [sɛ̃bal] NF cymbal
cynique [sinik] ADJ cynical
cyniquement [sinikmɑ̃] ADV cynically
cynisme [sinism] NM cynicism
cyprès [sipʁɛ] NM cypress
cypriote [sipʁijɔt] ADJ Cypriot ▸ NMF: **C~**
Cypriot
cyrillique [siʁilik] ADJ Cyrillic
cystite [sistit] NF cystitis
cytise [sitiz] NM laburnum
cytologie [sitɔlɔʒi] NF cytology

Dd

D, d [de] NM INV D, d ▶ ABR: **D** (*Météorologie:* = *dépression*) low, depression; **D comme Désiré** D for David (*Brit*) *ou* Dog (*US*); *voir* **système**

d' PRÉP, ART *voir* **de**

Dacca [daka] N Dacca

dactylo [daktilo] NF (*aussi:* **dactylographe**) typist; (*aussi:* **dactylographie**) typing, typewriting

dactylographier [daktilɔgʀafje] /**7**/ VT to type (out)

dada [dada] NM hobby-horse

dadais [dadɛ] NM ninny, lump

dague [dag] NF dagger

dahlia [dalja] NM dahlia

dahoméen, ne [daɔmeɛ̃, -ɛn] ADJ Dahomean

Dahomey [daɔme] NM: **le ~** Dahomey

daigner [deɲe] /**1**/ VT to deign

daim [dɛ̃] NM (fallow) deer *inv*; (*peau*) buckskin; (*cuir suédé*) suede

dais [dɛ] NM (*tenture*) canopy

Dakar [dakaʀ] N Dakar

dal. ABR (= *décalitre*) dal.

dallage [dalaʒ] NM paving

dalle [dal] NF slab; (*au sol*) paving stone, flag(stone); **que ~** nothing at all, damn all (*Brit*)

daller [dale] /**1**/ VT to pave

dalmatien, ne [dalmasjɛ̃, -ɛn] NM/F (*chien*) Dalmatian

daltonien, ne [daltɔnjɛ̃, -ɛn] ADJ colour-blind (*Brit*), color-blind (*US*)

daltonisme [daltɔnism] NM colour (*Brit*) *ou* color (*US*) blindness

dam [dam] NM: **au grand ~ de** much to the detriment (*ou* annoyance) of

Damas [dama] N Damascus

damas [dama] NM (*étoffe*) damask

damassé, e [damase] ADJ damask *cpd*

dame [dam] NF lady; (*Cartes, Échecs*) queen; **dames** NFPL (*jeu*) draughts *sg* (*Brit*), checkers *sg* (*US*); **les (toilettes des) dames** the ladies' (toilets); **~ de charité** benefactress; **~ de compagnie** lady's companion

dame-jeanne [damʒan] (*pl* **dames-jeannes**) NF demijohn

damer [dame] /**1**/ VT to ram *ou* pack down; **~ le pion à** (*fig*) to get the better of

damier [damje] NM draughts board (*Brit*),

checkerboard (*US*); (*dessin*) check (pattern); **en ~** check

damner [dɑne] /**1**/ VT to damn

dancing [dɑ̃siŋ] NM dance hall

dandiner [dɑ̃dine] /**1**/: **se dandiner** VI to sway about; (*en marchant*) to waddle along

Danemark [danmaʀk] NM: **le ~** Denmark

danger [dɑ̃ʒe] NM danger; **mettre en ~** (*personne*) to put in danger; (*projet, carrière*) to jeopardize; **être en ~** (*personne*) to be in danger; **être en ~ de mort** to be in peril of one's life; **être hors de ~** to be out of danger

dangereusement [dɑ̃ʒʀøzmɑ̃] ADV dangerously

dangereux, -euse [dɑ̃ʒʀø, -øz] ADJ dangerous

danois, e [danwa, -waz] ADJ Danish ▶ NM (*Ling*) Danish ▶ NM/F: **D~, e** Dane

---

(MOT-CLÉ)

dans [dɑ̃] PRÉP **1** (*position*) in; (: *à l'intérieur de*) inside; **c'est dans le tiroir/le salon** it's in the drawer/lounge; **dans la boîte** in *ou* inside the box; **marcher dans la ville/la rue** to walk about the town/along the street; **je l'ai lu dans le journal** I read it in the newspaper; **être dans les meilleurs** to be among *ou* one of the best

2 (*direction*) into; **elle a couru dans le salon** she ran into the lounge; **monter dans une voiture/le bus** to get into a car/on to the bus

3 (*provenance*) out of, from; **je l'ai pris dans le tiroir/salon** I took it out of *ou* from the drawer/lounge; **boire dans un verre** to drink out of *ou* from a glass

4 (*temps*) in; **dans deux mois** in two months, in two months' time

5 (*approximation*) about; **dans les 20 euros** about 20 euros

---

dansant, e [dɑ̃sɑ̃, -ɑ̃t] ADJ: **soirée ~** evening of dancing; (*bal*) dinner dance

danse [dɑ̃s] NF: **la ~** dancing; (*classique*) (ballet) dancing; **une ~** a dance; **~ du ventre** belly dancing

danser [dɑ̃se] /**1**/ VI, VT to dance

danseur, -euse [dɑ̃sœʀ, -øz] NM/F ballet dancer; (*au bal etc*) dancer; (: *cavalier*) partner; **~ de claquettes** tap-dancer; **en danseuse** (*à vélo*) standing on the pedals

Danube [danyb] NM: **le ~** the Danube

DAO SIGLE M (= *dessin assisté par ordinateur*) CAD

dard [daʀ] NM sting (*organ*)

darder [daʀde] /1/ VT to shoot, send forth

dare-dare [daʀdaʀ] ADV in double quick time

Dar-es-Salaam, Dar-es-Salam [daʀɛsalam] N Dar-es-Salaam

darne [daʀn] NF steak (*of fish*)

darse [daʀs] NF sheltered dock (*in a Mediterranean port*)

dartre [daʀtʀ] NF (*Méd*) sore

datation [datasjɔ̃] NF dating

date [dat] NF date; (*d'un aliment: aussi:* **date limite de vente**) sell-by date; **faire ~** to mark a milestone; **de longue ~** adj longstanding; **~ de naissance** date of birth; **~ limite** deadline

dater [date] /1/ VT, VI to date; **~ de** to date from, go back to; **à ~ de** (as) from

dateur [datœʀ] NM (*de montre*) date indicator; **timbre ~** date stamp

datif [datif] NM dative

datte [dat] NF date

dattier [datje] NM date palm

daube [dob] NF: **bœuf en ~** beef casserole

dauphin [dofɛ̃] NM (*Zool*) dolphin; (*du roi*) dauphin; (*fig*) heir apparent

Dauphiné [dofine] NM: **le ~** the Dauphiné

dauphinois, e [dofinwa, -waz] ADJ of *ou* from the Dauphiné

daurade [dɔʀad] NF sea bream

davantage [davɑ̃taʒ] ADV more; (*plus longtemps*) longer; **~ de** more; **~ que** more than

DB SIGLE F (*Mil*) = **division blindée**

DCA SIGLE F (= *défense contre avions*) anti-aircraft defence

DCT SIGLE M (= *diphtérie coqueluche tétanos*) DPT

DDASS [das] SIGLE F (= *Direction départementale d'action sanitaire et sociale*) ≈ DWP (= Department of Work and Pensions (BRIT)), ≈ SSA (= Social Security Administration (US))

DDT SIGLE M (= *dichloro-diphénol-trichloréthane*) DDT

[MOT-CLÉ]

de, d' [də, d] (*de + le =* **du**, *de + les =* **des**) PRÉP
1 (*appartenance*) of; **le toit de la maison** the roof of the house; **la voiture d'Elisabeth/de mes parents** Elisabeth's/my parents' car
2 (*provenance*) from; **il vient de Londres** he comes from London; **de Londres à Paris** from London to Paris; **elle est sortie du cinéma** she came out of the cinema
3 (*moyen*) with; **je l'ai fait de mes propres mains** I did it with my own two hands
4 (*caractérisation: mesure*): **un mur de brique/bureau d'acajou** a brick wall/mahogany desk; **un billet de 10 euros** a 10 euro note; **une pièce de 2 m de large** *ou* **large de 2 m** a room 2 m wide, a 2m-wide room; **un bébé de 10 mois** a 10-month-old baby; **12 mois de crédit/travail** 12 months' credit/work; **elle est payée 20 euros de l'heure** she's paid 20 euros an hour *ou* per hour; **augmenter de 10 euros** to increase by 10 euros; **trois jours de libres** three free days, three days free; **un verre d'eau** a glass of water; **il mange de tout** he'll eat anything
5 (*rapport*) from; **de quatre à six** from four to six
6 (*cause*): **mourir de faim** to die of hunger; **rouge de colère** red with fury
7 (*vb + de + infin*) to; **il m'a dit de rester** he told me to stay
8 (*de la part de*): **estimé de ses collègues** respected by his colleagues
9 (*en apposition*): **cet imbécile de Paul** that idiot Paul; **le terme de franglais** the term "franglais"
▶ ART **1** (*phrases affirmatives*) some (*souvent omis*); **du vin, de l'eau, des pommes** (some) wine, (some) water, (some) apples; **des enfants sont venus** some children came; **pendant des mois** for months
2 (*phrases interrogatives et négatives*) any; **a-t-il du vin?** has he got any wine?; **il n'a pas de pommes/d'enfants** he hasn't (got) any apples/children, he has no apples/children

dé [de] NM (*à jouer*) die *ou* dice; (*aussi:* **dé à coudre**) thimble; **dés** NMPL (*jeu*) (game of) dice; **un coup de dés** a throw of the dice; **couper en dés** (*Culin*) to dice

DEA SIGLE M (= *Diplôme d'études approfondies*) post-graduate diploma

dealer [dilœʀ] NM (*fam*) (drug) pusher

déambulateur [deɑ̃bylatœʀ] NM Zimmer®

déambuler [deɑ̃byle] /1/ VI to stroll about

déb. ABR = **débutant**; (*Comm*) = **à débattre**

débâcle [debɑkl] NF rout

déballage [debalaʒ] NM (*de marchandises*) display (*of loose goods*); (*fig: fam*) outpourings pl

déballer [debale] /1/ VT to unpack

débandade [debɑ̃dad] NF scattering; (*déroute*) rout

débander [debɑ̃de] /1/ VT to unbandage

débaptiser [debatize] /1/ VT (*rue*) to rename

débarbouiller [debaʀbuje] /1/ VT to wash; **se débarbouiller** VI to wash (one's face)

débarcadère [debaʀkadɛʀ] NM landing stage (BRIT), wharf

débardeur [debaʀdœʀ] NM docker, stevedore; (*maillot*) slipover; (*pour femme*) vest top; (*pour homme*) sleeveless top

débarquement [debaʀkəmɑ̃] NM unloading, landing; disembarkation; (*Mil*) landing; **le D~** the Normandy landings

débarquer [debaʀke] /1/ VT to unload, land ▶ VI to disembark; (*fig*) to turn up

débarras [debaʀɑ] NM (*pièce*) lumber room; (*placard*) junk cupboard; (*remise*) outhouse; **bon ~!** good riddance!

débarrasser [debaʀase] /1/ VT to clear ▶ VI (*enlever le couvert*) to clear away; **se débarrasser de** VT to get rid of; to rid o.s. of; **~ qn** (*vêtements, paquets*) to relieve sb of; (*habitude, ennemi*) to rid sb of; **~ qch de** (*fouillis etc*) to clear sth of

débat [deba] VB *voir* **débattre** ▶ NM discussion, debate; **débats** NMPL (*Pol*) proceedings, debates

débattre [debatʀ] /41/ VT to discuss, debate; **se**

débattre vi to struggle

débauchage [deboʃaʒ] NM (*licenciement*) laying off (of staff); (*par un concurrent*) poaching

débauche [deboʃ] NF debauchery; **une ~ de** (*fig*) a profusion of (: *de couleurs*) a riot of

débauché, e [deboʃe] ADJ debauched ▶ NM/F profligate

débaucher [deboʃe] /1/ VT (*licencier*) to lay off, dismiss; (*salarié d'une autre entreprise*) to poach; (*entraîner*) to lead astray, debauch; (*inciter à la grève*) to incite

débile [debil] ADJ weak, feeble; (*fam: idiot*) dim-witted

débilitant, e [debilitɑ̃, -ɑ̃t] ADJ debilitating

débilité [debilite] NF debility; (*fam: idiotie*) stupidity; **~ mentale** mental debility

débiner [debine] /1/: **se débiner** vi to do a bunk (BRIT), clear out

débit [debi] NM (*d'un liquide, fleuve*) (rate of) flow; (*d'un magasin*) turnover (of goods); (*élocution*) delivery; (*bancaire*) debit; **avoir un ~ de 10 euros** to be 10 euros in debit; **~ de boissons** drinking establishment; **~ de tabac** tobacconist's (shop) (BRIT), tobacco ou smoke shop (US)

débiter [debite] /1/ VT (*compte*) to debit; (*liquide, gaz*) to yield, produce, give out; (*couper: bois, viande*) to cut up; (*vendre*) to retail; (*péj: paroles etc*) to come out with, churn out

débiteur, -trice [debitœr, -tris] NM/F debtor ▶ ADJ in debit; (*compte*) debit cpd

déblai [deblɛ] NM (*nettoyage*) clearing; **déblais** NMPL (*terre*) earth; (*décombres*) rubble

déblaiement [deblɛmɑ̃] NM clearing; **travaux de ~** earth moving sg

déblatérer [deblatere] /6/ vi: **~ contre** to go on about

déblayer [debleje] /8/ VT to clear; **~ le terrain** (*fig*) to clear the ground

déblocage [deblɔkaʒ] NM (*des prix, cours*) unfreezing

débloquer [deblɔke] /1/ VT (*frein, fonds*) to release; (*prix, crédits*) to free ▶ VI (*fam*) to talk rubbish

débobiner [debɔbine] /1/ VT to unwind

déboires [debwar] NMPL setbacks

déboisement [debwazmɑ̃] NM deforestation

déboiser [debwaze] /1/ VT to clear of trees; (*région*) to deforest; **se déboiser** vi (*colline, montagne*) to become bare of trees

déboîter [debwate] /1/ VT (*Auto*) to pull out; **se ~ le genou** *etc* to dislocate one's knee *etc*

débonnaire [debɔnɛr] ADJ easy-going, good-natured

débordant, e [debɔrdɑ̃, -ɑ̃t] ADJ (*joie*) unbounded; (*activité*) exuberant

débordé, e [debɔrde] ADJ: **être ~ de** (*travail, demandes*) to be snowed under with

débordement [debɔrdəmɑ̃] NM overflowing

déborder [debɔrde] /1/ VI to overflow; (*lait etc*) to boil over ▶ VT (*Mil, Sport*) to outflank; **~ (de) qch** (*dépasser*) to extend beyond sth; **~ de** (*joie, zèle*) to be brimming over with ou bursting with

débouché [debuʃe] NM (*pour vendre*) outlet; (*perspective d'emploi*) opening; (*sortie*): **au ~ de la vallée** where the valley opens out (onto the plain)

déboucher [debuʃe] /1/ VT (*évier, tuyau etc*) to unblock; (*bouteille*) to uncork, open ▶ VI: **~ de** to emerge from, come out of; **~ sur** to come out onto; to open out onto; (*fig*) to arrive at, lead up to; (*études*) to lead on to

débouler [debule] /1/ VI to go (ou come) tumbling down; (*sans tomber*) to come careering down ▶ VT: **~ l'escalier** to belt down the stairs

déboulonner [debulɔne] /1/ VT to dismantle; (*fig: renvoyer*) to dismiss; (: *détruire le prestige de*) to discredit

débours [debur] NMPL outlay

débourser [deburse] /1/ VT to pay out, lay out

déboussoler [debusɔle] /1/ VT to disorientate, disorient

debout [dəbu] ADV: **être ~** (*personne*) to be standing, stand (: *levé, éveillé*) to be up (and about); (*chose*) to be upright; **être encore ~** (*fig: en état*) to be still going; to be still standing; to be still up; **mettre qn ~** to get sb to his feet; **mettre qch ~** to stand sth up; **se mettre ~** to get up (on one's feet); **se tenir ~** to stand; **~!** stand up!; (*du lit*) get up!; **cette histoire ne tient pas ~** this story doesn't hold water

débouter [debute] /1/ VT (*Jur*) to dismiss; **~ qn de sa demande** to dismiss sb's petition

déboutonner [debutɔne] /1/ VT to undo, unbutton; **se déboutonner** vi to come undone ou unbuttoned

débraillé, e [debraje] ADJ slovenly, untidy

débrancher [debrɑ̃ʃe] /1/ VT (*appareil électrique*) to unplug; (*téléphone, courant électrique*) to disconnect, cut off

débrayage [debrejaʒ] NM (*Auto*) clutch; (: *action*) disengaging the clutch; (*grève*) stoppage; **faire un double ~** to double-declutch

débrayer [debreje] /8/ VI (*Auto*) to declutch, disengage the clutch; (*cesser le travail*) to stop work

débridé, e [debride] ADJ unbridled, unrestrained

débrider [debride] /1/ VT (*cheval*) to unbridle; (*Culin: volaille*) to untruss

débris [debri] NM (*fragment*) fragment ▶ NMPL (*déchets*) pieces, debris sg; rubbish sg (BRIT), garbage sg (US); **des ~ de verre** bits of glass

débrouillard, e [debrujar, -ard] ADJ smart, resourceful

débrouillardise [debrujardiz] NF smartness, resourcefulness

débrouiller [debruje] /1/ VT to disentangle, untangle; (*fig*) to sort out, unravel; **se débrouiller** VI to manage; **débrouillez-vous** you'll have to sort things out yourself

débroussailler [debrusaje] /1/ VT to clear (of brushwood)

débusquer [debyske] /1/ VT to drive out (from cover)

début [deby] NM beginning, start; **débuts** NMPL beginnings; (*de carrière*) début sg; **faire ses débuts** to start out; **au ~** in ou at the beginning,

at first; **au ~ de** at the beginning *ou* start of;
dès le ~ from the start; **~ juin** in early June
débutant, e [debytã, -ãt] NM/F beginner, novice
débuter [debyte] /1/ VI to begin, start; *(faire ses débuts)* to start out
deçà [dəsa]: **en ~ de** *prép* this side of; **en ~** *adv* on this side
décacheter [dekaʃte] /4/ VT to unseal, open
décade [dekad] NF *(10 jours)* (period of) ten days; *(10 ans)* decade
décadence [dekadãs] NF decadence; decline
décadent, e [dekadã, -ãt] ADJ decadent
décaféiné, e [dekafeine] ADJ decaffeinated, caffeine-free
décalage [dekalaʒ] NM move forward *ou* back; shift forward *ou* back; *(écart)* gap; *(désaccord)* discrepancy; **~ horaire** time difference (between time zones), time-lag
décalaminer [dekalamine] /1/ VT to decoke
décalcification [dekalsifikasjɔ̃] NF decalcification
décalcifier [dekalsifje] /7/: **se décalcifier** VR to decalcify
décalcomanie [dekalkɔmani] NF transfer
décaler [dekale] /1/ VT *(dans le temps: avancer)* to bring forward; *(: retarder)* to put back; *(changer de position)* to shift forward *ou* back; **~ de 10 cm** to move forward *ou* back by 10 cm; **~ de deux heures** to bring *ou* move forward two hours; to put back two hours
décalitre [dekalitʀ] NM decalitre (BRIT), decaliter (US)
décalogue [dekalɔg] NM Decalogue
décalquer [dekalke] /1/ VT to trace; *(par pression)* to transfer
décamètre [dekamɛtʀ] NM decametre (BRIT), decameter (US)
décamper [dekãpe] /1/ VI to clear out *ou* off
décan [dekã] NM *(Astrologie)* decan
décanter [dekãte] /1/ VT to (allow to) settle (and decant); **se décanter** VI to settle
décapage [dekapaʒ] NM stripping; scouring; sanding
décapant [dekapã] NM acid solution; scouring agent; paint stripper
décaper [dekape] /1/ VT to strip; *(avec abrasif)* to scour; *(avec papier de verre)* to sand
décapiter [dekapite] /1/ VT to behead; *(par accident)* to decapitate; *(fig)* to cut the top off; *(: organisation)* to remove the top people from
décapotable [dekapɔtabl] ADJ convertible
décapoter [dekapɔte] /1/ VT to put down the top of
décapsuler [dekapsyle] /1/ VT to take the cap *ou* top off
décapsuleur [dekapsylœʀ] NM bottle-opener
décarcasser [dekaʀkase] /1/ VT: **se ~ pour qn/ pour faire qch** *(fam)* to slog one's guts out for sb/to do sth
décathlon [dekatlɔ̃] NM decathlon
décati, e [dekati] ADJ faded, aged
décédé, e [desede] ADJ deceased
décéder [desede] /6/ VI to die
décelable [des(ə)labl] ADJ discernible

déceler [desle] /5/ VT to discover, detect; *(révéler)* to indicate, reveal
décélération [deseleʀasjɔ̃] NF deceleration
décélérer [deseleʀe] /1/ VI to decelerate, slow down
décembre [desãbʀ] NM December; *voir aussi* **juillet**
décemment [desamã] ADV decently
décence [desãs] NF decency
décennal, e, -aux [desenal, -o] ADJ *(qui dure dix ans)* having a term of ten years, ten-year; *(qui revient tous les dix ans)* ten-yearly
décennie [deseni] NF decade
décent, e [desã, -ãt] ADJ decent
décentralisation [desãtʀalizasjɔ̃] NF decentralization
décentraliser [desãtʀalize] /1/ VT to decentralize
décentrer [desãtʀe] /1/ VT to throw off centre; **se décentrer** VI to move off-centre
déception [desɛpsjɔ̃] NF disappointment
décerner [desɛʀne] /1/ VT to award
décès [desɛ] NM death, decease; **acte de ~** death certificate
décevant, e [desvã, -ãt] ADJ disappointing
décevoir [des(ə)vwaʀ] /28/ VT to disappoint
déchaîné, e [deʃene] ADJ unbridled, raging
déchaînement [deʃenmã] NM *(de haine, violence)* outbreak, outburst
déchaîner [deʃene] /1/ VT *(passions, colère)* to unleash; *(rires etc)* to give rise to, arouse; **se déchaîner** VI to be unleashed; *(rires)* to burst out; *(se mettre en colère)* to fly into a rage; **se déchaîner contre qn** to unleash one's fury on sb
déchanter [deʃãte] /1/ VI to become disillusioned
décharge [deʃaʀʒ] NF *(dépôt d'ordures)* rubbish tip *ou* dump; *(électrique)* electrical discharge; *(salve)* volley of shots; **à la ~ de** in defence of
déchargement [deʃaʀʒəmã] NM unloading
décharger [deʃaʀʒe] /3/ VT *(marchandise, véhicule)* to unload; *(Élec)* to discharge; *(arme: neutraliser)* to unload; *(: faire feu)* to discharge, fire; **~ qn de** *(responsabilité)* to relieve sb of, release sb from; **~ sa colère (sur)** to vent one's anger (on); **~ sa conscience** to unburden one's conscience; **se ~ dans** *(se déverser)* to flow into; **se ~ d'une affaire sur qn** to hand a matter over to sb
décharné, e [deʃaʀne] ADJ bony, emaciated, fleshless
déchaussé, e [deʃose] ADJ *(dent)* loose
déchausser [deʃose] /1/ VT *(personne)* to take the shoes off; *(skis)* to take off; **se déchausser** VI to take off one's shoes; *(dent)* to come *ou* work loose
dèche [dɛʃ] NF *(fam)*: **être dans la ~** to be flat broke
déchéance [deʃeãs] NF *(déclin)* degeneration, decay, decline; *(chute)* fall
déchet [deʃɛ] NM *(de bois, tissu etc)* scrap; *(perte: gén: Comm)* wastage, waste; **déchets** NMPL *(ordures)* refuse *sg*, rubbish *sg* (BRIT), garbage *sg* (US); **déchets nucléaires** nuclear waste;

déchets radioactifs radioactive waste
déchiffrage [deʃifʀaʒ] NM sight-reading
déchiffrer [deʃifʀe] /1/ VT to decipher
déchiqueté, e [deʃikte] ADJ jagged(-edged), ragged
déchiqueter [deʃikte] /4/ VT to tear ou pull to pieces
déchirant, e [deʃiʀɑ̃, -ɑ̃t] ADJ heart-breaking, heart-rending
déchiré, e [deʃiʀe] ADJ torn; *(fig)* heart-broken
déchirement [deʃiʀmɑ̃] NM *(chagrin)* wrench, heartbreak; *(gén pl: conflit)* rift, split
déchirer [deʃiʀe] /1/ VT to tear, rip; *(mettre en morceaux)* to tear up; *(pour ouvrir)* to tear off; *(arracher)* to tear out; *(fig)* to tear apart; **se déchirer** VI to tear, rip; **se déchirer un muscle/tendon** to tear a muscle/tendon
déchirure [deʃiʀyʀ] NF *(accroc)* tear, rip; **~ musculaire** torn muscle
déchoir [deʃwaʀ] /25/ VI *(personne)* to lower o.s., demean o.s.; **~ de** to fall from
déchu, e [deʃy] PP *de* **déchoir** ▶ ADJ fallen; *(roi)* deposed
décibel [desibɛl] NM decibel
décidé, e [deside] ADJ *(personne, air)* determined; **c'est ~** it's decided; **être ~ à faire** to be determined to do
décidément [desidemɑ̃] ADV undoubtedly; really
décider [deside] /1/ VT: **~ qch** to decide on sth; **se décider** VI *(personne)* to decide, make up one's mind; *(problème, affaire)* to be resolved; **~ de faire/que** to decide to do/that; **~ qn (à faire qch)** to persuade ou induce sb (to do sth); **~ de qch** to decide upon sth; *(chose)* to determine sth; **se décider à qch** to decide on sth; **se décider à faire** to decide ou make up one's mind to do; **se décider pour qch** to decide on ou in favour of sth
décideur [desidœʀ] NM decision-maker
décilitre [desilitʀ] NM decilitre (BRIT), deciliter (US)
décimal, e, -aux [desimal, -o] ADJ, NF decimal
décimalisation [desimalizasjɔ̃] NF decimalization
décimaliser [desimalize] /1/ VT to decimalize
décimer [desime] /1/ VT to decimate
décimètre [desimɛtʀ] NM decimetre (BRIT), decimeter (US); **double ~ (20 cm)** ruler
décisif, -ive [desizif, -iv] ADJ decisive; *(qui l'emporte)*: **le facteur/l'argument ~** the deciding factor/argument
décision [desizjɔ̃] NF decision; *(fermeté)* decisiveness, decision; **prendre une ~** to make a decision; **prendre la ~ de faire** to take the decision to do; **emporter** ou **faire la ~** to be decisive
déclamation [deklamasjɔ̃] NF declamation; *(péj)* ranting, spouting
déclamatoire [deklamatwaʀ] ADJ declamatory
déclamer [deklame] /1/ VT to declaim; *(péj)* to spout ▶ VI: **~ contre** to rail against
déclarable [deklaʀabl] ADJ *(marchandise)* dutiable; *(revenus)* declarable

déclaration [deklaʀasjɔ̃] NF declaration; registration; *(discours: Pol etc)* statement; *(compte rendu)* report; **fausse ~** misrepresentation; **~ (d'amour)** declaration; **~ de décès** registration of death; **~ de guerre** declaration of war; **~ (d'impôts)** statement of income, tax declaration, ≈ tax return; **~ (de sinistre)** *(insurance)* claim; **~ de revenus** statement of income; **faire une ~ de vol** to report a theft
déclaré, e [deklaʀe] ADJ *(juré)* avowed
déclarer [deklaʀe] /1/ VT to declare, announce; *(revenus, employés, marchandises)* to declare; *(décès, naissance)* to register; *(vol etc: à la police)* to report; **rien à ~** nothing to declare; **se déclarer** VI *(feu, maladie)* to break out; **~ la guerre** to declare war
déclassé, e [deklɑse] ADJ relegated, downgraded; *(matériel)* (to be) sold off
déclassement [deklɑsmɑ̃] NM relegation, downgrading; *(Rail etc)* change of class
déclasser [deklɑse] /1/ VT to relegate, downgrade; *(déranger: fiches, livres)* to get out of order
déclenchement [deklɑ̃ʃmɑ̃] NM release; setting off
déclencher [deklɑ̃ʃe] /1/ VT *(mécanisme etc)* to release; *(sonnerie)* to set off, activate; *(attaque, grève)* to launch; *(provoquer)* to trigger off; **se déclencher** VI to release itself; *(sonnerie)* to go off
déclencheur [deklɑ̃ʃœʀ] NM release mechanism
déclic [deklik] NM trigger mechanism; *(bruit)* click
déclin [deklɛ̃] NM decline
déclinaison [deklinɛzɔ̃] NF declension
décliner [dekline] /1/ VI to decline ▶ VT *(invitation)* to decline, refuse; *(responsabilité)* to refuse to accept; *(nom, adresse)* to state; *(Ling)* to decline; **se décliner** *(Ling)* to decline
déclivité [deklivite] NF slope, incline; **en ~** sloping, on the incline
décloisonner [deklwazone] /1/ VT to decompartmentalize
déclouer [deklue] /1/ VT to unnail
décocher [dekɔʃe] /1/ VT to hurl; *(flèche, regard)* to shoot
décoction [dekɔksjɔ̃] NF decoction
décodage [dekɔdaʒ] NM deciphering, decoding
décoder [dekɔde] /1/ VT to decipher, decode
décodeur [dekɔdœʀ] NM decoder
décoiffé, e [dekwafe] ADJ: **elle est toute ~** her hair is in a mess
décoiffer [dekwafe] /1/ VT: **~ qn** to mess up sb's hair; to take sb's hat off; **se décoiffer** VI to take off one's hat; **je suis toute décoiffée** my hair is in a real mess
décoincer [dekwɛ̃se] /3/ VT to unjam, loosen
déçois *etc* [deswa], **déçoive** *etc* [deswav] VB *voir* **décevoir**
décolérer [dekɔleʀe] /6/ VI: **il ne décolère pas** he's still angry, he hasn't calmed down
décollage [dekɔlaʒ] NM *(Aviat, Écon)* takeoff
décollé, e [dekɔle] ADJ: **oreilles décollées** sticking-out ears
décollement [dekɔlmɑ̃] NM *(Méd)*: **~ de la**

rétine retinal detachment

décoller [dekɔle] /**1**/ vᴛ to unstick ▶ vi (*avion*) to take off; (*projet, entreprise*) to take off, get off the ground; **se décoller** vi to come unstuck

décolleté, e [dekɔlte] ᴀᴅᴊ low-necked, low-cut; (*femme*) wearing a low-cut dress ▶ ɴᴍ low neck(line); (*épaules*) (bare) neck and shoulders; (*plongeant*) cleavage

décolleter [dekɔlte] /**4**/ vᴛ (*vêtement*) to give a low neckline to; (*Tech*) to cut

décolonisation [dekɔlɔnizasjɔ̃] ɴF decolonization

décoloniser [dekɔlɔnize] /**1**/ vᴛ to decolonize

décolorant [dekɔlɔʀɑ̃] ɴᴍ decolorant, bleaching agent

décoloration [dekɔlɔʀasjɔ̃] ɴF: **se faire faire une ~** (*chez le coiffeur*) to have one's hair bleached *ou* lightened

décoloré, e [dekɔlɔʀe] ᴀᴅᴊ (*vêtement*) faded; (*cheveux*) bleached

décolorer [dekɔlɔʀe] /**1**/ vᴛ (*tissu*) to fade; (*cheveux*) to bleach, lighten; **se décolorer** vi to fade; **se faire décolorer les cheveux** to have one's hair bleached

décombres [dekɔ̃bʀ] ɴᴍᴘʟ rubble *sg*, debris *sg*

décommander [dekɔmɑ̃de] /**1**/ vᴛ to cancel; (*invités*) to put off; **se décommander** vi to cancel, cry off

décomposé, e [dekɔ̃poze] ᴀᴅᴊ (*pourri*) decomposed; (*visage*) haggard, distorted

décomposer [dekɔ̃poze] /**1**/ vᴛ to break up; (*Chimie*) to decompose; (*Math*) to factorize; **se décomposer** vi to decompose

décomposition [dekɔ̃pozisjɔ̃] ɴF breaking up; decomposition; factorization; **en ~** (*organisme*) in a state of decay, decomposing

décompresser [dekɔ̃pʀese] /**1**/ vi (*fam: se détendre*) to unwind

décompresseur [dekɔ̃pʀesœʀ] ɴᴍ decompressor

décompression [dekɔ̃pʀesjɔ̃] ɴF decompression

décomprimer [dekɔ̃pʀime] /**1**/ vᴛ to decompress

décompte [dekɔ̃t] ɴᴍ deduction; (*facture*) breakdown (of an account), detailed account

décompter [dekɔ̃te] /**1**/ vᴛ to deduct

déconcentration [dekɔ̃sɑ̃tʀasjɔ̃] ɴF (*des industries etc*) dispersal; **~ des pouvoirs** devolution

déconcentré, e [dekɔ̃sɑ̃tʀe] ᴀᴅᴊ (*sportif etc*) who has lost his/her) concentration

déconcentrer [dekɔ̃sɑ̃tʀe] /**1**/ vᴛ (*Admin*) to disperse; **se déconcentrer** vi to lose (one's) concentration

déconcertant, e [dekɔ̃sɛʀtɑ̃, -ɑ̃t] ᴀᴅᴊ disconcerting

déconcerter [dekɔ̃sɛʀte] /**1**/ vᴛ to disconcert, confound

déconditionner [dekɔ̃disjɔne] /**1**/ vᴛ: **~ l'opinion américaine** to change the way the Americans have been forced to think

déconfit, e [dekɔ̃fi, -it] ᴀᴅᴊ crestfallen, downcast

déconfiture [dekɔ̃fityʀ] ɴF collapse, ruin; (*morale*) defeat

décongélation [dekɔ̃ʒelasjɔ̃] ɴF defrosting, thawing

décongeler [dekɔ̃ʒ(ə)le] /**5**/ vᴛ to thaw (out)

décongestionner [dekɔ̃ʒɛstjɔne] /**1**/ vᴛ (*Méd*) to decongest; (*rues*) to relieve congestion in

déconnecter [dekɔnɛkte] /**1**/ vᴛ to disconnect

déconner [dekɔne] /**1**/ vi (!: *en parlant*) to talk (a load of) rubbish (BRIT) *ou* garbage (US); (: *faire des bêtises*) to muck about; **sans ~** no kidding

déconseiller [dekɔ̃seje] /**1**/ vᴛ: **~ qch (à qn)** to advise (sb) against sth; **~ à qn de faire** to advise sb against doing; **c'est déconseillé** it's not advised *ou* advisable

déconsidérer [dekɔ̃sidere] /**6**/ vᴛ to discredit

décontamination [dekɔ̃taminasjɔ̃] ɴF decontamination

décontaminer [dekɔ̃tamine] /**1**/ vᴛ to decontaminate

décontenancer [dekɔ̃tnɑ̃se] /**3**/ vᴛ to disconcert, discountenance

décontracté, e [dekɔ̃trakte] ᴀᴅᴊ relaxed, laid-back (*fam*)

décontracter [dekɔ̃trakte] /**1**/ vᴛ, **se décontracter** vi to relax

décontraction [dekɔ̃traksjɔ̃] ɴF relaxation

déconvenue [dekɔ̃vny] ɴF disappointment

décor [dekɔʀ] ɴᴍ décor; (*paysage*) scenery; **décors** ɴᴍᴘʟ (*Théât*) scenery *sg*, decor *sg*; (*Ciné*) set *sg*; **changement de ~** (*fig*) change of scene; **entrer dans le ~** (*fig*) to run off the road; **en ~ naturel** (*Ciné*) on location

décorateur, -trice [dekɔʀatœʀ, -tʀis] ɴᴍ/F (interior) decorator; (*Ciné*) set designer

décoratif, -ive [dekɔʀatif, -iv] ᴀᴅᴊ decorative

décoration [dekɔʀasjɔ̃] ɴF decoration

décorer [dekɔʀe] /**1**/ vᴛ to decorate

décortiqué, e [dekɔʀtike] ᴀᴅᴊ shelled; hulled

décortiquer [dekɔʀtike] /**1**/ vᴛ to shell; (*riz*) to hull; (*fig: texte*) to dissect

décorum [dekɔʀɔm] ɴᴍ decorum; etiquette

décote [dekɔt] ɴF tax relief

découcher [dekuʃe] /**1**/ vi to spend the night away

découdre [dekudʀ] /**48**/ vᴛ (*vêtement, couture*) to unpick, take the stitching out of; (*bouton*) to take off; **se découdre** vi to come unstitched; (*bouton*) to come off; **en ~** (*fig*) to fight, do battle

découler [dekule] /**1**/ vi: **~ de** to ensue *ou* follow from

découpage [dekupaʒ] ɴᴍ cutting up; carving; (*image*) cut-out (figure); **~ électoral** division into constituencies

découper [dekupe] /**1**/ vᴛ (*papier, tissu etc*) to cut up; (*volaille, viande*) to carve; (*détacher: manche, article*) to cut out; **se ~ sur** (*ciel, fond*) to stand out against

découplé, e [dekuple] ᴀᴅᴊ: **bien ~** well-built, well-proportioned

découpure [dekupyʀ] ɴF: **découpures** (*morceaux*) cut-out bits; (*d'une côte, arête*) indentations, jagged outline *sg*

décourageant, e [dekuʀaʒɑ̃, -ɑ̃t] ᴀᴅᴊ

discouraging; (*personne, attitude*) negative

découragement [dekuraʒmɑ̃] NM discouragement, despondency

décourager [dekuraʒe] /**3**/ VT to discourage, dishearten; (*dissuader*) to discourage, put off; **se décourager** VI to lose heart, become discouraged; **~ qn de faire/de qch** to discourage sb from doing/from sth, put sb off doing/sth

décousu, e [dekuzy] PP *de* **découdre** ▶ ADJ unstitched; (*fig*) disjointed, disconnected

découvert, e [dekuvɛR, -ɛRt] PP *de* **découvrir** ▶ ADJ (*tête*) bare, uncovered; (*lieu*) open, exposed ▶ NM (*bancaire*) overdraft ▶ NF discovery; **à ~** *adv* (*Mil*) exposed, without cover; (*fig*) openly; (*Comm*) *adj* overdrawn; **à visage ~** openly; **aller à la ~ de** to go in search of; **faire la ~ de** to discover

découvrir [dekuvRiR] /**18**/ VT to discover; (*apercevoir*) to see; (*enlever ce qui couvre ou protège*) to uncover; (*montrer, dévoiler*) to reveal; **se découvrir** VI (*chapeau*) to take off one's hat; (*se déshabiller*) to take something off; (*au lit*) to uncover o.s.; (*ciel*) to clear; **se découvrir des talents** to find hidden talents in o.s.

décrasser [dekrase] /**1**/ VT to clean

décrêper [dekrepe] /**1**/ VT (*cheveux*) to straighten

décrépi, e [dekrepi] ADJ peeling; with roughcast rendering removed

décrépit, e [dekrepi, -it] ADJ decrepit

décrépitude [dekrepityd] NF decrepitude; decay

decrescendo [dekreʃɛndo] NM (*Mus*) decrescendo; **aller ~** (*fig*) to decline, be on the wane

décret [dekrɛ] NM decree

décréter [dekrete] /**6**/ VT to decree; (*ordonner*) to order

décret-loi [dekrɛlwa] NM statutory order

décrié, e [dekrije] ADJ disparaged

décrire [dekRiR] /**39**/ VT to describe; (*courbe, cercle*) to follow, describe

décrisper [dekRispe] /**1**/ VT to defuse

décrit, e [dekRi, -it] PP *de* **décrire**

décrivais *etc* [dekRivɛ] VB *voir* **décrire**

décrochage [dekRɔʃaʒ] NM: **~ scolaire** (*Scol*) ≈ truancy

décrochement [dekRɔʃmɑ̃] NM (*d'un mur etc*) recess

décrocher [dekRɔʃe] /**1**/ VT (*dépendre*) to take down; (*téléphone*) to take off the hook; (: *pour répondre*) **~ (le téléphone)** to pick up ou lift the receiver; (*fig: contrat etc*) to get, land ▶ VI (*fam: abandonner*) to drop out; (: *cesser d'écouter*) to switch off; **se décrocher** VI (*tableau, rideau*) to fall down

décroîs *etc* [dekRwa] VB *voir* **décroître**

décroiser [dekRwaze] /**1**/ VT (*bras*) to unfold; (*jambes*) to uncross

décroissant, e [dekRwasɑ̃, -ɑ̃t] VB *voir* **décroître** ▶ ADJ decreasing, declining, diminishing; **par ordre ~** in descending order

décroître [dekRwatR] /**55**/ VI to decrease, decline, diminish

décrotter [dekRɔte] /**1**/ VT (*chaussures*) to clean the mud from; **se ~ le nez** to pick one's nose

décru, e [dekRy] PP *de* **décroître**

décrue [dekRy] NF drop in level (of the waters)

décrypter [dekRipte] /**1**/ VT to decipher; (*Inform, Tél*) to decrypt

déçu, e [desy] PP *de* **décevoir** ▶ ADJ disappointed

déculotter [dekylɔte] /**1**/ VT: **~ qn** to take off ou down sb's trousers; **se déculotter** VI to take off ou down one's trousers

déculpabiliser [dekylpabilize] /**1**/ VT (*personne*) to relieve of guilt; (*chose*) to decriminalize

décuple [dekypl] NM: **le ~ de** ten times; **au ~** tenfold

décupler [dekyple] /**1**/ VT, VI to increase tenfold

déçut *etc* [desy] VB *voir* **décevoir**

dédaignable [dedɛɲabl] ADJ: **pas ~** not to be despised

dédaigner [dedeɲe] /**1**/ VT to despise, scorn; (*négliger*) to disregard, spurn; **~ de faire** to consider it beneath one to do, not deign to do

dédaigneusement [dedɛɲøzmɑ̃] ADV scornfully, disdainfully

dédaigneux, -euse [dedɛɲø, -øz] ADJ scornful, disdainful

dédain [dedɛ̃] NM scorn, disdain

dédale [dedal] NM maze

dedans [dədɑ̃] ADV inside; (*pas en plein air*) indoors, inside ▶ NM inside; **au ~** on the inside; inside; **en ~** (*vers l'intérieur*) inwards; *voir aussi* **là**

dédicace [dedikas] NF (*imprimée*) dedication; (*manuscrite, sur une photo etc*) inscription

dédicacer [dedikase] /**3**/ VT: **~ (à qn)** to sign (for sb), autograph (for sb), inscribe (to sb)

dédié, e [dedje] ADJ: **ordinateur ~** dedicated computer

dédier [dedje] /**7**/ VT to dedicate; **~ à** to dedicate to

dédire [dediR] /**37**/: **se dédire** VI to go back on one's word; (*se rétracter*) to retract, recant

dédit, e [dedi, -it] PP *de* **dédire** ▶ NM (*Comm*) forfeit, penalty

dédommagement [dedɔmaʒmɑ̃] NM compensation

dédommager [dedɔmaʒe] /**3**/ VT: **~ qn (de)** to compensate sb (for); (*fig*) to repay sb (for)

dédouaner [dedwane] /**1**/ VT to clear through customs

dédoublement [dedubləmɑ̃] NM splitting; (*Psych*): **~ de la personnalité** split ou dual personality

dédoubler [deduble] /**1**/ VT (*classe, effectifs*) to split (into two); (*couverture etc*) to unfold; (*manteau*) to remove the lining of; **~ un train/les trains** to run a relief train/additional trains; **se dédoubler** VI (*Psych*) to have a split personality

dédramatiser [dedramatize] /**1**/ VT (*situation*) to defuse; (*événement*) to play down

déductible [dedyktibl] ADJ deductible

déduction [dedyksjɔ̃] NF (*d'argent*) deduction; (*raisonnement*) deduction, inference

déduire [deduiR] /**38**/ VT: **~ qch (de)** (*ôter*) to deduct sth (from); (*conclure*) to deduce ou infer sth (from)

déesse [dɛɛs] NF goddess

DEFA SIGLE M (= *Diplôme d'État relatif aux fonctions d'animation*) diploma for senior youth leaders

défaillance [defajɑ̃s] NF (*syncope*) blackout; (*fatigue*) (sudden) weakness *no pl*; (*technique*) fault, failure; (*morale etc*) weakness;
~ **cardiaque** heart failure

défaillant, e [defajɑ̃, -ɑ̃t] ADJ defective; (*Jur: témoin*) defaulting

défaillir [defajiʀ] /13/ VI to faint; to feel faint; (*mémoire etc*) to fail

défaire [defɛʀ] /60/ VT (*installation, échafaudage*) to take down, dismantle; (*paquet etc, nœud, vêtement*) to undo; (*bagages*) to unpack; (*ouvrage*) to undo, unpick; (*cheveux*) to take out; **se défaire** VI to come undone; **se défaire de** vt (*se débarrasser de*) to get rid of; (*se séparer de*) to part with; ~ **le lit** (*pour changer les draps*) to strip the bed; (*pour se coucher*) to turn back the bedclothes

défait, e [defɛ, -ɛt] PP *de* **défaire** ▶ ADJ (*visage*) haggard, ravaged ▶ NF defeat

défaites [defɛt] VB *voir* **défaire**

défaitisme [defetism] NM defeatism

défaitiste [defetist] ADJ, NMF defeatist

défalcation [defalkasjɔ̃] NF deduction

défalquer [defalke] /1/ VT to deduct

défasse *etc* [defas] VB *voir* **défaire**

défausser [defose] /1/ VT to get rid of; **se défausser** VI (*Cartes*) to discard

défaut [defo] NM (*moral*) fault, failing, defect; (*d'étoffe, métal*) fault, flaw, defect; (*manque: carence*): ~ **de** lack of; shortage of; (*Inform*) bug; ~ **de la cuirasse** (*fig*) chink in the armour (BRIT) *ou* armor (US); **en** ~ at fault; in the wrong; **prendre qn en** ~ to catch sb out; **faire** ~ (*manquer*) to be lacking; **à** ~ *adv* failing that; **à** ~ **de** for lack *ou* want of; **par** ~ (*Jur*) in his (*ou* her *etc*) absence

défaveur [defavœʀ] NF disfavour (BRIT), disfavor (US)

défavorable [defavɔʀabl] ADJ unfavourable (BRIT), unfavorable (US)

défavoriser [defavɔʀize] /1/ VT to put at a disadvantage

défectif, -ive [defɛktif, -iv] ADJ: **verbe** ~ defective verb

défection [defɛksjɔ̃] NF defection, failure to give support *ou* assistance; failure to appear; **faire** ~ (*d'un parti etc*) to withdraw one's support, leave

défectueux, -euse [defɛktɥø, -øz] ADJ faulty, defective

défectuosité [defɛktɥozite] NF defectiveness *no pl*; (*défaut*) defect, fault

défendable [defɑ̃dabl] ADJ defensible

défendeur, -eresse [defɑ̃dœʀ, -dʀɛs] NM/F (*Jur*) defendant

défendre [defɑ̃dʀ] /41/ VT to defend; (*interdire*) to forbid; **se défendre** VI to defend o.s.; ~ **à qn qch/de faire** to forbid sb sth/to do; **il est défendu de cracher** spitting (is) prohibited *ou* is not allowed; **c'est défendu** it is forbidden; **il se défend** (*fig*) he can hold his own; **ça se défend** (*fig*) it holds together; **se défendre de/**

contre (*se protéger*) to protect o.s. from/against; **se défendre de** (*se garder de*) to refrain from; (*nier*) **se défendre de vouloir** to deny wanting

défenestrer [defənɛstʀe] /1/ VT to throw out of the window

défense [defɑ̃s] NF defence (BRIT), defense (US); (*d'éléphant etc*) tusk; **ministre de la** ~ Minister of Defence (BRIT), Defence Secretary; **la** ~ **nationale** defence, the defence of the realm (BRIT); **la** ~ **contre avions** anti-aircraft defence; **"~ de fumer/cracher"** "no smoking/spitting", "smoking/spitting prohibited"; **prendre la** ~ **de qn** to stand up for sb; ~ **des consommateurs** consumerism

défenseur [defɑ̃sœʀ] NM defender; (*Jur*) counsel for the defence

défensif, -ive [defɑ̃sif, -iv] ADJ, NF defensive; **être sur la défensive** to be on the defensive

déféquer [defeke] /6/ VI to defecate

déferai *etc* [defʀe] VB *voir* **défaire**

déférence [defeʀɑ̃s] NF deference

déférent, e [defeʀɑ̃, -ɑ̃t] ADJ (*poli*) deferential, deferent

déférer [defeʀe] /6/ VT (*Jur*) to refer; ~ **à** vt (*requête, décision*) to defer to; ~ **qn à la justice** to hand sb over to justice

déferlant, e [defɛʀlɑ̃, -ɑ̃t] ADJ: **vague** ~ breaker

déferlement [defɛʀləmɑ̃] NM breaking; surge

déferler [defɛʀle] /1/ VI (*vagues*) to break; (*fig*) to surge

défi [defi] NM (*provocation*) challenge; (*bravade*) defiance; **mettre qn au** ~ **de faire qch** to challenge sb to do sth; **relever un** ~ to take up *ou* accept a challenge; **lancer un** ~ **à qn** to challenge sb; **sur un ton de** ~ defiantly

défiance [defjɑ̃s] NF mistrust, distrust

déficeler [defisle] /4/ VT (*paquet*) to undo, untie

déficience [defisjɑ̃s] NF deficiency

déficient, e [defisjɑ̃, -ɑ̃t] ADJ deficient

déficit [defisit] NM (*Comm*) deficit; (*Psych etc: manque*) defect; ~ **budgétaire** budget deficit; **être en** ~ to be in deficit

déficitaire [defisitɛʀ] ADJ (*année, récolte*) bad; **entreprise/budget** ~ business/budget in deficit

défier [defje] /7/ VT (*provoquer*) to challenge; (*fig*) to defy, brave; **se** ~ **de** (*se méfier de*) to distrust, mistrust; ~ **qn de faire** to challenge *ou* defy sb to do; ~ **qn à** to challenge sb to; ~ **toute comparaison/concurrence** to be incomparable/unbeatable

défigurer [defigyʀe] /1/ VT to disfigure; (*boutons etc*) to mar *ou* spoil (the looks of); (*fig: œuvre*) to mutilate, deface

défilé [defile] NM (*Géo*) (narrow) gorge *ou* pass; (*soldats*) parade; (*manifestants*) procession, march; **un** ~ **de** (*voitures, visiteurs etc*) a stream of

défiler [defile] /1/ VI (*troupes*) to march past; (*sportifs*) to parade; (*manifestants*) to march; (*visiteurs*) to pour, stream; **faire** ~ **un document** (*Inform*) to scroll a document; **se défiler** VI (*se dérober*) to slip away, sneak off; **faire** ~ (*bande, film*) to put on; (*Inform*) to scroll; **il s'est défilé** (*fam*) he wriggled out of it

défini, e [defini] ADJ definite

définir [definiʀ] /2/ VT to define

définissable [definisabl] ADJ definable

définitif, -ive [definitif, -iv] ADJ (final) final, definitive; (pour longtemps) permanent, definitive; (sans appel) final, definite ▶ NF: **en définitive** eventually; (somme toute) when all is said and done

définition [definisjɔ̃] NF definition; (de mots croisés) clue; (TV) (picture) resolution

définitivement [definitivmɑ̃] ADV definitively; permanently; definitely

défit etc [defi] VB voir **défaire**

déflagration [deflagʀasjɔ̃] NF explosion

déflation [deflasjɔ̃] NF deflation

déflationniste [deflasjɔnist] ADJ deflationist, deflationary

déflecteur [deflɛktœʀ] NM (Auto) quarterlight (BRIT), deflector (US)

déflorer [defloʀe] /1/ VT (jeune fille) to deflower; (fig) to spoil the charm of

défoncé, e [defɔ̃se] ADJ smashed in; broken down; (route) full of potholes ▶ NM/F addict

défoncer [defɔ̃se] /3/ VT (caisse) to stave in; (porte) to smash in ou down; (lit, fauteuil) to burst (the springs of); (terrain, route) to rip ou plough up; **se défoncer** VI (se donner à fond) to give it all one's got

défont [defɔ̃] VB voir **défaire**

déformant, e [defɔʀmɑ̃, -ɑ̃t] ADJ: **glace** ~ ou **miroir** ~ distorting mirror

déformation [defɔʀmasjɔ̃] NF loss of shape; deformation; distortion; ~ **professionnelle** conditioning by one's job

déformer [defɔʀme] /1/ VT to put out of shape; (corps) to deform; (pensée, fait) to distort; **se déformer** VI to lose its shape

défoulement [defulmɑ̃] NM release of tension; unwinding

défouler [defule] /1/: **se défouler** VI (Psych) to work off one's tensions, release one's pent-up feelings; (gén) to unwind, let off steam

défraîchi, e [defʀeʃi] ADJ faded; (article à vendre) shop-soiled

défraîchir [defʀeʃiʀ] /2/: **se défraîchir** VI to fade; to become shop-soiled

défrayer [defʀeje] /8/ VT: ~ **qn** to pay sb's expenses; ~ **la chronique** to be in the news; ~ **la conversation** to be the main topic of conversation

défrichement [defʀiʃmɑ̃] NM clearance

défricher [defʀiʃe] /1/ VT to clear (for cultivation)

défriser [defʀize] /1/ VT (cheveux) to straighten; (fig) to annoy

défroisser [defʀwase] /1/ VT to smooth out

défroque [defʀɔk] NF cast-off

défroqué [defʀɔke] NM former monk (ou priest)

défroquer [defʀɔke] /1/ VI (aussi: **se défroquer**) to give up the cloth, renounce one's vows

défunt, e [defœ̃, -œ̃t] ADJ: **son** ~ **père** his late father ▶ NM/F deceased

dégagé, e [degaʒe] ADJ (route, ciel) clear; (ton, air) casual, jaunty; **sur un ton** ~ casually

dégagement [degaʒmɑ̃] NM emission; freeing; clearing; (espace libre) clearing; passage; clearance; (Football) clearance; **voie de** ~ slip road; **itinéraire de** ~ alternative route (to relieve traffic congestion)

dégager [degaʒe] /3/ VT (exhaler) to give off, emit; (délivrer) to free, extricate; (Mil: troupes) to relieve; (désencombrer) to clear; (isoler, mettre en valeur) to bring out; (crédits) to release; **se dégager** VI (odeur) to emanate, be given off; (passage, ciel) to clear; ~ **qn de** (engagement, parole etc) to release ou free sb from; **se dégager de** (fig: engagement etc) to get out of (: promesse) to go back on

dégaine [degɛn] NF awkward way of walking

dégainer [degene] /1/ VT to draw

dégarni, e [degaʀni] ADJ bald

dégarnir [degaʀniʀ] /2/ VT (vider) to empty, clear; **se dégarnir** VI to empty; to be cleaned out ou cleared; (tempes, crâne) to go bald

dégâts [degɑ] NMPL damage sg; **faire des** ~ to damage

dégauchir [degoʃiʀ] /2/ VT (Tech) to surface

dégazer [degaze] /1/ VI (pétrolier) to clean its tanks

dégel [deʒɛl] NM thaw; (fig: des prix etc) unfreezing

dégeler [deʒle] /5/ VT to thaw (out); (fig) to unfreeze ▶ VI to thaw (out); **se dégeler** VI (fig) to thaw out

dégénéré, e [deʒeneʀe] ADJ, NM/F degenerate

dégénérer [deʒeneʀe] /6/ VI to degenerate; (empirer) to go from bad to worse; (devenir): ~ **en** to degenerate into

dégénérescence [deʒeneʀesɑ̃s] NF degeneration

dégingandé, e [deʒɛ̃gɑ̃de] ADJ gangling, lanky

dégivrage [deʒivʀaʒ] NM defrosting; de-icing

dégivrer [deʒivʀe] /1/ VT (frigo) to defrost; (vitres) to de-ice

dégivreur [deʒivʀœʀ] NM defroster; de-icer

déglinguer [deglɛ̃ge] /1/ VT to bust

déglutir [deglytiʀ] /2/ VT, VI to swallow

déglutition [deglytisjɔ̃] NF swallowing

dégonflé, e [degɔ̃fle] ADJ (pneu) flat; (fam) chicken ▶ NM/F (fam) chicken

dégonfler [degɔ̃fle] /1/ VT (pneu, ballon) to let down, deflate ▶ VI (désenfler) to go down; **se dégonfler** VI (fam) to chicken out

dégorger [degɔʀʒe] /3/ VI (Culin): **faire** ~ to leave to sweat; (rivière): (**se**) ~ **dans** to flow into ▶ VT to disgorge

dégoter [degɔte] /1/ VT (fam) to dig up, find

dégouliner [deguline] /1/ VI to trickle, drip; ~ **de** to be dripping with

dégoupiller [degupije] /1/ VT (grenade) to take the pin out of

dégourdi, e [deguʀdi] ADJ smart, resourceful

dégourdir [deguʀdiʀ] /2/ VT to warm (up); **se** ~ **(les jambes)** to stretch one's legs

dégoût [degu] NM disgust, distaste

dégoûtant, e [degutɑ̃, -ɑ̃t] ADJ disgusting

dégoûté, e [degute] ADJ disgusted; ~ **de** sick of

dégoûter [degute] /1/ VT to disgust; **cela me**

dégoutter – délectation

dégoûte I find this disgusting *ou* revolting; **~ qn de qch** to put sb off sth; **se ~ de** to get *ou* become sick of

dégoutter [degute] /1/ VI to drip; **~ de** to be dripping with

dégradant, e [degradã, -ãt] ADJ degrading

dégradation [degradasjɔ̃] NF reduction in rank; defacement; degradation, debasement; deterioration; *(aussi: **dégradations**: dégâts)* damage *no pl*

dégradé, e [degrade] ADJ *(couleur)* shaded off; *(teintes)* faded; *(cheveux)* layered ▸ NM *(Peinture)* gradation

dégrader [degrade] /1/ VT *(Mil: officier)* to degrade; *(abîmer)* to damage, deface; *(avilir)* to degrade, debase; **se dégrader** VI *(relations, situation)* to deteriorate

dégrafer [degrafe] /1/ VT to unclip, unhook, unfasten

dégraissage [degrɛsaʒ] NM *(Écon)* cutbacks *pl*; **~ et nettoyage à sec** dry cleaning

dégraissant [degrɛsã] NM spot remover

dégraisser [degrese] /1/ VT *(soupe)* to skim; *(vêtement)* to take the grease marks out of; *(Écon)* to cut back; *(: entreprise)* to slim down

degré [dəgre] NM degree; *(d'escalier)* step; **brûlure au 1er/2ème ~** 1st/2nd degree burn; **équation du 1er/2ème ~** linear/quadratic equation; **le premier ~** *(Scol)* primary level; **alcool à 90 degrés** surgical spirit; **vin de 10 degrés** 10° wine *(on Gay-Lussac scale)*; **par ~(s)** *adv* by degrees, gradually

dégressif, -ive [degresif, -iv] ADJ on a decreasing scale, degressive; **tarif ~** decreasing rate of charge

dégrèvement [degrɛvmã] NM tax relief

dégrever [degrəve] /5/ VT to grant tax relief to; to reduce the tax burden on

dégriffé, e [degrife] ADJ *(vêtement)* sold without the designer's label; **voyage ~** discount holiday

dégringolade [degrɛ̃gɔlad] NF tumble; *(fig)* collapse

dégringoler [degrɛ̃gɔle] /1/ VI to tumble (down); *(fig: prix, monnaie etc)* to collapse

dégriser [degrize] /1/ VT to sober up

dégrossir [degrosir] /2/ VT *(bois)* to trim; *(fig)* to work out roughly; *(: personne)* to knock the rough edges off

déguenillé, e [degnije] ADJ ragged, tattered

déguerpir [degɛrpir] /2/ VI to clear off

dégueulasse [degœlas] ADJ *(fam)* disgusting

dégueuler [degœle] /1/ VI *(fam)* to puke, throw up

déguisé, e [degize] ADJ disguised; dressed up; **~ en** disguised *(ou* dressed up) as

déguisement [degizmã] NM disguise; *(habits: pour s'amuser)* fancy dress; *(: pour tromper)* disguise

déguiser [degize] /1/ VT to disguise; **se déguiser (en)** VI *(se costumer)* to dress up (as); *(pour tromper)* to disguise o.s.

dégustation [degystasjɔ̃] NF tasting; *(de fromages etc)* sampling; savouring (BRIT), savoring (US); *(séance):* **~ de vin(s)** wine-tasting

déguster [degyste] /1/ VT *(vins)* to taste;

(fromages etc) to sample; *(savourer)* to enjoy, savour (BRIT), savor (US)

déhancher [deãʃe] /1/: **se déhancher** VI to sway one's hips; to lean (one's weight) on one hip

dehors [dəɔr] ADV outside; *(en plein air)* outdoors, outside ▸ NM outside ▸ NMPL *(apparences)* appearances, exterior *sg*; **mettre** *ou* **jeter ~** to throw out; **au ~** outside; *(en apparence)* outwardly; **au ~ de** outside; **de ~** from outside; **en ~** outside; outwards; **en ~ de** apart from

déifier [deifje] /7/ VT to deify

déjà [deʒa] ADV already; *(auparavant)* before, already; **as-tu ~ été en France?** have you been to France before?; **c'est ~ pas mal** that's not too bad (at all); **c'est ~ quelque chose** (at least) it's better than nothing; **quel nom, ~?** what was the name again?

déjanter [deʒãte] /1/: **se déjanter** VI *(pneu)* to come off the rim

déjà-vu [deʒavy] NM: **c'est du ~** there's nothing new in that

déjeté, e [deʒte] ADJ lop-sided, crooked

déjeuner [deʒœne] /1/ VI to (have) lunch; *(le matin)* to have breakfast ▸ NM lunch; *(petit déjeuner)* breakfast; **~ d'affaires** business lunch

déjouer [deʒwe] /1/ VT to elude, to foil, thwart

déjuger [deʒyʒe] /3/: **se déjuger** VI to go back on one's opinion

delà [dəla] ADV: **par ~, en ~ (de), au ~ (de)** beyond

délabré, e [delabre] ADJ dilapidated, broken-down

délabrement [delabrəmã] NM decay, dilapidation

délabrer [delabre] /1/: **se délabrer** VI to fall into decay, become dilapidated

délacer [delase] /3/ VT *(chaussures)* to undo, unlace

délai [delɛ] NM *(attente)* waiting period; *(sursis)* extension (of time); *(temps accordé: aussi: **délais**)* time limit; **sans ~** without delay; **à bref ~** shortly, very soon; at short notice; **dans les délais** within the time limit; **un ~ de 30 jours** a period of 30 days; **comptez un ~ de livraison de 10 jours** allow 10 days for delivery

délaissé, e [delese] ADJ abandoned, deserted; neglected

délaisser [delese] /1/ VT *(abandonner)* to abandon, desert; *(négliger)* to neglect

délassant, e [delasã, -ãt] ADJ relaxing

délassement [delasmã] NM relaxation

délasser [delase] /1/ VT *(reposer)* to relax; *(divertir)* to divert, entertain; **se délasser** VI to relax

délateur, -trice [delatœr, -tris] NM/F informer

délation [delasjɔ̃] NF denouncement, informing

délavé, e [delave] ADJ faded

délayage [delejaʒ] NM mixing; thinning down

délayer [deleje] /8/ VT *(Culin)* to mix (with water etc); *(peinture)* to thin down; *(fig)* to pad out, spin out

delco® [dɛlko] NM *(Auto)* distributor; **tête de ~** distributor cap

délectation [delɛktasjɔ̃] NF delight

délecter [delɛkte] /**1**/: **se délecter** VI: **se délecter de** to revel ou delight in

délégation [delegasjɔ̃] NF delegation; **~ de pouvoir** delegation of power

délégué, e [delege] ADJ delegated ▶ NM/F delegate; representative; **ministre ~ à** minister with special responsibility for

déléguer [delege] /**6**/ VT to delegate

délestage [delɛstaʒ] NM: **itinéraire de ~** alternative route (to relieve traffic congestion)

délester [delɛste] /**1**/ VT (navire) to unballast; **~ une route** to relieve traffic congestion on a road by diverting traffic

Delhi [dɛli] N Delhi

délibérant, e [deliberɑ̃, -ɑ̃t] ADJ: **assemblée ~** deliberative assembly

délibératif, -ive [deliberatif, -iv] ADJ: **avoir voix délibérative** to have voting rights

délibération [deliberasjɔ̃] NF deliberation

délibéré, e [delibere] ADJ (conscient) deliberate; (déterminé) determined, resolute; **de propos ~** (à dessein, exprès) intentionally

délibérément [deliberemɑ̃] ADV deliberately; (résolument) resolutely

délibérer [delibere] /**6**/ VI to deliberate

délicat, e [delika, -at] ADJ delicate; (plein de tact) tactful; (attentionné) thoughtful; (exigeant) fussy, particular; **procédés peu délicats** unscrupulous methods

délicatement [delikatmɑ̃] ADV delicately; (avec douceur) gently

délicatesse [delikatɛs] NF delicacy; tactfulness; thoughtfulness; **délicatesses** NFPL attentions, consideration sg

délice [delis] NM delight

délicieusement [delisjøzmɑ̃] ADV deliciously; delightfully

délicieux, -euse [delisjø, -øz] ADJ (au goût) delicious; (sensation, impression) delightful

délictueux, -euse [deliktɥø, -øz] ADJ criminal

délié, e [delje] ADJ nimble, agile; (mince) slender, fine ▶ NM: **les déliés** the upstrokes (in handwriting)

délier [delje] /**7**/ VT to untie; **~ qn de** (serment etc) to free ou release sb from

délimitation [delimitasjɔ̃] NF delimitation

délimiter [delimite] /**1**/ VT (terrain) to delimit, demarcate

délinquance [delɛ̃kɑ̃s] NF criminality; **~ juvénile** juvenile delinquency

délinquant, e [delɛ̃kɑ̃, -ɑ̃t] ADJ, NM/F delinquent

déliquescence [delikesɑ̃s] NF: **en ~** in a state of decay

déliquescent, e [delikesɑ̃, -ɑ̃t] ADJ decaying

délirant, e [delirɑ̃, -ɑ̃t] ADJ (Méd: fièvre) delirious; (: imagination) frenzied; (fam: déraisonnable) crazy

délire [delir] NM (fièvre) delirium; (fig) frenzy; (: folie) lunacy

délirer [delire] /**1**/ VI to be delirious; **tu délires!** (fam) you're crazy!

délit [deli] NM (criminal) offence; **~ de droit commun** violation of common law; **~ de fuite** failure to stop after an accident; **~ d'initiés** insider dealing ou trading; **~ de presse**

violation of the press laws

délivrance [delivrɑ̃s] NF freeing, release; (sentiment) relief

délivrer [delivre] /**1**/ VT (prisonnier) to (set) free, release; (passeport, certificat) to issue; **~ qn de** (ennemis) to set sb free from, deliver ou free sb from; (fig) to rid sb of

délocalisation [delɔkalizasjɔ̃] NF relocation

délocaliser [delɔkalize] /**1**/ VT (entreprise, emplois) relocate

déloger [delɔʒe] /**3**/ VT (locataire) to turn out; (objet coincé, ennemi) to dislodge

déloyal, e, -aux [delwajal, -o] ADJ (personne, conduite) disloyal; (procédé) unfair

Delphes [dɛlf] N Delphi

delta [dɛlta] NM (Géo) delta

deltaplane® [dɛltaplan] NM hang-glider

déluge [delyʒ] NM (biblique) Flood, Deluge; (grosse pluie) downpour, deluge; (grand nombre): **~ de** flood of

déluré, e [delyre] ADJ smart, resourceful; (péj) forward, pert

démagnétiser [demaɲetize] /**1**/ VT to demagnetize

démagogie [demagɔʒi] NF demagogy

démagogique [demagɔʒik] ADJ demagogic, popularity-seeking; (Pol) vote-catching

démagogue [demagɔg] ADJ demagogic ▶ NM demagogue

démaillé, e [demaje] ADJ (bas) laddered (BRIT), with a run (ou runs)

demain [d(ə)mɛ̃] ADV tomorrow; **~ matin/soir** tomorrow morning/evening; **~ midi** tomorrow at midday; **à ~!** see you tomorrow!

demande [d(ə)mɑ̃d] NF (requête) request; (revendication) demand; (Admin, formulaire) application; (Écon): **la ~** demand; **"demandes d'emploi"** "situations wanted"; **à la ~ générale** by popular request; **~ en mariage** (marriage) proposal; **faire sa ~ (en mariage)** to propose (marriage); **~ de naturalisation** application for naturalization; **~ de poste** job application

demandé, e [d(ə)mɑ̃de] ADJ (article etc): **très ~** (very) much in demand

demander [d(ə)mɑ̃de] /**1**/ VT to ask for; (question, date, heure, chemin) to ask; (requérir, nécessiter) to require, demand; **~ qch à qn** to ask sb for sth, ask sb sth; **ils demandent deux secrétaires et un ingénieur** they're looking for two secretaries and an engineer; **~ la main de qn** to ask for sb's hand (in marriage); **~ pardon à qn** to apologize to sb; **~ à ou de voir/faire** to ask to see/ask if one can do; **~ à qn de faire** to ask sb to do; **~ que/pourquoi** to ask that/why; **se ~ si/pourquoi** etc to wonder if/why etc; (sens purement réfléchi) to ask o.s. if/why etc; **on vous demande au téléphone** you're wanted on the phone, there's someone for you on the phone; **il ne demande que ça** that's all he wants; **je ne demande pas mieux** I'm asking nothing more; **il ne demande qu'à faire** all he wants is to do

demandeur, -euse [dəmɑ̃dœr, -øz] NM/F:

117

~ d'asile asylum-seeker; **~ d'emploi** job-seeker

démangeaison [demãʒɛzɔ̃] NF itching; **avoir des démangeaisons** to be itching

démanger [demãʒe] /3/ VI to itch; **la main me démange** my hand is itching; **l'envie** *ou* **ça me démange de faire** I'm itching to do

démantèlement [demãtɛlmã] NM breaking up

démanteler [demãtle] /5/ VT to break up; to demolish

démaquillant [demakijã] NM make-up remover

démaquiller [demakije] /1/: **se démaquiller** VT to remove one's make-up

démarcage [demarkaʒ] NM = **démarquage**

démarcation [demarkasjɔ̃] NF demarcation

démarchage [demarʃaʒ] NM (*Comm*) door-to-door selling

démarche [demarʃ] NF (*allure*) gait, walk; (*intervention*) step; approach; (*fig: intellectuelle*) thought processes *pl*; approach; **entreprendre des démarches** to take action; **faire des démarches auprès de qn** to approach sb; **faire les démarches nécessaires (pour obtenir qch)** to take the necessary steps (to obtain sth)

démarcheur, -euse [demarʃœr, -øz] NM/F (*Comm*) door-to-door salesman/woman; (*Pol etc*) canvasser

démarquage [demarkaʒ] NM marking down

démarque [demark] NF (*Comm: d'un article*) mark-down

démarqué, e [demarke] ADJ (*Football*) unmarked; (*Comm*) reduced; **prix démarqués** marked-down prices

démarquer [demarke] /1/ VT (*prix*) to mark down; (*joueur*) to stop marking; **se démarquer** VI (*Sport*) to shake off one's marker

démarrage [demaraʒ] NM starting *no pl*, start; **~ en côte** hill start

démarrer [demare] /1/ VT to start up ▶ VI (*conducteur*) to start (up); (*véhicule*) to move off; (*travaux, affaire*) to get moving; (*coureur: accélérer*) to pull away

démarreur [demarœr] NM (*Auto*) starter

démasquer [demaske] /1/ VT to unmask; **se démasquer** to unmask; (*fig*) to drop one's mask

démâter [demate] /1/ VT to dismast ▶ VI to be dismasted

démêlant, e [demelã, -ãt] ADJ: **baume ~, crème ~** (hair) conditioner ▶ NM conditioner

démêler [demele] /1/ VT to untangle, disentangle

démêlés [demele] NMPL problems

démembrement [demãbrəmã] NM dismemberment

démembrer [demãbre] /1/ VT to dismember

déménagement [demenaʒmã] NM (*du point de vue du locataire etc*) move; (: *du déménageur*) removal (BRIT), moving (US); **entreprise/camion de ~** removal (BRIT) *ou* moving (US) firm/van

déménager [demenaʒe] /3/ VT (*meubles*) to (re)move ▶ VI to move (house)

déménageur [demenaʒœr] NM removal man

(BRIT), (furniture) mover (US); (*entrepreneur*) furniture remover

démence [demãs] NF madness, insanity; (*Méd*) dementia

démener [demne] /5/: **se démener** VI to thrash about; (*fig*) to exert o.s.

dément, e [demã, -ãt] VB *voir* **démentir** ▶ ADJ (*fou*) mad (BRIT), crazy; (*fam*) brilliant, fantastic

démenti [demãti] NM refutation

démentiel, le [demãsjɛl] ADJ insane

démentir [demãtir] /16/ VT (*nouvelle, témoin*) to refute; (*faits etc*) to belie, refute; **~ que** to deny that; **ne pas se ~** not to fail, keep up

démerder [demɛrde] /1/: **se démerder** VI (!) to bloody well manage for o.s.

démériter [demerite] /1/ VI: **~ auprès de qn** to come down in sb's esteem

démesure [deməzyr] NF immoderation, immoderateness

démesuré, e [deməzyre] ADJ immoderate, disproportionate

démesurément [deməzyremã] ADV disproportionately

démettre [demɛtr] /56/ VT: **~ qn de** (*fonction, poste*) to dismiss sb from; **se ~ (de ses fonctions)** to resign (from) one's duties; **se ~ l'épaule** *etc* to dislocate one's shoulder *etc*

demeurant [dəmœrã]: **au ~** adv for all that

demeure [dəmœr] NF residence; **dernière ~** (*fig*) last resting place; **mettre qn en ~ de faire** to enjoin *ou* order sb to do; **à ~** adv permanently

demeuré, e [dəmœre] ADJ backward ▶ NM/F backward person

demeurer [d(ə)mœre] /1/ VI (*habiter*) to live; (*séjourner*) to stay; (*rester*) to remain; **en ~ là** (*personne*) to leave it at that (: *choses*) to be left at that

demi, e [dəmi] ADJ half; **et ~: trois heures/bouteilles et demies** three and a half hours/bottles ▶ NM (*bière: = 0.25 litre*) ≈ half-pint; (*Football*) half-back; **il est 2 heures et ~** it's half past 2; **il est midi et ~** it's half past 12; **~ de mêlée/d'ouverture** (*Rugby*) scrum/fly half; **à ~** adv half-; **ouvrir à ~** to half-open; **faire les choses à ~** to do things by halves; **à la ~** (*heure*) on the half-hour

demi... [dəmi] PRÉFIXE half-, semi..., demi-

demi-bas [dəmiba] NM INV (*chaussette*) knee-sock

demi-bouteille [dəmibutɛj] NF half-bottle

demi-cercle [dəmisɛrkl] NM semicircle; **en ~** adj semicircular ▶ ADV in a semicircle

demi-douzaine [dəmiduzɛn] NF half-dozen, half a dozen

demi-finale [dəmifinal] NF semifinal

demi-finaliste [dəmifinalist] NMF semifinalist

demi-fond [dəmifɔ̃] NM (*Sport*) medium-distance running

demi-frère [dəmifrɛr] NM half-brother

demi-gros [dəmigro] NM INV wholesale trade

demi-heure [dəmijœr] NF: **une ~** a half-hour, half an hour

demi-jour [dəmiʒur] NM half-light

demi-journée [dəmiʒurne] NF half-day, half a day

démilitariser [demilitaʀize] /**1**/ vт to demilitarize

demi-litre [dəmilitʀ] NM half-litre (BʀIт), half-liter (US), half a litre ou liter

demi-livre [dəmilivʀ] NF half-pound, half a pound

demi-longueur [dəmilɔ̃gœʀ] NF (Sport) half-length, half a length

demi-lune [dəmilyn]: **en ~** adj inv semicircular

demi-mal [dəmimal] NM: **il n'y a que ~** there's not much harm done

demi-mesure [dəmimzyʀ] NF half-measure

demi-mot [dəmimo]: **à ~** adv without having to spell things out

déminer [demine] /**1**/ vт to clear of mines

démineur [deminœʀ] NM bomb disposal expert

demi-pension [dəmipɑ̃sjɔ̃] NF half-board; **être en ~** (Scol) to take school meals

demi-pensionnaire [dəmipɑ̃sjɔnɛʀ] NMF: **être ~** to take school lunches

demi-place [dəmiplas] NF half-price; (Transports) half-fare

démis, e [demi, -iz] PP de **démettre** ▶ ADJ (épaule etc) dislocated

demi-saison [dəmisɛzɔ̃] NF: **vêtements de ~** spring ou autumn clothing

demi-sel [dəmisɛl] ADJ INV slightly salted

demi-sœur [dəmisœʀ] NF half-sister

demi-sommeil [dəmisɔmɛj] NM doze

demi-soupir [dəmisupiʀ] NM (Mus) quaver (BʀIт) ou eighth note (US) rest

démission [demisjɔ̃] NF resignation; **donner sa ~** to give ou hand in one's notice, hand in one's resignation

démissionnaire [demisjɔnɛʀ] ADJ outgoing ▶ NMF person resigning

démissionner [demisjɔne] /**1**/ vι (de son poste) to resign, give ou hand in one's notice

demi-tarif [dəmitaʀif] NM half-price; (Transports) half-fare; **voyager à ~** to travel half-fare

demi-ton [dəmitɔ̃] NM (Mus) semitone

demi-tour [dəmituʀ] NM about-turn; **faire un ~** (Mil etc) to make an about-turn; **faire ~** to turn (and go) back; (Auto) to U-turn

démobilisation [demɔbilizasjɔ̃] NF demobilization; (fig) demotivation, demoralization

démobiliser [demɔbilize] /**1**/ vт to demobilize; (fig) to demotivate, demoralize

démocrate [demɔkʀat] ADJ democratic ▶ NMF democrat

démocrate-chrétien, ne [demɔkʀatkʀetjɛ̃, -ɛn] NM/F Christian Democrat

démocratie [demɔkʀasi] NF democracy; **~ populaire/libérale** people's/liberal democracy

démocratique [demɔkʀatik] ADJ democratic

démocratiquement [demɔkʀatikmɑ̃] ADV democratically

démocratisation [demɔkʀatizasjɔ̃] NF democratization

démocratiser [demɔkʀatize] /**1**/ vт to democratize

démodé, e [demɔde] ADJ old-fashioned

démoder [demɔde] /**1**/: **se démoder** vι to go out of fashion

démographe [demɔgʀaf] NMF demographer

démographie [demɔgʀafi] NF demography

démographique [demɔgʀafik] ADJ demographic; **poussée ~** increase in population

demoiselle [d(ə)mwazɛl] NF (jeune fille) young lady; (célibataire) single lady, maiden lady; **~ d'honneur** bridesmaid

démolir [demɔliʀ] /**2**/ vт to demolish; (fig: personne) to do for

démolisseur [demɔlisœʀ] NM demolition worker

démolition [demɔlisjɔ̃] NF demolition

démon [demɔ̃] NM demon, fiend; evil spirit; (enfant turbulent) devil, demon; **le ~ du jeu/des femmes** a mania for gambling/women; **le D~** the Devil

démonétiser [demɔnetize] /**1**/ vт to demonetize

démoniaque [demɔnjak] ADJ fiendish

démonstrateur, -trice [demɔ̃stʀatœʀ, -tʀis] NM/F demonstrator

démonstratif, -ive [demɔ̃stʀatif, -iv] ADJ, NM (aussi Ling) demonstrative

démonstration [demɔ̃stʀasjɔ̃] NF demonstration; (aérienne, navale) display

démontable [demɔ̃tabl] ADJ folding

démontage [demɔ̃taʒ] NM dismantling

démonté, e [demɔ̃te] ADJ (fig) raging, wild

démonte-pneu [demɔ̃təpnø] NM tyre lever (BʀIт), tire iron (US)

démonter [demɔ̃te] /**1**/ vт (machine etc) to take down, dismantle; (pneu, porte) to take off; (cavalier) to throw, unseat; (fig: personne) to disconcert; **se démonter** vι (meuble) to be dismantled, be taken to pieces; (personne) to lose countenance

démontrable [demɔ̃tʀabl] ADJ demonstrable

démontrer [demɔ̃tʀe] /**1**/ vт to demonstrate, show

démoralisant, e [demɔʀalizɑ̃, -ɑ̃t] ADJ demoralizing

démoralisateur, -trice [demɔʀalizatœʀ, -tʀis] ADJ demoralizing

démoraliser [demɔʀalize] /**1**/ vт to demoralize

démordre [demɔʀdʀ] /**41**/ vι: **ne pas ~ de** to refuse to give up, stick to

démouler [demule] /**1**/ vт (gâteau) to turn out

démultiplication [demyltiplikasjɔ̃] NF reduction; reduction ratio

démuni, e [demyni] ADJ (sans argent) impoverished; **~ de** without, lacking in

démunir [demyniʀ] /**2**/ vт: **~ qn de** to deprive sb of; **se ~ de** to part with, give up

démuseler [demyzle] /**4**/ vт to unmuzzle

démystifier [demistifje] /**7**/ vт to demystify

démythifier [demitifje] /**7**/ vт to demythologize

dénatalité [denatalite] NF fall in the birth rate

dénationalisation [denasjɔnalizasjɔ̃] NF denationalization

dénationaliser [denasjɔnalize] /**1**/ vт to denationalize

119

dénaturé, e [denatyʀe] ADJ (*alcool*) denaturized; (*goûts*) unnatural

dénaturer [denatyʀe] /1/ VT (*goût*) to alter (completely); (*pensée, fait*) to distort, misrepresent

dénégations [denegasjɔ̃] NFPL denials

déneigement [denɛʒmɑ̃] NM snow clearance

déneiger [deneʒe] /3/ VT to clear snow from

déni [deni] NM: ~ **(de justice)** denial of justice

déniaiser [denjeze] /1/ VT: ~ **qn** to teach sb about life

dénicher [denise] /1/ VT (*fam: objet*) to unearth; (: *restaurant etc*) to discover

dénicotinisé, e [denikɔtinize] ADJ nicotine-free

denier [dənje] NM (*monnaie*) *formerly, a coin of small value*; (*de bas*) denier; ~ **du culte** contribution to parish upkeep; **deniers publics** public money; **de ses (propres) deniers** out of one's own pocket

dénier [denje] /7/ VT to deny; ~ **qch à qn** to deny sb sth

dénigrement [denigʀəmɑ̃] NM denigration; **campagne de** ~ smear campaign

dénigrer [denigʀe] /1/ VT to denigrate, run down

dénivelé, e [denivle] ADJ (*chaussée*) on a lower level ▶ NM difference in height

déniveler [denivle] /4/ VT to make uneven; to put on a lower level

dénivellation [denivelasjɔ̃] NF, **dénivellement** [denivɛlmɑ̃] NM difference in level; (*pente*) ramp; (*creux*) dip

dénombrer [denɔ̃bʀe] /1/ VT (*compter*) to count; (*énumérer*) to enumerate, list

dénominateur [denɔminatœʀ] NM denominator; ~ **commun** common denominator

dénomination [denɔminasjɔ̃] NF designation, appellation

dénommé, e [denɔme] ADJ: **le ~ Dupont** the man by the name of Dupont

dénommer [denɔme] /1/ VT to name

dénoncer [denɔ̃se] /3/ VT to denounce; **se dénoncer** VI to give o.s. up, come forward

dénonciation [denɔ̃sjasjɔ̃] NF denunciation

dénoter [denɔte] /1/ VT to denote

dénouement [denumɑ̃] NM outcome, conclusion; (*Théât*) dénouement

dénouer [denwe] /1/ VT to unknot, undo

dénoyauter [denwajote] /1/ VT to stone; **appareil à** ~ stoner

dénoyauteur [denwajotœʀ] NM stoner

denrée [dɑ̃ʀe] NF commodity; (*aussi:* **denrée alimentaire**) food(stuff)

dense [dɑ̃s] ADJ dense

densité [dɑ̃site] NF denseness; (*Physique*) density

dent [dɑ̃] NF tooth; **avoir/garder une ~ contre qn** to have/hold a grudge against sb; **se mettre qch sous la** ~ to eat sth; **être sur les dents** to be on one's last legs; **faire ses dents** to teethe, cut (one's) teeth; **en dents de scie** serrated; (*irrégulier*) jagged; **avoir les dents longues** (*fig*) to be ruthlessly ambitious; ~ **de lait/sagesse** milk/wisdom tooth

dentaire [dɑ̃tɛʀ] ADJ dental; **cabinet** ~ dental surgery; **école** ~ dental school

denté, e [dɑ̃te] ADJ: **roue** ~ cog wheel

dentelé, e [dɑ̃tle] ADJ jagged, indented

dentelle [dɑ̃tɛl] NF lace *no pl*

dentelure [dɑ̃tlyʀ] NF (*aussi:* **dentelures**) jagged outline

dentier [dɑ̃tje] NM denture

dentifrice [dɑ̃tifʀis] ADJ, NM: **(pâte)** ~ toothpaste; **eau** ~ mouthwash

dentiste [dɑ̃tist] NMF dentist

dentition [dɑ̃tisjɔ̃] NF teeth *pl*, dentition

dénucléariser [denykleaʀize] /1/ VT to make nuclear-free

dénudé, e [denyde] ADJ bare

dénuder [denyde] /1/ VT to bare; **se dénuder** (*personne*) to strip

dénué, e [denɥe] ADJ: ~ **de** lacking in; (*intérêt*) devoid of

dénuement [denymɑ̃] NM destitution

dénutrition [denytʀisjɔ̃] NF undernourishment

déodorant [deɔdɔʀɑ̃] NM deodorant

déodoriser [deɔdɔʀize] /1/ VT to deodorize

déontologie [deɔ̃tɔlɔʒi] NF code of ethics; (*professionnelle*) (professional) code of practice

dép. ABR (= *département*) dept; (= *départ*) dep.

dépannage [depanaʒ] NM: **service/camion de** ~ (*Auto*) breakdown service/truck

dépanner [depane] /1/ VT (*voiture, télévision*) to fix, repair; (*fig*) to bail out, help out

dépanneur [depanœʀ] NM (*Auto*) breakdown mechanic; (*TV*) television engineer

dépanneuse [depanøz] NF breakdown lorry (BRIT), tow truck (US)

dépareillé, e [depaʀeje] ADJ (*collection, service*) incomplete; (*gant, volume, objet*) odd

déparer [depaʀe] /1/ VT to spoil, mar

départ [depaʀ] NM leaving *no pl*, departure; (*Sport*) start; (*sur un horaire*) departure; **à son** ~ when he left; **au** ~ (*au début*) initially, at the start; **courrier au** ~ outgoing mail; **la veille de son** ~ the day before he leaves/left

départager [depaʀtaʒe] /3/ VT to decide between

département [depaʀtəmɑ̃] NM department; *see note*

> France is divided into 96 administrative units called *départements*. These local government divisions are headed by a state-appointed *préfet*, and administered by an elected *Conseil général*. *Départements* are usually named after prominent geographical features such as rivers or mountain ranges.

départemental, e, -aux [depaʀtəmɑ̃tal, -o] ADJ departmental

départementaliser [depaʀtəmɑ̃talize] /1/ VT to devolve authority to

départir [depaʀtiʀ] /16/: **se ~ de** vt to abandon, depart from

dépassé, e [depase] ADJ superseded, outmoded; (*fig*) out of one's depth

dépassement [depɑsmɑ̃] NM (*Auto*) overtaking
no pl

dépasser [depɑse] /**1**/ VT (*véhicule, concurrent*) to
overtake; (*endroit*) to pass, go past; (*somme,
limite*) to exceed; (*fig: en beauté etc*) to surpass,
outshine; (*être en saillie sur*) to jut out above (*ou* in
front of); (*dérouter*): **cela me dépasse** it's
beyond me ▸ VI (*Auto*) to overtake; (*jupon*) to
show; **se dépasser** VI to excel o.s.

dépassionner [depɑsjɔne] /**1**/ VT (*débat etc*) to
take the heat out of

dépaver [depave] /**1**/ VT to remove the
cobblestones from

dépaysé, e [depeize] ADJ disoriented

dépaysement [depeizmɑ̃] NM disorientation;
change of scenery

dépayser [depeize] /**1**/ VT (*désorienter*) to
disorientate; (*changer agréablement*) to provide
with a change of scenery.

dépecer [depəse] /**5**/ VT (*boucher*) to joint, cut up;
(*animal*) to dismember

dépêche [depɛʃ] NF dispatch;
~ **(télégraphique)** telegram, wire

dépêcher [depeʃe] /**1**/ VT to dispatch; **se
dépêcher** VI to hurry; **se dépêcher de faire
qch** to hasten to do sth, hurry (in order) to
do sth

dépeindre [depɛ̃dR] /**52**/ VT to depict

dépénalisation [depenalizasjɔ̃] NF
decriminalization

dépendance [depɑ̃dɑ̃s] NF (*interdépendance*)
dependence *no pl*, dependency; (*bâtiment*)
outbuilding

dépendant, e [depɑ̃dɑ̃, -ɑ̃t] VB *voir* **dépendre**
▸ ADJ (*financièrement*) dependent

dépendre [depɑ̃dR] /**41**/ VT (*tableau*) to take
down; ~ **de** *vt* to depend on, to depend on;
(*appartenir*) to belong to; **ça dépend** it depends

dépens [depɑ̃] NMPL: **aux ~ de** at the expense of

dépense [depɑ̃s] NF spending *no pl*, expense,
expenditure *no pl*, (*fig*) consumption; (: *de temps,
de forces*) expenditure; **pousser qn à la ~** to
make sb incur an expense; ~ **physique**
(physical) exertion; **dépenses de
fonctionnement** revenue expenditure;
dépenses d'investissement capital
expenditure; **dépenses publiques** public
expenditure

dépenser [depɑ̃se] /**1**/ VT to spend; (*gaz, eau*) to
use; (*fig*) to expend, use up; **se dépenser** VI (*se
fatiguer*) to exert o.s.

dépensier, -ière [depɑ̃sje, -jɛR] ADJ: **il est ~** he's
a spendthrift

déperdition [depɛRdisjɔ̃] NF loss

dépérir [depeRiR] /**2**/ VI (*personne*) to waste away;
(*plante*) to wither

dépersonnaliser [depɛRsɔnalize] /**1**/ VT to
depersonalize

dépêtrer [depetRe] /**1**/ VT: **se ~ de** (*situation*) to
extricate o.s. from

dépeuplé, e [depœple] ADJ depopulated

dépeuplement [depœpləmɑ̃] NM depopulation

dépeupler [depœple] /**1**/ VT to depopulate; **se
dépeupler** VI to become depopulated

déphasage [defazaʒ] NM (*fig*) being out of touch

déphasé, e [defaze] ADJ (*Élec*) out of phase; (*fig*)
out of touch

déphaser [defaze] /**1**/ VT (*fig*) to put out of touch

dépilation [depilasjɔ̃] NF hair loss; hair
removal

dépilatoire [depilatwaR] ADJ depilatory,
hair-removing; **crème ~** hair-removing *ou*
depilatory cream

dépiler [depile] /**1**/ VT (*épiler*) to depilate,
remove hair from

dépistage [depistaʒ] NM (*Méd*) screening

dépister [depiste] /**1**/ VT to detect; (*Méd*) to
screen; (*voleur*) to track down; (*poursuivants*) to
throw off the scent

dépit [depi] NM vexation, frustration; **en ~ de**
prép in spite of; **en ~ du bon sens** contrary to all
good sense

dépité, e [depite] ADJ vexed, frustrated

dépiter [depite] /**1**/ VT to vex, frustrate

déplacé, e [deplase] ADJ (*propos*) out of place,
uncalled-for; **personne ~** displaced person

déplacement [deplasmɑ̃] NM moving;
shifting; transfer; (*voyage*) trip, travelling *no pl*
(*Brit*), traveling *no pl* (*US*); **en ~** away (on a trip);
~ **d'air** displacement of air; ~ **de vertèbre**
slipped disc

déplacer [deplase] /**3**/ VT (*table, voiture*) to move,
shift; (*employé*) to transfer, move; **se déplacer**
VI, VT (*objet*) to move; (*organe*) to become
displaced; (*personne: bouger*) to move, walk;
(: *voyager*) to travel; **se déplacer une vertèbre**
to slip a disc

déplaire [deplɛR] /**54**/ VI: **ceci me déplaît** I
don't like this, I dislike this; **il cherche à nous
~** he's trying to displease us *ou* be disagreeable
to us; **se ~ quelque part** to dislike it *ou* be
unhappy somewhere

déplaisant, e [deplezɑ̃, -ɑ̃t] VB *voir* **déplaire** ▸ ADJ
disagreeable, unpleasant

déplaisir [depleziR] NM displeasure, annoyance

déplaît [deplɛ] VB *voir* **déplaire**

dépliant [deplijɑ̃] NM leaflet

déplier [deplije] /**7**/ VT to unfold; **se déplier** VI
(*parachute*) to open

déplisser [deplise] /**1**/ VT to smooth out

déploiement [deplwamɑ̃] NM (*voir déployer*)
deployment; display

déplomber [deplɔ̃be] /**1**/ VT (*caisse, compteur*) to
break (open) the seal of; (*Inform*) to hack into

déplorable [deplɔRabl] ADJ deplorable;
lamentable

déplorer [deplɔRe] /**1**/ VT (*regretter*) to deplore;
(*pleurer sur*) to lament

déployer [deplwaje] /**8**/ VT to open out, spread;
(*Mil*) to deploy; (*montrer*) to display, exhibit

déplu [deply] PP *de* **déplaire**

dépointer [depwɛ̃te] /**1**/ VI to clock out

dépoli, e [depɔli] ADJ: **verre ~** frosted glass

dépolitiser [depɔlitize] /**1**/ VT to depoliticize

dépopulation [depɔpylasjɔ̃] NF depopulation

déportation [depɔRtasjɔ̃] NF deportation

déporté, e [depɔRte] NM/F deportee; (*1939–45*)
concentration camp prisoner

déporter [depɔʀte] /**1**/ VT (Pol) to deport; (dévier) to carry off course; **se déporter** VI (voiture) to swerve

déposant, e [depozɑ̃, -ɑ̃t] NM/F (épargnant) depositor

dépose [depoz] NF taking out; taking down

déposé, e [depoze] ADJ registered; voir aussi **marque**

déposer [depoze] /**1**/ VT (gén: mettre, poser) to lay down, put down, set down; (à la banque, à la consigne) to deposit; (caution) to put down; (passager) to drop (off), set down; (démonter: serrure, moteur) to take out; (: rideau) to take down; (roi) to depose; (Admin: faire enregistrer) to file; (marque) to register; (plainte) to lodge ▶ VI to form a sediment ou deposit; (Jur): ~ (contre) to testify ou give evidence (against); **se déposer** VI to settle; ~ **son bilan** (Comm) to go into (voluntary) liquidation

dépositaire [depoziteʀ] NMF (Jur) depository; (Comm) agent; ~ **agréé** authorized agent

déposition [depozisjɔ̃] NF (Jur) deposition, statement

déposséder [deposede] /**6**/ VT to dispossess

dépôt [depo] NM (à la banque, sédiment) deposit; (entrepôt, réserve) warehouse, store; (gare) depot; (prison) cells pl; ~ **d'ordures** rubbish (BRIT) ou garbage (US) dump, tip (BRIT); ~ **de bilan** (voluntary) liquidation; ~ **légal** registration of copyright

dépoter [depɔte] /**1**/ VT (plante) to take from the pot, transplant

dépotoir [depɔtwaʀ] NM dumping ground, rubbish (BRIT) ou garbage (US) dump; ~ **nucléaire** nuclear (waste) dump

dépouille [depuj] NF (d'animal) skin, hide; (humaine): ~ (**mortelle**) mortal remains pl

dépouillé, e [depuje] ADJ (fig) bare, bald; ~ **de** stripped of; lacking in

dépouillement [depujmɑ̃] NM (de scrutin) count, counting no pl

dépouiller [depuje] /**1**/ VT (animal) to skin; (spolier) to deprive of one's possessions; (documents) to go through, peruse; ~ **qn/qch de** to strip sb/sth of; ~ **le scrutin** to count the votes

dépourvu, e [depuʀvy] ADJ: ~ **de** lacking in, without; **au** ~, adv **prendre qn au** ~ to catch sb unawares

dépoussiérer [depusjeʀe] /**6**/ VT to remove dust from

dépravation [depʀavasjɔ̃] NF depravity

dépravé, e [depʀave] ADJ depraved

dépraver [depʀave] /**1**/ VT to deprave

dépréciation [depʀesjasjɔ̃] NF depreciation

déprécier [depʀesje] /**7**/ VT to reduce the value of; **se déprécier** VI to depreciate

déprédations [depʀedasjɔ̃] NFPL damage sg

dépressif, -ive [depʀesif, -iv] ADJ depressive

dépression [depʀesjɔ̃] NF depression; ~ (**nerveuse**) (nervous) breakdown

déprimant, e [depʀimɑ̃, -ɑ̃t] ADJ depressing

déprime [depʀim] NF (fam): **la** ~ depression

déprimé, e [depʀime] ADJ (découragé) depressed

déprimer [depʀime] /**1**/ VT to depress

déprogrammer [depʀɔgʀame] /**1**/ VT (supprimer) to cancel

DEPS ABR (= dernier entré premier sorti) LIFO (= last in first out)

dépt ABR (= département) dept

dépuceler [depysle] /**4**/ VT (fam) to take the virginity of

MOT-CLÉ

depuis [dəpɥi] PRÉP **1** (point de départ dans le temps) since; **il habite Paris depuis 1983/l'an dernier** he has been living in Paris since 1983/last year; **depuis quand?** since when?; **depuis quand le connaissez-vous?** how long have you known him?; **depuis lors** since then
2 (temps écoulé) for; **il habite Paris depuis cinq ans** he has been living in Paris for five years; **je le connais depuis trois ans** I've known him for three years; **depuis combien de temps êtes-vous ici?** how long have you been here?
3 (lieu): **il a plu depuis Metz** it's been raining since Metz; **elle a téléphoné depuis Valence** she rang from Valence
4 (quantité, rang) from; **depuis les plus petits jusqu'aux plus grands** from the youngest to the oldest
▶ ADV (temps) since (then); **je ne lui ai pas parlé depuis** I haven't spoken to him since (then); **depuis que** conj (ever) since; **depuis qu'il m'a dit ça** (ever) since he said that to me

dépuratif, -ive [depyʀatif, -iv] ADJ depurative, purgative

députation [depytasjɔ̃] NF deputation; (fonction) position of deputy, ≈ parliamentary seat (BRIT), ≈ seat in Congress (US)

député, e [depyte] NM/F (Pol) deputy, ≈ Member of Parliament (BRIT), ≈ Congressman/woman (US)

députer [depyte] /**1**/ VT to delegate; ~ **qn auprès de** to send sb (as a representative) to

déracinement [deʀasinmɑ̃] NM (gén) uprooting; (d'un préjugé) eradication

déraciner [deʀasine] /**1**/ VT to uproot

déraillement [deʀɑjmɑ̃] NM derailment

dérailler [deʀɑje] /**1**/ VI (train) to be derailed, go off ou jump the rails; (fam) to be completely off the track; **faire** ~ to derail

dérailleur [deʀɑjœʀ] NM (de vélo) dérailleur gears pl

déraison [deʀezɔ̃] NF unreasonableness

déraisonnable [deʀezɔnabl] ADJ unreasonable

déraisonner [deʀezɔne] /**1**/ VI to talk nonsense, rave

dérangement [deʀɑ̃ʒmɑ̃] NM (gêne, déplacement) trouble; (gastrique etc) disorder; (mécanique) breakdown; **en** ~ (téléphone) out of order

déranger [deʀɑ̃ʒe] /**3**/ VT (personne) to trouble, bother, disturb; (projets) to disrupt, upset; (objets, vêtements) to disarrange; **se déranger** VI to put o.s. out; (se déplacer) to (take the trouble to) come (ou go) out; **surtout ne vous dérangez pas pour moi** please don't put yourself out on my account; **est-ce que cela vous dérange si ...?** do you mind if ...?; **ça te dérangerait de faire ...?** would you mind doing ...?; **ne vous dérangez pas** don't go to any trouble; don't disturb yourself

dérapage [deʀapaʒ] NM skid, skidding *no pl*; going out of control

déraper [deʀape] /1/ VI (*voiture*) to skid; (*personne, semelles, couteau*) to slip; (*fig: économie etc*) to go out of control

dératé, e [deʀate] NM/F: **courir comme un ~** to run like the clappers

dératiser [deʀatize] /1/ VT to rid of rats

déréglé, e [deʀegle] ADJ (*mœurs*) dissolute

dérèglement [deʀɛɡləmɑ̃] NM upsetting *no pl*, upset

déréglementation [deʀɛɡləmɑ̃tasjɔ̃] NF deregulation

dérégler [deʀegle] /6/ VT (*mécanisme*) to put out of order, cause to break down; (*estomac*) to upset; **se dérégler** VI to break down, go wrong

dérider [deʀide] /1/ VT, **se dérider** VI to cheer up

dérision [deʀizjɔ̃] NF derision; **tourner en ~** to deride; **par ~** in mockery

dérisoire [deʀizwaʀ] ADJ derisory

dérivatif [deʀivatif] NM distraction

dérivation [deʀivasjɔ̃] NF derivation; diversion

dérive [deʀiv] NF (*de dériveur*) centre-board; **aller à la ~** (*Navig, fig*) to drift; **~ des continents** (*Géo*) continental drift

dérivé, e [deʀive] ADJ derived ▶ NM (*Ling*) derivative; (*Tech*) by-product ▶ NF (*Math*) derivative

dériver [deʀive] /1/ VT (*Math*) to derive; (*cours d'eau etc*) to divert ▶ VI (*bateau*) to drift; **~ de** to derive from

dériveur [deʀivœʀ] NM sailing dinghy

dermatite [dɛʀmatit] NF dermatitis

dermato [dɛʀmato] NMF (*fam: = dermatologue*) dermatologist

dermatologie [dɛʀmatɔlɔʒi] NF dermatology

dermatologue [dɛʀmatɔlɔg] NMF dermatologist

dermatose [dɛʀmatoz] NF dermatosis

dermite [dɛʀmit] NF = **dermatite**

dernier, -ière [dɛʀnje, -jɛʀ] ADJ (*dans le temps, l'espace*) last; (*le plus récent: gén avant n*) latest, last; (*final, ultime: effort*) final; (*: échelon, grade*) top, highest ▶ NM (*étage*) top floor; **lundi/le mois ~** last Monday/month; **du ~ chic** extremely smart; **le ~ cri** the last word (in fashion); **les derniers honneurs** the last tribute; **le ~ soupir, rendre le ~ soupir** to breathe one's last; **en ~** *adv* last; **ce ~, cette dernière** the latter

dernièrement [dɛʀnjɛʀmɑ̃] ADV recently

dernier-né, dernière-née [dɛʀnjene, dɛʀnjɛʀne] NM/F (*enfant*) last-born

dérobade [deʀɔbad] NF side-stepping *no pl*

dérobé, e [deʀɔbe] ADJ (*porte*) secret, hidden; **à la ~** surreptitiously

dérober [deʀɔbe] /1/ VT to steal; (*cacher*): **~ qch à (la vue de) qn** to conceal *ou* hide sth from sb's (view); **se dérober** VI (*s'esquiver*) to slip away; (*fig*)

to shy away; **se dérober sous** (*s'effondrer*) to give way beneath; **se dérober à** (*justice, regards*) to hide from; (*obligation*) to shirk

dérogation [deʀɔgasjɔ̃] NF (special) dispensation

déroger [deʀɔʒe] /3/: **~ à** vt to go against, depart from

dérouiller [deʀuje] /1/: VT: **se ~ les jambes** to stretch one's legs (*fig*)

déroulement [deʀulmɑ̃] NM (*d'une opération etc*) progress

dérouler [deʀule] /1/ VT (*ficelle*) to unwind; (*papier*) to unroll; **se dérouler** VI to unwind; to unroll, come unrolled; (*avoir lieu*) to take place; (*se passer*) to go; **tout s'est déroulé comme prévu** everything went as planned

déroutant, e [deʀutɑ̃, -ɑ̃t] ADJ disconcerting

déroute [deʀut] NF (*Mil*) rout; (*fig*) total collapse; **mettre en ~** to rout; **en ~** routed

dérouter [deʀute] /1/ VT (*avion, train*) to reroute, divert; (*étonner*) to disconcert, throw (out)

derrick [deʀik] NM derrick (*over oil well*)

derrière [dɛʀjɛʀ] ADV, PRÉP behind ▶ NM (*d'une maison*) back; (*postérieur*) behind, bottom; **les pattes de ~** the back legs, the hind legs; **par ~** from behind; (*fig*) in an underhand way, behind one's back

derviche [dɛʀviʃ] NM dervish

DES SIGLE M (= *diplôme d'études supérieures*) *university post-graduate degree*

des [de] ART *voir* **de**

dès [dɛ] PRÉP from; **~ que** *conj* as soon as; **~ à présent** here and now; **~ son retour** as soon as he was (*ou* is) back; **~ réception** upon receipt; **~ lors** *adv* from then on; **~ lors que** *conj* from the moment (that)

désabusé, e [dezabyze] ADJ disillusioned

désaccord [dezakɔʀ] NM disagreement

désaccordé, e [dezakɔʀde] ADJ (*Mus*) out of tune

désacraliser [desakʀalize] /1/ VT to deconsecrate; (*fig: profession, institution*) to take the mystique out of

désaffecté, e [dezafɛkte] ADJ disused

désaffection [dezafɛksjɔ̃] NF: **~ pour** estrangement from

désagréable [dezagʀeabl] ADJ unpleasant, disagreeable

désagréablement [dezagʀeabləmɑ̃] ADV disagreeably, unpleasantly

désagrégation [dezagʀegasjɔ̃] NF disintegration

désagréger [dezagʀeʒe] /3/: **se désagréger** VI to disintegrate, break up

désagrément [dezagʀemɑ̃] NM annoyance, trouble *no pl*

désaltérant, e [dezalteʀɑ̃, -ɑ̃t] ADJ thirst-quenching

désaltérer [dezalteʀe] /6/: **se désaltérer** VT to quench one's thirst; **ça désaltère** it's thirst-quenching, it quenches your thirst

désamorcer [dezamɔʀse] /3/ VT to remove the primer from; (*fig*) to defuse; (*: prévenir*) to forestall

désappointé, e [dezapwɛ̃te] ADJ disappointed

désapprobateur, -trice [dezapʀɔbatœʀ, -tʀis] ADJ disapproving
désapprobation [dezapʀɔbasjɔ̃] NF disapproval
désapprouver [dezapʀuve] /1/ VT to disapprove of
désarçonner [dezaʀsɔne] /1/ VT to unseat, throw; (fig) to throw, nonplus (BRIT), disconcert
désargenté, e [dezaʀʒɑ̃te] ADJ impoverished
désarmant, e [dezaʀmɑ̃, -ɑ̃t] ADJ disarming
désarmé, e [dezaʀme] ADJ (fig) disarmed
désarmement [dezaʀməmɑ̃] NM disarmament
désarmer [dezaʀme] /1/ VT (Mil, aussi fig) to disarm; (Navig) to lay up; (fusil) to unload; (: mettre le cran de sûreté) to put the safety catch on ▶ VI (pays) to disarm; (haine) to wane; (personne) to give up
désarroi [dezaʀwa] NM helplessness, disarray
désarticulé, e [dezaʀtikyle] ADJ (pantin, corps) dislocated
désarticuler [dezaʀtikyle] /1/: **se désarticuler** VT to contort (o.s.)
désassorti, e [dezasɔʀti] ADJ non-matching, unmatched; (magasin, marchand) sold out
désastre [dezastʀ] NM disaster
désastreux, -euse [dezastʀø, -øz] ADJ disastrous
désavantage [dezavɑ̃taʒ] NM disadvantage; (inconvénient) drawback, disadvantage
désavantager [dezavɑ̃taʒe] /3/ VT to put at a disadvantage
désavantageux, -euse [dezavɑ̃taʒø, -øz] ADJ unfavourable, disadvantageous
désaveu [dezavø] NM repudiation; (déni) disclaimer
désavouer [dezavwe] /1/ VT to disown, repudiate, disclaim
désaxé, e [dezakse] ADJ (fig) unbalanced
désaxer [dezakse] /1/ VT (roue) to put out of true; (personne) to throw off balance
desceller [desele] /1/ VT (pierre) to pull free
descendance [desɑ̃dɑ̃s] NF (famille) descendants pl, issue; (origine) descent
descendant, e [desɑ̃dɑ̃, -ɑ̃t] VB voir **descendre** ▶ NM/F descendant
descendeur, -euse [desɑ̃dœʀ, -øz] NM/F (Sport) downhiller
descendre [desɑ̃dʀ] /41/ VT (escalier, montagne) to go (ou come) down; (valise, paquet) to take ou get down; (étagère etc) to lower; (fam: abattre) to shoot down; (: boire) to knock back ▶ VI to go (ou come) down; (passager: s'arrêter) to get out, alight; (niveau, température) to go ou come down, fall, drop; (marée) to go out; **~ à pied/en voiture** to walk/drive down, go down on foot/by car; **~ de** (famille) to be descended from; **~ du train** to get out of ou off the train; **~ d'un arbre** to climb down from a tree; **~ de cheval** to dismount, get off one's horse; **~ à l'hôtel** to stay at a hotel; **~ dans la rue** (manifester) to take to the streets; **~ en ville** to go into town, go down town
descente [desɑ̃t] NF descent, going down; (chemin) way down; (Ski) downhill (race); **au**

milieu de la ~ halfway down; **freinez dans les descentes** use the brakes going downhill; **~ de lit** bedside rug; **~ (de police)** (police) raid
descriptif, -ive [dɛskʀiptif, -iv] ADJ descriptive ▶ NM explanatory leaflet
description [dɛskʀipsjɔ̃] NF description
désembourber [dezɑ̃buʀbe] /1/ VT to pull out of the mud
désembourgeoiser [dezɑ̃buʀʒwaze] /1/ VT: **~ qn** to get sb out of his (ou her) middle-class attitudes
désembuer [dezɑ̃bɥe] /1/ VT to demist
désemparé, e [dezɑ̃paʀe] ADJ bewildered, distraught; (bateau, avion) crippled
désemparer [dezɑ̃paʀe] /1/ VI: **sans ~** without stopping
désemplir [dezɑ̃pliʀ] /2/ VI: **ne pas ~** to be always full
désenchanté, e [dezɑ̃ʃɑ̃te] ADJ disenchanted, disillusioned
désenchantement [dezɑ̃ʃɑ̃tmɑ̃] NM disenchantment, disillusion
désenclaver [dezɑ̃klave] /1/ VT to open up
désencombrer [dezɑ̃kɔ̃bʀe] /1/ VT to clear
désenfler [dezɑ̃fle] /1/ VI to become less swollen
désengagement [dezɑ̃gaʒmɑ̃] NM (Pol) disengagement
désensabler [dezɑ̃sable] /1/ VT to pull out of the sand
désensibiliser [desɑ̃sibilize] /1/ VT (Méd) to desensitize
désenvenimer [dezɑ̃vnime] /1/ VT (plaie) to remove the poison from; (fig) to take the sting out of
désépaissir [dezepesiʀ] /2/ VT to thin (out)
déséquilibre [dezekilibʀ] NM (position): **être en ~** to be unsteady; (fig: des forces, du budget) imbalance; (Psych) unbalance
déséquilibré, e [dezekilibʀe] NM/F (Psych) unbalanced person
déséquilibrer [dezekilibʀe] /1/ VT to throw off balance
désert, e [dezɛʀ, -ɛʀt] ADJ deserted ▶ NM desert
déserter [dezɛʀte] /1/ VI, VT to desert
déserteur [dezɛʀtœʀ] NM deserter
désertion [dezɛʀsjɔ̃] NF desertion
désertique [dezɛʀtik] ADJ desert cpd; (inculte) barren, empty
désescalade [dezɛskalad] NF (Mil) de-escalation
désespérant, e [dezɛspeʀɑ̃, -ɑ̃t] ADJ hopeless, despairing
désespéré, e [dezɛspeʀe] ADJ desperate; (regard) despairing; **état ~** (Méd) hopeless condition
désespérément [dezɛspeʀemɑ̃] ADV desperately
désespérer [dezɛspeʀe] /6/ VT to drive to despair ▶ VI: **~ de** to despair of; **se désespérer** VI to despair
désespoir [dezɛspwaʀ] NM despair; **être ou faire le ~ de qn** to be the despair of sb; **en ~ de cause** in desperation
déshabillé, e [dezabije] ADJ undressed ▶ NM négligée

déshabiller [dezabije] /**1**/ vt to undress; **se déshabiller** vi to undress (o.s.)

déshabituer [dezabitɥe] /**1**/ vt: **se ~ de** to get out of the habit of

désherbant [dezɛʀbɑ̃] NM weed-killer

désherber [dezɛʀbe] /**1**/ vt to weed

déshérité, e [dezeʀite] ADJ disinherited ▶ NM/F: **les déshérités** (*pauvres*) the underprivileged, the deprived

déshériter [dezeʀite] /**1**/ vt to disinherit

déshonneur [dezɔnœʀ] NM dishonour (BRIT), dishonor (US), disgrace

déshonorer [dezɔnɔʀe] /**1**/ vt to dishonour (BRIT), dishonor (US), bring disgrace upon; **se déshonorer** vi to bring dishono(u)r on o.s.

déshumaniser [dezymanize] /**1**/ vt to dehumanize

déshydratation [dezidʀatasjɔ̃] NF dehydration

déshydraté, e [dezidʀate] ADJ dehydrated

déshydrater [dezidʀate] /**1**/ vt to dehydrate

desiderata [dezideʀata] NMPL requirements

design [dizajn] ADJ (*mobilier*) designer cpd ▶ NM (industrial) design

désignation [deziɲasjɔ̃] NF naming, appointment; (*signe, mot*) name, designation

designer [dizajnɛʀ] NM designer

désigner [deziɲe] /**1**/ vt (*montrer*) to point out, indicate; (*dénommer*) to denote, refer to; (*nommer: candidat etc*) to name, appoint

désillusion [dezilyzjɔ̃] NF disillusion(ment)

désillusionner [dezilyzjɔne] /**1**/ vt to disillusion

désincarné, e [dezɛ̃kaʀne] ADJ disembodied

désinence [dezinɑ̃s] NF ending, inflexion

désinfectant, e [dezɛ̃fɛktɑ̃, -ɑ̃t] ADJ, NM disinfectant

désinfecter [dezɛ̃fɛkte] /**1**/ vt to disinfect

désinfection [dezɛ̃fɛksjɔ̃] NF disinfection

désinformation [dezɛ̃fɔʀmasjɔ̃] NF disinformation

désintégration [dezɛ̃tegʀasjɔ̃] NF disintegration

désintégrer [dezɛ̃tegʀe] /**6**/ vt to break up; **se désintégrer** vi to disintegrate

désintéressé, e [dezɛ̃teʀese] ADJ (*généreux, bénévole*) disinterested, unselfish

désintéressement [dezɛ̃teʀesmɑ̃] NM (*générosité*) disinterestedness

désintéresser [dezɛ̃teʀese] /**1**/: **se désintéresser (de)** vt to lose interest (in)

désintérêt [dezɛ̃teʀɛ] NM (*indifférence*) disinterest

désintoxication [dezɛ̃tɔksikasjɔ̃] NF treatment for alcoholism (*ou* drug addiction); **faire une cure de ~** to have *ou* undergo treatment for alcoholism (*ou* drug addiction)

désintoxiquer [dezɛ̃tɔksike] /**1**/ vt to treat for alcoholism (*ou* drug addiction)

désinvolte [dezɛ̃vɔlt] ADJ casual, off-hand

désinvolture [dezɛ̃vɔltyʀ] NF casualness

désir [deziʀ] NM wish; (*fort, sensuel*) desire

désirable [deziʀabl] ADJ desirable

désirer [deziʀe] /**1**/ vt to want, wish for; (*sexuellement*) to desire; **je désire ...** (*formule de*

politesse) I would like ...; **il désire que tu l'aides** he would like *ou* he wants you to help him; **~ faire** to want *ou* wish to do; **ça laisse à ~** it leaves something to be desired

désireux, -euse [deziʀø, -øz] ADJ: **~ de faire** anxious to do

désistement [dezistəmɑ̃] NM withdrawal

désister [deziste] /**1**/: **se désister** vi to stand down, withdraw

désobéir [dezɔbeiʀ] /**2**/ vi: **~ (à qn/qch)** to disobey (sb/sth)

désobéissance [dezɔbeisɑ̃s] NF disobedience

désobéissant, e [dezɔbeisɑ̃, -ɑ̃t] ADJ disobedient

désobligeant, e [dezɔbliʒɑ̃, -ɑ̃t] ADJ disagreeable, unpleasant

désobliger [dezɔbliʒe] /**3**/ vt to offend

désodorisant [dezɔdɔʀizɑ̃] NM air freshener, deodorizer

désodoriser [dezɔdɔʀize] /**1**/ vt to deodorize

désœuvré, e [dezœvʀe] ADJ idle

désœuvrement [dezœvʀəmɑ̃] NM idleness

désolant, e [dezɔlɑ̃, -ɑ̃t] ADJ distressing

désolation [dezɔlasjɔ̃] NF (*affliction*) distress, grief; (*d'un paysage etc*) desolation, devastation

désolé, e [dezɔle] ADJ (*paysage*) desolate; **je suis ~** I'm sorry

désoler [dezɔle] /**1**/ vt to distress, grieve; **se désoler** vi to be upset

désolidariser [desɔlidaʀize] /**1**/ vt: **se ~ de** *ou* **d'avec** to dissociate o.s. from

désopilant, e [dezɔpilɑ̃, -ɑ̃t] ADJ screamingly funny, hilarious

désordonné, e [dezɔʀdɔne] ADJ untidy, disorderly

désordre [dezɔʀdʀ] NM disorder(liness), untidiness; (*anarchie*) disorder; **désordres** NMPL (Pol) disturbances, disorder sg; **en ~** in a mess, untidy

désorganiser [dezɔʀganize] /**1**/ vt to disorganize

désorienté, e [dezɔʀjɑ̃te] ADJ disorientated; (*fig*) bewildered

désorienter [dezɔʀjɑ̃te] /**1**/ vt (*fig*) to confuse

désormais [dezɔʀmɛ] ADV in future, from now on

désosser [dezɔse] /**1**/ vt to bone

despote [dɛspɔt] NM despot; (*fig*) tyrant

despotique [dɛspɔtik] ADJ despotic

despotisme [dɛspɔtism] NM despotism

desquamer [dɛskwame] /**1**/: **se desquamer** vi to flake off

desquels, desquelles [dekɛl] *voir* **lequel**

DESS SIGLE M (= *Diplôme d'études supérieures spécialisées*) post-graduate diploma

dessaisir [deseziʀ] /**2**/ vt: **~ un tribunal d'une affaire** to remove a case from a court; **se ~ de** vt to give up, part with

dessaler [desale] /**1**/ vt (*eau de mer*) to desalinate; (*Culin: morue etc*) to soak; (*fig: fam: délurer*): **~ qn** to teach sb a thing or two ▶ vi (*voilier*) to capsize

Desse ABR = **duchesse**

desséché, e [deseʃe] ADJ dried up

dessèchement [desɛʃmɑ̃] NM drying out; dryness; hardness

125

dessécher [desefe] /6/ vᴛ (*terre, plante*) to dry out, parch; (*peau*) to dry out; (*volontairement: aliments etc*) to dry, dehydrate; (*fig: cœur*) to harden; **se dessécher** vɪ to dry out; (*peau, lèvres*) to go dry

dessein [desɛ̃] ɴᴍ design; **dans le ~ de** with the intention of; **à ~** intentionally, deliberately

desseller [desele] /1/ vᴛ to unsaddle

desserrer [desere] /1/ vᴛ to loosen; (*frein*) to release; (*poing, dents*) to unclench; (*objets alignés*) to space out; **ne pas ~ les dents** not to open one's mouth

dessert [desɛʀ] ᴠʙ *voir* **desservir** ▶ ɴᴍ dessert, pudding

desserte [desɛʀt] ɴꜰ (*table*) side table; (*transport*): **la ~ du village est assurée par autocar** there is a coach service to the village; **chemin** *ou* **voie de ~** service road

desservir [desɛʀviʀ] /14/ vᴛ (*ville, quartier*) to serve; (: *voie de communication*) to lead into; (*vicaire, paroisse*) to serve; (*nuire à: personne*) to do a disservice to; (*débarrasser*): ~ (**la table**) to clear the table

dessiller [desije] /1/ vᴛ (*fig*): ~ **les yeux à qn** to open sb's eyes

dessin [desɛ̃] ɴᴍ (*œuvre, art*) drawing; (*motif*) pattern, design; (*contour*) (out)line; **le ~ industriel** draughtsmanship (ʙʀɪᴛ), draftsmanship (ᴜꜱ); **~ animé** cartoon (film); **~ humoristique** cartoon

dessinateur, -trice [desinatœʀ, -tʀis] ɴᴍ/ꜰ drawer; (*de bandes dessinées*) cartoonist; (*industriel*) draughtsman (ʙʀɪᴛ), draftsman (ᴜꜱ); **dessinatrice de mode** fashion designer

dessiner [desine] /1/ vᴛ to draw; (*concevoir: carrosserie, maison*) to design; (*robe, taille*) to show off; **se dessiner** vɪ (*forme*) to be outlined; (*fig: solution*) to emerge

dessoûler [desule] /1/ vᴛ, vɪ to sober up

dessous [d(ə)su] ᴀᴅᴠ underneath, beneath ▶ ɴᴍ underside; (*étage inférieur*): **les voisins du ~** the downstairs neighbours ▶ ɴᴍᴘʟ (*sous-vêtements*) underwear *sg*; (*fig*) hidden aspects; **en ~** underneath; below; (*fig: en catimini*) slyly, on the sly; **par ~** underneath; below; **de ~ le lit** from under the bed; **au-~** *adv* below; **au-~ de** *prép* below; (*peu digne de*) beneath; **au-~ de tout** the (absolute) limit; **avoir le ~** to get the worst of it

dessous-de-bouteille [dəsudbutɛj] ɴᴍ bottle mat

dessous-de-plat [dəsudpla] ɴᴍ ɪɴᴠ tablemat

dessous-de-table [dəsudtabl] ɴᴍ (*fig*) bribe, under-the-counter payment

dessus [d(ə)sy] ᴀᴅᴠ on top; (*collé, écrit*) on it ▶ ɴᴍ top; (*étage supérieur*): **les voisins/l'appartement du ~** the upstairs neighbours/flat; **en ~** above; **par ~** *adv* over it; *prép* over; **au-~** above; **au-~ de** above; **avoir/prendre le ~** to have/get the upper hand; **reprendre le ~** to get over it; **bras ~ bras dessous** arm in arm; **sens ~ dessous** upside down; *voir* **ci-dessus**; **là-dessus**

dessus-de-lit [dəsydli] ɴᴍ ɪɴᴠ bedspread

déstabiliser [destabilize] /1/ vᴛ (*Pol*) to destabilize

destin [dɛstɛ̃] ɴᴍ fate; (*avenir*) destiny

destinataire [dɛstinatɛʀ] ɴᴍꜰ (*Postes*) addressee; (*d'un colis*) consignee; (*d'un mandat*) payee; **aux risques et périls du ~** at owner's risk

destination [dɛstinasjɔ̃] ɴꜰ (*lieu*) destination; (*usage*) purpose; **à ~ de** (*avion etc*) bound for; (*voyageur*) bound for, travelling to

destinée [dɛstine] ɴꜰ fate; (*existence, avenir*) destiny

destiner [dɛstine] /1/ vᴛ: ~ **qn à** (*poste, sort*) to destine sb for; ~ **qn/qch à** (*prédestiner*) to mark sb/sth out for; ~ **qch à** (*envisager d'affecter*) to intend to use sth for; ~ **qch à qn** (*envisager de donner*) to intend sb to have sth, intend to give sth to sb; (*adresser*) to intend sth for sb; **se ~ à l'enseignement** to intend to become a teacher; **être destiné à** (*sort*) to be destined to + *verbe*; (*usage*) to be intended *ou* meant for; (*sort*) to be in store for

destituer [dɛstitɥe] /1/ vᴛ to depose; ~ **qn de ses fonctions** to relieve sb of his duties

destitution [dɛstitysjɔ̃] ɴꜰ deposition

destructeur, -trice [dɛstʀyktœʀ, -tʀis] ᴀᴅᴊ destructive

destructif, -ive [dɛstʀyktif, -iv] ᴀᴅᴊ destructive

destruction [dɛstʀyksjɔ̃] ɴꜰ destruction

déstructuré, e [destʀyktyʀe] ᴀᴅᴊ: **vêtements déstructurés** casual clothes

déstructurer [destʀyktyʀe] /1/ vᴛ to break down, take to pieces

désuet, -ète [desɥɛ, -ɛt] ᴀᴅᴊ outdated, outmoded

désuétude [desɥetyd] ɴꜰ: **tomber en ~** to fall into disuse, become obsolete

désuni, e [dezyni] ᴀᴅᴊ divided, disunited

désunion [dezynjɔ̃] ɴꜰ disunity

désunir [dezyniʀ] /2/ vᴛ to disunite; **se désunir** vɪ (*athlète*) to get out of one's stride

détachable [detaʃabl] ᴀᴅᴊ (*coupon etc*) tear-off *cpd*; (*capuche etc*) detachable

détachant [detaʃɑ̃] ɴᴍ stain remover

détaché, e [detaʃe] ᴀᴅᴊ (*fig*) detached ▶ ɴᴍ/ꜰ (*représentant*) person on secondment (ʙʀɪᴛ) *ou* a posting

détachement [detaʃmɑ̃] ɴᴍ detachment; (*fonctionnaire, employé*): **être en ~** to be on secondment (ʙʀɪᴛ) *ou* a posting

détacher [detaʃe] /1/ vᴛ (*enlever*) to detach, remove; (*délier*) to untie; (*Admin*): ~ **qn (auprès de** *ou* **à)** to post sb (to), send sb on secondment (to) (ʙʀɪᴛ); (*Mil*) to detail; (*vêtement: nettoyer*) to remove the stains from; **se détacher** vɪ (*se séparer*) to come off; (*page*) to come out; (*se défaire*) to come undone; (*Sport*) to pull *ou* break away; (*se délier: chien, prisonnier*) to break loose; **se détacher sur** to stand out against; **se détacher de** (*se désintéresser*) to grow away from

détail [detaj] ɴᴍ detail; (*Comm*): **le ~** retail; **prix de ~** retail price; **au ~** *adv* (*Comm*) retail (: *individuellement*) separately; **donner le ~ de** to give a detailed account of; (*compte*) to give a breakdown of; **en ~** in detail

détaillant, e [detajɑ̃, -ɑ̃t] ɴᴍ/ꜰ retailer

détaillé, e [detaje] ADJ (récit, plan, explications) detailed; (facture) itemized

détailler [detaje] /1/ VT (Comm) to sell retail; to sell separately; (expliquer) to explain in detail; to detail; (examiner) to look over, examine

détaler [detale] /1/ VI (lapin) to scamper off; (fam: personne) to make off, scarper (fam)

détartrant [detartrã] NM descaling agent (BRIT), scale remover

détartrer [detartre] /1/ VT to descale; (dents) to scale

détaxe [detaks] NF (réduction) reduction in tax; (suppression) removal of tax; (remboursement) tax refund

détaxer [detakse] /1/ VT (réduire) to reduce the tax on; (ôter) to remove the tax on

détecter [detɛkte] /1/ VT to detect

détecteur [detɛktœr] NM detector, sensor; ~ **de mensonges** lie detector; ~ **(de mines)** mine detector

détection [detɛksjɔ̃] NF detection

détective [detɛktiv] NM detective; ~ **(privé)** private detective ou investigator

déteindre [detɛ̃dr] /52/ VI to fade; (au lavage) to run; ~ **sur** (vêtement) to run into; (fig) to rub off on

déteint, e [detɛ̃, -ɛ̃t] PP de **déteindre**

dételer [detle] /4/ VT to unharness; (voiture, wagon) to unhitch ▶ VI (fig: s'arrêter) to leave off (working)

détendeur [detãdœr] NM (de bouteille à gaz) regulator

détendre [detãdr] /41/ VT (fil) to slacken, loosen; (personne, atmosphère, corps, esprit) to relax; (: situation) to relieve; **se détendre** VI (ressort) to lose its tension; (personne) to relax

détendu, e [detãdy] ADJ relaxed

détenir [det(ə)nir] /22/ VT (fortune, objet, secret) to be in possession of; (prisonnier) to detain; (record) to hold; ~ **le pouvoir** to be in power

détente [detãt] NF relaxation; (Pol) détente; (d'une arme) trigger; (d'un athlète qui saute) spring

détenteur, -trice [detãtœr, -tris] NM/F holder

détention [detãsjɔ̃] NF (de fortune, objet, secret) possession; (captivité) detention; (de record) holding; ~ **préventive** (pre-trial) custody

détenu, e [det(ə)ny] PP de **détenir** ▶ NM/F prisoner

détergent [detɛrʒã] NM detergent

détérioration [deterjɔrasjɔ̃] NF damaging; deterioration

détériorer [deterjɔre] /1/ VT to damage; **se détériorer** VI to deteriorate

déterminant, e [detɛrminã, -ãt] ADJ: **un facteur** ~ a determining factor ▶ NM (Ling) determiner

détermination [detɛrminasjɔ̃] NF determining; (résolution) decision; (fermeté) determination

déterminé, e [detɛrmine] ADJ (résolu) determined; (précis) specific, definite

déterminer [detɛrmine] /1/ VT (fixer) to determine; (décider): ~ **qn à faire** to decide sb to do; **se** ~ **à faire** to make up one's mind to do

déterminisme [detɛrminism] NM determinism

déterré, e [detere] NM/F: **avoir une mine de** ~ to look like death warmed up (BRIT) ou warmed over (US)

déterrer [detere] /1/ VT to dig up

détersif, -ive [detɛrsif, -iv] ADJ, NM detergent

détestable [detɛstabl] ADJ foul, detestable

détester [detɛste] /1/ VT to hate, detest

détiendrai [detjɛ̃dre], **détiens** etc [detjɛ̃] VB voir **détenir**

détonant, e [detɔnã, -ãt] ADJ: **mélange** ~ explosive mixture

détonateur [detɔnatœr] NM detonator

détonation [detɔnasjɔ̃] NF detonation, bang, report (of a gun)

détoner [detɔne] /1/ VI to detonate, explode

détonner [detɔne] /1/ VI (Mus) to go out of tune; (fig) to clash

détordre [detɔrdr] /41/ VT to untwist, unwind

détour [detur] NM detour; (tournant) bend, curve; (fig: subterfuge) roundabout means; **ça vaut le** ~ it's worth the trip; **sans** ~ (fig) plainly

détourné, e [deturne] ADJ (sentier, chemin, moyen) roundabout

détournement [deturnəmã] NM diversion, rerouting; ~ **d'avion** hijacking; ~ **(de fonds)** embezzlement ou misappropriation (of funds); ~ **de mineur** corruption of a minor

détourner [deturne] /1/ VT to divert; (avion) to divert, reroute; (: par la force) to hijack; (yeux, tête) to turn away; (de l'argent) to embezzle, misappropriate; **se détourner** VI to turn away; ~ **la conversation** to change the subject; ~ **qn de son devoir** to divert sb from his duty; ~ **l'attention (de qn)** to distract ou divert (sb's) attention

détracteur, -trice [detraktœr, -tris] NM/F disparager, critic

détraqué, e [detrake] ADJ (machine, santé) broken-down ▶ NM/F (fam): **c'est un** ~ he's unhinged

détraquer [detrake] /1/ VT to put out of order; (estomac) to upset; **se détraquer** VI to go wrong

détrempe [detrãp] NF (Art) tempera

détrempé, e [detrãpe] ADJ (sol) sodden, waterlogged

détremper [detrãpe] /1/ VT (peinture) to water down

détresse [detrɛs] NF distress; **en** ~ (avion etc) in distress; **appel/signal de** ~ distress call/signal

détriment [detrimã] NM: **au** ~ **de** to the detriment of

détritus [detritys] NMPL rubbish sg, refuse sg, garbage sg (US)

détroit [detrwa] NM strait; **le** ~ **de Bering** ou **Behring** the Bering Strait; **le** ~ **de Gibraltar** the Straits of Gibraltar; **le** ~ **du Bosphore** the Bosphorus; **le** ~ **de Magellan** the Strait of Magellan, the Magellan Strait

détromper [detrɔ̃pe] /1/ VT to disabuse; **se détromper** VI: **détrompez-vous** don't believe it

détrôner [detrone] /1/ VT to dethrone, depose; (fig) to oust, dethrone

127

détrousser [detʀuse] /**1**/ vt to rob
détruire [detʀɥiʀ] /**38**/ vt to destroy; (fig: santé, réputation) to ruin; (documents) to shred
détruit, e [detʀɥi, -it] pp de **détruire**
dette [dɛt] nf debt; **~ publique** ou **de l'État** national debt
DEUG [dœg] sigle m = **Diplôme d'études universitaires générales**; see note

French students sit their DEUG (diplôme d'études universitaires générales) after two years at university. They can then choose to leave university altogether, or go on to study for their licence. The certificate specifies the student's major subject and may be awarded with distinction.

deuil [dœj] nm (perte) bereavement; (période) mourning; (chagrin) grief; **porter le ~** to wear mourning; **prendre le/être en ~** to go into/be in mourning
DEUST [dœst] sigle m = **Diplôme d'études universitaires scientifiques et techniques**
deux [dø] num two; **les ~** both; **ses ~ mains** both his hands, his two hands; **à ~ pas** a short distance away; **tous les ~ mois** every two months, every other month; **deudx fois** twice
deuxième [døzjɛm] num second
deuxièmement [døzjɛmmã] adv secondly, in the second place
deux-pièces [døpjɛs] nm inv (tailleur) two-piece (suit); (de bain) two-piece (swimsuit); (appartement) two-roomed flat (Brit) ou apartment (US)
deux-points [døpwɛ̃] nm inv colon sg
deux-roues [døʀu] nm inv two-wheeled vehicle
deux-temps [døtã] adj inv two-stroke
devais etc [dəvɛ] vb voir **devoir**
dévaler [devale] /**1**/ vt to hurtle down
dévaliser [devalize] /**1**/ vt to rob, burgle
dévalorisant, e [devalɔʀizã, -ãt] adj depreciatory
dévalorisation [devalɔʀizasjɔ̃] nf depreciation
dévaloriser [devalɔʀize] /**1**/ vt to reduce the value of; **se dévaloriser** vi to depreciate
dévaluation [devalɥasjɔ̃] nf depreciation; (Écon: mesure) devaluation
dévaluer [devalɥe] /**1**/ vt, **se dévaluer** vi to devalue
devancer [d(ə)vɑ̃se] /**3**/ vt to be ahead of; (distancer) to get ahead of; (arriver avant) to arrive before; (prévenir) to anticipate; **~ l'appel** (Mil) to enlist before call-up
devancier, -ière [dəvãsje, -jɛʀ] nm/f precursor
devant [d(ə)vã] vb voir **devoir** ▶ adv in front; (à distance: en avant) ahead ▶ prép in front of; (en avant) ahead of; (avec mouvement: passer) past; (fig) before, in front of; (: face à) faced with, in the face of; (: vu) in view of ▶ nm front; **prendre les devants** to make the first move; **de ~** (roue, porte) front; **les pattes de ~** the front legs, the forelegs; **par ~** (boutonner) at the front; (entrer) the front way; **par-~ notaire** in the presence of a notary; **aller au-~ de qn** to go out to meet sb; **aller au-~ de** (désirs de qn) to anticipate; **aller au-~ des ennuis** ou **difficultés** to be asking for trouble

devanture [d(ə)vãtyʀ] nf (façade) (shop) front; (étalage) display; (vitrine) (shop) window
dévastateur, -trice [devastatœʀ, -tʀis] adj devastating
dévastation [devastasjɔ̃] nf devastation
dévaster [devaste] /**1**/ vt to devastate
déveine [devɛn] nf rotten luck no pl
développement [dev(ə)lɔpmã] nm development; **pays en voie de ~** developing countries; **~ durable** sustainable development
développer [dev(ə)lɔpe] /**1**/ vt to develop; **se développer** vi to develop
devenir [dəv(ə)niʀ] /**22**/ vi to become; **~ instituteur** to become a teacher; **que sont-ils devenus?** what has become of them?
devenu, e [dəvny] pp de **devenir**
dévergondé, e [devɛʀgɔ̃de] adj wild, shameless
dévergonder [devɛʀgɔ̃de] /**1**/ vt, **se dévergonder** vi to get into bad ways
déverrouiller [devɛʀuje] /**1**/ vt to unbolt
devers [dəvɛʀ] adv: **par ~ soi** to oneself
déverser [devɛʀse] /**1**/ vt (liquide) to pour (out); (ordures) to tip (out); **se ~ dans** (fleuve, mer) to flow into
déversoir [devɛʀswaʀ] nm overflow
dévêtir [devetiʀ] /**20**/ vt, **se dévêtir** vi to undress
devez [dəve] vb voir **devoir**
déviation [devjasjɔ̃] nf deviation; (Auto) diversion (Brit), detour (US); **~ de la colonne (vertébrale)** curvature of the spine
dévider [devide] /**1**/ vt to unwind
dévidoir [devidwaʀ] nm reel
deviendrai [dəvjɛ̃dʀe], **deviens** etc [dəvjɛ̃] vb voir **devenir**
devienne etc [dəvjɛn] vb voir **devenir**
dévier [devje] /**7**/ vt (fleuve, circulation) to divert; (coup) to deflect ▶ vi to veer (off course); **(faire) ~** (projectile) to deflect; (véhicule) to push off course
devin [dəvɛ̃] nm soothsayer, seer
deviner [d(ə)vine] /**1**/ vt to guess; (prévoir) to foretell, foresee; (apercevoir) to distinguish
devinette [davinɛt] nf riddle
devint etc [dəvɛ̃] vb voir **devenir**
devis [d(ə)vi] nm estimate, quotation; **~ descriptif/estimatif** detailed/preliminary estimate
dévisager [devizaʒe] /**3**/ vt to stare at
devise [dəviz] nf (formule) motto, watchword; (Écon: monnaie) currency; **devises** nfpl (argent) currency sg
deviser [dəvize] /**1**/ vi to converse
dévisser [devise] /**1**/ vt to unscrew, undo; **se dévisser** vi to come unscrewed
de visu [devizy] adv: **se rendre compte de qch ~** to see sth for o.s.
dévitaliser [devitalize] /**1**/ vt (dent) to remove the nerve from
dévoiler [devwale] /**1**/ vt to unveil
devoir [d(ə)vwaʀ] /**28**/ nm duty; (Scol) piece of homework, homework no pl; (: en classe) exercise ▶ vt (argent, respect): **~ qch (à qn)** to owe (sb) sth; **combien est-ce que je vous dois?** how much

do I owe you?; **il doit le faire** (*obligation*) he has to do it, he must do it; **cela devait arriver un jour** (*fatalité*) it was bound to happen; **il doit partir demain** (*intention*) he is due to leave tomorrow; **il doit être tard** (*probabilité*) it must be late; **se faire un ~ de faire qch** to make it one's duty to do sth; **devoirs de vacances** homework set for the holidays; **se ~ de faire qch** to be duty bound to do sth; **je devrais faire** I ought to *ou* should do; **tu n'aurais pas dû** you ought not to have *ou* shouldn't have; **comme il se doit** (*comme il faut*) as is right and proper

dévolu, e [devɔly] ADJ: **~ à** allotted to ▶ NM: **jeter son ~ sur** to fix one's choice on

devons [dəvɔ̃] VB *voir* **devoir**

dévorant, e [devɔʀɑ̃, -ɑ̃t] ADJ (*faim, passion*) raging

dévorer [devɔʀe] /1/ VT to devour; (*feu, soucis*) to consume; **~ qn/qch des yeux** *ou* **du regard** (*fig*) to eye sb/sth intently; (*convoitise*) to eye sb/sth greedily

dévot, e [devo, -ɔt] ADJ devout, pious ▶ NM/F devout person; **un faux ~** a falsely pious person

dévotion [devɔsjɔ̃] NF devoutness; **être à la ~ de qn** to be totally devoted to sb; **avoir une ~ pour qn** to worship sb

dévoué, e [devwe] ADJ devoted

dévouement [devumɑ̃] NM devotion, dedication

dévouer [devwe] /1/: **se dévouer** VI (*se sacrifier*): **se dévouer (pour)** to sacrifice o.s. (for); (*se consacrer*): **se dévouer à** to devote *ou* dedicate o.s. to

dévoyé, e [devwaje] ADJ delinquent

dévoyer [devwaje] /8/ VT to lead astray; **se dévoyer** VI to go off the rails; **~ l'opinion publique** to influence public opinion

devrai *etc* [dəvʀe] VB *voir* **devoir**

dextérité [dɛksteʀite] NF skill, dexterity

dézipper [dezipe] /1/ VT (*Inform*) to unzip

dfc ABR (= *désire faire connaissance*) *in personal column of newspaper*

DG SIGLE M = **directeur général**

dg. ABR (= *décigramme*) dg.

DGE SIGLE F (= *Dotation globale d'équipement*) *state contribution to local government budget*

DGSE SIGLE F (= *Direction générale de la sécurité extérieure*) ≈ MI6 (*BRIT*), ≈ CIA (*US*)

diabète [djabɛt] NM diabetes *sg*

diabétique [djabetik] NMF diabetic

diable [djabl] NM devil; **une musique du ~** an unholy racket; **il fait une chaleur du ~** it's fiendishly hot; **avoir le ~ au corps** to be the very devil

diablement [djabləmɑ̃] ADV fiendishly

diableries [djabləʀi] NFPL (*d'enfant*) devilment *sg*, mischief *sg*

diablesse [djablɛs] NF (*petite fille*) little devil

diablotin [djablɔtɛ̃] NM imp; (*pétard*) cracker

diabolique [djabɔlik] ADJ diabolical

diabolo [djabɔlo] NM (*jeu*) diabolo; (*boisson*) lemonade and fruit cordial; **~(-menthe)** lemonade and mint cordial

diacre [djakʀ] NM deacon

diadème [djadɛm] NM diadem

diagnostic [djagnɔstik] NM diagnosis *sg*

diagnostiquer [djagnɔstike] /1/ VT to diagnose

diagonal, e, -aux [djagɔnal, -o] ADJ, NF diagonal; **en ~** diagonally; **lire en ~** (*fig*) to skim through

diagramme [djagʀam] NM chart, graph

dialecte [djalɛkt] NM dialect

dialectique [djalɛktik] ADJ dialectic(al)

dialogue [djalɔg] NM dialogue; **~ de sourds** dialogue of the deaf

dialoguer [djalɔge] /1/ VI to converse; (*Pol*) to have a dialogue

dialoguiste [djalɔgist] NMF dialogue writer

dialyse [djaliz] NF dialysis

diamant [djamɑ̃] NM diamond

diamantaire [djamɑ̃tɛʀ] NM diamond dealer

diamétralement [djametʀalmɑ̃] ADV diametrically; **~ opposés** (*opinions*) diametrically opposed

diamètre [djamɛtʀ] NM diameter

diapason [djapazɔ̃] NM tuning fork; (*fig*): **être/se mettre au ~ (de)** to be/get in tune (with)

diaphane [djafan] ADJ diaphanous

diaphragme [djafʀagm] NM (*Anat, Photo*) diaphragm; (*contraceptif*) diaphragm, cap; **ouverture du ~** (*Photo*) aperture

diapo [djapo], **diapositive** [djapozitiv] NF transparency, slide

diaporama [djapɔʀama] NM slide show

diapré, e [djapʀe] ADJ many-coloured (*BRIT*), many-colored (*US*)

diarrhée [djaʀe] NF diarrhoea (*BRIT*), diarrhea (*US*)

diatribe [djatʀib] NF diatribe

dichotomie [dikɔtɔmi] NF dichotomy

dictaphone [diktafɔn] NM Dictaphone®

dictateur [diktatœʀ] NM dictator

dictatorial, e, -aux [diktatɔʀjal, -o] ADJ dictatorial

dictature [diktatyʀ] NF dictatorship

dictée [dikte] NF dictation; **prendre sous ~** to take down (*sth dictated*)

dicter [dikte] /1/ VT to dictate

diction [diksjɔ̃] NF diction, delivery; **cours de ~** speech production lesson(s)

dictionnaire [diksjɔnɛʀ] NM dictionary; **~ géographique** gazetteer

dicton [diktɔ̃] NM saying, dictum

didacticiel [didaktisjɛl] NM educational software

didactique [didaktik] ADJ didactic

dièse [djɛz] NM (*Mus*) sharp

diesel [djezɛl] NM, ADJ INV diesel

diète [djɛt] NF (*jeûne*) starvation diet; (*régime*) diet; **être à la ~** to be on a diet

diététicien, ne [djetetisjɛ̃, -ɛn] NM/F dietician

diététique [djetetik] NF dietetics *sg* ▶ ADJ: **magasin ~** health food shop (*BRIT*) *ou* store (*US*)

dieu, x [djø] NM god; **D~** God; **le bon D~** the good Lord; **mon D~!** good heavens!

diffamant, e [difamɑ̃, -ɑ̃t] ADJ slanderous, defamatory; libellous

diffamation [difamasjɔ̃] NF slander; (*écrite*) libel; **attaquer qn en ~** to sue sb for slander (*ou* libel)

diffamatoire [difamatwaʀ] ADJ slanderous, defamatory; libellous

diffamer [difame] /1/ VT to slander, defame; to libel

différé [difeʀe] ADJ: **crédit ~** deferred credit ▶ NM (*TV*): **en ~** (pre-)recorded; **traitement ~** (*Inform*) batch processing

différemment [difeʀamɑ̃] ADV differently

différence [difeʀɑ̃s] NF difference; **à la ~ de** unlike

différenciation [difeʀɑ̃sjasjɔ̃] NF differentiation

différencier [difeʀɑ̃sje] /7/ VT to differentiate; **se différencier** VI (*organisme*) to become differentiated; **se différencier de** to differentiate o.s. from; (*être différent*) to differ from

différend [difeʀɑ̃] NM difference (of opinion), disagreement

différent, e [difeʀɑ̃, -ɑ̃t] ADJ (*dissemblable*) different; **~ de** different from; **différents objets** different *ou* various objects; **à différentes reprises** on various occasions

différentiel, le [difeʀɑ̃sjɛl] ADJ, NM differential

différer [difeʀe] /6/ VT to postpone, put off ▶ VI: **~ (de)** to differ (from); **~ de faire** (*tarder*) to delay doing

difficile [difisil] ADJ difficult; (*exigeant*) hard to please, difficult (to please); **faire le** *ou* **la ~** to be hard to please, be difficult

difficilement [difisilmɑ̃] ADV (*marcher, s'expliquer etc*) with difficulty; **~ lisible/compréhensible** difficult *ou* hard to read/understand

difficulté [difikylte] NF difficulty; **en ~** (*bateau, alpiniste*) in trouble *ou* difficulties; **avoir de la ~ à faire** to have difficulty (in) doing

difforme [difɔʀm] ADJ deformed, misshapen

difformité [difɔʀmite] NF deformity

diffracter [difʀakte] /1/ VT to diffract

diffus, e [dify, -yz] ADJ diffuse

diffuser [difyze] /1/ VT (*chaleur, bruit, lumière*) to diffuse; (*émission, musique*) to broadcast; (*nouvelle, idée*) to circulate; (*Comm: livres, journaux*) to distribute

diffuseur [difyzœʀ] NM diffuser; distributor

diffusion [difyzjɔ̃] NF diffusion; broadcast(ing); circulation; distribution

digérer [diʒeʀe] /6/ VT (*personne*) to digest; (: *machine*) to process; (*fig: accepter*) to stomach, put up with

digeste [diʒɛst] ADJ easily digestible

digestible [diʒɛstibl] ADJ digestible

digestif, -ive [diʒɛstif, -iv] ADJ digestive ▶ NM (after-dinner) liqueur

digestion [diʒɛstjɔ̃] NF digestion

digit [didʒit] NM: **~ binaire** binary digit

digital, e, -aux [diʒital, -o] ADJ digital

digitale [diʒital] NF digitalis, foxglove

digne [diɲ] ADJ dignified; **~ de** worthy of; **~ de foi** trustworthy

dignitaire [diɲitɛʀ] NM dignitary

dignité [diɲite] NF dignity

digression [digʀesjɔ̃] NF digression

digue [dig] NF dike, dyke; (*pour protéger la côte*) sea wall

dijonnais, e [diʒɔnɛ, -ɛz] ADJ of *ou* from Dijon ▶ NM/F: **D~, e** inhabitant *ou* native of Dijon

diktat [diktat] NM diktat

dilapidation [dilapidasjɔ̃] NF (*voir vb*) squandering; embezzlement; misappropriation

dilapider [dilapide] /1/ VT to squander, waste; (*détourner: biens, fonds publics*) to embezzle, misappropriate

dilater [dilate] /1/ VT to dilate; (*gaz, métal*) to cause to expand; (*ballon*) to distend; **se dilater** VI to expand

dilemme [dilɛm] NM dilemma

dilettante [diletɑ̃t] NMF dilettante; **en ~** in a dilettantish way

dilettantisme [diletɑ̃tism] NM dilettant(e)ism

diligence [diliʒɑ̃s] NF stagecoach, diligence; (*empressement*) despatch; **faire ~** to make haste

diligent, e [diliʒɑ̃, -ɑ̃t] ADJ prompt and efficient; diligent

diluant [dilɥɑ̃] NM thinner(s)

diluer [dilɥe] /1/ VT to dilute

dilution [dilysjɔ̃] NF dilution

diluvien, ne [dilyvjɛ̃, -ɛn] ADJ: **pluie ~** torrential rain

dimanche [dimɑ̃ʃ] NM Sunday; **le ~ des Rameaux/de Pâques** Palm/Easter Sunday; *voir aussi* **lundi**

dîme [dim] NF tithe

dimension [dimɑ̃sjɔ̃] NF (*grandeur*) size; (*gén pl: cotes, Math: de l'espace*) dimension; (*dimensions*) dimensions

diminué, e [diminɥe] ADJ (*personne: physiquement*) run-down; (: *mentalement*) less alert

diminuer [diminɥe] /1/ VT to reduce, decrease; (*ardeur etc*) to lessen; (*personne: physiquement*) to undermine; (*dénigrer*) to belittle ▶ VI to decrease, diminish

diminutif [diminytif] NM (*Ling*) diminutive; (*surnom*) pet name

diminution [diminysjɔ̃] NF decreasing, diminishing

dînatoire [dinatwaʀ] ADJ: **goûter ~** ≈ high tea (*BRIT*); **apéritif ~** ≈ evening buffet

dinde [dɛ̃d] NF turkey; (*femme stupide*) goose

dindon [dɛ̃dɔ̃] NM turkey

dindonneau, x [dɛ̃dɔno] NM turkey poult

dîner [dine] /1/ VI dinner ▶ VI to have dinner; **~ d'affaires/de famille** business/family dinner

dînette [dinɛt] NF (*jeu*): **jouer à la ~** to play at tea parties

dingue [dɛ̃g] ADJ (*fam*) crazy

dinosaure [dinɔzɔʀ] NM dinosaur

diocèse [djɔsɛz] NM diocese

diode [djɔd] NF diode

diphasé, e [difaze] ADJ (*Élec*) two-phase

diphtérie [difteʀi] NF diphtheria

diphtongue [diftɔ̃g] NF diphthong

diplomate [diplɔmat] ADJ diplomatic ▶ NM

diplomat; (fig: personne habile) diplomatist; (Culin: gâteau) dessert made of sponge cake, candied fruit and custard, ≈ trifle (BRIT)

diplomatie [diplɔmasi] NF diplomacy

diplomatique [diplɔmatik] ADJ diplomatic

diplôme [diplom] NM diploma certificate; (examen) (diploma) examination; **avoir des diplômes** to have qualifications

diplômé, e [diplome] ADJ qualified

dire [diʀ] /37/ VT to say; (secret, mensonge) to tell; **se dire** VI (à soi-même) to say to oneself ▶ NM: **au ~ de** according to; **leurs dires** what they say; **~ l'heure/la vérité** to tell the time/the truth; **dis pardon/merci** say sorry/thank you; **~ qch à qn** to tell sb sth; **~ à qn qu'il fasse** ou **de faire** to tell sb to do; **~ que** to say that; **on dit que** they say that; **comme on dit** as they say; **on dirait que** it looks (ou sounds etc) as though; **on dirait du vin** you'd ou one would think it was wine; **que dites-vous de** (penser) what do you think of; **si cela lui dit** if he feels like it, if he fancies it; **cela ne me dit rien** that doesn't appeal to me; **à vrai ~** truth to tell; **pour ainsi ~** so to speak; **cela va sans ~** that goes without saying; **dis donc!, dites donc!** (pour attirer l'attention) hey!; (au fait) by the way; **et ~ que …** and to think that …; **ceci** ou **cela dit** that being said; (à ces mots) whereupon; **c'est dit, voilà qui est dit** so that's settled; **il n'y a pas à ~** there's no getting away from it; **c'est ~ si …** that just shows that …; **c'est beaucoup/peu ~** that's saying a lot/not saying much; **ça se dit … en anglais** that is … in English; **ça ne se dit pas** (impoli) you shouldn't say that; (pas en usage) you don't say that; **cela ne se dit pas comme ça** you don't say it like that; **se dire au revoir** to say goodbye (to each other)

direct, e [diʀɛkt] ADJ direct ▶ NM (train) through train; **en ~** (émission) live; **train/bus ~** express train/bus

directement [diʀɛktəmã] ADV directly

directeur, -trice [diʀɛktœʀ, -tʀis] NM/F (d'entreprise) director; (de service) manager/eress; (d'école) head(teacher) (BRIT), principal (US); **comité ~** management ou steering committee; **~ général** general manager; **~ de thèse** ≈ PhD supervisor

direction [diʀɛksjɔ̃] NF (d'entreprise) management; conducting; supervision; (Auto) steering; (sens) direction; **sous la ~ de** (Mus) conducted by; **en ~ de** (avion, train, bateau) for; **"toutes directions"** (Auto) "all routes"

directive [diʀɛktiv] NF directive, instruction; **directives anticipées** (Méd) living will

directorial, e, -aux [diʀɛktɔʀjal, -o] ADJ (bureau) director's; manager's; head teacher's

directrice [diʀɛktʀis] ADJ F, NF voir **directeur**

dirent [diʀ] VB voir **dire**

dirigeable [diʀiʒabl] ADJ, NM: **(ballon) ~** dirigible

dirigeant, e [diʀiʒã, -ãt] ADJ managerial; (classes) ruling ▶ NM/F (d'un parti etc) leader; (d'entreprise) manager, member of the management

diriger [diʀiʒe] /3/ VT (entreprise) to manage, run; (véhicule) to steer; (orchestre) to conduct; (recherches, travaux) to supervise, be in charge of; (braquer: arme): **~ sur** to point ou level ou aim at; (fig: critiques): **~ contre** to aim at; **se diriger** VI (s'orienter) to find one's way; **~ son regard sur** to look in the direction of; **se diriger vers** ou **sur** to make ou head for

dirigisme [diʀiʒism] NM (Écon) state intervention, interventionism

dirigiste [diʀiʒist] ADJ interventionist

dis [di], **disais** etc [dize] VB voir **dire**

discal, e, -aux [diskal, -o] ADJ (Méd): **hernie ~** slipped disc

discernement [disɛʀnəmã] NM discernment, judgment

discerner [disɛʀne] /1/ VT to discern, make out

disciple [disipl] NMF disciple

disciplinaire [disiplinɛʀ] ADJ disciplinary

discipline [disiplin] NF discipline

discipliné, e [disipline] ADJ (well-)disciplined

discipliner [disipline] /1/ VT to discipline; (cheveux) to control

discobole [diskɔbɔl] NMF discus thrower

discographie [diskɔgʀafi] NF discography

discontinu, e [diskɔ̃tiny] ADJ intermittent; (bande: sur la route) broken

discontinuer [diskɔ̃tinɥe] /1/ VI: **sans ~** without stopping, without a break

disconvenir [diskɔ̃vəniʀ] /22/ VI: **ne pas ~ de qch/que** not to deny sth/that

discophile [diskɔfil] NMF record enthusiast

discordance [diskɔʀdãs] NF discordance; conflict

discordant, e [diskɔʀdã, -ãt] ADJ discordant; conflicting

discorde [diskɔʀd] NF discord, dissension

discothèque [diskɔtɛk] NF (boîte de nuit) disco(thèque); (disques) record collection; (dans une bibliothèque): **~ (de prêt)** record library

discourais etc [diskuʀɛ] VB voir **discourir**

discourir [diskuʀiʀ] /11/ VI to discourse, hold forth

discours [diskuʀ] VB voir **discourir** ▶ NM speech; **~ direct/indirect** (Ling) direct/indirect ou reported speech

discourtois, e [diskuʀtwa, -waz] ADJ discourteous

discrédit [diskʀedi] NM: **jeter le ~ sur** to discredit

discréditer [diskʀedite] /1/ VT to discredit

discret, -ète [diskʀɛ, -ɛt] ADJ discreet; (fig: musique, style, maquillage) unobtrusive; (: endroit) quiet

discrètement [diskʀɛtmã] ADV discreetly

discrétion [diskʀesjɔ̃] NF discretion; **à la ~ de qn** at sb's discretion; in sb's hands; **à ~** (boisson etc) unlimited, as much as one wants

discrétionnaire [diskʀesjɔnɛʀ] ADJ discretionary

discrimination [diskʀiminasjɔ̃] NF discrimination; **sans ~** indiscriminately

discriminatoire [diskʀiminatwaʀ] ADJ discriminatory

d

131

disculper [diskylpe] /**1**/ VT to exonerate
discussion [diskysjɔ̃] NF discussion
discutable [diskytabl] ADJ (*contestable*) doubtful; (*à débattre*) debatable
discuté, e [diskyte] ADJ controversial
discuter [diskyte] /**1**/ VT (*contester*) to question, dispute; (*débattre: prix*) to discuss ▶ VI to talk; (*protester*) to argue; **~ de** to discuss
dise *etc* [diz] VB *voir* **dire**
disert, e [dizɛʀ, -ɛʀt] ADJ loquacious
disette [dizet] NF food shortage
diseuse [dizøz] NF: **~ de bonne aventure** fortune-teller
disgrâce [disgʀɑs] NF disgrace; **être en ~** to be in disgrace
disgracié, e [disgʀasje] ADJ (*en disgrâce*) disgraced
disgracieux, -euse [disgʀasjø, -øz] ADJ ungainly, awkward
disjoindre [disʒwɛ̃dʀ] /**49**/ VT to take apart; **se disjoindre** VI to come apart
disjoint, e [disʒwɛ̃, -wɛ̃t] PP *de* **disjoindre** ▶ ADJ loose
disjoncteur [disʒɔ̃ktœʀ] NM (*Élec*) circuit breaker
dislocation [dislɔkasjɔ̃] NF dislocation
disloquer [dislɔke] /**1**/ VT (*membre*) to dislocate; (*chaise*) to dismantle; (*troupe*) to disperse; **se disloquer** VI (*parti, empire*) to break up; (*meuble*) to come apart; **se disloquer l'épaule** to dislocate one's shoulder
disons *etc* [dizɔ̃] VB *voir* **dire**
disparaître [dispaʀɛtʀ] /**57**/ VI to disappear; (*à la vue*) to vanish, disappear; to be hidden *ou* concealed; (*être manquant*) to go missing, disappear; (*se perdre: traditions etc*) to die out; (*personne: mourir*) to die; **faire ~** (*objet, tache, trace*) to remove; (*personne, douleur*) to get rid of
disparate [dispaʀat] ADJ disparate; (*couleurs*) ill-assorted
disparité [dispaʀite] NF disparity
disparition [dispaʀisjɔ̃] NF disappearance; **espèce en voie de ~** endangered species
disparu, e [dispaʀy] PP *de* **disparaître** ▶ NM/F missing person; (*défunt*) departed; **être porté ~** to be reported missing
dispendieux, -euse [dispɑ̃djø, -øz] ADJ extravagant, expensive
dispensaire [dispɑ̃sɛʀ] NM community clinic
dispense [dispɑ̃s] NF exemption; (*permission*) special permission; **~ d'âge** special exemption from age limit
dispenser [dispɑ̃se] /**1**/ VT (*donner*) to lavish, bestow; (*exempter*): **~ qn de** to exempt sb from; **se ~ de** VT to avoid, get out of
disperser [dispɛʀse] /**1**/ VT to scatter; (*fig: son attention*) to dissipate; **se disperser** VI to scatter; (*fig*) to dissipate one's efforts
dispersion [dispɛʀsjɔ̃] NF scattering; (*des efforts*) dissipation
disponibilité [dispɔnibilite] NF availability; (*Admin*): **être en ~** to be on leave of absence; **disponibilités** NFPL (*Comm*) liquid assets
disponible [dispɔnibl] ADJ available
dispos [dispo] ADJ M: **(frais et) ~** fresh (as a daisy)

disposé, e [dispoze] ADJ (*d'une certaine manière*) arranged, laid-out; **bien/mal ~** (*humeur*) in a good/bad mood; **bien/mal ~ pour** *ou* **envers qn** well/badly disposed towards sb; **~ à** (*prêt à*) willing *ou* prepared to
disposer [dispoze] /**1**/ VT (*arranger, placer*) to arrange; (*inciter*): **~ qn à qch/faire qch** to dispose *ou* incline sb towards sth/to do sth ▶ VI: **vous pouvez ~** you may leave; **~ de** VT to have (at one's disposal); **se ~ à faire** to prepare to do, be about to do
dispositif [dispozitif] NM device; (*fig*) system, plan of action; set-up; (*d'un texte de loi*) operative part; **~ de sûreté** safety device
disposition [dispozisjɔ̃] NF (*arrangement*) arrangement, layout; (*humeur*) mood; (*tendance*) tendency; **dispositions** NFPL (*mesures*) steps, measures; (*préparatifs*) arrangements; (*de loi, testament*) provisions; (*aptitudes*) bent *sg*, aptitude *sg*; **prendre ses dispositions** to make arrangements; **avoir des dispositions pour la musique** *etc* to have a special aptitude for music *etc*; **à la ~ de qn** at sb's disposal; **je suis à votre ~** I am at your service
disproportion [dispʀɔpɔʀsjɔ̃] NF disproportion
disproportionné, e [dispʀɔpɔʀsjɔne] ADJ disproportionate, out of all proportion
dispute [dispyt] NF quarrel, argument
disputer [dispyte] /**1**/ VT (*match*) to play; (*combat*) to fight; (*course*) to run; **se disputer** VI to quarrel, have a quarrel; (*match, combat, course*) to take place; **~ qch à qn** to fight with sb for *ou* over sth
disquaire [diskɛʀ] NMF record dealer
disqualification [diskalifikasjɔ̃] NF disqualification
disqualifier [diskalifje] /**7**/ VT to disqualify; **se disqualifier** VI to bring discredit on o.s.
disque [disk] NM (*Mus*) record; (*Inform*) disk, disc; (*forme, pièce*) disc; (*Sport*) discus; **~ compact** compact disc; **~ compact interactif** CD-I®; **~ dur** hard drive; **~ d'embrayage** (*Auto*) clutch plate; **~ laser** compact disc; **~ de stationnement** parking disc; **~ système** system disk
disquette [diskɛt] NF floppy (disk), diskette
dissection [disɛksjɔ̃] NF dissection
dissemblable [disɑ̃blabl] ADJ dissimilar
dissemblance [disɑ̃blɑ̃s] NF dissimilarity, difference
dissémination [diseminasjɔ̃] NF (*voir vb*) scattering; dispersal; (*des armes*) proliferation
disséminer [disemine] /**1**/ VT to scatter; (*troupes: sur un territoire*) to disperse
dissension [disɑ̃sjɔ̃] NF dissension; **dissensions** NFPL dissension
disséquer [diseke] /**6**/ VT to dissect
dissertation [disɛʀtasjɔ̃] NF (*Scol*) essay
disserter [disɛʀte] /**1**/ VI: **~ sur** to discourse upon
dissidence [disidɑ̃s] NF (*concept*) dissidence; **rejoindre la ~** to join the dissidents
dissident, e [disidɑ̃, -ɑ̃t] ADJ, NM/F dissident
dissimilitude [disimilityd] NF dissimilarity

dissimulateur, -trice [disimylatœr, -tʀis] ADJ dissembling ▸ NM/F dissembler

dissimulation [disimylasjɔ̃] NF concealing; *(duplicité)* dissimulation; **~ de bénéfices/de revenus** concealment of profits/income

dissimulé, e [disimyle] ADJ *(personne: secret)* secretive; *(: fourbe, hypocrite)* deceitful

dissimuler [disimyle] /1/ VT to conceal; **se dissimuler** VI to conceal o.s.; to be concealed

dissipation [disipasjɔ̃] NF squandering; unruliness; *(débauche)* dissipation

dissipé, e [disipe] ADJ *(indiscipliné)* unruly

dissiper [disipe] /1/ VT to dissipate; *(fortune)* to squander, fritter away; **se dissiper** VI *(brouillard)* to clear, disperse; *(doutes)* to disappear, melt away; *(élève)* to become undisciplined *ou* unruly

dissociable [disɔsjabl] ADJ separable

dissocier [disɔsje] /7/ VT to dissociate; **se dissocier** VI *(éléments, groupe)* to break up, split up; **se dissocier de** *(groupe, point de vue)* to dissociate o.s. from

dissolu, e [disɔly] ADJ dissolute

dissoluble [disɔlybl] ADJ *(Pol: assemblée)* dissolvable

dissolution [disɔlysjɔ̃] NF dissolving; *(Pol, Jur)* dissolution

dissolvant, e [disɔlvɑ̃, -ɑ̃t] VB *voir* **dissoudre** ▸ NM *(Chimie)* solvent; **~ (gras)** nail polish remover

dissonant, e [disɔnɑ̃, -ɑ̃t] ADJ discordant

dissoudre [disudʀ] /51/ VT, **se dissoudre** VI to dissolve

dissous, -oute [disu, -ut] PP *de* **dissoudre**

dissuader [disɥade] /1/ VT: **~ qn de faire/de qch** to dissuade sb from doing/from sth

dissuasif, -ive [disɥazif, -iv] ADJ dissuasive

dissuasion [disɥazjɔ̃] NF dissuasion; **force de ~** deterrent power

distance [distɑ̃s] NF distance; *(fig: écart)* gap; **à ~** at *ou* from a distance; *(mettre en marche, commander)* by remote control; **(situé) à ~** *(Inform)* remote; **tenir qn à ~** to keep sb at a distance; **se tenir à ~** to keep one's distance; **à une ~ de 10 km, à 10 km de ~** 10 km away, at a distance of 10 km; **à deux ans de ~** with a gap of two years; **prendre ses distances** to space out; **garder ses distances** to keep one's distance; **tenir la ~** *(Sport)* to cover the distance, last the course; **~ focale** *(Photo)* focal length

distancer [distɑ̃se] /3/ VT to outdistance, leave behind

distancier [distɑ̃sje] /7/: **se distancier** VI to distance o.s.

distant, e [distɑ̃, -ɑ̃t] ADJ *(réservé)* distant, aloof; *(éloigné)* distant, far away; **~ de** *(lieu)* far away *ou* a long way from; **~ de 5 km (d'un lieu)** 5 km away (from a place)

distendre [distɑ̃dʀ] /41/ VT, **se distendre** VI to distend

distillation [distilasjɔ̃] NF distillation, distilling

distillé, e [distile] ADJ: **eau ~** distilled water

distiller [distile] /1/ VT to distil; *(fig)* to exude; to elaborate

distillerie [distilʀi] NF distillery

distinct, e [distɛ̃(kt), distɛ̃kt] ADJ distinct

distinctement [distɛ̃ktəmɑ̃] ADV distinctly

distinctif, -ive [distɛ̃ktif, -iv] ADJ distinctive

distinction [distɛ̃ksjɔ̃] NF distinction

distingué, e [distɛ̃ge] ADJ distinguished

distinguer [distɛ̃ge] /1/ VT to distinguish; **se distinguer** VI *(s'illustrer)* to distinguish o.s.; *(différer)*: **se distinguer (de)** to distinguish o.s. *ou* be distinguished (from)

distinguo [distɛ̃go] NM distinction

distorsion [distɔʀsjɔ̃] NF *(gén)* distortion; *(fig: déséquilibre)* disparity, imbalance

distraction [distʀaksjɔ̃] NF *(manque d'attention)* absent-mindedness; *(oubli)* lapse (in concentration *ou* attention); *(détente)* diversion, recreation; *(passe-temps)* distraction, entertainment

distraire [distʀɛʀ] /50/ VT *(déranger)* to distract; *(divertir)* to entertain, divert; *(détourner: somme d'argent)* to divert, misappropriate; **se distraire** VI to amuse *ou* enjoy o.s.

distrait, e [distʀɛ, -ɛt] PP *de* **distraire** ▸ ADJ absent-minded

distraitement [distʀɛtmɑ̃] ADV absent-mindedly

distrayant, e [distʀɛjɑ̃, -ɑ̃t] VB *voir* **distraire** ▸ ADJ entertaining

distribuer [distʀibɥe] /1/ VT to distribute; to hand out; *(Cartes)* to deal (out); *(courrier)* to deliver

distributeur [distʀibytœʀ] NM *(Auto, Comm)* distributor; *(automatique)* (vending) machine; **~ de billets** *(Rail)* ticket machine; *(Banque)* cash dispenser

distribution [distʀibysjɔ̃] NF distribution; *(postale)* delivery; *(choix d'acteurs)* casting; **circuits de ~** *(Comm)* distribution network; **~ des prix** *(Scol)* prize giving

district [distʀik(t)] NM district

dit, e [di, dit] PP *de* **dire** *(fixé)*: **le jour ~** the arranged day; *(surnommé)* **X, ~ Pierrot** X, known as *ou* called Pierrot

dites [dit] VB *voir* **dire**

dithyrambique [ditiʀɑ̃bik] ADJ eulogistic

DIU SIGLE M *(= dispositif intra-utérin)* IUD

diurétique [djyʀetik] ADJ, NM diuretic

diurne [djyʀn] ADJ diurnal, daytime *cpd*

divagations [divagasjɔ̃] NFPL ramblings; ravings

divaguer [divage] /1/ VI to ramble; *(malade)* to rave

divan [divɑ̃] NM divan

divan-lit [divɑ̃li] NM divan (bed)

divergence [divɛʀʒɑ̃s] NF divergence; **des divergences d'opinion au sein de …** differences of opinion within …

divergent, e [divɛʀʒɑ̃, -ɑ̃t] ADJ divergent

diverger [divɛʀʒe] /3/ VI to diverge

divers, e [divɛʀ, -ɛʀs] ADJ *(varié)* diverse, varied; *(différent)* different, various; **(frais) ~** *(Comm)* sundries, miscellaneous (expenses); **"~"** *(rubrique)* "miscellaneous"; **diverses personnes** various *ou* several people

diversement [divɛʀsəmɑ̃] ADV in various ou diverse ways

diversification [divɛʀsifikasjɔ̃] NF diversification

diversifier [divɛʀsifje] /7/ VT, **se diversifier** VI to diversify

diversion [divɛʀsjɔ̃] NF diversion; **faire ~** to create a diversion

diversité [divɛʀsite] NF diversity, variety

divertir [divɛʀtiʀ] /2/ VT to amuse, entertain; **se divertir** VI to amuse ou enjoy o.s.

divertissant, e [divɛʀtisɑ̃, -ɑ̃t] ADJ entertaining

divertissement [divɛʀtismɑ̃] NM entertainment; (Mus) divertimento, divertissement

dividende [dividɑ̃d] NM (Math, Comm) dividend

divin, e [divɛ̃, -in] ADJ divine; (fig: excellent) heavenly, divine

divinateur, -trice [divinatœʀ, -tʀis] ADJ perspicacious

divinatoire [divinatwaʀ] ADJ (art, science) divinatory; **baguette ~** divining rod

diviniser [divinize] /1/ VT to deify

divinité [divinite] NF divinity

divisé, e [divize] ADJ divided

diviser [divize] /1/ VT (gén, Math) to divide; (morceler, subdiviser) to divide (up), split (up); **se ~ en** to divide into; **~ par** to divide by

diviseur [divizœʀ] NM (Math) divisor

divisible [divizibl] ADJ divisible

division [divizjɔ̃] NF (gén) division; **~ du travail** (Écon) division of labour

divisionnaire [divizjɔnɛʀ] ADJ: **commissaire ~** ≈ chief superintendent (BRIT), ≈ police chief (US)

divorce [divɔʀs] NM divorce

divorcé, e [divɔʀse] NM/F divorcee

divorcer [divɔʀse] /3/ VI to get a divorce, get divorced; **~ de** ou **d'avec qn** to divorce sb

divulgation [divylgasjɔ̃] NF disclosure

divulguer [divylge] /1/ VT to disclose, divulge

dix [di, dis, diz] NUM ten

dix-huit [dizɥit] NUM eighteen

dix-huitième [dizɥitjɛm] NUM eighteenth

dixième [dizjɛm] NUM tenth

dix-neuf [diznœf] NUM nineteen

dix-neuvième [diznœvjɛm] NUM nineteenth

dix-sept [disɛt] NUM seventeen

dix-septième [disɛtjɛm] NUM seventeenth

dizaine [dizɛn] NF (10) ten; (environ 10): **une ~ (de)** about ten, ten or so

Djakarta [dʒakaʀta] N Djakarta

Djibouti [dʒibuti] N Djibouti

dl ABR (= décilitre) dl

DM ABR (= Deutschmark) DM

dm. ABR (= décimètre) dm.

do [do] NM (note) C; (en chantant la gamme) do(h)

docile [dɔsil] ADJ docile

docilement [dɔsilmɑ̃] ADV docilely

docilité [dɔsilite] NF docility

dock [dɔk] NM dock; (hangar, bâtiment) warehouse

docker [dɔkɛʀ] NM docker

docte [dɔkt] ADJ (péj) learned

docteur, e [dɔktœʀ] NM/F doctor; **~ en médecine** doctor of medicine

doctoral, e, -aux [dɔktɔʀal, -o] ADJ pompous, bombastic

doctorat [dɔktɔʀa] NM: **~ (d'Université)** ≈ doctorate; **~ d'État** ≈ PhD; **~ de troisième cycle** ≈ doctorate

doctoresse [dɔktɔʀɛs] NF lady doctor

doctrinaire [dɔktʀinɛʀ] ADJ doctrinaire; (sentencieux) pompous, sententious

doctrinal, e, -aux [dɔktʀinal, -o] ADJ doctrinal

doctrine [dɔktʀin] NF doctrine

document [dɔkymɑ̃] NM document

documentaire [dɔkymɑ̃tɛʀ] ADJ, NM documentary

documentaliste [dɔkymɑ̃talist] NMF archivist; (Presse, TV) researcher

documentation [dɔkymɑ̃tasjɔ̃] NF documentation, literature; (Presse, TV: service) research

documenté, e [dɔkymɑ̃te] ADJ well-informed, well-documented; well-researched

documenter [dɔkymɑ̃te] /1/ VT: **se ~ (sur)** to gather information ou material (on ou about)

Dodécanèse [dɔdekanɛz] NM Dodecanese (Islands)

dodeliner [dɔdline] /1/ VI: **~ de la tête** to nod one's head gently

dodo [dɔdo] NM: **aller faire ~** to go to beddy-byes

dodu, e [dɔdy] ADJ plump

dogmatique [dɔgmatik] ADJ dogmatic

dogmatisme [dɔgmatism] NM dogmatism

dogme [dɔgm] NM dogma

dogue [dɔg] NM mastiff

doigt [dwa] NM finger; **à deux doigts de** within an ace (BRIT) ou an inch of; **un ~ de lait/whisky** a drop of milk/whisky; **désigner** ou **montrer du ~** to point at; **au ~ et à l'œil** to the letter; **connaître qch sur le bout du ~** to know sth backwards; **mettre le ~ sur la plaie** (fig) to find the sensitive spot; **~ de pied** toe

doigté [dwate] NM (Mus) fingering; (fig: habileté) diplomacy, tact

doigtier [dwatje] NM fingerstall

dois etc [dwa] VB voir **devoir**

doit etc [dwa] VB voir **devoir**

doive etc [dwav] VB voir **devoir**

doléances [dɔleɑ̃s] NFPL complaints; (réclamations) grievances

dolent, e [dɔlɑ̃, -ɑ̃t] ADJ doleful, mournful

dollar [dɔlaʀ] NM dollar

dolmen [dɔlmɛn] NM dolmen

DOM [dɔm] SIGLE M, SIGLE MPL = **Département(s) d'outre-mer**

domaine [dɔmɛn] NM estate, property; (fig) domain, field; **tomber dans le ~ public** (livre etc) to be out of copyright; **dans tous les domaines** in all areas

domanial, e, -aux [dɔmanjal, -o] ADJ national, state cpd

dôme [dom] NM dome

domestication [dɔmɛstikasjɔ̃] NF (voir domestiquer) domestication; harnessing

domesticité [dɔmɛstisite] NF (domestic) staff

domestique [dɔmɛstik] ADJ domestic ▸ NMF servant, domestic

domestiquer [dɔmɛstike] /1/ VT to domesticate; (*vent, marées*) to harness

domicile [dɔmisil] NM home, place of residence; **à ~** at home; **élire ~ à** to take up residence in; **sans ~ fixe** of no fixed abode; **~ conjugal** marital home; **~ légal** domicile; **livrer à ~** to deliver

domicilié, e [dɔmisilje] ADJ: **être ~ à** to have one's home in *ou* at

dominant, e [dɔminɑ̃, -ɑ̃t] ADJ dominant; (*plus important: opinion*) predominant ▸ NF (*caractéristique*) dominant characteristic; (*couleur*) dominant colour

dominateur, -trice [dɔminatœR, -tRis] ADJ dominating; (*qui aime à dominer*) domineering

domination [dɔminasjɔ̃] NF domination

dominer [dɔmine] /1/ VT to dominate; (*passions etc*) to control, master; (*sujet*) to master; (*surpasser*) to outclass, surpass; (*surplomber*) to tower above, dominate ▸ VI to be in the dominant position; **se dominer** VI to control o.s.

dominicain, e [dɔminikɛ̃, -ɛn] ADJ Dominican

dominical, e, -aux [dɔminikal, -o] ADJ Sunday *cpd*, dominical

Dominique [dɔminik] NF: **la ~** Dominica

domino [dɔmino] NM domino; **dominos** NMPL (*jeu*) dominoes *sg*

dommage [dɔmaʒ] NM (*préjudice*) harm, injury; **dommages** (*dégâts, pertes*) damage *no pl*; **c'est ~ de faire/que** it's a shame *ou* pity to do/that; **quel ~!, c'est ~!** what a pity *ou* shame!; **dommages corporels** physical injury

dommages-intérêts [dɔmaʒ(əz)ɛ̃teRɛ] NMPL damages

dompter [dɔ̃(p)te] /1/ VT to tame

dompteur, -euse [dɔ̃tœR, -øz] NM/F trainer; (*de lion*) lion tamer

DOM-ROM [dɔmRɔm], **DOM-TOM** [dɔmtɔm] SIGLE M, SIGLE MPL (= *Département(s) et Région(s)/Territoire(s) d'outre-mer*) *French overseas departments and regions; see note*

> There are four *Départements d'outre-mer* or *DOMs*: Guadeloupe, Martinique, La Réunion and French Guyana. They are run in the same way as metropolitan *départements* and their inhabitants are French citizens. In administrative terms they are also *Régions*, and in this regard are also referred to as *ROM* (*Régions d'outre-mer*). The term *DOM-TOM* is still commonly used, but the term *Territoire d'outre-mer* has been superseded by that of *Collectivité d'outre-mer* (COM). The COMs include French Polynesia, Wallis-and-Futuna, New Caledonia and polar territories. They are independent, but each is supervised by a representative of the French government.

don [dɔ̃] NM (*cadeau*) gift; (*charité*) donation; (*aptitude*) gift, talent; **avoir des dons pour** to have a gift *ou* talent for; **faire ~ de** to make a gift of; **~ en argent** cash donation; **elle a le ~**

de m'énerver she's got a knack of getting on my nerves

donateur, -trice [dɔnatœR, -tRis] NM/F donor

donation [dɔnasjɔ̃] NF donation

donc [dɔ̃k] CONJ therefore, so; (*après une digression*) so, then; (*intensif*): **voilà ~ la solution** so there's the solution; **je disais ~ que ...** as I was saying, ...; **venez ~ dîner à la maison** do come for dinner; **allons ~!** come now!; **faites ~** go ahead

dongle [dɔ̃gl] NM dongle

donjon [dɔ̃ʒɔ̃] NM keep

don Juan [dɔ̃ʒɥɑ̃] NM Don Juan

donnant, e [dɔnɑ̃, -ɑ̃t] ADJ: **~, ~** fair's fair

donne [dɔn] NF (*Cartes*): **il y a mauvaise** *ou* **fausse ~** there's been a misdeal

donné, e [dɔne] ADJ (*convenu: lieu, heure*) given; (*pas cher*) very cheap; **données** NFPL (*Math, Inform, gén*) data; **c'est ~** it's a gift; **étant ~ que ...** given that ...

données [dɔne] NFPL data

donner [dɔne] /1/ VT to give; (*vieux habits etc*) to give away; (*spectacle*) to put on; (*film*) to show; **~ qch à qn** to give sb sth, give sth to sb; **~ sur** (*fenêtre, chambre*) to look (out) onto; **~ dans** (*piège etc*) to fall into; **faire ~ l'infanterie** (*Mil*) to send in the infantry; **~ l'heure à qn** to tell sb the time; **~ le ton** (*fig*) to set the tone; **~ à penser/entendre que ...** to make one think/give one to understand that ...; **ça donne soif/faim** it makes you (feel) thirsty/hungry; **se ~ à fond** (**à son travail**) to give one's all (to one's work); **se ~ du mal** *ou* **de la peine** (**pour faire qch**) to go to a lot of trouble (to do sth); **s'en ~ à cœur joie** (*fam*) to have a great time (of it)

donneur, -euse [dɔnœR, -øz] NM/F (*Méd*) donor; (*Cartes*) dealer; **~ de sang** blood donor

MOT-CLÉ

dont [dɔ̃] PRON RELATIF **1** (*appartenance: objets*) whose, of which; (: *êtres animés*) whose; **la maison dont le toit est rouge** the house the roof of which is red, the house whose roof is red; **l'homme dont je connais la sœur** the man whose sister I know

2 (*parmi lesquel(le)s*): **deux livres, dont l'un est ...** two books, one of which is ...; **il y avait plusieurs personnes, dont Gabrielle** there were several people, among them Gabrielle; **10 blessés, dont 2 grièvement** 10 injured, 2 of them seriously

3 (*complément d'adjectif: de verbe*): **le fils dont il est si fier** the son he's so proud of; **le pays dont il est originaire** the country he's from; **ce dont je parle** what I'm talking about; **la façon dont il l'a fait** the way (in which) he did it

donzelle [dɔ̃zɛl] NF (*péj*) young madam

dopage [dɔpaʒ] NM (*Sport*) drug use; (*de cheval*) doping

dopant [dɔpɑ̃] NM dope

doper [dɔpe] /1/ VT to dope; **se doper** VI to take dope

doping [dɔpiŋ] NM doping; (*excitant*) dope

d

dorade [dɔʀad] NF = **daurade**

doré, e [dɔʀe] ADJ golden; (avec dorure) gilt, gilded

dorénavant [dɔʀenavɑ̃] ADV from now on, henceforth

dorer [dɔʀe] /1/ VT (cadre) to gild; (faire) ~ (Culin) to brown (: gâteau) to glaze; **se ~ au soleil** to sunbathe; **~ la pilule à qn** to sugar the pill for sb

dorloter [dɔʀlɔte] /1/ VT to pamper, cosset (BRIT); **se faire ~** to be pampered ou cosseted

dormant, e [dɔʀmɑ̃, -ɑ̃t] ADJ: **eau ~** still water

dorme etc [dɔʀm] VB voir **dormir**

dormeur, -euse [dɔʀmœʀ, -øz] NM/F sleeper

dormir [dɔʀmiʀ] /16/ VI to sleep; (être endormi) to be asleep; **~ à poings fermés** to sleep very soundly

dorsal, e, -aux [dɔʀsal, -o] ADJ dorsal; voir **rouleau**

dortoir [dɔʀtwaʀ] NM dormitory

dorure [dɔʀyʀ] NF gilding

doryphore [dɔʀifɔʀ] NM Colorado beetle

dos [do] NM back; (de livre) spine; "**voir au ~**" "see over"; **robe décolletée dans le ~** low-backed dress; **de ~** from the back, from behind; **~ à ~** back to back; **sur le ~** on one's back; **à ~ de chameau** riding on a camel; **avoir bon ~** to be a good excuse; **se mettre qn à ~** to turn sb against one

dosage [dozaʒ] NM mixture

dos-d'âne [dodɑn] NM humpback; **pont en ~** humpbacked bridge

dose [doz] NF (Méd) dose; **forcer la ~** (fig) to overstep the mark

doser [doze] /1/ VT to measure out; (mélanger) to mix in the correct proportions; (fig) to expend in the right amounts ou proportions; to strike a balance between; **il faut savoir ~ ses efforts** you have to be able to pace yourself

doseur [dozœʀ] NM measure; **bouchon ~** measuring cap

dossard [dosaʀ] NM number (worn by competitor)

dossier [dosje] NM (renseignements, fichier) file; (enveloppe) folder, file; (de chaise) back; (Presse) feature; (Inform) folder; **un ~ scolaire** a school report; **le ~ social/monétaire** (fig) the social/financial question; **~ suspendu** suspension file

dot [dɔt] NF dowry

dotation [dɔtasjɔ̃] NF block grant; endowment

doté, e [dɔte] ADJ: **~ de** equipped with

doter [dɔte] /1/ VT: **~ qn/qch de** to equip sb/sth with

douairière [dwɛʀjɛʀ] NF dowager

douane [dwan] NF (poste, bureau) customs pl; (taxes) (customs) duty; **passer la ~** to go through customs; **en ~** (marchandises, entrepôt) bonded

douanier, -ière [dwanje, -jɛʀ] ADJ customs cpd ▶ NM customs officer

doublage [dublaʒ] NM (Ciné) dubbing

double [dubl] ADJ, ADV double ▶ NM (autre exemplaire) duplicate, copy; (sosie) double; (Tennis) doubles sg; (2 fois plus) **le ~ (de)** twice as much (ou many) (as), double the amount (ou number) (of); **voir ~** to see double; **en ~ (exemplaire)** in duplicate; **faire ~ emploi** to be redundant; **à ~ sens** with a double meaning; **à ~ tranchant** two-edged; **~ carburateur** twin carburettor; **à doubles commandes** dual-control; **~ messieurs/mixte** men's/mixed doubles sg; **~ toit** (de tente) fly sheet; **~ vue** second sight

doublé, e [duble] ADJ (vêtement): **~ (de)** lined (with)

double-cliquer [dubl(ə)klike] /1/ VI (Inform) to double-click

doublement [dubləmɑ̃] NM doubling; twofold increase ▶ ADV doubly; (pour deux raisons) in two ways, on two counts

doubler [duble] /1/ VT (multiplier par 2) to double; (vêtement) to line; (dépasser) to overtake, pass; (film) to dub; (acteur) to stand in for ▶ VI to double, increase twofold; **se ~ de** to be coupled with; **~ (la classe)** (Scol) to repeat a year; **~ un cap** (Navig) to round a cape; (fig) to get over a hurdle

doublure [dublyʀ] NF lining; (Ciné) stand-in

douce [dus] ADJ F voir **doux**

douceâtre [dusɑtʀ] ADJ sickly sweet

doucement [dusmɑ̃] ADV gently; (à voix basse) softly; (lentement) slowly

doucereux, -euse [dusʀø, -øz] ADJ (péj) sugary

douceur [dusœʀ] NF softness; sweetness; (de climat) mildness; (de quelqu'un) gentleness; **douceurs** NFPL (friandises) sweets (BRIT), candy sg (US); **en ~** gently

douche [duʃ] NF shower; **douches** NFPL shower room sg; **prendre une ~** to have ou take a shower; **~ écossaise**, (fig) **~ froide** (fig) let-down

doucher [duʃe] /1/ VT: **~ qn** to give sb a shower; (mouiller) to drench sb; (fig) to give sb a telling-off; **se doucher** VI to have ou take a shower

doudoune [dudun] NF padded jacket; (fam) boob

doué, e [dwe] ADJ gifted, talented; **~ de** endowed with; **être ~ pour** to have a gift for

douille [duj] NF (Élec) socket; (de projectile) case

douillet, te [dujɛ, -ɛt] ADJ cosy; (péj: à la douleur) soft

douleur [dulœʀ] NF pain; (chagrin) grief, distress; **ressentir des douleurs** to feel pain; **il a eu la ~ de perdre son père** he suffered the grief of losing his father

douloureux, -euse [duluʀø, -øz] ADJ painful

doute [dut] NM doubt; **sans ~** adv no doubt; (probablement) probably; **sans nul** ou **aucun ~** without (a) doubt; **hors de ~** beyond doubt; **nul ~** there's no doubt that; **mettre en ~** to call into question; **mettre en ~ que** to question whether

douter [dute] /1/ VT to doubt; **~ de** vt (allié, sincérité de qn) to have (one's) doubts about, doubt; (résultat, réussite) to be doubtful of; **~ que** to doubt whether ou if; **j'en doute** I have my doubts; **se ~ de qch/que** to suspect sth/that; **je m'en doutais** I suspected as much; **il ne se doutait de rien** he didn't suspect a thing

douteux, -euse [dutø, -øz] ADJ (*incertain*) doubtful; (*discutable*) dubious, questionable; (*péj*) dubious-looking

douve [duv] NF (*de château*) moat; (*de tonneau*) stave

Douvres [duvʀ] N Dover

doux, douce [du, dus] ADJ (*lisse, moelleux, pas vif: couleur, non calcaire: eau*) soft; (*sucré, agréable*) sweet; (*peu fort: moutarde etc, clément: climat*) mild; (*pas brusque*) gentle; **en douce** (*partir etc*) on the quiet

douzaine [duzɛn] NF (12) dozen; (*environ 12*): **une ~ (de)** a dozen or so, twelve or so

douze [duz] NUM twelve

douzième [duzjɛm] NUM twelfth

doyen, ne [dwajɛ̃, -ɛn] NM/F (*en âge, ancienneté*) most senior member; (*de faculté*) dean

DPLG ABR (= *diplômé par le gouvernement*) *extra certificate for architects, engineers etc*

Dr ABR (= *docteur*) Dr

dr. ABR (= *droit(e)*) R, r

draconien, ne [dʀakɔnjɛ̃, -ɛn] ADJ draconian, stringent

dragage [dʀagaʒ] NM dredging

dragée [dʀaʒe] NF sugared almond; (*Méd*) (sugar-coated) pill

dragéifié, e [dʀaʒeifje] ADJ (*Méd*) sugar-coated

dragon [dʀagɔ̃] NM dragon

drague [dʀag] NF (*filet*) dragnet; (*bateau*) dredger

draguer [dʀage] /1/ VT (*rivière: pour nettoyer*) to dredge; (*: pour trouver qch*) to drag; (*fam*) to try and pick up, chat up (BRIT) ▶ VI (*fam*) to try and pick sb up, chat sb up (BRIT)

dragueur [dʀagœʀ] NM (*aussi:* **dragueur de mines**) minesweeper; (*fam*): **quel ~!** he's a great one for picking up girls!

drain [dʀɛ̃] NM (*Méd*) drain

drainage [dʀɛnaʒ] NM drainage

drainer [dʀɛne] /1/ VT to drain; (*fig: visiteurs, région*) to drain off

dramatique [dʀamatik] ADJ dramatic; (*tragique*) tragic ▶ NF (*TV*) (television) drama

dramatisation [dʀamatizasjɔ̃] NF dramatization

dramatiser [dʀamatize] /1/ VT to dramatize

dramaturge [dʀamatyʀʒ] NM dramatist, playwright

drame [dʀam] NM (*Théât*) drama; (*catastrophe*) drama, tragedy; **~ familial** family drama

drap [dʀa] NM (*de lit*) sheet; (*tissu*) woollen fabric; **~ de plage** beach towel

drapé [dʀape] NM (*d'un vêtement*) hang

drapeau, x [dʀapo] NM flag; **sous les ~** with the colours (BRIT) *ou* colors (US), in the army

draper [dʀape] /1/ VT to drape; (*robe, jupe*) to arrange

draperies [dʀapʀi] NFPL hangings

drap-housse [dʀaus] (*pl* **draps-housses**) NM fitted sheet

drapier [dʀapje] NM (*woollen*) cloth manufacturer; (*marchand*) clothier

drastique [dʀastik] ADJ drastic

dressage [dʀesaʒ] NM training

dresser [dʀese] /1/ VT (*mettre vertical, monter: tente*) to put up, erect; (*fig: liste, bilan, contrat*) to draw up; (*animal*) to train; **se dresser** VI (*falaise, obstacle*) to stand; (*avec grandeur, menace*) to tower (up); (*personne*) to draw o.s. up; **~ l'oreille** to prick up one's ears; **~ la table** to set *ou* lay the table; **~ qn contre qn d'autre** to set sb against sb else; **~ un procès-verbal** *ou* **une contravention à qn** to book sb

dresseur, -euse [dʀesœʀ, -øz] NM/F trainer

dressoir [dʀeswaʀ] NM dresser

dribbler [dʀible] /1/ VT, VI (*Sport*) to dribble

drille [dʀij] NM: **joyeux ~** cheerful sort

drogue [dʀɔg] NF drug; **la ~** drugs *pl*; **~ dure/ douce** hard/soft drugs *pl*

drogué, e [dʀɔge] NM/F drug addict

droguer [dʀɔge] /1/ VT (*victime*) to drug; (*malade*) to give drugs to; **se droguer** VI (*aux stupéfiants*) to take drugs; (*péj: de médicaments*) to dose o.s. up

droguerie [dʀɔgʀi] NF ≈ hardware shop (BRIT) *ou* store (US)

droguiste [dʀɔgist] NM ≈ keeper (*ou* owner) of a hardware shop *ou* store

droit, e [dʀwa, dʀwat] ADJ (*non courbe*) straight; (*vertical*) upright, straight; (*fig: loyal, franc*) upright, straight(forward); (*opposé à gauche*) right, right-hand ▶ ADV straight ▶ NM (*prérogative, Boxe*) right; (*taxe*) duty, tax; (*: d'inscription*) fee; (*lois, branche*): **le ~** law ▶ NF (*Pol*) right (wing); (*ligne*) straight line; **~ au but** *ou* **au fait/cœur** straight to the point/heart; **avoir le ~ de** to be allowed to; **avoir ~ à** to be entitled to; **être en ~ de** to have a *ou* the right to; **faire ~ à** to grant, accede to; **être dans son ~** to be within one's rights; **à bon ~** (*justement*) with good reason; **de quel ~?** by what right?; **à qui de ~** to whom it may concern; **à ~** on the right; (*direction*) (to the) right; **à ~ de** to the right of; **de ~, sur votre ~** on your right; (*Pol*) right-wing; **~ d'auteur** copyright; **avoir ~ de cité (dans)** (*fig*) to belong (to); **~ coutumier** common law; **~ de regard** right of access *ou* inspection; **~ de réponse** right to reply; **~ de visite** (right of) access; **~ de vote** (right to) vote; **droits d'auteur** (*rémunération*) royalties; **droits de douane** customs duties; **droits de l'homme** human rights; **droits d'inscription** enrolment *ou* registration fees

droitement [dʀwatmã] ADV (*agir*) uprightly

droitier, -ière [dʀwatje, -jɛʀ] NM/F right-handed person ▶ ADJ right-handed

droiture [dʀwatyʀ] NF uprightness, straightness

drôle [dʀol] ADJ (*amusant*) funny, amusing; (*bizarre*) funny, peculiar; **un ~ de ...** (*bizarre*) a strange *ou* funny ...; (*intensif*) an incredible ..., a terrific ...

drôlement [dʀolmã] ADV funnily; peculiarly; (*très*) terribly, awfully; **il fait ~ froid** it's awfully cold

drôlerie [dʀolʀi] NF funniness; funny thing

dromadaire [dʀɔmadɛʀ] NM dromedary

dru, e [dʀy] ADJ (*cheveux*) thick, bushy; (*pluie*) heavy ▶ ADV (*pousser*) thickly; (*tomber*) heavily

drugstore [dʀœgstɔʀ] NM drugstore
druide [dʀɥid] NM Druid
ds ABR = **dans**
DST SIGLE F (= *Direction de la surveillance du territoire*)
internal security service, ≈ MI5 (BRIT)
DT SIGLE M (= *diphtérie tétanos*) *vaccine*
DTCP SIGLE M (= *diphtérie tétanos coqueluche polio*)
vaccine
DTP SIGLE M (= *diphtérie tétanos polio*) *vaccine*
DTTAB SIGLE M (= *diphtérie tétanos typhoïde A et B*)
vaccine
du [dy] ART *voir* **de = de + le**
dû, due [dy] PP *de* **devoir** ▸ ADJ (*somme*) owing,
owed; (: *venant à échéance*) due; (*causé par*):
dû à due to ▸ NM due; (*somme*) dues *pl*
dualisme [dɥalism] NM dualism
Dubaï, Dubay [dybaj] N Dubai
dubitatif, -ive [dybitatif, -iv] ADJ doubtful,
dubious
Dublin [dyblɛ̃] N Dublin
duc [dyk] NM duke
duché [dyʃe] NM dukedom, duchy
duchesse [dyʃɛs] NF duchess
duel [dɥɛl] NM duel
duettiste [dɥetist] NMF duettist
duffel-coat [dœfœlkot] NM duffel coat
dûment [dymɑ̃] ADV duly
dumping [dœmpiŋ] NM dumping
dune [dyn] NF dune
Dunkerque [dɔ̃kɛʀk] N Dunkirk
duo [dɥo] NM (*Mus*) duet; (*fig: couple*) duo, pair
dupe [dyp] NF dupe ▸ ADJ: (**ne pas**) **être ~ de**
(not) to be taken in by
duper [dype] /**1**/ VT to dupe, deceive
duperie [dypʀi] NF deception, dupery
duplex [dyplɛks] NM (*appartement*) split-level
apartment, duplex; (*TV*): **émission en ~**
link-up
duplicata [dyplikata] NM duplicate
duplicateur [dyplikatœʀ] NM duplicator; **~ à**
alcool spirit duplicator
duplicité [dyplisite] NF duplicity
duquel [dykɛl] *voir* **lequel**
dur, e [dyʀ] ADJ (*pierre, siège, travail, problème*) hard;
(*lumière, voix, climat*) harsh; (*sévère*) hard, harsh;
(*cruel*) hard(-hearted); (*porte, col*) stiff;

(*viande*) tough ▸ ADV hard ▸ NF: **à la ~** rough
▸ NM (*fam: meneur*) tough nut; **mener la vie ~ à**
qn to give sb a hard time; **~ d'oreille** hard of
hearing
durabilité [dyʀabilite] NF durability
durable [dyʀabl] ADJ lasting
durablement [dyʀabləmɑ̃] ADV for the long
term
durant [dyʀɑ̃] PRÉP (*au cours de*) during; (*pendant*)
for; **~ des mois, des mois ~** for months
durcir [dyʀsiʀ] /**2**/ VT, VI to harden; **se durcir** VI
to harden
durcissement [dyʀsismɑ̃] NM hardening
durée [dyʀe] NF length; (*d'une pile etc*) life;
(*déroulement: des opérations etc*) duration; **pour**
une ~ illimitée for an unlimited length of
time; **de courte ~** (*séjour, répit*) brief, short-term;
de longue ~ (*effet*) long-term; **pile de longue ~**
long-life battery
durement [dyʀmɑ̃] ADV harshly
durent [dyʀ] VB *voir* **devoir**
durer [dyʀe] /**1**/ VI to last
dureté [dyʀte] NF (*voir dur*) hardness;
harshness; stiffness; toughness
durillon [dyʀijɔ̃] NM callus
durit® [dyʀit] NF (car radiator) hose
DUT SIGLE M (= **Diplôme universitaire de**
technologie)
dut *etc* [dy] VB *voir* **devoir**
duvet [dyve] NM down; (**sac de couchage en**) **~**
down-filled sleeping bag
duveteux, -euse [dyvtø, -øz] ADJ downy
DVD SIGLE M (= *digital versatile disc*) DVD
dynamique [dinamik] ADJ dynamic
dynamiser [dinamize] /**1**/ VT to pep up, enliven;
(*équipe, service*) to inject some dynamism into
dynamisme [dinamism] NM dynamism
dynamite [dinamit] NF dynamite
dynamiter [dinamite] /**1**/ VT to (blow up with)
dynamite
dynamo [dinamo] NF dynamo
dynastie [dinasti] NF dynasty
dysenterie [disɑ̃tʀi] NF dysentery
dyslexie [dislɛksi] NF dyslexia, word blindness
dyslexique [dislɛksik] ADJ dyslexic
dyspepsie [dispɛpsi] NF dyspepsia

Ee

E, e [ə] NM INV E, e ▶ ABR (= *Est*) E; **E comme Eugène** E for Edward (*BRIT*) ou Easy (*US*)

EAO SIGLE M (= *enseignement assisté par ordinateur*) CAL (= *computer-aided learning*)

EAU SIGLE MPL (= *Émirats arabes unis*) UAE (= *United Arab Emirates*)

eau, x [o] NF water ▶ NFPL (*Méd*) waters; **prendre l'~** (*chaussure etc*) to leak, let in water; **prendre les ~** to take the waters; **faire ~** to leak; **tomber à l'~** (*fig*) to fall through; **à l'~ de rose** slushy, sentimental; **~ bénite** holy water; **~ de Cologne** eau de Cologne; **~ courante** running water; **~ distillée** distilled water; **~ douce** fresh water; **~ gazeuse** sparkling (mineral) water; **~ de Javel** bleach; **~ lourde** heavy water; **~ minérale** mineral water; **~ oxygénée** hydrogen peroxide; **~ plate** still water; **~ de pluie** rainwater; **~ salée** salt water; **~ de toilette** toilet water; **~ ménagères** dirty water (*from washing up etc*); **~ territoriales** territorial waters; **~ usées** liquid waste

eau-de-vie [odvi] (*pl* **eaux-de-vie**) NF brandy

eau-forte [ofɔrt] (*pl* **eaux-fortes**) NF etching

ébahi, e [ebai] ADJ dumbfounded, flabbergasted

ébahir [ebaiʀ] /**2**/ VT to astonish, astound

ébats [eba] VB *voir* **ébattre** ▶ NMPL frolics, gambols

ébattre [ebatʀ] /**41**/: **s'ébattre** VI to frolic

ébauche [eboʃ] NF (rough) outline, sketch

ébaucher [eboʃe] /**1**/ VT to sketch out, outline; (*fig*): **~ un sourire/geste** to give a hint of a smile/make a slight gesture; **s'ébaucher** VI to take shape

ébène [ebɛn] NF ebony

ébéniste [ebenist] NM cabinetmaker

ébénisterie [ebenistri] NF cabinetmaking; (*bâti*) cabinetwork

éberlué, e [ebɛʀlɥe] ADJ astounded, flabbergasted

éblouir [ebluiʀ] /**2**/ VT to dazzle

éblouissant, e [ebluisã, -ãt] ADJ dazzling

éblouissement [ebluismã] NM dazzle; (*faiblesse*) dizzy turn

ébonite [ebɔnit] NF vulcanite

éborgner [ebɔʀɲe] /**1**/ VT: **~ qn** to blind sb in one eye

éboueur [ebwœʀ] NM dustman (*BRIT*), garbage man (*US*)

ébouillanter [ebujãte] /**1**/ VT to scald; (*Culin*) to blanch; **s'ébouillanter** VI to scald o.s.

éboulement [ebulmã] NM falling rocks *pl*, rock fall; (*amas*) heap of boulders *etc*

ébouler [ebule] /**1**/: **s'ébouler** VI to crumble, collapse

éboulis [ebuli] NMPL fallen rocks

ébouriffé, e [eburife] ADJ tousled, ruffled

ébouriffer [eburife] /**1**/ VT to tousle, ruffle

ébranlement [ebʀãlmã] NM shaking

ébranler [ebʀãle] /**1**/ VT to shake; (*rendre instable: mur, santé*) to weaken; **s'ébranler** VI (*partir*) to move off

ébrécher [ebʀeʃe] /**6**/ VT to chip

ébriété [ebʀijete] NF: **en état d'~** in a state of intoxication

ébrouer [ebʀue] /**1**/: **s'ébrouer** VI (*souffler*) to snort; (*s'agiter*) to shake o.s.

ébruiter [ebʀɥite] /**1**/ VT, **s'ébruiter** VI to spread

ébullition [ebylisjɔ̃] NF boiling point; **en ~** boiling; (*fig*) in an uproar

écaille [ekaj] NF (*de poisson*) scale; (*de coquillage*) shell; (*matière*) tortoiseshell; (*de roc etc*) flake

écaillé, e [ekaje] ADJ (*peinture*) flaking

écailler [ekaje] /**1**/ VT (*poisson*) to scale; (*huître*) to open; **s'écailler** VI to flake ou peel (off)

écarlate [ekaʀlat] ADJ scarlet

écarquiller [ekaʀkije] /**1**/ VT: **~ les yeux** to stare wide-eyed

écart [ekaʀ] NM gap; (*embardée*) swerve; (*saut*) sideways leap; (*fig*) departure, deviation; **à l'~** *adv* out of the way; **à l'~ de** *prép* away from; (*fig*) out of; **faire un ~** (*voiture*) to swerve; **faire le grand ~** (*Danse, Gym*) to do the splits; **~ de conduite** misdemeanour

écarté, e [ekaʀte] ADJ (*lieu*) out-of-the-way, remote; (*ouvert*): **les jambes écartées** legs apart; **les bras écartés** arms outstretched

écarteler [ekaʀtəle] /**5**/ VT to quarter; (*fig*) to tear

écartement [ekaʀtəmã] NM space, gap; (*Rail*) gauge

écarter [ekaʀte] /**1**/ VT (*séparer*) to move apart, separate; (*éloigner*) to push back, move away; (*ouvrir: bras, jambes*) to spread, open; (: *rideau*) to draw (back); (*éliminer: candidat, possibilité*) to dismiss; (*Cartes*) to discard; **s'écarter** VI to part; (*personne*) to move away; **s'écarter de** to wander from

ecchymose [ekimoz] NF bruise

ecclésiastique [eklezjastik] ADJ ecclesiastical
▶ NM ecclesiastic

écervelé, e [esɛrvəle] ADJ scatterbrained,
featherbrained

ECG SIGLE M (= *électrocardiogramme*) ECG

échafaud [eʃafo] NM scaffold

échafaudage [eʃafodaʒ] NM scaffolding; (*fig*)
heap, pile

échafauder [eʃafode] /1/ VT (*plan*) to construct

échalas [eʃala] NM stake, pole; (*personne*)
beanpole

échalote [eʃalɔt] NF shallot

échancré, e [eʃɑ̃kre] ADJ (*robe, corsage*)
low-necked; (*côte*) indented

échancrure [eʃɑ̃kryr] NF (*de robe*) scoop
neckline; (*de côte, arête rocheuse*) indentation

échange [eʃɑ̃ʒ] NM exchange; **en ~** in exchange;
en ~ de in exchange *ou* return for; **libre ~** free
trade; **~ de lettres/politesses/vues** exchange
of letters/civilities/views; **échanges
commerciaux** trade; **échanges culturels**
cultural exchanges

échangeable [eʃɑ̃ʒabl] ADJ exchangeable

échanger [eʃɑ̃ʒe] /3/ VT: **~ qch (contre)** to
exchange sth (for)

échangeur [eʃɑ̃ʒœr] NM (*Auto*) interchange

échantillon [eʃɑ̃tijɔ̃] NM sample

échantillonnage [eʃɑ̃tijɔnaʒ] NM selection of
samples

échappatoire [eʃapatwar] NF way out

échappée [eʃape] NF (*vue*) vista; (*Cyclisme*)
breakaway

échappement [eʃapmɑ̃] NM (*Auto*) exhaust;
~ libre cutout

échapper [eʃape] /1/: **~ à** VT (*gardien*) to escape
(from); (*punition, péril*) to escape; **~ à qn** (*détail,
sens*) to escape sb; (*objet qu'on tient: aussi:* **échapper
des mains de qn**) to slip out of sb's hands;
laisser ~ to let fall; (*cri etc*) to let out; **l'~ belle** to
have a narrow escape

écharde [eʃard] NF splinter (of wood)

écharpe [eʃarp] NF scarf; (*de maire*) sash; (*Méd*)
sling; **avoir le bras en ~** to have one's arm in a
sling; **prendre en ~** (*dans une collision*) to hit
sideways on

écharper [eʃarpe] /1/ VT to tear to pieces

échasse [eʃas] NF stilt

échassier [eʃasje] NM wader

échauder [eʃode] /1/ VT: **se faire ~** (*fig*) to get
one's fingers burnt

échauffement [eʃofmɑ̃] NM overheating;
(*Sport*) warm-up

échauffer [eʃofe] /1/ VT (*métal, moteur*) to
overheat; (*fig: exciter*) to fire, excite; **s'échauffer**
VI (*Sport*) to warm up; (*discussion*) to become
heated

échauffourée [eʃofure] NF clash, brawl; (*Mil*)
skirmish

échéance [eʃeɑ̃s] NF (*d'un paiement: date*)
settlement date; (*: somme due*) financial
commitment(s); (*fig*) deadline; **à brève/
longue ~** *adj* short-/long-term; *adv* in the short/
long term

échéancier [eʃeɑ̃sje] NM schedule

échéant [eʃeɑ̃]: **le cas ~** *adv* if the case arises

échec [eʃɛk] NM failure; (*Échecs*): **~ et mat/au
roi** checkmate/check; **échecs** NMPL (*jeu*) chess
sg; **mettre en ~** to put in check; **tenir en ~** to
hold in check; **faire ~ à** to foil, thwart

échelle [eʃɛl] NF ladder; (*fig, d'une carte*) scale; **à
l'~ de** on the scale of; **sur une grande/petite ~**
on a large/small scale; **faire la courte ~ à qn** to
give sb a leg up; **~ de corde** rope ladder

échelon [eʃ(ə)lɔ̃] NM (*d'échelle*) rung; (*Admin*)
grade

échelonner [eʃ(ə)lɔne] /1/ VT to space out,
spread out; (*versement*) **échelonné**
(payment) by instalments

écheveau, x [eʃvo] NM skein, hank

échevelé, e [eʃəvle] ADJ tousled, dishevelled;
(*fig*) wild, frenzied

échine [eʃin] NF backbone, spine

échiner [eʃine] /1/: **s'échiner** VI (*se fatiguer*) to
work o.s. to the bone

échiquier [eʃikje] NM chessboard

écho [eko] NM echo; **échos** NMPL (*potins*) gossip
sg, rumours; (*Presse: rubrique*) "news in brief";
rester sans ~ (*suggestion etc*) to come to nothing;
se faire l'~ de to repeat, spread about

échographie [ekɔgrafi] NF ultrasound (scan);
passer une ~ to have a scan

échoir [eʃwar] VI (*dette*) to fall due; (*délais*) to
expire; **~ à** VT to fall to

échoppe [eʃɔp] NF stall, booth

échouer [eʃwe] /1/ VI to fail; (*débris etc: sur la plage*)
to be washed up; (*aboutir: personne dans un café etc*)
to arrive ▶ VT (*bateau*) to ground; **s'échouer** VI to
run aground

échu, e [eʃy] PP *de* **échoir** ▶ ADJ due, mature

échut *etc* [eʃy] VB *voir* **échoir**

éclabousser [eklabuse] /1/ VT to splash; (*fig*) to
tarnish

éclaboussure [eklabusyr] NF splash; (*fig*) stain

éclair [eklɛr] NM (*d'orage*) flash of lightning,
lightning *no pl*; (*Photo: de flash*) flash; (*fig*) flash,
spark; (*gâteau*) éclair

éclairage [eklɛraʒ] NM lighting

éclairagiste [eklɛraʒist] NMF lighting
engineer

éclaircie [eklɛrsi] NF bright *ou* sunny interval

éclaircir [eklɛrsir] /2/ VT to lighten; (*fig: mystère*)
to clear up; (*point*) to clarify; (*Culin*) to thin
(down); **s'éclaircir** VI (*ciel*) to brighten up, clear;
(*cheveux*) to go thin; (*situation etc*) to become
clearer; **s'éclaircir la voix** to clear one's throat

éclaircissement [eklɛrsismɑ̃] NM clearing up,
clarification

éclairer [eklere] /1/ VT (*lieu*) to light (up);
(*personne: avec une lampe de poche etc*) to light the
way for; (*fig: instruire*) to enlighten; (: *rendre
compréhensible*) to shed light on ▶ VI: **~ mal/bien**
to give a poor/good light; **s'éclairer** VI (*phare, rue*)
to light up; (*situation etc*) to become clearer;
s'éclairer à la bougie/l'électricité to use
candlelight/have electric lighting

éclaireur, -euse [eklɛrœr, -øz] NM/F (*scout*)
(boy) scout/(girl) guide ▶ NM (*Mil*) scout;

partir en ~ to go off to reconnoitre

éclat [ekla] NM (de bombe, de verre) fragment; (du soleil, d'une couleur etc) brightness, brilliance; (d'une cérémonie) splendour; (scandale): **faire un ~** to cause a commotion; **action d'~** outstanding action; **voler en éclats** to shatter; **des éclats de verre** broken glass; flying glass; **~ de rire** burst ou roar of laughter; **~ de voix** shout

éclatant, e [eklatɑ̃, -ɑ̃t] ADJ brilliant, bright; (succès) resounding; (revanche) devastating

éclater [eklate] /1/ VI (pneu) to burst; (bombe) to explode; (guerre, épidémie) to break out; (groupe, parti) to break up; **~ de rire/en sanglots** to burst out laughing/sobbing

éclectique [eklɛktik] ADJ eclectic

éclipse [eklips] NF eclipse

éclipser [eklipse] /1/ VT to eclipse; **s'éclipser** VI to slip away

éclopé, e [eklɔpe] ADJ lame

éclore [eklɔR] /45/ VI (œuf) to hatch; (fleur) to open (out)

éclosion [eklozjɔ̃] NF blossoming

écluse [eklyz] NF lock

éclusier [eklyzje] NM lock keeper

éco- [eko] PRÉFIXE eco-

écœurant, e [ekœRɑ̃, -ɑ̃t] ADJ sickening; (gâteau etc) sickly

écœurement [ekœRmɑ̃] NM disgust

écœurer [ekœRe] VT: **~ qn** (nourriture) to make sb feel sick; (fig: conduite, personne) to disgust sb

école [ekɔl] NF school; **aller à l'~** to go to school; **faire ~** to collect a following; **les grandes écoles** prestige university-level colleges with competitive entrance examinations; **~ maternelle** nursery school; see note; **~ primaire** primary (BRIT) ou grade (US) school; **~ secondaire** secondary (BRIT) ou high (US) school; **~ privée/publique/élémentaire** private/state/elementary school; **~ de dessin/danse/musique** art/dancing/music school; **~ hôtelière** catering college; **~ normale (d'instituteurs)** primary school teachers' training college; **~ normale supérieure** grande école for training secondary school teachers; **~ de secrétariat** secretarial college

Nursery school (kindergarten) (l'école maternelle) is publicly funded in France and, though not compulsory, is attended by most children between the ages of three and six. Statutory education begins with primary (grade) school (l'école primaire) and is attended by children between the ages of six and 10 or 11.

écolier, -ière [ekɔlje, -jɛR] NM/F schoolboy/girl

écolo [ekɔlo] NMF (fam) ecologist ▸ ADJ ecological

écologie [ekɔlɔʒi] NF ecology; (sujet scolaire) environmental studies pl

écologique [ekɔlɔʒik] ADJ ecological; environment-friendly

écologiste [ekɔlɔʒist] NMF ecologist; environmentalist

éconduire [ekɔ̃dɥiR] /38/ VT to dismiss

économat [ekɔnɔma] NM (fonction) bursarship

(BRIT), treasurership (US); (bureau) bursar's office (BRIT), treasury (US)

économe [ekɔnɔm] ADJ thrifty ▸ NMF (de lycée etc) bursar (BRIT), treasurer (US)

économétrie [ekɔnɔmetRi] NF econometrics sg

économie [ekɔnɔmi] NF (vertu) economy, thrift; (gain: d'argent, de temps etc) saving; (science) economics sg; (situation économique) economy; **économies** NFPL (pécule) savings; **faire des économies** to save up; **une ~ de temps/d'argent** a saving in time/of money; **~ dirigée** planned economy; **~ de marché** market economy

économique [ekɔnɔmik] ADJ (avantageux) economical; (Écon) economic

économiquement [ekɔnɔmikmɑ̃] ADV economically; **les ~ faibles** (Admin) the low-paid, people on low incomes

économiser [ekɔnɔmize] /1/ VT, VI to save

économiseur [ekɔnɔmizœR] NM: **~ d'écran** (Inform) screen saver

économiste [ekɔnɔmist] NMF economist

écoper [ekɔpe] /1/ VI to bale out; (fig) to cop it; **~ (de)** VT to get

écorce [ekɔRs] NF bark; (de fruit) peel

écorcer [ekɔRse] /3/ VT to bark

écorché, e [ekɔRʃe] ADJ: **~ vif** flayed alive ▸ NM cut-away drawing

écorcher [ekɔRʃe] /1/ VT (animal) to skin; (égratigner) to graze; **~ une langue** to speak a language brokenly; **s'~ le genou** etc to scrape ou graze one's knee etc

écorchure [ekɔRʃyR] NF graze

écorner [ekɔRne] /1/ VT (taureau) to dehorn; (livre) to make dog-eared

écossais, e [ekɔsɛ, -ɛz] ADJ Scottish, Scots; (whisky, confiture) Scotch; (écharpe, tissu) tartan ▸ NM (Ling) Scots; (: gaélique) Gaelic; (tissu) tartan (cloth) ▸ NM/F: **É~, e** Scot, Scotsman/woman; **les É~** the Scots

Écosse [ekɔs] NF: **l'~** Scotland

écosser [ekɔse] /1/ VT to shell

écosystème [ekɔsistɛm] NM ecosystem

écot [eko] NM: **payer son ~** to pay one's share

écotaxe [ekɔtaks] NF green tax

écoulement [ekulmɑ̃] NM (de faux billets) circulation; (de stock) selling

écouler [ekule] /1/ VT to dispose of; **s'écouler** VI (eau) to flow (out); (foule) to drift away; (jours, temps) to pass (by)

écourter [ekuRte] /1/ VT to curtail, cut short

écoute [ekut] NF (Navig: cordage) sheet; (Radio, TV): **temps d'~** (listening ou viewing) time; **heure de grande ~** peak listening ou viewing time; **prendre l'~** to tune in; **rester à l'~ (de)** to stay tuned in (to); **écoutes téléphoniques** phone tapping sg

écouter [ekute] /1/ VT to listen to; **s'écouter** (malade) to be a bit of a hypochondriac; **si je m'écoutais** if I followed my instincts

écouteur [ekutœR] NM (Tél) receiver; **écouteurs** NMPL (casque) headphones, headset sg

écoutille [ekutij] NF hatch

écr. ABR = **écrire**

écrabouiller [ekʀabuje] /1/ vt to squash, crush

écran [ekʀɑ̃] nm screen; (Inform) screen, VDU; **~ de fumée/d'eau** curtain of smoke/water; **porter à l'~** (Ciné) to adapt for the screen; **le petit ~** television, the small screen; **~ tactile** touchscreen; **~ total** sunblock

écrasant, e [ekʀazɑ̃, -ɑ̃t] adj overwhelming

écraser [ekʀaze] /1/ vt to crush; (piéton) to run over; (Inform) to overwrite; **se faire ~** to be run over; **écrase(-toi)!** shut up!; **s'~ (au sol)** vi to crash; **s'~ contre** to crash into

écrémé, e [ekʀeme] adj (lait) skimmed

écrémer [ekʀeme] /6/ vt to skim

écrevisse [ekʀəvis] nf crayfish inv

écrier [ekʀije] /7/: **s'écrier** vi to exclaim

écrin [ekʀɛ̃] nm case, box

écrire [ekʀiʀ] /39/ vt, vi to write; **s'écrire** vi to write to one another; **~ à qn que** to write and tell sb that; **ça s'écrit comment?** how is it spelt?

écrit, e [ekʀi, -it] pp de **écrire** ▶ adj: **bien/mal ~** well/badly written ▶ nm document; (examen) written paper; **par ~** in writing

écriteau, x [ekʀito] nm notice, sign

écritoire [ekʀitwaʀ] nf writing case

écriture [ekʀityʀ] nf writing; (Comm) entry; **écritures** nfpl (Comm) accounts, books; **l'É-(sainte), les Écritures** the Scriptures

écrivain [ekʀivɛ̃] nm writer

écrivais etc [ekʀivɛ] vb voir **écrire**

écrou [ekʀu] nm nut

écrouer [ekʀue] /1/ vt to imprison; (provisoirement) to remand in custody

écroulé, e [ekʀule] adj (de fatigue) exhausted; (par un malheur) overwhelmed; **~ (de rire)** in stitches

écroulement [ekʀulmɑ̃] nm collapse

écrouler [ekʀule] /1/: **s'écrouler** vi to collapse

écru, e [ekʀy] adj (toile) raw, unbleached; (couleur) off-white, écru

écu [eky] nm (bouclier) shield; (monnaie: ancienne) crown; (: de la CEE) ecu

écueil [ekœj] nm reef; (fig) pitfall; stumbling block

écuelle [ekɥɛl] nf bowl

éculé, e [ekyle] adj (chaussure) down-at-heel; (fig: péj) hackneyed

écume [ekym] nf foam; (Culin) scum; **~ de mer** meerschaum

écumer [ekyme] /1/ vt (Culin) to skim; (fig) to plunder ▶ vi (mer) to foam; (fig) to boil with rage

écumoire [ekymwaʀ] nf skimmer

écureuil [ekyʀœj] nm squirrel

écurie [ekyʀi] nf stable

écusson [ekysɔ̃] nm badge

écuyer, -ère [ekɥije, -ɛʀ] nm/f rider

eczéma [ɛgzema] nm eczema

éd. abr = **édition**

édam [edam] nm (fromage) Edam

edelweiss [edɛlvajs] nm inv edelweiss

éden [edɛn] nm Eden

édenté, e [edɑ̃te] adj toothless

EDF sigle f (= Électricité de France) national electricity company

édifiant, e [edifjɑ̃, -ɑ̃t] adj edifying

édification [edifikasjɔ̃] nf (d'un bâtiment) building, erection

édifice [edifis] nm building, edifice

édifier [edifje] /7/ vt to build, erect; (fig) to edify

édiles [edil] nmpl city fathers

Édimbourg [edɛ̃buʀ] n Edinburgh

édit [edi] nm edict

édit. abr = **éditeur**

éditer [edite] /1/ vt (publier) to publish; (: disque) to produce; (préparer: texte, Inform: annoter) to edit

éditeur, -trice [editœʀ, -tʀis] nm/f publisher; editor; **~ de textes** (Inform) text editor

édition [edisjɔ̃] nf editing no pl; (série d'exemplaires) edition; (industrie du livre): **l'~** publishing; **~ sur écran** (Inform) screen editing

édito [edito] nm (fam: éditorial) editorial, leader

éditorial, -aux [editɔʀjal, -o] nm editorial, leader

éditorialiste [editɔʀjalist] nmf editorial ou leader writer

édredon [edʀədɔ̃] nm eiderdown, comforter (US)

éducateur, -trice [edykatœʀ, -tʀis] nm/f teacher; (en école spécialisée) instructor; **~ spécialisé** specialist teacher

éducatif, -ive [edykatif, -iv] adj educational

éducation [edykasjɔ̃] nf education; (familiale) upbringing; (manières) (good) manners pl; **bonne/mauvaise ~** good/bad upbringing; **sans ~** bad-mannered, ill-bred; **l'É-(nationale)** ≈ the Department for Education; **~ permanente** continuing education; **~ physique** physical education

édulcorant [edylkɔʀɑ̃] nm sweetener

édulcorer [edylkɔʀe] /1/ vt to sweeten; (fig) to tone down

éduquer [edyke] /1/ vt to educate; (élever) to bring up; (faculté) to train; **bien/mal éduqué** well/badly brought up

EEG sigle m (= électroencéphalogramme) EEG

effacé, e [efase] adj (fig) retiring, unassuming

effacer [efase] /3/ vt to erase, rub out; (bande magnétique) to erase; (Inform: fichier, fiche) to delete; **s'effacer** vi (inscription etc) to wear off; (pour laisser passer) to step aside; **~ le ventre** to pull one's stomach in

effarant, e [efaʀɑ̃, -ɑ̃t] adj alarming

effaré, e [efaʀe] adj alarmed

effarement [efaʀmɑ̃] nm alarm

effarer [efaʀe] /1/ vt to alarm

effarouchement [efaʀuʃmɑ̃] nm alarm

effaroucher [efaʀuʃe] /1/ vt to frighten ou scare away; (personne) to alarm

effectif, -ive [efɛktif, -iv] adj real; effective ▶ nm (Mil) strength; (Scol) total number of pupils, size; **effectifs** numbers, strength sg; (Comm) manpower sg; **réduire l'~ de** to downsize

effectivement [efɛktivmɑ̃] adv effectively; (réellement) actually, really; (en effet) indeed

effectuer [efɛktɥe] /1/ vt (opération, mission) to carry out; (déplacement, trajet) to make, complete; (mouvement) to execute, make;

s'effectuer vɪ to be carried out

efféminé, e [efemine] ADJ effeminate

effervescence [efɛʀvesɑ̃s] NF (*fig*): **en ~** in a turmoil

effervescent, e [efɛʀvesɑ̃, -ɑ̃t] ADJ (*cachet, boisson*) effervescent; (*fig*) agitated, in a turmoil

effet [efɛ] NM (*résultat, artifice*) effect; (*impression*) impression; (*Comm*) bill; (*Jur: d'une loi, d'un jugement*): **avec ~ rétroactif** applied retrospectively; **effets** NMPL (*vêtements etc*) things; **~ de style/couleur/lumière** stylistic/colour/lighting effect; **effets de voix** dramatic effects with one's voice; **faire ~** (*médicament*) to take effect; **faire de l'~** (*médicament, menace*) to have an effect, be effective; (*impressionner*) to make an impression; **faire bon/mauvais ~ sur qn** to make a good/bad impression on sb; **sous l'~ de** under the effect of; **donner de l'~ à une balle** (*Tennis*) to put some spin on a ball; **à cet ~** to that end; **en ~** adv indeed; **~ (de commerce)** bill of exchange; **~ de serre** greenhouse effect; **effets spéciaux** (*Ciné*) special effects

effeuiller [efœje] /1/ VT to remove the leaves (*ou* petals) from

efficace [efikas] ADJ (*personne*) efficient; (*action, médicament*) effective

efficacité [efikasite] NF efficiency; effectiveness

effigie [efiʒi] NF effigy; **brûler qn en ~** to burn an effigy of sb

effilé, e [efile] ADJ slender; (*pointe*) sharp; (*carrosserie*) streamlined

effiler [efile] /1/ VT (*cheveux*) to thin (out); (*tissu*) to fray

effilocher [efilɔʃe] /1/: **s'effilocher** vɪ to fray

efflanqué, e [eflɑ̃ke] ADJ emaciated

effleurement [eflœʀmɑ̃] NM: **touche à ~** touch-sensitive control *ou* key

effleurer [eflœʀe] /1/ VT to brush (against); (*sujet*) to touch upon; (*idée, pensée*): **~ qn** to cross sb's mind

effluves [eflyv] NMPL exhalation(s)

effondré, e [efɔ̃dʀe] ADJ (*abattu: par un malheur, échec*) overwhelmed

effondrement [efɔ̃dʀəmɑ̃] NM collapse

effondrer [efɔ̃dʀe] /1/: **s'effondrer** vɪ to collapse

efforcer [efɔʀse] /3/: **s'efforcer de** VT: **s'efforcer de faire** to try hard to do

effort [efɔʀ] NM effort; **faire un ~** to make an effort; **faire tous ses efforts** to try one's hardest; **faire l'~ de ...** to make the effort to ...; **sans ~** adj effortless; adv effortlessly; **~ de mémoire** attempt to remember; **~ de volonté** effort of will

effraction [efʀaksjɔ̃] NF breaking-in; **s'introduire par ~ dans** to break into

effrangé, e [efʀɑ̃ʒe] ADJ fringed; (*effiloché*) frayed

effrayant, e [efʀɛjɑ̃, -ɑ̃t] ADJ frightening, fearsome; (*sens affaibli*) dreadful

effrayer [efʀeje] /8/ VT to frighten, scare; (*rebuter*) to put off; **s'effrayer (de)** vɪ to be frightened *ou* scared (by)

effréné, e [efʀene] ADJ wild

effritement [efʀitmɑ̃] NM crumbling; erosion; slackening off

effriter [efʀite] /1/: **s'effriter** vɪ to crumble; (*monnaie*) to be eroded; (*valeurs*) to slacken off

effroi [efʀwa] NM terror, dread *no pl*

effronté, e [efʀɔ̃te] ADJ insolent

effrontément [efʀɔ̃temɑ̃] ADV insolently

effronterie [efʀɔ̃tʀi] NF insolence

effroyable [efʀwajabl] ADJ horrifying, appalling

effusion [efyzjɔ̃] NF effusion; **sans ~ de sang** without bloodshed

égailler [egaje] /1/: **s'égailler** vɪ to scatter, disperse

égal, e, -aux [egal, -o] ADJ (*identique, ayant les mêmes droits*) equal; (*plan: surface*) even, level; (*constant: vitesse*) steady; (*équitable*) even ▶ NM/F equal; **être ~ à** (*prix, nombre*) to be equal to; **ça m'est ~** it's all the same to me, it doesn't matter to me, I don't mind; **c'est ~, ...** all the same, ...; **sans ~** matchless, unequalled; **à l'~ de** (*comme*) just like; **d'~ à ~** as equals

également [egalmɑ̃] ADV equally; evenly; steadily; (*aussi*) too, as well

égaler [egale] /1/ VT to equal

égalisateur, -trice [egalizatœʀ, -tʀis] ADJ (*Sport*): **but ~** equalizing goal, equalizer

égalisation [egalizasjɔ̃] NF (*Sport*) equalization

égaliser [egalize] /1/ VT (*sol, salaires*) to level (out); (*chances*) to equalize ▶ VI (*Sport*) to equalize

égalitaire [egalitɛʀ] ADJ egalitarian

égalitarisme [egalitaʀism] NM egalitarianism

égalité [egalite] NF equality; evenness; steadiness; (*Math*) identity; **être à ~ (de points)** to be level; **~ de droits** equality of rights; **~ d'humeur** evenness of temper

égard [egaʀ] NM, **égards** NMPL consideration *sg*; **à cet ~** in this respect; **à certains égards/tous égards** in certain respects/all respects; **eu ~ à** in view of; **par ~ pour** out of consideration for; **sans ~ pour** without regard for; **à l'~ de** *prép* towards; (*en ce qui concerne*) concerning, as regards

égaré, e [egaʀe] ADJ lost

égarement [egaʀmɑ̃] NM distraction; aberration

égarer [egaʀe] /1/ VT (*objet*) to mislay; (*moralement*) to lead astray; **s'égarer** vɪ to get lost, lose one's way; (*objet*) to go astray; (*fig: dans une discussion*) to wander

égayer [egeje] /8/ VT (*personne*) to amuse; (: *remonter*) to cheer up; (*récit, endroit*) to brighten up, liven up

Égée [eʒe] ADJ: **la mer ~** the Aegean (Sea)

égéen, ne [eʒeɛ̃, -ɛn] ADJ Aegean

égérie [eʒeʀi] NF: **l'~ de qn/qch** the brains behind sb/sth

égide [eʒid] NF: **sous l'~ de** under the aegis of

églantier [eglɑ̃tje] NM wild *ou* dog rose(-bush)

églantine [eglɑ̃tin] NF wild *ou* dog rose

églefin [egləfɛ̃] NM haddock

église [egliz] NF church; **aller à l'~** to go to church

égocentrique [egɔsɑ̃tʀik] ADJ egocentric, self-centred

égocentrisme [egɔsɑ̃tʀism] NM egocentricity

égoïne [egɔin] NF handsaw

égoïsme [egɔism] NM selfishness, egoism

égoïste [egɔist] ADJ selfish, egoistic ▸ NMF egoist

égoïstement [egɔistəmã] ADV selfishly

égorger [egɔʀʒe] /3/ VT to cut the throat of

égosiller [egozije] /1/: **s'égosiller** VI to shout o.s. hoarse

égotisme [egɔtism] NM egotism, egoism

égout [egu] NM sewer; **eaux d'~** sewage

égoutier [egutje] NM sewer worker

égoutter [egute] /1/ VT (linge) to wring out; (vaisselle, fromage) to drain ▸ VI to drip; **s'égoutter** VI to drip

égouttoir [egutwaʀ] NM draining board; (mobile) draining rack

égratigner [egratiɲe] /1/ VT to scratch; **s'égratigner** VI to scratch o.s.

égratignure [egratiɲyʀ] NF scratch

égrener [egʀəne] /5/ VT: **~ une grappe, ~ des raisins** to pick grapes off a bunch; **s'égrener** VI (fig: heures etc) to pass by; (: notes) to chime out

égrillard, e [egrijar, -ard] ADJ ribald, bawdy

Égypte [eʒipt] NF: **l'~** Egypt

égyptien, ne [eʒipsjẽ, -ɛn] ADJ Egyptian ▸ NM/F: **É~, ne** Egyptian

égyptologue [eʒiptɔlɔg] NMF Egyptologist

eh [e] EXCL hey!; **eh bien** well

éhonté, e [eõte] ADJ shameless, brazen (BRIT)

éjaculation [eʒakylasjõ] NF ejaculation

éjaculer [eʒakyle] /1/ VI to ejaculate

éjectable [eʒɛktabl] ADJ: **siège ~** ejector seat

éjecter [eʒɛkte] /1/ VT (Tech) to eject; (fam) to kick ou chuck out

éjection [eʒɛksjõ] NF ejection

élaboration [elabɔrasjõ] NF elaboration

élaboré, e [elabɔre] ADJ (complexe) elaborate

élaborer [elabɔre] /1/ VT to elaborate; (projet, stratégie) to work out; (rapport) to draft

élagage [elagaʒ] NM pruning

élaguer [elage] /1/ VT to prune

élan [elã] NM (Zool) elk, moose; (Sport: avant le saut) run up; (de véhicule) momentum; (fig: de tendresse etc) surge; **prendre son ~/de l'~** to take a run up/gather speed; **perdre son ~** to lose one's momentum

élancé, e [elãse] ADJ slender

élancement [elãsmã] NM shooting pain

élancer [elãse] /3/: **s'élancer** VI to dash, hurl o.s.; (fig: arbre, clocher) to soar (upwards)

élargir [elarʒir] /2/ VT to widen; (vêtement) to let out; (Jur) to release; **s'élargir** VI to widen; (vêtement) to stretch

élargissement [elarʒismã] NM widening; letting out

élasticité [elastisite] NF (aussi Écon) elasticity; **~ de l'offre/de la demande** flexibility of supply/demand

élastique [elastik] ADJ elastic ▸ NM (de bureau) rubber band; (pour la couture) elastic no pl

élastomère [elastɔmɛr] NM elastomer

Elbe [ɛlb] NF: **l'île d'~** (the Island of) Elba; (fleuve) **l'~** the Elbe

eldorado [ɛldɔrado] NM Eldorado

électeur, -trice [elɛktœr, -tris] NM/F elector, voter

électif, -ive [elɛktif, -iv] ADJ elective

élection [elɛksjõ] NF election; **élections** NFPL (Pol) election(s); **sa terre/patrie d'~** the land/country of one's choice; **~ partielle** ≈ by-election; **élections législatives/présidentielles** general/presidential election sg; see note

électoral, e, -aux [elɛktɔral, -o] ADJ electoral, election cpd

électoralisme [elɛktɔralism] NM electioneering

électorat [elɛktɔra] NM electorate

électricien, ne [elɛktrisjẽ, -ɛn] NM/F electrician

électricité [elɛktrisite] NF electricity; **allumer/éteindre l'~** to put on/off the light; **~ statique** static electricity

électrification [elɛktrifikasjõ] NF (Rail) electrification; (d'un village etc) laying on of electricity

électrifier [elɛktrifje] /7/ VT (Rail) to electrify

électrique [elɛktrik] ADJ electric(al)

électriser [elɛktrize] /1/ VT to electrify

électro... [elɛktro] PRÉFIXE electro...

électro-aimant [elɛktroemã] NM electromagnet

électrocardiogramme [elɛktrokardjɔgram] NM electrocardiogram

électrocardiographe [elɛktrokardjɔgraf] NM electrocardiograph

électrochoc [elɛktroʃɔk] NM electric shock treatment

électrocuter [elɛktrokyte] /1/ VT to electrocute

électrocution [elɛktrokysjõ] NF electrocution

électrode [elɛktrɔd] NF electrode

électro-encéphalogramme [elɛktroãsefalɔgram] NM electroencephalogram

électrogène [elɛktroʒɛn] ADJ: **groupe ~** generating set

électrolyse [elɛktroliz] NF electrolysis sg

électromagnétique [elɛktromaɲetik] ADJ electromagnetic

électroménager [elɛktromenaʒe] ADJ M: **appareils électroménagers** domestic (electrical) appliances ▸ NM: **l'~** household appliances

électron [elɛktrõ] NM electron

électronicien, ne [elɛktronisjẽ, -ɛn] NM/F electronics (BRIT) ou electrical (US) engineer

électronique [elɛktronik] ADJ electronic ▸ NF (science) electronics sg

électronucléaire [elɛktronykleer] ADJ nuclear power cpd ▸ NM: **l'~** nuclear power

électrophone [elɛktrofon] NM record player

électrostatique [elɛktrostatik] ADJ
electrostatic ▶ NF electrostatics *sg*

élégamment [elegamã] ADV elegantly

élégance [elegãs] NF elegance

élégant, e [elegã, -ãt] ADJ elegant; *(solution)*
neat, elegant; *(attitude, procédé)* courteous,
civilized

élément [elemã] NM element; *(pièce)*
component, part; **éléments** NMPL elements

élémentaire [elemãtɛr] ADJ elementary;
(Chimie) elemental

éléphant [elefã] NM elephant; **~ de mer**
elephant seal

éléphanteau, x [elefãto] NM baby elephant

éléphantesque [elefãtɛsk] ADJ elephantine

élevage [el(ə)vaʒ] NM breeding; *(de bovins)* cattle
breeding *ou* rearing; *(ferme)* cattle farm; **truite
d'~** farmed trout

élévateur [elevatœr] NM elevator

élévation [elevasjɔ̃] NF *(gén)* elevation; *(voir
élever)* raising; *(voir s'élever)* rise

élevé, e [el(ə)ve] ADJ *(prix, sommet)* high; *(fig:
noble)* elevated; **bien/mal ~** well-/ill-mannered

élève [elɛv] NMF pupil; **~ infirmière** student
nurse

élever [el(ə)ve] **/5/** VT *(enfant)* to bring up, raise;
(bétail, volaille) to breed; *(abeilles)* to keep;
(hausser: taux, niveau) to raise; *(fig: âme, esprit)* to
elevate; *(édifier: monument)* to put up, erect;
s'élever VI *(avion, alpiniste)* to go up; *(niveau,
température, aussi: cri etc)* to rise; *(survenir:
difficultés)* to arise; **s'élever à** *(frais, dégâts)* to
amount to, add up to; **s'élever contre** to rise
up against; **~ la voix** to raise one's voice; **~ une
protestation/critique** to raise a protest/make
a criticism; **~ qn au rang de** to raise *ou* elevate
sb to the rank of; **~ un nombre au carré/au
cube** to square/cube a number

éleveur, -euse [el(ə)vœr, -øz] NM/F stock
breeder

elfe [ɛlf] NM elf

élidé, e [elide] ADJ elided

élider [elide] **/1/** VT to elide

éligibilité [eliʒibilite] NF eligibility

éligible [eliʒibl] ADJ eligible

élimé, e [elime] ADJ worn (thin), threadbare

élimination [eliminasjɔ̃] NF elimination

éliminatoire [eliminatwar] ADJ eliminatory;
(Sport) disqualifying ▶ NF *(Sport)* heat

éliminer [elimine] **/1/** VT to eliminate

élire [elir] **/43/** VT to elect; **~ domicile à** to take
up residence in *ou* at

élision [elizjɔ̃] NF elision

élite [elit] NF elite; **tireur d'~** crack rifleman;
chercheur d'~ top-notch researcher

élitisme [elitism] NM elitism

élitiste [elitist] ADJ elitist

élixir [eliksir] NM elixir

elle [ɛl] PRON *(sujet)* she; *(: chose)* it; *(complément)*
her; it; **elles** *(sujet)* they; *(complément)* them;
~-même herself; itself; **elles-mêmes**
themselves; *voir* **il**

ellipse [elips] NF ellipse; *(Ling)* ellipsis *sg*

elliptique [eliptik] ADJ elliptical

élocution [elɔkysjɔ̃] NF delivery; **défaut d'~**
speech impediment

éloge [elɔʒ] NM praise *gen no pl*; **faire l'~ de** to
praise

élogieusement [elɔʒjøzmã] ADV very
favourably

élogieux, -euse [elɔʒjø, -øz] ADJ laudatory, full
of praise

éloigné, e [elwaɲe] ADJ distant, far-off; *(parent)*
distant

éloignement [elwaɲmã] NM removal; putting
off; estrangement; *(fig: distance)* distance

éloigner [elwaɲe] **/1/** VT *(échéance)* to put off,
postpone; *(soupçons, danger)* to ward off;
~ qch (de) to move *ou* take sth away (from);
s'éloigner (de) VI *(personne)* to go away (from);
(véhicule) to move away (from); *(affectivement)* to
become estranged (from); **~ qn (de)** to take sb
away *ou* remove sb (from)

élongation [elɔ̃gasjɔ̃] NF strained muscle

éloquence [elɔkãs] NF eloquence

éloquent, e [elɔkã, -ãt] ADJ eloquent

élu, e [ely] PP *de* **élire** ▶ NM/F *(Pol)* elected
representative

élucider [elyside] **/1/** VT to elucidate

élucubrations [elykybrasjɔ̃] NFPL wild
imaginings

éluder [elyde] **/1/** VT to evade

élus *etc* [ely] VB *voir* **élire**

élusif, -ive [elyzif, -iv] ADJ elusive

Élysée [elize] NM: **(le palais de) l'~** the Élysée
palace; *see note*; **les Champs Élysées** the
Champs Élysées

> The *palais de l'Élysée*, situated in the heart of
> Paris just off the Champs Élysées, is the
> official residence of the French President.
> Built in the eighteenth century, it has
> performed its present function since
> 1876. A shorter form of its name, l'*Élysée*, is
> frequently used to refer to the presidency
> itself.

émacié, e [emasje] ADJ emaciated

émail, -aux [emaj, -o] NM enamel

e-mail [imel] NM email; **envoyer qch par ~**
to email sth

émaillé, e [emaje] ADJ enamelled; *(fig)*: **~ de**
dotted with

émailler [emaje] **/1/** VT to enamel

émanation [emanasjɔ̃] NF emanation

émancipation [emãsipasjɔ̃] NF emancipation

émancipé, e [emãsipe] ADJ emancipated

émanciper [emãsipe] **/1/** VT to emancipate;
s'émanciper VI *(fig)* to become emancipated *ou*
liberated

émaner [emane] **/1/**: **~ de** VT to emanate from;
(Admin) to proceed from

émarger [emarʒe] **/3/** VT to sign; **~ de 1000
euros à un budget** to receive 1000 euros out of
a budget

émasculer [emaskyle] **/1/** VT to emasculate

emballage [ãbalaʒ] NM wrapping; packing;
(papier) wrapping; *(carton)* packaging

emballer [ãbale] **/1/** VT to wrap (up); *(dans un
carton)* to pack (up); *(fig: fam)* to thrill (to bits);

s'emballer VI (*moteur*) to race; (*cheval*) to bolt; (*fig: personne*) to get carried away

emballeur, -euse [ãbalœʀ, -øz] NM/F packer

embarcadère [ãbaʀkadɛʀ] NM landing stage (BRIT), pier

embarcation [ãbaʀkasjõ] NF (small) boat, (small) craft *inv*

embardée [ãbaʀde] NF swerve; **faire une ~** to swerve

embargo [ãbaʀgo] NM embargo; **mettre l'~ sur** to put an embargo on, embargo

embarquement [ãbaʀkəmã] NM embarkation; (*de marchandises*) loading; (*de passagers*) boarding

embarquer [ãbaʀke] /**1**/ VT (*personne*) to embark; (*marchandise*) to load; (*fam*) to cart off; (*: arrêter*) to nick ▶ VI (*passager*) to board; (*Navig*) to ship water; **s'embarquer** VI to board; **s'embarquer dans** (*affaire, aventure*) to embark upon

embarras [ãbaʀa] NM (*obstacle*) hindrance; (*confusion*) embarrassment; **être dans l'~** (*ennuis*) to be in a predicament *ou* an awkward position; (*gêne financière*) to be in difficulties; **~ gastrique** stomach upset; **vous n'avez que l'~ du choix** the only problem is choosing

embarrassant, e [ãbaʀasã, -ãt] ADJ cumbersome; embarrassing; awkward

embarrassé, e [ãbaʀase] ADJ (*encombré*) encumbered; (*gêné*) embarrassed; (*explications etc*) awkward

embarrasser [ãbaʀase] /**1**/ VT (*encombrer*) to clutter (up); (*gêner*) to hinder, hamper; (*fig*) to cause embarrassment to; to put in an awkward position; **s'embarrasser de** VI to burden o.s. with

embauche [ãboʃ] NF hiring; **bureau d'~** labour office

embaucher [ãboʃe] /**1**/ VT to take on, hire; **s'embaucher comme** VI to get (o.s.) a job as

embauchoir [ãboʃwaʀ] NM shoetree

embaumer [ãbome] /**1**/ VT to embalm; (*parfumer*) to fill with its fragrance; **~ la lavande** to be fragrant with (the scent of) lavender

embellie [ãbeli] NF bright spell, brighter period

embellir [ãbeliʀ] /**2**/ VT to make more attractive; (*une histoire*) to embellish ▶ VI to grow lovelier *ou* more attractive

embellissement [ãbelismã] NM embellishment

embêtant, e [ãbɛtã, -ãt] ADJ annoying

embêtement [ãbɛtmã] NM problem, difficulty; **embêtements** NMPL trouble *sg*

embêter [ãbete] /**1**/ VT to bother; **s'embêter** VI (*s'ennuyer*) to be bored; **ça m'embête** it bothers me; **il ne s'embête pas!** (*ironique*) he does all right for himself!

emblée [ãble]: **d'~** *adv* straightaway

emblème [ãblɛm] NM emblem

embobiner [ãbɔbine] /**1**/ VT (*enjôler*): **~ qn** to get round sb

emboîtable [ãbwatabl] ADJ interlocking

emboîter [ãbwate] /**1**/ VT to fit together; **s'emboîter dans** to fit into; **s'emboîter (l'un dans l'autre)** to fit together; **~ le pas à qn** to follow in sb's footsteps

embolie [ãbɔli] NF embolism

embonpoint [ãbõpwɛ̃] NM stoutness (BRIT), corpulence; **prendre de l'~** to grow stout (BRIT) *ou* corpulent

embouché, e [ãbuʃe] ADJ: **mal ~** foul-mouthed

embouchure [ãbuʃyʀ] NF (*Géo*) mouth; (*Mus*) mouthpiece

embourber [ãbuʀbe] /**1**/: **s'embourber** VI to get stuck in the mud; (*fig*): **s'embourber dans** to sink into

embourgeoiser [ãbuʀʒwaze] /**1**/: **s'embourgeoiser** VI to adopt a middle-class outlook

embout [ãbu] NM (*de canne*) tip; (*de tuyau*) nozzle

embouteillage [ãbutɛjaʒ] NM traffic jam, (traffic) holdup (BRIT)

embouteiller [ãbuteje] /**1**/ VT (*véhicules etc*) to block

emboutir [ãbutiʀ] /**2**/ VT (*Tech*) to stamp; (*heurter*) to crash into, ram

embranchement [ãbʀãʃmã] NM (*routier*) junction; (*classification*) branch

embrancher [ãbʀãʃe] /**1**/ VT (*tuyaux*) to join; **~ qch sur** to join sth to

embraser [ãbʀaze] /**1**/: **s'embraser** VI to flare up

embrassade [ãbʀasad] NF (*gén pl*) hugging and kissing *no pl*

embrasse [ãbʀas] NF (*de rideau*) tie-back, loop

embrasser [ãbʀase] /**1**/ VT to kiss; (*sujet, période*) to embrace, encompass; (*carrière*) to embark on; (*métier*) to go in for, take up; **s'embrasser** VI to kiss (each other); **~ du regard** to take in (with eyes)

embrasure [ãbʀazyʀ] NF: **dans l'~ de la porte** in the door(way)

embrayage [ãbʀɛjaʒ] NM clutch

embrayer [ãbʀeje] /**8**/ VI (*Auto*) to let in the clutch ▶ VT (*fig: affaire*) to set in motion; **~ sur qch** to begin on sth

embrigader [ãbʀigade] /**1**/ VT to recruit

embrocher [ãbʀɔʃe] /**1**/ VT to (put on a) spit (*ou* skewer)

embrouillamini [ãbʀujamini] NM (*fam*) muddle

embrouillé, e [ãbʀuje] ADJ (*affaire*) confused, muddled

embrouiller [ãbʀuje] /**1**/ VT (*fils*) to tangle (up); (*fiches, idées, personne*) to muddle up; **s'embrouiller** VI to get in a muddle

embroussaillé, e [ãbʀusaje] ADJ overgrown, scrubby; (*cheveux*) bushy, shaggy

embruns [ãbʀœ̃] NMPL sea spray *sg*

embryologie [ãbʀijɔlɔʒi] NF embryology

embryon [ãbʀijõ] NM embryo

embryonnaire [ãbʀijɔnɛʀ] ADJ embryonic

embûches [ãbyʃ] NFPL pitfalls, traps

embué, e [ãbɥe] ADJ misted up; **yeux embués de larmes** eyes misty with tears

embuscade [ãbyskad] NF ambush; **tendre une ~ à** to lay an ambush for

embusqué, e [ãbyske] ADJ in ambush ▶ NM (*péj*) shirker, skiver (BRIT)

embusquer [ãbyske] /**1**/: **s'embusquer** VI to take up position (for an ambush)

éméché, e [emeʃe] ADJ tipsy, merry

émeraude [em(ə)ʀod] NF emerald ▸ ADJ INV emerald-green

émergence [emɛʀʒɑ̃s] NF (fig) emergence

émerger [emɛʀʒe] /**3**/ VI to emerge; (faire saillie, aussi fig) to stand out

émeri [em(ə)ʀi] NM: **toile** ou **papier** ~ emery paper

émérite [emeʀit] ADJ highly skilled

émerveillement [emɛʀvɛjmɑ̃] NM wonderment

émerveiller [emɛʀveje] /**1**/ VT to fill with wonder; **s'émerveiller de** VI to marvel at

émet etc [emɛ] VB voir **émettre**

émétique [emetik] NM emetic

émetteur, -trice [emetœʀ, -tʀis] ADJ transmitting; **(poste)** ~ transmitter

émetteur-récepteur [emetœʀʀesɛptœʀ] (pl **émetteurs-récepteurs**) NM transceiver

émettre [emɛtʀ] /**56**/ VT (son, lumière) to give out, emit; (message etc: Radio) to transmit; (billet, timbre, emprunt, chèque) to issue; (hypothèse, avis) to voice, put forward; (vœu) to express ▸ VI to broadcast; ~ **sur ondes courtes** to broadcast on short wave

émeus etc [emø] VB voir **émouvoir**

émeute [emøt] NF riot

émeutier, -ière [emøtje, -jɛʀ] NM/F rioter

émeuve etc [emœv] VB voir **émouvoir**

émietter [emjete] /**1**/ VT (pain, terre) to crumble; (fig) to split up, disperse; **s'émietter** VI (pain, terre) to crumble

émigrant, e [emigʀɑ̃, -ɑ̃t] NM/F emigrant

émigration [emigʀasjɔ̃] NF emigration

émigré, e [emigʀe] NM/F expatriate

émigrer [emigʀe] /**1**/ VI to emigrate

émincer [emɛ̃se] /**3**/ VT (Culin) to slice thinly

éminemment [eminamɑ̃] ADV eminently

éminence [eminɑ̃s] NF distinction; (colline) knoll, hill; **Son É~** His Eminence; ~ **grise** éminence grise

éminent, e [eminɑ̃, -ɑ̃t] ADJ distinguished

émir [emiʀ] NM emir

émirat [emiʀa] NM emirate; **les Émirats arabes unis (EAU)** the United Arab Emirates (UAE)

émis, e [emi, -iz] PP de **émettre**

émissaire [emisɛʀ] NM emissary

émission [emisjɔ̃] NF (voir émettre) emission; (d'un message) transmission; (de billet, timbre, emprunt, chèque) issue; (Radio, TV) programme, broadcast

émit etc [emi] VB voir **émettre**

emmagasinage [ɑ̃magazinaʒ] NM storage; storing away

emmagasiner [ɑ̃magazine] /**1**/ VT to (put into) store; (fig) to store up

emmailloter [ɑ̃majɔte] /**1**/ VT to wrap up

emmanchure [ɑ̃mɑ̃ʃyʀ] NF armhole

emmêlement [ɑ̃mɛlmɑ̃] NM (état) tangle

emmêler [ɑ̃mele] /**1**/ VT to tangle (up); (fig) to muddle up; **s'emmêler** VI to get into a tangle

emménagement [ɑ̃menaʒmɑ̃] NM settling in

emménager [ɑ̃menaʒe] /**3**/ VI to move in; ~ **dans** to move into

emmener [ɑ̃m(ə)ne] /**5**/ VT to take (with one); (comme otage, capture) to take away; ~ **qn au cinéma** to take sb to the cinema

emmental, emmenthal [emɛ̃tal] NM (fromage) Emmenthal

emmerder [ɑ̃mɛʀde] /**1**/ (!) VT to bug, bother; **s'emmerder** VI (s'ennuyer) to be bored stiff; **je t'emmerde!** to hell with you!

emmitoufler [ɑ̃mitufle] /**1**/ VT to wrap up (warmly); **s'emmitoufler** VI to wrap (o.s.) up (warmly)

emmurer [ɑ̃myʀe] /**1**/ VT to wall up, immure

émoi [emwa] NM (agitation, effervescence) commotion; (trouble) agitation; **en ~** (sens) excited, stirred

émollient, e [emɔljɑ̃, -ɑ̃t] ADJ (Méd) emollient

émoluments [emɔlymɑ̃] NMPL remuneration sg, fee sg

émonder [emɔ̃de] /**1**/ VT (arbre etc) to prune; (amande etc) to blanch

émoticone [emɔticɔn] NM (Inform) smiley

émotif, -ive [emɔtif, -iv] ADJ emotional

émotion [emɔsjɔ̃] NF emotion; **avoir des émotions** (fig) to get a fright; **donner des émotions à** to give a fright to; **sans ~** without emotion, coldly

émotionnant, e [emɔsjɔnɑ̃, -ɑ̃t] ADJ upsetting

émotionnel, le [emɔsjɔnɛl] ADJ emotional

émotionner [emɔsjɔne] /**1**/ VT to upset

émoulu, e [emuly] ADJ: **frais ~ de** fresh from, just out of

émoussé, e [emuse] ADJ blunt

émousser [emuse] /**1**/ VT to blunt; (fig) to dull

émoustiller [emustije] /**1**/ VT to titillate, arouse

émouvant, e [emuvɑ̃, -ɑ̃t] ADJ moving

émouvoir [emuvwaʀ] /**27**/ VT (troubler) to stir, affect; (toucher, attendrir) to move; (indigner) to rouse; (effrayer) to disturb, worry; **s'émouvoir** VI to be affected; to be moved; to be roused; to be disturbed ou worried

empailler [ɑ̃paje] /**1**/ VT to stuff

empailleur, -euse [ɑ̃pajœʀ, -øz] NM/F (d'animaux) taxidermist

empaler [ɑ̃pale] /**1**/ VT to impale

empaquetage [ɑ̃paktaʒ] NM packing, packaging

empaqueter [ɑ̃pakte] /**4**/ VT to pack up

emparer [ɑ̃paʀe] /**1**/: **s'emparer de** VT (objet) to seize, grab; (comme otage, Mil) to seize; (peur etc) to take hold of

empâter [ɑ̃pate] /**1**/: **s'empâter** VI to thicken out

empattement [ɑ̃patmɑ̃] NM (Auto) wheelbase; (Typo) serif

empêché, e [ɑ̃peʃe] ADJ detained

empêchement [ɑ̃peʃmɑ̃] NM (unexpected) obstacle, hitch

empêcher [ɑ̃peʃe] /**1**/ VT to prevent; ~ **qn de faire** to prevent ou stop sb (from) doing; ~ **que qch (n')arrive/qn (ne) fasse** to prevent sth from happening/sb from doing; **il n'empêche que** nevertheless, be that as it may; **il n'a pas pu s'~ de rire** he couldn't help laughing

empêcheur [ɑ̃peʃœʀ] NM: ~ **de danser en rond** spoilsport, killjoy (BRIT)

empeigne [ɑ̃pɛɲ] NF upper (of shoe)

empennage [ɑ̃penaʒ] NM (Aviat) tailplane

empereur [ɑ̃pʀœʀ] NM emperor

empesé, e [ɑ̃pəze] ADJ (fig) stiff, starchy

empeser [ɑ̃pəze] /5/ VT to starch

empester [ɑ̃pɛste] /1/ VT (lieu) to stink out ▶ VI to stink, reek; ~ **le tabac/le vin** to stink ou reek of tobacco/wine

empêtrer [ɑ̃petʀe] /1/: **s'empêtrer dans** VT (fils etc, aussi fig) to get tangled up in

emphase [ɑ̃faz] NF pomposity, bombast; **avec ~** pompously

emphatique [ɑ̃fatik] ADJ emphatic

empiècement [ɑ̃pjɛsmɑ̃] NM (Couture) yoke

empierrer [ɑ̃pjeʀe] /1/ VT (route) to metal

empiéter [ɑ̃pjete] /6/: ~ **sur** vt to encroach upon

empiffrer [ɑ̃pifʀe] /1/: **s'empiffrer** VI (péj) to stuff o.s.

empiler [ɑ̃pile] /1/ VT to pile (up), stack (up); **s'empiler** VI to pile up

empire [ɑ̃piʀ] NM empire; (fig) influence; **style E~** Empire style; **sous l'~ de** in the grip of

empirer [ɑ̃piʀe] /1/ VI to worsen, deteriorate

empirique [ɑ̃piʀik] ADJ empirical

empirisme [ɑ̃piʀism] NM empiricism

emplacement [ɑ̃plasmɑ̃] NM site; **sur l'~ de** on the site of

emplâtre [ɑ̃plɑtʀ] NM plaster; (fam) twit

emplette [ɑ̃plɛt] NF: **faire l'~ de** to purchase; **emplettes** shopping sg; **faire des emplettes** to go shopping

emplir [ɑ̃pliʀ] /2/ VT to fill; **s'emplir (de)** VI to fill (with)

emploi [ɑ̃plwa] NM use; (poste) job, situation; **l'~** (Comm, Écon) employment; **d'~ facile** easy to use; **le plein ~** full employment; **mode d'~** directions for use; **~ du temps** timetable, schedule

emploie etc [ɑ̃plwa] VB voir **employer**

employé, e [ɑ̃plwaje] NM/F employee; **~ de bureau/banque** office/bank employee ou clerk; **~ de maison** domestic (servant)

employer [ɑ̃plwaje] /8/ VT (outil, moyen, méthode, mot) to use; (ouvrier, main-d'œuvre) to employ; **s'~ à qch/à faire** to apply ou devote o.s. to sth/to doing

employeur, -euse [ɑ̃plwajœʀ, -øz] NM/F employer

empocher [ɑ̃pɔʃe] /1/ VT to pocket

empoignade [ɑ̃pwaɲad] NF row, set-to

empoigne [ɑ̃pwaɲ] NF: **foire d'~** free-for-all

empoigner [ɑ̃pwaɲe] /1/ VT to grab; **s'empoigner** (fig) to have a row ou set-to

empois [ɑ̃pwa] NM starch

empoisonnement [ɑ̃pwazɔnmɑ̃] NM poisoning; (fam: ennui) annoyance, irritation

empoisonner [ɑ̃pwazɔne] /1/ VT to poison; (empester: air, pièce) to stink out; (fam): ~ **qn** to drive sb mad; **s'empoisonner** to poison o.s.; ~ **l'atmosphère** (aussi fig) to poison the atmosphere; **il nous empoisonne l'existence** he's the bane of our life

empoissonner [ɑ̃pwasɔne] /1/ VT (étang, rivière) to stock with fish

emporté, e [ɑ̃pɔʀte] ADJ (personne, caractère) fiery

emportement [ɑ̃pɔʀtəmɑ̃] NM fit of rage, anger no pl

emporte-pièce [ɑ̃pɔʀtəpjɛs] NM INV (Tech) punch; **à l'~** adj (fig) incisive

emporter [ɑ̃pɔʀte] /1/ VT to take (with one); (en dérobant ou enlevant, emmener: blessés, voyageurs) to take away; (entraîner) to carry away ou along; (arracher) to tear off; (rivière, vent) to carry away; (Mil: position) to take; (avantage, approbation) to win; **s'emporter** VI (de colère) to fly into a rage, lose one's temper; **la maladie qui l'a emporté** the illness which caused his death; **l'~ (sur)** to gain victory; **l'~ (sur)** to get the upper hand (of); (méthode etc) to prevail (over); **boissons à ~** take-away drinks; **plats à ~** take-away meals

empoté, e [ɑ̃pɔte] ADJ (maladroit) clumsy

empourpré, e [ɑ̃puʀpʀe] ADJ crimson

empreint, e [ɑ̃pʀɛ̃, -ɛ̃t] ADJ: ~ **de** marked with; tinged with ▶ NF (de pied, main) print; (fig) stamp, mark; ~ **(digitale)** fingerprint; ~ **écologique** carbon footprint

empressé, e [ɑ̃pʀese] ADJ attentive; (péj) overanxious to please, overattentive

empressement [ɑ̃pʀɛsmɑ̃] NM eagerness

empresser [ɑ̃pʀese] /1/: **s'empresser** VI: **s'empresser auprès de qn** to surround sb with attentions; **s'empresser de faire** to hasten to do

emprise [ɑ̃pʀiz] NF hold, ascendancy; **sous l'~ de** under the influence of

emprisonnement [ɑ̃pʀizɔnmɑ̃] NM imprisonment

emprisonner [ɑ̃pʀizɔne] /1/ VT to imprison, jail

emprunt [ɑ̃pʀœ̃] NM borrowing no pl, loan (from debtor's point of view); (Ling etc) borrowing; **nom d'~** assumed name; ~ **d'État** government ou state loan; ~ **public à 5%** 5% public loan

emprunté, e [ɑ̃pʀœ̃te] ADJ (fig) ill-at-ease, awkward

emprunter [ɑ̃pʀœ̃te] /1/ VT to borrow; (itinéraire) to take, follow; (style, manière) to adopt, assume

emprunteur, -euse [ɑ̃pʀœ̃tœʀ, -øz] NM/F borrower

empuantir [ɑ̃pɥɑ̃tiʀ] /2/ VT to stink out

EMT SIGLE F (= éducation manuelle et technique) handwork as a school subject

ému, e [emy] PP de **émouvoir** ▶ ADJ excited; (gratitude) touched; (compassion) moved

émulation [emylasjɔ̃] NF emulation

émule [emyl] NMF imitator

émulsion [emylsjɔ̃] NF emulsion; (cosmétique) (water-based) lotion

émut etc [emy] VB voir **émouvoir**

EN SIGLE F = **l'Éducation (nationale)**; voir **éducation**

MOT-CLÉ

en [ɑ̃] PRÉP **1** (endroit, pays) in; (: direction) to; **habiter en France/ville** to live in France/town; **aller en France/ville** to go to France/town

2 (*moment, temps*) in; **en été/juin** in summer/June; **en 3 jours/20 ans** in 3 days/20 years
3 (*moyen*) by; **en avion/taxi** by plane/taxi
4 (*composition*) made of; **c'est en verre/coton/laine** it's (made of) glass/cotton/wool; **en métal/plastique** made of metal/plastic; **un collier en argent** a silver necklace; **en deux volumes/une pièce** in two volumes/one piece
5 (*description: état*): **une femme (habillée) en rouge** a woman (dressed) in red; **peindre qch en rouge** to paint sth red; **en T/étoile** T-/star-shaped; **en chemise/chaussettes** in one's shirt sleeves/socks; **en soldat** as a soldier; **en civil** in civilian clothes; **cassé en plusieurs morceaux** broken into several pieces; **en réparation** being repaired, under repair; **en vacances** on holiday; **en bonne santé** healthy, in good health; **en deuil** in mourning; **le même en plus grand** the same but *ou* only bigger
6 (*avec gérondif*) while; on; **en dormant** while sleeping, as one sleeps; **en sortant** on going out, as he *etc* went out; **sortir en courant** to run out; **en apprenant la nouvelle, il s'est évanoui** he fainted at the news *ou* when he heard the news
7 (*matière*): **fort en math** good at maths; **expert en** expert in
8 (*conformité*): **en tant que** as; **en bon politicien, il …** good politician that he is, he …, like a good *ou* true politician, he …; **je te parle en ami** I'm talking to you as a friend
▶ PRON **1** (*indéfini*): **j'en ai/veux** I have/want some; **en as-tu?** have you got any?; **il n'y en a pas** there isn't *ou* aren't any; **je n'en veux pas** I don't want any; **j'en ai deux** I've got two; **combien y en a-t-il?** how many (of them) are there?; **j'en ai assez** I've got enough (of it *ou* them); (*j'en ai marre*) I've had enough; **où en étais-je?** where was I?
2 (*provenance*) from there; **j'en viens** I've come from there
3 (*cause*): **il en est malade/perd le sommeil** he is ill/can't sleep because of it
4 (*de la part de*): **elle en est aimée** she is loved by him (*ou* here *etc*)
5 (*complément de nom: d'adjectif: de verbe*): **j'en connais les dangers** I know its *ou* the dangers; **j'en suis fier/ai besoin** I am proud of it/need it; **il en est ainsi** *ou* **de même pour moi** it's the same for me, same here

ENA [ena] SIGLE F (= *École nationale d'administration*) *grande école for training civil servants*
énarque [enaʁk] NM/F former ENA student
encablure [ɑ̃kablyʁ] NF (*Navig*) cable's length
encadrement [ɑ̃kadʁəmɑ̃] NM framing; training; (*de porte*) frame; **~ du crédit** credit restrictions
encadrer [ɑ̃kadʁe] /**1**/ VT (*tableau, image*) to frame; (*fig: entourer*) to surround; (*personnel, soldats etc*) to train; (*Comm: crédit*) to restrict
encadreur [ɑ̃kadʁœʁ] NM (picture) framer
encaisse [ɑ̃kɛs] NF cash in hand; **~ or/**

métallique gold/gold and silver reserves
encaissé, e [ɑ̃kese] ADJ (*vallée*) steep-sided; (*rivière*) with steep banks
encaisser [ɑ̃kese] /**1**/ VT (*chèque*) to cash; (*argent*) to collect; (*fig: coup, défaite*) to take
encaisseur [ɑ̃kesœʁ] NM collector (*of debts etc*)
encan [ɑ̃kɑ̃]: **à l'~** *adv* by auction
encanailler [ɑ̃kanɑje] /**1**/: **s'encanailler** VI to become vulgar *ou* common; to mix with the riff-raff
encart [ɑ̃kaʁ] NM insert; **~ publicitaire** publicity insert
encarter [ɑ̃kaʁte] /**1**/ VT to insert
en-cas [ɑ̃kɑ] NM INV snack
encastrable [ɑ̃kastʁabl] ADJ (*four, élément*) that can be built in
encastré, e [ɑ̃kastʁe] ADJ (*four, baignoire*) built-in
encastrer [ɑ̃kastʁe] /**1**/ VT: **~ qch dans** (*mur*) to embed sth in(to); (*boîtier*) to fit sth into; **s'encastrer dans** VI to fit into; (*heurter*) to crash into
encaustique [ɑ̃kɔstik] NF polish, wax
encaustiquer [ɑ̃kɔstike] /**1**/ VT to polish, wax
enceinte [ɑ̃sɛ̃t] ADJ F: **~ (de six mois)** (six months) pregnant ▶ NF (*mur*) wall; (*espace*) enclosure; **~ (acoustique)** speaker
encens [ɑ̃sɑ̃] NM incense
encenser [ɑ̃sɑ̃se] /**1**/ VT to (in)cense; (*fig*) to praise to the skies
encensoir [ɑ̃sɑ̃swaʁ] NM thurible (BRIT), censer
encéphalogramme [ɑ̃sefalɔgʁam] NM encephalogram
encercler [ɑ̃sɛʁkle] /**1**/ VT to surround
enchaîné [ɑ̃ʃene] NM (*Ciné*) link shot
enchaînement [ɑ̃ʃɛnmɑ̃] NM (*fig*) linking
enchaîner [ɑ̃ʃene] /**1**/ VT to chain up; (*mouvements, séquences*) to link (together) ▶ VI to carry on
enchanté, e [ɑ̃ʃɑ̃te] ADJ (*ravi*) delighted; (*ensorcelé*) enchanted; **~ (de faire votre connaissance)** pleased to meet you, how do you do?
enchantement [ɑ̃ʃɑ̃tmɑ̃] NM delight; (*magie*) enchantment; **comme par ~** as if by magic
enchanter [ɑ̃ʃɑ̃te] /**1**/ VT to delight
enchanteur, -teresse [ɑ̃ʃɑ̃tœʁ, -tʁɛs] ADJ enchanting
enchâsser [ɑ̃ʃase] /**1**/ VT: **~ qch (dans)** to set sth (in)
enchère [ɑ̃ʃɛʁ] NF bid; **faire une ~** to (make a) bid; **mettre/vendre aux enchères** to put up for (sale by)/sell by auction; **les enchères montent** the bids are rising; **faire monter les enchères** (*fig*) to raise the bidding
enchérir [ɑ̃ʃeʁiʁ] /**2**/ VI: **~ sur qn** (*aux enchères, aussi fig*) to outbid sb
enchérisseur, -euse [ɑ̃ʃeʁisœʁ, -øz] NM/F bidder
enchevêtrement [ɑ̃ʃvɛtʁəmɑ̃] NM tangle
enchevêtrer [ɑ̃ʃvetʁe] /**1**/ VT to tangle (up)
enclave [ɑ̃klav] NF enclave
enclaver [ɑ̃klave] /**1**/ VT to enclose, hem in
enclencher [ɑ̃klɑ̃ʃe] /**1**/ VT (*mécanisme*) to engage; (*fig: affaire*) to set in motion; **s'enclencher** VI to engage

149

enclin, e [ãklɛ̃, -in] ADJ: ~ **à qch/à faire** inclined *ou* prone to sth/to do

enclore [ãklɔʀ] **/45/** VT to enclose

enclos [ãklo] NM enclosure; (*clôture*) fence

enclume [ãklym] NF anvil

encoche [ãkɔʃ] NF notch

encoder [ãkɔde] **/1/** VT to encode

encodeur [ãkɔdœʀ] NM encoder

encoignure [ãkɔɲyʀ] NF corner

encoller [ãkɔle] **/1/** VT to paste

encolure [ãkɔlyʀ] NF (*tour de cou*) collar size; (*col, cou*) neck

encombrant, e [ãkɔ̃bʀã, -ãt] ADJ cumbersome, bulky

encombre [ãkɔ̃bʀ]: **sans ~** adv without mishap *ou* incident

encombré, e [ãkɔ̃bʀe] ADJ (*pièce, passage*) cluttered; (*lignes téléphoniques*) engaged; (*marché*) saturated

encombrement [ãkɔ̃bʀəmã] NM (*d'un lieu*) cluttering (up); (*d'un objet: dimensions*) bulk; **être pris dans un ~** to be stuck in a traffic jam

encombrer [ãkɔ̃bʀe] **/1/** VT to clutter (up); (*gêner*) to hamper; **s'encombrer de** VI (*bagages etc*) to load *ou* burden o.s. with; **~ le passage** to block *ou* obstruct the way

encontre [ãkɔ̃tʀ]: **à l'~ de** prép against, counter to

encorbellement [ãkɔʀbɛlmã] NM: **fenêtre en ~** oriel window

encorder [ãkɔʀde] **/1/** VT, **s'encorder** VI (*Alpinisme*) to rope up

---

MOT-CLÉ

encore [ãkɔʀ] ADV **1** (*continuation*) still; **il y travaille encore** he's still working on it; **pas encore** not yet

2 (*de nouveau*) again; **j'irai encore demain** I'll go again tomorrow; **encore une fois** (once) again

3 (*en plus*) more; **encore un peu de viande?** a little more meat?; **encore un effort** one last effort; **encore deux jours** two more days

4 (*intensif*) even, still; **encore plus fort/mieux** even louder/better, louder/better still; **hier encore** even yesterday; **non seulement ..., mais encore ...** not only ..., but also ...; **encore!** (*insatisfaction*) not again!; **quoi encore?** what now?

5 (*restriction*) even so then, only; **encore pourrais-je le faire si ...** even so, I might be able to do it if ...; **si encore** if only; **encore que** conj although

---

encourageant, e [ãkuʀaʒã, -ãt] ADJ encouraging

encouragement [ãkuʀaʒmã] NM encouragement; (*récompense*) incentive

encourager [ãkuʀaʒe] **/3/** VT to encourage; **~ qn à faire qch** to encourage sb to do sth

encourir [ãkuʀiʀ] **/11/** VT to incur

encrasser [ãkʀase] **/1/** VT to foul up; (*Auto etc*) to soot up

encre [ãkʀ] NF ink; **~ de Chine** Indian ink;

~ indélébile indelible ink; **~ sympathique** invisible ink

encrer [ãkʀe] **/1/** VT to ink

encreur [ãkʀœʀ] ADJ M: **rouleau ~** inking roller

encrier [ãkʀije] NM inkwell

encroûter [ãkʀute] **/1/**: **s'encroûter** VI (*fig*) to get into a rut, get set in one's ways

encyclique [ãsiklik] NF encyclical

encyclopédie [ãsiklɔpedi] NF encyclopaedia (BRIT), encyclopedia (US)

encyclopédique [ãsiklɔpedik] ADJ encyclopaedic (BRIT), encyclopedic (US)

endémique [ãdemik] ADJ endemic

endetté, e [ãdete] ADJ in debt; (*fig*): **très ~ envers qn** deeply indebted to sb

endettement [ãdɛtmã] NM debts pl

endetter [ãdete] **/1/** VT, **s'endetter** VI to get into debt

endeuiller [ãdœje] **/1/** VT to plunge into mourning; **manifestation endeuillée par** event over which a tragic shadow was cast by

endiablé, e [ãdjable] ADJ furious; (*enfant*) boisterous

endiguer [ãdige] **/1/** VT to dyke (up); (*fig*) to check, hold back

endimanché, e [ãdimãʃe] ADJ in one's Sunday best

endimancher [ãdimãʃe] **/1/**: **s'endimancher** VT to put on one's Sunday best; **avoir l'air endimanché** to be all done up to the nines (*fam*)

endive [ãdiv] NF chicory no pl

endocrine [ãdɔkʀin] ADJ F: **glande ~** endocrine (gland)

endoctrinement [ãdɔktʀinmã] NM indoctrination

endoctriner [ãdɔktʀine] **/1/** VT to indoctrinate

endolori, e [ãdɔlɔʀi] ADJ painful

endommager [ãdɔmaʒe] **/3/** VT to damage

endormant, e [ãdɔʀmã, -ãt] ADJ dull, boring

endormi, e [ãdɔʀmi] PP de **endormir** ▶ ADJ (*personne*) asleep; (*fig: indolent, lent*) sluggish; (*engourdi: main, pied*) numb

endormir [ãdɔʀmiʀ] **/16/** VT to put to sleep; (*chaleur etc*) to send to sleep; (*Méd: dent, nerf*) to anaesthetize; (*fig: soupçons*) to allay; **s'endormir** VI to fall asleep, go to sleep

endoscope [ãdɔskɔp] NM (*Méd*) endoscope

endoscopie [ãdɔskɔpi] NF endoscopy

endosser [ãdose] **/1/** VT (*responsabilité*) to take, shoulder; (*chèque*) to endorse; (*uniforme, tenue*) to put on, don

endroit [ãdʀwa] NM place; (*localité*): **les gens de l'~** the local people; (*opposé à l'envers*) right side; **à cet ~** in this place; **à l'~** right side out; the right way up; (*vêtement*) the right way out; (*objet posé*) the right way round; **à l'~ de** prép regarding, with regard to; **par endroits** in places

enduire [ãdɥiʀ] **/38/** VT to coat; **~ qch de** to coat sth with

enduit, e [ãdɥi, -it] PP de **enduire** ▶ NM coating

endurance [ãdyʀãs] NF endurance

endurant, e [ãdyʀã, -ãt] ADJ tough, hardy

endurcir [ɑ̃dyʀsiʀ] /2/ vt (physiquement) to toughen; (moralement) to harden; **s'endurcir** vi (physiquement) to become tougher; (moralement) to become hardened

endurer [ɑ̃dyʀe] /1/ vt to endure, bear

énergétique [enɛʀʒetik] adj (ressources etc) energy cpd; (aliment) energizing

énergie [enɛʀʒi] nf (Physique) energy; (Tech) power; (fig: physique) energy; (: morale) vigour, spirit; ~ **éolienne/solaire** wind/solar power

énergique [enɛʀʒik] adj energetic; vigorous; (mesures) drastic, stringent

énergiquement [enɛʀʒikmɑ̃] adv energetically; drastically

énergisant, e [enɛʀʒizɑ̃, -ɑ̃t] adj energizing

énergumène [enɛʀgymɛn] nm rowdy character ou customer

énervant, e [enɛʀvɑ̃, -ɑ̃t] adj irritating, annoying

énervé, e [enɛʀve] adj nervy, on edge; (agacé) irritated

énervement [enɛʀvəmɑ̃] nm nerviness; irritation

énerver [enɛʀve] /1/ vt to irritate, annoy; **s'énerver** vi to get excited, get worked up

enfance [ɑ̃fɑ̃s] nf (âge) childhood; (fig) infancy; (enfants) children pl; **c'est l'~ de l'art** it's child's play; **petite ~** infancy; **souvenir/ami d'~** childhood memory/friend; **retomber en ~** to lapse into one's second childhood

enfant [ɑ̃fɑ̃] nmf child; ~ **adoptif/naturel** adopted/natural child; **bon ~** adj good-natured, easy-going; ~ **de chœur** nm (Rel) altar boy; ~ **prodige** child prodigy; ~ **unique** only child

enfanter [ɑ̃fɑ̃te] /1/ vi to give birth ▶ vt to give birth to

enfantillage [ɑ̃fɑ̃tijaʒ] nm (péj) childish behaviour no pl

enfantin, e [ɑ̃fɑ̃tɛ̃, -in] adj childlike; (péj) childish; (langage) children's cpd

enfer [ɑ̃fɛʀ] nm hell; **allure/bruit d'~** horrendous speed/noise

enfermer [ɑ̃fɛʀme] /1/ vt to shut up; (à clef, interner) to lock up; **s'enfermer** to shut o.s. away; **s'enfermer à clé** to lock o.s. in; **s'enfermer dans la solitude/le mutisme** to retreat into solitude/silence

enferrer [ɑ̃feʀe] /1/: **s'enferrer** vi: **s'enferrer dans** to tangle o.s. up in

enfiévré, e [ɑ̃fjevʀe] adj (fig) feverish

enfilade [ɑ̃filad] nf: **une ~ de** a series ou line of; **prendre des rues en ~** to cross directly from one street into the next

enfiler [ɑ̃file] /1/ vt (vêtement) to slip on; (rue, couloir) to take; (perles) to string; (aiguille) to thread; (insérer): ~ **qch dans** to stick sth into; **s'enfiler dans** vi to disappear into; ~ **un tee-shirt** to slip into a T-shirt

enfin [ɑ̃fɛ̃] adv at last; (en énumérant) lastly; (de restriction, résignation) still; (eh bien) well; (pour conclure) in a word; (somme toute) after all

enflammé, e [ɑ̃flame] adj (torche, allumette) burning; (Méd: plaie) inflamed; (fig: nature, discours, déclaration) fiery

enflammer [ɑ̃flame] /1/ vt to set fire to; (Méd) to inflame; **s'enflammer** vi to catch fire; (Méd) to become inflamed

enflé, e [ɑ̃fle] adj swollen; (péj: style) bombastic, turgid

enfler [ɑ̃fle] /1/ vi to swell (up); **s'enfler** vi to swell

enflure [ɑ̃flyʀ] nf swelling

enfoncé, e [ɑ̃fɔ̃se] adj staved-in, smashed-in; (yeux) deep-set

enfoncement [ɑ̃fɔ̃smɑ̃] nm (recoin) nook

enfoncer [ɑ̃fɔ̃se] /3/ vt (clou) to drive in; (faire pénétrer): ~ **qch dans** to push (ou drive) sth into; (forcer: porte) to break open; (: plancher) to cause to cave in; (défoncer: côtes etc) to smash; (fam: surpasser) to lick, beat (hollow) ▶ vi (dans la vase etc) to sink in; (sol, surface porteuse) to give way; **s'enfoncer** vi to sink; **s'enfoncer dans** to sink into; (forêt, ville) to disappear into; ~ **un chapeau sur la tête** to cram ou jam a hat on one's head; ~ **qn dans la dette** to drag sb into debt

enfouir [ɑ̃fwiʀ] /2/ vt (dans le sol) to bury; (dans un tiroir etc) to tuck away; **s'enfouir dans/sous** to bury o.s. in/under

enfourcher [ɑ̃fuʀʃe] /1/ vt to mount; ~ **son dada** (fig) to get on one's hobby-horse

enfourner [ɑ̃fuʀne] /1/ vt (poterie) to put in the oven, to put in the kiln; **s'enfourner dans** (personne) to dive into; ~ **qch dans** to shove ou stuff sth into

enfreignais etc [ɑ̃fʀɛɲɛ] vb voir **enfreindre**

enfreindre [ɑ̃fʀɛ̃dʀ] /52/ vt to infringe, break

enfuir [ɑ̃fɥiʀ] /17/: **s'enfuir** vi to run away ou off

enfumer [ɑ̃fyme] /1/ vt to smoke out

enfuyais etc [ɑ̃fɥijɛ] vb voir **enfuir**

engagé, e [ɑ̃gaʒe] adj (littérature etc) engagé, committed

engageant, e [ɑ̃gaʒɑ̃, -ɑ̃t] adj attractive, appealing

engagement [ɑ̃gaʒmɑ̃] nm taking on, engaging; starting; investing; (promesse) commitment; (Mil: combat) engagement; (: recrutement) enlistment; (Sport) entry; **prendre l'~ de faire** to undertake to do; **sans ~** (Comm) without obligation

engager [ɑ̃gaʒe] /3/ vt (embaucher) to take on; (: artiste) to engage; (commencer) to start; (lier) to bind, commit; (impliquer, entraîner) to involve; (investir) to invest, lay out; (faire intervenir) to engage; (Sport: concurrents, chevaux) to enter; (introduire: clé) to insert; (inciter): ~ **qn à faire** to urge sb to do; (faire pénétrer): ~ **qch dans** to insert sth into; ~ **qn à qch** to urge sth on sb; **s'engager** vi to get taken on; (Mil) to enlist; (promettre, politiquement) to commit o.s.; (débuter: conversation etc) to start (up); **s'engager à faire** to undertake to do; **s'engager dans** (rue, passage) to turn into, enter; (s'emboîter) to engage ou fit into; (fig: affaire, discussion) to enter into, embark on

engazonner [ɑ̃gazɔne] /1/ vt to turf

engeance [ɑ̃ʒɑ̃s] nf mob

engelures [ɑ̃ʒlyʀ] nfpl chilblains

engendrer [ɑ̃ʒɑ̃dʀe] /**1**/ vt to father; (fig) to create, breed

engin [ɑ̃ʒɛ̃] nm machine; (outil) instrument; (Auto) vehicle; (péj) gadget; (Aviat: avion) aircraft inv; (: missile) missile; ~ **blindé** armoured vehicle; ~ **(explosif)** (explosive) device; **engins (spéciaux)** missiles; ~ **explosif improvisé** improvised explosive device

englober [ɑ̃ɡlɔbe] /**1**/ vt to include

engloutir [ɑ̃ɡlutiʀ] /**2**/ vt to swallow up; (fig: dépenses) to devour; **s'engloutir** vi to be engulfed

englué, e [ɑ̃ɡlye] adj sticky

engoncé, e [ɑ̃ɡɔ̃se] adj: ~ **dans** cramped in

engorgement [ɑ̃ɡɔʀʒəmɑ̃] nm blocking; (Méd) engorgement

engorger [ɑ̃ɡɔʀʒe] /**3**/ vt to obstruct, block; **s'engorger** vi to become blocked

engouement [ɑ̃ɡumɑ̃] nm (sudden) passion

engouffrer [ɑ̃ɡufʀe] /**1**/ vt to swallow up, devour; **s'engouffrer dans** to rush into

engourdi, e [ɑ̃ɡuʀdi] adj numb

engourdir [ɑ̃ɡuʀdiʀ] /**2**/ vt to numb; (fig) to dull, blunt; **s'engourdir** vi to go numb

engrais [ɑ̃ɡʀɛ] nm manure; ~ **(chimique)** (chemical) fertilizer; ~ **organique/ inorganique** organic/inorganic fertilizer

engraisser [ɑ̃ɡʀese] /**1**/ vt to fatten (up); (terre: fertiliser) to fertilize ▶ vi (péj) to get fat(ter)

engranger [ɑ̃ɡʀɑ̃ʒe] /**3**/ vt (foin) to bring in; (fig) to store away

engrenage [ɑ̃ɡʀənaʒ] nm gears pl, gearing; (fig) chain

engueuler [ɑ̃ɡœle] /**1**/ vt (fam) to bawl at ou out

enguirlander [ɑ̃ɡiʀlɑ̃de] /**1**/ vt (fam) to give sb a bawling out, bawl at

enhardir [ɑ̃aʀdiʀ] /**2**/: **s'enhardir** vi to grow bolder

ENI [eni] sigle f = **école normale (d'instituteurs)**

énième [ɛnjɛm] adj = **nième**

énigmatique [enigmatik] adj enigmatic

énigmatiquement [enigmatikmɑ̃] adv enigmatically

énigme [enigm] nf riddle

enivrant, e [ɑ̃nivʀɑ̃, -ɑ̃t] adj intoxicating

enivrer [ɑ̃nivʀe] /**1**/: **s'enivrer** vt to get drunk; **s'enivrer de** (fig) to become intoxicated with

enjambée [ɑ̃ʒɑ̃be] nf stride; **d'une ~** with one stride

enjamber [ɑ̃ʒɑ̃be] /**1**/ vt to stride over; (pont etc) to span, straddle

enjeu, x [ɑ̃ʒø] nm stakes pl

enjoindre [ɑ̃ʒwɛ̃dʀ] /**49**/ vt: ~ **à qn de faire** to enjoin ou order sb to do

enjôler [ɑ̃ʒole] /**1**/ vt to coax, wheedle

enjôleur, -euse [ɑ̃ʒolœʀ, -øz] adj (sourire, paroles) winning

enjolivement [ɑ̃ʒolivmɑ̃] nm embellishment

enjoliver [ɑ̃ʒolive] /**1**/ vt to embellish

enjoliveur [ɑ̃ʒolivœʀ] nm (Auto) hub cap

enjoué, e [ɑ̃ʒwe] adj playful

enlacer [ɑ̃lase] /**3**/ vt (étreindre) to embrace, hug; (lianes) to wind round, entwine

enlaidir [ɑ̃lediʀ] /**2**/ vt to make ugly

▶ vi to become ugly

enlevé, e [ɑ̃lve] adj (morceau de musique) played brightly

enlèvement [ɑ̃lɛvmɑ̃] nm removal; (rapt) abduction, kidnapping; **l'~ des ordures ménagères** refuse collection

enlever [ɑ̃l(ə)ve] /**5**/ vt (ôter: gén) to remove; (: vêtement, lunettes) to take off; (: Méd: organe) to remove; (emporter: ordures etc) to collect, take away; (kidnapper) to abduct, kidnap; (obtenir: prix, contrat) to win; (Mil: position) to take; (morceau de piano etc) to execute with spirit ou brio; (prendre): ~ **qch à qn** to take sth (away) from sb; **s'enlever** vi (tache) to come out ou off; **la maladie qui nous l'a enlevé** (euphémisme) the illness which took him from us

enliser [ɑ̃lize] /**1**/: **s'enliser** vi to sink, get stuck; (dialogue etc) to get bogged down

enluminure [ɑ̃lyminyʀ] nf illumination

ENM sigle f (= École nationale de la magistrature) grande école for law students

enneigé, e [ɑ̃neʒe] adj snowy; (fam) snowed-up; (maison) snowed-in

enneigement [ɑ̃nɛʒmɑ̃] nm depth of snow, snowfall; **bulletin d'~** snow report

ennemi, e [ɛnmi] adj hostile; (Mil) enemy cpd ▶ nm/f enemy; **être ~ de** to be strongly averse ou opposed to

ennième [enjɛm] adj = **nième**

ennoblir [ɑ̃nɔbliʀ] /**2**/ vt to ennoble

ennui [ɑ̃nɥi] nm (lassitude) boredom; (difficulté) trouble no pl; **avoir des ennuis** to have problems; **s'attirer des ennuis** to cause problems for o.s.

ennuie etc [ɑ̃nɥi] vb voir **ennuyer**

ennuyé, e [ɑ̃nɥije] adj (air, personne) preoccupied, worried

ennuyer [ɑ̃nɥije] /**8**/ vt to bother; (lasser) to bore; **s'ennuyer** vi to be bored; (s'ennuyer de: regretter) to miss; **si cela ne vous ennuie pas** if it's no trouble to you

ennuyeux, -euse [ɑ̃nɥijø, -øz] adj boring, tedious; (agaçant) annoying

énoncé [enɔ̃se] nm terms pl; wording; (Ling) utterance

énoncer [enɔ̃se] /**3**/ vt to say, express; (conditions) to set out, lay down, state

énonciation [enɔ̃sjasjɔ̃] nf statement

enorgueillir [ɑ̃nɔʀɡœjiʀ] /**2**/: **s'enorgueillir de** vt to pride o.s. on; to boast

énorme [enɔʀm] adj enormous, huge

énormément [enɔʀmemɑ̃] adv enormously, tremendously; ~ **de neige/gens** an enormous amount of snow/number of people

énormité [enɔʀmite] nf enormity, hugeness; (propos) outrageous remark

en part. abr (= en particulier) esp.

enquérir [ɑ̃keʀiʀ] /**21**/: **s'enquérir de** vt to inquire about

enquête [ɑ̃kɛt] nf (de journaliste, de police) investigation; (judiciaire, administrative) inquiry; (sondage d'opinion) survey

enquêter [ɑ̃kete] /**1**/ vi to investigate; to hold an inquiry; (faire un sondage): ~ **(sur)** to do a survey (on), carry out an opinion poll (on); pollster

enquêteur, -euse, -trice [ākɛtœʀ, -øz, -tʀis] NM/F officer in charge of an investigation; person conducting a survey; pollster

enquiers, enquière etc [ākjɛʀ] VB voir **enquérir**

enquiquiner [ākikine] /1/ VT to rile, irritate

enquis, e [āki, -iz] PP de **enquérir**

enraciné, e [āʀasine] ADJ deep-rooted

enragé, e [āʀaʒe] ADJ (Méd) rabid, with rabies; (furieux) furiously angry; (fig) fanatical; **~ de** wild about

enrageant, e [āʀaʒā, -āt] ADJ infuriating

enrager [āʀaʒe] /3/ VI to be furious, be in a rage; **faire ~ qn** to make sb wild with anger

enrayer [āʀeje] /8/ VT to check, stop; **s'enrayer** VI (arme à feu) to jam

enrégimenter [āʀeʒimāte] /1/ VT (péj) to enlist

enregistrement [āʀ(ə)ʒistʀəmā] NM recording; (Admin) registration; (à l'aéroport) baggage check-in; **~ magnétique** tape-recording

enregistrer [āʀ(ə)ʒistʀe] /1/ VT (Mus) to record; (Inform) to save; (remarquer, noter) to note, record; (Comm: commande) to note, enter; (fig: mémoriser) to make a mental note of; (Admin) to register; (bagages: aussi: **faire enregistrer**: par train) to register; (: à l'aéroport) to check in

enregistreur, -euse [āʀ(ə)ʒistʀœʀ, -øz] ADJ (machine) recording cpd ▶ NM (appareil): **~ de vol** (Aviat) flight recorder

enrhumé, e [āʀyme] ADJ: **il est ~** he has a cold

enrhumer [āʀyme] /1/: **s'enrhumer** VI to catch a cold

enrichir [āʀiʃiʀ] /2/ VT to make rich(er); (fig) to enrich; **s'enrichir** VI to get rich(er)

enrichissant, e [āʀiʃisā, -āt] ADJ instructive

enrichissement [āʀiʃismā] NM enrichment

enrober [āʀɔbe] /1/ VT: **~ qch de** to coat sth with; (fig) to wrap sth up in

enrôlement [āʀolmā] NM enlistment

enrôler [āʀole] /1/ VT to enlist; **s'enrôler (dans)** VI to enlist (in)

enroué, e [āʀwe] ADJ hoarse

enrouer [āʀwe] /1/: **s'enrouer** VI to go hoarse

enrouler [āʀule] /1/ VT (fil, corde) to wind (up); **s'enrouler** to coil up; **~ qch autour de** to wind sth (a)round

enrouleur, -euse [āʀulœʀ, -øz] ADJ (Tech) winding ▶ NM voir **ceinture**

enrubanné, e [āʀybane] ADJ trimmed with ribbon

ENS SIGLE F = **école normale supérieure**

ensabler [āsable] /1/ VT (port, canal) to silt up, sand up; (embarcation) to strand (on a sandbank); **s'ensabler** VI to silt up; to get stranded

ensacher [āsaʃe] /1/ VT to pack into bags

ENSAM SIGLE F (= École nationale supérieure des arts et métiers) grande école for engineering students

ensanglanté, e [āsāglāte] ADJ covered with blood

enseignant, e [āsɛɲā, -āt] ADJ teaching ▶ NM/F teacher

enseigne [āsɛɲ] NF sign ▶ NM: **~ de vaisseau** lieutenant; **à telle ~ que** so much so that; **être logés à la même ~** (fig) to be in the same boat; **~ lumineuse** neon sign

enseignement [āsɛɲ(ə)mā] NM teaching; (Admin) education; **~ ménager** home economics; **~ primaire** primary (BRIT) ou grade school (US) education; **~ secondaire** secondary (BRIT) ou high school (US) education

enseigner [āsɛɲe] /1/ VT, VI to teach; **~ qch à qn/à qn que** to teach sb sth/sb that

ensemble [āsābl] ADV together ▶ NM (assemblage, Math) set; (vêtements) outfit; (vêtement féminin) ensemble, suit; (unité, harmonie) unity; (résidentiel) housing development; **l'~ du/ de la** (totalité) the whole ou entire; **aller ~** to go together; **impression/idée d'~** overall ou general impression/idea; **dans l'~** (en gros) on the whole; **dans son ~** overall, in general; **~ vocal/musical** vocal/musical ensemble

ensemblier [āsāblije] NM interior designer

ensemencer [āsmāse] /3/ VT to sow

enserrer [āseʀe] /1/ VT to hug (tightly)

ENSET [ɛnsɛt] SIGLE F (= École normale supérieure de l'enseignement technique) grande école for training technical teachers

ensevelir [āsəvliʀ] /2/ VT to bury

ensilage [āsilaʒ] NM (aliment) silage

ensoleillé, e [āsɔleje] ADJ sunny

ensoleillement [āsɔlɛjmā] NM period ou hours pl of sunshine

ensommeillé, e [āsɔmeje] ADJ sleepy, drowsy

ensorceler [āsɔʀsəle] /4/ VT to enchant, bewitch

ensuite [āsɥit] ADV then, next; (plus tard) afterwards, later; **~ de quoi** after which

ensuivre [āsɥivʀ] /40/: **s'ensuivre** VI to follow, ensue; **il s'ensuit que ...** it follows that ...; **et tout ce qui s'ensuit** and all that goes with it

entaché, e [ātaʃe] ADJ: **~ de** marred by; **~ de nullité** null and void

entacher [ātaʃe] /1/ VT to soil

entaille [ātaj] NF (encoche) notch; (blessure) cut; **se faire une ~** to cut o.s.

entailler [ātaje] /1/ VT to notch; to cut; **s'~ le doigt** to cut one's finger

entamer [ātame] /1/ VT (pain, bouteille) to start; (hostilités, pourparlers) to open; (fig: altérer) to make a dent in; to damage

entartrer [ātaʀtʀe] /1/: **s'entartrer** VI to fur up; (dents) to become covered with plaque

entassement [ātasmā] NM (tas) pile, heap

entasser [ātase] /1/ VT (empiler) to pile up, heap up; (tenir à l'étroit) to cram together; **s'entasser** VI (s'amonceler) to pile up; to cram; **s'entasser dans** to cram into

entendement [ātādmā] NM understanding

entendre [ātādʀ] /41/ VT to hear; (comprendre) to understand; (vouloir dire) to mean; (vouloir): **~ être obéi/que** to intend ou mean to be obeyed/that; **s'entendre** VI (sympathiser) to get on; (se mettre d'accord) to agree; **j'ai entendu dire que** I've heard (it said) that; **je suis heureux de vous l'~ dire** I'm pleased to hear you say it; **~ parler de** to hear of; **laisser ~ que**,

donner à ~ que to let it be understood that;
~ raison to see sense, listen to reason;
qu'est-ce qu'il ne faut pas ~! whatever next!;
j'ai mal entendu I didn't catch what was said;
je vous entends très mal I can hardly hear
you; **s'entendre à qch/à faire** (*être compétent*) to
be good at sth/doing; **ça s'entend** (*est audible*)
it's audible; **je m'entends** I mean;
entendons-nous! let's be clear what we mean

entendu, e [ɑ̃tɑ̃dy] PP *de* **entendre** ▶ ADJ (*réglé*)
agreed; (*au courant: air*) knowing; **étant ~ que**
since (it's understood *ou* agreed that); (**c'est**) ~
all right, agreed; **c'est ~** (*concession*) all right,
granted; **bien ~** of course

entente [ɑ̃tɑ̃t] NF (*entre amis, pays*)
understanding, harmony; (*accord, traité*)
agreement, understanding; **à double ~** (*sens*)
with a double meaning

entériner [ɑ̃teʀine] /1/ VT to ratify, confirm

entérite [ɑ̃teʀit] NF enteritis *no pl*

enterrement [ɑ̃tɛʀmɑ̃] NM burying; (*cérémonie*)
funeral, burial; (*cortège funèbre*) funeral
procession

enterrer [ɑ̃teʀe] /1/ VT to bury

entêtant, e [ɑ̃tɛtɑ̃, -ɑ̃t] ADJ heady

en-tête [ɑ̃tɛt] NM heading; (*de papier à lettres*)
letterhead; **papier à ~** headed notepaper

entêté, e [ɑ̃tete] ADJ stubborn

entêtement [ɑ̃tɛtmɑ̃] NM stubbornness

entêter [ɑ̃tete] /1/: **s'entêter** VI: **s'entêter (à
faire)** to persist (in doing)

enthousiasmant, e [ɑ̃tuzjasmɑ̃, -ɑ̃t] ADJ
exciting

enthousiasme [ɑ̃tuzjasm] NM enthusiasm;
avec ~ enthusiastically

enthousiasmé, e [ɑ̃tuzjasme] ADJ filled with
enthusiasm

enthousiasmer [ɑ̃tuzjasme] /1/ VT to fill with
enthusiasm; **s'~ (pour qch)** to get enthusiastic
(about sth)

enthousiaste [ɑ̃tuzjast] ADJ enthusiastic

enticher [ɑ̃tiʃe] /1/: **s'enticher de** VT to become
infatuated with

entier, -ière [ɑ̃tje, -jɛʀ] ADJ (*non entamé, en totalité*)
whole; (*total, complet: satisfaction etc*) complete;
(*fig: caractère*) unbending, averse to compromise
▶ NM (*Math*) whole; **en ~** totally, in its entirety;
se donner tout ~ à qch to devote o.s.
completely to sth; **lait ~** full-cream milk; **pain
~** wholemeal bread; **nombre ~** whole number

entièrement [ɑ̃tjɛʀmɑ̃] ADV entirely,
completely, wholly

entité [ɑ̃tite] NF entity

entomologie [ɑ̃tɔmɔlɔʒi] NF entomology

entonner [ɑ̃tɔne] /1/ VT (*chanson*) to strike up

entonnoir [ɑ̃tɔnwaʀ] NM (*ustensile*) funnel;
(*trou*) shell-hole, crater

entorse [ɑ̃tɔʀs] NF (*Méd*) sprain; (*fig*): **~ à la loi/
au règlement** infringement of the law/rule;
se faire une ~ à la cheville/au poignet to
sprain one's ankle/wrist

entortiller [ɑ̃tɔʀtije] /1/ VT: **~ qch dans/avec**
(*envelopper*) to wrap sth in/with; **s'entortiller** VI:
s'entortiller dans (*draps*) to roll o.s. up in;

(*réponses*) to get tangled up in

entourage [ɑ̃tuʀaʒ] NM circle; (*famille*) family
(circle); (*d'une vedette etc*) entourage; (*ce qui enclôt*)
surround

entouré, e [ɑ̃tuʀe] ADJ (*recherché, admiré*) popular;
~ de surrounded by

entourer [ɑ̃tuʀe] /1/ VT to surround; (*apporter son
soutien à*) to rally round; **~ de** to surround with;
(*trait*) to encircle with; **s'entourer de** VI to
surround o.s. with; **s'entourer de
précautions** to take all possible precautions

entourloupette [ɑ̃tuʀlupɛt] NF mean trick

entournures [ɑ̃tuʀnyʀ] NFPL: **gêné aux ~** in
financial difficulties; (*fig*) a bit awkward

entracte [ɑ̃tʀakt] NM interval

entraide [ɑ̃tʀɛd] NF mutual aid *ou* assistance

entraider [ɑ̃tʀede] /1/: **s'entraider** VI to help
each other

entrailles [ɑ̃tʀaj] NFPL entrails; (*humaines*)
bowels

entrain [ɑ̃tʀɛ̃] NM spirit; **avec ~** (*répondre,
travailler*) energetically; **faire qch sans ~** to do
sth half-heartedly *ou* without enthusiasm

entraînant, e [ɑ̃tʀɛnɑ̃, -ɑ̃t] ADJ (*musique*) stirring,
rousing

entraînement [ɑ̃tʀɛnmɑ̃] NM training; (*Tech*):
~ à chaîne/galet chain/wheel drive; **manquer
d'~** to be unfit; **~ par ergots/friction** (*Inform*)
tractor/friction feed

entraîner [ɑ̃tʀene] /1/ VT (*tirer: wagons*) to pull;
(*charrier*) to carry *ou* drag along; (*Tech*) to drive;
(*emmener: personne*) to take (off); (*mener à l'assaut,
influencer*) to lead; (*Sport*) to train; (*impliquer*) to
entail; (*causer*) to lead to, bring about; **~ qn à
faire** (*inciter*) to lead sb to do; **s'entraîner** VI
(*Sport*) to train; **s'entraîner à qch/à faire** to
train o.s. for sth/to do

entraîneur [ɑ̃tʀɛnœʀ] NMF (*Sport*) coach,
trainer ▶ NM (*Hippisme*) trainer

entraîneuse [ɑ̃tʀɛnøz] NF (*de bar*) hostess

entrapercevoir [ɑ̃tʀapɛʀsəvwaʀ] /28/ VT to
catch a glimpse of

entrave [ɑ̃tʀav] NF hindrance

entraver [ɑ̃tʀave] /1/ VT (*circulation*) to hold up;
(*action, progrès*) to hinder, hamper

entre [ɑ̃tʀ] PRÉP between; (*parmi*) among(st);
l'un d'~ eux/nous one of them/us; **le meilleur
d'~ eux/nous** the best of them/us; **ils
préfèrent rester ~ eux** they prefer to keep to
themselves; **~ autres (choses)** among other
things; **~ nous, ...** between ourselves ...,
between you and me ...; **ils se battent ~ eux**
they are fighting among(st) themselves

entrebâillé, e [ɑ̃tʀəbaje] ADJ half-open, ajar

entrebâillement [ɑ̃tʀəbajmɑ̃] NM: **dans l'~ (de
la porte)** in the half-open door

entrebâiller [ɑ̃tʀəbaje] /1/ VT to half open

entrechat [ɑ̃tʀəʃa] NM leap

entrechoquer [ɑ̃tʀəʃɔke] /1/: **s'entrechoquer** VI
to knock *ou* bang together

entrecôte [ɑ̃tʀəkot] NF entrecôte *ou* rib steak

entrecoupé, e [ɑ̃tʀəkupe] ADJ (*paroles, voix*)
broken

entrecouper [ɑ̃tʀəkupe] /1/ VT: **~ qch de** to

intersperse sth with; **s'entrecouper** VI (*traits, lignes*) to cut across each other; ~ **un récit/ voyage de** to interrupt a story/journey with

entrecroiser [ãtrəkrwaze] /**1**/ VT, **s'entrecroiser** VI to intertwine

entrée [ãtre] NF entrance; (*accès: au cinéma etc*) admission; (*billet*) (admission) ticket; (*Culin*) first course; (*Comm: de marchandises*) entry; (*Inform*) entry, input; **entrées** NFPL: **avoir ses entrées chez** *ou* **auprès de** to be a welcome visitor to; **d'~** *adv* from the outset; **erreur d'~** input error; **"~ interdite"** "no admittance *ou* entry"; ~ **des artistes** stage door; ~ **en matière** introduction; ~ **principale** main entrance; ~ **en scène** entrance; ~ **de service** service entrance

entrefaites [ãtrəfɛt]: **sur ces ~** *adv* at this juncture

entrefilet [ãtrəfilɛ] NM (*article*) paragraph, short report

entregent [ãtrəʒã] NM: **avoir de l'~** to have an easy manner

entrejambes [ãtrəʒãb] NM INV crotch

entrelacement [ãtrəlasmã] NM: **un ~ de …** a network of …

entrelacer [ãtrəlase] /**3**/ VT, **s'entrelacer** VI to intertwine

entrelarder [ãtrəlarde] /**1**/ VT to lard; (*fig*): **entrelardé de** interspersed with

entremêler [ãtrəmele] /**1**/ VT: ~ **qch de** to (inter)mingle sth with

entremets [ãtrəmɛ] NM (cream) dessert

entremetteur, -euse [ãtrəmetœr, -øz] NM/F go-between

entremettre [ãtrəmɛtr] /**56**/: **s'entremettre** VI to intervene

entremise [ãtrəmiz] NF intervention; **par l'~ de** through

entrepont [ãtrəpõ] NM steerage; **dans l'~** in steerage

entreposer [ãtrəpoze] /**1**/ VT to store, put into storage

entrepôt [ãtrəpo] NM warehouse

entreprenant, e [ãtrəprənã, -ãt] VB *voir* **entreprendre** ▶ ADJ (*actif*) enterprising; (*trop galant*) forward

entreprendre [ãtrəprãdr] /**58**/ VT (*se lancer dans*) to undertake; (*commencer*) to begin *ou* start (upon); (*personne*) to buttonhole; ~ **qn sur un sujet** to tackle sb on a subject; ~ **de faire** to undertake to do

entrepreneur, -euse [ãtrəprənœr, -øz] NM/F: ~ **(en bâtiment)** (building) contractor; ~ **de pompes funèbres** funeral director, undertaker

entreprenne *etc* [ãtrəprɛn] VB *voir* **entreprendre**

entrepris, e [ãtrəpri, -iz] PP *de* **entreprendre** ▶ NF (*société*) firm, business; (*action*) undertaking, venture

entrer [ãtre] /**1**/ VI to go (*ou* come) in, enter ▶ VT (*Inform*) to input, enter; ~ **dans** (*gén*) to enter; (*pièce*) to go (*ou* come) into; (*club*) to join; (*heurter*) to run into; (*partager: vues, craintes de qn*) to share; (*être une composante de*) to go into; (*faire*

partie de) to form part of; **(faire)** ~ **qch dans** to get sth into; ~ **au couvent** to enter a convent; ~ **à l'hôpital** to go into hospital; ~ **dans le système** (*Inform*) to log in; ~ **en fureur** to become angry; ~ **en ébullition** to start to boil; ~ **en scène** to come on stage; **laisser** ~ **qn/qch** to let sb/sth in; **faire** ~ (*visiteur*) to show in

entresol [ãtrəsɔl] NM entresol, mezzanine

entre-temps [ãtrətã] ADV meanwhile, (in the) meantime

entretenir [ãtrət(ə)nir] /**22**/ VT to maintain; (*amitié*) to keep alive; (*famille, maîtresse*) to support, keep; ~ **qn (de)** to speak to sb (about); **s'entretenir (de)** to converse (about); ~ **qn dans l'erreur** to let sb remain in ignorance

entretenu, e [ãtrətny] PP *de* **entretenir** ▶ ADJ (*femme*) kept; **bien/mal ~** (*maison, jardin*) well/ badly kept

entretien [ãtrətjɛ̃] NM maintenance; (*discussion*) discussion, talk; (*pour un emploi*) interview; **frais d'~** maintenance charges

entretiendrai [ãtrətjɛ̃dre], **entretiens** *etc* [ãtrətjɛ̃] VB *voir* **entretenir**

entretuer [ãtrətɥe] /**1**/: **s'entretuer** VI to kill one another

entreverrai [ãtrəvere], **entrevit** *etc* [ãtrəvi] VB *voir* **entrevoir**

entrevoir [ãtrəvwar] /**30**/ VT (*à peine*) to make out; (*brièvement*) to catch a glimpse of

entrevu, e [ãtrəvy] PP *de* **entrevoir** ▶ NF meeting; (*audience*) interview

entrouvert, e [ãtruver, -ɛrt] PP *de* **entrouvrir** ▶ ADJ half-open

entrouvrir [ãtruvrir] /**18**/ VT, **s'entrouvrir** VI to half open

énumération [enymerasjõ] NF enumeration

énumérer [enymere] /**6**/ VT to list, enumerate

envahir [ãvair] /**2**/ VT to invade; (*inquiétude, peur*) to come over

envahissant, e [ãvaisã, -ãt] ADJ (*péj: personne*) interfering, intrusive

envahissement [ãvaismã] NM invasion

envahisseur [ãvaisœr] NM (*Mil*) invader

envasement [ãvazmã] NM silting up

envaser [ãvaze] /**1**/: **s'envaser** VI to get bogged down (in the mud)

enveloppe [ãv(ə)lɔp] NF (*de lettre*) envelope; (*Tech*) casing; outer layer; (*crédits*) budget; **mettre sous ~** to put in an envelope; ~ **autocollante** self-seal envelope; ~ **budgétaire** budget; ~ **à fenêtre** window envelope

envelopper [ãv(ə)lɔpe] /**1**/ VT to wrap; (*fig*) to envelop, shroud; **s'~ dans un châle/une couverture** to wrap o.s. in a shawl/blanket

envenimer [ãvnime] /**1**/ VT to aggravate; **s'envenimer** VI (*plaie*) to fester; (*situation, relations*) to worsen

envergure [ãvergyr] NF (*d'un oiseau, avion*) wingspan; (*fig: étendue*) scope; (: *valeur*) calibre

enverrai *etc* [ãvere] VB *voir* **envoyer**

envers [ãver] PRÉP towards, to ▶ NM other side; (*d'une étoffe*) wrong side; **à l'~** (*verticalement*) upside down; (*pull*) back to front; (*vêtement*) inside out; **~ et contre tous** *ou* **tout** against all opposition

enviable [ɑ̃vjabl] ADJ enviable; **peu ~** unenviable

envie [ɑ̃vi] NF (*sentiment*) envy; (*souhait*) desire, wish; (*tache sur la peau*) birthmark; (*filet de peau*) hangnail; **avoir ~ de** to feel like; (*désir plus fort*) to want; **avoir ~ de faire** to feel like doing; to want to do; **avoir ~ que** to wish that; **donner à qn l' ~ de faire** to make sb want to do; **cette glace me fait ~** I fancy some of that ice cream

envier [ɑ̃vje] **/7/** VT to envy; **~ qch à qn** to envy sb sth; **n'avoir rien à ~ à** to have no cause to be envious of

envieux, -euse [ɑ̃vjø, -øz] ADJ envious

environ [ɑ̃viʁɔ̃] ADV: **~ 3 h/2 km, 3 h/2km ~** (around) about 3 o'clock/2 km, 3 o'clock/2 km or so; *voir aussi* **environs**

environnant, e [ɑ̃viʁɔnɑ̃, -ɑ̃t] ADJ surrounding

environnement [ɑ̃viʁɔnmɑ̃] NM environment

environnementaliste [ɑ̃viʁɔnmɑ̃talist] NMF environmentalist

environner [ɑ̃viʁɔne] **/1/** VT to surround

environs [ɑ̃viʁɔ̃] NMPL surroundings; **aux ~ de** around

envisageable [ɑ̃vizaʒabl] ADJ conceivable

envisager [ɑ̃vizaʒe] **/3/** VT (*examiner, considérer*) to contemplate, view; (*avoir en vue*) to envisage; **~ de faire** to consider doing

envoi [ɑ̃vwa] NM sending; (*paquet*) parcel, consignment; **~ contre remboursement** (*Comm*) cash on delivery

envoie *etc* [ɑ̃vwa] VB *voir* **envoyer**

envol [ɑ̃vɔl] NM takeoff

envolée [ɑ̃vɔle] NF (*fig*) flight

envoler [ɑ̃vɔle] **/1/**: **s'envoler** VI (*oiseau*) to fly away *ou* off; (*avion*) to take off; (*papier, feuille*) to blow away; (*fig*) to vanish (into thin air)

envoûtant, e [ɑ̃vutɑ̃, -ɑ̃t] ADJ enchanting

envoûtement [ɑ̃vutmɑ̃] NM bewitchment

envoûter [ɑ̃vute] **/1/** VT to bewitch

envoyé, e [ɑ̃vwaje] NM/F (*Pol*) envoy; (*Presse*) correspondent; **~ spécial** special correspondent ▶ ADJ: **bien ~** (*remarque, réponse*) well-aimed

envoyer [ɑ̃vwaje] **/8/** VT to send; (*lancer*) to hurl, throw; **~ une gifle/un sourire à qn** to aim a blow/flash a smile at sb; **~ les couleurs** to run up the colours; **~ chercher** to send for; **~ par le fond** (*bateau*) to send to the bottom; **~ promener qn** (*fam*) to send sb packing; **~ un SMS à qn** to text sb

envoyeur, -euse [ɑ̃vwajœʁ, -øz] NM/F sender

enzyme [ɑ̃zim] NM OU F enzyme

éolien, ne [eɔljɛ̃, -ɛn] ADJ wind *cpd* ▶ NF wind turbine; **pompe ~** windpump

EOR SIGLE M (= *élève officier de réserve*) ≈ military cadet

éosine [eɔzin] NF eosin (*antiseptic used in France to treat skin ailments*)

épagneul, e [epaɲœl] NM/F spaniel

épais, se [epɛ, -ɛs] ADJ thick

épaisseur [epesœʁ] NF thickness

épaissir [epesiʁ] **/2/** VT, **s'épaissir** VI to thicken

épaississement [epesismɑ̃] NM thickening

épanchement [epɑ̃ʃmɑ̃] NM: **un ~ de synovie** water on the knee; **épanchements** NMPL (*fig*) (sentimental) outpourings

épancher [epɑ̃ʃe] **/1/** VT to give vent to; **s'épancher** VI to open one's heart; (*liquide*) to pour out

épandage [epɑ̃daʒ] NM manure spreading

épanoui, e [epanwi] ADJ (*éclos, ouvert, développé*) blooming; (*radieux*) radiant

épanouir [epanwiʁ] **/2/**: **s'épanouir** VI (*fleur*) to bloom, open out; (*visage*) to light up; (*fig: se développer*) to blossom (out); (: *mentalement*) to open up

épanouissement [epanwismɑ̃] NM blossoming; opening up

épargnant, e [epaʁɲɑ̃, -ɑ̃t] NM/F saver, investor

épargne [epaʁɲ] NF saving; **l' ~-logement** property investment

épargner [epaʁɲe] **/1/** VT to save; (*ne pas tuer ou endommager*) to spare ▶ VI to save; **~ qch à qn** to spare sb sth

éparpillement [epaʁpijmɑ̃] NM (*de papier*) scattering; (*des efforts*) dissipation

éparpiller [epaʁpije] **/1/** VT to scatter; (*pour répartir*) to disperse; (*fig: efforts*) to dissipate; **s'éparpiller** VI to scatter; (*fig*) to dissipate one's efforts

épars, e [epaʁ, -aʁs] ADJ (*maisons*) scattered; (*cheveux*) sparse

épatant, e [epatɑ̃, -ɑ̃t] ADJ (*fam*) super, splendid

épaté, e [epate] ADJ: **nez ~** flat nose (with wide nostrils)

épater [epate] **/1/** VT (*fam*) to amaze; (: *impressionner*) to impress

épaule [epol] NF shoulder

épaulé-jeté [epoleʒəte] (*pl* **épaulés-jetés**) NM (*Sport*) clean-and-jerk

épaulement [epolmɑ̃] NM escarpment; (*mur*) retaining wall

épauler [epole] **/1/** VT (*aider*) to back up, support; (*arme*) to raise (to one's shoulder) ▶ VI (*take*) aim

épaulette [epolɛt] NF (*Mil, d'un veston*) epaulette; (*de combinaison*) shoulder strap

épave [epav] NF wreck

épée [epe] NF sword

épeler [ep(ə)le] **/4/** VT to spell

éperdu, e [epɛʁdy] ADJ (*personne*) overcome; (*sentiment*) passionate; (*fuite*) frantic

éperdument [epɛʁdymɑ̃] ADV (*aimer*) wildly; (*espérer*) fervently

éperlan [epɛʁlɑ̃] NM (*Zool*) smelt

éperon [epʁɔ̃] NM spur

éperonner [epʁɔne] **/1/** VT to spur (on); (*navire*) to ram

épervier [epɛʁvje] NM (*Zool*) sparrowhawk; (*Pêche*) casting net

éphèbe [efɛb] NM beautiful young man

éphémère [efemɛʁ] ADJ ephemeral, fleeting

éphéméride [efemeʁid] NF block *ou* tear-off calendar

épi [epi] NM (*de blé, d'orge*) ear; (*de maïs*) cob; **~ de cheveux** tuft of hair; **stationnement/se garer**

en ~ parking/to park at an angle to the kerb

épice [epis] NF spice

épicé, e [epise] ADJ highly spiced, spicy; *(fig)* spicy

épicéa [episea] NM spruce

épicentre [episɑ̃tʀ] NM epicentre

épicer [epise] /3/ VT to spice; *(fig)* to add spice to

épicerie [episʀi] NF *(magasin)* grocer's shop; *(denrées)* groceries pl; **~ fine** delicatessen (shop)

épicier, -ière [episje, -jɛʀ] NM/F grocer

épicurien, ne [epikyʀjɛ̃, -ɛn] ADJ epicurean

épidémie [epidemi] NF epidemic

épidémique [epidemik] ADJ epidemic

épiderme [epidɛʀm] NM skin, epidermis

épidermique [epidɛʀmik] ADJ skin cpd, epidermic

épier [epje] /7/ VT to spy on, watch closely; *(occasion)* to look out for

épieu, x [epjø] NM (hunting-)spear

épigramme [epigʀam] NF epigram

épigraphe [epigʀaf] NF epigraph

épilation [epilasjɔ̃] NF removal of unwanted hair

épilatoire [epilatwaʀ] ADJ depilatory, hair-removing

épilepsie [epilɛpsi] NF epilepsy

épileptique [epilɛptik] ADJ, NMF epileptic

épiler [epile] /1/ VT *(jambes)* to remove the hair from; *(sourcils)* to pluck; **s'~ les jambes** to remove the hair from one's legs; **s'~ les sourcils** to pluck one's eyebrows; **se faire ~** to get unwanted hair removed; **crème à ~** hair-removing *ou* depilatory cream; **pince à ~** eyebrow tweezers

épilogue [epilɔg] NM *(fig)* conclusion, dénouement

épiloguer [epilɔge] /1/ VI: **~ sur** to hold forth on

épinards [epinaʀ] NMPL spinach sg

épine [epin] NF thorn, prickle; *(d'oursin etc)* spine, prickle; **~ dorsale** backbone

épineux, -euse [epinø, -øz] ADJ thorny, prickly

épinglage [epɛ̃glaʒ] NM pinning

épingle [epɛ̃gl] NF pin; **tirer son ~ du jeu** to play one's game well; **tiré à quatre épingles** well turned-out; **monter qch en ~** to build sth up, make a thing of sth *(fam)*; **~ à chapeau** hatpin; **~ à cheveux** hairpin; **virage en ~ à cheveux** hairpin bend; **~ de cravate** tie pin; **~ de nourrice** *ou* **de sûreté** *ou* **double** safety pin, nappy *(BRIT)* *ou* diaper *(US)* pin

épingler [epɛ̃gle] /1/ VT *(badge, décoration)*: **~ qch sur** to pin sth on(to); *(Couture: tissu, robe)* to pin together; *(fam)* to catch, nick

épinière [epinjɛʀ] ADJ F voir **moelle**

Épiphanie [epifani] NF Epiphany

épique [epik] ADJ epic

épiscopal, e, -aux [episkɔpal, -o] ADJ episcopal

épiscopat [episkɔpa] NM bishopric, episcopate

épisiotomie [epizjɔtɔmi] NF *(Méd)* episiotomy

épisode [epizɔd] NM episode; **film/roman à épisodes** serialized film/novel, serial

épisodique [epizɔdik] ADJ occasional

épisodiquement [epizɔdikmɑ̃] ADV occasionally

épissure [episyʀ] NF splice

épistémologie [epistemɔlɔʒi] NF epistemology

épistolaire [epistɔlɛʀ] ADJ epistolary; **être en relations épistolaires avec qn** to correspond with sb

épitaphe [epitaf] NF epitaph

épithète [epitɛt] NF *(nom, surnom)* epithet; **adjectif ~** attributive adjective

épître [epitʀ] NF epistle

éploré, e [eplɔʀe] ADJ in tears, tearful

épluchage [eplyʃaʒ] NM peeling; *(de dossier etc)* careful reading *ou* analysis

épluche-légumes [eplyʃlegym] NM INV potato peeler

éplucher [eplyʃe] /1/ VT *(fruit, légumes)* to peel; *(comptes, dossier)* to go over with a fine-tooth comb

éplucheur [eplyʃœʀ] NM (automatic) peeler

épluchures [eplyʃyʀ] NFPL peelings

épointer [epwɛ̃te] /1/ VT to blunt

éponge [epɔ̃ʒ] NF sponge; **passer l'~ (sur)** *(fig)* to let bygones be bygones (with regard to); **jeter l'~** *(fig)* to throw in the towel; **~ métallique** scourer

éponger [epɔ̃ʒe] /3/ VT *(liquide)* to mop *ou* sponge up; *(surface)* to sponge; *(fig: déficit)* to soak up, absorb; **s'~ le front** to mop one's brow

épopée [epɔpe] NF epic

époque [epɔk] NF *(de l'histoire)* age, era; *(de l'année, la vie)* time; **d'~** *(meuble)* period cpd; **à cette ~** at this *(ou* that) time *ou* period; **faire ~** to make history

épouiller [epuje] /1/ VT to pick lice off; *(avec un produit)* to delouse

époumoner [epumɔne] /1/: **s'époumoner** VI to shout *(ou* sing) o.s. hoarse

épouse [epuz] NF wife

épouser [epuze] /1/ VT to marry; *(fig: idées)* to espouse; *(: forme)* to fit

époussetage [epustaʒ] NM dusting

épousseter [epuste] /4/ VT to dust

époustouflant, e [epustuflɑ̃, -ɑ̃t] ADJ staggering, mind-boggling

époustoufler [epustufle] /1/ VT to flabbergast, astound

épouvantable [epuvɑ̃tabl] ADJ appalling, dreadful

épouvantablement [epuvɑ̃tabləmɑ̃] ADV terribly, dreadfully

épouvantail [epuvɑ̃taj] NM *(à moineaux)* scarecrow; *(fig)* bog(e)y; bugbear

épouvante [epuvɑ̃t] NF terror; **film d'~** horror film

épouvanter [epuvɑ̃te] /1/ VT to terrify

époux [epu] NM husband ▶ NMPL: **les ~** the (married) couple, the husband and wife

éprendre [epʀɑ̃dʀ] /58/: **s'éprendre de** VT to fall in love with

épreuve [epʀœv] NF *(d'examen)* test; *(malheur, difficulté)* trial, ordeal; *(Photo)* print; *(Typo)* proof; *(Sport)* event; **à l'~ des balles/du feu** *(vêtement)* bulletproof/fireproof; **à toute ~** unfailing; **mettre à l'~** to put to the test; **~ de force** trial of strength; *(fig)* showdown; **~ de résistance**

test of resistance; ~ **de sélection** (*Sport*) heat

épris, e [epʀi, -iz] VB *voir* **éprendre** ▶ ADJ: ~ **de** in love with

éprouvant, e [epʀuvã, -ãt] ADJ trying

éprouvé, e [epʀuve] ADJ tested, proven

éprouver [epʀuve] /1/ VT (*tester*) to test; (*mettre à l'épreuve*) to put to the test; (*marquer, faire souffrir*) to afflict, distress; (*ressentir*) to experience

éprouvette [epʀuvɛt] NF test tube

EPS SIGLE F (= *Éducation physique et sportive*) ≈ PE

épuisant, e [epɥizã, -ãt] ADJ exhausting

épuisé, e [epɥize] ADJ exhausted; (*livre*) out of print

épuisement [epɥizmã] NM exhaustion; **jusqu'à ~ des stocks** while stocks last

épuiser [epɥize] /1/ VT (*fatiguer*) to exhaust, wear *ou* tire out; (*stock, sujet*) to exhaust; **s'épuiser** VI to wear *ou* tire o.s. out, exhaust o.s.; (*stock*) to run out

épuisette [epɥizɛt] NF landing net; shrimping net

épuration [epyʀasjɔ̃] NF purification; purging; refinement

épure [epyʀ] NF working drawing

épurer [epyʀe] /1/ VT (*liquide*) to purify; (*parti, administration*) to purge; (*langue, texte*) to refine

équarrir [ekaʀiʀ] /2/ VT (*pierre, arbre*) to square (off); (*animal*) to quarter

équateur [ekwatœʀ] NM equator; (**la république de**) **l'É~** Ecuador

équation [ekwasjɔ̃] NF equation; **mettre en ~** to equate; **~ du premier/second degré** simple/quadratic equation

équatorial, e, -aux [ekwatɔʀjal, -o] ADJ equatorial

équatorien, ne [ekwatɔʀjɛ̃, -ɛn] ADJ Ecuadorian ▶ NM/F: **É~, ne** Ecuadorian

équerre [ekɛʀ] NF (*à dessin*) (set) square; (*pour fixer*) brace; **en ~** at right angles; **à l'~, d'~** straight; **double ~** T-square

équestre [ekɛstʀ] ADJ equestrian

équeuter [ekøte] /1/ VT (*Culin*) to remove the stalk(s) from

équidé [ekide] NM (*Zool*) member of the horse family

équidistance [ekɥidistãs] NF: **à ~ (de)** equidistant (from)

équidistant, e [ekɥidistã, -ãt] ADJ: **~ (de)** equidistant (from)

équilatéral, e, -aux [ekɥilateʀal, -o] ADJ equilateral

équilibrage [ekilibʀaʒ] NM (*Auto*): **~ des roues** wheel balancing

équilibre [ekilibʀ] NM balance; (*d'une balance*) equilibrium; **~ budgétaire** balanced budget; **garder/perdre l'~** to keep/lose one's balance; **être en ~** to be balanced; **mettre en ~** to make steady; **avoir le sens de l'~** to be well-balanced

équilibré, e [ekilibʀe] ADJ (*fig*) well-balanced, stable

équilibrer [ekilibʀe] /1/ VT to balance; **s'équilibrer** VI (*poids*) to balance; (*fig: défauts etc*) to balance each other out

équilibriste [ekilibʀist] NMF tightrope walker

équinoxe [ekinɔks] NM equinox

équipage [ekipaʒ] NM crew; **en grand ~** in great array

équipe [ekip] NF team; (*bande: parfois péj*) bunch; **travailler par équipes** to work in shifts; **travailler en ~** to work as a team; **faire ~ avec** to team up with; **~ de chercheurs** research team; **~ de secours** *ou* **de sauvetage** rescue team

équipé, e [ekipe] ADJ (*cuisine etc*) equipped, fitted(-out) ▶ NF escapade; **bien/mal ~** well-/poorly-equipped

équipement [ekipmã] NM equipment; **équipements** NMPL amenities, facilities; installations; **biens/dépenses d'~** capital goods/expenditure; **ministère de l'É~** department of public works; **équipements sportifs/collectifs** sports/community facilities *ou* resources

équiper [ekipe] /1/ VT to equip; (*voiture, cuisine*) to equip, fit out; **~ qn/qch de** to equip sb/sth with; **s'équiper** VI (*sportif*) to equip o.s., kit o.s. out

équipier, -ière [ekipje, -jɛʀ] NM/F team member

équitable [ekitabl] ADJ fair

équitablement [ekitabləmã] ADV fairly, equitably

équitation [ekitasjɔ̃] NF (horse-)riding; **faire de l'~** to go (horse-)riding

équité [ekite] NF equity

équivaille *etc* [ekivaj] VB *voir* **équivaloir**

équivalence [ekivalãs] NF equivalence

équivalent, e [ekivalã, -ãt] ADJ, NM equivalent

équivaloir [ekivalwaʀ] /29/: **~ à** VT to be equivalent to; (*représenter*) to amount to

équivaut *etc* [ekivo] VB *voir* **équivaloir**

équivoque [ekivɔk] ADJ equivocal, ambiguous; (*louche*) dubious ▶ NF ambiguity

érable [eʀabl] NM maple

éradication [eʀadikasjɔ̃] NF eradication

éradiquer [eʀadike] /1/ VT to eradicate

érafler [eʀafle] /1/ VT to scratch; **s'~ la main/les jambes** to scrape *ou* scratch one's hand/legs

éraflure [eʀaflyʀ] NF scratch

éraillé, e [eʀaje] ADJ (*voix*) rasping, hoarse

ère [ɛʀ] NF era; **en l'an 1050 de notre ~** in the year 1050 A.D.

érection [eʀɛksjɔ̃] NF erection

éreintant, e [eʀɛ̃tã, -ãt] ADJ exhausting

éreinté, e [eʀɛ̃te] ADJ exhausted

éreintement [eʀɛ̃tmã] NM exhaustion

éreinter [eʀɛ̃te] /1/ VT to exhaust, wear out; (*fig: critiquer*) to slate; **s'~ (à faire qch/à qch)** to wear o.s. out (doing sth/with sth)

ergonomie [ɛʀɡɔnɔmi] NF ergonomics *sg*

ergonomique [ɛʀɡɔnɔmik] ADJ ergonomic

ergot [ɛʀɡo] NM (*de coq*) spur; (*Tech*) lug

ergoter [ɛʀɡɔte] /1/ VI to split hairs, argue over details

ergoteur, -euse [ɛʀɡɔtœʀ, -øz] NM/F hairsplitter

ériger [eʀiʒe] /3/ VT (*monument*) to erect; **~ qch en principe/loi** to make sth a principle/law;

s'~ en critique (de) to set o.s. up as a critic (of)
ermitage [ɛrmitaʒ] NM retreat
ermite [ɛrmit] NM hermit
éroder [erɔde] /1/ VT to erode
érogène [erɔʒɛn] ADJ erogenous
érosion [erozjɔ̃] NF erosion
érotique [erɔtik] ADJ erotic
érotiquement [erɔtikmɑ̃] ADV erotically
érotisme [erɔtism] NM eroticism
errance [ɛrɑ̃s] NF wandering
errant, e [ɛrɑ̃, -ɑ̃t] ADJ: **un chien** ~ a stray dog
erratum [ɛratɔm] (pl **errata**, [-a]) NM erratum
errements [ɛrmɑ̃] NMPL misguided ways
errer [ere] /1/ VI to wander
erreur [erœr] NF mistake, error; (Inform) error;
(morale): **erreurs** nfpl errors; **être dans l'**~ to be
wrong; **induire qn en** ~ to mislead sb; **par** ~ by
mistake; **sauf** ~ unless I'm mistaken; **faire** ~ to
be mistaken; ~ **de date** mistake in the date;
~ **de fait** error of fact; ~ **d'impression** (Typo)
misprint; ~ **judiciaire** miscarriage of justice;
~ **de jugement** error of judgment;
~ **matérielle** ou **d'écriture** clerical error;
~ **tactique** tactical error
erroné, e [erɔne] ADJ wrong, erroneous
ersatz [ɛrzats] NM substitute, ersatz; ~ **de café**
coffee substitute
éructer [erykte] /1/ VI to belch
érudit, e [erydi, -it] ADJ erudite, learned ▸ NM/F
scholar
érudition [erydisjɔ̃] NF erudition, scholarship
éruptif, -ive [eryptif, -iv] ADJ eruptive
éruption [erypsjɔ̃] NF eruption; (cutanée)
outbreak; (: boutons) rash; (fig: de joie, colère, folie)
outburst
E/S ABR (= entrée/sortie) I/O (= in/out)
es [ɛ] VB voir **être**
ès [ɛs] PRÉP: **licencié ès lettres/sciences**
≈ Bachelor of Arts/Science; **docteur ès lettres**
≈ doctor of philosophy, ≈ PhD
ESB SIGLE F (= encéphalopathie spongiforme bovine)
BSE
esbroufe [ɛsbruf] NF: **faire de l'**~ to have
people on
escabeau, x [ɛskabo] NM (tabouret) stool; (échelle)
stepladder
escadre [ɛskadr] NF (Navig) squadron; (Aviat)
wing
escadrille [ɛskadrij] NF (Aviat) flight
escadron [ɛskadrɔ̃] NM squadron
escalade [ɛskalad] NF climbing no pl; (Pol etc)
escalation
escalader [ɛskalade] /1/ VT to climb, scale
escalator [ɛskalatɔr] NM escalator
escale [ɛskal] NF (Navig: durée) call; (: port) port of
call; (Aviat) stop(over); **faire** ~ **à** (Navig) to put in
at, call in at; (Aviat) to stop over at; ~ **technique**
refuelling stop; **vol sans** ~ nonstop flight
escalier [ɛskalje] NM stairs pl; **dans l'**~ ou **les**
escaliers on the stairs; **descendre l'**~ ou **les**
escaliers to go downstairs; ~ **mécanique** ou
roulant escalator; ~ **de secours** fire escape;
~ **de service** backstairs; ~ **à vis** ou **en**
colimaçon spiral staircase

escalope [ɛskalɔp] NF escalope
escamotable [ɛskamɔtabl] ADJ (train
d'atterrissage, antenne) retractable; (table, lit)
fold-away
escamoter [ɛskamɔte] /1/ VT (esquiver) to get
round, evade; (faire disparaître) to conjure away;
(dérober: portefeuille etc) to snatch; (train
d'atterrissage) to retract; (mots) to miss out
escapade [ɛskapad] NF: **faire une** ~ to go on a
jaunt; (s'enfuir) to run away ou off
escarbille [ɛskarbij] NF bit of grit
escarcelle [ɛskarsɛl] NF: **faire tomber**
dans l'~ (argent) to bring in
escargot [ɛskargo] NM snail
escarmouche [ɛskarmuʃ] NF (Mil) skirmish;
(fig: propos hostiles) angry exchange
escarpé, e [ɛskarpe] ADJ steep
escarpement [ɛskarpəmɑ̃] NM steep slope
escarpin [ɛskarpɛ̃] NM flat(-heeled) shoe
escarre [ɛskar] NF bedsore
Escaut [ɛsko] NM: **l'**~ the Scheldt
escient [esjɑ̃] NM: **à bon** ~ advisedly
esclaffer [ɛsklafe] /1/: **s'esclaffer** VI to guffaw
esclandre [ɛsklɑ̃dr] NM scene, fracas
esclavage [ɛsklavaʒ] NM slavery
esclavagiste [ɛsklavaʒist] ADJ pro-slavery
▸ NMF supporter of slavery
esclave [ɛsklav] NMF slave; **être** ~ **de** (fig) to be a
slave of
escogriffe [ɛskɔgrif] NM (péj) beanpole
escompte [ɛskɔ̃t] NM discount
escompter [ɛskɔ̃te] /1/ VT (Comm) to discount;
(espérer) to expect, reckon upon; ~ **que** to reckon
ou expect that
escorte [ɛskɔrt] NF escort; **faire** ~ **à** to escort
escorter [ɛskɔrte] /1/ VT to escort
escorteur [ɛskɔrtœr] NM (Navig) escort (ship)
escouade [ɛskwad] NF squad; (fig: groupe de
personnes) group
escrime [ɛskrim] NF fencing; **faire de l'**~ to
fence
escrimer [ɛskrime] /1/: **s'escrimer** VI:
s'escrimer à faire to wear o.s. out doing
escrimeur, -euse [ɛskrimœr, -øz] NM/F fencer
escroc [ɛskro] NM swindler, con-man
escroquer [ɛskrɔke] /1/ VT: ~ **qn (de qch)/qch à**
qn to swindle sb (out of sth)/sth out of sb
escroquerie [ɛskrɔkri] NF swindle
ésotérique [ezɔterik] ADJ esoteric
espace [ɛspas] NM space; ~ **publicitaire**
advertising space; ~ **vital** living space
espacé, e [ɛspase] ADJ spaced out
espacement [ɛspasmɑ̃] NM: ~ **proportionnel**
proportional spacing (on printer)
espacer [ɛspase] /3/ VT to space out; **s'espacer**
VI (visites etc) to become less frequent
espadon [ɛspadɔ̃] NM swordfish inv
espadrille [ɛspadrij] NF rope-soled sandal
Espagne [ɛspaɲ] NF: **l'**~ Spain
espagnol, e [ɛspaɲɔl] ADJ Spanish ▸ NM (Ling)
Spanish ▸ NM/F: **E**~, **e** Spaniard
espagnolette [ɛspaɲɔlɛt] NF (window) catch;
fermé à l'~ resting on the catch
espalier [ɛspalje] NM (arbre fruitier) espalier

e

espèce [ɛspɛs] NF (*Bio, Bot, Zool*) species inv; (*gén: sorte*) sort, kind, type; (*péj*): **~ de maladroit/de brute!** you clumsy oaf/you brute!; **espèces** NFPL (*Comm*) cash sg; (*Rel*) species; **de toute ~** of all kinds ou sorts; **en l'~** adv in the case in point; **payer en espèces** to pay (in) cash; **cas d'~** individual case; **l'~ humaine** humankind

espérance [ɛsperɑ̃s] NF hope; **~ de vie** life expectancy

espéranto [ɛsperɑ̃to] NM Esperanto

espérer [ɛspere] /6/ VT to hope for; **j'espère (bien)** I hope so; **~ que/faire** to hope that/to do; **~ en** to trust in

espiègle [ɛspjɛgl] ADJ mischievous

espièglerie [ɛspjɛgləri] NF mischievousness; (*tour, farce*) piece of mischief, prank

espion, ne [ɛspjɔ̃, -ɔn] NM/F spy; **avion ~** spy plane

espionnage [ɛspjɔnaʒ] NM espionage, spying; **film/roman d'~** spy film/novel

espionner [ɛspjɔne] /1/ VT to spy (up)on

esplanade [ɛsplanad] NF esplanade

espoir [ɛspwaʀ] NM hope; **l'~ de qch/de faire qch** the hope of sth/of doing sth; **avoir bon ~ que ...** to have high hopes that ...; **garder l'~ que ...** to remain hopeful that ...; **dans l'~ de/que** in the hope of/that; **reprendre ~** not to lose hope; **un ~ de la boxe/du ski** one of boxing's/skiing's hopefuls, one of the hopes of boxing/skiing; **sans ~** adj hopeless

esprit [ɛspʀi] NM (*pensée, intellect*) mind; (*humour, ironie*) wit; (*mentalité, d'une loi etc, fantôme etc*) spirit; **l'~ d'équipe/de compétition** team/competitive spirit; **faire de l'~** to try to be witty; **reprendre ses esprits** to come to; **perdre l'~** to lose one's mind; **avoir bon/mauvais ~** to be of a good/bad disposition; **avoir l'~ à faire qch** to have a mind to do sth; **avoir l'~ critique** to be critical; **~ de contradiction** contrariness; **~ de corps** esprit de corps; **~ de famille** family loyalty; **l'~ malin** (*le diable*) the Evil One; **esprits chagrins** fault-finders

esquif [ɛskif] NM skiff

esquimau, de, x [ɛskimo, -od] ADJ Eskimo ▶ NM (*Ling*) Eskimo; (*glace*): **E~®** ice lolly (*Brit*), popsicle (*US*) ▶ NM/F: **E~, de** Eskimo; **chien ~** husky

esquinter [ɛskɛ̃te] /1/ VT (*fam*) to mess up; **s'esquinter** VI: **s'esquinter à faire qch** to knock o.s. out doing sth

esquisse [ɛskis] NF sketch; **l'~ d'un sourire/changement** a hint of a smile/of change

esquisser [ɛskise] /1/ VT to sketch; **s'esquisser** VI (*amélioration*) to begin to be detectable; **~ un sourire** to give a hint of a smile

esquive [ɛskiv] NF (*Boxe*) dodging; (*fig*) sidestepping

esquiver [ɛskive] /1/ VT to dodge; **s'esquiver** VI to slip away

essai [ɛsɛ] NM trying; (*tentative*) attempt, try; (*de produit*) testing; (*Rugby*) try; (*Littérature*) essay; **essais** NMPL (*Auto*) trials; **à l'~** on a trial basis; **mettre à l'~** to put to the test;

~ gratuit (*Comm*) free trial

essaim [ɛsɛ̃] NM swarm

essaimer [ɛseme] /1/ VI to swarm; (*fig*) to spread, expand

essayage [ɛsejaʒ] NM (*d'un vêtement*) trying on, fitting; **salon d'~** fitting room; **cabine d'~** fitting room (*cubicle*)

essayer [ɛseje] /8/ VT (*gén*) to try; (*vêtement, chaussures*) to try (on); (*restaurant, méthode, voiture*) to try (out) ▶ VI to try; **~ de faire** to try ou attempt to do; **s'~ à faire** to try one's hand at doing; **essayez un peu!** (*menace*) just you try!

essayeur, -euse [ɛsejœʀ, -øz] NM/F (*chez un tailleur etc*) fitter

essayiste [ɛsejist] NMF essayist

ESSEC [ɛsɛk] SIGLE F (= *École supérieure des sciences économiques et sociales*) *grande école* for management and business studies

essence [ɛsɑ̃s] NF (*de voiture*) petrol (*Brit*), gas(oline) (*US*); (*extrait de plante, Philosophie*) essence; (*espèce: d'arbre*) species inv; **prendre de l'~** to get (some) petrol ou gas; **par ~** (*essentiellement*) essentially; **~ de citron/rose** lemon/rose oil; **~ sans plomb** unleaded petrol; **~ de térébenthine** turpentine

essentiel, le [ɛsɑ̃sjɛl] ADJ essential ▶ NM: **l'~ d'un discours/d'une œuvre** the essence of a speech/work of art; **emporter l'~** to take the essentials; **c'est l'~** (*ce qui importe*) that's the main thing; **l'~ de** (*la majeure partie*) the main part of

essentiellement [ɛsɑ̃sjɛlmɑ̃] ADV essentially

esseulé, e [ɛsœle] ADJ forlorn

essieu, x [ɛsjø] NM axle

essor [ɛsɔʀ] NM (*de l'économie etc*) rapid expansion; **prendre son ~** (*oiseau*) to fly off

essorage [ɛsɔʀaʒ] NM wringing out; spin-drying; spinning; shaking

essorer [ɛsɔʀe] /1/ VT (*en tordant*) to wring (out); (*par la force centrifuge*) to spin-dry; (*salade*) to spin; (: *en secouant*) to shake dry

essoreuse [ɛsɔʀøz] NF mangle, wringer; (*à tambour*) spin-dryer

essoufflé, e [esufle] ADJ out of breath, breathless

essouffler [esufle] /1/ VT to make breathless; **s'essouffler** VI to get out of breath; (*fig: économie*) to run out of steam

essuie etc [ɛsɥi] VB voir **essuyer**

essuie-glace [ɛsɥiglas] NM windscreen (*Brit*) ou windshield (*US*) wiper

essuie-mains [ɛsɥimɛ̃] NM INV hand towel

essuierai etc [ɛsɥiʀe] VB voir **essuyer**

essuie-tout [ɛsɥitu] NM INV kitchen paper

essuyer [ɛsɥije] /8/ VT to wipe; (*fig: subir*) to suffer; **s'essuyer** (*après le bain*) to dry o.s.; **~ la vaisselle** to dry up, dry the dishes

est VB [ɛ] voir **être** ▶ NM [ɛst]: **l'~** the east ▶ ADJ INV [ɛst] east; (*région*) east(ern); **à l'~** in the east; (*direction*) to the east, east(wards); **à l'~ de** to the east of; **les pays de l'E~** the eastern countries

estafette [ɛstafɛt] NF (*Mil*) dispatch rider

estafilade [ɛstafilad] NF gash, slash

est-allemand, e [ɛstalmɑ̃, -ɑ̃d] ADJ East German

estaminet [ɛstaminɛ] NM tavern

estampe [ɛstɑ̃p] NF print, engraving

estamper [ɛstɑ̃pe] /1/ VT (*monnaies etc*) to stamp; (*fam: escroquer*) to swindle

estampille [ɛstɑ̃pij] NF stamp

est-ce que [ɛskə] ADV: ~ **c'est cher/c'était bon?** is it expensive/was it good?; **quand est-ce qu'il part?** when does he leave?, when is he leaving?; **où est-ce qu'il va?** where's he going?; *voir aussi* **que**

este [ɛst] ADJ Estonian ▸ NMF: **E~** Estonian

esthète [ɛstɛt] NMF aesthete

esthéticienne [ɛstetisjɛn] NF beautician

esthétique [ɛstetik] ADJ (*sens, jugement*) aesthetic; (*beau*) attractive, aesthetically pleasing ▸ NF aesthetics *sg*; **l'~ industrielle** industrial design

esthétiquement [ɛstetikmɑ̃] ADV aesthetically

estimable [ɛstimabl] ADJ respected

estimatif, -ive [ɛstimatif, -iv] ADJ estimated

estimation [ɛstimasjɔ̃] NF valuation; assessment; (*chiffre*) estimate; **d'après mes estimations** according to my calculations

estime [ɛstim] NF esteem, regard; **avoir de l'~ pour qn** to think highly of sb

estimer [ɛstime] /1/ VT (*respecter*) to esteem, hold in high regard; (*expertiser: bijou*) to value; (*évaluer: coût etc*) to assess, estimate; (*penser*): ~ **que** to consider that/o.s. to be; **s'estimer satisfait/heureux** VI to feel satisfied/happy; **j'estime la distance à 10 km** I reckon the distance to be 10 km

estival, e, -aux [ɛstival, -o] ADJ summer *cpd*; **station ~** (summer) holiday resort

estivant, e [ɛstivɑ̃, -ɑ̃t] NM/F (summer) holiday-maker

estoc [ɛstɔk] NM: **frapper d'~ et de taille** to cut and thrust

estocade [ɛstɔkad] NF death-blow

estomac [ɛstɔma] NM stomach; **avoir mal à l'~** to have stomach ache; **avoir l'~ creux** to have an empty stomach

estomaqué, e [ɛstɔmake] ADJ flabbergasted

estompe [ɛstɔ̃p] NF stump; (*dessin*) stump drawing

estompé, e [ɛstɔ̃pe] ADJ blurred

estomper [ɛstɔ̃pe] /1/ VT (*Art*) to shade off; (*fig*) to blur, dim; **s'estomper** VI (*sentiments*) to soften; (*contour*) to become blurred

Estonie [ɛstɔni] NF: **l'~** Estonia

estonien, ne [ɛstɔnjɛ̃, -ɛn] ADJ Estonian ▸ NM (*Ling*) Estonian ▸ NM/F: **E~, ne** Estonian

estrade [ɛstrad] NF platform, rostrum

estragon [ɛstragɔ̃] NM tarragon

estropié, e [ɛstrɔpje] NM/F cripple (*péj*)

estropier [ɛstrɔpje] /7/ VT to cripple, maim; (*fig*) to twist, distort

estuaire [ɛstɥɛr] NM estuary

estudiantin, e [ɛstydjɑ̃tɛ̃, -in] ADJ student *cpd*

esturgeon [ɛstyrʒɔ̃] NM sturgeon

et [e] CONJ and; **et lui?** what about him?; **et alors?, et (puis) après?** so what?; (*ensuite*) and then?

ét. ABR = **étage**

ETA [eta] SIGLE M (*Pol*) ETA

étable [etabl] NF cowshed

établi, e [etabli] ADJ established ▸ NM (work)bench

établir [etablir] /2/ VT (*papiers d'identité, facture*) to make out; (*liste, programme*) to draw up; (*gouvernement, artisan etc: aider à s'installer*) to set up, establish; (*entreprise, atelier, camp*) to set up; (*réputation, usage, fait, culpabilité, relations*) to establish; (*Sport: record*) to set; **s'établir** VI (*se faire: entente etc*) to be established; **s'établir (à son compte)** to set up in business; **s'établir à/près de** to settle in/near

établissement [etablismɑ̃] NM making out; drawing up; setting up, establishing; (*entreprise, institution*) establishment; ~ **de crédit** credit institution; ~ **hospitalier** hospital complex; ~ **industriel** industrial plant, factory; ~ **scolaire** school, educational establishment

étage [etaʒ] NM (*d'immeuble*) storey (BRIT), story (US), floor; (*de fusée*) stage; (*Géo: de culture, végétation*) level; **au 2ème ~** on the 2nd (BRIT) *ou* 3rd (US) floor; **à l'~** upstairs; **maison à deux étages** two-storey *ou* -story house; **c'est à quel ~?** what floor is it on?; **de bas ~** *adj* low-born; (*médiocre*) inferior

étager [etaʒe] /3/ VT (*cultures*) to lay out in tiers; **s'étager** VI (*prix*) to range; (*zones, cultures*) to lie on different levels

étagère [etaʒɛr] NF (*rayon*) shelf; (*meuble*) shelves *pl*, set of shelves

étai [etɛ] NM stay, prop

étain [etɛ̃] NM tin; (*Orfèvrerie*) pewter *no pl*

étais *etc* [etɛ] VB *voir* **être**

étal [etal] NM stall

étalage [etalaʒ] NM display; (*vitrine*) display window; **faire ~ de** to show off, parade

étalagiste [etalaʒist] NMF window-dresser

étale [etal] ADJ (*mer*) slack

étalement [etalmɑ̃] NM spreading; (*échelonnement*) staggering

étaler [etale] /1/ VT (*carte, nappe*) to spread (out); (*peinture, liquide*) to spread; (*échelonner: paiements, dates, vacances*) to spread, stagger; (*exposer: marchandises*) to display; (*richesses, connaissances*) to parade; **s'étaler** VI (*liquide*) to spread out; (*fam*) to fall flat on one's face, come a cropper (BRIT); **s'étaler sur** (*paiements etc*) to be spread over

étalon [etalɔ̃] NM (*mesure*) standard; (*cheval*) stallion; **l'~-or** the gold standard

étalonner [etalɔne] /1/ VT to calibrate

étamer [etame] /1/ VT (*casserole*) to tin(plate); (*glace*) to silver

étamine [etamin] NF (*Bot*) stamen; (*tissu*) butter muslin

étanche [etɑ̃ʃ] ADJ (*récipient, aussi fig*) watertight; (*montre, vêtement*) waterproof; ~ **à l'air** airtight

étanchéité [etɑ̃ʃeite] NF watertightness; airtightness

étancher [etɑ̃ʃe] /1/ VT (*liquide*) to stop (flowing); ~ **sa soif** to quench *ou* slake one's thirst

étançon [etɑ̃sɔ̃] NM (*Tech*) prop

étançonner [etɑ̃sɔne] /1/ VT to prop up

étang [etɑ̃] NM pond

étant [etɑ̃] VB *voir* **être**; **donné**

étape [etap] NF stage; (*lieu d'arrivée*) stopping place; (: *Cyclisme*) staging point; **faire ~ à** to stop off at; **brûler les étapes** (*fig*) to cut corners

état [eta] NM (*Pol, condition*) state; (*d'un article d'occasion etc*) condition, state; (*liste*) inventory, statement; (*condition: professionnelle*) profession, trade; (: *sociale*) status; **en bon/mauvais ~** in good/poor condition; **en ~ (de marche)** in (working) order; **remettre en ~** to repair; **hors d'~** out of order; **être en ~/hors d'~ de faire** to be in a state/in no fit state to do; **en tout ~ de cause** in any event; **être dans tous ses états** to be in a state; **faire ~ de** (*alléguer*) to put forward; **en ~ d'arrestation** under arrest; **~ de grâce** (*Rel*) state of grace; (*fig*) honeymoon period; **en ~ de grâce** (*fig*) inspired; **en ~ d'ivresse** under the influence of drink; **~ de choses** (*situation*) state of affairs; **l'É~** the State; **~ civil** civil status; (*bureau*) registry office (BRIT); **~ d'esprit** frame of mind; **~ des lieux** inventory of fixtures; **~ de santé** state of health; **~ de siège/d'urgence** state of siege/emergency; **~ de veille** (*Psych*) waking state; **états d'âme** moods; **les États barbaresques** the Barbary States; **les États du Golfe** the Gulf States; **états de service** service record *sg*

étatique [etatik] ADJ state *cpd*, State *cpd*

étatisation [etatizasjɔ̃] NF nationalization

étatiser [etatize] /1/ VT to bring under state control

étatisme [etatism] NM state control

étatiste [etatist] ADJ (*doctrine etc*) of state control ▸ NMF partisan of state control

état-major [etamaʒɔʀ] (*pl* **états-majors**) NM (*Mil*) staff; (*d'un parti etc*) top advisers *pl*; (*d'une entreprise*) top management

État-providence [etapʀɔvidɑ̃s] NM welfare state

États-Unis [etazyni] NMPL: **les ~ (d'Amérique)** the United States (of America)

étau, x [eto] NM vice (BRIT), vise (US)

étayer [eteje] /8/ VT to prop *ou* shore up; (*fig*) to back up

et cætera, et cetera, etc. [ɛtseteʀa] ADV et cetera, and so on, etc

été [ete] PP *de* **être** ▸ NM summer; **en ~** in summer

éteignais *etc* [etɛɲɛ] VB *voir* **éteindre**

éteignoir [etɛɲwaʀ] NM (candle) snuffer; (*péj*) killjoy, wet blanket

éteindre [etɛ̃dʀ] /52/ VT (*lampe, lumière, radio, chauffage*) to turn *ou* switch off; (*cigarette, incendie, bougie*) to put out, extinguish; (*Jur: dette*) to extinguish; **s'éteindre** VI to go off; (*feu, lumière*) to go out; (*mourir*) to pass away

éteint, e [etɛ̃, -ɛ̃t] PP *de* **éteindre** ▸ ADJ (*fig*) lacklustre, dull; (*volcan*) extinct; **tous feux éteints** (*Auto: rouler*) without lights

étendard [etɑ̃daʀ] NM standard

étendre [etɑ̃dʀ] /41/ VT (*appliquer: pâte, liquide*) to spread; (*déployer: carte etc*) to spread out; (*sur un fil: lessive, linge*) to hang up *ou* out; (*bras, jambes, par terre: blessé*) to stretch out; (*diluer*) to dilute, thin; (*fig: agrandir*) to extend; (*fam: adversaire*) to floor; **s'étendre** VI (*augmenter, se propager*) to spread; (*terrain, forêt etc*): **s'étendre jusqu'à/à … à** to stretch as far as/from … to; **s'étendre (sur)** (*s'allonger*) to stretch out (upon); (*se coucher*) to lie down (on); (*fig: expliquer*) to elaborate *ou* enlarge (upon)

étendu, e [etɑ̃dy] ADJ extensive ▸ NF (*d'eau, de sable*) stretch, expanse; (*importance*) extent

éternel, le [etɛʀnɛl] ADJ eternal; **les neiges éternelles** perpetual snow

éternellement [etɛʀnɛlmɑ̃] ADV eternally

éterniser [etɛʀnize] /1/: **s'éterniser** VI to last for ages; (*personne*) to stay for ages

éternité [etɛʀnite] NF eternity; **il y a** *ou* **ça fait une ~ que** it's ages since; **de toute ~** from time immemoral; **ça a duré une ~** it lasted for ages

éternuement [etɛʀnymɑ̃] NM sneeze

éternuer [etɛʀnɥe] /1/ VI to sneeze

êtes [ɛt(z)] VB *voir* **être**

étêter [etete] /1/ VT (*arbre*) to poll(ard); (*clou, poisson*) to cut the head off

éther [etɛʀ] NM ether

éthéré, e [etere] ADJ ethereal

Éthiopie [etjɔpi] NF: **l'~** Ethiopia

éthiopien, ne [etjɔpjɛ̃, -ɛn] ADJ Ethiopian

éthique [etik] ADJ ethical ▸ NF ethics *sg*

ethnie [ɛtni] NF ethnic group

ethnique [ɛtnik] ADJ ethnic

ethnographe [ɛtnɔgraf] NMF ethnographer

ethnographie [ɛtnɔgrafi] NF ethnography

ethnographique [ɛtnɔgrafik] ADJ ethnographic(al)

ethnologie [ɛtnɔlɔʒi] NF ethnology

ethnologique [ɛtnɔlɔʒik] ADJ ethnological

ethnologue [ɛtnɔlɔg] NMF ethnologist

éthylique [etilik] ADJ alcoholic

éthylisme [etilism] NM alcoholism

étiage [etjaʒ] NM low water

étiez [etje] VB *voir* **être**

étincelant, e [etɛ̃slɑ̃, -ɑ̃t] ADJ sparkling

étinceler [etɛ̃s(ə)le] /4/ VI to sparkle

étincelle [etɛ̃sɛl] NF spark

étioler [etjɔle] /1/: **s'étioler** VI to wilt

étions [etjɔ̃] VB *voir* **être**

étique [etik] ADJ skinny, bony

étiquetage [etiktaʒ] NM labelling

étiqueter [etikte] /4/ VT to label

étiquette [etikɛt] NF (*voir* **étiqueter** ▸ NF label; (*protocole*): **l'~** etiquette

étirer [etiʀe] /1/ VT to stretch; (*ressort*) to stretch out; **s'étirer** VI (*personne*) to stretch; (*convoi, route*): **s'étirer sur** to stretch out over

étoffe [etɔf] NF material, fabric; **avoir l'~ d'un chef** *etc* to be cut out to be a leader *etc*; **avoir de l'~** to be a forceful personality

étoffer [etɔfe] /1/ VT to flesh out; **s'étoffer** VI to fill out

étoile [etwal] NF star ▸ ADJ: **danseuse** *ou* **danseur ~** leading dancer; **la bonne/mauvaise ~ de qn** sb's lucky/unlucky star;

à la belle ~ (out) in the open; ~ **filante** shooting star; ~ **de mer** starfish; ~ **polaire** pole star

étoilé, e [etwale] ADJ starry

étole [etɔl] NF stole

étonnamment [etɔnamɑ̃] ADV amazingly

étonnant, e [etɔnɑ̃, -ɑ̃t] ADJ surprising

étonné, e [etɔne] ADJ surprised

étonnement [etɔnmɑ̃] NM surprise, amazing; **à mon grand ~ ...** to my great surprise *ou* amazement ...

étonner [etɔne] /**1**/ VT to surprise, amaze; **s'étonner que/de** to be surprised that/at; **cela m'étonnerait (que)** (*j'en doute*) I'd be (very) surprised (if)

étouffant, e [etufɑ̃, -ɑ̃t] ADJ stifling

étouffé, e [etufe] ADJ (*asphyxié*) suffocated; (*assourdi: cris, rires*) smothered ▶ NF: **à l'~** (*Culin: poisson, légumes*) steamed; (: *viande*) braised

étouffement [etufmɑ̃] NM suffocation

étouffer [etufe] /**1**/ VT to suffocate; (*bruit*) to muffle; (*scandale*) to hush up ▶ VI to suffocate; (*avoir trop chaud: aussi fig*) to feel stifled; **s'étouffer** VI (*en mangeant etc*) to choke; **on étouffe** it's stifling

étouffoir [etufwaʀ] NM (*Mus*) damper

étourderie [etuʀdəʀi] NF (*caractère*) absent-mindedness *no pl*; (*faute*) thoughtless blunder; **faute d'~** careless mistake

étourdi, e [etuʀdi] ADJ (*distrait*) scatterbrained, heedless

étourdiment [etuʀdimɑ̃] ADV rashly

étourdir [etuʀdiʀ] /**2**/ VT (*assommer*) to stun, daze; (*griser*) to make dizzy *ou* giddy

étourdissant, e [etuʀdisɑ̃, -ɑ̃t] ADJ staggering

étourdissement [etuʀdismɑ̃] NM dizzy spell

étourneau, x [etuʀno] NM starling

étrange [etʀɑ̃ʒ] ADJ strange

étrangement [etʀɑ̃ʒmɑ̃] ADV strangely

étranger, -ère [etʀɑ̃ʒe, -ɛʀ] ADJ foreign; (*pas de la famille, non familier*) strange ▶ NM/F foreigner; stranger ▶ NM: **l'~** foreign countries; **à l'~** abroad; **de l'~** from abroad; ~ **à** (*mal connu*) unfamiliar to; (*sans rapport*) irrelevant to

étrangeté [etʀɑ̃ʒte] NF strangeness

étranglé, e [etʀɑ̃gle] ADJ: **d'une voix ~** in a strangled voice

étranglement [etʀɑ̃gləmɑ̃] NM (*d'une vallée etc*) constriction, narrow passage

étrangler [etʀɑ̃gle] /**1**/ VT to strangle; (*fig: presse, libertés*) to stifle; **s'étrangler** VI (*en mangeant etc*) to choke; (*se resserrer*) to make a bottleneck

étrave [etʀav] NF stem

(MOT-CLÉ)

être [ɛtʀ] /**61**/ NM being; **être humain** human being

▶ VB COPULE **1** (*état, description*) to be; **il est instituteur** he is *ou* he's a teacher; **vous êtes grand/intelligent/fatigué** you are *ou* you're tall/clever/tired

2 (+à: *appartenir*) to be; **le livre est à Paul** the book is Paul's *ou* belongs to Paul; **c'est à moi/eux** it is *ou* it's mine/theirs

3 (+de: *provenance*): **il est de Paris** he is from Paris; (: *appartenance*): **il est des nôtres** he is one of us

4 (*date*): **nous sommes le 10 janvier** it's the 10th of January (today)

▶ VI to be; **je ne serai pas ici demain** I won't be here tomorrow

▶ VB AUX **1** to have; to be; **être arrivé/allé** to have arrived/gone; **il est parti** he has left, he has gone

2 (*forme passive*) to be; **être fait par** to be made by; **il a été promu** he has been promoted

3 (+à +inf: *obligation, but*): **c'est à réparer** it needs repairing; **c'est à essayer** it should be tried; **il est à espérer que ...** it is *ou* it's to be hoped that ...

▶ VB IMPERS **1**: **il est** (+*adj*) it is; **il est impossible de le faire** it's impossible to do it

2: **il est** (*heure, date*): **il est 10 heures** it is *ou* it's 10 o'clock

3 (*emphatique*): **c'est moi** it's me; **c'est à lui de le faire** it's up to him to do it; *voir aussi* **est-ce que; n'est-ce pas; c'est-à-dire; ce**

étreindre [etʀɛ̃dʀ] /**52**/ VT to clutch, grip; (*amoureusement, amicalement*) to embrace; **s'étreindre** to embrace

étreinte [etʀɛ̃t] NF clutch, grip; embrace; **resserrer son ~ autour de** (*fig*) to tighten one's grip on *ou* around

étrenner [etʀene] /**1**/ VT to use (*ou* wear) for the first time

étrennes [etʀɛn] NFPL (*cadeaux*) New Year's present; (*gratifications*) ≈ Christmas box *sg*, ≈ Christmas bonus

étrier [etʀije] NM stirrup

étriller [etʀije] /**1**/ VT (*cheval*) to curry; (*fam: battre*) to slaughter (*fig*)

étriper [etʀipe] /**1**/ VT to gut; (*fam*): ~ **qn** to tear sb's guts out

étriqué, e [etʀike] ADJ skimpy

étroit, e [etʀwa, -wat] ADJ narrow; (*vêtement*) tight; (*fig: liens, collaboration*) close, tight; **à l'~** cramped; ~ **d'esprit** narrow-minded

étroitement [etʀwatmɑ̃] ADV closely

étroitesse [etʀwatɛs] NF narrowness; ~ **d'esprit** narrow-mindedness

étrusque [etʀysk] ADJ Etruscan

étude [etyd] NF studying; (*ouvrage, rapport, Mus*) study; (*de notaire: bureau*) office; (: *charge*) practice; (*Scol: salle de travail*) study room; **études** NFPL (*Scol*) studies; **être à l'~** (*projet etc*) to be under consideration; **faire des études (de droit/médecine)** to study (law/medicine); **études secondaires/supérieures** secondary/higher education; ~ **de cas** case study; ~ **de faisabilité** feasibility study; ~ **de marché** (*Écon*) market research

étudiant, e [etydjɑ̃, -ɑ̃t] ADJ, NM/F student

étudié, e [etydje] ADJ (*démarche*) studied; (*système*) carefully designed; (*prix*) keen

étudier [etydje] /**7**/ VT, VI to study

étui [etɥi] NM case

étuve [etyv] NF steamroom; (*appareil*) sterilizer

étuvée [etyve]: **à l'~** adv braised
étymologie [etimɔlɔʒi] NF etymology
étymologique [etimɔlɔʒik] ADJ etymological
EU SIGLE MPL (= États-Unis) US
eu, eue [y] PP de avoir
EUA SIGLE MPL (= États-Unis d'Amérique) USA
eucalyptus [økaliptys] NM eucalyptus
Eucharistie [økaʀisti] NF: **l'~** the Eucharist, the Lord's Supper
eucharistique [økaʀistik] ADJ eucharistic
euclidien, ne [øklidjɛ̃, -ɛn] ADJ Euclidian
eugénique [øʒenik] ADJ eugenic ▸ NF eugenics sg
eugénisme [øʒenism] NM eugenics sg
euh [ø] EXCL er
eunuque [ønyk] NM eunuch
euphémique [øfemik] ADJ euphemistic
euphémisme [øfemism] NM euphemism
euphonie [øfɔni] NF euphony
euphorbe [øfɔʀb] NF (Bot) spurge
euphorie [øfɔʀi] NF euphoria
euphorique [øfɔʀik] ADJ euphoric
euphorisant, e [øfɔʀizɑ̃, -ɑ̃t] ADJ exhilarating
eurafricain, e [øʀafʀikɛ̃, -ɛn] ADJ Eurafrican
eurasiatique [øʀazjatik] ADJ Eurasiatic
Eurasie [øʀazi] NF: **l'~** Eurasia
eurasien, ne [øʀazjɛ̃, -ɛn] ADJ Eurasian
EURATOM [øʀatɔm] SIGLE F Euratom
eurent [yʀ] VB voir avoir
euro [øʀo] NM euro
euro- [øʀo] PRÉFIXE Euro-
eurocrate [øʀɔkʀat] NMF (péj) Eurocrat
eurodevise [øʀɔdəviz] NF Eurocurrency
eurodollar [øʀɔdɔlaʀ] NM Eurodollar
Euroland [øʀɔlɑ̃d] NM Euroland
euromonnaie [øʀɔmɔnɛ] NF Eurocurrency
Europe [øʀɔp] NF: **l'~** Europe; **l'~ centrale** Central Europe; **l'~ verte** European agriculture
européanisation [øʀɔpeanizasjɔ̃] NF Europeanization
européaniser [øʀɔpeanize] /1/ VT to Europeanize
européen, ne [øʀɔpeɛ̃, -ɛn] ADJ European ▸ NM/F: **E~, ne** European
eurosceptique [øʀoseptik] NMF Eurosceptic
Eurovision [øʀovizjɔ̃] NF Eurovision; **émission en ~** Eurovision broadcast
eus etc [y] VB voir avoir
euthanasie [øtanazi] NF euthanasia
eux [ø] PRON (sujet) they; (objet) them; **~, ils ont fait ...** THEY did ...
évacuation [evakɥasjɔ̃] NF evacuation
évacué, e [evakɥe] NM/F evacuee
évacuer [evakɥe] /1/ VT (salle, région) to evacuate, clear; (occupants, population) to evacuate; (toxine etc) to evacuate, discharge
évadé, e [evade] ADJ escaped ▸ NM/F escapee
évader [evade] /1/: **s'évader** VI to escape
évaluation [evalɥasjɔ̃] NF assessment, evaluation
évaluer [evalɥe] /1/ VT (expertiser) to assess, evaluate; (juger approximativement) to estimate
évanescent, e [evanesɑ̃, -ɑ̃t] ADJ evanescent
évangélique [evɑ̃ʒelik] ADJ evangelical

évangélisation [evɑ̃ʒelizasjɔ̃] NF evangelization
évangéliser [evɑ̃ʒelize] /1/ VT to evangelize
évangéliste [evɑ̃ʒelist] NM evangelist
évangile [evɑ̃ʒil] NM gospel; (texte de la Bible): **l'É~** the Gospel; **ce n'est pas l'É~** (fig) it's not gospel
évanoui, e [evanwi] ADJ in a faint; **tomber ~** to faint
évanouir [evanwiʀ] /2/: **s'évanouir** VI to faint, pass out; (disparaître) to vanish, disappear
évanouissement [evanwismɑ̃] NM (syncope) fainting fit; (Méd) loss of consciousness
évaporation [evapɔʀasjɔ̃] NF evaporation
évaporé, e [evapɔʀe] ADJ giddy, scatterbrained
évaporer [evapɔʀe] /1/: **s'évaporer** VI to evaporate
évasé, e [evaze] ADJ (jupe etc) flared
évaser [evaze] /1/ VT (tuyau) to widen, open out; (jupe, pantalon) to flare; **s'évaser** VI to widen, open out
évasif, -ive [evazif, -iv] ADJ evasive
évasion [evazjɔ̃] NF escape; **littérature d'~** escapist literature; **~ des capitaux** (Écon) flight of capital; **~ fiscale** tax avoidance
évasivement [evazivmɑ̃] ADV evasively
évêché [eveʃe] NM (fonction) bishopric; (palais) bishop's palace
éveil [evɛj] NM awakening; **être en ~** to be alert; **mettre qn en ~, donner l'~ à qn** to arouse sb's suspicions; **activités d'~** early-learning activities
éveillé, e [eveje] ADJ awake; (vif) alert, sharp
éveiller [eveje] /1/ VT to (a)waken; (soupçons etc) to arouse; **s'éveiller** VI to (a)waken; (fig) to be aroused
événement [evɛnmɑ̃] NM event
éventail [evɑ̃taj] NM fan; (choix) range; **en ~** fanned out; fan-shaped
éventaire [evɑ̃tɛʀ] NM stall, stand
éventé, e [evɑ̃te] ADJ (parfum, vin) stale
éventer [evɑ̃te] /1/ VT (secret, complot) to uncover; (avec un éventail) to fan; **s'éventer** VI (parfum, vin) to go stale
éventrer [evɑ̃tʀe] /1/ VT to disembowel; (fig) to tear ou rip open
éventualité [evɑ̃tɥalite] NF eventuality; possibility; **dans l'~ de** in the event of; **parer à toute ~** to guard against all eventualities
éventuel, le [evɑ̃tɥɛl] ADJ possible
éventuellement [evɑ̃tɥɛlmɑ̃] ADV possibly
évêque [evɛk] NM bishop
Everest [evʀɛst] NM: **(mont) ~** (Mount) Everest
évertuer [evɛʀtɥe] /1/: **s'évertuer** VI: **s'évertuer à faire** to try very hard to do
éviction [eviksjɔ̃] NF ousting, supplanting; (de locataire) eviction
évidemment [evidamɑ̃] ADV (bien sûr) of course; (certainement) obviously
évidence [evidɑ̃s] NF obviousness; (fait) obvious fact; **se rendre à l'~** to bow before the evidence; **nier l'~** to deny the evidence; **à l'~** evidently; **de toute ~** quite obviously ou evidently; **en ~** conspicuous; **être en ~** to be

clearly visible; **mettre en ~** (*fait*) to highlight
évident, e [evidɑ̃, -ɑ̃t] ADJ obvious, evident; **ce n'est pas ~** (*cela pose des problèmes*) it's not (all that) straightforward, it's not as simple as all that
évider [evide] /1/ VT to scoop out
évier [evje] NM (kitchen) sink
évincer [evɛ̃se] /3/ VT to oust, supplant
évitable [evitabl] ADJ avoidable
évitement [evitmɑ̃] NM: **place d'~** (*Auto*) passing place
éviter [evite] /1/ VT to avoid; **~ de faire/que qch ne se passe** to avoid doing/sth happening; **~ qch à qn** to spare sb sth
évocateur, -trice [evokatœʀ, -tʀis] ADJ evocative, suggestive
évocation [evɔkasjɔ̃] NF evocation
évolué, e [evɔlɥe] ADJ advanced; (*personne*) broad-minded
évoluer [evɔlɥe] /1/ VI (*enfant, maladie*) to develop; (*situation, moralement*) to evolve, develop; (*aller et venir: danseur etc*) to move about, circle
évolutif, -ive [evɔlytif, -iv] ADJ evolving
évolution [evɔlysjɔ̃] NF development; evolution; **évolutions** NFPL movements
évolutionnisme [evɔlysjɔnism] NM evolutionism
évoquer [evɔke] /1/ VT to call to mind, evoke; (*mentionner*) to mention
ex. ABR (= *exemple*) ex.
ex- [ɛks] PRÉFIXE ex-; **son ~mari** her ex-husband; **son ~femme** his ex-wife
exacerbé, e [ɛgzasɛʀbe] ADJ (*orgueil, sensibilité*) exaggerated
exacerber [ɛgzasɛʀbe] /1/ VT to exacerbate
exact, e [ɛgza(kt), ɛgzakt] ADJ (*précis*) exact, accurate, precise; (*correct*) correct; (*ponctuel*) punctual; **l'heure ~** the right *ou* exact time
exactement [ɛgzaktəmɑ̃] ADV exactly, accurately, precisely; correctly; (*c'est cela même*) exactly
exaction [ɛgzaksjɔ̃] NF (*d'argent*) exaction; (*gén pl: actes de violence*) abuse(s)
exactitude [ɛgzaktityd] NF exactitude, accurateness, precision
ex aequo [ɛgzeko] ADJ INV equally placed; **classé 1er ~** placed equal first; **arriver ~** to finish neck and neck
exagération [ɛgzaʒeʀasjɔ̃] NF exaggeration
exagéré, e [ɛgzaʒeʀe] ADJ (*prix etc*) excessive
exagérément [ɛgzaʒeʀemɑ̃] ADV excessively
exagérer [ɛgzaʒeʀe] /6/ VT to exaggerate ▶ VI (*abuser*) to go too far; (*dépasser les bornes*) to overstep the mark; (*déformer les faits*) to exaggerate; **s'exagérer qch** to exaggerate sth
exaltant, e [ɛgzaltɑ̃, -ɑ̃t] ADJ exhilarating
exaltation [ɛgzaltasjɔ̃] NF exaltation
exalté, e [ɛgzalte] ADJ (over)excited ▶ NM/F (*péj*) fanatic
exalter [ɛgzalte] /1/ VT (*enthousiasmer*) to excite, elate; (*glorifier*) to exalt
examen [ɛgzamɛ̃] NM examination; (*Scol*) exam, examination; **à l'~** (*dossier, projet*) under

consideration; (*Comm*) on approval; **~ blanc** mock exam(ination); **~ de la vue** sight test; **~ médical** (medical) examination; (*analyse*) test
examinateur, -trice [ɛgzaminatœʀ, -tʀis] NM/F examiner
examiner [ɛgzamine] /1/ VT to examine
exaspérant, e [ɛgzaspeʀɑ̃, -ɑ̃t] ADJ exasperating
exaspération [ɛgzaspeʀasjɔ̃] NF exasperation
exaspéré, e [ɛgzaspeʀe] ADJ exasperated
exaspérer [ɛgzaspeʀe] /6/ VT to exasperate; (*aggraver*) to exacerbate
exaucer [ɛgzose] /3/ VT (*vœu*) to grant, fulfil; **~ qn** to grant sb's wishes
ex cathedra [ɛkskatedʀa] ADJ INV, ADV ex cathedra
excavateur [ɛkskavatœʀ] NM excavator, mechanical digger
excavation [ɛkskavasjɔ̃] NF excavation
excavatrice [ɛkskavatʀis] NF = **excavateur**
excédent [ɛksedɑ̃] NM surplus; **en ~** surplus; **payer 60 euros d'~** (*de bagages*) to pay 60 euros excess baggage; **~ de bagages** excess baggage; **~ commercial** trade surplus
excédentaire [ɛksedɑ̃tɛʀ] ADJ surplus, excess
excéder [ɛksede] /6/ VT (*dépasser*) to exceed; (*agacer*) to exasperate; **excédé de fatigue** exhausted; **excédé de travail** worn out with work
excellence [ɛksɛlɑ̃s] NF excellence; (*titre*) Excellency; **par ~** par excellence
excellent, e [ɛksɛlɑ̃, -ɑ̃t] ADJ excellent
exceller [ɛksele] /1/ VI: **~ (dans)** to excel (in)
excentricité [ɛksɑ̃tʀisite] NF eccentricity
excentrique [ɛksɑ̃tʀik] ADJ eccentric; (*quartier*) outlying ▶ NMF eccentric
excentriquement [ɛksɑ̃tʀikmɑ̃] ADV eccentrically
excepté, e [ɛksɛpte] ADJ, PRÉP: **les élèves exceptés, ~ les élèves** except for *ou* apart from the pupils; **~ si/quand** except if/when; **~ que** except that
excepter [ɛksɛpte] /1/ VT to except
exception [ɛksɛpsjɔ̃] NF exception; **faire ~** to be an exception; **faire une ~** to make an exception; **sans ~** without exception; **à l'~ de** except for, with the exception of; **d'~** (*mesure, loi*) special, exceptional
exceptionnel, le [ɛksɛpsjɔnɛl] ADJ exceptional; (*prix*) special
exceptionnellement [ɛksɛpsjɔnɛlmɑ̃] ADV exceptionally; (*par exception*) by way of an exception, on this occasion
excès [ɛksɛ] NM surplus ▶ NMPL excesses; **à l'~** (*méticuleux, généreux*) to excess; **avec ~** to excess; **sans ~** in moderation; **tomber dans l'~ inverse** to go to the opposite extreme; **~ de langage** immoderate language; **~ de pouvoir** abuse of power; **faire des ~** to overindulge; **~ de vitesse** speeding *no pl*, exceeding the speed limit; **~ de zèle** overzealousness *no pl*
excessif, -ive [ɛksesif, -iv] ADJ excessive
excessivement [ɛksesivmɑ̃] ADV (*trop: cher*) excessively, inordinately; (*très: riche, laid*) extremely, incredibly; **manger/boire ~** to eat/drink to excess

exciper [ɛksipe] /1/: ~ **de** vt to plead
excipient [ɛksipjɑ̃] NM (Méd) inert base, excipient
exciser [ɛksize] /1/ VT (Méd) to excise
excision [ɛksizjɔ̃] NF (Méd) excision; (rituelle) circumcision
excitant, e [ɛksitɑ̃, -ɑ̃t] ADJ exciting ▶ NM stimulant
excitation [ɛksitasjɔ̃] NF (état) excitement
excité, e [ɛksite] ADJ excited
exciter [ɛksite] /1/ VT to excite; (café etc) to stimulate; **s'exciter** VI to get excited; ~ **qn à** (révolte etc) to incite sb to
exclamation [ɛksklamasjɔ̃] NF exclamation
exclamer [ɛksklame] /1/: **s'exclamer** VI to exclaim
exclu, e [ɛkskly] PP de **exclure** ▶ ADJ: **il est/n'est pas ~ que …** it's out of the question/not impossible that …; **ce n'est pas ~** it's not impossible, I don't rule that out
exclure [ɛksklyʀ] /35/ VT (faire sortir) to expel; (ne pas compter) to exclude, leave out; (rendre impossible) to exclude, rule out
exclusif, -ive [ɛksklyzif, -iv] ADJ exclusive; **avec la mission exclusive/dans le but ~ de …** with the sole mission/aim of …; **agent ~** sole agent
exclusion [ɛksklyzjɔ̃] NF expulsion; **à l'~ de** with the exclusion ou exception of
exclusivement [ɛksklyzivmɑ̃] ADV exclusively
exclusivité [ɛksklyzivite] NF exclusiveness; (Comm) exclusive rights pl; **film passant en ~ à** film showing only at
excommunier [ɛkskɔmynje] /7/ VT to excommunicate
excréments [ɛkskʀemɑ̃] NMPL excrement sg, faeces
excréter [ɛkskʀete] /6/ VT to excrete
excroissance [ɛkskʀwasɑ̃s] NF excrescence, outgrowth
excursion [ɛkskyʀsjɔ̃] NF (en autocar) excursion, trip; (à pied) walk, hike; **faire une ~** to go on an excursion ou a trip; to go on a walk ou hike
excursionniste [ɛkskyʀsjɔnist] NMF tripper; hiker
excusable [ɛkskyzabl] ADJ excusable
excuse [ɛkskyz] NF excuse; **excuses** NFPL (regret) apology sg, apologies; **faire des excuses** to apologize; **faire ses excuses** to offer one's apologies; **mot d'~** (Scol) note from one's parent(s) (to explain absence etc); **lettre d'excuses** letter of apology
excuser [ɛkskyze] /1/ VT to excuse; **s'excuser (de)** to apologize (for); ~ **qn de qch** (dispenser) to excuse sb from sth; "**excusez-moi**" "I'm sorry"; (pour attirer l'attention) "excuse me"; **se faire excuser** to ask to be excused
exécrable [ɛgzekʀabl] ADJ atrocious
exécrer [ɛgzekʀe] /6/ VT to loathe, abhor
exécutant, e [ɛgzekytɑ̃, -ɑ̃t] NM/F performer
exécuter [ɛgzekyte] /1/ VT (prisonnier) to execute; (tâche etc) to execute, carry out; (Mus: jouer) to perform, execute; (Inform) to run; **s'exécuter** VI to comply
exécuteur, -trice [ɛgzekytœʀ, -tʀis] NM/F (testamentaire) executor ▶ NM (bourreau) executioner
exécutif, -ive [ɛgzekytif, -iv] ADJ, NM (Pol) executive
exécution [ɛgzekysjɔ̃] NF execution; carrying out; **mettre à ~** to carry out
exécutoire [ɛgzekytwaʀ] ADJ (Jur) (legally) binding
exégèse [ɛgzeʒɛz] NF exegesis
exégète [ɛgzeʒɛt] NM exegete
exemplaire [ɛgzɑ̃plɛʀ] ADJ exemplary ▶ NM copy
exemple [ɛgzɑ̃pl] NM example; **par ~** for instance, for example; (valeur intensive) really!; **sans ~** (bêtise, gourmandise etc) unparalleled; **donner l'~** to set an example; **prendre ~ sur** to take as a model; **à l'~ de** just like; **pour l'~** (punir) as an example
exempt, e [ɛgzɑ̃, -ɑ̃t] ADJ: ~ **de** (dispensé de) exempt from; (sans) free from; ~ **de taxes** tax-free
exempter [ɛgzɑ̃te] /1/ VT: ~ **de** to exempt from
exercé, e [ɛgzɛʀse] ADJ trained
exercer [ɛgzɛʀse] /3/ VT (pratiquer) to exercise, practise; (faire usage de: prérogative) to exercise; (effectuer: influence, contrôle, pression) to exert; (former) to exercise, train; **s'exercer** VI (médecin) to be in practice; (sportif, musicien) to practise; (se faire sentir: pression etc): **s'exercer (sur** ou **contre)** to be exerted (on); **s'exercer à faire qch** to train o.s. to do sth
exercice [ɛgzɛʀsis] NM practice; exercising; (tâche, travail) exercise; (Comm, Admin: période) accounting period; (Mil) drill; **l'~** (sportif etc) exercise; **en ~** (juge) in office; (médecin) practising; **dans l'~ de ses fonctions** in the discharge of his duties; **exercices d'assouplissement** limbering-up (exercises)
exergue [ɛgzɛʀg] NM: **mettre en ~** (inscription) to inscribe; **porter en ~** to be inscribed with
exhalaison [ɛgzalɛzɔ̃] NF exhalation
exhaler [ɛgzale] /1/ VT (parfum) to exhale; (souffle, son, soupir) to utter, breathe; **s'exhaler** VI to rise (up)
exhausser [ɛgzose] /1/ VT to raise (up)
exhausteur [ɛgzostœʀ] NM extractor fan
exhaustif, -ive [ɛgzostif, -iv] ADJ exhaustive
exhiber [ɛgzibe] /1/ VT (montrer: papiers, certificat) to present, produce; (péj) to display, flaunt; **s'exhiber** VI (personne) to parade; (exhibitionniste) to expose o.s.
exhibitionnisme [ɛgzibisjɔnism] NM exhibitionism
exhibitionniste [ɛgzibisjɔnist] NMF exhibitionist
exhortation [ɛgzɔʀtasjɔ̃] NF exhortation
exhorter [ɛgzɔʀte] /1/ VT: ~ **qn à faire** to urge sb to do
exhumer [ɛgzyme] /1/ VT to exhume
exigeant, e [ɛgziʒɑ̃, -ɑ̃t] ADJ demanding; (péj) hard to please
exigence [ɛgziʒɑ̃s] NF demand, requirement
exiger [ɛgziʒe] /3/ VT to demand, require
exigible [ɛgziʒibl] ADJ (Comm, Jur) payable

exigu, ë [ɛgzigy] ADJ cramped, tiny
exiguité [ɛgzigɥite] NF (*d'un lieu*) cramped nature
exil [ɛgzil] NM exile; **en ~** in exile
exilé, e [ɛgzile] NM/F exile
exiler [ɛgzile] /1/ VT to exile; **s'exiler** VI to go into exile
existant, e [ɛgzistɑ̃, -ɑ̃t] ADJ (*actuel, présent*) existing
existence [ɛgzistɑ̃s] NF existence; **dans l'~** in life
existentialisme [ɛgzistɑ̃sjalism] NM existentialism
existentiel, le [ɛgzistɑ̃sjɛl] ADJ existential
exister [ɛgziste] /1/ VI to exist; **il existe un/des** there is a/are (some)
exode [ɛgzɔd] NM exodus
exonération [ɛgzɔnerasjɔ̃] NF exemption
exonéré, e [ɛgzɔnere] ADJ: **~ de TVA** zero-rated (for VAT)
exonérer [ɛgzɔnere] /6/ VT: **~ de** to exempt from
exorbitant, e [ɛgzɔrbitɑ̃, -ɑ̃t] ADJ exorbitant
exorbité, e [ɛgzɔrbite] ADJ: **yeux exorbités** bulging eyes
exorciser [ɛgzɔrsize] /1/ VT to exorcize
exorde [ɛgzɔrd] NM introduction
exotique [ɛgzɔtik] ADJ exotic; **yaourt aux fruits exotiques** tropical fruit yoghurt
exotisme [ɛgzɔtism] NM exoticism
expansif, -ive [ɛkspɑ̃sif, -iv] ADJ expansive, communicative
expansion [ɛkspɑ̃sjɔ̃] NF expansion
expansionniste [ɛkspɑ̃sjɔnist] ADJ expansionist
expansivité [ɛkspɑ̃sivite] NF expansiveness
expatrié, e [ɛkspatrije] NM/F expatriate
expatrier [ɛkspatrije] /7/ VT (*argent*) to take *ou* send out of the country; **s'expatrier** to leave one's country
expectative [ɛkspɛktativ] NF: **être dans l'~** to be waiting to see
expectorant, e [ɛkspɛktɔrɑ̃, -ɑ̃t] ADJ: **sirop ~** expectorant (syrup)
expectorer [ɛkspɛktɔre] /1/ VI to expectorate
expédient [ɛkspedjɑ̃] NM (*parfois péj*) expedient; **vivre d'expédients** to live by one's wits
expédier [ɛkspedje] /7/ VT (*lettre, paquet*) to send; (*troupes, renfort*) to dispatch; (*péj: travail etc*) to dispose of, dispatch
expéditeur, -trice [ɛkspeditœr, -tris] NM/F (*Postes*) sender
expéditif, -ive [ɛkspeditif, -iv] ADJ quick, expeditious
expédition [ɛkspedisjɔ̃] NF sending; (*scientifique, sportive, Mil*) expedition; **~ punitive** punitive raid
expéditionnaire [ɛkspedisjɔnɛr] ADJ: **corps ~** (*Mil*) task force
expérience [ɛksperjɑ̃s] NF (*de la vie, des choses*) experience; (*scientifique*) experiment; **avoir de l'~** to have experience, be experienced; **avoir l'~ de** to have experience of; **faire l'~ de qch** to experience sth; **~ de chimie/d'électricité** chemical/electrical experiment

expérimental, e, -aux [ɛksperimɑ̃tal, -o] ADJ experimental
expérimentalement [ɛksperimɑ̃talmɑ̃] ADV experimentally
expérimenté, e [ɛksperimɑ̃te] ADJ experienced
expérimenter [ɛksperimɑ̃te] /1/ VT (*machine, technique*) to test out, experiment with
expert, e [ɛkspɛr, -ɛrt] ADJ: **~ en** expert in ▶ NM (*spécialiste*) expert; **~ en assurances** insurance valuer
expert-comptable [ɛkspɛrkɔ̃tabl] (*pl* **experts-comptables**) NM ≈ chartered (*BRIT*) *ou* certified public (*US*) accountant
expertise [ɛkspɛrtiz] NF valuation; assessment; valuer's (*ou* assessor's) report; (*Jur*) (forensic) examination
expertiser [ɛkspɛrtize] /1/ VT (*objet de valeur*) to value; (*voiture accidentée etc*) to assess damage to
expier [ɛkspje] /7/ VT to expiate, atone for
expiration [ɛkspirasjɔ̃] NF expiry (*BRIT*), expiration; breathing out
expirer [ɛkspire] /1/ VI (*prendre fin, lit: mourir*) to expire; (*respirer*) to breathe out
explétif, -ive [ɛkspletif, -iv] ADJ (*Ling*) expletive
explicable [ɛksplikabl] ADJ: **pas ~** inexplicable
explicatif, -ive [ɛksplikatif, -iv] ADJ (*mot, texte, note*) explanatory
explication [ɛksplikasjɔ̃] NF explanation; (*discussion*) discussion; (*dispute*) argument; **~ de texte** (*Scol*) critical analysis (of a text)
explicite [ɛksplisit] ADJ explicit
explicitement [ɛksplisitmɑ̃] ADV explicitly
expliciter [ɛksplisite] /1/ VT to make explicit
expliquer [ɛksplike] /1/ VT to explain; **~ (à qn) comment/que** to point out *ou* explain (to sb) how/that; **s'expliquer** (*se faire comprendre: personne*) to explain o.s.; (*se disputer*) to have it out; (*comprendre*): **je m'explique son retard/absence** I understand his lateness/absence; **son erreur s'explique** one can understand his mistake; **s'expliquer avec qn** (*discuter*) to explain o.s. to sb
exploit [ɛksplwa] NM exploit, feat
exploitable [ɛksplwatabl] ADJ (*gisement etc*) that can be exploited; **~ par une machine** machine-readable
exploitant [ɛksplwatɑ̃] NMF: **~ (agricole)** farmer
exploitation [ɛksplwatasjɔ̃] NF exploitation; (*d'une entreprise*) running; (*entreprise*): **~ agricole** farming concern
exploiter [ɛksplwate] /1/ VT (*personne, don*) to exploit; (*entreprise, ferme*) to run, operate; (*mine*) to exploit, work
exploiteur, -euse [ɛksplwatœr, -øz] NM/F (*péj*) exploiter
explorateur, -trice [ɛksplɔratœr, -tris] NM/F explorer
exploration [ɛksplɔrasjɔ̃] NF exploration
explorer [ɛksplɔre] /1/ VT to explore
exploser [ɛksploze] /1/ VI to explode, blow up; (*engin explosif*) to go off; (*fig: joie, colère*) to burst out, explode; (: *personne: de colère*) to explode, flare up; **faire ~** (*bombe*) to explode, detonate; (*bâtiment, véhicule*) to blow up

explosif, -ive [ɛksplozif, -iv] ADJ, NM explosive

explosion [ɛksplozjɔ̃] NF explosion; **~ de joie/colère** outburst of joy/rage; **~ démographique** population explosion

exponentiel, le [ɛkspɔnɑ̃sjɛl] ADJ exponential

exportateur, -trice [ɛkspɔrtatœr, -tris] ADJ export *cpd*, exporting ▶ NM exporter

exportation [ɛkspɔrtasjɔ̃] NF (*action*) exportation; (*produit*) export

exporter [ɛkspɔrte] /1/ VT to export

exposant [ɛkspozɑ̃] NM exhibitor; (*Math*) exponent

exposé, e [ɛkspoze] NM (*écrit*) exposé; (*oral*) talk ▶ ADJ: **~ au sud** facing south, with a southern aspect; **bien ~** well situated; **très ~** very exposed

exposer [ɛkspoze] /1/ VT (*montrer: marchandise*) to display; (: *peinture*) to exhibit, show; (*parler de: problème, situation*) to explain, expose, set out; (*mettre en danger, orienter: Photo*) to expose; **s'exposer à** (*soleil, danger*) to expose o.s. to; (*critiques, punition*) to lay o.s. open to; **~ qn/qch à** to expose sb/sth to; **~ sa vie** to risk one's life

exposition [ɛkspozisjɔ̃] NF (*voir exposer*) displaying; exhibiting; explanation, exposition; exposure; (*voir exposé*) aspect, situation; (*manifestation*) exhibition; (*Photo*) exposure; (*introduction*) exposition

exprès¹ [ɛksprɛ] ADV (*délibérément*) on purpose; (*spécialement*) specially; **faire ~ de faire qch** to do sth on purpose

exprès², -esse [ɛksprɛs] ADJ (*ordre, défense*) express, formal ▶ ADJ INV, ADV (*Postes: lettre, colis*) express; **envoyer qch en ~** to send sth express

express [ɛksprɛs] ADJ INV, NM INV: (**café**) **~** espresso; (**train**) **~** fast train

expressément [ɛksprɛsemɑ̃] ADV expressly, specifically

expressif, -ive [ɛksprɛsif, -iv] ADJ expressive

expression [ɛksprɛsjɔ̃] NF expression; **réduit à sa plus simple ~** reduced to its simplest terms; **liberté/moyens d'~** freedom/means of expression; **~ toute faite** set phrase

expressionnisme [ɛksprɛsjɔnism] NM expressionism

expressivité [ɛksprɛsivite] NF expressiveness

exprimer [ɛksprime] /1/ VT (*sentiment, idée*) to express; (*faire sortir: jus, liquide*) to press out; **s'exprimer** VI (*personne*) to express o.s.

expropriation [ɛksprɔprijasjɔ̃] NF expropriation; **frapper d'~** to put a compulsory purchase order on

exproprier [ɛksprɔprije] /7/ VT to buy up (*ou* buy the property of) by compulsory purchase, expropriate

expulser [ɛkspylse] /1/ VT (*d'une salle, d'un groupe*) to expel; (*locataire*) to evict; (*Football*) to send off

expulsion [ɛkspylsjɔ̃] NF expulsion; eviction; sending off

expurger [ɛkspyrʒe] /3/ VT to expurgate, bowdlerize

exquis, e [ɛkski, -iz] ADJ (*gâteau, parfum, élégance*) exquisite; (*personne, temps*) delightful

exsangue [ɛksɑ̃g] ADJ bloodless, drained of blood

exsuder [ɛksyde] /1/ VT to exude

extase [ɛkstɑz] NF ecstasy; **être en ~** to be in raptures

extasier [ɛkstɑzje] /7/: **s'extasier** VI: **s'extasier sur** to go into raptures over

extatique [ɛkstatik] ADJ ecstatic

extenseur [ɛkstɑ̃sœr] NM (*Sport*) chest expander

extensible [ɛkstɑ̃sibl] ADJ extensible

extensif, -ive [ɛkstɑ̃sif, -iv] ADJ extensive

extension [ɛkstɑ̃sjɔ̃] NF (*d'un muscle, ressort*) stretching; (*fig*) extension; expansion; **à l'~** (*Méd*) in traction

exténuant, e [ɛkstenɥɑ̃, -ɑ̃t] ADJ exhausting

exténuer [ɛkstenɥe] /1/ VT to exhaust

extérieur, e [ɛksterjœr] ADJ (*de dehors: porte, mur etc*) outer, outside; (: *commerce, politique*) foreign; (: *influences, pressions*) external; (*au dehors: escalier, w.-c.*) outside; (*apparent: calme, gaieté etc*) outer ▶ NM (*d'une maison, d'un récipient etc*) outside, exterior; (*d'une personne: apparence*) exterior; (*d'un pays, d'un groupe social*): **l'~** the outside world; **à l'~** (*dehors*) outside; (*fig: à l'étranger*) abroad

extérieurement [ɛksterjœrmɑ̃] ADV (*de dehors*) on the outside; (*en apparence*) on the surface

extérioriser [ɛksterjɔrize] /1/ VT to exteriorize

extermination [ɛksterminasjɔ̃] NF extermination, wiping out

exterminer [ɛkstermine] /1/ VT to exterminate, wipe out

externat [ɛksterna] NM day school

externe [ɛkstern] ADJ external, outer ▶ NMF (*Méd*) non-resident medical student, extern (*US*); (*Scol*) day pupil

extincteur [ɛkstɛ̃ktœr] NM (fire) extinguisher

extinction [ɛkstɛ̃ksjɔ̃] NF extinction; (*Jur: d'une dette*) extinguishment; **~ de voix** (*Méd*) loss of voice

extirper [ɛkstirpe] /1/ VT (*tumeur*) to extirpate; (*plante*) to root out, pull up; (*préjugés*) to eradicate

extorquer [ɛkstɔrke] /1/ VT (*de l'argent, un renseignement*): **~ qch à qn** to extort sth from sb

extorsion [ɛkstɔrsjɔ̃] NF: **~ de fonds** extortion of money

extra [ɛkstra] ADJ INV first-rate; (*fam*) fantastic; (*marchandises*) top-quality ▶ NM INV extra help ▶ PRÉFIXE extra(-)

extraction [ɛkstraksjɔ̃] NF extraction

extrader [ɛkstrade] /1/ VT to extradite

extradition [ɛkstradisjɔ̃] NF extradition

extra-fin, e [ɛkstrafɛ̃, -in] ADJ extra-fine

extra-fort, e [ɛkstrafɔr] ADJ extra strong

extraire [ɛkstrɛr] /50/ VT to extract; **~ qch de** to extract sth from

extrait, e [ɛkstrɛ, -ɛt] PP *de* **extraire** ▶ NM (*de plante*) extract; (*de film, livre*) extract, excerpt; **~ de naissance** birth certificate

extra-lucide [ɛkstralysid] ADJ: **voyante ~** clairvoyant

extraordinaire [ɛkstraɔrdinɛr] ADJ extraordinary; (*Pol, Admin: mesures etc*) special; **ambassadeur ~** ambassador extraordinary; **assemblée ~** extraordinary meeting; **par ~** by some unlikely chance

extraordinairement [ɛkstraɔrdinɛrmɑ̃] ADV extraordinarily

extrapoler [ɛkstrapɔle] /1/ VT, VI to extrapolate

extra-sensoriel, le [ɛkstrasɑ̃sɔrjɛl] ADJ extrasensory

extra-terrestre [ɛkstratɛrɛstr] NMF extraterrestrial

extra-utérin, e [ɛkstrayterɛ̃, -in] ADJ extrauterine

extravagance [ɛkstravagɑ̃s] NF extravagance no pl; extravagant behaviour no pl

extravagant, e [ɛkstravagɑ̃, -ɑ̃t] ADJ (personne, attitude) extravagant; (idée) wild

extraverti, e [ɛkstravɛrti] ADJ extrovert

extrayais etc [ɛkstrɛjɛ] VB voir **extraire**

extrême [ɛkstrɛm] ADJ, NM extreme; (intensif): **d'une ~ simplicité/brutalité** extremely simple/brutal; **d'un ~ à l'autre** from one extreme to another; **à l'~** in the extreme; **à l'~ rigueur** in the absolute extreme

extrêmement [ɛkstrɛmmɑ̃] ADV extremely

extrême-onction [ɛkstrɛmɔ̃ksjɔ̃] (pl **extrêmes-onctions**) NF (Rel) last rites pl, Extreme Unction

Extrême-Orient [ɛkstrɛmɔrjɑ̃] NM: **l'~** the Far East

extrême-oriental, e, -aux [ɛkstrɛmɔrjɑ̃tal, -o] ADJ Far Eastern

extrémisme [ɛkstremism] NM extremism

extrémiste [ɛkstremist] ADJ, NMF extremist

extrémité [ɛkstremite] NF (bout) end; (situation) straits pl, plight; (geste désespéré) extreme action; **extrémités** NFPL (pieds et mains) extremities; **à la dernière ~** (à l'agonie) on the point of death

extroverti, e [ɛkstrɔvɛrti] ADJ = **extraverti**

exubérance [ɛgzyberɑ̃s] NF exuberance

exubérant, e [ɛgzyberɑ̃, -ɑ̃t] ADJ exuberant

exulter [ɛgzylte] /1/ VI to exult

exutoire [ɛgzytwar] NM outlet, release

ex-voto [ɛksvoto] NM INV ex-voto

eye-liner [ajlajnœr] NM eyeliner

e

169

Ff

F, f [ɛf] NM INV F, f ▶ ABR = **féminin**; (= *franc*) fr.; (*appartement*) **un F2/F3** a 2-/3-roomed flat (BRIT) ou apartment (US); (= *Fahrenheit*) F; (= *frère*) Br(o).; (= *femme*) W; **F comme François** F for Frederick (BRIT) ou Fox (US)

fa [fa] NM INV (*Mus*) F; (*en chantant la gamme*) fa

fable [fabl] NF fable; (*mensonge*) story, tale

fabricant, e [fabʀikɑ̃, -ɑ̃t] NM/F manufacturer, maker

fabrication [fabʀikasjɔ̃] NF manufacture, making

fabrique [fabʀik] NF factory

fabriquer [fabʀike] /1/ VT to make; (*industriellement*) to manufacture, make; (*construire: voiture*) to manufacture, build; (: *maison*) to build; (*fig: inventer: histoire, alibi*) to make up; (*fam*): **qu'est-ce qu'il fabrique?** what is he up to?; **~ en série** to mass-produce

fabulateur, -trice [fabylatœʀ, -tʀis] NM/F: **c'est un ~** he fantasizes, he makes up stories

fabulation [fabylasjɔ̃] NF (*Psych*) fantasizing

fabuleusement [fabyløzmɑ̃] ADV fabulously, fantastically

fabuleux, -euse [fabylø, -øz] ADJ fabulous, fantastic

fac [fak] NF (*fam: Scol*: = *faculté*) Uni (BRIT *fam*), ≈ college (US)

façade [fasad] NF front, façade; (*fig*) façade

face [fas] NF face; (*fig: aspect*) side ▶ ADJ: **le côté ~** heads; **perdre/sauver la ~** to lose/save face; **regarder qn en ~** to look sb in the face; **la maison/le trottoir d'en ~** the house/pavement opposite; **en ~ de** *prép* opposite; (*fig*) in front of; **de ~** *adv* from the front; face on; **~ à** *prép* facing; (*fig*) faced with, in the face of; **faire ~ à** to face; **faire ~ à la demande** (*Comm*) to meet the demand; **~ à ~** *adv* facing each other

face-à-face [fasafas] NM INV encounter

face-à-main [fasamɛ̃] (*pl* **faces-à-main**) NM lorgnette

Facebook® [feɪsbuk] M Facebook®; **elle m'a envoyé un message sur ~** she facebooked me

facéties [fasesi] NFPL jokes, pranks

facétieux, -euse [fasesjø, -øz] ADJ mischievous

facette [fasɛt] NF facet

fâché, e [fɑʃe] ADJ angry; (*désolé*) sorry

fâcher [fɑʃe] /1/ VT to anger; **se fâcher** VI to get angry; **se fâcher avec** (*se brouiller*) to fall out with

fâcherie [fɑʃʀi] NF quarrel

fâcheusement [fɑʃøzmɑ̃] ADV unpleasantly; (*impressionné etc*) badly; **avoir ~ tendance à** to have an irritating tendency to

fâcheux, -euse [fɑʃø, -øz] ADJ unfortunate, regrettable

facho [faʃo] ADJ, NMF (*fam*: = *fasciste*) fascist

facial, e, -aux [fasjal, -o] ADJ facial

faciès [fasjɛs] NM (*visage*) features *pl*

facile [fasil] ADJ easy; (*accommodant: caractère*) easy-going

facilement [fasilmɑ̃] ADV easily

facilité [fasilite] NF easiness; (*disposition, don*) aptitude; (*moyen, occasion, possibilité*): **il a la ~ de rencontrer les gens** he has every opportunity to meet people; **facilités** NFPL (*possibilités*) facilities; (*Comm*) terms; **facilités de crédit** credit terms; **facilités de paiement** easy terms

faciliter [fasilite] /1/ VT to make easier

façon [fasɔ̃] NF (*manière*) way; (*d'une robe etc*) making-up; cut; (*main-d'œuvre*) labour (BRIT), labor (US); **façons** NFPL (*péj*) fuss *sg*; **faire des façons** (*péj: être affecté*) to be affected; (: *faire des histoires*) to make a fuss; **châle ~ cachemire** (*imitation*) cashmere-style shawl; **de quelle ~?** (in) what way?; **sans ~** *adv* without fuss; *adj* unaffected; **non merci, sans ~** no thanks, honestly; **d'une autre ~** in another way; **en aucune ~** in no way; **de ~ à** so as to; **de ~ à ce que, de (telle) ~ que** so that; **de toute ~** anyway, in any case; **(c'est une) ~ de parler** it's a way of putting it; **travail à ~** tailoring

façonner [fasɔne] /1/ VT (*fabriquer*) to manufacture; (*travailler: matière*) to shape, fashion; (*fig*) to mould, shape

fac-similé [faksimile] NM facsimile

facteur, -trice [faktœʀ, -tʀis] NM/F postman/woman (BRIT), mailman/woman (US) ▶ NM (*Math, gén: élément*) factor; **~ d'orgues** organ builder; **~ de pianos** piano maker; **~ rhésus** rhesus factor

factice [faktis] ADJ artificial

faction [faksjɔ̃] NF (*groupe*) faction; (*Mil*) guard ou sentry (duty); watch; **en ~** on guard; standing watch

factionnaire [faksjɔnɛʀ] NM guard, sentry
factoriel, le [faktɔʀjɛl] ADJ, NF factorial
factotum [faktɔtɔm] NM odd-job man, dogsbody (BRIT)
factuel, le [faktɥɛl] ADJ factual
facturation [faktyʀasjɔ̃] NF invoicing; (*bureau*) invoicing (office)
facture [faktyʀ] NF (*à payer: gén*) bill; (: *Comm*) invoice; (*d'un artisan, artiste*) technique, workmanship
facturer [faktyʀe] /**1**/ VT to invoice
facturier, -ière [faktyʀje, -jɛʀ] NM/F invoice clerk
facultatif, -ive [fakyltatif, -iv] ADJ optional; (*arrêt de bus*) request *cpd*
faculté [fakylte] NF (*intellectuelle, d'université*) faculty; (*pouvoir, possibilité*) power
fadaises [fadɛz] NFPL twaddle *sg*
fade [fad] ADJ insipid
fading [fadiŋ] NM (*Radio*) fading
fagot [fago] NM (*de bois*) bundle of sticks
fagoté, e [fagɔte] ADJ (*fam*): **drôlement ~** oddly dressed
faible [fɛbl] ADJ weak; (*voix, lumière, vent*) faint; (*élève, copie*) poor; (*rendement, intensité, revenu etc*) low ▶ NM weak point; (*pour quelqu'un*) weakness, soft spot; **~ d'esprit** feeble-minded
faiblement [fɛbləmɑ̃] ADV weakly; (*peu: éclairer etc*) faintly
faiblesse [fɛblɛs] NF weakness
faiblir [febliʀ] /**2**/ VI to weaken; (*lumière*) to dim; (*vent*) to drop
faïence [fajɑ̃s] NF earthenware *no pl*; (*objet*) piece of earthenware
faignant, e [fɛɲɑ̃, -ɑ̃t] NM/F = **fainéant**
faille [faj] VB *voir* **falloir** ▶ NF (*Géo*) fault; (*fig*) flaw, weakness
failli, e [faji] ADJ, NM/F bankrupt
faillible [fajibl] ADJ fallible
faillir [fajiʀ] /**2**/ VI: **j'ai failli tomber/lui dire** I almost *ou* nearly fell/told him; **~ à une promesse/un engagement** to break a promise/an agreement
faillite [fajit] NF bankruptcy; (*échec: d'une politique etc*) collapse; **être en ~** to be bankrupt; **faire ~** to go bankrupt
faim [fɛ̃] NF hunger; (*fig*): **~ d'amour/de richesse** hunger *ou* yearning for love/wealth; **avoir ~** to be hungry; **rester sur sa ~** (*aussi fig*) to be left wanting more
fainéant, e [fɛneɑ̃, -ɑ̃t] NM/F idler, loafer
fainéantise [fɛneɑ̃tiz] NF idleness, laziness

MOT-CLÉ

faire [fɛʀ] /**60**/ VT **1** (*fabriquer, être l'auteur de*) to make; (: *produire*) to produce; (: *construire: maison, bateau*) to build; **faire du vin/une offre/un film** to make wine/an offer/a film; **faire du bruit** to make a noise
2 (*effectuer: travail, opération*) to do; **que faites-vous?** (*quel métier etc*) what do you do?; (*quelle activité: au moment de la question*) what are you doing?; **que faire?** what are we going to do?, what can be done (about it)?; **faire la**

lessive/le ménage to do the washing/the housework
3 (*études*) to do; (*sport, musique*) to play; **faire du droit/du français** to do law/French; **faire du rugby/piano** to play rugby/the piano; **faire du cheval/du ski** to go riding/skiing
4 (*visiter*): **faire les magasins** to go shopping; **faire l'Europe** to tour *ou* do Europe
5 (*vitesse, distance*): **faire du 50 (à l'heure)** to do 50 (km an hour); **nous avons fait 1000 km en 2 jours** we did *ou* covered 1000 km in 2 days
6 (*simuler*): **faire le malade/l'ignorant** to act the invalid/the fool
7 (*transformer, avoir un effet sur*): **faire de qn un frustré/avocat** to make sb frustrated/a lawyer; **ça ne me fait rien** (*m'est égal*) I don't care *ou* mind; (*me laisse froid*) it has no effect on me; **ça ne fait rien** it doesn't matter; **faire que** (*impliquer*) to mean that
8 (*calculs, prix, mesures*): **deux et deux font quatre** two and two are *ou* make four; **ça fait 10 m/15 euros** it's 10 m/15 euros; **je vous le fais 10 euros** I'll let you have it for 10 euros; **je fais du 40** I take a size 40
9 (*vb +de*): **qu'a-t-il fait de sa valise/de sa sœur?** what has he done with his case/his sister?
10: **ne faire que**: **il ne fait que critiquer** (*sans cesse*) all he (ever) does is criticize; (*seulement*) he's only criticizing
11 (*dire*) to say; **vraiment? fit-il** really? he said
12 (*maladie*) to have; **faire du diabète/de la tension** to have diabetes *sg*/high blood pressure
▶ VI **1** (*agir, s'y prendre*) to act, do; **il faut faire vite** we (*ou* you *etc*) must act quickly; **comment a-t-il fait pour?** how did he manage to?; **faites comme chez vous** make yourself at home; **je n'ai pas pu faire autrement** there was nothing else I could do
2 (*paraître*) to look; **faire vieux/démodé** to look old/old-fashioned; **ça fait bien** it looks good; **tu fais jeune dans cette robe** that dress makes you look young(er)
3 (*remplaçant un autre verbe*) to do; **ne le casse pas comme je l'ai fait** don't break it as I did; **je peux le voir? — faites!** can I see it? — please do!; **remets-le en place — je viens de le faire** put it back in its place — I just have (done)
▶ VB IMPERS **1**: **il fait beau** *etc* the weather is fine *etc*; *voir aussi* **jour**; **froid** *etc*
2 (*temps écoulé: durée*): **ça fait deux ans qu'il est parti** it's two years since he left; **ça fait deux ans qu'il y est** he's been there for two years
▶ VB AUX **1**: **faire** (+*infinitif: action directe*) to make; **faire tomber/bouger qch** to make sth fall/move; **faire démarrer un moteur/chauffer de l'eau** to start up an engine/heat some water; **cela fait dormir** it makes you sleep; **faire travailler les enfants** to make the children work *ou* get the children to work; **il m'a fait traverser la rue** he helped me to cross the road
2: **faire** (+*infinitif: indirectement, par un intermédiaire*): **faire réparer qch** to get *ou* have sth repaired;

f

faire punir les enfants to have the children punished; **il m'a fait ouvrir la porte** he got me to open the door

se faire VR **1** (*vin, fromage*) to mature **2** (*être convenable*): **cela se fait beaucoup/ne se fait pas** it's done a lot/not done **3** (*+nom ou pron*): **se faire une jupe** to make o.s. a skirt; **se faire des amis** to make friends; **se faire du souci** to worry; **se faire des illusions** to delude o.s.; **se faire beaucoup d'argent** to make a lot of money; **il ne s'en fait pas** he doesn't worry

4 (*+adj: devenir*): **se faire vieux** to be getting old; (: *délibérément*): **se faire beau** to do o.s. up **5**: **se faire à** (*s'habituer*) to get used to; **je n'arrive pas à me faire à la nourriture/au climat** I can't get used to the food/climate **6** (*+infinitif*): **se faire examiner la vue/opérer** to have one's eyes tested/have an operation; **se faire couper les cheveux** to get one's hair cut; **il va se faire tuer/punir** he's going to get himself killed/get (himself) punished; **il s'est fait aider** he got somebody to help him; **il s'est fait aider par Simon** he got Simon to help him; **se faire faire un vêtement** to get a garment made for o.s.

7 (*impersonnel*): **comment se fait-il/faisait-il que?** how is it/was it that?; **il peut se faire que nous utilisions …** it's possible that we could use …

faire-part [fɛʀpaʀ] NM INV announcement (*of birth, marriage etc*)
fair-play [fɛʀplɛ] ADJ INV fair play
fais [fɛ] VB *voir* **faire**
faisabilité [fəzabilite] NF feasibility
faisable [fəzabl] ADJ feasible
faisais *etc* [fəzɛ] VB *voir* **faire**
faisan, e [fəzɑ̃, -an] NM/F pheasant
faisandé, e [fəzɑ̃de] ADJ high (*bad*); (*fig: péj*) corrupt, decadent
faisceau, x [fɛso] NM (*de lumière etc*) beam; (*de branches etc*) bundle
faiseur, -euse [fəzœʀ, -øz] NM/F (*gén: péj*): **~ de** maker of ▸ NM (*bespoke*) tailor; **~ d'embarras** fusspot; **~ de projets** schemer
faisons *etc* [fəzɔ̃] VB *voir* **faire**
faisselle [fɛsɛl] NF cheese strainer
fait¹ [fɛ] VB *voir* **faire** ▸ NM (*événement*) event, occurrence; (*réalité, donnée*) fact; **le ~ que/de manger** the fact that/of eating; **être le ~ de** (*causé par*) to be the work of; **être au ~ (de)** to be informed (of); **mettre qn au ~** to inform sb, put sb in the picture; **au ~** (*à propos*) by the way; **en venir au ~** to get to the point; **de ~ adj** (*opposé à: de droit*) de facto; *adv* in fact; **du ~ de ceci/qu'il a menti** because of *ou* on account of this/his having lied; **de ce ~** therefore, for this reason; **en ~** in fact; **en ~ de repas** by way of a meal; **prendre ~ et cause pour qn** to support sb, side with sb; **prendre qn sur le ~** to catch sb in the act; **dire à qn son ~** to give sb a piece of one's mind; **hauts faits** (*exploits*) exploits; **~ d'armes** feat of arms; **~ divers** (*short*) news item; **les**

faits et gestes de qn sb's actions *ou* doings
fait², e [fɛ, fɛt] PP *de* **faire** ▸ ADJ (*mûr: fromage, melon*) ripe; (*maquillé: yeux*) made-up; (*vernis: ongles*) painted, polished; **un homme ~** a grown man; **tout(e) ~(e)** (*préparé à l'avance*) ready-made; **c'en est ~ de notre tranquillité** that's the end of our peace; **c'est bien ~** (**pour lui** *ou* **eux** *etc*) it serves him (*ou* them *etc*) right
faîte [fɛt] NM top; (*fig*) pinnacle, height
faites [fɛt] VB *voir* **faire**
faîtière [fɛtjɛʀ] NF (*de tente*) ridge pole
faitout [fɛtu] NM stewpot
fakir [fakiʀ] NM (*Théât*) wizard
falaise [falɛz] NF cliff
falbalas [falbala] NMPL fripperies, frills
fallacieux, -euse [fa(l)lasjø, -øz] ADJ (*raisonnement*) fallacious; (*apparences*) deceptive; (*espoir*) illusory
falloir [falwaʀ] /**29**/ VB IMPERS: **il faut faire les lits** we (*ou* you *etc*) have to *ou* must make the beds; **il faut que je fasse les lits** I have to *ou* must make the beds; **il a fallu qu'il parte** he had to leave; **il faudrait qu'elle rentre** she should *ou* go back, she ought to come up *ou* go back; **il faut faire attention** you have to be careful; **il me faudrait 100 euros** I would need 100 euros; **il doit ~ du temps** that must take time; **il vous faut tourner à gauche après l'église** you have to turn left past the church; **nous avons ce qu'il (nous) faut** we have what we need; **il faut qu'il ait oublié** he must have forgotten; **il a fallu qu'il l'apprenne** he would have to hear about it; **il ne fallait pas** (*pour remercier*) you shouldn't have (done); **faut le faire!** (it) takes some doing!; **s'en falloir** VI: **il s'en est fallu de 10 euros/5 minutes** we (*ou* they *etc*) were 10 euros short/5 minutes late (*ou* early); **il s'en faut de beaucoup qu'il soit …** he is far from being …; **il s'en est fallu de peu que cela n'arrive** it very nearly happened; **ou peu s'en faut** or just about, or as good as; **comme il faut** *adj* proper; *adv* properly
fallu [faly] PP *de* **falloir**
falot, e [falo, -ɔt] ADJ dreary, colourless (BRIT), colorless (US) ▸ NM lantern
falsification [falsifikasjɔ̃] NF falsification
falsifier [falsifje] /**7**/ VT to falsify
famé, e [fame] ADJ: **mal ~** disreputable, of ill repute
famélique [famelik] ADJ half-starved
fameux, -euse [famø, -øz] ADJ (*illustre: parfois péj*) famous; (*bon: repas, plat etc*) first-rate, first-class; (*intensif*): **un ~ problème** *etc* a real problem *etc*; **pas ~** not great, not much good
familial, e, -aux [familjal, -o] ADJ family *cpd* ▸ NF (*Auto*) family estate car (BRIT), station wagon (US)
familiariser [familjaʀize] /**1**/ VT: **~ qn avec** to familiarize sb with; **se ~ avec** to familiarize o.s. with
familiarité [familjaʀite] NF familiarity; informality; **familiarités** NFPL familiarities; **~ avec** (*sujet, science*) familiarity with
familier, -ière [familje, -jɛʀ] ADJ (*connu,*

impertinent) familiar; (*atmosphère*) informal, friendly; (*Ling*) informal, colloquial ▶ NM regular (visitor)

familièrement [familjɛʀmɑ̃] ADV (*sans façon: s'entretenir*) informally; (*cavalièrement*) familiarly

famille [famij] NF family; **il a de la ~ à Paris** he has relatives in Paris

famine [famin] NF famine

fan [fan] NMF fan

fana [fana] ADJ, NMF (*fam*) = **fanatique**

fanal, -aux [fanal, -o] NM beacon; lantern

fanatique [fanatik] ADJ: **~ (de)** fanatical (about) ▶ NMF fanatic

fanatisme [fanatism] NM fanaticism

fane [fan] NF top

fané, e [fane] ADJ faded

faner [fane] /1/: **se faner** VI to fade

faneur, -euse [fanœʀ, -øz] NM/F haymaker ▶ NF (*Tech*) tedder

fanfare [fɑ̃faʀ] NF (*orchestre*) brass band; (*musique*) fanfare; **en ~** (*avec bruit*) noisily

fanfaron, ne [fɑ̃faʀɔ̃, -ɔn] NM/F braggart

fanfaronnades [fɑ̃faʀɔnad] NFPL bragging *no pl*

fanfreluches [fɑ̃fʀəlyʃ] NFPL trimming *no pl*

fange [fɑ̃ʒ] NF mire

fanion [fanjɔ̃] NM pennant

fanon [fanɔ̃] NM (*de baleine*) plate of baleen; (*repli de peau*) dewlap, wattle

fantaisie [fɑ̃tezi] NF (*spontanéité*) fancy, imagination; (*caprice*) whim; extravagance; (*Mus*) fantasia ▶ ADJ: **bijou (de) ~** (piece of) costume jewellery (*BRIT*) *ou* jewelry (*US*); **pain (de) ~** fancy bread

fantaisiste [fɑ̃tezist] ADJ (*péj*) unorthodox, eccentric ▶ NMF (*de music-hall*) variety artist *ou* entertainer

fantasmagorique [fɑ̃tasmagɔʀik] ADJ phantasmagorical

fantasme [fɑ̃tasm] NM fantasy

fantasmer [fɑ̃tasme] /1/ VI to fantasize

fantasque [fɑ̃task] ADJ whimsical, capricious; fantastic

fantassin [fɑ̃tasɛ̃] NM infantryman

fantastique [fɑ̃tastik] ADJ fantastic

fantoche [fɑ̃tɔʃ] NM (*péj*) puppet

fantomatique [fɑ̃tɔmatik] ADJ ghostly

fantôme [fɑ̃tom] NM ghost, phantom

FAO SIGLE F (= *Food and Agricultural Organization*) FAO

faon [fɑ̃] NM fawn (*deer*)

FAQ SIGLE F (= *foire aux questions*) FAQ *pl* (= *frequently asked questions*)

faramineux, -euse [faʀaminø, -øz] ADJ (*fam*) fantastic

farandole [faʀɑ̃dɔl] NF farandole

farce [faʀs] NF (*viande*) stuffing; (*blague*) (practical) joke; (*Théât*) farce; **faire une ~ à qn** to play a (practical) joke on sb; **farces et attrapes** jokes and novelties

farceur, -euse [faʀsœʀ, -øz] NM/F practical joker; (*fumiste*) clown

farci, e [faʀsi] ADJ (*Culin*) stuffed

farcir [faʀsiʀ] /2/ VT (*viande*) to stuff; (*fig*): **~ qch de** to stuff sth with; **se farcir** (*fam*): **je me suis**

farci la vaisselle I've got stuck *ou* landed with the washing-up

fard [faʀ] NM make-up; **~ à joues** blusher

fardeau, x [faʀdo] NM burden

farder [faʀde] /1/ VT to make up; (*vérité*) to disguise; **se farder** VI to make o.s. up

farfelu, e [faʀfəly] ADJ wacky (*fam*), harebrained

farfouiller [faʀfuje] /1/ VI (*péj*) to rummage around

fariboles [faʀibɔl] NFPL nonsense *no pl*

farine [faʀin] NF flour; **~ de blé** wheatflour; **~ de maïs** cornflour (*BRIT*), cornstarch (*US*); **~ lactée** (*pour bouillie*) baby cereal

fariner [faʀine] /1/ VT to flour

farineux, -euse [faʀinø, -øz] ADJ (*sauce, pomme*) floury ▶ NMPL (*aliments*) starchy foods

farniente [faʀnjɛnte] NM idleness

farouche [faʀuʃ] ADJ shy, timid; (*sauvage*) savage, wild; (*violent*) fierce

farouchement [faʀuʃmɑ̃] ADV fiercely

fart [faʀt] NM (ski) wax

farter [faʀte] /1/ VT to wax

fascicule [fasikyl] NM volume

fascinant, e [fasinɑ̃, -ɑ̃t] ADJ fascinating

fascination [fasinasjɔ̃] NF fascination

fasciner [fasine] /1/ VT to fascinate

fascisant, e [faʃizɑ̃, -ɑ̃t] ADJ fascistic

fascisme [faʃism] NM fascism

fasciste [faʃist] ADJ, NMF fascist

fasse *etc* [fas] VB *voir* **faire**

faste [fast] NM splendour (*BRIT*), splendor (*US*) ▶ ADJ: **c'est un jour ~** it's his (*ou* our *etc*) lucky day

fastidieux, -euse [fastidjø, -øz] ADJ tedious, tiresome

fastueux, -euse [fastɥø, -øz] ADJ sumptuous, luxurious

fat [fa(t)] ADJ M conceited, smug

fatal, e [fatal] ADJ fatal; (*inévitable*) inevitable

fatalement [fatalmɑ̃] ADV inevitably

fatalisme [fatalism] NM fatalism

fataliste [fatalist] ADJ fatalistic

fatalité [fatalite] NF (*destin*) fate; (*coïncidence*) fateful coincidence; (*caractère inévitable*) inevitability

fatidique [fatidik] ADJ fateful

fatigant, e [fatigɑ̃, -ɑ̃t] ADJ tiring; (*agaçant*) tiresome

fatigue [fatig] NF tiredness, fatigue; (*détérioration*) fatigue; **les fatigues du voyage** the wear and tear of the journey

fatigué, e [fatige] ADJ tired

fatiguer [fatige] /1/ VT to tire, make tired; (*Tech*) to put a strain on, strain; (*fig: agacer*) to annoy ▶ VI (*moteur*) to labour (*BRIT*), labor (*US*), strain; **se fatiguer** VI to get tired; to tire o.s. (out); **se fatiguer à faire qch** to tire o.s. out doing sth

fatras [fatʀa] NM jumble, hotchpotch

fatuité [fatɥite] NF conceitedness, smugness

faubourg [fobuʀ] NM suburb

faubourien, ne [fobuʀjɛ̃, -ɛn] ADJ (*accent*) working-class

fauché, e [foʃe] ADJ (*fam*) broke

faucher [foʃe] /1/ VT (herbe) to cut; (champs, blés) to reap; (fig) to cut down; (véhicule) to mow down; (fam: voler) to pinch, nick

faucheur, -euse [foʃœʀ, -øz] NM/F reaper, mower

faucille [fosij] NF sickle

faucon [fokɔ̃] NM falcon, hawk

faudra etc [fodʀa] VB voir **falloir**

faufil [fofil] NM (Couture) tacking thread

faufilage [fofilaʒ] NM (Couture) tacking

faufiler [fofile] /1/ VT to tack, baste; **se faufiler** VI: **se faufiler dans** to edge one's way into; **se faufiler parmi/entre** to thread one's way among/between

faune [fon] NF (Zool) wildlife, fauna; (fig: péj) set, crowd ▶ NM faun; ~ **marine** marine (animal) life

faussaire [fosɛʀ] NMF forger

fausse [fos] ADJ F voir **faux²**

faussement [fosmɑ̃] ADV (accuser) wrongly, wrongfully; (croire) falsely, erroneously

fausser [fose] /1/ VT (objet) to bend, buckle; (fig) to distort; ~ **compagnie à qn** to give sb the slip

fausset [fosɛ] NM: **voix de** ~ falsetto voice

fausseté [foste] NF wrongness; falseness

faut [fo] VB voir **falloir**

faute [fot] NF (erreur) mistake, error; (péché, manquement) misdemeanour; (Football etc) offence; (Tennis) fault; (responsabilité): **par la ~ de** through the fault of, because of; **c'est de sa/ma ~** it's his/my fault; **être en ~** to be in the wrong; **prendre qn en ~** to catch sb out; ~ **de** (temps, argent) for ou through lack of; ~ **de mieux** for want of anything ou something better; **sans ~** adv without fail; ~ **de frappe** typing error; ~ **d'inattention** careless mistake; ~ **d'orthographe** spelling mistake; ~ **professionnelle** professional misconduct no pl

fauteuil [fotœj] NM armchair; ~ **à bascule** rocking chair; ~ **club** (big) easy chair; ~ **d'orchestre** seat in the front stalls (BRIT) ou the orchestra (US); ~ **roulant** wheelchair

fauteur [fotœʀ] NM: ~ **de troubles** trouble-maker

fautif, -ive [fotif, -iv] ADJ (incorrect) incorrect, inaccurate; (responsable) at fault, in the wrong; (coupable) guilty ▶ NM/F culprit; **il se sentait ~** he felt guilty

fauve [fov] NM wildcat; (peintre) Fauve ▶ ADJ (couleur) fawn

fauvette [fovɛt] NF warbler

fauvisme [fovism] NM (Art) Fauvism

faux¹ [fo] NF scythe

faux², fausse [fo, fos] ADJ (inexact) wrong; (piano, voix) out of tune; (falsifié: billet) fake, forged; (sournois, postiche) false ▶ ADV (Mus) out of tune ▶ NM (copie) fake, forgery; (opposé au vrai): **le** ~ falsehood; ~ **ami** (Ling) faux ami; **faire** ~ **bond à qn** to let sb down; ~ **col** detachable collar; ~ **départ** (Sport, fig) false start; **faire fausse route** to go the wrong way; **le** ~ **numéro/la fausse clé** the wrong number/key; ~ **frais** nmpl extras, incidental expenses; ~ **frère** (fig: péj)

false friend; ~ **mouvement** awkward movement; ~ **nez** false nose; ~ **nom** assumed name; ~ **pas** tripping no pl; (fig) faux pas; **faire un** ~ **pas** to trip; (fig) to make a faux pas; ~ **témoignage** (délit) perjury; **fausse alerte** false alarm; **fausse clé** skeleton key; **fausse couche** (Méd) miscarriage; **fausse joie** vain joy; **fausse note** wrong note

faux-filet [fofilɛ] NM sirloin

faux-fuyant [fofɥijɑ̃] NM equivocation

faux-monnayeur [fomɔnɛjœʀ] NM counterfeiter, forger

faux-semblant [fosɑ̃blɑ̃] NM pretence (BRIT), pretense (US)

faux-sens [fosɑ̃s] NM mistranslation

faveur [favœʀ] NF favour (BRIT), favor (US); **traitement de** ~ preferential treatment; **à la ~ de** under cover of; (grâce à) thanks to; **en** ~ **de** in favo(u)r of

favorable [favɔʀabl] ADJ favo(u)rable

favori, te [favɔʀi, -it] ADJ, NM/F favo(u)rite

favoris [favɔʀi] NMPL (barbe) sideboards (BRIT), sideburns

favoriser [favɔʀize] /1/ VT to favour (BRIT), favor (US)

favoritisme [favɔʀitism] NM (péj) favo(u)ritism

fax [faks] NM fax

faxer [fakse] /1/ VT to fax

fayot [fajo] NM (fam) crawler

FB ABR (= franc belge) BF, FB

FBI SIGLE M FBI

FC SIGLE M (= Football Club) FC

fébrile [febʀil] ADJ feverish, febrile; **capitaux fébriles** (Écon) hot money

fébrilement [febʀilmɑ̃] ADV feverishly

fécal, e, -aux [fekal, -o] ADJ voir **matière**

fécond, e [fekɔ̃, -ɔ̃d] ADJ fertile

fécondation [fekɔ̃dasjɔ̃] NF fertilization

féconder [fekɔ̃de] /1/ VT to fertilize

fécondité [fekɔ̃dite] NF fertility

fécule [fekyl] NF potato flour

féculent [fekylɑ̃] NM starchy food

fédéral, e, -aux [fedeʀal, -o] ADJ federal

fédéralisme [fedeʀalism] NM federalism

fédéraliste [fedeʀalist] ADJ federalist

fédération [fedeʀasjɔ̃] NF federation; **la F~ française de football** the French football association

fée [fe] NF fairy

féerie [feʀi] NF enchantment

féerique [feʀik] ADJ magical, fairytale cpd

feignant, e [fɛɲɑ̃, -ɑ̃t] NM/F = **fainéant**

feindre [fɛ̃dʀ] /52/ VT to feign ▶ VI to dissemble; ~ **de faire** to pretend to do

feint, e [fɛ̃, fɛ̃t] PP de **feindre** ▶ ADJ feigned ▶ NF (Sport: escrime) feint; (: Football, Rugby) dummy (BRIT), fake (US); (fam: ruse) sham

feinter [fɛ̃te] /1/ VI (Sport: escrime) to feint; (: Football, Rugby) to dummy (BRIT), fake (US) ▶ VT (fam: tromper) to fool

fêlé, e [fele] ADJ (aussi fig) cracked

fêler [fele] /1/ VT to crack

félicitations [felisitasjɔ̃] NFPL congratulations

félicité [felisite] NF bliss

féliciter [felisite] /**1**/ VT: ~ **qn (de)** to congratulate sb (on)

félin, e [felɛ̃, -in] ADJ feline ▶ NM (big) cat

félon, ne [felɔ̃, -ɔn] ADJ perfidious, treacherous

félonie [felɔni] NF treachery

fêlure [felyʀ] NF crack

femelle [fəmɛl] ADJ (aussi Élec, Tech) female ▶ NF female

féminin, e [feminɛ̃, -in] ADJ feminine; (sexe) female; (équipe, vêtements etc) women's; (parfois péj: homme) effeminate ▶ NM (Ling) feminine

féminiser [feminize] /**1**/ VT to feminize; (rendre efféminé) to make effeminate; **se féminiser** VI: **cette profession se féminise** this profession is attracting more women

féminisme [feminism] NM feminism

féministe [feminist] ADJ, NF feminist

féminité [feminite] NF femininity

femme [fam] NF woman; (épouse) wife; **être très ~** to be very much a woman; **devenir ~** to attain womanhood; ~ **d'affaires** businesswoman; ~ **de chambre** chambermaid; ~ **fatale** femme fatale; ~ **au foyer** housewife; ~ **d'intérieur** (real) homemaker; ~ **de ménage** domestic help, cleaning lady; ~**du monde** society woman; ~**-objet** sex object; ~ **de tête** determined, intellectual woman

fémoral, e, -aux [femɔral, -o] ADJ femoral

fémur [femyʀ] NM femur, thighbone

FEN [fɛn] SIGLE F (= Fédération de l'Éducation nationale) teachers' trades union

fenaison [fənɛzɔ̃] NF haymaking

fendillé, e [fɑ̃dije] ADJ (terre etc) crazed

fendre [fɑ̃dʀ] /**41**/ VT (couper en deux) to split; (fissurer) to crack; (fig: traverser) to cut through; to push one's way through; **se fendre** VI to crack

fendu, e [fɑ̃dy] ADJ (sol, mur) cracked; (jupe) slit

fenêtre [f(ə)nɛtʀ] NF window; ~ **à guillotine** sash window

fennec [fenɛk] NM fennec

fenouil [fənuj] NM fennel

fente [fɑ̃t] NF (fissure) crack; (de boîte à lettres etc) slit

féodal, e, -aux [feɔdal, -o] ADJ feudal

féodalisme [feɔdalism] NM feudalism

féodalité [feɔdalite] NF feudalism

fer [fɛʀ] NM iron; (de cheval) shoe; **fers** NMPL (Méd) forceps; **mettre aux fers** (enchaîner) to put in chains; **au ~ rouge** with a red-hot iron; **santé/main de ~** iron constitution/hand; ~ **à cheval** horseshoe; **en ~ à cheval** (fig) horseshoe-shaped; ~ **forgé** wrought iron; ~ **à friser** curling tongs; ~ **de lance** spearhead; ~ **(à repasser)** iron; ~ **à souder** soldering iron

ferai etc [fəʀe] VB voir **faire**

fer-blanc [fɛʀblɑ̃] NM tin(plate)

ferblanterie [fɛʀblɑ̃tʀi] NF tinplate making; (produit) tinware

ferblantier [fɛʀblɑ̃tje] NM tinsmith

férié, e [feʀje] ADJ: **jour ~** public holiday

ferions etc [fəʀjɔ̃] VB voir **faire**

férir [feʀiʀ]: **sans coup ~** adv without

meeting any opposition

fermage [fɛʀmaʒ] NM tenant farming

ferme [fɛʀm] ADJ firm ▶ ADV (travailler etc) hard; (discuter) ardently ▶ NF (exploitation) farm; (maison) farmhouse; **tenir ~** to stand firm

fermé, e [fɛʀme] ADJ closed, shut; (gaz, eau etc) off; (fig: personne) uncommunicative; (: milieu) exclusive

fermement [fɛʀməmɑ̃] ADV firmly

ferment [fɛʀmɑ̃] NM ferment

fermentation [fɛʀmɑ̃tasjɔ̃] NF fermentation

fermenter [fɛʀmɑ̃te] /**1**/ VI to ferment

fermer [fɛʀme] /**1**/ VT to close, shut; (cesser l'exploitation de) to close down, shut down; (eau, lumière, électricité, robinet) to turn off; (aéroport, route) to close ▶ VI to close, shut; (magasin: définitivement) to close down, shut down; **se fermer** VI (yeux) to close, shut; (fleur, blessure) to close up; ~ **à clef** to lock; ~ **au verrou** to bolt; ~ **les yeux (sur qch)** (fig) to close one's eyes (to sth); **se fermer à** (pitié, amour) to close one's heart ou mind to

fermeté [fɛʀməte] NF firmness

fermette [fɛʀmɛt] NF farmhouse

fermeture [fɛʀmətyʀ] NF closing; shutting; closing ou shutting down; putting ou turning off; (dispositif) catch; fastening, fastener; **heure de ~** (Comm) closing time; **jour de ~** (Comm) day on which the shop (etc) is closed; ~ **éclair®**, ~ **à glissière** zip (fastener) (BRIT), zipper (US); voir **fermer**

fermier, -ière [fɛʀmje, -jɛʀ] NM/F farmer ▶ NF (femme de fermier) farmer's wife ▶ ADJ: **beurre/cidre ~** farm butter/cider

fermoir [fɛʀmwaʀ] NM clasp

féroce [feʀɔs] ADJ ferocious, fierce

férocement [feʀɔsmɑ̃] ADV ferociously

férocité [feʀɔsite] NF ferocity, ferociousness

ferons etc [fəʀɔ̃] VB voir **faire**

ferraille [feʀaj] NF scrap iron; **mettre à la ~** to scrap; **bruit de ~** clanking

ferrailler [feʀaje] /**1**/ VI to clank

ferrailleur [feʀajœʀ] NM scrap merchant

ferrant [feʀɑ̃] ADJ M voir **maréchal-ferrant**

ferré, e [feʀe] ADJ (chaussure) hobnailed; (canne) steel-tipped; ~ **sur** (fam: savant) well up on

ferrer [feʀe] /**1**/ VT (cheval) to shoe; (chaussure) to nail; (canne) to tip; (poisson) to strike

ferreux, -euse [feʀø, -øz] ADJ ferrous

ferronnerie [feʀɔnʀi] NF ironwork; ~ **d'art** wrought iron work

ferronnier [feʀɔnje] NM craftsman in wrought iron; (marchand) ironware merchant

ferroviaire [feʀɔvjɛʀ] ADJ rail cpd, railway cpd (BRIT), railroad cpd (US)

ferrugineux, -euse [feʀyʒinø, -øz] ADJ ferruginous

ferrure [feʀyʀ] NF (ornamental) hinge

ferry(-boat) [feʀe(bot)] NM ferry

fertile [fɛʀtil] ADJ fertile; ~ **en incidents** eventful, packed with incidents

fertilisant [fɛʀtilizɑ̃] NM fertilizer

fertilisation [fɛʀtilizasjɔ̃] NF fertilization

fertiliser [fɛʀtilize] /**1**/ VT to fertilize

f

fertilité [fɛʀtilite] NF fertility

féru, e [feʀy] ADJ: ~ **de** with a keen interest in

férule [feʀyl] NF: **être sous la ~ de qn** to be under sb's (iron) rule

fervent, e [fɛʀvɑ̃, -ɑ̃t] ADJ fervent

ferveur [fɛʀvœʀ] NF fervour (BRIT), fervor (US)

fesse [fɛs] NF buttock; **les fesses** the bottom sg, the buttocks

fessée [fese] NF spanking

fessier [fesje] NM (fam) behind

festin [fɛstɛ̃] NM feast

festival [fɛstival] NM festival

festivalier [fɛstivalje] NM festival-goer

festivités [fɛstivite] NFPL festivities, merrymaking sg

feston [fɛstɔ̃] NM (Archit) festoon; (Couture) scallop

festoyer [fɛstwaje] /8/ VI to feast

fêtard, e [fɛtaʀ, -aʀd] NM/F (fam, péj) high liver, merrymaker

fête [fɛt] NF (religieuse) feast; (publique) holiday; (en famille etc) celebration; (réception) party; (kermesse) fête, fair, festival; (du nom) feast day, name day; **faire la ~** to live it up; **faire ~ à qn** to give sb a warm welcome; **se faire une ~ de** to look forward to; to enjoy; **ça va être sa ~!** (fam) he's going to get it!; **jour de ~** holiday; **les fêtes (de fin d'année)** the festive season; **la salle/le comité des fêtes** the village hall/ festival committee; **la ~ des Mères/Pères** Mother's/Father's Day; **~ de charité** charity fair ou fête; **~ foraine** (fun)fair; **la ~ de la musique** see note; **~ mobile** movable feast (day); **la F~ Nationale** the national holiday

The Fête de la Musique is a music festival which has taken place every year since 1981. On 21 June throughout France local musicians perform free of charge in parks, streets and squares.

Fête-Dieu [fɛtdjø] NF: **la ~** Corpus Christi

fêter [fete] /1/ VT to celebrate; (personne) to have a celebration for

fétiche [fetiʃ] NM fetish; **animal ~, objet ~** mascot

fétichisme [fetiʃism] NM fetishism

fétichiste [fetiʃist] ADJ fetishist

fétide [fetid] ADJ fetid

fétu [fety] NM: **~ de paille** wisp of straw

feu¹ [fø] ADJ INV: **~ son père** his late father

feu², x [fø] NM (gén) fire; (signal lumineux) light; (de cuisinière) ring; (sensation de brûlure) burning (sensation); **feux** NMPL fire sg; (Auto) (traffic) lights; **tous ~ éteints** (Navig, Auto) without lights; **au ~!** (incendie) fire!; **à ~ doux/vif** over a slow/brisk heat; **à petit ~** (Culin) over a gentle heat; (fig) slowly; **faire ~** to fire; **ne pas faire long ~** (fig) not to last long; **commander le ~** (Mil) to give the order to (open) fire; **tué au ~** (Mil) killed in action; **mettre à ~** (fusée) to fire off; **pris entre deux ~** caught in the crossfire; **en ~** on fire; **être tout ~ tout flamme (pour)** (passion) to be aflame with passion (for); (enthousiasme) to be fired with enthusiasm (for); **prendre ~** to catch fire; **mettre le ~ à** to set fire

to, set on fire; **faire du ~** to make a fire; **avez-vous du ~?** (pour cigarette) have you (got) a light?; **~ rouge/vert/orange** (Auto) red/green/ amber (BRIT) ou yellow (US) light; **donner le ~ vert à qch/qn** (fig) to give sth/sb the go-ahead ou green light; **~ arrière** (Auto) rear light; **~ d'artifice** firework; (spectacle) fireworks pl; **~ de camp** campfire; **~ de cheminée** chimney fire; **~ de joie** bonfire; **~ de paille** (fig) flash in the pan; **~ de brouillard** (Auto) fog lights ou lamps; **~ de croisement** (Auto) dipped (BRIT) ou dimmed (US) headlights; **~ de position** (Auto) sidelights; **~ de route** (Auto) headlights (on full (BRIT) ou high (US) beam); **~ de stationnement** parking lights

feuillage [fœjaʒ] NM foliage, leaves pl

feuille [fœj] NF (d'arbre) leaf; **~ (de papier)** sheet (of paper); **rendre ~ blanche** (Scol) to give in a blank paper; **~ de calcul** spreadsheet; **~ d'or/ de métal** gold/metal leaf; **~ de chou** (péj: journal) rag; **~ d'impôts** tax form; **~ de maladie** medical expenses claim form; **~ morte** dead leaf; **~ de paie**, **~ de paye** pay slip; **~ de présence** attendance sheet; **~ de température** temperature chart; **~ de vigne** (Bot) vine leaf; (sur statue) fig leaf; **~ volante** loose sheet

feuillet [fœjɛ] NM leaf, page

feuilletage [fœjtaʒ] NM (aspect feuilleté) flakiness

feuilleté, e [fœjte] ADJ (Culin) flaky; (verre) laminated; **pâte ~** flaky pastry

feuilleter [fœjte] /4/ VT (livre) to leaf through

feuilleton [fœjtɔ̃] NM serial

feuillette etc [fœjɛt] VB voir **feuilleter**

feuillu, e [fœjy] ADJ leafy ▸ NM broad-leaved tree

feulement [følmɑ̃] NM growl

feutre [føtʀ] NM felt; (chapeau) felt hat; (stylo) felt-tip(ped pen)

feutré, e [føtʀe] ADJ feltlike; (pas, voix, atmosphère) muffled

feutrer [føtʀe] /1/ VT to felt; (fig: bruits) to muffle ▸ VI, **se feutrer** (tissu) to felt

feutrine [føtʀin] NF (lightweight) felt

fève [fɛv] NF broad bean; (dans la galette des Rois) charm (hidden in cake eaten on Twelfth Night)

février [fevʀije] NM February; voir aussi **juillet**

fez [fɛz] NM fez

FF ABR (= franc français) FF

FFA SIGLE FPL (= Forces françaises en Allemagne) French forces in Germany

FFF ABR = **Fédération française de football**

FFI SIGLE FPL = **Forces françaises de l'intérieur (1942–45)** ▸ SIGLE M member of the FFI

FFL SIGLE FPL (= Forces françaises libres) Free French Army

Fg ABR = **faubourg**

FGA SIGLE M (= Fonds de garantie automobile) fund financed through insurance premiums, to compensate victims of uninsured losses

FGEN SIGLE F (= Fédération générale de l'éducation nationale) teachers' trade union

fi [fi] EXCL: **faire fi de** to snap one's fingers at

fiabilité [fjabilite] NF reliability

fiable [fjabl] ADJ reliable

fiacre [fjakʀ] NM (hackney) cab ou carriage

fiançailles [fjɑ̃sɑj] NFPL engagement *sg*
fiancé, e [fjɑ̃se] NM/F fiancé (fiancée) ▸ ADJ:
  être ~ (à) to be engaged (to)
fiancer [fjɑ̃se] **/3/: se fiancer** VI: **se fiancer
  (avec)** to become engaged (to)
fiasco [fjasko] NM fiasco
fibranne [fibʀan] NF bonded fibre *ou* fiber (US)
fibre [fibʀ] NF fibre, fiber (US); **avoir la ~
  paternelle/militaire** to be a born father/
  soldier; **~ optique** optical fibre *ou* fiber; **~ de
  verre** fibreglass (BRIT), fiberglass (US), glass
  fibre *ou* fiber
fibreux, -euse [fibʀø, -øz] ADJ fibrous; (*viande*)
  stringy
fibrome [fibʀom] NM (*Méd*) fibroma
ficelage [fis(ə)laʒ] NM tying (up)
ficelé, e [fis(ə)le] ADJ (*fam*): **être mal ~** (*habillé*) to
  be badly got up; **bien/mal ~** (*conçu: roman, projet*)
  well/badly put together
ficeler [fis(ə)le] **/4/** VT to tie up
ficelle [fisɛl] NF string *no pl*; (*morceau*) piece *ou*
  length of string; (*pain*) stick of French bread;
  ficelles NFPL (*fig*) strings; **tirer sur la ~** (*fig*) to
  go too far
fiche [fiʃ] NF (*carte*) (index) card; (*formulaire*)
  form; (*Élec*) plug; **~ de paye** pay slip;
  ~ signalétique (*Police*) identification card;
  ~ technique data sheet, specification *ou* spec
  sheet
ficher [fiʃe] **/1/** VT (*dans un fichier*) to file; (: *Police*) to
  put on file; (*fam: faire*) to do; (: *donner*) to give;
  (: *mettre*) to stick *ou* shove; (*planter*): **~ qch dans**
  to stick *ou* drive sth into; **~ qn à la porte** (*fam*)
  to chuck sb out; **fiche(-moi) le camp** (*fam*)
  clear off; **fiche-moi la paix** (*fam*) leave me
  alone; **se ~ dans** (*s'enfoncer*) to get stuck in,
  embed itself in; **se ~ de** (*fam: rire de*) to make fun
  of; (: *être indifférent à*) not to care about
fichier [fiʃje] NM (*gén, Inform*) file; (*à cartes*) card
  index; **~ actif** *ou* **en cours d'utilisation**
  (*Inform*) active file; **~ d'adresses** mailing list;
  ~ d'archives (*Inform*) archive file; **~ joint**
  (*Inform*) attachment
fichu, e [fiʃy] PP *de* **ficher** ▸ ADJ (*fam: fini,
  inutilisable*) bust, done for; (: *intensif*) wretched,
  darned ▸ NM (*foulard*) (head)scarf; **être ~ de** to
  be capable of; **mal ~** feeling lousy; useless;
  bien ~ great
fictif, -ive [fiktif, -iv] ADJ fictitious
fiction [fiksjɔ̃] NF fiction; (*fait imaginé*)
  invention
fictivement [fiktivmɑ̃] ADV fictitiously
fidèle [fidɛl] ADJ: **~ (à)** faithful (to) ▸ NMF (*Rel*):
  les fidèles the faithful; (*à l'église*) the
  congregation
fidèlement [fidɛlmɑ̃] ADV faithfully
fidélité [fidelite] NF (*d'un conjoint*) fidelity,
  faithfulness; (*d'un ami, client*) loyalty
Fidji [fidʒi] NFPL: **(les îles)** ~ Fiji
fiduciaire [fidysjɛʀ] ADJ fiduciary; **héritier ~**
  heir, trustee; **monnaie ~** flat money
fief [fjɛf] NM fief; (*fig*) preserve; stronghold
fieffé, e [fjefe] ADJ (*ivrogne, menteur*) arrant,
  out-and-out

fiel [fjɛl] NM gall
fiente [fjɑ̃t] NF (*bird*) droppings *pl*
fier¹ [fje]: **se ~ à** VT to trust
fier², fière [fjɛʀ] ADJ proud; **~ de** proud of;
  avoir fière allure to cut a fine figure
fièrement [fjɛʀmɑ̃] ADV proudly
fierté [fjɛʀte] NF pride
fièvre [fjɛvʀ] NF fever; **avoir de la ~/39 de ~** to
  have a high temperature/a temperature of 39°C;
  ~ typhoïde typhoid fever
fiévreusement [fjevʀøzmɑ̃] ADV (*fig*) feverishly
fiévreux, -euse [fjevʀø, -øz] ADJ feverish
FIFA [fifa] SIGLE F (= *Fédération internationale de
  Football association*) FIFA
fifre [fifʀ] NM fife; (*personne*) fife-player
fig ABR (= *figure*) fig
figé, e [fiʒe] ADJ (*manières*) stiff; (*société*) rigid;
  (*sourire*) set
figer [fiʒe] **/3/** VT to congeal; (*fig: personne*) to freeze,
  root to the spot; **se figer** VI to congeal; (*personne*) to
  freeze; (*institutions etc*) to become set, stop evolving
fignoler [fiɲɔle] **/1/** VT to put the finishing
  touches to
figue [fig] NF fig
figuier [figje] NM fig tree
figurant, e [figyʀɑ̃, -ɑ̃t] NM/F (*Théât*) walk-on;
  (*Ciné*) extra
figuratif, -ive [figyʀatif, -iv] ADJ
  representational, figurative
figuration [figyʀasjɔ̃] NF walk-on parts *pl*;
  extras *pl*
figure [figyʀ] NF (*visage*) face; (*image, tracé, forme,
  personnage*) figure; (*illustration*) picture, diagram;
  faire ~ de to look like; **faire bonne ~** to put up a
  good show; **faire triste ~** to be a sorry sight;
  ~ de rhétorique figure of speech
figuré, e [figyʀe] ADJ (*sens*) figurative
figurer [figyʀe] **/1/** VI to appear ▸ VT to
  represent; **se ~ que** to imagine that;
  figurez-vous que … would you believe that …?
figurine [figyʀin] NF figurine
fil [fil] NM (*brin, fig: d'une histoire*) thread; (*du
  téléphone*) cable, wire; (*textile de lin*) linen; (*d'un
  couteau: tranchant*) edge; **au ~ des années** with
  the passing of the years; **au ~ de l'eau** with the
  stream *ou* current; **de ~ en aiguille** one thing
  leading to another; **ne tenir qu'à un ~** (*vie,
  réussite etc*) to hang by a thread; **donner du ~ à
  retordre à qn** to make life difficult for sb;
  coup de ~ (*fam*) phone call; **donner/recevoir
  un coup de ~** to make/get a phone call; **~ à
  coudre** (sewing) thread *ou* yarn; **~ dentaire**
  dental floss; **~ électrique** electric wire; **~ de
  fer** wire; **~ de fer barbelé** barbed wire; **~ à
  pêche** fishing line; **~ à plomb** plumb line; **~ à
  souder** soldering wire
filament [filamɑ̃] NM (*Élec*) filament; (*de liquide*)
  trickle, thread
filandreux, -euse [filɑ̃dʀø, -øz] ADJ stringy
filant, e [filɑ̃, -ɑ̃t] ADJ: **étoile ~** shooting star
filasse [filas] ADJ INV white blond
filature [filatyʀ] NF (*fabrique*) mill; (*policière*)
  shadowing *no pl*, tailing *no pl*; **prendre qn en ~**
  to shadow *ou* tail sb

file [fil] NF line; (Auto) lane; ~ **(d'attente)** queue (BRIT), line (US); **prendre la ~** to join the (end of the) queue ou line; **prendre la ~ de droite** (Auto) to move into the right-hand lane; **se mettre en ~** to form a line; (Auto) to get into lane; **stationner en double ~** (Auto) to double-park; **à la ~** adv (d'affilée) in succession; (à la suite) one after another; **à la** ou **en ~ indienne** in single file

filer [file] /1/ VT (tissu, toile, verre) to spin; (dérouler: câble etc) to pay ou let out; (prendre en filature) to shadow, tail; (fam: donner): ~ **qch à qn** to slip sb sth ▶ VI (bas, maille, liquide, pâte) to run; (aller vite) to fly past ou by; (fam: partir) to make off; ~ **à l'anglaise** to take French leave; ~ **doux** to behave o.s., toe the line; ~ **un mauvais coton** to be in a bad way

filet [file] NM net; (Culin) fillet; (d'eau, de sang) trickle; **tendre un ~** (police) to set a trap; ~ **(à bagages)** (Rail) luggage rack; ~ **(à provisions)** string bag

filetage [filtaʒ] NM threading; thread

fileter [filte] /5/ VT to thread

filial, e, -aux [filjal, -o] ADJ filial ▶ NF (Comm) subsidiary; affiliate

filiation [filjasjɔ̃] NF filiation

filière [filjɛʀ] NF (carrière) path; **passer par la ~** to go through the (administrative) channels; **suivre la ~** to work one's way up (through the hierarchy)

filiforme [filifɔʀm] ADJ spindly; threadlike

filigrane [filigʀan] NM (d'un billet, timbre) watermark; **en ~** (fig) showing just beneath the surface

filin [filɛ̃] NM (Navig) rope

fille [fij] NF girl; (opposé à fils) daughter; **vieille ~** old maid; ~ **de joie** prostitute; ~ **de salle** waitress

fille-mère [fijmɛʀ] (pl **filles-mères**) NF unmarried mother

fillette [fijɛt] NF (little) girl

filleul, e [fijœl] NM/F godchild, godson (goddaughter)

film [film] NM (pour photo) (roll of) film; (œuvre) film, picture, movie; (couche) film; ~ **muet/parlant** silent/talking picture ou movie; ~ **alimentaire** clingfilm; ~ **d'amour/d'animation/d'horreur** romantic/animated/horror film; ~ **comique** comedy; ~ **policier** thriller

filmer [filme] /1/ VT to film

filon [filɔ̃] NM vein, lode; (fig) lucrative line, money-spinner

filou [filu] NM (escroc) swindler

fils [fis] NM son; ~ **de famille** moneyed young man; ~ **à papa** (péj) daddy's boy

filtrage [filtʀaʒ] NM filtering

filtrant, e [filtʀɑ̃, -ɑ̃t] ADJ (huile solaire etc) filtering

filtre [filtʀ] NM filter; **"~ ou sans ~?"** (cigarettes) "tipped or plain?"; ~ **à air** air filter

filtrer [filtʀe] /1/ VT to filter; (fig: candidats, visiteurs) to screen ▶ VI to filter (through)

fin¹ [fɛ̃] NF end; **fins** NFPL (but) ends; **à (la) ~ mai**,

~ **mai** at the end of May; **en ~ de semaine** at the end of the week; **prendre ~** to come to an end; **toucher à sa ~** to be drawing to a close; **mettre ~ à** to put an end to; **mener à bonne ~** to bring to a successful conclusion; **à cette ~** to this end; **à toutes fins utiles** for your information; **à la ~** in the end, eventually; **en ~ de compte** in the end; **sans ~** adj endless; adv endlessly; ~ **de non-recevoir** (Jur, Admin) objection; ~ **de section** (de ligne d'autobus) (fare) stage

fin², e [fɛ̃, fin] ADJ (papier, couche, fil) thin; (cheveux, poudre, pointe, visage) fine; (taille) neat, slim; (esprit, remarque) subtle; shrewd ▶ ADV (moudre, couper) finely ▶ NM: **vouloir jouer au plus ~ (avec qn)** to try to outsmart sb ▶ NF (alcool) liqueur brandy; **c'est ~!** (ironique) how clever!; ~ **prêt/soûl** quite ready/drunk; **un ~ gourmet** a gourmet; **un ~ tireur** a crack shot; **avoir la vue/l'ouïe ~** to have keen eyesight/hearing, have sharp eyes/ears; **or/linge/vin ~** fine gold/linen/wine; **le ~ fond de** the very depths of; **le ~ mot de** the real story behind; **la ~ fleur de** the flower of; **une ~ mouche** (fig) a sly customer; **fines herbes** mixed herbs

final, e [final] ADJ, NF final ▶ NM (Mus) finale; **quarts de ~** quarter finals; **8èmes/16èmes de ~** 2nd/1st round (in 5 round knock-out competition)

finalement [finalmɑ̃] ADV finally, in the end; (après tout) after all

finaliste [finalist] NMF finalist

finalité [finalite] NF (but) aim, goal; (fonction) purpose

finance [finɑ̃s] NF finance; **finances** NFPL (situation financière) finances; (activités financières) finance sg; **moyennant ~** for a fee ou consideration

financement [finɑ̃smɑ̃] NM financing

financer [finɑ̃se] /3/ VT to finance

financier, -ière [finɑ̃sje, -jɛʀ] ADJ financial ▶ NM financier

financièrement [finɑ̃sjɛʀmɑ̃] ADV financially

finasser [finase] /1/ VI (péj) to wheel and deal

finaud, e [fino, -od] ADJ wily

fine [fin] ADJ F, NF voir **fin²**

finement [finmɑ̃] ADV thinly; finely; neatly, slimly; subtly; shrewdly

finesse [fines] NF thinness; (raffinement) fineness; neatness, slimness; (subtilité) subtlety; shrewdness; **finesses** NFPL (subtilités) niceties; finer points

fini, e [fini] ADJ finished; (Math) finite; (intensif): **un menteur ~** a liar through and through ▶ NM (d'un objet manufacturé) finish

finir [finiʀ] /2/ VT to finish ▶ VI to finish, end; ~ **quelque part** to end ou finish up somewhere; ~ **de faire** to finish doing; (cesser) to stop doing; ~ **par faire** to end ou finish up doing; **il finit par m'agacer** he's beginning to get on my nerves; ~ **en pointe/tragédie** to end in a point/in tragedy; **en ~ avec** to be ou have done with; **à n'en plus ~** (route, discussions) never-ending; **il va mal ~** he will come to a bad end; **c'est bientôt fini?** (reproche) have you quite finished?

finish [finiʃ] NM (*Sport*) finish
finissage [finisaʒ] NM finishing
finisseur, -euse [finisœʀ, -øz] NM/F (*Sport*) strong finisher
finition [finisjɔ̃] NF finishing; (*résultat*) finish
finlandais, e [fɛ̃lɑ̃dɛ, -ɛz] ADJ Finnish ▶ NM/F: **F~, e** Finn
Finlande [fɛ̃lɑ̃d] NF: **la ~** Finland
finnois, e [finwa, -waz] ADJ Finnish ▶ NM (*Ling*) Finnish
fiole [fjɔl] NF phial
fiord [fjɔʀ(d)] NM = **fjord**
fioriture [fjɔʀityʀ] NF embellishment, flourish
fioul [fjul] NM fuel oil
firent [fiʀ] VB *voir* **faire**
firmament [fiʀmamɑ̃] NM firmament, skies *pl*
firme [fiʀm] NF firm
fis [fi] VB *voir* **faire**
fisc [fisk] NM tax authorities *pl*, ≈ Inland Revenue (*Brit*), ≈ Internal Revenue Service (*US*)
fiscal, e, -aux [fiskal, -o] ADJ tax *cpd*, fiscal
fiscaliser [fiskalize] /1/ VT to subject to tax
fiscaliste [fiskalist] NMF tax specialist
fiscalité [fiskalite] NF tax system; (*charges*) taxation
fissible [fisibl] ADJ fissile
fission [fisjɔ̃] NF fission
fissure [fisyʀ] NF crack
fissurer [fisyʀe] /1/ VT to crack; **se fissurer** VI to crack
fiston [fistɔ̃] NM (*fam*) son, lad
fit [fi] VB *voir* **faire**
FIV SIGLE F (= *fécondation in vitro*) IVF
fixage [fiksaʒ] NM (*Photo*) fixing
fixateur [fiksatœʀ] NM (*Photo*) fixer; (*pour cheveux*) hair cream
fixatif [fiksatif] NM fixative
fixation [fiksasjɔ̃] NF fixing; (*attache*) fastening; setting; (*de ski*) binding; (*Psych*) fixation
fixe [fiks] ADJ fixed; (*emploi*) steady, regular ▶ NM (*salaire*) basic salary; (*téléphone*) landline; **à heure ~** at a set time; **menu à prix ~** set menu
fixé, e [fikse] ADJ (*heure, jour*) appointed; **être ~ (sur)** (*savoir à quoi s'en tenir*) to have made up one's mind (about); to know for certain (about)
fixement [fiksəmɑ̃] ADV fixedly, steadily
fixer [fikse] /1/ VT (*attacher*): **~ qch (à/sur)** to fix *ou* fasten sth (to/onto); (*déterminer*) to fix, set; (*Chimie, Photo*) to fix; (*poser son regard sur*) to stare at, look hard at; **se fixer** (*s'établir*) to settle down; **~ son choix sur qch** to decide on sth; **se fixer sur** (*attention*) to focus on
fixité [fiksite] NF fixedness
fjord [fjɔʀ(d)] NM fjord, fiord
fl. ABR (= *fleuve*) r, R; (= *florin*) fl
flacon [flakɔ̃] NM bottle
flagada [flagada] ADJ INV (*fam: fatigué*) shattered
flagellation [flaʒelasjɔ̃] NF flogging
flageller [flaʒele] /1/ VT to flog, scourge
flageoler [flaʒɔle] /1/ VI to have knees like jelly
flageolet [flaʒɔlɛ] NM (*Mus*) flageolet; (*Culin*) dwarf kidney bean
flagornerie [flagɔʀnəʀi] NF toadying, fawning

flagorneur, -euse [flagɔʀnœʀ, -øz] NM/F toady, fawner
flagrant, e [flagʀɑ̃, -ɑ̃t] ADJ flagrant, blatant; **en ~ délit** in the act, in flagrante delicto
flair [flɛʀ] NM sense of smell; (*fig*) intuition
flairer [fleʀe] /1/ VT (*humer*) to sniff (at); (*détecter*) to scent
flamand, e [flamɑ̃, -ɑ̃d] ADJ Flemish ▶ NM (*Ling*) Flemish ▶ NM/F: **F~, e** Fleming; **les Flamands** the Flemish
flamant [flamɑ̃] NM flamingo
flambant [flɑ̃bɑ̃] ADV: **~ neuf** brand new
flambé, e [flɑ̃be] ADJ (*Culin*) flambé ▶ NF blaze; (*fig*) flaring-up, explosion
flambeau, x [flɑ̃bo] NM (*flaming*) torch; **se passer le ~** (*fig*) to hand down the (*ou* a) tradition
flambée [flɑ̃be] NF (*feu*) blaze; (*Comm*): **~ des prix** (sudden) shooting up of prices
flamber [flɑ̃be] /1/ VI to blaze (up) ▶ VT (*poulet*) to singe; (*aiguille*) to sterilize
flambeur, -euse [flɑ̃bœʀ, -øz] NM/F big-time gambler
flamboyant, e [flɑ̃bwajɑ̃, -ɑ̃t] ADJ blazing, flaming
flamboyer [flɑ̃bwaje] /8/ VI to blaze (up); (*fig*) to flame
flamenco [flamɛnko] NM flamenco
flamingant, e [flamɛ̃gɑ̃, -ɑ̃t] ADJ Flemish-speaking ▶ NM/F: **F~, e** Flemish speaker; (*Pol*) Flemish nationalist
flamme [flam] NF flame; (*fig*) fire, fervour; **en flammes** on fire, ablaze
flammèche [flamɛʃ] NF (*flying*) spark
flammerole [flamʀɔl] NF will-o'-the-wisp
flan [flɑ̃] NM (*Culin*) custard tart *ou* pie
flanc [flɑ̃] NM side; (*Mil*) flank; **à ~ de colline** on the hillside; **prêter le ~ à** (*fig*) to lay o.s. open to
flancher [flɑ̃ʃe] /1/ VI (*cesser de fonctionner*) to fail, pack up; (*armée*) to quit
Flandre [flɑ̃dʀ] NF: **la ~** (*aussi*: **les Flandres**) Flanders
flanelle [flanɛl] NF flannel
flâner [flɑne] /1/ VI to stroll
flânerie [flɑnʀi] NF stroll
flâneur, -euse [flɑnœʀ, -øz] ADJ idle ▶ NM/F stroller
flanquer [flɑ̃ke] /1/ VT to flank; (*fam: mettre*) to chuck, shove; **~ par terre/à la porte** (*jeter*) to fling to the ground/chuck out; **~ la frousse à qn** (*donner*) to put the wind up sb, give sb an awful fright
flapi, e [flapi] ADJ dog-tired
flaque [flak] NF (*d'eau*) puddle; (*d'huile, de sang etc*) pool
flash [flaʃ] (*pl* **flashes**) NM (*Photo*) flash; **~ (d'information)** newsflash
flasque [flask] ADJ flabby ▶ NF (*flacon*) flask
flatter [flate] /1/ VT to flatter; (*caresser*) to stroke; **se ~ de qch** to pride o.s. on sth
flatterie [flatʀi] NF flattery
flatteur, -euse [flatœʀ, -øz] ADJ flattering ▶ NM/F flatterer
flatulence [flatylɑ̃s], **flatuosité** [flatyozite] NF (*Méd*) flatulence, wind

FLB ABR (= *franco long du bord*) FAS ▶ SIGLE M (*Pol*) = **Front de libération de la Bretagne**
FLC SIGLE M = **Front de libération de la Corse**
fléau, x [fleo] NM scourge, curse; (*de balance*) beam; (*pour le blé*) flail
fléchage [fleʃaʒ] NM (*d'un itinéraire*) signposting
flèche [flɛʃ] NF arrow; (*de clocher*) spire; (*de grue*) jib; (*trait d'esprit, critique*) shaft; **monter en ~** (*fig*) to soar, rocket; **partir en ~** (*fig*) to be off like a shot; **à ~ variable** (*avion*) swing-wing *cpd*
flécher [fleʃe] /**1**/ VT to arrow, mark with arrows
fléchette [fleʃɛt] NF dart; **fléchettes** NFPL (*jeu*) darts *sg*
fléchir [fleʃiʀ] /**2**/ VT (*corps, genou*) to bend; (*fig*) to sway, weaken ▶ VI (*poutre*) to sag, bend; (*fig*) to weaken, flag; (: *baisser: prix*) to fall off
fléchissement [fleʃismã] NM bending; sagging; flagging; (*de l'économie*) dullness
flegmatique [flɛgmatik] ADJ phlegmatic
flegme [flɛgm] NM composure
flemmard, e [flemaʀ, -aʀd] NM/F lazybones *sg*, loafer
flemme [flɛm] NF (*fam*): **j'ai la ~ de le faire** I can't be bothered
flétan [fletã] NM (*Zool*) halibut
flétrir [fletʀiʀ] /**2**/ VT to wither; (*stigmatiser*) to condemn (in the most severe terms); **se flétrir** VI to wither
fleur [flœʀ] NF flower; (*d'un arbre*) blossom; **être en ~** (*arbre*) to be in blossom; **tissu à fleurs** flowered ou flowery fabric; **la (fine) ~ de** (*fig*) the flower of; **être ~ bleue** to be soppy ou sentimental; **à ~ de terre** just above the ground; **faire une ~ à qn** to do sb a favour (BRIT) ou favor (US); **~ de lis** fleur-de-lis
fleurer [flœʀe] /**1**/ VT: **~ la lavande** to have the scent of lavender
fleuret [flœʀɛ] NM (*arme*) foil; (*sport*) fencing
fleurette [flœʀɛt] NF: **conter ~ à qn** to whisper sweet nothings to sb
fleuri, e [flœʀi] ADJ (*jardin*) in flower ou bloom; surrounded by flowers; (*fig: style, tissu, papier*) flowery; (: *teint*) glowing
fleurir [flœʀiʀ] /**2**/ VI (*rose*) to flower; (*arbre*) to blossom; (*fig*) to flourish ▶ VT (*tombe*) to put flowers on; (*chambre*) to decorate with flowers
fleuriste [flœʀist] NMF florist
fleuron [flœʀɔ̃] NM jewel (*fig*)
fleuve [flœv] NM river; **roman-~** saga; **discours-~** interminable speech
flexibilité [flɛksibilite] NF flexibility
flexible [flɛksibl] ADJ flexible
flexion [flɛksjɔ̃] NF flexing, bending; (*Ling*) inflection
flibustier [flibystje] NM buccaneer
flic [flik] NM (*fam, péj*) cop
flingue [flɛ̃g] NM (*fam*) shooter
flipper [flipœʀ] NM pinball (machine) ▶ VI [flipe] /**1**/ (*fam: être déprimé*) to feel down, be on a downer; (: *être exalté*) to freak out
flirt [flœʀt] NM flirting; (*personne*) boyfriend, girlfriend
flirter [flœʀte] /**1**/ VI to flirt
FLN SIGLE M = **Front de libération nationale**

FLNKS SIGLE M (= *Front de libération nationale kanak et socialiste*) *political movement in New Caledonia*
flocon [flɔkɔ̃] NM flake; (*de laine etc: boulette*) flock; **flocons d'avoine** oat flakes, porridge oats
floconneux, -euse [flɔkɔnø, -øz] ADJ fluffy, fleecy
flonflons [flɔ̃flɔ̃] NMPL blare *sg*
flopée [flɔpe] NF: **une ~ de** loads of
floraison [flɔʀɛzɔ̃] NF flowering; blossoming; flourishing; *voir* **fleurir**
floral, e, -aux [flɔʀal, -o] ADJ floral, flower *cpd*
floralies [flɔʀali] NFPL flower show *sg*
flore [flɔʀ] NF flora
Florence [flɔʀãs] N (*ville*) Florence
florentin, e [flɔʀãtɛ̃, -in] ADJ Florentine
floriculture [flɔʀikyltyʀ] NF flower-growing
florissant, e [flɔʀisã, -ãt] VB *voir* **fleurir** ▶ ADJ (*économie*) flourishing; (*santé, teint, mine*) blooming
flot [flo] NM flood, stream; (*marée*) flood tide; **flots** NMPL (*de la mer*) waves; **être à ~** (*Navig*) to be afloat; (*fig*) to be on an even keel; **à flots** (*couler*) in torrents; **entrer à flots** to stream ou pour in
flottage [flɔtaʒ] NM (*du bois*) floating
flottaison [flɔtɛzɔ̃] NF: **ligne de ~** waterline
flottant, e [flɔtã, -ãt] ADJ (*vêtement*) loose(-fitting); (*cours, barème*) floating
flotte [flɔt] NF (*Navig*) fleet; (*fam: eau*) water; (: *pluie*) rain
flottement [flɔtmã] NM (*fig*) wavering, hesitation; (*Écon*) floating
flotter [flɔte] /**1**/ VI to float; (*nuage, odeur*) to drift; (*drapeau*) to fly; (*vêtements*) to hang loose ▶ VB IMPERS (*fam: pleuvoir*): **il flotte** it's raining ▶ VT to float; **faire ~** to float
flotteur [flɔtœʀ] NM float
flottille [flɔtij] NF flotilla
flou, e [flu] ADJ fuzzy, blurred; (*fig*) woolly (BRIT), vague; (*non ajusté: robe*) loose(-fitting)
flouer [flue] /**1**/ VT to swindle
FLQ ABR (= *franco long du quai*) FAQ
fluctuant, e [flyktɥã, -ãt] ADJ (*prix, cours*) fluctuating; (*opinions*) changing
fluctuation [flyktɥasjɔ̃] NF fluctuation
fluctuer [flyktɥe] /**1**/ VI to fluctuate
fluet, te [flyɛ, -ɛt] ADJ thin, slight; (*voix*) thin
fluide [flɥid] ADJ fluid; (*circulation etc*) flowing freely ▶ NM fluid; (*force*) (mysterious) power
fluidifier [flɥidifje] /**7**/ VT to make fluid
fluidité [flɥidite] NF fluidity; free flow
fluor [flyɔʀ] NM fluorine; **dentifrice au ~** fluoride toothpaste
fluoré, e [flyɔʀe] ADJ fluoridated
fluorescent, e [flyɔʀesã, -ãt] ADJ fluorescent
flûte [flyt] NF (*aussi*: **flûte traversière**) flute; (*verre*) flute glass; (*pain*) (thin) baguette; **petite ~** piccolo; **~!** drat it!; **~ (à bec)** recorder; **~ de Pan** panpipes *pl*
flûtiste [flytist] NMF flautist, flute player
fluvial, e, -aux [flyvjal, -o] ADJ river *cpd*, fluvial
flux [fly] NM incoming tide; (*écoulement*) flow; **le ~ et le reflux** the ebb and flow

fluxion [flyksjɔ̃] NF: ~ **de poitrine** pneumonia
FM SIGLE F (= *frequency modulation*) FM
Fme ABR (= *femme*) W
FMI SIGLE M (= *Fonds monétaire international*) IMF
FN SIGLE M (= *Front national*) ≈ NF (= *National Front*)
FNAC [fnak] SIGLE F (= *Fédération nationale des achats des cadres*) chain of discount shops (hi-fi, photo etc)
FNSEA SIGLE F (= *Fédération nationale des syndicats d'exploitants agricoles*) farmers' union
FO SIGLE F (= *Force ouvrière*) trades union
foc [fɔk] NM jib
focal, e, -aux [fɔkal, -o] ADJ focal ▶ NF focal length
focaliser [fɔkalize] /1/ VT to focus
foehn [føn] NM foehn, föhn
fœtal, e, -aux [fetal, -o] ADJ fetal, foetal (BRIT)
fœtus [fetys] NM fetus, foetus (BRIT)
foi [fwa] NF faith; **sous la ~ du serment** under *ou* on oath; **ajouter ~ à** to lend credence to; **faire ~** (*prouver*) to be evidence; **digne de ~** reliable; **sur la ~ de** on the word *ou* strength of; **être de bonne/mauvaise ~** to be in good faith/ not to be in good faith; **ma ~!** well!
foie [fwa] NM liver; **~ gras** foie gras; **crise de ~** stomach upset
foin [fwɛ̃] NM hay; **faire les foins** to make hay; **faire du ~** (*fam*) to kick up a row
foire [fwaR] NF fair; (*fête foraine*) (fun) fair; (*fig: désordre, confusion*) bear garden; **~ aux questions** (*Internet*) frequently asked questions; **faire la ~** to whoop it up; **~ (exposition)** trade fair
fois [fwa] NF time; **une/deux ~** once/twice; **trois/vingt ~** three/twenty times; **deux ~ deux** twice two; **deux/quatre ~ plus grand (que)** twice/four times as big (as); **une ~** (*passé*) once; (*futur*) sometime; **une (bonne) ~ pour toutes** once and for all; **encore une ~** again, once more; **il était une ~** once upon a time; **une ~ que c'est fait** once it's done; **une ~ parti** once he (*ou* I etc) had left; **des ~** (*parfois*) sometimes; **si des ~ …** (*fam*) if ever …; **non mais des ~!** (*fam*) (now) look here!; **à la ~** (*ensemble*) (all) at once; **à la ~ grand et beau** both tall and handsome
foison [fwazɔ̃] NF: **une ~ de** an abundance of; **à ~** adv in plenty
foisonnant, e [fwazɔnɑ̃, -ɑ̃t] ADJ teeming
foisonnement [fwazɔnmɑ̃] NM profusion, abundance
foisonner [fwazɔne] /1/ VI to abound; **~ en** *ou* **de** to abound in
fol [fɔl] ADJ M voir **fou**
folâtre [fɔlɑtR] ADJ playful
folâtrer [fɔlɑtRe] /1/ VI to frolic (about)
folichon, ne [fɔliʃɔ̃, -ɔn] ADJ: **ça n'a rien de ~** it's not a lot of fun
folie [fɔli] NF (*d'une décision, d'un acte*) madness, folly; (*état*) madness, insanity; (*acte*) folly; **la ~ des grandeurs** delusions of grandeur; **faire des folies** (*en dépenses*) to be extravagant
folklore [fɔlklɔR] NM folklore
folklorique [fɔlklɔrik] ADJ folk cpd; (*fam*) weird
folle [fɔl] ADJ F, NF voir **fou**
follement [fɔlmɑ̃] ADV (*très*) madly, wildly

follet [fɔlɛ] ADJ M: **feu ~** will-o'-the-wisp
fomentateur, -trice [fɔmɑ̃tatœR, -tRis] NM/F agitator
fomenter [fɔmɑ̃te] /1/ VT to stir up, foment
foncé, e [fɔ̃se] ADJ dark; **bleu ~** dark blue
foncer [fɔ̃se] /3/ VT to make darker; (*Culin: moule etc*) to line ▶ VI to go darker; (*fam: aller vite*) to tear *ou* belt along; **~ sur** to charge at
fonceur, -euse [fɔ̃sœR, -øz] NM/F whizz kid
foncier, -ière [fɔ̃sje, -jɛR] ADJ (*honnêteté etc*) basic, fundamental; (*malhonnêteté*) deep-rooted; (*Comm*) real estate cpd
foncièrement [fɔ̃sjɛRmɑ̃] ADV basically; (*absolument*) thoroughly
fonction [fɔ̃ksjɔ̃] NF (*rôle, Math, Ling*) function; (*emploi, poste*) post, position; **fonctions** NFPL (*professionnelles*) duties; **entrer en fonctions** to take up one's post *ou* duties; to take up office; **voiture de ~** company car; **être ~ de** (*dépendre de*) to depend on; **en ~ de** (*par rapport à*) according to; **faire ~ de** to serve as; **la ~ publique** the state *ou* civil (BRIT) service
fonctionnaire [fɔ̃ksjɔnɛR] NMF state employee *ou* official; (*dans l'administration*) ≈ civil servant (BRIT)
fonctionnariser [fɔ̃ksjɔnaRize] /1/ VT (*Admin: personne*) to give the status of a state employee to
fonctionnel, le [fɔ̃ksjɔnɛl] ADJ functional
fonctionnellement [fɔ̃ksjɔnɛlmɑ̃] ADV functionally
fonctionnement [fɔ̃ksjɔnmɑ̃] NM working; functioning; operation
fonctionner [fɔ̃ksjɔne] /1/ VI to work, function; (*entreprise*) to operate, function; **faire ~** to work, operate
fond [fɔ̃] NM voir aussi **fonds**; (*d'un récipient, trou*) bottom; (*d'une salle, scène*) back; (*d'un tableau, décor*) background; (*opposé à la forme*) content; (*petite quantité*): **un ~ de verre** a drop; (*Sport*): **le ~** long distance (running); **course/épreuve de ~** long-distance race/trial; **au ~ de** at the bottom of; at the back of; **aller au ~ des choses** to get to the root of things; **le ~ de sa pensée** his (*ou* her) true thoughts *ou* feelings; **sans ~** bottomless; **envoyer par le ~** (*Navig: couler*) to sink, scuttle; **à ~** adv (*connaître, soutenir*) thoroughly; (*appuyer, visser*) right down *ou* home; **à ~ (de train)** adv (*fam*) full tilt; **dans le ~, au ~** adv (*en somme*) basically, really; **de ~ en comble** adv from top to bottom; **~ sonore** background noise; background music; **~ de teint** foundation
fondamental, e, -aux [fɔ̃damɑ̃tal, -o] ADJ fundamental
fondamentalement [fɔ̃damɑ̃talmɑ̃] ADV fundamentally
fondamentalisme [fɔ̃damɑ̃talism] NM fundamentalism
fondamentaliste [fɔ̃damɑ̃talist] ADJ, NMF fundamentalist
fondant, e [fɔ̃dɑ̃, -ɑ̃t] ADJ (*neige*) melting; (*poire*) that melts in the mouth; (*chocolat*) fondant
fondateur, -trice [fɔ̃datœR, -tRis] NM/F

f

181

founder; **membre ~** founder (BRIT) *ou* founding (US) member

fondation [fɔ̃dasjɔ̃] NF founding; (*établissement*) foundation; **fondations** NFPL (*d'une maison*) foundations; **travail de ~** foundation works *pl*

fondé, e [fɔ̃de] ADJ (*accusation etc*) well-founded ▶ NM: **~ de pouvoir** authorized representative; **mal ~** unfounded; **être ~ à croire** to have grounds for believing *ou* good reason to believe

fondement [fɔ̃dmã] NM (*derrière*) behind; **fondements** NMPL foundations; **sans ~** *adj* (*rumeur etc*) groundless, unfounded

fonder [fɔ̃de] /**1**/ VT to found; (*fig*): **~ qch sur** to base sth on; **se ~ sur** (*personne*) to base o.s. on; **~ un foyer** (*se marier*) to set up home

fonderie [fɔ̃dri] NF smelting works *sg*

fondeur, -euse [fɔ̃dœʀ, -øz] NM/F (*skieur*) long-distance skier ▶ NM: (**ouvrier**) **~** caster

fondre [fɔ̃dʀ] /**41**/ VT (*aussi*: **faire fondre**) (*: dans l'eau: sucre, sel*) to dissolve; (*fig: mélanger*) to merge, blend ▶ VI (*à la chaleur*) to melt; to dissolve; (*fig*) to melt away; (*se précipiter*): **~ sur** to swoop down on; **se fondre** VI (*se combiner, se confondre*) to merge into each other; to dissolve; **~ en larmes** to dissolve into tears

fondrière [fɔ̃dʀijɛʀ] NF rut

fonds [fɔ̃] NM (*de bibliothèque*) collection; (*Comm*): **~ (de commerce)** business; (*fig*): **~ de probité** *etc* fund of integrity *etc* ▶ NMPL (*argent*) funds; **à ~ perdus** with little or no hope of getting the money back; **être en ~** to be in funds; **mise de ~** investment, (capital) outlay; **F~ monétaire international (FMI)** International Monetary Fund (IMF); **~ de roulement** NM float

fondu, e [fɔ̃dy] ADJ (*beurre, neige*) melted; (*métal*) molten ▶ NM (*Ciné*): **~ (enchaîné)** dissolve ▶ NF (*Culin*) fondue

fongicide [fɔ̃ʒisid] NM fungicide

font [fɔ̃] VB *voir* **faire**

fontaine [fɔ̃tɛn] NF fountain; (*source*) spring

fontanelle [fɔ̃tanɛl] NF fontanelle

fonte [fɔ̃t] NF melting; (*métal*) cast iron; **la ~ des neiges** the (spring) thaw

fonts baptismaux [fɔ̃batismo] NMPL (baptismal) font *sg*

foot [fut], **football** [futbol] NM football, soccer

footballeur, -euse [futbolœʀ, -øz] NM/F footballer (BRIT), football *ou* soccer player

footing [futiŋ] NM jogging; **faire du ~** to go jogging

for [fɔʀ] NM: **dans** *ou* **en son ~ intérieur** in one's heart of hearts

forage [fɔʀaʒ] NM drilling, boring

forain, e [fɔʀɛ̃, -ɛn] ADJ fairground *cpd* ▶ NM (*marchand*) stallholder; (*acteur etc*) fairground entertainer

forban [fɔʀbã] NM (*pirate*) pirate; (*escroc*) crook

forçat [fɔʀsa] NM convict

force [fɔʀs] NF strength; (*puissance: surnaturelle etc*) power; (*Physique, Mécanique*) force; **forces** NFPL (*physiques*) strength *sg*; (*Mil*) forces; (*effectifs*): **d'importantes forces de police** large contingents of police; **avoir de la ~** to be strong; **être à bout de ~** to have no strength

left; **à la ~ du poignet** (*fig*) by the sweat of one's brow; **à ~ de faire** by dint of doing; **arriver en ~** (*nombreux*) to arrive in force; **cas de ~ majeure** case of absolute necessity; (*Assurances*) act of God; **~ de la nature** natural force; **de ~** *adv* forcibly, by force; **de toutes mes/ses forces** with all my/his strength; **par la ~** using force; **par la ~ des choses/d'habitude** by force of circumstances/habit; **à toute ~** (*absolument*) at all costs; **faire ~ de rames/voiles** to ply the oars/cram on sail; **être de ~ à faire** to be up to doing; **de première ~** first class; **la ~ armée** (*les troupes*) the army; **~ d'âme** fortitude; **~ de frappe** strike force; **~ d'inertie** force of inertia; **la ~ publique** the authorities responsible for public order; **forces d'intervention** (*Mil, Police*) peace-keeping force *sg*; **dans la ~ de l'âge** in the prime of life; **les forces de l'ordre** the police

forcé, e [fɔʀse] ADJ forced; (*bain*) unintended; (*inévitable*): **c'est ~!** it's inevitable!, it HAS to be!

forcément [fɔʀsemã] ADV necessarily; inevitably; (*bien sûr*) of course; **pas ~** not necessarily

forcené, e [fɔʀsəne] ADJ frenzied ▶ NM/F maniac

forceps [fɔʀsɛps] NM forceps *pl*

forcer [fɔʀse] /**3**/ VT (*contraindre: porte, serrure, plante*) to force; (*moteur, voix*) to strain ▶ VI (*Sport*) to overtax o.s.; **~ qn à faire** to force sb to do; **se ~ à faire qch** to force o.s. to do sth; **~ la dose/l'allure** to overdo it/increase the pace; **~ l'attention/le respect** to command attention/respect; **~ la consigne** to bypass orders

forcing [fɔʀsiŋ] NM (*Sport*): **faire le ~** to pile on the pressure

forcir [fɔʀsiʀ] /**2**/ VI (*grossir*) to broaden out; (*vent*) to freshen

forclore [fɔʀklɔʀ] /**45**/ VT (*Jur: personne*) to debar

forclusion [fɔʀklyzjɔ̃] NF (*Jur*) debarment

forer [fɔʀe] /**1**/ VT to drill, bore

forestier, -ière [fɔʀɛstje, -jɛʀ] ADJ forest *cpd*

foret [fɔʀɛ] NM drill

forêt [fɔʀɛ] NF forest; **Office National des Forêts** (*Admin*) ≈ Forestry Commission (BRIT), ≈ National Forest Service (US); **la F~ Noire** the Black Forest

foreuse [fɔʀøz] NF (electric) drill

forfait [fɔʀfɛ] NM (*Comm: prix fixe*) fixed *ou* set price; (*: prix tout compris*) all-in deal *ou* price; (*crime*) infamy; **déclarer ~** to withdraw; **gagner par ~** to win by a walkover; **travailler à ~** to work for a lump sum

forfaitaire [fɔʀfɛtɛʀ] ADJ set; inclusive

forfait-vacances [fɔʀfɛvakãs] (*pl* **forfaits-vacances**) NM package holiday

forfanterie [fɔʀfãtʀi] NF boastfulness *no pl*

forge [fɔʀʒ] NF forge, smithy

forgé, e [fɔʀʒe] ADJ: **~ de toutes pièces** (*histoire*) completely fabricated

forger [fɔʀʒe] /**3**/ VT to forge; (*fig: personnalité*) to form; (*: prétexte*) to contrive, make up

forgeron [fɔʀʒəʀɔ̃] NM (black)smith

formaliser [fɔʀmalize] /1/: **se formaliser** vi: **se formaliser (de)** to take offence (at)

formalisme [fɔʀmalism] NM formality

formalité [fɔʀmalite] NF formality; **simple ~** mere formality

format [fɔʀma] NM size; **petit ~** small size; (Photo) 35 mm (film)

formater [fɔʀmate] /1/ VT (disque) to format; **non formaté** unformatted

formateur, -trice [fɔʀmatœʀ, -tʀis] ADJ formative

formation [fɔʀmasjɔ̃] NF forming; (éducation) training; (Mus) group; (Mil, Aviat, Géo) formation; **la ~ permanente** ou **continue** continuing education; **la ~ professionnelle** vocational training

forme [fɔʀm] NF (gén) form; (d'un objet) shape, form; **formes** NFPL (bonnes manières) proprieties; (d'une femme) figure sg; **en ~ de poire** pear-shaped, in the shape of a pear; **sous ~ de** in the form of; in the guise of; **sous ~ de cachets** in the form of tablets; **être en (bonne** ou **pleine) ~, avoir la ~** (Sport etc) to be on form; **en bonne et due ~** in due form; **pour la ~** for the sake of form; **sans autre ~ de procès** (fig) without further ado; **prendre ~** to take shape

formel, le [fɔʀmɛl] ADJ (preuve, décision) definite, positive; (logique) formal

formellement [fɔʀmɛlmɑ̃] ADV (interdit) strictly; (absolument) positively

former [fɔʀme] /1/ VT (gén) to form; (éduquer: soldat, ingénieur etc) to train; **se former** vi to form; to train

formidable [fɔʀmidabl] ADJ tremendous

formidablement [fɔʀmidabləmɑ̃] ADV tremendously

formol [fɔʀmɔl] NM formalin, formol

formosan, e [fɔʀmozɑ̃, -an] ADJ Formosan

Formose [fɔʀmoz] NM Formosa

formulaire [fɔʀmylɛʀ] NM form

formulation [fɔʀmylasjɔ̃] NF formulation; expression; voir **formuler**

formule [fɔʀmyl] NF (gén) formula; (formulaire) form; (expression) phrase; **selon la ~ consacrée** as one says; **~ de politesse** polite phrase; (en fin de lettre) letter ending

formuler [fɔʀmyle] /1/ VT (émettre: réponse, vœux) to formulate; (expliciter: sa pensée) to express

forniquer [fɔʀnike] /1/ VI to fornicate

fort, e [fɔʀ, fɔʀt] ADJ strong; (intensité, rendement) high, great; (corpulent) large; (doué): **être ~ (en)** to be good (at) ▶ ADV (serrer, frapper) hard; (sonner) loud(ly); (beaucoup) greatly, very much; (très) very ▶ NM (édifice) fort; (point fort) strong point, forte; (gén pl: personne, pays): **le ~, les forts** the strong; **c'est un peu ~!** it's a bit much!; **à plus ~ raison** even more so, all the more reason; **avoir ~ à faire avec qn** to have a hard job with sb; **se faire ~ de faire** to claim one can do; **~ bien/peu** very well/few; **au plus ~ de** (au milieu de) in the thick of, at the height of; **~ tête** rebel

fortement [fɔʀtəmɑ̃] ADV strongly; (s'intéresser) deeply

forteresse [fɔʀtəʀɛs] NF fortress

fortifiant [fɔʀtifjɑ̃] NM tonic

fortifications [fɔʀtifikasjɔ̃] NFPL fortifications

fortifier [fɔʀtifje] /7/ VT to strengthen, fortify; (Mil) to fortify; **se fortifier** vi (personne, santé) to grow stronger

fortin [fɔʀtɛ̃] NM (small) fort

fortiori [fɔʀtjɔʀi]: **à ~** adv all the more so

FORTRAN [fɔʀtʀɑ̃] NM FORTRAN

fortuit, e [fɔʀtɥi, -it] ADJ fortuitous, chance cpd

fortuitement [fɔʀtɥitmɑ̃] ADV fortuitously

fortune [fɔʀtyn] NF fortune; **faire ~** to make one's fortune; **de ~** adj makeshift; (compagnon) chance cpd

fortuné, e [fɔʀtyne] ADJ wealthy, well-off

forum [fɔʀɔm] NM forum; **~ de discussion** (Internet) message board

fosse [fos] NF (grand trou) pit; (tombe) grave; **la ~ aux lions/ours** the lions' den/bear pit; **~ commune** common ou communal grave; **~ (d'orchestre)** (orchestra) pit; **~ à purin** cesspit; **~ septique** septic tank; **fosses nasales** nasal fossae

fossé [fose] NM ditch; (fig) gulf, gap

fossette [fosɛt] NF dimple

fossile [fosil] NM fossil ▶ ADJ fossilized, fossil cpd

fossilisé, e [fosilize] ADJ fossilized

fossoyeur [foswajœʀ] NM gravedigger

fou, fol, folle [fu, fɔl] ADJ mad, crazy; (déréglé etc) wild, erratic; (mèche) stray; (herbe) wild; (fam: extrême, très grand) terrific, tremendous ▶ NM/F madman/woman ▶ NM (du roi) jester, fool; (Échecs) bishop; **~ à lier, ~ furieux (folle furieuse)** raving mad; **être ~ de** to be mad ou crazy about; (chagrin, joie, colère) to be wild with; **faire le ~** to play ou act the fool; **avoir le ~ rire** to have the giggles

foucade [fukad] NF caprice

foudre [fudʀ] NF: **la ~** lightning; **foudres** NFPL (fig: colère) wrath sg

foudroyant, e [fudʀwajɑ̃, -ɑ̃t] ADJ devastating; (progrès) lightning cpd; (succès) stunning; (maladie, poison) violent

foudroyer [fudʀwaje] /8/ VT to strike down; **~ qn du regard** to look daggers at sb; **il a été foudroyé** he was struck by lightning

fouet [fwɛ] NM whip; (Culin) whisk; **de plein ~** adv (se heurter) head on

fouettement [fwɛtmɑ̃] NM lashing no pl

fouetter [fwete] /1/ VT to whip; (crème) to whisk

fougasse [fugas] NF type of flat pastry

fougère [fuʒɛʀ] NF fern

fougue [fug] NF ardour (Brit), ardor (US), spirit

fougueusement [fugøzmɑ̃] ADV ardently

fougueux, -euse [fugø, -øz] ADJ fiery, ardent

fouille [fuj] NF search; **fouilles** NFPL (archéologiques) excavations; **passer à la ~** to be searched

fouillé, e [fuje] ADJ detailed

fouiller [fuje] /1/ VT to search; (creuser) to dig; (: archéologue) to excavate; (approfondir: étude etc) to go into ▶ VI (archéologue) to excavate; **~ dans/parmi** to rummage in/among

fouillis [fuji] NM jumble, muddle

fouine [fwin] NF stone marten

fouiner [fwine] /1/ VI (péj): ~ **dans** to nose around ou about in

fouineur, -euse [fwinœR, -øz] ADJ nosey ▶ NM/F nosey parker, snooper

fouir [fwiR] /2/ VT to dig

fouisseur, -euse [fwisœR, -øz] ADJ burrowing

foulage [fulaʒ] NM pressing

foulante [fulɑ̃t] ADJ F: **pompe** ~ force pump

foulard [fulaR] NM scarf

foule [ful] NF crowd; **la** ~ crowds pl; **une** ~ **de** masses of; **venir en** ~ to come in droves

foulée [fule] NF stride; **dans la** ~ **de** on the heels of

fouler [fule] /1/ VT to press; (sol) to tread upon; **se fouler** VI (fam) to overexert o.s.; **se fouler la cheville** to sprain one's ankle; **ne pas se fouler** not to overexert o.s.; **il ne se foule pas** he doesn't put himself out; ~ **aux pieds** to trample underfoot

foulure [fulyR] NF sprain

four [fuR] NM oven; (de potier) kiln; (Théât: échec) flop; **allant au** ~ ovenproof

fourbe [fuRb] ADJ deceitful

fourberie [fuRbəRi] NF deceit

fourbi [fuRbi] NM (fam) gear, junk

fourbir [fuRbiR] /2/ VT: ~ **ses armes** (fig) to get ready for the fray

fourbu, e [fuRby] ADJ exhausted

fourche [fuRʃ] NF pitchfork; (de bicyclette) fork

fourcher [fuRʃe] /1/ VI: **ma langue a fourché** it was a slip of the tongue

fourchette [fuRʃɛt] NF fork; (Statistique) bracket, margin

fourchu, e [fuRʃy] ADJ split; (arbre etc) forked

fourgon [fuRgɔ̃] NM van; (Rail) wag(g)on; ~ **mortuaire** hearse

fourgonnette [fuRgɔnɛt] NF (delivery) van

fourmi [fuRmi] NF ant; **avoir des fourmis dans les jambes/mains** to have pins and needles in one's legs/hands

fourmilière [fuRmiljɛR] NF ant-hill; (fig) hive of activity

fourmillement [fuRmijmɑ̃] NM (démangeaison) pins and needles pl; (grouillement) swarming no pl

fourmiller [fuRmije] /1/ VI to swarm; ~ **de** to be teeming with, be swarming with

fournaise [fuRnɛz] NF blaze; (fig) furnace, oven

fourneau, x [fuRno] NM stove

fournée [fuRne] NF batch

fourni, e [fuRni] ADJ (barbe, cheveux) thick; (magasin): **bien ~ (en)** well stocked (with)

fournil [fuRni] NM bakehouse

fournir [fuRniR] /2/ VT to supply; (preuve, exemple) to provide, supply; (effort) to put in; ~ **qch à qn** to supply sth to sb, supply ou provide sb with sth; ~ **qn en** (Comm) to supply sb with; **se ~ chez** to shop at

fournisseur, -euse [fuRnisœR, -øz] NM/F supplier; (Internet): ~ **d'accès à Internet** (Internet) service provider, ISP

fourniture [fuRnityR] NF supply(ing); **fournitures** NFPL supplies; **fournitures de bureau** office supplies, stationery; **fournitures scolaires** school stationery

fourrage [fuRaʒ] NM fodder

fourrager¹ [fuRaʒe] VI: ~ **dans/parmi** to rummage through/among

fourrager², -ère [fuRaʒe, -ɛR] ADJ fodder cpd ▶ NF (Mil) fourragère

fourré, e [fuRe] ADJ (bonbon, chocolat) filled; (manteau, botte) fur-lined ▶ NM thicket

fourreau, x [fuRo] NM sheath; (de parapluie) cover; **robe** ~ figure-hugging dress

fourrer [fuRe] /1/ VT (fam) to stick, shove; ~ **qch dans** to stick ou shove sth into; **se ~ dans/sous** to get into/under; **se ~ dans** (une mauvaise situation) to land o.s. in

fourre-tout [fuRtu] NM INV (sac) holdall; (péj) junk room (ou cupboard); (fig) rag-bag

fourreur [fuRœR] NM furrier

fourrière [fuRjɛR] NF pound

fourrure [fuRyR] NF fur; (sur l'animal) coat; **manteau/col de** ~ fur coat/collar

fourvoyer [fuRvwaje] /8/: **se fourvoyer** VI to go astray, stray; **se fourvoyer dans** to stray into

foutre [futR] VT (!) = **ficher**

foutu, e [futy] ADJ (!) = **fichu**

foyer [fwaje] NM (de cheminée) hearth; (fig) seat, centre; (famille) family; (domicile) home; (local de réunion) (social) club; (résidence) hostel; (salon) foyer; (Optique, Photo) focus; **lunettes à double** ~ bi-focal glasses

FP SIGLE F (= franchise postale) exemption from postage

FPA SIGLE F (= Formation professionnelle pour adultes) adult education

FPLP SIGLE M (= Front populaire de la libération de la Palestine) PFLP (= Popular Front for the Liberation of Palestine)

fracas [fRaka] NM din; crash

fracassant, e [fRakasɑ̃, -ɑ̃t] ADJ (succès) sensational, staggering

fracasser [fRakase] /1/ VT to smash; **se fracasser contre** ou **sur** to crash against

fraction [fRaksjɔ̃] NF fraction

fractionnement [fRaksjɔnmɑ̃] NM division

fractionner [fRaksjɔne] /1/ VT to divide (up), split (up)

fracture [fRaktyR] NF fracture; ~ **du crâne** fractured skull; ~ **de la jambe** broken leg

fracturer [fRaktyRe] /1/ VT (coffre, serrure) to break open; (os, membre) to fracture; **se ~ le crâne** to fracture one's skull

fragile [fRaʒil] ADJ fragile, delicate; (fig) frail

fragiliser [fRaʒilize] /1/ VT to weaken, make fragile

fragilité [fRaʒilite] NF fragility

fragment [fRagmɑ̃] NM (d'un objet) fragment, piece; (d'un texte) passage, extract

fragmentaire [fRagmɑ̃tɛR] ADJ sketchy

fragmenter [fRagmɑ̃te] /1/ VT to split up

frai [fRɛ] NM spawn; (ponte) spawning

fraîche [fRɛʃ] ADJ F voir **frais**

fraîchement [fRɛʃmɑ̃] ADV (sans enthousiasme) coolly; (récemment) freshly, newly

fraîcheur [fʀɛʃœʀ] NF coolness; (*d'un aliment*) freshness; *voir* **frais**

fraîchir [fʀeʃiʀ] /2/ VI to get cooler; (*vent*) to freshen

frais, fraîche [fʀɛ, fʀɛʃ] ADJ (*air, eau, accueil*) cool; (*petit pois, œufs, nouvelles, couleur, troupes*) fresh ▶ ADV (*récemment*) newly, fresh(ly) ▶ NM: **mettre au ~** to put in a cool place; **prendre le ~** to take a breath of cool air ▶ NMPL (*débours*) expenses; (*Comm*) costs; charges; **le voilà ~!** he's in a (right) mess!; **il fait ~** it's cool; **servir ~** chill before serving, serve chilled; **faire des ~** to spend; to go to a lot of expense; **faire les ~ de** to bear the brunt of; **faire les ~ de la conversation** (*parler*) to do most of the talking; (*en être le sujet*) to be the topic of conversation; **il en a été pour ses ~** he could have spared himself the trouble; **rentrer dans ses ~** to recover one's expenses; **~ de déplacement** travel(ling) expenses; **~ d'entretien** upkeep; **~ généraux** overheads; **~ de scolarité** school fees (*Brit*), tuition (*US*)

fraise [fʀɛz] NF strawberry; (*Tech*) countersink (bit); (*de dentiste*) drill; **~ des bois** wild strawberry

fraiser [fʀeze] /1/ VT to countersink; (*Culin: pâte*) to knead

fraiseuse [fʀɛzøz] NF (*Tech*) milling machine

fraisier [fʀezje] NM strawberry plant

framboise [fʀɑ̃bwaz] NF raspberry

framboisier [fʀɑ̃bwazje] NM raspberry bush

franc, franche [fʀɑ̃, fʀɑ̃ʃ] ADJ (*personne*) frank, straightforward; (*visage*) open; (*net: refus, couleur*) clear; (*: coupure*) clean; (*intensif*) downright; (*exempt*): **~ de port** post free, postage paid; (*zone, port*) free; (*boutique*) duty-free ▶ ADV: **parler ~** to be frank *ou* candid ▶ NM franc

français, e [fʀɑ̃sɛ, -ɛz] ADJ French ▶ NM (*Ling*) French ▶ NM/F: **F~, e** Frenchman/woman; **les F~** the French

franc-comtois, e [fʀɑ̃kɔ̃twa, -waz] (*mpl* **francs-comtois**) ADJ *ou* from (the) Franche-Comté

France [fʀɑ̃s] NF: **la ~** France; **en ~** in France; **~ 2, ~ 3** *public-sector television channels*; *see note*

> France 2 and France 3 are public-sector television channels. France 2 is a national general interest and entertainment channel; France 3 provides regional news and information as well as programmes for the national network.

Francfort [fʀɑ̃kfɔʀ] N Frankfurt

franche [fʀɑ̃ʃ] ADJ F *voir* **franc**

Franche-Comté [fʀɑ̃ʃkɔ̃te] NF Franche-Comté

franchement [fʀɑ̃ʃmɑ̃] ADV frankly; clearly; (*nettement*) definitely; (*tout à fait*) downright ▶ EXCL well, really!; *voir* **franc**

franchir [fʀɑ̃ʃiʀ] /2/ VT (*obstacle*) to clear, get over; (*seuil, ligne, rivière*) to cross; (*distance*) to cover

franchisage [fʀɑ̃ʃizaʒ] NM (*Comm*) franchising

franchise [fʀɑ̃ʃiz] NF frankness; (*douanière, d'impôt*) exemption; (*Assurances*) excess; (*Comm*)
franchise; **~ de bagages** baggage allowance

franchissable [fʀɑ̃ʃisabl] ADJ (*obstacle*) surmountable

francilien, ne [fʀɑ̃siljɛ̃, -ɛn] ADJ of *ou* from the Île-de-France region ▶ NM/F: **F~, ne** person from the Île-de-France region

franciscain, e [fʀɑ̃siskɛ̃, -ɛn] ADJ Franciscan

franciser [fʀɑ̃size] /1/ VT to gallicize, Frenchify

franc-jeu [fʀɑ̃ʒø] NM: **jouer ~** to play fair

franc-maçon [fʀɑ̃masɔ̃] (*pl* **francs-maçons**) NM Freemason

franc-maçonnerie [fʀɑ̃masɔnʀi] NF Freemasonry

franco [fʀɑ̃ko] ADV (*Comm*): **~ (de port)** postage paid

franco... [fʀɑ̃ko] PRÉFIXE franco-

franco-canadien [fʀɑ̃kokanadjɛ̃] NM (*Ling*) Canadian French

francophile [fʀɑ̃kɔfil] ADJ Francophile

francophobe [fʀɑ̃kɔfɔb] ADJ Francophobe

francophone [fʀɑ̃kɔfɔn] ADJ French-speaking ▶ NMF French speaker

francophonie [fʀɑ̃kɔfɔni] NF French-speaking communities *pl*

franco-québécois [fʀɑ̃kokebekwa] NM (*Ling*) Quebec French

franc-parler [fʀɑ̃paʀle] NM INV outspokenness; **avoir son ~** to speak one's mind

franc-tireur [fʀɑ̃tiʀœʀ] NM (*Mil*) irregular; (*fig*) freelance

frange [fʀɑ̃ʒ] NF fringe; (*cheveux*) fringe (*Brit*), bangs (*US*)

frangé, e [fʀɑ̃ʒe] ADJ (*tapis, nappe*): **~ de** trimmed with

frangin [fʀɑ̃ʒɛ̃] NM (*fam*) brother

frangine [fʀɑ̃ʒin] NF (*fam*) sis, sister

frangipane [fʀɑ̃ʒipan] NF almond paste

franglais [fʀɑ̃glɛ] NM Franglais

franquette [fʀɑ̃kɛt]: **à la bonne ~** *adv* without any fuss

frappant, e [fʀapɑ̃, -ɑ̃t] ADJ striking

frappe [fʀap] NF (*d'une dactylo, pianiste, machine à écrire*) touch; (*Boxe*) punch; (*péj*) hood, thug

frappé, e [fʀape] ADJ (*Culin*) iced; **~ de panique** panic-stricken; **~ de stupeur** thunderstruck, dumbfounded

frapper [fʀape] /1/ VT to hit, strike; (*étonner*) to strike; (*monnaie*) to strike, stamp; **se frapper** VI (*s'inquiéter*) to get worked up; **~ à la porte** to knock at the door; **~ dans ses mains** to clap one's hands; **~ du poing sur** to bang one's fist on; **~ un grand coup** (*fig*) to strike a blow; **frappé de stupeur** dumbfounded

frasques [fʀask] NFPL escapades; **faire des ~** to get up to mischief

fraternel, le [fʀatɛʀnɛl] ADJ brotherly, fraternal

fraternellement [fʀatɛʀnɛlmɑ̃] ADV in a brotherly way

fraterniser [fʀatɛʀnize] /1/ VI to fraternize

fraternité [fʀatɛʀnite] NF brotherhood

fratricide [fʀatʀisid] ADJ fratricidal

fraude [fʀod] NF fraud; (*Scol*) cheating; **passer qch en ~** to smuggle sth in (*ou* out); **~ fiscale** tax evasion

frauder [fʀode] /**1**/ vi, vt to cheat; **~ le fisc** to evade paying tax(es)

fraudeur, -euse [fʀodœʀ, -øz] NM/F person guilty of fraud; (candidat) candidate who cheats; (au fisc) tax evader

frauduleusement [fʀodyløzmɑ̃] ADV fraudulently

frauduleux, -euse [fʀodylø, -øz] ADJ fraudulent

frayer [fʀeje] /**8**/ vt to open up, clear ▶ vi to spawn; (fréquenter): **~ avec** to mix ou associate with; **se ~ un passage dans** to clear o.s. a path through, force one's way through

frayeur [fʀɛjœʀ] NF fright

fredaines [fʀədɛn] NFPL mischief sg, escapades

fredonner [fʀədɔne] /**1**/ vt to hum

freezer [fʀizœʀ] NM freezing compartment

frégate [fʀegat] NF frigate

frein [fʀɛ̃] NM brake; **mettre un ~ à** (fig) to put a brake on, check; **sans ~** (sans limites) unchecked; **~ à main** handbrake; **~ moteur** engine braking; **freins à disques** disc brakes; **freins à tambour** drum brakes

freinage [fʀɛnaʒ] NM braking; **distance de ~** braking distance; **traces de ~** tyre (BRIT) ou tire (US) marks

freiner [fʀene] /**1**/ vi to brake ▶ vt (progrès etc) to check

frelaté, e [fʀəlate] ADJ adulterated; (fig) tainted

frêle [fʀɛl] ADJ frail, fragile

frelon [fʀəlɔ̃] NM hornet

freluquet [fʀəlykɛ] NM (péj) whippersnapper

frémir [fʀemiʀ] /**2**/ vi (de froid, de peur) to shudder, shiver; (de colère) to shake; (de joie, feuillage) to quiver; (eau) to (begin to) bubble

frémissement [fʀemismɑ̃] NM shiver; quiver; bubbling no pl

frêne [fʀɛn] NM ash (tree)

frénésie [fʀenezi] NF frenzy

frénétique [fʀenetik] ADJ frenzied, frenetic

frénétiquement [fʀenetikmɑ̃] ADV frenetically

fréon® [fʀeɔ̃] NM Freon®

fréquemment [fʀekamɑ̃] ADV frequently

fréquence [fʀekɑ̃s] NF frequency

fréquent, e [fʀekɑ̃, -ɑ̃t] ADJ frequent

fréquentable [fʀekɑ̃tabl] ADJ: **il est peu ~** he's not the type one can associate oneself with

fréquentation [fʀekɑ̃tasjɔ̃] NF frequenting; seeing; **fréquentations** NFPL (relations) company sg; **avoir de mauvaises fréquentations** to be in with the wrong crowd, keep bad company

fréquenté, e [fʀekɑ̃te] ADJ: **très ~** (very) busy; **mal ~** patronized by disreputable elements

fréquenter [fʀekɑ̃te] /**1**/ vt (lieu) to frequent; (personne) to see; **se fréquenter** to see a lot of each other

frère [fʀɛʀ] NM brother ▶ ADJ: **partis/pays frères** sister parties/countries

fresque [fʀɛsk] NF (Art) fresco

fret [fʀɛ(t)] NM freight

fréter [fʀete] /**6**/ vt to charter

frétiller [fʀetije] /**1**/ vi to wriggle; to quiver; **~ de la queue** to wag its tail

fretin [fʀətɛ̃] NM: **le menu ~** the small fry

freudien, ne [fʀødjɛ̃, -ɛn] ADJ Freudian

freux [fʀø] NM (Zool) rook

friable [fʀijabl] ADJ crumbly

friand, e [fʀijɑ̃, -ɑ̃d] ADJ: **~ de** very fond of ▶ NM (Culin) small minced-meat (BRIT) ou ground-meat (US) pie; (: sucré) small almond cake; **~ au fromage** cheese puff

friandise [fʀijɑ̃diz] NF sweet

fric [fʀik] NM (fam) cash, bread

fricassée [fʀikase] NF fricassee

fric-frac [fʀikfʀak] NM break-in

friche [fʀiʃ] : **en ~** adj, adv (lying) fallow

friction [fʀiksjɔ̃] NF (massage) rub, rub-down; (chez le coiffeur) scalp massage; (Tech, fig) friction

frictionner [fʀiksjɔne] /**1**/ vt to rub (down); to massage

frigidaire® [fʀiʒidɛʀ] NM refrigerator

frigide [fʀiʒid] ADJ frigid

frigidité [fʀiʒidite] NF frigidity

frigo [fʀigo] NM (= frigidaire) fridge

frigorifier [fʀigɔʀifje] /**7**/ vt to refrigerate; (fig: personne) to freeze

frigorifique [fʀigɔʀifik] ADJ refrigerating

frileusement [fʀiløzmɑ̃] ADV with a shiver

frileux, -euse [fʀilø, -øz] ADJ sensitive to (the) cold; (fig) overcautious

frimas [fʀimɑ] NMPL wintry weather sg

frime [fʀim] NF (fam): **c'est de la ~** it's all put on; **pour la ~** just for show

frimer [fʀime] /**1**/ vi (fam) to show off

frimeur, -euse [fʀimœʀ, -øz] NM/F poser

frimousse [fʀimus] NF (sweet) little face

fringale [fʀɛ̃gal] NF (fam): **avoir la ~** to be ravenous

fringant, e [fʀɛ̃gɑ̃, -ɑ̃t] ADJ dashing

fringues [fʀɛ̃g] NFPL (fam) clothes, gear no pl

fripé, e [fʀipe] ADJ crumpled

friperie [fʀipʀi] NF (commerce) secondhand clothes shop; (vêtements) secondhand clothes

fripes [fʀip] NFPL secondhand clothes

fripier, -ière [fʀipje, -jɛʀ] NM/F secondhand clothes dealer

fripon, ne [fʀipɔ̃, -ɔn] ADJ roguish, mischievous ▶ NM/F rascal, rogue

fripouille [fʀipuj] NF scoundrel

frire [fʀiʀ] vt to fry ▶ vi to fry

Frisbee® [fʀizbi] NM Frisbee®

frise [fʀiz] NF frieze

frisé, e [fʀize] ADJ (cheveux) curly; (personne) curly-haired ▶ NF: **(chicorée) ~** curly endive

friser [fʀize] /**1**/ vt to curl; (fig: surface) to skim, graze; (: mort) to come within a hair's breadth of; (: hérésie) to verge on ▶ vi (cheveux) to curl; (personne) to have curly hair; **se faire ~** to have one's hair curled

frisette [fʀizɛt] NF little curl

frisotter [fʀizɔte] /**1**/ vi (cheveux) to curl tightly

frisquet [fʀiskɛ] ADJ M chilly

frisson [fʀisɔ̃], **frissonnement** [fʀisɔnmɑ̃] NM (de froid) shiver; (de peur) shudder; quiver

frissonner [fʀisɔne] /**1**/ vi (de fièvre, froid) to shiver; (d'horreur) to shudder; (feuilles) to quiver

frit, e [fʀi, fʀit] PP de **frire** ▶ ADJ fried ▶ NF: **(pommes) frites** chips (BRIT), French fries

friterie [fʀitʀi] NF ≈ chip shop (BRIT), ≈ hamburger stand (US)

friteuse [fʀitøz] NF deep fryer, chip pan (BRIT); ~ **électrique** electric fryer

friture [fʀityʀ] NF (huile) (deep) fat; (plat): ~ **(de poissons)** fried fish; (Radio) crackle, crackling no pl; **fritures** NFPL (aliments frits) fried food sg

frivole [fʀivɔl] ADJ frivolous

frivolité [fʀivɔlite] NF frivolity

froc [fʀɔk] NM (Rel) habit; (fam: pantalon) trousers pl, pants pl

froid, e [fʀwa, fʀwad] ADJ cold ▸ NM cold; (absence de sympathie) coolness no pl; **il fait** ~ it's cold; **avoir** ~ to be cold; **prendre** ~ to catch a chill ou cold; **à** ~ adv (démarrer) (from) cold; **(pendant) les grands froids** (in) the depths of winter, (during) the cold season; **jeter un** ~ (fig) to cast a chill; **être en** ~ **avec** to be on bad terms with; **battre** ~ **à qn** to give sb the cold shoulder

froidement [fʀwadmɑ̃] ADV (accueillir) coldly; (décider) coolly

froideur [fʀwadœʀ] NF coolness no pl

froisser [fʀwase] /1/ VT to crumple (up), crease; (fig) to hurt, offend; **se froisser** VI to crumple, crease; (personne) to take offence (BRIT) ou offense (US); **se froisser un muscle** to strain a muscle

frôlement [fʀolmɑ̃] NM (contact) light touch

frôler [fʀole] /1/ VT to brush against; (projectile) to skim past; (fig) to come very close to, come within a hair's breadth of

fromage [fʀɔmaʒ] NM cheese; ~ **blanc** soft white cheese; ~ **de tête** pork brawn

fromager, -ère [fʀɔmaʒe, -ɛʀ] NM/F cheese merchant ▸ ADJ (industrie) cheese cpd

fromagerie [fʀɔmaʒʀi] NF cheese dairy

froment [fʀɔmɑ̃] NM wheat

fronce [fʀɔ̃s] NF (de tissu) gather

froncement [fʀɔ̃smɑ̃] NM: ~ **de sourcils** frown

froncer [fʀɔ̃se] /3/ VT to gather; ~ **les sourcils** to frown

frondaisons [fʀɔ̃dɛzɔ̃] NFPL foliage sg

fronde [fʀɔ̃d] NF sling; (fig) rebellion, rebelliousness

frondeur, -euse [fʀɔ̃dœʀ, -øz] ADJ rebellious

front [fʀɔ̃] NM forehead, brow; (Mil, Météorologie, Pol) front; **avoir le** ~ **de faire** to have the effrontery to do; **de** ~ adv (se heurter) head-on; (rouler) together (2 or 3 abreast); (simultanément) at once; **faire** ~ **à** to face up to; ~ **de mer** (sea) front

frontal, e, -aux [fʀɔ̃tal, -o] ADJ frontal

frontalier, -ière [fʀɔ̃talje, -jɛʀ] ADJ border cpd, frontier cpd ▸ NM/F: **(travailleurs) frontaliers** workers who cross the border to go to work, commuters from across the border

frontière [fʀɔ̃tjɛʀ] NF (Géo, Pol) frontier, border; (fig) frontier, boundary

frontispice [fʀɔ̃tispis] NM frontispiece

fronton [fʀɔ̃tɔ̃] NM pediment; (de pelote basque) (front) wall

frottement [fʀɔtmɑ̃] NM rubbing, scraping; **frottements** NMPL (fig: difficultés) friction sg

frotter [fʀɔte] /1/ VI to rub, scrape ▸ VT to rub; (pour nettoyer) to rub (up); (: avec une brosse: pommes de terre, plancher) to scrub; ~ **une allumette** to strike a match; **se** ~ **à qn** to cross swords with sb; **se** ~ **à qch** to come up against sth; **se** ~ **les mains** (fig) to rub one's hands (gleefully)

frottis [fʀɔti] NM (Méd) smear

frottoir [fʀɔtwaʀ] NM (d'allumettes) friction strip; (pour encaustiquer) (long-handled) brush

frou-frou [fʀufʀu] (pl **frous-frous**) NM rustle

frousse [fʀus] NF (fam: peur): **avoir la** ~ to be in a blue funk

fructifier [fʀyktifje] /7/ VI to yield a profit; **faire** ~ to turn to good account

fructueux, -euse [fʀyktɥø, -øz] ADJ fruitful; profitable

frugal, e, -aux [fʀygal, -o] ADJ frugal

frugalement [fʀygalmɑ̃] ADV frugally

frugalité [fʀygalite] NF frugality

fruit [fʀɥi] NM fruit no pl; **fruits de mer** (Culin) seafood(s); **fruits secs** dried fruit sg

fruité, e [fʀɥite] ADJ (vin) fruity

fruiterie [fʀɥitʀi] NF (boutique) greengrocer's (BRIT), fruit (and vegetable) store (US)

fruitier, -ière [fʀɥitje, -jɛʀ] ADJ: **arbre** ~ fruit tree ▸ NM/F fruiterer (BRIT), fruit merchant (US)

fruste [fʀyst] ADJ unpolished, uncultivated

frustrant, e [fʀystʀɑ̃, -ɑ̃t] ADJ frustrating

frustration [fʀystʀasjɔ̃] NF frustration

frustré, e [fʀystʀe] ADJ frustrated

frustrer [fʀystʀe] /1/ VT to frustrate; (priver): ~ **qn de qch** to deprive sb of sth

FS ABR (= franc suisse) FS, SF

FSE SIGLE M (= foyer socio-éducatif) community home

FTP SIGLE MPL (= Francs-tireurs et partisans) Communist Resistance in 1940–45

fuchsia [fyʃja] NM fuchsia

fuel(-oil) [fjul(ɔjl)] NM fuel oil; (pour chauffer) heating oil

fugace [fygas] ADJ fleeting

fugitif, -ive [fyʒitif, -iv] ADJ (lueur, amour) fleeting; (prisonnier etc) runaway ▸ NM/F fugitive, runaway

fugue [fyg] NF (d'un enfant) running away no pl; (Mus) fugue; **faire une** ~ to run away, abscond

fuir [fɥiʀ] /17/ VT to flee from; (éviter) to shun ▸ VI to run away; (gaz, robinet) to leak

fuite [fɥit] NF flight; (écoulement) leak, leakage; (divulgation) leak; **être en** ~ to be on the run; **mettre en** ~ to put to flight; **prendre la** ~ to take flight

fulgurant, e [fylgyʀɑ̃, -ɑ̃t] ADJ lightning cpd, dazzling

fulminant, e [fylminɑ̃, -ɑ̃t] ADJ (lettre, regard) furious; ~ **de colère** raging with anger

fulminer [fylmine] /1/ VI: ~ **(contre)** to thunder forth (against)

fumant, e [fymɑ̃, -ɑ̃t] ADJ smoking; (liquide) steaming; **un coup** ~ (fam) a master stroke

fumé, e [fyme] ADJ (Culin) smoked; (verre) tinted ▸ NF smoke; **partir en** ~ to go up in smoke

fume-cigarette [fymsigaʀɛt] NM INV cigarette holder

f

fumer [fyme] /**1**/ vi to smoke; (*liquide*) to steam ▶ vt to smoke; (*terre, champ*) to manure

fumerie [fymʀi] nf: **~ d'opium** opium den

fumerolles [fymʀɔl] nfpl gas and smoke (*from volcano*)

fûmes [fym] vb *voir* **être**

fumet [fymɛ] nm aroma

fumeur, -euse [fymœʀ, -øz] nm/f smoker; **(compartiment) fumeurs** smoking compartment

fumeux, -euse [fymø, -øz] adj *péj* woolly (Brit), hazy

fumier [fymje] nm manure

fumigation [fymigasjɔ̃] nf fumigation

fumigène [fymiʒɛn] adj smoke cpd

fumiste [fymist] nm (*ramoneur*) chimney sweep ▶ nmf (*péj: paresseux*) shirker; (*: charlatan*) phoney

fumisterie [fymistəʀi] nf (*péj*) fraud, con

fumoir [fymwaʀ] nm smoking room

funambule [fynãbyl] nm tightrope walker

funèbre [fynɛbʀ] adj funeral cpd; (*fig*) doleful; funereal

funérailles [fyneʀaj] nfpl funeral sg

funéraire [fyneʀɛʀ] adj funeral cpd, funerary

funeste [fynɛst] adj disastrous; deathly

funiculaire [fynikylɛʀ] nm funicular (railway)

FUNU [fyny] sigle f (= *Force d'urgence des Nations unies*) UNEF (= *United Nations Emergency Forces*)

fur [fyʀ]: **au ~ et à mesure** adv as one goes along; **au ~ et à mesure que** as; **au ~ et à mesure de leur progression** as they advance (*ou* advanced)

furax [fyʀaks] adj inv (*fam*) livid

furent [fyʀ] vb *voir* **être**

furet [fyʀɛ] nm ferret

fureter [fyʀ(ə)te] /**5**/ vi (*péj*) to nose about

fureur [fyʀœʀ] nf fury; (*passion*): **~ de** passion for; **être en ~** to be infuriated; **faire ~** to be all the rage

furibard, e [fyʀibaʀ, -aʀd] adj (*fam*) livid, absolutely furious

furibond, e [fyʀibɔ̃, -ɔ̃d] adj livid, absolutely furious

furie [fyʀi] nf fury; (*femme*) shrew, vixen; **en ~** (*mer*) raging

furieusement [fyʀjøzmã] adv furiously

furieux, -euse [fyʀjø, -øz] adj furious

furoncle [fyʀɔ̃kl] nm boil

furtif, -ive [fyʀtif, -iv] adj furtive

furtivement [fyʀtivmã] adv furtively

fus [fy] vb *voir* **être**

fusain [fyzɛ̃] nm (*Bot*) spindle-tree; (*Art*) charcoal

fuseau, x [fyzo] nm (*pantalon*) (ski-)pants pl; (*pour filer*) spindle; **en ~** (*jambes*) tapering; (*colonne*) bulging; **~ horaire** time zone

fusée [fyze] nf rocket; **~ éclairante** flare

fuselage [fyz(ə)laʒ] nm fuselage

fuselé, e [fyz(ə)le] adj slender; (*galbé*) tapering

fuser [fyze] /**1**/ vi (*rires etc*) to burst forth

fusible [fyzibl] nm (*Élec: fil*) fuse wire; (*: fiche*) fuse

fusil [fyzi] nm (*de guerre, à canon rayé*) rifle, gun; (*de chasse, à canon lisse*) shotgun, gun; **~ à deux coups** double-barrelled rifle *ou* shotgun; **~ sous-marin** spear-gun

fusilier [fyzilje] nm (*Mil*) rifleman

fusillade [fyzijad] nf gunfire no pl, shooting no pl; (*combat*) gun battle

fusiller [fyzije] /**1**/ vt to shoot; **~ qn du regard** to look daggers at sb

fusil-mitrailleur [fyzimitʀajœʀ] (pl **fusils-mitrailleurs**) nm machine gun

fusion [fyzjɔ̃] nf fusion, melting; (*fig*) merging; (*Comm*) merger; **en ~** (*métal, roches*) molten

fusionnement [fyzjɔnmã] nm merger

fusionner [fyzjɔne] /**1**/ vi to merge

fustiger [fystiʒe] /**3**/ vt to denounce

fut [fy] vb *voir* **être**

fût [fy] vb *voir* **être** ▶ nm (*tonneau*) barrel, cask; (*de canon*) stock; (*d'arbre*) bole, trunk; (*de colonne*) shaft

futaie [fytɛ] nf forest, plantation

futé, e [fyte] adj crafty; **Bison ~®** TV and radio traffic monitoring service

fûtes [fyt] vb *voir* **être**

futile [fytil] adj (*inutile*) futile; (*frivole*) frivolous

futilement [fytilmã] adv frivolously

futilité [fytilite] nf futility; frivolousness; (*chose futile*) futile pursuit (*ou* thing *etc*)

futon [fytɔ̃] nm futon

futur, e [fytyʀ] adj, nm future; **son ~ époux** her husband-to-be; **au ~** (*Ling*) in the future

futuriste [fytyʀist] adj futuristic

futurologie [fytyʀɔlɔʒi] nf futurology

fuyant, e [fɥijã, -ãt] vb *voir* **fuir** ▶ adj (*regard etc*) evasive; (*lignes etc*) receding; (*perspective*) vanishing

fuyard, e [fɥijaʀ, -aʀd] nm/f runaway

fuyons *etc* [fɥijɔ̃] vb *voir* **fuir**

Gg

G, g [ʒe] NM INV G, g ▸ ABR (= *gramme*) g; (= *gauche*)
L, l; **G comme Gaston** G for George; **le G8** (Pol)
the G8 nations, the Group of Eight

gabardine [gabaʁdin] NF gabardine

gabarit [gabaʁi] NM (*fig: dimension, taille*) size;
(: *valeur*) calibre; (*Tech*) template; **du même ~**
(*fig*) of the same type, of that ilk

gabegie [gabʒi] NF (*péj*) chaos

Gabon [gabɔ̃] NM: **le ~** Gabon

gabonais, e [gabɔnɛ, -ɛz] ADJ Gabonese

gâcher [gɑʃe] /**1**/ VT (*gâter*) to spoil, ruin; (*gaspiller*)
to waste; (*plâtre*) to temper; (*mortier*) to mix

gâchette [gɑʃɛt] NF trigger

gâchis [gɑʃi] NM (*désordre*) mess; (*gaspillage*)
waste *no pl*

gadget [gadʒɛt] NM thingumajig; (*nouveauté*)
gimmick

gadin [gadɛ̃] NM (*fam*): **prendre un ~** to come a
cropper (BRIT)

gadoue [gadu] NF sludge

gaélique [gaelik] ADJ Gaelic ▸ NM (*Ling*) Gaelic

gaffe [gaf] NF (*instrument*) boat hook; (*fam: erreur*)
blunder; **faire ~** (*fam*) to watch out

gaffer [gafe] /**1**/ VI to blunder

gaffeur, -euse [gafœʁ, -øz] NM/F blunderer

gag [gag] NM gag

gaga [gaga] ADJ (*fam*) gaga

gage [gaʒ] NM (*dans un jeu*) forfeit; (*fig: de fidélité*)
token; **gages** NMPL (*salaire*) wages; (*garantie*)
guarantee *sg*; **mettre en ~** to pawn; **laisser en
~** to leave as security

gager [gaʒe] /**3**/ VT: **~ que** to bet *ou* wager that

gageure [gaʒyʁ] NF: **c'est une ~** it's attempting
the impossible

gagnant, e [gaɲɑ̃, -ɑ̃t] ADJ: **billet/numéro ~**
winning ticket/number ▸ ADV: **jouer ~** (*aux
courses*) to be bound to win ▸ NM/F winner

gagne-pain [gaɲpɛ̃] NM INV job

gagne-petit [gaɲpəti] NM INV low wage earner

gagner [gaɲe] /**1**/ VT (*concours, procès, pari*) to win;
(*somme d'argent, revenu*) to earn; (*aller vers, atteindre*)
to reach; (*s'emparer de*) to overcome; (*envahir*) to
spread to; (*se concilier*): **~ qn** to win sb over ▸ VI to
win; (*fig*) to gain; **~ du temps/de la place** to
gain time/save space; **~ sa vie** to earn one's
living; **~ du terrain** (*aussi fig*) to gain ground;
~ qn de vitesse to outstrip sb; (*aussi fig*) **~ à faire**
(*s'en trouver bien*) to be better off doing; **il y gagne**

it's in his interest, it's to his advantage

gagneur [gaɲœʁ] NM winner

gai, e [ge] ADJ cheerful; (*livre, pièce de théâtre*)
light-hearted; (*un peu ivre*) merry

gaiement [gemɑ̃] ADV cheerfully

gaieté [gete] NF cheerfulness; **gaietés** NFPL
(*souvent ironique*) delights; **de ~ de cœur** with a
light heart

gaillard, e [gajaʁ, -aʁd] ADJ (*robuste*) sprightly;
(*grivois*) bawdy, ribald ▸ NM/F (*strapping*)
fellow/wench

gaillardement [gajaʁdəmɑ̃] ADV cheerfully

gain [gɛ̃] NM (*revenu*) earnings pl; (*bénéfice: gén pl*)
profits pl; (*au jeu: gén pl*) winnings pl; (*fig: de
temps, place*) saving; (: *avantage*) benefit; (: *lucre*)
gain; **avoir ~ de cause** to win the case; (*fig*) to
be proved right; **obtenir ~ de cause** (*fig*) to win
out

gaine [gɛn] NF (*corset*) girdle; (*fourreau*) sheath;
(*de fil électrique etc*) outer covering

gaine-culotte [gɛnkylɔt] (*pl* **gaines-culottes**)
NF pantie girdle

gainer [gene] /**1**/ VT to cover

gala [gala] NM official reception; **soirée de ~**
gala evening

galamment [galamɑ̃] ADV courteously

galant, e [galɑ̃, -ɑ̃t] ADJ (*courtois*) courteous,
gentlemanly; (*entreprenant*) flirtatious, gallant;
(*aventure, poésie*) amorous; (*scène, rendez-vous*)
romantic; **en ~ compagnie** (*homme*) with a lady
friend; (*femme*) with a gentleman friend

galanterie [galɑ̃tʁi] NF gallantry

galantine [galɑ̃tin] NF galantine

Galapagos [galapagos] NFPL: **les (îles) ~** the
Galapagos Islands

galaxie [galaksi] NF galaxy

galbe [galb] NM curve(s); shapeliness

galbé, e [galbe] ADJ (*jambes*) (well-)rounded;
bien ~ shapely

gale [gal] NF (*Méd*) scabies *sg*; (*de chien*) mange

galéjade [galeʒad] NF tall story

galère [galɛʁ] NF galley

galérer [galeʁe] /**6**/ VI (*fam*) to work hard, slave
(away)

galerie [galʁi] NF gallery; (*Théât*) circle; (*de
voiture*) roof rack; (*fig: spectateurs*) audience;
~ marchande shopping mall; **~ de peinture**
(private) art gallery

galérien [galerjɛ̃] NM galley slave

galet [galɛ] NM pebble; (*Tech*) wheel; **galets** NMPL pebbles, shingle *sg*

galette [galɛt] NF (*gâteau*) flat pastry cake; (*crêpe*) savoury pancake; **la ~ des Rois** *cake traditionally eaten on Twelfth Night*

> A *galette des Rois* is a cake eaten on Twelfth Night containing a figurine. The person who finds it is the king (or queen) and gets a paper crown. They then choose someone else to be their queen (or king).

galeux, -euse [galø, -øz] ADJ: **un chien ~** a mangy dog

Galice [galis] NF: **la ~** Galicia (*in Spain*)

Galicie [galisi] NF: **la ~** Galicia (*in Central Europe*)

galiléen, ne [galileɛ̃, -ɛn] ADJ Galilean

galimatias [galimatja] NM (*péj*) gibberish

galipette [galipɛt] NF somersault; **faire des galipettes** to turn somersaults

Galles [gal] NFPL: **le pays de ~** Wales

gallicisme [galisism] NM French idiom; (*tournure fautive*) gallicism

gallois, e [galwa, -waz] ADJ Welsh ▶ NM (*Ling*) Welsh ▶ NM/F: **G~, e** Welshman(-woman)

gallo-romain, e [galorɔmɛ̃, -ɛn] ADJ Gallo-Roman

galoche [galɔʃ] NF clog

galon [galɔ̃] NM (*Mil*) stripe; (*décoratif*) piece of braid; **prendre du ~** to be promoted

galop [galo] NM gallop; **au ~** at a gallop; **~ d'essai** (*fig*) trial run

galopade [galopad] NF stampede

galopant, e [galopɑ̃, -ɑ̃t] ADJ: **inflation ~** galloping inflation; **démographie ~** exploding population

galoper [galope] /1/ VI to gallop

galopin [galopɛ̃] NM urchin, ragamuffin

galvaniser [galvanize] /1/ VT to galvanize

galvaudé, e [galvode] ADJ (*expression*) hackneyed; (*mot*) clichéd

galvauder [galvode] /1/ VT to debase

gambade [gɑ̃bad] NF: **faire des gambades** to skip *ou* frisk about

gambader [gɑ̃bade] /1/ VI (*animal, enfant*) to leap about

gamberger [gɑ̃bɛrʒe] /3/ (*fam*) VI to (have a) think ▶ VT to dream up

Gambie [gɑ̃bi] NF: **la ~** (*pays*) Gambia; (*fleuve*) the Gambia

gamelle [gamɛl] NF mess tin; billy can; (*fam*): **ramasser une ~** to fall flat on one's face

gamin, e [gamɛ̃, -in] NM/F kid ▶ ADJ mischievous, playful

gaminerie [gaminri] NF mischievousness, playfulness

gamme [gam] NF (*Mus*) scale; (*fig*) range

gammé, e [game] ADJ: **croix ~** swastika

Gand [gɑ̃] N Ghent

gang [gɑ̃g] NM (*de criminels*) gang

Gange [gɑ̃ʒ] NM: **le ~** the Ganges

ganglion [gɑ̃glijɔ̃] NM ganglion; (*lymphatique*) gland; **avoir des ganglions** to have swollen glands

gangrène [gɑ̃grɛn] NF gangrene; (*fig*)

corruption; corrupting influence

gangster [gɑ̃gstɛr] NM gangster

gangstérisme [gɑ̃gsterism] NM gangsterism

gangue [gɑ̃g] NF coating

ganse [gɑ̃s] NF braid

gant [gɑ̃] NM glove; **prendre des gants** (*fig*) to handle the situation with kid gloves; **relever le ~** (*fig*) to take up the gauntlet; **~ de crin** massage glove; **~ de toilette** (face) flannel (*Brit*), face cloth; **gants de boxe** boxing gloves; **gants de caoutchouc** rubber gloves

ganté, e [gɑ̃te] ADJ: **~ de blanc** wearing white gloves

ganterie [gɑ̃tri] NF glove trade; (*magasin*) glove shop

garage [garaʒ] NM garage; **~ à vélos** bicycle shed

garagiste [garaʒist] NMF (*propriétaire*) garage owner; (*mécanicien*) garage mechanic

garant, e [garɑ̃, -ɑ̃t] NM/F guarantor ▶ NM guarantee; **se porter ~ de** to vouch for; to be answerable for

garantie [garɑ̃ti] NF guarantee, warranty; (*gage*) security, surety; **(bon de) ~** guarantee *ou* warranty slip; **~ de bonne exécution** performance bond

garantir [garɑ̃tir] /2/ VT to guarantee; (*protéger*): **~ de** to protect from; **je vous garantis que** I can assure you that; **garanti pure laine/2 ans** guaranteed pure wool/for 2 years

garce [gars] NF (*péj*) bitch (!)

garçon [garsɔ̃] NM boy; (*jeune homme*) boy, lad; (*aussi*: **garçon de café**) waiter; **vieux ~** (*célibataire*) bachelor; **~ boucher/coiffeur** butcher's/hairdresser's assistant; **~ de courses** messenger; **~ d'écurie** stable lad; **~ manqué** tomboy

garçonnet [garsɔnɛ] NM small boy

garçonnière [garsɔnjɛr] NF bachelor flat

garde [gard] NM (*de prisonnier*) guard; (*de domaine etc*) warden; (*soldat, sentinelle*) guardsman ▶ NF guarding; looking after; (*soldats, Boxe, Escrime*) guard; (*faction*) watch; (*d'une arme*) hilt; (*Typo*: *aussi*: **page** *ou* **feuille de garde**) flyleaf; (: *collée*) endpaper; **de ~** *adj, adv* on duty; **monter la ~** to stand guard; **être sur ses gardes** to be on one's guard; **mettre en ~** to warn; **mise en ~** warning; **prendre ~ (à)** to be careful (of); **avoir la ~ des enfants** (*après divorce*) to have custody of the children; **~ champêtre** *nm* rural policeman; **~ du corps** *nm* bodyguard; **~ d'enfants** *nf* child minder; **~ forestier** *nm* forest warden; **~ mobile** *nmf* mobile guard; **~ des Sceaux** *nm* ≈ Lord Chancellor (*Brit*), ≈ Attorney General (*US*); **~ à vue** *nf* (*Jur*) ≈ police custody

garde-à-vous [gardavu] NM INV: **être/se mettre au ~** to be at/stand to attention; **~ (fixe)!** (*Mil*) attention!

garde-barrière [gardəbarjɛr] (*pl* **gardes-barrière(s)**) NM/F level-crossing keeper

garde-boue [gardəbu] NM INV mudguard

garde-chasse [gardəʃas] (*pl* **gardes-chasse(s)**) NM gamekeeper

garde-côte [gaʀdəkot] NM (*vaisseau*) coastguard boat

garde-feu [gaʀdəfø] NM INV fender

garde-fou [gaʀdəfu] NM railing, parapet

garde-malade [gaʀdəmalad] (*pl* **gardes-malade(s)**) NF home nurse

garde-manger [gaʀdəmãʒe] NM INV (*boîte*) meat safe; (*placard*) pantry, larder

garde-meuble [gaʀdəmœbl] NM furniture depository

garde-pêche [gaʀdəpɛʃ] NM INV (*personne*) water bailiff; (*navire*) fisheries protection ship

garder [gaʀde] /**1**/ VT (*conserver*) to keep; (: *sur soi*: *vêtement, chapeau*) to keep on; (*surveiller*: *enfants*) to look after; (: *immeuble, lieu, prisonnier*) to guard; **se garder** VI (*aliment*: *se conserver*) to keep; **se garder de faire** to be careful not to do; **~ le lit/ la chambre** to stay in bed/indoors; **~ le silence** to keep silent *ou* quiet; **~ la ligne** to keep one's figure; **~ à vue** to keep in custody; **pêche/ chasse gardée** private fishing/hunting (ground)

garderie [gaʀdəʀi] NF day nursery, crèche

garde-robe [gaʀdəʀɔb] NF wardrobe

gardeur, -euse [gaʀdœʀ, -øz] NM/F (*de vaches*) cowherd; (*de chèvres*) goatherd

gardian [gaʀdjã] NM cowboy (*in the Camargue*)

gardien, ne [gaʀdjɛ̃, -ɛn] NM/F (*garde*) guard; (*de prison*) warder; (*de domaine, réserve*) warden; (*de musée etc*) attendant; (*de phare, cimetière*) keeper; (*d'immeuble*) caretaker; (*fig*) guardian; **~ de but** goalkeeper; **~ de nuit** night watchman; **~ de la paix** policeman

gardiennage [gaʀdjɛnaʒ] NM (*emploi*) caretaking; **société de ~** security firm

gardon [gaʀdɔ̃] NM roach

gare [gaʀ] NF (*railway*) station, train station (US) ▶ EXCL: **~ à ... mind ...!, watch out for ...!; ~ à ne pas ...** mind you don't ...; **à toi!** watch out!; **sans crier ~** without warning; **~ maritime** harbour station; **~ routière** bus station; (*de camions*) haulage (BRIT) *ou* trucking (US) depot; **~ de triage** marshalling yard

garenne [gaʀɛn] NF *voir* **lapin**

garer [gaʀe] /**1**/ VT to park; **se garer** VI to park; (*pour laisser passer*) to draw into the side

gargantuesque [gaʀgɑ̃tɥɛsk] ADJ gargantuan

gargariser [gaʀgaʀize] /**1**/: **se gargariser** VI to gargle; **se gargariser de** (*fig*) to revel in

gargarisme [gaʀgaʀism] NM gargling *no pl*; (*produit*) gargle

gargote [gaʀgɔt] NF cheap restaurant, greasy spoon (*fam*)

gargouille [gaʀguj] NF gargoyle

gargouillement [gaʀgujmã] NM = **gargouillis**

gargouiller [gaʀguje] /**1**/ VI (*estomac*) to rumble; (*eau*) to gurgle

gargouillis [gaʀguji] NM (*gén pl*: *voir vb*) rumbling; gurgling

garnement [gaʀnəmã] NM rascal, scallywag

garni, e [gaʀni] ADJ (*plat*) served with vegetables (*and chips, pasta or rice*) ▶ NM (*appartement*) furnished accommodation *no pl* (BRIT) *ou* accommodations *pl* (US)

garnir [gaʀniʀ] /**2**/ VT to decorate; (*remplir*) to fill; (*recouvrir*) to cover; **se garnir** VI (*pièce, salle*) to fill up; **~ qch de** (*orner*) to decorate sth with; to trim sth with; (*approvisionner*) to fill *ou* stock sth with; (*protéger*) to fit sth with; (*Culin*) to garnish sth with

garnison [gaʀnizɔ̃] NF garrison

garniture [gaʀnityʀ] NF (*Culin*: *légumes*) vegetables *pl*; (: *persil etc*) garnish; (: *farce*) filling; (*décoration*) trimming; (*protection*) fittings *pl*; **~ de cheminée** mantelpiece ornaments *pl*; **~ de frein** (*Auto*) brake lining; **~ intérieure** (*Auto*) interior trim; **~ périodique** sanitary towel (BRIT) *ou* napkin (US)

garrigue [gaʀig] NF scrubland

garrot [gaʀo] NM (*Méd*) tourniquet; (*torture*) garrotte

garrotter [gaʀɔte] /**1**/ VT to tie up; (*fig*) to muzzle

gars [gɑ] NM lad; (*type*) guy

Gascogne [gaskɔɲ] NF: **la ~** Gascony; **le golfe de ~** the Bay of Biscay

gascon, ne [gaskɔ̃, -ɔn] ADJ Gascon ▶ NM: **G~** (*hâbleur*) braggart

gas-oil [gazojl] NM diesel oil

gaspillage [gaspijaʒ] NM waste

gaspiller [gaspije] /**1**/ VT to waste

gaspilleur, -euse [gaspijœʀ, -øz] ADJ wasteful

gastrique [gastʀik] ADJ gastric, stomach *cpd*

gastro-entérite [gastʀoɑ̃teʀit] NF (*Méd*) gastro-enteritis

gastro-intestinal, e, -aux [gastʀoɛ̃tɛstinal, -o] ADJ gastrointestinal

gastronome [gastʀɔnɔm] NMF gourmet

gastronomie [gastʀɔnɔmi] NF gastronomy

gastronomique [gastʀɔnɔmik] ADJ gastronomic; **menu ~** gourmet menu

gâteau, x [gɑto] NM cake ▶ ADJ INV (*fam*: *trop indulgent*): **papa-/maman-~** doting father/ mother; **~ d'anniversaire** birthday cake; **~ de riz** ≈ rice pudding; **~ sec** biscuit

gâter [gɑte] /**1**/ VT to spoil; **se gâter** VI (*dent, fruit*) to go bad; (*temps, situation*) to change for the worse

gâterie [gɑtʀi] NF little treat

gâteux, -euse [gɑtø, -øz] ADJ senile

gâtisme [gɑtism] NM senility

GATT [gat] SIGLE M (= *General Agreement on Tariffs and Trade*) GATT

gauche [goʃ] ADJ left, left-hand; (*maladroit*) awkward, clumsy ▶ NF (*Pol*) left (wing); (*Boxe*) left; **le bras ~** the left arm; **le côté ~** the left-hand side; **à ~** on the left; (*direction*) (to the) left; **à ~ de** (*on ou* to the) left of; **à la ~ de** to the left of; **sur votre ~** on your left; **de ~** (*Pol*) left-wing

gauchement [goʃmã] ADV awkwardly, clumsily

gaucher, -ère [goʃe, -ɛʀ] ADJ left-handed

gaucherie [goʃʀi] NF awkwardness, clumsiness

gauchir [goʃiʀ] /**2**/ VT (*planche, objet*) to warp; (*fig*: *fait, idée*) to distort

gauchisant, e [goʃizɑ̃, -ɑ̃t] ADJ with left-wing tendencies

gauchisme [goʃism] NM leftism

191

gauchiste [goʃist] ADJ, NMF leftist

gaufre [gofʀ] NF (*pâtisserie*) waffle; (*de cire*) honeycomb

gaufrer [gofʀe] /1/ VT (*papier*) to emboss; (*tissu*) to goffer

gaufrette [gofʀɛt] NF wafer

gaufrier [gofʀije] NM (*moule*) waffle iron

Gaule [gol] NF: **la ~** Gaul

gaule [gol] NF (*perche*) (long) pole; (*canne à pêche*) fishing rod

gauler [gole] /1/ VT (*arbre*) to beat (*using a long pole to bring down fruit*); (*fruits*) to beat down (*with a pole*)

gaullisme [golism] NM Gaullism

gaulliste [golist] ADJ, NMF Gaullist

gaulois, e [golwa, -waz] ADJ Gallic; (*grivois*) bawdy ▸ NM/F: **G~, e** Gaul

gauloiserie [golwazʀi] NF bawdiness

gausser [gose] /1/: **se ~ de** vt to deride

gaver [gave] /1/ VT to force-feed; (*fig*) **~ de** to cram with, fill up with; **se ~ de** to stuff o.s. with

gay [gɛ] ADJ, NM (*fam*) gay

gaz [gaz] NM INV gas; **mettre les ~** (*Auto*) to put one's foot down; **chambre/masque à ~** gas chamber/mask; **~ en bouteille** bottled gas; **~ butane** Calor gas® (*BRIT*), butane gas; **~ carbonique** carbon dioxide; **~ hilarant** laughing gas; **~ lacrymogène** tear gas; **~ naturel** natural gas; **~ de ville** town gas (*BRIT*), manufactured domestic gas; **ça sent le ~** I can smell gas, there's a smell of gas

gaze [gaz] NF gauze

gazéifié, e [gazeifje] ADJ carbonated, aerated

gazelle [gazɛl] NF gazelle

gazer [gaze] /1/ VT to gas ▸ VI (*fam*) to be going ou working well

gazette [gazɛt] NF news sheet

gazeux, -euse [gazø, -øz] ADJ gaseous; (*eau*) sparkling; (*boisson*) fizzy

gazoduc [gazodyk] NM gas pipeline

gazole [gazɔl] NM = **gas-oil**

gazomètre [gazɔmɛtʀ] NM gasometer

gazon [gazɔ̃] NM (*herbe*) turf, grass; (*pelouse*) lawn

gazonner [gazone] /1/ VT (*terrain*) to grass over

gazouillement [gazujmɑ̃] NM (*voir vb*) chirping; babbling

gazouiller [gazuje] /1/ VI (*oiseau*) to chirp; (*enfant*) to babble

gazouillis [gazuji] NMPL chirp *sg*

GB SIGLE F (= *Grande-Bretagne*) GB

gd ABR (= *grand*) L

GDF SIGLE M (= *Gaz de France*) national gas company

geai [ʒɛ] NM jay

géant, e [ʒeɑ̃, -ɑ̃t] ADJ gigantic, giant; (*Comm*) giant-size ▸ NM/F giant

geignement [ʒɛɲmɑ̃] NM groaning, moaning

geindre [ʒɛ̃dʀ] /52/ VI to groan, moan

gel [ʒɛl] NM frost; (*de l'eau*) freezing; (*fig: des salaires, prix*) freeze; freezing; (*produit de beauté*) gel; **~ douche** shower gel

gélatine [ʒelatin] NF gelatine

gélatineux, -euse [ʒelatinø, -øz] ADJ jelly-like, gelatinous

gelé, e [ʒəle] ADJ frozen ▸ NF jelly; (*gel*) frost; **~ blanche** hoarfrost, white frost

geler [ʒ(ə)le] /5/ VT, VI to freeze; **il gèle** it's freezing

gélule [ʒelyl] NF (*Méd*) capsule

gelures [ʒəlyʀ] NFPL frostbite *sg*

Gémeaux [ʒemo] NMPL: **les ~** Gemini, the Twins; **être des ~** to be Gemini

gémir [ʒemiʀ] /2/ VI to groan, moan

gémissement [ʒemismɑ̃] NM groan, moan

gemme [ʒɛm] NF gem(stone)

gémonies [ʒemɔni] NFPL: **vouer qn aux ~** to subject sb to public scorn

gén. ABR (= *généralement*) gen.

gênant, e [ʒɛnɑ̃, -ɑ̃t] ADJ (*objet*) awkward, in the way; (*histoire, personne*) embarrassing

gencive [ʒɑ̃siv] NF gum

gendarme [ʒɑ̃daʀm] NM gendarme

gendarmer [ʒɑ̃daʀme] /1/: **se gendarmer** VI to kick up a fuss

gendarmerie [ʒɑ̃daʀməʀi] NF military police force in countryside and small towns; their police station or barracks

gendre [ʒɑ̃dʀ] NM son-in-law

gène [ʒɛn] NM (*Bio*) gene

gêne [ʒɛn] NF (*à respirer, bouger*) discomfort, difficulty; (*dérangement*) bother, trouble; (*manque d'argent*) financial difficulties *pl ou* straits *pl*; (*confusion*) embarrassment; **sans ~** *adj* inconsiderate

gêné, e [ʒene] ADJ embarrassed; (*dépourvu d'argent*) short (of money)

généalogie [ʒenealɔʒi] NF genealogy

généalogique [ʒenealɔʒik] ADJ genealogical

gêner [ʒene] /1/ VT (*incommoder*) to bother; (*encombrer*) to hamper; (*bloquer le passage*) to be in the way of; (*déranger*) to bother; (*embarrasser*): **~ qn** to make sb feel ill-at-ease; **se gêner** to put o.s. out; **ne vous gênez pas!** (*ironique*) go right ahead!, don't mind me!; **je vais me ~!** (*ironique*) why should I care?

général, e, -aux [ʒeneʀal, -o] ADJ, NM general ▸ NF: (*répétition*) ~ final dress rehearsal; **en ~** usually, in general; **à la satisfaction ~** to everyone's satisfaction

généralement [ʒeneʀalmɑ̃] ADV generally

généralisable [ʒeneʀalizabl] ADJ generally applicable

généralisation [ʒeneʀalizasjɔ̃] NF generalization

généraliser [ʒeneʀalize] /1/ VT, VI to generalize; **se généraliser** VI to become widespread

généraliste [ʒeneʀalist] NMF (*Méd*) general practitioner, GP

généralité [ʒeneʀalite] NF: **la ~ des ...** the majority of ...; **généralités** NFPL generalities; (*introduction*) general points

générateur, -trice [ʒeneʀatœʀ, -tʀis] ADJ: **~ de** which causes ou brings about ▸ NF (*Élec*) generator

génération [ʒeneʀasjɔ̃] NF generation

généreusement [ʒeneʀøzmɑ̃] ADV
generously

généreux, -euse [ʒeneʀø, -øz] ADJ generous

générique [ʒeneʀik] ADJ generic ▶ NM (Ciné, TV)
credits pl, credit titles pl

générosité [ʒeneʀozite] NF generosity

Gênes [ʒɛn] N Genoa

genèse [ʒənɛz] NF genesis

genêt [ʒ(ə)nɛ] NM (Bot) broom no pl

généticien, ne [ʒenetisjɛ̃, -ɛn] NM/F
geneticist

génétique [ʒenetik] ADJ genetic ▶ NF
genetics sg

génétiquement [ʒenetikmɑ̃] ADV genetically

gêneur, -euse [ʒɛnœʀ, -øz] NM/F (personne qui
gêne) obstacle; (importun) intruder

Genève [ʒ(ə)nɛv] N Geneva

genevois, e [ʒənəvwa, -waz] ADJ Genevan

genévrier [ʒənevʀije] NM juniper

génial, e, -aux [ʒenjal, -o] ADJ of genius; (fam:
formidable) fantastic, brilliant

génie [ʒeni] NM genius; (Mil): **le ~ ≈** the
Engineers pl; **avoir du ~** to have genius; **~ civil**
civil engineering; **~ génétique** genetic
engineering

genièvre [ʒənjɛvʀ] NM (Bot) juniper (tree);
(boisson) Dutch gin; **grain de ~** juniper berry

génisse [ʒenis] NF heifer; **foie de ~** ox liver

génital, e, -aux [ʒenital, -o] ADJ genital; **les
parties génitales** the genitals

génitif [ʒenitif] NM genitive

génocide [ʒenɔsid] NM genocide

génois, e [ʒenwa, -waz] ADJ Genoese ▶ NF
(gâteau) ≈ sponge cake

génome [ʒenom] NM genome

genou, x [ʒ(ə)nu] NM knee; **à ~** on one's knees;
se mettre à ~ to kneel down

genouillère [ʒənujɛʀ] NF (Sport) kneepad

genre [ʒɑ̃ʀ] NM (espèce, sorte) kind, type, sort;
(allure) manner; (Ling) gender; (Art) genre; (Zool
etc) genus; **se donner du ~** to give o.s. airs;
avoir bon ~ to look a nice sort; **avoir mauvais ~**
to be coarse-looking; **ce n'est pas son ~** it's not
like him

gens [ʒɑ̃] NMPL (f in some phrases) people pl; **les ~
d'Église** the clergy; **les ~ du monde** society
people; **~ de maison** domestics

gentiane [ʒɑ̃sjan] NF gentian

gentil, le [ʒɑ̃ti, -ij] ADJ kind; (enfant: sage) good;
(sympathique: endroit etc) nice; **c'est très ~ à vous**
it's very kind ou good ou nice of you

gentilhommière [ʒɑ̃tijɔmjɛʀ] NF (small)
manor house ou country seat

gentillesse [ʒɑ̃tijɛs] NF kindness

gentillet, te [ʒɑ̃tijɛ, -ɛt] ADJ nice little

gentiment [ʒɑ̃timɑ̃] ADV kindly

génuflexion [ʒenyflɛksjɔ̃] NF genuflexion

géo ABR (= géographie) geography

géodésique [ʒeodezik] ADJ geodesic

géographe [ʒeogʀaf] NMF geographer

géographie [ʒeogʀafi] NF geography

géographique [ʒeogʀafik] ADJ geographical

geôlier [ʒolje] NM jailer

géologie [ʒeolɔʒi] NF geology

géologique [ʒeolɔʒik] ADJ geological

géologiquement [ʒeolɔʒikmɑ̃] ADV
geologically

géologue [ʒeolɔg] NMF geologist

géomètre [ʒeomɛtʀ] NM: **(arpenteur-)~** (land)
surveyor

géométrie [ʒeometʀi] NF geometry; **à ~
variable** (Aviat) swing-wing

géométrique [ʒeometʀik] ADJ geometric

géophysique [ʒeofizik] NF geophysics sg

géopolitique [ʒeopolitik] NF geopolitics sg

Géorgie [ʒeoʀʒi] NF: **la ~** (Caucase, USA) Georgia;
la ~ du Sud South Georgia

géorgien, ne [ʒeoʀʒjɛ̃, -ɛn] ADJ Georgian

géostationnaire [ʒeostasjɔnɛʀ] ADJ
geostationary

géothermique [ʒeotɛʀmik] ADJ: **énergie ~**
geothermal energy

gérance [ʒeʀɑ̃s] NF management; **mettre en ~**
to appoint a manager for; **prendre en ~** to take
over (the management of)

géranium [ʒeʀanjɔm] NM geranium

gérant, e [ʒeʀɑ̃, -ɑ̃t] NM/F manager/
manageress; **~ d'immeuble** managing agent

gerbe [ʒɛʀb] NF (de fleurs, d'eau) spray; (de blé)
sheaf; (fig) shower, burst

gercé, e [ʒɛʀse] ADJ chapped

gercer [ʒɛʀse] /3/ VI, **se gercer** to chap

gerçure [ʒɛʀsyʀ] NF crack

gérer [ʒeʀe] /6/ VT to manage

gériatrie [ʒeʀjatʀi] NF geriatrics sg

gériatrique [ʒeʀjatʀik] ADJ geriatric

germain, e [ʒɛʀmɛ̃, -ɛn] ADJ: **cousin ~** first
cousin

germanique [ʒɛʀmanik] ADJ Germanic

germaniste [ʒɛʀmanist] NMF German scholar

germe [ʒɛʀm] NM germ

germer [ʒɛʀme] /1/ VI to sprout; (semence, aussi
fig) to germinate

gérondif [ʒeʀɔ̃dif] NM gerund; (en latin)
gerundive

gérontologie [ʒeʀɔ̃tɔlɔʒi] NF gerontology

gérontologue [ʒeʀɔ̃tɔlɔg] NMF gerontologist

gésier [ʒezje] NM gizzard

gésir [ʒeziʀ] VI to be lying (down); voir aussi **ci-gît**

gestation [ʒɛstasjɔ̃] NF gestation

geste [ʒɛst] NM gesture; move; motion; **il fit
un ~ de la main pour m'appeler** he signed to
me to come over, he waved me over; **ne faites
pas un ~** (ne bougez pas) don't move

gesticuler [ʒɛstikyle] /1/ VI to gesticulate

gestion [ʒɛstjɔ̃] NF management; **~ des
disques** (Inform) housekeeping; **~ de fichier(s)**
(Inform) file management

gestionnaire [ʒɛstjɔnɛʀ] NMF administrator;
~ de fichiers (Inform) file manager

geyser [ʒezɛʀ] NM geyser

Ghana [gana] NM: **le ~** Ghana

ghetto [gɛto] NM ghetto

gibecière [ʒibsjɛʀ] NF (de chasseur) gamebag; (sac
en bandoulière) shoulder bag

gibelotte [ʒiblɔt] NF rabbit fricassee in white wine

gibet [ʒibɛ] NM gallows pl

gibier [ʒibje] NM (animaux) game; (fig) prey

193

giboulée [ʒibule] NF sudden shower

giboyeux, -euse [ʒibwajø, -øz] ADJ well-stocked with game

Gibraltar [ʒibʀaltaʀ] NM Gibraltar

gibus [ʒibys] NM opera hat

giclée [ʒikle] NF spurt, squirt

gicler [ʒikle] /1/ VI to spurt, squirt

gicleur [ʒiklœʀ] NM (Auto) jet

GIE SIGLE M = **groupement d'intérêt économique**

gifle [ʒifl] NF slap (in the face)

gifler [ʒifle] /1/ VT to slap (in the face)

gigantesque [ʒigɑ̃tɛsk] ADJ gigantic

gigantisme [ʒigɑ̃tism] NM (Méd) gigantism; (des mégalopoles) vastness

gigaoctet [ʒigaɔktɛ] NM gigabyte

GIGN SIGLE M (= Groupe d'intervention de la gendarmerie nationale) special crack force of the gendarmerie, ≈ SAS (BRIT)

gigogne [ʒigɔɲ] ADJ: **lits gigognes** truckle (BRIT) ou trundle (US) beds; **tables/poupées gigognes** nest of tables/dolls

gigolo [ʒigɔlo] NM gigolo

gigot [ʒigo] NM leg (of mutton ou lamb)

gigoter [ʒigɔte] /1/ VI to wriggle (about)

gilet [ʒilɛ] NM waistcoat; (pull) cardigan; (de corps) vest; **~ pare-balles** bulletproof jacket; **~ de sauvetage** life jacket

gin [dʒin] NM gin; **~-tonic** gin and tonic

gingembre [ʒɛ̃ʒɑ̃bʀ] NM ginger

gingivite [ʒɛ̃ʒivit] NF inflammation of the gums, gingivitis

ginseng [ʒinsɛŋ] NM ginseng

girafe [ʒiʀaf] NF giraffe

giratoire [ʒiʀatwaʀ] ADJ: **sens ~** roundabout

girofle [ʒiʀɔfl] NM: **clou de ~** clove

giroflée [ʒiʀɔfle] NF wallflower

girolle [ʒiʀɔl] NF chanterelle

giron [ʒiʀɔ̃] NM (genoux) lap; (fig: sein) bosom

Gironde [ʒiʀɔ̃d] NF: **la ~** the Gironde

girophare [ʒiʀɔfaʀ] NM revolving (flashing) light

girouette [ʒiʀwɛt] NF weather vane ou cock

gis [ʒi], **gisais** etc [ʒizɛ] VB voir **gésir**

gisement [ʒizmɑ̃] NM deposit

gît [ʒi] VB voir **gésir**

gitan, e [ʒitɑ̃, -an] NM/F gipsy

gîte [ʒit] NM (maison) home; (abri) shelter; (du lièvre) form; **~ (rural)** (country) holiday cottage ou apartment, gîte (self-catering accommodation in the country)

gîter [ʒite] /1/ VI (Navig) to list

givrage [ʒivʀaʒ] NM icing

givrant, e [ʒivʀɑ̃, -ɑ̃t] ADJ: **brouillard ~** freezing fog

givre [ʒivʀ] NM (hoar) frost

givré, e [ʒivʀe] ADJ covered in frost; (fam: fou) nuts; **citron ~/orange ~** lemon/orange sorbet (served in fruit skin)

glabre [glabʀ] ADJ hairless; (menton) clean-shaven

glaçage [glasaʒ] NM (au sucre) icing; (au blanc d'œuf, de la viande) glazing

glace [glas] NF ice; (crème glacée) ice cream; (verre) sheet of glass; (miroir) mirror; (de voiture) window; **glaces** NFPL (Géo) ice sheets, ice sg; **de ~** (fig: accueil, visage) frosty, icy; **rester de ~** to remain unmoved

glacé, e [glase] ADJ (mains, vent, pluie) freezing; (lac) frozen; (boisson) iced

glacer [glase] /3/ VT to freeze; (boisson) to chill, ice; (gâteau) to ice (BRIT), frost (US); (papier, tissu) to glaze; (fig): **~ qn** (: intimider) to chill sb; (: effrayer) to make sb's blood run cold

glaciaire [glasjɛʀ] ADJ (période) ice cpd; (relief) glacial

glacial, e [glasjal] ADJ icy

glacier [glasje] NM (Géo) glacier; (marchand) ice-cream maker

glacière [glasjɛʀ] NF icebox

glaçon [glasɔ̃] NM icicle; (pour boisson) ice cube

gladiateur [gladjatœʀ] NM gladiator

glaïeul [glajœl] NM gladiola

glaire [glɛʀ] NF (Méd) phlegm no pl

glaise [glɛz] NF clay

glaive [glɛv] NM two-edged sword

gland [glɑ̃] NM (de chêne) acorn; (décoration) tassel; (Anat) glans

glande [glɑ̃d] NF gland

glander [glɑ̃de] /1/ VI (fam) to fart around (BRIT!), screw around (US!)

glaner [glane] /1/ VT, VI to glean

glapir [glapiʀ] /2/ VI to yelp

glapissement [glapismɑ̃] NM yelping

glas [gla] NM knell, toll

glauque [glok] ADJ dull blue-green

glissade [glisad] NF (par jeu) slide; (chute) slip; (dérapage) skid; **faire des glissades** to slide

glissant, e [glisɑ̃, -ɑ̃t] ADJ slippery

glisse [glis] NF: **sports de ~** sports involving sliding or gliding (eg skiing, surfing, windsurfing)

glissement [glismɑ̃] NM sliding; (fig) shift; **~ de terrain** landslide

glisser [glise] /1/ VI (avancer) to glide ou slide along; (coulisser, tomber) to slide; (déraper) to slip; (être glissant) to be slippery ▶ VT to slip; **~ qch sous/dans/à** to slip sth under/into/to; **~ sur** (fig: détail etc) to skate over; **se ~ dans/entre** to slip into/between

glissière [glisjɛʀ] NF slide channel; **à ~** (porte, fenêtre) sliding; **~ de sécurité** (Auto) crash barrier

glissoire [gliswaʀ] NF slide

global, e, -aux [glɔbal, -o] ADJ overall

globalement [glɔbalmɑ̃] ADV taken as a whole

globe [glɔb] NM globe; **sous ~** under glass; **~ oculaire** eyeball; **le ~ terrestre** the globe

globe-trotter [glɔbtʀɔtœʀ] NM globe-trotter

globule [glɔbyl] NM (du sang): **~ blanc/rouge** white/red corpuscle

globuleux, -euse [glɔbylø, -øz] ADJ: **yeux ~** protruding eyes

gloire [glwaʀ] NF glory; (mérite) distinction, credit; (personne) celebrity

glorieux, -euse [glɔʀjø, -øz] ADJ glorious

glorifier [glɔʀifje] /7/ VT to glorify, extol; **se ~ de** to glory in

gloriole [glɔʀjɔl] NF vainglory

glose [gloz] NF gloss

glossaire [glɔsɛʀ] NM glossary

glotte [glɔt] NF (Anat) glottis

glouglouter [gluglute] /1/ VI to gurgle

gloussement [glusmã] NM (de poule) cluck; (rire) chuckle

glousser [gluse] /1/ VI to cluck; (rire) to chuckle

glouton, ne [glutɔ̃, -ɔn] ADJ gluttonous, greedy

gloutonnerie [glutɔnʀi] NF gluttony

glu [gly] NF birdlime

gluant, e [glyã, -ãt] ADJ sticky, gummy

glucide [glysid] NM carbohydrate, (fam) carb; **alimentation** ou **régime pauvre en glucides** low-carb diet

glucose [glykoz] NM glucose

gluten [glytɛn] NM gluten

glycérine [gliseʀin] NF glycerine

glycine [glisin] NF wisteria

GMT SIGLE ADJ (= Greenwich Mean Time) GMT

gnangnan [nãnã] ADJ INV (fam: livre, film) soppy

GNL SIGLE M (= gaz naturel liquéfié) LNG (= liquefied natural gas)

gnôle [njol] NF (fam) booze no pl; **un petit verre de** ~ a drop of the hard stuff

gnome [gnom] NM gnome

gnon [ɲɔ̃] NM (fam: coup de poing) bash; (: marque) dent

GO SIGLE FPL (= grandes ondes) LW ▶ SIGLE M (= gentil organisateur) title given to leaders on Club Méditerranée holidays; extended to refer to easy-going leader of any group

Go ABR (= gigaoctet) GB

go [go]: **tout de go** adv straight out

goal [gol] NM goalkeeper

gobelet [gɔblɛ] NM (en métal) tumbler; (en plastique) beaker; (à dés) cup

gober [gɔbe] /1/ VT to swallow

goberger [gɔbɛʀʒe] /3/: **se goberger** VI to cosset o.s.

Gobi [gɔbi] N: **désert de** ~ Gobi Desert

godasse [gɔdas] NF (fam) shoe

godet [gɔdɛ] NM pot; (Couture) unpressed pleat

godiller [gɔdije] /1/ VI (Navig) to scull; (Ski) to wedeln

goéland [gɔelã] NM (sea)gull

goélette [gɔelɛt] NF schooner

goémon [gɔemɔ̃] NM wrack

gogo [gɔgo] NM (péj) mug, sucker; **à** ~ adv galore

goguenard, e [gɔgnaʀ, -aʀd] ADJ mocking

goguette [gɔgɛt] NF: **en** ~ on the binge

goinfre [gwɛ̃fʀ] NM glutton

goinfrer [gwɛ̃fʀe] /1/: **se goinfrer** VI to make a pig of o.s.; **se goinfrer de** to guzzle

goitre [gwatʀ] NM goitre

golf [gɔlf] NM (jeu) golf; (terrain) golf course; ~ **miniature** crazy ou miniature golf

golfe [gɔlf] NM gulf; (petit) bay; **le** ~ **d'Aden** the Gulf of Aden; **le** ~ **de Gascogne** the Bay of Biscay; **le** ~ **du Lion** the Gulf of Lions; **le** ~ **Persique** the Persian Gulf

golfeur, -euse [gɔlfœʀ, -øz] NM/F golfer

gominé, e [gɔmine] ADJ slicked down

gomme [gɔm] NF (à effacer) rubber (BRIT), eraser; (résine) gum; **boule** ou **pastille de** ~ throat pastille

gommé, e [gɔme] ADJ: **papier** ~ gummed paper

gommer [gɔme] /1/ VT (effacer) to rub out (BRIT), erase; (enduire de gomme) to gum

gond [gɔ̃] NM hinge; **sortir de ses gonds** (fig) to fly off the handle

gondole [gɔ̃dɔl] NF gondola; (pour l'étalage) shelves pl, gondola

gondoler [gɔ̃dɔle] /1/: **se gondoler** VI to warp, buckle; (fam: rire) to hoot with laughter; to be in stitches

gondolier [gɔ̃dɔlje] NM gondolier

gonflable [gɔ̃flabl] ADJ inflatable

gonflage [gɔ̃flaʒ] NM inflating, blowing up

gonflé, e [gɔ̃fle] ADJ swollen; (ventre) bloated; **il est** ~ (fam: courageux) he's got some nerve; (: impertinent) he's got a nerve

gonflement [gɔ̃fləmã] NM inflation; (Méd) swelling

gonfler [gɔ̃fle] /1/ VT (pneu, ballon) to inflate, blow up; (nombre, importance) to inflate ▶ VI (pied etc) to swell (up); (Culin: pâte) to rise

gonfleur [gɔ̃flœʀ] NM air pump

gong [gɔ̃g] NM gong

gonzesse [gɔ̃zɛs] NF (fam) chick, bird (BRIT)

googler [gugle] /1/ VT to google

goret [gɔʀɛ] NM piglet

gorge [gɔʀʒ] NF (Anat) throat; (poitrine) breast; (Géo) gorge; (rainure) groove; **avoir mal à la** ~ to have a sore throat; **avoir la** ~ **serrée** to have a lump in one's throat

gorgé, e [gɔʀʒe] ADJ: ~ **de** filled with; (eau) saturated with ▶ NF mouthful; (petite) sip; (grande) gulp; **boire à petites/grandes gorgées** to take little sips/big gulps

gorille [gɔʀij] NM gorilla; (fam) bodyguard

gosier [gozje] NM throat

gosse [gɔs] NMF kid

gothique [gɔtik] ADJ Gothic

gouache [gwaʃ] NF gouache

gouaille [gwaj] NF street wit, cocky humour (BRIT) ou humor (US)

goudron [gudʀɔ̃] NM (asphalte) tar(mac) (BRIT), asphalt; (du tabac) tar

goudronner [gudʀɔne] /1/ VT to tar(mac) (BRIT), asphalt (US)

gouffre [gufʀ] NM abyss, gulf

goujat [guʒa] NM boor

goujon [guʒɔ̃] NM gudgeon

goulée [gule] NF gulp

goulet [gulɛ] NM bottleneck

goulot [gulo] NM neck; **boire au** ~ to drink from the bottle

goulu, e [guly] ADJ greedy

goulûment [gulymã] ADV greedily

goupille [gupij] NF (metal) pin

goupiller [gupije] /1/ VT to pin (together)

goupillon [gupijɔ̃] NM (Rel) sprinkler; (brosse) bottle brush; (fig) the cloth, the clergy

gourd, e [guʀ, guʀd] ADJ numb (with cold)

gourde [guʀd] NF (récipient) flask; (fam) (clumsy) clot ou oaf ▶ ADJ oafish

g

gourdin [guʀdɛ̃] NM club, bludgeon
gourer [guʀe] /1/ *(fam)*: **se gourer** VI to boob
gourmand, e [guʀmɑ̃, -ɑ̃d] ADJ greedy
gourmandise [guʀmɑ̃diz] NF greed; *(bonbon)* sweet *(BRIT)*, piece of candy *(US)*
gourmet [guʀmɛ] NM epicure
gourmette [guʀmɛt] NF chain bracelet
gourou [guʀu] NM guru
gousse [gus] NF *(de vanille etc)* pod; **~ d'ail** clove of garlic
gousset [gusɛ] NM *(de gilet)* fob
goût [gu] NM taste; *(fig: appréciation)* taste, liking; **le (bon) ~** good taste; **de bon ~** in good taste, tasteful; **de mauvais ~** in bad taste, tasteless; **avoir bon/mauvais ~** *(aliment)* to taste nice/nasty; *(personne)* to have good/bad taste; **avoir du/manquer de ~** to have/lack taste; **avoir du ~ pour** to have a liking for; **prendre ~ à** to develop a taste ou a liking for
goûter [gute] /1/ VT *(essayer)* to taste; *(apprécier)* to enjoy ▶ VI to have *(afternoon)* tea ▶ NM *(afternoon)* tea; **~ à** to taste, sample; **~ de** to have a taste of; **~ d'enfants/d'anniversaire** children's tea/birthday party; **je peux ~?** can I have a taste?
goutte [gut] NF drop; *(Méd)* gout; *(alcool)* nip *(BRIT)*, tot *(BRIT)*, drop *(US)*; **gouttes** NFPL *(Méd)* drops; **~ à ~** adv a drop at a time; **tomber ~ à ~** to drip
goutte-à-goutte [gutagut] NM INV *(Méd)* drip; **alimenter au ~** to drip-feed
gouttelette [gutlɛt] NF droplet
goutter [gute] /1/ VI to drip
gouttière [gutjɛʀ] NF gutter
gouvernail [guvɛʀnaj] NM rudder; *(barre)* helm, tiller
gouvernant, e [guvɛʀnɑ̃, -ɑ̃t] ADJ ruling cpd ▶ NF housekeeper; *(d'un enfant)* governess
gouverne [guvɛʀn] NF: **pour sa ~** for his guidance
gouvernement [guvɛʀnəmɑ̃] NM government
gouvernemental, e, -aux [guvɛʀnəmɑ̃tal, -o] ADJ *(politique)* government cpd; *(journal, parti)* pro-government
gouverner [guvɛʀne] /1/ VT to govern; *(diriger)* to steer; *(fig)* to control
gouverneur [guvɛʀnœʀ] NM governor; *(Mil)* commanding officer
goyave [gɔjav] NF guava
GPL SIGLE M *(= gaz de pétrole liquéfié)* LPG *(= liquefied petroleum gas)*
GQG SIGLE M *(= grand quartier général)* GHQ
grabataire [gʀabatɛʀ] ADJ bedridden ▶ NMF bedridden invalid
grâce [gʀɑs] NF *(charme, Rel)* grace; *(faveur)* favour; *(Jur)* pardon; **grâces** NFPL *(Rel)* grace sg; **de bonne/mauvaise ~** with (a) good/bad grace; **dans les bonnes grâces de qn** in favour with sb; **faire ~ à qn de qch** to spare sb sth; **rendre ~(s) à** to give thanks to; **demander ~** to beg for mercy; **droit de ~** right of reprieve; **recours en ~** plea for pardon; **~ à** prép thanks to
gracier [gʀasje] /7/ VT to pardon

gracieusement [gʀasjøzmɑ̃] ADV graciously, kindly; *(gratuitement)* freely; *(avec grâce)* gracefully
gracieux, -euse [gʀasjø, -øz] ADJ *(charmant, élégant)* graceful; *(aimable)* gracious, kind; **à titre ~** free of charge
gracile [gʀasil] ADJ slender
gradation [gʀadasjɔ̃] NF gradation
grade [gʀad] NM *(Mil)* rank; *(Scol)* degree; **monter en ~** to be promoted
gradé [gʀade] NM *(Mil)* officer
gradin [gʀadɛ̃] NM *(dans un théâtre)* tier; *(de stade)* step; **gradins** NMPL *(de stade)* terracing no pl *(BRIT)*, standing area; **en gradins** terraced
graduation [gʀaduasjɔ̃] NF graduation
gradué, e [gʀadue] ADJ *(exercices)* graded (for difficulty); *(thermomètre)* graduated; **verre ~** measuring jug
graduel, le [gʀaduɛl] ADJ gradual; progressive
graduer [gʀadue] /1/ VT *(effort etc)* to increase gradually; *(règle, verre)* to graduate
graffiti [gʀafiti] NMPL graffiti
grain [gʀɛ̃] NM *(gén)* grain; *(de chapelet)* bead; *(Navig)* squall; *(averse)* heavy shower; *(fig: petite quantité)*: **un ~ de** a touch of; **~ de beauté** beauty spot; **~ de café** coffee bean; **~ de poivre** peppercorn; **~ de poussière** speck of dust; **~ de raisin** grape
graine [gʀɛn] NF seed; **mauvaise ~** *(mauvais sujet)* bad lot; **une ~ de voyou** a hooligan in the making
graineterie [gʀɛntʀi] NF seed merchant's (shop)
grainetier, -ière [gʀɛntje, -jɛʀ] NM/F seed merchant
graissage [gʀesaʒ] NM lubrication, greasing
graisse [gʀɛs] NF fat; *(lubrifiant)* grease; **~ saturée** saturated fat
graisser [gʀese] /1/ VT to lubricate, grease; *(tacher)* to make greasy
graisseux, -euse [gʀesø, -øz] ADJ greasy; *(Anat)* fatty
grammaire [gʀamɛʀ] NF grammar
grammatical, e, -aux [gʀamatikal, -o] ADJ grammatical
gramme [gʀam] NM gramme
grand, e [gʀɑ̃, gʀɑ̃d] ADJ *(haut)* tall; *(gros, vaste, large)* big, large; *(long)* long; *(plus âgé)* big; *(adulte)* grown-up; *(important, brillant)* great ▶ ADV: **~ ouvert** wide open; **un ~ buveur** a heavy drinker; **un ~ homme** a great man; **son ~ frère** his big ou older brother; **avoir ~ besoin de** to be in dire ou desperate need of; **il est ~ temps de** it's high time to; **il est assez ~ pour** he's big ou old enough to; **voir ~** to think big; **en ~** on a large scale; **au ~ air** in the open (air); **les grands blessés/brûlés** the severely injured/burned; **de ~ matin** at the crack of dawn; **~ écart** splits pl; **~ ensemble** housing scheme; **~ jour** broad daylight; **~ livre** *(Comm)* ledger; **~ magasin** department store; **~ malade** very sick person; **~ public** general public; **~ personne** grown-up; **~ surface** hypermarket, superstore; **grandes écoles** prestige university-

level colleges with competitive entrance examinations; see note; **grandes lignes** (*Rail*) main lines; **grandes vacances** summer holidays (*Brit*) *ou* vacation (*US*)

> The *grandes écoles* are highly-respected institutes of higher education which train students for specific careers. Students who have spent two years after the *baccalauréat* in the *classes préparatoires* are recruited by competitive entry examination. The prestigious *grandes écoles* have a strong corporate identity and tend to furnish France with its intellectual, administrative and political élite.

grand-angle [gʀɑ̃tɑ̃gl] (*pl* **grands-angles**) NM (*Photo*) wide-angle lens

grand-angulaire [gʀɑ̃tɑ̃gylɛʀ] (*pl* **grands-angulaires**) NM (*Photo*) wide-angle lens

grand-chose [gʀɑ̃ʃoz] NMF INV: **pas** ~ not much

Grande-Bretagne [gʀɑ̃dbʀətaɲ] NF: **la ~** (Great) Britain; **en ~** in (Great) Britain

grandement [gʀɑ̃dmɑ̃] ADV (*tout à fait*) greatly; (*largement*) easily; (*généreusement*) lavishly

grandeur [gʀɑ̃dœʀ] NF (*dimension*) size; (*fig: ampleur, importance*) magnitude; (: *gloire, puissance*) greatness; **~ nature** *adj* life-size

grand-guignolesque [gʀɑ̃giɲɔlɛsk] ADJ gruesome

grandiloquent, e [gʀɑ̃dilɔkɑ̃, -ɑ̃t] ADJ bombastic, grandiloquent

grandiose [gʀɑ̃djoz] ADJ (*paysage, spectacle*) imposing

grandir [gʀɑ̃diʀ] /2/ VI (*enfant, arbre*) to grow; (*bruit, hostilité*) to increase, grow ▶ VT: **~ qn** (*vêtement, chaussure*) to make sb look taller; (*fig*) to make sb grow in stature

grandissant, e [gʀɑ̃disɑ̃, -ɑ̃t] ADJ growing

grand-mère [gʀɑ̃mɛʀ] (*pl* **grand(s)-mères**) NF grandmother

grand-messe [gʀɑ̃mɛs] NF high mass

grand-oncle [gʀɑ̃tɔ̃kl(ə)] (*pl* **grands-oncles** [gʀɑ̃zɔ̃kl]) NM great-uncle

grand-peine [gʀɑ̃pɛn]: **à ~** *adv* with (great) difficulty

grand-père [gʀɑ̃pɛʀ] (*pl* **grands-pères**) NM grandfather

grand-route [gʀɑ̃ʀut] NF main road

grand-rue [gʀɑ̃ʀy] NF high street

grands-parents [gʀɑ̃paʀɑ̃] NMPL grandparents

grand-tante [gʀɑ̃tɑ̃t] (*pl* **grand(s)-tantes**) NF great-aunt

grand-voile [gʀɑ̃vwal] NF mainsail

grange [gʀɑ̃ʒ] NF barn

granit, granite [gʀanit] NM granite

granitique [gʀanitik] ADJ granite; (*terrain*) granitic

granule [gʀanyl] NM small pill

granulé [gʀanyle] NM granule

granuleux, -euse [gʀanylø, -øz] ADJ granular

graphe [gʀaf] NM graph

graphie [gʀafi] NF written form

graphique [gʀafik] ADJ graphic ▶ NM graph

graphisme [gʀafism] NM graphic arts *pl*; graphics *sg*; (*écriture*) handwriting

graphiste [gʀafist] NMF graphic designer

graphologie [gʀafɔlɔʒi] NF graphology

graphologue [gʀafɔlɔg] NMF graphologist

grappe [gʀap] NF cluster; **~ de raisin** bunch of grapes

grappiller [gʀapije] /1/ VT to glean

grappin [gʀapɛ̃] NM grapnel; **mettre le ~ sur** (*fig*) to get one's claws on

gras, se [gʀɑ, gʀɑs] ADJ (*viande, soupe*) fatty; (*personne*) fat; (*surface, main, cheveux*) greasy; (*terre*) sticky; (*toux*) loose, phlegmy; (*rire*) throaty; (*plaisanterie*) coarse; (*crayon*) soft-lead; (*Typo*) bold ▶ NM (*Culin*) fat; **faire la ~ matinée** to have a lie-in (*Brit*), sleep late; **matière ~** fat (content)

gras-double [gʀɑdubl] NM (*Culin*) tripe

grassement [gʀɑsmɑ̃] ADV (*généreusement*): **~ payé** handsomely paid; (*grossièrement: rire*) coarsely

grassouillet, te [gʀasujɛ, -ɛt] ADJ podgy, plump

gratifiant, e [gʀatifjɑ̃, -ɑ̃t] ADJ gratifying, rewarding

gratification [gʀatifikasjɔ̃] NF bonus

gratifier [gʀatifje] /7/ VT: **~ qn de** to favour (*Brit*) *ou* favor (*US*) sb with; to reward sb with; (*sourire etc*) to favo(u)r sb with

gratin [gʀatɛ̃] NM (*Culin*) cheese- (*ou* crumb-)topped dish; (: *croûte*) topping; **au ~** au gratin; **tout le ~ parisien** all the best people of Paris

gratiné [gʀatine] ADJ (*Culin*) au gratin; (*fam*) hellish ▶ NF (*soupe*) onion soup au gratin

gratis [gʀatis] ADV, ADJ INV free

gratitude [gʀatityd] NF gratitude

gratte-ciel [gʀatsjɛl] NM INV skyscraper

grattement [gʀatmɑ̃] NM (*bruit*) scratching (noise)

gratte-papier [gʀatpapje] NM INV (*péj*) penpusher

gratter [gʀate] /1/ VT (*frotter*) to scrape; (*avec un ongle: bras, bouton*) to scratch; (*enlever: avec un outil*) to scrape off; (: *avec un ongle*) to scratch off ▶ VI (*irriter*) to be scratchy; (*démanger*) to itch; **se gratter** to scratch o.s.

grattoir [gʀatwaʀ] NM scraper

gratuit, e [gʀatɥi, -ɥit] ADJ (*entrée*) free; (*billet*) free, complimentary; (*fig*) gratuitous

gratuité [gʀatɥite] NF being free (of charge); gratuitousness

gratuitement [gʀatɥitmɑ̃] ADV (*sans payer*) free; (*sans preuve, motif*) gratuitously

gravats [gʀava] NMPL rubble *sg*

grave [gʀav] ADJ (*dangereux: maladie, accident*) serious, bad; (*sérieux: sujet, problème*) serious, grave; (*personne, air*) grave, solemn; (*voix, son*) deep, low-pitched ▶ NM (*Mus*) low register; **ce n'est pas ~!** it's all right, don't worry; **blessé ~** seriously injured person

graveleux, -euse [gʀavlø, -øz] ADJ (*terre*) gravelly; (*fruit*) gritty; (*contes, propos*) smutty

gravement [gʀavmɑ̃] ADV seriously; badly; (*parler, regarder*) gravely

graver [gʀave] /1/ VT (*plaque, nom*) to engrave;

g

(CD, DVD) to burn; (fig): ~ **qch dans son esprit/ sa mémoire** to etch sth in one's mind/memory

graveur [gʀavœʀ] NM engraver; ~ **de CD/DVD** CD/DVD burner ou writer

gravier [gʀavje] NM (loose) gravel no pl

gravillons [gʀavijɔ̃] NMPL gravel sg, loose chippings ou gravel

gravir [gʀaviʀ] /2/ VT to climb (up)

gravitation [gʀavitasjɔ̃] NF gravitation

gravité [gʀavite] NF (de maladie, d'accident) seriousness; (de sujet, problème) gravity; (Physique) gravity

graviter [gʀavite] /1/ VI to revolve; ~ **autour de** to revolve around

gravure [gʀavyʀ] NF engraving; (reproduction) print; plate

gré [gʀe] NM: **à son** ~ adj to his liking; adv as he pleases; **au** ~ **de** according to, following; **contre le** ~ **de qn** against sb's will; **de son (plein)** ~ of one's own free will; **de** ~ **ou de force** whether one likes it or not; **de bon** ~ willingly; **bon** ~ **mal** ~ like it or not; willy-nilly; **de** ~ **à** ~ (Comm) by mutual agreement; **savoir (bien)** ~ **à qn de qch** to be (most) grateful to sb for sth

grec, grecque [gʀɛk] ADJ Greek; (classique: vase etc) Grecian ▶ NM (Ling) Greek ▶ NM/F: **G~, Grecque** Greek

Grèce [gʀɛs] NF: **la** ~ Greece

gredin, e [gʀədɛ̃, -in] NM/F rogue, rascal

gréement [gʀemɑ̃] NM rigging

greffe [gʀɛf] NF (Bot, Méd: de tissu) graft; (Méd: d'organe) transplant ▶ NM (Jur) office

greffer [gʀefe] /1/ VT (Bot, Méd: tissu) to graft; (Méd: organe) to transplant

greffier [gʀefje] NM clerk of the court

grégaire [gʀegɛʀ] ADJ gregarious

grège [gʀɛʒ] ADJ: **soie** ~ raw silk

grêle [gʀɛl] ADJ (very) thin ▶ NF hail

grêlé, e [gʀele] ADJ pockmarked

grêler [gʀele] /1/ VB IMPERS: **il grêle** it's hailing ▶ VT: **la région a été grêlée** the region was damaged by hail

grêlon [gʀɛlɔ̃] NM hailstone

grelot [gʀəlo] NM little bell

grelottant, e [gʀəlɔtɑ̃, -ɑ̃t] ADJ shivering, shivery

grelotter [gʀəlɔte] /1/ VI (trembler) to shiver

Grenade [gʀənad] N Granada ▶ NF (île) Grenada

grenade [gʀənad] NF (explosive) grenade; (Bot) pomegranate; ~ **lacrymogène** teargas grenade

grenadier [gʀənadje] NM (Mil) grenadier; (Bot) pomegranate tree

grenadine [gʀənadin] NF grenadine

grenat [gʀəna] ADJ INV dark red

grenier [gʀənje] NM (de maison) attic; (de ferme) loft

grenouille [gʀənuj] NF frog

grenouillère [gʀənujɛʀ] NF (de bébé) leggings; (: combinaison) sleepsuit

grenu, e [gʀəny] ADJ grainy, grained

grès [gʀɛ] NM (roche) sandstone; (poterie) stoneware

grésil [gʀezi] NM (fine) hail

grésillement [gʀezijmɑ̃] NM sizzling; crackling

grésiller [gʀezije] /1/ VI to sizzle; (Radio) to crackle

grève [gʀɛv] NF (d'ouvriers) strike; (plage) shore; **se mettre en/faire** ~ to go on/be on strike; ~ **bouchon** partial strike (in key areas of a company); ~ **de la faim** hunger strike; ~ **perlée** go-slow (BRIT), slowdown (US); ~ **sauvage** wildcat strike; ~ **de solidarité** sympathy strike; ~ **surprise** lightning strike; ~ **sur le tas** sit down strike; ~ **tournante** strike by rota; ~ **du zèle** work-to-rule (BRIT), slowdown (US)

grever [gʀəve] /5/ VT (budget, économie) to put a strain on; **grevé d'impôts** crippled by taxes; **grevé d'hypothèques** heavily mortgaged

gréviste [gʀevist] NMF striker

gribouillage [gʀibujaʒ] NM scribble, scrawl

gribouiller [gʀibuje] /1/ VT to scribble, scrawl ▶ VI to doodle

gribouillis [gʀibuji] NM (dessin) doodle; (action) doodling no pl; (écriture) scribble

grief [gʀijɛf] NM grievance; **faire** ~ **à qn de** to reproach sb for

grièvement [gʀijɛvmɑ̃] ADV seriously

griffe [gʀif] NF claw; (fig) signature; (: d'un couturier, parfumeur) label, signature

griffé, e [gʀife] ADJ designer(-label) cpd

griffer [gʀife] /1/ VT to scratch

griffon [gʀifɔ̃] NM (chien) griffon

griffonnage [gʀifɔnaʒ] NM scribble

griffonner [gʀifɔne] /1/ VT to scribble

griffure [gʀifyʀ] NF scratch

grignoter [gʀiɲɔte] /1/ VT (personne) to nibble at; (souris) to gnaw at ▶ VI to nibble

gril [gʀil] NM steak ou grill pan

grillade [gʀijad] NF grill

grillage [gʀijaʒ] NM (treillis) wire netting; (clôture) wire fencing

grillager [gʀijaʒe] /3/ VT (objet) to put wire netting on; (périmètre, jardin) to put wire fencing around

grille [gʀij] NF (portail) (metal) gate; (clôture) railings pl; (d'égout) (metal) grate; (fig) grid

grille-pain [gʀijpɛ̃] NM INV toaster

griller [gʀije] /1/ VT (aussi: **faire griller**: pain) to toast; (: viande) to grill (BRIT), broil (US); (: café, châtaignes) to roast; (fig: ampoule etc) to burn out, blow ▶ VI (brûler) to be roasting; ~ **un feu rouge** to jump the lights (BRIT), run a stoplight (US)

grillon [gʀijɔ̃] NM (Zool) cricket

grimace [gʀimas] NF grimace; (pour faire rire): **faire des grimaces** to pull ou make faces

grimacer [gʀimase] /3/ VI to grimace

grimacier, -ière [gʀimasje, -jɛʀ] ADJ: **c'est un enfant** ~ that child is always pulling faces

grimer [gʀime] /1/ VT to make up

grimoire [gʀimwaʀ] NM (illisible) unreadable scribble; (livre de magie) book of magic spells

grimpant, e [gʀɛ̃pɑ̃, -ɑ̃t] ADJ: **plante** ~ climbing plant, climber

grimper [gʀɛ̃pe] /1/ VI, VT to climb ▶ NM: **le** ~ (Sport) rope-climbing; ~ **à/sur** to climb (up)/ climb onto

grimpeur, -euse [gʀɛ̃pœʀ, -øz] NM/F climber

grinçant, e [gʀɛ̃sɑ̃, -ɑ̃t] ADJ grating

grincement [gʀɛ̃smɑ̃] NM grating (noise); creaking (noise)

grincer [gʀɛ̃se] /**3**/ VI (*porte, roue*) to grate; (*plancher*) to creak; **~ des dents** to grind one's teeth

grincheux, -euse [gʀɛ̃ʃø, -øz] ADJ grumpy

gringalet [gʀɛ̃galɛ] ADJ M puny ▸ NM weakling

griotte [gʀijɔt] NF Morello cherry

grippal, e, -aux [gʀipal, -o] ADJ (*état*) flu-like

grippe [gʀip] NF flu, influenza; **prendre qn/qch en ~** (*fig*) to take a sudden dislike to sb/sth; **~ A** swine flu; **~ aviaire** bird flu; **~ porcine** swine flu

grippé, e [gʀipe] ADJ: **être ~** to have (the) flu; (*moteur*) to have seized up (BRIT) *ou* jammed

gripper [gʀipe] /**1**/ VT, VI to jam

grippe-sou [gʀipsu] NMF penny pincher

gris, e [gʀi, gʀiz] ADJ grey (BRIT), gray (US); (*ivre*) tipsy ▸ NM (*couleur*) grey (BRIT), gray (US); **il fait ~** it's a dull *ou* grey day; **faire ~ mine** to look miserable *ou* morose; **faire ~ mine à qn** to give sb a cool reception

grisaille [gʀizaj] NF greyness (BRIT), grayness (US), dullness

grisant, e [gʀizɑ̃, -ɑ̃t] ADJ intoxicating, exhilarating

grisâtre [gʀizɑtʀ] ADJ greyish (BRIT), grayish (US)

griser [gʀize] /**1**/ VT to intoxicate; **se ~ de** (*fig*) to become intoxicated with

griserie [gʀizʀi] NF intoxication

grisonnant, e [gʀizɔnɑ̃, -ɑ̃t] ADJ greying (BRIT), graying (US)

grisonner [gʀizɔne] /**1**/ VI to be going grey (BRIT) *ou* gray (US)

Grisons [gʀizɔ̃] NMPL: **les ~** Graubünden

grisou [gʀizu] NM firedamp

gris-vert [gʀivɛʀ] ADJ grey-green

grive [gʀiv] NF (*Zool*) thrush

grivois, e [gʀivwa, -waz] ADJ saucy

grivoiserie [gʀivwazʀi] NF sauciness

Groenland [gʀɔɛnlɑ̃d] NM: **le ~** Greenland

grog [gʀɔg] NM grog

groggy [gʀɔgi] ADJ INV dazed

grogne [gʀɔɲ] NF grumble

grognement [gʀɔɲmɑ̃] NM grunt; growl

grogner [gʀɔɲe] /**1**/ VI to growl; (*fig*) to grumble

grognon, ne [gʀɔɲɔ̃, -ɔn] ADJ grumpy, grouchy

groin [gʀwɛ̃] NM snout

grommeler [gʀɔmle] /**4**/ VI to mutter to o.s.

grondement [gʀɔ̃dmɑ̃] NM rumble; growl

gronder [gʀɔ̃de] /**1**/ VI (*canon, moteur, tonnerre*) to rumble; (*animal*) to growl; (*fig: révolte*) to be brewing ▸ VT to scold; **se faire ~** to get a telling-off

groom [gʀum] NM page, bellhop (US)

gros, se [gʀo, gʀos] ADJ big, large; (*obèse*) fat; (*problème, quantité*) great; (*travaux, dégâts*) extensive; (*large: trait, fil*) thick; (*rhume, averse*) heavy ▸ ADV: **risquer/gagner ~** to risk/win a lot ▸ NM/F fat man/woman ▸ NM (*Comm*): **le ~** the wholesale business; **écrire ~** to write in big

letters; **prix de ~** wholesale price; **par ~ temps/~ mer** in rough weather/heavy seas; **le ~ de** the main body of; (*du travail etc*) the bulk of; **en avoir ~ sur le cœur** to be upset; **en ~** roughly; (*Comm*) wholesale; **~ intestin** large intestine; **~ lot** jackpot; **~ mot** swearword, vulgarity; **~ œuvre** shell (of building); **~ plan** (*Photo*) close-up; **~ porteur** wide-bodied aircraft, jumbo (jet); **~ sel** cooking salt; **~ titre** headline; **~ caisse** big drum

groseille [gʀozɛj] NF: **~ (rouge)/(blanche)** red/ white currant; **~ à maquereau** gooseberry

groseillier [gʀozeje] NM red *ou* white currant bush; gooseberry bush

grosse [gʀos] ADJ F *voir* **gros** ▸ NF (*Comm*) gross

grossesse [gʀosɛs] NF pregnancy; **~ nerveuse** phantom pregnancy

grosseur [gʀosœʀ] NF size; fatness; (*tumeur*) lump

grossier, -ière [gʀosje, -jɛʀ] ADJ coarse; (*insolent*) rude; (*dessin*) rough; (*travail*) roughly done; (*imitation, instrument*) crude; (*évident: erreur*) gross

grossièrement [gʀosjɛʀmɑ̃] ADV (*vulgairement*) coarsely; (*sommairement*) roughly; crudely; (*en gros*) roughly

grossièreté [gʀosjɛʀte] NF coarseness; rudeness; (*mot*): **dire des grossièretés** to use coarse language

grossir [gʀosiʀ] /**2**/ VI (*personne*) to put on weight; (*fig*) to grow, get bigger; (*rivière*) to swell ▸ VT to increase; (*exagérer*) to exaggerate; (*au microscope*) to magnify, enlarge; (*vêtement*): **~ qn** to make sb look fatter

grossissant, e [gʀosisɑ̃, -ɑ̃t] ADJ magnifying, enlarging

grossissement [gʀosismɑ̃] NM (*optique*) magnification

grossiste [gʀosist] NMF wholesaler

grosso modo [gʀosomodo] ADV roughly

grotesque [gʀɔtɛsk] ADJ (*extravagant*) grotesque; (*ridicule*) ludicrous

grotte [gʀɔt] NF cave

grouiller [gʀuje] /**1**/ VI (*foule*) to mill about; (*fourmis*) to swarm about; **~ de** to be swarming with

groupe [gʀup] NM group; **cabinet de ~** group practice; **médecine de ~** group practice; **~ électrogène** generator; **~ de parole** support group; **~ de pression** pressure group; **~ sanguin** blood group; **~ scolaire** school complex

groupement [gʀupmɑ̃] NM grouping; (*groupe*) group; **~ d'intérêt économique** ≈ trade association

grouper [gʀupe] /**1**/ VT to group; (*ressources, moyens*) to pool; **se grouper** VI to get together

groupuscule [gʀupyskyl] NM clique

gruau [gʀyo] NM: **pain de ~** wheaten bread

grue [gʀy] NF crane; **faire le pied de ~** (*fam*) to hang around (waiting), kick one's heels (BRIT)

gruger [gʀyʒe] /**3**/ VT to cheat, dupe

grumeaux [gʀymo] NMPL (*Culin*) lumps

grumeleux, -euse [gʀymlø, -øz] ADJ (*sauce etc*) lumpy; (*peau etc*) bumpy

grutier [gʀytje] NM crane driver

gruyère [gʀyjɛʀ] NM gruyère (BRIT) *ou* Swiss cheese

GSM [ʒeɛsɛm] NM, ADJ GSM

Guadeloupe [gwadlup] NF: **la** ~ Guadeloupe

guadeloupéen, ne [gwadlupeɛ̃, -ɛn] ADJ Guadelupian

Guatémala [gwatemala] NM: **le** ~ Guatemala

guatémalien, ne [gwatemaljɛ̃, -ɛn] ADJ Guatemalan

guatémaltèque [gwatemaltɛk] ADJ Guatemalan

gué [ge] NM ford; **passer à** ~ to ford

guenilles [gənij] NFPL rags

guenon [gənɔ̃] NF female monkey

guépard [gepaʀ] NM cheetah

guêpe [gɛp] NF wasp

guêpier [gepje] NM (*fig*) trap

guère [gɛʀ] ADV (*avec adjectif, adverbe*): **ne ... ~** hardly; (*avec verbe: pas beaucoup*) **ne ... ~** (*tournure négative*) much; (*pas souvent*) hardly ever; (*tournure négative*) (very) long; **il n'y a ~ que/de** there's hardly anybody (*ou* anything) but/hardly any; **ce n'est ~ difficile** it's hardly difficult; **nous n'avons ~ de temps** we have hardly any time

guéridon [geʀidɔ̃] NM pedestal table

guérilla [geʀija] NF guerrilla warfare

guérillero [geʀijeʀo] NM guerrilla

guérir [geʀiʀ] /2/ VT (*personne, maladie*) to cure; (*membre, plaie*) to heal ▶ VI (*personne, malade*) to recover, be cured; (*maladie*) to be cured; (*plaie, chagrin, blessure*) to heal; ~ **de** to be cured of, recover from; ~ **qn de** to cure sb of

guérison [geʀizɔ̃] NF (*de maladie*) curing; (*de membre, plaie*) healing; (*de malade*) recovery

guérissable [geʀisabl] ADJ curable

guérisseur, -euse [geʀisœʀ, -øz] NM/F healer

guérite [geʀit] NF (*Mil*) sentry box; (*sur un chantier*) (workman's) hut

Guernesey [gɛʀnəze] NF Guernsey

guernesiais, e [gɛʀnəzjɛ, -ɛz] ADJ of *ou* from Guernsey

guerre [gɛʀ] NF war; (*méthode*): ~ **atomique/de tranchées** atomic/trench warfare *no pl*; **en** ~ at war; **faire la** ~ **à** to wage war against; **de** ~ **lasse** (*fig*) tired of fighting *ou* resisting; **de bonne** ~ fair and square; ~ **civile/mondiale** civil/world war; ~ **froide/sainte** cold/holy war; ~ **d'usure** war of attrition

guerrier, -ière [gɛʀje, -jɛʀ] ADJ warlike ▶ NM/F warrior

guerroyer [gɛʀwaje] /8/ VI to wage war

guet [gɛ] NM: **faire le** ~ to be on the watch *ou* look-out

guet-apens [gɛtapɑ̃] (*pl* **guets-apens**) NM ambush

guêtre [gɛtʀ] NF gaiter

guetter [gete] /1/ VT (*épier*) to watch (intently); (*attendre*) to watch (out) for; (: *pour surprendre*) to be lying in wait for

guetteur [gɛtœʀ] NM look-out

gueule [gœl] NF (*d'animal*) mouth; (*fam: visage*) mug; (: *bouche*) gob (!), mouth; **ta ~!** (*fam*)

shut up!; **avoir la ~ de bois** (*fam*) to have a hangover, be hung over

gueule-de-loup [gœldəlu] (*pl* **gueules-de-loup**) NF snapdragon

gueuler [gœle] /1/ VI (*fam*) to bawl

gueuleton [gœltɔ̃] NM (*fam*) blowout (BRIT), big meal

gueux [gø] NM beggar; (*coquin*) rogue

gui [gi] NM mistletoe

guibole [gibɔl] NF (*fam*) leg

guichet [giʃɛ] NM (*de bureau, banque*) counter, window; (*d'une porte*) wicket, hatch; **les guichets** (*à la gare, au théâtre*) the ticket office; **jouer à guichets fermés** to play to a full house

guichetier, -ière [giʃtje, -jɛʀ] NM/F counter clerk

guide [gid] NM (*personne*) guide; (*livre*) guide(book) ▶ NF (*fille scout*) (girl) guide (BRIT), girl scout (US); **guides** NFPL (*d'un cheval*) reins

guider [gide] /1/ VT to guide

guidon [gidɔ̃] NM handlebars *pl*

guigne [giɲ] NF (*fam*): **avoir la** ~ to be jinxed

guignol [giɲɔl] NM ≈ Punch and Judy show; (*fig*) clown

guillemets [gijmɛ] NMPL: **entre** ~ in inverted commas *ou* quotation marks; ~ **de répétition** ditto marks

guilleret, te [gijʀɛ, -ɛt] ADJ perky, bright

guillotine [gijɔtin] NF guillotine

guillotiner [gijɔtine] /1/ VT to guillotine

guimauve [gimov] NF (*Bot*) marshmallow; (*fig*) sentimentality, sloppiness

guimbarde [gɛ̃baʀd] NF old banger (BRIT), jalopy

guindé, e [gɛ̃de] ADJ (*personne, air*) stiff, starchy; (*style*) stilted

Guinée [gine] NF: **la (République de)** ~ (the Republic of) Guinea; **la** ~ **équatoriale** Equatorial Guinea

Guinée-Bissau [ginebiso] NF: **la** ~ Guinea-Bissau

guinéen, ne [gineɛ̃, -ɛn] ADJ Guinean

guingois [gɛ̃gwa]: **de** ~ *adv* askew

guinguette [gɛ̃gɛt] NF open-air café or dance hall

guirlande [giʀlɑ̃d] NF (*fleurs*) garland; (*de papier*) paper chain; ~ **lumineuse** lights *pl*, fairy lights *pl* (BRIT); ~ **de Noël** tinsel *no pl*

guise [giz] NF: **à votre** ~ as you wish *ou* please; **en** ~ **de** by way of

guitare [gitaʀ] NF guitar

guitariste [gitaʀist] NMF guitarist, guitar player

gustatif, -ive [gystatif, -iv] ADJ gustatory; *voir* **papille**

guttural, e, -aux [gytyʀal, -o] ADJ guttural

guyanais, e [gɥijanɛ, -ɛz] ADJ Guyanese, Guyanan; (*français*) Guianese, Guianan

Guyane [gɥijan] NF: **la** ~ Guyana; **la** ~ **(française)** (French) Guiana

gvt ABR (= *gouvernement*) govt

gym [ʒim] NF (*exercices*) gym

gymkhana [ʒimkana] NM rally; ~ **motocycliste** (motorbike) scramble (BRIT), motocross

gymnase [ʒimnɑz] NM gym(nasium)
gymnaste [ʒimnast] NMF gymnast
gymnastique [ʒimnastik] NF gymnastics *sg*;
　(*au réveil etc*) keep-fit exercises *pl*; ~ **corrective**
　remedial gymnastics
gynécologie [ʒinekɔlɔʒi] NF gynaecology
　(*BRIT*), gynecology (*US*)

gynécologique [ʒinekɔlɔʒik] ADJ
　gynaecological (*BRIT*), gynecological (*US*)
gynécologue [ʒinekɔlɔg] NMF gynaecologist
　(*BRIT*), gynecologist (*US*)
gypse [ʒips] NM gypsum
gyrophare [ʒiʀɔfaʀ] NM (*sur une voiture*)
　revolving (flashing) light

g

Hh

H, h [aʃ] NM INV H, h ▸ ABR (= *homme*) M;
(= *hydrogène*) H; = **heure**; **à l'heure H** at zero
hour; **bombe H** H bomb; **H comme Henri**
H for Harry (BRIT) *ou* How (US)

ha. ABR (= *hectare*) ha.

hab. ABR = **habitant**

habile [abil] ADJ skilful; (*malin*) clever

habilement [abilmɑ̃] ADV skilfully; cleverly

habileté [abilte] NF skill, skilfulness;
cleverness

habilité, e [abilite] ADJ: **~ à faire** entitled to do,
empowered to do

habiliter [abilite] /1/ VT to empower, entitle

habillage [abijaʒ] NM dressing

habillé, e [abije] ADJ dressed; (*chic*) dressy;
~ de (*Tech*) covered with; encased in

habillement [abijmɑ̃] NM clothes *pl*; (*profession*)
clothing industry

habiller [abije] /1/ VT to dress; (*fournir en
vêtements*) to clothe; (*couvrir*) to cover; **s'habiller**
VI to dress (o.s.); (*se déguiser, mettre des vêtements
chic*) to dress up; **s'habiller de/en** to dress in/
dress up as; **s'habiller chez/à** to buy one's
clothes from/at

habilleuse [abijøz] NF (*Ciné, Théât*) dresser

habit [abi] NM outfit; **habits** NMPL (*vêtements*)
clothes; **~ (de soirée)** evening dress; (*pour
homme*) tails *pl*; **prendre l'~** (*Rel: entrer en religion*)
to enter (holy) orders

habitable [abitabl] ADJ (in)habitable

habitacle [abitakl] NM cockpit; (*Auto*)
passenger cell

habitant, e [abitɑ̃, -ɑ̃t] NM/F inhabitant; (*d'une
maison*) occupant, occupier; **loger chez l'~** to
stay with the locals

habitat [abita] NM housing conditions *pl*;
(*Bot, Zool*) habitat

habitation [abitasjɔ̃] NF living; (*demeure*)
residence, home; (*maison*) house; **habitations
à loyer modéré (HLM)** low-rent, state-owned
housing, ≈ council flats (BRIT), ≈ public housing
units (US)

habité, e [abite] ADJ inhabited; lived in

habiter [abite] /1/ VT to live in; (*sentiment*) to
dwell in ▸ VI: **~ à/dans** to live in *ou* at/in; **~ chez
ou avec qn** to live with sb; **~ 16 rue Montmartre**
to live at number 16 rue Montmartre; **~ rue
Montmartre** to live in rue Montmartre

habitude [abityd] NF habit; **avoir l'~ de faire**
to be in the habit of doing; (*expérience*) to be used
to doing; **avoir l'~ des enfants** to be used to
children; **prendre l'~ de faire qch** to get into
the habit of doing sth; **perdre une ~** to get out
of a habit; **d'~** usually; **comme d'~** as usual;
par ~ out of habit

habitué, e [abitye] ADJ: **être ~ à** to be used *ou*
accustomed to ▸ NM/F (*de maison*) regular
visitor; (*client*) regular (customer)

habituel, le [abityɛl] ADJ usual

habituellement [abityɛlmɑ̃] ADV usually

habituer [abitye] /1/ VT: **~ qn à** to get sb used to;
s'habituer à to get used to

'hâbleur, -euse ['ɑblœr, -øz] ADJ boastful

'hache ['aʃ] NF axe

'haché, e ['aʃe] ADJ minced (BRIT), ground (US);
(*persil*) chopped; (*fig*) jerky

'hache-légumes ['aʃlegym] NM INV vegetable
chopper

'hacher ['aʃe] /1/ VT (*viande*) to mince (BRIT), grind
(US); (*persil*) to chop; **~ menu** to mince *ou* grind
finely; to chop finely

'hachette ['aʃɛt] NF hatchet

'hache-viande ['aʃvjɑ̃d] NM INV (meat) mincer
(BRIT) *ou* grinder (US); (*couteau*) (meat) cleaver

'hachis ['aʃi] NM mince *no pl* (BRIT), hamburger
meat (US); **~ de viande** minced (BRIT) *ou* ground
(US) meat; **~ Parmentier** ≈ shepherd's pie

'hachisch ['aʃiʃ] NM hashish

'hachoir ['aʃwar] NM chopper; (meat) mincer
(BRIT) *ou* grinder (US); (*planche*) chopping board

'hachurer ['aʃyre] /1/ VT to hatch

'hachures ['aʃyr] NFPL hatching *sg*

'hagard, e ['agar, -ard] ADJ wild, distraught

'haie ['ɛ] NF hedge; (*Sport*) hurdle; (*fig: rang*) line,
row; **200 m haies** 200 m hurdles; **~ d'honneur**
guard of honour

'haillons ['ajɔ̃] NMPL rags

'haine ['ɛn] NF hatred

'haineux, -euse ['ɛnø, -øz] ADJ full of hatred

'haïr ['air] /10/ VT to detest, hate; **se 'haïr** to hate
each other

'hais ['ɛ], **'haïs** *etc* ['ai] VB *voir* **'haïr**

'haïssable ['aisabl] ADJ detestable

Haïti [aiti] N Haiti

haïtien, ne [aisjɛ̃, -ɛn] ADJ Haitian

'halage ['alaʒ] NM: **chemin de ~** towpath

'**hâle** ['ɑl] NM (sun)tan
'**hâlé, e** ['ɑle] ADJ (sun)tanned, sunburnt
haleine [alɛn] NF breath; **perdre ~** to get out of breath; **à perdre ~** until one is gasping for breath; **avoir mauvaise ~** to have bad breath; **reprendre ~** to get one's breath back; **hors d'~** out of breath; **tenir en ~** (*attention*) to hold spellbound; (*en attente*) to keep in suspense; **de longue ~** *adj* long-term
'**haler** ['ale] /**1**/ VT to haul in; (*remorquer*) to tow
'**haleter** ['alte] /**5**/ VI to pant
'**hall** ['ol] NM hall
'**hallali** [alali] NM kill
'**halle** ['al] NF (covered) market; **halles** NFPL (*d'une grande ville*) central food market *sg*
'**hallebarde** ['albard] NF halberd; **il pleut des hallebardes** (*fam*) it's bucketing down
hallucinant, e [alysinā, -āt] ADJ staggering
hallucination [alysinasjɔ̃] NF hallucination
hallucinatoire [alysinatwaʀ] ADJ hallucinatory
halluciné, e [alysine] NM/F person suffering from hallucinations; (*fou*) (raving) lunatic
hallucinogène [a(l)lysinɔʒɛn] ADJ hallucinogenic ▶ NM hallucinogen
'**halo** ['alo] NM halo
halogène [alɔʒɛn] NM: **lampe (à) ~** halogen lamp
'**halte** ['alt] NF stop, break; (*escale*) stopping place; (*Rail*) halt ▶ EXCL stop!; **faire ~** to stop
'**halte-garderie** ['altgardəri] (*pl* '**haltes-garderies**) NF crèche
haltère [altɛʀ] NM (*à boules, disques*) dumbbell, barbell; (**poids et) haltères** (*activité*) weightlifting *sg*
haltérophile [alterɔfil] NMF weightlifter
haltérophilie [alterɔfili] NF weightlifting
'**hamac** ['amak] NM hammock
'**Hambourg** ['ābuʀ] N Hamburg
'**hamburger** ['āburgœʀ] NM hamburger
'**hameau, x** ['amo] NM hamlet
hameçon [amsɔ̃] NM (fish) hook
'**hampe** ['āp] NF (*de drapeau etc*) pole; (*de lance*) shaft
'**hamster** ['amstɛʀ] NM hamster
'**hanche** ['āʃ] NF hip
'**hand-ball** ['ādbal] NM handball
'**handballeur, -euse** ['ādbalœʀ, -øz] NM/F handball player
'**handicap** ['ādikap] NM handicap
'**handicapé, e** ['ādikape] ADJ disabled ▶ NM/F person with a disability; **~ mental/physique** person with learning difficulties/a physical disability; **~ moteur** person with a movement disorder
'**handicaper** ['ādikape] /**1**/ VT to handicap
'**hangar** ['āgar] NM shed; (*Aviat*) hangar
'**hanneton** ['antɔ̃] NM cockchafer
'**Hanovre** ['anɔvʀ] N Hanover
'**hanter** ['āte] /**1**/ VT to haunt
'**hantise** ['ātiz] NF obsessive fear
'**happer** ['ape] /**1**/ VT to snatch; (*train etc*) to hit
'**harangue** ['arāg] NF harangue
'**haranguer** ['arāge] /**1**/ VT to harangue
'**haras** ['arɑ] NM stud farm

'**harassant, e** ['arasā, -āt] ADJ exhausting
'**harcèlement** ['arsɛlmā] NM harassment; **~ sexuel** sexual harassment
'**harceler** ['arsəle] /**5**/ VT (*Mil, Chasse*) to harass, harry; (*importuner*) to plague; **~ qn de questions** to plague sb with questions
'**hardes** ['ard] NFPL rags
'**hardi, e** ['ardi] ADJ bold, daring
'**hardiesse** ['ardjɛs] NF audacity; **avoir la ~ de** to have the audacity *ou* effrontery to
'**harem** ['arɛm] NM harem
'**hareng** ['arā] NM herring; **~ saur** kipper, smoked herring
'**hargne** ['arɲ] NF aggressivity, aggressiveness
'**hargneusement** ['arɲøzmā] ADV belligerently, aggressively
'**hargneux, -euse** ['arɲø, -øz] ADJ (*propos, personne*) belligerent, aggressive; (*chien*) fierce
'**haricot** ['ariko] NM bean; **~ blanc/rouge** haricot/kidney bean; **~ vert** French (BRIT) *ou* green bean
harmonica [armɔnika] NM mouth organ
harmonie [armɔni] NF harmony
harmonieux, -euse [armɔnjø, -øz] ADJ harmonious; (*couleurs, couple*) well-matched
harmonique [armɔnik] ADJ, NM *ou* F harmonic
harmoniser [armɔnize] /**1**/ VT to harmonize; **s'harmoniser** (*couleurs, teintes*) to go well together
harmonium [armɔnjɔm] NM harmonium
'**harnaché, e** ['arnaʃe] ADJ (*fig*) rigged out
'**harnachement** ['arnaʃmā] NM (*habillement*) rig-out; (*équipement*) harness, equipment
'**harnacher** ['arnaʃe] /**1**/ VT to harness
'**harnais** ['arnɛ] NM harness
'**haro** ['aro] NM: **crier ~ sur qn/qch** to inveigh against sb/sth
'**harpe** ['arp] NF harp
'**harpie** ['arpi] NF harpy
'**harpiste** ['arpist] NMF harpist
'**harpon** ['arpɔ̃] NM harpoon
'**harponner** ['arpɔne] /**1**/ VT to harpoon; (*fam*) to collar
'**hasard** ['azar] NM: **le ~** chance, fate; **un ~** a coincidence; (*aubaine, chance*) a stroke of luck; **au ~** (*sans but*) aimlessly; (*à l'aveuglette*) at random, haphazardly; **par ~** by chance; **comme par ~** as if by chance; **à tout ~** (*en espérant trouver ce qu'on cherche*) on the off chance; (*en cas de besoin*) just in case
'**hasarder** ['azarde] /**1**/ VT (*mot*) to venture; (*fortune*) to risk; **se ~ à faire** to risk doing, venture to do
'**hasardeux, -euse** ['azardø, -øz] ADJ hazardous, risky; (*hypothèse*) rash
'**haschisch** ['aʃiʃ] NM hashish
'**hâte** ['ɑt] NF haste; **à la ~** hurriedly, hastily; **en ~** posthaste, with all possible speed; **avoir ~ de** to be eager *ou* anxious to
'**hâter** ['ɑte] /**1**/ VT to hasten; **se 'hâter** to hurry; **se ~ de** to hurry *ou* hasten to
'**hâtif, -ive** ['ɑtif, -iv] ADJ (*travail*) hurried; (*décision*) hasty; (*légume*) early
'**hâtivement** ['ɑtivmā] ADV hurriedly; hastily

'**hauban** ['obā] NM (*Navig*) shroud

'**hausse** ['os] NF rise, increase; (*de fusil*) backsight adjuster; **à la ~** upwards; **en ~** rising; **être en ~** to be going up

'**hausser** ['ose] /1/ VT to raise; **~ les épaules** to shrug (one's shoulders); **se ~ sur la pointe des pieds** to stand (up) on tiptoe *ou* tippy-toe (*US*)

'**haut, e** ['o, 'ot] ADJ high; (*grand*) tall; (*son, voix*) high(-pitched) ▶ ADV high ▶ NM top (part); **de 3 m de ~, ~ de 3 m** 3 m high, 3 m in height; **en haute montagne** high up in the mountains; **en ~ lieu** in high places; **à haute voix, (tout) ~** aloud, out loud; **des hauts et des bas** ups and downs; **du ~ de** from the top of; **tomber de ~** to fall from a height; (*fig*) to have one's hopes dashed; **dire qch bien ~** to say sth plainly; **prendre qch de (très) ~** to react haughtily to sth; **traiter qn de ~** to treat sb with disdain; **de ~ en bas** from top to bottom; downwards; **~ en couleur** (*chose*) highly coloured; (*personne*) **un personnage ~ en couleur** a colourful character; **plus ~** higher up, further up; (*dans un texte*) above; (*parler*) louder; **en ~** up above; (*être/aller*) at (*ou* to) the top; (*dans une maison*) upstairs; **en ~ de** at the top of; **~ les mains!** hands up!, stick 'em up!; **la haute couture/coiffure** haute couture/coiffure; **~ débit** (*Inform*) broadband; **haute fidélité** hi-fi, high fidelity; **la haute finance** high finance; **haute trahison** high treason

'**hautain, e** ['otɛ̃, -ɛn] ADJ (*personne, regard*) haughty

'**hautbois** ['obwa] NM oboe

'**hautboïste** ['oboist] NMF oboist

'**haut-de-forme** ['odfɔrm] (*pl* '**hauts-de-forme**) NM top hat

'**haute-contre** ['otkɔ̃tr] (*pl* '**hautes-contre**) NF counter-tenor

'**hautement** ['otmā] ADV (*ouvertement*) openly; (*supérieurement*) **~ qualifié** highly qualified

'**hauteur** ['otœr] NF height; (*Géo*) height, hill; (*fig*) loftiness; haughtiness; **à ~ de** up to (the level of); **à ~ des yeux** at eye level; **à la ~ de** (*sur la même ligne*) level with; by; (*fig: tâche, situation*) equal to; **à la ~** (*fig*) up to it, equal to the task

'**Haute-Volta** ['otvolta] NF: **la ~** Upper Volta

'**haut-fond** ['ofɔ̃] (*pl* '**hauts-fonds**) NM shallow

'**haut-fourneau** ['ofurno] (*pl* '**hauts-fourneaux**) NM blast *ou* smelting furnace

'**haut-le-cœur** ['olkœr] NM INV retch, heave

'**haut-le-corps** ['olkɔr] NM INV start, jump

'**haut-parleur** ['oparlœr] (*pl* '**haut-parleurs**) NM (loud)speaker

'**hauturier, -ière** ['otyrje, -jɛr] ADJ (*Navig*) deep-sea

'**havanais, e** ['avanɛ, -ɛz] ADJ of *ou* from Havana

'**Havane** ['avan] NF: **la ~** Havana ▶ NM: **havane** (*cigare*) Havana

'**hâve** ['av] ADJ gaunt

'**havrais, e** ['avrɛ, -ɛz] ADJ of *ou* from Le Havre

'**havre** ['avr] NM haven

'**havresac** ['avrəsak] NM haversack

Hawaï [awai] N Hawaii; **les îles ~** the Hawaiian Islands

hawaïen, ne [awajɛ̃, -ɛn] ADJ Hawaiian

▶ NM (*Ling*) Hawaiian

'**Haye** ['ɛ] N: **la ~** the Hague

'**hayon** ['ɛjɔ̃] NM tailgate

HCR SIGLE M (= *Haut-Commissariat des Nations unies pour les réfugiés*) UNHCR

hdb. ABR (= *heures de bureau*) o.h. (= *office hours*)

'**hé** ['e] EXCL hey!

hebdo [ɛbdo] NM (*fam*) weekly

hebdomadaire [ɛbdɔmadɛr] ADJ, NM weekly

hébergement [ebɛrʒəmɑ̃] NM accommodation, lodging; taking in

héberger [ebɛrʒe] /3/ VT (*touristes*) to accommodate, lodge; (*amis*) to put up; (*réfugiés*) to take in

hébergeur [ebɛrʒœr] NM (*Internet*) host

hébété, e [ebete] ADJ dazed

hébétude [ebetyd] NF stupor

hébraïque [ebraik] ADJ Hebrew, Hebraic

hébreu, x [ebrø] ADJ M, NM Hebrew

Hébrides [ebrid] NF: **les ~** the Hebrides

HEC SIGLE FPL (= *École des hautes études commerciales*) grande école for management and business studies

hécatombe [ekatɔ̃b] NF slaughter

hectare [ɛktar] NM hectare, 10,000 square metres

hecto... [ɛkto] PRÉFIXE hecto...

hectolitre [ɛktɔlitr] NM hectolitre

hédoniste [edɔnist] ADJ hedonistic

hégémonie [eʒemɔni] NF hegemony

'**hein** ['ɛ̃] EXCL eh?; (*sollicitant l'approbation*): **tu m'approuves, ~?** so I did the right thing then?; **Paul est venu, ~?** Paul came, did he?; **que fais-tu, ~?** hey! what are you doing?

'**hélas** ['elas] EXCL alas! ▶ ADV unfortunately

'**héler** ['ele] /6/ VT to hail

hélice [elis] NF propeller

hélicoïdal, e, -aux [elikɔidal, -o] ADJ helical; helicoid

hélicoptère [elikɔptɛr] NM helicopter

héliogravure [eljɔgravyr] NF heliogravure

héliomarin, e [eljɔmarɛ̃, -in] ADJ: **centre ~** centre offering sea and sun therapy

héliotrope [eljɔtrɔp] NM (*Bot*) heliotrope

héliport [elipɔr] NM heliport

héliporté, e [elipɔrte] ADJ transported by helicopter

hélium [eljɔm] NM helium

hellénique [elenik] ADJ Hellenic

hellénisant, e [elenizɑ̃, -ɑ̃t], **helléniste** [elenist] NM/F hellenist

Helsinki [ɛlzinki] N Helsinki

helvète [ɛlvɛt] ADJ Helvetian ▶ NMF: **H~** Helvetian

Helvétie [ɛlvesi] NF: **la ~** Helvetia

helvétique [ɛlvetik] ADJ Swiss

hématologie [ematɔlɔʒi] NF (*Méd*) haematology.

hématome [ematom] NM haematoma

hémicycle [emisikl] NM semicircle; (*Pol*): **l'~** the benches (in French parliament)

hémiplégie [emipleʒi] NF paralysis of one side, hemiplegia

hémisphère [emisfɛr] NM: **~ nord/sud** northern/southern hemisphere

hémisphérique [emisferik] ADJ hemispherical
hémoglobine [emɔglɔbin] NF haemoglobin (BRIT), hemoglobin (US)
hémophile [emɔfil] ADJ haemophiliac (BRIT), hemophiliac (US)
hémophilie [emɔfili] NF haemophilia (BRIT), hemophilia (US)
hémorragie [emɔraʒi] NF bleeding no pl, haemorrhage (BRIT), hemorrhage (US); **~ cérébrale** cerebral haemorrhage; **~ interne** internal bleeding ou haemorrhage
hémorroïdes [emɔrɔid] NFPL piles, haemorrhoids (BRIT), hemorrhoids (US)
hémostatique [emɔstatik] ADJ haemostatic (BRIT), hemostatic (US)
henné ['ene] NM henna
hennir ['enir] /2/ VI to neigh, whinny
hennissement ['enismɑ̃] NM neighing, whinnying
hep ['ɛp] EXCL hey!
hépatite [epatit] NF hepatitis, liver infection
héraldique [eraldik] ADJ heraldry
herbacé, e [ɛrbase] ADJ herbaceous
herbage [ɛrbaʒ] NM pasture
herbe [ɛrb] NF grass; (Culin, Méd) herb; **herbes de Provence** mixed herbs; **en ~** unripe; (fig) budding; **touffe/brin d'~** clump/blade of grass
herbeux, -euse [ɛrbø, -øz] ADJ grassy
herbicide [ɛrbisid] NM weed-killer
herbier [ɛrbje] NM herbarium
herbivore [ɛrbivɔr] NM herbivore
herboriser [ɛrbɔrize] /1/ VI to collect plants
herboriste [ɛrbɔrist] NMF herbalist
herboristerie [ɛrbɔristri] NF (magasin) herbalist's shop; (commerce) herb trade
herculéen, ne [ɛrkyleɛ̃, -ɛn] ADJ (fig) herculean
hère ['ɛr] NM: **pauvre ~** poor wretch
héréditaire [erediter] ADJ hereditary
hérédité [eredite] NF heredity
hérésie [erezi] NF heresy
hérétique [eretik] NMF heretic
hérissé, e ['erise] ADJ bristling; **~ de** spiked with; (fig) bristling with
hérisser ['erise] /1/ VT: **~ qn** (fig) to ruffle sb; **se hérisser** VI to bristle, bristle up
hérisson ['erisɔ̃] NM hedgehog
héritage [eritaʒ] NM inheritance; (fig: coutumes, système) heritage; (: legs) legacy; **faire un (petit) ~** to come into (a little) money
hériter [erite] /1/ VI: **~ de qch (de qn)** to inherit sth (from sb); **~ de qn** to inherit sb's property
héritier, -ière [eritje, -jɛr] NM/F heir/heiress
hermaphrodite [ɛrmafrɔdit] ADJ (Bot, Zool) hermaphrodite
hermétique [ɛrmetik] ADJ (à l'air) airtight; (à l'eau) watertight; (fig: écrivain, style) abstruse; (: visage) impenetrable
hermétiquement [ɛrmetikmɑ̃] ADV hermetically
hermine [ɛrmin] NF ermine
hernie ['ɛrni] NF hernia
héroïne [erɔin] NF heroine; (drogue) heroin
héroïnomane [erɔinɔman] NMF heroin addict
héroïque [erɔik] ADJ heroic

héroïquement [erɔikmɑ̃] ADV heroically
héroïsme [erɔism] NM heroism
héron ['erɔ̃] NM heron
héros ['ero] NM hero
herpès [ɛrpɛs] NM herpes
herse ['ɛrs] NF harrow; (de château) portcullis
hertz [ɛrts] NM (Élec) hertz
hertzien, ne [ɛrtsjɛ̃, -ɛn] ADJ (Élec) Hertzian
hésitant, e [ezitɑ̃, -ɑ̃t] ADJ hesitant
hésitation [ezitasjɔ̃] NF hesitation
hésiter [ezite] /1/ VI: **~ (à faire)** to hesitate (to do); **~ sur qch** to hesitate over sth
hétéro [etero] ADJ (hétérosexuel(le)) hetero
hétéroclite [eterɔklit] ADJ heterogeneous; (objets) sundry
hétérogène [eterɔʒɛn] ADJ heterogeneous
hétérosexuel, le [eterɔsɛkɥɛl] ADJ heterosexual
hêtre ['ɛtr] NM beech
heure [œr] NF hour; (Scol) period; (moment, moment fixé) time; **c'est l'~** it's time; **pourriez-vous me donner l'~, s'il vous plaît?** could you tell me the time, please?; **quelle ~ est-il?** what time is it?; **2 heures (du matin)** 2 o'clock (in the morning); **à la bonne ~!** (parfois ironique) splendid!; **être à l'~** to be on time; (montre) to be right; **le bus passe à l'~** the bus runs on the hour; **mettre à l'~** to set right; **100 km à l'~** ≈ 60 miles an ou per hour; **à toute ~** at any time; **24 heures sur 24** round the clock, 24 hours a day; **à l'~ qu'il est** at this time (of day); (fig) now; **à l'~ actuelle** at the present time; **sur l'~** at once; **pour l'~** for the time being; **d'~ en ~** from one hour to the next; (régulièrement) hourly; **d'une ~ à l'autre** from hour to hour; **à une ~ avancée (de la nuit)** at a late hour (of the night); **de bonne ~** early; **deux heures de marche/travail** two hours' walking/work; **une ~ d'arrêt** an hour's break ou stop; **~ d'été** summer time (BRIT), daylight saving time (US); **~ de pointe** rush hour; (téléphone) peak period; **heures de bureau** office hours; **heures supplémentaires** overtime sg
heureusement [œrøzmɑ̃] ADV (par bonheur) fortunately, luckily; **~ que ...** it's a good job that ..., fortunately ...
heureux, -euse [œrø, -øz] ADJ happy; (chanceux) lucky, fortunate; (judicieux) felicitous, fortunate; **être ~ de qch** to be pleased ou happy about sth; **être ~ de faire/que** to be pleased ou happy to do/that; **s'estimer ~ de qch/que** to consider o.s. fortunate with sth/that; **encore ~ que ...** just as well that ...
heurt ['œr] NM (choc) collision; **heurts** NMPL (fig) clashes
heurté, e ['œrte] ADJ (fig) jerky, uneven; (: couleurs) clashing
heurter ['œrte] /1/ VT (mur) to strike, hit; (personne) to collide with; (fig) to go against, upset; **se heurter** (couleurs, tons) to clash; **se ~ à** to collide with; (fig) to come up against; **~ qn de front** to clash head-on with sb
heurtoir ['œrtwar] NM door knocker
hévéa [evea] NM rubber tree

205

hexagonal, e, -aux [ɛgzagɔnal, -o] ADJ
hexagonal; *(français)* French *(see note at hexagone)*

hexagone [ɛgzagɔn] NM hexagon; **l'H~** *(la France)* France *(because of its roughly hexagonal shape)*

HF SIGLE F *(= haute fréquence)* HF

hiatus [jatys] NM hiatus

hibernation [ibɛʀnasjɔ̃] NF hibernation

hiberner [ibɛʀne] /1/ VI to hibernate

hibiscus [ibiskys] NM hibiscus

'hibou, x ['ibu] NM owl

'hic ['ik] NM *(fam)* snag

'hideusement ['idøzmɑ̃] ADV hideously

'hideux, -euse ['idø, -øz] ADJ hideous

hier [jɛʀ] ADV yesterday; **~ matin/soir/midi** yesterday morning/evening/lunchtime; **toute la journée d'~** all day yesterday; **toute la matinée d'~** all yesterday morning

'hiérarchie ['jeʀaʀʃi] NF hierarchy

'hiérarchique ['jeʀaʀʃik] ADJ hierarchic

'hiérarchiquement ['jeʀaʀʃikmɑ̃] ADV hierarchically

'hiérarchiser ['jeʀaʀʃize] /1/ VT to organize into a hierarchy

'hiéroglyphe ['jeʀɔglif] NM hieroglyphic

'hiéroglyphique ['jeʀɔglifik] ADJ hieroglyphic

'hi-fi ['ifi] NF INV hi-fi

hilarant, e [ilaʀɑ̃, -ɑ̃t] ADJ hilarious

hilare [ilaʀ] ADJ mirthful

hilarité [ilaʀite] NF hilarity, mirth

Himalaya [imalaja] NM: **l'~** the Himalayas *pl*

himalayen, ne [imalajɛ̃, -ɛn] ADJ Himalayan

hindou, e [ɛ̃du] ADJ Hindu ▶ NM/F: **H~, e** Hindu; *(Indien)* Indian

hindouisme [ɛ̃duism] NM Hinduism

Hindoustan [ɛ̃dustɑ̃] NM: **l'~** Hindustan

'hippie ['ipi] NMF hippy

hippique [ipik] ADJ equestrian, horse *cpd*; **un club ~** a riding centre; **un concours ~** a horse show

hippisme [ipism] NM (horse-)riding

hippocampe [ipɔkɑ̃p] NM sea horse

hippodrome [ipɔdʀom] NM racecourse

hippophagique [ipɔfaʒik] ADJ: **boucherie ~** horse butcher's

hippopotame [ipɔpɔtam] NM hippopotamus

hirondelle [iʀɔ̃dɛl] NF swallow

hirsute [iʀsyt] ADJ *(personne)* hairy; *(barbe)* shaggy; *(tête)* tousled

hispanique [ispanik] ADJ Hispanic

hispanisant, e [ispanizɑ̃, -ɑ̃t], **hispaniste** [ispanist] NM/F Hispanist

hispano-américain, e [ispanɔameʀikɛ̃, -ɛn] ADJ Spanish-American

hispano-arabe [ispanɔaʀab] ADJ Hispano-Moresque

'hisser ['ise] /1/ VT to hoist, haul up; **se 'hisser sur** to haul o.s. up onto

histoire [istwaʀ] NF *(science, événements)* history; *(anecdote, récit, mensonge)* story; *(affaire)* business *no pl*; *(chichis: gén pl)* fuss *no pl*; **histoires** NFPL *(ennuis)* trouble *sg*; **l'~ de France** French history, the history of France; **l'~ sainte** biblical history; **~ géo** humanities *pl*;

une ~ de *(fig)* a question of

histologie [istɔlɔʒi] NF histology

historien, ne [istɔʀjɛ̃, -ɛn] NM/F historian

historique [istɔʀik] ADJ historical; *(important)* historic ▶ NM *(exposé, récit)*: **faire l'~ de** to give the background to

historiquement [istɔʀikmɑ̃] ADV historically

'hit-parade ['itpaʀad] NM: **le ~** the charts

HIV SIGLE M *(= human immunodeficiency virus)* HIV

hiver [ivɛʀ] NM winter; **en ~** in winter

hivernal, e, -aux [ivɛʀnal, -o] ADJ *(de l'hiver)* winter *cpd*; *(comme en hiver)* wintry

hivernant, e [ivɛʀnɑ̃, -ɑ̃t] NM/F winter holiday-maker

hiverner [ivɛʀne] /1/ VI to winter

HLM SIGLE MF *(= habitations à loyer modéré)* low-rent, state-owned housing; **un(e) ~** ≈ a council flat *(ou* house) *(BRIT)*, ≈ a public housing unit *(US)*

Hme ABR *(= homme)* M

HO ABR *(= hors œuvre)* labour not included *(on invoices)*

'hobby ['ɔbi] NM hobby

'hochement ['ɔʃmɑ̃] NM: **~ de tête** nod; shake of the head

'hocher ['ɔʃe] /1/ VT: **~ la tête** to nod; *(signe négatif ou dubitatif)* to shake one's head

'hochet ['ɔʃɛ] NM rattle

'hockey ['ɔkɛ] NM: **~ (sur glace/gazon)** (ice/field) hockey

'hockeyeur, -euse ['ɔkɛjœʀ, -øz] NM/F hockey player

'holà ['ɔla] NM: **mettre le ~ à qch** to put a stop to sth

'holding ['ɔldiŋ] NM holding company

'hold-up ['ɔldœp] NM INV hold-up

'hollandais, e ['ɔlɑ̃dɛ, -ɛz] ADJ Dutch ▶ NM *(Ling)* Dutch ▶ NM/F: **H~, e** Dutchman/woman; **les H~** the Dutch

'Hollande ['ɔlɑ̃d] NF: **la H~** Holland ▶ NM: **h~** *(fromage)* Dutch cheese

holocauste [ɔlɔkost] NM holocaust

hologramme [ɔlɔgʀam] NM hologram

'homard ['ɔmaʀ] NM lobster

homéopathe [ɔmeɔpat] N homoeopath

homéopathie [ɔmeɔpati] NF homoeopathy

homéopathique [ɔmeɔpatik] ADJ homoeopathic

homérique [ɔmeʀik] ADJ Homeric

homicide [ɔmisid] NM murder ▶ NMF murderer/eress; **~ involontaire** manslaughter

hommage [ɔmaʒ] NM tribute; **hommages** NMPL: **présenter ses hommages** to pay one's respects; **rendre ~ à** to pay tribute *ou* homage to; **en ~ de** as a token of; **faire ~ de qch à qn** to present sb with sth

homme [ɔm] NM man; *(espèce humaine)*: **l'~** man, mankind; **~ d'affaires** businessman; **~ des cavernes** caveman; **~ d'Église** churchman, clergyman; **~ d'État** statesman; **~ de loi** lawyer; **~ de main** hired man; **~ de paille** stooge; **~ politique** politician; **l'~ de la rue** the man in the street; **~ à tout faire** odd-job man

homme-grenouille [ɔmgʀənuj] *(pl* **hommes-grenouilles)** NM frogman

homme-orchestre [ɔmɔʀkɛstʀ] (pl **hommes-orchestres**) NM one-man band

homme-sandwich [ɔmsɑ̃dwitʃ] (pl **hommes-sandwichs**) NM sandwich (board) man

homo [ɔmo] ADJ, NMF = **homosexuel**

homogène [ɔmɔʒɛn] ADJ homogeneous

homogénéisé, e [ɔmɔʒeneize] ADJ: **lait ~** homogenized milk

homogénéité [ɔmɔʒeneite] NF homogeneity

homologation [ɔmɔlɔgasjɔ̃] NF ratification; official recognition

homologue [ɔmɔlɔg] NMF counterpart, opposite number

homologué, e [ɔmɔlɔge] ADJ (Sport) officially recognized, ratified; (tarif) authorized

homologuer [ɔmɔlɔge] /1/ VT (Jur) to ratify; (Sport) to recognize officially, ratify

homonyme [ɔmɔnim] NM (Ling) homonym; (d'une personne) namesake

homosexualité [ɔmɔsɛksɥalite] NF homosexuality

homosexuel, le [ɔmɔsɛksɥɛl] ADJ homosexual

'**Honduras** [ɔ̃dyʀas] NM: **le ~** Honduras

'**hondurien, ne** [ɔ̃dyʀjɛ̃, -ɛn] ADJ Honduran

'**Hong-Kong** [ɔ̃gkɔ̃g] N Hong Kong

'**hongre** [ɔ̃gʀ] ADJ (cheval) gelded ▶ NM gelding

'**Hongrie** [ɔ̃gʀi] NF: **la ~** Hungary

'**hongrois, e** [ɔ̃gʀwa, -waz] ADJ Hungarian ▶ NM (Ling) Hungarian ▶ NM/F: **H~, e** Hungarian

honnête [ɔnɛt] ADJ (intègre) honest; (juste, satisfaisant) fair

honnêtement [ɔnɛtmɑ̃] ADV honestly

honnêteté [ɔnɛtte] NF honesty

honneur [ɔnœʀ] NM honour; (mérite): **l'~ lui revient** the credit is his; **à qui ai-je l'~?** to whom have I the pleasure of speaking?; "**j'ai l'~ de …**" "I have the honour of …"; **en l'~ de** (personne) in honour of; (événement) on the occasion of; **faire ~ à** (engagements) to honour; (famille, professeur) to be a credit to; (fig: repas etc) to do justice to; **être à l'~** to be in the place of honour; **être en ~** to be in favour; **membre d'~** honorary member; **table d'~** top table

Honolulu [ɔnɔlyly] N Honolulu

honorable [ɔnɔʀabl] ADJ worthy, honourable; (suffisant) decent

honorablement [ɔnɔʀabləmɑ̃] ADV honourably; decently

honoraire [ɔnɔʀɛʀ] ADJ honorary; **honoraires** NMPL fees; **professeur ~** professor emeritus

honorer [ɔnɔʀe] /1/ VT to honour; (estimer) to hold in high regard; (faire honneur à) to do credit to; **~ qn de** to honour sb with; **s'honorer de** to pride o.s. upon

honorifique [ɔnɔʀifik] ADJ honorary

'**honte** [ɔ̃t] NF shame; **avoir ~ de** to be ashamed of; **faire H~ à qn** to make sb (feel) ashamed

'**honteusement** [ɔ̃tøzmɑ̃] ADV ashamedly; shamefully

'**honteux, -euse** [ɔ̃tø, -øz] ADJ ashamed; (conduite, acte) shameful, disgraceful

hôpital, -aux [ɔpital, -o] NM hospital; **où est l'~ le plus proche?** where is the nearest hospital?

'**hoquet** [ɔkɛ] NM hiccup, hiccough; **avoir le ~**

to have (the) hiccups ou hiccoughs

'**hoqueter** ['ɔkte] /4/ VI to hiccough

horaire [ɔʀɛʀ] ADJ hourly ▶ NM timetable, schedule; **horaires** NMPL (heures de travail) hours; **~ flexible** ou **mobile** ou **à la carte** ou **souple** flex(i)time

'**horde** ['ɔʀd] NF horde

'**horions** ['ɔʀjɔ̃] NMPL blows

horizon [ɔʀizɔ̃] NM horizon; (paysage) landscape, view; **sur l'~** on the skyline ou horizon

horizontal, e, -aux [ɔʀizɔ̃tal, -o] ADJ horizontal ▶ NF: **à l'~** on the horizontal

horizontalement [ɔʀizɔ̃talmɑ̃] ADV horizontally

horloge [ɔʀlɔʒ] NF clock; **l'~ parlante** the speaking clock; **~ normande** grandfather clock; **~ physiologique** biological clock

horloger, -ère [ɔʀlɔʒe, -ɛʀ] NM/F watchmaker; clockmaker

horlogerie [ɔʀlɔʒʀi] NF watchmaking; watchmaker's (shop); clockmaker's (shop); **pièces d'~** watch parts ou components

'**hormis** ['ɔʀmi] PRÉP save

hormonal, e, -aux [ɔʀmɔnal, -o] ADJ hormonal

hormone [ɔʀmɔn] NF hormone

horodaté, e [ɔʀɔdate] ADJ (ticket) time- and date-stamped; (stationnement) pay and display

horodateur, -trice [ɔʀɔdatœʀ, -tʀis] ADJ (appareil) for stamping the time and date ▶ NM/F (parking) ticket machine

horoscope [ɔʀɔskɔp] NM horoscope

horreur [ɔʀœʀ] NF horror; **avoir ~ de** to loathe, detest; **quelle ~!** how awful!; **avoir ~ de** to loathe ou detest

horrible [ɔʀibl] ADJ horrible

horriblement [ɔʀibləmɑ̃] ADV horribly

horrifiant, e [ɔʀifjɑ̃, -ɑ̃t] ADJ horrifying

horrifier [ɔʀifje] /7/ VT to horrify

horrifique [ɔʀifik] ADJ horrific

horripilant, e [ɔʀipilɑ̃, -ɑ̃t] ADJ exasperating

horripiler [ɔʀipile] /1/ VT to exasperate

'**hors** ['ɔʀ] PRÉP except (for); **~ de** out of; **~ ligne** (Inform) off line; **~ pair** outstanding; **~ de propos** inopportune; **~ série** (sur mesure) made-to-order; (exceptionnel) exceptional; **~ service (HS)**, **~ d'usage** out of service; **être ~ de soi** to be beside o.s.

'**hors-bord** ['ɔʀbɔʀ] NM INV outboard motor; (canot) speedboat (with outboard motor)

'**hors-concours** ['ɔʀkɔ̃kuʀ] ADJ INV ineligible to compete; (fig) in a class of one's own

'**hors-d'œuvre** ['ɔʀdœvʀ] NM INV hors d'œuvre

'**hors-jeu** ['ɔʀʒø] NM INV being offside no pl

'**hors-la-loi** ['ɔʀlalwa] NM INV outlaw

'**hors-piste**, '**hors-pistes** ['ɔʀpist] NM INV (Ski) cross-country

'**hors-taxe** [ɔʀtaks] ADJ (sur une facture, prix) excluding VAT; (boutique, marchandises) duty-free

'**hors-texte** ['ɔʀtɛkst] NM INV plate

hortensia [ɔʀtɑ̃sja] NM hydrangea

horticole [ɔʀtikɔl] ADJ horticultural

horticulteur, -trice [ɔʀtikyltœʀ, -tʀis] NM/F horticulturalist (BRIT), horticulturist (US)

h

horticulture [ɔʀtikyltyʀ] NF horticulture

hospice [ɔspis] NM (*de vieillards*) home; (*asile*) hospice

hospitalier, -ière [ɔspitalje, -jɛʀ] ADJ (*accueillant*) hospitable; (*Méd: service, centre*) hospital cpd

hospitalisation [ɔspitalizasjɔ̃] NF hospitalization

hospitaliser [ɔspitalize] /1/ VT to take (*ou* send) to hospital, hospitalize

hospitalité [ɔspitalite] NF hospitality

hospitalo-universitaire [ɔspitaloynivɛʀsitɛʀ] ADJ: **centre ~ (CHU)** ≈ (teaching) hospital

hostie [ɔsti] NF host

hostile [ɔstil] ADJ hostile

hostilité [ɔstilite] NF hostility; **hostilités** NFPL hostilities

hôte [ot] NM (*maître de maison*) host; (*client*) patron; (*fig*) inhabitant, occupant ▶ NMF (*invité*) guest; **~ payant** paying guest

hôtel [otɛl] NM hotel; **aller à l'~** to stay in a hotel; **~ (particulier)** (private) mansion; *see note*; **~ de ville** town hall

> There are six categories of hotel in France, from zero (*non classé*) to four stars and luxury four stars (*quatre étoiles luxe*). Prices include VAT but not breakfast. In some towns, guests pay a small additional tourist tax, the *taxe de séjour*.

hôtelier, -ière [otəlje, -jɛʀ] ADJ hotel cpd ▶ NM/F hotelier, hotel-keeper

hôtellerie [otɛlʀi] NF (*profession*) hotel business; (*auberge*) inn

hôtesse [otɛs] NF hostess; **~ de l'air** flight attendant; **~ (d'accueil)** receptionist

'hotte ['ɔt] NF (*panier*) basket (*carried on the back*); (*de cheminée*) hood; **~ aspirante** cooker hood

'houblon ['ublɔ̃] NM (*Bot*) hop; (*pour la bière*) hops pl

'houe ['u] NF hoe

'houille ['uj] NF coal; **~ blanche** hydroelectric power

'houiller, -ère ['uje, -ɛʀ] ADJ coal cpd; (*terrain*) coal-bearing ▶ NF coal mine

'houle ['ul] NF swell

'houlette [ulɛt] NF: **sous la ~ de** under the guidance of

'houleux, -euse ['ulø, -øz] ADJ heavy, swelling; (*fig*) stormy, turbulent

'houppe ['up], **'houppette** ['upɛt] NF powder puff; (*cheveux*) tuft

'hourra ['uʀa] NM cheer ▶ EXCL hurrah!

'houspiller ['uspije] /1/ VT to scold

'housse ['us] NF cover; (*pour protéger provisoirement*) dust cover; (*pour recouvrir à neuf*) loose *ou* stretch cover; **~ (penderie)** hanging wardrobe

'houx ['u] NM holly

hovercraft [ovœʀkʀaft] NM hovercraft

HS ABR = **hors service**

HT ABR = **'hors taxe**

'hublot ['yblo] NM porthole

'huche ['yʃ] NF: **~ à pain** bread bin

'huées ['ɥe] NFPL boos

'huer ['ɥe] /1/ VT to boo; (*hibou, chouette*) to hoot

huile [ɥil] NF oil; (*Art*) oil painting; (*fam*) bigwig; **mer d'~** (*très calme*) glassy sea, sea of glass; **faire tache d'~** (*fig*) to spread; **~ d'arachide** groundnut oil; **~ essentielle** essential oil; **~ de foie de morue** cod-liver oil; **~ de ricin** castor oil; **~ solaire** suntan oil; **~ de table** salad oil

huiler [ɥile] /1/ VT to oil

huilerie [ɥilʀi] NF (*usine*) oil-works

huileux, -euse [ɥilø, -øz] ADJ oily

huilier [ɥilje] NM (oil and vinegar) cruet

huis [ɥi] NM: **à ~ clos** in camera

huissier [ɥisje] NM usher; (*Jur*) ≈ bailiff

'huit ['ɥi(t)] NUM eight; **samedi en ~** a week on Saturday; **dans ~ jours** in a week('s time)

'huitaine ['ɥitɛn] NF: **une ~ de** about eight, eight or so; **une ~ de jours** a week or so

'huitante ['ɥitɑ̃t] NUM (*SUISSE*) eighty

'huitième ['ɥitjɛm] NUM eighth

huître [ɥitʀ] NF oyster

'hululement ['ylylmɑ̃] NM hooting

'huluer ['ylyle] /1/ VI to hoot

humain, e [ymɛ̃, -ɛn] ADJ human; (*compatissant*) humane ▶ NM human (being)

humainement [ymɛnmɑ̃] ADV humanly; humanely

humanisation [ymanizasjɔ̃] NF humanization

humaniser [ymanize] /1/ VT to humanize

humaniste [ymanist] NMF (*Ling*) classicist; humanist

humanitaire [ymanitɛʀ] ADJ humanitarian

humanitarisme [ymanitaʀism] NM humanitarianism

humanité [ymanite] NF humanity

humanoïde [ymanɔid] NMF humanoid

humble [œ̃bl] ADJ humble

humblement [œ̃bləmɑ̃] ADV humbly

humecter [ymɛkte] /1/ VT to dampen; **s'~ les lèvres** to moisten one's lips

humer ['yme] /1/ VT (*parfum*) to inhale; (*pour sentir*) to smell

humérus [ymeʀys] NM (*Anat*) humerus

humeur [ymœʀ] NF mood; (*tempérament*) temper; (*irritation*) bad temper; **de bonne/mauvaise ~** in a good/bad mood; **être d'~ à faire qch** to be in the mood for doing sth

humide [ymid] ADJ (*linge*) damp; (*main, yeux*) moist; (*climat, chaleur*) humid; (*saison, route*) wet

humidificateur [ymidifikatœʀ] NM humidifier

humidifier [ymidifje] /7/ VT to humidify

humidité [ymidite] NF humidity; dampness; **traces d'~** traces of moisture *ou* damp

humiliant, e [ymiljɑ̃, -ɑ̃t] ADJ humiliating

humiliation [ymiljasjɔ̃] NF humiliation

humilier [ymilje] /7/ VT to humiliate; **s'~ devant qn** to humble o.s. before sb

humilité [ymilite] NF humility, humbleness

humoriste [ymɔʀist] NMF humorist

humoristique [ymɔʀistik] ADJ humorous; humoristic

humour [ymuʀ] NM humour; **avoir de l'~** to have a sense of humour; **~ noir** sick humour

humus [ymys] NM humus

'huppé, e ['ype] ADJ crested; (*fam*) posh

'**hurlement** ['yʀləmɑ̃] NM howling *no pl*, howl; yelling *no pl*, yell

'**hurler** ['yʀle] /**1**/ vi to howl, yell; (*fig: vent*) to howl; (*: couleurs etc*) to clash; ~ **à la mort** (*chien*) to bay at the moon

hurluberlu [yʀlybɛʀly] NM (*péj*) crank ▸ ADJ cranky

'**hutte** ['yt] NF hut

hybride [ibʀid] ADJ hybrid

hydratant, e [idʀatɑ̃, -ɑ̃t] ADJ (*crème*) moisturizing

hydrate [idʀat] NM: **hydrates de carbone** carbohydrates

hydrater [idʀate] /**1**/ vt to hydrate

hydraulique [idʀolik] ADJ hydraulic

hydravion [idʀavjɔ̃] NM seaplane, hydroplane

hydro... [idʀo] PRÉFIXE hydro...

hydrocarbure [idʀokaʀbyʀ] NM hydrocarbon

hydrocution [idʀokysjɔ̃] NF immersion syncope

hydro-électrique [idʀoelɛktʀik] ADJ hydroelectric

hydrogène [idʀoʒɛn] NM hydrogen

hydroglisseur [idʀoglisœʀ] NM hydroplane

hydrographie [idʀogʀafi] NF (*fleuves*) hydrography

hydrophile [idʀofil] ADJ *voir* **coton**

hyène [jɛn] NF hyena

hygiène [iʒjɛn] NF hygiene; ~ **intime** personal hygiene

hygiénique [iʒjenik] ADJ hygienic

hymne [imn] NM hymn; ~ **national** national anthem

hyper... [ipɛʀ] PRÉFIXE hyper...

hyperlien [ipɛʀljɛ̃] NM (*Inform*) hyperlink

hypermarché [ipɛʀmaʀʃe] NM hypermarket

hypermétrope [ipɛʀmetʀop] ADJ long-sighted

hypernerveux, -euse [ipɛʀnɛʀvø, -øz] ADJ highly-strung

hypersensible [ipɛʀsɑ̃sibl] ADJ hypersensitive

hypertendu, e [ipɛʀtɑ̃dy] ADJ having high blood pressure, hypertensive

hypertension [ipɛʀtɑ̃sjɔ̃] NF high blood pressure, hypertension

hypertexte [ipɛʀtɛkst] NM (*Inform*) hypertext

hypertrophié, e [ipɛʀtʀofje] ADJ hypertrophic

hypnose [ipnoz] NF hypnosis

hypnotique [ipnotik] ADJ hypnotic

hypnotiser [ipnotize] /**1**/ vt to hypnotize

hypnotiseur [ipnotizœʀ] NM hypnotist

hypnotisme [ipnotism] NM hypnotism

hypocondriaque [ipokɔ̃dʀijak] ADJ hypochondriac

hypocrisie [ipokʀizi] NF hypocrisy

hypocrite [ipokʀit] ADJ hypocritical ▸ NMF hypocrite

hypocritement [ipokʀitmɑ̃] ADV hypocritically

hypotendu, e [ipotɑ̃dy] ADJ having low blood pressure, hypotensive

hypotension [ipotɑ̃sjɔ̃] NF low blood pressure, hypotension

hypoténuse [ipotenyz] NF hypotenuse

hypothécaire [ipotekɛʀ] ADJ mortgage; **garantie/prêt** ~ mortgage security/loan

hypothèque [ipotɛk] NF mortgage

hypothéquer [ipoteke] /**6**/ vt to mortgage

hypothermie [ipotɛʀmi] NF hypothermia

hypothèse [ipotɛz] NF hypothesis; **dans l'** ~ **où** assuming that

hypothétique [ipotetik] ADJ hypothetical

hypothétiquement [ipotetikmɑ̃] ADV hypothetically

hystérectomie [isteʀɛktomi] NF hysterectomy

hystérie [isteʀi] NF hysteria; ~ **collective** mass hysteria

hystérique [isteʀik] ADJ hysterical

Hz ABR (= *Hertz*) Hz

h

I i

I, i [i] NM INV I, i; **I comme Irma** I for Isaac (BRIT) *ou* Item (US)

IAC SIGLE F (= *insémination artificielle entre conjoints*) AIH

IAD SIGLE F (= *insémination artificielle par donneur extérieur*) AID

ibère [ibɛʀ] ADJ Iberian ▶ NMF: **I~** Iberian

ibérique [ibeʀik] ADJ: **la péninsule ~** the Iberian peninsula

ibid. [ibid] ABR (= *ibidem*) ibid., ib.

iceberg [isbɛʀg] NM iceberg

ici [isi] ADV here; **jusqu'~** as far as this; (*temporel*) until now; **d'~ là** by then; **d'~ demain** by tomorrow; (*en attendant*) in the meantime; **d'~ peu** before long

icône [ikon] NF (*aussi Inform*) icon

iconoclaste [ikɔnɔklast] NMF iconoclast

iconographie [ikɔnɔgʀafi] NF iconography; (*illustrations*) (collection of) illustrations

id. [id] ABR (= *idem*) id.

idéal, e, -aux [ideal, -o] ADJ ideal ▶ NM ideal; (*système de valeurs*) ideals *pl*

idéalement [idealmɑ̃] ADV ideally

idéalisation [idealizasjɔ̃] NF idealization

idéaliser [idealize] /1/ VT to idealize

idéalisme [idealism] NM idealism

idéaliste [idealist] ADJ idealistic ▶ NMF idealist

idée [ide] NF idea; (*illusion*): **se faire des idées** to imagine things, get ideas into one's head; **avoir dans l'~ que** to have an idea that; **mon ~, c'est que ...** I suggest that ..., I think that ...; **à l'~ de/que** at the idea of/that, at the thought of/that; **je n'ai pas la moindre ~** I haven't the faintest idea; **avoir ~ que** to have an idea that; **avoir des idées larges/étroites** to be broad-/narrow-minded; **venir à l'~ de qn** to occur to sb; **en voilà des idées!** the very idea!; **~ fixe** idée fixe, obsession; **idées noires** black *ou* dark thoughts; **idées reçues** accepted ideas *ou* wisdom

identifiable [idɑ̃tifjabl] ADJ identifiable

identifiant [idɑ̃tifjɑ̃] NM (*Inform*) login

identification [idɑ̃tifikasjɔ̃] NF identification

identifier [idɑ̃tifje] /7/ VT to identify; **~ qch/qn à** to identify sth/sb with; **s'identifier** VI: **s'identifier avec** *ou* **à qn/qch** (*héros etc*) to identify with sb/sth

identique [idɑ̃tik] ADJ: **~ (à)** identical (to)

identité [idɑ̃tite] NF identity; **~ judiciaire** (*Police*) ≈ Criminal Records Office

idéogramme [ideɔgʀam] NM ideogram

idéologie [ideɔlɔʒi] NF ideology

idéologique [ideɔlɔʒik] ADJ ideological

idiomatique [idjɔmatik] ADJ: **expression ~** idiom, idiomatic expression

idiome [idjom] NM (*Ling*) idiom

idiot, e [idjo, idjɔt] ADJ idiotic ▶ NM/F idiot

idiotie [idjɔsi] NF idiocy; (*propos*) idiotic remark

idiotisme [idjɔtism] NM idiom, idiomatic phrase

idoine [idwan] ADJ fitting

idolâtrer [idolɑtʀe] /1/ VT to idolize

idolâtrie [idolɑtʀi] NF idolatry

idole [idɔl] NF idol

idylle [idil] NF idyll

idyllique [idilik] ADJ idyllic

if [if] NM yew

IFOP [ifɔp] SIGLE M (= *Institut français d'opinion publique*) French market research institute

IGH SIGLE M = **immeuble de grande hauteur**

igloo [iglu] NM igloo

IGN SIGLE M = **Institut géographique national**

ignare [iɲaʀ] ADJ ignorant

ignifuge [iɲifyʒ] ADJ fireproofing ▶ NM fireproofing (substance)

ignifuger [iɲifyʒe] /3/ VT to fireproof

ignoble [iɲɔbl] ADJ vile

ignominie [iɲɔmini] NF ignominy; (*acte*) ignominious *ou* base act

ignominieux, -euse [iɲɔminjø, -øz] ADJ ignominious

ignorance [iɲɔʀɑ̃s] NF ignorance; **dans l'~ de** in ignorance of, ignorant of

ignorant, e [iɲɔʀɑ̃, -ɑ̃t] ADJ ignorant ▶ NM/F: **faire l'~** to pretend one doesn't know; **~ de** ignorant of, not aware of; **~ en** ignorant of, knowing nothing of

ignoré, e [iɲɔʀe] ADJ unknown

ignorer [iɲɔʀe] /1/ VT (*ne pas connaître*) not to know, be unaware *ou* ignorant of; (*être sans expérience de: plaisir, guerre etc*) not to have experienced, have no experience of; (*bouder: personne*) to ignore; **j'ignore comment/si** I do not know how/if; **~ que** to be unaware that, not to know that; **je n'ignore pas que ...** I'm not forgetting that ..., I'm not unaware that ...; **je l'ignore** I don't know

IGPN SIGLE F (= *Inspection générale de la police nationale*) police disciplinary body

IGS SIGLE F (= *Inspection générale des services*) police disciplinary body for Paris

iguane [igwan] NM iguana

il [il] PRON he; *(animal, chose, en tournure impersonnelle)* it, NB: *en anglais les navires et les pays sont en général assimilés aux femelles, et les bébés aux choses, si le sexe n'est pas spécifié*; **ils** they; **il neige** it's snowing; **Pierre est-il arrivé?** has Pierre arrived?; **il a gagné** he won; *voir aussi* **avoir**

île [il] NF island; **les Îles** the West Indies; **l'~ de Beauté** Corsica; **l'~ Maurice** Mauritius; **les îles anglo-normandes** the Channel Islands; **les îles Britanniques** the British Isles; **les îles Cocos** ou **Keeling** the Cocos ou Keeling Islands; **les îles Cook** the Cook Islands; **les îles Scilly** the Scilly Isles, the Scillies; **les îles Shetland** the Shetland Islands, Shetland; **les îles Sorlingues** = **les îles Scilly**; **les îles Vierges** the Virgin Islands

iliaque [iljak] ADJ *(Anat)*: **os/artère ~** iliac bone/artery

illégal, e, -aux [ilegal, -o] ADJ illegal, unlawful *(Admin)*

illégalement [ilegalmɑ̃] ADV illegally

illégalité [ilegalite] NF illegality; unlawfulness; **être dans l'~** to be outside the law

illégitime [ileʒitim] ADJ illegitimate; *(optimisme, sévérité)* unjustified, unwarranted

illégitimement [ileʒitimmɑ̃] ADV illegitimately

illégitimité [ileʒitimite] NF illegitimacy; **gouverner dans l'~** to rule illegally

illettré, e [iletre] ADJ, NM/F illiterate

illicite [ilisit] ADJ illicit

illicitement [ilisitmɑ̃] ADV illicitly

illico [iliko] ADV *(fam)* pronto

illimité, e [ilimite] ADJ *(immense)* boundless, unlimited; *(congé, durée)* indefinite, unlimited

illisible [ilizibl] ADJ illegible; *(roman)* unreadable

illisiblement [iliziblmɑ̃] ADV illegibly

illogique [ilɔʒik] ADJ illogical

illogisme [ilɔʒism] NM illogicality

illumination [ilyminasjɔ̃] NF illumination, floodlighting; *(inspiration)* flash of inspiration; **illuminations** NFPL illuminations, lights

illuminé, e [ilymine] ADJ lit up; illuminated, floodlit ▶ NM/F *(fig: péj)* crank

illuminer [ilymine] /1/ VT to light up; *(monument, rue; pour une fête)* to illuminate; *(: au moyen de projecteurs)* floodlight; **s'illuminer** VI to light up

illusion [ilyzjɔ̃] NF illusion; **se faire des illusions** to delude o.s.; **faire ~** to delude ou fool people; **~ d'optique** optical illusion

illusionner [ilyzjɔne] /1/ VT to delude; **s'~ (sur qn/qch)** to delude o.s. (about sb/sth)

illusionnisme [ilyzjɔnism] NM conjuring

illusionniste [ilyzjɔnist] NMF conjuror

illusoire [ilyzwar] ADJ illusory, illusive

illustrateur, -trice [ilystratœr, -tris] NM/F illustrator

illustratif, -ive [ilystratif, -iv] ADJ illustrative

illustration [ilystrasjɔ̃] NF illustration; *(d'un ouvrage: photos)* illustrations pl

illustre [ilystr] ADJ illustrious, renowned

illustré, e [ilystre] ADJ illustrated ▶ NM illustrated magazine; *(pour enfants)* comic

illustrer [ilystre] /1/ VT to illustrate; **s'illustrer** to become famous, win fame

îlot [ilo] NM small island, islet; *(de maisons)* block; *(petite zone)*: **un ~ de verdure** an island of greenery, a patch of green

ils [il] PRON they

image [imaʒ] NF *(gén)* picture; *(comparaison, ressemblance, Optique)* image; **~ de** picture ou image of; **~ d'Épinal** (social) stereotype; **~ de marque** brand image; *(d'une personne)* (public) image; *(d'une entreprise)* corporate image; **~ pieuse** holy picture

imagé, e [imaʒe] ADJ *(texte)* full of imagery; *(langage)* colourful

imaginable [imaʒinabl] ADJ imaginable; **difficilement ~** hard to imagine

imaginaire [imaʒiner] ADJ imaginary

imaginatif, -ive [imaʒinatif, -iv] ADJ imaginative

imagination [imaʒinasjɔ̃] NF imagination; *(chimère)* fancy, imagining; **avoir de l'~** to be imaginative, have a good imagination

imaginer [imaʒine] /1/ VT to imagine; *(croire)*: **qu'allez-vous ~ là?** what on earth are you thinking of?; *(inventer: expédient, mesure)* to devise, think up; **s'imaginer** VT *(se figurer: scène etc)* to imagine, picture; **s'imaginer à 60 ans** to picture ou imagine o.s. at 60; **s'imaginer que** to imagine that; **s'imaginer pouvoir faire qch** to think one can do sth; **j'imagine qu'il a voulu plaisanter** I suppose he was joking; **~ de faire** *(se mettre dans l'idée de)* to dream up the idea of doing

imam [imam] NM imam

imbattable [ɛ̃batabl] ADJ unbeatable

imbécile [ɛ̃besil] ADJ idiotic ▶ NMF idiot; *(Méd)* imbecile

imbécillité [ɛ̃besilite] NF idiocy; imbecility; idiotic action *(ou remark etc)*

imberbe [ɛ̃bɛrb] ADJ beardless

imbiber [ɛ̃bibe] /1/ VT: **~ qch de** to moisten ou wet sth with; **s'imbiber de** to become saturated with; **imbibé(e) d'eau** *(chaussures, étoffe)* saturated; *(terre)* waterlogged

imbriqué, e [ɛ̃brike] ADJ overlapping

imbriquer [ɛ̃brike] /1/: **s'imbriquer** VI to overlap (each other); *(fig)* to become interlinked ou interwoven

imbroglio [ɛ̃brɔljo] NM imbroglio

imbu, e [ɛ̃by] ADJ: **~ de** full of; **~ de soi-même/sa supériorité** full of oneself/one's superiority

imbuvable [ɛ̃byvabl] ADJ undrinkable

imitable [imitabl] ADJ imitable; **facilement ~** easily imitated

imitateur, -trice [imitatœr, -tris] NM/F *(gén)* imitator; *(Music-Hall: d'une personnalité)* impersonator

imitation [imitasjɔ̃] NF imitation; *(de personnalité)* impersonation; **sac ~ cuir** bag in imitation *ou* simulated leather; **à l'~ de** in imitation of

imiter [imite] /1/ VT to imitate; (*personne*) to imitate, impersonate; (*contrefaire: signature, document*) to forge, copy; (*ressembler à*) to look like; **il se leva et je l'imitai** he got up and I did likewise

imm. ABR = **immeuble**

immaculé, e [imakyle] ADJ spotless, immaculate; **l'I- Conception** (*Rel*) the Immaculate Conception

immanent, e [imanā, -āt] ADJ immanent

immangeable [ēmāʒabl] ADJ inedible, uneatable

immanquable [ēmākabl] ADJ (*cible*) impossible to miss; (*fatal, inévitable*) bound to happen, inevitable

immanquablement [ēmākabləmā] ADV inevitably

immatériel, le [imaterjɛl] ADJ ethereal; (*Philosophie*) immaterial

immatriculation [imatrikylasjɔ̃] NF registration

> The last two numbers on vehicle licence plates used to show which *département* of France the vehicle was registered in. For example, a car registered in Paris had the number 75 on its licence plates. In 2009, a new alphanumeric system was introduced, in which the *département* number no longer features. Displaying this number to the right of the plate is now optional.

immatriculer [imatrikyle] /1/ VT to register; **faire/se faire ~** to register; **voiture immatriculée dans la Seine** car with a Seine registration (number)

immature [imatyr] ADJ immature

immaturité [imatyrite] NF immaturity

immédiat, e [imedja, -at] ADJ immediate ▶ NM: **dans l'~** for the time being; **dans le voisinage ~ de** in the immediate vicinity of

immédiatement [imedjatmā] ADV immediately

immémorial, e, -aux [imemɔrjal, -o] ADJ ancient, age-old

immense [imās] ADJ immense

immensément [imāsemā] ADV immensely

immensité [imāsite] NF immensity

immerger [imɛrʒe] /3/ VT to immerse, submerge; (*câble etc*) to lay under water; (*déchets*) to dump at sea; **s'immerger** VI (*sous-marin*) to dive, submerge

immérité, e [imerite] ADJ undeserved

immersion [imɛrsjɔ̃] NF immersion

immettable [ēmetabl] ADJ unwearable

immeuble [imœbl] NM building ▶ ADJ (*Jur*) immovable, real; **~ locatif** block of rented flats (BRIT), rental building (US); **~ de rapport** investment property

immigrant, e [imigrā, -āt] NM/F immigrant

immigration [imigrasjɔ̃] NF immigration

immigré, e [imigre] NM/F immigrant

immigrer [imigre] /1/ VI to immigrate

imminence [iminās] NF imminence

imminent, e [iminā, -āt] ADJ imminent, impending

immiscer [imise] /3/: **s'immiscer** VI: **s'immiscer dans** to interfere in *ou* with

immixtion [imiksjɔ̃] NF interference

immobile [imɔbil] ADJ still, motionless; (*pièce de machine*) fixed; (*fig*) unchanging; **rester/se tenir ~** to stay/keep still

immobilier, -ière [imɔbilje, -jɛr] ADJ property *cpd*, in real property ▶ NM: **l'~** the property *ou* the real estate business

immobilisation [imɔbilizasjɔ̃] NF immobilization; **immobilisations** NFPL (*Jur*) fixed assets

immobiliser [imɔbilize] /1/ VT (*gén*) to immobilize; (*circulation, véhicule, affaires*) to bring to a standstill; **s'immobiliser** (*personne*) to stand still; (*machine, véhicule*) to come to a halt *ou* a standstill

immobilisme [imɔbilism] NM strong resistance *ou* opposition to change

immobilité [imɔbilite] NF immobility

immodéré, e [imɔdere] ADJ immoderate, inordinate

immodérément [imɔderemā] ADV immoderately

immoler [imɔle] /1/ VT to sacrifice

immonde [imɔ̃d] ADJ foul; (*sale: ruelle, taudis*) squalid

immondices [imɔ̃dis] NFPL (*ordures*) refuse *sg*; (*saletés*) filth *sg*

immoral, e, -aux [imɔral, -o] ADJ immoral

immoralisme [imɔralism] NM immoralism

immoralité [imɔralite] NF immorality

immortaliser [imɔrtalize] /1/ VT to immortalize

immortel, le [imɔrtɛl] ADJ immortal ▶ NF (*Bot*) everlasting (flower)

immuable [imɥabl] ADJ (*inébranlable*) immutable; (*qui ne change pas*) unchanging; (*personne*): **~ dans ses convictions** immoveable (in one's convictions)

immunisation [imynizasjɔ̃] NF immunization

immunisé, e [im(m)ynize] ADJ: **~ contre** immune to

immuniser [imynize] /1/ VT (*Méd*) to immunize; **~ qn contre** to immunize sb against; (*fig*) to make sb immune to

immunitaire [imynitɛr] ADJ immune

immunité [imynite] NF immunity; **~ diplomatique** diplomatic immunity; **~ parlementaire** parliamentary privilege

immunologie [imynɔlɔʒi] NF immunology

immutabilité [imytabilite] NF immutability

impact [ēpakt] NM impact; **point d'~** point of impact

impair, e [ēpɛr] ADJ odd ▶ NM faux pas, blunder; **numéros impairs** odd numbers

impalpable [ēpalpabl] ADJ impalpable

impaludation [ēpalydasjɔ̃] NF inoculation against malaria

imparable [ēparabl] ADJ unstoppable

impardonnable [ēpardɔnabl] ADJ unpardonable, unforgivable; **vous êtes ~**

d'avoir fait cela it's unforgivable of you to have done that

imparfait, e [ɛ̃paʀfɛ, -ɛt] ADJ imperfect ▶ NM (*Ling*) imperfect (tense)

imparfaitement [ɛ̃paʀfɛtmɑ̃] ADV imperfectly

impartial, e, -aux [ɛ̃paʀsjal, -o] ADJ impartial, unbiased

impartialité [ɛ̃paʀsjalite] NF impartiality

impartir [ɛ̃paʀtiʀ] /2/ VT: **~ qch à qn** to assign sth to sb; (*dons*) to bestow sth upon sb; **dans les délais impartis** in the time allowed

impasse [ɛ̃pɑs] NF dead-end, cul-de-sac; (*fig*) deadlock; **être dans l'~** (*négociations*) to have reached deadlock; **~ budgétaire** budget deficit

impassibilité [ɛ̃pasibilite] NF impassiveness

impassible [ɛ̃pasibl] ADJ impassive

impassiblement [ɛ̃pasibləmɑ̃] ADV impassively

impatiemment [ɛ̃pasjamɑ̃] ADV impatiently

impatience [ɛ̃pasjɑ̃s] NF impatience

impatient, e [ɛ̃pasjɑ̃, -ɑ̃t] ADJ impatient; **~ de faire qch** keen *ou* impatient to do sth

impatienter [ɛ̃pasjɑ̃te] /1/ VT to irritate, annoy; **s'impatienter** VI to get impatient; **s'impatienter de/contre** to lose patience at/with, grow impatient at/with

impayable [ɛ̃pɛjabl] ADJ (*drôle*) priceless

impayé, e [ɛ̃peje] ADJ unpaid, outstanding

impeccable [ɛ̃pekabl] ADJ faultless, impeccable; (*propre*) spotlessly clean; (*chic*) impeccably dressed; (*fam*) smashing

impeccablement [ɛ̃pekabləmɑ̃] ADV impeccably

impénétrable [ɛ̃penetrabl] ADJ impenetrable

impénitent, e [ɛ̃penitɑ̃, -ɑ̃t] ADJ unrepentant

impensable [ɛ̃pɑ̃sabl] ADJ (*événement hypothétique*) unthinkable; (*événement qui a eu lieu*) unbelievable

imper [ɛ̃pɛʀ] NM (*imperméable*) mac

impératif, -ive [ɛ̃peʀatif, -iv] ADJ imperative; (*Jur*) mandatory ▶ NM (*Ling*) imperative; **impératifs** NMPL (*exigences: d'une fonction, d'une charge*) requirements; (: *de la mode*) demands

impérativement [ɛ̃peʀativmɑ̃] ADV imperatively

impératrice [ɛ̃peʀatʀis] NF empress

imperceptible [ɛ̃pɛʀsɛptibl] ADJ imperceptible

imperceptiblement [ɛ̃pɛʀsɛptibləmɑ̃] ADV imperceptibly

imperdable [ɛ̃pɛʀdabl] ADJ that cannot be lost

imperfectible [ɛ̃pɛʀfɛktibl] ADJ which cannot be perfected

imperfection [ɛ̃pɛʀfɛksjɔ̃] NF imperfection

impérial, e, -aux [ɛ̃peʀjal, -o] ADJ imperial ▶ NF upper deck; **autobus à ~** double-decker bus

impérialisme [ɛ̃peʀjalism] NM imperialism

impérialiste [ɛ̃peʀjalist] ADJ, NMF imperialist

impérieusement [ɛ̃peʀjøzmɑ̃] ADV: **avoir ~ besoin de qch** to have urgent need of sth

impérieux, -euse [ɛ̃peʀjø, -øz] ADJ (*caractère, ton*) imperious; (*obligation, besoin*) pressing, urgent

impérissable [ɛ̃peʀisabl] ADJ undying, imperishable

imperméabilisation [ɛ̃pɛʀmeabilizasjɔ̃] NF waterproofing

imperméabiliser [ɛ̃pɛʀmeabilize] /1/ VT to waterproof

imperméable [ɛ̃pɛʀmeabl] ADJ waterproof; (*Géo*) impermeable; (*fig*): **~ à** impervious to ▶ NM raincoat; **~ à l'air** airtight

impersonnel, le [ɛ̃pɛʀsɔnɛl] ADJ impersonal

impertinemment [ɛ̃pɛʀtinamɑ̃] ADV impertinently

impertinence [ɛ̃pɛʀtinɑ̃s] NF impertinence

impertinent, e [ɛ̃pɛʀtinɑ̃, -ɑ̃t] ADJ impertinent

imperturbable [ɛ̃pɛʀtyʀbabl] ADJ (*personne*) imperturbable; (*sang-froid*) unshakeable; **rester ~** to remain unruffled

imperturbablement [ɛ̃pɛʀtyʀbabləmɑ̃] ADV imperturbably; unshakeably

impétrant, e [ɛ̃petʀɑ̃, -ɑ̃t] NM/F (*Jur*) applicant

impétueux, -euse [ɛ̃petɥø, -øz] ADJ fiery

impétuosité [ɛ̃petɥozite] NF fieriness

impie [ɛ̃pi] ADJ impious, ungodly

impiété [ɛ̃pjete] NF impiety

impitoyable [ɛ̃pitwajabl] ADJ pitiless, merciless

impitoyablement [ɛ̃pitwajabləmɑ̃] ADV mercilessly

implacable [ɛ̃plakabl] ADJ implacable

implacablement [ɛ̃plakabləmɑ̃] ADV implacably

implant [ɛ̃plɑ̃] NM (*Méd*) implant

implantation [ɛ̃plɑ̃tasjɔ̃] NF establishment; settling; implantation

implanter [ɛ̃plɑ̃te] /1/ VT (*usine, industrie, usage*) to establish; (*colons etc*) to settle; (*idée, préjugé*) to implant; **s'implanter dans** VI to be established in; to settle in; to become implanted in

implémenter [ɛ̃plemɑ̃te] /1/ VT (*aussi Inform*) to implement

implication [ɛ̃plikasjɔ̃] NF implication

implicite [ɛ̃plisit] ADJ implicit

implicitement [ɛ̃plisitmɑ̃] ADV implicitly

impliquer [ɛ̃plike] /1/ VT to imply; **~ qn (dans)** to implicate sb (in)

implorant, e [ɛ̃plɔʀɑ̃, -ɑ̃t] ADJ imploring

implorer [ɛ̃plɔʀe] /1/ VT to implore

imploser [ɛ̃ploze] /1/ VI to implode

implosion [ɛ̃plozjɔ̃] NF implosion

impoli, e [ɛ̃pɔli] ADJ impolite, rude

impoliment [ɛ̃pɔlimɑ̃] ADV impolitely

impolitesse [ɛ̃pɔlitɛs] NF impoliteness, rudeness; (*propos*) impolite *ou* rude remark

impondérable [ɛ̃pɔ̃deʀabl] NM imponderable

impopulaire [ɛ̃pɔpylɛʀ] ADJ unpopular

impopularité [ɛ̃pɔpylaʀite] NF unpopularity

importable [ɛ̃pɔʀtabl] ADJ (*Comm: marchandise*) importable; (*vêtement: immettable*) unwearable

importance [ɛ̃pɔʀtɑ̃s] NF importance; (*de somme*) size; **avoir de l'~** to be important; **sans ~** unimportant; **d'~** important, considerable; **quelle ~?** what does it matter?

important, e [ɛ̃pɔʀtɑ̃, -ɑ̃t] ADJ important; (*en quantité: somme, retard*) considerable, sizeable; (: *gamme, dégâts*) extensive; (*péj: airs, ton*) self-important ▶ NM: **l'~** the important thing

importateur, -trice [ɛ̃pɔʀtatœʀ, -tʀis] ADJ importing ▶ NM/F importer; **pays ~ de blé** wheat-importing country

importation [ɛ̃pɔʀtasjɔ̃] NF import; introduction; (produit) import

importer [ɛ̃pɔʀte] /1/ VT (Comm) to import; (maladies, plantes) to introduce ▸ VI (être important) to matter; **~ à qn** to matter to sb; **il importe de** it is important to; **il importe qu'il fasse** he must do, it is important that he should do; **peu m'importe** (je n'ai pas de préférence) I don't mind; (je m'en moque) I don't care; **peu importe** it doesn't matter; **peu importe (que)** it doesn't matter (if); **peu importe le prix** never mind the price; voir aussi **n'importe**

import-export [ɛ̃pɔʀɛkspɔʀ] NM import-export business

importun, e [ɛ̃pɔʀtœ̃, -yn] ADJ irksome, importunate; (arrivée, visite) inopportune, ill-timed ▸ NM intruder

importuner [ɛ̃pɔʀtyne] /1/ VT to bother

imposable [ɛ̃pozabl] ADJ taxable

imposant, e [ɛ̃pozɑ̃, -ɑ̃t] ADJ imposing

imposé, e [ɛ̃poze] ADJ (soumis à l'impôt) taxed; (Gym etc: figures) set

imposer [ɛ̃poze] /1/ VT (taxer) to tax; (Rel): **~ les mains** to lay on hands; **~ qch à qn** to impose sth on sb; **s'imposer** VI (être nécessaire) to be imperative; (montrer sa proéminence) to stand out, emerge; (artiste: se faire connaître) to win recognition, come to the fore; **en ~** to be imposing; **en ~ à** to impress; **s'imposer comme** to emerge as; **s'imposer par** to win recognition through; **ça s'impose** it's essential, it's vital

imposition [ɛ̃pozisjɔ̃] NF (Admin) taxation

impossibilité [ɛ̃posibilite] NF impossibility; **être dans l'~ de faire** to be unable to do, find it impossible to do

impossible [ɛ̃posibl] ADJ impossible ▸ NM: **l'~** the impossible; **~ à faire** impossible to do; **il m'est ~ de le faire** it is impossible for me to do it, I can't possibly do it; **faire l'~ (pour que)** to do one's utmost (so that); **si, par ~ ...** if, by some miracle ...

imposteur [ɛ̃pɔstœʀ] NM impostor

imposture [ɛ̃pɔstyʀ] NF imposture, deception

impôt [ɛ̃po] NM tax; (taxes) taxation, taxes pl; **impôts** NMPL (contributions) (income) tax sg; **payer 1000 euros d'impôts** to pay 1,000 euros in tax; **~ direct/indirect** direct/indirect tax; **~ sur le chiffre d'affaires** corporation (BRIT) ou corporate (US) tax; **~ foncier** land tax; **~ sur la fortune** wealth tax; **~ sur les plus-values** capital gains tax; **~ sur le revenu** income tax; **~ sur le RPP** personal income tax; **~ sur les sociétés** tax on companies; **impôts locaux** rates, local taxes (US), ≈ council tax (BRIT)

impotence [ɛ̃pɔtɑ̃s] NF disability

impotent, e [ɛ̃pɔtɑ̃, -ɑ̃t] ADJ disabled

impraticable [ɛ̃pʀatikabl] ADJ (projet) impracticable, unworkable; (piste) impassable

imprécation [ɛ̃pʀekasjɔ̃] NF imprecation

imprécis, e [ɛ̃pʀesi, -iz] ADJ (contours, souvenir) imprecise, vague; (tir) inaccurate, imprecise

imprécision [ɛ̃pʀesizjɔ̃] NF imprecision

imprégner [ɛ̃pʀeɲe] /6/ VT (amertume, ironie) to pervade; **~ (de)** (tissu, tampon) to soak ou impregnate (with); (lieu, air) to fill (with); **s'imprégner de** VI to become impregnated with; to be filled with; (fig) to absorb

imprenable [ɛ̃pʀənabl] ADJ (forteresse) impregnable; **vue ~** unimpeded outlook

impresario [ɛ̃pʀesaʀjo] NM manager, impresario

impression [ɛ̃pʀesjɔ̃] NF impression; (d'un ouvrage, tissu) printing; (Photo) exposure; **faire bonne/mauvaise ~** to make a good/bad impression; **donner une ~ de/l'~ que** to give the impression of/that; **avoir l'~ de/que** to have the impression of/that; **faire ~** to make an impression; **impressions de voyage** impressions of one's journey

impressionnable [ɛ̃pʀesjɔnabl] ADJ impressionable

impressionnant, e [ɛ̃pʀesjɔnɑ̃, -ɑ̃t] ADJ (imposant) impressive; (bouleversant) upsetting

impressionner [ɛ̃pʀesjɔne] /1/ VT (frapper) to impress; (troubler) to upset; (Photo) to expose

impressionnisme [ɛ̃pʀesjɔnism] NM impressionism

impressionniste [ɛ̃pʀesjɔnist] ADJ, NMF impressionist

imprévisible [ɛ̃pʀevizibl] ADJ unforeseeable; (réaction, personne) unpredictable

imprévoyance [ɛ̃pʀevwajɑ̃s] NF lack of foresight

imprévoyant, e [ɛ̃pʀevwajɑ̃, -ɑ̃t] ADJ lacking in foresight; (en matière d'argent) improvident

imprévu, e [ɛ̃pʀevy] ADJ unforeseen, unexpected ▸ NM (incident) unexpected incident; **l'~** the unexpected; **des vacances pleines d'~** holidays full of surprises; **en cas d'~** if anything unexpected happens; **sauf ~** unless anything unexpected crops up

imprimante [ɛ̃pʀimɑ̃t] NF (Inform) printer; **~ à bulle d'encre** bubble jet printer; **~ à jet d'encre** ink-jet printer; **~ à laser** laser printer; **~ (ligne par) ligne** line printer; **~ à marguerite** daisy-wheel printer

imprimé [ɛ̃pʀime] NM (formulaire) printed form; (Postes) printed matter no pl; (tissu) printed fabric; **un ~ à fleurs/pois** (tissu) a floral/polka-dot print

imprimer [ɛ̃pʀime] /1/ VT to print; (Inform) to print (out); (apposer: visa, cachet) to stamp; (: empreinte etc) to imprint; (publier) to publish; (communiquer: mouvement, impulsion) to impart, transmit

imprimerie [ɛ̃pʀimʀi] NF printing; (établissement) printing works sg; (atelier) printing house, printery

imprimeur [ɛ̃pʀimœʀ] NM printer; **~-éditeur/-libraire** printer and publisher/bookseller

improbable [ɛ̃pʀɔbabl] ADJ unlikely, improbable

improductif, -ive [ɛ̃pʀɔdyktif, -iv] ADJ unproductive

impromptu, e [ɛ̃pʀɔ̃pty] ADJ impromptu; (départ) sudden

imprononçable [ɛ̃pʀɔnɔ̃sabl] ADJ unpronounceable

impropre [ɛ̃pʀɔpʀ] ADJ inappropriate; **~ à** unsuitable for

improprement [ɛ̃pʀɔpʀəmɑ̃] ADV improperly

impropriété [ɛ̃pʀɔpʀijete] NF: **~ (de langage)** incorrect usage *no pl*

improvisation [ɛ̃pʀɔvizasjɔ̃] NF improvisation

improvisé, e [ɛ̃pʀɔvize] ADJ makeshift, improvised; *(jeu etc)* scratch, improvised; **avec des moyens improvisés** using whatever comes to hand

improviser [ɛ̃pʀɔvize] /1/ VT, VI to improvise; **s'improviser** *(secours, réunion)* to be improvised; **s'improviser cuisinier** to *(decide to)* act as cook; **~ qn cuisinier** to get sb to act as cook

improviste [ɛ̃pʀɔvist]: **à l'~** *adv* unexpectedly, without warning

imprudemment [ɛ̃pʀydamɑ̃] ADV carelessly; unwisely, imprudently

imprudence [ɛ̃pʀydɑ̃s] NF *(d'une personne, d'une action)* carelessness *no pl*; *(d'une remarque)* imprudence *no pl*; act of carelessness; foolish *ou* unwise action; **commettre une ~** to do something foolish

imprudent, e [ɛ̃pʀydɑ̃, -ɑ̃t] ADJ *(conducteur, geste, action)* careless; *(remarque)* unwise, imprudent; *(projet)* foolhardy

impubère [ɛ̃pybɛʀ] ADJ below the age of puberty

impubliable [ɛ̃pyblijabl] ADJ unpublishable

impudemment [ɛ̃pydamɑ̃] ADV impudently

impudence [ɛ̃pydɑ̃s] NF impudence

impudent, e [ɛ̃pydɑ̃, -ɑ̃t] ADJ impudent

impudeur [ɛ̃pydœʀ] NF shamelessness

impudique [ɛ̃pydik] ADJ shameless

impuissance [ɛ̃pɥisɑ̃s] NF helplessness; ineffectualness; impotence

impuissant, e [ɛ̃pɥisɑ̃, -ɑ̃t] ADJ helpless; *(sans effet)* ineffectual; *(sexuellement)* impotent ▶ NM impotent man; **~ à faire qch** powerless to do sth

impulsif, -ive [ɛ̃pylsif, -iv] ADJ impulsive

impulsion [ɛ̃pylsjɔ̃] NF *(Élec, instinct)* impulse; *(élan, influence)* impetus

impulsivement [ɛ̃pylsivmɑ̃] ADV impulsively

impulsivité [ɛ̃pylsivite] NF impulsiveness

impunément [ɛ̃pynemɑ̃] ADV with impunity

impuni, e [ɛ̃pyni] ADJ unpunished

impunité [ɛ̃pynite] NF impunity

impur, e [ɛ̃pyʀ] ADJ impure

impureté [ɛ̃pyʀte] NF impurity

imputable [ɛ̃pytabl] ADJ *(attribuable)*: **~ à** imputable to, ascribable to; *(Comm: somme)* **~ sur** chargeable to

imputation [ɛ̃pytasjɔ̃] NF imputation, charge

imputer [ɛ̃pyte] /1/ VT *(attribuer)*: **~ qch à** to ascribe *ou* impute sth to; *(Comm)* **~ qch à** *ou* **sur** to charge sth to

imputrescible [ɛ̃pytʀesibl] ADJ rotproof

in [in] ADJ INV in, trendy

INA [ina] SIGLE M *(= Institut national de l'audio-visuel)* library of television archives

inabordable [inabɔʀdabl] ADJ *(lieu)* inaccessible; *(cher)* prohibitive

inaccentué, e [inaksɑ̃tɥe] ADJ *(Ling)* unstressed

inacceptable [inaksɛptabl] ADJ unacceptable

inaccessible [inaksesibl] ADJ inaccessible; *(objectif)* unattainable; *(insensible)*: **~ à** impervious to

inaccoutumé, e [inakutyme] ADJ unaccustomed

inachevé, e [inaʃve] ADJ unfinished

inactif, -ive [inaktif, -iv] ADJ inactive, idle; *(remède)* ineffective; *(Bourse: marché)* slack

inaction [inaksjɔ̃] NF inactivity

inactivité [inaktivite] NF *(Admin)*: **en ~** out of active service

inadaptation [inadaptasjɔ̃] NF *(Psych)* maladjustment

inadapté, e [inadapte] ADJ *(Psych: adulte, enfant)* maladjusted ▶ NM/F *(péj: adulte: asocial)* misfit; **~ à** not adapted to, unsuited to

inadéquat, e [inadekwa, -wat] ADJ inadequate

inadéquation [inadekwasjɔ̃] NF inadequacy

inadmissible [inadmisibl] ADJ inadmissible

inadvertance [inadvɛʀtɑ̃s]: **par ~** *adv* inadvertently

inaliénable [inaljenabl] ADJ inalienable

inaltérable [inalteʀabl] ADJ *(matière)* stable; *(fig)* unchanging; **~ à** unaffected by; **couleur ~ (au lavage/à la lumière)** fast colour/fade-resistant colour

inamovible [inamɔvibl] ADJ fixed; *(Jur)* irremovable

inanimé, e [inanime] ADJ *(matière)* inanimate; *(évanoui)* unconscious; *(sans vie)* lifeless

inanité [inanite] NF futility

inanition [inanisjɔ̃] NF: **tomber d'~** to faint with hunger (and exhaustion)

inaperçu, e [inapɛʀsy] ADJ: **passer ~** to go unnoticed

inappétence [inapetɑ̃s] NF lack of appetite

inapplicable [inaplikabl] ADJ inapplicable

inapplication [inaplikasjɔ̃] NF lack of application

inappliqué, e [inaplike] ADJ lacking in application

inappréciable [inapʀesjabl] ADJ *(service)* invaluable; *(différence, nuance)* inappreciable

inapte [inapt] ADJ: **~ à** incapable of; *(Mil)* unfit for

inaptitude [inaptityd] NF inaptitude; unfitness

inarticulé, e [inaʀtikyle] ADJ inarticulate

inassimilable [inasimilabl] ADJ that cannot be assimilated

inassouvi, e [inasuvi] ADJ unsatisfied, unfulfilled

inattaquable [inatakabl] ADJ *(Mil)* unassailable; *(texte, preuve)* irrefutable

inattendu, e [inatɑ̃dy] ADJ unexpected ▶ NM: **l'~** the unexpected

inattentif, -ive [inatɑ̃tif, -iv] ADJ inattentive; **~ à** *(dangers, détails)* heedless of

inattention [inatɑ̃sjɔ̃] NF inattention; *(inadvertance)*: **une minute d'~** a minute of inattention, a minute's carelessness; **par ~** inadvertently; **faute d'~** careless mistake

inaudible [inodibl] ADJ inaudible
inaugural, e, -aux [inɔgyʀal, -o] ADJ (cérémonie) inaugural, opening; (vol, voyage) maiden
inauguration [inɔgyʀasjɔ̃] NF unveiling; opening; **discours/cérémonie d'~** inaugural speech/ceremony
inaugurer [inɔgyʀe] /1/ VT (monument) to unveil; (exposition, usine) to open; (fig) to inaugurate
inauthenticité [inɔtɑ̃tisite] NF inauthenticity
inavouable [inavwabl] ADJ (bénéfices) undisclosable; (honteux) shameful
inavoué, e [inavwe] ADJ unavowed
INC SIGLE M (= Institut national de la consommation) consumer research organization
inca [ɛ̃ka] ADJ Inca ▶ NMF: **I~** Inca
incalculable [ɛ̃kalkylabl] ADJ incalculable; **un nombre ~ de** countless numbers of
incandescence [ɛ̃kɑ̃desɑ̃s] NF incandescence; **en ~** incandescent, white-hot; **porter à ~** to heat white-hot; **lampe/manchon à ~** incandescent lamp/(gas) mantle
incandescent, e [ɛ̃kɑ̃desɑ̃, -ɑ̃t] ADJ incandescent, white-hot
incantation [ɛ̃kɑ̃tasjɔ̃] NF incantation
incantatoire [ɛ̃kɑ̃tatwaʀ] ADJ: **formule ~** incantation
incapable [ɛ̃kapabl] ADJ incapable; **~ de faire** incapable of doing; (empêché) unable to do
incapacitant, e [ɛ̃kapasitɑ̃, -ɑ̃t] ADJ (Mil) incapacitating
incapacité [ɛ̃kapasite] NF (incompétence) incapability; (Jur: impossibilité) incapacity; **être dans l'~ de faire** to be unable to do; **~ permanente/de travail** permanent/industrial disablement; **~ électorale** ineligibility to vote
incarcération [ɛ̃kaʀseʀasjɔ̃] NF incarceration
incarcérer [ɛ̃kaʀseʀe] /6/ VT to incarcerate, imprison
incarnat, e [ɛ̃kaʀna, -at] ADJ (rosy) pink
incarnation [ɛ̃kaʀnasjɔ̃] NF incarnation
incarné, e [ɛ̃kaʀne] ADJ incarnate; (ongle) ingrown
incarner [ɛ̃kaʀne] /1/ VT to embody, personify; (Théât) to play; (Rel) to incarnate; **s'incarner dans** VI (Rel) to be incarnate in
incartade [ɛ̃kaʀtad] NF prank, escapade
incassable [ɛ̃kasabl] ADJ unbreakable
incendiaire [ɛ̃sɑ̃djɛʀ] ADJ incendiary; (fig: discours) inflammatory ▶ NMF fire-raiser, arsonist
incendie [ɛ̃sɑ̃di] NM fire; **~ criminel** arson no pl; **~ de forêt** forest fire
incendier [ɛ̃sɑ̃dje] /7/ VT (mettre le feu à) to set fire to, set alight; (brûler complètement) to burn down
incertain, e [ɛ̃sɛʀtɛ̃, -ɛn] ADJ uncertain; (temps) uncertain, unsettled; (imprécis: contours) indistinct, blurred
incertitude [ɛ̃sɛʀtityd] NF uncertainty
incessamment [ɛ̃sesamɑ̃] ADV very shortly
incessant, e [ɛ̃sesɑ̃, -ɑ̃t] ADJ incessant, unceasing
incessible [ɛ̃sesibl] ADJ (Jur) non-transferable
inceste [ɛ̃sɛst] NM incest

incestueux, -euse [ɛ̃sɛstɥø, -øz] ADJ incestuous
inchangé, e [ɛ̃ʃɑ̃ʒe] ADJ unchanged, unaltered
inchantable [ɛ̃ʃɑ̃tabl] ADJ unsingable
inchauffable [ɛ̃ʃofabl] ADJ impossible to heat
incidemment [ɛ̃sidamɑ̃] ADV in passing
incidence [ɛ̃sidɑ̃s] NF (effet, influence) effect; (Physique) incidence
incident [ɛ̃sidɑ̃] NM incident; **~ de frontière** border incident; **~ de parcours** minor hitch ou setback; **~ technique** technical difficulties pl, technical hitch
incinérateur [ɛ̃sineʀatœʀ] NM incinerator
incinération [ɛ̃sineʀasjɔ̃] NF (d'ordures) incineration; (crémation) cremation
incinérer [ɛ̃sineʀe] /6/ VT (ordures) to incinerate; (mort) to cremate
incise [ɛ̃siz] NF (Ling) interpolated clause
inciser [ɛ̃size] /1/ VT to make an incision in; (abcès) to lance
incisif, -ive [ɛ̃sizif, -iv] ADJ incisive, cutting ▶ NF incisor
incision [ɛ̃sizjɔ̃] NF incision; (d'un abcès) lancing
incitation [ɛ̃sitasjɔ̃] NF (encouragement) incentive; (provocation) incitement
inciter [ɛ̃site] /1/ VT: **~ qn à (faire) qch** to prompt ou encourage sb to do sth; (à la révolte etc) to incite sb to do sth
incivil, e [ɛ̃sivil] ADJ uncivil
incivilité [ɛ̃sivilite] NF (grossièreté) incivility; **incivilités** NFPL antisocial behaviour sg
inclinable [ɛ̃klinabl] ADJ (dossier etc) tilting; **siège à dossier ~** reclining seat
inclinaison [ɛ̃klinɛzɔ̃] NF (déclivité: d'une route etc) incline; (d'un toit) slope; (état penché: d'un mur) lean; (: de la tête) tilt; (: d'un navire) list
inclination [ɛ̃klinasjɔ̃] NF (penchant) inclination, tendency; **montrer de l'~ pour les sciences** etc to show an inclination for the sciences etc; **inclinations égoïstes/altruistes** egoistic/altruistic tendencies; **~ de (la) tête** nod (of the head); **~ (de buste)** bow
incliner [ɛ̃kline] /1/ VT (bouteille) to tilt; (tête) to incline; (inciter): **~ qn à qch/à faire** to encourage sb towards sth/to do ▶ VI: **~ à qch/à faire** (tendre à, pencher pour) to incline towards sth/doing, tend towards sth/to do; **s'incliner** VI (route) to slope; (toit) to be sloping; **s'incliner (devant)** to bow (before)
inclure [ɛ̃klyʀ] /35/ VT to include; (joindre à un envoi) to enclose; **jusqu'au 10 mars inclus** until 10th March inclusive
inclus, e [ɛ̃kly, -yz] PP de **inclure** ▶ ADJ included; (joint à un envoi) enclosed; (compris: frais, dépense) included; (Math: ensemble): **~ dans** included in; **jusqu'au troisième chapitre ~** up to and including the third chapter; **jusqu'au 10 mars ~** until 10th March inclusive
inclusion [ɛ̃klyzjɔ̃] NF (voir inclure) inclusion; enclosing
inclusivement [ɛ̃klyzivmɑ̃] ADV inclusively
inclut [ɛ̃kly] VB voir **inclure**
incoercible [ɛ̃kɔɛʀsibl] ADJ uncontrollable
incognito [ɛ̃kɔɲito] ADV incognito ▶ NM: **garder l'~** to remain incognito

incohérence [ɛ̃kɔeʀɑ̃s] NF inconsistency; incoherence

incohérent, e [ɛ̃kɔeʀɑ̃, -ɑ̃t] ADJ (comportement) inconsistent; (geste, langage, texte) incoherent

incollable [ɛ̃kɔlabl] ADJ (riz) that does not stick; (fam: personne): **il est ~** he's got all the answers

incolore [ɛ̃kɔlɔʀ] ADJ colourless

incomber [ɛ̃kɔ̃be] /1/: **~ à** vt (devoirs, responsabilité) to rest ou be incumbent upon; (: frais, travail) to be the responsibility of

incombustible [ɛ̃kɔ̃bystibl] ADJ incombustible

incommensurable [ɛ̃kɔmɑ̃syʀabl] ADJ immeasurable

incommodant, e [ɛ̃kɔmɔdɑ̃, -ɑ̃t] ADJ (bruit) annoying; (chaleur) uncomfortable

incommode [ɛ̃kɔmɔd] ADJ inconvenient; (posture, siège) uncomfortable

incommodément [ɛ̃kɔmɔdemɑ̃] ADV (installé, assis) uncomfortably; (logé, situé) inconveniently

incommoder [ɛ̃kɔmɔde] /1/ VT: **~ qn** (chaleur, odeur) to bother ou inconvenience sb; (embarrasser) to make sb feel uncomfortable ou ill at ease

incommodité [ɛ̃kɔmɔdite] NF inconvenience

incommunicable [ɛ̃kɔmynikabl] ADJ (Jur: droits, privilèges) non-transferable; (: pensée) incommunicable

incomparable [ɛ̃kɔ̃paʀabl] ADJ not comparable; (inégalable) incomparable, matchless

incomparablement [ɛ̃kɔ̃paʀabləmɑ̃] ADV incomparably

incompatibilité [ɛ̃kɔ̃patibilite] NF incompatibility; **~ d'humeur** (mutual) incompatibility

incompatible [ɛ̃kɔ̃patibl] ADJ incompatible

incompétence [ɛ̃kɔ̃petɑ̃s] NF lack of expertise; incompetence

incompétent, e [ɛ̃kɔ̃petɑ̃, -ɑ̃t] ADJ (ignorant) inexpert; (incapable) incompetent, not competent

incomplet, -ète [ɛ̃kɔ̃plɛ, -ɛt] ADJ incomplete

incomplètement [ɛ̃kɔ̃plɛtmɑ̃] ADV not completely, incompletely

incompréhensible [ɛ̃kɔ̃pʀeɑ̃sibl] ADJ incomprehensible

incompréhensif, -ive [ɛ̃kɔ̃pʀeɑ̃sif, -iv] ADJ lacking in understanding, unsympathetic

incompréhension [ɛ̃kɔ̃pʀeɑ̃sjɔ̃] NF lack of understanding

incompressible [ɛ̃kɔ̃pʀesibl] ADJ (Physique) incompressible; (fig: dépenses) that cannot be reduced; (Jur: peine) irreducible

incompris, e [ɛ̃kɔ̃pʀi, -iz] ADJ misunderstood

inconcevable [ɛ̃kɔ̃svabl] ADJ (conduite etc) inconceivable; (mystère) incredible

inconciliable [ɛ̃kɔ̃siljabl] ADJ irreconcilable

inconditionnel, le [ɛ̃kɔ̃disjɔnɛl] ADJ unconditional; (partisan) unquestioning ▶ NM/F (partisan) unquestioning supporter

inconditionnellement [ɛ̃kɔ̃disjɔnɛlmɑ̃] ADV unconditionally

inconduite [ɛ̃kɔ̃dɥit] NF bad ou unsuitable behaviour no pl

inconfort [ɛ̃kɔ̃fɔʀ] NM lack of comfort, discomfort

inconfortable [ɛ̃kɔ̃fɔʀtabl] ADJ uncomfortable

inconfortablement [ɛ̃kɔ̃fɔʀtabləmɑ̃] ADV uncomfortably

incongru, e [ɛ̃kɔ̃gʀy] ADJ unseemly; (remarque) ill-chosen, incongruous

incongruité [ɛ̃kɔ̃gʀyite] NF unseemliness; incongruity; (parole incongrue) ill-chosen remark

inconnu, e [ɛ̃kɔny] ADJ unknown; (sentiment, plaisir) new, strange ▶ NM/F stranger; unknown person (ou artist etc) ▶ NM: **l'~** the unknown ▶ NF (Math) unknown; (fig) unknown factor

inconsciemment [ɛ̃kɔ̃sjamɑ̃] ADV unconsciously

inconscience [ɛ̃kɔ̃sjɑ̃s] NF unconsciousness; recklessness

inconscient, e [ɛ̃kɔ̃sjɑ̃, -ɑ̃t] ADJ unconscious; (irréfléchi) thoughtless, reckless; (sentiment) subconscious ▶ NM (Psych): **l'~** the subconscious, the unconscious; **~ de** unaware of

inconséquence [ɛ̃kɔ̃sekɑ̃s] NF inconsistency; thoughtlessness; (action, parole) thoughtless thing to do (ou say)

inconséquent, e [ɛ̃kɔ̃sekɑ̃, -ɑ̃t] ADJ (illogique) inconsistent; (irréfléchi) thoughtless

inconsidéré, e [ɛ̃kɔ̃sidere] ADJ ill-considered

inconsidérément [ɛ̃kɔ̃sideremɑ̃] ADV thoughtlessly

inconsistant, e [ɛ̃kɔ̃sistɑ̃, -ɑ̃t] ADJ flimsy, weak; (crème etc) runny

inconsolable [ɛ̃kɔ̃sɔlabl] ADJ inconsolable

inconstance [ɛ̃kɔ̃stɑ̃s] NF inconstancy, fickleness

inconstant, e [ɛ̃kɔ̃stɑ̃, -ɑ̃t] ADJ inconstant, fickle

inconstitutionnel, le [ɛ̃kɔ̃stitysjɔnɛl] ADJ unconstitutional

incontestable [ɛ̃kɔ̃tɛstabl] ADJ unquestionable, indisputable

incontestablement [ɛ̃kɔ̃tɛstabləmɑ̃] ADV unquestionably, indisputably

incontesté, e [ɛ̃kɔ̃tɛste] ADJ undisputed

incontinence [ɛ̃kɔ̃tinɑ̃s] NF (Méd) incontinence

incontinent, e [ɛ̃kɔ̃tinɑ̃, -ɑ̃t] ADJ (Méd) incontinent ▶ ADV (tout de suite) forthwith

incontournable [ɛ̃kɔ̃tuʀnabl] ADJ unavoidable

incontrôlable [ɛ̃kɔ̃tʀolabl] ADJ unverifiable; (irrépressible) uncontrollable

incontrôlé, e [ɛ̃kɔ̃tʀole] ADJ uncontrolled

inconvenance [ɛ̃kɔ̃vnɑ̃s] NF (parole, action) impropriety

inconvenant, e [ɛ̃kɔ̃vnɑ̃, -ɑ̃t] ADJ unseemly, improper

inconvénient [ɛ̃kɔ̃venjɑ̃] NM (d'une situation, d'un projet) disadvantage, drawback; (d'un remède, changement etc) risk, inconvenience; **si vous n'y voyez pas d'~** if you have no objections; **y a-t-il un ~ à ...?** (risque) is there a risk in ...?; (objection) is there any objection to ...?

inconvertible [ɛ̃kɔ̃vɛʀtibl] ADJ inconvertible

incorporation [ɛ̃kɔʀpɔʀasjɔ̃] NF (Mil) call-up

incorporé, e [ɛ̃kɔʀpɔʀe] ADJ (micro etc) built-in

incorporel, le [ɛ̃kɔʀpɔʀɛl] ADJ (Jur): **biens incorporels** intangible property

217

incorporer [ɛ̃kɔʀpɔʀe] /**1**/ vt: ~ **(à)** to mix in (with); ~ **(dans)** (*paragraphe etc*) to incorporate (in); (*territoire, immigrants*) to incorporate (into); (*Mil: appeler*) to recruit (into), call up; (: *affecter*): ~ **qn dans** to enlist sb into; **s'incorporer** vi: **il a très bien su s'incorporer à notre groupe** he was very easily incorporated into our group

incorrect, e [ɛ̃kɔʀɛkt] ADJ (*impropre, inconvenant*) improper; (*défectueux*) faulty; (*inexact*) incorrect; (*impoli*) impolite; (*déloyal*) underhand

incorrectement [ɛ̃kɔʀɛktəmɑ̃] ADV improperly; faultily; incorrectly; impolitely; in an underhand way

incorrection [ɛ̃kɔʀɛksjɔ̃] NF impropriety; incorrectness; underhand nature; (*terme impropre*) impropriety; (*action, remarque*) improper behaviour (*ou* remark)

incorrigible [ɛ̃kɔʀiʒibl] ADJ incorrigible

incorruptible [ɛ̃kɔʀyptibl] ADJ incorruptible

incrédibilité [ɛ̃kʀedibilite] NF incredibility

incrédule [ɛ̃kʀedyl] ADJ incredulous; (*Rel*) unbelieving

incrédulité [ɛ̃kʀedylite] NF incredulity; **avec ~** incredulously

increvable [ɛ̃kʀəvabl] ADJ (*pneu*) puncture-proof; (*fam*) tireless

incriminer [ɛ̃kʀimine] /**1**/ vt (*personne*) to incriminate; (*action, conduite*) to bring under attack; (*bonne foi, honnêteté*) to call into question; **livre/article incriminé** offending book/article

incrochetable [ɛ̃kʀɔʃtabl] ADJ (*serrure*) that can't be picked, burglarproof

incroyable [ɛ̃kʀwajabl] ADJ incredible, unbelievable

incroyablement [ɛ̃kʀwajabləmɑ̃] ADV incredibly, unbelievably

incroyant, e [ɛ̃kʀwajɑ̃, -ɑ̃t] NM/F non-believer

incrustation [ɛ̃kʀystasjɔ̃] NF inlaying *no pl*; inlay; (*dans une chaudière etc*) fur *no pl*, scale *no pl*

incruster [ɛ̃kʀyste] /**1**/ vt (*radiateur etc*) to coat with scale *ou* fur; **s'incruster** vi (*invité*) to take root; (*radiateur etc*) to become coated with scale *ou* fur; ~ **qch dans/qch de** (*Art*) to inlay sth into/sth with; **s'incruster dans** (*corps étranger, caillou*) to become embedded in

incubateur [ɛ̃kybatœʀ] NM incubator

incubation [ɛ̃kybasjɔ̃] NF incubation

inculpation [ɛ̃kylpasjɔ̃] NF charging *no pl*; charge; **sous l'~ de** on a charge of

inculpé, e [ɛ̃kylpe] NM/F accused

inculper [ɛ̃kylpe] /**1**/ vt: ~ **(de)** to charge (with)

inculquer [ɛ̃kylke] /**1**/ vt: ~ **qch à** to inculcate sth in, instil sth into

inculte [ɛ̃kylt] ADJ uncultivated; (*esprit, peuple*) uncultured; (*barbe*) unkempt

incultivable [ɛ̃kyltivabl] ADJ (*terrain*) unworkable

inculture [ɛ̃kyltyʀ] NF lack of education

incurable [ɛ̃kyʀabl] ADJ incurable

incurie [ɛ̃kyʀi] NF carelessness

incursion [ɛ̃kyʀsjɔ̃] NF incursion, foray

incurvé, e [ɛ̃kyʀve] ADJ curved

incurver [ɛ̃kyʀve] /**1**/ vt (*barre de fer*) to bend into a curve; **s'incurver** vi (*planche, route*) to bend

Inde [ɛ̃d] NF: **l'~** India

indécemment [ɛ̃desamɑ̃] ADV indecently

indécence [ɛ̃desɑ̃s] NF indecency; (*propos, acte*) indecent remark (*ou* act *etc*)

indécent, e [ɛ̃desɑ̃, -ɑ̃t] ADJ indecent

indéchiffrable [ɛ̃deʃifʀabl] ADJ indecipherable

indéchirable [ɛ̃deʃiʀabl] ADJ tear-proof

indécis, e [ɛ̃desi, -iz] ADJ (*par nature*) indecisive; (*perplexe*) undecided

indécision [ɛ̃desizjɔ̃] NF indecision, indecisiveness

indéclinable [ɛ̃deklinabl] ADJ (*Ling: mot*) indeclinable

indécomposable [ɛ̃dekɔ̃pozabl] ADJ that cannot be broken down

indécrottable [ɛ̃dekʀɔtabl] ADJ (*fam*) hopeless

indéfectible [ɛ̃defɛktibl] ADJ (*attachement*) indestructible

indéfendable [ɛ̃defɑ̃dabl] ADJ indefensible

indéfini, e [ɛ̃defini] ADJ (*imprécis, incertain*) undefined; (*illimité, Ling*) indefinite

indéfiniment [ɛ̃definimɑ̃] ADV indefinitely

indéfinissable [ɛ̃definisabl] ADJ indefinable

indéformable [ɛ̃defɔʀmabl] ADJ that keeps its shape

indélébile [ɛ̃delebil] ADJ indelible

indélicat, e [ɛ̃delika, -at] ADJ tactless; (*malhonnête*) dishonest

indélicatesse [ɛ̃delikatɛs] NF tactlessness; dishonesty

indémaillable [ɛ̃demajabl] ADJ run-resist

indemne [ɛ̃dɛmn] ADJ unharmed

indemnisable [ɛ̃dɛmnizabl] ADJ entitled to compensation

indemnisation [ɛ̃dɛmnizasjɔ̃] NF (*somme*) indemnity, compensation

indemniser [ɛ̃dɛmnize] /**1**/ vt: ~ **qn (de)** to compensate sb (for); **se faire ~** to get compensation

indemnité [ɛ̃dɛmnite] NF (*dédommagement*) compensation *no pl*; (*allocation*) allowance; ~ **de licenciement** redundancy payment; ~ **de logement** housing allowance; ~ **parlementaire** ≈ MP's (BRIT) *ou* Congressman's (US) salary

indémontable [ɛ̃demɔ̃tabl] ADJ (*meuble etc*) that cannot be dismantled, in one piece

indéniable [ɛ̃denjabl] ADJ undeniable, indisputable

indéniablement [ɛ̃denjabləmɑ̃] ADV undeniably

indépendamment [ɛ̃depɑ̃damɑ̃] ADV independently; ~ **de** independently of; (*abstraction faite de*) irrespective of; (*en plus de*) over and above

indépendance [ɛ̃depɑ̃dɑ̃s] NF independence; ~ **matérielle** financial independence

indépendant, e [ɛ̃depɑ̃dɑ̃, -ɑ̃t] ADJ independent; ~ **de** independent of; **chambre ~** room with private entrance; **travailleur ~** self-employed worker

indépendantiste [ɛ̃depɑ̃dɑ̃tist] ADJ, NMF separatist

indéracinable [ɛ̃deʀasinabl] ADJ (*fig: croyance etc*) ineradicable

indéréglable [ɛ̃deʀeglabl] ADJ which will not break down

indescriptible [ɛ̃dɛskʀiptibl] ADJ indescribable

indésirable [ɛ̃dezirabl] ADJ undesirable

indestructible [ɛ̃dɛstʀyktibl] ADJ indestructible; (marque, impression) indelible

indéterminable [ɛ̃detɛʀminabl] ADJ indeterminable

indétermination [ɛ̃detɛʀminasjɔ̃] NF indecision, indecisiveness

indéterminé, e [ɛ̃detɛʀmine] ADJ (date, cause, nature) unspecified; (forme, longueur, quantité) indeterminate; indeterminable

index [ɛ̃dɛks] NM (doigt) index finger; (d'un livre etc) index; **mettre à l'~** to blacklist

indexation [ɛ̃dɛksasjɔ̃] NF indexing

indexé, e [ɛ̃dɛkse] ADJ (Écon): **~ (sur)** index-linked (to)

indexer [ɛ̃dɛkse] /1/ VT (salaire, emprunt): **~ (sur)** to index (on)

indicateur, -trice [ɛ̃dikatœʀ, -tʀis] NM (Police) informer; (livre) guide; (: liste) directory; (Tech) gauge; indicator; (Écon) indicator ▶ADJ: **poteau ~** signpost; **tableau ~** indicator (board); **~ des chemins de fer** railway timetable; **~ de direction** (Auto) indicator; **~ immobilier** property gazette; **~ de niveau** level, gauge; **~ de pression** pressure gauge; **~ de rues** street directory; **~ de vitesse** speedometer

indicatif, -ive [ɛ̃dikatif, -iv] ADJ: **à titre ~** for (your) information ▶ NM (Ling) indicative; (d'une émission) theme ou signature tune; (Tél) dialling code (BRIT), area code (US); **~ d'appel** (Radio) call sign; **quel est l'~ de …** what's the code for …?

indication [ɛ̃dikasjɔ̃] NF indication; (renseignement) information no pl; **indications** NFPL (directives) instructions; **~ d'origine** (Comm) place of origin

indice [ɛ̃dis] NM (marque, signe) indication, sign; (Police: lors d'une enquête) clue; (Jur: présomption) piece of evidence; (Science, Écon, Tech) index; (Admin) grading; rating; **~ du coût de la vie** cost-of-living index; **~ inférieur** subscript; **~ d'octane** octane rating; **~ des prix** price index; **~ de traitement** salary grading; **~ de protection** (sun protection) factor

indicible [ɛ̃disibl] ADJ inexpressible

indien, ne [ɛ̃djɛ̃, -ɛn] ADJ Indian ▶ NM/F: **I~, ne** (d'Amérique) Native American; (d'Inde) Indian

indifféremment [ɛ̃difeʀamɑ̃] ADV (sans distinction) equally; indiscriminately

indifférence [ɛ̃difeʀɑ̃s] NF indifference

indifférencié, e [ɛ̃difeʀɑ̃sje] ADJ undifferentiated

indifférent, e [ɛ̃difeʀɑ̃, -ɑ̃t] ADJ (peu intéressé) indifferent; **~ à** (insensible à) indifferent to, unconcerned about; (peu intéressant pour) indifferent to; immaterial to; **ça m'est ~ (que …)** it doesn't matter to me (whether …); **elle m'est ~** I am indifferent to her

indifférer [ɛ̃difeʀe] /6/ VT: **cela m'indiffère** I'm indifferent about it

indigence [ɛ̃diʒɑ̃s] NF poverty; **être dans l'~** to be destitute

indigène [ɛ̃diʒɛn] ADJ native, indigenous; (de la région) local ▶ NMF native

indigent, e [ɛ̃diʒɑ̃, -ɑ̃t] ADJ destitute, poverty-stricken; (fig) poor

indigeste [ɛ̃diʒɛst] ADJ indigestible

indigestion [ɛ̃diʒɛstjɔ̃] NF indigestion no pl; **avoir une ~** to have indigestion

indignation [ɛ̃diɲasjɔ̃] NF indignation; **avec ~** indignantly

indigne [ɛ̃diɲ] ADJ: **~ (de)** unworthy (of)

indigné, e [ɛ̃diɲe] ADJ indignant

indignement [ɛ̃diɲmɑ̃] ADV shamefully

indigner [ɛ̃diɲe] /1/ VT to make indignant; **s'indigner (de/contre)** VI to be (ou become) indignant (at)

indignité [ɛ̃diɲite] NF unworthiness no pl; (acte) shameful act

indigo [ɛ̃digo] NM indigo

indiqué, e [ɛ̃dike] ADJ (date, lieu) given, appointed; (adéquat) appropriate, suitable; (conseillé) advisable; (remède, traitement) appropriate

indiquer [ɛ̃dike] /1/ VT: **~ qch/qn à qn** (désigner) to point sth/sb out to sb; (faire connaître: médecin, lieu, restaurant) to tell sb of sth/sb; (pendule, aiguille) to show; (étiquette, plan) to show, indicate; (renseigner sur) to point out, tell; (déterminer: date, lieu) to give, state; (dénoter) to indicate, point to; **~ du doigt** to point out; **~ de la main** to indicate with one's hand; **~ du regard** to glance towards ou in the direction of; **pourriez-vous m'~ les toilettes/l'heure?** could you direct me to the toilets/tell me the time?

indirect, e [ɛ̃diʀɛkt] ADJ indirect

indirectement [ɛ̃diʀɛktəmɑ̃] ADV indirectly; (apprendre) in a roundabout way

indiscernable [ɛ̃disɛʀnabl] ADJ undiscernable

indiscipline [ɛ̃disiplin] NF lack of discipline

indiscipliné, e [ɛ̃disipline] ADJ undisciplined; (fig) unmanageable

indiscret, -ète [ɛ̃diskʀɛ, -ɛt] ADJ indiscreet

indiscrétion [ɛ̃diskʀesjɔ̃] NF indiscretion; **sans ~, …** without wishing to be indiscreet, …

indiscutable [ɛ̃diskytabl] ADJ indisputable

indiscutablement [ɛ̃diskytabləmɑ̃] ADV indisputably

indiscuté, e [ɛ̃diskyte] ADJ (incontesté: droit, chef) undisputed

indispensable [ɛ̃dispɑ̃sabl] ADJ indispensable, essential; **~ à qn/pour faire qch** essential for sb/to do sth

indisponibilité [ɛ̃disponibilite] NF unavailability

indisponible [ɛ̃disponibl] ADJ unavailable

indisposé, e [ɛ̃dispoze] ADJ indisposed, unwell

indisposer [ɛ̃dispoze] /1/ VT (incommoder) to upset; (déplaire à) to antagonize

indisposition [ɛ̃dispozisjɔ̃] NF (slight) illness, indisposition

indissociable [ɛ̃disɔsjabl] ADJ indissociable

indissoluble [ɛ̃disɔlybl] ADJ indissoluble

i

indissolublement [ɛ̃disɔlybləmɑ̃] ADV indissolubly

indistinct, e [ɛ̃distɛ̃, -ɛ̃kt] ADJ indistinct

indistinctement [ɛ̃distɛ̃ktəmɑ̃] ADV (*voir, prononcer*) indistinctly; (*sans distinction*) without distinction, indiscriminately

individu [ɛ̃dividy] NM individual

individualiser [ɛ̃dividɥalize] /1/ VT to individualize; (*personnaliser*) to tailor to individual requirements; **s'individualiser** VI to develop one's own identity

individualisme [ɛ̃dividɥalism] NM individualism

individualiste [ɛ̃dividɥalist] NMF individualist

individualité [ɛ̃dividɥalite] NF individuality

individuel, le [ɛ̃dividɥɛl] ADJ (*gén*) individual; (*opinion, livret, contrôle, avantages*) personal; **chambre ~** single room; **maison ~** detached house; **propriété ~** personal *ou* private property

individuellement [ɛ̃dividɥɛlmɑ̃] ADV individually

indivis, e [ɛ̃divi, -iz] ADJ (*Jur: bien, succession*) indivisible; (*: cohéritiers, propriétaires*) joint

indivisible [ɛ̃divizibl] ADJ indivisible

Indochine [ɛ̃dɔʃin] NF: **l'~** Indochina

indochinois, e [ɛ̃dɔʃinwa, -waz] ADJ Indochinese

indocile [ɛ̃dɔsil] ADJ unruly

indo-européen, ne [ɛ̃dɔœʀɔpeɛ̃, -ɛn] ADJ Indo-European ▶ NM (*Ling*) Indo-European

indolence [ɛ̃dɔlɑ̃s] NF indolence

indolent, e [ɛ̃dɔlɑ̃, -ɑ̃t] ADJ indolent

indolore [ɛ̃dɔlɔʀ] ADJ painless

indomptable [ɛ̃dɔ̃tabl] ADJ untameable; (*fig*) invincible, indomitable

indompté, e [ɛ̃dɔ̃te] ADJ (*cheval*) unbroken

Indonésie [ɛ̃dɔnezi] NF: **l'~** Indonesia

indonésien, ne [ɛ̃dɔnezjɛ̃, -ɛn] ADJ Indonesian ▶ NM/F: **I~, ne** Indonesian

indu, e [ɛ̃dy] ADJ: **à une heure ~** at some ungodly hour

indubitable [ɛ̃dybitabl] ADJ indubitable

indubitablement [ɛ̃dybitabləmɑ̃] ADV indubitably

induction [ɛ̃dyksjɔ̃] NF induction

induire [ɛ̃dɥiʀ] /38/ VT: **~ qch de** to induce sth from; **~ qn en erreur** to lead sb astray, mislead sb

indulgence [ɛ̃dylʒɑ̃s] NF indulgence; leniency; **avec ~** indulgently; leniently

indulgent, e [ɛ̃dylʒɑ̃, -ɑ̃t] ADJ (*parent, regard*) indulgent; (*juge, examinateur*) lenient

indûment [ɛ̃dymɑ̃] ADV without due cause; (*illégitimement*) wrongfully

industrialisation [ɛ̃dystʀijalizasjɔ̃] NF industrialization

industrialisé, e [ɛ̃dystʀijalize] ADJ industrialized

industrialiser [ɛ̃dystʀijalize] /1/ VT to industrialize; **s'industrialiser** VI to become industrialized

industrie [ɛ̃dystʀi] NF industry; **~ automobile/textile** car/textile industry; **~ du spectacle** entertainment business

industriel, le [ɛ̃dystʀijɛl] ADJ industrial; (*produit industriellement: pain etc*) mass-produced, factory-produced ▶ NM industrialist; (*fabricant*) manufacturer

industriellement [ɛ̃dystʀijɛlmɑ̃] ADV industrially

industrieux, -euse [ɛ̃dystʀijø, -øz] ADJ industrious

inébranlable [inebʀɑ̃labl] ADJ (*masse, colonne*) solid; (*personne, certitude, foi*) steadfast, unwavering

inédit, e [inedi, -it] ADJ (*correspondance etc*) (hitherto) unpublished; (*spectacle, moyen*) novel, original; (*film*) unreleased

ineffable [inefabl] ADJ inexpressible, ineffable

ineffaçable [inefasabl] ADJ indelible

inefficace [inefikas] ADJ (*remède, moyen*) ineffective; (*machine, employé*) inefficient

inefficacité [inefikasite] NF ineffectiveness; inefficiency

inégal, e, -aux [inegal, -o] ADJ unequal; (*irrégulier*) uneven

inégalable [inegalabl(e)] ADJ matchless

inégalé, e [inegale] ADJ (*record*) unmatched, unequalled; (*beauté*) unrivalled

inégalement [inegalmɑ̃] ADV unequally

inégalité [inegalite] NF inequality; unevenness *no pl*; **~ de deux hauteurs** difference *ou* disparity between two heights; **inégalités de terrain** uneven ground

inélégance [inelegɑ̃s] NF inelegance

inélégant, e [inelegɑ̃, -ɑ̃t] ADJ inelegant; (*indélicat*) discourteous

inéligible [ineliʒibl] ADJ ineligible

inéluctable [inelyktabl] ADJ inescapable

inéluctablement [inelyktabləmɑ̃] ADV inescapably

inemployable [inɑ̃plwajabl] ADJ unusable

inemployé, e [inɑ̃plwaje] ADJ unused

inénarrable [inenaʀabl] ADJ hilarious

inepte [inɛpt] ADJ inept

ineptie [inɛpsi] NF ineptitude; (*propos*) nonsense *no pl*

inépuisable [inepɥizabl] ADJ inexhaustible

inéquitable [inekitabl] ADJ inequitable

inerte [inɛʀt] ADJ (*immobile*) lifeless; (*apathique*) passive, inert; (*Physique, Chimie*) inert

inertie [inɛʀsi] NF inertia

inescompté, e [inɛskɔ̃te] ADJ unexpected, unhoped-for

inespéré, e [inɛspeʀe] ADJ unhoped-for, unexpected

inesthétique [inɛstetik] ADJ unsightly

inestimable [inɛstimabl] ADJ priceless; (*fig: bienfait*) invaluable

inévitable [inevitabl] ADJ unavoidable; (*fatal, habituel*) inevitable

inévitablement [inevitabləmɑ̃] ADV inevitably

inexact, e [inɛgzakt] ADJ inaccurate, inexact; (*non ponctuel*) unpunctual

inexactement [inɛgzaktəmɑ̃] ADV inaccurately

inexactitude [inɛgzaktityd] NF inaccuracy

inexcusable [inɛkskyzabl] ADJ inexcusable, unforgivable

inexécutable [inɛgzekytabl] ADJ impracticable, unworkable; (Mus) unplayable

inexistant, e [inɛgzistɑ̃, -ɑ̃t] ADJ non-existent

inexorable [inɛgzɔRabl] ADJ inexorable; (personne: dur): ~ (**à**) unmoved (by)

inexorablement [inɛgzɔRabləmɑ̃] ADV inexorably

inexpérience [inɛkspeRjɑ̃s] NF inexperience, lack of experience

inexpérimenté, e [inɛkspeRimɑ̃te] ADJ inexperienced; (arme, procédé) untested

inexplicable [inɛksplikabl] ADJ inexplicable

inexplicablement [inɛksplikabləmɑ̃] ADV inexplicably

inexpliqué, e [inɛksplike] ADJ unexplained

inexploitable [inɛksplwatabl] ADJ (gisement, richesse) unexploitable; (données, renseignements) unusable

inexploité, e [inɛksplwate] ADJ unexploited, untapped

inexploré, e [inɛksplɔRe] ADJ unexplored

inexpressif, -ive [inɛksprɛsif, -iv] ADJ inexpressive; (regard etc) expressionless

inexpressivité [inɛkspRɛsivite] NF expressionlessness

inexprimable [inɛkspRimabl] ADJ inexpressible

inexprimé, e [inɛkspRime] ADJ unspoken, unexpressed

inexpugnable [inɛkspygnabl] ADJ impregnable

inextensible [inɛkstɑ̃sibl] ADJ (tissu) non-stretch

in extenso [inɛkstɛ̃so] ADV in full

inextinguible [inɛkstɛ̃gibl] ADJ (soif) unquenchable; (rire) uncontrollable

in extremis [inɛkstRemis] ADV at the last minute ▶ ADJ INV last-minute; (testament) death bed cpd

inextricable [inɛkstRikabl] ADJ inextricable

inextricablement [inɛkstRikabləmɑ̃] ADV inextricably

infaillibilité [ɛ̃fajibilite] NF infallibility

infaillible [ɛ̃fajibl] ADJ infallible; (instinct) infallible, unerring

infailliblement [ɛ̃fajibləmɑ̃] ADV (certainement) without fail

infaisable [ɛ̃fəzabl] ADJ (travail etc) impossible, impractical

infamant, e [ɛ̃famɑ̃, -ɑ̃t] ADJ libellous, defamatory

infâme [ɛ̃fɑm] ADJ vile

infamie [ɛ̃fami] NF infamy

infanterie [ɛ̃fɑ̃tRi] NF infantry

infanticide [ɛ̃fɑ̃tisid] NMF child-murderer, murderess ▶ NM (meurtre) infanticide

infantile [ɛ̃fɑ̃til] ADJ (Méd) infantile, child cpd; (péj: ton, réaction) infantile, childish

infantilisme [ɛ̃fɑ̃tilism] NM infantilism

infarctus [ɛ̃faRktys] NM: ~ (**du myocarde**) coronary (thrombosis)

infatigable [ɛ̃fatigabl] ADJ tireless, indefatigable

infatigablement [ɛ̃fatigabləmɑ̃] ADV tirelessly, indefatigably

infatué, e [ɛ̃fatɥe] ADJ conceited; ~ **de** full of

infécond, e [ɛ̃fekɔ̃, -ɔ̃d] ADJ infertile, barren

infect, e [ɛ̃fɛkt] ADJ revolting; (repas, vin) revolting, foul; (personne) obnoxious; (temps) foul

infecter [ɛ̃fɛkte] /1/ VT (atmosphère, eau) to contaminate; (Méd) to infect; **s'infecter** VI to become infected ou septic

infectieux, -euse [ɛ̃fɛksjø, -øz] ADJ infectious

infection [ɛ̃fɛksjɔ̃] NF infection; (puanteur) stench

inféoder [ɛ̃feɔde] /1/: **s'inféoder à** VT to pledge allegiance to

inférer [ɛ̃feRe] /6/ VT: ~ **qch de** to infer sth from

inférieur, e [ɛ̃feRjœR] ADJ lower; (en qualité, intelligence) inferior ▶ NM/F inferior; ~ **à** (somme, quantité) less ou smaller than; (moins bon que) inferior to; (tâche: pas à la hauteur de) unequal to

infériorité [ɛ̃feRjɔRite] NF inferiority; ~ **en nombre** inferiority in numbers

infernal, e, -aux [ɛ̃fɛRnal, -o] ADJ (insupportable: chaleur, rythme) infernal; (: enfant) horrid; (méchanceté, complot) diabolical

infester [ɛ̃fɛste] /1/ VT to infest; **infesté de moustiques** infested with mosquitoes, mosquito-ridden

infidèle [ɛ̃fidɛl] ADJ unfaithful; (Rel) infidel

infidélité [ɛ̃fidelite] NF unfaithfulness no pl

infiltration [ɛ̃filtRasjɔ̃] NF infiltration

infiltrer [ɛ̃filtRe] /1/: **s'infiltrer** VI: **s'infiltrer dans** to penetrate into; (liquide) to seep into; (fig: noyauter) to infiltrate

infime [ɛ̃fim] ADJ minute, tiny; (inférieur) lowly

infini, e [ɛ̃fini] ADJ infinite ▶ NM infinity; **à l'~** (Math) to infinity; (discourir) ad infinitum, endlessly; (agrandir, varier) infinitely; (à perte de vue) endlessly (into the distance)

infiniment [ɛ̃finimɑ̃] ADV infinitely; ~ **grand/ petit** (Math) infinitely great/infinitesimal

infinité [ɛ̃finite] NF: **une ~ de** an infinite number of

infinitésimal, e, -aux [ɛ̃finitezimal, -o] ADJ infinitesimal

infinitif, -ive [ɛ̃finitif, -iv] ADJ, NM infinitive

infirme [ɛ̃fiRm] ADJ disabled ▶ NMF person with a disability; ~ **de guerre** person disabled in the war; ~ **du travail** industrially disabled person

infirmer [ɛ̃fiRme] /1/ VT to invalidate

infirmerie [ɛ̃fiRməRi] NF sick bay

infirmier, -ière [ɛ̃fiRmje, -jɛR] NM/F nurse ▶ ADJ: **élève** ~ student nurse; **infirmière chef** sister; **infirmière diplômée** registered nurse; **infirmière visiteuse** visiting nurse, ≈ district nurse (BRIT)

infirmité [ɛ̃fiRmite] NF disability

inflammable [ɛ̃flamabl] ADJ (in)flammable

inflammation [ɛ̃flamasjɔ̃] NF inflammation

inflammatoire [ɛ̃flamatwaR] ADJ (Méd) inflammatory

inflation [ɛ̃flasjɔ̃] NF inflation; ~ **rampante/ galopante** creeping/galloping inflation

inflationniste [ɛ̃flasjɔnist] ADJ inflationist

infléchir [ɛ̃fleʃiR] /2/ VT (fig: politique) to reorientate, redirect; **s'infléchir** VI (poutre, tringle) to bend, sag

i

221

inflexibilité [ɛ̃flɛksibilite] NF inflexibility
inflexible [ɛ̃flɛksibl] ADJ inflexible
inflexion [ɛ̃flɛksjɔ̃] NF inflexion; **~ de la tête** slight nod (of the head)
infliger [ɛ̃fliʒe] /3/ VT: **~ qch (à qn)** to inflict sth (on sb); (amende, sanction) to impose sth (on sb)
influençable [ɛ̃flyɑ̃sabl] ADJ easily influenced
influence [ɛ̃flyɑ̃s] NF influence; (d'un médicament) effect
influencer [ɛ̃flyɑ̃se] /3/ VT to influence
influent, e [ɛ̃flyɑ̃, -ɑ̃t] ADJ influential
influer [ɛ̃flye] /1/: **~ sur** vt to have an influence upon
influx [ɛ̃fly] NM: **~ nerveux** (nervous) impulse
infobulle [ɛ̃fobyl] NF (Inform) help bubble
infographie [ɛ̃fɔgrafi] NF computer graphics sg
informateur, -trice [ɛ̃fɔrmatœr, -tris] NM/F informant
informaticien, ne [ɛ̃fɔrmatisjɛ̃, -ɛn] NM/F computer scientist
informatif, -ive [ɛ̃fɔrmatif, -iv] ADJ informative
information [ɛ̃fɔrmasjɔ̃] NF (renseignement) piece of information; (Presse, TV: nouvelle) item of news; (diffusion de renseignements, Inform) information; (Jur) inquiry, investigation; **informations** NFPL (TV) news sg; **voyage d'~** fact-finding trip; **agence d'~** news agency; **journal d'~** quality (BRIT) ou serious newspaper
informatique [ɛ̃fɔrmatik] NF (technique) data processing; (science) computer science ▶ ADJ computer cpd; **~ en nuage** cloud computing
informatisation [ɛ̃fɔrmatizasjɔ̃] NF computerization
informatiser [ɛ̃fɔrmatize] /1/ VT to computerize
informe [ɛ̃fɔrm] ADJ shapeless
informé, e [ɛ̃fɔrme] ADJ: **jusqu'à plus ample ~** until further information is available
informel, le [ɛ̃fɔrmɛl] ADJ informal
informer [ɛ̃fɔrme] /1/ VT: **~ qn (de)** to inform sb (of) ▶ VI (Jur): **~ contre qn/sur qch** to initiate inquiries about sb/sth; **s'informer (sur)** to inform o.s. (about); **s'informer (de qch/si)** to inquire ou find out (about sth/whether ou if)
informulé, e [ɛ̃fɔrmyle] ADJ unformulated
infortune [ɛ̃fɔrtyn] NF misfortune
infos [ɛ̃fo] NFPL (= informations) news
infraction [ɛ̃fraksjɔ̃] NF offence; **~ à** violation ou breach of; **être en ~** to be in breach of the law
infranchissable [ɛ̃frɑ̃ʃisabl] ADJ impassable; (fig) insuperable
infrarouge [ɛ̃fraruʒ] ADJ, NM infrared
infrason [ɛ̃frasɔ̃] NM infrasonic vibration
infrastructure [ɛ̃frastryktyr] NF (d'une route etc) substructure; (Aviat, Mil) ground installations pl; (Écon: touristique etc) facilities pl
infréquentable [ɛ̃frekɑ̃tabl] ADJ not to be associated with
infroissable [ɛ̃frwasabl] ADJ crease-resistant
infructueux, -euse [ɛ̃fryktɥø, -øz] ADJ fruitless, unfruitful
infus, e [ɛ̃fy, -yz] ADJ: **avoir la science ~** to have innate knowledge

infuser [ɛ̃fyze] /1/ VT (aussi: **faire infuser**: thé) to brew; (: tisane) to infuse ▶ VI to brew; to infuse; **laisser ~** (to leave) to brew
infusion [ɛ̃fyzjɔ̃] NF (tisane) infusion, herb tea
ingambe [ɛ̃gɑ̃b] ADJ spry, nimble
ingénier [ɛ̃ʒenje] /7/: **s'ingénier** VI: **s'ingénier à faire** to strive to do
ingénierie [ɛ̃ʒeniri] NF engineering
ingénieur [ɛ̃ʒenjœr] NM engineer; **~ agronome/chimiste** agricultural/chemical engineer; **~ conseil** consulting engineer; **~ du son** sound engineer
ingénieusement [ɛ̃ʒenjøzmɑ̃] ADV ingeniously
ingénieux, -euse [ɛ̃ʒenjø, -øz] ADJ ingenious, clever
ingéniosité [ɛ̃ʒenjozite] NF ingenuity
ingénu, e [ɛ̃ʒeny] ADJ ingenuous, artless ▶ NF (Théât) ingénue
ingénuité [ɛ̃ʒenɥite] NF ingenuousness
ingénument [ɛ̃ʒenymɑ̃] ADV ingenuously
ingérence [ɛ̃ʒerɑ̃s] NF interference
ingérer [ɛ̃ʒere] /6/: **s'ingérer** VI: **s'ingérer dans** to interfere in
ingouvernable [ɛ̃guvɛrnabl] ADJ ungovernable
ingrat, e [ɛ̃gra, -at] ADJ (personne) ungrateful; (sol) poor; (travail, sujet) arid, thankless; (visage) unprepossessing
ingratitude [ɛ̃gratityd] NF ingratitude
ingrédient [ɛ̃gredjɑ̃] NM ingredient
inguérissable [ɛ̃gerisabl] ADJ incurable
ingurgiter [ɛ̃gyrʒite] /1/ VT to swallow; **faire ~ qch à qn** to make sb swallow sth; (fig: connaissances) to force sth into sb
inhabile [inabil] ADJ clumsy; (fig) inept
inhabitable [inabitabl] ADJ uninhabitable
inhabité, e [inabite] ADJ (régions) uninhabited; (maison) unoccupied
inhabituel, le [inabitɥɛl] ADJ unusual
inhalateur [inalatœr] NM inhaler; **~ d'oxygène** oxygen mask
inhalation [inalasjɔ̃] NF (Méd) inhalation; **faire des inhalations** to use an inhalation bath
inhaler [inale] /1/ VT to inhale
inhérent, e [inerɑ̃, -ɑ̃t] ADJ: **~ à** inherent in
inhiber [inibe] /1/ VT to inhibit
inhibition [inibisjɔ̃] NF inhibition
inhospitalier, -ière [inɔspitalje, -jɛr] ADJ inhospitable
inhumain, e [inymɛ̃, -ɛn] ADJ inhuman
inhumation [inymasjɔ̃] NF interment, burial
inhumer [inyme] /1/ VT to inter, bury
inimaginable [inimaʒinabl] ADJ unimaginable
inimitable [inimitabl] ADJ inimitable
inimitié [inimitje] NF enmity
ininflammable [inɛ̃flamabl] ADJ non-flammable
inintelligent, e [inɛ̃teliʒɑ̃, -ɑ̃t] ADJ unintelligent
inintelligible [inɛ̃teliʒibl] ADJ unintelligible
inintelligiblement [inɛ̃teliʒibləmɑ̃] ADV unintelligibly
inintéressant, e [inɛ̃teresɑ̃, -ɑ̃t] ADJ uninteresting
ininterrompu, e [inɛ̃terɔ̃py] ADJ (file, série) unbroken; (flot, vacarme) uninterrupted,

non-stop; (*effort*) unremitting, continuous; (*suite, ligne*) unbroken

iniquité [inikite] NF iniquity

initial, e, -aux [inisjal, -o] ADJ initial; **initiales** NFPL initials

initialement [inisjalmɑ̃] ADV initially

initialiser [inisjalize] /1/ VT to initialize

initiateur, -trice [inisjatœʀ, -tʀis] NM/F initiator; (*d'une mode, technique*) innovator, pioneer

initiation [inisjasjɔ̃] NF initiation; **~ à** introduction to

initiatique [inisjatik] ADJ (*rites, épreuves*) initiatory

initiative [inisjativ] NF initiative; **prendre l'~ de qch/de faire** to take the initiative for sth/of doing; **avoir de l'~** to have initiative, show enterprise; **esprit/qualités d'~** spirit/qualities of initiative; **à** *ou* **sur l'~ de qn** on sb's initiative; **de sa propre ~** on one's own initiative

initié, e [inisje] ADJ initiated ▶ NM/F initiate

initier [inisje] /7/ VT to initiate; **~ qn à** to initiate sb into; (*faire découvrir: art, jeu*) to introduce sb to; **s'initier à** VI (*métier, profession, technique*) to become initiated into

injectable [ɛ̃ʒɛktabl] ADJ injectable

injecté, e [ɛ̃ʒɛkte] ADJ: **yeux injectés de sang** bloodshot eyes

injecter [ɛ̃ʒɛkte] /1/ VT to inject

injection [ɛ̃ʒɛksjɔ̃] NF injection; **à ~** (*Auto*) fuel injection *cpd*

injonction [ɛ̃ʒɔ̃ksjɔ̃] NF injunction, order; **~ de payer** (*Jur*) order to pay

injouable [ɛ̃ʒwabl] ADJ unplayable

injure [ɛ̃ʒyʀ] NF insult, abuse *no pl*

injurier [ɛ̃ʒyʀje] /7/ VT to insult, abuse

injurieux, -euse [ɛ̃ʒyʀjø, -øz] ADJ abusive, insulting

injuste [ɛ̃ʒyst] ADJ unjust, unfair

injustement [ɛ̃ʒystəmɑ̃] ADV unjustly, unfairly

injustice [ɛ̃ʒystis] NF injustice

injustifiable [ɛ̃ʒystifjabl] ADJ unjustifiable

injustifié, e [ɛ̃ʒystifje] ADJ unjustified, unwarranted

inlassable [ɛ̃lɑsabl] ADJ tireless, indefatigable

inlassablement [ɛ̃lɑsabləmɑ̃] ADV tirelessly

inné, e [ine] ADJ innate, inborn

innocemment [inɔsamɑ̃] ADV innocently

innocence [inɔsɑ̃s] NF innocence

innocent, e [inɔsɑ̃, -ɑ̃t] ADJ innocent ▶ NM/F innocent person; **faire l'~** to play *ou* come the innocent

innocenter [inɔsɑ̃te] /1/ VT to clear, prove innocent

innocuité [inɔkɥite] NF innocuousness

innombrable [inɔ̃bʀabl] ADJ innumerable

innommable [inɔmabl] ADJ unspeakable

innovateur, -trice [inɔvatœʀ, -tʀis] ADJ innovatory

innovation [inɔvasjɔ̃] NF innovation

innover [inɔve] /1/ VI: **~ en matière d'art** to break new ground in the field of art

inobservance [inɔpsɛʀvɑ̃s] NF non-observance

inobservation [inɔpsɛʀvasjɔ̃] NF non-observation, inobservance

inoccupé, e [inɔkype] ADJ unoccupied

inoculer [inɔkyle] /1/ VT: **~ qch à qn** (*volontairement*) to inoculate sb with sth; (*accidentellement*) to infect sb with sth; **~ qn contre** to inoculate sb against

inodore [inɔdɔʀ] ADJ (*gaz*) odourless; (*fleur*) scentless

inoffensif, -ive [inɔfɑ̃sif, -iv] ADJ harmless, innocuous

inondable [inɔ̃dabl] ADJ (*zone etc*) liable to flooding

inondation [inɔ̃dasjɔ̃] NF flooding *no pl*; (*torrent, eau*) flood

inonder [inɔ̃de] /1/ VT to flood; (*fig*) to inundate, overrun; **~ de** (*fig*) to flood *ou* swamp with

inopérable [inɔpeʀabl] ADJ inoperable

inopérant, e [inɔpeʀɑ̃, -ɑ̃t] ADJ inoperative, ineffective

inopiné, e [inɔpine] ADJ unexpected, sudden

inopinément [inɔpinemɑ̃] ADV unexpectedly

inopportun, e [inɔpɔʀtœ̃, -yn] ADJ ill-timed, untimely; inappropriate; (*moment*) inopportune

inorganisation [inɔʀganizasjɔ̃] NF lack of organization

inorganisé, e [inɔʀganize] ADJ (*travailleurs*) non-organized

inoubliable [inublijabl] ADJ unforgettable

inouï, e [inwi] ADJ unheard-of, extraordinary

inox [inɔks] ADJ INV, NM (= *inoxydable*) stainless (steel)

inoxydable [inɔksidabl] ADJ stainless; (*couverts*) stainless steel *cpd*

inqualifiable [ɛ̃kalifjabl] ADJ unspeakable

inquiet, -ète [ɛ̃kjɛ, -ɛt] ADJ (*par nature*) anxious; (*momentanément*) worried; **~ de qch/au sujet de qn** worried about sth/sb

inquiétant, e [ɛ̃kjetɑ̃, -ɑ̃t] ADJ worrying, disturbing

inquiéter [ɛ̃kjete] /6/ VT to worry, disturb; (*harceler*) to harass; **s'inquiéter** to worry, become anxious; **s'inquiéter de** to worry about; (*s'enquérir de*) to inquire about

inquiétude [ɛ̃kjetyd] NF anxiety; **donner de l'~** *ou* **des inquiétudes à** to worry; **avoir de l'~** *ou* **des inquiétudes au sujet de** to feel anxious *ou* worried about

inquisiteur, -trice [ɛ̃kizitœʀ, -tʀis] ADJ (*regards, questions*) inquisitive, prying

inquisition [ɛ̃kizisjɔ̃] NF inquisition

INRA [inʀa] SIGLE M = **Institut national de la recherche agronomique**

inracontable [ɛ̃ʀakɔ̃tabl] ADJ (*trop osé*) unrepeatable; (*trop compliqué*): **l'histoire est ~** the story is too complicated to relate

insaisissable [ɛ̃sezisabl] ADJ (*fugitif, ennemi*) elusive; (*différence, nuance*) imperceptible

insalubre [ɛ̃salybʀ] ADJ unhealthy, insalubrious

insalubrité [ɛ̃salybʀite] NF unhealthiness, insalubrity

insanité [ɛ̃sanite] NF madness *no pl*, insanity *no pl*

insatiable [ɛ̃sasjabl] ADJ insatiable

insatisfaction [ɛ̃satisfaksjɔ̃] NF dissatisfaction

insatisfait, e [ɛ̃satisfɛ, -ɛt] ADJ *(non comblé)* unsatisfied; *(: passion, envie)* unfulfilled; *(mécontent)* dissatisfied

inscription [ɛ̃skʀipsjɔ̃] NF *(sur un mur, écriteau etc)* inscription; *(à une institution: voir s'inscrire)* enrolment; registration

inscrire [ɛ̃skʀiʀ] **/39/** VT *(marquer: sur son calepin etc)* to note *ou* write down; *(: sur un mur, une affiche etc)* to write; *(: dans la pierre, le métal)* to inscribe; *(mettre: sur une liste, un budget etc)* to put down; *(enrôler: soldat)* to enlist; **~ qn à** *(club, école etc)* to enrol sb at; **s'inscrire** VI *(pour une excursion etc)* to put one's name down; **s'inscrire (à)** *(club, parti)* to join; *(université)* to register *ou* enrol (at); *(examen, concours)* to register *ou* enter (for); **s'inscrire dans** *(se situer: négociations etc)* to come within the scope of; **s'inscrire en faux contre** to deny (strongly); *(Jur)* to challenge

inscrit, e [ɛ̃skʀi, -it] PP *de* **inscrire** ▶ ADJ *(étudiant, électeur etc)* registered

insécable [ɛ̃sekabl] ADJ *(Inform)* indivisible; **espace ~** hard space

insecte [ɛ̃sɛkt] NM insect

insecticide [ɛ̃sɛktisid] NM insecticide

insécurité [ɛ̃sekyʀite] NF insecurity, lack of security

INSEE [inse] SIGLE M (= *Institut national de la statistique et des études économiques*) national institute of statistical and economic information

insémination [ɛ̃seminasjɔ̃] NF insemination

insensé, e [ɛ̃sɑ̃se] ADJ insane, mad

insensibiliser [ɛ̃sɑ̃sibilize] **/1/** VT to anaesthetize; *(à une allergie)* to desensitize; **~ à qch** *(fig)* to cause to become insensitive to sth

insensibilité [ɛ̃sɑ̃sibilite] NF insensitivity

insensible [ɛ̃sɑ̃sibl] ADJ *(nerf, membre)* numb; *(dur, indifférent)* insensitive; *(imperceptible)* imperceptible

insensiblement [ɛ̃sɑ̃sibləmɑ̃] ADV *(doucement, peu à peu)* imperceptibly

inséparable [ɛ̃sepaʀabl] ADJ: **~ (de)** inseparable (from) ▶ NMPL: **inséparables** *(oiseaux)* lovebirds

insérer [ɛ̃seʀe] **/6/** VT to insert; **s'~ dans** to fit into; *(fig)* to come within

INSERM [insɛʀm] SIGLE M (= *Institut national de la santé et de la recherche médicale*) national institute for medical research

insert [ɛ̃sɛʀ] NM *enclosed fireplace burning solid fuel*

insertion [ɛ̃sɛʀsjɔ̃] NF *(d'une personne)* integration

insidieusement [ɛ̃sidjøzmɑ̃] ADV insidiously

insidieux, -euse [ɛ̃sidjø, -øz] ADJ insidious

insigne [ɛ̃siɲ] NM *(d'un parti, club)* badge ▶ ADJ distinguished; **insignes** NMPL *(d'une fonction)* insignia *pl*

insignifiant, e [ɛ̃siɲifjɑ̃, -ɑ̃t] ADJ insignificant; *(somme, affaire, détail)* trivial, insignificant

insinuant, e [ɛ̃sinɥɑ̃, -ɑ̃t] ADJ ingratiating

insinuation [ɛ̃sinɥasjɔ̃] NF innuendo, insinuation

insinuer [ɛ̃sinɥe] **/1/** VT to insinuate, imply; **s'insinuer dans** VI to seep into; *(fig)* to worm one's way into, creep into

insipide [ɛ̃sipid] ADJ insipid

insistance [ɛ̃sistɑ̃s] NF insistence; **avec ~** insistently

insistant, e [ɛ̃sistɑ̃, -ɑ̃t] ADJ insistent

insister [ɛ̃siste] **/1/** VI to insist; *(s'obstiner)* to keep on; **~ sur** *(détail, note)* to stress; **~ pour qch/ pour faire qch** to be insistent about sth/about doing sth

insociable [ɛ̃sɔsjabl] ADJ unsociable

insolation [ɛ̃sɔlasjɔ̃] NF *(Méd)* sunstroke *no pl*; *(ensoleillement)* period of sunshine

insolence [ɛ̃sɔlɑ̃s] NF insolence *no pl*; **avec ~** insolently

insolent, e [ɛ̃sɔlɑ̃, -ɑ̃t] ADJ insolent

insolite [ɛ̃sɔlit] ADJ strange, unusual

insoluble [ɛ̃sɔlybl] ADJ insoluble

insolvable [ɛ̃sɔlvabl] ADJ insolvent

insomniaque [ɛ̃sɔmnjak] ADJ, NMF insomniac

insomnie [ɛ̃sɔmni] NF insomnia *no pl*, sleeplessness *no pl*; **avoir des insomnies** to sleep badly, suffer from insomnia

insondable [ɛ̃sɔ̃dabl] ADJ unfathomable

insonore [ɛ̃sɔnɔʀ] ADJ soundproof

insonorisation [ɛ̃sɔnɔʀizasjɔ̃] NF soundproofing

insonoriser [ɛ̃sɔnɔʀize] **/1/** VT to soundproof

insouciance [ɛ̃susjɑ̃s] NF carefree attitude; heedless attitude

insouciant, e [ɛ̃susjɑ̃, -ɑ̃t] ADJ carefree; *(imprévoyant)* heedless; **~ du danger** heedless of (the) danger

insoumis, e [ɛ̃sumi, -iz] ADJ *(caractère, enfant)* rebellious, refractory; *(contrée, tribu)* unsubdued; *(Mil: soldat)* absent without leave ▶ NM *(Mil: soldat)* absentee

insoumission [ɛ̃sumisjɔ̃] NF rebelliousness; *(Mil)* absence without leave

insoupçonnable [ɛ̃supsɔnabl] ADJ unsuspected; *(personne)* above suspicion

insoupçonné, e [ɛ̃supsɔne] ADJ unsuspected

insoutenable [ɛ̃sutnabl] ADJ *(argument)* untenable; *(chaleur)* unbearable

inspecter [ɛ̃spɛkte] **/1/** VT to inspect

inspecteur, -trice [ɛ̃spɛktœʀ, -tʀis] NM/F inspector; *(des assurances)* assessor; **~ d'Académie** (regional) director of education; **~ (de l'enseignement) primaire** primary school inspector; **~ des finances** ≈ tax inspector (BRIT), ≈ Internal Revenue Service agent (US); **~ (de police)** (police) inspector

inspection [ɛ̃spɛksjɔ̃] NF inspection

inspirateur, -trice [ɛ̃spiʀatœʀ, -tʀis] NM/F *(instigateur)* instigator; *(animateur)* inspirer

inspiration [ɛ̃spiʀasjɔ̃] NF inspiration; breathing in *no pl*; *(idée)* flash of inspiration, brainwave; **sous l'~ de** prompted by

inspiré, e [ɛ̃spiʀe] ADJ: **être bien/mal ~ de faire qch** to be well-advised/ill-advised to do sth

inspirer [ɛ̃spiʀe] **/1/** VT *(gén)* to inspire ▶ VI *(aspirer)* to breathe in; **s'inspirer de** *(artiste)* to draw one's inspiration from; *(tableau)* to be inspired by; **~ qch à qn** *(œuvre, projet, action)* to inspire sb with sth; *(dégoût, crainte, horreur)* to fill sb with sth; **ça ne m'inspire pas** I'm not keen on the idea

instabilité [ɛ̃stabilite] NF instability

instable [ɛ̃stabl] ADJ (*meuble, équilibre*) unsteady; (*population, temps*) unsettled; (*paix, régime, caractère*) unstable

installateur [ɛ̃stalatœʀ] NM fitter

installation [ɛ̃stalasjɔ̃] NF (*mise en place*) installation; putting in *ou* up; fitting out; settling in; (*appareils etc*) fittings *pl*, installations *pl*; **installations** NFPL installations; (*industrielles*) plant *sg*; (*de sport, dans un camping*) facilities; **l'~ électrique** wiring

installé, e [ɛ̃stale] ADJ: **bien/mal ~** well/poorly equipped; (*personne*) well/not very well set up *ou* organized

installer [ɛ̃stale] /1/ VT (*asseoir, coucher*) to settle (down); (*placer*) to put, place; (*meuble*) to put in; (*rideau, étagère, tente*) to put up; (*gaz, électricité etc*) to put in, install; (*appartement*) to fit out; **s'installer** VI (*s'établir: artisan, dentiste etc*) to set o.s. up; (*emménager*) to settle in; (*sur un siège, à un emplacement*) to settle (down); (*fig: maladie, grève*) to take a firm hold *ou* grip; **~ qn** (*loger*) to get sb settled, install sb; **~ une salle de bains dans une pièce** to fit out a room with a bathroom suite; **s'installer à l'hôtel/chez qn** to move into a hotel/in with sb

instamment [ɛ̃stamɑ̃] ADV urgently

instance [ɛ̃stɑ̃s] NF (*Jur: procédure*) (legal) proceedings *pl*; (*Admin: autorité*) authority; **instances** NFPL (*prières*) entreaties; **affaire en ~** matter pending; **courrier en ~** mail ready for posting; **être en ~ de divorce** to be awaiting a divorce; **train en ~ de départ** train on the point of departure; **tribunal de première ~** court of first instance; **en seconde ~** on appeal

instant [ɛ̃stɑ̃] NM moment, instant; **dans un ~** in a moment; **à l'~** this instant; **je l'ai vu à l'~** I've just this minute seen him, I saw him a moment ago; **à l'~ (même) où** at the (very) moment that *ou* when, (just) as; **à chaque ~, à tout ~** at any moment; constantly; **pour l'~** for the moment, for the time being; **par instants** at times; **de tous les instants** perpetual; **dès l'~ *ou* que ...** from the moment when ..., since that moment when ...

instantané, e [ɛ̃stɑ̃tane] ADJ (*lait, café*) instant; (*explosion, mort*) instantaneous ▶ NM snapshot

instantanément [ɛ̃stɑ̃tanemɑ̃] ADV instantaneously

instar [ɛ̃staʀ]: **à l'~ de** prép following the example of, like

instaurer [ɛ̃stɔʀe] /1/ VT to institute; (*couvre-feu*) to impose; **s'instaurer** VI to set o.s. up; (*collaboration, paix etc*) to be established; (*doute*) to set in

instigateur, -trice [ɛ̃stigatœʀ, -tʀis] NM/F instigator

instigation [ɛ̃stigasjɔ̃] NF: **à l'~ de qn** at sb's instigation

instiller [ɛ̃stile] /1/ VT to instil, apply

instinct [ɛ̃stɛ̃] NM instinct; **d'~** (*spontanément*) instinctively; **~ grégaire** herd instinct; **~ de conservation** instinct of self-preservation

instinctif, -ive [ɛ̃stɛ̃ktif, -iv] ADJ instinctive

instinctivement [ɛ̃stɛ̃ktivmɑ̃] ADV instinctively

instit [ɛ̃stit] (*fam*) NMF (primary school) teacher

instituer [ɛ̃stitɥe] /1/ VT to establish, institute; **s'~ défenseur d'une cause** to set o.s. up as defender of a cause

institut [ɛ̃stity] NM institute; **~ de beauté** beauty salon; **~ médico-légal** mortuary; **I~ universitaire de technologie** ≈ Institute of technology

instituteur, -trice [ɛ̃stitytœʀ, -tʀis] NM/F (primary (BRIT) *ou* grade (US) school) teacher

institution [ɛ̃stitysjɔ̃] NF institution; (*collège*) private school; **institutions** NFPL (*structures politiques et sociales*) institutions

institutionnaliser [ɛ̃stitysjɔnalize] /1/ VT to institutionalize

instructeur, -trice [ɛ̃stʀyktœʀ, -tʀis] ADJ (*Mil*): **sergent ~** drill sergeant; (*Jur*): **juge ~** examining (BRIT) *ou* committing (US) magistrate ▶ NM/F instructor

instructif, -ive [ɛ̃stʀyktif, -iv] ADJ instructive

instruction [ɛ̃stʀyksjɔ̃] NF (*enseignement, savoir*) education; (*Jur*) (preliminary) investigation and hearing; (*directive*) instruction; (*Admin: document*) directive; **instructions** NFPL instructions; (*mode d'emploi*) directions, instructions; **~ civique** civics *sg*; **~ primaire/ publique** primary/public education; **~ religieuse** religious instruction; **~ professionnelle** vocational training

instruire [ɛ̃stʀɥiʀ] /38/ VT (*élèves*) to teach; (*recrues*) to train; (*Jur: affaire*) to conduct the investigation for; **s'instruire** to educate o.s.; **s'instruire auprès de qn de qch** (*s'informer*) to find sth out from sb; **~ qn de qch** (*informer*) to inform *ou* advise sb of sth; **~ contre qn** (*Jur*) to investigate sb

instruit, e [ɛ̃stʀɥi, -it] PP *de* **instruire** ▶ ADJ educated

instrument [ɛ̃stʀymɑ̃] NM instrument; **~ à cordes/vent** stringed/wind instrument; **~ de mesure** measuring instrument; **~ de musique** musical instrument; **~ de travail** (working) tool

instrumental, e, -aux [ɛ̃stʀymɑ̃tal, -o] ADJ instrumental

instrumentation [ɛ̃stʀymɑ̃tasjɔ̃] NF instrumentation

instrumentiste [ɛ̃stʀymɑ̃tist] NMF instrumentalist

insu [ɛ̃sy] NM: **à l'~ de qn** without sb knowing

insubmersible [ɛ̃sybmɛʀsibl] ADJ unsinkable

insubordination [ɛ̃sybɔʀdinasjɔ̃] NF rebelliousness; (*Mil*) insubordination

insubordonné, e [ɛ̃sybɔʀdɔne] ADJ insubordinate

insuccès [ɛ̃syksɛ] NM failure

insuffisamment [ɛ̃syfizamɑ̃] ADV insufficiently

insuffisance [ɛ̃syfizɑ̃s] NF insufficiency; inadequacy; **insuffisances** NFPL (*lacunes*) inadequacies; **~ cardiaque** cardiac insufficiency *no pl*; **~ hépatique** liver deficiency

insuffisant, e [ɛ̃syfizɑ̃, -ɑ̃t] ADJ *(en quantité)* insufficient; *(en qualité: élève, travail)* inadequate; *(sur une copie)* poor

insuffler [ɛ̃syfle] /1/ VT: ~ **qch dans** to blow sth into; ~ **qch à qn** to inspire sb with sth

insulaire [ɛ̃sylɛʀ] ADJ island cpd; *(attitude)* insular

insularité [ɛ̃sylaʀite] NF insularity

insuline [ɛ̃sylin] NF insulin

insultant, e [ɛ̃syltɑ̃, -ɑ̃t] ADJ insulting

insulte [ɛ̃sylt] NF insult

insulter [ɛ̃sylte] /1/ VT to insult

insupportable [ɛ̃sypɔʀtabl] ADJ unbearable

insurgé, e [ɛ̃syʀʒe] ADJ, NM/F insurgent, rebel

insurger [ɛ̃syʀʒe] /3/: **s'insurger** VI: **s'insurger (contre)** to rise up ou rebel (against)

insurmontable [ɛ̃syʀmɔ̃tabl] ADJ *(difficulté)* insuperable; *(aversion)* unconquerable

insurpassable [ɛ̃syʀpasabl] ADJ unsurpassable, unsurpassed

insurrection [ɛ̃syʀɛksjɔ̃] NF insurrection, revolt

insurrectionnel, le [ɛ̃syʀɛksjɔnɛl] ADJ insurrectionary

intact, e [ɛ̃takt] ADJ intact

intangible [ɛ̃tɑ̃ʒibl] ADJ intangible; *(principe)* inviolable

intarissable [ɛ̃taʀisabl] ADJ inexhaustible

intégral, e, -aux [ɛ̃tegʀal, -o] ADJ complete ▶ NF *(Math)* integral; *(œuvres complètes)* complete works; **texte** ~ unabridged version; **bronzage** ~ all-over suntan

intégralement [ɛ̃tegʀalmɑ̃] ADV in full, fully

intégralité [ɛ̃tegʀalite] NF *(d'une somme, d'un revenu)* whole *(ou* full) amount; **dans son** ~ in its entirety

intégrant, e [ɛ̃tegʀɑ̃, -ɑ̃t] ADJ: **faire partie** ~ **de** to be an integral part of, be part and parcel of

intégration [ɛ̃tegʀasjɔ̃] NF integration

intégrationniste [ɛ̃tegʀasjɔnist] ADJ, NMF integrationist

intégré, e [ɛ̃tegʀe] ADJ: **circuit** ~ integrated circuit

intègre [ɛ̃tegʀ] ADJ perfectly honest, upright

intégrer [ɛ̃tegʀe] /6/ VT: ~ **qch à** ou **dans** to integrate sth into; **s'intégrer** VR: **s'intégrer à** ou **dans** to become integrated into; **bien s'intégrer** to fit in

intégrisme [ɛ̃tegʀism] NM fundamentalism

intégriste [ɛ̃tegʀist] ADJ, NMF fundamentalist

intégrité [ɛ̃tegʀite] NF integrity

intellect [ɛ̃telɛkt] NM intellect

intellectuel, le [ɛ̃telɛktɥɛl] ADJ, NM/F intellectual; *(péj)* highbrow

intellectuellement [ɛ̃telɛktɥɛlmɑ̃] ADV intellectually

intelligemment [ɛ̃teliʒamɑ̃] ADV intelligently

intelligence [ɛ̃teliʒɑ̃s] NF intelligence; *(compréhension)*: **l'~ de** the understanding of; *(complicité)*: **regard d'~** glance of complicity, meaningful ou knowing look; *(accord)*: **vivre en bonne ~ avec qn** to be on good terms with sb; **intelligences** NFPL *(Mil, fig)* secret contacts; **être d'~** to have an understanding;

~ **artificielle** artificial intelligence (A.I.)

intelligent, e [ɛ̃teliʒɑ̃, -ɑ̃t] ADJ intelligent; *(capable)*: ~ **en affaires** competent in business

intelligentsia [ɛ̃telidʒɛnsja] NF intelligentsia

intelligible [ɛ̃teliʒibl] ADJ intelligible

intello [ɛ̃telo] ADJ, NMF *(fam)* highbrow

intempérance [ɛ̃tɑ̃peʀɑ̃s] NF overindulgence *no pl*; intemperance *no pl*

intempérant, e [ɛ̃tɑ̃peʀɑ̃, -ɑ̃t] ADJ overindulgent; *(moralement)* intemperate

intempéries [ɛ̃tɑ̃peʀi] NFPL bad weather *sg*

intempestif, -ive [ɛ̃tɑ̃pɛstif, -iv] ADJ untimely

intenable [ɛ̃tnabl] ADJ unbearable

intendance [ɛ̃tɑ̃dɑ̃s] NF *(Mil)* supply corps; *(: bureau)* supplies office; *(Scol)* bursar's office

intendant, e [ɛ̃tɑ̃dɑ̃, -ɑ̃t] NM/F *(Mil)* quartermaster; *(Scol)* bursar; *(d'une propriété)* steward

intense [ɛ̃tɑ̃s] ADJ intense

intensément [ɛ̃tɑ̃semɑ̃] ADV intensely

intensif, -ive [ɛ̃tɑ̃sif, -iv] ADJ intensive; **cours** ~ crash course; ~ **en main-d'œuvre** labour-intensive; ~ **en capital** capital-intensive

intensification [ɛ̃tɑ̃sifikasjɔ̃] NF intensification

intensifier [ɛ̃tɑ̃sifje] /7/ VT, **s'intensifier** VI to intensify

intensité [ɛ̃tɑ̃site] NF intensity

intensivement [ɛ̃tɑ̃sivmɑ̃] ADV intensively

intenter [ɛ̃tɑ̃te] /1/ VT: ~ **un procès contre** ou **à qn** to start proceedings against sb

intention [ɛ̃tɑ̃sjɔ̃] NF intention; *(Jur)* intent; **avoir l'~ de faire** to intend to do, have the intention of doing; **dans l'~ de faire qch** with a view to doing sth; **à l'~ de** *prép* for; *(renseignement)* for the benefit ou information of; *(film, ouvrage)* aimed at; **à cette ~** with this aim in view; **sans ~** unintentionally; **faire qch sans mauvaise ~** to do sth without ill intent; **agir dans une bonne ~** to act with good intentions

intentionné, e [ɛ̃tɑ̃sjɔne] ADJ: **bien ~** well-meaning ou -intentioned; **mal ~** ill-intentioned

intentionnel, le [ɛ̃tɑ̃sjɔnɛl] ADJ intentional, deliberate

intentionnellement [ɛ̃tɑ̃sjɔnɛlmɑ̃] ADV intentionally, deliberately

inter [ɛ̃tɛʀ] NM *(Tél: interurbain)* long-distance call service; *(Sport)*: ~ **gauche/droit** inside-left/-right

interactif, -ive [ɛ̃tɛʀaktif, -iv] ADJ *(aussi Inform)* interactive

interaction [ɛ̃tɛʀaksjɔ̃] NF interaction

interbancaire [ɛ̃tɛʀbɑ̃kɛʀ] ADJ interbank

intercalaire [ɛ̃tɛʀkalɛʀ] ADJ, NM: **(feuillet)** ~ insert; **(fiche)** ~ divider

intercaler [ɛ̃tɛʀkale] /1/ VT to insert; **s'intercaler entre** VI to come in between; to slip in between

intercéder [ɛ̃tɛʀsede] /6/ VI: ~ **(pour qn)** to intercede (on behalf of sb)

intercepter [ɛ̃tɛʀsɛpte] /1/ VT to intercept; *(lumière, chaleur)* to cut off

intercepteur [ɛ̃tɛʀsɛptœʀ] NM (Aviat) interceptor

interception [ɛ̃tɛʀsɛpsjɔ̃] NF interception; **avion d'~** interceptor

intercession [ɛ̃tɛʀsesjɔ̃] NF intercession

interchangeable [ɛ̃tɛʀʃɑ̃ʒabl] ADJ interchangeable

interclasse [ɛ̃tɛʀklɑs] NM (Scol) break (between classes)

interclubs [ɛ̃tɛʀklœb] ADJ INV interclub

intercommunal, e, -aux [ɛ̃tɛʀkɔmynal, -o] ADJ intervillage, intercommunity

intercommunautaire [ɛ̃tɛʀkɔmynotɛʀ] ADJ intercommunity

intercontinental, e, -aux [ɛ̃tɛʀkɔ̃tinɑtal, -o] ADJ intercontinental

intercostal, e, -aux [ɛ̃tɛʀkɔstal, -o] ADJ intercostal, between the ribs

interdépartemental, e, -aux [ɛ̃tɛʀdepaʀtəmɑtal, -o] ADJ interdepartmental

interdépendance [ɛ̃tɛʀdepɑ̃dɑ̃s] NF interdependence

interdépendant, e [ɛ̃tɛʀdepɑ̃dɑ̃, -ɑt] ADJ interdependent

interdiction [ɛ̃tɛʀdiksjɔ̃] NF ban; **~ de faire qch** ban on doing sth; **~ de séjour** (Jur) order banning ex-prisoner from frequenting specified places; **~ de fumer** no smoking

interdire [ɛ̃tɛʀdiʀ] /37/ VT to forbid; (Admin: stationnement, meeting, passage) to ban, prohibit; (: journal, livre) to ban; **s'interdire qch** VI (éviter) to refrain ou abstain from sth; (se refuser): **il s'interdit d'y penser** he doesn't allow himself to think about it; **~ qch à qn** to forbid sb sth; **~ à qn de faire** to forbid sb to do, prohibit sb from doing; (empêcher) to prevent ou preclude sb from doing

interdisciplinaire [ɛ̃tɛʀdisiplinɛʀ] ADJ interdisciplinary

interdit, e [ɛ̃tɛʀdi, -it] PP de **interdire** ▶ ADJ (stupéfait) taken aback; (défendu) forbidden, prohibited ▶ NM interdict, prohibition; **film ~ aux moins de 18/12 ans** ≈ 18-/12A-rated film; **sens ~** one way; **stationnement ~** no parking; **~ de chéquier** having cheque book facilities suspended; **~ de séjour** subject to an "interdiction de séjour"

intéressant, e [ɛ̃teresɑ̃, -ɑt] ADJ interesting; (avantageux) attractive; **faire l'~** to draw attention to o.s.

intéressé, e [ɛ̃terese] ADJ (parties) involved, concerned; (amitié, motifs) self-interested ▶ NM: **l'~** the interested party; **les intéressés** those concerned ou involved

intéressement [ɛ̃teresmɑ̃] NM (Comm) profit-sharing

intéresser [ɛ̃terese] /1/ VT (captiver) to interest; (toucher) to be of interest ou concern to; (Admin: concerner) to affect, concern; (Comm: travailleur) to give a share in the profits to; (: partenaire) to interest (in the business); **s'intéresser à** VI to take an interest in, be interested in; **~ qn à qch** to get sb interested in sth

intérêt [ɛ̃terɛ] NM (aussi Comm) interest; (égoïsme) self-interest; **porter de l'~ à qn** to take an interest in sb; **agir par ~** to act out of self-interest; **avoir des intérêts dans** (Comm) to have a financial interest ou a stake in; **avoir ~ à faire** to do well to do; **tu as ~ à accepter** it's in your interest to accept; **tu as ~ à te dépêcher** you'd better hurry; **il y a ~ à ...** it would be a good thing to ...; **~ composé** compound interest

interface [ɛ̃tɛʀfas] NF (Inform) interface

interférence [ɛ̃tɛʀfeʀɑ̃s] NF interference

interférer [ɛ̃tɛʀfeʀe] /6/ VI: **~ (avec)** to interfere (with)

intergouvernemental, e, -aux [ɛ̃tɛʀguvɛʀnəmɑtal, -o] ADJ intergovernmental

intérieur, e [ɛ̃teʀjœʀ] ADJ (mur, escalier, poche) inside; (commerce, politique) domestic; (cour, calme, vie) inner; (navigation) inland ▶ NM (d'une maison, d'un récipient etc) inside; (d'un pays, aussi décor, mobilier) interior; (Pol): **l'I~** (the Department of) the Interior, ≈ the Home Office (BRIT); **à l'~ (de)** inside; (fig) within; **de l'~** (fig) from the inside; **en ~** (Ciné) in the studio; **vêtement d'~** indoor garment

intérieurement [ɛ̃teʀjœʀmɑ̃] ADV inwardly

intérim [ɛ̃teʀim] NM (période) interim period; (travail) temping; **agence d'~** temping agency; **assurer l'~ (de)** to deputize (for); **président par ~** interim president; **travailler en ~, faire de l'~** to temp

intérimaire [ɛ̃teʀimɛʀ] ADJ (directeur, ministre) acting; (secrétaire, personnel) temporary, interim ▶ NMF (secrétaire etc) temporary, temp (BRIT); (suppléant) deputy

intérioriser [ɛ̃teʀjɔʀize] /1/ VT to internalize

interjection [ɛ̃tɛʀʒɛksjɔ̃] NF interjection

interjeter [ɛ̃tɛʀʒəte] /4/ VT (Jur): **~ appel** to lodge an appeal

interligne [ɛ̃tɛʀliɲ] NM inter-line space ▶ NF (Typo) lead, leading; **simple/double ~** single/double spacing

interlocuteur, -trice [ɛ̃tɛʀlɔkytœʀ, -tʀis] NM/F speaker; (Pol): **~ valable** valid representative; **son ~** the person he ou she was speaking to

interlope [ɛ̃tɛʀlɔp] ADJ illicit; (milieu, bar) shady

interloquer [ɛ̃tɛʀlɔke] /1/ VT to take aback

interlude [ɛ̃tɛʀlyd] NM interlude

intermède [ɛ̃tɛʀmɛd] NM interlude

intermédiaire [ɛ̃tɛʀmedjɛʀ] ADJ intermediate; middle; half-way; (solution) temporary ▶ NMF intermediary; (Comm) middleman; **sans ~** directly; **par l'~ de** through

interminable [ɛ̃tɛʀminabl] ADJ never-ending

interminablement [ɛ̃tɛʀminabləmɑ̃] ADV interminably

interministériel, le [ɛ̃tɛʀministeʀjɛl] ADJ: **comité ~** interdepartmental committee

intermittence [ɛ̃tɛʀmitɑ̃s] NF: **par ~** intermittently, sporadically

intermittent, e [ɛ̃tɛʀmitɑ̃, -ɑt] ADJ intermittent, sporadic

internat [ɛ̃tɛʀna] NM (Scol) boarding school

international, e, -aux [ɛ̃tɛʀnasjɔnal, -o] ADJ, NM/F international

i

internationalisation [ɛ̃tɛʀnasjɔnalizasjɔ̃] NF internationalization

internationaliser [ɛ̃tɛʀnasjɔnalize] /**1**/ VT to internationalize

internationalisme [ɛ̃tɛʀnasjɔnalism] NM internationalism

internaute [ɛ̃tɛʀnot] NMF Internet user

interne [ɛ̃tɛʀn] ADJ internal ▶ NMF (Scol) boarder; (Méd) houseman (BRIT), intern (US)

internement [ɛ̃tɛʀnəmɑ̃] NM (Pol) internment; (Méd) confinement

interner [ɛ̃tɛʀne] /**1**/ VT (Pol) to intern; (Méd) to confine to a psychiatric hospital

Internet [ɛ̃tɛʀnɛt] NM: l'~ the Internet

interparlementaire [ɛ̃tɛʀpaʀləmɑ̃tɛʀ] ADJ interparliamentary

interpellation [ɛ̃tɛʀpelasjɔ̃] NF interpellation; (Pol) question

interpeller [ɛ̃tɛʀpele] /**1**/ VT (appeler) to call out to; (apostropher) to shout at; (Police) to take in for questioning; (Pol) to question; (concerner) to concern; **s'interpeller** VI to exchange insults

interphone [ɛ̃tɛʀfɔn] NM intercom; (d'immeuble) entry phone

interplanétaire [ɛ̃tɛʀplanetɛʀ] ADJ interplanetary

Interpol [ɛ̃tɛʀpɔl] SIGLE M Interpol

interpoler [ɛ̃tɛʀpɔle] /**1**/ VT to interpolate

interposer [ɛ̃tɛʀpoze] /**1**/ VT to interpose; **s'interposer** VI to intervene; **par personnes interposées** through a third party

interprétariat [ɛ̃tɛʀpʀetaʀja] NM interpreting

interprétation [ɛ̃tɛʀpʀetasjɔ̃] NF interpretation

interprète [ɛ̃tɛʀpʀɛt] NMF interpreter; (porte-parole) spokesman

interpréter [ɛ̃tɛʀpʀete] /**6**/ VT to interpret; (jouer) to play; (chanter) to sing

interprofessionnel, le [ɛ̃tɛʀpʀɔfesjɔnɛl] ADJ interprofessional

interrogateur, -trice [ɛ̃teʀɔgatœʀ, -tʀis] ADJ questioning, inquiring ▶ NM/F (Scol) (oral) examiner

interrogatif, -ive [ɛ̃teʀɔgatif, -iv] ADJ (Ling) interrogative

interrogation [ɛ̃teʀɔgasjɔ̃] NF question; (Scol) (written ou oral) test

interrogatoire [ɛ̃teʀɔgatwaʀ] NM (Police) questioning no pl; (Jur, aussi fig) cross-examination, interrogation

interroger [ɛ̃teʀɔʒe] /**3**/ VT to question; (Inform) to search; (Scol: candidat) to test; **~ qn (sur qch)** to question sb (about sth); **~ qn du regard** to look questioningly at sb, give sb a questioning look; **s'~ sur qch** to ask o.s. about sth, ponder (about) sth

interrompre [ɛ̃teʀɔ̃pʀ] /**41**/ VT (gén) to interrupt; (travail, voyage) to break off, interrupt; (négociations) to break off; (match) to stop; **s'interrompre** VI to break off

interrupteur [ɛ̃teʀyptœʀ] NM switch

interruption [ɛ̃teʀypsjɔ̃] NF interruption; (pause) break; **sans ~** without a break; **~ de grossesse** termination of pregnancy;

~ volontaire de grossesse voluntary termination of pregnancy, abortion

interscolaire [ɛ̃tɛʀskɔlɛʀ] ADJ interschool(s)

intersection [ɛ̃tɛʀsɛksjɔ̃] NF intersection

intersidéral, e, -aux [ɛ̃tɛʀsideʀal, -o] ADJ interstellar

interstice [ɛ̃tɛʀstis] NM crack, slit

intersyndical, e, -aux [ɛ̃tɛʀsɛ̃dikal, -o] ADJ interunion

interurbain, e [ɛ̃tɛʀyʀbɛ̃, -ɛn] (Tél) NM long-distance call service ▶ ADJ long-distance

intervalle [ɛ̃tɛʀval] NM (espace) space; (de temps) interval; **dans l'~** in the meantime; **à deux jours d'~** two days apart; **à intervalles rapprochés** at close intervals; **par intervalles** at intervals

intervenant, e [ɛ̃tɛʀvənɑ̃, -ɑ̃t] VB voir **intervenir** ▶ NM/F speaker (at conference)

intervenir [ɛ̃tɛʀvəniʀ] /**22**/ VI (gén) to intervene; (survenir) to take place; (faire une conférence) to give a talk ou lecture; **~ auprès de/en faveur de qn** to intervene with/on behalf of sb; **la police a dû ~** police had to step in ou intervene; **les médecins ont dû ~** the doctors had to operate

intervention [ɛ̃tɛʀvɑ̃sjɔ̃] NF intervention; (conférence) talk, paper; (discours) speech; **~ (chirurgicale)** operation

interventionnisme [ɛ̃tɛʀvɑ̃sjɔnism] NM interventionism

interventionniste [ɛ̃tɛʀvɑ̃sjɔnist] ADJ interventionist

intervenu, e [ɛ̃tɛʀv(ə)ny] PP de **intervenir**

intervertible [ɛ̃tɛʀvɛʀtibl] ADJ interchangeable

intervertir [ɛ̃tɛʀvɛʀtiʀ] /**2**/ VT to invert (the order of), reverse

interviendrai [ɛ̃tɛʀvjɛ̃dʀe], **interviens** etc [ɛ̃tɛʀvjɛ̃] VB voir **intervenir**

interview [ɛ̃tɛʀvju] NF interview

interviewer [ɛ̃tɛʀvjuve] /**1**/ VT to interview ▶ NM [ɛ̃tɛʀvjuvɔœʀ] (journaliste) interviewer

intervins etc [ɛ̃tɛʀvɛ̃] VB voir **intervenir**

intestat [ɛ̃tɛsta] ADJ (Jur): **décéder ~** to die intestate

intestin, e [ɛ̃tɛstɛ̃, -in] ADJ internal ▶ NM intestine; **~ grêle** small intestine

intestinal, e, -aux [ɛ̃tɛstinal, -o] ADJ intestinal

intime [ɛ̃tim] ADJ intimate; (vie, journal) private; (convictions) inmost; (dîner, cérémonie) held among friends, quiet ▶ NMF close friend; **un journal ~** a diary

intimement [ɛ̃timmɑ̃] ADV (profondément) deeply, firmly; (étroitement) intimately

intimer [ɛ̃time] /**1**/ VT (Jur) to notify; **~ à qn l'ordre de faire** to order sb to do

intimidant, e [ɛ̃timidɑ̃, -ɑ̃t] ADJ intimidating

intimidation [ɛ̃timidasjɔ̃] NF intimidation; **manœuvres d'~** (action) acts of intimidation; (stratégie) intimidatory tactics

intimider [ɛ̃timide] /**1**/ VT to intimidate

intimité [ɛ̃timite] NF intimacy; (vie privée) privacy; private life; **dans l'~** in private; (sans formalités) with only a few friends, quietly

intitulé [ɛ̃tityle] NM title

intituler [ɛ̃tityle] /**1**/ VT: **comment a-t-il**

intitulé son livre? what title did he give his book?; **s'intituler** VI to be entitled; (*personne*) to call o.s.

intolérable [ɛ̃tɔleʀabl] ADJ intolerable

intolérance [ɛ̃tɔleʀɑ̃s] NF intolerance; **~ aux antibiotiques** intolerance to antibiotics

intolérant, e [ɛ̃tɔleʀɑ̃, -ɑ̃t] ADJ intolerant

intonation [ɛ̃tɔnasjɔ̃] NF intonation

intouchable [ɛ̃tuʃabl] ADJ (*fig*) above the law, sacrosanct; (*Rel*) untouchable

intox [ɛ̃tɔks] (*fam*) NF brainwashing

intoxication [ɛ̃tɔksikasjɔ̃] NF poisoning *no pl*; (*toxicomanie*) drug addiction; (*fig*) brainwashing; **~ alimentaire** food poisoning

intoxiqué, e [ɛ̃tɔksike] NM/F addict

intoxiquer [ɛ̃tɔksike] /**1**/ VT to poison; (*fig*) to brainwash; **s'intoxiquer** to poison o.s.

intradermique [ɛ̃tʀadɛʀmik] ADJ, NF: **(injection) ~** intradermal *ou* intracutaneous injection

intraduisible [ɛ̃tʀadyizibl] ADJ untranslatable; (*fig*) inexpressible

intraitable [ɛ̃tʀɛtabl] ADJ inflexible, uncompromising

intramusculaire [ɛ̃tʀamyskylɛʀ] ADJ, NF: **(injection) ~** intramuscular injection

intranet [ɛ̃tʀanɛt] NM intranet

intransigeance [ɛ̃tʀɑ̃ziʒɑ̃s] NF intransigence

intransigeant, e [ɛ̃tʀɑ̃ziʒɑ̃, -ɑ̃t] ADJ intransigent; (*morale, passion*) uncompromising

intransitif, -ive [ɛ̃tʀɑ̃zitif, -iv] ADJ (*Ling*) intransitive

intransportable [ɛ̃tʀɑ̃spɔʀtabl] ADJ (*blessé*) unable to travel

intraveineux, -euse [ɛ̃tʀavɛnø, -øz] ADJ intravenous

intrépide [ɛ̃tʀepid] ADJ dauntless, intrepid

intrépidité [ɛ̃tʀepidite] NF dauntlessness

intrigant, e [ɛ̃tʀigɑ̃, -ɑ̃t] NM/F schemer

intrigue [ɛ̃tʀig] NF intrigue; (*scénario*) plot

intriguer [ɛ̃tʀige] /**1**/ VI to scheme ▶ VT to puzzle, intrigue

intrinsèque [ɛ̃tʀɛ̃sɛk] ADJ intrinsic

introductif, -ive [ɛ̃tʀɔdyktif, -iv] ADJ introductory

introduction [ɛ̃tʀɔdyksjɔ̃] NF introduction; **paroles/chapitre d'~** introductory words/chapter; **lettre/mot d'~** letter/note of introduction

introduire [ɛ̃tʀɔdyiʀ] /**38**/ VT to introduce; (*visiteur*) to show in; (*aiguille, clef*): **~ qch dans** to insert *ou* introduce sth into; (*personne*): **à qch** to introduce to sth; (: *présenter*): **~ qn à qn/dans un club** to introduce sb to sb/to a club; **s'introduire** VI (*techniques, usages*) to be introduced; **s'introduire dans** to gain entry into; (*dans un groupe*) to get o.s. accepted into; (*eau, fumée*) to get into

introduit, e [ɛ̃tʀɔdyi, -it] PP *de* **introduire** ▶ ADJ: **bien ~** (*personne*) well-received

introniser [ɛ̃tʀɔnize] /**1**/ VT to enthrone

introspection [ɛ̃tʀɔspɛksjɔ̃] NF introspection

introuvable [ɛ̃tʀuvabl] ADJ which cannot be found; (*Comm*) unobtainable

introverti, e [ɛ̃tʀɔvɛʀti] NM/F introvert

intrus, e [ɛ̃tʀy, -yz] NM/F intruder

intrusion [ɛ̃tʀyzjɔ̃] NF intrusion; (*ingérence*) interference

intuitif, -ive [ɛ̃tyitif, -iv] ADJ intuitive

intuition [ɛ̃tyisjɔ̃] NF intuition; **avoir une ~** to have a feeling; **avoir l'~ de qch** to have an intuition of sth; **avoir de l'~** to have intuition

intuitivement [ɛ̃tyitivmɑ̃] ADV intuitively

inusable [inyzabl] ADJ hard-wearing

inusité, e [inyzite] ADJ rarely used

inutile [inytil] ADJ useless; (*superflu*) unnecessary

inutilement [inytilmɑ̃] ADV needlessly

inutilisable [inytilizabl] ADJ unusable

inutilisé, e [inytilize] ADJ unused

inutilité [inytilite] NF uselessness

invaincu, e [ɛ̃vɛ̃ky] ADJ unbeaten; (*armée, peuple*) unconquered

invalide [ɛ̃valid] ADJ disabled ▶ NM/F: **~ de guerre** disabled ex-serviceman; **~ du travail** industrially disabled person

invalider [ɛ̃valide] /**1**/ VT to invalidate

invalidité [ɛ̃validite] NF disability

invariable [ɛ̃vaʀjabl] ADJ invariable

invariablement [ɛ̃vaʀjablemɑ̃] ADV invariably

invasion [ɛ̃vazjɔ̃] NF invasion

invective [ɛ̃vɛktiv] NF invective

invectiver [ɛ̃vɛktive] /**1**/ VT to hurl abuse at ▶ VI: **~ contre** to rail against

invendable [ɛ̃vɑ̃dabl] ADJ unsaleable, unmarketable

invendu, e [ɛ̃vɑ̃dy] ADJ unsold ▶ NM return; **invendus** NMPL unsold goods

inventaire [ɛ̃vɑ̃tɛʀ] NM inventory; (*Comm: liste*) stocklist; (: *opération*) stocktaking *no pl*; (*fig*) survey; **faire un ~** to make an inventory; (*Comm*) to take stock; **faire** *ou* **procéder à l'~** to take stock

inventer [ɛ̃vɑ̃te] /**1**/ VT to invent; (*subterfuge*) to devise, invent; (*histoire, excuse*) to make up, invent; **~ de faire** to hit on the idea of doing

inventeur, -trice [ɛ̃vɑ̃tœʀ, -tʀis] NM/F inventor

inventif, -ive [ɛ̃vɑ̃tif, -iv] ADJ inventive

invention [ɛ̃vɑ̃sjɔ̃] NF invention; (*imagination, inspiration*) inventiveness

inventivité [ɛ̃vɑ̃tivite] NF inventiveness

inventorier [ɛ̃vɑ̃tɔʀje] /**7**/ VT to make an inventory of

invérifiable [ɛ̃veʀifjabl] ADJ unverifiable

inverse [ɛ̃vɛʀs] ADJ (*ordre*) reverse; (*sens*) opposite; (*rapport*) inverse ▶ NM reverse; inverse; **l'~ the** opposite; **dans l'ordre ~** in the reverse order; **en proportion ~** in inverse proportion; **dans le sens ~ des aiguilles d'une montre** anti-clockwise; **en sens ~** in (*ou* from) the opposite direction; **à l'~** conversely

inversement [ɛ̃vɛʀsemɑ̃] ADV conversely

inverser [ɛ̃vɛʀse] /**1**/ VT to reverse, invert; (*Élec*) to reverse

inversion [ɛ̃vɛʀsjɔ̃] NF reversal; inversion

invertébré, e [ɛ̃vɛʀtebʀe] ADJ, NM invertebrate

inverti, e [ɛ̃vɛʀti] NM/F homosexual

investigation [ɛ̃vɛstigasjɔ̃] NF investigation, inquiry

investir [ɛ̃vɛstiʀ] /2/ VT to invest; ~ **qn de** (d'une fonction, d'un pouvoir) to vest ou invest sb with; **s'investir** VI (Psych) to involve o.s.; **s'investir dans** to put a lot into

investissement [ɛ̃vɛstismɑ̃] NM investment; (Psych) involvement

investisseur [ɛ̃vɛstisœʀ] NM investor

investiture [ɛ̃vɛstityʀ] NF investiture; (à une élection) nomination

invétéré, e [ɛ̃veteʀe] ADJ (habitude) ingrained; (bavard, buveur) inveterate

invincible [ɛ̃vɛ̃sibl] ADJ invincible, unconquerable

invinciblement [ɛ̃vɛ̃sibləmɑ̃] ADV (fig) invincibly

inviolabilité [ɛ̃vjɔlabilite] NF: ~ **parlementaire** parliamentary immunity

inviolable [ɛ̃vjɔlabl] ADJ inviolable

invisible [ɛ̃vizibl] ADJ invisible; (fig: personne) not available

invitation [ɛ̃vitasjɔ̃] NF invitation; **à/sur l'~ de qn** at/on sb's invitation; **carte/lettre d'~** invitation card/letter

invite [ɛ̃vit] NF invitation

invité, e [ɛ̃vite] NM/F guest

inviter [ɛ̃vite] /1/ VT to invite; ~ **qn à faire qch** to invite sb to do sth; (chose) to induce ou tempt sb to do sth

invivable [ɛ̃vivabl] ADJ unbearable, impossible

involontaire [ɛ̃vɔlɔ̃tɛʀ] ADJ (mouvement) involuntary; (insulte) unintentional; (complice) unwitting

involontairement [ɛ̃vɔlɔ̃tɛʀmɑ̃] ADV involuntarily

invoquer [ɛ̃vɔke] /1/ VT (Dieu, muse) to call upon, invoke; (prétexte) to put forward (as an excuse); (témoignage) to call upon; (loi, texte) to refer to; ~ **la clémence de qn** to beg sb ou appeal to sb for clemency

invraisemblable [ɛ̃vʀɛsɑ̃blabl] ADJ (fait, nouvelle) unlikely, improbable; (bizarre) incredible

invraisemblance [ɛ̃vʀɛsɑ̃blɑ̃s] NF unlikelihood no pl, improbability

invulnérable [ɛ̃vylneʀabl] ADJ invulnerable

iode [jɔd] NM iodine

iodé, e [jɔde] ADJ iodized

ion [jɔ̃] NM ion

ionique [jɔnik] ADJ (Archit) Ionic; (Science) ionic

ioniseur [jɔnizœʀ] NM ionizer

iota [jɔta] NM: **sans changer un ~** without changing one iota ou the tiniest bit

iPad® [aipad] M iPad®

IPC SIGLE M (= Indice des prix à la consommation) CPI

iPhone® [aifɔn] M iPhone®

IR. ABR = **infrarouge**

IRA SIGLE F (= Irish Republican Army) IRA

irai etc [iʀe] VB voir **aller**

Irak [iʀak] NM: **l'~** Iraq ou Irak

irakien, ne [iʀakjɛ̃, -ɛn] ADJ Iraqi ▶ NM/F: **I~, ne** Iraqi

Iran [iʀɑ̃] NM: **l'~** Iran

iranien, ne [iʀanjɛ̃, -ɛn] ADJ Iranian ▶ NM (Ling) Iranian ▶ NM/F: **I~, ne** Iranian

Iraq [iʀak] NM = **Irak**

iraquien, ne [iʀakjɛ̃, -ɛn] ADJ, NM/F = **irakien**

irascible [iʀasibl] ADJ short-tempered, irascible

irions etc [iʀjɔ̃] VB voir **aller**

iris [iʀis] NM iris

irisé, e [iʀize] ADJ iridescent

irlandais, e [iʀlɑ̃dɛ, -ɛz] ADJ, NM (Ling) Irish ▶ NM/F: **I~, e** Irishman/woman; **les I~** the Irish

Irlande [iʀlɑ̃d] NF: **l'~** (pays) Ireland; **la République d'~** the Irish Republic, the Republic of Ireland, Eire; ~ **du Nord** Northern Ireland, Ulster; ~ **du Sud** Southern Ireland, Irish Republic, Eire; **la mer d'~** the Irish Sea

ironie [iʀɔni] NF irony

ironique [iʀɔnik] ADJ ironical

ironiquement [iʀɔnikmɑ̃] ADV ironically

ironiser [iʀɔnize] /1/ VI to be ironical

irons etc [iʀɔ̃] VB voir **aller**

IRPP SIGLE M (= impôt sur le revenu des personnes physiques) income tax

irradiation [iʀadjasjɔ̃] NF irradiation

irradier [iʀadje] /7/ VI to radiate ▶ VT to irradiate

irraisonné, e [iʀezɔne] ADJ irrational, unreasoned

irrationnel, le [iʀasjɔnɛl] ADJ irrational

irrattrapable [iʀatʀapabl] ADJ (retard) that cannot be made up; (bévue) that cannot be made good

irréalisable [iʀealizabl] ADJ unrealizable; (projet) impracticable

irréalisme [iʀealism] NM lack of realism

irréaliste [iʀealist] ADJ unrealistic

irréalité [iʀealite] NF unreality

irrecevable [iʀsəvabl] ADJ unacceptable

irréconciliable [iʀekɔ̃siljabl] ADJ irreconcilable

irrécouvrable [iʀekuvʀabl] ADJ irrecoverable

irrécupérable [iʀekypeʀabl] ADJ unreclaimable, beyond repair; (personne) beyond redemption ou recall

irrécusable [iʀekyzabl] ADJ (témoignage) unimpeachable; (preuve) incontestable, indisputable

irréductible [iʀedyktibl] ADJ indomitable, implacable; (Math: fraction, équation) irreducible

irréductiblement [iʀedyktibləmɑ̃] ADV implacably

irréel, le [iʀeɛl] ADJ unreal

irréfléchi, e [iʀefleʃi] ADJ thoughtless

irréfutable [iʀefytabl] ADJ irrefutable

irréfutablement [iʀefytabləmɑ̃] ADV irrefutably

irrégularité [iʀegylaʀite] NF irregularity; (de travail, d'effort, de qualité) unevenness no pl

irrégulier, -ière [iʀegylje, -jɛʀ] ADJ irregular; (surface, rythme, écriture) uneven, irregular; (travail, effort, qualité) uneven; (élève, athlète) erratic

irrégulièrement [iʀegyljɛʀmɑ̃] ADV irregularly

irrémédiable [iʀemedjabl] ADJ irreparable

irrémédiablement [iʀemedjabləmɑ̃] ADV irreparably

irremplaçable [iʀɑ̃plasabl] ADJ irreplaceable

irréparable [iʀepaʀabl] ADJ beyond repair, irreparable; (fig) irreparable

irrépréhensible [iʀepʀeɑ̃sibl] ADJ irreproachable

irrépressible [iʀepʀesibl] ADJ irrepressible
irréprochable [iʀepʀɔʃabl] ADJ irreproachable, beyond reproach; (tenue, toilette) impeccable
irrésistible [iʀezistibl] ADJ irresistible; (preuve, logique) compelling; (amusant) hilarious
irrésistiblement [iʀezistibləmɑ̃] ADV irresistibly
irrésolu, e [iʀezɔly] ADJ irresolute
irrésolution [iʀezɔlysjɔ̃] NF irresoluteness
irrespectueux, -euse [iʀɛspɛktɥø, -øz] ADJ disrespectful
irrespirable [iʀɛspiʀabl] ADJ unbreathable; (fig) oppressive, stifling
irresponsabilité [iʀɛspɔ̃sabilite] NF irresponsibility
irresponsable [iʀɛspɔ̃sabl] ADJ irresponsible
irrévérencieux, -euse [iʀeveʀɑ̃sjø, -øz] ADJ irreverent
irréversible [iʀevɛʀsibl] ADJ irreversible
irréversiblement [iʀevɛʀsibləmɑ̃] ADV irreversibly
irrévocable [iʀevɔkabl] ADJ irrevocable
irrévocablement [iʀevɔkabləmɑ̃] ADV irrevocably
irrigation [iʀigasjɔ̃] NF irrigation
irriguer [iʀige] /1/ VT to irrigate
irritabilité [iʀitabilite] NF irritability
irritable [iʀitabl] ADJ irritable
irritant, e [iʀitɑ̃, -ɑ̃t] ADJ irritating; (Méd) irritant
irritation [iʀitasjɔ̃] NF irritation
irrité, e [iʀite] ADJ irritated
irriter [iʀite] /1/ VT (agacer) to irritate, annoy; (Méd: enflammer) to irritate; **s'~ contre qn/de qch** to get annoyed ou irritated with sb/at sth
irruption [iʀypsjɔ̃] NF irruption no pl; **faire ~ dans** to burst into; **faire ~ chez qn** to burst in on sb
ISBN SIGLE M (= International Standard Book Number) ISBN
ISF SIGLE M (= impôt de solidarité sur la fortune) wealth tax
Islam [islam] NM: **l'~** Islam
islamique [islamik] ADJ Islamic
islamiste [islamist] ADJ, NMF Islamist
islamophobie NF Islamophobia
islandais, e [islɑ̃dɛ, -ɛz] ADJ Icelandic ▶ NM (Ling) Icelandic ▶ NM/F: **I~, e** Icelander
Islande [islɑ̃d] NF: **l'~** Iceland
ISMH SIGLE M = **Inventaire supplémentaire des monuments historiques; monument inscrit à l'~** ≈ listed building
isocèle [izɔsɛl] ADJ isoceles
isolant, e [izɔlɑ̃, -ɑ̃t] ADJ insulating; (insonorisant) soundproofing ▶ NM insulator
isolateur [izɔlatœʀ] NM (Élec) insulator
isolation [izɔlasjɔ̃] NF insulation; **~ thermique**

thermal insulation; **~ acoustique** soundproofing
isolationnisme [izɔlasjɔnism] NM isolationism
isolé, e [izɔle] ADJ isolated; (Élec) insulated; (contre le froid) insulated
isolement [izɔlmɑ̃] NM isolation; solitary confinement
isolément [izɔlemɑ̃] ADV in isolation
isoler [izɔle] /1/ VT to isolate; (prisonnier) to put in solitary confinement; (ville) to cut off, isolate; (Élec) to insulate; (contre le froid) to insulate; **s'isoler** VI to isolate o.s.
isoloir [izɔlwaʀ] NM polling booth
isorel® [izɔʀɛl] NM hardboard
isotherme [izɔtɛʀm] ADJ (camion) refrigerated
Israël [isʀaɛl] NM: **l'~** Israel
israélien, ne [isʀaeljɛ̃, -ɛn] ADJ Israeli ▶ NM/F: **I~, ne** Israeli
israélite [isʀaelit] ADJ Jewish; (dans l'Ancien Testament) Israelite ▶ NMF: **I~** Jew m, Jewess f (péj); Israelite
issu, e [isy] ADJ: **~ de** (né de) descended from; (résultant de) stemming from ▶ NF (ouverture, sortie) exit; (solution) way out, solution; (dénouement) outcome; **à l'~ de** at the conclusion ou close of; **rue sans ~, voie sans ~** dead end, no through road (BRIT), no outlet (US); **~ de secours** emergency exit
Istamboul, Istanbul [istɑ̃bul] N Istanbul
isthme [ism] NM isthmus
Italie [itali] NF: **l'~** Italy
italien, ne [italjɛ̃, -ɛn] ADJ Italian ▶ NM (Ling) Italian ▶ NM/F: **I~, ne** Italian
italique [italik] NM: **en ~(s)** in italics
item [itɛm] NM item; (question) question, test
itinéraire [itineʀɛʀ] NM itinerary, route; **~ bis** alternative route
itinérant, e [itineʀɑ̃, -ɑ̃t] ADJ itinerant, travelling
ITP SIGLE M (= ingénieur des travaux publics) civil engineer
IUT SIGLE M = **Institut universitaire de technologie**
IVG SIGLE F (= interruption volontaire de grossesse) abortion
ivoire [ivwaʀ] NM ivory
ivoirien, ne [ivwaʀjɛ̃, -ɛn] ADJ of ou from the Ivory Coast
ivraie [ivʀɛ] NF: **séparer le bon grain de l'~** (fig) to separate the wheat from the chaff
ivre [ivʀ] ADJ drunk; **~ de** (colère) wild with; (bonheur) drunk ou intoxicated with; **~ mort** dead drunk
ivresse [ivʀɛs] NF drunkenness; (euphorie) intoxication
ivrogne [ivʀɔɲ] NMF drunkard

i

Jj

J, j [ʒi] NM INV J, j ▸ ABR (= *Joule*) J; **=jour; jour J** D-day; **J comme Joseph** J for Jack (BRIT) ou Jig (US)

j' [ʒ] PRON *voir* **je**

jabot [ʒabo] NM (*Zool*) crop; (*de vêtement*) jabot

jacasser [ʒakase] /**1**/ VI to chatter

jachère [ʒaʃɛʀ] NF: **(être) en ~** (to lie) fallow

jacinthe [ʒasɛ̃t] NF hyacinth; **~ des bois** bluebell

jack [dʒak] NM jack plug

jacquard [ʒakaʀ] ADJ INV Fair Isle

jacquerie [ʒakʀi] NF riot

jade [ʒad] NM jade

jadis [ʒadis] ADV in times past, formerly

jaguar [ʒagwaʀ] NM (*Zool*) jaguar

jaillir [ʒajiʀ] /**2**/ VI (*liquide*) to spurt out, gush out; (*lumière*) to flood out; (*fig*) to rear up; (*cris, réponses*) to burst out

jaillissement [ʒajismɑ̃] NM spurt, gush

jais [ʒɛ] NM jet; **(d'un noir) de ~** jet-black

jalon [ʒalɔ̃] NM range pole; (*fig*) milestone; **poser des jalons** (*fig*) to pave the way

jalonner [ʒalɔne] /**1**/ VT to mark out; (*fig*) to mark, punctuate

jalousement [ʒaluzmɑ̃] ADV jealously

jalouser [ʒaluze] /**1**/ VT to be jealous of

jalousie [ʒaluzi] NF jealousy; (*store*) (venetian) blind

jaloux, -ouse [ʒalu, -uz] ADJ jealous; **être ~ de qn/qch** to be jealous of sb/sth

jamaïquain, e [ʒamaikɛ̃, -ɛn] ADJ Jamaican ▸ NM/F: **J~, e** Jamaican

Jamaïque [ʒamaik] NF: **la ~** Jamaica

jamais [ʒamɛ] ADV never; (*sans négation*) ever; **ne … ~** never; **~ de la vie!** never!; **si ~ …** if ever …; **à (tout) ~, pour ~** for ever, for ever and ever; **je ne suis ~ allé en Espagne** I've never been to Spain

jambage [ʒɑ̃baʒ] NM (*de lettre*) downstroke; (*de porte*) jamb

jambe [ʒɑ̃b] NF leg; **à toutes jambes** as fast as one's legs can carry one

jambières [ʒɑ̃bjɛʀ] NFPL legwarmers; (*Sport*) shin pads

jambon [ʒɑ̃bɔ̃] NM ham

jambonneau, x [ʒɑ̃bɔno] NM knuckle of ham

jante [ʒɑ̃t] NF (*wheel*) rim

janvier [ʒɑ̃vje] NM January; *voir aussi* **juillet**

Japon [ʒapɔ̃] NM: **le ~** Japan

japonais, e [ʒapɔnɛ, -ɛz] ADJ Japanese ▸ NM (*Ling*) Japanese ▸ NM/F: **J~, e** Japanese

japonaiserie [ʒapɔnɛzʀi] NF (*bibelot*) Japanese curio

jappement [ʒapmɑ̃] NM yap, yelp

japper [ʒape] /**1**/ VI to yap, yelp

jaquette [ʒakɛt] NF (*de cérémonie*) morning coat; (*de femme*) jacket; (*de livre*) dust cover, (dust) jacket

jardin [ʒaʀdɛ̃] NM garden; **~ d'acclimatation** zoological gardens *pl*; **~ botanique** botanical gardens *pl*; **~ d'enfants** nursery school; **~ potager** vegetable garden; **~ public** (public) park, public gardens *pl*; **jardins suspendus** hanging gardens; **~ zoologique** zoological gardens

jardinage [ʒaʀdinaʒ] NM gardening

jardiner [ʒaʀdine] /**1**/ VI to garden, do some gardening

jardinet [ʒaʀdinɛ] NM little garden

jardinier, -ière [ʒaʀdinje, -jɛʀ] NM/F gardener ▸ NF (*de fenêtre*) window box; **jardinière d'enfants** nursery school teacher; **jardinière (de légumes)** (*Culin*) mixed vegetables

jargon [ʒaʀgɔ̃] NM (*charabia*) gibberish; (*publicitaire, scientifique etc*) jargon

jarre [ʒaʀ] NF (*earthenware*) jar

jarret [ʒaʀɛ] NM back of knee; (*Culin*) knuckle, shin

jarretelle [ʒaʀtɛl] NF suspender (BRIT), garter (US)

jarretière [ʒaʀtjɛʀ] NF garter

jars [ʒaʀ] NM (*Zool*) gander

jaser [ʒaze] /**1**/ VI to chatter, prattle; (*indiscrètement*) to gossip

jasmin [ʒasmɛ̃] NM jasmine

jaspe [ʒasp] NM jasper

jaspé, e [ʒaspe] ADJ marbled, mottled

jatte [ʒat] NF basin, bowl

jauge [ʒoʒ] NF (*capacité*) capacity, tonnage; (*instrument*) gauge; **~ (de niveau) d'huile** (*Auto*) dipstick

jauger [ʒoʒe] /**3**/ VT to gauge the capacity of; (*fig*) to size up; **~ 3 000 tonneaux** to measure 3,000 tons

jaunâtre [ʒonɑtʀ] ADJ (*couleur, teint*) yellowish

jaune [ʒon] ADJ, NM yellow ▸ NMF Asiatic;

(*briseur de grève*) blackleg ▶ ADV (*fam*): **rire ~ to** laugh on the other side of one's face; **~ d'œuf** (egg) yolk

jaunir [ʒoniʀ] **/2/** VI, VT to turn yellow

jaunisse [ʒonis] NF jaundice

Java [ʒava] NF Java

java [ʒava] NF (*fam*): **faire la ~ to live it up, have** a real party

javanais, e [ʒavanɛ, -ɛz] ADJ Javanese

Javel [ʒavɛl] NF *voir* **eau**

javelliser [ʒavelize] **/1/** VT (*eau*) to chlorinate

javelot [ʒavlo] NM javelin; (*Sport*): **faire du ~ to** throw the javelin

jazz [dʒaz] NM jazz

J.-C. ABR = **Jésus-Christ**

je, j' [ʒə, ʒ] PRON I

jean [dʒin] NM jeans pl

jeannette [ʒanɛt] NF (*planchette*) sleeve board; (*petite fille scout*) Brownie

jeep® [(d)ʒip] NF (*Auto*) Jeep®

jérémiades [ʒeʀemjad] NFPL moaning *sg*

jerrycan [ʒeʀikan] NM jerry can

Jersey [ʒɛʀze] NF Jersey

jersey [ʒɛʀze] NM jersey; (*Tricot*): **pointe de ~** stocking stitch

jersiais, e [ʒɛʀzjɛ, -ɛz] ADJ Jersey cpd, of *ou* from Jersey

Jérusalem [ʒeʀyzalɛm] N Jerusalem

jésuite [ʒezɥit] NM Jesuit

Jésus-Christ [ʒezykʀi(st)] N Jesus Christ; **600 avant/après ~** 600 B.C./A.D.

jet¹ [ʒɛ] NM (*lancer: action*) throwing *no pl*; (*: résultat*) throw; (*jaillissement: d'eaux*) jet; (*: de sang*) spurt; (*de tuyau*) nozzle; (*fig*): **premier ~** (*ébauche*) rough outline; **arroser au ~ to hose;** **d'un (seul) ~** (*d'un seul coup*) at (*ou* in) one go; **du premier ~** at the first attempt *ou* shot; **~ d'eau** spray; (*fontaine*) fountain

jet² [dʒɛt] NM (*avion*) jet

jetable [ʒətabl] ADJ disposable

jeté [ʒəte] NM (*Tricot*): **un ~ make one; ~ de table** (table) runner; **~ de lit** bedspread

jetée [ʒəte] NF jetty; (*grande*) pier

jeter [ʒəte] **/4/** VT (*gén*) to throw; (*se défaire de*) to throw away *ou* out; (*son, lueur etc*) to give out; **~ qch à qn** to throw sth to sb; (*de façon agressive*) to throw sth at sb; **~ l'ancre** (*Navig*) to cast anchor; **~ un coup d'œil (à)** to take a look (at); **~ les bras en avant/la tête en arrière** to throw one's arms forward/one's head back(ward); **~ l'effroi parmi** to spread fear among; **~ un sort à qn** to cast a spell on sb; **~ qn dans la misère** to reduce sb to poverty; **~ qn dehors/en prison** to throw sb out/into prison; **~ l'éponge** (*fig*) to throw in the towel; **~ des fleurs à qn** (*fig*) to say lovely things to sb; **~ la pierre à qn** (*accuser, blâmer*) to accuse sb; **se ~ sur** to throw o.s. onto; **se ~ dans** (*fleuve*) to flow into; **se ~ par la fenêtre** to throw o.s. out of the window; **se ~ à l'eau** (*fig*) to take the plunge

jeton [ʒətɔ̃] NM (*au jeu*) counter; (*de téléphone*) token; **jetons de présence** (director's) fees

jette *etc* [ʒɛt] VB *voir* **jeter**

jeu, x [ʒø] NM (*divertissement, Tech: d'une pièce*) play;

(*défini par des règles, Tennis: partie, Football etc: façon de jouer*) game; (*Théât etc*) acting; (*fonctionnement*) working, interplay; (*série d'objets, jouet*) set; (*Cartes*) hand; (*au casino*): **le ~** gambling; **cacher son ~** (*fig*) to keep one's cards hidden, conceal one's hand; **c'est un ~ d'enfant!** (*fig*) it's child's play!; **en ~** at stake; at work; (*Football*) in play; **remettre en ~** to throw in; **entrer/ mettre en ~** to come/bring into play; **par ~** (*pour s'amuser*) for fun; **d'entrée de ~** (*tout de suite, dès le début*) from the outset; **entrer dans le ~/le ~ de qn** (*fig*) to play the game/sb's game; **jouer gros ~** to play for high stakes; **se piquer/se prendre au ~** to get excited over/get caught up in the game; **~ d'arcade** video game; **~ de boules** game of bowls; (*endroit*) bowling pitch; (*boules*) set of bowls; **~ de cartes** card game; (*paquet*) pack of cards; **~ de construction** building set; **~ d'échecs** chess set; **~ d'écritures** (*Comm*) paper transaction; **~ électronique** electronic game; **~ de hasard** game of chance; **~ de mots** pun; **le ~ de l'oie** snakes and ladders *sg*; **~ d'orgue(s)** organ stop; **~ de patience** puzzle; **~ de physionomie** facial expressions *pl*; **~ de société** board game; **~ télévisé** television quiz; **~ vidéo** video game; **~ de lumière** lighting effects; **J~ olympiques** Olympic Games

jeu-concours [ʒøkɔ̃kuʀ] (*pl* **jeux-concours**) NM competition

jeudi [ʒødi] NM Thursday; **~ saint** Maundy Thursday; *voir aussi* **lundi**

jeun [ʒœ̃]: **à ~ adv** on an empty stomach; **être à ~** to have eaten nothing; **rester à ~** not to eat anything

jeune [ʒœn] ADJ young ▶ ADV: **faire/s'habiller ~** to look/dress young; **les jeunes** young people, the young; **~ fille** *nf* girl; **~ homme** *nm* young man; **~ loup** *nm* (*Pol, Écon*) young go-getter; **~ premier** leading man; **jeunes gens** *nmpl* young people; **jeunes mariés** *nmpl* newly weds

jeûne [ʒøn] NM fast

jeûner [ʒøne] **/1/** VT to fast, go without food

jeunesse [ʒœnɛs] NF youth; (*aspect*) youthfulness; (*jeunes*) young people *pl*, youth

jf SIGLE F = **jeune fille**

jh SIGLE M = **jeune homme**

JI SIGLE M = **juge d'instruction**

jiu-jitsu [ʒyʒitsy] NM INV (*Sport*) jujitsu

JMF SIGLE F (= *Jeunesses musicales de France*) association to promote music among the young

JO SIGLE M = **le Journal officiel (de la République française)** ▶ SIGLE MPL = **Jeux olympiques**

joaillerie [ʒɔajʀi] NF jewel trade; jewellery (*BRIT*), jewelry (*US*)

joaillier, -ière [ʒɔaje, -jɛʀ] NM/F jeweller (*BRIT*), jeweler (*US*)

job [dʒɔb] NM job

jobard [ʒɔbaʀ] NM (*péj*) sucker, mug

jockey [ʒɔkɛ] NM jockey

jodler [ʒɔdle] **/1/** VI to yodel

jogging [dʒɔgiŋ] NM jogging; (*survêtement*) tracksuit (*BRIT*), sweatsuit (*US*); **faire du ~ to go** jogging, jog

j

joie [ʒwa] NF joy

joignais etc [ʒwaɲɛ] VB voir **joindre**

joindre [ʒwɛ̃dʀ] /49/ VT to join; (contacter) to contact, get in touch with; **se joindre** (mains etc) to come together; **~ qch à** (à une lettre) to enclose sth with; **~ un fichier à un mail** (Inform) to attach a file to an email; **~ les mains/talons** to put one's hands/heels together; **~ les deux bouts** (fig: du mois) to make ends meet; **se joindre à qn** to join sb; **se joindre à qch** to join in sth

joint, e [ʒwɛ̃, -ɛt] PP de **joindre** ▶ ADJ: **~ (à)** (lettre, paquet) attached (to), enclosed (with) ▶ NM joint; (ligne) join; (de ciment etc) pointing no pl; **pièce ~** (de lettre) enclosure; (de mail) attachment; **chercher/trouver le ~** (fig) to look for/come up with the answer; **~ de cardan** cardan joint; **~ de culasse** cylinder head gasket; **~ de robinet** washer; **~ universel** universal joint

jointure [ʒwɛ̃tyʀ] NF (Anat: articulation) joint; (Tech: assemblage) joint; (: ligne) join

joker [ʒɔkɛʀ] NM (Cartes) joker; (Inform): (caractère) ~ wild card

joli, e [ʒɔli] ADJ pretty, attractive; **une ~ somme/situation** a nice little sum/situation; **un ~ gâchis** etc a nice mess etc; **c'est du ~!** (ironique) that's very nice!; **tout ça, c'est bien ~ mais ...** that's all very well but ...

joliment [ʒɔlimɑ̃] ADV prettily, attractively; (fam: très) pretty

jonc [ʒɔ̃] NM (bul)rush; (bague, bracelet) band

joncher [ʒɔ̃ʃe] /1/ VT (choses) to be strewed on; **jonché de** strewn with

jonction [ʒɔ̃ksjɔ̃] NF junction, joining; **(point de) ~** (de routes) junction; (de fleuves) confluence; **opérer une ~** (Mil etc) to rendez-vous

jongler [ʒɔ̃gle] /1/ VI to juggle; (fig): **~ avec** to juggle with, play with

jongleur, -euse [ʒɔ̃glœʀ, -øz] NM/F juggler

jonquille [ʒɔ̃kij] NF daffodil

Jordanie [ʒɔʀdani] NF: **la ~** Jordan

jordanien, ne [ʒɔʀdanjɛ̃, -ɛn] ADJ Jordanian ▶ NM/F: **J~, ne** Jordanian

jouable [ʒwabl] ADJ playable

joue [ʒu] NF cheek; **mettre en ~** to take aim at

jouer [ʒwe] /1/ VT (partie, carte, coup, Mus: morceau) to play; (somme d'argent, réputation) to stake, wager; (pièce, rôle) to perform; (film) to show; (simuler: sentiment) to affect, feign ▶ VI to play; (Théât, Ciné) to act, perform; (au casino) to gamble; (bois, porte: se voiler) to warp; (clef, pièce: avoir du jeu) to be loose; (entrer ou être en jeu) to come into play, come into it; **~ sur** (miser) to gamble on; **~ de** (Mus) to play; **~ du couteau/des coudes** to use knives/one's elbows; **~ à** (jeu, sport, roulette) to play; **~ au héros** to act ou play the hero; **~ avec** (risquer) to gamble with; **se ~ de** (difficultés) to make light of; **se ~ de qn** to deceive ou dupe sb; **~ un tour à qn** to play a trick on sb; **~ la comédie** (fig) to put on an act, put it on; **~ aux courses** to back horses, bet on horses; **~ à la baisse/hausse** (Bourse) to play for a fall/rise; **~ serré** to play a close game; **~ de**

malchance to be dogged with ill-luck; **~ sur les mots** to play with words; **à toi/nous de ~** it's your/our go ou turn; **bien joué!** well done!; **on joue Hamlet au théâtre X** Hamlet is on at the X theatre

jouet [ʒwɛ] NM toy; **être le ~ de** (illusion etc) to be the victim of

joueur, -euse [ʒwœʀ, -øz] NM/F player ▶ ADJ (enfant, chat) playful; **être beau/mauvais ~** to be a good/bad loser

joufflu, e [ʒufly] ADJ chubby(-cheeked)

joug [ʒu] NM yoke

jouir [ʒwiʀ] /2/ VI (sexe: fam) to come ▶ VT: **~ de** to enjoy

jouissance [ʒwisɑ̃s] NF pleasure; (Jur) use

jouisseur, -euse [ʒwisœʀ, -øz] NM/F sensualist

joujou [ʒuʒu] NM (fam) toy

jour [ʒuʀ] NM day; (opposé à la nuit) day, daytime; (clarté) daylight; (fig: aspect, ouverture) opening; (Couture) openwork no pl; **sous un ~ favorable/nouveau** in a favourable/new light; **de ~** (crème, service) day cpd; **travailler de ~** to work during the day; **voyager de ~** to travel by day; **au ~ le ~** from day to day; **de nos jours** these days, nowadays; **tous les jours** every day; **de ~ en ~** day by day; **d'un ~ à l'autre** from one day to the next; **du ~ au lendemain** overnight; **il fait ~** it's daylight; **en plein ~** in broad daylight; **au ~** in daylight; **au petit ~** at daybreak; **au grand ~** (fig) in the open; **mettre au ~** to disclose, uncover; **être à ~** to be up to date; **mettre à ~** to bring up to date, update; **mise à ~** updating; **donner le ~ à** to give birth to; **voir le ~** to be born; **se faire ~** (fig) to become clear; **~ férié** public holiday; **le ~ J** D-day; **~ ouvrable** working day

Jourdain [ʒuʀdɛ̃] NM: **le ~** the (River) Jordan

journal, -aux [ʒuʀnal, -o] NM (news)paper; (personnel) journal; (intime) diary; **~ de bord** log; **~ de mode** fashion magazine; **le J~ officiel (de la République française)** bulletin giving details of laws and official announcements; **~ parlé** radio news sg; **~ télévisé** television news sg

journalier, -ière [ʒuʀnalje, -jɛʀ] ADJ daily; (banal) everyday ▶ NM day labourer

journalisme [ʒuʀnalism] NM journalism

journaliste [ʒuʀnalist] NMF journalist

journalistique [ʒuʀnalistik] ADJ journalistic

journée [ʒuʀne] NF day; **la ~ continue** the 9 to 5 working day (with short lunch break)

journellement [ʒuʀnɛlmɑ̃] ADV (tous les jours) daily; (souvent) every day

joute [ʒut] NF (tournoi) duel; (verbale) duel, battle of words

jouvence [ʒuvɑ̃s] NF: **bain de ~** rejuvenating experience

jouxter [ʒukste] /1/ VT to adjoin

jovial, e, -aux [ʒɔvjal, -o] ADJ jovial, jolly

jovialité [ʒɔvjalite] NF joviality

joyau, x [ʒwajo] NM gem, jewel

joyeusement [ʒwajøzmɑ̃] ADV joyfully, gladly

joyeux, -euse [ʒwajø, -øz] ADJ joyful, merry; **~ Noël!** Merry ou Happy Christmas!; **joyeuses**

Pâques! Happy Easter!; **~ anniversaire!** many happy returns!

JT SIGLE M = **journal télévisé**

jubilation [ʒybilasjɔ̃] NF jubilation

jubilé [ʒybile] NM jubilee

jubiler [ʒybile] /**1**/ VI to be jubilant, exult

jucher [ʒyʃe] /**1**/ VT: **~ qch sur** to perch sth (up)on ▶ VI (oiseau): **~ sur** to perch (up)on; **se ~ sur** to perch o.s. (up)on

judaïque [ʒydaik] ADJ (loi) Judaic; (religion) Jewish

judaïsme [ʒydaism] NM Judaism

judas [ʒyda] NM (trou) spy-hole

Judée [ʒyde] NF: **la ~** Jud(a)ea

judéo- [ʒydeɔ] PRÉFIXE Judeo-

judéo-allemand, e [ʒydeɔalmɑ̃, -ɑ̃d] ADJ, NM Yiddish

judéo-chrétien, ne [ʒydeɔkretjɛ̃, -ɛn] ADJ Judeo-Christian

judiciaire [ʒydisjɛʀ] ADJ judicial

judicieusement [ʒydisjøzmɑ̃] ADV judiciously

judicieux, -euse [ʒydisjø, -øz] ADJ judicious

judo [ʒydo] NM judo

judoka [ʒydɔka] NMF judoka

juge [ʒyʒ] NM judge; **~ d'instruction** examining (BRIT) ou committing (US) magistrate; **~ de paix** justice of the peace; **~ de touche** linesman

jugé [ʒyʒe]: **au ~** adv by guesswork

jugement [ʒyʒmɑ̃] NM judgment; (Jur: au pénal) sentence; (: au civil) decision; **~ de valeur** value judgment

jugeote [ʒyʒɔt] NF (fam) gumption

juger [ʒyʒe] /**3**/ VT to judge; (estimer) to consider ▶ NM: **au ~** by guesswork; **~ qn/qch satisfaisant** to consider sb/sth (to be) satisfactory; **~ que** to think ou consider that; **~ bon de faire** to consider it a good idea to do, see fit to do; **~ de** vt to judge; **jugez de ma surprise** imagine my surprise

jugulaire [ʒygylɛʀ] ADJ jugular ▶ NF (Mil) chinstrap

juguler [ʒygyle] /**1**/ VT (maladie) to halt; (révolte) to suppress; (inflation etc) to control, curb

juif, -ive [ʒɥif, -iv] ADJ Jewish ▶ NM/F: **J~, -ive** Jew/Jewess ou Jewish woman

juillet [ʒɥijɛ] NM July; **le premier ~** the first of July (BRIT), July first (US); **le deux/onze ~** the second/eleventh of July, July second/eleventh; **il est venu le 5 ~** he came on 5th July ou July 5th; **en ~** in July; **début/fin ~** at the beginning/end of July; see note

> Le 14 juillet is a national holiday in France and commemorates the storming of the Bastille during the French Revolution. Throughout the country there are celebrations, which feature parades, music, dancing and firework displays. In Paris a military parade along the Champs-Élysées is attended by the President.

juin [ʒɥɛ̃] NM June; voir aussi **juillet**

juive [ʒɥiv] ADJ, NF voir **juif**

jumeau, -elle, x [ʒymo, -ɛl] ADJ, NM/F twin; **maisons jumelles** semidetached houses

jumelage [ʒymlaʒ] NM twinning

jumeler [ʒymle] /**4**/ VT to twin; **roues jumelées** double wheels; **billets de loterie jumelés** double series lottery tickets; **pari jumelé** double bet

jumelle [ʒymɛl] ADJ F, NF voir **jumeau** ▶ VB voir **jumeler**

jumelles [ʒymɛl] NFPL binoculars

jument [ʒymɑ̃] NF mare

jungle [ʒɔ̃gl] NF jungle

junior [ʒynjɔʀ] ADJ junior

junte [ʒœ̃t] NF junta

jupe [ʒyp] NF skirt

jupe-culotte [ʒypkylɔt] (pl jupes-culottes) NF divided skirt, culotte(s)

jupette [ʒypɛt] NF short skirt

jupon [ʒypɔ̃] NM waist slip ou petticoat

Jura [ʒyʀa] NM: **le ~** the Jura (Mountains)

jurassien, ne [ʒyʀasjɛ̃, -ɛn] ADJ of ou from the Jura Mountains

juré, e [ʒyʀe] NM/F juror ▶ ADJ: **ennemi ~** sworn ou avowed enemy

jurer [ʒyʀe] /**1**/ VT (obéissance etc) to swear, vow ▶ VI (dire des jurons) to swear, curse; (dissoner): **~ (avec)** to clash (with); (s'engager): **~ de faire/que** to swear ou vow to do/that; (affirmer): **~ que** to swear ou vouch that; **~ de qch** (s'en porter garant) to swear to sth; **ils ne jurent que par lui** they swear by him; **je vous jure!** honestly!

juridiction [ʒyʀidiksjɔ̃] NF jurisdiction; (tribunal, tribunaux) court(s) of law

juridique [ʒyʀidik] ADJ legal

juridiquement [ʒyʀidikmɑ̃] ADV (devant la justice) juridically; (du point de vue du droit) legally

jurisconsulte [ʒyʀiskɔ̃sylt] NM jurisconsult

jurisprudence [ʒyʀispʀydɑ̃s] NF (Jur: décisions) (legal) precedents; (: principes juridiques) jurisprudence; **faire ~** (faire autorité) to set a precedent

juriste [ʒyʀist] NMF jurist; lawyer

juron [ʒyʀɔ̃] NM curse, swearword

jury [ʒyʀi] NM (Jur) jury; (Art, Sport) panel of judges; (Scol) board (of examiners), jury

jus [ʒy] NM juice; (de viande) gravy, (meat) juice; **~ de fruits** fruit juice; **~ de raisin/tomates** grape/tomato juice

jusant [ʒyzɑ̃] NM ebb (tide)

jusqu'au-boutiste [ʒyskobutist] NMF extremist, hardliner

jusque [ʒysk]: **jusqu'à** prép (endroit) as far as, (up) to; (moment) until, till; (limite) up to; **~ sur/dans** up to, as far as; (y compris) even on/in; **~ vers** until about; **jusqu'à ce que** conj until; **~-là** (temps) until then; (espace) up to there; **jusqu'ici** (temps) until now; (espace) up to here; **jusqu'à présent** ou **maintenant** until now, so far; **jusqu'où?** how far?

justaucorps [ʒystokɔʀ] NM INV (Danse, Sport) leotard

juste [ʒyst] ADJ (équitable) just, fair; (légitime) just, justified; (exact, vrai) right; (pertinent) apt; (étroit) tight; (insuffisant) on the short side ▶ ADV right; tight; (chanter) in tune; (seulement) just; **~ assez/au-dessus** just enough/above;

j

pouvoir tout ~ faire to be only just able to do; **au ~** exactly, actually; **comme de ~** of course, naturally; **le ~ milieu** the happy medium; **c'était ~** it was a close thing; **à ~ titre** rightfully

justement [ʒystəmɑ̃] ADV rightly; justly; (*précisément*) just, precisely; **c'est ~ ce qu'il fallait faire** that's just *ou* precisely what needed doing

justesse [ʒystɛs] NF (*précision*) accuracy; (*d'une remarque*) aptness; (*d'une opinion*) soundness; **de ~** only just, by a narrow margin

justice [ʒystis] NF (*équité*) fairness, justice; (*Admin*) justice; **rendre la ~** to dispense justice; **traduire en ~** to bring before the courts; **obtenir ~** to obtain justice; **rendre ~ à qn** to do sb justice; **se faire ~** to take the law into one's own hands; (*se suicider*) to take one's life

justiciable [ʒystisjabl] ADJ: **~ de** (*Jur*) answerable to

justicier, -ière [ʒystisje, -jɛʀ] NM/F judge, righter of wrongs

justifiable [ʒystifjabl] ADJ justifiable

justificatif, -ive [ʒystifikatif, -iv] ADJ (*document etc*) supporting ▶ NM supporting proof; **pièce justificative** written proof

justification [ʒystifikasjɔ̃] NF justification

justifier [ʒystifje] /**7**/ VT to justify; **~ de** VT to prove; **non justifié** unjustified; **justifié à droite/gauche** ranged right/left

jute [ʒyt] NM jute

juteux, -euse [ʒytø, -øz] ADJ juicy

juvénile [ʒyvenil] ADJ young, youthful

juxtaposer [ʒykstapoze] /**1**/ VT to juxtapose

juxtaposition [ʒykstapozisjɔ̃] NF juxtaposition

Kk

K, k [ka] NM INV K, k ▶ ABR (= *kilo*) kg; **K comme Kléber** K for King

K 7 [kasɛt] NF cassette

Kaboul, Kabul [kabul] N Kabul

kabyle [kabil] ADJ Kabyle ▶ NM (*Ling*) Kabyle ▶ NMF: **K~** Kabyle

Kabylie [kabili] NF: **la ~** Kabylia

kafkaïen, ne [kafkajɛ̃, -ɛn] ADJ Kafkaesque

kaki [kaki] ADJ INV khaki

Kalahari [kalaari] N: **désert de ~** Kalahari Desert

kaléidoscope [kaleidɔskɔp] NM kaleidoscope

Kampala [kɑ̃pala] N Kampala

Kampuchéa [kɑ̃putʃea] NM: **le ~ (démocratique)** (the People's Republic of) Kampuchea

kangourou [kɑ̃guru] NM kangaroo

kaolin [kaɔlɛ̃] NM kaolin

kapok [kapɔk] NM kapok

karaoke [karaɔke] NM karaoke

karaté [karate] NM karate

kart [kart] NM go-cart

karting [kartiŋ] NM go-carting, karting

kascher [kaʃɛr] ADJ INV kosher

kayak [kajak] NM kayak; **faire du ~** to go kayaking

Kazakhstan [kazakstɑ̃] NM Kazakhstan

Kenya [kenja] NM: **le ~** Kenya

kenyan, e [kenjɑ̃, -an] ADJ Kenyan ▶ NM/F: **K~, e** Kenyan

képi [kepi] NM kepi

Kerguelen [kɛrgelɛn] NFPL: **les (îles) ~** Kerguelen

kermesse [kɛrmɛs] NF bazaar, (charity) fête; village fair

kérosène [kerozɛn] NM jet fuel; rocket fuel

kg ABR (= *kilogramme*) kg

KGB SIGLE M KGB

khmer, -ère [kmɛr] ADJ Khmer ▶ NM (*Ling*) Khmer

khôl [kol] NM khol

kibboutz [kibuts] NM kibbutz

kidnapper [kidnape] /1/ VT to kidnap

kidnappeur, -euse [kidnapœr, -øz] NM/F kidnapper

kidnapping [kidnapiŋ] NM kidnapping

Kilimandjaro [kilimɑ̃dʒaro] NM: **le ~** Mount Kilimanjaro

kilo [kilo] NM kilo

kilogramme [kilɔgram] NM kilogramme (*BRIT*), kilogram (*US*)

kilométrage [kilɔmetraʒ] NM number of kilometres travelled, ≈ mileage

kilomètre [kilɔmɛtr] NM kilometre (*BRIT*), kilometer (*US*); **kilomètres-heure** kilometres per hour

kilométrique [kilɔmetrik] ADJ (*distance*) in kilometres; **compteur ~** ≈ mileage indicator

kilooctet [kilɔɔktɛ] NM kilobyte

kilowatt [kilɔwat] NM kilowatt

Kindle® [kindl] M Kindle®

kinésithérapeute [kineziterapøt] NMF physiotherapist

kinésithérapie [kineziterapi] NF physiotherapy

kiosque [kjɔsk] NM kiosk, stall; (*Tél etc*) telephone and/or videotext information service; **~ à journaux** newspaper kiosk

kir [kir] NM kir (*white wine with blackcurrant liqueur*)

Kirghizistan [kirgizistɑ̃] NM Kirghizia

kirsch [kirʃ] NM kirsch

kit [kit] NM kit; **~ piéton** *ou* **mains libres** hands-free kit; **en ~** in kit form

kitchenette [kitʃ(ə)nɛt] NF kitchenette

kiwi [kiwi] NM (*Zool*) kiwi; (*Bot*) kiwi (fruit)

klaxon [klaksɔn] NM horn

klaxonner [klaksɔne] /1/ VI, VT to hoot (*BRIT*), honk (one's horn) (*US*)

kleptomane [klɛptɔman] NMF kleptomaniac

km ABR (= *kilomètre*) km

km/h ABR (= *kilomètres/heure*) km/h, kph

knock-out [nɔkawt] NM knock-out

Ko ABR (*Inform*: = *kilooctet*) kB

K.-O. [kao] ADJ INV shattered, knackered

koala [kɔala] NM koala (bear)

kolkhoze [kɔlkoz] NM kolkhoz

Kosovo [kɔsɔvo] NM: **le ~** Kosovo

Koweit, Kuweit [kɔwɛt] NM: **le ~** Kuwait, Koweit

koweitien, ne [kɔwɛtjɛ̃, -ɛn] ADJ Kuwaiti ▶ NM/F: **K~, ne** Kuwaiti

krach [krak] NM (*Écon*) crash

kraft [kraft] NM brown *ou* kraft paper

Kremlin [krɛmlɛ̃] NM: **le ~** the Kremlin

Kuala Lumpur [kwalalympur] N Kuala Lumpur

k

kurde [kyʀd] ADJ Kurdish ▶ NM (*Ling*) Kurdish ▶ NMF: **K~** Kurd

Kurdistan [kyʀdistã] NM: **le ~** Kurdistan

Kuweit [kɔwɛt] NM = **Koweit**

kW ABR (= *kilowatt*) kW

k-way® [kawɛ] NM (lightweight nylon) cagoule

kW/h ABR (= *kilowatt/heure*) kW/h

kyrielle [kiʀjɛl] NF: **une ~ de** a stream of

kyste [kist] NM cyst

L, l [εl] NM INV L, l ▸ ABR (= *litre*) l; **L comme Louis** L for Lucy (BRIT) *ou* Love (US)

l' [l] ART DÉF *voir* **le**

la [la] ART DÉF, PRON *voir* **le** ▸ NM (*Mus*) A; (*en chantant la gamme*) la

là [la] ADV there; (*ici*) here; (*dans le temps*) then; **est-ce que Catherine est là?** is Catherine there (*ou* here)?; **elle n'est pas là** she isn't here; **c'est là que** this is where; **là où** where; **de là** (*fig*) hence; **par là** (*fig*) by that; **tout est là** (*fig*) that's what it's all about; *voir aussi* **-ci**; **celui**

là-bas [labɑ] ADV there

label [label] NM stamp, seal

labeur [labœR] NM toil *no pl*, toiling *no pl*

labo [labo] NM (= *laboratoire*) lab

laborantin, e [labɔRɑ̃tɛ̃, -in] NM/F laboratory assistant

laboratoire [labɔRatwaR] NM laboratory; **~ de langues/d'analyses** language/(medical) analysis laboratory

laborieusement [labɔRjøzmɑ̃] ADV laboriously

laborieux, -euse [labɔRjø, -øz] ADJ (*tâche*) laborious; **classes laborieuses** working classes

labour [labuR] NM ploughing *no pl* (BRIT), plowing *no pl* (US); **labours** NMPL (*champs*) ploughed fields; **cheval de ~** plough- *ou* cart-horse; **bœuf de ~** ox

labourage [labuRaʒ] NM ploughing (BRIT), plowing (US)

labourer [labuRe] /1/ VT to plough (BRIT), plow (US); (*fig*) to make deep gashes *ou* furrows in

laboureur [labuRœR] NM ploughman (BRIT), plowman (US)

labrador [labRadɔR] NM (*chien*) labrador; (*Géo*): **le L~** Labrador

labyrinthe [labiRɛ̃t] NM labyrinth, maze

lac [lak] NM lake; **le ~ Léman** Lake Geneva; **les Grands Lacs** the Great Lakes; *voir aussi* **lacs**

lacer [lase] /3/ VT to lace *ou* do up

lacérer [laseRe] /6/ VT to tear to shreds

lacet [lasɛ] NM (*de chaussure*) lace; (*de route*) sharp bend; (*piège*) snare; **chaussures à lacets** lace-up *ou* lacing shoes

lâche [lɑʃ] ADJ (*poltron*) cowardly; (*desserré*) loose, slack; (*morale, mœurs*) lax ▸ NMF coward

lâchement [lɑʃmɑ̃] ADV (*par peur*) like a coward; (*par bassesse*) despicably

lâcher [lɑʃe] /1/ NM (*de ballons, oiseaux*) release ▸ VT to let go of; (*ce qui tombe, abandonner*) to drop; (*oiseau, animal: libérer*) to release, set free; (*fig: mot, remarque*) to let slip, come out with; (*Sport: distancer*) to leave behind ▸ VI (*fil, amarres*) to break, give way; (*freins*) to fail; **~ les amarres** (*Navig*) to cast off (the moorings); **~ prise** to let go

lâcheté [lɑʃte] NF cowardice; (*bassesse*) lowness

lacis [lasi] NM (*de ruelles*) maze

laconique [lakɔnik] ADJ laconic

laconiquement [lakɔnikmɑ̃] ADV laconically

lacrymal, e, -aux [lakRimal, -o] ADJ (*canal, glande*) tear *cpd*

lacrymogène [lakRimɔʒɛn] ADJ: **grenade/gaz ~** tear gas grenade/tear gas

lacs [lɑ] NM (*piège*) snare

lactation [laktasjɔ̃] NF lactation

lacté, e [lakte] ADJ milk *cpd*

lactique [laktik] ADJ: **acide/ferment ~** lactic acid/ferment

lactose [laktoz] NM lactose, milk sugar

lacune [lakyn] NF gap

lacustre [lakystR] ADJ lake *cpd*, lakeside *cpd*

lad [lad] NM stable-lad

là-dedans [ladədɑ̃] ADV inside (there), in it; (*fig*) in that

là-dehors [ladəɔR] ADV out there

là-derrière [ladɛRjɛR] ADV behind there; (*fig*) behind that

là-dessous [ladsu] ADV underneath, under there; (*fig*) behind that

là-dessus [ladsy] ADV on there; (*fig: sur ces mots*) at that point; (: *à ce sujet*) about that

là-devant [ladvɑ̃] ADV there (in front)

ladite [ladit] ADJ *voir* **ledit**

ladre [ladR] ADJ miserly

lagon [lagɔ̃] NM lagoon

Lagos [lagɔs] N Lagos

lagune [lagyn] NF lagoon

là-haut [lao] ADV up there

laïc [laik] ADJ M, NM = **laïque**

laïciser [laisize] /1/ VT to secularize

laïcité [laisite] NF secularity, secularism

laid, e [lɛ, lɛd] ADJ ugly; (*fig: acte*) mean, cheap

laideron [lɛdRɔ̃] NM ugly girl

laideur [lɛdœR] NF ugliness *no pl*; meanness *no pl*

laie [lɛ] NF wild sow

lainage [lɛnaʒ] NM (*vêtement*) woollen garment; (*étoffe*) woollen material

laine [lɛn] NF wool; ~ **peignée** worsted (wool); ~ **à tricoter** knitting wool; ~ **de verre** glass wool; ~ **vierge** new wool

laineux, -euse [lɛnø, -øz] ADJ woolly

lainier, -ière [lenje, -jɛR] ADJ (*industrie etc*) woollen

laïque [laik] ADJ lay, civil; (*Scol*) state *cpd* (*as opposed to private and Roman Catholic*) ▶ NMF layman(-woman)

laisse [lɛs] NF (*de chien*) lead, leash; **tenir en** ~ to keep on a lead *ou* leash

laissé-pour-compte, laissée-, laissés- [lesepuʀkɔ̃t] ADJ (*Comm*) unsold; (: *refusé*) returned ▶ NM/F (*fig*) reject; **les laissés-pour-compte de la reprise économique** those who are left out of the economic upturn

laisser [lese] /1/ VT to leave ▶ VB AUX: ~ **qn faire** to let sb do; **se ~ exploiter** to let o.s. be exploited; **se ~ aller** to let o.s. go; ~ **qn tranquille** to let *ou* leave sb alone; **laisse-toi faire** let me (*ou* him) do it; **rien ne laisse penser que ...** there is no reason to think that ...; **cela ne laisse pas de surprendre** nonetheless it is surprising

laisser-aller [leseale] NM carelessness, slovenliness

laisser-faire [lesefɛR] NM laissez-faire

laissez-passer [lesepase] NM INV pass

lait [lɛ] NM milk; **frère/sœur de** ~ foster brother/sister; ~ **écrémé/entier/concentré/ condensé** skimmed/full-fat/condensed/ evaporated milk; ~ **en poudre** powdered milk, milk powder; ~ **de chèvre/vache** goat's/cow's milk; ~ **maternel** mother's milk; ~ **démaquillant/de beauté** cleansing/beauty lotion

laitage [lɛtaʒ] NM dairy product

laiterie [lɛtRi] NF dairy

laiteux, -euse [lɛtø, -øz] ADJ milky

laitier, -ière [letje, -jɛR] ADJ dairy *cpd* ▶ NM/F milkman (dairywoman)

laiton [lɛtɔ̃] NM brass

laitue [lety] NF lettuce

laïus [lajys] NM (*péj*) spiel

lama [lama] NM llama

lambeau, x [lɑ̃bo] NM scrap; **en** ~ in tatters, tattered

lambin, e [lɑ̃bɛ̃, -in] ADJ (*péj*) slow

lambiner [lɑ̃bine] /1/ VI (*péj*) to dawdle

lambris [lɑ̃bRi] NM panelling *no pl*

lambrissé, e [lɑ̃bRise] ADJ panelled

lame [lam] NF blade; (*vague*) wave; (*lamelle*) strip; ~ **de fond** ground swell *no pl*; ~ **de rasoir** razor blade

lamé [lame] NM lamé

lamelle [lamɛl] NF (*lame*) small blade; (*morceau*) sliver; (*de champignon*) gill; **couper en lamelles** to slice thinly

lamentable [lamɑ̃tabl] ADJ (*déplorable*) appalling; (*pitoyable*) pitiful

lamentablement [lamɑ̃tabləmɑ̃] ADV (*échouer*) miserably; (*se conduire*) appallingly

lamentation [lamɑ̃tasjɔ̃] NF wailing *no pl*, lamentation; moaning *no pl*

lamenter [lamɑ̃te] /1/: **se lamenter** VI: **se lamenter (sur)** to moan (over)

laminage [laminaʒ] NM lamination

laminer [lamine] /1/ VT to laminate; (*fig: écraser*) to wipe out

laminoir [laminwaR] NM rolling mill; **passer au** ~ (*fig*) to go (*ou* put) through the mill

lampadaire [lɑ̃padɛR] NM (*de salon*) standard lamp; (*dans la rue*) street lamp

lampe [lɑ̃p] NF lamp; (*Tech*) valve; ~ **à alcool** spirit lamp; ~ **à pétrole** oil lamp; ~ **à bronzer** sunlamp; ~ **de poche** torch (BRIT), flashlight (US); ~ **à souder** blowlamp; ~ **témoin** warning light; ~ **halogène** halogen lamp

lampée [lɑ̃pe] NF gulp, swig

lampe-tempête [lɑ̃ptɑ̃pɛt] NF (*pl* **lampes-tempête**) NF storm lantern

lampion [lɑ̃pjɔ̃] NM Chinese lantern

lampiste [lɑ̃pist] NM light (maintenance) man; (*fig*) underling

lamproie [lɑ̃pRwa] NF lamprey

lance [lɑ̃s] NF spear; ~ **d'arrosage** garden hose; ~ **à eau** water hose; ~ **d'incendie** fire hose

lancée [lɑ̃se] NF: **être/continuer sur sa** ~ to be under way/keep going

lance-flammes [lɑ̃sflam] NM INV flamethrower

lance-fusées [lɑ̃sfyze] NM INV rocket launcher

lance-grenades [lɑ̃sgRənad] NM INV grenade launcher

lancement [lɑ̃smɑ̃] NM launching *no pl*, launch; **offre de** ~ introductory offer

lance-missiles [lɑ̃smisil] NM INV missile launcher

lance-pierres [lɑ̃spjɛR] NM INV catapult

lancer [lɑ̃se] /3/ VT (*Sport*) throwing *no pl*, throw; (*Pêche*) rod and reel fishing ▶ VT to throw; (*émettre, projeter*) to throw out, send out; (*produit, fusée, bateau, artiste*) to launch; (*injure*) to hurl, fling; (*proclamation, mandat d'arrêt*) to issue; (*emprunt*) to float; (*moteur*) to send roaring away; **se lancer** VI (*prendre de l'élan*) to build up speed; (*se précipiter*): **se lancer sur** *ou* **contre** to rush at; ~ **du poids** *nm* putting the shot; ~ **qch à qn** to throw sth to sb; (*de façon agressive*) to throw sth at sb; ~ **un cri** *ou* **un appel** to shout *ou* call out; **se lancer dans** (*discussion*) to launch into; (*aventure*) to embark on; (*les affaires, la politique*) to go into

lance-roquettes [lɑ̃sRɔkɛt] NM INV rocket launcher

lance-torpilles [lɑ̃stɔRpij] NM INV torpedo tube

lanceur, -euse [lɑ̃sœR, -øz] NM/F bowler; (*Baseball*) pitcher ▶ NM (*Espace*) launcher

lancinant, e [lɑ̃sinɑ̃, -ɑ̃t] ADJ (*regrets etc*) haunting; (*douleur*) shooting

lanciner [lɑ̃sine] /1/ VI to throb; (*fig*) to nag

landais, e [lɑ̃dɛ, -ɛz] ADJ of *ou* from the Landes

landau [lɑ̃do] NM pram (BRIT), baby carriage (US)

lande [lɑ̃d] NF moor

Landes [lɑ̃d] NFPL: **les** ~ the Landes

langage [lɑ̃gaʒ] NM language; ~ **d'assemblage** (*Inform*) assembly language; ~ **du corps** body language; ~ **évolué/machine** (*Inform*) high-level/machine language; **~ de programmation** (*Inform*) programming language

lange [lɑ̃ʒ] NM flannel blanket; **langes** NMPL swaddling clothes

langer [lɑ̃ʒe] **/3/** VT to change (the nappy (*Brit*) *ou* diaper (*US*) of); **table à ~** changing table

langoureusement [lɑ̃ɡuʀøzmɑ̃] ADV languorously

langoureux, -euse [lɑ̃ɡuʀø, -øz] ADJ languorous

langouste [lɑ̃ɡust] NF crayfish *inv*

langoustine [lɑ̃ɡustin] NF Dublin Bay prawn

langue [lɑ̃ɡ] NF (*Anat, Culin*) tongue; (*Ling*) language; (*bande*): **~ de terre** spit of land; **tirer la ~ (à)** to stick out one's tongue (at); **donner sa ~ au chat** to give up, give in; **de ~ française** French-speaking; **~ de bois** officialese; **~ maternelle** native language, mother tongue; **~ verte** slang; **langues vivantes** modern languages

langue-de-chat [lɑ̃ɡdəʃa] NF finger biscuit

languedocien, ne [lɑ̃ɡdɔsjɛ̃, -ɛn] ADJ of *ou* from the Languedoc

languette [lɑ̃ɡɛt] NF tongue

langueur [lɑ̃ɡœʀ] NF languidness

languir [lɑ̃ɡiʀ] **/2/** VI to languish; (*conversation*) to flag; **se languir** VI to be languishing; **faire ~ qn** to keep sb waiting

languissant, e [lɑ̃ɡisɑ̃, -ɑ̃t] ADJ languid

lanière [lanjɛʀ] NF (*de fouet*) lash; (*de valise, bretelle*) strap

lanoline [lanɔlin] NF lanolin

lanterne [lɑ̃tɛʀn] NF (*portable*) lantern; (*électrique*) light, lamp; (*de voiture*) (side)light; **~ rouge** (*fig*) tail-ender; **~ vénitienne** Chinese lantern

lanterneau, x [lɑ̃tɛʀno] NM skylight

lanterner [lɑ̃tɛʀne] **/1/** VI: **faire ~ qn** to keep sb hanging around

Laos [laɔs] NM: **le ~** Laos

laotien, ne [laɔsjɛ̃, -ɛn] ADJ Laotian

lapalissade [lapalisad] NF statement of the obvious

La Paz [lapaz] N La Paz

laper [lape] **/1/** VT to lap up

lapereau, x [lapʀo] NM young rabbit

lapidaire [lapidɛʀ] ADJ stone *cpd*; (*fig*) terse

lapider [lapide] **/1/** VT to stone

lapin [lapɛ̃] NM rabbit; (*peau*) rabbitskin; (*fourrure*) cony; **coup du ~** rabbit punch; **poser un ~ à qn** to stand sb up; **~ de garenne** wild rabbit

lapis [lapis], **lapis-lazuli** [lapislazyli] NM INV lapis lazuli

lapon, e [lapɔ̃, -ɔn] ADJ Lapp, Lappish ▸ NM (*Ling*) Lapp, Lappish ▸ NM/F: **L~, e** Lapp, Laplander

Laponie [laponi] NF: **la ~** Lapland

laps [laps] NM: **~ de temps** space of time, time *no pl*

lapsus [lapsys] NM slip

laquais [lakɛ] NM lackey

laque [lak] NF (*vernis*) lacquer; (*brute*) shellac; (*pour cheveux*) hair spray ▸ NM lacquer; piece of lacquer ware

laqué, e [lake] ADJ lacquered

laquelle [lakɛl] PRON *voir* **lequel**

larbin [laʀbɛ̃] NM (*péj*) flunkey

larcin [laʀsɛ̃] NM theft

lard [laʀ] NM (*graisse*) fat; (*bacon*) (streaky) bacon

larder [laʀde] **/1/** VT (*Culin*) to lard

lardon [laʀdɔ̃] NM (*Culin*) piece of chopped bacon; (*fam: enfant*) kid

large [laʀʒ] ADJ wide; broad; (*fig*) generous ▸ ADV: **calculer/voir ~** to allow extra/think big ▸ NM (*largeur*): **5 m de ~** 5 m wide *ou* in width; (*mer*) **le ~** the open sea; **en ~** adv sideways; **au ~ de** off; **~ d'esprit** broad-minded; **ne pas en mener ~** to have one's heart in one's boots

largement [laʀʒəmɑ̃] ADV widely; (*de loin*) greatly; (*amplement, au minimum*) easily; (*sans compter: donner etc*) generously; **c'est ~ suffisant** that's ample

largesse [laʀʒɛs] NF generosity; **largesses** NFPL (*dons*) liberalities

largeur [laʀʒœʀ] NF (*qu'on mesure*) width; (*impression visuelle*) wideness, width; breadth; (*d'esprit*) broadness

larguer [laʀɡe] **/1/** VT to drop; (*fam: se débarrasser de*) to get rid of; **~ les amarres** to cast off (the moorings)

larme [laʀm] NF tear; (*fig*): **une ~ de** a drop of; **en larmes** in tears; **pleurer à chaudes larmes** to cry one's eyes out, cry bitterly

larmoyant, e [laʀmwajɑ̃, -ɑ̃t] ADJ tearful

larmoyer [laʀmwaje] **/8/** VI (*yeux*) to water; (*se plaindre*) to whimper

larron [laʀɔ̃] NM thief

larve [laʀv] NF (*Zool*) larva; (*fig*) worm

larvé, e [laʀve] ADJ (*fig*) latent

laryngite [laʀɛ̃ʒit] NF laryngitis

laryngologiste [laʀɛ̃ɡɔlɔʒist] NMF throat specialist

larynx [laʀɛ̃ks] NM larynx

las, lasse [lɑ, lɑs] ADJ weary

lasagne [lazaɲ] NF lasagne

lascar [laskaʀ] NM character; (*malin*) rogue

lascif, -ive [lasif, -iv] ADJ lascivious

laser [lazɛʀ] NM: **(rayon) ~** laser (beam); **chaîne** *ou* **platine ~** compact disc (player); **disque ~** compact disc

lassant, e [lɑsɑ̃, -ɑ̃t] ADJ tiresome, wearisome

lasse [lɑs] ADJ F *voir* **las**

lasser [lɑse] **/1/** VT to weary, tire; **se ~ de** to grow weary *ou* tired of

lassitude [lɑsityd] NF lassitude, weariness

lasso [laso] NM lasso; **prendre au ~** to lasso

latent, e [latɑ̃, -ɑ̃t] ADJ latent

latéral, e, -aux [lateʀal, -o] ADJ side *cpd*, lateral

latéralement [lateʀalmɑ̃] ADV edgeways; (*arriver, souffler*) from the side

latex [latɛks] NM INV latex

latin, e [latɛ̃, -in] ADJ Latin ▸ NM (*Ling*) Latin ▸ NM/F: **L~, e** Latin; **j'y perds mon ~** it's all Greek to me

latiniste [latinist] NMF Latin scholar (*ou* student)

latino-américain, e [latinɔameʀikɛ̃, -ɛn] ADJ Latin-American

latitude [latityd] NF latitude; (*fig*): **avoir la ~ de faire** to be left free *ou* be at liberty to do; **à 48° de ~ Nord** at latitude 48°North; **sous toutes les latitudes** (*fig*) world-wide, throughout the world

latrines [latʀin] NFPL latrines

latte [lat] NF lath, slat; (*de plancher*) board

lattis [lati] NM lathwork

laudanum [lodanɔm] NM laudanum

laudatif, -ive [lodatif, -iv] ADJ laudatory

lauréat, e [lɔʀea, -at] NM/F winner

laurier [lɔʀje] NM (*Bot*) laurel; (*Culin*) bay leaves *pl*; **lauriers** NMPL (*fig*) laurels

laurier-rose [lɔʀjeʀoz] (*pl* **lauriers-roses**) NM oleander

laurier-tin [lɔʀjetɛ̃] (*pl* **lauriers-tins**) NM laurustinus

lavable [lavabl] ADJ washable

lavabo [lavabo] NM washbasin; **lavabos** NMPL toilet *sg*

lavage [lavaʒ] NM washing *no pl*, wash; **~ d'estomac/d'intestin** stomach/intestinal wash; **~ de cerveau** brainwashing *no pl*

lavande [lavɑ̃d] NF lavender

lavandière [lavɑ̃djɛʀ] NF washerwoman

lave [lav] NF lava *no pl*

lave-glace [lavglas] NM (*Auto*) windscreen (BRIT) *ou* windshield (US) washer

lave-linge [lavlɛ̃ʒ] NM INV washing machine

lavement [lavmɑ̃] NM (*Méd*) enema

laver [lave] /1/ VT to wash; (*tache*) to wash off; (*fig: affront*) to avenge; **se laver** VI to have a wash, wash; **se laver les mains/dents** to wash one's hands/clean one's teeth; **~ la vaisselle/le linge** to wash the dishes/clothes; **~ qn de** (*accusation*) to clear sb of

laverie [lavʀi] NF: **~ (automatique)** Launderette® (BRIT), Laundromat® (US)

lavette [lavɛt] NF (*chiffon*) dish cloth; (*brosse*) dish mop; (*fam: homme*) wimp, drip

laveur, -euse [lavœʀ, -øz] NM/F cleaner

lave-vaisselle [lavvɛsɛl] NM INV dishwasher

lavis [lavi] NM (*technique*) washing; (*dessin*) wash drawing

lavoir [lavwaʀ] NM wash house; (*bac*) washtub; (*évier*) sink

laxatif, -ive [laksatif, -iv] ADJ, NM laxative

laxisme [laksism] NM laxity

laxiste [laksist] ADJ lax

layette [lɛjɛt] NF layette

layon [lɛjɔ̃] NM trail

lazaret [lazaʀɛ] NM quarantine area

lazzi [ladzi] NM gibe

LCR SIGLE F (= *Ligue communiste révolutionnaire*) political party

⸺ MOT-CLÉ ⸺

le, la, l' [lə, la, l] (*pl* **les**) ART DÉF **1** the; **le livre/la pomme/l'arbre** the book/the apple/the tree; **les étudiants** the students

2 (*noms abstraits*): **le courage/l'amour/la jeunesse** courage/love/youth

3 (*indiquant la possession*): **se casser la jambe** *etc* to break one's leg *etc*; **levez la main** put your hand up; **avoir les yeux gris/le nez rouge** to have grey eyes/a red nose

4 (*temps*): **le matin/soir** in the morning/evening; mornings/evenings; **le jeudi** *etc* (*d'habitude*) on Thursdays *etc*; (*ce jeudi-là etc*) on (the) Thursday; **nous venons le 3 décembre** (*parlé*) we're coming on the 3rd of December *ou* on December the 3rd; (*écrit*) we're coming (on) 3rd *ou* 3 December

5 (*distribution, évaluation*) a, an; **trois euros le mètre/kilo** three euros a *ou* per metre/kilo; **le tiers/quart de** a third/quarter of

▶ PRON **1** (*personne: mâle*) him; (: *femelle*) her; (: *pluriel*) them; **je le/la/les vois** I can see him/her/them

2 (*animal, chose: singulier*) it; (: *pluriel*) them; **je le (ou la) vois** I can see it; **je les vois** I can see them

3 (*remplaçant une phrase*): **je ne le savais pas** I didn't know (about it); **il était riche et ne l'est plus** he was once rich but no longer is

lé [le] NM (*de tissu*) width; (*de papier peint*) strip, length

leader [lidœʀ] NM leader

leadership [lidœʀʃip] NM (*Pol*) leadership

leasing [liziŋ] NM leasing

lèche-bottes [lɛʃbɔt] NM INV bootlicker

lèchefrite [lɛʃfʀit] NF dripping pan *ou* tray

lécher [leʃe] /6/ VT to lick; (*laper: lait, eau*) to lick *ou* lap up; (*finir, polir*) to over-refine; **se ~ les vitrines** to go window-shopping; **se ~ les doigts/lèvres** to lick one's fingers/lips

lèche-vitrines [lɛʃvitʀin] NM INV: **faire du ~** to go window-shopping

leçon [ləsɔ̃] NF lesson; **faire la ~** to teach; **faire la ~ à** (*fig*) to give a lecture to; **leçons de conduite** driving lessons; **leçons particulières** private lessons *ou* tuition *sg* (BRIT)

lecteur, -trice [lɛktœʀ, -tʀis] NM/F reader; (*d'université*) (foreign language) assistant (BRIT), (foreign) teaching assistant (US) ▶ NM (*Tech*): **~ de cassettes** cassette player; **~ de disquette(s)** disk drive; **~ de CD/DVD** (*d'ordinateur*) CD/DVD drive; (*de salon*) CD/DVD player; **~ MP3** MP3 player

lectorat [lɛktɔʀa] NM (foreign language *ou* teaching) assistantship

lecture [lɛktyʀ] NF reading

LED [lɛd] SIGLE F (= *light emitting diode*) LED

ledit, ladite [lədi, ladit] (*mpl* **lesdits** [ledi], *fpl* **lesdites** [ledit]) ADJ the aforesaid

légal, e, -aux [legal, -o] ADJ legal

légalement [legalmɑ̃] ADV legally

légalisation [legalizasjɔ̃] NF legalization

légaliser [legalize] /1/ VT to legalize

légalité [legalite] NF legality, lawfulness; **être dans/sortir de la ~** to be within/step outside the law

légat [lega] NM (*Rel*) legate

légataire [legatɛʀ] NM legatee

légendaire [leʒɑ̃dɛʀ] ADJ legendary

légende [leʒɑ̃d] NF (*mythe*) legend; (*de carte, plan*) key, legend; (de dessin) caption

léger, -ère [leʒe, -ɛʀ] ADJ light; (bruit, retard) slight; (boisson, parfum) weak; (couche, étoffe) thin; (superficiel) thoughtless; (volage) free and easy; flighty; (peu sérieux) lightweight; **blessé ~** slightly injured person; **à la légère** adv (parler, agir) rashly, thoughtlessly

légèrement [leʒɛʀmɑ̃] ADV (s'habiller, bouger) lightly; thoughtlessly, rashly; **~ plus grand** slightly bigger; **manger ~** to eat a light meal

légèreté [leʒɛʀte] NF lightness; thoughtlessness; (d'une remarque) flippancy

légiférer [leʒifeʀe] /6/ VI to legislate

légion [leʒjɔ̃] NF legion; **la L~ étrangère** the Foreign Legion; **la L~ d'honneur** the Legion of Honour; see note

> Created by Napoleon in 1802 to reward services to the French nation, the *Légion d'honneur* is a prestigious group of men and women headed by the President of the Republic, the *Grand Maître*. Members receive a nominal tax-free payment each year.

légionnaire [leʒjɔnɛʀ] NM (Mil) legionnaire; (de la Légion d'honneur) holder of the Legion of Honour

législateur [leʒislatœʀ] NM legislator, lawmaker

législatif, -ive [leʒislatif, -iv] ADJ legislative; **législatives** NFPL general election sg

législation [leʒislasjɔ̃] NF legislation

législature [leʒislatyʀ] NF legislature; (période) term (of office)

légiste [leʒist] NM jurist ▶ ADJ: **médecin ~** forensic scientist (BRIT), medical examiner (US)

légitime [leʒitim] ADJ (Jur) lawful, legitimate; (enfant) legitimate; (fig) rightful, legitimate; **en état de ~ défense** in self-defence

légitimement [leʒitimmɑ̃] ADV lawfully; legitimately; rightfully

légitimer [leʒitime] /1/ VT (enfant) to legitimize; (justifier: conduite etc) to justify

légitimité [leʒitimite] NF (Jur) legitimacy

legs [leg] NM legacy

léguer [lege] /6/ VT: **~ qch à qn** (Jur) to bequeath sth to sb; (fig) to hand sth down ou pass sth on to sb

légume [legym] NM vegetable; **légumes verts** green vegetables; **légumes secs** pulses

légumier [legymje] NM vegetable dish

leitmotiv [lejtmotiv] NM leitmotiv, leitmotif

Léman [lemɑ̃] NM voir **lac**

lendemain [lɑ̃dmɛ̃] NM: **le ~** the next ou following day; **le ~ matin/soir** the next ou following morning/evening; **le ~ de** the day after; **au ~ de** in the days following; in the wake of; **penser au ~** to think of the future; **sans ~** short-lived; **de beaux lendemains** bright prospects; **des lendemains qui chantent** a rosy future

lénifiant, e [lenifjɑ̃, -ɑ̃t] ADJ soothing

léniniste [leninist] ADJ, NMF Leninist

lent, e [lɑ̃, lɑ̃t] ADJ slow

lente [lɑ̃t] NF nit

lentement [lɑ̃tmɑ̃] ADV slowly

lenteur [lɑ̃tœʀ] NF slowness no pl; **lenteurs** NFPL (actions, décisions lentes) slowness sg

lentille [lɑ̃tij] NF (Optique) lens sg; (Bot) lentil; **~ d'eau** duckweed; **lentilles de contact** contact lenses

léonin, e [leɔnɛ̃, -in] ADJ (fig: contrat etc) one-sided

léopard [leɔpaʀ] NM leopard

LEP [lɛp] SIGLE M (= lycée d'enseignement professionnel) secondary school for vocational training, pre-1986

lèpre [lɛpʀ] NF leprosy

lépreux, -euse [lepʀø, -øz] NM/F leper ▶ ADJ (fig) flaking, peeling

(MOT-CLÉ)

lequel, laquelle [ləkɛl, lakɛl] (mpl **lesquels**, fpl **lesquelles**) (à + lequel = **auquel**, de + lequel = **duquel**) PRON **1** (interrogatif) which, which one; **lequel des deux?** which one?
2 (relatif: personne: sujet) who; (: objet, après préposition) whom; (: possessif) whose; (: chose) which; **je l'ai proposé au directeur, lequel est d'accord** I suggested it to the director, who agrees; **la femme à laquelle j'ai acheté mon chien** the woman from whom I bought my dog; **le pont sur lequel nous sommes passés** the bridge (over) which we crossed; **un homme sur la compétence duquel on peut compter** a man whose competence one can count on
▶ ADJ: **auquel cas** in which case

les [le] ART DÉF, PRON voir **le**

lesbienne [lɛsbjɛn] NF lesbian

lesdits, lesdites [ledi, ledit] ADJ voir **ledit**

lèse-majesté [lɛzmaʒɛste] NF INV: **crime de ~** crime of lese-majesty

léser [leze] /6/ VT to wrong; (Méd) to injure

lésiner [lezine] /1/ VI: **ne pas ~ sur les moyens** (pour mariage etc) to push the boat out

lésion [lezjɔ̃] NF lesion, damage no pl; **lésions cérébrales** brain damage

Lesotho [lezɔto] NM: **le ~** Lesotho

lesquels, lesquelles [lekɛl] PRON voir **lequel**

lessivable [lesivabl] ADJ washable

lessive [lesiv] NF (poudre) washing powder; (linge) washing no pl, wash; (opération) washing no pl; **faire la ~** to do the washing

lessivé, e [lesive] ADJ (fam) washed out

lessiver [lesive] /1/ VT to wash; (fam: fatiguer) to tire out, exhaust

lessiveuse [lesivøz] NF (récipient) washtub

lessiviel, le [lesivjɛl] ADJ detergent

lest [lɛst] NM ballast; **jeter** ou **lâcher du ~** (fig) to make concessions

leste [lɛst] ADJ (personne, mouvement) sprightly, nimble; (désinvolte: manières) offhand; (osé: plaisanterie) risqué

lestement [lɛstəmɑ̃] ADV nimbly

lester [lɛste] /1/ VT to ballast

letchi [lɛtʃi] NM = **litchi**

léthargie [letaʀʒi] NF lethargy

léthargique [letaʀʒik] ADJ lethargic

letton, ne [lɛtɔ̃, -ɔn] ADJ Latvian, Lett

Lettonie [lɛtɔni] NF: **la** ~ Latvia
lettre [lɛtʀ] NF letter; **lettres** NFPL (*étude, culture*) literature *sg*; (*Scol*) arts (subjects); **à la** ~ (*au sens propre*) literally; (*ponctuellement*) to the letter; **en lettres majuscules** *ou* **capitales** in capital letters, in capitals; **en toutes lettres** in words, in full; ~ **de change** bill of exchange; ~ **piégée** letter bomb; ~ **de voiture** (**aérienne**) (air) waybill, (air) bill of lading; **lettres de noblesse** pedigree
lettré, e [lɛtʀe] ADJ well-read, scholarly
lettre-transfert [lɛtʀətʀãsfɛʀ] (*pl* **lettres-transferts**) NF (*pressure*) transfer
leu [lø] NM *voir* **queue**
leucémie [løsemi] NF leukaemia

MOT-CLÉ

leur [lœʀ] ADJ POSS their; **leur maison** their house; **leurs amis** their friends; **à leur approche** as they came near; **à leur vue** at the sight of them
▶ PRON **1** (*objet indirect*) (to) them; **je leur ai dit la vérité** I told them the truth; **je le leur ai donné** I gave it to them, I gave them it
2 (*possessif*): **le (la) leur, les leurs** theirs

leurre [lœʀ] NM (*appât*) lure; (*fig*) delusion; (: *piège*) snare
leurrer [lœʀe] /**1**/ VT to delude, deceive
leurs [lœʀ] ADJ *voir* **leur**
levain [ləvɛ̃] NM leaven; **sans** ~ unleavened
levant, e [ləvã, -ãt] ADJ: **soleil** ~ rising sun ▶ NM: **le L~** the Levant; **au soleil** ~ at sunrise
levantin, e [ləvãtɛ̃, -in] ADJ Levantine ▶ NM/F: **L~, e** Levantine
levé, e [ləve] ADJ: **être** ~ to be up ▶ NM: ~ **de terrain** land survey; **à mains levées** (*vote*) by a show of hands; **au pied** ~ at a moment's notice
levée [ləve] NF (*Postes*) collection; (*Cartes*) trick; ~ **de boucliers** general outcry; ~ **du corps** *collection of the body from house of the deceased, before funeral*; ~ **d'écrou** release from custody; ~ **de terre** levee; ~ **de troupes** levy
lever [ləve] /**5**/ VT (*vitre, bras etc*) to raise; (*soulever de terre, supprimer: interdiction, siège*) to lift; (: *difficulté*) to remove; (*séance*) to close; (*impôts, armée*) to levy; (*Chasse: lièvre*) to start; (: *perdrix*) to flush; (*fam: fille*) to pick up ▶ VI (*Culin*) to rise ▶ NM: **au** ~ on getting up; **se lever** VI to get up; (*soleil*) to rise; (*jour*) to break; (*brouillard*) to lift; **levez-vous!, lève-toi!** stand up!, get up!; **ça va se lever** (*temps*) it's going to clear up; ~ **du jour** daybreak; ~ **du rideau** (*Théât*) curtain; ~ **de rideau** (*pièce*) curtain raiser; ~ **de soleil** sunrise
lève-tard [lɛvtaʀ] NMF INV late riser
lève-tôt [lɛvto] NMF INV early riser, early bird
levier [ləvje] NM lever; **faire** ~ **sur** to lever up (*ou* off); ~ **de changement de vitesse** gear lever
lévitation [levitasjɔ̃] NF levitation
levraut [ləvʀo] NM (*Zool*) leveret
lèvre [lɛvʀ] NF lip; **lèvres** NFPL (*d'une plaie*) edges; **petites/grandes lèvres** labia minora/majora; **du bout des lèvres** half-heartedly
lévrier [levʀije] NM greyhound

levure [ləvyʀ] NF yeast; ~ **chimique** baking powder
lexical, e, -aux [lɛksikal, -o] ADJ lexical
lexicographe [lɛksikɔgʀaf] NMF lexicographer
lexicographie [lɛksikɔgʀafi] NF lexicography, dictionary writing
lexicologie [lɛksikɔlɔʒi] NF lexicology
lexique [lɛksik] NM vocabulary, lexicon; (*glossaire*) vocabulary
lézard [lezaʀ] NM lizard; (*peau*) lizard skin
lézarde [lezaʀd] NF crack
lézarder [lezaʀde] /**1**/: **se lézarder** VI to crack
LGBT SIGLE PL (= *lesbiennes, gays, bisexuels et transgenres*) LGBT *abr*
liaison [ljɛzɔ̃] NF (*rapport*) connection, link; (*Rail, Aviat etc*) link; (*relation: d'amitié*) friendship; (: *d'affaires*) relationship; (: *amoureuse*) affair; (*Culin, Phonétique*) liaison; **entrer/être en** ~ **avec** to get/be in contact with; ~ **radio** radio contact; ~ (**de transmission de données**) (*Inform*) data link
liane [ljan] NF creeper
liant, e [ljã, -ãt] ADJ sociable
liasse [ljas] NF wad, bundle
Liban [libã] NM: **le** ~ (the) Lebanon
libanais, e [libanɛ, -ɛz] ADJ Lebanese ▶ NM/F: **L~, e** Lebanese
libations [libasjɔ̃] NFPL libations
libelle [libɛl] NM lampoon
libellé [libele] NM wording
libeller [libele] /**1**/ VT (*chèque, mandat*): ~ (**au nom de**) to make out (to); (*lettre*) to word
libellule [libelyl] NF dragonfly
libéral, e, -aux [liberal, -o] ADJ, NM/F liberal; **les professions libérales** liberal professions
libéralement [liberalmã] ADV liberally
libéralisation [liberalizasjɔ̃] NF liberalization; ~ **du commerce** easing of trade restrictions
libéraliser [liberalize] /**1**/ VT to liberalize
libéralisme [liberalism] NM liberalism
libéralité [liberalite] NF liberality *no pl*, generosity *no pl*
libérateur, -trice [liberatœʀ, -tʀis] ADJ liberating ▶ NM/F liberator
libération [liberasjɔ̃] NF liberation, freeing; release; discharge; ~ **conditionnelle** release on parole
libéré, e [libere] ADJ liberated; ~ **de** freed from; **être** ~ **sous caution/sur parole** to be released on bail/on parole
libérer [libere] /**6**/ VT (*délivrer*) to free, liberate; (: *moralement, Psych*) to liberate; (*relâcher: prisonnier*) to discharge, release; (: *soldat*) to discharge; (*dégager: gaz, cran d'arrêt*) to release; (*Écon: échanges commerciaux*) to ease restrictions on; **se libérer** VI (*de rendez-vous*) to get out of previous engagements, try and be free; ~ **qn de** (*liens, dette*) to free sb from; (*promesse*) to release sb from
Libéria [liberja] NM: **le** ~ Liberia
libérien, ne [liberjɛ̃, -ɛn] ADJ Liberian ▶ NM/F: **L~, ne** Liberian
libéro [libero] NM (*Football*) sweeper
libertaire [libɛʀtɛʀ] ADJ libertarian

liberté [libɛʀte] NF freedom; (loisir) free time; **libertés** NFPL (privautés) liberties; **mettre/être en ~** to set/be free; **en ~ provisoire/surveillée/conditionnelle** on bail/probation/parole; **~ d'association** right of association; **~ de conscience** freedom of conscience; **~ du culte** freedom of worship; **~ d'esprit** independence of mind; **~ d'opinion** freedom of thought; **~ de la presse** freedom of the press; **~ de réunion** right to hold meetings; **~ syndicale** union rights pl; **libertés individuelles** personal freedom sg; **libertés publiques** civil rights

libertin, e [libɛʀtɛ̃, -in] ADJ libertine, licentious

libertinage [libɛʀtinaʒ] NM licentiousness

libidineux, -euse [libidinø, -øz] ADJ lustful

libido [libido] NF libido

libraire [libʀɛʀ] NMF bookseller

libraire-éditeur [libʀɛʀeditœʀ] (pl **libraires-éditeurs**) NM publisher and bookseller

librairie [libʀɛʀi] NF bookshop

librairie-papeterie [libʀɛʀipapetʀi] (pl **librairies-papeteries**) NF bookseller's and stationer's

libre [libʀ] ADJ free; (route) clear; (place etc) vacant, free; (fig: propos, manières) open; (ligne) not engaged; (Scol) non-state, private and Roman Catholic (as opposed to "laïque"); **de ~** (place) free; **~ de qch/de faire** free from sth/to do; **vente ~** (Comm) unrestricted sale; **~ arbitre** free will; **~ concurrence** free-market economy; **~ entreprise** free enterprise

libre-échange [libʀeʃɑ̃ʒ] NM free trade

librement [libʀəmɑ̃] ADV freely

libre-penseur, -euse [libʀəpɑ̃sœʀ, -øz] NM/F free thinker

libre-service [libʀəsɛʀvis] NM INV (magasin) self-service store; (restaurant) self-service restaurant

librettiste [libʀetist] NMF librettist

Libye [libi] NF: **la ~** Libya

libyen, ne [libjɛ̃, -ɛn] ADJ Libyan ▶ NM/F: **L~, ne** Libyan

lice [lis] NF: **entrer en ~** (fig) to enter the lists

licence [lisɑ̃s] NF (permis) permit; (diplôme) (first) degree; see note; (liberté) liberty; (poétique, orthographique) licence (BRIT), license (US); (des mœurs) licentiousness; **~ ès lettres/en droit** arts/law degree

> After the DEUG, French university students undertake a third year of study to complete their *licence*. This is roughly equivalent to a bachelor's degree in Britain.

licencié, e [lisɑ̃sje] NM/F (Scol): **~ ès lettres/en droit** ≈ Bachelor of Arts/Law, arts/law graduate; (Sport) permit-holder

licenciement [lisɑ̃simɑ̃] NM dismissal; redundancy; laying off no pl

licencier [lisɑ̃sje] /7/ VT (renvoyer) to dismiss; (débaucher) to make redundant; to lay off

licencieux, -euse [lisɑ̃sjø, -øz] ADJ licentious

lichen [likɛn] NM lichen

licite [lisit] ADJ lawful

licorne [likɔʀn] NF unicorn

licou [liku] NM halter

lie [li] NF dregs pl, sediment

lié, e [lje] ADJ: **très ~ avec** (fig) very friendly with ou close to; **~ par** (serment, promesse) bound by; **avoir partie ~ (avec qn)** to be involved (with sb)

Liechtenstein [liftɛnʃtajn] NM: **le ~** Liechtenstein

lie-de-vin [lidvɛ̃] ADJ INV wine(-coloured)

liège [ljɛʒ] NM cork

liégeois, e [ljeʒwa, -waz] ADJ of ou from Liège ▶ NM/F: **L~, e** inhabitant ou native of Liège; **café/chocolat ~** coffee/chocolate ice cream topped with whipped cream

lien [ljɛ̃] NM (corde, fig: affectif, culturel) bond; (rapport) link, connection; (analogie) link; **~ de parenté** family tie; **~ hypertexte** hyperlink

lier [lje] /7/ VT (attacher) to tie up; (joindre) to link up; (fig: unir, engager) to bind; (Culin) to thicken; **~ qch à** (attacher) to tie sth to; (associer) to link sth to; **~ conversation (avec)** to strike up a conversation (with); **se ~ avec** to make friends with; **~ connaissance avec** to get to know

lierre [ljɛʀ] NM ivy

liesse [ljɛs] NF: **être en ~** to be jubilant

lieu, x [ljø] NM place; **lieux** NMPL (locaux) premises; (endroit: d'un accident etc) scene sg; **en ~ sûr** in a safe place; **en haut ~** in high places; **vider** ou **quitter les ~** to leave the premises; **arriver/être sur les ~** to arrive/be on the scene; **en premier ~** in the first place; **en dernier ~** lastly; **avoir ~** to take place; **avoir ~ de faire** to have grounds ou good reason for doing; **tenir ~ de** to take the place of; (servir de) to serve as; **donner ~ à** to give rise to, give cause for; **au ~ de** instead of; **au ~ qu'il y aille** instead of him going; **~ commun** commonplace; **~ géométrique** locus; **~ de naissance** place of birth

lieu-dit [ljødi] (pl **lieux-dits**) NM locality

lieue [ljø] NF league

lieutenant [ljøtnɑ̃] NM lieutenant; **~ de vaisseau** (Navig) lieutenant

lieutenant-colonel [ljøtnɑ̃kɔlɔnɛl] (pl **lieutenants-colonels**) NM (armée de terre) lieutenant colonel; (armée de l'air) wing commander (BRIT), lieutenant colonel (US)

lièvre [ljɛvʀ] NM hare; (coureur) pacemaker; **lever un ~** (fig) to bring up a prickly subject

liftier, -ière [liftje, -jɛʀ] NM/F lift (BRIT) ou elevator (US) attendant

lifting [liftiŋ] NM face lift

ligament [ligamɑ̃] NM ligament

ligature [ligatyʀ] NF ligature

lige [liʒ] ADJ: **homme ~** (péj) henchman

ligne [liɲ] NF (gén) line; (Transports: liaison) service; (: trajet) route; (silhouette) figure; **garder la ~** to keep one's figure; **en ~** (Inform) online; **en ~ droite** as the crow flies; **"à la ~"** "new paragraph"; **entrer en ~ de compte** to be taken into account; to come into it; **~ but/médiane** goal/halfway line; **~ d'arrivée/de départ** finishing/starting line; **~ de conduite** course of action; **~ directrice** guiding line; **~ fixe** (Tél) landline; **~ d'horizon** skyline; **~ de mire** line of sight; **~ de touche** touchline

ligné, e [liɲe] ADJ: **papier** ~ ruled paper ▶ NF (*race, famille*) line, lineage; (*postérité*) descendants pl

ligneux, -euse [liɲø, -øz] ADJ ligneous, woody

lignite [liɲit] NM lignite

ligoter [ligɔte] /1/ VT to tie up

ligue [lig] NF league

liguer [lige] /1/: **se liguer** VI to form a league; **se liguer contre** (*fig*) to combine against

lilas [lila] NM lilac

lillois, e [lilwa, -waz] ADJ of ou from Lille

Lima [lima] N Lima

limace [limas] NF slug

limaille [limaj] NF: ~ **de fer** iron filings pl

limande [limɑ̃d] NF dab

limande-sole [limɑ̃dsɔl] NF lemon sole

limbes [lɛ̃b] NMPL limbo sg; **être dans les** ~ (*fig: projet etc*) to be up in the air

lime [lim] NF (*Tech*) file; (*Bot*) lime; ~ **à ongles** nail file

limer [lime] /1/ VT (*bois, métal*) to file (down); (*ongles*) to file; (*fig: prix*) to pare down

limier [limje] NM (*Zool*) bloodhound; (*détective*) sleuth

liminaire [liminɛR] ADJ (*propos*) introductory

limitatif, -ive [limitatif, -iv] ADJ restrictive

limitation [limitasjɔ̃] NF limitation, restriction; **sans** ~ **de temps** with no time limit; ~ **des naissances** birth control; ~ **de vitesse** speed limit

limite [limit] NF (*de terrain*) boundary; (*partie ou point extrême*) limit; **dans la** ~ **de** within the limits of; **à la** ~ (*au pire*) if the worst comes to (*ou* came) to the worst; **sans limites** (*bêtise, richesse, pouvoir*) limitless, boundless; **vitesse/charge** ~ maximum speed/load; **cas** ~ borderline case; **date** ~ deadline; **date** ~ **de vente/consommation** sell-by/best-before date; **prix** ~ upper price limit; ~ **d'âge** maximum age, age limit

limiter [limite] /1/ VT (*restreindre*) to limit, restrict; (*délimiter*) to border, form the boundary of; **se** ~ **(à qch/à faire)** (*personne*) to limit ou confine o.s. (to sth/to doing sth); **se** ~ **à** (*chose*) to be limited to

limitrophe [limitRɔf] ADJ border cpd; ~ **de** bordering on

limogeage [limɔʒaʒ] NM dismissal

limoger [limɔʒe] /3/ VT to dismiss

limon [limɔ̃] NM silt

limonade [limɔnad] NF lemonade (BRIT), (lemon) soda (US)

limonadier, -ière [limɔnadje, -jɛR] NM/F (*commerçant*) café owner; (*fabricant de limonade*) soft drinks manufacturer

limoneux, -euse [limɔnø, -øz] ADJ muddy

limousin, e [limuzɛ̃, -in] ADJ of ou from Limousin ▶ NM (*région*): **le L**~ the Limousin ▶ NF limousine

limpide [lɛ̃pid] ADJ limpid

lin [lɛ̃] NM (*Bot*) flax; (*tissu, toile*) linen

linceul [lɛ̃sœl] NM shroud

linéaire [lineɛR] ADJ linear ▶ NM: ~ **(de vente)** shelves pl

linéament [lineamɑ̃] NM outline

linge [lɛ̃ʒ] NM (*serviettes etc*) linen; (*pièce de tissu*) cloth; (*aussi*: **linge de corps**) underwear; (*aussi*: **linge de toilette**) towel; (*lessive*) washing; ~ **sale** dirty linen

lingère [lɛ̃ʒɛR] NF linen maid

lingerie [lɛ̃ʒRi] NF lingerie, underwear

lingot [lɛ̃go] NM ingot

linguiste [lɛ̃gɥist] NMF linguist

linguistique [lɛ̃gɥistik] ADJ linguistic ▶ NF linguistics sg

lino [lino], **linoléum** [linɔleɔm] NM lino(leum)

linotte [linɔt] NF: **tête de** ~ bird brain

linteau, x [lɛ̃to] NM lintel

lion, ne [ljɔ̃, ljɔn] NM/F lion (lioness); (*signe*): **le L~** Leo, the Lion; **être du L~** to be Leo; ~ **de mer** sea lion

lionceau, x [ljɔ̃so] NM lion cub

liposuccion [lipɔsy(k)sjɔ̃] NF liposuction

lippu, e [lipy] ADJ thick-lipped

liquéfier [likefje] /7/ VT to liquefy; **se liquéfier** VI (*gaz etc*) to liquefy; (*fig: personne*) to succumb

liqueur [likœR] NF liqueur

liquidateur, -trice [likidatœR, -tRis] NM/F (*Jur*) receiver; ~ **judiciaire** official liquidator

liquidation [likidasjɔ̃] NF (*vente*) sale, liquidation; (*Comm*) clearance (sale); ~ **judiciaire** compulsory liquidation

liquide [likid] ADJ liquid ▶ NM liquid; (*Comm*): **en** ~ in ready money ou cash; **je n'ai pas de** ~ I haven't got any cash

liquider [likide] /1/ VT (*société, biens, témoin gênant*) to liquidate; (*compte, problème*) to settle; (*Comm: articles*) to clear, sell off

liquidités [likidite] NFPL (*Comm*) liquid assets

liquoreux, -euse [likɔRø, -øz] ADJ syrupy

lire [liR] /43/ NF (*monnaie*) lira ▶ VT, VI to read; ~ **qch à qn** to read sth (out) to sb

lis VB [li] *voir* **lire** ▶ NM [lis] = **lys**

lisais etc [lize] VB *voir* **lire**

Lisbonne [lizbɔn] N Lisbon

lise etc [liz] VB *voir* **lire**

liseré [lizRe] NM border, edging

liseron [lizRɔ̃] NM bindweed

liseuse [lizøz] NF book-cover; (*veste*) bed jacket ▶ NF e-reader n

lisible [lizibl] ADJ legible; (*digne d'être lu*) readable

lisiblement [lizibləmɑ̃] ADV legibly

lisière [lizjɛR] NF (*de forêt*) edge; (*de tissu*) selvage

lisons [lizɔ̃] VB *voir* **lire**

lisse [lis] ADJ smooth

lisser [lise] /1/ VT to smooth

lisseur [lisœR] NM straighteners pl

listage [listaʒ] NM (*Inform*) listing

liste [list] NF list; (*Inform*) listing; **faire la** ~ **de** to list, make out a list of; ~ **d'attente** waiting list; ~ **civile** civil list; ~ **électorale** electoral roll; ~ **de mariage** wedding (present) list; ~ **noire** black list

lister [liste] /1/ VT to list

listéria [listeRja] NF listeria

listing [listiŋ] NM (*Inform*) printout; **qualité** ~ draft quality

lit [li] NM (*gén*) bed; **petit** ~, ~ **à une place** single

bed; **grand ~, ~ à deux places** double bed;
faire son ~ to make one's bed; **aller/se mettre
au ~** to go to/get into bed; **chambre avec un
grand ~** room with a double bed; **prendre le ~**
to take to one's bed; **d'un premier ~** (Jur) of a
first marriage; **~ de camp** camp bed (BRIT), cot
(US); **~ d'enfant** cot (BRIT), crib (US)
litanie [litani] NF litany
lit-cage [likaʒ] (pl **lits-cages**) NM folding bed
litchi [litʃi] NM lychee
literie [litri] NF bedding; (linge) bedding,
bedclothes pl
litho [lito], **lithographie** [litɔgʀafi] NF
litho(graphy); (épreuve) litho(graph)
litière [litjɛʀ] NF litter
litige [litiʒ] NM dispute; **en ~** in contention
litigieux, -euse [litiʒjø, -øz] ADJ litigious,
contentious
litote [litɔt] NF understatement
litre [litʀ] NM litre; (récipient) litre measure
littéraire [liteʀɛʀ] ADJ literary ▶ NMF arts
student; **elle est très ~** she's very literary
littéral, e, -aux [liteʀal, -o] ADJ literal
littéralement [liteʀalmɑ̃] ADV literally
littérature [liteʀatyʀ] NF literature
littoral, e, -aux [litɔʀal, -o] ADJ coastal ▶ NM
coast
Lituanie [lituani] NF: **la ~** Lithuania
lituanien, ne [lituanjɛ̃, -ɛn] ADJ Lithuanian
▶ NM (Ling) Lithuanian ▶ NM/F: **L~, ne**
Lithuanian
liturgie [lityʀʒi] NF liturgy
liturgique [lityʀʒik] ADJ liturgical
livide [livid] ADJ livid, pallid
living [liviŋ], **living-room** [liviŋʀum] NM
living room
livrable [livʀabl] ADJ (Comm) that can be
delivered
livraison [livʀɛzɔ̃] NF delivery; **~ à domicile**
home delivery (service)
livre [livʀ] NM book; (imprimerie etc): **le ~** the book
industry ▶ NF (poids, monnaie) pound; **traduire
qch à ~ ouvert** to translate sth off the cuff ou at
sight; **~ blanc** official report (on war, natural
disaster etc, prepared by independent body); **~ de bord**
(Navig) logbook; **~ de comptes** account(s) book;
~ de cuisine cookery book (BRIT), cookbook;
~ de messe mass ou prayer book; **~ numérique**
e-book; **~ d'or** visitors' book; **~ de poche**
paperback; **~ sterling** pound sterling; **~ verte**
green pound
livré, e [livʀe] NF livery ▶ ADJ: **~ à** (l'anarchie etc)
given over to; **~ à soi-même** left to oneself ou
one's own devices
livrer [livʀe] /1/ VT (Comm) to deliver; (otage,
coupable) to hand over; (secret, information) to give
away; **se ~ à** (se confier) to confide in; (se rendre) to
give o.s. up to; (s'abandonner à: débauche etc) to give
o.s. up ou over to; (faire: pratiques, actes) to indulge
in; (: travail) to be engaged in, engage in; (: sport)
to practise; (: enquête) to carry out; **~ bataille** to
give battle
livresque [livʀɛsk] ADJ (péj) bookish
livret [livʀɛ] NM booklet; (d'opéra) libretto; **~ de**

caisse d'épargne (savings) bank-book; **~ de
famille** (official) family record book;
~ scolaire (school) report book
livreur, -euse [livʀœʀ, -øz] NM/F delivery boy ou
man/girl ou woman
LO SIGLE F (= Lutte ouvrière) political party
lob [lɔb] NM lob
lobe [lɔb] NM: **~ de l'oreille** ear lobe
lobé, e [lɔbe] ADJ (Archit) foiled
lober [lɔbe] /1/ VT to lob
local, e, -aux [lɔkal, -o] ADJ local ▶ NM (salle)
premises pl ▶ NMPL premises
localement [lɔkalmɑ̃] ADV locally
localisé, e [lɔkalize] ADJ localized
localiser [lɔkalize] /1/ VT (repérer) to locate, place;
(limiter) to localize, confine
localité [lɔkalite] NF locality
locataire [lɔkatɛʀ] NMF tenant; (de chambre)
lodger
locatif, -ive [lɔkatif, -iv] ADJ (charges, réparations)
incumbent upon the tenant; (valeur) rental;
(immeuble) with rented flats, used as a letting ou
rental (US) concern
location [lɔkasjɔ̃] NF (par le locataire) renting;
(par l'usager: de voiture etc) hiring (BRIT), renting
(US); (par le propriétaire) renting out, letting;
hiring out (BRIT); (de billets, places) booking;
(bureau) booking office; **"~ de voitures"** "car
hire (BRIT) ou rental (US)"; **habiter en ~** to live
in rented accommodation; **prendre une ~
(pour les vacances)** to rent a house etc (for the
holidays)
location-vente [lɔkasjɔ̃vɑ̃t] NF form of hire
purchase (BRIT) ou installment plan (US)
lock-out [lɔkawt] NM INV lockout
locomoteur, -trice [lɔkɔmɔtœʀ, -tʀis] ADJ, NF
locomotive
locomotion [lɔkɔmosjɔ̃] NF locomotion
locomotive [lɔkɔmɔtiv] NF locomotive, engine;
(fig) pacesetter, pacemaker
locuteur, -trice [lɔkytœʀ, -tʀis] NM/F (Ling)
speaker
locution [lɔkysjɔ̃] NF phrase
loden [lɔdɛn] NM loden
lofer [lɔfe] /1/ VI (Navig) to luff
logarithme [lɔgaʀitm] NM logarithm
loge [lɔʒ] NF (Théât: d'artiste) dressing room; (: de
spectateurs) box; (de concierge, franc-maçon) lodge
logeable [lɔʒabl] ADJ habitable; (spacieux) roomy
logement [lɔʒmɑ̃] NM flat (BRIT), apartment
(US); accommodation no pl (BRIT),
accommodations pl (US); (Pol, Admin): **le ~**
housing; **chercher un ~** to look for a flat ou
apartment, look for accommodation(s);
construire des logements bon marché to
build cheap housing sg; **crise du ~** housing
shortage; **~ de fonction** (Admin) company flat
ou apartment, accommodation(s) provided
with one's job
loger [lɔʒe] /3/ VT to accommodate ▶ VI to live;
se loger VR: **trouver à se loger** to find
accommodation; **se loger dans** (balle, flèche) to
lodge itself in; **être logé, nourri** to have board
and lodging

logeur, -euse [lɔʒœʀ, -øz] NM/F landlord (landlady)

loggia [lɔdʒja] NF loggia

logiciel [lɔʒisjɛl] NM (*Inform*) piece of software

logicien, ne [lɔʒisjɛ̃, -ɛn] NM/F logician

logique [lɔʒik] ADJ logical ▸ NF logic; **c'est ~** it stands to reason

logiquement [lɔʒikmɑ̃] ADV logically

logis [lɔʒi] NM home; abode, dwelling

logisticien, ne [lɔʒistisjɛ̃, -ɛn] NM/F logistician

logistique [lɔʒistik] NF logistics *sg* ▸ ADJ logistic

logo [lɔgo], **logotype** [lɔgotip] NM logo

loi [lwa] NF law; **faire la ~** to lay down the law; **les lois de la mode** (*fig*) the dictates of fashion; **proposition de ~** (private member's) bill; **projet de ~** (government) bill

loi-cadre [lwakadʀ] (*pl* **lois-cadres**) NF (*Pol*) blueprint law

loin [lwɛ̃] ADV far; (*dans le temps: futur*) a long way off; (: *passé*) a long time ago; **plus ~** further; **moins ~ (que)** not as far (as); **~ de** far from; **~ d'ici** a long way from here; **pas ~ de 100 euros** not far off 100 euros; **au ~** far off; **de ~** *adv* from a distance; (*fig: de beaucoup*) by far; **il vient de ~** he's come a long way; he comes from a long way away; **de ~ en ~** here and there; (*de temps en temps*) (every) now and then; **~ de là** (*au contraire*) far from it

lointain, e [lwɛ̃tɛ̃, -ɛn] ADJ faraway, distant; (*dans le futur, passé*) distant, far-off; (*cause, parent*) remote, distant ▸ NM: **dans le ~** in the distance

loi-programme [lwapʀɔgʀam] (*pl* **lois-programmes**) NF (*Pol*) act providing framework for government programme

loir [lwaʀ] NM dormouse

Loire [lwaʀ] NF: **la ~** the Loire

loisible [lwazibl] ADJ: **il vous est ~ de ...** you are free to ...

loisir [lwaziʀ] NM: **heures de ~** spare time; **loisirs** NMPL (*temps libre*) leisure *sg*; (*activités*) leisure activities; **avoir le ~ de faire** to have the time ou opportunity to do; (**tout) à ~** (*en prenant son temps*) at leisure; (*autant qu'on le désire*) at one's pleasure

lombaire [lɔ̃bɛʀ] ADJ lumbar

lombalgie [lɔ̃balʒi] NF back pain

londonien, ne [lɔ̃dɔnjɛ̃, -ɛn] ADJ London *cpd*, of London ▸ NM/F: **L~, ne** Londoner

Londres [lɔ̃dʀ] N London

long, longue [lɔ̃, lɔ̃g] ADJ long ▸ ADV: **en savoir ~** to know a great deal ▸ NM **de 3 m de ~** 3 m long, 3 m in length ▸ NF: **à la longue** in the end; **faire ~ feu** to fizzle out; **ne pas faire ~ feu** not to last long; **au ~ cours** (*Navig*) ocean *cpd*, ocean-going; **de longue date** *adj* long-standing; **longue durée** *adj* long-term; **de longue haleine** *adj* long-term; **être ~ à faire** to take a long time to do; **en ~** *adv* lengthwise, lengthways; (**tout) le ~ de** (all) along; **tout au ~ de** (*année, vie*) throughout; **de ~ en large** (*marcher*) to and fro, up and down; **en ~ et en large** (*fig*) in every detail

longanimité [lɔ̃ganimite] NF forbearance

long-courrier [lɔ̃kuʀje] NM (*Aviat*) long-haul aircraft

longe [lɔ̃ʒ] NF (*corde: pour attacher*) tether; (: *pour mener*) lead; (*Culin*) loin

longer [lɔ̃ʒe] /3/ VT to go (ou walk ou drive) along(side); (*mur, route*) to border

longévité [lɔ̃ʒevite] NF longevity

longiligne [lɔ̃ʒiliɲ] ADJ long-limbed

longitude [lɔ̃ʒityd] NF longitude; **à 45° de ~ ouest** at 45° longitude west

longitudinal, e, -aux [lɔ̃ʒitydinal, -o] ADJ longitudinal, lengthways; (*entaille, vallée*) running lengthways

longtemps [lɔ̃tɑ̃] ADV (for) a long time, (for) long; **ça ne va pas durer ~** it won't last long; **avant ~** before long; **pour/pendant ~** for a long time; **je n'en ai pas pour ~** I shan't be long; **mettre ~ à faire** to take a long time to do; **il en a pour ~** he'll be a long time; **il y a ~ que je travaille** I have been working (for) a long time; **il n'y a pas ~ que je l'ai rencontré** it's not long since I met him

longue [lɔ̃g] ADJ F *voir* **long** ▸ NF: **à la ~** in the end

longuement [lɔ̃gmɑ̃] ADV (*longtemps: parler, regarder*) for a long time; (*en détail: expliquer, raconter*) at length

longueur [lɔ̃gœʀ] NF length; **longueurs** NFPL (*fig: d'un film etc*) tedious parts; **sur une ~ de 10 km** for ou over 10 km; **en ~** *adv* lengthwise, lengthways; **tirer en ~** to drag on; **à ~ de journée** all day long; **d'une ~** (*gagner*) by a length; **~ d'onde** wavelength

longue-vue [lɔ̃gvy] NF telescope

look [luk] (*fam*) NM look, image

looping [lupiŋ] NM (*Aviat*): **faire des loopings** to loop the loop

lopin [lɔpɛ̃] NM: **~ de terre** patch of land

loquace [lɔkas] ADJ talkative, loquacious

loque [lɔk] NF (*personne*) wreck; **loques** NFPL (*habits*) rags; **être** ou **tomber en loques** to be in rags

loquet [lɔkɛ] NM latch

lorgner [lɔʀɲe] /1/ VT to eye; (*fig: convoiter*) to have one's eye on

lorgnette [lɔʀɲɛt] NF opera glasses *pl*

lorgnon [lɔʀɲɔ̃] NM (*face-à-main*) lorgnette; (*pince-nez*) pince-nez

loriot [lɔʀjo] NM (golden) oriole

lorrain, e [lɔʀɛ̃, -ɛn] ADJ of ou from Lorraine; **quiche ~** quiche

lors [lɔʀ]: **~ de** *prép* (*au moment de*) at the time of; (*pendant*) during; **~ même que** even though

lorsque [lɔʀsk] CONJ when, as

losange [lɔzɑ̃ʒ] NM diamond; (*Géom*) lozenge; **en ~** diamond-shaped

lot [lo] NM (*part*) share; (*de loterie*) prize; (*fig: destin*) fate, lot; (*Comm, Inform*) batch; **le gros ~** the jackpot; **~ de consolation** consolation prize

loterie [lɔtʀi] NF lottery; (*tombola*) raffle; **L~ nationale** French national lottery

loti, e [lɔti] ADJ: **bien/mal ~** well-/badly off, lucky/unlucky

lotion [losjɔ̃] NF lotion; **~ après rasage**

after-shave (lotion); **~ capillaire** hair lotion

lotir [lɔtiʀ] /**2**/ VT (*terrain: diviser*) to divide into plots; (*: vendre*) to sell by lots

lotissement [lɔtismɑ̃] NM (*groupe de maisons, d'immeubles*) housing development; (*parcelle*) (building) plot, lot

loto [lɔto] NM lotto

lotte [lɔt] NF (*Zool: de rivière*) burbot; (*: de mer*) monkfish

louable [lwabl] ADJ (*appartement, garage*) rentable; (*action, personne*) praiseworthy, commendable

louage [lwaʒ] NM: **voiture de ~** hired (BRIT) *ou* rented (US) car; (*à louer*) hire (BRIT) *ou* rental (US) car

louange [lwɑ̃ʒ] NF: **à la ~ de** in praise of; **louanges** NFPL praise *sg*

loubar(d) [lubaʀ] NM (*fam*) lout

louche [luʃ] ADJ shady, fishy, dubious ▸ NF ladle

loucher [luʃe] /**1**/ VI to squint; (*fig*): **~ sur** to have one's (beady) eye on

louer [lwe] /**1**/ VT (*maison: propriétaire*) to let, rent (out); (*: locataire*) to rent; (*voiture etc: entreprise*) to hire out (BRIT), rent (out); (*: locataire*) to hire (BRIT), rent; (*réserver*) to book; (*faire l'éloge de*) to praise; **"à ~"** "to let" (BRIT), "for rent" (US); **~ qn de** to praise sb for; **se ~ de** to congratulate o.s. on

loufoque [lufɔk] ADJ (*fam*) crazy, zany

loukoum [lukum] NM Turkish delight

loulou [lulu] NM (*chien*) spitz; **~ de Poméranie** Pomeranian (dog)

loup [lu] NM wolf; (*poisson*) bass; (*masque*) (eye) mask; **jeune ~** young go-getter; **~ de mer** (*marin*) old seadog

loupe [lup] NF magnifying glass; **~ de noyer** burr walnut; **à la ~** (*fig*) in minute detail

louper [lupe] /**1**/ VT (*fam: manquer*) to miss; (*gâcher*) to mess up, bungle; (*examen*) to flunk

lourd, e [luʀ, luʀd] ADJ heavy; (*chaleur, temps*) sultry; (*fig: personne, style*) heavy-handed ▸ ADV: **peser ~** to be heavy; **~ de** (*menaces*) charged with; (*conséquences*) fraught with; **artillerie/industrie ~** heavy artillery/industry

lourdaud, e [luʀdo, -od] ADJ clumsy

lourdement [luʀdəmɑ̃] ADV heavily; **se tromper ~** to make a big mistake

lourdeur [luʀdœʀ] NF heaviness; **~ d'estomac** indigestion *no pl*

loustic [lustik] NM (*fam, péj*) joker

loutre [lutʀ] NF otter; (*fourrure*) otter skin

louve [luv] NF she-wolf

louveteau, x [luvto] NM (*Zool*) wolf-cub; (*scout*) cub (scout)

louvoyer [luvwaje] /**8**/ VI (*Navig*) to tack; (*fig*) to hedge, evade the issue

lover [lɔve] /**1**/: **se lover** VI to coil up

loyal, e, -aux [lwajal, -o] ADJ (*fidèle*) loyal, faithful; (*fair-play*) fair

loyalement [lwajalmɑ̃] ADV loyally, faithfully; fairly

loyalisme [lwajalism] NM loyalty

loyauté [lwajote] NF loyalty, faithfulness; fairness

loyer [lwaje] NM rent; **~ de l'argent** interest rate

LP SIGLE M (= *lycée professionnel*) *secondary school for vocational training*

LPO SIGLE F (= *Ligue pour la protection des oiseaux*) *bird protection society*

LSD SIGLE M (= *Lyserg Säure Diäthylamid*) LSD

lu, e [ly] PP *de* lire

lubie [lybi] NF whim, craze

lubricité [lybʀisite] NF lust

lubrifiant [lybʀifjɑ̃] NM lubricant

lubrifier [lybʀifje] /**7**/ VT to lubricate

lubrique [lybʀik] ADJ lecherous

lucarne [lykaʀn] NF skylight

lucide [lysid] ADJ (*conscient*) lucid; (*accidenté*) conscious; (*perspicace*) clear-headed

lucidité [lysidite] NF lucidity

luciole [lysjɔl] NF firefly

lucratif, -ive [lykʀatif, -iv] ADJ lucrative; profitable; **à but non ~** non profit-making

ludique [lydik] ADJ play *cpd*, playing

ludothèque [lydɔtɛk] NF toy library

luette [lɥɛt] NF uvula

lueur [lɥœʀ] NF (*chatoyante*) glimmer *no pl*; (*métallique, mouillée*) gleam *no pl*; (*rougeoyante*) glow *no pl*; (*pâle*) (faint) light; (*fig*) spark; (*: d'espérance*) glimmer, gleam

luge [lyʒ] NF sledge (BRIT), sled (US); **faire de la ~** to sledge (BRIT), sled (US), toboggan

lugubre [lygybʀ] ADJ gloomy; dismal

(MOT-CLÉ)

lui [lɥi] PP *de* luire
▸ PRON **1** (*objet indirect: mâle*) (to) him; (*: femelle*) (to) her; (*: chose, animal*) (to) it; **je lui ai parlé** I have spoken to him (*ou* to her); **il lui a offert un cadeau** he gave him (*ou* her) a present; **je le lui ai donné** I gave it to him (*ou* her)
2 (*après préposition, comparatif: personne*) him; (*: chose, animal*) it; **elle est contente de lui** she is pleased with him; **je la connais mieux que lui** I know her better than he does; I know her better than him; **cette voiture est à lui** this car belongs to him, this is HIS car; **c'est à lui de jouer** it's his turn *ou* go
3 (*sujet, forme emphatique*) he; **lui, il est à Paris** HE is in Paris; **c'est lui qui l'a fait** HE did it
4 (*objet, forme emphatique*) him; **c'est lui que j'attends** I'm waiting for HIM
5: **lui-même** himself; itself

lui-même [lɥimɛm] PRON (*personne*) himself; (*chose*) itself

luire [lɥiʀ] /**38**/ VI (*gén*) to shine, gleam; (*surface mouillée*) to glisten; (*reflets chauds, cuivrés*) to glow

luisant, e [lɥizɑ̃, -ɑ̃t] VB *voir* luire ▸ ADJ shining, gleaming

lumbago [lɔ̃bago] NM lumbago

lumière [lymjɛʀ] NF light; **lumières** NFPL (*d'une personne*) knowledge *sg*, wisdom *sg*; **à la ~ de** by the light of; (*fig: événements*) in the light of; **fais de la ~** let's have some light, give us some light; **faire (toute) la ~ sur** (*fig*) to clarify (completely); **mettre en ~** (*fig*) to highlight; **~ du jour/soleil** day/sunlight

luminaire [lyminɛʀ] NM lamp, light
lumineux, -euse [lyminø, -øz] ADJ (*émettant de la lumière*) luminous; (*éclairé*) illuminated; (*ciel, journée, couleur*) bright; (*relatif à la lumière: rayon etc*) of light, light *cpd*; (*fig: regard*) radiant
luminosité [lyminɔzite] NF (*Tech*) luminosity
lump [lœp] NM: **œufs de ~** lump-fish roe
lunaire [lynɛʀ] ADJ lunar, moon *cpd*
lunatique [lynatik] ADJ whimsical, temperamental
lunch [lœntʃ] NM (*réception*) buffet lunch
lundi [lœdi] NM Monday; **on est ~** it's Monday; **le ~ 20 août** Monday 20th August; **il est venu ~** he came on Monday; **le(s) ~(s)** on Mondays; **à ~!** see you (on) Monday!; **~ de Pâques** Easter Monday; **~ de Pentecôte** Whit Monday (*BRIT*)
lune [lyn] NF moon; **pleine/nouvelle ~** full/new moon; **être dans la ~** (*distrait*) to have one's head in the clouds; **~ de miel** honeymoon
luné, e [lyne] ADJ: **bien/mal ~** in a good/bad mood
lunette [lynɛt] NF: **lunettes** glasses, spectacles; (*protectrices*) goggles; **~ d'approche** telescope; **~ arrière** (*Auto*) rear window; **lunettes noires** dark glasses; **lunettes de soleil** sunglasses
lurent [lyʀ] VB *voir* **lire**
lurette [lyʀɛt] NF: **il y a belle ~** ages ago
luron, ne [lyʀɔ̃, -ɔn] NM/F lad/lass; **joyeux** *ou* **gai ~** gay dog
lus *etc* [ly] VB *voir* **lire**
lustre [lystʀ] NM (*de plafond*) chandelier; (*fig: éclat*) lustre
lustrer [lystʀe] /1/ VT: **~ qch** (*faire briller*) to make sth shine; (*user*) to make sth shiny
lut [ly] VB *voir* **lire**
luth [lyt] NM lute
luthier [lytje] NM (stringed-)instrument maker
lutin [lytɛ̃] NM imp, goblin
lutrin [lytʀɛ̃] NM lectern
lutte [lyt] NF (*conflit*) struggle; (*Sport*): **la ~** wrestling; **de haute ~** after a hard-fought struggle; **~ des classes** class struggle; **~ libre** (*Sport*) all-in wrestling
lutter [lyte] /1/ VI to fight, struggle; (*Sport*) to wrestle
lutteur, -euse [lytœʀ, -øz] NM/F (*Sport*) wrestler; (*fig*) battler, fighter

luxation [lyksasjɔ̃] NF dislocation
luxe [lyks] NM luxury; **un ~ de** (*détails, précautions*) a wealth of; **de ~** *adj* luxury *cpd*
Luxembourg [lyksɑ̃buʀ] NM: **le ~** Luxembourg
luxembourgeois, e [lyksɑ̃buʀʒwa, -waz] ADJ of *ou* from Luxembourg ▶ NM/F: **L~, e** inhabitant *ou* native of Luxembourg
luxer [lykse] /1/ VT: **se ~ l'épaule** to dislocate one's shoulder
luxueusement [lyksɥøzmɑ̃] ADV luxuriously
luxueux, -euse [lyksɥø, -øz] ADJ luxurious
luxure [lyksyʀ] NF lust
luxuriant, e [lyksyʀjɑ̃, -ɑ̃t] ADJ luxuriant, lush
luzerne [lyzɛʀn] NF lucerne, alfalfa
lycée [lise] NM (*state*) secondary (*BRIT*) *ou* high (*US*) school; **~ technique** technical secondary *ou* high school; *see note*

> French pupils spend the last three years of their secondary education at a *lycée*, where they sit their *baccalauréat* before leaving school or going on to higher education. There are various types of *lycée*, including the *lycées d'enseignement technologique*, providing technical courses, and *lycées d'enseignement professionnel*, providing vocational courses. Some *lycées*, particularly those with a wide catchment area or those which run specialist courses, have boarding facilities.

lycéen, ne [liseɛ̃, -ɛn] NM/F secondary school pupil
Lycra® [likra] NM Lycra®
lymphatique [lɛ̃fatik] ADJ (*fig*) lethargic, sluggish
lymphe [lɛ̃f] NF lymph
lyncher [lɛ̃ʃe] /1/ VT to lynch
lynx [lɛ̃ks] NM lynx
Lyon [ljɔ̃] N Lyons
lyonnais, e [ljɔnɛ, -ɛz] ADJ of *ou* from Lyons; (*Culin*) Lyonnaise
lyophilisé, e [ljɔfilize] ADJ (*café*) freeze-dried
lyre [liʀ] NF lyre
lyrique [liʀik] ADJ lyrical; (*Opéra*) lyric; **artiste ~** opera singer; **comédie ~** comic opera; **théâtre ~** opera house (*for light opera*)
lyrisme [liʀism] NM lyricism
lys [lis] NM lily

Mm

M, m [ɛm] NM INV M, m ▸ ABR = **masculin**; **Monsieur**; **mètre**; (= *million*) M; **M comme Marcel** M for Mike

m' [m] PRON *voir* **me**

MA SIGLE M = **maître auxiliaire**

ma [ma] ADJ POSS *voir* **mon**

maboul, e [mabul] ADJ (*fam*) loony

macabre [makabʀ] ADJ macabre, gruesome

macadam [makadam] NM tarmac (BRIT), asphalt

macaron [makaʀɔ̃] NM (*gâteau*) macaroon; (*insigne*) (round) badge

macaronis [makaʀɔni] NMPL macaroni *sg*; **~ au gratin** macaroni cheese (BRIT), macaroni and cheese (US)

Macédoine [masedwan] NF Macedonia

macédoine [masedwan] NF: **~ de fruits** fruit salad; **~ de légumes** mixed vegetables *pl*

macérer [maseʀe] /6/ VI, VT to macerate; (*dans du vinaigre*) to pickle

mâchefer [maʃfɛʀ] NM clinker, cinders *pl*

mâcher [maʃe] /1/ VT to chew; **ne pas ~ ses mots** not to mince one's words; **~ le travail à qn** (*fig*) to spoon-feed sb, do half sb's work for him

machiavélique [makjavelik] ADJ Machiavellian

machin [maʃɛ̃] NM (*fam*) thingamajig, thing; (*personne*): **M~(e)** what's-his(*ou* her)-name

machinal, e, -aux [maʃinal, -o] ADJ mechanical, automatic

machinalement [maʃinalmɑ̃] ADV mechanically, automatically

machination [maʃinasjɔ̃] NF scheming, frame-up

machine [maʃin] NF machine; (*locomotive: de navire etc*) engine; (*fig: rouages*) machinery; (*fam: personne*): **M~** what's-her-name; **faire ~ arrière** (*Navig*) to go astern; (*fig*) to back-pedal; **~ à laver/coudre/tricoter** washing/sewing/ knitting machine; **~ à écrire** typewriter; **~ à sous** fruit machine; **~ à vapeur** steam engine

machine-outil [maʃinuti] (*pl* **machines-outils**) NF machine tool

machinerie [maʃinʀi] NF machinery, plant; (*d'un navire*) engine room

machinisme [maʃinism] NM mechanization

machiniste [maʃinist] NM (*Théât*) scene shifter; (*de bus, métro*) driver

macho [matʃo] (*fam*) NM male chauvinist

mâchoire [maʃwaʀ] NF jaw; **~ de frein** brake shoe

mâchonner [maʃone] /1/ VT to chew (at)

maçon [masɔ̃] NM bricklayer; (*constructeur*) builder

mâcon [makɔ̃] NM Mâcon wine

maçonner [masɔne] /1/ VT (*revêtir*) to face, render (with cement); (*boucher*) to brick up

maçonnerie [masɔnʀi] NF (*murs: de brique*) brickwork; (: *de pierre*) masonry, stonework; (*activité*) bricklaying; building; **~ de béton** concrete

maçonnique [masɔnik] ADJ masonic

macramé [makʀame] NM macramé

macrobiotique [makʀɔbjɔtik] ADJ macrobiotic

macrocosme [makʀɔkɔsm] NM macrocosm

macro-économie [makʀɔekɔnɔmi] NF macroeconomics *sg*

maculer [makyle] /1/ VT to stain; (*Typo*) to mackle

Madagascar [madagaskaʀ] NF Madagascar

Madame [madam] (*pl* **Mesdames** [medam]) NF: **~ X** Mrs X; **occupez-vous de ~/Monsieur/ Mademoiselle** please serve this lady/ gentleman/(young) lady; **bonjour ~/ Monsieur/Mademoiselle** good morning; (*ton déférent*) good morning Madam/Sir/Madam; (*le nom est connu*) good morning Mrs X/Mr X/Miss X; **~/Monsieur/Mademoiselle!** (*pour appeler*) excuse me!; (*ton déférent*) Madam/Sir/Miss!; **~/Monsieur/Mademoiselle** (*sur lettre*) Dear Madam/Sir/Madam; **chère ~/cher Monsieur/ chère Mademoiselle** Dear Mrs X/Mr X/Miss X; **~ la Directrice** the director; the manageress; the head teacher; **Mesdames** Ladies; **mesdames, mesdemoiselles, messieurs** ladies and gentlemen

Madeleine [madlɛn]: **îles de la ~** *nfpl* Magdalen Islands

madeleine [madlɛn] NF madeleine, ≈ sponge finger cake

Mademoiselle [madmwazɛl] (*pl* **Mesdemoiselles** [medmwazɛl]) NF Miss; *voir aussi* **Madame**

Madère [madɛʀ] NF Madeira ▸ NM: **madère** Madeira (wine)

madone [madɔn] NF Madonna

madré, e [madʀe] ADJ crafty, wily
Madrid [madʀid] N Madrid
madrier [madʀije] NM beam
madrigal, -aux [madʀigal, -o] NM madrigal
madrilène [madʀilɛn] ADJ of ou from Madrid
maestria [maɛstʀija] NF (masterly) skill
maestro [maɛstʀo] NM maestro
mafia, maffia [mafja] NF Maf(f)ia
magasin [magazɛ̃] NM (boutique) shop; (entrepôt) warehouse; (d'arme) magazine; **en ~** (Comm) in stock; **faire les magasins** to go (a)round the shops, do the shops; **~ d'alimentation** grocer's (shop) (BRIT), grocery store (US)

> French shops are usually open from 9am to noon and from 2pm to 7pm. Most shops are closed on Sunday and some do not open on Monday. In bigger towns and shopping centres, most shops are open throughout the day.

magasinier [magazinje] NM warehouseman
magazine [magazin] NM magazine
mage [maʒ] NM: **les Rois Mages** the Magi, the (Three) Wise Men
Maghreb [magʀɛb] NM: **le ~** the Maghreb, North(-West) Africa
maghrébin, e [magʀebɛ̃, -in] ADJ of ou from the Maghreb, North African ▶ NM/F: **M~, e** North African, Maghrebi
magicien, ne [maʒisjɛ̃, -ɛn] NM/F magician
magie [maʒi] NF magic; **~ noire** black magic
magique [maʒik] ADJ (occulte) magic; (fig) magical
magistral, e, -aux [maʒistʀal, -o] ADJ (œuvre, adresse) masterly; (ton) authoritative; (gifle etc) sound, resounding; (ex cathedra):
enseignement ~ lecturing, lectures pl; **cours ~** lecture
magistrat [maʒistʀa] NM magistrate
magistrature [maʒistʀatyʀ] NF magistracy, magistrature; **~ assise** judges pl, bench; **~ debout** state prosecutors pl
magma [magma] NM (Géo) magma; (fig) jumble
magnanime [maɲanim] ADJ magnanimous
magnanimité [maɲanimite] NF magnanimity
magnat [maɲa] NM tycoon, magnate
magner [maɲe] /1/: **se magner** VI (fam) to get a move on
magnésie [maɲezi] NF magnesia
magnésium [maɲezjɔm] NM magnesium
magnétique [maɲetik] ADJ magnetic
magnétiser [maɲetize] /1/ VT to magnetize; (fig) to mesmerize, hypnotize
magnétiseur, -euse [maɲetizœʀ, -øz] NM/F hypnotist
magnétisme [maɲetism] NM magnetism
magnéto [maɲeto] NM (à cassette) cassette deck; (magnétophone) tape recorder
magnétophone [maɲetɔfɔn] NM tape recorder; **~ à cassettes** cassette recorder
magnétoscope [maɲetɔskɔp] NM: **~ (à cassette)** video (recorder)
magnificence [maɲifisɑ̃s] NF (faste) magnificence, splendour (BRIT), splendor (US); (générosité) munificence, lavishness

magnifier [maɲifje] /7/ VT (glorifier) to glorify; (idéaliser) to idealize
magnifique [maɲifik] ADJ magnificent
magnifiquement [maɲifikmɑ̃] ADV magnificently
magnolia [maɲɔlja] NM magnolia
magnum [magnɔm] NM magnum
magot [mago] NM (argent) pile (of money); (économies) nest egg
magouille [maguj] NF (fam) scheming
magret [magʀɛ] NM: **~ de canard** duck breast
mahométan, e [maɔmetɑ̃, -an] ADJ Mohammedan, Mahometan
mai [mɛ] NM May; see note; voir aussi **juillet**

> Le premier mai is a public holiday in France and commemorates the trades union demonstrations in the United States in 1886 when workers demanded the right to an eight-hour working day. Sprigs of lily of the valley are traditionally exchanged. Le 8 mai is also a public holiday and commemorates the surrender of the German army to Eisenhower on 7 May, 1945. It is marked by parades of ex-servicemen and ex-servicewomen in most towns. The social upheavals of May and June 1968, with their student demonstrations, workers' strikes and general rioting, are usually referred to as les événements de mai 68. De Gaulle's Government survived, but reforms in education and a move towards decentralization ensued.

maigre [mɛgʀ] ADJ (very) thin, skinny; (viande) lean; (fromage) low-fat; (végétation) thin, sparse; (fig) poor, meagre, skimpy ▶ ADV: **faire ~** not to eat meat; **jours maigres** days of abstinence, fish days
maigrelet, te [mɛgʀəlɛ, -ɛt] ADJ skinny, scrawny
maigreur [mɛgʀœʀ] NF thinness
maigrichon, ne [mɛgʀiʃɔ̃, -ɔn] ADJ = **maigrelet**
maigrir [mɛgʀiʀ] /2/ VI to get thinner, lose weight ▶ VT: **~ qn** (vêtement) to make sb look slim(mer); **~ de 2 kilos** to lose 2 kilos
mail [mɛl] NM email
mailing [mɛliŋ] NM direct mail no pl; **un ~** a mailshot
maille [maj] NF (boucle) stitch; (ouverture) hole (in the mesh); **avoir ~ à partir avec qn** to have a brush with sb; **~ à l'endroit/à l'envers** knit one/purl one; (boucle) plain/purl stitch
maillechort [majʃɔʀ] NM nickel silver
maillet [majɛ] NM mallet
maillon [majɔ̃] NM link
maillot [majo] NM (aussi: **maillot de corps**) vest; (de danseur) leotard; (de sportif) jersey; **~ de bain** swimming ou bathing (BRIT) costume, swimsuit; (d'homme) (swimming ou bathing (BRIT)) trunks pl; **~ deux pièces** two-piece swimsuit, bikini; **~ jaune** yellow jersey
main [mɛ̃] NF hand; **la ~ dans la ~** hand in hand; **à deux mains** with both hands; **à une ~** with one hand; **à la ~** (tenir, avoir) in one's hand; (faire, tricoter etc) by hand; **se donner la ~** to hold hands; **donner** ou **tendre la ~ à qn** to hold out

one's hand to sb; **se serrer la ~** to shake hands; **serrer la ~ à qn** to shake hands with sb; **sous la ~** to *ou* at hand; **haut les mains!** hands up!; **à ~ levée** (*Art*) freehand; **à mains levées** (*voter*) with a show of hands; **attaque à ~ armée** armed attack; **à ~ droite/gauche** to the right/left; **à remettre en mains propres** to be delivered personally; **de première ~** (*renseignement*) first-hand; (*Comm: voiture etc*) with only one previous owner; **faire ~ basse sur** to help o.s. to; **mettre la dernière ~ à** to put the finishing touches to; **mettre la ~ à la pâte** (*fig*) to lend a hand; **avoir/passer la ~** (*Cartes*) to lead/hand over the lead; **s'en laver les mains** (*fig*) to wash one's hands of it; **se faire/perdre la ~** to get one's hand in/lose one's touch; **avoir qch bien en ~** to have got the hang of sth; **en un tour de ~** (*fig*) in the twinkling of an eye; **~ courante** handrail
mainate [mɛnat] NM myna(h) bird
main-d'œuvre [mɛ̃dœvʀ] NF manpower, labour (*Brit*), labor (*US*)
main-forte [mɛ̃fɔʀt] NF: **prêter ~ à qn** to come to sb's assistance
mainmise [mɛ̃miz] NF seizure; (*fig*): **avoir la ~ sur** to have a grip *ou* stranglehold on
mains-libres [mɛ̃libʀ] ADJ INV (*téléphone, kit*) hands-free
maint, e [mɛ̃, mɛ̃t] ADJ many a; **maints** many; **à maintes reprises** time and (time) again
maintenance [mɛ̃tnɑ̃s] NF maintenance, servicing
maintenant [mɛ̃tnɑ̃] ADV now; (*actuellement*) nowadays
maintenir [mɛ̃tniʀ] /**22**/ VT (*retenir, soutenir*) to support; (*contenir: foule etc*) to keep in check, hold back; (*conserver*) to maintain, uphold; (*affirmer*) to maintain; **se maintenir** VI (*paix, temps*) to hold; (*prix*) to keep steady; (*préjugé*) to persist; (*malade*) to remain stable
maintien [mɛ̃tjɛ̃] NM maintaining, upholding; (*attitude*) bearing; **~ de l'ordre** maintenance of law and order
maintiendrai [mɛ̃tjɛ̃dʀe], **maintiens** *etc* [mɛ̃tjɛ̃] VB *voir* **maintenir**
maire [mɛʀ] NM mayor
mairie [meʀi] NF (*bâtiment*) town hall; (*administration*) town council
mais [mɛ] CONJ but; **~ non!** of course not!; **~ enfin** but after all; (*indignation*) look here!; **~ encore?** is that all?
maïs [mais] NM maize (*Brit*), corn (*US*)
maison [mɛzɔ̃] NF (*bâtiment*) house; (*chez-soi*) home; (*Comm*) firm; (*famille*): **ami de la ~** friend of the family ▸ ADJ INV (*Culin*) home-made; (: *au restaurant*) made by the chef; (*Comm*) in-house, own; (*fam*) first-rate; **à la ~** at home; (*direction*) home; **~ d'arrêt** (short-stay) prison; **~ centrale** prison; **~ close** brothel; **~ de correction** ≈ remand home (*Brit*), ≈ reformatory (*US*); **~ de la culture** ≈ arts centre; **~ des jeunes** ≈ youth club; **~ mère** parent company; **~ de passe** = **maison close**; **~ de repos** convalescent home; **~ de retraite** old people's home; **~ de santé** psychiatric hospital
Maison-Blanche [mɛzɔ̃blɑ̃ʃ] NF: **la ~** the White House
maisonnée [mɛzɔne] NF household, family
maisonnette [mɛzɔnɛt] NF small house
maître, -esse [mɛtʀ, mɛtʀɛs] NM/F master (mistress); (*Scol*) teacher, schoolmaster(-mistress) ▸ NM (*peintre etc*) master; (*titre*): **M-** Maître (*term of address for lawyers etc*) ▸ NF (*amante*) mistress ▸ ADJ (*principal, essentiel*) main; **maison de ~** family seat; **être ~ de** (*soi-même, situation*) to be in control of; **se rendre ~ de** (*pays, ville*) to gain control of; (*situation, incendie*) to bring under control; **être passé ~ dans l'art de** to be a (past) master in the art of; **une maîtresse femme** a forceful woman; **~ d'armes** fencing master; **~ auxiliaire** (*Scol*) temporary teacher; **~ chanteur** blackmailer; **~ de chapelle** choirmaster; **~ de conférences** ≈ senior lecturer (*Brit*), ≈ assistant professor (*US*); **~/maîtresse d'école** teacher, schoolmaster/-mistress; **~ d'hôtel** (*domestique*) butler; (*d'hôtel*) head waiter; **~ de maison** host; **~ nageur** lifeguard; **~ d'œuvre** (*Constr*) project manager; **~ d'ouvrage** (*Constr*) client; **~ queux** chef; **maîtresse de maison** hostess; (*ménagère*) housewife
maître-assistant, e [mɛtʀasistɑ̃, -ɑ̃t] (*pl* **maîtres-assistants, es**) NM/F ≈ lecturer
maîtrise [mɛtʀiz] NF (*aussi:* **maîtrise de soi**) self-control, self-possession; (*habileté*) skill, mastery; (*suprématie*) mastery, command; (*diplôme*) ≈ master's degree; (*chefs d'équipe*) supervisory staff; *see note*

> The *maîtrise* is a French degree which is awarded to university students if they successfully complete two more years' study after the DEUG. Students wishing to go on to do research or to take the *agrégation* must hold a *maîtrise*.

maîtriser [mɛtʀize] /**1**/ VT (*cheval, incendie*) to (bring under) control; (*sujet*) to master; (*émotion*) to control, master; **se maîtriser** to control o.s.
majesté [maʒɛste] NF majesty
majestueux, -euse [maʒɛstɥø, -øz] ADJ majestic
majeur, e [maʒœʀ] ADJ (*important*) major; (*Jur*) of age; (*fig*) adult ▸ NM/F (*Jur*) person who has come of age *ou* attained his (*ou* her) majority ▸ NM (*doigt*) middle finger; **en ~ partie** for the most part; **la ~ partie de** most of
major [maʒɔʀ] NM adjutant; (*Scol*): **~ de la promotion** first in one's year
majoration [maʒɔʀasjɔ̃] NF increase
majordome [maʒɔʀdɔm] NM major-domo
majorer [maʒɔʀe] /**1**/ VT to increase
majorette [maʒɔʀɛt] NF majorette
majoritaire [maʒɔʀitɛʀ] ADJ majority *cpd*; **système/scrutin ~** majority system/ballot
majorité [maʒɔʀite] NF (*gén*) majority; (*parti*) party in power; **en ~** (*composé etc*) mainly; **avoir la ~** to have the majority

m

Majorque [maʒɔʀk] NF Majorca
majuscule [maʒyskyl] ADJ, NF: **(lettre)** ~ capital (letter)
mal, maux [mal, mo] NM (*opposé au bien*) evil; (*tort, dommage*) harm; (*douleur physique*) pain, ache; (*maladie*) illness, sickness *no pl*; (*difficulté, peine*) trouble; (*souffrance morale*) pain ▸ ADV badly ▸ ADJ: **c'est ~ (de faire)** it's bad *ou* wrong (to do); **être ~ (à l'aise)** to be uncomfortable; **être ~ avec qn** to be on bad terms with sb; **être au plus ~** (*malade*) to be very bad; (*brouillé*) to be at daggers drawn; **il comprend ~** he has difficulty in understanding; **il a ~ compris** he misunderstood; **se sentir** *ou* **se trouver ~** to feel ill *ou* unwell; **~ tourner** to go wrong; **dire/penser du ~ de** to speak/think ill of; **ne vouloir de ~ à personne** to wish nobody any ill; **il n'a rien fait de ~** he has done nothing wrong; **avoir du ~ à faire qch** to have trouble doing sth; **se donner du ~ pour faire qch** to go to a lot of trouble to do sth; **ne voir aucun ~ à** to see no harm in, see nothing wrong in; **craignant ~ faire** fearing he *etc* was doing the wrong thing; **sans penser** *ou* **songer à ~** without meaning any harm; **faire du ~ à qn** to hurt sb; to mahis *ou* harms); **se faire ~** to hurt o.s.; **se faire ~ au pied** to hurt one's foot; **ça fait ~** it hurts; **j'ai ~ (ici)** it hurts (here); **j'ai ~ au dos** my back aches, I've got a pain in my back; **avoir ~ à la tête/à la gorge** to have a headache/a sore throat; **avoir ~ aux dents/à l'oreille** to have toothache/earache; **avoir le ~ de l'air** to be airsick; **avoir le ~ du pays** to be homesick; **~ de mer** seasickness; **~ de la route** carsickness; **~ en point** *adj inv* in a bad state; **maux de ventre** stomach ache *sg*; *voir aussi* **cœur**
malabar [malabaʀ] NM (*fam*) muscle man
malade [malad] ADJ ill, sick; (*poitrine, jambe*) bad; (*plante*) diseased; (*fig: entreprise, monde*) ailing ▸ NMF invalid, sick person; (*à l'hôpital*) patient; **tomber ~** to fall ill; **être ~ du cœur** to have heart trouble *ou* a bad heart; **grand ~** seriously ill person; **~ mental** mentally sick *ou* ill person
maladie [maladi] NF (*spécifique*) disease, illness; (*mauvaise santé*) illness, sickness; (*fig: manie*) mania; **être rongé par la ~** to be wasting away (through illness); **~ d'Alzheimer** Alzheimer's disease; **~ de peau** skin disease
maladif, -ive [maladif, -iv] ADJ sickly; (*curiosité, besoin*) pathological
maladresse [maladʀɛs] NF clumsiness *no pl*; (*gaffe*) blunder
maladroit, e [maladʀwa, -wat] ADJ clumsy
maladroitement [maladʀwatmɑ̃] ADV clumsily
mal-aimé, e [maleme] NM/F unpopular person; (*de la scène politique, de la société*) persona non grata
malais, e [malɛ, -ɛz] ADJ Malay, Malayan ▸ NM (*Ling*) Malay ▸ NM/F: **M~, e** Malay, Malayan
malaise [malɛz] NM (*Méd*) feeling of faintness, feeling of discomfort; (*fig*) uneasiness, malaise; **avoir un ~** to feel faint *ou* dizzy

malaisé, e [maleze] ADJ difficult
Malaisie [malɛzi] NF: **la ~** Malaysia; **la péninsule de ~** the Malay Peninsula
malappris, e [malapʀi, -iz] NM/F ill-mannered *ou* boorish person
malaria [malaʀja] NF malaria
malavisé, e [malavize] ADJ ill-advised, unwise
Malawi [malawi] NM: **le ~** Malawi
malaxer [malakse] /1/ VT (*pétrir*) to knead; (*mêler*) to mix
Malaysia [malɛzja] NF: **la ~** Malaysia
malbouffe [malbuf] NF (*fam*): **la ~** junk food
malchance [malʃɑ̃s] NF misfortune, ill luck *no pl*; **par ~** unfortunately; **quelle ~!** what bad luck!
malchanceux, -euse [malʃɑ̃sø, -øz] ADJ unlucky
malcommode [malkɔmɔd] ADJ impractical, inconvenient
Maldives [maldiv] NFPL: **les ~** the Maldive Islands
maldonne [maldɔn] NF (*Cartes*) misdeal; **il y a ~** (*fig*) there's been a misunderstanding
mâle [mɑl] ADJ (*Élec, Tech*) male; (*viril: voix, traits*) manly ▸ NM male
malédiction [malediksjɔ̃] NF curse
maléfice [malefis] NM evil spell
maléfique [malefik] ADJ evil, baleful
malencontreusement [malɑ̃kɔ̃tʀøzmɑ̃] ADV (*arriver*) at the wrong moment; (*rappeler, mentionner*) inopportunely
malencontreux, -euse [malɑ̃kɔ̃tʀø, -øz] ADJ unfortunate, untoward
malentendant, e [malɑ̃tɑ̃dɑ̃, -ɑ̃t] NM/F: **les malentendants** the hard of hearing
malentendu [malɑ̃tɑ̃dy] NM misunderstanding; **il y a eu un ~** there's been a misunderstanding
malfaçon [malfasɔ̃] NF fault
malfaisant, e [malfəzɑ̃, -ɑ̃t] ADJ evil, harmful
malfaiteur [malfetœʀ] NM lawbreaker, criminal; (*voleur*) burglar, thief
malfamé, e [malfame] ADJ disreputable, of ill repute
malfrat [malfʀa] NM villain, crook
malgache [malgaʃ] ADJ Malagasy, Madagascan ▸ NM (*Ling*) Malagasy ▸ NM/F: **M~** Malagasy, Madagascan
malgré [malgʀe] PRÉP in spite of, despite; **~ tout** *adv* in spite of everything
malhabile [malabil] ADJ clumsy
malheur [malœʀ] NM (*situation*) adversity, misfortune; (*événement*) misfortune; (: *plus fort*) disaster, tragedy; **par ~** unfortunately; **quel ~!** what a shame *ou* pity!; **faire un ~** (*fam: un éclat*) to do something desperate; (: *avoir du succès*) to be a smash hit
malheureusement [malœʀøzmɑ̃] ADV unfortunately
malheureux, -euse [malœʀø, -øz] ADJ (*triste*) unhappy, miserable; (*infortuné, regrettable*) unfortunate; (*malchanceux*) unlucky; (*insignifiant*) wretched ▸ NM/F (*infortuné, misérable*) poor soul; (*indigent, miséreux*) unfortunate creature; **les ~** the destitute;

avoir la main **malheureuse** (*au jeu*) to be
unlucky; (*tout casser*) to be ham-fisted
malhonnête [malɔnɛt] ADJ dishonest
malhonnêtement [malɔnɛtmɑ̃] ADV
dishonestly
malhonnêteté [malɔnɛtte] NF dishonesty;
rudeness *no pl*
Mali [mali] NM: **le ~** Mali
malice [malis] NF mischievousness; (*méchanceté*):
par ~ out of malice *ou* spite; **sans ~** guileless
malicieusement [malisjøzmɑ̃] ADV
mischievously
malicieux, -euse [malisjø, -øz] ADJ mischievous
malien, ne [maljɛ̃, -ɛn] ADJ Malian
malignité [maliɲite] NF (*d'une tumeur, d'un mal*)
malignancy
malin, -igne [malɛ̃, -iɲ] ADJ (*futé: f gén:* **maline**)
smart, shrewd; (*: sourire*) knowing; (*Méd,
influence*) malignant; **faire le ~** to show off;
éprouver un ~ plaisir à to take malicious
pleasure in
malingre [malɛ̃gʀ] ADJ puny
malintentionné, e [malɛ̃tɑ̃sjɔne] ADJ
ill-intentioned, malicious
malle [mal] NF trunk; (*Auto*): **~ (arrière)** boot
(BRIT), trunk (US)
malléable [maleabl] ADJ malleable
malle-poste [malpɔst] (*pl* **malles-poste**) NF
mail coach
mallette [malɛt] NF (*valise*) (small) suitcase;
(*aussi:* **mallette de voyage**) overnight case;
(*pour documents*) attaché case
malmener [malmɘne] /5/ VT to manhandle;
(*fig*) to give a rough ride to
malnutrition [malnytʀisjɔ̃] NF malnutrition
malodorant, e [malɔdɔʀɑ̃, -ɑ̃t] ADJ foul-
smelling
malotru [malɔtʀy] NM lout, boor
Malouines [malwin] NFPL: **les ~** the Falklands,
the Falkland Islands
malpoli, e [malpɔli] NM/F rude individual ▶ ADJ
impolite
malpropre [malpʀɔpʀ] ADJ (*personne, vêtement*)
dirty; (*travail*) slovenly; (*histoire, plaisanterie*)
unsavoury (BRIT), unsavory (US), smutty;
(*malhonnête*) dishonest
malpropreté [malpʀɔpʀəte] NF dirtiness
malsain, e [malsɛ̃, -ɛn] ADJ unhealthy
malséant, e [malseɑ̃, -ɑ̃t] ADJ unseemly,
unbecoming
malsonnant, e [malsɔnɑ̃, -ɑ̃t] ADJ offensive
malt [malt] NM malt; **pur ~** (*whisky*) malt
(whisky)
maltais, e [maltɛ, -ɛz] ADJ Maltese
Malte [malt] NF Malta
malté, e [malte] ADJ (*lait etc*) malted
maltraiter [maltʀete] /1/ VT (*brutaliser*) to
manhandle, ill-treat; (*critiquer, éreinter*) to slate
(BRIT), roast
malus [malys] NM (*Assurances*) car insurance
weighting, penalty
malveillance [malvɛjɑ̃s] NF (*animosité*) ill will;
(*intention de nuire*) malevolence; (*Jur*) malicious
intent *no pl*

malveillant, e [malvɛjɑ̃, -ɑ̃t] ADJ malevolent,
malicious
malvenu, e [malvɘny] ADJ: **être ~ de** *ou* **à faire
qch** not to be in a position to do sth
malversation [malvɛʀsasjɔ̃] NF
embezzlement, misappropriation (of funds)
mal-vivre [malvivʀ] NM INV malaise
maman [mamɑ̃] NF mum(my) (BRIT), mom (US)
mamelle [mamɛl] NF teat
mamelon [mamlɔ̃] NM (*Anat*) nipple; (*colline*)
knoll, hillock
mamie [mami] NF (*fam*) granny
mammifère [mamifɛʀ] NM mammal
mammouth [mamut] NM mammoth
manager [manadʒɛʀ] NM (*Sport*) manager;
(*Comm*): **~ commercial** commercial director
manche [mɑ̃ʃ] NF (*de vêtement*) sleeve; (*d'un jeu,
tournoi*) round; (*Géo*): **la M~** the (English)
Channel ▶ NM (*d'outil, casserole*) handle; (*de pelle,
pioche etc*) shaft; (*de violon, guitare*) neck; (*fam*)
clumsy oaf; **faire la ~** to pass the hat; **~ à air** *nf*
(*Aviat*) wind-sock; **à manches courtes/
longues** short-/long-sleeved; **~ à balai** *nm*
broomstick; (*Aviat, Inform*) joystick *nm inv*
manchette [mɑ̃ʃɛt] NF (*de chemise*) cuff; (*coup*)
forearm blow; (*titre*) headline
manchon [mɑ̃ʃɔ̃] NM (*de fourrure*) muff; **~ à
incandescence** incandescent (gas) mantle
manchot [mɑ̃ʃo] NM one-armed man; armless
man; (*Zool*) penguin
mandarine [mɑ̃daʀin] NF mandarin (orange),
tangerine
mandat [mɑ̃da] NM (*postal*) postal *ou* money
order; (*d'un député etc*) mandate; (*procuration*)
power of attorney, proxy; (*Police*) warrant;
~ d'amener summons *sg*; **~ d'arrêt** warrant for
arrest; **~ de dépôt** committal order; **~ de
perquisition** (*Police*) search warrant
mandataire [mɑ̃datɛʀ] NMF (*représentant,
délégué*) representative; (*Jur*) proxy
mandat-carte [mɑ̃dakaʀt] (*pl* **mandats-cartes**)
NM money order (*in postcard form*)
mander [mɑ̃date] /1/ VT (*personne*) to appoint;
(*Pol: député*) to elect
mandat-lettre [mɑ̃dalɛtʀ] (*pl* **mandats-lettres**)
NM money order (*with space for correspondence*)
mandchou, e [mɑ̃tʃu] ADJ Manchu,
Manchurian ▶ NM (*Ling*) Manchu ▶ NM/F:
M~, e Manchu
Mandchourie [mɑ̃tʃuʀi] NF: **la ~** Manchuria
mander [mɑ̃de] /1/ VT to summon
mandibule [mɑ̃dibyl] NF mandible
mandoline [mɑ̃dɔlin] NF mandolin(e)
manège [manɛʒ] NM riding school; (*à la foire*)
roundabout (BRIT), merry-go-round; (*fig*) game,
ploy; **faire un tour de ~** to go for a ride on a *ou*
the roundabout *etc*; **~ (de chevaux de bois)**
roundabout (BRIT), merry-go-round
manette [manɛt] NF lever, tap; **~ de jeu** (*Inform*)
joystick
manganèse [mɑ̃ganɛz] NM manganese
mangeable [mɑ̃ʒabl] ADJ edible, eatable
mangeaille [mɑ̃ʒaj] NF (*péj*) grub
mangeoire [mɑ̃ʒwaʀ] NF trough, manger

manger [mɑ̃ʒe] /3/ vt to eat; (ronger: rouille etc) to eat into ou away; (utiliser, consommer) to eat up ▸ vi to eat; **donner à ~ à** (enfant) to feed

mange-tout [mɑ̃ʒtu] nm inv mange-tout

mangeur, -euse [mɑ̃ʒœʀ, -øz] nm/f eater

mangouste [mɑ̃gust] nf mongoose

mangue [mɑ̃g] nf mango

maniabilité [manjabilite] nf (d'un outil) handiness; (d'un véhicule, voilier) manoeuvrability

maniable [manjabl] adj (outil) handy; (voiture, voilier) easy to handle; manoeuvrable (Brit), maneuverable (US); (fig: personne) easily influenced, manipulable

maniaque [manjak] adj (pointilleux, méticuleux) finicky, fussy; (atteint de manie) suffering from a mania ▸ nm/f (méticuleux) fusspot; (fou) maniac

manie [mani] nf mania; (tic) odd habit; **avoir la ~ de** to be obsessive about

maniement [manimɑ̃] nm handling; **~ d'armes** arms drill

manier [manje] /7/ vt to handle; **se manier** vi (fam) to get a move on

maniéré, e [manjere] adj affected

manière [manjɛʀ] nf (façon) way, manner; (genre, style) style; **manières** nfpl (attitude) manners; (chichis) fuss sg; **de ~ à** so as to; **de telle ~ que** in such a way that; **de cette ~** in this way ou manner; **d'une ~ générale** generally speaking, as a general rule; **de toute ~** in any case; **d'une certaine ~** in a (certain) way; **faire des manières** to put on airs; **employer la ~ forte** to use strong-arm tactics

manif [manif] nf (manifestation) demo

manifestant, e [manifɛstɑ̃, -ɑ̃t] nm/f demonstrator

manifestation [manifɛstasjɔ̃] nf (de joie, mécontentement) expression, demonstration; (symptôme) outward sign; (fête etc) event; (Pol) demonstration

manifeste [manifɛst] adj obvious, evident ▸ nm manifesto

manifestement [manifɛstəmɑ̃] adv obviously

manifester [manifɛste] /1/ vt (volonté, intentions) to show, indicate; (joie, peur) to express, show ▸ vi (Pol) to demonstrate; **se manifester** vi (émotion) to show ou express itself; (difficultés) to arise; (symptômes) to appear; (témoin etc) to come forward

manigance [manigɑ̃s] nf scheme

manigancer [manigɑ̃se] /3/ vt to plot, devise

Manille [manij] n Manila

manioc [manjɔk] nm cassava, manioc

manipulateur, -trice [manipylatœʀ, -tʀis] nm/f (technicien) technician, operator; (prestidigitateur) conjurer; (péj) manipulator

manipulation [manipylasjɔ̃] nf handling; (Pol, génétique) manipulation

manipuler [manipyle] /1/ vt to handle; (fig) to manipulate

manivelle [manivɛl] nf crank

manne [man] nf (Rel) manna; (fig) godsend

mannequin [mankɛ̃] nm (Couture) dummy; (Mode) model

manœuvrable [manœvʀabl] adj (bateau, véhicule) manoeuvrable (Brit), maneuverable (US)

manœuvre [manœvʀ] nf (gén) manoeuvre (Brit), maneuver (US) ▸ nm (ouvrier) labourer (Brit), laborer (US)

manœuvrer [manœvʀe] /1/ vt to manoeuvre (Brit), maneuver (US); (levier, machine) to operate; (personne) to manipulate ▸ vi to manoeuvre ou maneuver

manoir [manwaʀ] nm manor ou country house

manomètre [manɔmɛtʀ] nm gauge, manometer

manquant, e [mɑ̃kɑ̃, -ɑ̃t] adj missing

manque [mɑ̃k] nm (insuffisance, vide) emptiness, gap; (Méd) withdrawal; **~ de** lack of; **manques** nmpl (lacunes) faults, defects; **par ~ de** for want of; **~ à gagner** loss of profit ou earnings; **être en état de ~** to suffer withdrawal symptoms

manqué [mɑ̃ke] adj failed; **garçon ~** tomboy

manquement [mɑ̃kmɑ̃] nm: **~ à** (discipline, règle) breach of

manquer [mɑ̃ke] /1/ vi (faire défaut) to be lacking; (être absent) to be missing; (échouer) to fail ▸ vt to miss ▸ vb impers: **il (nous) manque encore 10 euros** we are still 10 euros short; **il manque des pages (au livre)** there are some pages missing ou some pages are missing (from the book); **l'argent qui leur manque** the money they need ou are short of; **le pied/la voix lui manqua** he missed his footing/his voice failed him; **~ à qn** (absent etc): **il/cela me manque** I miss him/that; **~ à** vt (règles etc) to be in breach of, fail to observe; **~ de** vt to lack; (Comm) to be out of (stock of); **ne pas ~ de faire: je ne manquerai pas de le lui dire** I'll be sure to tell him; **~ (de) faire, il a manqué (de) se tuer** he very nearly got killed; **il ne manquerait plus qu'il fasse** all we need now is for him to do; **je n'y manquerai pas** leave it to me, I'll definitely do it

mansarde [mɑ̃saʀd] nf attic

mansardé, e [mɑ̃saʀde] adj: **chambre ~** attic room

mansuétude [mɑ̃sɥetyd] nf leniency

mante [mɑ̃t] nf: **~ religieuse** praying mantis

manteau, x [mɑ̃to] nm coat; **~ de cheminée** mantelpiece; **sous le ~** (fig) under cover

mantille [mɑ̃tij] nf mantilla

manucure [manykyʀ] nf manicurist

manuel, le [manɥɛl] adj manual ▸ nm/f manually gifted pupil (as opposed to intellectually gifted) ▸ nm (ouvrage) manual, handbook

manuellement [manɥɛlmɑ̃] adv manually

manufacture [manyfaktyʀ] nf (établissement) factory; (fabrication) manufacture

manufacturé, e [manyfaktyʀe] adj manufactured

manufacturier, -ière [manyfaktyʀje, -jɛʀ] nm/f factory owner

manuscrit, e [manyskʀi, -it] adj handwritten ▸ nm manuscript

manutention [manytɑ̃sjɔ̃] nf (Comm) handling; (local) storehouse

manutentionnaire [manytɑ̃sjɔnɛʀ] NMF warehouse man(-woman), packer

manutentionner [manytɑ̃sjɔne] /1/ VT to handle

mappemonde [mapmɔ̃d] NF (plane) map of the world; (sphère) globe

maquereau, x [makʀo] NM (Zool) mackerel inv; (fam: proxénète) pimp

maquerelle [makʀɛl] NF (fam) madam

maquette [makɛt] NF (d'un décor, bâtiment, véhicule) (scale) model; (Typo) mockup; (: d'une page illustrée, affiche) paste-up; (: prête à la reproduction) artwork

maquignon [makiɲɔ̃] NM horse-dealer

maquillage [makijaʒ] NM making up; faking; (produits) make-up

maquiller [makije] /1/ VT (personne, visage) to make up; (truquer: passeport, statistique) to fake; (: voiture volée) to do over (respray etc); **se maquiller** VI to make o.s. up

maquilleur, -euse [makijœʀ, -øz] NM/F make-up artist

maquis [maki] NM (Géo) scrub; (fig) tangle; (Mil) maquis, underground fighting no pl

maquisard, e [makizaʀ, -aʀd] NM/F maquis, member of the Resistance

marabout [maʀabu] NM (Zool) marabou(t)

maraîcher, -ère [maʀeʃe, maʀɛʃɛʀ] ADJ: **cultures maraîchères** market gardening sg ▶ NM/F market gardener

marais [maʀɛ] NM marsh, swamp; **~ salant** saltworks

marasme [maʀasm] NM (Pol, Écon) stagnation, sluggishness; (accablement) dejection, depression

marathon [maʀatɔ̃] NM marathon

marâtre [maʀɑtʀ] NF cruel mother

maraude [maʀod] NF pilfering, thieving (of poultry, crops); (dans un verger) scrumping; (vagabondage) prowling; **en ~** on the prowl; (taxi) cruising

maraudeur, -euse [maʀodœʀ, -øz] NM/F marauder; prowler

marbre [maʀbʀ] NM (pierre, statue) marble; (d'une table, commode) marble top; (Typo) stone, bed; **rester de ~** to remain stonily indifferent

marbrer [maʀbʀe] /1/ VT to mottle, blotch; (Tech: papier) to marble

marbrerie [maʀbʀəʀi] NF (atelier) marble mason's workshop; (industrie) marble industry

marbrures [maʀbʀyʀ] NFPL blotches pl; (Tech) marbling sg

marc [maʀ] NM (de raisin, pommes) marc; **~ de café** coffee grounds pl ou dregs pl

marcassin [maʀkasɛ̃] NM young wild boar

marchand, e [maʀʃɑ̃, -ɑ̃d] NM/F shopkeeper, tradesman(-woman); (au marché) stallholder; (spécifique): **~ de cycles/tapis** bicycle/carpet dealer; **~ de charbon/vins** coal/wine merchant ▶ ADJ: **prix/valeur marchand(e)** market price/value; **qualité ~** standard quality; **~ en gros/au détail** wholesaler/retailer; **~ de biens** real estate agent; **~ de canons** (péj) arms dealer; **~ de couleurs** ironmonger (BRIT), hardware

dealer (US); **~/e de fruits** fruiterer (BRIT), fruit seller (US); **~/e de journaux** newsagent; **~/e de légumes** greengrocer (BRIT), produce dealer (US); **~/e de poisson** fishmonger (BRIT), fish seller (US); **~/e de(s) quatre-saisons** costermonger (BRIT), street vendor (selling fresh fruit and vegetables); **~ de sable** (fig) sandman; **~ de tableaux** art dealer

marchandage [maʀʃɑ̃daʒ] NM bargaining; (péj: électoral) bargaining, manoeuvring

marchander [maʀʃɑ̃de] /1/ VT (article) to bargain ou haggle over; (éloges) to be sparing with ▶ VI to bargain, haggle

marchandisage [maʀʃɑ̃dizaʒ] NM merchandising

marchandise [maʀʃɑ̃diz] NF goods pl, merchandise no pl

marche [maʀʃ] NF (d'escalier) step; (activité) walking; (promenade, trajet, allure) walk; (démarche) walk, gait; (Mil, Mus) march; (fonctionnement) running; (progression) progress; (des événements) course; **à une heure de ~** an hour's walk (away); **ouvrir/fermer la ~** to lead the way/bring up the rear; **dans le sens de la ~** (Rail) facing the engine; **en ~** (monter etc) while the vehicle is moving ou in motion; **mettre en ~** to start; **remettre qch en ~** to set ou start sth going again; **se mettre en ~** (personne) to get moving; (machine) to start; **être en état de ~** to be in working order; **~ arrière** (Auto) reverse (gear); **faire ~ arrière** (Auto) to reverse; (fig) to backtrack, back-pedal; **~ à suivre** (correct) procedure; (sur notice) (step by step) instructions pl

marché [maʀʃe] NM (lieu, Comm, Écon) market; (ville) trading centre; (transaction) bargain, deal; **par-dessus le ~** into the bargain; **faire son ~** to do one's shopping; **mettre le ~ en main à qn** to tell sb to take it or leave it; **~ au comptant** (Bourse) spot market; **~ aux fleurs** flower market; **~ noir** black market; **faire du ~ noir** to buy and sell on the black market; **~ aux puces** flea market; **~ à terme** (Bourse) forward market; **~ du travail** labour market

marchepied [maʀʃəpje] NM (Rail) step; (Auto) running board; (fig) stepping stone

marcher [maʀʃe] /1/ VI to walk; (Mil) to march; (aller: voiture, train, affaires) to go; (prospérer) to go well; (fonctionner) to work, run; (fam: consentir) to go along, agree; (: croire naïvement) to be taken in; **~ sur** to walk on; (mettre le pied sur) to step on ou in; (Mil) to march upon; **~ dans** (herbe etc) to walk in ou on; (flaque) to step in; **faire ~ qn** (pour rire) to pull sb's leg; (pour tromper) to lead sb up the garden path

marcheur, -euse [maʀʃœʀ, -øz] NM/F walker

mardi [maʀdi] NM Tuesday; **M~ gras** Shrove Tuesday; voir aussi **lundi**

mare [maʀ] NF pond; (flaque) pool; **~ de sang** pool of blood

marécage [maʀekaʒ] NM marsh, swamp

marécageux, -euse [maʀekaʒø, -øz] ADJ marshy, swampy

maréchal, -aux [maʀeʃal, -o] NM marshal; **~ des logis** (Mil) sergeant

m

maréchal-ferrant [maʀeʃalferɑ̃] (pl **maréchaux-ferrants** [maʀeʃo-]) NM blacksmith
maréchaussée [maʀeʃose] NF (humoristique: gendarmes) constabulary (BRIT), police
marée [maʀe] NF tide; (poissons) fresh (sea) fish; ~ **haute/basse** high/low tide; ~ **montante/descendante** rising/ebb tide; ~ **noire** oil slick
marelle [maʀɛl] NF: (**jouer à**) **la** ~ (to play) hopscotch
marémotrice [maʀemɔtʀis] ADJ F tidal
mareyeur, -euse [maʀejœʀ, -øz] NM/F wholesale (sea) fish merchant
margarine [maʀɡaʀin] NF margarine
marge [maʀʒ] NF margin; **en** ~ in the margin; **en** ~ **de** (fig) on the fringe of; (en dehors de) cut off from; (qui se rapporte à) connected with; ~ **bénéficiaire** profit margin, mark-up; ~ **de sécurité** safety margin
margelle [maʀʒɛl] NF coping
margeur [maʀʒœʀ] NM margin stop
marginal, e, -aux [maʀʒinal, -o] ADJ marginal ▶ NM/F (original) eccentric; (déshérité) dropout
marguerite [maʀɡəʀit] NF marguerite, (oxeye) daisy; (d'imprimante) daisy-wheel
marguillier [maʀɡije] NM churchwarden
mari [maʀi] NM husband
mariage [maʀjaʒ] NM (union, état, fig) marriage; (noce) wedding; ~ **civil/religieux** registry office (BRIT) ou civil/church wedding; **un** ~ **de raison/d'amour** a marriage of convenience/a love match; ~ **blanc** unconsummated marriage; ~ **en blanc** white wedding; see note

Since May 2013 same sex marriage and adoption have been legal in France. The corresponding bill led to major nationwide protests from conservative, mostly Catholic citizens. Several times since the Revolution similar cultural struggles have taken place between the conservative and the revolutionary republicans in France. But ultimately president Hollande kept his campaign promise to allow same-sex couples to marry.

marié, e [maʀje] ADJ married ▶ NM/F (bride)groom/bride; **les mariés** the bride and groom; **les (jeunes) mariés** the newly-weds
marier [maʀje] /7/ VT to marry; (fig) to blend; **se** ~ **(avec)** to marry, get married (to); (fig) to blend (with)
marijuana [maʀiʒwana] NF marijuana
marin, e [maʀɛ̃, -in] ADJ sea cpd, marine ▶ NM sailor ▶ NF navy; (Art) seascape; (couleur) navy (blue); **avoir le pied** ~ to be a good sailor; (garder son équilibre) to have one's sea legs; ~ **de guerre** navy; ~ **marchande** merchant navy; ~ **à voiles** sailing ships pl
marina [maʀina] NF marina
marinade [maʀinad] NF marinade
marine [maʀin] ADJ F, NF voir **marin** ▶ ADJ INV navy (blue) ▶ NM (Mil) marine
mariner [maʀine] /1/ VI, VT to marinate, marinade
marinier [maʀinje] NM bargee
marinière [maʀinjɛʀ] NF (blouse) smock

▶ ADJ INV: **moules** ~ (Culin) mussels in white wine
marionnette [maʀjɔnɛt] NF puppet
marital, e, -aux [maʀital, -o] ADJ: **autorisation** ~ husband's permission
maritalement [maʀitalmɑ̃] ADV: **vivre** ~ to live together (as husband and wife)
maritime [maʀitim] ADJ sea cpd, maritime; (ville) coastal, seaside; (droit) shipping, maritime
marjolaine [maʀʒɔlɛn] NF marjoram
mark [maʀk] NM mark
marketing [maʀkətiŋ] NM (Comm) marketing
marmaille [maʀmaj] NF (péj) (gang of) brats pl
marmelade [maʀməlad] NF (compote) stewed fruit, compote; ~ **d'oranges** (orange) marmalade; **en** ~ (fig) crushed (to a pulp)
marmite [maʀmit] NF (cooking-)pot
marmiton [maʀmitɔ̃] NM kitchen boy
marmonner [maʀmɔne] /1/ VT, VI to mumble, mutter
marmot [maʀmo] NM (fam) brat
marmotte [maʀmɔt] NF marmot
marmotter [maʀmɔte] /1/ VT (prière) to mumble, mutter
marne [maʀn] NF (Géo) marl
Maroc [maʀɔk] NM: **le** ~ Morocco
marocain, e [maʀɔkɛ̃, -ɛn] ADJ Moroccan ▶ NM/F: **M**~, **e** Moroccan
maroquin [maʀɔkɛ̃] NM (peau) morocco (leather); (fig) (minister's) portfolio
maroquinerie [maʀɔkinʀi] NF (industrie) leather craft; (commerce) leather shop; (articles) fine leather goods pl
maroquinier [maʀɔkinje] NM (fabricant) leather craftsman; (marchand) leather dealer
marotte [maʀɔt] NF fad
marquant, e [maʀkɑ̃, -ɑ̃t] ADJ outstanding
marque [maʀk] NF mark; (Sport, Jeu) score; (Comm: de nourriture) brand; (: de voiture, produits manufacturés) make; (insigne: d'une fonction) badge; (fig): ~ **d'affection** token of affection; ~ **de joie** sign of joy; **à vos marques!** (Sport) on your marks!; **de** ~ adj (Comm) brand-name cpd; proprietary; (fig) high-class; (: personnage, hôte) distinguished; **produit de** ~ quality product; ~ **déposée** registered trademark; ~ **de fabrique** trademark; **une grande** ~ **de vin** a well-known brand of wine
marqué, e [maʀke] ADJ marked
marquer [maʀke] /1/ VT to mark; (inscrire) to write down; (bétail) to brand; (Sport: but etc) to score; (: joueur) to mark; (accentuer: taille etc) to emphasize; (manifester: refus, intérêt) to show ▶ VI (événement, personnalité) to stand out; (Sport) to score; ~ **qn de son influence/empreinte** to have an influence/leave its impression on sb; ~ **un temps d'arrêt** to pause momentarily; ~ **le pas** (fig) to mark time; **il a marqué ce jour-là d'une pierre blanche** that was a red-letter day for him; ~ **les points** (tenir la marque) to keep the score
marqueté, e [maʀkəte] ADJ inlaid
marqueterie [maʀkɛtʀi] NF inlaid work, marquetry

marqueur, -euse [maʁkœʁ, -øz] NM/F (*Sport: de but*) scorer ▶ NM (*crayon feutre*) marker pen

marquis, e [maʁki, -iz] NM/F marquis *ou* marquess (marchioness) ▶ NF (*auvent*) glass canopy *ou* awning

Marquises [maʁkiz] NFPL: **les (îles)** ~ the Marquesas Islands

marraine [maʁɛn] NF godmother; (*d'un navire, d'une rose etc*) namer

Marrakech [maʁakɛʃ] N Marrakech *ou* Marrakesh

marrant, e [maʁɑ̃, -ɑ̃t] ADJ (*fam*) funny

marre [maʁ] ADV (*fam*): **en avoir ~ de** to be fed up with

marrer [maʁe] /1/: **se marrer** VI (*fam*) to have a (good) laugh

marron, ne [maʁɔ̃, -ɔn] NM (*fruit*) chestnut ▶ ADJ INV brown ▶ ADJ (*péj*) crooked; (: *faux*) bogus; **marrons glacés** marrons glacés

marronnier [maʁɔnje] NM chestnut (tree)

Mars [maʁs] NM *ou* F Mars

mars [maʁs] NM March; *voir aussi* **juillet**

marseillais, e [maʁsɛjɛ, -ɛz] ADJ of *ou* from Marseilles ▶ NF: **la M~** *the French national anthem*; *see note*

> The *Marseillaise* has been France's national anthem since 1879. The words of the *Chant de guerre de l'armée du Rhin*, as the song was originally called, were written to an anonymous tune by an army captain called Rouget de Lisle in 1792. Adopted as a marching song by the Marseille battalion, it was finally popularized as the *Marseillaise*.

Marseille [maʁsɛj] N Marseilles

marsouin [maʁswɛ̃] NM porpoise

marsupiaux [maʁsypjo] NMPL marsupials

marteau, x [maʁto] NM hammer; (*de porte*) knocker; **~ pneumatique** pneumatic drill; **être ~** (*fam*) to be nuts

marteau-pilon [maʁtopilɔ̃] (*pl* **marteaux-pilons**) NM power hammer

marteau-piqueur [maʁtopikœʁ] (*pl* **marteaux-piqueurs**) NM pneumatic drill

martel [maʁtɛl] NM: **se mettre ~ en tête** to worry o.s.

martèlement [maʁtɛlmɑ̃] NM hammering

marteler [maʁtəle] /5/ VT to hammer; (*mots, phrases*) to rap out

martial, e, -aux [maʁsjal, -o] ADJ martial; **cour ~** court-martial

martien, ne [maʁsjɛ̃, -ɛn] ADJ Martian, of *ou* from Mars

martinet [maʁtinɛ] NM (*fouet*) small whip; (*Zool*) swift

martingale [maʁtɛ̃gal] NF (*Couture*) half-belt; (*Jeu*) winning formula

martiniquais, e [maʁtinikɛ, -ɛz] ADJ of *ou* from Martinique

Martinique [maʁtinik] NF: **la ~** Martinique

martin-pêcheur [maʁtɛ̃pɛʃœʁ] (*pl* **martins-pêcheurs**) NM kingfisher

martre [maʁtʁ] NF marten; **~ zibeline** sable

martyr, e [maʁtiʁ] NM/F martyr ▶ ADJ martyred; **enfants martyrs** battered children

martyre [maʁtiʁ] NM martyrdom; (*fig: sens affaibli*) agony, torture; **souffrir le ~** to suffer agonies

martyriser [maʁtiʁize] /1/ VT (*Rel*) to martyr; (*fig*) to bully; (: *enfant*) to batter

marxiste [maʁksist] ADJ, NMF Marxist

mas [ma(s)] NM traditional house or farm in Provence

mascara [maskaʁa] NM mascara

mascarade [maskaʁad] NF masquerade

mascotte [maskɔt] NF mascot

masculin, e [maskylɛ̃, -in] ADJ masculine; (*sexe, population*) male; (*équipe, vêtements*) men's; (*viril*) manly ▶ NM masculine

masochisme [mazɔʃism] NM masochism

masochiste [mazɔʃist] ADJ masochistic ▶ NMF masochist

masque [mask] NM mask; **~ de beauté** face pack; **~ à gaz** gas mask; **~ de plongée** diving mask

masqué, e [maske] ADJ masked

masquer [maske] /1/ VT (*cacher: porte, goût*) to hide, conceal; (*dissimuler: vérité, projet*) to mask, obscure

massacrant, e [masakʁɑ̃, -ɑ̃t] ADJ: **humeur ~** foul temper

massacre [masakʁ] NM massacre, slaughter; **jeu de ~** (*fig*) wholesale slaughter

massacrer [masakʁe] /1/ VT to massacre, slaughter; (*fig: adversaire*) to slaughter; (: *texte etc*) to murder

massage [masaʒ] NM massage

masse [mas] NF mass; (*Élec*) earth; (*maillet*) sledgehammer; **masses** NFPL masses; **une ~ de, des masses de** (*fam*) masses *ou* loads of; **la ~** (*péj*) the masses *pl*; **en ~** adv (*en bloc*) in bulk; (*en foule*) en masse; adj (*exécutions, production*) mass cpd; **~ monétaire** (*Écon*) money supply; **~ salariale** (*Comm*) wage(s) bill

massepain [maspɛ̃] NM marzipan

masser [mase] /1/ VT (*assembler: gens*) to gather; (*pétrir*) to massage; **se masser** VI (*foule*) to gather

masseur, -euse [masœʁ, -øz] NM/F (*personne*) masseur(-euse) ▶ NM (*appareil*) massager

massicot [masiko] NM (*Typo*) guillotine

massif, -ive [masif, -iv] ADJ (*porte*) solid, massive; (*visage*) heavy, large; (*bois, or*) solid; (*dose*) massive; (*déportations etc*) mass cpd ▶ NM (*montagneux*) massif; (*de fleurs*) clump, bank; **le M~ Central** the Massif Central

massivement [masivmɑ̃] ADV (*répondre*) en masse; (*administrer, injecter*) in massive doses

massue [masy] NF club, bludgeon ▶ ADJ INV: **argument ~** sledgehammer argument

mastectomie [mastɛktɔmi] NF mastectomy

mastic [mastik] NM (*pour vitres*) putty; (*pour fentes*) filler

masticage [mastikaʒ] NM (*d'une fente*) filling; (*d'une vitre*) puttying

mastication [mastikasjɔ̃] NF chewing, mastication

mastiquer [mastike] /1/ VT (*aliment*) to chew, masticate; (*fente*) to fill; (*vitre*) to putty

mastoc [mastɔk] ADJ INV hefty

mastodonte [mastɔdɔ̃t] NM monster (*fig*)

m

259

masturbation [mastyʀbasjɔ̃] NF masturbation
masturber [mastyʀbe] /1/: **se masturber** VI to masturbate
m'as-tu-vu [matyvy] NMF INV show-off
masure [mazyʀ] NF tumbledown cottage
mat, e [mat] ADJ (couleur, métal) mat(t); (bruit, son) dull ▸ ADJ INV (Échecs): **être ~** to be checkmate
mât [mɑ] NM (Navig) mast; (poteau) pole, post
matamore [matamɔʀ] NM braggart, blusterer
match [matʃ] NM match; **~ nul** draw, tie (US); **faire ~ nul** to draw (BRIT), tie (US); **~ aller** first leg; **~ retour** second leg, return match
matelas [matla] NM mattress; **~ pneumatique** air bed ou mattress; **~ à ressorts** spring ou interior-sprung mattress
matelassé, e ADJ padded; (tissu) quilted
matelasser [matlase] /1/ VT to pad
matelot [matlo] NM sailor, seaman
mater [mate] /1/ VT (personne) to bring to heel, subdue; (révolte) to put down; (fam) to watch, look at
matérialisation [mateʀjalizasjɔ̃] NF materialization
matérialiser [mateʀjalize] /1/: **se matérialiser** VI to materialize
matérialisme [mateʀjalism] NM materialism
matérialiste [mateʀjalist] ADJ materialistic ▸ NMF materialist
matériau, x [mateʀjo] NM material; **matériaux** NMPL material(s); **~ de construction** building materials
matériel, le [mateʀjɛl] ADJ material; (organisation, aide, obstacle) practical; (fig: péj: personne) materialistic ▸ NM equipment no pl; (de camping etc) gear no pl; (Inform) hardware; **il n'a pas le temps ~ de le faire** he doesn't have the time (needed) to do it; **~ d'exploitation** (Comm) plant; **~ roulant** rolling stock
matériellement [mateʀjɛlmɑ̃] ADV (financièrement) materially; **~ à l'aise** comfortably off; **je n'en ai ~ pas le temps** I simply do not have the time
maternel, le [matɛʀnɛl] ADJ (amour, geste) motherly, maternal; (grand-père, oncle) maternal ▸ NF (aussi: **école maternelle**) (state) nursery school
materner [matɛʀne] /1/ VT (personne) to mother
maternisé, e [matɛʀnize] ADJ: **lait ~** (infant) formula
maternité [matɛʀnite] NF (établissement) maternity hospital; (état de mère) motherhood, maternity; (grossesse) pregnancy; **congé de ~** maternity leave
math [mat] NFPL maths (BRIT), math (US)
mathématicien, ne [matematisjɛ̃, -ɛn] NM/F mathematician
mathématique [matematik] ADJ mathematical
mathématiques [matematik] NFPL mathematics sg
matheux, -euse [matø, -øz] NM/F (fam) maths (BRIT) ou math (US) student; (fort en math) mathematical genius
maths [mat] NFPL maths (BRIT), math (US)

matière [matjɛʀ] NF (Physique) matter; (Comm, Tech) material; matter no pl; (fig: d'un livre etc) subject matter, material; (Scol) subject; **en ~ de** as regards; **donner ~ à** to give cause to; **~ plastique** plastic; **matières fécales** faeces; **matières grasses** fat (content) sg; **matières premières** raw materials
MATIF [matif] SIGLE M (= Marché à terme des instruments financiers) body which regulates the activities of the French Stock Exchange
Matignon [matiɲɔ̃] NM: **(l'hôtel) ~** the French Prime Minister's residence; see note

> The hôtel Matignon is the Paris office and residence of the French Prime Minister. By extension, the term Matignon is often used to refer to the Prime Minister and his or her staff.

matin [matɛ̃] NM, ADV morning; **le ~** (pendant le matin) in the morning; **demain/hier/dimanche ~** tomorrow/yesterday/Sunday morning; **tous les matins** every morning; **le lendemain ~** (the) next morning; **du ~ au soir** from morning till night; **une heure du ~** one o'clock in the morning; **de grand** ou **bon ~** early in the morning
matinal, e, -aux [matinal, -o] ADJ (toilette, gymnastique) morning cpd; (de bonne heure) early; **être ~** (personne) to be up early; (: habituellement) to be an early riser
matinée [matine] NF morning; (spectacle) matinée, afternoon performance
matois, e [matwa, -waz] ADJ wily
matou [matu] NM tom(cat)
matraquage [matʀakaʒ] NM beating up; **~ publicitaire** plug, plugging
matraque [matʀak] NF (de malfaiteur) cosh (BRIT), club; (de policier) truncheon (BRIT), billy (US)
matraquer [matʀake] /1/ VT to beat up (with a truncheon ou billy); to cosh (BRIT), club; (fig: touristes etc) to rip off; (: disque) to plug
matriarcal, e, -aux [matʀijaʀkal, -o] ADJ matriarchal
matrice [matʀis] NF (Anat) womb; (Tech) mould; (Math etc) matrix
matricule [matʀikyl] NF (aussi: **registre matricule**) roll, register ▸ NM (aussi: **numéro matricule**: Mil) regimental number; (Admin) reference number
matrimonial, e, -aux [matʀimɔnjal, -o] ADJ marital, marriage cpd
matrone [matʀɔn] NF matron
mâture [mɑtyʀ] NF masts pl
maturité [matyʀite] NF maturity; (d'un fruit) ripeness, maturity
maudire [modiʀ] /2/ VT to curse
maudit, e [modi, -it] ADJ (fam: satané) blasted, confounded
maugréer [mogʀee] /1/ VI to grumble
mauresque [mɔʀɛsk] ADJ Moorish
Maurice [mɔʀis] NF: **(l'île) ~** Mauritius
mauricien, ne [mɔʀisjɛ̃, -ɛn] ADJ Mauritian
Mauritanie [mɔʀitani] NF: **la ~** Mauritania
mauritanien, ne [mɔʀitanjɛ̃, -ɛn] ADJ Mauritanian

mausolée [mozɔle] NM mausoleum
maussade [mosad] ADJ (air, personne) sullen; (ciel, temps) gloomy
mauvais, e [mɔvɛ, -ɛz] ADJ bad; (méchant, malveillant) malicious, spiteful; (faux): **le ~ numéro** the wrong number ▶ NM: **le ~** the bad side ▶ ADV: **il fait ~** the weather is bad; **sentir ~** to have a nasty smell, smell bad ou nasty; **la mer est ~** the sea is rough; **~ coucheur** awkward customer; **~ coup** (fig) criminal venture; **~ garçon** tough; **~ pas** tight spot; **~ plaisant** hoaxer; **~ plaisanterie** nasty trick; **~ traitements** ill treatment sg; **~ joueur** bad loser; **~ herbe** weed; **~ langue** gossip, scandalmonger (BRIT); **~ passe** difficult situation; (période) bad patch; **~ tête** rebellious ou headstrong customer
mauve [mov] ADJ (couleur) mauve ▶ NF (Bot) mallow
mauviette [movjɛt] NF (péj) weakling
maux [mo] NMPL voir **mal**
max. ABR (= maximum) max
maximal, e, -aux [maksimal, -o] ADJ maximal
maxime [maksim] NF maxim
maximum [maksimɔm] ADJ, NM maximum; **atteindre un/son ~** to reach a/his peak; **au ~** adv (le plus possible) to the full; as much as one can; (tout au plus) at the (very) most ou maximum; **faire le ~** to do one's level best
Mayence [majɑ̃s] N Mainz
mayonnaise [majɔnɛz] NF mayonnaise
Mayotte [majɔt] NF Mayotte
mazout [mazut] NM (fuel) oil; **chaudière/poêle à ~** oil-fired boiler/stove
mazouté, e [mazute] ADJ oil-polluted
MDM SIGLE MPL (= Médecins du Monde) medical association for aid to Third World countries
Me ABR = **Maître**
me, m' [mə, m] PRON (direct: téléphoner, attendre etc) me; (indirect: parler, donner etc) (to) me; (réfléchi) myself
méandres [meɑ̃dʀ] NMPL meanderings
mec [mɛk] NM (fam) guy, bloke (BRIT)
mécanicien, ne [mekanisjɛ̃, -ɛn] NM/F mechanic; (Rail) (train ou engine) driver; **~ navigant** ou **de bord** (Aviat) flight engineer
mécanique [mekanik] ADJ mechanical ▶ NF (science) mechanics sg; (technologie) mechanical engineering; (mécanisme) mechanism; engineering; works pl; **ennui ~** engine trouble no pl; **s'y connaître en ~** to be mechanically minded; **~ hydraulique** hydraulics sg; **~ ondulatoire** wave mechanics sg
mécaniquement [mekanikmɑ̃] ADV mechanically
mécanisation [mekanizasjɔ̃] NF mechanization
mécaniser [mekanize] /1/ VT to mechanize
mécanisme [mekanism] NM mechanism; **~ des taux de change** exchange rate mechanism
mécano [mekano] NM (fam) mechanic
mécène [mesɛn] NM patron
méchamment [meʃamɑ̃] ADV nastily,

maliciously; spitefully; viciously
méchanceté [meʃɑ̃ste] NF (d'une personne, d'une parole) nastiness, maliciousness, spitefulness; (parole, action) nasty ou spiteful ou malicious remark (ou action); **dire des méchancetés à qn** to say spiteful things to sb
méchant, e [meʃɑ̃, -ɑ̃t] ADJ nasty, malicious, spiteful; (enfant: pas sage) naughty; (animal) vicious; (avant le nom: péj) nasty
mèche [mɛʃ] NF (de lampe, bougie) wick; (d'un explosif) fuse; (Méd) pack, dressing; (de vilebrequin, perceuse) bit; (de dentiste) drill; (de fouet) lash; (de cheveux) lock; **se faire faire des mèches** (chez le coiffeur) to have highlights put in one's hair, have one's hair streaked; **vendre la ~** to give the game away; **de ~ avec** in league with
méchoui [meʃwi] NM whole sheep barbecue
mécompte [mekɔ̃t] NM (erreur) miscalculation; (déception) disappointment
méconnais etc [mekɔnɛ] VB voir **méconnaître**
méconnaissable [mekɔnɛsabl] ADJ unrecognizable
méconnaissais etc [mekɔnɛsɛ] VB voir **méconnaître**
méconnaissance [mekɔnɛsɑ̃s] NF ignorance
méconnaître [mekɔnɛtʀ] /57/ VT (ignorer) to be unaware of; (mésestimer) to misjudge
méconnu, e [mekɔny] PP de **méconnaître** ▶ ADJ (génie etc) unrecognized
mécontent, e [mekɔ̃tɑ̃, -ɑ̃t] ADJ: **~ (de)** (insatisfait) discontented ou dissatisfied ou displeased (with); (contrarié) annoyed (at) ▶ NM/F malcontent, dissatisfied person
mécontentement [mekɔ̃tɑ̃tmɑ̃] NM dissatisfaction, discontent, displeasure; (irritation) annoyance
mécontenter [mekɔ̃tɑ̃te] /1/ VT to displease
Mecque [mɛk] NF: **la ~** Mecca
mécréant, e [mekʀeɑ̃, -ɑ̃t] ADJ (peuple) infidel; (personne) atheistic
méd. ABR = **médecin**
médaille [medaj] NF medal
médaillé, e [medaje] NM/F (Sport) medal-holder
médaillon [medajɔ̃] NM (portrait) medallion; (bijou) locket; (Culin) médaillon; **en ~** adj (carte etc) inset
médecin [medsɛ̃] NM doctor; **~ du bord** (Navig) ship's doctor; **~ généraliste** general practitioner, GP; **~ légiste** forensic scientist (BRIT), medical examiner (US); **~ traitant** family doctor, GP
médecine [medsin] NF medicine; **~ générale** general medicine; **~ infantile** paediatrics sg (BRIT), pediatrics sg (US); **~ légale** forensic medicine; **~ préventive** preventive medicine; **~ du travail** occupational ou industrial medicine; **médecines parallèles** ou **douces** alternative medicine
MEDEF [medɛf] SIGLE M (= Mouvement des entreprises de France) French employers' confederation
média [medja] NMPL: **les ~** the media
médian, e [medjɑ̃, -an] ADJ median
médias [medja] NMPL: **les ~** the media

m

médiateur, -trice [medjatœʀ, -tʀis] NM/F *voir*
médiation mediator; arbitrator
médiathèque [medjatɛk] NF media library
médiation [medjasjɔ̃] NF mediation; (*dans
conflit social etc*) arbitration
médiatique [medjatik] ADJ media *cpd*
médiatisé, e [medjatize] ADJ reported in the
media; **ce procès a été très ~** (*péj*) this trial
was turned into a media event
médiator [medjatɔʀ] NM plectrum
médical, e, -aux [medikal, -o] ADJ medical;
visiteur *ou* **délégué ~** medical rep *ou*
representative; **passer une visite ~** to have
a medical
médicalement [medikalmɑ̃] ADV medically
médicament [medikamɑ̃] NM medicine, drug
médicamenteux, -euse [medikamɑ̃tø, -øz] ADJ
medicinal
médication [medikasjɔ̃] NF medication
médicinal, e, -aux [medisinal, -o] ADJ medicinal
médico-légal, e, -aux [medikolegal, -o] ADJ
forensic
médico-social, e, -aux [medikosɔsjal, -o] ADJ:
assistance ~ medical and social assistance
médiéval, e, -aux [medjeval, -o] ADJ medieval
médiocre [medjɔkʀ] ADJ mediocre, poor
médiocrité [medjɔkʀite] NF mediocrity
médire [mediʀ] **/37/** VI: **~ de** to speak ill of
médisance [medizɑ̃s] NF scandalmongering *no
pl* (BRIT), mud-slinging *no pl*; (*propos*) piece of
scandal *ou* malicious gossip
médisant, e [medizɑ̃, -ɑ̃t] VB *voir* **médire** ▸ ADJ
slanderous, malicious
médit, e [medi, -it] PP *de* **médire**
méditatif, -ive [meditatif, -iv] ADJ thoughtful
méditation [meditasjɔ̃] NF meditation
méditer [medite] **/1/** VT (*approfondir*) to meditate
on, ponder (over); (*combiner*) to meditate ▸ VI to
meditate; **~ de faire** to contemplate doing,
plan to do
Méditerranée [mediteʀane] NF: **la (mer) ~** the
Mediterranean (Sea)
méditerranéen, ne [mediteʀaneɛ̃, -ɛn] ADJ
Mediterranean ▸ NM/F: **M~, ne** Mediterranean
médium [medjɔm] NM medium (*spiritualist*)
médius [medjys] NM middle finger
méduse [medyz] NF jellyfish
méduser [medyze] **/1/** VT to dumbfound
meeting [mitiŋ] NM (*Pol, Sport*) rally, meeting;
~ d'aviation air show
méfait [mefɛ] NM (*faute*) misdemeanour,
wrongdoing; **méfaits** NMPL (*ravages*) ravages,
damage *sg*
méfiance [mefjɑ̃s] NF mistrust, distrust
méfiant, e [mefjɑ̃, -ɑ̃t] ADJ mistrustful,
distrustful
méfier [mefje] **/7/**: **se méfier** VI to be wary; (*faire
attention*) to be careful; **se méfier de** VT to
mistrust, distrust, be wary of; to be careful
about
mégalomane [megalɔman] ADJ megalomaniac
mégalomanie [megalɔmani] NF megalomania
mégalopole [megalɔpɔl] NF megalopolis
méga-octet [megaɔktɛ] NM megabyte

mégarde [megaʀd] NF: **par ~** (*accidentellement*)
accidentally; (*par erreur*) by mistake
mégatonne [megatɔn] NF megaton
mégère [meʒɛʀ] NF (*péj: femme*) shrew
mégot [mego] NM cigarette end *ou* butt
mégoter [megɔte] **/1/** VI to nitpick
meilleur, e [mɛjœʀ] ADJ, ADV better; (*valeur
superlative*) best ▸ NM: **le ~** (*celui qui ...*) the best
(one); (*ce qui ...*) the best ▸ NF: **la ~** the best (one);
le ~ des deux the better of the two; **il fait ~
qu'hier** it's better weather than yesterday; **de
~ heure** earlier; **~ marché** cheaper
méjuger [meʒyʒe] **/3/** VT to misjudge
mél [mɛl] NM email
mélancolie [melɑ̃kɔli] NF melancholy, gloom
mélancolique [melɑ̃kɔlik] ADJ melancholy,
gloomy
mélange [melɑ̃ʒ] NM (*opération*) mixing;
blending; (*résultat*) mixture; blend; **sans ~**
unadulterated
mélanger [melɑ̃ʒe] **/3/** VT (*substances*) to mix;
(*vins, couleurs*) to blend; (*mettre en désordre,
confondre*) to mix up, muddle (up); **se mélanger**
(*liquides, couleurs*) to blend, mix
mélanine [melanin] NF melanin
mélasse [melas] NF treacle, molasses *sg*
mêlée [mele] NF (*bataille, cohue*) mêlée, scramble;
(*lutte, conflit*) tussle, scuffle; (*Rugby*) scrum(mage)
mêler [mele] **/1/** VT (*substances, odeurs, races*) to
mix; (*embrouiller*) to muddle (up), mix up; **se
mêler** VI to mix; (*se joindre, s'allier*) to mingle; **se
mêler à** (*personne*) to join; (*s'associer à*) to mix
with; (*: odeurs etc*) to mingle with; **se mêler de**
(*personne*) to meddle with, interfere in;
mêle-toi de tes affaires! mind your own
business!; **~ à** *ou* **avec** *ou* **de** to mix with; to
mingle with; **~ qn à** (*affaire*) to get sb mixed up
ou involved in
mélo [melo] NM, ADJ = **mélodrame**;
mélodramatique
mélodie [melɔdi] NF melody
mélodieux, -euse [melɔdjø, -øz] ADJ melodious,
tuneful
mélodique [melɔdik] ADJ melodic
mélodramatique [melɔdʀamatik] ADJ
melodramatic
mélodrame [melɔdʀam] NM melodrama
mélomane [melɔman] NM music lover
melon [məlɔ̃] NM (*Bot*) (honeydew) melon;
(*aussi*: **chapeau melon**) bowler (hat); **~ d'eau**
watermelon
mélopée [melɔpe] NF monotonous chant
membrane [mɑ̃bʀan] NF membrane
membre [mɑ̃bʀ] NM (*Anat*) limb; (*personne, pays,
élément*) member ▸ ADJ member *cpd*; **être ~ de** to
be a member of ▸ **~ (viril)** (male) organ
mémé [meme] NF (*fam*) granny; (*: vieille femme*)
old dear

⎡ **MOT-CLÉ** ⎤

même [mɛm] ADJ **1** (*avant le nom*) same; **en
même temps** at the same time; **ils ont les
mêmes goûts** they have the same *ou* similar
tastes

2 (*après le nom: renforcement*): **il est la loyauté même** he is loyalty itself; **ce sont ses paroles même** they are his very words
▸ PRON: **le (la) même** the same one
▸ ADV **1** (*renforcement*): **il n'a même pas pleuré** he didn't even cry; **même lui l'a dit** even HE said it; **ici même** at this very place; **même si** even if
2: **à même**: **à même la bouteille** straight from the bottle; **à même la peau** next to the skin; **être à même de faire** to be in a position to do, be able to do; **mettre qn à même de faire** to enable sb to do
3: **de même** likewise; **faire de même** to do likewise *ou* the same; **lui de même** so does (*ou* did *ou* is) he; **de même que** just as; **il en va de même pour** the same goes for

mémento [memɛ̃to] NM (*agenda*) appointments diary; (*ouvrage*) summary
mémo [memo] (*fam*) NM memo
mémoire [memwaʀ] NF memory ▸ NM (*Admin, Jur*) memorandum; (*Scol*) dissertation, paper; **avoir la ~ des visages/chiffres** to have a (good) memory for faces/figures; **n'avoir aucune ~** to have a terrible memory; **avoir de la ~** to have a good memory; **à la ~ de** to the *ou* in memory of; **pour ~** *adv* for the record; **de ~** *adv* from memory; **de ~ d'homme** in living memory; **mettre en ~** (*Inform*) to store; **~ morte** read-only memory, ROM; **~ vive** random access memory, RAM
mémoires [memwaʀ] NMPL memoirs
mémorable [memɔʀabl] ADJ memorable
mémorandum [memɔʀɑ̃dɔm] NM memorandum; (*carnet*) notebook
mémorial, -aux [memɔʀjal, -o] NM memorial
mémoriser [memɔʀize] /1/ VT to memorize; (*Inform*) to store
menaçant, e [mənasɑ̃, -ɑ̃t] ADJ threatening, menacing
menace [mənas] NF threat; **~ en l'air** empty threat
menacer [mənase] /3/ VT to threaten; **~ qn de qch/de faire qch** to threaten sb with sth/to do sth
ménage [menaʒ] NM (*travail*) housekeeping, housework; (*couple*) (married) couple; (*famille, Admin*) household; **faire le ~** to do the housework; **faire des ménages** to work as a cleaner (*in private homes*); **monter son ~** to set up house; **se mettre en ~ (avec)** to set up house (with); **heureux en ~** happily married; **faire bon ~ avec** to get on well with; **~ de poupée** doll's kitchen set; **à trois** love triangle
ménagement [menaʒmɑ̃] NM care and attention; **ménagements** NMPL (*égards*) consideration *sg*, attention *sg*
ménager¹ [menaʒe] VT (*traiter avec mesure*) to handle with tact; (*traiter considérément*) to treat considerately; (*utiliser*) to use with care; (: *avec économie*) to use sparingly; (*prendre soin de*) to take (great) care of, look after; (*organiser*) to arrange; (*installer*) to put in; to make; **se ménager** to look after o.s.;

~ qch à qn (*réserver*) to have sth in store for sb
ménager², -ère [menaʒe, -ɛʀ] ADJ household *cpd*, domestic ▸ NF (*femme*) housewife; (*couverts*) canteen (of cutlery)
ménagerie [menaʒʀi] NF menagerie
mendiant, e [mɑ̃djɑ̃, -ɑ̃t] NM/F beggar
mendicité [mɑ̃disite] NF begging
mendier [mɑ̃dje] /7/ VI to beg ▸ VT to beg (for); (*fig: éloges, compliments*) to fish for
menées [məne] NFPL intrigues, manœuvres (*BRIT*), maneuvers (*US*); (*Comm*) activities
mener [məne] /5/ VT to lead; (*enquête*) to conduct; (*affaires*) to manage, conduct, run ▸ VI: **~ (à la marque)** to lead, be in the lead; **~ à/dans** (*emmener*) to take to/into; **~ qch à bonne fin** *ou* **à terme** *ou* **à bien** to see sth through (to a successful conclusion), complete sth successfully
meneur, -euse [mənœʀ, -øz] NM/F leader; (*péj: agitateur*) ringleader; **~ d'hommes** born leader; **~ de jeu** host, quizmaster (*BRIT*)
menhir [meniʀ] NM standing stone
méningite [menɛ̃ʒit] NF meningitis *no pl*
ménisque [menisk] NM (*Anat*) meniscus
ménopause [menopoz] NF menopause
menotte [mənɔt] NF (*langage enfantin*) handie; **menottes** NFPL handcuffs; **passer les menottes à** to handcuff
mens [mɑ̃] VB *voir* **mentir**
mensonge [mɑ̃sɔ̃ʒ] NM: **le ~** lying *no pl*; **un ~** a lie
mensonger, -ère [mɑ̃sɔ̃ʒe, -ɛʀ] ADJ false
menstruation [mɑ̃stʀyasjɔ̃] NF menstruation
menstruel, le [mɑ̃stʀyɛl] ADJ menstrual
mensualiser [mɑ̃syalize] /1/ VT to pay monthly
mensualité [mɑ̃syalite] NF (*somme payée*) monthly payment; (*somme perçue*) monthly salary
mensuel, le [mɑ̃syɛl] ADJ monthly ▸ NM/F (*employé*) employee paid monthly ▸ NM (*Presse*) monthly
mensuellement [mɑ̃syɛlmɑ̃] ADV monthly
mensurations [mɑ̃syʀasjɔ̃] NFPL measurements
mentais *etc* [mɑ̃tɛ] VB *voir* **mentir**
mental, e, -aux [mɑ̃tal, -o] ADJ mental
mentalement [mɑ̃talmɑ̃] ADV in one's head, mentally
mentalité [mɑ̃talite] NF mentality
menteur, -euse [mɑ̃tœʀ, -øz] NM/F liar
menthe [mɑ̃t] NF mint; **~ (à l'eau)** peppermint cordial
mentholé, e [mɑ̃tɔle] ADJ menthol *cpd*, mentholated
mention [mɑ̃sjɔ̃] NF (*note*) note, comment; (*Scol*): **~ (très) bien/passable** (very) good/ satisfactory pass; **faire ~ de** to mention; **"rayer la ~ inutile"** "delete as appropriate"
mentionner [mɑ̃sjɔne] /1/ VT to mention
mentir [mɑ̃tiʀ] /16/ VI to lie
menton [mɑ̃tɔ̃] NM chin
mentonnière [mɑ̃tɔnjɛʀ] NF chin strap
menu, e [məny] ADJ (*mince*) slim, slight; (*petit*) tiny; (*frais, difficulté*) minor ▸ ADV (*couper, hacher*)

m

very fine ▸ NM menu; **par le ~** (*raconter*) in minute detail; **~ touristique** popular *ou* tourist menu; **~ monnaie** small change

menuet [mənɥɛ] NM minuet

menuiserie [mənɥizʀi] NF (*travail*) joinery, carpentry; (*d'amateur*) woodwork; (*local*) joiner's workshop; (*ouvrages*) woodwork *no pl*

menuisier [mənɥizje] NM joiner, carpenter

méprendre [mepʀɑ̃dʀ] /58/: **se méprendre** VI: **se méprendre sur** to be mistaken about

mépris, e [mepʀi, -iz] PP *de* **méprendre** ▸ NM (*dédain*) contempt, scorn; (*indifférence*): **le ~ de** contempt *ou* disregard for; **au ~ de** regardless of, in defiance of

méprisable [mepʀizabl] ADJ contemptible, despicable

méprisant, e [mepʀizɑ̃, -ɑ̃t] ADJ contemptuous, scornful

méprise [mepʀiz] NF mistake, error; (*malentendu*) misunderstanding

mépriser [mepʀize] /1/ VT to scorn, despise; (*gloire, danger*) to scorn, spurn

mer [mɛʀ] NF sea; (*marée*) tide; **~ fermée** inland sea; **en ~** at sea; **prendre la ~** to put out to sea; **en haute** *ou* **pleine ~** off shore, on the open sea; **la ~ Adriatique** the Adriatic (Sea); **la ~ des Antilles** *ou* **des Caraïbes** the Caribbean (Sea); **la ~ Baltique** the Baltic (Sea); **la ~ Caspienne** the Caspian Sea; **la ~ de Corail** the Coral Sea; **la ~ Égée** the Aegean (Sea); **la ~ Ionienne** the Ionian Sea; **la ~ Morte** the Dead Sea; **la ~ Noire** the Black Sea; **la ~ du Nord** the North Sea; **la ~ Rouge** the Red Sea; **la ~ des Sargasses** the Sargasso Sea; **les mers du Sud** the South Seas; **la ~ Tyrrhénienne** the Tyrrhenian Sea

mercantile [mɛʀkɑ̃til] ADJ (*péj*) mercenary

mercantilisme [mɛʀkɑ̃tilism] NM (*esprit mercantile*) mercenary attitude

mercenaire [mɛʀsənɛʀ] NM mercenary, hired soldier

mercerie [mɛʀsəʀi] NF (*Couture*) haberdashery (BRIT), notions *pl* (US); (*boutique*) haberdasher's (shop) (BRIT), notions store (US)

merci [mɛʀsi] EXCL thank you ▸ NF: **à la ~ de qn/qch** at sb's mercy/the mercy of sth; **~ beaucoup** thank you very much; **~ de** *ou* **pour** thank you for; **sans ~** *adj* merciless; *adv* mercilessly

mercier, -ière [mɛʀsje, -jɛʀ] NM/F haberdasher

mercredi [mɛʀkʀədi] NM Wednesday; **~ des Cendres** Ash Wednesday; *voir aussi* **lundi**

mercure [mɛʀkyʀ] NM mercury

merde [mɛʀd] (!) NF shit (!) ▸ EXCL (bloody) hell (!)

merdeux, -euse [mɛʀdø, -øz] NM/F (!) little bugger (BRIT !), little devil

mère [mɛʀ] NF mother ▸ ADJ INV mother *cpd*; **~ célibataire** single parent, unmarried mother; **~ de famille** housewife, mother

merguez [mɛʀgɛz] NF *spicy North African sausage*

méridien [meʀidjɛ̃] NM meridian

méridional, e, -aux [meʀidjɔnal, -o] ADJ southern; (*du midi de la France*) Southern (French) ▸ NM/F Southerner

meringue [məʀɛ̃g] NF meringue

mérinos [meʀinos] NM merino

merisier [məʀizje] NM wild cherry (tree)

méritant, e [meʀitɑ̃, -ɑ̃t] ADJ deserving

mérite [meʀit] NM merit; **avoir du ~ (à faire qch)** to deserve credit (for doing sth); **le ~ (de ceci) lui revient** the credit (for this) is his

mériter [meʀite] /1/ VT to deserve; **il mérite qu'on fasse ...** he deserves people to do ...

méritocratie [meʀitɔkʀasi] NF meritocracy

méritoire [meʀitwaʀ] ADJ praiseworthy, commendable

merlan [mɛʀlɑ̃] NM whiting

merle [mɛʀl] NM blackbird

mérou [meʀu] NM grouper (*fish*)

merveille [mɛʀvɛj] NF marvel, wonder; **faire ~** *ou* **des merveilles** to work wonders; **à ~** perfectly, wonderfully

merveilleux, -euse [mɛʀvɛjø, -øz] ADJ marvellous, wonderful

mes [me] ADJ POSS *voir* **mon**

mésalliance [mezaljɑ̃s] NF misalliance, mismatch

mésallier [mezalje] /7/: **se mésallier** VI to marry beneath (*ou* above) o.s.

mésange [mezɑ̃ʒ] NF tit(mouse); **~ bleue** bluetit

mésaventure [mezavɑ̃tyʀ] NF misadventure, misfortune

Mesdames [medam] NFPL *voir* **Madame**

Mesdemoiselles [medmwazɛl] NFPL *voir* **Mademoiselle**

mésentente [mezɑ̃tɑ̃t] NF dissension, disagreement

mésestimer [mezɛstime] /1/ VT to underestimate, underrate

Mésopotamie [mezɔpɔtami] NF: **la ~** Mesopotamia

mesquin, e [mɛskɛ̃, -in] ADJ mean, petty

mesquinerie [mɛskinʀi] NF meanness *no pl*, pettiness *no pl*; (*procédé*) mean trick

mess [mɛs] NM mess

message [mesaʒ] NM message; **~ d'erreur** (*Inform*) error message; **~ électronique** (*Inform*) email; **~ publicitaire** ad, advertisement; **~ téléphoné** telegram dictated by telephone; **~ SMS** text message; **elle m'a envoyé un ~ sur Facebook** she messaged me on Facebook; **~ instantané** instant message

messager, -ère [mesaʒe, -ɛʀ] NM/F messenger

messagerie [mesaʒʀi] NF: **messageries aériennes/maritimes** air freight/shipping service *sg*; (*Internet*): **~ électronique** electronic mail, email; **messageries de presse** press distribution service; **~ instantanée** instant messenger, IM; **~ rose** *lonely hearts and contact service on videotext*; **~ vocale** voice mail

messe [mɛs] NF mass; **aller à la ~** to go to mass; **~ de minuit** midnight mass; **faire des messes basses** (*fig, péj*) to mutter

messie [mesi] NM: **le M~** the Messiah

Messieurs [mesjø] NMPL *voir* **Monsieur**

mesure [məzyʀ] NF (*évaluation, dimension*)

measurement; (*étalon, récipient, contenu*) measure; (*Mus: cadence*) time, tempo; (*: division*) bar; (*retenue*) moderation; (*disposition*) measure, step; **unité/système de ~** unit/system of measurement; **sur ~** (*costume*) made-to-measure; (*fig*) personally adapted; **à la ~ de** (*fig: personne*) worthy of; (*chambre etc*) on the same scale as; **dans la ~ où** insofar as, inasmuch as; **dans une certaine ~** to some *ou* a certain extent; **à ~ que** as; **en ~** (*Mus*) in time *ou* tempo; **être en ~ de** to be in a position to; **dépasser la ~** (*fig*) to overstep the mark

mesuré, e [məzyʀe] ADJ (*ton, effort*) measured; (*personne*) restrained

mesurer [məzyʀe] /**1**/ VT to measure; (*juger*) to weigh up, assess; (*limiter*) to limit, ration; (*modérer: ses paroles etc*) to moderate; (*proportionner*): **~ qch à** to match sth to, gear sth to; **se ~ avec** to have a confrontation with; to tackle; **il mesure 1 m 80** he's 1 m 80 tall

met [mɛ] VB *voir* **mettre**

métabolisme [metabɔlism] NM metabolism

métairie [meteʀi] NF smallholding

métal, -aux [metal, -o] NM metal

métalangage [metalɑ̃gaʒ] NM metalanguage

métallique [metalik] ADJ metallic

métallisé, e [metalize] ADJ metallic

métallurgie [metalyʀʒi] NF metallurgy

métallurgique [metalyʀʒik] ADJ steel *cpd*, metal *cpd*

métallurgiste [metalyʀʒist] NMF (*ouvrier*) steel *ou* metal worker; (*industriel*) metallurgist

métamorphose [metamɔʀfoz] NF metamorphosis

métamorphoser [metamɔʀfoze] /**1**/ VT to transform

métaphore [metafɔʀ] NF metaphor

métaphorique [metafɔʀik] ADJ metaphorical, figurative

métaphoriquement [metafɔʀikmɑ̃] ADV metaphorically

métaphysique [metafizik] NF metaphysics *sg* ▶ ADJ metaphysical

métapsychique [metapsiʃik] ADJ psychic, parapsychological

métayer, -ère [meteje, metejɛʀ] NM/F (*tenant*) farmer

météo [meteo] NF (*bulletin*) (weather) forecast; (*service*) ≈ Met Office (*BRIT*), ≈ National Weather Service (*US*)

météore [meteɔʀ] NM meteor

météorite [meteɔʀit] NM OU F meteorite

météorologie [meteɔʀɔlɔʒi] NF (*étude*) meteorology; (*service*) ≈ Meteorological Office (*BRIT*), ≈ National Weather Service (*US*)

météorologique [meteɔʀɔlɔʒik] ADJ meteorological, weather *cpd*

météorologue [meteɔʀɔlɔg], **météorologiste** [meteɔʀɔlɔʒist] NMF meteorologist, weather forecaster

métèque [metɛk] NM (*péj*) wop (!)

méthane [metan] NM methane

méthanier [metanje] NM (*bateau*) (liquefied)

gas carrier *ou* tanker

méthode [metɔd] NF method; (*livre, ouvrage*) manual, tutor

méthodique [metɔdik] ADJ methodical

méthodiquement [metɔdikmɑ̃] ADV methodically

méthodiste [metɔdist] ADJ, NMF (*Rel*) Methodist

méthylène [metilɛn] NM: **bleu de ~** methylene blue

méticuleux, -euse [metikylø, -øz] ADJ meticulous

métier [metje] NM (*profession: gén*) job; (*: manuel*) trade; (*: artisanal*) craft; (*technique, expérience*) (acquired) skill *ou* technique; (*aussi*: **métier à tisser**) (weaving) loom; **être du ~** to be in the trade *ou* profession

métisser [metise] /**1**/ VT to cross(breed)

métrage [metʀaʒ] NM (*de tissu*) length; (*Ciné*) footage, length; **long/moyen/court ~** feature *ou* full-length/medium-length/short film

mètre [mɛtʀ] NM metre (*BRIT*), meter (*US*); (*règle*) metre rule, meter rule; (*ruban*) tape measure; **~ carré/cube** square/cubic metre *ou* meter

métrer [metʀe] /**6**/ VT (*Tech*) to measure (in metres *ou* meters); (*Constr*) to survey

métreur, -euse [metʀœʀ, -øz] NM/F: **~ (vérificateur), métreuse (vérificatrice)** (quantity) surveyor

métrique [metʀik] ADJ metric ▶ NF metrics *sg*

métro [metʀo] NM underground (*BRIT*), subway (*US*)

métronome [metʀɔnɔm] NM metronome

métropole [metʀɔpɔl] NF (*capitale*) metropolis; (*pays*) home country

métropolitain, e [metʀɔpɔlitɛ̃, -ɛn] ADJ metropolitan

mets [mɛ] NM dish ▶ VB *voir* **mettre**

mettable [mɛtabl] ADJ fit to be worn, decent

metteur [metœʀ] NM: **~ en scène** (*Théât*) producer; (*Ciné*) director; **~ en ondes** (*Radio*) producer

---

MOT-CLÉ

---

mettre [mɛtʀ] /**56**/ VT **1** (*placer*) to put; **mettre en bouteille/en sac** to bottle/put in bags *ou* sacks; **mettre qch à la poste** to post sth (*BRIT*), mail sth (*US*); **mettre en examen (pour)** to charge (with) (*BRIT*), indict (for) (*US*); **mettre une note gaie/amusante** to inject a cheerful/an amusing note; **mettre qn debout/assis** to help sb up *ou* to their feet/help sb to sit down

2 (*vêtements: revêtir*) to put on; (*: porter*) to wear; **mets ton gilet** put your cardigan on; **je ne mets plus mon manteau** I no longer wear my coat

3 (*faire fonctionner: chauffage, électricité*) to put on; (*: réveil, minuteur*) to set; **mettre en marche** to start up

4 (*installer: gaz, eau*) to put in, lay on

5 (*consacrer*): **mettre du temps/deux heures à faire qch** to take time/two hours to do sth; **y mettre du sien** to pull one's weight

6 (*noter, écrire*) to say, put (down); **qu'est-ce qu'il a mis sur la carte?** what did he say *ou* write on the card?; **mettez au pluriel ...** put ... into the plural

7 (*supposer*): **mettons que ...** let's suppose *ou* say that ...

8 (*faire + vb*): **faire mettre le gaz/l'électricité** to have gas/electricity put in *ou* installed

se mettre VR **1** (*se placer*): **vous pouvez vous mettre là** you can sit (*ou* stand) there; **où ça se met?** where does it go?; **se mettre au lit** to get into bed; **se mettre au piano** to sit down at the piano; **se mettre à l'eau** to get into the water; **se mettre de l'encre sur les doigts** to get ink on one's fingers

2 (*s'habiller*): **se mettre en maillot de bain** to get into *ou* put on a swimsuit; **n'avoir rien à se mettre** to have nothing to wear

3 (*dans rapports*): **se mettre bien/mal avec qn** to get on the right/wrong side of sb; **se mettre qn à dos** to get on sb's bad side; **se mettre avec qn** (*prendre parti*) to side with sb; (*faire équipe*) to team up with sb; (*en ménage*) to move in with sb

4: **se mettre à** to begin, start; **se mettre à faire** to begin *ou* start doing *ou* to do; **se mettre au piano** to start learning the piano; **se mettre au régime** to go on a diet; **se mettre au travail/à l'étude** to get down to work/one's studies; **il est temps de s'y mettre** it's time we got down to it *ou* got on with it

meublant, e [mœblɑ̃, -ɑ̃t] ADJ (*tissus etc*) effective (in the room)
meuble [mœbl] NM (*objet*) piece of furniture; (*ameublement*) furniture *no pl* ▶ ADJ (*terre*) loose, friable; (*Jur*): **biens meubles** movables
meublé [mœble] NM (*pièce*) furnished room; (*appartement*) furnished flat (BRIT) *ou* apartment (US)
meubler [mœble] /**1**/ VT to furnish; (*fig*): ~ **qch (de)** to fill sth (with); **se meubler** to furnish one's house
meuf [mœf] NF (*fam*) woman
meugler [møgle] /**1**/ VI to low, moo
meule [møl] NF (*à broyer*) millstone; (*à aiguiser*) grindstone; (*à polir*) buff wheel; (*de foin, blé*) stack; (*de fromage*) round
meunerie [mønʀi] NF (*industrie*) flour trade; (*métier*) milling
meunier, -ière [mønje, -jɛʀ] NM miller ▶ NF miller's wife ▶ ADJ f (*Culin*) meunière
meurs *etc* [mœʀ] VB *voir* **mourir**
meurtre [mœʀtʀ] NM murder
meurtrier, -ière [mœʀtʀije, -jɛʀ] ADJ (*arme, épidémie, combat*) deadly; (*accident*) fatal; (*carrefour, route*) lethal; (*fureur, instincts*) murderous ▶ NM/F murderer(-ess) ▶ NF (*ouverture*) loophole
meurtrir [mœʀtʀiʀ] /**2**/ VT to bruise; (*fig*) to wound
meurtrissure [mœʀtʀisyʀ] NF bruise; (*fig*) scar
meus *etc* [mœ] VB *voir* **mouvoir**
Meuse [mœz] NF: **la** ~ the Meuse

meute [møt] NF pack
meuve *etc* [mœv] VB *voir* **mouvoir**
mévente [mevɑ̃t] NF slump (in sales)
mexicain, e [mɛksikɛ̃, -ɛn] ADJ Mexican ▶ NM/F: **M~, e** Mexican
Mexico [mɛksiko] N Mexico City
Mexique [mɛksik] NM: **le** ~ Mexico
mezzanine [mɛdzanin] NF mezzanine (floor)
MF SIGLE MPL = **millions de francs** ▶ SIGLE F (*Radio*: = *modulation de fréquence*) FM
Mgr ABR = **monseigneur**
mi [mi] NM (*Mus*) E; (*en chantant la gamme*) mi
mi... [mi] PRÉFIXE half(-), mid-; **à la mi-janvier** in mid-January; **mi-bureau, mi-chambre** half office, half bedroom; **à mi-jambes/-corps** (up *ou* down) to the knees/waist; **à mi-hauteur/-pente** halfway up (*ou* down)/up (*ou* down) the hill
miaou [mjau] NM miaow
miaulement [mjolmɑ̃] NM (*cri*) miaow; (*continu*) miaowing *no pl*
miauler [mjole] /**1**/ VI to miaow
mi-bas [miba] NM INV knee-length sock
mica [mika] NM mica
mi-carême [mikaʀɛm] NF: **la** ~ the third Thursday in Lent
miche [miʃ] NF round *ou* cob loaf
mi-chemin [miʃmɛ̃]: **à** ~ *adv* halfway, midway
mi-clos, e [miklo, -kloz] ADJ half-closed
micmac [mikmak] NM (*péj*) carry-on
mi-côte [mikot]: **à** ~ *adv* halfway up (*ou* down) the hill
mi-course [mikuʀs]: **à** ~ *adv* halfway through the race
micro [mikʀo] NM mike, microphone; (*Inform*) micro; ~ **cravate** lapel mike
microbe [mikʀɔb] NM germ, microbe
microbiologie [mikʀɔbjɔlɔʒi] NF microbiology
microchirurgie [mikʀoʃiʀyʀʒi] NF microsurgery
microclimat [mikʀoklima] NM microclimate
microcosme [mikʀɔkɔsm] NM microcosm
micro-édition [mikʀoedisjɔ̃] NF desktop publishing
micro-électronique [mikʀoelɛktʀonik] NF microelectronics *sg*
microfiche [mikʀofiʃ] NF microfiche
microfilm [mikʀofilm] NM microfilm
micro-onde [mikʀoɔ̃d] NF: **four à micro-ondes** microwave oven
micro-ordinateur [mikʀɔɔʀdinatœʀ] NM microcomputer
micro-organisme [mikʀɔɔʀganism] NM micro-organism
microphone [mikʀofɔn] NM microphone
microplaquette [mikʀoplakɛt] NF microchip
microprocesseur [mikʀoprosɛsœʀ] NM microprocessor
microscope [mikʀoskop] NM microscope; **au** ~ under *ou* through the microscope
microscopique [mikʀoskopik] ADJ microscopic
microsillon [mikʀosijɔ̃] NM long-playing record
MIDEM [midɛm] SIGLE M (= *Marché international*

du disque et de l'édition musicale) music industry
trade fair

midi [midi] NM (milieu du jour) midday, noon;
(moment du déjeuner) lunchtime; (sud) south; **le
M~** (de la France) the South (of France), the Midi;
à ~ at 12 (o'clock) ou midday ou noon; **tous les
midis** every lunchtime; **le repas de ~** lunch;
en plein ~ (right) in the middle of the day; (sud)
facing south

midinette [midinɛt] NF silly young townie

mie [mi] NF inside (of the loaf)

miel [mjɛl] NM honey; **être tout ~** (fig) to be all
sweetness and light

mielleux, -euse [mjɛlø, -øz] ADJ (péj: personne)
sugary, syrupy

mien, ne [mjɛ̃, mjɛn] ADJ, PRON: **le (la)
mien(ne), les miens** mine; **les miens** (ma
famille) my family

miette [mjɛt] NF (de pain, gâteau) crumb; (fig: de la
conversation etc) scrap; **en miettes** (fig) in pieces
ou bits

(MOT-CLÉ)

mieux [mjø] ADV **1** (d'une meilleure façon): **mieux
(que)** better (than); **elle travaille/mange
mieux** she works/eats better; **aimer mieux** to
prefer; **j'attendais mieux de vous** I expected
better of you; **elle va mieux** she is better; **de
mieux en mieux** better and better

2 (de la meilleure façon): **ce que je sais le
mieux** what I know best; **les livres les mieux
faits** the best made books

3 (intensif): **vous feriez mieux de faire ...** you
would be better to do ...; **crier à qui mieux
mieux** to try to shout each other down

▶ ADJ INV **1** (plus à l'aise, en meilleure forme) better;
se sentir mieux to feel better

2 (plus satisfaisant) better; **c'est mieux ainsi** it's
better like this; **c'est le mieux des deux** it's
the better of the two; **le/la mieux, les mieux**
the best; **demandez-lui, c'est le mieux** ask
him, it's the best thing

3 (plus joli) better-looking; (plus gentil) nicer;
il est mieux que son frère (plus beau) he's
better-looking than his brother; (plus gentil)
he's nicer than his brother; **il est mieux sans
moustache** he looks better without a
moustache

4: **au mieux** at best; **au mieux avec** on the best
of terms with; **pour le mieux** for the best; **qui
mieux est** even better, better still

▶ NM **1** (progrès) improvement

2: **de mon/ton mieux** as best I/you can (ou
could); **faire de son mieux** to do one's best;
du mieux qu'il peut the best he can; **faute de
mieux** for lack ou want of anything better,
failing anything better

mieux-être [mjøzɛtʀ] NM greater well-being;
(financier) improved standard of living

mièvre [mjɛvʀ] ADJ sickly sentimental

mignon, ne [miɲɔ̃, -ɔn] ADJ sweet, cute

migraine [migʀɛn] NF headache; (Méd)
migraine

migrant, e [migʀɑ̃, -ɑ̃t] ADJ, NM/F migrant

migrateur, -trice [migʀatœʀ, -tʀis] ADJ
migratory

migration [migʀasjɔ̃] NF migration

mijaurée [miʒɔʀe] NF pretentious (young)
madam

mijoter [miʒɔte] /1/ VT to simmer; (préparer avec
soin) to cook lovingly; (affaire, projet) to plot, cook
up ▶ VI to simmer

mil [mil] NUM = **mille**

Milan [milɑ̃] N Milan

milanais, e [milanɛ, -ɛz] ADJ Milanese

mildiou [mildju] NM mildew

milice [milis] NF militia

milicien, ne [milisjɛ̃, -ɛn] NM/F
militiaman(-woman)

milieu, x [miljø] NM (centre) middle; (fig) middle
course ou way; (aussi: **juste milieu**) happy
medium; (Bio, Géo) environment; (entourage
social) milieu; (familial) background; circle;
(pègre): **le ~** the underworld; **au ~ de** in the
middle of; **au beau ou en plein ~ (de)** right in
the middle (of); **~ de terrain** (Football: joueur)
midfield player; (: joueurs) midfield

militaire [militɛʀ] ADJ military, army cpd ▶ NM
serviceman; **service ~** military service

militant, e [militɑ̃, -ɑ̃t] ADJ, NM/F militant

militantisme [militɑ̃tism] NM militancy

militariser [militaʀize] /1/ VT to militarize

militarisme [militaʀism] NM (péj) militarism

militer [milite] /1/ VI to be a militant; **~ pour/
contre** to militate in favour of/against

milk-shake [milkʃɛk] NM milk shake

mille [mil] NUM a ou one thousand ▶ NM (mesure):
~ (marin) nautical mile; **mettre dans le ~** to
hit the bull's-eye; (fig) to be bang on (target)

millefeuille [milfœj] NM cream ou vanilla slice

millénaire [milenɛʀ] NM millennium ▶ ADJ
thousand-year-old; (fig) ancient

mille-pattes [milpat] NM INV centipede

millésime [milezim] NM year

millésimé, e [milezime] ADJ vintage cpd

millet [mijɛ] NM millet

milliard [miljaʀ] NM milliard, thousand
million (Brit), billion (US)

milliardaire [miljaʀdɛʀ] NMF multimillionaire
(Brit), billionaire (US)

millième [miljɛm] NUM thousandth

millier [milje] NM thousand; **un ~ (de)** a
thousand or so, about a thousand; **par
milliers** in (their) thousands, by the thousand

milligramme [miligʀam] NM milligramme
(Brit), milligram (US)

millimétré, e [milimetʀe] ADJ: **papier ~** graph
paper

millimètre [milimɛtʀ] NM millimetre (Brit),
millimeter (US)

million [miljɔ̃] NM million; **deux millions de**
two million; **riche à millions** worth millions

millionième [miljɔnjɛm] NUM millionth

millionnaire [miljɔnɛʀ] NMF millionaire

mi-lourd [miluʀ] ADJ M, NM light heavyweight

mime [mim] NMF (acteur) mime(r); (imitateur)
mimic ▶ NM (art) mime, miming

m

mimer [mime] /1/ VT to mime; (*singer*) to mimic, take off

mimétisme [mimetism] NM (*Bio*) mimicry

mimique [mimik] NF (*funny*) face; (*signes*) gesticulations *pl*, sign language *no pl*

mimosa [mimoza] NM mimosa

mi-moyen [mimwajɛ̃] ADJ M, NM welterweight

MIN SIGLE M (= *Marché d'intérêt national*) wholesale market for fruit, vegetables and agricultural produce

min. ABR (= *minimum*) min

minable [minabl] ADJ (*personne*) shabby(-looking); (*travail*) pathetic

minaret [minaʀɛ] NM minaret

minauder [minode] /1/ VI to mince, simper

minauderies [minodʀi] NFPL simpering *sg*

mince [mɛ̃s] ADJ thin; (*personne, taille*) slim, slender; (*fig: profit, connaissances*) slight, small; (*: prétexte*) weak ▶ EXCL: **~ (alors)!** darn it!

minceur [mɛ̃sœʀ] NF thinness; (*d'une personne*) slimness, slenderness

mincir [mɛ̃siʀ] /2/ VI to get slimmer *ou* thinner

mine [min] NF (*physionomie*) expression, look; (*extérieur*) exterior, appearance; (*de crayon*) lead; (*gisement, exploitation, explosif*) mine; **mines** NFPL (*péj*) simpering airs; **les Mines** (*Admin*) the national mining and geological service, the government vehicle testing department; **avoir bonne ~** (*personne*) to look well; (*ironique*) to look an utter idiot; **avoir mauvaise ~** to look unwell; **faire ~ de faire** to make a pretence of doing; **ne pas payer de ~** to be not much to look at; **~ de rien** *adv* with a casual air; although you wouldn't think so; **~ de charbon** coal mine; **~ à ciel ouvert** opencast (BRIT) *ou* open-air (US) mine

miner [mine] /1/ VT (*saper*) to undermine, erode; (*Mil*) to mine

minerai [minʀɛ] NM ore

minéral, e, -aux [mineʀal, -o] ADJ mineral; (*Chimie*) inorganic ▶ NM mineral

minéralier [mineʀalje] NM (*bateau*) ore tanker

minéralisé, e [mineʀalize] ADJ mineralized

minéralogie [mineʀalɔʒi] NF mineralogy

minéralogique [mineʀalɔʒik] ADJ mineralogical; **plaque ~** number (BRIT) *ou* license (US) plate; **numéro ~** registration (BRIT) *ou* license (US) number

minet, te [minɛ, -ɛt] NM/F (*chat*) pussy-cat; (*péj*) young trendy

mineur, e [minœʀ] ADJ minor ▶ NM/F (*Jur*) minor ▶ NM (*travailleur*) miner; (*Mil*) sapper; **~ de fond** face worker

miniature [minjatyʀ] ADJ, NF miniature

miniaturisation [minjatyʀizasjɔ̃] NF miniaturization

miniaturiser [minjatyʀize] /1/ VT to miniaturize

minibus [minibys] NM minibus

minichaîne [miniʃɛn] NF mini system

minier, -ière [minje, -jɛʀ] ADJ mining

mini-jupe [miniʒyp] NF mini-skirt

minimal, e, -aux [minimal, -o] ADJ minimum

minimaliste [minimalist] ADJ (*Art*) minimalist

minime [minim] ADJ minor, minimal ▶ NMF (*Sport*) junior

minimiser [minimize] /1/ VT to minimize; (*fig*) to play down

minimum [minimɔm] ADJ, NM minimum; **au ~** at the very least; **~ vital** (*salaire*) living wage; (*niveau de vie*) subsistence level

ministère [ministɛʀ] NM (*cabinet*) government; (*département*) ministry (BRIT), department; (*Rel*) ministry; **~ public** (*Jur*) Prosecution, State Prosecutor

ministériel, le [ministeʀjɛl] ADJ government *cpd*; ministerial, departmental; (*partisan*) pro-government

ministrable [ministʀabl] ADJ (*Pol*): **il est ~** he's a potential minister

ministre [ministʀ] NM minister (BRIT), secretary; (*Rel*) minister; **~ d'État** senior minister *ou* secretary

Minitel® [minitɛl] NM *videotext terminal and service*

minium [minjɔm] NM red lead paint

minois [minwa] NM little face

minorer [minɔʀe] /1/ VT to cut, reduce

minoritaire [minɔʀitɛʀ] ADJ minority *cpd*

minorité [minɔʀite] NF minority; **être en ~** to be in the *ou* a minority; **mettre en ~** (*Pol*) to defeat

Minorque [minɔʀk] NF Minorca

minorquin, e [minɔʀkɛ̃, -in] ADJ Minorcan

minoterie [minɔtʀi] NF flour-mill

minuit [minɥi] NM midnight

minuscule [minyskyl] ADJ minute, tiny ▶ NF: **(lettre) ~** small letter

minutage [minytaʒ] NM timing

minute [minyt] NF minute; (*Jur: original*) minute, draft ▶ EXCL just a minute!, hang on!; **à la ~** (*présent*) (just) this instant; (*passé*) there and then; **entrecôte** *ou* **steak ~** minute steak

minuter [minyte] /1/ VT to time

minuterie [minytʀi] NF time switch

minuteur [minytœʀ] NM timer

minutie [minysi] NF meticulousness; minute detail; **avec ~** meticulously; in minute detail

minutieusement [minysjøzmɑ̃] ADV (*organiser, travailler*) meticulously; (*examiner*) minutely

minutieux, -euse [minysjø, -øz] ADJ (*personne*) meticulous; (*inspection*) minutely detailed; (*travail*) requiring painstaking attention to detail

mioche [mjɔʃ] NM (*fam*) nipper, brat

mirabelle [miʀabɛl] NF (*fruit*) (cherry) plum; (*eau-de-vie*) plum brandy

miracle [miʀakl] NM miracle

miraculé, e [miʀakyle] ADJ who has been miraculously cured (*ou* rescued)

miraculeux, -euse [miʀakylø, -øz] ADJ miraculous

mirador [miʀadɔʀ] NM (*Mil*) watchtower

mirage [miʀaʒ] NM mirage

mire [miʀ] NF (*d'un fusil*) sight; (*TV*) test card; **point de ~** target; (*fig*) focal point; **ligne de ~** line of sight

mirent [miʀ] VB *voir* **mettre**

mirer [miʀe] /1/ VT (*œufs*) to candle; **se mirer** VI: **se mirer dans** (*personne*) to gaze at one's reflection in; (*chose*) to be mirrored in

mirifique [miʀifik] ADJ wonderful

mirobolant, e [miʀɔbɔlɑ̃, -ɑ̃t] ADJ fantastic

miroir [miʀwaʀ] NM mirror

miroiter [miʀwate] /**1**/ VI to sparkle, shimmer; **faire ~ qch à qn** to paint sth in glowing colours for sb, dangle sth in front of sb's eyes

miroiterie [miʀwatʀi] NF (*usine*) mirror factory; (*magasin*) mirror dealer's (shop)

Mis ABR = **marquis**

mis, e [mi, miz] PP *de* **mettre** ▶ ADJ (*couvert, table*) set, laid; (*personne*): **bien ~** well dressed ▶ NF (*argent: au jeu*) stake; (*tenue*) clothing; attire; **être de ~** to be acceptable *ou* in season; **~ en bouteilles** bottling; **~ en examen** charging, indictment; **~ à feu** blast-off; **~ de fonds** capital outlay; **~ à jour** (*Inform*) update; **~ à mort** kill; **~ à pied** (*d'un employé*) suspension; lay-off; **~ sur pied** (*d'une affaire, entreprise*) setting up; **~ en plis** set; **~ au point** (*Photo*) focusing; (*fig*) clarification; **~ à prix** reserve (BRIT) *ou* upset price; **~ en scène** production

misaine [mizɛn] NF: **mât de ~** foremast

misanthrope [mizɑ̃tʀɔp] NMF misanthropist

Mise ABR = **marquise**

mise [miz] ADJ F, NF *voir* **mis**

miser [mize] /**1**/ VT (*enjeu*) to stake, bet; **~ sur** VT (*cheval, numéro*) to bet on; (*fig*) to bank *ou* count on

misérable [mizeʀabl] ADJ (*lamentable, malheureux*) pitiful, wretched; (*pauvre*) poverty-stricken; (*insignifiant, mesquin*) miserable ▶ NMF wretch; (*miséreux*) poor wretch

misère [mizeʀ] NF (*pauvreté*) (extreme) poverty, destitution; **misères** NFPL (*malheurs*) woes, miseries; (*ennuis*) little troubles; **être dans la ~** to be destitute *ou* poverty-stricken; **salaire de ~** starvation wage; **faire des misères à qn** to torment sb; **~ noire** utter destitution, abject poverty

miséreux, -euse [mizeʀø, -øz] ADJ poverty-stricken ▶ NM/F down-and-out

miséricorde [mizeʀikɔʀd] NF mercy, forgiveness

miséricordieux, -euse [mizeʀikɔʀdjø, -øz] ADJ merciful, forgiving

misogyne [mizɔʒin] ADJ misogynous ▶ NMF misogynist

missel [misɛl] NM missal

missile [misil] NM missile

mission [misjɔ̃] NF mission; **partir en ~** (*Admin, Pol*) to go on an assignment

missionnaire [misjɔnɛʀ] NMF missionary

missive [misiv] NF missive

mistral [mistʀal] NM mistral (wind)

mit [mi] VB *voir* **mettre**

mitaine [mitɛn] NF mitt(en)

mite [mit] NF clothes moth

mité, e [mite] ADJ moth-eaten

mi-temps [mitɑ̃] NF INV (*Sport: période*) half; (: *pause*) half-time; **à ~** adj, adv part-time

miteux, -euse [mitø, -øz] ADJ seedy, shabby

mitigé, e [mitiʒe] ADJ (*conviction, ardeur*) lukewarm; (*sentiments*) mixed

mitonner [mitɔne] /**1**/ VT (*préparer*) to cook with loving care; (*fig*) to cook up quietly

mitoyen, ne [mitwajɛ̃, -ɛn] ADJ (*mur*) common, party cpd; **maisons mitoyennes** semi-detached houses; (*plus de deux*) terraced (BRIT) *ou* row (US) houses

mitraille [mitʀaj] NF (*balles de fonte*) grapeshot; (*décharge d'obus*) shellfire

mitrailler [mitʀaje] /**1**/ VT to machine-gun; (*fig: photographier*) to snap away at; **~ qn de** to pelt *ou* bombard sb with

mitraillette [mitʀajɛt] NF submachine gun

mitrailleur [mitʀajœʀ] NM machine gunner ▶ ADJ M: **fusil ~** machine gun

mitrailleuse [mitʀajøz] NF machine gun

mitre [mitʀ] NF mitre

mitron [mitʀɔ̃] NM baker's boy

mi-voix [mivwa]: **à ~** adv in a low *ou* hushed voice

mixage [miksaʒ] NM (*Ciné*) (sound) mixing

mixer, mixeur [miksœʀ] NM (*Culin*) (food) mixer

mixité [miksite] NF (*Scol*) coeducation

mixte [mikst] ADJ (*gén*) mixed; (*Scol*) mixed, coeducational; **à usage ~** dual-purpose; **cuisinière ~** combined gas and electric cooker; **équipe ~** combined team

mixture [mikstyʀ] NF mixture; (*fig*) concoction

MJC SIGLE F (= *maison des jeunes et de la culture*) *community arts centre and youth club*

ml ABR (= *millilitre*) ml

MLF SIGLE M (= *Mouvement de libération de la femme*) Women's Movement

Mlle (*pl* **Mlles**) ABR = **Mademoiselle**

MM ABR = **Messieurs**; *voir* **Monsieur**

Mme (*pl* **Mmes**) ABR = **Madame**

MMS SIGLE M (= *Multimedia messaging service*) MMS

mn. ABR (= *minute*) min

mnémotechnique [mnemɔtɛknik] ADJ mnemonic

MNS SIGLE M (= *maître nageur sauveteur*) ≈ lifeguard

MO SIGLE F (= *main-d'œuvre*) *labour costs (on invoices)*

Mo ABR = **méga-octet**; **métro**

mobile [mɔbil] ADJ mobile; (*amovible*) loose, removable; (*pièce de machine*) moving; (*élément de meuble etc*) movable ▶ NM (*motif*) motive; (*œuvre d'art*) mobile; (*Physique*) moving object *ou* body; (**téléphone**)**~** mobile (phone) (BRIT), cell (phone) (US)

mobilier, -ière [mɔbilje, -jɛʀ] ADJ (*Jur*) personal ▶ NM (*meubles*) furniture; **valeurs mobilières** transferable securities; **vente mobilière** sale of personal property *ou* chattels

mobilisation [mɔbilizasjɔ̃] NF mobilization

mobiliser [mɔbilize] /**1**/ VT (*Mil, gén*) to mobilize

mobilité [mɔbilite] NF mobility

mobylette® [mɔbilɛt] NF moped

mocassin [mɔkasɛ̃] NM moccasin

moche [mɔʃ] ADJ (*fam: laid*) ugly; (*mauvais, méprisable*) rotten

modalité [mɔdalite] NF form, mode; **modalités** NFPL (*d'un accord etc*) clauses, terms; **modalités de paiement** methods of payment

mode [mɔd] NF fashion; (*commerce*) fashion

m

trade *ou* industry ▶ NM (*manière*) form, mode, method; (*Ling*) mood; (*Inform, Mus*) mode; **travailler dans la ~** to be in the fashion business; **à la ~** fashionable, in fashion; **~ dialogué** (*Inform*) interactive *ou* conversational mode; **~ d'emploi** directions *pl* (for use); **~ de paiement** method of payment; **~ de vie** way of life

modelage [mɔdlaʒ] NM modelling

modelé [mɔdle] NM (*Géo*) relief; (*du corps etc*) contours *pl*

modèle [mɔdɛl] ADJ model ▶ NM model; (*qui pose: de peintre*) sitter; (*type*) type; (*gabarit, patron*) pattern; **~ courant** *ou* **de série** (*Comm*) production model; **~ déposé** registered design; **~ réduit** small-scale model

modeler [mɔdle] /5/ VT (*Art*) to model, mould; (*vêtement, érosion*) to mould, shape; **~ qch sur/d'après** to model sth on

modélisation [mɔdelizasjɔ̃] NF (*Math*) modelling

modéliste [mɔdelist] NMF (*Couture*) designer; (*de modèles réduits*) model maker

modem [mɔdɛm] NM (*Inform*) modem

modérateur, -trice [mɔdeʀatœʀ, -tʀis] ADJ moderating ▶ NM/F moderator

modération [mɔdeʀasjɔ̃] NF moderation; **~ de peine** reduction of sentence

modéré, e [mɔdeʀe] ADJ, NM/F moderate

modérément [mɔdeʀemɑ̃] ADV moderately, in moderation

modérer [mɔdeʀe] /6/ VT to moderate; **se modérer** VI to restrain o.s.

moderne [mɔdɛʀn] ADJ modern ▶ NM (*Art*) modern style; (*ameublement*) modern furniture

modernisation [mɔdɛʀnizasjɔ̃] NF modernization

moderniser [mɔdɛʀnize] /1/ VT to modernize

modernisme [mɔdɛʀnism] NM modernism

modernité [mɔdɛʀnite] NF modernity

modeste [mɔdɛst] ADJ modest; (*origine*) humble, lowly

modestement [mɔdɛstəmɑ̃] ADV modestly

modestie [mɔdɛsti] NF modesty; **fausse ~** false modesty

modicité [mɔdisite] NF: **la ~ des prix** *etc* the low prices *etc*

modificatif, -ive [mɔdifikatif, -iv] ADJ modifying

modification [mɔdifikasjɔ̃] NF modification

modifier [mɔdifje] /7/ VT to modify, alter; (*Ling*) to modify; **se modifier** VI to alter

modique [mɔdik] ADJ (*salaire, somme*) modest

modiste [mɔdist] NF milliner

modulaire [mɔdylɛʀ] ADJ modular

modulation [mɔdylasjɔ̃] NF modulation; **~ de fréquence** (**FM** *ou* **MF**) frequency modulation (FM)

module [mɔdyl] NM module

moduler [mɔdyle] /1/ VT to modulate; (*air*) to warble

moelle [mwal] NF marrow; (*fig*) pith, core; **~ épinière** spinal chord

moelleux, -euse [mwalø, -øz] ADJ soft; (*au goût, à l'ouïe*) mellow; (*gracieux, souple*) smooth; (*gâteau*) light and moist

moellon [mwalɔ̃] NM rubble stone

mœurs [mœʀ] NFPL (*conduite*) morals; (*manières*) manners; (*pratiques sociales*) habits; (*mode de vie*) life style *sg*; (*d'une espèce animale*) behaviour *sg* (BRIT), behavior *sg* (US); **femme de mauvaises ~** loose woman; **passer dans les ~** to become the custom; **contraire aux bonnes ~** contrary to proprieties

mohair [mɔɛʀ] NM mohair

moi [mwa] PRON me; (*emphatique*): **~, je …** for my part, I …, I myself … ▶ NM INV (*Psych*) ego, self; **c'est ~ qui l'ai fait** I did it, it was me who did it; **apporte-le-~** bring it to me; **à ~** mine; (*dans un jeu*) my turn; **à ~!** (*à l'aide*) help (me)!

moignon [mwaɲɔ̃] NM stump

moi-même [mwamɛm] PRON myself; (*emphatique*) I myself

moindre [mwɛ̃dʀ] ADJ lesser; lower; **le (la) ~, les moindres** the least; the slightest; **le (la) ~ de** the least of; **c'est la ~ des choses** it's nothing at all

moindrement [mwɛ̃dʀəmɑ̃] ADV: **pas le ~** not in the least

moine [mwan] NM monk, friar

moineau, x [mwano] NM sparrow

MOT-CLÉ

moins [mwɛ̃] ADV **1** *comparatif*: **moins (que)** less (than); **moins grand que** less tall than, not as tall as; **il a trois ans de moins que moi** he's three years younger than me; **il est moins intelligent que moi** he's not as clever as me, he's less clever than me; **moins je travaille, mieux je me porte** the less I work, the better I feel

2 *superlatif*: **le moins** (the) least; **c'est ce que j'aime le moins** it's what I like (the) least; **le (la) moins doué(e)** the least gifted; **au moins, du moins** at least; **pour le moins** at the very least

3: **moins de** (*quantité*) less (than); (*nombre*) fewer (than); **moins de sable/d'eau** less sand/water; **moins de livres/gens** fewer books/people; **moins de deux ans** less than two years; **moins de midi** not yet midday

4: **de moins, en moins**: **100 euros/3 jours de moins** 100 euros/3 days less; **trois livres en moins** three books fewer; three books too few; **de l'argent en moins** less money; **le soleil en moins** but for the sun, minus the sun; **de moins en moins** less and less; **en moins de deux** in a flash *ou* a trice

5: **à moins de, à moins que** unless; **à moins de faire** unless we do (*ou* he does *etc*); **à moins que tu ne fasses** unless you do; **à moins d'un accident** barring any accident

▶ PRÉP: **quatre moins deux** four minus two; **dix heures moins cinq** five to ten; **il fait moins cinq** it's five (degrees) below (freezing), it's minus five; **il est moins cinq** it's five to ▶ NM (*signe*) minus sign

moins-value [mwɛ̃valy] NF (*Écon, Comm*) depreciation

moire [mwaʀ] NF moiré

moiré, e [mwaʀe] ADJ (*tissu, papier*) moiré, watered; (*reflets*) shimmering

mois [mwa] NM month; (*salaire, somme due*) (monthly) pay *ou* salary; **treizième ~, double ~** extra month's salary

moïse [mɔiz] NM Moses basket

moisi, e [mwazi] ADJ mouldy (BRIT), moldy (US), mildewed ▸ NM mould, mold, mildew; **odeur de ~** musty smell

moisir [mwaziʀ] /2/ VI to go mouldy (BRIT) *ou* moldy (US); (*fig*) to rot; (*personne*) to hang about ▸ VT to make mouldy *ou* moldy

moisissure [mwazisyʀ] NF mould *no pl* (BRIT), mold *no pl* (US)

moisson [mwasɔ̃] NF harvest; (*époque*) harvest (time); (*fig*): **faire une ~ de** to gather a wealth of

moissonner [mwasɔne] /1/ VT to harvest, reap; (*fig*) to collect

moissonneur, -euse [mwasɔnœʀ, -øz] NM/F harvester, reaper ▸ NF (*machine*) harvester

moissonneuse (*machine*) harvester

moissonneuse-batteuse [mwasɔnøzbatøz] (*pl* **moissonneuses-batteuses**) NF combine harvester

moite [mwat] ADJ (*peau, mains*) sweaty, sticky; (*atmosphère*) muggy

moitié [mwatje] NF half; (*épouse*): **sa ~** his better half; **la ~** half; **la ~ de** half (of), half the amount (*ou* number) of; **la ~ du temps/des gens** half the time/the people; **à la ~ de** halfway through; **~ moins grand** half as tall; **~ plus long** half as long again, longer by half; **à ~** half (*avant le verbe*), half- (*avant l'adjectif*); **à ~ prix** (at) half price, half-price; **de ~** by half; **~ ~** half-and-half

moka [mɔka] NM (*café*) mocha coffee; (*gâteau*) mocha cake

mol [mɔl] ADJ M *voir* **mou**

molaire [mɔlɛʀ] NF molar

moldave [mɔldav] ADJ Moldavian

Moldavie [mɔldavi] NF: **la ~** Moldavia

môle [mol] NM jetty

moléculaire [mɔlekylɛʀ] ADJ molecular

molécule [mɔlekyl] NF molecule

moleskine [mɔlɛskin] NF imitation leather

molester [mɔlɛste] /1/ VT to manhandle, maul (about)

molette [mɔlɛt] NF toothed *ou* cutting wheel

mollasse [mɔlas] ADJ (*péj: sans énergie*) sluggish; (*: flasque*) flabby

molle [mɔl] ADJ F *voir* **mou**

mollement [mɔlmɑ̃] ADV softly; (*péj: travailler*) sluggishly; (*protester*) feebly

mollesse [mɔlɛs] NF (*voir* **mou**) softness; flabbiness; limpness; sluggishness; feebleness

mollet [mɔlɛ] NM calf ▸ ADJ M: **œuf ~** soft-boiled egg

molletière [mɔltjɛʀ] ADJ F: **bande ~** puttee

molleton [mɔltɔ̃] NM (*Textiles*) felt

molletonné, e [mɔltɔne] ADJ (*gants etc*) fleece-lined

mollir [mɔliʀ] /2/ VI (*jambes*) to give way; (*substance*) to go soft; (*Navig: vent*) to drop, die down; (*fig: personne*) to relent; (*: courage*) to fail, flag

mollusque [mɔlysk] NM (*Zool*) mollusc; (*fig: personne*) lazy lump

molosse [mɔlɔs] NM big ferocious dog

môme [mom] NMF (*fam: enfant*) brat; (*: fille*) bird (BRIT), chick

moment [mɔmɑ̃] NM moment; (*occasion*): **profiter du ~** to take (advantage of) the opportunity; **ce n'est pas le ~** this is not the right time; **à un certain ~** at some point; **à un ~ donné** at a certain point; **à quel ~?** when exactly?; **au même ~** at the same time; (*instant*) at the same moment; **pour un bon ~** for a good while; **pour le ~** for the moment, for the time being; **au ~ de** at the time of; **au ~ où** as; at a time when; **à tout ~** at any time *ou* moment; (*continuellement*) constantly, continually; **en ce ~** at the moment; (*aujourd'hui*) at present; **sur le ~** at the time; **par moments** now and then, at times; **d'un ~ à l'autre** from one minute (now); **du ~ où** *ou* **que** seeing that, since; **n'avoir pas un ~ à soi** not to have a minute to oneself

momentané, e [mɔmɑ̃tane] ADJ temporary, momentary

momentanément [mɔmɑ̃tanemɑ̃] ADV for a moment, for a while

momie [mɔmi] NF mummy

mon, ma [mɔ̃, ma] (*pl* **mes** [me]) ADJ POSS my

monacal, e, -aux [mɔnakal, -o] ADJ monastic

Monaco [mɔnako] NM: **le ~** Monaco

monarchie [mɔnaʀʃi] NF monarchy

monarchiste [mɔnaʀʃist] ADJ, NMF monarchist

monarque [mɔnaʀk] NM monarch

monastère [mɔnastɛʀ] NM monastery

monastique [mɔnastik] ADJ monastic

monceau, x [mɔ̃so] NM heap

mondain, e [mɔ̃dɛ̃, -ɛn] ADJ (*soirée, vie*) society *cpd*; (*obligations*) social; (*peintre, écrivain*) fashionable; (*personne*) society *cpd* ▸ NM/F society man/woman, socialite ▸ NF: **la M~, la police ~** the vice squad

mondanités [mɔ̃danite] NFPL (*vie mondaine*) society life *sg*; (*paroles*) (society) small talk *sg*; (*Presse*) (society) gossip column *sg*

monde [mɔ̃d] NM world; **le ~** (*personnes mondaines*) (high) society; **être du même ~** (*milieu*) to move in the same circles; **il y a du ~** (*beaucoup de gens*) there are a lot of people; (*quelques personnes*) there are some people; **y a-t-il du ~ dans le salon?** is there anybody in the lounge?; **beaucoup/peu de ~** many/few people; **le meilleur** *etc* **du ~** the best *etc* in the world; **mettre au ~** to bring into the world; **pas le moins du ~** not in the least; **se faire un ~ de qch** to make a great deal of fuss about sth; **tour du ~** round-the-world trip; **homme/femme du ~** society man/woman

mondial, e, -aux [mɔ̃djal, -o] ADJ (*population*) world *cpd*; (*influence*) world-wide

mondialement [mɔ̃djalmɑ̃] ADV throughout the world

mondialisation [mɔ̃djalizasjɔ̃] NF globalization; (d'une technique) global application; (d'un conflit) global spread

mondovision [mɔ̃dɔvizjɔ̃] NF (world coverage by) satellite television

monégasque [mɔnegask] ADJ Monegasque, of ou from Monaco ▶ NMF: **M~** Monegasque

monétaire [mɔnetɛʀ] ADJ monetary

monétarisme [mɔnetaʀism] NM monetarism

monétique [mɔnetik] NF electronic money

mongol, e [mɔ̃gɔl] ADJ Mongol, Mongolian ▶ NM (Ling) Mongolian ▶ NM/F: **M~, e** (de la Mongolie) Mongolian

Mongolie [mɔ̃gɔli] NF: **la ~** Mongolia

mongolien, ne [mɔ̃gɔljɛ̃, -ɛn] ADJ, NM/F mongol

mongolisme [mɔ̃gɔlism] NM mongolism, Down's syndrome

moniteur, -trice [mɔnitœʀ, -tʀis] NM/F (Sport) instructor (instructress); (de colonie de vacances) supervisor ▶ NM (écran) monitor; **~ cardiaque** cardiac monitor; **~ d'auto-école** driving instructor

monitorage [mɔnitɔʀaʒ] NM monitoring

monitorat [mɔnitɔʀa] NM (formation) instructor's training (course); (fonction) instructorship

monnaie [mɔnɛ] NF (pièce) coin; (Écon: moyen d'échange) currency; (petites pièces): **avoir de la ~** to have (some) change; **faire de la ~** to get (some) change; **avoir/faire la ~ de 20 euros** to have change/get change for 20 euros; **faire** ou **donner à qn la ~ de 20 euros** to give sb change for 20 euros, change 20 euros for sb; **rendre à qn la ~ (sur 20 euros)** to give sb the change (from ou out of 20 euros); **servir de ~ d'échange** (fig) to be used as a bargaining counter ou as bargaining counters; **payer en ~ de singe** to fob sb off with empty promises; **c'est ~ courante** it's a common occurrence; **~ légale** legal tender

monnayable [mɔnɛjabl] ADJ (vendable) convertible into cash; **mes services sont monnayables** my services are worth money

monnayer [mɔneje] /8/ VT to convert into cash; (talent) to capitalize on

monnayeur [mɔnɛjœʀ] NM voir **faux-monnayeur**

mono [mɔno] NF (monophonie) mono ▶ NM (monoski) monoski

monochrome [mɔnɔkʀom] ADJ monochrome

monocle [mɔnɔkl] NM monocle, eyeglass

monocoque [mɔnɔkɔk] ADJ (voiture) monocoque ▶ NM (voilier) monohull

monocorde [mɔnɔkɔʀd] ADJ monotonous

monoculture [mɔnɔkyltyʀ] NF single-crop farming, monoculture

monogamie [mɔnɔgami] NF monogamy

monogramme [mɔnɔgʀam] NM monogram

monokini [mɔnɔkini] NM one-piece bikini, bikini pants pl

monolingue [mɔnɔlɛ̃g] ADJ monolingual

monolithique [mɔnɔlitik] ADJ (lit, fig) monolithic

monologue [mɔnɔlɔg] NM monologue, soliloquy; **~ intérieur** stream of consciousness

monologuer [mɔnɔlɔge] /1/ VI to soliloquize

monôme [mɔnom] NM (Math) monomial; (d'étudiants) students' rag procession

monoparental, e, -aux [mɔnɔpaʀɑ̃tal, -o] ADJ: **famille ~** single-parent ou one-parent family

monophasé, e [mɔnɔfaze] ADJ single-phase cpd

monophonie [mɔnɔfɔni] NF monophony

monoplace [mɔnɔplas] ADJ, NMF single-seater, one-seater

monoplan [mɔnɔplɑ̃] NM monoplane

monopole [mɔnɔpɔl] NM monopoly

monopolisation [mɔnɔpɔlizasjɔ̃] NF monopolization

monopoliser [mɔnɔpɔlize] /1/ VT to monopolize

monorail [mɔnɔʀaj] NM monorail; monorail train

monoski [mɔnɔski] NM monoski

monosyllabe [mɔnɔsilab] NM monosyllable, word of one syllable

monosyllabique [mɔnɔsilabik] ADJ monosyllabic

monotone [mɔnɔtɔn] ADJ monotonous

monotonie [mɔnɔtɔni] NF monotony

monseigneur [mɔ̃sɛɲœʀ] NM (archevêque, évêque) Your (ou His) Grace; (cardinal) Your (ou His) Eminence; **M~ Thomas** Bishop Thomas; Cardinal Thomas

Monsieur [məsjø] (pl **Messieurs** [mesjø]) NM (titre) Mr; **un/le monsieur** (homme quelconque) a/the gentleman; **~, ...** (en tête de lettre) Dear Sir, ...; voir aussi **Madame**

monstre [mɔ̃stʀ] NM monster ▶ ADJ (fam: effet, publicité) massive; **un travail ~** a fantastic amount of work; an enormous job; **~ sacré** superstar

monstrueux, -euse [mɔ̃stʀyø, -øz] ADJ monstrous

monstruosité [mɔ̃stʀyozite] NF monstrosity

mont [mɔ̃] NM: **par monts et par vaux** up hill and down dale; **le M~ Blanc** Mont Blanc; **~ de Vénus** mons veneris

montage [mɔ̃taʒ] NM putting up; (d'un bijou) mounting, setting; (d'une machine etc) assembly; (Photo) photomontage; (Ciné) editing; **~ sonore** sound editing

montagnard, e [mɔ̃taɲaʀ, -aʀd] ADJ mountain cpd ▶ NM/F mountain-dweller

montagne [mɔ̃taɲ] NF (cime) mountain; (région): **la ~** the mountains pl; **la haute ~** the high mountains; **les montagnes Rocheuses** the Rocky Mountains, the Rockies; **montagnes russes** big dipper sg, switchback sg

montagneux, -euse [mɔ̃taɲø, -øz] ADJ mountainous; (basse montagne) hilly

montant, e [mɔ̃tɑ̃, -ɑ̃t] ADJ (mouvement, marée) rising; (chemin) uphill; (robe, corsage) high-necked ▶ NM (somme, total) (sum) total, (total) amount; (de fenêtre) upright; (de lit) post

mont-de-piété [mɔ̃dpjete] (pl **monts-de-piété**) NM pawnshop

monte [mɔ̃t] NF (accouplement): **la ~** stud; (d'un jockey) seat

monté, e [mɔ̃te] ADJ: **être ~ contre qn** to be angry with sb; (*fourni, équipé*) **~ en** equipped with

monte-charge [mɔ̃tʃaRʒ] NM INV goods lift, hoist

montée [mɔ̃te] NF rising, rise; (*escalade*) ascent, climb; (*chemin*) way up; (*côte*) hill; **au milieu de la ~** halfway up; **le moteur chauffe dans les montées** the engine overheats going uphill

Monténégro [mɔ̃tenegRo] NM: **le ~** Montenegro

monte-plats [mɔ̃tpla] NM INV service lift

monter [mɔ̃te] /1/ VT (*escalier, côte*) to go (*ou* come) up; (*valise, paquet*) to take (*ou* bring) up; (*cheval*) to mount; (*femelle*) to cover, serve; (*étagère*) to raise; (*tente, échafaudage*) to put up; (*machine*) to assemble; (*bijou*) to mount, set; (*Couture*) to sew on; (: *manche*) to set in; (*Ciné*) to edit; (*Théât*) to put on, stage; (*société, coup etc*) to set up; (*fournir, équiper*) to equip ▶ VI to go (*ou* come) up; (*avion, voiture*) to climb, go up; (*chemin, niveau, température, voix, prix*) to go up, rise; (*brouillard, bruit*) to rise, come up; (*passager*) to get on; (*à cheval*): **~ bien/mal** to ride well/badly; **se monter** (*s'équiper*) to equip o.s., get kitted out (BRIT); **~ à cheval** to get on *ou* mount a horse; (*faire du cheval*) to ride (a horse); **~ à bicyclette** to get on *ou* mount a bicycle, to (ride a) bicycle; **~ à pied/en voiture** to walk/ drive up, go up on foot/by car; **~ dans le train/l'avion** to get into the train/plane, board the train/plane; **~ sur** to climb up onto; **~ sur** *ou* **à un arbre/une échelle** to climb (up) a tree/ladder; **~ à bord** (get on) board; **~ à la tête de qn** to go to sb's head; **~ sur les planches** to go on the stage; **~ en grade** to be promoted; **se monter à** (*frais etc*) to add up to, come to; **~ qn contre qn** to set sb against sb; **~ la tête à qn** to give sb ideas

monteur, -euse [mɔ̃tœR, -øz] NM/F (*Tech*) fitter; (*Ciné*) (film) editor

montgolfière [mɔ̃golfjɛR] NF hot-air balloon

monticule [mɔ̃tikyl] NM mound

montmartrois, e [mɔ̃maRtRwa, -waz] ADJ of *ou* from Montmartre

montre [mɔ̃tR] NF watch; (*ostentation*): **pour la ~** for show; **~ en main** exactly, to the minute; **faire ~ de** to show, display; **contre la ~** (*Sport*) against the clock; **~ de plongée** diver's watch

Montréal [mɔ̃Real] N Montreal

montréalais, e [mɔ̃Reale, -ez] ADJ of *ou* from Montreal ▶ NM/F: **M~, e** Montrealer

montre-bracelet [mɔ̃tRəbRaslɛ] (*pl* **montres-bracelets**) NF wrist watch

montrer [mɔ̃tRe] /1/ VT to show; **se montrer** to appear; **~ qch à qn** to show sb sth; **~ qch du doigt** to point to sth, point one's finger at sth; **se montrer intelligent** to prove (to be) intelligent

montreur, -euse [mɔ̃tRœR, -øz] NM/F: **~ de marionnettes** puppeteer

monture [mɔ̃tyR] NF (*bête*) mount; (*d'une bague*) setting; (*de lunettes*) frame

monument [mɔnymɑ̃] NM monument; **~ aux morts** war memorial

monumental, e, -aux [mɔnymɑ̃tal, -o] ADJ monumental

moquer [mɔke] /1/: **se ~ de** VT to make fun of, laugh at; (*fam: se désintéresser de*) not to care about; (*tromper*) **se ~ de qn** to take sb for a ride

moquerie [mɔkRi] NF mockery *no pl*

moquette [mɔkɛt] NF fitted carpet, wall-to-wall carpeting *no pl*

moquetter [mɔkete] /1/ VT to carpet

moqueur, -euse [mɔkœR, -øz] ADJ mocking

moral, e, -aux [mɔral, -o] ADJ moral ▶ NM morale ▶ NF (*conduite*) morals *pl* (*règles*), moral code, ethic; (*valeurs*) moral standards *pl*, morality; (*science*) ethics *sg*, moral philosophy; (*conclusion: d'une fable etc*) moral; **au ~, sur le plan ~** morally; **avoir le ~** (*fam*) to be in good spirits; **avoir le ~ à zéro** to be really down; **faire la ~ à** to lecture, preach at

moralement [mɔralmɑ̃] ADV morally

moralisateur, -trice [mɔralizatœR, -tRis] ADJ moralizing, sanctimonious ▶ NM/F moralizer

moraliser [mɔralize] /1/ VT (*sermonner*) to lecture, preach at

moraliste [mɔralist] NMF moralist ▶ ADJ moralistic

moralité [mɔralite] NF (*d'une action, attitude*) morality; (*conduite*) morals *pl*; (*conclusion, enseignement*) moral

moratoire [mɔRatwaR] ADJ M: **intérêts moratoires** (*Écon*) interest on arrears

morbide [mɔRbid] ADJ morbid

morceau, x [mɔRso] NM piece, bit; (*d'une œuvre*) passage, extract; (*Mus*) piece; (*Culin: de viande*) cut; (: *de sucre*) lump; **mettre en ~** to pull to pieces *ou* bits; **manger un ~** to have a bite (to eat)

morceler [mɔRsəle] /4/ VT to break up, divide up

morcellement [mɔRsɛlmɑ̃] NM breaking up

mordant, e [mɔRdɑ̃, -ɑ̃t] ADJ (*ton, remarque*) scathing, cutting; (*froid*) biting ▶ NM (*dynamisme, énergie*) spirit; (*fougue*) bite, punch

mordicus [mɔRdikys] ADV (*fam*) obstinately, stubbornly

mordiller [mɔRdije] /1/ VT to nibble at, chew at

mordoré, e [mɔRdɔRe] ADJ lustrous bronze

mordre [mɔRdR] /41/ VT to bite; (*lime, vis*) to bite into ▶ VI (*poisson*) to bite; **~ dans** to bite into; **~ sur** (*fig*) to go over into, overlap into; **~ à qch** (*comprendre, aimer*) to take to; **~ à l'hameçon** to bite, rise to the bait

mordu, e [mɔRdy] PP *de* **mordre** ▶ ADJ (*amoureux*) smitten ▶ NM/F enthusiast; **un ~ du jazz/de la voile** a jazz/sailing fanatic *ou* buff

morfondre [mɔRfɔ̃dR] /41/: **se morfondre** VI to mope

morgue [mɔRg] NF (*arrogance*) haughtiness; (*lieu: de la police*) morgue; (: *à l'hôpital*) mortuary

moribond, e [mɔRibɔ̃, -ɔ̃d] ADJ dying, moribund

morille [mɔRij] NF morel (*mushroom*)

mormon, e [mɔRmɔ̃, -ɔn] ADJ, NM/F Mormon

morne [mɔRn] ADJ (*personne, visage*) glum, gloomy; (*temps, vie*) dismal, dreary

morose [mɔRoz] ADJ sullen, morose; (*marché*) sluggish

morphine – moucheté

morphine [mɔʀfin] NF morphine
morphinomane [mɔʀfinɔman] NMF morphine addict
morphologie [mɔʀfɔlɔʒi] NF morphology
morphologique [mɔʀfɔlɔʒik] ADJ morphological
mors [mɔʀ] NM bit
morse [mɔʀs] NM (Zool) walrus; (Tél) Morse (code)
morsure [mɔʀsyʀ] NF bite
mort¹ [mɔʀ] NF death; **se donner la ~** to take one's own life; **de ~** (silence, pâleur) deathly; **blessé à ~** fatally wounded ou injured; **à la vie, à la ~** for better, for worse; **~ clinique** brain death; **~ subite du nourrisson, ~ au berceau** cot death
mort², e [mɔʀ, mɔʀt] PP de mourir ▶ ADJ dead ▶ NM/F (défunt) dead man/woman; (victime): **il y a eu plusieurs morts** several people were killed, there were several killed ▶ NM (Cartes) dummy; **~ ou vif** dead or alive; **~ de peur/fatigue** frightened to death/dead tired; **morts et blessés** casualties; **faire le ~** to play dead; (fig) to lie low
mortadelle [mɔʀtadɛl] NF mortadella
mortalité [mɔʀtalite] NF mortality, death rate
mort-aux-rats [mɔʀ(t)oʀa] NF INV rat poison
mortel, le [mɔʀtɛl] ADJ (poison etc) deadly, lethal; (accident, blessure) fatal; (silence, ennemi) deadly; (Rel: danger, frayeur, péché) mortal; (fig: froid) deathly; (: ennui, soirée) deadly (boring) ▶ NM/F mortal
mortellement [mɔʀtɛlmɑ̃] ADV (blessé etc) fatally, mortally; (pâle etc) deathly; (fig: ennuyeux etc) deadly
morte-saison [mɔʀtəsɛzɔ̃] (pl **mortes-saisons**) NF slack ou off season
mortier [mɔʀtje] NM (gén) mortar
mortifier [mɔʀtifje] /7/ VT to mortify
mort-né, e [mɔʀne] ADJ (enfant) stillborn; (fig) abortive
mortuaire [mɔʀtɥɛʀ] ADJ funeral cpd; **avis mortuaires** death announcements, intimations; **chapelle ~** mortuary chapel; **couronne ~** (funeral) wreath; **domicile ~** house of the deceased; **drap ~** pall
morue [mɔʀy] NF (Zool) cod inv; (Culin: salée) salt-cod
morvandeau, -elle, x [mɔʀvɑ̃do, -ɛl] ADJ of ou from the Morvan region
morveux, -euse [mɔʀvø, -øz] ADJ (fam) snotty-nosed
mosaïque [mɔzaik] NF (Art) mosaic; (fig) patchwork
Moscou [mɔsku] N Moscow
moscovite [mɔskɔvit] ADJ of ou from Moscow, Moscow cpd ▶ NMF: **M~** Muscovite
mosquée [mɔske] NF mosque
mot [mo] NM word; (message) line, note; (bon mot etc) saying; **le ~ de la fin** the last word; **~ à ~** adj, adv word for word; **~ pour ~** word for word, verbatim; **sur ou à ces mots** with these words; **en un ~** in a word; **à mots couverts** in veiled terms; **prendre qn au ~** to take sb at his word;

se donner le ~ to send the word round; **avoir son ~ à dire** to have a say; **~ d'ordre** watchword; **~ de passe** password; **mots croisés** crossword (puzzle) sg
motard, e [mɔtaʀ, -aʀd] NM biker; (policier) motorcycle cop
motel [mɔtɛl] NM motel
moteur, -trice [mɔtœʀ, -tʀis] ADJ (Anat, Physiol) motor; (Tech) driving; (Auto): **à 4 roues motrices** 4-wheel drive ▶ NM engine, motor; (fig) mover, mainspring; **à ~** power-driven, motor cpd; **~ à deux temps** two-stroke engine; **~ à explosion** internal combustion engine; **~ à réaction** jet engine; **~ de recherche** search engine; **~ thermique** heat engine
motif [mɔtif] NM (cause) motive; (décoratif) design, pattern, motif; (d'un tableau) subject, motif; (Mus) figure, motif; **motifs** NMPL (Jur) grounds pl; **sans ~** adj groundless
motion [mosjɔ̃] NF motion; **~ de censure** motion de censure, vote of no confidence
motivation [mɔtivasjɔ̃] NF motivation
motivé, e [mɔtive] ADJ (acte) justified; (personne) motivated
motiver [mɔtive] /1/ VT (justifier) to justify, account for; (Admin, Jur, Psych) to motivate
moto [mɔto] NF (motor)bike; **~ verte ou de trial** trail (BRIT) ou dirt (US) bike
moto-cross [mɔtokʀɔs] NM motocross
motoculteur [mɔtokyltœʀ] NM (motorized) cultivator
motocyclette [mɔtosiklɛt] NF motorbike, motorcycle
motocyclisme [mɔtosiklism] NM motorcycle racing
motocycliste [mɔtosiklist] NM motorcyclist
motoneige [mɔtonɛʒ] NF snow bike
motorisé, e [mɔtoʀize] ADJ (troupe) motorized; (personne) having one's own transport
motrice [mɔtʀis] ADJ F voir **moteur**
motte [mɔt] NF: **~ de terre** lump of earth, clod (of earth); **~ de gazon** turf, sod; **~ de beurre** lump of butter
motus [mɔtys] EXCL: **~ (et bouche cousue)!** mum's the word!
mou, mol, molle [mu, mɔl] ADJ soft; (péj: visage, traits) flabby; (: geste) limp; (: personne) sluggish; (: résistance, protestations) feeble ▶ NM (homme mou) wimp; (abats) lights pl, lungs pl; (de la corde): **avoir du ~** to be slack; **donner du ~** to slacken, loosen; **avoir les jambes molles** to be weak at the knees
mouchard, e [muʃaʀ, -aʀd] NM/F (péj: Scol) sneak; (: Police) stool pigeon, grass (BRIT) ▶ NM (appareil) control device; (: de camion) tachograph
mouche [muʃ] NF fly; (Escrime) button; (de taffetas) patch; **prendre la ~** to go into a huff; **faire ~** to score a bull's-eye
moucher [muʃe] /1/ VT (enfant) to blow the nose of; (chandelle) to snuff (out); **se moucher** VI to blow one's nose
moucheron [muʃʀɔ̃] NM midge
moucheté, e [muʃte] ADJ (cheval) dappled; (laine) flecked; (Escrime) buttoned

mouchoir [muʃwaʀ] NM handkerchief, hanky; ~ **en papier** tissue, paper hanky

moudre [mudʀ] /47/ VT to grind

moue [mu] NF pout; **faire la ~** to pout; (fig) to pull a face

mouette [mwɛt] NF (sea)gull

moufette, mouffette [mufɛt] NF skunk

moufle [mufl] NF (gant) mitt(en); (Tech) pulley block

mouflon [muflɔ̃] NM mouf(f)lon

mouillage [mujaʒ] NM (Navig: lieu) anchorage, moorings pl

mouillé, e [muje] ADJ wet

mouiller [muje] /1/ VT (humecter) to wet, moisten; (tremper): ~ **qn/qch** to make sb/sth wet; (Culin: ragoût) to add stock ou wine to; (couper, diluer) to water down; (mine etc) to lay ▶ VI (Navig) to lie ou be at anchor; **se mouiller** to get wet; (fam: prendre des risques) to commit o.s; to get (o.s.) involved; ~ **l'ancre** to drop ou cast anchor

mouillette [mujɛt] NF (bread) finger

mouillure [mujyʀ] NF wet no pl; (tache) wet patch

moulage [mulaʒ] NM moulding (BRIT), molding (US); casting; (objet) cast

moulais etc [mulɛ] VB voir **moudre**

moulant, e [mulɑ̃, -ɑ̃t] ADJ figure-hugging

moule [mul] VB voir **moudre** ▶ NF (mollusque) mussel ▶ NM (creux, Culin) mould (BRIT), mold (US); (modèle plein) cast; ~ **à gâteau** nm cake tin (BRIT) ou pan (US); ~ **à gaufre** nm waffle iron; ~ **à tarte** nm pie ou flan dish

moulent [mul] VB voir **moudre**; **mouler**

mouler [mule] /1/ VT (brique) to mould (BRIT), mold (US); (statue) to cast; (visage, bas-relief) to make a cast of; (lettre) to shape with care; (vêtement) to hug, fit closely round; ~ **qch sur** (fig) to model sth on

moulin [mulɛ̃] NM mill; (fam) engine; ~ **à café** coffee mill; ~ **à eau** watermill; ~ **à légumes** (vegetable) shredder; ~ **à paroles** (fig) chatterbox; ~ **à poivre** pepper mill; ~ **à prières** prayer wheel; ~ **à vent** windmill

mouliner [muline] /1/ VT to shred

moulinet [mulinɛ] NM (de treuil) winch; (de canne à pêche) reel; (mouvement): **faire des moulinets avec qch** to whirl sth around

moulinette® [mulinɛt] NF (vegetable) shredder

moulons etc [mulɔ̃] VB voir **moudre**

moulu, e [muly] PP de **moudre** ▶ ADJ (café) ground

moulure [mulyʀ] NF (ornement) moulding (BRIT), molding (US)

mourant, e [muʀɑ̃, -ɑ̃t] VB voir **mourir** ▶ ADJ dying ▶ NM/F dying man/woman

mourir [muʀiʀ] /1/ VI to die; (civilisation) to die out; ~ **assassiné** to be murdered; ~ **de froid/ faim/vieillesse** to die of exposure/hunger/old age; ~ **de faim/d'ennui** (fig) to be starving/be bored to death; ~ **d'envie de faire** to be dying to do; **s'ennuyer à ~** to be bored to death

mousquetaire [muskətɛʀ] NM musketeer

mousqueton [muskətɔ̃] NM (fusil) carbine; (anneau) snap-link, karabiner

moussant, e [musɑ̃, -ɑ̃t] ADJ foaming; **bain ~** foam ou bubble bath, bath foam

mousse [mus] NF (Bot) moss; (de savon) lather; (écume: sur eau, bière) froth, foam; (: shampooing) lather; (de champagne) bubbles pl; (Culin) mousse; (en caoutchouc etc) foam ▶ NM (Navig) ship's boy; **bain de ~** bubble bath; **bas ~** stretch stockings; **balle ~** rubber ball; ~ **carbonique** (fire-fighting) foam; ~ **de nylon** nylon foam; (tissu) stretch nylon; ~ **à raser** shaving foam

mousseline [muslin] NF (Textiles) muslin; chiffon; **pommes ~** (Culin) creamed potatoes

mousser [muse] /1/ VI (bière, détergent) to foam; (savon) to lather

mousseux, -euse [musø, -øz] ADJ (chocolat) frothy; (eau) foamy, frothy; (vin) sparkling ▶ NM: (vin) ~ sparkling wine

mousson [musɔ̃] NF monsoon

moussu, e [musy] ADJ mossy

moustache [mustaʃ] NF moustache; **moustaches** NFPL (d'animal) whiskers pl

moustachu, e [mustaʃy] ADJ with a moustache

moustiquaire [mustikɛʀ] NF (rideau) mosquito net; (chassis) mosquito screen

moustique [mustik] NM mosquito

moutarde [mutaʀd] NF mustard ▶ ADJ INV mustard(-coloured)

moutardier [mutaʀdje] NM mustard jar

mouton [mutɔ̃] NM (Zool, péj) sheep inv; (peau) sheepskin; (Culin) mutton

mouture [mutyʀ] NF grinding; (péj) rehash

mouvant, e [muvɑ̃, -ɑ̃t] ADJ unsettled; changing; shifting

mouvement [muvmɑ̃] NM (gén, aussi: mécanisme) movement; (ligne courbe) contours pl; (fig: tumulte, agitation) activity, bustle; (: impulsion) impulse; (geste) gesture; (Mus: rythme) tempo; **en ~** in motion; on the move; **mettre qch en ~** to set sth in motion, set sth going; ~ **d'humeur** fit ou burst of temper; ~ **d'opinion** trend of (public) opinion; **le ~ perpétuel** perpetual motion

mouvementé, e [muvmɑ̃te] ADJ (vie, poursuite) eventful; (réunion) turbulent

mouvoir [muvwaʀ] /27/ VT (levier, membre) to move; (machine) to drive; **se mouvoir** VI to move

moyen, ne [mwajɛ̃, -ɛn] ADJ average; (tailles, prix) medium; (de grandeur moyenne) medium-sized ▶ NM (façon) means sg, way ▶ NF average; (Statistique) mean; (Scol: à l'examen) pass mark; (Auto) average speed; **moyens** NMPL (capacités) means; **très ~** (résultats) pretty poor; **je n'en ai pas les moyens** I can't afford it; **au ~ de** by means of; **y a-t-il ~ de ...?** is it possible to ...?, can one ...?; **par quel ~?** how?, which way?, by which means?; **par tous les moyens** by every possible means, every possible way; **avec les moyens du bord** (fig) with what's available ou what comes to hand; **employer les grands moyens** to resort to drastic measures; **par ses propres moyens** all by oneself; **en ~** on (an) average; **faire la ~** to work out the average; ~ **de locomotion/d'expression** means of transport/expression; **M~ âge** Middle Ages;

~ **de transport** means of transport; ~ **d'âge** average age; ~ **entreprise** (*Comm*) medium-sized firm

moyenâgeux, -euse [mwajɛnaʒø, -øz] ADJ medieval

moyen-courrier [mwajɛ̃kuʀje] NM (*Aviat*) medium-haul aircraft

moyennant [mwajɛnɑ̃] PRÉP (*somme*) for; (*service, conditions*) in return for; (*travail, effort*) with

moyennement [mwajɛnmɑ̃] ADV fairly, moderately; (*faire*) fairly ou moderately well

Moyen-Orient [mwajɛnɔʀjɑ̃] NM: **le** ~ the Middle East

moyeu, x [mwajø] NM hub

mozambicain, e [mɔzɑ̃bikɛ̃, -ɛn] ADJ Mozambican

Mozambique [mɔzɑ̃bik] NM: **le** ~ Mozambique

MRAP SIGLE M = **Mouvement contre le racisme et pour l'amitié entre les peuples**

MRG SIGLE M (= *Mouvement des radicaux de gauche*) political party

ms ABR (= *manuscrit*) MS., ms

MSF SIGLE MPL = **Médecins sans frontières**

MST SIGLE F (= *maladie sexuellement transmissible*) STD (= *sexually transmitted disease*)

mû, mue [my] PP *de* **mouvoir**

mucosité [mykozite] NF mucus *no pl*

mucus [mykys] NM mucus *no pl*

mue [my] PP *de* **mouvoir** ▶ NF moulting (*Brit*), molting (*US*); sloughing; breaking of the voice

muer [mɥe] /1/ VI (*oiseau, mammifère*) to moult (*Brit*), molt (*US*); (*serpent*) to slough (its skin); (*jeune garçon*): **il mue** his voice is breaking; **se** ~ **en** to transform into

muet, te [mɥɛ, -ɛt] ADJ dumb; (*fig*): ~ **d'admiration** *etc* speechless with admiration *etc*; (*joie, douleur, Ciné*) silent; (*Ling: lettre*) silent, mute; (*carte*) blank ▶ NM: **le** ~ (*Ciné*) the silent cinema ou (*esp US*) movies

mufle [myfl] NM muzzle; (*goujat*) boor ▶ ADJ boorish

mugir [myʒiʀ] /2/ VI (*bœuf*) to bellow; (*vache*) to low, moo; (*fig*) to howl

mugissement [myʒismɑ̃] NM (*voir mugir*) bellowing; lowing, mooing; howling

muguet [mygɛ] NM (*Bot*) lily of the valley; (*Méd*) thrush

mulâtre, tresse [mylɑtʀ(ə), -tʀɛs] NM/F mulatto (!)

mule [myl] NF (*Zool*) (she-)mule

mules [myl] NFPL (*pantoufles*) mules

mulet [mylɛ] NM (*Zool*) (he-)mule; (*poisson*) mullet

muletier, -ière [myltje, -jɛʀ] ADJ: **sentier** ou **chemin** ~ mule track

mulot [mylo] NM fieldmouse

multicolore [myltikɔlɔʀ] ADJ multicoloured (*Brit*), multicolored (*US*)

multicoque [myltikɔk] NM multihull

multidisciplinaire [myltidisiplinɛʀ] ADJ multidisciplinary

multiforme [myltifɔʀm] ADJ many-sided

multilatéral, e, -aux [myltilateʀal, -o] ADJ multilateral

multimilliardaire [myltimiljaʀdɛʀ], **multimillionnaire** [myltimiljɔnɛʀ] ADJ, NMF multimillionaire

multinational, e, -aux [myltinasjɔnal, -o] ADJ, NF multinational

multiple [myltipl] ADJ multiple, numerous; (*varié*) many, manifold ▶ NM (*Math*) multiple

multiplex [myltiplɛks] NM (*Radio*) live link-up

multiplicateur [myltiplikatœʀ] NM multiplier

multiplication [myltiplikasjɔ̃] NF multiplication

multiplicité [myltiplisite] NF multiplicity

multiplier [myltiplije] /7/ VT to multiply; **se multiplier** VI to multiply; (*fig: personne*) to be everywhere at once

multiprogrammation [myltipʀɔgʀamasjɔ̃] NF (*Inform*) multiprogramming

multipropriété [myltipʀɔpʀijete] NF timesharing *no pl*

multirisque [myltiʀisk] ADJ: **assurance** ~ multiple-risk insurance

multisalles [myltisal] ADJ INV: (**cinéma**) ~ multiplex (cinema)

multitraitement [myltitʀɛtmɑ̃] NM (*Inform*) multiprocessing

multitude [myltityd] NF multitude; mass; **une** ~ **de** a vast number of, a multitude of

Munich [mynik] N Munich

munichois, e [mynikwa, -waz] ADJ of ou from Munich

municipal, e, -aux [mynisipal, -o] ADJ (*élections, stade*) municipal; (*conseil*) town *cpd*; **piscine/ bibliothèque** ~ public swimming pool/library

municipalité [mynisipalite] NF (*corps municipal*) town council, corporation; (*commune*) town, municipality

munificence [mynifisɑ̃s] NF munificence

munir [myniʀ] /2/ VT: ~ **qn/qch de** to equip sb/ sth with; **se** ~ **de** to provide o.s. with

munitions [mynisjɔ̃] NFPL ammunition *sg*

muqueuse [mykøz] NF mucous membrane

mur [myʀ] NM wall; (*fig*) stone ou brick wall; **faire le** ~ (*interne, soldat*) to jump the wall; ~ **du son** sound barrier

mûr, e [myʀ] ADJ ripe; (*personne*) mature ▶ NF (*de la ronce*) blackberry; (*du mûrier*) mulberry

muraille [myʀaj] NF (high) wall

mural, e, -aux [myʀal, -o] ADJ wall *cpd* ▶ NM (*Art*) mural

mûre [myʀ] NF blackberry

mûrement [myʀmɑ̃] ADV: **ayant** ~ **réfléchi** having given the matter much thought

murène [myʀɛn] NF moray (eel)

murer [myʀe] /1/ VT (*enclos*) to wall (in); (*porte, issue*) to wall up; (*personne*) to wall up ou in

muret [myʀɛ] NM low wall

mûrier [myʀje] NM mulberry tree; (*ronce*) blackberry bush

mûrir [myʀiʀ] /2/ VI (*fruit, blé*) to ripen; (*abcès, furoncle*) to come to a head; (*fig: idée, personne*) to mature; (*projet*) to develop ▶ VT (*fruit, blé*) to ripen; *(personne)* to (make) mature; *(pensée, projet)* to nurture

murmure [myʀmyʀ] NM murmur; **murmures** NMPL *(plaintes)* murmurings, mutterings

murmurer [myʀmyʀe] /1/ VI to murmur; *(se plaindre)* to mutter, grumble

mus *etc* [my] VB *voir* **mouvoir**

musaraigne [myzaʀɛɲ] NF shrew

musarder [myzaʀde] /1/ VI to idle (about); *(en marchant)* to dawdle (along)

musc [mysk] NM musk

muscade [myskad] NF *(aussi:* **noix (de) muscade)** nutmeg

muscat [myska] NM *(raisin)* muscat grape; *(vin)* muscatel (wine)

muscle [myskl] NM muscle

musclé, e [myskle] ADJ *(personne, corps)* muscular; *(fig: politique, régime etc)* strong-arm *cpd*

muscler [myskle] /1/ VT to develop the muscles of

musculaire [myskylɛʀ] ADJ muscular

musculation [myskylasjɔ̃] NF: **exercices de ~** muscle-developing exercises

musculature [myskylatyʀ] NF muscle structure, muscles *pl*, musculature

muse [myz] NF muse

museau, x [myzo] NM muzzle; *(Culin)* brawn

musée [myze] NM museum; *(de peinture)* art gallery

museler [myzle] /4/ VT to muzzle

muselière [myzəljɛʀ] NF muzzle

musette [myzɛt] NF *(sac)* lunch bag ▸ ADJ INV *(orchestre etc)* accordion *cpd*

muséum [myzeɔm] NM museum

musical, e, -aux [myzikal, -o] ADJ musical

music-hall [myzikol] NM *(salle)* variety theatre; *(genre)* variety

musicien, ne [myzisjɛ̃, -ɛn] ADJ musical ▸ NM/F musician

musique [myzik] NF music; *(fanfare)* band; **faire de la ~** to make music; *(jouer d'un instrument)* to play an instrument; **~ de chambre** chamber music; **~ de fond** background music

musqué, e [myske] ADJ musky

must [mœst] NM must

musulman, e [myzylmɑ̃, -an] ADJ, NM/F Moslem, Muslim

mutant, e [mytɑ̃, -ãt] NM/F mutant

mutation [mytasjɔ̃] NF *(Admin)* transfer; *(Bio)* mutation

muter [myte] /1/ VT *(Admin)* to transfer, move

mutilation [mytilasjɔ̃] NF mutilation

mutilé, e [mytile] NM/F disabled person *(through loss of limbs)*; **~ de guerre** disabled ex-

serviceman; **grand ~** person with a severe disability

mutiler [mytile] /1/ VT to mutilate, maim; *(fig)* to mutilate, deface

mutin, e [mytɛ̃, -in] ADJ *(enfant, air, ton)* mischievous, impish ▸ NM/F *(Mil, Navig)* mutineer

mutiner [mytine] /1/: **se mutiner** VI to mutiny

mutinerie [mytinʀi] NF mutiny

mutisme [mytism] NM silence

mutualiste [mytɥalist] ADJ: **société ~** mutual benefit society, ≈ Friendly Society

mutualité [mytɥalite] NF *(assurance)* mutual (benefit) insurance scheme

mutuel, le [mytɥɛl] ADJ mutual ▸ NF mutual benefit society; *see note*

Additional insurance covers most health care costs that are not covered by basic national health insurance. It is based on the principle of solidarity. The *mutuelles*, which individuals can choose freely, are becoming proportionally more important as the amounts reimbursed by national health insurance decline.

mutuellement [mytɥɛlmɑ̃] ADV each other, one another

Myanmar [mjanmaʀ] NM Myanmar

myocarde [mjɔkaʀd] NM *voir* **infarctus**

myope [mjɔp] ADJ short-sighted

myopie [mjɔpi] NF short-sightedness, myopia

myosotis [mjɔzɔtis] NM forget-me-not

myriade [miʀjad] NF myriad

myrtille [miʀtij] NF blueberry, bilberry (BRIT)

mystère [mistɛʀ] NM mystery

mystérieusement [misteʀjøzmɑ̃] ADV mysteriously

mystérieux, -euse [misteʀjø, -øz] ADJ mysterious

mysticisme [mistisism] NM mysticism

mystificateur, -trice [mistifikatœʀ, -tʀis] NM/F hoaxer, practical joker

mystification [mistifikasjɔ̃] NF *(tromperie, mensonge)* hoax; *(mythe)* mystification

mystifier [mistifje] /7/ VT to fool, take in; *(tromper)* to mystify

mystique [mistik] ADJ mystic, mystical ▸ NMF mystic

mythe [mit] NM myth

mythifier [mitifje] /7/ VT to turn into a myth, mythologize

mythique [mitik] ADJ mythical

mythologie [mitɔlɔʒi] NF mythology

mythologique [mitɔlɔʒik] ADJ mythological

mythomane [mitɔman] ADJ, NMF mythomaniac

m

Nn

N, n [ɛn] NM INV N, n ▶ ABR (= *nord*) N; **N comme Nicolas** N for Nelly (BRIT) *ou* Nan (US)

n' [n] ADV *voir* **ne**

nabot [nabo] NM dwarf

nacelle [nasɛl] NF (*de ballon*) basket

nacre [nakʀ] NF mother-of-pearl

nacré, e [nakʀe] ADJ pearly

nage [naʒ] NF swimming; (*manière*) style of swimming, stroke; **traverser/s'éloigner à la ~** to swim across/away; **en ~** bathed in sweat; **~ indienne** sidestroke; **~ libre** freestyle; **~ papillon** butterfly

nageoire [naʒwaʀ] NF fin

nager [naʒe] /3/ VI to swim; (*fig: ne rien comprendre*) to be all at sea; **~ dans** to be swimming in; (*vêtements*) to be lost in; **~ dans le bonheur** to be overjoyed

nageur, -euse [naʒœʀ, -øz] NM/F swimmer

naguère [nagɛʀ] ADV (*il y a peu de temps*) not long ago; (*autrefois*) formerly

naïf, -ïve [naif, naiv] ADJ naïve

nain, e [nɛ̃, nɛn] ADJ, NM/F (*péj*) dwarf (!)

Nairobi [nɛʀɔbi] N Nairobi

nais [nɛ], **naissais** *etc* [nɛsɛ] VB *voir* **naître**

naissance [nɛsɑ̃s] NF birth; **donner ~ à** to give birth to; (*fig*) to give rise to; **prendre ~** to originate; **aveugle de ~** born blind; **Français de ~** French by birth; **à la ~ des cheveux** at the roots of the hair; **lieu de ~** place of birth

naissant, e [nɛsɑ̃, -ɑ̃t] VB *voir* **naître** ▶ ADJ budding, incipient; (*jour*) dawning

naît [nɛ] VB *voir* **naître**

naître [nɛtʀ] /59/ VI to be born; (*conflit, complications*): **~ de** to arise from, be born out of; **~ à** (*amour, poésie*) to awaken to; **je suis né en 1960** I was born in 1960; **il naît plus de filles que de garçons** there are more girls born than boys; **faire ~** (*fig*) to give rise to, arouse

naïvement [naivmɑ̃] ADV naïvely

naïveté [naivte] NF naivety

Namibie [namibi] NF: **la ~** Namibia

nana [nana] NF (*fam: fille*) bird (BRIT), chick

nantais, e [nɑ̃tɛ, -ɛz] ADJ of *ou* from Nantes

nantir [nɑ̃tiʀ] /2/ VT: **~ qn de** to provide sb with; **les nantis** (*péj*) the well-to-do

napalm [napalm] NM napalm

naphtaline [naftalin] NF: **boules de ~** mothballs

Naples [napl] N Naples

napolitain, e [napɔlitɛ̃, -ɛn] ADJ Neapolitan; **tranche ~** Neapolitan ice cream

nappe [nap] NF tablecloth; (*fig*) sheet; (*de pétrole, gaz*) layer; **~ de mazout** oil slick; **~ (phréatique)** water table

napper [nape] /1/ VT: **~ qch de** to coat sth with

napperon [napʀɔ̃] NM table-mat; **~ individuel** place mat

naquis *etc* [naki] VB *voir* **naître**

narcisse [naʀsis] NM narcissus

narcissique [naʀsisik] ADJ narcissistic

narcissisme [naʀsisism] NM narcissism

narcodollars [naʀkodɔlaʀ] NMPL drug money *no pl*

narcotique [naʀkɔtik] ADJ, NM narcotic

narguer [naʀge] /1/ VT to taunt

narine [naʀin] NF nostril

narquois, e [naʀkwa, -waz] ADJ derisive, mocking

narrateur, -trice [naʀatœʀ, -tʀis] NM/F narrator

narration [naʀasjɔ̃] NF narration, narrative; (*Scol*) essay

narrer [naʀe] /1/ VT to tell the story of, recount

NASA [naza] SIGLE F (= *National Aeronautics and Space Administration*) NASA

nasal, e, -aux [nazal, -o] ADJ nasal

naseau, x [nazo] NM nostril

nasillard, e [nazijaʀ, -aʀd] ADJ nasal

nasiller [nazije] /1/ VI to speak with a (nasal) twang

nasse [nas] NF fish-trap

natal, e [natal] ADJ native

nataliste [natalist] ADJ supporting a rising birth rate

natalité [natalite] NF birth rate

natation [natasjɔ̃] NF swimming; **faire de la ~** to go swimming (*regularly*)

natif, -ive [natif, -iv] ADJ native

nation [nasjɔ̃] NF nation; **les Nations unies (NU)** the United Nations (UN)

national, e, -aux [nasjɔnal, -o] ADJ national ▶ NF: **(route) ~** ≈ A road (BRIT), ≈ state highway (US); **obsèques nationales** state funeral

nationalisation [nasjɔnalizasjɔ̃] NF nationalization

nationaliser [nasjɔnalize] /1/ VT to nationalize

nationalisme [nasjɔnalism] NM nationalism
nationaliste [nasjɔnalist] ADJ, NMF nationalist
nationalité [nasjɔnalite] NF nationality; **de ~ française** of French nationality
natte [nat] NF (*tapis*) mat; (*cheveux*) plait
natter [nate] /1/ VT (*cheveux*) to plait
naturalisation [natyralizasjɔ̃] NF naturalization
naturaliser [natyralize] /1/ VT to naturalize; (*empailler*) to stuff
naturaliste [natyralist] NMF naturalist; (*empailleur*) taxidermist
nature [natyr] NF nature ▶ ADJ, ADV (*Culin*) plain, without seasoning or sweetening; (*café, thé: sans lait*) black; (: *sans sucre*) without sugar; (*yaourt*) natural; **payer en ~** to pay in kind; **peint d'après ~** painted from life; **être de ~ à faire qch** (*propre à*) to be the sort of thing (*ou* person) to do sth; **~ morte** still-life
naturel, le [natyrɛl] ADJ natural ▶ NM naturalness; (*caractère*) disposition, nature; (*autochtone*) native; **au ~** (*Culin*) in water; in its own juices
naturellement [natyrɛlmɑ̃] ADV naturally; (*bien sûr*) of course
naturisme [natyrism] NM naturism
naturiste [natyrist] NMF naturist
naufrage [nofraʒ] NM (*ship*)wreck; (*fig*) wreck; **faire ~** to be shipwrecked
naufragé, e [nofraʒe] NM/F shipwreck victim, castaway
nauséabond, e [nozeabɔ̃, -ɔ̃d] ADJ foul, nauseous
nausée [noze] NF nausea; **avoir la ~** to feel sick; **avoir des nausées** to have waves of nausea, feel nauseous *ou* sick
nautique [notik] ADJ nautical, water *cpd*; **sports nautiques** water sports
nautisme [notism] NM water sports *pl*
naval, e [naval] ADJ naval; (*industrie*) shipbuilding
navarrais, e [navarɛ, -ɛz] ADJ Navarrese
navet [navɛ] NM turnip; (*péj: film*) third-rate film
navette [navɛt] NF shuttle; (*en car etc*) shuttle (service); **faire la ~ (entre)** to go to and fro (between), shuttle (between); **~ spatiale** space shuttle
navigabilité [navigabilite] NF (*d'un navire*) seaworthiness; (*d'un avion*) airworthiness
navigable [navigabl] ADJ navigable
navigant, e [navigɑ̃, -ɑ̃t] ADJ (*Aviat: personnel*) flying ▶ NM/F: **les navigants** the flying staff *ou* personnel
navigateur [navigatœr] NM (*Navig*) seafarer, sailor; (*Aviat*) navigator; (*Inform*) browser
navigation [navigasjɔ̃] NF navigation, sailing; (*Comm*) shipping; **compagnie de ~** shipping company; **~ spatiale** space navigation
naviguer [navige] /1/ VI to navigate, sail; **~ sur Internet** to browse the Internet
navire [navir] NM ship; **~ de guerre** warship; **~ marchand** merchantman
navire-citerne [navirsitɛrn] (*pl* **navires-citernes**) NM tanker

navire-hôpital [navirɔpital] (*pl* **navires-hôpitaux** [-to]) NM hospital ship
navrant, e [navrɑ̃, -ɑ̃t] ADJ (*affligeant*) upsetting; (*consternant*) annoying
navrer [navre] /1/ VT to upset, distress; **je suis navré (de/de faire/que)** I'm so sorry (for/for doing/that)
NB ABR (= *nota bene*) NB
nbr. ABR = **nombre**
nbses ABR = **nombreuses**
ND SIGLE F = **Notre Dame**
NDA SIGLE F = **note de l'auteur**
NDE SIGLE F = **note de l'éditeur**
NDLR SIGLE F = **note de la rédaction**
NDT SIGLE F = **note du traducteur**
ne, n' [nə, n] ADV *voir* **pas¹**; **plus²**; **jamais** *etc*; (*sans valeur négative: non traduit*): **c'est plus loin que je ne le croyais** it's further than I thought
né, e [ne] PP *de* **naître** ▶ ADJ: **un comédien né** a born comedian; **né en 1960** born in 1960; **née Scott** née Scott; **né(e) de ... et de ...** son/daughter of ... and of ...; **né d'une mère française** having a French mother; **né pour commander** born to lead
néanmoins [neɑ̃mwɛ̃] ADV nevertheless, yet
néant [neɑ̃] NM nothingness; **réduire à ~** to bring to nought; (*espoir*) to dash
nébuleux, -euse [nebylø, -øz] ADJ (*ciel*) cloudy; (*fig*) nebulous ▶ NF (*Astronomie*) nebula
nébuliser [nebylize] /1/ VT (*liquide*) to spray
nébulosité [nebylozite] NF cloud cover; **~ variable** cloudy in places
nécessaire [neseser] ADJ necessary ▶ NM necessary; (*sac*) kit; **faire le ~** to do the necessary; **n'emporter que le strict ~** to take only what is strictly necessary; **~ de couture** sewing kit; **~ de toilette** toilet bag; **~ de voyage** overnight bag
nécessairement [nesesɛrmɑ̃] ADV necessarily
nécessité [nesesite] NF necessity; **se trouver dans la ~ de faire qch** to find it necessary to do sth; **par ~** out of necessity
nécessiter [nesesite] /1/ VT to require
nécessiteux, -euse [nesesitø, -øz] ADJ needy
nec plus ultra [nekplysyltra] NM: **le ~ de** the last word in
nécrologie [nekrɔlɔʒi] NF obituary
nécrologique [nekrɔlɔʒik] ADJ: **article ~** obituary; **rubrique ~** obituary column
nécromancie [nekrɔmɑ̃si] NF necromancy
nécrose [nekroz] NF necrosis
nectar [nɛktar] NM nectar
nectarine [nɛktarin] NF nectarine
néerlandais, e [neɛrlɑ̃dɛ, -ɛz] ADJ Dutch, of the Netherlands ▶ NM (*Ling*) Dutch ▶ NM/F: **N~, e** Dutchman/woman; **les N~** the Dutch
nef [nɛf] NF (*d'église*) nave
néfaste [nefast] ADJ (*nuisible*) harmful; (*funeste*) ill-fated
négatif, -ive [negatif, -iv] ADJ negative ▶ NM (*Photo*) negative
négation [negasjɔ̃] NF denial; (*Ling*) negation
négativement [negativmɑ̃] ADV: **répondre ~** to give a negative response

n

négligé, e [negliʒe] ADJ (*en désordre*) slovenly
▶ NM (*tenue*) negligee
négligeable [negliʒabl] ADJ insignificant,
negligible
négligemment [negliʒamɑ̃] ADV carelessly
négligence [negliʒɑ̃s] NF carelessness *no pl*;
(*faute*) careless omission
négligent, e [negliʒɑ̃, -ɑ̃t] ADJ careless; (*Jur etc*)
negligent
négliger [negliʒe] /3/ VT (*épouse, jardin*) to
neglect; (*tenue*) to be careless about; (*avis,
précautions*) to disregard, overlook; ~ **de faire** to
fail to do, not bother to do; **se négliger** to
neglect o.s.
négoce [negɔs] NM trade
négociable [negɔsjabl] ADJ negotiable
négociant, e [negɔsjɑ̃, -ɑ̃t] NM/F merchant
négociateur [negɔsjatœʀ] NM negotiator
négociation [negɔsjasjɔ̃] NF negotiation;
négociations collectives collective
bargaining *sg*
négocier [negɔsje] /7/ VI, VT to negotiate
nègre [nɛgʀ] NM (*péj*) Negro (!); (*péj: écrivain*)
ghost writer ▶ ADJ (*péj*) Negro (!)
négresse [negʀɛs] NF (*péj*) Negress (!)
négrier [negʀije] NM (*fig*) slave driver
neige [nɛʒ] NF snow; **battre les œufs en ~**
(*Culin*) to whip *ou* beat the egg whites until stiff;
~ **carbonique** dry ice; ~ **fondue** (*par terre*) slush;
(*qui tombe*) sleet; ~ **poudreuse** powdery snow
neiger [neʒe] /3/ VI to snow
neigeux, -euse [nɛʒø, -øz] ADJ snowy,
snow-covered
nénuphar [nenyfaʀ] NM water-lily
néo-calédonien, ne [neɔkaledɔnjɛ̃, -ɛn] ADJ
New Caledonian ▶ NM/F: **N~, ne** native of New
Caledonia
néocapitalisme [neokapitalism] NM
neocapitalism
néo-colonialisme [neokɔlɔnjalism] NM
neocolonialism
néologisme [neɔlɔʒism] NM neologism
néon [neɔ̃] NM neon
néo-natal, e [neonatal] ADJ neonatal
néophyte [neɔfit] NMF novice
néo-zélandais, e [neozelɑ̃dɛ, -ɛz] ADJ New
Zealand *cpd* ▶ NM/F: **N~, e** New Zealander
Népal [nepal] NM: **le ~** Nepal
népalais, e [nepalɛ, -ɛz] ADJ Nepalese, Nepali
▶ NM (*Ling*) Nepalese, Nepali ▶ NM/F: **N~, e**
Nepalese, Nepali
néphrétique [nefʀetik] ADJ (*Méd: colique*)
nephritic
néphrite [nefʀit] NF (*Méd*) nephritis
népotisme [nepɔtism] NM nepotism
nerf [nɛʀ] NM nerve; (*fig*) spirit; (: *forces*)
stamina; **nerfs** NMPL nerves; **être** *ou* **vivre sur
les nerfs** to live on one's nerves; **être à bout
de nerfs** to be at the end of one's tether;
passer ses nerfs sur qn to take it out on sb
nerveusement [nɛʀvøzmɑ̃] ADV nervously
nerveux, -euse [nɛʀvø, -øz] ADJ nervous;
(*cheval*) highly-strung; (*irritable*) touchy, nervy;
(*voiture*) nippy, responsive; (*tendineux*) sinewy

nervosité [nɛʀvozite] NF nervousness;
(*émotivité*) excitability, tenseness
nervure [nɛʀvyʀ] NF (*de feuille*) vein; (*Archit, Tech*)
rib
n'est-ce pas [nɛspɑ] ADV isn't it?, won't you? *etc*
(*selon le verbe qui précède*); **c'est bon, ~?** it's good,
isn't it?; **il a peur, ~?** he's afraid, isn't he?;
~ **que c'est bon?** don't you think it's good?;
lui, ~, il peut se le permettre he, of course,
can afford to do that, can't he?
Net [nɛt] NM (*Internet*): **le ~** the Net
net, nette [nɛt] ADJ (*sans équivoque, distinct*) clear;
(*photo*) sharp; (*évident*) definite; (*amélioration,
différence*) marked, distinct; (*propre*) neat, clean;
(*Comm: prix, salaire, poids*) net ▶ ADV (*refuser*) flatly
▶ NM: **mettre au ~** to copy out; **s'arrêter ~** to
stop dead; **la lame a cassé ~** the blade snapped
clean through; **faire place nette** to make a
clean sweep; ~ **d'impôt** tax free
netiquette [netiket] NF netiquette
nettement [nɛtmɑ̃] ADV (*distinctement*) clearly;
(*évidemment*) definitely; (*incontestablement*)
decidedly; (*avec comparatif: superlatif*): ~ **mieux**
definitely *ou* clearly better
netteté [nɛtte] NF clearness
nettoie *etc* [netwa] VB *voir* **nettoyer**
nettoiement [netwamɑ̃] NM (*Admin*) cleaning;
service du ~ refuse collection
nettoierai *etc* [netwaʀe] VB *voir* **nettoyer**
nettoyage [netwajaʒ] NM cleaning; ~ **à sec** dry
cleaning
nettoyant [netwajɑ̃] NM (*produit*) cleaning
agent
nettoyer [netwaje] /8/ VT to clean; (*fig*) to clean
out
neuf¹ [nœf] NUM nine
neuf², neuve [nœf, nœv] ADJ new ▶ NM:
repeindre à ~ to redecorate; **remettre à ~** to do
up (as good as new), refurbish; **n'acheter que
du ~** to buy everything new; **quoi de ~?** what's
new?
neurasthénique [nøʀastenik] ADJ
neurasthenic
neurochirurgie [nøʀoʃiʀyʀʒi] NF neurosurgery
neurochirurgien [nøʀoʃiʀyʀʒjɛ̃] NM
neurosurgeon
neuroleptique [nøʀolɛptik] ADJ neuroleptic
neurologie [nøʀolɔʒi] NF neurology
neurologique [nøʀolɔʒik] ADJ neurological
neurologue [nøʀolɔg] NMF neurologist
neurone [nøʀɔn] NM neuron(e)
neuropsychiatre [nøʀopsikjatʀ] NMF
neuropsychiatrist
neutralisation [nøtʀalizasjɔ̃] NF
neutralization
neutraliser [nøtʀalize] /1/ VT to neutralize
neutralisme [nøtʀalism] NM neutralism
neutraliste [nøtʀalist] ADJ neutralist
neutralité [nøtʀalite] NF neutrality
neutre [nøtʀ] ADJ, NM (*Ling*) neuter; ~ **en
carbone** carbon neutral
neutron [nøtʀɔ̃] NM neutron
neuve [nœv] ADJ F *voir* **neuf²**
neuvième [nœvjɛm] NUM ninth

neveu, x [nəvø] NM nephew

névralgie [nevralʒi] NF neuralgia

névralgique [nevralʒik] ADJ (fig: sensible) sensitive; **centre ~** nerve centre

névrite [nevrit] NF neuritis

névrose [nevroz] NF neurosis

névrosé, e [nevroze] ADJ, NM/F neurotic

névrotique [nevrɔtik] ADJ neurotic

New York [njujɔrk] N New York

new-yorkais, e [njujɔrkɛ, -ɛz] ADJ of ou from New York, New York cpd ▶ NM/F: **New-Yorkais, e** New Yorker

nez [ne] NM nose; **rire au ~ de qn** to laugh in sb's face; **avoir du ~** to have flair; **avoir le ~ fin** to have foresight; **~ à ~ avec** face to face with; **à vue de ~** roughly

NF SIGLE MPL = **nouveaux francs** ▶ SIGLE F (Industrie: = norme française) industrial standard

ni [ni] CONJ: **ni ... ni** neither ... nor; **je n'aime ni les lentilles ni les épinards** I like neither lentils nor spinach; **il n'a dit ni oui ni non** he didn't say either yes or no; **elles ne sont venues ni l'une ni l'autre** neither of them came; **il n'a rien vu ni entendu** he didn't see or hear anything

Niagara [njagara] NM: **les chutes du ~** the Niagara Falls

niais, e [njɛ, -ɛz] ADJ silly, thick

niaiserie [njɛzri] NF gullibility; (action, propos, futilité) silliness

Nicaragua [nikaragwa] NM: **le ~** Nicaragua

nicaraguayen, ne [nikaragwajɛ̃, -ɛn] ADJ Nicaraguan ▶ NM/F: **N~, ne** Nicaraguan

Nice [nis] N Nice

niche [niʃ] NF (du chien) kennel; (de mur) recess, niche; (farce) trick

nichée [niʃe] NF brood, nest

nicher [niʃe] /1/ VI to nest; **se ~ dans** (personne: se blottir) to snuggle into; (: se cacher) to hide in; (objet) to lodge itself in

nichon [niʃɔ̃] NM (fam) boob, tit

nickel [nikɛl] NM nickel

niçois, e [niswa, -waz] ADJ of ou from Nice; (Culin) Niçoise

nicotine [nikɔtin] NF nicotine

nid [ni] NM nest; (fig: repaire etc) den, lair; **~ d'abeilles** (Couture, Textiles) honeycomb stitch; **~ de poule** pothole

nièce [njɛs] NF niece

nième [ɛnjɛm] ADJ: **la ~ fois** the nth ou umpteenth time

nier [nje] /7/ VT to deny

nigaud, e [nigo, -od] NM/F booby, fool

Niger [niʒɛr] NM: **le ~** Niger; (fleuve) the Niger

Nigéria [niʒerja] NM ou F Nigeria

nigérian, e [niʒerjɑ̃, -an] ADJ Nigerian ▶ NM/F: **N~, e** Nigerian

nigérien, ne [niʒerjɛ̃, -ɛn] ADJ of ou from Niger

night-club [najtklœb] NM nightclub

nihilisme [niilism] NM nihilism

nihiliste [niilist] ADJ nihilist, nihilistic

Nil [nil] NM: **le ~** the Nile

n'importe [nɛ̃pɔrt] ADV: **~!** no matter!; **~ qui/quoi/où** anybody/anything/anywhere; **~ quoi!**
(fam: désapprobation) what rubbish!; **~ quand** any time; **~ quel/quelle** any; **~ lequel/laquelle** any (one); **~ comment** (sans soin) carelessly; **~ comment, il part ce soir** he's leaving tonight in any case

nippes [nip] NFPL (fam) togs

nippon, e ou **ne** [nipɔ̃, -ɔn] ADJ Japanese

nique [nik] NF: **faire la ~ à** to thumb one's nose at (fig)

nitouche [nituʃ] NF (péj): **c'est une sainte ~** she looks as if butter wouldn't melt in her mouth

nitrate [nitrat] NM nitrate

nitrique [nitrik] ADJ: **acide ~** nitric acid

nitroglycérine [nitrɔgliserin] NF nitroglycerin(e)

niveau, x [nivo] NM level; (des élèves, études) standard; **au ~ de** at the level of; (personne) on a level with; **de ~ (avec)** level (with); **le ~ de la mer** sea level; **~ (à bulle)** spirit level; **~ (d'eau)** water level; **~ de vie** standard of living

niveler [nivle] /4/ VT to level

niveleuse [nivløz] NF (Tech) grader

nivellement [nivɛlmɑ̃] NM levelling

nivernais, e [nivɛrnɛ, -ɛz] ADJ of ou from Nevers (and region) ▶ NM/F: **N~, e** inhabitant ou native of Nevers (and region)

NL SIGLE F = **nouvelle lune**

NN ABR (= nouvelle norme) revised standard of hotel classification

n° ABR (numéro)

nobiliaire [nɔbiljɛr] ADJ F voir **particule**

noble [nɔbl] ADJ noble; (de qualité: métal etc) precious ▶ NM F noble(man/-woman)

noblesse [nɔbles] NF (classe sociale) nobility; (d'une action etc) nobleness

noce [nɔs] NF wedding; (gens) wedding party (ou guests pl); **il l'a épousée en secondes noces** she was his second wife; **faire la ~** (fam) to go on a binge; **noces d'or/d'argent/de diamant** golden/silver/diamond wedding

noceur [nɔsœr] NM (fam): **c'est un sacré ~** he's a real party animal

nocif, -ive [nɔsif, -iv] ADJ harmful, noxious

noctambule [nɔktɑ̃byl] NM night-bird

nocturne [nɔktyrn] ADJ nocturnal ▶ NF (Sport) floodlit fixture; (d'un magasin) late opening

Noël [nɔɛl] NM Christmas; **la (fête de) ~** Christmas time

nœud [nø] NM (de corde, du bois, Navig) knot; (ruban) bow; (fig: liens) bond, tie; (: d'une question) crux; (: Théât etc): **le ~ de l'action** the web of events; **~ coulant** noose; **~ gordien** Gordian knot; **~ papillon** bow tie

noie etc [nwa] VB voir **noyer**

noir, e [nwar] ADJ black; (obscur, sombre) dark ▶ NM/F black man/woman ▶ NM: **dans le ~** in the dark ▶ NF (Mus) crotchet (BRIT), quarter note (US); **il fait ~** it is dark; **au ~** adv (acheter, vendre) on the black market; **travail au ~** moonlighting; **travailler au ~** to work on the side

noirâtre [nwaratr] ADJ (teinte) blackish

noirceur [nwarsœr] NF blackness; darkness

noircir [nwarsir] /2/ VT, VI to blacken

noise [nwaz] NF: **chercher ~ à** to try and pick a quarrel with

noisetier [nwaztje] NM hazel (tree)

noisette [nwazɛt] NF hazelnut; (*morceau: de beurre etc*) small knob ▶ ADJ (*yeux*) hazel

noix [nwa] NF walnut; (*fam*) twit; (*Culin*): **une ~ de beurre** a knob of butter; **à la ~** (*fam*) worthless; **~ de cajou** cashew nut; **~ de coco** coconut; **~ muscade** nutmeg; **~ de veau** (*Culin*) round fillet of veal

nom [nɔ̃] NM name; (*Ling*) noun; **connaître qn de ~** to know sb by name; **au ~ de** in the name of; **~ d'une pipe** *ou* **d'un chien!** (*fam*) for goodness' sake!; **~ de Dieu!** (!) bloody hell! (BRIT), my God!; **~ commun/propre** common/ proper noun; **~ composé** (*Ling*) compound noun; **~ déposé** trade name; **~ d'emprunt** assumed name; **~ de famille** surname; **~ de fichier** file name; **~ de jeune fille** maiden name; **~ d'utilisateur** username

nomade [nɔmad] ADJ nomadic ▶ NMF nomad

nombre [nɔ̃bʀ] NM number; **venir en ~** to come in large numbers; **depuis ~ d'années** for many years; **ils sont au ~ de trois** there are three of them; **au ~ de mes amis** among my friends; **sans ~** countless; **(bon) ~ de** (*beaucoup, plusieurs*) a (large) number of; **~ premier/entier** prime/ whole number

nombreux, -euse [nɔ̃bʀø, -øz] ADJ many, numerous; (*avec nom sg: foule etc*) large; **peu ~** few; small; **de ~ cas** many cases

nombril [nɔ̃bʀi(l)] NM navel

nomenclature [nɔmãklatyʀ] NF wordlist; list of items

nominal, e, -aux [nɔminal, -o] ADJ nominal; (*appel, liste*) of names

nominatif, -ive [nɔminatif, -iv] NM (*Ling*) nominative ▶ ADJ: **liste nominative** list of names; **carte nominative** calling card; **titre ~** registered name

nomination [nɔminasjɔ̃] NF nomination

nommément [nɔmemã] ADV (*désigner*) by name

nommer [nɔme] /1/ VT (*baptiser*) to name, give a name to; (*qualifier*) to call; (*mentionner*) to name, give the name of; (*élire*) to appoint, nominate; **se nommer** VR: **il se nomme Pascal** his name's Pascal, he's called Pascal

non [nɔ̃] ADV (*réponse*) no; (*suivi d'un adjectif, adverbe*) not; **Paul est venu, ~?** Paul came, didn't he?; **répondre** *ou* **dire que ~** to say no; **~ pas que** not that; **~ plus, moi ~ plus** neither do I, I don't either; **je préférerais que ~** I would prefer not; **il se trouve que ~** perhaps not; **je pense que ~** I don't think so; **~ mais!** well really!; **~ mais des fois!** you must be joking!; **~ alcoolisé** non-alcoholic; **~ loin/ seulement** not far/only

nonagénaire [nɔnaʒenɛʀ] NMF nonagenarian

non-agression [nɔnagʀesjɔ̃] NF: **pacte de ~** non-aggression pact

nonante [nɔnãt] NUM (BELGIQUE, SUISSE) ninety

non-assistance [nɔnasistãs] NF (*Jur*): **~ à personne en danger** *failure to render assistance to a person in danger*

nonce [nɔ̃s] NM (*Rel*) nuncio

nonchalamment [nɔ̃ʃalamã] ADV nonchalantly

nonchalance [nɔ̃ʃalãs] NF nonchalance, casualness

nonchalant, e [nɔ̃ʃalã, -ãt] ADJ nonchalant, casual

non-conformisme [nɔ̃kɔ̃fɔʀmism] NM nonconformism

non-conformiste [nɔ̃kɔ̃fɔʀmist] ADJ, NMF non-conformist

non-conformité [nɔ̃kɔ̃fɔʀmite] NF nonconformity

non-croyant, e [nɔ̃kʀwajã, -ãt] NM/F (*Rel*) non-believer

non-engagé, e [nɔ̃ãgaʒe] ADJ non-aligned

non-fumeur, -euse [nɔ̃fymœʀ, -øz] NM/F non-smoker

non-ingérence [nɔnɛ̃ʒeʀãs] NF non-interference

non-initié, e [nɔ̃ninisje] NM/F lay person; **les non-initiés** the uninitiated

non-inscrit, e [nɔnɛ̃skʀi, -it] NM/F (*Pol: député*) independent

non-intervention [nɔnɛ̃tɛʀvãsjɔ̃] NF non-intervention

non-lieu [nɔ̃ljø] NM: **il y a eu ~** the case was dismissed

nonne [nɔn] NF nun

nonobstant [nɔnɔpstã] PRÉP notwithstanding

non-paiement [nɔ̃pemã] NM non-payment

non-prolifération [nɔ̃pʀɔliferasjɔ̃] NF non-proliferation

non-résident [nɔ̃ʀezidã] NM (*Écon*) non-resident

non-retour [nɔ̃ʀətuʀ] NM: **point de ~** point of no return

non-sens [nɔ̃sãs] NM absurdity

non-spécialiste [nɔ̃spesjalist] NMF non-specialist

non-stop [nɔnstɔp] ADJ INV nonstop

non-syndiqué, e [nɔ̃sɛ̃dike] NM/F non-union member

non-violence [nɔ̃vjɔlãs] NF nonviolence

non-violent, e [nɔ̃vjɔlã, -ãt] ADJ non-violent

nord [nɔʀ] NM North ▶ ADJ INV northern; north; **au ~** (*situation*) in the north; (*direction*) to the north; **au ~ de** north of, to the north of; **perdre le ~** to lose one's way (*fig*)

nord-africain, e [nɔʀafʀikɛ̃, -ɛn] ADJ North-African ▶ NM/F: **Nord-Africain, e** North African

nord-américain, e [nɔʀamerikɛ̃, -ɛn] ADJ North American ▶ NM/F: **Nord-Américain, e** North American

nord-coréen, ne [nɔʀkɔʀeɛ̃, -ɛn] ADJ North Korean ▶ NM/F: **Nord-Coréen, ne** North Korean

nord-est [nɔʀɛst] NM North-East

nordique [nɔʀdik] ADJ (*pays, race*) Nordic; (*langues*) Scandinavian, Nordic ▶ NMF: **N~** Scandinavian

nord-ouest [nɔʀwɛst] NM North-West

nord-vietnamien, ne [nɔʀvjɛtnamjɛ̃, -ɛn] ADJ

North Vietnamese ▶ NM/F: **Nord-Vietnamien, ne** North Vietnamese

normal, e, -aux [nɔrmal, -o] ADJ normal ▶ NF: **la ~** the norm, the average; **c'est tout à fait ~** it's perfectly natural; **vous trouvez ça ~?** does it seem right to you?

normalement [nɔrmalmɑ̃] ADV (*en général*) normally; (*comme prévu*): **~, il le fera demain** he should be doing it tomorrow, he's supposed to do it tomorrow

normalien, ne [nɔrmaljɛ̃, -ɛn] NM/F *student of École normale supérieure*

normalisation [nɔrmalizasjɔ̃] NF standardization; normalization

normaliser [nɔrmalize] /**1**/ VT (*Comm, Tech*) to standardize; (*Pol*) to normalize

normand, e [nɔrmɑ̃, -ɑ̃d] ADJ (*de Normandie*) Norman ▶ NM/F: **N~, e** (*de Normandie*) Norman

Normandie [nɔrmɑ̃di] NF: **la ~** Normandy

norme [nɔrm] NF norm; (*Tech*) standard

Norvège [nɔrvɛʒ] NF: **la ~** Norway

norvégien, ne [nɔrveʒjɛ̃, -ɛn] ADJ Norwegian ▶ NM (*Ling*) Norwegian ▶ NM/F: **N~, ne** Norwegian

nos [no] ADJ POSS *voir* **notre**

nostalgie [nɔstalʒi] NF nostalgia

nostalgique [nɔstalʒik] ADJ nostalgic

notable [nɔtabl] ADJ notable, noteworthy; (*marqué*) noticeable, marked ▶ NM prominent citizen

notablement [nɔtabləmɑ̃] ADV notably; (*sensiblement*) noticeably

notaire [nɔtɛr] NM notary; solicitor

notamment [nɔtamɑ̃] ADV in particular, among others

notariat [nɔtarja] NM profession of notary (*ou* solicitor)

notarié, e [nɔtarje] ADJ: **acte ~** deed drawn up by a notary (*ou* solicitor)

notation [nɔtasjɔ̃] NF notation

note [nɔt] NF (*écrite, Mus*) note; (*Scol*) mark (BRIT), grade; (*facture*) bill; **prendre des notes** to take notes; **prendre ~ de** to note; (*par écrit*) to note, write down; **dans la ~** exactly right; **forcer la ~** to exaggerate; **une ~ de tristesse/de gaieté** a sad/happy note; **~ de service** memorandum

noté, e [nɔte] ADJ: **être bien/mal ~** (*employé etc*) to have a good/bad record

noter [nɔte] /**1**/ VT (*écrire*) to write down, note; (*remarquer*) to note, notice; (*Scol, Admin: donner une appréciation: devoir*) to mark, give a grade to; **notez bien que …** (please) note that …

notice [nɔtis] NF summary, short article; (*brochure*): **~ explicative** explanatory leaflet, instruction booklet

notification [nɔtifikasjɔ̃] NF notification

notifier [nɔtifje] /**7**/ VT: **~ qch à qn** to notify sb of sth, notify sth to sb

notion [nosjɔ̃] NF notion, idea; **notions** NFPL (*rudiments*) rudiments

notoire [nɔtwar] ADJ widely known; (*en mal*) notorious; **le fait est ~** the fact is common knowledge

notoriété [nɔtɔrjete] NF: **c'est de ~ publique** it's common knowledge

notre [nɔtr(ə)] (*pl* **nos** [no]) ADJ POSS our

nôtre [notr] ADJ ours ▶ PRON: **le/la ~** ours; **les nôtres** ours; (*alliés etc*) our own people; **soyez des nôtres** join us

nouba [nuba] NF (*fam*): **faire la ~** to live it up

nouer [nwe] /**1**/ VT to tie, knot; (*fig: alliance etc*) to strike up; **~ la conversation** to start a conversation; **se nouer** VI: **c'est là où l'intrigue se noue** it's at that point that the strands of the plot come together; **ma gorge se noua** a lump came to my throat

noueux, -euse [nwø, -øz] ADJ gnarled

nougat [nuga] NM nougat

nougatine [nugatin] NF *kind of nougat*

nouille [nuj] NF (*fam*) noodle (BRIT), fathead; **nouilles** NFPL (*pâtes*) noodles; pasta *sg*

nounou [nunu] NF nanny

nounours [nunurs] NM teddy (bear)

nourri, e [nuri] ADJ (*feu etc*) sustained

nourrice [nuris] NF ≈ child-minder; (*autrefois*) wet-nurse

nourrir [nurir] /**2**/ VT to feed; (*fig: espoir*) to harbour, nurse; **logé nourri** with board and lodging; **~ au sein** to breast-feed; **se ~ de légumes** to live on vegetables

nourrissant, e [nurisɑ̃, -ɑ̃t] ADJ nourishing, nutritious

nourrisson [nurisɔ̃] NM (*unweaned*) infant

nourriture [nurityr] NF food

nous [nu] PRON (*sujet*) we; (*objet*) us

nous-mêmes [numɛm] PRON ourselves

nouveau, nouvel, -elle, x [nuvo, -ɛl] ADJ new; (*original*) novel ▶ NM/F new pupil (*ou* employee) ▶ NM: **il y a du ~** there's something new ▶ NF (*piece of*) news *sg*; (*Littérature*) short story; **nouvelles** NFPL (*Presse, TV*) news; **de ~, à ~** again; **je suis sans nouvelles de lui** I haven't heard from him; **Nouvel An** New Year; **~ venu, nouvelle venue** newcomer; **nouveaux mariés** newly-weds; **nouvelle vague** new wave

nouveau-né, e [nuvone] NM/F newborn (baby)

nouveauté [nuvote] NF novelty; (*chose nouvelle*) innovation, something new; (*Comm*) new film (*ou* book *ou* creation *etc*)

nouvel, -elle [nuvɛl] ADJ ▶ NF *voir* **nouveau**

Nouvelle-Angleterre [nuvɛlɑ̃glətɛr] NF: **la ~** New England

Nouvelle-Calédonie [nuvɛlkaledɔni] NF: **la ~** New Caledonia

Nouvelle-Écosse [nuvɛlekɔs] NF: **la ~** Nova Scotia

Nouvelle-Galles du Sud [nuvɛlgaldysyd] NF: **la ~** New South Wales

Nouvelle-Guinée [nuvɛlgine] NF: **la ~** New Guinea

nouvellement [nuvɛlmɑ̃] ADV (*arrivé etc*) recently, newly

Nouvelle-Orléans [nuvɛlɔrleɑ̃] NF: **la ~** New Orleans

Nouvelles-Hébrides [nuvɛlsebrid] NFPL: **les ~** the New Hebrides

Nouvelle-Zélande [nuvɛlzelɑ̃d] NF: **la ~** New Zealand

n

nouvelliste [nuvelist] NMF editor *ou* writer of short stories

novateur, -trice [nɔvatœʀ, -tʀis] ADJ innovative ▶ NM/F innovator

novembre [nɔvɑ̃bʀ] NM November; *see note; voir aussi* **juillet**

> Le 11 *novembre* is a public holiday in France and commemorates the signing of the armistice, near Compiègne, at the end of the First World War.

novice [nɔvis] ADJ inexperienced ▶ NMF novice

noviciat [nɔvisja] NM (*Rel*) noviciate

noyade [nwajad] NF drowning *no pl*

noyau, x [nwajo] NM (*de fruit*) stone; (*Bio, Physique*) nucleus; (*Élec, Géo, fig: centre*) core; (*fig: d'artistes etc*) group; (*: de résistants etc*) cell

noyautage [nwajotaʒ] NM (*Pol*) infiltration

noyauter [nwajote] /1/ VT (*Pol*) to infiltrate

noyé, e [nwaje] NM/F drowning (*ou* drowned) man/woman ▶ ADJ (*fig: dépassé*) out of one's depth

noyer [nwaje] /8/ NM walnut (tree); (*bois*) walnut ▶ VT to drown; (*fig*) to flood; to submerge; (*Auto: moteur*) to flood; **se noyer** to be drowned, drown; (*suicide*) to drown o.s.; **~ son chagrin** to drown one's sorrows; **~ le poisson** to duck the issue

NSP SIGLE M (*Rel*) = **Notre Saint Père**; (*dans les sondages*: = *ne sais pas*) don't know

NT SIGLE M (= *Nouveau Testament*) NT

NU SIGLE FPL (= *Nations unies*) UN

nu, e [ny] ADJ naked; (*membres*) naked, bare; (*chambre, fil, plaine*) bare ▶ NM (*Art*) nude; **le nu intégral** total nudity; **tout nu** stark naked; **se mettre nu** to strip; **mettre à nu** to bare

nuage [nɥaʒ] NM cloud; **être dans les nuages** (*distrait*) to have one's head in the clouds; **~ de lait** drop of milk

nuageux, -euse [nɥaʒø, -øz] ADJ cloudy

nuance [nɥɑ̃s] NF (*de couleur, sens*) shade; **il y a une ~ (entre)** there's a slight difference (between); **une ~ de tristesse** a tinge of sadness

nuancé, e [nɥɑ̃se] ADJ (*opinion*) finely-shaded, subtly differing; **être ~ dans ses opinions** to have finely-shaded opinions

nuancer [nɥɑ̃se] /3/ VT (*pensée, opinion*) to qualify

nubile [nybil] ADJ nubile

nucléaire [nykleɛʀ] ADJ nuclear ▶ NM: **le ~** nuclear power

nudisme [nydism] NM nudism

nudiste [nydist] ADJ, NMF nudist

nudité [nydite] NF *voir* **nu** nudity, nakedness; bareness

nuée [nɥe] NF: **une ~ de** a cloud *ou* host *ou* swarm of

nues [ny] NFPL: **tomber des ~** to be taken aback; **porter qn aux ~** to praise sb to the skies

nui [nɥi] PP *de* **nuire**

nuire [nɥiʀ] /38/ VI to be harmful; **~ à** to harm, do damage to

nuisance [nɥizɑ̃s] NF nuisance; **nuisances**

NFPL pollution *sg*

nuisible [nɥizibl] ADJ harmful; (**animal**) **~** pest

nuisis *etc* [nɥizi] VB *voir* **nuire**

nuit [nɥi] NF night; **payer sa ~** to pay for one's overnight accommodation; **il fait ~** it's dark; **cette ~** (*hier*) last night; (*aujourd'hui*) tonight; **de ~** (*vol, service*) night *cpd*; **~ blanche** sleepless night; **~ de noces** wedding night; **~ de Noël** Christmas Eve

nuitamment [nɥitamɑ̃] ADV by night

nuitées [nɥite] NFPL overnight stays, beds occupied (*in statistics*)

nul, nulle [nyl] ADJ (*aucun*) no; (*minime*) nil, non-existent; (*non valable*) null; (*péj*) useless, hopeless ▶ PRON no one, no one; **résultat ~**, **match ~** draw; **nulle part** *adv* nowhere

nullement [nylmɑ̃] ADV by no means

nullité [nylite] NF nullity; (*péj*) hopelessness; (*: personne*) hopeless individual, nonentity

numéraire [nymeʀɛʀ] NM cash; metal currency

numéral, e, -aux [nymeʀal, -o] ADJ numeral

numérateur [nymeʀatœʀ] NM numerator

numération [nymeʀasjɔ̃] NF: **~ décimale/binaire** decimal/binary notation; **~ globulaire** blood count

numérique [nymeʀik] ADJ numerical; (*Inform, TV: affichage, son, télévision*) digital

numériquement [nymeʀikmɑ̃] ADV numerically; (*Inform*) digitally

numériser [nymeʀize] /1/ VT (*Inform*) to digitize

numéro [nymeʀo] NM number; (*spectacle*) act, turn; (*Presse*) issue, number; **faire** *ou* **composer un ~** to dial a number; **~ d'identification personnel** personal identification number (PIN); **~ d'immatriculation** *ou* **minéralogique** *ou* **de police** registration (BRIT) *ou* license (US) number; **~ de téléphone** (tele)phone number; **~ vert** ≈ Freefone® number (BRIT), ≈ toll-free number (US)

numérotage [nymeʀotaʒ] NM numbering

numérotation [nymeʀotasjɔ̃] NF numeration

numéroter [nymeʀote] /1/ VT to number

numerus clausus [nymeʀysklozys] NM INV restriction *ou* limitation of numbers

numismate [nymismat] NMF numismatist, coin collector

nu-pieds [nypje] NM INV sandal ▶ ADJ INV barefoot

nuptial, e, -aux [nypsjal, -o] ADJ nuptial; wedding *cpd*

nuptialité [nypsjalite] NF: **taux de ~** marriage rate

nuque [nyk] NF nape of the neck

nu-tête [nytɛt] ADJ INV bareheaded

nutritif, -ive [nytʀitif, -iv] ADJ (*besoins, valeur*) nutritional; (*aliment*) nutritious, nourishing

nutrition [nytʀisjɔ̃] NF nutrition

nutritionnel, le [nytʀisjɔnɛl] ADJ nutritional

nutritionniste [nytʀisjɔnist] NMF nutritionist

nylon [nilɔ̃] NM nylon

nymphomane [nɛ̃fɔman] ADJ, NF nymphomaniac

Oo

O, o [o] NM INV O, o ▶ ABR (= *ouest*) W;
O comme Oscar O for Oliver (*BRIT*) ou
Oboe (*US*)

OAS SIGLE F (= *Organisation de l'armée secrète*)
organization opposed to Algerian independence
(1961–63)

oasis [ɔazis] NM OU F oasis

obédience [ɔbedjɑ̃s] NF allegiance

obéir [ɔbeiʀ] /2/ VI to obey; ~ **à** to obey; (*moteur,
véhicule*) to respond to

obéissance [ɔbeisɑ̃s] NF obedience

obéissant, e [ɔbeisɑ̃, -ɑ̃t] ADJ obedient

obélisque [ɔbelisk] NM obelisk

obèse [ɔbɛz] ADJ obese

obésité [ɔbezite] NF obesity

objecter [ɔbʒɛkte] /1/ VT (*prétexter*) to plead,
put forward as an excuse; ~ **qch à** (*argument*) to
put forward sth against; ~ **(à qn) que** to object
(to sb) that

objecteur [ɔbʒɛktœʀ] NM: ~ **de conscience**
conscientious objector

objectif, -ive [ɔbʒɛktif, -iv] ADJ objective
▶ NM (*Optique, Photo*) lens *sg*; (*Mil, fig*) objective;
~ **grand angulaire/à focale variable**
wide-angle/zoom lens

objection [ɔbʒɛksjɔ̃] NF objection; ~ **de
conscience** conscientious objection

objectivement [ɔbʒɛktivmɑ̃] ADV objectively

objectivité [ɔbʒɛktivite] NF objectivity

objet [ɔbʒɛ] NM (*chose*) object; (*d'une discussion,
recherche*) subject; **être** ou **faire l'~ de** (*discussion*)
to be the subject of; (*soins*) to be given ou shown;
sans ~ *adj* purposeless; (*sans fondement*)
groundless; ~ **d'art** objet d'art; **objets
personnels** personal items; **objets de toilette**
toiletries; **objets trouvés** lost property *sg*
(*BRIT*), lost-and-found *sg* (*US*); **objets de valeur**
valuables

obligataire [ɔbligatɛʀ] ADJ bond *cpd* ▶ NMF
bondholder, debenture holder

obligation [ɔbligasjɔ̃] NF obligation; (*gén pl:
devoir*) duty; (*Comm*) bond, debenture; **sans ~
d'achat** with no obligation to buy; **être dans
l'~ de faire** to be obliged to do; **avoir l'~ de
faire** to be under an obligation to do;
obligations familiales family obligations ou
responsibilities; **obligations militaires**
military obligations ou duties

obligatoire [ɔbligatwaʀ] ADJ compulsory,
obligatory

obligatoirement [ɔbligatwaʀmɑ̃] ADV
compulsorily; (*fatalement*) necessarily; (*fam:
sans aucun doute*) inevitably

obligé, e [ɔbliʒe] ADJ (*redevable*): **être très ~ à qn**
to be most obliged to sb; (*contraint*): **je suis
(bien) ~ (de le faire)** I have to (do it); (*nécessaire:
conséquence*) necessary; **c'est ~!** it's inevitable!

obligeamment [ɔbliʒamɑ̃] ADV obligingly

obligeance [ɔbliʒɑ̃s] NF: **avoir l'~ de** to be kind
ou good enough to

obligeant, e [ɔbliʒɑ̃, -ɑ̃t] ADJ obliging; kind

obliger [ɔbliʒe] /3/ VT (*contraindre*): ~ **qn à faire** to
force ou oblige sb to do; (*Jur: engager*) to bind;
(*rendre service à*) to oblige; **je suis bien obligé
(de le faire)** I have to (do it)

oblique [ɔblik] ADJ oblique; **regard ~** sidelong
glance; **en ~** *adv* diagonally

obliquer [ɔblike] /1/ VI: ~ **vers** to turn off
towards

oblitération [ɔbliterasjɔ̃] NF cancelling *no pl*,
cancellation; obstruction

oblitérer [ɔblitere] /6/ VT (*timbre-poste*) to cancel;
(*Méd: canal, vaisseau*) to obstruct

oblong, oblongue [ɔblɔ̃, ɔblɔ̃g] ADJ oblong

obnubiler [ɔbnybile] /1/ VT to obsess

obole [ɔbɔl] NF offering

obscène [ɔpsɛn] ADJ obscene

obscénité [ɔpsenite] NF obscenity

obscur, e [ɔpskyʀ] ADJ (*sombre*) dark; (*fig: raisons*)
obscure; (*: sentiment, malaise*) vague; (*: personne,
vie*) humble, lowly

obscurcir [ɔpskyʀsiʀ] /2/ VT to darken; (*fig*) to
obscure; **s'obscurcir** VI to grow dark

obscurité [ɔpskyʀite] NF darkness; **dans l'~** in
the dark, in darkness; (*anonymat, médiocrité*) in
obscurity

obsédant, e [ɔpsedɑ̃, -ɑ̃t] ADJ obsessive

obsédé, e [ɔpsede] NM/F fanatic; ~**(e) sexuel(le)**
sex maniac

obséder [ɔpsede] /6/ VT to obsess, haunt

obsèques [ɔpsɛk] NFPL funeral *sg*

obséquieux, -euse [ɔpsekjø, -øz] ADJ
obsequious

observance [ɔpsɛʀvɑ̃s] NF observance

observateur, -trice [ɔpsɛʀvatœʀ, -tʀis] ADJ
observant, perceptive ▶ NM/F observer

o

observation [ɔpsɛrvasjɔ̃] NF observation; (d'un règlement etc) observance; (commentaire) observation, remark; (reproche) reproof; **en ~** (Méd) under observation

observatoire [ɔpsɛrvatwar] NM observatory; (lieu élevé) observation post, vantage point

observer [ɔpsɛrve] /**1**/ VT (regarder) to observe, watch; (examiner) to examine; (scientifiquement, aussi: règlement, jeûne etc) to observe; (surveiller) to watch; (remarquer) to observe, notice; **faire ~ qch à qn** (dire) to point out sth to sb; **s'observer** VI (se surveiller) to keep a check on o.s.

obsession [ɔpsesjɔ̃] NF obsession; **avoir l'~ de** to have an obsession with

obsessionnel, le [ɔpsesjɔnɛl] ADJ obsessive

obsolescent, e [ɔpsɔlesɑ̃, -ɑ̃t] ADJ obsolescent

obstacle [ɔpstakl] NM obstacle; (Équitation) jump, hurdle; **faire ~ à** (lumière) to block out; (projet) to hinder, put obstacles in the path of; **obstacles antichars** tank defences

obstétricien, ne [ɔpstetrisjɛ̃, -ɛn] NM/F obstetrician

obstétrique [ɔpstetrik] NF obstetrics sg

obstination [ɔpstinasjɔ̃] NF obstinacy

obstiné, e [ɔpstine] ADJ obstinate

obstinément [ɔpstinemɑ̃] ADV obstinately

obstiner [ɔpstine] /**1**/: **s'obstiner** VI to insist, dig one's heels in; **s'obstiner à faire** to persist (obstinately) in doing; **s'obstiner sur qch** to keep working at sth, labour away at sth

obstruction [ɔpstryksjɔ̃] NF obstruction, blockage; (Sport) obstruction; **faire de l'~** (fig) to be obstructive

obstruer [ɔpstrye] /**1**/ VT to block, obstruct; **s'obstruer** VI to become blocked

obtempérer [ɔptɑ̃pere] /**6**/ VI to obey; **~ à** to obey, comply with

obtenir [ɔptənir] /**22**/ VT to obtain, get; (total) to arrive at, reach; (résultat) to achieve, obtain; **~ de pouvoir faire** to obtain permission to do; **~ qch à qn** to obtain sth for sb; **~ de qn qu'il fasse** to get sb to agree to do(ing)

obtention [ɔptɑ̃sjɔ̃] NF obtaining

obtenu, e [ɔpt(ə)ny] PP de **obtenir**

obtiendrai [ɔptjɛ̃dre], **obtiens** [ɔptjɛ̃], **obtint** etc [ɔptɛ̃] VB voir **obtenir**

obturateur [ɔptyratœr] NM (Photo) shutter; **~ à rideau** focal plane shutter

obturation [ɔptyrasjɔ̃] NF closing (up); **~ (dentaire)** filling; **vitesse d'~** (Photo) shutter speed

obturer [ɔptyre] /**1**/ VT to close (up); (dent) to fill

obtus, e [ɔpty, -yz] ADJ obtuse

obus [ɔby] NM shell; **~ explosif** high-explosive shell; **~ incendiaire** incendiary device, fire bomb

obvier [ɔbvje] /**7**/: **~ à** VT to obviate

OC SIGLE FPL (= ondes courtes) SW

occasion [ɔkazjɔ̃] NF (aubaine, possibilité) opportunity; (circonstance) occasion; (Comm: article non neuf) secondhand buy; (: acquisition avantageuse) bargain; **à plusieurs occasions** on several occasions; **à la première ~** at the first ou earliest opportunity; **avoir l'~ de faire** to have the opportunity to do; **être l'~ de** to occasion, give rise to; **à l'~** adv sometimes, on occasions; (un jour) some time; **à l'~ de** on the occasion of; **d'~** adj, adv secondhand

occasionnel, le [ɔkazjɔnɛl] ADJ (fortuit) chance cpd; (non régulier) occasional; (: travail) casual

occasionnellement [ɔkazjɔnɛlmɑ̃] ADV occasionally, from time to time

occasionner [ɔkazjɔne] /**1**/ VT to cause, bring about; **~ qch à qn** to cause sb sth

occident [ɔksidɑ̃] NM: **l'O~** the West

occidental, e, -aux [ɔksidɑ̃tal, -o] ADJ western; (Pol) Western ▶ NM/F Westerner

occidentaliser [ɔksidɑ̃talize] /**1**/ VT (coutumes, mœurs) to westernize

occiput [ɔksipyt] NM back of the head, occiput

occire [ɔksir] VT to slay

occitan, e [ɔksitɑ̃, -an] ADJ of the langue d'oc, of Provençal French

occlusion [ɔklyzjɔ̃] NF: **~ intestinale** obstruction of the bowel

occulte [ɔkylt] ADJ occult, supernatural

occulter [ɔkylte] /**1**/ VT (fig) to overshadow

occupant, e [ɔkypɑ̃, -ɑ̃t] ADJ occupying ▶ NM/F (d'un appartement) occupier, occupant; (d'un véhicule) occupant ▶ NM (Mil) occupying forces pl; (Pol: d'usine etc) occupier

occupation [ɔkypasjɔ̃] NF occupation; **l'O~** the Occupation (of France)

occupationnel, le [ɔkypasjɔnɛl] ADJ: **thérapie ~** occupational therapy

occupé, e [ɔkype] ADJ (Mil, Pol) occupied; (personne: affairé, pris) busy; (esprit: absorbé) occupied; (place, sièges) taken; (toilettes) engaged; **la ligne est ~** the line's engaged (BRIT) ou busy (US)

occuper [ɔkype] /**1**/ VT to occupy; (poste, fonction) to hold; (main-d'œuvre) to employ; **s'~ (à qch)** to occupy o.s. ou keep o.s. busy (with sth); **s'~ de** (être responsable de) to be in charge of; (se charger de: affaire) to take charge of, deal with; (: clients etc) to attend to; (s'intéresser à, pratiquer: politique etc) to be involved in; **ça occupe trop de place** it takes up too much room

occurrence [ɔkyrɑ̃s] NF: **en l'~** in this case

OCDE SIGLE F (= Organisation de coopération et de développement économique) OECD

océan [ɔseɑ̃] NM ocean; **l'~ Indien** the Indian Ocean

Océanie [ɔseani] NF: **l'~** Oceania, South Sea Islands

océanique [ɔseanik] ADJ oceanic

océanographe [ɔseanɔgraf] NMF oceanographer

océanographie [ɔseanɔgrafi] NF oceanography

océanologie [ɔseanɔlɔʒi] NF oceanology

ocelot [ɔslo] NM (Zool) ocelot; (fourrure) ocelot fur

ocre [ɔkr] ADJ INV ochre

octane [ɔktan] NM octane

octante [ɔktɑ̃t] NUM (BELGIQUE, SUISSE) eighty

octave [ɔktav] NF octave

octet [ɔktɛ] NM byte

octobre [ɔktɔbr] NM October; voir aussi **juillet**

octogénaire [ɔktɔʒenɛʀ] ADJ, NMF octogenarian
octogonal, e, -aux [ɔktɔgɔnal, -o] ADJ octagonal
octogone [ɔktɔgɔn] NM octagon
octroi [ɔktʀwa] NM granting
octroyer [ɔktʀwaje] /8/ VT: ~ **qch à qn** to grant sth to sb, grant sb sth
oculaire [ɔkylɛʀ] ADJ ocular, eye *cpd* ▶ NM (*de microscope*) eyepiece
oculiste [ɔkylist] NMF eye specialist, oculist
ode [ɔd] NF ode
odeur [ɔdœʀ] NF smell
odieusement [ɔdjøzmɑ̃] ADV odiously
odieux, -euse [ɔdjø, -øz] ADJ odious, hateful
odontologie [ɔdɔ̃tɔlɔʒi] NF odontology
odorant, e [ɔdɔʀɑ̃, -ɑ̃t] ADJ sweet-smelling, fragrant
odorat [ɔdɔʀa] NM (sense of) smell; **avoir l'~ fin** to have a keen sense of smell
odoriférant, e [ɔdɔʀifeʀɑ̃, -ɑ̃t] ADJ sweet-smelling, fragrant
odyssée [ɔdise] NF odyssey
OEA SIGLE F (= *Organisation des États américains*) OAS
œcuménique [ekymenik] ADJ ecumenical
œdème [edɛm] NM oedema (BRIT), edema (US)
œil [œj] (*pl* **yeux** [jø]) NM eye; **avoir un ~ poché** *ou* **au beurre noir** to have a black eye; **à l'~** (*fam*) for free; **à l'~ nu** with the naked eye; **tenir qn à l'~** to keep an eye *ou* a watch on sb; **avoir l'~ à** to keep an eye on; **faire de l'~ à qn** to make eyes at sb; **voir qch d'un bon/mauvais ~** to view sth in a favourable/an unfavourable light; **à l'~ vif** with a lively expression; **à mes/ses yeux** in my/his eyes; **de ses propres yeux** with his own eyes; **fermer les yeux (sur)** (*fig*) to turn a blind eye (to); **les yeux fermés** (*aussi fig*) with one's eyes shut; **ouvrir l'~** (*fig*) to keep one's eyes open *ou* an eye out; **fermer l'~** to get a moment's sleep; **~ pour ~, dent pour dent** an eye for an eye, a tooth for a tooth; **pour les beaux yeux de qn** (*fig*) for love of sb; **~ de verre** glass eye
œil-de-bœuf [œjdəbœf] (*pl* **œils-de-bœuf**) NM bull's-eye (window)
œillade [œjad] NF: **lancer une ~ à qn** to wink at sb, give sb a wink; **faire des œillades à** to make eyes at
œillères [œjɛʀ] NFPL blinkers (BRIT), blinders (US); **avoir des ~** (*fig*) to be blinkered, wear blinders
œillet [œjɛ] NM (*Bot*) carnation; (*trou*) eyelet
œnologue [enɔlɔg] NMF wine expert
œsophage [ezɔfaʒ] NM oesophagus (BRIT), esophagus (US)
œstrogène [ɛstʀɔʒɛn] ADJ oestrogen (BRIT), estrogen (US)
œuf [œf] NM egg; **étouffer dans l'~** to nip in the bud; **~ à la coque/dur/mollet** boiled/hard-boiled/soft-boiled egg; **~ au plat/poché** fried/poached egg; **œufs brouillés** scrambled eggs; **~ de Pâques** Easter egg; **~ à repriser** darning egg
œuvre [œvʀ] NF (*tâche*) task, undertaking;

(*ouvrage achevé, livre, tableau etc*) work; (*ensemble de la production artistique*) works *pl*; (*organisation charitable*) charity ▶ NM (*d'un artiste*) works *pl*; (*Constr*): **le gros ~** the shell; **œuvres** NFPL (*actes*) deeds, works; **être/se mettre à l'~** to be at/get (down) to work; **mettre en ~** (*moyens*) to make use of; (*plan, loi, projet etc*) to implement; **~ d'art** work of art; **bonnes œuvres** good works *ou* deeds; **œuvres de bienfaisance** charitable works
OFCE SIGLE M (= *Observatoire français des conjonctures économiques*) economic research institute
offensant, e [ɔfɑ̃sɑ̃, -ɑ̃t] ADJ offensive, insulting
offense [ɔfɑ̃s] NF (*affront*) insult; (*Rel: péché*) transgression, trespass
offenser [ɔfɑ̃se] /1/ VT to offend, hurt; (*principes, Dieu*) to offend against; **s'offenser de** VI to take offence (BRIT) *ou* offense (US) at
offensif, -ive [ɔfɑ̃sif, -iv] ADJ (*armes, guerre*) offensive ▶ NF offensive; (*fig: du froid, de l'hiver*) onslaught; **passer à l'offensive** to go into the attack *ou* offensive
offert, e [ɔfɛʀ, -ɛʀt] PP *de* **offrir**
offertoire [ɔfɛʀtwaʀ] NM offertory
office [ɔfis] NM (*charge*) office; (*agence*) bureau, agency; (*Rel*) service ▶ NM *ou* F (*pièce*) pantry; **faire ~ de** to act as; to do duty as; **d'~** *adv* automatically; **bons offices** (*Pol*) good offices; **~ du tourisme** tourist office
officialiser [ɔfisjalize] /1/ VT to make official
officiel, le [ɔfisjɛl] ADJ, NM/F official
officiellement [ɔfisjɛlmɑ̃] ADV officially
officier [ɔfisje] /7/ NM officer ▶ VI (*Rel*) to officiate; **~ de l'état-civil** registrar; **~ ministériel** member of the legal profession; **~ de police** ≈ police officer
officieusement [ɔfisjøzmɑ̃] ADV unofficially
officieux, -euse [ɔfisjø, -øz] ADJ unofficial
officinal, e, -aux [ɔfisinal, -o] ADJ: **plantes officinales** medicinal plants
officine [ɔfisin] NF (*de pharmacie*) dispensary; (*Admin: pharmacie*) pharmacy; (*gén péj: bureau*) agency, office
offrais *etc* [ɔfʀɛ] VB *voir* **offrir**
offrande [ɔfʀɑ̃d] NF offering
offrant [ɔfʀɑ̃] NM: **au plus ~** to the highest bidder
offre [ɔfʀ] VB *voir* **offrir** ▶ NF offer; (*aux enchères*) bid; (*Admin: soumission*) tender; (*Écon*): **l'~ et la demande** supply and demand; **~ d'emploi** job advertised; **"offres d'emploi"** "situations vacant"; **~ publique d'achat** takeover bid; **offres de service** offer of service
offrir [ɔfʀiʀ] /18/ VT: **~ (à qn)** to offer (to sb); (*faire cadeau*) to give to (sb); **s'offrir** VI, VT (*se présenter: occasion, paysage*) to present itself; (*se payer: vacances, voiture*) to treat o.s. to; **~ (à qn) de faire qch** to offer to do sth (for sb); **~ à boire à qn** (*chez soi*) to offer sb a drink; **je vous offre un verre** I'll buy you a drink; **s'offrir à faire qch** to offer *ou* volunteer to do sth; **s'offrir comme guide/en otage** to offer one's services as (a) guide/offer o.s. as (a) hostage; **s'offrir aux regards** (*personne*) to expose o.s. to the public gaze

o

offset [ɔfsɛt] NM offset (printing)

offusquer [ɔfyske] /1/ VT to offend; **s'offusquer de** to take offence (BRIT) ou offense (US) at, be offended by

ogive [ɔʒiv] NF (Archit) diagonal rib; (d'obus, de missile) nose cone; **voûte en ~** rib vault; **arc en ~** lancet arch; **~ nucléaire** nuclear warhead

OGM SIGLE M (= organisme génétiquement modifié) GMO; **culture ~** GM crop

ogre [ɔgʀ] NM ogre

oh [o] EXCL oh!; **oh la la!** oh (dear)!; **pousser des oh! et des ah!** to gasp with admiration

oie [wa] NF (Zool) goose; **~ blanche** (fig) young innocent

oignon [ɔɲɔ̃] NM (Culin) onion; (de tulipe etc: bulbe) bulb; (Méd) bunion; **ce ne sont pas tes oignons** (fam) that's none of your business

oindre [wɛ̃dʀ] /49/ VT to anoint

oiseau, x [wazo] NM bird; **~ de proie** bird of prey

oiseau-mouche [wazomuʃ] (pl **oiseaux-mouches**) NM hummingbird

oiseleur [wazlœʀ] NM bird-catcher

oiselier, -ière [wazəlje, -jɛʀ] NM/F bird-seller

oisellerie [wazɛlʀi] NF bird shop

oiseux, -euse [wazø, -øz] ADJ pointless, idle; (sans valeur, importance) trivial

oisif, -ive [wazif, -iv] ADJ idle ▶ NM/F (péj) man/lady of leisure

oisillon [wazijɔ̃] NM little ou baby bird

oisiveté [wazivte] NF idleness

OIT SIGLE F (= Organisation internationale du travail) ILO

OK [oke] EXCL OK!, all right!

OL SIGLE FPL (= ondes longues) LW

oléagineux, -euse [ɔleaʒinø, -øz] ADJ oleaginous, oil-producing

oléiculture [ɔleikyltyʀ] NM olive growing

oléoduc [ɔleɔdyk] NM (oil) pipeline

olfactif, -ive [ɔlfaktif, -iv] ADJ olfactory

olibrius [ɔlibʀijys] NM oddball

oligarchie [ɔligaʀʃi] NF oligarchy

oligo-élément [ɔligɔelemɑ̃] NM trace element

oligopole [ɔligɔpɔl] NM oligopoly

olivâtre [ɔlivɑtʀ] ADJ olive-greenish; (teint) sallow

olive [ɔliv] NF (Bot) olive ▶ ADJ INV olive-green

oliveraie [ɔlivʀɛ] NF olive grove

olivier [ɔlivje] NM olive (tree); (bois) olive (wood)

olographe [ɔlɔgʀaf] ADJ: **testament ~** will written, dated and signed by the testator

OLP SIGLE F (= Organisation de libération de la Palestine) PLO

olympiade [ɔlɛ̃pjad] NF (période) Olympiad; **les olympiades** (jeux) the Olympiad sg

olympien, ne [ɔlɛ̃pjɛ̃, -ɛn] ADJ Olympian, of Olympian aloofness

olympique [ɔlɛ̃pik] ADJ Olympic

OM SIGLE FPL (= ondes moyennes) MW

Oman [ɔman] NM: **l'~, le sultanat d'~** (the Sultanate of) Oman

ombilical, e, -aux [ɔ̃bilikal, -o] ADJ umbilical

ombrage [ɔ̃bʀaʒ] NM (ombre) (leafy) shade; (fig): **prendre ~ de** to take umbrage at; **faire** ou **porter ~ à qn** to offend sb

ombragé, e [ɔ̃bʀaʒe] ADJ shaded, shady

ombrageux, -euse [ɔ̃bʀaʒø, -øz] ADJ (cheval) skittish, nervous; (personne) touchy, easily offended

ombre [ɔ̃bʀ] NF (espace non ensoleillé) shade; (ombre portée, tache) shadow; **à l'~** in the shade; (fam: en prison) behind bars; **à l'~ de** in the shade of; (tout près de, fig) in the shadow of; **tu me fais de l'~** you're in my light; **ça nous donne de l'~** it gives us (some) shade; **il n'y a pas l'~ d'un doute** there's not the shadow of a doubt; **dans l'~** in the shade; (fig) in the dark; **vivre dans l'~** (fig) to live in obscurity; **laisser dans l'~** (fig) to leave in the dark; **~ à paupières** eye shadow; **~ portée** shadow; **ombres chinoises** (spectacle) shadow show sg

ombrelle [ɔ̃bʀɛl] NF parasol, sunshade

ombrer [ɔ̃bʀe] /1/ VT to shade

OMC SIGLE F (= organisation mondiale du commerce) WTO

omelette [ɔmlɛt] NF omelette; **~ baveuse** runny omelette; **~ au fromage/au jambon** cheese/ham omelette; **~ aux herbes** omelette with herbs; **~ norvégienne** baked Alaska

omettre [ɔmɛtʀ] /56/ VT to omit, leave out; **~ de faire** to fail ou omit to do

omis, e [ɔmi, -iz] PP de **omettre**

omission [ɔmisjɔ̃] NF omission

omnibus [ɔmnibys] NM slow ou stopping train

omnipotent, e [ɔmnipɔtɑ̃, -ɑ̃t] ADJ omnipotent

omnipraticien, ne [ɔmnipʀatisjɛ̃, -ɛn] NM/F (Méd) general practitioner

omniprésent, e [ɔmnipʀezɑ̃, -ɑ̃t] ADJ omnipresent

omniscient, e [ɔmnisjɑ̃, -ɑ̃t] ADJ omniscient

omnisports [ɔmnispɔʀ] ADJ INV (club) general sports cpd; (salle) multi-purpose cpd; (terrain) all-purpose cpd

omnium [ɔmnjɔm] NM (Comm) corporation; (Cyclisme) omnium; (Courses) open handicap

omnivore [ɔmnivɔʀ] ADJ omnivorous

omoplate [ɔmɔplat] NF shoulder blade

OMS SIGLE F (= Organisation mondiale de la santé) WHO

MOT-CLÉ

on [ɔ̃] PRON **1** (indéterminé) you, one; **on peut le faire ainsi** you ou one can do it like this, it can be done like this; **on dit que ...** they say that ..., it is said that ..

2 (quelqu'un): **on les a attaqués** they were attacked; **on vous demande au téléphone** there's a phone call for you, you're wanted on the phone; **on frappe à la porte** someone's knocking at the door

3 (nous) we; **on va y aller demain** we're going tomorrow

4 (les gens) they; **autrefois, on croyait ...** they used to believe ..

5: **on ne peut plus** adv: **on ne peut plus stupide** as stupid as can be

once [ɔ̃s] NF: **une ~ de** an ounce of

oncle [ɔ̃kl] NM uncle

onction [ɔ̃ksjɔ̃] NF *voir* **extrême-onction**

onctueux, -euse [ɔ̃ktɥø, -øz] ADJ creamy, smooth; (*fig*) smooth, unctuous

onde [ɔ̃d] NF (*Physique*) wave; **sur l'~** on the waters; **sur les ondes** on the radio; **mettre en ondes** to produce for the radio; **~ de choc** shock wave; **ondes courtes (OC)** short wave *sg*; **petites ondes (PO), ondes moyennes (OM)** medium wave *sg*; **grandes ondes (GO), ondes longues (OL)** long wave *sg*; **ondes sonores** sound waves

ondée [ɔ̃de] NF shower

on-dit [ɔ̃di] NM INV rumour

ondoyer [ɔ̃dwaje] /8/ VI to ripple, wave ▶ VT (*Rel*) to baptize (*in an emergency*)

ondulant, e [ɔ̃dylɑ̃, -ɑ̃t] ADJ (*démarche*) swaying; (*ligne*) undulating

ondulation [ɔ̃dylasjɔ̃] NF undulation; wave

ondulé, e [ɔ̃dyle] ADJ undulating; wavy

onduler [ɔ̃dyle] /1/ VI to undulate; (*cheveux*) to wave

onéreux, -euse [ɔnerø, -øz] ADJ costly; **à titre ~** in return for payment

ONF SIGLE M (= *Office national des forêts*) ≈ Forestry Commission (*BRIT*), ≈ National Forest Service (*US*)

ONG SIGLE F (= *organisation non-gouvernementale*) NGO

ongle [ɔ̃gl] NM (*Anat*) nail; **manger** *ou* **ronger ses ongles** to bite one's nails; **se faire les ongles** to do one's nails

onglet [ɔ̃glɛ] NM (*rainure*) (thumbnail) groove; (*bande de papier*) tab

onguent [ɔ̃gɑ̃] NM ointment

onirique [ɔnirik] ADJ dreamlike, dream *cpd*

onirisme [ɔnirism] NM dreams *pl*

onomatopée [ɔnɔmatɔpe] NF onomatopoeia

ont [ɔ̃] VB *voir* **avoir**

ontarien, ne [ɔ̃taʀjɛ̃, -ɛn] ADJ Ontarian

ONU [ɔny] SIGLE F (= *Organisation des Nations unies*) UN(O)

onusien, ne [ɔnyzjɛ̃, -ɛn] ADJ of the UN(O), of the United Nations (Organization)

onyx [ɔniks] NM onyx

onze [ɔ̃z] NUM eleven

onzième [ɔ̃zjɛm] NUM eleventh

op [ɔp] NF (*opération*): **salle d'op** (operating) theatre

OPA SIGLE F = **offre publique d'achat**

opacité [ɔpasite] NF opaqueness

opale [ɔpal] NF opal

opalescent, e [ɔpalesɑ̃, -ɑ̃t] ADJ opalescent

opalin, e [ɔpalɛ̃, -in] ADJ, NF opaline

opaque [ɔpak] ADJ (*vitre, verre*) opaque; (*brouillard, nuit*) impenetrable

OPE SIGLE F (= *offre publique d'échange*) take-over bid where bidder offers shares in his company in exchange for shares in target company

OPEP [ɔpɛp] SIGLE F (= *Organisation des pays exportateurs de pétrole*) OPEC

opéra [ɔpera] NM opera; (*édifice*) opera house

opérable [ɔperabl] ADJ operable

opéra-comique [ɔperakɔmik] (*pl* **opéras-comiques**) NM light opera, opéra comique

opérant, e [ɔperɑ̃, -ɑ̃t] ADJ (*mesure*) effective

opérateur, -trice [ɔperatœr, -tris] NM/F operator; **~ (de prise de vues)** cameraman

opération [ɔperasjɔ̃] NF operation; (*Comm*) dealing; **salle/table d'~** operating theatre/ table; **~ de sauvetage** rescue operation; **~ à cœur ouvert** open-heart surgery *no pl*

opérationnel, le [ɔperasjɔnɛl] ADJ operational

opératoire [ɔperatwar] ADJ (*manœuvre, méthode*) operating; (*choc etc*) post-operative

opéré, e [ɔpere] NM/F post-operative patient

opérer [ɔpere] /6/ VT (*Méd*) to operate on; (*faire, exécuter*) to carry out, make ▶ VI (*remède: faire effet*) to act, work; (*procéder*) to proceed; (*Méd*) to operate; **s'opérer** VI (*avoir lieu*) to occur, take place; **se faire opérer** to have an operation; **se faire opérer des amygdales/du cœur** to have one's tonsils out/have a heart operation

opérette [ɔperɛt] NF operetta, light opera

ophtalmique [ɔftalmik] ADJ ophthalmic

ophtalmologie [ɔftalmɔlɔʒi] NF ophthalmology

ophtalmologue [ɔftalmɔlɔg] NMF ophthalmologist

opiacé, e [ɔpjase] ADJ opiate

opiner [ɔpine] /1/ VI: **~ de la tête** to nod assent ▶ VT: **~ à** to consent to

opiniâtre [ɔpinjɑtr] ADJ stubborn

opiniâtreté [ɔpinjɑtrəte] NF stubbornness

opinion [ɔpinjɔ̃] NF opinion; **l'~ (publique)** public opinion; **avoir bonne/mauvaise ~ de** to have a high/low opinion of

opiomane [ɔpjɔman] NMF opium addict

opium [ɔpjɔm] NM opium

OPJ SIGLE M (= *officier de police judiciaire*) ≈ DC (= *Detective Constable*)

opportun, e [ɔpɔrtœ̃, -yn] ADJ timely, opportune; **en temps ~** at the appropriate time

opportunément [ɔpɔrtynemɑ̃] ADV opportunely

opportunisme [ɔpɔrtynism] NM opportunism

opportuniste [ɔpɔrtynist] ADJ, NMF opportunist

opportunité [ɔpɔrtynite] NF timeliness, opportuneness

opposant, e [ɔpozɑ̃, -ɑ̃t] ADJ opposing ▶ NM/F opponent

opposé, e [ɔpoze] ADJ (*direction, rive*) opposite; (*faction*) opposing; (*couleurs*) contrasting; (*opinions, intérêts*) conflicting; (*contre*): **~ à** opposed to, against ▶ NM: **l'~** the other *ou* opposite side (*ou* direction); (*contraire*) the opposite; **être ~ à** to be opposed to; **à l'~** (*fig*) on the other hand; **à l'~ de** on the other *ou* opposite side from; (*fig*) contrary to, unlike

opposer [ɔpoze] /1/ VT (*meubles, objets*) to place opposite each other; (*personnes, armées, équipes*) to oppose; (*couleurs, termes, tons*) to contrast; (*comparer: livres, avantages*) to contrast; **~ qch à** (*comme obstacle, défense*) to set sth against; (*comme objection*) to put sth forward against; (*en contraste*) to set sth opposite; to match sth with; **s'opposer** VI (*équipes*) to confront each other; (*opinions*) to conflict; (*couleurs, styles*) to contrast;

s'opposer à (*interdire, empêcher*) to oppose; (*tenir tête à*) to rebel against; **sa religion s'y oppose** it's against his religion; **s'opposer à ce que qn fasse** to be opposed to sb's doing

opposition [ɔpozisjɔ̃] NF opposition; **par** ~ in contrast; **par** ~ **à** as opposed to, in contrast with; **entrer en** ~ **avec** to come into conflict with; **être en** ~ **avec** (*idées, conduite*) to be at variance with; **faire** ~ **à un chèque** to stop a cheque

oppressant, e [ɔpʀesɑ̃, -ɑ̃t] ADJ oppressive

oppresser [ɔpʀese] /1/ VT to oppress; **se sentir oppressé** to feel breathless

oppresseur [ɔpʀesœʀ] NM oppressor

oppressif, -ive [ɔpʀesif, -iv] ADJ oppressive

oppression [ɔpʀesjɔ̃] NF oppression; (*malaise*) feeling of suffocation

opprimer [ɔpʀime] /1/ VT (*asservir: peuple, faibles*) to oppress; (*étouffer: liberté, opinion*) to suppress, stifle; (*chaleur etc*) to suffocate, oppress

opprobre [ɔpʀɔbʀ] NM disgrace

opter [ɔpte] /1/ VI: ~ **pour** to opt for; ~ **entre** to choose between

opticien, ne [ɔptisjɛ̃, -ɛn] NM/F optician

optimal, e, -aux [ɔptimal, -o] ADJ optimal

optimisation [ɔptimizasjɔ̃] NF optimization

optimiser [ɔptimize] /1/ VT to optimize

optimisme [ɔptimism] NM optimism

optimiste [ɔptimist] ADJ optimistic ▶ NMF optimist

optimum [ɔptimɔm] ADJ, NM optimum

option [ɔpsjɔ̃] NF option; (*Auto: supplément*) optional extra; **matière à** ~ (*Scol*) optional subject (BRIT), elective (US); **prendre une** ~ **sur** to take (out) an option on; ~ **par défaut** (*Inform*) default (option)

optionnel, le [ɔpsjɔnɛl] ADJ optional

optique [ɔptik] ADJ (*nerf*) optic; (*verres*) optical ▶ NF (*Photo: lentilles etc*) optics pl; (*science, industrie*) optics sg; (*fig: manière de voir*) perspective

opulence [ɔpylɑ̃s] NF wealth, opulence

opulent, e [ɔpylɑ̃, -ɑ̃t] ADJ wealthy, opulent; (*formes, poitrine*) ample, generous

OPV SIGLE F (= *offre publique de vente*) public offer of sale

or [ɔʀ] NM gold ▶ CONJ now, but; **d'or** (*fig*) golden; **en or** gold cpd; (*occasion*) golden; **un mari/enfant en or** a treasure; **une affaire en or** (*achat*) a real bargain; (*commerce*) a gold mine; **plaqué or** gold-plated; **or noir** black gold; **il croyait gagner or il a perdu** he was sure he would win and yet he lost

oracle [ɔʀakl] NM oracle

orage [ɔʀaʒ] NM (thunder)storm

orageux, -euse [ɔʀaʒø, -øz] ADJ stormy

oraison [ɔʀɛzɔ̃] NF orison, prayer; ~ **funèbre** funeral oration

oral, e, -aux [ɔʀal, -o] ADJ (*déposition, promesse*) oral, verbal; (*Méd*): **par voie** ~ by mouth, orally ▶ NM (*Scol*) oral

oralement [ɔʀalmɑ̃] ADV orally

orange [ɔʀɑ̃ʒ] ADJ INV, NF orange; ~ **sanguine** blood orange; ~ **pressée** freshly-squeezed orange juice

orangé, e [ɔʀɑ̃ʒe] ADJ orangey, orange-coloured

orangeade [ɔʀɑ̃ʒad] NF orangeade

oranger [ɔʀɑ̃ʒe] NM orange tree

orangeraie [ɔʀɑ̃ʒʀɛ] NF orange grove

orangerie [ɔʀɑ̃ʒʀi] NF orangery

orang-outan, orang-outang [ɔʀɑ̃utɑ̃] NM orang-utan

orateur [ɔʀatœʀ] NM speaker; orator

oratoire [ɔʀatwaʀ] NM (*lieu, chapelle*) oratory; (*au bord du chemin*) wayside shrine ▶ ADJ oratorical

oratorio [ɔʀatɔʀjo] NM oratorio

orbital, e, -aux [ɔʀbital, -o] ADJ orbital; **station** ~ space station

orbite [ɔʀbit] NF (*Anat*) (eye-)socket; (*Physique*) orbit; **mettre sur** ~ to put into orbit; (*fig*) to launch; **dans l'** ~ **de** (*fig*) within the sphere of influence of

Orcades [ɔʀkad] NFPL: **les** ~ the Orkneys, the Orkney Islands

orchestral, e, -aux [ɔʀkɛstʀal, -o] ADJ orchestral

orchestrateur, -trice [ɔʀkɛstʀatœʀ, -tʀis] NM/F orchestrator

orchestration [ɔʀkɛstʀasjɔ̃] NF orchestration

orchestre [ɔʀkɛstʀ] NM orchestra; (*de jazz, danse*) band; (*places*) stalls pl (BRIT), orchestra (US)

orchestrer [ɔʀkɛstʀe] /1/ VT (*Mus*) to orchestrate; (*fig*) to mount, stage-manage

orchidée [ɔʀkide] NF orchid

ordinaire [ɔʀdinɛʀ] ADJ ordinary; (*coutumier: maladresse etc*) usual; (*de tous les jours*) everyday; (*modèle, qualité*) standard; (*péj: commun*) common ▶ NM ordinary; (*menus*) everyday fare ▶ NF (*essence*) ≈ two-star (petrol) (BRIT), ≈ regular (gas) (US); **d'** ~ usually, normally; **à l'** ~ usually, ordinarily; **comme à l'** ~ as usual

ordinairement [ɔʀdinɛʀmɑ̃] ADV ordinarily, usually

ordinal, e, -aux [ɔʀdinal, -o] ADJ ordinal

ordinateur [ɔʀdinatœʀ] NM computer; **mettre sur** ~ to computerize, put on computer; ~ **de bureau** desktop computer; ~ **individuel** *ou* **personnel** personal computer; ~ **portable** laptop (computer)

ordination [ɔʀdinasjɔ̃] NF ordination

ordonnance [ɔʀdɔnɑ̃s] NF organization; (*groupement, disposition*) layout; (*Méd*) prescription; (*Jur*) order; (*Mil*) orderly, batman (BRIT); **d'** ~ (*Mil*) regulation cpd; **officier d'** ~ aide-de-camp

ordonnateur, -trice [ɔʀdɔnatœʀ, -tʀis] NM/F (*d'une cérémonie, fête*) organizer; ~ **des pompes funèbres** funeral director

ordonné, e [ɔʀdɔne] ADJ tidy, orderly; (*Math*) ordered ▶ NF (*Math*) Y-axis, ordinate

ordonner [ɔʀdɔne] /1/ VT (*agencer*) to organize, arrange; (*meubles, appartement*) to lay out, arrange; (*donner un ordre*): ~ **à qn de faire** to order sb to do; (*Math*) to (arrange in) order; (*Rel*) to ordain; (*Méd*) to prescribe; (*Jur*) to order; **s'ordonner** VI (*faits*) to organize themselves

ordre [ɔʀdʀ] NM (*gén*) order; (*propreté et soin*) orderliness, tidiness; (*association professionnelle,* *honorifique*) association; (*Comm*): **à l'~ de** payable to; (*nature*): **d'~ pratique** of a practical nature; **ordres** NMPL (*Rel*) holy orders; **avoir de l'~** to be tidy *ou* orderly; **mettre en ~** to tidy (up), put in order; **mettre bon ~ à** to put to rights, sort out; **procéder par ~** to take things one at a time; **par ~ alphabétique/d'importance** in alphabetical order/in order of importance; **être aux ordres de qn/sous les ordres de qn** to be at sb's disposal/under sb's command; **rappeler qn à l'~** to call sb to order; **jusqu'à nouvel ~** until further notice; **dans le même ~ d'idées** in this connection; **par ~ d'entrée en scène** in order of appearance; **un ~ de grandeur** some idea of the size (*ou* amount); **de premier ~** first-rate; **~ de grève** strike call; **~ du jour** (*d'une réunion*) agenda; (*Mil*) order of the day; **à l'~ du jour** on the agenda; (*fig*) topical; (*Mil: citer*) in dispatches; **~ de mission** (*Mil*) orders *pl*; **~ public** law and order; **~ de route** marching orders *pl*

ordure [ɔʀdyʀ] NF filth *no pl*; (*propos, écrit*) obscenity, (piece of) filth; **ordures** NFPL (*balayures, déchets*) rubbish *sg*, refuse *sg*; **ordures ménagères** household refuse

ordurier, -ière [ɔʀdyʀje, -jɛʀ] ADJ lewd, filthy

oreille [ɔʀej] NF (*Anat*) ear; (*de marmite, tasse*) handle; (*Tech: d'un écrou*) wing; **avoir de l'~** to have a good ear (for music); **avoir l'~ fine** to have good *ou* sharp ears; **l'~ basse** crestfallen, dejected; **se faire tirer l'~** to take a lot of persuading; **dire qch à l'~ de qn** to have a word in sb's ear (about sth)

oreiller [ɔʀeje] NM pillow

oreillette [ɔʀejɛt] NF (*Anat*) auricle

oreillons [ɔʀejɔ̃] NMPL mumps *sg*

ores [ɔʀ]: **d'~ et déjà** *adv* already

orfèvre [ɔʀfɛvʀ] NM goldsmith; silversmith

orfèvrerie [ɔʀfɛvʀəʀi] NF (*art, métier*) goldsmith's (*ou* silversmith's) trade; (*ouvrage*) (silver *ou* gold) plate

orfraie [ɔʀfʀɛ] NM white-tailed eagle; **pousser des cris d'~** to yell at the top of one's voice

organe [ɔʀgan] NM organ; (*véhicule, instrument*) instrument; (*voix*) voice; (*porte-parole*) representative, mouthpiece; **organes de commande** (*Tech*) controls; **organes de transmission** (*Tech*) transmission system *sg*

organigramme [ɔʀganigʀam] NM (*hiérarchie, structure*) organization chart; (*des opérations*) flow chart

organique [ɔʀganik] ADJ organic

organisateur, -trice [ɔʀganizatœʀ, -tʀis] NM/F organizer

organisation [ɔʀganizasjɔ̃] NF organization; **O~ des Nations unies (ONU)** United Nations (Organization) (UN(O)); **O~ mondiale de la santé (OMS)** World Health Organization (WHO); **O~ du traité de l'Atlantique Nord (OTAN)** North Atlantic Treaty Organization (NATO)

organisationnel, le [ɔʀganizasjɔnɛl] ADJ organizational

organiser [ɔʀganize] /1/ VT to organize; (*mettre*

sur pied: service etc) to set up; **s'organiser** VI to get organized

organisme [ɔʀganism] NM (*Bio*) organism; (*corps humain*) body; (*Admin, Pol etc*) body, organism

organiste [ɔʀganist] NMF organist

orgasme [ɔʀgasm] NM orgasm, climax

orge [ɔʀʒ] NF barley

orgeat [ɔʀʒa] NM: **sirop d'~** barley water

orgelet [ɔʀʒəlɛ] NM sty(e)

orgie [ɔʀʒi] NF orgy

orgue [ɔʀg] NM organ; **orgues** NFPL organ *sg*; **~ de Barbarie** barrel *ou* street organ

orgueil [ɔʀgœj] NM pride

orgueilleux, -euse [ɔʀgœjø, -øz] ADJ proud

Orient [ɔʀjɑ̃] NM: **l'~** the East, the Orient

orientable [ɔʀjɑ̃tabl] ADJ (*phare, lampe etc*) adjustable

oriental, e, -aux [ɔʀjɑ̃tal, -o] ADJ (*langue, produit*) oriental, eastern; (*frontière*) eastern ▶ NM/F: **O~, e** Oriental

orientation [ɔʀjɑ̃tasjɔ̃] NF positioning; adjustment; (*de recherches*) orientation; direction; (*d'une maison etc*) aspect; (*d'un journal*) leanings *pl*; **avoir le sens de l'~** to have a (good) sense of direction; **course d'~** orienteering exercise; **~ professionnelle** careers advice *ou* guidance; (*service*) careers advisory service

orienté, e [ɔʀjɑ̃te] ADJ (*fig: article, journal*) slanted; **bien/mal ~** (*appartement*) well/badly positioned; **~ au sud** facing south, with a southern aspect

orienter [ɔʀjɑ̃te] /1/ VT (*situer*) to position; (*placer, disposer: pièce mobile*) to adjust, position; (*tourner: antenne*) to direct, turn; (*voyageur, touriste, recherches*) to direct; (*fig: élève*) to orientate; **s'orienter** VI (*se repérer*) to find one's bearings; **s'orienter vers** (*fig*) to turn towards

orienteur, -euse [ɔʀjɑ̃tœʀ, -øz] NM/F (*Scol*) careers adviser

orifice [ɔʀifis] NM opening, orifice

oriflamme [ɔʀiflam] NF banner, standard

origan [ɔʀigɑ̃] NM oregano

originaire [ɔʀiʒinɛʀ] ADJ original; **être ~ de** (*pays, lieu*) to be a native of; (*provenir de*) to originate from; to be native to

original, e, -aux [ɔʀiʒinal, -o] ADJ original; (*bizarre*) eccentric ▶ NM/F (*fam: excentrique*) eccentric; (*: fantaisiste*) joker ▶ NM (*document etc, Art*) original; (*dactylographie*) top copy

originalité [ɔʀiʒinalite] NF (*d'un nouveau modèle*) originality *no pl*; (*excentricité, bizarrerie*) eccentricity

origine [ɔʀiʒin] NF origin; (*d'un message, appel téléphonique*) source; (*d'une révolution, réussite*) root; **origines** (*d'une personne*) origins; **d'~** (*pays*) of origin; (*pneus etc*) original; (*bureau postal*) dispatching; **d'~ française** of French origin; **dès l'~** at *ou* from the outset; **à l'~** originally; **avoir son ~ dans** to have its origins in, originate in

originel, le [ɔʀiʒinɛl] ADJ original

originellement [ɔʀiʒinɛlmɑ̃] ADV (*à l'origine*) originally; (*dès l'origine*) from the beginning

oripeaux [ɔʀipo] NMPL rags

291

ORL SIGLE F (= *oto-rhino-laryngologie*) ENT ▶ SIGLE MF (= *oto-rhino-laryngologiste*) ENT specialist; **être en ~** (*malade*) to be in the ENT hospital *ou* department

orme [ɔRm] NM elm

orné, e [ɔRne] ADJ ornate; **~ de** adorned *ou* decorated with

ornement [ɔRnəmã] NM ornament; (*fig*) embellishment, adornment; **ornements sacerdotaux** vestments

ornemental, e, -aux [ɔRnəmãtal, -o] ADJ ornamental

ornementer [ɔRnəmãte] /1/ VT to ornament

orner [ɔRne] /1/ VT to decorate, adorn; **~ qch de** to decorate sth with

ornière [ɔRnjɛR] NF rut; (*fig*): **sortir de l'~** (*routine*) to get out of the rut; (*impasse*) to get out of a spot

ornithologie [ɔRnitɔlɔʒi] NF ornithology

ornithologue [ɔRnitɔlɔg] NMF ornithologist; **~ amateur** birdwatcher

orphelin, e [ɔRfǝlɛ̃, -in] ADJ orphan(ed) ▶ NM/F orphan; **~ de père/mère** fatherless/motherless

orphelinat [ɔRfǝlina] NM orphanage

ORSEC [ɔRsɛk] SIGLE F = **Organisation des secours**; **le plan ~** *disaster contingency plan*

ORSECRAD [ɔRsɛkRad] SIGLE M = **ORSEC en cas d'accident nucléaire**

orteil [ɔRtɛj] NM toe; **gros ~** big toe

ORTF SIGLE M (= *Office de radio-diffusion télévision française*) (*former*) French broadcasting corporation

orthodontiste [ɔRtɔdɔ̃tist] NMF orthodontist

orthodoxe [ɔRtɔdɔks] ADJ orthodox

orthodoxie [ɔRtɔdɔksi] NF orthodoxy

orthogénie [ɔRtɔʒeni] NF family planning

orthographe [ɔRtɔgRaf] NF spelling

orthographier [ɔRtɔgRafje] /7/ VT to spell; **mal orthographié** misspelt

orthopédie [ɔRtɔpedi] NF orthopaedics *sg* (BRIT), orthopedics *sg* (US)

orthopédique [ɔRtɔpedik] ADJ orthopaedic (BRIT), orthopedic (US)

orthopédiste [ɔRtɔpedist] NMF orthopaedic (BRIT) *ou* orthopedic (US) specialist

orthophonie [ɔRtɔfɔni] NF (*Méd*) speech therapy; (*Ling*) correct pronunciation

orthophoniste [ɔRtɔfɔnist] NMF speech therapist

ortie [ɔRti] NF (stinging) nettle; **~ blanche** white dead-nettle

OS SIGLE M = **ouvrier spécialisé**

os [ɔs] NM bone; **sans os** (*Boucherie*) off the bone, boned; **os à moelle** marrowbone

oscillation [ɔsilasjɔ̃] NF oscillation; **oscillations** NFPL (*fig*) fluctuations

osciller [ɔsile] /1/ VI (*pendule*) to swing; (*au vent etc*) to rock; (*Tech*) to oscillate; (*fig*): **~ entre** to waver *ou* fluctuate between

osé, e [oze] ADJ daring, bold

oseille [ozɛj] NF sorrel

oser [oze] /1/ VI, VT to dare; **~ faire** to dare (to) do

osier [ozje] NM (*Bot*) willow; **d'~, en ~** wicker(work) *cpd*

Oslo [ɔslo] N Oslo

osmose [ɔsmoz] NF osmosis

ossature [ɔsatyR] NF (*Anat: squelette*) frame, skeletal structure; (: *du visage*) bone structure; (*fig*) framework

osselet [ɔslɛ] NM (*Anat*) ossicle; **jouer aux osselets** to play jacks

ossements [ɔsmã] NMPL bones

osseux, -euse [ɔsø, -øz] ADJ bony; (*tissu, maladie, greffe*) bone *cpd*

ossifier [ɔsifje] /7/: **s'ossifier** VI to ossify

ossuaire [ɔsɥɛR] NM ossuary

Ostende [ɔstɑ̃d] N Ostend

ostensible [ɔstɑ̃sibl] ADJ conspicuous

ostensiblement [ɔstɑ̃sibləmã] ADV conspicuously

ostensoir [ɔstɑ̃swaR] NM monstrance

ostentation [ɔstɑ̃tasjɔ̃] NF ostentation; **faire ~ de** to parade, make a display of

ostentatoire [ɔstɑ̃tatwaR] ADJ ostentatious

ostracisme [ɔstRasism] NM ostracism; **frapper d'~** to ostracize

ostréicole [ɔstReikɔl] ADJ oyster *cpd*

ostréiculture [ɔstReikyltyR] NF oyster-farming

otage [ɔtaʒ] NM hostage; **prendre qn comme ~** to take sb hostage

OTAN [ɔtɑ̃] SIGLE F (= *Organisation du traité de l'Atlantique Nord*) NATO

otarie [ɔtaRi] NF sea-lion

ôter [ote] /1/ VT to remove; (*soustraire*) to take away; **~ qch à qn** to take sth (away) from sb; **~ qch de** to remove sth from; **six ôté de dix égale quatre** six from ten equals *ou* is four

otite [ɔtit] NF ear infection

oto-rhino, oto-rhino-laryngologiste [ɔtɔRino(-)] NM/F ear, nose and throat specialist.

ottomane [ɔtɔman] NF ottoman

ou [u] CONJ or; **ou … ou** either … or; **ou bien** or (else)

(MOT-CLÉ)

où [u] PRON RELATIF **1** (*position, situation*) where, that (*souvent omis*); **la chambre où il était** the room (that) he was in, the room where he was; **la ville où je l'ai rencontré** the town where I met him; **la pièce d'où il est sorti** the room he came out of; **le village d'où je viens** the village I come from; **les villes par où il est passé** the towns he went through

2 (*temps, état*) that (*souvent omis*); **le jour où il est parti** the day (that) he left; **au prix où c'est** at the price it is

▶ ADV **1** (*interrogation*) where; **où est-il/va-t-il?** where is he/is he going?; **par où?** which way?; **d'où vient que …?** how come …?

2 (*position*) where; **je sais où il est** I know where he is; **où que l'on aille** wherever you go

OUA SIGLE F (= *Organisation de l'unité africaine*) OAU (= *Organization of African Unity*)

ouais [wɛ] EXCL yeah

ouate [wat] NF cotton wool (BRIT), cotton (US); (*bourre*) padding, wadding; **~ (hydrophile)** cotton wool (BRIT), (absorbent) cotton (US)

ouaté, e [wate] ADJ cotton-wool; (*doublé*) padded; (*fig: atmosphère*) cocoon-like; (: *pas, bruit*) muffled

oubli [ubli] NM (*acte*): **l'~ de** forgetting; (*trou de mémoire*) lapse of memory; (*étourderie*) forgetfulness *no pl*; (*négligence*) omission, oversight; (*absence de souvenirs*) oblivion; **~ de soi** self-effacement, self-negation; **tomber dans l'~** to sink into oblivion

oublier [ublije] /7/ VT (*gén*) to forget; (*ne pas voir: erreurs etc*) to miss; (*ne pas mettre: virgule, nom*) to leave out, forget; (*laisser quelque part: chapeau etc*) to leave behind; **s'oublier** VI to forget o.s.; (*enfant, animal*) to have an accident (*euphemism*); **~ l'heure** to forget (about) the time

oubliettes [ublijɛt] NFPL dungeon *sg*; (**jeter**) **aux ~** (*fig*) (to put) completely out of mind

oublieux, -euse [ublijø, -øz] ADJ forgetful

oued [wɛd] NM wadi

ouest [wɛst] NM west ▸ ADJ INV west; (*région*) western; **à l'~** in the west; (*direction*) (to the) west, westwards; **à l'~ de** (to the) west of; **vent d'~** westerly wind

ouest-allemand, e [wɛstalmɑ̃, -ɑ̃d] ADJ West German

ouf [uf] EXCL phew!

Ouganda [ugɑ̃da] NM: **l'~** Uganda

ougandais, e [ugɑ̃dɛ, -ɛz] ADJ Ugandan

oui [wi] ADV yes; **répondre (par) ~** to answer yes; **mais ~, bien sûr** yes, of course; **je pense que ~** I think so; **pour un ~ ou pour un non** for no apparent reason

ouï-dire [widiʀ]: **par ~** *adv* by hearsay

ouïe [wi] NF hearing; **ouïes** NFPL (*de poisson*) gills; (*de violon*) sound-hole *sg*

ouïr [wiʀ] /10/ VT to hear; **avoir ouï dire que** to have heard it said that

ouistiti [wistiti] NM marmoset

ouragan [uʀagɑ̃] NM hurricane; (*fig*) storm

Oural [uʀal] NM: **l'~** (*fleuve*) the Ural; (*aussi:* **les monts Oural**) the Urals, the Ural Mountains

ourdir [uʀdiʀ] /2/ VT (*complot*) to hatch

ourdou, e [uʀdu] ADJ Urdu ▸ NM (*Ling*) Urdu

ourlé, e [uʀle] ADJ hemmed; (*fig*) rimmed

ourler [uʀle] /1/ VT to hem

ourlet [uʀlɛ] NM hem; (*de l'oreille*) rim; **faire un ~ à** to hem

ours [uʀs] NM bear; **~ brun/blanc** brown/polar bear; **~ marin** fur seal; **~ mal léché** uncouth fellow; **~ (en peluche)** teddy (bear)

ourse [uʀs] NF (*Zool*) she-bear; **la Grande/ Petite O~** the Great/Little Bear, Ursa Major/ Minor

oursin [uʀsɛ̃] NM sea urchin

ourson [uʀsɔ̃] NM (bear-)cub

ouste [ust] EXCL hop it!

outil [uti] NM tool

outillage [utijaʒ] NM set of tools; (*d'atelier*) equipment *no pl*

outiller [utije] /1/ VT (*ouvrier, usine*) to equip

outrage [utʀaʒ] NM insult; **faire subir les derniers outrages à** (*femme*) to ravish; **~ aux bonnes mœurs** (*Jur*) outrage to public decency; **~ à magistrat** (*Jur*) contempt of court; **~ à la**

pudeur (*Jur*) indecent behaviour *no pl*

outragé, e [utʀaʒe] ADJ offended; outraged

outrageant, e [utʀaʒɑ̃, -ɑ̃t] ADJ offensive

outrager [utʀaʒe] /3/ VT to offend gravely; (*fig: contrevenir à*) to outrage, insult

outrageusement [utʀaʒøzmɑ̃] ADV outrageously

outrance [utʀɑ̃s] NF excessiveness *no pl*, excess: **à ~** adv excessively, to excess

outrancier, -ière [utʀɑ̃sje, -jɛʀ] ADJ extreme

outre [utʀ] NF goatskin, water skin ▸ PRÉP besides ▸ ADV: **passer ~** to carry on regardless; **passer ~ à** to disregard, take no notice of; **en ~** besides, moreover; **~ que** apart from the fact that; **~ mesure** to excess; (*manger, boire*) immoderately

outré, e [utʀe] ADJ (*flatterie, éloge*) excessive, exaggerated; (*indigné, scandalisé*) outraged

outre-Atlantique [utʀatlɑ̃tik] ADV across the Atlantic

outrecuidance [utʀəkɥidɑ̃s] NF presumptuousness *no pl*

outre-Manche [utʀəmɑ̃ʃ] ADV across the Channel

outremer [utʀəmɛʀ] ADJ INV ultramarine

outre-mer [utʀəmɛʀ] ADV overseas; **d'~** overseas

outrepasser [utʀəpase] /1/ VT to go beyond, exceed

outrer [utʀe] /1/ VT (*pensée, attitude*) to exaggerate; (*indigner: personne*) to outrage

outre-Rhin [utʀəʀɛ̃] ADV across the Rhine, in Germany

outsider [awtsajdœʀ] NM outsider

ouvert, e [uvɛʀ, -ɛʀt] PP *de* **ouvrir** ▸ ADJ open; (*robinet, gaz etc*) on; **à bras ouverts** with open arms

ouvertement [uvɛʀtəmɑ̃] ADV openly

ouverture [uvɛʀtyʀ] NF opening; (*Mus*) overture; (*Pol*): **l'~** the widening of the political spectrum; (*Photo*): **~ (du diaphragme)** aperture; **ouvertures** NFPL (*propositions*) overtures; **~ d'esprit** open-mindedness; **heures d'~** (*Comm*) opening hours; **jours d'~** (*Comm*) days of opening

ouvrable [uvʀabl] ADJ: **jour ~** working day, weekday; **heures ouvrables** business hours

ouvrage [uvʀaʒ] NM (*tâche, de tricot etc, Mil*) work *no pl*; (*objet: Couture, Art*) (piece of) work; (*texte, livre*) work; **panier** *ou* **corbeille à ~** work basket; **~ d'art** (*Génie Civil*) bridge or tunnel etc

ouvragé, e [uvʀaʒe] ADJ finely embroidered (*ou* worked *ou* carved)

ouvrant, e [uvʀɑ̃, -ɑ̃t] VB *voir* **ouvrir** ▸ ADJ: **toit ~** sunroof

ouvré, e [uvʀe] ADJ finely-worked; **jour ~** working day

ouvre-boîte(s) [uvʀəbwat] NM INV tin (*Brit*) *ou* can opener

ouvre-bouteille(s) [uvʀəbutɛj] NM INV bottle-opener

ouvreuse [uvʀøz] NF usherette

ouvrier, -ière [uvʀije, -jɛʀ] NM/F worker ▸ NF (*Zool*) worker (bee) ▸ ADJ working-class;

(*problèmes, conflit*) industrial; (*mouvement*) labour *cpd* (BRIT), labor *cpd* (US); (*revendications*) workers'; **classe ouvrière** working class; **~ agricole** farmworker; **~ qualifié** skilled worker; **~ spécialisé** semiskilled worker; **~ d'usine** factory worker

ouvrir [uvRiR] /**18**/ VT (*gén*) to open; (*brèche, passage*) to open up; (*commencer l'exploitation de, créer*) to open (up); (*eau, électricité, chauffage, robinet*) to turn on; (*Méd: abcès*) to open up, cut open ▸ VI to open; to open up; (*Cartes*): **~ à trèfle** to open in clubs; **s'ouvrir** VI to open; **s'ouvrir à** (*art etc*) to open one's mind to; **s'ouvrir à qn (de qch)** to open one's heart to sb (about sth); **s'ouvrir les veines** to slash *ou* cut one's wrists; **~ sur** to open onto; **~ l'appétit à qn** to whet sb's appetite; **~ des horizons** to open up new horizons; **~ l'esprit** to broaden one's horizons; **~ une session** (*Inform*) to log in

ouvroir [uvRwaR] NM workroom, sewing room

ovaire [ɔvɛR] NM ovary

ovale [ɔval] ADJ oval

ovation [ɔvasjɔ̃] NF ovation

ovationner [ɔvasjɔne] /**1**/ VT: **~ qn** to give sb an ovation

ovin, e [ɔvɛ̃, -in] ADJ ovine

OVNI [ɔvni] SIGLE M (= *objet volant non identifié*) UFO

ovoïde [ɔvɔid] ADJ egg-shaped

ovulation [ɔvylasjɔ̃] NF (*Physiol*) ovulation

ovule [ɔvyl] NM (*Physiol*) ovum; (*Méd*) pessary

oxfordien, ne [ɔksfɔRdjɛ̃, -ɛn] ADJ Oxonian ▸ NM/F: **O~, ne** Oxonian

oxydable [ɔksidabl] ADJ liable to rust

oxyde [ɔksid] NM oxide; **~ de carbone** carbon monoxide

oxyder [ɔkside] /**1**/: **s'oxyder** VI to become oxidized

oxygéné, e [ɔksiʒene] ADJ: **eau ~** hydrogen peroxide; **cheveux oxygénés** bleached hair

oxygène [ɔksiʒɛn] NM oxygen; (*fig*): **cure d'~** fresh air cure

ozone [ozon] NM ozone; **trou dans la couche d'~** hole in the ozone layer

Pp

P, p [pe] NM INV P, p ▶ ABR (= *Père*) Fr; (= *page*) p; **P comme Pierre** P for Peter
PA SIGLE FPL = **les petites annonces**
PAC SIGLE F (= *Politique agricole commune*) CAP
pacage [pakaʒ] NM grazing, pasture
pacemaker [pɛsmekœʀ] NM pacemaker
pachyderme [paʃidɛʀm] NM pachyderm; elephant
pacificateur, -trice [pasifikatœʀ, -tʀis] ADJ pacificatory
pacification [pasifikasjɔ̃] NF pacification
pacifier [pasifje] /7/ VT to pacify
pacifique [pasifik] ADJ (*personne*) peaceable; (*intentions, coexistence*) peaceful ▶ NM: **le P~, l'océan P~** the Pacific (Ocean)
pacifiquement [pasifikmɑ̃] ADV peaceably; peacefully
pacifisme [pasifism] NM pacifism
pacifiste [pasifist] NMF pacifist
pack [pak] NM pack
pacotille [pakɔtij] NF (*péj*) cheap junk *pl*; **de ~** cheap
PACS [paks] SIGLE M (= *pacte civil de solidarité*) ≈ civil partnership
pacser [pakse] /1/: **se pacser** VI ≈ to form a civil partnership
pacte [pakt] NM pact, treaty
pactiser [paktize] /1/ VI: **~ avec** to come to terms with
pactole [paktɔl] NM gold mine (*fig*)
paddock [padɔk] NM paddock
Padoue [padu] N Padua
PAF SIGLE F (= *Police de l'air et des frontières*) police authority responsible for civil aviation, border control *etc* ▶ SIGLE M (= *paysage audiovisuel français*) French broadcasting scene
pagaie [pagɛ] NF paddle
pagaille [pagaj] NF mess, shambles *sg*; **il y en a en ~** there are loads *ou* heaps of them
paganisme [paganism] NM paganism
pagayer [pageje] /8/ VI to paddle
page [paʒ] NF page; (*passage: d'un roman*) passage ▶ NM page (boy); **mettre en pages** to make up (into pages); **mise en ~** layout; **à la ~** (*fig*) up-to-date; **~ d'accueil** (*Inform*) home page; **~ blanche** blank page; **~ de garde** endpaper; **~ Web** (*Inform*) web page
page-écran [paʒekʀɑ̃] (*pl* **pages-écrans**) NF (*Inform*) screen page
pagination [paʒinasjɔ̃] NF pagination
paginer [paʒine] /1/ VT to paginate
pagne [paɲ] NM loincloth
pagode [pagɔd] NF pagoda
paie [pɛ] NF = **paye**
paiement [pɛmɑ̃] NM = **payement**
païen, ne [pajɛ̃, -ɛn] ADJ, NM/F pagan, heathen
paillard, e [pajaʀ, -aʀd] ADJ bawdy
paillasse [pajas] NF (*matelas*) straw mattress; (*d'un évier*) draining board
paillasson [pajasɔ̃] NM doormat
paille [paj] NF straw; (*défaut*) flaw; **être sur la ~** to be ruined; **~ de fer** steel wool
paillé, e [paje] ADJ with a straw seat
pailleté, e [pajte] ADJ sequined
paillette [pajɛt] NF speck, flake; **paillettes** NFPL (*décoratives*) sequins, spangles; **lessive en paillettes** soapflakes *pl*
pain [pɛ̃] NM (*substance*) bread; (*unité*) loaf (of bread); (*morceau*): **~ de cire** *etc* bar of wax *etc*; (*Culin*): **~ de poisson/légumes** fish/vegetable loaf; **petit ~** (bread) roll; **~ bis/complet** brown/wholemeal (BRIT) *ou* wholewheat (US) bread; **~ de campagne** farmhouse bread; **~ d'épice** ≈ gingerbread; **~ grillé** toast; **~ de mie** sandwich loaf; **~ perdu** French toast; **~ de seigle** rye bread; **~ de sucre** sugar loaf; **~ au chocolat** pain au chocolat; **~ aux raisins** currant pastry
pair, e [pɛʀ] ADJ (*nombre*) even ▶ NM peer; **aller de ~ (avec)** to go hand in hand *ou* together (with); **au ~** (*Finance*) at par; **valeur au ~** par value; **jeune fille au ~** au pair
paire [pɛʀ] NF pair; **une ~ de lunettes/tenailles** a pair of glasses/pincers; **les deux font la ~** they are two of a kind
pais [pɛ] VB *voir* **paître**
paisible [pezibl] ADJ peaceful, quiet
paisiblement [peziblmɑ̃] ADV peacefully, quietly
paître [pɛtʀ] /57/ VI to graze
paix [pɛ] NF peace; (*fig*) peacefulness, peace; **faire la ~ avec** to make peace with; **avoir la ~** to have peace (and quiet); **fiche-lui la ~!** (*fam*) leave him alone!
Pakistan [pakistɑ̃] NM: **le ~** Pakistan
pakistanais, e [pakistanɛ, -ɛz] ADJ Pakistani

PAL SIGLE M (= *Phase Alternation Line*) PAL
palabrer [palabʀe] /**1**/ VI to argue endlessly
palabres [palabʀ] NFPL, NMPL endless discussions
palace [palas] NM luxury hotel
palais [palɛ] NM palace; (*Anat*) palate; **le P~ Bourbon** *the seat of the French National Assembly*; **le P~ de l'Élysée** the Élysée Palace; **~ des expositions** exhibition centre; **le P~ de Justice** the Law Courts *pl*
palan [palɑ̃] NM hoist
pale [pal] NF (*d'hélice, de rame*) blade; (*de roue*) paddle
pâle [pɑl] ADJ pale; (*fig*): **une ~ imitation** a pale imitation; **bleu ~** pale blue; **~ de colère** white *ou* pale with anger
palefrenier [palfʀənje] NM groom (*for horses*)
paléontologie [paleɔ̃tɔlɔʒi] NF paleontology
paléontologiste [paleɔ̃tɔlɔʒist], **paléontologue** [paleɔ̃tɔlɔg] NMF paleontologist
Palerme [palɛʀm] N Palermo
Palestine [palɛstin] NF: **la ~** Palestine
palestinien, ne [palɛstinjɛ̃, -ɛn] ADJ Palestinian ▶ NM/F: **P~, ne** Palestinian
palet [palɛ] NM disc; (*Hockey*) puck
paletot [palto] NM (short) coat
palette [palɛt] NF (*de peintre*) palette; (*de produits*) range
palétuvier [paletyvje] NM mangrove
pâleur [pɑlœʀ] NF paleness
palier [palje] NM (*d'escalier*) landing; (*fig*) level, plateau; (*: phase stable*) levelling (BRIT) *ou* leveling (US) off, new level; (*Tech*) bearing; **nos voisins de ~** our neighbo(u)rs across the landing (BRIT) *ou* the hall (US); **en ~** *adv* level; **par paliers** in stages
palière [paljɛʀ] ADJ F landing *cpd*
pâlir [paliʀ] /**2**/ VI to turn *ou* go pale; (*couleur*) to fade; **faire ~ qn** (*de jalousie*) to make sb green (with envy)
palissade [palisad] NF fence
palissandre [palisɑ̃dʀ] NM rosewood
palliatif [paljatif] NM palliative; (*expédient*) stopgap measure
pallier [palje] /**7**/ VT: **~ à** to offset, make up for
palmarès [palmaʀɛs] NM record (*of achievements*); (*Scol*) prize list; (*Sport*) list of winners
palme [palm] NF (*Bot*) palm leaf; (*symbole*) palm; (*de plongeur*) flipper; **palmes (académiques)** *decoration for services to education*
palmé, e [palme] ADJ (*pattes*) webbed
palmeraie [palməʀɛ] NF palm grove
palmier [palmje] NM palm tree; (*gâteau*) *heart-shaped biscuit made of flaky pastry*
palmipède [palmipɛd] NM palmiped, webfooted bird
palois, e [palwa, -waz] ADJ of *ou* from Pau ▶ NM/F: **P~, e** inhabitant *ou* native of Pau
palombe [palɔ̃b] NF woodpigeon, ringdove
pâlot, te [pɑlo, -ɔt] ADJ pale, peaky
palourde [paluʀd] NF clam
palpable [palpabl] ADJ tangible, palpable

palper [palpe] /**1**/ VT to feel, finger
palpitant, e [palpitɑ̃, -ɑ̃t] ADJ thrilling, gripping
palpitation [palpitasjɔ̃] NF palpitation
palpiter [palpite] /**1**/ VI (*cœur, pouls*) to beat; (*: plus fort*) to pound, throb; (*narines, chair*) to quiver
paludisme [palydism] NM malaria
palustre [palystʀ] ADJ (*coquillage etc*) marsh *cpd*; (*fièvre*) malarial
pâmer [pɑme] /**1**/: **se pâmer** VI to swoon; (*fig*): **se pâmer devant** to go into raptures over
pâmoison [pɑmwazɔ̃] NF: **tomber en ~** to swoon
pampa [pɑ̃pa] NF pampas *pl*
pamphlet [pɑ̃flɛ] NM lampoon, satirical tract
pamphlétaire [pɑ̃fletɛʀ] NMF lampoonist
pamplemousse [pɑ̃pləmus] NM grapefruit
pan [pɑ̃] NM section, piece; (*côté: d'un prisme, d'une tour*) side, face ▶ EXCL bang!; **~ de chemise** shirt tail; **~ de mur** section of wall
panacée [panase] NF panacea
panachage [panaʃaʒ] NM blend, mix; (*Pol*) *voting for candidates from different parties instead of for the set list of one party*
panache [panaʃ] NM plume; (*fig*) spirit, panache
panaché, e [panaʃe] ADJ: **œillet ~** variegated carnation ▶ NM (*bière*) shandy; **glace ~** mixed ice cream; **salade ~** mixed salad
panais [panɛ] NM parsnip
Panama [panama] NM: **le ~** Panama
panaméen, ne [panameɛ̃, -ɛn] ADJ Panamanian ▶ NM/F: **P~, ne** Panamanian
panaris [panaʀi] NM whitlow
pancarte [pɑ̃kaʀt] NF sign, notice; (*dans un défilé*) placard
pancréas [pɑ̃kʀeas] NM pancreas
panda [pɑ̃da] NM panda
pandémie [pɑ̃demi] NF pandemic
pané, e [pane] ADJ fried in breadcrumbs
panégyrique [paneʒiʀik] NM: **faire le ~ de qn** to extol sb's merits *ou* virtues
panier [panje] NM basket; (*à diapositives*) magazine; **mettre au ~** to chuck away; **~ de crabes: c'est un ~ de crabes** (*fig*) they're constantly at one another's throats; **~ percé** (*fig*) spendthrift; **~ à provisions** shopping basket; **~ à salade** (*Culin*) salad shaker; (*Police*) paddy wagon, police van
panier-repas [panje(ə)pɑ] (*pl* **paniers-repas**) NM packed lunch
panification [panifikasjɔ̃] NF bread-making
panique [panik] ADJ panicky ▶ NF panic
paniquer [panike] /**1**/ VI to panic
panne [pan] NF (*d'un mécanisme, moteur*) breakdown; **être/tomber en ~** to have broken down/break down; **être en ~ d'essence** *ou* **en ~ sèche** to have run out of petrol (BRIT) *ou* gas (US); **mettre en ~** (*Navig*) to bring to; **~ d'électricité** *ou* **de courant** power *ou* electrical failure
panneau, x [pano] NM (*écriteau*) sign, notice; (*de boiserie, de tapisserie etc*) panel; **tomber dans le ~** (*fig*) to walk into the trap; **~ d'affichage** notice (BRIT) *ou* bulletin (US) board; **~ électoral** board

for election poster; **~ indicateur** signpost;
~ publicitaire hoarding (BRIT), billboard (US);
~ de signalisation roadsign; **~ solaire** solar
panel
panonceau, x [panɔso] NM (*de magasin etc*) sign;
(*de médecin etc*) plaque
panoplie [panɔpli] NF (*jouet*) outfit; (*d'armes*)
display; (*fig*) array
panorama [panɔʀama] NM (*vue*) all-round
view, panorama; (*peinture*) panorama; (*fig: étude
complète*) complete overview
panoramique [panɔʀamik] ADJ panoramic;
(*carrosserie*) with panoramic windows ▶ NM
(*Ciné, TV*) panoramic shot
panse [pɑs] NF paunch
pansement [pɑsmɑ] NM dressing, bandage;
~ adhésif sticking plaster (BRIT), bandaid® (US)
panser [pɑse] /1/ VT (*plaie*) to dress, bandage;
(*bras*) to put a dressing on, bandage; (*cheval*) to
groom
pantacourt [pɑtakuʀ] NM cropped trousers pl
pantalon [pɑtalɔ] NM trousers pl (BRIT), pants pl
(US), pair of trousers ou pants; **~ de ski** ski pants pl
pantalonnade [pɑtalɔnad] NF slapstick
(comedy)
pantelant, e [pɑtlɑ, -ɑt] ADJ gasping for breath,
panting
panthère [pɑtɛʀ] NF panther
pantin [pɑtɛ] NM (*jouet*) jumping jack; (*péj:
personne*) puppet
pantois [pɑtwa] ADJ M: **rester ~** to be
flabbergasted
pantomime [pɑtɔmim] NF mime; (*pièce*) mime
show; (*péj*) fuss, carry-on
pantouflard, e [pɑtuflaʀ, -aʀd] ADJ (*péj*)
stay-at-home
pantoufle [pɑtufl] NF slipper
panure [panyʀ] NF breadcrumbs pl
PAO SIGLE F (= *publication assistée par ordinateur*) DTP
paon [pɑ] NM peacock
papa [papa] NM dad(dy)
papauté [papote] NF papacy
papaye [papaj] NF pawpaw
pape [pap] NM pope
paperasse [papʀas] NF (*péj*) bumf no pl, papers
pl; forms pl
paperasserie [papʀasʀi] NF (*péj*) red tape no pl;
paperwork no pl
papeterie [papɛtʀi] NF (*fabrication du papier*)
paper-making (industry); (*usine*) paper mill;
(*magasin*) stationer's (shop) (BRIT); (*articles*)
stationery
papetier, -ière [paptje, -jɛʀ] NM/F paper-
maker; stationer
papetier-libraire [paptjelibʀɛʀ] (*pl* **papetiers-
libraires**) NM bookseller and stationer
papi [papi] NM (*fam*) granddad
papier [papje] NM paper; (*feuille*) sheet ou piece
of paper; (*article*) article; (*écrit officiel*) document;
papiers NMPL (*aussi:* **papiers d'identité**)
(identity) papers; **sur le ~** (*théoriquement*) on
paper; **noircir du ~** to write page after page;
~ couché/glacé art/glazed paper;
~ (d')aluminium aluminium (BRIT) ou

aluminum (US) foil, tinfoil; **~ d'Arménie**
incense paper; **~ bible** India ou bible paper;
~ de brouillon rough ou scrap paper; **~ bulle**
manil(l)a paper; **~ buvard** blotting paper;
~ calque tracing paper; **~ carbone** carbon
paper; **~ collant** Sellotape® (BRIT), Scotch tape®
(US), sticky tape; **~ en continu** continuous
stationery; **~ à dessin** drawing paper;
~ d'emballage wrapping paper; **~ gommé**
gummed paper; **~ hygiénique** ou **(de) toilette**
toilet paper; **~ journal** newsprint; (*pour
emballer*) newspaper; **~ à lettres** writing paper,
notepaper; **~ mâché** papier-mâché; **~ machine**
typing paper; **~ peint** wallpaper; **~ pelure**
India paper; **~ à pliage accordéon** fanfold
paper; **~ de soie** tissue paper; **~ thermique**
thermal paper; **~ de tournesol** litmus paper;
~ de verre sandpaper
papier-filtre [papjefiltʀ] (*pl* **papiers-filtres**) NM
filter paper
papier-monnaie [papjemɔnɛ] (*pl* **papiers-
monnaies**) NM paper money
papille [papij] NF: **papilles gustatives** taste buds
papillon [papijɔ] NM butterfly; (*fam:
contravention*) (parking) ticket; (*Tech: écrou*) wing
ou butterfly nut; **~ de nuit** moth
papillonner [papijɔne] /1/ VI to flit from one
thing (ou person) to another
papillote [papijɔt] NF (*pour cheveux*) curlpaper;
(*de gigot*) (paper) frill; **en ~** cooked in tinfoil
papilloter [papijɔte] /1/ VI (*yeux*) to blink;
(*paupières*) to flutter; (*lumière*) to flicker
papotage [papɔtaʒ] NM chitchat
papoter [papɔte] /1/ VI to chatter
papou, e [papu] ADJ Papuan
Papouasie-Nouvelle-Guinée
[papwazinuvɛlgine] NF: **la ~** Papua-New-
Guinea
paprika [papʀika] NM paprika
papyrus [papiʀys] NM papyrus
pâque [pak] NF: **la ~** Passover; *voir aussi* **Pâques**
paquebot [pakbo] NM liner
pâquerette [pakʀɛt] NF daisy
Pâques [pak] NM, NFPL Easter; *see note;* **faire
ses ~** to do one's Easter duties; **l'île de ~** Easter
Island

> In France, Easter eggs are said to be brought
> by the Easter bells or *cloches de Pâques* which
> fly from Rome and drop them in people's
> gardens.

paquet [pakɛ] NM packet; (*colis*) parcel; (*ballot*)
bundle; (*dans négociations*) package (deal); (*fig:
tas*): **~ de pile** ou heap of; **paquets** NMPL (*bagages*)
bags; **mettre le ~** (*fam*) to give one's all; **~ de
mer** big wave
paquetage [pakta ʒ] NM (*Mil*) kit, pack
paquet-cadeau [pakɛkado] (*pl* **paquets-
cadeaux**) NM gift-wrapped parcel
par [paʀ] PRÉP by; **finir** *etc* **~** to end *etc* with;
~ amour out of love; **passer ~ Lyon/la côte** to
go via ou through Lyons/along by the coast; **~ la
fenêtre** (*jeter, regarder*) out of the window; **trois
~ jour/personne** three ou per day/head; **deux
~ deux** two at a time; (*marcher etc*) in twos; **~ où?**

which way?; **~ ici** this way; (*dans le coin*) round here; **~-ci, ~-là** here and there; **~ temps de pluie** in wet weather

para [paʀa] NM (*parachutiste*) para

parabole [paʀabɔl] NF (*Rel*) parable; (*Géom*) parabola

parabolique [paʀabɔlik] ADJ parabolic; **antenne ~** satellite dish

parachever [paʀaʃve] /5/ VT to perfect

parachutage [paʀaʃytaʒ] NM (*de soldats, vivres*) parachuting-in; **nous sommes contre le ~ d'un candidat parisien dans notre circonscription** (*Pol, fig*) we are against a Parisian candidate being landed on us

parachute [paʀaʃyt] NM parachute

parachuter [paʀaʃyte] /1/ VT (*soldat etc*) to parachute; (*fig*) to pitchfork; **il a été parachuté à la tête de l'entreprise** he was brought in from outside as head of the company

parachutisme [paʀaʃytism] NM parachuting

parachutiste [paʀaʃytist] NMF parachutist; (*Mil*) paratrooper

parade [paʀad] NF (*spectacle, défilé*) parade; (*Escrime, Boxe*) parry; (*ostentation*): **faire ~ de** to display, show off; (*défense, riposte*): **trouver la ~ à une attaque** to find the answer to an attack; **de ~** *adj* ceremonial; (*superficiel*) superficial, outward

parader [paʀade] /1/ VI to swagger (around), show off

paradis [paʀadi] NM heaven, paradise; **P~ terrestre** (*Rel*) Garden of Eden; (*fig*) heaven on earth

paradisiaque [paʀadizjak] ADJ heavenly, divine

paradoxal, e, -aux [paʀadɔksal, -o] ADJ paradoxical

paradoxalement [paʀadɔksalmɑ̃] ADV paradoxically

paradoxe [paʀadɔks] NM paradox

parafe [paʀaf] NM, **parafer** [paʀafe] VT = **paraphe; parapher**

paraffine [paʀafin] NF paraffin; paraffin wax

paraffiné, e [paʀafine] ADJ: **papier ~** wax(ed) paper

parafoudre [paʀafudʀ] NM (*Élec*) lightning conductor

parages [paʀaʒ] NMPL (*Navig*) waters; **dans les ~ (de)** in the area *ou* vicinity (of)

paragraphe [paʀagʀaf] NM paragraph

Paraguay [paʀagwɛ] NM: **le ~** Paraguay

paraguayen, ne [paʀagwajɛ̃, -ɛn] ADJ Paraguayan ▶ NM/F: **P~, ne** Paraguayan

paraître [paʀɛtʀ] /57/ VB COPULE to seem, look, appear ▶ VI to appear; (*être visible*) to show; (*Presse, Édition*) to be published, come out, appear; (*briller*) to show off; **laisser ~ qch** to let (sth) show ▶ VB IMPERS: **il paraît que** it seems *ou* appears that; **il me paraît que** it seems to me that; **il paraît absurde de** it seems absurd to; **il ne paraît pas son âge** he doesn't look his age; **~ en justice** to appear before the court(s); **~ en scène/en public/à l'écran** to appear on stage/in public/on the screen

parallèle [paʀalɛl] ADJ parallel; (*police, marché*) unofficial; (*société, énergie*) alternative ▶ NM (*comparaison*): **faire un ~ entre** to draw a parallel between; (*Géo*) parallel ▶ NF parallel (line); **en ~** in parallel; **mettre en ~** (*choses opposées*) to compare; (*choses semblables*) to parallel

parallèlement [paʀalɛlmɑ̃] ADV in parallel; (*fig: en même temps*) at the same time

parallélépipède [paʀalelepiped] NM parallelepiped

parallélisme [paʀalelism] NM parallelism; (*Auto*) wheel alignment

parallélogramme [paʀalelɔgʀam] NM parallelogram

paralyser [paʀalize] /1/ VT to paralyze

paralysie [paʀalizi] NF paralysis

paralytique [paʀalitik] ADJ, NMF paralytic

paramédical, e, -aux [paʀamedikal, -o] ADJ paramedical; **personnel ~** paramedics *pl*, paramedical workers *pl*

paramètre [paʀamɛtʀ] NM parameter

paramilitaire [paʀamilitɛʀ] ADJ paramilitary

paranoïa [paʀanɔja] NF paranoia

paranoïaque [paʀanɔjak] NMF paranoiac

paranormal, e, -aux [paʀanɔʀmal, -o] ADJ paranormal

parapet [paʀapɛ] NM parapet

paraphe [paʀaf] NM (*trait*) flourish; (*signature*) initials *pl*; signature

parapher [paʀafe] /1/ VT to initial; to sign

paraphrase [paʀafʀaz] NF paraphrase

paraphraser [paʀafʀaze] /1/ VT to paraphrase

paraplégie [paʀapleʒi] NF paraplegia

paraplégique [paʀapleʒik] ADJ, NMF paraplegic

parapluie [paʀaplɥi] NM umbrella; **~ atomique** *ou* **nucléaire** nuclear umbrella; **~ pliant** telescopic umbrella

parapsychique [paʀapsiʃik] ADJ parapsychological

parapsychologie [paʀapsikɔlɔʒi] NF parapsychology

parapublic, -ique [paʀapyblik] ADJ *partly state-controlled*

parascolaire [paʀaskɔlɛʀ] ADJ extracurricular

parasitaire [paʀazitɛʀ] ADJ parasitic(al)

parasite [paʀazit] NM parasite ▶ ADJ (*Bot, Bio*) parasitic(al); **parasites** NMPL (*Tél*) interference *sg*

parasitisme [paʀazitism] NM parasitism

parasol [paʀasɔl] NM parasol, sunshade

paratonnerre [paʀatɔnɛʀ] NM lightning conductor

paravent [paʀavɑ̃] NM folding screen; (*fig*) screen

parc [paʀk] NM (*public*) park, gardens *pl*; (*de château etc*) grounds *pl*; (*pour le bétail*) pen, enclosure; (*d'enfant*) playpen; (*Mil: entrepôt*) depot; (*ensemble d'unités*) stock; (*de voitures etc*) fleet; **~ d'attractions** amusement park; **~ automobile** (*d'un pays*) number of cars on the roads; **~ éolien** wind farm; **~ à huîtres** oyster bed; **~ national** national park; **~ naturel** nature reserve; **~ de stationnement** car park;

~ à thème theme park; **~ zoologique** zoological gardens *pl*

parcelle [paʀsɛl] NF fragment, scrap; *(de terrain)* plot, parcel

parceliser [paʀselize] /**1**/ VT to divide *ou* split up

parce que [paʀsk] CONJ because

parchemin [paʀʃəmɛ̃] NM parchment

parcheminé, e [paʀʃəmine] ADJ wrinkled; *(papier)* with a parchment finish

parcimonie [paʀsimɔni] NF parsimony, parsimoniousness

parcimonieux, -euse [paʀsimɔnjø, -øz] ADJ parsimonious, miserly

parc(o)mètre [paʀk(ɔ)mɛtʀ] NM parking meter

parcotrain [paʀkɔtʀɛ̃] NM station car park (BRIT) *ou* parking lot (US), park-and-ride car park (BRIT)

parcourir [paʀkuʀiʀ] /**11**/ VT *(trajet, distance)* to cover; *(article, livre)* to skim *ou* glance through; *(lieu)* to go all over, travel up and down; *(frisson, vibration)* to run through; **~ des yeux** to run one's eye over

parcours [paʀkuʀ] VB *voir* **parcourir** ▶ NM *(trajet)* journey; *(itinéraire)* route; *(Sport: terrain)* course; *(: tour)* round; run; lap; **~ du combattant** assault course

parcouru, e [paʀkuʀy] PP *de* **parcourir**

par-delà [paʀdəla] PRÉP beyond

par-dessous [paʀdəsu] PRÉP, ADV under(neath)

pardessus [paʀdəsy] NM overcoat

par-dessus [paʀdəsy] PRÉP over (the top of) ▶ ADV over (the top); **~ le marché** on top of it all; **~ tout** above all; **en avoir ~ la tête** to have had enough

par-devant [paʀdəvɑ̃] PRÉP in the presence of, before ▶ ADV at the front; *(passer)* round the front

pardon [paʀdɔ̃] NM forgiveness *no pl* ▶ EXCL *(excuses)* (I'm) sorry; *(pour interpeller etc)* excuse me; **demander ~ à qn (de)** to apologize to sb (for); **je vous demande ~** I'm sorry; *(pour interpeller)* excuse me; *(demander de répéter)* (I beg your) pardon? (BRIT), pardon me? (US)

pardonnable [paʀdɔnabl] ADJ forgivable, excusable

pardonner [paʀdɔne] /**1**/ VT to forgive; **~ qch à qn** to forgive sb for sth; **qui ne pardonne pas** *(maladie, erreur)* fatal

paré, e [paʀe] ADJ ready, prepared

pare-balles [paʀbal] ADJ INV bulletproof

pare-boue [paʀbu] NM INV mudflap

pare-brise [paʀbʀiz] NM INV windscreen (BRIT), windshield (US)

pare-chocs [paʀʃɔk] NM INV bumper (BRIT), fender (US)

pare-étincelles [paʀetɛ̃sɛl] NM INV fireguard

pare-feu [paʀfø] NM INV *(de foyer)* fireguard; *(Inform)* firewall ▶ ADJ INV: **portes ~** fire (resistant) doors

pareil, le [paʀɛj] ADJ *(identique)* the same, alike; *(similaire)* similar; *(tel)*: **un courage/livre ~** such courage/a book, courage/a book like this; **de pareils livres** such books ▶ ADV: **habillés ~** dressed the same (way), dressed alike; **faire ~** to do the same (thing); **j'en veux un ~** I'd like

one just like it; **rien de ~** no *(ou* any) such thing, nothing *(ou* anything) like it; **ses pareils** one's fellow men; one's peers; **ne pas avoir son (sa) ~(le)** to be second to none; **~ à** the same as; similar to; **sans ~** unparalleled, unequalled; **c'est du ~ au même** it comes to the same thing, it's six (of one) and half-a-dozen (of the other); **en ~ cas** in such a case; **rendre la ~ à qn** to pay sb back in his own coin

pareillement [paʀɛjmɑ̃] ADV the same, alike; in such a way; *(également)* likewise

parement [paʀmɑ̃] NM *(Constr: revers d'un col, d'une manche)* facing; *(Rel)*: **~ d'autel** antependium

parent, e [paʀɑ̃, -ɑ̃t] NM/F: **un/une ~/e** a relative *ou* relation ▶ ADJ: **être ~ de** to be related to; **parents** NMPL *(père et mère)* parents; *(famille, proches)* relatives, relations; **~ unique** lone parent; **parents par alliance** relatives *ou* relations by marriage; **parents en ligne directe** blood relations

parental, e, -aux [paʀɑ̃tal, -o] ADJ parental

parenté [paʀɑ̃te] NF *(lien)* relationship; *(personnes)* relatives *pl*, relations *pl*

parenthèse [paʀɑ̃tɛz] NF *(ponctuation)* bracket, parenthesis; *(Math)* bracket; *(digression)* parenthesis, digression; **ouvrir/fermer la ~** to open/close brackets; **entre parenthèses** in brackets; *(fig)* incidentally

parer [paʀe] /**1**/ VT to adorn; *(Culin)* to dress, trim; *(éviter)* to ward off; **~ à** *(danger)* to ward off; *(inconvénient)* to deal with; **se ~ de** *(fig: qualité, titre)* to assume; **~ à toute éventualité** to be ready for every eventuality; **~ au plus pressé** to attend to what's most urgent

pare-soleil [paʀsɔlɛj] NM INV sun visor

paresse [paʀɛs] NF laziness

paresser [paʀese] /**1**/ VI to laze around

paresseusement [paʀɛsøzmɑ̃] ADV lazily; sluggishly

paresseux, -euse [paʀesø, -øz] ADJ lazy; *(fig)* slow, sluggish ▶ NM *(Zool)* sloth

parfaire [paʀfɛʀ] /**60**/ VT to perfect, complete

parfait, e [paʀfɛ, -ɛt] PP *de* **parfaire** ▶ ADJ perfect ▶ NM *(Ling)* perfect (tense); *(Culin)* parfait ▶ EXCL fine, excellent

parfaitement [paʀfɛtmɑ̃] ADV perfectly ▶ EXCL (most) certainly

parfaites [paʀfɛt], **parfasse** [paʀfas], **parferai** *etc* [paʀfəʀe] VB *voir* **parfaire**

parfois [paʀfwa] ADV sometimes

parfum [paʀfœ̃] NM *(produit)* perfume, scent; *(odeur: de fleur)* scent, fragrance; *(: de tabac, vin)* aroma; *(goût: de glace, milk-shake)* flavour (BRIT), flavor (US)

parfumé, e [paʀfyme] ADJ *(fleur, fruit)* fragrant; *(papier à lettres etc)* scented; *(femme)* wearing perfume *ou* scent, perfumed; **~ au café** coffee-flavoured (BRIT) *ou* -flavored (US)

parfumer [paʀfyme] /**1**/ VT *(odeur, bouquet)* to perfume; *(mouchoir)* to put scent *ou* perfume on; *(crème, gâteau)* to flavour (BRIT), flavor (US); **se parfumer** to put on (some) perfume *ou* scent; *(d'habitude)* to use perfume *ou* scent

P

parfumerie [paʀfymʀi] NF *(commerce)* perfumery; *(produits)* perfumes; *(boutique)* perfume shop (BRIT) ou store (US)

pari [paʀi] NM bet, wager; *(Sport)* bet; **~ mutuel urbain (PMU)** *system of betting on horses*

paria [paʀja] NM outcast

parier [paʀje] /7/ VT to bet; **j'aurais parié que si/non** I'd have said he *(ou* you *etc)* would/wouldn't

parieur [paʀjœʀ] NM *(turfiste etc)* punter

Paris [paʀi] N Paris

parisien, ne [paʀizjɛ̃, -ɛn] ADJ Parisian; *(Géo, Admin)* Paris *cpd* ▸ NM/F: **P~, ne** Parisian

paritaire [paʀitɛʀ] ADJ: **commission ~** joint commission

parité [paʀite] NF parity; **~ de change** *(Écon)* exchange parity; **~ hommes-femmes** *(Pol)* balanced representation of men and women

parjure [paʀʒyʀ] NM *(faux serment)* false oath, perjury; *(violation de serment)* breach of oath, perjury ▸ NMF perjurer

parjurer [paʀʒyʀe] /1/: **se parjurer** VI to perjure o.s

parka [paʀka] NF parka

parking [paʀkiŋ] NM *(lieu)* car park (BRIT), parking lot (US); **~-relais** park and ride

parlant, e [paʀlɑ̃, -ɑ̃t] ADJ *(fig)* graphic, vivid; *(comparaison, preuve)* eloquent; *(Ciné)* talking ▸ ADV: **généralement ~** generally speaking

parlé, e [paʀle] ADJ: **langue ~** spoken language

parlement [paʀləmɑ̃] NM parliament; **le P~ européen** the European Parliament

parlementaire [paʀləmɑ̃tɛʀ] ADJ parliamentary ▸ NMF *(député)* ≈ Member of Parliament (BRIT) ou Congress (US); parliamentarian; *(négociateur)* negotiator, mediator

parlementarisme [paʀləmɑ̃taʀism] NM parliamentary government

parlementer [paʀləmɑ̃te] /1/ VI *(ennemis)* to negotiate, parley; *(s'entretenir, discuter)* to argue at length, have lengthy talks

parler [paʀle] NM speech; dialect ▸ VI to speak, talk; *(avouer)* to talk; **~ (à qn) de** to talk ou speak (to sb) about; **~ pour qn** *(intercéder)* to speak for sb; **~ en l'air** to say the first thing that comes into one's head; **~ le/en français** to speak French/in French; **~ affaires** to talk business; **~ en dormant/du nez** to talk in one's sleep/through one's nose; **sans ~ de** *(fig)* not to mention, to say nothing of; **tu parles!** you must be joking!; *(bien sûr)* you bet!; **n'en parlons plus!** let's forget it!

parleur [paʀlœʀ] NM: **beau ~** fine talker

parloir [paʀlwaʀ] NM *(d'une prison, d'un hôpital)* visiting room; *(Rel)* parlour (BRIT), parlor (US)

parlote [paʀlɔt] NF chitchat

Parme [paʀm] N Parma

parme [paʀm] ADJ violet (blue)

parmesan [paʀməzɑ̃] NM Parmesan (cheese)

parmi [paʀmi] PRÉP among(st)

parodie [paʀɔdi] NF parody

parodier [paʀɔdje] /7/ VT *(œuvre, auteur)* to parody

paroi [paʀwa] NF wall; *(cloison)* partition;

~ rocheuse rock face

paroisse [paʀwas] NF parish

paroissial, e, -aux [paʀwasjal, -o] ADJ parish *cpd*

paroissien, ne [paʀwasjɛ̃, -ɛn] NM/F parishioner ▸ NM prayer book

parole [paʀɔl] NF *(mot, promesse)* word; *(faculté):* **la ~** speech; **paroles** NFPL *(Mus)* words, lyrics; **la bonne ~** *(Rel)* the word of God; **tenir ~** to keep one's word; **avoir la ~** to have the floor; **n'avoir qu'une ~** to be true to one's word; **donner la ~ à qn** to hand over to sb; **prendre la ~** to speak; **demander la ~** to ask for permission to speak; **perdre la ~** to lose the power of speech; *(fig)* to lose one's tongue; **je le crois sur ~** I'll take his word for it, I'll take him at his word; **temps de ~** *(TV, Radio etc)* discussion time; **ma ~!** my word!, good heavens!; **~ d'honneur** word of honour (BRIT) ou honor (US)

parolier, -ière [paʀɔlje, -jɛʀ] NM/F lyricist; *(Opéra)* librettist

paroxysme [paʀɔksism] NM height, paroxysm

parpaing [paʀpɛ̃] NM bond-stone, parpen

parquer [paʀke] /1/ VT *(voiture, matériel)* to park; *(bestiaux)* to pen (in ou up); *(prisonniers)* to pack in

parquet [paʀkɛ] NM *(parquet)* floor; *(Jur: bureau)* public prosecutor's office; **le ~ (général)** *(magistrats)* ≈ the Bench

parqueter [paʀkəte] /4/ VT to lay a parquet floor in

parrain [paʀɛ̃] NM godfather; *(d'un navire)* namer; *(d'un nouvel adhérent)* sponsor, proposer

parrainage [paʀɛnaʒ] NM sponsorship

parrainer [paʀɛne] /1/ VT *(nouvel adhérent)* to sponsor, propose; *(entreprise)* to promote, sponsor

parricide [paʀisid] NMF parricide

pars [paʀ] VB *voir* **partir**

parsemer [paʀsəme] /5/ VT *(feuilles, papiers)* to be scattered over; **~ qch de** to scatter sth with

parsi, e [paʀsi] ADJ Parsee

part [paʀ] VB *voir* **partir** ▸ NF *(qui revient à qn)* share; *(fraction, partie)* part; *(de gâteau, fromage)* portion; *(Finance)* (non-voting) share; **prendre ~ à** *(débat etc)* to take part in; *(soucis, douleur de qn)* to share in; **faire ~ de qch à qn** to announce sth to sb, inform sb of sth; **pour ma ~** as for me, as far as I'm concerned; **à ~ entière** *adj* full; **de la ~ de** *(au nom de)* on behalf of; *(donné par)* from; **c'est de la ~ de qui?** *(au téléphone)* who's calling *ou* speaking (please)?; **de toute(s) ~(s)** from all sides *ou* quarters; **de ~ et d'autre** on both sides, on either side; **de ~ en ~** right through; **d'une ~ ... d'autre ~** on the one hand ... on the other hand; **d'autre ~** *(de plus)* moreover; **nulle/autre/quelque ~** nowhere/elsewhere/somewhere; **à ~** *adv* separately; *(de côté)* aside; *prép* apart from, except for; *adj* exceptional, special; **pour une large** *ou* **bonne ~** to a great extent; **prendre qch en bonne/mauvaise ~** to take sth well/badly; **faire la ~ des choses** to make allowances; **faire la ~ du feu** *(fig)* to cut one's losses; **faire la ~ (trop) belle à qn** to give sb more than his *(ou* her) share

part. ABR = **particulier**

partage [paʀtaʒ] NM sharing (out) *no pl*, share-out; sharing; dividing up; (*Pol: de suffrages*) share; **recevoir qch en ~** to receive sth as one's share (*ou* lot); **sans ~** undivided; **~ de fichiers** (*Inform*) file sharing

partagé, e [paʀtaʒe] ADJ (*opinions etc*) divided; (*amour*) shared; **être ~ entre** to be shared between; **être ~ sur** to be divided about

partager [paʀtaʒe] /3/ VT to share; (*distribuer, répartir*) to share (out); (*morceler, diviser*) to divide (up); **se partager** VT (*héritage etc*) to share between themselves (*ou* ourselves *etc*)

partance [paʀtɑ̃s] : **en ~** adv outbound, due to leave; **en ~ pour** (bound) for

partant, e [paʀtɑ̃, -ɑ̃t] VB *voir* **partir** ▶ ADJ: **être ~ pour qch** (*d'accord pour*) to be quite ready for sth ▶ NM (*Sport*) starter; (*Hippisme*) runner

partenaire [paʀtənɛʀ] NMF partner; **partenaires sociaux** management and workforce

parterre [paʀtɛʀ] NM (*de fleurs*) (flower) bed, border; (*Théât*) stalls *pl*

parti [paʀti] NM (*Pol*) party; (*décision*) course of action; (*personne à marier*) match; **tirer ~ de** to take advantage of, turn to good account; **prendre le ~ de faire** to make up one's mind to do, resolve to do; **prendre le ~ de qn** to stand up for sb, side with sb; **prendre ~ (pour/contre)** to take sides *ou* a stand (for/against); **prendre son ~ de** to come to terms with; **~ pris** bias

partial, e, -aux [paʀsjal, -o] ADJ biased, partial

partialement [paʀsjalmɑ̃] ADV in a biased way

partialité [paʀsjalite] NF bias, partiality

participant, e [paʀtisipɑ̃, -ɑ̃t] NM/F participant; (*à un concours*) entrant; (*d'une société*) member

participation [paʀtisipasjɔ̃] NF participation; (*financière*) contribution; sharing; (*Comm*) interest; **la ~ aux bénéfices** profit-sharing; **la ~ ouvrière** worker participation; **"avec la ~ de …"** "featuring …"

participe [paʀtisip] NM participle; **~ passé/présent** past/present participle

participer [paʀtisipe] /1/: **~ à** VT (*course, réunion*) to take part in; (*profits etc*) to share in; (*frais etc*) to contribute to; (*entreprise: financièrement*) to cooperate in; (*chagrin, succès de qn*) to share (in); **~ de** VT to partake of

particulariser [paʀtikylaʀize] /1/: **se particulariser** VT to mark o.s. (*ou* itself) out

particularisme [paʀtikylaʀism] NM sense of identity

particularité [paʀtikylaʀite] NF particularity; (*distinctive*) characteristic, feature

particule [paʀtikyl] NF particle; **~ (nobiliaire)** nobiliary particle

particulier, -ière [paʀtikylje, -jɛʀ] ADJ (*personnel, privé*) private; (*étrange*) peculiar, odd; (*spécial*) special, particular; (*caractéristique*) characteristic, distinctive; (*spécifique*) particular ▶ NM (*individu: Admin*) private individual; **"~ vend …"** (*Comm*) "for sale privately …", "for sale by owner …" (*US*); **~ à**

peculiar to; **en ~** adv (*surtout*) in particular, particularly; (*à part*) separately; (*en privé*) in private

particulièrement [paʀtikyljɛʀmɑ̃] ADV particularly

partie [paʀti] NF (*gén*) part; (*profession, spécialité*) field, subject; (*Jur etc: protagonistes*) party; (*de cartes, tennis etc*) game; (*fig: lutte, combat*) struggle, fight; **une ~ de campagne/de pêche** an outing in the country/a fishing party *ou* trip; **en ~** adv partly, in part; **faire ~ de** to belong to; (*chose*) to be part of; **prendre qn à ~** to take sb to task; (*malmener*) to set on sb; **en grande ~** largely, in the main; **ce n'est que ~ remise** it will be for another time *ou* the next time; **avoir ~ liée avec qn** to be in league with sb; **~ civile** (*Jur*) party claiming damages in a criminal case

partiel, le [paʀsjɛl] ADJ partial ▶ NM (*Scol*) class exam

partiellement [paʀsjɛlmɑ̃] ADV partially, partly

partir [paʀtiʀ] /16/ VI (*gén*) to go; (*quitter*) to go, leave; (*s'éloigner*) to go (*ou* drive off) away *ou* off; (*moteur*) to start; (*pétard*) to go off; (*bouchon*) to come out; (*bouton*) to come off; (*tache*) to go, come out; **~ de** (*lieu: quitter*) to leave; (: *commencer à*) to start from; (*date*) to run *ou* start from; **~ pour/à** (*lieu, pays etc*) to leave for/go off to; **à ~ de** from

partisan, e [paʀtizɑ̃, -an] NM/F partisan; (*d'un parti, régime etc*) supporter ▶ ADJ (*lutte, querelle*) partisan, one-sided; **être ~ de qch/faire** to be in favour (*Brit*) *ou* favor (*US*) of sth/doing

partitif, -ive [paʀtitif, -iv] ADJ: **article ~** partitive article

partition [paʀtisjɔ̃] NF (*Mus*) score

partout [paʀtu] ADV everywhere; **~ où il allait** everywhere *ou* wherever he went; **trente ~** (*Tennis*) thirty all

paru [paʀy] PP *de* **paraître**

parure [paʀyʀ] NF (*bijoux etc*) finery *no pl*; jewellery *no pl* (*Brit*), jewelry *no pl* (*US*); (*assortiment*) set

parus *etc* [paʀy] VB *voir* **paraître**

parution [paʀysjɔ̃] NF publication, appearance

parvenir [paʀvəniʀ] /22/: **~ à** VT (*atteindre*) to reach; (*obtenir, arriver à*) to attain; (*réussir*) **~ à faire** to manage to do, succeed in doing; **faire ~ qch à qn** to have sth sent to sb

parvenu, e [paʀvəny] PP *de* **parvenir** ▶ NM/F (*péj*) parvenu, upstart

parviendrai [paʀvjɛ̃dʀe], **parviens** *etc* [paʀvjɛ̃] VB *voir* **parvenir**

parvis [paʀvi] NM square (*in front of a church*)

┌─────────┐
│ MOT-CLÉ │
└─────────┘

pas¹ [pɑ] ADV **1** (*en corrélation avec ne, non etc*) not; **il ne pleure pas** (*habituellement*) he does not *ou* doesn't cry (: *maintenant*) he's not *ou* isn't crying; **je ne mange pas de viande** I don't *ou* do not eat meat; **il n'a pas pleuré/ne pleurera pas** he did not *ou* didn't/will not *ou* won't cry; **ils n'ont pas de voiture/d'enfants** they haven't got a car/any children, they have no car/children; **il m'a dit de ne pas le faire** he told me not to

P

do it; **non pas que ...** not that ..
2 (*employé sans ne etc*): **pas moi** not me, not I, I
don't (*ou* can't *etc*); **elle travaille, (mais) lui
pas** *ou* **pas lui** she works but he doesn't *ou* does
not; **une pomme pas mûre** an apple which
isn't ripe; **pas plus tard qu'hier** only
yesterday; **pas du tout** not at all; **pas de
sucre, merci** no sugar, thanks; **ceci est à vous
ou pas?** is this yours or not?, is this yours or
isn't it?
3: **pas mal** (*joli: personne, maison*) not bad; **pas
mal fait** not badly done *ou* made; **comment ça
va? — pas mal** how are things? — not bad; **pas
mal de** quite a lot of

pas² [pα] NM (*démarche*) tread; (*enjambée, Danse,
fig: étape*) step; (*bruit*) (foot)step; (*trace*) footprint;
(*allure, mesure*) pace; (*d'un cheval*) walk; (*Tech: de
vis, d'écrou*) thread; ~ **à** ~ step by step; **au** ~ at a
walking pace; **de ce** ~ (*à l'instant même*)
straightaway, at once; **marcher à grands** ~ to
stride along; **mettre qn au** ~ to bring sb to
heel; **au** ~ **de gymnastique/de course** at a jog
trot/at a run; **à** ~ **de loup** stealthily; **faire les
cent** ~ to pace up and down; **faire les
premiers** ~ to make the first move; **retourner
ou revenir sur ses** ~ to retrace one's steps; **se
tirer d'un mauvais** ~ to get o.s. out of a tight
spot; **sur le** ~ **de la porte** on the doorstep; **le** ~
de Calais (*détroit*) the Straits *pl* of Dover; ~ **de
porte** (*fig*) key money

pascal, e, -aux [paskal, -o] ADJ Easter *cpd*
passable [pαsabl] ADJ passable, tolerable
passablement [pαsabləmᾶ] ADV (*pas trop mal*)
reasonably well; (*beaucoup*) quite a lot
passade [pαsad] NF passing fancy, whim
passage [pαsaʒ] NM (*fait de passer*) *voir* **passer**;
(*lieu, prix de la traversée, extrait de livre etc*) passage;
(*chemin*) way; (*itinéraire*): **sur le** ~ **du cortège**
along the route of the procession;
"laissez/n'obstruez pas le ~**"** "keep clear/do
not obstruct"; **au** ~ (*en passant*) as I (*ou* he *etc*)
went by; **de** ~ (*touristes*) passing through;
(*amants etc*) casual; ~ **clouté** pedestrian
crossing; **"~ interdit"** "no entry"; **à niveau**
level (BRIT) *ou* grade (US) crossing; **"~ protégé"**
right of way over secondary road(s) on your right;
~ **souterrain** subway (BRIT), underpass; ~ **à
tabac** beating-up; ~ **à vide** (*fig*) bad patch
passager, -ère [pαsaʒe, -ɛR] ADJ passing; (*hôte*)
short-stay *cpd*; (*oiseau*) migratory ▶ NM/F
passenger; ~ **clandestin** stowaway
passagèrement [pαsaʒɛRmᾶ] ADV temporarily,
for a short time
passant, e [pαsᾶ, -ᾶt] ADJ (*rue, endroit*) busy
▶ NM/F passer-by ▶ NM (*pour ceinture etc*) loop;
remarquer qch en ~ to notice sth in passing
passation [pαsasjɔ̃] NF (*Jur: d'un acte*) signing;
~ **des pouvoirs** transfer *ou* handover of power
passe [pαs] NF (*Sport, magnétique*) pass; (*Navig*)
channel ▶ NM (*passe-partout*) master *ou* skeleton
key; **être en** ~ **de faire** to be on the way to
doing; **être dans une mauvaise** ~ (*fig*) to be
going through a bad patch; **être dans une**

bonne ~ (*fig*) to be in a healthy situation;
~ **d'armes** (*fig*) heated exchange
passé, e [pαse] ADJ (*événement, temps*) past;
(*dernier: semaine etc*) last; (*couleur, tapisserie*) faded
▶ PRÉP after ▶ NM past; (*Ling*) past (tense); **il est
~ midi** *ou* **midi ~** it's gone (BRIT) *ou* past twelve;
~ **de mode** out of fashion; ~ **composé** perfect
(tense); ~ **simple** past historic
passe-droit [pαsdRwa] NM special privilege
passéiste [pαseist] ADJ backward-looking
passementerie [pαsmᾶtRi] NF trimmings *pl*
passe-montagne [pαsmɔ̃taɲ] NM balaclava
passe-partout [pαspartu] NM INV master *ou*
skeleton key ▶ ADJ INV all-purpose
passe-passe [pαspαs] NM: **tour de** ~ trick,
sleight of hand *no pl*
passe-plat [pαspla] NM serving hatch
passeport [pαspɔR] NM passport
passer [pαse] /**1**/ VI (*se rendre, aller*) to go; (*voiture,
piétons: défiler*) to pass (by), go by; (*faire une halte
rapide: facteur, laitier etc*) to come, call; (*: pour rendre
visite*) to drop in; (*courant, air, lumière,
franchir un obstacle etc*) to get through; (*accusé,
projet de loi*): ~ **devant** to come before; (*film,
émission*) to be on; (*temps, jours*) to pass, go by;
(*liquide, café*) to go through; (*être digéré, avalé*) to
go down; (*couleur, papier*) to fade; (*mode*) to die
out; (*douleur*) to pass, go away; (*Cartes*) to pass;
(*Scol*): ~ **dans la classe supérieure** to go up (to
the next class); (*devenir*): ~ **président** to be
appointed *ou* become president ▶ VT (*frontière,
rivière etc*) to cross; (*douane*) to go through;
(*examen*) to sit, take; (*visite médicale etc*) to have;
(*journée, temps*) to spend; (*donner*): ~ **qch à qn** (*sel
etc*) to pass sth to sb; (*prêter*) to lend sb sth; (*lettre,
message*) to pass sth on to sb; (*tolérer*) to let sb get
away with sth; (*transmettre*) to pass sth on to sb;
(*enfiler: vêtement*) to slip on; (*faire entrer, mettre*):
(faire) ~ **qch dans/par** to get sth into/through;
(*café*) to pour the water on; (*thé, soupe*) to strain;
(*film, pièce*) to show, put on; (*disque*) to play, put
on; (*commande*) to place; (*marché, accord*) to agree
on; **se passer** VI (*avoir lieu: scène, action*) to take
place; (*se dérouler: entretien etc*) to go; (*arriver*): **que
s'est-il passé?** what happened?; (*s'écouler:
semaine etc*) to pass, go by; **se passer de** vt to go
ou do without; **se passer les mains sous l'eau/
de l'eau sur le visage** to put one's hands under
the tap/run water over one's face; **en passant**
in passing; ~ **par** to go through; **passez
devant/par ici** go in front/this way; ~ **sur** vt
(*faute, détail inutile*) to pass over; ~ **dans les
mœurs/l'usage** to become the custom/normal
usage; ~ **avant qch/qn** (*fig*) to come before sth/
sb; ~ **un coup de fil à qn** (*fam*) to give sb a ring;
laisser ~ (*air, lumière, personne*) to let through;
(*occasion*) to let slip, miss; (*erreur*) to overlook;
faire ~ (*message*) to get over *ou* across; **faire** ~ **à
qn le goût de qch** to cure sb of his (*ou* her) taste
for sth; ~ **à la radio/fouille** to be X-rayed/
searched; ~ **à la radio/télévision** to be on the
radio/on television; ~ **à table** to sit down to eat;
~ **au salon** to go through to *ou* into the sitting
room; ~ **son tour** to miss one's turn; ~ **à**

l'opposition to go over to the opposition; ~ aux aveux to confess, make a confession; ~ à l'action to go into action; ~ pour riche to be taken for a rich man; il passait pour avoir he was said to have; faire ~ qn/qch pour to make sb/sth out to be; passe encore de le penser, mais de le dire! it's one thing to think it, but to say it!; passons! let's say no more (about it); et j'en passe! and that's not all!; ~ en seconde, ~ la seconde (Auto) to change into second; ~ qch en fraude to smuggle sth in (ou out); ~ la main par la portière to stick one's hand out of the door; ~ le balai/l'aspirateur to sweep up/ hoover; ~ commande/la parole à qn to hand over to sb; je vous passe M. X (je vous mets en communication avec lui) I'm putting you through to Mr X; (je lui passe l'appareil) here is Mr X, I'll hand you over to Mr X; je vous passe M. Dupont (je vous mets en communication avec lui) I'm putting you through to Mr Dupont; (je lui passe l'appareil) here is Mr Dupont, I'll hand you over to Mr Dupont; ~ prendre to (come and) collect

passereau, x [pasʁo] NM sparrow

passerelle [pasʁɛl] NF footbridge; (de navire, avion) gangway; (Navig): ~ (de commandement) bridge

passe-temps [pastɑ̃] NM INV pastime

passette [pasɛt] NF (tea-)strainer

passeur, -euse [pasœʁ, -øz] NM/F smuggler

passible [pasibl] ADJ: ~ de liable to

passif, -ive [pasif, -iv] ADJ passive ▶ NM (Ling) passive; (Comm) liabilities pl

passion [pasjɔ̃] NF passion; avoir la ~ de to have a passion for; fruit de la ~ passion fruit

passionnant, e [pasjɔnɑ̃, -ɑ̃t] ADJ fascinating

passionné, e [pasjɔne] ADJ (personne, tempérament) passionate; (description, récit) impassioned ▶ NM/F: c'est un ~ d'échecs he's a chess fanatic; être ~ de ou pour qch to have a passion for sth

passionnel, le [pasjɔnɛl] ADJ of passion

passionnément [pasjɔnemɑ̃] ADV passionately

passionner [pasjɔne] /1/ VT (personne) to fascinate, grip; (débat, discussion) to inflame; se ~ pour to take an avid interest in; to have a passion for

passivement [pasivmɑ̃] ADV passively

passivité [pasivite] NF passivity, passiveness

passoire [paswaʁ] NF sieve; (à légumes) colander; (à thé) strainer

pastel [pastɛl] NM, ADJ INV (Art) pastel

pastèque [pastɛk] NF watermelon

pasteur [pastœʁ] NM (protestant) minister, pastor

pasteurisation [pastœʁizasjɔ̃] NF pasteurization

pasteurisé, e [pastœʁize] ADJ pasteurized

pasteuriser [pastœʁize] /1/ VT to pasteurize

pastiche [pastiʃ] NM pastiche

pastille [pastij] NF (à sucer) lozenge, pastille; (de papier etc) (small) disc; pastilles pour la toux cough drops ou lozenges

pastis [pastis] NM anise-flavoured alcoholic drink

pastoral, e, -aux [pastɔʁal, -o] ADJ pastoral

patagon, ne [patagɔ̃, -ɔn] ADJ Patagonian

Patagonie [patagɔni] NF: la ~ Patagonia

patate [patat] NF spud; ~ douce sweet potato

pataud, e [pato, -od] ADJ lumbering

patauger [patoʒe] /3/ VI (pour s'amuser) to splash about; (avec effort) to wade about; (fig) to flounder; ~ dans (en marchant) to wade through

patch [patʃ] NM nicotine patch

patchouli [patʃuli] NM patchouli

patchwork [patʃwœʁk] NM patchwork

pâte [pɑt] NF (à tarte) pastry; (à pain) dough; (à frire) batter; (substance molle) paste; cream; pâtes NFPL (macaroni etc) pasta sg; fromage à ~ dure/molle hard/soft cheese; ~ d'amandes almond paste, marzipan; ~ brisée shortcrust (BRIT) ou pie crust (US) pastry; ~ à choux/ feuilletée choux/puff ou flaky (BRIT) pastry; ~ de fruits crystallized fruit no pl; ~ à modeler modelling clay, Plasticine® (BRIT); ~ à papier paper pulp

pâté [pɑte] NM (charcuterie, terrine) pâté; (tache) ink blot; (de sable) sandpie; ~ (en croûte) ≈ meat pie; ~ de foie liver pâté; ~ de maisons block (of houses)

pâtée [pɑte] NF mash, feed

patelin [patlɛ̃] NM little place

patente [patɑ̃t] NF (Comm) trading licence (BRIT) ou license (US)

patenté, e [patɑ̃te] ADJ (Comm) licensed; (fig: attitré) registered, (officially) recognized

patère [patɛʁ] NF (coat-)peg

paternalisme [patɛʁnalism] NM paternalism

paternaliste [patɛʁnalist] ADJ paternalistic

paternel, le [patɛʁnɛl] ADJ (amour, soins) fatherly; (ligne, autorité) paternal

paternité [patɛʁnite] NF paternity, fatherhood

pâteux, -euse [pɑtø, -øz] ADJ thick; pasty; avoir la bouche ou langue pâteuse to have a furred (BRIT) ou coated tongue

pathétique [patetik] ADJ pathetic, moving

pathologie [patɔlɔʒi] NF pathology

pathologique [patɔlɔʒik] ADJ pathological

patibulaire [patibylɛʁ] ADJ sinister

patiemment [pasjamɑ̃] ADV patiently

patience [pasjɑ̃s] NF patience; être à bout de ~ to have run out of patience; perdre/prendre ~ to lose (one's)/have patience

patient, e [pasjɑ̃, -ɑ̃t] ADJ, NM/F patient

patienter [pasjɑ̃te] /1/ VI to wait

patin [patɛ̃] NM skate; (sport) skating; (de traîneau, luge) runner; (pièce de tissu) cloth pad (used as slippers to protect polished floor); ~ (de frein) brake block; patins (à glace) (ice) skates; patins à roulettes roller skates

patinage [patinaʒ] NM skating; ~ artistique/ de vitesse figure/speed skating

patine [patin] NF sheen

patiner [patine] /1/ VI to skate; (embrayage) to slip; (roue, voiture) to spin; se patiner VI (meuble, cuir) to acquire a sheen, become polished

patineur, -euse [patinœʁ, -øz] NM/F skater

patinoire [patinwaʁ] NF skating rink, (ice) rink

patio [patjo] NM patio

pâtir [pɑtiʁ] /2/: ~ de VT to suffer because of

P

pâtisserie [patisʀi] NF (boutique) cake shop; (métier) confectionery; (à la maison) pastry- ou cake-making, baking; **pâtisseries** NFPL (gâteaux) pastries, cakes

pâtissier, -ière [patisje, -jɛʀ] NM/F pastrycook; confectioner

patois [patwa] NM dialect, patois

patraque [patʀak] (fam) ADJ peaky, off-colour

patriarche [patʀijaʀʃ] NM patriarch

patrie [patʀi] NF homeland

patrimoine [patʀimwan] NM inheritance, patrimony; (culture) heritage; ~ **génétique** ou **héréditaire** genetic inheritance

> Once a year, important public buildings are open to the public for a weekend. During these *Journées du Patrimoine*, there are guided visits and talks based on a particular theme.

patriote [patʀijɔt] ADJ patriotic ▶ NMF patriot

patriotique [patʀijɔtik] ADJ patriotic

patriotisme [patʀijɔtism] NM patriotism

patron, ne [patʀɔ̃, -ɔn] NM/F (chef) boss, manager(-ess); (propriétaire) owner, proprietor(-tress); (employeur) employer; (Méd) ≈ senior consultant; (Rel) patron saint ▶ NM (Couture) pattern; ~ **de thèse** supervisor (of postgraduate thesis)

patronage [patʀɔnaʒ] NM patronage; (organisation, club) youth club; (parish) children's club

patronal, e, -aux [patʀɔnal, -o] ADJ (syndicat, intérêts) employers'

patronat [patʀɔna] NM employers pl

patronner [patʀɔne] /1/ VT to sponsor, support

patronnesse [patʀɔnɛs] ADJ F: **dame ~** patroness

patronyme [patʀɔnim] NM name

patronymique [patʀɔnimik] ADJ: **nom ~** patronymic (name)

patrouille [patʀuj] NF patrol

patrouiller [patʀuje] /1/ VI to patrol, be on patrol

patrouilleur [patʀujœʀ] NM (Aviat) scout (plane); (Navig) patrol boat

patte [pat] NF (jambe) leg; (pied: de chien, chat) paw; (: d'oiseau) foot; (languette) strap; (: de poche) flap; (favoris): **pattes (de lapin)** (short) sideburns; **à pattes d'éléphant** adj (pantalon) flared; **pattes de mouche** (fig) spidery scrawl sg; **pattes d'oie** (fig) crow's feet

pattemouille [patmuj] NF damp cloth (for ironing)

pâturage [pɑtyʀaʒ] NM pasture

pâture [pɑtyʀ] NF food

paume [pom] NF palm

paumé, e [pome] NM/F (fam) drop-out

paumer [pome] /1/ VT (fam) to lose

paupérisation [popeʀizasjɔ̃] NF pauperization

paupérisme [popeʀism] NM pauperism

paupière [popjɛʀ] NF eyelid

paupiette [popjɛt] NF: **paupiettes de veau** veal olives

pause [poz] NF (arrêt) break; (en parlant, Mus) pause; ~ **de midi** lunch break

pause-café [pozkafe] (pl **pauses-café**) NF coffee-break

pauvre [povʀ] ADJ poor ▶ NMF poor man/woman; **les pauvres** the poor; ~ **en calcium** low in calcium

pauvrement [povʀəmɑ̃] ADV poorly

pauvreté [povʀəte] NF (état) poverty; ~ **énergétique** fuel poverty

pavage [pavaʒ] NM paving; cobbles pl

pavaner [pavane] /1/: **se pavaner** VI to strut about

pavé, e [pave] ADJ (cour) paved; (rue) cobbled ▶ NM (bloc) paving stone; cobblestone; (pavage) paving; (bifteck) slab of steak; (fam: livre) hefty tome; **être sur le ~** (sans domicile) to be on the streets; (sans emploi) to be out of a job; ~ **numérique** (Inform) keypad

pavillon [pavijɔ̃] NM (de banlieue) small (detached) house; (kiosque) lodge; pavilion; (d'hôpital) ward; (Mus: de cor etc) bell; (Anat: de l'oreille) pavilion, pinna; (Navig) flag; ~ **de complaisance** flag of convenience

pavoiser [pavwaze] /1/ VT to deck with flags ▶ VI to put out flags; (fig) to rejoice, exult

pavot [pavo] NM poppy

payable [pejabl] ADJ payable

payant, e [pejɑ̃, -ɑ̃t] ADJ (spectateurs etc) paying; (billet) that you pay for, to be paid for; (fig: entreprise) profitable; (effort) which pays off; **c'est ~** you have to pay, there is a charge

paye [pɛj] NF pay, wages pl

payement [pɛjmɑ̃] NM payment

payer [peje] /8/ VT (créancier, employé, loyer) to pay; (achat, réparations, fig: faute) to pay for ▶ VI to pay; (métier) to be well-paid, pay; (effort, tactique etc) to pay off; **être bien/mal payé** to be well/badly paid; **il me l'a fait ~ 10 euros** he charged me 10 euros for it; ~ **qn de** (ses efforts, peines) to reward sb for; ~ **qch à qn** to buy sth for sb, buy sb sth; **ils nous ont payé le voyage** they paid for our trip; ~ **de sa personne** to give of oneself; ~ **d'audace** to act with great daring; ~ **cher qch** to pay dear(ly) for sth; **cela ne paie pas de mine** it doesn't look much; **se ~ qch** to buy o.s. sth; **se ~ de mots** to shoot one's mouth off; **se ~ la tête de qn** to take the mickey out of sb (BRIT), make a fool of sb; (duper) to take sb for a ride

payeur, -euse [pejœʀ, -øz] ADJ (organisme, bureau) payments cpd ▶ NM/F payer

pays [pei] NM (territoire, habitants) country, land; (région) region; (village) village; **du ~** adj local; **le ~ de Galles** Wales

paysage [peizaʒ] NM landscape

paysager, -ère [peizaʒe, -ɛʀ] ADJ (jardin, parc) landscaped

paysagiste [peizaʒist] NMF (de jardin) landscape gardener; (Art) landscapist, landscape painter

paysan, ne [peizɑ̃, -an] NM/F countryman/-woman; farmer; (péj) peasant ▶ ADJ (rural) country cpd; (agricole) farming, farmers'

paysannat [peizana] NM peasantry

Pays-Bas [peiba] NMPL: **les ~** the Netherlands

PC SIGLE M (Pol) = **parti communiste**; (Inform: = personal computer) PC; (Constr) = **permis de**

construire; (*Mil*) = **poste de commandement**; (= *prêt conventionné*) type of loan for house purchase

pcc ABR (= *pour copie conforme*) c.c

Pce ABR = **prince**

Pcesse ABR = **princesse**

PCV ABR = **percevoir**; *voir* **communication**

PDA SIGLE M (= *personal digital assistant*) PDA

p de p ABR = **pas de porte**

PDG SIGLE M = **président directeur général**

p.-ê. ABR = **peut-être**

PEA SIGLE M (= *plan d'épargne en actions*) building society savings plan

péage [peaʒ] NM toll; (*endroit*) tollgate; **pont à ~** toll bridge

peau, x [po] NF skin; (*cuir*): **gants de ~** leather gloves; **être bien/mal dans sa ~** to be at ease/ ill-at-ease; **se mettre dans la ~ de qn** to put o.s. in sb's place *ou* shoes; **faire ~ neuve** (*se renouveler*) to change one's image; **~ de chamois** (*chiffon*) chamois leather, shammy; **~ d'orange** orange peel

peaufiner [pofine] /**1**/ VT to polish (up)

Peau-Rouge [poruʒ] NMF Red Indian, red skin

peccadille [pekadij] NF trifle, peccadillo

péché [peʃe] NM sin; **~ mignon** weakness

pêche [pɛʃ] NF (*sport, activité*) fishing; (*poissons pêchés*) catch; (*fruit*) peach; **aller à la ~** to go fishing; **avoir la ~** (*fam*) to be on (top) form; **~ à la ligne** (*en rivière*) angling; **~ sous-marine** deep-sea fishing

pêche-abricot [pɛʃabriko] (*pl* **pêches-abricots**) NF yellow peach

pécher [peʃe] /**6**/ VI (*Rel*) to sin; (*fig: personne*) to err; (*: chose*) to be flawed; **~ contre la bienséance** to break the rules of good behaviour

pêcher [peʃe] /**1**/ VI to go fishing; (*en rivière*) to go angling ▸ VT (*attraper*) to catch, land; (*chercher*) to fish for ▸ NM peach tree; **~ au chalut** to trawl

pécheur, -eresse [peʃœr, peʃrɛs] NM/F sinner

pêcheur [peʃœr] NM *voir* **pêcher** fisherman; (*à la ligne*) angler; **~ de perles** pearl diver

pectine [pɛktin] NF pectin

pectoral, e, -aux [pɛktɔral, -o] ADJ (*Anat*) pectoral; (*sirop*) throat *cpd*, cough *cpd* ▸ NMPL pectoral muscles

pécule [pekyl] NM savings *pl*, nest egg; (*d'un détenu*) earnings *pl* (*paid on release*)

pécuniaire [pekynjɛr] ADJ financial

pédagogie [pedagoʒi] NF educational methods *pl*, pedagogy

pédagogique [pedagoʒik] ADJ educational; **formation ~** teacher training

pédagogue [pedagog] NMF teacher, education(al)ist

pédale [pedal] NF pedal; **mettre la ~ douce** to soft-pedal

pédaler [pedale] /**1**/ VI to pedal

pédalier [pedalje] NM pedal and gear mechanism

pédalo [pedalo] NM pedalo, pedal-boat

pédant, e [pedã, -ãt] ADJ (*péj*) pedantic ▸ NM/F pedant

pédantisme [pedãtism] NM pedantry

pédéraste [pederast] NM homosexual, pederast

pédérastie [pederasti] NF homosexuality, pederasty

pédestre [pedɛstr] ADJ: **tourisme ~** hiking; **randonnée ~** (*activité*) rambling; (*excursion*) ramble; **sentier ~** pedestrian footpath

pédiatre [pedjatr] NMF paediatrician (*BRIT*), pediatrician *ou* pediatrist (*US*), child specialist

pédiatrie [pedjatri] NF paediatrics *sg* (*BRIT*), pediatrics *sg* (*US*)

pédicure [pedikyr] NMF chiropodist

pedigree [pedigre] NM pedigree

peeling [piliŋ] NM exfoliation treatment

PEEP SIGLE F = **Fédération des parents d'élèves de l'enseignement public**

pègre [pɛgr] NF underworld

peignais *etc* [peɲɛ] VB *voir* **peindre**

peigne [peɲ] VB *voir* **peindre**; **peigner** ▸ NM comb

peigné, e [peɲe] ADJ: **laine ~** wool worsted; combed wool

peigner [peɲe] /**1**/ VT to comb (the hair of); **se peigner** VI to comb one's hair

peignez *etc* [peɲe] VB *voir* **peindre**

peignoir [peɲwar] NM dressing gown; **~ de bain** bathrobe; **~ de plage** beach robe

peignons [peɲɔ̃] VB *voir* **peindre**

peinard, e [penar, -ard] ADJ (*emploi*) cushy (*BRIT*), easy; (*personne*): **on est ~ ici** we're left in peace here

peindre [pɛ̃dr] /**52**/ VT to paint; (*fig*) to portray, depict

peine [pen] NF (*affliction*) sorrow, sadness *no pl*; (*mal, effort*) trouble *no pl*, effort; (*difficulté*) difficulty; (*punition, châtiment*) punishment; (*Jur*) sentence; **faire de la ~ à qn** to distress *ou* upset sb; **prendre la ~ de faire** to go to the trouble of doing; **se donner de la ~** to make an effort; **ce n'est pas la ~ de faire** there's no point in doing, it's not worth doing; **ce n'est pas la ~ que vous fassiez** there's no point (in) you doing; **avoir de la ~** to be sad; **avoir de la ~ à faire** to have difficulty doing; **donnez-vous** *ou* **veuillez vous donner la ~ d'entrer** please do come in; **c'est ~ perdue** it's a waste of time (and effort); **à ~** *adv* scarcely, hardly, barely; **à ~ ... que** hardly ... than, no sooner ... than; **c'est à ~ si ...** it's (*ou* it was) a job to ...; **sous ~:** **sous ~ d'être puni** for fear of being punished; **défense d'afficher sous ~ d'amende** billposters will be fined; **~ capitale** capital punishment; **~ de mort** death sentence *ou* penalty

peiner [pene] /**1**/ VI to work hard; to struggle; (*moteur, voiture*) to labour (*BRIT*), labor (*US*) ▸ VT to grieve, sadden

peint, e [pɛ̃, pɛ̃t] PP *de* **peindre**

peintre [pɛ̃tr] NM painter; **~ en bâtiment** house painter, painter and decorator; **~ d'enseignes** signwriter

peinture [pɛ̃tyr] NF painting; (*couche de couleur, couleur*) paint; (*surfaces peintes: aussi:* **peintures**)

p

paintwork; **je ne peux pas le voir en ~** I can't stand the sight of him; **~ mate/brillante** matt/gloss paint; **"~ fraîche"** "wet paint"

péjoratif, -ive [peʒɔʀatif, -iv] ADJ pejorative, derogatory

Pékin [pekɛ̃] N Beijing

pékinois, e [pekinwa, -waz] ADJ Pekin(g)ese ▸ NM (*chien*) peke, pekin(g)ese; (*Ling*) Mandarin, Pekin(g)ese ▸ NM/F: **P~, e** Pekin(g)ese

PEL SIGLE M (= *plan d'épargne logement*) *savings scheme providing lower-interest mortgages*

pelade [pəlad] NF alopecia

pelage [pəlaʒ] NM coat, fur

pelé, e [pəle] ADJ (*chien*) hairless; (*vêtement*) threadbare; (*terrain*) bare

pêle-mêle [pɛlmɛl] ADV higgledy-piggledy

peler [pəle] /**5**/ VT, VI to peel

pèlerin [pɛlʀɛ̃] NM pilgrim

pèlerinage [pɛlʀinaʒ] NM (*voyage*) pilgrimage; (*lieu*) place of pilgrimage, shrine

pèlerine [pɛlʀin] NF cape

pélican [pelikɑ̃] NM pelican

pelisse [pəlis] NF fur-lined cloak

pelle [pɛl] NF shovel; (*d'enfant, de terrassier*) spade; **~ à gâteau** cake slice; **~ mécanique** mechanical digger

pelletée [pɛlte] NF shovelful; spadeful

pelleter [pɛlte] /**4**/ VT to shovel (up)

pelleteuse [pɛltøz] NF mechanical digger, excavator

pelletier [pɛltje] NM furrier

pellicule [pelikyl] NF film; **pellicules** NFPL (*Méd*) dandruff *sg*

Péloponnèse [pelɔpɔnɛz] NM: **le ~** the Peloponnese

pelote [pəlɔt] NF (*de fil, laine*) ball; (*d'épingles*) pin cushion; **~ basque** pelota

peloter [pəlɔte] /**1**/ VT (*fam*) to feel (up); **se peloter** to pet

peloton [pəlɔtɔ̃] NM (*groupe: de personnes*) group; (: *de pompiers, gendarmes*) squad; (: *Sport*) pack; (*de laine*) ball; **~ d'exécution** firing squad

pelotonner [pəlɔtɔne] /**1**/: **se pelotonner** VI to curl (o.s.) up

pelouse [pəluz] NF lawn; (*Hippisme*) spectating area inside racetrack

peluche [pəlyʃ] NF (bit of) fluff; **animal en ~** soft toy, fluffy animal; **chien/lapin en ~** fluffy dog/rabbit

pelucher [p(ə)lyʃe] /**1**/ VI to become fluffy, fluff up

pelucheux, -euse [p(ə)lyʃø, -øz] ADJ fluffy

pelure [pəlyʀ] NF peeling, peel *no pl*; **~ d'oignon** onion skin

pénal, e, -aux [penal, -o] ADJ penal

pénalisation [penalizasjɔ̃] NF (*Sport*) sanction, penalty

pénaliser [penalize] /**1**/ VT to penalize

pénalité [penalite] NF penalty

penalty, -ies [penalti, -z] NM (*Sport*) penalty (kick)

pénard, e [penaʀ, -aʀd] ADJ = **peinard**

pénates [penat] NMPL: **regagner ses ~** to return to the bosom of one's family

penaud, e [pəno, -od] ADJ sheepish, contrite

penchant [pɑ̃ʃɑ̃] NM: **un ~ à faire/à qch** a tendency to do/to sth; **un ~ pour qch** a liking *ou* fondness for sth

penché, e [pɑ̃ʃe] ADJ slanting

pencher [pɑ̃ʃe] /**1**/ VI to tilt, lean over ▸ VT to tilt; **se pencher** VI to lean over; (*se baisser*) to bend down; **se pencher sur** to bend over; (*fig: problème*) to look into; **se pencher au dehors** to lean out; **~ pour** to be inclined to favour (BRIT) *ou* favor (US)

pendable [pɑ̃dabl] ADJ: **tour ~** rotten trick; **c'est un cas ~!** he (*ou* she) deserves to be shot!

pendaison [pɑ̃dezɔ̃] NF hanging

pendant, e [pɑ̃dɑ̃, -ɑ̃t] ADJ hanging (out); (*Admin, Jur*) pending ▸ NM counterpart; matching piece ▸ PRÉP (*au cours de*) during; (*indiquant la durée*) for; **faire ~ à** to match; to be the counterpart of; **~ que** while; **pendants d'oreilles** drop *ou* pendant earrings

pendeloque [pɑ̃dlɔk] NF pendant

pendentif [pɑ̃dɑ̃tif] NM pendant

penderie [pɑ̃dʀi] NF wardrobe; (*placard*) walk-in cupboard

pendiller [pɑ̃dije] /**1**/ VI to flap (about)

pendre [pɑ̃dʀ] /**41**/ VT, VI to hang; **se ~ (à)** (*se suicider*) to hang o.s. (on); **~ à** to hang (down) from; **~ qch à** (*mur*) to hang sth (up) on; (*plafond*) to hang sth (up) from; **se ~ à** (*se suspendre*) to hang from

pendu, e [pɑ̃dy] PP *de* **pendre** ▸ NM/F hanged man (*ou* woman)

pendulaire [pɑ̃dylɛʀ] ADJ pendular, of a pendulum

pendule [pɑ̃dyl] NF clock ▸ NM pendulum

pendulette [pɑ̃dylet] NF small clock

pêne [pɛn] NM bolt

pénétrant, e [penetʀɑ̃, -ɑ̃t] ADJ (*air, froid*) biting; (*pluie*) that soaks right through you; (*fig: odeur*) noticeable; (*œil, regard*) piercing; (*clairvoyant, perspicace*) perceptive ▸ NF (*route*) expressway

pénétration [penetʀasjɔ̃] NF (*fig: d'idées etc*) penetration; (*perspicacité*) perception

pénétré, e [penetʀe] ADJ (*air, ton*) earnest; **être ~ de soi-même/son importance** to be full of oneself/one's own importance

pénétrer [penetʀe] /**6**/ VI to come *ou* get in ▸ VT to penetrate; **~ dans** to enter; (*froid, projectile*) to penetrate; (: *air, eau*) to come into, get into; (*mystère, secret*) to fathom; **se ~ de qch** to get sth firmly set in one's mind

pénible [penibl] ADJ (*astreignant*) hard; (*affligeant*) painful; (*personne, caractère*) tiresome; **il m'est ~ de ...** I'm sorry to ...

péniblement [peniblǝmɑ̃] ADV with difficulty

péniche [peniʃ] NF barge; **~ de débarquement** landing craft *inv*

pénicilline [penisilin] NF penicillin

péninsulaire [penɛ̃sylɛʀ] ADJ peninsular

péninsule [penɛ̃syl] NF peninsula

pénis [penis] NM penis

pénitence [penitɑ̃s] NF (*repentir*) penitence; (*peine*) penance; (*punition, châtiment*) punishment; **mettre un enfant en ~** ≈ to make a child stand in the corner; **faire** ~ to do a penance

pénitencier [penitɑ̃sje] NM prison, penitentiary (US)

pénitent, e [penitɑ̃, -ɑ̃t] ADJ penitent

pénitentiaire [penitɑ̃sjɛʀ] ADJ prison cpd, penitentiary (US)

pénombre [penɔ̃bʀ] NF (faible clarté) half-light; (obscurité) darkness

pensable [pɑ̃sabl] ADJ: **ce n'est pas** ~ it's unthinkable

pensant, e [pɑ̃sɑ̃, -ɑ̃t] ADJ: **bien** ~ right-thinking

pense-bête [pɑ̃sbɛt] NM aide-mémoire, mnemonic device

pensée [pɑ̃se] NF thought; (démarche, doctrine) thinking no pl; (Bot) pansy; **se représenter qch par la** ~ to conjure up a mental picture of sth; **en** ~ in one's mind

penser [pɑ̃se] /1/ VI to think ▸ VT to think; (concevoir: problème, machine) to think out; ~ **à** (prévoir) to think of; (songer à: ami, vacances) to think of ou about; ~ **à faire qch** to think of doing sth; ~ **faire qch** to be thinking of doing sth, intend to do sth; **faire** ~ **à** to remind one of; **n'y pensons plus** let's forget it; **vous n'y pensez pas!** don't let it bother you!; **sans** ~ **à mal** without meaning any harm; **je le pense aussi** I think so too; **je pense que oui/non** I think so/don't think so

penseur [pɑ̃sœʀ] NM thinker; **libre** ~ free-thinker

pensif, -ive [pɑ̃sif, -iv] ADJ pensive, thoughtful

pension [pɑ̃sjɔ̃] NF (allocation) pension; (prix du logement) board and lodging, bed and board; (maison particulière) boarding house; (hôtel) guesthouse, hotel; (école) boarding school; **prendre** ~ **chez** to take board and lodging at; **prendre qn en** ~ to take sb (in) as a lodger; **mettre en** ~ to send to boarding school; ~ **alimentaire** (d'étudiant) living allowance; (de divorcée) maintenance allowance; alimony; ~ **complète** full board; ~ **de famille** boarding house, guesthouse; ~ **de guerre/d'invalidité** war/disablement pension

pensionnaire [pɑ̃sjɔnɛʀ] NMF (Scol) boarder; guest

pensionnat [pɑ̃sjɔna] NM boarding school

pensionné, e [pɑ̃sjɔne] NM/F pensioner

pensivement [pɑ̃sivmɑ̃] ADV pensively, thoughtfully

pensum [pɛ̃sɔm] NM (Scol) punishment exercise; (fig) chore

pentagone [pɛ̃tagon] NM pentagon; **le P**~ the Pentagon

pentathlon [pɛ̃tatlɔ̃] NM pentathlon

pente [pɑ̃t] NF slope; **en** ~ adj sloping

Pentecôte [pɑ̃tkot] NF: **la** ~ Whitsun (BRIT); Pentecost; (dimanche) Whitsunday (BRIT); **lundi de** ~ Whit Monday (BRIT)

pénurie [penyʀi] NF shortage; ~ **de main-d'œuvre** undermanning

PEP [pɛp] SIGLE M (= plan d'épargne populaire) individual savings plan

pépé [pepe] NM (fam) grandad

pépère [pepɛʀ] ADJ (fam) cushy; (fam) quiet ▸ NM (fam) grandad

pépier [pepje] /7/ VI to chirp, tweet

pépin [pepɛ̃] NM (Bot: graine) pip; (fam: ennui) snag, hitch; (: parapluie) brolly (BRIT), umbrella

pépinière [pepinjɛʀ] NF nursery; (fig) nest, breeding-ground

pépiniériste [pepinjeʀist] NM nurseryman

pépite [pepit] NF nugget

PEPS ABR (= premier entré premier sorti) first in first out

PER [pɛʀ] SIGLE M (= plan d'épargne retraite) type of personal pension plan

perçant, e [pɛʀsɑ̃, -ɑ̃t] ADJ (vue, regard, yeux) sharp, keen; (cri, voix) piercing, shrill

percée [pɛʀse] NF (trouée) opening; (Mil, Comm: fig) breakthrough; (Sport) break

perce-neige [pɛʀsənɛʒ] NM OU F INV snowdrop

perce-oreille [pɛʀsɔʀɛj] NM earwig

percepteur, -trice [pɛʀsɛptœʀ, -tʀis] NM/F tax collector

perceptible [pɛʀsɛptibl] ADJ (son, différence) perceptible; (impôt) payable, collectable

perception [pɛʀsɛpsjɔ̃] NF perception; (d'impôts etc) collection; (bureau) tax (collector's) office

percer [pɛʀse] /3/ VT to pierce; (ouverture etc) to make; (mystère, énigme) to penetrate ▸ VI to come through; (réussir) to break through; ~ **une dent** to cut a tooth

perceuse [pɛʀsøz] NF drill; ~ **à percussion** hammer drill

percevable [pɛʀsəvabl] ADJ collectable, payable

percevoir [pɛʀsəvwaʀ] /28/ VT (distinguer) to perceive, detect; (taxe, impôt) to collect; (revenu, indemnité) to receive

perche [pɛʀʃ] NF (Zool) perch; (bâton) pole; ~ **à son** (sound) boom

percher [pɛʀʃe] /1/ VT to perch; ~ **qch sur** to perch sth on; **se percher** VI (oiseau) to perch

perchiste [pɛʀʃist] NMF (Sport) pole vaulter; (TV etc) boom operator

perchoir [pɛʀʃwaʀ] NM perch; (fig) presidency of the French National Assembly

perclus, e [pɛʀkly, -yz] ADJ: ~ **de** (rhumatismes) crippled with

perçois etc [pɛʀswa] VB voir **percevoir**

percolateur [pɛʀkɔlatœʀ] NM percolator

perçu, e [pɛʀsy] PP de **percevoir**

percussion [pɛʀkysjɔ̃] NF percussion

percussionniste [pɛʀkysjɔnist] NMF percussionist

percutant, e [pɛʀkytɑ̃, -ɑ̃t] ADJ (article etc) resounding, forceful

percuter [pɛʀkyte] /1/ VT to strike; (véhicule) to crash into ▸ VI: ~ **contre** to crash into

percuteur [pɛʀkytœʀ] NM firing pin, hammer

perdant, e [pɛʀdɑ̃, -ɑ̃t] NM/F loser ▸ ADJ losing

perdition [pɛʀdisjɔ̃] NF (morale) ruin; **en** ~ (Navig) in distress; **lieu de** ~ den of vice

perdre [pɛʀdʀ] /41/ VT to lose; (gaspiller: temps, argent) to waste; (: occasion) to waste, miss; (personne: moralement etc) to ruin ▸ VI to lose; (sur une vente etc) to lose out; (récipient) to leak; **se perdre** VI (s'égarer) to get lost, lose one's way; (fig: se gâter) to go to waste; (disparaître) to disappear, vanish; **il ne perd rien pour attendre** he's got it coming to him; **je me suis perdu** *(et je le suis encore)* I'm lost; *(et je ne le suis plus)* I got lost

perdreau, x [pɛʀdʀo] NM (young) partridge

perdrix [pɛʀdʀi] NF partridge

perdu, e [pɛʀdy] PP *de* **perdre** ▸ ADJ *(enfant, cause, objet)* lost; *(isolé)* out-of-the-way; *(Comm: emballage)* non-returnable; *(récolte etc)* ruined; *(malade)*: **il est ~** there's no hope left for him; **à vos moments perdus** in your spare time

père [pɛʀ] NM father; **pères** NMPL *(ancêtres)* forefathers; **de ~ en fils** from father to son; **~ de famille** father; family man; **mon ~** *(Rel)* Father; **le ~ Noël** Father Christmas

pérégrinations [peʀegʀinasjɔ̃] NFPL travels

péremption [peʀɑ̃psjɔ̃] NF: **date de ~** expiry date

péremptoire [peʀɑ̃ptwaʀ] ADJ peremptory

pérennité [peʀenite] NF durability, lasting quality

péréquation [peʀekwasjɔ̃] NF *(des salaires)* realignment; *(des prix, impôts)* equalization

perfectible [pɛʀfɛktibl] ADJ perfectible

perfection [pɛʀfɛksjɔ̃] NF perfection; **à la ~** *adv* to perfection

perfectionné, e [pɛʀfɛksjɔne] ADJ sophisticated

perfectionnement [pɛʀfɛksjɔnmɑ̃] NM improvement

perfectionner [pɛʀfɛksjɔne] /1/ VT to improve, perfect; **se ~ en anglais** to improve one's English

perfectionniste [pɛʀfɛksjɔnist] NMF perfectionist

perfide [pɛʀfid] ADJ perfidious, treacherous

perfidie [pɛʀfidi] NF treachery

perforant, e [pɛʀfɔʀɑ̃, -ɑ̃t] ADJ *(balle)* armour-piercing (BRIT), armor-piercing (US)

perforateur, -trice [pɛʀfɔʀatœʀ, -tʀis] NM/F punch-card operator ▸ NM *(perceuse)* borer; drill ▸ NF *(perceuse)* borer; drill; *(pour cartes)* card-punch; *(de bureau)* punch

perforation [pɛʀfɔʀasjɔ̃] NF perforation; punching; *(trou)* hole

perforatrice [pɛʀfɔʀatʀis] NF *voir* **perforateur**

perforé, e [pɛʀfɔʀe] ADJ: **bande ~** punched tape; **carte ~** punch card

perforer [pɛʀfɔʀe] /1/ VT to perforate, punch a hole ou holes in; *(ticket, bande, carte)* to punch

perforeuse [pɛʀfɔʀøz] NF *(machine)* (card) punch; *(personne)* card punch operator

performance [pɛʀfɔʀmɑ̃s] NF performance

performant, e [pɛʀfɔʀmɑ̃, -ɑ̃t] ADJ *(Écon: produit, entreprise)* high-return *cpd*; *(Tech)*: **très ~** *(appareil, machine)* high-performance *cpd*

perfusion [pɛʀfyzjɔ̃] NF perfusion; **faire une ~ à qn** to put sb on a drip

péricliter [peʀiklite] /1/ VI to go downhill

péridurale [peʀidyʀal] NF epidural

périgourdin, e [peʀiguʀdɛ̃, -in] ADJ of ou from the Perigord

péril [peʀil] NM peril; **au ~ de sa vie** at the risk of his life; **à ses risques et périls** at his *(ou* her) own risk

périlleux, -euse [peʀijø, -øz] ADJ perilous

périmé, e [peʀime] ADJ (out)dated; *(Admin)* out-of-date, expired

périmètre [peʀimɛtʀ] NM perimeter

périnatal, e [peʀinatal] ADJ perinatal

période [peʀjɔd] NF period

périodique [peʀjɔdik] ADJ *(phases)* periodic; *(publication)* periodical; *(Math: fraction)* recurring ▸ NM periodical; **garniture ou serviette ~** sanitary towel (BRIT) ou napkin (US)

périodiquement [peʀjɔdikmɑ̃] ADV periodically

péripéties [peʀipesi] NFPL events, episodes

périphérie [peʀifeʀi] NF periphery; *(d'une ville)* outskirts *pl*

périphérique [peʀifeʀik] ADJ *(quartiers)* outlying; *(Anat, Tech)* peripheral; *(station de radio)* operating from a neighbouring country ▸ NM *(Inform)* peripheral; *(Auto)*: **(boulevard) ~** ring road (BRIT), beltway (US)

périphrase [peʀifʀɑz] NF circumlocution

périple [peʀipl] NM journey

périr [peʀiʀ] /2/ VI to die, perish

périscolaire [peʀiskɔlɛʀ] ADJ extracurricular

périscope [peʀiskɔp] NM periscope

périssable [peʀisabl] ADJ perishable

péristyle [peʀistil] NM peristyle

péritonite [peʀitɔnit] NF peritonitis

perle [pɛʀl] NF pearl; *(de plastique, métal, sueur)* bead; *(personne, chose)* gem, treasure; *(erreur)* gem, howler

perlé, e [pɛʀle] ADJ *(rire)* rippling, tinkling; *(travail)* exquisite; *(orge)* pearl *cpd*; **grève ~** go-slow, selective strike (action)

perler [pɛʀle] /1/ VI to form in droplets

perlier, -ière [pɛʀlje, -jɛʀ] ADJ pearl *cpd*

permanence [pɛʀmanɑ̃s] NF permanence; *(local)* (duty) office, strike headquarters; *(service des urgences)* emergency service; *(Scol)* study room; **assurer une ~** *(service public, bureaux)* to operate ou maintain a basic service; **être de ~** to be on call ou duty; **en ~** *adv (toujours)* permanently; *(continûment)* continuously

permanent, e [pɛʀmanɑ̃, -ɑ̃t] ADJ permanent; *(spectacle)* continuous; *(armée, comité)* standing ▸ NM perm ▸ NM/F *(d'un syndicat, parti)* paid official

perméable [pɛʀmeabl] ADJ *(terrain)* permeable; **~ à** *(fig)* receptive ou open to

permettre [pɛʀmɛtʀ] /56/ VT to allow, permit; **~ à qn de faire/qch** to allow sb to do/sth; **se ~ de faire qch** to take the liberty of doing sth; **permettez!** excuse me!

permis, e [pɛʀmi, -iz] PP *de* **permettre** ▸ NM permit, licence (BRIT), license (US); **~ de chasse** hunting permit; **~ (de conduire)** (driving) licence (BRIT), (driver's) license (US); **~ de construire** planning permission (BRIT), building permit (US); **~ d'inhumer** burial certificate; **~ poids lourds** ≈ HGV (driving) licence (BRIT), ≈ class E (driver's) license (US); **~ de séjour** residence permit; **~ de travail** work permit

permissif, -ive [pɛʀmisif, -iv] ADJ permissive

permission [pɛʀmisjɔ̃] NF permission; (Mil) leave; (: papier) pass; **en ~** on leave; **avoir la ~ de faire** to have permission to do, be allowed to do

permissionnaire [pɛʀmisjɔnɛʀ] NM soldier on leave

permutable [pɛʀmytabl] ADJ which can be changed ou switched around

permuter [pɛʀmyte] /1/ VT to change around, permutate ▶ VI to change, swap

pernicieux, -euse [pɛʀnisjø, -øz] ADJ pernicious

péroné [peʀɔne] NM fibula

pérorer [peʀɔʀe] /1/ VI to hold forth

Pérou [peʀu] NM: **le ~** Peru

perpendiculaire [pɛʀpɑ̃dikylɛʀ] ADJ, NF perpendicular

perpendiculairement [pɛʀpɑ̃dikylɛʀmɑ̃] ADV perpendicularly

perpète [pɛʀpɛt] NF: **à ~** (fam: loin) miles away; (: longtemps) forever

perpétrer [pɛʀpetʀe] /6/ VT to perpetrate

perpétuel, le [pɛʀpetɥɛl] ADJ perpetual; (Admin etc) permanent; for life

perpétuellement [pɛʀpetɥɛlmɑ̃] ADV perpetually, constantly

perpétuer [pɛʀpetɥe] /1/ VT to perpetuate; **se perpétuer** (usage, injustice) to be perpetuated; (espèces) to survive

perpétuité [pɛʀpetɥite] NF: **à ~** for life; **être condamné à ~** to be sentenced to life imprisonment, receive a life sentence

perplexe [pɛʀplɛks] ADJ perplexed, puzzled

perplexité [pɛʀpleksite] NF perplexity

perquisition [pɛʀkizisjɔ̃] NF (police) search

perquisitionner [pɛʀkizisjɔne] /1/ VI to carry out a search

perron [peʀɔ̃] NM steps pl (in front of mansion etc)

perroquet [peʀɔkɛ] NM parrot

perruche [peʀyʃ] NF budgerigar (Brit), budgie (Brit), parakeet (US)

perruque [peʀyk] NF wig

persan, e [pɛʀsɑ̃, -an] ADJ Persian ▶ NM (Ling) Persian

perse [pɛʀs] ADJ Persian ▶ NM (Ling) Persian ▶ NMF: **P~** Persian ▶ NF: **la P~** Persia

persécuter [pɛʀsekyte] /1/ VT to persecute

persécution [pɛʀsekysjɔ̃] NF persecution

persévérance [pɛʀseveʀɑ̃s] NF perseverance

persévérant, e [pɛʀseveʀɑ̃, -ɑ̃t] ADJ persevering

persévérer [pɛʀseveʀe] /6/ VI to persevere; **~ à croire que** to continue to believe that

persiennes [pɛʀsjɛn] NFPL (slatted) shutters

persiflage [pɛʀsiflaʒ] NM mockery no pl

persifleur, -euse [pɛʀsiflœʀ, -øz] ADJ mocking

persil [pɛʀsi] NM parsley

persillé, e [pɛʀsije] ADJ (sprinkled) with parsley; (fromage) veined; (viande) marbled, with fat running through

Persique [pɛʀsik] ADJ: **le golfe ~** the (Persian) Gulf

persistance [pɛʀsistɑ̃s] NF persistence

persistant, e [pɛʀsistɑ̃, -ɑ̃t] ADJ persistent; (feuilles) evergreen; **à feuillage ~** evergreen

persister [pɛʀsiste] /1/ VI to persist; **~ à faire qch** to persist in doing sth

personnage [pɛʀsɔnaʒ] NM (notable) personality; figure; (individu) character, individual; (Théât: de roman, film) character; (Peinture) figure

personnaliser [pɛʀsɔnalize] /1/ VT to personalize; (appartement) to give a personal touch to; (véhicule, téléphone) to customize

personnalité [pɛʀsɔnalite] NF personality; (personnage) prominent figure

personne [pɛʀsɔn] NF person ▶ PRON nobody, no one; (avec négation en anglais) anybody, anyone; **personnes** NFPL people pl; **il n'y a ~** there's nobody in ou there, there isn't anybody in ou there; **10 euros par ~** 10 euros per person ou a head; **en ~** personally, in person; **~ âgée** elderly person; **~ à charge** (Jur) dependent; **~ morale** ou **civile** (Jur) legal entity

personnel, le [pɛʀsɔnɛl] ADJ personal; (égoïste: personne) selfish, self-centred; (idée, opinion): **j'ai des idées personnelles à ce sujet** I have my own ideas about that ▶ NM personnel, staff; **service du ~** personnel department

personnellement [pɛʀsɔnɛlmɑ̃] ADV personally

personnification [pɛʀsɔnifikasjɔ̃] NF personification

personnifier [pɛʀsɔnifje] /7/ VT to personify; to typify; **c'est l'honnêteté personnifiée** he (ou she etc) is honesty personified

perspective [pɛʀspɛktiv] NF (Art) perspective; (vue, coup d'œil) view; (point de vue) viewpoint, angle; (chose escomptée, envisagée) prospect; **en ~** in prospect

perspicace [pɛʀspikas] ADJ clear-sighted, gifted with (ou showing) insight

perspicacité [pɛʀspikasite] NF insight, perspicacity

persuader [pɛʀsɥade] /1/ VT: **~ qn (de/de faire)** to persuade sb (of/to do); **j'en suis persuadé** I'm quite sure ou convinced (of it)

persuasif, -ive [pɛʀsɥazif, -iv] ADJ persuasive

persuasion [pɛʀsɥazjɔ̃] NF persuasion

perte [pɛʀt] NF loss; (de temps) waste; (fig: morale) ruin; **pertes** NFPL losses; **à ~** (Comm) at a loss; **à ~ de vue** as far as the eye can (ou could) see; (fig) interminably; **en pure ~** for absolutely nothing; **courir à sa ~** to be on the road to ruin; **être en ~ de vitesse** (fig) to be losing momentum; **avec ~ et fracas** forcibly; **~ de chaleur** heat loss; **~ sèche** dead loss; **pertes blanches** (vaginal) discharge sg

pertinemment [pɛʀtinamɑ̃] ADV to the point; (savoir) perfectly well, full well

pertinence [pɛʀtinɑ̃s] NF pertinence, relevance; discernment

pertinent, e [pɛʀtinɑ̃, -ɑ̃t] ADJ (remarque) apt, pertinent, relevant; (analyse) discerning, judicious

perturbateur, -trice [pɛʀtyʀbatœʀ, -tʀis] ADJ disruptive

perturbation [pɛʀtyʀbasjɔ̃] NF (dans un service public) disruption; (agitation, trouble) perturbation; **~ (atmosphérique)** atmospheric disturbance

perturber [pɛrtyrbe] /**1**/ vt to disrupt; (Psych) to perturb, disturb

péruvien, ne [peryvjɛ̃, -ɛn] ADJ Peruvian
▶ NM/F: **P~, ne** Peruvian

pervenche [pɛrvɑ̃ʃ] NF periwinkle; (fam) traffic warden (BRIT), meter maid (US)

pervers, e [pɛrvɛr, -ɛrs] ADJ perverted, depraved; (malfaisant) perverse

perversion [pɛrvɛrsjɔ̃] NF perversion

perversité [pɛrvɛrsite] NF depravity; perversity

perverti, e [pɛrvɛrti] NM/F pervert

pervertir [pɛrvɛrtir] /**2**/ vt to pervert

pesage [pəzaʒ] NM weighing; (Hippisme: action) weigh-in; (: salle) weighing room; (: enceinte) enclosure

pesamment [pəzamɑ̃] ADV heavily

pesant, e [pəzɑ̃, -ɑ̃t] ADJ heavy; (fig: présence) burdensome ▶ NM: **valoir son ~ de** to be worth one's weight in

pesanteur [pəzɑ̃tœr] NF gravity

pèse-bébé [pɛzbebe] NM (baby) scales pl

pesée [pəze] NF weighing; (Boxe) weigh-in; (pression) pressure

pèse-lettre [pɛzlɛtr] NM letter scales pl

pèse-personne [pɛzpɛrsɔn] NM (bathroom) scales pl

peser [pəze] /**5**/ vt to weigh; (considérer, comparer) to weigh up ▶ vi to be heavy; (fig: avoir de l'importance) to carry weight; **~ sur** (levier, bouton) to press, push; (fig: accabler) to lie heavy on (: influencer) to influence; **~ à qn** to weigh heavy on sb

pessaire [pɛsɛr] NM pessary

pessimisme [pesimism] NM pessimism

pessimiste [pesimist] ADJ pessimistic ▶ NMF pessimist

peste [pɛst] NF plague; (fig) pest, nuisance

pester [pɛste] /**1**/ vi: **~ contre** to curse

pesticide [pɛstisid] NM pesticide

pestiféré, e [pɛstifere] NM/F plague victim

pestilentiel, le [pɛstilɑ̃sjɛl] ADJ foul

pet [pɛ] NM (!) fart (!)

pétale [petal] NM petal

pétanque [petɑ̃k] NF type of bowls; see note

Pétanque is a version of the game of boules, played on a variety of hard surfaces. Standing with their feet together, players throw steel bowls at a wooden jack. Pétanque originated in the South of France and is still very much associated with that area.

pétarade [petarad] NF backfiring no pl

pétarader [petarade] /**1**/ vi to backfire

pétard [petar] NM (feu d'artifice) banger (BRIT), firecracker; (de cotillon) cracker; (Rail) detonator

pet-de-nonne [pɛdnɔn] (pl pets-de-nonne) NM ≈ choux bun

péter [pete] /**6**/ vi (fam: casser, sauter) to burst; to bust; (!) to fart (!)

pète-sec [pɛtsɛk] ADJ INV abrupt, sharp(-tongued)

pétillant, e [petijɑ̃, -ɑ̃t] ADJ (eau) sparkling

pétiller [petije] /**1**/ vi (flamme, bois) to crackle; (mousse, champagne) to bubble; (pierre, métal) to glisten; (yeux) to sparkle; (fig): **~ d'esprit** to sparkle with wit

petit, e [pəti, -it] ADJ (gén) small; (avec nuance affective) little; (main, objet, colline, en âge: enfant) small, little; (mince, fin: personne, taille, pluie) slight; (voyage) short, little; (bruit etc) faint, slight; (mesquin) mean; (peu important) minor ▶ NM/F (petit enfant) little one, child; **petits** NMPL (d'un animal) young pl; **faire des petits** to have kittens (ou puppies etc); **en ~** in miniature; **mon ~** son; little one; **ma ~** dear; little one; **pauvre ~** poor little thing; **la classe des petits** the infant class; **pour petits et grands** for children and adults; **les tout-petits** toddlers; **~ à** - bit by bit, gradually; **~(e) ami(e)** boyfriend/girlfriend; **les petites annonces** the small ads; **~ déjeuner** breakfast; **~ doigt** little finger; **le ~ écran** the small screen; **~ four** petit four; **~ pain** (bread) roll; **~ monnaie** small change; **~ vérole** smallpox; **petits pois** petit pois pl, garden peas; **petites gens** people of modest means

petit-beurre [pətibœr] (pl petits-beurre) NM sweet butter biscuit (BRIT) ou cookie (US)

petit-bourgeois, petite-bourgeoise [pətiburʒwa, pətitburʒwaz] (pl **petit(e)s-bourgeois(es)**) ADJ (péj) petit-bourgeois, middle-class

petite-fille [pətitfij] (pl **petites-filles**) NF granddaughter

petitement [pətitmɑ̃] ADV poorly; meanly; **être logé ~** to be in cramped accommodation

petitesse [pətitɛs] NF smallness; (d'un salaire, de revenus) modestness; (mesquinerie) meanness

petit-fils [pətifis] (pl **petits-fils**) NM grandson

pétition [petisjɔ̃] NF petition; **faire signer une ~** to get up a petition

pétitionnaire [petisjɔnɛr] NMF petitioner

pétitionner [petisjɔne] /**1**/ vi to petition

petit-lait [pətilɛ] (pl **petits-laits**) NM whey no pl

petit-nègre [pətinɛgr] NM (péj) pidgin French

petits-enfants [pətizɑ̃fɑ̃] NMPL grandchildren

petit-suisse [pətisɥis] (pl **petits-suisses**) NM small individual pot of cream cheese

pétoche [petɔʃ] NF (fam): **avoir la ~** to be scared out of one's wits

pétri, e [petri] ADJ: **~ d'orgueil** filled with pride

pétrifier [petrifje] /**7**/ vt to petrify; (fig) to paralyze, transfix

pétrin [petrɛ̃] NM kneading-trough; (fig): **dans le ~** in a jam ou fix

pétrir [petrir] /**2**/ vt to knead

pétrochimie [petrɔʃimi] NF petrochemistry

pétrochimique [petrɔʃimik] ADJ petrochemical

pétrodollar [petrodɔlar] NM petrodollar

pétrole [petrɔl] NM oil; (aussi: **pétrole lampant**: pour lampe, réchaud etc) paraffin (BRIT), kerosene (US)

pétrolier, -ière [petrɔlje, -jɛr] ADJ oil cpd; (pays) oil-producing ▶ NM (navire) oil tanker; (financier) oilman; (technicien) petroleum engineer

pétrolifère [petrɔlifɛr] ADJ oil(-bearing)

P et T SIGLE FPL = **postes et télécommunications**

pétulant, e [petylɑ̃, -ɑ̃t] ADJ exuberant

peu [pø] ADV **1** (*modifiant verbe: adjectif: adverbe*): **il boit peu** he doesn't drink (very) much; **il est peu bavard** he's not very talkative; **peu avant/après** shortly before/afterwards; **pour peu qu'il fasse** if he should do, if by any chance he does
2 (*modifiant nom*): **peu de**: **peu de gens/d'arbres** few *ou* not (very) many people/trees; **il a peu d'espoir** he hasn't (got) much hope, he has little hope; **pour peu de temps** for (only) a short while; **à peu de frais** for very little cost
3: **peu à peu** little by little; **à peu près** just about, more or less; **à peu près 10 kg/10 euros** approximately 10 kg/10 euros
▶ NM **1**: **le peu de gens qui** the few people who; **le peu de sable qui** what little sand, the little sand which
2: **un peu** a little; **un petit peu** a little bit; **un peu d'espoir** a little hope; **elle est un peu bavarde** she's rather talkative; **un peu plus de** slightly more than; **un peu moins de** slightly less than; (*avec pluriel*) slightly fewer than; **pour un peu il ..., un peu plus et il ...** he very nearly *ou* all but ...; **essayez un peu!** have a go!, just try it!
▶ PRON: **peu le savent** few know (it); **avant** *ou* **sous peu** shortly, before long; **depuis peu** for a short *ou* little while; (*au passé*) a short *ou* little while ago; **de peu** (only) just; **c'est peu de chose** it's nothing; **il est de peu mon cadet** he's just a little *ou* bit younger than me

peuplade [pœplad] NF (*horde, tribu*) tribe, people
peuple [pœpl] NM people; (*masse*): **un ~ de vacanciers** a crowd of holiday-makers; **il y a du ~** there are a lot of people
peuplé, e [pœple] ADJ: **très/peu ~** densely/sparsely populated
peupler [pœple] /**1**/ VT (*pays, région*) to populate; (*étang*) to stock; (*hommes, poissons*) to inhabit; (*fig: imagination, rêves*) to fill; **se peupler** VI (*ville, région*) to become populated; (*fig: s'animer*) to fill (up), be filled
peuplier [pøplije] NM poplar (tree)
peur [pœʀ] NF fear; **avoir ~ (de/de faire/que)** to be frightened *ou* afraid (of/of doing/that); **prendre ~** to take fright; **faire ~ à** to frighten; **de ~ de/que** for fear of/that; **j'ai ~ qu'il ne soit trop tard** I'm afraid it might be too late; **j'ai ~ qu'il (ne) vienne (pas)** I'm afraid he may (not) come
peureux, -euse [pœʀø, -øz] ADJ fearful, timorous
peut [pø] VB *voir* **pouvoir**
peut-être [pøtɛtʀ] ADV perhaps, maybe; **~ que** perhaps, maybe; **~ bien qu'il fera/est** he may well do/be
peuvent [pœv], **peux** *etc* [pø] VB *voir* **pouvoir**
p. ex. ABR (= *par exemple*) e.g.
phalange [falɑ̃ʒ] NF (*Anat*) phalanx; (*Mil: fig*) phalanx
phallique [falik] ADJ phallic
phallocrate [falɔkʀat] NM male chauvinist

phallocratie [falɔkʀasi] NF male chauvinism
phallus [falys] NM phallus
pharaon [faʀaɔ̃] NM Pharaoh
phare [faʀ] NM (*en mer*) lighthouse; (*d'aéroport*) beacon; (*de véhicule*) headlight, headlamp (BRIT)
▶ ADJ: **produit ~** leading product; **se mettre en phares**, **mettre ses phares** to put on one's headlights; **phares de recul** reversing (BRIT) *ou* back-up (US) lights
pharmaceutique [faʀmasøtik] ADJ pharmaceutic(al)
pharmacie [faʀmasi] NF (*science*) pharmacology; (*magasin*) chemist's (BRIT), pharmacy; (*officine*) dispensary; (*produits*) pharmaceuticals *pl*; (*armoire*) medicine chest *ou* cupboard, first-aid cupboard
pharmacien, ne [faʀmasjɛ̃, -ɛn] NM/F pharmacist, chemist (BRIT)
pharmacologie [faʀmakɔlɔʒi] NF pharmacology
pharyngite [faʀɛ̃ʒit] NF pharyngitis *no pl*
pharynx [faʀɛ̃ks] NM pharynx
phase [faz] NF phase
phénoménal, e, -aux [fenɔmenal, -o] ADJ phenomenal
phénomène [fenɔmɛn] NM phenomenon; (*monstre*) freak
philanthrope [filɑ̃tʀɔp] NMF philanthropist
philanthropie [filɑ̃tʀɔpi] NF philanthropy
philanthropique [filɑ̃tʀɔpik] ADJ philanthropic
philatélie [filateli] NF philately, stamp collecting
philatélique [filatelik] ADJ philatelic
philatéliste [filatelist] NMF philatelist, stamp collector
philharmonique [filaʀmɔnik] ADJ philharmonic
philippin, e [filipɛ̃, -in] ADJ Filipino
Philippines [filipin] NFPL: **les ~** the Philippines
philistin [filistɛ̃] NM philistine
philo [filo] NF (*fam: = philosophie*) philosophy
philosophe [filɔzɔf] NMF philosopher ▶ ADJ philosophical
philosopher [filɔzɔfe] /**1**/ VI to philosophize
philosophie [filɔzɔfi] NF philosophy
philosophique [filɔzɔfik] ADJ philosophical
philosophiquement [filɔzɔfikmɑ̃] ADV philosophically
philtre [filtʀ] NM philtre, love potion
phlébite [flebit] NF phlebitis
phlébologue [flebɔlɔg] NMF vein specialist
phobie [fɔbi] NF phobia
phonétique [fɔnetik] ADJ phonetic ▶ NF phonetics *sg*
phonétiquement [fɔnetikmɑ̃] ADV phonetically
phonographe [fɔnɔgʀaf] NM (wind-up) gramophone
phoque [fɔk] NM seal; (*fourrure*) sealskin
phosphate [fɔsfat] NM phosphate
phosphaté, e [fɔsfate] ADJ phosphate-enriched
phosphore [fɔsfɔʀ] NM phosphorus
phosphoré, e [fɔsfɔʀe] ADJ phosphorous

P

phosphorescent, e [fɔsfɔʀesɑ̃, -ɑ̃t] ADJ luminous

phosphorique [fɔsfɔʀik] ADJ: **acide ~** phosphoric acid

photo [fɔto] NF (*photographie*) photo ▶ ADJ: **appareil/pellicule ~** camera/film; **en ~** in *ou* on a photo; **prendre en ~** to take a photo of; **aimer la/faire de la ~** to like photography/ taking photos; **~ en couleurs** colour photo; **~ d'identité** passport photo

photo... [fɔtɔ] PRÉFIXE photo...

photocopie [fɔtɔkɔpi] NF (*procédé*) photocopying; (*document*) photocopy

photocopier [fɔtɔkɔpje] /7/ VT to photocopy

photocopieur [fɔtɔkɔpjœʀ] NM, **photocopieuse** [fɔtɔkɔpjøz] NF (photo)copier

photo-électrique [fɔtɔelektʀik] ADJ photo-electric

photo-finish [fɔtɔfiniʃ] (*pl* **photos-finish**) NF (*appareil*) photo finish camera; (*photo*) photo finish picture; **il y a eu ~ pour la troisième place** there was a photo finish for third place

photogénique [fɔtɔʒenik] ADJ photogenic

photographe [fɔtɔgʀaf] NMF photographer

photographie [fɔtɔgʀafi] NF (*procédé, technique*) photography; (*cliché*) photograph; **faire de la ~** to do photography as a hobby; (*comme métier*) to be a photographer

photographier [fɔtɔgʀafje] /7/ VT to photograph, take

photographique [fɔtɔgʀafik] ADJ photographic

photogravure [fɔtɔgʀavyʀ] NF photoengraving

photomaton® [fɔtɔmatɔ̃] NM photo-booth, photomat

photomontage [fɔtɔmɔ̃taʒ] NM photomontage

photophone [fɔtɔfɔn] NM camera phone

photo-robot [fɔtɔʀɔbo] NF Identikit® (picture)

photosensible [fɔtɔsɑ̃sibl] ADJ photosensitive

photostat [fɔtɔsta] NM photostat

phrase [fʀɑz] NF (*Ling*) sentence; (*propos, Mus*) phrase; **phrases** NFPL (*péj*) flowery language *sg*

phraséologie [fʀazeɔlɔʒi] NF phraseology; (*rhétorique*) flowery language

phraseur, -euse [fʀazœʀ, -øz] NM/F: **c'est un ~** he uses such flowery language

phrygien, ne [fʀiʒjɛ̃, -ɛn] ADJ: **bonnet ~** Phrygian cap

phtisie [ftizi] NF consumption

phylloxéra [filɔkseʀa] NM phylloxera

physicien, ne [fizisjɛ̃, -ɛn] NM/F physicist

physiologie [fizjɔlɔʒi] NF physiology

physiologique [fizjɔlɔʒik] ADJ physiological

physiologiquement [fizjɔlɔʒikmɑ̃] ADV physiologically

physionomie [fizjɔnɔmi] NF face; (*d'un paysage etc*) physiognomy

physionomiste [fizjɔnɔmist] NMF good judge of faces; person who has a good memory for faces

physiothérapie [fizjɔteʀapi] NF natural medicine, alternative medicine

physique [fizik] ADJ physical ▶ NM physique

▶ NF physics *sg*; **au ~** physically

physiquement [fizikmɑ̃] ADV physically

phytothérapie [fitɔteʀapi] NF herbal medicine

p.i. ABR = **par intérim**; *voir* **intérim**

piaffer [pjafe] /1/ VI to stamp

piaillement [pjɑjmɑ̃] NM squawking *no pl*

piailler [pjɑje] /1/ VI to squawk

pianiste [pjanist] NMF pianist

piano [pjano] NM piano; **~ à queue** grand piano

pianoter [pjanɔte] /1/ VI to tinkle away (at the piano); (*tapoter*): **~ sur** to drum one's fingers on

piaule [pjol] NF (*fam*) pad

piauler [pjole] /1/ VI (*enfant*) to whimper; (*oiseau*) to cheep

PIB SIGLE M (= *produit intérieur brut*) GDP

pic [pik] NM (*instrument*) pick(axe); (*montagne*) peak; (*Zool*) woodpecker; **à ~** *adv* vertically; (*fig: tomber, arriver*) just at the right time; **couler à ~** (*bateau*) to go straight down; **~ à glace** ice pick

picard, e [pikaʀ, -aʀd] ADJ of *ou* from Picardy

Picardie [pikaʀdi] NF: **la ~** Picardy

picaresque [pikaʀɛsk] ADJ picaresque

piccolo [pikɔlo] NM piccolo

pichenette [piʃnɛt] NF flick

pichet [piʃɛ] NM jug

pickpocket [pikpɔkɛt] NM pickpocket

pick-up [pikœp] NM INV record player

picorer [pikɔʀe] /1/ VT to peck

picot [piko] NM sprocket; **entraînement par roue à picots** sprocket feed

picotement [pikɔtmɑ̃] NM smarting *no pl*, prickling *no pl*

picoter [pikɔte] /1/ VT (*oiseau*) to peck ▶ VI (*irriter*) to smart, prickle

pictural, e, -aux [piktyʀal, -o] ADJ pictorial

pie [pi] NF magpie; (*fig*) chatterbox ▶ ADJ INV: **cheval ~** piebald; **vache ~** black and white cow

pièce [pjɛs] NF (*d'un logement*) room; (*Théât*) play; (*de mécanisme, machine*) part; (*de monnaie*) coin; (*Couture*) patch; (*document*) document; (*de drap, fragment, d'une collection*) piece; (*de bétail*) head; **mettre en pièces** to smash to pieces; **deux euros ~** two euros each; **vendre à la ~** to sell separately *ou* individually; **travailler/payer à la ~** to do piecework/pay piece rate; **c'est inventé de toutes pièces** it's a complete fabrication; **un maillot une ~** a one-piece swimsuit; **un deux-pièces cuisine** a two-room(ed) flat (BRIT) *ou* apartment (US) with kitchen; **tout d'une ~** (*personne: franc*) blunt; (*: sans souplesse*) inflexible; **~ à conviction** exhibit; **~ d'eau** ornamental lake *ou* pond; **~ d'identité: avez-vous une ~ d'identité?** have you got any (means of) identification?; **~ jointe** (*Inform*) attachment; **~ montée** tiered cake; **~ de rechange** spare (part); **~ de résistance** pièce de résistance; (*plat*) main dish; **pièces détachées** spares, (spare) parts; **en pièces détachées** (*à monter*) in kit form; **pièces justificatives** supporting documents

pied [pje] NM foot; (*de verre*) stem; (*de table*) leg; (*de lampe*) base; (*plante*) plant; **pieds nus** barefoot; **à ~** on foot; **à ~ sec** without getting one's feet wet; **à ~ d'œuvre** ready to start (work);

au ~ de la lettre literally; au ~ levé at a moment's notice; de ~ en cap from head to foot; en ~ (portrait) full-length; avoir ~ to be able to touch the bottom, not to be out of one's depth; avoir le ~ marin to be a good sailor; perdre ~ to lose one's footing; (fig) to get out of one's depth; sur ~ (Agr) on the stalk, uncut; (debout, rétabli) up and about; mettre sur ~ (entreprise) to set up; mettre à ~ to suspend; to lay off; mettre qn au ~ du mur to get sb with his (ou her) back to the wall; sur le ~ de guerre ready for action; sur un ~ d'égalité on an equal footing; sur ~ d'intervention on stand-by; faire du ~ à qn (prévenir) to give sb a (warning) kick; (galamment) to play footsie with sb; mettre les pieds quelque part to set foot somewhere; faire des pieds et des mains (fig) to move heaven and earth, pull out all the stops; c'est le ~! (fam) it's brilliant!; mettre les pieds dans le plat (fam) to put one's foot in it; il se débrouille comme un ~ (fam) he's completely useless; se lever du bon ~/du ~ gauche to get out of bed on the right/wrong side; ~ de lit footboard; faire un ~ de nez à to thumb one's nose at; ~ de vigne vine

pied-à-terre [pjetatɛʀ] NM INV pied-à-terre

pied-bot [pjebo] (pl pieds-bots) NM person with a club foot

pied-de-biche [pjedbiʃ] (pl pieds-de-biche) NM claw; (Couture) presser foot

pied-de-poule [pjedpul] ADJ INV hound's-tooth

piédestal, -aux [pjedɛstal, -o] NM pedestal

pied-noir [pjenwaʀ] (pl pieds-noirs) NM Algerian-born Frenchman

piège [pjɛʒ] NM trap; **prendre au ~** to trap

piéger [pjeʒe] /3, 6/ VT (animal, fig) to trap; (avec une bombe) to booby-trap; **lettre/voiture piégée** letter-/car-bomb

piercing [pjɛʀsiŋ] NM piercing

pierraille [pjɛʀaj] NF loose stones pl

pierre [pjɛʀ] NF stone; **première ~** (d'un édifice) foundation stone; **mur de pierres sèches** drystone wall; **faire d'une ~ deux coups** to kill two birds with one stone; **~ à briquet** flint; **~ fine** semiprecious stone; **~ ponce** pumice stone; **~ de taille** freestone no pl; **~ tombale** tombstone, gravestone; **~ de touche** touchstone

pierreries [pjɛʀʀi] NFPL gems, precious stones

pierreux, -euse [pjɛʀø, -øz] ADJ stony

piété [pjete] NF piety

piétinement [pjetinmɑ̃] NM stamping no pl

piétiner [pjetine] /1/ VI (trépigner) to stamp (one's foot); (marquer le pas) to stand about; (fig) to be at a standstill ▶ VT to trample on

piéton, ne [pjetɔ̃, -ɔn] NM/F pedestrian ▶ ADJ pedestrian cpd

piétonnier, -ière [pjetɔnje, -jɛʀ] ADJ pedestrian cpd

piètre [pjɛtʀ] ADJ poor, mediocre

pieu, x [pjø] NM (piquet) post; (pointu) stake; (fam: lit) bed

pieusement [pjøzmɑ̃] ADV piously

pieuvre [pjœvʀ] NF octopus

pieux, -euse [pjø, -øz] ADJ pious

pif [pif] NM (fam) conk (BRIT), beak; **au ~ = pifomètre**

piffer [pife] /1/ VT (fam): **je ne peux pas le ~** I can't stand him

pifomètre [pifɔmɛtʀ] NM (fam): **choisir etc au ~** to follow one's nose when choosing etc

pige [piʒ] NF piecework rate

pigeon [piʒɔ̃] NM pigeon; **~ voyageur** homing pigeon

pigeonnant, e [piʒɔnɑ̃, -ɑ̃t] ADJ full, well-developed

pigeonneau, x [piʒɔno] NM young pigeon

pigeonnier [piʒɔnje] NM pigeon loft, dovecot(e)

piger [piʒe] /3/ VI (fam) to get it ▶ VT (fam) to get, understand

pigiste [piʒist] NMF (typographe) typesetter on piecework; (journaliste) freelance journalist (paid by the line)

pigment [pigmɑ̃] NM pigment

pignon [piɲɔ̃] NM (de mur) gable; (d'engrenage) cog(wheel), gearwheel; (graine) pine kernel; **avoir ~ sur rue** (fig) to have a prosperous business

pile [pil] NF (tas, pilier) pile; (Élec) battery ▶ ADJ: **le côté ~** tails ▶ ADV (net, brusquement) dead; (à temps, à point nommé) just at the right time; **à deux heures ~** at two on the dot; **jouer à ~ ou face** to toss up (for it); **~ ou face?** heads or tails?

piler [pile] /1/ VT to crush, pound

pileux, -euse [pilø, -øz] ADJ: **système ~** (body) hair

pilier [pilje] NM (colonne, support) pillar; (personne) mainstay; (Rugby) prop (forward)

pillage [pijaʒ] NM pillaging, plundering, looting

pillard, e [pijaʀ, -aʀd] NM/F looter; plunderer

piller [pije] /1/ VT to pillage, plunder, loot

pilleur, -euse [pijœʀ, -øz] NM/F looter

pilon [pilɔ̃] NM (instrument) pestle; (de volaille) drumstick; **mettre un livre au ~** to pulp a book

pilonner [pilɔne] /1/ VT to pound

pilori [pilɔʀi] NM: **mettre ou clouer au ~** to pillory

pilotage [pilɔtaʒ] NM piloting; flying; **~ automatique** automatic piloting; **~ sans visibilité** blind flying

pilote [pilɔt] NM pilot; (de char, voiture) driver ▶ ADJ pilot cpd; **usine/ferme ~** experimental factory/farm; **~ de chasse/d'essai/de ligne** fighter/test/airline pilot; **~ de course** racing driver

piloter [pilɔte] /1/ VT (navire) to pilot; (avion) to fly; (automobile) to drive; (fig): **~ qn** to guide sb round

pilotis [pilɔti] NM pile; stilt

pilule [pilyl] NF pill; **prendre la ~** to be on the pill; **~ du lendemain** morning-after pill

pimbêche [pɛ̃bɛʃ] NF (péj) stuck-up girl

piment [pimɑ̃] NM (Bot) pepper, capsicum; (fig) spice, piquancy; **~ rouge** (Culin) chilli

pimenté, e [pimɑ̃te] ADJ (plat) hot and spicy

pimenter [pimɑ̃te] /1/ VT (plat) to season (with peppers ou chillis); (fig) to add ou give spice to

pimpant, e [pɛ̃pɑ̃, -ɑ̃t] ADJ spruce
pin [pɛ̃] NM pine (tree); (*bois*) pine(wood)
pinacle [pinakl] NM: **porter qn au ~** (*fig*) to praise sb to the skies
pinard [pinaʀ] NM (*fam*) (cheap) wine, plonk (BRIT)
pince [pɛ̃s] NF (*outil*) pliers pl; (*de homard, crabe*) pincer, claw; (*Couture: pli*) dart; **~ à sucre/glace** sugar/ice tongs pl; **~ à épiler** tweezers pl; **~ à linge** clothes peg (BRIT) ou pin (US); **~ universelle** (universal) pliers pl; **pinces de cycliste** bicycle clips
pincé, e [pɛ̃se] ADJ (*air*) stiff; (*mince: bouche*) pinched ► NF: **une ~ de** a pinch of
pinceau, x [pɛ̃so] NM (paint)brush
pincement [pɛ̃smɑ̃] NM: **~ au cœur** twinge of regret
pince-monseigneur [pɛ̃smɔ̃sɛɲœʀ] (*pl* **pinces-monseigneur**) NF crowbar
pince-nez [pɛ̃sne] NM INV pince-nez
pincer [pɛ̃se] /3/ VT to pinch; (*Mus: cordes*) to pluck; (*Couture*) to dart, put darts in; (*fam*) to nab; **se ~ le doigt** to squeeze ou nip one's finger; **se ~ le nez** to hold one's nose
pince-sans-rire [pɛ̃ssɑ̃ʀiʀ] ADJ INV deadpan
pincettes [pɛ̃sɛt] NFPL tweezers; (*pour le feu*) (fire) tongs
pinçon [pɛ̃sɔ̃] NM pinch mark
pinède [pined] NF pinewood, pine forest
pingouin [pɛ̃gwɛ̃] NM penguin
ping-pong [piŋpɔ̃g] NM table tennis
pingre [pɛ̃gʀ] ADJ niggardly
pinson [pɛ̃sɔ̃] NM chaffinch
pintade [pɛ̃tad] NF guinea-fowl
pin up [pinœp] NF INV pin-up (girl)
pioche [pjɔʃ] NF pickaxe
piocher [pjɔʃe] /1/ VT to dig up (with a pickaxe); (*fam*) to swot (BRIT) ou grind (US) at; **~ dans** to dig into
piolet [pjɔlɛ] NM ice axe
pion, ne [pjɔ̃, pjɔn] NM/F (*Scol*) student paid to supervise schoolchildren ► NM (*Échecs*) pawn; (*Dames*) piece, draught (BRIT), checker (US)
pionnier [pjɔnje] NM pioneer
pipe [pip] NF pipe; **fumer la** ou **une ~** to smoke a pipe; **~ de bruyère** briar pipe
pipeau, x [pipo] NM (reed-)pipe
pipe-line [piplin] NM pipeline
piper [pipe] /1/ VT (*dé*) to load; (*carte*) to mark; **sans ~ mot** (*fam*) without a squeak; **les dés sont pipés** (*fig*) the dice are loaded
pipette [pipɛt] NF pipette
pipi [pipi] NM (*fam*): **faire ~** to have a wee
piquant, e [pikɑ̃, -ɑ̃t] ADJ (*barbe, rosier etc*) prickly; (*saveur, sauce*) hot, pungent; (*fig: détail*) titillating; (: *mordant, caustique*) biting ► NM (*épine*) thorn, prickle; (*de hérisson*) quill, spine; (*fig*) spiciness, spice
pique [pik] NF (*arme*) pike, (*fig*): **envoyer** ou **lancer des piques à qn** to make cutting remarks to sb ► NM (*Cartes: couleur*) spades pl; (: *carte*) spade
piqué, e [pike] ADJ (*Couture*) (machine-)stitched; quilted; (*livre, glace*) mildewed; (*vin*) sour; (*Mus:*

note) staccato; (*fam: personne*) nuts ► NM (*Aviat*) dive; (*Textiles*) piqué
pique-assiette [pikasjɛt] NMF INV (*péj*) scrounger, sponger
pique-fleurs [pikflœʀ] NM INV flower holder
pique-nique [piknik] NM picnic
pique-niquer [piknike] /1/ VI to (have a) picnic
pique-niqueur, -euse [piknikœʀ, -øz] NM/F picnicker
piquer [pike] /1/ VT (*percer*) to prick; (*Méd*) to give an injection to; (: *animal blessé etc*) to put to sleep; (*insecte, fumée, ortie*) to sting; (*moustique*) to bite; (*poivre*) to burn; (*froid*) to bite; (*Couture*) to machine (stitch); (*intérêt etc*) to arouse; (*fam: prendre*) to pick up; (: *voler*) to pinch; (: *arrêter*) to nab; (*planter*): **~ qch dans** to stick sth into; (*fixer*): **~ qch à** ou **sur** to pin sth onto ► VI (*oiseau, avion*) to go into a dive; (*saveur*) to be pungent; to be sour; **se piquer** (*avec une aiguille*) to prick o.s.; (*se faire une piqûre*) to inject o.s.; (*se vexer*) to get annoyed; **se piquer de faire** to pride o.s. on doing; **~ sur** to swoop down on; to head straight for; **~ du nez** (*avion*) to go into a nose-dive; **~ une tête** (*plonger*) to dive headfirst; **~ un galop/un cent mètres** to break into a gallop/put on a sprint; **~ une crise** to throw a fit; **~ au vif** (*fig*) to sting
piquet [pikɛ] NM (*pieu*) post, stake; (*de tente*) peg; **mettre un élève au ~** to make a pupil stand in the corner; **~ de grève** (strike) picket; **~ d'incendie** fire-fighting squad
piqueté, e [pikte] ADJ: **~ de** dotted with
piquette [pikɛt] NF (*fam*) cheap wine, plonk (BRIT)
piqûre [pikyʀ] NF (*d'épingle*) prick; (*d'ortie*) sting; (*de moustique*) bite; (*Méd*) injection, shot (US); (*Couture*) (straight) stitch; straight stitching; (*de ver*) hole; (*tache*) spot of) mildew; **faire une ~ à qn** to give sb an injection
piranha [piʀana] NM piranha
piratage [piʀataʒ] NM (*Inform*) piracy
pirate [piʀat] ADJ pirate cpd ► NM pirate; (*fig: escroc*) crook, shark; (*Inform*) hacker; **~ de l'air** hijacker
pirater [piʀate] /1/ VI (*Inform*) to hack ► VT (*Inform*) to hack into
piraterie [piʀatʀi] NF (act of) piracy; **~ aérienne** hijacking
pire [piʀ] ADJ (*comparatif*) worse; (*superlatif*): **le (la) ~ ...** the worst ... ► NM: **le ~ (de)** the worst (of); **au ~** at (the very) worst
Pirée [piʀe] N Piraeus
pirogue [piʀɔg] NF dugout (canoe)
pirouette [piʀwɛt] NF pirouette; (*fig: volte-face*) about-turn
pis [pi] NM (*de vache*) udder; (*pire*): **le ~** the worst ► ADJ INV, ADV worse; **qui ~ est** what is worse; **au ~ aller** if the worst comes to the worst, at worst; **de mal en ~** from bad to worse
pis-aller [pizale] NM INV stopgap
pisciculture [pisikyltyʀ] NF fish farming
piscine [pisin] NF (swimming) pool; **~ couverte** indoor (swimming) pool
Pise [piz] N Pisa
pissenlit [pisɑ̃li] NM dandelion

pisser [pise] /**1**/ vi (!) to pee
pissotière [pisɔtjɛʀ] NF (fam) public urinal
pistache [pistaʃ] NF pistachio (nut)
pistard [pistaʀ] NM (Cyclisme) track cyclist
piste [pist] NF (d'un animal, sentier) track, trail; (indice) lead; (de stade, de magnétophone) track; (de cirque) ring; (de danse) floor; (de patinage) rink; (de ski) run; (Aviat) runway; ~ **cavalière** bridle path; ~ **cyclable** cycle track, bikeway (US); ~ **sonore** sound track
pister [piste] /**1**/ vt to track, trail
pisteur [pistœʀ] NM (Ski) member of the ski patrol
pistil [pistil] NM pistil
pistolet [pistɔlɛ] NM (arme) pistol, gun; (à peinture) spray gun; ~ **à bouchon/air comprimé** popgun/airgun; ~ **à eau** water pistol
pistolet-mitrailleur [pistɔlɛmitʀajœʀ] (pl **pistolets-mitrailleurs**) NM submachine gun
piston [pistɔ̃] NM (Tech) piston; (Mus) valve; (fig: appui) string-pulling; **avoir du** ~ (fam) to have friends in the right places
pistonner [pistɔne] /**1**/ vt (candidat) to pull strings for
pitance [pitɑ̃s] NF (péj) (means of) sustenance
piteusement [pitøzmɑ̃] ADV (échouer) miserably
piteux, -euse [pitø, -øz] ADJ pitiful, sorry (avant le nom); **en** ~ **état** in a sorry state
pitié [pitje] NF pity; **sans** ~ adj pitiless, merciless; **faire** ~ to inspire pity; **il me fait** ~ I pity him, I feel sorry for him; **avoir** ~ **de** (compassion) to pity, feel sorry for; (merci) to have pity ou mercy on; **par** ~! for pity's sake!
piton [pitɔ̃] NM (clou) peg, bolt; ~ **rocheux** rocky outcrop
pitoyable [pitwajabl] ADJ pitiful
pitre [pitʀ] NM clown
pitrerie [pitʀəʀi] NF tomfoolery no pl
pittoresque [pitɔʀɛsk] ADJ picturesque; (expression, détail) colourful (BRIT), colorful (US)
pivert [pivɛʀ] NM green woodpecker
pivoine [pivwan] NF peony
pivot [pivo] NM pivot; (d'une dent) post
pivoter [pivɔte] /**1**/ vi (fauteuil) to swivel; (porte) to revolve; ~ **sur ses talons** to swing round
pixel [piksɛl] NM pixel
pizza [pidza] NF pizza
PJ SIGLE F (= police judiciaire) ≈ CID (BRIT), ≈ FBI (US) ▸ SIGLE FPL (= pièces jointes) encl
PL SIGLE M (Auto) = **poids lourd**
Pl. ABR = **place**
placage [plakaʒ] NM (bois) veneer
placard [plakaʀ] NM (armoire) cupboard; (affiche) poster, notice; (Typo) galley; ~ **publicitaire** display advertisement
placarder [plakaʀde] /**1**/ vt (affiche) to put up; (mur) to stick posters on
place [plas] NF (emplacement, situation, classement) place; (de ville, village) square; (espace libre) room, space; (de parking) space; (siège: de train, cinéma, voiture) seat; (prix: au cinéma etc) price; (: dans un bus, taxi) fare; (emploi) job; ~ **financière/boursière** money/stock market; **en** ~ (mettre) in

its place; **de** ~ **en** ~, **par places** here and there, in places; **sur** ~ on the spot; **faire** ~ **à** to give way to; **faire de la** ~ **à** to make room for; **ça prend de la** ~ it takes up a lot of room ou space; **prendre** ~ to take one's place; **remettre qn à sa** ~ to put sb in his (ou her) place; **ne pas rester** ou **tenir en** ~ to be always on the go; **à la** ~ **de** in place of, instead of; **à votre** ~ ... if I were you ...; **se mettre à la** ~ **de qn** to put o.s. in sb's place ou in sb's shoes; **une quatre places** (Auto) a four-seater; **il y a 20 places assises/debout** there are 20 seats/there is standing room for 20; ~ **forte** fortified town; ~ **d'honneur** place (ou seat) of honour (BRIT) ou honor (US)
placé, e [plase] ADJ (Hippisme) placed; **haut** ~ (fig) high-ranking; **être bien/mal** ~ to be well/badly placed; (spectateur) to have a good/bad seat; **être bien/mal** ~ **pour faire** to be in/not to be in a position to do; **il est bien** ~ **pour le savoir** he is in a position to know
placebo [plasebo] NM placebo
placement [plasmɑ̃] NM placing; (Finance) investment; **agence** ou **bureau de** ~ employment agency
placenta [plasɑ̃ta] NM placenta
placer [plase] /**3**/ vt to place, put; (convive, spectateur) to seat; (capital, argent) to place, invest; (dans la conversation) to put ou get in; ~ **qn chez** to get sb a job at (ou with); **se** ~ **au premier rang** to go and stand (ou sit) in the first row
placide [plasid] ADJ placid
placidité [plasidite] NF placidity
placier, -ière [plasje, -jɛʀ] NM/F commercial rep(resentative), salesman/woman
Placoplâtre® [plakoplatʀ] NM plasterboard
plafond [plafɔ̃] NM ceiling
plafonner [plafɔne] /**1**/ vt (pièce) to put a ceiling (up) in ▸ vi to reach one's (ou a) ceiling
plafonnier [plafɔnje] NM ceiling light; (Auto) interior light
plage [plaʒ] NF beach; (station) (seaside) resort; (fig) band, bracket; (de disque) track, band; ~ **arrière** (Auto) parcel ou back shelf
plagiaire [plaʒjɛʀ] NMF plagiarist
plagiat [plaʒja] NM plagiarism
plagier [plaʒje] /**7**/ vt to plagiarize
plagiste [plaʒist] NMF beach attendant
plaid [plɛd] NM (tartan) car rug, lap robe (US)
plaidant, e [plɛdɑ̃, -ɑ̃t] ADJ litigant
plaider [plede] /**1**/ vi (avocat) to plead; (plaignant) to go to court, litigate ▸ vt to plead; ~ **pour** (fig) to speak for
plaideur, -euse [plɛdœʀ, -øz] NM/F litigant
plaidoirie [plɛdwaʀi] NF (Jur) speech for the defence (BRIT) ou defense (US)
plaidoyer [plɛdwaje] NM (Jur) speech for the defence (BRIT) ou defense (US); (fig) plea
plaie [plɛ] NF wound
plaignant, e [plɛɲɑ̃, -ɑ̃t] VB voir **plaindre** ▸ NM/F plaintiff
plaindre [plɛ̃dʀ] /**52**/ vt to pity, feel sorry for; **se plaindre** vi (gémir) to moan; (protester, rouspéter): **se plaindre (à qn) (de)** to complain (to sb) (about); **se plaindre de** (souffrir) to complain of

plaine [plɛn] NF plain
plain-pied [plɛ̃pje] ADV: **de** ~ at street-level; (fig) straight; **de** ~ **(avec)** on the same level (as)
plaint, e [plɛ̃, -ɛ̃t] PP de **plaindre** ▶ NF (gémissement) moan, groan; (doléance) complaint; **porter** ~ to lodge a complaint
plaintif, -ive [plɛ̃tif, -iv] ADJ plaintive
plaire [plɛʀ] /54/ VI to be a success, be successful; to please; **cela me plaît** I like it; **ça plaît beaucoup aux jeunes** it's very popular with young people; **essayer de** ~ **à qn** (en étant serviable etc) to try and please sb; **elle plaît aux hommes** she's a success with men, men like her; **se** ~ **quelque part** to like being somewhere, like it somewhere; **se** ~ **à faire** to take pleasure in doing; **ce qu'il vous plaira** what(ever) you like ou wish; **s'il vous plaît, s'il te plaît** please
plaisamment [plɛzamɑ̃] ADV pleasantly
plaisance [plɛzɑ̃s] NF (aussi: **navigation de plaisance**) (pleasure) sailing, yachting
plaisancier [plɛzɑ̃sje] NM amateur sailor, yachting enthusiast
plaisant, e [plɛzɑ̃, -ɑ̃t] ADJ pleasant; (histoire, anecdote) amusing
plaisanter [plɛzɑ̃te] /1/ VI to joke ▶ VT (personne) to tease, make fun of; **pour** ~ for a joke; **on ne plaisante pas avec cela** that's no joking matter; **tu plaisantes!** you're joking ou kidding!
plaisanterie [plɛzɑ̃tʀi] NF joke; joking no pl
plaisantin [plɛzɑ̃tɛ̃] NM joker; (fumiste) fly-by-night
plaise etc [plɛz] VB voir **plaire**
plaisir [plezi R] NM pleasure; **faire** ~ **à qn** (délibérément) to be nice to sb, please sb; **ça me fait** ~ (cadeau, nouvelle etc) I'm delighted ou very pleased with this; **j'espère que ça te fera** ~ I hope you'll like it; **prendre** ~ **à/à faire** to take pleasure in/in doing; **j'ai le** ~ **de** ... it is with great pleasure that I ...; **M. et Mme X ont le** ~ **de vous faire part de** ... M. and Mme X are pleased to announce ...; **se faire un** ~ **de faire qch** to be (only too) pleased to do sth; **faites-moi le** ~ **de** ... would you mind ..., would you be kind enough to ...; **à** ~ freely; for the sake of it; **au** ~ **(de vous revoir)** (I hope to) see you again; **pour le** ou **pour son** ou **par** ~ for pleasure
plaît [plɛ] VB voir **plaire**
plan, e [plɑ̃, -an] ADJ flat ▶ NM plan; (Géom) plane; (fig) level, plane; (Ciné) shot; **au premier/second** ~ in the foreground/middle distance; **à l'arrière** ~ in the background; **mettre qch au premier** ~ (fig) to consider sth to be of primary importance; **sur le** ~ **sexuel** sexually, as far as sex is concerned; **laisser/rester en** ~ to abandon/be abandoned; ~ **d'action** plan of action; ~ **directeur** (Écon) master plan; ~ **d'eau** lake; pond; ~ **de travail** work-top, work surface; ~ **de vol** (Aviat) flight plan
planche [plɑ̃ʃ] NF (pièce de bois) plank, (wooden) board; (illustration) plate; (de salades, radis,

poireaux) bed; (d'un plongeoir) (diving) board; **les planches** (Théât) the boards; **en planches** adj wooden; **faire la** ~ (dans l'eau) to float on one's back; **avoir du pain sur la** ~ to have one's work cut out; ~ **à découper** chopping board; ~ **à dessin** drawing board; ~ **à pain** breadboard; ~ **à repasser** ironing board; ~ **(à roulettes)** (planche) skateboard; (sport) skateboarding; ~ **de salut** (fig) sheet anchor; ~ **à voile** (planche) windsurfer, sailboard; (sport) windsurfing
plancher [plɑ̃ʃe] /1/ NM floor; (planches) floorboards pl; (fig) minimum level ▶ VI to work hard
planchiste [plɑ̃ʃist] NMF windsurfer
plancton [plɑ̃ktɔ̃] NM plankton
planer [plane] /1/ VI (oiseau, avion) to glide; (fumée, vapeur) to float, hover; (drogué) to be (on a) high; (fam: rêveur) to have one's head in the clouds; ~ **sur** (danger) to hang over; to hover above
planétaire [planetɛʀ] ADJ planetary
planétarium [planetaʀjɔm] NM planetarium
planète [planɛt] NF planet
planeur [planœʀ] NM glider
planification [planifikasjɔ̃] NF (economic) planning
planifier [planifje] /7/ VT to plan
planisphère [planisfɛʀ] NM planisphere
planning [planiŋ] NM programme (BRIT), program (US), schedule; ~ **familial** family planning
planque [plɑ̃k] NF (fam: combine, filon) cushy (BRIT) ou easy number; (: cachette) hideout
planquer [plɑ̃ke] /1/ VT (fam) to hide (away), stash away; **se planquer** to hide
plant [plɑ̃] NM seedling, young plant
plantage [plɑ̃taʒ] NM (d'ordinateur) crash
plantaire [plɑ̃tɛʀ] ADJ voir **voûte**
plantation [plɑ̃tasjɔ̃] NF planting; (de fleurs, légumes) bed; (exploitation) plantation
plante [plɑ̃t] NF plant; ~ **d'appartement** house ou pot plant; ~ **du pied** sole (of the foot); ~ **verte** house plant
planter [plɑ̃te] /1/ VT (plante) to plant; (enfoncer) to hammer ou drive in; (tente) to put up, pitch; (drapeau, échelle, décors) to put up; (fam: mettre) to dump; (: abandonner): ~ **là** to ditch; **se planter** VI (fam: se tromper) to get it wrong; ~ **qch dans** to hammer ou drive sth into; to stick sth into; **se planter dans** to sink into; to get stuck in; **se planter devant** to plant o.s. in front of
planteur [plɑ̃tœʀ] NM planter
planton [plɑ̃tɔ̃] NM orderly
plantureux, -euse [plɑ̃tyʀø, -øz] ADJ (repas) copious, lavish; (femme) buxom
plaquage [plakaʒ] NM (Rugby) tackle
plaque [plak] NF plate; (de verre) sheet; (de verglas, d'eczéma) patch; (dentaire) plaque; (avec inscription) plaque; ~ **(minéralogique** ou **police** ou **d'immatriculation)** number (BRIT) ou license (US) plate; ~ **de beurre** slab of butter; ~ **chauffante** hotplate; ~ **de chocolat** bar of chocolate; ~ **de cuisson** hob; ~ **d'identité** identity disc; ~ **tournante** (fig) centre (BRIT), center (US)

plaqué, e [plake] ADJ: **~ or/argent** gold-/silver-plated ▸ NM: **~ or/argent** gold/silver plate; **~ acajou** with a mahogany veneer

plaquer [plake] /1/ VT (bijou) to plate; (bois) to veneer; (aplatir): **~ qch sur/contre** to make sth stick ou cling to; (Rugby) to bring down; (fam: laisser tomber) to drop, ditch; **se ~ contre** to flatten o.s. against; **~ qn contre** to pin sb to

plaquette [plaket] NF tablet; (de chocolat) bar; (de beurre) slab, packet; (livre) small volume; (Méd: de pilules, gélules) pack, packet; **~ de frein** (Auto) brake pad

plasma [plasma] NM plasma

plastic [plastik] NM plastic explosive

plastifié, e [plastifje] ADJ plastic-coated

plastifier [plastifje] /7/ VT (document, photo) to laminate

plastiquage [plastikaʒ] NM bombing, bomb attack

plastique [plastik] ADJ plastic ▸ NM plastic ▸ NF plastic arts pl; (d'une statue) modelling

plastiquer [plastike] /1/ VT to blow up

plastiqueur [plastikœR] NM terrorist (planting a plastic bomb)

plastron [plastRɔ̃] NM shirt front

plastronner [plastRɔne] /1/ VI to swagger

plat, e [pla, -at] ADJ flat; (fade: vin) flat-tasting, insipid; (personne, livre) dull; (style) flat, dull ▸ NM (récipient, Culin) dish; (d'un repas) course; **le premier ~** the first course; (partie plate): **le ~ de la main** the flat of the hand; (: d'une route) flat (part); **à ~ ventre** adv face down; (tomber) flat on one's face; **à ~** adj (pneu, batterie) flat; (fam: fatigué) dead beat, tired out; **~ cuisiné** pre-cooked meal (ou dish); **~ du jour** dish of the day; **~ principal** ou **de résistance** main course; **plats préparés** convenience food(s)

platane [platan] NM plane tree

plateau, x [plato] NM (support) tray; (d'une table) top; (d'une balance) pan; (Géo) plateau; (de tourne-disques) turntable; (Ciné) set; (TV): **nous avons deux journalistes sur le ~ ce soir** we have two journalists with us tonight; **~ à fromages** cheeseboard

plateau-repas [platoRəpa] (pl **plateaux-repas**) NM tray meal, TV dinner (US)

plate-bande [platbɑ̃d] (pl **plates-bandes**) NF flower bed

platée [plate] NF dish(ful)

plate-forme [platfɔRm] (pl **plates-formes**) NF platform; **~ de forage/pétrolière** drilling/oil rig

platine [platin] NM platinum ▸ NF (d'un tourne-disque) turntable; **~ disque/cassette** record/cassette deck; **~ laser** ou **compact-disc** compact disc (player)

platitude [platityd] NF platitude

platonique [platɔnik] ADJ platonic

plâtras [plɑtRɑ] NM rubble no pl

plâtre [plɑtR] NM (matériau) plaster; (statue) plaster statue; (Méd) (plaster) cast; **plâtres** NMPL plasterwork sg; **avoir un bras dans le ~** to have an arm in plaster

plâtrer [plɑtRe] /1/ VT to plaster; (Méd) to set ou put in a (plaster) cast

plâtrier [plɑtRije] NM plasterer

plausible [plozibl] ADJ plausible

play-back [plɛbak] NM miming

play-boy [plɛbɔj] NM playboy

plébiscite [plebisit] NM plebiscite

plébisciter [plebisite] /1/ VT (approuver) to give overwhelming support to; (élire) to elect by an overwhelming majority

plectre [plɛktR] NM plectrum

plein, e [plɛ̃, -ɛn] ADJ full; (porte, roue) solid; (chienne, jument) big (with young) ▸ NM: **faire le ~ (d'essence)** to fill up (with petrol (BRIT) ou gas (US)) ▸ PRÉP: **avoir de l'argent ~ les poches** to have loads of money; **~ de** full of; **avoir les mains pleines** to have one's hands full; **à pleines mains** (ramasser) in handfuls; (empoigner) firmly; **à ~ régime** at maximum revs; (fig) at full speed; **à ~ temps** full-time; **en ~ air** in the open air; **jeux en ~ air** outdoor games; **en ~ mer** on the open sea; **en ~ soleil** in direct sunlight; **en ~ nuit/rue** in the middle of the night/street; **en ~ milieu** right in the middle; **en ~ jour** in broad daylight; **les pleins** the downstrokes (in handwriting); **faire le ~ des voix** to get the maximum number of votes possible; **en ~ sur** right on; **en avoir ~ le dos** (fam) to have had it up to here

pleinement [plɛnmɑ̃] ADV fully; to the full

plein-emploi [plɛnɑ̃plwa] NM full employment

plénière [plenjɛR] ADJ F: **assemblée ~** plenary assembly

plénipotentiaire [plenipɔtɑ̃sjɛR] NM plenipotentiary

plénitude [plenityd] NF fullness

pléthore [pletɔR] NF: **~ de** overabundance ou plethora of

pléthorique [pletɔRik] ADJ (classes) overcrowded; (documentation) excessive

pleurer [plœRe] /1/ VI to cry; (yeux) to water ▸ VT to mourn (for); **~ sur** vt to lament (over), bemoan; **~ de rire** to laugh till one cries

pleurésie [plœRezi] NF pleurisy

pleureuse [plœRøz] NF professional mourner

pleurnicher [plœRniʃe] /1/ VI to snivel, whine

pleurs [plœR] NMPL: **en ~** in tears

pleut [plø] VB voir **pleuvoir**

pleutre [pløtR] ADJ cowardly

pleuvait etc [pløvɛ] VB voir **pleuvoir**

pleuviner [pløvine] /1/ VB IMPERS to drizzle

pleuvoir [pløvwaR] /23/ VB IMPERS to rain ▸ VI (fig: coups) to rain down; (critiques, invitations) to shower down; **il pleut** it's raining; **il pleut des cordes** ou **à verse** ou **à torrents** it's pouring (down), it's raining cats and dogs

pleuvra etc [pløvRa] VB voir **pleuvoir**

plexiglas® [plɛksiglɑs] NM Plexiglas® (US)

pli [pli] NM fold; (de jupe) pleat; (de pantalon) crease; (aussi: **faux pli**) crease; (enveloppe) envelope; (lettre) letter; (Cartes) trick; **prendre le ~ de faire** to get into the habit of doing; **ça ne fait pas un ~!** don't you worry!; **~ d'aisance** inverted pleat

pliable [plijabl] ADJ pliable, flexible

P

317

pliage [plijaʒ] NM folding; (*Art*) origami
pliant, e [plijɑ̃, -ɑ̃t] ADJ folding ▶ NM folding stool, campstool
plier [plije] **/7/** VT to fold; (*pour ranger*) to fold up; (*table pliante*) to fold down; (*genou, bras*) to bend ▶ VI to bend; (*fig*) to yield; **se ~ à** to submit to; **~ bagages** (*fig*) to pack up (and go)
plinthe [plɛ̃t] NF skirting board
plissé, e [plise] ADJ (*jupe, robe*) pleated; (*peau*) wrinkled; (*Géo*) folded ▶ NM (*Couture*) pleats pl
plissement [plismɑ̃] NM (*Géo*) fold
plisser [plise] **/1/** VT (*chiffonner: papier, étoffe*) to crease; (*rider: yeux*) to screw up; (*: front*) to furrow, wrinkle; (*: bouche*) to pucker; (*jupe*) to put pleats in; **se plisser** VI (*vêtement, étoffe*) to crease
pliure [plijyʀ] NF (*du bras, genou*) bend; (*d'un ourlet*) fold
plomb [plɔ̃] NM (*métal*) lead; (*d'une cartouche*) (lead) shot; (*Pêche*) sinker; (*sceau*) (lead) seal; (*Élec*) fuse; **de ~** (*soleil*) blazing; **sans ~** (*essence*) unleaded; **sommeil de ~** heavy ou very deep sleep; **mettre à ~** to plumb
plombage [plɔ̃baʒ] NM (*de dent*) filling
plomber [plɔ̃be] **/1/** VT (*canne, ligne*) to weight (with lead); (*colis, wagon*) to put a lead seal on; (*Tech: mur*) to plumb; (*: dent*) to fill (BRIT), stop (US); (*Inform*) to protect
plomberie [plɔ̃bʀi] NF plumbing
plombier [plɔ̃bje] NM plumber
plonge [plɔ̃ʒ] NF: **faire la ~** to be a washer-up (BRIT) ou dishwasher (*person*)
plongeant, e [plɔ̃ʒɑ̃, -ɑ̃t] ADJ (*vue*) from above; (*tir, décolleté*) plunging
plongée [plɔ̃ʒe] NF (*Sport*) diving no pl; (*: sans scaphandre*) skin diving; (*de sous-marin*) submersion, dive; **en ~** (*sous-marin*) submerged; (*prise de vue*) high angle; **~ sous-marine** diving
plongeoir [plɔ̃ʒwaʀ] NM diving board
plongeon [plɔ̃ʒɔ̃] NM dive
plonger [plɔ̃ʒe] **/3/** VI to dive ▶ VT: **~ qch dans** to plunge sth into; **~ dans un sommeil profond** to sink straight into a deep sleep; **~ qn dans l'embarras** to throw sb into a state of confusion; **se ~ dans** (*études, lecture*) to bury ou immerse o.s. in
plongeur, -euse [plɔ̃ʒœʀ, -øz] NM/F diver; (*de café*) washer-up (BRIT), dishwasher (*person*)
plot [plo] NM (*Élec*) contact
ploutocratie [plutɔkʀasi] NF plutocracy
ploutocratique [plutɔkʀatik] ADJ plutocratic
ployer [plwaje] **/8/** VT to bend ▶ VI to bend; (*plancher*) to sag
plu [ply] PP *de* plaire; pleuvoir
pluie [plɥi] NF rain; (*averse, ondée*): **une ~ brève** a shower; (*fig*): **~ de** shower of; **une ~ fine** fine rain; **retomber en ~** to shower down; **sous la ~** in the rain
plumage [plymaʒ] NM plumage no pl, feathers pl
plume [plym] NF feather; (*pour écrire*) (pen) nib; (*fig*) pen; **dessin à la ~** pen and ink drawing
plumeau, x [plymo] NM feather duster
plumer [plyme] **/1/** VT to pluck
plumet [plymɛ] NM plume

plumier [plymje] NM pencil box
plupart [plypaʀ]: **la ~** pron the majority, most (of them); **la ~ des** most, the majority of; **la ~ du temps/d'entre nous** most of the time/of us; **pour la ~** adv for the most part, mostly
pluralisme [plyʀalism] NM pluralism
pluralité [plyʀalite] NF plurality
pluridisciplinaire [plyʀidisiplinɛʀ] ADJ multidisciplinary
pluriel [plyʀjɛl] NM plural; **au ~** in the plural
plus¹ [ply] VB *voir* plaire

MOT-CLÉ

plus² [ply] ADV **1** (*forme négative*): **ne ... plus** no more, no longer; **je n'ai plus d'argent** I've got no more money ou no money left; **il ne travaille plus** he's no longer working, he doesn't work any more
2 [ply, (+voyelle) plyz] (*comparatif*) more, ...+er; (*superlatif*): **le plus** the most, the ...+est; **plus grand/intelligent (que)** bigger/more intelligent (than); **le plus grand/intelligent** the biggest/most intelligent; **tout au plus** at the very most
3 [plys, (+voyelle) plyz] (*davantage*) more; **il travaille plus (que)** he works more (than); **plus il travaille, plus il est heureux** the more he works, the happier he is; **plus de pain** more bread; **plus de 10 personnes/trois heures/quatre kilos** more than ou over 10 people/three hours/four kilos; **trois heures de plus que** three hours more than; **plus de minuit** after ou past midnight; **de plus** what's more, moreover; **il a trois ans de plus que moi** he's three years older than me; **trois kilos en plus** three kilos more; **en plus de** in addition to; **de plus en plus** more and more; **en plus de cela** ... what is more ...; **plus ou moins** more or less; **ni plus ni moins** no more, no less; **sans plus** (but) no more than that, (but) that's all; **qui plus est** what is more
▶ PRÉP [plys]: **quatre plus deux** four plus two

plusieurs [plyzjœʀ] ADJ, PRON several; **ils sont ~** there are several of them
plus-que-parfait [plyskəpaʀfɛ] NM pluperfect, past perfect
plus-value [plyvaly] NF (*d'un bien*) appreciation; (*bénéfice*) capital gain; (*budgétaire*) surplus
plut [ply] VB *voir* plaire; pleuvoir
plutonium [plytɔnjɔm] NM plutonium
plutôt [plyto] ADV rather; **je ferais ~ ceci** I'd rather ou sooner do this; **fais ~ comme ça** try this way instead; **~ que (de) faire** rather than ou instead of doing
pluvial, e, -aux [plyvjal, -o] ADJ (*eaux*) rain cpd
pluvieux, -euse [plyvjø, -øz] ADJ rainy, wet
pluviosité [plyvjozite] NF rainfall
PM SIGLE F = **Police militaire**
p.m. ABR (= *pour mémoire*) for the record
PME SIGLE FPL (= *petites et moyennes entreprises*) small businesses
PMI SIGLE FPL = **petites et moyennes industries** ▶ SIGLE F = **protection maternelle et infantile**

PMU SIGLE M (= *pari mutuel urbain*) (*dans un café*) betting agency; *see note*

> The PMU (*pari mutuel urbain*) is a Government-regulated network of betting counters run from bars displaying the PMU sign. Punters buy fixed-price tickets predicting winners or finishing positions in horse races. The traditional bet is the *tiercé*, a triple bet, although other multiple bets (*quarté* and so on) are becoming increasingly popular.

PNB SIGLE M (= *produit national brut*) GNP

pneu [pnø] NM (*de roue*) tyre (BRIT), tire (US); (*message*) letter sent by pneumatic tube

pneumatique [pnømatik] ADJ pneumatic; (*gonflable*) inflatable ▶ NM tyre (BRIT), tire (US)

pneumonie [pnømɔni] NF pneumonia

PO SIGLE FPL (= *petites ondes*) MW

po [po] ABR *voir* **science**

Pô [po] NM: **le Pô** the Po

p.o. ABR (= *par ordre*) p.p. (*on letters etc*)

poche [pɔʃ] NF pocket; (*déformation*): **faire une/des ~(s)** to bag; (*sous les yeux*) bag, pouch; (*Zool*) pouch ▶ NM (*livre de poche*) (pocket-size) paperback; **de ~** pocket *cpd*; **en être de sa ~** to be out of pocket; **c'est dans la ~** it's in the bag; **argent de ~** pocket money

poché, e [pɔʃe] ADJ: **œuf ~** poached egg; **œil ~** black eye

pocher [pɔʃe] /1/ VT (*Culin*) to poach; (*Art*) to sketch ▶ VI (*vêtement*) to bag

poche-revolver [pɔʃʀəvɔlvɛʀ] (*pl* **poches-revolver**) NF hip pocket

pochette [pɔʃɛt] NF (*de timbres*) wallet, envelope; (*d'aiguilles etc*) case; (*sac: de femme*) clutch bag, purse; (: *d'homme*) bag; (*sur veston*) breast pocket; (*mouchoir*) breast pocket handkerchief; **~ d'allumettes** book of matches; **~ de disque** record sleeve; **~ surprise** lucky bag

pochoir [pɔʃwaʀ] NM (*Art: cache*) stencil; (: *tampon*) transfer

podcast [pɔdkast] NM (*Inform*) podcast

podcaster [pɔdkaste] /1/ VI (*Inform*) to podcast

podium [pɔdjɔm] NM podium

poêle [pwɑl] NM stove ▶ NF: **~ (à frire)** frying pan

poêlon [pwɑlɔ̃] NM casserole

poème [pɔɛm] NM poem

poésie [pɔezi] NF (*poème*) poem; (*art*): **la ~** poetry

poète [pɔɛt] NM poet; (*fig*) dreamer ▶ ADJ poetic

poétique [pɔetik] ADJ poetic

pognon [pɔɲɔ̃] NM (*fam: argent*) dough

poids [pwa] NM weight; (*Sport*) shot; **vendre au ~** to sell by weight; **de ~** adj (*argument etc*) weighty; **perdre/prendre du ~** to lose/put on weight; **faire le ~** (*fig*) to measure up; **~ plume/mouche/coq/moyen** (*Boxe*) feather/fly/bantam/middleweight; **~ et haltères** weight lifting *sg*; **~ lourd** (*Boxe*) heavyweight; (*camion: aussi*: **PL**) (big) lorry (BRIT), truck (US); (*Admin*) large goods vehicle (BRIT), truck (US); **~ mort** dead weight; **~ utile** net weight

poignant, e [pwaɲɑ̃, -ɑ̃t] ADJ poignant, harrowing

poignard [pwaɲaʀ] NM dagger

poignarder [pwaɲaʀde] /1/ VT to stab, knife

poigne [pwaɲ] NF grip; (*fig*) firm-handedness; **à ~** firm-handed; **avoir de la ~** (*fig*) to rule with a firm hand

poignée [pwaɲe] NF (*de sel etc, fig*) handful; (*de couvercle, porte*) handle; **~ de main** handshake

poignet [pwaɲɛ] NM (*Anat*) wrist; (*de chemise*) cuff

poil [pwal] NM (*Anat*) hair; (*de pinceau, brosse*) bristle; (*de tapis, tissu*) strand; (*pelage*) coat; (*ensemble des poils*): **avoir du ~ sur la poitrine** to have hair(s) on one's chest, have a hairy chest; **à ~** adj (*fam*) starkers; **au ~** adj (*fam*) hunky-dory; **de tout ~** of all kinds; **être de bon/mauvais ~** to be in a good/bad mood; **~ à gratter** itching powder

poilu, e [pwaly] ADJ hairy

poinçon [pwɛ̃sɔ̃] NM awl; bodkin; (*marque*) hallmark

poinçonner [pwɛ̃sɔne] /1/ VT (*marchandise*) to stamp; (*bijou etc*) to hallmark; (*billet, ticket*) to punch, clip

poinçonneuse [pwɛ̃sɔnøz] NF (*outil*) punch

poindre [pwɛ̃dʀ] /49/ VI (*fleur*) to come up; (*aube*) to break; (*jour*) to dawn

poing [pwɛ̃] NM fist; **coup de ~** punch; **dormir à poings fermés** to sleep soundly

point [pwɛ̃] VB *voir* **poindre** ▶ NM (*marque, signe*) dot; (*de ponctuation*) full stop, period (US); (*moment, de score etc, fig: question*) point; (*endroit*) spot; (*Couture, Tricot*) stitch ▶ ADV = **pas¹**; **ne … ~** not (at all); **faire le ~** (*Navig*) to take a bearing; (*fig*) to take stock (of the situation); **faire le ~ sur** to review; **en tout ~** in every respect; **sur le ~ de faire** (just) about to do; **au ~ que, à tel ~ que** so much so that; **mettre au ~** (*mécanisme, procédé*) to develop; (*appareil photo*) to focus; (*affaire*) to settle; **à ~** (*Culin: viande*) medium; **à ~ (nommé)** just at the right time; **~ de croix/tige/chaînette** (*Couture*) cross/stem/chain stitch; **~ mousse/jersey** (*Tricot*) garter/stocking stitch; **~ de départ/d'arrivée/d'arrêt** departure/arrival/stopping point; **~ chaud** (*Mil, Pol*) hot spot; **~ de chute** landing place; (*fig*) stopping-off point; **~ (de côté)** stitch (*pain*); **~ culminant** summit; (*fig*) height, climax; **~ d'eau** spring, water point; **~ d'exclamation** exclamation mark; **~ faible** weak spot; **~ final** full stop, period (US); **~ d'interrogation** question mark; **~ mort** (*Finance*) break-even point; **au ~ mort** (*Auto*) in neutral; (*affaire, entreprise*) at a standstill; **~ noir** (*sur le visage*) blackhead; (*Auto*) accident black spot; **~ de non-retour** point of no return; **~ de repère** landmark; (*dans le temps*) point of reference; **~ de vente** retail outlet; **~ de vue** viewpoint; (*fig: opinion*) point of view; **du ~ de vue de** from the point of view of; **points cardinaux** points of the compass, cardinal points; **points de suspension** suspension points

pointage [pwɛ̃taʒ] NM ticking off; checking in

pointe [pwɛ̃t] NF point; (*de la côte*) headland; (*allusion*) dig; sally; (*clou*) tack; **pointes** NFPL (*Danse*) points, point shoes; **une ~**

d'ail/d'accent a touch *ou* hint of garlic/of an accent; **être à la ~ de** (*fig*) to be in the forefront of; **faire** *ou* **pousser une ~ jusqu'à ...** to press on as far as ...; **sur la ~ des pieds** on tiptoe; **en ~** *adv* (*tailler*) into a point; *adj* pointed, tapered; **de ~** *adj* (*technique, technologie etc*) leading, cutting-edge; (: *vitesse*) maximum, top; **heures/ jours de ~** peak hours/days; **faire du 180 en ~** (*Auto*) to have a top *ou* maximum speed of 180; **faire des pointes** (*Danse*) to dance on points; **~ d'asperge** asparagus tip; **~ de courant** surge (of current); **~ de vitesse** burst of speed

pointer [pwēte] /1/ VT (*cocher*) to tick off; (*employés etc*) to check in; (*diriger: canon, longue-vue, doigt*): **~ vers qch, ~ sur qch** to point at sth; (*Mus: note*) to dot ▶ VI (*employé*) to clock in *ou* on; (*pousses*) to come through; (*jour*) to break; **~ les oreilles** (*chien*) to prick up its ears

pointeur, -euse [pwētœʀ, -øz] NM/F time-keeper ▶ NF timeclock ▶ NM (*Inform*) cursor

pointillé [pwētije] NM (*trait*) dotted line; (*Art*) stippling *no pl*

pointilleux, -euse [pwētijø, -øz] ADJ particular, pernickety

pointu, e [pwēty] ADJ pointed; (*clou*) sharp; (*voix*) shrill; (*analyse*) precise

pointure [pwētyʀ] NF size

point-virgule [pwēviʀgyl] (*pl* **points-virgules**) NM semi-colon

poire [pwaʀ] NF pear; (*fam, péj*) mug; **~ électrique** (*pear-shaped*) switch; **~ à injections** syringe

poireau, x [pwaʀo] NM leek

poireauter [pwaʀote] /1/ VI (*fam*) to hang about (waiting)

poirier [pwaʀje] NM pear tree; (*Sport*): **faire le ~** to do a headstand

pois [pwa] NM (*Bot*) pea; (*sur une étoffe*) dot, spot; **à ~** (*cravate etc*) spotted, polka-dot *cpd*; **~ chiche** chickpea; **~ de senteur** sweet pea; **~ cassés** split peas

poison [pwazɔ̃] NM poison

poisse [pwas] NF rotten luck

poisser [pwase] /1/ VT to make sticky

poisseux, -euse [pwasø, -øz] ADJ sticky

poisson [pwasɔ̃] NM fish *gen inv*; **les Poissons** (*Astrologie: signe*) Pisces, the Fish; **être des Poissons** to be Pisces; **pêcher** *ou* **prendre du ~** *ou* **des poissons** to fish; **~ d'avril** April fool; (*blague*) April fool's day trick; *see note*; **~ rouge** goldfish

> The traditional April Fools' Day prank in France involves attaching a cut-out paper fish, known as a *poisson d'avril*, to the back of one's victim, without being caught.

poisson-chat [pwasɔ̃ʃa] (*pl* **poissons-chats**) NM catfish

poissonnerie [pwasɔnʀi] NF fishmonger's (*Brit*), fish store (*US*)

poissonneux, -euse [pwasɔnø, -øz] ADJ abounding in fish

poissonnier, -ière [pwasɔnje, -jɛʀ] NM/F fishmonger (*Brit*), fish merchant (*US*) ▶ NF (*ustensile*) fish kettle

poisson-scie [pwasɔ̃si] (*pl* **poissons-scies**) NM sawfish

poitevin, e [pwatvɛ̃, -in] ADJ (*région*) of *ou* from Poitou; (*ville*) of *ou* from Poitiers

poitrail [pwatʀaj] NM (*d'un cheval etc*) breast

poitrine [pwatʀin] NF (*Anat*) chest; (*seins*) bust, bosom; (*Culin*) breast; **~ de bœuf** brisket

poivre [pwavʀ] NM pepper; **~ en grains/moulu** whole/ground pepper; **~ de cayenne** cayenne (pepper); **~ et sel** *adj* (*cheveux*) pepper-and-salt

poivré, e [pwavʀe] ADJ peppery

poivrer [pwavʀe] /1/ VT to pepper

poivrier [pwavʀije] NM (*Bot*) pepper plant

poivrière [pwavʀijɛʀ] NF pepperpot, pepper shaker (*US*)

poivron [pwavʀɔ̃] NM pepper, capsicum; **~ vert/ rouge** green/red pepper

poix [pwa] NF pitch (*tar*)

poker [pɔkɛʀ] NM: **le ~** poker; **partie de ~** (*fig*) gamble; **~ d'as** four aces

polaire [pɔlɛʀ] ADJ polar

polar [pɔlaʀ] (*fam*) NM detective novel

polarisation [pɔlaʀizasjɔ̃] NF (*Physique, Élec*) polarization; (*fig*) focusing

polariser [pɔlaʀize] /1/ VT to polarize; (*fig: attirer*) to attract; (: *réunir, concentrer*) to focus; **être polarisé sur** (*personne*) to be completely bound up with *ou* absorbed by

pôle [pol] NM (*Géo, Élec*) pole; **le ~ Nord/Sud** the North/South Pole; **~ d'attraction** (*fig*) centre of attraction

polémique [pɔlemik] ADJ controversial, polemic(al) ▶ NF controversy

polémiquer [pɔlemike] /1/ VI to be involved in controversy

polémiste [pɔlemist] NMF polemist, polemicist

poli, e [pɔli] ADJ polite; (*lisse*) smooth; polished

police [pɔlis] NF police; (*discipline*): **assurer la ~ de** *ou* **dans** to keep order in; **peine de simple ~** *sentence given by a magistrate's or police court*; **~ (d'assurance)** (insurance) policy; **~ (de caractères)** (*Typo, Inform*) font, typeface; **~ judiciaire (PJ)** ≈ Criminal Investigation Department (CID) (*Brit*), ≈ Federal Bureau of Investigation (FBI) (*US*); **~ des mœurs** ≈ vice squad; **~ secours** ≈ emergency services *pl* (*Brit*), ≈ paramedics *pl* (*US*)

polichinelle [pɔliʃinɛl] NM Punch; (*péj*) buffoon; **secret de ~** open secret

policier, -ière [pɔlisje, -jɛʀ] ADJ police *cpd* ▶ NM policeman; (*aussi: roman policier*) detective novel

policlinique [pɔliklinik] NF ≈ outpatients *sg* (clinic)

poliment [pɔlimɑ̃] ADV politely

polio [pɔljo] NF (*aussi: poliomyélite*) polio ▶ NMF (*aussi: poliomyélitique*) polio patient *ou* case

poliomyélite [pɔljɔmjelit] NF poliomyelitis

poliomyélitique [pɔljɔmjelitik] NMF polio patient *ou* case

polir [pɔliʀ] /2/ VT to polish

polisson, ne [pɔlisɔ̃, -ɔn] ADJ naughty

politesse [pɔlitɛs] NF politeness; **politesses** NFPL (exchange of) courtesies; **rendre une ~ à qn** to return sb's favour (*Brit*) *ou* favor (*US*)

politicard [pɔlitikaʀ] NM (*péj*) politico, political schemer

politicien, ne [pɔlitisjɛ̃, -ɛn] ADJ political ▶ NM/F (*péj*) politician

politique [pɔlitik] ADJ political ▶ NF (*science, activité*) politics *sg*; (*principes, tactique*) policy, policies *pl* ▶ NM (*politicien*) politician; ~ **étrangère/intérieure** foreign/domestic policy

politique-fiction [pɔlitikfiksjɔ̃] NF political fiction

politiquement [pɔlitikmɑ̃] ADV politically; ~ **correct** politically correct

politisation [pɔlitizasjɔ̃] NF politicization

politiser [pɔlitize] /1/ VT to politicize; ~ **qn** to make sb politically aware

pollen [pɔlɛn] NM pollen

polluant, e [pɔlɥɑ̃, -ɑ̃t] ADJ polluting ▶ NM polluting agent, pollutant; **non** ~ non-polluting

polluer [pɔlɥe] /1/ VT to pollute

pollueur, -euse [pɔlɥœʀ, -øz] NM/F polluter

pollution [pɔlysjɔ̃] NF pollution

polo [pɔlo] NM (*sport*) polo; (*tricot*) polo shirt

Pologne [pɔlɔɲ] NF: **la** ~ Poland

polonais, e [pɔlɔnɛ, -ɛz] ADJ Polish ▶ NM (*Ling*) Polish ▶ NM/F: **P~, e** Pole

poltron, ne [pɔltrɔ̃, -ɔn] ADJ cowardly

poly... [pɔli] PRÉFIXE poly...

polyamide [pɔliamid] NF polyamide

polychrome [pɔlikʀom] ADJ polychrome, polychromatic

polyclinique [pɔliklinik] NF (*private*) clinic (*treating different illnesses*)

polycopie [pɔlikɔpi] NF (*procédé*) duplicating; (*reproduction*) duplicated copy

polycopié, e [pɔlikɔpje] ADJ duplicated ▶ NM handout, duplicated notes *pl*

polycopier [pɔlikɔpje] /7/ VT to duplicate

polyculture [pɔlikyltyʀ] NF mixed farming

polyester [pɔliɛstɛʀ] NM polyester

polyéthylène [pɔlietilɛn] NM polyethylene

polygame [pɔligam] ADJ polygamous

polygamie [pɔligami] NF polygamy

polyglotte [pɔliglɔt] ADJ polyglot

polygone [pɔligɔn] NM polygon

Polynésie [pɔlinezi] NF: **la** ~ Polynesia; **la** ~ **française** French Polynesia

polynésien, ne [pɔlinezjɛ̃, -ɛn] ADJ Polynesian

polynôme [pɔlinom] NM polynomial

polype [pɔlip] NM polyp

polystyrène [pɔlistiʀɛn] NM polystyrene

polytechnicien, ne [pɔlitɛknisjɛ̃, -ɛn] NM/F *student or former student of the École polytechnique*

Polytechnique [pɔlitɛknik] NF: (**École**) ~ *prestigious military academy producing high-ranking officers and engineers*

polyvalent, e [pɔlivalɑ̃, -ɑ̃t] ADJ (*vaccin*) polyvalent; (*personne*) versatile; (*rôle*) varied; (*salle*) multi-purpose ▶ NM ≈ tax inspector

pomélo [pɔmelo] NM pomelo, grapefruit

pommade [pɔmad] NF ointment, cream

pomme [pɔm] NF (*Bot*) apple; (*boule décorative*) knob; (*pomme de terre*): **steak pommes (frites)**

steak and chips (*Brit*) *ou* (French) fries (*US*); **tomber dans les pommes** (*fam*) to pass out; ~ **d'Adam** Adam's apple; **pommes allumettes** French fries (*thin-cut*); ~ **d'arrosoir** (sprinkler) rose; ~ **de pin** pine *ou* fir cone; ~ **de terre** potato; **pommes vapeur** boiled potatoes

pommé, e [pɔme] ADJ (*chou etc*) firm

pommeau, x [pɔmo] NM (*boule*) knob; (*de selle*) pommel

pommelé, e [pɔmle] ADJ: **gris** ~ dapple grey

pommette [pɔmɛt] NF cheekbone

pommier [pɔmje] NM apple tree

pompe [pɔ̃p] NF pump; (*faste*) pomp (and ceremony); ~ **à eau/essence** water/petrol pump; ~ **à huile** oil pump; ~ **à incendie** fire engine (*apparatus*); **pompes funèbres** undertaker's *sg*, funeral parlour *sg* (*Brit*), mortician's *sg* (*US*)

Pompéi [pɔ̃pei] N Pompeii

pompéien, ne [pɔ̃pejɛ̃, -ɛn] ADJ Pompeiian

pomper [pɔ̃pe] /1/ VT to pump; (*évacuer*) to pump out; (*aspirer*) to pump up; (*absorber*) to soak up ▶ VI to pump

pompeusement [pɔ̃pøzmɑ̃] ADV pompously

pompeux, -euse [pɔ̃pø, -øz] ADJ pompous

pompier [pɔ̃pje] NM fireman ▶ ADJ M (*style*) pretentious, pompous

pompiste [pɔ̃pist] NMF petrol (*Brit*) *ou* gas (*US*) pump attendant

pompon [pɔ̃pɔ̃] NM pompom, bobble

pomponner [pɔ̃pɔne] /1/ VT to titivate (*Brit*), dress up

ponce [pɔ̃s] NF: **pierre** ~ pumice stone

poncer [pɔ̃se] /3/ VT to sand (down)

ponceuse [pɔ̃søz] NF sander

poncif [pɔ̃sif] NM cliché

ponction [pɔ̃ksjɔ̃] NF (*d'argent etc*) withdrawal; ~ **lombaire** lumbar puncture

ponctualité [pɔ̃ktɥalite] NF punctuality

ponctuation [pɔ̃ktɥasjɔ̃] NF punctuation

ponctuel, le [pɔ̃ktɥɛl] ADJ (*à l'heure, Tech*) punctual; (*fig: opération etc*) one-off, single; (*scrupuleux*) punctilious, meticulous

ponctuellement [pɔ̃ktɥɛlmɑ̃] ADV punctually; punctiliously, meticulously

ponctuer [pɔ̃ktɥe] /1/ VT to punctuate; (*Mus*) to phrase

pondéré, e [pɔ̃deʀe] ADJ level-headed, composed

pondérer [pɔ̃deʀe] /6/ VT to balance

pondeuse [pɔ̃døz] NF layer, laying hen

pondre [pɔ̃dʀ] /41/ VT to lay; (*fig*) to produce ▶ VI to lay

poney [pɔne] NM pony

pongiste [pɔ̃ʒist] NMF table tennis player

pont [pɔ̃] NM bridge; (*Auto*): ~ **arrière/avant** rear/front axle; (*Navig*) deck; **faire le** ~ to take the extra day off; *see note*; **faire un** ~ **d'or à qn** to offer sb a fortune to take a job; ~ **aérien** airlift; ~ **basculant** bascule bridge; ~ **d'envol** flight deck; ~ **élévateur** hydraulic ramp; ~ **de graissage** ramp (*in garage*); ~ **à péage** tollbridge; ~ **roulant** travelling crane; ~ **suspendu** suspension bridge; ~ **tournant** swing bridge;

Ponts et Chaussées highways department
The expression *faire le pont* refers to the
practice of taking a Monday or Friday off to
make a long weekend if a public holiday
falls on a Tuesday or Thursday. The French
commonly take an extra day off work to give
four consecutive days' holiday at *l'Ascension*,
le 14 juillet and *le 15 août*.

ponte [pɔ̃t] NF laying; (*œufs pondus*) clutch ▸ NM
(*fam*) big shot
pontife [pɔ̃tif] NM pontiff
pontifier [pɔ̃tifje] /**7**/ VI to pontificate
pont-levis [pɔ̃lvi] (*pl* ponts-levis) NM
drawbridge
ponton [pɔ̃tɔ̃] NM pontoon (*on water*)
pop [pɔp] ADJ INV pop ▸ NF: **la ~** pop (music)
pop-corn [pɔpkɔrn] NM popcorn
popeline [pɔplin] NF poplin
populace [pɔpylas] NF (*péj*) rabble
populaire [pɔpylɛr] ADJ popular; (*manifestation*)
mass *cpd*, of the people; (*milieux, clientèle*)
working-class; (*Ling*: *mot etc*) used by the lower
classes (of society)
populariser [pɔpylarize] /**1**/ VT to popularize
popularité [pɔpylarite] NF popularity
population [pɔpylasjɔ̃] NF population;
~ active/agricole working/farming population
populeux, -euse [pɔpylø, -øz] ADJ densely
populated
porc [pɔr] NM (*Zool*) pig; (*Culin*) pork; (*peau*)
pigskin
porcelaine [pɔrsəlɛn] NF (*substance*) porcelain,
china; (*objet*) piece of china(ware)
porcelet [pɔrsəlɛ] NM piglet
porc-épic [pɔrkepik] (*pl* porcs-épics) NM
porcupine
porche [pɔrʃ] NM porch
porcher, -ère [pɔrʃe, -ɛr] NM/F pig-keeper
porcherie [pɔrʃəri] NF pigsty
porcin, e [pɔrsɛ̃, -in] ADJ (*race*) porcine; (*élevage*)
pig *cpd*; (*fig*) piglike
pore [pɔr] NM pore
poreux, -euse [pɔrø, -øz] ADJ porous
porno [pɔrno] ADJ porno ▸ NM porn
pornographie [pɔrnɔgrafi] NF pornography
pornographique [pɔrnɔgrafik] ADJ
pornographic
port [pɔr] NM (*Navig*) harbour (*Brit*), harbor
(*US*), port; (*ville, Inform*) port; (*de l'uniforme etc*)
wearing; (*pour lettre*) postage; (*pour colis, aussi*:
posture) carriage; **~ de commerce/de pêche**
commercial/fishing port; **arriver à bon ~** to
arrive safe and sound; **~ d'arme** (*Jur*) carrying
of a firearm; **~ d'attache** (*Navig*) port of
registry; (*fig*) home base; **~ d'escale** port of call;
~ franc free port; **~ payé** postage paid
portable [pɔrtabl] ADJ (*vêtement*) wearable;
(*portatif*) portable; (*téléphone*) mobile (*Brit*), cell
(*US*) ▸ NM (*Inform*) laptop (computer); (*téléphone*)
mobile (phone) (*Brit*), cell (phone) (*US*)
portail [pɔrtaj] NM gate; (*de cathédrale*) portal
portant, e [pɔrtɑ̃, -ɑ̃t] ADJ (*murs*) structural,
supporting; (*roues*) running; **bien/mal ~** in
good/poor health

portatif, -ive [pɔrtatif, -iv] ADJ portable
porte [pɔrt] NF door; (*de ville, forteresse, Ski*) gate;
mettre à la ~ to throw out; **prendre la ~** to
leave, go away; **à ma/sa ~** (*tout près*) on my/his
(*ou* her) doorstep; **~ (d'embarquement)** (*Aviat*)
(departure) gate; **~ d'entrée** front door; **~ à ~**
nm door-to-door selling; **~ de secours**
emergency exit; **~ de service** service entrance
porté, e [pɔrte] ADJ: **être ~ à faire qch** to be apt
to do sth, tend to do sth; **être ~ sur qch** to be
partial to sth
porte-à-faux [pɔrtafo] NM: **en ~** cantilevered;
(*fig*) in an awkward position
porte-aiguilles [pɔrtegɥij] NM INV needle case
porte-avions [pɔrtavjɔ̃] NM INV aircraft carrier
porte-bagages [pɔrtbagaʒ] NM INV luggage
rack (*ou* basket *etc*)
porte-bébé [pɔrtbebe] NM baby sling *ou* carrier
porte-bonheur [pɔrtbɔnœr] NM INV lucky
charm
porte-bouteilles [pɔrtbutej] NM INV bottle
carrier; (*à casiers*) wine rack
porte-cartes [pɔrtəkart] NM INV (*de cartes
d'identité*) card holder; (*de cartes géographiques*)
map wallet
porte-cigarettes [pɔrtsigarɛt] NM INV
cigarette case
porte-clefs [pɔrtəkle] NM INV key ring
porte-conteneurs [pɔrtəkɔ̃tnœr] NM INV
container ship
porte-couteau, x [pɔrtkuto] NM knife rest
porte-crayon [pɔrtkrɛjɔ̃] NM pencil holder
porte-documents [pɔrtdɔkymɑ̃] NM INV
attaché *ou* document case
porte-drapeau, x [pɔrtdrapo] NM standard
bearer
portée [pɔrte] NF (*d'une arme*) range; (*fig*:
importance) impact, import; (: *capacités*) scope,
capability; (*de chatte etc*) litter; (*Mus*) stave,
staff; **à/hors de ~ (de)** within/out of reach (of);
à ~ de (la) main within (arm's) reach; **à ~ de
voix** within earshot; **à la ~ de qn** (*fig*) at sb's
level, within sb's capabilities; **à la ~ de toutes
les bourses** to suit every pocket, within
everyone's means
portefaix [pɔrtəfɛ] NM INV porter
porte-fenêtre [pɔrtfənɛtr] (*pl* portes-fenêtres)
NF French window
portefeuille [pɔrtəfœj] NM wallet; (*Pol, Bourse*)
portfolio; **faire un lit en ~** to make an
apple-pie bed
porte-jarretelles [pɔrtʒartɛl] NM INV
suspender belt (*Brit*), garter belt (*US*)
porte-jupe [pɔrtəʒyp] NM skirt hanger
portemanteau, x [pɔrtmɑ̃to] NM coat rack;
(*cintre*) coat hanger
porte-mine [pɔrtəmin] NM propelling (*Brit*) *ou*
mechanical (*US*) pencil
porte-monnaie [pɔrtmɔnɛ] NM INV purse
porte-parapluies [pɔrtparaplɥi] NM INV
umbrella stand
porte-parole [pɔrtparɔl] NM INV spokesperson
porte-plume [pɔrtəplym] NM INV penholder
porter [pɔrte] /**1**/ VT (*charge ou sac etc, aussi*: *fœtus*)

to carry; (*sur soi: vêtement, barbe, bague*) to wear; (*fig: responsabilité etc*) to bear, carry; (*inscription, marque, titre, patronyme, arbre, fruits, fleurs*) to bear; (*coup*) to deal; (*attention*) to turn; (*jugement*) to pass; (*apporter*): **~ qch quelque part/à qn** to take sth somewhere/to sb; (*inscrire*): **~ qch sur** to put sth down on; to enter sth in ▶ VI (*voix, regard, canon*) to carry; (*coup, argument*) to hit home; **se porter** VI (*se sentir*): **se porter bien/mal** to be well/unwell; (*aller*): **se porter vers** to go towards; **~ sur** (*peser*) to rest on; (*accent*) to fall on; (*conférence etc*) to concern; (*heurter*) to strike; **être porté à faire** to be apt *ou* inclined to do; **elle portait le nom de Rosalie** she was called Rosalie; **~ qn au pouvoir** to bring sb to power; **~ bonheur à qn** to bring sb luck; **~ qn à croire** to lead sb to believe; **~ son âge** to look one's age; **~ un toast** to drink a toast; **~ de l'argent au crédit d'un compte** to credit an account with some money; **se porter partie civile** *to associate in a court action with the public prosecutor*; **se porter garant de qch** to guarantee sth, vouch for sth; **se porter candidat à la députation** ≈ to stand for Parliament (*BRIT*) ≈ run for Congress (*US*); **se faire porter malade** to report sick; **~ la main à son chapeau** to raise one's hand to one's hat; **~ son effort sur** to direct one's efforts towards; **~ un fait à la connaissance de qn** to bring a fact to sb's attention *ou* notice

porte-savon [pɔʀtsavɔ̃] NM soap dish

porte-serviettes [pɔʀtsɛʀvjɛt] NM INV towel rail

portes-ouvertes [pɔʀtuvɛʀt] ADJ INV: **journée ~** open day

porteur, -euse [pɔʀtœʀ, -øz] ADJ (*Comm*) strong, promising; (*nouvelle, chèque etc*): **être ~ de** to be the bearer of ▶ NM/F (*de messages*) bearer ▶ NM (*de bagages*) porter; (*Comm: de chèque*) bearer; (*: d'actions*) holder; (**avion**) **gros ~** wide-bodied aircraft, jumbo (jet)

porte-voix [pɔʀtəvwa] NM INV megaphone, loudhailer (*BRIT*)

portier [pɔʀtje] NM doorman, commissionnaire (*BRIT*)

portière [pɔʀtjɛʀ] NF door

portillon [pɔʀtijɔ̃] NM gate

portion [pɔʀsjɔ̃] NF (*part*) portion, share; (*partie*) portion, section

portique [pɔʀtik] NM (*Sport*) crossbar; (*Archit*) portico; (*Rail*) gantry

porto [pɔʀto] NM port (wine)

portoricain, e [pɔʀtɔʀikɛ̃, -ɛn] ADJ Puerto Rican

Porto Rico [pɔʀtɔʀiko] NF Puerto Rico

portrait [pɔʀtʀɛ] NM portrait; (*photographie*) photograph; (*fig*): **elle est le ~ de sa mère** she's the image of her mother

portraitiste [pɔʀtʀetist] NMF portrait painter

portrait-robot [pɔʀtʀɛʀɔbo] NM Identikit® *ou* Photo-fit® (*BRIT*) picture

portuaire [pɔʀtɥɛʀ] ADJ port *cpd*, harbour *cpd* (*BRIT*), harbor *cpd* (*US*)

portugais, e [pɔʀtyɡɛ, -ɛz] ADJ Portuguese ▶ NM (*Ling*) Portuguese ▶ NM/F: **P~, e** Portuguese

Portugal [pɔʀtyɡal] NM: **le ~** Portugal

POS SIGLE M (= *plan d'occupation des sols*) zoning ordinances *ou* regulations

pose [poz] NF (*de moquette*) laying; (*de rideaux, papier peint*) hanging; (*attitude, d'un modèle*) pose; (*Photo*) exposure

posé, e [poze] ADJ calm, unruffled

posément [pozemɑ̃] ADV calmly

posemètre [pozmɛtʀ] NM exposure meter

poser [poze] /**1**/ VT (*place*) to put down, to put; (*déposer, installer: moquette, carrelage*) to lay; (*rideaux, papier peint*) to hang; (*Math: chiffre*) to put (down); (*question*) to ask; (*principe, conditions*) to lay *ou* set down; (*problème*) to formulate; (*difficulté*) to pose; (*personne: mettre en valeur*) to give standing to ▶ VI (*modèle*) to pose; to sit; **se poser** VI (*oiseau, avion*) to land; (*question*) to arise; **~ qch (sur)** to put sth down (on); **~ qn à** to drop sb at; **~ qch sur qch/quelque part** to put sth on sth/somewhere; **se poser en** to pass o.s. off as, pose as; **~ son ou un regard sur qn/qch** to turn one's gaze on sb/sth; **sa candidature à un poste** to apply for a post; (*Pol*) to put o.s. up for election

poseur, -euse [pozœʀ, -øz] NM/F (*péj*) show-off, poseur; **~ de parquets/carrelages** floor/tile layer

positif, -ive [pozitif, -iv] ADJ positive

position [pozisjɔ̃] NF position; **prendre ~** (*fig*) to take a stand

positionner [pozisjɔne] /**1**/ VT to position; (*compte en banque*) to calculate the balance of

positivement [pozitivmɑ̃] ADV positively

posologie [pozɔlɔʒi] NF directions *pl* for use, dosage

possédant, e [pɔsedɑ̃, -ɑ̃t] ADJ (*classe*) wealthy ▶ NM/F: **les possédants** the haves, the wealthy

possédé, e [pɔsede] NM/F person possessed

posséder [pɔsede] /**6**/ VT to own, possess; (*qualité, talent*) to have, possess; (*bien connaître: métier, langue*) to have mastered, have a thorough knowledge of; (*sexuellement, aussi: suj, colère*) to possess; (*fam: duper*) to take in

possesseur [pɔsesœʀ] NM owner

possessif, -ive [pɔsesif, -iv] ADJ, NM (*Ling*) possessive

possession [pɔsesjɔ̃] NF ownership *no pl*; possession; **être en ~ de qch** to be in possession of sth; **prendre ~ de qch** to take possession of sth

possibilité [pɔsibilite] NF possibility; **possibilités** NFPL (*moyens*) means; (*potentiel*) potential *sg*; **avoir la ~ de faire** to be in a position to do; to have the opportunity to do

possible [pɔsibl] ADJ possible; (*projet, entreprise*) feasible ▶ NM: **faire son ~** to do all one can, do one's utmost; (**ce n'est**) **pas ~!** impossible!; **le plus/moins de livres ~** as many/few books as possible; **le plus vite ~** as quickly as possible; **dès que ~** as soon as possible; **gentil** *etc* **au ~** as nice *etc* as it is possible to be

postal, e, -aux [pɔstal, -o] ADJ postal, post office *cpd*; **sac ~** mailbag, postbag

postdater [pɔstdate] /**1**/ VT to postdate

p

323

poste¹ [pɔst] NF (*service*) post, postal service; (*administration, bureau*) post office; **postes** NFPL post office *sg*; **mettre à la** ~ to post; ~ **restante** poste restante (BRIT), general delivery (US); **Postes télécommunications et télédiffusion** *postal and telecommunications service*; **agent** *ou* **employé des postes** post office worker

poste² [pɔst] NM (*fonction, Mil*) post; (*Tél*) extension; (*de radio etc*) set; (*de budget*) item; ~ **de commandement** (*Mil etc*) headquarters; ~ **contrôle** checkpoint; ~ **de douane** customs post; ~ **émetteur** transmitting set; ~ **d'essence** filling station; ~ **d'incendie** fire point; ~ **de péage** tollgate; ~ **de pilotage** cockpit, flight deck; ~ **(de police)** police station; ~ **de radio** radio set; ~ **de secours** first-aid post; ~ **de télévision** television set; ~ **de travail** work station

poster /1/ VT [pɔste] to post ▶ NM [pɔstɛʀ] poster; **se poster** to position o.s.

postérieur, e [pɔsteʀjœʀ] ADJ (*date*) later; (*partie*) back ▶ NM (*fam*) behind

postérieurement [pɔsteʀjœʀmɑ̃] ADV later, subsequently; ~ **à** after

posteriori [pɔsteʀjɔʀi]: **a** ~ *adv* with hindsight, a posteriori

postérité [pɔsteʀite] NF posterity

postface [pɔstfas] NF appendix

posthume [pɔstym] ADJ posthumous

postiche [pɔstiʃ] ADJ false ▶ NM hairpiece

postier, -ière [pɔstje, -jɛʀ] NM/F post office worker

postillon [pɔstijɔ̃] NM: **envoyer des postillons** to splutter

postillonner [pɔstijɔne] /1/ VI to splutter

post-natal, e [pɔstnatal] ADJ postnatal

postopératoire [pɔstɔpeʀatwaʀ] ADJ post-operative

postscolaire [pɔstskɔlɛʀ] ADJ further, continuing

post-scriptum [pɔstskʀiptɔm] NM INV postscript

postsynchronisation [pɔstsɛ̃kʀɔnizasjɔ̃] NF dubbing

postsynchroniser [pɔstsɛ̃kʀɔnize] /1/ VT to dub

postulant, e [pɔstylɑ̃, -ɑ̃t] NM/F (*candidat*) applicant; (*Rel*) postulant

postulat [pɔstyla] NM postulate

postuler [pɔstyle] /1/ VT (*emploi*) to apply for, put in for ▶ VI: ~ **à** *ou* **pour un emploi** to apply for a job

posture [pɔstyʀ] NF posture, position; (*fig*) position

pot [po] NM (*en verre*) jar; (*en terre*) pot; (*en plastique, carton*) carton; (*en métal*) tin; (*fam: chance*) luck; **avoir du** ~ (*fam*) to be lucky; **boire** *ou* **prendre un** ~ (*fam*) to have a drink; **petit** ~ **(pour bébé)** (jar of) baby food; **découvrir le** ~ **aux roses** to find out what's been going on; ~ **catalytique** catalytic converter; ~ **(de chambre)** (chamber)pot; ~ **d'échappement** exhaust pipe; ~ **de fleurs** plant pot, flowerpot; (*plante*) pot plant; ~ **à tabac** tobacco jar

potable [pɔtabl] ADJ (*fig: boisson*) drinkable; (: *travail, devoir*) decent; **eau (non)** ~ (not) drinking water

potache [pɔtaʃ] NM schoolboy

potage [pɔtaʒ] NM soup

potager, -ère [pɔtaʒe, -ɛʀ] ADJ (*plante*) edible, vegetable *cpd*; **(jardin)** ~ kitchen *ou* vegetable garden

potasse [pɔtas] NF potassium hydroxide; (*engrais*) potash

potasser [pɔtase] /1/ VT (*fam*) to swot up (BRIT), cram

potassium [pɔtasjɔm] NM potassium

pot-au-feu [pɔtofø] NM INV (beef) stew; (*viande*) stewing beef ▶ ADJ (*fam: personne*) stay-at-home

pot-de-vin [pɔdvɛ̃] (*pl* **pots-de-vin**) NM bribe

pote [pɔt] NM (*fam*) mate (BRIT), pal

poteau, x [pɔto] NM post; ~ **de départ/arrivée** starting/finishing post; ~ **(d'exécution)** execution post, stake; ~ **indicateur** signpost; ~ **télégraphique** telegraph pole; ~ **(de but)** goal-posts

potée [pɔte] NF hotpot (*of pork and cabbage*)

potelé, e [pɔtle] ADJ plump, chubby

potence [pɔtɑ̃s] NF gallows *sg*; **en** ~ T-shaped

potentat [pɔtɑ̃ta] NM potentate; (*fig: péj*) despot

potentiel, le [pɔtɑ̃sjɛl] ADJ, NM potential

potentiellement [pɔtɑ̃sjɛlmɑ̃] ADV potentially

poterie [pɔtʀi] NF (*fabrication*) pottery; (*objet*) piece of pottery

potiche [pɔtiʃ] NF large vase

potier, -ière [pɔtje, -jɛʀ] NM/F potter

potins [pɔtɛ̃] NMPL gossip *sg*

potion [posjɔ̃] NF potion

potiron [pɔtiʀɔ̃] NM pumpkin

pot-pourri [popuʀi] (*pl* **pots-pourris**) NM (*Mus*) medley

pou, x [pu] NM louse

pouah [pwa] EXCL ugh!, yuk!

poubelle [pubɛl] NF (dust)bin

pouce [pus] NM thumb; **se tourner** *ou* **se rouler les pouces** (*fig*) to twiddle one's thumbs; **manger sur le** ~ to eat on the run, snatch something to eat

poudre [pudʀ] NF powder; (*fard*) (face) powder; (*explosif*) gunpowder; **en** ~: **café en** ~ instant coffee; **savon en** ~ soap powder; **lait en** ~ dried *ou* powdered milk; ~ **à canon** gunpowder; ~ **à éternuer** sneezing powder; ~ **à récurer** scouring powder; ~ **de riz** face powder

poudrer [pudʀe] /1/ VT to powder

poudreux, -euse [pudʀø, -øz] ADJ dusty; (*neige*) powdery, powder *cpd*

poudrier [pudʀije] NM (powder) compact

poudrière [pudʀijɛʀ] NF powder magazine; (*fig*) powder keg

pouf [puf] NM pouffe

pouffer [pufe] /1/ VI: ~ **(de rire)** to burst out laughing

pouffiasse [pufjas] NF (*fam*) fat cow; (*prostituée*) tart

pouilleux, -euse [pujø, -øz] ADJ flea-ridden; (*fig*) seedy

poulailler [pulɑje] NM henhouse; (*Théât*): **le ~** the gods *sg*

poulain [pulɛ̃] NM foal; (*fig*) protégé

poularde [pulaʀd] NF fatted chicken

poule [pul] NF (*Zool*) hen; (*Culin*) (boiling) fowl; (*Sport*) (round-robin) tournament; (*Rugby*) group; (*fam*) bird (*BRIT*), chick, broad (*US*); (*prostituée*) tart; **~ d'eau** moorhen; **~ mouillée** coward; **~ pondeuse** laying hen, layer; **~ au riz** chicken and rice

poulet [pulɛ] NM chicken; (*fam*) cop

poulette [pulɛt] NF (*jeune poule*) pullet

pouliche [puliʃ] NF filly

poulie [puli] NF pulley

poulpe [pulp] NM octopus

pouls [pu] NM pulse; (*Anat*): **prendre le ~ de qn** to take sb's pulse

poumon [pumɔ̃] NM lung; **~ d'acier** *ou* **artificiel** iron *ou* artificial lung

poupe [pup] NF stern; **en ~** astern

poupée [pupe] NF doll; **jouer à la ~** to play with one's doll (*ou* dolls); **de ~** (*très petit*): **jardin de ~** doll's garden, pocket-handkerchief-sized garden

poupin, e [pupɛ̃, -in] ADJ chubby

poupon [pupɔ̃] NM babe-in-arms

pouponner [pupɔne] /1/ VI to fuss (around)

pouponnière [pupɔnjɛʀ] NF crèche, day nursery

pour [puʀ] PRÉP for ▶ NM: **le ~ et le contre** the pros and cons; **~ faire** (so as) to do, in order to do; **~ avoir fait** for having done; **~ que** so that, in order that; **fermé ~ (cause de) travaux** closed for refurbishment *ou* alterations; **c'est ~ ça que …** that's why …; **~ quoi faire?** what for?; **~ moi** (*à mon avis, pour ma part*) for my part, personally; **~ riche qu'il soit** rich though he may be; **~ 20 euros d'essence** 20 euros' worth of petrol; **~ cent** per cent; **~ ce qui est de** as for; **y être ~ quelque chose** to have something to do with it

pourboire [puʀbwaʀ] NM tip

pourcentage [puʀsɑ̃taʒ] NM percentage; **travailler au ~** to work on commission

pourchasser [puʀʃase] /1/ VT to pursue

pourfendeur [puʀfɑ̃dœʀ] NM sworn opponent

pourfendre [puʀfɑ̃dʀ] /41/ VT to assail

pourlécher [puʀleʃe] /6/: **se pourlécher** VI to lick one's lips

pourparlers [puʀpaʀle] NMPL talks, negotiations; **être en ~ avec** to be having talks with

pourpre [puʀpʀ] ADJ crimson

pourquoi [puʀkwa] ADV, CONJ why ▶ NM INV: **le ~ (de)** the reason (for)

pourrai *etc* [puʀe] VB *voir* **pouvoir**

pourri, e [puʀi] ADJ rotten; (*roche, pierre*) crumbling; (*temps, climat*) filthy, foul ▶ NM: **sentir le ~** to smell rotten

pourriel [puʀjɛl] NM (*Inform*) spam

pourrir [puʀiʀ] /2/ VI to rot; (*fruit*) to go rotten *ou* bad; (*fig: situation*) to deteriorate ▶ VT to rot; (*fig: corrompre: personne*) to corrupt; (: *gâter: enfant*) to spoil thoroughly

pourrissement [puʀismɑ̃] NM deterioration

pourriture [puʀityʀ] NF rot

pourrons *etc* [puʀɔ̃] VB *voir* **pouvoir**

poursuis *etc* [puʀsɥi] VB *voir* **poursuivre**

poursuite [puʀsɥit] NF pursuit, chase; **poursuites** NFPL (*Jur*) legal proceedings; **(course) ~** track race; (*fig*) chase

poursuivant, e [puʀsɥivɑ̃, -ɑ̃t] VB *voir* **poursuivre** ▶ NM/F pursuer; (*Jur*) plaintiff

poursuivre [puʀsɥivʀ] /40/ VT to pursue, chase (after); (*relancer*) to hound, harry; (*obséder*) to haunt; (*Jur*) to bring proceedings against, prosecute; (: *au civil*) to sue; (*but*) to strive towards; (*voyage, études*) to carry on with, continue ▶ VI to carry on, go on; **se poursuivre** VI to go on, continue

pourtant [puʀtɑ̃] ADV yet; **mais ~** but nevertheless, but even so; **c'est ~ facile** (and) yet it's easy

pourtour [puʀtuʀ] NM perimeter

pourvoi [puʀvwa] NM appeal

pourvoir [puʀvwaʀ] /25/ NM (*Comm*) supply; (*emploi*) to fill ▶ VT: **~ qch/qn de** to equip sth/sb with ▶ VI: **~ à** to provide for; **se pourvoir** VI (*Jur*): **se pourvoir en cassation** to take one's case to the Court of Appeal

pourvoyeur, -euse [puʀvwajœʀ, -øz] NM/F supplier

pourvu, e [puʀvy] PP *de* pourvoir ▶ ADJ: **~ de** equipped with; **~ que** *conj* (*si*) provided that, so long as; (*espérons que*) let's hope (that)

pousse [pus] NF growth; (*bourgeon*) shoot

poussé, e [puse] ADJ sophisticated, advanced; (*moteur*) souped-up

pousse-café [puskafe] NM INV (after-dinner) liqueur

poussée [puse] NF thrust; (*coup*) push; (*Méd: d'acné*) eruption; (*fig: prix*) upsurge

pousse-pousse [puspus] NM INV rickshaw

pousser [puse] /1/ VT to push; (*moteur, voiture*) to drive hard; (*émettre: cri etc*) to give; (*stimuler: élève*) to urge on; to drive hard; (*poursuivre: études, discussion*) to carry on ▶ VI to push; (*croître*) to grow; (*aller*): **~ plus loin** to push on a bit further; **se pousser** VI to move over; **~ qn à faire qch** (*inciter*) to urge *ou* press sb to do sth; (*acculer*) to drive sb to do sth; **faire ~** (*plante*) to grow; **~ le dévouement** *etc* **jusqu'à …** to take devotion *etc* as far as …

poussette [pusɛt] NF (*voiture d'enfant*) pushchair (*BRIT*), stroller (*US*)

poussette-canne [pusɛtkan] (*pl* **poussettes-cannes**) NF baby buggy (*BRIT*), (folding) stroller (*US*)

poussier [pusje] NM coal dust

poussière [pusjɛʀ] NF dust; (*grain*) speck of dust; **et des poussières** (*fig*) and a bit; **~ de charbon** coal dust

poussiéreux, -euse [pusjeʀø, -øz] ADJ dusty

poussif, -ive [pusif, -iv] ADJ wheezy, wheezing

poussin [pusɛ̃] NM chick

poussoir [puswaʀ] NM button

poutre [putʀ] NF beam; (*en fer, ciment armé*) girder; **poutres apparentes** exposed beams

p

poutrelle [putʀɛl] NF (*petite poutre*) small beam; (*barre d'acier*) girder

MOT-CLÉ

pouvoir [puvwaʀ] /**33**/ NM power; (*dirigeants*): **le pouvoir** those in power; **les pouvoirs publics** the authorities; **avoir pouvoir de faire** (*autorisation*) to have (the) authority to do; (*droit*) to have the right to do; **pouvoir absolu** absolute power; **pouvoir absorbant** absorbency; **pouvoir d'achat** purchasing power; **pouvoir calorifique** calorific value
▸ VB AUX **1** (*être en état de*) can, be able to; **je ne peux pas le réparer** I can't *ou* I am not able to repair it; **déçu de ne pas pouvoir le faire** disappointed not to be able to do it
2 (*avoir la permission*) can, may, be allowed to; **vous pouvez aller au cinéma** you can *ou* may go to the pictures
3 (*probabilité, hypothèse*) may, might, could; **il a pu avoir un accident** he may *ou* might *ou* could have had an accident; **il aurait pu le dire!** he might *ou* could have said (so)!
4 (*expressions*): **tu ne peux pas savoir!** you have no idea!; **tu peux le dire!** you can say that again!
▸ VB IMPERS may, might, could; **il peut arriver que** it may *ou* might *ou* could happen that; **il pourrait pleuvoir** it might rain
▸ VT **1** can, be able to; **j'ai fait tout ce que j'ai pu** I did all I could; **je n'en peux plus** (*épuisé*) I'm exhausted; (*à bout*) I can't take any more
2 (*vb+adj ou adv comparatif*): **je me porte on ne peut mieux** I'm absolutely fine, I couldn't be better; **elle est on ne peut plus gentille** she couldn't be nicer, she's as nice as can be
se pouvoir VI: **il se peut que** it may *ou* might be that; **cela se pourrait** that's quite possible

PP SIGLE F (= *préventive de la pellagre: vitamine*) niacin
▸ ABR (= *pages*) pp
p.p. ABR (= *par procuration*) p.p.
p.p.c.m. SIGLE M (*Math*: = *plus petit commun multiple*) LCM (= *lowest common multiple*)
PQ SIGLE F (CANADA: = *province de Québec*) PQ
PR ▸ SIGLE F = **poste restante**
pr ABR = **pour**
pragmatique [pʀagmatik] ADJ pragmatic
pragmatisme [pʀagmatism] NM pragmatism
Prague [pʀag] N Prague
prairie [pʀeʀi] NF meadow
praline [pʀalin] NF (*bonbon*) sugared almond; (*au chocolat*) praline
praliné, e [pʀaline] ADJ (*amande*) sugared; (*chocolat, glace*) praline cpd
praticable [pʀatikabl] ADJ (*route etc*) passable, practicable; (*projet*) practicable
praticien, ne [pʀatisjɛ̃, -ɛn] NM/F practitioner
pratiquant, e [pʀatikɑ̃, -ɑ̃t] ADJ practising (BRIT), practicing (US) ▸ NM/F (regular) churchgoer
pratique [pʀatik] NF practice ▸ ADJ practical; (*commode: horaire etc*) convenient; (: *outil*) handy, useful; **dans la ~** in (actual) practice;

mettre en ~ to put into practice
pratiquement [pʀatikmɑ̃] ADV (*dans la pratique*) in practice; (*pour ainsi dire*) practically, virtually
pratiquer [pʀatike] /**1**/ VT to practise (BRIT), practice (US); (*l'équitation, la pêche*) to go in for; (*le golf, football*) to play; (*appliquer: méthode, théorie*) to apply; (*intervention, opération*) to carry out; (*ouverture, abri*) to make ▸ VI (Rel) to be a churchgoer
pré [pʀe] NM meadow
préados [pʀeado] NMPL pre-teens
préalable [pʀealabl] ADJ preliminary; **condition ~ (de)** precondition (for), prerequisite (for); **sans avis ~** without prior *ou* previous notice; **au ~** first, beforehand
préalablement [pʀealabləmɑ̃] ADV first, beforehand
Préalpes [pʀealp] NFPL: **les ~** the Pre-Alps
préalpin, e [pʀealpɛ̃, -in] ADJ of the Pre-Alps
préambule [pʀeɑ̃byl] NM preamble; (*fig*) prelude; **sans ~** straight away
préau, x [pʀeo] NM (*d'une cour d'école*) covered playground; (*d'un monastère, d'une prison*) inner courtyard
préavis [pʀeavi] NM notice; **~ de congé** notice; **communication avec ~** (Tél) personal *ou* person-to-person call
prébende [pʀebɑ̃d] NF (*péj*) remuneration
précaire [pʀekɛʀ] ADJ precarious
précaution [pʀekosjɔ̃] NF precaution; **avec ~** cautiously; **prendre des** *ou* **ses précautions** to take precautions; **par ~** as a precaution; **pour plus de ~** to be on the safe side; **précautions oratoires** carefully phrased remarks
précautionneux, -euse [pʀekosjɔnø, -øz] ADJ cautious, careful
précédemment [pʀesedamɑ̃] ADV before, previously
précédent, e [pʀesedɑ̃, -ɑ̃t] ADJ previous ▸ NM precedent; **sans ~** unprecedented; **le jour ~** the day before, the previous day
précéder [pʀesede] /**6**/ VT to precede; (*marcher ou rouler devant*) to be in front of; (*arriver avant*) to get ahead of
précepte [pʀesɛpt] NM precept
précepteur, -trice [pʀesɛptœʀ, -tʀis] NM/F (private) tutor
préchauffer [pʀeʃofe] /**1**/ VT to preheat
prêcher [pʀeʃe] /**1**/ VT, VI to preach
prêcheur, -euse [pʀeʃœʀ, -øz] ADJ moralizing ▸ NM/F (Rel) preacher; (*fig*) moralizer
précieusement [pʀesjøzmɑ̃] ADV (*avec soin*) carefully; (*avec préciosité*) preciously
précieux, -euse [pʀesjø, -øz] ADJ precious; (*collaborateur, conseils*) invaluable; (*style, écrivain*) précieux, precious
préciosité [pʀesjozite] NF preciosity, preciousness
précipice [pʀesipis] NM drop, chasm; (*fig*) abyss; **au bord du ~** at the edge of the precipice
précipitamment [pʀesipitamɑ̃] ADV hurriedly, hastily
précipitation [pʀesipitasjɔ̃] NF (*hâte*) haste; **précipitations (atmosphériques)** precipitation sg

précipité, e [pʀesipite] ADJ (*respiration*) fast; (*pas*) hurried; (*départ*) hasty

précipiter [pʀesipite] /1/ VT (*hâter: marche*) to quicken; (: *départ*) to hasten; **se précipiter** VI (*événements*) to move faster; (*respiration*) to speed up; **~ qn/qch du haut de** (*faire tomber*) to throw *ou* hurl sb/sth off *ou* from; **se précipiter sur/ vers** to rush at/towards; **se précipiter au-devant de qn** to throw o.s. before sb

précis, e [pʀesi, -iz] ADJ precise; (*tir, mesures*) accurate, precise; **à 4 heures précises** at 4 o'clock sharp ▶ NM handbook

précisément [pʀesizemɑ̃] ADV precisely; **ma vie n'est pas ~ distrayante** my life is not exactly entertaining

préciser [pʀesize] /1/ VT (*expliquer*) to be more specific about, clarify; (*spécifier*) to state, specify; **se préciser** VI to become clear(er)

précision [pʀesizjɔ̃] NF precision; accuracy; (*détail*) point *ou* detail (*made clear or to be clarified*); **précisions** NFPL further details

précoce [pʀekɔs] ADJ early; (*enfant*) precocious; (*calvitie*) premature

précocité [pʀekɔsite] NF earliness; precociousness

préconçu, e [pʀekɔ̃sy] ADJ preconceived

préconiser [pʀekɔnize] /1/ VT to advocate

précuit, e [pʀekɥi, -it] ADJ precooked

précurseur [pʀekyʀsœʀ] ADJ M precursory ▶ NM forerunner, precursor

prédateur [pʀedatœʀ] NM predator

prédécesseur [pʀedesesœʀ] NM predecessor

prédécoupé, e [pʀedekupe] ADJ pre-cut

prédestiner [pʀedestine] /1/ VT: **~ qn à qch/à faire** to predestine sb for sth/to do

prédicateur [pʀedikatœʀ] NM preacher

prédiction [pʀediksjɔ̃] NF prediction

prédilection [pʀedileksjɔ̃] NF: **avoir une ~ pour** to be partial to; **de ~** favourite (*BRIT*), favorite (*US*)

prédire [pʀediʀ] /37/ VT to predict

prédisposer [pʀedispoze] /1/ VT: **~ qn à qch/à faire** to predispose sb to sth/to do

prédisposition [pʀedispozisjɔ̃] NF predisposition

prédit, e [pʀedi, -it] PP *de* **prédire**

prédominance [pʀedɔminɑ̃s] NF predominance

prédominant, e [pʀedɔminɑ̃, -ɑ̃t] ADJ predominant; prevailing

prédominer [pʀedɔmine] /1/ VI to predominate; (*avis*) to prevail

pré-électoral, e, -aux [pʀeelɛktɔʀal, -o] ADJ pre-election *cpd*

pré-emballé, e [pʀeɑ̃bale] ADJ pre-packed

prééminent, e [pʀeeminɑ̃, -ɑ̃t] ADJ pre-eminent

préemption [pʀeɑ̃psjɔ̃] NF: **droit de ~** (*Jur*) pre-emptive right

pré-encollé, e [pʀeɑ̃kɔle] ADJ pre-pasted

préétabli, e [pʀeetabli] ADJ pre-established

préexistant, e [pʀeɛɡzistɑ̃, -ɑ̃t] ADJ pre-existing

préfabriqué, e [pʀefabʀike] ADJ prefabricated; (*péj: sourire*) artificial ▶ NM prefabricated material

préface [pʀefas] NF preface

préfacer [pʀefase] /3/ VT to write a preface for

préfectoral, e, -aux [pʀefɛktɔʀal, -o] ADJ prefectorial

préfecture [pʀefɛktyʀ] NF prefecture; *see note*; **~ de police** police headquarters

> The *préfecture* is the administrative headquarters of the *département*. The *préfet*, a senior civil servant appointed by the government, is responsible for putting government policy into practice. France's 22 regions, each comprising a number of *départements*, also have a *préfet de région*.

préférable [pʀefeʀabl] ADJ preferable

préféré, e [pʀefeʀe] ADJ, NM/F favourite (*BRIT*), favorite (*US*)

préférence [pʀefeʀɑ̃s] NF preference; **de ~** preferably; **de** *ou* **par ~ à** in preference to, rather than; **donner la ~ à qn** to give preference to sb; **par ordre de ~** in order of preference; **obtenir la ~ sur** to have preference over

préférentiel, le [pʀefeʀɑ̃sjɛl] ADJ preferential

préférer [pʀefeʀe] /6/ VT: **~ qn/qch (à)** to prefer sb/sth (to), like sb/sth better (than); **~ faire** to prefer to do; **je préférerais du thé** I would rather have tea, I'd prefer tea

préfet [pʀefɛ] NM prefect; **~ de police** ≈ Chief Constable (*BRIT*), ≈ Police Commissioner (*US*)

préfigurer [pʀefigyʀe] /1/ VT to prefigure

préfixe [pʀefiks] NM prefix

préhistoire [pʀeistwaʀ] NF prehistory

préhistorique [pʀeistɔʀik] ADJ prehistoric

préjudice [pʀeʒydis] NM (*matériel*) loss; (*moral*) harm *no pl*; **porter ~ à** to harm, be detrimental to; **au ~ de** at the expense of

préjudiciable [pʀeʒydisjabl] ADJ: **~ à** prejudicial *ou* harmful to

préjugé [pʀeʒyʒe] NM prejudice; **avoir un ~ contre** to be prejudiced against; **bénéficier d'un ~ favorable** to be viewed favourably

préjuger [pʀeʒyʒe] /3/: **~ de** VT to prejudge

prélasser [pʀelase] /1/: **se prélasser** VI to lounge

prélat [pʀela] NM prelate

prélavage [pʀelavaʒ] NM pre-wash

prélèvement [pʀelɛvmɑ̃] NM (*montant*) deduction; withdrawal; **faire un ~ de sang** to take a blood sample

prélever [pʀelve] /5/ VT (*échantillon*) to take; **~ (sur)** (*argent*) to deduct (from); (: *sur son compte*) to withdraw (from)

préliminaire [pʀeliminɛʀ] ADJ preliminary; **préliminaires** NMPL preliminaries; (*négociations*) preliminary talks

prélude [pʀelyd] NM prelude; (*avant le concert*) warm-up

prématuré, e [pʀematyʀe] ADJ premature; (*retraite*) early ▶ NM premature baby

prématurément [pʀematyʀemɑ̃] ADV prematurely

préméditation [pʀemeditasjɔ̃] NF: **avec ~** *adj* premeditated; *adv* with intent

préméditer [pʀemedite] /1/ VT to premeditate, plan

prémices [pʀemis] NFPL beginnings
premier, -ière [pʀəmje, -jɛʀ] ADJ first; (rang) front; (branche, marche, grade) bottom; (fig: fondamental) basic; prime; (en importance) first, foremost ▶ NM (premier étage) first (BRIT) ou second (US) floor ▶ NF (Auto) first (gear); (Rail, Aviat etc) first class; (Scol) year 12 (BRIT), eleventh grade (US); (Théât) first night; (Ciné) première; (exploit) first; **au ~ abord** at first sight; **au** ou **du ~ coup** at the first attempt ou go; **de ~ ordre** first-class, first-rate; **de première qualité, de ~ choix** best ou top quality; **de première importance** of the highest importance; **de première nécessité** absolutely essential; **le ~ venu** the first person to come along; **jeune ~** leading man; **le ~ de l'an** New Year's Day; **enfant du ~ lit** child of a first marriage; **en ~ lieu** in the first place; **~ âge** (d'un enfant) the first three months (of life); **P~ Ministre** Prime Minister
premièrement [pʀəmjɛʀmɑ̃] ADV firstly
première-née [pʀəmjɛʀne] (pl **premières-nées**) NF first-born
premier-né [pʀəmjene] (pl **premiers-nés**) NM first-born
prémisse [pʀemis] NF premise
prémolaire [pʀemɔlɛʀ] NF premolar
prémonition [pʀemɔnisjɔ̃] NF premonition
prémonitoire [pʀemɔnitwaʀ] ADJ premonitory
prémunir [pʀemyniʀ] /2/: **se prémunir** VI: **se prémunir contre** to protect o.s. from, guard against
prenant, e [pʀənɑ̃, -ɑ̃t] VB voir prendre ▶ ADJ absorbing, engrossing
prénatal, e [pʀenatal] ADJ (Méd) antenatal; (allocation) maternity cpd
prendre [pʀɑ̃dʀ] /58/ VT to take; (repas) to have; (aller chercher) to take, fetch; (se procurer) to get; (réserver: place) to book; (acquérir: du poids, de la valeur) to put on, gain; (malfaiteur, poisson) to catch; (passager) to pick up; (personnel, aussi: couleur, goût) to take on; (locataire) to take in; (traiter: enfant, problème) to handle; (voix, ton) to put on; (prélever: pourcentage, argent) to take off; (ôter): **~ qch à** to take sth from; (coincer): **se ~ les doigts dans** to get one's fingers caught in ▶ VI (liquide, ciment) to set; (greffe, vaccin) to take; (mensonge) to be successful; (feu: foyer) to go; (: incendie) to start; (allumette) to light; (se diriger): **~ à gauche** to turn (to the) left; **~ froid** to catch cold; **~ son origine** ou **sa source** (mot, rivière) to have its source; **~ qn pour** to take sb for; **se ~ pour** to think one is; **~ sur soi de faire qch** to take it upon o.s. to do sth; **~ qn en sympathie/ horreur** to get to like/loathe sb; **à tout ~** all things considered; **s'en ~ à** (agresser) to set about; (passer sa colère sur) to take it out on; (critiquer) to attack; (remettre en question) to challenge; **se ~ d'amitié/d'affection pour** to befriend/ become fond of; **s'y ~** (procéder) to set about it; **s'y ~ à l'avance** to see to it in advance; **s'y ~ à deux fois** to try twice, make two attempts
preneur [pʀənœʀ] NM: **être ~** to be willing to buy; **trouver ~** to find a buyer

preniez [pʀənje] VB voir prendre
prenne etc [pʀɛn] VB voir prendre
prénom [pʀenɔ̃] NM first name
prénommer [pʀenɔme] /1/ VT: **elle se prénomme Claude** her (first) name is Claude
prénuptial, e, -aux [pʀenypsjal, -o] ADJ premarital
préoccupant, e [pʀeɔkypɑ̃, -ɑ̃t] ADJ worrying
préoccupation [pʀeɔkypasjɔ̃] NF (souci) concern; (idée fixe) preoccupation
préoccupé, e [pʀeɔkype] ADJ concerned; preoccupied
préoccuper [pʀeɔkype] /1/ VT (tourmenter, tracasser) to concern; (absorber, obséder) to preoccupy; **se ~ de qch** to be concerned about sth; to show concern about sth
préparateur, -trice [pʀepaʀatœʀ, -tʀis] NM/F assistant
préparatifs [pʀepaʀatif] NMPL preparations
préparation [pʀepaʀasjɔ̃] NF preparation; (Scol) piece of homework
préparatoire [pʀepaʀatwaʀ] ADJ preparatory
préparer [pʀepaʀe] /1/ VT to prepare; (café, repas) to make; (examen) to prepare for; (voyage, entreprise) to plan; **se préparer** VI (orage, tragédie) to brew, be in the air; **se préparer (à qch/à faire)** to prepare (o.s.) ou get ready (for sth/to do); **~ qch à qn** (surprise etc) to have sth in store for sb; **~ qn à qch** (nouvelle etc) to prepare sb for sth
prépondérance [pʀepɔ̃deʀɑ̃s] NF: **~ (sur)** predominance (over)
prépondérant, e [pʀepɔ̃deʀɑ̃, -ɑ̃t] ADJ major, dominating; **voix ~** casting vote
préposé, e [pʀepoze] ADJ: **~ à** in charge of ▶ NM/F (gén: employé) employee; (Admin: facteur) postman/woman (BRIT), mailman/woman (US); (de la douane etc) official; (de vestiaire) attendant
préposer [pʀepoze] /1/ VT: **~ qn à qch** to appoint sb to sth
préposition [pʀepozisjɔ̃] NF preposition
prérentrée [pʀeʀɑ̃tʀe] NF in-service training period before start of school term
préretraite [pʀeʀətʀɛt] NF early retirement
prérogative [pʀeʀɔgativ] NF prerogative
près [pʀɛ] ADV near, close; **~ de** prép near (to), close to; (environ) nearly, almost; **~ d'ici** near here; **de ~** adv closely; **à cinq kg ~** to within about five kg; **à cela ~ que** apart from the fact that; **je ne suis pas ~ de lui pardonner** I'm nowhere near ready to forgive him; **on n'est pas à un jour ~** one day (either way) won't make any difference, we're not going to quibble over the odd day; **il n'est pas à 10 minutes ~** he can spare 10 minutes
présage [pʀezaʒ] NM omen
présager [pʀezaʒe] /3/ VT (prévoir) to foresee; (annoncer) to portend
pré-salé [pʀesale] (pl **prés-salés**) NM (Culin) salt-meadow lamb
presbyte [pʀɛsbit] ADJ long-sighted (BRIT), far-sighted (US)
presbytère [pʀɛsbitɛʀ] NM presbytery
presbytérien, ne [pʀɛsbiteʀjɛ̃, -ɛn] ADJ, NM/F Presbyterian

presbytie [pʀɛsbisi] NF long-sightedness (BRIT), far-sightedness (US)

prescience [pʀesjɑ̃s] NF prescience, foresight

préscolaire [pʀeskɔlɛʀ] ADJ preschool *cpd*

prescription [pʀɛskʀipsjɔ̃] NF (*instruction*) order, instruction; (*Méd, Jur*) prescription

prescrire [pʀɛskʀiʀ] /**39**/ VT to prescribe; **se prescrire** VI (*Jur*) to lapse

prescrit, e [pʀɛskʀi, -it] PP *de* **prescrire** ▶ ADJ (*date etc*) stipulated

préséance [pʀeseɑ̃s] NF precedence *no pl*

présélection [pʀeselɛksjɔ̃] NF (*de candidats*) short-listing; **effectuer une ~** to draw up a shortlist

présélectionner [pʀeselɛksjɔne] /**1**/ VT to preselect; (*dispositif*) to preset; (*candidats*) to make an initial selection from among, short-list (BRIT)

présence [pʀezɑ̃s] NF presence; (*au bureau etc*) attendance; **en ~** face to face; **en ~ de** in (the) presence of; (*fig*) in the face of; **faire acte de ~** to put in a token appearance; **~ d'esprit** presence of mind

présent, e [pʀezɑ̃, -ɑ̃t] ADJ, NM present; (*Admin, Comm*): **la ~ lettre/loi** this letter/law ▶ NM/F: **les présents** (*personnes*) those present ▶ NF (*Comm: lettre*): **la ~** this letter; **à ~** now, at present; **dès à ~** here and now; **jusqu'à ~** up till now, until now; **à ~ que** now that

présentable [pʀezɑ̃tabl] ADJ presentable

présentateur, -trice [pʀezɑ̃tatœʀ, -tʀis] NM/F presenter

présentation [pʀezɑ̃tasjɔ̃] NF presentation; (*de nouveau venu*) introduction; (*allure*) appearance; **faire les présentations** to do the introductions

présenter [pʀezɑ̃te] /**1**/ VT to present; (*invité, candidat*) to introduce; (*félicitations, condoléances*) to offer; (*montrer: billet, pièce d'identité*) to show, produce; (*faire inscrire: candidat*) to put forward; (*soumettre*) to submit; **~ qn à** to introduce sb to ▶ VI: **~ mal/bien** to have an unattractive/a pleasing appearance; **se présenter** VI (*sur convocation*) to report, come; (*se faire connaître*) to come forward; (*à une élection*) to stand; (*occasion*) to arise; **se présenter à un examen** to sit an exam; **se présenter bien/mal** to look good/not too good; **je vous présente Nadine** this is Nadine

présentoir [pʀezɑ̃twaʀ] NM (*étagère*) display shelf; (*vitrine*) showcase; (*étal*) display stand

préservatif [pʀezɛʀvatif] NM condom, sheath

préservation [pʀezɛʀvasjɔ̃] NF protection, preservation

préserver [pʀezɛʀve] /**1**/ VT: **~ de** (*protéger*) to protect from; (*sauver*) to save from

présidence [pʀezidɑ̃s] NF presidency; chairmanship

président [pʀezidɑ̃] NM (*Pol*) president; (*d'une assemblée, Comm*) chairman; **~ directeur général** chairman and managing director (BRIT), chairman and president (US); **~ du jury** (*Jur*) foreman of the jury; (*d'examen*) chief examiner

présidente [pʀezidɑ̃t] NF president; (*femme du président*) president's wife; (*d'une réunion*) chairwoman

présidentiable [pʀezidɑ̃sjabl] ADJ, NMF potential president

présidentiel, le [pʀezidɑ̃sjɛl] ADJ presidential; **présidentielles** NFPL presidential election(s)

présider [pʀezide] /**1**/ VT to preside over; (*dîner*) to be the guest of honour (BRIT) *ou* honor (US) at; **~ à** VT to direct; to govern

présomption [pʀezɔ̃psjɔ̃] NF presumption

présomptueux, -euse [pʀezɔ̃ptɥø, -øz] ADJ presumptuous

presque [pʀɛsk] ADV almost, nearly; **~ rien** hardly anything; **~ pas** hardly (at all); **~ pas de** hardly any; **personne, ou ~** next to nobody, hardly anyone; **la ~ totalité (de)** almost *ou* nearly all

presqu'île [pʀɛskil] NF peninsula

pressant, e [pʀesɑ̃, -ɑ̃t] ADJ urgent; (*personne*) insistent; **se faire ~** to become insistent

presse [pʀɛs] NF press; (*affluence*): **heures de ~** busy times; **sous ~** gone to press; **mettre sous ~** to send to press; **avoir une bonne/mauvaise ~** to have a good/bad press; **~ féminine** women's magazines *pl*; **~ d'information** quality newspapers *pl*

pressé, e [pʀese] ADJ in a hurry; (*air*) hurried; (*besogne*) urgent ▶ NM: **aller au plus ~** to see to first things first; **être ~ de faire qch** to be in a hurry to do sth; **orange ~** freshly squeezed orange juice

presse-citron [pʀɛssitʀɔ̃] NM INV lemon squeezer

presse-fruits [pʀɛsfʀɥi] NM INV lemon squeezer

pressentiment [pʀesɑ̃timɑ̃] NM foreboding, premonition

pressentir [pʀesɑ̃tiʀ] /**16**/ VT to sense; (*prendre contact avec*) to approach

presse-papiers [pʀɛspapje] NM INV paperweight

presse-purée [pʀɛspyʀe] NM INV potato masher

presser [pʀese] /**1**/ VT (*fruit, éponge*) to squeeze; (*interrupteur, bouton*) to press, push; (*allure, affaire*) to speed up; (*débiteur etc*) to press; (*inciter*): **~ qn de faire** to urge *ou* press sb to do ▶ VI to be urgent; **se presser** VI (*se hâter*) to hurry (up); (*se grouper*) to crowd; **rien ne presse** there's no hurry; **se presser contre qn** to squeeze up against sb; **le temps presse** there's not much time; **~ le pas** to quicken one's step; **~ qn entre ses bras** to squeeze sb tight

pressing [pʀesiŋ] NM (*repassage*) steam-pressing; (*magasin*) dry-cleaner's

pression [pʀesjɔ̃] NF pressure; (*bouton*) press stud (BRIT), snap fastener (US); (*fam: bière*) draught beer; **faire ~ sur** to put pressure on; **sous ~** pressurized, under pressure; (*fig*) keyed up; **~ artérielle** blood pressure

pressoir [pʀeswaʀ] NM (*wine ou oil etc*) press

pressurer [pʀesyʀe] /**1**/ VT (*fig*) to squeeze

pressurisé, e [pʀesyʀize] ADJ pressurized

prestance [pʀɛstɑ̃s] NF presence, imposing bearing

p

prestataire [pʀɛstatɛʀ] NMF person receiving benefits; (*Comm*): ~ **de services** provider of services

prestation [pʀɛstasjɔ̃] NF (*allocation*) benefit; (*d'une assurance*) cover *no pl*; (*d'une entreprise*) service provided; (*d'un joueur, artiste*) performance; ~ **de serment** taking the oath; ~ **de service** provision of a service; **prestations familiales** ≈ child benefit

preste [pʀɛst] ADJ nimble

prestement [pʀɛstəmã] ADV nimbly

prestidigitateur, -trice [pʀɛstidiʒitatœʀ, -tʀis] NM/F conjurer

prestidigitation [pʀɛstidiʒitasjɔ̃] NF conjuring

prestige [pʀɛstiʒ] NM prestige

prestigieux, -euse [pʀɛstiʒjø, -øz] ADJ prestigious

présumer [pʀezyme] /1/ VT: ~ **que** to presume *ou* assume that; ~ **de** to overrate; ~ **qn coupable** to presume sb guilty

présupposé [pʀesypoze] NM presupposition

présupposer [pʀesypoze] /1/ VT to presuppose

présupposition [pʀesypozisjɔ̃] NF presupposition

présure [pʀezyʀ] NF rennet

prêt, e [pʀe, pʀɛt] ADJ ready ▶ NM lending *no pl*; (*somme prêtée*) loan; ~ **à faire** ready to do; ~ **à tout** ready for anything; ~ **sur gages** pawnbroking *no pl*

prêt-à-porter [pʀɛtapɔʀte] (*pl* **prêts-à-porter**) NM ready-to-wear *ou* off-the-peg (BRIT) clothes *pl*

prétendant [pʀetãdã] NM pretender; (*d'une femme*) suitor

prétendre [pʀetãdʀ] /41/ VT (*affirmer*): ~ **que** to claim that; ~ **faire qch** (*avoir l'intention de*) to mean *ou* intend to do sth; ~ **à** (*droit, titre*) to lay claim to

prétendu, e [pʀetãdy] ADJ (*supposé*) so-called

prétendument [pʀetãdymã] ADV allegedly

prête-nom [pʀɛtnɔ̃] NM (*péj*) figurehead; (*Comm etc*) dummy

prétentieux, -euse [pʀetãsjø, -øz] ADJ pretentious

prétention [pʀetãsjɔ̃] NF pretentiousness; (*exigence, ambition*) claim; **sans** ~ unpretentious

prêter [pʀete] /1/ VT: ~ **qch à qn** (*livres, argent*) to lend sth to sb; (*caractère, propos*) to attribute sth to sb; **se prêter** VI (*tissu, cuir*) to give; ~ **à** (*commentaires etc*) to be open to, give rise to; **se prêter à** to lend o.s. (*ou* itself) to; (*manigances etc*) to go along with; ~ **assistance à** to give help to; ~ **attention** to pay attention; ~ **serment** to take the oath; ~ **l'oreille** to listen

prêteur, -euse [pʀetœʀ, -øz] NM/F moneylender; ~ **sur gages** pawnbroker

prétexte [pʀetɛkst] NM pretext, excuse; **sous aucun** ~ on no account; **sous (le)** ~ **que/de** on the pretext that/of

prétexter [pʀetɛkste] /1/ VT to give as a pretext *ou* an excuse

prêtre [pʀɛtʀ] NM priest

prêtre-ouvrier [pʀɛtʀuvʀije] (*pl* **prêtres-ouvriers**) NM worker-priest

prêtrise [pʀetʀiz] NF priesthood

preuve [pʀœv] NF proof; (*indice*) proof, evidence *no pl*; **jusqu'à ~ du contraire** until proved otherwise; **faire ~ de** to show; **faire ses preuves** to prove o.s. (*ou* itself); ~ **matérielle** material evidence

prévaloir [pʀevalwaʀ] /29/ VI to prevail; **se ~ de** VT to take advantage of; (*tirer vanité de*) to pride o.s. on

prévarication [pʀevaʀikasjɔ̃] NF maladministration

prévaut *etc* [pʀevo] VB *voir* **prévaloir**

prévenances [pʀevnãs] NFPL thoughtfulness *sg*, kindness *sg*

prévenant, e [pʀevnã, -ãt] ADJ thoughtful, kind

prévenir [pʀevniʀ] /22/ VT (*éviter: catastrophe etc*) to avoid, prevent; (*anticiper: désirs, besoins*) to anticipate; ~ **qn (de)** (*avertir*) to warn sb (about); (*informer*) to tell *ou* inform sb (about); ~ **qn contre** (*influencer*) to prejudice sb against

préventif, -ive [pʀevãtif, -iv] ADJ preventive

prévention [pʀevãsjɔ̃] NF prevention; (*préjugé*) prejudice; (*Jur*) custody, detention; ~ **routière** road safety

prévenu, e [pʀevny] NM/F (*Jur*) defendant, accused

prévisible [pʀevizibl] ADJ foreseeable

prévision [pʀevizjɔ̃] NF: **prévisions** predictions; (*météorologiques, économiques*) forecast *sg*; **en ~ de** in anticipation of; **prévisions météorologiques** *ou* **du temps** weather forecast *sg*

prévisionnel, le [pʀevizjɔnɛl] ADJ concerned with future requirements

prévit *etc* [pʀevi] VB *voir* **prévoir**

prévoir [pʀevwaʀ] /24/ VT (*deviner*) to foresee; (*s'attendre à*) to expect, reckon on; (*prévenir*) to anticipate; (*organiser: voyage etc*) to plan; (*préparer, réserver*) to allow; **prévu pour quatre personnes** designed for four people; **prévu pour 10 h** scheduled for 10 o'clock; **comme prévu** as planned

prévoyance [pʀevwajãs] NF foresight; **société/caisse de** ~ provident society/contingency fund

prévoyant, e [pʀevwajã, -ãt] VB *voir* **prévoir** ▶ ADJ gifted with (*ou* showing) foresight, far-sighted

prévu, e [pʀevy] PP *de* **prévoir**

prier [pʀije] /7/ VI to pray ▶ VT (*Dieu*) to pray to; (*implorer*) to beg; (*demander*): ~ **qn de faire** to ask sb to do; ~ **qn à dîner** to invite sb to dinner; **se faire** ~ to need coaxing *ou* persuading; **je vous en prie** (*allez-y*) please do; (*de rien*) don't mention it; **je vous prie de faire** please (would you) do

prière [pʀijɛʀ] NF prayer; (*demande instante*) plea, entreaty; **"~ de faire …"** "please do …"

primaire [pʀimɛʀ] ADJ primary; (*péj: personne*) simple-minded; (: *idées*) simplistic ▶ NM (*Scol*) primary education

primauté [pʀimote] NF (*fig*) primacy

prime [pʀim] NF (*bonification*) bonus; (*subside*) allowance; (*Comm: cadeau*) free gift; (*Assurances*,

Bourse) premium ▶ ADJ: **de ~ abord** at first glance; **~ de risque** danger money *no pl*; **~ de transport** travel allowance

primer [pʀime] /**1**/ VT (*l'emporter sur*) to prevail over; (*récompenser*) to award a prize to ▶ VI to dominate, prevail

primesautier, -ière [pʀimsotje, -jɛʀ] ADJ impulsive

primeur [pʀimœʀ] NF: **avoir la ~ de** to be the first to hear (*ou see etc*); **primeurs** NFPL (*fruits, légumes*) early fruits and vegetables; **marchand de ~** greengrocer (BRIT), produce dealer (US)

primevère [pʀimvɛʀ] NF primrose

primitif, -ive [pʀimitif, -iv] ADJ primitive; (*originel*) original ▶ NM/F primitive

primo [pʀimo] ADV first (of all), firstly

primordial, e, -aux [pʀimɔʀdjal, -o] ADJ essential, primordial

prince [pʀɛ̃s] NM prince; **~ charmant** Prince Charming; **~ de Galles** *n inv* (*tissu*) check cloth; **~ héritier** crown prince

princesse [pʀɛ̃sɛs] NF princess

princier, -ière [pʀɛ̃sje, -jɛʀ] ADJ princely

principal, e, -aux [pʀɛ̃sipal, -o] ADJ principal, main ▶ NM (*Scol*) head (teacher) (BRIT), principal (US); (*essentiel*) main thing ▶ NF (*Ling*): **(proposition) ~** main clause

principalement [pʀɛ̃sipalmɑ̃] ADV principally, mainly

principauté [pʀɛ̃sipote] NF principality

principe [pʀɛ̃sip] NM principle; **partir du ~ que** to work on the principle *ou* assumption that; **pour le ~** on principle, for the sake of it; **de ~** *adj* (*hostilité*) automatic; (*accord*) in principle; **par ~** on principle; **en ~** (*habituellement*) as a rule; (*théoriquement*) in principle

printanier, -ière [pʀɛ̃tanje, -jɛʀ] ADJ spring, spring-like

printemps [pʀɛ̃tɑ̃] NM spring; **au ~** in spring

priori [pʀijɔʀi]: **a ~** *adv* at first glance, initially; a priori

prioritaire [pʀijɔʀitɛʀ] ADJ having priority; (*Auto*) having right of way; (*Inform*) foreground

priorité [pʀijɔʀite] NF priority; (*Auto*): **avoir la ~ (sur)** to have right of way (over); **~ à droite** right of way to vehicles coming from the right; **en ~** as a (matter of) priority

pris, e [pʀi, pʀiz] PP *de* **prendre** ▶ ADJ (*place*) taken; (*billets*) sold; (*journée, mains*) full; (*personne*) busy; (*crème, ciment*) set; **avoir le nez/ la gorge ~(e)** to have a stuffy nose/a bad throat; **être ~ de peur/de fatigue/de panique** to be stricken with fear/overcome with fatigue/panic-stricken

prise [pʀiz] NF (*d'une ville*) capture; (*Pêche, Chasse*) catch; (*de judo ou catch, point d'appui ou pour empoigner*) hold; (*Élec: fiche*) plug; (*: femelle*) socket; (*: au mur*) point; **en ~** (*Auto*) in gear; **être aux prises avec** to be grappling with; to be battling with; **lâcher ~** to let go; **donner ~ à** (*fig*) to give rise to; **avoir ~ sur qn** to have a hold over sb; **~ en charge** (*taxe*) pick-up charge (*par la sécurité sociale*) undertaking to reimburse costs; **~ de contact** initial meeting, first contact; **~ de**

courant power point; **~ d'eau** water (supply) point; tap; **~ multiple** adaptor; **~ d'otages** hostage-taking; **~ à partie** (*Jur*) action against a judge; **~ péritel** SCART socket; **~ de sang** blood test; **~ de son** sound recording; **~ de tabac** pinch of snuff; **~ de terre** earth; **~ de vue** (*photo*) shot; **~ de vue(s)** (*action*) filming, shooting

priser [pʀize] /**1**/ VT (*tabac, héroïne*) to take; (*estimer*) to prize, value ▶ VI to take snuff

prisme [pʀism] NM prism

prison [pʀizɔ̃] NF prison; **aller/être en ~** to go to/be in prison *ou* jail; **faire de la ~** to serve time; **être condamné à cinq ans de ~** to be sentenced to five years' imprisonment *ou* five years in prison

prisonnier, -ière [pʀizɔnje, -jɛʀ] NM/F prisoner ▶ ADJ captive; **faire qn ~** to take sb prisoner

prit [pʀi] VB *voir* **prendre**

privatif, -ive [pʀivatif, -iv] ADJ (*jardin etc*) private; (*peine*) which deprives one of one's liberties

privations [pʀivasjɔ̃] NFPL privations, hardships

privatisation [pʀivatizasjɔ̃] NF privatization

privatiser [pʀivatize] /**1**/ VT to privatize

privautés [pʀivote] NFPL liberties

privé, e [pʀive] ADJ private; (*en punition*): **tu es ~ de télé!** no TV for you!; (*dépourvu*): **~ de** without, lacking ▶ NM (*Comm*) private sector; **en ~, dans le ~** in private

priver [pʀive] /**1**/ VT: **~ qn de** to deprive sb of; **se ~ de** to go *ou* do without; **ne pas se ~ de faire** not to refrain from doing

privilège [pʀivilɛʒ] NM privilege

privilégié, e [pʀivileʒje] ADJ privileged

privilégier [pʀivileʒje] /**7**/ VT to favour (BRIT), favor (US)

prix [pʀi] NM (*valeur*) price; (*récompense, Scol*) prize; **mettre à ~** to set a reserve (BRIT) *ou* an upset (US) price on; **au ~ fort** at a very high price; **acheter qch à ~ d'or** to pay a (small) fortune for sth; **hors de ~** exorbitantly priced; **à aucun ~** not at any price; **à tout ~** at all costs; **grand ~** (*Sport*) Grand Prix; **~ d'achat/de vente/ de revient** purchasing/selling/cost price; **~ conseillé** manufacturer's recommended price (MRP)

pro [pʀo] NM (= *professionnel*) pro

probabilité [pʀobabilite] NF probability; **selon toute ~** in all probability

probable [pʀobabl] ADJ likely, probable

probablement [pʀobabləmɑ̃] ADV probably

probant, e [pʀobɑ̃, -ɑ̃t] ADJ convincing

probatoire [pʀobatwaʀ] ADJ (*examen, test*) preliminary; (*stage*) probationary, trial *cpd*

probité [pʀobite] NF integrity, probity

problématique [pʀoblematik] ADJ problematic(al) ▶ NF problematics *sg*; (*problème*) problem

problème [pʀoblɛm] NM problem

procédé [pʀosede] NM (*méthode*) process; (*comportement*) behaviour *no pl* (BRIT), behavior *no pl* (US)

procéder [pʀosede] /**6**/ VI to proceed;

P

(*moralement*) to behave; **~ à** *vt* to carry out

procédure [pʀɔsedyʀ] NF (*Admin, Jur*) procedure

procès [pʀɔsɛ] NM (*Jur*) trial; (: *poursuites*) proceedings *pl*; **être en ~ avec** to be involved in a lawsuit with; **faire le ~ de qn/qch** (*fig*) to put sb/sth on trial; **sans autre forme de ~** without further ado

processeur [pʀɔsesœʀ] NM processor

procession [pʀɔsesjɔ̃] NF procession

processus [pʀɔsesys] NM process

procès-verbal, -aux [pʀɔsɛvɛʀbal, -o] NM (*constat*) statement; (*de réunion*) minutes *pl*; (*aussi*: **PV**): **avoir un ~** to get a parking ticket, to be booked

prochain, e [pʀɔʃɛ̃, -ɛn] ADJ next; (*proche: départ, arrivée*) impending; near ▸ NM fellow man; **la ~ fois/semaine** ~ next time/week; **à la ~!**, (*fam*) **à la ~ fois** see you!, till the next time!; **un ~ jour** (some day) soon

prochainement [pʀɔʃɛnmɑ̃] ADV soon, shortly

proche [pʀɔʃ] ADJ nearby; (*dans le temps*) imminent; close at hand; (*parent, ami*) close; **proches** NMPL (*parents*) close relatives, next of kin; (*amis*): **l'un de ses proches** one of those close to him (*ou* her); **être ~ (de)** to be near, be close (to); **de ~ en ~** gradually

Proche-Orient [pʀɔʃɔʀjɑ̃] NM: **le ~** the Near East

proclamation [pʀɔklamasjɔ̃] NF proclamation

proclamer [pʀɔklame] /1/ VT to proclaim; (*résultat d'un examen*) to announce

procréer [pʀɔkʀee] /1/ VT to procreate

procuration [pʀɔkyʀasjɔ̃] NF proxy; power of attorney; **voter par ~** to vote by proxy

procurer [pʀɔkyʀe] /1/ VT (*fournir*): **~ qch à qn** (*obtenir*) to get *ou* obtain sth for sb; (*plaisir etc*) to bring *ou* give sb sth; **se procurer** VT to get

procureur [pʀɔkyʀœʀ] NM public prosecutor; **~ général** public prosecutor (*in appeal court*)

prodigalité [pʀɔdigalite] NF (*générosité*) generosity; (*extravagance*) extravagance, wastefulness

prodige [pʀɔdiʒ] NM (*miracle, merveille*) marvel, wonder; (*personne*) prodigy

prodigieusement [pʀɔdiʒjøzmɑ̃] ADV tremendously

prodigieux, -euse [pʀɔdiʒjø, -øz] ADJ prodigious; phenomenal

prodigue [pʀɔdig] ADJ (*généreux*) generous; (*dépensier*) extravagant, wasteful; **fils ~** prodigal son

prodiguer [pʀɔdige] /1/ VT (*argent, biens*) to be lavish with; (*soins, attentions*): **~ qch à qn** to lavish sth on sb

producteur, -trice [pʀɔdyktœʀ, -tʀis] ADJ: **~ de blé** wheat-producing ▸ NM/F producer; **société productrice** (*Ciné*) film *ou* movie company

productif, -ive [pʀɔdyktif, -iv] ADJ productive

production [pʀɔdyksjɔ̃] NF (*gén*) production; (*rendement*) output; (*produits*) products *pl*, goods *pl*; (*œuvres*): **la ~ dramatique du XVIIe siècle** the plays of the 17th century

productivité [pʀɔdyktivite] NF productivity

produire [pʀɔdɥiʀ] /38/ VT, VI to produce; **se produire** VI (*acteur*) to perform, appear; (*événement*) to happen, occur

produit, e [pʀɔdɥi, -it] PP *de* **produire** ▸ NM (*gén*) product; **~ chimique** chemical; **~ d'entretien** cleaning product; **~ national brut (PNB)** gross national product (GNP); **~ net** net profit; **~ (pour la) vaisselle** washing-up (*Brit*) *ou* dish-washing (*US*) liquid; **~ des ventes** income from sales; **produits agricoles** farm produce *sg*; **produits alimentaires** foodstuffs; **produits de beauté** beauty products, cosmetics

proéminent, e [pʀɔeminɑ̃, -ɑ̃t] ADJ prominent

prof [pʀɔf] NM (*fam*: = *professeur*) teacher; professor; lecturer

prof. [pʀɔf] ABR = **professeur; professionnel**

profane [pʀɔfan] ADJ (*Rel*) secular; (*ignorant, non initié*) uninitiated ▸ NMF layman

profaner [pʀɔfane] /1/ VT to desecrate; (*fig: sentiment*) to defile; (: *talent*) to debase

proférer [pʀɔfeʀe] /6/ VT to utter

professer [pʀɔfese] /1/ VT to profess

professeur, e [pʀɔfesœʀ] NM/F teacher; (*titulaire d'une chaire*) professor; **~ (de faculté)** (university) lecturer

profession [pʀɔfesjɔ̃] NF (*libérale*) profession; (*gén*) occupation; **faire ~ de** (*opinion, religion*) to profess; **de ~** by profession; **"sans ~"** "unemployed"; (*femme mariée*) "housewife"

professionnel, le [pʀɔfesjɔnɛl] ADJ professional ▸ NM/F professional; (*ouvrier qualifié*) skilled worker

professoral, e, -aux [pʀɔfesɔʀal, -o] ADJ professorial; **le corps ~** the teaching profession

professorat [pʀɔfesɔʀa] NM: **le ~** the teaching profession

profil [pʀɔfil] NM profile; (*d'une voiture*) line, contour; **de ~** in profile

profilé, e [pʀɔfile] ADJ shaped; (*aile etc*) streamlined

profiler [pʀɔfile] /1/ VT to streamline; **se profiler** VI (*arbre, tour*) to stand out, be silhouetted

profit [pʀɔfi] NM (*avantage*) benefit, advantage; (*Comm, Finance*) profit; **au ~ de** in aid of; **tirer** *ou* **retirer ~ de** to profit from; **mettre à ~** to take advantage of; to turn to good account; **profits et pertes** (*Comm*) profit and loss(es)

profitable [pʀɔfitabl] ADJ (*utile*) beneficial; (*lucratif*) profitable

profiter [pʀɔfite] /1/ VI: **~ de** (*situation, occasion*) to take advantage of; (*vacances, jeunesse etc*) to make the most of; **~ de ce que ...** to take advantage of the fact that ...; **~ à** to be of benefit to, benefit; to be profitable to

profiteur, -euse [pʀɔfitœʀ, -øz] NM/F (*péj*) profiteer

profond, e [pʀɔfɔ̃, -ɔ̃d] ADJ deep; (*méditation, mépris*) profound; **peu ~** (*eau, vallée, puits*) shallow; (*coupure*) superficial; **au plus ~ de** in the depths of, at the (very) bottom of; **la France ~** the heartlands of France

profondément [pʀɔfɔ̃demɑ̃] ADV deeply;

profoundly; **il dort ~** he is sound asleep
profondeur [prɔfɔ̃dœr] NF depth; **l'eau a quelle ~?** how deep is the water?
profusément [prɔfyzemɑ̃] ADV profusely
profusion [prɔfyzjɔ̃] NF profusion; **à ~** in plenty
progéniture [prɔʒenityr] NF offspring *inv*
progiciel [prɔʒisjɛl] NM (*Inform*) (software) package; **~ d'application** applications package, applications software *no pl*
progouvernemental, e, -aux [prɔguvɛrnəmɑ̃tal, -o] ADJ pro-government *cpd*
programmable [prɔgramabl] ADJ programmable
programmateur, -trice [prɔgramatœr, -tris] NM/F (*Ciné, TV*) programme (*BRIT*) *ou* program (*US*) planner ▸ NM (*de machine à laver etc*) timer
programmation [prɔgramasjɔ̃] NF programming
programme [prɔgram] NM programme (*BRIT*), program (*US*); (*TV, Radio*) program(me)s *pl*; (*Scol*) syllabus, curriculum; (*Inform*) program; **au ~ de ce soir** (*TV*) among tonight's program(me)s
programmé, e [prɔgrame] ADJ: **enseignement ~** programmed learning
programmer [prɔgrame] /1/ VT (*TV, Radio*) to put on, show; (*organiser, prévoir: émission*) to schedule; (*Inform*) to program
programmeur, -euse [prɔgramœr, -øz] NM/F (computer) programmer
progrès [prɔgrɛ] NM progress *no pl*; **faire des/être en ~** to make/be making progress
progresser [prɔgrese] /1/ VI to progress; (*troupes etc*) to make headway *ou* progress
progressif, -ive [prɔgresif, -iv] ADJ progressive
progression [prɔgresjɔ̃] NF progression; (*d'une troupe etc*) advance, progress
progressiste [prɔgresist] ADJ progressive
progressivement [prɔgresivmɑ̃] ADV progressively
prohiber [prɔibe] /1/ VT to prohibit, ban
prohibitif, -ive [prɔibitif, -iv] ADJ prohibitive
prohibition [prɔibisjɔ̃] NF ban, prohibition; (*Hist*) Prohibition
proie [prwa] NF prey *no pl*; **être la ~ de** to fall prey to; **être en ~ à** (*doutes, sentiment*) to be prey to; (*douleur, mal*) to be suffering
projecteur [prɔʒɛktœr] NM projector; (*de théâtre, cirque*) spotlight
projectile [prɔʒɛktil] NM missile; (*d'arme*) projectile, bullet (*ou shell etc*)
projection [prɔʒɛksjɔ̃] NF projection; (*séance*) showing; **conférence avec projections** lecture with slides (*ou a film*)
projectionniste [prɔʒɛksjɔnist] NMF (*Ciné*) projectionist
projet [prɔʒɛ] NM plan; (*ébauche*) draft; **faire des projets** to make plans; **~ de loi** bill
projeter [prɔʒte] /4/ VT (*envisager*) to plan; (*film, photos*) to project; (*passer*) to show; (*ombre, lueur*) to throw, cast, project; (*jeter*) to throw up (*ou off ou out*); **~ de faire qch** to plan to do sth
prolétaire [prɔletɛr] ADJ, NMF proletarian
prolétariat [prɔletarja] NM proletariat

prolétarien, ne [prɔletarjɛ̃, -ɛn] ADJ proletarian
prolifération [prɔliferasjɔ̃] NF proliferation
proliférer [prɔlifere] /6/ VI to proliferate
prolifique [prɔlifik] ADJ prolific
prolixe [prɔliks] ADJ verbose
prolo [prɔlo] NMF (*fam*: = *prolétaire*) prole (*péj*)
prologue [prɔlɔg] NM prologue
prolongateur [prɔlɔ̃gatœr] NM (*Élec*) extension cable
prolongation [prɔlɔ̃gasjɔ̃] NF prolongation; extension; **prolongations** NFPL (*Football*) extra time *sg*
prolongement [prɔlɔ̃ʒmɑ̃] NM extension; **prolongements** NMPL (*fig*) repercussions, effects; **dans le ~ de** running on from
prolonger [prɔlɔ̃ʒe] /3/ VT (*débat, séjour*) to prolong; (*délai, billet, rue*) to extend; (*chose*) to be a continuation *ou* an extension of; **se prolonger** VI to go on
promenade [prɔmnad] NF walk (*ou* drive *ou* ride); **faire une ~** to go for a walk; **une ~ (à pied)/en voiture/à vélo** a walk/drive/(bicycle) ride
promener [prɔmne] /5/ VT (*personne, chien*) to take out for a walk; (*fig*) to carry around; to trail round; (*doigts, regard*): **~ qch sur** to run sth over; **se promener** VI (*à pied*) to go for (*ou* be out for) a walk; (*en voiture*) to go for (*ou* be out for) a drive; (*fig*): **se promener sur** to wander over
promeneur, -euse [prɔmnœr, -øz] NM/F walker, stroller
promenoir [prɔmənwar] NM gallery, (covered) walkway
promesse [prɔmɛs] NF promise; **~ d'achat** commitment to buy
prometteur, -euse [prɔmɛtœr, -øz] ADJ promising
promettre [prɔmɛtr] /56/ VT to promise ▸ VI (*récolte, arbre*) to look promising; (*enfant, musicien*) to be promising; **se ~ de faire** to resolve *ou* mean to do; **~ à qn de faire** to promise sb that one will do
promeus *etc* [prɔmø] VB *voir* **promouvoir**
promis, e [prɔmi, -iz] PP *de* **promettre** ▸ ADJ: **être ~ à qch** (*destiné*) to be destined for sth
promiscuité [prɔmiskɥite] NF crowding; lack of privacy
promit [prɔmi] VB *voir* **promettre**
promontoire [prɔmɔ̃twar] NM headland
promoteur, -trice [prɔmɔtœr, -tris] NM/F (*instigateur*) instigator, promoter; **~ (immobilier)** property developer (*BRIT*), real estate promoter (*US*)
promotion [prɔmosjɔ̃] NF (*avancement*) promotion; (*Scol*) year (*BRIT*), class; **en ~ (*Comm*)** on promotion, on (special) offer
promotionnel, le [prɔmɔsjɔnɛl] ADJ (*article*) on promotion, on (special) offer; (*vente*) promotional
promouvoir [prɔmuvwar] /27/ VT to promote
prompt, e [prɔ̃, prɔ̃t] ADJ swift, rapid; (*intervention, changement*) sudden; **~ à faire qch** quick to do sth
promptement [prɔ̃ptəmɑ̃] ADV swiftly

p.

prompteur® [pʀɔ̃tœʀ] NM Autocue® (BRIT), Teleprompter® (US)

promptitude [pʀɔ̃tityd] NF swiftness, rapidity

promu, e [pʀɔmy] PP *de* **promouvoir**

promulguer [pʀɔmylge] /1/ VT to promulgate

prôner [pʀone] /1/ VT (*louer*) to laud, extol; (*préconiser*) to advocate, commend

pronom [pʀɔnɔ̃] NM pronoun

pronominal, e, -aux [pʀɔnɔminal, -o] ADJ pronominal; (*verbe*) reflexive, pronominal

prononcé, e [pʀɔnɔ̃se] ADJ pronounced, marked

prononcer [pʀɔnɔ̃se] /3/ VT (*son, mot, jugement*) to pronounce; (*dire*) to utter; (*discours*) to deliver ▶ VI (*Jur*) to deliver *ou* give a verdict; **~ bien/mal** to have good/poor pronunciation; **se prononcer** VI to be pronounced; **se prononcer (sur)** (*se décider*) to reach a decision (on *ou* about), give a verdict (on); **se prononcer contre** to come down against; **ça se prononce comment?** how do you pronounce this?

prononciation [pʀɔnɔ̃sjasjɔ̃] NF pronunciation

pronostic [pʀɔnɔstik] NM (*Méd*) prognosis; (*fig: aussi*: **pronostics**) forecast

pronostiquer [pʀɔnɔstike] /1/ VT (*Méd*) to prognosticate; (*annoncer, prévoir*) to forecast, foretell

pronostiqueur, -euse [pʀɔnɔstikœʀ, -øz] NM/F forecaster

propagande [pʀɔpagɑ̃d] NF propaganda; **faire de la ~ pour qch** to plug *ou* push sth

propagandiste [pʀɔpagɑ̃dist] NMF propagandist

propagation [pʀɔpagasjɔ̃] NF propagation

propager [pʀɔpaʒe] /3/ VT to spread; **se propager** VI to spread; (*Physique*) to be propagated

propane [pʀɔpan] NM propane

propension [pʀɔpɑ̃sjɔ̃] NF: **~ à (faire) qch** propensity to (do) sth

prophète, prophétesse [pʀɔfɛt, pʀɔfetɛs] NM/F prophet(ess)

prophétie [pʀɔfesi] NF prophecy

prophétique [pʀɔfetik] ADJ prophetic

prophétiser [pʀɔfetize] /1/ VT to prophesy

prophylactique [pʀɔfilaktik] ADJ prophylactic

propice [pʀɔpis] ADJ favourable (BRIT), favorable (US)

proportion [pʀɔpɔʀsjɔ̃] NF proportion; **il n'y a aucune ~ entre le prix demandé et le prix réel** the asking price bears no relation to the real price; **à ~ de** proportionally to, in proportion to; **en ~ (de)** in proportion (to); **hors de ~** out of proportion; **toute(s) ~(s) gardée(s)** making due allowance(s)

proportionné, e [pʀɔpɔʀsjɔne] ADJ: **bien ~** well-proportioned; **~ à** proportionate to

proportionnel, le [pʀɔpɔʀsjɔnɛl] ADJ proportional; **~ à** proportional to ▶ NF proportional representation

proportionnellement [pʀɔpɔʀsjɔnɛlmɑ̃] ADV proportionally, proportionately

proportionner [pʀɔpɔʀsjɔne] /1/ VT: **~ qch à** to proportion *ou* adjust sth to

propos [pʀɔpo] NM (*paroles*) talk *no pl*, remark; (*intention, but*) intention, aim; (*sujet*): **à quel ~?** what about?; **à ~ de** about, regarding; **à tout ~** for no reason at all; **à ce ~** on that subject, in this connection; **à ~** adv by the way; (*opportunément*) (just) at the right moment; **hors de ~, mal à ~** adv at the wrong moment

proposer [pʀɔpoze] /1/ VT (*loi, motion*) to propose; (*candidat*) to nominate, put forward; **~ qch (à qn)/de faire** (*suggérer*) to suggest sth (to sb)/ doing, propose sth (to sb)/to do; (*offrir*) to offer (sb) sth/to do; **se ~ (pour faire)** to offer one's services (to do); **se ~ de faire** to intend *ou* propose to do

proposition [pʀɔpozisjɔ̃] NF suggestion; proposal; offer; (*Ling*) clause; **sur la ~ de** at the suggestion of; **~ de loi** private bill

propre [pʀɔpʀ] ADJ clean; (*net*) neat, tidy; (*qui ne salit pas: chien, chat*) house-trained; (: *enfant*) toilet-trained; (*fig: honnête*) honest; (*possessif*) own; (*sens*) literal; (*particulier*): **~ à** peculiar to, characteristic of; (*approprié*): **~ à** suitable *ou* appropriate for; (*de nature à*): **~ à faire** likely to do, that will do ▶ NM: **recopier au ~** to make a fair copy of; (*particularité*): **le ~ de** the peculiarity of, the distinctive feature of; **au ~** (*Ling*) literally; **appartenir à qn en ~** to belong to sb (exclusively); **~ à rien** *nmf* (*péj*) good-for-nothing

proprement [pʀɔpʀəmɑ̃] ADV (*avec propreté*) cleanly; neatly, tidily; **à ~ parler** strictly speaking; **le village ~ dit** the actual village, the village itself

propret, te [pʀɔpʀɛ, -ɛt] ADJ neat and tidy, spick-and-span

propreté [pʀɔpʀəte] NF cleanliness, cleanness; neatness, tidiness

propriétaire [pʀɔpʀijetɛʀ] NMF owner; (*d'hôtel etc*) proprietor(-tress), owner; (*pour le locataire*) landlord(-lady); **~ (immobilier)** house-owner; householder; **~ récoltant** grower; **~ (terrien)** landowner

propriété [pʀɔpʀijete] NF (*droit*) ownership; (*objet, immeuble etc*) property *gen no pl*; (*villa*) residence, property; (*terres*) property *gen no pl*, land *gen no pl*; (*qualité, Chimie, Math*) property; (*correction*) appropriateness, suitability; **~ artistique et littéraire** artistic and literary copyright; **~ industrielle** patent rights *pl*

propulser [pʀɔpylse] /1/ VT (*missile*) to propel; (*projeter*) to hurl, fling

propulsion [pʀɔpylsjɔ̃] NF propulsion

prorata [pʀɔʀata] NM INV: **au ~ de** in proportion to, on the basis of

prorogation [pʀɔʀɔgasjɔ̃] NF deferment; extension; adjournment

proroger [pʀɔʀɔʒe] /3/ VT to put back, defer; (*prolonger*) to extend; (*assemblée*) to adjourn, prorogue

prosaïque [pʀɔzaik] ADJ mundane, prosaic

proscription [pʀɔskʀipsjɔ̃] NF banishment; (*interdiction*) banning; prohibition

proscrire [pʀɔskʀiʀ] /39/ VT (*bannir*) to banish; (*interdire*) to ban, prohibit

prose [pʀoz] NF prose (*style*)

prosélyte [prɔzelit] NMF proselyte, convert
prospecter [prɔspɛkte] /1/ VT to prospect;
(*Comm*) to canvass
prospecteur-placier [prɔspɛktœrplasje] (*pl*
prospecteurs-placiers) NM placement officer
prospectif, -ive [prɔspɛktif, -iv] ADJ prospective
prospectus [prɔspɛktys] NM (*feuille*) leaflet;
(*dépliant*) brochure, leaflet
prospère [prɔspɛr] ADJ prosperous; (*santé,
entreprise*) thriving, flourishing
prospérer [prɔspere] /6/ VI to thrive
prospérité [prɔsperite] NF prosperity
prostate [prɔstat] NF prostate (gland)
prosterner [prɔstɛrne] /1/: **se prosterner** VI to
bow low, prostrate o.s.
prostituée [prɔstitɥe] NF prostitute
prostitution [prɔstitysjɔ̃] NF prostitution
prostré, e [prɔstre] ADJ prostrate
protagoniste [prɔtagɔnist] NM protagonist
protecteur, -trice [prɔtɛktœr, -tris] ADJ
protective; (*air, ton: péj*) patronizing ▶ NM/F
(*défenseur*) protector; (*des arts*) patron
protection [prɔtɛksjɔ̃] NF protection; (*d'un
personnage influent: aide*) patronage; **écran de ~**
protective screen; **~ civile** state-financed civilian
rescue service; **~ maternelle et infantile** social
service concerned with child welfare
protectionnisme [prɔtɛksjɔnism] NM
protectionism
protectionniste [prɔtɛksjɔnist] ADJ
protectionist
protégé, e [prɔteʒe] NM/F protégé(e)
protège-cahier [prɔtɛʒkaje] NM exercise book
cover
protéger [prɔteʒe] /6, 3/ VT to protect; (*aider,
patronner: personne, arts*) to be a patron of;
(: *carrière*) to further; **se ~ de/contre** to protect
o.s. from
protège-slip [prɔtɛʒslip] NM panty liner
protéine [prɔtein] NF protein
protestant, e [prɔtɛstɑ̃, -ɑ̃t] ADJ, NM/F
Protestant
protestantisme [prɔtɛstɑ̃tism] NM
Protestantism
protestataire [prɔtɛstatɛr] NMF protestor
protestation [prɔtɛstasjɔ̃] NF (*plainte*) protest;
(*déclaration*) protestation, profession
protester [prɔtɛste] /1/ VI: **~ (contre)** to protest
(against *ou* about); **~ de** (*son innocence, sa loyauté*)
to protest
prothèse [prɔtɛz] NF artificial limb, prosthesis;
~ dentaire (*appareil*) denture; (*science*) dental
engineering
protocolaire [prɔtɔkɔlɛr] ADJ formal; (*questions,
règles*) of protocol
protocole [prɔtɔkɔl] NM protocol; (*fig*)
etiquette; **~ d'accord** draft treaty;
~ opératoire (*Méd*) operating procedure
prototype [prɔtɔtip] NM prototype
protubérance [prɔtyberɑ̃s] NF bulge,
protuberance
protubérant, e [prɔtyberɑ̃, -ɑ̃t] ADJ protruding,
bulging, protuberant
proue [pru] NF bow(s *pl*), prow

prouesse [prues] NF feat
prouver [pruve] /1/ VT to prove
provenance [prɔvnɑ̃s] NF origin; (*de mot,
coutume*) source; **avion en ~ de** plane (arriving)
from
provençal, e, -aux [prɔvɑ̃sal, -o] ADJ Provençal
▶ NM (*Ling*) Provençal
Provence [prɔvɑ̃s] NF: **la ~** Provence
provenir [prɔvnir] /22/: **~ de** VT to come from;
(*résulter de*) to be due to, be the result of
proverbe [prɔvɛrb] NM proverb
proverbial, e, -aux [prɔvɛrbjal, -o] ADJ
proverbial
providence [prɔvidɑ̃s] NF: **la ~** providence
providentiel, le [prɔvidɑ̃sjɛl] ADJ providential
province [prɔvɛ̃s] NF province
provincial, e, -aux [prɔvɛ̃sjal, -o] ADJ, NM/F
provincial
proviseur [prɔvizœr] NM ≈ head (teacher)
(*Brit*), ≈ principal (*US*)
provision [prɔvizjɔ̃] NF (*réserve*) stock, supply;
(*avance: à un avocat, avoué*) retainer, retaining fee;
(*Comm*) funds *pl* (in account); reserve;
provisions NFPL (*vivres*) provisions, food *no pl*;
faire ~ de to stock up with; **placard** *ou*
armoire à provisions food cupboard
provisoire [prɔvizwar] ADJ temporary; (*Jur*)
provisional; **mise en liberté ~** release on bail
provisoirement [prɔvizwarmɑ̃] ADV
temporarily, for the time being
provocant, e [prɔvɔkɑ̃, -ɑ̃t] ADJ provocative
provocateur, -trice [prɔvɔkatœr, -tris] ADJ
provocative ▶ NM (*meneur*) agitator
provocation [prɔvɔkasjɔ̃] NF provocation
provoquer [prɔvɔke] /1/ VT (*défier*) to provoke;
(*causer*) to cause, bring about; (: *curiosité*) to
arouse, give rise to; (: *aveux*) to prompt, elicit;
(*inciter*): **~ qn à** to incite sb to
prox. ABR = **proximité**
proxénète [prɔksenɛt] NM procurer
proxénétisme [prɔksenetism] NM procuring
proximité [prɔksimite] NF nearness, closeness,
proximity; (*dans le temps*) imminence,
closeness; **à ~** near *ou* close by; **à ~ de** near (to),
close to
prude [pryd] ADJ prudish
prudemment [prydamɑ̃] ADV (*voir prudent*)
carefully; cautiously; prudently; wisely,
sensibly
prudence [prydɑ̃s] NF carefulness; caution;
prudence; **avec ~** carefully; cautiously; wisely;
par (mesure de) ~ as a precaution
prudent, e [prydɑ̃, -ɑ̃t] ADJ (*pas téméraire*) careful,
cautious, prudent; (: *en général*) safety-
conscious; (*sage, conseillé*) wise, sensible;
(*réservé*) cautious; **c'est plus ~** it's wiser; **ce
n'est pas ~** it's risky; it's not sensible; **soyez ~**
take care, be careful
prune [pryn] NF plum
pruneau, x [pryno] NM prune
prunelle [prynɛl] NF pupil; (*œil*) eye; (*Bot*) sloe;
(*eau de vie*) sloe gin
prunier [prynje] NM plum tree
Prusse [prys] NF: **la ~** Prussia

P

PS SIGLE M = **parti socialiste**; (= *post-scriptum*) PS
psalmodier [psalmɔdje] /**7**/ VT to chant; (*fig*) to drone out
psaume [psom] NM psalm
pseudonyme [psødɔnim] NM (*gén*) fictitious name; (*d'écrivain*) pseudonym, pen name; (*de comédien*) stage name
PSIG SIGLE M (= *Peloton de surveillance et d'intervention de gendarmerie*) type of police commando squad
psy [psi] NMF (*fam*: = *psychiatre, psychologue*) shrink
psychanalyse [psikanaliz] NF psychoanalysis
psychanalyser [psikanalize] /**1**/ VT to psychoanalyze; **se faire ~** to undergo (psycho)analysis
psychanalyste [psikanalist] NMF psychoanalyst
psychanalytique [psikanalitik] ADJ psychoanalytical
psychédélique [psikedelik] ADJ psychedelic
psychiatre [psikjatʀ] NMF psychiatrist
psychiatrie [psikjatʀi] NF psychiatry
psychiatrique [psikjatʀik] ADJ psychiatric; (*hôpital*) mental, psychiatric
psychique [psiʃik] ADJ psychological
psychisme [psiʃism] NM psyche
psychologie [psikɔlɔʒi] NF psychology
psychologique [psikɔlɔʒik] ADJ psychological
psychologiquement [psikɔlɔʒikmɑ̃] ADV psychologically
psychologue [psikɔlɔg] NMF psychologist; **être ~** (*fig*) to be a good psychologist
psychomoteur, -trice [psikɔmɔtœʀ, -tʀis] ADJ psychomotor
psychopathe [psikɔpat] NMF psychopath
psychopédagogie [psikɔpedagɔʒi] NF educational psychology
psychose [psikoz] NF (*Méd*) psychosis; (*obsession, idée fixe*) obsessive fear
psychosomatique [psikɔsɔmatik] ADJ psychosomatic
psychothérapie [psikɔteʀapi] NF psychotherapy
psychotique [psikɔtik] ADJ psychotic
PTCA SIGLE M = **poids total en charge autorisé**
Pte ABR = **porte**
pte ABR (= *pointe*) pt
PTMA SIGLE M (= *poids total maximum autorisé*) maximum loaded weight
PTT SIGLE FPL = **poste**[1]
pu [py] PP *de* **pouvoir**
puanteur [pɥɑ̃tœʀ] NF stink, stench
pub [pyb] NF (*fam*: = *publicité*); **la ~** advertising
pubère [pybɛʀ] ADJ pubescent
puberté [pybɛʀte] NF puberty
pubis [pybis] NM (*bas-ventre*) pubes *pl*; (*os*) pubis
public, -ique [pyblik] ADJ public; (*école, instruction*) state *cpd*; (*scrutin*) open ▶ NM public; (*assistance*) audience; **en ~** in public; **le grand ~** the general public
publication [pyblikasjɔ̃] NF publication
publiciste [pyblisist] NMF adman
publicitaire [pyblisitɛʀ] ADJ advertising *cpd*; (*film, voiture*) publicity *cpd*; (*vente*) promotional ▶ NM adman; **rédacteur ~** copywriter

publicité [pyblisite] NF (*méthode, profession*) advertising; (*annonce*) advertisement; (*révélations*) publicity
publier [pyblije] /**7**/ VT to publish; (*nouvelle*) to publicize, make public
publipostage [pyblipɔstaʒ] NM mailshot, (mass) mailing
publique [pyblik] ADJ F *voir* **public**
publiquement [pyblikmɑ̃] ADV publicly
puce [pys] NF flea; (*Inform*) chip; **carte à ~** smart card; **(marché aux) puces** flea market *sg*; **mettre la ~ à l'oreille de qn** to give sb something to think about
puceau, x [pyso] ADJ M: **être ~** to be a virgin
pucelle [pysɛl] ADJ F: **être ~** to be a virgin
puceron [pysʀɔ̃] NM aphid
pudeur [pydœʀ] NF modesty
pudibond, e [pydibɔ̃, -ɔ̃d] ADJ prudish
pudique [pydik] ADJ (*chaste*) modest; (*discret*) discreet
pudiquement [pydikmɑ̃] ADV modestly
puer [pɥe] /**1**/ (*péj*) VI to stink ▶ VT to stink of, reek of
puéricultrice [pɥeʀikyltʀis] NF ≈ paediatric nurse
puériculture [pɥeʀikyltyʀ] NF infant care
puéril, e [pɥeʀil] ADJ childish
puérilement [pɥeʀilmɑ̃] ADV childishly
puérilité [pɥeʀilite] NF childishness; (*acte, idée*) childish thing
pugilat [pyʒila] NM (fist) fight
puis [pɥi] VB *voir* **pouvoir** ▶ ADV (*ensuite*) then; (*dans une énumération*) next; (*en outre*): **et ~** and (then); **et ~ (après** *ou* **quoi)?** so (what)?
puisard [pɥizaʀ] NM (*égout*) cesspool
puiser [pɥize] /**1**/ VT: **~ (dans)** to draw (from); **~ dans qch** to dip into sth
puisque [pɥisk] CONJ since; (*valeur intensive*): **~ je te le dis!** I'm telling you!
puissamment [pɥisamɑ̃] ADV powerfully
puissance [pɥisɑ̃s] NF power; **en ~** *adj* potential; **deux (à la) ~ cinq** two to the power (of) five
puissant, e [pɥisɑ̃, -ɑ̃t] ADJ powerful
puisse *etc* [pɥis] VB *voir* **pouvoir**
puits [pɥi] NM well; **~ artésien** artesian well; **~ de mine** mine shaft; **~ de science** fount of knowledge
pull(-over) [pyl(ɔvœʀ)] NM sweater, jumper (BRIT)
pulluler [pylyle] /**1**/ VI to swarm; (*fig: erreurs*) to abound, proliferate
pulmonaire [pylmɔnɛʀ] ADJ lung *cpd*; (*artère*) pulmonary
pulpe [pylp] NF pulp
pulsation [pylsasjɔ̃] NF (*Méd*) beat
pulsé [pylse] ADJ M: **chauffage à air ~** warm air heating
pulsion [pylsjɔ̃] NF (*Psych*) drive, urge
pulvérisateur [pylveʀizatœʀ] NM spray
pulvérisation [pylveʀizasjɔ̃] NF spraying
pulvériser [pylveʀize] /**1**/ VT (*solide*) to pulverize; (*liquide*) to spray; (*fig: anéantir: adversaire*) to pulverize; (: *record*) to smash, shatter; (: *argument*) to demolish
puma [pyma] NM puma, cougar

punaise [pynɛz] NF (Zool) bug; (clou) drawing pin (BRIT), thumb tack (US)

punch [pɔ̃ʃ] NM (boisson) punch; [pœnʃ] (Boxe) punching ability; (fig) punch

punching-ball [pœnʃiŋbol] NM punchball

punir [pyniR] /2/ VT to punish; ~ qn de qch to punish sb for sth

punitif, -ive [pynitif, -iv] ADJ punitive

punition [pynisjɔ̃] NF punishment

pupille [pypij] NF (Anat) pupil ▶ NMF (enfant) ward; ~ de l'État child in care; ~ de la Nation war orphan

pupitre [pypitR] NM (Scol) desk; (Rel) lectern; (de chef d'orchestre) rostrum; ~ de commande control panel

pur, e [pyR] ADJ pure; (vin) undiluted; (whisky) neat; (intentions) honourable (BRIT), honorable (US) ▶ NM (personne) hard-liner; en ~ perte fruitlessly, to no avail; c'est de la folie ~ it's sheer madness

purée [pyRe] NF: ~ (de pommes de terre) ≈ mashed potatoes pl; ~ de marrons chestnut purée; ~ de pois (fig) peasoup(er)

purement [pyRmɑ̃] ADV purely

pureté [pyRte] NF purity

purgatif [pyRgatif] NM purgative, purge

purgatoire [pyRgatwaR] NM purgatory

purge [pyR3] NF (Pol) purge; (Méd) purging no pl; purge

purger [pyR3e] /3/ VT (radiateur) to flush (out), drain; (circuit hydraulique) to bleed; (Méd, Pol) to purge; (Jur: peine) to serve

purification [pyRifikasjɔ̃] NF (de l'eau) purification; ~ ethnique ethnic cleansing

purifier [pyRifje] /7/ VT to purify; (Tech: métal) to refine

purin [pyRɛ̃] NM liquid manure

puriste [pyRist] NMF purist

puritain, e [pyRitɛ̃, -ɛn] ADJ, NM/F Puritan

puritanisme [pyRitanism] NM Puritanism

pur-sang [pyRsɑ̃] NM INV thoroughbred, pure-bred

purulent, e [pyRylɑ̃, -ɑ̃t] ADJ purulent

pus [py] VB voir **pouvoir** ▶ NM pus

pusillanime [pyzilanim] ADJ fainthearted

putain [pytɛ̃] NF (!) whore (!); ce/cette ~ de ... this bloody (BRIT) ou goddamn (US)... (!)

putois [pytwa] NM polecat; crier comme un ~ to yell one's head off

putréfaction [pytRefaksjɔ̃] NF putrefaction

putréfier [pytRefje] /7/ VT, se putréfier VI to putrefy, rot

putride [pytRid] ADJ putrid

putsch [putʃ] NM (Pol) putsch

puzzle [pœzl] NM jigsaw (puzzle)

PV SIGLE M = **procès-verbal**

PVC SIGLE F (= polychlorure de vinyle) PVC

PVD SIGLE MPL (= pays en voie de développement) developing countries

Px ABR = **prix**

pygmée [pigme] NM pygmy

pyjama [pi3ama] NM pyjamas pl (BRIT), pajamas pl (US)

pylône [pilon] NM pylon

pyramide [piRamid] NF pyramid

pyrénéen, ne [piReneɛ̃, -ɛn] ADJ Pyrenean

Pyrénées [piRene] NFPL: les ~ the Pyrenees

pyrex® [piRɛks] NM Pyrex®

pyrogravure [piRɔgRavyR] NF poker-work

pyromane [piRɔman] NMF arsonist

python [pitɔ̃] NM python

p

Qq

Q, q [ky] NM INV Q, q ▶ ABR (= *quintal*) q;
Q comme Quintal Q for Queen

Qatar [katar] NM: **le ~** Qatar

QCM SIGLE M (= *questionnaire à choix multiples*)
multiple-choice test

QG SIGLE M (= *quartier général*) HQ

QHS SIGLE M (= *quartier de haute sécurité*)
high-security wing *ou* prison

QI SIGLE M (= *quotient intellectuel*) IQ

qqch. ABR (= *quelque chose*) sth

qqe ABR = **quelque**

qqes ABR = **quelques**

qqn ABR (= *quelqu'un*) sb, s.o.

quadra [k(w)adra] (*fam*) NMF (= *quadragénaire*)
person in his (*ou* her) forties; **les quadras** forty
somethings (*fam*)

quadragénaire [kadraʒenɛr] NMF (*de quarante
ans*) forty-year-old; (*de quarante à cinquante ans*)
man/woman in his/her forties

quadrangulaire [kwadrɑ̃gylɛr] ADJ
quadrangular

quadrature [kwadratyr] NF: **c'est la ~ du
cercle** it's like trying to square the circle

quadrichromie [kwadrikrɔmi] NF four-colour
(*Brit*) *ou* -color (*US*) printing

quadrilatère [k(w)adrilatɛr] NM (*Géom, Mil*)
quadrilateral; (*terrain*) four-sided area

quadrillage [kadrijaʒ] NM (*lignes etc*) square
pattern, criss-cross pattern

quadrillé, e [kadrije] ADJ (*papier*) squared

quadriller [kadrije] /1/ VT (*papier*) to mark out in
squares; (*Police: ville, région etc*) to keep under
tight control, be positioned throughout

quadrimoteur [k(w)adrimɔtœr] NM
four-engined plane

quadripartite [kwadripartit] ADJ (*entre pays*)
four-power; (*entre partis*) four-party

quadriphonie [kadrifɔni] NF quadraphony

quadriréacteur [k(w)adrireaktœr] NM
four-engined jet

quadrupède [k(w)adrypɛd] NM quadruped

quadruple [k(w)adrypl] NM: **le ~ de** four times
as much as

quadrupler [k(w)adryple] /1/ VT, VI to
quadruple, increase fourfold

quadruplés, -ées [k(w)adryple] NM/FPL
quadruplets, quads

quai [ke] NM (*de port*) quay; (*de gare*) platform; (*de
cours d'eau, canal*) embankment; **être à ~** (*navire*)
to be alongside; (*train*) to be in the station; **le Q~
d'Orsay** *offices of the French Ministry for Foreign
Affairs*; **le Q~ des Orfèvres** *central police
headquarters*

qualifiable [kalifjabl] ADJ: **ce n'est pas ~** it
defies description

qualificatif, -ive [kalifikatif, -iv] ADJ (*Ling*)
qualifying ▶ NM (*terme*) term; (*Ling*) qualifier

qualification [kalifikasjɔ̃] NF qualification

qualifié, e [kalifje] ADJ qualified; (*main-d'œuvre*)
skilled

qualifier [kalifje] /7/ VT to qualify; (*appeler*):
~ qch/qn de to describe sth/sb as; **se qualifier**
VI (*Sport*) to qualify; **être qualifié pour** to be
qualified for

qualitatif, -ive [kalitatif, -iv] ADJ qualitative

qualité [kalite] NF quality; (*titre, fonction*)
position; **en ~ de** in one's capacity as; **ès
qualités** in an official capacity; **avoir ~ pour**
to have authority to; **de ~** *adj* quality *cpd*;
rapport ~-prix value (for money)

quand [kɑ̃] CONJ, ADV when; **~ je serai riche**
when I'm rich; **~ même** (*cependant, pourtant*)
nevertheless; (*tout de même*) all the same;
~ même, il exagère! really, he overdoes it!;
~ bien même even though

quant [kɑ̃]: **~ à** *prép* (*pour ce qui est de*) as for, as to;
(*au sujet de*) regarding

quant-à-soi [kɑ̃taswa] NM: **rester sur son ~**
to remain aloof

quantième [kɑ̃tjɛm] NM date, day (of the month)

quantifiable [kɑ̃tifjabl] ADJ quantifiable

quantifier [kɑ̃tifje] /7/ VT to quantify

quantitatif, -ive [kɑ̃titatif, -iv] ADJ quantitative

quantitativement [kɑ̃titativmɑ̃] ADV
quantitatively

quantité [kɑ̃tite] NF quantity, amount; (*Science*)
quantity; **une ou des ~(s) de** (*grand nombre*) a
great deal of; a lot of; **en grande ~** in large
quantities; **en quantités industrielles** in vast
amounts; **du travail en ~** a great deal of work;
~ de many

quarantaine [karɑ̃tɛn] NF (*isolement*)
quarantine; **une ~ (de)** forty or so, about forty;
avoir la ~ (*âge*) to be around forty; **mettre en ~**
to put into quarantine; (*fig*) to send to Coventry
(*Brit*), ostracize

quarante [kaʀɑ̃t] NUM forty
quarantième [kaʀɑ̃tjɛm] NUM fortieth
quark [kwaʀk] NM quark
quart [kaʀ] NM (fraction) quarter; (surveillance)
watch; (partie): **un ~ de poulet/fromage** a
chicken quarter/a quarter of a cheese; **un ~ de
beurre** a quarter kilo of butter, ≈ a half pound
of butter; **un ~ de vin** a quarter litre of wine;
une livre un ~ ou **et ~** one and a quarter
pounds; **le ~ de** a quarter of; **~ d'heure** quarter
of an hour; **deux heures et** ou **un ~** (a) quarter
past two, (a) quarter after two (US); **il est le ~ de**
it's (a) quarter past ou after (US); **une heure
moins le ~** (a) quarter to one, (a) quarter of one
(US); **il est moins le ~** it's (a) quarter to; **être
de/prendre le ~** to keep/take the watch; **~ de
tour** quarter turn; **au ~ de tour** (fig) straight
off; **quarts de finale** (Sport) quarter finals
quarté [kaʀte] NM (Courses) system of forecast
betting giving first four horses
quarteron [kaʀtəʀɔ̃] NM (péj) small bunch,
handful
quartette [kwaʀtɛt] NM quartet(te)
quartier [kaʀtje] NM (de ville) district, area; (de
bœuf, de la lune) quarter; (de fruit, fromage) piece;
quartiers NMPL (Mil) quarters; **cinéma/salle
de ~** local cinema/hall; **avoir ~ libre** to be free;
(Mil) to have leave from barracks; **ne pas faire
de ~** to spare no one, give no quarter;
~ commerçant/résidentiel shopping/
residential area; **~ général (QG)** headquarters
(HQ)
quartier-maître [kaʀtjemɛtʀ] NM ≈ leading
seaman
quartz [kwaʀts] NM quartz
quasi [kazi] ADV almost, nearly ▶ PRÉFIXE:
~-certitude near certainty
quasiment [kazimɑ̃] ADV almost, (very) nearly;
~ jamais hardly ever
quaternaire [kwatɛʀnɛʀ] ADJ (Géo) Quaternary
quatorze [katɔʀz] NUM fourteen
quatorzième [katɔʀzjɛm] NUM fourteenth
quatrain [katʀɛ̃] NM quatrain
quatre [katʀ] NUM four; **à ~ pattes** on all fours;
tiré à ~ épingles dressed up to the nines; **faire
les ~ cent coups** to be a bit wild; **se mettre en
~ pour qn** to go out of one's way for sb; **~ à ~**
(monter, descendre) four at a time; **à ~ mains**
(jouer) four-handed
quatre-vingt-dix [katʀəvɛ̃dis] NUM ninety
quatre-vingts [katʀəvɛ̃] NUM eighty
quatre-vingt-un [katʀəvɛ̃œ̃] NUM eighty-one
quatrième [katʀijɛm] NUM fourth ▶ NF (Scol)
year 9 (BRIT), eighth grade (US)
quatuor [kwatɥɔʀ] NM quartet(te)

(MOT-CLÉ)

que [kə] CONJ 1 (introduisant complétive) that; **il
sait que tu es là** he knows (that) you're here;
je veux que tu acceptes I want you to accept;
il a dit que oui he said he would (ou it was etc)
2 (reprise d'autres conjonctions): **quand il rentrera
et qu'il aura mangé** when he gets back and
(when) he has eaten; **si vous y allez ou que**

vous ... if you go there or if you ...
3 (en tête de phrase: hypothèse, souhait etc): **qu'il le
veuille ou non** whether he likes it or not; **qu'il
fasse ce qu'il voudra!** let him do as he pleases!
4 (but): **tenez-le qu'il ne tombe pas** hold it so
(that) it doesn't fall
5 (après comparatif) than; as; voir aussi **plus²**; **aussi**;
autant etc
6 (seulement): **ne ... que** only; **il ne boit que de
l'eau** he only drinks water
7 (temps): **elle venait à peine de sortir qu'il se
mit à pleuvoir** she had just gone out when it
started to rain, no sooner had she gone out
than it started to rain; **il y a quatre ans qu'il
est parti** it is four years since he left, he left
four years ago
▶ ADV (exclamation): **qu'il** ou **qu'est-ce qu'il est
bête/court vite!** he's so silly!/he runs so fast!;
que de livres! what a lot of books!
▶ PRON 1 (relatif: personne) whom; (: chose) that,
which; **l'homme que je vois** the man (whom)
I see; **le livre que tu vois** the book (that ou
which) you see; **un jour que j'étais ...** a day
when I was ...
2 (interrogatif) what; **que fais-tu?**, **qu'est-ce
que tu fais?** what are you doing?; **qu'est-ce
que c'est?** what is it?, what's that?; **que faire?**
what can one do?; **que préfères-tu, celui-ci
ou celui-là?** which (one) do you prefer, this one
or that one?

Québec [kebɛk] N (ville) Quebec ▶ NM: **le ~**
Quebec (Province)
québécois, e [kebekwa, -waz] ADJ Quebec cpd
▶ NM (Ling) Quebec French ▶ NM/F: **Q~, e**
Quebecois, Quebec(k)er

(MOT-CLÉ)

quel, quelle [kɛl] ADJ 1 (interrogatif: personne) who;
(: chose) what; which; **quel est cet homme?**
who is this man?; **quel est ce livre?** what is
this book?; **quel livre/homme?** what book/
man?; (parmi un certain choix) which book/man?;
quels acteurs préférez-vous? which actors do
you prefer?; **dans quels pays êtes-vous allé?**
which ou what countries did you go to?
2 (exclamatif): **quelle surprise/coïncidence!**
what a surprise/coincidence!
3: **quel que soit le coupable** whoever is guilty;
quel que soit votre avis whatever your
opinion (may be)

quelconque [kɛlkɔ̃k] ADJ (médiocre: repas)
indifferent, poor; (sans attrait) ordinary, plain;
(indéfini): **un ami/prétexte ~** some friend/
pretext or other; **un livre ~ suffira** any book
will do; **pour une raison ~** for some reason (or
other)

(MOT-CLÉ)

quelque [kɛlk] ADJ 1 (au singulier) some; (au pluriel)
a few, some; (tournure interrogative) any; **quelque
espoir** some hope; **il a quelques amis** he has a
few ou some friends; **a-t-il quelques amis?**

q

does he have any friends?; **les quelques livres qui** the few books which; **20 kg et quelque(s)** a bit over 20 kg; **il habite à quelque distance d'ici** he lives some distance *ou* way (away) from here

2: quelque … que whatever, whichever; **quelque livre qu'il choisisse** whatever (*ou* whichever) book he chooses; **par quelque temps qu'il fasse** whatever the weather

3: quelque chose something; (*tournure interrogative*) anything; **quelque chose d'autre** something else; anything else; **y être pour quelque chose** to have something to do with it; **faire quelque chose à qn** to have an effect on sb, do something to sb; **quelque part** somewhere; anywhere; **en quelque sorte** as it were

▶ ADV **1** (*environ*): **quelque 100 mètres** some 100 metres

2: quelque peu rather, somewhat

quelquefois [kɛlkəfwa] ADV sometimes

quelques-uns, -unes [kɛlkəzœ̃, -yn] PRON some, a few; **~ des lecteurs** some of the readers

quelqu'un [kɛlkœ̃] PRON someone, somebody; (+ *tournure interrogative ou négative*) anyone, anybody; **~ d'autre** someone *ou* somebody else; anybody else

quémander [kemɑ̃de] /1/ VT to beg for

qu'en dira-t-on [kɑ̃diratɔ̃] NM INV: **le ~** gossip, what people say

quenelle [kənɛl] NF quenelle

quenouille [kənuj] NF distaff

querelle [kərɛl] NF quarrel; **chercher ~ à qn** to pick a quarrel with sb

quereller [kərele] /1/: **se quereller** VI to quarrel

querelleur, -euse [kərɛlœʀ, -øz] ADJ quarrelsome

qu'est-ce que [kɛskə] *voir* **que**

qu'est-ce qui [kɛski] *voir* **qui**

question [kɛstjɔ̃] NF (*gén*) question; (*fig*) matter; issue; **il a été ~ de** we (*ou* they) spoke about; **il est ~ de les emprisonner** there's talk of them being jailed; **c'est une ~ de temps** it's a matter *ou* question of time; **de quoi est-il ~?** what is it about?; **il n'en est pas ~** there's no question of it; **en ~** in question; **hors de ~** out of the question; **je ne me suis jamais posé la ~** I've never thought about it; **(re)mettre en ~** (*autorité, science*) to question; **poser la ~ de confiance** (*Pol*) to ask for a vote of confidence; **~ piège** (*d'apparence facile*) trick question; (*pour nuire*) loaded question; **~ subsidiaire** tiebreaker

questionnaire [kɛstjɔnɛʀ] NM questionnaire

questionner [kɛstjɔne] /1/ VT to question

quête [kɛt] NF (*collecte*) collection; (*recherche*) quest, search; **faire la ~** (*à l'église*) to take the collection; (*artiste*) to pass the hat round; **se mettre en ~ de qch** to go in search of sth

quêter [kete] /1/ VI (*à l'église*) to take the collection; (*dans la rue*) to collect money (for charity) ▶ VT to seek

quetsche [kwɛtʃ] NF damson

queue [kø] NF tail; (*fig: du classement*) bottom; (: *de poêle*) handle; (: *de fruit, feuille*) stalk; (: *de train, colonne, file*) rear; (*file: de personnes*) queue (BRIT), line (US); **en ~ (de train)** at the rear (of the train); **faire la ~** to queue (up) (BRIT), line up (US); **se mettre à la ~** to join the queue *ou* line; **histoire sans ~ ni tête** cock and bull story; **à la ~ leu leu** in single file; (*fig*) one after the other; **~ de cheval** ponytail; **~ de poisson: faire une ~ de poisson à qn** (*Auto*) to cut in front of sb; **finir en ~ de poisson** (*film*) to come to an abrupt end

queue-de-pie [kødpi] (*pl* **queues-de-pie**) NF (*habit*) tails *pl*, tail coat

queux [kø] ADJ M *voir* **maître**

(MOT-CLÉ)

qui [ki] PRON **1** (*interrogatif: personne*) who; (: *avec préposition*) whom; (: *chose, animal*) which, that; (: *interrogatif indirect: sujet*): **je me demande qui est là** I wonder who is there; (: *objet*): **elle ne sait à qui se plaindre** she doesn't know who to complain to *ou* to whom to complain; (: *chose*): **qu'est-ce qui est sur la table?** what is on the table?; **qui est-ce qui?** who?; **qui est-ce que?** who?; **à qui est ce sac?** whose bag is this?; **à qui parlais-tu?** who were you talking to?, to whom were you talking?; **chez qui allez-vous?** whose house are you going to?

2 (*relatif: personne*) who; (+ *prép*) whom; **l'ami de qui je vous ai parlé** the friend I told you about; **la dame chez qui je suis allé** the lady whose house I went to

3 (*sans antécédent*): **amenez qui vous voulez** bring who you like; **qui que ce soit** whoever it may be

quiche [kiʃ] NF quiche; **~ lorraine** quiche Lorraine

quiconque [kikɔ̃k] PRON (*celui qui*) whoever, anyone who; (*n'importe qui, personne*) anyone, anybody

quidam [k(ɥ)idam] NM (*humoristique*) fellow

quiétude [kjetyd] NF (*d'un lieu*) quiet, tranquillity; (*d'une personne*) peace (of mind), serenity; **en toute ~** in complete peace; (*mentale*) with complete peace of mind

quignon [kiɲɔ̃] NM: **~ de pain** (*croûton*) crust of bread; (*morceau*) hunk of bread

quille [kij] NF bowling, skittle (BRIT); (*Navig: d'un bateau*) keel; **(jeu de) quilles** skittles *sg* (BRIT), bowling (US)

quincaillerie [kɛ̃kajʀi] NF (*ustensiles, métier*) hardware, ironmongery (BRIT); (*magasin*) hardware shop *ou* store (US), ironmonger's (BRIT)

quincaillier, -ière [kɛ̃kaje, -jɛʀ] NM/F hardware dealer, ironmonger (BRIT)

quinconce [kɛ̃kɔ̃s] NM: **en ~** in staggered rows

quinine [kinin] NF quinine

quinqua [kɛ̃ka] (*fam*) NMF (= *quinquagénaire*) person in his (*ou* her) fifties; **les quinquas** fifty somethings (*fam*)

quinquagénaire [kɛ̃kaʒenɛʀ] NMF (*de cinquante*

ans) fifty-year old; (*de cinquante à soixante ans*) man/woman in his/her fifties

quinquennal, e, -aux [kɛ̃kenal, -o] ADJ five-year, quinquennial

quinquennat [kɛ̃kena] NM *five year term of office (of French President)*

quintal, -aux [kɛ̃tal, -o] NM quintal (*100 kg*)

quinte [kɛ̃t] NF: **~ (de toux)** coughing fit

quintessence [kɛ̃tesɑ̃s] NF quintessence, very essence

quintette [kɛ̃tɛt] NM quintet(te)

quintuple [kɛ̃typl] NM: **le ~ de** five times as much as

quintupler [kɛ̃typle] /1/ VT, VI to increase fivefold

quintuplés, -ées [kɛ̃typle] NM/FPL quintuplets, quins

quinzaine [kɛ̃zɛn] NF: **une ~ (de)** about fifteen, fifteen or so; **une ~ (de jours)** (*deux semaines*) a fortnight (BRIT), two weeks; **~ publicitaire** ou **commerciale** (two-week) sale

quinze [kɛ̃z] NUM fifteen; **demain en ~** a fortnight (BRIT) ou two weeks tomorrow; **dans ~ jours** in a fortnight('s time) (BRIT), in two weeks(' time)

quinzième [kɛ̃zjɛm] NUM fifteenth

quiproquo [kiprɔko] NM (*méprise sur une personne*) mistake; (*malentendu sur un sujet*) misunderstanding; (*Théât*) (case of) mistaken identity

Quito [kito] N Quito

quittance [kitɑ̃s] NF (*reçu*) receipt; (*facture*) bill

quitte [kit] ADJ: **être ~ envers qn** to be no longer in sb's debt; (*fig*) to be quits with sb; **être ~ de** (*obligation*) to be clear of; **en être ~ à bon compte** to have got off lightly; **~ à faire** even if it means doing; **~ ou double** (*jeu*) double or quits; (*fig*) **c'est du ~ ou double** it's a big risk

quitter [kite] /1/ VT to leave; (*espoir, illusion*) to give up; (*vêtement*) to take off; (*couples, interlocuteurs*) to part; **ne quittez pas** (*au téléphone*) hold the line; **ne pas ~ qn d'une semelle** to stick to sb like glue

quitus [kitys] NM final discharge; **donner ~ à** to discharge

qui-vive [kiviv] NM INV: **être sur le ~** to be on the alert

(MOT-CLÉ)

quoi [kwa] PRON INTERROG **1** what; **quoi de neuf?** what's new?; **quoi?** (*qu'est-ce que tu dis?*) what?

2 (*avec prép*): **à quoi tu penses?** what are you thinking about?; **de quoi parlez-vous?** what are you talking about?; **à quoi bon?** what's the use?
▶ PRON RELATIF: **as-tu de quoi écrire?** do you have anything to write with?; **il n'a pas de quoi se l'acheter** he can't afford it, he hasn't got the money to buy it; **il y a de quoi être fier** that's something to be proud of; **il n'y a pas de quoi** (please) don't mention it; **il n'y a pas de quoi rire** there's nothing to laugh about
▶ PRON (*locutions*): **quoi qu'il arrive** whatever happens; **quoi qu'il en soit** be that as it may; **quoi que ce soit** anything at all; **en quoi puis-je vous aider?** how can I help you?; **et puis quoi encore!** what(ever) next!; **quoi faire?** what's to be done?; **sans quoi** (*ou sinon*) otherwise
▶ EXCL what!

quoique [kwak] CONJ (al)though

quolibet [kɔlibɛ] NM gibe, jeer

quorum [kɔrɔm] NM quorum

quota [kwɔta] NM quota

quote-part [kɔtpar] NF share

quotidien, ne [kɔtidjɛ̃, -ɛn] ADJ (*journalier*) daily; (*banal*) ordinary, everyday ▶ NM (*journal*) daily (paper); (*vie quotidienne*) daily life, day-to-day existence; **les grands quotidiens** the big (national) dailies

quotidiennement [kɔtidjɛnmɑ̃] ADV daily, every day

quotient [kɔsjɑ̃] NM (*Math*) quotient; **~ intellectuel (QI)** intelligence quotient (IQ)

quotité [kɔtite] NF (*Finance*) quota

Rr

R, r [ɛʀ] NM INV R, r ▶ ABR = **route; rue; R comme Raoul** R for Robert (BRIT) *ou* Roger (US)

rab [ʀab], **rabiot** [ʀabjo] NM (*fam: nourriture*) extra, more; **est-ce qu'il y a du ~?** are there any seconds?

rabâcher [ʀabaʃe] /**1**/ VI to harp on ▶ VT to keep on repeating

rabais [ʀabɛ] NM reduction, discount; **au ~** at a reduction *ou* discount

rabaisser [ʀabese] /**1**/ VT (*rabattre: prix*) to reduce; (*dénigrer*) to belittle

rabane [ʀaban] NF raffia (matting)

Rabat [ʀaba(t)] N Rabat

rabat [ʀaba] VB *voir* **rabattre** ▶ NM flap

rabat-joie [ʀabaʒwa] NMF INV killjoy (BRIT), spoilsport

rabatteur, -euse [ʀabatœʀ, -øz] NM/F (*de gibier*) beater; (*péj*) tout

rabattre [ʀabatʀ] /**41**/ VT (*couvercle, siège*) to pull down; (*fam*) to turn down; (*couture*) to stitch down; (*gibier*) to drive; (*somme d'un prix*) to deduct, take off; (*orgueil, prétentions*) to humble; (*Tricot*) to decrease; (*déduire*) to reduce; **se rabattre** VI (*bords, couvercle*) to fall shut; (*véhicule, coureur*) to cut in; **se rabattre sur** (*accepter*) to fall back on

rabattu, e [ʀabaty] PP *de* **rabattre** ▶ ADJ turned down

rabbin [ʀabɛ̃] NM rabbi

rabique [ʀabik] ADJ rabies *cpd*

râble [ʀɑbl] NM back; (*Culin*) saddle

râblé, e [ʀɑble] ADJ broad-backed, stocky

rabot [ʀabo] NM plane

raboter [ʀabɔte] /**1**/ VT to plane (down)

raboteux, -euse [ʀabɔtø, -øz] ADJ uneven, rough

rabougri, e [ʀabugʀi] ADJ stunted

rabrouer [ʀabʀue] /**1**/ VT to snub, rebuff

racaille [ʀakɑj] NF (*péj*) rabble, riffraff

raccommodage [ʀakɔmɔdaʒ] NM mending *no pl*, repairing *no pl*; darning *no pl*

raccommoder [ʀakɔmɔde] /**1**/ VT to mend, repair; (*chaussette etc*) to darn; (*fam: réconcilier: amis, ménage*) to bring together again; **se ~ (avec)** (*fam*) to patch it up (with)

raccompagner [ʀakɔ̃paɲe] /**1**/ VT to take *ou* see back

raccord [ʀakɔʀ] NM link; **~ de maçonnerie**

pointing *no pl*; **~ de peinture** join; (*retouche*) touch-up

raccordement [ʀakɔʀdəmɑ̃] NM joining up; connection

raccorder [ʀakɔʀde] /**1**/ VT to join (up), link up; (*pont etc*) to connect, link; **se ~** to join up with; (*fig: se rattacher à*) to tie in with; **~ au réseau du téléphone** to connect to the telephone service

raccourci [ʀakuʀsi] NM short cut; **en ~** in brief

raccourcir [ʀakuʀsiʀ] /**2**/ VT to shorten ▶ VI (*vêtement*) to shrink; (*jours*) to grow shorter, draw in

raccroc [ʀakʀo]: **par ~** *adv* by chance

raccrocher [ʀakʀɔʃe] /**1**/ VT (*tableau, vêtement*) to hang back up; (*récepteur*) to put down; (*fig: affaire*) to save ▶ VI (*Tél*) to hang up, ring off; **se ~ à** VT to cling to, hang on to; **ne raccrochez pas** (*Tél*) hold on, don't hang up

race [ʀas] NF race; (*d'animaux, fig: espèce*) breed; (*ascendance, origine*) stock, race; **de ~** *adj* purebred, pedigree

racé, e [ʀase] ADJ thoroughbred

rachat [ʀaʃa] NM buying; (*du même objet*) buying back; redemption; atonement

racheter [ʀaʃte] /**5**/ VT (*article perdu*) to buy another; (*davantage*) to buy more; (*après avoir vendu*) to buy back; (*d'occasion*) to buy; (*Comm: part, firme*) to buy up; (*pension, rente*) to redeem; (*Rel: pécheur*) to redeem; (*: péché*) to atone for, expiate; (*mauvaise conduite, oubli, défaut*) to make up for; **se racheter** (*Rel*) to redeem o.s.; (*gén*) to make amends, make up for it; **~ du lait/trois œufs** to buy more milk/another three eggs *ou* three more eggs

rachitique [ʀaʃitik] ADJ suffering from rickets; (*fig*) scraggy, scrawny

rachitisme [ʀaʃitism] NM rickets *sg*

racial, e, -aux [ʀasjal, -o] ADJ racial

racine [ʀasin] NF root; (*fig: attache*) roots *pl*; **~ carrée/cubique** square/cube root; **prendre ~** (*fig*) to take root; to put down roots

racisme [ʀasism] NM racism

raciste [ʀasist] ADJ, NMF racist

racket [ʀakɛt] NM racketeering *no pl*

racketteur [ʀakɛtœʀ] NM racketeer

raclée [ʀɑkle] NF (*fam*) hiding, thrashing

raclement [ʀɑkləmɑ̃] NM (*bruit*) scraping (noise)

racler [ʀɑkle] /**1**/ VT (os, plat) to scrape; (tache, boue) to scrape off; (fig: instrument) to scrape on; (chose: frotter contre) to scrape (against); **se ~ la gorge** to clear one's throat

raclette [ʀɑklɛt] NF (Culin) raclette (Swiss cheese dish)

racloir [ʀɑklwaʀ] NM (outil) scraper

racolage [ʀakɔlaʒ] NM soliciting; touting

racoler [ʀakɔle] /**1**/ VT (attirer: prostituée) to solicit; (: parti, marchand) to tout for; (attraper) to pick up

racoleur, -euse [ʀakɔlœʀ, -øz] ADJ (péj) cheap and alluring ▶ NM (péj: de clients etc) tout ▶ NF streetwalker

racontars [ʀakɔ̃taʀ] NMPL stories, gossip sg

raconter [ʀakɔ̃te] /**1**/ VT: **~ (à qn)** (décrire) to relate (to sb), tell (sb) about; (dire) to tell (sb); **~ une histoire** to tell a story

racorni, e [ʀakɔʀni] ADJ hard(ened)

racornir [ʀakɔʀniʀ] /**2**/ VT to harden

radar [ʀadaʀ] NM radar; **système ~** radar system; **écran ~** radar screen; **~ (automatique)** (Auto: contrôle de vitesse) speed camera

rade [ʀad] NF (natural) harbour; **en ~ de Toulon** in Toulon harbour; **rester en ~** (fig) to be left stranded

radeau, x [ʀado] NM raft; **~ de sauvetage** life raft

radial, e, -aux [ʀadjal, -o] ADJ radial

radiant, e [ʀadjɑ̃, -ɑ̃t] ADJ radiant

radiateur [ʀadjatœʀ] NM radiator, heater; (Auto) radiator; **~ électrique/à gaz** electric/gas heater ou fire

radiation [ʀadjasjɔ̃] NF (d'un nom etc) striking off no pl; (Physique) radiation

radical, e, -aux [ʀadikal, -o] ADJ radical ▶ NM (Ling) stem; (Math) root sign; (Pol) radical

radicalement [ʀadikalmɑ̃] ADV radically, completely

radicaliser [ʀadikalize] /**1**/ VT (durcir: opinions etc) to harden; **se radicaliser** VI (mouvement etc) to become more radical

radicalisme [ʀadikalism] NM (Pol) radicalism

radier [ʀadje] /**7**/ VT to strike off

radiesthésie [ʀadjɛstezi] NF divination (by radiation)

radiesthésiste [ʀadjɛstezist] NMF diviner

radieux, -euse [ʀadjø, -øz] ADJ (visage, personne) radiant; (journée, soleil) brilliant, glorious

radin, e [ʀadɛ̃, -in] ADJ (fam) stingy

radio [ʀadjo] NF radio; (Méd) X-ray ▶ NM (personne) radio operator; **à la ~** on the radio; **avoir la ~** to have a radio; **passer à la ~** to be on the radio; **se faire faire une ~/une ~ des poumons** to have an X-ray/a chest X-ray

radio... [ʀadjo] PRÉFIXE radio...

radioactif, -ive [ʀadjoaktif, -iv] ADJ radioactive

radioactivité [ʀadjoaktivite] NF radioactivity

radioamateur [ʀadjoamatœʀ] NM (radio) ham

radiobalise [ʀadjobaliz] NF radio beacon

radiocassette [ʀadjokasɛt] NF cassette radio

radiodiffuser [ʀadjodifyze] /**1**/ VT to broadcast

radiodiffusion [ʀadjodifyzjɔ̃] NF (radio) broadcasting

radioélectrique [ʀadjoelɛktʀik] ADJ radio cpd

radiographie [ʀadjɔgʀafi] NF radiography; (photo) X-ray photograph, radiograph

radiographier [ʀadjɔgʀafje] /**7**/ VT to X-ray; **se faire ~** to have an X-ray

radioguidage [ʀadjɔgidaʒ] NM (Navig, Aviat) radio control; (Auto) (broadcast of) traffic information

radioguider [ʀadjɔgide] /**1**/ VT (Navig, Aviat) to guide by radio, control by radio

radiologie [ʀadjɔlɔʒi] NF radiology

radiologique [ʀadjɔlɔʒik] ADJ radiological

radiologue [ʀadjɔlɔg] NMF radiologist

radiophonique [ʀadjɔfɔnik] ADJ radio cpd; **programme/émission/jeu ~** radio programme/broadcast/game

radio-réveil [ʀadjɔʀevɛj] (pl **radios-réveils**) NM radio alarm (clock)

radioscopie [ʀadjɔskɔpi] NF radioscopy

radio-taxi [ʀadjɔtaksi] NM radio taxi

radiotélescope [ʀadjɔtelɛskɔp] NM radio telescope

radiotélévisé, e [ʀadjɔtelevize] ADJ broadcast on radio and television

radiothérapie [ʀadjɔteʀapi] NF radiotherapy

radis [ʀadi] NM radish; **~ noir** horseradish no pl

radium [ʀadjɔm] NM radium

radoter [ʀadɔte] /**1**/ VI to ramble on

radoub [ʀadu] NM: **bassin** ou **cale de ~** dry dock

radouber [ʀadube] /**1**/ VT to repair, refit

radoucir [ʀadusiʀ] /**2**/: **se radoucir** VI (se réchauffer) to become milder; (se calmer) to calm down; to soften

radoucissement [ʀadusismɑ̃] NM milder period, better weather

rafale [ʀafal] NF (vent) gust (of wind); (de balles, d'applaudissements) burst; **~ de mitrailleuse** burst of machine-gun fire

raffermir [ʀafɛʀmiʀ] /**2**/ VT, **se raffermir** VI (tissus, muscle) to firm up; (fig) to strengthen

raffermissement [ʀafɛʀmismɑ̃] NM (fig) strengthening

raffinage [ʀafinaʒ] NM refining

raffiné, e [ʀafine] ADJ refined

raffinement [ʀafinmɑ̃] NM refinement

raffiner [ʀafine] /**1**/ VT to refine

raffinerie [ʀafinʀi] NF refinery

raffoler [ʀafɔle] /**1**/: **~ de** VT to be very keen on

raffut [ʀafy] NM (fam) row, racket

rafiot [ʀafjo] NM tub

rafistoler [ʀafistɔle] /**1**/ VT (fam) to patch up

rafle [ʀafl] NF (de police) roundup, raid

rafler [ʀafle] /**1**/ VT (fam) to swipe, nick

rafraîchir [ʀafʀeʃiʀ] /**2**/ VT (atmosphère, température) to cool (down); (boisson) to chill; (air, eau) to freshen up; (fig: rénover) to brighten up ▶ VI: **mettre du vin/une boisson à ~** to chill wine/a drink; **se rafraîchir** VI to grow cooler; (en se lavant) to freshen up; (personne: en buvant etc) to refresh o.s.; **~ la mémoire à qn** to refresh sb's memory

rafraîchissant, e [ʀafʀeʃisɑ̃, -ɑ̃t] ADJ refreshing

rafraîchissement [ʀafʀeʃismɑ̃] NM cooling; (boisson) cool drink; **rafraîchissements** NMPL (boissons, fruits etc) refreshments

r

ragaillardir [Ragajaʀdiʀ] /2/ VT (fam) to perk ou
buck up

rage [Raʒ] NF (Méd): **la ~** rabies; (fureur) rage,
fury; **faire ~** to rage; **~ de dents** (raging)
toothache

rager [Raʒe] /3/ VI to fume (with rage); **faire ~
qn** to enrage sb, get sb mad

rageur, -euse [Raʒœʀ, -øz] ADJ snarling;
ill-tempered

raglan [Raglɑ̃] ADJ INV raglan

ragot [Rago] NM (fam) malicious gossip no pl

ragoût [Ragu] NM (plat) stew

ragoûtant, e [Ragutɑ̃, -ɑ̃t] ADJ: **peu ~**
unpalatable

rai [Rɛ] NM: **un ~ de soleil/lumière** a shaft of
sunlight/light

raid [Rɛd] NM (Mil) raid; (attaque aérienne) air
raid; (Sport) long-distance trek

raide [Rɛd] ADJ (tendu) taut, tight; (escarpé) steep;
(droit: cheveux) straight; (ankylosé, dur, guindé) stiff;
(fam: cher) steep, stiff; (: sans argent) flat broke
▸ ADV (en pente) steeply; **~ mort** stone dead

raideur [Rɛdœʀ] NF steepness; (rigidité)
stiffness; **avec ~** (répondre) stiffly, abruptly

raidir [Rɛdiʀ] /2/ VT (muscles) to stiffen; (câble) to
pull taut, tighten; **se raidir** VI to stiffen; to
become taut; (personne: se crisper) to tense up; (: se
préparer moralement) to brace o.s.; (fig: devenir
intransigeant) to harden

raidissement [Redismɑ̃] NM stiffening;
tightening; hardening

raie [Rɛ] NF (Zool) skate, ray; (rayure) stripe; (des
cheveux) parting

raifort [Rɛfɔʀ] NM horseradish

rail [Raj] NM (barre d'acier) rail; (chemins de fer)
railways pl (Brit), railroads pl (US); **les rails** (la
voie ferrée) the rails, the track sg; **par ~** by rail;
~ conducteur live ou conductor rail

railler [Raje] /1/ VT to scoff at, jeer at

raillerie [Rajʀi] NF mockery

railleur, -euse [Rajœʀ, -øz] ADJ mocking

rainurage [RenyRaʒ] NM (Auto) uneven road
surface

rainure [Renyʀ] NF groove; slot

rais [Rɛ] NM INV = **rai**

raisin [Rɛzɛ̃] NM (aussi: **raisins**) grapes pl;
(variété): **~ blanc/noir** white (ou green)/black
grape; **~ muscat** muscat grape; **raisins secs**
raisins

raison [Rɛzɔ̃] NF reason; **avoir ~** to be right;
donner ~ à qn (personne) to agree with sb; (fait)
to prove sb right; **avoir ~ de qn/qch** to get the
better of sb/sth; **se faire une ~** to learn to live
with it; **perdre la ~** to become insane; (fig) to
take leave of one's senses; **recouvrer la ~** to
come to one's senses; **ramener qn à la ~** to
make sb see sense; **demander ~ à qn de** (affront
etc) to demand satisfaction from sb for;
entendre ~ to listen to reason, see reason; **plus
que de ~** too much, more than is reasonable;
~ de plus all the more reason; **à plus forte ~** all
the more so; **sans ~** for no reason; **en ~ de** (à
cause de) because of; (à proportion de) in proportion
to; **à ~ de** at the rate of; **~ d'État** reason of state;

~ d'être raison d'être; **~ sociale** corporate
name

raisonnable [Rɛzɔnabl] ADJ reasonable,
sensible

raisonnablement [Rɛzɔnabləmɑ̃] ADV
reasonably

raisonné, e [Rɛzɔne] ADJ reasoned

raisonnement [Rɛzɔnmɑ̃] NM reasoning;
arguing; argument

raisonner [Rɛzɔne] /1/ VI (penser) to reason;
(argumenter, discuter) to argue ▸ VT (personne) to
reason with; (attitude: justifier) to reason out; **se
raisonner** to reason with oneself

raisonneur, -euse [Rɛzɔnœʀ, -øz] ADJ (péj)
quibbling

rajeunir [Raʒœniʀ] /2/ VT (cure etc) to rejuvenate;
(fig: rafraîchir) to brighten up; (: moderniser) to give
a new look to; (: en recrutant) to inject new blood
into ▸ VI (personne) to become (ou look) younger;
(entreprise, quartier) to be modernized; **~ qn**
(coiffure, robe) to make sb look younger

rajout [Raʒu] NM addition

rajouter [Raʒute] /1/ VT (commentaire) to add;
~ du sel/un œuf to add some more salt/
another egg; **~ que** to add that; **en ~** to lay it on
thick

rajustement [Raʒystəmɑ̃] NM adjustment

rajuster [Raʒyste] /1/ VT (vêtement) to straighten,
tidy; (salaires) to adjust; (machine) to readjust;
se rajuster to tidy ou straighten o.s. up

râle [Rɑl] NM groan; **~ d'agonie** death rattle

ralenti [Ralɑ̃ti] NM: **au ~** (Ciné) in slow motion;
(fig) at a slower pace; **tourner au ~** (Auto) to tick
over, idle

ralentir [Ralɑ̃tiʀ] /2/ VT, VI, **se ralentir** VI to slow
down

ralentissement [Ralɑ̃tismɑ̃] NM slowing down

râler [Rɑle] /1/ VI to groan; (fam) to grouse, moan
(and groan)

ralliement [Ralimɑ̃] NM (rassemblement) rallying;
(adhésion: à une cause, une opinion) winning over;
point/signe de ~ rallying point/sign

rallier [Ralje] /7/ VT (rassembler) to rally; (rejoindre)
to rejoin; (gagner à sa cause) to win over; **se ~ à**
(avis) to come over ou round to

rallonge [Ralɔ̃ʒ] NF (de table) (extra) leaf; (argent
etc) extra no pl; (Élec) extension (cable ou flex);
(fig: de crédit etc) extension

rallonger [Ralɔ̃ʒe] /3/ VT to lengthen

rallumer [Ralyme] /1/ VT to light up again,
relight; (fig) to revive; **se rallumer** VI (lumière) to
come on again

rallye [Rali] NM rally; (Pol) march

ramages [Ramaʒ] NMPL (dessin) leaf pattern sg;
(chants) songs

ramassage [Ramasaʒ] NM: **~ scolaire** school
bus service

ramassé, e [Ramase] ADJ (trapu) squat, stocky;
(concis: expression etc) compact

ramasse-miettes [Ramasmjɛt] NM INV
table-tidy

ramasser [Ramase] /1/ VT (objet tombé ou par terre)
to pick up; (recueillir: copies, ordures) to collect;
(récolter) to gather; (: pommes de terre) to lift;

se ramasser VI (*sur soi-même*) to huddle up; to crouch

ramasseur, -euse [ʀamɑsœʀ, -øz] NM/F: **~ de balles** ballboy/girl

ramassis [ʀamɑsi] NM (*péj: de voyous*) bunch; (: *de choses*) jumble

rambarde [ʀɑ̃baʀd] NF guardrail

rame [ʀam] NF (*aviron*) oar; (*de métro*) train; (*de papier*) ream; **~ de haricots** bean support; **faire force de rames** to row hard

rameau, x [ʀamo] NM (small) branch; (*fig*) branch; **les R~** (*Rel*) Palm Sunday *sg*

ramener [ʀamne] /5/ VT to bring back; (*reconduire*) to take back; **~ qch sur** (*rabattre: couverture, visière*) to pull sth back over; **se ramener** VI (*fam*) to roll *ou* turn up; **~ qch à** (*réduire à: Math*) to reduce sth to; **~ qn à la vie/raison** to bring sb back to life/bring sb to his (*ou* her) senses; **se ramener à** (*se réduire à*) to come *ou* boil down to

ramequin [ʀamkɛ̃] NM ramekin

ramer [ʀame] /1/ VI to row

rameur, -euse [ʀamœʀ, -øz] NM/F rower

rameuter [ʀamøte] /1/ VT to gather together

ramier [ʀamje] NM: (**pigeon**) **~** woodpigeon

ramification [ʀamifikasjɔ̃] NF ramification

ramifier [ʀamifje] /7/: **se ramifier** VI: **se ramifier (en)** (*tige, secte, réseau*) to branch out (into); (*veines, nerfs*) to ramify

ramolli, e [ʀamɔli] ADJ soft

ramollir [ʀamɔliʀ] /2/ VT to soften; **se ramollir** VI (*os, tissus*) to get (*ou* go) soft; (*beurre, asphalte*) to soften

ramonage [ʀamɔnaʒ] NM (chimney-)sweeping

ramoner [ʀamɔne] /1/ VT (*cheminée*) to sweep; (*pipe*) to clean

ramoneur [ʀamɔnœʀ] NM (chimney) sweep

rampe [ʀɑ̃p] NF (*d'escalier*) banister(s *pl*); (*dans un garage, d'un terrain*) ramp; (*lampes: lumineuse, de balisage*) floodlights *pl*; **la ~** (*Théât*) the footlights *pl*; **passer la ~** (*toucher le public*) to get across to the audience; **~ de lancement** launching pad

ramper [ʀɑ̃pe] /1/ VI (*reptile, animal*) to crawl; (*plante*) to creep

rancard [ʀɑ̃kaʀ] NM (*fam*) date; tip

rancart [ʀɑ̃kaʀ] NM: **mettre au ~** (*article, projet*) to scrap; (*personne*) to put on the scrapheap

rance [ʀɑ̃s] ADJ rancid

rancir [ʀɑ̃siʀ] /2/ VI to go off, go rancid

rancœur [ʀɑ̃kœʀ] NF rancour (*Brit*), rancor (*US*), resentment

rançon [ʀɑ̃sɔ̃] NF ransom; (*fig*): **la ~ du succès** *etc* the price of success *etc*

rançonner [ʀɑ̃sɔne] /1/ VT to hold to ransom

rancune [ʀɑ̃kyn] NF grudge, rancour (*Brit*), rancor (*US*); **garder ~ à qn (de qch)** to bear sb a grudge (for sth); **sans ~!** no hard feelings!

rancunier, -ière [ʀɑ̃kynje, -jɛʀ] ADJ vindictive, spiteful

randonnée [ʀɑ̃dɔne] NF ride; (*à pied*) walk, ramble; (*en montagne*) hike, hiking *no pl*; **la ~** (*activité*) hiking, walking; **une ~ à cheval** a pony trek

randonneur, -euse [ʀɑ̃dɔnœʀ, -øz] NM/F hiker

rang [ʀɑ̃] NM (*rangée*) row; (*de perles*) row, string, rope; (*grade, condition sociale, classement*) rank; **rangs** NMPL (*Mil*) ranks; **se mettre en rangs/sur un ~** to get into *ou* form rows/a line; **sur trois rangs** (lined up) three deep; **se mettre en rangs par quatre** to form fours *ou* rows of four; **se mettre sur les rangs** (*fig*) to get into the running; **au premier ~** in the first row; (*fig*) ranking first; **rentrer dans le ~** to get into line; **au ~ de** (*au nombre de*) among (the ranks of); **avoir ~ de** to hold the rank of

rangé, e [ʀɑ̃ʒe] ADJ (*vie*) well-ordered; (*sérieux: personne*) orderly, steady

rangée [ʀɑ̃ʒe] NF row

rangement [ʀɑ̃ʒmɑ̃] NM tidying-up, putting-away; **faire des rangements** to tidy up

ranger [ʀɑ̃ʒe] /3/ VT (*classer, grouper*) to order, arrange; (*mettre à sa place*) to put away; (*voiture dans la rue*) to park; (*mettre de l'ordre dans*) to tidy up; (*arranger, disposer: en cercle etc*) to arrange; (*fig: classer*): **~ qn/qch parmi** to rank sb/sth among; **se ranger** VI (*se placer, se disposer: autour d'une table etc*) to take one's place, sit round; (*véhicule, conducteur: s'écarter*) to pull over *ou* in; (: *s'arrêter*) to pull in; (*piéton*) to step aside; (*s'assagir*) to settle down; **se ranger à** (*avis*) to come round to, fall in with

ranimer [ʀanime] /1/ VT (*personne évanouie*) to bring round; (*revigorer: forces, courage*) to restore; (*réconforter: troupes etc*) to kindle new life in; (*douleur, souvenir*) to revive; (*feu*) to rekindle

rap [ʀap] NM rap (music)

rapace [ʀapas] NM bird of prey ▶ ADJ (*péj*) rapacious, grasping; **~ diurne/nocturne** diurnal/nocturnal bird of prey

rapatrié, e [ʀapatʀije] NM/F repatriate (*esp French North African settler*)

rapatriement [ʀapatʀimɑ̃] NM repatriation

rapatrier [ʀapatʀije] /7/ VT to repatriate; (*capitaux*) to bring (back) into the country

râpe [ʀɑp] NF (*Culin*) grater; (*à bois*) rasp

râpé, e [ʀɑpe] ADJ (*tissu*) threadbare; (*Culin*) grated

râper [ʀɑpe] /1/ VT (*Culin*) to grate; (*gratter, râcler*) to rasp

rapetasser [ʀaptase] /1/ VT (*fam*) to patch up

rapetisser [ʀaptise] /1/ VT: **~ qch** to shorten sth; to make sth look smaller ▶ VI, **se rapetisser** to shrink

râpeux, -euse [ʀapø, -øz] ADJ rough

raphia [ʀafja] NM raffia

rapide [ʀapid] ADJ fast; (*prompt: intelligence, coup d'œil, mouvement*) quick ▶ NM express (train); (*de cours d'eau*) rapid

rapidement [ʀapidmɑ̃] ADV fast; quickly

rapidité [ʀapidite] NF speed; quickness

rapiécer [ʀapjese] /3, 6/ VT to patch

rappel [ʀapɛl] NM (*d'un ambassadeur, Mil*) recall; (*Théât*) curtain call; (*Méd: vaccination*) booster; (*Admin: de salaire*) back pay *no pl*; (*d'une aventure, d'un nom*) reminder; (*de limitation de vitesse: sur écriteau*) speed limit sign (*reminder*); (*Tech*) return; (*Navig*) sitting out; (*Alpinisme: aussi:*

rappel de corde) abseiling no pl, roping down no pl; abseil; **~ à l'ordre** call to order

rappeler [Raple] /**4**/ vt (pour faire revenir, retéléphoner) to call back; (ambassadeur, Mil) to recall; (acteur) to call back (onto the stage); (faire se souvenir): **~ qch à qn** to remind sb of sth; **se rappeler** vt (se souvenir de) to remember, recall; **~ qn à la vie** to bring sb back to life; **~ qn à la décence** to recall sb to a sense of decency; **ça rappelle la Provence** it's reminiscent of Provence, it reminds you of Provence; **se rappeler que…** to remember that…

rappelle etc [Rapɛl] vb voir **rappeler**

rappliquer [Raplike] /**1**/ vi (fam) to turn up

rapport [RapɔR] nm (compte rendu) report; (profit) yield, return; revenue; (lien, analogie) relationship; (corrélation) connection; (proportion: Math, Tech) ratio; **rapports** nmpl (entre personnes, pays) relations; **avoir ~ à** to have something to do with, concern; **être en ~ avec** (idée de corrélation) to be related to; **être/se mettre en ~ avec qn** to be/get in touch with sb; **par ~ à** (comparé à) in relation to; (à propos de) with regard to; **sous le ~ de** from the point of view of; **sous tous (les) rapports** in all respects; **rapports (sexuels)** (sexual) intercourse sg; **~ qualité-prix** value (for money)

rapporté, e [RapɔRte] adj: **pièce ~** (Couture) patch

rapporter [RapɔRte] /**1**/ vt (rendre, ramener) to bring back; (apporter davantage) to bring more; (Couture) to sew on; (investissement) to yield; (: activité) to bring in; (relater) to report; (Jur: annuler) to revoke ▸ vi (investissement) to give a good return ou yield; (activité) to be very profitable; (péj: moucharder) to tell; **~ qch à** (fig: rattacher) to relate sth to; **se ~ à** (correspondre à) to relate to; **s'en ~ à** to rely on

rapporteur, -euse [RapɔRtœR, -øz] nm/f (de procès, commission) reporter; (péj) telltale ▸ nm (Géom) protractor

rapproché, e [RapRoʃe] adj (proche) near, close at hand; **rapprochés** (l'un de l'autre) at close intervals

rapprochement [RapRoʃmã] nm (réconciliation: de nations, familles) reconciliation; (analogie, rapport) parallel

rapprocher [RapRoʃe] /**1**/ vt (deux objets) to bring closer together; (réunir: ennemis, partis etc) to bring together; (comparer) to establish a parallel between; (chaise d'une table): **~ qch (de)** to bring sth closer (to); **se rapprocher** vi to draw closer ou nearer; (fig: familles, pays) to come together; to come closer together; **se rapprocher de** to come closer to; (présenter une analogie avec) to be close to

rapt [Rapt] nm abduction

raquette [Rakɛt] nf (de tennis) racket; (de ping-pong) bat; (à neige) snowshoe

rare [RɑR] adj rare; (main-d'œuvre, denrées) scarce; (cheveux, herbe) sparse; **il est ~ que** it's rare that, it's unusual that; **se faire ~** to become scarce; (fig: personne) to make oneself scarce

raréfaction [Raʀefaksjɔ̃] nf scarcity; (de l'air) rarefaction

raréfier [Raʀefje] /**7**/: **se raréfier** vi to grow scarce; (air) to rarefy

rarement [RaʀRmã] adv rarely, seldom

rareté [RaʀRte] nf voir **rare** rarity; scarcity

rarissime [Raʀisim] adj extremely rare

RAS abr = **rien à signaler**

ras, e [Rɑ, Rɑz] adj (tête, cheveux) close-cropped; (poil, herbe) short; (mesure, cuillère) level ▸ adv short; **faire table ~** to make a clean sweep; **en ~ campagne** in open country; **à ~ bords** to the brim; **au ~ de** level with; **en avoir ~ le bol** (fam) to be fed up; **~ du cou** adj (pull, robe) crew-neck

rasade [Razad] nf glassful

rasant, e [Razã, -ãt] adj (Mil: balle, tir) grazing; (fam) boring

rascasse [Raskas] nf (Zool) scorpion fish

rasé, e [Raze] adj: **~ de frais** freshly shaven; **~ de près** close-shaven

rase-mottes [Razmɔt] nm inv: **faire du ~** to hedgehop; **vol en ~** hedgehopping

raser [Raze] /**1**/ vt (barbe, cheveux) to shave off; (menton, personne) to shave; (fam: ennuyer) to bore; (démolir) to raze (to the ground); (frôler) to graze, skim; **se raser** vi to shave; (fam) to be bored (to tears)

rasoir [RazwaR] nm razor; **~ électrique** electric shaver ou razor; **~ mécanique** ou **de sûreté** safety razor

rassasier [Rasazje] /**7**/ vt to satisfy; **être rassasié** (dégoûté) to be sated; to have had more than enough

rassemblement [Rasãbləmã] nm (groupe) gathering; (Pol) union; association; (Mil): **le ~** parade

rassembler [Rasãble] /**1**/ vt (réunir) to assemble, gather; (regrouper, amasser: documents, notes) to gather together, collect; **se rassembler** vi to gather; **~ ses idées/ses esprits/son courage** to collect one's thoughts/gather one's wits/screw up one's courage

rasseoir [RaswaR] /**26**/: **se rasseoir** vi to sit down again

rassir [RasiR] /**2**/ vi to go stale

rassis, e [Rasi, -iz] adj (pain) stale

rassurant, e [Rasyʀã, -ãt] adj (nouvelles etc) reassuring

rassuré, e [RasyʀRe] adj: **ne pas être très ~** to be rather ill at ease

rassurer [RasyʀRe] /**1**/ vt to reassure; **se rassurer** vi to be reassured; **rassure-toi** don't worry

rat [Ra] nm rat; **~ d'hôtel** hotel thief; **~ musqué** muskrat

ratatiné, e [Ratatine] adj shrivelled (up), wrinkled

ratatiner [Ratatine] /**1**/ vt to shrivel; (peau) to wrinkle; **se ratatiner** vi to shrivel; to become wrinkled

ratatouille [Ratatuj] nf (Culin) ratatouille

rate [Rat] nf female rat; (Anat) spleen

raté, e [Rate] adj (tentative) unsuccessful, failed ▸ nm/f (fam: personne) failure ▸ nm misfiring no pl

râteau, x [Rɑto] nm rake

râtelier [ʀɑtəlje] NM rack; (fam) false teeth pl
rater [ʀate] /**1**/ VI (ne pas partir: coup de feu) to fail to go off; (affaire, projet etc) to go wrong, fail ▶ VT (cible, train, occasion) to miss; (démonstration, plat) to spoil; (examen) to fail; **~ son coup** to fail, not to bring it off
raticide [ʀatisid] NM rat poison
ratification [ʀatifikasjɔ̃] NF ratification
ratifier [ʀatifje] /**7**/ VT to ratify
ratio [ʀasjo] NM ratio
ration [ʀasjɔ̃] NF ration; (fig) share; **~ alimentaire** food intake
rationalisation [ʀasjɔnalizasjɔ̃] NF rationalization
rationaliser [ʀasjɔnalize] /**1**/ VT to rationalize
rationnel, le [ʀasjɔnɛl] ADJ rational
rationnellement [ʀasjɔnɛlmɑ̃] ADV rationally
rationnement [ʀasjɔnmɑ̃] NM rationing; **ticket de ~** ration coupon
rationner [ʀasjɔne] /**1**/ VT to ration; (personne) to put on rations; **se rationner** to ration o.s.
ratisser [ʀatise] /**1**/ VT (allée) to rake; (feuilles) to rake up; (armée, police) to comb; **~ large** to cast one's net wide
raton [ʀatɔ̃] NM: **~ laveur** raccoon
RATP SIGLE F (= Régie autonome des transports parisiens) Paris transport authority
rattacher [ʀataʃe] /**1**/ VT (animal, cheveux) to tie up again; **~ qch à** (incorporer: Admin etc) to join sth to, unite sth with; (relier) to link sth with, relate sth to; **~ qn à** (fig: lier) to bind ou tie sb to; **se ~ à** (fig: avoir un lien avec) to be linked (ou connected) with
rattrapage [ʀatʀapaʒ] NM (Scol) remedial classes pl; (Écon) catching up
rattraper [ʀatʀape] /**1**/ VT (fugitif) to recapture; (retenir, empêcher de tomber) to catch (hold of); (atteindre, rejoindre) to catch up with; (réparer: erreur) to make up for; **se rattraper** VI (regagner: du temps) to make up for lost time; (: de l'argent etc) to make good one's losses; (réparer une gaffe etc) to make up for it; **se rattraper (à)** (se raccrocher) to stop o.s. falling (by catching hold of); **~ son retard/le temps perdu** to make up (for) lost time
rature [ʀatyʀ] NF deletion, erasure
raturer [ʀatyʀe] /**1**/ VT to cross out, delete, erase
rauque [ʀok] ADJ raucous; (voix) hoarse
ravagé, e [ʀavaʒe] ADJ (visage) harrowed
ravager [ʀavaʒe] /**3**/ VT to devastate, ravage
ravages [ʀavaʒ] NMPL ravages; **faire des ~** to wreak havoc; (fig: séducteur) to break hearts
ravalement [ʀavalmɑ̃] NM restoration
ravaler [ʀavale] /**1**/ VT (mur, façade) to restore; (déprécier) to lower; (avaler de nouveau) to swallow again; **~ sa colère/son dégoût** to stifle one's anger/swallow one's distaste
ravauder [ʀavode] /**1**/ VT to repair, mend
rave [ʀav] NF (Bot) rape
ravi, e [ʀavi] ADJ delighted; **être ~ de/que** to be delighted with/that
ravier [ʀavje] NM hors d'œuvre dish
ravigote [ʀavigɔt] ADJ: **sauce ~** oil and vinegar dressing with shallots

ravigoter [ʀavigɔte] /**1**/ VT (fam) to buck up
ravin [ʀavɛ̃] NM gully, ravine
raviner [ʀavine] /**1**/ VT to furrow, gully
ravioli [ʀavjɔli] NMPL ravioli sg
ravir [ʀaviʀ] /**2**/ VT (enchanter) to delight; (enlever): **~ qch à qn** to rob sb of sth; **à ~** adv delightfully, beautifully; **être beau à ~** to be ravishingly beautiful
raviser [ʀavize] /**1**/: **se raviser** VI to change one's mind
ravissant, e [ʀavisɑ̃, -ɑ̃t] ADJ delightful
ravissement [ʀavismɑ̃] NM (enchantement, délice) rapture
ravisseur, -euse [ʀavisœʀ, -øz] NM/F abductor, kidnapper
ravitaillement [ʀavitajmɑ̃] NM resupplying; refuelling; (provisions) supplies pl; **aller au ~** to go for fresh supplies; **~ en vol** (Aviat) in-flight refuelling
ravitailler [ʀavitaje] /**1**/ VT (en vivres, munitions) to provide with fresh supplies; (véhicule) to refuel; **se ravitailler** VI to get fresh supplies
raviver [ʀavive] /**1**/ VT (feu) to rekindle, revive; (douleur) to revive; (couleurs) to brighten up
ravoir [ʀavwaʀ] /**34**/ VT to get back
rayé, e [ʀeje] ADJ (à rayures) striped; (éraflé) scratched
rayer [ʀeje] /**8**/ VT (érafler) to scratch; (barrer) to cross ou score out; (d'une liste: radier) to cross ou strike off
rayon [ʀejɔ̃] NM (de soleil etc) ray; (Géom) radius; (de roue) spoke; (étagère) shelf; (de grand magasin) department; (fig: domaine) responsibility, concern; (de ruche) (honey)comb; **dans un ~ de** within a radius of; **rayons** NMPL (radiothérapie) radiation; **~ d'action** range; **~ de braquage** (Auto) turning circle; **~ laser** laser beam; **~ de soleil** sunbeam, ray of sunlight ou sunshine; **rayons X** X-rays
rayonnage [ʀejɔnaʒ] NM set of shelves
rayonnant, e [ʀejɔnɑ̃, -ɑ̃t] ADJ radiant
rayonne [ʀejɔn] NF rayon
rayonnement [ʀejɔnmɑ̃] NM radiation; (fig: éclat) radiance; (influence: d'une culture) influence
rayonner [ʀejɔne] /**1**/ VI (chaleur, énergie) to radiate; (fig: émotion) to shine forth; (: visage, personne) to be radiant; (avenues, axes) to radiate; (touriste) to go touring (from one base)
rayure [ʀejyʀ] NF (motif) stripe; (éraflure) scratch; (rainure, d'un fusil) groove; **à rayures** striped
raz-de-marée [ʀɑdmaʀe] NM INV tidal wave
razzia [ʀazja] NF raid, foray
RBE SIGLE M (= revenu brut d'exploitation) gross profit (of a farm)
R-D SIGLE F (= Recherche-Développement) R & D
RDA SIGLE F (Hist: = République démocratique allemande) GDR
rdc ABR = **rez-de-chaussée**
ré [ʀe] NM (Mus) D; (en chantant la gamme) re
réabonnement [ʀeabɔnmɑ̃] NM renewal of subscription
réabonner [ʀeabɔne] /**1**/ VT: **~ qn à** to renew sb's subscription to; **se ~ (à)** to renew one's subscription (to)

r

347

réac [Reak] ADJ, NMF (*fam*: = *réactionnaire*) reactionary

réacteur [Reaktœr] NM jet engine; ~ **nucléaire** nuclear reactor

réactif [Reaktif] NM reagent

réaction [Reaksjɔ̃] NF reaction; **par** ~ jet-propelled; **avion/moteur à** ~ jet (plane)/jet engine; ~ **en chaîne** chain reaction

réactionnaire [ReaksjɔnɛR] ADJ, NMF reactionary

réactualiser [Reaktɥalize] /**1**/ VT to update, bring up to date

réadaptation [Readaptasjɔ̃] NF readjustment; rehabilitation

réadapter [Readapte] /**1**/ VT to readjust; (*Méd*) to rehabilitate; **se** ~ **(à)** vi to readjust (to)

réaffirmer [Reafirme] /**1**/ VT to reaffirm, reassert

réagir [Reaʒir] /**2**/ VI to react

réajuster [Reaʒyste] /**1**/ VT = **rajuster**

réalisable [Realizabl] ADJ (*projet, plan*) feasible; (*Comm*: *valeur*) realizable

réalisateur, -trice [Realizatœr, -tRis] NM/F (TV, *Ciné*) director

réalisation [Realizasjɔ̃] NF carrying out; realization; fulfilment; achievement; (*Ciné*) production; (*œuvre*) production, work; (*création*) creation; **en cours de** ~ under way

réaliser [Realize] /**1**/ VT (*projet, opération*) to carry out, realize; (*rêve, souhait*) to realize, fulfil; (*exploit*) to achieve; (*achat, vente*) to make; (*film*) to produce; (*se rendre compte de, Comm: bien, capital*) to realize; **se réaliser** VI to be realized

réalisme [Realism] NM realism

réaliste [Realist] ADJ realistic; (*peintre, roman*) realist ▶ NMF realist

réalité [Realite] NF reality; **en** ~ in (actual) fact; **dans la** ~ in reality; ~ **virtuelle** virtual reality

réanimation [Reanimasjɔ̃] NF resuscitation; **service de** ~ intensive care unit

réanimer [Reanime] /**1**/ VT (*Méd*) to resuscitate

réapparaître [ReapaRɛtR] /**57**/ VI to reappear

réapparition [Reaparisjɔ̃] NF reappearance

réapprovisionner [ReapRovizjone] /**1**/ VT (*magasin*) to restock; **se** ~ **(en)** to restock (with)

réarmement [ReaRməmɑ̃] NM rearmament

réarmer [ReaRme] /**1**/ VT (*arme*) to reload ▶ VI (*état*) to rearm

réassortiment [ReasoRtimɑ̃] NM (*Comm*) restocking

réassortir [ReasoRtir] /**2**/ VT to match up

réassurance [Reasyrɑ̃s] NF reinsurance

réassurer [Reasyre] /**1**/ VT to reinsure

rebaptiser [Rəbatize] /**1**/ VT (*rue*) to rename

rébarbatif, -ive [Rebarbatif, -iv] ADJ forbidding; (*style*) off-putting (BRIT), crabbed

rebattre [RəbatR] /**41**/ VT: ~ **les oreilles à qn de qch** to keep harping on to sb about sth

rebattu, e [Rəbaty] PP de **rebattre** ▶ ADJ hackneyed

rebelle [Rəbɛl] NMF rebel ▶ ADJ (*troupes*) rebel; (*enfant*) rebellious; (*mèche etc*) unruly; ~ **à qch** unamenable to sth; ~ **à faire** unwilling to do

rebeller [Rəbele] /**1**/: **se rebeller** VI to rebel

rébellion [Rebeljɔ̃] NF rebellion; (*rebelles*) rebel forces pl

rebiffer [Rəbife] /**1**/: **se rebiffer** VR to fight back

reboisement [Rəbwazmɑ̃] NM reafforestation

reboiser [Rəbwaze] /**1**/ VT to replant with trees, reafforest

rebond [Rəbɔ̃] NM (*voir rebondir*) bounce; rebound

rebondi, e [Rəbɔ̃di] ADJ (*ventre*) rounded; (*joues*) chubby, well-rounded

rebondir [Rəbɔ̃dir] /**2**/ VI (*ballon*: *au sol*) to bounce; (: *contre un mur*) to rebound; (*fig*: *procès, action, conversation*) to get moving again, be suddenly revived

rebondissement [Rəbɔ̃dismɑ̃] NM new development

rebord [RəboR] NM edge; **le** ~ **de la fenêtre** the windowsill

reboucher [Rəbuʃe] /**1**/ VT (*flacon*) to put the stopper (*ou* top) back on, recork; (*trou*) to stop up

rebours [RəbuR] : **à** ~ adv the wrong way

rebouteux, -euse [Rəbutø, -øz] NM/F (*péj*) bonesetter

reboutonner [Rəbutone] /**1**/ VT (*vêtement*) to button up (again)

rebrousse-poil [RəbRuspwal] : **à** ~ adv the wrong way

rebrousser [RəbRuse] /**1**/ VT (*cheveux, poils*) to brush back, brush up; ~ **chemin** to turn back

rebuffade [Rəbyfad] NF rebuff

rébus [Rebys] NM INV (*jeu d'esprit*) rebus; (*fig*) puzzle

rebut [Rəby] NM: **mettre au** ~ to scrap, discard

rebutant, e [Rəbytɑ̃, -ɑ̃t] ADJ (*travail, démarche*) off-putting, disagreeable

rebuter [Rəbyte] /**1**/ VT to put off

récalcitrant, e [Rekalsitrɑ̃, -ɑ̃t] ADJ refractory, recalcitrant

recaler [Rəkale] /**1**/ VT (*Scol*) to fail

récapitulatif, -ive [Rekapitylatif, -iv] ADJ (*liste, tableau*) summary cpd, that sums up

récapituler [Rekapityle] /**1**/ VT to recapitulate; (*résumer*) to sum up

recel [Rəsɛl] NM receiving (stolen goods)

receler [Rəsəle] /**5**/ VT (*produit d'un vol*) to receive; (*malfaiteur*) to harbour; (*fig*) to conceal

receleur, -euse [Rəsəlœr, -øz] NM/F receiver

récemment [Resamɑ̃] ADV recently

recensement [Rəsɑ̃smɑ̃] NM census; inventory

recenser [Rəsɑ̃se] /**1**/ VT (*population*) to take a census of; (*inventorier*) to make an inventory of; (*dénombrer*) to list

récent, e [Resɑ̃, -ɑ̃t] ADJ recent

récépissé [Resepise] NM receipt

réceptacle [Resɛptakl] NM (*où les choses aboutissent*) recipient; (*où les choses sont stockées*) repository; (*Bot*) receptacle

récepteur, -trice [Resɛptœr, -tRis] ADJ receiving ▶ NM receiver; ~ **(de radio)** radio set *ou* receiver

réceptif, -ive [Resɛptif, -iv] ADJ: ~ **(à)** receptive (to)

réception [Resɛpsjɔ̃] NF receiving *no pl*; (*d'une marchandise, commande*) receipt; (*accueil*) reception, welcome; (*bureau*) reception (desk); (*réunion mondaine*) reception, party; (*pièces*) reception rooms *pl*; (*Sport: après un saut*) landing; (*du ballon*) catching *no pl*; **jour/heures de** ~ day/hours for receiving visitors (*ou students etc*)

réceptionner [ʀesɛpsjɔne] /**1**/ ᴠᴛ (*Comm*) to take delivery of; (*Sport: ballon*) to catch (and control)

réceptionniste [ʀesɛpsjɔnist] ɴᴍꜰ receptionist

réceptivité [ʀesɛptivite] ɴꜰ (*à une influence*) receptiveness; (*à une maladie*) susceptibility

récessif, -ive [ʀesesif, -iv] ᴀᴅᴊ (*Bio*) recessive

récession [ʀesesjɔ̃] ɴꜰ recession

recette [ʀəsɛt] ɴꜰ (*Culin*) recipe; (*fig*) formula, recipe; (*Comm*) takings *pl*; (*Admin: bureau*) tax *ou* revenue office; **recettes** ɴꜰᴘʟ (*Comm: rentrées*) receipts; **faire** ~ (*spectacle, exposition*) to be a winner

receveur, -euse [ʀəsvœʀ, -øz] ɴᴍ/ꜰ (*des contributions*) tax collector; (*des postes*) postmaster/mistress; (*d'autobus*) conductor/conductress; (*Méd: de sang, organe*) recipient

recevoir [ʀəsvwaʀ] /**28**/ ᴠᴛ to receive; (*lettre, prime*) to receive, get; (*client, patient, représentant*) to see; (*jour, soleil, pièce*) to get; (*Scol: candidat*) to pass ▶ ᴠɪ to receive visitors; to give parties; to see patients *etc*; **se recevoir** ᴠɪ (*athlète*) to land; ~ **qn à dîner** to invite sb to dinner; **il reçoit de huit à 10** he's at home from eight to 10, he will see visitors from eight to 10; (*docteur, dentiste etc*) he sees patients from eight to 10; **être reçu** (*à un examen*) to pass; **être bien/mal reçu** to be well/badly received

rechange [ʀəʃɑ̃ʒ]: **de** ~ *adj* (*pièces, roue*) spare; (*fig: solution*) alternative; **des vêtements de** ~ a change of clothes

rechaper [ʀəʃape] /**1**/ ᴠᴛ to remould (ʙʀɪᴛ), remold (ᴜs), retread

réchapper [ʀeʃape] /**1**/: ~ **de** *ou* **à** *vt* (*accident, maladie*) to come through; **va-t-il en** ~? is he going to get over it?, is he going to come through (it)?

recharge [ʀəʃaʀʒ] ɴꜰ refill

rechargeable [ʀəʃaʀʒabl] ᴀᴅᴊ (*stylo etc*) refillable; rechargeable

recharger [ʀəʃaʀʒe] /**3**/ ᴠᴛ (*camion, fusil, appareil photo*) to reload; (*briquet, stylo*) to refill; (*batterie*) to recharge

réchaud [ʀeʃo] ɴᴍ (portable) stove, plate-warmer

réchauffé [ʀeʃofe] ɴᴍ (*nourriture*) reheated food; (*fig*) stale news (*ou* joke *etc*)

réchauffement [ʀeʃofmɑ̃] ɴᴍ warming (up); **le** ~ **de la planète** global warming

réchauffer [ʀeʃofe] /**1**/ ᴠᴛ (*plat*) to reheat; (*mains, personne*) to warm; **se réchauffer** ᴠɪ (*température*) to get warmer; (*personne*) to warm o.s. (up); **se réchauffer les doigts** to warm (up) one's fingers

rêche [ʀɛʃ] ᴀᴅᴊ rough

recherche [ʀəʃɛʀʃ] ɴꜰ (*action*): **la** ~ **de** the search for; (*raffinement*) affectedness, studied elegance; (*scientifique etc*): **la** ~ research; **recherches** ɴꜰᴘʟ (*de la police*) investigations; (*scientifiques*) research *sg*; **être/se mettre à la** ~ **de** to be/go in search of

recherché, e [ʀəʃɛʀʃe] ᴀᴅᴊ (*rare, demandé*) much

sought-after; (*entouré: acteur, femme*) in demand; (*raffiné*) studied, affected; (*tenue*) elegant

rechercher [ʀəʃɛʀʃe] /**1**/ ᴠᴛ (*objet égaré, personne*) to look for, search for; (*témoins, coupable, main-d'œuvre*) to look for; (*causes d'un phénomène, nouveau procédé*) to try to find; (*bonheur etc, l'amitié de qn*) to seek; **"~ et remplacer"** (*Inform*) "find and replace"

rechigner [ʀəʃiɲe] /**1**/ ᴠɪ: ~ (**à**) to balk (at)

rechute [ʀəʃyt] ɴꜰ (*Méd*) relapse; (*dans le péché, le vice*) lapse; **faire une** ~ to have a relapse

rechuter [ʀəʃyte] /**1**/ ᴠɪ (*Méd*) to relapse

récidive [ʀesidiv] ɴꜰ (*Jur*) second (*ou* subsequent) offence; (*fig*) repetition; (*Méd*) recurrence

récidiver [ʀesidive] /**1**/ ᴠɪ to commit a second (*ou* subsequent) offence; (*fig*) to do it again

récidiviste [ʀesidivist] ɴᴍꜰ second (*ou* habitual) offender, recidivist

récif [ʀesif] ɴᴍ reef

récipiendaire [ʀesipjɑ̃dɛʀ] ɴᴍ recipient (*of diploma etc*); (*d'une société*) newly elected member

récipient [ʀesipjɑ̃] ɴᴍ container

réciproque [ʀesipʀɔk] ᴀᴅᴊ reciprocal ▶ ɴꜰ: **la** ~ (*l'inverse*) the converse

réciproquement [ʀesipʀɔkmɑ̃] ᴀᴅᴠ reciprocally; **et** ~ and vice versa

récit [ʀesi] ɴᴍ (*action de narrer*) telling; (*conte, histoire*) story

récital [ʀesital] ɴᴍ recital

récitant, e [ʀesitɑ̃, -ɑ̃t] ɴᴍ/ꜰ narrator

récitation [ʀesitasjɔ̃] ɴꜰ recitation

réciter [ʀesite] /**1**/ ᴠᴛ to recite

réclamation [ʀeklamasjɔ̃] ɴꜰ complaint; **réclamations** ɴꜰᴘʟ (*bureau*) complaints department *sg*

réclame [ʀeklam] ɴꜰ: **la** ~ advertising; **une** ~ an ad(vertisement), an advert (ʙʀɪᴛ); **faire de la** ~ (**pour qch/qn**) to advertise (sth/sb); **article en** ~ special offer

réclamer [ʀeklame] /**1**/ ᴠᴛ (*aide, nourriture etc*) to ask for; (*revendiquer: dû, part, indemnité*) to claim, demand; (*nécessiter*) to demand, require ▶ ᴠɪ to complain; **se** ~ **de** to give as one's authority; to claim filiation with

reclassement [ʀəklasmɑ̃] ɴᴍ reclassifying; regrading; rehabilitation

reclasser [ʀəklase] /**1**/ ᴠᴛ (*fiches, dossiers*) to reclassify; (*fig: fonctionnaire etc*) to regrade; (: *ouvrier licencié*) to place, rehabilitate

reclus, e [ʀəkly, -yz] ɴᴍ/ꜰ recluse

réclusion [ʀeklyzjɔ̃] ɴꜰ imprisonment; ~ **à perpétuité** life imprisonment

recoiffer [ʀəkwafe] /**1**/ ᴠᴛ: ~ **un enfant** to do a child's hair again; **se recoiffer** to do one's hair again

recoin [ʀəkwɛ̃] ɴᴍ nook, corner; (*fig*) hidden recess

reçois *etc* [ʀəswa] ᴠʙ *voir* **recevoir**

reçoive *etc* [ʀəswav] ᴠʙ *voir* **recevoir**

recoller [ʀəkɔle] /**1**/ ᴠᴛ (*enveloppe*) to stick back down

récolte [ʀekɔlt] ɴꜰ harvesting, gathering; (*produits*) harvest, crop; (*fig*) crop, collection; (: *d'observations*) findings

récolter [Rekɔlte] /**1**/ VT to harvest, gather (in); (*fig*) to get

recommandable [Rəkɔmɑ̃dabl] ADJ commendable; **peu ~** not very commendable

recommandation [Rəkɔmɑ̃dasjɔ̃] NF recommendation

recommandé [Rəkɔmɑ̃de] NM (*méthode etc*) recommended; (*Postes*): **en ~** by registered mail

recommander [Rəkɔmɑ̃de] /**1**/ VT to recommend; (*qualités etc*) to commend; (*Postes*) to register; **~ qch à qn** to recommend sth to sb; **~ à qn de faire** to recommend sb to do; **~ qn auprès de qn** *ou* **à qn** to recommend sb to sb; **il est recommandé de faire ...** it is recommended that one does ...; **se ~ à qn** to commend o.s. to sb; **se ~ de qn** to give sb's name as a reference

recommencer [Rəkɔmɑ̃se] /**3**/ VT (*reprendre: lutte, séance*) to resume, start again; (*refaire: travail, explications*) to start afresh, start (over) again; (*récidiver: erreur*) to make again ▶ VI to start again; (*récidiver*) to do it again; **~ à faire** to start doing again; **ne recommence pas!** don't do that again!

récompense [Rekɔ̃pɑ̃s] NF reward; (*prix*) award; **recevoir qch en ~** to get sth as a reward, be rewarded with sth

récompenser [Rekɔ̃pɑ̃se] /**1**/ VT: **~ qn (de** *ou* **pour)** to reward sb (for)

réconciliation [Rekɔ̃siljasjɔ̃] NF reconciliation

réconcilier [Rekɔ̃silje] /**7**/ VT to reconcile; **se réconcilier (avec)** to be reconciled (with); **~ qn avec qn** to reconcile sb with sb; **~ qn avec qch** to reconcile sb to sth

reconductible [Rəkɔ̃dyktibl] ADJ (*Jur: contrat, bail*) renewable

reconduction [Rəkɔ̃dyksjɔ̃] NF renewal; (*Pol: d'une politique*) continuation

reconduire [Rəkɔ̃dɥiʀ] /**38**/ VT (*raccompagner*) to take *ou* see back; (: *à la porte*) to show out; (: *à son domicile*) to see home, take home; (*Jur, Pol: renouveler*) to renew

réconfort [Rekɔ̃fɔʀ] NM comfort

réconfortant, e [Rekɔ̃fɔʀtɑ̃, -ɑ̃t] ADJ (*idée, paroles*) comforting; (*boisson*) fortifying

réconforter [Rekɔ̃fɔʀte] /**1**/ VT (*consoler*) to comfort; (*revigorer*) to fortify

reconnais *etc* [R(ə)kɔnɛ] VB *voir* **reconnaître**

reconnaissable [Rəkɔnɛsabl] ADJ recognizable

reconnaissance [Rəkɔnɛsɑ̃s] NF (*action de reconnaître*) recognition; acknowledgement; (*gratitude*) gratitude, gratefulness; (*Mil*) reconnaissance, recce; **en ~** (*Mil*) on reconnaissance; **~ de dette** acknowledgement of a debt, IOU

reconnaissant, e [Rəkɔnɛsɑ̃, -ɑ̃t] VB *voir* **reconnaître** ▶ ADJ grateful; **je vous serais ~ de bien vouloir** I should be most grateful if you would (kindly)

reconnaître [Rəkɔnɛtʀ] /**57**/ VT to recognize; (*Mil: lieu*) to reconnoitre; (*Jur: enfant, dette, droit*) to acknowledge; **~ que** to admit *ou* acknowledge that; **~ qn/qch à** (*l'identifier grâce à*) to recognize sb/sth by; **je lui reconnais**

certaines qualités I recognize certain qualities in him; **se ~ quelque part** (*s'y retrouver*) to find one's way around (a place)

reconnu, e [R(ə)kɔny] PP *de* **reconnaître** ▶ ADJ (*indiscuté, connu*) recognized

reconquérir [Rəkɔ̃keʀiʀ] /**21**/ VT to reconquer, recapture; (*sa dignité etc*) to recover

reconquête [Rəkɔ̃kɛt] NF recapture; recovery

reconsidérer [Rəkɔ̃sidere] /**6**/ VT to reconsider

reconstituant, e [Rəkɔ̃stitɥɑ̃, -ɑ̃t] ADJ (*régime*) strength-building ▶ NM tonic, pick-me-up

reconstituer [Rəkɔ̃stitɥe] /**1**/ VT (*monument ancien*) to recreate, build a replica of; (*fresque, vase brisé*) to piece together, reconstitute; (*événement, accident*) to reconstruct; (*fortune, patrimoine*) to rebuild; (*Bio: tissus etc*) to regenerate

reconstitution [Rəkɔ̃stitysjɔ̃] NF (*d'un accident etc*) reconstruction

reconstruction [Rəkɔ̃stʀyksjɔ̃] NF rebuilding, reconstruction

reconstruire [Rəkɔ̃stʀɥiʀ] /**38**/ VT to rebuild, reconstruct

reconversion [Rəkɔ̃vɛʀsjɔ̃] NF (*du personnel*) redeployment

reconvertir [Rəkɔ̃vɛʀtiʀ] /**2**/ VT (*usine*) to reconvert; (*personnel, troupes etc*) to redeploy; **se ~ dans** (*un métier, une branche*) to move into, be redeployed into

recopier [Rəkɔpje] /**7**/ VT (*transcrire*) to copy out again, write out again; (*mettre au propre: devoir*) to make a clean *ou* fair copy of

record [Rəkɔʀ] NM, ADJ record; **~ du monde** world record

recoucher [Rəkuʃe] /**1**/ VT (*enfant*) to put back to bed

recoudre [Rəkudʀ] /**48**/ VT (*bouton*) to sew back on; (*plaie, incision*) to sew (back) up, stitch up

recoupement [Rəkupmɑ̃] NM: **faire un ~** *ou* **des recoupements** to cross-check; **par ~** by cross-checking

recouper [Rəkupe] /**1**/ VT (*tranche*) to cut again; (*vêtement*) to recut ▶ VI (*Cartes*) to cut again; **se recouper** VI (*témoignages*) to tie *ou* match up

recourais *etc* [Rəkuʀɛ] VB *voir* **recourir**

recourbé, e [Rəkuʀbe] ADJ curved; hooked; bent

recourber [Rəkuʀbe] /**1**/ VT (*branche, tige de métal*) to bend; **se recourber** VI to curve (up), bend (up)

recourir [Rəkuʀiʀ] /**11**/ VI (*courir de nouveau*) to run again; (*refaire une course*) to race again; **~ à** VT (*ami, agence*) to turn *ou* appeal to; (*force, ruse, emprunt*) to resort to, have recourse to

recours [Rəkuʀ] VB *voir* **recourir** ▶ NM (*Jur*) appeal; **avoir ~ à** = **recourir à**; **en dernier ~** as a last resort; **sans ~** final; with no way out; **~ en grâce** plea for clemency (*ou* pardon)

recouru, e [Rəkuʀy] PP *de* **recourir**

recousu, e [Rəkuzy] PP *de* **recoudre**

recouvert, e [Rəkuvɛʀ, -ɛʀt] PP *de* **recouvrir**

recouvrable [Rəkuvʀabl] ADJ (*somme*) recoverable

recouvrais *etc* [Rəkuvʀɛ] VB *voir* **recouvrer**; **recouvrir**

recouvrement [Rəkuvʀəmɑ̃] NM recovery

recouvrer [ʀəkuvʀe] /**1**/ vt (*vue, santé etc*) to recover, regain; (*impôts*) to collect; (*créance*) to recover

recouvrir [ʀəkuvʀiʀ] /**18**/ vt (*couvrir à nouveau*) to re-cover; (*couvrir entièrement: aussi fig*) to cover; (*cacher, masquer*) to conceal, hide; **se recouvrir** (*se superposer*) to overlap

recracher [ʀəkʀaʃe] /**1**/ vt to spit out

récréatif, -ive [ʀekʀeatif, -iv] ADJ of entertainment; recreational

récréation [ʀekʀeasjɔ̃] NF recreation, entertainment; (*Scol*) break

recréer [ʀəkʀee] /**1**/ vt to recreate

récrier [ʀekʀije] /**7**/: **se récrier** vi to exclaim

récriminations [ʀekʀiminasjɔ̃] NFPL remonstrations, complaints

récriminer [ʀekʀimine] /**1**/ vi: **~ contre qn/qch** to remonstrate against sb/sth

recroqueviller [ʀəkʀɔkvije] /**1**/: **se recroqueviller** vi (*feuilles*) to curl ou shrivel up; (*personne*) to huddle up

recru, e [ʀəkʀy] ADJ: **~ de fatigue** exhausted ▶ NF recruit

recrudescence [ʀəkʀydesɑ̃s] NF fresh outbreak

recrutement [ʀəkʀytmɑ̃] NM recruiting, recruitment

recruter [ʀəkʀyte] /**1**/ vt to recruit

rectal, e, -aux [ʀɛktal, -o] ADJ: **par voie ~** rectally

rectangle [ʀɛktɑ̃gl] NM rectangle

rectangulaire [ʀɛktɑ̃gylɛʀ] ADJ rectangular

recteur [ʀɛktœʀ] NM ≈ (regional) director of education (BRIT), ≈ state superintendent of education (US)

rectificatif, -ive [ʀɛktifikatif, -iv] ADJ corrected ▶ NM correction

rectification [ʀɛktifikasjɔ̃] NF correction

rectifier [ʀɛktifje] /**7**/ vt (*tracé, virage*) to straighten; (*calcul, adresse*) to correct; (*erreur, faute*) to rectify, put right

rectiligne [ʀɛktiliɲ] ADJ straight; (*Géom*) rectilinear

rectitude [ʀɛktityd] NF rectitude, uprightness

recto [ʀɛkto] NM front (*of a sheet of paper*); **~ verso** on both sides (of the page)

rectorat [ʀɛktɔʀa] NM (*fonction*) position of recteur; (*bureau*) recteur's office; *voir aussi* **recteur**

rectum [ʀɛktɔm] NM rectum

reçu, e [ʀəsy] PP *de* **recevoir** ▶ ADJ (*candidat*) successful; (*admis, consacré*) accepted ▶ NM (*Comm*) receipt

recueil [ʀəkœj] NM collection

recueillement [ʀəkœjmɑ̃] NM meditation, contemplation

recueilli, e [ʀəkœji] ADJ contemplative

recueillir [ʀəkœjiʀ] /**12**/ vt to collect; (*voix, suffrages*) to win; (*accueillir: réfugiés, chat*) to take in; **se recueillir** vi to gather one's thoughts; to meditate

recuire [ʀəkɥiʀ] /**38**/ vi: **faire ~** to recook

recul [ʀəkyl] NM retreat; recession; (*déclin*) decline; (*éloignement*) distance; (*d'arme à feu*) recoil, kick; **avoir un mouvement de ~** to recoil, start back; **prendre du ~** to stand back;

être en ~ to be on the decline; **avec le ~** with the passing of time, in retrospect

reculade [ʀəkylad] NF (*péj*) climb-down

reculé, e [ʀəkyle] ADJ remote

reculer [ʀəkyle] /**1**/ vi to move back, back away; (*Auto*) to reverse, back (up); (*fig: civilisation, épidémie*) to be on the decline; (: *se dérober*) to shrink back ▶ vt to move back; (*véhicule*) to reverse, back (up); (*fig: possibilités, limites*) to extend; (: *date, décision*) to postpone; **~ devant** (*danger, difficulté*) to shrink from; **~ pour mieux sauter** (*fig*) to postpone the evil day

reculons [ʀəkylɔ̃]: **à ~** adv backwards

récupérable [ʀekypeʀabl] ADJ (*créance*) recoverable; (*heures*) which can be made up; (*ferraille*) salvageable

récupération [ʀekypeʀasjɔ̃] NF (*de métaux etc*) salvage, reprocessing; (*Pol*) hijacking (*of policies*)

récupérer [ʀekypeʀe] /**6**/ vt (*rentrer en possession de*) to recover, get back; (: *forces*) to recover; (*déchets etc*) to salvage (for reprocessing); (*remplacer: journée, heures de travail*) to make up; (*délinquant etc*) to rehabilitate; (*Pol*) to hijack (*policies*) ▶ vi to recover

récurer [ʀekyʀe] /**1**/ vt to scour; **poudre à ~** scouring powder

reçus *etc* [ʀəsy] VB *voir* **recevoir**

récusable [ʀekyzabl] ADJ (*témoin*) challengeable; (*témoignage*) impugnable

récuser [ʀekyze] /**1**/ vt to challenge; **se récuser** to decline to give an opinion

recyclage [ʀəsiklaʒ] NM reorientation; retraining; recycling; **cours de ~** retraining course

recycler [ʀəsikle] /**1**/ vt (*Scol*) to reorientate; (*employés*) to retrain; (*matériau*) to recycle; **se recycler** vi to retrain; to go on a retraining course

rédacteur, -trice [ʀedaktœʀ, -tʀis] NM/F (*journaliste*) writer; subeditor; (*d'ouvrage de référence*) editor, compiler; **~ en chef** chief editor; **~ publicitaire** copywriter

rédaction [ʀedaksjɔ̃] NF writing; (*rédacteurs*) editorial staff; (*bureau*) editorial office(s); (*Scol: devoir*) essay, composition

reddition [ʀedisjɔ̃] NF surrender

redéfinir [ʀədefiniʀ] /**2**/ vt to redefine

redemander [ʀədmɑ̃de] /**1**/ vt (*renseignement*) to ask again for; (*objet prêté*): **~ qch** to ask for sth back; **~ de** (*nourriture*) to ask for more (ou another)

redémarrer [ʀədemaʀe] /**1**/ vi (*véhicule*) to start again, get going again; (*fig: industrie etc*) to get going again

rédemption [ʀedɑ̃psjɔ̃] NF redemption

redéploiement [ʀədeplwamɑ̃] NM redeployment

redescendre [ʀədesɑ̃dʀ] /**41**/ vi (*à nouveau*) to go back down; (*après la montée*) to go down (again) ▶ vt (*pente etc*) to go down

redevable [ʀədvabl] ADJ: **être ~ de qch à qn** (*somme*) to owe sb sth; (*fig*) to be indebted to sb for sth

redevance [ʀədvɑ̃s] NF (*Tél*) rental charge; (*TV*) licence (BRIT) *ou* license (US) fee

r

redevenir [ʀədvəniʀ] /**22**/ vɪ to become again

rédhibitoire [ʀedibitwaʀ] ADJ: **vice ~** (Jur) latent defect in merchandise that renders the sales contract void; (fig: défaut) crippling

rediffuser [ʀədifyze] /**1**/ vᴛ (Radio, TV) to repeat, broadcast again

rediffusion [ʀədifyzjɔ̃] NF repeat (programme)

rédiger [ʀediʒe] /**3**/ vᴛ to write; (contrat) to draw up

redire [ʀədiʀ] /**37**/ vᴛ to repeat; **trouver à ~ à** to find fault with

redistribuer [ʀədistʀibɥe] /**1**/ vᴛ (cartes etc) to deal again; (richesses, tâches, revenus) to redistribute

redite [ʀədit] NF (needless) repetition

redondance [ʀədɔ̃dɑ̃s] NF redundancy

redonner [ʀədɔne] /**1**/ vᴛ (restituer) to give back, return; (du courage, des forces) to restore

redoublé, e [ʀəduble] ADJ: **à coups redoublés** even harder, twice as hard

redoubler [ʀəduble] /**1**/ vɪ (tempête, violence) to intensify, get even stronger ou fiercer etc; (Scol) to repeat a year ▸ vᴛ (Scol: classe) to repeat; (Ling: lettre) to double; **le vent redouble de violence** the wind is blowing twice as hard; **~ de patience/prudence** to be doubly patient/careful

redoutable [ʀədutabl] ADJ formidable, fearsome

redouter [ʀədute] /**1**/ vᴛ to fear; (appréhender) to dread; **~ de faire** to dread doing

redoux [ʀədu] NM milder spell

redressement [ʀədʀɛsmɑ̃] NM (économique) recovery; (de l'économie etc) putting right; **maison de ~** reformatory; **~ fiscal** repayment of back taxes

redresser [ʀədʀese] /**1**/ vᴛ (arbre, mât) to set upright, right; (pièce tordue) to straighten out; (Aviat, Auto) to straighten up; (situation, économie) to put right; **se redresser** vɪ (objet penché) to right itself; to straighten up; (personne) to sit (ou stand) up; to sit (ou stand) up straight; (fig: pays, situation) to recover; **~ (les roues)** (Auto) to straighten up

redresseur [ʀədʀesœʀ] NM: **~ de torts** righter of wrongs

réducteur, -trice [ʀedyktœʀ, -tʀis] ADJ simplistic

réduction [ʀedyksjɔ̃] NF reduction; **en ~** adv in miniature, scaled-down

réduire [ʀedɥiʀ] /**38**/ vᴛ (gén, Culin, Math) to reduce; (prix, dépenses) to cut, reduce; (carte) to scale down, reduce; (Méd: fracture) to set; **~ qn/qch à** to reduce sb/sth to; **se ~ à** (revenir à) to boil down to; **se ~ en** (se transformer en) to be reduced to; **en être réduit à** to be reduced to

réduit, e [ʀedɥi, -it] PP de **réduire** ▸ ADJ (prix, tarif, échelle) reduced; (mécanisme) scaled-down; (vitesse) reduced ▸ NM tiny room; recess

rééditer [ʀeedite] /**1**/ vᴛ to republish

réédition [ʀeedisjɔ̃] NF new edition

rééducation [ʀeedykasjɔ̃] NF (d'un membre) re-education; (de délinquants, d'un blessé) rehabilitation; **~ de la parole** speech therapy;

centre de ~ physiotherapy ou physical therapy (US) centre

rééduquer [ʀeedyke] /**1**/ vᴛ to reeducate; to rehabilitate

réel, le [ʀeɛl] ADJ real ▸ NM: **le ~** reality

réélection [ʀeelɛksjɔ̃] NF re-election

rééligible [ʀeeliʒibl] ADJ re-eligible

réélire [ʀeeliʀ] /**43**/ vᴛ to re-elect

réellement [ʀeɛlmɑ̃] ADV really

réembaucher [ʀeɑ̃boʃe] /**1**/ vᴛ to take on again

réemploi [ʀeɑ̃plwa] NM = **remploi**

réemployer [ʀeɑ̃plwaje] /**8**/ vᴛ (méthode, produit) to re-use; (argent) to reinvest; (personnel, employé) to re-employ

rééquilibrer [ʀeekilibʀe] /**1**/ vᴛ (budget) to balance (again)

réescompte [ʀeeskɔ̃t] NM rediscount

réessayer [ʀeeseje] /**8**/ vᴛ to try on again

réévaluation [ʀeevalɥasjɔ̃] NF revaluation

réévaluer [ʀeevalɥe] /**1**/ vᴛ to revalue

réexaminer [ʀeɛgzamine] /**1**/ vᴛ to re-examine

réexpédier [ʀeɛkspedje] /**7**/ vᴛ (à l'envoyeur) to return, send back; (au destinataire) to send on, forward

réexporter [ʀeɛkspɔʀte] /**1**/ vᴛ to re-export

réf. ABR = **référence(s)**; **V/réf.** Your ref

refaire [ʀəfɛʀ] /**60**/ vᴛ (faire de nouveau, recommencer) to do again; (sport) to take up again; (réparer, restaurer) to do up; **se refaire** vɪ (en argent) to make up one's losses; **se refaire une santé** to recuperate; **se refaire à qch** (se réhabituer à) to get used to sth again

refasse etc [ʀəfas] vʙ voir **refaire**

réfection [ʀefɛksjɔ̃] NF repair; **en ~** under repair

réfectoire [ʀefɛktwaʀ] NM refectory

referai etc [ʀ(ə)fʀe] vʙ voir **refaire**

référé [ʀefeʀe] NM (Jur) emergency interim proceedings ou ruling

référence [ʀefeʀɑ̃s] NF reference; **références** NFPL (recommandations) reference sg; **faire ~ à** to refer to; **ouvrage de ~** reference work; **ce n'est pas une ~** (fig) that's no recommendation

référendum [ʀefeʀɑ̃dɔm] NM referendum

référer [ʀefeʀe] /**6**/: **se ~ à** vᴛ to refer to; **en ~ à qn** to refer the matter to sb

refermer [ʀəfɛʀme] /**1**/ vᴛ to close again, shut again; **se refermer** vɪ (porte) to close ou shut (again)

refiler [ʀəfile] /**1**/ vᴛ (fam): **~ qch à qn** to palm (Bʀɪᴛ) ou fob sth off on sb; to pass sth on to sb

refit etc [ʀəfi] vʙ voir **refaire**

réfléchi, e [ʀefleʃi] ADJ (caractère) thoughtful; (action) well-thought-out; (Ling) reflexive; **c'est tout ~** my mind's made up

réfléchir [ʀefleʃiʀ] /**2**/ vᴛ to reflect ▸ vɪ to think; **~ à ou sur** to think about

réflecteur [ʀeflɛktœʀ] NM (Auto) reflector

reflet [ʀəflɛ] NM reflection; (sur l'eau etc) sheen no pl, glint; **reflets** NMPL gleam sg

refléter [ʀəflete] /**6**/ vᴛ to reflect; **se refléter** vɪ to be reflected

réflex [ʀeflɛks] ADJ INV (Photo) reflex

réflexe [Reflɛks] ADJ, NM reflex; ~ **conditionné** conditioned reflex

réflexion [Reflɛksjɔ̃] NF (*de la lumière etc, pensée*) reflection; (*fait de penser*) thought; (*remarque*) remark; **réflexions** NFPL (*méditations*) thought *sg*, reflection *sg*; **sans** ~ without thinking; ~ **faite, à la** ~, **après** ~ on reflection; **délai de** ~ cooling-off period; **groupe de** ~ think tank

réflexologie [Reflɛksɔlɔʒi] NF reflexology

refluer [Rəflye] /**1**/ VI to flow back; (*foule*) to surge back

reflux [Rəfly] NM (*de la mer*) ebb; (*fig*) backward surge

refondre [Rəfɔ̃dR] /**41**/ VT (*texte*) to recast

refont [R(ə)fɔ̃] VB *voir* **refaire**

reformater [RəfɔRmate] /**1**/ VT to reformat

réformateur, -trice [RefɔRmatœR, -tRis] NM/F reformer ▶ ADJ (*mesures*) reforming

Réformation [RefɔRmasjɔ̃] NF: **la** ~ the Reformation

réforme [RefɔRm] NF reform; (*Mil*) declaration of unfitness for service; discharge (*on health grounds*); (*Rel*): **la R**~ the Reformation

réformé, e [RefɔRme] ADJ, NM/F (*Rel*) Protestant

reformer [RəfɔRme] /**1**/ VT, **se reformer** VI to reform; ~ **les rangs** (*Mil*) to fall in again

réformer [RefɔRme] /**1**/ VT to reform; (*Mil: recrue*) to declare unfit for service; (*: soldat*) to discharge, invalid out; (*matériel*) to scrap

réformisme [RefɔRmism] NM reformism, policy of reform

réformiste [RefɔRmist] ADJ, NMF (*Pol*) reformist

refoulé, e [Rəfule] ADJ (*Psych*) repressed

refoulement [Rəfulmɑ̃] NM (*d'une armée*) driving back; (*Psych*) repression

refouler [Rəfule] /**1**/ VT (*envahisseurs*) to drive back, repulse; (*liquide, larmes*) to force back; (*fig*) to suppress; (*Psych: désir, colère*) to repress

réfractaire [RefRaktɛR] ADJ (*minerai*) refractory; (*brique*) fire *cpd*; (*maladie*) which is resistant to treatment; (*prêtre*) nonjuring; **soldat** ~ draft evader; **être** ~ **à** to resist

réfracter [RefRakte] /**1**/ VT to refract

réfraction [RefRaksjɔ̃] NF refraction

refrain [RəfRɛ̃] NM (*Mus*) refrain, chorus; (*air, fig*) tune

refréner, réfréner [RəfRene, RefRene] /**6**/ VT to curb, check

réfrigérant, e [RefRiʒeRɑ̃, -ɑ̃t] ADJ refrigerant, cooling

réfrigérateur [RefRiʒeRatœR] NM refrigerator; ~-**congélateur** fridge-freezer

réfrigération [RefRiʒeRasjɔ̃] NF refrigeration

réfrigéré, e [RefRiʒeRe] ADJ (*camion, wagon*) refrigerated

réfrigérer [RefRiʒeRe] /**6**/ VT to refrigerate; (*fam: glacer: aussi: fig*) to cool

refroidir [RəfRwadiR] /**2**/ VT to cool; (*fig*) to have a cooling effect on; (*: personne*) to put off ▶ VI to cool (down); **se refroidir** VI (*prendre froid*) to catch a chill; (*temps*) to get cooler *ou* colder; (*fig: ardeur*) to cool (off)

refroidissement [RəfRwadismɑ̃] NM cooling; (*grippe etc*) chill

refuge [Rəfyʒ] NM refuge; (*pour piétons*) (traffic) island; **demander** ~ **à qn** to ask sb for refuge

réfugié, e [Refyʒje] ADJ, NM/F refugee

réfugier [Refyʒje] /**7**/: **se réfugier** VI to take refuge

refus [Rəfy] NM refusal; **ce n'est pas de** ~ I won't say no, it's very welcome

refuser [Rəfyze] /**1**/ VT to refuse; (*Scol: candidat*) to fail ▶ VI to refuse; ~ **qch à qn/de faire** to refuse sb sth/to do; ~ **du monde** to have to turn people away; **se** ~ **à qch** *ou* **à faire qch** to refuse to do sth; **il ne se refuse rien** he doesn't stint himself; **se** ~ **à qn** to refuse sb

réfutable [Refytabl] ADJ refutable

réfuter [Refyte] /**1**/ VT to refute

regagner [Rəgaɲe] /**1**/ VT (*argent, faveur*) to win back; (*lieu*) to get back to; ~ **le temps perdu** to make up for lost time; ~ **du terrain** to regain ground

regain [Rəgɛ̃] NM (*herbe*) second crop of hay; (*renouveau*): ~ **de qch** renewed sth

régal [Regal] NM treat; **un** ~ **pour les yeux** a pleasure *ou* delight to look at

régalade [Regalad] ADV: **à la** ~ from the bottle (held away from the lips)

régaler [Regale] /**1**/ VT: ~ **qn** to treat sb to a delicious meal; ~ **qn de** to treat sb to; **se régaler** VI to have a delicious meal; (*fig*) to enjoy o.s.

regard [Rəgar] NM (*coup d'œil*) look, glance; (*expression*) look (in one's eye); **parcourir/menacer du** ~ to cast an eye over/look threateningly at; **au** ~ **de** (*loi, morale*) from the point of view of; **en** ~ (*vis à vis*) opposite; **en** ~ **de** in comparison with

regardant, e [Rəgardɑ̃, -ɑ̃t] ADJ: **très/peu** ~ (**sur**) quite fussy/very free (about); (*économe*) very tight-fisted/quite generous (with)

regarder [Rəgarde] /**1**/ VT (*examiner, observer, lire*) to look at; (*film, télévision, match*) to watch; (*envisager: situation, avenir*) to view; (*considérer: son intérêt etc*) to be concerned with; (*être orienté vers*): ~ (**vers**) to face; (*concerner*) to concern ▶ VI to look; ~ **à** VT (*dépense, qualité, détails*) to be fussy with *ou* over; ~ **à faire** to hesitate to do; **dépenser sans** ~ to spend freely; **ne pas** ~ **à la dépense** to spare no expense; ~ **qn/qch comme** to regard sb/sth as; ~ (**qch**) **dans le dictionnaire** to look (sth up) in the dictionary; ~ **par la fenêtre** to look out of the window; **cela me regarde** it concerns me, it's my business

régate [Regat] NF, **régates** FPL regatta

régénérer [Reʒenere] /**6**/ VT to regenerate; (*fig*) to revive

régent [Reʒɑ̃] NM regent

régenter [Reʒɑ̃te] /**1**/ VT to rule over; to dictate to

régie [Reʒi] NF (*Comm, Industrie*) state-owned company; (*Théât, Ciné*) production; (*Radio, TV*) control room; **la** ~ **de l'État** state control

regimber [Rəʒɛ̃be] /**1**/ VI to balk, jib

régime [Reʒim] NM (*Pol*) régime; (*Admin: carcéral, fiscal etc*) system; (*Méd*) diet; (*Tech*) (engine)

353

speed; (*fig*) rate, pace; (*de bananes, dattes*) bunch;
se mettre au/suivre un ~ to go on/be on a diet;
~ sans sel salt-free diet; **à bas/haut ~** (*Auto*) at
low/high revs; **à plein ~** flat out, at full speed;
~ matrimonial marriage settlement

régiment [ʀeʒimɑ̃] NM (*Mil: unité*) regiment;
(*fig: fam*): **un ~ de** an army of; **un copain de ~**
a pal from military service *ou* (one's) army
days

région [ʀeʒjɔ̃] NF region; **la ~ parisienne** the
Paris area

régional, e, -aux [ʀeʒjɔnal, -o] ADJ regional

régionalisation [ʀeʒjɔnalizasjɔ̃] NF
regionalisation

régionalisme [ʀeʒjɔnalism] NM regionalism

régir [ʀeʒiʀ] /2/ VT to govern

régisseur [ʀeʒisœʀ] NM (*d'un domaine*) steward;
(*Ciné, TV*) assistant director; (*Théât*) stage
manager

registre [ʀəʒistʀ] NM (*livre*) register; logbook;
ledger; (*Mus, Ling*) register; (*d'orgue*) stop; **~ de
comptabilité** ledger; **~ de l'état civil** register
of births, marriages and deaths

réglable [ʀeglabl] ADJ (*siège, flamme etc*)
adjustable; (*achat*) payable

réglage [ʀeglaʒ] NM (*d'une machine*) adjustment;
(*d'un moteur*) tuning

réglé, e [ʀegle] ADJ well-ordered; stable, steady;
(*papier*) ruled; (*arrangé*) settled

règle [ʀɛgl] NF (*instrument*) ruler; (*loi, prescription*)
rule; **règles** NFPL (*Physiol*) period *sg*; **avoir pour
~ de** to make it a rule that *ou* to; **en ~** (*papiers
d'identité*) in order; **être/se mettre en ~** to be/
put o.s. straight with the authorities; **en ~
générale** as a (general) rule; **être la ~** to be the
rule; **être de ~** to be usual; **~ à calcul** slide rule;
~ de trois (*Math*) rule of three

règlement [ʀɛglǝmɑ̃] NM settling; (*paiement*)
settlement; (*arrêté*) regulation; (*règles, statuts*)
regulations *pl*, rules *pl*; **~ à la commande** cash
with order; **~ de compte(s)** settling of scores;
~ en espèces/par chèque payment in cash/by
cheque; **~ intérieur** (*Scol*) school rules *pl*;
(*Admin*) by-laws *pl*; **~ judiciaire** compulsory
liquidation

réglementaire [ʀɛglǝmɑ̃tɛʀ] ADJ conforming to
the regulations; (*tenue, uniforme*) regulation *cpd*

réglementation [ʀɛglǝmɑ̃tasjɔ̃] NF regulation,
control; (*règlements*) regulations *pl*

réglementer [ʀɛglǝmɑ̃te] /1/ VT to regulate,
control

régler [ʀegle] /6/ VT (*mécanisme, machine*) to
regulate, adjust; (*moteur*) to tune; (*thermostat
etc*) to set, adjust; (*emploi du temps etc*) to
organize, plan; (*question, conflit, facture, dette*) to
settle; (*fournisseur*) to settle up with, pay; (*papier*)
to rule; **~ qch sur** to model sth on; **~ son
compte** to sort sb out, settle sb; **~ un compte**
to settle a score with sb

réglisse [ʀeglis] NM *ou* F liquorice; **bâton de ~**
liquorice stick

règne [ʀɛɲ] NM (*d'un roi etc, fig*) reign; (*Bio*): **le ~
végétal/animal** the vegetable/animal
kingdom

régner [ʀeɲe] /6/ VI (*roi*) to rule, reign; (*fig*) to
reign

regonfler [ʀ(ə)gɔ̃fle] /1/ VT (*ballon, pneu*) to
reinflate, blow up again

regorger [ʀəgɔʀʒe] /3/ VI to overflow; **~ de** to
overflow with, be bursting with

régresser [ʀegʀese] /1/ VI (*phénomène*) to decline;
(*enfant, malade*) to regress

régressif, -ive [ʀegʀesif, -iv] ADJ regressive

régression [ʀegʀesjɔ̃] NF decline; regression;
être en ~ to be on the decline

regret [ʀəgʀɛ] NM regret; **à ~** with regret; **avec
~** regretfully; **sans ~** with no regrets; **être au ~
de devoir/ne pas pouvoir faire** to regret to
have to/that one is unable to do; **j'ai le ~ de
vous informer que …** I regret to inform you
that …

regrettable [ʀəgʀɛtabl] ADJ regrettable

regretter [ʀəgʀete] /1/ VT to regret; (*personne*) to
miss; **~ d'avoir fait** to regret doing; **~ que** to
regret that, be sorry that; **non, je regrette** no,
I'm sorry

regroupement [ʀ(ə)gʀupmɑ̃] NM grouping
together; (*groupe*) group

regrouper [ʀəgʀupe] /1/ VT (*grouper*) to group
together; (*contenir*) to include, comprise; **se
regrouper** VI to gather (together)

régularisation [ʀegylaʀizasjɔ̃] NF (*de papiers,
passeport*) putting in order; (*de sa situation: par le
mariage*) regularization; (*d'un mécanisme*)
regulation

régulariser [ʀegylaʀize] /1/ VT (*fonctionnement,
trafic*) to regulate; (*passeport, papiers*) to put in
order; (*sa situation*) to straighten out, regularize

régularité [ʀegylaʀite] NF regularity

régulateur, -trice [ʀegylatœʀ, -tʀis] ADJ
regulating ▶ NM (*Tech*): **~ de vitesse/de
température** speed/temperature regulator

régulation [ʀegylasjɔ̃] NF (*du trafic*) regulation;
~ des naissances birth control

régulier, -ière [ʀegylje, -jɛʀ] ADJ (*gén*) regular;
(*vitesse, qualité*) steady; (*répartition, pression*) even;
(*Transports: ligne, service*) scheduled, regular;
(*légal, réglementaire*) lawful, in order; (*fam: correct*)
straight, on the level

régulièrement [ʀegyljɛʀmɑ̃] ADV regularly;
steadily; evenly; normally

régurgiter [ʀegyʀʒite] /1/ VT to regurgitate

réhabiliter [ʀeabilite] /1/ VT to rehabilitate; (*fig*)
to restore to favour (*BRIT*) *ou* favor (*US*)

réhabituer [ʀeabitɥe] /1/ VT: **se ~ à qch/à faire
qch** to get used to sth again/to doing sth again

rehausser [ʀəose] /1/ VT (*relever*) to heighten,
raise; (*fig: souligner*) to set off, enhance

réimporter [ʀeɛ̃pɔʀte] /1/ VT to reimport

réimposer [ʀeɛ̃poze] /1/ VT (*Finance*) to reimpose;
to tax again

réimpression [ʀeɛ̃pʀesjɔ̃] NF reprinting;
(*ouvrage*) reprint

réimprimer [ʀeɛ̃pʀime] /1/ VT to reprint

Reims [ʀɛ̃s] N Rheims

rein [ʀɛ̃] NM kidney; **reins** NMPL (*dos*) back *sg*;
avoir mal aux reins to have backache;
~ artificiel kidney machine

réincarnation [Reɛ̃kaRnasjɔ̃] NF
reincarnation

réincarner [Reɛ̃kaRne] /1/: **se réincarner** VR to be
reincarnated

reine [Rɛn] NF queen

reine-claude [Rɛnklod] NF greengage

reinette [Rɛnɛt] NF rennet, pippin

réinitialisation [Reinisjalizasjɔ̃] NF (*Inform*)
reset

réinscriptible [Reɛ̃skRiptibl] ADJ (*CD, DVD*)
rewritable

réinsérer [Reɛ̃seRe] /6/ VT (*délinquant, handicapé
etc*) to rehabilitate

réinsertion [Reɛ̃seRsjɔ̃] NF (*de délinquant*)
reintegration, rehabilitation

réintégrer [Reɛ̃tegRe] /6/ VT (*lieu*) to return to;
(*fonctionnaire*) to reinstate

réitérer [ReiteRe] /6/ VT to repeat, reiterate

rejaillir [RəʒajiR] /2/ VI to splash up; to fall
upon; ~ **sur** to splash up onto; (*fig: scandale*) to
rebound on; (: *gloire*) to be reflected on

rejet [Rəʒɛ] NM (*action, aussi Méd*) rejection;
(*Poésie*) enjambment, rejet; (*Bot*) shoot

rejeter [Rəʒte] /4/ VT (*relancer*) to throw back;
(*vomir*) to bring ou throw up; (*écarter*) to reject;
(*déverser*) to throw out, discharge; (*reporter*): ~ **un
mot à la fin d'une phrase** to transpose a word
to the end of a sentence; ~ **la tête/les épaules
en arrière** to throw one's head/pull one's
shoulders back; ~ **la responsabilité de qch
sur qn** to lay the responsibility for sth at sb's
door

rejeton [Rəʒtɔ̃] NM offspring

rejette *etc* [R(ə)ʒɛt] VB *voir* **rejeter**

rejoignais *etc* [R(ə)ʒwaɲɛ] VB *voir* **rejoindre**

rejoindre [Rəʒwɛ̃dR] /49/ VT (*famille, régiment*) to
rejoin, return to; (*lieu*) to get (back) to; (*route etc*)
to meet, join; (*rattraper*) to catch up (with);
se rejoindre VI to meet; **je te rejoins au café**
I'll see ou meet you at the café

réjoui, e [Reʒwi] ADJ joyous

réjouir [ReʒwiR] /2/ VT to delight; **se réjouir** VI
to be delighted; **se réjouir de qch/de faire** to
be delighted about sth/to do; **se réjouir que** to
be delighted that

réjouissances [Reʒwisɑ̃s] NFPL (*joie*) rejoicing
sg; (*fête*) festivities, merry-making *sg*

réjouissant, e [Reʒwisɑ̃, -ɑ̃t] ADJ heartening,
delighting

relâche [Rəlɑʃ]: **faire** ~ VI (*navire*) to put into port;
(*Ciné*) to be closed; **c'est le jour de** ~ (*Ciné*) it's
closed today; **sans** ~ *adv* without respite ou a
break

relâché, e [Rəlɑʃe] ADJ loose, lax

relâchement [Rəlɑʃmɑ̃] NM (*d'un prisonnier*)
release; (*de la discipline, musculaire*) relaxation

relâcher [Rəlɑʃe] /1/ VT (*ressort, prisonnier*) to
release; (*étreinte, cordes*) to loosen; (*discipline*) to
relax ▶ VI (*Navig*) to put into port; **se relâcher** VI
to loosen; (*discipline*) to become slack ou lax;
(*élève etc*) to slacken off

relais [Rəlɛ] NM (*Sport*): (**course de**) ~
relay (race); (*Radio, TV*) relay; (*intermédiaire*)
go-between; **équipe de** ~ shift team;

(*Sport*) relay team; **prendre le** ~ (**de**) to take
over (from); ~ **de poste** post house, coaching
inn; ~ **routier** ≈ transport café (*Brit*), ≈ truck
stop (*US*)

relance [Rəlɑ̃s] NF boosting, revival; (*Écon*)
reflation

relancer [Rəlɑ̃se] /3/ VT (*balle*) to throw back
(again); (*moteur*) to restart; (*fig*) to boost, revive;
(*personne*): ~ **qn** to pester sb; to get on to sb again

relater [Rəlate] /1/ VT to relate, recount

relatif, -ive [Rəlatif, -iv] ADJ relative

relation [Rəlasjɔ̃] NF (*récit*) account, report;
(*rapport*) relation(ship); (*connaissance*)
acquaintance; **relations** NFPL (*rapports*)
relations; relationship; (*connaissances*)
connections; **être/entrer en** ~(**s**) **avec** to be in
contact ou be dealing/get in contact with;
mettre qn en ~(**s**) **avec** to put sb in touch with;
relations internationales international
relations; **relations publiques** public
relations; **relations (sexuelles)** sexual
relations, (sexual) intercourse *sg*

relativement [Rəlativmɑ̃] ADV relatively; ~ **à**
in relation to

relativiser [Rəlativize] /1/ VT to see in relation
to; to put into context

relativité [Rəlativite] NF relativity

relax [Rəlaks] ADJ INV, **relaxe** [Rəlaks] ADJ
relaxed, informal, casual; easy-going;
(**fauteuil-**)~ *nm* reclining chair

relaxant, e [Rəlaksɑ̃, -ɑ̃t] ADJ (*cure, médicament*)
relaxant; (*ambiance*) relaxing

relaxation [R(ə)laksasjɔ̃] NF relaxation

relaxer [Rəlakse] /1/ VT to relax; (*Jur*) to
discharge; **se relaxer** VI to relax

relayer [Rəleje] /8/ VT (*collaborateur, coureur etc*)
to relieve, take over from; (*Radio, TV*) to relay;
se relayer VI (*dans une activité*) to take it in turns

relecture [R(ə)lɛktyR] NF rereading

relégation [Rəlegasjɔ̃] NF (*Sport*) relegation

reléguer [Rəlege] /6/ VT to relegate; ~ **au second
plan** to push into the background

relent [Rəlɑ̃] NM, **relents** NMPL stench *sg*

relevé, e [Rəlve] ADJ (*bord de chapeau*) turned-up;
(*manches*) rolled-up; (*fig: style*) elevated; (: *sauce*)
highly-seasoned ▶ NM (*lecture*) reading; (*de
cotes*) plotting; (*liste*) statement; list; (*facture*)
account; ~ **bancaire** ou **de compte** bank
statement; ~ **d'identité bancaire** (bank)
account number

relève [Rəlɛv] NF (*personne*) relief; (*équipe*) relief
team (ou troops *pl*); **prendre la** ~ to take over

relèvement [Rəlɛvmɑ̃] NM (*d'un taux, niveau*)
raising

relever [Rəlve] /5/ VT (*statue, meuble*) to stand up
again; (*personne tombée*) to help up; (*vitre, plafond,
niveau de vie*) to raise; (*pays, économie, entreprise*) to
put back on its feet; (*col*) to turn up; (*style,
conversation*) to elevate; (*plat, sauce*) to season;
(*sentinelle, équipe*) to relieve; (*souligner: fautes,
points*) to point out; (*constater: traces etc*) to find,
pick up; (*répliquer à: remarque*) to react to, reply to;
(: *défi*) to accept, take up; (*noter: adresse etc*) to
take down, note; (: *plan*) to sketch; (: *cotes etc*)

355

to plot; (*compteur*) to read; (*ramasser: cahiers, copies*) to collect, take in ▶ vɪ (*jupe, bord*) to ride up; ~ **de** vt (*maladie*) to be recovering from; (*être du ressort de*) to be a matter for; (Admin: *dépendre de*) to come under; (*fig*) to pertain to; **se relever** vɪ (*se remettre debout*) to get up; (*fig*): **se relever (de)** to recover (from); ~ **qn de** (*vœux*) to release sb from; (*fonctions*) to relieve sb of; ~ **la tête** to look up; to hold up one's head

relief [Rəljɛf] NM relief; (*de pneu*) tread pattern; **reliefs** NMPL (*restes*) remains; **en ~** in relief; (*photographie*) three-dimensional; **mettre en ~** (*fig*) to bring out, highlight

relier [Rəlje] /7/ vt to link up; (*livre*) to bind; ~ **qch à** to link sth to; **livre relié cuir** leather-bound book

relieur, -euse [Rəljœʀ, -øz] NM/F (book)binder

religieusement [R(ə)liʒjøzmɑ̃] ADV religiously; (*enterré, mariés*) in church; **vivre ~** to lead a religious life

religieux, -euse [Rəliʒjø, -øz] ADJ religious ▶ NM monk ▶ NF nun; (*gâteau*) cream bun

religion [Rəliʒjɔ̃] NF religion; (*piété, dévotion*) faith; **entrer en ~** to take one's vows

reliquaire [RəlikɛR] NM reliquary

reliquat [Rəlika] NM (*d'une somme*) balance; (Jur: *de succession*) residue

relique [Rəlik] NF relic

relire [RəliR] /43/ vt (*à nouveau*) to reread, read again; (*vérifier*) to read over; **se relire** to read through what one has written

reliure [RəljyR] NF binding; (*art, métier*): **la ~** book-binding

reloger [R(ə)lɔʒe] /3/ vt (*locataires, sinistrés*) to rehouse

relooker [Rəluke] /1/ vt: ~ **qn** to give sb a makeover

relu, e [Rəly] PP *de* **relire**

reluire [RəlɥiR] /38/ vɪ to gleam

reluisant, e [Rəlɥizɑ̃, -ɑ̃t] vb *voir* **reluire** ▶ ADJ gleaming; **peu ~** (*fig*) unattractive; unsavoury (BRIT), unsavory (US)

reluquer [R(ə)lyke] /1/ vt (*fam*) to eye (up), ogle

remâcher [Rəmɑʃe] /1/ vt to chew *ou* ruminate over

remailler [Rəmaje] /1/ vt (*tricot*) to darn; (*filet*) to mend

remaniement [Rəmanimɑ̃] NM: ~ **ministériel** Cabinet reshuffle

remanier [Rəmanje] /7/ vt to reshape, recast; (*Pol*) to reshuffle

remarier [R(ə)maRje] /7/: **se remarier** vɪ to remarry, get married again

remarquable [Rəmaʀkabl] ADJ remarkable

remarquablement [R(ə)maʀkabləmɑ̃] ADV remarkably

remarque [Rəmaʀk] NF remark; (*écrite*) note

remarquer [Rəmaʀke] /1/ vt (*voir*) to notice; (*dire*): ~ **que** to remark that; **se remarquer** vɪ to be noticeable; **se faire remarquer** to draw attention to o.s.; **faire ~ (à qn) que** to point out (to sb) that; **faire ~ qch (à qn)** to point sth out (to sb); **remarquez, ...** mark you, ..., mind you, ...

remballer [Rɑ̃bale] /1/ vt to wrap up (again); (*dans un carton*) to pack up (again)

rembarrer [Rɑ̃baRe] /1/ vt: ~ **qn** (*repousser*) to rebuff sb; (*remettre à sa place*) to put sb in his (*ou* her) place

remblai [Rɑ̃blɛ] NM embankment

remblayer [Rɑ̃bleje] /8/ vt to bank up; (*fossé*) to fill in

rembobiner [Rɑ̃bɔbine] /1/ vt to rewind

rembourrage [Rɑ̃buRaʒ] NM stuffing; padding

rembourré, e [Rɑ̃buRe] ADJ padded

rembourrer [Rɑ̃buRe] /1/ vt to stuff; (*dossier, vêtement, souliers*) to pad

remboursable [Rɑ̃buRsabl] ADJ repayable

remboursement [Rɑ̃buRsəmɑ̃] NM (*de dette, d'emprunt*) repayment; (*de frais*) refund; **envoi contre ~** cash on delivery

rembourser [Rɑ̃buRse] /1/ vt to pay back, repay; (*frais, billet etc*) to refund; **se faire ~** to get a refund

rembrunir [Rɑ̃bRyniR] /2/: **se rembrunir** vɪ to grow sombre (BRIT) *ou* somber (US)

remède [Rəmɛd] NM (*médicament*) medicine; (*traitement, fig*) remedy, cure; **trouver un ~ à** (*Méd, fig*) to find a cure for

remédier [Rəmedje] /7/: ~ **à** vt to remedy

remembrement [Rəmɑ̃bRəmɑ̃] NM (*Agr*) regrouping of lands

remémorer [RəmemɔRe] /1/: **se remémorer** vt to recall, recollect

remerciements [RəmɛRsimɑ̃] NMPL thanks; **(avec) tous mes ~** (with) grateful *ou* many thanks

remercier [RəmɛRsje] /7/ vt to thank; (*congédier*) to dismiss; ~ **qn de/d'avoir fait** to thank sb for/for having done; **non, je vous remercie** no thank you

remettre [RəmɛtR] /56/ vt (*vêtement*): ~ **qch** to put sth back on, put sth on again; (*replacer*): ~ **qch quelque part** to put sth back somewhere; (*ajouter*): ~ **du sel/un sucre** to add more salt/another lump of sugar; (*ajourner*): ~ **qch (à)** to postpone sth *ou* put sth off (until); (*rétablir: personne*): ~ **qn** to set sb back on his (*ou* her) feet; **se remettre** vɪ to get better, recover; ~ **qch à qn** (*rendre, restituer*) to give sth back to sb, return sth to sb; (*confier: paquet, argent*) to hand sth over to, deliver sth to sb; (*donner: lettre, clé etc*) to hand over sth to sb; (: *prix, décoration*) to present sb with sth; **se remettre de** to recover from, get over; **s'en remettre à** to leave it (up) to; **se remettre à faire/qch** to start doing/sth again; ~ **une pendule à l'heure** to put a clock right; ~ **un moteur/une machine en marche** to get an engine/a machine going again; ~ **en état/en ordre** to repair/sort out; ~ **en cause/question** to challenge/question again; ~ **sa démission** to hand in one's notice; ~ **qch à neuf** to make sth as good as new; ~ **qn à sa place** (*fig*) to put sb in his (*ou* her) place

réminiscence [Reminisɑ̃s] NF reminiscence

remis, e [Rəmi, -iz] PP *de* **remettre** ▶ NF delivery; presentation; (*rabais*) discount; (*local*) shed; ~ **en marche/en ordre** starting up again/

sorting out; **~ en cause/question** calling into
question/challenging; **~ de fonds** remittance;
~ en jeu (*Football*) throw-in; **~ à neuf**
restoration; **~ de peine** remission of sentence;
~ des prix prize-giving

remiser [ʀəmize] /**1**/ VT to put away

rémission [ʀemisjɔ̃]: **sans ~** *adj* irremediable
▶ ADV unremittingly

remodeler [ʀəmɔdle] /**5**/ VT to remodel; (*fig:
restructurer*) to restructure

rémois, e [ʀemwa, -waz] ADJ of ou from Rheims
▶ NM/F: **R~, e** inhabitant ou native of Rheims

remontant [ʀəmɔ̃tɑ̃] NM tonic, pick-me-up

remontée [ʀəmɔ̃te] NF rising; ascent;
remontées mécaniques (*Ski*) ski lifts,
ski tows

remonte-pente [ʀəmɔ̃tpɑ̃t] NM ski lift,
(ski) tow

remonter [ʀəmɔ̃te] /**1**/ VI (*à nouveau*) to go back
up; (*à cheval*) to remount; (*après une descente*) to
go up (again); (*prix, température*) to go up again;
(*en voiture*) to get back in; (*jupe*) to ride up ▶ VT
(*pente*) to go up; (*fleuve*) to sail (*ou* swim *etc*) up;
up; (*manches, pantalon*) to roll up; (*fam*) to turn
up; (*niveau, limite*) to raise; (*fig: personne*) to buck
up; (*moteur, meuble*) to put back together,
reassemble; (*garde-robe etc*) to renew, replenish;
(*montre, mécanisme*) to wind up; **~ le moral à qn**
to raise sb's spirits; **~ à** (*dater de*) to date ou go
back to; **~ en voiture** to get back into the car

remontoir [ʀəmɔ̃twaʀ] NM winding
mechanism, winder

remontrance [ʀəmɔ̃tʀɑ̃s] NF reproof,
reprimand

remontrer [ʀəmɔ̃tʀe] /**1**/ VT (*montrer de nouveau*):
~ qch (à qn) to show sth again (to sb); (*fig*) **en ~**
à to prove one's superiority over

remords [ʀəmɔʀ] NM remorse *no pl*; **avoir des ~**
to feel remorse, be conscience-stricken

remorque [ʀəmɔʀk] NF trailer; **prendre/être**
en ~ to tow/be on tow; **être à la ~** (*fig*) to tag
along (behind)

remorquer [ʀəmɔʀke] /**1**/ VT to tow

remorqueur [ʀəmɔʀkœʀ] NM tug(boat)

rémoulade [ʀemulad] NF *dressing with mustard
and herbs*

rémouleur [ʀemulœʀ] NM (knife- *ou* scissor-)
grinder

remous [ʀəmu] NM (*d'un navire*) (back)wash *no pl*;
(*de rivière*) swirl, eddy *pl*; (*fig*) stir *sg*

rempailler [ʀɑ̃paje] /**1**/ VT to reseat (*with straw*)

rempart [ʀɑ̃paʀ] NM rampart; **faire à qn un ~**
de son corps to shield sb with one's (own)
body

remparts [ʀɑ̃paʀ] NMPL walls, ramparts

rempiler [ʀɑ̃pile] /**1**/ VT (*dossiers, livres etc*) to pile
up again ▶ VI (*Mil: fam*) to join up again

remplaçant, e [ʀɑ̃plasɑ̃, -ɑ̃t] NM/F replacement,
substitute, stand-in; (*Théât*) understudy; (*Scol*)
supply (BRIT) ou substitute (US) teacher

remplacement [ʀɑ̃plasmɑ̃] NM replacement;
(*job*) replacement work *no pl*; (*suppléance: Scol*)
supply (BRIT) ou substitute (US) teacher;
assurer le ~ de qn (*remplaçant*) to stand in ou

substitute for sb; **faire des remplacements**
(*professeur*) to do supply ou substitute teaching;
(*médecin*) to do locum work; (*secrétaire*) to temp

remplacer [ʀɑ̃plase] /**3**/ VT to replace; (*prendre
temporairement la place de*) to stand in for; (*tenir lieu
de*) to take the place of, act as a substitute for;
~ qch/qn par to replace sth/sb with

rempli, e [ʀɑ̃pli] ADJ (*emploi du temps*) full, busy;
~ de full of, filled with

remplir [ʀɑ̃pliʀ] /**2**/ VT to fill (up); (*questionnaire*)
to fill out ou up; (*obligations, fonction, condition*) to
fulfil; **se remplir** VI to fill up; **~ qch de** to fill sth
with

remplissage [ʀɑ̃plisaʒ] NM (*fig: péj*) padding

remploi [ʀɑ̃plwa] NM re-use

rempocher [ʀɑ̃pɔʃe] /**1**/ VT to put back into one's
pocket

remporter [ʀɑ̃pɔʀte] /**1**/ VT (*marchandise*) to take
away; (*fig*) to win, achieve

rempoter [ʀɑ̃pɔte] /**1**/ VT to repot

remuant, e [ʀəmɥɑ̃, -ɑ̃t] ADJ restless

remue-ménage [ʀəmymenaʒ] NM INV
commotion

remuer [ʀəmɥe] /**1**/ VT to move; (*café, sauce*) to
stir ▶ VI to move; (*fig: opposants*) to show signs of
unrest; **se remuer** VI to move; (*se démener*) to bestir
o.s.; (*fam: s'activer*) to get a move on

rémunérateur, -trice [ʀemyneʀatœʀ, -tʀis] ADJ
remunerative, lucrative

rémunération [ʀemyneʀasjɔ̃] NF
remuneration

rémunérer [ʀemyneʀe] /**6**/ VT to remunerate,
pay

renâcler [ʀənɑkle] /**1**/ VI to snort; (*fig*) to
grumble, balk

renaissance [ʀənɛsɑ̃s] NF rebirth, revival; **la
R~** the Renaissance

renaître [ʀənɛtʀ] /**59**/ VI to be revived; **~ à la vie**
to take on a new lease of life; **~ à l'espoir** to
find fresh hope

rénal, e, -aux [ʀenal, -o] ADJ renal, kidney *cpd*

renard [ʀənaʀ] NM fox

renardeau [ʀənaʀdo] NM fox cub

rencard [ʀɑ̃kaʀ] NM = **rancard**

rencart [ʀɑ̃kaʀ] NM = **rancart**

renchérir [ʀɑ̃ʃeʀiʀ] /**2**/ VI to become more
expensive; (*fig*): **~ (sur)** (*en paroles*) to add
something (to)

renchérissement [ʀɑ̃ʃeʀismɑ̃] NM increase (in
the cost *ou* price of)

rencontre [ʀɑ̃kɔ̃tʀ] NF (*de cours d'eau*)
confluence; (*de véhicules*) collision; (*entrevue,
congrès, match etc*) meeting; (*imprévue*) encounter;
faire la ~ de qn to meet sb; **aller à la ~ de qn** to
go and meet sb; **amours de ~** casual love
affairs

rencontrer [ʀɑ̃kɔ̃tʀe] /**1**/ VT to meet; (*mot,
expression*) to come across; (*difficultés*) to meet
with; **se rencontrer** VI to meet; (*véhicules*) to
collide

rendement [ʀɑ̃dmɑ̃] NM (*d'un travailleur, d'une
machine*) output; (*d'une culture, d'un champ*) yield;
(*d'un investissement*) return; **à plein ~** at full
capacity

rendez-vous [Rɑ̃devu] NM (*rencontre*) appointment; (: *d'amoureux*) date; (*lieu*) meeting place; **donner ~ à qn** to arrange to meet sb; **recevoir sur ~** to have an appointment system; **fixer un ~ à qn** to give sb an appointment; **avoir/prendre ~ (avec)** to have/make an appointment (with); **prendre ~ chez le médecin** to make an appointment with the doctor; **~ spatial** *ou* **orbital** docking (in space)

rendormir [Rɑ̃dɔRmiR] /16/: **se rendormir** VR to go back to sleep

rendre [Rɑ̃dR] /41/ VT (*livre, argent etc*) to give back, return; (*otages, visite, politesse, invitation, Jur: verdict*) to return; (*honneurs*) to pay; (*sang, aliments*) to bring up; (*sons, instrument*) to produce, make; (*exprimer, traduire*) to render; (*jugement*) to pronounce, render; (*faire devenir*): **~ qn célèbre/qch possible** to make sb famous/sth possible; **se rendre** VI (*capituler*) to surrender, give o.s. up; (*aller*): **se rendre quelque part** to go somewhere; **se rendre à** (*arguments etc*) to bow to; (*ordres*) to comply with; **se rendre compte de qch** to realize sth; **~ la vue/la santé à qn** to restore sb's sight/health; **~ la liberté à qn** to set sb free; **~ la monnaie** to give change; **se rendre insupportable/malade** to become unbearable/make o.s. ill

rendu, e [Rɑ̃dy] PP *de* **rendre** ▸ ADJ (*fatigué*) exhausted

renégat, e [Rənega, -at] NM/F renegade

renégocier [Rənegɔsje] /7/ VT to renegotiate

rênes [Rɛn] NFPL reins

renfermé, e [Rɑ̃fɛRme] ADJ (*fig*) withdrawn ▸ NM: **sentir le ~** to smell stuffy

renfermer [Rɑ̃fɛRme] /1/ VT to contain; **se renfermer (sur soi-même)** to withdraw into o.s.

renfiler [Rɑ̃file] /1/ VT (*collier*) to rethread; (*pull*) to slip on

renflé, e [Rɑ̃fle] ADJ bulging, bulbous

renflement [Rɑ̃fləmɑ̃] NM bulge

renflouer [Rɑ̃flue] /1/ VT to refloat; (*fig*) to set back on its (*ou* his/her *etc*) feet (again)

renfoncement [Rɑ̃fɔ̃smɑ̃] NM recess

renforcer [Rɑ̃fɔRse] /3/ VT to reinforce; **~ qn dans ses opinions** to confirm sb's opinion

renfort [Rɑ̃fɔR] NM: **renforts** *nmpl* reinforcements; **en ~** as a back-up; **à grand ~ de** with a great deal of

renfrogné, e [Rɑ̃fRɔɲe] ADJ sullen, scowling

renfrogner [Rɑ̃fRɔɲe] /1/: **se renfrogner** VI to scowl

rengager [Rɑ̃gaʒe] /3/ VT (*personnel*) to take on again; **se rengager** (*Mil*) to re-enlist

rengaine [Rɑ̃gɛn] NF (*péj*) old tune

rengainer [Rɑ̃gene] /1/ VT (*revolver*) to put back in its holster; (*épée*) to sheathe; (*fam: compliment, discours*) to save, withhold

rengorger [Rɑ̃gɔRʒe] /3/: **se rengorger** VI (*fig*) to puff o.s. up

renier [Rənje] /7/ VT (*parents*) to disown, repudiate; (*engagements*) to go back on; (*foi*) to renounce

renifler [Rənifle] /1/ VI to sniff ▸ VT (*tabac*) to sniff up; (*odeur*) to sniff

rennais, e [Rɛnɛ, -ɛz] ADJ of *ou* from Rennes ▸ NM/F: **R~, e** inhabitant *ou* native of Rennes

renne [Rɛn] NM reindeer *inv*

renom [Rənɔ̃] NM reputation; (*célébrité*) renown; **vin de grand ~** celebrated *ou* highly renowned wine

renommé, e [R(ə)nɔme] ADJ celebrated, renowned ▸ NF fame

renoncement [Rənɔ̃smɑ̃] NM abnegation, renunciation

renoncer [Rənɔ̃se] /3/: **~ à** vt to give up; **~ à faire** to give up the idea of doing; **j'y renonce!** I give up!

renouer [Rənwe] /1/ VT (*cravate etc*) to retie; (*fig: conversation, liaison*) to renew, resume; **~ avec** (*tradition*) to revive; (*habitude*) to take up again; **~ avec qn** to take up with sb again

renouveau, x [Rənuvo] NM revival; **~ de succès** renewed success

renouvelable [R(ə)nuvlabl] ADJ (*contrat, bail, énergie*) renewable; (*expérience*) which can be renewed

renouveler [Rənuvle] /4/ VT to renew; (*exploit, méfait*) to repeat; **se renouveler** VI (*incident*) to recur, happen again, be repeated; (*cellules etc*) to be renewed *ou* replaced; (*artiste, écrivain*) to try something new

renouvellement [R(ə)nuvelmɑ̃] NM renewal; recurrence

rénovation [Renɔvasjɔ̃] NF renovation; restoration; reform(ing); redevelopment

rénover [Renɔve] /1/ VT (*immeuble*) to renovate, do up; (*meuble*) to restore; (*enseignement*) to reform; (*quartier*) to redevelop

renseignement [Rɑ̃sɛɲmɑ̃] NM information *no pl*, piece of information; (*Mil*) intelligence *no pl*; **prendre des renseignements sur** to make inquiries about, ask for information about; **(guichet des) renseignements** information desk; **(service des) renseignements** (*Tél*) directory inquiries (BRIT), information (US); **service de renseignements** (*Mil*) intelligence service; **les renseignements généraux** ≈ the secret police

renseigner [Rɑ̃seɲe] /1/ VT: **~ qn (sur)** to give information to sb (about); **se renseigner** VI to ask for information, make inquiries

rentabiliser [Rɑ̃tabilize] /1/ VT (*capitaux, production*) to make profitable

rentabilité [Rɑ̃tabilite] NF profitability; cost-effectiveness; (*d'un investissement*) return; **seuil de ~** break-even point

rentable [Rɑ̃tabl] ADJ profitable; cost-effective

rente [Rɑ̃t] NF income; (*pension*) pension; (*titre*) government stock *ou* bond; **~ viagère** life annuity

rentier, -ière [Rɑ̃tje, -jɛR] NM/F person of private *ou* independent means

rentrée [Rɑ̃tRe] NF: **~ (d'argent)** cash *no pl* coming in; **la ~ (des classes** *ou* **scolaire)** the start of the new school year; **la ~**

(parlementaire) the reopening *ou* reassembly of parliament; *see note*

> La rentrée in September each year has wider connotations than just the start of the new school year. It is also the time when political and social life pick up again after the long summer break, and so marks an important point in the French calendar.

rentrer [Rɑ̃tRe] /**1**/ vi (*entrer de nouveau*) to go (*ou* come) back in; (*entrer*) to go (*ou* come) in; (*revenir chez soi*) to go (*ou* come) (back) home; (*air, clou: pénétrer*) to go in; (*revenu, argent*) to come in ▸ vt (*foins*) to bring in; (*véhicule*) to put away; (*chemise dans pantalon etc*) to tuck in; (*griffes*) to draw in; (*train d'atterrissage*) to raise; (*fig: larmes, colère etc*) to hold back; **~ le ventre** to pull in one's stomach; **~ dans** to go (*ou* come) back into; to go (*ou* come) into; (*famille, patrie*) to go back *ou* return to; (*heurter*) to crash into; (*appartenir à*) to be included in; (*: catégorie etc*) to fall into; **~ dans l'ordre** to get back to normal; **~ dans ses frais** to recover one's expenses (*ou* initial outlay)

renverrai *etc* [Rɑ̃vRe] vb *voir* **renvoyer**

renversant, e [Rɑ̃vɛRsɑ̃, -ɑ̃t] ADJ amazing, astounding

renverse [Rɑ̃vɛRs]: **à la ~** adv backwards

renversé, e [Rɑ̃vɛRse] ADJ (*écriture*) backhand; (*image*) reversed; (*stupéfait*) staggered

renversement [Rɑ̃vɛRsəmɑ̃] NM (*d'un régime, des traditions*) overthrow; **~ de la situation** reversal of the situation

renverser [Rɑ̃vɛRse] /**1**/ vt (*faire tomber: chaise, verre*) to knock over, overturn; (*: piéton*) to knock down; (*: liquide, contenu*) to spill, upset; (*retourner: verre, image*) to turn upside down, invert; (*: ordre des mots etc*) to reverse; (*fig: gouvernement etc*) to overthrow; (*stupéfier*) to bowl over, stagger; **se renverser** vi (*verre, vase*) to fall over; to overturn; (*contenu*) to spill; **se renverser (en arrière)** to lean back; **~ la tête/le corps (en arrière)** to tip one's head back/throw oneself back; **~ la vapeur** (*fig*) to change course

renvoi [Rɑ̃vwa] NM (*d'employé*) dismissal; return; reflection; postponement; (*d'élève*) expulsion; (*référence*) cross-reference; (*éructation*) belch

renvoyer [Rɑ̃vwaje] /**8**/ vt to send back; (*congédier*) to dismiss; (*Tennis*) to return; (*élève: définitivement*) to expel; (*lumière*) to reflect; (*son*) to echo; (*ajourner*): **~ qch (à)** to postpone sth (until); **~ qch à qn** (*rendre*) to return sth to sb; **~ qn à** (*fig*) to refer sb to

réorganisation [ReɔRganizasjɔ̃] NF reorganization

réorganiser [ReɔRganize] /**1**/ vt to reorganize

réorienter [ReɔRjɑ̃te] /**1**/ vt to reorient(ate), redirect

réouverture [ReuvɛRtyR] NF reopening

repaire [RəpɛR] NM den

repaître [RəpɛtR] /**57**/ vt to feast; to feed; **se ~ de** vt (*animal*) to feed on; (*fig*) to wallow *ou* revel in

répandre [Repɑ̃dR] /**41**/ vt (*renverser*) to spill; (*étaler, diffuser*) to spread; (*lumière*) to shed;

(*chaleur, odeur*) to give off; **se répandre** vi to spill; to spread; **se répandre en** (*injures etc*) to pour out

répandu, e [Repɑ̃dy] PP *de* **répandre** ▸ ADJ (*opinion, usage*) widespread

réparable [RepaRabl] ADJ (*montre etc*) repairable; (*perte etc*) which can be made up for

reparaître [RəpaRɛtR] /**57**/ vi to reappear

réparateur, -trice [RepaRatœR, -tRis] NM/F repairer

réparation [RepaRasjɔ̃] NF repairing *no pl*, repair; **en ~** (*machine etc*) under repair; **demander à qn ~ de** (*offense etc*) to ask sb to make amends for

réparer [RepaRe] /**1**/ vt to repair; (*fig: offense*) to make up for, atone for; (*: oubli, erreur*) to put right

reparler [RəpaRle] /**1**/ vi: **~ de qn/qch** to talk about sb/sth again; **~ à qn** to speak to sb again

repars *etc* [RəpaR] vb *voir* **repartir**

repartie [RəpaRti] NF retort; **avoir de la ~** to be quick at repartee

repartir [RəpaRtiR] /**16**/ vi to set off again; (*voyageur*) to leave again; (*fig*) to get going again, pick up again; **~ à zéro** to start from scratch (again)

répartir [RepaRtiR] /**2**/ vt (*pour attribuer*) to share out; (*pour disperser, disposer*) to divide up; (*poids, chaleur*) to distribute; (*étaler: dans le temps*): **~ sur** to spread over; (*classer, diviser*): **~ en** to divide into, split up into; **se répartir** vt (*travail, rôles*) to share out between themselves

répartition [RepaRtisjɔ̃] NF sharing out; dividing up; (*des richesses etc*) distribution

repas [Rəpɑ] NM meal; **à l'heure des ~** at mealtimes

repassage [Rəpɑsaʒ] NM ironing

repasser [Rəpɑse] /**1**/ vi to come (*ou* go) back ▸ vt (*vêtement, tissu*) to iron; (*examen*) to retake, resit; (*film*) to show again; (*lame*) to sharpen; (*leçon, rôle: revoir*) to go over (again); (*plat, pain*): **~ qch à qn** to pass sth back to sb

repasseuse [Rəpɑsøz] NF (*machine*) ironing machine

repayer [Rəpeje] /**8**/ vt to pay again

repêchage [Rəpɛʃaʒ] NM (*Scol*): **question de ~** question to give candidates a second chance

repêcher [Rəpɛʃe] /**1**/ vt (*noyé*) to recover the body of, fish out; (*fam: candidat*) to pass (*by inflating marks*); to give a second chance to

repeindre [Rəpɛ̃dR] /**52**/ vt to repaint

repentir [Rəpɑ̃tiR] /**16**/ NM repentance; **se repentir** vi to repent; **se repentir d'avoir fait qch** (*regretter*) to regret having done sth

répercussions [RepɛRkysjɔ̃] NFPL repercussions

répercuter [RepɛRkyte] /**1**/ vt (*réfléchir, renvoyer: son, voix*) to reflect; (*faire transmettre: consignes, charges etc*) to pass on; **se répercuter** vi (*bruit*) to reverberate; (*fig*): **se répercuter sur** to have repercussions on

repère [RəpɛR] NM mark; (*monument etc*) landmark; **(point de)** ~ point of reference

repérer [RəpeRe] /**6**/ vt (*erreur, connaissance*) to spot; (*abri, ennemi*) to locate; **se repérer** vi to get one's bearings; **se faire repérer** to be spotted

répertoire [ʀepɛʀtwaʀ] NM (*liste*) (alphabetical) list; (*carnet*) index notebook; (*Inform*) directory; (*de carnet*) thumb index; (*indicateur*) directory, index; (*d'un théâtre, artiste*) repertoire

répertorier [ʀepɛʀtɔʀje] /7/ VT to itemize, list

répéter [ʀepete] /6/ VT to repeat; (*préparer: leçon*) to learn, go over; (*Théât*) to rehearse; **se répéter** (*redire*) to repeat o.s.; (*se reproduire*) to be repeated, recur

répéteur [ʀepetœʀ] NM (*Tél*) repeater

répétitif, -ive [ʀepetitif, -iv] ADJ repetitive

répétition [ʀepetisjɔ̃] NF repetition; (*Théât*) rehearsal; **répétitions** NFPL (*leçons*) private coaching *sg*; **armes à ~** repeater weapons; **~ générale** final dress rehearsal

repeupler [ʀəpœple] /1/ VT to repopulate; (*forêt, rivière*) to restock

repiquage [ʀəpika3] NM pricking out, planting out; re-recording

repiquer [ʀəpike] /1/ VT (*plants*) to prick out, plant out; (*enregistrement*) to re-record

répit [ʀepi] NM respite; **sans ~** without letting up

replacer [ʀəplase] /3/ VT to replace, put back

replanter [ʀəplɑ̃te] /1/ VT to replant

replat [ʀəpla] NM ledge

replâtrer [ʀəplɑtʀe] /1/ VT (*mur*) to replaster

replet, -ète [ʀəplɛ, -ɛt] ADJ chubby, fat

repli [ʀəpli] NM (*d'une étoffe*) fold; (*Mil, fig*) withdrawal

replier [ʀəplije] /7/ VT (*rabattre*) to fold down *ou* over; **se replier** VI (*armée*) to withdraw, fall back; **se replier sur soi-même** to withdraw into oneself

réplique [ʀeplik] NF (*repartie, fig*) reply; (*objection*) retort; (*Théât*) line; (*copie*) replica; **donner la ~ à** to play opposite; **sans ~** *adj* no-nonsense; irrefutable

répliquer [ʀeplike] /1/ VI to reply; (*avec impertinence*) to answer back; (*riposter*) to retaliate

replonger [ʀəplɔ̃3e] /3/ VT: **~ qch dans** to plunge sth back into; **se ~ dans** (*journal etc*) to immerse o.s. in again

répondant, e [ʀepɔ̃dɑ̃, -ɑ̃t] NM/F (*garant*) guarantor, surety

répondeur [ʀepɔ̃dœʀ] NM: **~ (automatique)** (*Tél*) answering machine

répondre [ʀepɔ̃dʀ] /41/ VI to answer, reply; (*freins, mécanisme*) to respond; **~ à** VT to reply to, answer; (*invitation, convocation*) to reply to; (*affection, salut*) to return; (*provocation, mécanisme etc*) to respond to; (*correspondre à: besoin*) to answer; (*: conditions*) to meet; (*: description*) to match; **~ à qn** (*avec impertinence*) to answer sb back; **~ que** to answer *ou* reply that; **~ de** to answer for

réponse [ʀepɔ̃s] NF answer, reply; **avec ~ payée** (*Postes*) reply-paid, post-paid (*US*); **avoir ~ à tout** to have an answer for everything; **en ~ à** in reply to; **carte-/bulletin-~** reply card/slip

report [ʀəpɔʀ] NM postponement; transfer; **~ d'incorporation** (*Mil*) deferment

reportage [ʀəpɔʀta3] NM (*bref*) report; (*écrit:*

documentaire) story; article; (*en direct*) commentary; (*genre, activité*): **le ~** reporting

reporter¹ [ʀəpɔʀtɛʀ] NM reporter

reporter² [ʀəpɔʀte] VT (*total*): **~ qch sur** to carry sth forward *ou* over to; (*ajourner*): **~ qch (à)** to postpone sth (until); (*transférer*): **~ qch sur** to transfer sth to; **se ~ à** (*époque*) to think back to; (*document*) to refer to

repos [ʀəpo] NM rest; (*fig*) peace (and quiet); (*mental*) peace of mind; (*Mil*): **~!** (stand) at ease!; **en ~** at rest; **au ~** at rest; (*soldat*) at ease; **de tout ~** safe; **ce n'est pas de tout ~!** it's no picnic!

reposant, e [ʀ(ə)pozɑ̃, -ɑ̃t] ADJ restful; (*sommeil*) refreshing

repose [ʀəpoz] NF refitting

reposé, e [ʀəpoze] ADJ fresh, rested; **à tête ~** in a leisurely way, taking time to think

repose-pied [ʀəpozpje] NM INV footrest

reposer [ʀəpoze] /1/ VT (*verre, livre*) to put down; (*rideaux, carreaux*) to put back; (*délasser*) to rest; (*problème*) to reformulate ▶ VI (*liquide, pâte*) to settle, rest; **se reposer** VI to rest; **laisser ~** (*pâte*) to leave to stand; **ici repose ...** (*personne*) here lies ...; **~ sur** to be built on; (*fig*) to rest on; **se reposer sur qn** to rely on sb

repoussant, e [ʀəpusɑ̃, -ɑ̃t] ADJ repulsive

repoussé, e [ʀəpuse] ADJ (*cuir*) embossed (by hand)

repousser [ʀəpuse] /1/ VI to grow again ▶ VT to repel, repulse; (*offre*) to turn down, reject; (*tiroir, personne*) to push back; (*différer*) to put back

répréhensible [ʀepʀeɑ̃sibl] ADJ reprehensible

reprendre [ʀəpʀɑ̃dʀ] /58/ VT (*prisonnier, ville*) to recapture; (*objet prêté, donné*) to take back; (*Comm: article usagé*) to take back; to take in part exchange; (*: firme, entreprise*) to take over; (*emprunter: argument, idée*) to take up, use; (*refaire: article etc*) to go over again; (*jupe etc*) to alter; (*émission, pièce*) to put on again; (*réprimander*) to tell off; (*corriger*) to correct; (*travail, promenade*) to resume; (*chercher*): **je viendrai te ~ à 4 h** I'll come and fetch you *ou* I'll come back for you at 4; (*se resservir de*): **~ du pain/un œuf** to take (*ou* eat) more bread/another egg ▶ VI (*classes, pluie*) to start (up) again; (*activités, travaux, combats*) to resume, start (up) again; (*affaires, industrie*) to pick up; (*dire*): **reprit-il** he went on; **se reprendre** (*se ressaisir*) to recover, pull o.s. together; **s'y reprendre** to make another attempt; **~ des forces** to recover one's strength; **~ courage** to take new heart; **~ ses habitudes/sa liberté** to get back into one's old habits/regain one's freedom; **~ la route** to resume one's journey, set off again; **~ connaissance** to come to, regain consciousness; **~ haleine** *ou* **son souffle** to get one's breath back; **~ la parole** to speak again

repreneur [ʀəpʀənœʀ] NM company fixer *ou* doctor

reprenne *etc* [ʀəpʀɛn] VB *voir* **reprendre**

représailles [ʀəpʀezaj] NFPL reprisals, retaliation *sg*

représentant, e [ʀəpʀezɑ̃tɑ̃, -ɑ̃t] NM/F representative

représentatif, -ive [ʀəpʀezɑ̃tatif, -iv] ADJ
representative

représentation [ʀəpʀezɑ̃tasjɔ̃] NF
representation; (*symbole, image*) representation;
(*spectacle*) performance; **la ~** (*Comm*) commercial
travelling; sales representation; **frais de ~** (*d'un
diplomate*) entertainment allowance

représenter [ʀəpʀezɑ̃te] /1/ VT to represent;
(*donner: pièce, opéra*) to perform; **se représenter**
VT, VI (*se figurer*) to imagine; to visualize; **se
représenter à** (*Pol*) to stand *ou* run again at;
(*Scol*) to resit

répressif, -ive [ʀepʀesif, -iv] ADJ repressive

répression [ʀepʀesjɔ̃] NF *voir* **réprimer**
suppression; repression; (*Pol*): **la ~** repression;
mesures de ~ repressive measures

réprimande [ʀepʀimɑ̃d] NF reprimand, rebuke

réprimander [ʀepʀimɑ̃de] /1/ VT to reprimand,
rebuke

réprimer [ʀepʀime] /1/ VT (*émotions*) to suppress;
(*peuple etc*) to repress

repris, e [ʀəpʀi, -iz] PP *de* **reprendre** ▶ NM: **~ de
justice** ex-prisoner, ex-convict

reprise [ʀəpʀiz] NF (*recommencement*)
resumption; (*économique*) recovery; (*TV*) repeat;
(*Ciné*) rerun; (*Auto*) acceleration
no pl; (*Comm*) trade-in, part exchange; (*de
location*) *sum asked for any extras or improvements
made to the property*; (*raccommodage*) darn, mend;
la ~ des hostilités the resumption of
hostilities; **à plusieurs reprises** on several
occasions, several times

repriser [ʀəpʀize] /1/ VT (*chaussette, lainage*) to
darn; (*tissu*) to mend; **aiguille/coton à ~**
darning needle/thread

réprobateur, -trice [ʀepʀɔbatœʀ, -tʀis] ADJ
reproving

réprobation [ʀepʀɔbasjɔ̃] NF reprobation

reproche [ʀəpʀɔʃ] NM (*remontrance*) reproach;
ton/air de ~ reproachful tone/look; **faire des
reproches à qn** to reproach sb; **faire ~ à qn de
qch** to reproach sb for sth; **sans ~(s)** beyond *ou*
above reproach

reprocher [ʀəpʀɔʃe] /1/ VT: **~ qch à qn** to
reproach *ou* blame sb for sth; **~ qch à** (*machine,
théorie*) to have sth against; **se ~ qch/d'avoir
fait qch** to blame o.s. for sth/for doing sth

reproducteur, -trice [ʀəpʀɔdyktœʀ, -tʀis] ADJ
reproductive

reproduction [ʀəpʀɔdyksjɔ̃] NF reproduction;
~ interdite all rights (of reproduction)
reserved

reproduire [ʀəpʀɔdɥiʀ] /38/ VT to reproduce; **se
reproduire** VI (*Bio*) to reproduce; (*recommencer*) to
recur, re-occur

reprographie [ʀəpʀɔgʀafi] NF (photo)copying

réprouvé, e [ʀepʀuve] NM/F reprobate

réprouver [ʀepʀuve] /1/ VT to reprove

reptation [ʀɛptasjɔ̃] NF crawling

reptile [ʀɛptil] NM reptile

repu, e [ʀəpy] PP *de* **repaître** ▶ ADJ satisfied,
sated

républicain, e [ʀepyblikɛ̃, -ɛn] ADJ, NM/F
republican

république [ʀepyblik] NF republic; **R~ arabe
du Yémen** Yemen Arab Republic; **R~
Centrafricaine** Central African Republic;
R~ de Corée South Korea; **R~ dominicaine**
Dominican Republic; **R~ d'Irlande** Irish
Republic, Eire; **R~ populaire de Chine**
People's Republic of China; **R~ populaire
démocratique de Corée** Democratic People's
Republic of Korea; **R~ populaire du Yémen**
People's Democratic Republic of Yemen

répudier [ʀepydje] /7/ VT (*femme*) to repudiate;
(*doctrine*) to renounce

répugnance [ʀepyɲɑ̃s] NF repugnance,
loathing; **avoir** *ou* **éprouver de la ~ pour**
(*médicament, comportement, travail etc*) to have an
aversion to; **avoir** *ou* **éprouver de la ~ à faire
qch** to be reluctant to do sth

répugnant, e [ʀepyɲɑ̃, -ɑ̃t] ADJ repulsive,
loathsome

répugner [ʀepyɲe] /1/: **~ à** VT: **~ à qn** to repel *ou*
disgust sb; **~ à faire** to be loath *ou* reluctant to do

répulsion [ʀepylsjɔ̃] NF repulsion

réputation [ʀepytasjɔ̃] NF reputation; **avoir la
~ d'être ...** to have a reputation for being ...;
connaître qn/qch de ~ to know sb/sth by
repute; **de ~ mondiale** world-renowned

réputé, e [ʀepyte] ADJ renowned; **être ~ pour** to
have a reputation for, be renowned for

requérir [ʀəkeʀiʀ] /21/ VT (*nécessiter*) to require,
call for; (*au nom de la loi*) to call upon; (*Jur: peine*)
to call for, demand

requête [ʀəkɛt] NF request, petition; (*Jur*)
petition

requiem [ʀekɥijɛm] NM requiem

requiers *etc* [ʀəkjɛʀ] VB *voir* **requérir**

requin [ʀəkɛ̃] NM shark

requinquer [ʀəkɛ̃ke] /1/ VT to set up, pep up

requis, e [ʀəki, -iz] PP *de* **requérir** ▶ ADJ required

réquisition [ʀekizisjɔ̃] NF requisition

réquisitionner [ʀekizisjɔne] /1/ VT to requisition

réquisitoire [ʀekizitwaʀ] NM (*Jur*) closing
speech for the prosecution; (*fig*): **~ contre**
indictment of

RER SIGLE M (= *Réseau express régional*) *Greater Paris
high-speed train service*

rescapé, e [ʀɛskape] NM/F survivor

rescousse [ʀɛskus] NF: **aller à la ~ de qn** to go
to sb's aid *ou* rescue; **appeler qn à la ~** to call on
sb for help

réseau, x [ʀezo] NM network; **~ social** social
network

réseautage [ʀezotaʒ] NM social networking

réséda [ʀezeda] NM (*Bot*) reseda, mignonette

réservation [ʀezɛʀvasjɔ̃] NF reservation;
booking

réserve [ʀezɛʀv] NF (*retenue*) reserve; (*entrepôt*)
storeroom; (*restriction, aussi: d'Indiens*)
reservation; (*de pêche, chasse*) preserve;
(*restrictions*): **faire des réserves** to have
reservations; **officier de ~** reserve officer; **sous
toutes réserves** with all reserve; (*dire*) with
reservations; **sous ~ de** subject to; **sans ~** *adv*
unreservedly; **en ~** in reserve; **de ~** (*provisions
etc*) in reserve

réservé, e [RezeRve] ADJ (*discret*) reserved; (*chasse, pêche*) private; **~ à** qn **pour** reserved for

réserver [RezeRve] /**1**/ VT (*gén*) to reserve; (*chambre, billet etc*) to book, reserve; (*mettre de côté, garder*): **~** qch **pour** ou **à** to keep ou save sth for; **~** qch **à** qn to reserve (*ou* book) sth for sb; (*fig: destiner*) to have sth in store for sb; **se ~ le droit de faire** to reserve the right to do

réserviste [RezeRvist] NM reservist

réservoir [RezeRvwaR] NM tank

résidence [Rezidɑ̃s] NF residence; **~ principale/ secondaire** main/second home; **~ universitaire** hall of residence (*BRIT*), dormitory (*US*); **(en) ~ surveillée** (under) house arrest

résident, e [Rezidɑ̃, -ɑ̃t] NM/F (*ressortissant*) foreign resident; (*d'un immeuble*) resident ▶ ADJ (*Inform*) resident

résidentiel, le [Rezidɑ̃sjɛl] ADJ residential

résider [Rezide] /**1**/ VI: **~ à** ou **dans** ou **en** to reside in; **~ dans** (*fig*) to lie in

résidu [Rezidy] NM residue *no pl*

résiduel, le [Reziduɛl] ADJ residual

résignation [Reziɲasjɔ̃] NF resignation

résigné, e [Reziɲe] ADJ resigned

résigner [Reziɲe] /**1**/ VT to relinquish, resign; **se résigner** VI: **se résigner (à** qch**/à faire)** to resign o.s. (to sth/to doing)

résiliable [Reziljabl] ADJ which can be terminated

résilier [Rezilje] /**7**/ VT to terminate

résille [Rezij] NF (hair)net

résine [Rezin] NF resin

résiné, e [Rezine] ADJ: **vin ~** retsina

résineux, -euse [Rezinø, -øz] ADJ resinous ▶ NM coniferous tree

résistance [Rezistɑ̃s] NF resistance; (*de réchaud, bouilloire: fil*) element

résistant, e [Rezistɑ̃, -ɑ̃t] ADJ (*personne*) robust, tough; (*matériau*) strong, hard-wearing ▶ NM/F (*patriote*) Resistance worker ou fighter

résister [Reziste] /**1**/ VI to resist; **~ à** vt (*assaut, tentation*) to resist; (*effort, souffrance*) to withstand; (*matériau, plante*) to withstand, stand up to; (*personne: désobéir à*) to stand up to, oppose

résolu, e [Rezɔly] PP *de* **résoudre** ▶ ADJ (*ferme*) resolute; **être ~ à** qch**/faire** to be set upon sth/ doing

résolument [Rezɔlymɑ̃] ADV resolutely, steadfastly; **~ contre** qch firmly against sth

résolution [Rezɔlysjɔ̃] NF solving; (*fermeté, décision, Inform*) resolution; (*d'un problème*) solution; **prendre la ~ de** to make a resolution to

résolvais *etc* [Rezɔlve] VB *voir* **résoudre**

résonance [Rezɔnɑ̃s] NF resonance

résonner [Rezɔne] /**1**/ VI (*cloche, pas*) to reverberate, resound; (*salle*) to be resonant; **~ de** to resound with

résorber [RezɔRbe] /**1**/: **se résorber** VI (*Méd*) to be resorbed; (*fig*) to be absorbed

résoudre [RezudR] /**51**/ VT to solve; **~** qn **à faire** qch to get sb to make up his (*ou* her) mind to do

sth; **~ de faire** to resolve to do; **se ~ à faire** to bring o.s. to do

respect [Rεspε] NM respect; **tenir en ~** to keep at bay; **présenter ses respects à** qn to pay one's respects to sb

respectabilité [Rεspεktabilite] NF respectability

respectable [Rεspεktabl] ADJ respectable

respecter [Rεspεkte] /**1**/ VT to respect; **faire ~** to enforce; **le lexicographe qui se respecte** (*fig*) any self-respecting lexicographer

respectif, -ive [Rεspεktif, -iv] ADJ respective

respectivement [Rεspεktivmɑ̃] ADV respectively

respectueusement [Rεspεktɥøzmɑ̃] ADV respectfully

respectueux, -euse [Rεspεktɥø, -øz] ADJ respectful; **~ de** respectful of

respirable [Rεspirabl] ADJ: **peu ~** unbreathable

respiration [Rεspirasjɔ̃] NF breathing *no pl*; **faire une ~ complète** to breathe in and out; **retenir sa ~** to hold one's breath; **~ artificielle** artificial respiration

respiratoire [RεspiratwaR] ADJ respiratory

respirer [Rεspire] /**1**/ VI to breathe; (*fig: se reposer*) to get one's breath, have a break; (: *être soulagé*) to breathe again ▶ VT to breathe (in), inhale; (*manifester: santé, calme etc*) to exude

resplendir [Rεsplɑ̃diR] /**2**/ VI to shine; (*fig*): **~ (de)** to be radiant (with)

resplendissant, e [Rεsplɑ̃disɑ̃, -ɑ̃t] ADJ radiant

responsabilité [Rεspɔ̃sabilite] NF responsibility; (*légale*) liability; **refuser la ~ de** to deny responsibility (*ou* liability) for; **prendre ses responsabilités** to assume responsibility for one's actions; **~ civile** civil liability; **~ pénale/morale/collective** criminal/moral/collective responsibility

responsable [Rεspɔ̃sabl] ADJ responsible ▶ NMF (*personne coupable*) person responsible; (*du ravitaillement etc*) person in charge; (*de parti, syndicat*) official; **~ de** responsible for; (*légalement: de dégâts etc*) liable for; (*chargé de*) in charge of, responsible for

resquiller [Rεskije] /**1**/ VI (*au cinéma, au stade*) to get in on the sly; (*dans le train*) to fiddle a free ride

resquilleur, -euse [RεskijœR, -øz] NM/F (*qui n'est pas invité*) gatecrasher; (*qui ne paie pas*) fare dodger

ressac [Rəsak] NM backwash

ressaisir [RəseziR] /**2**/: **se ressaisir** VI to regain one's self-control; (*équipe sportive*) to rally

ressasser [Rəsase] /**1**/ VT (*remâcher*) to keep turning over; (*redire*) to keep trotting out

ressemblance [Rəsɑ̃blɑ̃s] NF (*visuelle*) resemblance, similarity, likeness; (: *Art*) likeness; (*analogie, trait commun*) similarity

ressemblant, e [Rəsɑ̃blɑ̃, -ɑ̃t] ADJ (*portrait*) lifelike, true to life

ressembler [Rəsɑ̃ble] /**1**/: **~ à** vt to be like, resemble; (*visuellement*) to look like; **se ressembler** VI to be (*ou* look) alike

ressemeler [Rəsəmle] /**4**/ VT to (re)sole

ressens etc [ʀ(ə)sɑ̃] VB voir **ressentir**

ressentiment [ʀəsɑ̃timɑ̃] NM resentment

ressentir [ʀəsɑ̃tiʀ] /16/ VT to feel; **se ~ de** to feel (ou show) the effects of

resserre [ʀəsɛʀ] NF shed

resserrement [ʀ(ə)sɛʀmɑ̃] NM narrowing; strengthening; (goulet) narrow part

resserrer [ʀəsɛʀe] /1/ VT (pores) to close; (nœud, boulon) to tighten (up); (fig: liens) to strengthen; **se resserrer** VI (route, vallée) to narrow; (liens) to strengthen; **se resserrer (autour de)** to draw closer (around), to close in (on)

ressers etc [ʀ(ə)sɛʀ] VB voir **resservir**

resservir [ʀəsɛʀviʀ] /14/ VI to do ou serve again ▶ VT: ~ **qch (à qn)** to serve sth up again (to sb); ~ **de qch (à qn)** to give (sb) a second helping of sth; ~ **qn (d'un plat)** to give sb a second helping (of a dish); **se ~ (de)** (plat) to take a second helping of; (outil etc) to use again

ressort [ʀəsɔʀ] VB voir **ressortir** ▶ NM (pièce) spring; (force morale) spirit; **en dernier ~** as a last resort; **être du ~ de** to fall within the competence of

ressortir [ʀəsɔʀtiʀ] /16/ VI to go (ou come) out (again); (contraster) to stand out; ~ **de** (résulter de): **il ressort de ceci que** it emerges from this that; ~ **à** (Jur) to come under the jurisdiction of; (Admin) to be the concern of; **faire ~** (fig: souligner) to bring out

ressortissant, e [ʀəsɔʀtisɑ̃, -ɑ̃t] NM/F national

ressouder [ʀəsude] /1/ VT to solder together again

ressource [ʀəsuʀs] NF: **avoir la ~ de** to have the possibility of; **ressources** NFPL resources; (fig) possibilities; **leur seule ~ était de** the only course open to them was to; **ressources d'énergie** energy resources

ressusciter [ʀesysite] /1/ VT to resuscitate, restore to life; (fig) to revive, bring back ▶ VI to rise (from the dead); (fig: pays) to come back to life

restant, e [ʀɛstɑ̃, -ɑ̃t] ADJ remaining ▶ NM: **le ~ (de)** the remainder (of); **un ~ de** (de trop) some leftover; (fig) a remnant ou last trace of

restaurant [ʀɛstɔʀɑ̃] NM restaurant; **manger au ~** to eat out; ~ **d'entreprise** staff canteen ou cafeteria (US); ~ **universitaire** university refectory ou cafeteria (US)

restaurateur, -trice [ʀɛstɔʀatœʀ, -tʀis] NM/F restaurant owner, restaurateur; (de tableaux) restorer

restauration [ʀɛstɔʀasjɔ̃] NF restoration; (hôtellerie) catering; ~ **rapide** fast food

restaurer [ʀɛstɔʀe] /1/ VT to restore; **se restaurer** VI to have something to eat

restauroute [ʀɛstɔʀut] NM = **restoroute**

reste [ʀɛst] NM (Math) remainder; (restant): **le ~ (de)** the rest (of); (de trop): **un ~ (de)** some leftover; (vestige): **un ~ de** a remnant ou last trace of; **restes** NMPL leftovers; (d'une cité etc, dépouille mortelle) remains; **avoir du temps de ~** to have time to spare; **ne voulant pas être en ~** not wishing to be outdone; **partir sans attendre** ou **demander son ~** (fig) to leave

without waiting to hear more; **du ~, au ~** adv besides, moreover; **pour le ~, quant au ~** adv as for the rest

rester [ʀɛste] /1/ VI (dans un lieu, un état, une position) to stay, remain; (subsister) to remain, be left; (durer) to last, live on ▶ VB IMPERS: **il reste du pain/deux œufs** there's some bread/there are two eggs left (over); **il reste du temps/10 minutes** there's some time/there are 10 minutes left; **il me reste assez de temps** I have enough time left; **il ne me reste plus qu'à** ... I've just got to ...; **voilà tout ce qui (me) reste** that's all I've got left; **ce qui reste à faire** what remains to be done; **ce qui me reste à faire** what remains for me to do; **(il) reste à savoir/établir si** ... it remains to be seen/established if ou whether ...; **il n'en reste pas moins que** ... the fact remains that ..., it's nevertheless a fact that ...; **en ~ à** (stade, menaces) to go no further than, only go as far as; **restons-en là** let's leave it at that; ~ **sur une impression** to retain an impression; **il a failli y ~** he nearly met his end

restituer [ʀɛstitɥe] /1/ VT (objet, somme): ~ **qch (à qn)** to return ou restore sth (to sb); (énergie) to release; (son) to reproduce

restitution [ʀɛstitysjɔ̃] NF restoration

restoroute [ʀɛstɔʀut] NM motorway (BRIT) ou highway (US) restaurant

restreindre [ʀɛstʀɛ̃dʀ] /52/ VT to restrict, limit; **se restreindre** (dans ses dépenses etc) to cut down; (champ de recherches) to narrow

restreint, e [ʀɛstʀɛ̃, -ɛ̃t] PP de **restreindre** ▶ ADJ restricted, limited

restrictif, -ive [ʀɛstʀiktif, -iv] ADJ restrictive, limiting

restriction [ʀɛstʀiksjɔ̃] NF restriction; (condition) qualification; **restrictions** NFPL (mentales) reservations; **sans ~** adv unreservedly

restructuration [ʀəstʀyktyʀasjɔ̃] NF restructuring

restructurer [ʀəstʀyktyʀe] /1/ VT to restructure

résultante [ʀezyltɑ̃t] NF (conséquence) result, consequence

résultat [ʀezylta] NM result; (conséquence) outcome no pl, result; (d'élection etc) results pl; **résultats** NMPL (d'une enquête) findings; **résultats sportifs** sports results

résulter [ʀezylte] /1/: ~ **de** vt to result from, be the result of; **il résulte de ceci que** ... the result of this is that ...

résumé [ʀezyme] NM summary, résumé; **faire le ~ de** to summarize; **en ~** adv in brief; (pour conclure) to sum up

résumer [ʀezyme] /1/ VT (texte) to summarize; (récapituler) to sum up; (fig) to epitomize, typify; **se résumer** VI (personne) to sum up (one's ideas); **se résumer à** to come down to

resurgir [ʀəsyʀʒiʀ] /2/ VI to reappear, re-emerge

résurrection [ʀezyʀɛksjɔ̃] NF resurrection; (fig) revival

rétablir [ʀetabliʀ] /2/ VT to restore, re-establish; (personne: traitement): ~ **qn** to restore sb to health, help sb recover; (Admin): ~ **qn dans son**

r

emploi/ses droits to reinstate sb in his post/restore sb's rights; **se rétablir** VI (*guérir*) to recover; (*silence, calme*) to return, be restored; (*Gym etc*): **se rétablir (sur)** to pull o.s. up (onto)

rétablissement [Retablismã] NM restoring; (*guérison*) recovery; pull-up

rétamer [Retame] /1/ VT to re-coat, re-tin

rétameur [RetamœR] NM tinker

retaper [Rətape] /1/ VT (*maison, voiture etc*) to do up; (*fam: revigorer*) to buck up; (*redactylographier*) to retype

retard [RətaR] NM (*d'une personne attendue*) lateness *no pl*; (*sur l'horaire, un programme, une échéance*) delay; (*fig (!): scolaire, mental etc*) backwardness; **être en ~** (*pays*) to be backward; (*dans paiement, travail*) to be behind; **en ~ (de deux heures)** (two hours) late; **désolé d'être en ~** sorry I'm late; **avoir un ~ de deux km** (*Sport*) to be two km behind; **rattraper son ~** to catch up; **avoir du ~** to be late; (*sur un programme*) to be behind (schedule); **prendre du ~** (*train, avion*) to be delayed; (*montre*) to lose (time); **sans ~** without delay; **~ à l'allumage** (*Auto*) retarded spark; **~ scolaire** backwardness at school

retardataire [RətaRdatɛR] ADJ late; (*enfant, idées*) backward (*péj*) ▶ NMF latecomer; backward child

retardé, e [RətaRde] ADJ backward

retardement [RətaRdəmã]: **à ~** *adj* delayed action *cpd*; **bombe à ~** time bomb

retarder [RətaRde] /1/ VT to delay; (*horloge*) to put back; (*sur un horaire*): **~ qn (d'une heure)** to delay sb (an hour); (*sur un programme*): **~ qn (de trois mois)** to set sb back *ou* delay sb (three months); (*départ, date*): **~ qch (de deux jours)** to put sth back (two days), delay sth (for *ou* by two days) ▶ VI (*montre*) to be slow; (: *habituellement*) to lose (time); **je retarde (d'une heure)** I'm (an hour) slow

retendre [Rətãdr] /41/ VT (*câble etc*) to stretch again; (*Mus: cordes*) to retighten

retenir [RətniR] /22/ VT (*garder, retarder*) to keep, detain; (*maintenir: objet qui glisse, fig: colère, larmes, rire*) to hold back; (: *objet suspendu*) to hold; (: *chaleur, odeur*) to retain; (*se rappeler*) to retain; (*réserver*) to reserve; (*accepter*) to accept; (*fig: empêcher d'agir*): **~ qn (de faire)** to hold sb back (from doing); (*prélever*): **~ qch (sur)** to deduct sth (from); **se retenir** VI (*euphémisme*) to hold on; (*se raccrocher*): **se retenir à** to hold onto; (*se contenir*): **se retenir de faire** to restrain o.s. from doing; **~ son souffle** *ou* **haleine** to hold one's breath; **~ qn à dîner** to ask sb to stay for dinner; **je pose trois et je retiens deux** put down three and carry two

rétention [Retãsjɔ̃] NF: **~ d'urine** urine retention

retentir [RətãtiR] /2/ VI to ring out; (*salle*): **~ de** to ring *ou* resound with; **~ sur** vt (*fig*) to have an effect upon

retentissant, e [Rətãtisã, -ãt] ADJ resounding; (*fig*) impact-making

retentissement [Rətãtismã] NM (*retombées*) repercussions *pl*; effect, impact

retenu, e [Rətny] PP *de* **retenir** ▶ ADJ (*place*) reserved; (*personne: empêché*) held up; (*propos: contenu, discret*) restrained ▶ NF (*prélèvement*) deduction; (*Math*) number to carry over; (*Scol*) detention; (*modération*) (self-)restraint; (*réserve*) reserve, reticence; (*Auto*) tailback

réticence [Retisãs] NF reticence *no pl*, reluctance *no pl*; **sans ~** without hesitation

réticent, e [Retisã, -ãt] ADJ reticent, reluctant

retiendrai [Rətjɛ̃dRe], **retiens** etc [Rətjɛ̃] VB *voir* **retenir**

rétif, -ive [Retif, -iv] ADJ restive

rétine [Retin] NF retina

retint etc [Rətɛ̃] VB *voir* **retenir**

retiré, e [Rətire] ADJ (*solitaire*) secluded; (*éloigné*) remote

retirer [Rətire] /1/ VT (*argent, plainte*) to withdraw; (*vêtement, lunettes*) to take off, remove; (*reprendre: bagages, billets*) to collect, pick up; (*enlever*): **~ qch à qn** to take sth from sb; (*extraire*): **~ qn/qch de** to take sb away from/sth out of, remove sb/sth from; **~ des avantages de** to derive advantages from; **se retirer** VI (*partir, reculer*) to withdraw; (*prendre sa retraite*) to retire; **se retirer de** to withdraw from; to retire from

retombées [Rətɔ̃be] NFPL (*radioactives*) fallout *sg*; (*fig*) fallout; spin-offs

retomber [Rətɔ̃be] /1/ VI (*à nouveau*) to fall again; (*atterrir: après un saut etc*) to land; (*tomber, redescendre*) to fall back; (*pendre*) to fall, hang (down); (*rechuter*): **~ malade/dans l'erreur** to fall ill again/fall back into error; (*échoir*): **~ sur qn** to fall on sb

retordre [RətɔRdR] /41/ VT: **donner du fil à ~ à qn** to make life difficult for sb

rétorquer [RetɔRke] /1/ VT: **~ (à qn) que** to retort (to sb) that

retors, e [RətɔR, -ɔRs] ADJ wily

rétorsion [RetɔRsjɔ̃] NF: **mesures de ~** reprisals

retouche [Rətuʃ] NF touching up *no pl*; (*sur vêtement*) alteration; **faire une ~** *ou* **des retouches à** to touch up

retoucher [Rətuʃe] /1/ VT (*photographie, tableau*) to touch up; (*texte, vêtement*) to alter

retour [RətuR] NM return; **au ~** (*en arrivant*) when we (*ou* they *etc*) get (*ou* got) back; (*en route*) on the way back; **pendant le ~** on the way *ou* journey back; **à mon/ton ~** on my/your return; **au ~ de** on the return of; **être de ~ (de)** to be back (from); **de ~ à .../chez moi** back at .../back home; **quand serons-nous de ~?** when do we get back?; **en ~** *adv* in return; **par ~ du courrier** by return of post; **par un juste ~ des choses** by a favourable twist of fate; **match ~** return match; **~ en arrière** (*Ciné*) flashback; (*mesure*) backward step; **~ de bâton** kickback; **~ de chariot** carriage return; **~ à l'envoyeur** (*Postes*) return to sender; **~ de flamme** backfire; **~ (automatique) à la ligne** (*Inform*) wordwrap; **~ de manivelle** (*fig*) backfire; **~ offensif** renewed attack; **~ aux sources** (*fig*) return to basics

retournement [RətuRnəmã] NM (*d'une personne: revirement*) turning (round); **~ de la situation** reversal of the situation

retourner [RətuRne] /**1**/ VT (*dans l'autre sens: matelas, crêpe*) to turn (over); (: *caisse*) to turn upside down; (: *sac, vêtement*) to turn inside out; (*fig: argument*) to turn back; (*en remuant: terre, sol, foin*) to turn over; (*émouvoir: personne*) to shake; (*renvoyer, restituer*): **~ qch à qn** to return sth to sb ▶ VI (*aller, revenir*): **~ quelque part/à** to go back ou return somewhere/to; **~ à** (*état, activité*) to return to, go back to; **se retourner** VI to turn over; (*tourner la tête*) to turn round; **s'en retourner** to go back; **se retourner contre** (*fig*) to turn against; **savoir de quoi il retourne** to know what it is all about; **~ sa veste** (*fig*) to turn one's coat; **~ en arrière** ou **sur ses pas** to turn back, retrace one's steps; **~ aux sources** to go back to basics

retracer [RətRase] /**3**/ VT to relate, recount

rétracter [RetRakte] /**1**/ VT, **se rétracter** VI to retract

retraduire [RətRadɥiR] /**38**/ VT to translate again; (*dans la langue de départ*) to translate back

retrait [RətRɛ] NM (*d'argent*) withdrawal; collection; (*rétrécissement*) shrinkage; **en ~** *adj* set back; **écrire en ~** to indent; **~ du permis (de conduire)** disqualification from driving (BRIT), revocation of driver's license (US)

retraite [RətRɛt] NF (*d'une armée, Rel, refuge*) retreat; (*d'un employé*) retirement; (*revenu*) (retirement) pension; **être/mettre à la ~** to be retired/pension off *ou* retire; **prendre sa ~** to retire; **~ anticipée** early retirement; **~ aux flambeaux** torchlight tattoo

retraité, e [RətRete] ADJ retired ▶ NM/F (old age) pensioner

retraitement [RətRɛtmã] NM reprocessing

retraiter [RətRɛte] /**1**/ VT to reprocess

retranchement [RətRãʃmã] NM entrenchment; **pousser qn dans ses derniers retranchements** to drive sb into a corner

retrancher [RətRãʃe] /**1**/ VT (*passage, détails*) to take out, remove; (*couper*) to cut off; **~ qch de** (*nombre, somme*) to take *ou* deduct sth from; **se ~ derrière/dans** to entrench o.s. behind/in; (*fig*) to take refuge behind/in

retranscrire [RətRãskRiR] /**39**/ VT to retranscribe

retransmettre [RətRãsmɛtR] /**56**/ VT (*Radio*) to broadcast, relay; (*TV*) to show

retransmission [RətRãsmisjõ] NF broadcast; showing

retravailler [RətRavaje] /**1**/ VI to start work again ▶ VT to work on again

retraverser [RətRavɛRse] /**1**/ VT (*dans l'autre sens*) to cross back over

rétréci, e [RetResi] ADJ (*idées, esprit*) narrow

rétrécir [RetResiR] /**2**/ VT (*vêtement*) to take in ▶ VI to shrink; **se rétrécir** VI (*route, vallée*) to narrow

rétrécissement [RetResismã] NM narrowing

retremper [RətRãpe] /**1**/ VT: **se ~ dans** (*fig*) to reimmerse o.s. in

rétribuer [RetRibɥe] /**1**/ VT (*travail*) to pay for; (*personne*) to pay

rétribution [RetRibysjõ] NF payment

rétro [RetRo] ADJ old-style ▶ NM (*rétroviseur*) (rear-view) mirror; **la mode ~** the nostalgia vogue

rétroactif, -ive [RetRoaktif, -iv] ADJ retroactive

rétrocéder [RetRosede] /**6**/ VT to retrocede

rétrocession [RetRosesjõ] NF retrocession

rétrofusée [RetRofyze] NF retrorocket

rétrograde [RetRogRad] ADJ reactionary, backward-looking

rétrograder [RetRogRade] /**1**/ VI (*élève*) to fall back; (*économie*) to regress; (*Auto*) to change down

rétroprojecteur [RetRopRoʒɛktœR] NM overhead projector

rétrospectif, -ive [RetRospɛktif, -iv] ADJ retrospective ▶ NF (*Art*) retrospective; (*Ciné*) season, retrospective

rétrospectivement [RetRospɛktivmã] ADV in retrospect

retroussé, e [RətRuse] ADJ: **nez ~** turned-up nose

retrousser [RətRuse] /**1**/ VT to roll up; (*fig: nez*) to wrinkle; (: *lèvres*) to curl

retrouvailles [RətRuvaj] NFPL reunion *sg*

retrouver [RətRuve] /**1**/ VT (*fugitif, objet perdu*) to find; (*occasion*) to find again; (*calme, santé*) to regain; (*reconnaître: expression, style*) to recognize; (*revoir*) to see again; (*rejoindre*) to meet (again), join; **se retrouver** VI to meet; (*s'orienter*) to find one's way; **se retrouver quelque part** to find o.s. somewhere; to end up somewhere; **se retrouver seul/sans argent** to find o.s. alone/with no money; **se retrouver dans** (*calculs, dossiers, désordre*) to make sense of; **s'y retrouver** (*y voir clair*) to make sense of it; (*rentrer dans ses frais*) to break even

rétroviseur [RetRovizœR] NM (rear-view) mirror

réunifier [Reynifje] /**7**/ VT to reunify

Réunion [Reynjõ] NF: **la ~, l'île de la ~** Réunion

réunion [Reynjõ] NF bringing together; joining; (*séance*) meeting

réunionnais, e [Reynjonɛ, -ɛz] ADJ of *ou* from Réunion

réunir [ReyniR] /**2**/ VT (*convoquer*) to call together; (*rassembler*) to gather together; (*inviter: amis, famille*) to have round, have in; (*cumuler: qualités etc*) to combine; (*rapprocher: ennemis*) to bring together (again), reunite; (*rattacher: parties*) to join (together); **se réunir** VI (*se rencontrer*) to meet; (*s'allier*) to unite

réussi, e [Reysi] ADJ successful

réussir [ReysiR] /**2**/ VI to succeed, be successful; (*à un examen*) to pass; (*plante, culture*) to thrive, do well ▶ VT to make a success of; to bring off; **~ à faire** to succeed in doing; **~ à qn** to go right for sb; (*être bénéfique à*) to agree with sb; **le travail/le mariage lui réussit** work/married life agrees with him

réussite [Reysit] NF success; (*Cartes*) patience

réutiliser [Reytilize] /**1**/ VT to re-use

revaloir [RəvalwaR] /**29**/ VT: **je vous revaudrai cela** I'll repay you some day; (*en mal*) I'll pay you back for this

revalorisation [RəvaloRizasjõ] NF revaluation; raising

r

revaloriser [ʀəvalɔʀize] /1/ ᴠᴛ (*monnaie*) to revalue; (*salaires, pensions*) to raise the level of; (*institution, tradition*) to reassert the value of

revanche [ʀəvɑ̃ʃ] ɴꜰ revenge; (*sport*) revenge match; **prendre sa ~ (sur)** to take one's revenge (on); **en ~** (*par contre*) on the other hand; (*en compensation*) in return

rêvasser [ʀɛvase] /1/ ᴠɪ to daydream

rêve [ʀɛv] ɴᴍ dream; (*activité psychique*): **le ~** dreaming; **de ~** dream *cpd*; **faire un ~** to have a dream; **~ éveillé** daydreaming *no pl*, daydream

rêvé, e [ʀɛve] ᴀᴅᴊ (*endroit, mari etc*) ideal

revêche [ʀəvɛʃ] ᴀᴅᴊ surly, sour-tempered

réveil [ʀevɛj] ɴᴍ (*d'un dormeur*) waking up *no pl*; (*fig*) awakening; (*pendule*) alarm (clock); **au ~** when I (*ou you etc*) wake (*ou* woke) up, on waking (up); **sonner le ~** (*Mil*) to sound the reveille

réveille-matin [ʀevɛjmatɛ̃] ɴᴍ ɪɴᴠ alarm clock

réveiller [ʀeveje] /1/ ᴠᴛ (*personne*) to wake up; (*fig*) to awaken, revive; **se réveiller** ᴠɪ to wake up; (*fig*) to be revived, reawaken

réveillon [ʀevɛjɔ̃] ɴᴍ Christmas Eve; (*de la Saint-Sylvestre*) New Year's Eve; Christmas Eve (*ou* New Year's Eve) party *ou* dinner

réveillonner [ʀevɛjɔne] /1/ ᴠɪ to celebrate Christmas Eve (*ou* New Year's Eve)

révélateur, -trice [ʀevelatœʀ, -tʀis] ᴀᴅᴊ: **~ (de qch)** revealing (sth) ▶ ɴᴍ (*Photo*) developer

révélation [ʀevelasjɔ̃] ɴꜰ revelation

révéler [ʀevele] /6/ ᴠᴛ (*gén*) to reveal; (*divulguer*) to disclose, reveal; (*dénoter*) to reveal, show; (*faire connaître au public*): **~ qn/qch** to make sb/sth widely known, bring sb/sth to the public's notice; **se révéler** ᴠɪ to be revealed, reveal itself; **se révéler facile/faux** to prove (to be) easy/false; **se révéler cruel/un allié sûr** to show o.s. to be cruel/a trustworthy ally

revenant, e [ʀəvnɑ̃, -ɑ̃t] ɴᴍ/ꜰ ghost

revendeur, -euse [ʀəvɑ̃dœʀ, -øz] ɴᴍ/ꜰ (*détaillant*) retailer; (*d'occasions*) secondhand dealer; (*de drogue*) (drug-)dealer

revendicatif, -ive [ʀəvɑ̃dikatif, -iv] ᴀᴅᴊ (*mouvement*) protest *cpd*

revendication [ʀəvɑ̃dikasjɔ̃] ɴꜰ claim, demand; **journée de ~** day of action (in support of one's claims)

revendiquer [ʀəvɑ̃dike] /1/ ᴠᴛ to claim, demand; (*responsabilité*) to claim ▶ ᴠɪ to agitate in favour of one's claims

revendre [ʀəvɑ̃dʀ] /41/ ᴠᴛ (*d'occasion*) to resell; (*détailler*) to sell; (*vendre davantage de*): **~ du sucre/un foulard/deux bagues** to sell more sugar/another scarf/another two rings; **à ~** *adv* (*en abondance*) to spare

revenir [ʀəvniʀ] /22/ ᴠɪ to come back; **faire ~** (*Culin*) to brown; **~ cher/à 100 euros (à qn)** to cost (sb) a lot/100 euros; **~ à** (*reprendre: études, projet*) to return to, go back to; (*équivaloir à*) to amount to; **~ à qn** (*rumeur, nouvelle*) to get back to sb, reach sb's ears; (*part, honneur*) to go to sb, be sb's; (*souvenir, nom*) to come back to sb; **~ de** (*fig: maladie, étonnement*) to recover from; **~ sur** (*question, sujet*) to go back over; (*engagement*) to go

back on; **~ à la charge** to return to the attack; **~ à soi** to come round; **je n'en reviens pas** I can't get over it; **~ sur ses pas** to retrace one's steps; **cela revient à dire que/au même** it amounts to saying that/to the same thing; **~ de loin** (*fig*) to have been at death's door

revente [ʀəvɑ̃t] ɴꜰ resale

revenu, e [ʀəvny] ᴘᴘ *de* **revenir** ▶ ɴᴍ income; (*de l'État*) revenue; (*d'un capital*) yield; **revenus** ɴᴍᴘʟ income *sg*; **~ national brut** gross national income

rêver [ʀeve] /1/ ᴠɪ, ᴠᴛ to dream; (*rêvasser*) to (day)dream; **~ de** (*voir en rêve*) to dream of *ou* about; **~ de qch/de faire** to dream of sth/of doing; **~ à** to dream of

réverbération [ʀevɛʀbeʀasjɔ̃] ɴꜰ reflection

réverbère [ʀevɛʀbɛʀ] ɴᴍ street lamp *ou* light

réverbérer [ʀevɛʀbeʀe] /6/ ᴠᴛ to reflect

reverdir [ʀəvɛʀdiʀ] /2/ ᴠɪ (*arbre etc*) to turn green again

révérence [ʀeveʀɑ̃s] ɴꜰ (*vénération*) reverence; (*salut: d'homme*) bow; (: *de femme*) curtsey

révérencieux, -euse [ʀeveʀɑ̃sjø, -øz] ᴀᴅᴊ reverent

révérend, e [ʀeveʀɑ̃, -ɑ̃d] ᴀᴅᴊ: **le ~ père Pascal** the Reverend Father Pascal

révérer [ʀeveʀe] /6/ ᴠᴛ to revere

rêverie [ʀɛvʀi] ɴꜰ daydreaming *no pl*, daydream

reverrai *etc* [ʀəveʀe] ᴠʙ *voir* **revoir**

revers [ʀəvɛʀ] ɴᴍ (*de feuille, main*) back; (*d'étoffe*) wrong side; (*de pièce, médaille*) back, reverse; (*Tennis, Ping-Pong*) backhand; (*de veston*) lapel; (*de pantalon*) turn-up; (*fig: échec*) setback; **~ de fortune** reverse of fortune; **d'un ~ de main** with the back of one's hand; **le ~ de la médaille** (*fig*) the other side of the coin; **prendre à ~** (*Mil*) to take from the rear

reverser [ʀəvɛʀse] /1/ ᴠᴛ (*reporter: somme etc*): **~ sur** to put back into; (*liquide*) **~ (dans)** to pour some more (into)

réversible [ʀevɛʀsibl] ᴀᴅᴊ reversible

revêtement [ʀəvɛtmɑ̃] ɴᴍ (*de paroi*) facing; (*des sols*) flooring; (*de chaussée*) surface; (*de tuyau etc: enduit*) coating

revêtir [ʀəvetiʀ] /20/ ᴠᴛ (*habit*) to don, put on; (*prendre: importance, apparence*) to take on; **~ qn de** to dress sb in; (*fig*) to endow *ou* invest sb with; **~ qch de** to cover sth with; (*fig*) to cloak sth in; **~ d'un visa** to append a visa to

rêveur, -euse [ʀɛvœʀ, -øz] ᴀᴅᴊ dreamy ▶ ɴᴍ/ꜰ dreamer

reviendrai *etc* [ʀəvjɛ̃dʀe] ᴠʙ *voir* **revenir**

revienne *etc* [ʀəvjɛn] ᴠʙ *voir* **revenir**

revient [ʀəvjɛ̃] ᴠʙ *voir* **revenir** ▶ ɴᴍ: **prix de ~** cost price

revigorer [ʀəvigɔʀe] /1/ ᴠᴛ (*air frais*) to invigorate, brace up; (*repas, boisson*) to revive, buck up

revint *etc* [ʀəvɛ̃] ᴠʙ *voir* **revenir**

revirement [ʀəviʀmɑ̃] ɴᴍ change of mind; (*d'une situation*) reversal

revis *etc* [ʀəvi] ᴠʙ *voir* **revoir**

révisable [ʀevizabl] ᴀᴅᴊ (*procès, taux etc*) reviewable, subject to review

réviser [Revize] /**1**/ VT (*texte, Scol: matière*) to revise; (*comptes*) to audit; (*machine, installation, moteur*) to overhaul, service; (*Jur: procès*) to review

révision [Revizjɔ̃] NF revision; auditing *no pl*; (*de voiture*) overhaul, servicing *no pl*; review; **conseil de ~** (*Mil*) recruiting board; **faire ses révisions** (*Scol*) to do one's revision (BRIT), revise (BRIT), review (US); **la ~ des 10 000 km** (*Auto*) the 10,000 km service

révisionnisme [Revizjɔnism] NM revisionism

revisser [Revise] /**1**/ VT to screw back again

revit [Revi] VB *voir* **revoir**

revitaliser [Revitalize] /**1**/ VT to revitalize

revivifier [Revivifje] /**7**/ VT to revitalize

revivre [RevivR] /**46**/ VI (*reprendre des forces*) to come alive again; (*traditions*) to be revived ▶ VT (*épreuve, moment*) to relive; **faire ~** (*mode, institution, usage*) to bring back to life

révocable [Revɔkabl] ADJ (*délégué*) dismissible; (*contrat*) revocable

révocation [Revɔkasjɔ̃] NF dismissal; revocation

revoir [RevwaR] /**30**/ VT to see again; (*réviser*) to revise (BRIT), review (US) ▶ NM: **au ~** goodbye; **se revoir** (*amis*) to meet (again), see each other again; **dire au ~ à qn** to say goodbye to sb

révoltant, e [Revɔltɑ̃, -ɑ̃t] ADJ revolting, appalling

révolte [Revɔlt] NF rebellion, revolt

révolter [Revɔlte] /**1**/ VT to revolt, outrage; **se révolter** VI: **se révolter (contre)** to rebel (against); **se révolter (à)** to be outraged (by)

révolu, e [Revɔly] ADJ past; (*Admin*): **âgé de 18 ans révolus** over 18 years of age; **après trois ans révolus** when three full years have passed

révolution [Revɔlysjɔ̃] NF revolution; **être en ~** (*pays etc*) to be in revolt; **la ~ industrielle** the industrial revolution

révolutionnaire [RevɔlysjɔnɛR] ADJ, NMF revolutionary

révolutionner [Revɔlysjɔne] /**1**/ VT to revolutionize; (*fig*) to stir up

revolver [RevɔlvɛR] NM gun; (*à barillet*) revolver

révoquer [Revɔke] /**1**/ VT (*fonctionnaire*) to dismiss, remove from office; (*arrêt, contrat*) to revoke

revoyais *etc* [Revwajɛ] VB *voir* **revoir**

revu, e [Revy] PP *de* **revoir** ▶ NF (*inventaire, examen*) review; (*Mil: défilé*) review, march past; (: *inspection*) inspection, review; (*périodique*) review, magazine; (*pièce satirique*) revue; (*de music-hall*) variety show; **passer en ~** to review, inspect; (*fig: mentalement*) to review, to go through; **~ de (la) presse** press review

révulsé, e [Revylse] ADJ (*yeux*) rolled upwards; (*visage*) contorted

Reykjavik [Rekjavik] N Reykjavik

rez-de-chaussée [Redʃose] NM INV ground floor

rez-de-jardin [RedʒaRdɛ̃] NM INV garden level

RF SIGLE F = **République française**

RFA SIGLE F (= *République fédérale d'Allemagne*) FRG

RFO SIGLE F (= *Radio-Télévision Française d'Outre-mer*) French overseas broadcasting service

RG SIGLE MPL (= *renseignements généraux*) security section of the police force

rhabiller [Rabije] /**1**/: **se rhabiller** VT to get dressed again, put one's clothes on again

rhapsodie [Rapsɔdi] NF rhapsody

rhéostat [Reɔsta] NM rheostat

rhésus [Rezys] ADJ INV, NM rhesus; **~ positif/ négatif** rhesus positive/negative

rhétorique [RetɔRik] NF rhetoric ▶ ADJ rhetorical

Rhin [Rɛ̃] NM: **le ~** the Rhine

rhinite [Rinit] NF rhinitis

rhinocéros [RinɔseRɔs] NM rhinoceros

rhinopharyngite [RinɔfaRɛ̃ʒit] NF throat infection

rhodanien, ne [Rɔdanjɛ̃, -ɛn] ADJ Rhône *cpd*, of the Rhône

Rhodes [Rɔd] N: (**l'île de**) **~** (the island of) Rhodes

Rhodésie [Rɔdezi] NF: **la ~** Rhodesia

rhodésien, ne [Rɔdezjɛ̃, -ɛn] ADJ Rhodesian

rhododendron [Rɔdɔdɛ̃dRɔ̃] NM rhododendron

Rhône [Ron] NM: **le ~** the Rhone

rhubarbe [RybaRb] NF rhubarb

rhum [Rɔm] NM rum

rhumatisant, e [Rymatizɑ̃, -ɑ̃t] ADJ, NM/F rheumatic

rhumatismal, e, -aux [Rymatismal, -o] ADJ rheumatic

rhumatisme [Rymatism] NM rheumatism *no pl*

rhumatologie [Rymatɔlɔʒi] NF rheumatology

rhumatologue [Rymatɔlɔg] NMF rheumatologist

rhume [Rym] NM cold; **~ de cerveau** head cold; **le ~ des foins** hay fever

rhumerie [RɔmRi] NF (*distillerie*) rum distillery

RI SIGLE M (*Mil*) = **régiment d'infanterie**

ri [Ri] PP *de* **rire**

riant, e [Rjɑ̃, -ɑ̃t] VB *voir* **rire** ▶ ADJ smiling, cheerful; (*campagne, paysage*) pleasant

RIB SIGLE M = **relevé d'identité bancaire**

ribambelle [Ribɑ̃bɛl] NF: **une ~ de** a herd *ou* swarm of

ricain, e [Rikɛ̃, -ɛn] ADJ (*fam*) Yank, Yankee

ricanement [Rikanmɑ̃] NM snigger; giggle

ricaner [Rikane] /**1**/ VI (*avec méchanceté*) to snigger; (*bêtement, avec gêne*) to giggle

riche [Riʃ] ADJ (*gén*) rich; (*personne, pays*) rich, wealthy; **~ en** rich in; **~ de** full of; rich in

richement [Riʃmɑ̃] ADV richly

richesse [Riʃɛs] NF wealth; (*fig: de sol, musée etc*) richness; **richesses** NFPL (*ressources, argent*) wealth *sg*; (*fig: trésors*) treasures; **~ en vitamines** high vitamin content

richissime [Riʃisim] ADJ extremely rich *ou* wealthy

ricin [Risɛ̃] NM: **huile de ~** castor oil

ricocher [Rikɔʃe] /**1**/ VI: **~ (sur)** to rebound (off); (*sur l'eau*) to bounce (on *ou* off); **faire ~** (*galet*) to skim

ricochet [Rikɔʃɛ] NM rebound; bounce; **faire ~** to rebound, bounce; (*fig*) to rebound; **faire des ricochets** to skip stones; **par ~** *adv* on the rebound; (*fig*) as an indirect result

rictus [Riktys] NM grin, (snarling) grimace
ride [Rid] NF wrinkle; (fig) ripple
ridé, e [Ride] ADJ wrinkled
rideau, x [Rido] NM curtain; **tirer/ouvrir les ~** to draw/open the curtains; **~ de fer** (lit) metal shutter; **le ~ de fer** (Pol) the Iron Curtain
ridelle [Ridɛl] NF slatted side (of truck)
rider [Ride] /1/ VT to wrinkle; (fig) to ripple, ruffle the surface of; **se rider** VI to become wrinkled
ridicule [Ridikyl] ADJ ridiculous ▶ NM ridiculousness no pl; (travers: gén pl) absurdities pl; **le ~ ridicule**; **tourner en ~** to ridicule
ridiculement [Ridikylmã] ADV ridiculously
ridiculiser [Ridikylize] /1/ VT to ridicule; **se ridiculiser** VI to make a fool of o.s.
ridule [Ridyl] NF (euph: ride) little wrinkle
rie etc [Ri] VB voir **rire**

[MOT-CLÉ]

rien [Rjɛ̃] PRON **1: (ne) … rien** nothing; (tournure négative) anything; **qu'est-ce que vous avez? — rien** what have you got? — nothing; **il n'a rien dit/fait** he said/did nothing, he hasn't said/done anything; **n'avoir peur de rien** to be afraid ou frightened of nothing, not to be afraid ou frightened of anything; **il n'a rien** (n'est pas blessé) he's all right; **ça ne fait rien** it doesn't matter; **il n'y est pour rien** he's got nothing to take up boxing
2 (quelque chose): **a-t-il jamais rien fait pour nous?** has he ever done anything for us?
3: rien de: rien d'intéressant nothing interesting; **rien d'autre** nothing else; **rien du tout** nothing at all; **il n'a rien d'un champion** he's no champion, there's nothing of the champion about him
4: rien que just, only; nothing but; **rien que pour lui faire plaisir** only ou just to please him; **rien que la vérité** nothing but the truth; **rien que cela** that alone
▶ EXCL: **de rien!** not at all!, don't mention it!; **il n'en est rien!** nothing of the sort!; **rien à faire!** it's no good!, it's no use!
▶ NM: **un petit rien** (cadeau) a little something; **des riens** trivia pl; **un rien de** a hint of; **en un rien de temps** in no time at all; **avoir peur d'un rien** to be frightened of the slightest thing

rieur, -euse [Rjœr, -øz] ADJ cheerful
rigide [Riʒid] ADJ stiff; (fig) rigid; (moralement) strict
rigidité [Riʒidite] NF stiffness; **la ~ cadavérique** rigor mortis
rigolade [Rigolad] NF: **la ~** fun; (fig): **c'est de la ~** it's a big farce; (c'est facile) it's a cinch
rigole [Rigɔl] NF (conduit) channel; (filet d'eau) rivulet
rigoler [Rigɔle] /1/ VI (rire) to laugh; (s'amuser) to have (some) fun; (plaisanter) to be joking ou kidding
rigolo, rigolote [Rigolo, -ɔt] ADJ (fam) funny ▶ NM/F comic; (péj) fraud, phoney

rigorisme [Rigorism] NM (moral) rigorism
rigoriste [Rigorist] ADJ rigorist
rigoureusement [Rigurøzmã] ADV rigorously; **~ vrai/interdit** strictly true/forbidden
rigoureux, -euse [Riguro, -øz] ADJ (morale) rigorous, strict; (personne) stern, strict; (climat, châtiment) rigorous, harsh, severe; (interdiction, neutralité) strict; (preuves, analyse, méthode) rigorous
rigueur [Rigœr] NF rigour (BRIT), rigor (US); strictness; harshness; **"tenue de soirée de ~"** "evening dress (to be worn)"; **être de ~** to be the usual thing, be the rule; **à la ~** at a pinch; possibly; **tenir ~ à qn de qch** to hold sth against sb
riions etc [Rijɔ̃] VB voir **rire**
rillettes [Rijɛt] NFPL ≈ potted meat sg (made from pork or goose)
rime [Rim] NF rhyme; **n'avoir ni ~ ni raison** to have neither rhyme nor reason
rimer [Rime] /1/ VI: **~ (avec)** to rhyme (with); **ne ~ à rien** not to make sense
Rimmel® [Rimɛl] NM mascara
rinçage [Rɛ̃saʒ] NM rinsing (out); (opération) rinse
rince-doigts [Rɛ̃sdwa] NM INV finger-bowl
rincer [Rɛ̃se] /3/ VT to rinse; (récipient) to rinse out; **se ~ la bouche** to rinse one's mouth out
ring [Riŋ] NM (boxing) ring; **monter sur le ~** (aussi fig) to enter the ring; (faire carrière de boxeur) to take up boxing
ringard, e [Rɛ̃gar, -ard] ADJ (péj) old-fashioned
Rio de Janeiro [Riodʒanero] N Rio de Janeiro
rions [Rijɔ̃] VB voir **rire**
ripaille [Ripaj] NF: **faire ~** to feast
riper [Ripe] /1/ VI to slip, slide
ripoliné, e [Ripoline] ADJ enamel-painted
riposte [Ripost] NF retort, riposte; (fig) counter-attack, reprisal
riposter [Riposte] /1/ VI to retaliate ▶ VT: **~ que** to retort that; **~ à** VT to counter; to reply to
ripper [Ripe] /1/ VT (Inform) to rip
rire [Rir] /36/ VI to laugh; (se divertir) to have fun; (plaisanter) to joke ▶ NM laugh; **le ~** laughter; **~ de** VT to laugh at; **se ~ de** to make light of; **tu veux ~!** you must be joking!; **~ aux éclats/aux larmes** to roar with laughter/laugh until one cries; **~ jaune** to force oneself to laugh; **~ sous cape** to laugh up one's sleeve; **~ au nez de qn** to laugh in sb's face; **pour ~** (pas sérieusement) for a joke ou a laugh
ris [Ri] VB voir **rire** ▶ NM: **~ de veau** (calf) sweetbread
risée [Rize] NF: **être la ~ de** to be the laughing stock of
risette [Rizɛt] NF: **faire ~ (à)** to give a nice little smile (to)
risible [Rizibl] ADJ laughable, ridiculous
risque [Risk] NM risk; **le ~** danger; **l'attrait du ~** the lure of danger; **prendre des risques** to take risks; **à ses risques et périls** at his own risk; **au ~ de** at the risk of; **~ d'incendie** fire risk; **~ calculé** calculated risk
risqué, e [Riske] ADJ risky; (plaisanterie) risqué, daring

risquer [Riske] /**1**/ VT to risk; (*allusion, question*) to venture, hazard; **se risquer** VI: **se risquer dans** (*s'aventurer*) to venture into; **tu risques qu'on te renvoie** you risk being dismissed; **ça ne risque rien** it's quite safe; **il risque de se tuer** he could get *ou* risks getting himself killed; **il a risqué de se tuer** he almost got himself killed; **ce qui risque de se produire** what might *ou* could well happen; **il ne risque pas de recommencer** there's no chance of him doing that again; **se risquer à faire** (*tenter*) to dare to do; ~ **le tout pour le tout** to risk the lot

risque-tout [Riskətu] NMF INV daredevil

rissoler [Risɔle] /**1**/ VI, VT: (**faire**) ~ to brown

ristourne [Risturn] NF rebate; discount

rit *etc* [Ri] VB *voir* **rire**

rite [Rit] NM rite; (*fig*) ritual

ritournelle [Riturnel] NF (*fig*) tune; **c'est toujours la même** ~ (*fam*) it's always the same old story

rituel, le [Rityɛl] ADJ, NM ritual

rituellement [Rityɛlmɑ̃] ADV religiously

riv. ABR (= *rivière*) R

rivage [Rivaʒ] NM shore

rival, e, -aux [Rival, -o] ADJ, NM/F rival; **sans** ~ *adj* unrivalled

rivaliser [Rivalize] /**1**/ VI: ~ **avec** to rival, vie with; (*être comparable*) to hold its own against, compare with; ~ **avec qn de** (*élégance etc*) to vie with *ou* rival sb in

rivalité [Rivalite] NF rivalry

rive [Riv] NF shore; (*de fleuve*) bank

river [Rive] /**1**/ VT (*clou, pointe*) to clinch; (*plaques*) to rivet together; **être rivé sur/à** to be riveted on/to

riverain, e [Rivrɛ̃, -ɛn] ADJ riverside *cpd*; lakeside *cpd*; roadside *cpd* ▸ NM/F riverside (*ou* lakeside) resident; (*d'une route*) local *ou* roadside resident

rivet [Rivɛ] NM rivet

riveter [Rivte] /**4**/ VT to rivet (together)

Riviera [Rivjɛra] NF: **la** ~ **(italienne)** the Italian Riviera

rivière [Rivjɛr] NF river; ~ **de diamants** diamond rivière

rixe [Riks] NF brawl, scuffle

Riyad [Rijad] N Riyadh

riz [Ri] NM rice; ~ **au lait** ≈ rice pudding

rizière [Rizjɛr] NF paddy field

RMC SIGLE F = **Radio Monte Carlo**

RMI SIGLE M (= *revenu minimum d'insertion*) ≈ income support (*BRIT*), ≈ welfare (*US*)

RN SIGLE F = **route nationale**

robe [Rɔb] NF dress; (*de juge, d'ecclésiastique*) robe; (*de professeur*) gown; (*pelage*) coat; ~ **de soirée/de mariée** evening/wedding dress; ~ **de baptême** christening robe; ~ **de chambre** dressing gown; ~ **de grossesse** maternity dress

robinet [Rɔbinɛ] NM tap (*BRIT*), faucet (*US*); ~ **du gaz** gas tap; ~ **mélangeur** mixer tap

robinetterie [Rɔbinɛtri] NF taps *pl*, plumbing

roboratif, -ive [Rɔbɔratif, -iv] ADJ bracing, invigorating

robot [Rɔbo] NM robot; ~ **de cuisine** food processor

robotique [Rɔbɔtik] NF robotics *sg*

robotiser [Rɔbɔtize] /**1**/ VT (*personne, travailleur*) to turn into a robot; (*monde, vie*) to automate

robuste [Rɔbyst] ADJ robust, sturdy

robustesse [Rɔbystɛs] NF robustness, sturdiness

roc [Rɔk] NM rock

rocade [Rɔkad] NF (*Auto*) bypass

rocaille [Rɔkaj] NF (*pierres*) loose stones *pl*; (*terrain*) rocky *ou* stony ground; (*jardin*) rockery, rock garden ▸ ADJ (*style*) rocaille

rocailleux, -euse [Rɔkajø, -øz] ADJ rocky, stony; (*voix*) harsh

rocambolesque [Rɔkɑ̃bɔlɛsk] ADJ fantastic, incredible

roche [Rɔʃ] NF rock

rocher [Rɔʃe] NM rock; (*Anat*) petrosal bone

rochet [Rɔʃɛ] NM: **roue à** ~ ratchet wheel

rocheux, -euse [Rɔʃø, -øz] ADJ rocky; **les (montagnes) Rocheuses** the Rockies, the Rocky Mountains

rock [Rɔk], **rock and roll** [Rɔkɛnrɔl] NM (*musique*) rock(-'n'-roll); (*danse*) rock

rocker [Rɔkœr] NM (*chanteur*) rock musician; (*adepte*) rock fan

rocking-chair [Rɔkiŋ(t)ʃɛr] NM rocking chair

rococo [Rɔkɔko] NM rococo ▸ ADJ INV rococo

rodage [Rɔdaʒ] NM running in (*BRIT*), breaking in (*US*); **en** ~ (*Auto*) running *ou* breaking in

rodé, e [Rɔde] ADJ run in (*BRIT*), broken in (*US*); (*personne*): ~ **à qch** having got the hang of sth

rodéo [Rɔdeo] NM rodeo

roder [Rɔde] /**1**/ VT (*moteur, voiture*) to run in (*BRIT*), break in (*US*); ~ **un spectacle** to iron out the initial problems of a show

rôder [Rode] /**1**/ VI to roam *ou* wander about; (*de façon suspecte*) to lurk (about *ou* around)

rôdeur, -euse [Rodœr, -øz] NM/F prowler

rodomontades [Rɔdɔmɔ̃tad] NFPL bragging *sg*; sabre rattling *sg*

rogatoire [Rɔgatwar] ADJ: **commission** ~ letters rogatory

rogne [Rɔɲ] NF: **être en** ~ to be mad *ou* in a temper; **se mettre en** ~ to get mad *ou* in a temper

rogner [Rɔɲe] /**1**/ VT to trim; (*fig*) to whittle down; ~ **sur** (*fig*) to cut down *ou* back on

rognons [Rɔɲɔ̃] NMPL kidneys

rognures [Rɔɲyr] NFPL trimmings

rogue [Rɔg] ADJ arrogant

roi [Rwa] NM king; **les Rois mages** the Three Wise Men, the Magi; **le jour** *ou* **la fête des Rois**, **les Rois** Twelfth Night; *see note*

> The *fête des Rois* is celebrated on 6 January. Figurines representing the Three Wise Men are traditionally added to the Christmas crib (*crèche*) and people eat *galette des Rois*, a flat cake in which a porcelain charm (*la fève*) is hidden. Whoever finds the charm is king or queen for the day and can choose a partner.

roitelet [Rwatlɛ] NM wren; (*péj*) kinglet

rôle [Rol] NM role; (*contribution*) part

r

rollers [ʀɔlœʀ] NMPL Rollerblades®

rollmops [ʀɔlmɔps] NM rollmop

romain, e [ʀɔmɛ̃, -ɛn] ADJ Roman ▶ NM/F: **R~, e** Roman ▶ NF (*Culin*) cos (lettuce)

roman, e [ʀɔmã, -an] ADJ (*Archit*) Romanesque; (*Ling*) Romance *cpd*, Romanic ▶ NM novel; **~ d'amour** love story; **~ d'espionnage** spy novel *ou* story; **~ noir** thriller; **~ policier** detective novel

romance [ʀɔmãs] NF ballad

romancer [ʀɔmãse] /3/ VT to romanticize

romanche [ʀɔmãʃ] ADJ, NM Romansh

romancier, -ière [ʀɔmãsje, -jɛʀ] NM/F novelist

romand, e [ʀɔmã, -ãd] ADJ *of ou* from French-speaking Switzerland ▶ NM/F: **R~, e** French-speaking Swiss

romanesque [ʀɔmanɛsk] ADJ (*fantastique*) fantastic; (*amours, aventures*) storybook *cpd*; (*sentimental: personne*) romantic; (*Littérature*) novelistic

roman-feuilleton [ʀɔmãfœjtɔ̃] (*pl* **romans-feuilletons**) NM serialized novel

roman-fleuve [ʀɔmãflœv] (*pl* **romans-fleuves**) NM saga, roman-fleuve

romanichel, le [ʀɔmaniʃɛl] NM/F gipsy (*péj*)

roman-photo [ʀɔmãfɔto] (*pl* **romans-photos**) NM (*romantic*) picture story

romantique [ʀɔmãtik] ADJ romantic

romantisme [ʀɔmãtism] NM romanticism

romarin [ʀɔmaʀɛ̃] NM rosemary

rombière [ʀɔ̃bjɛʀ] NF (*péj*) old bag

Rome [ʀɔm] N Rome

rompre [ʀɔ̃pʀ] /41/ VT to break; (*entretien, fiançailles*) to break off ▶ VI (*fiancés*) to break it off; **se rompre** VI to break; (*Méd*) to burst, rupture; **se rompre les os** *ou* **le cou** to break one's neck; **~ avec** to break with; **à tout ~** *adv* wildly; **applaudir à tout ~** to bring down the house, applaud wildly; **rompez (les rangs)!** (*Mil*) dismiss!, fall out!

rompu, e [ʀɔ̃py] PP *de* **rompre** ▶ ADJ (*fourbu*) exhausted, worn out; **~ à** with wide experience of; inured to

romsteck [ʀɔ̃mstɛk] NM rump steak *no pl*

ronce [ʀɔ̃s] NF (*Bot*) bramble branch; (*Menuiserie*): **~ de noyer** burr walnut; **ronces** NFPL brambles, thorns

ronchonner [ʀɔ̃ʃɔne] /1/ VI (*fam*) to grouse, grouch

rond, e [ʀɔ̃, ʀɔ̃d] ADJ round; (*joues, mollets*) well-rounded; (*fam: ivre*) tight; (*sincère, décidé*): **être ~ en affaires** to be on the level in business, do an honest deal ▶ NM (*cercle*) ring; (*fam: sou*): **je n'ai plus un ~** I haven't a penny left ▶ NF (*gén: de surveillance*) rounds *pl*, patrol; (*danse*) round (dance); (*Mus*) semibreve (BRIT), whole note (US) ▶ ADV: **tourner ~** (*moteur*) to run smoothly; **ça ne tourne pas ~** (*fig*) there's something not quite right about it; **pour faire un compte ~** to make (it) a round figure, to round (it) off; **avoir le dos ~** to be round-shouldered; **en ~** (*s'asseoir, danser*) in a ring; **à la ~** (*alentour*): **à 10 km à la ~** for 10 km round; (*à chacun son tour*) **passer qch à la ~** to pass sth

(a)round; **faire des ronds de jambe** to bow and scrape; **~ de serviette** napkin ring

rond-de-cuir [ʀɔ̃dkɥiʀ] (*pl* **ronds-de-cuir**) NM (*péj*) penpusher

rondelet, te [ʀɔ̃dlɛ, -ɛt] ADJ plump; (*fig: somme*) tidy; (: *bourse*) well-lined, fat

rondelle [ʀɔ̃dɛl] NF (*Tech*) washer; (*tranche*) slice, round

rondement [ʀɔ̃dmã] ADV (*avec décision*) briskly; (*loyalement*) frankly

rondeur [ʀɔ̃dœʀ] NF (*d'un bras, des formes*) plumpness; (*bonhomie*) friendly straightforwardness; **rondeurs** NFPL (*d'une femme*) curves

rondin [ʀɔ̃dɛ̃] NM log

rond-point [ʀɔ̃pwɛ̃] (*pl* **ronds-points**) NM roundabout (BRIT), traffic circle (US)

ronflant, e [ʀɔ̃flã, -ãt] ADJ (*péj*) high-flown, grand

ronflement [ʀɔ̃fləmã] NM snore, snoring *no pl*

ronfler [ʀɔ̃fle] /1/ VI to snore; (*moteur, poêle*) to hum; (: *plus fort*) to roar

ronger [ʀɔ̃ʒe] /3/ VT to gnaw (at); (*vers, rouille*) to eat into; **~ son frein** to champ (at) the bit; **se ~ de souci, se ~ les sangs** to worry o.s. sick, fret; **se ~ les ongles** to bite one's nails

rongeur, -euse [ʀɔ̃ʒœʀ, -øz] NM/F rodent

ronronnement [ʀɔ̃ʀɔnmã] NM purring; (*bruit*) purr

ronronner [ʀɔ̃ʀɔne] /1/ VI to purr

roque [ʀɔk] NM (*Échecs*) castling

roquefort [ʀɔkfɔʀ] NM Roquefort

roquer [ʀɔke] /1/ VI to castle

roquet [ʀɔkɛ] NM nasty little lap-dog

roquette [ʀɔkɛt] NF rocket; **~ antichar** antitank rocket

rosace [ʀɔzas] NF (*vitrail*) rose window, rosace; (*motif: de plafond etc*) rose

rosaire [ʀɔzɛʀ] NM rosary

rosbif [ʀɔsbif] NM: **du ~** roasting beef; (*cuit*) roast beef; **un ~** a joint of (roasting) beef

rose [ʀoz] NF rose; (*vitrail*) rose window ▶ ADJ pink; **~ bonbon** *adj inv* candy pink; **~ des vents** compass card

rosé, e [ʀoze] ADJ pinkish; (*vin*) **~ rosé** (wine)

roseau, x [ʀozo] NM reed

rosée [ʀoze] ADJ F *voir* **rosé** ▶ NF dew; **goutte de ~** dewdrop

roseraie [ʀozʀɛ] NF rose garden; (*plantation*) rose nursery

rosette [ʀozɛt] NF rosette (*gen of the Légion d'honneur*)

rosier [ʀozje] NM rosebush, rose tree

rosir [ʀoziʀ] /2/ VI to go pink

rosse [ʀɔs] NF (*péj: cheval*) nag ▶ ADJ nasty, vicious

rosser [ʀɔse] /1/ VT (*fam*) to thrash

rossignol [ʀɔsiɲɔl] NM (*Zool*) nightingale; (*crochet*) picklock

rot [ʀo] NM belch; (*de bébé*) burp

rotatif, -ive [ʀɔtatif, -iv] ADJ rotary ▶ NF rotary press

rotation [ʀɔtasjɔ̃] NF rotation; (*fig*) rotation, swap-around; (*renouvellement*) turnover; **par ~**

on a rota (BRIT) *ou* rotation (US) basis; **~ des cultures** crop rotation; **~ des stocks** stock turnover

rotatoire [ʀɔtatwaʀ] ADJ: **mouvement ~** rotary movement

roter [ʀɔte] /1/ VI (*fam*) to burp, belch

rôti [ʀoti] NM: **du ~** roasting meat; (*cuit*) roast meat; **un ~ de bœuf/porc** a joint of beef/pork

rotin [ʀɔtɛ̃] NM rattan (cane); **fauteuil en ~** cane (arm)chair

rôtir [ʀotiʀ] /2/ VT (*aussi*: **faire rôtir**) to roast ▶ VI to roast; **se ~ au soleil** to bask in the sun

rôtisserie [ʀotisʀi] NF (*restaurant*) steakhouse; (*comptoir, magasin*) roast meat counter (*ou* shop); (*traiteur*) roast meat shop

rôtissoire [ʀotiswaʀ] NF (roasting) spit

rotonde [ʀɔtɔ̃d] NF (*Archit*) rotunda; (*Rail*) engine shed

rotondité [ʀɔtɔ̃dite] NF roundness

rotor [ʀɔtɔʀ] NM rotor

Rotterdam [ʀɔtɛʀdam] N Rotterdam

rotule [ʀɔtyl] NF kneecap, patella

roturier, -ière [ʀɔtyʀje, -jɛʀ] NM/F commoner

rouage [ʀwaʒ] NM cog(wheel), gearwheel; (*de montre*) part; (*fig*) cog; **rouages** NMPL (*fig*) internal structure *sg*; **les rouages de l'État** the wheels of State

Rouanda [ʀwɑ̃da] NM: **le ~** Rwanda

roubaisien, ne [ʀubezjɛ̃, -ɛn] ADJ *of ou* from Roubaix

roublard, e [ʀublaʀ, -aʀd] ADJ (*péj*) crafty, wily

rouble [ʀubl] NM rouble

roucoulement [ʀukulmɑ̃] NM (*de pigeons, fig*) coo, cooing

roucouler [ʀukule] /1/ VI to coo; (*fig: péj*) to warble; (: *amoureux*) to bill and coo

roue [ʀu] NF wheel; **faire la ~** (*paon*) to spread *ou* fan its tail; (*Gym*) to do a cartwheel; **descendre en ~ libre** to freewheel *ou* coast down; **pousser à la ~** to put one's shoulder to the wheel; **grande ~** (*à la foire*) big wheel; **~ à aubes** paddle wheel; **~ dentée** cogwheel; **~ de secours** spare wheel

roué, e [ʀwe] ADJ wily

rouennais, e [ʀwanɛ, -ɛz] ADJ *of ou* from Rouen

rouer [ʀwe] /1/ VT: **~ qn de coups** to give sb a thrashing

rouet [ʀwɛ] NM spinning wheel

rouge [ʀuʒ] ADJ, NM/F red ▶ NM red; (*fard*) rouge; (**vin**) **~** red wine; **passer au ~** (*signal*) to go red; (*automobiliste*) to go through a red light; **porter au ~** (*métal*) to bring to red heat; **sur la liste ~** (*Tél*) ex-directory (BRIT), unlisted (US); **~ de honte/colère** red with shame/anger; **se fâcher tout/voir ~** to blow one's top/see red; **~ à joue** blusher; **~ à lèvres** lipstick

rougeâtre [ʀuʒɑtʀ] ADJ reddish

rougeaud, e [ʀuʒo, -od] ADJ (*teint*) red; (*personne*) red-faced

rouge-gorge [ʀuʒgɔʀʒ] NM robin (redbreast)

rougeoiement [ʀuʒwamɑ̃] NM reddish glow

rougeole [ʀuʒɔl] NF measles *sg*

rougeoyant, e [ʀuʒwajɑ̃, -ɑ̃t] ADJ (*ciel, braises*) glowing; (*aube, reflets*) glowing red

rougeoyer [ʀuʒwaje] /8/ VI to glow red

rouget [ʀuʒɛ] NM mullet

rougeur [ʀuʒœʀ] NF redness; (*du visage*) red face; **rougeurs** NFPL (*Méd*) red blotches

rougir [ʀuʒiʀ] /2/ VI to turn red; (*de honte, timidité*) to blush, flush; (*de plaisir, colère*) to flush; (*fraise, tomate*) to go *ou* turn red; (*ciel*) to redden

rouille [ʀuj] ADJ INV rust-coloured, rusty ▶ NF rust; (*Culin*) spicy (Provençal) sauce served with fish dishes

rouillé, e [ʀuje] ADJ rusty

rouiller [ʀuje] /1/ VT to rust ▶ VI to rust, go rusty; **se rouiller** VI to rust; (*fig: mentalement*) to become rusty; (: *physiquement*) to grow stiff

roulade [ʀulad] NF (*Gym*) roll; (*Culin*) rolled meat *no pl*; (*Mus*) roulade, run

roulage [ʀulaʒ] NM (*transport*) haulage

roulant, e [ʀulɑ̃, -ɑ̃t] ADJ (*meuble*) on wheels; (*surface, trottoir, tapis*) moving; **matériel ~** (*Rail*) rolling stock; **escalier ~** escalator; **personnel ~** (*Rail*) train crews *pl*

roulé, e [ʀule] ADJ: **bien ~** (*fam: femme*) shapely, curvy

rouleau, x [ʀulo] NM (*de papier, tissu, pièces de monnaie, Sport*) roll; (*de machine à écrire*) roller, platen; (*à mise en plis, à peinture, vague*) roller; **être au bout du ~** (*fig*) to be at the end of the line; **~ compresseur** steamroller; **~ à pâtisserie** rolling pin; **~ de pellicule** roll of film

roulé-boulé [ʀulebule] (*pl* roulés-boulés) N (*Sport*) roll

roulement [ʀulmɑ̃] NM (*bruit*) rumbling *no pl*, rumble; (*rotation*) rotation; turnover; (*de capitaux*) circulation; **par ~** on a rota (BRIT) *ou* rotation (US) basis; **~ (à billes)** ball bearings *pl*; **~ de tambour** drum roll; **~ d'yeux** roll(ing) of the eyes

rouler [ʀule] /1/ VT to roll; (*papier, tapis*) to roll up; (*Culin: pâte*) to roll out; (*fam: duper*) to do, con ▶ VI (*bille, boule*) to roll; (*voiture, train*) to go, run; (*automobiliste*) to drive; (*cycliste*) to ride; (*bateau*) to roll; (*tonnerre*) to rumble, roll; (*dégringoler*): **~ en bas de** to roll down; **~ sur** (*conversation*) to turn on; **se ~ dans** (*boue*) to roll in; (*couverture*) to roll o.s. (up) in; **~ dans la farine** (*fam*) to con; **~ les épaules/hanches** to sway one's shoulders/wiggle one's hips; **~ les "r"** to roll one's r's; **~ sur l'or** to be rolling in money, be rolling in it; **~ (sa bosse)** to go places

roulette [ʀulɛt] NF (*de table, fauteuil*) castor; (*de dentiste*) drill; (*de pâtissier*) pastry wheel; (*jeu*): **la ~ roulette**; **à roulettes** on castors; **la ~ russe** Russian roulette; **ça a marché comme sur des roulettes** (*fam*) it went off very smoothly

roulis [ʀuli] NM roll(ing)

roulotte [ʀulɔt] NF caravan

roumain, e [ʀumɛ̃, -ɛn] ADJ Rumanian, Romanian ▶ NM (*Ling*) Rumanian, Romanian ▶ NM/F: **R~, e** Rumanian, Romanian

Roumanie [ʀumani] NF: **la ~** Rumania, Romania

roupiller [ʀupije] /1/ VI (*fam*) to sleep

rouquin, e [ʀukɛ̃, -in] NM/F (*péj*) redhead

rouspéter [ʀuspete] /6/ VI (*fam*) to moan, grouse

r

rousse [ʀus] ADJ F *voir* **roux**

rousseur [ʀusœʀ] NF: **tache de ~** freckle

roussi [ʀusi] NM: **ça sent le ~** there's a smell of burning; (*fig*) I can smell trouble

roussir [ʀusiʀ] /2/ VT to scorch ▶ VI (*feuilles*) to go *ou* turn brown; (*Culin*): **faire ~** to brown

routage [ʀutaʒ] NM (collective) mailing

routard, e [ʀutaʀ, -aʀd] NM/F traveller

route [ʀut] NF road; (*fig: chemin*) way; (*itinéraire, parcours*) route; (*fig: voie*) road, path; **par (la) ~** by road; **il y a trois heures de ~** it's a three-hour ride *ou* journey; **en ~** *adv* on the way; **en ~!** let's go!; **en cours de ~** en route; **mettre en ~** to start up; **se mettre en ~** to set off; **faire ~ vers** to head towards; **faire fausse ~** (*fig*) to be on the wrong track; **~ nationale** ≈ A-road (BRIT), ≈ state highway (US)

routier, -ière [ʀutje, -jɛʀ] ADJ road *cpd* ▶ NM (*camionneur*) (long-distance) lorry (BRIT) *ou* truck (US) driver; (*restaurant*) ≈ transport café (BRIT), ≈ truck stop (US); (*scout*) ≈ rover; (*cycliste*) road racer ▶ NF (*voiture*) touring car; **vieux ~** old stager; **carte routière** road map

routine [ʀutin] NF routine; **visite/contrôle de ~** routine visit/check

routinier, -ière [ʀutinje, -jɛʀ] ADJ (*péj: travail*) humdrum, routine; (*: personne*) addicted to routine

rouvert, e [ʀuvɛʀ, -ɛʀt] PP *de* **rouvrir**

rouvrir [ʀuvʀiʀ] /18/ VT, VI to reopen, open again; **se rouvrir** VI (*blessure*) to open up again

roux, rousse [ʀu, ʀus] ADJ red; (*personne*) red-haired ▶ NM/F redhead ▶ NM (*Culin*) roux

royal, e, -aux [ʀwajal, -o] ADJ royal; (*fig*) fit for a king, princely; blissful; thorough

royalement [ʀwajalmɑ̃] ADV royally

royaliste [ʀwajalist] ADJ, NMF royalist

royaume [ʀwajom] NM kingdom; (*fig*) realm; **le ~ des cieux** the kingdom of heaven

Royaume-Uni [ʀwajomyni] NM: **le ~** the United Kingdom

royauté [ʀwajote] NF (*dignité*) kingship; (*régime*) monarchy

RP SIGLE F (= *recette principale*) ≈ main post office; = **la région parisienne** ▶ SIGLE FPL (= *relations publiques*) PR

R.S.V.P. ABR (= *répondez s'il vous plaît*) R.S.V.P

RTB SIGLE F = **Radio-Télévision belge**

Rte ABR = **route**

RTL SIGLE F = **Radio-Télévision Luxembourg**

RU [ʀy] SIGLE M = **restaurant universitaire**

ruade [ʀɥad] NF kick

Ruanda [ʀwɑ̃da] NM: **le ~** Rwanda

ruban [ʀybɑ̃] NM (*gén*) ribbon; (*pour ourlet, couture*) binding; (*de téléscripteur etc*) tape; (*d'acier*) strip; **~ adhésif** adhesive tape; **~ carbone** carbon ribbon

rubéole [ʀybeɔl] NF German measles *sg*, rubella

rubicond, e [ʀybikɔ̃, -ɔ̃d] ADJ rubicund, ruddy

rubis [ʀybi] NM ruby; (*Horlogerie*) jewel; **payer ~ sur l'ongle** to pay cash on the nail

rubrique [ʀybʀik] NF (*titre, catégorie*) heading, rubric; (*Presse: article*) column

ruche [ʀyʃ] NF hive

rucher [ʀyʃe] NM apiary

rude [ʀyd] ADJ (*barbe, toile*) rough; (*métier, tâche*) hard, tough; (*climat*) severe, harsh; (*bourru*) harsh, rough; (*fruste: manières*) rugged, tough; (*fam: fameux*) jolly good; **être mis à ~ épreuve** to be put through the mill

rudement [ʀydmɑ̃] ADV (*tomber, frapper*) hard; (*traiter, reprocher*) harshly; (*fam: très*) terribly; (*: beaucoup*) terribly hard

rudesse [ʀydɛs] NF roughness; toughness; severity; harshness

rudimentaire [ʀydimɑ̃tɛʀ] ADJ rudimentary, basic

rudiments [ʀydimɑ̃] NMPL rudiments; basic knowledge *sg*; basic principles; **avoir des ~ d'anglais** to have a smattering of English

rudoyer [ʀydwaje] /8/ VT to treat harshly

rue [ʀy] NF street; **être/jeter qn à la ~** to be on the streets/throw sb out onto the street

ruée [ʀɥe] NF rush; **la ~ vers l'or** the gold rush

ruelle [ʀɥɛl] NF alley(way)

ruer [ʀɥe] /1/ VI (*cheval*) to kick out; **se ruer** VI: **se ruer sur** to pounce on; **se ruer vers/dans/hors de** to rush *ou* dash towards/into/out of; **~ dans les brancards** to become rebellious

rugby [ʀygbi] NM rugby (football); **~ à treize/quinze** rugby league/union

rugir [ʀyʒiʀ] /2/ VI to roar

rugissement [ʀyʒismɑ̃] NM roar, roaring *no pl*

rugosité [ʀygozite] NF roughness; (*aspérité*) rough patch

rugueux, -euse [ʀygø, -øz] ADJ rough

ruine [ʀɥin] NF ruin; **ruines** NFPL ruins; **tomber en ~** to fall into ruin(s)

ruiner [ʀɥine] /1/ VT to ruin

ruineux, -euse [ʀɥinø, -øz] ADJ terribly expensive to buy (*ou* run), ruinous; extravagant

ruisseau, x [ʀɥiso] NM stream, brook; (*caniveau*) gutter; (*fig*): **~ de larmes/sang** floods of tears/streams of blood

ruisselant, e [ʀɥislɑ̃, -ɑ̃t] ADJ streaming

ruisseler [ʀɥisle] /4/ VI to stream; **~ (d'eau)** to be streaming (with water); **~ de lumière** to stream with light

ruissellement [ʀɥisɛlmɑ̃] NM streaming; **~ de lumière** stream of light

rumeur [ʀymœʀ] NF (*bruit confus*) rumbling; hubbub *no pl*; (*protestation*) murmur(ing); (*nouvelle*) rumour (BRIT), rumor (US)

ruminer [ʀymine] /1/ VT (*herbe*) to ruminate; (*fig*) to ruminate on *ou* over, chew over ▶ VI (*vache*) to chew the cud, ruminate

rumsteck [ʀɔ̃mstɛk] NM = **romsteck**

rupestre [ʀypɛstʀ] ADJ (*plante*) rock *cpd*; (*art*) wall *cpd*

rupture [ʀyptyʀ] NF (*de câble, digue*) breaking; (*de tendon*) rupture, tearing; (*de négociations etc*) breakdown; (*de contrat*) breach; (*dans continuité*) break; (*séparation, désunion*) break-up, split; **en ~ de ban** at odds with authority; **en ~ de stock** (*Comm*) out of stock

rural, e, -aux [ʀyʀal, -o] ADJ rural, country *cpd* ▶ NMPL: **les ruraux** country people

ruse [ʀyz] NF: **la ~** cunning, craftiness; (*pour tromper*) trickery; **une ~** a trick, a ruse; **par ~** by trickery

rusé, e [ʀyze] ADJ cunning, crafty

russe [ʀys] ADJ Russian ▶ NM (*Ling*) Russian ▶ NMF: **R~** Russian

Russie [ʀysi] NF: **la ~** Russia; **la ~ blanche** White Russia; **la ~ soviétique** Soviet Russia

rustine [ʀystin] NF repair patch (*for bicycle inner tube*)

rustique [ʀystik] ADJ rustic; (*plante*) hardy

rustre [ʀystʀ] NM boor

rut [ʀyt] NM: **être en ~** (*animal domestique*) to be in *ou* on heat; (*animal sauvage*) to be rutting

rutabaga [ʀytabaga] NM swede

rutilant, e [ʀytilɑ̃, -ɑ̃t] ADJ gleaming

RV SIGLE M = **rendez-vous**

Rwanda [ʀwɑ̃da] NM: **le ~** Rwanda

rythme [ʀitm] NM rhythm; (*vitesse*) rate; (: *de la vie*) pace, tempo; **au ~ de 10 par jour** at the rate of 10 a day

rythmé, e [ʀitme] ADJ rhythmic(al)

rythmer [ʀitme] /1/ VT to give rhythm to

rythmique [ʀitmik] ADJ rhythmic(al) ▶ NF rhythmics *sg*

Ss

S, s [ɛs] NM INV S, s ▸ ABR (= *sud*) S; (= *seconde*) sec; (= *siècle*) c., century; **S comme Suzanne** S for Sugar

s/ ABR = **sur¹**

s' [s] PRON *voir* **se**

SA SIGLE F = **société anonyme**; (= *Son Altesse*) HH

sa [sa] ADJ POSS *voir* **son¹**

sabbatique [sabatik] ADJ: **année ~** sabbatical year

sable [sabl] NM sand; **sables mouvants** quicksand(s)

sablé [sable] ADJ (*allée*) sandy ▸ NM shortbread biscuit; **pâte sablée** (*Culin*) shortbread dough

sabler [sable] /1/ VT to sand; (*contre le verglas*) to grit; **~ le champagne** to drink champagne

sableux, -euse [sablø, -øz] ADJ sandy

sablier [sablije] NM hourglass; (*de cuisine*) egg timer

sablière [sablijɛʀ] NF sand quarry

sablonneux, -euse [sablɔnø, -øz] ADJ sandy

saborder [sabɔʀde] /1/ VT (*navire*) to scuttle; (*fig*) to wind up, shut down

sabot [sabo] NM clog; (*de cheval, bœuf*) hoof; **~ (de Denver)** (*wheel*) clamp; **~ de frein** brake shoe

sabotage [sabɔtaʒ] NM sabotage

saboter [sabɔte] /1/ VT (*travail, morceau de musique*) to botch, make a mess of; (*machine, installation, négociation etc*) to sabotage

saboteur, -euse [sabɔtœʀ, -øz] NM/F saboteur

sabre [sabʀ] NM sabre; **le ~** (*fig*) the sword, the army

sabrer [sabʀe] /1/ VT to cut down

sac [sak] NM bag; (*à charbon etc*) sack; (*pillage*) sack(ing); **mettre à ~** to sack; **~ à provisions/ de voyage** shopping/travelling bag; **~ de couchage** sleeping bag; **~ à dos** rucksack; **~ à main** handbag; **~ de plage** beach bag

saccade [sakad] NF jerk; **par saccades** jerkily; haltingly

saccadé, e [sakade] ADJ jerky; (*respiration*) spasmodic

saccage [sakaʒ] NM havoc

saccager [sakaʒe] /3/ VT (*piller*) to sack, lay waste; (*dévaster*) to create havoc in, wreck

saccharine [sakaʀin] NF saccharin(e)

saccharose [sakaʀoz] NM sucrose

SACEM [sasɛm] SIGLE F (= *Société des auteurs, compositeurs et éditeurs de musique*) body responsible for collecting and distributing royalties

sacerdoce [sasɛʀdɔs] NM priesthood; (*fig*) calling, vocation

sacerdotal, e, -aux [sasɛʀdɔtal, -o] ADJ priestly, sacerdotal

sachant *etc* [saʃɑ̃] VB *voir* **savoir**

sache *etc* [saʃ] VB *voir* **savoir**

sachet [saʃɛ] NM (small) bag; (*de lavande, poudre, shampooing*) sachet; **thé en sachets** tea bags; **~ de thé** tea bag; **du potage en ~** packet soup

sacoche [sakɔʃ] NF (*gén*) bag; (*de bicyclette*) saddlebag; (*du facteur*) (post)bag; (*d'outils*) toolbag

sacquer [sake] /1/ VT (*fam: candidat, employé*) to sack; (: *réprimander, mal noter*) to plough

sacraliser [sakʀalize] /1/ VT to make sacred

sacre [sakʀ] NM coronation; consecration

sacré, e [sakʀe] ADJ sacred; (*fam: satané*) blasted; (: *fameux*): **un ~ ...** a heck of a ...; (*Anat*) sacral

sacrement [sakʀəmɑ̃] NM sacrament; **les derniers sacrements** the last rites

sacrer [sakʀe] /1/ VT (*roi*) to crown; (*évêque*) to consecrate ▸ VI to curse, swear

sacrifice [sakʀifis] NM sacrifice; **faire le ~ de** to sacrifice

sacrificiel, le [sakʀifisjɛl] ADJ sacrificial

sacrifier [sakʀifje] /7/ VT to sacrifice; **~ à** VT to conform to; **se sacrifier** to sacrifice o.s.; **articles sacrifiés** (*Comm*) items sold at rock-bottom *ou* give-away prices

sacrilège [sakʀilɛʒ] NM sacrilege ▸ ADJ sacrilegious

sacristain [sakʀistɛ̃] NM sexton; sacristan

sacristie [sakʀisti] NF sacristy; (*culte protestant*) vestry

sacro-saint, e [sakʀosɛ̃, -ɛ̃t] ADJ sacrosanct

sadique [sadik] ADJ sadistic ▸ NMF sadist

sadisme [sadism] NM sadism

sadomasochisme [sadomazoʃism] NM sadomasochism

sadomasochiste [sadomazoʃist] NMF sadomasochist

safari [safaʀi] NM safari; **faire un ~** to go on safari

safari-photo [safaʀifoto] NM photographic safari

SAFER [safɛʀ] SIGLE F (= *Société d'aménagement foncier et d'établissement rural*) organization with the right to buy land in order to retain it for agricultural use

safran [safʀɑ̃] NM saffron

saga [saga] NF saga

sagace [sagas] ADJ sagacious, shrewd

sagacité [sagasite] NF sagacity, shrewdness

sagaie [sagɛ] NF assegai

sage [saʒ] ADJ wise; (*enfant*) good ▸ NM wise man; sage

sage-femme [saʒfam] NF midwife

sagement [saʒmɑ̃] ADV (*raisonnablement*) wisely, sensibly; (*tranquillement*) quietly

sagesse [saʒɛs] NF wisdom

Sagittaire [saʒitɛʀ] NM: **le ~** Sagittarius, the Archer; **être du ~** to be Sagittarius

Sahara [saaʀa] NM: **le ~** the Sahara (Desert); **le ~ occidental** (*pays*) Western Sahara

saharien, ne [saaʀjɛ̃, -ɛn] ADJ Saharan ▸ NF safari jacket

Sahel [saɛl] NM: **le ~** the Sahel

sahélien, ne [saeljɛ̃, -ɛn] ADJ Sahelian

saignant, e [sɛɲɑ̃, -ɑ̃t] ADJ (*viande*) rare; (*blessure, plaie*) bleeding

saignée [seɲe] NF (*Méd*) bleeding *no pl*, bloodletting *no pl*; (*fig: Mil*) heavy losses *pl*; (: *prélèvement*) savage cut; **la ~ du bras** the bend of the arm

saignement [sɛɲmɑ̃] NM bleeding; **~ de nez** nosebleed

saigner [seɲe] /1/ VI to bleed ▸ VT to bleed; (*animal*) to bleed to death; **~ qn à blanc** (*fig*) to bleed sb white; **~ du nez** to have a nosebleed

Saigon [sajgɔ̃] N Saigon

saillant, e [sajɑ̃, -ɑ̃t] ADJ (*pommettes, menton*) prominent; (*corniche etc*) projecting; (*fig*) salient, outstanding

saillie [saji] NF (*sur un mur etc*) projection; (*trait d'esprit*) witticism; (*accouplement*) covering, serving; **faire ~** to project, stick out; **en ~, formant ~** projecting, overhanging

saillir [sajiʀ] /13/ VI to project, stick out; (*veine, muscle*) to bulge ▸ VT (*Agr*) to cover, serve

sain, e [sɛ̃, sɛn] ADJ healthy; (*dents, constitution*) healthy, sound; (*lectures*) wholesome; **~ et sauf** safe and sound, unharmed; **~ d'esprit** sound in mind, sane

saindoux [sɛ̃du] NM lard

sainement [sɛnmɑ̃] ADV (*vivre*) healthily; (*raisonner*) soundly

saint, e [sɛ̃, sɛ̃t] ADJ holy; (*fig*) saintly ▸ NM/F saint; **la S~ Vierge** the Blessed Virgin

saint-bernard [sɛ̃bɛʀnaʀ] NM INV (*chien*) St Bernard

Sainte-Hélène [sɛ̃telɛn] NF St Helena

Sainte-Lucie [sɛ̃tlysi] NF Saint Lucia

Saint-Esprit [sɛ̃tɛspʀi] NM: **le ~** the Holy Spirit *ou* Ghost

sainteté [sɛ̃te] NF holiness; saintliness

Saint-Laurent [sɛ̃lɔʀɑ̃] NM: **le ~** the St Lawrence

Saint-Marin [sɛ̃maʀɛ̃] NM: **le ~** San Marino

Saint-Père [sɛ̃pɛʀ] NM: **le ~** the Holy Father, the Pontiff

Saint-Pierre [sɛ̃pjɛʀ] NM Saint Peter; (*église*) Saint Peter's

Saint-Pierre-et-Miquelon [sɛ̃pjɛʀemiklɔ̃] NM Saint Pierre and Miquelon

Saint-Siège [sɛ̃sjɛʒ] NM: **le ~** the Holy See

Saint-Sylvestre [sɛ̃silvɛstʀ] NF: **la ~** New Year's Eve

Saint-Thomas [sɛ̃tɔma] NF Saint Thomas

Saint-Vincent et les Grenadines [sɛ̃vɛ̃sɑ̃elegʀənadin] NM St Vincent and the Grenadines

sais *etc* [sɛ] VB *voir* **savoir**

saisie [sezi] NF seizure; **à la ~** (*texte*) being keyed; **~ (de données)** (data) capture

saisine [sezin] NF (*Jur*) submission of a case to the court

saisir [seziʀ] /2/ VT to take hold of, grab; (*fig: occasion*) to seize; (*comprendre*) to grasp; (*entendre*) to get, catch; (*émotions*) to take hold of, come over; (*Inform*) to capture, keyboard; (*Culin*) to fry quickly; (*Jur: biens, publication*) to seize; (: *juridiction*): **~ un tribunal d'une affaire** to submit *ou* refer a case to a court; **se ~ de** VT to seize; **être saisi** (*frappé de*) to be overcome

saisissant, e [sezisɑ̃, -ɑ̃t] ADJ startling, striking; (*froid*) biting

saisissement [sezismɑ̃] NM: **muet/figé de ~** speechless/frozen with emotion

saison [sɛzɔ̃] NF season; **la belle/mauvaise ~** the summer/winter months; **être de ~** to be in season; **en/hors ~** in/out of season; **haute/basse/morte ~** high/low/slack season; **la ~ des pluies/des amours** the rainy/mating season

saisonnier, -ière [sɛzɔnje, -jɛʀ] ADJ seasonal ▸ NM (*travailleur*) seasonal worker; (*vacancier*) seasonal holidaymaker

sait [sɛ] VB *voir* **savoir**

salace [salas] ADJ salacious

salade [salad] NF (*Bot*) lettuce *etc* (*generic term*); (*Culin*) (green) salad; (*fam: confusion*) tangle, muddle; **salades** NFPL (*fam*): **raconter des salades** to tell tales (*fam*); **haricots en ~** bean salad; **~ composée** mixed salad; **~ de concombres** cucumber salad; **~ de fruits** fruit salad; **~ niçoise** salade niçoise; **~ russe** Russian salad; **~ de tomates** tomato salad; **~ verte** green salad

saladier [saladje] NM (salad) bowl

salaire [salɛʀ] NM (*annuel, mensuel*) salary; (*hebdomadaire, journalier*) pay, wages *pl*; (*fig*) reward; **~ de base** basic salary (*ou* wage); **~ de misère** starvation wage; **~ minimum interprofessionnel de croissance** index-linked guaranteed minimum wage

salaison [salɛzɔ̃] NF salting; **salaisons** NFPL salt meat *sg*

salamandre [salamɑ̃dʀ] NF salamander

salami [salami] NM salami *no pl*, salami sausage

salant [salɑ̃] ADJ M: **marais ~** salt pan

salarial, e, -aux [salaʀjal, -o] ADJ salary *cpd*, wage(s) *cpd*

salariat [salaʀja] NM salaried staff

salarié, e [salaʀje] ADJ salaried; wage-earning ▸ NM/F salaried employee; wage-earner

S

salaud [salo] NM (!) sod (!), bastard (!)
sale [sal] ADJ dirty, filthy; (fig: mauvais: avant le nom) nasty
salé, e [sale] ADJ (liquide, saveur, mer, goût) salty; (Culin: amandes, beurre etc) salted; (: gâteaux) savoury; (fig: grivois) spicy, juicy; (: note, facture) steep, stiff ▶ NM (porc salé) salt pork; **petit ~** ≈ boiling bacon
salement [salmɑ̃] ADV (manger etc) dirtily, messily
saler [sale] /1/ VT to salt
saleté [salte] NF (état) dirtiness; (crasse) dirt, filth; (tache etc) dirt no pl, something dirty, dirty mark; (fig: tour) filthy trick; (: chose sans valeur) rubbish no pl; (: obscénité) filth no pl; (: microbe etc) bug; **vivre dans la ~** to live in squalor
salière [saljɛʀ] NF saltcellar
saligaud [saligo] NM (!) bastard (!), sod (!)
salin, e [salɛ̃, -in] ADJ saline ▶ NF saltworks sg
salinité [salinite] NF salinity, salt-content
salir [saliʀ] /2/ VT to (make) dirty; (fig) to soil the reputation of; **se salir** VI to get dirty
salissant, e [salisɑ̃, -ɑ̃t] ADJ (tissu) which shows the dirt; (métier) dirty, messy
salissure [salisyʀ] NF dirt no pl; (tache) dirty mark
salive [saliv] NF saliva
saliver [salive] /1/ VI to salivate
salle [sal] NF room; (d'hôpital) ward; (de restaurant) dining room; (d'un cinéma) auditorium; (: public) audience; **faire ~ comble** to have a full house; **~ d'armes** (pour l'escrime) arms room; **~ d'attente** waiting room; **~ de bain(s)** bathroom; **~ de bal** ballroom; **~ de cinéma** cinema; **~ de classe** classroom; **~ commune** (d'hôpital) ward; **~ de concert** concert hall; **~ de consultation** consulting room (BRIT), office (US); **~ de danse** dance hall; **~ de douches** shower-room; **~ d'eau** shower-room; **~ d'embarquement** (à l'aéroport) departure lounge; **~ d'exposition** showroom; **~ de jeux** games room; (pour enfants) playroom; **~ des machines** engine room; **~ à manger** dining room; (mobilier) dining room suite; **~ obscure** cinema (BRIT), movie theater (US); **~ d'opération** (d'hôpital) operating theatre; **~ des professeurs** staffroom; **~ de projection** film theatre; **~ de séjour** living room; **~ de spectacle** theatre; cinema; **~ des ventes** saleroom
salmonellose [salmɔneloz] NF (Méd) salmonella poisoning
Salomon [salɔmɔ̃] NM: **les îles ~** the Solomon Islands
salon [salɔ̃] NM lounge, sitting room; (mobilier) lounge suite; (exposition) exhibition, show; (mondain, littéraire) salon; **~ de coiffure** hairdressing salon; **~ de discussion** (Inform) chatroom; **~ de thé** tearoom
salopard [salɔpaʀ] NM (!) bastard (!)
salope [salɔp] NF (!) bitch (!)
saloper [salɔpe] /1/ VT (!) to muck up, mess up
saloperie [salɔpʀi] NF (!) filth no pl; (: action) dirty trick; (: chose sans valeur) rubbish no pl

salopette [salɔpɛt] NF dungarees pl; (d'ouvrier) overall(s)
salpêtre [salpɛtʀ] NM saltpetre
salsifis [salsifi] NM salsify, oyster plant
SALT [salt] ABR (= Strategic Arms Limitation Talks ou Treaty) SALT
saltimbanque [saltɛ̃bɑ̃k] NMF (travelling) acrobat
salubre [salybʀ] ADJ healthy, salubrious
salubrité [salybʀite] NF healthiness, salubrity; **~ publique** public health
saluer [salɥe] /1/ VT (pour dire bonjour, fig) to greet; (pour dire au revoir) to take one's leave; (Mil) to salute
salut [saly] NM (sauvegarde) safety; (Rel) salvation; (geste) wave; (parole) greeting; (Mil) salute ▶ EXCL (fam: pour dire bonjour) hi (there); (: pour dire au revoir) see you!, bye!
salutaire [salytɛʀ] ADJ (remède) beneficial; (conseils) salutary
salutations [salytasjɔ̃] NFPL greetings; **recevez mes ~ distinguées ou respectueuses** yours faithfully
salutiste [salytist] NMF Salvationist
Salvador [salvadɔʀ] NM: **le ~** El Salvador
salve [salv] NF salvo; volley of shots; **~ d'applaudissements** burst of applause
Samarie [samaʀi] NF: **la ~** Samaria
samaritain [samaʀitɛ̃] NM: **le bon S~** the Good Samaritan
samedi [samdi] NM Saturday; voir aussi **lundi**
Samoa [samɔa] NFPL: **les (îles) ~** Samoa, the Samoa Islands
SAMU [samy] SIGLE M (= service d'assistance médicale d'urgence) ≈ ambulance (service) (BRIT), ≈ paramedics (US)
sanatorium [sanatɔʀjɔm] NM sanatorium
sanctifier [sɑ̃ktifje] /7/ VT to sanctify
sanction [sɑ̃ksjɔ̃] NF sanction; (fig) penalty; **prendre des sanctions contre** to impose sanctions on
sanctionner [sɑ̃ksjɔne] /1/ VT (loi, usage) to sanction; (punir) to punish
sanctuaire [sɑ̃ktɥɛʀ] NM sanctuary
sandale [sɑ̃dal] NF sandal; **sandales à lanières** strappy sandals
sandalette [sɑ̃dalɛt] NF sandal
sandwich [sɑ̃dwitʃ] NM sandwich; **pris en ~** sandwiched
sang [sɑ̃] NM blood; **en ~** covered in blood; **jusqu'au ~** (mordre, pincer) till the blood comes; **se faire du mauvais ~** to fret, get in a state
sang-froid [sɑ̃fʀwa] NM calm, sangfroid; **garder/perdre/reprendre son ~** to keep/lose/regain one's cool; **de ~** in cold blood
sanglant, e [sɑ̃glɑ̃, -ɑ̃t] ADJ bloody, covered in blood; (combat) bloody; (fig: reproche, affront) cruel
sangle [sɑ̃gl] NF strap; **sangles** NFPL (pour lit etc) webbing sg
sangler [sɑ̃gle] /1/ VT to strap up; (animal) to girth
sanglier [sɑ̃glije] NM (wild) boar
sanglot [sɑ̃glo] NM sob
sangloter [sɑ̃glɔte] /1/ VI to sob

sangsue [sɑ̃sy] NF leech
sanguin, e [sɑ̃gɛ̃, -in] ADJ blood *cpd*; *(fig)* fiery ▶ NF blood orange; *(Art)* red pencil drawing
sanguinaire [sɑ̃ginɛʀ] ADJ *(animal, personne)* bloodthirsty; *(lutte)* bloody
sanguinolent, e [sɑ̃ginɔlɑ̃, -ɑ̃t] ADJ streaked with blood
Sanisette® [sanizɛt] NF coin-operated public lavatory
sanitaire [sanitɛʀ] ADJ health *cpd*; **sanitaires** NMPL *(salle de bain et w.-c.)* bathroom *sg*; **installation/appareil ~** bathroom plumbing/ appliance
sans [sɑ̃] PRÉP without; **~ qu'il s'en aperçoive** without him *ou* his noticing; **~ scrupules** unscrupulous; **~ manches** sleeveless; **un pull ~ manches** a sleeveless jumper; **~ faute** without fail; **~ arrêt** without a break; **~ ça** *(fam)* otherwise
sans-abri [sɑ̃zabʀi] NMPL homeless
sans-emploi [sɑ̃zɑ̃plwa] NMF INV unemployed person; **les ~** the unemployed
sans-façon [sɑ̃fasɔ̃] ADJ INV fuss-free; free and easy
sans-gêne [sɑ̃ʒɛn] ADJ INV inconsiderate ▶ NM INV *(attitude)* lack of consideration
sans-logis [sɑ̃lɔʒi] NMPL homeless
sans-souci [sɑ̃susi] ADJ INV carefree
sans-travail [sɑ̃tʀavaj] NMPL unemployed, jobless
santal [sɑ̃tal] NM sandal(wood)
santé [sɑ̃te] NF health; **avoir une ~ de fer** to be bursting with health; **être en bonne ~** to be in good health, be healthy; **boire à la ~ de qn** to drink (to) sb's health; **"à la ~ de"** "here's to"; **à ta** *ou* **votre ~!** cheers!; **service de ~** *(dans un port etc)* quarantine service; **la ~ publique** public health
Santiago [sɑ̃tjago], **Santiago du Chili** [sɑ̃tjagodyʃili] N Santiago (de Chile)
santon [sɑ̃tɔ̃] NM *ornamental figure at a Christmas crib*
saoudien, ne [saudjɛ̃, -ɛn] ADJ Saudi (Arabian) ▶ NM/F: **S~, ne** Saudi (Arabian)
saoul, e [su, sul] ADJ = **soûl**
sape [sap] NF: **travail de ~** *(Mil)* sap; *(fig)* insidious undermining process *ou* work; **sapes** NFPL *(fam)* gear *sg*, togs
saper [sape] /1/ VT to undermine, sap; **se saper** VI *(fam)* to dress
sapeur [sapœʀ] NM sapper
sapeur-pompier [sapœʀpɔ̃pje] NM fireman
saphir [safiʀ] NM sapphire; *(d'électrophone)* needle, sapphire
sapin [sapɛ̃] NM fir (tree); *(bois)* fir; **~ de Noël** Christmas tree
sapinière [sapinjɛʀ] NF fir plantation *ou* forest
SAR SIGLE F *(= Son Altesse Royale)* HRH
sarabande [saʀabɑ̃d] NF saraband; *(fig)* hullabaloo; whirl
sarbacane [saʀbakan] NF blowpipe, blowgun; *(jouet)* peashooter
sarcasme [saʀkasm] NM sarcasm *no pl*; *(propos)* piece of sarcasm

sarcastique [saʀkastik] ADJ sarcastic
sarcastiquement [saʀkastikmɑ̃] ADV sarcastically
sarclage [saʀklaʒ] NM weeding
sarcler [saʀkle] /1/ VT to weed
sarcloir [saʀklwaʀ] NM (weeding) hoe, spud
sarcophage [saʀkɔfaʒ] NM sarcophagus
Sardaigne [saʀdɛɲ] NF: **la ~** Sardinia
sarde [saʀd] ADJ Sardinian
sardine [saʀdin] NF sardine; **sardines à l'huile** sardines in oil
sardinerie [saʀdinʀi] NF sardine cannery
sardinier, -ière [saʀdinje, -jɛʀ] ADJ *(pêche, industrie)* sardine *cpd* ▶ NM *(bateau)* sardine boat
sardonique [saʀdɔnik] ADJ sardonic
sari [saʀi] NM sari
SARL [saʀl] SIGLE F *(= société à responsabilité limitée)* ≈ plc *(BRIT)*, ≈ Inc. *(US)*
sarment [saʀmɑ̃] NM: **~ (de vigne)** vine shoot
sarrasin [saʀazɛ̃] NM buckwheat
sarrau [saʀo] NM smock
Sarre [saʀ] NF: **la ~** the Saar
sarriette [saʀjɛt] NF savory
sarrois, e [saʀwa, -waz] ADJ Saar *cpd* ▶ NM/F: **S~, e** inhabitant *ou* native of the Saar
sas [sas] NM *(de sous-marin, d'engin spatial)* airlock; *(d'écluse)* lock
satané, e [satane] ADJ *(fam)* confounded
satanique [satanik] ADJ satanic, fiendish
satelliser [satelize] /1/ VT *(fusée)* to put into orbit; *(fig: pays)* to make into a satellite
satellite [satelit] NM satellite; **pays ~** satellite country
satellite-espion [satelitɛspjɔ̃] *(pl* **satellites-espions)** NM spy satellite
satellite-observatoire [satelitɔpsɛʀvatwaʀ] *(pl* **satellites-observatoires)** NM observation satellite
satellite-relais [satelitʀəlɛ] *(pl* **satellites-relais)** NM *(TV)* relay satellite
satiété [sasjete] NF: **à ~** *adv* to satiety *ou* satiation; *(répéter)* ad nauseam
satin [satɛ̃] NM satin
satiné, e [satine] ADJ satiny; *(peau)* satin-smooth
satinette [satinɛt] NF satinet, sateen
satire [satiʀ] NF satire; **faire la ~ de** to satirize
satirique [satiʀik] ADJ satirical
satiriser [satiʀize] /1/ VT to satirize
satiriste [satiʀist] NMF satirist
satisfaction [satisfaksjɔ̃] NF satisfaction; **à ma grande ~** to my great satisfaction; **obtenir ~** to obtain *ou* get satisfaction; **donner ~ (à)** to give satisfaction (to)
satisfaire [satisfɛʀ] /60/ VT to satisfy; **se satisfaire de** to be satisfied *ou* content with; **~ à** *vt (engagement)* to fulfil; *(revendications, conditions)* to meet, satisfy
satisfaisant, e [satisfəzɑ̃, -ɑ̃t] VB *voir* **satisfaire** ▶ ADJ *(acceptable)* satisfactory; *(qui fait plaisir)* satisfying
satisfait, e [satisfɛ, -ɛt] PP *de* **satisfaire** ▶ ADJ satisfied; **~ de** happy *ou* satisfied with
satisfasse [satisfas], **satisferai** *etc* [satisfʀe] VB *voir* **satisfaire**

saturation [satyʀasjɔ̃] NF saturation; **arriver à ~** to reach saturation point

saturer [satyʀe] /1/ VT to saturate; **~ qn/qch de** to saturate sb/sth with

saturnisme [satyʀnism] NM (Méd) lead poisoning

satyre [satiʀ] NM satyr; (péj) lecher

sauce [sos] NF sauce; (avec un rôti) gravy; **en ~** in a sauce; **~ blanche** white sauce; **~ chasseur** sauce chasseur; **~ tomate** tomato sauce

saucer [sose] /3/ VT (assiette) to soak up the sauce from

saucière [sosjɛʀ] NF sauce boat; gravy boat

saucisse [sosis] NF sausage

saucisson [sosisɔ̃] NM (slicing) sausage; **~ à l'ail** garlic sausage

saucissonner [sosisɔne] /1/ VT to cut up, slice ▶ VI to picnic

sauf¹ [sof] PRÉP except; **~ si** (à moins que) unless; **~ avis contraire** unless you hear to the contrary; **~ empêchement** barring (any) problems; **~ erreur** if I'm not mistaken; **~ imprévu** unless anything unforeseen arises, barring accidents

sauf², sauve [sof, sov] ADJ unharmed, unhurt; (fig: honneur) intact, saved; **laisser la vie sauve à qn** to spare sb's life

sauf-conduit [sofkɔ̃dɥi] NM safe-conduct

sauge [soʒ] NF sage

saugrenu, e [sogʀəny] ADJ preposterous, ludicrous

saule [sol] NM willow (tree); **~ pleureur** weeping willow

saumâtre [somɑtʀ] ADJ briny; (désagréable: plaisanterie) unsavoury (BRIT), unsavory (US)

saumon [somɔ̃] NM salmon inv ▶ ADJ INV salmon (pink)

saumoné, e [somɔne] ADJ: **truite ~** salmon trout

saumure [somyʀ] NF brine

sauna [sona] NM sauna

saupoudrer [sopudʀe] /1/ VT: **~ qch de** to sprinkle sth with

saupoudreuse [sopudʀøz] NF dredger

saur [sɔʀ] ADJ M: **hareng ~** smoked ou red herring, kipper

saurai etc [sɔʀe] VB voir **savoir**

saut [so] NM jump; (discipline sportive) jumping; **faire un ~** to (make a) jump ou leap; **faire un ~ chez qn** to pop over to sb's (place); **au ~ du lit** on getting out of bed; **~ en hauteur/longueur** high/long jump; **~ à la corde** skipping; **~ en page/ligne** (Inform) page/line break; **~ en parachute** parachuting no pl; **~ à la perche** pole vaulting; **~ à l'élastique** bungee jumping; **~ périlleux** somersault

saute [sot] NF: **~ de vent/température** sudden change of wind direction/in the temperature; **avoir des sautes d'humeur** to have sudden changes of mood

sauté, e [sote] ADJ (Culin) sauté ▶ NM: **~ de veau** sauté of veal

saute-mouton [sotmutɔ̃] NM: **jouer à ~** to play leapfrog

sauter [sote] /1/ VI to jump, leap; (exploser) to blow up, explode; (: fusibles) to blow; (se rompre) to snap, burst; (se détacher) to pop out (ou off) ▶ VT to jump (over), leap (over); (fig: omettre) to skip, miss (out); **faire ~** to blow up; to burst open; (Culin) to sauté; **~ à pieds joints/à cloche-pied** to make a standing jump/to hop; **~ en parachute** to make a parachute jump; **~ à la corde** to skip; **~ de joie** to jump for joy; **~ de colère** to be hopping with rage ou hopping mad; **~ au cou de qn** to fly into sb's arms; **~ sur une occasion** to jump at an opportunity; **~ aux yeux** to be quite obvious; **~ au plafond** (fig) to hit the roof

sauterelle [sotʀɛl] NF grasshopper

sauterie [sotʀi] NF party, hop

sauteur, -euse [sotœʀ, -øz] NM/F (athlète) jumper ▶ NF (casserole) shallow pan, frying pan; **~ à la perche** pole vaulter; **~ à skis** ski jumper

sautillement [sotijmɑ̃] NM hopping; skipping

sautiller [sotije] /1/ VI (oiseau) to hop; (enfant) to skip

sautoir [sotwaʀ] NM chain; (Sport: emplacement) jumping pit; **~ (de perles)** string of pearls

s'automutiler [sɔtomytile] VR to self-harm

sauvage [sovaʒ] ADJ (gén) wild; (peuplade) savage; (farouche) unsociable; (barbare) wild, savage; (non officiel) unauthorized, unofficial; **faire du camping ~** to camp in the wild ▶ NMF savage; (timide) unsociable type, recluse

sauvagement [sovaʒmɑ̃] ADV savagely

sauvageon, ne [sovaʒɔ̃, -ɔn] NM/F little savage

sauvagerie [sovaʒʀi] NF wildness; savagery; unsociability

sauve [sov] ADJ F voir **sauf²**

sauvegarde [sovgaʀd] NF safeguard; **sous la ~ de** under the protection of; **disquette/fichier de ~** (Inform) backup disk/file

sauvegarder [sovgaʀde] /1/ VT to safeguard; (Inform: enregistrer) to save; (: copier) to back up

sauve-qui-peut [sovkipø] NM INV stampede, mad rush ▶ EXCL run for your life!

sauver [sove] /1/ VT to save; (porter secours à) to rescue; (récupérer) to salvage, rescue; **se sauver** VI (s'enfuir) to run away; (fam: partir) to be off; **~ qn de** to save sb from; **~ la vie à qn** to save sb's life; **~ les apparences** to keep up appearances

sauvetage [sovtaʒ] NM rescue; (de banque, d'entreprise) bailout; **~ en montagne** mountain rescue; **ceinture de ~** lifebelt (BRIT), life preserver (US); **brassière ou gilet de ~** life jacket (BRIT), life preserver (US)

sauveteur [sovtœʀ] NM rescuer

sauvette [sovɛt]: **à la ~** adv (vendre) without authorization; (se marier etc) hastily, hurriedly; **vente à la ~** (unauthorized) street trading, (street) peddling

sauveur [sovœʀ] NM saviour (BRIT), savior (US)

SAV SIGLE M = **service après-vente**

savais etc [save] VB voir **savoir**

savamment [savamɑ̃] ADV (avec érudition) learnedly; (habilement) skilfully, cleverly

savane [savan] NF savannah

savant, e [savɑ̃, -ɑ̃t] ADJ scholarly, learned; (calé) clever ▶ NM scientist; **animal ~** performing animal

savate [savat] NF worn-out shoe; (Sport) French boxing

saveur [savœʀ] NF flavour (BRIT), flavor (US); (fig) savour (BRIT), savor (US)

Savoie [savwa] NF: **la ~** Savoy

savoir [savwaʀ] /32/ VT to know; (être capable de): **il sait nager** he knows how to swim, he can swim ▶ NM knowledge; **se savoir** VI (être connu) to be known; **se savoir malade/incurable** to know that one is ill/incurably ill; **il est petit: tu ne peux pas ~!** you won't believe how small he is!; **vous n'êtes pas sans ~ que** you are not ou will not be unaware of the fact that; **je crois ~ que …** I believe that …, I think I know that …; **je n'en sais rien** I (really) don't know; **à ~ (que)** that is, namely; **faire ~ qch à qn** to let sb know sth, inform sb about sth; **pas que je sache** not as far as I know; **sans le ~** adv unknowingly, unwittingly; **en ~ long** to know a lot

savoir-faire [savwaʀfɛʀ] NM INV savoir-faire, know-how

savoir-vivre [savwaʀvivʀ] NM INV: **le ~** savoir-faire, good manners pl

savon [savɔ̃] NM (produit) soap; (morceau) bar ou tablet of soap; (fam): **passer un ~ à qn** to give sb a good dressing-down

savonner [savɔne] /1/ VT to soap

savonnerie [savɔnʀi] NF soap factory

savonnette [savɔnɛt] NF bar of soap

savonneux, -euse [savɔnø, -øz] ADJ soapy

savons [savɔ̃] VB voir **savoir**

savourer [savuʀe] /1/ VT to savour (BRIT), savor (US)

savoureux, -euse [savuʀø, -øz] ADJ tasty; (fig: anecdote) spicy, juicy

savoyard, e [savwajaʀ, -aʀd] ADJ Savoyard

Saxe [saks] NF: **la ~** Saxony

saxo(phone) [saksɔ(fɔn)] NM sax(ophone)

saxophoniste [saksɔfɔnist] NMF saxophonist, sax(ophone) player

saynète [sɛnɛt] NF playlet

SBB SIGLE F (= Schweizerische Bundesbahn) Swiss federal railways

sbire [sbiʀ] NM (péj) henchman

sc. ABR = **scène**

s/c ABR (= sous couvert de) ≈ c/o

scabreux, -euse [skabʀø, -øz] ADJ risky; (indécent) improper, shocking

scalpel [skalpɛl] NM scalpel

scalper [skalpe] /1/ VT to scalp

scampi [skɑ̃pi] NMPL scampi

scandale [skɑ̃dal] NM scandal; **faire un ~** (scène) to make a scene; (Jur) create a disturbance; **faire ~** to scandalize people; **au grand ~ de …** to the great indignation of …

scandaleusement [skɑ̃daløzmɑ̃] ADV scandalously, outrageously

scandaleux, -euse [skɑ̃dalø, -øz] ADJ scandalous, outrageous

scandaliser [skɑ̃dalize] /1/ VT to scandalize; **se ~ (de)** to be scandalized (by)

scander [skɑ̃de] /1/ VT (vers) to scan; (mots, syllabes) to stress separately; (slogans) to chant

scandinave [skɑ̃dinav] ADJ Scandinavian ▶ NMF: **S~** Scandinavian

Scandinavie [skɑ̃dinavi] NF: **la ~** Scandinavia

scanner [skanɛʀ] NM (Méd) scanner

scanographie [skanɔgʀafi] NF (Méd) scanning; (image) scan

scaphandre [skafɑ̃dʀ] NM (de plongeur) diving suit; (de cosmonaute) spacesuit; **~ autonome** aqualung

scaphandrier [skafɑ̃dʀije] NM diver

scarabée [skaʀabe] NM beetle

scarlatine [skaʀlatin] NF scarlet fever

scarole [skaʀɔl] NF endive

scatologique [skatɔlɔʒik] ADJ scatological, lavatorial

sceau, x [so] NM seal; (fig) stamp, mark; **sous le ~ du secret** under the seal of secrecy

scélérat, e [seleʀa, -at] NM/F villain, blackguard ▶ ADJ villainous, blackguardly

sceller [sele] /1/ VT to seal

scellés [sele] NMPL seals

scénario [senaʀjo] NM (Ciné) screenplay, script; (: idée, plan) scenario; (fig) pattern; scenario

scénariste [senaʀist] NMF scriptwriter

scène [sɛn] NF (gén) scene; (estrade, fig: théâtre) stage; **entrer en ~** to come on stage; **mettre en ~** (Théât) to stage; (Ciné) to direct; (fig) to present, introduce; **sur le devant de la ~** (en pleine actualité) in the forefront; **porter à la ~** to adapt for the stage; **faire une ~ (à qn)** to make a scene (with sb); **~ de ménage** domestic fight ou scene

scénique [senik] ADJ (effets) theatrical; (art) scenic

scepticisme [sɛptisism] NM scepticism

sceptique [sɛptik] ADJ sceptical ▶ NMF sceptic

sceptre [sɛptʀ] NM sceptre

schéma [ʃema] NM (diagramme) diagram, sketch; (fig) outline

schématique [ʃematik] ADJ diagrammatic(al), schematic; (fig) oversimplified

schématiquement [ʃematikmɑ̃] ADV schematically, diagrammatically

schématisation [ʃematizasjɔ̃] NF schematization; oversimplification

schématiser [ʃematize] /1/ VT to schematize; to (over)simplify

schismatique [ʃismatik] ADJ schismatic

schisme [ʃism] NM schism; rift, split

schiste [ʃist] NM schist

schizophrène [skizɔfʀɛn] NMF schizophrenic

schizophrénie [skizɔfʀeni] NF schizophrenia

sciatique [sjatik] ADJ: **nerf ~** sciatic nerve ▶ NF sciatica

scie [si] NF saw; (fam: rengaine) catch-tune; (: personne) bore; **~ à bois** wood saw; **~ circulaire** circular saw; **~ à découper** fretsaw; **~ à métaux** hacksaw; **~ sauteuse** jigsaw

sciemment [sjamɑ̃] ADV knowingly, wittingly

science [sjɑ̃s] NF science; (savoir) knowledge; (savoir-faire) art, skill; **sciences économiques**

S

economics; **sciences humaines/sociales** social sciences; **sciences naturelles** (*Scol*) natural science *sg*, biology *sg*; **sciences po** political science *ou* studies *pl*

science-fiction [sjãsfiksjõ] NF science fiction

scientifique [sjãtifik] ADJ scientific ▸ NMF (*savant*) scientist; (*étudiant*) science student

scientifiquement [sjãtifikmã] ADV scientifically

scier [sje] /7/ VT to saw; (*retrancher*) to saw off

scierie [siRi] NF sawmill

scieur [sjœR] NM: **~ de long** pit sawyer

Scilly [sili]: **les îles ~** the Scilly Isles, the Scillies, the Isles of Scilly

scinder [sẽde] /1/ VT, **se scinder** VI to split (up)

scintillant, e [sẽtijã, -ãt] ADJ sparkling

scintillement [sẽtijmã] NM sparkling *no pl*

scintiller [sẽtije] /1/ VI to sparkle; (*étoile*) to twinkle

scission [sisjõ] NF split

sciure [sjyR] NF: **~ (de bois)** sawdust

sclérose [skleRoz] NF sclerosis; (*fig*) ossification; **~ en plaques (SEP)** multiple sclerosis (MS)

sclérosé, e [skleRoze] ADJ sclerosed, sclerotic; ossified

scléroser [skleRoze] /1/: **se scléroser** VI to become sclerosed; (*fig*) to become ossified

scolaire [skɔlɛR] ADJ school *cpd*; (*péj*) schoolish; **l'année ~** the school year; (*à l'université*) the academic year; **en âge ~** of school age

scolarisation [skɔlaRizasjõ] NF (*d'un enfant*) schooling; **la ~ d'une région** the provision of schooling in a region; **le taux de ~** the proportion of children in full-time education

scolariser [skɔlaRize] /1/ VT to provide with schooling (*ou* schools)

scolarité [skɔlaRite] NF schooling; **frais de ~** school fees (BRIT), tuition (US)

scolastique [skɔlastik] ADJ (*péj*) scholastic

scoliose [skɔljoz] NF curvature of the spine, scoliosis

scoop [skup] NM (*Presse*) scoop, exclusive

scooter [skutœR] NM (motor) scooter

scorbut [skɔRbyt] NM scurvy

score [skɔR] NM score; (*électoral etc*) result

scories [skɔRi] NFPL scoria *pl*

scorpion [skɔRpjõ] NM (*signe*): **le S~** Scorpio, the Scorpion; **être du S~** to be Scorpio

scotch [skɔtʃ] NM (*whisky*) scotch, whisky; **Scotch®** (*adhésif*) Sellotape® (BRIT), Scotch tape® (US)

scotcher [skɔtʃe] /1/ VT to sellotape® (BRIT), scotchtape® (US)

scout, e [skut] ADJ, NM scout

scoutisme [skutism] NM (boy) scout movement; (*activités*) scouting

scribe [skRib] NM scribe; (*péj*) penpusher

scribouillard [skRibujaR] NM penpusher

script [skRipt] NM (*écriture*) printing; (*Ciné*) (shooting) script

scripte [skRipt] NF continuity girl

script-girl [skRiptgœRl] NF continuity girl

scriptural, e, -aux [skRiptyRal, -o] ADJ: **monnaie ~** bank money

scrupule [skRypyl] NM scruple; **être sans scrupules** to be unscrupulous; **se faire un ~ de qch** to have scruples *ou* qualms about doing sth

scrupuleusement [skRypyløzmã] ADV scrupulously

scrupuleux, -euse [skRypylø, -øz] ADJ scrupulous

scrutateur, -trice [skRytatœR, -tRis] ADJ searching ▸ NM/F scrutineer

scruter [skRyte] /1/ VT to scrutinize, search; (*l'obscurité*) to peer into; (*motifs, comportement*) to examine, scrutinize

scrutin [skRytẽ] NM (*vote*) ballot; (*ensemble des opérations*) poll; **~ proportionnel/majoritaire** election on a proportional/majority basis; **~ à deux tours** poll with two ballots *ou* rounds; **~ de liste** list system

sculpter [skylte] /1/ VT to sculpt; (*érosion*) to carve

sculpteur [skyltœR] NM sculptor

sculptural, e, -aux [skyltyRal, -o] ADJ sculptural; (*fig*) statuesque

sculpture [skyltyR] NF sculpture; **~ sur bois** wood carving

sdb. ABR = **salle de bain**

SDF SIGLE M (= *sans domicile fixe*) homeless person; **les ~** the homeless

SDN SIGLE F (= *Société des Nations*) League of Nations

SE SIGLE F (= *Son Excellence*) HE

(MOT-CLÉ)

se, s' [sə, s] PRON **1** (*emploi réfléchi*) oneself; (*: masc*) himself; (*: fém*) herself; (*: sujet non humain*) itself; (*: pl*) themselves; **se voir comme l'on est** to see o.s. as one is; **se savonner** to soap o.s.

2 (*réciproque*) one another, each other; **ils s'aiment** they love one another *ou* each other

3 (*passif*): **cela se répare facilement** it is easily repaired

4 (*possessif*): **se casser la jambe/se laver les mains** to break one's leg/wash one's hands

séance [seãs] NF (*d'assemblée, récréative*) meeting, session; (*de tribunal*) sitting, session; (*musicale, Ciné, Théât*) performance; **ouvrir/lever la ~** to open/close the meeting; **~ tenante** forthwith

séant, e [seã, -ãt] ADJ seemly, fitting ▸ NM posterior

seau, x [so] NM bucket, pail; **~ à glace** ice bucket

sébum [sebɔm] NM sebum

sec, sèche [sɛk, sɛʃ] ADJ dry; (*raisins, figues*) dried; (*insensible: cœur, personne*) hard, cold; (*maigre, décharné*) spare, lean; (*réponse, ton*) sharp, curt; (*démarrage*) sharp, sudden ▸ NM: **tenir au ~** to keep in a dry place ▸ ADV hard; (*démarrer*) sharply; **boire ~** to be a heavy drinker; **je le bois ~** I drink it straight *ou* neat; **à pied ~** without getting one's feet wet; **à ~** *adj* (*puits*) dried up; (*à court d'argent*) broke

SECAM [sekam] SIGLE M (= *procédé séquentiel à mémoire*) SECAM

sécante [sekɑ̃t] NF secant
sécateur [sekatœʀ] NM secateurs pl (BRIT), shears pl, pair of secateurs ou shears
sécession [sesesjɔ̃] NF: **faire** ~ to secede; **la guerre de S~** the American Civil War
séchage [seʃaʒ] NM drying; (de bois) seasoning
sèche [sɛʃ] ADJ F voir **sec** ▶ NF (fam) cigarette, fag (BRIT)
sèche-cheveux [sɛʃʃəvø] NM INV hair-drier
sèche-linge [sɛʃlɛ̃ʒ] NM INV tumble dryer
sèche-mains [sɛʃmɛ̃] NM INV hand drier
sèchement [sɛʃmɑ̃] ADV (frapper etc) sharply; (répliquer etc) drily, sharply
sécher [seʃe] /6/ VT to dry; (dessécher: peau, blé) to dry (out); (: étang) to dry up; (bois) to season; (fam: classe, cours) to skip, miss ▶ VI to dry; to dry out; to dry up; (fam: candidat) to be stumped; **se sécher** VI (après le bain) to dry o.s.
sécheresse [seʃʀɛs] NF dryness; (absence de pluie) drought
séchoir [seʃwaʀ] NM drier
second, e [səɡɔ̃, -ɔ̃d] ADJ second ▶ NM (assistant) second in command; (étage) second floor (BRIT), third floor (US); (Navig) first mate ▶ NF second; (Scol) ≈ year 11 (BRIT), ≈ tenth grade (US); (Aviat, Rail etc) second class; **en ~** (en second rang) in second place; **voyager en ~** to travel second-class; **doué de ~ vue** having (the gift of) second sight; **trouver son ~ souffle** (Sport, fig) to get one's second wind; **être dans un état ~** to be in a daze (ou trance); **de ~ main** second-hand
secondaire [səɡɔ̃dɛʀ] ADJ secondary
seconder [səɡɔ̃de] /1/ VT to assist; (favoriser) to back
secouer [səkwe] /1/ VT to shake; (passagers) to rock; (traumatiser) to shake (up); **se secouer** (chien) to shake itself; (fam: se démener) to shake o.s. up; ~ **la poussière d'un tapis** to shake the dust off a carpet; ~ **la tête** to shake one's head
secourable [səkuʀabl] ADJ helpful
secourir [səkuʀiʀ] /11/ VT (aller sauver) to (go and) rescue; (prodiguer des soins à) to help, assist; (venir en aide à) to assist, aid
secourisme [səkuʀism] NM (premiers soins) first aid; (sauvetage) life saving
secouriste [səkuʀist] NMF first-aid worker
secourons etc [səkuʀɔ̃] VB voir **secourir**
secours [səkuʀ] VB voir **secourir** ▶ NM help, aid, assistance ▶ NMPL aid sg; **cela lui a été d'un grand ~** this was a great help to him; **au ~!** help!; **appeler au ~** to shout ou call for help; **appeler qn à son ~** to call sb to one's assistance; **porter ~ à qn** to give sb assistance, help sb; **les premiers ~** first aid sg; **le ~ en montagne** mountain rescue

> Emergency phone numbers can be dialled free from public phones. For the police (la police) dial 17; for medical services (le SAMU) dial 15; for the fire brigade (les sapeurs-pompiers), dial 18.

secouru, e [səkuʀy] PP de **secourir**
secousse [səkus] NF jolt, bump; (électrique) shock; (fig: psychologique) jolt, shock; ~ **sismique** ou **tellurique** earth tremor

secret, -ète [səkʀɛ, -ɛt] ADJ secret; (fig: renfermé) reticent, reserved ▶ NM secret; (discrétion absolue): **le ~** secrecy; **en ~** in secret, secretly; **au ~** in solitary confinement; ~ **de fabrication** trade secret; ~ **professionnel** professional secrecy
secrétaire [səkʀetɛʀ] NMF secretary ▶ NM (meuble) writing desk, secretaire; ~ **d'ambassade** embassy secretary; ~ **de direction** private ou personal secretary; ~ **d'État** ≈ junior minister; ~ **général** Secretary-General; (Comm) company secretary; ~ **de mairie** town clerk; ~ **médicale** medical secretary; ~ **de rédaction** sub-editor
secrétariat [s(ə)kʀetaʀja] NM (profession) secretarial work; (bureau: d'entreprise, d'école) (secretary's) office; (: d'organisation internationale) secretariat; (Pol etc: fonction) secretaryship, office of Secretary
secrètement [səkʀɛtmɑ̃] ADV secretly
sécréter [sekʀete] /6/ VT to secrete
sécrétion [sekʀesjɔ̃] NF secretion
sectaire [sɛktɛʀ] ADJ sectarian, bigoted
sectarisme [sɛktaʀism] NM sectarianism
secte [sɛkt] NF sect
secteur [sɛktœʀ] NM sector; (Admin) district; (Élec): **branché sur le ~** plugged into the mains (supply); **fonctionne sur pile et ~** battery or mains operated; **le ~ privé/public** (Écon) the private/public sector; **le ~ primaire/tertiaire** the primary/tertiary sector
section [sɛksjɔ̃] NF section; (de parcours d'autobus) fare stage; (Mil: unité) platoon; ~ **rythmique** rhythm section
sectionner [sɛksjɔne] /1/ VT to sever; **se sectionner** VI to be severed
sectionneur [sɛksjɔnœʀ] NM (Élec) isolation switch
sectoriel, le [sɛktɔʀjɛl] ADJ sector-based
sectorisation [sɛktɔʀizasjɔ̃] NF division into sectors
sectoriser [sɛktɔʀize] /1/ VT to divide into sectors
sécu [seky] NF (fam: = sécurité sociale) ≈ dole (BRIT), ≈ Welfare (US)
séculaire [sekylɛʀ] ADJ secular; (très vieux) age-old
séculariser [sekylaʀize] /1/ VT to secularize
séculier, -ière [sekylje, -jɛʀ] ADJ secular
sécurisant, e [sekyʀizɑ̃, -ɑ̃t] ADJ secure, giving a sense of security
sécuriser [sekyʀize] /1/ VT to give a sense of security to
sécurité [sekyʀite] NF (absence de troubles) security; (absence de danger) safety; **impression de ~** sense of security; **la ~ internationale** international security; **système de ~** security (ou safety) system; **être en ~** to be safe; **la ~ de l'emploi** job security; **la ~ routière** road safety; **la ~ sociale** ≈ (the) Social Security (BRIT), ≈ (the) Welfare (US)
sédatif, -ive [sedatif, -iv] ADJ, NM sedative
sédentaire [sedɑ̃tɛʀ] ADJ sedentary
sédiment [sedimɑ̃] NM sediment; **sédiments** NMPL (alluvions) sediment sg

S

sédimentaire [sedimɑ̃tɛʀ] ADJ sedimentary
sédimentation [sedimɑ̃tasjɔ̃] NF sedimentation
séditieux, -euse [sedisjø, -øz] ADJ insurgent; seditious
sédition [sedisjɔ̃] NF insurrection; sedition
séducteur, -trice [sedyktœʀ, -tʀis] ADJ seductive ▶ NM/F seducer (seductress)
séduction [sedyksjɔ̃] NF seduction; (*charme, attrait*) appeal, charm
séduire [seduiʀ] /**38**/ VT to charm; (*femme: abuser de*) to seduce; (*chose*) to appeal to
séduisant, e [seduizɑ̃, -ɑ̃t] VB *voir* **séduire** ▶ ADJ (*femme*) seductive; (*homme, offre*) very attractive
séduit, e [sedui, -it] PP *de* **séduire**
segment [sɛɡmɑ̃] NM segment; (*Auto*): ~ **(de piston)** piston ring; ~ **de frein** brake shoe
segmenter [sɛɡmɑ̃te] /**1**/ VT, **se segmenter** VI to segment
ségrégation [seɡʀeɡasjɔ̃] NF segregation
ségrégationnisme [seɡʀeɡasjɔnism] NM segregationism
ségrégationniste [seɡʀeɡasjɔnist] ADJ segregationist
seiche [sɛʃ] NF cuttlefish
séide [seid] NM (*péj*) henchman
seigle [sɛɡl] NM rye
seigneur [sɛɲœʀ] NM lord; **le S~** the Lord
seigneurial, e, -aux [sɛɲœʀjal, -o] ADJ lordly, stately
sein [sɛ̃] NM breast; (*entrailles*) womb; **au ~ de** *prép* (*équipe, institution*) within; (*flots, bonheur*) in the midst of; **donner le ~ à** (*bébé*) to feed (at the breast); to breast-feed; **nourrir au ~ to** breast-feed
Seine [sɛn] NF: **la ~** the Seine
séisme [seism] NM earthquake
séismique *etc* [seismik] ADJ *voir* **sismique** *etc*
SEITA [seita] SIGLE F = **Société d'exploitation industrielle des tabacs et allumettes**
seize [sɛz] NUM sixteen
seizième [sɛzjɛm] NUM sixteenth
séjour [seʒuʀ] NM stay; (*pièce*) living room
séjourner [seʒuʀne] /**1**/ VI to stay
sel [sɛl] NM salt; (*fig*) wit; (: *piquant*) spice; ~ **de cuisine/de table** cooking/table salt; ~ **gemme** rock salt; **sels de bain** bath salts
sélect, e [selɛkt] ADJ select
sélectif, -ive [selɛktif, -iv] ADJ selective
sélection [selɛksjɔ̃] NF selection; **faire/opérer une ~ parmi** to make a selection from among; **épreuve de ~** (*Sport*) trial (for selection); ~ **naturelle** natural selection; ~ **professionnelle** professional recruitment
sélectionné, e [selɛksjɔne] ADJ (*joueur*) selected; (*produit*) specially selected
sélectionner [selɛksjɔne] /**1**/ VT to select
sélectionneur, -euse [selɛksjɔnœʀ, -øz] NM/F selector
sélectivement [selɛktivmɑ̃] ADV selectively
sélectivité [selɛktivite] NF selectivity
self [sɛlf] NM (*fam*) self-service
self-service [sɛlfsɛʀvis] ADJ self-service ▶ NM self-service (restaurant); (*magasin*) self-service shop

selle [sɛl] NF saddle; **selles** NFPL (*Méd*) stools; **aller à la ~** (*Méd*) to have a bowel movement; **se mettre en ~** to mount, get into the saddle
seller [sele] /**1**/ VT to saddle
sellette [sɛlɛt] NF: **être sur la ~** to be on the carpet (*fig*)
sellier [selje] NM saddler
selon [səlɔ̃] PRÉP according to; (*en se conformant à*) in accordance with; ~ **moi** as I see it; ~ **que** according to, depending on whether
SEm SIGLE F (= *Son Éminence*) HE
semailles [səmaj] NFPL sowing *sg*
semaine [səmɛn] NF week; (*salaire*) week's wages *ou* pay, weekly wages *ou* pay; **en ~** during the week, on weekdays; **à la petite ~** from day to day; **la ~ sainte** Holy Week
semainier [səmenje] NM (*bracelet*) bracelet made up of seven bands; (*calendrier*) desk diary; (*meuble*) chest of (seven) drawers
sémantique [semɑ̃tik] ADJ semantic ▶ NF semantics *sg*
sémaphore [semafɔʀ] NM (*Rail*) semaphore signal
semblable [sɑ̃blabl] ADJ similar; (*de ce genre*): **de semblables mésaventures** such mishaps ▶ NM fellow creature *ou* man; ~ **à** similar to, like
semblant [sɑ̃blɑ̃] NM: **un ~ de vérité** a semblance of truth; **faire ~ (de faire)** to pretend (to do)
sembler [sɑ̃ble] /**1**/ VB COPULE to seem ▶ VB IMPERS: **il semble (bien) que/inutile de** it (really) seems *ou* appears that/useless to; **il me semble (bien) que** it (really) seems to me that, I (really) think that; **il me semble le connaître** I think *ou* I've a feeling I know him; ~ **être** to seem to be; **comme bon lui semble** as he sees fit; **me semble-t-il, à ce qu'il me semble** it seems to me, to my mind
semelle [səmɛl] NF sole; (*intérieure*) insole, inner sole; **battre la ~** to stamp one's feet (to keep them warm); (*fig*) to hang around (waiting); **semelles compensées** platform soles
semence [səmɑ̃s] NF (*graine*) seed; (*clou*) tack
semer [səme] /**5**/ VT to sow; (*fig: éparpiller*) to scatter; (: *confusion*) to spread; (*fam: poursuivants*) to lose, shake off; ~ **la discorde parmi** to sow discord among; **semé de** (*difficultés*) riddled with
semestre [səmɛstʀ] NM half-year; (*Scol*) semester
semestriel, le [səmɛstʀijɛl] ADJ half-yearly; semestral
semeur, -euse [səmœʀ, -øz] NM/F sower
semi-automatique [səmiɔtɔmatik] ADJ semiautomatic
semiconducteur [səmikɔ̃dyktœʀ] NM (*Inform*) semiconductor
semi-conserve [səmikɔ̃sɛʀv] NF semi-perishable foodstuff
semi-fini [səmifini] ADJ M (*produit*) semi-finished
semi-liberté [səmilibɛʀte] NF (*Jur*) partial release from prison (*in order to follow a profession or undergo medical treatment*)

sémillant, e [semijɑ̃, -ɑ̃t] ADJ vivacious; dashing
séminaire [seminɛʀ] NM seminar; (Rel) seminary
séminariste [seminarist] NM seminarist
sémiologie [semjɔlɔʒi] NF semiology
semi-public, -ique [səmipyblik] ADJ (Jur) semipublic
semi-remorque [səmiʀəmɔʀk] NF trailer ▶ NM articulated lorry (BRIT), semi(trailer) (US)
semis [səmi] NM (terrain) seedbed, seed plot; (plante) seedling
sémite [semit] ADJ Semitic
sémitique [semitik] ADJ Semitic
semoir [səmwaʀ] NM seed-bag; seeder
semonce [səmɔ̃s] NF: **un coup de ~** a shot across the bows
semoule [səmul] NF semolina; **~ de riz** ground rice
sempiternel, le [sɛ̃pitɛʀnɛl] ADJ eternal, never-ending
sénat [sena] NM senate; see note
| The *Sénat* is the upper house of the French parliament and is housed in the Palais du Luxembourg in Paris. One-third of its members, *sénateurs* are elected for a nine-year term every three years by an electoral college consisting of the *députés* and other elected representatives. The *Sénat* has a wide range of powers but can be overridden by the lower house, the *Assemblée nationale* in case of dispute.
sénateur, -trice [senatœʀ, -tʀis] NM/F senator
sénatorial, e, -aux [senatɔʀjal, -o] ADJ senatorial, Senate cpd
Sénégal [senegal] NM: **le ~** Senegal
sénégalais, e [senegalɛ, -ɛz] ADJ Senegalese
sénevé [sɛnve] NM (Bot) mustard; (graine) mustard seed
sénile [senil] ADJ senile
sénilité [senilite] NF senility
senior [senjɔʀ] NMF (Sport) senior
sens [sɑ̃s] VB voir **sentir** ▶ NM (Physiol: instinct) sense; (signification) meaning, sense; (direction) direction, way ▶ NMPL (sensualité) senses; **reprendre ses ~** to regain consciousness; **avoir le ~ des affaires/de la mesure** to have business sense/a sense of moderation; **ça n'a pas de ~** that doesn't make (any) sense; **en dépit du bon ~** contrary to all good sense; **tomber sous le ~** to stand to reason, be perfectly obvious; **en un ~, dans un ~** in a way; **en ce ~ que** in the sense that; **à mon ~** to my mind; **dans le ~ des aiguilles d'une montre** clockwise; **dans le ~ contraire des aiguilles d'une montre** anticlockwise; **dans le ~ de la longueur/largeur** lengthways/widthways; **dans le mauvais ~** (aller) the wrong way; in the wrong direction; **bon ~** good sense; **~ commun** common sense; **~ dessus dessous** upside down; **~ interdit, ~ unique** one-way street
sensass [sɑ̃sas] ADJ INV (fam) fantastic
sensation [sɑ̃sasjɔ̃] NF sensation; **faire ~**

to cause a sensation, create a stir; **à ~** (péj) sensational
sensationnel, le [sɑ̃sasjɔnɛl] ADJ sensational, fantastic
sensé, e [sɑ̃se] ADJ sensible
sensibilisation [sɑ̃sibilizasjɔ̃] NF consciousness-raising; **une campagne de ~ de l'opinion** a campaign to raise public awareness
sensibiliser [sɑ̃sibilize] /1/ VT to sensitize; **~ qn (à)** to make sb sensitive (to)
sensibilité [sɑ̃sibilite] NF sensitivity; (affectivité, émotivité) sensitivity, sensibility
sensible [sɑ̃sibl] ADJ sensitive; (aux sens) perceptible; (appréciable: différence, progrès) appreciable, noticeable; (quartier) problem cpd; **~ à** sensitive to
sensiblement [sɑ̃sibləmɑ̃] ADV (notablement) appreciably, noticeably; (à peu près): **ils ont ~ le même poids** they weigh approximately the same
sensiblerie [sɑ̃sibləʀi] NF sentimentality; squeamishness
sensitif, -ive [sɑ̃sitif, -iv] ADJ (nerf) sensory; (personne) oversensitive
sensoriel, le [sɑ̃sɔʀjɛl] ADJ sensory, sensorial
sensualité [sɑ̃sɥalite] NF sensuality, sensuousness
sensuel, le [sɑ̃sɥɛl] ADJ (personne) sensual; (musique) sensuous
sent [sɑ̃] VB voir **sentir**
sente [sɑ̃t] NF path
sentence [sɑ̃tɑ̃s] NF (jugement) sentence; (adage) maxim
sentencieusement [sɑ̃tɑ̃sjøzmɑ̃] ADV sententiously
sentencieux, -euse [sɑ̃tɑ̃sjø, -øz] ADJ sententious
senteur [sɑ̃tœʀ] NF scent, perfume
senti, e [sɑ̃ti] ADJ: **bien ~** (mots etc) well-chosen
sentier [sɑ̃tje] NM path
sentiment [sɑ̃timɑ̃] NM feeling; (conscience, impression): **avoir le ~ de/que** to be aware of/have the feeling that; **recevez mes sentiments respectueux** (personne nommée) yours sincerely; (personne non nommée) yours faithfully; **faire du ~** (péj) to be sentimental; **si vous me prenez par les sentiments** if you appeal to my feelings
sentimental, e, -aux [sɑ̃timɑ̃tal, -o] ADJ sentimental; (vie, aventure) love cpd
sentimentalisme [sɑ̃timɑ̃talism] NM sentimentalism
sentimentalité [sɑ̃timɑ̃talite] NF sentimentality
sentinelle [sɑ̃tinɛl] NF sentry; **en ~** standing guard; (soldat: en faction) on sentry duty
sentir [sɑ̃tiʀ] /16/ VT (par l'odorat) to smell; (par le goût) to taste; (au toucher, fig) to feel; (répandre une odeur de) to smell of; (: ressemblance) to smell like; (avoir la saveur de) to taste of; to taste like; (fig: dénoter, annoncer) to be indicative of; to smack of; to foreshadow ▶ VI to smell; **~ mauvais** to smell bad; **se ~ bien** to feel good; **se ~ mal**

S

(être indisposé) to feel unwell ou ill; **se ~ le courage/la force de faire** to feel brave/strong enough to do; **ne plus se ~ de joie** to be beside o.s. with joy; **il ne peut pas le ~** (fam) he can't stand him; **je ne me sens pas bien** I don't feel well

seoir [swar] /26/: **~ à** vt to become, befit; **comme il (leur) sied** as it is fitting (to them)

Séoul [seul] N Seoul

SEP SIGLE F (= sclérose en plaques) MS

séparation [separasjɔ̃] NF separation; (cloison) division, partition; **~ de biens** division of property (in marriage settlement); **~ de corps** legal separation

séparatisme [separatism] NM separatism

séparatiste [separatist] ADJ, NMF (Pol) separatist

séparé, e [separe] ADJ (appartements, pouvoirs) separate; (époux) separated; **~ de** separate from; separated from

séparément [separemã] ADV separately

séparer [separe] /1/ VT (gén) to separate; (désunir: divergences etc) to divide; to drive apart; (: différences, obstacles) to stand between; (détacher): **~ qch de** to pull sth (off) from; (dissocier) to distinguish between; (diviser): **~ qch par** to divide sth (up) with; **~ une pièce en deux** to divide a room into two; **se séparer** VI (époux) to separate, part; (prendre congé: amis etc) to part, leave each other; (: adversaires) to separate; (se diviser: route, tige etc) to divide; (se détacher): **se séparer (de)** to split off (from); to come off; **se séparer de** (époux) to separate ou part from; (employé, objet personnel) to part with

sépia [sepja] NF sepia

sept [sɛt] NUM seven

septante [sɛptɑ̃t] NUM (BELGIQUE, SUISSE) seventy

septembre [sɛptɑ̃bʀ] NM September; voir aussi **juillet**

septennal, e, -aux [sɛptenal, -o] ADJ seven-year; (festival) seven-year, septennial

septennat [sɛptena] NM seven-year term (of office)

septentrional, e, -aux [sɛptɑ̃tʀijɔnal, -o] ADJ northern

septicémie [sɛptisemi] NF blood poisoning, septicaemia

septième [sɛtjɛm] NUM seventh; **être au ~ ciel** to be on cloud nine

septique [sɛptik] ADJ: **fosse ~** septic tank

septuagénaire [sɛptɥaʒenɛʀ] ADJ, NMF septuagenarian

sépulcral, e, -aux [sepylkʀal, -o] ADJ (voix) sepulchral

sépulcre [sepylkʀ] NM sepulchre

sépulture [sepyltyʀ] NF burial; (tombeau) burial place, grave

séquelles [sekɛl] NFPL after-effects; (fig) aftermath sg; consequences

séquence [sekɑ̃s] NF sequence

séquentiel, le [sekɑ̃sjɛl] ADJ sequential

séquestration [sekɛstʀasjɔ̃] NF illegal confinement; impounding

séquestre [sekɛstʀ] NM impoundment; **mettre sous ~** to impound

séquestrer [sekɛstʀe] /1/ VT (personne) to confine illegally; (biens) to impound

serai etc [səʀe] VB voir **être**

sérail [seʀaj] NM seraglio; harem; **rentrer au ~** to return to the fold

serbe [sɛʀb] ADJ Serbian ▶ NM (Ling) Serbian ▶ NMF: **S~** Serb

Serbie [sɛʀbi] NF: **la ~** Serbia

serbo-croate [sɛʀbɔkʀɔat] ADJ Serbo-Croat, Serbo-Croatian ▶ NM (Ling) Serbo-Croat

serein, e [səʀɛ̃, -ɛn] ADJ serene; (jugement) dispassionate

sereinement [səʀɛnmɑ̃] ADV serenely

sérénade [seʀenad] NF serenade; (fam) hullabaloo

sérénité [seʀenite] NF serenity

serez [səʀe] VB voir **être**

serf, serve [sɛʀ, sɛʀv] NM/F serf

serfouette [sɛʀfwɛt] NF weeding hoe

serge [sɛʀʒ] NF serge

sergent [sɛʀʒɑ̃] NM sergeant

sergent-chef [sɛʀʒɑ̃ʃɛf] NM staff sergeant

sergent-major [sɛʀʒɑ̃maʒɔʀ] NM ≈ quartermaster sergeant

sériciculture [seʀisikyltyʀ] NF silkworm breeding, sericulture

série [seʀi] NF (de questions, d'accidents, TV) series inv; (de clés, casseroles, outils) set; (catégorie: Sport) rank; class; **en ~** in quick succession; (Comm) mass cpd; **de ~** adj (voiture) standard; **hors ~** (Comm) custom-built; (fig) outstanding; **imprimante ~** (Inform) serial printer; **soldes de fin de séries** end of line special offers; **~ noire** nm (crime) thriller; nf (suite de malheurs) run of bad luck

sérier [seʀje] /7/ VT to classify, sort out

sérieusement [seʀjøzmɑ̃] ADV seriously; reliably; responsibly; **il parle ~** he's serious, he means it; **~?** are you serious?, do you mean it?

sérieux, -euse [seʀjø, -øz] ADJ serious; (élève, employé) reliable, responsible; (client, maison) reliable, dependable; (offre, proposition) genuine, serious; (grave, sévère) serious, solemn; (maladie, situation) serious, grave; (important) considerable ▶ NM seriousness; (d'une entreprise etc) reliability; **ce n'est pas ~** (raisonnable) that's not on; **garder son ~** to keep a straight face; **manquer de ~** not to be very responsible (ou reliable); **prendre qch/qn au ~** to take sth/sb seriously

sérigraphie [seʀigʀafi] NF silk screen printing

serin [səʀɛ̃] NM canary

seriner [səʀine] /1/ VT: **~ qch à qn** to drum sth into sb

seringue [səʀɛ̃g] NF syringe

serions etc [səʀjɔ̃] VB voir **être**

serment [sɛʀmɑ̃] NM (juré) oath; (promesse) pledge, vow; **prêter ~** to take the ou an oath; **faire le ~ de** to take a vow to, swear to; **sous ~** on ou under oath

sermon [sɛʀmɔ̃] NM sermon; (péj) sermon, lecture

sermonner [sɛʀmɔne] /1/ VT to lecture

SERNAM [sɛʁnam] SIGLE M (= *Service national de messageries*) rail delivery service

sérologie [seʁɔlɔʒi] NF serology

séronégatif, -ive [seʁonegatif, -iv] ADJ HIV negative

séropositif, -ive [seʁopozitif, -iv] ADJ HIV positive

serpe [sɛʁp] NF billhook

serpent [sɛʁpɑ̃] NM snake; ~ **à sonnettes** rattlesnake; ~ **monétaire (européen)** (European) monetary snake

serpenter [sɛʁpɑ̃te] /**1**/ VI to wind

serpentin [sɛʁpɑ̃tɛ̃] NM (*tube*) coil; (*ruban*) streamer

serpillière [sɛʁpijɛʁ] NF floorcloth

serrage [seʁaʒ] NM tightening; **collier de ~** clamp

serre [sɛʁ] NF (*Agr*) greenhouse; **serres** NFPL (*griffes*) claws, talons; ~ **chaude** hothouse; ~ **froide** unheated greenhouse

serré, e [seʁe] ADJ (*tissu*) closely woven; (*réseau*) dense; (*écriture*) close; (*habits*) tight; (*fig: lutte, match*) tight, close-fought; (*passagers etc*) (tightly) packed; (*café*) strong ► ADV: **jouer ~** to play it close, play a close game; **écrire ~** to write a cramped hand; **avoir la gorge ~** to have a lump in one's throat; **avoir le cœur ~** to have a heavy heart

serre-livres [sɛʁlivʁ] NM INV book ends pl

serrement [sɛʁmɑ̃] NM: ~ **de main** handshake; ~ **de cœur** pang of anguish

serrer [seʁe] /**1**/ VT (*tenir*) to grip ou hold tight; (*comprimer, coincer*) to squeeze; (*poings, mâchoires*) to clench; (*vêtement*) to be too tight for; to fit tightly; (*rapprocher*) to close up, move closer together; (*ceinture, nœud, frein, vis*) to tighten ► VI: ~ **à droite** to keep to the right; to move into the right-hand lane; **se serrer** (*se rapprocher*) to squeeze up; **se serrer contre qn** to huddle up to sb; **se serrer les coudes** to stick together, back one another up; **se serrer la ceinture** to tighten one's belt; ~ **la main à qn** to shake sb's hand; ~ **qn dans ses bras** to hug sb, clasp sb in one's arms; ~ **la gorge à qn** (*chagrin*) to bring a lump to sb's throat; ~ **les dents** to clench ou grit one's teeth; ~ **qn de près** to follow close behind sb; ~ **le trottoir** to hug the kerb; ~ **sa droite** to keep well to the right; ~ **la vis à qn** to crack down harder on sb; ~ **les rangs** to close ranks

serres [sɛʁ] NFPL (*griffes*) claws, talons

serre-tête [sɛʁtɛt] NM INV (*bandeau*) headband; (*bonnet*) skullcap

serrure [seʁyʁ] NF lock

serrurerie [seʁyʁʁi] NF (*métier*) locksmith's trade; (*ferronnerie*) ironwork; ~ **d'art** ornamental ironwork

serrurier [seʁyʁje] NM locksmith

sers, sert [sɛʁ] VB *voir* servir

sertir [sɛʁtiʁ] /**2**/ VT (*pierre*) to set; (*pièces métalliques*) to crimp

sérum [seʁɔm] NM serum; ~ **antivenimeux** snakebite serum; ~ **sanguin** (blood) serum

servage [sɛʁvaʒ] NM serfdom

servant [sɛʁvɑ̃] NM server

servante [sɛʁvɑ̃t] NF (maid)servant

serve [sɛʁv] NF *voir* **serf** ► VB *voir* **servir**

serveur, -euse [sɛʁvœʁ, -øz] NM/F waiter (waitress) ► NM (*Inform*) server ► ADJ: **centre ~** (*Inform*) service centre

servi, e [sɛʁvi] ADJ: **être bien ~** to get a large helping (ou helpings); **vous êtes ~?** are you being served?

serviable [sɛʁvjabl] ADJ obliging, willing to help

service [sɛʁvis] NM (*gén*) service; (*série de repas*): **premier ~** first sitting; (*pourboire*) service (charge); (*assortiment de vaisselle*) set, service; (*linge de table*) set; (*bureau: de la vente etc*) department, section; (*travail*): **pendant le ~** on duty; **services** NMPL (*travail, Écon*) services; **faire le ~** to serve; **être en ~ chez qn** (*domestique*) to be in sb's service; **être au ~ de** (*patron, patrie*) to be in the service of; **être au ~ de qn** (*collaborateur, voiture*) to be at sb's service; **porte de ~** tradesman's entrance; **rendre ~ à qn** to help sb; (*objet: s'avérer utile*) to come in useful ou handy for sb; **il aime rendre ~** he likes to help; **rendre un ~ à qn** to do sb a favour; **heures de ~** hours of duty; **être de ~** to be on duty; **reprendre du ~** to get back into action; **avoir 25 ans de ~** to have completed 25 years' service; **être/mettre en ~** to be in/put into service ou operation; ~ **compris/non compris** service included/not included, inclusive/exclusive of service; **hors ~** not in use; out of order; ~ **à thé/café** tea/coffee set ou service; ~ **après-vente** after-sales service; **en ~ commandé** on an official assignment; ~ **funèbre** funeral service; ~ **militaire** military service; *see note*; ~ **d'ordre** police (ou stewards) in charge of maintaining order; **services publics** public services, (public) utilities; **services secrets** secret service sg; **services sociaux** social services

> Until 1997, French men over the age of 18 who were passed as fit, and who were not in full-time higher education, were required to do ten months' *service militaire*. Conscientious objectors were required to do two years' community service. Since 1997, military service has been suspended in France. However, all sixteen- or seventeen-year-olds, both male and female, are required to register for a compulsory one-day training course, the JAPD (*journée d'appel de préparation à la défense*), which covers basic information on the principles and organization of defence in France, and also advises on career opportunities in the military and in the voluntary sector. Young people must attend the training day before their eighteenth birthday.

serviette [sɛʁvjet] NF (*de table*) (table) napkin, serviette; (*de toilette*) towel; (*porte-documents*) briefcase; ~ **éponge** terry towel; ~ **hygiénique** sanitary towel

servile [sɛʀvil] ADJ servile

servir [sɛʀviʀ] /**14**/ VT (gén) to serve; (dîneur: au restaurant) to wait on; (client: au magasin) to serve, attend to; (fig: aider) : **~ qn** to aid sb; to serve sb's interests; to stand sb in good stead; (Comm: rente) to pay ▶ VI (Tennis) to serve; (Cartes) to deal; (être militaire) to serve; **se servir** VI (prendre d'un plat) to help o.s.; (s'approvisionner) : **se servir chez** to shop at; **se servir de** (plat) to help o.s. to; (voiture, outil, relations) to use; **vous êtes servi?** are you being served?; **sers-toi!** help yourself; **~ qch à qn** to serve sb with sth, help sb to sth; **qu'est-ce que je vous sers?** what can I get you?; **~ à qn** (diplôme, livre) to be of use to sb; **ça m'a servi pour faire** it was useful to me when I did; I used it to do; **~ à qch/à faire** (outil etc) to be used for sth/for doing; **ça peut ~** it may come in handy; **à quoi cela sert-il (de faire)?** what's the use (of doing)?; **ça ne sert à rien** it's no use; **~ (à qn) de ...** to serve as ... (for sb); **~ à dîner (à qn)** to serve dinner (to sb)

serviteur [sɛʀvitœʀ] NM servant

servitude [sɛʀvityd] NF servitude; (fig) constraint; (Jur) easement

servofrein [sɛʀvofʀɛ̃] NM servo(-assisted) brake

servomécanisme [sɛʀvomekanism] NM servo system

ses [se] ADJ POSS voir **son**[1]

sésame [sezam] NM (Bot) sesame; (graine) sesame seed

session [sesjɔ̃] NF session

set [sɛt] NM set; (napperon) placemat; **~ de table** set of placemats

seuil [sœj] NM doorstep; (fig) threshold; **sur le ~ de la maison** in the doorway of his house, on his doorstep; **au ~ de** (fig) on the threshold ou brink ou edge of; **~ de rentabilité** (Comm) breakeven point

seul, e [sœl] ADJ (sans compagnie) alone; (avec nuance affective: isolé) lonely; (unique) : **un ~ livre** only one book, a single book; **le ~ livre** the only book; **~ ce livre, ce livre ~** this book alone, only this book ▶ ADV (vivre) alone, on one's own; **faire qch (tout) ~** to do sth (all) on one's own ou (all) by oneself ▶ NM/F: **il en reste un(e) ~(e)** there's only one left; **pas un(e) ~(e)** not a single; **à lui (tout) ~** single-handed, on his own; **~ à ~** in private; **se sentir ~** to feel lonely; **d'un ~ coup** (soudainement) all at once; (à la fois) at one blow; **parler tout ~** to talk to oneself

seulement [sœlmɑ̃] ADV only; **~ cinq, cinq ~** only five; **~ eux** only them, them alone; **~ hier/à 10h** only yesterday/at 10 o'clock; **il consent, ~ il demande des garanties** he agrees, only he wants guarantees; **non ~ ... mais aussi** ou **encore** not only ... but also

sève [sɛv] NF sap

sévère [seveʀ] ADJ severe

sévèrement [seveʀmɑ̃] ADV severely

sévérité [seveʀite] NF severity

sévices [sevis] NMPL (physical) cruelty sg, ill treatment sg

Séville [sevil] N Seville

sévir [seviʀ] /**2**/ VI (punir) to use harsh measures, crack down; (fléau) to rage, be rampant; **~ contre** (abus) to deal ruthlessly with, crack down on

sevrage [səvʀaʒ] NM weaning; deprivation; (d'un toxicomane) withdrawal

sevrer [səvʀe] /**5**/ VT to wean; (fig) : **~ qn de** to deprive sb of

sexagénaire [sɛgzaʒenɛʀ] ADJ, NMF sexagenarian

SExc SIGLE F (= Son Excellence) HE

sexe [sɛks] NM sex; (organe mâle) member

sexisme [sɛksism] NM sexism

sexiste [sɛksist] ADJ, NM sexist

sexologie [sɛksɔlɔʒi] NF sexology

sexologue [sɛksɔlɔg] NMF sexologist, sex specialist

sextant [sɛkstɑ̃] NM sextant

sexualité [sɛksɥalite] NF sexuality

sexué, e [sɛksɥe] ADJ sexual

sexuel, le [sɛksɥɛl] ADJ sexual; **acte ~** sex act

sexuellement [sɛksɥɛlmɑ̃] ADV sexually

seyait [sɛjɛ] VB voir **seoir**

seyant, e [sɛjɑ̃, -ɑ̃t] VB voir **seoir** ▶ ADJ becoming

Seychelles [seʃɛl] NFPL: **les ~** the Seychelles

SG SIGLE M = **secrétaire général**

SGEN SIGLE M (= Syndicat général de l'éducation nationale) (main) teachers' trades union

shaker [ʃɛkœʀ] NM (cocktail) shaker

shampooiner [ʃɑ̃pwine] /**1**/ VT to shampoo

shampooineur, -euse [ʃɑ̃pwinœʀ, -øz] NM/F (personne) junior (who does the shampooing)

shampooing [ʃɑ̃pwɛ̃] NM shampoo; **se faire un ~** to shampoo one's hair; **~ colorant** (colour) rinse; **~ traitant** medicated shampoo

Shetland [ʃɛtlɑ̃d] N: **les îles ~** the Shetland Islands, Shetland

shoot [ʃut] NM (Football) shot

shooter [ʃute] /**1**/ VI (Football) to shoot; **se shooter** (drogué) to mainline

shopping [ʃɔpiŋ] NM: **faire du ~** to go shopping

short [ʃɔʀt] NM (pair of) shorts pl

SI SIGLE M = **syndicat d'initiative**

(MOT-CLÉ)

si [si] ADV **1** (oui) yes; "Paul n'est pas venu" — "si!" "Paul hasn't come" — "Yes he has!"; **je vous assure que si** I assure you he did/she is etc

2 (tellement) so; **si gentil/rapidement** so kind/fast; (tant et) **si bien que** so much so that; **si rapide qu'il soit** however fast he may be ▶ CONJ if; **si tu veux** if you want; **je me demande si** I wonder if ou whether; **si j'étais toi** if I were you; **si seulement** if only; **si ce n'est que** apart from; **une des plus belles, si ce n'est la plus belle** one of the most beautiful, if not THE most beautiful; **s'il est aimable, eux par contre ...** while ou whereas he's nice, they (on the other hand) ... ▶ NM (Mus) B; (: en chantant la gamme) ti

siamois, e [sjamwa, -waz] ADJ Siamese; **frères/sœurs ~(es)** Siamese twins

Sibérie [sibeʀi] NF: **la ~** Siberia

sibérien, ne [siberjɛ̃, -ɛn] ADJ Siberian ▶ NM/F:
S~, ne Siberian
sibyllin, e [sibilɛ̃, -in] ADJ sibylline
SICAV [sikav] SIGLE F (= *société d'investissement à
capital variable*) open-ended investment trust, *share in
such a trust*
Sicile [sisil] NF: **la** ~ Sicily
sicilien, ne [sisiljɛ̃, -ɛn] ADJ Sicilian
sida [sida] NM (= *syndrome immuno-déficitaire acquis*)
AIDS *sg*
sidéral, e, -aux [sideral, -o] ADJ sideral
sidérant, e [siderɑ̃, -ɑ̃t] ADJ staggering
sidéré, e [sidere] ADJ staggered
sidérurgie [sideryrʒi] NF steel industry
sidérurgique [sideryrʒik] ADJ steel *cpd*
sidérurgiste [sideryrʒist] NMF steel worker
siècle [sjɛkl] NM century; (*époque*): **le ~ des
lumières/de l'atome** the age of
enlightenment/atomic age; (*Rel*): **le ~** the
world
sied [sje] VB *voir* **seoir**
siège [sjɛʒ] NM seat; (*d'entreprise*) head office;
(*d'organisation*) headquarters *pl*; (*Mil*) siege;
lever le ~ to raise the siege; **mettre le ~
devant** to besiege; **présentation par le ~** (*Méd*)
breech presentation; **~ avant/arrière** (*Auto*)
front/back seat; **~ baquet** bucket seat; **~ social**
registered office
siéger [sjeʒe] /3, 6/ VI (*assemblée, tribunal*) to sit;
(*résider, se trouver*) to lie, be located
sien, ne [sjɛ̃, sjɛn] PRON: **le (la) ~(ne), les ~(ne)s**
(*d'un homme*) his; (*d'une femme*) hers; (*d'une chose*)
its; **y mettre du ~** to pull one's weight; **faire
des siennes** (*fam*) to be up to one's (usual)
tricks; **les siens** (*sa famille*) one's family
siérait *etc* [sjere] VB *voir* **seoir**
Sierra Leone [sjɛraleone] NF: **la ~** Sierra Leone
sieste [sjɛst] NF (afternoon) snooze *ou* nap,
siesta; **faire la ~** to have a snooze *ou* nap
sieur [sjœr] NM: **le ~ Thomas** Mr Thomas; (*en
plaisantant*) Master Thomas
sifflant, e [siflɑ̃, -ɑ̃t] ADJ (*bruit*) whistling; (*toux*)
wheezing; **(consonne) ~** sibilant
sifflement [sifləmɑ̃] NM whistle, whistling *no
pl*; wheezing *no pl*; hissing *no pl*
siffler [sifle] /1/ VI (*gén*) to whistle; (*avec un sifflet*)
to blow (on) one's whistle; (*en respirant*) to
wheeze; (*serpent, vapeur*) to hiss ▶ VT (*chanson*) to
whistle; (*chien etc*) to whistle for; (*fille*) to
whistle at; (*pièce, orateur*) to hiss, boo; (*faute*) to
blow one's whistle at; (*fin du match, départ*) to
blow one's whistle for; (*fam: verre, bouteille*) to
guzzle, knock back (BRIT)
sifflet [siflɛ] NM whistle; **sifflets** NMPL (*de
mécontentement*) whistles, boos; **coup de ~**
whistle
siffloter [siflɔte] /1/ VI, VT to whistle
sigle [sigl] NM acronym, (set of) initials *pl*
signal, -aux [siɲal, -o] NM (*signe convenu, appareil*)
signal; (*indice, écriteau*) sign; **donner le ~ de** to
give the signal for; **~ d'alarme** alarm signal;
~ d'alerte/de détresse warning/distress
signal; **~ horaire** time signal; **~ optique/
sonore** warning light/sound; visual/acoustic

signal; **signaux (lumineux)** (*Auto*) traffic
signals; **signaux routiers** road signs;
(*lumineux*) traffic lights
signalement [siɲalmɑ̃] NM description,
particulars *pl*
signaler [siɲale] /1/ VT to indicate; to announce;
(*vol, perte*) to report; (*personne: faire un signe*) to
signal; (*être l'indice de*) to indicate; **~ qch à qn/à
qn que** to point out sth to sb/to sb that; **~ qn à
la police** to bring sb to the notice of the police;
se ~ par to distinguish o.s. by; **se ~ à
l'attention de qn** to attract sb's attention
signalétique [siɲaletik] ADJ: **fiche ~**
identification sheet
signalisation [siɲalizasjɔ̃] NF signalling,
signposting; signals *pl*; roadsigns *pl*; **panneau
de ~** roadsign
signaliser [siɲalize] /1/ VT to put up roadsigns
on; to put signals on
signataire [siɲatɛr] NMF signatory
signature [siɲatyr] NF signature; (*action*)
signing
signe [siɲ] NM sign; (*Typo*) mark; **ne pas
donner ~ de vie** to give no sign of life; **c'est
bon ~** it's a good sign; **c'est ~ que** it's a sign
that; **faire un ~ de la main/tête** to give a sign
with one's hand/shake one's head; **faire ~ à qn**
(*fig: contacter*) to get in touch with sb; **faire ~ à
qn d'entrer** to motion (to) sb to come in; **en ~
de** as a sign *ou* mark of; **le ~ de la croix** the sign
of the Cross; **~ de ponctuation** punctuation
mark; **~ du zodiaque** sign of the zodiac;
signes particuliers distinguishing marks
signer [siɲe] /1/ VT to sign; **se signer** VI to
cross o.s.
signet [siɲɛ] NM bookmark
significatif, -ive [siɲifikatif, -iv] ADJ significant
signification [siɲifikasjɔ̃] NF meaning
signifier [siɲifje] /7/ (*vouloir dire*) to mean,
signify; (*faire connaître*): **~ qch (à qn)** to make
sth known (to sb); (*Jur*): **~ qch à qn** to serve
notice of sth on sb
silence [silɑ̃s] NM silence; (*Mus*) rest; **garder le
~ (sur qch)** to keep silent (about sth), say
nothing (about sth); **passer sous ~** to pass over
(in silence); **réduire au ~** to silence
silencieusement [silɑ̃sjøzmɑ̃] ADV silently
silencieux, -euse [silɑ̃sjø, -øz] ADJ quiet, silent
▶ NM silencer (BRIT), muffler (US)
silex [silɛks] NM flint
silhouette [silwɛt] NF outline, silhouette;
(*lignes, contour*) outline; (*figure*) figure
silice [silis] NF silica
siliceux, -euse [silisø, -øz] ADJ (*terrain*) chalky
silicium [silisjɔm] NM silicon; **plaquette de ~**
silicon chip
silicone [silikɔn] NF silicone
silicose [silikoz] NF silicosis, dust disease
sillage [sijaʒ] NM wake; (*fig*) trail; **dans le ~ de**
(*fig*) in the wake of
sillon [sijɔ̃] NM (*d'un champ*) furrow; (*de disque*)
groove
sillonner [sijɔne] /1/ VT (*creuser*) to furrow;
(*traverser*) to criss-cross, cross

S

silo [silo] NM silo

simagrées [simagʀe] NFPL fuss *sg*; airs and graces

simiesque [simjɛsk] ADJ monkey-like, ape-like

similaire [similɛʀ] ADJ similar

similarité [similaʀite] NF similarity

simili [simili] NM imitation; (*Typo*) half-tone ▸ NF half-tone engraving

simili... [simili] PRÉFIXE imitation *cpd*, artificial

similicuir [similikɥiʀ] NM imitation leather

similigravure [similiɡʀavyʀ] NF half-tone engraving

similitude [similityd] NF similarity

simple [sɛ̃pl] ADJ (*gén*) simple; (*non multiple*) single; **simples** NMPL (*Méd*) medicinal plants; **~ messieurs/dames** *nm* (*Tennis*) men's/ladies' singles *sg*; **un ~ particulier** an ordinary citizen; **une ~ formalité** a mere formality; **cela varie du ~ au double** it can double, it can double the price *etc*; **dans le plus ~ appareil** in one's birthday suit; **~ course** *adj* single; **~ d'esprit** *nmf* simpleton; **~ soldat** private

simplement [sɛ̃pləmɑ̃] ADV simply

simplet, te [sɛ̃plɛ, -ɛt] ADJ (*personne*) simple-minded

simplicité [sɛ̃plisite] NF simplicity; **en toute ~** quite simply

simplification [sɛ̃plifikasjɔ̃] NF simplification

simplifier [sɛ̃plifje] **/7/** VT to simplify

simpliste [sɛ̃plist] ADJ simplistic

simulacre [simylakʀ] NM enactment; (*péj*): **un ~ de** a pretence of, a sham

simulateur, -trice [simylatœʀ, -tʀis] NM/F shammer, pretender; (*qui se prétend malade*) malingerer ▸ NM: **~ de vol** flight simulator

simulation [simylasjɔ̃] NF shamming, simulation; malingering

simuler [simyle] **/1/** VT to sham, simulate

simultané, e [simyltane] ADJ simultaneous

simultanéité [simyltaneite] NF simultaneity

simultanément [simyltanemɑ̃] ADV simultaneously

Sinaï [sinai] NM: **le ~** Sinai

sinapisme [sinapism] NM (*Méd*) mustard poultice

sincère [sɛ̃sɛʀ] ADJ sincere; genuine; heartfelt; **mes sincères condoléances** my deepest sympathy

sincèrement [sɛ̃sɛʀmɑ̃] ADV sincerely; genuinely

sincérité [sɛ̃seʀite] NF sincerity; **en toute ~** in all sincerity

sinécure [sinekyʀ] NF sinecure

sine die [sinedje] ADV sine die, indefinitely

sine qua non [sinekwanɔn] ADJ: **condition ~** indispensable condition

Singapour [sɛ̃ɡapuʀ] NM: **le ~** Singapore

singe [sɛ̃ʒ] NM monkey; (*de grande taille*) ape

singer [sɛ̃ʒe] **/3/** VT to ape, mimic

singeries [sɛ̃ʒʀi] NFPL antics; (*simagrées*) airs and graces

singulariser [sɛ̃ɡylaʀize] **/1/** VT to mark out; **se singulariser** VI to call attention to o.s.

singularité [sɛ̃ɡylaʀite] NF peculiarity

singulier, -ière [sɛ̃ɡylje, -jɛʀ] ADJ remarkable, singular; (*Ling*) singular ▸ NM singular

singulièrement [sɛ̃ɡyljɛʀmɑ̃] ADV singularly, remarkably

sinistre [sinistʀ] ADJ sinister; (*intensif*): **un ~ imbécile** an incredible idiot ▸ NM (*incendie*) blaze; (*catastrophe*) disaster; (*Assurances*) damage (*giving rise to a claim*)

sinistré, e [sinistʀe] ADJ disaster-stricken ▸ NM/F disaster victim

sinistrose [sinistʀoz] NF pessimism

sino... [sino] PRÉFIXE: **~-indien** Sino-Indian, Chinese-Indian

sinon [sinɔ̃] CONJ (*autrement, sans quoi*) otherwise, or else; (*sauf*) except, other than; (*si ce n'est*) if not

sinueux, -euse [sinɥø, -øz] ADJ winding; (*fig*) tortuous

sinuosités [sinɥozite] NFPL winding *sg*, curves

sinus [sinys] NM (*Anat*) sinus; (*Géom*) sine

sinusite [sinyzit] NF sinusitis, sinus infection

sinusoïdal, e, -aux [sinyzɔidal, -o] ADJ sinusoidal

sinusoïde [sinyzɔid] NF sinusoid

sionisme [sjɔnism] NM Zionism

sioniste [sjɔnist] ADJ, NMF Zionist

siphon [sifɔ̃] NM (*tube, d'eau gazeuse*) siphon; (*d'évier etc*) U-bend

siphonner [sifɔne] **/1/** VT to siphon

sire [siʀ] NM (*titre*): **S~** Sire; **un triste ~** an unsavoury individual

sirène [siʀɛn] NF siren; **~ d'alarme** fire alarm; (*pendant la guerre*) air-raid siren

sirop [siʀo] NM (*à diluer: de fruit etc*) syrup, cordial (BRIT); (*boisson*) fruit drink; (*pharmaceutique*) syrup, mixture; **~ de menthe** mint syrup *ou* cordial; **~ contre la toux** cough syrup *ou* mixture

siroter [siʀɔte] **/1/** VT to sip

sirupeux, -euse [siʀypø, -øz] ADJ syrupy

sis, e [si, siz] ADJ: **~ rue de la Paix** located in the rue de la Paix

sisal [sizal] NM (*Bot*) sisal

sismique [sismik] ADJ seismic

sismographe [sismɔɡʀaf] NM seismograph

sismologie [sismɔlɔʒi] NF seismology

site [sit] NM (*paysage, environnement*) setting; (*d'une ville etc: emplacement*) site; **~ (pittoresque)** beauty spot; **sites touristiques** places of interest; **sites naturels/historiques** natural/historic sites; **~ web** (*Inform*) website

sitôt [sito] ADV: **~ parti** as soon as he *etc* had left; **~ après** straight after; **pas de ~** not for a long time; **~ (après) que** as soon as

situation [sitɥasjɔ̃] NF (*gén*) situation; (*d'un édifice, d'une ville*) situation, position; (*emplacement*) location; **être en ~ de faire qch** to be in a position to do sth; **~ de famille** marital status

situé, e [sitɥe] ADJ: **bien ~** well situated, in a good location; **~ à/près de** situated at/near

situer [sitɥe] **/1/** VT to site, situate; (*en pensée*) to set, place; **se situer** VI: **se situer à/près de** to be situated at/near

SIVOM [sivɔm] SIGLE M (= *Syndicat intercommunal à vocation multiple*) association of "communes"

six [sis] NUM six

sixième [sizjɛm] NUM sixth ▶ NF (*Scol: classe*) year 7 (BRIT), sixth grade (US); **en ~** in year 7 (BRIT), in sixth grade (US)

skaï® [skaj] NM ≈ Leatherette®

skate [skɛt], **skate-board** [skɛtbɔrd] NM (*sport*) skateboarding; (*planche*) skateboard

sketch [skɛtʃ] NM (*variety*) sketch

ski [ski] NM (*objet*) ski; (*sport*) skiing; **faire du ~** to ski; **~ alpin** Alpine skiing; **~ court** short ski; **~ évolutif** short ski method; **~ de fond** cross-country skiing; **~ nautique** water-skiing; **~ de piste** downhill skiing; **~ de randonnée** cross-country skiing

ski-bob [skibɔb] NM skibob

skier [skje] /7/ VI to ski

skieur, -euse [skjœr, -øz] NM/F skier

skif, skiff [skif] NM skiff

slalom [slalɔm] NM slalom; **faire du ~ entre** to slalom between

slalomer [slalɔme] /1/ VI (*entre des obstacles*) to weave in and out; (*Ski*) to slalom

slalomeur, -euse [slalɔmœr, -øz] NM/F (*Ski*) slalom skier

slave [slav] ADJ Slav(onic), Slavic ▶ NM (*Ling*) Slavonic ▶ NMF: **S~** Slav

slip [slip] NM (*sous-vêtement*) underpants pl, pants pl (BRIT), briefs pl; (*de bain: d'homme*) trunks pl; (: *du bikini*) (bikini) briefs pl

slogan [slɔgɑ̃] NM slogan

slovaque [slɔvak] ADJ Slovak ▶ NM (*Ling*) Slovak ▶ NMF: **S~** Slovak

Slovaquie [slɔvaki] NF: **la ~** Slovakia

slovène [slɔvɛn] ADJ Slovene ▶ NM (*Ling*) Slovene ▶ NMF: **S~** Slovene

Slovénie [slɔveni] NF: **la ~** Slovenia

slow [slo] NM (*danse*) slow number

SM SIGLE F (= *Sa Majesté*) HM

SMAG [smag] SIGLE M = **salaire minimum agricole garanti**

smasher [smaʃe] /1/ VI to smash the ball ▶ VT (*balle*) to smash

SMIC [smik] SIGLE M = **salaire minimum interprofessionnel de croissance**; *see note*

> In France, the SMIC (*salaire minimum interprofessionnel de croissance*) is the minimum hourly rate which workers over the age of 18 must legally be paid. It is index-linked and is raised each time the cost of living rises by 2 per cent.

smicard, e [smikar, -ard] NM/F minimum wage earner

smocks [smɔk] NMPL (*Couture*) smocking *no pl*

smoking [smɔkiŋ] NM dinner *ou* evening suit

SMS SIGLE M (= *short message service*) (*service*) SMS; (: *message*) text (message)

SMUR [smyr] SIGLE M (= *service médical d'urgence et de réanimation*) specialist mobile emergency unit

snack [snak] NM snack bar

SNC ABR = **service non compris**

SNCB SIGLE F (= *Société nationale des chemins de fer belges*) Belgian railways

SNCF SIGLE F (= *Société nationale des chemins de fer français*) French railways

SNES [snɛs] SIGLE M (= *Syndicat national de l'enseignement secondaire*) secondary teachers' union

SNE-sup [ɛsɛnəsyp] SIGLE M (= *Syndicat national de l'enseignement supérieur*) university teachers' union

SNJ SIGLE M (= *Syndicat national des journalistes*) journalists' union

snob [snɔb] ADJ snobbish ▶ NMF snob

snober [snɔbe] /1/ VT: **~ qn** to give sb the cold shoulder, treat sb with disdain

snobinard, e [snɔbinar, -ard] NM/F snooty *ou* stuck-up person

snobisme [snɔbism] NM snobbery, snobbishness

SNSM SIGLE F (= *Société nationale de sauvetage en mer*) national sea-rescue association

s.o. ABR (= *sans objet*) no longer applicable

sobre [sɔbr] ADJ (*personne*) temperate, abstemious; (*élégance, style*) restrained, sober; **~ de** (*gestes, compliments*) sparing of

sobrement [sɔbrəmɑ̃] ADV in moderation, abstemiously; soberly

sobriété [sɔbrijete] NF temperance, abstemiousness; sobriety

sobriquet [sɔbrikɛ] NM nickname

soc [sɔk] NM ploughshare

sociabilité [sɔsjabilite] NF sociability

sociable [sɔsjabl] ADJ sociable

social, e, -aux [sɔsjal, -o] ADJ social

socialisant, e [sɔsjalizɑ̃, -ɑ̃t] ADJ with socialist tendencies

socialisation [sɔsjalizasjɔ̃] NF socialisation

socialiser [sɔsjalize] /1/ VT to socialize

socialisme [sɔsjalism] NM socialism

socialiste [sɔsjalist] ADJ, NMF socialist

sociétaire [sɔsjetɛr] NMF member

société [sɔsjete] NF society; (*d'abeilles, de fourmis*) colony; (*sportive*) club; (*Comm*) company; **la bonne ~** polite society; **se plaire dans la ~ de** to enjoy the society of; **l'archipel de la S~** the Society Islands; **la ~ d'abondance/de consommation** the affluent/consumer society; **~ par actions** joint stock company; **~ anonyme** ≈ limited company (BRIT), ≈ incorporated company (US); **~ d'investissement à capital variable** ≈ investment trust (BRIT), ≈ mutual fund (US); **~ à responsabilité limitée** *type of limited liability company (with non-negotiable shares)*; **~ savante** learned society; **~ de services** service company

socioculturel, le [sɔsjokyltyrɛl] ADJ sociocultural

socio-économique [sɔsjoekɔnɔmik] ADJ socioeconomic

socio-éducatif, -ive [sɔsjoedykatif, -iv] ADJ socio-educational

sociolinguistique [sɔsjolɛ̃ɡɥistik] ADJ sociolinguistic

sociologie [sɔsjɔlɔʒi] NF sociology

sociologique [sɔsjɔlɔʒik] ADJ sociological

sociologue [sɔsjɔlɔg] NMF sociologist

socio-professionnel, le [sɔsjoprɔfɛsjɔnɛl] ADJ socio professional

S

socle [sɔkl] NM (*de colonne, statue*) plinth, pedestal; (*de lampe*) base

socquette [sɔkɛt] NF ankle sock

soda [sɔda] NM (*boisson*) fizzy drink, soda (*US*)

sodium [sɔdjɔm] NM sodium

sodomie [sɔdɔmi] NF sodomy; buggery

sodomiser [sɔdɔmize] /**1**/ VT to sodomize; to bugger

sœur [sœʀ] NF sister; (*religieuse*) nun, sister; **~ Élisabeth** (*Rel*) Sister Elizabeth; **~ de lait** foster sister

sofa [sɔfa] NM sofa

Sofia [sɔfja] N Sofia

SOFRES [sɔfʀɛs] SIGLE F (= *Société française d'enquête par sondage*) *company which conducts opinion polls*

soi [swa] PRON oneself; **en ~** (*intrinsèquement*) in itself; **cela va de ~** that *ou* it goes without saying, it stands to reason

soi-disant [swadizɑ̃] ADJ INV so-called ▶ ADV supposedly

soie [swa] NF silk; (*de porc, sanglier: poil*) bristle

soient [swa] VB *voir* **être**

soierie [swaʀi] NF (*industrie*) silk trade; (*tissu*) silk

soif [swaf] NF thirst; (*fig*): **~ de** thirst *ou* craving for; **avoir ~** to be thirsty; **donner ~ à qn** to make sb thirsty

soigné, e [swaɲe] ADJ (*tenue*) well-groomed, neat; (*travail*) careful, meticulous; (*fam*) whopping; stiff

soigner [swaɲe] /**1**/ VT (*malade, maladie: docteur*) to treat; (: *infirmière, mère*) to nurse, look after; (*blessé*) to tend; (*travail, détails*) to take care over; (*jardin, chevelure, invités*) to look after

soigneur [swaɲœʀ] NM (*Cyclisme, Football*) trainer; (*Boxe*) second

soigneusement [swaɲøzmɑ̃] ADV carefully

soigneux, -euse [swaɲø, -øz] ADJ (*propre*) tidy, neat; (*méticuleux*) painstaking, careful; **~ de** careful with

soi-même [swamɛm] PRON oneself

soin [swɛ̃] NM (*application*) care; (*propreté, ordre*) tidiness, neatness; (*responsabilité*): **le ~ de qch** the care of sth; **soins** NMPL (*à un malade, blessé*) treatment *sg*, medical attention *sg*; (*attentions, prévenance*) care and attention *sg*; (*hygiène*) care *sg*; **soins de la chevelure/de beauté** hair/beauty care; **soins du corps/ménage** care of one's body/the home; **avoir** *ou* **prendre ~ de** to take care of, look after; **avoir** *ou* **prendre ~ de faire** to take care to do; **faire qch avec (grand) ~** to do sth (very) carefully; **sans ~** *adj* careless, untidy; **les premiers soins** first aid *sg*; **aux bons soins de** c/o, care of; **être aux petits soins pour qn** to wait on sb hand and foot, see to sb's every need; **confier qn aux soins de qn** to hand sb over to sb's care

soir [swaʀ] NM, ADV evening; **le ~** in the evening(s); **ce ~** this evening, tonight; **à ce ~!** see you this evening (*ou* tonight)!; **la veille au ~** the previous evening; **sept/dix heures du ~** seven in the evening/ten at night; **le repas/journal du ~** the evening meal/newspaper;

dimanche ~ Sunday evening; **hier ~** yesterday evening; **demain ~** tomorrow evening, tomorrow night

soirée [swaʀe] NF evening; (*réception*) party; **donner en ~** (*film, pièce*) to give an evening performance of

soit [swa] VB *voir* **être** ▶ CONJ (*à savoir*) namely, to wit; (*ou*): **~ ... ~** either ... or ▶ ADV so be it, very well; **~ un triangle ABC** let ABC be a triangle; **~ que ... ~ que** *ou* **ou que** whether ... or whether

soixantaine [swasɑ̃tɛn] NF: **une ~ (de)** sixty or so, about sixty; **avoir la ~** (*âge*) to be around sixty

soixante [swasɑ̃t] NUM sixty

soixante-dix [swasɑ̃tdis] NUM seventy

soixante-dixième [swasɑ̃tdizjɛm] NUM seventieth

soixante-huitard, e [swasɑ̃tɥitaʀ, -aʀd] ADJ relating to the demonstrations of May 1968 ▶ NM/F participant in the demonstrations of May 1968

soixantième [swasɑ̃tjɛm] NUM sixtieth

soja [sɔʒa] NM soya; (*graines*) soya beans *pl*; **germes de ~** beansprouts

sol [sɔl] NM ground; (*de logement*) floor; (*revêtement*) flooring *no pl*; (*territoire, Agr, Géo*) soil; (*Mus*) G; (: *en chantant la gamme*) so(h)

solaire [sɔlɛʀ] ADJ (*énergie etc*) solar; (*crème etc*) sun *cpd*

solarium [sɔlaʀjɔm] NM solarium

soldat [sɔlda] NM soldier; **S~ inconnu** Unknown Warrior *ou* Soldier; **~ de plomb** tin *ou* toy soldier

solde [sɔld] NF pay ▶ NM (*Comm*) balance; **soldes** NMPL, NFPL (*Comm*) sales; (*articles*) sale goods; **à la ~ de qn** (*péj*) in sb's pay; **~ créditeur/débiteur** credit/debit balance; **~ à payer** balance outstanding; **en ~** at sale price; **aux soldes** at the sales

solder [sɔlde] /**1**/ VT (*compte*) to settle; (*marchandise*) to sell at sale price, sell off; **se ~ par** (*fig*) to end in; **article soldé (à) 10 euros** item reduced to 10 euros

soldeur, -euse [sɔldœʀ, -øz] NM/F (*Comm*) discounter

sole [sɔl] NF sole *inv* (*fish*)

soleil [sɔlɛj] NM sun; (*lumière*) sun(light); (*temps ensoleillé*) sun(shine); (*feu d'artifice*) Catherine wheel; (*d'acrobate*) grand circle; (*Bot*) sunflower; **il y a** *ou* **il fait du ~** it's sunny; **au ~** in the sun; **en plein ~** in full sun; **le ~ levant/couchant** the rising/setting sun; **le ~ de minuit** the midnight sun

solennel, le [sɔlanɛl] ADJ solemn; ceremonial

solennellement [sɔlanɛlmɑ̃] ADV solemnly

solennité [sɔlanite] NF (*d'une fête*) solemnity; **solennités** NFPL (*formalités*) formalities

solénoïde [sɔlenɔid] NM (*Élec*) solenoid

solfège [sɔlfɛʒ] NM rudiments *pl* of music; (*exercices*) ear training *no pl*

solfier [sɔlfje] /**7**/ VT: **~ un morceau** to sing a piece using the sol-fa

soli [sɔli] NMPL *de* **solo**

solidaire [sɔlidɛʀ] ADJ: **être solidaires** (*personnes*) to show solidarity, stand *ou* stick together; (*pièces mécaniques*) interdependent; (*Jur: engagement*) binding on all parties; (: *débiteurs*) jointly liable; **être ~ de** (*collègues*) to stand by; (*mécanisme*) to be bound up with, be dependent on

solidairement [sɔlidɛʀmɑ̃] ADV jointly

solidariser [sɔlidaʀize] /1/: **se ~ avec** vt to show solidarity with

solidarité [sɔlidaʀite] NF (*entre personnes*) solidarity; (*de mécanisme, phénomènes*) interdependence; **par ~ (avec)** (*cesser le travail etc*) in sympathy (with)

solide [sɔlid] ADJ solid; (*mur, maison, meuble*) solid, sturdy; (*connaissances, argument*) sound; (*personne*) robust, sturdy; (*estomac*) strong ▶ NM solid; **avoir les reins solides** (*fig*) to be in a good financial position; to have sound financial backing

solidement [sɔlidmɑ̃] ADV solidly; (*fermement*) firmly

solidifier [sɔlidifje] /7/ VT, **se solidifier** VI to solidify

solidité [sɔlidite] NF solidity; sturdiness

soliloque [sɔlilɔk] NM soliloquy

soliste [sɔlist] NMF soloist

solitaire [sɔlitɛʀ] ADJ (*sans compagnie*) solitary, lonely; (*isolé*) solitary, isolated, lone; (*lieu*) lonely ▶ NMF (*ermite*) recluse; (*fig: ours*) loner ▶ NM (*diamant, jeu*) solitaire

solitude [sɔlityd] NF loneliness; (*paix*) solitude

solive [sɔliv] NF joist

sollicitations [sɔlisitasjɔ̃] NFPL (*requêtes*) entreaties, appeals; (*attractions*) enticements; (*Tech*) stress *sg*

solliciter [sɔlisite] /1/ VT (*personne*) to appeal to; (*emploi, faveur*) to seek; (*moteur*) to prompt; (*occupations, attractions etc*): ~ **qn** to appeal to sb's curiosity *etc*; to entice sb; to make demands on sb's time; ~ **qn de faire** to appeal to sb *ou* request sb to do

sollicitude [sɔlisityd] NF concern

solo [sɔlo] NM (*pl* **soli**) (*Mus*) solo

sol-sol [sɔlsɔl] ADJ INV surface-to-surface

solstice [sɔlstis] NM solstice; ~ **d'hiver/d'été** winter/summer solstice

solubilisé, e [sɔlybilize] ADJ soluble

solubilité [sɔlybilite] NF solubility

soluble [sɔlybl] ADJ (*sucre, cachet*) soluble; (*problème etc*) soluble, solvable

soluté [sɔlyte] NM solution

solution [sɔlysjɔ̃] NF solution; ~ **de continuité** gap, break; ~ **de facilité** easy way out

solutionner [sɔlysjɔne] /1/ VT to solve, find a solution for

solvabilité [sɔlvabilite] NF solvency

solvable [sɔlvabl] ADJ solvent

solvant [sɔlvɑ̃] NM solvent

Somalie [sɔmali] NF: **la ~** Somalia

somalien, ne [sɔmaljɛ̃, -ɛn] ADJ Somalian

somatique [sɔmatik] ADJ somatic

sombre [sɔ̃bʀ] ADJ dark; (*fig*) sombre, gloomy; (*sinistre*) awful, dreadful

sombrer [sɔ̃bʀe] /1/ VI (*bateau*) to sink, go down; ~ **corps et biens** to go down with all hands; ~ **dans** (*misère, désespoir*) to sink into

sommaire [sɔmɛʀ] ADJ (*simple*) basic; (*expéditif*) summary ▶ NM summary; **faire le ~ de** to make a summary of, summarize; **exécution ~** summary execution

sommairement [sɔmɛʀmɑ̃] ADV basically; summarily

sommation [sɔmasjɔ̃] NF (*Jur*) summons *sg*; (*avant de faire feu*) warning

somme [sɔm] NF (*Math*) sum; (*fig*) amount; (*argent*) sum, amount ▶ NM: **faire un ~** to have a (short) nap; **faire la ~ de** to add up; **en ~, ~ toute** adv all in all

sommeil [sɔmɛj] NM sleep; **avoir ~** to be sleepy; **avoir le ~ léger** to be a light sleeper; **en ~** (*fig*) dormant

sommeiller [sɔmeje] /1/ VI to doze; (*fig*) to lie dormant

sommelier [sɔməlje] NM wine waiter

sommer [sɔme] /1/ VT: ~ **qn de faire** to command *ou* order sb to do; (*Jur*) to summon sb to do

sommes [sɔm] VB *voir* **être**; *voir aussi* **somme**

sommet [sɔmɛ] NM top; (*d'une montagne*) summit, top; (*fig: de la perfection, gloire*) height; (*Géom: d'angle*) vertex; (*conférence*) summit (conference)

sommier [sɔmje] NM bed base, bedspring (US); (*Admin: registre*) register; ~ **à ressorts** (interior sprung) divan base (BRIT), box spring (US); ~ **à lattes** slatted bed base

sommité [sɔmite] NF prominent person, leading light

somnambule [sɔmnɑ̃byl] NMF sleepwalker

somnambulisme [sɔmnɑ̃bylism] NM sleepwalking

somnifère [sɔmnifɛʀ] NM sleeping drug; (*comprimé*) sleeping pill *ou* tablet

somnolence [sɔmnɔlɑ̃s] NF drowsiness

somnolent, e [sɔmnɔlɑ̃, -ɑ̃t] ADJ sleepy, drowsy

somnoler [sɔmnɔle] /1/ VI to doze

somptuaire [sɔ̃ptɥɛʀ] ADJ: **lois somptuaires** sumptuary laws; **dépenses somptuaires** extravagant expenditure *sg*

somptueusement [sɔ̃ptɥøzmɑ̃] ADV sumptuously

somptueux, -euse [sɔ̃ptɥø, -øz] ADJ sumptuous; (*cadeau*) lavish

somptuosité [sɔ̃ptɥozite] NF sumptuousness; (*d'un cadeau*) lavishness

son¹, sa [sɔ̃, sa] (*pl* **ses** [se]) ADJ POSS (*antécédent humain: mâle*) his; (: *femelle*) her; (: *valeur indéfinie*) one's, his (her); (: *non humain*) its; *voir* **il**

son² [sɔ̃] NM sound; (*de blé etc*) bran; ~ **et lumière** adj inv son et lumière

sonar [sɔnaʀ] NM (*Navig*) sonar

sonate [sɔnat] NF sonata

sondage [sɔ̃daʒ] NM (*de terrain*) boring, drilling; (*de mer, atmosphère*) sounding; probe; (*enquête*) survey, sounding out of opinion; ~ **(d'opinion)** (opinion) poll

sonde [sɔ̃d] NF (*Navig*) lead *ou* sounding line;

sonder – sortir

(*Météorologie*) sonde; (*Méd*) probe; catheter; (: *d'alimentation*) feeding tube; (*Tech*) borer, driller; (: *de forage, sondage*) drill; (*pour fouiller etc*) probe; **~ à avalanche** pole (*for probing snow and locating victims*); **~ spatiale** probe

sonder [sɔ̃de] /**1**/ VT (*Navig*) to sound; (*atmosphère, plaie, bagages etc*) to probe; (*Tech*) to bore, drill; (*fig: personne*) to sound out; (: *opinion*) to probe; **~ le terrain** (*fig*) to see how the land lies

songe [sɔ̃ʒ] NM dream

songer [sɔ̃ʒe] /**3**/ VI to dream; **~ à** (*rêver à*) to think over, muse over; (*penser à*) to think of; (*envisager*) to contemplate, think of, consider; **~ que** to consider that; to think that

songerie [sɔ̃ʒʀi] NF reverie

songeur, -euse [sɔ̃ʒœʀ, -øz] ADJ pensive; **ça me laisse ~** that makes me wonder

sonnailles [sɔnaj] NFPL jingle of bells

sonnant, e [sɔnɑ̃, -ɑ̃t] ADJ: **en espèces sonnantes et trébuchantes** in coin of the realm; **à huit heures sonnantes** on the stroke of eight

sonné, e [sɔne] ADJ (*fam*) cracked; (*passé*): **il est midi ~** it's gone twelve; **il a quarante ans bien sonnés** he's well into his forties

sonner [sɔne] /**1**/ VI (*retentir*) to ring; (*donner une impression*) to sound ▸ VT (*cloche*) to ring; (*glas, tocsin*) to sound; (*portier, infirmière*) to ring for; (*messe*) to ring the bell for; (*fam: choc, coup*) to knock out; **~ du clairon** to sound the bugle; **~ bien/mal/creux** to sound good/bad/hollow; **~ faux** (*instrument*) to sound out of tune; (*rire*) to ring false; **~ les heures** to strike the hours; **minuit vient de ~** midnight has just struck; **~ chez qn** to ring sb's doorbell, ring at sb's door

sonnerie [sɔnʀi] NF (*son*) ringing; (*sonnette*) bell; (*mécanisme d'horloge*) striking mechanism; (*de portable*) ringtone; **~ d'alarme** alarm bell; **~ de clairon** bugle call

sonnet [sɔnɛ] NM sonnet

sonnette [sɔnɛt] NF bell; **~ d'alarme** alarm bell; **~ de nuit** night-bell

sono [sɔno] NF (= *sonorisation*) PA (system); (*d'une discothèque*) sound system

sonore [sɔnɔʀ] ADJ (*voix*) sonorous, ringing; (*salle, métal*) resonant; (*ondes, film, signal*) sound cpd; (*Ling*) voiced; **effets sonores** sound effects

sonorisation [sɔnɔʀizasjɔ̃] NF (*équipement: de salle de conférences*) public address system, PA system; (: *de discothèque*) sound system

sonoriser [sɔnɔʀize] /**1**/ VT (*film, spectacle*) to add the sound track to; (*salle*) to fit with a public address system

sonorité [sɔnɔʀite] NF (*de piano, violon*) tone; (*de voix, mot*) sonority; (*d'une salle*) resonance, acoustics pl

sonothèque [sɔnɔtɛk] NF sound library

sont [sɔ̃] VB *voir* **être**

sophisme [sɔfism] NM sophism

sophiste [sɔfist] NMF sophist

sophistication [sɔfistikasjɔ̃] NF sophistication

sophistiqué, e [sɔfistike] ADJ sophisticated

soporifique [sɔpɔʀifik] ADJ soporific

soprano [sɔpʀano] NMF soprano

sorbet [sɔʀbɛ] NM water ice, sorbet

sorbetière [sɔʀbɛtjɛʀ] NF ice-cream maker

sorbier [sɔʀbje] NM service tree

sorcellerie [sɔʀsɛlʀi] NF witchcraft no pl, sorcery no pl

sorcier, -ière [sɔʀsje, -jɛʀ] NM/F sorcerer (witch ou sorceress) ▸ ADJ: **ce n'est pas ~** (*fam*) it's as easy as pie

sordide [sɔʀdid] ADJ (*lieu*) squalid; (*action*) sordid

Sorlingues [sɔʀlɛ̃g] NFPL: **les (îles) ~** the Scilly Isles, the Isles of Scilly, the Scillies

sornettes [sɔʀnɛt] NFPL twaddle sg

sort [sɔʀ] VB *voir* **sortir** ▸ NM (*fortune, destinée*) fate; (*condition, situation*) lot; (*magique*): **jeter un ~** to cast a spell; **un coup du ~** a blow dealt by fate; **le ~ en est jeté** the die is cast; **tirer au ~** to draw lots; **tirer qch au ~** to draw lots for sth

sortable [sɔʀtabl] ADJ: **il n'est pas ~** you can't take him anywhere

sortant, e [sɔʀtɑ̃, -ɑ̃t] VB *voir* **sortir** ▸ ADJ (*numéro*) which comes up (*in a draw etc*); (*député, président*) outgoing

sorte [sɔʀt] VB *voir* **sortir** ▸ NF sort, kind; **une ~ de** a sort of; **de la ~** adv in that way; **en quelque ~** in a way; **de ~ à** so as to, in order to; **de (telle) ~ que, en ~ que** (*de manière que*) so that; (*si bien que*) so much so that; **faire en ~ que** to see to it that

sortie [sɔʀti] NF (*issue*) way out, exit; (*Mil*) sortie; (*fig: verbale*) outburst; sally; (: *parole incongrue*) odd remark; (*d'un gaz, de l'eau*) outlet; (*promenade*) outing; (*le soir: au restaurant etc*) night out; (*de produits*) export; (*de capitaux*) outflow; (*Inform*) output; (*d'imprimante*) printout; (*Comm: d'un disque*) release; (: *d'un livre*) publication; (: *d'un modèle*) launching; **sorties** NFPL (*Comm: somme*) items of expenditure; outgoings; **à sa ~** as he went out ou left; **à la ~ de l'école/l'usine** (*moment*) after school/work; when school/the factory comes out; (*lieu*) at the school/factory gates; **à la ~ de ce nouveau modèle** when this new model comes (*ou* came) out, when they bring (*ou* brought) out this new model; **~ de bain** (*vêtement*) bathrobe; **"~ de camions"** "vehicle exit"; **~ papier** hard copy; **~ de secours** emergency exit

sortilège [sɔʀtilɛʒ] NM (*magic*) spell

sortir [sɔʀtiʀ] /**16**/ VI (*gén*) to come out; (*partir, se promener, aller au spectacle etc*) to go out; (*bourgeon, plante, numéro gagnant*) to come up ▸ VT (*gén*) to take out; (*produit, ouvrage, modèle*) to bring out; (*fam: dire: boniments, incongruités*) to come out with; (*Inform*) to output; (: *sur papier*) to print out; (*fam: expulser*) to throw out ▸ NM: **au ~ de l'hiver/l'enfance** as winter/childhood nears its end; **~ qch de** to take sth out of; **~ qn d'embarras** to get sb out of trouble; **~ avec qn** to be going out with sb; **~ de** (*gén*) to leave; (*endroit*) to go (*ou* come) out of, leave; (*rainure etc*) to come out of; (*maladie*) to get over; (*époque*) to get through; (*cadre, compétence*) to be outside; (*provenir de: famille etc*) to come from; **~ de table** to leave the table; **~ du système** (*Inform*) to log out; **~ de ses gonds** (*fig*) to fly off the handle;

se ~ de (*affaire, situation*) to get out of; **s'en ~** (*malade*) to pull through; (*d'une difficulté etc*) to come through all right; to get through, be able to manage

SOS SIGLE M mayday, SOS

sosie [sɔzi] NM double

sot, sotte [so, sɔt] ADJ silly, foolish ▶ NM/F fool

sottement [sɔtmɑ̃] ADV foolishly

sottise [sɔtiz] NF silliness *no pl*, foolishness *no pl*; (*propos, acte*) silly *ou* foolish thing (to do *ou* say)

sou [su] NM: **près de ses sous** tight-fisted; **sans le ~** penniless; **~ à ~** penny by penny; **pas un ~ de bon sens** not a scrap *ou* an ounce of good sense; **de quatre sous** worthless

souahéli, e [swaeli] ADJ Swahili ▶ NM (*Ling*) Swahili

soubassement [subɑsmɑ̃] NM base

soubresaut [subrəso] NM (*de peur etc*) start; (*cahot: d'un véhicule*) jolt

soubrette [subrɛt] NF soubrette, maidservant

souche [suʃ] NF (*d'arbre*) stump; (*de carnet*) counterfoil (BRIT), stub; **dormir comme une ~** to sleep like a log; **de vieille ~** of old stock

souci [susi] NM (*inquiétude*) worry; (*préoccupation*) concern; (*Bot*) marigold; **se faire du ~** to worry; **avoir (le) ~ de** to have concern for; **par ~ de** for the sake of, out of concern for

soucier [susje] /7/: **se ~ de** *vt* to care about

soucieux, -euse [susjø, -øz] ADJ concerned, worried; **~ de** concerned about; **peu ~ de/que** caring little about/whether

soucoupe [sukup] NF saucer; **~ volante** flying saucer

soudain, e [sudɛ̃, -ɛn] ADJ (*douleur, mort*) sudden ▶ ADV suddenly, all of a sudden

soudainement [sudɛnmɑ̃] ADV suddenly

soudaineté [sudɛnte] NF suddenness

Soudan [sudɑ̃] NM: **le ~** Sudan

soudanais, e [sudanɛ, -ɛz] ADJ Sudanese

soude [sud] NF soda

soudé, e [sude] ADJ (*fig: pétales, organes*) joined (together)

souder [sude] /1/ VT (*avec fil à souder*) to solder; (*par soudure autogène*) to weld; (*fig*) to bind *ou* knit together; to fuse (together); **se souder** VI (*os*) to knit (together)

soudeur, -euse [sudœr, -øz] NM/F (*ouvrier*) welder

soudoyer [sudwaje] /8/ VT (*péj*) to bribe, buy over

soudure [sudyr] NF soldering; welding; (*joint*) soldered joint; weld; **faire la ~** (*Comm*) to fill a gap; (*fig: assurer une transition*) to bridge the gap

souffert, e [sufɛr, -ɛrt] PP *de* **souffrir**

soufflage [suflaʒ] NM (*du verre*) glass-blowing

souffle [sufl] NM (*en expirant*) breath; (*en soufflant*) puff, blow; (*respiration*) breathing; (*d'explosion, de ventilateur*) blast; (*du vent*) blowing; (*fig*) inspiration; **retenir son ~** to hold one's breath; **avoir du/manquer de ~** to have a lot of puff/be short of breath; **être à bout de ~** to be out of breath; **avoir le ~ court** to be short-winded; **un ~ d'air** *ou* **de vent** a breath of air, a puff of wind; **~ au cœur** (*Méd*) heart murmur

soufflé, e [sufle] ADJ (*Culin*) soufflé; (*fam: ahuri, stupéfié*) staggered ▶ NM (*Culin*) soufflé

souffler [sufle] /1/ VI (*gén*) to blow; (*haleter*) to puff (and blow) ▶ VT (*feu, bougie*) to blow out; (*chasser: poussière etc*) to blow away; (*Tech: verre*) to blow; (*explosion*) to destroy (with its blast); (*dire*): **~ qch à qn** to whisper sth to sb; (*fam: voler*): **~ qch à qn** to pinch sth from sb; **~ son rôle à qn** to prompt sb; **ne pas ~ mot** not to breathe a word; **laisser ~ qn** (*fig*) to give sb a breather

soufflet [suflɛ] NM (*instrument*) bellows *pl*; (*entre wagons*) vestibule; (*Couture*) gusset; (*gifle*) slap (in the face)

souffleur, -euse [suflœr, -øz] NM/F (*Théât*) prompter; (*Tech*) glass-blower

souffrance [sufrɑ̃s] NF suffering; **en ~** (*marchandise*) awaiting delivery; (*affaire*) pending

souffrant, e [sufrɑ̃, -ɑ̃t] ADJ unwell

souffre-douleur [sufrədulœr] NM INV whipping boy (BRIT), butt, underdog

souffreteux, -euse [sufrətø, -øz] ADJ sickly

souffrir [sufrir] /18/ VI to suffer; (*éprouver des douleurs*) to be in pain ▶ VT to suffer, endure; (*supporter*) to bear, stand; (*admettre: exception etc*) to allow ou admit of; **~ de** (*maladie, froid*) to suffer from; **~ des dents** to have trouble with one's teeth; **ne pas pouvoir ~ qch/que …** not to be able to endure *ou* bear sth/that …; **elle ne peut pas le ~** she can't stand *ou* bear him; **faire ~ qn** (*personne*) to make sb suffer; (: *dents, blessure etc*) to hurt sb

soufre [sufr] NM sulphur (BRIT), sulfur (US)

soufrer [sufre] /1/ VT (*vignes*) to treat with sulphur *ou* sulfur

souhait [swɛ] NM wish; **tous nos souhaits de** good wishes *ou* our best wishes for; **tous nos souhaits pour la nouvelle année** (our) best wishes for the New Year; **riche** *etc* **à ~** as rich *etc* as one could wish; **à vos souhaits!** bless you!

souhaitable [swɛtabl] ADJ desirable

souhaiter [swete] /1/ VT to wish for; **~ le bonjour à qn** to bid sb good day; **~ la bonne année à qn** to wish sb a happy New Year; **~ que** to hope that; **il est à ~ que** it is to be hoped that

souiller [suje] /1/ VT to dirty, soil; (*fig*) to sully, tarnish

souillure [sujyr] NF stain

soûl, e [su, sul] ADJ drunk; (*fig*): **~ de musique/plaisirs** drunk with music/pleasure ▶ NM: **tout son ~** to one's heart's content

soulagement [sulaʒmɑ̃] NM relief

soulager [sulaʒe] /3/ VT to relieve; **~ qn de** to relieve sb of

soûler [sule] /1/ VT: **~ qn** to get sb drunk; (*boisson*) to make sb drunk; (*fig*) to make sb's head spin *ou* reel; **se soûler** VI to get drunk; **se soûler de** (*fig*) to intoxicate o.s. with

soûlerie [sulri] NF (*péj*) drunken binge

soulèvement [sulɛvmɑ̃] NM uprising; (*Géo*) upthrust

soulever [sulve] /5/ VT to lift; (*vagues, poussière*) to send up; (*peuple*) to stir up (to revolt); (*enthousiasme*) to arouse; (*question, débat,*

S

393

protestations, difficultés) to raise; **se soulever** VI
(*peuple*) to rise up; (*personne couchée*) to lift o.s. up;
(*couvercle etc*) to lift; **cela me soulève le cœur** it
makes me feel sick

soulier [sulje] NM shoe; **souliers bas**
low-heeled shoes; **souliers plats/à talons** flat/
heeled shoes

souligner [suliɲe] /1/ VT to underline; (*fig*) to
emphasize, stress

soumettre [sumɛtR] /56/ VT (*pays*) to subject,
subjugate; (*rebelles*) to put down, subdue; **~ qn/
qch à** to subject sb/sth to; **~ qch à qn** (*projet etc*)
to submit sth to sb; **se ~ (à)** (*se rendre, obéir*) to
submit (to); **se ~ à** (*formalités etc*) to submit to;
(*régime etc*) to submit o.s. to

soumis, e [sumi, -iz] PP *de* **soumettre** ▶ ADJ
submissive; **revenus ~ à l'impôt** taxable
income

soumission [sumisjɔ̃] NF (*voir se soumettre*)
submission; (*docilité*) submissiveness; (*Comm*)
tender

soumissionner [sumisjɔne] /1/ VT (*Comm:
travaux*) to bid for, tender for

soupape [supap] NF valve; **~ de sûreté** safety
valve

soupçon [supsɔ̃] NM suspicion; (*petite quantité*):
un ~ de a hint *ou* touch of; **avoir ~ de** to
suspect; **au dessus de tout ~** above (all)
suspicion

soupçonner [supsɔne] /1/ VT to suspect; **~ qn de
qch/d'être** to suspect sb of sth/of being

soupçonneux, -euse [supsɔnø, -øz] ADJ
suspicious

soupe [sup] NF soup; **~ au lait** *adj inv* quick-
tempered; **~ à l'oignon/de poisson** onion/fish
soup; **~ populaire** soup kitchen

soupente [supɑ̃t] NF (*mansarde*) attic; (*placard*)
cupboard (BRIT) *ou* closet (US) under the stairs

souper [supe] /1/ VI to have supper ▶ NM supper;
avoir soupé de (*fam*) to be sick and tired of

soupeser [supəze] /5/ VT to weigh in one's
hand(s), feel the weight of; (*fig*) to weigh up

soupière [supjɛR] NF (*soup*) tureen

soupir [supiR] NM sigh; (*Mus*) crotchet rest
(BRIT), quarter note rest (US); **rendre le dernier
~** to breathe one's last; **pousser un ~ de
soulagement** to heave a sigh of relief

soupirail, -aux [supiRaj, -o] NM (small)
basement window

soupirant [supiRɑ̃] NM (*péj*) suitor, wooer

soupirer [supiRe] /1/ VI to sigh; **~ après qch** to
yearn for sth

souple [supl] ADJ supple; (*fam*) soft; (*fig:
règlement, caractère*) flexible; (: *démarche, taille*)
lithe, supple

souplesse [suplɛs] NF suppleness; (*de caractère*)
flexibility

source [suRs] NF (*point d'eau*) spring; (*d'un cours
d'eau, fig*) source; **prendre sa ~ à/dans** (*cours
d'eau*) to have its source at/in; **tenir qch de
bonne ~/de ~ sûre** to have sth on good
authority/from a reliable source;
~ thermale/d'eau minérale hot *ou* thermal/
mineral spring

sourcier, -ière [suRsje, -jɛR] NM water diviner

sourcil [suRsij] NM (*eye*)brow

sourcilière [suRsiljɛR] ADJ F *voir* **arcade**

sourciller [suRsije] /1/ VI: **sans ~** without
turning a hair *ou* batting an eyelid

sourcilleux, -euse [suRsijø, -øz] ADJ (*hautain,
sévère*) haughty, supercilious; (*pointilleux*)
finicky, pernickety

sourd, e [suR, suRd] ADJ deaf; (*bruit, voix*)
muffled; (*couleur*) muted; (*douleur*) dull; (*lutte*)
silent, hidden; (*Ling*) voiceless ▶ NM/F deaf
person; **être ~ à** to be deaf to; **faire la ~ oreille**
to turn a deaf ear

sourdement [suRdəmɑ̃] ADV (*avec un bruit sourd*)
dully; (*secrètement*) silently

sourdine [suRdin] NF (*Mus*) mute; **en ~** *adv*
softly, quietly; **mettre une ~ à** (*fig*) to tone
down

sourd-muet, sourde-muette [suRmɥɛ,
suRdmɥɛt] ADJ with a speech and hearing
impairment

sourdre [suRdR] VI (*eau*) to spring up; (*fig*) to rise

souriant, e [suRjɑ̃, -ɑ̃t] VB *voir* **sourire** ▶ ADJ
cheerful

souricière [suRisjɛR] NF mousetrap; (*fig*) trap

sourie *etc* [suRi] VB *voir* **sourire**

sourire [suRiR] /36/ NM smile ▶ VI to smile; **~ à
qn** to smile at sb; (*fig: plaire à*) to appeal to sb;
(: *chance*) to smile on sb; **faire un ~ à qn** to give
sb a smile; **garder le ~** to keep smiling

souris [suRi] NF (*aussi Inform*) mouse

sournois, e [suRnwa, -waz] ADJ deceitful,
underhand

sournoisement [suRnwazmɑ̃] ADV deceitfully

sournoiserie [suRnwazRi] NF deceitfulness,
underhandedness

sous [su] PRÉP (*gén*) under; **~ la pluie/le soleil**
in the rain/sunshine; **~ mes yeux** before my
eyes; **~ terre** *adj, adv* underground;
~ l'influence/l'action de under the influence
of/by the action of; **~ antibiotiques/perfusion**
on antibiotics/a drip; **~ cet angle/ce rapport**
from this angle/in this respect; **~ vide** *adj, adv*
vacuum-packed; **~ peu** *adv* shortly, before long

sous... [su, suz +*vowel*] PRÉFIXE sub-; under...

sous-alimentation [suzalimɑ̃tasjɔ̃] NF
undernourishment

sous-alimenté, e [suzalimɑ̃te] ADJ
undernourished

sous-bois [subwa] NM INV undergrowth

sous-catégorie [sukategɔRi] NF subcategory

sous-chef [suʃɛf] NM deputy chief, second in
command; **~ de bureau** deputy head clerk

sous-comité [sukɔmite] NM subcommittee

sous-commission [sukɔmisjɔ̃] NF
subcommittee

sous-continent [sukɔ̃tinɑ̃] NM subcontinent

sous-couche [sukuʃ] NF (*de peinture*) undercoat

souscripteur, -trice [suskRiptœR, -tRis] NM/F
subscriber

souscription [suskRipsjɔ̃] NF subscription;
offert en ~ available on subscription

souscrire [suskRiR] /39/: **~ à** vt to subscribe to

sous-cutané, e [sukytane] ADJ subcutaneous

sous-développé, e [sudevlɔpe] ADJ underdeveloped

sous-développement [sudevlɔpmɑ̃] NM underdevelopment

sous-directeur, -trice [sudiʀɛktœʀ, -tʀis] NM/F assistant manager/manageress, submanager/manageress

sous-emploi [suzɑ̃plwa] NM underemployment

sous-employé, e [suzɑ̃plwaje] ADJ underemployed

sous-ensemble [suzɑ̃sɑ̃bl] NM subset

sous-entendre [suzɑ̃tɑ̃dʀ] /41/ VT to imply, infer

sous-entendu, e [suzɑ̃tɑ̃dy] ADJ implied; (*Ling*) understood ▶ NM innuendo, insinuation

sous-équipé, e [suzekipe] ADJ under-equipped; **~ en infrastructures industrielles** (*Écon: pays, région*) with an insufficient industrial infrastructure

sous-estimer [suzɛstime] /1/ VT to underestimate

sous-exploiter [suzɛksplwate] /1/ VT to underexploit

sous-exposer [suzɛkspoze] /1/ VT to underexpose

sous-fifre [sufifʀ] NM (*péj*) underling

sous-groupe [sugʀup] NM subgroup

sous-homme [suzɔm] NM sub-human

sous-jacent, e [suʒasɑ̃, -ɑ̃t] ADJ underlying

sous-lieutenant [suljøtnɑ̃] NM sub-lieutenant

sous-locataire [sulɔkatɛʀ] NMF subtenant

sous-location [sulɔkasjɔ̃] NF subletting

sous-louer [sulwe] /1/ VT to sublet

sous-main [sumɛ̃] NM INV desk blotter; **en ~** adv secretly

sous-marin, e [sumaʀɛ̃, -in] ADJ (*flore, volcan*) submarine; (*navigation, pêche, explosif*) underwater ▶ NM submarine

sous-médicalisé, e [sumedikalize] ADJ lacking adequate medical care

sous-nappe [sunap] NF undercloth

sous-officier [suzɔfisje] NM = non-commissioned officer (NCO)

sous-ordre [suzɔʀdʀ] NM subordinate; **créancier en ~** creditor's creditor

sous-payé, e [supeje] ADJ underpaid

sous-préfecture [supʀefɛktyʀ] NF sub-prefecture

sous-préfet [supʀefɛ] NM sub-prefect

sous-production [supʀɔdyksjɔ̃] NF underproduction

sous-produit [supʀɔdɥi] NM by-product; (*fig: péj*) pale imitation

sous-programme [supʀɔgʀam] NM (*Inform*) subroutine

sous-pull [supul] NM thin polo-neck sweater

sous-secrétaire [susəkʀetɛʀ] NM: **~ d'État** Under-Secretary of State

soussigné, e [susiɲe] ADJ: **je ~** I the undersigned

sous-sol [susɔl] NM basement; (*Géo*) subsoil

sous-tasse [sutas] NF saucer

sous-tendre [sutɑ̃dʀ] /41/ VT to underlie

sous-titre [sutitʀ] NM subtitle

sous-titré, e [sutitʀe] ADJ with subtitles

soustraction [sustʀaksjɔ̃] NF subtraction

soustraire [sustʀɛʀ] /50/ VT to subtract, take away; (*dérober*): **~ qch à qn** to remove sth from sb; **~ qn à** (*danger*) to shield sb from; **se ~ à** (*autorité, obligation, devoir*) to elude, escape from

sous-traitance [sutʀɛtɑ̃s] NF subcontracting

sous-traitant [sutʀɛtɑ̃] NM subcontractor

sous-traiter [sutʀete] /1/ VT, VI to subcontract

soustrayais etc [sustʀeje] VB voir **soustraire**

sous-verre [suvɛʀ] NM INV glass mount

sous-vêtement [suvɛtmɑ̃] NM undergarment, item of underwear; **sous-vêtements** NMPL underwear sg

soutane [sutan] NF cassock, soutane

soute [sut] NF hold; **~ à bagages** baggage hold

soutenable [sutnabl] ADJ (*opinion*) tenable, defensible

soutenance [sutnɑ̃s] NF: **~ de thèse** ≈ viva (voce)

soutènement [sutɛnmɑ̃] NM: **mur de ~** retaining wall

souteneur [sutnœʀ] NM procurer

soutenir [sutniʀ] /22/ VT to support; (*assaut, choc, regard*) to stand up to, withstand; (*intérêt, effort*) to keep up; (*assurer*): **~ que** to maintain that; **se soutenir** (*dans l'eau etc*) to hold o.s. up; (*être soutenable: point de vue*) to be tenable; (*s'aider mutuellement*) to stand by each other; **~ la comparaison avec** to bear ou stand comparison with; **~ le regard de qn** to be able to look sb in the face

soutenu, e [sutny] PP de **soutenir** ▶ ADJ (*efforts*) sustained, unflagging; (*style*) elevated; (*couleur*) strong

souterrain, e [sutɛʀɛ̃, -ɛn] ADJ underground; (*fig*) subterranean ▶ NM underground passage

soutien [sutjɛ̃] NM support; **apporter son ~ à** to lend one's support to; **~ de famille** breadwinner

soutiendrai etc [sutjɛ̃dʀe] VB voir **soutenir**

soutien-gorge [sutjɛ̃gɔʀʒ] (*pl* **soutiens-gorge**) NM bra; (*de maillot de bain*) top

soutiens [sutjɛ̃], **soutint** etc [sutɛ̃] VB voir **soutenir**

soutirer [sutiʀe] /1/ VT: **~ qch à qn** to squeeze ou get sth out of sb

souvenance [suvnɑ̃s] NF: **avoir ~ de** to recollect

souvenir [suvniʀ] /22/ NM (*réminiscence*) memory; (*cadeau*) souvenir, keepsake; (*de voyage*) souvenir ▶ VB: **se ~ de** vt to remember; **se ~ que** to remember that; **garder le ~ de** to retain the memory of; **en ~ de** in memory ou remembrance of; **avec mes affectueux/meilleurs souvenirs, ...** with love from, .../regards, ...

souvent [suvɑ̃] ADV often; **peu ~** seldom, infrequently; **le plus ~** more often than not, most often

souvenu, e [suvny] PP = **se souvenir**

souverain, e [suvʀɛ̃, -ɛn] ADJ sovereign; (*fig: mépris*) supreme ▶ NM/F sovereign, monarch

souverainement [suvʀɛnmɑ̃] ADV (*sans appel*) with sovereign power; (*extrêmement*) supremely, intensely

S

395

souveraineté [suvʀɛnte] NF sovereignty
souviendrai [suvjɛ̃dʀe], **souviens** [suvjɛ̃],
souvint etc [suvɛ̃] VB voir **souvenir**
soviétique [sɔvjetik] ADJ Soviet ▶ NMF: **S~**
Soviet citizen
soviétologue [sɔvjetɔlɔg] NMF Kremlinologist
soyeux, -euse [swajø, -øz] ADJ silky
soyez etc [swaje] VB voir **être**
soyons etc [swajɔ̃] VB voir **être**
SPA SIGLE F (= Société protectrice des animaux)
≈ RSPCA (BRIT), ≈ SPCA (US)
spacieux, -euse [spasjø, -øz] ADJ spacious;
roomy
spaciosité [spasjɔzite] NF spaciousness
spaghettis [spageti] NMPL spaghetti sg
sparadrap [spaʀadʀa] NM adhesive ou sticking
(BRIT) plaster, bandaid® (US)
Sparte [spaʀt] NF Sparta
spartiate [spaʀsjat] ADJ Spartan; **spartiates**
NFPL (sandales) Roman sandals
spasme [spazm] NM spasm
spasmodique [spazmɔdik] ADJ spasmodic
spatial, e, -aux [spasjal, -o] ADJ (Aviat) space cpd;
(Psych) spatial
spatule [spatyl] NF (ustensile) slice; spatula;
(bout) tip
speaker, ine [spikœʀ, -kʀin] NM/F announcer
spécial, e, -aux [spesjal, -o] ADJ special; (bizarre)
peculiar
spécialement [spesjalmɑ̃] ADV especially,
particularly; (tout exprès) specially; **pas ~** not
particularly
spécialisation [spesjalizasjɔ̃] NF specialization
spécialisé, e [spesjalize] ADJ specialised;
ordinateur ~ dedicated computer
spécialiser [spesjalize] /1/: **se spécialiser** VI to
specialize
spécialiste [spesjalist] NMF specialist
spécialité [spesjalite] NF speciality; (Scol)
special field; **~ pharmaceutique** patent
medicine
spécieux, -euse [spesjø, -øz] ADJ specious
spécification [spesifikasjɔ̃] NF specification
spécificité [spesifisite] NF specificity
spécifier [spesifje] /7/ VT to specify, state
spécifique [spesifik] ADJ specific
spécifiquement [spesifikmɑ̃] ADV (typiquement)
typically; (tout exprès) specifically
spécimen [spesimɛn] NM specimen; (revue etc)
specimen ou sample copy
spectacle [spɛktakl] NM (tableau, scène) sight;
(représentation) show; (industrie) show business,
entertainment; **se donner en ~** (péj) to make a
spectacle ou an exhibition of o.s.; **pièce/revue**
à grand ~ spectacular (play/revue); **au ~ de ...**
at the sight of ...
spectaculaire [spɛktakylɛʀ] ADJ spectacular
spectateur, -trice [spɛktatœʀ, -tʀis] NM/F (Ciné
etc) member of the audience; (Sport) spectator;
(d'un événement) onlooker, witness
spectre [spɛktʀ] NM (fantôme, fig) spectre;
(Physique) spectrum; **~ solaire** solar spectrum
spéculateur, -trice [spekylatœʀ, -tʀis] NM/F
speculator

spéculatif, -ive [spekylatif, -iv] ADJ speculative
spéculation [spekylasjɔ̃] NF speculation
spéculer [spekyle] /1/ VI to speculate; **~ sur**
(Comm) to speculate in; (réfléchir) to speculate on;
(tabler sur) to bank ou rely on
spéléologie [speleɔlɔʒi] NF (étude) speleology;
(activité) potholing
spéléologue [speleɔlɔg] NMF speleologist;
potholer
spermatozoïde [spɛʀmatozɔid] NM sperm,
spermatozoon
sperme [spɛʀm] NM semen, sperm
spermicide [spɛʀmisid] ADJ, NM spermicide
sphère [sfɛʀ] NF sphere
sphérique [sferik] ADJ spherical
sphincter [sfɛ̃ktɛʀ] NM sphincter
sphinx [sfɛ̃ks] NM INV sphinx; (Zool) hawkmoth
spiral, -aux [spiral, -o] NM hairspring
spirale [spiral] NF spiral; **en ~** in a spiral
spire [spiʀ] NF (d'une spirale) turn; (d'une coquille)
whorl
spiritisme [spiʀitism] NM spiritualism,
spiritism
spirituel, le [spiʀituɛl] ADJ spiritual; (fin,
piquant) witty; **musique ~** sacred music;
concert ~ concert of sacred music
spirituellement [spiʀituɛlmɑ̃] ADV spiritually;
wittily
spiritueux [spiʀituø] NM spirit
splendeur [splɑ̃dœʀ] NF splendour (BRIT),
splendor (US)
splendide [splɑ̃did] ADJ splendid, magnificent
spolier [spɔlje] /7/ VT: **~ qn (de)** to despoil sb (of)
spongieux, -euse [spɔ̃ʒjø, -øz] ADJ spongy
sponsor [spɔ̃sɔʀ] NM sponsor
sponsoriser [spɔ̃sɔʀize] /1/ VT to sponsor
spontané, e [spɔ̃tane] ADJ spontaneous
spontanéité [spɔ̃taneite] NF spontaneity
spontanément [spɔ̃tanemɑ̃] ADV
spontaneously
sporadique [spɔʀadik] ADJ sporadic
sporadiquement [spɔʀadikmɑ̃] ADV
sporadically
sport [spɔʀ] NM sport ▶ ADJ INV (vêtement) casual;
(fair-play) sporting; **faire du ~** to do sport;
~ individuel/d'équipe individual/team sport;
~ de combat combative sport; **sports d'hiver**
winter sports
sportif, -ive [spɔʀtif, -iv] ADJ (journal, association,
épreuve) sports cpd; (allure, démarche) athletic;
(attitude, esprit) sporting; **les résultats sportifs**
the sports results
sportivement [spɔʀtivmɑ̃] ADV sportingly
sportivité [spɔʀtivite] NF sportsmanship
spot [spɔt] NM (lampe) spot(light); (annonce):
~ (publicitaire) commercial (break)
spray [spʀɛ] NM spray, aerosol
sprint [spʀint] NM sprint; **piquer un ~** to put
on a (final) spurt
sprinter /1/ NM [spʀintœʀ] sprinter ▶ VI
[spʀinte] to sprint
squale [skwal] NM (type of) shark
square [skwaʀ] NM public garden(s)
squash [skwaʃ] NM squash

squat [skwat] NM (*lieu*) squat
squatter /1/ NM [skwatœr] squatter ▶ VT [skwate] to squat
squelette [skəlɛt] NM skeleton
squelettique [skəletik] ADJ scrawny; (*fig*) skimpy
SRAS [sras] SIGLE M (= *syndrome respiratoire aigu sévère*) SARS
Sri Lanka [srilɑ̃ka] NM: **le ~** Sri Lanka
sri-lankais, e [srilɑ̃kɛ, -ɛz] ADJ Sri-Lankan
SS SIGLE F = **la sécurité sociale**; (= *Sa Sainteté*) HH
ss ABR = **sous**
SSR SIGLE F (= *Société suisse romande*) the Swiss French-language broadcasting company
St, Ste ABR (= *Saint(e)*) St
stabilisateur, -trice [stabilizatœr, -tris] ADJ stabilizing ▶ NM stabilizer; (*d'un véhicule*) anti-roll device; (*d'un avion*) tailplane
stabiliser [stabilize] /1/ VT to stabilize; (*terrain*) to consolidate
stabilité [stabilite] NF stability
stable [stabl] ADJ stable, steady
stade [stad] NM (*Sport*) stadium; (*phase, niveau*) stage
stadier [stadje] NM steward (*working in a stadium*), stage
stage [staʒ] NM training period; (*cours*) training course; (*d'avocat stagiaire*) articles pl; **~ en entreprise** work experience placement; **~ de formation (professionnelle)** vocational (training) course; **~ de perfectionnement** advanced training course
stagiaire [staʒjɛr] NMF, ADJ trainee
stagnant, e [stagnɑ̃, -ɑ̃t] ADJ stagnant
stagnation [stagnasjɔ̃] NF stagnation
stagner [stagne] /1/ VI to stagnate
stalactite [stalaktit] NF stalactite
stalagmite [stalagmit] NF stalagmite
stalle [stal] NF stall, box
stand [stɑ̃d] NM (*d'exposition*) stand; (*de foire*) stall; **~ de tir** (*à la foire, Sport*) shooting range; **~ de ravitaillement** pit
standard [stɑ̃dar] ADJ INV standard ▶ NM (*type, norme*) standard; (*téléphonique*) switchboard
standardisation [stɑ̃dardizasjɔ̃] NF standardization
standardiser [stɑ̃dardize] /1/ VT to standardize
standardiste [stɑ̃dardist] NMF switchboard operator
standing [stɑ̃diŋ] NM standing; **de grand ~** luxury; **immeuble de grand ~** block of luxury flats (*Brit*), condo(minium) (*US*)
star [star] NF star
starlette [starlɛt] NF starlet
starter [starter] NM (*Auto*) choke; (*Sport: personne*) starter; **mettre le ~** to pull out the choke
station [stasjɔ̃] NF station; (*de bus*) stop; (*de villégiature*) resort; (*posture*): **la ~ debout** standing, an upright posture; **~ balnéaire** seaside resort; **~ de graissage** lubrication bay; **~ de lavage** carwash; **~ de ski** ski resort; **~ de sports d'hiver** winter sports resort; **~ de taxis** taxi rank (*Brit*) *ou* stand (*US*); **~ thermale** thermal spa; **~ de travail** workstation

stationnaire [stasjɔnɛr] ADJ stationary
stationnement [stasjɔnmɑ̃] NM parking; **zone de ~ interdit** no parking area; **~ alterné** parking on alternate sides
stationner [stasjɔne] /1/ VI to park
station-service [stasjɔ̃sɛrvis] NF service station
statique [statik] ADJ static
statisticien, ne [statistisjɛ̃, -ɛn] NM/F statistician
statistique [statistik] NF (*science*) statistics sg; (*rapport, étude*) statistic ▶ ADJ statistical; **statistiques** NFPL (*données*) statistics pl
statistiquement [statistikmɑ̃] ADV statistically
statue [staty] NF statue
statuer [statɥe] /1/ VI: **~ sur** to rule on, give a ruling on
statuette [statɥɛt] NF statuette
statu quo [statykwo] NM status quo
stature [statyr] NF stature; **de haute ~** of great stature
statut [staty] NM status; **statuts** NMPL (*Jur, Admin*) statutes
statutaire [statytɛr] ADJ statutory
Sté ABR (= *société*) SOC
steak [stɛk] NM steak; **~ haché** hamburger
stèle [stɛl] NF stela, stele
stellaire [stelɛr] ADJ stellar
stencil [stɛnsil] NM stencil
sténo [steno] NMF (*aussi:* **sténographe**) shorthand typist (*Brit*), stenographer (*US*) ▶ NF (*aussi:* **sténographie**) shorthand; **prendre en ~** to take down in shorthand
sténodactylo [stenodaktilo] NMF shorthand typist (*Brit*), stenographer (*US*)
sténodactylographie [stenodaktilografi] NF shorthand typing (*Brit*), stenography (*US*)
sténographe [stenograf] NMF shorthand typist (*Brit*), stenographer (*US*)
sténographie [stenografi] NF shorthand
sténographier [stenografje] /7/ VT to take down in shorthand
sténographique [stenografik] ADJ shorthand cpd
stentor [stɑ̃tɔr] NM: **voix de ~** stentorian voice
step® [stɛp] NM step aerobics® sg, step Reebok®
stéphanois, e [stefanwa, -waz] ADJ of *ou* from Saint-Étienne
steppe [stɛp] NF steppe
stère [stɛr] NM stere
stéréo NF (*aussi:* **stéréophonie**) stereo; **émission en ~** stereo broadcast ▶ ADJ (*aussi:* **stéréophonique**) stereo
stéréophonie [stereofɔni] NF stereo(phony)
stéréophonique [stereofɔnik] ADJ stereo(phonic)
stéréoscope [stereoskɔp] NM stereoscope
stéréoscopique [stereoskɔpik] ADJ stereoscopic
stéréotype [stereotip] NM stereotype
stéréotypé, e [stereotipe] ADJ stereotyped
stérile [steril] ADJ sterile; (*terre*) barren; (*fig*) fruitless, futile

S

stérilement [steʀilmɑ̃] ADV fruitlessly
stérilet [steʀilɛ] NM coil, loop
stérilisateur [steʀilizatœʀ] NM sterilizer
stérilisation [steʀilizasjɔ̃] NF sterilization
stériliser [steʀilize] /1/ VT to sterilize
stérilité [steʀilite] NF sterility
sternum [stɛʀnɔm] NM breastbone, sternum
stéthoscope [stetɔskɔp] NM stethoscope
stick [stik] NM stick
stigmates [stigmat] NMPL scars, marks; (Rel) stigmata pl
stigmatiser [stigmatize] /1/ VT to denounce, stigmatize
stimulant, e [stimylɑ̃, -ɑ̃t] ADJ stimulating ▶ NM (Méd) stimulant; (fig) stimulus, incentive
stimulateur [stimylatœʀ] NM: ~ **cardiaque** pacemaker
stimulation [stimylasjɔ̃] NF stimulation
stimuler [stimyle] /1/ VT to stimulate
stimulus [stimylys] NM (pl **stimuli** [stimyli]) stimulus
stipulation [stipylasjɔ̃] NF stipulation
stipuler [stipyle] /1/ VT to stipulate, specify
stock [stɔk] NM stock; **en ~** in stock
stockage [stɔkaʒ] NM stocking; storage
stocker [stɔke] /1/ VT to stock; (déchets) to store
Stockholm [stɔkɔlm] N Stockholm
stockiste [stɔkist] NM stockist
stoïcisme [stɔisism] NM stoicism
stoïque [stɔik] ADJ stoic, stoical
stoïquement [stɔikmɑ̃] ADV stoically
stomacal, e, -aux [stɔmakal, -o] ADJ gastric, stomach cpd
stomatologie [stɔmatɔlɔʒi] NF stomatology
stomatologue [stɔmatɔlɔg] NMF stomatologist
stop [stɔp] NM (Auto: écriteau) stop sign; (: signal) brake-light; (dans un télégramme) stop ▶ EXCL stop!; **faire du ~** (fam) to hitch(hike)
stoppage [stɔpaʒ] NM invisible mending
stopper [stɔpe] /1/ VT to stop, halt; (Couture) to mend ▶ VI to stop, halt
store [stɔʀ] NM blind; (de magasin) shade, awning
strabisme [stʀabism] NM squint(ing)
strangulation [stʀɑ̃gylasjɔ̃] NF strangulation
strapontin [stʀapɔ̃tɛ̃] NM jump ou foldaway seat
Strasbourg [stʀazbuʀ] N Strasbourg
strass [stʀas] NM paste, strass
stratagème [stʀataʒɛm] NM stratagem
strate [stʀat] NF (Géo) stratum, layer
stratège [stʀatɛʒ] NM strategist
stratégie [stʀateʒi] NF strategy
stratégique [stʀateʒik] ADJ strategic
stratégiquement [stʀateʒikmɑ̃] ADV strategically
stratifié, e [stʀatifje] ADJ (Géo) stratified; (Tech) laminated
stratosphère [stʀatɔsfɛʀ] NF stratosphere
stress [stʀɛs] NM INV stress
stressant, e [stʀɛsɑ̃, -ɑ̃t] ADJ stressful
stresser [stʀɛse] /1/ VT to stress, cause stress in; **~ qn** to make sb (feel) tense
strict, e [stʀikt] ADJ strict; (tenue, décor) severe,

plain; **son droit le plus ~** his most basic right; **dans la plus ~ intimité** strictly in private; **le ~ nécessaire/minimum** the bare essentials/minimum
strictement [stʀiktəmɑ̃] ADV strictly; plainly
strident, e [stʀidɑ̃, -ɑ̃t] ADJ shrill, strident
stridulations [stʀidylasjɔ̃] NFPL stridulations, chirrings
strie [stʀi] NF streak; (Anat, Géo) stria
strier [stʀije] /7/ VT to streak; to striate
strip-tease [stʀiptiz] NM striptease
strip-teaseuse [stʀiptizøz] NF stripper, striptease artist
striures [stʀijyʀ] NFPL streaking sg
strophe [stʀɔf] NF verse, stanza
structure [stʀyktyʀ] NF structure; **structures d'accueil/touristiques** reception/tourist facilities
structurer [stʀyktyʀe] /1/ VT to structure
strychnine [stʀiknin] NF strychnine
stuc [styk] NM stucco
studieusement [stydjøzmɑ̃] ADV studiously
studieux, -euse [stydjø, -øz] ADJ (élève) studious; (vacances) study cpd
studio [stydjo] NM (logement) studio flat (BRIT) ou apartment (US); (d'artiste, TV etc) studio
stupéfaction [stypefaksjɔ̃] NF stupefaction, astonishment
stupéfait, e [stypefɛ, -ɛt] ADJ astonished
stupéfiant, e [stypefjɑ̃, -ɑ̃t] ADJ (étonnant) stunning, astonishing ▶ NM (Méd) drug, narcotic
stupéfier [stypefje] /7/ VT to stupefy; (étonner) to stun, astonish
stupeur [stypœʀ] NF (inertie, insensibilité) stupor; (étonnement) astonishment, amazement
stupide [stypid] ADJ stupid; (hébété) stunned
stupidement [stypidmɑ̃] ADV stupidly
stupidité [stypidite] NF stupidity no pl; (parole, acte) stupid thing (to say ou do)
stups [styp] NMPL = **stupéfiants**; **brigade des ~** narcotics bureau ou squad
style [stil] NM style; **meuble/robe de ~** piece of period furniture/period dress; **~ de vie** lifestyle
stylé, e [stile] ADJ well-trained
stylet [stilɛ] NM (poignard) stiletto; (Chirurgie) stylet
stylisé, e [stilize] ADJ stylized
styliste [stilist] NMF designer; stylist
stylistique [stilistik] NF stylistics sg ▶ ADJ stylistic
stylo [stilo] NM: **~ (à encre)** (fountain) pen; **~ (à) bille** ballpoint pen
stylo-feutre [stiloføtʀ] NM felt-tip pen
su, e [sy] PP de **savoir** ▶ NM: **au su de** with the knowledge of
suaire [sɥɛʀ] NM shroud
suant, e [sɥɑ̃, -ɑ̃t] ADJ sweaty
suave [sɥav] ADJ (odeur) sweet; (voix) suave, smooth; (coloris) soft, mellow
subalterne [sybaltɛʀn] ADJ (employé, officier) junior; (rôle) subordinate, subsidiary ▶ NMF subordinate, inferior
subconscient [sypkɔ̃sjɑ̃] NM subconscious

subdiviser [sybdivize] /**1**/ VT to subdivide
subdivision [sybdivizjɔ̃] NF subdivision
subir [sybiʀ] /**2**/ VT (affront, dégâts, mauvais traitements) to suffer; (influence, charme) to be under, be subjected to; (traitement, opération, châtiment) to undergo; (personne) to suffer, be subjected to
subit, e [sybi, -it] ADJ sudden
subitement [sybitmɑ̃] ADV suddenly, all of a sudden
subjectif, -ive [sybʒɛktif, -iv] ADJ subjective
subjectivement [sybʒɛktivmɑ̃] ADV subjectively
subjectivité [sybʒɛktivite] NF subjectivity
subjonctif [sybʒɔ̃ktif] NM subjunctive
subjuguer [sybʒyge] /**1**/ VT to subjugate
sublime [syblim] ADJ sublime
sublimer [syblime] /**1**/ VT to sublimate
submergé, e [sybmɛʀʒe] ADJ submerged; ~ de (fig) snowed under with; overwhelmed with
submerger [sybmɛʀʒe] /**3**/ VT to submerge; (foule) to engulf; (fig) to overwhelm
submersible [sybmɛʀsibl] NM submarine
subordination [sybɔʀdinasjɔ̃] NF subordination
subordonné, e [sybɔʀdɔne] ADJ, NM/F subordinate; ~ à (personne) subordinate to; (résultats etc) subject to, depending on
subordonner [sybɔʀdɔne] /**1**/ VT: ~ qn/qch à to subordinate sb/sth to
subornation [sybɔʀnasjɔ̃] NF bribing
suborner [sybɔʀne] /**1**/ VT to bribe
subrepticement [sybʀɛptismɑ̃] ADV surreptitiously
subroger [sybʀɔʒe] /**3**/ VT (Jur) to subrogate
subside [sypsid] NM grant
subsidiaire [sypsidjɛʀ] ADJ subsidiary; **question** ~ deciding question
subsistance [sybzistɑ̃s] NF subsistence; **pourvoir à la ~ de qn** to keep sb, provide for sb's subsistence ou keep
subsister [sybziste] /**1**/ VI (rester) to remain, subsist; (vivre) to live; (survivre) to live on
subsonique [sybsɔnik] ADJ subsonic
substance [sypstɑ̃s] NF substance; **en ~** in substance
substantiel, le [sypstɑ̃sjɛl] ADJ substantial
substantif [sypstɑ̃tif] NM noun, substantive
substantiver [sypstɑ̃tive] /**1**/ VT to nominalize
substituer [sypstitɥe] /**1**/ VT: ~ qn/qch à to substitute sb/sth for; **se ~ à qn** (représenter) to substitute for sb; (évincer) to substitute o.s. for sb
substitut [sypstity] NM (Jur) deputy public prosecutor; (succédané) substitute
substitution [sypstitysjɔ̃] NF substitution
subterfuge [syptɛʀfyʒ] NM subterfuge
subtil, e [syptil] ADJ subtle
subtilement [syptilmɑ̃] ADV subtly
subtiliser [syptilize] /**1**/ VT: ~ qch (à qn) to spirit sth away (from sb)
subtilité [syptilite] NF subtlety
subtropical, e, -aux [sybtʀɔpikal, -o] ADJ subtropical

suburbain, e [sybyʀbɛ̃, -ɛn] ADJ suburban
subvenir [sybvəniʀ] /**22**/: ~ **à** VT to meet
subvention [sybvɑ̃sjɔ̃] NF subsidy, grant
subventionner [sybvɑ̃sjɔne] /**1**/ VT to subsidize
subversif, -ive [sybvɛʀsif, -iv] ADJ subversive
subversion [sybvɛʀsjɔ̃] NF subversion
suc [syk] NM (Bot) sap; (de viande, fruit) juice; **sucs gastriques** gastric juices
succédané [syksedane] NM substitute
succéder [syksede] /**6**/: ~ **à** VT (directeur, roi etc) to succeed; (venir après: dans une série) to follow, succeed; **se succéder** VI (accidents, années) to follow one another
succès [syksɛ] NM success; **avec ~** successfully; **sans ~** unsuccessfully; **avoir du ~** to be a success, be successful; **à ~** successful; **livre à ~** bestseller; **~ de librairie** bestseller; **~ (féminins)** conquests
successeur [syksesœʀ] NM successor
successif, -ive [syksesif, -iv] ADJ successive
succession [syksesjɔ̃] NF (série, Pol) succession; (Jur: patrimoine) estate, inheritance; **prendre la ~ de** (directeur) to succeed, take over from; (entreprise) to take over
successivement [syksesivmɑ̃] ADV successively
succinct, e [syksɛ̃, -ɛ̃t] ADJ succinct
succinctement [syksɛ̃tmɑ̃] ADV succinctly
succion [syksjɔ̃] NF: **bruit de ~** sucking noise
succomber [sykɔ̃be] /**1**/ VI to die, succumb; (fig): ~ **à** to succumb to, give way to
succulent, e [sykylɑ̃, -ɑ̃t] ADJ delicious
succursale [sykyʀsal] NF branch; **magasin à succursales multiples** chain ou multiple store
sucer [syse] /**3**/ VT to suck
sucette [sysɛt] NF (bonbon) lollipop; (de bébé) dummy (BRIT), comforter, pacifier (US)
suçoter [sysɔte] /**1**/ VT to suck
sucre [sykʀ] NM (substance) sugar; (morceau) lump of sugar, sugar lump ou cube; **~ de canne/betterave** cane/beet sugar; **~ en morceaux/cristallisé/en poudre** lump ou cube/granulated/caster sugar; **~ glace** icing sugar (BRIT), confectioner's sugar (US); **~ d'orge** barley sugar
sucré, e [sykʀe] ADJ (produit alimentaire) sweetened; (au goût) sweet; (péj) sugary, honeyed
sucrer [sykʀe] /**1**/ VT (thé, café) to sweeten, put sugar in; ~ **qn** to put sugar in sb's tea (ou coffee etc); **se sucrer** to help o.s. to sugar, have some sugar; (fam) to line one's pocket(s)
sucrerie [sykʀəʀi] NF (usine) sugar refinery; **sucreries** NFPL (bonbons) sweets, sweet things
sucrier, -ière [sykʀije, -jɛʀ] ADJ (industrie) sugar cpd; (région) sugar-producing ▶ NM (fabricant) sugar producer; (récipient) sugar bowl ou basin
sud [syd] NM: **le ~** the south ▶ ADJ INV south; (côte) south, southern; **au ~** (situation) in the south; (direction) to the south; **au ~ de** (to the) south of
sud-africain, e [sydafʀikɛ̃, -ɛn] ADJ South African ▶ NM/F: **Sud-Africain, e** South African
sud-américain, e [sydamerikɛ̃, -ɛn] ADJ South American ▶ NM/F: **Sud-Américain, e** South American

S

sudation [sydasjɔ̃] NF sweating, sudation

sud-coréen, ne [sydkɔʀeɛ̃, -ɛn] ADJ South Korean ▶ NM/F: **Sud-Coréen, ne** South Korean

sud-est [sydɛst] NM, ADJ INV south-east

sud-ouest [sydwɛst] NM, ADJ INV south-west

sud-vietnamien, ne [sydvjɛtnamjɛ̃, -ɛn] ADJ South Vietnamese ▶ NM/F: **Sud-Vietnamien, ne** South Vietnamese

Suède [sɥɛd] NF: **la ~** Sweden

suédois, e [sɥedwa, -waz] ADJ Swedish ▶ NM (Ling) Swedish ▶ NM/F: **S~, e** Swede

suer [sɥe] /1/ VI to sweat; (suinter) to ooze ▶ VT (fig) to exude; **~ à grosses gouttes** to sweat profusely

sueur [sɥœʀ] NF sweat; **en ~** sweating, in a sweat; **avoir des sueurs froides** to be in a cold sweat

suffire [syfiʀ] /37/ VI (être assez): **~ (à qn/pour qch/pour faire)** to be enough ou sufficient (for sb/for sth/to do); **se suffire** VI to be self-sufficient; **cela lui suffit** he's content with this, this is enough for him; **cela suffit pour les irriter/qu'ils se fâchent** it's enough to annoy them/for them to get angry; **il suffit d'une négligence/qu'on oublie pour que ...** it only takes one act of carelessness/one only needs to forget for ...; **ça suffit!** that's enough!, that'll do!

suffisamment [syfizamɑ̃] ADV sufficiently, enough; **~ de** sufficient, enough

suffisance [syfizɑ̃s] NF (vanité) self-importance, bumptiousness; (quantité): **en ~** in plenty

suffisant, e [syfizɑ̃, -ɑ̃t] ADJ (temps, ressources) sufficient; (résultats) satisfactory; (vaniteux) self-important, bumptious

suffisons etc [syfizɔ̃] VB voir **suffire**

suffixe [syfiks] NM suffix

suffocant, e [syfɔkɑ̃, -ɑ̃t] ADJ (étouffant) suffocating; (stupéfiant) staggering

suffocation [syfɔkasjɔ̃] NF suffocation

suffoquer [syfɔke] /1/ VT to choke, suffocate; (stupéfier) to stagger, astound ▶ VI to choke, suffocate; **~ de colère/d'indignation** to choke with anger/indignation

suffrage [syfʀaʒ] NM (Pol: voix) vote; (du public etc) approval no pl; **~ universel/direct/indirect** universal/direct/indirect suffrage; **suffrages exprimés** valid votes

suggérer [sygʒeʀe] /6/ VT to suggest; **~ que/de faire** to suggest that/doing

suggestif, -ive [sygʒɛstif, -iv] ADJ suggestive

suggestion [sygʒɛstjɔ̃] NF suggestion

suggestivité [sygʒɛstivite] NF suggestiveness, suggestive nature

suicidaire [sɥisideʀ] ADJ suicidal

suicide [sɥisid] NM suicide ▶ ADJ: **opération ~** suicide mission

suicidé, e [sɥiside] NM/F suicide

suicider [sɥiside] /1/: **se suicider** VI to commit suicide

suie [sɥi] NF soot

suif [sɥif] NM tallow

suinter [sɥɛ̃te] /1/ VI to ooze

suis [sɥi] VB voir **être**; **suivre**

suisse [sɥis] ADJ Swiss ▶ NM (bedeau) ≈ verger ▶ NMF: **S~** Swiss inv ▶ NF: **la S~** Switzerland; **la S~ romande/allemande** French-speaking/German-speaking Switzerland; **~ romand** Swiss French

suisse-allemand, e [sɥisalmɑ̃, -ɑ̃d] ADJ, NM/F Swiss German

Suissesse [sɥisɛs] NF Swiss (woman ou girl)

suit [sɥi] VB voir **suivre**

suite [sɥit] NF (continuation: d'énumération etc) rest, remainder; (: de feuilleton) continuation; (: second film etc sur le même thème) sequel; (série) series, succession; (Math) series sg; (conséquence) result; (ordre, liaison logique) coherence; (appartement, Mus) suite; (escorte) retinue, suite; **suites** NFPL (d'une maladie etc) effects; **une ~ de** (de maisons, succès) a series ou succession of; **prendre la ~ de** (directeur etc) to succeed, take over from; **donner ~ à** (requête, projet) to follow up; **faire ~ à** to follow; **(faisant) ~ à votre lettre du** further to your letter of the; **sans ~** adj incoherent, disjointed; adv incoherently, disjointedly; **de ~** adv (d'affilée) in succession; (: immédiatement) at once; **par la ~** afterwards, subsequently; **à la ~** adv one after the other; **à la ~ de** (derrière) behind; (en conséquence de) following; **par ~ de** owing to, as a result of; **avoir de la ~ dans les idées** to show great singleness of purpose; **attendre la ~ des événements** to (wait and see) what happens

suivant, e [sɥivɑ̃, -ɑ̃t] VB voir **suivre** ▶ ADJ next, following; (ci-après): **l'exercice ~** the following exercise ▶ PRÉP (selon) according to; **~ que** according to whether; **au ~!** next!

suive etc [sɥiv] VB voir **suivre**

suiveur [sɥivœʀ] NM (Cyclisme) (official) follower; (péj) (camp) follower

suivi, e [sɥivi] PP de suivre ▶ ADJ (régulier) regular; (Comm: article) in general production; (effort, qualité) consistent; (cohérent) coherent ▶ NM follow-up; **très/peu ~** (cours) well-/poorly-attended; (mode) widely/not widely adopted; (feuilleton etc) widely/not widely followed

suivre [sɥivʀ] /40/ VT (gén) to follow; (Scol: cours) to attend; (: leçon) to follow, attend to; (: programme) to keep up with; (Comm: article) to continue to stock ▶ VI to follow; (élève: écouter) to attend, pay attention; (: assimiler le programme) to keep up, follow; **se suivre** VI (accidents, personnes, voitures etc) to follow one after the other; (raisonnement) to be coherent; **~ des yeux** to follow with one's eyes; **faire ~** (lettre) to forward; **~ son cours** (enquête etc) to run ou take its course; **"à ~"** "to be continued"

sujet, te [syʒɛ, -ɛt] ADJ: **être ~ à** (accidents) to be prone to; (vertige etc) to be liable ou subject to ▶ NM/F (d'un souverain) subject ▶ NM subject; **un ~ de dispute/discorde/mécontentement** a cause for argument/dissension/dissatisfaction; **c'est à quel ~?** what is it about?; **avoir ~ de se plaindre** to have cause for complaint; **au ~ de** prép about; **à ~ caution** questionable; **~ de conversation** topic ou subject of conversation; **~ d'examen** (Scol)

examination question; examination paper;
~ **d'expérience** (Bio etc) experimental subject

sujétion [syʒesjɔ̃] NF subjection; (fig) constraint

sulfater [sylfate] /1/ VT to spray with copper
sulphate

sulfureux, -euse [sylfyrø, -øz] ADJ sulphurous
(BRIT), sulfurous (US)

sulfurique [sylfyʀik] ADJ: **acide** ~ sulphuric
(BRIT) ou sulfuric (US) acid

sulfurisé, e [sylfyʀize] ADJ: **papier** ~ greaseproof
(BRIT) ou wax (US) paper

Sumatra [symatra] NF Sumatra

summum [sɔmɔm] NM: **le – de** the height of

super [sypɛʀ] ADJ INV great, fantastic ▶ NM
(= supercarburant) ≈ 4-star (BRIT), ≈ premium (US)

superbe [sypɛʀb] ADJ magnificent, superb ▶ NF
arrogance

superbement [sypɛʀbəmɑ̃] ADV superbly

supercarburant [sypɛʀkaʀbyʀɑ̃] NM ≈ 4-star
petrol (BRIT), ≈ premium gas (US)

supercherie [sypɛʀʃəʀi] NF trick, trickery no pl;
(fraude) fraud

supérette [sypeʀɛt] NF minimarket

superfétatoire [sypɛʀfetatwaʀ] ADJ
superfluous

superficie [sypɛʀfisi] NF (surface) area; (fig)
surface

superficiel, le [sypɛʀfisjɛl] ADJ superficial

superficiellement [sypɛʀfisjɛlmɑ̃] ADV
superficially

superflu, e [sypɛʀfly] ADJ superfluous ▶ NM: **le** ~
the superfluous

superforme [sypɛʀfɔʀm] NF (fam) top form,
excellent shape

super-grand [sypɛʀgʀɑ̃] NM superpower

super-huit [sypɛʀɥit] ADJ INV: **camera/film** ~
super-eight camera/film

supérieur, e [sypeʀjœʀ] ADJ (lèvre, étages, classes)
upper; ~ **(à)** (plus élevé: température, niveau) higher
(than); (meilleur: qualité, produit) superior (to);
(excellent, hautain) superior ▶ NM/F superior;
Mère ~ Mother Superior; **à l'étage** ~ on the
next floor up; ~ **en nombre** superior in
number

supérieurement [sypeʀjœʀmɑ̃] ADV
exceptionally well; (avec adjectif) exceptionally

supériorité [sypeʀjɔʀite] NF superiority

superlatif [sypɛʀlatif] NM superlative

supermarché [sypɛʀmaʀʃe] NM supermarket

supernova [sypɛʀnɔva] NF supernova

superposable [sypɛʀpozabl] ADJ (figures) that
may be superimposed; (lits) stackable

superposer [sypɛʀpoze] /1/ VT to superpose;
(meubles, caisses) to stack; (faire chevaucher) to
superimpose; **se superposer** (images, souvenirs)
to be superimposed; **lits superposés** bunk
beds

superposition [sypɛʀpozisjɔ̃] NF
superposition; superimposition

superpréfet [sypɛʀpʀefe] NM prefect in charge
of a region

superproduction [sypɛʀpʀɔdyksjɔ̃] NF (film)
spectacular

superpuissance [sypɛʀpɥisɑ̃s] NF superpower

supersonique [sypɛʀsɔnik] ADJ supersonic

superstitieux, -euse [sypɛʀstisjø, -øz] ADJ
superstitious

superstition [sypɛʀstisjɔ̃] NF superstition

superstructure [sypɛʀstʀyktyʀ] NF
superstructure

supertanker [sypɛʀtɑ̃kœʀ] NM supertanker

superviser [sypɛʀvize] /1/ VT to supervise

supervision [sypɛʀvizjɔ̃] NF supervision

suppl. ABR = **supplément**

supplanter [syplɑ̃te] /1/ VT to supplant

suppléance [sypleɑ̃s] NF (poste) supply post
(BRIT), substitute teacher's post (US)

suppléant, e [sypleɑ̃, -ɑ̃t] ADJ (juge, fonctionnaire)
deputy cpd; (professeur) supply cpd (BRIT),
substitute cpd (US) ▶ NM/F deputy; (professeur)
supply ou substitute teacher; **médecin** ~ locum

suppléer [syplee] /1/ VT (ajouter: mot manquant etc)
to supply, provide; (compenser: lacune) to fill in;
(: défaut) to make up for; (remplacer: professeur) to
stand in for; (: juge) to deputize for; ~ **à** vt to
make up for; to substitute for

supplément [syplemɑ̃] NM supplement; **un** ~
de travail extra ou additional work; **un** ~ **de
frites** etc an extra portion of chips etc; **un** ~ **de
10 euros** a supplement of 10 euros, an extra ou
additional 10 euros; **ceci est en** ~ (au menu etc)
this is extra, there is an extra charge for this;
le vin est en ~ wine is extra; **payer un** ~ to pay
an additional charge; ~ **d'information**
additional information

supplémentaire [syplemɑ̃tɛʀ] ADJ additional,
further; (train, bus) relief cpd, extra

supplétif, -ive [sypletif, -iv] ADJ (Mil) auxiliary

suppliant, e [syplijɑ̃, -ɑ̃t] ADJ imploring

supplication [syplikasjɔ̃] NF (Rel) supplication;
supplications NFPL (adjurations) pleas, entreaties

supplice [syplis] NM (peine corporelle) torture no pl;
form of torture; (douleur physique, morale) torture,
agony; **être au** ~ to be in agony

supplier [syplije] /7/ VT to implore, beseech

supplique [syplik] NF petition

support [sypɔʀ] NM support; (pour livre, outils)
stand; ~ **audiovisuel** audio-visual aid;
~ **publicitaire** advertising medium

supportable [sypɔʀtabl] ADJ (douleur, température)
bearable; (procédé, conduite) tolerable

supporter¹ [sypɔʀtɛʀ] NM supporter, fan

supporter² [sypɔʀte] VT (poids, poussée, Sport:
concurrent, équipe) to support; (conséquences,
épreuve) to bear, endure; (défauts, personne) to
tolerate, put up with; (chose, chaleur etc) to
withstand; (personne, chaleur, vin) to take

supposé, e [sypoze] ADJ (nombre) estimated;
(auteur) supposed

supposer [sypoze] /1/ VT to suppose; (impliquer)
to presuppose; **en supposant** ou **à** ~ **que**
supposing (that)

supposition [sypozisjɔ̃] NF supposition

suppositoire [sypozitwaʀ] NM suppository

suppôt [sypo] NM (péj) henchman

suppression [sypʀesjɔ̃] NF (voir supprimer)
removal; deletion; cancellation; suppression

supprimer [sypʀime] /1/ VT (cloison, cause, anxiété)

to remove; (*clause, mot*) to delete; (*congés, service d'autobus etc*) to cancel; (*publication, article*) to suppress; (*emplois, privilèges, témoin gênant*) to do away with; **~ qch à qn** to deprive sb of sth

suppurer [sypyʀe] /**1**/ vi to suppurate

supputations [sypytasjɔ̃] NFPL calculations, reckonings

supputer [sypyte] /**1**/ vt to calculate, reckon

supranational, e, -aux [sypʀanasjɔnal, -o] ADJ supranational

suprématie [sypʀemasi] NF supremacy

suprême [sypʀɛm] ADJ supreme

suprêmement [sypʀɛmmɑ̃] ADV supremely

(MOT-CLÉ)

sur¹ [syʀ] PRÉP **1** (*position*) on; (: *par-dessus*) over; (: *au-dessus*) above; **pose-le sur la table** put it on the table; **je n'ai pas d'argent sur moi** I haven't any money on me
2 (*direction*) towards; **en allant sur Paris** going towards Paris; **sur votre droite** on *ou* to your right
3 (*à propos de*) on, about; **un livre/une conférence sur Balzac** a book/lecture on *ou* about Balzac
4 (*proportion, mesures*) out of; by; **un sur 10** one in 10; (*Scol*) one out of 10; **sur 20, deux sont venus** out of 20, two came; **4 m sur 2** 4 m by 2; **avoir accident sur accident** to have one accident after another
5 (*cause*): **sur sa recommandation** on *ou* at his recommendation; **sur son invitation** at his invitation
6: sur ce *adv* whereupon; **sur ce, il faut que je vous quitte** and now I must leave you

sur², e [syʀ] ADJ sour

sûr, e [syʀ] ADJ sure, certain; (*digne de confiance*) reliable; (*sans danger*) safe; **peu ~** unreliable; **~ de qch** sure *ou* certain of sth; **être ~ de qn** to be sure of sb; **~ et certain** absolutely certain; **~ de soi** self-assured, self-confident; **le plus ~ est de** the safest thing is to

surabondance [syʀabɔ̃dɑ̃s] NF overabundance

surabondant, e [syʀabɔ̃dɑ̃, -ɑ̃t] ADJ overabundant

surabonder [syʀabɔ̃de] /**1**/ vi to be overabundant; **~ de** to abound with, have an overabundance of

suractivité [syʀaktivite] NF hyperactivity

suraigu, ë [syʀegy] ADJ very shrill

surajouter [syʀaʒute] /**1**/ vt: **~ qch à** to add sth to

suralimentation [syʀalimɑ̃tasjɔ̃] NF overfeeding; (*Tech: d'un moteur*) supercharging

suralimenté, e [syʀalimɑ̃te] ADJ (*personne*) overfed; (*moteur*) supercharged

suranné, e [syʀane] ADJ outdated, outmoded

surarmement [syʀaʀməmɑ̃] NM (excess) stockpiling of arms (*ou* weapons)

surbaissé, e [syʀbese] ADJ lowered, low

surcapacité [syʀkapasite] NF overcapacity

surcharge [syʀʃaʀʒ] NF (*de passagers, marchandises*) excess load; (*de détails, d'ornements*)

overabundance, excess; (*correction*) alteration; (*Postes*) surcharge; **prendre des passagers en ~** to take on excess *ou* extra passengers; **~ de bagages** excess luggage; **~ de travail** extra work

surchargé, e [syʀʃaʀʒe] ADJ (*décoration, style*) over-elaborate, overfussy; (*voiture, emploi du temps*) overloaded

surcharger [syʀʃaʀʒe] /**3**/ vt to overload; (*timbre-poste*) to surcharge; (*décoration*) to overdo

surchauffe [syʀʃof] NF overheating

surchauffé, e [syʀʃofe] ADJ overheated; (*fig: imagination*) overactive

surchoix [syʀʃwa] ADJ INV top-quality

surclasser [syʀklase] /**1**/ vt to outclass

surconsommation [syʀkɔ̃sɔmasjɔ̃] NF (*Écon*) overconsumption

surcoté, e [syʀkɔte] ADJ overpriced

surcouper [syʀkupe] /**1**/ vt to overtrump

surcroît [syʀkʀwa] NM: **~ de qch** additional sth; **par** *ou* **de ~** moreover; **en ~** in addition

surdi-mutité [syʀdimytite] NF: **atteint de ~** person with a hearing and speech impairment

surdité [syʀdite] NF deafness; **atteint de ~ totale** profoundly deaf

surdoué, e [syʀdwe] ADJ gifted

sureau, x [syʀo] NM elder (tree)

sureffectif [syʀefɛktif] NM overmanning

surélever [syʀɛlve] /**5**/ vt to raise, heighten

sûrement [syʀmɑ̃] ADV reliably; (*sans risques*) safely, securely; (*certainement*) certainly; **~ pas** certainly not

suremploi [syʀɑ̃plwa] NM (*Écon*) overemployment

surenchère [syʀɑ̃ʃeʀ] NF (*aux enchères*) higher bid; (*sur prix fixe*) overbid; (*fig*) overstatement; outbidding tactics *pl*; **~ de violence** build-up of violence; **~ électorale** political (*ou* electoral) one-upmanship

surenchérir [syʀɑ̃ʃeʀiʀ] /**2**/ vi to bid higher; raise one's bid; (*fig*) to try and outbid each other

surendettement [syʀɑ̃dɛtmɑ̃] NM excessive debt

surent [syʀ] VB *voir* **savoir**

surentraîné, e [syʀɑ̃tʀene] ADJ overtrained

suréquipé, e [syʀekipe] ADJ overequipped

surestimer [syʀɛstime] /**1**/ vt (*tableau*) to overvalue; (*possibilité, personne*) to overestimate

sûreté [syʀte] NF (*voir sûr: exactitude: de renseignements etc*) reliability; (*sécurité*) safety; (*d'un geste*) steadiness; (*Jur*) guaranty; surety; **mettre en ~** to put in a safe place; **pour plus de ~** as an extra precaution; to be on the safe side; **la ~ de l'État** State security; **la S~ (nationale)** division of the Ministère de l'Intérieur heading all police forces except the gendarmerie and the Paris préfecture de police

surexcité, e [syʀɛksite] ADJ overexcited

surexciter [syʀɛksite] /**1**/ vt (*personne*) to overexcite

surexploiter [syʀɛksplwate] /**1**/ vt to overexploit

surexposer [syʀɛkspoze] /**1**/ vt to overexpose

surf [sœʀf] NM surfing; **faire du ~** to go surfing

surface [syʀfas] NF surface; *(superficie)* surface area; **une grande ~** a supermarket; **faire ~** to surface; **en ~** *adv* near the surface; *(fig)* superficially; **la pièce fait 100 m² de ~** the room has a surface area of 100m²; **~ de réparation** *(Sport)* penalty area; **~ porteuse** *ou* **de sustentation** *(Aviat)* aerofoil

surfait, e [syʀfɛ, -ɛt] ADJ overrated

surfer [sœʀfe] /1/ VI to surf; **~ sur Internet** to surf *ou* browse the Internet

surfeur, -euse [sœʀfœʀ, -øz] NM/F surfer

surfiler [syʀfile] /1/ VT *(Couture)* to oversew

surfin, e [syʀfɛ̃, -in] ADJ superfine

surgélateur [syʀʒelatœʀ] NM deep freeze

surgélation [syʀʒelasjɔ̃] NF deep-freezing

surgelé, e [syʀʒəle] ADJ (deep-)frozen ▶ NM: **les surgelés** (deep-)frozen food

surgeler [syʀʒəle] /5/ VT to (deep-)freeze

surgir [syʀʒiʀ] /2/ VI *(personne, véhicule)* to appear suddenly; *(jaillir)* to shoot up; *(montagne etc)* to rise up, loom up; *(fig: problème, conflit)* to arise

surhomme [syʀɔm] NM superman

surhumain, e [syʀymɛ̃, -ɛn] ADJ superhuman

surimposer [syʀɛ̃poze] /1/ VT to overtax

surimpression [syʀɛ̃pʀesjɔ̃] NF *(Photo)* double exposure; **en ~** superimposed

surimprimer [syʀɛ̃pʀime] /1/ VT to overstrike, overprint

Surinam [syʀinam] NM: **le ~** Surinam

surinfection [syʀɛ̃fɛksjɔ̃] NF *(Méd)* secondary infection

surjet [syʀʒɛ] NM *(Couture)* overcast seam

sur-le-champ [syʀləʃɑ̃] ADV immediately

surlendemain [syʀlɑ̃dmɛ̃] NM: **le ~ (soir)** two days later (in the evening); **le ~ de** two days after

surligneur [syʀliɲœʀ] NM *(feutre)* highlighter (pen)

surmenage [syʀmənaʒ] NM overwork; **le ~ intellectuel** mental fatigue

surmené, e [syʀməne] ADJ overworked

surmener [syʀməne] /5/ VT to overwork; **se surmener** VI to overwork

surmonter [syʀmɔ̃te] /1/ VT *(coupole etc)* to surmount, top; *(vaincre)* to overcome, surmount; *(être au-dessus de)* to top

surmultiplié, e [syʀmyltiplije] ADJ, NF: **(vitesse) ~** overdrive

surnager [syʀnaʒe] /3/ VI to float

surnaturel, le [syʀnatyʀɛl] ADJ, NM supernatural

surnom [syʀnɔ̃] NM nickname

surnombre [syʀnɔ̃bʀ] NM: **être en ~** to be too many *(ou* one too many)

surnommer [syʀnɔme] /1/ VT to nickname

surnuméraire [syʀnymeʀɛʀ] NMF supernumerary

suroît [syʀwa] NM sou'wester

surpasser [syʀpɑse] /1/ VT to surpass; **se surpasser** VI to surpass o.s., excel o.s.

surpayer [syʀpeje] /8/ VT *(personne)* to overpay; *(article etc)* to pay too much for

surpeuplé, e [syʀpœple] ADJ overpopulated

surpeuplement [syʀpœpləmɑ̃] NM overpopulation

surpiquer [syʀpike] /1/ VT *(Couture)* to overstitch

surpiqûre [syʀpikyʀ] NF *(Couture)* overstitching

surplace [syʀplas] NM: **faire du ~** to mark time

surplis [syʀpli] NM surplice

surplomb [syʀplɔ̃] NM overhang; **en ~** overhanging

surplomber [syʀplɔ̃be] /1/ VI to be overhanging ▶ VT to overhang; *(dominer)* to tower above

surplus [syʀply] NM *(Comm)* surplus; *(reste)*: **~ de bois** wood left over; **au ~** moreover; **~ américains** American army surplus *sg*

surpopulation [syʀpɔpylasjɔ̃] NF overpopulation

surprenant, e [syʀpʀənɑ̃, -ɑ̃t] VB *voir* **surprendre** ▶ ADJ amazing

surprendre [syʀpʀɑ̃dʀ] /58/ VT *(étonner, prendre à l'improviste)* to amaze, surprise; *(secret)* to discover; *(tomber sur: intrus etc)* to catch; *(fig)* to detect; to chance *ou* happen upon; *(clin d'œil)* to intercept; *(conversation)* to overhear; *(orage, nuit etc)* to catch out, take by surprise; **~ la vigilance/bonne foi de qn** to catch sb out/ betray sb's good faith; **se ~ à faire** to catch *ou* find o.s. doing

surprime [syʀpʀim] NF additional premium

surpris, e [syʀpʀi, -iz] PP *de* **surprendre** ▶ ADJ: **~ (de/que)** amazed *ou* surprised (at/that)

surprise [syʀpʀiz] NF surprise; **faire une ~ à qn** to give sb a surprise; **voyage sans surprises** uneventful journey; **par ~** *adv* by surprise

surprise-partie [syʀpʀizpaʀti] NF party

surprit [syʀpʀi] VB *voir* **surprendre**

surproduction [syʀpʀɔdyksjɔ̃] NF overproduction

surréaliste [syʀʀealist] ADJ, NMF surrealist

sursaut [syʀso] NM start, jump; **~ de** *(énergie, indignation)* sudden fit *ou* burst of; **en ~** *adv* with a start

sursauter [syʀsote] /1/ VI to (give a) start, jump

surseoir [syʀswaʀ] /26/: **~ à** VT to defer; *(Jur)* to stay

sursis [syʀsi] NM *(Jur: gén)* suspended sentence; *(: à l'exécution capitale: aussi fig)* reprieve; *(Mil)*: **~ (d'appel** *ou* **d'incorporation)** deferment; **condamné à cinq mois (de prison) avec ~** given a five-month suspended (prison) sentence

sursitaire [syʀsitɛʀ] NM *(Mil)* deferred conscript

sursois [syʀswa], **sursoyais** *etc* [syʀswaje] VB *voir* **surseoir**

surtaxe [syʀtaks] NF surcharge

surtension [syʀtɑ̃sjɔ̃] NF *(Élec)* overvoltage

surtout [syʀtu] ADV *(avant tout, d'abord)* above all; *(spécialement, particulièrement)* especially; **il aime le sport, ~ le football** he likes sport, especially football; **cet été, il a ~ fait de la pêche** this summer he went fishing more than anything (else); **~ pas d'histoires!** no fuss now!; **~, ne dites rien!** whatever you do, don't say anything!; **~ pas!** certainly *ou* definitely not!; **~ que …** especially as …

survécu, e [syʀveky] PP *de* **survivre**

surveillance [syʀvejɑ̃s] NF watch; (*Police, Mil*) surveillance; **sous ~ médicale** under medical supervision; **la ~ du territoire** internal security; *voir aussi* DST

surveillant, e [syʀvejɑ̃, -ɑ̃t] NM/F (*de prison*) warder; (*Scol*) monitor; (*de travaux*) supervisor, overseer

surveiller [syʀveje] /1/ VT (*enfant, élèves, bagages*) to watch, keep an eye on; (*malade*) to watch over; (*prisonnier, suspect*) to keep (a) watch on; (*territoire, bâtiment*) to (keep) watch over; (*travaux, cuisson*) to supervise; (*Scol: examen*) to invigilate; **se surveiller** to keep a check *ou* watch on o.s.; **~ son langage/sa ligne** to watch one's language/figure

survenir [syʀvəniʀ] /22/ VI (*incident, retards*) to occur, arise; (*événement*) to take place; (*personne*) to appear, arrive

survenu, e [syʀv(ə)ny] PP *de* **survenir**

survêt [syʀvɛt], **survêtement** [syʀvɛtmɑ̃] NM tracksuit (BRIT), sweat suit (US)

survie [syʀvi] NF survival; (*Rel*) afterlife; **équipement de ~** survival equipment; **une ~ de quelques mois** a few more months of life

surviens [syʀvjɛ̃], **survint** etc [syʀvɛ̃] VB *voir* **survenir**

survit etc [syʀvi] VB *voir* **survivre**

survitrage [syʀvitʀaʒ] NM double-glazing

survivance [syʀvivɑ̃s] NF relic

survivant, e [syʀvivɑ̃, -ɑ̃t] VB *voir* **survivre** ▶ NM/F survivor

survivre [syʀvivʀ] /46/ VI to survive; **~ à** vt (*accident etc*) to survive; (*personne*) to outlive; **la victime a peu de chance de ~** the victim has little hope of survival

survol [syʀvɔl] NM flying over

survoler [syʀvɔle] /1/ VT to fly over; (*fig: livre*) to skim through; (: *question, problèmes*) to skim over

survolté, e [syʀvɔlte] ADJ (*Élec*) stepped up, boosted; (*fig*) worked up

sus [sy(s)]: **en ~** *prép* in addition to, over and above; **en ~** *adv* in addition; **~ à** *excl*: **~ au tyran!** at the tyrant!; *voir* **savoir**

susceptibilité [syseptibilite] NF sensitivity *no pl*

susceptible [syseptibl] ADJ touchy, sensitive; **~ de faire** (*capacité*) able to do; (*probabilité*) liable to do; **~ d'amélioration** *ou* **d'être amélioré** that can be improved, open to improvement

susciter [sysite] /1/ VT (*admiration*) to arouse; (*obstacles, ennuis*): **~ (à qn)** to create (for sb)

susdit, e [sysdi, -dit] ADJ foresaid

susmentionné, e [sysmɑ̃sjɔne] ADJ abovementioned

susnommé, e [sysnɔme] ADJ above-named

suspect, e [syspɛ(kt), -ɛkt] ADJ suspicious; (*témoignage, opinions, vin etc*) suspect ▶ NM/F suspect; **peu ~ de** most unlikely to be suspected of

suspecter [syspɛkte] /1/ VT to suspect; (*honnêteté de qn*) to question, have one's suspicions about; **~ qn d'être/d'avoir fait qch** to suspect sb of being/having done sth

suspendre [syspɑ̃dʀ] /41/ VT (*interrompre, démettre*) to suspend; (*remettre*) to defer; (*accrocher: vêtement*): **~ qch (à)** to hang sth up (on); (*fixer: lustre etc*): **~ qch à** to hang sth from; **se ~ à** to hang from

suspendu, e [syspɑ̃dy] PP *de* **suspendre** ▶ ADJ (*accroché*): **~ à** hanging on (ou from); (*perché*) **~ au-dessus de** suspended over; (*Auto*) **bien/mal ~** with good/poor suspension; **être ~ aux lèvres de qn** to hang upon sb's every word

suspens [syspɑ̃]: **en ~** *adv* (*affaire*) in abeyance; **tenir en ~** to keep in suspense

suspense [syspɑ̃s] NM suspense

suspension [syspɑ̃sjɔ̃] NF suspension; deferment; (*Auto*) suspension; (*lustre*) pendant light fitting; **en ~** in suspension, suspended; **~ d'audience** adjournment

suspicieux, -euse [syspisjø, -øz] ADJ suspicious

suspicion [syspisjɔ̃] NF suspicion

sustentation [systɑ̃tasjɔ̃] NF (*Aviat*) lift; **base** *ou* **polygone de ~** support polygon

sustenter [systɑ̃te] /1/: **se sustenter** VI to take sustenance

susurrer [sysyʀe] /1/ VT to whisper

sut [sy] VB *voir* **savoir**

suture [sytyʀ] NF: **point de ~** stitch

suturer [sytyʀe] /1/ VT to stitch up, suture

suzeraineté [syzʀɛnte] NF suzerainty

svelte [svɛlt] ADJ slender, svelte

SVP ABR (= *s'il vous plaît*) please

Swaziland [swazilɑ̃d] NM: **le ~** Swaziland

sweat [swit] NM (*fam*) sweatshirt

sweat-shirt [switʃœʀt] (*pl* **sweat-shirts**) NM sweatshirt

syllabe [silab] NF syllable

sylphide [silfid] NF (*fig*): **sa taille de ~** her sylph-like figure

sylvestre [silvɛstʀ] ADJ: **pin ~** Scots pine, Scotch fir

sylvicole [silvikɔl] ADJ forestry *cpd*

sylviculteur [silvikyltœʀ] NM forester

sylviculture [silvikyltyʀ] NF forestry, sylviculture

symbole [sɛ̃bɔl] NM symbol

symbolique [sɛ̃bɔlik] ADJ symbolic; (*geste, offrande*) token *cpd*; (*salaire, dommages-intérêts*) nominal

symboliquement [sɛ̃bɔlikmɑ̃] ADV symbolically

symboliser [sɛ̃bɔlize] /1/ VT to symbolize

symétrie [simetʀi] NF symmetry

symétrique [simetʀik] ADJ symmetrical

symétriquement [simetʀikmɑ̃] ADV symmetrically

sympa [sɛ̃pa] ADJ INV (*fam*: = *sympathique*) nice; friendly; good; **sois ~, prête-le moi** be a pal and lend it to me

sympathie [sɛ̃pati] NF (*inclination*) liking; (*affinité*) fellow feeling; (*condoléances*) sympathy; **accueillir avec ~** (*projet*) to receive favourably; **avoir de la ~ pour qn** to like sb, have a liking for sb; **témoignages de ~** expressions of sympathy; **croyez à toute ma ~** you have my deepest sympathy

sympathique [sɛ̃patik] ADJ (*personne, figure*) nice, friendly, likeable; (*geste*) friendly; (*livre*) good; (*déjeuner*) nice; (*réunion, endroit*) pleasant, nice

sympathisant, e [sɛ̃patizɑ̃, -ɑ̃t] NM/F sympathizer
sympathiser [sɛ̃patize] /1/ VI (*voisins etc*: *s'entendre*) to get on (BRIT) *ou* along (US) (well); (: *se fréquenter*) to socialize, see each other; ~ **avec** to get on *ou* along (well) with, to see, socialize with
symphonie [sɛ̃fɔni] NF symphony
symphonique [sɛ̃fɔnik] ADJ (*orchestre, concert*) symphony *cpd*; (*musique*) symphonic
symposium [sɛ̃pozjɔm] NM symposium
symptomatique [sɛ̃ptɔmatik] ADJ symptomatic
symptôme [sɛ̃ptom] NM symptom
synagogue [sinagɔg] NF synagogue
synchrone [sɛ̃kʀɔn] ADJ synchronous
synchronique [sɛ̃kʀɔnik] ADJ: **tableau ~** synchronic table of events
synchronisation [sɛ̃kʀɔnizasjɔ̃] NF synchronization; (*Auto*): ~ **des vitesses** synchromesh
synchronisé, e [sɛ̃kʀɔnize] ADJ synchronized
synchroniser [sɛ̃kʀɔnize] /1/ VT to synchronize
syncope [sɛ̃kɔp] NF (*Méd*) blackout; (*Mus*) syncopation; **tomber en ~** to faint, pass out
syncopé, e [sɛ̃kɔpe] ADJ syncopated
syndic [sɛ̃dik] NM managing agent
syndical, e, -aux [sɛ̃dikal, -o] ADJ (trade-)union *cpd*; **centrale ~** group of affiliated trade unions
syndicalisme [sɛ̃dikalism] NM (*mouvement*) trade unionism; (*activités*) union(ist) activities *pl*
syndicaliste [sɛ̃dikalist] NMF trade unionist
syndicat [sɛ̃dika] NM (*d'ouvriers, employés*) (trade(s)) union; (*autre association d'intérêts*) union, association; ~ **d'initiative** tourist office *ou* bureau; ~ **patronal** employers' syndicate, federation of employers; ~ **de propriétaires** association of property owners
syndiqué, e [sɛ̃dike] ADJ belonging to a (trade) union; **non ~** non-union
syndiquer [sɛ̃dike] /1/: **se syndiquer** VI to form a trade union; (*adhérer*) to join a trade union
syndrome [sɛ̃dʀom] NM syndrome; ~ **prémenstruel** premenstrual syndrome (PMS)
synergie [sinɛʀʒi] NF synergy
synode [sinɔd] NM synod
synonyme [sinɔnim] ADJ synonymous ▶ NM synonym; ~ **de** synonymous with
synopsis [sinɔpsis] NMF synopsis
synoptique [sinɔptik] ADJ: **tableau ~** synoptic table
synovie [sinɔvi] NF synovia; **épanchement de** ~ water on the knee
syntaxe [sɛ̃taks] NF syntax
synthèse [sɛ̃tɛz] NF synthesis; **faire la ~ de** to synthesize
synthétique [sɛ̃tetik] ADJ synthetic
synthétiser [sɛ̃tetize] /1/ VT to synthesize
synthétiseur [sɛ̃tetizœʀ] NM (*Mus*) synthesizer
syphilis [sifilis] NF syphilis
Syrie [siʀi] NF: **la ~** Syria
syrien, ne [siʀjɛ̃, -ɛn] ADJ Syrian ▶ NM/F: **S~, ne** Syrian
systématique [sistematik] ADJ systematic
systématiquement [sistematikmɑ̃] ADV systematically
systématiser [sistematize] /1/ VT to systematize
système [sistɛm] NM system; **le ~ D** resourcefulness; ~ **décimal** decimal system; ~ **expert** expert system; ~ **d'exploitation** (*Inform*) operating system; ~ **immunitaire** immune system; ~ **métrique** metric system; ~ **solaire** solar system

S

405

Tt

T, t [te] NM INV T, t ▶ ABR (= *tonne*) t; **T comme Thérèse** T for Tommy

t' [t] PRON *voir* **te**

ta [ta] ADJ POSS *voir* **ton¹**

tabac [taba] NM tobacco; (*aussi*: **débit** *ou* **bureau de tabac**) tobacconist's (shop) ▶ ADJ INV: (**couleur**) ~ buff, tobacco *cpd*; **passer qn à** ~ to beat sb up; **faire un** ~ (*fam*) to be a big hit; ~ **blond/brun** light/dark tobacco; ~ **gris** shag; ~ **à priser** snuff

tabagie [tabaʒi] NF smoke den

tabagisme [tabaʒism] NM nicotine addiction; ~ **passif** passive smoking

tabasser [tabase] /1/ VT to beat up

tabatière [tabatjɛʀ] NF snuffbox

tabernacle [tabɛʀnakl] NM tabernacle

table [tabl] NF table; **avoir une bonne** ~ to keep a good table; **à** ~! dinner *etc* is ready!; **se mettre à** ~ to sit down to eat; (*fig: fam*) to come clean; **mettre** *ou* **dresser/desservir la** ~ to lay *ou* set/clear the table; **faire** ~ **rase de** to make a clean sweep of; ~ **à repasser** ironing board; ~ **basse** coffee table; ~ **de cuisson** (*à l'électricité*) hob, hotplate; (*au gaz*) hob, gas ring; ~ **d'écoute** wire-tapping set; ~ **d'harmonie** sounding board; ~ **d'hôte** set menu; ~ **de lecture** turntable; ~ **des matières** (table of) contents *pl*; ~ **de multiplication** multiplication table; ~ **des négociations** negotiating table; ~ **de nuit** *ou* **de chevet** bedside table; ~ **d'orientation** viewpoint indicator; ~ **ronde** (*débat*) round table; ~ **roulante** (tea) trolley (BRIT), tea wagon (US); ~ **de toilette** washstand; ~ **traçante** (*Inform*) plotter

tableau, x [tablo] NM (*Art*) painting; (*reproduction, fig*) picture; (*panneau*) board; (*schéma*) table, chart; ~ **d'affichage** notice board; ~ **de bord** dashboard; (*Aviat*) instrument panel; ~ **de chasse** tally; ~ **de contrôle** console, control panel; ~ **de maître** masterpiece; ~ **noir** blackboard

tablée [table] NF (*personnes*) table

tabler [table] /1/ VI: ~ **sur** to count *ou* bank on

tablette [tablɛt] NF (*planche*) shelf; ~ **de chocolat** bar of chocolate; ~ **tactile** (*Inform*) tablet

tableur [tablœʀ] NM (*Inform*) spreadsheet

tablier [tablije] NM apron; (*de pont*) roadway; (*de cheminée*) (flue-)shutter

tabou, e [tabu] ADJ, NM taboo

tabouret [tabuʀɛ] NM stool

tabulateur [tabylatœʀ] NM (*Tech*) tabulator

tac [tak] NM: **du** ~ **au** ~ tit for tat

tache [taʃ] NF (*saleté*) stain, mark; (*Art, de couleur, lumière*) spot; splash, patch; **faire** ~ **d'huile** to spread, gain ground; ~ **de rousseur** *ou* **de son** freckle; ~ **de vin** (*sur la peau*) strawberry mark

tâche [taʃ] NF task; **travailler à la** ~ to do piecework

tacher [taʃe] /1/ VT to stain, mark; (*fig*) to sully, stain; **se tacher** VI (*fruits*) to become marked

tâcher [taʃe] /1/ VI: ~ **de faire** to try to do, endeavour (BRIT) *ou* endeavor (US) to do

tâcheron [taʃʀɔ̃] NM (*fig*) drudge

tacheté, e [taʃte] ADJ: ~ **de** speckled *ou* spotted with

tachisme [taʃism] NM (*Peinture*) tachisme

tachygraphe [takigʀaf] NM tachograph

tachymètre [takimɛtʀ] NM tachometer

tacite [tasit] ADJ tacit

tacitement [tasitmɑ̃] ADV tacitly

taciturne [tasityʀn] ADJ taciturn

tacot [tako] NM (*péj: voiture*) banger (BRIT), clunker (US)

tact [takt] NM tact; **avoir du** ~ to be tactful, have tact

tacticien, ne [taktisjɛ̃, -ɛn] NM/F tactician

tactile [taktil] ADJ tactile

tactique [taktik] ADJ tactical ▶ NF (*technique*) tactics *sg*; (*plan*) tactic

Tadjikistan [tadʒikistɑ̃] NM Tajikistan

taffetas [tafta] NM taffeta

Tage [taʒ] NM: **le** ~ the (river) Tagus

Tahiti [taiti] NF Tahiti

tahitien, ne [taisjɛ̃, -ɛn] ADJ Tahitian

taie [tɛ] NF: ~ (**d'oreiller**) pillowslip, pillowcase

taillader [tajade] /1/ VT to gash

taille [taj] NF cutting; (*d'arbre*) pruning; (*milieu du corps*) waist; (*hauteur*) height; (*grandeur*) size; **de** ~ **à faire** capable of doing; **de** ~ *adj* sizeable; **quelle** ~ **faites- vous?** what size are you?

taillé, e [taje] ADJ (*moustache, ongles, arbre*) trimmed; ~ **pour** (*fait pour, apte à*) cut out for; tailor-made for; ~ **en pointe** sharpened to a point

taille-crayon(s) [tɑjkʀɛjɔ̃] NM INV pencil sharpener

tailler [tɑje] /1/ VT (*pierre, diamant*) to cut; (*arbre, plante*) to prune; (*vêtement*) to cut out; (*crayon*) to sharpen; **se tailler** VT, VI (*ongles, barbe*) to trim, cut; (*fig: réputation*) to gain, win; (*fam: s'enfuir*) to beat it; **~ dans** (*chair, bois*) to cut into; **~ grand/petit** to be on the large/small side

tailleur [tɑjœʀ] NM (*couturier*) tailor; (*vêtement*) suit, costume; **en ~** (*assis*) cross-legged; **~ de diamants** diamond-cutter

taillis [tɑji] NM copse

tain [tɛ̃] NM silvering; **glace sans ~** two-way mirror

taire [tɛʀ] /54/ VT to keep to o.s., conceal ▶ VI: **faire ~ qn** to make sb be quiet; (*fig*) to silence sb; **se taire** VI (*s'arrêter de parler*) to fall silent, stop talking; (*ne pas parler*) to be silent *ou* quiet; (*s'abstenir de s'exprimer*) to keep quiet; (*bruit, voix*) to disappear; **tais-toi!**, **taisez-vous!** be quiet!

Taiwan [tajwan] NF Taiwan

talc [talk] NM talc, talcum powder

talé, e [tale] ADJ (*fruit*) bruised

talent [talɑ̃] NM talent; **avoir du ~** to be talented, have talent

talentueux, -euse [talɑ̃tɥø, -øz] ADJ talented

talion [taljɔ̃] NM: **la loi du ~** an eye for an eye

talisman [talismɑ̃] NM talisman

talkie-walkie [tɔkiwɔki] NM walkie-talkie

taloche [talɔʃ] NF (*fam: claque*) slap; (*Tech*) plaster float

talon [talɔ̃] NM heel; (*de chèque, billet*) stub, counterfoil (BRIT); **talons plats/aiguilles** flat/stiletto heels; **être sur les talons de qn** to be on sb's heels; **tourner les talons** to turn on one's heel; **montrer les talons** (*fig*) to show a clean pair of heels

talonner [talɔne] /1/ VT to follow hard behind; (*fig*) to hound; (*Rugby*) to heel

talonnette [talɔnɛt] NF (*de chaussure*) heelpiece; (*de pantalon*) stirrup

talquer [talke] /1/ VT to put talc(um powder) on

talus [taly] NM embankment; **~ de remblai/déblai** embankment/excavation slope

tamarin [tamaʀɛ̃] NM (*Bot*) tamarind

tambour [tɑ̃buʀ] NM (*Mus, Tech*) drum; (*musicien*) drummer; (*porte*) revolving door(s pl); **sans ~ ni trompette** unobtrusively

tambourin [tɑ̃buʀɛ̃] NM tambourine

tambouriner [tɑ̃buʀine] /1/ VI: **~ contre** to drum against *ou* on

tambour-major [tɑ̃buʀmaʒɔʀ] (*pl* **tambours-majors**) NM drum major

tamis [tami] NM sieve

Tamise [tamiz] NF: **la ~** the Thames

tamisé, e [tamize] ADJ (*fig*) subdued, soft

tamiser [tamize] /1/ VT to sieve, sift

tampon [tɑ̃pɔ̃] NM (*de coton, d'ouate*) pad; (*aussi*: **tampon hygiénique** *ou* **périodique**) tampon; (*amortisseur, Inform: aussi*: **mémoire tampon**) buffer; (*bouchon*) plug, stopper; (*cachet, timbre*) stamp; (*Chimie*) buffer; **~ buvard** blotter; **~ encreur** inking pad; **~ (à récurer)** scouring pad

tamponné, e [tɑ̃pɔne] ADJ: **solution ~** buffer solution

tamponner [tɑ̃pɔne] /1/ VT (*timbres*) to stamp; (*heurter*) to crash *ou* ram into; (*essuyer*) to mop up; **se tamponner** (*voitures*) to crash (into each other)

tamponneuse [tɑ̃pɔnøz] ADJ F: **autos tamponneuses** dodgems, bumper cars

tam-tam [tamtam] NM tomtom

tancer [tɑ̃se] /3/ VT to scold

tanche [tɑ̃ʃ] NF tench

tandem [tɑ̃dɛm] NM tandem; (*fig*) duo, pair

tandis [tɑ̃di]: **~ que** conj while

tangage [tɑ̃gaʒ] NM pitching (and tossing)

tangent, e [tɑ̃ʒɑ̃, -ɑ̃t] ADJ (*Math*): **(à)** tangential (to); (*de justesse: fam*) close ▶ NF (*Math*) tangent

Tanger [tɑ̃ʒe] N Tangier

tango [tɑ̃go] NM (*Mus*) tango ▶ ADJ INV (*couleur*) dark orange

tanguer [tɑ̃ge] /1/ VI to pitch (and toss)

tanière [tanjɛʀ] NF lair, den

tanin [tanɛ̃] NM tannin

tank [tɑ̃k] NM tank

tanker [tɑ̃kɛʀ] NM tanker

tankini [tɑ̃kini] NM tankini

tanné, e [tane] ADJ weather-beaten

tanner [tane] /1/ VT to tan

tannerie [tanʀi] NF tannery

tanneur [tanœʀ] NM tanner

tant [tɑ̃] ADV so much; **~ de** (*sable, eau*) so much; (*gens, livres*) so many; **~ que** conj as long as; **~ que** (*comparatif*) as much as; **~ mieux** that's great; (*avec une certaine réserve*) so much the better; **~ mieux pour lui** good for him; **~ pis** too bad; (*conciliant*) never mind; **un ~ soit peu** (*un peu*) a little bit; (*même un peu*) (even) remotely; **~ bien que mal** as well as can be expected; **~ s'en faut** far from it, not by a long way

tante [tɑ̃t] NF aunt

tantinet [tɑ̃tinɛ]: **un ~** adv a tiny bit

tantôt [tɑ̃to] ADV (*parfois*): **tantôt ... tantôt** now ... now; (*cet après-midi*) this afternoon

Tanzanie [tɑ̃zani] NF: **la ~** Tanzania

tanzanien, ne [tɑ̃zanjɛ̃, -ɛn] ADJ Tanzanian

TAO SIGLE F (= *traduction assistée par ordinateur*) MAT (= *machine-aided translation*)

taon [tɑ̃] NM horsefly, gadfly

tapage [tapaʒ] NM uproar, din; (*fig*) fuss, row; **~ nocturne** (*Jur*) disturbance of the peace (*at night*)

tapageur, -euse [tapaʒœʀ, -øz] ADJ (*bruyant: enfants etc*) noisy; (*voyant: toilette*) loud, flashy; (*publicité*) obtrusive

tape [tap] NF slap

tape-à-l'œil [tapalœj] ADJ INV flashy, showy

taper [tape] /1/ VT (*personne*) to clout; (*porte*) to bang, slam; (*enfant*) to slap; (*dactylographier*) to type (out); (*Inform*) to key(board); (*fam: emprunter*): **~ qn de 10 euros** to touch sb for 10 euros, cadge 10 euros off sb ▶ VI (*soleil*) to beat down; **se taper** VT (*fam: travail*) to get landed with; (: *boire, manger*) to down; **~ sur qn** to thump sb; (*fig*) to run sb down; **~ sur qch** (*clou etc*) to hit sth; (*table etc*) to bang on sth;

~ **à** (*porte etc*) to knock on; ~ **dans** (*se servir*) to dig into; ~ **des mains/pieds** to clap one's hands/stamp one's feet; ~ (**à la machine**) to type

tapi, e [tapi] ADJ: ~ **dans/derrière** (*blotti*) crouching *ou* cowering in/behind; (*caché*) hidden away in/behind

tapinois [tapinwa]: **en** ~ adv stealthily

tapioca [tapjɔka] NM tapioca

tapir [tapiʀ] /**2**/: **se tapir** VI to hide away

tapis [tapi] NM carpet; (*petit*) rug; (*de table*) cloth; **mettre sur le** ~ (*fig*) to bring up for discussion; **aller au** ~ (*Boxe*) to go down; **envoyer au** ~ (*Boxe*) to floor; ~ **roulant** conveyor belt; (*pour piétons*) moving walkway; (*pour bagages*) carousel; ~ **de sol** (*de tente*) groundsheet; ~ **de souris** (*Inform*) mouse mat

tapis-brosse [tapibʀɔs] NM doormat

tapisser [tapise] /**1**/ VT (*avec du papier peint*) to paper; (*recouvrir*): ~ **qch** (**de**) to cover sth (with)

tapisserie [tapisʀi] NF (*tenture, broderie*) tapestry; (: *travail*) tapestry-making; (: *ouvrage*) tapestry work; (*papier peint*) wallpaper; (*fig*): **faire** ~ to sit out, be a wallflower

tapissier, -ière [tapisje, -jɛʀ] NM/F: ~-**décorateur** interior decorator

tapoter [tapɔte] /**1**/ VT (*joue, main*) to pat; (*objet*) to tap

taquet [takɛ] NM (*cale*) wedge; (*cheville*) peg

taquin, e [takɛ̃, -in] ADJ teasing

taquiner [takine] /**1**/ VT to tease

taquinerie [takinʀi] NF teasing *no pl*

tarabiscoté, e [taʀabiskɔte] ADJ over-ornate, fussy

tarabuster [taʀabyste] /**1**/ VT to bother, worry

tarama [taʀama] NM (*Culin*) taramasalata

tarauder [taʀode] /**1**/ VT (*Tech*) to tap; to thread; (*fig*) to pierce

tard [taʀ] ADV late ▶ NM: **sur le** ~ (*à une heure avancée*) late in the day; (*vers la fin de la vie*) late in life; **plus** ~ later (on); **au plus** ~ at the latest; **il est trop** ~ it's too late

tarder [taʀde] /**1**/ VI (*chose*) to be a long time coming; (*personne*): ~ **à faire** to delay doing; **il me tarde d'être** I am longing to be; **sans** (**plus**) ~ without (further) delay

tardif, -ive [taʀdif, -iv] ADJ (*heure, repas, fruit*) late; (*talent, goût*) late in developing

tardivement [taʀdivmɑ̃] ADV late

tare [taʀ] NF (*Comm*) tare; (*fig*) defect; blemish

taré, e [taʀe] NM/F cretin

targette [taʀʒɛt] NF (*verrou*) bolt

targuer [taʀge] /**1**/: **se** ~ **de** vt to boast about

tarif [taʀif] NM: ~ **des consommations** price list; **tarifs postaux/douaniers** postal/ customs rates; ~ **des taxis** taxi fares; ~ **plein/réduit** (*train*) full/reduced fare; (*téléphone*) peak/off-peak rate; **voyager à plein** ~/**à** ~ **réduit** to travel at full/ reduced fare

tarifaire [taʀifɛʀ] ADJ (*voir tarif*) relating to price lists *etc*

tarifé, e [taʀife] ADJ: ~ **10 euros** priced at 10 euros

tarifer [taʀife] /**1**/ VT to fix the price *ou* rate for

tarification [taʀifikasjɔ̃] NF *fixing of a price scale*

tarir [taʀiʀ] /**2**/ VI to dry up, run dry ▶ VT to dry up

tarot [taʀo] NM, **tarots** NMPL tarot cards

tartare [taʀtaʀ] ADJ (*Culin*) tartar(e)

tarte [taʀt] NF tart; ~ **aux pommes/à la crème** apple/custard tart; ~ **Tatin** ≈ apple upside-down tart

tartelette [taʀtəlɛt] NF tartlet

tartine [taʀtin] NF slice of bread (and butter (*ou* jam)); ~ **de miel** slice of bread and honey; ~ **beurrée** slice of bread and butter

tartiner [taʀtine] /**1**/ VT to spread; **fromage à** ~ cheese spread

tartre [taʀtʀ] NM (*des dents*) tartar; (*de chaudière*) fur, scale

tas [ta] NM heap, pile; **un** ~ **de** (*fig*) heaps of, lots of; **en** ~ in a heap *ou* pile; **dans le** ~ (*fig*) in the crowd; among them; **formé sur le** ~ trained on the job

Tasmanie [tasmani] NF: **la** ~ Tasmania

tasmanien, ne [tasmanjɛ̃, -ɛn] ADJ Tasmanian

tasse [tas] NF cup; **boire la** ~ (*en se baignant*) to swallow a mouthful; ~ **à café/thé** coffee/ teacup

tassé, e [tase] ADJ: **bien** ~ (*café etc*) strong

tasseau, x [taso] NM length of wood

tassement [tasmɑ̃] NM (*de vertèbres*) compression; (*Écon, Pol: ralentissement*) fall-off, slowdown; (*Bourse*) dullness

tasser [tase] /**1**/ VT (*terre, neige*) to pack down; (*entasser*): ~ **qch dans** to cram sth into; **se tasser** VI (*se serrer*) to squeeze up; (*s'affaisser*) to settle; (*personne: avec l'âge*) to shrink; (*fig*) to sort itself out, settle down

tâter [tate] /**1**/ VT to feel; (*fig*) to try out; ~ **de** (*prison etc*) to have a taste of; **se tâter** (*hésiter*) to be in two minds; ~ **le terrain** (*fig*) to test the ground

tatillon, ne [tatijɔ̃, -ɔn] ADJ pernickety

tâtonnement [tɑtɔnmɑ̃] NM: **par tâtonnements** (*fig*) by trial and error

tâtonner [tɑtɔne] /**1**/ VI to grope one's way along; (*fig*) to grope around (in the dark)

tâtons [tɑtɔ̃]: **à** ~ adv: **chercher/avancer à** ~ to grope around for/grope one's way forward

tatouage [tatwaʒ] NM tattooing; (*dessin*) tattoo

tatouer [tatwe] /**1**/ VT to tattoo

taudis [todi] NM hovel, slum

taule [tol] NF (*fam*) nick (BRIT), jail

taupe [top] NF mole; (*peau*) moleskin

taupinière [topinjɛʀ] NF molehill

taureau, x [tɔʀo] NM bull; (*signe*): **le T**~ Taurus, the Bull; **être du T**~ to be Taurus

taurillon [tɔʀijɔ̃] NM bull-calf

tauromachie [tɔʀɔmaʃi] NF bullfighting

taux [to] NM rate; (*d'alcool*) level; ~ **d'escompte** discount rate; ~ **d'intérêt** interest rate; ~ **de mortalité** mortality rate

tavelé, e [tavle] ADJ marked

taverne [tavɛʀn] NF inn, tavern

taxable [taksabl] ADJ taxable

taxation [taksasjɔ̃] NF taxation; (Tél) charges pl

taxe [taks] NF tax; (douanière) duty; **toutes taxes comprises** inclusive of tax; **la boutique hors taxes** the duty-free shop; **~ de base** (Tél) unit charge; **~ de séjour** tourist tax; **~ à** ou **sur la valeur ajoutée** value added tax

taxer [takse] /1/ VT (personne) to tax; (produit) to put a tax on, tax; **~ qn de qch** (qualifier) to call sb sth; (accuser) to accuse sb of sth, tax sb with sth

taxi [taksi] NM taxi; (chauffeur: fam) taxi driver

taxidermie [taksidɛʀmi] NF taxidermy

taxidermiste [taksidɛʀmist] NMF taxidermist

taximètre [taksimɛtʀ] NM (taxi)meter

taxiphone [taksifɔn] NM pay phone

TB ABR = **très bien; très bon**

tbe ABR (= très bon état) VGC, vgc

TCF SIGLE M (= Touring Club de France) ≈ AA ou RAC (BRIT), ≈ AAA (US)

Tchad [tʃad] NM: **le ~** Chad

tchadien, ne [tʃadjɛ̃, -ɛn] ADJ Chad(ian), of ou from Chad

tchao [tʃao] EXCL (fam) bye(-bye)!

tchécoslovaque [tʃekɔslɔvak] (Hist) ADJ Czechoslovak(ian) ▶ NMF: **T~** Czechoslovak(ian)

Tchécoslovaquie [tʃekɔslɔvaki] NF (Hist): **la ~** Czechoslovakia

tchèque [tʃɛk] ADJ Czech ▶ NM (Ling) Czech ▶ NMF: **T~** Czech; **la République ~** the Czech Republic

Tchétchénie [tʃetʃeni] NF: **la ~** Chechnya

TCS SIGLE M (= Touring Club de Suisse) ≈ AA ou RAC (BRIT), ≈ AAA (US)

TD SIGLE MPL = **travaux dirigés**

te, t' [tə] PRON you; (réfléchi) yourself

té [te] NM T-square

technicien, ne [tɛknisjɛ̃, -ɛn] NM/F technician

technicité [tɛknisite] NF technical nature

technico-commercial, e, -aux [tɛknikokɔmɛʀsjal, -o] ADJ: **agent ~** sales technician

technique [tɛknik] ADJ technical ▶ NF technique

techniquement [tɛknikmɑ̃] ADV technically

techno [tɛkno] NF (fam: Mus): **la (musique) ~** techno (music); = **technologie**

technocrate [tɛknɔkʀat] NMF technocrat

technocratie [tɛknɔkʀasi] NF technocracy

technologie [tɛknɔlɔʒi] NF technology

technologique [tɛknɔlɔʒik] ADJ technological

technologue [tɛknɔlɔg] NMF technologist

teck [tɛk] NM teak

teckel [tekɛl] NM dachshund

tee-shirt [tiʃœʀt] NM T-shirt, tee-shirt

Téhéran [teeʀɑ̃] N Teheran

teigne [tɛɲ] VB voir **teindre** ▶ NF (Zool) moth; (Méd) ringworm

teigneux, -euse [tɛɲø, -øz] ADJ (péj) nasty, scabby

teindre [tɛ̃dʀ] /52/ VT to dye; **se ~ (les cheveux)** to dye one's hair

teint, e [tɛ̃, tɛ̃t] PP de **teindre** ▶ ADJ dyed ▶ NM (du visage: permanent) complexion, colouring (BRIT), coloring (US); (: momentané) colour (BRIT), color (US) ▶ NF shade, colour, color; (fig: petite dose): **une ~ de** a hint of; **grand ~** adj inv colourfast; **bon ~** adj inv (couleur) fast; (tissu) colourfast; (personne) staunch, firm

teinté, e [tɛ̃te] (verres) tinted; (bois) stained; **~ acajou** mahogany-stained; **~ de** (fig) tinged with

teinter [tɛ̃te] /1/ VT (verre) to tint; (bois) to stain; (fig: d'ironie etc) to tinge

teinture [tɛ̃tyʀ] NF dyeing; (substance) dye; (Méd): **~ d'iode** tincture of iodine

teinturerie [tɛ̃tyʀʀi] NF dry cleaner's

teinturier, -ière [tɛ̃tyʀje, -jɛʀ] NM/F dry cleaner

tel, telle [tɛl] ADJ (pareil) such; (comme): **~ un/des ...** like a/like ...; (indéfini) such-and-such a, a given; (intensif): **un ~/de tels ...** such (a)/such ...; **venez ~ jour** come on such-and-such a day; **rien de ~** nothing like it, no such thing; **~ que** conj like, such as; **~ quel** as it is ou stands (ou was etc)

tél. ABR = **téléphone**

Tel Aviv [tɛlaviv] N Tel Aviv

télé [tele] NF (fam: télévision) TV, telly (BRIT); **à la ~** on TV ou telly

télébenne [telebɛn] NMF telecabine, gondola

télécabine [telekabin] NMF (benne) cable car

télécarte [telekaʀt] NF phonecard

téléchargeable [teleʃaʀʒabl] ADJ downloadable

téléchargement [teleʃaʀʒemɑ̃] NM (action) downloading; (fichier) download

télécharger [teleʃaʀʒe] /3/ VT (Inform: recevoir) to download; (: transmettre) to upload

TELECOM [telekɔm] ABR (= Télécommunications) ≈ Telecom.

télécommande [telekɔmɑ̃d] NF remote control

télécommander [telekɔmɑ̃de] /1/ VT to operate by remote control, radio-control

télécommunications [telekɔmynikasjɔ̃] NFPL telecommunications

télécopie [telekɔpi] NF fax, telefax

télécopieur [telekɔpjœʀ] NM fax (machine)

télédétection [teledetɛksjɔ̃] NF remote sensing

télédiffuser [teledifyze] /1/ VT to broadcast (on television)

télédiffusion [teledifyzjɔ̃] NF television broadcasting

télédistribution [teledistʀibysjɔ̃] NF cable TV

téléenseignement [teleɑ̃sɛɲmɑ̃] NM distance teaching (ou learning)

téléférique [telefeʀik] NM = **téléphérique**

téléfilm [telefilm] NM film made for TV, TV film

télégramme [telegʀam] NM telegram

télégraphe [telegʀaf] NM telegraph

télégraphie [telegʀafi] NF telegraphy

télégraphier [telegʀafje] /7/ VT to telegraph, cable

télégraphique [telegʀafik] ADJ telegraph cpd, telegraphic; (fig) telegraphic

télégraphiste [telegʀafist] NMF telegraphist

téléguider [telegide] /1/ VT to operate by remote control, radio-control

t

téléinformatique [teleɛ̃fɔʀmatik] NF remote access computing

téléjournal, -aux [teleʒuʀnal, -o] NM television news magazine programme

télématique [telematik] NF telematics *sg* ▸ ADJ telematic

téléobjectif [teleɔbʒɛktif] NM telephoto lens *sg*

téléopérateur, trice [teleɔpeʀatœʀ, -tʀis] NM/F call-centre operator

télépathie [telepati] NF telepathy

téléphérique [teleferik] NM cable-car

téléphone [telefɔn] NM telephone; **avoir le ~** to be on the (tele)phone; **au ~** on the phone; **~ arabe** bush telegraph; **~ à carte** cardphone; **~ avec appareil photo** camera phone; **~ mobile** *ou* **portable** mobile (phone) (BRIT), cell (phone) (US); **~ rouge** hotline; **~ sans fil** cordless (tele)phone

téléphoner [telefɔne] /1/ VT to telephone ▸ VI to telephone; to make a phone call; **~ à** to phone, ring up, call up

téléphonie [telefɔni] NF telephony

téléphonique [telefɔnik] ADJ (tele)phone *cpd*, phone *cpd*; **cabine ~** call box (BRIT), (tele)phone box (BRIT) *ou* booth; **conversation/appel ~** (tele)phone conversation/call

téléphoniste [telefɔnist] NMF telephonist, telephone operator; (*d'entreprise*) switchboard operator

téléport [telepɔʀ] NM teleport

téléprospection [teleprɔspɛksjɔ̃] NF telesales

téléréalité [telerealite] NF reality TV

télescopage [telɛskɔpaʒ] NM crash

télescope [telɛskɔp] NM telescope

télescoper [telɛskɔpe] /1/ VT to smash up; **se télescoper** (*véhicules*) to concertina, crash into each other

télescopique [telɛskɔpik] ADJ telescopic

téléscripteur [teleskriptœʀ] NM teleprinter

télésiège [telesjɛʒ] NM chairlift

téléski [teleski] NM ski-tow; **~ à archets** T-bar tow; **~ à perche** button lift

téléspectateur, -trice [telespɛktatœʀ, -tʀis] NM/F (television) viewer

télétexte® [teletɛkst] NM Teletext®

téléthon [teletɔ̃] NM telethon

télétransmission [teletrɑ̃smisjɔ̃] NF remote transmission

télétravail NM telecommuting

télétype [teletip] NM teleprinter

télévente [televɑ̃t] NF telesales

téléviser [televize] /1/ VT to televise

téléviseur [televizœʀ] NM television set

télévision [televizjɔ̃] NF television; **(poste de) ~** television (set); **avoir la ~** to have a television; **à la ~** on television; **~ numérique** digital TV; **~ par câble/satellite** cable/satellite television

télex [telɛks] NM telex

télexer [telɛkse] /1/ VT to telex

télexiste [telɛksist] NMF telex operator

telle [tɛl] ADJ F *voir* **tel**

tellement [tɛlmɑ̃] ADV (*tant*) so much; (*si*) so; **~ plus grand (que)** so much bigger (than); **~ de** (*sable, eau*) so much; (*gens, livres*) so many;

il s'est endormi ~ il était fatigué he was so tired (that) he fell asleep; **pas ~** not really; **pas ~ fort/lentement** not (all) that strong/slowly; **il ne mange pas ~** he doesn't eat (all that) much

tellurique [telyʀik] ADJ: **secousse ~** earth tremor

téméraire [temeʀɛʀ] ADJ reckless, rash

témérité [temerite] NF recklessness, rashness

témoignage [temwaɲaʒ] NM (Jur: *déclaration*) testimony *no pl*, evidence *no pl*; (: *faits*) evidence *no pl*; (*gén: rapport, récit*) account; (*fig: d'affection etc*) token, mark; (*geste*) expression

témoigner [temwaɲe] /1/ VT (*manifester: intérêt, gratitude*) to show ▸ VI (Jur) to testify, give evidence; **~ que** to testify that; (*fig: démontrer*) to reveal that, testify to the fact that; **~ de** VT (*confirmer*) to bear witness to, testify to

témoin [temwɛ̃] NM witness; (*fig*) testimony; (Sport) baton; (Constr) telltale ▸ ADJ control *cpd*, test *cpd*; **~ le fait que ...** (as) witness the fact that ...; **appartement-~** show flat (BRIT), model apartment (US); **être ~ de** (*voir*) to witness; **prendre à ~** to call to witness; **~ à charge** witness for the prosecution; **~ de connexion** (Inform) cookie; **T~ de Jehovah** Jehovah's Witness; **~ de moralité** character reference; **~ oculaire** eyewitness

tempe [tɑ̃p] NF (Anat) temple

tempérament [tɑ̃peʀamɑ̃] NM temperament, disposition; (*santé*) constitution; **à ~** (*vente*) on deferred (payment) terms; (*achat*) by instalments, hire purchase *cpd*; **avoir du ~** to be hot-blooded

tempérance [tɑ̃peʀɑ̃s] NF temperance; **société de ~** temperance society

tempérant, e [tɑ̃peʀɑ̃, -ɑ̃t] ADJ temperate

température [tɑ̃peʀatyʀ] NF temperature; **prendre la ~ de** to take the temperature of; (*fig*) to gauge the feeling of; **avoir** *ou* **faire de la ~** to be running *ou* have a temperature

tempéré, e [tɑ̃peʀe] ADJ temperate

tempérer [tɑ̃peʀe] /6/ VT to temper

tempête [tɑ̃pɛt] NF storm; **~ de sable/neige** sand/snowstorm; **vent de ~** gale

tempêter [tɑ̃pete] /1/ VI to rant and rave

temple [tɑ̃pl] NM temple; (*protestant*) church

tempo [tɛmpo] NM tempo

temporaire [tɑ̃pɔʀɛʀ] ADJ temporary

temporairement [tɑ̃pɔʀɛʀmɑ̃] ADV temporarily

temporel, le [tɑ̃pɔʀɛl] ADJ temporal

temporisateur, -trice [tɑ̃pɔʀizatœʀ, -tʀis] ADJ temporizing, delaying

temporisation [tɑ̃pɔʀizasjɔ̃] NF temporizing, playing for time

temporiser [tɑ̃pɔʀize] /1/ VI to temporize, play for time

temps [tɑ̃] NM (*atmosphérique*) weather; (*durée*) time; (*époque*) time, times *pl*; (Ling) tense; (Mus) beat; (Tech) stroke; **un ~ de chien** (*fam*) rotten weather; **quel ~ fait-il?** what's the weather like?; **il fait beau/mauvais ~** the weather is fine/bad; **avoir le ~/tout le ~/juste le ~** to have time/plenty of time/just enough time; **les ~ changent/sont durs** times are changing/hard; **avoir fait son ~** (fig) to have had its (ou his etc) day; **en ~ de paix/guerre** in peacetime/wartime; **en ~ utile** ou **voulu** in due time ou course; **ces derniers ~** lately; **dans quelque ~** in a (little) while; **de ~ en ~**, **de ~ à autre** from time to time, now and again; **en même ~** at the same time; **à ~** (partir, arriver) in time; **à ~ complet**, **à plein ~** adv, adj full-time; **à ~ partiel**, **à mi-~** adv, adj part-time; **dans le ~** at one time; **de tout ~** always; **du ~ que** at the time when, in the days when; **dans le** ou **du** ou **au ~ où** at the time when; **pendant ce ~** in the meantime; **~ d'accès** (Inform) access time; **~ d'arrêt** pause, halt; **~ libre** free ou spare time; **~ mort** (Sport) stoppage (time); (Comm) slack period; **~ partagé** (Inform) time-sharing; **~ réel** (Inform) real time

tenable [tənabl] ADJ bearable

tenace [tənas] ADJ tenacious, persistent

ténacité [tenasite] NF tenacity, persistence

tenailler [tənaje] /1/ VT (fig) to torment, torture

tenailles [tənaj] NFPL pincers

tenais etc [t(ə)nɛ] VB voir **tenir**

tenancier, -ière [tənãsje, -jɛR] NM/F (d'hôtel, de bistro) manager (manageress)

tenant, e [tənã, -ãt] ADJ voir **séance** ▶ NM/F (Sport): **~ du titre** title-holder ▶ NM: **d'un seul ~** in one piece; **les tenants et les aboutissants** (fig) the ins and outs

tendance [tãdãs] NF (opinions) leanings pl, sympathies pl; (inclination) tendency; (évolution) trend; **~ à la hausse/baisse** upward/downward trend; **avoir ~ à** to have a tendency to, tend to

tendancieux, -euse [tãdãsjø, -øz] ADJ tendentious

tendeur [tãdœR] NM (de vélo) chain-adjuster; (de câble) wire-strainer; (de tente) runner; (attache) elastic strap

tendinite [tãdinit] NF tendinitis, tendonitis

tendon [tãdɔ̃] NM tendon, sinew; **~ d'Achille** Achilles' tendon

tendre [tãdR] /41/ ADJ (viande, légumes) tender; (bois, roche, couleur) soft; (affectueux) tender, loving ▶ VT (élastique, peau) to stretch, draw tight; (corde) to tighten; (muscle) to tense; (donner): **~ qch à qn** to hold sth out to sb; (offrir) to offer sb sth; (fig: piège) to set, lay; (tapisserie): **tendu de soie** hung with silk, with silk hangings; **se tendre** VI (corde) to tighten; (relations) to become strained; **~ à qch/à faire** to tend towards sth/to do; **~ l'oreille** to prick up one's ears; **~ la main/le bras** to hold out one's hand/stretch out one's arm; **~ la perche à qn** (fig) to throw sb a line

tendrement [tãdRəmã] ADV tenderly, lovingly

tendresse [tãdRɛs] NF tenderness; **tendresses** NFPL (caresses etc) tenderness no pl, caresses

tendu, e [tãdy] PP de **tendre** ▶ ADJ (corde) tight; (muscles) tensed; (relations) strained

ténèbres [tenɛbR] NFPL darkness sg

ténébreux, -euse [tenebRø, -øz] ADJ obscure, mysterious; (personne) saturnine

Ténérife [tenerif] NF Tenerife

teneur [tənœR] NF content, substance; (d'une lettre) terms pl, content; **~ en cuivre** copper content

ténia [tenja] NM tapeworm

tenir [təniR] /22/ VT to hold; (magasin, hôtel) to run; (promesse) to keep ▶ VI to hold; (neige, gel) to last; (survivre) to survive; **se tenir** VI (avoir lieu) to be held, take place; (être: personne) to stand; **se tenir droit** to stand up (ou sit up) straight; **bien se tenir** to behave well; **se tenir à qch** to hold on to sth; **s'en tenir à qch** to confine o.s. to sth; to stick to sth; **~ à** vt (personne, objet) to be attached to, care about (ou for); (réputation) to care about; (avoir pour cause) to be due to, stem from; **~ à faire** to want to do, be keen to do; **~ à ce que qn fasse qch** to be anxious that sb should do sth; **~ de** vt to partake of; (ressembler à) to take after; **ça ne tient qu'à lui** it is entirely up to him; **~ qn pour** to take sb for; **~ qch de qn** (histoire) to have heard ou learnt sth from sb; (qualité, défaut) to have inherited ou got sth from sb; **~ dans** to fit into; **~ compte de qch** to take sth into account; **~ les comptes** to keep the books; **~ un rôle** to play a part; **~ de la place** to take up space ou room; **~ l'alcool** to be able to hold a drink; **~ le coup** to hold out; **~ bon** to stand ou hold fast; **~ trois jours/deux mois** (résister) to hold out ou last three days/two months; **~ au chaud/à l'abri** to keep hot/ under shelter ou cover; **un manteau qui tient chaud** a warm coat; **~ prêt** to have ready; **~ sa langue** (fig) to hold one's tongue; **tiens** (ou **tenez**), **voilà le stylo** there's the pen!; **tiens, voilà Alain!** look, here's Alain!; **tiens?** (surprise) really?; **tiens-toi bien!** (pour informer) brace yourself!, take a deep breath!

tennis [tenis] NM tennis; (aussi: **court de tennis**) tennis court ▶ NMPL ou FPL (aussi: **chaussures de tennis**) tennis ou gym shoes; **~ de table** table tennis

tennisman [tenisman] NM tennis player

ténor [tenɔR] NM tenor

tension [tãsjɔ̃] NF tension; (fig: des relations, de la situation) tension; (: concentration, effort) strain; (Méd) blood pressure; **faire** ou **avoir de la ~** to have high blood pressure; **~ nerveuse/raciale** nervous/racial tension

tentaculaire [tãtakylɛR] ADJ (fig) sprawling

tentacule [tãtakyl] NM tentacle

tentant, e [tãtã, -ãt] ADJ tempting

tentateur, -trice [tãtatœR, -tRis] ADJ tempting ▶ NM (Rel) tempter

tentation [tãtasjɔ̃] NF temptation

tentative [tãtativ] NF attempt, bid; **~ d'évasion** escape bid; **~ de suicide** suicide attempt

tente [tãt] NF tent; **~ à oxygène** oxygen tent

tenter [tãte] /1/ VT (éprouver, attirer) to tempt; (essayer): **~ qch/de faire** to attempt ou try sth/to do; **être tenté de** to be tempted to; **~ sa chance** to try one's luck

tenture [tɑ̃tyʀ] NF hanging

tenu, e [təny] PP *de* **tenir** ▸ ADJ: **bien ~** (*maison, comptes*) well-kept; **~ de faire** (*obligé*) under an obligation to do ▸ NF (*action de tenir*) running; keeping; holding; (*vêtements*) clothes *pl*, gear; (*allure*) dress *no pl*, appearance; (*comportement*) manners *pl*, behaviour (BRIT), behavior (US); (*d'une maison*) upkeep; **être en ~** to be dressed (up); **se mettre en ~** to dress (up); **en grande ~** in full dress; **en petite ~** scantily dressed *ou* clad; **avoir de la ~** to have good manners; (*journal*) to have a high standard; **~ de combat** combat gear *ou* dress; **~ de pompier** fireman's uniform; **~ de route** (*Auto*) road-holding; **~ de soirée** evening dress; **~ de sport/voyage** sports/travelling clothes *pl ou* gear *no pl*

ténu, e [təny] ADJ (*indice, nuance*) tenuous, subtle; (*fil, objet*) fine; (*voix*) thin

TER SIGLE M (= *Train Express Régional*) local train

ter [tɛʀ] ADV: **16 ~ 16b** *ou* **B**

térébenthine [teʀebɑ̃tin] NF: (**essence de**) **~** (oil of) turpentine

tergal® [tɛʀgal] NM Terylene®

tergiversations [tɛʀʒivɛʀsasjɔ̃] NFPL shilly-shallying *no pl*

tergiverser [tɛʀʒivɛʀse] /1/ VI to shilly-shally

terme [tɛʀm] NM term; (*fin*) end; **être en bons/mauvais termes avec qn** to be on good/bad terms with sb; **vente/achat à ~** (*Comm*) forward sale/purchase; **au ~ de** at the end of; **en d'autres termes** in other words; **moyen ~** (*solution intermédiaire*) middle course; **à court/long ~** *adj* short-/long-term *ou* -range; *adv* in the short/long term; **à ~** (*Méd*) *adj* full-term; *adv* sooner or later, eventually; (*Méd*) at term; **avant ~** (*Méd*) *adj* premature; *adv* prematurely; **mettre un ~ à** to put an end *ou* a stop to; **toucher à son ~** to be nearing its end

terminaison [tɛʀminɛzɔ̃] NF (*Ling*) ending

terminal, e, -aux [tɛʀminal, -o] ADJ (*partie, phase*) final; (*Méd*) terminal ▸ NM terminal ▸ NF (*Scol*) ≈ year 13 (BRIT), ≈ twelfth grade (US)

terminer [tɛʀmine] /1/ VT to end; (*travail, repas*) to finish; **se terminer** VI to end; **se terminer par** to end with

terminologie [tɛʀminɔlɔʒi] NF terminology

terminus [tɛʀminys] NM terminus; **~!** all change!

termite [tɛʀmit] NM termite, white ant

termitière [tɛʀmitjɛʀ] NF ant-hill

ternaire [tɛʀnɛʀ] ADJ compound

terne [tɛʀn] ADJ dull

ternir [tɛʀniʀ] /2/ VT to dull; (*fig*) to sully, tarnish; **se ternir** VI to become dull

terrain [teʀɛ̃] NM (*sol, fig*) ground; (*Comm: étendue de terre*) land *no pl*; (: *parcelle*) plot (of land); (: *à bâtir*) site; **sur le ~** (*fig*) on the field; **~ de football/rugby** football/rugby pitch (BRIT) *ou* field (US); **~ d'atterrissage** landing strip; **~ d'aviation** airfield; **~ de camping** campsite; **un ~ d'entente** an area of agreement; **~ de golf** golf course; **~ de jeu** (*pour les petits*) playground; (*Sport*) games field; **~ de sport** sports ground; **~ vague** waste ground *no pl*

terrasse [teʀas] NF terrace; (*de café*) pavement area, terrasse; **à la ~** (*café*) outside

terrassement [teʀasmɑ̃] NM earth-moving, earthworks *pl*; embankment

terrasser [teʀase] /1/ VT (*adversaire*) to floor, bring down; (*maladie etc*) to lay low

terrassier [teʀasje] NM navvy, roadworker

terre [tɛʀ] NF (*gén, aussi Élec*) earth; (*substance*) soil, earth; (*opposé à mer*) land *no pl*; (*contrée*) land; **terres** NFPL (*terrains*) lands, land *sg*; **travail de la ~** work on the land; **en ~** (*pipe, poterie*) clay *cpd*; **mettre en ~** (*plante etc*) to plant; (*personne: enterrer*) to bury; **à** *ou* **par ~** (*mettre, être, s'asseoir*) on the ground (*ou* floor); (*jeter, tomber*) to the ground, down; **~ à ~** *adj inv* down-to-earth, matter-of-fact; **la T~ Adélie** Adélie Coast *ou* Land; **~ de bruyère** (heath-)peat; **~ cuite** earthenware; terracotta; **la ~ ferme** dry land, terra firma; **la T~ de Feu** Tierra del Fuego; **~ glaise** clay; **la T~ promise** the Promised Land; **la T~ Sainte** the Holy Land

terreau [teʀo] NM compost

Terre-Neuve [tɛʀnœv] NF: **la ~** Newfoundland

terre-plein [tɛʀplɛ̃] NM platform; (*sur chaussée*) central reservation

terrer [teʀe] /1/: **se terrer** VI to hide away; to go to ground

terrestre [teʀɛstʀ] ADJ (*surface*) earth's, of the earth; (*Bot, Zool, Mil*) land *cpd*; (*Rel*) earthly, worldly

terreur [teʀœʀ] NF terror *no pl*, fear

terreux, -euse [teʀø, -øz] ADJ muddy; (*goût*) earthy

terrible [teʀibl] ADJ terrible, dreadful; (*fam: fantastique*) terrific; **pas ~** nothing special

terriblement [teʀibləmɑ̃] ADV (*très*) terribly, awfully

terrien, ne [teʀjɛ̃, -ɛn] ADJ: **propriétaire ~** landowner ▸ NM/F countryman/woman, man/woman of the soil; (*non martien etc*) earthling; (*non marin*) landsman

terrier [teʀje] NM burrow, hole; (*chien*) terrier

terrifiant, e [teʀifjɑ̃, -ɑ̃t] ADJ (*effrayant*) terrifying; (*extraordinaire*) terrible, awful

terrifier [teʀifje] /7/ VT to terrify

terril [teʀil] NM slag heap

terrine [teʀin] NF (*récipient*) terrine; (*Culin*) pâté

territoire [teʀitwaʀ] NM territory; **T~ des Afars et des Issas** French Territory of Afars and Issas

territorial, e, -aux [teʀitɔʀjal, -o] ADJ territorial; **eaux territoriales** territorial waters; **armée ~** regional defence force, ≈ Territorial Army (BRIT); **collectivités territoriales** local and regional authorities

terroir [teʀwaʀ] NM (*Agr*) soil; (*région*) region; **accent du ~** country *ou* rural accent

terroriser [teʀɔʀize] /1/ VT to terrorize

terrorisme [teʀɔʀism] NM terrorism

terroriste [teʀɔʀist] NMF terrorist

tertiaire [tɛʀsjɛʀ] ADJ tertiary ▸ NM (*Écon*) tertiary sector, service industries *pl*

tertiarisation [tɛʀsjaʀizasjɔ̃] NF *expansion or development of the service sector*

tertre [tɛʀtʀ] NM hillock, mound
tes [te] ADJ POSS *voir* **ton¹**
tesson [tesɔ̃] NM: ~ **de bouteille** piece of broken bottle
test [tɛst] NM test; ~ **de grossesse** pregnancy test
testament [tɛstamɑ̃] NM (*Jur*) will; (*fig*) legacy; (*Rel*) **T~** Testament; **faire son ~** to make one's will
testamentaire [tɛstamɑ̃tɛʀ] ADJ of a will
tester [tɛste] /1/ VT to test
testicule [tɛstikyl] NM testicle
tétanie [tetani] NF tetany
tétanos [tetanos] NM tetanus
têtard [tɛtaʀ] NM tadpole
tête [tɛt] NF head; (*cheveux*) hair *no pl*; (*visage*) face; (*longueur*): **gagner d'une (courte) ~** to win by a (short) head; (*Football*) header; **de ~** *adj* (*wagon etc*) front *cpd*; (*concurrent*) leading ▶ ADV (*calculer*) in one's head, mentally; **par ~** (*par personne*) per head; **se mettre en ~ que** to get it into one's head that; **se mettre en ~ de faire** to take it into one's head to do; **prendre la ~ de qch** to take the lead in sth; **perdre la ~** (*fig: s'affoler*) to lose one's head; (*: devenir fou*) to go off one's head; **ça ne va pas, la ~?** (*fam*) are you crazy?; **tenir ~ à qn** to stand up to *ou* defy sb; **la ~ en bas** with one's head down; **la ~ la première** (*tomber*) head-first; **la ~ basse** hanging one's head; **avoir la ~ dure** (*fig*) to be thickheaded; **faire une ~** (*Football*) to head the ball; **faire la ~** (*fig*) to sulk; **en ~** (*Sport*) in the lead; at the front *ou* head; **à la ~ de** at the head of; **à ~ reposée** in a more leisurely moment; **n'en faire qu'à sa ~** to do as one pleases; **en avoir par-dessus la ~** to be fed up; **~ à ~** in private, alone together; **de la ~ aux pieds** from head to toe; **~ d'affiche** (*Théât etc*) top of the bill; **~ de bétail** head of cattle; **~ brûlée** desperado; **~ chercheuse** homing device; **~ d'enregistrement** recording head; **~ d'impression** printhead; **~ de lecture** (playback) head; **~ de ligne** (*Transports*) start of the line; **~ de liste** (*Pol*) chief candidate; **~ de mort** skull and crossbones; **~ de pont** (*Mil*) bridge- *ou* beachhead; **~ de série** (*Tennis*) seeded player, seed; **~ de Turc** (*fig*) whipping boy (*BRIT*), butt; **~ de veau** (*Culin*) calf's head
tête-à-queue [tɛtakø] NM INV: **faire un ~** to spin round
tête-à-tête [tɛtatɛt] NM INV tête-à-tête; (*service*) breakfast set for two; **en ~** in private, alone together
tête-bêche [tɛtbɛʃ] ADV head to tail
tétée [tete] NF (*action*) sucking; (*repas*) feed
téter [tete] /6/ VT: ~ **(sa mère)** to suck at one's mother's breast, feed
tétine [tetin] NF teat; (*sucette*) dummy (*BRIT*), pacifier (*US*)
téton [tetɔ̃] NM breast
têtu, e [tety] ADJ stubborn, pigheaded
texte [tɛkst] NM text; (*morceau choisi*) passage; (*Scol: d'un devoir*) subject, topic; **apprendre son ~** (*Théât*) to learn one's lines; **un ~ de loi** the wording of a law

textile [tɛkstil] ADJ textile *cpd* ▶ NM textile; (*industrie*) textile industry
Texto® [tɛksto] NM text (message)
texto [tɛksto] ADV (*fam*) word for word
textuel, le [tɛkstɥɛl] ADJ literal, word for word
textuellement [tɛkstɥɛlmɑ̃] ADV literally
texture [tɛkstyʀ] NF texture; (*fig: d'un texte, livre*) feel
TF1 SIGLE F (= *Télévision française 1*) TV channel
TG SIGLE F = **trésorerie générale**
TGI SIGLE M = **tribunal de grande instance**
TGV SIGLE M = **train à grande vitesse**
thaï, e [taj] ADJ Thai ▶ NM (*Ling*) Thai
thaïlandais, e [tailɑ̃dɛ, -ɛz] ADJ Thai ▶ NM/F: **T~, e** Thai
Thaïlande [tailɑ̃d] NF: **la ~** Thailand
thalassothérapie [talasɔteʀapi] NF sea-water therapy
thé [te] NM tea; (*réunion*) tea party; **prendre le ~** to have tea; ~ **au lait/citron** tea with milk/lemon; **faire le ~** to make the tea
théâtral, e, -aux [teatʀal, -o] ADJ theatrical
théâtre [teatʀ] NM theatre; (*techniques, genre*) drama, theatre; (*activité*) stage, theatre; (*œuvres*) plays *pl*, dramatic works *pl*; (*péj*) histrionics *pl*, playacting; (*fig: lieu*): **le ~ de** the scene of; **faire du ~** (*en professionnel*) to be on the stage; (*en amateur*) to act; ~ **filmé** filmed stage productions *pl*
thébain, e [tebɛ̃, -ɛn] ADJ Theban
Thèbes [tɛb] N Thebes
théière [tejɛʀ] NF teapot
théine [tein] NF theine
théisme [teism] NM theism
thématique [tematik] ADJ thematic
thème [tɛm] NM theme; (*Scol: traduction*) prose (composition); ~ **astral** birth chart
théocratie [teɔkʀasi] NF theocracy
théologie [teɔlɔʒi] NF theology
théologien, ne [teɔlɔʒjɛ̃, -ɛn] NM theologian
théologique [teɔlɔʒik] ADJ theological
théorème [teɔʀɛm] NM theorem
théoricien, ne [teɔʀisjɛ̃, -ɛn] NM/F theoretician, theorist
théorie [teɔʀi] NF theory; **en ~** in theory
théorique [teɔʀik] ADJ theoretical
théoriquement [teɔʀikmɑ̃] ADV theoretically
théoriser [teɔʀize] /1/ VI to theorize
thérapeutique [teʀapøtik] ADJ therapeutic ▶ NF (*Méd: branche*) therapeutics *sg*; (*: traitement*) therapy
thérapie [teʀapi] NF therapy; ~ **de groupe** group therapy
thermal, e, -aux [tɛʀmal, -o] ADJ thermal; **station ~** spa; **cure ~** water cure
thermes [tɛʀm] NMPL thermal baths; (*romains*) thermae *pl*
thermique [tɛʀmik] ADJ (*énergie*) thermic; (*unité*) thermal
thermodynamique [tɛʀmɔdinamik] NF thermodynamics *sg*

thermoélectrique [tɛʀmoelɛktʀik] ADJ
thermoelectric

thermomètre [tɛʀmɔmɛtʀ] NM thermometer

thermonucléaire [tɛʀmɔnykleɛʀ] ADJ
thermonuclear

thermos® [tɛʀmos] NM OU F: **(bouteille)** ~
vacuum ou Thermos® flask (BRIT) ou bottle (US)

thermostat [tɛʀmɔsta] NM thermostat

thésauriser [tezɔʀize] /1/ VI to hoard money

thèse [tɛz] NF thesis

Thessalie [tesali] NF: **la** ~ Thessaly

thibaude [tibod] NF carpet underlay

thon [tɔ̃] NM tuna (fish)

thonier [tɔnje] NM tuna boat

thoracique [tɔʀasik] ADJ thoracic

thorax [tɔʀaks] NM thorax

thrombose [tʀɔ̃boz] NF thrombosis

thym [tɛ̃] NM thyme

thyroïde [tiʀɔid] NF thyroid (gland)

TI SIGLE M = **tribunal d'instance**

tiare [tjaʀ] NF tiara

Tibet [tibɛ] NM: **le** ~ Tibet

tibétain, e [tibetɛ̃, -ɛn] ADJ Tibetan

tibia [tibja] NM shin; (os) shinbone, tibia

Tibre [tibʀ] NM: **le** ~ the Tiber

TIC SIGLE FPL (= technologies de l'information et de la
communication) ICT sg

tic [tik] NM tic, (nervous) twitch; (de langage etc)
mannerism

ticket [tikɛ] NM ticket; ~ **de caisse** till receipt;
~ **modérateur** patient's contribution towards
medical costs; ~ **de quai** platform ticket; ~ **repas**
luncheon voucher

tic-tac [tiktak] NM INV tick-tock

tictaquer [tiktake] /1/ VI to tick (away)

tiède [tjɛd] ADJ (bière etc) lukewarm; (thé, café etc)
tepid; (bain, accueil, sentiment) lukewarm; (vent,
air) mild, warm ▶ ADV: **boire** ~ to drink things
lukewarm

tièdement [tjɛdmɑ̃] ADV coolly, half-heartedly

tiédeur [tjedœʀ] NF lukewarmness; (du vent, de
l'air) mildness

tiédir [tjediʀ] /2/ VI (se réchauffer) to grow
warmer; (refroidir) to cool

tien, tienne [tjɛ̃, tjɛn] PRON: **le (la)** ~**(ne)** yours;
les ~**(ne)s** yours; **à la tienne!** cheers!

tiendrai etc [tjɛ̃dʀe] VB voir **tenir**

tienne [tjɛn] VB voir **tenir** ▶ PRON voir **tien**

tiens [tjɛ̃] VB, EXCL voir **tenir**

tierce [tjɛʀs] ADJ F, NF voir **tiers**

tiercé [tjɛʀse] NM system of forecast betting giving
first three horses

tiers, tierce [tjɛʀ, tjɛʀs] ADJ third ▶ NM (Jur)
third party; (fraction) third ▶ NF (Mus) third;
(Cartes) tierce; **une tierce personne** a third
party; **assurance au** ~ third-party insurance;
le ~ **monde** the third world; ~ **payant** direct
payment by insurers of medical expenses;
~ **provisionnel** interim payment of tax

tifs [tif] (fam) NMPL hair

TIG SIGLE M = **travail d'intérêt général**

tige [tiʒ] NF stem; (baguette) rod

tignasse [tiɲas] NF (péj) shock ou mop of hair

Tigre [tigʀ] NM: **le** ~ the Tigris

tigre [tigʀ] NM tiger

tigré, e [tigʀe] ADJ (rayé) striped; (tacheté)
spotted; (chat) tabby

tigresse [tigʀɛs] NF tigress

tilleul [tijœl] NM lime (tree), linden (tree);
(boisson) lime(-blossom) tea

tilt [tilt] NM: **faire** ~ (fig: inspirer) to ring a bell

timbale [tɛ̃bal] NF (metal) tumbler; **timbales**
NFPL (Mus) timpani, kettledrums

timbrage [tɛ̃bʀaʒ] NM: **dispensé de** ~ post(age)
paid

timbre [tɛ̃bʀ] NM (tampon) stamp; (aussi:
timbre-poste) (postage) stamp; (cachet de la
poste) postmark; (sonnette) bell; (Mus: de voix,
instrument) timbre, tone; ~ **anti-tabac** nicotine
patch; ~ **dateur** date stamp

timbré, e [tɛ̃bʀe] ADJ (enveloppe) stamped; (voix)
resonant; (fam: fou) cracked, nuts

timbrer [tɛ̃bʀe] VT to stamp

timide [timid] ADJ (emprunté) shy, timid; (timoré)
timid, timorous

timidement [timidmɑ̃] ADV shyly; timidly

timidité [timidite] NF shyness; timidity

timonerie [timɔnʀi] NF wheelhouse

timonier [timɔnje] NM helmsman

timoré, e [timɔʀe] ADJ timorous

tint etc [tɛ̃] VB voir **tenir**

tintamarre [tɛ̃tamaʀ] NM din, uproar

tintement [tɛ̃tmɑ̃] NM ringing, chiming;
tintements d'oreilles ringing in the ears

tinter [tɛ̃te] /1/ VI to ring, chime; (argent, clés) to
jingle

Tipp-Ex® [tipɛks] NM Tipp-Ex®

tique [tik] NF tick (insect)

tiquer [tike] /1/ VI (personne) to make a face

TIR SIGLE MPL (= Transports internationaux routiers)
TIR

tir [tiʀ] NM (sport) shooting; (fait ou manière de tirer)
firing no pl; (Football) shot; (rafale) fire; (stand)
shooting gallery; ~ **d'obus/de mitraillette**
shell/machine gun fire; ~ **à l'arc** archery; ~ **de
barrage** barrage fire; ~ **au fusil** (rifle)
shooting; ~ **au pigeon** (d'argile) clay pigeon
shooting

tirade [tiʀad] NF tirade

tirage [tiʀaʒ] NM (action) printing; (Photo) print;
(Inform) printout; (de journal) circulation; (de
livre) (print-)run; edition; (de cheminée) draught
(BRIT), draft (US); (de loterie) draw; (fig: désaccord)
friction; ~ **au sort** drawing lots

tiraillement [tiʀajmɑ̃] NM (douleur) sharp pain;
(fig: doutes) agony no pl of indecision; (conflits)
friction no pl

tirailler [tiʀaje] /1/ VT to pull at, tug at; (fig) to
gnaw at ▶ VI to fire at random

tirailleur [tiʀajœʀ] NM skirmisher

tirant [tiʀɑ̃] NM: ~ **d'eau** draught (BRIT), draft
(US)

tire [tiʀ] NF: **vol à la** ~ pickpocketing

tiré, e [tiʀe] ADJ (visage, traits) drawn ▶ NM (Comm)
drawee; ~ **par les cheveux** far-fetched; ~ **à
part** off-print

tire-au-flanc [tiʀoflɑ̃] NM INV (péj) skiver

tire-bouchon [tiʀbuʃɔ̃] NM corkscrew

tire-bouchonner [tiʀbuʃɔne] /1/ vт to twirl
tire-d'aile [tiʀdɛl]: **à ~** adv swiftly
tire-fesses [tiʀfɛs] NM INV ski-tow
tire-lait [tiʀlɛ] NM INV breast-pump
tire-larigot [tiʀlaʀigo]: **à ~** adv as much as one
  likes, to one's heart's content
tirelire [tiʀliʀ] NF moneybox
tirer [tiʀe] /1/ vт (gén) to pull; (tracer: ligne, trait) to
  draw, trace; (fermer: volet, porte, trappe) to pull to,
  close; (: rideau) to draw; (choisir: carte, conclusion:
  Comm: chèque) to draw; (en faisant feu: balle, coup)
  to fire; (: animal) to shoot; (journal, livre, photo) to
  print; (Football: corner etc) to take ▶ vι (faire feu) to
  fire; (faire du tir, Football) to shoot; (cheminée) to
  draw; **se tirer** vι (fam) to push off; (aussi: **s'en
  tirer**: éviter le pire) to get off; (: survivre) to pull
  through; (: se débrouiller) to manage; (extraire):
  ~ qch de to take ou pull sth out of; to get sth out
  of; to extract sth from; **~ sur** (corde, poignée) to
  pull on ou at; (faire feu sur) to shoot ou fire at; (pipe)
  to draw on; (fig: avoisiner) to verge ou border on; **~
  six mètres** (Navig) to draw six metres of
  water; **~ son nom de** to take ou get its name
  from; **~ la langue** to stick out one's tongue;
  ~ qn de (embarras etc) to help ou get sb out of; **~ à
  l'arc/la carabine** to shoot with a bow and
  arrow/with a rifle; **~ en longueur** to drag on;
  ~ à sa fin to be drawing to an end; **~ qch au
  clair** to clear sth up; **~ au sort** to draw lots;
  ~ parti de to take advantage of; **~ profit de** to
  profit from; **~ les cartes** to read ou tell the
  cards
tiret [tiʀɛ] NM dash; (en fin de ligne) hyphen
tireur [tiʀœʀ] NM gunman; (Comm) drawer;
  bon ~ good shot; **~ d'élite** marksman; **~ de
  cartes** fortuneteller
tiroir [tiʀwaʀ] NM drawer
tiroir-caisse [tiʀwaʀkɛs] NM till
tisane [tizan] NF herb tea
tison [tizɔ̃] NM brand
tisonner [tizɔne] /1/ vт to poke
tisonnier [tizɔnje] NM poker
tissage [tisaʒ] NM weaving no pl
tisser [tise] /1/ vт to weave
tisserand, e [tisʀɑ̃, -ɑ̃d] NM/F weaver
tissu¹ [tisy] NM fabric, material, cloth no pl; (fig)
  fabric; (Anat, Bio) tissue; **~ de mensonges** web
  of lies
tissu², e [tisy] ADJ: **~ de** woven through with
tissu-éponge [tisyepɔ̃ʒ] NM (terry) towelling no
  pl
titane [titan] NM titanium
titanesque [titanɛsk] ADJ titanic
titiller [titile] /1/ vт to titillate
titrage [titʀaʒ] NM (d'un film) titling; (d'un alcool)
  determination of alcohol content
titre [titʀ] NM (gén) title; (de journal) headline;
  (diplôme) qualification; (Comm) security;
  (Chimie) titre; **en ~** (champion, responsable) official,
  recognized; **à juste ~** with just cause, rightly;
  à quel ~? on what grounds?; **à aucun ~** on no
  account; **au même ~ (que)** in the same way
  (as); **au ~ de la coopération** etc in the name of
  cooperation etc; **à ~ d'exemple** as an ou by way

of an example; **à ~ exceptionnel** exceptionally;
  à ~ d'information for (your) information; **à ~
  gracieux** free of charge; **à ~ d'essai** on a trial
  basis; **à ~ privé** in a private capacity; **~ courant**
  running head; **~ de propriété** title deed; **~ de
  transport** ticket
titré, e [titʀe] ADJ (livre, film) entitled; (personne)
  titled
titrer [titʀe] /1/ vт (Chimie) to titrate; to assay;
  (Presse) to run as a headline; (vin): **~ 10°** to be 10°
  proof
titubant, e [titybɑ̃, -ɑ̃t] ADJ staggering, reeling
tituber [titybe] /1/ vι to stagger ou reel (along)
titulaire [titylɛʀ] ADJ (Admin) appointed, with
  tenure ▶ NMF (Admin) incumbent; (de permis)
  holder; **être ~ de** (diplôme, permis) to hold
titularisation [titylaʀizasjɔ̃] NF granting of
  tenure
titulariser [titylaʀize] /1/ vт to give tenure to
TNP SIGLE M = **Théâtre national populaire**
TNT SIGLE M (= Trinitrotoluène) TNT ▶ SIGLE F
  (= Télévision numérique terrestre) digital television
toast [tost] NM slice ou piece of toast; (de
  bienvenue) (welcoming) toast; **porter un ~ à qn**
  to propose ou drink a toast to sb
toboggan [tɔbɔgɑ̃] NM toboggan; (jeu) slide;
  (Auto) flyover (BRIT), overpass (US); **~ de secours**
  (Aviat) escape chute
toc [tɔk] NM: **en toc** imitation cpd ▶ EXCL: **toc,
  toc** knock knock
tocsin [tɔksɛ̃] NM alarm (bell)
toge [tɔʒ] NF toga; (de juge) gown
Togo [tɔgo] NM: **le ~** Togo
togolais, e [tɔgɔlɛ, -ɛz] ADJ Togolese
tohu-bohu [tɔybɔy] NM (désordre) confusion;
  (tumulte) commotion
toi [twa] PRON you; **~, tu l'as fait?** did YOU do
  it?
toile [twal] NF (matériau) cloth no pl; (bâche) piece
  of canvas; (tableau) canvas; **grosse ~** canvas;
  de ou **en ~** (pantalon) cotton; (sac) canvas; **tisser
  sa ~** (araignée) to spin its web; **~ d'araignée**
  spider's web; (au plafond etc: à enlever) cobweb; **la
  T~** (Internet) the Web; **~ cirée** oilcloth; **~ émeri**
  emery cloth; **~ de fond** (fig) backdrop; **~ de jute**
  hessian; **~ de lin** linen; **~ de tente** canvas
toilettage [twalɛtaʒ] NM grooming no pl; (d'un
  texte) tidying up
toilette [twalɛt] NF wash; (s'habiller et se préparer)
  getting ready, washing and dressing; (habits)
  outfit; dress no pl; **toilettes** NFPL toilet sg; **les
  toilettes des dames/messieurs** the ladies'/
  gents' (toilets) (BRIT), the ladies'/men's
  (rest)room (US); **faire sa ~** to have a wash, get
  washed; **faire la ~ de** (animal) to groom; (voiture
  etc) to clean, wash; (texte) to tidy up; **articles de
  ~** toiletries; **~ intime** personal hygiene
toi-même [twamɛm] PRON yourself
toise [twaz] NF: **passer à la ~** to have one's
  height measured
toiser [twaze] /1/ vт to eye up and down
toison [twazɔ̃] NF (de mouton) fleece; (cheveux)
  mane
toit [twa] NM roof; **~ ouvrant** sun roof

toiture [twatyʀ] NF roof

Tokyo [tɔkjo] N Tokyo

tôle [tol] NF sheet metal *no pl*; *(plaque)* steel *(ou* iron*)* sheet; **tôles** NFPL *(carrosserie)* bodywork *sg* (BRIT), body *sg*; panels; ~ **d'acier** sheet steel *no pl*; ~ **ondulée** corrugated iron

Tolède [tɔlɛd] N Toledo

tolérable [tɔleʀabl] ADJ tolerable, bearable

tolérance [tɔleʀɑ̃s] NF tolerance; *(hors taxe)* allowance

tolérant, e [tɔleʀɑ̃, -ɑ̃t] ADJ tolerant

tolérer [tɔleʀe] /6/ VT to tolerate; *(Admin: hors taxe etc)* to allow

tôlerie [tolʀi] NF sheet metal manufacture; *(atelier)* sheet metal workshop; *(ensemble des tôles)* panels *pl*

tollé [tɔle] NM: **un ~ (de protestations)** a general outcry

TOM [tɔm] SIGLE NM(PL) = **territoire(s) d'outre-mer**

tomate [tɔmat] NF tomato; **tomates farcies** stuffed tomatoes

tombal, e [tɔ̃bal] ADJ: **pierre ~** tombstone, gravestone

tombant, e [tɔ̃bɑ̃, -ɑ̃t] ADJ *(fig)* drooping, sloping

tombe [tɔ̃b] NF *(sépulture)* grave; *(avec monument)* tomb

tombeau, x [tɔ̃bo] NM tomb; **à ~ ouvert** at breakneck speed

tombée [tɔ̃be] NF: **à la ~ du jour** *ou* **de la nuit** at the close of day, at nightfall

tomber [tɔ̃be] /1/ VI to fall; *(fièvre, vent)* to drop ▶ VT: ~ **la veste** to slip off one's jacket; **laisser ~** *(objet)* to drop; *(personne)* to let down; *(activité)* to give up; **laisse ~!** forget it!; **faire ~** to knock over; ~ **sur** VT *(rencontrer)* to come across; *(attaquer)* to set about; ~ **de fatigue/sommeil** to drop from exhaustion/be falling asleep on one's feet; **à l'eau** *(fig: projet etc)* to fall through; ~ **en panne** to break down; ~ **juste** *(opération, calcul)* to come out right; ~ **en ruine** to fall into ruins; **ça tombe bien/mal** *(fig)* that's come at the right/wrong time; **il est bien/mal tombé** *(fig)* he's been lucky/unlucky

tombereau, x [tɔ̃bʀo] NM tipcart

tombeur [tɔ̃bœʀ] NM *(péj)* Casanova

tombola [tɔ̃bɔla] NF raffle

Tombouctou [tɔ̃buktu] N Timbuktu

tome [tɔm] NM volume

tommette [tɔmɛt] NF hexagonal floor tile

ton¹, ta [tɔ̃, ta] *(pl* **tes** [te]*)* ADJ POSS your

ton² [tɔ̃] NM *(gén)* tone; *(Mus)* key; *(couleur)* shade, tone; *(de la voix: hauteur)* pitch; **donner le ~** to set the tone; **élever** *ou* **hausser le ~** to raise one's voice; **de bon ~** in good taste; **si vous le prenez sur ce ~** if you're going to take it like that; ~ **sur ~** in matching shades

tonal, e [tɔnal] ADJ tonal

tonalité [tɔnalite] NF *(au téléphone)* dialling tone; *(Mus)* tonality; *(: ton)* key; *(fig)* tone

tondeuse [tɔ̃døz] NF *(à gazon)* (lawn)mower; *(du coiffeur)* clippers *pl*; *(pour la tonte)* shears *pl*

tondre [tɔ̃dʀ] /41/ VT *(pelouse, herbe)* to mow; *(haie)* to cut, clip; *(mouton, toison)* to shear; *(cheveux)* to crop

tondu, e [tɔ̃dy] PP *de* **tondre** ▶ ADJ *(cheveux)* cropped; *(mouton, crâne)* shorn

Tonga [tɔ̃ga] NM: **les îles ~** Tonga

tongs [tɔ̃g] NFPL flip-flops (BRIT), thongs (US)

tonicité [tɔnisite] NF *(Méd: des tissus)* tone; *(fig: de l'air, la mer)* bracing effect

tonifiant, e [tɔnifjɑ̃, -ɑ̃t] ADJ invigorating, revivifying

tonifier [tɔnifje] /7/ VT *(air, eau)* to invigorate; *(peau, organisme)* to tone up

tonique [tɔnik] ADJ fortifying; *(personne)* dynamic ▶ NMF tonic

tonitruant, e [tɔnitʀyɑ̃, -ɑ̃t] ADJ: **voix ~** thundering voice

Tonkin [tɔ̃kɛ̃] NM: **le ~** Tonkin, Tongking

tonkinois, e [tɔ̃kinwa, -waz] ADJ Tonkinese

tonnage [tɔnaʒ] NM tonnage

tonnant, e [tɔnɑ̃, -ɑ̃t] ADJ thunderous

tonne [tɔn] NF metric ton, tonne

tonneau, x [tɔno] NM *(à vin, cidre)* barrel; *(Navig)* ton; **faire des ~** *(voiture, avion)* to roll over

tonnelet [tɔnlɛ] NM keg

tonnelier [tɔnəlje] NM cooper

tonnelle [tɔnɛl] NF bower, arbour (BRIT), arbor (US)

tonner [tɔne] /1/ VI to thunder; *(parler avec véhémence)*: ~ **contre qn/qch** to inveigh against sb/sth; **il tonne** it is thundering, there's some thunder

tonnerre [tɔnɛʀ] NM thunder; **coup de ~** *(fig)* thunderbolt, bolt from the blue; **un ~ d'applaudissements** thunderous applause; **du ~** *adj (fam)* terrific

tonsure [tɔ̃syʀ] NF bald patch; *(de moine)* tonsure

tonte [tɔ̃t] NF shearing

tonton [tɔ̃tɔ̃] NM uncle

tonus [tɔnys] NM energy; *(des muscles)* tone; *(d'une personne)* dynamism

top [tɔp] NM: **au troisième ~** at the third stroke ▶ ADJ INV: ~ **secret** top secret ▶ EXCL go!

topaze [tɔpaz] NF topaz

toper [tɔpe] /1/ VI: **tope-/topez-là** it's a deal!, you're on!

topinambour [tɔpinɑ̃buʀ] NM Jerusalem artichoke

topo [tɔpo] NM *(discours, exposé)* talk; *(fam)* spiel

topographie [tɔpɔgʀafi] NF topography

topographique [tɔpɔgʀafik] ADJ topographical

toponymie [tɔpɔnimi] NF study of place names, toponymy

toquade [tɔkad] NF fad, craze

toque [tɔk] NF *(de fourrure)* fur hat; ~ **de jockey/juge** jockey's/judge's cap; ~ **de cuisinier** chef's hat

toqué, e [tɔke] ADJ *(fam)* touched, cracked

torche [tɔʀʃ] NF torch; **se mettre en ~** *(parachute)* to candle

torcher [tɔʀʃe] /1/ VT *(fam)* to wipe

torchère [tɔʀʃɛʀ] NF flare

torchon [tɔʀʃɔ̃] NM cloth, duster; (à vaisselle) tea towel ou cloth

tordre [tɔʀdʀ] /41/ VT (chiffon) to wring; (barre, fig: visage) to twist; **se tordre** VI (barre) to bend; (roue) to twist, buckle; (ver, serpent) to writhe; **se tordre le poignet/la cheville** to twist one's wrist/ankle; **se tordre de douleur/rire** to writhe in pain/be doubled up with laughter

tordu, e [tɔʀdy] PP de **tordre** ▶ ADJ (fig) warped, twisted; (fig) crazy

torero [tɔʀeʀo] NM bullfighter

tornade [tɔʀnad] NF tornado

toron [tɔʀɔ̃] NM strand (of rope)

Toronto [tɔʀɔ̃to] N Toronto

torontois, e [tɔʀɔ̃twa, -waz] ADJ Torontonian ▶ NM/F: **T~, e** Torontonian

torpeur [tɔʀpœʀ] NF torpor, drowsiness

torpille [tɔʀpij] NF torpedo

torpiller [tɔʀpije] /1/ VT to torpedo

torpilleur [tɔʀpijœʀ] NM torpedo boat

torréfaction [tɔʀefaksjɔ̃] NF roasting

torréfier [tɔʀefje] /7/ VT to roast

torrent [tɔʀɑ̃] NM torrent, mountain stream; (fig): **un ~ de** a torrent ou flood of; **il pleut à torrents** the rain is lashing down

torrentiel, le [tɔʀɑ̃sjɛl] ADJ torrential

torride [tɔʀid] ADJ torrid

tors, e [tɔʀ, tɔʀs(ə)] ADJ twisted

torsade [tɔʀsad] NF twist; (Archit) cable moulding (BRIT) ou molding (US); **un pull à torsades** a cable sweater

torsader [tɔʀsade] /1/ VT to twist

torse [tɔʀs] NM chest; (Anat, Sculpture) torso; (poitrine) chest; **~ nu** stripped to the waist

torsion [tɔʀsjɔ̃] NF (action) twisting; (Tech, Physique) torsion

tort [tɔʀ] NM (défaut) fault; (préjudice) wrong no pl; **torts** NMPL (Jur) fault sg; **avoir ~** to be wrong; **être dans son ~** to be in the wrong; **donner ~ à qn** to lay the blame on sb; (fig) to prove sb wrong; **causer du ~ à** to harm; to be harmful ou detrimental to; **en ~** in the wrong, at fault; **à ~** wrongly; **à ~ ou à raison** rightly or wrongly; **à ~ et à travers** wildly

torte [tɔʀt] ADJ F voir **tors**

torticolis [tɔʀtikɔli] NM stiff neck

tortiller [tɔʀtije] /1/ VT (corde, mouchoir) to twist; (doigts) to twiddle; (moustache) to twirl; **se tortiller** VI to wriggle, squirm; (en dansant) to wiggle

tortionnaire [tɔʀsjɔnɛʀ] NM torturer

tortue [tɔʀty] NF tortoise; (fig) slowcoach (BRIT), slowpoke (US); (d'eau douce) terrapin; (d'eau de mer) turtle

tortueux, -euse [tɔʀtɥø, -øz] ADJ (rue) twisting; (fig) tortuous

torture [tɔʀtyʀ] NF torture

torturer [tɔʀtyʀe] /1/ VT to torture; (fig) to torment

torve [tɔʀv] ADJ: **regard ~** menacing ou grim look

toscan, e [tɔskɑ̃, -an] ADJ Tuscan

Toscane [tɔskan] NF: **la ~** Tuscany

tôt [to] ADV early; **~ ou tard** sooner or later; **si ~** so early; (déjà) so soon; **au plus ~** at the earliest, as soon as possible; **plus ~** earlier; **il eut ~ fait de faire ...** he soon did ...

total, e, -aux [tɔtal, -o] ADJ, NM total; **au ~** in total ou all; (fig) all in all, on the whole; **faire le ~** to work out the total

totalement [tɔtalmɑ̃] ADV totally, completely

totalisateur [tɔtalizatœʀ] NM adding machine

totaliser [tɔtalize] /1/ VT to total (up)

totalitaire [tɔtalitɛʀ] ADJ totalitarian

totalitarisme [tɔtalitaʀism] NM totalitarianism

totalité [tɔtalite] NF: **la ~ de**: **la ~ des élèves** all (of) the pupils; **la ~ de la population/classe** the whole population/class; **en ~** entirely

totem [tɔtɛm] NM totem

toubib [tubib] NM (fam) doctor

touchant, e [tuʃɑ̃, -ɑ̃t] ADJ touching

touche [tuʃ] NF (de piano, de machine à écrire) key; (de violon) fingerboard; (de télécommande etc) key, button; (de téléphone) button; (Peinture etc) stroke, touch; (fig: de couleur, nostalgie) touch, hint; (Rugby) line-out; (Football: aussi: **remise en touche**) throw-in; (aussi: **ligne de touche**) touch-line; (Escrime) hit; **en ~** in (ou into) touch; **avoir une drôle de ~** to look a sight; **~ de commande/de fonction/de retour** (Inform) control/function/return key; **~ dièse** (de téléphone, clavier) hash key; **~ à effleurement** ou **sensitive** touch-sensitive control ou key

touche-à-tout [tuʃatu] NM INV (péj: gén: enfant) meddler; (: fig: inventeur etc) dabbler

toucher [tuʃe] /1/ NM touch ▶ VT to touch; (palper) to feel; (atteindre: d'un coup de feu etc) to hit; (affecter) to touch, affect; (concerner) to concern, affect; (contacter) to reach, contact; (recevoir: récompense) to receive, get; (: salaire) to draw, get; (chèque) to cash; (aborder: problème, sujet) to touch on; **au ~** to the touch; by the feel; **se toucher** (être en contact) to touch; **~ à** to touch; (modifier) to touch, tamper ou meddle with; (traiter de, concerner) to have to do with, concern; **je vais lui en ~ un mot** I'll have a word with him about it; **~ au but** (fig) to near one's goal; **~ à sa fin** to be drawing to a close

touffe [tuf] NF tuft

touffu, e [tufy] ADJ thick, dense; (fig) complex, involved

toujours [tuʒuʀ] ADV always; (encore) still; (constamment) forever; **depuis ~** always; **essaie ~ (you can) try anyway; **pour ~** forever; **~ est-il que** the fact remains that; **~ plus** more and more

toulonnais, e [tulɔnɛ, -ɛz] ADJ of ou from Toulon

toulousain, e [tuluzɛ̃, -ɛn] ADJ of ou from Toulouse

toupet [tupɛ] NM quiff (BRIT), tuft; (fam) nerve, cheek (BRIT)

toupie [tupi] NF (spinning) top

tour [tuʀ] NF tower; (immeuble) high-rise block (BRIT) ou building (US), tower block (BRIT); (Échecs) castle, rook ▶ NM (excursion: à pied) stroll, walk; (: en voiture etc) run, ride; (: plus long) trip; (Sport: aussi: **tour de piste**) lap; (d'être servi ou de *jouer etc, tournure, de vis ou clef*) turn; (*de roue etc*) revolution; (*Pol: aussi*: **tour de scrutin**) ballot; (*ruse, de prestidigitation, de cartes*) trick; (*de potier*) wheel; (*à bois, métaux*) lathe; (*circonférence*): **de 3 m de ~** 3 m round, with a circumference *ou* girth of 3 m; **faire le ~ de** to go (a)round; (*à pied*) to walk (a)round; (*fig*) to review; **faire le ~ de l'Europe** to tour Europe; **faire un ~** to go for a walk; (*en voiture etc*) to go for a ride; **faire 2 tours** to go (a)round twice; (*hélice etc*) to turn *ou* revolve twice; **fermer à double ~** *vi* to double-lock the door; **c'est au ~ de Renée** it's Renée's turn; **à ~ de rôle, ~ à ~** in turn; **à ~ de bras** with all one's strength; (*fig*) non-stop, relentlessly; **~ de taille/tête** waist/head measurement; **~ de chant** *nm* song recital; **~ de contrôle** *nf* control tower; **la ~ Eiffel** the Eiffel Tower; **le T~ de France** the Tour de France; *see note*; **~ de force** *nm* tour de force; **~ de garde** *nm* spell of duty; **un 33 tours** an LP; **un 45 tours** a single; **~ d'horizon** *nm* (*fig*) general survey; **~ de lit** *nm* valance; **~ de main** *nm* dexterity, knack; **en un ~ de main** (as) quick as a flash; **~ de passe-passe** *nm* trick, sleight of hand; **~ de reins** *nm* sprained back

> The *Tour de France* is an annual road race for professional cyclists. It takes about three weeks to complete and is divided into daily stages, or *étapes* of approximately 175km (110 miles) over terrain of varying levels of difficulty. The leading cyclist wears a yellow jersey, the *maillot jaune*. The route varies; it is not usually confined to France but always ends in Paris. In addition, there are a number of time trials.

tourangeau, -elle, x [turɑ̃ʒo, -ɛl] ADJ (*de la région*) of *ou* from Touraine; (*de la ville*) of *ou* from Tours

tourbe [turb] NF peat

tourbière [turbjɛr] NF peat-bog

tourbillon [turbijɔ̃] NM whirlwind; (*d'eau*) whirlpool; (*fig*) whirl, swirl

tourbillonner [turbijɔne] /1/ VI to whirl, swirl; (*objet, personne*) to whirl *ou* twirl round

tourelle [turɛl] NF turret

tourisme [turism] NM tourism; **agence de ~** tourist agency; **avion/voiture de ~** private plane/car; **faire du ~** to go touring; (*en ville*) to go sightseeing

touriste [turist] NMF tourist

touristique [turistik] ADJ tourist *cpd*; (*région*) touristic (*péj*), with tourist appeal

tourment [turmɑ̃] NM torment

tourmente [turmɑ̃t] NF storm

tourmenté, e [turmɑ̃te] ADJ tormented, tortured; (*mer, période*) turbulent

tourmenter [turmɑ̃te] /1/ VT to torment; **se tourmenter** VI to fret, worry o.s.

tournage [turnaʒ] NM (*d'un film*) shooting

tournant, e [turnɑ̃, -ɑ̃t] ADJ (*feu, scène*) revolving; (*chemin*) winding; (*escalier*) spiral *cpd*; (*mouvement*) circling ▸ NM (*de route*) bend (BRIT), curve (US); (*fig*) turning point; *voir* **plaque**; **grève**

tourné, e [turne] ADJ (*lait, vin*) sour, off; (*Menuiserie: bois*) turned; **bien ~** (*compliment*) well-phrased; (*femme*) shapely; **mal ~** (*lettre*) badly expressed; **avoir l'esprit mal ~** to have a dirty mind

tournebroche [turnəbrɔʃ] NM roasting spit

tourne-disque [turnədisk] NM record player

tournedos [turnədo] NM tournedos

tournée [turne] NF (*du facteur etc*) round; (*d'artiste, politicien*) tour; (*au café*) round (of drinks); **faire la ~ de** to go (a)round

tournemain [turnəmɛ̃]: **en un ~** *adv* in a flash

tourner [turne] /1/ VT to turn; (*sauce, mélange*) to stir; (*contourner*) to get (a)round; (*Ciné: faire les prises de vues*) to shoot; (*: produire*) to make ▸ VI to turn; (*moteur*) to run; (*compteur*) to tick away; (*lait etc*) to turn (sour); (*fig: chance, vie*) to turn out; **se tourner** VI to turn (a)round; **se tourner vers** to turn to; to turn towards; **bien ~** to turn out well; **mal ~** to go wrong; **~ autour de** to go (a)round; (*planète*) to revolve (a)round; (*péj*) to hang (a)round; **~ autour du pot** (*fig*) to go (a)round in circles; **~ à/en** to turn into; **~ à la pluie/au rouge** to turn rainy/red; **~ en ridicule** to ridicule; **~ le dos à** (*mouvement*) to turn one's back on; (*position*) to have one's back to; **~ court** to come to a sudden end; **se tourner les pouces** to twiddle one's thumbs; **~ la tête** to look away; **~ la tête à qn** (*fig*) to go to sb's head; **~ de l'œil** to pass out; **~ la page** (*fig*) to turn the page

tournesol [turnəsɔl] NM sunflower

tourneur [turnœr] NM turner; lathe-operator

tournevis [turnəvis] NM screwdriver

tourniquer [turnike] /1/ VI to go (a)round in circles

tourniquet [turnikɛ] NM (*pour arroser*) sprinkler; (*portillon*) turnstile; (*présentoir*) revolving stand, spinner; (*Chirurgie*) tourniquet

tournis [turni] NM: **avoir/donner le ~** to feel/make dizzy

tournoi [turnwa] NM tournament

tournoyer [turnwaje] /8/ VI (*oiseau*) to wheel (a)round; (*fumée*) to swirl (a)round

tournure [turnyr] NF (*Ling: syntaxe*) turn of phrase; form; (*d'une phrase*) phrasing; **la ~ de qch** (*évolution*) the way sth is developing; (*aspect*) the look of sth; **la ~ des événements** the turn of events; **prendre ~** to take shape; **~ d'esprit** turn *ou* cast of mind

tour-opérateur [turɔperatœr] NM tour operator

tourte [turt] NF pie

tourteau, x [turto] NM (*Agr*) oilcake, cattle-cake; (*Zool*) edible crab

tourtereaux [turtəro] NMPL lovebirds

tourterelle [turtərɛl] NF turtledove

tourtière [turtjɛr] NF pie dish *ou* plate

tous [tu, tus] ADJ, PRON *voir* **tout**

Toussaint [tusɛ̃] NF: **la ~** All Saints' Day; *see note*

> *La Toussaint*, 1 November, or All Saints' Day, is a public holiday in France. People traditionally visit the graves of friends and relatives to lay chrysanthemums on them.

tousser [tuse] /1/ VI to cough
toussoter [tusɔte] /1/ VI to have a slight cough; (*pour avertir*) to give a slight cough

[MOT-CLÉ]

tout, e [tu, tut] (*mpl* **tous** [tus], *fpl* **toutes** [tut])
ADJ **1** (*avec article singulier*) all; **tout le lait** all the milk; **toute la nuit** all night, the whole night; **tout le livre** the whole book; **tout un pain** a whole loaf; **tout le temps** all the time, the whole time; **c'est tout le contraire** it's quite the opposite; **c'est toute une affaire** *ou* **histoire** it's quite a business, it's a whole rigmarole
2 (*avec article pluriel*) every, all; **tous les livres** all the books; **toutes les nuits** every night; **toutes les fois** every time; **toutes les trois/deux semaines** every third/other *ou* second week, every three/two weeks; **tous les deux** both *ou* each of us (*ou* them *ou* you); **toutes les trois** all three of us (*ou* them *ou* you)
3 (*sans article*): **à tout âge** at any age; **pour toute nourriture, il avait ...** his only food was ...; **de tous côtés, de toutes parts** from everywhere, from every side
▶ PRON everything, all; **il a tout fait** he's done everything; **je les vois tous** I can see them all *ou* all of them; **nous y sommes tous allés** all of us went, we all went; **c'est tout** that's all; **en tout** in all; **en tout et pour tout** all in all; **tout ce qu'il sait** all he knows; **c'était tout ce qu'il y a de chic** it was the last word *ou* the ultimate in chic
▶ NM whole; **le tout** all of it (*ou* them); **le tout est de ...** the main thing is to ...; **pas du tout** not at all; **elle a tout d'une mère/d'une intrigante** she's a real *ou* true mother/schemer; **du tout au tout** utterly
▶ ADV **1** (*très, complètement*) very; **tout près** *ou* **à côté** very near; **le tout premier** the very first; **tout seul** all alone; **il était tout rouge** he was really *ou* all red; **parler tout bas** to speak very quietly; **le livre tout entier** the whole book; **tout en haut** right at the top; **tout droit** straight ahead
2: tout en while; **tout en travaillant** while working, as he *etc* works
3: tout d'abord first of all; **tout à coup** suddenly; **tout à fait** absolutely; **tout à fait!** exactly!; **tout à l'heure** a short while ago; (*futur*) in a short while, shortly; **à tout à l'heure!** see you later!; **il répondit tout court que non** he just answered no (and that was all); **tout de même** all the same; **tout le monde** everybody; **tout ou rien** all or nothing; **tout simplement** quite simply; **tout de suite** immediately, straight away

tout-à-l'égout [tutalegu] NM INV mains drainage
toutefois [tutfwa] ADV however
toutes [tut] ADJ, PRON *voir* **tout**
toutou [tutu] NM (*fam*) doggie
tout-petit [tup(ə)ti] NM toddler

tout-puissant, toute-puissante [tupɥisɑ̃, tutpɥisɑ̃t] ADJ all-powerful, omnipotent
tout-terrain [tuterɛ̃] ADJ INV: **vélo** ~ mountain bike; **véhicule** ~ four-wheel drive
tout-venant [tuvnɑ̃] NM: **le** ~ everyday stuff
toux [tu] NF cough
toxémie [tɔksemi] NF toxaemia (BRIT), toxemia (US)
toxicité [tɔksisite] NF toxicity
toxicologie [tɔksikɔlɔʒi] NF toxicology
toxicomane [tɔksikɔman] NMF drug addict
toxicomanie [tɔksikɔmani] NF drug addiction
toxine [tɔksin] NF toxin
toxique [tɔksik] ADJ toxic, poisonous
toxoplasmose [tɔksoplasmoz] NF toxoplasmosis
TP SIGLE MPL = **travaux pratiques**; **travaux publics** ▶ SIGLE M = **trésor (public)**
TPG SIGLE M = **Trésorier-payeur général**
tps ABR = **temps**
trac [trak] NM (*aux examens*) nerves *pl*; (*Théât*) stage fright; **avoir le** ~ (*aux examens*) to get an attack of nerves; (*Théât*) to have stage fright; **tout à** ~ all of a sudden
traçant, e [trasɑ̃, -ɑ̃t] ADJ: **table** ~ (*Inform*) (graph) plotter
tracas [traka] NM bother *no pl*, worry *no pl*
tracasser [trakase] /1/ VT to worry, bother; (*harceler*) to harass; **se tracasser** VI to worry (o.s.), fret
tracasserie [trakasri] NF annoyance *no pl*; harassment *no pl*
tracassier, -ière [trakasje, -jɛr] ADJ irksome
trace [tras] NF (*empreintes*) tracks *pl*; (*marques: fig*) mark; (*restes, vestige*) trace; (*indice*) sign; (*aussi:* **suivre à la trace**) to track; **traces de pas** footprints
tracé [trase] NM (*contour*) line; (*plan*) layout
tracer [trase] /3/ VT to draw; (*mot*) to trace; (*piste*) to open up; (*fig: chemin*) to show
traceur [trasœr] NM (*Inform*) plotter
trachée [trase], **trachée-artère** [traseartɛr] NF windpipe, trachea
trachéite [trakeit] NF tracheitis
tract [trakt] NM tract, pamphlet; (*publicitaire*) handout
tractations [traktasjɔ̃] NFPL dealings, bargaining *sg*
tracter [trakte] /1/ VT to tow
tracteur [traktœr] NM tractor
traction [traksjɔ̃] NF traction; (*Gym*) pull-up; ~ **avant/arrière** front-wheel/rear-wheel drive; ~ **électrique** electric(al) traction *ou* haulage
trad. ABR (= *traduit*) translated; (= *traduction*) translation; (= *traducteur*) translator
tradition [tradisjɔ̃] NF tradition
traditionalisme [tradisjɔnalism] NM traditionalism
traditionaliste [tradisjɔnalist] ADJ, NMF traditionalist
traditionnel, le [tradisjɔnɛl] ADJ traditional
traditionnellement [tradisjɔnɛlmɑ̃] ADV traditionally

t

traducteur, -trice [tʀadyktœʀ, -tʀis] NM/F translator

traduction [tʀadyksjɔ̃] NF translation

traduire [tʀadɥiʀ] **/38/** VT to translate; (*exprimer*) to convey, render; **se ~ par** to find expression in; **~ en français** to translate into French; **~ en justice** to bring before the courts

traduis *etc* [tʀadɥi] VB *voir* **traduire**

traduisible [tʀadɥizibl] ADJ translatable

traduit, e [tʀadɥi, -it] PP *de* **traduire**

trafic [tʀafik] NM traffic; **~ d'armes** arms dealing; **~ de drogue** drug peddling

trafiquant, e [tʀafikɑ̃, -ɑ̃t] NM/F trafficker; (*d'armes*) dealer

trafiquer [tʀafike] **/1/** VT (*péj: vin*) to doctor; (: *moteur, document*) to tamper with ▶ VI to traffic, be engaged in trafficking

tragédie [tʀaʒedi] NF tragedy

tragédien, ne [tʀaʒedjɛ̃, -ɛn] NM/F tragedian/tragedienne

tragi-comique [tʀaʒikomik] ADJ tragi-comic

tragique [tʀaʒik] ADJ tragic ▶ NM: **prendre qch au ~** to make a tragedy out of sth

tragiquement [tʀaʒikmɑ̃] ADV tragically

trahir [tʀaiʀ] **/2/** VT to betray; (*fig*) to give away, reveal; **se trahir** to betray o.s., give o.s. away

trahison [tʀaizɔ̃] NF betrayal; (*Jur*) treason

traie *etc* [tʀɛ] VB *voir* **traire**

train [tʀɛ̃] NM (*Rail*) train; (*allure*) pace; (*fig: ensemble*) set; **être en ~ de faire qch** to be doing sth; **mettre qch en ~** to get sth under way; **mettre qn en ~** to put sb in good spirits; **se mettre en ~** (*commencer*) to get started; (*faire de la gymnastique*) to warm up; **se sentir en ~** to feel in good form; **aller bon ~** to make good progress; **~ avant/arrière** front-wheel/rear-wheel axle unit; **~ à grande vitesse** high-speed train; **~ d'atterrissage** undercarriage; **~ autos-couchettes** car-sleeper train; **~ électrique** (*jouet*) (electric) train set; **~ de pneus** set of tyres *ou* tires; **~ de vie** style of living

traînailler [tʀɛnaje] **/1/** VI = **traînasser**

traînant, e [tʀɛnɑ̃, -ɑ̃t] ADJ (*voix, ton*) drawling

traînard, e [tʀɛnaʀ, -aʀd] NM/F (*péj*) slowcoach (BRIT), slowpoke (US)

traînasser [tʀɛnase] **/1/** VI to dawdle

traîne [tʀɛn] NF (*de robe*) train; **être à la ~** to be in tow; (*en arrière*) to lag behind; (*en désordre*) to be lying around

traîneau, x [tʀɛno] NM sleigh, sledge

traînée [tʀene] NF streak, trail; (*péj*) slut

traîner [tʀene] **/1/** VT (*remorque*) to pull; (*enfant, chien*) to drag *ou* trail along; (*maladie*): **il traîne un rhume depuis l'hiver** he has a cold which has been dragging on since winter ▶ VI (*robe, manteau*) to trail; (*être en désordre*) to lie around; (*marcher lentement*) to dawdle (along); (*vagabonder*) to hang about; (*agir lentement*) to idle about; (*durer*) to drag on; **se traîner** VI (*ramper*) to crawl along; (*marcher avec difficulté*) to drag o.s. along; (*durer*) to drag on; **se traîner par terre** to crawl (on the ground); **~ qn au cinéma** to drag sb to the cinema; **~ les pieds** to drag one's feet; **~ par terre** to trail on the ground; **~ en longueur** to drag out

training [tʀɛniŋ] NM (*pull*) tracksuit top; (*chaussure*) trainer (BRIT), sneaker (US)

train-train [tʀɛ̃tʀɛ̃] NM humdrum routine

traire [tʀɛʀ] **/50/** VT to milk

trait, e [tʀɛ, -ɛt] PP *de* **traire** ▶ NM (*ligne*) line; (*de dessin*) stroke; (*caractéristique*) feature, trait; (*flèche*) dart, arrow; shaft; **traits** NMPL (*du visage*) features; **d'un ~** (*boire*) in one gulp; **de ~** *adj* (*animal*) draught (BRIT), draft (US); **avoir ~ à** to concern; **~ pour ~** line for line; **~ de caractère** characteristic, trait; **~ d'esprit** flash of wit; **~ de génie** brainwave; **~ d'union** hyphen; (*fig*) link

traitable [tʀɛtabl] ADJ (*personne*) accommodating; (*sujet*) manageable

traitant, e [tʀɛtɑ̃, -ɑ̃t] ADJ: **votre médecin ~** your usual *ou* family doctor; **shampooing ~** medicated shampoo; **crème ~** conditioning cream, conditioner

traite [tʀɛt] NF (*Comm*) draft; (*Agr*) milking; (*trajet*) stretch; **d'une (seule) ~** without stopping (once); **la ~ des noirs** the slave trade; **la ~ des blanches** the white slave trade

traité [tʀete] NM treaty

traitement [tʀɛtmɑ̃] NM treatment; processing; (*salaire*) salary; **suivre un ~** to undergo treatment; **mauvais ~** ill-treatment; **~ de données** *ou* **de l'information** (*Inform*) data processing; **~ hormono-supplétif** hormone replacement therapy; **~ par lots** (*Inform*) batch processing; **~ de texte** (*Inform*) word processing; (*logiciel*) word processing package

traiter [tʀete] **/1/** VT (*gén*) to treat; (*Tech: matériaux*) to process, treat; (*Inform*) to process; (*affaire*) to deal with, handle; (*qualifier*): **~ qn d'idiot** to call sb a fool ▶ VI to deal; **~ de** *vt* to deal with; **bien/mal ~** to treat well/ill-treat

traiteur [tʀɛtœʀ] NM caterer

traître, -esse [tʀɛtʀ, -tʀɛs] ADJ (*dangereux*) treacherous ▶ NM/F traitor (traitress); **prendre qn en ~** to make an insidious attack on sb

traîtrise [tʀɛtʀiz] NF treachery

trajectoire [tʀaʒɛktwaʀ] NF trajectory, path

trajet [tʀaʒɛ] NM (*parcours, voyage*) journey; (*itinéraire*) route; (*fig*) path, course; (*distance à parcourir*) distance; **il y a une heure de ~** the journey takes one hour

tralala [tʀalala] NM (*péj*) fuss

tram [tʀam] NM tram (BRIT), streetcar (US)

trame [tʀam] NF (*de tissu*) weft; (*fig*) framework; texture; (*Typo*) screen

tramer [tʀame] **/1/** VT to plot, hatch

trampoline [tʀɑ̃pɔlin], **trampolino** [tʀɑ̃polino] NM trampoline; (*Sport*) trampolining

tramway [tʀamwɛ] NM tram(way); (*voiture*) tram(car) (BRIT), streetcar (US)

tranchant, e [tʀɑ̃ʃɑ̃, -ɑ̃t] ADJ sharp; (*fig: personne*) peremptory; (: *couleurs*) striking ▶ NM (*d'un couteau*) cutting edge; (*de la main*) edge; **à double ~** (*argument, procédé*) double-edged

tranche [trɑ̃ʃ] NF (*morceau*) slice; (*arête*) edge; (*partie*) section; (*série*) block; (*d'impôts, revenus etc*) bracket; (*loterie*) issue; ~ **d'âge/de salaires** age/ wage bracket; ~ **(de silicium)** wafer

tranché, e [trɑ̃ʃe] ADJ (*couleurs*) distinct, sharply contrasted; (*opinions*) clear-cut, definite ▶ NF trench

trancher [trɑ̃ʃe] /1/ VT to cut, sever; (*fig: résoudre*) to settle ▶ VI to be decisive; (*entre deux choses*) to settle the argument; ~ **avec** to contrast sharply with

tranchet [trɑ̃ʃɛ] NM knife

tranchoir [trɑ̃ʃwar] NM chopper

tranquille [trɑ̃kil] ADJ calm, quiet; (*enfant, élève*) quiet; (*rassuré*) easy in one's mind, with one's mind at rest; **se tenir ~** (*enfant*) to be quiet; **avoir la conscience ~** to have an easy conscience; **laisse-moi/laisse-ça ~** leave me/ it alone

tranquillement [trɑ̃kilmɑ̃] ADV calmly

tranquillisant, e [trɑ̃kilizɑ̃, -ɑ̃t] ADJ (*nouvelle*) reassuring ▶ NM tranquillizer

tranquilliser [trɑ̃kilize] /1/ VT to reassure; **se tranquilliser** to calm (o.s.) down

tranquillité [trɑ̃kilite] NF quietness, peace (and quiet); **en toute ~** with complete peace of mind; ~ **d'esprit** peace of mind

transaction [trɑ̃zaksjɔ̃] NF (*Comm*) transaction, deal

transafricain, e [trɑ̃safrikɛ̃, -ɛn] ADJ transafrican

transalpin, e [trɑ̃zalpɛ̃, -in] ADJ transalpine

transaméricain, e [trɑ̃zamerikɛ̃, -ɛn] ADJ transamerican

transat [trɑ̃zat] NM deckchair ▶ NF = **course transatlantique**

transatlantique [trɑ̃zatlɑ̃tik] ADJ transatlantic ▶ NM transatlantic liner

transborder [trɑ̃sbɔrde] /1/ VT to tran(s)ship

transcendant, e [trɑ̃sɑ̃dɑ̃, -ɑ̃t] ADJ (*Philosophie, Math*) transcendental; (*supérieur*) transcendent

transcodeur [trɑ̃skɔdœr] NM compiler

transcontinental, e, -aux [trɑ̃skɔ̃tinɑtal, -o] ADJ transcontinental

transcription [trɑ̃skripsjɔ̃] NF transcription

transcrire [trɑ̃skrir] /39/ VT to transcribe

transe [trɑ̃s] NF: **entrer en ~** to go into a trance; **transes** NFPL agony *sg*

transférable [trɑ̃sferabl] ADJ transferable

transfèrement [trɑ̃sfɛrmɑ̃] NM transfer

transférer [trɑ̃sfere] /6/ VT to transfer

transfert [trɑ̃sfɛr] NM transfer

transfiguration [trɑ̃sfigyrasjɔ̃] NF transformation, transfiguration

transfigurer [trɑ̃sfigyre] /1/ VT to transform

transfo [trɑ̃sfo] NM (= *transformateur*) transformer

transformable [trɑ̃sfɔrmabl] ADJ convertible

transformateur [trɑ̃sfɔrmatœr] NM transformer

transformation [trɑ̃sfɔrmasjɔ̃] NF change, alteration; (*radicale*) transformation; (*Rugby*) conversion; **transformations** NFPL (*travaux*) alterations; **industries de ~** processing industries

transformer [trɑ̃sfɔrme] /1/ VT to change; (*radicalement*) to transform, alter ("*alter*" *implique un changement moins radical*); (*vêtement*) alter; (*matière première, appartement, Rugby*) to convert; ~ **en** to transform into; to turn into; to convert into; **se transformer** VI to be transformed; to alter

transfuge [trɑ̃sfyʒ] NM renegade

transfuser [trɑ̃sfyze] /1/ VT to transfuse

transfusion [trɑ̃sfyzjɔ̃] NF: ~ **sanguine** blood transfusion

transgénique [trɑ̃sʒenik] ADJ transgenic

transgresser [trɑ̃sgrese] /1/ VT to contravene, disobey

transhumance [trɑ̃zymɑ̃s] NF transhumance, seasonal move to new pastures

transi, e [trɑ̃zi] ADJ numb (with cold), chilled to the bone

transiger [trɑ̃ziʒe] /3/ VI to compromise, come to an agreement; ~ **sur** *ou* **avec qch** to compromise on sth

transistor [trɑ̃zistɔr] NM transistor

transistorisé, e [trɑ̃zistɔrize] ADJ transistorized

transit [trɑ̃zit] NM transit; **de ~** transit *cpd*; **en ~** in transit

transitaire [trɑ̃zitɛr] NMF forwarding agent

transiter [trɑ̃zite] /1/ VI to pass in transit

transitif, -ive [trɑ̃zitif, -iv] ADJ transitive

transition [trɑ̃zisjɔ̃] NF transition; **de ~** transitional

transitoire [trɑ̃zitwar] ADJ (*mesure, gouvernement*) transitional, provisional; (*fugitif*) transient

translucide [trɑ̃slysid] ADJ translucent

transmet *etc* [trɑ̃smɛ] VB *voir* **transmettre**

transmettais *etc* [trɑ̃smɛtɛ] VB *voir* **transmettre**

transmetteur [trɑ̃smɛtœr] NM transmitter

transmettre [trɑ̃smɛtr] /56/ VT (*passer*): ~ **qch à qn** to pass sth on to sb; (*Tech, Tél, Méd*) to transmit; (*TV, Radio: retransmettre*) to broadcast

transmis, e [trɑ̃smi, -iz] PP *de* **transmettre**

transmissible [trɑ̃smisibl] ADJ transmissible

transmission [trɑ̃smisjɔ̃] NF transmission, passing on; (*Auto*) transmission; **transmissions** NFPL (*Mil*) ≈ signals corps *sg*; ~ **de données** (*Inform*) data transmission; ~ **de pensée** thought transmission

transocéanien, ne [trɑ̃zɔseanjɛ̃, -ɛn], **transocéanique** [trɑ̃zɔseanik] ADJ transoceanic

transparaître [trɑ̃sparɛtr] /57/ VI to show (through)

transparence [trɑ̃sparɑ̃s] NF transparency; **par ~** (*regarder*) against the light; (*voir*) showing through

transparent, e [trɑ̃sparɑ̃, -ɑ̃t] ADJ transparent

transpercer [trɑ̃spɛrse] /3/ VT (*froid, pluie*) to go through, pierce; (*balle*) to go through

transpiration [trɑ̃spirasjɔ̃] NF perspiration

t

transpirer [tʀɑ̃spiʀe] /1/ vi to perspire; (*information, nouvelle*) to come to light

transplant [tʀɑ̃splɑ̃] NM transplant

transplantation [tʀɑ̃splɑ̃tasjɔ̃] NF transplant

transplanter [tʀɑ̃splɑ̃te] /1/ vt (*Méd, Bot*) to transplant; (*personne*) to uproot, move

transport [tʀɑ̃spɔʀ] NM transport; (*émotions*): ~ **de colère** fit of rage; ~ **de joie** transport of delight; ~ **de voyageurs/marchandises** passenger/goods transportation; **transports en commun** public transport sg; **transports routiers** haulage (*BRIT*), trucking (*US*)

transportable [tʀɑ̃spɔʀtabl] ADJ (*marchandises*) transportable; (*malade*) fit (enough) to be moved

transporter [tʀɑ̃spɔʀte] /1/ vt to carry, move; (*Comm*) to transport, convey; (*fig*): ~ **qn (de joie)** to send sb into raptures; **se ~ quelque part** (*fig*) to let one's imagination carry one away (somewhere)

transporteur [tʀɑ̃spɔʀtœʀ] NM haulage contractor (*BRIT*), trucker (*US*)

transposer [tʀɑ̃spoze] /1/ vt to transpose

transposition [tʀɑ̃spozisjɔ̃] NF transposition

transrhénan, e [tʀɑ̃sʀenɑ̃, -an] ADJ transrhenane

transsaharien, ne [tʀɑ̃ssaaʀjɛ̃, -ɛn] ADJ trans-Saharan

transsexuel, le [tʀɑ̃ssɛksɥɛl] ADJ, NM/F transsexual

transsibérien, ne [tʀɑ̃ssibeʀjɛ̃, -ɛn] ADJ trans-Siberian

transvaser [tʀɑ̃svaze] /1/ vt to decant

transversal, e, -aux [tʀɑ̃sveʀsal, -o] ADJ transverse, cross(-); (*route etc*) cross-country; (*mur, chemin, rue*) running at right angles; (*Auto*): **axe ~** main cross-country road (*BRIT*) *ou* highway (*US*); **coupe ~** cross section

transversalement [tʀɑ̃sveʀsalmɑ̃] ADV crosswise

trapèze [tʀapɛz] NM (*Géom*) trapezium; (*au cirque*) trapeze

trapéziste [tʀapezist] NMF trapeze artist

trappe [tʀap] NF (*de cave, grenier*) trap door; (*piège*) trap

trappeur [tʀapœʀ] NM trapper, fur trader

trapu, e [tʀapy] ADJ squat, stocky

traquenard [tʀaknaʀ] NM trap

traquer [tʀake] /1/ vt to track down; (*harceler*) to hound

traumatisant, e [tʀomatizɑ̃, -ɑ̃t] ADJ traumatic

traumatiser [tʀomatize] /1/ vt to traumatize

traumatisme [tʀomatism] NM traumatism

traumatologie [tʀomatɔlɔʒi] NF *branch of medicine concerned with accidents*

travail, -aux [tʀavaj, -o] NM (*gén*) work; (*tâche, métier*) work *no pl*, job; (*Écon, Méd*) labour (*BRIT*), labor (*US*); (*Inform*) job; **travaux** NMPL (*de réparation, agricoles etc*) work sg; (*sur route*) roadworks; (*de construction*) building (work) sg; **être/entrer en ~** (*Méd*) to be in/go into labour; **être sans ~** (*employé*) to be out of work, be unemployed; ~ **d'intérêt général** ≈ community service; ~ **(au) noir**

moonlighting; ~ **posté** shiftwork; **travaux des champs** farm work sg; **travaux dirigés** (*Scol*) supervised practical work sg; **travaux forcés** hard labour sg; **travaux manuels** (*Scol*) handicrafts; **travaux ménagers** housework sg; **travaux pratiques** (*gén*) practical work pl; (*en laboratoire*) lab work pl (*BRIT*), lab (*US*); **travaux publics** ≈ public works sg

travaillé, e [tʀavaje] ADJ (*style*) polished

travailler [tʀavaje] /1/ vi to work; (*bois*) to warp ▶ vt (*bois, métal*) to work; (*pâte*) to knead; (*objet d'art, discipline, fig: influencer*) to work on; **cela le travaille** it is on his mind; ~ **la terre** to work the land; ~ **son piano** to do one's piano practice; ~ **à** to work on; (*fig: contribuer à*) to work towards; ~ **à faire** to endeavour (*BRIT*) *ou* endeavor (*US*) to do

travailleur, -euse [tʀavajœʀ, -øz] ADJ hard-working ▶ NM/F worker; ~ **de force** labourer (*BRIT*), laborer (*US*); ~ **intellectuel** non-manual worker; ~ **social** social worker; **travailleuse familiale** home help

travailliste [tʀavajist] ADJ ≈ Labour cpd ▶ NMF member of the Labour party

travaux [tʀavo] NMPL *voir* **travail**

travée [tʀave] NF row; (*Archit*) bay; span

traveller's [tʀavlœʀs], **traveller's chèque** [tʀavlœʀsʃɛk] NM traveller's cheque

travelling [tʀavliŋ] NM (*chariot*) dolly; (*technique*) tracking; ~ **optique** zoom shots pl

travelo [tʀavlo] NM (*fam*) (drag) queen

travers [tʀavɛʀ] NM fault, failing ▶ ADV sideways; (*fig*) the wrong way; **en ~ (de)** across; **au ~ (de)** through; **de ~** adj (*nez, bouche*) crooked; (*chapeau*) askew; **à ~** through; **regarder de ~** (*fig*) to look askance at; **comprendre de ~** to misunderstand

traverse [tʀavɛʀs] NF (*de voie ferrée*) sleeper; **chemin de ~** shortcut

traversée [tʀavɛʀse] NF crossing

traverser [tʀavɛʀse] /1/ vt (*gén*) to cross; (*ville, tunnel: aussi: percer, fig*) to go through; (*ligne, trait*) to run across

traversin [tʀavɛʀsɛ̃] NM bolster

travesti [tʀavesti] NM (*comme mode de vie*) transvestite; (*artiste de cabaret*) female impersonator, drag artist; (*costume*) fancy dress

travestir [tʀavestiʀ] /2/ vt (*vérité*) to misrepresent; **se travestir** (*se costumer*) to dress up; (*artiste*) to put on drag; (*Psych*) to dress as a woman

trayais *etc* [tʀɛje] vB *voir* **traire**

trayeuse [tʀɛjøz] NF milking machine

trébucher [tʀebyʃe] /1/ vi: ~ **(sur)** to stumble (over), trip (over)

trèfle [tʀɛfl] NM (*Bot*) clover; (*Cartes: couleur*) clubs pl; (: *carte*) club; ~ **à quatre feuilles** four-leaf clover

treillage [tʀɛjaʒ] NM lattice work

treille [tʀɛj] NF (*tonnelle*) vine arbour (*BRIT*) *ou* arbor (*US*); (*vigne*) climbing vine

treillis [tʀeji] NM (*métallique*) wire-mesh; (*toile*) canvas; (*Mil: tenue*) combat uniform; (: *pantalon*) combat trousers pl

treize [tʀɛz] NUM thirteen
treizième [tʀɛzjɛm] NUM thirteenth; *see note*

> The *treizième mois* is an end-of-year bonus roughly corresponding to one month's salary. For many employees it is a standard part of their salary package.

tréma [tʀema] NM diaeresis
tremblant, e [tʀɑ̃blɑ̃, -ɑ̃t] ADJ trembling, shaking
tremble [tʀɑ̃bl] NM (*Bot*) aspen
tremblé, e [tʀɑ̃ble] ADJ shaky
tremblement [tʀɑ̃bləmɑ̃] NM trembling *no pl*, shaking *no pl*, shivering *no pl*; **~ de terre** earthquake
trembler [tʀɑ̃ble] /**1**/ VI to tremble, shake; **~ de** (*froid, fièvre*) to shiver *ou* tremble with; (*peur*) to shake *ou* tremble with; **~ pour qn** to fear for sb
tremblotant, e [tʀɑ̃blɔtɑ̃, -ɑ̃t] ADJ trembling
trembloter [tʀɑ̃blɔte] /**1**/ VI to tremble *ou* shake slightly
trémolo [tʀemɔlo] NM (*d'un instrument*) tremolo; (*de la voix*) quaver
trémousser [tʀemuse] /**1**/: **se trémousser** VI to jig about, wriggle about
trempe [tʀɑ̃p] NF (*fig*): **de cette/sa ~** of this/his calibre (*BRIT*) *ou* caliber (*US*)
trempé, e [tʀɑ̃pe] ADJ soaking (wet), drenched; (*Tech*): **acier ~** tempered steel
tremper [tʀɑ̃pe] /**1**/ VT to soak, drench; (*aussi*: **faire tremper**, **mettre à tremper**) to soak ▶ VI to soak; (*fig*): **~ dans** to be involved *ou* have a hand in; **se tremper** VI to have a quick dip; **se faire tremper** to get soaked *ou* drenched
trempette [tʀɑ̃pɛt] NF: **faire ~** to go paddling
tremplin [tʀɑ̃plɛ̃] NM springboard; (*Ski*) ski jump
trentaine [tʀɑ̃tɛn] NF (*âge*): **avoir la ~** to be around thirty; **une ~ (de)** thirty or so, about thirty
trente [tʀɑ̃t] NUM thirty; **voir ~-six chandelles** (*fig*) to see stars; **être/se mettre sur son ~ et un** to be wearing/put on one's Sunday best; **~-trois tours** *nm* long-playing record, LP
trentième [tʀɑ̃tjɛm] NUM thirtieth
trépanation [tʀepanasjɔ̃] NF trepan
trépaner [tʀepane] /**1**/ VT to trepan, trephine
trépasser [tʀepase] /**1**/ VI to pass away
trépidant, e [tʀepidɑ̃, -ɑ̃t] ADJ (*fig: rythme*) pulsating; (: *vie*) hectic
trépidation [tʀepidasjɔ̃] NF (*d'une machine, d'un moteur*) vibration; (*fig: de la vie*) whirl
trépider [tʀepide] /**1**/ VI to vibrate
trépied [tʀepje] NM (*d'appareil*) tripod; (*meuble*) trivet
trépignement [tʀepiɲmɑ̃] NM stamping (of feet)
trépigner [tʀepiɲe] /**1**/ VI to stamp (one's feet)
très [tʀɛ] ADV very; **~ beau/bien** very beautiful/well; **~ critiqué** much criticized; **~ industrialisé** highly industrialized; **j'ai ~ faim** I'm very hungry
trésor [tʀezɔʀ] NM treasure; (*Admin*) finances *pl*; (*d'une organisation*) funds *pl*; **~ (public)** public revenue; (*service*) public revenue office

trésorerie [tʀezɔʀʀi] NF (*fonds*) funds *pl*; (*gestion*) accounts *pl*; (*bureaux*) accounts department; (*poste*) treasurership; **difficultés de ~** cash problems, shortage of cash *ou* funds; **~ générale** local government finance office
trésorier, -ière [tʀezɔʀje, -jɛʀ] NM/F treasurer
Trésorier-payeur [tʀezɔʀjepɛjœʀ] NM: **~ général** paymaster
tressaillement [tʀesajmɑ̃] NM shiver, shudder; quiver
tressaillir [tʀesajiʀ] /**13**/ VI (*de peur etc*) to shiver, shudder; (*de joie*) to quiver
tressauter [tʀesote] /**1**/ VI to start, jump
tresse [tʀɛs] NF (*de cheveux*) braid, plait; (*cordon, galon*) braid
tresser [tʀese] /**1**/ VT (*cheveux*) to braid, plait; (*fil, jonc*) to plait; (*corbeille*) to weave; (*corde*) to twist
tréteau, x [tʀeto] NM trestle; **les ~** (*fig: Théât*) the boards
treuil [tʀœj] NM winch
trêve [tʀɛv] NF (*Mil, Pol*) truce; (*fig*) respite; **sans ~** unremittingly; **~ de ...** enough of this ...; **les États de la T~** the Trucial States
tri [tʀi] NM (*voir trier*) sorting (out) *no pl*; selection; screening; (*Inform*) sort; (*Postes: action*) sorting; **faire le ~ (de)** to sort out; **le (bureau de) ~** (*Postes*) the sorting office
triage [tʀijaʒ] NM (*Rail*) shunting; (*gare*) marshalling yard
trial [tʀijal] NM (*Sport*) scrambling
triangle [tʀijɑ̃gl] NM triangle; **~ isocèle/ équilatéral** isosceles/equilateral triangle; **~ rectangle** right-angled triangle
triangulaire [tʀijɑ̃gylɛʀ] ADJ triangular
triathlon [tʀi(j)atlɔ̃] NM triathlon
tribal, e, -aux [tʀibal, -o] ADJ tribal
tribord [tʀibɔʀ] NM: **à ~** to starboard, on the starboard side
tribu [tʀiby] NF tribe
tribulations [tʀibylasjɔ̃] NFPL tribulations, trials
tribunal, -aux [tʀibynal, -o] NM (*Jur*) court; (*Mil*) tribunal; **~ de police/pour enfants** police/juvenile court; **~ d'instance** ≈ magistrates' court (*BRIT*), ≈ district court (*US*); **~ de grande instance** ≈ High Court (*BRIT*), ≈ Supreme Court (*US*)
tribune [tʀibyn] NF (*estrade*) platform, rostrum; (*débat*) forum; (*d'église, de tribunal*) gallery; (*de stade*) stand; **~ libre** (*Presse*) opinion column
tribut [tʀiby] NM tribute
tributaire [tʀibytɛʀ] ADJ: **être ~ de** to be dependent on; (*Géo*) to be a tributary of
tricentenaire [tʀisɑ̃tnɛʀ] NM tercentenary, tricentennial
tricher [tʀiʃe] /**1**/ VI to cheat
tricherie [tʀiʃʀi] NF cheating *no pl*
tricheur, -euse [tʀiʃœʀ, -øz] NM/F cheat
trichromie [tʀikʀɔmi] NF three-colour (*BRIT*) *ou* -color (*US*) printing
tricolore [tʀikɔlɔʀ] ADJ three-coloured (*BRIT*), three-colored (*US*); (*français: drapeau*) red, white and blue; (: *équipe etc*) French

t

tricot [tʀiko] NM (*technique, ouvrage*) knitting *no pl*; (*tissu*) knitted fabric; (*vêtement*) jersey, sweater; **~ de corps, ~ de peau** vest (BRIT), undershirt (US)

tricoter [tʀikɔte] /1/ VT to knit; **machine/ aiguille à ~** knitting machine/needle (BRIT) *ou* pin (US)

trictrac [tʀiktʀak] NM backgammon

tricycle [tʀisikl] NM tricycle

tridimensionnel, le [tʀidimɑ̃sjɔnɛl] ADJ three-dimensional

triennal, e, -aux [tʀiɛnal, -o] ADJ (*prix, foire, élection*) three-yearly; (*charge, mandat, plan*) three-year

trier [tʀije] /7/ VT (*classer*) to sort (out); (*choisir*) to select; (*visiteurs*) to screen; (*Postes, Inform, fruits*) to sort

trieur, -euse [tʀijœʀ, -øz] NM/F sorter

trigonométrie [tʀigɔnɔmetʀi] NF trigonometry

trigonométrique [tʀigɔnɔmetʀik] ADJ trigonometric

trilingue [tʀilɛ̃g] ADJ trilingual

trilogie [tʀilɔʒi] NF trilogy

trimaran [tʀimaʀɑ̃] NM trimaran

trimbaler [tʀɛ̃bale] /1/ VT to cart around, trail along

trimer [tʀime] /1/ VI to slave away

trimestre [tʀimɛstʀ] NM (*Scol*) term; (*Comm*) quarter

trimestriel, le [tʀimɛstʀijɛl] ADJ quarterly; (*Scol*) end-of-term

trimoteur [tʀimɔtœʀ] NM three-engined aircraft

tringle [tʀɛ̃gl] NF rod

Trinité [tʀinite] NF Trinity

Trinité et Tobago [tʀiniteetɔbago] NF Trinidad and Tobago

trinquer [tʀɛ̃ke] /1/ VI to clink glasses; (*fam*) to cop it; **~ à qch/la santé de qn** to drink to sth/sb

trio [tʀijo] NM trio

triolet [tʀijɔlɛ] NM (*Mus*) triplet

triomphal, e, -aux [tʀijɔ̃fal, -o] ADJ triumphant, triumphal

triomphalement [tʀijɔ̃falmɑ̃] ADV triumphantly

triomphant, e [tʀijɔ̃fɑ̃, -ɑ̃t] ADJ triumphant

triomphateur, -trice [tʀijɔ̃fatœʀ, -tʀis] NM/F (*triumphant*) victor

triomphe [tʀijɔ̃f] NM triumph; **être reçu/ porté en ~** to be given a triumphant welcome/ be carried shoulder-high in triumph

triompher [tʀijɔ̃fe] /1/ VI to triumph, win; **~ de** to triumph over, overcome

triparti, e [tʀipaʀti] ADJ (*aussi*: **tripartite**: *réunion, assemblée*) tripartite, three-party

triperie [tʀipʀi] NF tripe shop

tripes [tʀip] NFPL (*Culin*) tripe *sg*; (*fam*) guts

triplace [tʀiplas] ADJ three-seater *cpd*

triple [tʀipl] ADJ (*à trois éléments*) triple; (*trois fois plus grand*) treble ▸ NM: **le ~ (de)** (*comparaison*) three times as much (as); **en ~ exemplaire** in triplicate; **~ saut** (*Sport*) triple jump

triplé [tʀiple] NM hat-trick (BRIT), triple success

triplement [tʀipləmɑ̃] ADV (*à un degré triple*) three times over; (*de trois façons*) in three ways; (*pour trois raisons*) on three counts ▸ NM trebling, threefold increase

tripler [tʀiple] /1/ VI, VT to triple, treble, increase threefold

triplés, -ées [tʀiple] NM/FPL triplets

Tripoli [tʀipɔli] N Tripoli

triporteur [tʀipɔʀtœʀ] NM delivery tricycle

tripot [tʀipo] NM (*péj*) dive

tripotage [tʀipɔtaʒ] NM (*péj*) jiggery-pokery

tripoter [tʀipɔte] /1/ VT to fiddle with, finger ▸ VI (*fam*) to rummage about

trique [tʀik] NF cudgel

trisannuel, le [tʀizanɥɛl] ADJ triennial

trisomie [tʀizɔmi] NF Down's syndrome

triste [tʀist] ADJ sad; (*couleur, temps, journée*) dreary; (*péj*): **~ personnage/affaire** sorry individual/affair; **c'est pas ~!** (*fam*) it's something else!

tristement [tʀistəmɑ̃] ADV sadly

tristesse [tʀistɛs] NF sadness

triton [tʀitɔ̃] NM triton

triturer [tʀityʀe] /1/ VT (*pâte*) to knead; (*objets*) to manipulate

trivial, e, -aux [tʀivjal, -o] ADJ coarse, crude; (*commun*) mundane

trivialité [tʀivjalite] NF coarseness, crudeness; mundaneness

troc [tʀɔk] NM (*Écon*) barter; (*transaction*) exchange, swap

troène [tʀɔɛn] NM privet

troglodyte [tʀɔglɔdit] NMF cave dweller, troglodyte

trognon [tʀɔɲɔ̃] NM (*de fruit*) core; (*de légume*) stalk

trois [tʀwa] NUM three

trois-huit [tʀwaɥit] NMPL: **faire les ~** to work eight-hour shifts (round the clock)

troisième [tʀwazjɛm] NUM third ▸ NF (*Scol*) year 10 (BRIT), ninth grade (US); **le ~ âge** (*période de vie*) one's retirement years; (*personnes âgées*) senior citizens *pl*

troisièmement [tʀwazjɛmmɑ̃] ADV thirdly

trois quarts [tʀwakaʀ] NMPL: **les ~ de** three-quarters of

trolleybus [tʀɔlɛbys] NM trolley bus

trombe [tʀɔ̃b] NF waterspout; **des trombes d'eau** a downpour; **en ~** (*arriver, passer*) like a whirlwind

trombone [tʀɔ̃bɔn] NM (*Mus*) trombone; (*de bureau*) paper clip; **~ à coulisse** slide trombone

tromboniste [tʀɔ̃bɔnist] NMF trombonist

trompe [tʀɔ̃p] NF (*d'éléphant*) trunk; (*Mus*) trumpet, horn; **~ d'Eustache** Eustachian tube; **trompes utérines** Fallopian tubes

trompe-l'œil [tʀɔ̃plœj] NM: **en ~** in trompe-l'œil style

tromper [tʀɔ̃pe] /1/ VT to deceive; (*fig: espoir, attente*) to disappoint; (*vigilance, poursuivants*) to elude; **se tromper** VI to make a mistake, be mistaken; **se tromper de voiture/jour** to take the wrong car/get the day wrong; **se tromper de 3 cm/20 euros** to be out by 3 cm/20 euros

tromperie [tʀɔ̃pʀi] NF deception, trickery *no pl*

trompette [tʀɔ̃pɛt] NF trumpet; **en ~** (*nez*) turned-up

trompettiste [tʀɔ̃petist] NMF trumpet player

trompeur, -euse [tʀɔ̃pœʀ, -øz] ADJ deceptive, misleading

tronc [tʀɔ̃] NM (*Bot, Anat*) trunk; (*d'église*) collection box; **~ d'arbre** tree trunk; **~ commun** (*Scol*) common-core syllabus; **~ de cône** truncated cone

tronche [tʀɔ̃ʃ] NF (*fam*) mug, face

tronçon [tʀɔ̃sɔ̃] NM section

tronçonner [tʀɔ̃sɔne] /1/ VT (*arbre*) to saw up; (*pierre*) to cut up

tronçonneuse [tʀɔ̃sɔnøz] NF chainsaw

trône [tʀon] NM throne; **monter sur le ~** to ascend the throne

trôner [tʀone] /1/ VI (*fig*) to have (*ou* take) pride of place (*BRIT*), have the place of honour (*BRIT*) *ou* honor (*US*)

tronquer [tʀɔ̃ke] /1/ VT to truncate; (*fig*) to curtail

trop [tʀo] ADV too; (*avec verbe*) too much; (*aussi:* **trop nombreux**) too many; (*aussi:* **trop souvent**) too often; **~ peu (nombreux)** too few; **~ longtemps** (for) too long; **~ de** (*nombre*) too many; (*quantité*) too much; **de ~, en ~: des livres en ~** a few books too many, a few extra books; **du lait en ~** too much milk; **trois livres/cinq euros de ~** three books too many/five euros too much; **ça coûte ~ cher** it's too expensive

trophée [tʀɔfe] NM trophy

tropical, e, -aux [tʀɔpikal, -o] ADJ tropical

tropique [tʀɔpik] NM tropic; **tropiques** NMPL tropics; **~ du Cancer/Capricorne** Tropic of Cancer/Capricorn

trop-plein [tʀoplɛ̃] NM (*tuyau*) overflow *ou* outlet (pipe); (*liquide*) overflow

troquer [tʀɔke] /1/ VT: **~ qch contre** to barter *ou* trade sth for; (*fig*) to swap sth for

trot [tʀo] NM trot; **aller au ~** to trot along; **partir au ~** to set off at a trot

trotter [tʀɔte] /1/ VI to trot; (*fig*) to scamper along (*ou* about)

trotteuse [tʀɔtøz] NF (*de montre*) second hand

trottiner [tʀɔtine] /1/ VI (*fig*) to scamper along (*ou* about)

trottinette [tʀɔtinɛt] NF (child's) scooter

trottoir [tʀɔtwaʀ] NM pavement (*BRIT*), sidewalk (*US*); **faire le ~** (*péj*) to walk the streets; **~ roulant** moving walkway, travelator

trou [tʀu] NM hole; (*fig*) gap; (*Comm*) deficit; **~ d'aération** (air) vent; **~ d'air** air pocket; **~ de mémoire** blank, lapse of memory; **~ noir** black hole; **~ de la serrure** keyhole

troublant, e [tʀublɑ̃, -ɑ̃t] ADJ disturbing

trouble [tʀubl] ADJ (*liquide*) cloudy; (*image, photo*) blurred; (*mémoire*) indistinct, hazy; (*affaire*) shady, murky ▸ ADV indistinctly; **voir ~** to have blurred vision ▸ NM (*désarroi*) distress, agitation; (*émoi sensuel*) turmoil, agitation; (*embarras*) confusion; (*zizanie*) unrest, discord; **troubles** NMPL (*Pol*) disturbances, troubles, unrest *sg*; (*Méd*) trouble *sg*, disorders; **troubles de la personnalité** personality problems; **troubles de la vision** eye trouble

trouble-fête [tʀubləfɛt] NMF INV spoilsport

troubler [tʀuble] /1/ VT (*embarrasser*) to confuse, disconcert; (*émouvoir*) to agitate; to disturb; to perturb; (*perturber: ordre etc*) to disrupt, disturb; (*: liquide*) to make cloudy; (*intriguer*) to bother; **se troubler** VI (*personne*) to become flustered *ou* confused; **~ l'ordre public** to cause a breach of the peace

troué, e [tʀue] ADJ with a hole (*ou* holes) in it ▸ NF gap; (*Mil*) breach

trouer [tʀue] /1/ VT to make a hole (*ou* holes) in; (*fig*) to pierce

trouille [tʀuj] NF (*fam*): **avoir la ~** to be scared stiff, be scared out of one's wits

troupe [tʀup] NF (*Mil*) troop; (*groupe*) troop, group; **la ~** (*Mil: l'armée*) the army; (*: les simples soldats*) the troops *pl*; **~ (de théâtre)** (theatrical) company; **troupes de choc** shock troops

troupeau, x [tʀupo] NM (*de moutons*) flock; (*de vaches*) herd

trousse [tʀus] NF case, kit; (*d'écolier*) pencil case; (*de docteur*) instrument case; **aux trousses de** (*fig*) on the heels *ou* tail of; **~ à outils** toolkit; **~ de toilette** toilet bag

trousseau, x [tʀuso] NM (*de mariée*) trousseau; **~ de clefs** bunch of keys

trouvaille [tʀuvaj] NF find; (*fig: idée, expression etc*) brainwave

trouvé, e [tʀuve] ADJ: **tout ~** ready-made

trouver [tʀuve] /1/ VT to find; (*rendre visite*): **aller/venir ~ qn** to go/come and see sb; **se trouver** VI (*être*) to be; (*être soudain*) to find o.s.; **je trouve que** I find *ou* think that; **~ à boire/critiquer** to find something to drink/criticize; **~ asile/refuge** to find refuge/shelter; **se trouver être/avoir** to happen to be/have; **il se trouve que** it happens that, it turns out that; **se trouver bien** to feel well; **se trouver mal** to pass out

truand [tʀyɑ̃] NM villain, crook

truander [tʀyɑ̃de] /1/ VI (*fam*) to cheat, do ▸ VT: **se faire ~** to be swindled

trublion [tʀyblijɔ̃] NM troublemaker

truc [tʀyk] NM (*astuce*) way, device; (*de cinéma, prestidigitateur*) trick effect; (*chose*) thing; (*machin*) thingumajig, whatsit (*BRIT*); **avoir le ~** to have the knack; **c'est pas son** (*ou* **mon** *etc*) **~** (*fam*) it's not really his (*ou* my *etc*) thing

truchement [tʀyʃmɑ̃] NM: **par le ~ de qn** through (the intervention of) sb

trucider [tʀyside] /1/ VT (*fam*) to do in, bump off

truculence [tʀykylɑ̃s] NF colourfulness (*BRIT*), colorfulness (*US*)

truculent, e [tʀykylɑ̃, -ɑ̃t] ADJ colourful (*BRIT*), colorful (*US*)

truelle [tʀyɛl] NF trowel

truffe [tʀyf] NF truffle; (*nez*) nose

truffé, e [tʀyfe] ADJ (*Culin*) garnished with truffles; *voir aussi* **truffer**

truffer [tʀyfe] /1/ VT (*Culin*) to garnish with truffles; **truffé de** (*citations*) peppered with; (*fautes*) riddled with; (*pièges*) bristling with

t

truie [tʀ૫i] NF SOW

truite [tʀ૫it] NF trout *inv*

truquage [tʀykaʒ] NM fixing; (*Ciné*) special effects *pl*

truquer [tʀyke] /**1**/ VT (*élections, serrure, dés*) to fix; (*Ciné*) to use special effects in

trust [tʀœst] NM (*Comm*) trust

truster [tʀœste] /**1**/ VT (*Comm*) to monopolize

ts ABR = **tous**

tsar [dzaʀ] NM tsar

tsé-tsé [tsetse] NF: **mouche ~** tsetse fly

TSF SIGLE F (= *télégraphie sans fil*) wireless

tsigane [tsigan] ADJ, NMF = **tzigane**

TSVP ABR (= *tournez s'il vous plaît*) PTO

TT, TTA SIGLE M (= *transit temporaire (autorisé)*) vehicle registration for cars etc bought in France for export tax-free by non-residents

tt ABR = **tout**

TTC ABR (= *toutes taxes comprises*) inclusive of tax

ttes ABR = **toutes**

TU SIGLE M = **temps universel**

tu[1] [ty] PRON you ▶ NM: **employer le tu** to use the "tu" form

tu[2]**, e** [ty] PP *de* taire

tuant, e [t૫ɑ̃, -ɑ̃t] ADJ (*épuisant*) killing; (*énervant*) infuriating

tuba [tyba] NM (*Mus*) tuba; (*Sport*) snorkel

tubage [tybaʒ] NM (*Méd*) intubation

tube [tyb] NM tube; (*de canalisation, métallique etc*) pipe; (*chanson, disque*) hit song *ou* record; **~ digestif** alimentary canal, digestive tract; **~ à essai** test tube

tuberculeux, -euse [tybɛʀkylø, -øz] ADJ tubercular ▶ NM/F tuberculosis *ou* TB patient

tuberculose [tybɛʀkyloz] NF tuberculosis, TB

tubulaire [tybylɛʀ] ADJ tubular

tubulure [tybylyʀ] NF pipe; piping *no pl*; (*Auto*): **~ d'échappement/d'admission** exhaust/inlet manifold

tué, e [t૫e] NM/F: **cinq tués** five killed *ou* dead

tue-mouche [tymuʃ] ADJ: **papier ~(s)** flypaper

tuer [t૫e] /**1**/ VT to kill; **se tuer** (*se suicider*) to kill o.s.; (*dans un accident*) to be killed; **se tuer au travail** (*fig*) to work o.s. to death

tuerie [tyʀi] NF slaughter *no pl*, massacre

tue-tête [tytɛt]: **à ~** adv at the top of one's voice

tueur [t૫œʀ] NM killer; **~ à gages** hired killer

tuile [t૫il] NF tile; (*fam*) spot of bad luck, blow

tulipe [tylip] NF tulip

tulle [tyl] NM tulle

tuméfié, e [tymefje] ADJ puffy, swollen

tumeur [tymœʀ] NF growth, tumour (*Brit*), tumor (*US*)

tumulte [tymylt] NM commotion, hubbub

tumultueux, -euse [tymyltɥø, -øz] ADJ stormy, turbulent

tuner [tynɛʀ] NM tuner

tungstène [tœ̃kstɛn] NM tungsten

tunique [tynik] NF tunic; (*de femme*) smock, tunic

Tunis [tynis] N Tunis

Tunisie [tynizi] NF: **la ~** Tunisia

tunisien, ne [tynizjɛ̃, -ɛn] ADJ Tunisian ▶ NM/F: **T~, ne** Tunisian

tunisois, e [tynizwa, -waz] ADJ *ou* from Tunis

tunnel [tynel] NM tunnel; **le ~ sous la Manche** the Channel Tunnel

TUP SIGLE M (= *titre universel de paiement*) = payment slip

turban [tyʀbɑ̃] NM turban

turbin [tyʀbɛ̃] NM (*fam*) work *no pl*

turbine [tyʀbin] NF turbine

turbo [tyʀbo] NM turbo; **un moteur ~** a turbo(-charged) engine

turbomoteur [tyʀbɔmɔtœʀ] NM turbo(-boosted) engine

turbopropulseur [tyʀbɔpʀɔpylsœʀ] NM turboprop

turboréacteur [tyʀbɔʀeaktœʀ] NM turbojet

turbot [tyʀbo] NM turbot

turbotrain [tyʀbɔtʀɛ̃] NM turbotrain

turbulences [tyʀbylɑ̃s] NFPL (*Aviat*) turbulence *sg*

turbulent, e [tyʀbylɑ̃, -ɑ̃t] ADJ boisterous, unruly

turc, turque [tyʀk] ADJ Turkish; (*w.-c.*) seatless ▶ NM (*Ling*) Turkish ▶ NM/F: **T~, Turque** Turk/ Turkish woman; **à la turque** adv (*assis*) cross-legged

turf [tyʀf] NM racing

turfiste [tyʀfist] NMF racegoer

Turks et Caïques [tyʀkekaik], **Turks et Caicos** [tyʀkekaikɔs] NFPL Turks and Caicos Islands

turpitude [tyʀpityd] NF base act, baseness *no pl*

turque [tyʀk] ADJ F, NF *voir* **turc**

Turquie [tyʀki] NF: **la ~** Turkey

turquoise [tyʀkwaz] NF, ADJ INV turquoise

tus *etc* [ty] VB *voir* **taire**

tut *etc* [ty] VB *voir* **taire**

tutelle [tytel] NF (*Jur*) guardianship; (*Pol*) trusteeship; **sous la ~ de** (*fig*) under the supervision of

tuteur, -trice [tytœʀ, -tʀis] NM/F (*Jur*) guardian; (*de plante*) stake, support

tutoiement [tytwamɑ̃] NM use of familiar "tu" form

tutoyer [tytwaje] /**8**/ VT: **~ qn** to address sb as "tu"

tutti quanti [tutikwɑ̃ti] NMPL: **et ~** and all the rest (of them)

tutu [tyty] NM (*Danse*) tutu

tuyau, x [t૫ijo] NM pipe; (*flexible*) tube; (*fam: conseil*) tip; (: *mise au courant*) gen *no pl*; **~ d'arrosage** hosepipe; **~ d'échappement** exhaust pipe; **~ d'incendie** fire hose

tuyauté, e [t૫ijote] ADJ fluted

tuyauterie [t૫ijotʀi] NF piping *no pl*

tuyère [t૫ijɛʀ] NF nozzle

TV [teve] NF TV, telly (*Brit*)

TVA SIGLE F (= *taxe à ou sur la valeur ajoutée*) VAT

TVHD SIGLE F (= *télévision haute définition*) HDTV

tweed [twid] NM tweed

tweet [twit] NM tweet

tympan [tɛ̃pɑ̃] NM (*Anat*) eardrum

type [tip] NM type; (*personne, chose, représentant*) classic example, epitome; (*fam*) chap, guy ▶ ADJ typical, standard; **avoir le ~ nordique** to be Nordic-looking

typé, e [tipe] ADJ ethnic (*euphémisme*)

typhoïde [tifɔid] NF typhoid (fever)
typhon [tifɔ̃] NM typhoon
typhus [tifys] NM typhus (fever)
typique [tipik] ADJ typical
typiquement [tipikmɑ̃] ADV typically
typographe [tipɔgʀaf] NMF typographer
typographie [tipɔgʀafi] NF typography;
(*procédé*) letterpress (printing)
typographique [tipɔgʀafik] ADJ typographical;
letterpress *cpd*

typologie [tipɔlɔʒi] NF typology
tyran [tiʀɑ̃] NM tyrant
tyrannie [tiʀani] NF tyranny
tyrannique [tiʀanik] ADJ tyrannical
tyranniser [tiʀanize] /1/ VT to tyrannize
Tyrol [tiʀɔl] NM: **le ~** the Tyrol
tyrolien, ne [tiʀɔljɛ̃, -ɛn] ADJ Tyrolean
tzar [dzaʀ] NM = **tsar**
tzigane [dzigan] ADJ gipsy (*péj*), tzigane ▶ NMF
(Hungarian) gipsy, Tzigane

t

Uu

U, u [y] NM INV U, u; **U comme Ursule** U for Uncle

ubiquité [ybikɥite] NF: **avoir le don d'~** to be everywhere at once, be ubiquitous

UDF SIGLE F (= *Union pour la démocratie française*) *political party*

UE SIGLE F (= *Union européenne*) EU

UEFA [yefa] SIGLE F (= *Union of European Football Associations*) UEFA

UEM SIGLE F (= *Union économique et monétaire*) EMU

UER SIGLE F (= *unité d'enseignement et de recherche*) old title of UFR; (= *Union européenne de radio-télévision*) EBU

UFC SIGLE F (= *Union fédérale des consommateurs*) *national consumer group*

UFR SIGLE F (= *unité de formation et de recherche*) ≈ university department

UHF SIGLE F (= *ultra-haute fréquence*) UHF

UHT ABR (= *ultra-haute température*) UHT

UIT SIGLE F (= *Union internationale des télécommunications*) ITU (= *International Telecommunications Union*)

Ukraine [ykʀɛn] NF: **l'~** the Ukraine

ukrainien, ne [ykʀɛnjɛ̃, -ɛn] ADJ Ukrainian ▶ NM (*Ling*) Ukrainian ▶ NM/F: **U~, ne** Ukrainian

ulcère [ylsɛʀ] NM ulcer; **~ à l'estomac** stomach ulcer

ulcérer [ylseʀe] /6/ VT (*Méd*) to ulcerate; (*fig*) to sicken, appal

ulcéreux, -euse [ylseʀø, -øz] ADJ (*plaie, lésion*) ulcerous; (*membre*) ulcerated

ULM SIGLE M (= *ultra léger motorisé*) microlight

ultérieur, e [ylteʀjœʀ] ADJ later, subsequent; **remis à une date ~** postponed to a later date

ultérieurement [ylteʀjœʀmɑ̃] ADV later, subsequently

ultimatum [yltimatɔm] NM ultimatum

ultime [yltim] ADJ final

ultra... [yltʀa] PRÉFIXE ultra...

ultramoderne [yltʀamɔdɛʀn] ADJ ultra-modern

ultra-rapide [yltʀaʀapid] ADJ ultra-fast

ultra-sensible [yltʀasɑ̃sibl] ADJ (*Photo*) high-speed

ultrason, ultra-son [yltʀasɔ̃] NM ultrasound *no pl*; **ultra(-)sons** NMPL ultrasonics

ultraviolet, ultra-violet, te [yltʀavjɔlɛ, -ɛt]

ADJ ultraviolet ▶ NM: **les ultra(-)violets** ultraviolet rays

ululer [ylyle] /1/ VI = **hululer**

UME SIGLE F (= *Union monétaire européenne*) EMU

UMP SIGLE F (= *Union pour un mouvement populaire*) *political party*

⸻ MOT-CLÉ ⸻

un, une [œ̃, yn] ART INDÉF a; (*devant voyelle*) an; **un garçon/vieillard** a boy/an old man; **une fille** a girl
▶ PRON one; **l'un des meilleurs** one of the best; **l'un..., l'autre** (the) one..., the other; **les uns..., les autres** some..., others; **l'un et l'autre** both (of them); **l'un ou l'autre** either (of them); **l'un l'autre, les uns les autres** each other, one another; **pas un seul** not a single one; **un par un** one by one
▶ NUM one; **une pomme seulement** one apple only, just one apple
▶ NF: **la une** (*Presse*) the front page

unanime [ynanim] ADJ unanimous; **ils sont unanimes (à penser que)** they are unanimous (in thinking that)

unanimement [ynanimmɑ̃] ADV (*par tous*) unanimously; (*d'un commun accord*) with one accord

unanimité [ynanimite] NF unanimity; **à l'~** unanimously; **faire l'~** to be approved unanimously

UNEF [ynɛf] SIGLE F = **Union nationale des étudiants de France**

UNESCO [ynɛsko] SIGLE F (= *United Nations Educational, Scientific and Cultural Organization*) UNESCO

Unetelle [yntɛl] NF *voir* **Untel**

UNI SIGLE F = **Union nationale inter-universitaire**

uni, e [yni] ADJ (*ton, tissu*) plain; (*surface*) smooth, even; (*famille*) close(-knit); (*pays*) united

UNICEF [ynisɛf] SIGLE MF (= *United Nations International Children's Emergency Fund*) UNICEF

unidirectionnel, le [ynidiʀɛksjɔnɛl] ADJ unidirectional, one-way

unième [ynjɛm] NUM: **vingt/trente et ~** twenty-/thirty-first; **cent ~** (one) hundred and first

unificateur, -trice [ynifikatœʀ, -tʀis] ADJ unifying

unification [ynifikasjɔ̃] NF uniting; unification; standardization

unifier [ynifje] /**7**/ VT to unite, unify; (*systèmes*) to standardize, unify; **s'unifier** VI to become united

uniforme [ynifɔʀm] ADJ (*mouvement*) regular, uniform; (*surface, ton*) even; (*objets, maisons*) uniform; (*fig: vie, conduite*) unchanging ▶ NM uniform; **être sous l'~** (*Mil*) to be serving

uniformément [ynifɔʀmemɑ̃] ADV uniformly

uniformisation [ynifɔʀmizasjɔ̃] NF standardization

uniformiser [ynifɔʀmize] /**1**/ VT to make uniform; (*systèmes*) to standardize

uniformité [ynifɔʀmite] NF regularity; uniformity; evenness

unijambiste [yniʒɑ̃bist] NMF one-legged man/woman

unilatéral, e, -aux [ynilateʀal, -o] ADJ unilateral; **stationnement ~** parking on one side only

unilatéralement [ynilateʀalmɑ̃] ADV unilaterally

uninominal, e, -aux [yninɔminal, -o] ADJ uncontested

union [ynjɔ̃] NF union; **~ conjugale** union of marriage; **~ de consommateurs** consumers' association; **~ libre** free love; **vivre en ~ libre** (*en concubinage*) to cohabit; **l'U~ européenne** the European Union; **l'U~ des Républiques socialistes soviétiques (URSS)** the Union of Soviet Socialist Republics (USSR); **l'U~ soviétique** the Soviet Union

unique [ynik] ADJ (*seul*) only; (*exceptionnel*) unique; **un prix/système ~** a single price/system; **ménage à salaire ~** one-salary family; **route à voie ~** single-lane road; **fils/fille ~** only son/daughter, only child; **sens ~** one-way street; **~ en France** the only one of its kind in France

uniquement [ynikmɑ̃] ADV only, solely; (*juste*) only, merely

unir [yniʀ] /**2**/ VT (*nations*) to unite; (*éléments, couleurs*) to combine; (*en mariage*) to unite, join together; **~ qch à** to unite sth with; to combine sth with; **s'unir** VI to unite; (*en mariage*) to be joined together; **s'unir à** *ou* **avec** to unite with

unisexe [yniseks] ADJ unisex

unisson [ynisɔ̃]: **à l'~** *adv* in unison

unitaire [yniteʀ] ADJ unitary; (*Pol*) unitarian; **prix ~** unit price

unité [ynite] NF (*harmonie, cohésion*) unity; (*Comm, Mil, de mesure, Math*) unit; **~ centrale de traitement** central processing unit; **~ de valeur** (university) course, credit

univers [yniveʀ] NM universe

universalisation [yniveʀsalizasjɔ̃] NF universalization

universaliser [yniveʀsalize] /**1**/ VT to universalize

universalité [yniveʀsalite] NF universality

universel, le [yniveʀsɛl] ADJ universal; (*esprit*) all-embracing

universellement [yniveʀsɛlmɑ̃] ADV universally

universitaire [yniveʀsiteʀ] ADJ university *cpd*; (*diplôme, études*) academic, university *cpd* ▶ NMF academic

université [yniveʀsite] NF university

univoque [ynivɔk] ADJ unambiguous; (*Math*) one-to-one

UNR SIGLE F (= *Union pour la nouvelle république*) *former political party*

UNSS SIGLE F = **Union nationale de sport scolaire**

Untel, Unetelle [œ̃tɛl, yntɛl] NM/F: **Monsieur ~** Mr so-and-so

uranium [yʀanjɔm] NM uranium

urbain, e [yʀbɛ̃, -ɛn] ADJ urban, city *cpd*; (*poli*) urbane

urbanisation [yʀbanizasjɔ̃] NF urbanization

urbaniser [yʀbanize] /**1**/ VT to urbanize

urbanisme [yʀbanism] NM town planning

urbaniste [yʀbanist] NMF town planner

urbanité [yʀbanite] NF urbanity

urée [yʀe] NF urea

urémie [yʀemi] NF uraemia (BRIT), uremia (US)

urgence [yʀʒɑ̃s] NF urgency; (*Méd etc*) emergency; **d'~** *adj* emergency *cpd* ▶ ADV as a matter of urgency; **en cas d'~** in case of emergency; **service des urgences** emergency service

urgent, e [yʀʒɑ̃, -ɑ̃t] ADJ urgent

urinaire [yʀineʀ] ADJ urinary

urinal, -aux [yʀinal, -o] NM (bed) urinal

urine [yʀin] NF urine

uriner [yʀine] /**1**/ VI to urinate

urinoir [yʀinwaʀ] NM (public) urinal

urne [yʀn] NF (*électorale*) ballot box; (*vase*) urn; **aller aux urnes** (*voter*) to go to the polls

urologie [yʀɔlɔʒi] NF urology

URSS [parfois : yʀs] SIGLE F (*Hist*: = *Union des Républiques Socialistes Soviétiques*) USSR

URSSAF [yʀsaf] SIGLE F (= *Union pour le recouvrement de la sécurité sociale et des allocations familiales*) *administrative body responsible for social security funds and payments*

urticaire [yʀtikɛʀ] NF nettle rash, urticaria

Uruguay [yʀygwɛ] NM: **l'~** Uruguay

uruguayen, ne [yʀygwajɛ̃, -ɛn] ADJ Uruguayan ▶ NM/F: **U~, ne** Uruguayan

us [ys] NMPL: **us et coutumes** (habits and) customs

USA SIGLE MPL (= *United States of America*) USA

usage [yzaʒ] NM (*emploi, utilisation*) use; (*coutume*) custom; (*éducation*) (good) manners *pl*, (good) breeding; (*Ling*): **l'~** usage; **faire ~ de** (*pouvoir, droit*) to exercise; **avoir l'~ de** to have the use of; **à l'~** *adv* with use; **à l'~ de** (*pour*) for (use of); **en ~** in use; **hors d'~** out of service; **à ~ interne** (*Méd*) to be taken (internally); **à ~ externe** (*Méd*) for external use only

usagé, e [yzaʒe] ADJ (*usé*) worn; (*d'occasion*) used

usager, -ère [yzaʒe, -ɛʀ] NM/F user

usé, e [yze] ADJ worn (down *ou* out *ou* away);

u

ruined; (*banal: argument etc*) hackneyed

user [yze] /1/ vT (*outil*) to wear down; (*vêtement*) to wear out; (*matière*) to wear away; (*consommer: charbon etc*) to use; (*fig: santé*) to ruin; (*: personne*) to wear out; **s'user** vi to wear; (*tissu, vêtement*) to wear out; (*fig*) to decline; **s'user à la tâche** to wear o.s. out with work; **~ de** vt (*moyen, procédé*) to use, employ; (*droit*) to exercise

usine [yzin] NF factory; **~ atomique** nuclear power plant; **~ à gaz** gasworks *sg*; **~ marémotrice** tidal power station

usiner [yzine] /1/ vT (*Tech*) to machine; (*fabriquer*) to manufacture

usité, e [yzite] ADJ in common use, common; **peu ~** rarely used

ustensile [ystãsil] NM implement; **~ de cuisine** kitchen utensil

usuel, le [yzɥɛl] ADJ everyday, common

usufruit [yzyfRɥi] NM usufruct

usuraire [yzyRɛR] ADJ usurious

usure [yzyR] NF wear; worn state; (*de l'usurier*) usury; **avoir qn à l'~** to wear sb down; **~ normale** fair wear and tear

usurier, -ière [yzyRje, -jɛR] NM/F usurer

usurpateur, -trice [yzyRpatœR, -tRis] NM/F usurper

usurpation [yzyRpasjɔ̃] NF usurpation

usurper [yzyRpe] /1/ vT to usurp

ut [yt] NM (*Mus*) C

UTA SIGLE F = **Union des transporteurs aériens**

utérin, e [yteRɛ̃, -in] ADJ uterine

utérus [yteRys] NM uterus, womb

utile [ytil] ADJ useful; **~ à qn/qch** of use to sb/sth

utilement [ytilmã] ADV usefully

utilisable [ytilizabl] ADJ usable

utilisateur, -trice [ytilizatœR, -tRis] NM/F user

utilisation [ytilizasjɔ̃] NF use

utiliser [ytilize] /1/ vT to use

utilitaire [ytilitɛR] ADJ utilitarian; (*objets*) practical ▶ NM (*Inform*) utility

utilité [ytilite] NF usefulness *no pl*; use; **jouer les utilités** (*Théât*) to play bit parts; **reconnu d'~ publique** state-approved; **c'est d'une grande ~** it's extremely useful; **il n'y a aucune ~ à ...** there's no use in ...; **de peu d'~** of little use *ou* help

utopie [ytɔpi] NF (*idée, conception*) utopian idea *ou* view; (*société etc idéale*) utopia

utopique [ytɔpik] ADJ utopian

utopiste [ytɔpist] NMF utopian

UV SIGLE F (*Scol*) = **unité de valeur** ▶ SIGLE MPL (= *ultra-violets*) UV

uvule [yvyl] NF uvula

Vv

V, v [ve] NM INV V, v ▶ ABR (= *voir, verset*) v = **vers**; (*de poésie*) l.; (: *en direction de*) toward(s); **V comme Victor** V for Victor; **en V** V-shaped; **encolure en V** V-neck; **décolleté en V** plunging neckline

va [va] VB *voir* **aller**

vacance [vakɑ̃s] NF (*Admin*) vacancy; **vacances** NFPL holiday(s) *pl* (BRIT), vacation *sg* (US); **les grandes vacances** the summer holidays *ou* vacation; **prendre des/ses vacances** to take a holiday *ou* vacation/one's holiday(s) *ou* vacation; **aller en vacances** to go on holiday *ou* vacation

vacancier, -ière [vakɑ̃sje, -jɛʀ] NM/F holidaymaker (BRIT), vacationer (US)

vacant, e [vakɑ̃, -ɑ̃t] ADJ vacant

vacarme [vakaʀm] NM row, din

vacataire [vakatɛʀ] NMF temporary (employee); (*enseignement*) supply (BRIT) *ou* substitute (US) teacher; (*Université*) part-time temporary lecturer

vaccin [vaksɛ̃] NM vaccine; (*opération*) vaccination

vaccination [vaksinasjɔ̃] NF vaccination

vacciner [vaksine] /1/ VT to vaccinate; (*fig*) to make immune; **être vacciné** (*fig*) to be immune

vache [vaʃ] NF (*Zool*) cow; (*cuir*) cowhide ▶ ADJ (*fam*) rotten, mean; **~ à eau** (canvas) water bag; (**manger de la**) **~ enragée** (to go through) hard times; **~ à lait** (*péj*) mug, sucker; **~ laitière** dairy cow; **période de vaches maigres** lean times *pl*, lean period

vachement [vaʃmɑ̃] ADV (*fam*) damned, really

vacher, -ère [vaʃe, -ɛʀ] NM/F cowherd

vacherie [vaʃʀi] NF (*fam*) meanness *no pl*; (: *action*) dirty trick; (: *propos*) nasty remark

vacherin [vaʃʀɛ̃] NM (*fromage*) vacherin cheese; (*gâteau*): **~ glacé** vacherin (*type of cream gâteau*)

vachette [vaʃɛt] NF calfskin

vacillant, e [vasijɑ̃, -ɑ̃t] ADJ wobbly; flickering; failing, faltering

vaciller [vasije] /1/ VI to sway, wobble; (*bougie, lumière*) to flicker; (*fig*) to be failing, falter; **~ dans ses réponses** to falter in one's replies; **~ dans ses résolutions** to waver in one's resolutions

vacuité [vakɥite] NF emptiness, vacuity

vade-mecum [vademekɔm] NM INV pocketbook

vadrouille [vadʀuj] NF: **être/partir en ~** to be on/go for a wander

vadrouiller [vadʀuje] /1/ VI to wander around *ou* about

va-et-vient [vaevjɛ̃] NM INV (*de pièce mobile*) to and fro (*ou* up and down) movement; (*de personnes, véhicules*) comings and goings *pl*, to-ings and fro-ings *pl*; (*Élec*) two-way switch

vagabond, e [vagabɔ̃, -ɔ̃d] ADJ wandering; (*imagination*) roaming, roving ▶ NM (*rôdeur*) tramp, vagrant; (*voyageur*) wanderer

vagabondage [vagabɔ̃daʒ] NM roaming, wandering; (*Jur*) vagrancy

vagabonder [vagabɔ̃de] /1/ VI to roam, wander

vagin [vaʒɛ̃] NM vagina

vaginal, e, -aux [vaʒinal, -o] ADJ vaginal

vagissement [vaʒismɑ̃] NM cry (*of newborn baby*)

vague [vag] NF wave ▶ ADJ vague; (*regard*) faraway; (*manteau, robe*) loose(-fitting); (*quelconque*): **un ~ bureau/cousin** some office/ cousin or other ▶ NM: **être dans le ~** to be rather in the dark; **rester dans le ~** to keep things rather vague; **regarder dans le ~** to gaze into space; **~ à l'âme** *nm* vague melancholy; **~ d'assaut** *nf* (*Mil*) wave of assault; **~ de chaleur** *nf* heatwave; **~ de fond** *nf* ground swell; **~ de froid** *nf* cold spell

vaguelette [vaglɛt] NF ripple

vaguement [vagmɑ̃] ADV vaguely

vaillamment [vajamɑ̃] ADV bravely, gallantly

vaillant, e [vajɑ̃, -ɑ̃t] ADJ (*courageux*) brave, gallant; (*robuste*) vigorous, hale and hearty; **n'avoir plus un sou ~** to be penniless

vaille [vaj] VB *voir* **valoir**

vain, e [vɛ̃, vɛn] ADJ vain; **en ~** *adv* in vain

vaincre [vɛ̃kʀ] /42/ VT to defeat; (*fig*) to conquer, overcome

vaincu, e [vɛ̃ky] PP *de* **vaincre** ▶ NM/F defeated party

vainement [vɛnmɑ̃] ADV vainly

vainquais *etc* [vɛ̃kɛ] VB *voir* **vaincre**

vainqueur [vɛ̃kœʀ] NM victor; (*Sport*) winner ▶ ADJ M victorious

vais [vɛ] VB *voir* **aller**

vaisseau, x [veso] NM (*Anat*) vessel; (*Navig*) ship, vessel; **~ spatial** spaceship

vaisselier [vesəlje] NM dresser

V

vaisselle [vɛsɛl] NF (service) crockery; (plats etc à laver) (dirty) dishes pl; **faire la ~** to do the washing-up (BRIT) ou the dishes

val [val] (pl **vaux** ou **vals**) NM valley

valable [valabl] ADJ valid; (acceptable) decent, worthwhile

valablement [valabləmɑ̃] ADV legitimately; (de façon satisfaisante) satisfactorily

Valence [valɑ̃s] N (en Espagne) Valencia; (en France) Valence

valent etc [val] VB voir **valoir**

valet [valɛ] NM valet; (péj) lackey; (Cartes) jack, knave (BRIT); **~ de chambre** manservant, valet; **~ de ferme** farmhand; **~ de pied** footman

valeur [valœʀ] NF (gén) value; (mérite) worth, merit; (Comm: titre) security; **valeurs** NFPL (morales) values; **mettre en ~** (bien) to exploit; (terrain, région) to develop; (fig) to highlight; to show off to advantage; **avoir de la ~** to be valuable; **prendre de la ~** to go up ou gain in value; **sans ~** worthless; **~ absolue** absolute value; **~ d'échange** exchange value; **~ nominale** face value; **valeurs mobilières** transferable securities

valeureux, -euse [valœʀø, -øz] ADJ valorous

validation [validasjɔ̃] NF validation

valide [valid] ADJ (en bonne santé) fit, well; (indemne) able-bodied, fit; (valable) valid

valider [valide] /1/ VT to validate

validité [validite] NF validity

valions etc [valjɔ̃] VB voir **valoir**

valise [valiz] NF (suit)case; **faire sa ~** to pack one's (suit)case; **la ~ (diplomatique)** the diplomatic bag

vallée [vale] NF valley

vallon [valɔ̃] NM small valley

vallonné, e [valɔne] ADJ undulating

vallonnement [valɔnmɑ̃] NM undulation

valoir [valwaʀ] /29/ VI (être valable) to hold, apply ▶ VT (prix, valeur, effort) to be worth; (causer): **~ qch à qn** to earn sb sth; **se valoir** to be of equal merit; (péj) to be two of a kind; **faire ~** (droits, prérogatives) to assert; (domaine, capitaux) to exploit; **faire ~ que** to point out that; **se faire valoir** to make the most of o.s.; **à ~ on** account; **à ~ sur** to be deducted from; **vaille que vaille** somehow or other; **cela ne me dit rien qui vaille** I don't like the look of it at all; **ce climat ne me vaut rien** this climate doesn't suit me; **~ la peine** to be worth the trouble, be worth it; **~ mieux: il vaut mieux se taire** it's better to say nothing; **il vaut mieux que je fasse/comme ceci** it's better if I do/like this; **ça ne vaut rien** it's worthless; **que vaut ce candidat?** how good is this applicant?

valorisation [valɔʀizasjɔ̃] NF (économic) development; increased standing

valoriser [valɔʀize] /1/ VT (Écon) to develop (the economy of); (produit) to increase the value of; (Psych) to increase the standing of; (fig) to highlight, bring out

valse [vals] NF waltz; **c'est la ~ des étiquettes** the prices don't stay the same from one moment to the next

valser [valse] /1/ VI to waltz; (fig): **aller ~** to go flying

valu, e [valy] PP de **valoir**

valve [valv] NF valve

vamp [vɑ̃p] NF vamp

vampire [vɑ̃piʀ] NM vampire

van [vɑ̃] NM horse box (BRIT) ou trailer (US)

vandale [vɑ̃dal] NMF vandal

vandalisme [vɑ̃dalism] NM vandalism

vanille [vanij] NF vanilla; **glace à la ~** vanilla ice cream

vanillé, e [vanije] ADJ vanilla cpd

vanité [vanite] NF vanity

vaniteux, -euse [vanitø, -øz] ADJ vain, conceited

vanity-case [vaniti(e)kɛz] NM vanity case

vanne [van] NF gate; (fam: remarque) dig, (nasty) crack; **lancer une ~ à qn** to have a go at sb (BRIT), knock sb

vanneau, x [vano] NM lapwing

vanner [vane] /1/ VT to winnow

vannerie [vanʀi] NF basketwork

vantail, -aux [vɑ̃taj, -o] NM door, leaf

vantard, e [vɑ̃taʀ, -aʀd] ADJ boastful

vantardise [vɑ̃taʀdiz] NF boastfulness no pl; boast

vanter [vɑ̃te] /1/ VT to speak highly of, praise; **se vanter** VI to boast, brag; **se vanter de** to pride o.s. on; (péj) to boast of

va-nu-pieds [vanypje] NMF INV tramp, beggar

vapeur [vapœʀ] NF steam; (émanation) vapour (BRIT), vapor (US), fumes pl; (brouillard, buée) haze; **vapeurs** NFPL (bouffées) vapours, vapors; **à ~** steam-powered, steam cpd; **à toute ~** full steam ahead; (fig) at full tilt; **renverser la ~** to reverse engines; (fig) to backtrack, backpedal; **cuit à la ~** steamed

vapocuiseur [vapɔkyizœʀ] NM pressure cooker

vaporeux, -euse [vapɔʀø, -øz] ADJ (flou) hazy, misty; (léger) filmy, gossamer cpd

vaporisateur [vapɔʀizatœʀ] NM spray

vaporiser [vapɔʀize] /1/ VT (Chimie) to vaporize; (parfum etc) to spray

vaquer [vake] /1/ VI (Admin) to be on vacation; **~ à ses occupations** to attend to one's affairs, go about one's business

varappe [vaʀap] NF rock climbing

varappeur, -euse [vaʀapœʀ, -øz] NM/F (rock) climber

varech [vaʀɛk] NM wrack, varec

vareuse [vaʀøz] NF (blouson) pea jacket; (d'uniforme) tunic

variable [vaʀjabl] ADJ variable; (temps, humeur) changeable; (Tech: à plusieurs positions etc) adaptable; (Ling) inflectional; (divers: résultats) varied, various ▶ NF (Inform, Math) variable

variante [vaʀjɑ̃t] NF variant

variation [vaʀjasjɔ̃] NF variation; changing no pl, change; (Mus) variation

varice [vaʀis] NF varicose vein

varicelle [vaʀisɛl] NF chickenpox

varié, e [vaʀje] ADJ varied; (divers) various; **hors-d'œuvre variés** selection of hors d'œuvres

varier [vaʀje] /**7**/ VI to vary; (temps, humeur) to change ▶ VT to vary

variété [vaʀjete] NF variety; **spectacle de variétés** variety show

variole [vaʀjɔl] NF smallpox

variqueux, -euse [vaʀikø, -øz] ADJ varicose

Varsovie [vaʀsɔvi] N Warsaw

vas [va] VB voir **aller**; **~-y!** go on!

vasculaire [vaskylɛʀ] ADJ vascular

vase [vɑz] NM vase ▶ NF silt, mud; **en ~ clos** in isolation; **~ de nuit** chamberpot; **vases communicants** communicating vessels

vasectomie [vazɛktɔmi] NF vasectomy

vaseline [vazlin] NF Vaseline®

vaseux, -euse [vɑzø, -øz] ADJ silty, muddy; (fig: confus) woolly, hazy; (: fatigué) peaky; (: étourdi) woozy

vasistas [vazistas] NM fanlight

vasque [vask] NF (bassin) basin; (coupe) bowl

vassal, e, -aux [vasal, -o] NM/F vassal

vaste [vast] ADJ vast, immense

Vatican [vatikɑ̃] NM: **le ~** the Vatican

vaticiner [vatisine] /**1**/ VI (péj) to make pompous predictions

va-tout [vatu] NM: **jouer son ~** to stake one's all

vaudeville [vodvil] NM vaudeville, light comedy

vaudrai etc [vodʀe] VB voir **valoir**

vau-l'eau [volo]: **à ~** adv with the current; **s'en aller à ~** (fig: projets) to be adrift

vaurien, ne [voʀjɛ̃, -ɛn] NM/F good-for-nothing, guttersnipe

vaut [vo] VB voir **valoir**

vautour [votuʀ] NM vulture

vautrer [votʀe] /**1**/: **se vautrer** VI: **se vautrer dans** to wallow in; **se vautrer sur** to sprawl on

vaux [vo] PL de **val** ▶ VB voir **valoir**

va-vite [vavit]: **à la ~** adv in a rush

vd ABR = **vend**

VDQS SIGLE M (= vin délimité de qualité supérieure) label guaranteeing quality of wine

vds ABR = **vends**

veau, x [vo] NM (Zool) calf; (Culin) veal; (peau) calfskin; **tuer le ~ gras** to kill the fatted calf

vecteur [vɛktœʀ] NM vector; (Mil, Bio) carrier

vécu, e [veky] PP de **vivre** ▶ ADJ real(-life)

vedettariat [vədetaʀja] NM stardom; (attitude) acting like a star

vedette [vədɛt] NF (artiste etc) star; (canot) patrol boat; (police) launch; **avoir la ~** to top the bill, get star billing; **mettre qn en ~** (Ciné etc) to give sb the starring role; (fig) to push sb into the limelight; **voler la ~ à qn** to steal the show from sb

végétal, e, -aux [veʒetal, -o] ADJ vegetable ▶ NM vegetable, plant

végétalien, ne [veʒetaljɛ̃, -ɛn] ADJ, NM/F vegan

végétalisme [veʒetalism] NM veganism

végétarien, ne [veʒetaʀjɛ̃, -ɛn] ADJ, NM/F vegetarian

végétarisme [veʒetaʀism] NM vegetarianism

végétatif, -ive [veʒetatif, -iv] ADJ: **une vie végétative** a vegetable existence

végétation [veʒetasjɔ̃] NF vegetation; **végétations** NFPL (Méd) adenoids

végéter [veʒete] /**6**/ VI (fig) to vegetate

véhémence [veemɑ̃s] NF vehemence

véhément, e [veemɑ̃, -ɑ̃t] ADJ vehement

véhicule [veikyl] NM vehicle; **~ utilitaire** commercial vehicle

véhiculer [veikyle] /**1**/ VT (personnes, marchandises) to transport, convey; (fig: idées, substances) to convey, serve as a vehicle for

veille [vɛj] NF (garde) watch; (Psych) wakefulness; (jour): **la ~** the day before, the previous day; **la ~ au soir** the previous evening; **la ~ de** the day before; **la ~ de Noël** Christmas Eve; **la ~ du jour de l'An** New Year's Eve; **à la ~ de** on the eve of; **l'état de ~** the waking state

veillée [veje] NF (soirée) evening; (réunion) evening gathering; **~ d'armes** night before combat; (fig) vigil; **~ (funèbre)** wake; **~ (mortuaire)** watch

veiller [veje] /**1**/ VI (rester debout) to stay ou sit up; (ne pas dormir) to be awake; (être de garde) to be on watch; (être vigilant) to be watchful ▶ VT (malade, mort) to watch over, sit up with; **~ à** vt to attend to, see to; **~ à ce que** to make sure that, see to it that; **~ sur** vt to keep a watch ou an eye on

veilleur [vɛjœʀ] NM: **~ de nuit** night watchman

veilleuse [vɛjøz] NF (lampe) night light; (Auto) sidelight; (flamme) pilot light; **en ~** adj (lampe) dimmed; (fig: affaire) shelved, set aside

veinard, e [vɛnaʀ, -aʀd] NM/F (fam) lucky devil

veine [vɛn] NF (Anat, du bois etc) vein; (filon) vein, seam; (inspiration) inspiration; **avoir de la ~** (fam: chance) to be lucky

veiné, e [vene] ADJ veined; (bois) grained

veineux, -euse [venø, -øz] ADJ venous

Velcro® [vɛlkʀo] NM Velcro®

vêler [vele] /**1**/ VI to calve

vélin [velɛ̃] NM: **(papier) ~** vellum (paper)

véliplanchiste [veliplɑ̃ʃist] NMF windsurfer

velléitaire [veleitɛʀ] ADJ irresolute, indecisive

velléités [veleite] NFPL vague impulses

vélo [velo] NM bike, cycle; **faire du ~** to go cycling

véloce [velɔs] ADJ swift

vélocité [velɔsite] NF (Mus) nimbleness, swiftness; (vitesse) velocity

vélodrome [velɔdʀom] NM velodrome

vélomoteur [velɔmɔtœʀ] NM moped

véloski [veloski] NM skibob

velours [v(ə)luʀ] NM velvet; **~ côtelé** corduroy

velouté, e [vəlute] ADJ (au toucher) velvety; (à la vue) soft, mellow; (au goût) smooth, mellow ▶ NM: **~ d'asperges/de tomates** cream of asparagus/tomato soup

velouteux, -euse [vəlutø, -øz] ADJ velvety

velu, e [vəly] ADJ hairy

venais etc [vənɛ] VB voir **venir**

venaison [vənɛzɔ̃] NF venison

vénal, e, -aux [venal, -o] ADJ venal

vénalité [venalite] NF venality

venant [vənɑ̃]: **à tout ~** adv to all and sundry

vendable [vɑ̃dabl] ADJ saleable, marketable

V

vendange [vɑ̃dɑ̃ʒ] NF (*opération, période: aussi:* **vendanges**) grape harvest; (*raisins*) grape crop, grapes *pl*

vendanger [vɑ̃dɑ̃ʒe] /3/ VI to harvest the grapes

vendangeur, -euse [vɑ̃dɑ̃ʒœʀ, -øz] NM/F grape-picker

vendéen, ne [vɑ̃deɛ̃, -ɛn] ADJ of *ou* from the Vendée

vendeur, -euse [vɑ̃dœʀ, -øz] NM/F (*de magasin*) shop *ou* sales assistant (BRIT), sales clerk (US); (*Comm*) salesman/woman ▶ NM (*Jur*) vendor, seller; ~ **de journaux** newspaper seller

vendre [vɑ̃dʀ] /41/ VT to sell; ~ **qch à qn** to sell sb sth; **cela se vend à la douzaine** these are sold by the dozen; **"à ~"** "for sale"

vendredi [vɑ̃dʀədi] NM Friday; **V~ saint** Good Friday; *voir aussi* **lundi**

vendu, e [vɑ̃dy] PP *de* **vendre** ▶ ADJ (*péj*) corrupt

venelle [vənɛl] NF alley

vénéneux, -euse [venenø, -øz] ADJ poisonous

vénérable [veneʀabl] ADJ venerable

vénération [veneʀasjɔ̃] NF veneration

vénérer [veneʀe] /6/ VT to venerate

vénerie [venʀi] NF hunting

vénérien, ne [veneʀjɛ̃, -ɛn] ADJ venereal

Venezuela [venezɥela] NM: **le ~** Venezuela

vénézuélien, ne [venezɥeljɛ̃, -ɛn] ADJ Venezuelan ▶ NM/F: **V~, ne** Venezuelan

vengeance [vɑ̃ʒɑ̃s] NF vengeance *no pl*, revenge *no pl*; (*acte*) act of vengeance *ou* revenge

venger [vɑ̃ʒe] /3/ VT to avenge; **se venger** VI to avenge o.s.; (*par rancune*) to take revenge; **se venger de qch** to avenge o.s. for sth; to take one's revenge for sth; **se venger de qn** to take revenge on sb; **se venger sur** to wreak vengeance upon; to take revenge on; to take it out on

vengeur, -eresse [vɑ̃ʒœʀ, -ʒʀɛs] ADJ vengeful ▶ NM/F avenger

véniel, le [venjɛl] ADJ venial

venimeux, -euse [vənimø, -øz] ADJ poisonous, venomous; (*fig: haineux*) venomous, vicious

venin [vənɛ̃] NM venom, poison; (*fig*) venom

venir [v(ə)niʀ] /22/ VI to come; ~ **de** to come from; ~ **de faire: je viens d'y aller/de le voir** I've just been there/seen him; **s'il vient à pleuvoir** if it should rain, if it happens to rain; **j'en viens à croire que** I am coming to believe that; **où veux-tu en ~?** what are you getting at?; **il en est venu à mendier** he has been reduced to begging; **en ~ aux mains** to come to blows; **les années/générations à ~** the years/ generations to come; **il me vient une idée** an idea has just occurred to me; **il me vient des soupçons** I'm beginning to be suspicious; **je te vois ~** I know what you're after; **faire ~** (*docteur, plombier*) to call (out); **d'où vient que ...?** how is it that ...?; ~ **au monde** to come into the world

Venise [vəniz] N Venice

vénitien, ne [venisjɛ̃, -ɛn] ADJ Venetian

vent [vɑ̃] NM wind; **il y a du ~** it's windy; **c'est du ~** it's all hot air; **au ~** to windward; **sous le ~** to leeward; **avoir le ~ debout/arrière** to head into the wind/have the wind astern; **dans le ~** (*fam*) trendy; **prendre le ~** (*fig*) to see which way the wind blows; **avoir ~ de** to get wind of; **contre vents et marées** come hell or high water

vente [vɑ̃t] NF sale; **la ~** (*activité*) selling; (*secteur*) sales *pl*; **mettre en ~** to put on sale; (*objets personnels*) to put up for sale; ~ **aux enchères** auction sale; ~ **de charité** jumble (BRIT) *ou* rummage (US) sale; ~ **par correspondance** (**VPC**) mail-order selling

venté, e [vɑ̃te] ADJ windswept, windy

venter [vɑ̃te] /1/ VB IMPERS: **il vente** the wind is blowing

venteux, -euse [vɑ̃tø, -øz] ADJ windswept, windy

ventilateur [vɑ̃tilatœʀ] NM fan

ventilation [vɑ̃tilasjɔ̃] NF ventilation

ventiler [vɑ̃tile] /1/ VT to ventilate; (*total, statistiques*) to break down

ventouse [vɑ̃tuz] NF (*ampoule*) cupping glass; (*de caoutchouc*) suction pad; (*Zool*) sucker

ventre [vɑ̃tʀ] NM (*Anat*) stomach; (*fig*) belly; **prendre du ~** to be getting a paunch; **avoir mal au ~** to have (a) stomach ache

ventricule [vɑ̃tʀikyl] NM ventricle

ventriloque [vɑ̃tʀilɔk] NMF ventriloquist

ventripotent, e [vɑ̃tʀipɔtɑ̃, -ɑ̃t] ADJ potbellied

ventru, e [vɑ̃tʀy] ADJ potbellied

venu, e [v(ə)ny] PP *de* **venir** ▶ ADJ: **être mal ~ à** *ou* **de faire** to have no grounds for doing, be in no position to do; **mal ~** ill-timed, unwelcome; **bien ~** timely, welcome ▶ NF coming

vêpres [vɛpʀ] NFPL vespers

ver [vɛʀ] NM worm; (*des fruits etc*) maggot; (*du bois*) woodworm *no pl*; ~ **blanc** May beetle grub; ~ **luisant** glow-worm; ~ **à soie** silkworm; ~ **solitaire** tapeworm; ~ **de terre** earthworm

véracité [veʀasite] NF veracity

véranda [veʀɑ̃da] NF veranda(h)

verbal, e, -aux [vɛʀbal, -o] ADJ verbal

verbalement [vɛʀbalmɑ̃] ADV verbally

verbaliser [vɛʀbalize] /1/ VI (*Police*) to book *ou* report an offender; (*Psych*) to verbalize

verbe [vɛʀb] NM (*Ling*) verb; (*voix*): **avoir le ~ sonore** to have a sonorous tone (of voice); **la magie du ~** the magic of language *ou* the word; **le V~** (*Rel*) the Word

verbeux, -euse [vɛʀbø, -øz] ADJ verbose, wordy

verbiage [vɛʀbjaʒ] NM verbiage

verbosité [vɛʀbozite] NF verbosity

verdâtre [vɛʀdɑtʀ] ADJ greenish

verdeur [vɛʀdœʀ] NF (*vigueur*) vigour (BRIT), vigor (US), vitality; (*crudité*) forthrightness; (*défaut de maturité*) tartness, sharpness

verdict [vɛʀdik(t)] NM verdict

verdir [vɛʀdiʀ] /2/ VI, VT to turn green

verdoyant, e [vɛʀdwajɑ̃, -ɑ̃t] ADJ green, verdant

verdure [vɛʀdyʀ] NF (*arbres, feuillages*) greenery; (*légumes verts*) green vegetables *pl*, greens *pl*

véreux, -euse [veʀø, -øz] ADJ worm-eaten; (*malhonnête*) shady, corrupt

verge [vɛʀʒ] NF (*Anat*) penis; (*baguette*) stick, cane

verger [vɛʀʒe] NM orchard

vergeture [vɛʀʒətyʀ] NF stretch mark *gen pl*
verglacé, e [vɛʀglase] ADJ icy, iced-over
verglas [vɛʀgla] NM (black) ice
vergogne [vɛʀgɔɲ]: **sans** ~ *adv* shamelessly
véridique [veʀidik] ADJ truthful
vérificateur, -trice [veʀifikatœʀ, -tʀis] NM/F
controller, checker ▶ NF (*machine*) verifier; ~ **des
comptes** (*Finance*) auditor
vérification [veʀifikasjɔ̃] NF checking *no pl*,
check; ~ **d'identité** identity check
vérifier [veʀifje] /7/ VT to check; (*corroborer*) to
confirm, bear out; **se vérifier** VI to be confirmed
ou verified
vérin [veʀɛ̃] NM jack
véritable [veʀitabl] ADJ real; (*ami, amour*) true;
un ~ désastre an absolute disaster
véritablement [veʀitabləmɑ̃] ADV (*effectivement*)
really; (*absolument*) absolutely
vérité [veʀite] NF truth; (*d'un portrait*)
lifelikeness; (*sincérité*) truthfulness, sincerity;
en ~, à la ~ to tell the truth
verlan [vɛʀlɑ̃] NM (back) slang; *see note*

> Verlan is a form of slang popularized in the
> 1950's. It consists of inverting a word's
> syllables, the term *verlan* itself coming from
> *l'envers* (*à l'envers* = back to front). Typical
> examples are *féca* (*café*), *ripou* (*pourri*), *meuf*
> (*femme*), and *beur* (*Arabe*).

vermeil, le [vɛʀmɛj] ADJ bright red, ruby red
▶ NM (*substance*) vermeil
vermicelles [vɛʀmisɛl] NMPL vermicelli *sg*
vermifuge [vɛʀmifyʒ] NM: **poudre** ~ worm
powder
vermillon [vɛʀmijɔ̃] ADJ INV vermilion, scarlet
vermine [vɛʀmin] NF vermin *pl*
vermoulu, e [vɛʀmuly] ADJ worm-eaten, with
woodworm
vermout, vermouth [vɛʀmut] NM vermouth
verni, e [vɛʀni] ADJ varnished; glazed; (*fam*)
lucky; **cuir** ~ patent leather; **souliers vernis**
patent (leather) shoes
vernir [vɛʀniʀ] /2/ VT (*bois, tableau, ongles*) to
varnish; (*poterie*) to glaze
vernis [vɛʀni] NM (*enduit*) varnish; glaze; (*fig*)
veneer; ~ **à ongles** nail varnish (BRIT) *ou* polish
vernissage [vɛʀnisaʒ] NM varnishing; glazing;
(*d'une exposition*) preview
vernisser [vɛʀnise] /1/ VT to glaze
vérole [veʀɔl] NF (*variole*) smallpox; (*fam: syphilis*)
pox
Vérone [veʀon] N Verona
verrai *etc* [veʀe] VB *voir* **voir**
verre [vɛʀ] NM glass; (*de lunettes*) lens *sg*; **verres**
NMPL (*lunettes*) glasses; **boire** *ou* **prendre un** ~
to have a drink; **à vin/à liqueur** wine/liqueur
glass; ~ **à dents** tooth mug; ~ **dépoli** frosted
glass; ~ **de lampe** lamp glass *ou* chimney; ~ **de
montre** watch glass; ~ **à pied** stemmed glass;
verres de contact contact lenses; **verres
fumés** tinted lenses
verrerie [vɛʀʀi] NF (*fabrique*) glassworks *sg*;
(*activité*) glass-making, glass-working; (*objets*)
glassware
verrier [vɛʀje] NM glass-blower

verrière [vɛʀjɛʀ] NF (*grand vitrage*) window;
(*toit vitré*) glass roof
verrons *etc* [veʀɔ̃] VB *voir* **voir**
verroterie [veʀɔtʀi] NF glass beads *pl*, glass
jewellery (BRIT) *ou* jewelry (US)
verrou [veʀu] NM (*targette*) bolt; (*fig*)
constriction; **mettre le** ~ to bolt the door;
mettre qn sous les verrous to put sb behind
bars
verrouillage [veʀujaʒ] NM (*dispositif*) locking
mechanism; (*Auto*): ~ **central** *ou* **centralisé**
central locking
verrouiller [veʀuje] /1/ VT to bolt; to lock;
(*Mil: brèche*) to close
verrue [veʀy] NF wart; (*plantaire*) verruca;
(*fig*) eyesore
vers [vɛʀ] NM line ▶ NMPL (*poésie*) verse *sg*
▶ PRÉP (*en direction de*) toward(s); (*près de*) around
(about); (*temporel*) about, around
versant [vɛʀsɑ̃] NM slopes *pl*, side
versatile [vɛʀsatil] ADJ fickle, changeable
verse [vɛʀs]: **à** ~ *adv*: **il pleut à** ~ it's pouring
(with rain)
versé, e [vɛʀse] ADJ: **être** ~ **dans** (*science*) to be
(well-)versed in
Verseau [vɛʀso] NM: **le** ~ Aquarius, the
water-carrier; **être du** ~ to be Aquarius
versement [vɛʀsəmɑ̃] NM payment; (*sur un
compte*) deposit, remittance; **en trois
versements** in three instalments
verser [vɛʀse] /1/ VT (*liquide, grains*) to pour;
(*larmes, sang*) to shed; (*argent*) to pay; (*soldat:
affecter*): ~ **qn dans** to assign sb to ▶ VI (*véhicule*)
to overturn; (*fig*): ~ **dans** to lapse into; ~ **sur un
compte** to pay into an account
verset [vɛʀsɛ] NM verse; versicle
verseur [vɛʀsœʀ] ADJ M *voir* **bec**; **bouchon**
versification [vɛʀsifikasjɔ̃] NF versification
versifier [vɛʀsifje] /7/ VT to put into verse ▶ VI to
versify, write verse
version [vɛʀsjɔ̃] NF version; (*Scol*) translation
(*into the mother tongue*); **film en** ~ **originale** film
in the original language
verso [vɛʀso] NM back; **voir au** ~ see over(leaf)
vert, e [vɛʀ, vɛʀt] ADJ green; (*vin*) young;
(*vigoureux*) sprightly; (*cru*) forthright ▶ NM
green; **dire des vertes (et des pas mûres)** to
say some pretty spicy things; **il en a vu des
vertes** he's seen a thing or two; ~ **bouteille** *adj
inv* bottle-green; ~ **d'eau** *adj inv* sea-green;
~ **pomme** *adj inv* apple-green; **les Verts** (*Pol*)
the Greens
vert-de-gris [vɛʀdəgʀi] NM verdigris ▶ ADJ INV
grey(ish)-green
vertébral, e, -aux [vɛʀtebʀal, -o] ADJ back *cpd*;
voir **colonne**
vertébré, e [vɛʀtebʀe] ADJ, NM vertebrate
vertèbre [vɛʀtɛbʀ] NF vertebra
vertement [vɛʀtəmɑ̃] ADV (*réprimander*) sharply
vertical, e, -aux [vɛʀtikal, -o] ADJ vertical
verticale [vɛʀtikal] NF vertical; **à la** ~ *adv* vertically
verticalement [vɛʀtikalmɑ̃] ADV vertically
verticalité [vɛʀtikalite] NF verticalness,
verticality

V

vertige [vɛʀtiʒ] NM (peur du vide) vertigo; (étourdissement) dizzy spell; (fig) fever; **ça me donne le ~** it makes me dizzy; (fig) it makes my head spin ou reel

vertigineux, -euse [vɛʀtiʒinø, -øz] ADJ (hausse, vitesse) breathtaking; (altitude, gorge) breathtakingly high (ou deep)

vertu [vɛʀty] NF virtue; **une ~** a saint, a paragon of virtue; **avoir la ~ de faire** to have the virtue of doing; **en ~ de** prép in accordance with

vertueusement [vɛʀtɥøzmɑ̃] ADV virtuously

vertueux, -euse [vɛʀtɥø, -øz] ADJ virtuous

verve [vɛʀv] NF witty eloquence; **être en ~** to be in brilliant form

verveine [vɛʀvɛn] NF (Bot) verbena, vervain; (infusion) verbena tea

vésicule [vezikyl] NF vesicle; **~ biliaire** gall-bladder

vespasienne [vɛspazjɛn] NF urinal

vespéral, e, -aux [vɛspeʀal, -o] ADJ vespertine, evening cpd

vessie [vesi] NF bladder

veste [vɛst] NF jacket; **~ droite/croisée** single-/double-breasted jacket; **retourner sa ~** (fig) to change one's colours

vestiaire [vɛstjɛʀ] NM (au théâtre etc) cloakroom; (de stade etc) changing-room (BRIT), locker-room (US); (métallique): **(armoire) ~** locker

vestibule [vɛstibyl] NM hall

vestige [vɛstiʒ] NM (objet) relic; (fragment) trace; (fig) remnant, vestige; **vestiges** NMPL (d'une ville) remains; (d'une civilisation, du passé) remnants, relics

vestimentaire [vɛstimɑ̃tɛʀ] ADJ (dépenses) clothing; (détail) of dress; (élégance) sartorial; **dépenses vestimentaires** clothing expenditure

veston [vɛstɔ̃] NM jacket

Vésuve [vezyv] NM: **le ~** Vesuvius

vêtais etc [vɛtɛ] VB voir **vêtir**

vêtement [vɛtmɑ̃] NM garment, item of clothing; (Comm): **le ~** the clothing industry; **vêtements** NMPL clothes; **vêtements de sport** sportswear sg, sports clothes

vétéran [veteʀɑ̃] NM veteran

vétérinaire [veteʀinɛʀ] ADJ veterinary ▸ NMF vet, veterinary surgeon (BRIT), veterinarian (US)

vétille [vetij] NF trifle, triviality

vétilleux, -euse [vetijø, -øz] ADJ punctilious

vêtir [vetiʀ] /20/ VT to clothe, dress; **se vêtir** to dress (o.s.)

vêtit etc [veti] VB voir **vêtir**

vétiver [vetivɛʀ] NM (Bot) vetiver

veto [veto] NM veto; **droit de ~** right of veto; **mettre** ou **opposer un ~ à** to veto

vêtu, e [vety] PP de **vêtir** ▸ ADJ: **~ de** dressed in, wearing; **chaudement ~** warmly dressed

vétuste [vetyst] ADJ ancient, timeworn

vétusté [vetyste] NF age, dilapidation

veuf, veuve [vœf, vœv] ADJ widowed ▸ NM widower ▸ NF widow

veuille [vœj], **veuillez** etc [vœje] VB voir **vouloir**

veule [vøl] ADJ spineless

veulent etc [vœl] VB voir **vouloir**

veulerie [vølʀi] NF spinelessness

veut [vø] VB voir **vouloir**

veuvage [vœvaʒ] NM widowhood

veuve [vœv] ADJ F, NF voir **veuf**

veux [vø] VB voir **vouloir**

vexant, e [vɛksɑ̃, -ɑ̃t] ADJ (contrariant) annoying; (blessant) upsetting

vexation [vɛksasjɔ̃] NF humiliation

vexations [vɛksasjɔ̃] NFPL humiliations

vexatoire [vɛksatwaʀ] ADJ: **mesures vexatoires** harassment sg

vexer [vɛkse] /1/ VT to hurt, upset; **se vexer** VI to be offended, get upset

VF SIGLE F (Ciné) = **version française**

VHF SIGLE F (= Very High Frequency) VHF

via [vja] PRÉP via

viabiliser [vjabilize] /1/ VT to provide with services (water etc)

viabilité [vjabilite] NF viability; (d'un chemin) practicability

viable [vjabl] ADJ viable; (économie, industrie etc) sustainable

viaduc [vjadyk] NM viaduct

viager, -ère [vjaʒe, -ɛʀ] ADJ: **rente viagère** life annuity ▸ NM: **mettre en ~** to sell in return for a life annuity

viande [vjɑ̃d] NF meat; **je ne mange pas de ~** I don't eat meat

viatique [vjatik] NM (Rel) viaticum; (fig) provisions pl ou money for the journey

vibrant, e [vibʀɑ̃, -ɑ̃t] ADJ vibrating; (voix) vibrant; (émouvant) emotive

vibraphone [vibʀafɔn] NM vibraphone, vibes pl

vibraphoniste [vibʀafɔnist] NMF vibraphone player

vibration [vibʀasjɔ̃] NF vibration

vibratoire [vibʀatwaʀ] ADJ vibratory

vibrer [vibʀe] /1/ VI to vibrate; (son, voix) to be vibrant; (fig) to be stirred; **faire ~** to (cause to) vibrate; to stir, thrill

vibromasseur [vibʀɔmasœʀ] NM vibrator

vicaire [vikɛʀ] NM curate

vice [vis] NM vice; (défaut) fault; **~ caché** (Comm) latent ou inherent defect; **~ de forme** legal flaw ou irregularity

vice... [vis] PRÉFIXE vice-

vice-consul [viskɔ̃syl] NM vice-consul

vice-présidence [vispʀezidɑ̃s] NF (d'un pays) vice-presidency; (d'une société) vice-presidency, vice-chairmanship (BRIT)

vice-président, e [vispʀezidɑ̃, -ɑ̃t] NM/F vice-president; vice-chairman

vice-roi [visʀwa] NM viceroy

vice-versa [visevɛʀsa] ADV vice versa

vichy [viʃi] NM (toile) gingham; (eau) Vichy water; **carottes V~** boiled carrots

vichyssois, e [viʃiswa, -waz] ADJ of ou from Vichy, Vichy cpd ▸ NF (soupe) vichyssoise (soup), cream of leek and potato soup ▸ NM/F: **V~, e** native ou inhabitant of Vichy

vicié, e [visje] ADJ (air) polluted, tainted; (Jur) invalidated

vicier [visje] /7/ VT (Jur) to invalidate

vicieux, -euse [visjø, -øz] ADJ (*pervers*) dirty(-minded); (*méchant*) nasty; (*fautif*) incorrect, wrong ► NM/F lecher

vicinal, e, -aux [visinal, -o] ADJ: **chemin ~** byroad, byway

vicissitudes [visisityd] NFPL (trials and) tribulations

vicomte [vikɔ̃t] NM viscount

vicomtesse [vikɔ̃tɛs] NF viscountess

victime [viktim] NF victim; (*d'accident*) casualty; **être (la) ~ de** to be the victim of; **être ~ d'une attaque/d'un accident** to suffer a stroke/be involved in an accident

victoire [viktwaʀ] NF victory

victorieusement [viktɔʀjøzmã] ADV triumphantly, victoriously

victorieux, -euse [viktɔʀjø, -øz] ADJ victorious; (*sourire, attitude*) triumphant

victuailles [viktɥaj] NFPL provisions

vidange [vidãʒ] NF (*d'un fossé, réservoir*) emptying; (*Auto*) oil change; (*de lavabo: bonde*) waste outlet; **vidanges** NFPL (*matières*) sewage *sg*; **faire la ~** (*Auto*) to change the oil, do an oil change; **tuyau de ~** drainage pipe

vidanger [vidãʒe] /**3**/ VT to empty; **faire ~ la voiture** to have the oil changed in one's car

vide [vid] ADJ empty ► NM (*Physique*) vacuum; (*espace*) (empty) space, gap; (*sous soi: dans une falaise etc*) drop; (*futilité, néant*) void; **~ de** empty of; (*de sens etc*) devoid of; **sous ~** adv in a vacuum; **emballé sous ~** vacuum-packed; **regarder dans le ~** to stare into space; **avoir peur du ~** to be afraid of heights; **parler dans le ~** to waste one's breath; **faire le ~** (*dans son esprit*) to make one's mind go blank; **faire le ~ autour de qn** to isolate sb; **à ~** adv (*sans occupants*) empty; (*sans charge*) unladen; (*Tech*) without gripping *ou* being in gear

vidé, e [vide] ADJ (*épuisé*) done in, all in

vidéo [video] NF, ADJ INV video; **cassette ~** video cassette; **~ inverse** reverse video

vidéocassette [videokasɛt] NF video cassette

vidéoclip [videoklip] NM music video

vidéoclub [videoklœb] NM video club

vidéoconférence [videokɔ̃feʀãs] NF video conference

vidéodisque [videodisk] NM videodisc

vide-ordures [vidɔʀdyʀ] NM INV (rubbish) chute

vidéotex® [videotɛks] NM teletext

vidéothèque [videotɛk] NF video library

vide-poches [vidpɔʃ] NM INV tidy; (*Auto*) glove compartment

vide-pomme [vidpɔm] NM INV apple-corer

vider [vide] /**1**/ VT to empty; (*Culin: volaille, poisson*) to gut, clean out; (*régler: querelle*) to settle; (*fatiguer*) to wear out; (*fam: expulser*) to throw out, chuck out; **se vider** VI to empty; **~ les lieux** to quit *ou* vacate the premises

videur [vidœʀ] NM (*de boîte de nuit*) bouncer

vie [vi] NF life; **être en ~** to be alive; **sans ~** lifeless; **à ~** for life; **membre à ~** life member; **dans la ~ courante** in everyday life; **avoir la ~ dure** to have nine lives; to die hard; **mener la ~ dure à qn** to make life a misery for sb; **que faites-vous dans la ~?** what do you do?

vieil [vjɛj] ADJ M *voir* **vieux**

vieillard [vjɛjaʀ] NM old man; **les vieillards** old people

vieille [vjɛj] ADJ F, NF *voir* **vieux**

vieilleries [vjɛjʀi] NFPL old things *ou* stuff *sg*

vieillesse [vjɛjɛs] NF old age; (*vieillards*): **la ~** old people, elderly people

vieilli, e [vjeji] ADJ (*marqué par l'âge*) aged; (*suranné*) dated

vieillir [vjejiʀ] /**2**/ VI (*prendre de l'âge*) to grow old; (*population, vin*) to age; (*doctrine, auteur*) to become dated ► VT to age; **il a beaucoup vieilli** he has aged a lot; **se vieillir** to make o.s. older

vieillissement [vjejismã] NM growing old; ageing

vieillot, te [vjɛjo, -ɔt] ADJ antiquated, quaint

vielle [vjɛl] NF hurdy-gurdy

viendrai *etc* [vjɛ̃dʀe] VB *voir* **venir**

Vienne [vjɛn] N (*en Autriche*) Vienna

vienne [vjɛn], **viens** *etc* [vjɛ̃] VB *voir* **venir**

viennois, e [vjɛnwa, -waz] ADJ Viennese

viens [vjɛ̃] VB *voir* **venir**

vierge [vjɛʀʒ] ADJ virgin; (*film*) blank; (*page*) clean, blank; (*jeune fille*): **être ~** to be a virgin ► NF virgin; (*signe*): **la V~** Virgo, the Virgin; **être de la V~** to be Virgo; **~ de** (*sans*) free from, unsullied by

Viêtnam, Vietnam [vjɛtnam] NM: **le ~** Vietnam; **le ~ du Nord/du Sud** North/South Vietnam

vietnamien, ne [vjɛtnamjɛ̃, -ɛn] ADJ Vietnamese ► NM (*Ling*) Vietnamese ► NM/F: **V~, ne** Vietnamese; **V~, ne du Nord/Sud** North/South Vietnamese

vieux, vieil, vieille [vjø, vjɛj] ADJ old ► NM/F old man/woman ► NMPL: **les ~** the old, old people; (*fam: parents*) the old folk *ou* ones; **un petit ~** a little old man; **mon ~/ma vieille** (*fam*) old man/girl; **pauvre ~** poor old soul; **prendre un coup de ~** to put years on; **se faire ~** to be old, to be getting on; **un ~ de la vieille** one of the old brigade; **~ garçon** *nm* bachelor; **~ jeu** *adj inv* old-fashioned; **~ rose** *adj inv* old rose; **vieil or** *adj inv* old gold; **vieille fille** *nf* spinster

vif, vive [vif, viv] ADJ (*animé*) lively; (*alerte*) sharp, quick; (*brusque*) sharp, brusque; (*aigu*) sharp; (*lumière, couleur*) brilliant; (*air*) crisp; (*vent, émotion*) keen; (*froid*) bitter; (*fort: regret, déception*) great, deep; (*vivant*): **brûlé ~** burnt alive; **eau vive** running water; **de vive voix** personally; **avoir l'esprit ~** to be quick-witted; **piquer qn au ~** to cut sb to the quick; **tailler dans le ~** to cut into the living flesh; **à ~** (*plaie*) open; **avoir les nerfs à ~** to be on edge; **sur le ~** (*Art*) from life; **entrer dans le ~ du sujet** to get to the very heart of the matter

vif-argent [vifaʀʒã] NM INV quicksilver

vigie [viʒi] NF (*matelot*) look-out; (*poste*) look-out post, crow's nest

vigilance [viʒilãs] NF vigilance

vigilant, e [viʒilã, -ãt] ADJ vigilant

v

437

vigile [viʒil] NM (*veilleur de nuit*) (night) watchman; (*police privée*) vigilante

vigne [viɲ] NF (*plante*) vine; (*plantation*) vineyard; **~ vierge** Virginia creeper

vigneron [viɲ(ɔ)Rɔ̃] NM wine grower

vignette [viɲɛt] NF (*motif*) vignette; (*de marque*) manufacturer's label *ou* seal; (*petite illustration*) (small) illustration; (*pour voiture*) ≈ (road) tax disc (BRIT), ≈ license plate sticker (US); (*sur médicament*) price label (*on medicines for reimbursement by Social Security*)

vignoble [viɲɔbl] NM (*plantation*) vineyard; (*vignes d'une région*) vineyards pl

vigoureusement [viguRøzmɑ̃] ADV vigorously

vigoureux, -euse [viguRø, -øz] ADJ vigorous, robust

vigueur [vigœR] NF vigour (BRIT), vigor (US); **être/entrer en ~** to be in/come into force; **en ~** current

vil, e [vil] ADJ vile, base; **à ~ prix** at a very low price

vilain, e [vilɛ̃, -ɛn] ADJ (*laid*) ugly; (*affaire, blessure*) nasty; (*pas sage: enfant*) naughty ▶ NM (*paysan*) villein, villain; **ça va tourner au ~** things are going to turn nasty; **~ mot** bad word

vilainement [vilɛnmɑ̃] ADV badly

vilebrequin [vilbRəkɛ̃] NM (*outil*) (bit-)brace; (*Auto*) crankshaft

vilenie [vilni] NF vileness *no pl*, baseness *no pl*

vilipender [vilipɑ̃de] /1/ VT to revile, vilify

villa [vila] NF (detached) house; **~ en multipropriété** time-share villa

village [vilaʒ] NM village; **~ de toile** tent village; **~ de vacances** holiday village

villageois, e [vilaʒwa, -waz] ADJ village cpd ▶ NM/F villager

ville [vil] NF town; (*importante*) city; (*administration*): **la ~** ≈ the Corporation, ≈ the (town) council; **aller en ~** to go to town; **habiter en ~** to live in town; **~ jumelée** twin town; **~ d'eaux** spa; **~ nouvelle** new town

ville-champignon [vilʃɑ̃piɲɔ̃] (*pl* **villes-champignons**) NF boom town

ville-dortoir [vildɔRtwaR] (*pl* **villes-dortoirs**) NF dormitory town

villégiature [vileʒjatyR] NF (*séjour*) holiday; (*lieu*) (holiday) resort

vin [vɛ̃] NM wine; **avoir le ~ gai/triste** to get happy/miserable after a few drinks; **~ blanc/rosé/rouge** white/rosé/red wine; **~ d'honneur** reception (*with wine and snacks*); **~ de messe** altar wine; **~ ordinaire** *ou* **de table** table wine; **~ de pays** local wine; *voir aussi* **AOC; VDQS**

vinaigre [vinɛgR] NM vinegar; **tourner au ~** (*fig*) to turn sour; **~ de vin/d'alcool** wine/spirit vinegar

vinaigrette [vinɛgRɛt] NF vinaigrette, French dressing

vinaigrier [vinɛgRije] NM (*fabricant*) vinegar-maker; (*flacon*) vinegar cruet *ou* bottle

vinasse [vinas] NF (*péj*) cheap wine, plonk (BRIT)

vindicatif, -ive [vɛ̃dikatif, -iv] ADJ vindictive

vindicte [vɛ̃dikt] NF: **désigner qn à la ~ publique** to expose sb to public condemnation

vineux, -euse [vinø, -øz] ADJ win(e)y

vingt [vɛ̃, vɛ̃t] (*2nd pron used when followed by a vowel*) NUM twenty; **~-quatre heures sur ~-quatre** twenty-four hours a day, round the clock

vingtaine [vɛ̃tɛn] NF: **une ~ (de)** around twenty, twenty or so

vingtième [vɛ̃tjɛm] NUM twentieth

vinicole [vinikɔl] ADJ (*production*) wine cpd; (*région*) wine-growing

vinification [vinifikasjɔ̃] NF wine-making, wine production; (*des sucres*) vinification

vins *etc* [vɛ̃] VB *voir* **venir**

vinyle [vinil] NM vinyl

viol [vjɔl] NM (*d'une femme*) rape; (*d'un lieu sacré*) violation

violacé, e [vjɔlase] ADJ purplish, mauvish

violation [vjɔlasjɔ̃] NF desecration; violation; (*d'un droit*) breach

violemment [vjɔlamɑ̃] ADV violently

violence [vjɔlɑ̃s] NF violence; **violences** NFPL acts of violence; **faire ~ à qn** to do violence to sb; **se faire ~** to force o.s.

violent, e [vjɔlɑ̃, -ɑ̃t] ADJ violent; (*remède*) drastic; (*besoin, désir*) intense, urgent

violenter [vjɔlɑ̃te] /1/ VT to assault (sexually)

violer [vjɔle] /1/ VT (*femme*) to rape; (*sépulture*) to desecrate, violate; (*loi, traité*) to violate

violet, te [vjɔlɛ, -ɛt] ADJ, NM purple, mauve ▶ NF (*fleur*) violet

violeur [vjɔlœR] NM rapist

violine [vjɔlin] NF deep purple

violon [vjɔlɔ̃] NM violin; (*dans la musique folklorique etc*) fiddle; (*fam: prison*) lock-up; **premier ~** first violin; **~ d'Ingres** (artistic) hobby

violoncelle [vjɔlɔ̃sɛl] NM cello

violoncelliste [vjɔlɔ̃selist] NMF cellist

violoniste [vjɔlɔnist] NMF violinist, violin-player; (*folklorique etc*) fiddler

VIP SIGLE M (= *Very Important Person*) VIP

vipère [vipɛR] NF viper, adder

virage [viraʒ] NM (*d'un véhicule*) turn; (*d'une route, piste*) bend; (*Chimie*) change in colour (BRIT) *ou* color (US); (*de cuti-réaction*) positive reaction; (*Photo*) toning; (*fig: Pol*) about-turn; **prendre un ~** to go into a bend, take a bend; **~ sans visibilité** blind bend

viral, e, -aux [viRal, -o] ADJ viral

virée [viRe] NF (*courte*) run; (: *à pied*) walk; (*longue*) hike, trip, walking tour

virement [viRmɑ̃] NM (*Comm*) transfer; **~ bancaire** (bank) credit transfer, ≈ (bank) giro transfer (BRIT); **~ postal** Post office credit transfer, ≈ Girobank® transfer (BRIT)

virent [viR] VB *voir* **voir**

virer [viRe] /1/ VT (*Comm*) to transfer; (*Photo*) to tone; (*fam: renvoyer*) to sack, boot out ▶ VI to turn; (*Chimie*) to change colour (BRIT) *ou* color (US); (*cuti-réaction*) to come up positive; (*Photo*) to tone; **~ au bleu** to turn blue; **~ de bord** to tack; (*fig*) to change tack; **~ sur l'aile** to bank

virevolte [viRvɔlt] NF twirl; (*d'avis, d'opinion*) about-turn

virevolter [viʀvɔlte] /**1**/ vi to twirl around
virginal, e, -aux [viʀʒinal, -o] ADJ virginal
virginité [viʀʒinite] NF virginity; (*fig*) purity
virgule [viʀgyl] NF comma; (*Math*) point; **quatre ~ deux** four point two; **~ flottante** floating decimal
viril, e [viʀil] ADJ (*propre à l'homme*) masculine; (*énergique, courageux*) manly, virile
viriliser [viʀilize] /**1**/ VT to make (more) manly *ou* masculine
virilité [viʀilite] NF (*attributs masculins*) masculinity; (*fermeté, courage*) manliness; (*sexuelle*) virility
virologie [viʀɔlɔʒi] NF virology
virtualité [viʀtɥalite] NF virtuality; potentiality
virtuel, le [viʀtɥɛl] ADJ potential; (*théorique*) virtual
virtuellement [viʀtɥɛlmɑ̃] ADV potentially; (*presque*) virtually
virtuose [viʀtɥoz] NMF (*Mus*) virtuoso; (*gén*) master
virtuosité [viʀtɥozite] NF virtuosity; masterliness, masterful skills *pl*
virulence [viʀylɑ̃s] NF virulence
virulent, e [viʀylɑ̃, -ɑ̃t] ADJ virulent
virus [viʀys] NM virus
vis VB [vi] *voir* **voir; vivre** ▶ NF [vis] screw; **~ à tête plate/ronde** flat-headed/round-headed screw; **~ platinées** (*Auto*) (contact) points; **~ sans fin** worm, endless screw
visa [viza] NM (*sceau*) stamp; (*validation de passeport*) visa; **~ de censure** (censor's) certificate
visage [vizaʒ] NM face; **à ~ découvert** (*franchement*) openly
visagiste [vizaʒist] NMF beautician
vis-à-vis [vizavi] ADV face to face ▶ NM person opposite; house *etc* opposite; **~** *prép* opposite; (*fig*) towards, vis-à-vis; **en ~** facing *ou* opposite each other; **sans ~** (*immeuble*) with an open outlook
viscéral, e, -aux [viseʀal, -o] ADJ (*fig*) deep-seated, deep-rooted
viscères [viseʀ] NMPL intestines, entrails
viscose [viskoz] NF viscose
viscosité [viskozite] NF viscosity
visée [vize] NF (*avec une arme*) aiming; (*Arpentage*) sighting; **visées** NFPL (*intentions*) designs; **avoir des visées sur qn/qch** to have designs on sb/sth
viser [vize] /**1**/ vi to aim ▶ VT to aim at; (*concerner*) to be aimed *ou* directed at; (*apposer un visa sur*) to stamp, visa; **~ à qch/faire** to aim at sth/at doing *ou* to do
viseur [vizœʀ] NM (*d'arme*) sights *pl*; (*Photo*) viewfinder
visibilité [vizibilite] NF visibility; **sans ~** (*pilotage, virage*) blind *cpd*
visible [vizibl] ADJ visible; (*disponible*): **est-il ~?** can he see me?, will he see visitors?
visiblement [vizibləmɑ̃] ADV visibly, obviously
visière [vizjɛʀ] NF (*de casquette*) peak; (*qui s'attache*) eyeshade

vision [vizjɔ̃] NF vision; (*sens*) (eye)sight, vision; (*fait de voir*): **la ~ de** the sight of; **première ~** (*Ciné*) first showing
visionnaire [vizjɔnɛʀ] ADJ, NMF visionary
visionner [vizjɔne] /**1**/ VT to view
visionneuse [vizjɔnøz] NF viewer
visiophone [vizjɔfɔn] NM videophone
visite [vizit] NF visit; (*visiteur*) visitor; (*touristique: d'un musée etc*) tour; (*Comm: de représentant*) call; (*expertise, d'inspection*) inspection; (*médicale, à domicile*) visit, call; **~ médicale** medical examination; (*Mil: d'entrée*) medicals *pl*; (: *quotidienne*) sick parade; **~ accompagnée** *ou* **guidée** guided tour; **faire une ~ à qn** to call on sb, pay sb a visit; **rendre ~ à qn** to visit sb, pay sb a visit; **être en ~ (chez qn)** to be visiting (sb); **avoir de la ~** to have visitors; **heures de ~** (*hôpital, prison*) visiting hours; **le droit de ~** (*Jur: aux enfants*) right of access, access; **~ de douane** customs inspection *ou* examination; **~ guidée** guided tour
visiter [vizite] /**1**/ VT to visit; (*musée, ville*) to visit, go round
visiteur, -euse [vizitœʀ, -øz] NM/F visitor; **~ des douanes** customs inspector; **~ médical** medical rep(resentative); **~ de prison** prison visitor
vison [vizɔ̃] NM mink
visqueux, -euse [viskø, -øz] ADJ viscous; (*péj*) gooey; (: *manières*) slimy
visser [vise] /**1**/ VT: **~ qch** (*fixer, serrer*) to screw sth on
visu [vizy]: **de ~** *adv* with one's own eyes
visualisation [vizɥalizasjɔ̃] NF (*Inform*) display; **écran de ~** visual display unit (VDU)
visualiser [vizɥalize] /**1**/ VT to visualize; (*Inform*) to display, bring up on screen
visuel, le [vizɥɛl] ADJ visual
visuellement [vizɥɛlmɑ̃] ADV visually
vit [vi] VB *voir* **vivre; voir**
vital, e, -aux [vital, -o] ADJ vital
vitalité [vitalite] NF vitality
vitamine [vitamin] NF vitamin
vitaminé, e [vitamine] ADJ with (added) vitamins
vitaminique [vitaminik] ADJ vitamin *cpd*
vite [vit] ADV (*rapidement*) quickly, fast; (*sans délai*) quickly; soon; **~!** quick!; **faire ~** (*agir rapidement*) to act fast; (*se dépêcher*) to be quick; **ce sera ~ fini** this will soon be finished; **viens ~** come quick(ly)
vitesse [vitɛs] NF speed; (*Auto: dispositif*) gear; **faire de la ~** to drive fast *ou* at speed; **prendre qn de ~** to outstrip sb, get ahead of sb; **prendre de la ~** to pick up *ou* gather speed; **à toute ~** at full *ou* top speed; **en perte de ~** (*avion*) losing lift; (*fig*) losing momentum; **changer de ~** (*Auto*) to change gear; **~ acquise** momentum; **~ de croisière** cruising speed; **~ de pointe** top speed; **~ du son** speed of sound; **en ~** quickly

The speed limit in France is 50 km/h in built-up areas, 90 km/h on main roads, and 130 km/h on motorways (110 km/h when it is raining).

V

viticole [vitikɔl] ADJ (*industrie*) wine *cpd*; (*région*) wine-growing

viticulteur [vitikyltœR] NM wine grower

viticulture [vitikyltyR] NF wine growing

vitrage [vitRaʒ] NM (*cloison*) glass partition; (*toit*) glass roof; (*rideau*) net curtain; **double ~** double glazing

vitrail, -aux [vitRaj, -o] NM stained-glass window

vitre [vitR] NF (*window*) pane; (*de portière, voiture*) window

vitré, e [vitRe] ADJ glass *cpd*

vitrer [vitRe] /**1**/ VT to glaze

vitreux, -euse [vitRø, -øz] ADJ vitreous; (*terne*) glassy

vitrier [vitRije] NM glazier

vitrifier [vitRifje] /**7**/ VT to vitrify; (*parquet*) to glaze

vitrine [vitRin] NF (*devanture*) (shop) window; (*étalage*) display; (*petite armoire*) display cabinet; **en ~** in the window, on display; **~ publicitaire** display case, showcase

vitriol [vitRijɔl] NM vitriol; **au ~** (*fig*) vitriolic

vitupérations [vityperasjɔ̃] NFPL invective *sg*

vitupérer [vitypeRe] /**6**/ VI to rant and rave; **~ contre** to rail against

vivable [vivabl] ADJ (*personne*) livable-with; (*maison*) fit to live in

vivace [vivas] ADJ (*arbre, plante*) hardy; (*fig*) enduring ▸ ADV [vivatʃe] (*Mus*) vivace

vivacité [vivasite] NF (*voir vif*) liveliness, vivacity; sharpness; brilliance

vivant, e [vivɑ̃, -ɑ̃t] VB *voir* vivre ▸ ADJ (*qui vit*) living, alive; (*animé*) lively; (*preuve, exemple*) living; (*langue*) modern ▸ NM: **du ~ de qn** in sb's lifetime; **les vivants et les morts** the living and the dead

vivarium [vivaRjɔm] NM vivarium

vivats [viva] NMPL cheers

vive [viv] ADJ F *voir* vif ▸ VB *voir* vivre ▸ EXCL: **~ le roi!** long live the king!; **~ les vacances!** hurrah for the holidays!

vivement [vivmɑ̃] ADV vivaciously; sharply ▸ EXCL: **~ les vacances!** I can't wait for the holidays!, roll on the holidays!

viveur [vivœR] NM (*péj*) high liver, pleasure-seeker

vivier [vivje] NM (*au restaurant etc*) fish tank; (*étang*) fishpond

vivifiant, e [vivifjɑ̃, -ɑ̃t] ADJ invigorating

vivifier [vivifje] /**7**/ VT to invigorate; (*fig: souvenirs, sentiments*) to liven up, enliven

vivions [vivjɔ̃] VB *voir* vivre

vivipare [vivipaR] ADJ viviparous

vivisection [viviseksjɔ̃] NF vivisection

vivoter [vivɔte] /**1**/ VI (*personne*) to scrape a living, get by; (*fig: affaire etc*) to struggle along

vivre [vivR] /**46**/ VI, VT to live ▸ NM: **le ~ et le logement** board and lodging; **vivres** NMPL provisions, food supplies; **il vit encore** he is still alive; **se laisser ~** to take life as it comes; **ne plus ~** (*être anxieux*) to live on one's nerves; **il a vécu** (*eu une vie aventureuse*) he has seen life; **ce régime a vécu** this regime has had its day;

être facile à ~ to be easy to get on with; **faire ~ qn** (*pourvoir à sa subsistance*) to provide (a living) for sb; **~ mal** (*chichement*) to have a meagre existence; **~ de** (*salaire etc*) to live on

vivrier, -ière [vivRije, -jɛR] ADJ food-producing *cpd*

vlan [vlɑ̃] EXCL wham!, bang!

VO SIGLE F (*Ciné*) = **version originale**; **voir un film en VO** to see a film in its original language

v° ABR = **verso**

vocable [vɔkabl] NM term

vocabulaire [vɔkabylɛR] NM vocabulary

vocal, e, -aux [vɔkal, -o] ADJ vocal

vocalique [vɔkalik] ADJ vocalic, vowel *cpd*

vocalise [vɔkaliz] NF singing exercise

vocaliser [vɔkalize] /**1**/ VI (*Ling*) to vocalize; (*Mus*) to do one's singing exercises

vocation [vɔkasjɔ̃] NF vocation, calling; **avoir la ~** to have a vocation

vociférations [vɔsiferasjɔ̃] NFPL cries of rage, screams

vociférer [vɔsifeRe] /**6**/ VI, VT to scream

vodka [vɔdka] NF vodka

vœu, x [vø] NM wish; (*à Dieu*) vow; **faire ~ de** to take a vow of; **avec tous nos ~** with every good wish *ou* our best wishes; **meilleurs ~** best wishes; (*sur une carte*) "Season's Greetings"; **~ de bonheur** best wishes for your future happiness; **~ de bonne année** best wishes for the New Year

vogue [vɔg] NF fashion, vogue; **en ~** in fashion, in vogue

voguer [vɔge] /**1**/ VI to sail

voici [vwasi] PRÉP (*pour introduire, désigner*) here is (+*sg*); here are (+*pl*); **et ~ que …** and now it (*ou* he) …; **il est parti ~ trois ans** he left three years ago; **~ une semaine que je l'ai vue** it's a week since I've seen her; **me ~** here I am; *voir aussi* **voilà**

voie [vwa] VB *voir* voir ▸ NF way; (*Rail*) track, line; (*Auto*) lane; **par ~ buccale** *ou* **orale** orally; **par ~ rectale** rectally; **suivre la ~ hiérarchique** to go through official channels; **ouvrir/montrer la ~** to open up/show the way; **être en bonne ~** to be shaping *ou* going well; **mettre qn sur la ~** to put sb on the right track; **être en ~ d'achèvement/de rénovation** to be nearing completion/in the process of renovation; **à ~ étroite** narrow-gauge; **à ~ unique** single-track; **route à deux/trois voies** two-/three-lane road; **par la ~ aérienne/maritime** by air/sea; **~ d'eau** (*Navig*) leak; **~ express** expressway; **~ de fait** (*Jur*) assault (and battery); **~ ferrée** track; railway line (*BRIT*), railroad (*US*); **par ~ ferrée** by rail, by railroad; **~ de garage** (*Rail*) siding; **la ~ lactée** the Milky Way; **~ navigable** waterway; **~ prioritaire** (*Auto*) road with right of way; **~ privée** private road; **la ~ publique** the public highway

voilà [vwala] PRÉP (*en désignant*) there is (+*sg*); there are (+*pl*); **les ~** *ou* **voici** here *ou* there they are; **en ~** *ou* **voici un** here's one, there's one;

voici mon frère et ~ ma sœur this is my brother and that's my sister; **~ ou voici deux ans** two years ago; **~ ou voici deux ans que** it's two years since; **et ~!** there we are!; **~ tout** that's all; **"~ ou voici"** (*en offrant etc*) "there *ou* here you are"; **tiens! ~ Paul** look! there's Paul

voilage [vwalaʒ] NM (*rideau*) net curtain; (*tissu*) net

voile [vwal] NM veil; (*tissu léger*) net ▶ NF sail; (*sport*) sailing; **prendre le ~** to take the veil; **mettre à la ~** to make way under sail; **~ du palais** *nm* soft palate, velum; **~ au poumon** *nm* shadow on the lung

voiler [vwale] /**1**/ VT to veil; (*Photo*) to fog; (*fausser: roue*) to buckle; (: *bois*) to warp; **se voiler** VI (*lune, regard*) to mist over; (*ciel*) to grow hazy; (*voix*) to become husky; (*roue, disque*) to buckle; (*planche*) to warp; **se voiler la face** to hide one's face

voilette [vwalɛt] NF (*hat*) veil

voilier [vwalje] NM sailing ship; (*de plaisance*) sailing boat

voilure [vwalyʀ] NF (*de voilier*) sails *pl*; (*d'avion*) aerofoils *pl* (BRIT), airfoils *pl* (US); (*de parachute*) canopy

voir [vwaʀ] /**30**/ VI, VT to see; **se voir** VI: **cela se voit** (*cela arrive*) it happens; (*c'est visible*) it's obvious, it shows; **se voir critiquer/transformer** to be criticized/transformed; **~ à faire qch** to see to it that sth is done; **~ loin** (*fig*) to be far-sighted; **~ venir** (*fig*) to wait and see; **faire ~ qch à qn** to show sb sth; **en faire ~ à qn** (*fig*) to give sb a hard time; **ne pas pouvoir ~ qn** (*fig*) not to be able to stand sb; **regardez ~** just look; **montrez ~** show (me); **dites ~** tell me; **voyons!** let's see now!; (*indignation etc*) come (along) now!; **c'est à ~!** we'll see!; **c'est ce qu'on va ~!** we'll see about that!; **avoir quelque chose à ~ avec** to have something to do with; **ça n'a rien à ~ avec lui** that has nothing to do with him

voire [vwaʀ] ADV indeed; nay; or even

voirie [vwaʀi] NF highway maintenance; (*administration*) highways department; (*enlèvement des ordures*) refuse (BRIT) *ou* garbage (US) collection

vois [vwa] VB *voir* **voir**

voisin, e [vwazɛ̃, -in] ADJ (*proche*) neighbouring (BRIT), neighboring (US); (*contigu*) next; (*ressemblant*) connected ▶ NM/F neighbour (BRIT), neighbor (US); (*de table, de dortoir etc*) person next to me (*ou* him *etc*); **~ de palier** neighbo(u)r across the landing (BRIT) *ou* hall (US)

voisinage [vwazinaʒ] NM (*proximité*) proximity; (*environs*) vicinity; (*quartier, voisins*) neighbourhood (BRIT), neighborhood (US); **relations de bon ~** neighbo(u)rly terms

voisiner [vwazine] /**1**/ VI: **~ avec** to be side by side with

voit [vwa] VB *voir* **voir**

voiture [vwatyʀ] NF car; (*wagon*) coach, carriage; **en ~!** all aboard!; **~ à bras** handcart; **~ d'enfant** pram (BRIT), baby carriage (US);

~ d'infirme invalid carriage; **~ de course** racing car; **~ de sport** sports car

voiture-lit [vwatyʀli] (*pl* **voitures-lits**) NF sleeper

voiture-restaurant [vwatyʀʀɛstoʀɑ̃] (*pl* **voitures-restaurants**) NF dining car

voix [vwa] NF voice; (*Pol*) vote; **la ~ de la conscience/raison** the voice of conscience/reason; **à haute ~** aloud; **à ~ basse** in a low voice; **faire la grosse ~** to speak gruffly; **avoir de la ~** to have a good voice; **rester sans ~** to be speechless; **~ de basse/ténor** *etc* bass/tenor *etc* voice; **à deux/quatre ~** (*Mus*) in two/four parts; **avoir ~ au chapitre** to have a say in the matter; **mettre aux ~** to put to the vote; **~ off** voice-over

vol [vɔl] NM (*mode de locomotion*) flying; (*trajet, voyage, groupe d'oiseaux*) flight; (*mode d'appropriation*) theft, stealing; (*larcin*) theft; **à ~ d'oiseau** as the crow flies; **au ~: attraper qch au ~** to catch sth as it flies past; **saisir une remarque au ~** to pick up a passing remark; **prendre son ~** to take flight; **de haut ~** (*fig*) of the highest order; **en ~** in flight; **~ avec effraction** breaking and entering *no pl*, break-in; **à l'étalage** shoplifting *no pl*; **~ libre** hang-gliding; **~ à main armée** armed robbery; **~ de nuit** night flight; **~ régulier** scheduled flight; **~ plané** (*Aviat*) glide, gliding *no pl*; **à la tire** pickpocketing *no pl*; **~ à voile** gliding

vol. ABR (= *volume*) vol

volage [vɔlaʒ] ADJ fickle

volaille [vɔlaj] NF (*oiseaux*) poultry *pl*; (*viande*) poultry *no pl*; (*oiseau*) fowl

volailler [vɔlaje] NM poulterer

volant, e [vɔlɑ̃, -ɑ̃t] ADJ flying; *voir* **feuille** *etc* ▶ NM (*d'automobile*) (steering) wheel; (*de commande*) wheel; (*objet lancé*) shuttlecock; (*jeu*) battledore and shuttlecock; (*bande de tissu*) flounce; (*feuillet détachable*) tear-off portion; **le personnel ~**, **les volants** (*Aviat*) the flight staff; **~ de sécurité** (*fig*) reserve, margin, safeguard

volatil, e [vɔlatil] ADJ volatile

volatile [vɔlatil] NM (*volaille*) bird; (*tout oiseau*) winged creature

volatiliser [vɔlatilize] /**1**/: **se volatiliser** VI (*Chimie*) to volatilize; (*fig*) to vanish into thin air

vol-au-vent [vɔlovɑ̃] NM INV vol-au-vent

volcan [vɔlkɑ̃] NM volcano; (*fig: personne*) hothead

volcanique [vɔlkanik] ADJ volcanic; (*fig: tempérament*) volatile

volcanologie [vɔlkanɔlɔʒi] NF vulcanology

volcanologue [vɔlkanɔlɔg] NMF vulcanologist

volée [vɔle] NF (*groupe d'oiseaux*) flight, flock; (*Tennis*) volley; **~ de coups/de flèches** volley of blows/arrows; **à la ~: rattraper à la ~** to catch in midair; **lancer à la ~** to fling about; **semer à la ~** to (sow) broadcast; **à toute ~** (*sonner les cloches*) vigorously; (*lancer un projectile*) with full force; **de haute ~** (*fig*) of the highest order

voler [vɔle] /**1**/ VI (*avion, oiseau, fig*) to fly; (*voleur*) to steal ▶ VT (*objet*) to steal; (*personne*) to rob; **~ en éclats** to smash to smithereens; **~ de ses**

V

propres ailes (fig) to stand on one's own two feet; ~ **au vent** to fly in the wind; ~ **qch à qn** to steal sth from sb; **on m'a volé mon portefeuille** my wallet (BRIT) ou billfold (US) has been stolen; **il ne l'a pas volé!** he asked for it!

volet [vɔlɛ] NM (de fenêtre) shutter; (Aviat) flap; (de feuillet, document) section; (fig: d'un plan) facet; **trié sur le** ~ hand-picked

voleter [vɔlte] /4/ VI to flutter (about)

voleur, -euse [vɔlœʀ, -øz] NM/F thief ▶ ADJ thieving; **"au ~!"** "stop thief!"

volière [vɔljɛʀ] NF aviary

volley [vɔlɛ], **volley-ball** [vɔlɛbol] NM volleyball

volleyeur, -euse [vɔlɛjœʀ, -øz] NM/F volleyball player

volontaire [vɔlɔ̃tɛʀ] ADJ (acte, activité) voluntary; (délibéré) deliberate; (caractère, personne: décidé) self-willed ▶ NMF volunteer

volontairement [vɔlɔ̃tɛʀmɑ̃] ADV voluntarily; deliberately

volontariat [vɔlɔ̃taʀja] NM voluntary service

volontarisme [vɔlɔ̃taʀism] NM voluntarism

volontariste [vɔlɔ̃taʀist] ADJ, NMF voluntarist

volonté [vɔlɔ̃te] NF (faculté de vouloir) will; (énergie, fermeté) will(power); (souhait, désir) wish; **se servir/boire à** ~ to take/drink as much as one likes; **bonne** ~ goodwill, willingness; **mauvaise** ~ lack of goodwill, unwillingness

volontiers [vɔlɔ̃tje] ADV (de bonne grâce) willingly; (avec plaisir) willingly, gladly; (habituellement, souvent) readily, willingly; **"~"** "with pleasure", "I'd be glad to"

volt [vɔlt] NM volt

voltage [vɔltaʒ] NM voltage

volte-face [vɔltəfas] NF INV about-turn; (fig) about-turn, U-turn; **faire** ~ to do an about-turn; to do a U-turn

voltige [vɔltiʒ] NF (Équitation) trick riding; (au cirque) acrobatics sg; (Aviat) (aerial) acrobatics sg; **numéro de haute** ~ acrobatic act

voltiger [vɔltiʒe] /3/ VI to flutter (about)

voltigeur [vɔltiʒœʀ] NM (au cirque) acrobat; (Mil) light infantryman

voltmètre [vɔltmɛtʀ] NM voltmeter

volubile [vɔlybil] ADJ voluble

volubilis [vɔlybilis] NM convolvulus

volume [vɔlym] NM volume; (Géom: solide) solid

volumineux, -euse [vɔlyminø, -øz] ADJ voluminous, bulky

volupté [vɔlypte] NF sensual delight ou pleasure

voluptueusement [vɔlyptɥøzmɑ̃] ADV voluptuously

voluptueux, -euse [vɔlyptɥø, -øz] ADJ voluptuous

volute [vɔlyt] NF (Archit) volute; ~ **de fumée** curl of smoke

vomi [vɔmi] NM vomit

vomir [vɔmiʀ] /2/ VI to vomit, be sick ▶ VT to vomit, bring up; (fig) to belch out, spew out; (exécrer) to loathe, abhor

vomissements [vɔmismɑ̃] NMPL (action) vomiting no pl; **des** ~ vomit sg

vomissure [vɔmisyʀ] NF vomit no pl

vomitif [vɔmitif] NM emetic

vont [vɔ̃] VB voir **aller**

vorace [vɔʀas] ADJ voracious

voracement [vɔʀasmɑ̃] ADV voraciously

voracité [vɔʀasite] NF voracity

vos [vo] ADJ POSS voir **votre**

Vosges [voʒ] NFPL: **les** ~ the Vosges

vosgien, ne [voʒjɛ̃, -ɛn] ADJ of ou from the Vosges ▶ NM/F inhabitant ou native of the Vosges

VOST SIGLE F (Ciné: = version originale sous-titrée) sub-titled version

votant, e [vɔtɑ̃, -ɑ̃t] NM/F voter

vote [vɔt] NM vote; ~ **par correspondance/procuration** postal/proxy vote; ~ **à main levée** vote by show of hands; ~ **secret**, ~ **à bulletins secrets** secret ballot

voter [vɔte] /1/ VI to vote ▶ VT (loi, décision) to vote for

votre [vɔtʀ] (pl **vos** [vo]) ADJ POSS your

vôtre [vɔtʀ] PRON: **le** ~, **la** ~, **les vôtres** yours; **les vôtres** (fig) your family ou folks; **à la** ~ (toast) your (good) health!

voudrai etc [vudʀe] VB voir **vouloir**

voué, e [vwe] ADJ: ~ **à** doomed to, destined for

vouer [vwe] /1/ VT: ~ **qch à** (Dieu/un saint) to dedicate sth to; **je voue ma vie/son temps à** (étude, cause etc) to devote one's life/time to; ~ **une haine/amitié éternelle à qn** to vow undying hatred/friendship to sb

MOT-CLÉ

vouloir [vulwaʀ] /31/ VT **1** (exiger, désirer) to want; **vouloir faire/que qn fasse** to want to do/sb to do; **voulez-vous du thé?** would you like ou do you want some tea?; **vouloir qch à qn** to wish sth for sb; **que me veut-il?** what does he want with me?; **que veux-tu que je te dise?** what do you want me to say?; **sans le vouloir** (involontairement) without meaning to, unintentionally; **je voudrais ceci/faire** I would ou I'd like this/to do; **le hasard a voulu que ...** as fate would have it, ...; **la tradition veut que ...** tradition demands that ...; **... qui se veut moderne** ... which purports to be modern

2 (consentir): **je veux bien** (bonne volonté) I'll be happy to; (concession) fair enough, that's fine; **oui, si on veut** (en quelque sorte) yes, if you like; **comme tu veux** as you wish; (en quelque sorte) if you like; **veuillez attendre** please wait; **veuillez agréer ...** (formule épistolaire) yours faithfully

3: **en vouloir** (être ambitieux) to be out to win; **en vouloir à qn** to bear sb a grudge; **je lui en veux d'avoir fait ça** I resent his having done that; **s'en vouloir (de)** to be annoyed with o.s. (for); **il en veut à mon argent** he's after my money

4: **vouloir de** to want; **l'entreprise ne veut plus de lui** the firm doesn't want him any

more; **elle ne veut pas de son aide** she doesn't want his help
5: **vouloir dire** to mean
▶ NM: **le bon vouloir de qn** sb's goodwill; sb's pleasure

voulu, e [vuly] PP *de* **vouloir** ▶ ADJ *(requis)* required, requisite; *(délibéré)* deliberate, intentional

voulus *etc* [vuly] VB *voir* **vouloir**

vous [vu] PRON you; *(objet indirect)* (to) you; *(réfléchi: sg)* yourself; *(: pl)* yourselves; *(réciproque)* each other ▶ NM: **employer le ~** *(vouvoyer)* to use the "vous" form; **~-même** yourself; **~-mêmes** yourselves

voûte [vut] NF vault; **la ~ céleste** the vault of heaven; **~ du palais** *(Anat)* roof of the mouth; **~ plantaire** arch (of the foot)

voûté, e [vute] ADJ vaulted, arched; *(dos, personne)* bent, stooped

voûter [vute] /**1**/ VT *(Archit)* to arch, vault; **se voûter** VI *(dos, personne)* to become stooped

vouvoiement [vuvwamɑ̃] NM use of formal "vous" form

vouvoyer [vuvwaje] /**8**/ VT: **~ qn** to address sb as "vous"

voyage [vwajaʒ] NM journey, trip; *(fait de voyager)*: **le ~** travel(ling); **partir/être en ~** to go off/be away on a journey *ou* trip; **faire un ~** to go on *ou* make a trip *ou* journey; **faire bon ~** to have a good journey; **les gens du ~** travelling people; **~ d'agrément/d'affaires** pleasure/business trip; **~ de noces** honeymoon; **~ organisé** package tour

voyager [vwajaʒe] /**3**/ VI to travel

voyageur, -euse [vwajaʒœr, -øz] NM/F traveller; *(passager)* passenger ▶ ADJ *(tempérament)* nomadic, wayfaring; **~ (de commerce)** commercial traveller

voyagiste [vwajaʒist] NM tour operator

voyais *etc* [vwajɛ] VB *voir* **voir**

voyance [vwajɑ̃s] NF clairvoyance

voyant, e [vwajɑ̃, -ɑ̃t] ADJ *(couleur)* loud, gaudy ▶ NM/F *(personne qui voit)* sighted person ▶ NM *(signal)* (warning) light ▶ NF clairvoyant

voyelle [vwajɛl] NF vowel

voyeur, -euse [vwajœr, -øz] NM/F voyeur; peeping Tom

voyeurisme [vwajœrism] NM voyeurism

voyons *etc* [vwajɔ̃] VB *voir* **voir**

voyou [vwaju] NM lout, hoodlum; *(enfant)* guttersnipe

VPC SIGLE F (= *vente par correspondance*) mail order selling

vrac [vrak]: **en ~** *adv* loose; *(Comm)* in bulk

vrai, e [vrɛ] ADJ *(véridique: récit, faits)* true; *(non factice, authentique)* real ▶ NM: **le ~** the truth; **à ~ dire** to tell the truth; **il est ~ que** it is true that; **être dans le ~** to be right

vraiment [vrɛmɑ̃] ADV really

vraisemblable [vrɛsɑ̃blabl] ADJ *(plausible)* likely;

(excuse) plausible; *(probable)* likely, probable

vraisemblablement [vrɛsɑ̃blabləmɑ̃] ADV in all likelihood, very likely

vraisemblance [vrɛsɑ̃blɑ̃s] NF likelihood, plausibility; *(romanesque)* verisimilitude; **selon toute ~** in all likelihood

vraquier [vrakje] NM freighter

vrille [vrij] NF *(de plante)* tendril; *(outil)* gimlet; *(spirale)* spiral; *(Aviat)* spin

vriller [vrije] /**1**/ VT to bore into, pierce

vrombir [vrɔ̃bir] /**2**/ VI to hum

vrombissant, e [vrɔ̃bisɑ̃, -ɑ̃t] ADJ humming

vrombissement [vrɔ̃bismɑ̃] NM hum(ming)

VRP SIGLE M (= *voyageur, représentant, placier*) (sales) rep *(fam)*

VTT SIGLE M (= *vélo tout-terrain*) mountain bike

vu¹ [vy] PRÉP *(en raison de)* in view of; **vu que** in view of the fact that

vu², e [vy] PP *de* **voir** ▶ ADJ: **bien/mal vu** *(personne)* well/poorly thought of; *(conduite)* good/bad form ▶ NM: **au vu et au su de tous** openly and publicly; **ni vu ni connu** what the eye doesn't see …!, no one will be any the wiser; **c'est tout vu** it's a foregone conclusion

vue [vy] NF *(sens, faculté)* (eye)sight; *(panorama, image, photo)* view; *(spectacle)* sight; **la ~ de** *(spectacle)* the sight of; **vues** NFPL *(idées)* views; *(dessein)* designs; **perdre la ~** to lose one's (eye)sight; **perdre de ~** to lose sight of; **à la ~ de tous** in full view of everybody; **hors de ~** out of sight; **à première ~** at first sight; **connaître de ~** to know by sight; **à ~** *(Comm)* at sight; **tirer à ~** to shoot on sight; **à ~ d'œil** *adv* visibly; *(à première vue)* at a quick glance; **avoir ~ sur** to have a view of; **en ~** *(visible)* in sight; *(Comm: célèbre)* in the public eye; **avoir qch en ~** *(intentions)* to have one's sights on sth; **en ~ de faire** with the intention of doing, with a view to doing; **~ d'ensemble** overall view; **~ de l'esprit** theoretical view

vulcanisation [vylkanizasjɔ̃] NF vulcanization

vulcaniser [vylkanize] /**1**/ VT to vulcanize

vulcanologie [vylkanɔlɔʒi] NF = **volcanologie**

vulcanologue [vylkanɔlɔg] NMF = **volcanologue**

vulgaire [vylgɛr] ADJ *(grossier)* vulgar, coarse; *(trivial)* commonplace, mundane; *(péj: quelconque)*: **de vulgaires touristes/chaises de cuisine** common tourists/kitchen chairs; *(Bot, Zool: non latin)* common

vulgairement [vylgɛrmɑ̃] ADV vulgarly, coarsely; *(communément)* commonly

vulgariser [vylgarize] /**1**/ VT to popularize

vulgarité [vylgarite] NF vulgarity, coarseness

vulnérabilité [vylnerabilite] NF vulnerability

vulnérable [vylnerabl] ADJ vulnerable

vulve [vylv] NF vulva

Vve ABR = **veuve**

VVF SIGLE M (= *village vacances famille*) state-subsidized holiday village

vx ABR = **vieux**

V

Ww

W, w [dubləve] NM INV W, w ▶ ABR (= *watt*) W; **W comme William** W for William

wagon [vagɔ̃] NM (*de voyageurs*) carriage; (*de marchandises*) truck, wagon

wagon-citerne [vagɔ̃sitɛʀn] (*pl* **wagons-citernes**) NM tanker

wagon-lit [vagɔ̃li] (*pl* **wagons-lits**) NM sleeper, sleeping car

wagonnet [vagɔnɛ] NM small truck

wagon-poste [vagɔ̃pɔst] (*pl* **wagons-postes**) NM mail van

wagon-restaurant [vagɔ̃ʀɛstɔʀɑ̃] (*pl* **wagons-restaurants**) NM restaurant *ou* dining car

Walkman® [wɔkman] NM Walkman®, personal stereo

Wallis et Futuna [walisefytyna] N: **les îles ~** the Wallis and Futuna Islands

wallon, ne [walɔ̃, -ɔn] ADJ Walloon ▶ NM (*Ling*) Walloon ▶ NM/F: **W~, ne** Walloon

Wallonie [walɔni] NF: **la ~** French-speaking (part of) Belgium

water-polo [watɛʀpolo] NM water polo

waters [watɛʀ] NMPL toilet *sg*, loo *sg* (BRIT)

watt [wat] NM watt

WC [vese] NMPL toilet *sg*, lavatory *sg*

Web [wɛb] NM INV: **le ~** the (World Wide) Web

webcam [wɛbkam] NF webcam

webmaster [-mastœʀ], **webmestre** [-mɛstʀ] NMF webmaster

week-end [wikɛnd] NM weekend

western [wɛstɛʀn] NM western

Westphalie [vɛsfali] NF: **la ~** Westphalia

whisky [wiski] (*pl* **whiskies**) NM whisky

white-spirit [wajtspiʀit] NM white spirit

widget [widʒɛt] NM (*Inform*) widget

wifi, Wi-Fi [wifi] NM INV (= *wireless fidelity*) wifi, Wi-Fi

wok [wɔk] NM wok

WWW SIGLE M (= *World Wide Web*) WWW

X, x [iks] NM INV X, x ▸ SIGLE M: **l'X** *the École polytechnique (prestigious engineering college in France)*; **plainte contre X** *(Jur)* action against person or persons unknown; **X comme Xavier** X for Xmas

xénophobe [gzenɔfɔb] ADJ xenophobic

▸ NMF xenophobe

xénophobie [gzenɔfɔbi] NF xenophobia

xérès [gzeʀɛs] NM sherry

xylographie [gzilɔgʀafi] NF xylography; *(image)* xylograph

xylophone [gzilɔfɔn] NM xylophone

Yy

Y, y [igʀɛk] NM INV Y, y; **Y comme Yvonne** Y for Yellow (BRIT) ou Yoke (US)

y [i] ADV (*à cet endroit*) there; (*dessus*) on it (ou them); (*dedans*) in it (ou them) ▶ PRON (about ou on ou of) it (*vérifier la syntaxe du verbe employé*); **j'y pense** I'm thinking about it; **ça y est!** that's it!; *voir aussi* **aller**; **avoir**

yacht [jɔt] NM yacht

yaourt [jauʀt] NM yogurt; ~ **nature/aux fruits** plain/fruit yogurt

yaourtière [jauʀtjɛʀ] NF yoghurt-maker

Yémen [jemɛn] NM: **le** ~ Yemen

yéménite [jemenit] ADJ Yemeni

yeux [jø] NMPL *de* **œil**

yoga [jɔga] NM yoga

yoghourt [jɔguʀt] NM = **yaourt**

yole [jɔl] NF skiff

yougoslave [jugɔslav] ADJ Yugoslav(ian) ▶ NMF: **Y~** Yugoslav(ian)

Yougoslavie [jugɔslavi] NF: **la** ~ Yugoslavia; **l'ex-~** the former Yugoslavia

youyou [juju] NM dinghy

yo-yo [jojo] NM INV yo-yo

yucca [juka] NM yucca (tree ou plant)

Zz

Z, z [zɛd] NM INV Z, z; **Z comme Zoé** Z for Zebra
ZAC [zak] SIGLE F (= *zone d'aménagement concerté*) urban development zone
ZAD [zad] SIGLE F (= *zone d'aménagement différé*) future development zone
Zaïre [zaiʀ] NM: **le ~** Zaïre
zaïrois, e [zaiʀwa, -waz] ADJ Zairian
Zambèze [zɑ̃bɛz] NM: **le ~** the Zambezi
Zambie [zɑ̃bi] NF: **la ~** Zambia
zambien, ne [zɑ̃bjɛ̃, -ɛn] ADJ Zambian
zapper [zape] /1/ VI to zap
zapping [zapiŋ] NM: **faire du ~** to flick through the channels
zébré, e [zebʀe] ADJ striped, streaked
zèbre [zɛbʀ] NM (*Zool*) zebra
zébrure [zebʀyʀ] NF stripe, streak
zélateur, -trice [zelatœʀ, -tʀis] NM/F partisan, zealot
zélé, e [zele] ADJ zealous
zèle [zɛl] NM zeal, diligence, assiduousness; **faire du ~** (*péj*) to be over-zealous
zénith [zenit] NM zenith
ZEP [zɛp] SIGLE F (= *zone d'éducation prioritaire*) area targeted for special help in education
zéro [zeʀo] NM zero, nought (*BRIT*); **au-dessous de ~** below zero (Centigrade), below freezing; **partir de ~** to start from scratch; **réduire à ~** to reduce to nothing; **trois (buts) à ~** three (goals to) nil
zeste [zɛst] NM peel, zest; **un ~ de citron** a piece of lemon peel
zézaiement [zezɛmɑ̃] NM lisp
zézayer [zezeje] /8/ VI to have a lisp
ZI SIGLE F = **zone industrielle**
zibeline [ziblin] NF sable
ZIF [zif] SIGLE F (= *zone d'intervention foncière*) intervention zone
zigouiller [ziguje] /1/ VT (*fam*) to do in
zigzag [zigzag] NM zigzag

zigzaguer [zigzage] /1/ VI to zigzag (along)
Zimbabwe [zimbabwe] NM: **le ~** Zimbabwe
zimbabwéen, ne [zimbabweɛ̃, -ɛn] ADJ Zimbabwean
zinc [zɛ̃g] NM (*Chimie*) zinc; (*comptoir*) bar, counter
zinguer [zɛ̃ge] /1/ VT to cover with zinc
zipper [zipe] /1/ VT (*Inform*) to zip
zircon [ziʀkɔ̃] NM zircon
zizanie [zizani] NF: **semer la ~** to stir up ill-feeling
zizi [zizi] NM (*fam*) willy (*BRIT*), peter (*US*)
zodiacal, e, -aux [zɔdjakal, -o] ADJ (*signe*) of the zodiac
zodiaque [zɔdjak] NM zodiac
zona [zona] NM shingles *sg*
zonage [zonaʒ] NM (*Admin*) zoning
zonard, e [zonaʀ, -aʀd] NM/F (*fam*) (young) hooligan *ou* thug
zone [zon] NF zone, area; (*quartiers pauvres*): **la ~** the slums; **de seconde ~** (*fig*) second-rate; **~ d'action** (*Mil*) sphere of activity; **~ bleue** ≈ restricted parking area; **~ d'extension** *ou* **d'urbanisation** urban development area; **~ franche** free zone; **~ industrielle** industrial estate; **~ piétonne** pedestrian precinct; **~ résidentielle** residential area; **~ tampon** buffer zone
zoner [zone] /1/ VI (*fam*) to hang around
zoo [zoo] NM zoo
zoologie [zɔɔlɔʒi] NF zoology
zoologique [zɔɔlɔʒik] ADJ zoological
zoologiste [zɔɔlɔʒist] NMF zoologist
zoom [zum] NM (*Photo*) zoom (lens)
ZUP [zyp] SIGLE F (= *zone à urbaniser en priorité*) = **ZAC**
Zurich [zyʀik] N Zürich
zut [zyt] EXCL dash (it)! (*BRIT*), nuts! (*US*)

z

Aa

A¹, a [eɪ] N (letter) A, a m; (Scol: mark) A; (Mus): A la m; **A for Andrew, A for Able** (US) A comme Anatole; **A shares** npl (BRIT Stock Exchange) actions fpl prioritaires

(KEYWORD)

a² [eɪ, ə] (before vowel and silent h **an**) INDEF ART
1 un(e); **a book** un livre; **an apple** une pomme; **she's a doctor** elle est médecin
2 (instead of the number "one") un(e); **a year ago** il y a un an; **a hundred/thousand** etc **pounds** cent/mille etc livres
3 (in expressing ratios: prices etc): **three a day/week** trois par jour/semaine; **10 km an hour** 10 km à l'heure; **£5 a person** 5£ par personne; **30p a kilo** 30p le kilo

a. ABBR = **acre**
A2 N (BRIT Scol) deuxième partie de l'examen équivalent au baccalauréat
A.A. N ABBR (BRIT: = Automobile Association) ≈ ACF m; (US: = Associate in/of Arts) diplôme universitaire; (= Alcoholics Anonymous) AA; (= anti-aircraft) AA
A.A.A. N ABBR (= American Automobile Association) ≈ ACF m; (BRIT) = **Amateur Athletics Association**
A & R N ABBR (Mus) = **artists and repertoire**; **~ man** découvreur m de talent
AAUP N ABBR (= American Association of University Professors) syndicat universitaire
AB ABBR (BRIT) = **able-bodied seaman**; (CANADA) = **Alberta**
aback [ə'bæk] ADV: **to be taken ~** être décontenancé(e)
abacus ['æbəkəs] (pl abaci [-saɪ]) N boulier m
abandon [ə'bændən] VT abandonner ▶ N abandon m; **to ~ ship** évacuer le navire
abandoned [ə'bændənd] ADJ (child, house etc) abandonné(e); (unrestrained) sans retenue
abase [ə'beɪs] VT: **to ~ o.s. (so far as to do)** s'abaisser (à faire)
abashed [ə'bæʃt] ADJ confus(e), embarrassé(e)
abate [ə'beɪt] VI s'apaiser, se calmer
abatement [ə'beɪtmənt] N: **noise ~** lutte f contre le bruit
abattoir ['æbətwɑːʳ] N (BRIT) abattoir m
abbey ['æbɪ] N abbaye f
abbot ['æbət] N père supérieur

abbreviate [ə'briːvɪeɪt] VT abréger
abbreviation [əbriːvɪ'eɪʃən] N abréviation f
ABC N ABBR (= American Broadcasting Company) chaîne de télévision
abdicate ['æbdɪkeɪt] VT, VI abdiquer
abdication [æbdɪ'keɪʃən] N abdication f
abdomen ['æbdəmən] N abdomen m
abdominal [æb'dɔmɪnl] ADJ abdominal(e)
abduct [æb'dʌkt] VT enlever
abduction [æb'dʌkʃən] N enlèvement m
Aberdonian [æbə'dəunɪən] ADJ d'Aberdeen ▶ N habitant(e) d'Aberdeen, natif(-ive) d'Aberdeen
aberration [æbə'reɪʃən] N anomalie f; **in a moment of mental ~** dans un moment d'égarement
abet [ə'bet] VT see **aid**
abeyance [ə'beɪəns] N: **in ~** (law) en désuétude; (matter) en suspens
abhor [əb'hɔːʳ] VT abhorrer, exécrer
abhorrent [əb'hɔrənt] ADJ odieux(-euse), exécrable
abide [ə'baɪd] VT souffrir, supporter; **I can't ~ it/him** je ne le supporte pas
▶ **abide by** VT FUS observer, respecter
abiding [ə'baɪdɪŋ] ADJ (memory etc) durable
ability [ə'bɪlɪtɪ] N compétence f; capacité f; (skill) talent m; **to the best of my ~** de mon mieux
abject ['æbdʒekt] ADJ (poverty) sordide; (coward) méprisable; **an ~ apology** les excuses les plus plates
ablaze [ə'bleɪz] ADJ en feu, en flammes; **~ with light** resplendissant de lumière
able ['eɪbl] ADJ compétent(e); **to be ~ to do sth** pouvoir faire qch, être capable de faire qch
able-bodied ['eɪbl'bɔdɪd] ADJ robuste; **~ seaman** (BRIT) matelot breveté
ably ['eɪblɪ] ADV avec compétence or talent, habilement
ABM N ABBR = **anti-ballistic missile**
abnormal [æb'nɔːməl] ADJ anormal(e)
abnormality [æbnɔː'mælɪtɪ] N (condition) caractère anormal; (instance) anomalie f
aboard [ə'bɔːd] ADV à bord ▶ PREP à bord de; (train) dans
abode [ə'bəud] N (old) demeure f; (Law): **of no fixed ~** sans domicile fixe
abolish [ə'bɔlɪʃ] VT abolir
abolition [æbə'lɪʃən] N abolition f

abominable [ə'bɒmɪnəbl] ADJ abominable

aborigine [æbə'rɪdʒɪnɪ] N aborigène *mf*

abort [ə'bɔːt] VT (*Med*) faire avorter; (*Comput, fig*) abandonner

abortion [ə'bɔːʃən] N avortement *m*; **to have an ~** se faire avorter

abortionist [ə'bɔːʃənɪst] N avorteur(-euse)

abortive [ə'bɔːtɪv] ADJ manqué(e)

abound [ə'baund] VI abonder; **to ~ in** abonder en, regorger de

(KEYWORD)

about [ə'baut] ADV 1 (*approximately*) environ, à peu près; **about a hundred/thousand** *etc* environ cent/mille *etc*, une centaine (de)/un millier (de) *etc*; **it takes about 10 hours** ça prend environ *or* à peu près 10 heures; **at about 2 o'clock** vers 2 heures; **I've just about finished** j'ai presque fini

2 (*referring to place*) çà et là, de-ci de-là; **to run about** courir çà et là; **to walk about** se promener, aller et venir; **is Paul about?** (*BRIT*) est-ce que Paul est là?; **it's about here** c'est par ici, c'est dans les parages; **they left all their things lying about** ils ont laissé traîner toutes leurs affaires

3: **to be about to do sth** être sur le point de faire qch; **I'm not about to do all that for nothing** (*inf*) je ne vais quand même pas faire tout ça pour rien

4 (*opposite*): **it's the other way about** (*BRIT*) c'est l'inverse

▶ PREP 1 (*relating to*) au sujet de, à propos de; **a book about London** un livre sur Londres; **what is it about?** de quoi s'agit-il?; **we talked about it** nous en avons parlé; **do something about it!** faites quelque chose!; **what** *or* **how about doing this?** et si nous faisions ceci?

2 (*referring to place*) dans; **to walk about the town** se promener dans la ville

above [ə'bʌv] ADV au-dessus ▶ PREP au-dessus de; (*more than*) plus de; **mentioned ~** mentionné ci-dessus; **costing ~ £10** coûtant plus de 10 livres; **~ all** par-dessus tout, surtout

aboveboard [ə'bʌv'bɔːd] ADJ franc (franche), loyal(e); honnête

abrasion [ə'breɪʒən] N frottement *m*; (*on skin*) écorchure *f*

abrasive [ə'breɪzɪv] ADJ abrasif(-ive); (*fig*) caustique, agressif(-ive)

abreast [ə'brɛst] ADV de front; **to keep ~ of** se tenir au courant de

abridge [ə'brɪdʒ] VT abréger

abroad [ə'brɔːd] ADV à l'étranger; **there is a rumour ~ that …** (*fig*) le bruit court que …

abrupt [ə'brʌpt] ADJ (*steep, blunt*) abrupt(e); (*sudden, gruff*) brusque

abruptly [ə'brʌptlɪ] ADV (*speak, end*) brusquement

abscess ['æbsɪs] N abcès *m*

abscond [əb'skɒnd] VI disparaître, s'enfuir

absence ['æbsəns] N absence *f*; **in the ~ of** (*person*) en l'absence de; (*thing*) faute de

absent ['æbsənt] ADJ absent(e); **~ without leave (AWOL)** (*Mil*) en absence irrégulière

absentee [æbsən'tiː] N absent(e)

absenteeism [æbsən'tiːɪzəm] N absentéisme *m*

absent-minded ['æbsənt'maɪndɪd] ADJ distrait(e)

absent-mindedness ['æbsənt'maɪndɪdnɪs] N distraction *f*

absolute ['æbsəluːt] ADJ absolu(e)

absolutely [æbsə'luːtlɪ] ADV absolument

absolve [əb'zɒlv] VT: **to ~ sb (from)** (*sin etc*) absoudre qn (de); **to ~ sb from** (*oath*) délier qn de

absorb [əb'zɔːb] VT absorber; **to be absorbed in a book** être plongé(e) dans un livre

absorbent [əb'zɔːbənt] ADJ absorbant(e)

absorbent cotton [əb'zɔːbənt-] N (*US*) coton *m* hydrophile

absorbing [əb'zɔːbɪŋ] ADJ absorbant(e); (*book, film etc*) captivant(e)

absorption [əb'sɔːpʃən] N absorption *f*

abstain [əb'steɪn] VI: **to ~ (from)** s'abstenir (de)

abstemious [əb'stiːmɪəs] ADJ sobre, frugal(e)

abstention [əb'stɛnʃən] N abstention *f*

abstinence ['æbstɪnəns] N abstinence *f*

abstract ['æbstrækt] ADJ abstrait(e) ▶ N (*summary*) résumé *m* ▶ VT [æb'strækt] extraire

absurd [əb'səːd] ADJ absurde

absurdity [əb'səːdɪtɪ] N absurdité *f*

ABTA ['æbtə] N ABBR = **Association of British Travel Agents**

Abu Dhabi ['æbuː'dɑːbɪ] N Ab(o)u Dhabî *m*

abundance [ə'bʌndəns] N abondance *f*

abundant [ə'bʌndənt] ADJ abondant(e)

abuse N [ə'bjuːs] (*insults*) insultes *fpl*, injures *fpl*; (*ill-treatment*) mauvais traitements *mpl*; (*of power etc*) abus *m* ▶ VT [ə'bjuːz] (*insult*) insulter; (*ill-treat*) malmener; (*power etc*) abuser de; **to be open to ~** se prêter à des abus

abusive [ə'bjuːsɪv] ADJ grossier(-ière), injurieux(-euse)

abysmal [ə'bɪzməl] ADJ exécrable; (*ignorance etc*) sans bornes

abyss [ə'bɪs] N abîme *m*, gouffre *m*

AC N ABBR (*US*) = **athletic club**

a/c ABBR (*Banking etc*) = **account; account current**

academic [ækə'dɛmɪk] ADJ universitaire; (*person: scholarly*) intellectuel(le); (*pej: issue*) oiseux(-euse), purement théorique ▶ N universitaire *mf*; **~ freedom** liberté *f* académique

academic year N (*University*) année *f* universitaire; (*Scol*) année scolaire

academy [ə'kædəmɪ] N (*learned body*) académie *f*; (*school*) collège *m*; **military/naval ~** école militaire/navale; **~ of music** conservatoire *m*

ACAS ['eɪkæs] N ABBR (*BRIT*: = *Advisory, Conciliation and Arbitration Service*) organisme de conciliation et d'arbitrage des conflits du travail

accede [æk'siːd] VI: **to ~ to** (*request, throne*) accéder à

accelerate [æk'sɛləreɪt] VT, VI accélérer

acceleration [æksɛlə'reɪʃən] N accélération *f*

accelerator [æk'sɛləreɪtəʳ] N (BRIT)
accélérateur m
accent ['æksɛnt] N accent m
accentuate [æk'sɛntjueɪt] VT (syllable)
accentuer; (need, difference etc) souligner
accept [ək'sɛpt] VT accepter
acceptable [ək'sɛptəbl] ADJ acceptable
acceptance [ək'sɛptəns] N acceptation f; **to
meet with general ~** être favorablement
accueilli par tous
access ['æksɛs] N accès m ▶ VT (Comput) accéder
à; **to have ~ to** (information, library etc) avoir accès
à, pouvoir utiliser or consulter; (person) avoir
accès auprès de; **the burglars gained ~
through a window** les cambrioleurs sont
entrés par une fenêtre
accessible [æk'sɛsəbl] ADJ accessible
accession [æk'sɛʃən] N accession f; (of king)
avènement m; (to library) acquisition f
accessory [æk'sɛsərɪ] N accessoire m; **toilet
accessories** (BRIT) articles mpl de toilette; **~ to**
(Law) accessoire à
access road N voie f d'accès; (to motorway)
bretelle f de raccordement
access time N (Comput) temps m d'accès
accident ['æksɪdənt] N accident m; (chance)
hasard m; **to meet with** or **to have an ~** avoir
un accident; **I've had an ~** j'ai eu un accident;
accidents at work accidents du travail; **by ~**
(by chance) par hasard; (not deliberately)
accidentellement
accidental [æksɪ'dɛntl] ADJ accidentel(le)
accidentally [æksɪ'dɛntəlɪ] ADV
accidentellement
Accident and Emergency Department N
(BRIT) service m des urgences
accident insurance N assurance f accident
accident-prone ['æksɪdənt'prəun] ADJ sujet(te)
aux accidents
acclaim [ə'kleɪm] VT acclamer ▶ N acclamations
fpl
acclamation [æklə'meɪʃən] N (approval)
acclamation f; (applause) ovation f
acclimatize [ə'klaɪmətaɪz], (US) **acclimate**
[ə'klaɪmət] VT: **to become acclimatized**
s'acclimater
accolade ['ækəleɪd] N accolade f; (fig) marque f
d'honneur
accommodate [ə'kɔmədeɪt] VT loger, recevoir;
(oblige, help) obliger; (car etc) contenir; (adapt): **to
~ one's plans to** adapter ses projets à
accommodating [ə'kɔmədeɪtɪŋ] ADJ
obligeant(e), arrangeant(e)
accommodation N, (US) **accommodations**
NPL [əkɔmə'deɪʃən(z)] logement m; **he's found
~** il a trouvé à se loger; **"~ to let"** (BRIT)
"appartement or studio etc à louer"; **they have
~ for 500** ils peuvent recevoir 500 personnes, il
y a de la place pour 500 personnes; **the hall
has seating ~ for 600** (BRIT) la salle contient
600 places assises
accompaniment [ə'kʌmpənɪmənt] N
accompagnement m
accompanist [ə'kʌmpənɪst] N

accompagnateur(-trice)
accompany [ə'kʌmpənɪ] VT accompagner
accomplice [ə'kʌmplɪs] N complice mf
accomplish [ə'kʌmplɪʃ] VT accomplir
accomplished [ə'kʌmplɪʃt] ADJ accompli(e)
accomplishment [ə'kʌmplɪʃmənt] N (skill: gen
pl) talent m; (completion) accomplissement m;
(achievement) réussite f
accord [ə'kɔːd] N accord m ▶ VT accorder; **of his
own ~** de son plein gré; **with one ~** d'un
commun accord
accordance [ə'kɔːdəns] N: **in ~ with**
conformément à
according [ə'kɔːdɪŋ]: **~ to** prep selon; **~ to plan**
comme prévu
accordingly [ə'kɔːdɪŋlɪ] ADV (appropriately) en
conséquence; (as a result) par conséquent
accordion [ə'kɔːdɪən] N accordéon m
accost [ə'kɔst] VT accoster, aborder
account [ə'kaunt] N (Comm) compte m; (report)
compte rendu, récit m; **accounts** NPL (Comm:
records) comptabilité f, comptes; **"~ payee only"**
(BRIT) "chèque non endossable"; **to keep an ~
of** noter; **to bring sb to ~ for sth/for having
done sth** amener qn à rendre compte de
qch/d'avoir fait qch; **by all accounts** au dire de
tous; **of little ~** de peu d'importance; **of no ~**
sans importance; **on ~** en acompte; **to buy sth
on ~** acheter qch à crédit; **on no ~** en aucun cas;
on ~ of à cause de; **to take into ~**, **take ~ of**
tenir compte de
▶ **account for** VT FUS (explain) expliquer, rendre
compte de; (represent) représenter; **all the
children were accounted for** aucun enfant ne
manquait; **four people are still not
accounted for** on n'a toujours pas retrouvé
quatre personnes
accountability [əkauntə'bɪlɪtɪ] N
responsabilité f; (financial, political)
transparence f
accountable [ə'kauntəbl] ADJ: **~ (for/to)**
responsable (de/devant)
accountancy [ə'kauntənsɪ] N comptabilité f
accountant [ə'kauntənt] N comptable mf
accounting [ə'kauntɪŋ] N comptabilité f
accounting period N exercice financier,
période f comptable
account number N numéro m de compte
account payable N compte m fournisseurs
account receivable N compte m clients
accredited [ə'krɛdɪtɪd] ADJ (person) accrédité(e)
accretion [ə'kriːʃən] N accroissement m
accrue [ə'kruː] VI s'accroître; (mount up)
s'accumuler; **to ~ to** s'ajouter à; **accrued
interest** intérêt couru
accumulate [ə'kjuːmjuleɪt] VT accumuler,
amasser ▶ VI s'accumuler, s'amasser
accumulation [əkjuːmju'leɪʃən] N
accumulation f
accuracy ['ækjurəsɪ] N exactitude f, précision f
accurate ['ækjurɪt] ADJ exact(e), précis(e);
(device) précis
accurately ['ækjurɪtlɪ] ADV avec précision
accusation [ækju'zeɪʃən] N accusation f

accusative [əˈkjuːzətɪv] N (Ling) accusatif m
accuse [əˈkjuːz] VT: **to ~ sb (of sth)** accuser qn (de qch)
accused [əˈkjuːzd] N (Law) accusé(e)
accuser [əˈkjuːzər] N accusateur(-trice)
accustom [əˈkʌstəm] VT accoutumer, habituer; **to ~ o.s. to sth** s'habituer à qch
accustomed [əˈkʌstəmd] ADJ (usual) habituel(le); **~ to** habitué(e) or accoutumé(e) à
AC/DC ABBR = **alternating current/direct current**
ACE [eɪs] N ABBR = **American Council on Education**
ace [eɪs] N as m; **within an ~ of** (BRIT) à deux doigts or un cheveu de
acerbic [əˈsəːbɪk] ADJ (also fig) acerbe
acetate [ˈæsɪteɪt] N acétate m
ache [eɪk] N mal m, douleur f ▶ VI (be sore) faire mal, être douloureux(-euse); (yearn): **to ~ to do sth** mourir d'envie de faire qch; **I've got stomach ~** or (US) **a stomach ~** j'ai mal à l'estomac; **my head aches** j'ai mal à la tête; **I'm aching all over** j'ai mal partout
achieve [əˈtʃiːv] VT (aim) atteindre; (victory, success) remporter, obtenir; (task) accomplir
achievement [əˈtʃiːvmənt] N exploit m, réussite f; (of aims) réalisation f
Achilles heel [əˈkɪliːz-] N talon m d'Achille
acid [ˈæsɪd] ADJ, N acide (m)
acidity [əˈsɪdɪtɪ] N acidité f
acid rain N pluies fpl acides
acid test N (fig) épreuve décisive
acknowledge [əkˈnɔlɪdʒ] VT (also: **acknowledge receipt of**) accuser réception de; (fact) reconnaître
acknowledgement [əkˈnɔlɪdʒmənt] N (of letter) accusé m de réception; **acknowledgements** (in book) remerciements mpl
ACLU N ABBR (= American Civil Liberties Union) ligue des droits de l'homme
acme [ˈækmɪ] N point culminant
acne [ˈæknɪ] N acné m
acorn [ˈeɪkɔːn] N gland m
acoustic [əˈkuːstɪk] ADJ acoustique
acoustics [əˈkuːstɪks] N, NPL acoustique f
acquaint [əˈkweɪnt] VT: **to ~ sb with sth** mettre qn au courant de qch; **to be acquainted with** (person) connaître; (fact) savoir
acquaintance [əˈkweɪntəns] N connaissance f; **to make sb's ~** faire la connaissance de qn
acquiesce [ækwɪˈɛs] VI (agree): **to ~ (in)** acquiescer (à)
acquire [əˈkwaɪər] VT acquérir
acquired [əˈkwaɪəd] ADJ acquis(e); **an ~ taste** un goût acquis
acquisition [ækwɪˈzɪʃən] N acquisition f
acquisitive [əˈkwɪzɪtɪv] ADJ qui a l'instinct de possession or le goût de la propriété
acquit [əˈkwɪt] VT acquitter; **to ~ o.s. well** s'en tirer très honorablement
acquittal [əˈkwɪtl] N acquittement m
acre [ˈeɪkər] N acre f (= 4047 m²)
acreage [ˈeɪkərɪdʒ] N superficie f
acrid [ˈækrɪd] ADJ (smell) âcre; (fig) mordant(e)

acrimonious [ækrɪˈməʊnɪəs] ADJ acrimonieux(-euse), aigre
acrobat [ˈækrəbæt] N acrobate mf
acrobatic [ækrəˈbætɪk] ADJ acrobatique
acrobatics [ækrəˈbætɪks] N, NPL acrobatie f
acronym [ˈækrənɪm] N acronyme m
Acropolis [əˈkrɔpəlɪs] N: **the ~** l'Acropole f
across [əˈkrɔs] PREP (on the other side) de l'autre côté de; (crosswise) en travers de ▶ ADV de l'autre côté; en travers; **to walk ~ (the road)** traverser (la route); **to run/swim ~** traverser en courant/à la nage; **to take sb ~ the road** faire traverser la route à qn; **a road ~ the wood** une route qui traverse le bois; **the lake is 12 km ~** le lac fait 12 km de large; **~ from** en face de; **to get sth ~ (to sb)** faire comprendre qch (à qn)
acrylic [əˈkrɪlɪk] ADJ, N acrylique m
ACT N ABBR (= American College Test) examen de fin d'études secondaires
act [ækt] N acte m, action f; (Theat: part of play) acte; (: of performer) numéro m; (Law) loi f ▶ VI agir; (Theat) jouer; (pretend) jouer la comédie ▶ VT (role) jouer, tenir; **~ of God** (Law) catastrophe naturelle; **to catch sb in the ~** prendre qn sur le fait or en flagrant délit; **it's only an ~** c'est du cinéma; **to ~ Hamlet** (BRIT) tenir or jouer le rôle d'Hamlet; **to ~ the fool** (BRIT) faire l'idiot; **to ~ as** servir de; **it acts as a deterrent** cela a un effet dissuasif; **acting in my capacity as chairman, I …** en ma qualité de président, je …
  ▶ **act on** VT: **to ~ on sth** agir sur la base de qch
  ▶ **act out** VT (event) raconter en mimant; (fantasies) réaliser
  ▶ **act up** (inf) VI (person) se conduire mal; (knee, back, injury) jouer des tours; (machine) être capricieux(-euse)
acting [ˈæktɪŋ] ADJ suppléant(e), par intérim ▶ N (of actor) jeu m; (activity): **to do some ~** faire du théâtre (or du cinéma); **he is the ~ manager** il remplace (provisoirement) le directeur
action [ˈækʃən] N action f; (Mil) combat(s) m(pl); (Law) procès m, action en justice ▶ VT (Comm) mettre en œuvre; (to put into effect): **to bring an ~ against sb** (Law) poursuivre qn en justice, intenter un procès contre qn; **killed in ~** (Mil) tué au champ d'honneur; **out of ~** hors de combat; (machine etc) hors d'usage; **to take ~** agir, prendre des mesures; **to put a plan into ~** mettre un projet à exécution
action replay N (BRIT TV) ralenti m
activate [ˈæktɪveɪt] VT (mechanism) actionner, faire fonctionner; (Chem, Physics) activer
active [ˈæktɪv] ADJ actif(-ive); (volcano) en activité; **to play an ~ part in** jouer un rôle actif dans
active duty N (US Mil) campagne f
actively [ˈæktɪvlɪ] ADV activement; (discourage) vivement
active partner N (Comm) associé(e) m/f
active service N (BRIT Mil) campagne f
activist [ˈæktɪvɪst] N activiste mf
activity [ækˈtɪvɪtɪ] N activité f
activity holiday N vacances actives

actor ['æktə'] N acteur m
actress ['æktrɪs] N actrice f
actual ['æktjuəl] ADJ réel(le), véritable; (emphatic use) lui-même (elle-même)
actually ['æktjuəlɪ] ADV réellement, véritablement; (in fact) en fait
actuary ['æktjuərɪ] N actuaire m
actuate ['æktjueɪt] VT déclencher, actionner
acuity [ə'kju:ɪtɪ] N acuité f
acumen ['ækjumən] N perspicacité f; **business ~** sens m des affaires
acupuncture ['ækjupʌŋktʃə'] N acuponcture f
acute [ə'kju:t] ADJ aigu(ë); (mind, observer) pénétrant(e)
ad [æd] N ABBR = **advertisement**
A.D. ADV ABBR (= Anno Domini) ap. J.-C. ▶ N ABBR (US Mil) = **active duty**
adamant ['ædəmənt] ADJ inflexible
Adam's apple ['ædəmz-] N pomme f d'Adam
adapt [ə'dæpt] VT adapter ▶ VI: **to ~ (to)** s'adapter (à)
adaptability [ədæptə'bɪlɪtɪ] N faculté f d'adaptation
adaptable [ə'dæptəbl] ADJ (device) adaptable; (person) qui s'adapte facilement
adaptation [ædæp'teɪʃən] N adaptation f
adapter, adaptor [ə'dæptə'] N (Elec) adaptateur m; (for several plugs) prise f multiple
ADC N ABBR (Mil) = **aide-de-camp**; (US: = Aid to Dependent Children) aide pour enfants assistés
add [æd] VT ajouter; (figures: also: **to add up**) additionner ▶ VI: **to ~ to** (increase) ajouter à, accroître ▶ N (Internet): **thanks for the ~** merci pour l'ajout; **it doesn't ~ up** (fig) cela ne rime à rien
  ▶ **add on** VT ajouter
  ▶ **add up to** VT FUS (Math) s'élever à; (fig: mean) signifier; **it doesn't ~ up to much** ça n'est pas grand'chose
adder ['ædə'] N vipère f
addict ['ædɪkt] N toxicomane mf; (fig) fanatique mf; **heroin ~** héroïnomane mf; **drug ~** drogué(e) m/f
addicted [ə'dɪktɪd] ADJ: **to be ~ to** (drink, drugs) être adonné(e) à; (fig: football etc) être un(e) fanatique de
addiction [ə'dɪkʃən] N (Med) dépendance f
addictive [ə'dɪktɪv] ADJ qui crée une dépendance
adding machine ['ædɪŋ-] N machine f à calculer
Addis Ababa ['ædɪs'æbəbə] N Addis Abeba, Addis Ababa
addition [ə'dɪʃən] N (adding up) addition f; (thing added) ajout m; **in ~** de plus, de surcroît; **in ~ to** en plus de
additional [ə'dɪʃənl] ADJ supplémentaire
additive ['ædɪtɪv] N additif m
address [ə'drɛs] N adresse f; (talk) discours m, allocution f ▶ VT adresser; (speak to) s'adresser à; **my ~ is ...** mon adresse, c'est ...; **form of ~** titre m; **what form of ~ do you use for ...?** comment s'adresse-t-on à ...?; **to ~ (o.s. to)** sth (problem, issue) aborder qch; **absolute/relative ~**

(Comput) adresse absolue/relative
address book N carnet m d'adresses
addressee [ædrɛ'si:] N destinataire mf
Aden ['eɪdən] N: **Gulf of ~** Golfe m d'Aden
adenoids ['ædɪnɔɪdz] NPL végétations fpl
adept ['ædɛpt] ADJ: **~ at** expert(e) à or en
adequate ['ædɪkwɪt] ADJ (enough) suffisant(e); (satisfactory) satisfaisant(e); **to feel ~ to the task** se sentir à la hauteur de la tâche
adequately ['ædɪkwɪtlɪ] ADV de façon adéquate
adhere [əd'hɪə'] VI: **to ~ to** adhérer à; (fig: rule, decision) se tenir à
adhesion [əd'hi:ʒən] N adhésion f
adhesive [əd'hi:zɪv] ADJ adhésif(-ive) ▶ N adhésif m
adhesive tape N (BRIT) ruban m adhésif; (US Med) sparadrap m
ad hoc ['æd'hɔk] ADJ (decision) de circonstance; (committee) ad hoc
ad infinitum ['ædɪnfɪ'naɪtəm] ADV à l'infini
adjacent [ə'dʒeɪsənt] ADJ adjacent(e), contigu(ë); **~ to** adjacent à
adjective ['ædʒɛktɪv] N adjectif m
adjoin [ə'dʒɔɪn] VT jouxter
adjoining [ə'dʒɔɪnɪŋ] ADJ voisin(e), adjacent(e), attenant(e) ▶ PREP voisin de, adjacent à
adjourn [ə'dʒə:n] VT ajourner ▶ VI suspendre la séance; lever la séance; clore la session; (go) se retirer; **to ~ a meeting till the following week** reporter une réunion à la semaine suivante; **they adjourned to the pub** (BRIT inf) ils ont filé au pub
adjournment [ə'dʒə:nmənt] N (period) ajournement m
Adjt ABBR (Mil: = adjutant) Adj
adjudicate [ə'dʒu:dɪkeɪt] VT (contest) juger; (claim) statuer (sur) ▶ VI se prononcer
adjudication [ədʒu:dɪ'keɪʃən] N (Law) jugement m
adjust [ə'dʒʌst] VT (machine) ajuster, régler; (prices, wages) rajuster ▶ VI: **to ~ (to)** s'adapter (à)
adjustable [ə'dʒʌstəbl] ADJ réglable
adjuster [ə'dʒʌstə'] N see **loss**
adjustment [ə'dʒʌstmənt] N (of machine) ajustage m, réglage m; (of prices, wages) rajustement m; (of person) adaptation f
adjutant ['ædʒətənt] N adjudant m
ad-lib [æd'lɪb] VT, VI improviser ▶ N improvisation f ▶ ADV: **ad lib** à volonté, à discrétion
adman ['ædmæn] N (irreg) (inf) publicitaire m
admin ['ædmɪn] N ABBR (inf) = **administration**
administer [əd'mɪnɪstə'] VT administrer; (justice) rendre
administration [ədmɪnɪs'treɪʃən] N (management) administration f; (government) gouvernement m
administrative [əd'mɪnɪstrətɪv] ADJ administratif(-ive)
administrator [əd'mɪnɪstreɪtə'] N administrateur(-trice)
admirable ['ædmərəbl] ADJ admirable
admiral ['ædmərəl] N amiral m
Admiralty ['ædmərəltɪ] N (BRIT: also: **Admiralty**

Board) ministère m de la Marine

admiration [ædmə'reɪʃən] N admiration f

admire [əd'maɪə^r] VT admirer

admirer [əd'maɪərə^r] N (fan) admirateur(-trice)

admiring [əd'maɪərɪŋ] ADJ admiratif(-ive)

admissible [əd'mɪsəbl] ADJ acceptable, admissible; (evidence) recevable

admission [əd'mɪʃən] N admission f; (to exhibition, night club etc) entrée f; (confession) aveu m; **"~ free"**, **"free ~"** "entrée libre"; **by his own ~** de son propre aveu

admission charge N droits mpl d'admission

admit [əd'mɪt] VT laisser entrer; admettre; (agree) reconnaître, admettre; (crime) reconnaître avoir commis; **"children not admitted"** "entrée interdite aux enfants"; **this ticket admits two** ce billet est valable pour deux personnes; **I must ~ that ...** je dois admettre or reconnaître que ...

▶ **admit of** VT FUS admettre, permettre

▶ **admit to** VT FUS reconnaître, avouer

admittance [əd'mɪtəns] N admission f, (droit m d')entrée f; **"no ~"** "défense d'entrer"

admittedly [əd'mɪtɪdlɪ] ADV il faut en convenir

admonish [əd'mɔnɪʃ] VT donner un avertissement à; réprimander

ad nauseam [æd'nɔːsɪæm] ADV à satiété

ado [ə'duː] N: **without (any) more ~** sans plus de cérémonies

adolescence [ædəu'lɛsns] N adolescence f

adolescent [ædəu'lɛsnt] ADJ, N adolescent(e)

adopt [ə'dɔpt] VT adopter

adopted [ə'dɔptɪd] ADJ adoptif(-ive), adopté(e)

adoption [ə'dɔpʃən] N adoption f

adore [ə'dɔː^r] VT adorer

adoring [ə'dɔːrɪŋ] ADJ: **his ~ wife** sa femme qui est en adoration devant lui

adoringly [ə'dɔːrɪŋlɪ] ADV avec adoration

adorn [ə'dɔːn] VT orner

adornment [ə'dɔːnmənt] N ornement m

ADP N ABBR = **automatic data processing**

adrenalin [ə'drenəlɪn] N adrénaline f; **to get the ~ going** faire monter le taux d'adrénaline

Adriatic [eɪdrɪ'ætɪk], **Adriatic Sea** N: **the ~ (Sea)** la mer Adriatique, l'Adriatique f

adrift [ə'drɪft] ADV à la dérive; **to come ~** (boat) aller à la dérive; (wire, rope, fastening etc) se défaire

adroit [ə'drɔɪt] ADJ adroit(e), habile

ADSL N ABBR (= asymmetric digital subscriber line) ADSL m

ADT ABBR (US: = Atlantic Daylight Time) heure d'été de New York

adult ['ædʌlt] N adulte mf ▶ ADJ (grown-up) adulte; (for adults) pour adultes

adult education N éducation f des adultes

adulterate [ə'dʌltəreɪt] VT frelater, falsifier

adulterer [ə'dʌltərə^r] N homme m adultère

adulteress [ə'dʌltərɪs] N femme f adultère

adultery [ə'dʌltərɪ] N adultère m

adulthood ['ædʌlthud] N âge m adulte

advance [əd'vɑːns] N avance f ▶ VT avancer ▶ VI s'avancer; **in ~** en avance, d'avance; **to make advances to sb** (gen) faire des propositions à qn; (amorously) faire des avances à qn; **~ booking**

location f; **~ notice**, **~ warning** préavis m; (verbal) avertissement m; **do I need to book in ~?** est-ce qu'il faut réserver à l'avance?

advanced [əd'vɑːnst] ADJ avancé(e); (Scol: studies) supérieur(e); **~ in years** d'un âge avancé

advancement [əd'vɑːnsmənt] N avancement m

advantage [əd'vɑːntɪdʒ] N (also Tennis) avantage m; **to take ~ of** (person) exploiter; (opportunity) profiter de; **it's to our ~** c'est notre intérêt; **it's to our ~ to ...** nous avons intérêt à ...

advantageous [ædvən'teɪdʒəs] ADJ avantageux(-euse)

advent ['ædvənt] N avènement m, venue f; **A~** (Rel) Avent m

Advent calendar N calendrier m de l'Avent

adventure [əd'vɛntʃə^r] N aventure f

adventure playground N aire f de jeux

adventurous [əd'vɛntʃərəs] ADJ aventureux(-euse)

adverb ['ædvə:b] N adverbe m

adversary ['ædvəsərɪ] N adversaire mf

adverse ['ædvə:s] ADJ adverse; (effect) négatif(-ive); (weather, publicity) mauvais(e); (wind) contraire; **~ to** hostile à; **in ~ circumstances** dans l'adversité

adversity [əd'və:sɪtɪ] N adversité f

advert ['ædvə:t] N ABBR (BRIT) = **advertisement**

advertise ['ædvətaɪz] VI faire de la publicité or de la réclame; (in classified ads etc) mettre une annonce ▶ VT faire de la publicité or de la réclame pour; (in classified ads etc) mettre une annonce pour vendre; **to ~ for** (staff) recruter par (voie d')annonce

advertisement [əd'və:tɪsmənt] N publicité f, réclame f; (in classified ads etc) annonce f

advertiser ['ædvətaɪzə^r] N annonceur m

advertising ['ædvətaɪzɪŋ] N publicité f

advertising agency N agence f de publicité

advertising campaign N campagne f de publicité

advice [əd'vaɪs] N conseils mpl; (notification) avis m; **a piece of ~** un conseil; **to ask (sb) for ~** demander conseil (à qn); **to take legal ~** consulter un avocat

advice note N (BRIT) avis m d'expédition

advisable [əd'vaɪzəbl] ADJ recommandable, indiqué(e)

advise [əd'vaɪz] VT conseiller; **to ~ sb of sth** aviser or informer qn de qch; **to ~ against sth/ doing sth** déconseiller qch/conseiller de ne pas faire qch; **you would be well/ill advised to go** vous feriez mieux d'y aller/de ne pas y aller, vous auriez intérêt à y aller/à ne pas y aller

advisedly [əd'vaɪzɪdlɪ] ADV (deliberately) délibérément

adviser, advisor [əd'vaɪzə^r] N conseiller(-ère)

advisory [əd'vaɪzərɪ] ADJ consultatif(-ive); **in an ~ capacity** à titre consultatif

advocate N ['ædvəkɪt] (lawyer) avocat (plaidant); (upholder) défenseur m, avocat(e) ▶ VT ['ædvəkeɪt] recommander, prôner; **to be an ~ of** être partisan(e) de

advt. ABBR = **advertisement**

AEA N ABBR (BRIT: = Atomic Energy Authority) ≈ AEN f

(= *Agence pour l'énergie nucléaire*)

AEC N ABBR (*US: = Atomic Energy Commission*) CEA m (= *Commissariat à l'énergie atomique*)

AEEU N ABBR (BRIT: = *Amalgamated Engineering and Electrical Union*) syndicat de techniciens et d'électriciens

Aegean [iː'dʒiːən] N, ADJ: **the ~ (Sea)** la mer Égée, l'Égée f

aegis ['iːdʒɪs] N: **under the ~ of** sous l'égide de

aeon ['iːən] N éternité f

aerial ['ɛərɪəl] N antenne f ▶ ADJ aérien(ne)

aerobatics ['ɛərəu'bætɪks] NPL acrobaties aériennes

aerobics [ɛə'rəubɪks] N aérobic m

aerodrome ['ɛərədrəum] N (BRIT) aérodrome m

aerodynamic ['ɛərəudaɪ'næmɪk] ADJ aérodynamique

aeronautics [ɛərə'nɔːtɪks] N aéronautique f

aeroplane ['ɛərəpleɪn] N (BRIT) avion m

aerosol ['ɛərəsɔl] N aérosol m

aerospace industry ['ɛərəuspeɪs-] N (industrie) aérospatiale f

aesthetic [ɪs'θɛtɪk] ADJ esthétique

afar [ə'fɑːʳ] ADV: **from ~** de loin

AFB N ABBR (*US*) = **Air Force Base**

AFDC N ABBR (*US: = Aid to Families with Dependent Children*) aide pour enfants assistés

affable ['æfəbl] ADJ affable

affair [ə'fɛəʳ] N affaire f; (*also:* **love affair**) liaison f; aventure f; **affairs** (*business*) affaires

affect [ə'fɛkt] VT affecter; (*subj: disease*) atteindre

affectation [æfɛk'teɪʃən] N affectation f

affected [ə'fɛktɪd] ADJ affecté(e)

affection [ə'fɛkʃən] N affection f

affectionate [ə'fɛkʃənɪt] ADJ affectueux(-euse)

affectionately [ə'fɛkʃənɪtlɪ] ADV affectueusement

affidavit [æfɪ'deɪvɪt] N (*Law*) déclaration écrite sous serment

affiliated [ə'fɪlɪeɪtɪd] ADJ affilié(e); **~ company** filiale f

affinity [ə'fɪnɪtɪ] N affinité f

affirm [ə'fəːm] VT affirmer

affirmation [æfə'meɪʃən] N affirmation f, assertion f

affirmative [ə'fəːmətɪv] ADJ affirmatif(-ive) ▶ N: **in the ~** dans or par l'affirmative

affix [ə'fɪks] VT apposer, ajouter

afflict [ə'flɪkt] VT affliger

affliction [ə'flɪkʃən] N affliction f

affluence ['æfluəns] N aisance f, opulence f

affluent ['æfluənt] ADJ opulent(e); (*person, family, surroundings*) aisé(e), riche; **the ~ society** la société d'abondance

afford [ə'fɔːd] VT (*goods etc*) avoir les moyens d'acheter or d'entretenir; (*behaviour*) se permettre; (*provide*) fournir, procurer; **can we ~ a car?** avons-nous de quoi acheter or les moyens d'acheter une voiture?; **I can't ~ the time** je n'ai vraiment pas le temps

affordable [ə'fɔːdəbl] ADJ abordable

affray [ə'freɪ] N (BRIT *Law*) échauffourée f, rixe f

affront [ə'frʌnt] N affront m

affronted [ə'frʌntɪd] ADJ insulté(e)

Afghan ['æfgæn] ADJ afghan(e) ▶ N Afghan(e)

Afghanistan [æf'gænɪstæn] N Afghanistan m

afield [ə'fiːld] ADV: **far ~** loin

AFL-CIO N ABBR (= *American Federation of Labor and Congress of Industrial Organizations*) confédération syndicale

afloat [ə'fləut] ADJ à flot ▶ ADV: **to stay ~** surnager; **to keep/get a business ~** maintenir à flot/lancer une affaire

afoot [ə'fut] ADV: **there is something ~** il se prépare quelque chose

aforementioned [ə'fɔːmɛnʃənd], **aforesaid** [ə'fɔːsɛd] ADJ susdit(e), susmentionné(e)

afraid [ə'freɪd] ADJ effrayé(e); **to be ~ of** or **to** avoir peur de; **I am ~ that** je crains que + *sub*; **I'm ~ so/not** oui/non, malheureusement

afresh [ə'frɛʃ] ADV de nouveau

Africa ['æfrɪkə] N Afrique f

African ['æfrɪkən] ADJ africain(e) ▶ N Africain(e)

African-American ['æfrɪkənə'mɛrɪkən] ADJ afro-américain(e) ▶ N Afro-Américain(e)

Afrikaans [æfrɪ'kɑːns] N afrikaans m

Afrikaner [æfrɪ'kɑːnəʳ] N Afrikaner mf

Afro-American ['æfrəuə'mɛrɪkən] ADJ afro-américain(e)

AFT N ABBR (= *American Federation of Teachers*) syndicat enseignant

aft [ɑːft] ADV à l'arrière, vers l'arrière

after ['ɑːftəʳ] PREP, ADV après ▶ CONJ après que, après avoir or être + *pp*; **~ dinner** après (le) dîner; **the day ~ tomorrow** après demain; **it's quarter ~ two** (*US*) il est deux heures et quart; **~ having done/~ he left** après avoir fait/après son départ; **to name sb ~ sb** donner à qn le nom de qn; **to ask ~ sb** demander des nouvelles de qn; **what/who are you ~?** que/qui cherchez-vous?; **the police are ~ him** la police est à ses trousses; **~ you!** après vous!; **~ all** après tout

afterbirth ['ɑːftəbəːθ] N placenta m

aftercare ['ɑːftəkɛəʳ] N (BRIT *Med*) post-cure f

after-effects ['ɑːftərɪfɛkts] NPL (*of disaster, radiation, drink etc*) répercussions fpl; (*of illness*) séquelles fpl, suites fpl

afterlife ['ɑːftəlaɪf] N vie future

aftermath ['ɑːftəmɑːθ] N conséquences fpl; **in the ~ of** dans les mois or années *etc* qui suivirent, au lendemain de

afternoon ['ɑːftə'nuːn] N après-midi mf; **good ~!** bonjour!; (*goodbye*) au revoir!

afterparty ['ɑːftəpɑːtɪ] N after m

afters ['ɑːftəz] N (BRIT *inf: dessert*) dessert m

after-sales service [ɑːftə'seɪlz-] N service m après-vente, SAV m

after-shave ['ɑːftəʃeɪv], **after-shave lotion** N lotion f après-rasage

aftershock ['ɑːftəʃɔk] N réplique f (sismique)

aftersun (cream/lotion) ['ɑːftəsʌn-] N après-soleil m inv

aftertaste ['ɑːftəteɪst] N arrière-goût m

afterthought ['ɑːftəθɔːt] N: **I had an ~** il m'est venu une idée après coup

afterwards ['ɑːftəwədz], (*US*) **afterward** ['ɑːftəwəd] ADV après

again [ə'gɛn] ADV de nouveau, encore (une fois); **to do sth ~** refaire qch; **not ... ~** ne ... plus; **~ and ~** à plusieurs reprises; **he's opened it ~** il l'a rouvert, il l'a de nouveau or l'a encore ouvert; **now and ~** de temps à autre

against [ə'gɛnst] PREP contre; (*compared to*) par rapport à; **~ a blue background** sur un fond bleu; **(as) ~** (BRIT) contre

age [eɪdʒ] N âge m ▸ VT, VI vieillir; **what ~ is he?** quel âge a-t-il?; **he is 20 years of ~** il a 20 ans; **under ~** mineur(e); **to come of ~** atteindre sa majorité; **it's ages since I saw you** ça fait une éternité que je ne t'ai pas vu

aged ['eɪdʒd] ADJ âgé(e); **~ 10** âgé de 10 ans ▸ NPL ['eɪdʒɪd]: **the ~** les personnes âgées

age group N tranche f d'âge; **the 40 to 50 ~** la tranche d'âge des 40 à 50 ans

ageing ['eɪdʒɪŋ] ADJ vieillissant(e)

ageless ['eɪdʒlɪs] ADJ sans âge

age limit N limite f d'âge

agency ['eɪdʒənsɪ] N agence f; **through** or **by the ~ of** par l'entremise or l'action de

agenda [ə'dʒɛndə] N ordre m du jour; **on the ~** à l'ordre du jour

agent ['eɪdʒənt] N agent m; (*firm*) concessionnaire m

aggravate ['ægrəveɪt] VT (*situation*) aggraver; (*annoy*) exaspérer, agacer

aggravation [ægrə'veɪʃən] N agacements mpl

aggregate ['ægrɪgɪt] N ensemble m, total m; **on ~** (*Sport*) au total des points

aggression [ə'grɛʃən] N agression f

aggressive [ə'grɛsɪv] ADJ agressif(-ive)

aggressiveness [ə'grɛsɪvnɪs] N agressivité f

aggressor [ə'grɛsəʳ] N agresseur m

aggrieved [ə'griːvd] ADJ chagriné(e), affligé(e)

aggro ['ægrəʊ] N (BRIT inf: *physical*) grabuge m; (: *hassle*) embêtements mpl

aghast [ə'gɑːst] ADJ consterné(e), atterré(e)

agile ['ædʒaɪl] ADJ agile

agility [ə'dʒɪlɪtɪ] N agilité f, souplesse f

agitate ['ædʒɪteɪt] VT rendre inquiet(-ète) or agité(e) ▸ VI faire de l'agitation (politique); **to ~ for** faire campagne pour

agitator ['ædʒɪteɪtəʳ] N agitateur(-trice) (politique)

AGM N ABBR (= *annual general meeting*) AG f

ago [ə'gəʊ] ADV: **two days ~** il y a deux jours; **not long ~** il n'y a pas longtemps; **as long ~ as 1960** déjà en 1960; **how long ~?** il y a combien de temps (de cela)?

agog [ə'gɔg] ADJ: **(all) ~** en émoi

agonize ['ægənaɪz] VI: **he agonized over the problem** ce problème lui a causé bien du tourment

agonizing ['ægənaɪzɪŋ] ADJ angoissant(e); (*cry*) déchirant(e)

agony ['ægənɪ] N (*pain*) douleur f atroce; (*distress*) angoisse f; **to be in ~** souffrir le martyre

agony aunt N (BRIT inf) journaliste qui tient la rubrique du courrier du cœur

agony column N courrier m du cœur

agree [ə'griː] VT (*price*) convenir de ▸ VI: **to ~ with** (*person*) être d'accord avec; (*statements etc*) concorder avec; (*Ling*) s'accorder avec; **to ~ to do** accepter de or consentir à faire; **to ~ to sth** consentir à qch; **to ~ that** (*admit*) convenir or reconnaître que; **it was agreed that ...** il a été convenu que ...; **they ~ on this** ils sont d'accord sur ce point; **they agreed on going/a price** ils se mirent d'accord pour y aller/sur un prix; **garlic doesn't ~ with me** je ne supporte pas l'ail

agreeable [ə'griːəbl] ADJ (*pleasant*) agréable; (*willing*) consentant(e), d'accord; **are you ~ to this?** est-ce que vous êtes d'accord?

agreed [ə'griːd] ADJ (*time, place*) convenu(e); **to be ~** être d'accord

agreement [ə'griːmənt] N accord m; **in ~** d'accord; **by mutual ~** d'un commun accord

agricultural [ægrɪ'kʌltʃərəl] ADJ agricole

agriculture ['ægrɪkʌltʃəʳ] N agriculture f

aground [ə'graʊnd] ADV: **to run ~** s'échouer

ahead [ə'hɛd] ADV en avant; devant; **go right** or **straight ~** (*direction*) allez tout droit; **go ~!** (*permission*) allez-y!; **~ of** devant; (*fig: schedule etc*) en avance sur; **~ of time** en avance; **they were (right) ~ of us** ils nous précédaient (de peu), ils étaient (juste) devant nous

AI N ABBR = **Amnesty International**; (*Comput*) = **artificial intelligence**

AIB N ABBR (BRIT: = *Accident Investigation Bureau*) commission d'enquête sur les accidents

AID N ABBR (= *artificial insemination by donor*) IAD f; (US: = *Agency for International Development*) agence pour le développement international

aid [eɪd] N aide f; (*device*) appareil m ▸ VT aider; **with the ~ of** avec l'aide de; **in ~ of** en faveur de; **to ~ and abet** (*Law*) se faire le complice de

aide [eɪd] N (*person*) assistant(e)

AIDS [eɪdz] N ABBR (= *acquired immune* (or *immuno-)deficiency syndrome*) SIDA m

AIH N ABBR (= *artificial insemination by husband*) IAC f

ailing ['eɪlɪŋ] ADJ (*person*) souffreteux(euse); (*economy*) malade

ailment ['eɪlmənt] N affection f

aim [eɪm] N (*objective*) but m; (*skill*): **his ~ is bad** il vise mal ▸ VI (*also*: **to take aim**) viser ▸ VT: **to ~ sth (at)** (*gun, camera*) braquer or pointer qch (sur); (*missile*) lancer qch (à or contre or en direction de); (*remark, blow*) destiner or adresser qch (à); **to ~ at** viser (à); (*fig*) viser (à); avoir pour but or ambition; **to ~ to do** avoir l'intention de faire

aimless ['eɪmlɪs] ADJ sans but

aimlessly ['eɪmlɪslɪ] ADV sans but

ain't [eɪnt] (*inf*) = **am not; aren't; isn't**

air [ɛəʳ] N air m ▸ VT aérer; (*idea, grievance, views*) mettre sur le tapis; (*knowledge*) faire étalage de ▸ CPD (*currents, attack etc*) aérien(ne); **to throw sth into the ~** (*ball etc*) jeter qch en l'air; **by ~** par avion; **to be on the ~** (*Radio, TV: programme*) être diffusé(e); (: *station*) émettre

airbag ['ɛəbæg] N airbag m

air base N base aérienne

airbed ['ɛəbɛd] N (BRIT) matelas m pneumatique

airborne ['ɛəbɔːn] ADJ (*plane*) en vol; (*troops*) aéroporté(e); (*particles*) dans l'air; **as soon as**

the plane was ~ dès que l'avion eut décollé
air cargo N fret aérien
air-conditioned ['ɛəkən'dɪʃənd] ADJ
climatisé(e), à air conditionné
air conditioning [-kən'dɪʃnɪŋ] N climatisation f
air-cooled ['ɛəkuːld] ADJ à refroidissement à air
aircraft ['ɛəkrɑːft] N INV avion m
aircraft carrier N porte-avions m inv
air cushion N coussin m d'air
airdrome ['ɛədrəum] N (US) aérodrome m
airfield ['ɛəfiːld] N terrain m d'aviation
Air Force N Armée f de l'air
air freight N fret aérien
air freshener [-'frɛʃnər] N désodorisant m
airgun ['ɛəgʌn] N fusil m à air comprimé
air hostess N (BRIT) hôtesse f de l'air
airily ['ɛərɪlɪ] ADV d'un air dégagé
airing ['ɛərɪŋ] N: **to give an ~ to** aérer; (fig: ideas,
views etc) mettre sur le tapis
airing cupboard N (BRIT) placard qui contient la
chaudière et dans lequel on met le linge à sécher
air letter N (BRIT) aérogramme m
airlift ['ɛəlɪft] N pont aérien
airline ['ɛəlaɪn] N ligne aérienne, compagnie
aérienne
airliner ['ɛəlaɪnər] N avion m de ligne
airlock ['ɛəlɔk] N sas m
airmail ['ɛəmeɪl] N: **by ~** par avion
air mattress N matelas m pneumatique
air mile N air mile m
airplane ['ɛəpleɪn] N (US) avion m
air pocket N trou m d'air
airport ['ɛəpɔːt] N aéroport m
air raid N attaque aérienne
air rifle N carabine f à air comprimé
airsick ['ɛəsɪk] ADJ: **to be ~** avoir le mal de l'air
airspace ['ɛəspeɪs] N espace m aérien
airspeed ['ɛəspiːd] N vitesse relative
airstrip ['ɛəstrɪp] N terrain m d'atterrissage
air terminal N aérogare f
airtight ['ɛətaɪt] ADJ hermétique
air time N (Radio, TV) temps m d'antenne
air traffic control N contrôle m de la navigation
aérienne
air-traffic controller N aiguilleur m du ciel
airway ['ɛəweɪ] N (Aviat) voie aérienne; **airways**
(Anat) voies aériennes
airy ['ɛərɪ] ADJ bien aéré(e); (manners) dégagé(e)
aisle [aɪl] N (of church: central) allée f centrale;
(: side) nef f latérale, bas-côté m; (in theatre,
supermarket) allée; (on plane) couloir m
aisle seat N place f côté couloir
ajar [ə'dʒɑːr] ADJ entrouvert(e)
AK ABBR (US) = **Alaska**
aka ABBR (= also known as) alias
akin [ə'kɪn] ADJ: **~ to** semblable à, du même
ordre que
AL ABBR (US) = **Alabama**
ALA N ABBR = **American Library Association**
Ala. ABBR (US) = **Alabama**
à la carte [ælæ'kɑːt] ADV à la carte
alacrity [ə'lækrɪtɪ] N: **with ~** avec
empressement, promptement
alarm [ə'lɑːm] N alarme f ▶ VT alarmer

alarm call N coup m de fil pour réveiller; **could I
have an ~ at 7 am, please?** pouvez-vous me
réveiller à 7 heures, s'il vous plaît?
alarm clock N réveille-matin m inv, réveil m
alarmed [ə'lɑːmd] ADJ (frightened) alarmé(e);
(protected by an alarm) protégé(e) par un système
d'alarme; **to become ~** prendre peur
alarming [ə'lɑːmɪŋ] ADJ alarmant(e)
alarmingly [ə'lɑːmɪŋlɪ] ADV d'une manière
alarmante; **~ close** dangereusement proche;
~ quickly à une vitesse inquiétante
alarmist [ə'lɑːmɪst] N alarmiste mf
alas [ə'læs] EXCL hélas
Alas. ABBR (US) = **Alaska**
Alaska [ə'læskə] N Alaska m
Albania [æl'beɪnɪə] N Albanie f
Albanian [æl'beɪnɪən] ADJ albanais(e) ▶ N
Albanais(e); (Ling) albanais m
albatross ['ælbətrɔs] N albatros m
albeit [ɔːl'biːɪt] CONJ bien que + sub, encore que
+ sub
album ['ælbəm] N album m
albumen ['ælbjumɪn] N albumine f; (of egg)
albumen m
alchemy ['ælkɪmɪ] N alchimie f
alcohol ['ælkəhɔl] N alcool m
alcohol-free ['ælkəhɔlfriː] ADJ sans alcool
alcoholic [ælkə'hɔlɪk] ADJ, N alcoolique mf
alcoholism ['ælkəhɔlɪzəm] N alcoolisme m
alcove ['ælkəuv] N alcôve f
Ald. ABBR = **alderman**
alderman ['ɔːldəmən] N (irreg) conseiller
municipal (en Angleterre)
ale [eɪl] N bière f
alert [ə'ləːt] ADJ alerte, vif (vive); (watchful)
vigilant(e) ▶ N alerte f ▶ VT alerter; **to ~ sb (to
sth)** attirer l'attention de qn (sur qch); **to ~ sb
to the dangers of sth** avertir qn des dangers
de qch; **on the ~** sur le qui-vive; (Mil) en état
d'alerte
Aleutian Islands [ə'luːʃən-] NPL îles
Aléoutiennes
A levels NPL ≈ baccalauréat msg
Alexandria [ælɪg'zɑːndrɪə] N Alexandrie
alfresco [æl'frɛskəu] ADJ, ADV en plein air
algebra ['ældʒɪbrə] N algèbre m
Algeria [æl'dʒɪərɪə] N Algérie f
Algerian [æl'dʒɪərɪən] ADJ algérien(ne) ▶ N
Algérien(ne)
Algiers [æl'dʒɪəz] N Alger
algorithm ['ælgərɪðəm] N algorithme m
alias ['eɪlɪəs] ADV alias ▶ N faux nom, nom
d'emprunt
alibi ['ælɪbaɪ] N alibi m
alien ['eɪlɪən] N (from abroad) étranger(-ère); (from
outer space) extraterrestre ▶ ADJ: **~ (to)**
étranger(-ère) (à)
alienate ['eɪlɪəneɪt] VT aliéner; (subj: person)
s'aliéner
alienation [eɪlɪə'neɪʃən] N aliénation f
alight [ə'laɪt] ADJ, ADV en feu ▶ VI mettre pied à
terre; (passenger) descendre; (bird) se poser
align [ə'laɪn] VT aligner
alignment [ə'laɪnmənt] N alignement m; **it's**

out of ~ (with) ce n'est pas aligné (avec)
alike [ə'laɪk] ADJ semblable, pareil(le) ▶ ADV de même; **to look ~** se ressembler
alimony ['ælɪmənɪ] N (payment) pension f alimentaire
alive [ə'laɪv] ADJ vivant(e); (active) plein(e) de vie; **~ with** grouillant(e) de; **~ to** sensible à
alkali ['ælkəlaɪ] N alcali m

(KEYWORD)

all [ɔːl] ADJ (singular) tout(e); (plural) tous (toutes); **all day** toute la journée; **all night** toute la nuit; **all men** tous les hommes; **all five** tous les cinq; **all the food** toute la nourriture; **all the books** tous les livres; **all the time** tout le temps; **all his life** toute sa vie
▶ PRON **1** tout; **I ate it all, I ate all of it** j'ai tout mangé; **all of us went** nous y sommes tous allés; **all of the boys went** tous les garçons y sont allés; **is that all?** c'est tout?; (in shop) ce sera tout?
2 (in phrases): **above all** surtout, par-dessus tout; **after all** après tout; **at all**: **not at all** (in answer to question) pas du tout; (in answer to thanks) je vous en prie!; **I'm not at all tired** je ne suis pas du tout fatigué(e); **anything at all will do** n'importe quoi fera l'affaire; **all in all** tout bien considéré, en fin de compte
▶ ADV: **all alone** tout(e) seul(e); **it's not as hard as all that** ce n'est pas si difficile que ça; **all the more the better** d'autant plus/mieux; **all but** presque, pratiquement; **to be all in** (BRIT inf) être complètement à plat; **the score is 2 all** le score est de 2 partout

Allah ['ælə] N Allah m
all-around [ɔːlə'raund] ADJ (US) = **all-round**
allay [ə'leɪ] VT (fears) apaiser, calmer
all clear N (also fig) fin f d'alerte
allegation [ælɪ'ɡeɪʃən] N allégation f
allege [ə'ledʒ] VT alléguer, prétendre; **he is alleged to have said** il aurait dit
alleged [ə'ledʒd] ADJ prétendu(e)
allegedly [ə'ledʒɪdlɪ] ADV à ce que l'on prétend, paraît-il
allegiance [ə'liːdʒəns] N fidélité f, obéissance f
allegory ['ælɪɡərɪ] N allégorie f
all-embracing ['ɔːlɪm'breɪsɪŋ] ADJ universel(le)
allergic [ə'lə:dʒɪk] ADJ: **~ to** allergique à; **I'm ~ to penicillin** je suis allergique à la pénicilline
allergy ['ælədʒɪ] N allergie f
alleviate [ə'liːvɪeɪt] VT soulager, adoucir
alley ['ælɪ] N ruelle f; (in garden) allée f
alleyway ['ælɪweɪ] N ruelle f
alliance [ə'laɪəns] N alliance f
allied ['ælaɪd] ADJ allié(e)
alligator ['ælɪɡeɪtə*] N alligator m
all-important ['ɔːlɪm'pɔːtənt] ADJ capital(e), crucial(e)
all-in ['ɔːlɪn] ADJ, ADV (BRIT: charge) tout compris
all-in wrestling N (BRIT) catch m
alliteration [əlɪtə'reɪʃən] N allitération f
all-night ['ɔːl'naɪt] ADJ ouvert(e) or qui dure toute la nuit

allocate ['æləkeɪt] VT (share out) répartir, distribuer; **to ~ sth to** (duties) assigner or attribuer qch à; (sum, time) allouer qch à; **to ~ sth for** affecter qch à
allocation [æləu'keɪʃən] N (see vb) répartition f; attribution f; allocation f; affectation f; (money) crédit(s) m(pl), somme(s) allouée(s)
allot [ə'lɔt] VT (share out) répartir, distribuer; **to ~ sth to** (time) allouer qch à; (duties) assigner qch à; **in the allotted time** dans le temps imparti
allotment [ə'lɔtmənt] N (share) part f; (garden) lopin m de terre (loué à la municipalité)
all-out ['ɔːlaut] ADJ (effort etc) total(e)
allow [ə'lau] VT (practice, behaviour) permettre, autoriser; (sum to spend etc) accorder, allouer; (sum, time estimated) compter, prévoir; (claim, goal) admettre; (concede): **to ~ that** convenir que; **to ~ sb to do** permettre à qn de faire, autoriser qn à faire; **he is allowed to ...** on lui permet de ...; **smoking is not allowed** il est interdit de fumer; **we must ~ three days for the journey** il faut compter trois jours pour le voyage
▶ **allow for** VT FUS tenir compte de
allowance [ə'lauəns] N (money received) allocation f; (: from parent etc) subside m; (: for expenses) indemnité f; (US: pocket money) argent m de poche; (Tax) somme f déductible du revenu imposable, abattement m; **to make allowances for** (person) essayer de comprendre; (thing) tenir compte de
alloy ['ælɔɪ] N alliage m
all right ADV (feel, work) bien; (as answer) d'accord
all-round ['ɔːl'raund] ADJ compétent(e) dans tous les domaines; (athlete etc) complet(-ète)
all-rounder [ɔːl'raundə*] N (BRIT): **to be a good ~** être doué(e) en tout
allspice ['ɔːlspaɪs] N poivre m de la Jamaïque
all-time ['ɔːl'taɪm] ADJ (record) sans précédent, absolu(e)
allude [ə'luːd] VI: **to ~ to** faire allusion à
alluring [ə'ljuərɪŋ] ADJ séduisant(e), alléchant(e)
allusion [ə'luːʒən] N allusion f
alluvium [ə'luːvɪəm] N alluvions fpl
ally ['ælaɪ] N allié m ▶ VT [ə'laɪ]: **to ~ o.s. with** s'allier avec
almighty [ɔːl'maɪtɪ] ADJ tout(e)-puissant(e); (tremendous) énorme
almond ['ɑːmənd] N amande f
almost ['ɔːlməust] ADV presque; **he ~ fell** il a failli tomber
alms [ɑːmz] N aumône(s) f(pl)
aloft [ə'lɔft] ADV en haut, en l'air; (Naut) dans la mâture
alone [ə'ləun] ADJ, ADV seul(e); **to leave sb ~** laisser qn tranquille; **to leave sth ~** ne pas toucher à qch; **let ~ ...** sans parler de ...; encore moins ...
along [ə'lɔŋ] PREP le long de ▶ ADV: **is he coming ~ with us?** vient-il avec nous?; **he was hopping/limping ~** il venait or avançait en sautillant/boitant; **~ with** avec, en plus de; (person) en compagnie de; **all ~** (all the time)

depuis le début

alongside [ə'lɔŋ'saɪd] PREP (*along*) le long de; (*beside*) à côté de ▸ ADV bord à bord; côte à côte; **we brought our boat ~** (*of a pier, shore etc*) nous avons accosté

aloof [ə'lu:f] ADJ distant(e) ▸ ADV à distance, à l'écart; **to stand ~** se tenir à l'écart *or* à distance

aloofness [ə'lu:fnɪs] N réserve (hautaine), attitude distante

aloud [ə'laud] ADV à haute voix

alphabet [ælfəbɛt] N alphabet *m*

alphabetical [ælfə'bɛtɪkl] ADJ alphabétique; **in ~ order** par ordre alphabétique

alphanumeric [ælfənju:'mɛrɪk] ADJ alphanumérique

alpine ['ælpaɪn] ADJ alpin(e), alpestre; **~ hut** cabane *f or* refuge *m* de montagne; **~ pasture** pâturage *m* (de montagne); **~ skiing** ski alpin

Alps [ælps] NPL: **the ~** les Alpes *fpl*

already [ɔːl'rɛdɪ] ADV déjà

alright ['ɔːl'raɪt] ADV (*BRIT*) = **all right**

Alsace [æl'sæs] N Alsace *f*

Alsatian [æl'seɪʃən] ADJ alsacien(ne), d'Alsace ▸ N Alsacien(ne); (*BRIT: dog*) berger allemand

also ['ɔːlsəu] ADV aussi

Alta. ABBR (*CANADA*) = **Alberta**

altar ['ɔltər] N autel *m*

alter ['ɔltər] VT, VI changer

alteration [ɔltə'reɪʃən] N changement *m*, modification *f*; **alterations** NPL (*Sewing*) retouches *fpl*; (*Archit*) modifications *fpl*; **timetable subject to ~** horaires sujets à modifications

altercation [ɔltə'keɪʃən] N altercation *f*

alternate ADJ [ɔl'tə:nɪt] alterné(e), alternant(e), alternatif(-ive); (*US*) = **alternative** ▸ VI ['ɔltə:neɪt] alterner; **to ~ with** alterner avec; **on ~ days** un jour sur deux, tous les deux jours

alternately [ɔl'tə:nɪtlɪ] ADV alternativement, en alternant

alternating ['ɔltə:neɪtɪŋ] ADJ (*current*) alternatif(-ive)

alternative [ɔl'tə:nətɪv] ADJ (*solution, plan*) autre, de remplacement; (*energy*) doux (douce); (*lifestyle*) parallèle ▸ N (*choice*) alternative *f*; (*other possibility*) autre possibilité *f*; **~ medicine** médecine alternative, médecine douce

alternatively [ɔl'tə:nətɪvlɪ] ADV: **~ one could ...** une autre *or* l'autre solution serait de ...

alternative medicine N médecines *fpl* parallèles *or* douces

alternator ['ɔltə:neɪtər] N (*Aut*) alternateur *m*

although [ɔːl'ðəu] CONJ bien que + *sub*

altitude ['æltɪtju:d] N altitude *f*

alto ['æltəu] N (*female*) contralto *m*; (*male*) haute-contre *f*

altogether [ɔːltə'gɛðər] ADV entièrement, tout à fait; (*on the whole*) tout compte fait; (*in all*) en tout; **how much is that ~?** ça fait combien en tout?

altruism ['æltruɪzəm] N altruisme *m*

altruistic [æltru'ɪstɪk] ADJ altruiste

aluminium [ælju'mɪnɪəm], (*US*) **aluminum** [ə'lu:mɪnəm] N aluminium *m*

alumna [ə'lʌmnə] (*pl* **alumnae** [-niː]) N (*US Scol*) ancienne élève; (*University*) ancienne étudiante

alumnus [ə'lʌmnəs] (*pl* **alumni** [-naɪ]) N (*US Scol*) ancien élève; (*University*) ancien étudiant

always ['ɔːlweɪz] ADV toujours

Alzheimer's ['æltshaɪməz], **Alzheimer's disease** N maladie *f* d'Alzheimer

AM ABBR = **amplitude modulation** ▸ N ABBR (= *Assembly Member*) député *m* au Parlement gallois

am [æm] VB *see* **be**

a.m. ADV ABBR (= *ante meridiem*) du matin

AMA N ABBR = **American Medical Association**

amalgam [ə'mælgəm] N amalgame *m*

amalgamate [ə'mælgəmeɪt] VT, VI fusionner

amalgamation [əmælgə'meɪʃən] N fusion *f*; (*Comm*) fusionnement *m*

amass [ə'mæs] VT amasser

amateur ['æmətər] N amateur *m* ▸ ADJ (*Sport*) amateur *inv*; **~ dramatics** le théâtre amateur

amateurish ['æmətərɪʃ] ADJ (*pej*) d'amateur, un peu amateur

amaze [ə'meɪz] VT stupéfier; **to be amazed (at)** être stupéfait(e) (de)

amazed [ə'meɪzd] ADJ stupéfait(e)

amazement [ə'meɪzmənt] N surprise *f*, étonnement *m*

amazing [ə'meɪzɪŋ] ADJ étonnant(e), incroyable; (*bargain, offer*) exceptionnel(le)

amazingly [ə'meɪzɪŋlɪ] ADV incroyablement

Amazon ['æməzən] N (*Geo, Mythology*) Amazone *f* ▸ CPD amazonien(ne), de l'Amazone; **the ~ basin** le bassin de l'Amazone; **the ~ jungle** la forêt amazonienne

Amazonian [æmə'zəunɪən] ADJ amazonien(ne)

ambassador [æm'bæsədər] N ambassadeur *m*

amber ['æmbər] N ambre *m*; **at ~** (*BRIT Aut*) à l'orange

ambidextrous [æmbɪ'dɛkstrəs] ADJ ambidextre

ambience ['æmbɪəns] N ambiance *f*

ambiguity [æmbɪ'gjuɪtɪ] N ambiguïté *f*

ambiguous [æm'bɪguəs] ADJ ambigu(ë)

ambition [æm'bɪʃən] N ambition *f*

ambitious [æm'bɪʃəs] ADJ ambitieux(-euse)

ambivalent [æm'bɪvələnt] ADJ (*attitude*) ambivalent(e)

amble ['æmbl] VI (*also*: **to amble along**) aller d'un pas tranquille

ambulance ['æmbjuləns] N ambulance *f*; **call an ~!** appelez une ambulance!

ambush ['æmbuʃ] N embuscade *f* ▸ VT tendre une embuscade à

ameba [ə'mi:bə] N (*US*) = **amoeba**

ameliorate [ə'mi:lɪəreɪt] VT améliorer

amen ['ɑː'mɛn] EXCL amen

amenable [ə'mi:nəbl] ADJ: **~ to** (*advice etc*) disposé(e) à écouter *or* suivre; **~ to the law** responsable devant la loi

amend [ə'mɛnd] VT (*law*) amender; (*text*) corriger; (*habits*) réformer ▸ VI s'amender, se corriger; **to make amends** réparer ses torts, faire amende honorable

amendment [ə'mɛndmənt] N (*to law*) amendement *m*; (*to text*) correction *f*

amenities [ə'miːnɪtɪz] NPL aménagements *mpl*, équipements *mpl*

amenity [ə'miːnɪtɪ] N charme *m*, agrément *m*

America [ə'mɛrɪkə] N Amérique *f*

American [ə'mɛrɪkən] ADJ américain(e) ► N Américain(e)

American football N (BRIT) football *m* américain

Americanize [ə'mɛrɪkənaɪz] VT américaniser

amethyst ['æmɪθɪst] N améthyste *f*

Amex ['æmɛks] N ABBR = **American Stock Exchange**

amiable ['eɪmɪəbl] ADJ aimable, affable

amicable ['æmɪkəbl] ADJ amical(e); (*Law*) à l'amiable

amicably ['æmɪkəblɪ] ADV amicalement

amid [ə'mɪd], **amidst** [ə'mɪdst] PREP parmi, au milieu de

amiss [ə'mɪs] ADJ, ADV: **there's something ~** il y a quelque chose qui ne va pas *or* qui cloche; **to take sth ~** prendre qch mal *or* de travers

ammo ['æməʊ] N ABBR (*inf*) = **ammunition**

ammonia [ə'məʊnɪə] N (*gas*) ammoniac *m*; (*liquid*) ammoniaque *f*

ammunition [æmju'nɪʃən] N munitions *fpl*; (*fig*) arguments *mpl*

ammunition dump N dépôt *m* de munitions

amnesia [æm'niːzɪə] N amnésie *f*

amnesty ['æmnɪstɪ] N amnistie *f*; **to grant an ~ to** accorder une amnistie à

Amnesty International N Amnesty International

amoeba, (US) **ameba** [ə'miːbə] N amibe *f*

amok [ə'mɔk] ADV: **to run ~** être pris(e) d'un accès de folie furieuse

among [ə'mʌŋ], **amongst** [ə'mʌŋst] PREP parmi, entre

amoral [eɪ'mɔrəl] ADJ amoral(e)

amorous ['æmərəs] ADJ amoureux(-euse)

amorphous [ə'mɔːfəs] ADJ amorphe

amortization [əmɔːtaɪ'zeɪʃən] N (*Comm*) amortissement *m*

amount [ə'maʊnt] N (*sum of money*) somme *f*; (*total*) montant *m*; (*quantity*) quantité *f*; nombre *m* ► VI: **to ~ to** (*total*) s'élever à; (*be same as*) équivaloir à, revenir à; **this amounts to a refusal** cela équivaut à un refus; **the total ~** (*of money*) le montant total

amp ['æmp], **ampère** ['æmpɛə'] N ampère *m*; **a 13 ~ plug** une fiche de 13 A

ampersand ['æmpəsænd] N signe &, "et" commercial

amphetamine [æm'fɛtəmiːn] N amphétamine *f*

amphibian [æm'fɪbɪən] N batracien *m*

amphibious [æm'fɪbɪəs] ADJ amphibie

amphitheatre, (US) **amphitheater** ['æmfɪθɪətə'] N amphithéâtre *m*

ample ['æmpl] ADJ ample, spacieux(-euse); (*enough*): **this is ~** c'est largement suffisant; **to have ~ time/room** avoir bien assez de temps/place, avoir largement le temps/la place

amplifier ['æmplɪfaɪə'] N amplificateur *m*

amplify ['æmplɪfaɪ] VT amplifier

amply ['æmplɪ] ADV amplement, largement

ampoule, (US) **ampule** ['æmpuːl] N (*Med*) ampoule *f*

amputate ['æmpjuteɪt] VT amputer

amputee [æmpju'tiː] N amputé(e)

Amsterdam ['æmstədæm] N Amsterdam

amt ABBR = **amount**

Amtrak® ['æmtræk] (US) N *société mixte de transports ferroviaires interurbains pour voyageurs*

amuck [ə'mʌk] ADV = **amok**

amuse [ə'mjuːz] VT amuser; **to ~ o.s. with sth/ by doing sth** se divertir avec qch/à faire qch; **to be amused at** être amusé par; **he was not amused** il n'a pas apprécié

amusement [ə'mjuːzmənt] N amusement *m*; (*pastime*) distraction *f*

amusement arcade N salle *f* de jeu

amusement park N parc *m* d'attractions

amusing [ə'mjuːzɪŋ] ADJ amusant(e), divertissant(e)

an [æn, ən, n] INDEF ART *see* **a**

ANA N ABBR = **American Newspaper Association; American Nurses Association**

anachronism [ə'nækrənɪzəm] N anachronisme *m*

anaemia, (US) **anemia** [ə'niːmɪə] N anémie *f*

anaemic, (US) **anemic** [ə'niːmɪk] ADJ anémique

anaesthetic, (US) **anesthetic** [ænɪs'θɛtɪk] ADJ, N anesthésique *m*; **under the ~** sous anesthésie; **local/general ~** anesthésie locale/générale

anaesthetist [æ'niːsθɪtɪst] N anesthésiste *mf*

anagram ['ænəgræm] N anagramme *m*

anal ['eɪnl] ADJ anal(e)

analgesic [ænæl'dʒiːsɪk] ADJ, N analgésique (*m*)

analog, analogue ['ænəlɔg] ADJ (*watch, computer*) analogique

analogous [ə'næləgəs] ADJ: **~ (to** *or* **with)** analogue (à)

analogy [ə'nælədʒɪ] N analogie *f*; **to draw an ~ between** établir une analogie entre

analyse, (US) **analyze** ['ænəlaɪz] VT analyser

analysis [ə'næləsɪs] (*pl* **analyses** [-siːz]) N analyse *f*; **in the last ~** en dernière analyse

analyst ['ænəlɪst] N (*political analyst etc*) analyste *mf*; (US) psychanalyste *mf*

analytic [ænə'lɪtɪk], **analytical** [ænə'lɪtɪkəl] ADJ analytique

analyze ['ænəlaɪz] VT (US) = **analyse**

anarchic [æ'nɑːkɪk] ADJ anarchique

anarchist ['ænəkɪst] ADJ, N anarchiste (*mf*)

anarchy ['ænəkɪ] N anarchie *f*

anathema [ə'næθɪmə] N: **it is ~ to him** il a cela en abomination

anatomical [ænə'tɔmɪkəl] ADJ anatomique

anatomy [ə'nætəmɪ] N anatomie *f*

ANC N ABBR (= *African National Congress*) ANC *m*

ancestor ['ænsɪstə'] N ancêtre *m*, aïeul *m*

ancestral [æn'sɛstrəl] ADJ ancestral(e)

ancestry ['ænsɪstrɪ] N ancêtres *mpl*; ascendance *f*

anchor ['æŋkə'] N ancre *f* ► VI (*also*: **to drop anchor**) jeter l'ancre, mouiller ► VT mettre à l'ancre; (*fig*): **to ~ sth to** fixer qch à; **to weigh ~**

lever l'ancre

anchorage ['æŋkərɪdʒ] N mouillage m, ancrage m

anchor man, anchor woman N (irreg) (TV, Radio) présentateur(-trice)

anchovy ['æntʃəvɪ] N anchois m

ancient ['eɪnʃənt] ADJ ancien(ne), antique; (person) d'un âge vénérable; (car) antédiluvien(ne); **~ monument** monument m historique

ancillary [æn'sɪlərɪ] ADJ auxiliaire

and [ænd] CONJ et; **~ so on** et ainsi de suite; **try ~ come** tâchez de venir; **come ~ sit here** venez vous asseoir ici; **he talked ~ talked** il a parlé pendant des heures; **better ~ better** de mieux en mieux; **more ~ more** de plus en plus

Andes ['ændiːz] NPL: **the ~** les Andes fpl

Andorra [æn'dɔːrə] N (principauté f d')Andorre f

anecdote ['ænɪkdəut] N anecdote f

anemia etc [ə'niːmɪə] N (US) = **anaemia** etc

anemic [ə'niːmɪk] ADJ = **anaemic**

anemone [ə'nɛmənɪ] N (Bot) anémone f; **sea ~** anémone de mer

anesthesiologist [ænɪsθiːzɪ'ɒlədʒɪst] N (US) anesthésiste mf

anesthetic [ænɪs'θɛtɪk] N, ADJ (US) = **anaesthetic**

anesthetist [æ'niːsθɪtɪst] N = **anaesthetist**

anew [ə'njuː] ADV à nouveau

angel ['eɪndʒəl] N ange m

angel dust N poussière f d'ange

anger ['æŋgəʳ] N colère f ▶ VT mettre en colère, irriter

angina [æn'dʒaɪnə] N angine f de poitrine

angle ['æŋgl] N angle m ▶ VI: **to ~ for** (trout) pêcher; (compliments) chercher, quêter; **from their ~** de leur point de vue

angler ['æŋgləʳ] N pêcheur(-euse) à la ligne

Anglican ['æŋglɪkən] ADJ, N anglican(e)

anglicize ['æŋglɪsaɪz] VT angliciser

angling ['æŋglɪŋ] N pêche f à la ligne

Anglo- ['æŋgləu] PREFIX anglo(-)

Anglo-French ['æŋgləu'frentʃ] ADJ anglo-français(e)

Anglo-Saxon ['æŋgləu'sæksən] ADJ, N anglo-saxon(ne)

Angola [æŋ'gəulə] N Angola m

Angolan [æŋ'gəulən] ADJ angolais(e) ▶ N Angolais(e)

angrily ['æŋgrɪlɪ] ADV avec colère

angry ['æŋgrɪ] ADJ en colère, furieux(-euse); (wound) enflammé(e); **to be ~ with sb/at sth** être furieux contre qn/de qch; **to get ~** se fâcher, se mettre en colère; **to make sb ~** mettre qn en colère

anguish ['æŋgwɪʃ] N angoisse f

anguished ['æŋgwɪʃt] ADJ (mentally) angoissé(e); (physically) plein(e) de souffrance

angular ['æŋgjuləʳ] ADJ anguleux(-euse)

animal ['ænɪməl] N animal m ▶ ADJ animal(e)

animal rights NPL droits mpl de l'animal

animate VT ['ænɪmeɪt] animer ▶ ADJ ['ænɪmɪt] animé(e), vivant(e)

animated ['ænɪmeɪtɪd] ADJ animé(e)

animation [ænɪ'meɪʃən] N (of person) entrain m; (of street, Cine) animation f

animosity [ænɪ'mɒsɪtɪ] N animosité f

aniseed ['ænɪsiːd] N anis m

Ankara ['æŋkərə] N Ankara

ankle ['æŋkl] N cheville f

ankle socks NPL socquettes fpl

annex ['ænɛks] N (BRIT: also: **annexe**) annexe f ▶ VT [ə'nɛks] annexer

annexation [ænɛks'eɪʃən] N annexion f

annihilate [ə'naɪəleɪt] VT annihiler, anéantir

annihilation [ənaɪə'leɪʃən] N anéantissement m

anniversary [ænɪ'vəːsərɪ] N anniversaire m

anniversary dinner N dîner commémoratif or anniversaire

annotate ['ænəuteɪt] VT annoter

announce [ə'nauns] VT annoncer; (birth, death) faire part de; **he announced that he wasn't going** il a déclaré qu'il n'irait pas

announcement [ə'naunsmənt] N annonce f; (for births etc: in newspaper) avis m de faire-part; (: letter, card) faire-part m; **I'd like to make an ~** j'ai une communication à faire

announcer [ə'naunsəʳ] N (Radio, TV: between programmes) speaker(ine); (: in a programme) présentateur(-trice)

annoy [ə'nɔɪ] VT agacer, ennuyer, contrarier; **to be annoyed (at sth/with sb)** être en colère or irrité (contre qch/qn); **don't get annoyed!** ne vous fâchez pas!

annoyance [ə'nɔɪəns] N mécontentement m, contrariété f

annoying [ə'nɔɪɪŋ] ADJ agaçant(e), contrariant(e)

annual ['ænjuəl] ADJ annuel(le) ▶ N (Bot) plante annuelle; (book) album m

annual general meeting N (BRIT) assemblée générale annuelle

annually ['ænjuəlɪ] ADV annuellement

annual report N rapport annuel

annuity [ə'njuːɪtɪ] N rente f; **life ~** rente viagère

annul [ə'nʌl] VT annuler; (law) abroger

annulment [ə'nʌlmənt] N (see vb) annulation f; abrogation f

annum ['ænəm] N see **per**

Annunciation [ənʌnsɪ'eɪʃən] N Annonciation f

anode ['ænəud] N anode f

anoint [ə'nɔɪnt] VT oindre

anomalous [ə'nɒmələs] ADJ anormal(e)

anomaly [ə'nɒməlɪ] N anomalie f

anon. [ə'nɒn] ABBR = **anonymous**

anonymity [ænə'nɪmɪtɪ] N anonymat m

anonymous [ə'nɒnɪməs] ADJ anonyme; **to remain ~** garder l'anonymat

anorak ['ænəræk] N anorak m

anorexia [ænə'rɛksɪə] N (also: **anorexia nervosa**) anorexie f

anorexic [ænə'rɛksɪk] ADJ, N anorexique (mf)

another [ə'nʌðəʳ] ADJ: **~ book** (one more) un autre livre, encore un livre, un livre de plus; (a different one) un autre livre ▶ PRON un(e) autre, encore un(e), un(e) de plus; **~ drink?** encore un verre?; **in ~ five years** dans cinq ans; see also **one**

ANSI ['ænsɪ] N ABBR (= American National Standards

Institution) ANSI m (= Institut américain de normalisation)

answer ['ɑːnsəʳ] N réponse f; (to problem) solution f ▶ vi répondre ▶ vt (reply to) répondre à; (problem) résoudre; (prayer) exaucer; **in ~ to your letter** suite à or en réponse à votre lettre; **to ~ the phone** répondre (au téléphone); **to ~ the bell** or **the door** aller or venir ouvrir (la porte)
▶ **answer back** vi répondre, répliquer
▶ **answer for** vt fus répondre de, se porter garant de; (crime, one's actions) répondre de
▶ **answer to** vt fus (description) répondre or correspondre à

answerable ['ɑːnsərəbl] ADJ: **~ (to sb/for sth)** responsable (devant qn/de qch); **I am ~ to no-one** je n'ai de comptes à rendre à personne

answering machine ['ɑːnsərɪŋ-] N répondeur m

answerphone ['ɑːnsəʳfəun] N (esp BRIT) répondeur m (téléphonique)

ant [ænt] N fourmi f

ANTA N ABBR = **American National Theater and Academy**

antagonism [æn'tægənɪzəm] N antagonisme m

antagonist [æn'tægənɪst] N antagoniste mf, adversaire mf

antagonistic [æntægə'nɪstɪk] ADJ (attitude, feelings) hostile

antagonize [æn'tægənaɪz] vt éveiller l'hostilité de, contrarier

Antarctic [ænt'ɑːktɪk] ADJ antarctique, austral(e) ▶ N: **the ~** l'Antarctique m

Antarctica [ænt'ɑːktɪkə] N Antarctique m, Terres Australes

Antarctic Circle N cercle m Antarctique

Antarctic Ocean N océan m Antarctique or Austral

ante ['æntɪ] N: **to up the ~** faire monter les enjeux

ante... ['æntɪ] PREFIX anté..., anti..., pré...

anteater ['æntiːtəʳ] N fourmilier m, tamanoir m

antecedent [æntɪ'siːdənt] N antécédent m

antechamber ['æntɪtʃeɪmbəʳ] N antichambre f

antelope ['æntɪləup] N antilope f

antenatal ['æntɪ'neɪtl] ADJ prénatal(e)

antenatal clinic N service m de consultation prénatale

antenna [æn'tɛnə] (pl **antennae** [-niː]) N antenne f

anthem ['ænθəm] N motet m; **national ~** hymne national

ant-hill ['ænthɪl] N fourmilière f

anthology [æn'θɔlədʒɪ] N anthologie f

anthrax ['ænθræks] N anthrax m

anthropologist [ænθrə'pɔlədʒɪst] N anthropologue mf

anthropology [ænθrə'pɔlədʒɪ] N anthropologie f

anti ['æntɪ] PREFIX anti-

anti-aircraft ['æntɪ'ɛəkrɑːft] ADJ antiaérien(ne)

anti-aircraft defence N défense f contre avions, DCA f

antiballistic ['æntɪbə'lɪstɪk] ADJ antibalistique

antibiotic ['æntɪbaɪ'ɔtɪk] ADJ, N antibiotique m

antibody ['æntɪbɔdɪ] N anticorps m

anticipate [æn'tɪsɪpeɪt] vt s'attendre à, prévoir; (wishes, request) aller au devant de, devancer; **this is worse than I anticipated** c'est pire que je ne pensais; **as anticipated** comme prévu

anticipation [æntɪsɪ'peɪʃən] N attente f; **thanking you in ~** en vous remerciant d'avance, mes remerciements anticipés

anticlimax ['æntɪ'klaɪmæks] N déception f

anticlockwise ['æntɪ'klɔkwaɪz] (BRIT) ADV dans le sens inverse des aiguilles d'une montre

antics ['æntɪks] NPL singeries fpl

anticyclone ['æntɪ'saɪkləun] N anticyclone m

antidepressant ['æntɪ'prɛsnt] N antidépresseur m

antidote ['æntɪdəut] N antidote m, contrepoison m

antifreeze ['æntɪfriːz] N antigel m

anti-globalization [æntɪgləubəlaɪ'zeɪʃən] N antimondialisation f

antihistamine [æntɪ'hɪstəmɪn] N antihistaminique m

Antilles [æn'tɪliːz] NPL: **the ~** les Antilles fpl

antipathy [æn'tɪpəθɪ] N antipathie f

antiperspirant [æntɪ'pə:spɪrənt] N déodorant m

Antipodean [æntɪpə'diːən] ADJ australien(ne) et néozélandais(e), d'Australie et de Nouvelle-Zélande

Antipodes [æn'tɪpədiːz] NPL: **the ~** l'Australie f et la Nouvelle-Zélande

antiquarian [æntɪ'kwɛərɪən] ADJ: **~ bookshop** librairie f d'ouvrages anciens ▶ N expert m en objets or livres anciens; amateur m d'antiquités

antiquated ['æntɪkweɪtɪd] ADJ vieilli(e), suranné(e), vieillot(te)

antique [æn'tiːk] N (ornament) objet m d'art ancien; (furniture) meuble ancien ▶ ADJ ancien(ne); (pre-mediaeval) antique

antique dealer N antiquaire mf

antique shop N magasin m d'antiquités

antiquity [æn'tɪkwɪtɪ] N antiquité f

anti-Semitic ['æntɪsɪ'mɪtɪk] ADJ antisémite

anti-Semitism ['æntɪ'sɛmɪtɪzəm] N antisémitisme m

antiseptic [æntɪ'sɛptɪk] ADJ, N antiseptique (m)

antisocial ['æntɪ'səuʃəl] ADJ (unfriendly) peu liant(e), insociable; (against society) antisocial(e)

antitank [æntɪ'tæŋk] ADJ antichar

antithesis [æn'tɪθɪsɪs] (pl **antitheses** [-siːz]) N antithèse f

antitrust [æntɪ'trʌst] ADJ: **~ legislation** loi f anti-trust

antiviral [æntɪ'vaɪərəl] ADJ (Med) antiviral

antivirus [æntɪ'vaɪrəs] ADJ (Comput) antivirus inv; **~ software** (logiciel m) antivirus

antlers ['æntləz] NPL bois mpl, ramure f

Antwerp ['æntwəːp] N Anvers

anus ['eɪnəs] N anus m

anvil ['ænvɪl] N enclume f

anxiety [æŋ'zaɪətɪ] N anxiété f; (keenness): **~ to do** grand désir or impatience f de faire

anxious ['æŋkʃəs] ADJ (très) inquiet(-ète); (always worried) anxieux(-euse); (worrying) angoissant(e); **~ to do/that** (keen) qui tient beaucoup à faire/à ce que + sub; impatient(e) de faire/que + sub; **I'm very ~ about you** je me fais beaucoup de souci pour toi

anxiously ['æŋkʃəslɪ] ADV anxieusement

(KEYWORD)

any ['ɛnɪ] ADJ **1** (in questions etc: singular) du, de l', de la; (: plural) des; **do you have any butter/children/ink?** avez-vous du beurre/des enfants/de l'encre?
2 (with negative) de, d'; **I don't have any money/books** je n'ai pas d'argent/de livres; **without any difficulty** sans la moindre difficulté
3 (no matter which) n'importe quel(le); (each and every) tout(e), chaque; **choose any book you like** vous pouvez choisir n'importe quel livre; **any teacher you ask will tell you** n'importe quel professeur vous le dira
4 (in phrases): **in any case** de toute façon; **any day now** d'un jour à l'autre; **at any moment** à tout moment, d'un instant à l'autre; **at any rate** en tout cas; **any time** n'importe quand; **he might come (at) any time** il pourrait venir n'importe quand; **come (at) any time** venez quand vous voulez
▶ PRON **1** (in questions etc) en; **have you got any?** est-ce que vous en avez?; **can any of you sing?** est-ce que parmi vous il y a qui savent chanter?
2 (with negative) en; **I don't have any (of them)** je n'en ai pas, je n'en ai aucun
3 (no matter which one(s)) n'importe lequel (or laquelle); (anybody) n'importe qui; **take any of those books (you like)** vous pouvez prendre n'importe lequel de ces livres
▶ ADV **1** (in questions etc): **do you want any more soup/sandwiches?** voulez-vous encore de la soupe/des sandwichs?; **are you feeling any better?** est-ce que vous vous sentez mieux?
2 (with negative): **I can't hear him any more** je ne l'entends plus; **don't wait any longer** n'attendez pas plus longtemps

anybody ['ɛnɪbɔdɪ] PRON n'importe qui; (in interrogative sentences) quelqu'un; (in negative sentences): **I don't see ~** je ne vois personne; **if ~ should phone ...** si quelqu'un téléphone ...
anyhow ['ɛnɪhau] ADV quoi qu'il en soit; (haphazardly) n'importe comment; **do it ~ you like** faites-le comme vous voulez; **she leaves things just ~** elle laisse tout traîner; **I shall go ~** j'irai de toute façon
anyone ['ɛnɪwʌn] PRON = **anybody**
anyplace ['ɛnɪpleɪs] ADV (US) = **anywhere**
anything ['ɛnɪθɪŋ] PRON (no matter what) n'importe quoi; (in questions etc) quelque chose; (with negative) ne ... rien; **I don't want ~** je ne veux rien; **can you see ~?** tu vois quelque chose?; **if ~ happens to me ...** s'il m'arrive quoi que ce soit ...; **you can say ~ you like** vous pouvez dire ce que vous voulez; **~ will do** n'importe quoi fera l'affaire; **he'll eat ~** il mange de tout; **~ else?** (in shop) avec ceci?; **it**

can cost ~ between £15 and £20 (BRIT) ça peut coûter dans les 15 à 20 livres
anytime ['ɛnɪtaɪm] ADV (at any moment) d'un moment à l'autre; (whenever) n'importe quand
anyway ['ɛnɪweɪ] ADV de toute façon; **~, I couldn't come even if I wanted to** de toute façon, je ne pouvais pas venir même si je le voulais; **I shall go ~** j'irai quand même; **why are you phoning, ~?** au fait, pourquoi tu me téléphones?
anywhere ['ɛnɪwɛəʳ] ADV n'importe où; (in interrogative sentences) quelque part; (in negative sentences): **I can't see him ~** je ne le vois nulle part; **can you see him ~?** tu le vois quelque part?; **put the books down ~** pose les livres n'importe où; **~ in the world** (no matter where) n'importe où dans le monde
Anzac ['ænzæk] N ABBR (= Australia-New Zealand Army Corps) soldat du corps ANZAC
Anzac Day N voir article

> Anzac Day est le 25 avril, jour férié en Australie et en Nouvelle-Zélande commémorant le débarquement des soldats du corps ANZAC à Gallipoli en 1915, pendant la Première Guerre mondiale. C'est la plus célèbre des campagnes du corps ANZAC.

apart [ə'pɑːt] ADV (to one side) à part; de côté; à l'écart; (separately) séparément; **to take/pull ~** démonter; **10 miles/a long way ~** à 10 miles/très éloignés l'un de l'autre; **they are living ~** ils sont séparés; **~ from** prep à part, excepté
apartheid [ə'pɑːteɪt] N apartheid m
apartment [ə'pɑːtmənt] N (US) appartement m, logement m; (room) chambre f
apartment building N (US) immeuble m; maison divisée en appartements
apathetic [æpə'θɛtɪk] ADJ apathique, indifférent(e)
apathy ['æpəθɪ] N apathie f, indifférence f
APB N ABBR (US: = all points bulletin) expression de la police signifiant "découvrir et appréhender le suspect"
ape [eɪp] N (grand) singe ▶ VT singer
Apennines ['æpənaɪnz] NPL: **the ~** les Apennins mpl
aperitif [ə'pɛrɪtɪf] N apéritif m
aperture ['æpətʃjuəʳ] N orifice m, ouverture f; (Phot) ouverture (du diaphragme)
APEX ['eɪpɛks] N ABBR (Aviat: = advance purchase excursion) APEX m
apex ['eɪpɛks] N sommet m
aphid ['eɪfɪd] N puceron m
aphrodisiac [æfrəu'dɪzɪæk] ADJ, N aphrodisiaque (m)
API N ABBR = **American Press Institute**
apiece [ə'piːs] ADV (for each person) chacun(e), par tête; (for each item) chacun(e), la pièce
aplomb [ə'plɔm] N sang-froid m, assurance f
APO N ABBR (US: = Army Post Office) service postal de l'armée
apocalypse [ə'pɔkəlɪps] N apocalypse f
apolitical [eɪpə'lɪtɪk] ADJ apolitique
apologetic [əpɔlə'dʒɛtɪk] ADJ (tone, letter) d'excuse; **to be very ~ about** s'excuser vivement de

apologetically [əpɔləˈdʒɛtɪkəlɪ] ADV (*say*) en s'excusant

apologize [əˈpɔlədʒaɪz] VI: **to ~ (for sth to sb)** s'excuser (de qch auprès de qn), présenter des excuses (à qn pour qch)

apology [əˈpɔlədʒɪ] N excuses *fpl*; **to send one's apologies** envoyer une lettre or un mot d'excuse, s'excuser (de ne pas pouvoir venir); **please accept my apologies** vous voudrez bien m'excuser

apoplectic [æpəˈplɛktɪk] ADJ (*Med*) apoplectique; (*inf*): **~ with rage** fou (folle) de rage

apoplexy [ˈæpəplɛksɪ] N apoplexie *f*

apostle [əˈpɔsl] N apôtre *m*

apostrophe [əˈpɔstrəfɪ] N apostrophe *f*

app N ABBR (*inf: Comput: = application*) appli *f*

appal, (*US*) **appall** [əˈpɔːl] VT consterner, atterrer; horrifier

Appalachian Mountains [æpəˈleɪʃən-] NPL: **the ~** les (monts *mpl*) Appalaches *mpl*

appalling [əˈpɔːlɪŋ] ADJ épouvantable; (*stupidity*) consternant(e); **she's an ~ cook** c'est une très mauvaise cuisinière

apparatus [æpəˈreɪtəs] N appareil *m*, dispositif *m*; (*in gymnasium*) agrès *mpl*

apparel [əˈpærl] N (*US*) habillement *m*, confection *f*

apparent [əˈpærənt] ADJ apparent(e); **it is ~ that** il est évident que

apparently [əˈpærəntlɪ] ADV apparemment

apparition [æpəˈrɪʃən] N apparition *f*

appeal [əˈpiːl] VI (*Law*) faire or interjeter appel ▶ N (*Law*) appel *m*; (*request*) appel; prière *f*; (*charm*) attrait *m*, charme *m*; **to ~ for** demander (instamment); implorer; **to ~ to** (*beg*) faire appel à; (*be attractive*) plaire à; **to ~ to sb for mercy** implorer la pitié de qn, prier or adjurer qn d'avoir pitié; **it doesn't ~ to me** cela ne m'attire pas; **right of ~** droit *m* de recours

appealing [əˈpiːlɪŋ] ADJ (*attractive*) attrayant(e); (*touching*) attendrissant(e)

appear [əˈpɪəʳ] VI apparaître, se montrer; (*Law*) comparaître; (*publication*) paraître, sortir, être publié(e); (*seem*) paraître, sembler; **it would ~ that** il semble que; **to ~ in Hamlet** jouer dans Hamlet; **to ~ on TV** passer à la télé

appearance [əˈpɪərəns] N apparition *f*; parution *f*; (*look, aspect*) apparence *f*, aspect *m*; **to put in** or **make an ~** faire acte de présence; **by order of ~** (*Theat*) par ordre d'entrée en scène; **to keep up appearances** sauver les apparences; **to all appearances** selon toute apparence

appease [əˈpiːz] VT apaiser, calmer

appeasement [əˈpiːzmənt] N (*Pol*) apaisement *m*

append [əˈpɛnd] VT (*Comput*) ajouter (à la fin d'un fichier)

appendage [əˈpɛndɪdʒ] N appendice *m*

appendices [əˈpɛndɪsiːz] NPL *of* **appendix**

appendicitis [əpɛndɪˈsaɪtɪs] N appendicite *f*

appendix [əˈpɛndɪks] (*pl* **appendices** [-siːz]) N appendice *m*; **to have one's ~ out** se faire

opérer de l'appendicite

appetite [ˈæpɪtaɪt] N appétit *m*; **that walk has given me an ~** cette promenade m'a ouvert l'appétit

appetizer [ˈæpɪtaɪzəʳ] N (*food*) amuse-gueule *m*; (*drink*) apéritif *m*

appetizing [ˈæpɪtaɪzɪŋ] ADJ appétissant(e)

applaud [əˈplɔːd] VT, VI applaudir

applause [əˈplɔːz] N applaudissements *mpl*

apple [ˈæpl] N pomme *f*; (*also:* **apple tree**) pommier *m*; **it's the ~ of my eye** j'y tiens comme à la prunelle de mes yeux

apple pie N tarte *f* aux pommes

apple turnover N chausson *m* aux pommes

appliance [əˈplaɪəns] N appareil *m*; **electrical appliances** l'électroménager *m*

applicable [əˈplɪkəbl] ADJ applicable; **the law is ~ from January** la loi entre en vigueur au mois de janvier; **to be ~ to** (*relevant*) valoir pour

applicant [ˈæplɪkənt] N: **~ (for)** (*Admin: for benefit etc*) demandeur(-euse) (de); (: *for post*) candidat(e) (à)

application [æplɪˈkeɪʃən] N application *f*; (*for a job, a grant etc*) demande *f*; candidature *f*; (*Comput*) application *f*, (logiciel *m*) applicatif *m*; **on ~** sur demande

application form N formulaire *m* de demande

application program N (*Comput*) (logiciel *m*) applicatif *m*

applications package N (*Comput*) progiciel *m* d'application

applied [əˈplaɪd] ADJ appliqué(e); **~ arts** *npl* arts décoratifs

apply [əˈplaɪ] VT: **to ~ (to)** (*paint, ointment*) appliquer (sur); (*law, etc*) appliquer (à) ▶ VI: **to ~ to** (*ask*) s'adresser à; (*be suitable for, relevant to*) s'appliquer à, être valable pour; **to ~ (for)** (*permit, grant*) faire une demande (en vue d'obtenir); (*job*) poser sa candidature (pour), faire une demande d'emploi (concernant); **to ~ the brakes** actionner les freins, freiner; **to ~ o.s. to** s'appliquer à

appoint [əˈpɔɪnt] VT (*to post*) nommer, engager; (*date, place*) fixer, désigner

appointee [əpɔɪnˈtiː] N personne nommée; candidat retenu

appointment [əˈpɔɪntmənt] N (*to post*) nomination *f*; (*job*) poste *m*; (*arrangement to meet*) rendez-vous *m*; **to have an ~** avoir un rendez-vous; **to make an ~ (with)** prendre rendez-vous (avec); **I'd like to make an ~** je voudrais prendre rendez-vous; **"appointments (vacant)"** (*Press*) "offres d'emploi"; **by ~** sur rendez-vous

apportion [əˈpɔːʃən] VT (*share out*) répartir, distribuer; **to ~ sth to sb** attribuer or assigner or allouer qch à qn

appraisal [əˈpreɪzl] N évaluation *f*

appraise [əˈpreɪz] VT (*value*) estimer; (*situation etc*) évaluer

appreciable [əˈpriːʃəbl] ADJ appréciable

appreciably [əˈpriːʃəblɪ] ADV sensiblement, de façon appréciable

appreciate [əˈpriːʃɪeɪt] VT (*like*) apprécier, faire

cas de; (be grateful for) être reconnaissant(e) de; (assess) évaluer; (be aware of) comprendre, se rendre compte de ▸ vı (Finance) prendre de la valeur; **I ~ your help** je vous remercie pour votre aide

appreciation [əpriːʃɪˈeɪʃən] N appréciation f; (gratitude) reconnaissance f; (Finance) hausse f, valorisation f

appreciative [əˈpriːʃɪətɪv] ADJ (person) sensible; (comment) élogieux(-euse)

apprehend [æprɪˈhɛnd] vт appréhender, arrêter; (understand) comprendre

apprehension [æprɪˈhɛnʃən] N appréhension f, inquiétude f

apprehensive [æprɪˈhɛnsɪv] ADJ inquiet(-ète), appréhensif(-ive)

apprentice [əˈprɛntɪs] N apprenti m ▸ vт: **to be apprenticed to** être en apprentissage chez

apprenticeship [əˈprɛntɪʃɪp] N apprentissage m; **to serve one's ~** faire son apprentissage

appro. [ˈæprəʊ] ABBR (BRIT Comm: inf) = **approval**

approach [əˈprəʊtʃ] vı approcher ▸ vт (come near) approcher de; (ask, apply to) s'adresser à; (subject, passer-by) aborder ▸ N approche f; accès m, abord m; démarche f (auprès de qn); (intellectual) démarche f; **to ~ sb about sth** aller or venir voir qn pour qch

approachable [əˈprəʊtʃəbl] ADJ accessible

approach road N voie f d'accès

approbation [æprəˈbeɪʃən] N approbation f

appropriate ADJ [əˈprəʊprɪɪt] (tool etc) qui convient, approprié(e); (moment, remark) opportun(e) ▸ vт [əˈprəʊprɪeɪt] (take) s'approprier; (allot): **to ~ sth for** affecter qch à; **~ for or to** approprié à; **it would not be ~ for me to comment** il ne me serait pas approprié de commenter

appropriately [əˈprəʊprɪɪtlɪ] ADV pertinemment, avec à-propos

appropriation [əprəʊprɪˈeɪʃən] N dotation f, affectation f

approval [əˈpruːvəl] N approbation f; **to meet with sb's ~** (proposal etc) recueillir l'assentiment de qn; **on ~** (Comm) à l'examen

approve [əˈpruːv] vт approuver
▸ **approve of** vт FUS (thing) approuver; (person): **they don't ~ of her** ils n'ont pas bonne opinion d'elle

approved school [əˈpruːvd-] N (BRIT) centre m d'éducation surveillée

approvingly [əˈpruːvɪŋlɪ] ADV d'un air approbateur

approx. ABBR (= approximately) env

approximate [əˈprɒksɪmɪt] ADJ approximatif(-ive) ▸ vт [əˈprɒksɪmeɪt] se rapprocher de; être proche de

approximately [əˈprɒksɪmətlɪ] ADV approximativement

approximation [əˈprɒksɪˈmeɪʃən] N approximation f

apr N ABBR (= annual percentage rate) taux (d'intérêt) annuel

Apr. ABBR = **April**

apricot [ˈeɪprɪkɒt] N abricot m

April [ˈeɪprəl] N avril m; **~ fool!** poisson d'avril!; see also **July**

April Fools' Day N le premier avril; voir article

> April Fools' Day est le 1er avril, à l'occasion duquel on fait des farces de toutes sortes. Les victimes de ces farces sont les April fools. Traditionnellement, on n'est censé faire des farces que jusqu'à midi.

apron [ˈeɪprən] N tablier m; (Aviat) aire f de stationnement

apse [æps] N (Archit) abside f

APT N ABBR (BRIT: = advanced passenger train) ≈ TGV m

apt [æpt] ADJ (suitable) approprié(e); **~ (at)** (able) doué(e) (pour); apte (à); **~ to do** (likely) susceptible de faire; ayant tendance à faire

Apt. ABBR (= apartment) appt

aptitude [ˈæptɪtjuːd] N aptitude f

aptitude test N test m d'aptitude

aptly [ˈæptlɪ] ADV (fort) à propos

aqualung [ˈækwəlʌŋ] N scaphandre m autonome

aquarium [əˈkwɛərɪəm] N aquarium m

Aquarius [əˈkwɛərɪəs] N le Verseau; **to be ~** être du Verseau

aquatic [əˈkwætɪk] ADJ aquatique; (sport) nautique

aqueduct [ˈækwɪdʌkt] N aqueduc m

AR ABBR (US) = **Arkansas**

ARA N ABBR (BRIT) = **Associate of the Royal Academy**

Arab [ˈærəb] N Arabe mf ▸ ADJ arabe

Arabia [əˈreɪbɪə] N Arabie f

Arabian [əˈreɪbɪən] ADJ arabe

Arabian Desert N désert m d'Arabie

Arabian Sea N mer f d'Arabie

Arabic [ˈærəbɪk] ADJ, N arabe (m)

Arabic numerals NPL chiffres mpl arabes

arable [ˈærəbl] ADJ arable

ARAM N ABBR (BRIT) = **Associate of the Royal Academy of Music**

arbiter [ˈɑːbɪtər] N arbitre m

arbitrary [ˈɑːbɪtrərɪ] ADJ arbitraire

arbitrate [ˈɑːbɪtreɪt] vı arbitrer; trancher

arbitration [ɑːbɪˈtreɪʃən] N arbitrage m; **the dispute went to ~** le litige a été soumis à arbitrage

arbitrator [ˈɑːbɪtreɪtər] N arbitre m, médiateur(-trice)

ARC N ABBR = **American Red Cross**

arc [ɑːk] N arc m

arcade [ɑːˈkeɪd] N arcade f; (passage with shops) passage m, galerie f; (with games) salle f de jeu

arch [ɑːtʃ] N arche f; (of foot) cambrure f, voûte f plantaire ▸ vт arquer, cambrer ▸ ADJ malicieux(-euse) ▸ PREFIX: (-) achevé(e); par excellence; **pointed ~** ogive f

archaeological [ɑːkɪəˈlɒdʒɪkl] ADJ archéologique

archaeologist [ɑːkɪˈɒlədʒɪst] N archéologue mf

archaeology, (US) archeology [ɑːkɪˈɒlədʒɪ] N archéologie f

archaic [ɑːˈkeɪɪk] ADJ archaïque

archangel [ˈɑːkeɪndʒəl] N archange m

465

archbishop [ɑːtʃˈbɪʃəp] N archevêque m
archenemy [ˈɑːtʃˈɛnɪmɪ] N ennemi m de
toujours or par excellence
archeology [ɑːkɪˈɔlədʒɪ] (US) N = **archaeology**
archer [ˈɑːtʃəʳ] N archer m
archery [ˈɑːtʃərɪ] N tir m à l'arc
archetypal [ˈɑːkɪtaɪpəl] ADJ archétype
archetype [ˈɑːkɪtaɪp] N prototype m,
archétype m
archipelago [ɑːkɪˈpɛlɪɡəu] N archipel m
architect [ˈɑːkɪtɛkt] N architecte m
architectural [ɑːkɪˈtɛktʃərəl] ADJ
architectural(e)
architecture [ˈɑːkɪtɛktʃəʳ] N architecture f
archive [ˈɑːkaɪv] N (often pl) archives fpl
archive file N (Comput) fichier m d'archives
archives [ˈɑːkaɪvz] NPL archives fpl
archivist [ˈɑːkɪvɪst] N archiviste mf
archway [ˈɑːtʃweɪ] N voûte f, porche voûté or
cintré
ARCM N ABBR (BRIT) = **Associate of the Royal
College of Music**
Arctic [ˈɑːktɪk] ADJ arctique ▶ N: **the ~**
l'Arctique m
Arctic Circle N cercle m Arctique
Arctic Ocean N océan m Arctique
ARD N ABBR (US Med) = **acute respiratory
disease**
ardent [ˈɑːdənt] ADJ fervent(e)
ardour, (US) **ardor** [ˈɑːdəʳ] N ardeur f
arduous [ˈɑːdjuəs] ADJ ardu(e)
are [ɑːʳ] VB see **be**
area [ˈɛərɪə] N (Geom) superficie f; (zone) région f;
(: smaller) secteur m; (in room) coin m; (knowledge,
research) domaine m; **the London ~** la région
Londonienne
area code (US) N (Tel) indicatif m de zone
arena [əˈriːnə] N arène f
aren't [ɑːnt] = **are not**
Argentina [ɑːdʒənˈtiːnə] N Argentine f
Argentinian [ɑːdʒənˈtɪnɪən] ADJ argentin(e) ▶ N
Argentin(e)
arguable [ˈɑːɡjuəbl] ADJ discutable, contestable;
it is ~ whether on peut se demander si
arguably [ˈɑːɡjuəblɪ] ADV: **it is ~ …** on peut
soutenir que c'est …
argue [ˈɑːɡjuː] VI (quarrel) se disputer; (reason)
argumenter ▶ VT (debate: case, matter) débattre;
to ~ about sth (with sb) se disputer (avec qn)
au sujet de qch; **to ~ that** objecter or alléguer
que, donner comme argument que
argument [ˈɑːɡjumənt] N (quarrel) dispute f,
discussion f; (reasons) argument m; (debate)
discussion, controverse f; **~ for/against**
argument pour/contre
argumentative [ɑːɡjuˈmɛntətɪv] ADJ
ergoteur(-euse), raisonneur(-euse)
aria [ˈɑːrɪə] N aria f
ARIBA [əˈriːbə] N ABBR (BRIT) = **Associate of the
Royal Institute of British Architects**
arid [ˈærɪd] ADJ aride
aridity [əˈrɪdɪtɪ] N aridité f
Aries [ˈɛərɪz] N le Bélier; **to be ~** être du Bélier
arise [əˈraɪz] (pt **arose** [əˈrəuz], pp **arisen** [əˈrɪzn])

VI survenir, se présenter; **to ~ from** résulter de;
should the need ~ en cas de besoin
aristocracy [ærɪsˈtɔkrəsɪ] N aristocratie f
aristocrat [ˈærɪstəkræt] N aristocrate mf
aristocratic [ærɪstəˈkrætɪk] ADJ aristocratique
arithmetic [əˈrɪθmətɪk] N arithmétique f
arithmetical [ærɪθˈmɛtɪkl] ADJ arithmétique
Ariz. ABBR (US) = **Arizona**
ark [ɑːk] N: **Noah's A~** l'Arche f de Noé
Ark. ABBR (US) = **Arkansas**
arm [ɑːm] N bras m ▶ VT armer; **arms** NPL
(weapons, Heraldry) armes fpl; **~ in ~** bras dessus
bras dessous
armaments [ˈɑːməmənts] NPL (weapons)
armement m
armband [ˈɑːmbænd] N brassard m
armchair [ˈɑːmtʃɛəʳ] N fauteuil m
armed [ɑːmd] ADJ armé(e)
armed forces NPL: **the ~** les forces armées
armed robbery N vol m à main armée
Armenia [ɑːˈmiːnɪə] N Arménie f
Armenian [ɑːˈmiːnɪən] ADJ arménien(ne) ▶ N
Arménien(ne); (Ling) arménien m
armful [ˈɑːmful] N brassée f
armistice [ˈɑːmɪstɪs] N armistice m
armour, (US) **armor** [ˈɑːməʳ] N armure f; (also:
armour-plating) blindage m; (Mil: tanks)
blindés mpl
armoured car, (US) **armored car** [ˈɑːməd-] N
véhicule blindé
armoury, (US) **armory** [ˈɑːmərɪ] N arsenal m
armpit [ˈɑːmpɪt] N aisselle f
armrest [ˈɑːmrɛst] N accoudoir m
arms control N contrôle m des armements
arms race N course f aux armements
army [ˈɑːmɪ] N armée f
A road N (BRIT) ≈ route nationale
aroma [əˈrəumə] N arôme m
aromatherapy [ərəumə'θɛrəpɪ] N
aromathérapie f
aromatic [ærəˈmætɪk] ADJ aromatique
arose [əˈrəuz] PT of **arise**
around [əˈraund] ADV (tout) autour; (nearby)
dans les parages ▶ PREP autour de; (near) près
de; (fig: about) environ; (: date, time) vers; **is he ~?**
est-il dans les parages or là?
arousal [əˈrauzəl] N (sexual) excitation sexuelle,
éveil m
arouse [əˈrauz] VT (sleeper) éveiller; (curiosity,
passions) éveiller, susciter; (anger) exciter
arrange [əˈreɪndʒ] VT arranger; (programme)
arrêter, convenir de ▶ VI: **we have arranged for
a car to pick you up** nous avons prévu qu'une
voiture vienne vous prendre; **it was arranged
that …** il a été convenu que …, il a été décidé
que …; **to ~ to do sth** prévoir de faire qch
arrangement [əˈreɪndʒmənt] N arrangement
m; **arrangements** NPL (plans etc) arrangements
mpl, dispositions fpl; **to come to an ~ (with sb)**
se mettre d'accord (avec qn); **home deliveries
by ~** livraison à domicile sur demande; **I'll
make arrangements for you to be met** je
vous enverrai chercher
arrant [ˈærənt] ADJ: **he's talking ~ nonsense** il

raconte vraiment n'importe quoi

array [ə'reɪ] N (*of objects*) déploiement *m*, étalage *m*; (*Math, Comput*) tableau *m*

arrears [ə'rɪəz] NPL arriéré *m*; **to be in ~ with one's rent** devoir un arriéré de loyer, être en retard pour le paiement de son loyer

arrest [ə'rɛst] VT arrêter; (*sb's attention*) retenir, attirer ▶ N arrestation *f*; **under ~** en état d'arrestation

arresting [ə'rɛstɪŋ] ADJ (*fig: beauty*) saisissant(e); (*: charm, candour*) désarmant(e)

arrival [ə'raɪvl] N arrivée *f*; (*Comm*) arrivage *m*; (*person*) arrivant(e); **new ~** nouveau venu/ nouvelle venue; (*baby*) nouveau-né(e)

arrive [ə'raɪv] VI arriver
  ▶ **arrive at** VT FUS (*decision, solution*) parvenir à

arrogance ['ærəgəns] N arrogance *f*

arrogant ['ærəgənt] ADJ arrogant(e)

arrow ['ærəʊ] N flèche *f*

arse [ɑːs] N (*BRIT inf!*) cul *m* (!)

arsenal ['ɑːsɪnl] N arsenal *m*

arsenic ['ɑːsnɪk] N arsenic *m*

arson ['ɑːsn] N incendie criminel

art [ɑːt] N art *m*; (*craft*) métier *m*; **work of ~** œuvre *f* d'art; **Arts** NPL (*Scol*) les lettres *fpl*

art college N école *f* des beaux-arts

artefact ['ɑːtɪfækt] N objet fabriqué

arterial [ɑː'tɪərɪəl] ADJ (*Anat*) artériel(le); (*road etc*) à grande circulation

artery ['ɑːtərɪ] N artère *f*

artful ['ɑːtful] ADJ rusé(e)

art gallery N musée *m* d'art; (*saleroom*) galerie *f* de peinture

arthritis [ɑː'θraɪtɪs] N arthrite *f*

artichoke ['ɑːtɪtʃəʊk] N artichaut *m*; **Jerusalem ~** topinambour *m*

article ['ɑːtɪkl] N article *m*; **articles** NPL (*training*) ≈ stage *m*; **articles of clothing** vêtements *mpl*

articles of association NPL (*Comm*) statuts *mpl* d'une société

articulate ADJ [ɑː'tɪkjulɪt] (*person*) qui s'exprime clairement et aisément; (*speech*) bien articulé(e), prononcé(e) clairement ▶ VI [ɑː'tɪkjuleɪt] articuler, parler distinctement
  ▶ VT articuler

articulated lorry [ɑː'tɪkjuleɪtɪd-] N (*BRIT*) (camion *m*) semi-remorque *m*

artifact ['ɑːtɪfækt] N (*US*) objet fabriqué

artifice ['ɑːtɪfɪs] N ruse *f*

artificial [ɑːtɪ'fɪʃəl] ADJ artificiel(le)

artificial insemination [-ɪnsɛmɪ'neɪʃən] N insémination artificielle

artificial intelligence N intelligence artificielle

artificial respiration N respiration artificielle

artillery [ɑː'tɪlərɪ] N artillerie *f*

artisan ['ɑːtɪzæn] N artisan(e)

artist ['ɑːtɪst] N artiste *mf*

artistic [ɑː'tɪstɪk] ADJ artistique

artistry ['ɑːtɪstrɪ] N art *m*, talent *m*

artless ['ɑːtlɪs] ADJ naïf (naïve), simple, ingénu(e)

arts [ɑːts] NPL (*Scol*) lettres *fpl*

art school N ≈ école *f* des beaux-arts

artwork ['ɑːtwəːk] N maquette *f* (*prête pour la photogravure*)

ARV N ABBR (= *American Revised Version*) traduction américaine de la Bible

AS N ABBR (*US Scol*: = *Associate in/of Science*) diplôme universitaire ▶ ABBR (*US*) = **American Samoa**

(KEYWORD)

as [æz] CONJ **1** (*time: moment*) comme, alors que; à mesure que; (*: duration*) tandis que; **he came in as I was leaving** il est arrivé comme je partais; **as the years went by** à mesure que les années passaient; **as from tomorrow** à partir de demain

2 (*because*) comme, puisque; **he left early as he had to be home by 10** comme il *or* puisqu'il devait être de retour avant 10h, il est parti de bonne heure

3 (*referring to manner, way*) comme; **do as you wish** faites comme vous voudrez; **as she said** comme elle disait

  ▶ ADV **1** (*in comparisons*): **as big as** aussi grand que; **twice as big as** deux fois plus grand que; **big as it is** si grand que ce soit; **much as I like them, I …** je les aime bien, mais je …; **as much** *or* **many as** autant que; **as much money/many books as** autant d'argent/de livres que; **as soon as** dès que

2 (*concerning*): **as for** *or* **to that** quant à cela, pour ce qui est de cela

3: **as if** *or* **though** comme si; **he looked as if he was ill** il avait l'air d'être malade; *see also* **long**; **such**; **well**

  ▶ PREP (*in the capacity of*) en tant que, en qualité de; **he works as a driver** il travaille comme chauffeur; **as chairman of the company, he …** en tant que président de la société, il …; **dressed up as a cowboy** déguisé en cow-boy; **he gave me it as a present** il me l'a offert, il m'en a fait cadeau

ASA N ABBR (= *American Standards Association*) association de normalisation

a.s.a.p. ABBR = **as soon as possible**

asbestos [æz'bɛstəs] N asbeste *m*, amiante *m*

ascend [ə'sɛnd] VT gravir

ascendancy [ə'sɛndənsɪ] N ascendant *m*

ascendant [ə'sɛndənt] N: **to be in the ~** monter

ascension [ə'sɛnʃən] N: **the A~** (*Rel*) l'Ascension *f*

Ascension Island N Île *f* de l'Ascension

ascent [ə'sɛnt] N (*climb*) ascension *f*

ascertain [æsə'teɪn] VT s'assurer de, vérifier; établir

ascetic [ə'sɛtɪk] ADJ ascétique

asceticism [ə'sɛtɪsɪzəm] N ascétisme *m*

ASCII ['æskiː] N ABBR (= *American Standard Code for Information Interchange*) ASCII

ascribe [ə'skraɪb] VT: **to ~ sth to** attribuer qch à; (*blame*) imputer qch à

ASCU N ABBR (*US*) = **Association of State Colleges and Universities**

ASE N ABBR = **American Stock Exchange**

ASH [æʃ] N ABBR (*BRIT*: = *Action on Smoking and*

Health) ligue anti-tabac

ash [æʃ] N (*dust*) cendre f; (*also*: **ash tree**) frêne m

ashamed [ə'ʃeɪmd] ADJ honteux(-euse), confus(e); **to be ~ of** avoir honte de; **to be ~ (of o.s.) for having done** avoir honte d'avoir fait

ashen ['æʃən] ADJ (*pale*) cendreux(-euse), blême

ashore [ə'ʃɔː'] ADV à terre; **to go ~** aller à terre, débarquer

ashtray ['æʃtreɪ] N cendrier m

Ash Wednesday N mercredi m des Cendres

Asia ['eɪʃə] N Asie f

Asia Minor N Asie Mineure

Asian ['eɪʃən] N (*from Asia*) Asiatique mf; (BRIT: *from Indian subcontinent*) Indo-Pakistanais(e) ▶ ADJ asiatique; indo-pakistanais(e)

Asiatic [eɪsɪ'ætɪk] ADJ asiatique

aside [ə'saɪd] ADV de côté; à l'écart ▶ N aparté m; **~ from** prep à part, excepté

ask [ɑːsk] VT demander; (*invite*) inviter; **to ~ sb sth/to do sth** demander à qn qch/de faire qch; **to ~ sb the time** demander l'heure à qn; **to ~ sb about sth** questionner qn au sujet de qch; se renseigner auprès de qn au sujet de qch; **to ~ about the price** s'informer du prix, se renseigner au sujet du prix; **to ~ (sb) a question** poser une question (à qn); **to ~ sb out to dinner** inviter qn au restaurant
▶ **ask after** VT FUS demander des nouvelles de
▶ **ask for** VT FUS demander; **it's just asking for trouble** or **for it** ce serait chercher des ennuis

askance [ə'skɑːns] ADV: **to look ~ at sb** regarder qn de travers or d'un œil désapprobateur

askew [ə'skjuː] ADV de travers, de guingois

asking price ['ɑːskɪŋ-] N prix demandé

asleep [ə'sliːp] ADJ endormi(e); **to be ~** dormir, être endormi; **to fall ~** s'endormir

ASLEF ['æzlɛf] N ABBR (BRIT: = *Associated Society of Locomotive Engineers and Firemen*) syndicat de cheminots

AS level N ABBR (= *Advanced Subsidiary level*) première partie de l'examen équivalent au baccalauréat

asp [æsp] N aspic m

asparagus [əs'pærəgəs] N asperges fpl

asparagus tips NPL pointes fpl d'asperges

ASPCA N ABBR (= *American Society for the Prevention of Cruelty to Animals*) ≈ SPA f

aspect ['æspɛkt] N aspect m; (*direction in which a building etc faces*) orientation f, exposition f

aspersions [əs'pəːʃənz] NPL: **to cast ~ on** dénigrer

asphalt ['æsfælt] N asphalte m

asphyxiate [æs'fɪksɪeɪt] VT asphyxier

asphyxiation [æsfɪksɪ'eɪʃən] N asphyxie f

aspiration [æspə'reɪʃən] N aspiration f

aspirations [æspə'reɪʃənz] NPL (*hopes, ambition*) aspirations fpl

aspire [əs'paɪə'] VI: **to ~ to** aspirer à

aspirin ['æsprɪn] N aspirine f

aspiring [əs'paɪərɪŋ] ADJ (*artist, writer*) en herbe; (*manager*) potentiel(le)

ass [æs] N âne m; (*inf*) imbécile mf; (US inf!) cul m (!)

assail [ə'seɪl] VT assaillir

assailant [ə'seɪlənt] N agresseur m; assaillant m

assassin [ə'sæsɪn] N assassin m

assassinate [ə'sæsɪneɪt] VT assassiner

assassination [əsæsɪ'neɪʃən] N assassinat m

assault [ə'sɔːlt] N (*Mil*) assaut m; (*gen: attack*) agression f; (*Law*): **~ (and battery)** voies fpl de fait, coups mpl et blessures fpl ▶ VT attaquer; (*sexually*) violenter

assemble [ə'sɛmbl] VT assembler ▶ VI s'assembler, se rassembler

assembly [ə'sɛmblɪ] N (*meeting*) rassemblement m; (*parliament*) assemblée f; (*construction*) assemblage m

assembly language N (*Comput*) langage m d'assemblage

assembly line N chaîne f de montage

assent [ə'sɛnt] N assentiment m, consentement m ▶ VI: **to ~ (to sth)** donner son assentiment (à qch), consentir (à qch)

assert [ə'səːt] VT affirmer, déclarer; établir; (*authority*) faire valoir; (*innocence*) protester de; **to ~ o.s.** s'imposer

assertion [ə'səːʃən] N assertion f, affirmation f

assertive [ə'səːtɪv] ADJ assuré(e); péremptoire

assess [ə'sɛs] VT évaluer, estimer; (*tax, damages*) établir or fixer le montant de; (*property etc: for tax*) calculer la valeur imposable de; (*person*) juger la valeur de

assessment [ə'sɛsmənt] N évaluation f, estimation f; (*of tax*) fixation f; (*of property*) calcul m de la valeur imposable; (*judgment*): **~ (of)** jugement m or opinion f (sur)

assessor [ə'sɛsə'] N expert m (*en matière d'impôt et d'assurance*)

asset ['æsɛt] N avantage m, atout m; (*person*) atout m; **assets** NPL (*Comm*) capital m; avoir(s) m(pl); actif m

asset-stripping ['æsɛt'strɪpɪŋ] N (*Comm*) récupération f (et démantèlement m) d'une entreprise en difficulté

assiduous [ə'sɪdjuəs] ADJ assidu(e)

assign [ə'saɪn] VT (*date*) fixer, arrêter; **to ~ sth to** (*task*) assigner qch à; (*resources*) affecter qch à; (*cause, meaning*) attribuer qch à

assignment [ə'saɪnmənt] N (*task*) mission f; (*homework*) devoir m

assimilate [ə'sɪmɪleɪt] VT assimiler

assimilation [əsɪmɪ'leɪʃən] N assimilation f

assist [ə'sɪst] VT aider, assister; (*injured person etc*) secourir

assistance [ə'sɪstəns] N aide f, assistance f; secours mpl

assistant [ə'sɪstənt] N assistant(e), adjoint(e); (BRIT: *also*: **shop assistant**) vendeur(-euse)

assistant manager N sous-directeur m

assizes [ə'saɪzɪz] NPL assises fpl

associate ADJ, N [ə'səuʃɪɪt] associé(e) ▶ VT [ə'səuʃɪeɪt] associer ▶ VI [ə'səuʃɪeɪt]: **to ~ with sb** fréquenter qn; **~ director** directeur adjoint; **associated company** société affiliée

association [əsəusɪ'eɪʃən] N association f; **in ~ with** en collaboration avec

association football N (BRIT) football m

assorted [ə'sɔːtɪd] ADJ assorti(e); **in ~ sizes** en plusieurs tailles

assortment [ə'sɔ:tmənt] N assortiment *m*; *(of people)* mélange *m*

Asst. ABBR = **assistant**

assuage [ə'sweɪdʒ] VT *(grief, pain)* soulager; *(thirst, appetite)* assouvir

assume [ə'sjuːm] VT supposer; *(responsibilities etc)* assumer; *(attitude, name)* prendre, adopter

assumed name [ə'sjuːmd-] N nom *m* d'emprunt

assumption [ə'sʌmpʃən] N supposition *f*, hypothèse *f*; *(of power)* assomption *f*, prise *f*; **on the ~ that** dans l'hypothèse où; *(on condition that)* à condition que

assurance [ə'ʃuərəns] N assurance *f*; **I can give you no assurances** je ne peux rien vous garantir

assure [ə'ʃuəʳ] VT assurer

assured [ə'ʃuəd] ADJ assuré(e)

AST ABBR *(US: = Atlantic Standard Time)* heure d'hiver de New York

asterisk ['æstərɪsk] N astérisque *m*

astern [ə'stəːn] ADV à l'arrière

asteroid ['æstərɔɪd] N astéroïde *m*

asthma ['æsmə] N asthme *m*

asthmatic [æs'mætɪk] ADJ, N asthmatique *mf*

astigmatism [ə'stɪgmətɪzəm] N astigmatisme *m*

astir [ə'stəːʳ] ADV en émoi

astonish [ə'stɒnɪʃ] VT étonner, stupéfier

astonished [ə'stɒnɪʃd] ADJ étonné(e); **to be ~ at** être étonné(e) de

astonishing [ə'stɒnɪʃɪŋ] ADJ étonnant(e), stupéfiant(e); **I find it ~ that ...** je trouve incroyable que ...+*sub*

astonishingly [ə'stɒnɪʃɪŋlɪ] ADV incroyablement

astonishment [ə'stɒnɪʃmənt] N *(grand)* étonnement, stupéfaction *f*

astound [ə'staund] VT stupéfier, sidérer

astray [ə'streɪ] ADV: **to go ~** s'égarer; *(fig)* quitter le droit chemin; **to lead ~** *(morally)* détourner du droit chemin; **to go ~ in one's calculations** faire fausse route dans ses calculs

astride [ə'straɪd] ADV à cheval ▶ PREP à cheval sur

astringent [əs'trɪndʒənt] ADJ astringent(e) ▶ N astringent *m*

astrologer [əs'trɒlədʒəʳ] N astrologue *m*

astrology [əs'trɒlədʒɪ] N astrologie *f*

astronaut ['æstrənɔːt] N astronaute *mf*

astronomer [əs'trɒnəməʳ] N astronome *m*

astronomical [æstrə'nɒmɪkl] ADJ astronomique

astronomy [əs'trɒnəmɪ] N astronomie *f*

astrophysics ['æstrəu'fɪzɪks] N astrophysique *f*

astute [əs'tjuːt] ADJ astucieux(-euse), malin(-igne)

asunder [ə'sʌndəʳ] ADV: **to tear ~** déchirer

ASV N ABBR *(= American Standard Version)* traduction de la Bible

asylum [ə'saɪləm] N asile *m*; **to seek political ~** demander l'asile politique

asylum seeker [-siːkəʳ] N demandeur(-euse) d'asile

asymmetric [eɪsɪ'mɛtrɪk], **asymmetrical** [eɪsɪ'mɛtrɪkl] ADJ asymétrique

(KEYWORD)

at [æt] PREP **1** *(referring to position, direction)* à; **at the top** au sommet; **at home/school** à la maison or chez soi/à l'école; **at the baker's** à la boulangerie, chez le boulanger; **to look at sth** regarder qch

2 *(referring to time)*: **at 4 o'clock** à 4 heures; **at Christmas** à Noël; **at night** la nuit; **at times** par moments, parfois

3 *(referring to rates, speed etc)* à; **at £1 a kilo** une livre le kilo; **two at a time** deux à la fois; **at 50 km/h** à 50 km/h; **at full speed** à toute vitesse

4 *(referring to manner)*: **at a stroke** d'un seul coup; **at peace** en paix

5 *(referring to activity)*: **to be at work** *(in the office etc)* être au travail; *(working)* travailler; **to play at cowboys** jouer aux cow-boys; **to be good at sth** être bon en qch

6 *(referring to cause)*: **shocked/surprised/ annoyed at sth** choqué par/étonné de/agacé par qch; **I went at his suggestion** j'y suis allé sur son conseil

▶ N *(@ symbol)* arobase *f*

ate [eɪt] PT *of* **eat**

atheism ['eɪθɪɪzəm] N athéisme *m*

atheist ['eɪθɪɪst] N athée *mf*

Athenian [ə'θiːnɪən] ADJ athénien(ne) ▶ N Athénien(ne)

Athens ['æθɪnz] N Athènes

athlete ['æθliːt] N athlète *mf*

athletic [æθ'lɛtɪk] ADJ athlétique

athletics [æθ'lɛtɪks] N athlétisme *m*

Atlantic [ət'læntɪk] ADJ atlantique ▶ N: **the ~ (Ocean)** l'(océan *m*) Atlantique *m*

atlas ['ætləs] N atlas *m*

Atlas Mountains NPL: **the ~** les monts *mpl* de l'Atlas, l'Atlas *m*

A.T.M. N ABBR *(= Automated Telling Machine)* guichet *m* automatique

atmosphere ['ætməsfɪəʳ] N *(air)* atmosphère *f*; *(fig: of place etc)* atmosphère, ambiance *f*

atmospheric [ætməs'fɛrɪk] ADJ atmosphérique

atmospherics [ætməs'fɛrɪks] N *(Radio)* parasites *mpl*

atoll ['ætɔl] N atoll *m*

atom ['ætəm] N atome *m*

atom bomb, atomic bomb N bombe *f* atomique

atomic [ə'tɒmɪk] ADJ atomique

atomizer ['ætəmaɪzəʳ] N atomiseur *m*

atone [ə'təun] VI: **to ~ for** expier, racheter

atonement [ə'təunmənt] N expiation *f*

ATP N ABBR *(= Association of Tennis Professionals)* ATP *f* *(= Association des tennismen professionnels)*

atrocious [ə'trəuʃəs] ADJ *(very bad)* atroce, exécrable

atrocity [ə'trɒsɪtɪ] N atrocité *f*

atrophy ['ætrəfɪ] N atrophie *f* ▶ VT atrophier ▶ VI s'atrophier

attach [ə'tætʃ] VT *(gen)* attacher; *(document, letter)* joindre; (*employee, troops*) affecter; **to be attached to sb/sth** (*to like*) être attaché à qn/qch; **to ~ a file to an email** joindre un fichier à un e-mail; **the attached letter** la lettre ci-jointe

attaché [ə'tæʃeɪ] N attaché *m*

attaché case [ə'tæʃeɪ-] N mallette *f*, attaché-case *m*

attachment [ə'tætʃmənt] N (*tool*) accessoire *m*; (*Comput*) fichier *m* joint; (*love*): **~ (to)** affection *f* (pour), attachement *m* (à)

attack [ə'tæk] VT attaquer; (*task etc*) s'attaquer à ▶ N attaque *f*; **heart ~** crise *f* cardiaque

attacker [ə'tækər] N attaquant *m*; agresseur *m*

attain [ə'teɪn] VT (*also*: **to attain to**) parvenir à, atteindre; (*knowledge*) acquérir

attainments [ə'teɪnmənts] NPL connaissances *fpl*, résultats *mpl*

attempt [ə'tɛmpt] N tentative *f* ▶ VT essayer, tenter; **attempted theft** *etc* (*Law*) tentative de vol *etc*; **to make an ~ on sb's life** attenter à la vie de qn; **he made no ~ to help** il n'a rien fait pour m'aider *or* l'aider *etc*

attempted [ə'tɛmptɪd] ADJ: **~ murder/suicide** tentative *f* de meurtre/suicide

attend [ə'tɛnd] VT (*course*) suivre; (*meeting, talk*) assister à; (*school, church*) aller à, fréquenter; (*patient*) soigner, s'occuper de; **to ~ (up)on** servir; être au service de

▶ **attend to** VT FUS (*needs, affairs etc*) s'occuper de; (*customer*) s'occuper de, servir

attendance [ə'tɛndəns] N (*being present*) présence *f*; (*people present*) assistance *f*

attendant [ə'tɛndənt] N employé(e); gardien(ne) ▶ ADJ concomitant(e), qui accompagne *or* s'ensuit

attention [ə'tɛnʃən] N attention *f* ▶ EXCL (*Mil*) garde-à-vous!; **attentions** NPL attentions *fpl*, prévenances *fpl*; **at ~** (*Mil*) au garde-à-vous; **for the ~ of** (*Admin*) à l'attention de; **it has come to my ~ that …** je constate que …

attentive [ə'tɛntɪv] ADJ attentif(-ive); (*kind*) prévenant(e)

attentively [ə'tɛntɪvlɪ] ADV attentivement, avec attention

attenuate [ə'tɛnjueɪt] VT atténuer ▶ VI s'atténuer

attest [ə'tɛst] VI: **to ~ to** témoigner de attester (de)

attic ['ætɪk] N grenier *m*, combles *mpl*

attire [ə'taɪər] N habit *m*, atours *mpl*

attitude ['ætɪtjuːd] N (*behaviour*) attitude *f*, manière *f*; (*posture*) pose *f*, attitude; (*view*): **~ (to)** attitude (envers)

attorney [ə'təːnɪ] N (*US: lawyer*) avocat *m*; (*having proxy*) mandataire *m*; **power of ~** procuration *f*

Attorney General N (*Brit*) ≈ procureur général; (*US*) ≈ garde *m* des Sceaux, ministre *m* de la Justice

attract [ə'trækt] VT attirer

attraction [ə'trækʃən] N (*gen pl: pleasant things*) attraction *f*, attrait *m*; (*Physics*) attraction; (*fig: towards sb, sth*) attirance *f*

attractive [ə'træktɪv] ADJ séduisant(e), attrayant(e)

attribute N ['ætrɪbjuːt] attribut *m* ▶ VT [ə'trɪbjuːt]: **to ~ sth to** attribuer qch à

attrition [ə'trɪʃən] N: **war of ~** guerre *f* d'usure

Atty. Gen. ABBR = **Attorney General**

ATV N ABBR (= *all terrain vehicle*) véhicule *m* tout-terrain

atypical [eɪ'tɪpɪkl] ADJ atypique

aubergine ['əubəʒiːn] N aubergine *f*

auburn ['ɔːbən] ADJ auburn *inv*, châtain roux *inv*

auction ['ɔːkʃən] N (*also*: **sale by auction**) vente *f* aux enchères ▶ VT (*also*: **to sell by auction**) vendre aux enchères; (*also*: **to put up for auction**) mettre aux enchères

auctioneer [ɔːkʃə'nɪər] N commissaire-priseur *m*

auction room N salle *f* des ventes

audacious [ɔː'deɪʃəs] ADJ impudent(e); audacieux(-euse), intrépide

audacity [ɔː'dæsɪtɪ] N impudence *f*; audace *f*

audible ['ɔːdɪbl] ADJ audible

audience ['ɔːdɪəns] N (*people*) assistance *f*, public *m*; (*on radio*) auditeurs *mpl*; (*at theatre*) spectateurs *mpl*; (*interview*) audience *f*

audiovisual [ɔːdɪəu'vɪzjuəl] ADJ audio-visuel(le); **~ aids** supports *or* moyens audiovisuels

audit ['ɔːdɪt] N vérification *f* des comptes, apurement *m* ▶ VT vérifier, apurer

audition [ɔː'dɪʃən] N audition *f* ▶ VI auditionner

auditor ['ɔːdɪtər] N vérificateur *m* des comptes

auditorium [ɔːdɪ'tɔːrɪəm] N auditorium *m*, salle *f* de concert *or* de spectacle

Aug. ABBR = **August**

augment [ɔːg'mɛnt] VT, VI augmenter

augur ['ɔːgər] VT (*be a sign of*) présager, annoncer ▶ VI: **it augurs well** c'est bon signe *or* de bon augure, cela s'annonce bien

August ['ɔːgəst] N août *m*; *see also* **July**

august [ɔː'gʌst] ADJ majestueux(-euse), imposant(e)

aunt [ɑːnt] N tante *f*

auntie, aunty ['ɑːntɪ] N DIMINUTIVE *of* **aunt**

au pair ['əu'pɛər] N (*also*: **au pair girl**) jeune fille *f* au pair

aura ['ɔːrə] N atmosphère *f*; (*of person*) aura *f*

auspices ['ɔːspɪsɪz] NPL: **under the ~ of** sous les auspices de

auspicious [ɔːs'pɪʃəs] ADJ de bon augure, propice

austere [ɔs'tɪər] ADJ austère

austerity [ɔs'tɛrɪtɪ] N austérité *f*

Australasia [ɔːstrə'leɪzɪə] N Australasie *f*

Australia [ɔs'treɪlɪə] N Australie *f*

Australian [ɔs'treɪlɪən] ADJ australien(ne) ▶ N Australien(ne)

Austria ['ɔstrɪə] N Autriche *f*

Austrian ['ɔstrɪən] ADJ autrichien(ne) ▶ N Autrichien(ne)

AUT N ABBR (*Brit*: = *Association of University Teachers*) syndicat universitaire

authentic [ɔː'θɛntɪk] ADJ authentique

authenticate [ɔː'θɛntɪkeɪt] VT établir l'authenticité de

authenticity [ɔːθɛn'tɪsɪtɪ] N authenticité *f*

author ['ɔ:θəʳ] N auteur m
authoritarian [ɔ:θɔrɪ'tɛərɪən] ADJ autoritaire
authoritative [ɔ:'θɔrɪtətɪv] ADJ (account) digne de foi; (study, treatise) qui fait autorité; (manner) autoritaire
authority [ɔ:'θɔrɪtɪ] N autorité f; (permission) autorisation (formelle); **the authorities** les autorités fpl, l'administration f; **to have ~ to do sth** être habilité à faire qch
authorization [ɔ:θəraɪ'zeɪʃən] N autorisation f
authorize ['ɔ:θəraɪz] VT autoriser
authorized capital ['ɔ:θəraɪzd-] N (Comm) capital social
authorship ['ɔ:θəʃɪp] N paternité f (littéraire etc)
autistic [ɔ:'tɪstɪk] ADJ autistique
auto ['ɔ:təʊ] N (US) auto f, voiture f
autobiography [ɔ:təbaɪ'ɒgrəfɪ] N autobiographie f
autocratic [ɔ:tə'krætɪk] ADJ autocratique
autograph ['ɔ:təgrɑ:f] N autographe m ▶ VT signer, dédicacer
autoimmune [ɔ:təʊɪ'mju:n] ADJ auto-immune
automat ['ɔ:təmæt] N (vending machine) distributeur m (automatique); (US: place) cafétéria f avec distributeurs automatiques
automated ['ɔ:təmeɪtɪd] ADJ automatisé(e)
automatic [ɔ:tə'mætɪk] ADJ automatique ▶ N (gun) automatique m; (washing machine) lave-linge m automatique; (car) voiture f à transmission automatique
automatically [ɔ:tə'mætɪklɪ] ADV automatiquement
automatic data processing N traitement m automatique des données
automation [ɔ:tə'meɪʃən] N automatisation f
automaton [ɔ:'tɔmətən] (pl **automata** [-tə]) N automate m
automobile ['ɔ:təməbi:l] N (US) automobile f
autonomous [ɔ:'tɔnəməs] ADJ autonome
autonomy [ɔ:'tɔnəmɪ] N autonomie f
autopsy ['ɔ:tɔpsɪ] N autopsie f
autumn ['ɔ:təm] N automne m
auxiliary [ɔ:g'zɪlɪərɪ] ADJ, N auxiliaire (mf)
AV N ABBR (= Authorized Version) traduction anglaise de la Bible ▶ ABBR = **audiovisual**
Av. ABBR (= avenue) Av
avail [ə'veɪl] VT: **to ~ o.s. of** user de; profiter de ▶ N: **to no ~** sans résultat, en vain, en pure perte
availability [əveɪlə'bɪlɪtɪ] N disponibilité f
available [ə'veɪləbl] ADJ disponible; **every ~ means** tous les moyens possibles or à sa (or notre etc) disposition; **is the manager ~?** est-ce que le directeur peut (me) recevoir?; (on phone) pourrais-je parler au directeur?; **to make sth ~ to sb** mettre qch à la disposition de qn
avalanche ['ævəlɑ:nʃ] N avalanche f
avant-garde ['ævãŋ'gɑ:d] ADJ d'avant-garde
avaricious [ævə'rɪʃəs] ADJ âpre au gain
avdp. ABBR = **avoirdupoids**
Ave. ABBR = **avenue**
avenge [ə'vɛndʒ] VT venger
avenue ['ævənju:] N avenue f; (fig) moyen m
average ['ævərɪdʒ] N moyenne f ▶ ADJ moyen(ne) ▶ VT (a certain figure) atteindre or faire

etc en moyenne; **on ~** en moyenne; **above/below (the) ~** au-dessus/en-dessous de la moyenne
  ▶ **average out** VI: **to ~ out at** représenter en moyenne, donner une moyenne de
averse [ə'və:s] ADJ: **to be ~ to sth/doing** éprouver une forte répugnance envers qch/à faire; **I wouldn't be ~ to a drink** un petit verre ne serait pas de refus, je ne dirais pas non à un petit verre
aversion [ə'və:ʃən] N aversion f, répugnance f
avert [ə'və:t] VT (danger) prévenir, écarter; (one's eyes) détourner
aviary ['eɪvɪərɪ] N volière f
aviation [eɪvɪ'eɪʃən] N aviation f
avid ['ævɪd] ADJ avide
avidly ['ævɪdlɪ] ADV avidement, avec avidité
avocado [ævə'kɑ:dəʊ] N (BRIT: also: **avocado pear**) avocat m
avoid [ə'vɔɪd] VT éviter
avoidable [ə'vɔɪdəbl] ADJ évitable
avoidance [ə'vɔɪdəns] N le fait d'éviter
avowed [ə'vaʊd] ADJ déclaré(e)
AVP N ABBR (US) = **assistant vice-president**
AWACS ['eɪwæks] N ABBR (= airborne warning and control system) AWACS (système aéroporté d'alerte et de contrôle)
await [ə'weɪt] VT attendre; **awaiting attention/delivery** (Comm) en souffrance; **long awaited** tant attendu(e)
awake [ə'weɪk] (pt **awoke** [ə'wəʊk], pp **awoken** [ə'wəʊkən]) ADJ éveillé(e); (fig) en éveil ▶ VT éveiller ▶ VI s'éveiller; **~ to** conscient de; **to be ~** être réveillé(e); **he was still ~** il ne dormait pas encore
awakening [ə'weɪknɪŋ] N réveil m
award [ə'wɔ:d] N (for bravery) récompense f; (prize) prix m; (Law: damages) dommages-intérêts mpl ▶ VT (prize) décerner; (Law: damages) accorder
aware [ə'wɛəʳ] ADJ: **~ of** (conscious) conscient(e) de; (informed) au courant de; **to become ~ of/ that** prendre conscience de/que; se rendre compte de/que; **politically/socially ~** sensibilisé(e) aux or ayant pris conscience des problèmes politiques/sociaux; **I am fully ~ that** je me rends parfaitement compte que
awareness [ə'wɛənɪs] N conscience f, connaissance f; **to develop people's ~ (of)** sensibiliser le public (à)
awash [ə'wɔʃ] ADJ recouvert(e) (d'eau); **~ with** inondé(e) de
away [ə'weɪ] ADV (au) loin; (movement): **she went ~** elle est partie ▶ ADJ (not in, not here) absent(e); **far ~** (au) loin; **two kilometres ~** à (une distance de) deux kilomètres, à deux kilomètres de distance; **two hours ~ by car** à deux heures de voiture or de route; **the holiday was two weeks ~** il restait deux semaines jusqu'aux vacances; **~ from** loin de; **he's ~ for a week** il est parti (pour) une semaine; **he's ~ in Milan** il est (parti) à Milan; **to take sth ~ from sb** prendre qch à qn; **to take sth ~ from sth** (subtract) ôter qch de qch; **to work/pedal ~** travailler/pédaler à cœur joie; **to fade ~** (colour)

s'estomper; (*sound*) s'affaiblir
away game N (*Sport*) match *m* à l'extérieur
awe [ɔː] N respect mêlé de crainte, effroi mêlé d'admiration
awe-inspiring [ˈɔːɪnspaɪərɪŋ], **awesome** [ˈɔːsəm] ADJ impressionnant(e)
awesome [ˈɔːsəm] (*US*) ADJ (*inf: excellent*) génial(e)
awestruck [ˈɔːstrʌk] ADJ frappé(e) d'effroi
awful [ˈɔːfəl] ADJ affreux(-euse); **an ~ lot of** énormément de
awfully [ˈɔːfəlɪ] ADV (*very*) terriblement, vraiment
awhile [əˈwaɪl] ADV un moment, quelque temps
awkward [ˈɔːkwəd] ADJ (*clumsy*) gauche, maladroit(e); (*inconvenient*) peu pratique; (*embarrassing*) gênant; **I can't talk just now, it's a bit ~** je ne peux pas parler tout de suite, c'est un peu difficile
awkwardness [ˈɔːkwədnɪs] N (*embarrassment*) gêne *f*
awl [ɔːl] N alêne *f*
awning [ˈɔːnɪŋ] N (*of tent*) auvent *m*; (*of shop*) store *m*; (*of hotel etc*) marquise *f* (de toile)
awoke [əˈwəuk] PT *of* **awake**

awoken [əˈwəukən] PP *of* **awake**
AWOL [ˈeɪwɔl] ABBR (*Mil*) = **absent without leave**
awry [əˈraɪ] ADV, ADJ de travers; **to go ~** mal tourner
axe, (*US*) **ax** [æks] N hache *f* ▶ VT (*employee*) renvoyer; (*project etc*) abandonner; (*jobs*) supprimer; **to have an ~ to grind** (*fig*) prêcher pour son saint
axes [ˈæksiːz] NPL *of* **axis**
axiom [ˈæksɪəm] N axiome *m*
axiomatic [æksɪəuˈmætɪk] ADJ axiomatique
axis [ˈæksɪs] (*pl* **axes** [-siːz]) N axe *m*
axle [ˈæksl] N (*also:* **axle-tree**) essieu *m*
ay, aye [aɪ] EXCL (*yes*) oui ▶ N: **the ay(e)s** les oui
AYH N ABBR = **American Youth Hostels**
AZ ABBR (*US*) = **Arizona**
azalea [əˈzeɪlɪə] N azalée *f*
Azerbaijan [æzəbaɪˈdʒɑːn] N Azerbaïdjan *m*
Azerbaijani [æzəbaɪˈdʒɑːnɪ], **Azeri** [əˈzeərɪ] ADJ azerbaïdjanais(e) ▶ N Azerbaïdjanais(e)
Azores [əˈzɔːz] NPL: **the ~** les Açores *fpl*
AZT N ABBR (= *azidothymidine*) AZT *f*
Aztec [ˈæztɛk] ADJ aztèque ▶ N Aztèque *mf*
azure [ˈeɪʒəʳ] ADJ azuré(e)

Bb

B, b [biː] N (*letter*) B, b *m*; (*Scol: mark*) B; (*Mus*): **B** si *m*; **B for Benjamin**, (*US*) **B for Baker** B comme Berthe; **B road** *n* (*BRIT Aut*) route départementale

b. ABBR = **born**

B.A. ABBR = **British Academy**; (*Scol*) = **Bachelor of Arts**

babble ['bæbl] VI babiller ▸ N babillage *m*

baboon [bə'buːn] N babouin *m*

baby ['beɪbɪ] N bébé *m*

baby carriage N (*US*) voiture *f* d'enfant

baby food N aliments *mpl* pour bébé(s)

baby grand N (*also:* **baby grand piano**) (piano *m*) demi-queue *m*

babyish ['beɪbɪɪʃ] ADJ enfantin(e), de bébé

baby-minder ['beɪbɪmaɪndə'] N (*BRIT*) gardienne *f* (d'enfants)

baby-sit ['beɪbɪsɪt] VI garder les enfants

baby-sitter ['beɪbɪsɪtə'] N baby-sitter *mf*

baby wipe N lingette *f* (pour bébé)

bachelor ['bætʃələ'] N célibataire *m*; **B~ of Arts/ Science (BA/BSc)** ≈ licencié(e) ès *or* en lettres/ sciences; **B~ of Arts/Science degree (BA/BSc)** *n* ≈ licence *f* ès *or* en lettres/sciences; *voir article*

Un *Bachelor's degree* est un diplôme accordé après trois ou quatre années d'université. Les *Bachelor's degrees* les plus courants sont le *BA* (*Bachelor of Arts*), le *BSc* (*Bachelor of Science*), le *BEd* (*Bachelor of Education*) et le *LLB* (*Bachelor of Laws*).

bachelor party N (*US*) enterrement *m* de vie de garçon

back [bæk] N (*of person, horse*) dos *m*; (*of hand*) dos, revers *m*; (*of house*) derrière *m*; (*of car, train*) arrière *m*; (*of chair*) dossier *m*; (*of page*) verso *m*; (*Football*) arrière *m* ▸ VT (*financially*) soutenir (financièrement); (*candidate: also:* **back up**) soutenir, appuyer; (*horse: at races*) parier *or* miser sur; (*car*) (faire) reculer ▸ VI reculer; (*car etc*) faire marche arrière ▸ ADJ (*in compounds*) de derrière, à l'arrière ▸ ADV (*not forward*) en arrière; (*returned*): **he's** ~ il est rentré, il est de retour; **can the people at the ~ hear me properly?** est-ce que les gens du fond m'entendent?; **to have one's ~ to the wall** (*fig*) être au pied du mur; **to break the ~ of a job** (*BRIT*) faire le gros d'un travail; ~ **to front** à l'envers; ~ **seat/ wheel** (*Aut*) siège *m*/roue *f* arrière *inv*;
~ **payments/rent** arriéré *m* de paiements/ loyer; ~ **garden/room** jardin/pièce sur l'arrière; **to take a** ~ **seat** (*fig*) se contenter d'un second rôle, être relégué(e) au second plan; **when will you be** ~? quand seras-tu de retour?; **he ran** ~ il est revenu en courant; **throw the ball** ~ renvoie la balle; **can I have it** ~? puis-je le ravoir?, peux-tu me le rendre?; **he called** ~ (*again*) il a rappelé

▸ **back down** VI rabattre de ses prétentions

▸ **back on to** VT FUS: **the house backs on to the golf course** la maison donne derrière sur le terrain de golf

▸ **back out** VI (*of promise*) se dédire

▸ **back up** VT (*person*) soutenir; (*Comput*) faire une copie de sauvegarde de

backache ['bækeɪk] N mal *m* au dos

backbencher [bæk'bentʃə'] N (*BRIT*) membre du parlement sans portefeuille

back benches NPL (*BRIT*); *voir article*

Le terme *back benches* désigne les bancs les plus éloignés de l'allée centrale de la Chambre des communes. Les députés qui occupent ces bancs sont les *backbenchers* et ils n'ont pas de portefeuille ministériel.

backbiting ['bækbaɪtɪŋ] N médisance(s) *f(pl)*

backbone ['bækbəʊn] N colonne vertébrale, épine dorsale; **he's the ~ of the organization** c'est sur lui que repose l'organisation

backchat ['bæktʃæt] N (*BRIT inf*) impertinences *fpl*

backcloth ['bækklɔθ] N (*BRIT*) toile *f* de fond

backcomb ['bækkəʊm] VT (*BRIT*) crêper

backdate [bæk'deɪt] VT (*letter*) antidater; **backdated pay rise** augmentation *f* avec effet rétroactif

back door N porte *f* de derrière

backdrop ['bækdrɔp] N = **backcloth**

backer ['bækə'] N partisan *m*; (*Comm*) commanditaire *m*

backfire [bæk'faɪə'] VI (*Aut*) pétarader; (*plans*) mal tourner

backgammon ['bækgæmən] N trictrac *m*

background ['bækgraʊnd] N arrière-plan *m*; (*of events*) situation *f*, conjoncture *f*; (*basic knowledge*) éléments *mpl* de base; (*experience*) formation *f* ▸ CPD (*noise, music*) de fond;
~ **reading** lecture(s) générale(s) (sur un sujet);

family ~ milieu familial

backhand ['bækhænd] N (*Tennis: also:* **backhand stroke**) revers *m*

backhanded ['bæk'hændɪd] ADJ (*fig*) déloyal(e); équivoque

backhander ['bæk'hændə'] N (*BRIT: bribe*) pot-de-vin *m*

backing ['bækɪŋ] N (*fig*) soutien *m*, appui *m*; (*Comm*) soutien (financier); (*Mus*) accompagnement *m*

backlash ['bæklæʃ] N contre-coup *m*, répercussion *f*

backlog ['bæklɔg] N: ~ **of work** travail *m* en retard

back number N (*of magazine etc*) vieux numéro

backpack ['bækpæk] N sac *m* à dos

backpacker ['bækpækə'] N randonneur(-euse)

back pain N mal *m* de dos

back pay N rappel *m* de salaire

backpedal ['bækpɛdl] VI (*fig*) faire marche arrière

backseat driver ['bæksi:t-] N *passager qui donne des conseils au conducteur*

backside ['bæksaɪd] N (*inf*) derrière *m*, postérieur *m*

backslash ['bækslæʃ] N barre oblique inversée

backslide ['bækslaɪd] VI retomber dans l'erreur

backspace ['bækspeɪs] VI (*in typing*) appuyer sur la touche retour

backstage [bæk'steɪdʒ] ADV dans les coulisses

back-street ['bækstri:t] ADJ (*abortion*) clandestin(e); ~ **abortionist** avorteur(-euse) (*clandestin*)

backstroke ['bækstrəuk] N dos crawlé

backtrack ['bæktræk] VI (*fig*) = **backpedal**

backup ['bækʌp] ADJ (*train, plane*) supplémentaire, de réserve; (*Comput*) de sauvegarde ▶ N (*support*) appui *m*, soutien *m*; (*Comput: also:* **backup file**) sauvegarde *f*

backward ['bækwəd] ADJ (*movement*) en arrière; (*measure*) rétrograde; (*person, country*) arriéré(e), attardé(e); (*shy*) hésitant(e); ~ **and forward movement** mouvement de va-et-vient

backwards ['bækwədz] ADV (*move, go*) en arrière; (*read a list*) à l'envers, à rebours; (*fall*) à la renverse; (*walk*) à reculons; (*in time*) en arrière, vers le passé; **to know sth** ~ or (*US*) ~ **and forwards** (*inf*) connaître qch sur le bout des doigts

backwater ['bækwɔ:tə'] N (*fig*) coin reculé; bled perdu

backyard [bæk'jɑ:d] N arrière-cour *f*

bacon ['beɪkən] N bacon *m*, lard *m*

bacteria [bæk'tɪərɪə] NPL bactéries *fpl*

bacteriology [bæktɪərɪ'ɔlədʒɪ] N bactériologie *f*

bad [bæd] ADJ mauvais(e); (*child*) vilain(e); (*mistake, accident*) grave; (*meat, food*) gâté(e), avarié(e); **his** ~ **leg** sa jambe malade; **to go** ~ (*meat, food*) se gâter; (*milk*) tourner; **to have a ~ time of it** traverser une mauvaise passe; **I feel** ~ **about it** (*guilty*) j'ai un peu mauvaise conscience; ~ **debt** créance douteuse; **in** ~ **faith** de mauvaise foi

baddie, baddy ['bædɪ] N (*inf: Cine etc*)

méchant *m*

bade [bæd] PT *of* **bid**

badge [bædʒ] N insigne *m*; (*of policeman*) plaque *f*; (*stick-on, sew-on*) badge *m*

badger ['bædʒə'] N blaireau *m* ▶ VT harceler

badly ['bædlɪ] ADV (*work, dress etc*) mal; **to reflect** ~ **on sb** donner une mauvaise image de qn; ~ **wounded** grièvement blessé; **he needs it** ~ il en a absolument besoin; **things are going** ~ les choses vont mal; ~ **off** *adj, adv* dans la gêne

bad-mannered ['bæd'mænəd] ADJ mal élevé(e)

badminton ['bædmɪntən] N badminton *m*

bad-mouth ['bæd'mauθ] VT (*US inf*) débiner

bad-tempered ['bæd'tɛmpəd] ADJ (*by nature*) ayant mauvais caractère; (*on one occasion*) de mauvaise humeur

baffle ['bæfl] VT (*puzzle*) déconcerter

baffling ['bæflɪŋ] ADJ déroutant(e), déconcertant(e)

bag [bæg] N sac *m*; (*of hunter*) gibecière *f*, chasse *f* ▶ VT (*inf: take*) empocher; s'approprier; (*Tech*) mettre en sacs; **bags of** (*inf: lots of*) des tas de; **to pack one's bags** faire ses valises or bagages; **bags under the eyes** poches *fpl* sous les yeux

bagful ['bægful] N plein sac

baggage ['bægɪdʒ] N bagages *mpl*

baggage allowance N franchise *f* de bagages

baggage reclaim N (*at airport*) livraison *f* des bagages

baggy ['bægɪ] ADJ avachi(e), qui fait des poches

Baghdad [bæg'dæd] N Baghdâd, Bagdad

bag lady N (*inf*) clocharde *f*

bagpipes ['bægpaɪps] NPL cornemuse *f*

bag-snatcher ['bægsnætʃə'] N (*BRIT*) voleur *m* à l'arraché

bag-snatching ['bægsnætʃɪŋ] N (*BRIT*) vol *m* à l'arraché

Bahamas [bə'hɑːməz] NPL: **the** ~ les Bahamas *fpl*

Bahrain [bɑː'reɪn] N Bahreïn *m*

bail [beɪl] N caution *f* ▶ VT (*prisoner: also:* **grant bail to**) mettre en liberté sous caution; (*boat: also:* **bail out**) écoper; **to be released on** ~ être libéré(e) sous caution; *see* **bale** ▶ **bail out** VT (*prisoner*) payer la caution de

bailiff ['beɪlɪf] N huissier *m*

bailout ['beɪlaut] N sauvetage *m* (*de banque, d'entreprise*)

bait [beɪt] N appât *m* ▶ VT appâter; (*fig: tease*) tourmenter

bake [beɪk] VT (*faire*) cuire au four ▶ VI (*bread etc*) cuire (au four); (*make cakes etc*) faire de la pâtisserie

baked beans [beɪkt-] NPL haricots blancs à la sauce tomate

baked potato N pomme *f* de terre en robe des champs

baker ['beɪkə'] N boulanger *m*

bakery ['beɪkərɪ] N boulangerie *f*; boulangerie industrielle

baking ['beɪkɪŋ] N (*process*) cuisson *f*

baking powder N levure *f* (chimique)

baking tin N (*for cake*) moule *m* à gâteaux; (*for meat*) plat *m* pour le four

baking tray N plaque f à gâteaux
balaclava [bælə'klɑːvə] N (also: **balaclava helmet**) passe-montagne m
balance ['bæləns] N équilibre m; (Comm: sum) solde m; (remainder) reste m; (scales) balance f
▶ VT mettre or faire tenir en équilibre; (pros and cons) peser; (budget) équilibrer; (account) balancer; (compensate) compenser, contrebalancer; **~ of trade/payments** balance commerciale/des comptes or paiements; **~ carried forward** solde m à reporter; **~ brought forward** solde reporté; **to ~ the books** arrêter les comptes, dresser le bilan
balanced ['bælənst] ADJ (personality, diet) équilibré(e); (report) objectif(-ive)
balance sheet N bilan m
balcony ['bælkənɪ] N balcon m; **do you have a room with a ~?** avez-vous une chambre avec balcon?
bald [bɔːld] ADJ chauve; (tyre) lisse
baldness ['bɔːldnɪs] N calvitie f
bale [beɪl] N balle f, ballot m
▶ **bale out** VI (of a plane) sauter en parachute
▶ VT (Naut: water, boat) écoper
Balearic Islands [bælɪ'ærɪk-] NPL: **the ~** les (îles fpl) Baléares fpl
baleful ['beɪlful] ADJ funeste, maléfique
balk [bɔːk] VI: **to ~ (at)** (person) regimber (contre); (horse) se dérober (devant)
Balkan ['bɔːlkən] ADJ balkanique ▶ N: **the Balkans** les Balkans mpl
ball [bɔːl] N boule f; (football) ballon m; (for tennis, golf) balle f; (dance) bal m; **to play ~** jouer au ballon (or à la balle); (fig) coopérer; **to be on the ~** (fig: competent) être à la hauteur; (: alert) être éveillé(e), être vif (vive); **to start the ~ rolling** (fig) commencer; **the ~ is in their court** (fig) la balle est dans leur camp
ballad ['bæləd] N ballade f
ballast ['bæləst] N lest m
ball bearings N roulement m à billes
ball cock N robinet m à flotteur
ballerina [bælə'riːnə] N ballerine f
ballet ['bæleɪ] N ballet m; (art) danse f (classique)
ballet dancer N danseur(-euse) de ballet
ballet shoe N chausson m de danse
ballistic [bə'lɪstɪk] ADJ balistique
ballistics [bə'lɪstɪks] N balistique f
balloon [bə'luːn] N ballon m; (in comic strip) bulle f ▶ VI gonfler
balloonist [bə'luːnɪst] N aéronaute mf
ballot ['bælət] N scrutin m
ballot box N urne (électorale)
ballot paper N bulletin m de vote
ballpark ['bɔːlpɑːk] N (US) stade m de base-ball
ballpark figure N (inf) chiffre approximatif
ballpoint ['bɔːlpɔɪnt], **ballpoint pen** N stylo m à bille
ballroom ['bɔːlrum] N salle f de bal
balls [bɔːlz] NPL (inf!) couilles fpl (!)
balm [bɑːm] N baume m
balmy ['bɑːmɪ] ADJ (breeze, air) doux (douce); (Brit inf) = **barmy**

BALPA ['bælpə] N ABBR (= British Airline Pilots' Association) syndicat des pilotes de ligne
balsa ['bɔːlsə], **balsa wood** N balsa m
balsam ['bɔːlsəm] N baume m
Baltic [bɔːltɪk] ADJ, N: **the ~ (Sea)** la (mer) Baltique
balustrade [bæləs'treɪd] N balustrade f
bamboo [bæm'buː] N bambou m
bamboozle [bæm'buːzl] VT (inf) embobiner
ban [bæn] N interdiction f ▶ VT interdire; **he was banned from driving** (Brit) on lui a retiré le permis (de conduire)
banal [bə'nɑːl] ADJ banal(e)
banana [bə'nɑːnə] N banane f
band [bænd] N bande f; (at a dance) orchestre m; (Mil) musique f, fanfare f
▶ **band together** VI se liguer
bandage ['bændɪdʒ] N bandage m, pansement m ▶ VT (wound, leg) mettre un pansement or un bandage sur; (person) mettre un pansement or un bandage à
Band-Aid® ['bændeɪd] N (US) pansement adhésif
B. & B. N ABBR = **bed and breakfast**
bandit ['bændɪt] N bandit m
bandstand ['bændstænd] N kiosque m (à musique)
bandwagon ['bændwægən] N: **to jump on the ~** (fig) monter dans or prendre le train en marche
bandy ['bændɪ] VT (jokes, insults) échanger
▶ **bandy about** VT employer à tout bout de champ or à tort et à travers
bandy-legged ['bændɪ'lɛgɪd] ADJ aux jambes arquées
bane [beɪn] N: **it** (or **he** etc) **is the ~ of my life** c'est (or il est etc) le drame de ma vie
bang [bæŋ] N détonation f; (of door) claquement m; (blow) coup (violent) ▶ VT frapper (violemment); (door) claquer ▶ VI détoner; claquer ▶ ADV: **to be ~ on time** (Brit inf) être à l'heure pile; **to ~ at the door** cogner à la porte; **to ~ into sth** se cogner contre qch
banger ['bæŋə'] N (Brit inf: car: also: **old banger**) (vieux) tacot m; (inf: sausage) saucisse f; (firework) pétard m
Bangkok [bæŋ'kɔk] N Bangkok
Bangladesh [bæŋglə'dɛʃ] N Bangladesh m
Bangladeshi [bæŋglə'dɛʃɪ] ADJ du Bangladesh
▶ N habitant(e) du Bangladesh
bangle ['bæŋgl] N bracelet m
bangs [bæŋz] NPL (US: fringe) frange f
banish ['bænɪʃ] VT bannir
banister ['bænɪstə'] N, **banisters** ['bænɪstəz] NPL rampe f (d'escalier)
banjo ['bændʒəu] (pl **banjoes** or **banjos**) N banjo m
bank [bæŋk] N banque f; (of river, lake) bord m, rive f; (of earth) talus m, remblai m ▶ VI (Aviat) virer sur l'aile; (Comm): **they ~ with Pitt's** leur banque or banquier est Pitt's
▶ **bank on** VT FUS miser or tabler sur
bank account N compte m en banque
bank balance N solde m bancaire
bank card (Brit) N carte f d'identité bancaire

bank charges NPL (*BRIT*) frais *mpl* de banque
bank draft N traite *f* bancaire
banker ['bæŋkə'] N banquier *m*; **~'s card** (*BRIT*) carte *f* d'identité bancaire; **~'s order** (*BRIT*) ordre *m* de virement
bank giro N paiement *m* par virement
bank holiday N (*BRIT*) jour férié (*où les banques sont fermées*); *voir article*

> Le terme *bank holiday* s'applique au Royaume-Uni aux jours fériés pendant lesquels banques et commerces sont fermés. Les principaux *bank holidays* à part Noël et Pâques se situent au mois de mai et fin août, et contrairement aux pays de tradition catholique, ne coïncident pas nécessairement avec une fête religieuse.

banking ['bæŋkɪŋ] N opérations *fpl* bancaires; profession *f* de banquier
banking hours NPL heures *fpl* d'ouverture des banques
bank loan N prêt *m* bancaire
bank manager N directeur *m* d'agence (bancaire)
banknote ['bæŋknəut] N billet *m* de banque
bank rate N taux *m* de l'escompte
bankrupt ['bæŋkrʌpt] N failli(e) ▶ ADJ en faillite; **to go ~** faire faillite
bankruptcy ['bæŋkrʌptsɪ] N faillite *f*
bank statement N relevé *m* de compte
banner ['bænə'] N bannière *f*
bannister ['bænɪstə'] N, **bannisters** ['bænɪstəz] NPL = **banister**
banns [bænz] NPL bans *mpl* (de mariage)
banquet ['bæŋkwɪt] N banquet *m*, festin *m*
bantam-weight ['bæntəmweɪt] N poids *m* coq *inv*
banter ['bæntə'] N badinage *m*
baptism ['bæptɪzəm] N baptême *m*
Baptist ['bæptɪst] N baptiste *mf*
baptize ['bæptaɪz] VT baptiser
bar [baː'] N (*pub*) bar *m*; (*counter*) comptoir *m*, bar; (*rod: of metal etc*) barre *f*; (: *of window etc*) barreau *m*; (*of chocolate*) tablette *f*, plaque *f*; (*fig: obstacle*) obstacle *m*; (*prohibition*) mesure *f* d'exclusion; (*Mus*) mesure *f* ▶ VT (*road*) barrer; (*window*) munir de barreaux; (*person*) exclure; (*activity*) interdire; **~ of soap** savonnette *f*; **behind bars** (*prisoner*) derrière les barreaux; **the B~** (*Law*) le barreau; **~ none** sans exception
Barbados [baː'beɪdɔs] N Barbade *f*
barbaric [baː'bærɪk] ADJ barbare
barbarous ['baːbərəs] ADJ barbare, cruel(le)
barbecue ['baːbɪkjuː] N barbecue *m*
barbed wire ['baːbd-] N fil *m* de fer barbelé
barber ['baːbə'] N coiffeur *m* (pour hommes)
barber's (shop) ['baːbəz-], (*US*) **barber shop** N salon *m* de coiffure (pour hommes); **to go to the barber's** aller chez le coiffeur
barbiturate [baː'bɪtjurɪt] N barbiturique *m*
Barcelona [baːsə'ləunə] N Barcelone
bar chart N diagramme *m* en bâtons
bar code N code *m* à barres, code-barre *m*
bare [bɛə'] ADJ nu(e) ▶ VT mettre à nu, dénuder; (*teeth*) montrer; **the ~ essentials**

le strict nécessaire
bareback ['bɛəbæk] ADV à cru, sans selle
barefaced ['bɛəfeɪst] ADJ impudent(e), effronté(e)
barefoot ['bɛəfut] ADJ, ADV nu-pieds, (les) pieds nus
bareheaded [bɛə'hɛdɪd] ADJ, ADV nu-tête, (la) tête nue
barely ['bɛəlɪ] ADV à peine
Barents Sea ['bærənts-] N: **the ~** la mer de Barents
bargain ['baːgɪn] N (*transaction*) marché *m*; (*good buy*) affaire *f*, occasion *f* ▶ VI (*haggle*) marchander; (*negotiate*) négocier, traiter; **into the ~** par-dessus le marché
▶ **bargain for** VT FUS (*inf*): **he got more than he bargained for!** il en a eu pour son argent!
bargaining ['baːgənɪŋ] N marchandage *m*; négociations *fpl*
bargaining position N: **to be in a weak/strong ~** être en mauvaise/bonne position pour négocier
barge [baːdʒ] N péniche *f*
▶ **barge in** VI (*walk in*) faire irruption; (*interrupt talk*) intervenir mal à propos
▶ **barge into** VT FUS rentrer dans
baritone ['bærɪtəun] N baryton *m*
barium meal ['bɛərɪəm-] N (bouillie *f* de) sulfate *m* de baryum
bark [baːk] N (*of tree*) écorce *f*; (*of dog*) aboiement *m* ▶ VI aboyer
barley ['baːlɪ] N orge *f*
barley sugar N sucre *m* d'orge
barmaid ['baːmeɪd] N serveuse *f* (de bar), barmaid *f*
barman ['baːmən] N (*irreg*) serveur *m* (de bar), barman *m*
bar meal N repas *m* de bistrot; **to go for a ~** aller manger au bistrot
barmy ['baːmɪ] ADJ (*BRIT inf*) timbré(e), cinglé(e)
barn [baːn] N grange *f*
barnacle ['baːnəkl] N anatife *m*, bernache *f*
barn owl N chouette-effraie *f*, chat-huant *m*
barometer [bə'rɔmɪtə'] N baromètre *m*
baron ['bærən] N baron *m*; **the press/oil barons** les magnats *mpl* or barons *mpl* de la presse/du pétrole
baroness ['bærənɪs] N baronne *f*
barrack ['bærək] VT (*BRIT*) chahuter
barracking ['bærəkɪŋ] N (*BRIT*): **to give sb a ~** chahuter qn
barracks ['bærəks] NPL caserne *f*
barrage ['bæraːʒ] N (*Mil*) tir *m* de barrage; (*dam*) barrage *m*; (*of criticism*) feu *m*
barrel ['bærəl] N tonneau *m*; (*of gun*) canon *m*
barrel organ N orgue *m* de Barbarie
barren ['bærən] ADJ stérile; (*hills*) aride
barrette [bə'ret] (*US*) N barrette *f*
barricade [bærɪ'keɪd] N barricade *f* ▶ VT barricader
barrier ['bærɪə'] N barrière *f*; (*BRIT: also:* **crash barrier**) rail *m* de sécurité
barrier cream N (*BRIT*) crème protectrice
barring ['baːrɪŋ] PREP sauf

barrister [ˈbærɪstər] N (*BRIT*) avocat (plaidant); *voir article*

> En Angleterre, un *barrister*, que l'on appelle également *barrister-at-law*, est un avocat qui représente ses clients devant la cour et plaide pour eux. Le client doit d'abord passer par l'intermédiaire d'un *solicitor*. On obtient le diplôme de *barrister* après avoir fait des études dans l'une des *Inns of Court*, les quatre écoles de droit londoniennes.

barrow [ˈbærəu] N (*cart*) charrette f à bras
barstool [ˈbɑːstuːl] N tabouret m de bar
Bart. ABBR (*BRIT*) = **baronet**
bartender [ˈbɑːtɛndər] N (*US*) serveur m (*de bar*), barman m
barter [ˈbɑːtər] N échange m, troc m ▶ VT: **to ~ sth for** échanger qch contre
base [beɪs] N base f ▶ VT (*troops*): **to be based at** être basé(e) à; (*opinion, belief*): **to ~ sth on** baser or fonder qch sur ▶ ADJ vil(e), bas(se); **coffee-based** à base de café; **a Paris-based firm** une maison opérant de Paris or dont le siège est à Paris; **I'm based in London** je suis basé(e) à Londres
baseball [ˈbeɪsbɔːl] N base-ball m
baseball cap N casquette f de base-ball
baseboard [ˈbeɪsbɔːd] N (*US*) plinthe f
base camp N camp m de base
Basel [ˈbɑːl] N = **Basle**
baseline [ˈbeɪslaɪn] N (*Tennis*) ligne f de fond
basement [ˈbeɪsmənt] N sous-sol m
base rate N taux m de base
bases [ˈbeɪsiːz] NPL of **basis**; [ˈbeɪsɪz] NPL of **base**
bash [bæʃ] VT (*inf*) frapper, cogner ▶ N: **I'll have a ~ (at it)** (*BRIT inf*) je vais essayer un coup; **bashed in** adj enfoncé(e), défoncé(e) ▶ **bash up** VT (*inf: car*) bousiller, (: *BRIT: person*) tabasser
bashful [ˈbæʃful] ADJ timide; modeste
bashing [ˈbæʃɪŋ] N (*inf*) raclée f
BASIC [ˈbeɪsɪk] N (*Comput*) BASIC m
basic [ˈbeɪsɪk] ADJ (*precautions, rules*) élémentaire; (*principles, research*) fondamental(e); (*vocabulary, salary*) de base; (*minimal*) réduit(e) au minimum, rudimentaire
basically [ˈbeɪsɪklɪ] ADV (*in fact*) en fait; (*essentially*) fondamentalement
basic rate N (*of tax*) première tranche d'imposition
basics [ˈbeɪsɪks] NPL: **the ~** l'essentiel m
basil [ˈbæzl] N basilic m
basin [ˈbeɪsn] N (*vessel, also Geo*) cuvette f, bassin m; (*BRIT: for food*) bol m; (: *bigger*) saladier m; (*also:* **washbasin**) lavabo m
basis [ˈbeɪsɪs] (*pl* **bases** [-siːz]) N base f; **on a part-time/trial ~** à temps partiel/à l'essai; **on the ~ of what you've said** d'après or compte tenu de ce que vous dites
bask [bɑːsk] VI: **to ~ in the sun** se chauffer au soleil
basket [ˈbɑːskɪt] N corbeille f; (*with handle*) panier m
basketball [ˈbɑːskɪtbɔːl] N basket-ball m

basketball player N basketteur(-euse)
Basle [bɑːl] N Bâle
basmati rice [bəzˈmætɪ-] N riz m basmati
Basque [bæsk] ADJ basque ▶ N Basque mf; **the ~ Country** le Pays basque
bass [beɪs] N (*Mus*) basse f
bass clef N clé f de fa
bass drum N grosse caisse f
bassoon [bəˈsuːn] N basson m
bastard [ˈbɑːstəd] N enfant naturel(le), bâtard(e); (*inf!*) salaud m (!)
baste [beɪst] VT (*Culin*) arroser; (*Sewing*) bâtir, faufiler
bat [bæt] N chauve-souris f; (*for baseball etc*) batte f; (*for table tennis*) raquette f ▶ VT: **he didn't ~ an eyelid** il n'a pas sourcillé or bronché; **off one's own ~** de sa propre initiative
batch [bætʃ] N (*of bread*) fournée f; (*of papers*) liasse f; (*of applicants, letters*) paquet m; (*of work*) monceau m; (*of goods*) lot m
bated [ˈbeɪtɪd] ADJ: **with ~ breath** en retenant son souffle
bath [bɑːθ] (*pl* **baths** [bɑːðz]) N bain m; (*bathtub*) baignoire f ▶ VT baigner, donner un bain à; **to have a ~** prendre un bain; *see also* **baths**
bathe [beɪð] VI se baigner ▶ VT baigner; (*wound etc*) laver
bather [ˈbeɪðər] N baigneur(-euse)
bathing [ˈbeɪðɪŋ] N baignade f
bathing cap N bonnet m de bain
bathing costume, (*US*) **bathing suit** N maillot m (de bain)
bathmat [ˈbɑːθmæt] N tapis m de bain
bathrobe [ˈbɑːθrəub] N peignoir m de bain
bathroom [ˈbɑːθrum] N salle f de bains
baths [bɑːðz] NPL (*BRIT: also:* **swimming baths**) piscine f
bath towel N serviette f de bain
bathtub [ˈbɑːθtʌb] N baignoire f
batman [ˈbætmən] N (*irreg*) (*BRIT Mil*) ordonnance f
baton [ˈbætən] N bâton m; (*Mus*) baguette f; (*club*) matraque f
battalion [bəˈtæliən] N bataillon m
batten [ˈbætn] N (*Carpentry*) latte f; (*Naut: on sail*) latte de voile ▶ **batten down** VT (*Naut*): **to ~ down the hatches** fermer les écoutilles
batter [ˈbætər] VT battre ▶ N pâte f à frire
battered [ˈbætəd] ADJ (*hat, pan*) cabossé(e); **~ wife/child** épouse/enfant maltraité(e) or martyr(e)
battering ram [ˈbætərɪŋ-] N bélier m (*fig*)
battery [ˈbætərɪ] N (*for torch, radio*) pile f; (*Aut, Mil*) batterie f
battery charger N chargeur m
battery farming N élevage m en batterie
battle [ˈbætl] N bataille f, combat m ▶ VI se battre, lutter; **that's half the ~** (*fig*) c'est déjà bien; **it's a** or **we're fighting a losing ~** (*fig*) c'est perdu d'avance, c'est peine perdue
battle dress N tenue f de campagne or d'assaut
battlefield [ˈbætlfiːld] N champ m de bataille
battlements [ˈbætlmənts] NPL remparts mpl

b

battleship ['bætlʃɪp] N cuirassé m
batty ['bætɪ] ADJ (inf: person) toqué(e), (: idea, behaviour) loufoque
bauble ['bɔːbl] N babiole f
baulk [bɔːlk] VI = **balk**
bauxite ['bɔːksaɪt] N bauxite f
Bavaria [bə'vɛərɪə] N Bavière f
Bavarian [bə'vɛərɪən] ADJ bavarois(e) ▶ N Bavarois(e)
bawdy ['bɔːdɪ] ADJ paillard(e)
bawl [bɔːl] VI hurler, brailler
bay [beɪ] N (of sea) baie f; (BRIT: for parking) place f de stationnement; (: for loading) aire f de chargement; (horse) bai(e) m/f; B~ **of Biscay** golfe m de Gascogne; **to hold sb at ~** tenir qn à distance or en échec
bay leaf N laurier m
bayonet ['beɪənɪt] N baïonnette f
bay tree N laurier m
bay window N baie vitrée
bazaar [bə'zɑːʳ] N (shop, market) bazar m; (sale) vente f de charité
bazooka [bə'zuːkə] N bazooka m
BB N ABBR (BRIT: = Boys' Brigade) mouvement de garçons
BBB N ABBR (US: = Better Business Bureau) organisme de défense du consommateur
BBC N ABBR (= British Broadcasting Corporation) office de la radiodiffusion et télévision britannique; voir article

> La BBC est un organisme centralisé dont les membres, nommés par l'État, gèrent les chaînes de télévision publiques (BBC1, qui présente des émissions d'intérêt général, et BBC2, qui est plutôt orientée vers les émissions plus culturelles, et les chaînes numériques) et les stations de radio publiques. Bien que non contrôlée par l'État, la BBC est responsable devant le Parliament quant au contenu des émissions qu'elle diffuse. Par ailleurs, la BBC offre un service mondial de diffusion d'émissions, en anglais et dans 43 autres langues, appelé BBC World Service. La BBC est financée par la redevance télévision et par l'exportation d'émissions.

B.C. ADV ABBR (= before Christ) av. J.-C. ▶ ABBR (CANADA) = **British Columbia**
BCG N ABBR (= Bacillus Calmette-Guérin) BCG m
BD N ABBR (= Bachelor of Divinity) diplôme universitaire
B/D ABBR = **bank draft**
BDS N ABBR (= Bachelor of Dental Surgery) diplôme universitaire

(KEYWORD)

be [biː] (pt **was, were**, pp **been**) AUX VB **1** (with present participle: forming continuous tenses): **what are you doing?** que faites-vous?; **they're coming tomorrow** ils viennent demain; **I've been waiting for you for 2 hours** je t'attends depuis 2 heures
2 (with pp: forming passives) être; **to be killed** être tué(e); **the box had been opened** la boîte avait

été ouverte; **he was nowhere to be seen** on ne le voyait nulle part
3 (in tag questions): **it was fun, wasn't it?** c'était drôle, n'est-ce pas?; **he's good-looking, isn't he?** il est beau, n'est-ce pas?; **she's back, is she?** elle est rentrée, n'est-ce pas or alors?
4 (+to+infinitive): **the house is to be sold** (necessity) la maison doit être vendue; (future) la maison va être vendue; **he's not to open it** il ne doit pas l'ouvrir; **am I to understand that ...?** dois-je comprendre que ...?; **he was to have come yesterday** il devait venir hier
5 (possibility: supposition): **if I were you, I ...** à votre place, je ..., si j'étais vous, je ...
▶ VB + COMPLEMENT **1** (gen) être; **I'm English** je suis anglais(e); **I'm tired** je suis fatigué(e); **I'm hot/cold** j'ai chaud/froid; **he's a doctor** il est médecin; **be careful/good/quiet!** faites attention/soyez sages/taisez-vous!; **2 and 2 are 4** 2 et 2 font 4
2 (of health) aller; **how are you?** comment allez-vous?; **I'm better now** je vais mieux maintenant; **he's fine now** il va bien maintenant; **he's very ill** il est très malade
3 (of age) avoir; **how old are you?** quel âge avez-vous?; **I'm sixteen (years old)** j'ai seize ans
4 (cost) coûter; **how much was the meal?** combien a coûté le repas?; **that'll be £5, please** ça fera 5 livres, s'il vous plaît; **this shirt is £17** cette chemise coûte 17 livres
▶ VI **1** (exist, occur etc) être, exister; **the prettiest girl that ever was** la fille la plus jolie qui ait jamais existé; **is there a God?** y a-t-il un dieu?; **be that as it may** quoi qu'il en soit; **so be it** soit
2 (referring to place) être, se trouver; **I won't be here tomorrow** je ne serai pas là demain; **Edinburgh is in Scotland** Édimbourg est or se trouve en Écosse
3 (referring to movement) aller; **where have you been?** où êtes-vous allé(s)?
▶ IMPERS VB **1** (referring to time) être; **it's 5 o'clock** il est 5 heures; **it's the 28th of April** c'est le 28 avril
2 (referring to distance): **it's 10 km to the village** le village est à 10 km
3 (referring to the weather) faire; **it's too hot/cold** il fait trop chaud/froid; **it's windy today** il y a du vent aujourd'hui
4 (emphatic): **it's me/the postman** c'est moi/le facteur; **it was Maria who paid the bill** c'est Maria qui a payé la note

B/E ABBR = **bill of exchange**
beach [biːtʃ] N plage f ▶ VT échouer
beachcomber ['biːtʃkəuməʳ] N ramasseur m d'épaves; (fig) bon(ne) m/f à rien
beachwear ['biːtʃwɛəʳ] N tenues fpl de plage
beacon ['biːkən] N (lighthouse) fanal m; (marker) balise f; (also: **radio beacon**) radiophare m
bead [biːd] N perle f; (of dew, sweat) goutte f; **beads** NPL (necklace) collier m
beady ['biːdɪ] ADJ: **~ eyes** yeux mpl de fouine

beagle [biːgl] N beagle *m*
beak [biːk] N bec *m*
beaker ['biːkəʳ] N gobelet *m*
beam [biːm] N (*Archit*) poutre *f*; (*of light*) rayon *m*; (*Radio*) faisceau *m* radio ▶ VI rayonner; **to drive on full** *or* **main** *or* (*US*) **high** ~ rouler en pleins phares
beaming ['biːmɪŋ] ADJ (*sun, smile*) radieux(-euse)
bean [biːn] N haricot *m*; (*of coffee*) grain *m*
beanpole ['biːnpəul] N (*inf*) perche *f*
beansprouts ['biːnsprauts] NPL pousses *fpl* or germes *mpl* de soja
bear [bɛəʳ] (*pt* **bore** [bɔːʳ], *pp* **borne** [bɔːn]) N ours *m*; (*Stock Exchange*) baissier *m* ▶ VT porter; (*endure*) supporter; (*traces, signs*) porter; (*Comm: interest*) rapporter ▶ VI: **to ~ right/left** obliquer à droite/gauche, se diriger vers la droite/gauche; **to ~ the responsibility of** assumer la responsabilité de; **to ~ comparison with** soutenir la comparaison avec; **I can't ~ him** je ne peux pas le supporter *or* souffrir; **to bring pressure to ~ on sb** faire pression sur qn
▶ **bear out** VT (*theory, suspicion*) confirmer
▶ **bear up** VI supporter, tenir le coup; **he bore up well** il a tenu le coup
▶ **bear with** VT FUS (*sb's moods, temper*) supporter; **~ with me a minute** un moment, s'il vous plaît
bearable ['bɛərəbl] ADJ supportable
beard [bɪəd] N barbe *f*
bearded ['bɪədɪd] ADJ barbu(e)
bearer ['bɛərəʳ] N porteur *m*; (*of passport etc*) titulaire *mf*
bearing ['bɛərɪŋ] N maintien *m*, allure *f*; (*connection*) rapport *m*; **(ball) bearings** NPL (*Tech*) roulement *m* (à billes); **to take a ~** faire le point; **to find one's bearings** s'orienter
beast [biːst] N bête *f*; (*inf: person*) brute *f*
beastly ['biːstlɪ] ADJ infect(e)
beat [biːt] (*pt* **~**, *pp* **beaten** [biːtn]) N battement *m*; (*Mus*) temps *m*, mesure *f*; (*of policeman*) ronde *f* ▶ VT, VI battre; **off the beaten track** hors des chemins *or* sentiers battus; **to ~ it** (*inf*) ficher le camp; **to ~ about the bush** tourner autour du pot; **that beats everything!** c'est le comble!
▶ **beat down** VT (*door*) enfoncer; (*price*) faire baisser; (*seller*) faire descendre ▶ VI (*rain*) tambouriner; (*sun*) taper
▶ **beat off** VT repousser
▶ **beat up** VT (*eggs*) battre; (*inf: person*) tabasser
beater ['biːtəʳ] N (*for eggs, cream*) fouet *m*, batteur *m*
beating ['biːtɪŋ] N raclée *f*
beat-up ['biːtʌp] ADJ (*inf*) déglingué(e)
beautician [bjuːˈtɪʃən] N esthéticien(ne)
beautiful ['bjuːtɪful] ADJ beau (belle)
beautifully ['bjuːtɪflɪ] ADV admirablement
beautify ['bjuːtɪfaɪ] VT embellir
beauty ['bjuːtɪ] N beauté *f*; **the ~ of it is that ...** le plus beau, c'est que ...
beauty contest N concours *m* de beauté
beauty parlour, (*US*) **beauty parlor** N institut *m* de beauté
beauty queen N reine *f* de beauté

beauty salon N institut *m* de beauté
beauty sleep N: **I need my ~** j'ai besoin de faire un gros dodo
beauty spot N (*on skin*) grain *m* de beauté; (*BRIT Tourism*) site naturel (d'une grande beauté)
beaver ['biːvəʳ] N castor *m*
becalmed [bɪˈkɑːmd] ADJ immobilisé(e) par le calme plat
became [bɪˈkeɪm] PT *of* **become**
because [bɪˈkɔz] CONJ parce que; **~ of** prep à cause de
beck [bɛk] N: **to be at sb's ~ and call** être à l'entière disposition de qn
beckon ['bɛkən] VT (*also*: **beckon to**) faire signe (de venir) à
become [bɪˈkʌm] VI (*irreg: like* **come**) devenir; **to ~ fat/thin** grossir/maigrir; **to ~ angry** se mettre en colère; **it became known that** on apprit que; **what has ~ of him?** qu'est-il devenu?
becoming [bɪˈkʌmɪŋ] ADJ (*behaviour*) convenable, bienséant(e); (*clothes*) seyant(e)
BECTU ['bɛktu] N ABBR (*BRIT*) = **Broadcasting, Entertainment, Cinematographic and Theatre Union**
BEd N ABBR (= *Bachelor of Education*) diplôme d'aptitude à l'enseignement
bed [bɛd] N lit *m*; (*of flowers*) parterre *m*; (*of coal, clay*) couche *f*; (*of sea, lake*) fond *m*; **to go to ~** aller se coucher
▶ **bed down** VI se coucher
bed and breakfast N (*terms*) chambre et petit déjeuner; (*place*) = chambre f d'hôte; *voir article*

Un *bed and breakfast* est une petite pension dans une maison particulière ou une ferme où l'on peut louer une chambre avec petit déjeuner compris pour un prix modique par rapport à ce que l'on paierait dans un hôtel. Ces établissements sont communément appelés *B&B*, et sont signalés par une pancarte dans le jardin ou au-dessus de la porte.

bedbug ['bɛdbʌg] N punaise *f*
bedclothes ['bɛdkləuðz] NPL couvertures *fpl* et draps *mpl*
bedcover ['bɛdkʌvəʳ] N couvre-lit *m*, dessus-de-lit *m*
bedding ['bɛdɪŋ] N literie *f*
bedevil [bɪˈdɛvl] VT (*harass*) harceler; **to be bedevilled by** être victime de
bedfellow ['bɛdfɛləu] N: **they are strange bedfellows** (*fig*) ça fait un drôle de mélange
bedlam ['bɛdləm] N chahut *m*, cirque *m*
bed linen N draps *mpl* de lit (et taies *fpl* d'oreillers), literie *f*
bedpan ['bɛdpæn] N bassin *m* (hygiénique)
bedpost ['bɛdpəust] N colonne *f* de lit
bedraggled [bɪˈdrægld] ADJ dépenaillé(e), les vêtements en désordre
bedridden ['bɛdrɪdn] ADJ cloué(e) au lit
bedrock ['bɛdrɔk] N (*fig*) principes essentiels *or* de base, essentiel *m*; (*Geo*) roche *f* en place, socle *m*
bedroom ['bɛdrum] N chambre *f* (à coucher)

Beds ABBR (*BRIT*) = Bedfordshire
bed settee N canapé-lit *m*
bedside ['bɛdsaɪd] N: **at sb's ~** au chevet de qn ▶ CPD (*book, lamp*) de chevet
bedside lamp N lampe *f* de chevet
bedside table N table *f* de chevet
bedsit ['bɛdsɪt], **bedsitter** ['bɛdsɪtə'] N (*BRIT*) chambre meublée, studio *m*
bedspread ['bɛdsprɛd] N couvre-lit *m*, dessus-de-lit *m*
bedtime ['bɛdtaɪm] N: **it's ~** c'est l'heure de se coucher
bee [bi:] N abeille *f*; **to have a ~ in one's bonnet (about sth)** être obnubilé(e) (par qch)
beech [bi:tʃ] N hêtre *m*
beef [bi:f] N bœuf *m*; **roast ~** rosbif *m*
▶ **beef up** VT (*inf: support*) renforcer; (: *essay*) étoffer
beefburger ['bi:fbə:gə'] N hamburger *m*
beehive ['bi:haɪv] N ruche *f*
bee-keeping ['bi:ki:pɪŋ] N apiculture *f*
beeline ['bi:laɪn] N: **to make a ~ for** se diriger tout droit vers
been [bi:n] PP *of* **be**
beep [bi:p] N bip *m*
beeper ['bi:pə'] N (*pager*) bip *m*
beer [bɪə'] N bière *f*
beer belly N (*inf*) bedaine *f* (*de buveur de bière*)
beer can N canette *f* de bière
beer garden N (*BRIT*) jardin *m* d'un pub (*où l'on peut emmener ses consommations*)
beet [bi:t] N (*vegetable*) betterave *f*; (*US: also*: **red beet**) betterave (*potagère*)
beetle ['bi:tl] N scarabée *m*, coléoptère *m*
beetroot ['bi:tru:t] N (*BRIT*) betterave *f*
befall [bɪ'fɔ:l] VI, VT (*irreg: like* **fall**) advenir (à)
befit [bɪ'fɪt] VT seoir à
before [bɪ'fɔ:'] PREP (*of time*) avant; (*of space*) devant ▶ CONJ avant que + *sub*; avant de ▶ ADV avant; **~ going** avant de partir; **~ she goes** avant qu'elle (ne) parte; **the week ~** la semaine précédente *or* d'avant; **I've seen it ~** je l'ai déjà vu; **I've never seen it ~** c'est la première fois que je le vois
beforehand [bɪ'fɔ:hænd] ADV au préalable, à l'avance
befriend [bɪ'frɛnd] VT venir en aide à; traiter en ami
befuddled [bɪ'fʌdld] ADJ: **to be ~** avoir les idées brouillées
beg [bɛg] VI mendier ▶ VT mendier; (*favour*) quémander, solliciter; (*forgiveness, mercy etc*) demander; (*entreat*) supplier; **to ~ sb to do sth** supplier qn de faire qch; **I ~ your pardon** (*apologizing*) excusez-moi; (: *not hearing*) pardon?; **that begs the question of ...** cela soulève la question de ..., cela suppose réglée la question de ...; *see also* **pardon**
began [bɪ'gæn] PT *of* **begin**
beggar ['bɛgə'] N (*also*: **beggarman**, **beggarwoman**) mendiant(e)
begin [bɪ'gɪn] (*pt* **began** [bɪ'gæn], *pp* **begun** [bɪ'gʌn]) VT, VI commencer; **to ~ doing** *or* **to do sth** commencer à faire qch; **beginning (from)**

Monday à partir de lundi; **I can't ~ to thank you** je ne saurais vous remercier; **to ~ with** d'abord, pour commencer
beginner [bɪ'gɪnə'] N débutant(e)
beginning [bɪ'gɪnɪŋ] N commencement *m*, début *m*; **right from the ~** dès le début
begrudge [bɪ'grʌdʒ] VT: **to ~ sb sth** envier qch à qn; donner qch à contrecœur *or* à regret à qn
beguile [bɪ'gaɪl] VT (*enchant*) enjôler
beguiling [bɪ'gaɪlɪŋ] ADJ (*charming*) séduisant(e), enchanteur(-eresse)
begun [bɪ'gʌn] PP *of* **begin**
behalf [bɪ'hɑ:f] N: **on ~ of**, (*US*) **in ~ of** (*representing*) de la part de; au nom de; (*for benefit of*) pour le compte de; **on my/his ~** de ma/sa part
behave [bɪ'heɪv] VI se conduire, se comporter; (*well: also*: **behave o.s.**) se conduire bien *or* comme il faut
behaviour, (*US*) **behavior** [bɪ'heɪvjə'] N comportement *m*, conduite *f*
behead [bɪ'hɛd] VT décapiter
beheld [bɪ'hɛld] PT, PP *of* **behold**
behind [bɪ'haɪnd] PREP derrière; (*time*) en retard sur; (*supporting*): **to be ~ sb** soutenir qn ▶ ADV derrière; en retard ▶ N derrière *m*; **~ the scenes** dans les coulisses; **to leave sth ~** (*forget*) oublier de prendre qch; **to be ~ (schedule) with sth** être en retard dans qch
behold [bɪ'həuld] VT (*irreg: like* **hold**) apercevoir, voir
beige [beɪʒ] ADJ beige
Beijing ['beɪdʒɪŋ] N Pékin
being [bi:ɪŋ] N être *m*; **to come into ~** prendre naissance
Beirut [beɪ'ru:t] N Beyrouth
Belarus [bɛlə'rus] N Biélorussie *f*, Bélarus *m*
Belarussian [bɛlə'rʌʃən] ADJ biélorusse ▶ N Biélorusse *mf*; (*Ling*) biélorusse *m*
belated [bɪ'leɪtɪd] ADJ tardif(-ive)
belch [bɛltʃ] VI avoir un renvoi, roter ▶ VT (*smoke etc: also*: **belch out**) vomir, cracher
beleaguered [bɪ'li:gɪd] ADJ (*city*) assiégé(e); (*army*) cerné(e); (*fig*) sollicité(e) de toutes parts
Belfast ['bɛlfɑ:st] N Belfast
belfry ['bɛlfrɪ] N beffroi *m*
Belgian ['bɛldʒən] ADJ belge, de Belgique ▶ N Belge *mf*
Belgium ['bɛldʒəm] N Belgique *f*
Belgrade [bɛl'greɪd] N Belgrade
belie [bɪ'laɪ] VT démentir; (*give false impression of*) occulter
belief [bɪ'li:f] N (*opinion*) conviction *f*; (*trust, faith*) foi *f*; (*acceptance as true*) croyance *f*; **it's beyond ~** c'est incroyable; **in the ~ that** dans l'idée que
believable [bɪ'li:vəbl] ADJ croyable
believe [bɪ'li:v] VT, VI croire, estimer; **to ~ in** (*God*) croire en; (*ghosts, method*) croire à; **I don't ~ in corporal punishment** je ne suis pas partisan des châtiments corporels; **he is believed to be abroad** il serait à l'étranger
believer [bɪ'li:və'] N (*in idea, activity*) partisan(e); **~ in** partisan(e) de; (*Rel*) croyant(e)
belittle [bɪ'lɪtl] VT déprécier, rabaisser

Belize [bɛ'liːz] N Bélize m

bell [bɛl] N cloche f; (small) clochette f, grelot m; (on door) sonnette f; (electric) sonnerie f; **that rings a ~** (fig) cela me rappelle qch

bell-bottoms ['bɛlbɔtəmz] NPL pantalon m à pattes d'éléphant

bellboy ['bɛlbɔɪ], (US) **bellhop** ['bɛlhɔp] N groom m, chasseur m

belligerent [bɪ'lɪdʒərənt] ADJ (at war) belligérant(e); (fig) agressif(-ive)

bellow ['bɛləu] VI (bull) meugler; (person) brailler ▶ VT (orders) hurler

bellows ['bɛləuz] NPL soufflet m

bell pepper N (esp US) poivron m

bell push N (BRIT) bouton m de sonnette

belly ['bɛlɪ] N ventre m

bellyache ['bɛlɪeɪk] (inf) N colique f ▶ VI ronchonner

belly button (inf) N nombril m

bellyful ['bɛlɪful] N (inf): **I've had a ~** j'en ai ras le bol

belong [bɪ'lɔŋ] VI: **to ~ to** appartenir à; (club etc) faire partie de; **this book belongs here** ce livre va ici, la place de ce livre est ici

belongings [bɪ'lɔŋɪŋz] NPL affaires fpl, possessions fpl; **personal ~** effets personnels

Belorussia [bɛlə'rʌʃə] N Biélorussie f

Belorussian [bɛlə'rʌʃən] ADJ, N = **Belarussian**

beloved [bɪ'lʌvɪd] ADJ (bien-)aimé(e), chéri(e) ▶ N bien-aimé(e)

below [bɪ'ləu] PREP sous, au-dessous de ▶ ADV en dessous; en contre-bas; **see ~** voir plus bas or plus loin or ci-dessous; **temperatures ~ normal** températures inférieures à la normale

belt [bɛlt] N ceinture f; (Tech) courroie f ▶ VT (thrash) donner une raclée à ▶ VI (BRIT inf) filer (à toutes jambes); **industrial ~** zone industrielle
▶ **belt out** VT (song) chanter à tue-tête or à pleins poumons
▶ **belt up** VI (BRIT inf) la boucler

beltway ['bɛltweɪ] N (US Aut) route f de ceinture; (: motorway) périphérique m

bemoan [bɪ'məun] VT se lamenter sur

bemused [bɪ'mjuːzd] ADJ médusé(e)

bench [bɛntʃ] N banc m; (in workshop) établi m; **the B~** (Law: judges) la magistrature, la Cour

bench mark N repère m

bend [bɛnd] (pt, pp **bent** [bɛnt]) VT courber; (leg, arm) plier ▶ VI se courber ▶ N (in road) virage m, tournant m; (in pipe, river) coude m
▶ **bend down** VI se baisser
▶ **bend over** VI se pencher

bends [bɛndz] NPL (Med) maladie f des caissons

beneath [bɪ'niːθ] PREP sous, au-dessous de; (unworthy of) indigne de ▶ ADV dessous, au-dessous, en bas

benefactor ['bɛnɪfæktər] N bienfaiteur m

benefactress ['bɛnɪfæktrɪs] N bienfaitrice f

beneficial [bɛnɪ'fɪʃəl] ADJ: **~ (to)** salutaire (pour), bénéfique (à)

beneficiary [bɛnɪ'fɪʃərɪ] N (Law) bénéficiaire mf

benefit ['bɛnɪfɪt] N avantage m, profit m; (allowance of money) allocation f ▶ VT faire du bien à, profiter à ▶ VI: **he'll ~ from it** cela lui

fera du bien, il y gagnera or s'en trouvera bien

benefit performance N représentation f or gala m de bienfaisance

Benelux ['bɛnɪlʌks] N Bénélux m

benevolent [bɪ'nɛvələnt] ADJ bienveillant(e)

BEng N ABBR (= Bachelor of Engineering) diplôme universitaire

benign [bɪ'naɪn] ADJ (person, smile) bienveillant(e), affable; (Med) bénin(-igne)

bent [bɛnt] PT, PP of **bend** ▶ N inclination f, penchant m ▶ ADJ (wire, pipe) coudé(e); (inf: dishonest) véreux(-euse); **to be ~ on** être résolu(e) à

bequeath [bɪ'kwiːð] VT léguer

bequest [bɪ'kwɛst] N legs m

bereaved [bɪ'riːvd] N: **the ~** la famille du disparu ▶ ADJ endeuillé(e)

bereavement [bɪ'riːvmənt] N deuil m

beret ['bɛreɪ] N béret m

Bering Sea ['beɪrɪŋ-] N: **the ~** la mer de Béring

berk [bəːk] N (BRIT inf) andouille mf

Berks ABBR (BRIT) = **Berkshire**

Berlin [bəː'lɪn] N Berlin; **East/West ~** Berlin Est/Ouest

berm [bəːm] N (US Aut) accotement m

Bermuda [bəː'mjuːdə] N Bermudes fpl

Bermuda shorts NPL bermuda m

Bern [bəːn] N Berne

berry ['bɛrɪ] N baie f

berserk [bə'səːk] ADJ: **to go ~** être pris(e) d'une rage incontrôlable; se déchaîner

berth [bəːθ] N (bed) couchette f; (for ship) poste m d'amarrage, mouillage m ▶ VI (in harbour) venir à quai; (at anchor) mouiller; **to give sb a wide ~** (fig) éviter qn

beseech [bɪ'siːtʃ] (pt, pp **besought** [-'sɔːt]) VT implorer, supplier

beset [bɪ'sɛt] (pt, pp **~**) VT assaillir ▶ ADJ: **~ with** semé(e) de

besetting [bɪ'sɛtɪŋ] ADJ: **his ~ sin** son vice, son gros défaut

beside [bɪ'saɪd] PREP à côté de; (compared with) par rapport à; **that's ~ the point** ça n'a rien à voir; **to be ~ o.s. (with anger)** être hors de soi

besides [bɪ'saɪdz] ADV en outre, de plus ▶ PREP en plus de; (except) excepté

besiege [bɪ'siːdʒ] VT (town) assiéger; (fig) assaillir

besotted [bɪ'sɔtɪd] ADJ (BRIT): **~ with** entiché(e) de

besought [bɪ'sɔːt] PT, PP of **beseech**

bespectacled [bɪ'spɛktɪkld] ADJ à lunettes

bespoke [bɪ'spəuk] ADJ (BRIT: garment) fait(e) sur mesure; **~ tailor** tailleur m à façon

best [bɛst] ADJ meilleur(e) ▶ ADV le mieux; **the ~ part of** (quantity) le plus clair de, la plus grande partie de; **at ~** au mieux; **to make the ~ of sth** s'accommoder de qch (du mieux que l'on peut); **to do one's ~** faire de son mieux; **to the ~ of my knowledge** pour autant que je sache; **to the ~ of my ability** du mieux que je pourrai; **he's not exactly patient at the ~ of times** il n'est jamais spécialement patient; **the ~ thing to do is …** le mieux, c'est de …

b

481

best-before date N date f de limite
d'utilisation or de consommation
best man N (irreg) garçon m d'honneur
bestow [bɪ'stəu] VT accorder; (title) conférer
bestseller ['bɛst'sɛlər] N best-seller m, succès m
de librairie
bet [bɛt] (pt, pp ~ or **betted**) N pari m ▶ VT, VI
parier; **it's a safe ~** (fig) il y a de fortes chances;
to ~ sb sth parier qch à qn
Bethlehem ['bɛθlɪhɛm] N Bethléem
betray [bɪ'treɪ] VT trahir
betrayal [bɪ'treɪəl] N trahison f
better ['bɛtər] ADJ meilleur(e) ▶ ADV mieux ▶ VT
améliorer ▶ N: **to get the ~ of** triompher de,
l'emporter sur; **a change for the ~** une
amélioration; **I had ~ go** il faut que je m'en
aille; **you had ~ do it** vous feriez mieux de le
faire; **he thought ~ of it** il s'est ravisé; **to get ~**
(Med) aller mieux; (improve) s'améliorer; **that's**
~! c'est mieux!; **~ off** adj plus à l'aise
financièrement; (fig) **you'd be ~ off this way**
vous vous en trouveriez mieux ainsi, ce serait
mieux or plus pratique ainsi
betting ['bɛtɪŋ] N paris mpl
betting shop N (BRIT) bureau m de paris
between [bɪ'twiːn] PREP entre ▶ ADV au milieu,
dans l'intervalle; **the road ~ here and London**
la route d'ici à Londres; **we only had 5 ~ us**
nous n'en avions que 5 en tout
bevel ['bɛvəl] N (also: **bevel edge**) biseau m
beverage ['bɛvərɪdʒ] N boisson f (gén sans alcool)
bevy ['bɛvɪ] N: **a ~ of** un essaim or une volée de
bewail [bɪ'weɪl] VT se lamenter sur
beware [bɪ'wɛər] VT, VI: **to ~ (of)** prendre garde
(à); **"~ of the dog"** "(attention) chien
méchant"
bewildered [bɪ'wɪldəd] ADJ dérouté(e), ahuri(e)
bewildering [bɪ'wɪldrɪŋ] ADJ déroutant(e),
ahurissant(e)
bewitching [bɪ'wɪtʃɪŋ] ADJ enchanteur(-teresse)
beyond [bɪ'jɒnd] PREP (in space, time) au-delà de;
(exceeding) au-dessus de ▶ ADV au-delà; **~ doubt**
hors de doute; **~ repair** irréparable
b/f ABBR = **brought forward**
BFPO N ABBR (= British Forces Post Office) service
postal de l'armée
bhp N ABBR (Aut: = brake horsepower) puissance f
aux freins
bi... [baɪ] PREFIX bi...
biannual [baɪ'ænjuəl] ADJ semestriel(le)
bias ['baɪəs] N (prejudice) préjugé m, parti pris;
(preference) prévention f
biased, biassed ['baɪəst] ADJ partial(e),
montrant un parti pris; **to be bias(s)ed**
against avoir un préjugé contre
biathlon [baɪ'æθlən] N biathlon m
bib [bɪb] N bavoir m, bavette f
Bible ['baɪbl] N Bible f
bibliography [bɪblɪ'ɒɡrəfɪ] N bibliographie f
bicarbonate of soda [baɪ'kɑːbənɪt-] N
bicarbonate m de soude
bicentenary [baɪsɛn'tiːnərɪ], **bicentennial**
[baɪsɛn'tɛnɪəl] N bicentenaire m
biceps ['baɪsɛps] N biceps m

bicker ['bɪkər] VI se chamailler
bicycle ['baɪsɪkl] N bicyclette f
bicycle path, bicycle track N piste f cyclable
bicycle pump N pompe f à vélo
bid [bɪd] N offre f; (at auction) enchère f; (attempt)
tentative f ▶ VI (pt, pp ~) faire une enchère or
offre ▶ VT (pt **bade** [bæd], pp **bidden** ['bɪdn]) faire
une enchère or offre de; **to ~ sb good day**
souhaiter le bonjour à qn
bidden ['bɪdn] PP of **bid**
bidder ['bɪdər] N: **the highest ~** le plus offrant
bidding ['bɪdɪŋ] N enchères fpl
bide [baɪd] VT: **to ~ one's time** attendre son
heure
bidet ['biːdeɪ] N bidet m
bidirectional ['baɪdɪ'rɛkʃənl] ADJ
bidirectionnel(le)
biennial [baɪ'ɛnɪəl] ADJ biennal(e), bisannuel(le)
▶ N biennale f; (plant) plante bisannuelle
bier [bɪər] N bière f (cercueil)
bifocals [baɪ'fəʊklz] NPL lunettes fpl à double
foyer
big [bɪɡ] ADJ (in height: person, building, tree)
grand(e); (in bulk, amount: person, parcel, book)
gros(se); **to do things in a ~ way** faire les
choses en grand
bigamy ['bɪɡəmɪ] N bigamie f
Big Apple N voir article

> Si l'on sait que *The Big Apple* désigne la ville
> de New York (apple est en réalité un terme
> d'argot signifiant "grande ville"), on
> connaît moins les surnoms donnés aux
> autres grandes villes américaines. Chicago
> est surnommée *Windy City* à cause des rafales
> soufflant du lac Michigan, La Nouvelle-
> Orléans doit son sobriquet de *Big Easy* à son
> style de vie décontracté, et l'industrie
> automobile a donné à Detroit son surnom
> de *Motown*.

big dipper [-'dɪpər] N montagnes fpl russes
big end N (Aut) tête f de bielle
biggish ['bɪɡɪʃ] ADJ (see big) assez grand(e), assez
gros(se)
bigheaded ['bɪɡ'hɛdɪd] ADJ prétentieux(-euse)
big-hearted ['bɪɡ'hɑːtɪd] ADJ au grand cœur
bigot ['bɪɡət] N fanatique mf, sectaire mf
bigoted ['bɪɡətɪd] ADJ fanatique, sectaire
bigotry ['bɪɡətrɪ] N fanatisme m, sectarisme m
big toe N gros orteil
big top N grand chapiteau
big wheel N (at fair) grande roue
bigwig ['bɪɡwɪɡ] N (inf) grosse légume, huile f
bike [baɪk] N vélo m, bécane f
bike lane N piste f cyclable
bikini [bɪ'kiːnɪ] N bikini m
bilateral [baɪ'lætərl] ADJ bilatéral(e)
bile [baɪl] N bile f
bilingual [baɪ'lɪŋɡwəl] ADJ bilingue
bilious ['bɪlɪəs] ADJ bilieux(-euse); (fig)
maussade, irritable
bill [bɪl] N note f, facture f; (in restaurant) addition
f, note f; (Pol) projet m de loi; (US: banknote) billet
m (de banque); (notice) affiche f; (of bird) bec m;
(Theat): **on the ~** à l'affiche ▶ VT (item) facturer;

(customer) remettre la facture à; **may I have the ~ please?** (est-ce que je peux avoir) l'addition, s'il vous plaît?; **put it on my ~** mettez-le sur mon compte; **"post no bills"** "défense d'afficher"; **to fit** or **fill the ~** *(fig)* faire l'affaire; **~ of exchange** lettre *f* de change; **~ of lading** connaissement *m*; **~ of sale** contrat *m* de vente

billboard ['bɪlbɔːd] N *(US)* panneau *m* d'affichage

billet ['bɪlɪt] N cantonnement *m* (chez l'habitant) ▶ VT *(troops)* cantonner

billfold ['bɪlfəuld] N *(US)* portefeuille *m*

billiards ['bɪljədz] N (jeu *m* de) billard *m*

billion ['bɪljən] N *(BRIT)* billion *m* *(million de millions)*; *(US)* milliard *m*

billow ['bɪləu] N nuage *m* ▶ VI *(smoke)* s'élever en nuage; *(sail)* se gonfler

billy goat ['bɪlɪgəut] N bouc *m*

bimbo ['bɪmbəu] N *(inf)* ravissante idiote *f*

bin [bɪn] N boîte *f*; *(BRIT: also:* **dustbin, litter bin)** poubelle *f*; *(for coal)* coffre *m*

binary ['baɪnərɪ] ADJ binaire

bind [baɪnd] *(pt, pp* **bound** [baund]*)* VT attacher; *(book)* relier; *(oblige)* obliger, contraindre ▶ N *(inf: nuisance)* scie *f*
▶ **bind over** VT *(Law)* mettre en liberté conditionnelle
▶ **bind up** VT *(wound)* panser; **to be bound up in** *(work, research etc)* être complètement absorbé par, être accroché par; **to be bound up with** *(person)* être accroché à

binder ['baɪndər] N *(file)* classeur *m*

binding ['baɪndɪŋ] N *(of book)* reliure *f* ▶ ADJ *(contract)* qui constitue une obligation

binge [bɪndʒ] N *(inf)*: **to go on a ~** faire la bringue

bingo ['bɪŋgəu] N sorte de jeu de loto pratiqué dans des établissements publics

bin liner N sac *m* poubelle

binoculars [bɪˈnɔkjuləz] NPL jumelles *fpl*

biochemistry [baɪəˈkemɪstrɪ] N biochimie *f*

biodegradable ['baɪəudɪˈɡreɪdəbl] ADJ biodégradable

biodiesel ['baɪəudiːzl] N biodiesel *m*; biogazole *m*

biodiversity ['baɪəudaɪˈvɜːsɪtɪ] N biodiversité *f*

biofuel ['baɪəufjuəl] N biocarburant *m*

biographer [baɪˈɔɡrəfər] N biographe *mf*

biographic [baɪəˈɡræfɪk], **biographical** [baɪəˈɡræfɪkl] ADJ biographique

biography [baɪˈɔɡrəfɪ] N biographie *f*

biological [baɪəˈlɔdʒɪkl] ADJ biologique

biological clock N horloge *f* physiologique

biologist [baɪˈɔlədʒɪst] N biologiste *mf*

biology [baɪˈɔlədʒɪ] N biologie *f*

biometric [baɪəˈmetrɪk] ADJ biométrique

biophysics ['baɪəuˈfɪzɪks] N biophysique *f*

biopic ['baɪəupɪk] N film *m* biographique

biopsy ['baɪɔpsɪ] N biopsie *f*

biosphere ['baɪəsfɪər] N biosphère *f*

biotechnology ['baɪəutekˈnɔlədʒɪ] N biotechnologie *f*

birch [bəːtʃ] N bouleau *m*

bird [bəːd] N oiseau *m*; *(BRIT inf: girl)* nana *f*

bird flu N grippe *f* aviaire

bird of prey N oiseau *m* de proie

bird's-eye view ['bəːdzaɪ-] N vue *f* à vol d'oiseau; *(fig)* vue d'ensemble or générale

bird watcher [-wɔtʃər] N ornithologue *mf* amateur

birdwatching ['bəːdwɔtʃɪŋ] N ornithologie *f* *(d'amateur)*

Biro® ['baɪərəu] N stylo *m* à bille

birth [bəːθ] N naissance *f*; **to give ~ to** donner naissance à, mettre au monde; *(animal)* mettre bas

birth certificate N acte *m* de naissance

birth control N *(policy)* limitation *f* des naissances; *(methods)* méthode(s) contraceptive(s)

birthday ['bəːθdeɪ] N anniversaire *m* ▶ CPD *(cake, card etc)* d'anniversaire

birthmark ['bəːθmaːk] N envie *f*, tache *f* de vin

birthplace ['bəːθpleɪs] N lieu *m* de naissance

birth rate N (taux *m* de) natalité *f*

Biscay ['bɪskeɪ] N: **the Bay of ~** le golfe de Gascogne

biscuit ['bɪskɪt] N *(BRIT)* biscuit *m*; *(US)* petit pain au lait

bisect [baɪˈsekt] VT couper or diviser en deux

bisexual ['baɪˈseksjuəl] ADJ, N bisexuel(le)

bishop ['bɪʃəp] N évêque *m*; *(Chess)* fou *m*

bistro ['biːstrəu] N petit restaurant *m*, bistrot *m*

bit [bɪt] PT *of* **bite** ▶ N morceau *m*; *(Comput)* bit *m*, élément *m* binaire; *(of tool)* mèche *f*; *(of horse)* mors *m*; **a ~ of** un peu de; **a ~ mad/dangerous** un peu fou/risqué; **~ by ~** petit à petit; **to come to bits** *(break)* tomber en morceaux, se déglinguer; **bring all your bits and pieces** apporte toutes tes affaires; **to do one's ~** y mettre du sien

bitch [bɪtʃ] N *(dog)* chienne *f*; *(offensive)* salope *f* *(!)*, garce *f*

bite [baɪt] *(pt* **bit** [bɪt]*, pp* **bitten** ['bɪtn]*)* VT, VI mordre; *(insect)* piquer ▶ N morsure *f*; *(insect bite)* piqûre *f*; *(mouthful)* bouchée *f*; **let's have a ~ (to eat)** mangeons un morceau; **to ~ one's nails** se ronger les ongles

biting ['baɪtɪŋ] ADJ mordant(e)

bit part N *(Theat)* petit rôle

bitten ['bɪtn] PP *of* **bite**

bitter ['bɪtər] ADJ amer(-ère); *(criticism)* cinglant(e); *(icy: weather, wind)* glacial(e) ▶ N *(BRIT: beer)* bière *f* (à forte teneur en houblon); **to the ~ end** jusqu'au bout

bitterly ['bɪtəlɪ] ADV *(complain, weep)* amèrement; *(oppose, criticise)* durement, âprement; *(jealous, disappointed)* horriblement; **it's ~ cold** il fait un froid de loup

bitterness ['bɪtənɪs] N amertume *f*; goût amer

bittersweet ['bɪtəswiːt] ADJ aigre-doux (douce)

bitty ['bɪtɪ] ADJ *(BRIT inf)* décousu(e)

bitumen ['bɪtjumɪn] N bitume *m*

bivouac ['bɪvuæk] N bivouac *m*

bizarre [bɪˈzaːr] ADJ bizarre

bk ABBR = **bank; book**

BL N ABBR (= *Bachelor of Law(s), Bachelor of Letters)*

diplôme universitaire; (US: = Bachelor of Literature) diplôme universitaire

bl ABBR = **bill of lading**

blab [blæb] VI jaser, trop parler ▶ VT (also: **blab out**) laisser échapper, aller raconter

black [blæk] ADJ noir(e) ▶ N (colour) noir m ▶ VT (shoes) cirer; (BRIT Industry) boycotter; **to give sb a ~ eye** pocher l'œil à qn, faire un œil au beurre noir à qn; **there it is in ~ and white** (fig) c'est écrit noir sur blanc; **to be in the ~** (in credit) avoir un compte créditeur; **~ and blue** (bruised) couvert(e) de bleus
  ▶ **black out** VI (faint) s'évanouir

black belt N (Judo etc) ceinture noire; **he's a ~** il est ceinture noire

blackberry ['blækbərɪ] N mûre f

blackbird ['blækbəːd] N merle m

blackboard ['blækbɔːd] N tableau noir

black box N (Aviat) boîte noire

black coffee N café noir

Black Country N (BRIT): **the ~** le Pays Noir (dans les Midlands)

blackcurrant ['blæk'kʌrənt] N cassis m

black economy N (BRIT) travail m au noir

blacken ['blækn] VT noircir

Black Forest N: **the ~** la Forêt Noire

blackhead ['blækhɛd] N point noir

black hole N (Astronomy) trou noir

black ice N verglas m

blackjack ['blækdʒæk] N (Cards) vingt-et-un m; (US: truncheon) matraque f

blackleg ['blækleg] N (BRIT) briseur m de grève, jaune m

blacklist ['blæklɪst] N liste noire ▶ VT mettre sur la liste noire

blackmail ['blækmeɪl] N chantage m ▶ VT faire chanter, soumettre au chantage

blackmailer ['blækmeɪlər] N maître-chanteur m

black market N marché noir

blackout ['blækaut] N panne f d'électricité; (in wartime) black-out m; (TV) interruption f d'émission; (fainting) syncope f

black pepper N poivre noir

black pudding N boudin (noir)

Black Sea N: **the ~** la mer Noire

black sheep N brebis galeuse

blacksmith ['blæksmɪθ] N forgeron m

black spot N (Aut) point noir

bladder ['blædər] N vessie f

blade [bleɪd] N lame f; (of oar) plat m; (of propeller) pale f; **a ~ of grass** un brin d'herbe

blame [bleɪm] N faute f, blâme m ▶ VT: **to ~ sb/sth for sth** attribuer à qn/qch la responsabilité de qch; reprocher qch à qn/qch; **who's to ~?** qui est le fautif or coupable or responsable?; **I'm not to ~** ce n'est pas ma faute

blameless ['bleɪmlɪs] ADJ irréprochable

blanch [blɑːntʃ] VI (person, face) blêmir ▶ VT (Culin) blanchir

bland [blænd] ADJ affable; (taste, food) doux (douce), fade

blank [blæŋk] ADJ blanc (blanche); (look) sans expression, dénué(e) d'expression ▶ N espace m vide, blanc m; (cartridge) cartouche f à blanc; **his mind was a ~** il avait la tête vide; **we drew a ~** (fig) nous n'avons abouti à rien

blank cheque, (US) **blank check** N chèque m en blanc; **to give sb a ~ to do …** (fig) donner carte blanche à qn pour faire …

blanket ['blæŋkɪt] N couverture f; (of snow, cloud) couche f ▶ ADJ (statement, agreement) global(e), de portée générale; **to give ~ cover** (insurance policy) couvrir tous les risques

blare [blɛər] VI (brass band, horns, radio) beugler

blasé ['blɑːzeɪ] ADJ blasé(e)

blasphemous ['blæsfɪməs] ADJ (words) blasphématoire; (person) blasphémateur(-trice)

blasphemy ['blæsfɪmɪ] N blasphème m

blast [blɑːst] N explosion f; (shock wave) souffle m; (of air, steam) bouffée f ▶ VT faire sauter or exploser ▶ EXCL (BRIT inf) zut!; **(at) full ~** (play music etc) à plein volume
  ▶ **blast off** VI (Space) décoller

blast-off ['blɑːstɔf] N (Space) lancement m

blatant ['bleɪtənt] ADJ flagrant(e), criant(e)

blatantly ['bleɪtəntlɪ] ADV (lie) ouvertement; **it's ~ obvious** c'est l'évidence même

blaze [bleɪz] N (fire) incendie m; (flames: of fire, sun etc) embrasement m; (: in hearth) flamme f, flambée f; (fig) flamboiement m ▶ VI (fire) flamber; (fig) flamboyer, resplendir ▶ VT: **to ~ a trail** (fig) montrer la voie; **in a ~ of publicity** à grand renfort de publicité

blazer ['bleɪzər] N blazer m

bleach [bliːtʃ] N (also: **household bleach**) eau f de Javel ▶ VT (linen) blanchir

bleached [bliːtʃt] ADJ (hair) oxygéné(e), décoloré(e)

bleachers ['bliːtʃəz] NPL (US Sport) gradins mpl (en plein soleil)

bleak [bliːk] ADJ morne, désolé(e); (weather) triste, maussade; (smile) lugubre; (prospect, future) morose

bleary-eyed ['blɪərɪ'aɪd] ADJ aux yeux pleins de sommeil

bleat [bliːt] N bêlement m ▶ VI bêler

bled [blɛd] PT, PP of **bleed**

bleed [bliːd] (pt, pp **bled** [blɛd]) VT saigner; (brakes, radiator) purger ▶ VI saigner; **my nose is bleeding** je saigne du nez

bleep [bliːp] N (Radio, TV) top m; (of pocket device) bip m ▶ VI émettre des signaux ▶ VT (doctor etc) appeler (au moyen d'un bip)

bleeper ['bliːpər] N (of doctor etc) bip m

blemish ['blɛmɪʃ] N défaut m; (on reputation) tache f

blend [blɛnd] N mélange m ▶ VT mélanger ▶ VI (colours etc: also: **blend in**) se mélanger, se fondre, s'allier

blender ['blɛndər] N (Culin) mixeur m

bless [blɛs] (pt, pp **blessed** or **blest** [blɛst]) VT bénir; **to be blessed with** avoir le bonheur de jouir de or d'avoir; **~ you!** (after sneeze) à tes souhaits!

blessed ['blɛsɪd] ADJ (Rel: holy) béni(e); (: happy) bienheureux(-euse); **it rains every ~ day** il ne

se passe pas de jour sans qu'il ne pleuve
blessing ['blɛsɪŋ] N bénédiction f; (godsend)
bienfait m; **to count one's blessings** s'estimer
heureux; **it was a ~ in disguise** c'est un bien
pour un mal
blew [blu:] PT of **blow**
blight [blaɪt] N (of plants) rouille f ▶ VT (hopes etc)
anéantir, briser
blimey ['blaɪmɪ] EXCL (BRIT inf) mince alors!
blind [blaɪnd] ADJ aveugle ▶ N (for window) store
m ▶ VT aveugler; **to turn a ~ eye (on or to)**
fermer les yeux (sur); **blind ~ les** aveugles mpl
blind alley N impasse f
blind corner N (BRIT) virage m sans visibilité
blind date N rendez-vous galant (avec un(e)
inconnu(e))
blindfold ['blaɪndfəʊld] N bandeau m ▶ ADJ, ADV
les yeux bandés ▶ VT bander les yeux à
blindly ['blaɪndlɪ] ADV aveuglément
blindness ['blaɪndnɪs] N cécité f; (fig)
aveuglement m
blind spot N (Aut etc) angle m aveugle; (fig) angle
mort
blink [blɪŋk] VI cligner des yeux; (light) clignoter
▶ N: **the TV's on the ~** (inf) la télé ne va pas
tarder à nous lâcher
blinkers ['blɪŋkəz] NPL œillères fpl
blinking ['blɪŋkɪŋ] ADJ (BRIT inf): **this ~ ...** ce
fichu or sacré ...
blip [blɪp] N (on radar etc) spot m; (on graph) petite
aberration; (fig) petite anomalie (passagère)
bliss [blɪs] N félicité f, bonheur m sans mélange
blissful ['blɪsful] ADJ (event, day)
merveilleux(-euse); (smile) de bonheur; **a ~ sigh**
un soupir d'aise; **in ~ ignorance** dans une
ignorance béate
blissfully ['blɪsfulɪ] ADV (smile) béatement;
(happy) merveilleusement
blister ['blɪstə'] N (on skin) ampoule f, cloque f;
(on paintwork) boursouflure f ▶ VI (paint) se
boursoufler, se cloquer
BLit, BLitt N ABBR (= Bachelor of Literature) diplôme
universitaire
blithely ['blaɪðlɪ] ADV (unconcernedly)
tranquillement; (joyfully) gaiement
blithering ['blɪðərɪŋ] ADJ (inf): **this ~ idiot** cet
espèce d'idiot
blitz [blɪts] N bombardement (aérien); **to have
a ~ on sth** (fig) s'attaquer à qch
blizzard ['blɪzəd] N blizzard m, tempête f de
neige
BLM N ABBR (US: = Bureau of Land Management) ≈ les
domaines
bloated ['bləʊtɪd] ADJ (face) bouffi(e); (stomach,
person) gonflé(e)
blob [blɔb] N (drop) goutte f; (stain, spot) tache f
bloc [blɔk] N (Pol) bloc m
block [blɔk] N bloc m; (in pipes) obstruction f;
(toy) cube m; (of buildings) pâté m (de maisons)
▶ VT bloquer; (fig) faire obstacle à; (Comput)
grouper; **the sink is blocked** l'évier est
bouché; **~ of flats** (BRIT) immeuble (locatif); **3
blocks from here** à trois rues d'ici; **mental ~**
blocage m; **~ and tackle** (Tech) palan m

▶ **block up** VT boucher
blockade [blɔ'keɪd] N blocus m ▶ VT faire le
blocus de
blockage ['blɔkɪdʒ] N obstruction f
block booking N réservation f en bloc
blockbuster ['blɔkbʌstə'] N (film, book) grand
succès
block capitals NPL majuscules fpl d'imprimerie
blockhead ['blɔkhɛd] N imbécile mf
block letters NPL majuscules fpl
block release N (BRIT) congé m de formation
block vote N (BRIT) vote m de délégation
blog [blɔg] N blog m, blogue m ▶ VI bloguer
blogger ['blɔgə'] N blogueur(-euse)
blogging ['blɔgɪŋ] N blogging m
blogosphere ['blɔgəsfɪə'] N blogosphère f
bloke [bləʊk] N (BRIT inf) type m
blond, blonde [blɔnd] ADJ, N blond(e)
blood [blʌd] N sang m
blood bank N banque f du sang
blood count N numération f globulaire
bloodcurdling ['blʌdkə:dlɪŋ] ADJ à vous glacer
le sang
blood donor N donneur(-euse) de sang
blood group N groupe sanguin
bloodhound ['blʌdhaund] N limier m
bloodless ['blʌdlɪs] ADJ (victory) sans effusion de
sang; (pale) anémié(e)
bloodletting ['blʌdlɛtɪŋ] N (Med) saignée f; (fig)
effusion f de sang, représailles fpl
blood poisoning N empoisonnement m du
sang
blood pressure N tension (artérielle);
to have high/low ~ faire de l'hypertension/
l'hypotension
bloodshed ['blʌdʃɛd] N effusion f de sang,
carnage m
bloodshot ['blʌdʃɔt] ADJ: **~ eyes** yeux injectés de
sang
blood sports NPL sports mpl sanguinaires
bloodstained ['blʌdsteɪnd] ADJ taché(e) de sang
bloodstream ['blʌdstri:m] N sang m, système
sanguin
blood test N analyse f de sang
bloodthirsty ['blʌdθə:stɪ] ADJ sanguinaire
blood transfusion N transfusion f de sang
blood type N groupe sanguin
blood vessel N vaisseau sanguin
bloody ['blʌdɪ] ADJ sanglant(e); (BRIT inf!): **this ~
... ce foutu ...,** ce putain de ... (!) ▶ ADV:
~ strong/good (BRIT inf!) vachement or
sacrément fort/bon
bloody-minded ['blʌdɪ'maɪndɪd] ADJ (BRIT inf)
contrariant(e), obstiné(e)
bloom [blu:m] N fleur f; (fig) épanouissement m
▶ VI être en fleur; (fig) s'épanouir; être
florissant(e)
blooming ['blu:mɪŋ] ADJ (inf): **this ~ ...** ce fichu
or sacré ...
blossom ['blɔsəm] N fleur(s) f(pl) ▶ VI être en
fleurs; (fig) s'épanouir; **to ~ into** (fig) devenir
blot [blɔt] N tache f ▶ VT tacher; (ink) sécher; **to
be a ~ on the landscape** gâcher le paysage; **to
~ one's copy book** (fig) faire un impair

▶ **blot out** vt (*memories*) effacer; (*view*) cacher, masquer; (*nation, city*) annihiler

blotchy ['blɒtʃɪ] ADJ (*complexion*) couvert(e) de marbrures

blotting paper ['blɒtɪŋ-] N buvard *m*

blotto ['blɒtəu] ADJ (*inf*) bourré(e)

blouse [blauz] N (*feminine garment*) chemisier *m*, corsage *m*

blow [bləu] (*pt* **blew** [blu:], *pp* **blown** [bləun]) N coup *m* ▶ vi souffler ▶ vt (*glass*) souffler; (*instrument*) jouer de; (*fuse*) faire sauter; **to ~ one's nose** se moucher; **to ~ a whistle** siffler; **to come to blows** en venir aux coups

▶ **blow away** vi s'envoler ▶ vt chasser, faire s'envoler

▶ **blow down** vt faire tomber, renverser

▶ **blow off** vi s'envoler ▶ vt (*hat*) emporter; (*ship*): **to ~ off course** faire dévier

▶ **blow out** vi (*fire, flame*) s'éteindre; (*tyre*) éclater; (*fuse*) sauter

▶ **blow over** vi s'apaiser

▶ **blow up** vi exploser, sauter ▶ vt faire sauter; (*tyre*) gonfler; (*Phot*) agrandir

blow-dry ['bləudraɪ] N (*hairstyle*) brushing *m* ▶ vt faire un brushing à

blowlamp ['bləulæmp] N (*Brit*) chalumeau *m*

blown [bləun] PP of **blow**

blow-out ['bləuaut] N (*of tyre*) éclatement *m*; (*Brit inf: big meal*) gueuleton *m*

blowtorch ['bləutɔ:tʃ] N chalumeau *m*

blowzy ['blauzɪ] ADJ (*Brit*) peu soigné(e)

BLS N ABBR (*US*) = **Bureau of Labor Statistics**

blubber ['blʌbəʳ] N blanc *m* de baleine ▶ vi (*pej*) pleurer comme un veau

bludgeon ['blʌdʒən] N gourdin *m*, trique *f*

blue [blu:] ADJ bleu(e); (*depressed*) triste; **~ film/joke** film *m*/histoire *f* pornographique; (**only**) **once in a ~ moon** tous les trente-six du mois; **out of the ~** (*fig*) à l'improviste, sans qu'on s'y attende

blue baby N enfant bleu(e)

bluebell ['blu:bɛl] N jacinthe *f* des bois

blueberry ['blu:bərɪ] N myrtille *f*, airelle *f*

bluebottle ['blu:bɒtl] N mouche *f* à viande

blue cheese N (*fromage*) bleu *m*

blue-chip ['blu:tʃɪp] ADJ: **~ investment** investissement *m* de premier ordre

blue-collar worker ['blu:kɒləʳ-] N ouvrier(-ère) col bleu

blue jeans NPL blue-jeans *mpl*

blueprint ['blu:prɪnt] N bleu *m*; (*fig*) projet *m*, plan directeur

blues [blu:z] NPL: **the ~** (*Mus*) le blues; **to have the ~** (*inf: feeling*) avoir le cafard

bluff [blʌf] vi bluffer ▶ N bluff *m*; (*cliff*) promontoire *m*, falaise *f* ▶ ADJ (*person*) bourru(e), brusque; **to call sb's ~** mettre qn au défi d'exécuter ses menaces

blunder ['blʌndəʳ] N gaffe *f*, bévue *f* ▶ vi faire une gaffe or une bévue; **to ~ into sb/sth** buter contre qn/qch

blunt [blʌnt] ADJ (*knife*) émoussé(e), peu tranchant(e); (*pencil*) mal taillé(e); (*person*) brusque, ne mâchant pas ses mots ▶ vt

émousser; **~ instrument** (*Law*) instrument contondant

bluntly ['blʌntlɪ] ADV carrément, sans prendre de gants

bluntness ['blʌntnɪs] N (*of person*) brusquerie *f*, franchise brutale

blur [bləːʳ] N (*shape*): **to become a ~** devenir flou ▶ vt brouiller, rendre flou(e)

blurb [bləːb] N (*for book*) texte *m* de présentation; (*pej*) baratin *m*

blurred [bləːd] ADJ flou(e)

blurt [bləːt]: **to ~ out** vt (*reveal*) lâcher; (*say*) balbutier, dire d'une voix entrecoupée

blush [blʌʃ] vi rougir ▶ N rougeur *f*

blusher ['blʌʃəʳ] N rouge *m* à joues

bluster ['blʌstəʳ] N paroles *fpl* en l'air; (*boasting*) fanfaronnades *fpl*; (*threats*) menaces *fpl* en l'air ▶ vi parler en l'air; fanfaronner

blustering ['blʌstərɪŋ] ADJ fanfaron(ne)

blustery ['blʌstərɪ] ADJ (*weather*) à bourrasques

Blvd ABBR (= *boulevard*) Bd

BM N ABBR = **British Museum**; (*Scol*: = *Bachelor of Medicine*) diplôme universitaire

BMA N ABBR = **British Medical Association**

BMJ N ABBR = **British Medical Journal**

BMus N ABBR (= *Bachelor of Music*) diplôme universitaire

BMX N ABBR (= *bicycle motorcross*) BMX *m*

BO N ABBR (*inf*: = *body odour*) odeurs corporelles; (*US*) = **box office**

boar [bɔːʳ] N sanglier *m*

board [bɔːd] N (*wooden*) planche *f*; (*on wall*) panneau *m*; (*for chess etc*) plateau *m*; (*cardboard*) carton *m*; (*committee*) conseil *m*, comité *m*; (*in firm*) conseil d'administration; (*Naut, Aviat*): **on ~** à bord ▶ vt (*ship*) monter à bord de; (*train*) monter dans; **full ~** (*Brit*) pension complète; **half ~** (*Brit*) demi-pension *f*; **~ and lodging** *n* chambre *f* avec pension; **with ~ and lodging** logé nourri; **above ~** (*fig*) régulier(-ère); **across the ~** (*fig: adv*) systématiquement (: *adj*) de portée générale; **to go by the ~** (*hopes, principles*) être abandonné(e); (*be unimportant*) compter pour rien, n'avoir aucune importance

▶ **board up** vt (*door*) condamner (*au moyen de planches, de tôle*)

boarder ['bɔːdəʳ] N pensionnaire *mf*; (*Scol*) interne *mf*, pensionnaire

board game N jeu *m* de société

boarding card ['bɔːdɪŋ-] N (*Aviat, Naut*) carte *f* d'embarquement

boarding house ['bɔːdɪŋ-] N pension *f*

boarding party ['bɔːdɪŋ-] N section *f* d'abordage

boarding pass ['bɔːdɪŋ-] N (*Brit*) = **boarding card**

boarding school ['bɔːdɪŋ-] N internat *m*, pensionnat *m*

board meeting N réunion *f* du conseil d'administration

board room N salle *f* du conseil d'administration

boardwalk ['bɔːdwɔːk] N (*US*) cheminement *m* en planches

boast [bəʊst] vi: **to ~ (about** or **of)** se vanter (de) ▸ vt s'enorgueillir de ▸ n vantardise f; sujet m d'orgueil or de fierté

boastful ['bəʊstful] adj vantard(e)

boastfulness ['bəʊstfulnıs] n vantardise f

boat [bəʊt] n bateau m; (small) canot m; barque f; **to go by ~** aller en bateau; **to be in the same ~** (fig) être logé à la même enseigne

boater ['bəʊtəʳ] n (hat) canotier m

boating ['bəʊtɪŋ] n canotage m

boat people npl boat people mpl

boatswain ['bəʊsn] n maître m d'équipage

bob [bɒb] vi (boat, cork on water: also: **bob up and down**) danser, se balancer ▸ n (Brit inf) = **shilling**
▸ **bob up** vi surgir or apparaître brusquement

bobbin ['bɒbɪn] n bobine f; (of sewing machine) navette f

bobby ['bɒbɪ] n (Brit inf) ≈ agent m (de police)

bobby pin ['bɒbɪ-] n (US) pince f à cheveux

bobsleigh ['bɒbsleɪ] n bob m

bode [bəʊd] vi: **to ~ well/ill (for)** être de bon/ mauvais augure (pour)

bodice ['bɒdɪs] n corsage m

bodily ['bɒdɪlɪ] adj corporel(le); (pain, comfort) physique; (needs) matériel(le) ▸ adv (carry, lift) dans ses bras

body ['bɒdɪ] n corps m; (of car) carrosserie f; (of plane) fuselage m; (fig: society) organe m, organisme m; (: quantity) ensemble m, masse f; (of wine) corps m; (also: **body stocking**) body m, justaucorps m; **ruling ~** organe directeur; **in a ~** en masse, ensemble; (speak) comme un seul et même homme

body blow n (fig) coup dur, choc m

body-building ['bɒdɪbɪldɪŋ] n body-building m, culturisme m

bodyguard ['bɒdɪgɑːd] n garde m du corps

body language n langage m du corps

body repairs npl travaux mpl de carrosserie

body search n fouille f (corporelle); **to carry out a ~ on sb** fouiller qn; **to submit to** or **undergo a ~** se faire fouiller

bodywork ['bɒdɪwɜːk] n carrosserie f

boffin ['bɒfɪn] n (Brit) savant m

bog [bɒg] n tourbière f ▸ vt: **to get bogged down (in)** (fig) s'enliser (dans)

boggle ['bɒgl] vi: **the mind boggles** c'est incroyable, on en reste sidéré

bogie ['bəʊgɪ] n bogie m

Bogotá [bəʊgə'tɑː] n Bogotá

bogus ['bəʊgəs] adj bidon inv; fantôme

Bohemia [bəʊ'hiːmɪə] n Bohême f

Bohemian [bəʊ'hiːmɪən] adj bohémien(ne) ▸ n Bohémien(ne); (gipsy: also: **bohemian**) bohémien(ne)

boil [bɔɪl] vt (faire) bouillir ▸ vi bouillir ▸ n (Med) furoncle m; **to come to the** or (US) **a ~** bouillir; **to bring to the** or (US) **a ~** porter à ébullition
▸ **boil down** vi (fig): **to ~ down to** se réduire or ramener à
▸ **boil over** vi déborder

boiled egg n œuf m à la coque

boiler ['bɔɪləʳ] n chaudière f

boiler suit n (Brit) bleu m de travail, combinaison f

boiling ['bɔɪlɪŋ] adj: **I'm ~ (hot)** (inf) je crève de chaud

boiling point n point m d'ébullition

boil-in-the-bag [bɔɪlɪnðə'bæg] adj (rice etc) en sachet cuisson

boisterous ['bɔɪstərəs] adj bruyant(e), tapageur(-euse)

bold [bəʊld] adj hardi(e), audacieux(-euse); (pej) effronté(e); (outline, colour) franc (franche), tranché(e), marqué(e)

boldness ['bəʊldnɪs] n hardiesse f, audace f; aplomb m, effronterie f

bold type n (Typ) caractères mpl gras

Bolivia [bə'lɪvɪə] n Bolivie f

Bolivian [bə'lɪvɪən] adj bolivien(ne) ▸ n Bolivien(ne)

bollard ['bɒləd] n (Naut) bitte f d'amarrage; (Brit Aut) borne lumineuse or de signalisation

Bollywood ['bɒlɪwud] n Bollywood m

bolshy ['bɒlʃɪ] adj râleur(-euse); **to be in a ~ mood** être peu coopératif(-ive)

bolster ['bəʊlstəʳ] n traversin m
▸ **bolster up** vt soutenir

bolt [bəʊlt] n verrou m; (with nut) boulon m ▸ adv: **~ upright** droit(e) comme un piquet ▸ vt (door) verrouiller; (food) engloutir ▸ vi se sauver, filer (comme une flèche); (horse) s'emballer; **a ~ from the blue** (fig) un coup de tonnerre dans un ciel bleu

bomb [bɒm] n bombe f ▸ vt bombarder

bombard [bɒm'bɑːd] vt bombarder

bombardment [bɒm'bɑːdmənt] n bombardement m

bombastic [bɒm'bæstɪk] adj grandiloquent(e), pompeux(-euse)

bomb disposal n: **~ unit** section f de déminage; **~ expert** artificier m

bomber ['bɒməʳ] n caporal m d'artillerie; (Aviat) bombardier m; (terrorist) poseur m de bombes

bombing ['bɒmɪŋ] n bombardement m

bomb scare n alerte f à la bombe

bombshell ['bɒmʃel] n obus m; (fig) bombe f

bomb site n zone f de bombardement

bona fide ['bəʊnə'faɪdɪ] adj de bonne foi; (offer) sérieux(-euse)

bonanza [bə'nænzə] n filon m

bond [bɒnd] n lien m; (binding promise) engagement m, obligation f; (Finance) obligation f; **bonds** npl (chains) chaînes fpl; **in ~** (of goods) en entrepôt

bondage ['bɒndɪdʒ] n esclavage m

bonded warehouse ['bɒndɪd-] n entrepôt m sous douanes

bone [bəʊn] n os m; (of fish) arête f ▸ vt désosser; ôter les arêtes de

bone china n porcelaine f tendre

bone-dry ['bəʊn'draɪ] adj absolument sec (sèche)

bone idle adj fainéant(e)

bone marrow n moelle osseuse

boner ['bəʊnəʳ] n (US) gaffe f, bourde f

bonfire ['bɒnfaɪə^r] N feu m (de joie); (for rubbish) feu

bonk [bɒŋk] (inf!) VT s'envoyer (!), sauter (!) ▶ VI s'envoyer en l'air (!)

bonkers ['bɒŋkəz] ADJ (BRITinf) cinglé(e), dingue

Bonn [bɒn] N Bonn

bonnet ['bɒnɪt] N bonnet m; (BRIT: of car) capot m

bonny [bɒnɪ] ADJ (SCOTTISH) joli(e)

bonus ['bəunəs] N (money) prime f; (advantage) avantage m

bony ['bəunɪ] ADJ (arm, face: Med: tissue) osseux(-euse); (thin: person) squelettique; (: meat) plein(e) d'os; (: fish) plein d'arêtes

boo [bu:] EXCL hou!, peuh! ▶ VT huer ▶ N huée f

boob [bu:b] N (inf: breast) nichon m; (: BRIT: mistake) gaffe f

booby prize ['bu:bɪ-] N timbale f (ironic)

booby trap ['bu:bɪ-] N guet-apens m

booby-trapped ['bu:bɪtræpt] ADJ piégé(e)

book [buk] N livre m; (of stamps, tickets etc) carnet m ▶ VT (ticket) prendre; (seat, room) réserver; (football player) prendre le nom de, donner un carton à; (driver) dresser un procès-verbal à; **books** NPL (Comm) comptes mpl, comptabilité f; **I booked a table in the name of ...** j'ai réservé une table au nom de ...; **to keep the books** tenir la comptabilité; **by the ~** à la lettre, selon les règles; **to throw the ~ at sb** passer un savon à qn
  ▶ **book in** VI (BRIT: at hotel) prendre sa chambre
  ▶ **book up** VT réserver; **all seats are booked up** tout est pris, c'est complet; **the hotel is booked up** l'hôtel est complet

bookable ['bukəbl] ADJ: **seats are ~** on peut réserver ses places

bookcase ['bukkeɪs] N bibliothèque f (meuble)

book ends NPL serre-livres m inv

booking ['bukɪŋ] N (BRIT) réservation f; **I confirmed my ~ by fax/email** j'ai confirmé ma réservation par fax/e-mail

booking office N (BRIT) bureau m de location

book-keeping ['buk'ki:pɪŋ] N comptabilité f

booklet ['buklɪt] N brochure f

bookmaker ['bukmeɪkə^r] N bookmaker m

bookmark ['bukmɑ:k] N (for book) marque-page m; (Comput) signet m

bookseller ['bukselə^r] N libraire mf

bookshelf ['bukʃelf] N (single) étagère f (à livres); (bookcase) bibliothèque f; **bookshelves** rayons mpl (de bibliothèque)

bookshop ['bukʃɒp], **bookstore** ['bukstɔ:^r] N librairie f

bookstall ['bukstɔ:l] N kiosque m à journaux

book store N = **bookshop**

book token N bon-cadeau m (pour un livre)

book value N valeur f comptable

bookworm ['bukwə:m] N dévoreur(-euse) de livres

boom [bu:m] N (noise) grondement m; (in prices, population) forte augmentation; (busy period) boom m, vague f de prospérité ▶ VI gronder; prospérer

boomerang ['bu:məræŋ] N boomerang m

boom town N ville f en plein essor

boon [bu:n] N bénédiction f, grand avantage

boorish ['buərɪʃ] ADJ grossier(-ère), rustre

boost [bu:st] N stimulant m, remontant m ▶ VT stimuler; **to give a ~ to sb's spirits** or **to sb** remonter le moral à qn

booster ['bu:stə^r] N (TV) amplificateur m (de signal); (Elec) survolteur m; (also: **booster rocket**) booster m; (: Med: vaccine) rappel m

booster seat N (Aut: for children) siège m rehausseur

boot [bu:t] N botte f; (for hiking) chaussure f (de marche); (ankle boot) bottine f; (BRIT: of car) coffre m ▶ VT (Comput) lancer, mettre en route; **to ~** (in addition) par-dessus le marché, en plus; **to give sb the ~** (inf) flanquer qn dehors, virer qn

booth [bu:ð] N (at fair) baraque (foraine); (of telephone etc) cabine f; (also: **voting booth**) isoloir m

bootleg ['bu:tleg] ADJ de contrebande; **~ record** enregistrement m pirate

booty ['bu:tɪ] N butin m

booze [bu:z] (inf) N boissons fpl alcooliques, alcool m ▶ VI boire, picoler

boozer ['bu:zə^r] N (inf: person): **he's a ~** il picole pas mal; (: BRIT: pub) pub m

border ['bɔ:də^r] N bordure f; bord m; (of a country) frontière f; **the Borders** la région frontière entre l'Écosse et l'Angleterre
  ▶ **border on** VT FUS être voisin(e) de, toucher à

borderline ['bɔ:dəlaɪn] N (fig) ligne f de démarcation ▶ ADJ: **~ case** cas m limite

bore [bɔ:^r] PT of **bear** ▶ VT (person) ennuyer, raser; (hole) percer; (well, tunnel) creuser ▶ N (person) raseur(-euse); (boring thing) barbe f; (of gun) calibre m

bored ['bɔ:d] ADJ: **to be ~** s'ennuyer; **he's ~ to tears** or **to death** or **stiff** il s'ennuie à mourir

boredom ['bɔ:dəm] N ennui m

boring ['bɔ:rɪŋ] ADJ ennuyeux(-euse)

born [bɔ:n] ADJ: **to be ~** naître; **I was ~ in 1960** je suis né en 1960; **~ blind** aveugle de naissance; **a ~ comedian** un comédien-né

born-again [bɔ:nə'gɛn] ADJ: **~ Christian** ≈ évangéliste mf

borne [bɔ:n] PP of **bear**

Borneo ['bɔ:nɪəu] N Bornéo f

borough ['bʌrə] N municipalité f

borrow ['bɒrəu] VT: **to ~ sth (from sb)** emprunter qch (à qn); **may I ~ your car?** est-ce que je peux vous emprunter votre voiture?

borrower ['bɒrəuə^r] N emprunteur(-euse)

borrowing ['bɒrəuɪŋ] N emprunt(s) mpl

borstal ['bɔ:stl] N (BRIT) maison f de correction

Bosnia ['bɒznɪə] N Bosnie f

Bosnia-Herzegovina, Bosnia-Hercegovina ['bɒznɪəhɛrtsə'gəuvi:nə] N Bosnie-Herzégovine f

Bosnian ['bɒznɪən] ADJ bosniaque, bosnien(ne) ▶ N Bosniaque mf, Bosnien(ne)

bosom ['buzəm] N poitrine f; (fig) sein m

bosom friend N ami(e) intime

boss [bɒs] N patron(ne) ▶ VT (also: **boss about**, **boss around**) mener à la baguette

b

bossy ['bɔsɪ] ADJ autoritaire
bosun ['bəʊsn] N maître m d'équipage
botanical [bə'tænɪkl] ADJ botanique
botanist ['bɔtənɪst] N botaniste mf
botany ['bɔtənɪ] N botanique f
botch [bɔtʃ] VT (also: **botch up**) saboter, bâcler
both [bəʊθ] ADJ les deux, l'un(e) et l'autre
▸ PRON: **~ (of them)** les deux, tous (toutes) (les) deux, l'un(e) et l'autre; **~ of us went, we ~ went** nous y sommes allés tous les deux ▸ ADV: **~ A and B** A et B; **they sell ~ the fabric and the finished curtains** ils vendent (et) le tissu et les rideaux (finis), ils vendent à la fois le tissu et les rideaux (finis)
bother ['bɔðəʳ] VT (worry) tracasser; (needle, bait) importuner, ennuyer; (disturb) déranger ▸ VI (also: **bother o.s.**) se tracasser, se faire du souci ▸ N (trouble) ennuis mpl; **it is a ~ to have to do** c'est vraiment ennuyeux d'avoir à faire ▸ EXCL zut!; **to ~ doing** prendre la peine de faire; **I'm sorry to ~ you** excusez-moi de vous déranger; **please don't ~** ne vous dérangez pas; **don't ~** ce n'est pas la peine; **it's no ~** aucun problème
Botswana [bɔt'swɑːnə] N Botswana m
bottle ['bɔtl] N bouteille f; (baby's) biberon m; (of perfume, medicine) flacon m ▸ VT mettre en bouteille(s); **~ of wine/milk** bouteille de vin/lait; **wine/milk ~** bouteille à vin/lait
▸ **bottle up** VT refouler, contenir
bottle bank N conteneur m (de bouteilles)
bottleneck ['bɔtlnɛk] N (in traffic) bouchon m; (in production) goulet m d'étranglement
bottle-opener ['bɔtləʊpnəʳ] N ouvre-bouteille m
bottom ['bɔtəm] N (of container, sea etc) fond m; (buttocks) derrière m; (of page, list) bas m; (of chair) siège m; (of mountain, tree, hill) pied m ▸ ADJ (shelf, step) du bas; **to get to the ~ of sth** (fig) découvrir le fin fond de qch
bottomless ['bɔtəmlɪs] ADJ sans fond, insondable
bottom line N: **the ~ is that …** l'essentiel, c'est que …
botulism ['bɔtjulɪzəm] N botulisme m
bough [baʊ] N branche f, rameau m
bought [bɔːt] PT, PP of **buy**
boulder ['bəʊldəʳ] N gros rocher (gén lisse, arrondi)
bounce [baʊns] VI (ball) rebondir; (cheque) être refusé (étant sans provision); (also: **to bounce forward/out** etc) bondir, s'élancer ▸ VT faire rebondir ▸ N (rebound) rebond m; **he's got plenty of ~** (fig) il est plein d'entrain or d'allant
bouncer ['baʊnsəʳ] N (inf: at dance, club) videur m
bound [baʊnd] PT, PP of **bind** ▸ N (gen pl) limite f; (leap) bond m ▸ VI (limit) borner ▸ ADJ: **to be ~ to do sth** (obliged) être obligé(e) or avoir obligation de faire qch; **he's ~ to fail** (likely) il est sûr d'échouer, son échec est inévitable or assuré; **~ by** (law, regulation) engagé(e) par; **~ for** à destination de; **out of bounds** dont l'accès est interdit
boundary ['baʊndrɪ] N frontière f
boundless ['baʊndlɪs] ADJ illimité(e), sans bornes

bountiful ['baʊntɪful] ADJ (person) généreux(-euse); (God) bienfaiteur(-trice); (supply) ample
bounty ['baʊntɪ] N (generosity) générosité f
bouquet ['bukeɪ] N bouquet m
bourbon ['buəbən] N (US: also: **bourbon whiskey**) bourbon m
bourgeois ['buəʒwɑː] ADJ, N bourgeois(e)
bout [baʊt] N période f; (of malaria etc) accès m, crise f, attaque f; (Boxing etc) combat m, match m
boutique [buːˈtiːk] N boutique f
bow¹ [bəʊ] N nœud m; (weapon) arc m; (Mus) archet m
bow² [baʊ] N (with body) révérence f, inclination f (du buste or corps); (Naut: also: **bows**) proue f ▸ VI faire une révérence, s'incliner; (yield): **to ~ to or before** s'incliner devant, se soumettre à; **to ~ to the inevitable** accepter l'inévitable or l'inéluctable
bowels [baʊəlz] NPL intestins mpl; (fig) entrailles fpl
bowl [bəʊl] N (for eating) bol m; (for washing) cuvette f; (ball) boule f; (of pipe) fourneau m ▸ VI (Cricket) lancer (la balle)
▸ **bowl over** VT (fig) renverser
bow-legged ['bəʊ'lɛɡɪd] ADJ aux jambes arquées
bowler ['bəʊləʳ] N joueur m de boules; (Cricket) lanceur m (de la balle); (Brit: also: **bowler hat**) (chapeau m) melon m
bowling ['bəʊlɪŋ] N (game) jeu m de boules, jeu de quilles
bowling alley N bowling m
bowling green N terrain m de boules (gazonné et carré)
bowls [bəʊlz] N (jeu m de) boules fpl
bow tie [bəʊ-] N nœud m papillon
box [bɔks] N boîte f; (also: **cardboard box**) carton m; (crate) caisse f; (Theat) loge f ▸ VT mettre en boîte; (Sport) boxer avec ▸ VI boxer, faire de la boxe
boxer ['bɔksəʳ] N (person) boxeur m; (dog) boxer m
boxer shorts NPL caleçon m
boxing ['bɔksɪŋ] N (sport) boxe f
Boxing Day N (Brit) le lendemain de Noël; voir article

> Boxing Day est le lendemain de Noël, férié en Grande-Bretagne. Ce nom vient d'une coutume du XIXᵉ siècle qui consistait à donner des cadeaux de Noël (dans des boîtes) à ses employés etc le 26 décembre.

boxing gloves NPL gants mpl de boxe
boxing ring N ring m
box number N (for advertisements) numéro m d'annonce
box office N bureau m de location
box room N débarras m; chambrette f
boy [bɔɪ] N garçon m
boy band N boys band m
boycott ['bɔɪkɔt] N boycottage m ▸ VT boycotter
boyfriend ['bɔɪfrɛnd] N (petit) ami
boyish ['bɔɪɪʃ] ADJ d'enfant, de garçon; **to look ~** (man: appear youthful) faire jeune
Bp ABBR = **bishop**
BR ABBR = **British Rail**

Br. ABBR (Rel) = **brother**

bra [brɑ:] N soutien-gorge m

brace [breɪs] N (support) attache f, agrafe f; (BRIT: also: **braces**: on teeth) appareil m (dentaire); (tool) vilebrequin m; (Typ: also: **brace bracket**) accolade f ▶ VT (support) consolider, soutenir; **braces** NPL (BRIT: for trousers) bretelles fpl; **to ~ o.s.** (fig) se préparer mentalement

bracelet ['breɪslɪt] N bracelet m

bracing ['breɪsɪŋ] ADJ tonifiant(e), tonique

bracken ['brækən] N fougère f

bracket ['brækɪt] N (Tech) tasseau m, support m; (group) classe f, tranche f; (also: **brace bracket**) accolade f; (also: **round bracket**) parenthèse f; (also: **square bracket**) crochet m ▶ VT mettre entre parenthèses; (fig: also: **bracket together**) regrouper; **income ~** tranche f des revenus; **in brackets** entre parenthèses or crochets

brackish ['brækɪʃ] ADJ (water) saumâtre

brag [bræg] VI se vanter

braid [breɪd] N (trimming) galon m; (of hair) tresse f, natte f

Braille [breɪl] N braille m

brain [breɪn] N cerveau m; **brains** NPL (intellect, food) cervelle f; **he's got brains** il est intelligent

brainchild ['breɪntʃaɪld] N trouvaille (personnelle), invention f

braindead ['breɪndɛd] ADJ (Med) dans un coma dépassé; (inf) demeuré(e)

brainless ['breɪnlɪs] ADJ sans cervelle, stupide

brainstorm ['breɪnstɔ:m] N (fig) moment m d'égarement; (US: **brainwave**) idée f de génie

brainwash ['breɪnwɔʃ] VT faire subir un lavage de cerveau à

brainwave ['breɪnweɪv] N idée f de génie

brainy ['breɪnɪ] ADJ intelligent(e), doué(e)

braise [breɪz] VT braiser

brake [breɪk] N frein m ▶ VT, VI freiner

brake light N feu m de stop

brake pedal N pédale f de frein

bramble ['bræmbl] N ronces fpl; (fruit) mûre f

bran [bræn] N son m

branch [brɑ:ntʃ] N branche f; (Comm) succursale f; (: of bank) agence f; (of association) section locale ▶ VI bifurquer
▶ **branch off** VI (road) bifurquer
▶ **branch out** VI diversifier ses activités; **to ~ out into** étendre ses activités à

branch line N (Rail) bifurcation f, embranchement m

branch manager N directeur(-trice) de succursale (or d'agence)

brand [brænd] N marque (commerciale) ▶ VT (cattle) marquer (au fer rouge); (fig: pej): **to ~ sb a communist** etc traiter or qualifier qn de communiste etc

brandish ['brændɪʃ] VT brandir

brand name N nom m de marque

brand-new ['brænd'nju:] ADJ tout(e) neuf (neuve), flambant neuf (neuve)

brandy ['brændɪ] N cognac m, fine f

brash [bræʃ] ADJ effronté(e)

Brasilia [brə'zɪlɪə] N Brasilia

brass [brɑ:s] N cuivre m (jaune), laiton m;

the ~ (Mus) les cuivres

brass band N fanfare f

brass tacks NPL: **to get down to ~** en venir au fait

brat [bræt] N (pej) mioche mf, môme mf

bravado [brə'vɑ:dəʊ] N bravade f

brave [breɪv] ADJ courageux(-euse), brave ▶ N guerrier indien ▶ VT braver, affronter

bravery ['breɪvərɪ] N bravoure f, courage m

brawl [brɔ:l] N rixe f, bagarre f ▶ VI se bagarrer

brawn [brɔ:n] N muscle m; (meat) fromage m de tête

brawny ['brɔ:nɪ] ADJ musclé(e), costaud(e)

bray [breɪ] N braiement m ▶ VI braire

brazen ['breɪzn] ADJ impudent(e), effronté(e) ▶ VT: **to ~ it out** payer d'effronterie, crâner

brazier ['breɪzɪər] N brasero m

Brazil [brə'zɪl] N Brésil m

Brazilian [brə'zɪljən] ADJ brésilien(ne) ▶ N Brésilien(ne)

Brazil nut N noix f du Brésil

breach [bri:tʃ] VT ouvrir une brèche dans ▶ N (gap) brèche f; (estrangement) brouille f; (breaking): **~ of contract** rupture f de contrat; **~ of the peace** attentat m à l'ordre public; **~ of trust** abus m de confiance

bread [brɛd] N pain m; (inf: money) fric m; **~ and butter** n tartines (beurrées); (fig) subsistance f; **to earn one's daily ~** gagner son pain; **to know which side one's ~ is buttered (on)** savoir où est son avantage or intérêt

breadbin ['brɛdbɪn] N (BRIT) boîte f or huche f à pain

breadboard ['brɛdbɔ:d] N planche f à pain; (Comput) montage expérimental

breadbox ['brɛdbɔks] N (US) boîte f or huche f à pain

breadcrumbs ['brɛdkrʌmz] NPL miettes fpl de pain; (Culin) chapelure f, panure f

breadline ['brɛdlaɪn] N: **to be on the ~** être sans le sou or dans l'indigence

breadth [brɛtθ] N largeur f

breadwinner ['brɛdwɪnər] N soutien m de famille

break [breɪk] (pt **broke** [brəʊk], pp **broken** ['brəʊkən]) VT casser, briser; (promise) rompre; (law) violer ▶ VI se casser, se briser; (weather) tourner; (storm) éclater; (day) se lever ▶ N (gap) brèche f; (fracture) cassure f; (rest) interruption f, arrêt m; (: short) pause f; (: at school) récréation f; (chance) chance f, occasion f favorable; **to ~ one's leg** etc se casser la jambe etc; **to ~ a record** battre un record; **to ~ the news to sb** annoncer la nouvelle à qn; **to ~ with sb** rompre avec qn; **to ~ even** vi rentrer dans ses frais; **to ~ free** or **loose** vi se dégager, s'échapper; **to take a ~** (few minutes) faire une pause, s'arrêter cinq minutes; (holiday) prendre un peu de repos; **without a ~** sans interruption, sans arrêt
▶ **break down** VT (door etc) enfoncer; (resistance) venir à bout de; (figures, data) décomposer, analyser ▶ VI s'effondrer; (Med) faire une dépression (nerveuse); (Aut) tomber en panne; **my car has broken down** ma voiture est en panne

▶ **break in** VT (*horse etc*) dresser ▶ VI (*burglar*) entrer par effraction; (*interrupt*) interrompre

▶ **break into** VT FUS (*house*) s'introduire *or* pénétrer par effraction dans

▶ **break off** VI (*speaker*) s'interrompre; (*branch*) se rompre ▶ VT (*talks, engagement*) rompre

▶ **break open** VT (*door etc*) forcer, fracturer

▶ **break out** VI éclater, se déclarer; (*prisoner*) s'évader; **to ~ out in spots** se couvrir de boutons

▶ **break through** VI: **the sun broke through** le soleil a fait son apparition ▶ VT FUS (*defences, barrier*) franchir; (*crowd*) se frayer un passage à travers

▶ **break up** VI (*partnership*) cesser, prendre fin; (*marriage*) se briser; (*crowd, meeting*) se séparer; (*ship*) se disloquer; (*Scol: pupils*) être en vacances; (*line*) couper ▶ VT fracasser, casser; (*fight etc*) interrompre, faire cesser; (*marriage*) désunir; **the line's** *or* **you're breaking up** ça coupe

breakable ['breɪkəbl] ADJ cassable, fragile ▶ N: **breakables** objets *mpl* fragiles

breakage ['breɪkɪdʒ] N casse *f*; **to pay for breakages** payer la casse

breakaway ['breɪkəweɪ] ADJ (*group etc*) dissident(e)

breakdown ['breɪkdaʊn] N (*Aut*) panne *f*; (*in communications, marriage*) rupture *f*; (*Med: also*: **nervous breakdown**) dépression (nerveuse); (*of figures*) ventilation *f*, répartition *f*

breakdown service N (*BRIT*) service *m* de dépannage

breakdown van, (*US*) **breakdown truck** N dépanneuse *f*

breaker ['breɪkə'] N brisant *m*

breakeven ['breɪk'i:vn] CPD: **~ chart** graphique *m* de rentabilité; **~ point** seuil *m* de rentabilité

breakfast ['brekfəst] N petit déjeuner *m*; **what time is ~?** le petit déjeuner est à quelle heure?

breakfast cereal N céréales *fpl*

break-in ['breɪkɪn] N cambriolage *m*

breaking and entering N (*Law*) effraction *f*

breaking point ['breɪkɪŋ-] N limites *fpl*

breakthrough ['breɪkθru:] N percée *f*

break-up ['breɪkʌp] N (*of partnership, marriage*) rupture *f*

break-up value N (*Comm*) valeur *f* de liquidation

breakwater ['breɪkwɔ:tə'] N brise-lames *m inv*, digue *f*

breast [brest] N (*of woman*) sein *m*; (*chest*) poitrine *f*; (*of chicken, turkey*) blanc *m*

breast-feed ['brestfi:d] VT, VI (*irreg: like* **feed**) allaiter

breast pocket N poche *f* (de) poitrine

breast-stroke ['breststrəʊk] N brasse *f*

breath [breθ] N haleine *f*, souffle *m*; **to go out for a ~ of air** sortir prendre l'air; **to take a deep ~** respirer à fond; **out of ~** à bout de souffle, essoufflé(e)

breathalyse ['breθəlaɪz] VT faire subir l'alcootest à

Breathalyser® ['breθəlaɪzə'] (*BRIT*) N alcootest *m*

breathe [bri:ð] VT, VI respirer; **I won't ~ a word**

about it je n'en soufflerai pas mot, je n'en dirai rien à personne

▶ **breathe in** VI inspirer ▶ VT aspirer

▶ **breathe out** VT, VI expirer

breather ['bri:ðə'] N moment *m* de repos *or* de répit

breathing ['bri:ðɪŋ] N respiration *f*

breathing space N (*fig*) (moment *m* de) répit *m*

breathless ['breθlɪs] ADJ essoufflé(e), haletant(e), oppressé(e); **~ with excitement** le souffle coupé par l'émotion

breathtaking ['breθteɪkɪŋ] ADJ stupéfiant(e), à vous couper le souffle

breath test N alcootest *m*

bred [bred] PT, PP *of* **breed**

-bred [bred] SUFFIX: **well/ill~** bien/mal élevé(e)

breed [bri:d] (*pt, pp* **bred** [bred]) VT élever, faire l'élevage de; (*fig: hate, suspicion*) engendrer ▶ VI se reproduire ▶ N race *f*, variété *f*

breeder ['bri:də'] N (*person*) éleveur *m*; (*Physics: also*: **breeder reactor**) (réacteur *m*) surrégénérateur *m*

breeding ['bri:dɪŋ] N reproduction *f*; élevage *m*; (*upbringing*) éducation *f*

breeze [bri:z] N brise *f*

breeze-block ['bri:zblɔk] N (*BRIT*) parpaing *m*

breezy ['bri:zɪ] ADJ (*day, weather*) venteux(-euse); (*manner*) désinvolte; (*person*) jovial(e)

Breton ['bretən] ADJ breton(ne) ▶ N Breton(ne); (*Ling*) breton *m*

brevity ['brevɪtɪ] N brièveté *f*

brew [bru:] VT (*tea*) faire infuser; (*beer*) brasser; (*plot*) tramer, préparer ▶ VI (*tea*) infuser; (*beer*) fermenter; (*fig*) se préparer, couver

brewer ['bru:ə'] N brasseur *m*

brewery ['bru:ərɪ] N brasserie *f* (*fabrique*)

briar ['braɪə'] N (*thorny bush*) ronces *fpl*; (*wild rose*) églantine *f*

bribe [braɪb] N pot-de-vin *m* ▶ VT acheter; soudoyer; **to ~ sb to do sth** soudoyer qn pour qu'il fasse qch

bribery ['braɪbərɪ] N corruption *f*

bric-a-brac ['brɪkəbræk] N bric-à-brac *m*

brick [brɪk] N brique *f*

bricklayer ['brɪkleɪə'] N maçon *m*

brickwork ['brɪkwə:k] N briquetage *m*, maçonnerie *f*

brickworks ['brɪkwə:ks] N briqueterie *f*

bridal ['braɪdl] ADJ nuptial(e); **~ party** noce *f*

bride [braɪd] N mariée *f*, épouse *f*

bridegroom ['braɪdgru:m] N marié *m*, époux *m*

bridesmaid ['braɪdzmeɪd] N demoiselle *f* d'honneur

bridge [brɪdʒ] N pont *m*; (*Naut*) passerelle *f* (de commandement); (*of nose*) arête *f*; (*Cards, Dentistry*) bridge *m* ▶ VT (*river*) construire un pont sur; (*gap*) combler

bridging loan ['brɪdʒɪŋ-] N (*BRIT*) prêt *m* relais

bridle ['braɪdl] N bride *f* ▶ VT refréner, mettre la bride à; (*horse*) brider

bridle path N piste *or* allée cavalière

brief [bri:f] ADJ bref (brève) ▶ N (*Law*) dossier *m*, cause *f*; (*gen*) tâche *f* ▶ VT mettre au courant; (*Mil*) donner des instructions à; **briefs** NPL slip *m*; **in ~ ...** (en) bref ...

briefcase ['bri:keɪs] N serviette f; porte-documents m inv
briefing ['bri:fɪŋ] N instructions fpl; (Press) briefing m
briefly ['bri:flɪ] ADV brièvement; (visit) en coup de vent; **to glimpse ~** entrevoir
briefness ['bri:fnɪs] N brièveté f
Brig. ABBR = **brigadier**
brigade [brɪ'geɪd] N (Mil) brigade f
brigadier [brɪgə'dɪəʳ] N brigadier général
bright [braɪt] ADJ brillant(e); (room, weather) clair(e); (person: clever) intelligent(e), doué(e); (: cheerful) gai(e); (idea) génial(e); (colour) vif (vive); **to look on the ~ side** regarder le bon côté des choses
brighten ['braɪtn], **brighten up** VT (room) éclaircir; égayer ▶ VI s'éclaircir; (person) retrouver un peu de sa gaieté
brightly ['braɪtlɪ] ADV brillamment
brill [brɪl] ADJ (BRIT inf) super inv
brilliance ['brɪljəns] N éclat m; (fig: of person) brio m
brilliant ['brɪljənt] ADJ brillant(e); (light, sunshine) éclatant(e); (inf: great) super
brim [brɪm] N bord m
brimful ['brɪm'fʊl] ADJ plein(e) à ras bord; (fig) débordant(e)
brine [braɪn] N eau salée; (Culin) saumure f
bring [brɪŋ] (pt, pp brought [brɔ:t]) VT (thing) apporter; (person) amener; **to ~ sth to an end** mettre fin à qch; **I can't ~ myself to fire him** je ne peux me résoudre à le mettre à la porte
▶ **bring about** VT provoquer, entraîner
▶ **bring back** VT rapporter; (person) ramener
▶ **bring down** VT (lower) abaisser; (shoot down) abattre; (government) faire s'effondrer
▶ **bring forward** VT avancer; (Book-keeping) reporter
▶ **bring in** VT (person) faire entrer; (object) rentrer; (Pol: legislation) introduire; (Law: verdict) rendre; (produce: income) rapporter
▶ **bring off** VT (task, plan) réussir, mener à bien; (deal) mener à bien
▶ **bring on** VT (illness, attack) provoquer; (player, substitute) amener
▶ **bring out** VT sortir; (meaning) faire ressortir, mettre en relief; (new product, book) sortir
▶ **bring round, bring to** VT (unconscious person) ranimer
▶ **bring up** VT élever; (carry up) monter; (question) soulever; (food: vomit) vomir, rendre
brink [brɪŋk] N bord m; **on the ~ of doing** sur le point de faire, à deux doigts de faire; **she was on the ~ of tears** elle était au bord des larmes
brisk [brɪsk] ADJ vif (vive); (abrupt) brusque; (trade etc) actif(-ive); **to go for a ~ walk** se promener d'un bon pas; **business is ~** les affaires marchent (bien)
bristle ['brɪsl] N poil m ▶ VI se hérisser; **bristling with** hérissé(e) de
bristly ['brɪslɪ] ADJ (beard, hair) hérissé(e); **your chin's all ~** ton menton gratte
Brit [brɪt] N ABBR (inf: = British person) Britannique mf

Britain ['brɪtən] N (also: **Great Britain**) la Grande-Bretagne; **in ~** en Grande-Bretagne
British ['brɪtɪʃ] ADJ britannique ▶ NPL: **the ~** les Britanniques mpl
British Isles NPL: **the ~** les îles fpl Britanniques
British Rail N compagnie ferroviaire britannique, ≈ SNCF f
British Summer Time N heure f d'été britannique
Briton ['brɪtən] N Britannique mf
Brittany ['brɪtənɪ] N Bretagne f
brittle ['brɪtl] ADJ cassant(e), fragile
Bro. ABBR (Rel) = **brother**
broach [brəutʃ] VT (subject) aborder
broad [brɔ:d] ADJ large; (distinction) général(e); (accent) prononcé(e) ▶ N (US inf) nana f; **~ hint** allusion transparente; **in ~ daylight** en plein jour; **the ~ outlines** les grandes lignes
B road N (BRIT) ≈ route départementale
broadband ['brɔ:dbænd] N transmission f à haut débit
broad bean N fève f
broadcast ['brɔ:dkɑ:st] (pt, pp ~) N émission f ▶ VT (Radio) radiodiffuser; (TV) téléviser ▶ VI émettre
broadcaster ['brɔ:dkɑ:stəʳ] N personnalité f de la radio or de la télévision
broadcasting ['brɔ:dkɑ:stɪŋ] N radiodiffusion f; télévision f
broadcasting station N station f de radio (or de télévision)
broaden ['brɔ:dn] VT élargir; **to ~ one's mind** élargir ses horizons ▶ VI s'élargir
broadly ['brɔ:dlɪ] ADV en gros, généralement
broad-minded ['brɔ:d'maɪndɪd] ADJ large d'esprit
broadsheet ['brɔ:dʃi:t] N (BRIT) journal m grand format
broccoli ['brɔkəlɪ] N brocoli m
brochure ['brəuʃjuəʳ] N prospectus m, dépliant m
brogue ['brəug] N (accent) accent régional; (shoe) (sorte de) chaussure basse de cuir épais
broil [brɔɪl] VT (US) rôtir
broke [brəuk] PT of **break** ▶ ADJ (inf) fauché(e); **to go ~** (business) faire faillite
broken ['brəukn] PP of **break** ▶ ADJ (stick, leg etc) cassé(e); (machine: also: **broken down**) fichu(e); (promise, vow) rompu(e); **a ~ marriage** un couple dissocié; **a ~ home** un foyer désuni; **in ~ French/English** dans un français/anglais approximatif or hésitant
broken-down ['brəukn'daun] ADJ (car) en panne; (machine) fichu(e); (house) en ruines
broken-hearted ['brəukn'hɑ:tɪd] ADJ (ayant) le cœur brisé
broker ['brəukəʳ] N courtier m
brokerage ['brəukrɪdʒ] N courtage m
brolly ['brɔlɪ] N (BRIT inf) pépin m, parapluie m
bronchitis [brɔŋ'kaɪtɪs] N bronchite f
bronze [brɔnz] N bronze m
bronzed ['brɔnzd] ADJ bronzé(e), hâlé(e)
brooch [brəutʃ] N broche f
brood [bru:d] N couvée f ▶ VI (hen, storm) couver;

(person) méditer (sombrement), ruminer

broody ['bruːdɪ] ADJ (fig) taciturne, mélancolique

brook [brʊk] N ruisseau m

broom [brʊm] N balai m; (Bot) genêt m

broomstick ['brʊmstɪk] N manche m à balai

Bros. ABBR (Comm: = brothers) Frères

broth [brɒθ] N bouillon m de viande et de légumes

brothel ['brɒθl] N maison close, bordel m

brother ['brʌðə^r] N frère m

brotherhood ['brʌðəhʊd] N fraternité f

brother-in-law ['brʌðərɪn'lɔː] N beau-frère m

brotherly ['brʌðəlɪ] ADJ fraternel(le)

brought [brɔːt] PT, PP of **bring**

brow [braʊ] N front m; (rare: eyebrow) sourcil m; (of hill) sommet m

browbeat ['braʊbiːt] VT (irreg: like **beat**) intimider, brusquer

brown [braʊn] ADJ brun(e), marron inv; (hair) châtain inv; (tanned) bronzé(e); (rice, bread, flour) complet(-ète) ▶ N (colour) brun m, marron m ▶ VT brunir; (Culin) faire dorer, faire roussir; **to go ~** (person) bronzer; (leaves) jaunir

brown bread N pain m bis

Brownie ['braʊnɪ] N jeannette f éclaireuse (cadette)

brown paper N papier m d'emballage, papier kraft

brown rice N riz m complet

brown sugar N cassonade f

browse [braʊz] VI (in shop) regarder (sans acheter); (among books) bouquiner, feuilleter les livres; (animal) paître; **to ~ through a book** feuilleter un livre

browser ['braʊzə^r] N (Comput) navigateur m

bruise [bruːz] N bleu m, ecchymose f, contusion f ▶ VT contusionner, meurtrir ▶ VI (fruit) se taler, se meurtrir; **to ~ one's arm** se faire un bleu au bras

Brum [brʌm] N ABBR, **Brummagem** ['brʌmədʒəm] N (inf) Birmingham

Brummie ['brʌmɪ] N (inf) habitant(e) de Birmingham; natif(-ive) de Birmingham

brunch [brʌntʃ] N brunch m

brunette [bruːˈnɛt] N (femme) brune

brunt [brʌnt] N: **the ~ of** (attack, criticism etc) le plus gros de

brush [brʌʃ] N brosse f; (for painting) pinceau m; (for shaving) blaireau m; (quarrel) accrochage m, prise f de bec ▶ VT brosser; (also: **brush past**, **brush against**) effleurer, frôler; **to have a ~ with sb** s'accrocher avec qn; **to have a ~ with the police** avoir maille à partir avec la police
  ▶ **brush aside** VT écarter, balayer
  ▶ **brush up** VT (knowledge) rafraîchir, réviser

brushed [brʌʃt] ADJ (Tech: steel, chrome etc) brossé(e); (: nylon, denim etc) gratté(e)

brush-off ['brʌʃɔf] N (inf): **to give sb the ~** envoyer qn promener

brushwood ['brʌʃwʊd] N broussailles fpl, taillis m

brusque [bruːsk] ADJ (person, manner) brusque, cassant(e); (tone) sec (sèche), cassant(e)

Brussels ['brʌslz] N Bruxelles

Brussels sprout N chou m de Bruxelles

brutal ['bruːtl] ADJ brutal(e)

brutality [bruːˈtælɪtɪ] N brutalité f

brutalize ['bruːtəlaɪz] VT (harden) rendre brutal(e); (ill-treat) brutaliser

brute [bruːt] N brute f ▶ ADJ: **by ~ force** par la force

brutish ['bruːtɪʃ] ADJ grossier(-ère), brutal(e)

BS N ABBR (US: = Bachelor of Science) diplôme universitaire

bs ABBR = **bill of sale**

BSA N ABBR = **Boy Scouts of America**

B.Sc. N ABBR = **Bachelor of Science**

BSE N ABBR (= bovine spongiform encephalopathy) ESB f, BSE f

BSI N ABBR (= British Standards Institution) association de normalisation

BST ABBR (= British Summer Time) heure f d'été

Bt. ABBR (BRIT) = **baronet**

btu N ABBR (= British thermal unit) btu (= 1054,2 joules)

bubble ['bʌbl] N bulle f ▶ VI bouillonner, faire des bulles; (sparkle, fig) pétiller

bubble bath N bain moussant

bubble gum N chewing-gum m

bubble jet printer ['bʌbldʒɛt-] N imprimante f à bulle d'encre

bubbly ['bʌblɪ] ADJ (drink) pétillant(e); (person) plein(e) de vitalité ▶ N (inf) champ m

Bucharest [buːkəˈrɛst] N Bucarest

buck [bʌk] N mâle m (d'un lapin, lièvre, daim etc); (US inf) dollar m ▶ VI ruer, lancer une ruade; **to pass the ~ (to sb)** se décharger de la responsabilité (sur qn)
  ▶ **buck up** VI (cheer up) reprendre du poil de la bête, se remonter ▶ VT: **to ~ one's ideas up** se reprendre

bucket ['bʌkɪt] N seau m ▶ VI (BRIT inf): **the rain is bucketing (down)** il pleut à verse

Buckingham Palace ['bʌkɪŋhəm-] N le palais de Buckingham; voir article

> Buckingham Palace est la résidence officielle londonienne du souverain britannique depuis 1762. Construit en 1703, il fut à l'origine le palais du duc de Buckingham. Il a été partiellement reconstruit au début du XXe siècle.

buckle ['bʌkl] N boucle f ▶ VT (belt etc) boucler, attacher ▶ VI (warp) tordre, gauchir; (: wheel) se voiler
  ▶ **buckle down** VI s'y mettre

Bucks [bʌks] ABBR (BRIT) = **Buckinghamshire**

bud [bʌd] N bourgeon m; (of flower) bouton m ▶ VI bourgeonner; (flower) éclore

Buddha ['bʊdə] N Bouddha m

Buddhism ['bʊdɪzəm] N bouddhisme m

Buddhist ['bʊdɪst] ADJ bouddhiste ▶ N Bouddhiste mf

budding ['bʌdɪŋ] ADJ (flower) en bouton; (poet etc) en herbe; (passion etc) naissant(e)

buddy ['bʌdɪ] N (US) copain m

budge [bʌdʒ] VT faire bouger ▶ VI bouger

budgerigar ['bʌdʒərɪgɑː^r] N perruche f

budget ['bʌdʒɪt] N budget m ▶ VI: **to ~ for sth**

inscrire qch au budget; **I'm on a tight ~** je dois faire attention à mon budget

budgie ['bʌdʒɪ] N = **budgerigar**

Buenos Aires ['bweɪnɔs'aɪrɪz] N Buenos Aires

buff [bʌf] ADJ (couleur f) chamois m ▶ N (inf: enthusiast) mordu(e)

buffalo ['bʌfələu] (pl ~ or **buffaloes**) N (BRIT) buffle m; (US) bison m

buffer ['bʌfər] N tampon m; (Comput) mémoire f tampon ▶ VT, VI (Comput) mettre en mémoire tampon

buffering ['bʌfərɪŋ] N (Comput) mise f en mémoire tampon

buffer state N état m tampon

buffer zone N zone f tampon

buffet N ['bufeɪ] (food: BRIT: bar) buffet m ▶ VT ['bʌfɪt] gifler, frapper; secouer, ébranler

buffet car N (BRIT Rail) voiture-bar f

buffet lunch N lunch m

buffoon [bə'fu:n] N bouffon m, pitre m

bug [bʌg] N (bedbug etc) punaise f; (esp US: any insect) insecte m, bestiole f; (fig: germ) virus m, microbe m; (spy device) dispositif m d'écoute (électronique), micro clandestin; (Comput: of program) erreur f; (: of equipment) défaut m ▶ VT (room) poser des micros dans; (inf: annoy) embêter; **I've got the travel ~** (fig) j'ai le virus du voyage

bugbear ['bʌgbɛər] N cauchemar m, bête noire

bugger ['bʌgər] (inf!) N salaud m (!), connard m (!) ▶ VI: ~ **off!** tire-toi! (!); ~ **(it)!** merde! (!)

buggy ['bʌgɪ] N poussette f

bugle ['bju:gl] N clairon m

build [bɪld] (pt, pp **built** [bɪlt]) N (of person) carrure f, charpente f ▶ VT construire, bâtir
  ▶ **build on** VT FUS (fig) tirer parti de, partir de
  ▶ **build up** VT accumuler, amasser; (business) développer; (reputation) bâtir

builder ['bɪldər] N entrepreneur m

building ['bɪldɪŋ] N (trade) construction f; (structure) bâtiment m, construction f; (: residential, offices) immeuble m

building contractor N entrepreneur m (en bâtiment)

building industry N (industrie f du) bâtiment m

building site N chantier m (de construction)

building society N (BRIT) société f de crédit immobilier; voir article

> Une building society est une mutuelle dont les épargnants et emprunteurs sont les propriétaires. Ces mutuelles offrent deux services principaux: on peut y avoir un compte d'épargne duquel on peut retirer son argent sur demande ou moyennant un court préavis et on peut également y faire des emprunts à long terme, par exemple pour acheter une maison. Les building societies ont eu jusqu'en 1985 le quasi-monopole des comptes d'épargne et des prêts immobiliers, mais les banques ont maintenant une part importante de ce marché.

building trade N = **building industry**

build-up ['bɪldʌp] N (of gas etc) accumulation f; (publicity): **to give sb/sth a good ~** faire de la pub pour qn/qch

built [bɪlt] PT, PP of **build**

built-in ['bɪlt'ɪn] ADJ (cupboard) encastré(e); (device) incorporé(e); intégré(e)

built-up ['bɪlt'ʌp] ADJ: ~ **area** agglomération (urbaine); zone urbanisée

bulb [bʌlb] N (Bot) bulbe m, oignon m; (Elec) ampoule f

bulbous ['bʌlbəs] ADJ bulbeux(-euse)

Bulgaria [bʌl'gɛərɪə] N Bulgarie f

Bulgarian [bʌl'gɛərɪən] ADJ bulgare ▶ N Bulgare mf; (Ling) bulgare m

bulge [bʌldʒ] N renflement m, gonflement m; (in birth rate, sales) brusque augmentation f ▶ VI faire saillie; présenter un renflement; (pocket, file): **to be bulging with** être plein(e) à craquer de

bulimia [bə'lɪmɪə] N boulimie f

bulimic [bju:'lɪmɪk] ADJ, N boulimique mf

bulk [bʌlk] N masse f, volume m; **in ~** (Comm) en gros, en vrac; **the ~ of** la plus grande or grosse partie de

bulk buying [-'baɪɪŋ] N achat m en gros

bulk carrier N cargo m

bulkhead ['bʌlkhɛd] N cloison f (étanche)

bulky ['bʌlkɪ] ADJ volumineux(-euse), encombrant(e)

bull [bul] N taureau m; (male elephant, whale) mâle m; (Stock Exchange) haussier m; (Rel) bulle f

bulldog ['buldɔg] N bouledogue m

bulldoze ['buldəuz] VT passer or raser au bulldozer; **I was bulldozed into doing it** (fig: inf) on m'a forcé la main

bulldozer ['buldəuzər] N bulldozer m

bullet ['bulɪt] N balle f (de fusil etc)

bulletin ['bulɪtɪn] N bulletin m, communiqué m; (also: **news bulletin**) (bulletin d')informations fpl

bulletin board N (Comput) messagerie f (électronique)

bulletproof ['bulɪtpru:f] ADJ à l'épreuve des balles; ~ **vest** gilet m pare-balles

bullfight ['bulfaɪt] N corrida f, course f de taureaux

bullfighter ['bulfaɪtər] N torero m

bullfighting ['bulfaɪtɪŋ] N tauromachie f

bullion ['buljən] N or m or argent m en lingots

bullock ['bulək] N bœuf m

bullring ['bulrɪŋ] N arène f

bull's-eye ['bulzaɪ] N centre m (de la cible)

bullshit ['bulʃɪt] (inf!) N connerie(s) f(pl) (!) ▶ VT raconter des conneries à (!) ▶ VI déconner (!)

bully ['bulɪ] N brute f, tyran m ▶ VT tyranniser, rudoyer; (frighten) intimider

bullying ['bulɪɪŋ] N brimades fpl

bum [bʌm] N (inf: BRIT: backside) derrière m; (esp US: tramp) vagabond(e), traîne-savates mf; (: idler) glandeur m
  ▶ **bum around** VI (inf) vagabonder

bumblebee ['bʌmblbi:] N bourdon m

bumf [bʌmf] N (inf: forms etc) paperasses fpl

bump [bʌmp] N (blow) coup m, choc m; (jolt) cahot m; (on road etc, on head) bosse f ▶ VT heurter, cogner; (car) emboutir

▶ **bump along** VI avancer en cahotant

▶ **bump into** VT FUS rentrer dans, tamponner; (*inf: meet*) tomber sur

bumper ['bʌmpəʳ] N pare-chocs *m inv* ▶ ADJ: **~ crop/harvest** récolte/moisson exceptionnelle

bumper cars NPL (*US*) autos tamponneuses

bumph [bʌmf] N = **bumf**

bumptious ['bʌmpʃəs] ADJ suffisant(e), prétentieux(-euse)

bumpy ['bʌmpɪ] ADJ (*road*) cahoteux(-euse); **it was a ~ flight/ride** on a été secoués dans l'avion/la voiture

bun [bʌn] N (*cake*) petit gâteau; (*bread*) petit pain au lait; (*of hair*) chignon *m*

bunch [bʌntʃ] N (*of flowers*) bouquet *m*; (*of keys*) trousseau *m*; (*of bananas*) régime *m*; (*of people*) groupe *m*; **bunches** NPL (*in hair*) couettes *fpl*; **~ of grapes** grappe *f* de raisin

bundle ['bʌndl] N paquet *m* ▶ VT (*also*: **bundle up**) faire un paquet de; (*put*): **to ~ sth/sb into** fourrer or enfourner qch/qn dans

▶ **bundle off** VT (*person*) faire sortir (en toute hâte); expédier

▶ **bundle out** VT éjecter, sortir (sans ménagements)

bun fight N (*BRIT inf*) réception *f*; (*tea party*) thé *m*

bung [bʌŋ] N bonde *f*, bouchon *m* ▶ VT (*BRIT*: *throw*: *also*: **bung into**) flanquer; (*also*: **bung up**: *pipe, hole*) boucher; **my nose is bunged up** j'ai le nez bouché

bungalow ['bʌŋɡələu] N bungalow *m*

bungee jumping ['bʌndʒiː'dʒʌmpɪŋ] N saut *m* à l'élastique

bungle ['bʌŋɡl] VT bâcler, gâcher

bunion ['bʌnjən] N oignon *m* (*au pied*)

bunk [bʌŋk] N couchette *f*; (*BRIT inf*): **to do a ~** mettre les bouts or les voiles

▶ **bunk off** VI (*BRIT inf: Scol*) sécher (les cours); **I'll ~ off at 3 o'clock this afternoon** je vais mettre les bouts or les voiles à 3 heures cet après-midi

bunk beds NPL lits superposés

bunker ['bʌŋkəʳ] N (*coal store*) soute *f* à charbon; (*Mil, Golf*) bunker *m*

bunny ['bʌnɪ] N (*also*: **bunny rabbit**) lapin *m*

bunny girl N (*BRIT*) hôtesse de cabaret

bunny hill N (*US Ski*) piste *f* pour débutants

bunting ['bʌntɪŋ] N pavoisement *m*, drapeaux *mpl*

buoy [bɔɪ] N bouée *f*

▶ **buoy up** VT faire flotter; (*fig*) soutenir, épauler

buoyancy ['bɔɪənsɪ] N (*of ship*) flottabilité *f*

buoyant ['bɔɪənt] ADJ (*ship*) flottable; (*carefree*) gai(e), plein(e) d'entrain; (*Comm: market, economy*) actif(-ive); (: *prices, currency*) soutenu(e)

burden ['bə:dn] N fardeau *m*, charge *f* ▶ VT charger; (*oppress*) accabler, surcharger; **to be a ~ to sb** être un fardeau pour qn

bureau ['bjuərəu] N (*pl* **bureaux** [-z]) (*BRIT*: *writing desk*) bureau *m*, secrétaire *m*; (*US: chest of drawers*) commode *f*; (*office*) bureau, office *m*

bureaucracy [bjuə'rɔkrəsɪ] N bureaucratie *f*

bureaucrat ['bjuərəkræt] N bureaucrate *mf*, rond-de-cuir *m*

bureaucratic [bjuərə'krætɪk] ADJ bureaucratique

bureau de change [-də'ʃɑ̃ʒ] (*pl* **bureaux de change**) N bureau *m* de change

bureaux ['bjuərəuz] NPL *of* **bureau**

burgeon ['bə:dʒən] VI (*fig*) être en expansion rapide

burger ['bə:ɡəʳ] N hamburger *m*

burglar ['bə:ɡləʳ] N cambrioleur *m*

burglar alarm N sonnerie *f* d'alarme

burglarize ['bə:ɡləraɪz] VT (*US*) cambrioler

burglary ['bə:ɡlərɪ] N cambriolage *m*

burgle ['bə:ɡl] VT cambrioler

Burgundy ['bə:ɡəndɪ] N Bourgogne *f*

burial ['berɪəl] N enterrement *m*

burial ground N cimetière *m*

burly ['bə:lɪ] ADJ de forte carrure, costaud(e)

Burma ['bə:mə] N Birmanie *f*; *see also* **Myanmar**

Burmese [bə:'mi:z] ADJ birman(e), de Birmanie ▶ N (*pl inv*) Birman(e); (*Ling*) birman *m*

burn [bə:n] (*pt, pp* **burned** *or* **burnt** [bə:nt]) VT, VI brûler ▶ N brûlure *f*; **the cigarette burnt a hole in her dress** la cigarette a fait un trou dans sa robe; **I've burnt myself!** je me suis brûlé(e)!

▶ **burn down** VT incendier, détruire par le feu

▶ **burn out** VT (*writer etc*): **to ~ o.s.** out s'user (à force de travailler)

burner ['bə:nəʳ] N brûleur *m*

burning ['bə:nɪŋ] ADJ (*building, forest*) en flammes; (*issue, question*) brûlant(e); (*ambition*) dévorant(e)

burnish ['bə:nɪʃ] VT polir

Burns' Night [bə:nz-] N fête écossaise à la mémoire du poète Robert Burns; *voir article*

> Burns' Night est une fête qui a lieu le 25 janvier, à la mémoire du poète écossais Robert Burns (1759–1796), à l'occasion de laquelle les Écossais partout dans le monde organisent un souper, en général arrosé de whisky. Le plat principal est toujours le haggis, servi avec de la purée de pommes de terre et de la purée de rutabagas. On apporte le haggis au son des cornemuses et au cours du repas on lit des poèmes de Burns et on chante ses chansons.

burnt [bə:nt] PT, PP *of* **burn**

burnt sugar N (*BRIT*) caramel *m*

burp [bə:p] (*inf*) N rot *m* ▶ VI roter

burrow ['bʌrəu] N terrier *m* ▶ VT creuser ▶ VI (*rabbit*) creuser un terrier; (*rummage*) fouiller

bursar ['bə:səʳ] N économe *mf*; (*BRIT*: *student*) boursier(-ère)

bursary ['bə:sərɪ] N (*BRIT*) bourse *f* (d'études)

burst [bə:st] (*pt, pp* **~**) VT faire éclater; (*river, banks etc*) rompre ▶ VI éclater; (*tyre*) crever ▶ N explosion *f*; (*also*: **burst pipe**) fuite *f* (*due à une rupture*); **a ~ of enthusiasm/energy** un accès d'enthousiasme/d'énergie; **~ of laughter** éclat *m* de rire; **a ~ of applause** une salve d'applaudissement; **a ~ of gunfire** une rafale de tir; **a ~ of speed** une pointe de vitesse;

~ **blood vessel** rupture *f* de vaisseau sanguin; **the river has ~ its banks** le cours d'eau est sorti de son lit; **to ~ into flames** s'enflammer soudainement; **to ~ out laughing** éclater de rire; **to ~ into tears** fondre en larmes; **to ~ open** *vi* s'ouvrir violemment *or* soudainement; **to be bursting with** (*container*) être plein(e) (à craquer) de, regorger de; (*fig*) être débordant(e) de

▶ **burst into** VT FUS (*room etc*) faire irruption dans

▶ **burst out of** VT FUS sortir précipitamment de

bury ['bɛrɪ] VT enterrer; **to ~ one's face in one's hands** se couvrir le visage de ses mains; **to ~ one's head in the sand** (*fig*) pratiquer la politique de l'autruche; **to ~ the hatchet** (*fig*) enterrer la hache de guerre

bus [bʌs] (*pl* **buses** ['bʌsɪz]) N (*auto*)bus *m*

busboy ['bʌsbɔɪ] N (*US*) aide-serveur *m*

bus conductor N receveur(-euse) *m/f* de bus

bush [buʃ] N buisson *m*; (*scrub land*) brousse *f*; **to beat about the ~** tourner autour du pot

bushed [buʃt] ADJ (*inf*) crevé(e), claqué(e)

bushel ['buʃl] N boisseau *m*

bushfire ['buʃfaɪə^r] N feu *m* de brousse

bushy ['buʃɪ] ADJ broussailleux(-euse), touffu(e)

busily ['bɪzɪlɪ] ADV: **to be ~ doing sth** s'affairer à faire qch

business ['bɪznɪs] N (*matter, firm*) affaire *f*; (*trading*) affaires *fpl*; (*job, duty*) travail *m*; **to be away on ~** être en déplacement d'affaires; **I'm here on ~** je suis là pour affaires; **he's in the insurance ~** il est dans les assurances; **to do ~ with sb** traiter avec qn; **it's none of my ~** cela ne me regarde pas, ce ne sont pas mes affaires; **he means ~** il ne plaisante pas, il est sérieux

business address N adresse professionnelle *or* au bureau

business card N carte *f* de visite (professionnelle)

business class N (*on plane*) classe *f* affaires

businesslike ['bɪznɪslaɪk] ADJ sérieux(-euse), efficace

businessman ['bɪznɪsmən] N (*irreg*) homme *m* d'affaires

business trip N voyage *m* d'affaires

businesswoman ['bɪznɪswumən] N (*irreg*) femme *f* d'affaires

busker ['bʌskə^r] N (*BRIT*) artiste ambulant(e)

bus lane N (*BRIT*) voie réservée aux autobus

bus pass N carte *f* de bus

bus shelter N abribus *m*

bus station N gare routière

bus stop N arrêt *m* d'autobus

bust [bʌst] N buste *m*; (*measurement*) tour *m* de poitrine ▶ ADJ (*inf: broken*) fichu(e), fini(e) ▶ VT (*inf: Police: arrest*) pincer; **to go ~** (*inf*) faire faillite

bustle ['bʌsl] N remue-ménage *m*, affairement *m* ▶ VI s'affairer, se démener

bustling ['bʌslɪŋ] ADJ (*person*) affairé(e); (*town*) très animé(e)

bust-up ['bʌstʌp] N (*BRIT inf*) engueulade *f*

busty ['bʌstɪ] ADJ (*inf*) à la poitrine plantureuse

busy ['bɪzɪ] ADJ occupé(e); (*shop, street*) très fréquenté(e); (*US: telephone, line*) occupé ▶ VT: **to ~ o.s.** s'occuper; **he's a ~ man** (*normally*) c'est un homme très pris; (*temporarily*) il est très pris

busybody ['bɪzɪbɔdɪ] N mouche *f* du coche, âme *f* charitable

busy signal N (*US*) tonalité *f* occupé *inv*

[KEYWORD]

but [bʌt] CONJ mais; **I'd love to come, but I'm busy** j'aimerais venir mais je suis occupé; **he's not English but French** il n'est pas anglais mais français; **but that's far too expensive!** mais c'est bien trop cher!

▶ PREP (*apart from, except*) sauf, excepté; **nothing but** rien d'autre que; **we've had nothing but trouble** nous n'avons eu que des ennuis; **no-one but him can do it** lui seul peut le faire; **who but a lunatic would do such a thing?** qui sinon un fou ferait une chose pareille?; **but for you/your help** sans toi/ton aide; **anything but that** tout sauf *or* excepté ça, tout mais pas ça; **the last but one** (*BRIT*) l'avant-dernier(-ère)

▶ ADV (*just, only*) ne ... que; **she's but a child** elle n'est qu'une enfant; **had I but known** si seulement j'avais su; **I can but try** je peux toujours essayer; **all but finished** pratiquement terminé; **anything but finished** tout sauf fini, très loin d'être fini

butane ['bjuːteɪn] N (*also*: **butane gas**) butane *m*

butch [butʃ] ADJ (*inf: man*) costaud, viril; (: *woman*) costaude, masculine

butcher ['butʃə^r] N boucher *m* ▶ VT massacrer; (*cattle etc for meat*) tuer

butcher's ['butʃəz], **butcher's shop** N boucherie *f*

butler ['bʌtlə^r] N maître *m* d'hôtel

butt [bʌt] N (*cask*) gros tonneau; (*thick end*) (gros) bout; (*of gun*) crosse *f*; (*of cigarette*) mégot *m*; (*BRIT fig: target*) cible *f* ▶ VT donner un coup de tête à

▶ **butt in** VI (*interrupt*) interrompre

butter ['bʌtə^r] N beurre *m* ▶ VT beurrer

buttercup ['bʌtəkʌp] N bouton *m* d'or

butter dish N beurrier *m*

butterfingers ['bʌtəfɪŋɡəz] N (*inf*) maladroit(e)

butterfly ['bʌtəflaɪ] N papillon *m*; (*Swimming: also*: **butterfly stroke**) brasse *f* papillon

buttocks ['bʌtəks] NPL fesses *fpl*

button ['bʌtn] N bouton *m*; (*US: badge*) pin *m* ▶ VT (*also*: **button up**) boutonner ▶ VI se boutonner

buttonhole ['bʌtnhəul] N boutonnière *f* ▶ VT accrocher, arrêter, retenir

buttress ['bʌtrɪs] N contrefort *m*

buxom ['bʌksəm] ADJ aux formes avantageuses *or* épanouies, bien galbé(e)

buy [baɪ] (*pt, pp* **bought** [bɔːt]) VT acheter; (*Comm: company*) (r)acheter ▶ N achat *m*; **that was a good/bad ~** c'était un bon/mauvais achat; **to ~ sb sth/sth from sb** acheter qch à qn; **to ~ sb a drink** offrir un verre *or* à boire à qn; **can I ~ you a drink?** je vous offre un verre?;

where can I ~ some postcards? où est-ce que je peux acheter des cartes postales?
▶ **buy back** ᴠᴛ racheter
▶ **buy in** ᴠᴛ (*Brit*: *goods*) acheter, faire venir
▶ **buy into** ᴠᴛ ꜰᴜꜱ (*Brit Comm*) acheter des actions de
▶ **buy off** ᴠᴛ (*bribe*) acheter
▶ **buy out** ᴠᴛ (*partner*) désintéresser; (*business*) racheter
▶ **buy up** ᴠᴛ acheter en bloc, rafler
buyer ['baɪə'] ɴ acheteur(-euse) *m/f*; **~'s market** marché *m* favorable aux acheteurs
buy-out ['baɪaut] ɴ (*Comm*) rachat *m* (*d'entreprise*)
buzz [bʌz] ɴ bourdonnement *m*; (*inf*: *phone call*): **to give sb a ~** passer un coup de fil à qn ▶ ᴠɪ bourdonner ▶ ᴠᴛ (*call on intercom*) appeler; (*with buzzer*) sonner; (*Aviat*: *plane, building*) raser; **my head is buzzing** j'ai la tête qui bourdonne
▶ **buzz off** ᴠɪ (*inf*) s'en aller, ficher le camp
buzzard ['bʌzəd] ɴ buse *f*
buzzer ['bʌzə'] ɴ timbre *m* électrique
buzz word ɴ (*inf*) mot *m* à la mode *or* dans le vent

[KEYWORD]

by [baɪ] ᴘʀᴇᴘ **1** (*referring to cause, agent*) par, de; **killed by lightning** tué par la foudre; **surrounded by a fence** entouré d'une barrière; **a painting by Picasso** un tableau de Picasso
2 (*referring to method: manner: means*): **by bus/car** en autobus/voiture; **by train** par le *or* en train; **to pay by cheque** payer par chèque; **by moonlight/candlelight** à la lueur de la lune/d'une bougie; **by saving hard, he …** à force d'économiser, il …
3 (*via, through*) par; **we came by Dover** nous sommes venus par Douvres
4 (*close to, past*) à côté de; **the house by the school** la maison à côté de l'école; **a holiday by the sea** des vacances au bord de la mer; **she sat by his bed** elle était assise à son chevet; **she went by me** elle est passée à côté de moi; **I go by the post office every day** je passe devant la poste tous les jours
5 (*with time: not later than*) avant; (: *during*): **by daylight** à la lumière du jour; **by night** la nuit, de nuit; **by 4 o'clock** avant 4 heures; **by this**

time tomorrow d'ici demain à la même heure; **by the time I got here it was too late** lorsque je suis arrivé il était déjà trop tard
6 (*amount*) à; **by the kilo/metre** au kilo/au mètre; **paid by the hour** payé à l'heure; **to increase** *etc* **by the hour** augmenter *etc* d'heure en heure
7 (*Math: measure*): **to divide/multiply by 3** diviser/multiplier par 3; **a room 3 metres by 4** une pièce de 3 mètres sur 4; **it's broader by a metre** c'est plus large d'un mètre; **the bullet missed him by inches** la balle est passée à quelques centimètres de lui; **one by one** un à un; **little by little** petit à petit, peu à peu
8 (*according to*) d'après, selon; **it's 3 o'clock by my watch** il est 3 heures à ma montre; **it's all right by me** je n'ai rien contre
9: (**all**) **by oneself** *etc* tout(e) seul(e)
▶ ᴀᴅᴠ **1** *see* **go**; **pass** *etc*
2: **by and by** un peu plus tard, bientôt; **by and large** dans l'ensemble

bye ['baɪ], **bye-bye** ['baɪ'baɪ] ᴇxᴄʟ au revoir!, salut!
bye-law ['baɪlɔ:] ɴ = **by-law**
by-election ['baɪɪlɛkʃən] ɴ (*Brit*) élection (législative) partielle
Byelorussia [bjɛləu'rʌʃə] ɴ Biélorussie *f*
Byelorussian [bjɛləu'rʌʃən] ᴀᴅᴊ, ɴ = **Belorussian**
bygone ['baɪgɔn] ᴀᴅᴊ passé(e) ▶ ɴ: **let bygones be bygones** passons l'éponge, oublions le passé
by-law ['baɪlɔ:] ɴ arrêté municipal
bypass ['baɪpɑ:s] ɴ rocade *f*; (*Med*) pontage *m*
▶ ᴠᴛ éviter
by-product ['baɪprɔdʌkt] ɴ sous-produit *m*, dérivé *m*; (*fig*) conséquence *f* secondaire, retombée *f*
byre ['baɪə'] ɴ (*Brit*) étable *f* (à vaches)
bystander ['baɪstændə'] ɴ spectateur(-trice), badaud(e)
byte [baɪt] ɴ (*Comput*) octet *m*
byway ['baɪweɪ] ɴ chemin détourné
byword ['baɪwə:d] ɴ: **to be a ~ for** être synonyme de (*fig*)
by-your-leave ['baɪjɔ:'li:v] ɴ: **without so much as a ~** sans même demander la permission

Cc

C¹, c [si:] N (*letter*) C, c *m*; (*Scol: mark*) C; (*Mus*): **C do** *m*; **C for Charlie** C comme Célestin

C² ABBR (= *Celsius, centigrade*) C

c² ABBR (= *century*) s.; (*US etc*) = **cent**; (= *circa*) v.

CA N ABBR = **Central America**; (*BRIT*) = **chartered accountant** ▶ ABBR (*US*) = **California**

ca. ABBR (= *circa*) v

c/a ABBR = **capital account; credit account; current account**

CAA N ABBR *BRIT*: = **Civil Aviation Authority**; (*US*: = *Civil Aeronautics Authority*) direction de l'aviation civile

CAB N ABBR (*BRIT*) = **Citizens' Advice Bureau**

cab [kæb] N taxi *m*; (*of train, truck*) cabine *f*; (*horse-drawn*) fiacre *m*

cabaret ['kæbəreɪ] N attractions *fpl*; (*show*) spectacle *m* de cabaret

cabbage ['kæbɪdʒ] N chou *m*

cabbie, cabby ['kæbɪ], **cab driver** N (*inf*) taxi *m*, chauffeur *m* de taxi

cabin ['kæbɪn] N (*house*) cabane *f*, hutte *f*; (*on ship*) cabine *f*; (*on plane*) compartiment *m*

cabin crew N (*Aviat*) équipage *m*

cabin cruiser N yacht *m* (à moteur)

cabinet ['kæbɪnɪt] N (*Pol*) cabinet *m*; (*furniture*) petit meuble à tiroirs et rayons; (*also:* **display cabinet**) vitrine *f*, petite armoire vitrée

cabinet-maker ['kæbɪnɪtmeɪkə'] N ébéniste *m*

cabinet minister N ministre *m* (*membre du cabinet*)

cable ['keɪbl] N câble *m* ▶ VT câbler, télégraphier

cable car ['keɪblkɑ:'] N téléphérique *m*

cablegram ['keɪblɡræm] N câblogramme *m*

cable railway N (*BRIT*) funiculaire *m*

cable television N télévision *f* par câble

cache [kæʃ] N cachette *f*; **a ~ of food** *etc* un dépôt secret de provisions *etc*, une cachette contenant des provisions *etc*

cackle ['kækl] VI caqueter

cactus ['kæktəs] (*pl* **cacti** [-taɪ]) N cactus *m*

CAD N ABBR (= *computer-aided design*) CAO *f*

caddie ['kædɪ] N caddie *m*

cadet [kə'dɛt] N (*Mil*) élève *m* officier; **police ~** élève agent de police

cadge [kædʒ] VT (*inf*) se faire donner; **to ~ a meal (off sb)** se faire inviter à manger (par qn)

cadre ['kædrɪ] N cadre *m*

Caesarean, (*US*) **Cesarean** [si:'zɛərɪən] ADJ:

~ (section) césarienne *f*

CAF ABBR (*BRIT*: = *cost and freight*) C et F

café ['kæfeɪ] N ≈ café(-restaurant) *m* (*sans alcool*)

cafeteria [kæfɪ'tɪərɪə] N cafétéria *f*

caffeine ['kæfi:n] N caféine *f*

cage [keɪdʒ] N cage *f* ▶ VT mettre en cage

cagey ['keɪdʒɪ] ADJ (*inf*) réticent(e), méfiant(e)

cagoule [kə'ɡu:l] N K-way® *m*

cahoots [kə'hu:ts] N: **to be in ~ (with)** être de mèche (avec)

CAI N ABBR (= *computer-aided instruction*) EAO *m*

Cairo ['kaɪərəʊ] N Le Caire

cajole [kə'dʒəʊl] VT couvrir de flatteries *or* de gentillesses

cake [keɪk] N gâteau *m*; **~ of soap** savonnette *f*; **it's a piece of ~** (*inf*) c'est un jeu d'enfant; **he wants to have his ~ and eat it (too)** (*fig*) il veut tout avoir

caked [keɪkt] ADJ: **~ with** raidi(e) par, couvert(e) d'une croûte de

cake shop N pâtisserie *f*

Cal. ABBR (*US*) = **California**

calamitous [kə'læmɪtəs] ADJ catastrophique, désastreux(-euse)

calamity [kə'læmɪtɪ] N calamité *f*, désastre *m*

calcium ['kælsɪəm] N calcium *m*

calculate ['kælkjuleɪt] VT calculer; (*estimate: chances, effect*) évaluer

▶ **calculate on** VT FUS: **to ~ on sth/on doing sth** compter sur qch/faire qch

calculated ['kælkjuleɪtɪd] ADJ (*insult, action*) délibéré(e); **a ~ risk** un risque pris en toute connaissance de cause

calculating ['kælkjuleɪtɪŋ] ADJ calculateur(-trice)

calculation [kælkju'leɪʃən] N calcul *m*

calculator ['kælkjuleɪtə'] N machine *f* à calculer, calculatrice *f*

calculus ['kælkjuləs] N analyse *f* (mathématique), calcul *m* infinitésimal; **integral/differential ~** calcul intégral/différentiel

calendar ['kæləndə'] N calendrier *m*

calendar year N année civile

calf [kɑ:f] (*pl* **calves** [kɑ:vz]) N (*of cow*) veau *m*; (*of other animals*) petit *m*; (*also:* **calfskin**) veau *m*, vachette *f*; (*Anat*) mollet *m*

caliber ['kælɪbə'] N (*US*) = **calibre**

calibrate ['kælɪbreɪt] VT (*gun etc*) calibrer; (*scale of measuring instrument*) étalonner
calibre, (*US*) **caliber** ['kælɪbəʳ] N calibre *m*
calico ['kælɪkəu] N (*BRIT*) calicot *m*; (*US*) indienne *f*
Calif. ABBR (*US*) = **California**
California [kælɪ'fɔ:nɪə] N Californie *f*
calipers ['kælɪpəz] NPL (*US*) = **callipers**
call [kɔ:l] VT (*gen, also Tel*) appeler; (*announce: flight*) annoncer; (: *meeting*) convoquer; (: *strike*) lancer ▸ VI appeler; (*visit: also*: **call in, call round**) passer ▸ N (*shout*) appel *m*, cri *m*; (*summons: for flight etc, fig: lure*) appel; (*visit*) visite *f*; (*also*: **telephone call**) coup *m* de téléphone; communication *f*; **to be on** ~ être de permanence; **to be called** s'appeler; **she's called Suzanne** elle s'appelle Suzanne; **who is calling?** (*Tel*) qui est à l'appareil?; **London calling** (*Radio*) ici Londres; **please give me a** ~ **at 7** appelez-moi à 7 heures; **to make a** ~ téléphoner, passer un coup de fil; **can I make a** ~ **from here?** est-ce que je peux téléphoner d'ici?; **to pay a** ~ **on sb** rendre visite à qn, passer voir qn; **there's not much** ~ **for these items** ces articles ne sont pas très demandés
▸ **call at** VT FUS (*ship*) faire escale à; (*train*) s'arrêter à
▸ **call back** VI (*return*) repasser; (*Tel*) rappeler
▸ VT (*Tel*) rappeler; **can you** ~ **back later?** pouvez-vous rappeler plus tard?
▸ **call for** VT FUS (*demand*) demander; (*fetch*) passer prendre
▸ **call in** VT (*doctor, expert, police*) appeler, faire venir
▸ **call off** VT annuler; **the strike was called off** l'ordre de grève a été rapporté
▸ **call on** VT FUS (*visit*) rendre visite à, passer voir; (*request*): **to** ~ **on sb to do** inviter qn à faire
▸ **call out** VI pousser un cri *or* des cris ▸ VT (*doctor, police, troops*) appeler
▸ **call up** VT (*Mil*) appeler, mobiliser; (*Tel*) appeler
call box ['kɔ:lbɔks] N (*BRIT*) cabine *f* téléphonique
call centre, (*US*) **call center** N centre *m* d'appels
caller ['kɔ:ləʳ] N (*Tel*) personne *f* qui appelle; (*visitor*) visiteur *m*; **hold the line,** ~! (*Tel*) ne quittez pas, Monsieur (*or* Madame)!
call girl N call-girl *f*
call-in ['kɔ:lɪn] N (*US Radio, TV*) programme *m* à ligne ouverte
calling ['kɔ:lɪŋ] N vocation *f*; (*trade, occupation*) état *m*
calling card N (*US*) carte *f* de visite
callipers, (*US*) **calipers** ['kælɪpəz] NPL (*Math*) compas *m*; (*Med*) appareil *m* orthopédique; gouttière *f*; étrier *m*
callous ['kæləs] ADJ dur(e), insensible
callousness ['kæləsnɪs] N dureté *f*, manque *m* de cœur, insensibilité *f*
callow ['kæləu] ADJ sans expérience (de la vie)
calm [kɑ:m] ADJ calme ▸ N calme *m* ▸ VT calmer, apaiser
▸ **calm down** VI se calmer, s'apaiser ▸ VT

calmer, apaiser
calmly ['kɑ:mlɪ] ADV calmement, avec calme
calmness ['kɑ:mnɪs] N calme *m*
Calor gas® ['kælə-] N (*BRIT*) butane *m*, butagaz® *m*
calorie ['kælərɪ] N calorie *f*; **low** ~ **product** produit *m* pauvre en calories
calve [kɑ:v] VI vêler, mettre bas
calves [kɑ:vz] NPL of **calf**
CAM N ABBR (= *computer-aided manufacturing*) FAO *f*
camber ['kæmbəʳ] N (*of road*) bombement *m*
Cambodia [kæm'bəudɪə] N Cambodge *m*
Cambodian [kæm'bəudɪən] ADJ cambodgien(ne) ▸ N Cambodgien(ne)
Cambs ABBR (*BRIT*) = **Cambridgeshire**
camcorder ['kæmkɔ:dəʳ] N caméscope *m*
came [keɪm] PT of **come**
camel ['kæməl] N chameau *m*
cameo ['kæmɪəu] N camée *m*
camera ['kæmərə] N appareil photo *m*; (*Cine, TV*) caméra *f*; **digital** ~ appareil numérique; **in** ~ à huis clos, en privé
cameraman ['kæmərəmæn] N (*irreg*) caméraman *m*
camera phone N téléphone *m* avec appareil photo
Cameroon, Cameroun [kæmə'ru:n] N Cameroun *m*
camouflage ['kæməflɑ:ʒ] N camouflage *m* ▸ VT camoufler
camp [kæmp] N camp *m* ▸ VI camper ▸ ADJ (*man*) efféminé(e)
campaign [kæm'peɪn] N (*Mil, Pol*) campagne *f* ▸ VI (*also fig*) faire campagne; **to** ~ **for/against** militer pour/contre
campaigner [kæm'peɪnəʳ] N: ~ **for** partisan(e) de; ~ **against** opposant(e) à
camp bed ['kæmp'bed] N (*BRIT*) lit *m* de camp
camper ['kæmpəʳ] N campeur(-euse); (*vehicle*) camping-car *m*
camping ['kæmpɪŋ] N camping *m*; **to go** ~ faire du camping
camping gas® N butane *m*
campsite ['kæmpsaɪt] N (terrain *m* de) camping *m*
campus ['kæmpəs] N campus *m*
camshaft ['kæmʃɑ:ft] N arbre *m* à came
can¹ [kæn] N (*of milk, oil, water*) bidon *m*; (*tin*) boîte *f* (de conserve) ▸ VT mettre en conserve; **a** ~ **of beer** une canette de bière; **he had to carry the** ~ (*BRIT inf*) on lui a fait porter le chapeau; *see also* **can²**

(KEYWORD)

can² [kæn] (*negative* **cannot, can't,** *conditional, pt* **could**) AUX VB **1** (*be able to*) pouvoir; **you can do it if you try** vous pouvez le faire si vous essayez; **I can't hear you** je ne t'entends pas
2 (*know how to*) savoir; **I can swim/play tennis/drive** je sais nager/jouer au tennis/conduire; **can you speak French?** parlez-vous français?
3 (*may*) pouvoir; **can I use your phone?** puis-je me servir de votre téléphone?
4 (*expressing disbelief, puzzlement etc*): **it can't be**

499

true! ce n'est pas possible!; **what** CAN **he want?** qu'est-ce qu'il peut bien vouloir?
5 (*expressing possibility, suggestion etc*): **he could be in the library** il est peut-être dans la bibliothèque; **she could have been delayed** il se peut qu'elle ait été retardée; **they could have forgotten** ils ont pu oublier

Canada ['kænədə] N Canada m
Canadian [kə'neɪdɪən] ADJ canadien(ne) ▶ N Canadien(ne)
canal [kə'næl] N canal m
canary [kə'nɛərɪ] N canari m, serin m
Canary Islands, Canaries [kə'nɛərɪz] NPL: **the ~** les (îles fpl) Canaries fpl
Canberra ['kænbərə] N Canberra
cancel ['kænsəl] VT annuler; (*train*) supprimer; (*party, appointment*) décommander; (*cross out*) barrer, rayer; (*stamp*) oblitérer; (*cheque*) faire opposition à; **I would like to ~ my booking** je voudrais annuler ma réservation
▶ **cancel out** VT annuler; **they ~ each other out** ils s'annulent
cancellation [kænsə'leɪʃən] N annulation f; suppression f; oblitération f; (*Tourism*) réservation annulée, client etc qui s'est décommandé
Cancer ['kænsər] N (*Astrology*) le Cancer; **to be ~** être du Cancer
cancer ['kænsər] N cancer m
cancerous ['kænsrəs] ADJ cancéreux(-euse)
cancer patient N cancéreux(-euse)
cancer research N recherche f contre le cancer
C and F ABBR (BRIT: = *cost and freight*) C et F
candid ['kændɪd] ADJ (très) franc (franche), sincère
candidacy ['kændɪdəsɪ] N candidature f
candidate ['kændɪdeɪt] N candidat(e)
candidature ['kændɪdətʃər] N (BRIT) = **candidacy**
candied ['kændɪd] ADJ confit(e); **~ apple** (US) pomme caramélisée
candle ['kændl] N bougie f; (*of tallow*) chandelle f; (*in church*) cierge m
candlelight ['kændllaɪt] N: **by ~** à la lumière d'une bougie; (*dinner*) aux chandelles
candlestick ['kændlstɪk] N (*also*: **candle holder**) bougeoir m; (*: bigger, ornate*) chandelier m
candour, (US) **candor** ['kændər] N (grande) franchise or sincérité
C & W N ABBR = **country and western**
candy ['kændɪ] N sucre candi; (US) bonbon m
candy bar (US) N barre f chocolatée
candyfloss ['kændɪflɔs] N (BRIT) barbe f à papa
candy store N (US) confiserie f
cane [keɪn] N canne f; (*for baskets, chairs etc*) rotin m ▶ VT (BRIT Scol) administrer des coups de bâton à
canine ['kænaɪn] ADJ canin(e)
canister ['kænɪstər] N boîte f (gén en métal); (*of gas*) bombe f
cannabis ['kænəbɪs] N (*drug*) cannabis m; (*cannabis plant*) chanvre indien
canned ['kænd] ADJ (*food*) en boîte, en conserve; (*inf: music*) enregistré(e); (BRIT inf: drunk) bourré(e); (US inf: worker) mis(e) à la porte

cannibal ['kænɪbəl] N cannibale mf, anthropophage mf
cannibalism ['kænɪbəlɪzəm] N cannibalisme m, anthropophagie f
cannon ['kænən] (pl ~ or **cannons**) N (*gun*) canon m
cannonball ['kænənbɔːl] N boulet m de canon
cannon fodder N chair f à canon
cannot ['kænɔt] = **can not**
canny ['kænɪ] ADJ madré(e), finaud(e)
canoe [kə'nuː] N pirogue f; (*Sport*) canoë m
canoeing [kə'nuːɪŋ] N (*sport*) canoë m
canoeist [kə'nuːɪst] N canoéiste mf
canon ['kænən] N (*clergyman*) chanoine m; (*standard*) canon m
canonize ['kænənaɪz] VT canoniser
can-opener [-'əupnər] N ouvre-boîte m
canopy ['kænəpɪ] N baldaquin m; dais m
cant [kænt] N jargon m ▶ VT, VI pencher
can't [kɑːnt] = **can not**
Cantab. ABBR (BRIT: = *cantabrigiensis*) *of Cambridge*
cantankerous [kæn'tæŋkərəs] ADJ querelleur(-euse), acariâtre
canteen [kæn'tiːn] N (*eating place*) cantine f; (BRIT: *of cutlery*) ménagère f
canter ['kæntər] N petit galop ▶ VI aller au petit galop
cantilever ['kæntɪliːvər] N porte-à-faux m inv
canvas ['kænvəs] N (*gen*) toile f; **under ~** (*camping*) sous la tente; (*Naut*) toutes voiles dehors
canvass ['kænvəs] VI (*Pol*): **to ~ for** faire campagne pour ▶ VT (*Pol: district*) faire la tournée électorale dans; (: *person*) solliciter le suffrage de; (*Comm: district*) prospecter; (: *citizens, opinions*) sonder
canvasser ['kænvəsər] N (*Pol*) agent électoral; (*Comm*) démarcheur m
canvassing ['kænvəsɪŋ] N (*Pol*) prospection électorale, démarchage électoral; (*Comm*) démarchage, prospection
canyon ['kænjən] N cañon m, gorge (profonde)
CAP N ABBR (= *Common Agricultural Policy*) PAC f
cap [kæp] N casquette f; (*for swimming*) bonnet m de bain; (*of pen*) capuchon m; (*of bottle*) capsule f; (BRIT: *contraceptive: also*: **Dutch cap**) diaphragme m; (*Football*) sélection f pour l'équipe nationale ▶ VT capsuler; (*outdo*) surpasser; (*put limit on*) plafonner; **capped with** coiffé(e) de; **and to ~ it all, he …** (BRIT) pour couronner le tout, il …
capability [keɪpə'bɪlɪtɪ] N aptitude f, capacité f
capable ['keɪpəbl] ADJ capable; **~ of** (*interpretation etc*) susceptible de
capacious [kə'peɪʃəs] ADJ vaste
capacity [kə'pæsɪtɪ] N (*of container*) capacité f, contenance f; (*ability*) aptitude f; **filled to ~** plein(e); **in his ~ as** en sa qualité de; **in an advisory ~** à titre consultatif; **to work at full ~** travailler à plein rendement
cape [keɪp] N (*garment*) cape f; (*Geo*) cap m
Cape of Good Hope N cap m de Bonne Espérance
caper ['keɪpər] N (*Culin: gen pl*) câpre f; (*prank*) farce f

Cape Town N Le Cap
capita ['kæpɪtə] N *see* **per capita**
capital ['kæpɪtl] N (*also*: **capital city**) capitale *f*; (*money*) capital *m*; (*also*: **capital letter**) majuscule *f*
capital account N balance *f* des capitaux; (*of country*) compte capital
capital allowance N provision *f* pour amortissement
capital assets NPL immobilisations *fpl*
capital expenditure N dépenses *fpl* d'équipement
capital gains tax N impôt *m* sur les plus-values
capital goods N biens *mpl* d'équipement
capital-intensive ['kæpɪtlɪn'tensɪv] ADJ à forte proportion de capitaux
capitalism ['kæpɪtəlɪzəm] N capitalisme *m*
capitalist ['kæpɪtəlɪst] ADJ, N capitaliste *mf*
capitalize ['kæpɪtəlaɪz] VT (*provide with capital*) financer
▸ **capitalize on** VT FUS (*fig*) profiter de
capital punishment N peine capitale
capital transfer tax N (*BRIT*) impôt *m* sur le transfert de propriété
Capitol ['kæpɪtl] N: **the** ~ le Capitole; *voir article*

> Le *Capitol* est le siège du *Congress*, à Washington. Il est situé sur Capitol Hill.

capitulate [kə'pɪtjuleɪt] VI capituler
capitulation [kəpɪtju'leɪʃən] N capitulation *f*
capricious [kə'prɪʃəs] ADJ capricieux(-euse), fantasque
Capricorn ['kæprɪkɔːn] N le Capricorne; **to be** ~ être du Capricorne
caps [kæps] ABBR = **capital letters**
capsize [kæp'saɪz] VT faire chavirer ▸ VI chavirer
capstan ['kæpstən] N cabestan *m*
capsule ['kæpsjuːl] N capsule *f*
Capt. ABBR (= *captain*) Cne
captain ['kæptɪn] N capitaine *m* ▸ VT commander, être le capitaine de
caption ['kæpʃən] N légende *f*
captivate ['kæptɪveɪt] VT captiver, fasciner
captive ['kæptɪv] ADJ, N captif(-ive)
captivity [kæp'tɪvɪtɪ] N captivité *f*
captor ['kæptər] N (*unlawful*) ravisseur *m*; (*lawful*): **his captors** les gens (*or* ceux *etc*) qui l'ont arrêté
capture ['kæptʃər] VT (*prisoner, animal*) capturer; (*town*) prendre; (*attention*) capter; (*Comput*) saisir ▸ N capture *f*; (*of data*) saisie *f* de données
car [kɑːʳ] N voiture *f*, auto *f*; (*US Rail*) wagon *m*, voiture; **by** ~ en voiture
carafe [kə'ræf] N carafe *f*
carafe wine N (*in restaurant*) ≈ vin ouvert
caramel ['kærəməl] N caramel *m*
carat ['kærət] N carat *m*; **18** ~ **gold** or *m* à 18 carats
caravan ['kærəvæn] N caravane *f*
caravan site N (*BRIT*) camping *m* pour caravanes
caraway ['kærəweɪ] N: ~ **seed** graine *f* de cumin, cumin *m*
carbohydrate [kɑːbəu'haɪdreɪt] N hydrate *m* de carbone; (*food*) féculent *m*
carbolic acid [kɑː'bɔlɪk-] N phénol *m*
car bomb N voiture piégée
carbon ['kɑːbən] N carbone *m*
carbonated ['kɑːbəneɪtɪd] ADJ (*drink*) gazeux(-euse)
carbon copy N carbone *m*
carbon credit N crédit *m* carbone
carbon dioxide [-daɪ'ɔksaɪd] N gaz *m* carbonique, dioxyde *m* de carbone
carbon footprint N empreinte *f* carbone
carbon monoxide [-mɔ'nɔksaɪd] N oxyde *m* de carbone
carbon-neutral ADJ neutre en carbone
carbon offset N compensation *f* carbone; ~ **credit** crédit de compensation carbone
carbon paper N papier *m* carbone
carbon ribbon N ruban *m* carbone
car boot sale N *voir article*

> Type de brocante très populaire, où chacun vide sa cave ou son grenier. Les articles sont présentés dans des coffres de voitures et la vente a souvent lieu sur un parking ou dans un champ. Les brocanteurs d'un jour doivent s'acquitter d'une petite contribution pour participer à la vente.

carburettor, (*US*) **carburetor** [kɑː'bju'rɛtəʳ] N carburateur *m*
carcass ['kɑːkəs] N carcasse *f*
carcinogenic [kɑːsɪnə'dʒenɪk] ADJ cancérigène
card [kɑːd] N carte *f*; (*material*) carton *m*; (*membership card*) carte d'adhérent; **to play cards** jouer aux cartes
cardamom ['kɑːdəməm] N cardamome *f*
cardboard ['kɑːdbɔːd] N carton *m*
cardboard box N (boîte *f* en) carton *m*
cardboard city N endroit de la ville où dorment les *SDF dans des boîtes en carton*
card-carrying member ['kɑːdkærɪɪŋ-] N membre actif
card game N jeu *m* de cartes
cardiac ['kɑːdɪæk] ADJ cardiaque
cardigan ['kɑːdɪgən] N cardigan *m*
cardinal ['kɑːdɪnl] ADJ cardinal(e); (*importance*) capital(e) ▸ N cardinal *m*
card index N fichier *m* (alphabétique)
cardphone ['kɑːdfəun] N téléphone *m* à carte (magnétique)
cardsharp ['kɑːdʃɑːp] N tricheur(-euse) professionnel(le)
card vote N (*BRIT*) vote *m* de délégués
CARE [kɛəʳ] N ABBR (= *Cooperative for American Relief Everywhere*) association charitable
care [kɛəʳ] N soin *m*, attention *f*; (*worry*) souci *m* ▸ VI: **to** ~ **about** (*feel interest for*) se soucier de, s'intéresser à; (*person: love*) être attaché(e) à; **in sb's** ~ à la garde de qn, confié à qn; ~ **of** (*on letter*) chez; **"with** ~**"** "fragile"; **to take** ~ (**to do**) faire attention (à faire); **to take** ~ **of** vt s'occuper de; **the child has been taken into** ~ l'enfant a été placé en institution; **would you** ~ **to/for ...?** voulez-vous ...?; **I wouldn't** ~ **to do it** je n'aimerais pas le faire; **I don't** ~ ça m'est bien égal, peu m'importe; **I couldn't** ~ **less** cela

m'est complètement égal, je m'en fiche complètement
▸ **care for** VT FUS s'occuper de; (*like*) aimer
careen [kə'riːn] VI (*ship*) donner de la bande ▸ VT caréner, mettre en carène
career [kə'rɪə'] N carrière f ▸ VI (*also*: **career along**) aller à toute allure
career girl N jeune fille f or femme f qui veut faire carrière
careers officer N conseiller(-ère) d'orientation (professionnelle)
career woman N (*irreg*) femme ambitieuse
carefree ['kɛəfriː] ADJ sans souci, insouciant(e)
careful ['kɛəful] ADJ soigneux(-euse); (*cautious*) prudent(e); (**be**) ~! (fais) attention!; **to be ~ with one's money** regarder à la dépense
carefully ['kɛəfəlɪ] ADV avec soin, soigneusement; prudemment
caregiver ['kɛəgɪvə'] N (US: *professional*) travailleur social; (*unpaid*) *personne qui s'occupe d'un proche qui est malade*
careless ['kɛəlɪs] ADJ négligent(e); (*heedless*) insouciant(e)
carelessly ['kɛəlɪslɪ] ADV négligemment; avec insouciance
carelessness ['kɛəlɪsnɪs] N manque m de soin, négligence f; insouciance f
carer ['kɛərə'] N (*professional*) travailleur social; (*unpaid*) *personne qui s'occupe d'un proche qui est malade*
caress [kə'rɛs] N caresse f ▸ VT caresser
caretaker ['kɛəteɪkə'] N gardien(ne), concierge mf
caretaker government N (BRIT) gouvernement m intérimaire
car-ferry ['kɑːfɛrɪ] N (*on sea*) ferry(-boat) m; (*on river*) bac m
cargo ['kɑːgəu] (*pl* **cargoes**) N cargaison f, chargement m
cargo boat N cargo m
cargo plane N avion-cargo m
car hire N (BRIT) location f de voitures
Caribbean [kærɪ'biːən] ADJ, N: **the ~ (Sea)** la mer des Antilles or des Caraïbes
caricature ['kærɪkətjuə'] N caricature f
caring ['kɛərɪŋ] ADJ (*person*) bienveillant(e); (*society, organization*) humanitaire
carnage ['kɑːnɪdʒ] N carnage m
carnal ['kɑːnl] ADJ charnel(le)
carnation [kɑː'neɪʃən] N œillet m
carnival ['kɑːnɪvl] N (*public celebration*) carnaval m; (US: *funfair*) fête foraine
carnivorous [kɑː'nɪvərəs] ADJ carnivore, carnassier(-ière)
carol ['kærəl] N: (**Christmas**) ~ chant m de Noël
carouse [kə'rauz] VI faire la bringue
carousel [kærə'sɛl] N (*for luggage*) carrousel m; (US) manège m
carp [kɑːp] N (*fish*) carpe f
▸ **carp at** VT FUS critiquer
car park (BRIT) N parking m, parc m de stationnement
carpenter ['kɑːpɪntə'] N charpentier m; (*joiner*) menuisier m

carpentry ['kɑːpɪntrɪ] N charpenterie f, métier m de charpentier; (*woodwork: at school etc*) menuiserie f
carpet ['kɑːpɪt] N tapis m ▸ VT recouvrir (d'un tapis); **fitted ~** (BRIT) moquette f
carpet bombing N bombardement intensif
carpet slippers NPL pantoufles fpl
carpet sweeper [-'swiːpə'] N balai m mécanique
car phone N téléphone m de voiture
car rental N (US) location f de voitures
carriage ['kærɪdʒ] N (BRIT Rail) wagon m; (*horse-drawn*) voiture f; (*of goods*) transport m; (: *cost*) port m; (*of typewriter*) chariot m; (*bearing*) maintien m, port m; **~ forward** port dû; **~ free** franco de port; **~ paid** (en) port payé
carriage return N retour m à la ligne
carriageway ['kærɪdʒweɪ] N (BRIT: *part of road*) chaussée f
carrier ['kærɪə'] N transporteur m, camionneur m; (*company*) entreprise f de transport; (*Med*) porteur(-euse); (*Naut*) porte-avions m inv
carrier bag N (BRIT) sac m en papier or en plastique
carrier pigeon N pigeon voyageur
carrion ['kærɪən] N charogne f
carrot ['kærət] N carotte f
carry ['kærɪ] VT (*subj: person*) porter; (: *vehicle*) transporter; (*a motion, bill*) voter, adopter; (*Math: figure*) retenir; (*Comm: interest*) rapporter; (*involve: responsibilities etc*) comporter, impliquer; (*Med: disease*) être porteur de ▸ VI (*sound*) porter; **to get carried away** (*fig*) s'emballer, s'enthousiasmer; **this loan carries 10% interest** ce prêt est à 10% (d'intérêt)
▸ **carry forward** VT (*gen, Book-keeping*) reporter
▸ **carry on** VI (*continue*) continuer; (*inf: make a fuss*) faire des histoires ▸ VT (*conduct: business*) diriger; (: *conversation*) entretenir; (*continue: business, conversation*) continuer; **to ~ on with sth/doing** continuer qch/à faire
▸ **carry out** VT (*orders*) exécuter; (*investigation*) effectuer; (*idea, threat*) mettre à exécution
carrycot ['kærɪkɔt] N (BRIT) porte-bébé m
carry-on ['kærɪ'ɔn] N (*inf: fuss*) histoires fpl; (: *annoying behaviour*) cirque m, cinéma m
cart [kɑːt] N charrette f ▸ VT (*inf*) transporter
carte blanche ['kɑːt'blɔnʃ] N: **to give sb ~** donner carte blanche à qn
cartel [kɑː'tɛl] N (*Comm*) cartel m
cartilage ['kɑːtɪlɪdʒ] N cartilage m
cartographer [kɑː'tɔgrəfə'] N cartographe mf
cartography [kɑː'tɔgrəfɪ] N cartographie f
carton ['kɑːtən] N (*box*) carton m; (*of yogurt*) pot m (en carton); (*of cigarettes*) cartouche f
cartoon [kɑː'tuːn] N (*Press*) dessin m (humoristique); (*satirical*) caricature f; (*comic strip*) bande dessinée; (*Cine*) dessin animé
cartoonist [kɑː'tuːnɪst] N dessinateur(-trice) humoristique; caricaturiste mf; auteur m de dessins animés; auteur de bandes dessinées
cartridge ['kɑːtrɪdʒ] N (*for gun, pen*) cartouche f; (*for camera*) chargeur m; (*music tape*) cassette f; (*of record player*) cellule f

cartwheel ['kɑ:twi:l] N roue f; **to turn a ~** faire la roue
carve [kɑ:v] VT (*meat: also:* **carve up**) découper; (*wood, stone*) tailler, sculpter
carving ['kɑ:vɪŋ] N (*in wood etc*) sculpture f
carving knife N couteau m à découper
car wash N station f de lavage (de voitures)
Casablanca [kæsə'blæŋkə] N Casablanca
cascade [kæs'keɪd] N cascade f ▸ VI tomber en cascade
case [keɪs] N cas m; (*Law*) affaire f, procès m; (*box*) caisse f, boîte f; (*for glasses*) étui m; (*BRIT also:* **suitcase**) valise f; (*Typ*): **lower/upper ~** minuscule f/majuscule f; **to have a good ~** avoir de bons arguments; **there's a strong ~ for reform** il y aurait lieu d'engager une réforme; **in ~ of** en cas de; **in ~ he** au cas où il; **just in ~** à tout hasard; **in any ~** en tout cas, de toute façon
case history N (*Med*) dossier médical, antécédents médicaux
case study N étude f de cas
cash [kæʃ] N argent m; (*Comm*) (argent m) liquide m, numéraire m; liquidités fpl; (*in payment*) argent comptant, espèces fpl ▸ VT encaisser; **to pay (in) ~** payer (en argent) comptant *or* en espèces; **~ with order/on delivery** (*Comm*) payable *or* paiement à la commande/livraison; **to be short of ~** être à court d'argent; **I haven't got any ~** je n'ai pas de liquide
▸ **cash in** VT (*insurance policy etc*) toucher
▸ **cash in on** VT FUS profiter de
cash account N compte m caisse
cash and carry N libre-service m de gros, cash and carry m inv
cashback ['kæʃbæk] N (*discount*) remise f; (*at supermarket etc*) retrait m (à la caisse)
cashbook ['kæʃbuk] N livre m de caisse
cash box N caisse f
cash card N carte f de retrait
cash desk N (*BRIT*) caisse f
cash discount N escompte m de caisse (pour paiement au comptant), remise f au comptant
cash dispenser N distributeur m automatique de billets
cashew [kæ'ʃu:] N (*also:* **cashew nut**) noix f de cajou
cash flow N cash-flow m, marge brute d'autofinancement
cashier [kæ'ʃɪər] N caissier(-ère) ▸ VT (*Mil*) destituer, casser
cashmere ['kæʃmɪər] N cachemire m
cash payment N paiement comptant, versement m en espèces
cash point N distributeur m automatique de billets
cash price N prix comptant
cash register N caisse enregistreuse
cash sale N vente f au comptant
casing ['keɪsɪŋ] N revêtement (protecteur), enveloppe (protectrice)
casino [kə'si:nəu] N casino m
cask [kɑ:sk] N tonneau m

casket ['kɑ:skɪt] N coffret m; (*US: coffin*) cercueil m
Caspian Sea ['kæspɪən-] N: **the ~** la mer Caspienne
casserole ['kæsərəul] N (*pot*) cocotte f; (*food*) ragoût m (en cocotte)
cassette [kæ'set] N cassette f
cassette deck N platine f cassette
cassette player N lecteur m de cassettes
cassette recorder N magnétophone m à cassettes
cast [kɑ:st] (*vb: pt, pp* ~) VT (*throw*) jeter; (*shadow: lit*) projeter; (*: fig*) jeter; (*glance*) jeter; (*shed*) perdre; se dépouiller de; (*metal*) couler, fondre ▸ N (*Theat*) distribution f; (*mould*) moule m; (*also:* **plaster cast**) plâtre m; **to ~ sb as Hamlet** attribuer à qn le rôle d'Hamlet; **to ~ one's vote** voter, exprimer son suffrage; **to ~ doubt on** jeter un doute sur
▸ **cast aside** VT (*reject*) rejeter
▸ **cast off** VI (*Naut*) larguer les amarres; (*Knitting*) arrêter les mailles ▸ VT (*Knitting*) arrêter
▸ **cast on** (*Knitting*) VT monter ▸ VI monter les mailles
castanets [kæstə'nets] NPL castagnettes fpl
castaway ['kɑ:stəweɪ] N naufragé(e)
caste [kɑ:st] N caste f, classe sociale
caster sugar ['kɑ:stə-] N (*BRIT*) sucre m semoule
casting vote ['kɑ:stɪŋ-] N (*BRIT*) voix prépondérante (*pour départager*)
cast iron N fonte f
cast-iron ['kɑ:staɪən] ADJ (*lit*) de *or* en fonte; (*fig: will*) de fer; (*alibi*) en béton
castle ['kɑ:sl] N château m; (*fortress*) château-fort m; (*Chess*) tour f
cast-offs ['kɑ:stɔfs] NPL vêtements mpl dont on ne veut plus
castor ['kɑ:stər] N (*wheel*) roulette f
castor oil N huile f de ricin
castrate [kæs'treɪt] VT châtrer
casual ['kæʒjul] ADJ (*by chance*) de hasard, fait(e) au hasard, fortuit(e); (*irregular: work etc*) temporaire; (*unconcerned*) désinvolte; **~ wear** vêtements mpl sport inv
casual labour N main-d'œuvre f temporaire
casually ['kæʒjulɪ] ADV avec désinvolture, négligemment; (*by chance*) fortuitement
casualty ['kæʒjultɪ] N accidenté(e), blessé(e); (*dead*) victime f, mort(e); (*BRIT Med: department*) urgences fpl; **heavy casualties** lourdes pertes
casualty ward N (*BRIT*) service m des urgences
cat [kæt] N chat m
catacombs ['kætəku:mz] NPL catacombes fpl
Catalan ['kætəlæn] ADJ catalan(e)
catalogue, (*US*) **catalog** ['kætəlɔg] N catalogue m ▸ VT cataloguer
catalyst ['kætəlɪst] N catalyseur m
catalytic converter [kætə'lɪtɪkkən'vɜ:tər] N pot m catalytique
catapult ['kætəpʌlt] N lance-pierres m inv, fronde f; (*Hist*) catapulte f
cataract ['kætərækt] N (*also Med*) cataracte f
catarrh [kə'tɑ:r] N rhume m chronique, catarrhe f
catastrophe [kə'tæstrəfɪ] N catastrophe f
catastrophic [kætə'strɔfɪk] ADJ catastrophique

catcall ['kætkɔːl] N (*at meeting etc*) sifflet m
catch [kætʃ] (*pt, pp* **caught** [kɔːt]) VT (*ball, train, thief, cold*) attraper; (*person: by surprise*) prendre, surprendre; (*understand*) saisir; (*get entangled*) accrocher ▶ VI (*fire*) prendre; (*get entangled*) s'accrocher ▶ N (*fish etc*) prise f; (*thief etc*) capture f; (*hidden problem*) attrape f; (*Tech*) loquet m; cliquet m; **to ~ sb's attention** *or* **eye** attirer l'attention de qn; **to ~ fire** prendre feu; **to ~ sight of** apercevoir; **to play ~** jouer à chat; (*with ball*) jouer à attraper le ballon
▶ **catch on** VI (*become popular*) prendre; (*understand*) **to ~ on (to sth)** saisir (qch)
▶ **catch out** VT (*BRIT fig: with trick question*) prendre en défaut
▶ **catch up** VI (*with work*) se rattraper, combler son retard ▶ VT (*also:* **catch up with**) rattraper
catch-22 ['kætʃtwentɪ'tuː] N: **it's a ~ situation** c'est (une situation) sans issue
catching ['kætʃɪŋ] ADJ (*Med*) contagieux(-euse)
catchment area ['kætʃmənt-] N (*BRIT Scol*) aire f de recrutement; (*Geo*) bassin m hydrographique
catch phrase N slogan m, expression toute faite
catchy ['kætʃɪ] ADJ (*tune*) facile à retenir
catechism ['kætɪkɪzəm] N catéchisme m
categoric [kætɪ'gɔrɪk], **categorical** [kætɪ'gɔrɪkl] ADJ catégorique
categorize ['kætɪgəraɪz] VT classer par catégories
category ['kætɪgərɪ] N catégorie f
cater ['keɪtər] VI: **to ~ for** (*BRIT: needs*) satisfaire, pourvoir à; (*: readers, consumers*) s'adresser à, pourvoir aux besoins de; (*: Comm: parties etc*) préparer des repas pour
caterer ['keɪtərər] N traiteur m; fournisseur m
catering ['keɪtərɪŋ] N restauration f; approvisionnement m, ravitaillement m
caterpillar ['kætəpɪlər] N chenille f ▶ CPD (*vehicle*) à chenille; **~ track** n chenille f
cat flap N chatière f
cathedral [kə'θiːdrəl] N cathédrale f
cathode ['kæθəʊd] N cathode f
cathode ray tube N tube m cathodique
Catholic ['kæθəlɪk] (*Rel*) ADJ catholique ▶ N catholique mf
catholic ['kæθəlɪk] ADJ (*wide-ranging*) éclectique; universel(le); libéral(e)
catsup ['kætsəp] N (*US*) ketchup m
cattle ['kætl] NPL bétail m, bestiaux mpl
catty ['kætɪ] ADJ méchant(e)
catwalk ['kætwɔːk] N passerelle f; (*for models*) podium m (*de défilé de mode*)
Caucasian [kɔː'keɪzɪən] ADJ, N caucasien(ne)
Caucasus ['kɔːkəsəs] N Caucase m
caucus ['kɔːkəs] N (*US Pol*) comité électoral (pour désigner des candidats); *voir article*; (*BRIT Pol: group*) comité local (*d'un parti politique*)

> Un *caucus* aux États-Unis est une réunion restreinte des principaux dirigeants d'un parti politique, précédant souvent une assemblée générale, dans le but de choisir des candidats ou de définir une ligne d'action. Par extension, ce terme désigne également l'état-major d'un parti politique.

caught [kɔːt] PT, PP *of* **catch**
cauliflower ['kɒlɪflaʊər] N chou-fleur m
cause [kɔːz] N cause f ▶ VT causer; **there is no ~ for concern** il n'y a pas lieu de s'inquiéter; **to ~ sth to be done** faire faire qch; **to ~ sb to do sth** faire faire qch à qn
causeway ['kɔːzweɪ] N chaussée (surélevée)
caustic ['kɔːstɪk] ADJ caustique
caution ['kɔːʃən] N prudence f; (*warning*) avertissement m ▶ VT avertir, donner un avertissement à
cautious ['kɔːʃəs] ADJ prudent(e)
cautiously ['kɔːʃəslɪ] ADV prudemment, avec prudence
cautiousness ['kɔːʃəsnɪs] N prudence f
cavalier [kævə'lɪər] ADJ cavalier(-ère), désinvolte ▶ N (*knight*) cavalier m
cavalry ['kævəlrɪ] N cavalerie f
cave [keɪv] N caverne f, grotte f ▶ VI: **to go caving** faire de la spéléo(logie)
▶ **cave in** VI (*roof etc*) s'effondrer
caveman ['keɪvmæn] N (*irreg*) homme m des cavernes
cavern ['kævən] N caverne f
caviar, caviare ['kævɪɑːr] N caviar m
cavity ['kævɪtɪ] N cavité f; (*Med*) carie f
cavity wall insulation N isolation f des murs creux
cavort [kə'vɔːt] VI cabrioler, faire des cabrioles
cayenne [keɪ'ɛn] N (*also:* **cayenne pepper**) poivre m de cayenne
CB N ABBR (= *Citizens' Band (Radio)*) CB f; (*BRIT:* = *Companion of (the Order of) the Bath*) titre honorifique
CBC N ABBR (= *Canadian Broadcasting Corporation*) organisme de radiodiffusion
CBE N ABBR (= *Companion of (the Order of) the British Empire*) titre honorifique
CBI N ABBR (= *Confederation of British Industry*) ≈ MEDEF m (= *Mouvement des entreprises de France*)
CBS N ABBR (*US:* = *Columbia Broadcasting System*) chaîne de télévision
CC ABBR (*BRIT*) = **county council**
cc ABBR (= *cubic centimetre*) cm³; (*on letter etc:* = *carbon copy*) cc
CCA N ABBR (*US:* = *Circuit Court of Appeals*) cour d'appel itinérante
CCTV N ABBR = **closed-circuit television**
CCTV camera N caméra f de vidéosurveillance
CCU N ABBR (*US:* = *coronary care unit*) unité f de soins cardiologiques
CD N ABBR (= *compact disc*) CD m; (*Mil: BRIT*) = **Civil Defence (Corps)**; (*: US*) = **Civil Defense** ▶ ABBR (*BRIT:* = *Corps Diplomatique*) CD
CD burner N graveur m de CD
CDC N ABBR (*US*) = **center for disease control**
CD player N platine f laser
Cdr. ABBR (= *commander*) Cdt
CD-ROM [siːdiː'rɒm] N ABBR (= *compact disc read-only memory*) CD-ROM m inv
CDT ABBR (*US:* = *Central Daylight Time*) heure d'été du centre
CDW N ABBR = **collision damage waiver**
CD writer N graveur m de CD

cease [siːs] VT, VI cesser
ceasefire ['siːsfaɪə'] N cessez-le-feu m
ceaseless ['siːslɪs] ADJ incessant(e), continuel(le)
CED N ABBR (US) = **Committee for Economic Development**
cedar ['siːdə'] N cèdre m
cede [siːd] VT céder
cedilla [sɪ'dɪlə] N cédille f
CEEB N ABBR (US: = College Entrance Examination Board) commission d'admission dans l'enseignement supérieur
ceilidh ['keɪlɪ] N bal m folklorique écossais or irlandais
ceiling ['siːlɪŋ] N (also fig) plafond m
celebrate ['sɛlɪbreɪt] VT, VI célébrer
celebrated ['sɛlɪbreɪtɪd] ADJ célèbre
celebration [sɛlɪ'breɪʃən] N célébration f
celebrity [sɪ'lɛbrɪtɪ] N célébrité f
celeriac [sə'lɛrɪæk] N céleri(-rave) m
celery ['sɛlərɪ] N céleri m (en branches)
celestial [sɪ'lɛstɪəl] ADJ céleste
celibacy ['sɛlɪbəsɪ] N célibat m
cell [sɛl] N (gen) cellule f; (Elec) élément m (de pile)
cellar ['sɛlə'] N cave f
'cellist ['tʃɛlɪst] N violoncelliste mf
cello ['tʃɛləu] N violoncelle m
Cellophane® ['sɛləfeɪn] N cellophane® f
cellphone ['sɛlfəun] N (téléphone m) portable m, mobile m
cell tower N (US Tel) antenne-relais f
cellular ['sɛljulə'] ADJ cellulaire
cellulose ['sɛljuləus] N cellulose f
Celsius ['sɛlsɪəs] ADJ Celsius inv
Celt [kɛlt, sɛlt] N Celte mf
Celtic ['kɛltɪk, 'sɛltɪk] ADJ celte, celtique ▶ N (Ling) celtique m
cement [sə'mɛnt] N ciment m ▶ VT cimenter
cement mixer N bétonnière f
cemetery ['sɛmɪtrɪ] N cimetière m
cenotaph ['sɛnətɑːf] N cénotaphe m
censor ['sɛnsə'] N censeur m ▶ VT censurer
censorship ['sɛnsəʃɪp] N censure f
censure ['sɛnʃə'] VT blâmer, critiquer
census ['sɛnsəs] N recensement m
cent [sɛnt] N (unit of dollar, euro) cent m (= un centième du dollar, de l'euro); see also **per cent**
centenary [sɛn'tiːnərɪ], (US) **centennial** [sɛn'tɛnɪəl] N centenaire m
center ['sɛntə'] N, VT (US) = **centre**
centigrade ['sɛntɪgreɪd] ADJ centigrade
centilitre, (US) **centiliter** ['sɛntiliːtə'] N centilitre m
centimetre, (US) **centimeter** ['sɛntimiːtə'] N centimètre m
centipede ['sɛntipiːd] N mille-pattes m inv
central ['sɛntrəl] ADJ central(e)
Central African Republic N République Centrafricaine
Central America N Amérique centrale
central heating N chauffage central
centralize ['sɛntrəlaɪz] VT centraliser
central processing unit N (Comput) unité centrale (de traitement)

central reservation N (Brit Aut) terre-plein central
centre, (US) **center** ['sɛntə'] N centre m ▶ VT centrer; (Phot) cadrer; (concentrate): **to ~ (on)** centrer (sur)
centrefold, (US) **centerfold** ['sɛntəfəuld] N (Press) pages centrales détachables (avec photo de pin up)
centre-forward ['sɛntə'fɔːwəd] N (Sport) avant-centre m
centre-half ['sɛntə'hɑːf] N (Sport) demi-centre m
centrepiece, (US) **centerpiece** ['sɛntəpiːs] N milieu m de table; (fig) pièce maîtresse
centre spread N (Brit) publicité f en double page
centre-stage [sɛntə'steɪdʒ] N: **to take ~** occuper le centre de la scène
centrifugal [sɛn'trɪfjugl] ADJ centrifuge
centrifuge ['sɛntrɪfjuːʒ] N centrifugeuse f
century ['sɛntjurɪ] N siècle m; **in the twentieth ~** au vingtième siècle
CEO N ABBR (US) = **chief executive officer**
ceramic [sɪ'ræmɪk] ADJ céramique
cereal ['siːrɪəl] N céréale f
cerebral ['sɛrɪbrəl] ADJ cérébral(e)
ceremonial [sɛrɪ'məunɪəl] N cérémonial m; (rite) rituel m
ceremony ['sɛrɪmənɪ] N cérémonie f; **to stand on ~** faire des façons
cert [sə:t] N (Brit inf): **it's a dead ~** ça ne fait pas un pli
certain ['sə:tən] ADJ certain(e); **to make ~ of** s'assurer de; **for ~** certainement, sûrement
certainly ['sə:tənlɪ] ADV certainement
certainty ['sə:təntɪ] N certitude f
certificate [sə'tɪfɪkɪt] N certificat m
certified letter ['sə:tɪfaɪd-] N (US) lettre recommandée
certified public accountant ['sə:tɪfaɪd-] N (US) expert-comptable m
certify ['sə:tɪfaɪ] VT certifier; (award diploma to) conférer un diplôme etc à; (declare insane) déclarer malade mental(e) ▶ VI: **to ~ to** attester
cervical ['sə:vɪkl] ADJ: **~ cancer** cancer m du col de l'utérus; **~ smear** frottis vaginal
cervix ['sə:vɪks] N col m de l'utérus
Cesarean [siːˈzɛərɪən] ADJ, N (US) = **Caesarean**
cessation [sə'seɪʃən] N cessation f, arrêt m
cesspit ['sɛspɪt] N fosse f d'aisance
CET ABBR (= Central European Time) heure d'Europe centrale
Ceylon [sɪ'lɔn] N Ceylan m
cf. ABBR (= compare) cf., voir
c/f ABBR (Comm) = **carried forward**
CFC N ABBR (= chlorofluorocarbon) CFC m
CG N ABBR (US) = **coastguard**
cg ABBR (= centigram) cg
CH N ABBR (Brit: = Companion of Honour) titre honorifique
ch ABBR (Brit: = central heating) cc
ch. ABBR (= chapter) chap
Chad [tʃæd] N Tchad m
chafe [tʃeɪf] VT irriter, frotter contre ▶ VI (fig): **to ~ against** se rebiffer contre, regimber contre

chaffinch ['tʃæfɪntʃ] N pinson m
chagrin ['ʃægrɪn] N contrariété f, déception f
chain [tʃeɪn] N (gen) chaîne f ▶ VT (also: **chain up**) enchaîner, attacher (avec une chaîne)
chain reaction N réaction f en chaîne
chain-smoke ['tʃeɪnsməuk] VI fumer cigarette sur cigarette
chain store N magasin m à succursales multiples
chair [tʃɛəʳ] N chaise f; (armchair) fauteuil m; (of university) chaire f; (of meeting) présidence f ▶ VT (meeting) présider; **the ~** (US: electric chair) la chaise électrique
chairlift ['tʃɛəlɪft] N télésiège m
chairman ['tʃɛəmən] N (irreg) président m
chairperson ['tʃɛəpə:sn] N président(e)
chairwoman ['tʃɛəwumən] N (irreg) présidente f
chalet ['ʃæleɪ] N chalet m
chalice ['tʃælɪs] N calice m
chalk [tʃɔːk] N craie f
▶ **chalk up** VT écrire à la craie; (fig: success etc) remporter
challenge ['tʃælɪndʒ] N défi m ▶ VT défier; (statement, right) mettre en question, contester; **to ~ sb to a fight/game** inviter qn à se battre/à jouer (sous forme d'un défi); **to ~ sb to do** mettre qn au défi de faire
challenger ['tʃælɪndʒəʳ] N (Sport) challenger m
challenging ['tʃælɪndʒɪŋ] ADJ (task, career) qui représente un défi or une gageure; (tone, look) de défi, provocateur(-trice)
chamber ['tʃeɪmbəʳ] N chambre f; (BRIT Law: gen pl) cabinet m; **~ of commerce** chambre de commerce
chambermaid ['tʃeɪmbəmeɪd] N femme f de chambre
chamber music N musique f de chambre
chamberpot ['tʃeɪmbəpɔt] N pot m de chambre
chameleon [kə'mi:lɪən] N caméléon m
chamois ['ʃæmwɑ:] N chamois m
chamois leather ['ʃæmɪ-] N peau f de chamois
champagne [ʃæm'peɪn] N champagne m
champers ['ʃæmpəz] N (inf) champ m
champion ['tʃæmpɪən] N (also of cause) champion(ne) ▶ VT défendre
championship ['tʃæmpɪənʃɪp] N championnat m
chance [tʃɑ:ns] N (luck) hasard m; (opportunity) occasion f, possibilité f; (hope, likelihood) chance f; (risk) risque m ▶ VT (risk) risquer; (happen): **to ~ to do** faire par hasard ▶ ADJ fortuit(e), de hasard; **there is little ~ of his coming** il est peu probable or il y a peu de chances qu'il vienne; **to take a ~** prendre un risque; **it's the ~ of a lifetime** c'est une occasion unique; **by ~** par hasard; **to ~ doing sth** se risquer à faire qch; **to ~ it** risquer le coup, essayer
▶ **chance on, chance upon** VT FUS (person) tomber sur, rencontrer par hasard; (thing) trouver par hasard
chancel ['tʃɑ:nsəl] N chœur m
chancellor ['tʃɑ:nsələʳ] N chancelier m
Chancellor of the Exchequer [-ɪks'tʃɛkəʳ] (BRIT) N chancelier m de l'Échiquier

change [tʃeɪndʒ] VT (alter, replace: Comm: money) changer; (switch, substitute: hands, trains, clothes, one's name etc) changer de; (transform): **to ~ sb into** changer or transformer qn en ▶ VI (gen) changer; (change clothes) se changer; (be transformed): **to ~ into** se changer or transformer en ▶ N changement m; (money) monnaie f; **to ~ gear** (Aut) changer de vitesse; **to ~ one's mind** changer d'avis; **she changed into an old skirt** elle (s'est changée et) a enfilé une vieille jupe; **a ~ of clothes** des vêtements de rechange; **to ~ a ~** pour changer; **small ~** petite monnaie; **to give sb ~ for** or **of £10** faire à qn la monnaie de 10 livres; **do you have ~ for £10?** vous avez la monnaie de 10 livres?; **where can I ~ some money?** où est-ce que je peux changer de l'argent?; **keep the ~!** gardez la monnaie!
▶ **change over** VI (swap) échanger; (change: drivers etc) changer; (change sides: players etc) changer de côté; **to ~ over from sth to sth** passer de qch à qch
changeable ['tʃeɪndʒəbl] ADJ (weather) variable; (person) d'humeur changeante
change machine N distributeur m de monnaie
changeover ['tʃeɪndʒəuvəʳ] N (to new system) changement m, passage m
changing ['tʃeɪndʒɪŋ] ADJ changeant(e)
changing room N (BRIT: in shop) salon m d'essayage; (: Sport) vestiaire m
channel ['tʃænl] N (TV) chaîne f; (waveband, groove, fig: medium) canal m; (of river, sea) chenal m ▶ VT canaliser; (fig: interest, energies): **to ~ into** diriger vers; **through the usual channels** en suivant la filière habituelle; **green/red ~** (Customs) couloir m or sortie f "rien à déclarer"/"marchandises à déclarer"; **the (English) C~** la Manche
channel-hopping ['tʃænl'hɔpɪŋ] N (TV) zapping m
Channel Islands NPL: **the ~** les îles fpl Anglo-Normandes
Channel Tunnel N: **the ~** le tunnel sous la Manche
chant [tʃɑ:nt] N chant m; mélopée f; (Rel) psalmodie f ▶ VT chanter, scander; psalmodier
chaos ['keɪɔs] N chaos m
chaos theory N théorie f du chaos
chaotic [keɪ'ɔtɪk] ADJ chaotique
chap [tʃæp] N (BRIT inf: man) type m; (term of address): **old ~** mon vieux ▶ VT (skin) gercer, crevasser
chapel ['tʃæpl] N chapelle f
chaperon ['ʃæpərəun] N chaperon m ▶ VT chaperonner
chaplain ['tʃæplɪn] N aumônier m
chapped [tʃæpt] ADJ (skin, lips) gercé(e)
chapter ['tʃæptəʳ] N chapitre m
char [tʃɑ:ʳ] VT (burn) carboniser ▶ VI (BRIT: cleaner) faire des ménages ▶ N (BRIT) = **charlady**
character ['kærɪktəʳ] N caractère m; (in novel, film) personnage m; (eccentric person) numéro m, phénomène m; **a person of good ~** une personne bien

character code N (*Comput*) code *m* de caractère

characteristic ['kærɪktə'rɪstɪk] ADJ, N caractéristique (*f*)

characterize ['kærɪktəraɪz] VT caractériser; **to ~ (as)** définir (comme)

charade [ʃə'rɑːd] N charade *f*

charcoal ['tʃɑːkəul] N charbon *m* de bois; (*Art*) charbon

charge [tʃɑːdʒ] N (*accusation*) accusation *f*; (*Law*) inculpation *f*; (*cost*) prix (demandé); (*of gun, battery, Mil: attack*) charge *f* ▸ VT (*gun, battery, Mil: enemy*) charger; (*customer, sum*) faire payer ▸ VI (*gen with: up, along etc*) foncer; **charges** NPL (*costs*) frais *mpl*; **to reverse the charges** (*BRIT Tel*) téléphoner en PCV; **bank/labour charges** frais *mpl* de banque/main-d'œuvre; **is there a ~?** doit-on payer?; **there's no ~** c'est gratuit, on ne fait pas payer; **extra ~** supplément *m*; **to take ~ of** se charger de; **to be in ~ of** être responsable de, s'occuper de; **to ~ in/out** entrer/sortir en trombe; **to ~ down/up** dévaler/grimper à toute allure; **to ~ sb (with)** (*Law*) inculper qn (de); **to have ~ of sb** avoir la charge de qn; **they charged us £10 for the meal** ils nous ont fait payer le repas 10 livres, ils nous ont compté 10 livres pour le repas; **how much do you ~ for this repair?** combien demandez-vous pour cette réparation?; **to ~ an expense (up) to sb** mettre une dépense sur le compte de qn; **~ it to my account** facturez-le sur mon compte

charge account N compte *m* client

charge card N carte *f* de client (*émise par un grand magasin*)

chargehand ['tʃɑːdʒhænd] N (*BRIT*) chef *m* d'équipe

charger ['tʃɑːdʒə'] N (*also*: **battery charger**) chargeur *m*; (*old: warhorse*) cheval *m* de bataille

charismatic [kærɪz'mætɪk] ADJ charismatique

charitable ['tʃærɪtəbl] ADJ charitable

charity ['tʃærɪtɪ] N charité *f*; (*organization*) institution *f* charitable *or* de bienfaisance, œuvre *f* (de charité)

charity shop N (*BRIT*) boutique vendant des articles d'occasion au profit d'une organisation caritative

charlady ['tʃɑːleɪdɪ] N (*BRIT*) femme *f* de ménage

charm [tʃɑːm] N charme *m*; (*on bracelet*) breloque *f* ▸ VT charmer, enchanter

charm bracelet N bracelet *m* à breloques

charming ['tʃɑːmɪŋ] ADJ charmant(e)

chart [tʃɑːt] N tableau *m*, diagramme *m*; graphique *m*; (*map*) carte marine; (*weather chart*) carte *f* du temps ▸ VT dresser *or* établir la carte de; (*sales, progress*) établir la courbe de; **charts** NPL (*Mus*) hit-parade *m*; **to be in the charts** (*record, pop group*) figurer au hit-parade

charter ['tʃɑːtə'] VT (*plane*) affréter ▸ N (*document*) charte *f*; **on ~** (*plane*) affrété(e)

chartered accountant ['tʃɑːtəd-] N (*BRIT*) expert-comptable *m*

charter flight N charter *m*

charwoman ['tʃɑːwumən] N (*irreg*) = **charlady**

chase [tʃeɪs] VT poursuivre, pourchasser; (*also*: **chase away**) chasser ▸ N poursuite *f*, chasse *f* ▸ **chase down** VT (*US*) = **chase up**

▸ **chase up** VT (*BRIT: person*) relancer; (*: information*) rechercher

chasm ['kæzəm] N gouffre *m*, abîme *m*

chassis ['ʃæsɪ] N châssis *m*

chastened ['tʃeɪsnd] ADJ assagi(e), rappelé(e) à la raison

chastening ['tʃeɪsnɪŋ] ADJ qui fait réfléchir

chastise [tʃæs'taɪz] VT punir, châtier; corriger

chastity ['tʃæstɪtɪ] N chasteté *f*

chat [tʃæt] VI (*also*: **have a chat**) bavarder, causer; (: *on Internet*) chatter ▸ N conversation *f*; (*on Internet*) chat *m*

▸ **chat up** VT (*BRIT inf: girl*) baratiner

chatline ['tʃætlaɪn] N *numéro téléphonique qui permet de bavarder avec plusieurs personnes en même temps*

chat room N (*Internet*) salon *m* de discussion

chat show N (*BRIT*) talk-show *m*

chattel ['tʃætl] N *see* **good**

chatter ['tʃætə'] VI (*person*) bavarder, papoter ▸ N bavardage *m*, papotage *m*; **my teeth are chattering** je claque des dents

chatterbox ['tʃætəbɔks] N moulin *m* à paroles, babillard(e)

chattering classes ['tʃætərɪŋ-] NPL: **the ~** (*inf, pej*) les intellos *mpl*

chatty ['tʃætɪ] ADJ (*style*) familier(-ière); (*person*) enclin(e) à bavarder *or* au papotage

chauffeur ['ʃəufə'] N chauffeur *m* (de maître)

chauvinism ['ʃəuvɪnɪzəm] N (*also*: **male chauvinism**) phallocratie *f*, machisme *m*; (*nationalism*) chauvinisme *m*

chauvinist ['ʃəuvɪnɪst] N (*also*: **male chauvinist**) phallocrate *m*, macho *m*; (*nationalist*) chauvin(e)

ChE ABBR = **chemical engineer**

cheap [tʃiːp] ADJ bon marché *inv*, pas cher (chère); (*reduced: ticket*) à prix réduit; (: *fare*) réduit(e); (*joke*) facile, d'un goût douteux; (*poor quality*) à bon marché, de qualité médiocre ▸ ADV à bon marché, pour pas cher; **cheaper** *adj* moins cher (chère); **can you recommend a ~ hotel/restaurant, please?** pourriez-vous m'indiquer un hôtel/restaurant bon marché?

cheap day return N billet *m* d'aller et retour réduit (*valable pour la journée*)

cheapen ['tʃiːpn] VT rabaisser, déprécier

cheaply ['tʃiːplɪ] ADV à bon marché, à bon compte

cheat [tʃiːt] VI tricher; (*in exam*) copier ▸ VT tromper, duper; (*rob*): **to ~ sb out of sth** escroquer qch à qn ▸ N tricheur(-euse) *m/f*; escroc *m*; (*trick*) duperie *f*, tromperie *f* ▸ **cheat on** VT FUS tromper

cheating ['tʃiːtɪŋ] N tricherie *f*

Chechnya [tʃɪtʃ'njɑː] N Tchétchénie *f*

check [tʃek] VT vérifier; (*passport, ticket*) contrôler; (*halt*) enrayer; (*restrain*) maîtriser ▸ VI (*official etc*) se renseigner ▸ N vérification *f*; contrôle *m*; (*curb*) frein *m*; (*BRIT: bill*) addition *f*; (*US*) = **cheque**; (*pattern: gen pl*) carreaux *mpl* ▸ ADJ (*also*: **checked**: *pattern, cloth*) à carreaux; **to ~ with sb** demander à qn; **to keep a ~ on sb/sth** surveiller qn/qch

▸ **check in** VI (*in hotel*) remplir sa fiche (d'hôtel);

(at airport) se présenter à l'enregistrement ▶ VT (luggage) (faire) enregistrer
▶ **check off** VT (tick off) cocher
▶ **check out** VI (in hotel) régler sa note ▶ VT (luggage) retirer; (investigate: story) vérifier; (: person) prendre des renseignements sur
▶ **check up** VI: **to ~ to** (**on sth**) vérifier (qch); **to ~ up on sb** se renseigner sur le compte de qn
checkbook ['tʃɛkbuk] N (US) = **chequebook**
checked ['tʃɛkt] ADJ (pattern, cloth) à carreaux
checkered ['tʃɛkəd] ADJ (US) = **chequered**
checkers ['tʃɛkəz] N (US) jeu m de dames
check guarantee card N (US) carte f (d'identité) bancaire
check-in ['tʃɛkin] N (at airport: also: **check-in desk**) enregistrement m
checking account ['tʃɛkin-] N (US) compte courant
checklist ['tʃɛklɪst] N liste f de contrôle
checkmate ['tʃɛkmeɪt] N échec et mat m
checkout ['tʃɛkaut] N (in supermarket) caisse f
checkpoint ['tʃɛkpɔint] N contrôle m
checkroom ['tʃɛkruːm] (US) N consigne f
checkup ['tʃɛkʌp] N (Med) examen médical, check-up m
cheddar ['tʃɛdər] N (also: **cheddar cheese**) cheddar m
cheek [tʃiːk] N joue f; (impudence) toupet m, culot m; **what a ~!** quel toupet!
cheekbone ['tʃiːkbəun] N pommette f
cheeky ['tʃiːki] ADJ effronté(e), culotté(e)
cheep [tʃiːp] N (of bird) piaulement m ▶ VI piauler
cheer [tʃiər] VT acclamer, applaudir; (gladden) réjouir, réconforter ▶ VI applaudir ▶ N (gen pl) acclamations fpl, applaudissements mpl; bravos mpl, hourras mpl; **cheers!** à la vôtre!
▶ **cheer on** VT encourager (par des cris etc)
▶ **cheer up** VI se dérider, reprendre courage ▶ VT remonter le moral à or de, dérider, égayer
cheerful ['tʃiəful] ADJ gai(e), joyeux(-euse)
cheerfulness ['tʃiəfulnis] N gaieté f, bonne humeur
cheerio [tʃiəri'əu] EXCL (BRIT) salut!, au revoir!
cheerleader ['tʃiːlidər] N membre d'un groupe de majorettes qui chantent et dansent pour soutenir leur équipe pendant les matchs de football américain
cheerless ['tʃiəlis] ADJ sombre, triste
cheese [tʃiːz] N fromage m
cheeseboard ['tʃiːzbɔːd] N plateau m à fromages; (with cheese on it) plateau m de fromages
cheeseburger ['tʃiːzbəːgər] N cheeseburger m
cheesecake ['tʃiːzkeɪk] N tarte f au fromage
cheetah ['tʃiːtə] N guépard m
chef [ʃɛf] N chef (cuisinier)
chemical ['kɛmɪkl] ADJ chimique ▶ N produit m chimique
chemist ['kɛmɪst] N (BRIT: pharmacist) pharmacien(ne); (scientist) chimiste mf
chemistry ['kɛmɪstrɪ] N chimie f
chemist's ['kɛmɪsts], **chemist's shop** N (BRIT) pharmacie f
chemotherapy [kiːmou'θɛrəpɪ] N chimiothérapie f

cheque, (US) **check** [tʃɛk] N chèque m; **to pay by ~** payer par chèque
chequebook, (US) **checkbook** ['tʃɛkbuk] N chéquier m, carnet m de chèques
cheque card N (BRIT) carte f (d'identité) bancaire
chequered, (US) **checkered** ['tʃɛkəd] ADJ (fig) varié(e)
cherish ['tʃɛrɪʃ] VT chérir; (hope etc) entretenir
cheroot [ʃə'ruːt] N cigare m de Manille
cherry ['tʃɛrɪ] N cerise f; (also: **cherry tree**) cerisier m
Ches ABBR (BRIT) = **Cheshire**
chess [tʃɛs] N échecs mpl
chessboard ['tʃɛsbɔːd] N échiquier m
chessman ['tʃɛsmən] (irreg) pièce f (de jeu d'échecs)
chessplayer ['tʃɛspleɪər] N joueur(-euse) d'échecs
chest [tʃɛst] N poitrine f; (box) coffre m, caisse f; **to get sth off one's ~** (inf) vider son sac
chest measurement N tour m de poitrine
chestnut ['tʃɛsnʌt] N châtaigne f; (also: **chestnut tree**) châtaignier m; (colour) châtain m ▶ ADJ (hair) châtain inv; (horse) alezan
chest of drawers N commode f
chesty ['tʃɛstɪ] ADJ (cough) de poitrine
chew [tʃuː] VT mâcher
chewing gum ['tʃuːɪŋ-] N chewing-gum m
chic [ʃiːk] ADJ chic inv, élégant(e)
chick [tʃɪk] N poussin m; (inf) fille f
chicken ['tʃɪkɪn] N poulet m; (inf: coward) poule mouillée
▶ **chicken out** VI (inf) se dégonfler
chicken feed N (fig) broutilles fpl, bagatelle f
chickenpox ['tʃɪkɪnpɔks] N varicelle f
chickpea ['tʃɪkpiː] N pois m chiche
chicory ['tʃɪkərɪ] N chicorée f; (salad) endive f
chide [tʃaɪd] VT réprimander, gronder
chief [tʃiːf] N chef m ▶ ADJ principal(e); **C~ of Staff** (Mil) chef d'État-major
chief constable N (BRIT) ≈ préfet m de police
chief executive, (US) **chief executive officer** N directeur(-trice) général(e)
chiefly ['tʃiːflɪ] ADV principalement, surtout
chiffon ['ʃɪfɔn] N mousseline f de soie
chilblain ['tʃɪlbleɪn] N engelure f
child [tʃaɪld] N (pl **children** ['tʃɪldrən]) N enfant mf
child abuse N maltraitance f d'enfants; (sexual) abus mpl sexuels sur des enfants
child benefit N (BRIT) ≈ allocations familiales
childbirth ['tʃaɪldbəːθ] N accouchement m
childcare ['tʃaɪldkɛər] N (for working parents) garde f des enfants (pour les parents qui travaillent)
childhood ['tʃaɪldhud] N enfance f
childish ['tʃaɪldɪʃ] ADJ puéril(e), enfantin(e)
childless ['tʃaɪldlɪs] ADJ sans enfants
childlike ['tʃaɪldlaɪk] ADJ innocent(e), pur(e)
child minder N (BRIT) garde f d'enfants
child prodigy N enfant mf prodige
children ['tʃɪldrən] NPL of **child**
children's home ['tʃɪldrənz-] N ≈ foyer m d'accueil (pour enfants)
Chile ['tʃɪlɪ] N Chili m

Chilean ['tʃɪlɪən] ADJ chilien(ne) ▶ N Chilien(ne)
chili, chilli ['tʃɪlɪ] N piment *m* (rouge)
chill [tʃɪl] N (*of water*) froid *m*; (*of air*) fraîcheur *f*; (*Med*) refroidissement *m*, coup *m* de froid ▶ ADJ froid(e), glacial(e) ▶ VT (*person*) faire frissonner; refroidir; (*Culin*) mettre au frais, rafraîchir; **"serve chilled"** "à servir frais"
▶ **chill out** VI (*inf: esp US*) se relaxer
chilling ['tʃɪlɪŋ] ADJ (*wind*) frais (fraîche), froid(e); (*look, smile*) glacé(e); (*thought*) qui donne le frisson
chilly ['tʃɪlɪ] ADJ froid(e), glacé(e); (*sensitive to cold*) frileux(-euse); **to feel ~** avoir froid
chime [tʃaɪm] N carillon *m* ▶ VI carillonner, sonner
chimney ['tʃɪmnɪ] N cheminée *f*
chimney sweep N ramoneur *m*
chimpanzee [tʃɪmpæn'zi:] N chimpanzé *m*
chin [tʃɪn] N menton *m*
China ['tʃaɪnə] N Chine *f*
china ['tʃaɪnə] N (*material*) porcelaine *f*; (*crockery*) (vaisselle *f* en) porcelaine
Chinese [tʃaɪ'ni:z] ADJ chinois(e) ▶ N (*pl inv*) Chinois(e); (*Ling*) chinois *m*
chink [tʃɪŋk] N (*opening*) fente *f*, fissure *f*; (*noise*) tintement *m*
chinwag ['tʃɪnwæg] N (*BRIT inf*): **to have a ~** tailler une bavette
chip [tʃɪp] N (*gen pl: Culin: BRIT*) frites *fpl*, (: *US: also*: **potato chip**) chip *m*; (*of wood*) copeau *m*; (*of glass, stone*) éclat *m*; (*also*: **microchip**) puce *f*; (*in gambling*) fiche *f* ▶ VT (*cup, plate*) ébrécher; **when the chips are down** (*fig*) au moment critique
▶ **chip in** VI (*inf*) mettre son grain de sel
chip and PIN N carte *f* à puce; **~ machine** machine *f* à carte (à puce)
chipboard ['tʃɪpbɔːd] N aggloméré *m*, panneau *m* de particules
chipmunk ['tʃɪpmʌŋk] N suisse *m* (*animal*)
chippings ['tʃɪpɪŋz] NPL: **loose ~** gravillons *mpl*
chip shop N (*BRIT*) friterie *f*; *voir article*

Un *chip shop*, que l'on appelle également un *fish-and-chip shop*, est un magasin où l'on vend des plats à emporter. Les *chip shops* sont d'ailleurs à l'origine des *takeaways*. On y achète en particulier du poisson frit et des frites, mais on y trouve également des plats traditionnels britanniques (*steak pies*, saucisses, etc). Tous les plats étaient à l'origine emballés dans du papier journal. Dans certains de ces magasins, on peut s'asseoir pour consommer sur place.

chiropodist [kɪ'rɔpədɪst] N (*BRIT*) pédicure *mf*
chirp [tʃəːp] N pépiement *m*, gazouillis *m*; (*of crickets*) stridulation *f* ▶ VI pépier, gazouiller; chanter, striduler
chirpy ['tʃəːpɪ] ADJ (*inf*) plein(e) d'entrain, tout guilleret(te)
chisel ['tʃɪzl] N ciseau *m*
chit [tʃɪt] N mot *m*, note *f*
chitchat ['tʃɪttʃæt] N bavardage *m*, papotage *m*
chivalrous ['ʃɪvəlrəs] ADJ chevaleresque
chivalry ['ʃɪvəlrɪ] N chevalerie *f*; esprit *m* chevaleresque

chives [tʃaɪvz] NPL ciboulette *f*, civette *f*
chloride ['klɔːraɪd] N chlorure *m*
chlorinate ['klɔrɪneɪt] VT chlorer
chlorine ['klɔːriːn] N chlore *m*
choc-ice ['tʃɔkaɪs] N (*BRIT*) esquimau® *m*
chock [tʃɔk] N cale *f*
chock-a-block ['tʃɔkə'blɔk], **chock-full** [tʃɔk'ful] ADJ plein(e) à craquer
chocolate ['tʃɔklɪt] N chocolat *m*
choice [tʃɔɪs] N choix *m* ▶ ADJ de choix; **by** *or* **from ~** par choix; **a wide ~** un grand choix
choir ['kwaɪər] N chœur *m*, chorale *f*
choirboy ['kwaɪəbɔɪ] N jeune choriste *m*, petit chanteur
choke [tʃəuk] VI étouffer ▶ VT étrangler; étouffer; (*block*) boucher, obstruer ▶ N (*Aut*) starter *m*
cholera ['kɔlərə] N choléra *m*
cholesterol [kə'lestərɔl] N cholestérol *m*
chook [tʃuk] N (*AUSTRALIA, NEW ZEALAND inf*) poule *f*
choose [tʃuːz] (*pt* **chose** [tʃəuz], *pp* **chosen** ['tʃəuzn]) VT choisir ▶ VI: **to ~ between** choisir entre; **to ~ from** choisir parmi; **to ~ to do** décider de faire, juger bon de faire
choosy ['tʃuːzɪ] ADJ: (**to be**) **~** (faire le) difficile
chop [tʃɔp] VT (*wood*) couper (à la hache); (*Culin: also*: **chop up**) couper (fin), émincer, hacher (en morceaux) ▶ N coup *m* (*de hache, du tranchant de la main*); (*Culin*) côtelette *f*; **to get the ~** (*BRIT inf: project*) tomber à l'eau; (: *person: be sacked*) se faire renvoyer
▶ **chop down** VT (*tree*) abattre
▶ **chop off** VT trancher
chopper ['tʃɔpər] N (*helicopter*) hélicoptère *m*, hélico *m*
choppy ['tʃɔpɪ] ADJ (*sea*) un peu agité(e)
chops [tʃɔps] NPL (*jaws*) mâchoires *fpl*; babines *fpl*
chopsticks ['tʃɔpstɪks] NPL baguettes *fpl*
choral ['kɔːrəl] ADJ choral(e), chanté(e) en chœur
chord [kɔːd] N (*Mus*) accord *m*
chore [tʃɔːr] N travail *m* de routine; **household chores** travaux *mpl* du ménage
choreographer [kɔrɪ'ɔgrəfər] N chorégraphe *mf*
choreography [kɔrɪ'ɔgrəfɪ] N chorégraphie *f*
chorister ['kɔrɪstər] N choriste *mf*
chortle ['tʃɔːtl] VI glousser
chorus ['kɔːrəs] N chœur *m*; (*repeated part of song, also fig*) refrain *m*
chose [tʃəuz] PT *of* **choose**
chosen ['tʃəuzn] PP *of* **choose**
chow [tʃau] N (*dog*) chow-chow *m*
chowder ['tʃaudər] N soupe *f* de poisson
Christ [kraɪst] N Christ *m*
christen ['krɪsn] VT baptiser
christening ['krɪsnɪŋ] N baptême *m*
Christian ['krɪstɪən] ADJ, N chrétien(ne)
Christianity [krɪstɪ'ænɪtɪ] N christianisme *m*
Christian name N prénom *m*
Christmas ['krɪsməs] N Noël *mf*; **happy** *or* **merry ~!** joyeux Noël!
Christmas card N carte *f* de Noël

Christmas carol N chant *m* de Noël
Christmas Day N le jour de Noël
Christmas Eve N la veille de Noël; la nuit de Noël
Christmas Island N île *f* Christmas
Christmas pudding N (*esp BRIT*) Christmas *m* pudding
Christmas tree N arbre *m* de Noël
chrome [krəum] N chrome *m*
chromium ['krəumɪəm] N chrome *m*; (*also:* **chromium plating**) chromage *m*
chromosome ['krəuməsəum] N chromosome *m*
chronic ['krɒnɪk] ADJ chronique; (*fig: liar, smoker*) invétéré(e)
chronicle ['krɒnɪkl] N chronique *f*
chronological [krɒnə'lɒdʒɪkl] ADJ chronologique
chrysanthemum [krɪ'sænθəməm] N chrysanthème *m*
chubby ['tʃʌbɪ] ADJ potelé(e), rondelet(te)
chuck [tʃʌk] VT (*inf*) lancer, jeter; (*job*) lâcher; (*person*) plaquer
▶ **chuck out** VT (*inf: person*) flanquer dehors *or* à la porte; (*: rubbish etc*) jeter
chuckle ['tʃʌkl] VI glousser
chuffed [tʃʌft] ADJ (*BRIT inf*): **to be ~ about sth** être content(e) de qch
chug [tʃʌg] VI faire teuf-teuf; souffler
chum [tʃʌm] N copain (copine)
chump [tʃʌmp] N (*inf*) imbécile *mf*, crétin(e)
chunk [tʃʌŋk] N gros morceau; (*of bread*) quignon *m*
chunky ['tʃʌŋkɪ] ADJ (*furniture etc*) massif(-ive); (*person*) trapu(e); (*knitwear*) en grosse laine
Chunnel ['tʃʌnəl] N = **Channel Tunnel**
church [tʃəːtʃ] N église *f*; **the C~ of England** l'Église anglicane
churchyard ['tʃəːtʃjɑːd] N cimetière *m*
churlish ['tʃəːlɪʃ] ADJ grossier(-ère); hargneux(-euse)
churn [tʃəːn] N (*for butter*) baratte *f*; (*also:* **milk churn**) (grand) bidon à lait
▶ **churn out** VT débiter
chute [ʃuːt] N goulotte *f*; (*also:* **rubbish chute**) vide-ordures *m inv*; (*BRIT: children's slide*) toboggan *m*
chutney ['tʃʌtnɪ] N chutney *m*
CIA N ABBR (= *Central Intelligence Agency*) CIA *f*
CID N ABBR (= *Criminal Investigation Department*) ≈ P.J. *f*
cider ['saɪdə'] N cidre *m*
CIF ABBR (= *cost, insurance and freight*) CAF
cigar [sɪ'gɑː'] N cigare *m*
cigarette [sɪgə'rɛt] N cigarette *f*
cigarette case N étui *m* à cigarettes
cigarette end N mégot *m*
cigarette holder N fume-cigarettes *m inv*
cigarette lighter N briquet *m*
C-in-C ABBR = **commander-in-chief**
cinch [sɪntʃ] N (*inf*): **it's a ~** c'est du gâteau, c'est l'enfance de l'art
Cinderella [sɪndə'rɛlə] N Cendrillon
cine-camera ['sɪnɪ'kæmərə] N (*BRIT*) caméra *f*
cine-film ['sɪnɪfɪlm] N (*BRIT*) film *m*

cinema ['sɪnəmə] N cinéma *m*
cine-projector ['sɪnɪprə'dʒɛktə'] N (*BRIT*) projecteur *m* de cinéma
cinnamon ['sɪnəmən] N cannelle *f*
cipher ['saɪfə'] N code secret; (*fig: faceless employee etc*) numéro *m*; **in ~** codé(e)
circa ['səːkə] PREP circa, environ
circle ['səːkl] N cercle *m*; (*in cinema*) balcon *m* ▶ VI faire *or* décrire des cercles ▶ VT (*surround*) entourer, encercler; (*move round*) faire le tour de, tourner autour de
circuit ['səːkɪt] N circuit *m*; (*lap*) tour *m*
circuit board N plaquette *f*
circuitous [səː'kjuɪtəs] ADJ indirect(e), qui fait un détour
circular ['səːkjulə'] ADJ circulaire ▶ N circulaire *f*; (*as advertisement*) prospectus *m*
circulate ['səːkjuleɪt] VI circuler ▶ VT faire circuler
circulation [səːkju'leɪʃən] N circulation *f*; (*of newspaper*) tirage *m*
circumcise ['səːkəmsaɪz] VT circoncire
circumference [sə'kʌmfərəns] N circonférence *f*
circumflex ['səːkəmflɛks] N (*also:* **circumflex accent**) accent *m* circonflexe
circumscribe ['səːkəmskraɪb] VT circonscrire
circumspect ['səːkəmspɛkt] ADJ circonspect(e)
circumstances ['səːkəmstənsɪz] NPL circonstances *fpl*; (*financial condition*) moyens *mpl*, situation financière; **in** *or* **under the ~** dans ces conditions; **under no ~** en aucun cas, sous aucun prétexte
circumstantial [səːkəm'stænʃl] ADJ (*report, statement*) circonstancié(e); **~ evidence** preuve indirecte
circumvent [səːkəm'vɛnt] VT (*rule etc*) tourner
circus ['səːkəs] N cirque *m*; (*also:* **Circus**: *in place names*) place *f*
cirrhosis [sɪ'rəusɪs] N (*also:* **cirrhosis of the liver**) cirrhose *f* (du foie)
CIS N ABBR (= *Commonwealth of Independent States*) CEI *f*
cissy ['sɪsɪ] N = **sissy**
cistern ['sɪstən] N réservoir *m* (d'eau); (*in toilet*) réservoir de la chasse d'eau
citation [saɪ'teɪʃən] N citation *f*; (*US*) P.-V *m*
cite [saɪt] VT citer
citizen ['sɪtɪzn] N (*Pol*) citoyen(ne); (*resident*): **the citizens of this town** les habitants de cette ville
Citizens' Advice Bureau ['sɪtɪznz-] N (*BRIT*) ≈ Bureau *m* d'aide sociale
citizenship ['sɪtɪznʃɪp] N citoyenneté *f*; (*BRIT Scol*) ≈ éducation *f* civique
citric ['sɪtrɪk] ADJ: **~ acid** acide *m* citrique
citrus fruits ['sɪtrəs-] NPL agrumes *mpl*
city ['sɪtɪ] N (grande) ville *f*; **the C~** la Cité de Londres (*centre des affaires*)
city centre N centre ville *m*
City Hall N (*US*) ≈ hôtel *m* de ville
city technology college N (*BRIT*) établissement *m* d'enseignement technologique (*situé dans un quartier défavorisé*)

civic ['sɪvɪk] ADJ civique; (*authorities*) municipal(e)

civic centre N (*BRIT*) centre administratif (municipal)

civil ['sɪvɪl] ADJ civil(e); (*polite*) poli(e), civil(e)

civil engineer N ingénieur civil

civil engineering N génie civil, travaux publics

civilian [sɪ'vɪlɪən] ADJ, N civil(e)

civilization [sɪvɪlaɪ'zeɪʃən] N civilisation f

civilized ['sɪvɪlaɪzd] ADJ civilisé(e); (*fig*) où règnent les bonnes manières, empreint(e) d'une courtoisie de bon ton

civil law N code civil; (*study*) droit civil

civil liberties NPL libertés fpl civiques

civil rights NPL droits mpl civiques

civil servant N fonctionnaire mf

Civil Service N fonction publique, administration f

civil war N guerre civile

civvies ['sɪvɪz] NPL (*inf*): **in ~** en civil

CJD N ABBR (= *Creutzfeldt-Jakob disease*) MCJ f

cl ABBR (= *centilitre*) cl

clad [klæd] ADJ: **~ (in)** habillé(e) de, vêtu(e) de

claim [kleɪm] VT (*rights etc*) revendiquer; (*compensation*) réclamer; (*assert*) déclarer, prétendre ▶ VI (*for insurance*) faire une déclaration de sinistre ▶ N revendication f; prétention f; (*right*) droit m; (*for expenses*) note f de frais; (**insurance**) ~ demande f d'indemnisation, déclaration f de sinistre; **to put in a ~ for** (*pay rise etc*) demander

claimant ['kleɪmənt] N (*Admin, Law*) requérant(e)

claim form N (*gen*) formulaire m de demande

clairvoyant [klɛə'vɔɪənt] N voyant(e), extra-lucide mf

clam [klæm] N palourde f
▶ **clam up** VI (*inf*) la boucler

clamber ['klæmbər] VI grimper, se hisser

clammy ['klæmɪ] ADJ humide et froid(e) (au toucher), moite

clamour, (*US*) **clamor** ['klæmər] N (*noise*) clameurs fpl; (*protest*) protestations bruyantes ▶ VI: **to ~ for sth** réclamer qch à grands cris

clamp [klæmp] N crampon m; (*on workbench*) valet m; (*on car*) sabot m de Denver ▶ VT attacher; (*car*) mettre un sabot à
▶ **clamp down on** VT FUS sévir contre, prendre des mesures draconiennes à l'égard de

clampdown ['klæmpdaʊn] N: **there has been a ~ on …** des mesures énergiques ont été prises contre …

clan [klæn] N clan m

clandestine [klæn'dɛstɪn] ADJ clandestin(e)

clang [klæŋ] N bruit m or fracas m métallique
▶ VI émettre un bruit or fracas métallique

clanger ['klæŋər] N (*BRIT inf*): **to drop a ~** faire une boulette

clansman ['klænzmən] N (*irreg*) membre m d'un clan (écossais)

clap [klæp] VI applaudir ▶ VT: **to ~ (one's hands)** battre des mains ▶ N claquement m; tape f; **a ~ of thunder** un coup de tonnerre

clapping ['klæpɪŋ] N applaudissements mpl

claptrap ['klæptræp] N (*inf*) baratin m

claret ['klærət] N (vin m de) bordeaux m (rouge)

clarification [klærɪfɪ'keɪʃən] N (*fig*) clarification f, éclaircissement m

clarify ['klærɪfaɪ] VT clarifier

clarinet [klærɪ'nɛt] N clarinette f

clarity ['klærɪtɪ] N clarté f

clash [klæʃ] N (*sound*) choc m, fracas m; (*with police*) affrontement m; (*fig*) conflit m ▶ VI se heurter; être or entrer en conflit; (*colours*) jurer; (*dates, events*) tomber en même temps

clasp [klɑːsp] N (*of necklace, bag*) fermoir m ▶ VT serrer, étreindre

class [klɑːs] N (*gen*) classe f; (*group, category*) catégorie f ▶ VT classer, classifier

class-conscious ['klɑːs'kɔnʃəs] ADJ conscient(e) de son appartenance sociale

class consciousness N conscience f de classe

classic ['klæsɪk] ADJ classique ▶ N (*author, work*) classique m; (*race etc*) classique f

classical ['klæsɪkl] ADJ classique

classics ['klæsɪks] NPL (*Scol*) lettres fpl classiques

classification [klæsɪfɪ'keɪʃən] N classification f

classified ['klæsɪfaɪd] ADJ (*information*) secret(-ète); **~ ads** petites annonces

classify ['klæsɪfaɪ] VT classifier, classer

classless society ['klɑːslɪs-] N société f sans classes

classmate ['klɑːsmeɪt] N camarade mf de classe

classroom ['klɑːsrum] N (salle f de) classe f

classroom assistant N assistant(e) d'éducation

classy ['klɑːsɪ] (*inf*) ADJ classe (*inf*)

clatter ['klætər] N cliquetis m ▶ VI cliqueter

clause [klɔːz] N clause f; (*Ling*) proposition f

claustrophobia [klɔːstrə'fəʊbɪə] N claustrophobie f

claustrophobic [klɔːstrə'fəʊbɪk] ADJ (*person*) claustrophobe; (*place*) où l'on se sent claustrophobe

claw [klɔː] N griffe f; (*of bird of prey*) serre f; (*of lobster*) pince f ▶ VT griffer; déchirer

clay [kleɪ] N argile f

clean [kliːn] ADJ propre; (*clear, smooth*) net(te); (*record, reputation*) sans tache; (*joke, story*) correct(e) ▶ VT nettoyer ▶ ADV: **he ~ forgot** il a complètement oublié; **to come ~** (*inf: admit guilt*) se mettre à table; **to ~ one's teeth** se laver les dents; **~ driving licence** or (*US*) **record** permis où n'est portée aucune indication de contravention
▶ **clean off** VT enlever
▶ **clean out** VT nettoyer (à fond)
▶ **clean up** VT nettoyer; (*fig*) remettre de l'ordre dans ▶ VI (*fig: make profit*): **to ~ up on** faire son beurre avec

clean-cut ['kliːn'kʌt] ADJ (*man*) soigné; (*situation etc*) bien délimité(e), net(te), clair(e)

cleaner ['kliːnər] N (*person*) nettoyeur(-euse), femme f de ménage; (*also:* **dry cleaner**) teinturier(-ière); (*product*) détachant m

cleaner's ['kliːnəz] N (*also:* **dry cleaner's**) teinturier m

cleaning ['kliːnɪŋ] N nettoyage m

cleaning lady N femme f de ménage
cleanliness ['klɛnlɪnɪs] N propreté f
cleanly ['kli:nlɪ] ADV proprement; nettement
cleanse [klɛnz] VT nettoyer; purifier
cleanser ['klɛnzəʳ] N détergent m; (for face) démaquillant m
clean-shaven ['kli:n'ʃeɪvn] ADJ rasé(e) de près
cleansing department ['klɛnzɪŋ-] N (BRIT) service m de voirie
clean sweep N: **to make a ~** (Sport) rafler tous les prix
clean technology N technologie f propre
clean-up ['kli:nʌp] N nettoyage m
clear [klɪəʳ] ADJ clair(e); (glass, plastic) transparent(e); (road, way) libre, dégagé(e); (profit, majority) net(te); (conscience) tranquille; (skin) frais (fraîche); (sky) dégagé(e) ▶ VT (road) dégager, déblayer; (table) débarrasser; (room etc: of people) faire évacuer; (woodland) défricher; (cheque) compenser; (Comm: goods) liquider; (Law: suspect) innocenter; (obstacle) franchir or sauter sans heurter ▶ VI (weather) s'éclaircir; (fog) se dissiper ▶ ADV: **~ of** à distance de, à l'écart de ▶ N: **to be in the ~** (out of debt) être dégagé(e) de toute dette; (out of suspicion) être lavé(e) de tout soupçon; (out of danger) être hors de danger; **to ~ the table** débarrasser la table, desservir; **to ~ one's throat** s'éclaircir la gorge; **to ~ a profit** faire un bénéfice net; **to make o.s. ~** se faire bien comprendre; **to make it ~ to sb that ...** bien faire comprendre à qn que ...; **I have a ~ day tomorrow** (BRIT) je n'ai rien de prévu demain; **to keep ~ of sb/sth** éviter qn/qch
▶ **clear away** VT (things, clothes etc) enlever, retirer; **to ~ away the dishes** débarrasser la table
▶ **clear off** VI (inf: leave) dégager
▶ **clear up** VI s'éclaircir, se dissiper ▶ VT ranger, mettre en ordre; (mystery) éclaircir, résoudre
clearance ['klɪərəns] N (removal) déblayage m; (free space) dégagement m; (permission) autorisation f
clearance sale N (Comm) liquidation f
clear-cut ['klɪə'kʌt] ADJ précis(e), nettement défini(e)
clearing ['klɪərɪŋ] N (in forest) clairière f; (BRIT Banking) compensation f, clearing m
clearing bank N (BRIT) banque f qui appartient à une chambre de compensation
clearly ['klɪəlɪ] ADV clairement; (obviously) de toute évidence
clearway ['klɪəweɪ] N (BRIT) route f à stationnement interdit
cleavage ['kli:vɪdʒ] N (of dress) décolleté m
cleaver ['kli:vəʳ] N fendoir m, couperet m
clef [klɛf] N (Mus) clé f
cleft [klɛft] N (in rock) crevasse f, fissure f
clemency ['klɛmənsɪ] N clémence f
clement ['klɛmənt] ADJ (weather) clément(e)
clementine ['klɛməntaɪn] N clémentine f
clench [klɛntʃ] VT serrer
clergy ['klə:dʒɪ] N clergé m
clergyman ['klə:dʒɪmən] N (irreg) ecclésiastique m
clerical ['klɛrɪkl] ADJ de bureau, d'employé de

bureau; (Rel) clérical(e), du clergé
clerk [klɑ:k, (US) klə:rk] N (BRIT) employé(e) de bureau; (US: salesman/woman) vendeur(-euse); **C~ of Court** (Law) greffier m (du tribunal)
clever ['klɛvəʳ] ADJ (intelligent) intelligent(e); (skilful) habile, adroit(e); (device, arrangement) ingénieux(-euse), astucieux(-euse)
cleverly ['klɛvəlɪ] ADV (skilfully) habilement; (craftily) astucieusement
clew [klu:] N (US) = **clue**
cliché ['kli:ʃeɪ] N cliché m
click [klɪk] VI faire un bruit sec or un déclic; (Comput) cliquer ▶ VT: **to ~ one's tongue** faire claquer sa langue; **to ~ one's heels** claquer des talons; **to ~ on an icon** cliquer sur une icône
client ['klaɪənt] N client(e)
clientele [kli:ɑ̃:n'tɛl] N clientèle f
cliff [klɪf] N falaise f
cliffhanger ['klɪfhæŋəʳ] N (TV, fig) histoire pleine de suspense
climactic [klaɪ'mæktɪk] ADJ à son point culminant, culminant(e)
climate ['klaɪmɪt] N climat m
climate change N changement m climatique
climax ['klaɪmæks] N apogée m, point culminant; (sexual) orgasme m
climb [klaɪm] VI grimper, monter; (plane) prendre de l'altitude ▶ VT (stairs) monter; (mountain) escalader; (tree) grimper à ▶ N montée f, escalade f; **to ~ over a wall** passer par dessus un mur
▶ **climb down** VI (re)descendre; (BRIT fig) rabattre de ses prétentions
climb-down ['klaɪmdaun] N (BRIT) reculade f
climber ['klaɪmə'] N (also: **rock climber**) grimpeur(-euse), varappeur(-euse); (plant) plante grimpante
climbing ['klaɪmɪŋ] N (also: **rock climbing**) escalade f, varappe f
clinch [klɪntʃ] VT (deal) conclure, sceller
clincher ['klɪntʃəʳ] N: **that was the ~** c'est ce qui a fait pencher la balance
cling [klɪŋ] (pt, pp **clung** [klʌŋ]) VI: **to ~ (to)** se cramponner (à), s'accrocher (à); (clothes) coller (à)
Clingfilm® ['klɪŋfɪlm] N film m alimentaire
clinic ['klɪnɪk] N clinique f; centre médical; (session: Med) consultation(s) f(pl), séance(s) f(pl); (: Sport) séance(s) de perfectionnement
clinical ['klɪnɪkl] ADJ clinique; (fig) froid(e)
clink [klɪŋk] VI tinter, cliqueter
clip [klɪp] N (for hair) barrette f; (also: **paper clip**) trombone m; (BRIT: also: **bulldog clip**) pince f de bureau; (holding hose etc) collier m or bague f (métallique) de serrage; (TV, Cine) clip m ▶ VT (papers: also: **clip together**) attacher; (hair, nails) couper; (hedge) tailler
clippers ['klɪpəz] NPL tondeuse f; (also: **nail clippers**) coupe-ongles m inv
clipping ['klɪpɪŋ] N (from newspaper) coupure f de journal
clique [kli:k] N clique f, coterie f
cloak [kləuk] N grande cape ▶ VT (fig) masquer, cacher

cloakroom ['kləukrum] N (*for coats etc*) vestiaire *m*; (BRIT: W.C.) toilettes *fpl*

clock [klɔk] N (*large*) horloge *f*; (*small*) pendule *f*; **round the ~** (*work etc*) vingt-quatre heures sur vingt-quatre; **to sleep round the ~** *or* **the ~ round** faire le tour du cadran; **30,000 on the ~** (BRIT Aut) 30 000 milles au compteur; **to work against the ~** faire la course contre la montre
▶ **clock in, clock on** (BRIT) VI (*with card*) pointer (en arrivant); (*start work*) commencer à travailler
▶ **clock off, clock out** (BRIT) VI (*with card*) pointer (en partant); (*leave work*) quitter le travail
▶ **clock up** VT (*miles, hours etc*) faire

clockwise ['klɔkwaɪz] ADV dans le sens des aiguilles d'une montre

clockwork ['klɔkwə:k] N rouages *mpl*, mécanisme *m*; (*of clock*) mouvement *m* (d'horlogerie) ▶ ADJ (*toy, train*) mécanique

clog [klɔg] N sabot *m* ▶ VT boucher, encrasser ▶ VI (*also*: **clog up**) se boucher, s'encrasser

cloister ['klɔɪstə^r] N cloître *m*

clone [kləun] N clone *m* ▶ VT cloner

close¹ [kləus] ADJ (*writing, texture*) serré(e); (*contact, link, watch*) étroit(e); (*examination*) attentif(-ive), minutieux(-euse); (*contest*) très serré(e); (*weather*) lourd(e), étouffant(e); (*room*) mal aéré(e); (*near*): **~ (to)** près (de), proche (de) ▶ ADV près, à proximité; **~ to** *prep* près de; **~ by, ~ at hand** *adj, adv* tout(e) près; **how ~ is Edinburgh to Glasgow?** combien de kilomètres y a-t-il entre Édimbourg et Glasgow?; **a ~ friend** un ami intime; **to have a ~ shave** (*fig*) l'échapper belle; **at ~ quarters** tout près, à côté

close² [kləuz] VT fermer; (*bargain, deal*) conclure ▶ VI (*shop etc*) fermer; (*lid, door etc*) se fermer; (*end*) se terminer, se conclure ▶ N (*end*) conclusion *f*; **to bring sth to a ~** mettre fin à qch; **what time do you ~?** à quelle heure fermez-vous?
▶ **close down** VT, VI fermer (*définitivement*)
▶ **close in** VI (*hunters*) approcher; (*night, fog*) tomber; **the days are closing in** les jours raccourcissent; **to ~ in on sb** cerner qn
▶ **close off** VT (*area*) boucler

closed [kləuzd] ADJ (*shop etc*) fermé(e); (*road*) fermé à la circulation

closed-circuit ['kləuzd'sə:kɪt] ADJ: **~ television** télévision *f* en circuit fermé

closed shop N organisation *f* qui n'admet que des travailleurs syndiqués

close-knit ['kləus'nɪt] ADJ (*family, community*) très uni(e)

closely ['kləuslɪ] ADV (*examine, watch*) de près; **we are ~ related** nous sommes proches parents; **a ~ guarded secret** un secret bien gardé

close season [kləus-] N (BRIT: Hunting) fermeture *f* de la chasse/pêche; (: Football) trêve *f*

closet ['klɔzɪt] N (*cupboard*) placard *m*, réduit *m*

close-up ['kləusʌp] N gros plan

closing ['kləuzɪŋ] ADJ (*stages, remarks*) final(e); **~ price** (Stock Exchange) cours *m* de clôture

closing time N heure *f* de fermeture

closure ['kləuʒə^r] N fermeture *f*

clot [klɔt] N (*of blood, milk*) caillot *m*; (*inf: person*) ballot *m* ▶ VI (*blood*) former des caillots; (: *external bleeding*) se coaguler

cloth [klɔθ] N (*material*) tissu *m*, étoffe *f*; (BRIT: *also*: **tea cloth**) torchon *m*; lavette *f*; (*also*: **tablecloth**) nappe *f*

clothe [kləuð] VT habiller, vêtir

clothes [kləuðz] NPL vêtements *mpl*, habits *mpl*; **to put one's ~ on** s'habiller; **to take one's ~ off** enlever ses vêtements

clothes brush N brosse *f* à habits

clothes line N corde *f* (à linge)

clothes peg, (US) clothes pin N pince *f* à linge

clothing ['kləuðɪŋ] N = **clothes**

clotted cream ['klɔtɪd-] N (BRIT) crème caillée

cloud [klaud] N nuage *m* ▶ VT (*liquid*) troubler; **to ~ the issue** brouiller les cartes; **every ~ has a silver lining** (*proverb*) à quelque chose malheur est bon (*proverbe*)
▶ **cloud over** VI se couvrir; (*fig*) s'assombrir

cloudburst ['klaudbə:st] N violente averse

cloud computing N cloud computing *m*; informatique *f* dans le nuage

cloud-cuckoo-land ['klaud'kuku:'lænd] N (BRIT) monde *m* imaginaire

cloudy ['klaudɪ] ADJ nuageux(-euse), couvert(e); (*liquid*) trouble

clout [klaut] N (*blow*) taloche *f*; (*fig*) pouvoir *m* ▶ VT flanquer une taloche à

clove [kləuv] N clou *m* de girofle; **a ~ of garlic** une gousse d'ail

clover ['kləuvə^r] N trèfle *m*

cloverleaf ['kləuvəli:f] N feuille *f* de trèfle; (Aut) croisement *m* en trèfle

clown [klaun] N clown *m* ▶ VI (*also*: **clown about, clown around**) faire le clown

cloying ['klɔɪɪŋ] ADJ (*taste, smell*) écœurant(e)

club [klʌb] N (*society*) club *m*; (*weapon*) massue *f*, matraque *f*; (*also*: **golf club**) club *m* ▶ VT matraquer ▶ VI: **to ~ together** s'associer; **clubs** NPL (*Cards*) trèfle *m*

club car N (US Rail) wagon-restaurant *m*

club class N (Aviat) classe *f* club

clubhouse ['klʌbhaus] N pavillon *m*

club soda N (US) eau *f* de seltz

cluck [klʌk] VI glousser

clue [klu:] N indice *m*; (*in crosswords*) définition *f*; **I haven't a ~** je n'en ai pas la moindre idée

clued up, (US) clued in [klu:d-] ADJ (*inf*) (*vachement*) calé(e)

clump [klʌmp] N: **~ of trees** bouquet *m* d'arbres

clumsy ['klʌmzɪ] ADJ (*person*) gauche, maladroit(e); (*object*) malcommode, peu maniable

clung [klʌŋ] PT, PP *of* **cling**

cluster ['klʌstə^r] N (petit) groupe; (*of flowers*) grappe *f* ▶ VI se rassembler

clutch [klʌtʃ] N (Aut) embrayage *m*; (*grasp*): **clutches** étreinte *f*, prise *f* ▶ VT (*grasp*) agripper; (*hold tightly*) serrer fort; (*hold on to*) se cramponner à

clutter ['klʌtə^r] VT (*also*: **clutter up**) encombrer ▶ N désordre *m*, fouillis *m*

C

cm ABBR (= *centimetre*) cm
CNAA N ABBR (BRIT: = *Council for National Academic Awards*) organisme non universitaire délivrant des diplômes
CND N ABBR = **Campaign for Nuclear Disarmament**
CO N ABBR (= *commanding officer*) Cdt; (BRIT) = **Commonwealth Office** ▶ ABBR (US) = **Colorado**
Co. ABBR = **company, county**
c/o ABBR (= *care of*) c/o, aux bons soins de
coach [kəutʃ] N (*bus*) autocar m; (*horse-drawn*) diligence f; (*of train*) voiture f, wagon m; (*Sport: trainer*) entraîneur(-euse); (*school: tutor*) répétiteur(-trice) ▶ VT (*Sport*) entraîner; (*student*) donner des leçons particulières à
coach station (BRIT) N gare routière
coach trip N excursion f en car
coagulate [kəu'ægjuleɪt] VT coaguler ▶ VI se coaguler
coal [kəul] N charbon m
coal face N front m de taille
coalfield ['kəulfi:ld] N bassin houiller
coalition [kəuə'lɪʃən] N coalition f
coalman ['kəulmən] N (*irreg*) charbonnier m, marchand m de charbon
coal mine N mine f de charbon
coarse [kɔ:s] ADJ grossier(-ère), rude; (*vulgar*) vulgaire
coast [kəust] N côte f ▶ VI (*car, cycle*) descendre en roue libre
coastal ['kəustl] ADJ côtier(-ère)
coaster ['kəustər] N (*Naut*) caboteur m; (*for glass*) dessous m de verre
coastguard ['kəustgɑ:d] N garde-côte m
coastline ['kəustlaɪn] N côte f, littoral m
coat [kəut] N manteau m; (*of animal*) pelage m, poil m; (*of paint*) couche f ▶ VT couvrir, enduire; **~ of arms** n blason m, armoiries fpl
coat hanger N cintre m
coating ['kəutɪŋ] N couche f, enduit m
co-author ['kəu'ɔ:θər] N co-auteur m
coax [kəuks] VT persuader par des cajoleries
cob [kɔb] N *see* **corn**
cobbled ['kɔbld] ADJ pavé(e)
cobbler ['kɔblər] N cordonnier m
cobbles, cobblestones ['kɔblz, 'kɔblstəunz] NPL pavés (ronds)
COBOL ['kəubɔl] N COBOL m
cobra ['kəubrə] N cobra m
cobweb ['kɔbweb] N toile f d'araignée
cocaine [kə'keɪn] N cocaïne f
cock [kɔk] N (*rooster*) coq m; (*male bird*) mâle m ▶ VT (*gun*) armer; **to ~ one's ears** (*fig*) dresser l'oreille
cock-a-hoop [kɔkə'hu:p] ADJ jubilant(e)
cockerel ['kɔkərl] N jeune coq m
cock-eyed ['kɔkaɪd] ADJ (*fig*) de travers; qui louche; qui ne tient pas debout (*fig*)
cockle ['kɔkl] N coque f
cockney ['kɔknɪ] N cockney mf (*habitant des quartiers populaires de l'East End de Londres*), ≈ faubourien(ne)
cockpit ['kɔkpɪt] N (*in aircraft*) poste m de

pilotage, cockpit m
cockroach ['kɔkrəutʃ] N cafard m, cancrelat m
cocktail ['kɔkteɪl] N cocktail m; **prawn ~**, (US) **shrimp ~** cocktail de crevettes
cocktail cabinet N (meuble-)bar m
cocktail party N cocktail m
cocktail shaker [-'ʃeɪkər] N shaker m
cocky ['kɔkɪ] ADJ trop sûr(e) de soi
cocoa ['kəukəu] N cacao m
coconut ['kəukənʌt] N noix f de coco
cocoon [kə'ku:n] N cocon m
cod [kɔd] N morue fraîche, cabillaud m
C.O.D. ABBR = **cash on delivery**; (US) = **collect on delivery**
code [kəud] N code m; (*Tel: area code*) indicatif m; **~ of behaviour** règles fpl de conduite; **~ of practice** déontologie f
codeine ['kəudi:n] N codéine f
codger ['kɔdʒər] N: **an old ~** (BRIT inf) un drôle de vieux bonhomme
codicil ['kɔdɪsɪl] N codicille m
codify ['kəudɪfaɪ] VT codifier
cod-liver oil ['kɔdlɪvər-] N huile f de foie de morue
co-driver ['kəu'draɪvər] N (*in race*) copilote m; (*of lorry*) deuxième chauffeur m
co-ed ['kəu'ɛd] ADJ ABBR = **coeducational** ▶ N ABBR (US: *female student*) étudiante d'une université mixte; (BRIT: *school*) école f mixte
coeducational ['kəuɛdju'keɪʃənl] ADJ mixte
coerce [kəu'ə:s] VT contraindre
coercion [kəu'ə:ʃən] N contrainte f
coexistence ['kəuɪg'zɪstəns] N coexistence f
C. of C. N ABBR = **chamber of commerce**
C of E N ABBR = **Church of England**
coffee ['kɔfɪ] N café m; **white ~**, (US) **~ with cream** (café-)crème m
coffee bar N (BRIT) café m
coffee bean N grain m de café
coffee break N pause-café f
coffee cake ['kɔfɪkeɪk] N (US) ≈ petit pain aux raisins
coffee cup N tasse f à café
coffee maker N cafetière f
coffeepot ['kɔfɪpɔt] N cafetière f
coffee shop N café m
coffee table N (petite) table basse
coffin ['kɔfɪn] N cercueil m
C of I N ABBR = **Church of Ireland**
C of S N ABBR = **Church of Scotland**
cog [kɔg] N (*wheel*) roue dentée; (*tooth*) dent f (d'engrenage)
cogent ['kəudʒənt] ADJ puissant(e), convaincant(e)
cognac ['kɔnjæk] N cognac m
cognitive ['kɔgnɪtɪv] ADJ cognitif(-ive)
cogwheel ['kɔgwi:l] N roue dentée
cohabit [kəu'hæbɪt] VI (*formal*): **to ~ (with sb)** cohabiter (avec qn)
coherent [kəu'hɪərənt] ADJ cohérent(e)
cohesion [kəu'hi:ʒən] N cohésion f
cohesive [kəu'hi:sɪv] ADJ (*fig*) cohésif(-ive)
COI N ABBR (BRIT: = *Central Office of Information*) service d'information gouvernemental

coil [kɔɪl] N rouleau m, bobine f; (one loop)
anneau m, spire f; (of smoke) volute f;
(contraceptive) stérilet m ▶ VT enrouler

coin [kɔɪn] N pièce f (de monnaie) ▶ VT (word)
inventer

coinage ['kɔɪnɪdʒ] N monnaie f, système m
monétaire

coinbox ['kɔɪnbɒks] N (BRIT) cabine f
téléphonique

coincide [kəʊɪn'saɪd] VI coïncider

coincidence [kəʊ'ɪnsɪdəns] N coïncidence f

coin-operated ['kɔɪn'ɒpəreɪtɪd] ADJ (machine,
launderette) automatique

Coke® [kəʊk] N coca m

coke [kəʊk] N (coal) coke m

Col. ABBR (= colonel) Col; (US) = **Colorado**

COLA N ABBR (US: = cost-of-living adjustment)
réajustement (des salaires, indemnités etc) en fonction
du coût de la vie

colander ['kɒləndəʳ] N passoire f (à légumes)

cold [kəʊld] ADJ froid(e) ▶ N froid m; (Med)
rhume m; **it's** ~ il fait froid; **to be** ~ (person)
avoir froid; **to catch** ~ prendre or attraper froid;
to catch a ~ s'enrhumer, attraper un rhume;
in ~ **blood** de sang-froid; **to have** ~ **feet** avoir
froid aux pieds; (fig) avoir la frousse or la
trouille; **to give sb the** ~ **shoulder** battre froid
à qn

cold-blooded ['kəʊld'blʌdɪd] ADJ (Zool) à sang
froid

cold cream N crème f de soins

coldly ['kəʊldlɪ] ADV froidement

cold sore N bouton m de fièvre

cold sweat N: **to be in a** ~ **(about sth)** avoir des
sueurs froides (au sujet de qch)

cold turkey N (inf) manque m; **to go** ~ être en
manque

Cold War N: **the** ~ la guerre froide

coleslaw ['kəʊlslɔ:] N sorte de salade de chou cru

colic ['kɒlɪk] N colique(s) f(pl)

colicky ['kɒlɪkɪ] ADJ qui souffre de coliques

collaborate [kə'læbəreɪt] VI collaborer

collaboration [kəlæbə'reɪʃən] N collaboration f

collaborator [kə'læbəreɪtəʳ] N
collaborateur(-trice)

collage [kɔ'lɑ:ʒ] N (Art) collage m

collagen ['kɒlədʒən] N collagène m

collapse [kə'læps] VI s'effondrer, s'écrouler;
(Med) avoir un malaise ▶ N effondrement m,
écroulement m; (of government) chute f

collapsible [kə'læpsəbl] ADJ pliant(e),
télescopique

collar ['kɒləʳ] N (of coat, shirt) col m; (for dog) collier
m; (Tech) collier, bague f ▶ VT (inf: person) pincer

collarbone ['kɒləbəʊn] N clavicule f

collate [kɔ'leɪt] VT collationner

collateral [kə'lætərl] N nantissement m

collation [kə'leɪʃən] N collation f

colleague ['kɒli:g] N collègue mf

collect [kə'lɛkt] VT rassembler; (pick up)
ramasser; (as a hobby) collectionner; (BRIT: call
for) (passer) prendre; (mail) faire la levée de,
ramasser; (money owed) encaisser; (donations,
subscriptions) recueillir ▶ VI (people) se

rassembler; (dust, dirt) s'amasser; **to** ~ **one's
thoughts** réfléchir, réunir ses idées; ~ **on
delivery (COD)** (US Comm) payable or paiement
à la livraison; **to call** ~ (US Tel) téléphoner en
PCV

collected [kə'lɛktɪd] ADJ: ~ **works** œuvres
complètes

collection [kə'lɛkʃən] N collection f; (of mail)
levée f; (for money) collecte f, quête f

collective [kə'lɛktɪv] ADJ collectif(-ive) ▶ N
collectif m

collective bargaining N convention collective

collector [kə'lɛktəʳ] N collectionneur m; (of
taxes) percepteur m; (of rent, cash) encaisseur m;
~'s item or **piece** pièce f de collection

college ['kɒlɪdʒ] N collège m; (of technology,
agriculture etc) institut m; **to go to** ~ faire des
études supérieures; ~ **of education** ≈ école
normale

collide [kə'laɪd] VI: **to** ~ **(with)** entrer en
collision (avec)

collie ['kɒlɪ] N (dog) colley m

colliery ['kɒlɪərɪ] N (BRIT) mine f de charbon,
houillère f

collision [kə'lɪʒən] N collision f, heurt m; **to be
on a** ~ **course** aller droit à la collision; (fig) aller
vers l'affrontement

collision damage waiver N (Insurance) rachat m
de franchise

colloquial [kə'ləʊkwɪəl] ADJ familier(-ère)

collusion [kə'lu:ʒən] N collusion f; **in** ~ **with** en
complicité avec

Colo. ABBR (US) = **Colorado**

cologne [kə'ləʊn] N (also: **eau de cologne**) eau f
de cologne

Colombia [kə'lɒmbɪə] N Colombie f

Colombian [kə'lɒmbɪən] ADJ colombien(ne) ▶ N
Colombien(ne)

colon ['kəʊlən] N (sign) deux-points mpl; (Med)
côlon m

colonel ['kə:nl] N colonel m

colonial [kə'ləʊnɪəl] ADJ colonial(e)

colonize ['kɒlənaɪz] VT coloniser

colony ['kɒlənɪ] N colonie f

color ['kʌləʳ] N (US) = **colour**

Colorado beetle [kɒlə'rɑ:dəʊ-] N doryphore m

colossal [kə'lɒsl] ADJ colossal(e)

colour, (US) **color** ['kʌləʳ] N couleur f ▶ VT
colorer; (dye) teindre; (paint) peindre; (with
crayons) colorier; (news) fausser, exagérer ▶ VI
(blush) rougir ▶ CPD (film, photograph, television) en
couleur; **colours** NPL (of party, club) couleurs fpl;
I'd like a different ~ je le voudrais dans un
autre coloris
  ▶ **colour in** VT colorier

colour bar, (US) **color bar** N discrimination
raciale (dans un établissement etc)

colour-blind, (US) **color-blind** ['kʌləblaɪnd] ADJ
daltonien(ne)

coloured, (US) **colored** ['kʌləd] ADJ (person, race:
offensive) coloré(e); (photo) en couleur

colour film, (US) **color film** N (for camera)
pellicule f (en) couleur

colourful, (US) **colorful** ['kʌləful] ADJ coloré(e),

vif (vive); (*personality*) pittoresque, haut(e) en couleurs

colouring, (*US*) **coloring** [ˈkʌlərɪŋ] N colorant *m*; (*complexion*) teint *m*

colour scheme, (*US*) **color scheme** N combinaison *f* de(s) couleur(s)

colour supplement N (*Brit Press*) supplément *m* magazine

colour television, (*US*) **color television** N télévision *f* (en) couleur

colt [kəult] N poulain *m*

column [ˈkɔləm] N colonne *f*; (*fashion column, sports column etc*) rubrique *f*; **the editorial ~** l'éditorial *m*

columnist [ˈkɔləmnɪst] N rédacteur(-trice) d'une rubrique

coma [ˈkəumə] N coma *m*

comb [kəum] N peigne *m* ▶ VT (*hair*) peigner; (*area*) ratisser, passer au peigne fin

combat [ˈkɔmbæt] N combat *m* ▶ VT combattre, lutter contre

combination [kɔmbɪˈneɪʃən] N (*gen*) combinaison *f*

combination lock N serrure *f* à combinaison

combine [kəmˈbaɪn] VT combiner ▶ VI s'associer; (*Chem*) se combiner ▶ N [ˈkɔmbaɪn] association *f*; (*Econ*) trust *m*; (*also:* **combine harvester**) moissonneuse-batteuse(-lieuse) *f*; **to ~ sth with sth** (*one quality with another*) joindre *or* allier qch à qch; **a combined effort** un effort conjugué

combine harvester N moissonneuse-batteuse(-lieuse) *f*

combo [ˈkɔmbəu] N (*Jazz etc*) groupe *m* de musiciens

combustible [kəmˈbʌstɪbl] ADJ combustible

combustion [kəmˈbʌstʃən] N combustion *f*

(KEYWORD)

come [kʌm] (*pt* **came** [keɪm], *pp* **come** [kʌm]) VI
1 (*movement towards*) venir; **to come running** arriver en courant; **he's come here to work** il est venu ici pour travailler; **come with me** suivez-moi; **to come into sight** *or* **view** apparaître
2 (*arrive*) arriver; **we've just come from Paris** nous arrivons de Paris; **coming!** j'arrive!
3 (*reach*): **to come to** (*decision etc*) parvenir à, arriver à; **the bill came to £40** la note s'est élevée à 40 livres; **if it comes to it** s'il le faut, dans le pire des cas
4 (*occur*): **an idea came to me** il m'est venu une idée; **what might come of it** ce qui pourrait en résulter, ce qui pourrait advenir *or* se produire
5 (*be, become*): **to come loose/undone** se défaire/desserrer; **I've come to like him** j'ai fini par bien l'aimer
6 (*inf: sexually*) jouir
▶ **come about** VI se produire, arriver
▶ **come across** VT FUS rencontrer par hasard, tomber sur ▶ VI: **to come across well/badly** faire une bonne/mauvaise impression
▶ **come along** VI (*Brit: pupil, work*) faire des progrès, avancer; **come along!** viens!; allons!, allez!
▶ **come apart** VI s'en aller en morceaux; se détacher
▶ **come away** VI partir, s'en aller; (*become detached*) se détacher
▶ **come back** VI revenir; (*reply*): **can I come back to you on that one?** est-ce qu'on peut revenir là-dessus plus tard?
▶ **come by** VT FUS (*acquire*) obtenir, se procurer
▶ **come down** VI descendre; (*prices*) baisser; (*buildings*) s'écrouler; (: *be demolished*) être démoli(e)
▶ **come forward** VI s'avancer; (*make o.s. known*) se présenter, s'annoncer
▶ **come from** VT FUS (*source*) venir de; (*place*) venir de, être originaire de
▶ **come in** VI entrer; (*train*) arriver; (*fashion*) entrer en vogue; (*on deal etc*) participer
▶ **come in for** VT FUS (*criticism etc*) être l'objet de
▶ **come into** VT FUS (*money*) hériter de
▶ **come off** VI (*button*) se détacher; (*attempt*) réussir
▶ **come on** VI (*lights, electricity*) s'allumer; (*central heating*) se mettre en marche; (*pupil, work, project*) faire des progrès, avancer; **come on!** viens!; allons!, allez!
▶ **come out** VI sortir; (*sun*) se montrer; (*book*) paraître; (*stain*) s'enlever; (*strike*) cesser le travail, se mettre en grève
▶ **come over** VT FUS: **I don't know what's come over him!** je ne sais pas ce qui lui a pris!
▶ **come round** VI (*after faint, operation*) revenir à soi, reprendre connaissance
▶ **come through** VI (*survive*) s'en sortir; (*telephone call*): **the call came through** l'appel est bien parvenu
▶ **come to** VI revenir à soi ▶ VT (*add up to: amount*): **how much does it come to?** ça fait combien?
▶ **come under** VT FUS (*heading*) se trouver sous; (*influence*) subir
▶ **come up** VI monter; (*sun*) se lever; (*problem*) se poser; (*event*) survenir; (*in conversation*) être soulevé
▶ **come up against** VT FUS (*resistance, difficulties*) rencontrer
▶ **come upon** VT FUS tomber sur
▶ **come up to** VT FUS arriver à; **the film didn't come up to our expectations** le film nous a déçu
▶ **come up with** VT FUS (*money*) fournir; **he came up with an idea** il a eu une idée, il a proposé quelque chose

comeback [ˈkʌmbæk] N (*Theat*) rentrée *f*; (*reaction*) réaction *f*; (*response*) réponse *f*

Comecon [ˈkɔmikɔn] N ABBR (= *Council for Mutual Economic Aid*) COMECON *m*

comedian [kəˈmiːdɪən] N (*comic*) comique *m*; (*Theat*) comédien *m*

comedienne [kəmiːdɪˈɛn] N comique *f*

comedown [ˈkʌmdaun] N déchéance *f*

comedy [ˈkɔmɪdɪ] N comédie *f*; (*humour*) comique *m*

comet ['kɔmɪt] N comète f
comeuppance [kʌm'ʌpəns] N: **to get one's ~** recevoir ce qu'on mérite
comfort ['kʌmfət] N confort m, bien-être m; (*solace*) consolation f, réconfort m ▶ VT consoler, réconforter
comfortable ['kʌmfətəbl] ADJ confortable; (*person*) à l'aise; (*financially*) aisé(e); (*patient*) dont l'état est stationnaire; **I don't feel very ~ about it** cela m'inquiète un peu
comfortably ['kʌmfətəblɪ] ADV (*sit*) confortablement; (*live*) à l'aise
comforter ['kʌmfətəʳ] N (*US*) édredon m
comforts ['kʌmfəts] NPL aises fpl
comfort station N (*US*) toilettes fpl
comic ['kɔmɪk] ADJ (*also*: **comical**) comique ▶ N (*person*) comique m; (*BRIT*: *magazine: for children*) magazine m de bandes dessinées or de BD; (: *for adults*) illustré m
comical ['kɔmɪkl] ADJ amusant(e)
comic book N (*US: for children*) magazine m de bandes dessinées or de BD; (: *for adults*) illustré m
comic strip N bande dessinée
coming ['kʌmɪŋ] N arrivée f ▶ ADJ (*next*) prochain(e); (*future*) à venir; **in the ~ weeks** dans les prochaines semaines
Comintern ['kɔmɪntəːn] N Comintern m
comma ['kɔmə] N virgule f
command [kə'mɑːnd] N ordre m, commandement m; (*Mil: authority*) commandement; (*mastery*) maîtrise f; (*Comput*) commande f ▶ VT (*troops*) commander; (*be able to get*) (pouvoir) disposer de, avoir à sa disposition; (*deserve*) avoir droit à; **to ~ sb to do** donner l'ordre or commander à qn de faire; **to have/ take ~ of** avoir/prendre le commandement de; **to have at one's ~** (*money, resources etc*) disposer de
command economy N économie planifiée
commandeer [kɔmən'dɪəʳ] VT réquisitionner (par la force)
commander [kə'mɑːndəʳ] N chef m; (*Mil*) commandant m
commander-in-chief [kə'mɑːndərɪn'tʃiːf] N (*Mil*) commandant m en chef
commanding [kə'mɑːndɪŋ] ADJ (*appearance*) imposant(e); (*voice, tone*) autoritaire; (*lead, position*) dominant(e)
commanding officer N commandant m
commandment [kə'mɑːndmənt] N (*Rel*) commandement m
command module N (*Space*) module m de commande
commando [kə'mɑːndəu] N commando m; membre m d'un commando
commemorate [kə'mɛmɔreɪt] VT commémorer
commemoration [kəmɛmə'reɪʃən] N commémoration f
commemorative [kə'mɛmərətɪv] ADJ commémoratif(-ive)
commence [kə'mɛns] VT, VI commencer
commend [kə'mɛnd] VT louer; (*recommend*) recommander
commendable [kə'mɛndəbl] ADJ louable

commendation [kɔmɛn'deɪʃən] N éloge m; recommandation f
commensurate [kə'mɛnʃərɪt] ADJ: **~ with/to** en rapport avec/selon
comment ['kɔmɛnt] N commentaire m ▶ VI faire des remarques or commentaires; **to ~ on** faire des remarques sur; **to ~ that** faire remarquer que; **"no ~"** "je n'ai rien à déclarer"
commentary ['kɔməntərɪ] N commentaire m; (*Sport*) reportage m (en direct)
commentator ['kɔmənteɪtəʳ] N commentateur m; (*Sport*) reporter m
commerce ['kɔməːs] N commerce m
commercial [kə'məːʃəl] ADJ commercial(e) ▶ N (*Radio, TV*) annonce f publicitaire, spot m (publicitaire)
commercial bank N banque f d'affaires
commercial break N (*Radio, TV*) spot m (publicitaire)
commercial college N école f de commerce
commercialism [kə'məːʃəlɪzəm] N mercantilisme m
commercial television N publicité f à la télévision, chaînes privées (financées par la publicité)
commercial traveller N voyageur m de commerce
commercial vehicle N véhicule m utilitaire
commiserate [kə'mɪzəreɪt] VI: **to ~ with sb** témoigner de la sympathie pour qn
commission [kə'mɪʃən] N (*committee, fee*) commission f; (*order for work of art etc*) commande f ▶ VT (*Mil*) nommer (à un commandement); (*work of art*) commander, charger un artiste de l'exécution de; **out of ~** (*Naut*) hors de service; (*machine*) hors service; **I get 10% ~** je reçois une commission de 10%; **~ of inquiry** (*BRIT*) commission d'enquête
commissionaire [kəmɪʃə'nɛəʳ] N (*BRIT: at shop, cinema etc*) portier m (en uniforme)
commissioner [kə'mɪʃənəʳ] N membre m d'une commission; (*Police*) préfet m (de police)
commit [kə'mɪt] VT (*act*) commettre; (*resources*) consacrer; (*to sb's care*) confier (à); **to ~ o.s. (to do)** s'engager (à faire); **to ~ suicide** se suicider; **to ~ to writing** coucher par écrit; **to ~ sb for trial** traduire qn en justice
commitment [kə'mɪtmənt] N engagement m; (*obligation*) responsabilité(s) f(pl)
committed [kə'mɪtɪd] ADJ (*writer, politician etc*) engagé(e)
committee [kə'mɪtɪ] N comité m; commission f; **to be on a ~** siéger dans un comité or une commission)
committee meeting N réunion f de comité or commission
commodity [kə'mɔdɪtɪ] N produit m, marchandise f, article m; (*food*) denrée f
commodity exchange N bourse f de marchandises
common ['kɔmən] ADJ (*gen*) commun(e); (*usual*) courant(e) ▶ N terrain communal; **in ~** en commun; **in ~ use** d'un usage courant; **it's ~ knowledge that** il est bien connu or notoire

que; **to the ~ good** pour le bien de tous, dans l'intérêt général

common cold N: **the ~** le rhume

common denominator N dénominateur commun

commoner ['kɔmənəʳ] N roturier(-ière)

common ground N (fig) terrain m d'entente

common land N terrain communal

common law N droit coutumier

common-law ['kɔmənlɔː] ADJ: **~ wife** épouse f de facto

commonly ['kɔmənlɪ] ADV communément, généralement; couramment

Common Market N Marché commun

commonplace ['kɔmənpleɪs] ADJ banal(e), ordinaire

common room N salle commune; (Scol) salle des professeurs

Commons ['kɔmənz] NPL (Brit Pol): **the (House of)** ~ la chambre des Communes

common sense N bon sens

Commonwealth ['kɔmənwɛlθ] N: **the ~** le Commonwealth; voir article

▌ Le Commonwealth regroupe 50 États indépendants et plusieurs territoires qui reconnaissent tous le souverain britannique comme chef de cette association.

commotion [kə'məuʃən] N désordre m, tumulte m

communal ['kɔmjuːnl] ADJ (life) communautaire; (for common use) commun(e)

commune N ['kɔmjuːn] (group) communauté f ▶ VI [kə'mjuːn]: **to ~ with** converser intimement avec; (nature) communier avec

communicate [kə'mjuːnɪkeɪt] VT communiquer, transmettre ▶ VI: **to ~ (with)** communiquer (avec)

communication [kəmjuːnɪ'keɪʃən] N communication f

communication cord N (Brit) sonnette f d'alarme

communications network N réseau m de communications

communications satellite N satellite m de télécommunications

communicative [kə'mjuːnɪkətɪv] ADJ communicatif(-ive)

communion [kə'mjuːnɪən] N (also: **Holy Communion**) communion f

communism ['kɔmjunɪzəm] N communisme m

communist ['kɔmjunɪst] ADJ, N communiste mf

community [kə'mjuːnɪtɪ] N communauté f

community centre, (US) **community center** N foyer socio-éducatif, centre m de loisirs

community chest N (US) fonds commun

community health centre N centre médico-social

community service N ≈ travail m d'intérêt général, TIG m

community spirit N solidarité f

commutation ticket [kɔmjuː'teɪʃən-] N (US) carte f d'abonnement

commute [kə'mjuːt] VI faire le trajet journalier (de son domicile à un lieu de travail assez éloigné) ▶ VT

(Law) commuer; (Math: terms etc) opérer la commutation de

commuter [kə'mjuːtəʳ] N banlieusard(e) (qui fait un trajet journalier pour se rendre à son travail)

compact ADJ [kəm'pækt] compact(e) ▶ N ['kɔmpækt] contrat m, entente f; (also: **powder compact**) poudrier m

compact disc N disque compact

compact disc player N lecteur m de disques compacts

companion [kəm'pænjən] N compagnon (compagne)

companionship [kəm'pænjənʃɪp] N camaraderie f

companionway [kəm'pænjənweɪ] N (Naut) escalier m des cabines

company ['kʌmpənɪ] N (also Comm, Mil, Theat) compagnie f; **he's good** ~ il est d'une compagnie agréable; **we have** ~ nous avons de la visite; **to keep sb** ~ tenir compagnie à qn; **to part** ~ **with** se séparer de; **Smith and C~** Smith et Compagnie

company car N voiture f de fonction

company director N administrateur(-trice)

company secretary N (Brit Comm) secrétaire général (d'une société)

comparable ['kɔmpərəbl] ADJ comparable

comparative [kəm'pærətɪv] ADJ (study) comparatif(-ive); (relative) relatif(-ive)

comparatively [kəm'pærətɪvlɪ] ADV (relatively) relativement

compare [kəm'pɛəʳ] VT: **to ~ sth/sb with** or **to** comparer qch/qn avec or à ▶ VI: **to ~ (with)** se comparer (à); **être comparable** (à); **how do the prices ~?** comment sont les prix?, est-ce que les prix sont comparables?; **compared with** or **to** par rapport à

comparison [kəm'pærɪsn] N comparaison f; **in ~ (with)** en comparaison (de)

compartment [kəm'pɑːtmənt] N (also Rail) compartiment m; **a non-smoking** ~ un compartiment non-fumeurs

compass ['kʌmpəs] N boussole f; **compasses** NPL (Math) compas m; **within the ~ of** dans les limites de

compassion [kəm'pæʃən] N compassion f, humanité f

compassionate [kəm'pæʃənɪt] ADJ accessible à la compassion, au cœur charitable et bienveillant; **on ~ grounds** pour raisons personnelles or de famille

compassionate leave N congé exceptionnel (pour raisons de famille)

compatibility [kəmpætɪ'bɪlɪtɪ] N compatibilité f

compatible [kəm'pætɪbl] ADJ compatible

compel [kəm'pɛl] VT contraindre, obliger

compelling [kəm'pɛlɪŋ] ADJ (fig: argument) irrésistible

compendium [kəm'pɛndɪəm] N (summary) abrégé m

compensate ['kɔmpənseɪt] VT indemniser, dédommager ▶ VI: **to ~ for** compenser

compensation [kɔmpən'seɪʃən] N

compensation *f*; *(money)* dédommagement *m*, indemnité *f*

compere ['kɔmpɛəʳ] N présentateur(-trice), animateur(-trice)

compete [kəm'piːt] VI *(take part)* concourir; *(vie)*: **to ~ (with)** rivaliser (avec), faire concurrence (à)

competence ['kɔmpɪtəns] N compétence *f*, aptitude *f*

competent ['kɔmpɪtənt] ADJ compétent(e), capable

competing [kəm'piːtɪŋ] ADJ *(ideas, theories)* opposé(e); *(companies)* concurrent(e)

competition [kɔmpɪ'tɪʃən] N *(contest)* compétition *f*, concours *m*; *(Econ)* concurrence *f*; **in ~ with** en concurrence avec

competitive [kəm'pɛtɪtɪv] ADJ *(Econ)* concurrentiel(le); *(sports)* de compétition; *(person)* qui a l'esprit de compétition

competitive examination N concours *m*

competitor [kəm'pɛtɪtəʳ] N concurrent(e)

compile [kəm'paɪl] VT compiler

complacency [kəm'pleɪsnsɪ] N contentement *m* de soi, autosatisfaction *f*

complacent [kəm'pleɪsnt] ADJ *(trop)* content(e) de soi

complain [kəm'pleɪn] VI: **to ~ (about)** se plaindre (de); *(in shop etc)* réclamer (au sujet de) ▶ **complain of** VT FUS *(Med)* se plaindre de

complaint [kəm'pleɪnt] N plainte *f*; *(in shop etc)* réclamation *f*; *(Med)* affection *f*

complement ['kɔmplɪmənt] N complément *m*; *(esp of ship's crew etc)* effectif complet ▶ VT *(enhance)* compléter

complementary [kɔmplɪ'mɛntərɪ] ADJ complémentaire

complete [kəm'pliːt] ADJ complet(-ète); *(finished)* achevé(e) ▶ VT achever, parachever; *(set, group)* compléter; *(a form)* remplir

completely [kəm'pliːtlɪ] ADV complètement

completion [kəm'pliːʃən] N achèvement *m*; *(of contract)* exécution *f*; **to be nearing ~** être presque terminé

complex ['kɔmplɛks] ADJ complexe ▶ N *(Psych, buildings etc)* complexe *m*

complexion [kəm'plɛkʃən] N *(of face)* teint *m*; *(of event etc)* aspect *m*, caractère *m*

complexity [kəm'plɛksɪtɪ] N complexité *f*

compliance [kəm'plaɪəns] N *(submission)* docilité *f*; *(agreement)*: **~ with** le fait de se conformer à; **in ~ with** en conformité avec, conformément à

compliant [kəm'plaɪənt] ADJ docile, très accommodant(e)

complicate ['kɔmplɪkeɪt] VT compliquer

complicated ['kɔmplɪkeɪtɪd] ADJ compliqué(e)

complication [kɔmplɪ'keɪʃən] N complication *f*

compliment N ['kɔmplɪmənt] compliment *m* ▶ VT ['kɔmplɪmɛnt] complimenter; **compliments** NPL compliments *mpl*, hommages *mpl*; vœux *mpl*; **to pay sb a ~** faire *or* adresser un compliment à qn; **to ~ sb (on sth/ on doing sth)** féliciter qn (pour qch/de faire qch)

complimentary [kɔmplɪ'mɛntərɪ] ADJ

flatteur(-euse); *(free)* à titre gracieux

complimentary ticket N billet *m* de faveur

compliments slip N fiche *f* de transmission

comply [kəm'plaɪ] VI: **to ~ with** se soumettre à, se conformer à

component [kəm'pəunənt] ADJ composant(e), constituant(e) ▶ N composant *m*, élément *m*

compose [kəm'pəuz] VT composer; *(form)*: **to be composed of** se composer de; **to ~ o.s.** se calmer, se maîtriser; **to ~ one's features** prendre une contenance

composed [kəm'pəuzd] ADJ calme, posé(e)

composer [kəm'pəuzəʳ] N *(Mus)* compositeur *m*

composite ['kɔmpəzɪt] ADJ composite; *(Bot, Math)* composé(e)

composition [kɔmpə'zɪʃən] N composition *f*

compost ['kɔmpɔst] N compost *m*

composure [kəm'pəuʒəʳ] N calme *m*, maîtrise *f* de soi

compound ['kɔmpaund] N *(Chem, Ling)* composé *m*; *(enclosure)* enclos *m*, enceinte *f* ▶ ADJ composé(e); *(fracture)* compliqué(e) ▶ VT [kəm'paund] *(fig: problem etc)* aggraver

compound fracture N fracture compliquée

compound interest N intérêt composé

comprehend [kɔmprɪ'hɛnd] VT comprendre

comprehension [kɔmprɪ'hɛnʃən] N compréhension *f*

comprehensive [kɔmprɪ'hɛnsɪv] ADJ *(très)* complet(-ète); **~ policy** *(Insurance)* assurance *f* tous risques

comprehensive [kɔmprɪ'hɛnsɪv], **comprehensive school** N *(Brit)* école secondaire non sélective avec libre circulation d'une section à l'autre, ≈ CES *m*

compress VT [kəm'prɛs] comprimer; *(text, information)* condenser ▶ N ['kɔmprɛs] *(Med)* compresse *f*

compression [kəm'prɛʃən] N compression *f*

comprise [kəm'praɪz] VT *(also:* **be comprised of**) comprendre; *(constitute)* constituer, représenter

compromise ['kɔmprəmaɪz] N compromis *m* ▶ VT compromettre ▶ VI transiger, accepter un compromis ▶ CPD *(decision, solution)* de compromis

compulsion [kəm'pʌlʃən] N contrainte *f*, force *f*; **under ~** sous la contrainte

compulsive [kəm'pʌlsɪv] ADJ *(Psych)* compulsif(-ive); *(book, film etc)* captivant(e); **he's a ~ smoker** c'est un fumeur invétéré

compulsory [kəm'pʌlsərɪ] ADJ obligatoire

compulsory purchase N expropriation *f*

compunction [kəm'pʌŋkʃən] N scrupule *m*; **to have no ~ about doing sth** n'avoir aucun scrupule à faire qch

computer [kəm'pjuːtəʳ] N ordinateur *m*; *(mechanical)* calculatrice *f*

computer game N jeu *m* vidéo

computer-generated [kəm'pjuːtə'dʒɛnəreɪtɪd] ADJ de synthèse

computerize [kəm'pjuːtəraɪz] VT *(data)* traiter par ordinateur; *(system, office)* informatiser

computer language N langage *m* machine *or* informatique

computer literate ADJ initié(e) à l'informatique

computer peripheral N périphérique m

computer program N programme m informatique

computer programmer N programmeur(-euse)

computer programming N programmation f

computer science N informatique f

computer scientist N informaticien(ne)

computer studies NPL informatique f

computing [kəm'pju:tɪŋ] N informatique f

comrade ['kɔmrɪd] N camarade mf

comradeship ['kɔmrɪdʃɪp] N camaraderie f

Comsat ['kɔmsæt] N ABBR = **communications satellite**

con [kɔn] VT duper; (cheat) escroquer ▶ N escroquerie f; **to ~ sb into doing sth** tromper qn pour lui faire faire qch

concave ['kɔn'keɪv] ADJ concave

conceal [kən'si:l] VT cacher, dissimuler

concede [kən'si:d] VT concéder ▶ VI céder

conceit [kən'si:t] N vanité f, suffisance f, prétention f

conceited [kən'si:tɪd] ADJ vaniteux(-euse), suffisant(e)

conceivable [kən'si:vəbl] ADJ concevable, imaginable; **it is ~ that** il est concevable que

conceivably [kən'si:vəblɪ] ADV: **he may ~ be right** il n'est pas impossible qu'il ait raison

conceive [kən'si:v] VT, VI concevoir; **to ~ of sth/ of doing sth** imaginer qch/de faire qch

concentrate ['kɔnsəntreɪt] VI se concentrer ▶ VT concentrer

concentration [kɔnsən'treɪʃən] N concentration f

concentration camp N camp m de concentration

concentric [kɔn'sɛntrɪk] ADJ concentrique

concept ['kɔnsɛpt] N concept m

conception [kən'sɛpʃən] N conception f; (idea) idée f

concern [kən'sə:n] N affaire f; (Comm) entreprise f, firme f; (anxiety) inquiétude f, souci m ▶ VT (worry) inquiéter; (involve) concerner; (relate to) se rapporter à; **to be concerned (about)** s'inquiéter (de), être inquiet(-ète) (au sujet de); **"to whom it may ~"** "à qui de droit"; **as far as I am concerned** en ce qui me concerne; **to be concerned with** (person: involved with) s'occuper de; **the department concerned** (under discussion) le service en question; (involved) le service concerné

concerning [kən'sə:nɪŋ] PREP en ce qui concerne, à propos de

concert ['kɔnsət] N concert m; **in ~** à l'unisson, en chœur; ensemble

concerted [kən'sə:tɪd] ADJ concerté(e)

concert hall N salle f de concert

concertina [kɔnsə'ti:nə] N concertina m ▶ VI se télescoper, se caramboler

concerto [kən'tʃə:təu] N concerto m

concession [kən'sɛʃən] N (compromise) concession f; (reduced price) réduction f; **tax ~** dégrèvement fiscal; **"concessions"** tarif réduit

concessionaire [kənsɛʃə'nɛər] N concessionnaire mf

concessionary [kən'sɛʃənrɪ] ADJ (ticket, fare) à tarif réduit

conciliation [kənsɪlɪ'eɪʃən] N conciliation f, apaisement m

conciliatory [kən'sɪlɪətrɪ] ADJ conciliateur(-trice); conciliant(e)

concise [kən'saɪs] ADJ concis(e)

conclave ['kɔnkleɪv] N assemblée secrète; (Rel) conclave m

conclude [kən'klu:d] VT conclure ▶ VI (speaker) conclure; (events) se terminer (par)

concluding [kən'klu:dɪŋ] ADJ (remarks etc) final(e)

conclusion [kən'klu:ʒən] N conclusion f; **to come to the ~ that** (en) conclure que

conclusive [kən'klu:sɪv] ADJ concluant(e), définitif(-ive)

concoct [kən'kɔkt] VT confectionner, composer

concoction [kən'kɔkʃən] N (food, drink) mélange m

concord ['kɔŋkɔ:d] N (harmony) harmonie f; (treaty) accord m

concourse ['kɔŋkɔ:s] N (hall) hall m, salle f des pas perdus; (crowd) affluence f; multitude f

concrete ['kɔŋkri:t] N béton m ▶ ADJ concret(-ète); (Constr) en béton

concrete mixer N bétonnière f

concur [kən'kə:r] VI être d'accord

concurrently [kən'kʌrntlɪ] ADV simultanément

concussion [kən'kʌʃən] N (Med) commotion (cérébrale)

condemn [kən'dɛm] VT condamner

condemnation [kɔndɛm'neɪʃən] N condamnation f

condensation [kɔndɛn'seɪʃən] N condensation f

condense [kən'dɛns] VI se condenser ▶ VT condenser

condensed milk [kən'dɛnst-] N lait concentré (sucré)

condescend [kɔndɪ'sɛnd] VI condescendre, s'abaisser; **to ~ to do sth** daigner faire qch

condescending [kɔndɪ'sɛndɪŋ] ADJ condescendant(e)

condition [kən'dɪʃən] N condition f; (disease) maladie f ▶ VT déterminer, conditionner; **in good/poor ~** en bon/mauvais état; **a heart ~** une maladie cardiaque; **weather conditions** conditions fpl météorologiques; **on ~ that** à condition que + sub, à condition de

conditional [kən'dɪʃənl] ADJ conditionnel(le); **to be ~ upon** dépendre de

conditioner [kən'dɪʃənər] N (for hair) baume démêlant; (for fabrics) assouplissant m

condo ['kɔndəu] N (US inf) = **condominium**

condolences [kən'dəulənsɪz] NPL condoléances fpl

condom ['kɔndəm] N préservatif m

condominium [kɔndə'mɪnɪəm] N (US: building) immeuble m (en copropriété); (: rooms) appartement *m* (dans un immeuble en copropriété)

condone [kən'dəun] VT fermer les yeux sur, approuver (tacitement)

conducive [kən'dju:sɪv] ADJ: ~ **to** favorable à, qui contribue à

conduct N ['kɔndʌkt] conduite *f* ▶ VT [kən'dʌkt] conduire; (*manage*) mener, diriger; (*Mus*) diriger; **to ~ o.s.** se conduire, se comporter

conductor [kən'dʌktə^r] N (*of orchestra*) chef *m* d'orchestre; (*on bus*) receveur *m*; (*US: on train*) chef *m* de train; (*Elec*) conducteur *m*

conductress [kən'dʌktrɪs] N (*on bus*) receveuse *f*

conduit ['kɔndɪt] N conduit *m*, tuyau *m*; tube *m*

cone [kəun] N cône *m*; (*for ice-cream*) cornet *m*; (*Bot*) pomme *f* de pin, cône

confectioner [kən'fɛkʃənə^r] N (*of cakes*) pâtissier(-ière); (*of sweets*) confiseur(-euse); **~'s (shop)** confiserie(-pâtisserie) *f*

confectionery [kən'fɛkʃənrɪ] N (*sweets*) confiserie *f*; (*cakes*) pâtisserie *f*

confederate [kən'fɛdrɪt] ADJ confédéré(e) ▶ N (*pej*) acolyte *m*; (*US Hist*) confédéré(e)

confederation [kənfɛdə'reɪʃən] N confédération *f*

confer [kən'fə:^r] VT: **to ~ sth on** conférer qch à ▶ VI conférer, s'entretenir; **to ~ (with sb about sth)** s'entretenir (de qch avec qn)

conference ['kɔnfərns] N conférence *f*; **to be in ~** être en réunion *or* en conférence

conference room N salle *f* de conférence

confess [kən'fɛs] VT confesser, avouer ▶ VI (*admit sth*) avouer; (*Rel*) se confesser

confession [kən'fɛʃən] N confession *f*

confessional [kən'fɛʃənl] N confessional *m*

confessor [kən'fɛsə^r] N confesseur *m*

confetti [kən'fɛtɪ] N confettis *mpl*

confide [kən'faɪd] VI: **to ~ in** s'ouvrir à, se confier à

confidence ['kɔnfɪdns] N confiance *f*; (*also:* **self-confidence**) assurance *f*, confiance en soi; (*secret*) confidence *f*; **to have (every) ~ that** être certain que; **motion of no ~** motion *f* de censure; **in ~** (*speak, write*) en confidence, confidentiellement; **to tell sb sth in strict ~** dire qch à qn en toute confidence

confidence trick N escroquerie *f*

confident ['kɔnfɪdənt] ADJ (*self-assured*) sûr(e) de soi; (*sure*) sûr

confidential [kɔnfɪ'dɛnʃəl] ADJ confidentiel(le); (*secretary*) particulier(-ère)

confidentiality ['kɔnfɪdɛnʃɪ'ælɪtɪ] N confidentialité *f*

configuration [kən'fɪgju'reɪʃən] N (*also Comput*) configuration *f*

confine [kən'faɪn] VT limiter, borner; (*shut up*) confiner, enfermer; **to ~ o.s. to doing sth/to sth** se contenter de faire qch/se limiter à qch

confined [kən'faɪnd] ADJ (*space*) restreint(e), réduit(e)

confinement [kən'faɪnmənt] N emprisonnement *m*, détention *f*; (*Mil*) consigne *f* (au quartier); (*Med*) accouchement *m*

confines ['kɔnfaɪnz] NPL confins *mpl*, bornes *fpl*

confirm [kən'fə:m] VT (*report, Rel*) confirmer; (*appointment*) ratifier

confirmation [kɔnfə'meɪʃən] N confirmation *f*; ratification *f*

confirmed [kən'fə:md] ADJ invétéré(e), incorrigible

confiscate ['kɔnfɪskeɪt] VT confisquer

confiscation [kɔnfɪs'keɪʃən] N confiscation *f*

conflagration [kɔnflə'greɪʃən] N incendie *m*; (*fig*) conflagration *f*

conflict N ['kɔnflɪkt] conflit *m*, lutte *f* ▶ VI [kən'flɪkt] être *or* entrer en conflit; (*opinions*) s'opposer, se heurter

conflicting [kən'flɪktɪŋ] ADJ contradictoire

conform [kən'fɔ:m] VI: **to ~ (to)** se conformer (à)

conformist [kən'fɔ:mɪst] N (*gen, Rel*) conformiste *mf*

confound [kən'faund] VT confondre; (*amaze*) rendre perplexe

confounded [kən'faundɪd] ADJ maudit(e), sacré(e)

confront [kən'frʌnt] VT (*two people*) confronter; (*enemy, danger*) affronter, faire face à; (*problem*) faire face à

confrontation [kɔnfrən'teɪʃən] N confrontation *f*

confrontational [kɔnfrən'teɪʃənl] ADJ conflictuel(le)

confuse [kən'fju:z] VT (*person*) troubler; (*situation*) embrouiller; (*one thing with another*) confondre

confused [kən'fju:zd] ADJ (*person*) dérouté(e), désorienté(e); (*situation*) embrouillé(e)

confusing [kən'fju:zɪŋ] ADJ peu clair(e), déroutant(e)

confusion [kən'fju:ʒən] N confusion *f*

congeal [kən'dʒi:l] VI (*oil*) se figer; (*blood*) se coaguler

congenial [kən'dʒi:nɪəl] ADJ sympathique, agréable

congenital [kən'dʒenɪtl] ADJ congénital(e)

conger eel ['kɔngər-] N congre *m*, anguille *f* de roche

congested [kən'dʒestɪd] ADJ (*Med*) congestionné(e); (*fig*) surpeuplé(e); congestionné; bloqué(e); (*telephone lines*) encombré(e)

congestion [kən'dʒestʃən] N (*Med*) congestion *f*; (*fig: traffic*) encombrement *m*

conglomerate [kən'glɔmərɪt] N (*Comm*) conglomérat *m*

conglomeration [kənglɔmə'reɪʃən] N groupement *m*; agglomération *f*

Congo ['kɔŋgəu] N (*state*) (république *f* du) Congo

congratulate [kən'grætjuleɪt] VT: **to ~ sb (on)** féliciter qn (de)

congratulations [kəngrætju'leɪʃənz] NPL: **~ (on)** félicitations *fpl* (pour) ▶ EXCL: **~!** (toutes mes) félicitations!

congregate ['kɔŋgrɪgeɪt] VI se rassembler, se réunir

congregation [kɔŋgrɪ'geɪʃən] N assemblée *f* (des fidèles)

congress ['kɔŋgrɛs] N congrès *m*; (*Pol*): **C~** Congrès *m*; *voir article*

> Le *Congress* est le parlement des États-Unis. Il comprend la *House of Representatives* et le *Senate*. Représentants et sénateurs sont élus au suffrage universel direct. Le Congrès se réunit au *Capitol*, à Washington.

congressman ['kɔŋgrɛsmən] N (*irreg*) membre *m* du Congrès

congresswoman ['kɔŋgrɛswumən] N (*irreg*) membre *m* du Congrès

conical ['kɔnɪkl] ADJ (de forme) conique

conifer ['kɔnɪfə'] N conifère *m*

coniferous [kə'nɪfərəs] ADJ (*forest*) de conifères

conjecture [kən'dʒɛktʃə'] N conjecture *f* ▶ VT, VI conjecturer

conjugal ['kɔndʒugl] ADJ conjugal(e)

conjugate ['kɔndʒugeɪt] VT conjuguer

conjugation [kɔndʒə'geɪʃən] N conjugaison *f*

conjunction [kən'dʒʌŋkʃən] N conjonction *f*; **in ~ with** (conjointement) avec

conjunctivitis [kəndʒʌŋktɪ'vaɪtɪs] N conjonctivite *f*

conjure ['kʌndʒə'] VT (*by magic*) faire apparaître (par la prestidigitation); [kən'dʒuə'] conjurer, supplier ▶ VI faire des tours de passe-passe ▶ **conjure up** VT (*ghost, spirit*) faire apparaître; (*memories*) évoquer

conjurer ['kʌndʒərə'] N prestidigitateur *m*, illusionniste *mf*

conjuring trick ['kʌndʒərɪŋ-] N tour *m* de prestidigitation

conker ['kɔŋkə'] N (BRIT) marron *m* (d'Inde)

conk out [kɔŋk-] VI (*inf*) tomber *or* rester en panne

conman ['kɔnmæn] N (*irreg*) escroc *m*

Conn. ABBR (*US*) = **Connecticut**

connect [kə'nɛkt] VT joindre, relier; (*Elec*) connecter; (*Tel: caller*) mettre en connexion; (*: subscriber*) brancher; (*fig*) établir un rapport entre, faire un rapprochement entre ▶ VI (*train*): **to ~ with** assurer la correspondance avec; **to be connected with** avoir un rapport avec; (*have dealings with*) avoir des rapports avec, être en relation avec; **I am trying to ~ you** (*Tel*) j'essaie d'obtenir votre communication

connecting flight N (vol *m* de) correspondance *f*

connection [kə'nɛkʃən] N relation *f*, lien *m*; (*Elec*) connexion *f*; (*Tel*) communication *f*; (*train etc*) correspondance *f*; **in ~ with** à propos de; **what is the ~ between them?** quel est le lien entre eux?; **business connections** relations d'affaires; **to miss/get one's ~** (*train etc*) rater/ avoir sa correspondance

connexion [kə'nɛkʃən] N (BRIT) = **connection**

conning tower ['kɔnɪŋ-] N kiosque *m* (de sous-marin)

connive [kə'naɪv] VI: **to ~ at** se faire le complice de

connoisseur [kɔnɪ'sə:'] N connaisseur *m*

connotation [kɔnə'teɪʃən] N connotation *f*, implication *f*

connubial [kə'nju:bɪəl] ADJ conjugal(e)

conquer ['kɔŋkə'] VT conquérir; (*feelings*) vaincre, surmonter

conqueror ['kɔŋkərə'] N conquérant *m*, vainqueur *m*

conquest ['kɔŋkwɛst] N conquête *f*

cons [kɔnz] NPL *see* **convenience**; **pro**

conscience ['kɔnʃəns] N conscience *f*; **in all ~** en conscience

conscientious [kɔnʃɪ'ɛnʃəs] ADJ consciencieux(-euse); (*scruple, objection*) de conscience

conscientious objector N objecteur *m* de conscience

conscious ['kɔnʃəs] ADJ conscient(e); (*deliberate: insult, error*) délibéré(e); **to become ~ of sth/ that** prendre conscience de qch/que

consciousness ['kɔnʃəsnɪs] N conscience *f*; (*Med*) connaissance *f*; **to lose/regain ~** perdre/ reprendre connaissance

conscript ['kɔnskrɪpt] N conscrit *m*

conscription [kən'skrɪpʃən] N conscription *f*

consecrate ['kɔnsɪkreɪt] VT consacrer

consecutive [kən'sɛkjutɪv] ADJ consécutif(-ive); **on three ~ occasions** trois fois de suite

consensus [kən'sɛnsəs] N consensus *m*; **the ~ (of opinion)** le consensus (d'opinion)

consent [kən'sɛnt] N consentement *m* ▶ VI: **to ~ (to)** consentir (à); **age of ~** âge nubile (légal); **by common ~** d'un commun accord

consenting adults [kən'sɛntɪŋ-] NPL personnes consentantes

consequence ['kɔnsɪkwəns] N suites *fpl*, conséquence *f*; (*significance*) importance *f*; **in ~** en conséquence, par conséquent

consequently ['kɔnsɪkwəntlɪ] ADV par conséquent, donc

conservation [kɔnsə'veɪʃən] N préservation *f*, protection *f*; (*also*: **nature conservation**) défense *f* de l'environnement; **energy ~** économies *fpl* d'énergie

conservationist [kɔnsə'veɪʃnɪst] N protecteur(-trice) de la nature

Conservative [kən'sə:vətɪv] ADJ, N (BRIT Pol) conservateur(-trice); **the ~ Party** le parti conservateur

conservative [kən'sə:vətɪv] ADJ conservateur(-trice); (*cautious*) prudent(e)

conservatory [kən'sə:vətrɪ] N (*room*) jardin *m* d'hiver; (*Mus*) conservatoire *m*

conserve [kən'sə:v] VT conserver, préserver; (*supplies, energy*) économiser ▶ N confiture *f*, conserve *f* (de fruits)

consider [kən'sɪdə'] VT (*study*) considérer, réfléchir à; (*take into account*) penser à, prendre en considération; (*regard, judge*) considérer, estimer; **to ~ doing sth** envisager de faire qch; **~ yourself lucky** estimez-vous heureux; **all things considered** (toute) réflexion faite

considerable [kən'sɪdərəbl] ADJ considérable

considerably [kən'sɪdərəblɪ] ADV nettement

considerate [kən'sɪdərɪt] ADJ prévenant(e), plein(e) d'égards

consideration [kənsɪdə'reɪʃən] N considération *f*; (*reward*) rétribution *f*, rémunération *f*; **out of ~ for** par égard pour; **under ~** à l'étude; **my first ~ is my family**

ma famille passe avant tout le reste

considered [kənˈsɪdəd] ADJ: **it is my ~ opinion that ...** après avoir mûrement réfléchi, je pense que ...

considering [kənˈsɪdərɪŋ] PREP: **~ (that)** étant donné (que)

consign [kənˈsaɪn] VT expédier, livrer

consignee [kɒnsaɪˈniː] N destinataire mf

consignment [kənˈsaɪnmənt] N arrivage m, envoi m

consignment note N (Comm) bordereau m d'expédition

consignor [kənˈsaɪnəʳ] N expéditeur(-trice)

consist [kənˈsɪst] VI: **to ~ of** consister en, se composer de

consistency [kənˈsɪstənsɪ] N (thickness) consistance f; (fig) cohérence f

consistent [kənˈsɪstənt] ADJ logique, cohérent(e); **~ with** compatible avec, en accord avec

consolation [kɒnsəˈleɪʃən] N consolation f

console¹ [kənˈsəul] VT consoler

console² [ˈkɒnsəul] N console f

consolidate [kənˈsɒlɪdeɪt] VT consolider

consols [ˈkɒnsɒlz] NPL (Brit Stock Exchange) rente f d'État

consommé [kənˈsɒmeɪ] N consommé m

consonant [ˈkɒnsənənt] N consonne f

consort [ˈkɒnsɔːt] N époux (épouse); **prince ~** prince m consort ▶ VI [kənˈsɔːt] (often pej): **to ~ with sb** frayer avec qn

consortium [kənˈsɔːtɪəm] N consortium m, comptoir m

conspicuous [kənˈspɪkjuəs] ADJ voyant(e), qui attire l'attention; **to make o.s. ~** se faire remarquer

conspiracy [kənˈspɪrəsɪ] N conspiration f, complot m

conspiratorial [kənspɪrəˈtɔːrɪəl] ADJ (behaviour) de conspirateur; (glance) conspirateur(-trice)

conspire [kənˈspaɪəʳ] VI conspirer, comploter

constable [ˈkʌnstəbl] N (Brit) ≈ agent m de police, gendarme m; **chief ~** préfet m de police

constabulary [kənˈstæbjulərɪ] N ≈ police f, gendarmerie f

constant [ˈkɒnstənt] ADJ constant(e); incessant(e)

constantly [ˈkɒnstəntlɪ] ADV constamment, sans cesse

constellation [kɒnstəˈleɪʃən] N constellation f

consternation [kɒnstəˈneɪʃən] N consternation f

constipated [ˈkɒnstɪpeɪtɪd] ADJ constipé(e)

constipation [kɒnstɪˈpeɪʃən] N constipation f

constituency [kənˈstɪtjuənsɪ] N (Pol: area) circonscription électorale; (: electors) électorat m; voir article

Une *constituency* est à la fois une région qui élit un député au parlement et l'ensemble des électeurs dans cette région. En Grande-Bretagne, les députés font régulièrement des permanences dans leur circonscription électorale lors desquelles les électeurs peuvent venir les voir pour parler de leurs problèmes de logement etc.

constituency party N section locale (d'un parti)

constituent [kənˈstɪtjuənt] N électeur(-trice); (part) élément constitutif, composant m

constitute [ˈkɒnstɪtjuːt] VT constituer

constitution [kɒnstɪˈtjuːʃən] N constitution f

constitutional [kɒnstɪˈtjuːʃənl] ADJ constitutionnel(le)

constitutional monarchy N monarchie constitutionnelle

constrain [kənˈstreɪn] VT contraindre, forcer

constrained [kənˈstreɪnd] ADJ contraint(e), gêné(e)

constraint [kənˈstreɪnt] N contrainte f; (embarrassment) gêne f

constrict [kənˈstrɪkt] VT rétrécir, resserrer; gêner, limiter

construct [kənˈstrʌkt] VT construire

construction [kənˈstrʌkʃən] N construction f; (fig: interpretation) interprétation f; **under ~** (building etc) en construction

construction industry N (industrie f du) bâtiment

constructive [kənˈstrʌktɪv] ADJ constructif(-ive)

construe [kənˈstruː] VT analyser, expliquer

consul [ˈkɒnsl] N consul m

consulate [ˈkɒnsjulɪt] N consulat m

consult [kənˈsʌlt] VT consulter; **to ~ sb (about sth)** consulter qn (à propos de qch)

consultancy [kənˈsʌltənsɪ] N service m de conseils

consultancy fee N honoraires mpl d'expert

consultant [kənˈsʌltənt] N (Med) médecin consultant; (other specialist) consultant m, (expert-)conseil m ▶ CPD: **~ engineer** n ingénieur-conseil m; **~ paediatrician** n pédiatre m; **legal/management ~** conseiller m juridique/en gestion

consultation [kɒnsəlˈteɪʃən] N consultation f; **in ~ with** en consultation avec

consultative [kənˈsʌltətɪv] ADJ consultatif(-ive)

consulting room [kənˈsʌltɪŋ-] N (Brit) cabinet m de consultation

consume [kənˈsjuːm] VT consommer; (subj: flames, hatred, desire) consumer; **to be consumed with hatred** être dévoré par la haine; **to be consumed with desire** brûler de désir

consumer [kənˈsjuːməʳ] N consommateur(-trice); (of electricity, gas etc) usager m

consumer credit N crédit m aux consommateurs

consumer durables NPL biens mpl de consommation durables

consumer goods NPL biens mpl de consommation

consumerism [kənˈsjuːmərɪzəm] N (consumer protection) défense f du consommateur; (Econ) consumérisme m

consumer society N société f de consommation

consumer watchdog N organisme m pour la défense des consommateurs

consummate ['kɔnsʌmeɪt] VT consommer
consumption [kən'sʌmpʃən] N consommation
f; **not fit for human** ~ non comestible
cont. ABBR (= *continued*) suite
contact ['kɔntækt] N contact m; (*person*)
connaissance f, relation f ▶ VT se mettre en
contact or en rapport avec; **to be in** ~ **with sb/**
sth être en contact avec qn/qch; **business**
contacts relations fpl d'affaires, contacts mpl;
~ **number** numéro m de téléphone
contact lenses NPL verres mpl de contact
contagious [kən'teɪdʒəs] ADJ contagieux(-euse)
contain [kən'teɪn] VT contenir; **to** ~ **o.s.** se
contenir, se maîtriser
container [kən'teɪnər] N récipient m; (*for shipping*
etc) conteneur m
containerize [kən'teɪnəraɪz] VT conteneuriser
container ship N porte-conteneurs m inv
contaminate [kən'tæmɪneɪt] VT contaminer
contamination [kəntæmɪ'neɪʃən] N
contamination f
cont'd ABBR (= *continued*) suite
contemplate ['kɔntəmpleɪt] VT contempler;
(*consider*) envisager
contemplation [kɔntəm'pleɪʃən] N
contemplation f
contemporary [kən'tɛmpərərɪ] ADJ
contemporain(e); (*design, wallpaper*) moderne
▶ N contemporain(e)
contempt [kən'tɛmpt] N mépris m, dédain m;
~ **of court** (*Law*) outrage m à l'autorité de la
justice
contemptible [kən'tɛmptəbl] ADJ méprisable,
vil(e)
contemptuous [kən'tɛmptjuəs] ADJ
dédaigneux(-euse), méprisant(e)
contend [kən'tɛnd] VT: **to** ~ **that** soutenir or
prétendre que ▶ VI: **to** ~ **with** (*compete*) rivaliser
avec; (*struggle*) lutter avec; **to have to** ~ **with** (*be*
faced with) avoir affaire à, être aux prises avec
contender [kən'tɛndər] N prétendant(e);
candidat(e)
content [kən'tɛnt] ADJ content(e), satisfait(e)
▶ VT contenter, satisfaire ▶ N ['kɔntɛnt]
contenu m; (*of fat, moisture*) teneur f; **contents**
NPL (*of container etc*) contenu m; (**table of**)
contents table f des matières; **to be** ~ **with** se
contenter de; **to** ~ **o.s. with sth/with doing**
sth se contenter de qch/de faire qch
contented [kən'tɛntɪd] ADJ content(e),
satisfait(e)
contentedly [kən'tɛntɪdlɪ] ADV avec un
sentiment de (profonde) satisfaction
contention [kən'tɛnʃən] N dispute f,
contestation f; (*argument*) assertion f,
affirmation f; **bone of** ~ sujet m de discorde
contentious [kən'tɛnʃəs] ADJ querelleur(-euse);
litigieux(-euse)
contentment [kən'tɛntmənt] N contentement
m, satisfaction f
contest N ['kɔntɛst] combat m, lutte f;
(*competition*) concours m ▶ VT [kən'tɛst]
contester, discuter; (*compete for*) disputer;
(*Law*) attaquer

contestant [kən'tɛstənt] N concurrent(e); (*in*
fight) adversaire mf
context ['kɔntɛkst] N contexte m; **in/out of** ~
dans le/hors contexte
continent ['kɔntɪnənt] N continent m; **the C~**
(BRIT) l'Europe continentale; **on the C~** en
Europe (continentale)
continental [kɔntɪ'nɛntl] ADJ continental(e)
▶ N (BRIT) Européen(ne) (continental(e))
continental breakfast N café (or thé) complet
continental quilt N (BRIT) couette f
contingency [kən'tɪndʒənsɪ] N éventualité f,
événement imprévu
contingency plan N plan m d'urgence
contingent [kən'tɪndʒənt] ADJ contingent(e)
▶ N contingent m; **to be** ~ **upon** dépendre de
continual [kən'tɪnjuəl] ADJ continuel(le)
continually [kən'tɪnjuəlɪ] ADV
continuellement, sans cesse
continuation [kəntɪnju'eɪʃən] N continuation
f; (*after interruption*) reprise f; (*of story*) suite f
continue [kən'tɪnju:] VI continuer ▶ VT
continuer; (*start again*) reprendre; **to be**
continued (*story*) à suivre; **continued on page**
10 suite page 10
continuing education [kən'tɪnjuɪŋ-] N
formation permanente or continue
continuity [kɔntɪ'nju:ɪtɪ] N continuité f; (*TV*)
enchaînement m; (*Cine*) script m
continuity girl N (*Cine*) script-girl f
continuous [kən'tɪnjuəs] ADJ continu(e),
permanent(e); (*Ling*) progressif(-ive);
~ **performance** (*Cine*) séance permanente;
~ **stationery** (*Comput*) papier m en continu
continuous assessment (BRIT) N contrôle
continu
continuously [kən'tɪnjuəslɪ] ADV (*repeatedly*)
continuellement; (*uninterruptedly*) sans
interruption
contort [kən'tɔ:t] VT tordre, crisper
contortion [kən'tɔ:ʃən] N crispation f, torsion f;
(*of acrobat*) contorsion f
contortionist [kən'tɔ:ʃənɪst] N contorsionniste
mf
contour ['kɔntuər] N contour m, profil m; (*also:*
contour line) courbe f de niveau
contraband ['kɔntrəbænd] N contrebande f
▶ ADJ de contrebande
contraception [kɔntrə'sɛpʃən] N
contraception f
contraceptive [kɔntrə'sɛptɪv] ADJ
contraceptif(-ive), anticonceptionnel(le) ▶ N
contraceptif m
contract N ['kɔntrækt] contrat m ▶ CPD (*price,*
date) contractuel(le); (*work*) à forfait ▶ VI
[kən'trækt] (*become smaller*) se contracter, se
resserrer ▶ VT contracter; (*Comm*): **to** ~ **to do**
sth s'engager (par contrat) à faire qch; ~ **of**
employment/service contrat de travail/de
service
▶ **contract in** VI s'engager (par contrat); (BRIT
Admin) s'affilier au régime de retraite
complémentaire
▶ **contract out** VI se dégager; (BRIT *Admin*) opter

pour la non-affiliation au régime de retraite complémentaire

contraction [kən'trækʃən] N contraction f; (*Ling*) forme contractée

contractor [kən'træktəʳ] N entrepreneur m

contractual [kən'træktʃuəl] ADJ contractuel(le)

contradict [kɔntrə'dɪkt] VT contredire; (*be contrary to*) démentir, être en contradiction avec

contradiction [kɔntrə'dɪkʃən] N contradiction f; **to be in ~ with** contredire, être en contradiction avec

contradictory [kɔntrə'dɪktərɪ] ADJ contradictoire

contraflow ['kɔntrəfləu] N (*Aut*): **~ lane** voie f à contresens; **there's a ~ system in operation on …** une voie a été mise en sens inverse sur …

contralto [kən'træltəu] N contralto m

contraption [kən'træpʃən] N (*pej*) machin m, truc m

contrary[1] ['kɔntrərɪ] ADJ contraire, opposé(e) ▸ N contraire m; **on the ~** au contraire; **unless you hear to the ~** sauf avis contraire; **~ to what we thought** contrairement à ce que nous pensions

contrary[2] [kən'trɛərɪ] ADJ (*perverse*) contrariant(e), entêté(e)

contrast N ['kɔntrɑːst] contraste m ▸ VT [kən'trɑːst] mettre en contraste, contraster; **in ~ to** or **with** contrairement à, par opposition à

contrasting [kən'trɑːstɪŋ] ADJ opposé(e), contrasté(e)

contravene [kɔntrə'viːn] VT enfreindre, violer, contrevenir à

contravention [kɔntrə'vɛnʃən] N: **~ (of)** infraction f (à)

contribute [kən'trɪbjuːt] VI contribuer ▸ VT: **to ~ £10/an article to** donner 10 livres/un article à; **to ~ to** (*gen*) contribuer à; (*newspaper*) collaborer à; (*discussion*) prendre part à

contribution [kɔntrɪ'bjuːʃən] N contribution f; (*Brit: for social security*) cotisation f; (*to publication*) article m

contributor [kən'trɪbjutəʳ] N (*to newspaper*) collaborateur(-trice); (*of money, goods*) donateur(-trice)

contributory [kən'trɪbjutərɪ] ADJ (*cause*) annexe; **it was a ~ factor in …** ce facteur a contribué à …

contributory pension scheme N (*Brit*) régime m de retraite salariale

contrite ['kɔntraɪt] ADJ contrit(e)

contrivance [kən'traɪvəns] N (*scheme*) machination f, combinaison f; (*device*) appareil m, dispositif m

contrive [kən'traɪv] VT combiner, inventer ▸ VI: **to ~ to do** s'arranger pour faire, trouver le moyen de faire

control [kən'trəul] VT (*process, machinery*) commander; (*temper*) maîtriser; (*disease*) enrayer; (*check*) contrôler ▸ N maîtrise f; (*power*) autorité f; **controls** NPL (*of machine etc*) commandes fpl; (*on radio*) boutons mpl de réglage; **to take ~ of** se rendre maître de; (*Comm*) acquérir une participation majoritaire

dans; **to be in ~ of** être maître de, maîtriser; (*in charge of*) être responsable de; **to ~ o.s.** se contrôler; **everything is under ~** j'ai (*or* il a *etc*) la situation en main; **the car went out of ~** j'ai (*or* il a *etc*) perdu le contrôle du véhicule; **beyond our ~** indépendant(e) de notre volonté

control key N (*Comput*) touche f de commande

controller [kən'trəuləʳ] N contrôleur m

controlling interest [kən'trəulɪŋ-] N (*Comm*) participation f majoritaire

control panel N (*on aircraft, ship, TV etc*) tableau m de commandes

control point N (poste m de) contrôle m

control room N (*Naut, Mil*) salle f des commandes; (*Radio, TV*) régie f

control tower N (*Aviat*) tour f de contrôle

control unit N (*Comput*) unité f de contrôle

controversial [kɔntrə'vəːʃl] ADJ discutable, controversé(e)

controversy ['kɔntrəvəːsɪ] N controverse f, polémique f

conurbation [kɔnə'beɪʃən] N conurbation f

convalesce [kɔnvə'lɛs] VI relever de maladie, se remettre (d'une maladie)

convalescence [kɔnvə'lɛsns] N convalescence f

convalescent [kɔnvə'lɛsnt] ADJ, N convalescent(e)

convector [kən'vɛktəʳ] N radiateur m à convection, appareil m de chauffage par convection

convene [kən'viːn] VT convoquer, assembler ▸ VI se réunir, s'assembler

convener [kən'viːnəʳ] N organisateur m

convenience [kən'viːnɪəns] N commodité f; **at your ~** quand or comme cela vous convient; **at your earliest ~** (*Comm*) dans les meilleurs délais, le plus tôt possible; **all modern conveniences**, **all mod cons** (*Brit*) avec tout le confort moderne, tout confort

convenience foods NPL plats cuisinés

convenient [kən'viːnɪənt] ADJ commode; **if it is ~ to you** si cela vous convient, si cela ne vous dérange pas

conveniently [kən'viːnɪəntlɪ] ADV (*happen*) à pic; (*situated*) commodément

convent ['kɔnvənt] N couvent m

convention [kən'vɛnʃən] N convention f; (*custom*) usage m

conventional [kən'vɛnʃənl] ADJ conventionnel(le)

convent school N couvent m

converge [kən'vəːdʒ] VI converger

conversant [kən'vəːsnt] ADJ: **to be ~ with** s'y connaître en; être au courant de

conversation [kɔnvə'seɪʃən] N conversation f

conversational [kɔnvə'seɪʃənl] ADJ de la conversation; (*Comput*) conversationnel(le)

conversationalist [kɔnvə'seɪʃnəlɪst] N brillant(e) causeur(-euse)

converse ['kɔnvəːs] N contraire m, inverse m ▸ VI [kən'vəːs]: **to ~ (with sb about sth)** s'entretenir (avec qn de qch)

conversely [kɔn'vəːslɪ] ADV inversement, réciproquement

conversion [kən'vəːʃən] N conversion f; (BRIT: of house) transformation f, aménagement m; (Rugby) transformation f

conversion table N table f de conversion

convert VT [kən'vəːt] (Rel, Comm) convertir; (alter) transformer; (house) aménager; (Rugby) transformer ▶ N ['kɔnvəːt] converti(e)

convertible [kən'vəːtəbl] ADJ convertible ▶ N (voiture f) décapotable f

convex ['kɔn'vɛks] ADJ convexe

convey [kən'veɪ] VT transporter; (thanks) transmettre; (idea) communiquer

conveyance [kən'veɪəns] N (of goods) transport m de marchandises; (vehicle) moyen m de transport

conveyancing [kən'veɪənsɪŋ] N (Law) rédaction f des actes de cession de propriété

conveyor belt [kən'veɪəʳ-] N convoyeur m tapis roulant

convict VT [kən'vɪkt] déclarer (or reconnaître) coupable ▶ N ['kɔnvɪkt] forçat m, convict m

conviction [kən'vɪkʃən] N (Law) condamnation f; (belief) conviction f

convince [kən'vɪns] VT convaincre, persuader; **to ~ sb (of sth/that)** persuader qn (de qch/que)

convinced [kən'vɪnst] ADJ: **~ of/that** convaincu(e) de/que

convincing [kən'vɪnsɪŋ] ADJ persuasif(-ive), convaincant(e)

convincingly [kən'vɪnsɪŋlɪ] ADV de façon convaincante

convivial [kən'vɪvɪəl] ADJ joyeux(-euse), plein(e) d'entrain

convoluted ['kɔnvəluːtɪd] ADJ (shape) tarabiscoté(e); (argument) compliqué(e)

convoy ['kɔnvɔɪ] N convoi m

convulse [kən'vʌls] VT ébranler; **to be convulsed with laughter** se tordre de rire

convulsion [kən'vʌlʃən] N convulsion f

coo [kuː] VI roucouler

cook [kuk] VT (faire) cuire ▶ VI cuire; (person) faire la cuisine ▶ N cuisinier(-ière)
▶ **cook up** VT (inf: excuse, story) inventer

cookbook ['kukbuk] N livre m de cuisine

cooker ['kukəʳ] N cuisinière f

cookery ['kukərɪ] N cuisine f

cookery book N (BRIT) = **cookbook**

cookie ['kukɪ] N (US) biscuit m, petit gâteau sec; (Comput) cookie m, témoin m de connexion

cooking ['kukɪŋ] N cuisine f ▶ CPD (apples, chocolate) à cuire; (utensils, salt) de cuisine

cookout ['kukaut] N (US) barbecue m

cool [kuːl] ADJ frais (fraîche); (not afraid) calme; (unfriendly) froid(e); (impertinent) effronté(e); (inf: trendy) cool inv (inf); (: great) super inv (inf) ▶ VT, VI rafraîchir, refroidir; **it's ~** (weather) il fait frais; **to keep sth ~** or **in a ~ place** garder or conserver qch au frais
▶ **cool down** VI refroidir; (fig: person, situation) se calmer
▶ **cool off** VI (become calmer) se calmer; (lose enthusiasm) perdre son enthousiasme

coolant ['kuːlənt] N liquide m de refroidissement

cool box, (US) **cooler** ['kuːləʳ] N boîte f isotherme

cooling ['kuːlɪŋ] ADJ (breeze) rafraîchissant(e)

cooling tower N refroidisseur m

coolly ['kuːlɪ] ADV (calmly) calmement; (audaciously) sans se gêner; (unenthusiastically) froidement

coolness ['kuːlnɪs] N fraîcheur f; sang-froid m, calme m; froideur f

coop [kuːp] N poulailler m ▶ VT: **to ~ up** (fig) cloîtrer, enfermer

co-op ['kəuɔp] N ABBR (= cooperative (society)) coop f

cooperate [kəu'ɔpəreɪt] VI coopérer, collaborer

cooperation [kəuɔpə'reɪʃən] N coopération f, collaboration f

cooperative [kəu'ɔpərətɪv] ADJ coopératif(-ive) ▶ N coopérative f

coopt [kəu'ɔpt] VT: **to ~ sb onto a committee** coopter qn pour faire partie d'un comité

coordinate VT [kəu'ɔːdɪneɪt] coordonner ▶ N [kəu'ɔːdɪnət] (Math) coordonnée f; **coordinates** NPL (clothes) ensemble m, coordonnés mpl

coordination [kəuɔːdɪ'neɪʃən] N coordination f

coot [kuːt] N foulque f

co-ownership ['kəu'əunəʃɪp] N copropriété f

cop [kɔp] N (inf) flic m

cope [kəup] VI s'en sortir, tenir le coup; **to ~ with** (problem) faire face à; (take care of) s'occuper de

Copenhagen ['kəupn'heɪgən] N Copenhague

copier ['kɔpɪəʳ] N (also: **photocopier**) copieur m

co-pilot ['kəu'paɪlət] N copilote m

copious ['kəupɪəs] ADJ copieux(-euse), abondant(e)

copper ['kɔpəʳ] N cuivre m; (BRIT inf: policeman) flic m; **coppers** NPL petite monnaie

coppice ['kɔpɪs], **copse** [kɔps] N taillis m

copulate ['kɔpjuleɪt] VI copuler

copy ['kɔpɪ] N copie f; (book etc) exemplaire m; (material: for printing) copie ▶ VT copier; (imitate) imiter; **rough ~** (gen) premier jet; (Scol) brouillon m; **fair ~** version définitive; propre m; **to make good ~** (Press) faire un bon sujet d'article
▶ **copy out** VT copier

copycat ['kɔpɪkæt] N (pej) copieur(-euse)

copyright ['kɔpɪraɪt] N droit m d'auteur, copyright m; **~ reserved** tous droits (de reproduction) réservés

copy typist N dactylo mf

copywriter ['kɔpɪraɪtəʳ] N rédacteur(-trice) publicitaire

coral ['kɔrəl] N corail m

coral reef N récif m de corail

Coral Sea N: **the ~** la mer de Corail

cord [kɔːd] N corde f; (fabric) velours côtelé; whipcord m; corde f; (Elec) cordon m (d'alimentation), fil m (électrique); **cords** NPL (trousers) pantalon m de velours côtelé

cordial ['kɔːdɪəl] ADJ cordial(e), chaleureux(-euse) ▶ N sirop m; cordial m

cordless ['kɔːdlɪs] ADJ sans fil

cordon ['kɔːdn] N cordon m

▶ **cordon off** VT (*area*) interdire l'accès à; (*crowd*) tenir à l'écart

corduroy ['kɔːdərɔɪ] N velours côtelé

CORE [kɔːʳ] N ABBR (*US*) = **Congress of Racial Equality**

core [kɔːʳ] N (*of fruit*) trognon *m*, cœur *m*; (*Tech: also of earth*) noyau *m*; (: *of nuclear reactor*) cœur; (*fig: of problem etc*) cœur ▶ VT enlever le trognon *or* le cœur de; **rotten to the ~** complètement pourri

Corfu [kɔː'fuː] N Corfou

coriander [kɔrɪ'ændəʳ] N coriandre *f*

cork [kɔːk] N (*material*) liège *m*; (*of bottle*) bouchon *m*

corkage ['kɔːkɪdʒ] N *droit payé par le client qui apporte sa propre bouteille de vin*

corked [kɔːkt], (*US*) **corky** ['kɔːkɪ] ADJ (*wine*) qui sent le bouchon

corkscrew ['kɔːkskruː] N tire-bouchon *m*

cormorant ['kɔːmərnt] N cormoran *m*

corn [kɔːn] N (*BRIT: wheat*) blé *m*; (*US: maize*) maïs *m*; (*on foot*) cor *m*; **~ on the cob** (*Culin*) épi *m* de maïs au naturel

cornea ['kɔːnɪə] N cornée *f*

corned beef ['kɔːnd-] N corned-beef *m*

corner ['kɔːnəʳ] N coin *m*; (*in road*) tournant *m*, virage *m*; (*Football: also:* **corner kick**) corner *m* ▶ VT (*trap: prey*) acculer; (*fig*) coincer; (*Comm: market*) accaparer ▶ VI prendre un virage; **to cut corners** (*fig*) prendre des raccourcis

corner flag N (*Football*) piquet *m* de coin

corner kick N (*Football*) corner *m*

corner shop (*BRIT*) N magasin *m* du coin

cornerstone ['kɔːnəstəun] N pierre *f* angulaire

cornet ['kɔːnɪt] N (*Mus*) cornet *m* à pistons; (*BRIT: of ice-cream*) cornet (de glace)

cornflakes ['kɔːnfleɪks] NPL cornflakes *mpl*

cornflour ['kɔːnflauəʳ] N (*BRIT*) farine *f* de maïs, maïzena® *f*

cornice ['kɔːnɪs] N corniche *f*

Cornish ['kɔːnɪʃ] ADJ de Cornouailles, cornouaillais(e)

corn oil N huile *f* de maïs

cornstarch ['kɔːnstaːtʃ] N (*US*) farine *f* de maïs, maïzena® *f*

cornucopia [kɔːnju'kəupɪə] N corne *f* d'abondance

Cornwall ['kɔːnwəl] N Cornouailles *f*

corny ['kɔːnɪ] ADJ (*inf*) rebattu(e), galvaudé(e)

corollary [kə'rɔlərɪ] N corollaire *m*

coronary ['kɔrənərɪ] N: **~ (thrombosis)** infarctus *m* (du myocarde), thrombose *f* coronaire

coronation [kɔrə'neɪʃən] N couronnement *m*

coroner ['kɔrənəʳ] N coroner *m*, officier de police judiciaire chargé de déterminer les causes d'un décès

coronet ['kɔrənɪt] N couronne *f*

Corp. ABBR = **corporation**

corporal ['kɔːpərl] N caporal *m*, brigadier *m* ▶ ADJ: **~ punishment** châtiment corporel

corporate ['kɔːpərɪt] ADJ (*action, ownership*) en commun; (*Comm*) de la société

corporate hospitality N *arrangement selon lequel une société offre des places de théâtre, concert etc à ses clients*

corporate identity, corporate image N (*of organization*) image *f* de la société

corporation [kɔːpə'reɪʃən] N (*of town*) municipalité *f*, conseil municipal; (*Comm*) société *f*

corporation tax N ≈ impôt *m* sur les bénéfices

corps [kɔːʳ] (*pl* **~** [kɔːz]) N corps *m*; **the diplomatic ~** le corps diplomatique; **the press ~** la presse

corpse [kɔːps] N cadavre *m*

corpuscle ['kɔːpʌsl] N corpuscule *m*

corral [kə'rɑːl] N corral *m*

correct [kə'rɛkt] ADJ (*accurate*) correct(e), exact(e); (*proper*) correct, convenable ▶ VT corriger; **you are ~** vous avez raison

correction [kə'rɛkʃən] N correction *f*

correlate ['kɔrɪleɪt] VT mettre en corrélation ▶ VI: **to ~ with** correspondre à

correlation [kɔrɪ'leɪʃən] N corrélation *f*

correspond [kɔrɪs'pɔnd] VI correspondre; **to ~ to sth** (*be equivalent to*) correspondre à qch

correspondence [kɔrɪs'pɔndəns] N correspondance *f*

correspondence course N cours *m* par correspondance

correspondent [kɔrɪs'pɔndənt] N correspondant(e)

corresponding [kɔrɪs'pɔndɪŋ] ADJ correspondant(e)

corridor ['kɔrɪdɔːʳ] N couloir *m*, corridor *m*

corroborate [kə'rɔbəreɪt] VT corroborer, confirmer

corrode [kə'rəud] VT corroder, ronger ▶ VI se corroder

corrosion [kə'rəuʒən] N corrosion *f*

corrosive [kə'rəuzɪv] ADJ corrosif(-ive)

corrugated ['kɔrəgeɪtɪd] ADJ plissé(e); ondulé(e)

corrugated iron N tôle ondulée

corrupt [kə'rʌpt] ADJ corrompu(e); (*Comput*) altéré(e) ▶ VT corrompre; (*Comput*) altérer; **~ practices** (*dishonesty, bribery*) malversation *f*

corruption [kə'rʌpʃən] N corruption *f*; (*Comput*) altération *f* (de données)

corset ['kɔːsɪt] N corset *m*

Corsica ['kɔːsɪkə] N Corse *f*

Corsican ['kɔːsɪkən] ADJ corse ▶ N Corse *mf*

cortège [kɔː'teɪʒ] N cortège *m* (*gén funèbre*)

cortisone ['kɔːtɪzəun] N cortisone *f*

coruscating ['kɔrəskeɪtɪŋ] ADJ scintillant(e)

cosh [kɔʃ] N (*BRIT*) matraque *f*

cosignatory ['kəu'sɪgnətərɪ] N cosignataire *mf*

cosiness ['kəuzɪnɪs] N atmosphère douillette, confort *m*

cos lettuce ['kɔs-] N (laitue *f*) romaine *f*

cosmetic [kɔz'mɛtɪk] N produit *m* de beauté, cosmétique *m* ▶ ADJ (*preparation*) cosmétique; (*fig: reforms*) symbolique, superficiel(le)

cosmetic surgery N chirurgie *f* esthétique

cosmic ['kɔzmɪk] ADJ cosmique

cosmonaut ['kɔzmənɔːt] N cosmonaute *mf*

cosmopolitan [kɔzmə'pɔlɪtn] ADJ cosmopolite

cosmos ['kɔzmɔs] N cosmos *m*

cosset ['kɔsɪt] VT choyer, dorloter

cost [kɔst] (*pt, pp* ~) N coût *m* ▶ VI coûter ▶ VT établir *or* calculer le prix de revient de; **costs** NPL (*Comm*) frais *mpl*; (*Law*) dépens *mpl*; **how much does it ~?** combien ça coûte?; **it costs £5/too much** cela coûte 5 livres/trop cher; **what will it ~ to have it repaired?** combien cela coûtera de le faire réparer?; **to ~ sb time/ effort** demander du temps/un effort à qn; **it ~ him his life/job** ça lui a coûté la vie/son emploi; **at all costs** coûte que coûte, à tout prix

cost accountant N analyste *mf* de coûts

co-star ['kəustɑː'] N partenaire *mf*

Costa Rica ['kɔstə'riːkə] N Costa Rica *m*

cost centre N centre *m* de coût

cost control N contrôle *m* des coûts

cost-effective ['kɔstɪ'fɛktɪv] ADJ rentable

cost-effectiveness ['kɔstɪ'fɛktɪvnɪs] N rentabilité *f*

costing ['kɔstɪŋ] N calcul *m* du prix de revient

costly ['kɔstlɪ] ADJ coûteux(-euse)

cost of living ['kɔstəv'lɪvɪŋ] N coût *m* de la vie ▶ ADJ: ~ **allowance** indemnité *f* de vie chère; ~ **index** indice *m* du coût de la vie

cost price N (*Brit*) prix coûtant *or* de revient

costume ['kɔstjuːm] N costume *m*; (*lady's suit*) tailleur *m*; (*Brit: also:* **swimming costume**) maillot *m* (de bain)

costume jewellery N bijoux *mpl* de fantaisie

cosy, (*US*) **cozy** ['kəuzɪ] ADJ (*room, bed*) douillet(te); (*scarf, gloves*) bien chaud(e); (*atmosphere*) chaleureux(-euse); **to be ~** (*person*) être bien (au chaud)

cot [kɔt] N (*Brit: child's*) lit *m* d'enfant, petit lit; (*US: campbed*) lit de camp

cot death N mort subite du nourrisson

Cotswolds ['kɔtswəuldz] NPL: **the ~** région de collines du Gloucestershire

cottage ['kɔtɪdʒ] N petite maison (à la campagne), cottage *m*

cottage cheese N fromage blanc (*maigre*)

cottage industry N industrie familiale *or* artisanale

cottage pie N ≈ hachis *m* Parmentier

cotton ['kɔtn] N coton *m*; (*thread*) fil *m* (de coton); ~ **dress** *etc* robe *etc* en *or* de coton ▶ **cotton on** VI (*inf*): **to ~ on (to sth)** piger (qch)

cotton bud N (*Brit*) coton-tige® *m*

cotton candy N (*US*) barbe *f* à papa

cotton wool N (*Brit*) ouate *f*, coton *m* hydrophile

couch [kautʃ] N canapé *m*; divan *m*; (*doctor's*) table *f* d'examen; (*psychiatrist's*) divan ▶ VT formuler, exprimer

couchette [kuːˈʃɛt] N couchette *f*

couch potato N (*inf*) mollasson(ne) (*qui passe son temps devant la télé*)

cough [kɔf] VI tousser ▶ N toux *f*; **I've got a ~** j'ai la toux

cough drop N pastille *f* pour *or* contre la toux

cough mixture, cough syrup N sirop *m* pour la toux

cough sweet N pastille *f* pour *or* contre la toux

could [kud] PT *of* **can²**

couldn't = **could not**

council ['kaunsl] N conseil *m*; **city** *or* **town ~** conseil municipal; **C~ of Europe** Conseil de l'Europe

council estate N (*Brit*) (quartier *m or* zone *f* de) logements loués à/par la municipalité

council house N (*Brit*) maison *f* (à loyer modéré) louée par la municipalité

councillor, (*US*) **councilor** ['kaunslə'] N conseiller(-ère)

council tax N (*Brit*) impôts locaux

counsel ['kaunsl] N conseil *m*; (*lawyer*) avocat(e) ▶ VT: **to ~ (sb to do sth)** conseiller (à qn de faire qch); ~ **for the defence/the prosecution** (avocat de la) défense/avocat du ministère public

counselling, (*US*) **counseling** ['kaunslɪŋ] N (*Psych*) aide psychosociale

counsellor, (*US*) **counselor** ['kaunslə'] N conseiller(-ère); (*US Law*) avocat *m*

count [kaunt] VT, VI compter ▶ N compte *m*; (*nobleman*) comte *m*; **to ~ (up) to 10** compter jusqu'à 10; **to keep ~ of sth** tenir le compte de qch; **not counting the children** sans compter les enfants; **10 counting him** 10 avec lui, 10 en le comptant; **to ~ the cost of** établir le coût de; **it counts for very little** cela n'a pas beaucoup d'importance; ~ **yourself lucky** estimez-vous heureux ▶ **count in** VT (*inf*): **to ~ sb in on sth** inclure qn dans qch ▶ **count on** VT FUS compter sur; **to ~ on doing sth** compter faire qch ▶ **count up** VT compter, additionner

countdown ['kauntdaun] N compte *m* à rebours

countenance ['kauntɪnəns] N expression *f* ▶ VT approuver

counter ['kauntə'] N comptoir *m*; (*in post office, bank*) guichet *m*; (*in game*) jeton *m* ▶ VT aller à l'encontre de, opposer; (*blow*) parer ▶ ADV: ~ **to** à l'encontre de; contrairement à; **to buy under the ~** (*fig*) acheter sous le manteau *or* en sous-main; **to ~ sth with sth/by doing sth** contrer *or* riposter à qch par qch/en faisant qch

counteract ['kauntər'ækt] VT neutraliser, contrebalancer

counterattack ['kauntərə'tæk] N contre-attaque *f* ▶ VI contre-attaquer

counterbalance ['kauntə'bæləns] VT contrebalancer, faire contrepoids à

counterclockwise ['kauntə'klɔkwaɪz] ADV (*US*) en sens inverse des aiguilles d'une montre

counter-espionage ['kauntər'ɛspɪənɑːʒ] N contre-espionnage *m*

counterfeit ['kauntəfɪt] N faux *m*, contrefaçon *f* ▶ VT contrefaire ▶ ADJ faux (fausse)

counterfoil ['kauntəfɔɪl] N talon *m*, souche *f*

counterintelligence ['kauntərɪn'tɛlɪdʒəns] N contre-espionnage *m*

countermand ['kauntəmɑːnd] VT annuler

countermeasure ['kauntəmɛʒə'] N contre-mesure *f*

counteroffensive ['kauntərə'fɛnsɪv] N contre-offensive *f*

counterpane ['kauntəpeɪn] N dessus-de-lit *m*

counterpart ['kauntəpɑːt] N (of document etc) double m; (of person) homologue mf
counterproductive ['kauntəprə'dʌktɪv] ADJ contre-productif(-ive)
counterproposal ['kauntəprə'pəuzl] N contre-proposition f
countersign ['kauntəsaɪn] VT contresigner
countersink ['kauntəsɪŋk] VT (hole) fraiser
counterterrorism [kauntə'tɛrərɪzəm] N contre-terrorisme m
countess ['kauntɪs] N comtesse f
countless ['kauntlɪs] ADJ innombrable
countrified ['kʌntrɪfaɪd] ADJ rustique, à l'air campagnard
country ['kʌntrɪ] N pays m; (native land) patrie f; (as opposed to town) campagne f; (region) région f, pays; **in the ~** à la campagne; **mountainous ~** pays de montagne, région montagneuse
country and western, country and western music N musique f country
country dancing N (BRIT) danse f folklorique
country house N manoir m, (petit) château
countryman ['kʌntrɪmən] N (irreg) (national) compatriote m; (rural) habitant m de la campagne, campagnard m
countryside ['kʌntrɪsaɪd] N campagne f
countrywide ['kʌntrɪ'waɪd] ADJ s'étendant à l'ensemble du pays; (problem) à l'échelle nationale ▶ ADV à travers or dans tout le pays
county ['kauntɪ] N comté m
county council N (BRIT) ≈ conseil régional
county town N (BRIT) chef-lieu m
coup [kuː] (pl coups [kuːz]) N (achievement) beau coup; (also: **coup d'état**) coup d'État
coupé [kuː'peɪ] N (Aut) coupé m
couple ['kʌpl] N couple m ▶ VT (carriages) atteler; (Tech) coupler; (ideas, names) associer; **a ~ of** (two) deux; (a few) deux ou trois
couplet ['kʌplɪt] N distique m
coupling ['kʌplɪŋ] N (Rail) attelage m
coupon ['kuːpɔn] N (voucher) bon m de réduction; (detachable form) coupon m détachable, coupon-réponse m; (Finance) coupon
courage ['kʌrɪdʒ] N courage m
courageous [kə'reɪdʒəs] ADJ courageux(-euse)
courgette [kuə'ʒɛt] N (BRIT) courgette f
courier ['kurɪəʳ] N messager m, courrier m; (for tourists) accompagnateur(-trice)
course [kɔːs] N cours m; (of ship) route f; (for golf) terrain m; (part of meal) plat m; **first ~** entrée f; **of ~** adv bien sûr; **(no,) of ~ not!** bien sûr que non!, évidemment que non!; **in the ~ of** au cours de; **in the ~ of the next few days** au cours des prochains jours; **in due ~** en temps utile or voulu; **~ of action** parti m, ligne f de conduite; **the best ~ would be to ...** le mieux serait de ...; **we have no other ~ but to ...** nous n'avons pas d'autre solution que de ...; **~ of lectures** série f de conférences; **~ of treatment** (Med) traitement m
court [kɔːt] N cour f; (Law) cour, tribunal m; (Tennis) court m ▶ VT (woman) courtiser, faire la cour à; (fig: favour, popularity) rechercher; (: death, disaster) courir après, flirter avec; **out of ~** (Law:

settle) à l'amiable; **to take to ~** actionner or poursuivre en justice; **~ of appeal** cour d'appel
courteous ['kəːtɪəs] ADJ courtois(e), poli(e)
courtesan [kɔːtɪ'zæn] N courtisane f
courtesy ['kəːtəsɪ] N courtoisie f, politesse f; **(by) ~ of** avec l'aimable autorisation de
courtesy bus, courtesy coach N navette gratuite
courtesy light N (Aut) plafonnier m
court-house ['kɔːthaus] N (US) palais m de justice
courtier ['kɔːtɪəʳ] N courtisan m, dame f de cour
court martial (pl **courts martial**) N cour martiale, conseil m de guerre
courtroom ['kɔːtrum] N salle f de tribunal
court shoe N escarpin m
courtyard ['kɔːtjɑːd] N cour f
cousin ['kʌzn] N cousin(e); **first ~** cousin(e) germain(e)
cove [kəuv] N petite baie, anse f
covenant ['kʌvənənt] N contrat m, engagement m ▶ VT: **to ~ £200 per year to a charity** s'engager à verser 200 livres par an à une œuvre de bienfaisance
Coventry ['kɔvəntrɪ] N: **to send sb to ~** (fig) mettre qn en quarantaine
cover ['kʌvəʳ] VT couvrir; (Press: report on) faire un reportage sur; (feelings, mistake) cacher; (include) englober; (discuss) traiter ▶ N (of book, Comm) couverture f; (of pan) couvercle m; (over furniture) housse f; (shelter) abri m; **covers** NPL (on bed) couvertures; **to take ~** se mettre à l'abri; **under ~** à l'abri; **under ~ of darkness** à la faveur de la nuit; **under separate ~** (Comm) sous pli séparé; **£10 will ~ everything** 10 livres suffiront (pour tout payer)
▶ **cover up** VT (truth, facts) occulter; (person, object): **to ~ up (with)** couvrir (de) ▶ VI: **to ~ up for sb** (fig) couvrir qn
coverage ['kʌvərɪdʒ] N (in media) reportage m; (Insurance) couverture f
cover charge N couvert m (supplément à payer)
covering ['kʌvərɪŋ] N couverture f, enveloppe f
covering letter, (US) cover letter N lettre explicative
cover note N (Insurance) police f provisoire
cover price N prix m de l'exemplaire
covert ['kʌvət] ADJ (threat) voilé(e), caché(e); (attack) indirect(e); (glance) furtif(-ive)
cover-up ['kʌvərʌp] N tentative f pour étouffer une affaire
covet ['kʌvɪt] VT convoiter
cow [kau] N vache f ▶ CPD femelle ▶ VT effrayer, intimider
coward ['kauəd] N lâche mf
cowardice ['kauədɪs] N lâcheté f
cowardly ['kauədlɪ] ADJ lâche
cowboy ['kaubɔɪ] N cow-boy m
cower ['kauəʳ] VI se recroqueviller; trembler
cowshed ['kauʃɛd] N étable f
cowslip ['kauslɪp] N (Bot) (fleur f de) coucou m
coy [kɔɪ] ADJ faussement effarouché(e) or timide
coyote [kɔɪ'əutɪ] N coyote m
cozy ['kəuzɪ] ADJ (US) = **cosy**

529

CP N ABBR (= *Communist Party*) PC *m*
cp. ABBR (= *compare*) cf
CPA N ABBR (*US*) = **certified public accountant**
CPI N ABBR (= *Consumer Price Index*) IPC *m*
Cpl. ABBR (= *corporal*) C/C
CP/M N ABBR (= *Central Program for Microprocessors*) CP/M *m*
c.p.s. ABBR (= *characters per second*) caractères/seconde
CPSA N ABBR (*BRIT*: = *Civil and Public Services Association*) syndicat de la fonction publique
CPU N ABBR = **central processing unit**
cr. ABBR = **credit; creditor**
crab [kræb] N crabe *m*
crab apple N pomme *f* sauvage
crack [kræk] N (*split*) fente *f*, fissure *f*; (*in cup, bone*) fêlure *f*; (*in wall*) lézarde *f*; (*noise*) craquement *m*, coup (sec); (*joke*) plaisanterie *f*; (*inf: attempt*): **to have a ~ (at sth)** essayer (qch); (*Drugs*) crack *m* ▶ VT fendre, fissurer; fêler; lézarder; (*whip*) faire claquer; (*nut*) casser; (*problem*) résoudre, trouver la clef de; (*code*) déchiffrer ▶ CPD (*athlete*) de première classe, d'élite; **to ~ jokes** (*inf*) raconter des blagues; **to get cracking** (*inf*) s'y mettre, se magner
▶ **crack down on** VT FUS (*crime*) sévir contre, réprimer; (*spending*) mettre un frein à
▶ **crack up** VI être au bout de son rouleau, flancher
crackdown ['krækdaun] N: **~ (on)** (*on crime*) répression *f* (de); (*on spending*) restrictions *fpl* (de)
cracked [krækt] ADJ (*cup, bone*) fêlé(e); (*broken*) cassé(e); (*wall*) lézardé(e); (*surface*) craquelé(e); (*inf*) toqué(e), timbré(e)
cracker ['krækə'] N (*also*: **Christmas cracker**) pétard *m*; (*biscuit*) biscuit (salé), craquelin *m*; **a ~ of a ...** (*BRIT inf*) un(e) ... formidable; **he's crackers** (*BRIT inf*) il est cinglé
crackle ['krækl] VI crépiter, grésiller
crackling ['kræklɪŋ] N crépitement *m*, grésillement *m*; (*on radio, telephone*) grésillement *m*, friture *f*; (*of pork*) couenne *f*
crackpot ['krækpɒt] N (*inf*) tordu(e)
cradle ['kreɪdl] N berceau *m* ▶ VT (*child*) bercer; (*object*) tenir dans ses bras
craft [krɑːft] N métier (artisanal); (*cunning*) ruse *f*, astuce *f*; (*boat: pl inv*) embarcation *f*, barque *f*; (*plane: pl inv*) appareil *m*
craftsman ['krɑːftsmən] N (*irreg*) artisan *m*, ouvrier (qualifié)
craftsmanship ['krɑːftsmənʃɪp] N métier *m*, habileté *f*
crafty ['krɑːftɪ] ADJ rusé(e), malin(-igne), astucieux(-euse)
crag [kræg] N rocher escarpé
cram [kræm] VT: **to ~ sth with** (*fill*) bourrer qch de; **to ~ sth into** (*put*) fourrer qch dans ▶ VI (*for exams*) bachoter
cramming ['kræmɪŋ] N (*for exams*) bachotage *m*
cramp [kræmp] N crampe *f* ▶ VT gêner, entraver; **I've got ~ in my leg** j'ai une crampe à la jambe
cramped [kræmpt] ADJ à l'étroit, très serré(e)
crampon ['kræmpən] N crampon *m*

cranberry ['krænbərɪ] N canneberge *f*
crane [kreɪn] N grue *f* ▶ VT, VI: **to ~ forward, to ~ one's neck** allonger le cou
cranium ['kreɪnɪəm] (*pl* **crania** ['kreɪnɪə]) N boîte crânienne
crank [kræŋk] N manivelle *f*; (*person*) excentrique *mf*
crankshaft ['kræŋkʃɑːft] N vilebrequin *m*
cranky ['kræŋkɪ] ADJ excentrique, loufoque; (*bad-tempered*) grincheux(-euse), revêche
cranny ['krænɪ] N *see* **nook**
crap [kræp] N (*inf!: nonsense*) conneries *fpl* (!); (*: excrement*) merde *f* (!); **the party was ~** la fête était merdique (!); **to have a ~** chier (!)
crappy ['kræpɪ] ADJ (*inf*) merdique (!)
crash [kræʃ] N (*noise*) fracas *m*; (*of car, plane*) collision *f*; (*of business*) faillite *f*; (*Stock Exchange*) krach *m* ▶ VT (*plane*) écraser ▶ VI (*plane*) s'écraser; (*two cars*) se percuter, s'emboutir; (*business*) s'effondrer; **to ~ into** se jeter *or* se fracasser contre; **he crashed the car into a wall** il s'est écrasé contre un mur avec sa voiture
crash barrier N (*BRIT Aut*) rail *m* de sécurité
crash course N cours intensif
crash helmet N casque (protecteur)
crash landing N atterrissage forcé *or* en catastrophe
crass [kræs] ADJ grossier(-ière), crasse
crate [kreɪt] N cageot *m*; (*for bottles*) caisse *f*
crater ['kreɪtə'] N cratère *m*
cravat [krə'væt] N foulard (*noué autour du cou*)
crave [kreɪv] VT, VI: **to ~ (for)** désirer violemment, avoir un besoin physiologique de, avoir une envie irrésistible de
craving ['kreɪvɪŋ] N: **~ (for)** (*for food, cigarettes etc*) envie *f* irrésistible (de)
crawl [krɔːl] VI ramper; (*vehicle*) avancer au pas ▶ N (*Swimming*) crawl *m*; **to ~ on one's hands and knees** aller à quatre pattes; **to ~ to sb** (*inf*) faire de la lèche à qn
crawler lane ['krɔːlə-] N (*BRIT Aut*) file *f or* voie *f* pour véhicules lents
crayfish ['kreɪfɪʃ] N (*pl inv: freshwater*) écrevisse *f*; (*: saltwater*) langoustine *f*
crayon ['kreɪən] N crayon *m* (de couleur)
craze [kreɪz] N engouement *m*
crazed [kreɪzd] ADJ (*look, person*) affolé(e); (*pottery, glaze*) craquelé(e)
crazy ['kreɪzɪ] ADJ fou (folle); **to go ~** devenir fou; **to be ~ about sb/sth** (*inf*) être fou de qn/qch
crazy paving N (*BRIT*) dallage irrégulier (en pierres plates)
creak [kriːk] VI (*hinge*) grincer; (*floor, shoes*) craquer
cream [kriːm] N crème *f* ▶ ADJ (*colour*) crème *inv*; **whipped ~** crème fouettée
▶ **cream off** VT (*fig*) prélever
cream cake N (*petit*) gâteau à la crème
cream cheese N fromage *m* à la crème, fromage blanc
creamery ['kriːmərɪ] N (*shop*) crémerie *f*; (*factory*) laiterie *f*
creamy ['kriːmɪ] ADJ crémeux(-euse)

crease [kriːs] N pli *m* ▸ VT froisser, chiffonner
▸ VI se froisser, se chiffonner
crease-resistant ['kriːsrɪzɪstənt] ADJ
infroissable
create [kriːˈeɪt] VT créer; (*impression, fuss*) faire
creation [kriːˈeɪʃən] N création *f*
creative [kriːˈeɪtɪv] ADJ créatif(-ive)
creativity [kriːeɪˈtɪvɪtɪ] N créativité *f*
creator [kriːˈeɪtəʳ] N créateur(-trice)
creature ['kriːtʃəʳ] N créature *f*
creature comforts NPL petit confort
crèche [krɛʃ] N garderie *f*, crèche *f*
credence ['kriːdns] N croyance *f*, foi *f*
credentials [krɪˈdɛnʃlz] NPL (*references*)
références *fpl*; (*identity papers*) pièce *f* d'identité;
(*letters of reference*) pièces justificatives
credibility [krɛdɪˈbɪlɪtɪ] N crédibilité *f*
credible ['krɛdɪbl] ADJ digne de foi, crédible
credit ['krɛdɪt] N crédit *m*; (*recognition*) honneur
m; (*Scol*) unité *f* de valeur ▸ VT (*Comm*) créditer;
(*believe: also:* **give credit to**) ajouter foi à, croire;
credits NPL (*Cine*) générique *m*; **to be in** ~ (*person,
bank account*) être créditeur(-trice); **on** ~ à crédit;
to one's ~ à son honneur; à son actif; **to take
the** ~ **for** s'attribuer le mérite de; **it does him** ~
cela lui fait honneur; **to** ~ **sb with** (*fig*) prêter or
attribuer à qn; **to** ~ **£5 to sb** créditer (le compte
de) qn de 5 livres
creditable ['krɛdɪtəbl] ADJ honorable, estimable
credit account N compte *m* client
credit agency N (*Brit*) agence *f* de
renseignements commerciaux
credit balance N solde créditeur
credit bureau N (*US*) agence *f* de
renseignements commerciaux
credit card N carte *f* de crédit; **do you take
credit cards?** acceptez-vous les cartes de
crédit?
credit control N suivi *m* des factures
credit crunch N crise *f* du crédit
credit facilities NPL facilités *fpl* de paiement
credit limit N limite *f* de crédit
credit note N (*Brit*) avoir *m*
creditor ['krɛdɪtəʳ] N créancier(-ière)
credit transfer N virement *m*
creditworthy ['krɛdɪtwəːðɪ] ADJ solvable
credulity [krɪˈdjuːlɪtɪ] N crédulité *f*
creed [kriːd] N croyance *f*; credo *m*, principes
mpl
creek [kriːk] N (*inlet*) crique *f*, anse *f*; (*US: stream*)
ruisseau *m*, petit cours d'eau
creel ['kriːl] N panier *m* de pêche; (*also:* **lobster
creel**) panier à homards
creep [kriːp] (*pt, pp* **crept** [krɛpt]) VI ramper;
(*silently*) se faufiler, se glisser; (*plant*) grimper
▸ N (*inf: flatterer*) lèche-botte *m*; **he's a** ~ c'est un
type puant; **it gives me the creeps** cela me
fait froid dans le dos; **to** ~ **up on sb** s'approcher
furtivement de qn
creeper ['kriːpəʳ] N plante grimpante
creepers ['kriːpəz] NPL (*US: for baby*) barboteuse *f*
creepy ['kriːpɪ] ADJ (*frightening*) qui fait
frissonner, qui donne la chair de poule
creepy-crawly ['kriːpɪ'krɔːlɪ] N (*inf*) bestiole *f*

cremate [krɪˈmeɪt] VT incinérer
cremation [krɪˈmeɪʃən] N incinération *f*
crematorium [krɛməˈtɔːrɪəm] (*pl* **crematoria**
[-ˈtɔːrɪə]) N four *m* crématoire
creosote ['krɪəsəut] N créosote *f*
crepe [kreɪp] N crêpe *m*
crepe bandage N (*Brit*) bande *f* Velpeau®
crepe paper N papier *m* crépon
crept [krɛpt] PT, PP *of* **creep**
crescendo [krɪˈʃɛndəu] N crescendo *m*
crescent ['krɛsnt] N croissant *m*; (*street*) rue *f* (*en
arc de cercle*)
cress [krɛs] N cresson *m*
crest [krɛst] N crête *f*; (*of helmet*) cimier *m*; (*of
coat of arms*) timbre *m*
crestfallen ['krɛstfɔːlən] ADJ déconfit(e),
découragé(e)
Crete ['kriːt] N Crète *f*
crevasse [krɪˈvæs] N crevasse *f*
crevice ['krɛvɪs] N fissure *f*, lézarde *f*, fente *f*
crew [kruː] N équipage *m*; (*Cine*) équipe *f* (de
tournage); (*gang*) bande *f*
crew-cut ['kruːkʌt] N: **to have a** ~ avoir les
cheveux en brosse
crew-neck ['kruːnɛk] N col ras
crib [krɪb] N lit *m* d'enfant; (*for baby*) berceau *m*
▸ VT (*inf*) copier
cribbage ['krɪbɪdʒ] N *sorte de jeu de cartes*
crick [krɪk] N crampe *f*; ~ **in the neck** torticolis *m*
cricket ['krɪkɪt] N (*insect*) grillon *m*, cri-cri *m inv*;
(*game*) cricket *m*
cricketer ['krɪkɪtəʳ] N joueur *m* de cricket
crime [kraɪm] N crime *m*; **minor** ~ délit mineur,
infraction mineure
crime wave N poussée *f* de la criminalité
criminal ['krɪmɪnl] ADJ, N criminel(le)
crimp [krɪmp] VT friser, frisotter
crimson ['krɪmzn] ADJ cramoisi(e)
cringe [krɪndʒ] VI avoir un mouvement de recul;
(*fig*) s'humilier, ramper
crinkle ['krɪŋkl] VT froisser, chiffonner
cripple ['krɪpl] N (*pej*) boiteux(-euse), infirme *mf*
▸ VT (*person*) estropier, paralyser; (*ship, plane*)
immobiliser; (*production, exports*) paralyser;
crippled with rheumatism perclus(e) de
rhumatismes
crippling ['krɪplɪŋ] ADJ (*disease*) handicapant(e);
(*taxation, debts*) écrasant(e)
crisis ['kraɪsɪs] (*pl* **crises** [-siːz]) N crise *f*
crisp [krɪsp] ADJ croquant(e); (*weather*) vif (vive);
(*manner etc*) brusque
crisps [krɪsps] (*Brit*) NPL (pommes *fpl*) chips *fpl*
crispy ['krɪspɪ] ADJ croustillant(e)
crisscross ['krɪskrɔs] ADJ entrecroisé(e), en
croisillons ▸ VT sillonner; ~ **pattern** croisillons
mpl
criterion [kraɪˈtɪərɪən] (*pl* **criteria** [-ˈtɪərɪə]) N
critère *m*
critic ['krɪtɪk] N critique *mf*
critical ['krɪtɪkl] ADJ critique; **to be** ~ **of sb/sth**
critiquer qn/qch
critically ['krɪtɪklɪ] ADV (*examine*) d'un œil
critique; (*speak*) sévèrement; ~ **ill** gravement
malade

531

criticism ['krɪtɪsɪzəm] N critique f
criticize ['krɪtɪsaɪz] VT critiquer
croak [krəuk] VI (frog) coasser; (raven) croasser
Croat ['krəuæt] ADJ, N = **Croatian**
Croatia [krəu'eɪʃə] N Croatie f
Croatian [krəu'eɪʃən] ADJ croate ▸ N Croate mf;
(Ling) croate m
crochet ['krəuʃeɪ] N travail m au crochet
crock [krɔk] N cruche f; (inf: also: **old crock**)
épave f
crockery ['krɔkərɪ] N vaisselle f
crocodile ['krɔkədaɪl] N crocodile m
crocus ['krəukəs] N crocus m
croft [krɔft] N (BRIT) petite ferme
crofter ['krɔftə'] N (BRIT) fermier m
croissant ['krwasã] N croissant m
crone [krəun] N vieille bique, (vieille) sorcière
crony ['krəunɪ] N copain (copine)
crook [kruk] N (inf) escroc m; (of shepherd)
houlette f
crooked ['krukɪd] ADJ courbé(e), tordu(e);
(action) malhonnête
crop [krɔp] N (produce) culture f; (amount produced)
récolte f; (riding crop) cravache f; (of bird) jabot m
▸ VT (hair) tondre; (animals, grass) brouter
▸ **crop up** VI surgir, se présenter, survenir
cropper ['krɔpə'] N: **to come a ~** (inf) faire la
culbute, s'étaler
crop spraying [-spreɪɪŋ] N pulvérisation f des
cultures
croquet ['krəukeɪ] N croquet m
cross [krɔs] N croix f; (Biol) croisement m ▸ VT
(street etc) traverser; (arms, legs, Biol) croiser;
(cheque) barrer; (thwart: person, plan) contrarier
▸ VI: **the boat crosses from ... to ...** le bateau
fait la traversée de ... à ... ▸ ADJ en colère,
fâché(e); **to ~ o.s.** se signer, faire le signe de (la)
croix; **we have a crossed line** (BRIT: on telephone)
il y a des interférences; **they've got their lines
crossed** (fig) il y a un malentendu entre eux; **to
be/get ~ with sb (about sth)** être en colère/(se)
fâcher contre qn (à propos de qch)
▸ **cross off, cross out** VT barrer, rayer
▸ **cross over** VI traverser
crossbar ['krɔsbɑ:'] N barre transversale
crossbow ['krɔsbəu] N arbalète f
crossbreed ['krɔsbri:d] N hybride m
cross-Channel ferry ['krɔs'tʃænl-] N ferry m qui
fait la traversée de la Manche
cross-check ['krɔstʃɛk] N recoupement m ▸ VI
vérifier par recoupement
cross-country ['krɔs'kʌntrɪ], **cross-country
race** N cross(-country) m
cross-dressing [krɔs'drɛsɪŋ] N travestisme m
cross-examination ['krɔsɪgzæmɪ'neɪʃən] N
(Law) examen m contradictoire (d'un témoin)
cross-examine ['krɔsɪg'zæmɪn] VT (Law) faire
subir un examen contradictoire à
cross-eyed ['krɔsaɪd] ADJ qui louche
crossfire ['krɔsfaɪə'] N feux croisés
crossing ['krɔsɪŋ] N croisement m, carrefour m;
(sea passage) traversée f; (also: **pedestrian
crossing**) passage clouté; **how long does the ~
take?** combien de temps dure la traversée?

crossing guard N (US) contractuel qui fait traverser
la rue aux enfants
crossing point N poste frontalier
cross-purposes ['krɔs'pə:pəsɪz] NPL: **to be at ~
with sb** comprendre qn de travers; **we're
(talking) at ~** on ne parle pas de la même chose
cross-question ['krɔs'kwɛstʃən] VT faire subir
un interrogatoire à
cross-reference ['krɔs'rɛfrəns] N renvoi m,
référence f
crossroads ['krɔsrəudz] N carrefour m
cross section N (Biol) coupe transversale; (in
population) échantillon m
crosswalk ['krɔswɔ:k] N (US) passage clouté
crosswind ['krɔswɪnd] N vent m de travers
crosswise ['krɔswaɪz] ADV en travers
crossword ['krɔswə:d] N mots mpl croisés
crotch [krɔtʃ] N (of garment) entrejambe m; (Anat)
entrecuisse m
crotchet ['krɔtʃɪt] N (Mus) noire f
crotchety ['krɔtʃɪtɪ] ADJ (person) grognon(ne),
grincheux(-euse)
crouch [krautʃ] VI s'accroupir; (hide) se tapir;
(before springing) se ramasser
croup [kru:p] N (Med) croup m
crouton ['kru:tɔn] N croûton m
crow [krəu] N (bird) corneille f; (of cock) chant m
du coq, cocorico m ▸ VI (cock) chanter; (fig)
pavoiser, chanter victoire
crowbar ['krəubɑ:'] N levier m
crowd [kraud] N foule f ▸ VT bourrer, remplir
▸ VI affluer, s'attrouper, s'entasser; **crowds of
people** une foule de gens
crowded ['kraudɪd] ADJ bondé(e), plein(e);
~ with plein de
crowd scene N (Cine, Theat) scène f de foule
crowdsource ['kraudsɔ:s] VT crowdsourcer
crowdsourcing ['kraudsɔ:sɪŋ] N crowdsourcing
m; Procédé par lequel un individu, une entreprise ou un
organisme confie une partie de son activité à une
multitude d'internautes volontaires.
crown [kraun] N couronne f; (of head) sommet m
de la tête, calotte crânienne; (of hat) fond m; (of
hill) sommet m ▸ VT (also tooth) couronner
crown court N (BRIT) ≈ Cour f d'assises; voir
article

En Angleterre et au pays de Galles, une crown
court est une cour de justice où sont jugées
les affaires très graves, telles que le meurtre,
l'homicide, le viol et le vol, en présence d'un
jury. Tous les crimes et délits, quel que soit
leur degré de gravité, doivent d'abord passer
devant une magistrates' court. Il existe environ
90 crown courts.

crowning ['kraunɪŋ] ADJ (achievement, glory)
suprême
crown jewels NPL joyaux mpl de la Couronne
crown prince N prince héritier
crow's-feet ['krəuzfi:t] NPL pattes fpl d'oie (fig)
crow's-nest ['krəuznɛst] N (on sailing-ship) nid m
de pie
crucial ['kru:ʃl] ADJ crucial(e), décisif(-ive); (also:
crucial to) essentiel(le) à
crucifix ['kru:sɪfɪks] N crucifix m

crucifixion [kruːsɪˈfɪkʃən] N crucifiement *m*, crucifixion *f*

crucify ['kruːsɪfaɪ] VT crucifier, mettre en croix; (*fig*) crucifier

crude [kruːd] ADJ (*materials*) brut(e); non raffiné(e); (*basic*) rudimentaire, sommaire; (*vulgar*) cru(e), grossier(-ière) ▸ N (*also*: **crude oil**) (pétrole *m*) brut *m*

cruel ['kruːəl] ADJ cruel(le)

cruelty ['kruːəltɪ] N cruauté *f*

cruet ['kruːɪt] N huilier *m*; vinaigrier *m*

cruise [kruːz] N croisière *f* ▸ VI (*ship*) croiser; (*car*) rouler; (*aircraft*) voler; (*taxi*) être en maraude

cruise missile N missile *m* de croisière

cruiser ['kruːzəʳ] N croiseur *m*

cruising speed ['kruːzɪŋ-] N vitesse *f* de croisière

crumb [krʌm] N miette *f*

crumble ['krʌmbl] VT émietter ▸ VI s'émietter; (*plaster etc*) s'effriter; (*land, earth*) s'ébouler; (*building*) s'écrouler, crouler; (*fig*) s'effondrer

crumbly ['krʌmblɪ] ADJ friable

crummy ['krʌmɪ] ADJ (*inf*) minable; (: *unwell*) mal fichu(e), patraque

crumpet ['krʌmpɪt] N petite crêpe (épaisse)

crumple ['krʌmpl] VT froisser, friper

crunch [krʌntʃ] VT croquer; (*underfoot*) faire craquer, écraser; faire crisser ▸ N (*fig*) instant *m* or moment *m* critique, moment de vérité

crunchy ['krʌntʃɪ] ADJ croquant(e), croustillant(e)

crusade [kruːˈseɪd] N croisade *f* ▸ VI (*fig*): **to ~ for/against** partir en croisade pour/contre

crusader [kruːˈseɪdəʳ] N croisé *m*; (*fig*): **~ (for)** champion *m* (de)

crush [krʌʃ] N (*crowd*) foule *f*, cohue *f*; (*love*): **to have a ~ on sb** avoir le béguin pour qn; (*drink*): **lemon ~** citron pressé ▸ VT écraser; (*crumple*) froisser; (*grind, break up: garlic, ice*) piler; (: *grapes*) presser; (*hopes*) anéantir

crush barrier N (BRIT) barrière *f* de sécurité

crushing ['krʌʃɪŋ] ADJ écrasant(e)

crust [krʌst] N croûte *f*

crustacean [krʌsˈteɪʃən] N crustacé *m*

crusty ['krʌstɪ] ADJ (*bread*) croustillant(e); (*inf: person*) revêche, bourru(e); (: *remark*) irrité(e)

crutch [krʌtʃ] N béquille *f*; (*Tech*) support *m*; (*of garment*) entrejambe *m*; (*Anat*) entrecuisse *m*

crux [krʌks] N point crucial

cry [kraɪ] VI pleurer; (*shout: also*: **cry out**) crier ▸ N cri *m*; **why are you crying?** pourquoi pleures-tu?; **to ~ for help** appeler à l'aide; **she had a good ~** elle a pleuré un bon coup; **it's a far ~ from ...** (*fig*) on est loin de ...
▸ **cry off** VI se dédire; se décommander
▸ **cry out** VI (*call out, shout*) pousser un cri ▸ VT crier

crying ['kraɪɪŋ] ADJ (*fig*) criant(e), flagrant(e)

crypt [krɪpt] N crypte *f*

cryptic ['krɪptɪk] ADJ énigmatique

crystal ['krɪstl] N cristal *m*

crystal-clear ['krɪstl'klɪəʳ] ADJ clair(e) comme de l'eau de roche

crystallize ['krɪstəlaɪz] VT cristalliser ▸ VI (se)

cristalliser; **crystallized fruits** (BRIT) fruits confits

CSA N ABBR = **Confederate States of America**; (BRIT: = *Child Support Agency*) *organisme pour la protection des enfants de parents séparés, qui contrôle le versement des pensions alimentaires.*

CSC N ABBR (= *Civil Service Commission*) commission de recrutement des fonctionnaires

CS gas N (BRIT) gaz *m* C.S.

CST ABBR (US: = *Central Standard Time*) fuseau horaire

CT ABBR (US) = **Connecticut**

ct ABBR = **carat**

CTC N ABBR (BRIT) = **city technology college**

CT scanner N ABBR (*Med*: = *computerized tomography scanner*) scanner *m*, tomodensitomètre *m*

cu. ABBR = **cubic**

cub [kʌb] N petit *m* (*d'un animal*); (*also*: **cub scout**) louveteau *m*

Cuba ['kjuːbə] N Cuba *m*

Cuban ['kjuːbən] ADJ cubain(e) ▸ N Cubain(e)

cubbyhole ['kʌbɪhəul] N cagibi *m*

cube [kjuːb] N cube *m* ▸ VT (*Math*) élever au cube

cube root N racine *f* cubique

cubic ['kjuːbɪk] ADJ cubique; **~ metre** *etc* mètre *m etc* cube; **~ capacity** (*Aut*) cylindrée *f*

cubicle ['kjuːbɪkl] N (*in hospital*) box *m*; (*at pool*) cabine *f*

cuckoo ['kuːkuː] N coucou *m*

cuckoo clock N (pendule *f* à) coucou *m*

cucumber ['kjuːkʌmbəʳ] N concombre *m*

cud [kʌd] N: **to chew the ~** ruminer

cuddle ['kʌdl] VT câliner, caresser ▸ VI se blottir l'un contre l'autre

cuddly ['kʌdlɪ] ADJ câlin(e)

cudgel ['kʌdʒl] N gourdin *m* ▸ VT: **to ~ one's brains** se creuser la tête

cue [kjuː] N queue *f* de billard; (*Theat etc*) signal *m*

cuff [kʌf] N (BRIT: *of shirt, coat etc*) poignet *m*, manchette *f*; (US: *on trousers*) revers *m*; (*blow*) gifle *f* ▸ VT gifler; **off the ~** *adv* à l'improviste

cufflinks ['kʌflɪŋks] N boutons *m* de manchette

cu. in. ABBR = **cubic inches**

cuisine [kwɪˈziːn] N cuisine *f*, art *m* culinaire

cul-de-sac ['kʌldəsæk] N cul-de-sac *m*, impasse *f*

culinary ['kʌlɪnərɪ] ADJ culinaire

cull [kʌl] VT sélectionner; (*kill selectively*) pratiquer l'abattage sélectif de ▸ N (*of animals*) abattage sélectif

culminate ['kʌlmɪneɪt] VI: **to ~ in** finir or se terminer par; (*lead to*) mener à

culmination [kʌlmɪˈneɪʃən] N point culminant

culottes [kjuːˈlɔts] NPL jupe-culotte *f*

culpable ['kʌlpəbl] ADJ coupable

culprit ['kʌlprɪt] N coupable *mf*

cult [kʌlt] N culte *m*

cult figure N idole *f*

cultivate ['kʌltɪveɪt] VT (*also fig*) cultiver

cultivation [kʌltɪˈveɪʃən] N culture *f*

cultural ['kʌltʃərəl] ADJ culturel(le)

culture ['kʌltʃəʳ] N (*also fig*) culture *f*

cultured ['kʌltʃəd] ADJ cultivé(e) (*fig*)

cumbersome ['kʌmbəsəm] ADJ encombrant(e), embarrassant(e)

cumin ['kʌmɪn] N (*spice*) cumin *m*

cumulative ['kjuːmjulətɪv] ADJ cumulatif(-ive)

cunning ['kʌnɪŋ] N ruse *f*, astuce *f* ▶ ADJ rusé(e), malin(-igne); (*clever: device, idea*) astucieux(-euse)

cunt [kʌnt] N (*inf!*) chatte *f*(!); (*insult*) salaud *m* (!), salope *f*(!)

cup [kʌp] N tasse *f*; (*prize, event*) coupe *f*; (*of bra*) bonnet *m*; **a ~ of tea** une tasse de thé

cupboard ['kʌbəd] N placard *m*

cup final N (*BRIT Football*) finale *f* de la coupe

Cupid ['kjuːpɪd] N Cupidon *m*; (*figurine*) amour *m*

cupidity [kjuː'pɪdɪtɪ] N cupidité *f*

cupola ['kjuːpələ] N coupole *f*

cuppa ['kʌpə] N (*BRIT inf*) tasse *f* de thé

cup tie ['kʌptaɪ] N (*BRIT Football*) match *m* de coupe

curable ['kjuərəbl] ADJ guérissable, curable

curate ['kjuərɪt] N vicaire *m*

curator [kjuə'reɪtər] N conservateur *m* (*d'un musée etc*)

curb [kəːb] VT refréner, mettre un frein à; (*expenditure*) limiter, juguler ▶ N (*fig*) frein *m*; (*US*) bord *m* du trottoir

curd cheese N ≈ fromage blanc

curdle ['kəːdl] VI (se) cailler

curds [kəːdz] NPL lait caillé

cure [kjuər] VT guérir; (*Culin: salt*) saler; (*: smoke*) fumer; (*: dry*) sécher ▶ N remède *m*; **to be cured of sth** être guéri de qch

cure-all ['kjuərɔːl] N (*also fig*) panacée *f*

curfew ['kəːfjuː] N couvre-feu *m*

curio ['kjuərɪəu] N bibelot *m*, curiosité *f*

curiosity [kjuərɪ'ɔsɪtɪ] N curiosité *f*

curious ['kjuərɪəs] ADJ curieux(-euse); **I'm ~ about him** il m'intrigue

curiously ['kjuərɪəslɪ] ADV curieusement; (*inquisitively*) avec curiosité; **~ enough, ...** bizarrement, ...

curl [kəːl] N boucle *f* (de cheveux); (*of smoke etc*) volute *f* ▶ VT, VI boucler; (*tightly*) friser ▶ **curl up** VI s'enrouler; (*person*) se pelotonner

curler ['kəːlər] N bigoudi *m*, rouleau *m*; (*Sport*) joueur(-euse) de curling

curlew ['kəːluː] N courlis *m*

curling ['kəːlɪŋ] N (*sport*) curling *m*

curling tongs, (*US*) **curling irons** NPL fer *m* à friser

curly ['kəːlɪ] ADJ bouclé(e); (*tightly curled*) frisé(e)

currant ['kʌrnt] N raisin *m* de Corinthe, raisin sec; (*fruit*) groseille *f*

currency ['kʌrnsɪ] N monnaie *f*; **foreign ~** devises étrangères, monnaie étrangère; **to gain ~** (*fig*) s'accréditer

current ['kʌrnt] N courant *m* ▶ ADJ (*common*) courant(e); (*tendency, price, event*) actuel(le); **direct/alternating ~** (*Elec*) courant continu/ alternatif; **the ~ issue of a magazine** le dernier numéro d'un magazine; **in ~ use** d'usage courant

current account N (*BRIT*) compte courant

current affairs NPL (questions *fpl* d')actualité *f*

current assets NPL (*Comm*) actif *m* disponible

current liabilities NPL (*Comm*) passif *m* exigible

currently ['kʌrntlɪ] ADV actuellement

curriculum [kə'rɪkjuləm] (*pl* **curriculums** or **curricula** [-lə]) N programme *m* d'études

curriculum vitae [-'viːtaɪ] N curriculum vitae (CV) *m*

curry ['kʌrɪ] N curry *m* ▶ VT: **to ~ favour with** chercher à gagner la faveur or à s'attirer les bonnes grâces de; **chicken ~** curry de poulet, poulet *m* au curry

curry powder N poudre *f* de curry

curse [kəːs] VI jurer, blasphémer ▶ VT maudire ▶ N (*spell*) malédiction *f*; (*problem, scourge*) fléau *m*; (*swearword*) juron *m*

cursor ['kəːsər] N (*Comput*) curseur *m*

cursory ['kəːsərɪ] ADJ superficiel(le), hâtif(-ive)

curt [kəːt] ADJ brusque, sec (sèche)

curtail [kəː'teɪl] VT (*visit etc*) écourter; (*expenses etc*) réduire

curtain ['kəːtn] N rideau *m*; **to draw the curtains** (*together*) fermer or tirer les rideaux; (*apart*) ouvrir les rideaux

curtain call N (*Theat*) rappel *m*

curtsey, curtsy ['kəːtsɪ] N révérence *f* ▶ VI faire une révérence

curvature ['kəːvətʃər] N courbure *f*

curve [kəːv] N courbe *f*; (*in the road*) tournant *m*, virage *m* ▶ VT courber ▶ VI se courber; (*road*) faire une courbe

curved [kəːvd] ADJ courbe

cushion ['kuʃən] N coussin *m* ▶ VT (*seat*) rembourrer; (*fall, shock*) amortir

cushy ['kuʃɪ] ADJ (*inf*): **a ~ job** un boulot de tout repos; **to have a ~ time** se la couler douce

custard ['kʌstəd] N (*for pouring*) crème anglaise

custard powder N (*BRIT*) ≈ crème pâtissière instantanée

custodial sentence [kʌs'təudɪəl-] N peine *f* de prison

custodian [kʌs'təudɪən] N gardien(ne); (*of collection etc*) conservateur(-trice)

custody ['kʌstədɪ] N (*of child*) garde *f*; (*for offenders*) détention préventive; **to take sb into ~** placer qn en détention préventive; **in the ~ of** sous la garde de

custom ['kʌstəm] N coutume *f*, usage *m*; (*Law*) droit coutumier, coutume *f*; (*Comm*) clientèle *f*

customary ['kʌstəmərɪ] ADJ habituel(le); **it is ~ to do it** l'usage veut qu'on le fasse

custom-built ['kʌstəm'bɪlt] ADJ *see* **custom-made**

customer ['kʌstəmər] N client(e); **he's an awkward ~** (*inf*) ce n'est pas quelqu'un de facile

customer profile N profil *m* du client

customize ['kʌstəmaɪz] VT personnaliser; customiser

customized ['kʌstəmaɪzd] ADJ personnalisé(e); (*car etc*) construit(e) sur commande

custom-made ['kʌstəm'meɪd] ADJ (*clothes*) fait(e) sur mesure; (*other goods: also:* **custom-built**) hors série, fait(e) sur commande

customs ['kʌstəmz] NPL douane *f*; **to go through (the) ~** passer la douane

Customs and Excise N (*BRIT*) administration *f* des douanes

customs officer N douanier *m*

cut [kʌt] (*pt, pp* ~) VT couper; (*meat*) découper; (*shape, make*) tailler; couper; creuser; graver; (*reduce*) réduire; (*inf: lecture, appointment*) manquer ▶ VI couper; (*intersect*) se couper ▶ N (*gen*) coupure *f*; (*of clothes*) coupe *f*; (*of jewel*) taille *f*; (*in salary etc*) réduction *f*; (*of meat*) morceau *m*; **to ~ teeth** (*baby*) faire ses dents; **to ~ a tooth** percer une dent; **to ~ one's finger** se couper le doigt; **to get one's hair ~** se faire couper les cheveux; **I've ~ myself** je me suis coupé; **to ~ sth short** couper court à qch; **to ~ sb dead** ignorer (complètement) qn
  ▶ **cut back** VT (*plants*) tailler; (*production, expenditure*) réduire
  ▶ **cut down** VT (*tree*) abattre; (*reduce*) réduire; **to ~ sb down to size** (*fig*) remettre qn à sa place
  ▶ **cut down on** VT FUS réduire
  ▶ **cut in** VI (*interrupt: conversation*): **to ~ in (on)** couper la parole (à); (*Aut*) faire une queue de poisson
  ▶ **cut off** VT couper; (*fig*) isoler; **we've been ~ off** (*Tel*) nous avons été coupés
  ▶ **cut out** VT (*picture etc*) découper; (*remove*) supprimer
  ▶ **cut up** VT découper

cut-and-dried ['kʌtən'draɪd] ADJ (*also:* **cut-and-dry**) tout(e) fait(e), tout(e) décidé(e)

cutaway ['kʌtəweɪ] ADJ, N: ~ **(drawing)** écorché *m*

cutback ['kʌtbæk] N réduction *f*

cute [kjuːt] ADJ mignon(ne), adorable; (*clever*) rusé(e), astucieux(-euse)

cut glass N cristal taillé

cuticle ['kjuːtɪkl] N (*on nail*): ~ **remover** repousse-peaux *m inv*

cutlery ['kʌtləri] N couverts *mpl*; (*trade*) coutellerie *f*

cutlet ['kʌtlɪt] N côtelette *f*

cutoff ['kʌtɔf] N (*also:* **cutoff point**) seuil-limite *m*

cutoff switch N interrupteur *m*

cutout ['kʌtaʊt] N coupe-circuit *m inv*; (*paper figure*) découpage *m*

cut-price ['kʌt'praɪs], (*US*) **cut-rate** ['kʌt'reɪt] ADJ au rabais, à prix réduit

cut-throat ['kʌtθrəʊt] N assassin *m* ▶ ADJ: ~ **competition** concurrence *f* sauvage

cutting ['kʌtɪŋ] ADJ tranchant(e), coupant(e); (*fig*) cinglant(e) ▶ N (*BRIT: from newspaper*) coupure *f* (de journal); (*from plant*) bouture *f*; (*Rail*) tranchée *f*; (*Cine*) montage *m*

cutting edge N (*of knife*) tranchant *m*; **on** *or* **at the ~ of** à la pointe de

cutting-edge [kʌtɪŋ'ɛdʒ] ADJ (*technology, research*) de pointe

cuttlefish ['kʌtlfɪʃ] N seiche *f*

cut-up ['kʌtʌp] ADJ affecté(e), démoralisé(e)

CV N ABBR = **curriculum vitae**

cwo ABBR (*Comm*) = **cash with order**

cwt ABBR = **hundredweight**

cyanide ['saɪənaɪd] N cyanure *m*

cyberattack ['saɪbərətæk] N cyber-attaque *f*

cyberbullying ['saɪbəbuliɪŋ] N harcèlement *m* virtuel

cybernetics [saɪbə'nɛtɪks] N cybernétique *f*

cybersecurity [saɪbəsɪ'kjʊrɪti] N cyber-sécurité *f*

cyberspace ['saɪbəspeɪs] N cyberespace *m*

cyclamen ['sɪkləmən] N cyclamen *m*

cycle ['saɪkl] N cycle *m*; (*bicycle*) bicyclette *f*, vélo *m* ▶ VI faire de la bicyclette

cycle hire N location *f* de vélos

cycle lane, cycle path N piste *f* cyclable

cycle race N course *f* cycliste

cycle rack N râtelier *m* à bicyclette

cycling ['saɪklɪŋ] N cyclisme *m*; **to go on a ~ holiday** (*BRIT*) faire du cyclotourisme

cyclist ['saɪklɪst] N cycliste *mf*

cyclone ['saɪkləʊn] N cyclone *m*

cygnet ['sɪgnɪt] N jeune cygne *m*

cylinder ['sɪlɪndə'] N cylindre *m*

cylinder capacity N cylindrée *f*

cylinder head N culasse *f*

cymbals ['sɪmblz] NPL cymbales *fpl*

cynic ['sɪnɪk] N cynique *mf*

cynical ['sɪnɪkl] ADJ cynique

cynicism ['sɪnɪsɪzəm] N cynisme *m*

CYO N ABBR (*US*: = *Catholic Youth Organization*) ≈ JC *f*

cypress ['saɪprɪs] N cyprès *m*

Cypriot ['sɪprɪət] ADJ cypriote, chypriote ▶ N Cypriote *mf*, Chypriote *mf*

Cyprus ['saɪprəs] N Chypre *f*

cyst [sɪst] N kyste *m*

cystitis [sɪs'taɪtɪs] N cystite *f*

CZ N ABBR (*US*: = *Central Zone*) zone du canal de Panama

czar [zɑː'] N tsar *m*

Czech [tʃɛk] ADJ tchèque ▶ N Tchèque *mf*; (*Ling*) tchèque *m*

Czechoslovak [tʃɛkə'sləʊvæk] ADJ, N (*Hist*) = **Czechoslovakian**

Czechoslovakia [tʃɛkəslə'vækɪə] N (*Hist*) Tchécoslovaquie *f*

Czechoslovakian [tʃɛkəslə'vækɪən] (*Hist*) ADJ tchécoslovaque ▶ N Tchécoslovaque *mf*

Czech Republic N: **the ~** la République tchèque

C

Dd

D¹, d [diː] N (*letter*) D, d *m*; (*Mus*) **D** ré *m*; **D for David**, (*US*) **D for Dog** D comme Désirée

D² ABBR (*US Pol*) = **democrat; democratic**

d² ABBR (*Brit old*) = **penny**

d. ABBR = **died**

DA N ABBR (*US*) = **district attorney**

dab [dæb] VT (*eyes, wound*) tamponner; (*paint, cream*) appliquer (par petites touches *or* rapidement); **a ~ of paint** un petit coup de peinture

dabble ['dæbl] VI: **to ~ in** faire *or* se mêler *or* s'occuper un peu de

Dacca ['dækə] N Dacca

dachshund ['dækshund] N teckel *m*

dad, daddy [dæd, 'dædɪ] N papa *m*

daddy-long-legs [dædɪ'lɒŋlɛgz] N tipule *f*; faucheux *m*

daffodil ['dæfədɪl] N jonquille *f*

daft [dɑːft] ADJ (*inf*) idiot(e), stupide; **to be ~ about** être toqué(e) *or* mordu(e) de

dagger ['dægər] N poignard *m*; **to be at daggers drawn with sb** être à couteaux tirés avec qn; **to look daggers at sb** foudroyer qn du regard

dahlia ['deɪljə] N dahlia *m*

daily ['deɪlɪ] ADJ quotidien(ne), journalier(-ière) ▶ N quotidien *m*; (*Brit: servant*) femme *f* de ménage (*à la journée*) ▶ ADV tous les jours; **twice ~** deux fois par jour

dainty ['deɪntɪ] ADJ délicat(e), mignon(ne)

dairy ['dɛərɪ] N (*shop*) crémerie *f*, laiterie *f*; (*on farm*) laiterie ▶ ADJ laitier(-ière)

dairy cow N vache laitière

dairy farm N exploitation *f* pratiquant l'élevage laitier

dairy produce N produits laitiers

dairy products NPL produits laitier

dais ['deɪɪs] N estrade *f*

daisy ['deɪzɪ] N pâquerette *f*

daisy wheel N (*on printer*) marguerite *f*

daisy-wheel printer ['deɪzɪwiːl-] N imprimante *f* à marguerite

Dakar ['dækə] N Dakar

dale [deɪl] N vallon *m*

dally ['dælɪ] VI musarder, flâner

dalmatian [dæl'meɪʃən] N (*dog*) dalmatien(ne)

dam [dæm] N (*wall*) barrage *m*; (*water*) réservoir *m*, lac *m* de retenue ▶ VT endiguer

damage ['dæmɪdʒ] N dégâts *mpl*, dommages

mpl; (*fig*) tort *m* ▶ VT endommager, abîmer; (*fig*) faire du tort à; **damages** NPL (*Law*) dommages-intérêts *mpl*; **to pay £5000 in damages** payer 5000 livres de dommages- intérêts; **~ to property** dégâts matériels

damaging ['dæmɪdʒɪŋ] ADJ: **~ (to)** préjudiciable (à), nuisible (à)

Damascus [də'mɑːskəs] N Damas

dame [deɪm] N (*title*) titre porté par une femme décorée de l'ordre de l'Empire Britannique ou d'un ordre de chevalerie, titre porté par la femme ou la veuve d'un chevalier ou baronnet; (*US inf*) nana *f*; (*Theat*) vieille dame (*rôle comique joué par un homme*)

damn [dæm] VT condamner; (*curse*) maudire ▶ N (*inf*): **I don't give a ~** je m'en fous ▶ ADJ (*inf: also:* **damned**): **this ~ ...** ce sacré *or* foutu ...; **~ (it)!** zut!

damnable ['dæmnəbl] ADJ (*inf: behaviour*) odieux(-euse), détestable; (: *weather*) épouvantable, abominable

damnation [dæm'neɪʃən] N (*Rel*) damnation *f* ▶ EXCL (*inf*) malédiction!, merde!

damning ['dæmɪŋ] ADJ (*evidence*) accablant(e)

damp [dæmp] ADJ humide ▶ N humidité *f* ▶ VT (*also:* **dampen**: *cloth, rag*) humecter; (: *enthusiasm etc*) refroidir

dampcourse ['dæmpkɔːs] N couche isolante (contre l'humidité)

damper ['dæmpər] N (*Mus*) étouffoir *m*; (*of fire*) registre *m*; **to put a ~ on** (*fig: atmosphere, enthusiasm*) refroidir

dampness ['dæmpnɪs] N humidité *f*

damson ['dæmzən] N prune *f* de Damas

dance [dɑːns] N danse *f*; (*ball*) bal *m* ▶ VI danser; **to ~ about** sautiller, gambader

dance floor N piste *f* de danse

dance hall N salle *f* de bal, dancing *m*

dancer ['dɑːnsər] N danseur(-euse)

dancing ['dɑːnsɪŋ] N danse *f*

D and C N ABBR (*Med:* = *dilation and curettage*) curetage *m*

dandelion ['dændɪlaɪən] N pissenlit *m*

dandruff ['dændrəf] N pellicules *fpl*

D & T N ABBR (*Brit Scol*) = **design and technology**

dandy ['dændɪ] N dandy *m*, élégant *m* ▶ ADJ (*US inf*) fantastique, super

Dane [deɪn] N Danois(e)

danger ['deɪndʒər] N danger *m*; **~!** (*on sign*)

danger!; **there is a ~ of fire** il y a (un) risque d'incendie; **in ~** en danger; **he was in ~ of falling** il risquait de tomber; **out of ~** hors de danger

danger list N (*Med*): **on the ~** dans un état critique

danger money N (*Brit*) prime f de risque

dangerous ['deɪndʒrəs] ADJ dangereux(-euse)

dangerously ['deɪndʒrəslɪ] ADV dangereusement; **~ ill** très gravement malade, en danger de mort

danger zone N zone dangereuse

dangle ['dæŋgl] VT balancer; (*fig*) faire miroiter ▶ VI pendre, se balancer

Danish ['deɪnɪʃ] ADJ danois(e) ▶ N (*Ling*) danois m

Danish pastry N feuilleté m (*recouvert d'un glaçage et fourré aux fruits etc*)

dank [dæŋk] ADJ froid(e) et humide

Danube ['dænjuːb] N: **the ~** le Danube

dapper ['dæpə^r] ADJ pimpant(e)

Dardanelles [daːdə'nɛlz] NPL Dardanelles fpl

dare [dɛə^r] VT: **to ~ sb to do** défier qn *or* mettre qn au défi de faire ▶ VI: **to ~ (to) do sth** oser faire qch; **I daren't tell him** (*Brit*) je n'ose pas le lui dire; **I ~ say he'll turn up** il est probable qu'il viendra

daredevil ['dɛədɛvl] N casse-cou m inv

Dar-es-Salaam ['daːrɛssə'laːm] N Dar-es-Salaam, Dar-es-Salam

daring ['dɛərɪŋ] ADJ hardi(e), audacieux(-euse) ▶ N audace f, hardiesse f

dark [daːk] ADJ (*night, room*) obscur(e), sombre; (*colour, complexion*) foncé(e), sombre; (*fig*) sombre ▶ N: **in the ~** dans le noir; **to be in the ~ about** (*fig*) ignorer tout de; **after ~** après la tombée de la nuit; **it is/is getting ~** il fait nuit/commence à faire nuit

darken [daːkn] VT obscurcir, assombrir ▶ VI s'obscurcir, s'assombrir

dark glasses NPL lunettes noires

dark horse N (*fig*): **he's a ~** on ne sait pas grand-chose de lui

darkly ['daːklɪ] ADV (*gloomily*) mélancoliquement; (*in a sinister way*) lugubrement

darkness ['daːknɪs] N obscurité f

darkroom ['daːkrʊm] N chambre noire

darling ['daːlɪŋ] ADJ, N chéri(e)

darn [daːn] VT repriser

dart [daːt] N fléchette f; (*in sewing*) pince f ▶ VI: **to ~ towards** (*also*: **make a dart towards**) se précipiter *or* s'élancer vers; **to ~ away/along** partir/passer comme une flèche

dartboard ['daːtbɔːd] N cible f (de jeu de fléchettes)

darts [daːts] N jeu m de fléchettes

dash [dæʃ] N (*sign*) tiret m; (*small quantity*) goutte f, larme f ▶ VT (*throw*) jeter *or* lancer violemment; (*hopes*) anéantir ▶ VI: **to ~ towards** (*also*: **make a dash towards**) se précipiter *or* se ruer vers; **a ~ of soda** un peu d'eau gazeuse

▶ **dash away** VI partir à toute allure

▶ **dash off** VI = **dash away**

dashboard ['dæʃbɔːd] N (*Aut*) tableau m de bord

dashing ['dæʃɪŋ] ADJ fringant(e)

dastardly ['dæstədlɪ] ADJ lâche

DAT N ABBR (= *digital audio tape*) cassette f audio digitale

data ['deɪtə] NPL données fpl

database ['deɪtəbeɪs] N base f de données

data capture N saisie f de données

data processing N traitement m des données

data transmission N transmission f de données

date [deɪt] N date f; (*with sb*) rendez-vous m; (*fruit*) datte f ▶ VT dater; (*person*) sortir avec; **what's the ~ today?** quelle date sommes-nous aujourd'hui?; **~ of birth** date de naissance; **closing ~** date de clôture; **to ~** adv à ce jour; **out of ~** périmé(e); **up to ~** à la page, mis(e) à jour, moderne; **to bring up to ~** (*correspondence, information*) mettre à jour; (*method*) moderniser; (*person*) mettre au courant; **letter dated 5th July** *or* **July 5th** (*US*) lettre (datée) du 5 juillet

dated ['deɪtɪd] ADJ démodé(e)

dateline ['deɪtlaɪn] N ligne f de changement de date

date rape N viol m (*à l'issue d'un rendez-vous galant*)

date stamp N timbre-dateur m

daub [dɔːb] VT barbouiller

daughter ['dɔːtə^r] N fille f

daughter-in-law ['dɔːtərɪnlɔː] N belle-fille f, bru f

daunt [dɔːnt] VT intimider, décourager

daunting ['dɔːntɪŋ] ADJ décourageant(e), intimidant(e)

dauntless ['dɔːntlɪs] ADJ intrépide

dawdle ['dɔːdl] VI traîner, lambiner; **to ~ over one's work** traînasser *or* lambiner sur son travail

dawn [dɔːn] N aube f, aurore f ▶ VI (*day*) se lever, poindre; (*fig*) naître, se faire jour; **at ~** à l'aube; **from ~ to dusk** du matin au soir; **it dawned on him that ...** il lui vint à l'esprit que ...

dawn chorus N (*Brit*) chant m des oiseaux à l'aube

day [deɪ] N jour m; (*as duration*) journée f; (*period of time, age*) époque f, temps m; **the ~ before** la veille, le jour précédent; **the ~ after, the following ~** le lendemain, le jour suivant; **the ~ before yesterday** avant-hier; **the ~ after tomorrow** après-demain; **(on) the ~ that ...** le jour où ...; **~ by ~** jour après jour; **by ~** de jour; **paid by the ~** payé(e) à la journée; **these days, in the present ~** de nos jours, à l'heure actuelle

daybook ['deɪbʊk] N (*Brit*) main courante, brouillard m, journal m

day boy N (*Scol*) externe m

daybreak ['deɪbreɪk] N point m du jour

day-care centre ['deɪkɛə-] N (*for elderly etc*) centre m d'accueil de jour; (*for children*) garderie f

daydream ['deɪdriːm] N rêverie f ▶ VI rêver (tout éveillé)

day girl N (*Scol*) externe f

daylight ['deɪlaɪt] N (lumière f du) jour m

d

537

daylight robbery N: **it's ~** (fig: inf) c'est du vol caractérisé or manifeste

daylight saving time N (US) heure f d'été

day release N: **to be on ~** avoir une journée de congé pour formation professionnelle

day return N (BRIT) billet m d'aller-retour (valable pour la journée)

day shift N équipe f de jour

daytime ['deɪtaɪm] N jour m, journée f

day-to-day ['deɪtə'deɪ] ADJ (routine, expenses) journalier(-ière); **on a ~ basis** au jour le jour

day trip N excursion f (d'une journée)

day tripper N excursionniste mf

daze [deɪz] VT (drug) hébéter; (blow) étourdir ▶ N: **in a ~** hébété(e), étourdi(e)

dazed [deɪzd] ADJ abruti(e)

dazzle ['dæzl] VT éblouir, aveugler

dazzling ['dæzlɪŋ] ADJ (light) aveuglant(e), éblouissant(e); (fig) éblouissant(e)

DC ABBR (Elec) = **direct current**; (US) = **District of Columbia**

DD N ABBR (= Doctor of Divinity) titre universitaire

dd. ABBR (Comm) = **delivered**

D/D ABBR = **direct debit**

D-day ['di:deɪ] N le jour J

DDS N ABBR US: = **Doctor of Dental Science**; (BRIT: = Doctor of Dental Surgery) titres universitaires

DDT N ABBR (= dichlorodiphenyl trichloroethane) DDT m

DE ABBR (US) = **Delaware**

DEA N ABBR (US: = Drug Enforcement Administration) ≈ brigade f des stupéfiants

deacon ['di:kən] N diacre m

dead [dɛd] ADJ mort(e); (numb) engourdi(e), insensible; (battery) à plat ▶ ADV (completely) absolument, complètement; (exactly) juste; **the dead** NPL les morts; **he was shot ~** il a été tué d'un coup de revolver; **~ on time** à l'heure pile; **~ tired** éreinté(e), complètement fourbu(e); **to stop ~** s'arrêter pile or net; **the line is ~** (Tel) la ligne est coupée

dead beat ADJ (inf) claqué(e), crevé(e)

deaden [dɛdn] VT (blow, sound) amortir; (make numb) endormir, rendre insensible

dead end N impasse f

dead-end ['dɛdɛnd] ADJ: **a ~ job** un emploi or poste sans avenir

dead heat N (Sport): **to finish in a ~** terminer ex aequo

dead-letter office [dɛd'lɛtər-] N ≈ centre m de recherche du courrier

deadline ['dɛdlaɪn] N date f or heure f limite; **to work to a ~** avoir des délais stricts à respecter

deadlock ['dɛdlɔk] N impasse f (fig)

dead loss N (inf): **to be a ~** (person) n'être bon (bonne à rien); (thing) ne rien valoir

deadly ['dɛdlɪ] ADJ mortel(le); (weapon) meurtrier(-ière); **~ dull** ennuyeux(-euse) à mourir, mortellement ennuyeux

deadpan ['dɛdpæn] ADJ impassible; (humour) pince-sans-rire inv

Dead Sea N: **the ~** la mer Morte

deaf [dɛf] ADJ sourd(e); **to turn a ~ ear to sth** faire la sourde oreille à qch

deaf-aid ['dɛfeɪd] N (BRIT) appareil auditif

deaf-and-dumb ['dɛfən'dʌm] (pej) ADJ sourd(e)-muet(te); **~ alphabet** alphabet m des sourds-muets

deafen ['dɛfn] VT rendre sourd(e); (fig) assourdir

deafening ['dɛfnɪŋ] ADJ assourdissant(e)

deaf-mute ['dɛfmjuːt] (pej) N sourd(e)-muet(te)

deafness ['dɛfnɪs] N surdité f

deal [diːl] (pt, pp **dealt** [dɛlt]) N affaire f, marché m ▶ VT (blow) porter; (cards) donner, distribuer; **to strike a ~ with sb** faire or conclure un marché avec qn; **it's a ~!** (inf) marché conclu!, tope-là!, topez-là!; **he got a bad ~ from them** ils ont mal agi envers lui; **he got a fair ~ from them** ils ont agi loyalement envers lui; **a good ~** (a lot) beaucoup; **a good ~ of**, **a great ~ of** beaucoup de, énormément de

▶ **deal in** VT FUS (Comm) faire le commerce de, être dans le commerce de

▶ **deal with** VT FUS (Comm) traiter avec; (handle) s'occuper or se charger de; (be about: book etc) traiter de

dealer ['diːlər] N (Comm) marchand m; (Cards) donneur m

dealership ['diːləʃɪp] N concession f

dealings ['diːlɪŋz] NPL (in goods, shares) opérations fpl, transactions fpl; (relations) relations fpl, rapports mpl

dealt [dɛlt] PT, PP of **deal**

dean [diːn] N (Rel, BRIT Scol) doyen m; (US Scol) conseiller principal (conseillère principale) d'éducation

dear [dɪər] ADJ cher (chère); (expensive) cher, coûteux(-euse) ▶ N: **my ~** mon cher (ma chère) ▶ EXCL: **~ me!** mon Dieu!; **D~ Sir/Madam** (in letter) Monsieur/Madame; **D~ Mr/Mrs X** Cher Monsieur/Chère Madame X

dearly ['dɪəlɪ] ADV (love) tendrement; (pay) cher

dearth [dəːθ] N disette f, pénurie f

death [dɛθ] N mort f; (Admin) décès m

deathbed ['dɛθbɛd] N lit m de mort

death certificate N acte m de décès

deathly ['dɛθlɪ] ADJ de mort ▶ ADV comme la mort

death penalty N peine f de mort

death rate N taux m de mortalité

death row [-'rəu] N (US) quartier m des condamnés à mort; **to be on ~** être condamné à la peine de mort

death sentence N condamnation f à mort

death squad N escadron m de la mort

death toll N nombre m de morts

death trap N endroit or véhicule etc dangereux

deb [dɛb] N ABBR (inf) = **debutante**

debar [dɪ'bɑːr] VT: **to ~ sb from a club** etc exclure qn d'un club etc; **to ~ sb from doing** interdire à qn de faire

debase [dɪ'beɪs] VT (currency) déprécier, dévaloriser; (person) abaisser, avilir

debatable [dɪ'beɪtəbl] ADJ discutable, contestable; **it is ~ whether ...** il est douteux que ...

debate [dɪ'beɪt] N discussion f, débat m ▶ VT discuter, débattre ▶ VI (consider): **to ~ whether**

se demander si

debauchery [dɪ'bɔ:tʃərɪ] N débauche f

debenture [dɪ'bɛntʃəʳ] N (Comm) obligation f

debilitate [dɪ'bɪlɪteɪt] VT débiliter

debit ['dɛbɪt] N débit m ▶ VT: **to ~ a sum to sb** or **to sb's account** porter une somme au débit de qn, débiter qn d'une somme

debit balance N solde débiteur

debit card N carte f de paiement

debit note N note f de débit

debrief [di:'bri:f] VT demander un compte rendu de fin de mission à

debriefing [di:'bri:fɪŋ] N compte rendu m

debris ['dɛbri:] N débris mpl, décombres mpl

debt [dɛt] N dette f; **to be in ~** avoir des dettes, être endetté(e); **bad ~** créance f irrécouvrable

debt collector N agent m de recouvrements

debtor ['dɛtəʳ] N débiteur(-trice)

debug [di:'bʌg] VT (Comput) déboguer

debunk [di:'bʌŋk] VT (inf: theory, claim) montrer le ridicule de

debut ['deɪbju:] N début(s) m(pl)

debutante ['dɛbjutænt] N débutante f

Dec. ABBR (= December) déc

decade ['dɛkeɪd] N décennie f, décade f

decadence ['dɛkədəns] N décadence f

decadent ['dɛkədənt] ADJ décadent(e)

decaf ['di:kæf] N (inf) déca m

decaffeinated [dɪ'kæfɪneɪtɪd] ADJ décaféiné(e)

decamp [dɪ'kæmp] VI (inf) décamper, filer

decant [dɪ'kænt] VT (wine) décanter

decanter [dɪ'kæntəʳ] N carafe f

decarbonize [di:'kɑ:bənaɪz] VT (Aut) décalaminer

decathlon [dɪ'kæθlən] N décathlon m

decay [dɪ'keɪ] N (of food, wood etc) décomposition f, pourriture f; (of building) délabrement m; (fig) déclin m; (also: **tooth decay**) carie f (dentaire) ▶ VI (rot) se décomposer, pourrir; (teeth) se carier; (fig: city, district, building) se délabrer; (: civilization) décliner; (: system) tomber en ruine

decease [dɪ'si:s] N décès m

deceased [dɪ'si:st] N: **the ~** le (la) défunt(e)

deceit [dɪ'si:t] N tromperie f, supercherie f

deceitful [dɪ'si:tful] ADJ trompeur(-euse)

deceive [dɪ'si:v] VT tromper; **to ~ o.s.** s'abuser

decelerate [di:'sɛləreɪt] VT, VI ralentir

December [dɪ'sɛmbəʳ] N décembre m; see also July

decency ['di:sənsɪ] N décence f

decent ['di:sənt] ADJ (proper) décent(e), convenable; **they were very ~ about it** ils se sont montrés très chics

decently ['di:səntlɪ] ADV (respectably) décemment, convenablement; (kindly) décemment

decentralization [di:sɛntrəlaɪ'zeɪʃən] N décentralisation f

decentralize [di:'sɛntrəlaɪz] VT décentraliser

deception [dɪ'sɛpʃən] N tromperie f

deceptive [dɪ'sɛptɪv] ADJ trompeur(-euse)

decibel ['dɛsɪbɛl] N décibel m

decide [dɪ'saɪd] VT (subj: person) décider; (question, argument) trancher, régler ▶ VI se décider,

décider; **to ~ to do/that** décider de faire/que; **to ~ on** décider, se décider pour; **to ~ on doing** décider de faire; **to ~ against doing** décider de ne pas faire

decided [dɪ'saɪdɪd] ADJ (resolute) résolu(e), décidé(e); (clear, definite) net(te), marqué(e)

decidedly [dɪ'saɪdɪdlɪ] ADV résolument; incontestablement, nettement

deciding [dɪ'saɪdɪŋ] ADJ décisif(-ive)

deciduous [dɪ'sɪdjuəs] ADJ à feuilles caduques

decimal ['dɛsɪməl] ADJ décimal(e) ▶ N décimale f; **to three ~ places** (jusqu')à la troisième décimale

decimalize ['dɛsɪməlaɪz] VT (Brit) décimaliser

decimal point N ≈ virgule f

decimate ['dɛsɪmeɪt] VT décimer

decipher [dɪ'saɪfəʳ] VT déchiffrer

decision [dɪ'sɪʒən] N décision f; **to make a ~** prendre une décision

decisive [dɪ'saɪsɪv] ADJ décisif(-ive); (influence) décisif, déterminant(e); (manner, person) décidé(e), catégorique; (reply) ferme, catégorique

deck [dɛk] N (Naut) pont m; (of cards) jeu m; (record deck) platine f; (of bus): **top ~** impériale f; **to go up on ~** monter sur le pont; **below ~** dans l'entrepont

deckchair ['dɛktʃɛəʳ] N chaise longue

deck hand N matelot m

declaration [dɛklə'reɪʃən] N déclaration f

declare [dɪ'klɛəʳ] VT déclarer

declassify [di:'klæsɪfaɪ] VT rendre accessible au public or à tous

decline [dɪ'klaɪn] N (decay) déclin m; (lessening) baisse f ▶ VT refuser, décliner ▶ VI décliner; (business) baisser; **~ in living standards** baisse du niveau de vie; **to ~ to do sth** refuser (poliment) de faire qch

declutch ['di:'klʌtʃ] VI (Brit) débrayer

decode ['di:'kəud] VT décoder

decoder ['di:'kəudəʳ] N (Comput, TV) décodeur m

decompose [di:kəm'pəuz] VI se décomposer

decomposition [di:kɔmpə'zɪʃən] N décomposition f

decompression [di:kəm'prɛʃən] N décompression f

decompression chamber N caisson m de décompression

decongestant [di:kən'dʒɛstənt] N décongestif m

decontaminate [di:kən'tæmɪneɪt] VT décontaminer

decontrol [di:kən'trəul] VT (prices etc) libérer

décor ['deɪkɔ:ʳ] N décor m

decorate ['dɛkəreɪt] VT (adorn, give a medal to) décorer; (paint and paper) peindre et tapisser

decoration [dɛkə'reɪʃən] N (medal etc, adornment) décoration f

decorative ['dɛkərətɪv] ADJ décoratif(-ive)

decorator ['dɛkəreɪtəʳ] N peintre m en bâtiment

decorum [dɪ'kɔ:rəm] N décorum m, bienséance f

decoy ['di:kɔɪ] N piège m; **they used him as a ~ for the enemy** ils se sont servis de lui pour attirer l'ennemi

decrease N ['diːkriːs] diminution f ▶ VT, VI [diːˈkriːs] diminuer; **to be on the ~** diminuer, être en diminution

decreasing [diːˈkriːsɪŋ] ADJ en voie de diminution

decree [dɪˈkriː] N (Pol, Rel) décret m; (Law) arrêt m, jugement m ▶ VT: **to ~ (that)** décréter (que), ordonner (que); **~ absolute** jugement définitif (de divorce); **~ nisi** jugement provisoire de divorce

decrepit [dɪˈkrɛpɪt] ADJ (person) décrépit(e); (building) délabré(e)

decry [dɪˈkraɪ] VT condamner ouvertement, déplorer; (disparage) dénigrer, décrier

decrypt [diːˈkrɪpt] VT (Comput, Tel) décrypter

dedicate ['dɛdɪkeɪt] VT consacrer; (book etc) dédier

dedicated ['dɛdɪkeɪtɪd] ADJ (person) dévoué(e); (Comput) spécialisé(e), dédié(e); **~ word processor** station f de traitement de texte

dedication [dɛdɪˈkeɪʃən] N (devotion) dévouement m; (in book) dédicace f

deduce [dɪˈdjuːs] VT déduire, conclure

deduct [dɪˈdʌkt] VT: **to ~ sth (from)** déduire qch (de), retrancher qch (de); (from wage etc) prélever qch (sur), retenir qch (sur)

deduction [dɪˈdʌkʃən] N (deducting, deducing) déduction f; (from wage etc) prélèvement m, retenue f

deed [diːd] N action f, acte m; (Law) acte notarié, contrat m; **~ of covenant** (acte m de) donation f

deem [diːm] VT (formal) juger, estimer; **to ~ it wise to do** juger bon de faire

deep [diːp] ADJ (water, sigh, sorrow, thoughts) profond(e); (voice) grave ▶ ADV: **~ in snow** recouvert(e) d'une épaisse couche de neige; **spectators stood 20 ~** il y avait 20 rangs de spectateurs; **knee-~ in water** dans l'eau jusqu'aux genoux; **4 metres ~** de 4 mètres de profondeur; **how ~ is the water?** l'eau a quelle profondeur?; **he took a ~ breath** il inspira profondément, il prit son souffle

deepen [diːpn] VT (hole) approfondir ▶ VI s'approfondir; (darkness) s'épaissir

deepfreeze ['diːpˈfriːz] N congélateur m ▶ VT surgeler

deep-fry ['diːpˈfraɪ] VT faire frire (dans une friteuse)

deeply ['diːplɪ] ADV profondément; (dig) en profondeur; (regret, interested) vivement

deep-rooted ['diːpˈruːtɪd] ADJ (prejudice) profondément enraciné(e); (affection) profond(e); (habit) invétéré(e)

deep-sea ['diːpˈsiː] ADJ: **~ diver** plongeur sous-marin; **~ diving** plongée sous-marine; **~ fishing** pêche hauturière

deep-seated ['diːpˈsiːtɪd] ADJ (belief) profondément enraciné(e)

deep-set ['diːpsɛt] ADJ (eyes) enfoncé(e)

deep vein thrombosis N thrombose f veineuse profonde

deer [dɪəʳ] N pl inv: **the ~** les cervidés mpl; (**red**) **~** cerf m; (**fallow**) **~** daim m; (**roe**) **~** chevreuil m

deerskin ['dɪəskɪn] N peau f de daim

deerstalker ['dɪəstɔːkəʳ] N (person) chasseur m de cerf; (hat) casquette f à la Sherlock Holmes

deface [dɪˈfeɪs] VT dégrader; barbouiller rendre illisible

defamation [dɛfəˈmeɪʃən] N diffamation f

defamatory [dɪˈfæmətrɪ] ADJ diffamatoire, diffamant(e)

default [dɪˈfɔːlt] VI (Law) faire défaut; (gen) manquer à ses engagements ▶ N (Comput: also: **default value**) valeur f par défaut; **by ~** (Law) par défaut, par contumace; (Sport) par forfait; **to ~ on a debt** ne pas s'acquitter d'une dette

defaulter [dɪˈfɔːltəʳ] N (on debt) débiteur défaillant

default option N (Comput) option f par défaut

defeat [dɪˈfiːt] N défaite f ▶ VT (team, opponents) battre; (fig: plans, efforts) faire échouer

defeatism [dɪˈfiːtɪzəm] N défaitisme m

defeatist [dɪˈfiːtɪst] ADJ, N défaitiste mf

defecate ['dɛfəkeɪt] VI déféquer

defect N ['diːfɛkt] défaut m ▶ VI [dɪˈfɛkt]: **to ~ to the enemy/the West** passer à l'ennemi/l'Ouest; **physical ~** malformation f, vice m de conformation; **mental ~** anomalie or déficience mentale

defective [dɪˈfɛktɪv] ADJ défectueux(-euse)

defector [dɪˈfɛktəʳ] N transfuge mf

defence, (US) **defense** [dɪˈfɛns] N défense f; **in ~ of** pour défendre; **witness for the ~** témoin m à décharge; **the Ministry of D~,** (US) **the Department of Defense** le ministère de la Défense nationale

defenceless [dɪˈfɛnslɪs] ADJ sans défense

defend [dɪˈfɛnd] VT défendre; (decision, action, opinion) justifier, défendre

defendant [dɪˈfɛndənt] N défendeur(-deresse); (in criminal case) accusé(e), prévenu(e)

defender [dɪˈfɛndəʳ] N défenseur m

defending champion [dɪˈfɛndɪŋ-] N (Sport) champion(ne) en titre

defending counsel [dɪˈfɛndɪŋ-] N (Law) avocat m de la défense

defense [dɪˈfɛns] N (US) = **defence**

defensive [dɪˈfɛnsɪv] ADJ défensif(-ive) ▶ N défensive f; **on the ~** sur la défensive

defer [dɪˈfəːʳ] VT (postpone) différer, ajourner ▶ VI (submit): **to ~ to sb/sth** déférer à qn/qch, s'en remettre à qn/qch

deference ['dɛfərəns] N déférence f, égards mpl; **out of** or **in ~ to** par déférence or égards pour

defiance [dɪˈfaɪəns] N défi m; **in ~ of** au mépris de

defiant [dɪˈfaɪənt] ADJ provocant(e), de défi; (person) rebelle, intraitable

defiantly [dɪˈfaɪəntlɪ] ADV d'un air (or d'un ton) de défi

deficiency [dɪˈfɪʃənsɪ] N (lack) insuffisance f; (: Med) carence f; (flaw) faiblesse f; (Comm) déficit m, découvert m

deficiency disease N maladie f de carence

deficient [dɪˈfɪʃənt] ADJ (inadequate) insuffisant(e); (defective) défectueux(-euse); **to be ~ in** manquer de

deficit ['dɛfɪsɪt] N déficit m

defile [dɪ'faɪl] ᴠᴛ souiller ▸ ᴠɪ défiler ▸ ɴ ['di:faɪl] défilé *m*
define [dɪ'faɪn] ᴠᴛ définir
definite ['dɛfɪnɪt] ᴀᴅᴊ (*fixed*) défini(e), (bien) déterminé(e); (*clear, obvious*) net(te), manifeste; (*Ling*) défini(e); (*certain*) sûr(e); **he was ~ about it** il a été catégorique; il était sûr de son fait
definitely ['dɛfɪnɪtlɪ] ᴀᴅᴠ sans aucun doute
definition [dɛfɪ'nɪʃən] ɴ définition *f*; (*clearness*) netteté *f*
definitive [dɪ'fɪnɪtɪv] ᴀᴅᴊ définitif(-ive)
deflate [di:'fleɪt] ᴠᴛ dégonfler; (*pompous person*) rabattre le caquet à; (*Econ*) provoquer la déflation de; (: *prices*) faire tomber *or* baisser
deflation [di:'fleɪʃən] ɴ (*Econ*) déflation *f*
deflationary [di:'fleɪʃənrɪ] ᴀᴅᴊ (*Econ*) déflationniste
deflect [dɪ'flɛkt] ᴠᴛ détourner, faire dévier
defog ['di:'fɔg] ᴠᴛ (*US Aut*) désembuer
defogger ['di:'fɔgər] ɴ (*US Aut*) dispositif *m* anti-buée *inv*
deform [dɪ'fɔ:m] ᴠᴛ déformer
deformed [dɪ'fɔ:md] ᴀᴅᴊ difforme
deformity [dɪ'fɔ:mɪtɪ] ɴ difformité *f*
defraud [dɪ'frɔ:d] ᴠᴛ frauder; **to ~ sb of sth** soutirer qch malhonnêtement à qn; escroquer qch à qn; frustrer qn de qch
defray [dɪ'freɪ] ᴠᴛ: **to ~ sb's expenses** défrayer qn (de ses frais), rembourser *or* payer à qn ses frais
defriend [di:'frɛnd] ᴠᴛ (*Internet*) supprimer de sa liste d'amis
defrost [di:'frɔst] ᴠᴛ (*fridge*) dégivrer; (*frozen food*) décongeler
deft [dɛft] ᴀᴅᴊ adroit(e), preste
defunct [dɪ'fʌŋkt] ᴀᴅᴊ défunt(e)
defuse [di:'fju:z] ᴠᴛ désamorcer
defy [dɪ'faɪ] ᴠᴛ défier; (*efforts etc*) résister à; **it defies description** cela défie toute description
degenerate ᴠɪ [dɪ'dʒɛnəreɪt] dégénérer ▸ ᴀᴅᴊ [dɪ'dʒɛnərɪt] dégénéré(e)
degradation [dɛgrə'deɪʃən] ɴ dégradation *f*
degrade [dɪ'greɪd] ᴠᴛ dégrader
degrading [dɪ'greɪdɪŋ] ᴀᴅᴊ dégradant(e)
degree [dɪ'gri:] ɴ degré *m*; (*Scol*) diplôme *m* (universitaire); **10 degrees below (zero)** 10 degrés au-dessous de zéro; **a (first) ~ in maths** (*Brit*) une licence en maths; **a considerable ~ of risk** un considérable facteur *or* élément de risque; **by degrees** (*gradually*) par degrés; **to some ~, to a certain ~** jusqu'à un certain point, dans une certaine mesure
dehydrated [di:haɪ'dreɪtɪd] ᴀᴅᴊ déshydraté(e); (*milk, eggs*) en poudre
dehydration [di:haɪ'dreɪʃən] ɴ déshydratation *f*
de-ice ['di:'aɪs] ᴠᴛ (*windscreen*) dégivrer
de-icer ['di:'aɪsər] ɴ dégivreur *m*
deign [deɪn] ᴠɪ: **to ~ to do** daigner faire
deity ['di:ɪtɪ] ɴ divinité *f*; dieu *m*, déesse *f*
déjà vu [deɪʒɑ:'vu:] ɴ: **I had a sense of ~** j'ai eu une impression de déjà-vu
dejected [dɪ'dʒɛktɪd] ᴀᴅᴊ abattu(e), déprimé(e)
dejection [dɪ'dʒɛkʃən] ɴ abattement *m*, découragement *m*

Del. ᴀʙʙʀ (*US*) = **Delaware**
del. ᴀʙʙʀ = **delete**
delay [dɪ'leɪ] ᴠᴛ (*journey, operation*) retarder, différer; (*traveller, train*) retarder; (*payment*) différer ▸ ᴠɪ s'attarder ▸ ɴ délai *m*, retard *m*; **to be delayed** être en retard; **without ~** sans délai, sans tarder
delayed-action [dɪ'leɪd'ækʃən] ᴀᴅᴊ à retardement
delectable [dɪ'lɛktəbl] ᴀᴅᴊ délicieux(-euse)
delegate ɴ ['dɛlɪgɪt] délégué(e) ▸ ᴠᴛ ['dɛlɪgeɪt] déléguer; **to ~ sth to sb/sb to do sth** déléguer qch à qn/qn pour faire qch
delegation [dɛlɪ'geɪʃən] ɴ délégation *f*
delete [dɪ'li:t] ᴠᴛ rayer, supprimer; (*Comput*) effacer
Delhi ['dɛlɪ] ɴ Delhi
deli ['dɛlɪ] ɴ épicerie fine
deliberate ᴀᴅᴊ [dɪ'lɪbərɪt] (*intentional*) délibéré(e); (*slow*) mesuré(e) ▸ ᴠɪ [dɪ'lɪbəreɪt] délibérer, réfléchir
deliberately [dɪ'lɪbərɪtlɪ] ᴀᴅᴠ (*on purpose*) exprès, délibérément
deliberation [dɪlɪbə'reɪʃən] ɴ délibération *f*, réflexion *f*; (*gen pl: discussion*) délibérations, débats *mpl*
delicacy ['dɛlɪkəsɪ] ɴ délicatesse *f*; (*choice food*) mets fin *or* délicat, friandise *f*
delicate ['dɛlɪkɪt] ᴀᴅᴊ délicat(e)
delicately ['dɛlɪkɪtlɪ] ᴀᴅᴠ délicatement; (*act, express*) avec délicatesse, avec tact
delicatessen [dɛlɪkə'tɛsn] ɴ épicerie fine
delicious [dɪ'lɪʃəs] ᴀᴅᴊ délicieux(-euse), exquis(e)
delight [dɪ'laɪt] ɴ (grande) joie, grand plaisir ▸ ᴠᴛ enchanter; **she's a ~ to work with** c'est un plaisir de travailler avec elle; **a ~ to the eyes** un régal *or* plaisir pour les yeux; **to take ~ in** prendre grand plaisir à; **to be the ~ of** faire les délices *or* la joie de
delighted [dɪ'laɪtɪd] ᴀᴅᴊ: **~ (at or with sth)** ravi(e) (de qch); **to be ~ to do sth/that** être enchanté(e) *or* ravi(e) de faire qch/que; **I'd be ~** j'en serais enchanté *or* ravi
delightful [dɪ'laɪtful] ᴀᴅᴊ (*person*) absolument charmant(e), adorable; (*meal, evening*) merveilleux(-euse)
delimit [di:'lɪmɪt] ᴠᴛ délimiter
delineate [dɪ'lɪnɪeɪt] ᴠᴛ tracer, esquisser; (*fig*) dépeindre, décrire
delinquency [dɪ'lɪŋkwənsɪ] ɴ délinquance *f*
delinquent [dɪ'lɪŋkwənt] ᴀᴅᴊ, ɴ délinquant(e)
delirious [dɪ'lɪrɪəs] ᴀᴅᴊ (*Med: fig*) délirant(e); **to be ~** délirer
delirium [dɪ'lɪrɪəm] ɴ délire *m*
deliver [dɪ'lɪvər] ᴠᴛ (*mail*) distribuer; (*goods*) livrer; (*message*) remettre; (*speech*) prononcer; (*warning, ultimatum*) lancer; (*free*) délivrer; (*Med: baby*) mettre au monde; (: *woman*) accoucher; **to ~ the goods** (*fig*) tenir ses promesses
deliverance [dɪ'lɪvrəns] ɴ délivrance *f*, libération *f*
delivery [dɪ'lɪvərɪ] ɴ (*of mail*) distribution *f*; (*of goods*) livraison *f*; (*of speaker*) élocution *f*; (*Med*)

d

accouchement *m*; **to take ~ of** prendre livraison de

delivery note N bon *m* de livraison

delivery van, (*US*) **delivery truck** N fourgonnette *f* or camionnette *f* de livraison

delta ['dɛltə] N delta *m*

delude [dɪ'luːd] VT tromper, leurrer; **to ~ o.s.** se leurrer, se faire des illusions

deluge ['dɛljuːdʒ] N déluge *m* ▶ VT (*fig*): **to ~ (with)** inonder (de)

delusion [dɪ'luːʒən] N illusion *f*; **to have delusions of grandeur** être un peu mégalomane

de luxe [də'lʌks] ADJ de luxe

delve [dɛlv] VI: **to ~ into** fouiller dans

Dem. ABBR (*US Pol*) = **democrat; democratic**

demagogue ['dɛməgɒg] N démagogue *mf*

demand [dɪ'mɑːnd] VT réclamer, exiger; (*need*) exiger, requérir ▶ N exigence *f*; (*claim*) revendication *f*; (*Econ*) demande *f*; **to ~ sth (from** *or* **of sb)** exiger qch (de qn), réclamer qch (à qn); **in ~** demandé(e), recherché(e); **on ~** sur demande

demanding [dɪ'mɑːndɪŋ] ADJ (*person*) exigeant(e); (*work*) astreignant(e)

demarcation [diːmɑː'keɪʃən] N démarcation *f*

demarcation dispute N (*Industry*) conflit *m* d'attributions

demean [dɪ'miːn] VT: **to ~ o.s.** s'abaisser

demeanour, (*US*) **demeanor** [dɪ'miːnər] N comportement *m*; maintien *m*

demented [dɪ'mɛntɪd] ADJ dément(e), fou (folle)

demilitarized zone [diː'mɪlɪtəraɪzd-] N zone démilitarisée

demise [dɪ'maɪz] N décès *m*

demist [diː'mɪst] VT (*BRIT Aut*) désembuer

demister [diː'mɪstər] N (*BRIT Aut*) dispositif *m* anti-buée *inv*

demo ['dɛməu] N ABBR (*inf*) = **demonstration**; (*protest*) manif *f*; (*Comput*) démonstration *f*

demobilize [diː'məubɪlaɪz] VT démobiliser

democracy [dɪ'mɒkrəsɪ] N démocratie *f*

democrat ['dɛməkræt] N démocrate *mf*

democratic [dɛmə'krætɪk] ADJ démocratique; **the D~ Party** (*US*) le parti démocrate

demography [dɪ'mɒgrəfɪ] N démographie *f*

demolish [dɪ'mɒlɪʃ] VT démolir

demolition [dɛmə'lɪʃən] N démolition *f*

demon ['diːmən] N démon *m* ▶ CPD: **a ~ squash player** un crack en squash; **a ~ driver** un fou du volant

demonstrate ['dɛmənstreɪt] VT démontrer, prouver; (*show*) faire une démonstration de ▶ VI: **to ~ (for/against)** manifester (en faveur de/contre)

demonstration [dɛmən'streɪʃən] N démonstration *f*; (*Pol etc*) manifestation *f*; **to hold a ~** (*Pol etc*) organiser une manifestation, manifester

demonstrative [dɪ'mɒnstrətɪv] ADJ démonstratif(-ive)

demonstrator ['dɛmənstreɪtər] N (*Pol etc*) manifestant(e); (*Comm: sales person*)

vendeur(-euse); (: *car, computer etc*) modèle *m* de démonstration

demoralize [dɪ'mɒrəlaɪz] VT démoraliser

demote [dɪ'məut] VT rétrograder

demotion [dɪ'məuʃən] N rétrogradation *f*

demur [dɪ'məːr] VI: **to ~ (at sth)** hésiter (devant qch); (*object*) élever des objections (contre qch) ▶ N: **without ~** sans hésiter; sans faire de difficultés

demure [dɪ'mjuər] ADJ sage, réservé(e), d'une modestie affectée

demurrage [dɪ'mʌrɪdʒ] N droits *mpl* de magasinage; surestarie *f*

den [dɛn] N (*of lion*) tanière *f*; (*room*) repaire *m*

denationalization [diːnæʃnəlaɪ'zeɪʃən] N dénationalisation *f*

denationalize [diː'næʃnəlaɪz] VT dénationaliser

denial [dɪ'naɪəl] N (*of accusation*) démenti *m*; (*of rights, guilt, truth*) dénégation *f*

denier ['dɛnɪər] N denier *m*; **15 ~ stockings** bas de 15 deniers

denigrate ['dɛnɪgreɪt] VT dénigrer

denim ['dɛnɪm] N jean *m*; **denims** NPL (blue-)jeans *mpl*

denim jacket N veste *f* en jean

denizen ['dɛnɪzn] N (*inhabitant*) habitant(e); (*foreigner*) étranger(-ère)

Denmark ['dɛnmɑːk] N Danemark *m*

denomination [dɪnɒmɪ'neɪʃən] N (*money*) valeur *f*; (*Rel*) confession *f*; culte *m*

denominator [dɪ'nɒmɪneɪtər] N dénominateur *m*

denote [dɪ'nəut] VT dénoter

denounce [dɪ'nauns] VT dénoncer

dense [dɛns] ADJ dense; (*inf: stupid*) obtus(e), dur(e) or lent(e) à la comprenette

densely ['dɛnslɪ] ADV: **~ wooded** couvert(e) d'épaisses forêts; **~ populated** à forte densité (de population), très peuplé(e)

density ['dɛnsɪtɪ] N densité *f*

dent [dɛnt] N bosse *f* ▶ VT (*also:* **make a dent in**) cabosser; **to make a ~ in** (*fig*) entamer

dental ['dɛntl] ADJ dentaire

dental floss [-flɒs] N fil *m* dentaire

dental surgeon N (chirurgien(ne)) dentiste

dental surgery N cabinet *m* de dentiste

dentist ['dɛntɪst] N dentiste *mf*; **~'s surgery** (*BRIT*) cabinet *m* de dentiste

dentistry ['dɛntɪstrɪ] N art *m* dentaire

dentures ['dɛntʃəz] NPL dentier *msg*

denunciation [dɪnʌnsɪ'eɪʃən] N dénonciation *f*

deny [dɪ'naɪ] VT nier; (*refuse*) refuser; (*disown*) renier; **he denies having said it** il nie l'avoir dit

deodorant [diː'əudərənt] N désodorisant *m*, déodorant *m*

depart [dɪ'pɑːt] VI partir; **to ~ from** (*leave*) quitter, partir de; (*fig: differ from*) s'écarter de

departed [dɪ'pɑːtɪd] ADJ (*dead*) défunt(e); **the (dear) ~** le défunt/la défunte/les défunts

department [dɪ'pɑːtmənt] N (*Comm*) rayon *m*; (*Scol*) section *f*; (*Pol*) ministère *m*, département *m*; **that's not my ~** (*fig*) ce n'est pas mon domaine *or* ma compétence, ce n'est pas mon rayon; **D~ of State** (US) Département d'État

departmental [diːpɑːt'mɛntl] ADJ d'une or de la section; d'un or du ministère, d'un or du département; **~ manager** chef m de service; (in shop) chef de rayon

department store N grand magasin

departure [dɪ'pɑːtʃəʳ] N départ m; (fig): **~ from** écart m par rapport à; **a new ~** une nouvelle voie

departure lounge N salle f de départ

depend [dɪ'pɛnd] VI: **to ~ (up)on** dépendre de; (rely on) compter sur; (financially) dépendre (financièrement) de, être à la charge de; **it depends** cela dépend; **depending on the result …** selon le résultat …

dependable [dɪ'pɛndəbl] ADJ sûr(e), digne de confiance

dependant [dɪ'pɛndənt] N personne f à charge

dependence [dɪ'pɛndəns] N dépendance f

dependent [dɪ'pɛndənt] ADJ: **to be ~ (on)** dépendre (de) ▶ N = **dependant**

depict [dɪ'pɪkt] VT (in picture) représenter; (in words) (dé)peindre, décrire

depilatory [dɪ'pɪlətrɪ] N (also: **depilatory cream**) dépilatoire m, crème f à épiler

depleted [dɪ'pliːtɪd] ADJ (considérablement) réduit(e) or diminué(e)

deplorable [dɪ'plɔːrəbl] ADJ déplorable, lamentable

deplore [dɪ'plɔːʳ] VT déplorer

deploy [dɪ'plɔɪ] VT déployer

depopulate [diː'pɔpjuleɪt] VT dépeupler

depopulation ['diːpɔpjuˈleɪʃən] N dépopulation f, dépeuplement m

deport [dɪ'pɔːt] VT déporter, expulser

deportation [diːpɔːˈteɪʃən] N déportation f, expulsion f

deportation order N arrêté m d'expulsion

deportee [diːpɔːˈtiː] N déporté(e)

deportment [dɪ'pɔːtmənt] N maintien m, tenue f

depose [dɪ'pəuz] VT déposer

deposit [dɪ'pɔzɪt] N (Chem, Comm, Geo) dépôt m; (of ore, oil) gisement m; (part payment) arrhes fpl, acompte m; (on bottle etc) consigne f; (for hired goods etc) cautionnement m, garantie f ▶ VT déposer; (valuables) mettre or laisser en dépôt; **to put down a ~ of £50** verser 50 livres d'arrhes or d'acompte; laisser 50 livres en garantie

deposit account N compte m sur livret

depositor [dɪ'pɔzɪtəʳ] N déposant(e)

depository [dɪ'pɔzɪtərɪ] N (person) dépositaire mf; (place) dépôt m

depot ['dɛpəu] N dépôt m; (US Rail) gare f

depraved [dɪ'preɪvd] ADJ dépravé(e), perverti(e)

depravity [dɪ'prævɪtɪ] N dépravation f

deprecate ['dɛprɪkeɪt] VT désapprouver

deprecating ['dɛprɪkeɪtɪŋ] ADJ (disapproving) désapprobateur(-trice); (apologetic): **a ~ smile** un sourire d'excuse

depreciate [dɪ'priːʃɪeɪt] VT déprécier ▶ VI se déprécier, se dévaloriser

depreciation [dɪpriːʃɪ'eɪʃən] N dépréciation f

depress [dɪ'prɛs] VT déprimer; (press down)

appuyer sur, abaisser; (wages etc) faire baisser

depressant [dɪ'prɛsnt] N (Med) dépresseur m

depressed [dɪ'prɛst] ADJ (person) déprimé(e), abattu(e); (area) en déclin, touché(e) par le sous-emploi; (Comm: market, trade) maussade; **to get ~** se démoraliser, se laisser abattre

depressing [dɪ'prɛsɪŋ] ADJ déprimant(e)

depression [dɪ'prɛʃən] N (Econ) dépression f

deprivation [dɛprɪ'veɪʃən] N privation f; (loss) perte f

deprive [dɪ'praɪv] VT: **to ~ sb of** priver qn de

deprived [dɪ'praɪvd] ADJ déshérité(e)

dept. ABBR (= department) dép, dépt

depth [dɛpθ] N profondeur f; **in the depths of** au fond de; au cœur de; au plus profond de; **to be in the depths of despair** être au plus profond du désespoir; **at a ~ of 3 metres** à 3 mètres de profondeur; **to be out of one's ~** (BRIT: swimmer) ne plus avoir pied; (fig) être dépassé(e), nager; **to study sth in ~** étudier qch en profondeur

depth charge N grenade sous-marine

deputation [dɛpju'teɪʃən] N députation f, délégation f

deputize ['dɛpjutaɪz] VI: **to ~ for** assurer l'intérim de

deputy ['dɛpjutɪ] N (replacement) suppléant(e), intérimaire mf; (second in command) adjoint(e); (Pol) député m; (US: also: **deputy sheriff**) shérif adjoint ▶ ADJ: **~ chairman** vice-président m; **~ head** (Scol) directeur(-trice) adjoint(e), sous-directeur(-trice); **~ leader** (BRIT Pol) vice-président(e), secrétaire adjoint(e)

derail [dɪ'reɪl] VT faire dérailler; **to be derailed** dérailler

derailment [dɪ'reɪlmənt] N déraillement m

deranged [dɪ'reɪndʒd] ADJ: **to be (mentally) ~** avoir le cerveau dérangé

derby ['dəːrbɪ] N (US) (chapeau m) melon m

deregulate [dɪ'rɛgjuleɪt] VT libérer, dérégler

deregulation [dɪrɛgju'leɪʃən] N libération f, dérèglement m

derelict ['dɛrɪlɪkt] ADJ abandonné(e), à l'abandon

deride [dɪ'raɪd] VT railler

derision [dɪ'rɪʒən] N dérision f

derisive [dɪ'raɪsɪv] ADJ moqueur(-euse), railleur(-euse)

derisory [dɪ'raɪsərɪ] ADJ (sum) dérisoire; (smile, person) moqueur(-euse), railleur(-euse)

derivation [dɛrɪ'veɪʃən] N dérivation f

derivative [dɪ'rɪvətɪv] N dérivé m ▶ ADJ dérivé(e)

derive [dɪ'raɪv] VT: **to ~ sth from** tirer qch de; trouver qch dans ▶ VI: **to ~ from** provenir de, dériver de

dermatitis [dəːmə'taɪtɪs] N dermatite f

dermatology [dəːmə'tɔlədʒɪ] N dermatologie f

derogatory [dɪ'rɔgətərɪ] ADJ désobligeant(e), péjoratif(-ive)

derrick ['dɛrɪk] N mât m de charge, derrick m

derv [dəːv] N (BRIT) gas-oil m, diesel m

DES N ABBR (BRIT: = Department of Education and Science) ministère de l'éducation nationale et des sciences

desalination [di:sælɪ'neɪʃən] N dessalement m, dessalage m

descend [dɪ'sɛnd] VT, VI descendre; **to ~ from** descendre de, être issu(e) de; **to ~ to** s'abaisser à; **in descending order of importance** par ordre d'importance décroissante
▶ **descend on** VT FUS (*enemy, angry person*) tomber or sauter sur; (*misfortune*) s'abattre sur; (*gloom, silence*) envahir; **visitors descended (up)on us** des gens sont arrivés chez nous à l'improviste

descendant [dɪ'sɛndənt] N descendant(e)

descent [dɪ'sɛnt] N descente f; (*origin*) origine f

describe [dɪs'kraɪb] VT décrire

description [dɪs'krɪpʃən] N description f; (*sort*) sorte f, espèce f; **of every ~** de toutes sortes

descriptive [dɪs'krɪptɪv] ADJ descriptif(-ive)

desecrate ['dɛsɪkreɪt] VT profaner

desert N [dɛzət] désert m ▶ VT [dɪ'zə:t] déserter, abandonner ▶ VI (*Mil*) déserter

deserted [dɪ'zə:tɪd] ADJ désert(e)

deserter [dɪ'zə:tə'] N déserteur m

desertion [dɪ'zə:ʃən] N désertion f

desert island N île déserte

deserts [dɪ'zə:ts] NPL: **to get one's just ~** n'avoir que ce qu'on mérite

deserve [dɪ'zə:v] VT mériter

deservedly [dɪ'zə:vɪdlɪ] ADV à juste titre, à bon droit

deserving [dɪ'zə:vɪŋ] ADJ (*person*) méritant(e); (*action, cause*) méritoire

desiccated ['dɛsɪkeɪtɪd] ADJ séché(e)

design [dɪ'zaɪn] N (*sketch*) plan m, dessin m; (*layout, shape*) conception f, ligne f; (*pattern*) dessin, motif(s) m(pl); (*of dress, car*) modèle m; (*art*) design m, stylisme m; (*intention*) dessein m ▶ VT dessiner; (*plan*) concevoir; **to have designs on** avoir des visées sur; **well-designed** adj bien conçu(e); **industrial ~** esthétique industrielle

design and technology N (BRIT Scol) technologie f

designate VT ['dɛzɪgneɪt] désigner ▶ ADJ ['dɛzɪgnɪt] désigné(e)

designation [dɛzɪg'neɪʃən] N désignation f

designer [dɪ'zaɪnə'] N (*Archit, Art*) dessinateur(-trice); (*Industry*) concepteur m, designer m; (*Fashion*) styliste mf

desirability [dɪzaɪərə'bɪlɪtɪ] N avantage m; attrait m

desirable [dɪ'zaɪərəbl] ADJ (*property, location, purchase*) attrayant(e); **it is ~ that** il est souhaitable que

desire [dɪ'zaɪə'] N désir m ▶ VT désirer, vouloir; **to ~ to do sth/that** désirer faire qch/que

desirous [dɪ'zaɪərəs] ADJ: **~ of** désireux(-euse) de

desk [dɛsk] N (*in office*) bureau m; (*for pupil*) pupitre m; (BRIT: *in shop, restaurant*) caisse f; (*in hotel, at airport*) réception f

desktop N ADJ de bureau; **~ computer** ordinateur de bureau

desk-top publishing ['dɛsktɔp-] N publication assistée par ordinateur, PAO f

desolate ['dɛsəlɪt] ADJ désolé(e)

desolation [dɛsə'leɪʃən] N désolation f

despair [dɪs'pɛə'] N désespoir m ▶ VI: **to ~ of**

désespérer de; **to be in ~** être au désespoir

despatch [dɪs'pætʃ] N, VT = **dispatch**

desperate ['dɛspərɪt] ADJ désespéré(e); (*fugitive*) prêt(e) à tout; (*measures*) désespéré, extrême; **to be ~ for sth/to do sth** avoir désespérément besoin de qch/de faire qch; **we are getting ~** nous commençons à désespérer

desperately ['dɛspərɪtlɪ] ADV désespérément; (*very*) terriblement, extrêmement; **~ ill** très gravement malade

desperation [dɛspə'reɪʃən] N désespoir m; **in (sheer) ~** en désespoir de cause

despicable [dɪs'pɪkəbl] ADJ méprisable

despise [dɪs'paɪz] VT mépriser, dédaigner

despite [dɪs'paɪt] PREP malgré, en dépit de

despondent [dɪs'pɔndənt] ADJ découragé(e), abattu(e)

despot ['dɛspɔt] N despote mf

dessert [dɪ'zə:t] N dessert m

dessertspoon [dɪ'zə:tspu:n] N cuiller f à dessert

destabilize [di:'steɪbɪlaɪz] VT déstabiliser

destination [dɛstɪ'neɪʃən] N destination f

destine ['dɛstɪn] VT destiner

destined ['dɛstɪnd] ADJ: **to be ~ to do sth** être destiné(e) à faire qch; **~ for London** à destination de Londres

destiny ['dɛstɪnɪ] N destinée f, destin m

destitute ['dɛstɪtju:t] ADJ indigent(e), dans le dénuement; **~ of** dépourvu(e) or dénué(e) de

destroy [dɪs'trɔɪ] VT détruire; (*injured horse*) abattre; (*dog*) faire piquer

destroyer [dɪs'trɔɪə'] N (*Naut*) contre-torpilleur m

destruction [dɪs'trʌkʃən] N destruction f

destructive [dɪs'trʌktɪv] ADJ destructeur(-trice)

desultory ['dɛsəltərɪ] ADJ (*reading, conversation*) décousu(e); (*contact*) irrégulier(-ière)

detach [dɪ'tætʃ] VT détacher

detachable [dɪ'tætʃəbl] ADJ amovible, détachable

detached [dɪ'tætʃt] ADJ (*attitude*) détaché(e)

detached house N pavillon m maison(nette) (individuelle)

detachment [dɪ'tætʃmənt] N (*Mil*) détachement m; (*fig*) détachement, indifférence f

detail ['di:teɪl] N détail m; (*Mil*) détachement m ▶ VT raconter en détail, énumérer; (*Mil*): **to ~ sb (for)** affecter qn (à), détacher qn (pour); **in ~** en détail; **to go into ~(s)** entrer dans les détails

detailed ['di:teɪld] ADJ détaillé(e)

detain [dɪ'teɪn] VT retenir; (*in captivity*) détenir; (*in hospital*) hospitaliser

detainee [di:teɪ'ni:] N détenu(e)

detect [dɪ'tɛkt] VT déceler, percevoir; (*Med, Police*) dépister; (*Mil, Radar, Tech*) détecter

detection [dɪ'tɛkʃən] N découverte f; (*Med, Police*) dépistage m; (*Mil, Radar, Tech*) détection f; **to escape ~** échapper aux recherches, éviter d'être découvert(e); (*mistake*) passer inaperçu(e); **crime ~** le dépistage des criminels

detective [dɪ'tɛktɪv] N agent m de la sûreté, policier m; **private ~** détective privé

detective story N roman policier

detector [dɪ'tɛktə^r] N détecteur m
détente [deɪ'tɑːnt] N détente f
detention [dɪ'tɛnʃən] N détention f; (Scol) retenue f, consigne f
deter [dɪ'tə:^r] VT dissuader
detergent [dɪ'tə:dʒənt] N détersif m, détergent m
deteriorate [dɪ'tɪərɪəreɪt] VI se détériorer, se dégrader
deterioration [dɪtɪərɪə'reɪʃən] N détérioration f
determination [dɪtə:mɪ'neɪʃən] N détermination f
determine [dɪ'tə:mɪn] VT déterminer; **to ~ to do** résoudre de faire, se déterminer à faire
determined [dɪ'tə:mɪnd] ADJ (person) déterminé(e), décidé(e); (quantity) déterminé, établi(e); (effort) très gros(se); **~ to do** bien décidé à faire
deterrence [dɪ'tɛrns] N dissuasion f
deterrent [dɪ'tɛrənt] N effet m de dissuasion; force f de dissuasion; **to act as a ~** avoir un effet dissuasif
detest [dɪ'tɛst] VT détester, avoir horreur de
detestable [dɪ'tɛstəbl] ADJ détestable odieux(-euse)
detonate ['dɛtəneɪt] VI exploser ▶ VT faire exploser or détoner
detonator ['dɛtəneɪtə^r] N détonateur m
detour ['diːtuə^r] N détour m; (US Aut: diversion) déviation f
detox ['diːtɔks] VI se détoxifier; (body) détoxifier ▶ N détox f
detoxification [diːtɔksɪfɪ'keɪʃən] N détox f
detoxify [diː'tɔksɪfaɪ] VI se détoxifier; (body) détoxifier
detract [dɪ'trækt] VT: **to ~ from** (quality, pleasure) diminuer; (reputation) porter atteinte à
detractor [dɪ'træktə^r] N détracteur(-trice)
detriment ['dɛtrɪmənt] N: **to the ~ of** au détriment de, au préjudice de; **without ~ to** sans porter atteinte or préjudice à, sans conséquences fâcheuses pour
detrimental [dɛtrɪ'mɛntl] ADJ: **~ to** préjudiciable or nuisible à
deuce [djuːs] N (Tennis) égalité f
devaluation [dɪvæljuːeɪʃən] N dévaluation f
devalue ['diː'væljuː] VT dévaluer
devastate ['dɛvəsteɪt] VT dévaster; **he was devastated by the news** cette nouvelle lui a porté un coup terrible
devastating ['dɛvəsteɪtɪŋ] ADJ dévastateur(-trice); (news) accablant(e)
devastation [dɛvəs'teɪʃən] N dévastation f
develop [dɪ'vɛləp] VT (gen) développer; (disease) commencer à souffrir de; (habit) contracter; (resources) mettre en valeur, exploiter; (land) aménager ▶ VI se développer; (situation, disease: evolve) évoluer; (facts, symptoms: appear) se manifester, se produire; **can you ~ this film?** pouvez-vous développer cette pellicule?; **to ~ a taste for sth** prendre goût à qch; **to ~ into** devenir
developer [dɪ'vɛləpə^r] N (Phot) révélateur m; (of land) promoteur m; (also: **property developer**)

promoteur immobilier
developing country [dɪ'vɛləpɪŋ-] N pays m en voie de développement
development [dɪ'vɛləpmənt] N développement m; (of land) exploitation f; (new fact, event) rebondissement m, fait(s) nouveau(x)
development area N zone f à urbaniser
deviate ['diːvɪeɪt] VI: **to ~ (from)** dévier (de)
deviation [diːvɪ'eɪʃən] N déviation f
device [dɪ'vaɪs] N (scheme) moyen m, expédient m; (apparatus) appareil m, dispositif m; **explosive ~** engin explosif; **improvised explosive ~** engin explosif improvisé
devil ['dɛvl] N diable m; démon m
devilish ['dɛvlɪʃ] ADJ diabolique
devil-may-care ['dɛvlmeɪ'kɛə^r] ADJ je-m'en-foutiste
devil's advocate N: **to play ~** se faire avocat du diable
devious ['diːvɪəs] ADJ (means) détourné(e); (person) sournois(e), dissimulé(e)
devise [dɪ'vaɪz] VT imaginer, concevoir
devoid [dɪ'vɔɪd] ADJ: **~ of** dépourvu(e) de, dénué(e) de
devolution [diːvə'luːʃən] N (Pol) décentralisation f
devolve [dɪ'vɔlv] VI: **to ~ (up)on** retomber sur
devote [dɪ'vəut] VT: **to ~ sth to** consacrer qch à
devoted [dɪ'vəutɪd] ADJ dévoué(e); **to be ~ to** être dévoué(e) or très attaché(e) à; (book etc) être consacré(e) à
devotee [dɛvəu'tiː] N (Rel) adepte mf; (Mus, Sport) fervent(e)
devotion [dɪ'vəuʃən] N dévouement m, attachement m; (Rel) dévotion f, piété f
devour [dɪ'vauə^r] VT dévorer
devout [dɪ'vaut] ADJ pieux(-euse), dévot(e)
dew [djuː] N rosée f
dexterity [dɛks'tɛrɪtɪ] N dextérité f, adresse f
DfEE N ABBR (BRIT: = Department for Education and Employment) Ministère de l'éducation et de l'emploi
dg ABBR (= decigram) dg
diabetes [daɪə'biːtiːz] N diabète m
diabetic [daɪə'bɛtɪk] N diabétique mf ▶ ADJ (person) diabétique; (chocolate, jam) pour diabétiques
diabolical [daɪə'bɔlɪkl] ADJ diabolique; (inf: dreadful) infernal(e), atroce
diagnose [daɪəg'nəuz] VT diagnostiquer
diagnosis [daɪəg'nəusɪs] (pl **diagnoses** [-siːz]) N diagnostic m
diagonal [daɪ'ægənl] ADJ diagonal(e) ▶ N diagonale f
diagram ['daɪəgræm] N diagramme m, schéma m
dial ['daɪəl] N cadran m ▶ VT (number) faire, composer; **to ~ a wrong number** faire un faux numéro; **can I ~ London direct?** puis-je or est-ce-que je peux avoir Londres par l'automatique?
dial. ABBR = **dialect**
dialect ['daɪəlɛkt] N dialecte m
dialling code ['daɪəlɪŋ-], (US) **dial code** N

indicatif *m* (téléphonique); **what's the ~ for Paris?** quel est l'indicatif de Paris?

dialling tone ['daɪəlɪŋ-], (*US*) **dial tone** N tonalité *f*

dialogue, (*US*) **dialog** ['daɪəlɔg] N dialogue *m*

dialysis [daɪˈælɪsɪs] N dialyse *f*

diameter [daɪˈæmɪtəʳ] N diamètre *m*

diametrically [daɪəˈmetrɪklɪ] ADV: **~ opposed (to)** diamétralement opposé(e) (à)

diamond ['daɪəmənd] N diamant *m*; (*shape*) losange *m*; **diamonds** NPL (*Cards*) carreau *m*

diamond ring N bague *f* de diamant(s)

diaper ['daɪəpəʳ] N (*US*) couche *f*

diaphragm ['daɪəfræm] N diaphragme *m*

diarrhoea, (*US*) **diarrhea** [daɪəˈriːə] N diarrhée *f*

diary ['daɪərɪ] N (*daily account*) journal *m*; (*book*) agenda *m*; **to keep a ~** tenir un journal

diatribe ['daɪətraɪb] N diatribe *f*

dice [daɪs] N (*pl inv*) dé *m* ► VT (*Culin*) couper en dés *or* en cubes

dicey ['daɪsɪ] ADJ (*inf*): **it's a bit ~** c'est un peu risqué

dichotomy [daɪˈkɔtəmɪ] N dichotomie *f*

dickhead ['dɪkhɛd] N (*Brit inf!*) tête *f* de nœud (!)

Dictaphone® ['dɪktəfəun] N Dictaphone® *m*

dictate VT [dɪkˈteɪt] dicter ► VI: **to ~ to** (*person*) imposer sa volonté à, régenter; **I won't be dictated to** je n'ai d'ordres à recevoir de personne ► N ['dɪkteɪt] injonction *f*

dictation [dɪkˈteɪʃən] N dictée *f*; **at ~ speed** à une vitesse de dictée

dictator [dɪkˈteɪtəʳ] N dictateur *m*

dictatorship [dɪkˈteɪtəʃɪp] N dictature *f*

diction ['dɪkʃən] N diction *f*, élocution *f*

dictionary ['dɪkʃənrɪ] N dictionnaire *m*

did [dɪd] PT *of* **do**

didactic [daɪˈdæktɪk] ADJ didactique

didn't ['dɪdnt] = **did not**

die [daɪ] N (*pl dice*) dé *m*; (*pl dies*) coin *m*; matrice *f*; étampe *f* ► VI mourir; **to ~ of** *or* **from** mourir de; **to be dying** être mourant(e); **to be dying for sth** avoir une envie folle de qch; **to be dying to do sth** mourir d'envie de faire qch
  ► **die away** VI s'éteindre
  ► **die down** VI se calmer, s'apaiser
  ► **die out** VI disparaître, s'éteindre

diehard ['daɪhɑːd] N réactionnaire *mf*, jusqu'au-boutiste *mf*

diesel ['diːzl] N (*vehicle*) diesel *m*; (*also*: **diesel oil**) carburant *m* diesel, gas-oil *m*

diesel engine N moteur *m* diesel

diesel fuel, diesel oil N carburant *m* diesel

diet ['daɪət] N alimentation *f*; (*restricted food*) régime *m* ► VI (*also*: **be on a diet**) suivre un régime; **to live on a ~ of** se nourrir de

dietician [daɪəˈtɪʃən] N diététicien(ne)

differ ['dɪfəʳ] VI: **to ~ from sth** (*be different*) être différent(e) de qch, différer de qch; **to ~ from sb over sth** ne pas être d'accord avec qn au sujet de qch

difference ['dɪfrəns] N différence *f*; (*quarrel*) différend *m*, désaccord *m*; **it makes no ~ to me** cela m'est égal, cela m'est indifférent; **to settle one's differences** résoudre la situation

different ['dɪfrənt] ADJ différent(e)

differential [dɪfəˈrɛnʃəl] N (*Aut, wages*) différentiel *m*

differentiate [dɪfəˈrɛnʃɪeɪt] VT différencier ► VI se différencier; **to ~ between** faire une différence entre

differently ['dɪfrəntlɪ] ADV différemment

difficult ['dɪfɪkəlt] ADJ difficile; **to ~ understand** difficile à comprendre

difficulty ['dɪfɪkəltɪ] N difficulté *f*; **to have difficulties with** avoir des ennuis *or* problèmes avec; **to be in ~** avoir des difficultés, avoir des problèmes

diffidence ['dɪfɪdəns] N manque *m* de confiance en soi, manque d'assurance

diffident ['dɪfɪdənt] ADJ qui manque de confiance *or* d'assurance, peu sûr(e) de soi

diffuse ADJ [dɪˈfjuːs] diffus(e) ► VT [dɪˈfjuːz] diffuser, répandre

dig [dɪg] (*pt, pp* **dug** [dʌg]) VT (*hole*) creuser; (*garden*) bêcher ► N (*prod*) coup *m* de coude; (*fig: remark*) coup de griffe *or* de patte; (*Archaeology*) fouille *f*; **to ~ into** (*snow, soil*) creuser; **to ~ into one's pockets for sth** fouiller dans ses poches pour chercher *or* prendre qch; **to ~ one's nails into** enfoncer ses ongles dans
  ► **dig in** VI (*Mil*) se retrancher; (*fig*) tenir bon, se braquer; (*inf: eat*) attaquer (un repas *or* un plat *etc*) ► VT (*compost*) bien mélanger à la bêche; (*knife, claw*) enfoncer; **to ~ in one's heels** (*fig*) se braquer, se buter
  ► **dig out** VT (*survivors, car from snow*) sortir *or* dégager (à coups de pelles *or* pioches)
  ► **dig up** VT déterrer

digest VT [daɪˈdʒɛst] digérer ► N ['daɪdʒɛst] sommaire *m*, résumé *m*

digestible [dɪˈdʒɛstəbl] ADJ digestible

digestion [dɪˈdʒɛstʃən] N digestion *f*

digestive [dɪˈdʒɛstɪv] ADJ digestif(-ive)

digit ['dɪdʒɪt] N (*number*) chiffre *m* (*de 0 à 9*); (*finger*) doigt *m*

digital ['dɪdʒɪtl] ADJ (*system, recording, radio*) numérique, digital(e); (*watch*) à affichage numérique *or* digital

digital camera N appareil *m* photo numérique

digital compact cassette N cassette *f* numérique

digital TV N télévision *f* numérique

dignified ['dɪgnɪfaɪd] ADJ digne

dignitary ['dɪgnɪtərɪ] N dignitaire *m*

dignity ['dɪgnɪtɪ] N dignité *f*

digress [daɪˈgrɛs] VI: **to ~ from** s'écarter de, s'éloigner de

digression [daɪˈgrɛʃən] N digression *f*

digs [dɪgz] NPL (*Brit inf*) piaule *f*, chambre meublée

dilapidated [dɪˈlæpɪdeɪtɪd] ADJ délabré(e)

dilate [daɪˈleɪt] VT dilater ► VI se dilater

dilatory ['dɪlətərɪ] ADJ dilatoire

dilemma [daɪˈlɛmə] N dilemme *m*; **to be in a ~** être pris dans un dilemme

diligent ['dɪlɪdʒənt] ADJ appliqué(e), assidu(e)

dill [dɪl] N aneth *m*

dilly-dally ['dɪlɪ'dælɪ] VI hésiter, tergiverser;

traînasser, lambiner

dilute [daɪˈluːt] VT diluer ▸ ADJ dilué(e)

dim [dɪm] ADJ (*light, eyesight*) faible; (*memory, outline*) vague, indécis(e); (*room*) sombre; (*inf: stupid*) borné(e), obtus(e) ▸ VT (*light*) réduire, baisser; (*US Aut*) mettre en code, baisser; **to take a ~ view of sth** voir qch d'un mauvais œil

dime [daɪm] N (*US*) pièce f de 10 cents

dimension [daɪˈmɛnʃən] N dimension f

-dimensional [dɪˈmɛnʃənl] ADJ SUFFIX: **two~** à deux dimensions

diminish [dɪˈmɪnɪʃ] VT, VI diminuer

diminished [dɪˈmɪnɪʃt] ADJ: **~ responsibility** (*Law*) responsabilité atténuée

diminutive [dɪˈmɪnjutɪv] ADJ minuscule, tout(e) petit(e) ▸ N (*Ling*) diminutif m

dimly [ˈdɪmlɪ] ADV faiblement; vaguement

dimmer [ˈdɪməʳ] N (*also*: **dimmer switch**) variateur m; **dimmers** NPL (*US Aut*: dipped headlights) phares mpl, code inv; (*parking lights*) feux mpl de position

dimple [ˈdɪmpl] N fossette f

dim-witted [ˈdɪmˈwɪtɪd] ADJ (*inf*) stupide, borné(e)

din [dɪn] N vacarme m ▸ VT: **to ~ sth into sb** (*inf*) enfoncer qch dans la tête or la caboche de qn

dine [daɪn] VI dîner

diner [ˈdaɪnəʳ] N (*person*) dîneur(-euse); (*Rail*) = **dining car**; (*US: eating place*) petit restaurant

dinghy [ˈdɪŋgɪ] N youyou m; (*inflatable*) canot m pneumatique; (*also*: **sailing dinghy**) voilier m, dériveur m

dingy [ˈdɪndʒɪ] ADJ miteux(-euse), minable

dining car [ˈdaɪnɪŋ-] N (*Brit*) voiture-restaurant f, wagon-restaurant m

dining room [ˈdaɪnɪŋ-] N salle f à manger

dining table [ˈdaɪnɪŋ-] N table f de (la) salle à manger

dinkum [ˈdɪŋkʌm] ADJ (*Australia, New Zealand inf*) vrai(e); **fair ~** vrai(e)

dinner [ˈdɪnəʳ] N (*evening meal*) dîner m; (*lunch*) déjeuner m; (*public*) banquet m; **~'s ready!** à table!

dinner jacket N smoking m

dinner party N dîner m

dinner time N (*evening*) heure f du dîner; (*midday*) heure du déjeuner

dinosaur [ˈdaɪnəsɔːʳ] N dinosaure m

dint [dɪnt] N: **by ~ of (doing) sth** à force de (faire) qch

diocese [ˈdaɪəsɪs] N diocèse m

dioxide [daɪˈɔksaɪd] N dioxyde m

dip [dɪp] N (*slope*) déclivité f; (*in sea*) baignade f, bain m; (*Culin*) ≈ sauce f ▸ VT tremper, plonger; (*Brit Aut*: *lights*) mettre en code, baisser ▸ VI plonger

Dip. ABBR (*Brit*) = **diploma**

diphtheria [dɪfˈθɪərɪə] N diphtérie f

diphthong [ˈdɪfθɔŋ] N diphtongue f

diploma [dɪˈpləumə] N diplôme m

diplomacy [dɪˈpləuməsɪ] N diplomatie f

diplomat [ˈdɪpləmæt] N diplomate m

diplomatic [dɪpləˈmætɪk] ADJ diplomatique; **to break off ~ relations (with)** rompre les relations diplomatiques (avec)

diplomatic corps N corps m diplomatique

diplomatic immunity N immunité f diplomatique

dipstick [ˈdɪpstɪk] N (*Brit Aut*) jauge f de niveau d'huile

dipswitch [ˈdɪpswɪtʃ] N (*Brit Aut*) commutateur m de code

dire [daɪəʳ] ADJ (*poverty*) extrême; (*awful*) affreux(-euse)

direct [daɪˈrɛkt] ADJ direct(e); (*manner, person*) direct, franc (franche) ▸ VT (*tell way*) diriger, orienter; (*letter, remark*) adresser; (*Cine, TV*) réaliser; (*Theat*) mettre en scène; (*order*): **to ~ sb to do sth** ordonner à qn de faire qch ▸ ADV directement; **can you ~ me to …?** pouvez-vous m'indiquer le chemin de …?

direct cost N (*Comm*) coût m variable

direct current N (*Elec*) courant continu

direct debit N (*Brit Banking*) prélèvement m automatique

direct dialling N (*Tel*) automatique m

direct hit N (*Mil*) coup m au but, touché m

direction [dɪˈrɛkʃən] N direction f; (*Theat*) mise f en scène; (*Cine, TV*) réalisation f; **directions** NPL (*to a place*) indications fpl; **directions for use** mode m d'emploi; **to ask for directions** demander sa route or son chemin; **sense of ~** sens m de l'orientation; **in the ~ of** dans la direction de, vers

directive [dɪˈrɛktɪv] N directive f; **a government ~** une directive du gouvernement

direct labour N main-d'œuvre directe; employés municipaux

directly [dɪˈrɛktlɪ] ADV (*in straight line*) directement, tout droit; (*at once*) tout de suite, immédiatement

direct mail N vente f par publicité directe

direct mailshot N (*Brit*) publicité postale

directness [daɪˈrɛktnɪs] N (*of person, speech*) franchise f

director [dɪˈrɛktəʳ] N directeur m; (*board member*) administrateur m; (*Theat*) metteur m en scène; (*Cine, TV*) réalisateur(-trice); **D~ of Public Prosecutions** (*Brit*) ≈ procureur général

directory [dɪˈrɛktərɪ] N annuaire m; (*also*: **street directory**) indicateur m de rues; (*also*: **trade directory**) annuaire du commerce; (*Comput*) répertoire m

directory enquiries, (*US*) **directory assistance** N (*Tel: service*) renseignements mpl

dirt [dəːt] N saleté f; (*mud*) boue f; **to treat sb like ~** traiter qn comme un chien

dirt-cheap [ˈdəːtˈtʃiːp] ADJ (ne) coûtant presque rien

dirt road N chemin non macadamisé or non revêtu

dirty [ˈdəːtɪ] ADJ sale; (*joke*) cochon(ne) ▸ VT salir; **~ story** histoire cochonne; **~ trick** coup tordu

disability [dɪsəˈbɪlɪtɪ] N invalidité f, infirmité f

disability allowance N allocation f d'invalidité or d'infirmité

disable [dɪsˈeɪbl] VT (*illness, accident*) rendre or

laisser infirme; *(tank, gun)* mettre hors d'action

disabled [dɪs'eɪbld] ADJ handicapé(e); *(maimed)* mutilé(e); *(through illness, old age)* impotent(e)

disadvantage [dɪsəd'vɑ:ntɪdʒ] N désavantage *m*, inconvénient *m*

disadvantaged [dɪsəd'vɑ:ntɪdʒd] ADJ *(person)* désavantagé(e)

disadvantageous [dɪsædvɑ:n'teɪdʒəs] ADJ désavantageux(-euse)

disaffected [dɪsə'fɛktɪd] ADJ: ~ **(to** or **towards)** mécontent(e) (de)

disaffection [dɪsə'fɛkʃən] N désaffection *f*, mécontentement *m*

disagree [dɪsə'gri:] VI *(differ)* ne pas concorder; *(be against, think otherwise)*: **to ~ (with)** ne pas être d'accord (avec); **garlic disagrees with me** l'ail ne me convient pas, je ne supporte pas l'ail

disagreeable [dɪsə'gri:əbl] ADJ désagréable

disagreement [dɪsə'gri:mənt] N désaccord *m*, différend *m*

disallow ['dɪsə'lau] VT rejeter, désavouer; *(Brit Football: goal)* refuser

disappear [dɪsə'pɪəʳ] VI disparaître

disappearance [dɪsə'pɪərəns] N disparition *f*

disappoint [dɪsə'pɔɪnt] VT décevoir

disappointed [dɪsə'pɔɪntɪd] ADJ déçu(e)

disappointing [dɪsə'pɔɪntɪŋ] ADJ décevant(e)

disappointment [dɪsə'pɔɪntmənt] N déception *f*

disapproval [dɪsə'pru:vəl] N désapprobation *f*

disapprove [dɪsə'pru:v] VI: **to ~ of** désapprouver

disapproving [dɪsə'pru:vɪŋ] ADJ désapprobateur(-trice), de désapprobation

disarm [dɪs'ɑ:m] VT désarmer

disarmament [dɪs'ɑ:məmənt] N désarmement *m*

disarming [dɪs'ɑ:mɪŋ] ADJ *(smile)* désarmant(e)

disarray [dɪsə'reɪ] N désordre *m*, confusion *f*; **in ~** *(troops)* en déroute; *(thoughts)* embrouillé(e); *(clothes)* en désordre; **to throw into ~** semer la confusion or le désordre dans (or parmi)

disaster [dɪ'zɑ:stəʳ] N catastrophe *f*, désastre *m*

disastrous [dɪ'zɑ:strəs] ADJ désastreux(-euse)

disband [dɪs'bænd] VT démobiliser; disperser ▶ VI se séparer, se disperser

disbelief ['dɪsbə'li:f] N incrédulité *f*; **in ~** avec incrédulité

disbelieve ['dɪsbə'li:v] VT *(person)* ne pas croire; *(story)* mettre en doute; **I don't ~ you** je veux bien vous croire

disc [dɪsk] N disque *m*; *(Comput)* = **disk**

disc. ABBR *(Comm)* = **discount**

discard [dɪs'kɑ:d] VT *(old things)* se débarrasser de, mettre au rencart or au rebut; *(fig)* écarter, renoncer à

disc brake N frein *m* à disque

discern [dɪ'sə:n] VT discerner, distinguer

discernible [dɪ'sə:nəbl] ADJ discernable, perceptible; *(object)* visible

discerning [dɪ'sə:nɪŋ] ADJ judicieux(-euse), perspicace

discharge VT [dɪs'tʃɑ:dʒ] *(duties)* s'acquitter de; *(settle: debt)* s'acquitter de, régler; *(waste etc)* déverser; décharger; *(Elec, Med)* émettre; *(patient)* renvoyer (chez lui); *(employee, soldier)*

congédier, licencier; *(defendant)* relaxer, élargir ▶ N ['dɪstʃɑ:dʒ] *(Elec, Med)* émission *f*; *(also:* **vaginal discharge)** pertes blanches; *(dismissal)* renvoi *m*, licenciement *m*, élargissement *m*; **to ~ one's gun** faire feu; **discharged bankrupt** failli(e), réhabilité(e)

disciple [dɪ'saɪpl] N disciple *m*

disciplinary ['dɪsɪplɪnərɪ] ADJ disciplinaire; **to take ~ action against sb** prendre des mesures disciplinaires à l'encontre de qn

discipline ['dɪsɪplɪn] N discipline *f* ▶ VT discipliner; *(punish)* punir; **to ~ o.s. to do sth** s'imposer or s'astreindre à une discipline pour faire qch

disc jockey N disque-jockey *m* (DJ)

disclaim [dɪs'kleɪm] VT désavouer, dénier

disclaimer [dɪs'kleɪməʳ] N démenti *m*, dénégation *f*; **to issue a ~** publier un démenti

disclose [dɪs'kləuz] VT révéler, divulguer

disclosure [dɪs'kləuʒəʳ] N révélation *f*, divulgation *f*

disco ['dɪskəu] N ABBR discothèque *f*

discolour, *(US)* **discolor** [dɪs'kʌləʳ] VT décolorer; *(sth white)* jaunir ▶ VI se décolorer; jaunir

discolouration, *(US)* **discoloration** [dɪskʌlə'reɪʃən] N décoloration *f*; jaunissement *m*

discoloured, *(US)* **discolored** [dɪs'kʌləd] ADJ décoloré(e), jauni(e)

discomfort [dɪs'kʌmfət] N malaise *m*, gêne *f*; *(lack of comfort)* manque *m* de confort

disconcert [dɪskən'sə:t] VT déconcerter, décontenancer

disconnect [dɪskə'nɛkt] VT détacher; *(Elec, Radio)* débrancher; *(gas, water)* couper

disconnected [dɪskə'nɛktɪd] ADJ *(speech, thoughts)* décousu(e), peu cohérent(e)

disconsolate [dɪs'kɔnsəlɪt] ADJ inconsolable

discontent [dɪskən'tɛnt] N mécontentement *m*

discontented [dɪskən'tɛntɪd] ADJ mécontent(e)

discontinue [dɪskən'tɪnju:] VT cesser, interrompre; **"discontinued"** *(Comm)* "fin de série"

discord ['dɪskɔ:d] N discorde *f*, dissension *f*; *(Mus)* dissonance *f*

discordant [dɪs'kɔ:dənt] ADJ discordant(e), dissonant(e)

discount N ['dɪskaunt] remise *f*, rabais *m* ▶ VT [dɪs'kaunt] *(report etc)* ne pas tenir compte de; **to give sb a ~ on sth** faire une remise or un rabais à qn sur qch; **~ for cash** escompte *f* au comptant; **at a ~** avec une remise or réduction, au rabais

discount house N *(Finance)* banque *f* d'escompte; *(Comm: also:* **discount store)** magasin *m* de discount

discount rate N taux *m* de remise

discourage [dɪs'kʌrɪdʒ] VT décourager; *(dissuade, deter)* dissuader, décourager

discouragement [dɪs'kʌrɪdʒmənt] N *(depression)* découragement *m*; **to act as a ~ to sb** dissuader qn

discouraging [dɪs'kʌrɪdʒɪŋ] ADJ décourageant(e)

discourteous [dɪs'kəːtɪəs] ADJ incivil(e), discourtois(e)

discover [dɪs'kʌvəʳ] VT découvrir

discovery [dɪs'kʌvərɪ] N découverte f

discredit [dɪs'krɛdɪt] VT (idea) mettre en doute; (person) discréditer ▶ N discrédit m

discreet [dɪ'skriːt] ADJ discret(-ète)

discreetly [dɪ'skriːtlɪ] ADV discrètement

discrepancy [dɪ'skrɛpənsɪ] N divergence f, contradiction f

discretion [dɪ'skrɛʃən] N discrétion f; **at the ~ of** à la discrétion de; **use your own ~** à vous de juger

discretionary [dɪ'skrɛʃənrɪ] ADJ (powers) discrétionnaire

discriminate [dɪ'skrɪmɪneɪt] VI: **to ~ between** établir une distinction entre, faire la différence entre; **to ~ against** pratiquer une discrimination contre

discriminating [dɪ'skrɪmɪneɪtɪŋ] ADJ qui a du discernement

discrimination [dɪskrɪmɪ'neɪʃən] N discrimination f; (judgment) discernement m; **racial/sexual ~** discrimination raciale/ sexuelle

discus ['dɪskəs] N disque m

discuss [dɪ'skʌs] VT discuter de; (debate) discuter

discussion [dɪ'skʌʃən] N discussion f; **under ~** en discussion

disdain [dɪs'deɪn] N dédain m

disease [dɪ'ziːz] N maladie f

diseased [dɪ'ziːzd] ADJ malade

disembark [dɪsɪm'baːk] VT, VI débarquer

disembarkation [dɪsɛmbaː'keɪʃən] N débarquement m

disembodied ['dɪsɪm'bɔdɪd] ADJ désincarné(e)

disembowel ['dɪsɪm'bauəl] VT éviscérer, étriper

disenchanted ['dɪsɪn'tʃaːntɪd] ADJ: **~ (with)** désenchanté(e) (de), désabusé(e) (de)

disenfranchise ['dɪsɪn'fræntʃaɪz] VT priver du droit de vote; (Comm) retirer la franchise à

disengage [dɪsɪn'geɪdʒ] VT dégager; (Tech) déclencher; **to ~ the clutch** (Aut) débrayer

disentangle [dɪsɪn'tæŋgl] VT démêler

disfavour, (US) **disfavor** [dɪs'feɪvəʳ] N défaveur f; disgrâce f

disfigure [dɪs'fɪgəʳ] VT défigurer

disgorge [dɪs'gɔːdʒ] VT déverser

disgrace [dɪs'greɪs] N honte f; (disfavour) disgrâce f ▶ VT déshonorer, couvrir de honte

disgraceful [dɪs'greɪsful] ADJ scandaleux(-euse), honteux(-euse)

disgruntled [dɪs'grʌntld] ADJ mécontent(e)

disguise [dɪs'gaɪz] N déguisement m ▶ VT déguiser; (voice) déguiser, contrefaire; (feelings etc) masquer, dissimuler; **in ~** déguisé(e); **to ~ o.s. as** se déguiser en; **there's no disguising the fact that …** on ne peut pas se dissimuler que …

disgust [dɪs'gʌst] N dégoût m, aversion f ▶ VT dégoûter, écœurer

disgusted [dɪs'gʌstɪd] ADJ dégoûté(e), écœuré(e)

disgusting [dɪs'gʌstɪŋ] ADJ dégoûtant(e), révoltant(e)

dish [dɪʃ] N plat m; **to do** or **wash the dishes** faire la vaisselle
▶ **dish out** VT distribuer
▶ **dish up** VT servir; (facts, statistics) sortir, débiter

dishcloth ['dɪʃklɔθ] N (for drying) torchon m; (for washing) lavette f

dishearten [dɪs'haːtn] VT décourager

dishevelled, (US) **disheveled** [dɪ'ʃɛvəld] ADJ ébouriffé(e), décoiffé(e), débraillé(e)

dishonest [dɪs'ɔnɪst] ADJ malhonnête

dishonesty [dɪs'ɔnɪstɪ] N malhonnêteté f

dishonour, (US) **dishonor** [dɪs'ɔnəʳ] N déshonneur m

dishonourable, (US) **dishonorable** [dɪs'ɔnərəbl] ADJ déshonorant(e)

dish soap N (US) produit m pour la vaisselle

dishtowel ['dɪʃtauəl] N (US) torchon m (à vaisselle)

dishwasher ['dɪʃwɔʃəʳ] N lave-vaisselle m; (person) plongeur(-euse)

dishy ['dɪʃɪ] ADJ (BRIT inf) séduisant(e), sexy inv

disillusion [dɪsɪ'luːʒən] VT désabuser, désenchanter ▶ N désenchantement m; **to become disillusioned (with)** perdre ses illusions (en ce qui concerne)

disillusionment [dɪsɪ'luːʒənmənt] N désillusionnement m, désillusion f

disincentive [dɪsɪn'sɛntɪv] N: **it's a ~** c'est démotivant; **to be a ~ to sb** démotiver qn

disinclined ['dɪsɪn'klaɪnd] ADJ: **to be ~ to do sth** être peu disposé(e) or peu enclin(e) à faire qch

disinfect [dɪsɪn'fɛkt] VT désinfecter

disinfectant [dɪsɪn'fɛktənt] N désinfectant m

disinflation [dɪsɪn'fleɪʃən] N désinflation f

disinformation [dɪsɪnfə'meɪʃən] N désinformation f

disinherit [dɪsɪn'hɛrɪt] VT déshériter

disintegrate [dɪs'ɪntɪgreɪt] VI se désintégrer

disinterested [dɪs'ɪntrəstɪd] ADJ désintéressé(e)

disjointed [dɪs'dʒɔɪntɪd] ADJ décousu(e), incohérent(e)

disk [dɪsk] N (Comput) disquette f; **single-/ double-sided ~** disquette une face/double face

disk drive N lecteur m de disquette

diskette [dɪs'kɛt] N (Comput) disquette f

disk operating system N système m d'exploitation à disques

dislike [dɪs'laɪk] N aversion f, antipathie f ▶ VT ne pas aimer; **to take a ~ to sb/sth** prendre qn/ qch en grippe; **I ~ the idea** l'idée me déplaît

dislocate ['dɪsləkeɪt] VT disloquer, déboîter; (services etc) désorganiser; **he has dislocated his shoulder** il s'est disloqué l'épaule

dislodge [dɪs'lɔdʒ] VT déplacer, faire bouger; (enemy) déloger

disloyal [dɪs'lɔɪəl] ADJ déloyal(e)

dismal ['dɪzml] ADJ (gloomy) lugubre, maussade; (very bad) lamentable

dismantle [dɪs'mæntl] VT démonter; (fort, warship) démanteler

dismast [dɪs'maːst] VT démâter

dismay [dɪs'meɪ] N consternation f ▶ VT consterner; **much to my ~** à ma grande consternation, à ma grande inquiétude

dismiss [dɪsˈmɪs] vt congédier, renvoyer; *(idea)* écarter; *(Law)* rejeter ▸ vi *(Mil)* rompre les rangs

dismissal [dɪsˈmɪsl] N renvoi *m*

dismount [dɪsˈmaunt] vi mettre pied à terre

disobedience [dɪsəˈbiːdɪəns] N désobéissance *f*

disobedient [dɪsəˈbiːdɪənt] ADJ désobéissant(e), indiscipliné(e)

disobey [dɪsəˈbeɪ] vt désobéir à; *(rule)* transgresser, enfreindre

disorder [dɪsˈɔːdəʳ] N désordre *m*; *(rioting)* désordres *mpl*; *(Med)* troubles *mpl*

disorderly [dɪsˈɔːdəlɪ] ADJ *(room)* en désordre; *(behaviour, retreat, crowd)* désordonné(e)

disorderly conduct N *(Law)* conduite *f* contraire aux bonnes mœurs

disorganized [dɪsˈɔːgənaɪzd] ADJ désorganisé(e)

disorientated [dɪsˈɔːrɪenteɪtɪd] ADJ désorienté(e)

disown [dɪsˈəun] vt renier

disparaging [dɪsˈpærɪdʒɪŋ] ADJ désobligeant(e); **to be ~ about sb/sth** faire des remarques désobligeantes sur qn/qch

disparate [ˈdɪspərɪt] ADJ disparate

disparity [dɪsˈpærɪtɪ] N disparité *f*

dispassionate [dɪsˈpæʃənət] ADJ calme, froid(e), impartial(e), objectif(-ive)

dispatch [dɪsˈpætʃ] vt expédier, envoyer; *(deal with: business)* régler, en finir avec ▸ N envoi *m*, expédition *f*; *(Mil, Press)* dépêche *f*

dispatch department N service *m* des expéditions

dispatch rider N *(Mil)* estafette *f*

dispel [dɪsˈpɛl] vt dissiper, chasser

dispensary [dɪsˈpɛnsərɪ] N pharmacie *f*; *(in chemist's)* officine *f*

dispense [dɪsˈpɛns] vt distribuer, administrer; *(medicine)* préparer (et vendre); **to ~ sb from** dispenser qn de
▸ **dispense with** vt FUS se passer de; *(make unnecessary)* rendre superflu(e)

dispenser [dɪsˈpɛnsəʳ] N *(device)* distributeur *m*

dispensing chemist [dɪsˈpɛnsɪŋ-] N *(BRIT)* pharmacie *f*

dispersal [dɪsˈpəːsl] N dispersion *f*; *(Admin)* déconcentration *f*

disperse [dɪsˈpəːs] vt disperser; *(knowledge)* disséminer ▸ vi se disperser

dispirited [dɪsˈpɪrɪtɪd] ADJ découragé(e), déprimé(e)

displace [dɪsˈpleɪs] vt déplacer

displaced person [dɪsˈpleɪst-] N *(Pol)* personne déplacée

displacement [dɪsˈpleɪsmənt] N déplacement *m*

display [dɪsˈpleɪ] N *(of goods)* étalage *m*; affichage *m*; *(Comput: information)* visualisation *f*; *(: device)* visuel *m*; *(of feeling)* manifestation *f*; *(pej)* ostentation *f*; *(show, spectacle)* spectacle *m*; *(military display)* parade *f* militaire ▸ vt montrer; *(goods)* mettre à l'étalage, exposer; *(results, departure times)* afficher; *(pej)* faire étalage de; **on ~** *(exhibits)* exposé(e), exhibé(e); *(goods)* à l'étalage

display advertising N publicité rédactionnelle

displease [dɪsˈpliːz] vt mécontenter, contrarier; **displeased with** mécontent(e) de

displeasure [dɪsˈplɛʒəʳ] N mécontentement *m*

disposable [dɪsˈpəuzəbl] ADJ *(pack etc)* jetable; *(income)* disponible; **~ nappy** *(BRIT)* couche *f* à jeter, couche-culotte *f*

disposal [dɪsˈpəuzl] N *(of rubbish)* évacuation *f*, destruction *f*; *(of property etc: by selling)* vente *f*; *(: by giving away)* cession *f*; *(availability, arrangement)* disposition *f*; **at one's ~** à sa disposition; **to put sth at sb's ~** mettre qch à la disposition de qn

dispose [dɪsˈpəuz] vt disposer ▸ vi: **to ~ of** *(time, money)* disposer de; *(unwanted goods)* se débarrasser de, se défaire de; *(Comm: stock)* écouler, vendre; *(problem)* expédier

disposed [dɪsˈpəuzd] ADJ: **~ to do** disposé(e) à faire

disposition [dɪspəˈzɪʃən] N disposition *f*; *(temperament)* naturel *m*

dispossess [ˈdɪspəˈzɛs] vt: **to ~ sb (of)** déposséder qn (de)

disproportion [dɪsprəˈpɔːʃən] N disproportion *f*

disproportionate [dɪsprəˈpɔːʃənət] ADJ disproportionné(e)

disprove [dɪsˈpruːv] vt réfuter

dispute [dɪsˈpjuːt] N discussion *f*; *(also: industrial dispute)* conflit *m* ▸ vt *(question)* contester; *(matter)* discuter; *(victory)* disputer; **to be in** or **under ~** *(matter)* être en discussion; *(territory)* être contesté(e)

disqualification [dɪskwɔlɪfɪˈkeɪʃən] N disqualification *f*; **~ (from driving)** *(BRIT)* retrait *m* du permis (de conduire)

disqualify [dɪsˈkwɔlɪfaɪ] vt *(Sport)* disqualifier; **to ~ sb for sth/from doing** *(status, situation)* rendre qn inapte à qch/à faire; *(authority)* signifier à qn l'interdiction de qch/de faire; **to ~ sb (from driving)** *(BRIT)* retirer à qn son permis (de conduire)

disquiet [dɪsˈkwaɪət] N inquiétude *f*, trouble *m*

disquieting [dɪsˈkwaɪətɪŋ] ADJ inquiétant(e), alarmant(e)

disregard [dɪsrɪˈgɑːd] vt ne pas tenir compte de ▸ N: **~ (for)** *(feelings)* indifférence *f* (pour), insensibilité *f* (à); *(danger, money)* mépris *m* (pour)

disrepair [ˈdɪsrɪˈpɛəʳ] N mauvais état; **to fall into ~** *(building)* tomber en ruine; *(street)* se dégrader

disreputable [dɪsˈrɛpjutəbl] ADJ *(person)* de mauvaise réputation, peu recommandable; *(behaviour)* déshonorant(e); *(area)* mal famé(e), louche

disrepute [ˈdɪsrɪˈpjuːt] N déshonneur *m*, discrédit *m*; **to bring into ~** faire tomber dans le discrédit

disrespectful [dɪsrɪˈspɛktful] ADJ irrespectueux(-euse)

disrupt [dɪsˈrʌpt] vt *(plans, meeting, lesson)* perturber, déranger

disruption [dɪsˈrʌpʃən] N perturbation *f*, dérangement *m*

disruptive [dɪs'rʌptɪv] ADJ perturbateur(-trice)
dissatisfaction [dɪssætɪs'fækʃən] N
mécontentement *m*, insatisfaction *f*
dissatisfied [dɪs'sætɪsfaɪd] ADJ: ~ **(with)**
insatisfait(e) (de)
dissect [dɪ'sɛkt] VT disséquer; (*fig*) disséquer,
éplucher
disseminate [dɪ'sɛmɪneɪt] VT disséminer
dissent [dɪ'sɛnt] N dissentiment *m*, différence *f*
d'opinion
dissenter [dɪ'sɛntər] N (*Rel, Pol etc*) dissident(e)
dissertation [dɪsə'teɪʃən] N (*Scol*) mémoire *m*
disservice [dɪs'sə:vɪs] N: **to do sb a ~** rendre un
mauvais service à qn; desservir qn
dissident ['dɪsɪdnt] ADJ, N dissident(e)
dissimilar [dɪ'sɪmɪlər] ADJ: ~ **(to)** dissemblable
(à), différent(e) (de)
dissipate ['dɪsɪpeɪt] VT dissiper; (*energy, efforts*)
disperser
dissipated ['dɪsɪpeɪtɪd] ADJ dissolu(e),
débauché(e)
dissociate [dɪ'səuʃɪeɪt] VT dissocier; **to ~ o.s.
from** se désolidariser de
dissolute ['dɪsəluːt] ADJ débauché(e), dissolu(e)
dissolve [dɪ'zɔlv] VT dissoudre ▶ VI se dissoudre,
fondre; (*fig*) disparaître; **to ~ in(to) tears**
fondre en larmes
dissuade [dɪ'sweɪd] VT: **to ~ sb (from)** dissuader
qn (de)
distance ['dɪstns] N distance *f*; **what's the ~ to
London?** à quelle distance se trouve Londres?;
it's within walking ~ on peut y aller à pied; **in
the ~** au loin
distant ['dɪstnt] ADJ lointain(e), éloigné(e);
(*manner*) distant(e), froid(e)
distaste [dɪs'teɪst] N dégoût *m*
distasteful [dɪs'teɪstful] ADJ déplaisant(e),
désagréable
Dist. Atty. ABBR (*US*) = **district attorney**
distemper [dɪs'tɛmpər] N (*paint*) détrempe *f*,
badigeon *m*; (*of dogs*) maladie *f* de Carré
distended [dɪs'tɛndɪd] ADJ (*stomach*) dilaté(e)
distil, (*US*) **distill** [dɪs'tɪl] VT distiller
distillery [dɪs'tɪləri] N distillerie *f*
distinct [dɪs'tɪŋkt] ADJ distinct(e); (*clear*)
marqué(e); **as ~ from** par opposition à, en
contraste avec
distinction [dɪs'tɪŋkʃən] N distinction *f*; (*in
exam*) mention *f* très bien; **to draw a ~ between**
faire une distinction entre; **a writer of ~** un
écrivain réputé
distinctive [dɪs'tɪŋktɪv] ADJ distinctif(-ive)
distinctly [dɪs'tɪŋktlɪ] ADV distinctement;
(*specify*) expressément
distinguish [dɪs'tɪŋgwɪʃ] VT distinguer
▶ VI: **to ~ between** (*concepts*) distinguer entre,
faire une distinction entre; **to ~ o.s.** se
distinguer
distinguished [dɪs'tɪŋgwɪʃt] ADJ (*eminent, refined*)
distingué(e); (*career*) remarquable, brillant(e)
distinguishing [dɪs'tɪŋgwɪʃɪŋ] ADJ (*feature*)
distinctif(-ive), caractéristique
distort [dɪs'tɔːt] VT déformer
distortion [dɪs'tɔːʃən] N déformation *f*

distract [dɪs'trækt] VT distraire, déranger
distracted [dɪs'træktɪd] ADJ (*not concentrating*)
distrait(e); (*worried*) affolé(e)
distraction [dɪs'trækʃən] N distraction *f*,
dérangement *m*; **to drive sb to ~** rendre qn
fou (folle)
distraught [dɪs'trɔːt] ADJ éperdu(e)
distress [dɪs'trɛs] N détresse *f*; (*pain*) douleur *f*
▶ VT affliger; **in ~** (*ship*) en perdition; (*plane*)
en détresse; **distressed area** (*BRIT*) zone
sinistrée
distressing [dɪs'trɛsɪŋ] ADJ douloureux(-euse),
pénible, affligeant(e)
distress signal N signal *m* de détresse
distribute [dɪs'trɪbjuːt] VT distribuer
distribution [dɪstrɪ'bjuːʃən] N distribution *f*
distribution cost N coût *m* de distribution
distributor [dɪs'trɪbjutər] N (*gen: Tech*)
distributeur *m*; (*Comm*) concessionnaire *mf*
district ['dɪstrɪkt] N (*of country*) région *f*; (*of town*)
quartier *m*; (*Admin*) district *m*
district attorney N (*US*) ≈ procureur *m* de la
République
district council N (*BRIT*) ≈ conseil municipal;
voir article

> En Grande-Bretagne, un *district council* est
> une administration locale qui gère un
> *district*. Les conseillers (*councillors*) sont élus
> au niveau local, en général tous les 4 ans.
> Le *district council* est financé par des impôts
> locaux et par des subventions du
> gouvernement.

district nurse N (*BRIT*) infirmière visiteuse
distrust [dɪs'trʌst] N méfiance *f*, doute *m* ▶ VT se
méfier de
distrustful [dɪs'trʌstful] ADJ méfiant(e)
disturb [dɪs'tə:b] VT troubler; (*inconvenience*)
déranger; **sorry to ~ you** excusez-moi de vous
déranger
disturbance [dɪs'tə:bəns] N dérangement *m*;
(*political etc*) troubles *mpl*; (*by drunks etc*) tapage *m*;
to cause a ~ troubler l'ordre public; **~ of the
peace** (*Law*) tapage injurieux *or* nocturne
disturbed [dɪs'tə:bd] ADJ (*worried, upset*) agité(e),
troublé(e); **to be emotionally ~** avoir des
problèmes affectifs
disturbing [dɪs'tə:bɪŋ] ADJ troublant(e),
inquiétant(e)
disuse [dɪs'juːs] N: **to fall into ~** tomber en
désuétude
disused [dɪs'juːzd] ADJ désaffecté(e)
ditch [dɪtʃ] N fossé *m*; (*for irrigation*) rigole *f* ▶ VT
(*inf*) abandonner; (*person*) plaquer
dither ['dɪðər] VI hésiter
ditto ['dɪtəu] ADV idem
divan [dɪ'væn] N divan *m*
divan bed N divan-lit *m*
dive [daɪv] N plongeon *m*; (*of submarine*) plongée
f; (*Aviat*) piqué *m*; (*pej: café, bar etc*) bouge *m* ▶ VI
plonger; **to ~ into** (*bag etc*) plonger la main
dans; (*place*) se précipiter dans
diver ['daɪvər] N plongeur *m*
diverge [daɪ'və:dʒ] VI diverger
diverse [daɪ'və:s] ADJ divers(e)

diversification – do

diversification [daɪvəːsɪfɪˈkeɪʃən] N
diversification f
diversify [daɪˈvəːsɪfaɪ] VT diversifier
diversion [daɪˈvəːʃən] N (BRIT Aut) déviation f;
(distraction, Mil) diversion f
diversionary tactics [daɪˈvəːʃənrɪ-] NPL
tactique fsg de diversion
diversity [daɪˈvəːsɪtɪ] N diversité f, variété f
divert [daɪˈvəːt] VT (BRIT: traffic) dévier; (plane)
dérouter; (train, river) détourner; (amuse) divertir
divest [daɪˈvɛst] VT: **to ~ sb of** dépouiller qn de
divide [dɪˈvaɪd] VT diviser; (separate) séparer ▸ VI
se diviser; **to ~ (between** or **among)** répartir or
diviser (entre); **40 divided by 5** 40 divisé par 5
▸ **divide out** VT: **to ~ out (between** or **among)**
distribuer or répartir (entre)
divided [dɪˈvaɪdɪd] ADJ (fig: country, couple)
désuni(e); (opinions) partagé(e)
divided highway N (US) route f à quatre voies
divided skirt N jupe-culotte f
dividend [ˈdɪvɪdɛnd] N dividende m
dividend cover N rapport m dividendes-
résultat
dividers [dɪˈvaɪdəz] NPL compas m à pointes
sèches; (between pages) feuillets mpl intercalaires
divine [dɪˈvaɪn] ADJ divin(e) ▸ VT (future) prédire;
(truth) deviner, entrevoir; (water, metal) détecter
la présence de (par l'intermédiaire de la radiesthésie)
diving [ˈdaɪvɪŋ] N plongée (sous-marine)
diving board N plongeoir m
diving suit N scaphandre m
divinity [dɪˈvɪnɪtɪ] N divinité f; (as study)
théologie f
division [dɪˈvɪʒən] N division f; (BRIT Football)
division f; (separation) séparation f; (Comm)
service m; (BRIT Pol) vote m; (also: **division of
labour**) division du travail
divisive [dɪˈvaɪsɪv] ADJ qui entraîne la division,
qui crée des dissensions
divorce [dɪˈvɔːs] N divorce m ▸ VT divorcer d'avec
divorced [dɪˈvɔːst] ADJ divorcé(e)
divorcee [dɪvɔːˈsiː] N divorcé(e)
divot [ˈdɪvət] N (Golf) motte f de gazon
divulge [daɪˈvʌldʒ] VT divulguer, révéler
DIY ADJ, N ABBR (BRIT) = **do-it-yourself**
dizziness [ˈdɪzɪnɪs] N vertige m,
étourdissement m
dizzy [ˈdɪzɪ] ADJ (height) vertigineux(-euse); **to
make sb ~** donner le vertige à qn; **I feel ~** la tête
me tourne, j'ai la tête qui tourne
DJ N ABBR = **disc jockey**
d.j. N ABBR = **dinner jacket**
Djakarta [dʒəˈkɑːtə] N Djakarta
DJIA N ABBR (US Stock Exchange) = **Dow-Jones
Industrial Average**
dl ABBR (= decilitre) dl
DLit, DLitt N ABBR (= Doctor of Literature, Doctor of
Letters) titre universitaire
DMus N ABBR (= Doctor of Music) titre universitaire
DMZ N ABBR = **demilitarized zone**
DNA N ABBR (= deoxyribonucleic acid) ADN m
DNA fingerprinting [-ˈfɪŋɡəprɪntɪŋ] N
technique f des empreintes génétiques

(KEYWORD)

do [duː] (pt **did**, pp **done**) N (inf: party etc) soirée f,
fête f; (: formal gathering) réception f
▸ AUX VB **1** (in negative constructions) non traduit; **I
don't understand** je ne comprends pas
2 (to form questions) non traduit; **didn't you know?**
vous ne le saviez pas?; **what do you think?**
qu'en pensez-vous?; **why didn't you come?**
pourquoi n'êtes-vous pas venu?
3 (for emphasis: in polite expressions): **people do
make mistakes sometimes** on peut toujours
se tromper; **she does seem rather late** je
trouve qu'elle est bien en retard; **do sit down/
help yourself** asseyez-vous/servez-vous je vous
en prie; **do take care!** faites bien attention à
vous!; **I DO wish I could go** j'aimerais tant y
aller; **but I DO like it!** mais si, je l'aime!
4 (used to avoid repeating vb): **she swims better
than I do** elle nage mieux que moi; **do you
agree? — yes, I do/no I don't** vous êtes
d'accord? — oui/non; **she lives in Glasgow —
so do I** elle habite Glasgow — moi aussi; **he
didn't like it and neither did we** il n'a pas
aimé ça, et nous non plus; **who broke it? — I
did** qui l'a cassé? — c'est moi; **he asked me to
help him and I did** il m'a demandé de l'aider,
et c'est ce que j'ai fait
5 (in question tags): **you like him, don't you?**
vous l'aimez bien, n'est-ce pas?; **he laughed,
didn't he?** il a ri, n'est-ce pas?; **I don't know
him, do I?** je ne crois pas le connaître
▸ VT **1** (gen: carry out, perform etc) faire; (: visit: city,
museum) faire, visiter; **what are you doing
tonight?** qu'est-ce que vous faites ce soir?;
what do you do? (job) que faites-vous dans la
vie?; **what did he do with the cat?** qu'a-t-il
fait du chat?; **what can I do for you?** que
puis-je faire pour vous?; **to do the cooking/
washing-up** faire la cuisine/la vaisselle; **to do
one's teeth/hair/nails** se brosser les dents/se
coiffer/se faire les ongles
2 (Aut etc: distance) faire; (: speed) faire du; **we've
done 200 km already** nous avons déjà fait 200
km; **the car was doing 100** la voiture faisait
du 100 (à l'heure); **he can do 100 in that car** il
peut faire du 100 (à l'heure) dans cette
voiture-là
▸ VI **1** (act, behave) faire; **do as I do** faites comme
moi
2 (get on, fare) marcher; **the firm is doing well**
l'entreprise marche bien; **he's doing well/
badly at school** ça marche bien/mal pour lui à
l'école; **how do you do?** comment allez-vous?;
(on being introduced) enchanté(e)!
3 (suit) aller; **will it do?** est-ce que ça ira?
4 (be sufficient) suffire, aller; **will £10 do?** est-ce
que 10 livres suffiront?; **that'll do** ça suffit, ça
ira; **that'll do!** (in annoyance) ça va or suffit
comme ça!; **to make do (with)** se contenter
(de)
▸ **do away with** VT FUS abolir; (inf: kill)
supprimer
▸ **do for** VT FUS (BRIT inf: clean for) faire le
ménage chez

▶**do up** VT (*laces, dress*) attacher; (*buttons*) boutonner; (*zip*) fermer; (*renovate: room*) refaire; (: *house*) remettre à neuf; **to do o.s. up** se faire beau (belle)

▶**do with** VT FUS (*need*): **I could do with a drink/some help** quelque chose à boire/un peu d'aide ne serait pas de refus; **it could do with a wash** ça ne lui ferait pas de mal d'être lavé; (*be connected with*): **that has nothing to do with you** cela ne vous concerne pas; **I won't have anything to do with it** je ne veux pas m'en mêler; **what has that got to do with it?** quel est le rapport?, qu'est-ce que cela vient faire là-dedans?

▶**do without** VI s'en passer; **if you're late for tea then you'll do without** si vous êtes en retard pour le dîner il faudra vous en passer
▶VT FUS se passer de; **I can do without a car** je peux me passer de voiture

do. ABBR (= *ditto*) d

DOA ABBR (= *dead on arrival*) décédé(e) à l'admission

d.o.b. ABBR = **date of birth**

doc [dɔk] N (*inf*) toubib *m*

docile ['dəʊsaɪl] ADJ docile

dock [dɔk] N dock *m*; (*wharf*) quai *m*; (*Law*) banc *m* des accusés ▶VI se mettre à quai; (*Space*) s'arrimer ▶VT: **they docked a third of his wages** ils lui ont retenu *or* décompté un tiers de son salaire; **docks** NPL (*Naut*) docks

dock dues NPL droits *mpl* de bassin

docker ['dɔkə']ʳ N docker *m*

docket ['dɔkɪt] N bordereau *m*; (*on parcel etc*) étiquette *f or* fiche *f* (*décrivant le contenu d'un paquet etc*)

dockyard ['dɔkjɑːd] N chantier *m* de construction navale

doctor ['dɔktə']ʳ N médecin *m*, docteur *m*; (*PhD etc*) docteur ▶VT (*cat*) couper; (*interfere with: food*) altérer; (: *drink*) frelater; (: *text, document*) arranger; **~'s office** (*US*) cabinet *m* de consultation; **call a ~!** appelez un docteur *or* un médecin!

doctorate ['dɔktərɪt] N doctorat *m*; *voir article*

> Le *doctorate* est le diplôme universitaire le plus prestigieux. Il est le résultat d'au minimum trois années de recherche et est accordé après soutenance d'une thèse devant un jury. Le *doctorat* le plus courant est le *PhD* (Doctor of Philosophy), accordé en lettres, en sciences et en ingénierie, bien qu'il existe également d'autres doctorats spécialisés (en musique, en droit, etc); voir *Bachelor's degree*, *Master's degree*

Doctor of Philosophy N (*degree*) doctorat *m*; (*person*) titulaire *mf* d'un doctorat

docudrama ['dɔkjudrɑːmə] N (*TV*) docudrame *m*

document ['dɔkjumənt] N document *m* ▶VT ['dɔkjument] documenter

documentary [dɔkju'mɛntərɪ] ADJ, N documentaire (*m*)

documentation [dɔkjumən'teɪʃən] N documentation *f*

DOD N ABBR (*US*) = **Department of Defense**

doddering ['dɔdərɪŋ] ADJ (*senile*) gâteux(-euse)

doddery ['dɔdərɪ] ADJ branlant(e)

doddle ['dɔdl] N: **it's a ~** (*inf*) c'est simple comme bonjour, c'est du gâteau

Dodecanese [dəʊdɪkə'niːz] N, **Dodecanese Islands** NPL Dodécanèse *m*

dodge [dɔdʒ] N truc *m*; combine *f* ▶VT esquiver, éviter ▶VI faire un saut de côté; (*Sport*) faire une esquive; **to ~ out of the way** s'esquiver; **to ~ through the traffic** se faufiler *or* faire de savantes manœuvres entre les voitures

Dodgems® ['dɔdʒəmz] NPL (*BRIT*) autos tamponneuses

dodgy ['dɔdʒɪ] ADJ (*BRIT inf: uncertain*) douteux(-euse); (: *shady*) louche

DOE N ABBR (*BRIT*) = **Department of the Environment**; (*US*) = **Department of Energy**

doe [dəʊ] N (*deer*) biche *f*; (*rabbit*) lapine *f*

does [dʌz] VB *see* **do**

doesn't ['dʌznt]= **does not**

dog [dɔg] N chien(ne) *f* ▶VT (*follow closely*) suivre de près, ne pas lâcher d'une semelle; (*fig: memory etc*) poursuivre, harceler; **to go to the dogs** (*nation etc*) aller à vau-l'eau

dog biscuits NPL biscuits *mpl* pour chien

dog collar N collier *m* de chien; (*fig*) faux-col *m* d'ecclésiastique

dog-eared ['dɔgɪəd] ADJ corné(e)

dog food N nourriture *f* pour les chiens *or* le chien

dogged ['dɔgɪd] ADJ obstiné(e), opiniâtre

doggy ['dɔgɪ] N (*inf*) toutou *m*

doggy bag ['dɔgɪ-] N petit sac pour emporter les restes

dogma ['dɔgmə] N dogme *m*

dogmatic [dɔg'mætɪk] ADJ dogmatique

do-gooder [duː'gʊdə']ʳ N (*pej*) faiseur(-euse) de bonnes œuvres

dogsbody ['dɔgzbɔdɪ] N (*BRIT*) bonne *f* à tout faire, tâcheron *m*

doily ['dɔɪlɪ] N dessus *m* d'assiette

doing ['duːɪŋ] N: **this is your ~** c'est votre travail, c'est vous qui avez fait ça

doings ['duːɪŋz] NPL activités *fpl*

do-it-yourself ['duːɪtjɔː'sɛlf] N bricolage *m*

doldrums ['dɔldrəmz] NPL: **to be in the ~** avoir le cafard; être dans le marasme

dole [dəʊl] N (*BRIT: payment*) allocation *f* de chômage; **on the ~** au chômage
▶**dole out** VT donner au compte-goutte

doleful ['dəʊlful] ADJ triste, lugubre

doll [dɔl] N poupée *f*
▶**doll up** VT: **to ~ o.s. up** se faire beau (belle)

dollar ['dɔlə']ʳ N dollar *m*

dollop ['dɔləp] N (*of butter, cheese*) bon morceau; (*of cream*) bonne cuillerée

dolly ['dɔlɪ] N poupée *f*

dolphin ['dɔlfɪn] N dauphin *m*

domain [də'meɪn] N (*also fig*) domaine *m*

dome [dəʊm] N dôme *m*

domestic [də'mɛstɪk] ADJ (*duty, happiness*) familial(e); (*policy, affairs, flight*) intérieur(e); (*news*) national(e); (*animal*) domestique

d

domesticated [dəˈmɛstɪkeɪtɪd] ADJ
domestiqué(e); (pej) d'intérieur; **he's very ~** il
participe volontiers aux tâches ménagères;
question ménage, il est très organisé
domesticity [dəʊmɛsˈtɪsɪtɪ] N vie f de famille
domestic servant N domestique mf
domicile [ˈdɒmɪsaɪl] N domicile m
dominant [ˈdɒmɪnənt] ADJ dominant(e)
dominate [ˈdɒmɪneɪt] VT dominer
domination [dɒmɪˈneɪʃən] N domination f
domineering [dɒmɪˈnɪərɪŋ] ADJ
dominateur(-trice), autoritaire
Dominican Republic [dəˈmɪnɪkən-] N
République Dominicaine
dominion [dəˈmɪnɪən] N domination f;
territoire m; dominion m
domino [ˈdɒmɪnəʊ] (pl **dominoes**) N domino m
dominoes [ˈdɒmɪnəʊz] N (game) dominos mpl
don [dɒn] N (BRIT) professeur m d'université
▶ VT revêtir
donate [dəˈneɪt] VT faire don de, donner
donation [dəˈneɪʃən] N donation f, don m
done [dʌn] PP of **do**
dongle [ˈdɒŋgl] N (Comput) dongle m
donkey [ˈdɒŋkɪ] N âne m
donkey-work [ˈdɒŋkɪwəːk] N (BRIT inf) le gros du
travail, le plus dur (du travail)
donor [ˈdəʊnəʳ] N (of blood etc) donneur(-euse);
(to charity) donateur(-trice)
donor card N carte f de don d'organes
don't [dəʊnt] = **do not**
donut [ˈdəʊnʌt] (US) N = **doughnut**
doodle [ˈduːdl] N griffonnage m, gribouillage m
▶ VI griffonner, gribouiller
doom [duːm] N (fate) destin m; (ruin) ruine f
▶ VT: **to be doomed to failure** être voué(e) à
l'échec
doomsday [ˈduːmzdeɪ] N le Jugement dernier
door [dɔːʳ] N porte f; (Rail, car) portière f; **to go
from ~ to ~** aller de porte en porte
doorbell [ˈdɔːbɛl] N sonnette f
door handle N poignée f de porte; (of car)
poignée de portière
doorknob [ˈdɔːnɒb] N poignée f or bouton m de
porte
doorman [ˈdɔːmən] N (irreg) (in hotel) portier m;
(in block of flats) concierge m
doormat [ˈdɔːmæt] N paillasson m
doorpost [ˈdɔːpəʊst] N montant m de porte
doorstep [ˈdɔːstɛp] N pas m de (la) porte, seuil m
door-to-door [ˈdɔːtəˈdɔːʳ] ADJ: **~ selling** vente f à
domicile
doorway [ˈdɔːweɪ] N (embrasure f de) porte f
dope [dəʊp] N (inf: drug) drogue f; (: person)
andouille f; (: information) tuyaux mpl, rancards
mpl ▶ VT (horse etc) doper
dopey [ˈdəʊpɪ] ADJ (inf) à moitié endormi(e)
dormant [ˈdɔːmənt] ADJ assoupi(e), en
veilleuse; (rule, law) inappliqué(e)
dormer [ˈdɔːməʳ] N (also: **dormer window**)
lucarne f
dormice [ˈdɔːmaɪs] NPL of **dormouse**
dormitory [ˈdɔːmɪtrɪ] N (BRIT) dortoir m; (US:
hall of residence) résidence f universitaire

dormouse [ˈdɔːmaʊs] (pl **dormice** [-maɪs]) N
loir m
DOS [dɒs] N ABBR (= disk operating system) DOS m
dosage [ˈdəʊsɪdʒ] N dose f; dosage m; (on label)
posologie f
dose [dəʊs] N dose f; (BRIT: bout) attaque f ▶ VT:
to ~ o.s. se bourrer de médicaments; **a ~ of flu**
une belle or bonne grippe
dosh [dɒʃ] N (inf) fric m
dosser [ˈdɒsəʳ] N (BRIT inf) clochard(e)
doss house [ˈdɒs-] N (BRIT) asile m de nuit
DOT N ABBR (US) = **Department of
Transportation**
dot [dɒt] N point m; (on material) pois m ▶ VT:
dotted with parsemé(e) de; **on the ~** à l'heure
tapante
dotcom N point com m, pointcom m
dot command N (Comput) commande précédée
d'un point
dote [dəʊt]: **to ~ on** vt fus être fou (folle) de
dot-matrix printer [dɒtˈmeɪtrɪks-] N
imprimante matricielle
dotted line [ˈdɒtɪd-] N ligne pointillée; (Aut)
ligne discontinue; **to sign on the ~** signer à
l'endroit indiqué or sur la ligne pointillée; (fig)
donner son consentement
dotty [ˈdɒtɪ] ADJ (inf) loufoque, farfelu(e)
double [ˈdʌbl] ADJ double ▶ ADV (fold) en deux;
(twice): **to cost ~ (sth)** coûter le double (de qch)
or deux fois plus (que qch) ▶ N double m; (Cine)
doublure f ▶ VT doubler; (fold) plier en deux ▶ VI
doubler; (have two uses): **to ~ as** servir aussi de;
~ five two six (5526) (BRIT Tel) cinquante-cinq –
vingt-six; **it's spelt with a ~ "l"** ça s'écrit avec
deux "l"; **on the ~, at the ~** au pas de course
▶ **double back** VI (person) revenir sur ses pas
▶ **double up** VI (bend over) se courber, se plier;
(share room) partager la chambre
double bass N contrebasse f
double bed N grand lit
double-breasted [ˈdʌblˈbrɛstɪd] ADJ croisé(e)
double-check [ˈdʌblˈtʃɛk] VT, VI revérifier
double-click [ˈdʌblˈklɪk] VI (Comput) double-
cliquer
double-clutch [ˈdʌblˈklʌtʃ] VI (US) faire un
double débrayage
double cream N (BRIT) crème fraîche épaisse
double-cross [ˈdʌblˈkrɒs] VT doubler, trahir
double-decker [ˈdʌblˈdɛkəʳ] N autobus m à
impériale
double declutch VI (BRIT) faire un double
débrayage
double exposure N (Phot) surimpression f
double glazing N (BRIT) double vitrage m
double-page [ˈdʌblpeɪdʒ] ADJ: **~ spread**
publicité f en double page
double parking N stationnement m en double
file
double room N chambre f pour deux
doubles [ˈdʌblz] N (Tennis) double m
double whammy [-ˈwæmɪ] N (inf) double
contretemps m
double yellow lines NPL (BRIT Aut) double bande
jaune marquant l'interdiction de stationner

doubly ['dʌblɪ] ADV doublement, deux fois plus
doubt [daut] N doute m ▶ VT douter de; **no ~** sans doute; **without (a) ~** sans aucun doute; **beyond ~** adv indubitablement; **adj** indubitable; **I - it very much** j'en doute fort; **to ~ that** douter que + sub
doubtful ['dautful] ADJ douteux(-euse); (person) incertain(e); **to be ~ about sth** avoir des doutes sur qch, ne pas être convaincu de qch; **I'm a bit ~** je n'en suis pas certain or sûr
doubtless ['dautlɪs] ADV sans doute, sûrement
dough [dəu] N pâte f; (inf: money) fric m, pognon m
doughnut, (US) **donut** ['dəunʌt] N beignet m
dour [duə^r] ADJ austère
douse [dauz] VT (with water) tremper, inonder; (flames) éteindre
dove [dʌv] N colombe f
Dover ['dəuvə^r] N Douvres
dovetail ['dʌvteɪl] N: ~ **joint** assemblage m à queue d'aronde ▶ VI (fig) concorder
dowager ['dauədʒə^r] N douairière f
dowdy ['daudɪ] ADJ démodé(e), mal fagoté(e)
Dow-Jones average ['dau'dʒəunz-] N (US) indice m Dow-Jones
down [daun] N (fluff) duvet m; (hill) colline (dénudée) ▶ ADV en bas, vers le bas; (on the ground) par terre ▶ PREP en bas de; (along) le long de ▶ VT (enemy) abattre; (inf: drink) siffler; **to fall ~** tomber; **she's going ~ to Bristol** elle descend à Bristol; **to write sth ~** écrire qch; **~ there** là-bas (en bas), là au fond; **~ here** ici en bas; **the price of meat is ~** le prix de la viande a baissé; **I've got it ~ in my diary** c'est inscrit dans mon agenda; **to pay £2 ~** verser 2 livres d'arrhes or en acompte; **England is two goals ~** l'Angleterre a deux buts de retard; **to walk ~ a hill** descendre une colline; **to run ~ the street** descendre la rue en courant; **to ~ tools** (BRIT) cesser le travail; **~ with X!** à bas X!
down-and-out ['daunəndaut] N (tramp) clochard(e)
down-at-heel ['daunət'hi:l] ADJ (fig) miteux(-euse)
downbeat ['daunbi:t] N (Mus) temps frappé ▶ ADJ sombre, négatif(-ive)
downcast ['daunka:st] ADJ démoralisé(e)
downer ['daunə^r] N (inf: drug) tranquillisant m; **to be on a ~** (depressed) flipper
downfall ['daunfɔ:l] N chute f; ruine f
downgrade ['daungreɪd] VT déclasser
downhearted ['daun'hɑ:tɪd] ADJ découragé(e)
downhill ['daun'hɪl] ADV (face, look) en aval, vers l'aval; (roll, go) vers le bas, en bas ▶ N (Ski: also: **downhill race**) descente f; **to go ~** descendre; (business) péricliter, aller à vau-l'eau
Downing Street ['daunɪŋ-] N (BRIT): **10 ~** résidence du Premier ministre; voir article

> Downing Street est une rue de Westminster (à Londres) où se trouvent la résidence officielle du Premier ministre et celle du ministre des Finances. Le nom Downing Street est souvent utilisé pour désigner le gouvernement britannique.

download ['daunləud] N téléchargement m ▶ VT (Comput) télécharger
downloadable [daun'ləudəbl] ADJ (Comput) téléchargeable
down-market ['daun'mɑ:kɪt] ADJ (product) bas de gamme inv
down payment N acompte m
downplay ['daunpleɪ] VT (US) minimiser (l'importance de)
downpour ['daunpɔ:^r] N pluie torrentielle, déluge m
downright ['daunraɪt] ADJ (lie etc) effronté(e); (refusal) catégorique
Downs [daunz] NPL (BRIT): **the ~** collines crayeuses du sud-est de l'Angleterre
downsize [daun'saɪz] VT réduire l'effectif de
Down's syndrome [daunz-] N mongolisme m, trisomie f; **a ~ baby** un bébé mongolien or trisomique
downstairs ['daun'stɛəz] ADV (on or to ground floor) au rez-de-chaussée; (on or to floor below) à l'étage inférieur; **to come ~, to go ~** descendre (l'escalier)
downstream ['daunstri:m] ADV en aval
downtime ['dauntaɪm] N (of machine etc) temps mort; (of person) temps d'arrêt
down-to-earth ['dauntu'ə:θ] ADJ terre à terre inv
downtown ['daun'taun] ADV en ville ▶ ADJ (US): **~ Chicago** le centre commerçant de Chicago
downtrodden ['dauntrɔdn] ADJ opprimé(e)
down under ADV en Australie or Nouvelle Zélande
downward ['daunwəd] ADJ, ADV vers le bas; **a ~ trend** une tendance à la baisse, une diminution progressive
downwards ['daunwədz] ADV vers le bas
dowry ['dauɪ] N dot f
doz. ABBR = **dozen**
doze [dəuz] VI sommeiller ▶ **doze off** VI s'assoupir
dozen ['dʌzn] N douzaine f; **a ~ books** une douzaine de livres; **80p a ~** 80p la douzaine; **dozens of** des centaines de
DPh, DPhil N ABBR (= Doctor of Philosophy) titre universitaire
DPP N ABBR (BRIT) = **Director of Public Prosecutions**
DPT N ABBR (Med: = diphtheria, pertussis, tetanus) DCT m
DPW N ABBR (US) = **Department of Public Works**
dr ABBR (Comm) = **debtor**
Dr. ABBR (= doctor) Dr; (in street names) = **drive**
drab [dræb] ADJ terne, morne
draft [drɑ:ft] N (of letter, school work) brouillon m; (of literary work) ébauche f; (of contract, document) version f préliminaire; (Comm) traite f; (US Mil) contingent m; (: call-up) conscription f ▶ VT faire le brouillon de; (document, report) rédiger une version préliminaire de; (Mil: send) détacher; see also **draught**
drag [dræg] VT traîner; (river) draguer ▶ VI traîner ▶ N (Aviat, Naut) résistance f; (inf) casse-pieds mf; (: women's clothing): **in ~** (en)

travesti; **to ~ and drop** (*Comput*) glisser-poser
▶ **drag away** VT: **to ~ away (from)** arracher or emmener de force (de)
▶ **drag on** VI s'éterniser
dragnet ['drægnɛt] N drège f; (*fig*) piège m, filets mpl
dragon ['drægn] N dragon m
dragonfly ['drægənflaɪ] N libellule f
dragoon [drə'gu:n] N (*cavalryman*) dragon m
▶ VT: **to ~ sb into doing sth** (*BRIT*) forcer qn à faire qch
drain [dreɪn] N égout m; (*on resources*) saignée f
▶ VT (*land, marshes*) drainer, assécher; (*vegetables*) égoutter; (*reservoir etc*) vider ▶ VI (*water*) s'écouler; **to feel drained (of energy** or **emotion)** être miné(e)
drainage ['dreɪnɪdʒ] N (*system*) système m d'égouts; (*act*) drainage m
draining board ['dreɪnɪŋ-], (*US*) **drainboard** ['dreɪnbɔ:d] N égouttoir m
drainpipe ['dreɪnpaɪp] N tuyau m d'écoulement
drake [dreɪk] N canard m (mâle)
dram [dræm] N petit verre
drama ['drɑ:mə] N (*art*) théâtre m, art m dramatique; (*play*) pièce f; (*event*) drame m
dramatic [drə'mætɪk] ADJ (*Theat*) dramatique; (*impressive*) spectaculaire
dramatically [drə'mætɪklɪ] ADV de façon spectaculaire
dramatist ['dræmətɪst] N auteur m dramatique
dramatize ['dræmətaɪz] VT (*events etc*) dramatiser; (*adapt*) adapter pour la télévision (or pour l'écran)
drank [dræŋk] PT of **drink**
drape [dreɪp] VT draper; **drapes** NPL (*US*) rideaux mpl
draper ['dreɪpər] N (*BRIT*) marchand(e) de nouveautés
drastic ['dræstɪk] ADJ (*measures*) d'urgence, énergique; (*change*) radical(e)
drastically ['dræstɪklɪ] ADV radicalement
draught, (*US*) **draft** [drɑ:ft] N courant m d'air; (*of chimney*) tirage m; (*Naut*) tirant m d'eau; **on ~** (*beer*) à la pression
draught beer N bière f (à la) pression
draughtboard ['drɑ:ftbɔ:d] N (*BRIT*) damier m
draughts [drɑ:fts] N (*BRIT*: *game*) (jeu m de) dames fpl
draughtsman, (*US*) **draftsman** ['drɑ:ftsmən] N (*irreg*) dessinateur(-trice) (industriel(le))
draughtsmanship, (*US*) **draftsmanship** ['drɑ:ftsmənʃɪp] N (*technique*) dessin industriel; (*art*) graphisme m
draw [drɔ:] (*vb*: *pt* **drew** [dru:], *pp* **drawn** [drɔ:n]) VT tirer; (*picture*) dessiner; (*attract*) attirer; (*line, circle*) tracer; (*money*) retirer; (*wages*) toucher; (*comparison, distinction*): **to ~ (between)** faire (entre) ▶ VI (*Sport*) faire match nul; (*move, come*): **to ~ to a close** toucher à or tirer à sa fin; **to ~ near** s'approcher; approcher ▶ N match nul; (*lottery*) loterie f; (*picking of ticket*) tirage m au sort
▶ **draw back** VI (*move back*): **to ~ back (from)** reculer (de)
▶ **draw in** VI (*BRIT*: *car*) s'arrêter le long du

trottoir; (*train*) entrer en gare or dans la station
▶ **draw on** VT (*resources*) faire appel à; (*imagination, person*) avoir recours à, faire appel à
▶ **draw out** VI (*lengthen*) s'allonger ▶ VT (*money*) retirer
▶ **draw up** VI (*stop*) s'arrêter ▶ VT (*document*) établir, dresser; (*plan*) formuler, dessiner; (*chair*) approcher
drawback ['drɔ:bæk] N inconvénient m, désavantage m
drawbridge ['drɔ:brɪdʒ] N pont-levis m
drawee [drɔ:'i:] N tiré m
drawer [drɔ:r] N tiroir m; ['drɔ:ər] (*of cheque*) tireur m
drawing ['drɔ:ɪŋ] N dessin m
drawing board N planche f à dessin
drawing pin N (*BRIT*) punaise f
drawing room N salon m
drawl [drɔ:l] N accent traînant
drawn [drɔ:n] PP of **draw** ▶ ADJ (*haggard*) tiré(e), crispé(e)
drawstring ['drɔ:strɪŋ] N cordon m
dread [drɛd] N épouvante f, effroi m ▶ VT redouter, appréhender
dreadful ['drɛdful] ADJ épouvantable, affreux(-euse)
dream [dri:m] (*pt*, *pp* **dreamed** or **dreamt** [drɛmt]) N rêve m ▶ VT, VI rêver; **to have a ~ about sb/sth** rêver à qn/qch; **sweet dreams!** faites de beaux rêves!
▶ **dream up** VT inventer
dreamer ['dri:mər] N rêveur(-euse)
dreamt [drɛmt] PT, PP of **dream**
dreamy ['dri:mɪ] ADJ (*absent-minded*) rêveur(-euse)
dreary ['drɪərɪ] ADJ triste; monotone
dredge [drɛdʒ] VT draguer
▶ **dredge up** VT draguer; (*fig*: *unpleasant facts*) (faire) ressortir
dredger ['drɛdʒər] N (*ship*) dragueur m; (*machine*) drague f; (*BRIT*: *also*: **sugar dredger**) saupoudreuse f
dregs [drɛgz] NPL lie f
drench [drɛntʃ] VT tremper; **drenched to the skin** trempé(e) jusqu'aux os
dress [drɛs] N robe f; (*clothing*) habillement m, tenue f ▶ VT habiller; (*wound*) panser; (*food*) préparer ▶ VI: **she dresses very well** elle s'habille très bien; **to ~ o.s.,** **to get dressed** s'habiller; **to ~ a shop window** faire l'étalage or la vitrine
▶ **dress up** VI s'habiller; (*in fancy dress*) se déguiser
dress circle N (*BRIT*) premier balcon
dress designer N modéliste mf, dessinateur(-trice) de mode
dresser ['drɛsər] N (*Theat*) habilleur(-euse); (*also*: **window dresser**) étalagiste mf; (*furniture*) vaisselier m; (: *US*) coiffeuse f, commode f
dressing ['drɛsɪŋ] N (*Med*) pansement m; (*Culin*) sauce f, assaisonnement m
dressing gown N (*BRIT*) robe f de chambre
dressing room N (*Theat*) loge f; (*Sport*) vestiaire m

dressing table N coiffeuse f
dressmaker ['drɛsmeɪkə^r] N couturière f
dressmaking ['drɛsmeɪkɪŋ] N couture f;
travaux mpl de couture
dress rehearsal N (répétition f) générale f
dress shirt N chemise f à plastron
dressy ['drɛsɪ] ADJ (inf: clothes) (qui fait)
habillé(e)
drew [druː] PT of **draw**
dribble ['drɪbl] VI tomber goutte à goutte; (baby)
baver ▶ VT (ball) dribbler
dried [draɪd] ADJ (fruit, beans) sec (sèche); (eggs,
milk) en poudre
drier ['draɪə^r] N = **dryer**
drift [drɪft] N (of current etc) force f; direction f;
(of sand etc) amoncellement m; (of snow) rafale f;
coulée f; (on ground) congère f; (general meaning)
sens général ▶ VI (boat) aller à la dérive, dériver;
(sand, snow) s'amonceler, s'entasser; **to let
things ~** laisser les choses aller à la dérive; **to ~
apart** (friends, lovers) s'éloigner l'un de l'autre;
I get or **catch your ~** je vois en gros ce que vous
voulez dire
drifter ['drɪftə^r] N personne f sans but dans la vie
driftwood ['drɪftwud] N bois flotté
drill [drɪl] N perceuse f; (bit) foret m; (of dentist)
roulette f, fraise f; (Mil) exercice m ▶ VT percer;
(troops) entraîner; (pupils: in grammar) faire faire
des exercices à ▶ VI (for oil) faire un or des
forage(s)
drilling ['drɪlɪŋ] N (for oil) forage m
drilling rig N (on land) tour f (de forage), derrick
m; (at sea) plate-forme f de forage
drily ['draɪlɪ] ADV = **dryly**
drink [drɪŋk] (pt **drank** [dræŋk], pp **drunk**
[drʌŋk]) N boisson f; (alcoholic) verre m ▶ VT, VI
boire; **to have a ~** boire quelque chose, boire un
verre; **a ~ of water** un verre d'eau; **would you
like a ~?** tu veux boire quelque chose?; **we had
drinks before lunch** on a pris l'apéritif
▶ **drink in** VT (fresh air) inspirer profondément;
(story) avaler, ne pas perdre une miette de;
(sight) se remplir la vue de
drinkable ['drɪŋkəbl] ADJ (not dangerous) potable;
(palatable) buvable
drink-driving ['drɪŋk'draɪvɪŋ] N conduite f en
état d'ivresse
drinker ['drɪŋkə^r] N buveur(-euse)
drinking ['drɪŋkɪŋ] N (drunkenness) boisson f,
alcoolisme m
drinking fountain N (in park etc) fontaine
publique; (in building) jet m d'eau potable
drinking water N eau f potable
drip [drɪp] N (drop) goutte f; (sound: of water etc)
bruit m de l'eau qui tombe goutte à goutte;
(Med: device) goutte-à-goutte m inv; (: liquid)
perfusion f; (inf: person) lavette f, nouille f ▶ VI
tomber goutte à goutte; (tap) goutter; (washing)
s'égoutter; (wall) suinter
drip-dry ['drɪp'draɪ] ADJ (shirt) sans repassage
drip-feed ['drɪpfiːd] VT alimenter au goutte-à-
goutte or par perfusion
dripping ['drɪpɪŋ] N graisse f de rôti ▶ ADJ: **~ wet**
trempé(e)

drive [draɪv] (pt **drove** [drəuv], pp **driven** ['drɪvn])
N promenade f or trajet m en voiture; (also:
driveway) allée f; (energy) dynamisme m,
énergie f; (Psych) besoin m, pulsion f; (push)
effort (concerté), campagne f; (Sport) drive m;
(Tech) entraînement m; traction f;
transmission f; (Comput: also: **disk drive**) lecteur
m de disquette ▶ VT conduire; (nail) enfoncer;
(push) chasser, pousser; (Tech: motor) actionner;
entraîner ▶ VI (be at the wheel) conduire; (travel by
car) aller en voiture; **to go for a ~** aller faire une
promenade en voiture; **it's 3 hours' ~ from
London** Londres est à 3 heures de route; **left-/
right-hand ~** (Aut) conduite f à gauche/droite;
front-/rear-wheel ~ (Aut) traction f avant/
arrière; **to ~ sb to (do) sth** pousser or conduire
qn à (faire) qch; **to ~ sb mad** rendre qn fou
(folle)
▶ **drive at** VT FUS (fig: intend, mean) vouloir dire,
en venir à
▶ **drive on** VI poursuivre sa route, continuer;
(after stopping) reprendre sa route, repartir ▶ VT
(incite, encourage) inciter
▶ **drive out** VT (force out) chasser
drive-by ['draɪvbaɪ] N (also: **drive-by shooting**)
tentative d'assassinat par coups de feu tirés d'une
voiture
drive-in ['draɪvɪn] ADJ, N (esp US) drive-in m
drive-in window N (US) guichet-auto m
drivel ['drɪvl] N (inf) idioties fpl, imbécillités fpl
driven ['drɪvn] PP of **drive**
driver ['draɪvə^r] N conducteur(-trice); (of taxi,
bus) chauffeur m
driver's license N (US) permis m de conduire
driveway ['draɪvweɪ] N allée f
driving ['draɪvɪŋ] ADJ: **~ rain** pluie battante ▶ N
conduite f
driving force N locomotive f, élément m
dynamique
driving instructor N moniteur m d'auto-école
driving lesson N leçon f de conduite
driving licence N (BRIT) permis m de conduire
driving school N auto-école f
driving test N examen m du permis de conduire
drizzle ['drɪzl] N bruine f, crachin m ▶ VI bruiner
droll [drəul] ADJ drôle
dromedary ['drɔmədərɪ] N dromadaire m
drone [drəun] VI (bee) bourdonner; (engine etc)
ronronner; (also: **drone on**) parler d'une voix
monocorde ▶ N bourdonnement m;
ronronnement m; (male bee) faux-bourdon m
drool [druːl] VI baver; **to ~ over sb/sth** (fig)
baver d'admiration or être en extase devant qn/
qch
droop [druːp] VI (flower) commencer à se faner;
(shoulders, head) tomber
drop [drɔp] N (of liquid) goutte f; (fall) baisse f; (: in
salary) réduction f; (also: **parachute drop**) saut
m; (of cliff) dénivellation f; à-pic m ▶ VT laisser
tomber; (voice, eyes, price) baisser; (passenger)
déposer ▶ VI (wind, temperature, price, voice)
tomber; (numbers, attendance) diminuer; **drops**
NPL (Med) gouttes; **cough drops** pastilles fpl
pour la toux; **a ~ of 10%** une baisse or réduction)

de 10%; **to ~ anchor** jeter l'ancre; **to ~ sb a line** mettre un mot à qn

▶ **drop in** vi (inf: visit): **to ~ in (on)** faire un saut (chez), passer (chez)

▶ **drop off** vi (sleep) s'assoupir ▶ vt (passenger) déposer; **to ~ sb off** déposer qn

▶ **drop out** vi (withdraw) se retirer; (student etc) abandonner, décrocher

droplet ['drɔplɪt] N gouttelette f

dropout ['drɔpaut] N (from society) marginal(e); (from university) drop-out mf, dropé(e)

dropper ['drɔpə'] N (Med etc) compte-gouttes m inv

droppings ['drɔpɪŋz] NPL crottes fpl

dross [drɔs] N déchets mpl; rebut m

drought [draut] N sécheresse f

drove [drəuv] PT of **drive** ▶ N: **droves of people** une foule de gens

drown [draun] vt noyer; (also: **drown out**: sound) couvrir, étouffer ▶ vi se noyer

drowse [drauz] vi somnoler

drowsy ['drauzɪ] ADJ somnolent(e)

drudge [drʌdʒ] N bête f de somme (fig)

drudgery ['drʌdʒərɪ] N corvée f

drug [drʌg] N médicament m; (narcotic) drogue f ▶ vt droguer; **to be on drugs** se droguer; **he's on drugs** il se drogue; (Med) il est sous médication

drug addict N toxicomane mf

drug dealer N revendeur(-euse) de drogue

drug-driving [drʌg'draɪvɪŋ] N conduite f sous l'emprise de stupéfiants

druggist ['drʌgɪst] N (US) pharmacien(ne)-droguiste

drug peddler N revendeur(-euse) de drogue

drugstore ['drʌgstɔː'] N (US) pharmacie-droguerie f, drugstore m

drum [drʌm] N tambour m; (for oil, petrol) bidon m ▶ vt: **to ~ one's fingers on the table** pianoter or tambouriner sur la table; **drums** NPL (Mus) batterie f

▶ **drum up** vt (enthusiasm, support) susciter, rallier

drummer ['drʌmə'] N (joueur m de) tambour m

drum roll N roulement m de tambour

drumstick ['drʌmstɪk] N (Mus) baguette f de tambour; (of chicken) pilon m

drunk [drʌŋk] PP of **drink** ▶ ADJ ivre, soûl(e) ▶ N (also: **drunkard**) ivrogne mf; **to get ~** s'enivrer, se soûler

drunkard ['drʌŋkəd] N ivrogne mf

drunken ['drʌŋkən] ADJ ivre, soûl(e); (rage, stupor) ivrogne, d'ivrogne; **~ driving** conduite f en état d'ivresse

drunkenness ['drʌŋkənnɪs] N ivresse f; ivrognerie f

dry [draɪ] ADJ sec (sèche); (day) sans pluie; (humour) pince-sans-rire; (uninteresting) aride, rébarbatif(-ive) ▶ vt sécher; (clothes) faire sécher ▶ vi sécher; **on ~ land** sur la terre ferme; **to ~ one's hands/hair/eyes** se sécher les mains/les cheveux/les yeux

▶ **dry off** vi, vt sécher

▶ **dry up** vi (river, supplies) se tarir; (: speaker) sécher, rester sec

dry-clean ['draɪ'kliːn] vt nettoyer à sec

dry-cleaner ['draɪ'kliːnə'] N teinturier m

dry-cleaner's ['draɪ'kliːnəz] N teinturerie f

dry-cleaning ['draɪ'kliːnɪŋ] N (process) nettoyage m à sec

dry dock N (Naut) cale sèche, bassin m de radoub

dryer ['draɪə'] N (tumble-dryer) sèche-linge m inv; (for hair) sèche-cheveux m inv

dry goods NPL (Comm) textiles mpl, mercerie f

dry goods store N (US) magasin m de nouveautés

dry ice N neige f carbonique

dryly ['draɪlɪ] ADV sèchement, d'un ton sec

dryness ['draɪnɪs] N sécheresse f

dry rot N pourriture sèche (du bois)

dry run N (fig) essai m

dry ski slope N piste (de ski) artificielle

DSc N ABBR (= Doctor of Science) titre universitaire

DSS N ABBR (BRIT) = **Department of Social Security**

DST ABBR (US: = Daylight Saving Time) heure d'été

DT N ABBR (Comput) = **data transmission**

DTI N ABBR (BRIT) = **Department of Trade and Industry**

DTP N ABBR (= desktop publishing) PAO f

DT's [diː'tiːz] N ABBR (inf: = delirium tremens) delirium tremens m

dual ['djuəl] ADJ double

dual carriageway N (BRIT) route f à quatre voies

dual-control ['djuəlkən'trəul] ADJ à doubles commandes

dual nationality N double nationalité f

dual-purpose ['djuəl'pəːpəs] ADJ à double emploi

dubbed [dʌbd] ADJ (Cine) doublé(e); (nicknamed) surnommé(e)

dubious ['djuːbɪəs] ADJ hésitant(e), incertain(e); (reputation, company) douteux(-euse); **I'm very about it** j'ai des doutes sur la question, je n'en suis pas sûr du tout

Dublin ['dʌblɪn] N Dublin

Dubliner ['dʌblɪnə'] N habitant(e) de Dublin, originaire mf de Dublin

duchess ['dʌtʃɪs] N duchesse f

duck [dʌk] N canard m ▶ vi se baisser vivement, baisser subitement la tête ▶ vt plonger dans l'eau

duckling ['dʌklɪŋ] N caneton m

duct [dʌkt] N conduite f, canalisation f; (Anat) conduit m

dud [dʌd] N (shell) obus non éclaté; (object, tool): **it's a ~** c'est de la camelote, ça ne marche pas ▶ ADJ (BRIT: cheque) sans provision; (: note, coin) faux (fausse)

due [djuː] ADJ (money, payment) dû (due); (expected) attendu(e); (fitting) qui convient ▶ N dû m ▶ ADV: **~ north** droit vers le nord; **dues** NPL (for club, union) cotisation f; (in harbour) droits mpl (de port); **~ to** (because of) en raison de; (caused by) dû à; **in ~ course** en temps utile or voulu; (in the end) finalement; **the rent is ~ on the 30th** il faut payer le loyer le 30; **the train is ~ at 8 a.m.**

le train est attendu à 8 h; **she is ~ back tomorrow** elle doit rentrer demain; **he is ~ £10** on lui doit 10 livres; **I am ~ 6 days' leave** j'ai droit à 6 jours de congé; **to give sb his** or **her ~** être juste envers qn

due date N date f d'échéance

duel ['djuəl] N duel m

duet [dju:'ɛt] N duo m

duff [dʌf] ADJ (*BRIT inf*) nullard(e), nul(le)

duffel bag, duffle bag ['dʌfl-] N sac marin

duffel coat, duffle coat ['dʌfl-] N duffel-coat m

duffer ['dʌfər] N (*inf*) nullard(e)

dug [dʌg] PT, PP *of* **dig**

dugout ['dʌgaut] N (*Sport*) banc m de touche

duke [dju:k] N duc m

dull [dʌl] ADJ (*boring*) ennuyeux(-euse); (*slow*) borné(e); (*not bright*) morne, terne; (*sound, pain*) sourd(e); (*weather, day*) gris(e), maussade; (*blade*) émoussé(e) ▶ VT (*pain, grief*) atténuer; (*mind, senses*) engourdir

duly ['dju:lɪ] ADV (*on time*) en temps voulu; (*as expected*) comme il se doit

dumb [dʌm] ADJ muet(te); (*stupid*) bête; **to be struck ~** (*fig*) rester abasourdi(e), être sidéré(e)

dumbbell ['dʌmbɛl] N (*Sport*) haltère m

dumbfounded [dʌm'faundɪd] ADJ sidéré(e)

dummy ['dʌmɪ] N (*tailor's model*) mannequin m; (*mock-up*) factice m, maquette f; (*Sport*) feinte f; (*BRIT: for baby*) tétine f ▶ ADJ faux (fausse), factice

dummy run N essai m

dump [dʌmp] N tas m d'ordures; (*also:* **rubbish dump**) décharge (publique); (*Mil*) dépôt m; (*Comput*) listage m (de la mémoire); (*inf: place*) trou m ▶ VT (*put down*) déposer; déverser; (*get rid of*) se débarrasser de; (*Comput*) lister; (*Comm: goods*) vendre à perte (*sur le marché extérieur*); **to be (down) in the dumps** (*inf*) avoir le cafard, broyer du noir

dumping ['dʌmpɪŋ] N (*Econ*) dumping m; (*of rubbish*): **"no ~"** "décharge interdite"

dumpling ['dʌmplɪŋ] N boulette f (de pâte)

dumpy ['dʌmpɪ] ADJ courtaud(e), boulot(te)

dunce [dʌns] N âne m, cancre m

dune [dju:n] N dune f

dung [dʌŋ] N fumier m

dungarees [dʌŋgə'ri:z] NPL bleu(s) m(pl); (*for child, woman*) salopette f

dungeon ['dʌndʒən] N cachot m

dunk [dʌŋk] VT tremper

Dunkirk [dʌn'kə:k] N Dunkerque

duo ['dju:əu] N (*gen: Mus*) duo m

duodenal [dju:əu'di:nl] ADJ duodénal(e); **~ ulcer** ulcère m du duodénum

dupe [dju:p] N dupe f ▶ VT duper, tromper

duplex ['dju:plɛks] N (*US: also:* **duplex apartment**) duplex m

duplicate N ['dju:plɪkət] double m, copie exacte; (*copy of letter etc*) duplicata m ▶ ADJ (*copy*) en double ▶ VT ['dju:plɪkeɪt] faire un double de; (*on machine*) polycopier; **in ~** en deux exemplaires, en double; **~ key** double m de la (or d'une) clé

duplicating machine ['dju:plɪkeɪtɪŋ-], **duplicator** ['dju:plɪkeɪtər] N duplicateur m

duplicity [dju:'plɪsɪtɪ] N duplicité f, fausseté f

durability [djuərə'bɪlɪtɪ] N solidité f; durabilité f

durable ['djuərəbl] ADJ durable; (*clothes, metal*) résistant(e), solide

duration [djuə'reɪʃən] N durée f

duress [djuə'rɛs] N: **under ~** sous la contrainte

Durex® ['djuərɛks] N (*BRIT*) préservatif (masculin)

during ['djuərɪŋ] PREP pendant, au cours de

dusk [dʌsk] N crépuscule m

dusky ['dʌskɪ] ADJ sombre

dust [dʌst] N poussière f ▶ VT (*furniture*) essuyer, épousseter; (*cake etc*): **to ~ with** saupoudrer de ▶ **dust off** VT (*also fig*) dépoussiérer

dustbin ['dʌstbɪn] N (*BRIT*) poubelle f

duster ['dʌstər] N chiffon m

dust jacket N jacquette f

dustman ['dʌstmən] N (*irreg*) (*BRIT*) boueux m, éboueur m

dustpan ['dʌstpæn] N pelle f à poussière

dusty ['dʌstɪ] ADJ poussiéreux(-euse)

Dutch [dʌtʃ] ADJ hollandais(e), néerlandais(e) ▶ N (*Ling*) hollandais m, néerlandais m ▶ ADV: **to go ~** or **dutch** (*inf*) partager les frais; **the Dutch** NPL les Hollandais, les Néerlandais

Dutch auction N enchères fpl à la baisse

Dutchman ['dʌtʃmən] N (*irreg*) Hollandais m

Dutchwoman ['dʌtʃwumən] N (*irreg*) Hollandaise f

dutiable ['dju:tɪəbl] ADJ taxable, soumis(e) à des droits de douane

dutiful ['dju:tɪful] ADJ (*child*) respectueux(-euse); (*husband, wife*) plein(e) d'égards, prévenant(e); (*employee*) consciencieux(-euse)

duty ['dju:tɪ] N devoir m; (*tax*) droit m, taxe f; **duties** NPL fonctions fpl; **to make it one's ~ to do sth** se faire un devoir de faire qch; **to pay ~ on sth** payer un droit or une taxe sur qch; **on ~** de service; (*at night etc*) de garde; **off ~** libre, pas de service or de garde

duty-free ['dju:tɪ'fri:] ADJ exempté(e) de douane, hors-taxe; **~ shop** boutique f hors-taxe

duty officer N (*Mil etc*) officier m de permanence

duvet ['du:veɪ] N (*BRIT*) couette f

DV ABBR (= *Deo volente*) si Dieu le veut

DVD N ABBR (= *digital versatile or video disc*) DVD m

DVD burner N graveur m de DVD

DVD player N lecteur m de DVD

DVD writer N graveur m de DVD

DVLA N ABBR (*BRIT*: = *Driver and Vehicle Licensing Agency*) *service qui délivre les cartes grises et les permis de conduire*

DVM N ABBR (*US*: = *Doctor of Veterinary Medicine*) *titre universitaire*

DVT N ABBR = **deep vein thrombosis**

dwarf [dwɔ:f] (*pl* **dwarves** [dwɔ:vz]) N (*offensive*) nain(e) ▶ VT écraser

dwell [dwɛl] (*pt, pp* **dwelt** [dwɛlt]) VI demeurer ▶ **dwell on** VT FUS s'étendre sur

dweller ['dwɛlər] N habitant(e)

dwelling ['dwɛlɪŋ] N habitation f, demeure f

dwelt [dwɛlt] PT, PP *of* **dwell**

dwindle ['dwɪndl] VI diminuer, décroître

dwindling ['dwɪndlɪŋ] ADJ décroissant(e), en diminution

dye [daɪ] N teinture f ▶ VT teindre; **hair ~** teinture pour les cheveux

dyestuffs ['daɪstʌfs] NPL colorants mpl

dying ['daɪɪŋ] ADJ mourant(e), agonisant(e)

dyke [daɪk] N (embankment) digue f

dynamic [daɪ'næmɪk] ADJ dynamique

dynamics [daɪ'næmɪks] N, NPL dynamique f

dynamite ['daɪnəmaɪt] N dynamite f ▶ VT dynamiter, faire sauter à la dynamite

dynamo ['daɪnəməu] N dynamo f

dynasty ['dɪnəstɪ] N dynastie f

dysentery ['dɪsntrɪ] N dysenterie f

dyslexia [dɪs'lɛksɪə] N dyslexie f

dyslexic [dɪs'lɛksɪk] ADJ, N dyslexique mf

dyspepsia [dɪs'pɛpsɪə] N dyspepsie f

dystrophy ['dɪstrəfɪ] N dystrophie f; **muscular ~** dystrophie musculaire

Ee

E, e [i:] N (*letter*) E, e *m*; (*Mus*): **E** mi *m* ▶ ABBR
(= *east*) E ▶ N ABBR (*Drugs*) = **ecstasy**; **E for
Edward**, (*US*) **E for Easy** E comme Eugène

ea. ABBR = **each**

E.A. N ABBR (*US*: = *educational age*) niveau scolaire

each [i:tʃ] ADJ chaque ▶ PRON chacun(e); **~ one**
chacun(e); **~ other** l'un l'autre; **they hate ~
other** ils se détestent (mutuellement); **you are
jealous of ~ other** vous êtes jaloux l'un de
l'autre; **~ day** chaque jour, tous les jours; **they
have 2 books ~** ils ont 2 livres chacun; **they
cost £5 ~** ils coûtent 5 livres (la) pièce; **~ of us**
chacun(e) de nous

eager ['i:gə'] ADJ (*person, buyer*) empressé(e);
(*lover*) ardent(e), passionné(e); (*keen: pupil,
worker*) enthousiaste; **to be ~ to do sth**
(*impatient*) brûler de faire qch; (*keen*) désirer
vivement faire qch; **to be ~ for** (*event*) désirer
vivement; (*vengeance, affection, information*) être
avide de

eagle ['i:gl] N aigle *m*

E and OE ABBR = **errors and omissions excepted**

ear [ɪə'] N oreille *f*; (*of corn*) épi *m*; **up to one's
ears in debt** endetté(e) jusqu'au cou

earache ['ɪəreɪk] N mal *m* aux oreilles

eardrum ['ɪədrʌm] N tympan *m*

earful ['ɪəful] N (*inf*): **to give sb an ~** passer un
savon à qn

earl [ə:l] N comte *m*

earlier ['ə:lɪə'] ADJ (*date etc*) plus rapproché(e);
(*edition etc*) plus ancien(ne), antérieur(e) ▶ ADV
plus tôt

early ['ə:lɪ] ADV tôt, de bonne heure; (*ahead of
time*) en avance; (*near the beginning*) au début
▶ ADJ précoce, qui se manifeste (*or* se fait) tôt *or*
de bonne heure; (*Christians, settlers*)
premier(-ière); (*reply*) rapide; (*death*)
prématuré(e); (*work*) de jeunesse; **to have an ~
night/start** se coucher/partir tôt *or* de bonne
heure; **take the ~ train** prenez le premier
train; **in the ~ or ~ in the spring/19th century**
au début *or* commencement du
printemps/19ème siècle; **you're ~!** tu es en
avance!; **~ in the morning** tôt le matin; **she's
in her ~ forties** elle a un peu plus de quarante
ans *or* de la quarantaine; **at your earliest
convenience** (*Comm*) dans les meilleurs délais

early retirement N retraite anticipée

early warning system N système *m* de
première alerte

earmark ['ɪəmɑ:k] VT: **to ~ sth for** réserver *or*
destiner qch à

earn [ə:n] VT gagner; (*Comm: yield*) rapporter; **to
~ one's living** gagner sa vie; **this earned him
much praise, he earned much praise for
this** ceci lui a valu de nombreux éloges; **he's
earned his rest/reward** il mérite *or* a bien
mérité *or* a bien gagné son repos/sa récompense

earned income [ə:nd-] N revenu *m* du travail

earnest ['ə:nɪst] ADJ sérieux(-euse) ▶ N (*also:*
earnest money) acompte *m*, arrhes *fpl*; **in ~** *adv*
sérieusement, pour de bon

earnings ['ə:nɪŋz] NPL salaire *m*; gains *mpl*;
(*of company etc*) profits *mpl*, bénéfices *mpl*

ear, nose and throat specialist N oto-rhino-
laryngologiste *mf*

earphones ['ɪəfəunz] NPL écouteurs *mpl*

earplugs ['ɪəplʌgz] NPL boules *fpl* Quiès®;
(*to keep out water*) protège-tympans *mpl*

earring ['ɪərɪŋ] N boucle *f* d'oreille

earshot ['ɪəʃɔt] N: **out of/within ~** hors de
portée/à portée de voix

earth [ə:θ] N (*gen, also* BRIT *Elec*) terre *f*; (*of fox etc*)
terrier *m* ▶ VT (BRIT *Elec*) relier à la terre

earthenware ['ə:θnwɛə'] N poterie *f*; faïence *f*
▶ ADJ de *or* en faïence

earthly ['ə:θlɪ] ADJ terrestre; (*also:* **earthly
paradise**) paradis *m* terrestre; **there is no ~
reason to think that …** il n'y a absolument
aucune raison *or* pas la moindre raison de
penser que …

earthquake ['ə:θkweɪk] N tremblement *m* de
terre, séisme *m*

earth-shattering ['ə:θʃætərɪŋ] ADJ stupéfiant(e)

earth tremor N secousse *f* sismique

earthworks ['ə:θwə:ks] NPL travaux *mpl* de
terrassement

earthy ['ə:θɪ] ADJ (*fig*) terre à terre *inv*,
truculent(e)

earwax ['ɪəwæks] N cérumen *m*

earwig ['ɪəwɪg] N perce-oreille *m*

ease [i:z] N facilité *f*, aisance *f*; (*comfort*)
bien-être *m* ▶ VT (*soothe: mind*) tranquilliser;
(*reduce: pain, problem*) atténuer; (*: tension*) réduire;
(*loosen*) relâcher, détendre; (*help pass*): **to ~ sth
in/out** faire pénétrer/sortir qch délicatement *or*

avec douceur, faciliter la pénétration/la sortie de qch ▶ VI (*situation*) se détendre; **with ~** sans difficulté, aisément; **life of ~** vie oisive; **at ~** à l'aise; (*Mil*) au repos
▶ **ease off, ease up** VI diminuer; (*slow down*) ralentir; (*relax*) se détendre
easel ['i:zl] N chevalet *m*
easily ['i:zɪlɪ] ADV facilement; (*by far*) de loin
easiness ['i:sɪnɪs] N facilité *f*; (*of manner*) aisance *f*; nonchalance *f*
east [i:st] N est *m* ▶ ADJ (*wind*) d'est; (*side*) est *inv* ▶ ADV à l'est, vers l'est; **the E~** l'Orient *m*; (*Pol*) les pays *mpl* de l'Est
eastbound ['i:stbaund] ADJ en direction de l'est; (*carriageway*) est *inv*
Easter ['i:stə^r] N Pâques *fpl* ▶ ADJ (*holidays*) de Pâques, pascal(e)
Easter egg N œuf *m* de Pâques
Easter Island N île *f* de Pâques
easterly ['i:stəlɪ] ADJ d'est
Easter Monday N le lundi de Pâques
eastern ['i:stən] ADJ de l'est, oriental(e); **E~ Europe** l'Europe de l'Est; **the E~ bloc** (*Pol*) les pays *mpl* de l'est
Easter Sunday N le dimanche de Pâques
East Germany N (*formerly*) Allemagne *f* de l'Est
eastward ['i:stwəd], **eastwards** ['i:stwədz] ADV vers l'est, à l'est
easy ['i:zɪ] ADJ facile; (*manner*) aisé(e) ▶ ADV: **to take it ~** (*rest*) ne pas se fatiguer; (*not worry*) ne pas (trop) s'en faire; **to have an ~ life** avoir la vie facile; **payment on ~ terms** (*Comm*) facilités *fpl* de paiement; **that's easier said than done** c'est plus facile à dire qu'à faire, c'est vite dit; **I'm ~** (*inf*) ça m'est égal
easy chair N fauteuil *m*
easy-going ['i:zɪ'gəuɪŋ] ADJ accommodant(e), facile à vivre
easy touch N (*inf*): **he's an ~** c'est une bonne poire
eat [i:t] (*pt* **ate** [eɪt], *pp* **eaten** ['i:tn]) VT, VI manger; **can we have something to ~?** est-ce qu'on peut manger quelque chose?
▶ **eat away** VT (*sea*) saper, éroder; (*acid*) ronger, corroder
▶ **eat away at, eat into** VT FUS ronger, attaquer
▶ **eat out** VI manger au restaurant
▶ **eat up** VT (*food*) finir (de manger); **it eats up electricity** ça bouffe du courant, ça consomme beaucoup d'électricité
eatable ['i:təbl] ADJ mangeable; (*safe to eat*) comestible
eaten ['i:tn] PP *of* **eat**
eau de Cologne ['əudəkə'ləun] N eau *f* de Cologne
eaves [i:vz] NPL avant-toit *m*
eavesdrop ['i:vzdrɔp] VI: **to ~ (on)** écouter de façon indiscrète
ebb [ɛb] N reflux *m* ▶ VI refluer; (*fig: also*: **ebb away**) décliner; **the ~ and flow** le flux et le reflux; **to be at a low ~** (*fig*) être bien bas(se), ne pas aller bien fort
ebb tide N marée descendante, reflux *m*
ebony ['ɛbənɪ] N ébène *f*

e-book ['i:buk] N livre *m* électronique
ebullient [ɪ'bʌlɪənt] ADJ exubérant(e)
e-business ['i:bɪznɪs] N (*company*) entreprise *f* électronique; (*commerce*) commerce *m* électronique
e-card ['i:kɑːd] N carte *f* virtuelle
ECB N ABBR (= *European Central Bank*) BCE *f* (= *Banque centrale européenne*)
eccentric [ɪk'sɛntrɪk] ADJ, N excentrique *mf*
ecclesiastic [ɪkliːzɪ'æstɪk], **ecclesiastical** [ɪkliːzɪ'æstɪkl] ADJ ecclésiastique
ECG N ABBR = **electrocardiogram**
echo ['ɛkəu] (*pl* **echoes**) N écho *m* ▶ VT répéter; faire chorus avec ▶ VI résonner; faire écho
éclair ['eɪklɛə^r] N éclair *m* (*Culin*)
eclipse [ɪ'klɪps] N éclipse *f* ▶ VT éclipser
eco- ['i:kəu] PREFIX éco-
eco-friendly [i:kəu'frɛndlɪ] ADJ non nuisible à *or* qui ne nuit pas à l'environnement
ecological [i:kə'lɔdʒɪkəl] ADJ écologique
ecologist [ɪ'kɔlədʒɪst] N écologiste *mf*
ecology [ɪ'kɔlədʒɪ] N écologie *f*
e-commerce [i:kɔmə:s] N commerce *m* électronique
economic [i:kə'nɔmɪk] ADJ économique; (*profitable*) rentable
economical [i:kə'nɔmɪkl] ADJ économique; (*person*) économe
economically [i:kə'nɔmɪklɪ] ADV économiquement
economics [i:kə'nɔmɪks] N (*Scol*) économie *f* politique ▶ NPL (*of project etc*) côté *m* or aspect *m* économique
economist [ɪ'kɔnəmɪst] N économiste *mf*
economize [ɪ'kɔnəmaɪz] VI économiser, faire des économies
economy [ɪ'kɔnəmɪ] N économie *f*; **economies of scale** économies d'échelle
economy class N (*Aviat*) classe *f* touriste
economy class syndrome N syndrome *m* de la classe économique
economy size N taille *f* économique
ecosystem ['i:kəusɪstəm] N écosystème *m*
eco-tourism [i:kəu'tuərɪzəm] N écotourisme *m*
ECSC N ABBR (= *European Coal & Steel Community*) CECA *f* (= *Communauté européenne du charbon et de l'acier*)
ecstasy ['ɛkstəsɪ] N extase *f*; (*Drugs*) ecstasy *m*; **to go into ecstasies over** s'extasier sur
ecstatic [ɛks'tætɪk] ADJ extatique, en extase
ECT N ABBR = **electroconvulsive therapy**
Ecuador ['ɛkwədɔː^r] N Équateur *m*
ecumenical [i:kju'mɛnɪkl] ADJ œcuménique
eczema ['ɛksɪmə] N eczéma *m*
eddy ['ɛdɪ] N tourbillon *m*
edge [ɛdʒ] N bord *m*; (*of knife etc*) tranchant *m*, fil *m* ▶ VT border ▶ VI: **to ~ forward** avancer petit à petit; **to ~ away from** s'éloigner furtivement de; **on ~** (*fig*) crispé(e), tendu(e); **to have the ~ on** (*fig*) l'emporter (de justesse) sur, être légèrement meilleur que
edgeways ['ɛdʒweɪz] ADV latéralement; **he couldn't get a word in ~** il ne pouvait pas placer un mot

edging ['ɛdʒɪŋ] N bordure f
edgy ['ɛdʒɪ] ADJ crispé(e), tendu(e)
edible ['ɛdɪbl] ADJ comestible; (meal) mangeable
edict ['iːdɪkt] N décret m
edifice ['ɛdɪfɪs] N édifice m
edifying ['ɛdɪfaɪɪŋ] ADJ édifiant(e)
Edinburgh ['ɛdɪnbərə] N Édimbourg; voir article

Le Festival d'Édimbourg, qui se tient chaque
année durant trois semaines au mois
d'août, est l'un des grands festivals
européens. Il est réputé pour son
programme officiel mais aussi pour son
festival off (the Fringe) qui propose des
spectacles aussi bien traditionnels que
résolument d'avant-garde. Pendant la durée
du Festival se tient par ailleurs, sur
l'esplanade du château, un grand spectacle
de musique militaire, le Military Tattoo.

edit ['ɛdɪt] VT (text, book) éditer; (report) préparer; (film) monter; (broadcast) réaliser; (magazine) diriger; (newspaper) être le rédacteur or la rédactrice en chef de
edition [ɪ'dɪʃən] N édition f
editor ['ɛdɪtə'] N (of newspaper) rédacteur(-trice), rédacteur(-trice) en chef; (of sb's work) éditeur(-trice); (also: **film editor**) monteur(-euse); **political/ foreign** ~ rédacteur politique/au service étranger
editorial [ɛdɪ'tɔːrɪəl] ADJ de la rédaction, éditorial(e) ▶ N éditorial m; **the** ~ **staff** la rédaction
EDP N ABBR = **electronic data processing**
EDT ABBR (US: = Eastern Daylight Time) heure d'été de New York
educate ['ɛdjukeɪt] VT (teach) instruire; (bring up) éduquer; **educated at ...** qui a fait ses études à ...
educated ['ɛdjukeɪtɪd] ADJ (person) cultivé(e)
educated guess N supposition éclairée
education [ɛdju'keɪʃən] N éducation f; (studies) études fpl; (teaching) enseignement m, instruction f; (at university: subject etc) pédagogie f; **primary** or (US) **elementary/secondary** ~ instruction f primaire/secondaire
educational [ɛdju'keɪʃənl] ADJ pédagogique; (institution) scolaire; (useful) instructif(-ive); (game, toy) éducatif(-ive); ~ **technology** technologie f de l'enseignement
Edwardian [ɛd'wɔːdɪən] ADJ de l'époque du roi Édouard VII, des années 1900
EE ABBR = **electrical engineer**
EEG N ABBR = **electroencephalogram**
eel [iːl] N anguille f
EENT N ABBR (US Med) = **eye, ear, nose and throat**
EEOC N ABBR (US) = **Equal Employment Opportunity Commission**
eerie ['ɪərɪ] ADJ inquiétant(e), spectral(e), surnaturel(le)
EET ABBR (= Eastern European Time) HEO (= heure d'Europe orientale)
effect [ɪ'fɛkt] N effet m ▶ VT effectuer; **effects** NPL (Theat) effets mpl; (property) effets, affaires fpl; **to take** ~ (Law) entrer en vigueur, prendre

effet; (drug) agir, faire son effet; **to put into** ~ (plan) mettre en application or à exécution; **to have an** ~ **on sb/sth** avoir or produire un effet sur qn/qch; **in** ~ en fait; **his letter is to the** ~ **that ...** sa lettre nous apprend que ...
effective [ɪ'fɛktɪv] ADJ efficace; (striking: display, outfit) frappant(e), qui produit or fait de l'effet; (actual) véritable; **to become** ~ (Law) entrer en vigueur, prendre effet; ~ **date** date f d'effet or d'entrée en vigueur
effectively [ɪ'fɛktɪvlɪ] ADV efficacement; (strikingly) d'une manière frappante, avec beaucoup d'effet; (in reality) effectivement, en fait
effectiveness [ɪ'fɛktɪvnɪs] N efficacité f
effeminate [ɪ'fɛmɪnɪt] ADJ efféminé(e)
effervescent [ɛfə'vɛsnt] ADJ effervescent(e)
efficacy ['ɛfɪkəsɪ] N efficacité f
efficiency [ɪ'fɪʃənsɪ] N efficacité f; (of machine, car) rendement m
efficiency apartment N (US) studio m avec coin cuisine
efficient [ɪ'fɪʃənt] ADJ efficace; (machine, car) d'un bon rendement
efficiently [ɪ'fɪʃəntlɪ] ADV efficacement
effigy ['ɛfɪdʒɪ] N effigie f
effluent ['ɛfluənt] N effluent m
effort ['ɛfət] N effort m; **to make an** ~ **to do sth** faire or fournir un effort pour faire qch
effortless ['ɛfətlɪs] ADJ sans effort, aisé(e); (achievement) facile
effrontery [ɪ'frʌntərɪ] N effronterie f
effusive [ɪ'fjuːsɪv] ADJ (person) expansif(-ive); (welcome) chaleureux(-euse)
EFL N ABBR (Scol) = **English as a Foreign Language**
EFTA ['ɛftə] N ABBR (= European Free Trade Association) AELE f (= Association européenne de libre-échange)
e.g. ADV ABBR (= exempli gratia) par exemple, p. ex.
egalitarian [ɪgælɪ'tɛərɪən] ADJ égalitaire
egg [ɛg] N œuf m; **hard-boiled/soft-boiled** ~ œuf dur/à la coque
▶ **egg on** VT pousser
eggcup ['ɛgkʌp] N coquetier m
egg plant (US) N aubergine f
eggshell ['ɛgʃɛl] N coquille f d'œuf ▶ ADJ (colour) blanc cassé inv
egg-timer ['ɛgtaɪmə'] N sablier m
egg white N blanc m d'œuf
egg yolk N jaune m d'œuf
ego ['iːgəu] N (self-esteem) amour-propre m; (Psych) moi m
egoism ['ɛgəuɪzəm] N égoïsme m
egoist ['ɛgəuɪst] N égoïste mf
egotism ['ɛgəutɪzəm] N égotisme m
egotist ['ɛgəutɪst] N égocentrique mf
ego trip N: **to be on an** ~ être en plein délire d'autosatisfaction
Egypt ['iːdʒɪpt] N Égypte f
Egyptian [ɪ'dʒɪpʃən] ADJ égyptien(ne) ▶ N Égyptien(ne)
EHIC N ABBR (= European Health Insurance Card) CEAM f

eiderdown ['aɪdədaun] N édredon *m*
Eiffel Tower ['aɪfəl-] N tour *f* Eiffel
eight [eɪt] NUM huit
eighteen [eɪ'tiːn] NUM dix-huit
eighteenth [eɪ'tiːnθ] NUM dix-huitième
eighth [eɪtθ] NUM huitième
eightieth ['eɪtɪɪθ] NUM quatre-vingtième
eighty ['eɪtɪ] NUM quatre-vingt(s)
Eire ['εərə] N République *f* d'Irlande
EIS N ABBR (= *Educational Institute of Scotland*)
  syndicat enseignant
either ['aɪðə**ʳ**] ADJ l'un ou l'autre; (*both, each*)
  chaque ▶ PRON: ~ **(of them)** l'un ou l'autre
  ▶ ADV non plus ▶ CONJ: ~ **good or bad** ou bon ou
  mauvais, soit bon soit mauvais; **I haven't seen**
  ~ **one or the other** je n'ai vu ni l'un ni l'autre;
  on ~ side de chaque côté; **I don't like ~** je
  n'aime ni l'un ni l'autre; **no, I don't ~** moi non
  plus; **which bike do you want?** — ~ **will do**
  quel vélo voulez-vous? — n'importe lequel;
  answer with ~ yes or no répondez par oui ou
  par non
ejaculation [ɪdʒækjuˈleɪʃən] N (*Physiol*)
  éjaculation *f*
eject [ɪ'dʒεkt] VT (*tenant etc*) expulser; (*object*)
  éjecter ▶ VI (*pilot*) s'éjecter
ejector seat [ɪ'dʒεktə-] N siège *m* éjectable
eke [iːk]: **to ~ out** VT faire durer; augmenter
EKG N ABBR (*US*) = **electrocardiogram**
el [εl] N ABBR (*US inf*) = **elevated railroad**
elaborate ADJ [ɪ'læbərɪt] compliqué(e),
  recherché(e), minutieux(-euse) ▶ VT
  [ɪ'læbəreɪt] élaborer ▶ VI entrer dans les
  détails
elapse [ɪ'læps] VI s'écouler, passer
elastic [ɪ'læstɪk] ADJ, N élastique (*m*)
elastic band N (*BRIT*) élastique *m*
elasticity [ɪlæs'tɪsɪtɪ] N élasticité *f*
elated [ɪ'leɪtɪd] ADJ transporté(e) de joie
elation [ɪ'leɪʃən] N (grande) joie, allégresse *f*
elbow ['εlbəu] N coude *m* ▶ VT: **to ~ one's way**
  through the crowd se frayer un passage à
  travers la foule (en jouant des coudes)
elbow grease N: **to use a bit of ~** mettre de
  l'huile de coude
elder ['εldə**ʳ**] ADJ aîné(e) ▶ N (*tree*) sureau *m*;
  one's elders ses aînés
elderly ['εldəlɪ] ADJ âgé(e)
elder statesman N (*irreg*) vétéran *m* de la
  politique
eldest ['εldɪst] ADJ, N: **the ~ (child)** l'aîné(e)
  (des enfants)
elect [ɪ'lεkt] VT élire; (*choose*): **to ~ to do** choisir
  de faire ▶ ADJ: **the president ~** le président
  désigné
election [ɪ'lεkʃən] N élection *f*; **to hold an ~**
  procéder à une élection
election campaign N campagne électorale
electioneering [ɪlεkʃə'nɪərɪŋ] N propagande
  électorale, manœuvres électorales
elector [ɪ'lεktə**ʳ**] N électeur(-trice)
electoral [ɪ'lεktərəl] ADJ électoral(e)
electoral college N collège électoral
electoral roll N (*BRIT*) liste électorale

electorate [ɪ'lεktərɪt] N électorat *m*
electric [ɪ'lεktrɪk] ADJ électrique
electrical [ɪ'lεktrɪkl] ADJ électrique
electrical engineer N ingénieur électricien
electrical failure N panne *f* d'électricité *or* de
  courant
electric blanket N couverture chauffante
electric chair N chaise *f* électrique
electric cooker N cuisinière *f* électrique
electric current N courant *m* électrique
electric fire N (*BRIT*) radiateur *m* électrique
electrician [ɪlεk'trɪʃən] N électricien *m*
electricity [ɪlεk'trɪsɪtɪ] N électricité *f*; **to switch**
  on/off the ~ rétablir/couper le courant
electricity board N (*BRIT*) ≈ agence régionale de
  l'E.D.F.
electric light N lumière *f* électrique
electric shock N choc *m* or décharge *f* électrique
electrify [ɪ'lεktrɪfaɪ] VT (*Rail*) électrifier;
  (*audience*) électriser
electro... [ɪ'lεktrəu] PREFIX électro...
electrocardiogram [ɪ'lεktrə] N
  électrocardiogramme *m*
electro-convulsive therapy [ɪ'lεktrə] N
  électrochocs *mpl*
electrocute [ɪ'lεktrəkjuːt] VT électrocuter
electrode [ɪ'lεktrəud] N électrode *f*
electroencephalogram [ɪ'lεktrəu] N
  électroencéphalogramme *m*
electrolysis [ɪlεk'trɔlɪsɪs] N électrolyse *f*
electromagnetic [ɪ'lεktrəmæg'nεtɪk] ADJ
  électromagnétique
electron [ɪ'lεktrɔn] N électron *m*
electronic [ɪlεk'trɔnɪk] ADJ électronique
electronic data processing N traitement *m*
  électronique des données
electronic mail N courrier *m* électronique
electronics [ɪlεk'trɔnɪks] N électronique *f*
electron microscope N microscope *m*
  électronique
electroplated [ɪ'lεktrə'pleɪtɪd] ADJ plaqué(e) or
  doré(e) or argenté(e) par galvanoplastie
electrotherapy [ɪ'lεktrə'θεrəpɪ] N
  électrothérapie *f*
elegance ['εlɪgəns] N élégance *f*
elegant ['εlɪgənt] ADJ élégant(e)
element ['εlɪmənt] N (*gen*) élément *m*; (*of heater,*
  kettle etc) résistance *f*
elementary [εlɪ'mεntərɪ] ADJ élémentaire;
  (*school, education*) primaire
elementary school N (*US*) école *f* primaire; *voir*
  article

> Aux États-Unis et au Canada, une *elementary*
> *school* (également appelée *grade school* ou
> *grammar school* aux États-Unis) est une école
> publique où les enfants passent les six à
> huit premières années de leur scolarité.

elephant ['εlɪfənt] N éléphant *m*
elevate ['εlɪveɪt] VT élever
elevated railroad ['εlɪveɪtɪd-] N (*US*) métro *m*
  aérien
elevation [εlɪ'veɪʃən] N élévation *f*; (*height*)
  altitude *f*
elevator ['εlɪveɪtə**ʳ**] N (*in warehouse etc*) élévateur *m*,

monte-charge *m inv*; *(US: lift)* ascenseur *m*

eleven [ɪ'lɛvn] NUM onze

elevenses [ɪ'lɛvnzɪz] NPL *(BRIT)* ≈ pause-café *f*

eleventh [ɪ'lɛvnθ] NUM onzième; **at the ~ hour** *(fig)* à la dernière minute

elf [ɛlf] *(pl* **elves** [ɛlvz]*)* N lutin *m*

elicit [ɪ'lɪsɪt] VT: **to ~ (from)** obtenir (de); tirer (de)

eligible ['ɛlɪdʒəbl] ADJ éligible; *(for membership)* admissible; **an ~ young man** un beau parti; **to be ~ for sth** remplir les conditions requises pour qch; **~ for a pension** ayant droit à la retraite

eliminate [ɪ'lɪmɪneɪt] VT éliminer

elimination [ɪlɪmɪ'neɪʃən] N élimination *f*; **by process of ~** par élimination

elitist [ɛ'li:tɪst] ADJ *(pej)* élitiste

Elizabethan [ɪlɪzə'bi:θən] ADJ élisabéthain(e)

ellipse [ɪ'lɪps] N ellipse *f*

elliptical [ɪ'lɪptɪkl] ADJ elliptique

elm [ɛlm] N orme *m*

elocution [ɛlə'kju:ʃən] N élocution *f*

elongated ['i:lɔŋgeɪtɪd] ADJ étiré(e), allongé(e)

elope [ɪ'ləup] VI *(lovers)* s'enfuir (ensemble)

elopement [ɪ'ləupmənt] N fugue amoureuse

eloquence ['ɛləkwəns] N éloquence *f*

eloquent ['ɛləkwənt] ADJ éloquent(e)

else [ɛls] ADV d'autre; **something ~** quelque chose d'autre, autre chose; **somewhere ~** ailleurs, autre part; **everywhere ~** partout ailleurs; **everyone ~** tous les autres; **nothing ~** rien d'autre; **is there anything ~ I can do?** est-ce que je peux faire quelque chose d'autre?; **where ~?** à quel autre endroit?; **little ~** pas grand-chose d'autre

elsewhere [ɛls'wɛəʳ] ADV ailleurs, autre part

ELT N ABBR *(Scol)* = **English Language Teaching**

elucidate [ɪ'lu:sɪdeɪt] VT élucider

elude [ɪ'lu:d] VT échapper à; *(question)* éluder

elusive [ɪ'lu:sɪv] ADJ insaisissable; *(answer)* évasif(-ive)

elves [ɛlvz] NPL *of* **elf**

emaciated [ɪ'meɪsɪeɪtɪd] ADJ émacié(e), décharné(e)

email ['i:meɪl] N ABBR *(= electronic mail)* (e-)mail *m*, courriel *m* ▶ VT: **to ~ sb** envoyer un (e-)mail or un courriel à qn

email account N compte *m* (e-)mail

email address N adresse *f* (e-)mail or électronique

emanate ['ɛməneɪt] VI: **to ~ from** émaner de

emancipate [ɪ'mænsɪpeɪt] VT émanciper

emancipation [ɪmænsɪ'peɪʃən] N émancipation *f*

emasculate [ɪ'mæskjuleɪt] VT émasculer

embalm [ɪm'bɑ:m] VT embaumer

embankment [ɪm'bæŋkmənt] N *(of road, railway)* remblai *m*, talus *m*; *(of river)* berge *f*, quai *m*; *(dyke)* digue *f*

embargo [ɪm'bɑ:gəu] *(pl* **embargoes**) N *(Comm, Naut)* embargo *m*; *(prohibition)* interdiction *f* ▶ VT frapper d'embargo, mettre l'embargo sur; **to put an ~ on sth** mettre l'embargo sur qch

embark [ɪm'bɑ:k] VI embarquer; **to ~ on** (s')embarquer à bord de or sur ▶ VT embarquer; **to ~ on** *(journey etc)* commencer, entreprendre; *(fig)* se lancer or s'embarquer dans

embarkation [ɛmbɑ:'keɪʃən] N embarquement *m*

embarkation card N carte *f* d'embarquement

embarrass [ɪm'bærəs] VT embarrasser, gêner

embarrassed [ɪm'bærəst] ADJ gêné(e); **to be ~** être gêné(e)

embarrassing [ɪm'bærəsɪŋ] ADJ gênant(e), embarrassant(e)

embarrassment [ɪm'bærəsmənt] N embarras *m*, gêne *f*; *(embarrassing thing, person)* source *f* d'embarras

embassy ['ɛmbəsɪ] N ambassade *f*; **the French E~** l'ambassade de France

embed [ɪm'bɛd] VT enfoncer; sceller

embellish [ɪm'bɛlɪʃ] VT embellir; enjoliver

embers ['ɛmbəz] NPL braise *f*

embezzle [ɪm'bɛzl] VT détourner

embezzlement [ɪm'bɛzlmənt] N détournement *m* (de fonds)

embezzler [ɪm'bɛzləʳ] N escroc *m*

embitter [ɪm'bɪtəʳ] VT aigrir; envenimer

emblem ['ɛmbləm] N emblème *m*

embodiment [ɪm'bɔdɪmənt] N personnification *f*, incarnation *f*

embody [ɪm'bɔdɪ] VT *(features)* réunir, comprendre; *(ideas)* formuler, exprimer

embolden [ɪm'bəuldn] VT enhardir

embolism ['ɛmbəlɪzəm] N embolie *f*

embossed [ɪm'bɔst] ADJ repoussé(e), gaufré(e); **~ with** où figure(nt) en relief

embrace [ɪm'breɪs] VT embrasser, étreindre; *(include)* embrasser, couvrir, comprendre ▶ VI s'embrasser, s'étreindre ▶ N étreinte *f*

embroider [ɪm'brɔɪdəʳ] VT broder; *(fig: story)* enjoliver

embroidery [ɪm'brɔɪdərɪ] N broderie *f*

embroil [ɪm'brɔɪl] VT: **to become embroiled (in sth)** se retrouver mêlé(e) (à qch), se laisser entraîner (dans qch)

embryo ['ɛmbrɪəu] N *(also fig)* embryon *m*

emcee [ɛm'si:] N maître *m* de cérémonie

emend [ɪ'mɛnd] VT *(text)* corriger

emerald ['ɛmərəld] N émeraude *f*

emerge [ɪ'mə:dʒ] VI apparaître; *(from room, car)* surgir; *(from sleep, imprisonment)* sortir; **it emerges that** *(BRIT)* il ressort que

emergence [ɪ'mə:dʒəns] N apparition *f*; *(of nation)* naissance *f*

emergency [ɪ'mə:dʒənsɪ] N *(crisis)* cas *m* d'urgence; *(Med)* urgence *f*; **in an ~** en cas d'urgence; **state of ~** état *m* d'urgence

emergency brake *(US)* N frein *m* à main

emergency exit N sortie *f* de secours

emergency landing N atterrissage forcé

emergency lane N *(US Aut)* accotement stabilisé

emergency road service N *(US)* service *m* de dépannage

emergency room N *(US Med)* urgences *fpl*

emergency services NPL: **the ~** *(fire, police, ambulance)* les services *mpl* d'urgence

emergency stop N (BRIT Aut) arrêt m d'urgence
emergent [ɪ'mə:dʒənt] ADJ: ~ **nation** pays m en voie de développement
emery board ['ɛmərɪ-] N lime f à ongles (en carton émerisé)
emery paper ['ɛmərɪ-] N papier m (d')émeri
emetic [ɪ'mɛtɪk] N vomitif m, émétique m
emigrant ['ɛmɪɡrənt] N émigrant(e)
emigrate ['ɛmɪɡreɪt] VI émigrer
emigration [ɛmɪ'ɡreɪʃən] N émigration f
émigré ['ɛmɪɡreɪ] N émigré(e)
eminence ['ɛmɪnəns] N éminence f
eminent ['ɛmɪnənt] ADJ éminent(e)
eminently ['ɛmɪnəntlɪ] ADV éminemment, admirablement
emissions [ɪ'mɪʃənz] NPL émissions fpl
emit [ɪ'mɪt] VT émettre
emolument [ɪ'mɔljumənt] N (often pl: formal) émoluments mpl; (fee) honoraires mpl; (salary) traitement m
emoticon [ɪ'məutɪkən] N (Comput) émoticone m
emotion [ɪ'məuʃən] N sentiment m; (as opposed to reason) émotion f, sentiments
emotional [ɪ'məuʃənl] ADJ (person) émotif(-ive), très sensible; (needs) affectif(-ive); (scene) émouvant(e); (tone, speech) qui fait appel aux sentiments
emotionally [ɪ'məuʃnəlɪ] ADV (behave) émotivement; (be involved) affectivement; (speak) avec émotion; ~ **disturbed** qui souffre de troubles de l'affectivité
emotive [ɪ'məutɪv] ADJ émotif(-ive); ~ **power** capacité f d'émouvoir or de toucher
empathy ['ɛmpəθɪ] N communion f d'idées or de sentiments, empathie f; **to feel ~ with sb** se mettre à la place de qn
emperor ['ɛmpərər] N empereur m
emphasis ['ɛmfəsɪs] (pl **emphases** [-siːz]) N accent m; **to lay** or **place ~ on sth** (fig) mettre l'accent sur, insister sur; **the ~ is on reading** la lecture tient une place primordiale, on accorde une importance particulière à la lecture
emphasize ['ɛmfəsaɪz] VT (syllable, word, point) appuyer or insister sur; (feature) souligner, accentuer
emphatic [ɛm'fætɪk] ADJ (strong) énergique, vigoureux(-euse); (unambiguous, clear) catégorique
emphatically [ɛm'fætɪklɪ] ADV avec vigueur or énergie; catégoriquement
empire ['ɛmpaɪər] N empire m
empirical [ɛm'pɪrɪkl] ADJ empirique
employ [ɪm'plɔɪ] VT employer; **he's employed in a bank** il est employé de banque, il travaille dans une banque
employee [ɪmplɔɪ'iː] N employé(e)
employer [ɪm'plɔɪər] N employeur(-euse)
employment [ɪm'plɔɪmənt] N emploi m; **to find ~** trouver un emploi or du travail; **without ~** au chômage, sans emploi; **place of ~** lieu m de travail
employment agency N agence f or bureau m de placement
employment exchange N (BRIT) agence f

pour l'emploi
empower [ɪm'pauər] VT: **to ~ sb to do** autoriser or habiliter qn à faire
empress ['ɛmprɪs] N impératrice f
emptiness ['ɛmptɪnɪs] N vide m; (of area) aspect m désertique
empty ['ɛmptɪ] ADJ vide; (street, area) désert(e); (threat, promise) en l'air, vain(e) ▶ N (bottle) bouteille f vide ▶ VT vider ▶ VI se vider; (liquid) s'écouler; **on an ~ stomach** à jeun; **to ~ into** (river) se jeter dans, se déverser dans
empty-handed ['ɛmptɪ'hændɪd] ADJ les mains vides
empty-headed ['ɛmptɪ'hɛdɪd] ADJ écervelé(e), qui n'a rien dans la tête
EMS N ABBR (= European Monetary System) SME m
EMT N ABBR = **emergency medical technician**
EMU N ABBR (= European Monetary Union) UME f
emulate ['ɛmjuleɪt] VT rivaliser avec, imiter
emulsion [ɪ'mʌlʃən] N émulsion f; (also: **emulsion paint**) peinture mate
enable [ɪ'neɪbl] VT: **to ~ sb to do** permettre à qn de faire, donner à qn la possibilité de faire
enact [ɪ'nækt] VT (Law) promulguer; (play, scene) jouer, représenter
enamel [ɪ'næməl] N émail m; (also: **enamel paint**) (peinture f) laque f
enamoured [ɪ'næməd] ADJ: ~ **of** amoureux(-euse) de; (idea) enchanté(e) par
encampment [ɪn'kæmpmənt] N campement m
encased [ɪn'keɪst] ADJ: ~ **in** enfermé(e) dans, recouvert(e) de
enchant [ɪn'tʃɑːnt] VT enchanter
enchanting [ɪn'tʃɑːntɪŋ] ADJ ravissant(e), enchanteur(-eresse)
encircle [ɪn'sə:kl] VT entourer, encercler
encl. ABBR (on letters etc: = enclosed) ci-joint(e); (= enclosure) PJ f
enclose [ɪn'kləuz] VT (land) clôturer; (space, object) entourer; (letter etc): **to ~ (with)** joindre (à); **please find enclosed** veuillez trouver ci-joint
enclosure [ɪn'kləuʒər] N enceinte f; (in letter etc) annexe f
encoder [ɪn'kəudər] N (Comput) encodeur m
encompass [ɪn'kʌmpəs] VT encercler, entourer; (include) contenir, inclure
encore [ɔŋ'kɔːr] EXCL, N bis (m)
encounter [ɪn'kauntər] N rencontre f ▶ VT rencontrer
encourage [ɪn'kʌrɪdʒ] VT encourager; (industry, growth) favoriser; **to ~ sb to do sth** encourager qn à faire qch
encouragement [ɪn'kʌrɪdʒmənt] N encouragement m
encouraging [ɪn'kʌrɪdʒɪŋ] ADJ encourageant(e)
encroach [ɪn'krəutʃ] VI: **to ~ (up)on** empiéter sur
encrusted [ɪn'krʌstɪd] ADJ: ~ **(with)** incrusté(e) (de)
encrypt [ɪn'krɪpt] VT (Comput, Tel) crypter
encyclopaedia, encyclopedia [ɛnsaɪkləu'piːdɪə] N encyclopédie f
end [ɛnd] N fin f; (of table, street, rope etc) bout m,

extrémité f; (of pointed object) pointe f; (of town) bout; (Sport) côté m ▶ VT terminer; (also: **bring to an end, put an end to**) mettre fin à ▶ VI se terminer, finir; **from ~ to ~** d'un bout à l'autre; **to come to an ~** prendre fin; **to be at an ~** être fini(e), être terminé(e); **in the ~** finalement; **on ~** (object) debout, dressé(e); **to stand on ~** (hair) se dresser sur la tête; **for 5 hours on ~** durant 5 heures d'affilée or de suite; **for hours on ~** pendant des heures (et des heures); **at the ~ of the day** (BRIT fig) en fin de compte; **to this ~, with this ~ in view** à cette fin, dans ce but
▶ **end up** VI: **to ~ up in** (condition) finir or se terminer par; (place) finir or aboutir à

endanger [ɪnˈdeɪndʒəʳ] VT mettre en danger; **an endangered species** une espèce en voie de disparition

endear [ɪnˈdɪəʳ] VT: **to ~ o.s. to sb** se faire aimer de qn

endearing [ɪnˈdɪərɪŋ] ADJ attachant(e)

endearment [ɪnˈdɪəmənt] N: **to whisper endearments** murmurer des mots or choses tendres; **term of ~** terme m d'affection

endeavour, (US) **endeavor** [ɪnˈdɛvəʳ] N effort m; (attempt) tentative f ▶ VT: **to ~ to do** tenter or s'efforcer de faire

endemic [ɛnˈdɛmɪk] ADJ endémique

ending [ˈɛndɪŋ] N dénouement m, conclusion f; (Ling) terminaison f

endive [ˈɛndaɪv] N (curly) chicorée f; (smooth, flat) endive f

endless [ˈɛndlɪs] ADJ sans fin, interminable; (patience, resources) inépuisable, sans limites; (possibilities) illimité(e)

endorse [ɪnˈdɔːs] VT (cheque) endosser; (approve) appuyer, approuver, sanctionner

endorsee [ɪndɔːˈsiː] N bénéficiaire mf, endossataire mf

endorsement [ɪnˈdɔːsmənt] N (approval) appui m, aval m; (signature) endossement m; (BRIT: on driving licence) contravention f (portée au permis de conduire)

endorser [ɪnˈdɔːsəʳ] N avaliste m, endosseur m

endow [ɪnˈdau] VT (provide with money) faire une donation à, doter; (equip): **to ~ with** gratifier de, doter de

endowment [ɪnˈdaumənt] N dotation f

endowment mortgage N hypothèque liée à une assurance-vie

endowment policy N assurance f à capital différé

end product N (Industry) produit fini; (fig) résultat m, aboutissement m

end result N résultat final

endurable [ɪnˈdjuərəbl] ADJ supportable

endurance [ɪnˈdjuərəns] N endurance f

endurance test N test m d'endurance

endure [ɪnˈdjuəʳ] VT (bear) supporter, endurer ▶ VI (last) durer

end user N (Comput) utilisateur final

enema [ˈɛnɪmə] N (Med) lavement m

enemy [ˈɛnəmɪ] ADJ, N ennemi(e); **to make an ~ of sb** se faire un(e) ennemi(e) de qn, se mettre qn à dos

energetic [ɛnəˈdʒɛtɪk] ADJ énergique; (activity) très actif(-ive), qui fait se dépenser (physiquement)

energy [ˈɛnədʒɪ] N énergie f; **Department of E~** ministère m de l'Énergie

energy crisis N crise f de l'énergie

energy drink N boisson f énergisante

energy-saving [ˈɛnədʒɪˈseɪvɪŋ] ADJ (policy) d'économie d'énergie; (device) qui permet de réaliser des économies d'énergie

enervating [ˈɛnəveɪtɪŋ] ADJ débilitant(e), affaiblissant(e)

enforce [ɪnˈfɔːs] VT (law) appliquer, faire respecter

enforced [ɪnˈfɔːst] ADJ forcé(e)

enfranchise [ɪnˈfræntʃaɪz] VT accorder le droit de vote à; (set free) affranchir

engage [ɪnˈgeɪdʒ] VT engager; (Mil) engager le combat avec; (lawyer) prendre ▶ VI (Tech) s'enclencher, s'engrener; **to ~ in** se lancer dans; **to ~ sb in conversation** engager la conversation avec qn

engaged [ɪnˈgeɪdʒd] ADJ (BRIT: busy, in use) occupé(e); (betrothed) fiancé(e); **to get ~** se fiancer; **the line's ~** la ligne est occupée; **he is ~ in research/a survey** il fait de la recherche/une enquête

engaged tone N (BRIT Tel) tonalité f occupé inv

engagement [ɪnˈgeɪdʒmənt] N (undertaking) obligation f, engagement m; (appointment) rendez-vous m inv; (to marry) fiançailles fpl; (Mil) combat m; **I have a previous ~** j'ai déjà un rendez-vous, je suis déjà pris(e)

engagement ring N bague f de fiançailles

engaging [ɪnˈgeɪdʒɪŋ] ADJ engageant(e), attirant(e)

engender [ɪnˈdʒɛndəʳ] VT produire, causer

engine [ˈɛndʒɪn] N (Aut) moteur m; (Rail) locomotive f

engine driver N (BRIT: of train) mécanicien m

engineer [ɛndʒɪˈnɪəʳ] N ingénieur m; (BRIT: repairer) dépanneur m; (Navy, US Rail) mécanicien m; **civil/mechanical ~** ingénieur des Travaux Publics or des Ponts et Chaussées/mécanicien

engineering [ɛndʒɪˈnɪərɪŋ] N engineering m, ingénierie f; (of bridges, ships) génie m; (of machine) mécanique f ▶ CPD: **~ works** or **factory** atelier m de construction mécanique

engine failure N panne f

engine trouble N ennuis mpl mécaniques

England [ˈɪŋglənd] N Angleterre f

English [ˈɪŋglɪʃ] ADJ anglais(e) ▶ N (Ling) anglais m; **the ~** npl les Anglais; **an ~ speaker** un anglophone

English Channel N: **the ~** la Manche

Englishman [ˈɪŋglɪʃmən] N (irreg) Anglais m

English-speaking [ˈɪŋglɪʃˈspiːkɪŋ] ADJ qui parle anglais; anglophone

Englishwoman [ˈɪŋglɪʃwumən] N (irreg) Anglaise f

engrave [ɪnˈgreɪv] VT graver

engraving [ɪnˈgreɪvɪŋ] N gravure f

engrossed [ɪnˈgrəust] ADJ: **~ in** absorbé(e) par, plongé(e) dans

e

engulf [ɪnˈɡʌlf] VT engloutir
enhance [ɪnˈhɑːns] VT rehausser, mettre en valeur; (*position*) améliorer; (*reputation*) accroître
enigma [ɪˈnɪɡmə] N énigme f
enigmatic [ɛnɪɡˈmætɪk] ADJ énigmatique
enjoy [ɪnˈdʒɔɪ] VT aimer, prendre plaisir à; (*have benefit of: health, fortune*) jouir de; (: *success*) connaître; **to ~ o.s.** s'amuser
enjoyable [ɪnˈdʒɔɪəbl] ADJ agréable
enjoyment [ɪnˈdʒɔɪmənt] N plaisir m
enlarge [ɪnˈlɑːdʒ] VT accroître; (*Phot*) agrandir
▶ **to ~ on** (*subject*) s'étendre sur
enlarged [ɪnˈlɑːdʒd] ADJ (*edition*) augmenté(e); (*Med: organ, gland*) anormalement gros(se), hypertrophié(e)
enlargement [ɪnˈlɑːdʒmənt] N (*Phot*) agrandissement m
enlighten [ɪnˈlaɪtn] VT éclairer
enlightened [ɪnˈlaɪtnd] ADJ éclairé(e)
enlightening [ɪnˈlaɪtnɪŋ] ADJ instructif(-ive), révélateur(-trice)
enlightenment [ɪnˈlaɪtnmənt] N édification f; éclaircissements mpl; (*Hist*): **the E~** = le Siècle des lumières
enlist [ɪnˈlɪst] VT recruter; (*support*) s'assurer
▶ VI s'engager; **enlisted man** (US Mil) simple soldat m
enliven [ɪnˈlaɪvn] VT animer, égayer
enmity [ˈɛnmɪtɪ] N inimitié f
ennoble [ɪˈnəʊbl] VT (*with title*) anoblir
enormity [ɪˈnɔːmɪtɪ] N énormité f
enormous [ɪˈnɔːməs] ADJ énorme
enormously [ɪˈnɔːməslɪ] ADV (*increase*) dans des proportions énormes; (*rich*) extrêmement
enough [ɪˈnʌf] ADJ: **~ time/books** assez or suffisamment de temps/livres ▶ ADV: **big ~** assez or suffisamment grand ▶ PRON: **have you got ~?** (en) avez-vous assez?; **will five be ~?** est-ce que cinq suffiront?, est-ce qu'il y en aura assez avec cinq?; **~ to eat** assez à manger; **(that's) ~!** ça suffit!, assez!; **that's ~ , thanks** cela suffit or c'est assez, merci; **I've had ~!** je n'en peux plus!; **I've had ~ of him** j'en ai assez de lui; **he has not worked ~** il n'a pas assez or suffisamment travaillé, il n'a pas travaillé assez or suffisamment; **it's hot ~ (as it is)!** il fait assez chaud comme ça!; **he was kind ~ to lend me the money** il a eu la gentillesse de me prêter l'argent; **... which, funnily** or **oddly or strangely ~ ...** qui, chose curieuse, ...
enquire [ɪnˈkwaɪə^r] VT, VI = **inquire**
enquiry [ɪnˈkwaɪərɪ] N = **inquiry**
enrage [ɪnˈreɪdʒ] VT mettre en fureur or en rage, rendre furieux(-euse)
enrich [ɪnˈrɪtʃ] VT enrichir
enrol, (US) **enroll** [ɪnˈrəʊl] VT inscrire ▶ VI s'inscrire
enrolment, (US) **enrollment** [ɪnˈrəʊlmənt] N inscription f
en route [ɔnˈruːt] ADV en route, en chemin; **~ for** or **to** en route vers, à destination de
ensconced [ɪnˈskɒnst] ADJ: **~ in** bien calé(e) dans
enshrine [ɪnˈʃraɪn] VT (*fig*) préserver

ensign N (Naut) [ˈɛnsən] enseigne f, pavillon m; (Mil) [ˈɛnsaɪn] porte-étendard m
enslave [ɪnˈsleɪv] VT asservir
ensue [ɪnˈsjuː] VI s'ensuivre, résulter
en suite [ˈɔnswiːt] ADJ: **with ~ bathroom** avec salle de bains en attenante
ensure [ɪnˈʃʊə^r] VT assurer, garantir; **to ~ that** s'assurer que
ENT N ABBR (= *Ear, Nose and Throat*) ORL f
entail [ɪnˈteɪl] VT entraîner, nécessiter
entangle [ɪnˈtæŋɡl] VT emmêler, embrouiller; **to become entangled in sth** (*fig*) se laisser entraîner or empêtrer dans qch
enter [ˈɛntə^r] VT (*room*) entrer dans, pénétrer dans; (*club, army*) entrer à; (*profession*) embrasser; (*competition*) s'inscrire à or pour; (*sb for a competition*) (faire) inscrire; (*write down*) inscrire, noter; (*Comput*) entrer, introduire ▶ VI entrer
▶ **enter for** VT FUS s'inscrire à, se présenter pour or à
▶ **enter into** VT FUS (*explanation*) se lancer dans; (*negotiations*) entamer; (*debate*) prendre part à; (*agreement*) conclure
▶ **enter on** VT FUS commencer
▶ **enter up** VT inscrire
▶ **enter upon** VT FUS = **enter on**
enteritis [ɛntəˈraɪtɪs] N entérite f
enterprise [ˈɛntəpraɪz] N (*company, undertaking*) entreprise f; (*initiative*) (esprit m d')initiative f; **free ~** libre entreprise; **private ~** entreprise privée
enterprising [ˈɛntəpraɪzɪŋ] ADJ entreprenant(e), dynamique; (*scheme*) audacieux(-euse)
entertain [ɛntəˈteɪn] VT amuser, distraire; (*invite*) recevoir (à dîner); (*idea, plan*) envisager
entertainer [ɛntəˈteɪnə^r] N artiste mf de variétés
entertaining [ɛntəˈteɪnɪŋ] ADJ amusant(e), distrayant(e) ▶ N: **to do a lot of ~** beaucoup recevoir
entertainment [ɛntəˈteɪnmənt] N (*amusement*) distraction f, divertissement m, amusement m; (*show*) spectacle m
entertainment allowance N frais mpl de représentation
enthralled [ɪnˈθrɔːld] ADJ captivé(e)
enthralling [ɪnˈθrɔːlɪŋ] ADJ captivant(e), enchanteur(-eresse)
enthuse [ɪnˈθuːz] VI: **to ~ about** or **over** parler avec enthousiasme de
enthusiasm [ɪnˈθuːzɪæzəm] N enthousiasme m
enthusiast [ɪnˈθuːzɪæst] N enthousiaste mf; **a jazz etc ~** un fervent or passionné du jazz etc
enthusiastic [ɪnθuːzɪˈæstɪk] ADJ enthousiaste; **to be ~ about** être enthousiasmé(e) par
entice [ɪnˈtaɪs] VT attirer, séduire
enticing [ɪnˈtaɪsɪŋ] ADJ (*person, offer*) séduisant(e); (*food*) alléchant(e)
entire [ɪnˈtaɪə^r] ADJ (tout) entier(-ère)
entirely [ɪnˈtaɪəlɪ] ADV entièrement, complètement
entirety [ɪnˈtaɪərətɪ] N: **in its ~** dans sa totalité
entitle [ɪnˈtaɪtl] VT (*allow*): **to ~ sb to do** donner

(le) droit à qn de faire; **to ~ sb to sth** donner droit à qch à qn

entitled [ɪnˈtaɪtld] ADJ *(book)* intitulé(e); **to be ~ to do** avoir le droit de faire

entity [ˈɛntɪtɪ] N entité *f*

entrails [ˈɛntreɪlz] NPL entrailles *fpl*

entrance N [ˈɛntrns] entrée *f* ▶ VT [ɪnˈtrɑːns] enchanter, ravir; **where's the ~?** où est l'entrée?; **to gain ~ to** *(university etc)* être admis à

entrance examination N examen *m* d'entrée *or* d'admission

entrance fee N *(to museum etc)* prix *m* d'entrée; *(to join club etc)* droit *m* d'inscription

entrance ramp N *(US Aut)* bretelle *f* d'accès

entrancing [ɪnˈtrɑːnsɪŋ] ADJ enchanteur(-eresse), ravissant(e)

entrant [ˈɛntrnt] N *(in race etc)* participant(e), concurrent(e); *(Brit: in exam)* candidat(e)

entreat [ɛnˈtriːt] VT supplier

entreaty [ɛnˈtriːtɪ] N supplication *f*, prière *f*

entrée [ˈɔntreɪ] N *(Culin)* entrée *f*

entrenched [ɛnˈtrɛntʃt] ADJ retranché(e)

entrepreneur [ˈɔntrəprəˈnəːʳ] N entrepreneur *m*

entrepreneurial [ˈɔntrəprəˈnəːrɪəl] ADJ animé(e) d'un esprit d'entreprise

entrust [ɪnˈtrʌst] VT: **to ~ sth to** confier qch à

entry [ˈɛntrɪ] N entrée *f*; *(in register, diary)* inscription *f*; *(in ledger)* écriture *f*; **"no ~"** "défense d'entrer", "entrée interdite"; *(Aut)* "sens interdit"; **single/double - book-keeping** comptabilité *f* en partie simple/double

entry form N feuille *f* d'inscription

entry phone N *(Brit)* interphone *m* *(à l'entrée d'un immeuble)*

entwine [ɪnˈtwaɪn] VT entrelacer

E-number [ˈiːnʌmbəʳ] N additif *m* (alimentaire)

enumerate [ɪˈnjuːməreɪt] VT énumérer

enunciate [ɪˈnʌnsɪeɪt] VT énoncer; prononcer

envelop [ɪnˈvɛləp] VT envelopper

envelope [ˈɛnvələup] N enveloppe *f*

enviable [ˈɛnvɪəbl] ADJ enviable

envious [ˈɛnvɪəs] ADJ envieux(-euse)

environment [ɪnˈvaɪərnmənt] N *(social, moral)* milieu *m*; *(natural world)*: **the ~** l'environnement *m*; **Department of the E~** *(Brit)* ministère de l'Équipement et de l'Aménagement du territoire

environmental [ɪnvaɪərnˈmɛntl] ADJ *(of surroundings)* du milieu; *(issue, disaster)* écologique; **~ studies** *(in school etc)* écologie *f*

environmentalist [ɪnvaɪərnˈmɛntlɪst] N écologiste *mf*

environmentally [ɪnvaɪərnˈmɛntlɪ] ADV: **~ sound/friendly** qui ne nuit pas à l'environnement

Environmental Protection Agency N *(US)* ≈ ministère *m* de l'Environnement

envisage [ɪnˈvɪzɪdʒ] VT *(imagine)* envisager; *(foresee)* prévoir

envision [ɪnˈvɪʒən] VT envisager, concevoir

envoy [ˈɛnvɔɪ] N envoyé(e); *(diplomat)* ministre *m* plénipotentiaire

envy [ˈɛnvɪ] N envie *f* ▶ VT envier; **to ~ sb sth** envier qch à qn

enzyme [ˈɛnzaɪm] N enzyme *m*

EPA N ABBR *(US)* = **Environmental Protection Agency**

ephemeral [ɪˈfɛmərl] ADJ éphémère

epic [ˈɛpɪk] N épopée *f* ▶ ADJ épique

epicentre, *(US)* **epicenter** [ˈɛpɪsɛntəʳ] N épicentre *m*

epidemic [ɛpɪˈdɛmɪk] N épidémie *f*

epilepsy [ˈɛpɪlɛpsɪ] N épilepsie *f*

epileptic [ɛpɪˈlɛptɪk] ADJ, N épileptique *mf*

epileptic fit N crise *f* d'épilepsie

epilogue [ˈɛpɪlɔg] N épilogue *m*

episcopal [ɪˈpɪskəpl] ADJ épiscopal(e)

episode [ˈɛpɪsəud] N épisode *m*

epistle [ɪˈpɪsl] N épître *f*

epitaph [ˈɛpɪtɑːf] N épitaphe *f*

epithet [ˈɛpɪθɛt] N épithète *f*

epitome [ɪˈpɪtəmɪ] N *(fig)* quintessence *f*, type *m*

epitomize [ɪˈpɪtəmaɪz] VT *(fig)* illustrer, incarner

epoch [ˈiːpɔk] N époque *f*, ère *f*

epoch-making [ˈiːpɔkmeɪkɪŋ] ADJ qui fait époque

eponymous [ɪˈpɔnɪməs] ADJ de ce *or* du même nom, éponyme

equable [ˈɛkwəbl] ADJ égal(e), de tempérament égal

equal [ˈiːkwl] ADJ égal(e) ▶ N égal(e) ▶ VT égaler; **~ to** *(task)* à la hauteur de; **~ to doing** de taille à *or* capable de faire

equality [iːˈkwɔlɪtɪ] N égalité *f*

equalize [ˈiːkwəlaɪz] VT, VI *(Sport)* égaliser

equalizer [ˈiːkwəlaɪzəʳ] N but égalisateur

equally [ˈiːkwəlɪ] ADV également; *(share)* en parts égales; *(treat)* de la même façon; *(pay)* autant; *(just as)* tout aussi; **they are ~ clever** ils sont tout aussi intelligents

Equal Opportunities Commission, *(US)* **Equal Employment Opportunity Commission** N commission pour la non discrimination dans l'emploi

equal sign, equals sign N signe *m* d'égalité

equanimity [ɛkwəˈnɪmɪtɪ] N égalité *f* d'humeur

equate [ɪˈkweɪt] VT: **to ~ sth with** comparer qch à; assimiler qch à; **to ~ sth to** mettre qch en équation avec; égaler qch à

equation [ɪˈkweɪʒən] N *(Math)* équation *f*

equator [ɪˈkweɪtəʳ] N équateur *m*

Equatorial Guinea [ˌɛkwəˈtɔːrɪəl-] N Guinée équatoriale

equestrian [ɪˈkwɛstrɪən] ADJ équestre ▶ N écuyer(-ère), cavalier(-ère)

equilibrium [iːkwɪˈlɪbrɪəm] N équilibre *m*

equinox [ˈiːkwɪnɔks] N équinoxe *m*

equip [ɪˈkwɪp] VT équiper; **to ~ sb/sth with** équiper *or* munir qn/qch de; **he is well equipped for the job** il a les compétences *or* les qualités requises pour ce travail

equipment [ɪˈkwɪpmənt] N équipement *m*; *(electrical etc)* appareillage *m*, installation *f*

equitable [ˈɛkwɪtəbl] ADJ équitable

equities [ˈɛkwɪtɪz] NPL *(Brit Comm)* actions cotées en Bourse

equity [ˈɛkwɪtɪ] N équité *f*

equity capital N capitaux *mpl* propres

equivalent [ɪˈkwɪvəlnt] ADJ équivalent(e) ▸ N équivalent *m*; **to be ~ to** équivaloir à, être équivalent(e) à

equivocal [ɪˈkwɪvəkl] ADJ équivoque; (*open to suspicion*) douteux(-euse)

equivocate [ɪˈkwɪvəkeɪt] VI user de faux-fuyants; éviter de répondre

equivocation [ɪkwɪvəˈkeɪʃən] N équivoque *f*

ER ABBR (BRIT: = *Elizabeth Regina*) la reine Élisabeth; (*US Med*: = *emergency room*) urgences *fpl*

ERA N ABBR (*US Pol*: = *Equal Rights Amendment*) amendement sur l'égalité des droits des femmes

era [ˈɪərə] N ère *f*, époque *f*

eradicate [ɪˈrædɪkeɪt] VT éliminer

erase [ɪˈreɪz] VT effacer

eraser [ɪˈreɪzəʳ] N gomme *f*

e-reader, eReader [ˈiːriːdəʳ] N liseuse *f*

erect [ɪˈrɛkt] ADJ droit(e) ▸ VT construire; (*monument*) ériger, élever; (*tent etc*) dresser

erection [ɪˈrɛkʃən] N (*Physiol*) érection *f*; (*of building*) construction *f*; (*of machinery etc*) installation *f*

ergonomics [əːgəˈnɔmɪks] N ergonomie *f*

ERISA N ABBR (*US*: = *Employee Retirement Income Security Act*) loi sur les pensions de retraite

Eritrea [ɛrɪˈtreɪə] N Érythrée *f*

ERM N ABBR (= *Exchange Rate Mechanism*) mécanisme *m* des taux de change

ermine [ˈəːmɪn] N hermine *f*

ERNIE [ˈəːnɪ] N ABBR (BRIT: = *Electronic Random Number Indicator Equipment*) ordinateur servant au tirage des bons à lots gagnants

erode [ɪˈrəud] VT éroder; (*metal*) ronger

erogenous zone [ɪˈrɔdʒənəs-] N zone *f* érogène

erosion [ɪˈrəuʒən] N érosion *f*

erotic [ɪˈrɔtɪk] ADJ érotique

eroticism [ɪˈrɔtɪsɪzəm] N érotisme *m*

err [əːʳ] VI se tromper; (*Rel*) pécher

errand [ˈɛrnd] N course *f*, commission *f*; **to run errands** faire des courses; **~ of mercy** mission *f* de charité, acte *m* charitable

errand boy N garçon *m* de courses

erratic [ɪˈrætɪk] ADJ irrégulier(-ière), inconstant(e)

erroneous [ɪˈrəunɪəs] ADJ erroné(e)

error [ˈɛrəʳ] N erreur *f*; **typing/spelling ~** faute *f* de frappe/d'orthographe; **in ~** par erreur, par méprise; **errors and omissions excepted** sauf erreur ou omission

error message N (*Comput*) message *m* d'erreur

erstwhile [ˈəːstwaɪl] ADJ précédent(e), d'autrefois

erudite [ˈɛrjudaɪt] ADJ savant(e)

erupt [ɪˈrʌpt] VI entrer en éruption; (*fig*) éclater, exploser

eruption [ɪˈrʌpʃən] N éruption *f*; (*of anger, violence*) explosion *f*

ESA N ABBR (= *European Space Agency*) ASE *f* (= *Agence spatiale européenne*)

escalate [ˈɛskəleɪt] VI s'intensifier; (*costs*) monter en flèche

escalation [ɛskəˈleɪʃən] N escalade *f*

escalation clause N clause *f* d'indexation

escalator [ˈɛskəleɪtəʳ] N escalier roulant

escapade [ɛskəˈpeɪd] N fredaine *f*; équipée *f*

escape [ɪˈskeɪp] N évasion *f*, fuite *f*; (*of gas etc*) fuite; (*Tech*) échappement *m* ▸ VI s'échapper, fuir; (*from jail*) s'évader; (*fig*) s'en tirer, en réchapper; (*leak*) fuir, s'échapper ▸ VT échapper à; **to ~ from** (*person*) échapper à; (*place*) s'échapper de; (*fig*) fuir; **to ~ to** (*another place*) fuir à, s'enfuir à; **to ~ to safety** se réfugier dans *or* gagner un endroit sûr; **to ~ notice** passer inaperçu(e); **his name escapes me** son nom m'échappe

escape artist N virtuose *mf* de l'évasion

escape clause N clause *f* dérogatoire

escapee [ɪskeɪˈpiː] N évadé(e)

escape key N (*Comput*) touche *f* d'échappement

escape route N (*from fire*) issue *f* de secours; (*of prisoners etc*) voie empruntée pour s'échapper

escapism [ɪˈskeɪpɪzəm] N évasion *f* (*fig*)

escapist [ɪˈskeɪpɪst] ADJ (*literature*) d'évasion ▸ N personne *f* qui se réfugie hors de la réalité

escapologist [ɛskəˈpɔlədʒɪst] N (BRIT) = **escape artist**

escarpment [ɪsˈkɑːpmənt] N escarpement *m*

eschew [ɪsˈtʃuː] VT éviter

escort VT [ɪˈskɔːt] escorter ▸ N [ˈɛskɔːt] (*Mil*) escorte *f*; (*to dance etc*): **her ~** son compagnon *or* cavalier; **his ~** sa compagne

escort agency N bureau *m* d'hôtesses

Eskimo [ˈɛskɪməu] ADJ esquimau(de), eskimo ▸ N Esquimau(de); (*Ling*) esquimau *m*

ESL N ABBR (*Scol*) = **English as a Second Language**

esophagus [iːˈsɔfəgəs] N (*US*) = **oesophagus**

esoteric [ɛsəˈtɛrɪk] ADJ ésotérique

ESP N ABBR = **extrasensory perception**; (*Scol*) = **English for Special Purposes**

esp. ABBR = **especially**

especially [ɪˈspɛʃlɪ] ADV (*particularly*) particulièrement; (*above all*) surtout

espionage [ˈɛspɪənɑːʒ] N espionnage *m*

esplanade [ɛspləˈneɪd] N esplanade *f*

espouse [ɪˈspauz] VT épouser, embrasser

Esquire [ɪˈskwaɪəʳ] N (BRIT: *abbr* **Esq.**): **J. Brown, ~** Monsieur J. Brown

essay [ˈɛseɪ] N (*Scol*) dissertation *f*; (*Literature*) essai *m*; (*attempt*) tentative *f*

essence [ˈɛsns] N essence *f*; (*Culin*) extrait *m*; **in ~** en substance; **speed is of the ~** l'essentiel, c'est la rapidité

essential [ɪˈsɛnʃl] ADJ essentiel(le); (*basic*) fondamental(e); **essentials** NPL éléments essentiels; **it is ~ that** il est essentiel *or* primordial que

essentially [ɪˈsɛnʃlɪ] ADV essentiellement

EST ABBR (*US*: = *Eastern Standard Time*) heure d'hiver de New York

est. ABBR = **established; estimate(d)**

establish [ɪˈstæblɪʃ] VT établir; (*business*) fonder, créer; (*one's power etc*) asseoir, affermir

established [ɪˈstæblɪʃt] ADJ bien établi(e)

establishment [ɪˈstæblɪʃmənt] N établissement *m*; (*founding*) création *f*; (*institution*) établissement; **the E~** les pouvoirs établis; l'ordre établi

estate [ɪ'steɪt] N (*land*) domaine *m*, propriété *f*; (*Law*) biens *mpl*, succession *f*; (*BRIT: also:* **housing estate**) lotissement *m*

estate agency N (*BRIT*) agence immobilière

estate agent N (*BRIT*) agent immobilier

estate car N (*BRIT*) break *m*

esteem [ɪ'sti:m] N estime *f* ▶ VT estimer; apprécier; **to hold sb in high ~** tenir qn en haute estime

esthetic [ɪs'θɛtɪk] ADJ (*US*) = **aesthetic**

estimate N ['ɛstɪmət] estimation *f*; (*Comm*) devis *m* ▶ VT ['ɛstɪmeɪt] estimer ▶ VI (*BRIT Comm*): **to ~ for** estimer, faire une estimation de; (*bid for*) faire un devis pour; **to give sb an ~ of** faire *or* donner un devis à qn pour; **at a rough ~** approximativement

estimation [ɛstɪ'meɪʃən] N opinion *f*; estime *f*; **in my ~** à mon avis, selon moi

Estonia [ɛ'stəʊnɪə] N Estonie *f*

Estonian [ɛ'stəʊnɪən] ADJ estonien(ne) ▶ N Estonien(ne); (*Ling*) estonien *m*

estranged [ɪs'treɪndʒd] ADJ (*couple*) séparé(e); (*husband, wife*) dont on s'est séparé(e)

estrangement [ɪs'treɪndʒmənt] N (*from wife, family*) séparation *f*

estrogen ['i:strəʊdʒən] N (*US*) = **oestrogen**

estuary ['ɛstjʊərɪ] N estuaire *m*

ET N ABBR (*BRIT: = Employment Training*) *formation professionnelle pour les demandeurs d'emploi* ▶ ABBR (*US: = Eastern Time*) *heure de New York*

ETA N ABBR (*= estimated time of arrival*) HPA *f* (*= heure probable d'arrivée*)

et al. ABBR (*= et alii: and others*) et coll

etc ABBR (*= et cetera*) etc

etch [ɛtʃ] VT graver à l'eau forte

etching ['ɛtʃɪŋ] N eau-forte *f*

ETD N ABBR (*= estimated time of departure*) HPD *f* (*= heure probable de départ*)

eternal [ɪ'tə:nl] ADJ éternel(le)

eternity [ɪ'tə:nɪtɪ] N éternité *f*

ether ['i:θə^r] N éther *m*

ethereal [ɪ'θɪərɪəl] ADJ éthéré(e)

ethical ['ɛθɪkl] ADJ moral(e)

ethics ['ɛθɪks] N éthique *f* ▶ NPL moralité *f*

Ethiopia [i:θɪ'əʊpɪə] N Éthiopie *f*

Ethiopian [i:θɪ'əʊpɪən] ADJ éthiopien(ne) ▶ N Éthiopien(ne)

ethnic ['ɛθnɪk] ADJ ethnique; (*clothes, food*) folklorique, exotique, *propre aux minorités ethniques non-occidentales*

ethnic cleansing [-'klɛnzɪŋ] N purification *f* ethnique

ethnic minority N minorité *f* ethnique

ethnology [ɛθ'nɔlədʒɪ] N ethnologie *f*

ethos ['i:θɔs] N (*système m de*) valeurs *fpl*

e-ticket ['i:tɪkɪt] N billet *m* électronique

etiquette ['ɛtɪkɛt] N convenances *fpl*, étiquette *f*

ETV N ABBR (*US: = Educational Television*) *télévision scolaire*

etymology [ɛtɪ'mɔlədʒɪ] N étymologie *f*

EU N ABBR (*= European Union*) UE *f*

eucalyptus [ju:kə'lɪptəs] N eucalyptus *m*

eulogy ['ju:lədʒɪ] N éloge *m*

euphemism ['ju:fəmɪzəm] N euphémisme *m*

euphemistic [ju:fə'mɪstɪk] ADJ euphémique

euphoria [ju:'fɔ:rɪə] N euphorie *f*

Eurasia [juə'reɪʃə] N Eurasie *f*

Eurasian [juə'reɪʃən] ADJ eurasien(ne); (*continent*) eurasiatique ▶ N Eurasien(ne)

Euratom [juə'rætəm] N ABBR (*= European Atomic Energy Community*) EURATOM *f*

euro ['juərəʊ] N (*currency*) euro *m*

Euro- ['juərəʊ] PREFIX euro-

Eurocrat ['juərəʊkræt] N eurocrate *mf*

Euroland ['juərəʊlænd] N Euroland *m*

Europe ['juərəp] N Europe *f*

European [juərə'pi:ən] ADJ européen(ne) ▶ N Européen(ne)

European Community N Communauté européenne

European Court of Justice N Cour *f* de Justice de la CEE

European Union N Union européenne

Euro-sceptic ['juərəʊskɛptɪk] N eurosceptique *mf*

Eurostar® ['juərəʊsta:^r] N Eurostar® *m*

euthanasia [ju:θə'neɪzɪə] N euthanasie *f*

evacuate [ɪ'vækjueɪt] VT évacuer

evacuation [ɪvækju'eɪʃən] N évacuation *f*

evacuee [ɪvækju'i:] N évacué(e)

evade [ɪ'veɪd] VT échapper à; (*question etc*) éluder; (*duties*) se dérober à

evaluate [ɪ'væljueɪt] VT évaluer

evangelist [ɪ'vændʒəlɪst] N évangéliste *m*

evangelize [ɪ'vændʒəlaɪz] VT évangéliser, prêcher l'Évangile à

evaporate [ɪ'væpəreɪt] VI s'évaporer; (*fig: hopes, fear*) s'envoler; (: *anger*) se dissiper ▶ VT faire évaporer

evaporated milk [ɪ'væpəreɪtɪd-] N lait condensé (non sucré)

evaporation [ɪvæpə'reɪʃən] N évaporation *f*

evasion [ɪ'veɪʒən] N dérobade *f*; (*excuse*) faux-fuyant *m*

evasive [ɪ'veɪsɪv] ADJ évasif(-ive)

eve [i:v] N: **on the ~ of** à la veille de

even ['i:vn] ADJ (*level, smooth*) régulier(-ière); (*equal*) égal(e); (*number*) pair(e) ▶ ADV même; **~ if** même si + *indic*; **~ though** quand (bien) même + *cond*, alors même que + *cond*; **~ more** encore plus; **~ faster** encore plus vite; **~ so** quand même; **not ~** pas même; **~ he was there** même lui était là; **~ on Sundays** même le dimanche; **to break ~** s'y retrouver, équilibrer ses comptes; **to get ~ with sb** prendre sa revanche sur qn ▶ **even out** VI s'égaliser

even-handed [i:vn'hændɪd] ADJ équitable

evening ['i:vnɪŋ] N soir *m*; (*as duration, event*) soirée *f*; **in the ~** le soir; **this ~** ce soir; **tomorrow/yesterday ~** demain/hier soir

evening class N cours *m* du soir

evening dress N (*man's*) tenue *f* de soirée, smoking *m*; (*woman's*) robe *f* de soirée

evenly ['i:vnlɪ] ADV uniformément, également; (*space*) régulièrement

evensong ['i:vnsɔŋ] N office *m* du soir

event [ɪ'vɛnt] N événement *m*; (*Sport*) épreuve *f*;

in the course of events par la suite; **in the ~ of** en cas de; **in the ~** en réalité, en fait; **at all events**, (BRIT) **in any ~** en tout cas, de toute manière

eventful [ɪ'vɛntful] ADJ mouvementé(e)

eventing [ɪ'vɛntɪŋ] N (Horse-Riding) concours complet (équitation)

eventual [ɪ'vɛntʃuəl] ADJ final(e)

eventuality [ɪvɛntʃu'ælɪtɪ] N possibilité f, éventualité f

eventually [ɪ'vɛntʃuəlɪ] ADV finalement

ever ['ɛvə'] ADV jamais; (at all times) toujours; **why ~ not?** mais enfin, pourquoi pas?; **the best ~** le meilleur qu'on ait jamais vu; **have you ~ seen it?** l'as-tu déjà vu?, as-tu eu l'occasion or t'est-il arrivé de le voir?; **did you ~ meet him?** est-ce qu'il vous est arrivé de le rencontrer?; **have you ~ been there?** y êtes-vous déjà allé?; **for ~** pour toujours; **hardly ~** ne ... presque jamais; **~ since** (as adv) depuis; (as conj) depuis que; **~ so pretty** si joli; **thank you ~ so much** merci mille fois

Everest ['ɛvərɪst] N (also: **Mount Everest**) le mont Everest, l'Everest m

evergreen ['ɛvəgri:n] N arbre m à feuilles persistantes

everlasting [ɛvə'la:stɪŋ] ADJ éternel(le)

(KEYWORD)

every ['ɛvrɪ] ADJ **1** (each) chaque; **every one of them** tous (sans exception); **every shop in town was closed** tous les magasins en ville étaient fermés

2 (all possible) tous (toutes) les; **I gave you every assistance** j'ai fait tout mon possible pour vous aider; **I have every confidence in him** j'ai entièrement or pleinement confiance en lui; **we wish you every success** nous vous souhaitons beaucoup de succès

3 (showing recurrence) tous les; **every day** tous les jours, chaque jour; **every other car** une voiture sur deux; **every other/third day** tous les deux/trois jours; **every now and then** de temps en temps

everybody PRON = **everyone**

everyday ['ɛvrɪdeɪ] ADJ (expression) courant(e), d'usage courant; (use) courant; (clothes, life) de tous les jours; (occurrence, problem) quotidien(ne)

everyone ['ɛvrɪwʌn] PRON tout le monde, tous pl; **~ knows about it** tout le monde le sait; **~ else** tous les autres

everything ['ɛvrɪθɪŋ] PRON tout; **~ is ready** tout est prêt; **he did ~ possible** il a fait tout son possible

everywhere ['ɛvrɪwɛə'] ADV partout; **~ you go you meet ...** où qu'on aille on rencontre ...

evict [ɪ'vɪkt] VT expulser

eviction [ɪ'vɪkʃən] N expulsion f

eviction notice N préavis m d'expulsion

evidence ['ɛvɪdns] N (proof) preuve(s) f(pl); (of witness) témoignage m; (sign) to **show ~ of** donner des signes de; **to give ~** témoigner, déposer; **in ~** (obvious) en évidence; en vue

evident ['ɛvɪdnt] ADJ évident(e)

evidently ['ɛvɪdntlɪ] ADV de toute évidence; (apparently) apparemment

evil ['i:vl] ADJ mauvais(e) ▶ N mal m

evince [ɪ'vɪns] VT manifester

evocative [ɪ'vɔkətɪv] ADJ évocateur(-trice)

evoke [ɪ'vəuk] VT évoquer; (admiration) susciter

evolution [i:və'lu:ʃən] N évolution f

evolve [ɪ'vɔlv] VT élaborer ▶ VI évoluer, se transformer

ewe [ju:] N brebis f

ex [ɛks] N (inf): **my ex** mon ex

ex- [ɛks] PREFIX (former: husband, president etc) ex-; (out of): **the price ~works** le prix départ usine

exacerbate [ɪg'zæsəbeɪt] VT (pain) exacerber, accentuer; (fig) aggraver

exact [ɪg'zækt] ADJ exact(e) ▶ VT: **to ~ sth (from)** (signature, confession) extorquer qch (à); (apology) exiger qch (de)

exacting [ɪg'zæktɪŋ] ADJ exigeant(e); (work) fatigant(e)

exactitude [ɪg'zæktɪtju:d] N exactitude f, précision f

exactly [ɪg'zæktlɪ] ADV exactement; **~!** parfaitement!, précisément!

exaggerate [ɪg'zædʒəreɪt] VT, VI exagérer

exaggeration [ɪgzædʒə'reɪʃən] N exagération f

exalted [ɪg'zɔ:ltɪd] ADJ (rank) élevé(e); (person) haut placé(e); (elated) exalté(e)

exam [ɪg'zæm] N ABBR (Scol) = **examination**

examination [ɪgzæmɪ'neɪʃən] N (Scol, Med) examen m; **to take** or **sit an ~** (BRIT) passer un examen; **the matter is under ~** la question est à l'examen

examine [ɪg'zæmɪn] VT (gen) examiner; (Scol, Law: person) interroger; (inspect: machine, premises) inspecter; (: passport) contrôler; (: luggage) fouiller

examiner [ɪg'zæmɪnə'] N examinateur(-trice)

example [ɪg'zɑ:mpl] N exemple m; **for ~** par exemple; **to set a good/bad ~** donner le bon/mauvais exemple

exasperate [ɪg'zɑ:spəreɪt] VT exaspérer, agacer

exasperated [ɪg'zɑ:spəreɪtɪd] ADJ exaspéré(e)

exasperation [ɪgzɑ:spə'reɪʃən] N exaspération f, irritation f

excavate ['ɛkskəveɪt] VT (site) fouiller, excaver; (object) mettre au jour

excavation [ɛkskə'veɪʃən] N excavation f

excavator ['ɛkskəveɪtə'] N excavateur m, excavatrice f

exceed [ɪk'si:d] VT dépasser; (one's powers) outrepasser

exceedingly [ɪk'si:dɪŋlɪ] ADV extrêmement

excel [ɪk'sɛl] VI exceller ▶ VT surpasser; **to ~ o.s.** se surpasser

excellence ['ɛksələns] N excellence f

Excellency ['ɛksələnsɪ] N: **His ~** son Excellence f

excellent ['ɛksələnt] ADJ excellent(e)

except [ɪk'sɛpt] PREP (also: **except for**, **excepting**) sauf, excepté, à l'exception de ▶ VT excepter; **~ if/when** sauf si/quand; **~ that** excepté que, si ce n'est que

exception [ɪk'sɛpʃən] N exception f; **to take ~**

to s'offusquer de; **with the ~ of** à l'exception de

exceptional [ɪkˈsɛpʃənl] ADJ exceptionnel(le)

exceptionally [ɪkˈsɛpʃənəlɪ] ADV exceptionnellement

excerpt [ˈɛksəːpt] N extrait *m*

excess [ɪkˈsɛs] N excès *m*; **in ~ of** plus de

excess baggage N excédent *m* de bagages

excess fare N supplément *m*

excessive [ɪkˈsɛsɪv] ADJ excessif(-ive)

excess supply N suroffre *f*, offre *f* excédentaire

exchange [ɪksˈtʃeɪndʒ] N échange *m*; (*also:* **telephone exchange**) central *m* ▶ VT: **to ~ (for)** échanger (contre); **could I ~ this, please?** est-ce que je peux échanger ceci, s'il vous plaît?; **in ~ for** en échange de; **foreign ~** (*Comm*) change *m*

exchange control N contrôle *m* des changes

exchange market N marché *m* des changes

exchange rate N taux *m* de change

excisable [ɪkˈsaɪzəbl] ADJ taxable

excise N [ˈɛksaɪz] taxe *f* ▶ VT [ɛkˈsaɪz] exciser

excise duties NPL impôts indirects

excitable [ɪkˈsaɪtəbl] ADJ excitable, nerveux(-euse)

excite [ɪkˈsaɪt] VT exciter

excited [ɪkˈsaɪtəd] ADJ (tout (toute)) excité(e); **to get ~** s'exciter

excitement [ɪkˈsaɪtmənt] N excitation *f*

exciting [ɪkˈsaɪtɪŋ] ADJ passionnant(e)

excl. ABBR = **excluding; exclusive (of)**

exclaim [ɪkˈskleɪm] VI s'exclamer

exclamation [ɛkskləˈmeɪʃən] N exclamation *f*

exclamation mark, (*US*) **exclamation point** N point *m* d'exclamation

exclude [ɪkˈskluːd] VT exclure

excluding [ɪkˈskluːdɪŋ] PREP: **~ VAT** la TVA non comprise

exclusion [ɪkˈskluːʒən] N exclusion *f*; **to the ~ of** à l'exclusion de

exclusion clause N clause *f* d'exclusion

exclusion zone N zone interdite

exclusive [ɪkˈskluːsɪv] ADJ exclusif(-ive); (*club, district*) sélect(e); (*item of news*) en exclusivité ▶ ADV (*Comm*) exclusivement, non inclus; **~ of VAT** TVA non comprise; **~ of postage** (les) frais de poste non compris; **from 1st to 15th March ~** du 1er au 15 mars exclusivement *or* exclu; **~ rights** (*Comm*) exclusivité *f*

exclusively [ɪkˈskluːsɪvlɪ] ADV exclusivement

excommunicate [ɛkskəˈmjuːnɪkeɪt] VT excommunier

excrement [ˈɛkskrəmənt] N excrément *m*

excruciating [ɪkˈskruːʃɪeɪtɪŋ] ADJ (*pain*) atroce, déchirant(e); (*embarrassing*) pénible

excursion [ɪkˈskəːʃən] N excursion *f*

excursion ticket N billet *m* tarif excursion

excusable [ɪkˈskjuːzəbl] ADJ excusable

excuse N [ɪkˈskjuːs] excuse *f* ▶ VT [ɪkˈskjuːz] (*forgive*) excuser; (*justify*) excuser, justifier; **to ~ sb from** (*activity*) dispenser qn de; **~ me!** excusez-moi!, pardon!; **now if you will ~ me,** ... maintenant, si vous (le) permettez ...; **to make excuses for sb** trouver des excuses à qn;

to ~ o.s. for sth/for doing sth s'excuser de/d'avoir fait qch

ex-directory [ˈɛksdɪˈrɛktərɪ] ADJ (*BRIT*) sur la liste rouge

execute [ˈɛksɪkjuːt] VT exécuter

execution [ɛksɪˈkjuːʃən] N exécution *f*

executioner [ɛksɪˈkjuːnəʳ] N bourreau *m*

executive [ɪgˈzɛkjutɪv] N (*person*) cadre *m*; (*managing group*) bureau *m*; (*Pol*) exécutif *m* ▶ ADJ exécutif(-ive); (*position, job*) de cadre; (*secretary*) de direction; (*offices*) de la direction; (*car, plane*) de fonction

executive director N administrateur(-trice)

executor [ɪgˈzɛkjutəʳ] N exécuteur(-trice) testamentaire

exemplary [ɪgˈzɛmplərɪ] ADJ exemplaire

exemplify [ɪgˈzɛmplɪfaɪ] VT illustrer

exempt [ɪgˈzɛmpt] ADJ: **~ from** exempté(e) *or* dispensé(e) de ▶ VT: **to ~ sb from** exempter *or* dispenser qn de

exemption [ɪgˈzɛmpʃən] N exemption *f*, dispense *f*

exercise [ˈɛksəsaɪz] N exercice *m* ▶ VT exercer; (*patience etc*) faire preuve de; (*dog*) promener ▶ VI (*also:* **to take exercise**) prendre de l'exercice

exercise bike N vélo *m* d'appartement

exercise book N cahier *m*

exert [ɪgˈzəːt] VT exercer, employer; (*strength, force*) employer; **to ~ o.s.** se dépenser

exertion [ɪgˈzəːʃən] N effort *m*

ex gratia [ˈɛksˈgreɪʃə] ADJ: **~ payment** gratification *f*

exhale [ɛksˈheɪl] VT (*breathe out*) expirer; exhaler ▶ VI expirer

exhaust [ɪgˈzɔːst] N (*also:* **exhaust fumes**) gaz *mpl* d'échappement; (*also:* **exhaust pipe**) tuyau *m* d'échappement ▶ VT épuiser; **to ~ o.s.** s'épuiser

exhausted [ɪgˈzɔːstɪd] ADJ épuisé(e)

exhausting [ɪgˈzɔːstɪŋ] ADJ épuisant(e)

exhaustion [ɪgˈzɔːstʃən] N épuisement *m*; **nervous ~** fatigue nerveuse

exhaustive [ɪgˈzɔːstɪv] ADJ très complet(-ète)

exhibit [ɪgˈzɪbɪt] N (*Art*) objet exposé, pièce exposée; (*Law*) pièce à conviction ▶ VT (*Art*) exposer; (*courage, skill*) faire preuve de

exhibition [ɛksɪˈbɪʃən] N exposition *f*; **~ of temper** manifestation *f* de colère

exhibitionist [ɛksɪˈbɪʃənɪst] N exhibitionniste *mf*

exhibitor [ɪgˈzɪbɪtəʳ] N exposant(e)

exhilarating [ɪgˈzɪləreɪtɪŋ] ADJ grisant(e), stimulant(e)

exhilaration [ɪgzɪləˈreɪʃən] N euphorie *f*, ivresse *f*

exhort [ɪgˈzɔːt] VT exhorter

ex-husband [ˈɛksˈhʌzbənd] N ex-mari *m*

exile [ˈɛksaɪl] N exil *m*; (*person*) exilé(e) ▶ VT exiler; **in ~** en exil

exist [ɪgˈzɪst] VI exister

existence [ɪgˈzɪstəns] N existence *f*; **to be in ~** exister

existentialism [ɛgzɪsˈtɛnʃlɪzəm] N existentialisme *m*

existing [ɪɡˈzɪstɪŋ] ADJ (laws) existant(e); (system, regime) actuel(le)

exit [ˈɛksɪt] N sortie f ▶ VI (Comput, Theat) sortir; **where's the ~?** où est la sortie?

exit poll N sondage m (fait à la sortie de l'isoloir)

exit ramp N (US Aut) bretelle f d'accès

exit visa N visa m de sortie

exodus [ˈɛksədəs] N exode m

ex officio [ˈɛksəˈfɪʃɪəu] ADJ, ADV d'office, de droit

exonerate [ɪɡˈzɔnəreɪt] VT: **to ~ from** disculper de

exorbitant [ɪɡˈzɔːbɪtnt] ADJ (price) exorbitant(e), excessif(-ive); (demands) exorbitant, démesuré(e)

exorcize [ˈɛksɔːsaɪz] VT exorciser

exotic [ɪɡˈzɔtɪk] ADJ exotique

expand [ɪkˈspænd] VT (area) agrandir; (quantity) accroître; (influence etc) étendre ▶ VI (population, production) s'accroître; (trade, etc) se développer, s'accroître; (gas, metal) se dilater, dilater; **to ~ on** (notes, story etc) développer

expanse [ɪkˈspæns] N étendue f

expansion [ɪkˈspænʃən] N (territorial, economic) expansion f; (of trade, influence etc) développement m; (of production) accroissement m; (of population) croissance f; (of gas, metal) expansion, dilatation f

expansionism [ɪkˈspænʃənɪzəm] N expansionnisme m

expansionist [ɪkˈspænʃənɪst] ADJ expansionniste

expatriate N [ɛksˈpætrɪət] expatrié(e) ▶ VT [ɛksˈpætrɪeɪt] expatrier, exiler

expect [ɪkˈspɛkt] VT (anticipate) s'attendre à, s'attendre à ce que+sub; (count on) compter sur, escompter; (hope for) espérer; (require) demander, exiger; (suppose) supposer; (await: also baby) attendre ▶ VI: **to be expecting** (pregnant woman) être enceinte; **to ~ sb to do** (anticipate) s'attendre à ce que qn fasse; (demand) attendre de qn qu'il fasse; **to ~ to do sth** penser or compter faire qch, s'attendre à faire qch; **as expected** comme prévu; **I ~ so** je crois que oui, je crois bien

expectancy [ɪkˈspɛktənsɪ] N attente f; **life ~** espérance f de vie

expectant [ɪkˈspɛktənt] ADJ qui attend (quelque chose); **~ mother** future maman

expectantly [ɪkˈspɛktəntlɪ] ADV (look, listen) avec l'air d'attendre quelque chose

expectation [ɛkspɛkˈteɪʃən] N (hope) attente f, espérance(s) f(pl); (belief) attente; **in ~ of** dans l'attente de, en prévision de; **against** or **contrary to all ~(s)** contre toute attente, contrairement à ce qu'on attendait; **to come** or **live up to sb's expectations** répondre à l'attente or aux espérances de qn

expedience [ɛkˈspiːdɪəns], **expediency** [ɛkˈspiːdɪənsɪ] N opportunité f; convenance f (du moment); **for the sake of ~** parce que c'est (or c'était) plus simple or plus commode

expedient [ɪkˈspiːdɪənt] ADJ indiqué(e), opportun(e), commode ▶ N expédient m

expedite [ˈɛkspədaɪt] VT hâter; expédier

expedition [ɛkspəˈdɪʃən] N expédition f

expeditionary force [ɛkspəˈdɪʃənrɪ-] N corps m expéditionnaire

expeditious [ɛkspəˈdɪʃəs] ADJ expéditif(-ive), prompt(e)

expel [ɪkˈspɛl] VT chasser, expulser; (Scol) renvoyer, exclure

expend [ɪkˈspɛnd] VT consacrer; (use up) dépenser

expendable [ɪkˈspɛndəbl] ADJ remplaçable

expenditure [ɪkˈspɛndɪtʃəʳ] N (act of spending) dépense f; (money spent) dépenses fpl

expense [ɪkˈspɛns] N (high cost) coût m; (spending) dépense f, frais mpl; **expenses** NPL frais mpl; dépenses; **to go to the ~ of** faire la dépense de; **at great/little ~** à grands/peu de frais; **at the ~ of** aux frais de; (fig) aux dépens de

expense account N (note f de) frais mpl

expensive [ɪkˈspɛnsɪv] ADJ cher (chère), coûteux(-euse); **to be ~** coûter cher; **it's too ~** ça coûte trop cher; **~ tastes** goûts mpl de luxe

experience [ɪkˈspɪərɪəns] N expérience f ▶ VT connaître; (feeling) éprouver; **to know by ~** savoir par expérience

experienced [ɪkˈspɪərɪənst] ADJ expérimenté(e)

experiment [ɪkˈspɛrɪmənt] N expérience f ▶ VI faire une expérience; **to ~ with** expérimenter; **to perform** or **carry out an ~** faire une expérience; **as an ~** à titre d'expérience

experimental [ɪkspɛrɪˈmɛntl] ADJ expérimental(e)

expert [ˈɛkspəːt] ADJ expert(e) ▶ N expert m; **~ in** or **at doing sth** spécialiste de qch; **an ~ on sth** un spécialiste de qch; **~ witness** (Law) expert m

expertise [ɛkspəːˈtiːz] N (grande) compétence

expire [ɪkˈspaɪəʳ] VI expirer

expiry [ɪkˈspaɪərɪ] N expiration f

expiry date N date f d'expiration; (on label) à utiliser avant …

explain [ɪkˈspleɪn] VT expliquer ▶ **explain away** VT justifier, excuser

explanation [ɛkspləˈneɪʃən] N explication f; **to find an ~ for sth** trouver une explication à qch

explanatory [ɪkˈsplænətrɪ] ADJ explicatif(-ive)

expletive [ɪkˈspliːtɪv] N juron m

explicit [ɪkˈsplɪsɪt] ADJ explicite; (definite) formel(le)

explode [ɪkˈspləud] VI exploser ▶ VT faire exploser; (fig: theory) démolir; **to ~ a myth** détruire un mythe

exploit N [ˈɛksplɔɪt] exploit m ▶ VT [ɪkˈsplɔɪt] exploiter

exploitation [ɛksplɔɪˈteɪʃən] N exploitation f

exploration [ɛkspləˈreɪʃən] N exploration f

exploratory [ɪkˈsplɔrətrɪ] ADJ (fig: talks) préliminaire; **~ operation** (Med) intervention f (à visée) exploratrice

explore [ɪkˈsplɔːʳ] VT explorer; (possibilities) étudier, examiner

explorer [ɪkˈsplɔːrəʳ] N explorateur(-trice)

explosion [ɪkˈspləuʒən] N explosion f

explosive [ɪkˈspləusɪv] ADJ explosif(-ive) ▶ N explosif m

exponent [ɪkˈspəunənt] N (of school of thought etc)

interprète *m*, représentant *m*; (*Math*) exposant *m*

export VT [ɛk'spɔːt] exporter ▶ N ['ɛkspɔːt] exportation *f* ▶ CPD ['ɛkspɔːt] d'exportation

exportation [ɛkspɔː'teɪʃən] N exportation *f*

exporter [ɛk'spɔːtəʳ] N exportateur *m*

export licence N licence *f* d'exportation

expose [ɪk'spəʊz] VT exposer; (*unmask*) démasquer, dévoiler; **to ~ o.s.** (*Law*) commettre un outrage à la pudeur

exposed [ɪk'spəʊzd] ADJ (*land, house*) exposé(e); (*Elec: wire*) à nu; (: *pipe, beam*) apparent(e)

exposition [ɛkspə'zɪʃən] N exposition *f*

exposure [ɪk'spəʊʒəʳ] N exposition *f*; (*publicity*) couverture *f*; (*Phot: speed*) (temps *m* de) pose *f*; (: *shot*) pose; **suffering from ~** (*Med*) souffrant des effets du froid et de l'épuisement; **to die of ~** (*Med*) mourir de froid

exposure meter N posemètre *m*

expound [ɪk'spaʊnd] VT exposer, expliquer

express [ɪk'sprɛs] ADJ (*definite*) formel(le), exprès(-esse); (*BRIT: letter etc*) exprès *inv* ▶ N (*train*) rapide *m* ▶ ADV (*send*) exprès ▶ VT exprimer; **to ~ o.s.** s'exprimer

expression [ɪk'sprɛʃən] N expression *f*

expressionism [ɪk'sprɛʃənɪzəm] N expressionnisme *m*

expressive [ɪk'sprɛsɪv] ADJ expressif(-ive)

expressly [ɪk'sprɛslɪ] ADV expressément, formellement

expressway [ɪk'sprɛsweɪ] N (*US*) voie *f* express (à plusieurs files)

expropriate [ɛks'prəʊprɪeɪt] VT exproprier

expulsion [ɪk'spʌlʃən] N expulsion *f*; renvoi *m*

exquisite [ɛk'skwɪzɪt] ADJ exquis(e)

ex-serviceman ['ɛks'səːvɪsmən] N (*irreg*) ancien combattant

ext. ABBR (*Tel*) = **extension**

extemporize [ɪk'stɛmpəraɪz] VI improviser

extend [ɪk'stɛnd] VT (*visit, street*) prolonger; (*deadline*) reporter, remettre; (*building*) agrandir; (*offer*) présenter, offrir; (*Comm: credit*) accorder; (*hand, arm*) tendre ▶ VI (*land*) s'étendre

extension [ɪk'stɛnʃən] N (*of visit, street*) prolongation *f*; (*of building*) agrandissement *m*; (*building*) annexe *f*; (*to wire, table*) rallonge *f*; (*telephone: in offices*) poste *m*; (: *in private house*) téléphone *m* supplémentaire; **~ 3718** (*Tel*) poste 3718

extension cable, extension lead N (*Elec*) rallonge *f*

extensive [ɪk'stɛnsɪv] ADJ étendu(e), vaste; (*damage, alterations*) considérable; (*inquiries*) approfondi(e); (*use*) largement répandu(e)

extensively [ɪk'stɛnsɪvlɪ] ADV (*altered, damaged etc*) considérablement; **he's travelled ~** il a beaucoup voyagé

extent [ɪk'stɛnt] N étendue *f*; (*degree: of damage, loss*) importance *f*; **to some ~** dans une certaine mesure; **to a certain ~** dans une certaine mesure, jusqu'à un certain point; **to a large ~** en grande partie; **to the ~ of …** au point de …; **to what ~?** dans quelle mesure?, jusqu'à quel point?; **to such an ~ that …** à tel point que …

extenuating [ɪk'stɛnjueɪtɪŋ] ADJ: **~ circumstances** circonstances atténuantes

exterior [ɛk'stɪərɪəʳ] ADJ extérieur(e) ▶ N extérieur *m*

exterminate [ɪk'stəːmɪneɪt] VT exterminer

extermination [ɪkstəːmɪ'neɪʃən] N extermination *f*

external [ɛk'stəːnl] ADJ externe ▶ N: **the externals** les apparences *fpl*; **for ~ use only** (*Med*) à usage externe

externally [ɛk'stəːnəlɪ] ADV extérieurement

extinct [ɪk'stɪŋkt] ADJ (*volcano*) éteint(e); (*species*) disparu(e)

extinction [ɪk'stɪŋkʃən] N extinction *f*

extinguish [ɪk'stɪŋgwɪʃ] VT éteindre

extinguisher [ɪk'stɪŋgwɪʃəʳ] N extincteur *m*

extol, (*US*) **extoll** [ɪk'stəʊl] VT (*merits*) chanter, prôner; (*person*) chanter les louanges de

extort [ɪk'stɔːt] VT: **to ~ sth (from)** extorquer qch (à)

extortion [ɪk'stɔːʃən] N extorsion *f*

extortionate [ɪk'stɔːʃnɪt] ADJ exorbitant(e)

extra ['ɛkstrə] ADJ supplémentaire, de plus ▶ ADV (*in addition*) en plus ▶ N supplément *m*; (*perk*) à-coté *m*; (*Cine, Theat*) figurant(e); **wine will cost ~** le vin sera en supplément; **~ large sizes** très grandes tailles

extra… ['ɛkstrə] PREFIX extra…

extract VT [ɪk'strækt] extraire; (*tooth*) arracher; (*money, promise*) soutirer ▶ N ['ɛkstrækt] extrait *m*

extraction [ɪk'strækʃən] N extraction *f*

extractor fan [ɪk'stræktə-] N exhausteur *m*, ventilateur *m* extracteur

extracurricular ['ɛkstrəkə'rɪkjuləʳ] ADJ (*Scol*) parascolaire

extradite ['ɛkstrədaɪt] VT extrader

extradition [ɛkstrə'dɪʃən] N extradition *f*

extramarital ['ɛkstrə'mærɪtl] ADJ extraconjugal(e)

extramural ['ɛkstrə'mjuərl] ADJ hors-faculté *inv*

extraneous [ɛk'streɪnɪəs] ADJ: **~ to** étranger(-ère) à

extraordinary [ɪk'strɔːdnrɪ] ADJ extraordinaire; **the ~ thing is that …** le plus étrange or étonnant c'est que …

extraordinary general meeting N assemblée *f* générale extraordinaire

extrapolation [ɛkstræpə'leɪʃən] N extrapolation *f*

extrasensory perception ['ɛkstrə'sɛnsərɪ-] N perception *f* extrasensorielle

extra time N (*Football*) prolongations *fpl*

extravagance [ɪk'strævəgəns] N (*excessive spending*) prodigalités *fpl*; (*thing bought*) folie *f*, dépense excessive

extravagant [ɪk'strævəgənt] ADJ extravagant(e); (*in spending: person*) prodigue, dépensier(-ière); (: *tastes*) dispendieux(-euse)

extreme [ɪk'striːm] ADJ, N extrême (*m*); **the ~ left/right** (*Pol*) l'extrême gauche/droite *f*; **extremes of temperature** différences *fpl* extrêmes de température

extremely [ɪk'striːmlɪ] ADV extrêmement

e

575

extremist [ɪk'stri:mɪst] ADJ, N extrémiste mf

extremity [ɪk'strɛmɪtɪ] N extrémité f

extricate ['ɛkstrɪkeɪt] VT: **to ~ sth (from)** dégager qch (de)

extrovert ['ɛkstrəvə:t] N extraverti(e)

exuberance [ɪg'zju:bərns] N exubérance f

exuberant [ɪg'zju:bərnt] ADJ exubérant(e)

exude [ɪg'zju:d] VT exsuder; (fig) respirer; **the charm** etc **he exudes** le charme etc qui émane de lui

exult [ɪg'zʌlt] VI exulter, jubiler

exultant [ɪg'zʌltənt] ADJ (shout, expression) de triomphe; **to be ~** jubiler, triompher

exultation [ɛgzʌl'teɪʃən] N exultation f, jubilation f

ex-wife ['ɛkswaɪf] N ex-femme f

eye [aɪ] N œil m; (of needle) trou m, chas m ▶ VT examiner; **as far as the ~ can see** à perte de vue; **to keep an ~ on** surveiller; **to have an ~ for sth** avoir l'œil pour qch; **in the public ~** en vue; **with an ~ to doing sth** (BRIT) en vue de faire qch; **there's more to this than meets the ~** ce n'est pas aussi simple que cela paraît

eyeball ['aɪbɔ:l] N globe m oculaire

eyebath ['aɪbɑ:θ] N (BRIT) œillère f (pour bains d'œil)

eyebrow ['aɪbrau] N sourcil m

eyebrow pencil N crayon m à sourcils

eye-catching ['aɪkætʃɪŋ] ADJ voyant(e), accrocheur(-euse)

eye cup N (US) = **eyebath**

eye drops ['aɪdrɔps] NPL gouttes fpl pour les yeux

eyeful ['aɪful] N: **to get an ~ (of sth)** se rincer l'œil (en voyant qch)

eyeglass ['aɪglɑ:s] N monocle m

eyelash ['aɪlæʃ] N cil m

eyelet ['aɪlɪt] N œillet m

eye-level ['aɪlɛvl] ADJ en hauteur

eyelid ['aɪlɪd] N paupière f

eyeliner ['aɪlaɪnər] N eye-liner m

eye-opener ['aɪəupnər] N révélation f

eye shadow ['aɪʃædəu] N ombre f à paupières

eyesight ['aɪsaɪt] N vue f

eyesore ['aɪsɔ:r] N horreur f, chose f qui dépare or enlaidit

eyestrain ['aɪstreɪn] ADJ: **to get ~** se fatiguer la vue or les yeux

eyewash ['aɪwɔʃ] N bain m d'œil; (fig) frime f

eye witness N témoin m oculaire

eyrie ['ɪərɪ] N aire f

Ff

F¹, f [ɛf] N (*letter*) F, f *m*; (*Mus*): **F** fa *m*; **F for Frederick**, (*US*) **F for Fox** F comme François

F² ABBR (= *Fahrenheit*) F

FA N ABBR (*BRIT*: = *Football Association*) fédération de football

FAA N ABBR (*US*) = **Federal Aviation Administration**

fable ['feɪbl] N fable *f*

fabric ['fæbrɪk] N tissu *m* ► CPD: **~ ribbon** (*for typewriter*) ruban *m* (en) tissu

fabricate ['fæbrɪkeɪt] VT fabriquer, inventer

fabrication [fæbrɪ'keɪʃən] N fabrication *f*, invention *f*

fabulous ['fæbjuləs] ADJ fabuleux(-euse); (*inf*: *super*) formidable, sensationnel(le)

façade [fə'sɑːd] N façade *f*

face [feɪs] N visage *m*, figure *f*; (*expression*) air *m*; grimace *f*; (*of clock*) cadran *m*; (*of cliff*) paroi *f*; (*of mountain*) face *f*; (*of building*) façade *f*; (*side, surface*) face *f* ► VT faire face à; (*facts etc*) accepter; **~ down** (*person*) à plat ventre; (*card*) face en dessous; **to lose/save ~** perdre/sauver la face; **to pull a ~** faire une grimace; **in the ~ of** (*difficulties etc*) face à, devant; **on the ~ of it** à première vue; **~ to ~** face à face
► **face up to** VT FUS faire face à, affronter

Facebook® ['feɪs,bʊk] N Facebook® *m*

facebook® ['feɪs,bʊk] VT envoyer un message sur Facebook (à qn); **she facebooked him** elle lui a envoyé un message sur Facebook

face cloth N (*BRIT*) gant *m* de toilette

face cream N crème *f* pour le visage

face lift N lifting *m*; (*of façade etc*) ravalement *m*, retapage *m*

face pack N (*BRIT*) masque *m* (de beauté)

face powder N poudre *f* (pour le visage)

face-saving ['feɪsseɪvɪŋ] ADJ qui sauve la face

facet ['fæsɪt] N facette *f*

facetious [fə'siːʃəs] ADJ facétieux(-euse)

face-to-face ['feɪstə'feɪs] ADV face à face

face value N (*of coin*) valeur nominale; **to take sth at ~** (*fig*) prendre qch pour argent comptant

facia ['feɪʃə] N = **fascia**

facial ['feɪʃl] ADJ facial(e) ► N soin complet du visage

facile ['fæsaɪl] ADJ facile

facilitate [fə'sɪlɪteɪt] VT faciliter

facilities [fə'sɪlɪtɪz] NPL installations *fpl*, équipement *m*; **credit ~** facilités *fpl* de paiement

facility [fə'sɪlɪtɪ] N facilité *f*

facing ['feɪsɪŋ] PREP face à, en face de ► N (*of wall etc*) revêtement *m*; (*Sewing*) revers *m*

facsimile [fæk'sɪmɪlɪ] N (*exact replica*) facsimilé *m*; (*also*: **facsimile machine**) télécopieur *m*; (*transmitted document*) télécopie *f*

fact [fækt] N fait *m*; **in ~** en fait; **to know for a ~ that ...** savoir pertinemment que ...

fact-finding ['fæktfaɪndɪŋ] ADJ: **a ~ tour** *or* **mission** une mission d'enquête

faction ['fækʃən] N faction *f*

factional ['fækʃnl] ADJ de factions

factor ['fæktəʳ] N facteur *m*; (*of sun cream*) indice *m* (de protection); (*Comm*) factor *m*, société *f* d'affacturage; (: *agent*) dépositaire *mf* ► VI faire du factoring; **safety ~** facteur de sécurité; **I'd like a ~ 15 suntan lotion** je voudrais une crème solaire d'indice 15

factory ['fæktərɪ] N usine *f*, fabrique *f*

factory farming N (*BRIT*) élevage industriel

factory floor N: **the ~** (*workers*) les ouvriers *mpl*; (*workshop*) l'usine *f*; **on the ~** dans les ateliers

factory ship N navire-usine *m*

factual ['fæktjuəl] ADJ basé(e) sur les faits

faculty ['fækəltɪ] N faculté *f*; (*US*: *teaching staff*) corps enseignant

fad [fæd] N (*personal*) manie *f*; (*craze*) engouement *m*

fade [feɪd] VI se décolorer, passer; (*light, sound*) s'affaiblir, disparaître; (*flower*) se faner
► **fade away** VI (*sound*) s'affaiblir
► **fade in** VT (*picture*) ouvrir en fondu; (*sound*) monter progressivement
► **fade out** VT (*picture*) fermer en fondu; (*sound*) baisser progressivement

faeces, (*US*) **feces** ['fiːsiːz] NPL fèces *fpl*

fag [fæg] N (*BRIT inf*: *cigarette*) clope *f*; (: *chore*): **what a ~!** quelle corvée!; (*US offensive*: *gay*) pédé *m*

fag end N (*BRIT inf*) mégot *m*

fagged out [fægd-] ADJ (*BRIT inf*) crevé(e)

Fahrenheit ['fɑːrənhaɪt] N Fahrenheit *m inv*

fail [feɪl] VT (*exam*) échouer à; (*candidate*) recaler; (*subj*: *courage, memory*) faire défaut à ► VI échouer; (*supplies*) manquer; (*eyesight, health, light*: *also*: **be failing**) baisser, s'affaiblir; (*brakes*) lâcher; **to ~**

to do sth (neglect) négliger de or ne pas faire qch; (be unable) ne pas arriver or parvenir à faire qch; **without ~** à coup sûr; sans faute

failing ['feɪlɪŋ] N défaut m ▸ PREP faute de; **~ that** à défaut, sinon

failsafe ['feɪlseɪf] ADJ (device etc) à sûreté intégrée

failure ['feɪljə'] N échec m; (person) raté(e); (mechanical etc) défaillance f; **his ~ to turn up** le fait de n'être pas venu or qu'il ne soit pas venu

faint [feɪnt] ADJ faible; (recollection) vague; (mark) à peine visible; (smell, breeze, trace) léger(-ère) ▸ N évanouissement m ▸ VI s'évanouir; **to feel ~** défaillir

faintest ['feɪntɪst] ADJ: **I haven't the ~ idea** je n'en ai pas la moindre idée

faint-hearted ['feɪnt'hɑːtɪd] ADJ pusillanime

faintly ['feɪntlɪ] ADV faiblement; (vaguely) vaguement

faintness ['feɪntnɪs] N faiblesse f

fair [fɛə'] ADJ équitable, juste; (reasonable) correct(e), honnête; (hair) blond(e); (skin, complexion) pâle, blanc (blanche); (weather) beau (belle); (good enough) assez bon(ne); (sizeable) considérable ▸ ADV: **to play ~** jouer franc jeu ▸ N foire f; (BRIT: funfair) fête (foraine); (also: **trade fair**) foire-(exposition) commerciale; **it's not ~!** ce n'est pas juste!; **a ~ amount of** une quantité considérable de

fair copy N copie f au propre, corrigé m

fair game N: **to be ~ (for)** être une cible légitime (pour)

fairground ['fɛəgraund] N champ m de foire

fair-haired [fɛə'hɛəd] ADJ (person) aux cheveux clairs, blond(e)

fairly ['fɛəlɪ] ADV (justly) équitablement; (quite) assez; **I'm ~ sure** j'en suis quasiment or presque sûr

fairness ['fɛənɪs] N (of trial etc) justice f, équité f; (of person) sens m de la justice; **in all ~** en toute justice

fair play N fair play m

fair trade N commerce m équitable

fairway ['fɛəweɪ] N (Golf) fairway m

fairy ['fɛərɪ] N fée f

fairy godmother N bonne fée

fairy lights NPL (BRIT) guirlande f électrique

fairy tale N conte m de fées

faith [feɪθ] N foi f; (trust) confiance f; (sect) culte m, religion f; **to have ~ in sb/sth** avoir confiance en qn/qch

faithful ['feɪθful] ADJ fidèle

faithfully ['feɪθfəlɪ] ADV fidèlement; **yours ~** (BRIT: in letters) veuillez agréer l'expression de mes salutations les plus distinguées

faith healer [-hiːlə'] N guérisseur(-euse)

fake [feɪk] N (painting etc) faux m; (photo) trucage m; (person) imposteur m ▸ ADJ faux (fausse) ▸ VT (emotions) simuler; (painting) faire un faux de; (photo) truquer; (story) fabriquer; **his illness is a ~** sa maladie est une comédie or de la simulation

falcon ['fɔːlkən] N faucon m

Falkland Islands ['fɔːlklənd-] NPL: **the ~** les Malouines fpl, les îles fpl Falkland

fall [fɔːl] (pt **fell** [fɛl], pp **fallen** ['fɔːlən]) N chute f; (decrease) baisse f; (US: autumn) automne m ▸ VI tomber; (price, temperature, dollar) baisser; **falls** NPL (waterfall) chute f d'eau, cascade f; **to ~ flat** vi (on one's face) tomber de tout son long, s'étaler; (joke) tomber à plat; (plan) échouer; **to ~ short of** (sb's expectations) ne pas répondre à; **a ~ of snow** (BRIT) une chute de neige

▸ **fall apart** VI (object) tomber en morceaux; (inf: emotionally) craquer

▸ **fall back** VI reculer, se retirer

▸ **fall back on** VT FUS se rabattre sur; **to have something to ~ back on** (money etc) avoir quelque chose en réserve; (job etc) avoir une solution de rechange

▸ **fall behind** VI prendre du retard

▸ **fall down** VI (person) tomber; (building) s'effondrer, s'écrouler

▸ **fall for** VT FUS (trick) se laisser prendre à; (person) tomber amoureux(-euse) de

▸ **fall in** VI s'effondrer; (Mil) se mettre en rangs

▸ **fall in with** VT FUS (sb's plans etc) accepter

▸ **fall off** VI tomber; (diminish) baisser, diminuer

▸ **fall out** VI (friends etc) se brouiller; (hair, teeth) tomber

▸ **fall over** VI tomber (par terre)

▸ **fall through** VI (plan, project) tomber à l'eau

fallacy ['fæləsɪ] N erreur f, illusion f

fallback ['fɔːlbæk] ADJ: **~ position** position f de repli

fallen ['fɔːlən] PP of **fall**

fallible ['fæləbl] ADJ faillible

fallopian tube [fə'ləupɪən-] N (Anat) trompe f de Fallope

fallout ['fɔːlaut] N retombées (radioactives)

fallout shelter NPL abri m anti-atomique

fallow ['fæləu] ADJ en jachère; en friche

false [fɔːls] ADJ faux (fausse); **under ~ pretences** sous un faux prétexte

false alarm N fausse alerte

falsehood ['fɔːlshud] N mensonge m

falsely ['fɔːlslɪ] ADV (accuse) à tort

false teeth NPL (BRIT) fausses dents, dentier m

falsify ['fɔːlsɪfaɪ] VT falsifier; (accounts) maquiller

falter ['fɔːltə'] VI chanceler, vaciller

fame [feɪm] N renommée f, renom m

familiar [fə'mɪlɪə'] ADJ familier(-ière); **to be ~ with sth** connaître qch; **to make o.s. ~ with sth** se familiariser avec qch; **to be on ~ terms with sb** bien connaître qn

familiarity [fəmɪlɪ'ærɪtɪ] N familiarité f

familiarize [fə'mɪlɪəraɪz] VT familiariser; **to ~ o.s. with** se familiariser avec

family ['fæmɪlɪ] N famille f

family allowance N (BRIT) allocations familiales

family business N entreprise familiale

family credit N (BRIT) complément familial

family doctor N médecin m de famille

family life N vie f de famille

family man N (irreg) père m de famille

family planning N planning familial

family planning clinic N centre m de planning familial

family tree N arbre *m* généalogique

famine ['fæmɪn] N famine *f*

famished ['fæmɪʃt] ADJ affamé(e); **I'm ~!** (*inf*) je meurs de faim!

famous ['feɪməs] ADJ célèbre

famously ['feɪməslɪ] ADV (*get on*) fameusement, à merveille

fan [fæn] N (*folding*) éventail *m*; (*Elec*) ventilateur *m*; (*person*) fan *m*, admirateur(-trice); (*Sport*) supporter *mf* ► VT éventer; (*fire, quarrel*) attiser
► **fan out** VI se déployer (en éventail)

fanatic [fə'nætɪk] N fanatique *mf*

fanatical [fə'nætɪkl] ADJ fanatique

fan belt N courroie *f* de ventilateur

fancied ['fænsɪd] ADJ imaginaire

fanciful ['fænsɪful] ADJ fantaisiste

fan club N fan-club *m*

fancy ['fænsɪ] N (*whim*) fantaisie *f*, envie *f*; (*imagination*) imagination *f* ► ADJ (*luxury*) de luxe; (*elaborate: jewellery, packaging*) fantaisie *inv*; (*showy*) tape-à-l'œil *inv*; (*pretentious: words*) recherché(e) ► VT (*feel like, want*) avoir envie de; (*imagine*) imaginer; **to take a ~ to** se prendre d'affection pour; s'enticher de; **it took** or **caught my ~** ça m'a plu; **when the ~ takes him** quand ça lui prend; **to ~ that ...** se figurer or s'imaginer que ...; **he fancies her** elle lui plaît

fancy dress N déguisement *m*, travesti *m*

fancy-dress ball [fænsɪ'drɛs-] N bal masqué or costumé

fancy goods NPL articles *mpl* (de) fantaisie

fanfare ['fænfɛər] N fanfare *f* (*musique*)

fanfold paper ['fænfəuld-] N papier *m* à pliage accordéon

fang [fæŋ] N croc *m*; (*of snake*) crochet *m*

fan heater N (*Brit*) radiateur soufflant

fanlight ['fænlaɪt] N imposte *f*

fanny ['fænɪ] N (*Brit inf!*) chatte *f*(!); (*US inf*) cul *m*(!)

fantasize ['fæntəsaɪz] VI fantasmer

fantastic [fæn'tæstɪk] ADJ fantastique

fantasy ['fæntəsɪ] N imagination *f*, fantaisie *f*; (*unreality*) fantasme *m*

fanzine ['fænzi:n] N fanzine *m*

FAO N ABBR (= *Food and Agriculture Organization*) FAO *f*

FAQ N ABBR (= *frequently asked question*) FAQ *f inv*, faq *f inv* ► ABBR (= *free alongside quay*) FLQ

far [fɑ:ʳ] ADJ (*distant*) lointain(e), éloigné(e) ► ADV loin; **the ~ side/end** l'autre côté/bout; **the ~ left/right** (*Pol*) l'extrême gauche *f*/droite *f*; **is it ~ to London?** est-ce qu'on est loin de Londres?; **it's not ~ (from here)** ce n'est pas loin (d'ici); **~ away, ~ off** au loin, dans le lointain; **~ better** beaucoup mieux; **~ from** loin de; **by ~** de loin, de beaucoup; **as ~ back as the 13th century** dès le 13e siècle; **go as ~ as the bridge** allez jusqu'au pont; **as ~ as I know** pour autant que je sache; **how ~ is it to ...?** combien y a-t-il jusqu'à ...?; **as ~ as possible** dans la mesure du possible; **how ~ have you got with your work?** où en êtes-vous dans votre travail?

faraway ['fɑ:rəweɪ] ADJ lointain(e); (*look*) absent(e)

farce [fɑ:s] N farce *f*

farcical ['fɑ:sɪkl] ADJ grotesque

fare [fɛəʳ] N (*on trains, buses*) prix *m* du billet; (*in taxi*) prix de la course; (*passenger in taxi*) client *m*; (*food*) table *f*, chère *f* ► VI se débrouiller; **half ~** demi-tarif; **full ~** plein tarif

Far East N: **the ~** l'Extrême-Orient *m*

farewell [fɛə'wɛl] EXCL, N adieu *m* ► CPD (*party etc*) d'adieux

far-fetched ['fɑ:'fɛtʃt] ADJ exagéré(e), poussé(e)

farm [fɑ:m] N ferme *f* ► VT cultiver
► **farm out** VT (*work etc*) distribuer

farmer ['fɑ:məʳ] N fermier(-ière), cultivateur(-trice)

farmhand ['fɑ:mhænd] N ouvrier(-ière) agricole

farmhouse ['fɑ:mhaus] N (maison *f* de) ferme *f*

farming ['fɑ:mɪŋ] N agriculture *f*; (*of animals*) élevage *m*; **intensive ~** culture intensive; **sheep ~** élevage du mouton

farm labourer N = **farmhand**

farmland ['fɑ:mlænd] N terres cultivées or arables

farm produce N produits *mpl* agricoles

farm worker N = **farmhand**

farmyard ['fɑ:mjɑ:d] N cour *f* de ferme

Faroe Islands ['fɛərəu-], **Faroes** ['fɛərəuz] NPL: **the ~** les îles *fpl* Féroé or Faeroe

far-reaching ['fɑ:'ri:tʃɪŋ] ADJ d'une grande portée

far-sighted ['fɑ:'saɪtɪd] ADJ presbyte; (*fig*) prévoyant(e), qui voit loin

fart [fɑ:t] (*inf!*) N pet *m* ► VI péter

farther ['fɑ:ðəʳ] ADV plus loin ► ADJ plus éloigné(e), plus lointain(e)

farthest ['fɑ:ðɪst] SUPERLATIVE *of* **far**

FAS ABBR (*Brit*: = *free alongside ship*) FLB

fascia ['feɪʃə] N (*Aut*) (garniture *f* du) tableau *m* de bord

fascinate ['fæsɪneɪt] VT fasciner, captiver

fascinated ['fæsɪneɪtəd] ADJ fasciné(e)

fascinating ['fæsɪneɪtɪŋ] ADJ fascinant(e)

fascination [fæsɪ'neɪʃən] N fascination *f*

fascism ['fæʃɪzəm] N fascisme *m*

fascist ['fæʃɪst] ADJ, N fasciste *mf*

fashion ['fæʃən] N mode *f*; (*manner*) façon *f*, manière *f* ► VT façonner; **in ~** à la mode; **out of ~** démodé(e); **in the Greek ~** à la grecque; **after a ~** (*finish, manage etc*) tant bien que mal

fashionable ['fæʃnəbl] ADJ à la mode

fashion designer N (grand(e)) couturier(-ière)

fashionista [fæʃə'nɪstə] N fashionista *mf*

fashion show N défilé *m* de mannequins or de mode

fast [fɑ:st] ADJ rapide; (*clock*): **to be ~** avancer; (*dye, colour*) grand or bon teint *inv* ► ADV vite, rapidement; (*stuck, held*) solidement ► N jeûne *m* ► VI jeûner; **my watch is 5 minutes ~** ma montre avance de 5 minutes; **~ asleep** profondément endormi; **as ~ as I can** aussi vite que je peux; **to make a boat ~** (*Brit*) amarrer un bateau

fasten ['fɑːsn] vt attacher, fixer; (coat) attacher, fermer ▶ vi se fermer, s'attacher
▶ **fasten on, fasten upon** vt fus (idea) se cramponner à

fastener ['fɑːsnər], **fastening** ['fɑːsnɪŋ] n fermeture f, attache f; (Brit: zip fastener) fermeture éclair® inv or à glissière

fast food n fast food m, restauration f rapide

fastidious [fæs'tɪdɪəs] adj exigeant(e), difficile

fast lane n (Aut: in Britain) voie f de droite

fat [fæt] adj gros(se) ▶ n graisse f; (on meat) gras m; (for cooking) matière grasse; **to live off the ~ of the land** vivre grassement

fatal ['feɪtl] adj (mistake) fatal(e); (injury) mortel(le)

fatalism ['feɪtlɪzəm] n fatalisme m

fatality [fə'tælɪtɪ] n (road death etc) victime f, décès m

fatally ['feɪtəlɪ] adv fatalement; (injured) mortellement

fate [feɪt] n destin m; (of person) sort m; **to meet one's ~** trouver la mort

fated ['feɪtɪd] adj (person) condamné(e); (project) voué(e) à l'échec

fateful ['feɪtful] adj fatidique

fat-free ['fæt'friː] adj sans matières grasses

father ['fɑːðər] n père m

Father Christmas n le Père Noël

fatherhood ['fɑːðəhud] n paternité f

father-in-law ['fɑːðərənlɔː] n beau-père m

fatherland ['fɑːðəlænd] n (mère f) patrie f

fatherly ['fɑːðəlɪ] adj paternel(le)

fathom ['fæðəm] n brasse f (= 1828 mm) ▶ vt (mystery) sonder, pénétrer

fatigue [fə'tiːg] n fatigue f; (Mil) corvée f; **metal ~** fatigue du métal

fatness ['fætnɪs] n corpulence f, grosseur f

fatten ['fætn] vt, vi engraisser

fattening ['fætnɪŋ] adj (food) qui fait grossir; **chocolate is ~** le chocolat fait grossir

fatty ['fætɪ] adj (food) gras(se) ▶ n (inf) gros (grosse)

fatuous ['fætjuəs] adj stupide

faucet ['fɔːsɪt] n (US) robinet m

fault [fɔːlt] n faute f; (defect) défaut m; (Geo) faille f ▶ vt trouver des défauts à, prendre en défaut; **it's my ~** c'est de ma faute; **to find ~ with** trouver à redire or à critiquer à; **at ~** fautif(-ive), coupable; **to a ~** à l'excès

faultless ['fɔːltlɪs] adj impeccable; irréprochable

faulty ['fɔːltɪ] adj défectueux(-euse)

fauna ['fɔːnə] n faune f

faux pas ['fəu'pɑː] n impair m, bévue f, gaffe f

favour, (US) **favor** ['feɪvər] n faveur f; (help) service m ▶ vt (proposition) être en faveur de; (pupil etc) favoriser; (team, horse) donner gagnant; **to do sb a ~** rendre un service à qn; **in ~ of** en faveur de; **to be in ~ of sth/of doing sth** être partisan de qch/de faire qch; **to find ~ with sb** trouver grâce aux yeux de qn

favourable, (US) **favorable** ['feɪvrəbl] adj favorable; (price) avantageux(-euse)

favourably, (US) **favorably** ['feɪvrəblɪ] adv favorablement

favourite, (US) **favorite** ['feɪvrɪt] adj, n favori(te)

favouritism, (US) **favoritism** ['feɪvrɪtɪzəm] n favoritisme m

fawn [fɔːn] n (deer) faon m ▶ adj (also: **fawn-coloured**) fauve ▶ vi: **to ~ (up)on** flatter servilement

fax [fæks] n (document) télécopie f; (machine) télécopieur m ▶ vt envoyer par télécopie

FBI n abbr (US: = Federal Bureau of Investigation) FBI m

FCC n abbr (US) = **Federal Communications Commission**

FCO n abbr (Brit: = Foreign and Commonwealth Office) ministère des Affaires étrangères et du Commonwealth

FD n abbr (US) = **fire department**

FDA n abbr (US: = Food and Drug Administration) office de contrôle des produits pharmaceutiques et alimentaires

FE n abbr = **further education**

fear [fɪər] n crainte f, peur f ▶ vt craindre ▶ vi: **to ~ for** craindre pour; **to ~ that** craindre que; **~ of heights** vertige m; **for ~ of** de peur que + sub or de + infinitive

fearful ['fɪəful] adj craintif(-ive); (sight, noise) affreux(-euse), épouvantable; **to be ~ of** avoir peur de, craindre

fearfully ['fɪəfəlɪ] adv (timidly) craintivement; (inf: very) affreusement

fearless ['fɪəlɪs] adj intrépide, sans peur

fearsome ['fɪəsəm] adj (opponent) redoutable; (sight) épouvantable

feasibility [fiːzə'bɪlɪtɪ] n (of plan) possibilité f de réalisation, faisabilité f

feasibility study n étude f de faisabilité

feasible ['fiːzəbl] adj faisable, réalisable

feast [fiːst] n festin m, banquet m; (Rel: also: **feast day**) fête f ▶ vi festoyer; **to ~ on** se régaler de

feat [fiːt] n exploit m, prouesse f

feather ['feðər] n plume f ▶ vt: **to ~ one's nest** (fig) faire sa pelote ▶ cpd (bed etc) de plumes

feather-weight ['feðəweɪt] n poids m plume inv

feature ['fiːtʃər] n caractéristique f; (article) chronique f, rubrique f ▶ vt (film) avoir pour vedette(s) ▶ vi figurer (en bonne place); **features** npl (of face) traits mpl; **a (special) ~ on sth/sb** un reportage sur qch/qn; **it featured prominently in ...** cela a figuré en bonne place sur or dans ...

feature film n long métrage

featureless ['fiːtʃəlɪs] adj anonyme, sans traits distinctifs

Feb. abbr (= February) fév

February ['februərɪ] n février m; see also **July**

feces ['fiːsiːz] npl (US) = **faeces**

feckless ['feklɪs] adj inepte

Fed abbr (US) = **federal; federation**

fed [fed] pt, pp of **feed**

Fed. [fed] n abbr (US inf) = **Federal Reserve Board**

federal ['fɛdərəl] ADJ fédéral(e)
Federal Reserve Board N (US) organe de contrôle de la banque centrale américaine
Federal Trade Commission N (US) organisme de protection contre les pratiques commerciales abusives
federation [fɛdə'reɪʃən] N fédération f
fed up [fɛd'ʌp] ADJ: **to be ~ (with)** en avoir marre or plein le dos (de)
fee [fi:] N rémunération f; (of doctor, lawyer) honoraires mpl; (of school, college etc) frais mpl de scolarité; (for examination) droits mpl; **entrance/ membership ~** droit d'entrée/d'inscription; **for a small ~** pour une somme modique
feeble ['fi:bl] ADJ faible; (attempt, excuse) pauvre; (joke) piteux(-euse)
feeble-minded ['fi:bl'maɪndɪd] ADJ faible d'esprit
feed [fi:d] (pt, pp **fed** [fɛd]) N (of baby) tétée f; (of animal) nourriture f, pâture f; (on printer) mécanisme m d'alimentation ▶ VT (person) nourrir; (BRIT: baby: breastfeed) allaiter; (: with bottle) donner le biberon à; (horse etc) donner à manger à; (machine) alimenter; (data etc): **to ~ sth into** enregistrer qch dans
  ▶ **feed back** VT (results) donner en retour
  ▶ **feed on** VT FUS se nourrir de
feedback ['fi:dbæk] N (Elec) effet m Larsen; (from person) réactions fpl
feeder ['fi:dər] N (bib) bavette f
feeding bottle ['fi:dɪŋ-] N (BRIT) biberon m
feel [fi:l] (pt, pp **felt** [fɛlt]) N (sensation) sensation f; (impression) impression f ▶ VT (touch) toucher; (explore) tâter, palper; (cold, pain) sentir; (grief, anger) ressentir, éprouver; (think, believe): **to ~ (that)** trouver que; **I ~ that you ought to do it** il me semble que vous devriez le faire; **to ~ hungry/cold** avoir faim/froid; **to ~ lonely/ better** se sentir seul/mieux; **I don't ~ well** je ne me sens pas bien; **to ~ sorry for** avoir pitié de; **it feels soft** c'est doux au toucher; **it feels colder here** je trouve qu'il fait plus froid ici; **it feels like velvet** on dirait du velours, ça ressemble au velours; **to ~ like** (want) avoir envie de; **to ~ about** or **around** fouiller, tâtonner; **to get the ~ of sth** (fig) s'habituer à qch
feeler ['fi:lər] N (of insect) antenne f; (fig): **to put out a ~** or **feelers** tâter le terrain
feeling ['fi:lɪŋ] N (physical) sensation f; (emotion, impression) sentiment m; **to hurt sb's feelings** froisser qn; **feelings ran high about it** cela a déchaîné les passions; **what are your feelings about the matter?** quel est votre sentiment sur cette question?; **my ~ is that** ... j'estime que ...; **I have a ~ that** ... j'ai l'impression que ...
fee-paying school ['fi:peɪɪŋ-] N établissement (d'enseignement) privé
feet [fi:t] NPL of **foot**
feign [feɪn] VT feindre, simuler
felicitous [fɪ'lɪsɪtəs] ADJ heureux(-euse)
fell [fɛl] PT of **fall** ▶ VT (tree) abattre ▶ N (BRIT: mountain) montagne f; (: moorland): **the fells** la lande ▶ ADJ: **with one ~ blow** d'un seul coup

fellow ['fɛləu] N type m; (comrade) compagnon m; (of learned society) membre m; (of university) universitaire mf (membre du conseil) ▶ CPD: **their ~ prisoners/students** leurs camarades prisonniers/étudiants; **his ~ workers** ses collègues mpl (de travail)
fellow citizen N concitoyen(ne)
fellow countryman N (irreg) compatriote m
fellow feeling N sympathie f
fellow men NPL semblables mpl
fellowship ['fɛləuʃɪp] N (society) association f; (comradeship) amitié f, camaraderie f; (Scol) sorte de bourse universitaire
fellow traveller N compagnon (compagne) de route; (Pol) communisant m
fell-walking ['fɛlwɔ:kɪŋ] N (BRIT) randonnée f en montagne
felon ['fɛlən] N (Law) criminel(le)
felony ['fɛlənɪ] N crime m, forfait m
felt [fɛlt] PT, PP of **feel** ▶ N feutre m
felt-tip ['fɛlttɪp] N (also: **felt-tip pen**) stylo-feutre m
female ['fi:meɪl] N (Zool) femelle f; (pej: woman) bonne femme ▶ ADJ (Biol, Elec) femelle; (sex, character) féminin(e); (vote etc) des femmes; (child etc) du sexe féminin; **male and ~ students** étudiants et étudiantes
female impersonator N (Theat) travesti m
feminine ['fɛmɪnɪn] ADJ féminin(e) ▶ N féminin m
femininity [fɛmɪ'nɪnɪtɪ] N féminité f
feminism ['fɛmɪnɪzəm] N féminisme m
feminist ['fɛmɪnɪst] N féministe mf
fen [fɛn] N (BRIT): **the Fens** les plaines fpl du Norfolk (anciennement marécageuses)
fence [fɛns] N barrière f; (Sport) obstacle m; (inf: person) receleur(-euse) ▶ VT (also: **fence in**) clôturer ▶ VI faire de l'escrime; **to sit on the ~** (fig) ne pas se mouiller
fencing ['fɛnsɪŋ] N (Sport) escrime m
fend [fɛnd] VI: **to ~ for o.s.** se débrouiller (tout seul)
  ▶ **fend off** VT (attack etc) parer; (questions) éluder
fender ['fɛndər] N garde-feu m inv; (on boat) défense f; (US: of car) aile f
fennel ['fɛnl] N fenouil m
ferment VI [fə'mɛnt] fermenter ▶ N ['fə:mɛnt] (fig) agitation f, effervescence f
fermentation [fə:mɛn'teɪʃən] N fermentation f
fern [fə:n] N fougère f
ferocious [fə'rəuʃəs] ADJ féroce
ferocity [fə'rɔsɪtɪ] N férocité f
ferret ['fɛrɪt] N furet m
  ▶ **ferret about, ferret around** VI fureter
  ▶ **ferret out** VT dénicher
ferry ['fɛrɪ] N (small) bac m; (large: also: **ferryboat**) ferry(-boat m) m ▶ VT transporter; **to ~ sth/sb across** or **over** faire traverser qch/qn
ferryman ['fɛrɪmən] N (irreg) passeur m
fertile ['fə:taɪl] ADJ fertile; (Biol) fécond(e); **~ period** période f de fécondité
fertility [fə'tɪlɪtɪ] N fertilité f; fécondité f
fertility drug N médicament m contre la stérilité

fertilize ['fɜːtɪlaɪz] VT fertiliser; (Biol) féconder

fertilizer ['fɜːtɪlaɪzəʳ] N engrais m

fervent ['fɜːvənt] ADJ fervent(e), ardent(e)

fervour, (US) **fervor** ['fɜːvəʳ] N ferveur f

fester ['fɛstəʳ] VI suppurer

festival ['fɛstɪvəl] N (Rel) fête f; (Art, Mus) festival m

festive ['fɛstɪv] ADJ de fête; **the ~ season** (BRIT: Christmas) la période des fêtes

festivities [fɛs'tɪvɪtɪz] NPL réjouissances fpl

festoon [fɛs'tuːn] VT: **to ~ with** orner de

fetch [fɛtʃ] VT aller chercher; (BRIT: sell for) rapporter; **how much did it ~?** ça a atteint quel prix?

▸ **fetch up** VI (BRIT) se retrouver

fetching ['fɛtʃɪŋ] ADJ charmant(e)

fête [feɪt] N fête f, kermesse f

fetid ['fɛtɪd] ADJ fétide

fetish ['fɛtɪʃ] N fétiche m

fetter ['fɛtəʳ] VT entraver

fetters ['fɛtəz] NPL chaînes fpl

fettle ['fɛtl] N (BRIT): **in fine ~** en bonne forme

fetus ['fiːtəs] N (US) = **foetus**

feud [fjuːd] N querelle f, dispute f ▸ VI se quereller, se disputer; **a family ~** une querelle de famille

feudal ['fjuːdl] ADJ féodal(e)

feudalism ['fjuːdlɪzəm] N féodalité f

fever ['fiːvəʳ] N fièvre f; **he has a ~** il a de la fièvre

feverish ['fiːvərɪʃ] ADJ fiévreux(-euse), fébrile

few [fjuː] ADJ (not many) peu de ▸ PRON peu; **~ succeed** il y en a peu qui réussissent, (bien) peu réussissent; **they were ~** ils étaient peu (nombreux), il y en avait peu; **a ~** (as adj) quelques; (as pron) quelques-uns(-unes); **I know a ~** j'en connais quelques-uns; **quite a ~ ...** adj un certain nombre de ..., pas mal de ...; **in the next ~ days** dans les jours qui viennent; **in the past ~ days** ces derniers jours; **every ~ days/months** tous les deux ou trois jours/mois; **a ~ more ...** encore quelques ..., quelques ... de plus

fewer ['fjuːəʳ] ADJ moins de ▸ PRON moins; **they are ~ now** il y en a moins maintenant, ils sont moins (nombreux) maintenant

fewest ['fjuːɪst] ADJ le moins nombreux

FFA N ABBR = **Future Farmers of America**

FH ABBR (BRIT) = **fire hydrant**

FHA N ABBR (US: = Federal Housing Administration) office fédéral du logement

fiancé [fɪ'ãːŋseɪ] N fiancé m

fiancée [fɪ'ãːŋseɪ] N fiancée f

fiasco [fɪ'æskəu] N fiasco m

fib [fɪb] N bobard m

fibre, (US) **fiber** ['faɪbəʳ] N fibre f

fibreboard, (US) **fiberboard** ['faɪbəbɔːd] N panneau m de fibres

fibreglass, (US) **Fiberglass**® ['faɪbəglɑːs] N fibre f de verre

fibrositis [faɪbrə'saɪtɪs] N aponévrosite f

FICA N ABBR (US) = **Federal Insurance Contributions Act**

fickle ['fɪkl] ADJ inconstant(e), volage, capricieux(-euse)

fiction ['fɪkʃən] N romans mpl, littérature f romanesque; (invention) fiction f

fictional ['fɪkʃənl] ADJ fictif(-ive)

fictionalize ['fɪkʃnəlaɪz] VT romancer

fictitious [fɪk'tɪʃəs] ADJ fictif(-ive), imaginaire

fiddle ['fɪdl] N (Mus) violon m; (cheating) combine f; escroquerie f ▸ VT (BRIT: accounts) falsifier, maquiller; **tax ~** fraude fiscale, combine f pour échapper au fisc; **to work a ~** traficoter

▸ **fiddle with** VT FUS tripoter

fiddler ['fɪdləʳ] N violoniste mf

fiddly ['fɪdlɪ] ADJ (task) minutieux(-euse)

fidelity [fɪ'dɛlɪtɪ] N fidélité f

fidget ['fɪdʒɪt] VI se trémousser, remuer

fidgety ['fɪdʒɪtɪ] ADJ agité(e), qui a la bougeotte

fiduciary [fɪ'djuːʃɪərɪ] N agent m fiduciaire

field [fiːld] N champ m; (fig) domaine m, champ; (Sport: ground) terrain m; (Comput) champ, zone f; **to lead the ~** (Sport, Comm) dominer; **the children had a ~ day** (fig) c'était un grand jour pour les enfants

field glasses NPL jumelles fpl

field hospital N antenne chirurgicale

field marshal N maréchal m

fieldwork ['fiːldwəːk] N travaux mpl pratiques (or recherches fpl) sur le terrain

fiend [fiːnd] N démon m

fiendish ['fiːndɪʃ] ADJ diabolique

fierce [fɪəs] ADJ (look, animal) féroce, sauvage; (wind, attack, person) (très) violent(e); (fighting, enemy) acharné(e)

fiery ['faɪərɪ] ADJ ardent(e), brûlant(e), fougueux(-euse)

FIFA ['fiːfə] N ABBR (= Fédération Internationale de Football Association) FIFA f

fifteen [fɪf'tiːn] NUM quinze

fifteenth [fɪf'tiːnθ] NUM quinzième

fifth [fɪfθ] NUM cinquième

fiftieth ['fɪftɪɪθ] NUM cinquantième

fifty ['fɪftɪ] NUM cinquante

fifty-fifty ['fɪftɪ'fɪftɪ] ADV moitié-moitié; **to share ~ with sb** partager moitié-moitié avec qn ▸ ADJ: **to have a ~ chance (of success)** avoir une chance sur deux (de réussir)

fig [fɪg] N figue f

fight [faɪt] (pt, pp fought [fɔːt]) N (between persons) bagarre f; (argument) dispute f; (Mil) combat m; (against cancer etc) lutte f ▸ VT se battre contre; (cancer, alcoholism, emotion) combattre, lutter contre; (election) se présenter à; (Law: case) défendre ▸ VI se battre; (argue) se disputer; (fig): **to ~ (for/against)** lutter (pour/contre)

▸ **fight back** VI rendre les coups; (after illness) reprendre le dessus ▸ VT (tears) réprimer

▸ **fight off** VT repousser; (disease, sleep, urge) lutter contre

fighter ['faɪtəʳ] N lutteur m; (fig: plane) chasseur m

fighter pilot N pilote m de chasse

fighting ['faɪtɪŋ] N combats mpl; (brawls) bagarres fpl

figment ['fɪgmənt] N: **a ~ of the imagination** une invention

figurative ['fɪgjurətɪv] ADJ figuré(e)

figure ['fɪgəʳ] N (*Drawing, Geom*) figure *f*; (*number*) chiffre *m*; (*body, outline*) silhouette *f*; (*person's shape*) ligne *f*, formes *fpl*; (*person*) personnage *m* ▶ VT (*US: think*) supposer ▶ VI (*appear*) figurer; (*US: make sense*) s'expliquer; **public ~** personnalité *f*; **~ of speech** figure *f* de rhétorique

▶ **figure on** VT FUS (*US*): **to ~ on doing** compter faire

▶ **figure out** VT (*understand*) arriver à comprendre; (*plan*) calculer

figurehead ['fɪgəhed] N (*Naut*) figure *f* de proue; (*pej*) prête-nom *m*

figure skating N figures imposées (*en patinage*), patinage *m* artistique

Fiji ['fi:dʒi:] N, **Fiji Islands** NPL (îles *fpl*) Fi(d)ji *fpl*

filament ['fɪləmənt] N filament *m*

filch [fɪltʃ] VT (*inf: steal*) voler, chiper

file [faɪl] N (*tool*) lime *f*; (*dossier*) dossier *m*; (*folder*) dossier, chemise *f*; (*: binder*) classeur *m*; (*Comput*) fichier *m*; (*row*) file *f* ▶ VT (*nails, wood*) limer; (*papers*) classer; (*Law: claim*) faire enregistrer; déposer ▶ VI: **to ~ in/out** entrer/sortir l'un derrière l'autre; **to ~ past** défiler devant; **to ~ a suit against sb** (*Law*) intenter un procès à qn

file name N (*Comput*) nom *m* de fichier

file sharing [-ʃɛərɪŋ] N (*Comput*) partage *m* de fichiers

filibuster ['fɪlɪbʌstəʳ] (*esp US Pol*) N (*also*: **filibusterer**) obstructionniste *mf* ▶ VI faire de l'obstructionnisme

filing ['faɪlɪŋ] N (*travaux mpl de*) classement *m*; **filings** NPL limaille *f*

filing cabinet N classeur *m* (*meuble*)

filing clerk N documentaliste *mf*

Filipino [fɪlɪ'pi:nəu] ADJ philippin(e) ▶ N (*person*) Philippin(e); (*Ling*) tagalog *m*

fill [fɪl] VT remplir; (*vacancy*) pourvoir à ▶ N: **to eat one's ~** manger à sa faim; **to ~ with** remplir de

▶ **fill in** VT (*hole*) boucher; (*form*) remplir; (*details, report*) compléter

▶ **fill out** VT (*form, receipt*) remplir

▶ **fill up** VT remplir ▶ VI (*Aut*) faire le plein; **~ it up, please** (*Aut*) le plein, s'il vous plaît

fillet ['fɪlɪt] N filet *m* ▶ VT préparer en filets

fillet steak N filet *m* de bœuf, tournedos *m*

filling ['fɪlɪŋ] N (*Culin*) garniture *f*, farce *f*; (*for tooth*) plombage *m*

filling station N station-service *f*, station *f* d'essence

fillip ['fɪlɪp] N coup *m* de fouet (*fig*)

filly ['fɪlɪ] N pouliche *f*

film [fɪlm] N film *m*; (*Phot*) pellicule *f*, film; (*of powder, liquid*) couche *f*, pellicule ▶ VT (*scene*) filmer ▶ VI tourner; **I'd like a 36-exposure ~** je voudrais une pellicule de 36 poses

film star N vedette *f* de cinéma

filmstrip ['fɪlmstrɪp] N (film *m* pour) projection *f* fixe

film studio N studio *m* (de cinéma)

Filofax® ['faɪləufæks] N Filofax® *m*

filter ['fɪltəʳ] N filtre *m* ▶ VT filtrer

filter coffee N café *m* filtre

filter lane N (BRIT *Aut*: *at traffic lights*) voie *f* de dégagement; (*: on motorway*) voie *f* de sortie

filter tip N bout *m* filtre

filth [fɪlθ] N saleté *f*

filthy ['fɪlθɪ] ADJ sale, dégoûtant(e); (*language*) ordurier(-ière), grossier(-ière)

fin [fɪn] N (*of fish*) nageoire *f*; (*of shark*) aileron *m*; (*of diver*) palme *f*

final ['faɪnl] ADJ final(e), dernier(-ière); (*decision, answer*) définitif(-ive) ▶ N (BRIT *Sport*) finale *f*; **finals** NPL (*US Scol*) examens *mpl* de dernière année; (*Sport*) finale *f*; **~ demand** (*on invoice etc*) dernier rappel

finale [fɪ'nɑ:lɪ] N finale *m*

finalist ['faɪnəlɪst] N (*Sport*) finaliste *mf*

finalize ['faɪnəlaɪz] VT mettre au point

finally ['faɪnəlɪ] ADV (*eventually*) enfin, finalement; (*lastly*) en dernier lieu; (*irrevocably*) définitivement

finance [faɪ'næns] N finance *f* ▶ VT financer; **finances** NPL finances *fpl*

financial [faɪ'nænʃəl] ADJ financier(-ière); **~ statement** bilan *m*, exercice financier

financially [faɪ'nænʃəlɪ] ADV financièrement

financial year N année *f* budgétaire

financier [faɪ'nænsɪəʳ] N financier *m*

find [faɪnd] (*pt, pp* **found** [faund]) VT trouver; (*lost object*) retrouver ▶ N trouvaille *f*, découverte *f*; **to ~ sb guilty** (*Law*) déclarer qn coupable; **to ~ (some) difficulty in doing sth** avoir du mal à faire qch

▶ **find out** VT se renseigner sur; (*truth, secret*) découvrir; (*person*) démasquer ▶ VI: **to ~ out about** (*make enquiries*) se renseigner sur; (*by chance*) apprendre

findings ['faɪndɪŋz] NPL (*Law*) conclusions *fpl*, verdict *m*; (*of report*) constatations *fpl*

fine [faɪn] ADJ (*weather*) beau (belle); (*excellent*) excellent(e); (*thin, subtle, not coarse*) fin(e); (*acceptable*) bien *inv* ▶ ADV (*well*) très bien; (*small*) fin, finement ▶ N (*Law*) amende *f*; contravention *f* ▶ VT (*Law*) condamner à une amende; donner une contravention à; **he's ~** il va bien; **the weather is ~** il fait beau; **you're doing ~** c'est bien, vous vous débrouillez bien; **to cut it ~** calculer un peu juste

fine arts NPL beaux-arts *mpl*

fine print N: **the ~** ce qui est imprimé en tout petit

finery ['faɪnərɪ] N parure *f*

finesse [fɪ'nɛs] N finesse *f*, élégance *f*

fine-tooth comb ['faɪntu:θ-] N: **to go through sth with a ~** (*fig*) passer qch au peigne fin *or* au crible

finger ['fɪŋgəʳ] N doigt *m* ▶ VT palper, toucher; **index ~** index *m*

fingernail ['fɪŋgəneɪl] N ongle *m* (de la main)

fingerprint ['fɪŋgəprɪnt] N empreinte digitale ▶ VT (*person*) prendre les empreintes digitales de

fingerstall ['fɪŋgəstɔ:l] N doigtier *m*

fingertip ['fɪŋgətɪp] N bout *m* du doigt; (*fig*): **to have sth at one's fingertips** avoir qch à sa disposition; (*knowledge*) savoir qch sur le bout du doigt

f

finicky ['fɪnɪkɪ] ADJ tatillon(ne),
méticuleux(-euse), minutieux(-euse)
finish ['fɪnɪʃ] N fin f; (Sport) arrivée f; (polish etc)
finition f ▶ VT finir, terminer ▶ VI finir, se
terminer; (session) s'achever; **to ~ doing sth**
finir de faire qch; **to ~ third** arriver or terminer
troisième; **when does the show ~?** quand
est-ce que le spectacle se termine?
▶ **finish off** VT finir, terminer; (kill) achever
▶ **finish up** VI, VT finir
finishing line ['fɪnɪʃɪŋ-] N ligne f d'arrivée
finishing school ['fɪnɪʃɪŋ-] N institution privée
(pour jeunes filles)
finite ['faɪnaɪt] ADJ fini(e); (verb) conjugué(e)
Finland ['fɪnlənd] N Finlande f
Finn [fɪn] N Finnois(e), Finlandais(e)
Finnish ['fɪnɪʃ] ADJ finnois(e), finlandais(e) ▶ N
(Ling) finnois m
fiord [fjɔːd] N fjord m
fir [fəːʳ] N sapin m
fire ['faɪəʳ] N feu m; (accidental) incendie m;
(heater) radiateur m ▶ VT (discharge): **to ~ a gun**
tirer un coup de feu; (fig: interest) enflammer,
animer; (inf: dismiss) mettre à la porte, renvoyer
▶ VI (shoot) tirer, faire feu ▶ CPD: ~ **hazard**,
~ **risk: that's a ~ risk** or **hazard** cela présente
un risque d'incendie; **~!** au feu!; **on ~** en feu; **to
set ~ to sth, set sth on ~** mettre le feu à qch;
insured against ~ assuré contre l'incendie
fire alarm N avertisseur m d'incendie
firearm ['faɪərɑːm] N arme f à feu
fire brigade N (régiment m de
sapeurs-)pompiers mpl
fire chief N (US) = **fire master**
fire department N (US) = **fire brigade**
fire door N porte f coupe-feu
fire engine N (BRIT) pompe f à incendie
fire escape N escalier m de secours
fire exit N issue f or sortie f de secours
fire extinguisher N extincteur m
fireguard ['faɪəgɑːd] N (BRIT) garde-feu m inv
fire insurance N assurance f incendie
fireman ['faɪəmən] N (irreg) pompier m
fire master N (BRIT) capitaine m des pompiers
fireplace ['faɪəpleɪs] N cheminée f
fireproof ['faɪəpruːf] ADJ ignifuge
fire regulations NPL consignes fpl en cas
d'incendie
fire screen N (decorative) écran m de cheminée;
(for protection) garde-feu m inv
fireside ['faɪəsaɪd] N foyer m, coin m du feu
fire station N caserne f de pompiers
fire truck N (US) = **fire engine**
firewall ['faɪəwɔːl] N (Internet) pare-feu m
firewood ['faɪəwud] N bois m de chauffage
fireworks ['faɪəwəːks] NPL (display) feu(x) m(pl)
d'artifice
firing ['faɪərɪŋ] N (Mil) feu m, tir m
firing squad N peloton m d'exécution
firm [fəːm] ADJ ferme ▶ N compagnie f, firme f;
it is my ~ belief that … je crois fermement
que …
firmly ['fəːmlɪ] ADV fermement
firmness ['fəːmnɪs] N fermeté f

first [fəːst] ADJ premier(-ière) ▶ ADV (before other
people) le premier, la première; (before other
things) en premier, d'abord; (when listing reasons
etc) en premier lieu, premièrement; (in the
beginning) au début ▶ N (person: in race)
premier(-ière); (BRIT Scol) mention f très bien;
(Aut) première f; **the ~ of January** le premier
janvier; **at ~** au commencement, au début; **~ of
all** tout d'abord, pour commencer; **in the ~
instance** en premier lieu; **I'll do it ~ thing
tomorrow** je le ferai tout de suite demain
matin
first aid N premiers secours or soins
first-aid kit [fəːst'eɪd-] N trousse f à pharmacie
first-class ['fəːst'klɑːs] ADJ (ticket etc) de première
classe; (excellent) excellent(e), exceptionnel(le);
(post) en tarif prioritaire
first-class mail N courrier m rapide
first-hand ['fəːst'hænd] ADJ de première main
first lady N (US) femme f du président
firstly ['fəːstlɪ] ADV premièrement, en premier
lieu
first name N prénom m
first night N (Theat) première f
first-rate ['fəːst'reɪt] ADJ excellent(e)
first-time buyer ['fəːsttaɪm-] N personne
achetant une maison ou un appartement pour la
première fois
fir tree N sapin m
fiscal ['fɪskl] ADJ fiscal(e)
fiscal year N exercice financier
fish [fɪʃ] N (pl inv) poisson m; poissons mpl ▶ VT, VI
pêcher; **to ~ a river** pêcher dans une rivière;
~ and chips poisson frit et frites
fisherman ['fɪʃəmən] N (irreg) pêcheur m
fishery ['fɪʃərɪ] N pêcherie f
fish factory N (BRIT) conserverie f de poissons
fish farm N établissement m piscicole
fish fingers NPL (BRIT) bâtonnets mpl de poisson
(congelés)
fish hook N hameçon m
fishing ['fɪʃɪŋ] N pêche f; **to go ~** aller à la pêche
fishing boat N barque f de pêche
fishing industry N industrie f de la pêche
fishing line N ligne f (de pêche)
fishing rod N canne f à pêche
fishing tackle N attirail m de pêche
fish market N marché m au poisson
fishmonger ['fɪʃmʌŋgəʳ] N (BRIT) marchand m
de poisson
fishmonger's ['fɪʃmʌŋgəz], **fishmonger's
shop** N (BRIT) poissonnerie f
fish slice N (BRIT) pelle f à poisson
fish sticks NPL (US) = **fish fingers**
fishy ['fɪʃɪ] ADJ (inf) suspect(e), louche
fission ['fɪʃən] N fission f; **atomic** or **nuclear ~**
fission nucléaire
fissure ['fɪʃəʳ] N fissure f
fist [fɪst] N poing m
fistfight ['fɪstfaɪt] N pugilat m, bagarre f (à
coups de poing)
fit [fɪt] ADJ (Med, Sport) en (bonne) forme; (proper)
convenable; approprié(e) ▶ VT (subj: clothes) aller
à; (adjust) ajuster; (put in, attach) installer, poser;

adapter; (*equip*) équiper, garnir, munir; (*suit*) convenir à ▸ vi (*clothes*) aller; (*parts*) s'adapter; (*in space, gap*) entrer, s'adapter ▸ n (*Med*) accès *m*, crise *f*; (*of anger*) accès; (*of hysterics, jealousy*) crise; ~ **to** (*ready to*) en état de; ~ **for** (*worthy*) digne de; (*capable*) apte à; **to keep** ~ se maintenir en forme; **this dress is a tight/good** ~ cette robe est un peu juste/(me) va très bien; **a** ~ **of coughing** une quinte de toux; **to have a** ~ (*Med*) faire *or* avoir une crise; (*inf*) piquer une crise; **by fits and starts** par à-coups
▸ **fit in** vi (*add up*) cadrer; (*integrate*) s'intégrer; (*to new situation*) s'adapter
▸ **fit out** vt (*Brit: also:* **fit up**) équiper
fitful ['fɪtful] adj intermittent(e)
fitment ['fɪtmənt] n meuble encastré, élément *m*
fitness ['fɪtnɪs] n (*Med*) forme *f* physique; (*of remark*) à-propos *m*, justesse *f*
fitness instructor n professeur *mf* de fitness
fitted ['fɪtɪd] adj (*jacket, shirt*) ajusté(e)
fitted carpet n moquette *f*
fitted kitchen n (*Brit*) cuisine équipée
fitted sheet n drap-housse *m*
fitter ['fɪtər] n monteur *m*; (*Dress*) essayeur(-euse)
fitting ['fɪtɪŋ] adj approprié(e) ▸ n (*of dress*) essayage *m*; (*of piece of equipment*) pose *f*, installation *f*
fitting room n (*in shop*) cabine *f* d'essayage
fittings ['fɪtɪŋz] npl installations *fpl*
five [faɪv] num cinq
five-day week ['faɪvdeɪ-] n semaine *f* de cinq jours
fiver ['faɪvər] n (*inf: US*) billet de cinq dollars; (: *Brit*) billet *m* de cinq livres
fix [fɪks] vt (*date, amount etc*) fixer; (*sort out*) arranger; (*mend*) réparer; (*make ready: meal, drink*) préparer; (*inf: game etc*) truquer ▸ n: **to be in a** ~ être dans le pétrin
▸ **fix up** vt (*meeting*) arranger; **to** ~ **sb up with sth** faire avoir qch à qn
fixation [fɪk'seɪʃən] n (*Psych*) fixation *f*; (*fig*) obsession *f*
fixed [fɪkst] adj (*prices etc*) fixe; **there's a** ~ **charge** il y a un prix forfaitaire; **how are you** ~ **for money?** (*inf*) question fric, ça va?
fixed assets npl immobilisations *fpl*
fixture ['fɪkstʃər] n installation *f* (fixe); (*Sport*) rencontre *f* (au programme)
fizz [fɪz] vi pétiller
fizzle ['fɪzl] vi pétiller
▸ **fizzle out** vi rater
fizzy ['fɪzɪ] adj pétillant(e), gazeux(-euse)
fjord [fjɔːd] n = **fiord**
FL, Fla. abbr (*US*) = **Florida**
flabbergasted ['flæbəgɑːstɪd] adj sidéré(e), ahuri(e)
flabby ['flæbɪ] adj mou (molle)
flag [flæg] n drapeau *m*; (*also:* **flagstone**) dalle *f* ▸ vi faiblir; fléchir; ~ **of convenience** pavillon *m* de complaisance
▸ **flag down** vt héler, faire signe (de s'arrêter) à
flagon ['flægən] n bonbonne *f*

flagpole ['flægpəul] n mât *m*
flagrant ['fleɪgrənt] adj flagrant(e)
flagship ['flægʃɪp] n vaisseau *m* amiral; (*fig*) produit *m* vedette
flag stop n (*US: for bus*) arrêt facultatif
flair [fleər] n flair *m*
flak [flæk] n (*Mil*) tir antiaérien; (*inf: criticism*) critiques *fpl*
flake [fleɪk] n (*of rust, paint*) écaille *f*; (*of snow, soap powder*) flocon *m* ▸ vi (*also:* **flake off**) s'écailler
flaky ['fleɪkɪ] adj (*paintwork*) écaillé(e); (*skin*) desquamé(e); (*pastry*) feuilleté(e)
flamboyant [flæm'bɔɪənt] adj flamboyant(e), éclatant(e); (*person*) haut(e) en couleur
flame [fleɪm] n flamme *f*
flamingo [flə'mɪŋgəu] n flamant *m* (rose)
flammable ['flæməbl] adj inflammable
flan [flæn] n (*Brit*) tarte *f*
Flanders ['flɑːndəz] n Flandre(s) *f(pl)*
flange [flændʒ] n boudin *m*; collerette *f*
flank [flæŋk] n flanc *m* ▸ vt flanquer
flannel ['flænl] n (*Brit: also:* **face flannel**) gant *m* de toilette; (*fabric*) flanelle *f*; (*Brit inf*) baratin *m*; **flannels** npl pantalon *m* de flanelle
flap [flæp] n (*of pocket, envelope*) rabat *m* ▸ vt (*wings*) battre (de) ▸ vi (*sail, flag*) claquer; (*inf: also:* **be in a flap**) paniquer
flapjack ['flæpdʒæk] n (*US: pancake*) ≈ crêpe *f*; (*Brit: biscuit*) galette *f*
flare [fleər] n (*signal*) signal lumineux; (*Mil*) fusée éclairante; (*in skirt etc*) évasement *m*; **flares** npl (*trousers*) pantalon *m* à pattes d'éléphant
▸ **flare up** vi s'embraser; (*fig: person*) se mettre en colère, s'emporter; (: *revolt*) éclater
flared ['fleəd] adj (*trousers*) à jambes évasées; (*skirt*) évasé(e)
flash [flæʃ] n éclair *m*; (*also:* **news flash**) flash *m* (d'information); (*Phot*) flash ▸ vt (*switch on*) allumer (brièvement); (*direct*): **to** ~ **sth at** braquer qch sur; (*flaunt*) étaler, exhiber; (*send: message*) câbler; (*smile*) lancer ▸ vi briller; jeter des éclairs; (*light on ambulance etc*) clignoter; **a** ~ **of lightning** un éclair; **in a** ~ en un clin d'œil; **to** ~ **one's headlights** faire un appel de phares; **he flashed by** *or* **past** il passa (devant nous) comme un éclair
flashback ['flæʃbæk] n flashback *m*, retour *m* en arrière
flashbulb ['flæʃbʌlb] n ampoule *f* de flash
flash card n (*Scol*) carte *f* (support visuel)
flashcube ['flæʃkjuːb] n cube-flash *m*
flash drive n (*Comput*) clé *f* USB
flasher ['flæʃər] n (*Aut*) clignotant *m*
flashlight ['flæʃlaɪt] n lampe *f* de poche
flashpoint ['flæʃpɔɪnt] n point *m* d'ignition; (*fig*): **to be at** ~ être sur le point d'exploser
flashy ['flæʃɪ] adj (*pej*) tape-à-l'œil *inv*, tapageur(-euse)
flask [flɑːsk] n flacon *m*, bouteille *f*; (*Chem*) ballon *m*; (*also:* **vacuum flask**) bouteille *f* thermos®
flat [flæt] adj plat(e); (*tyre*) dégonflé(e), à plat; (*beer*) éventé(e); (*battery*) à plat; (*denial*)

catégorique; (*Mus*) bémol *inv*; (: *voice*) faux (fausse) ▶ N (*Brit*: *apartment*) appartement *m*; (*Aut*) crevaison *f*, pneu crevé; (*Mus*) bémol *m*; ~ **out** (*work*) sans relâche; (*race*) à fond; ~ **rate of pay** (*Comm*) salaire *m* fixe

flat-footed ['flæt'futɪd] ADJ: **to be** ~ avoir les pieds plats

flatly ['flætlɪ] ADV catégoriquement

flatmate ['flætmeɪt] N (*Brit*): **he's my** ~ il partage l'appartement avec moi

flatness ['flætnɪs] N (*of land*) absence *f* de relief, aspect plat

flat-screen ['flætskri:n] ADJ à écran plat

flatten ['flætn] VT (*also*: **flatten out**) aplatir; (*crop*) coucher; (*house, city*) raser

flatter ['flætə**ʳ**] VT flatter

flatterer ['flætərə**ʳ**] N flatteur *m*

flattering ['flætərɪŋ] ADJ flatteur(-euse); (*clothes etc*) seyant(e)

flattery ['flætərɪ] N flatterie *f*

flatulence ['flætjuləns] N flatulence *f*

flaunt [flɔ:nt] VT faire étalage de

flavour, (*US*) **flavor** ['fleɪvə**ʳ**] N goût *m*, saveur *f*; (*of ice cream etc*) parfum *m* ▶ VT parfumer, aromatiser; **vanilla-flavoured** à l'arôme de vanille, vanillé(e); **what flavours do you have?** quels parfums avez-vous?; **to give** *or* **add** ~ **to** donner du goût à, relever

flavouring, (*US*) **flavoring** ['fleɪvərɪŋ] N arôme *m* (synthétique)

flaw [flɔ:] N défaut *m*

flawless ['flɔ:lɪs] ADJ sans défaut

flax [flæks] N lin *m*

flaxen ['flæksən] ADJ blond(e)

flea [fli:] N puce *f*

flea market N marché *m* aux puces

fleck [flɛk] N (*of dust*) particule *f*; (*of mud, paint, colour*) tacheture *f*, moucheture *f* ▶ VT tacher, éclabousser; **brown flecked with white** brun moucheté de blanc

fled [flɛd] PT, PP *of* **flee**

fledgeling, fledgling ['flɛdʒlɪŋ] N oisillon *m*

flee [fli:] (*pt, pp* **fled** [flɛd]) VT fuir, s'enfuir de ▶ VI fuir, s'enfuir

fleece [fli:s] N (*of sheep*) toison *f*; (*top*) (laine *f*) polaire *f* ▶ VT (*inf*) voler, filouter

fleecy ['fli:sɪ] ADJ (*blanket*) moelleux(-euse); (*cloud*) floconneux(-euse)

fleet [fli:t] N flotte *f*; (*of lorries, cars etc*) parc *m*; convoi *m*

fleeting ['fli:tɪŋ] ADJ fugace, fugitif(-ive); (*visit*) très bref (brève)

Flemish ['flɛmɪʃ] ADJ flamand(e) ▶ N (*Ling*) flamand *m*; **the** ~ *npl* les Flamands

flesh [flɛʃ] N chair *f*

flesh wound [-wu:nd] N blessure superficielle

flew [flu:] PT *of* **fly**

flex [flɛks] N fil *m or* câble *m* électrique (souple) ▶ VT (*knee*) fléchir; (*muscles*) bander

flexibility [flɛksɪ'bɪlɪtɪ] N flexibilité *f*

flexible ['flɛksəbl] ADJ flexible; (*person, schedule*) souple

flexitime ['flɛksɪtaɪm], (*US*) **flextime** ['flɛkstaɪm] N horaire *m* variable *or* à la carte

flick [flɪk] N petit coup; (*with finger*) chiquenaude *f* ▶ VT donner un petit coup à; (*switch*) appuyer sur

▶ **flick through** VT FUS feuilleter

flicker ['flɪkə**ʳ**] VI (*light, flame*) vaciller ▶ N vacillement *m*; **a** ~ **of light** une brève lueur

flick knife N (*Brit*) couteau *m* à cran d'arrêt

flicks [flɪks] NPL (*inf*) ciné *m*

flier ['flaɪə**ʳ**] N aviateur *m*

flies [flaɪz] NPL *of* **fly**

flight [flaɪt] N vol *m*; (*escape*) fuite *f*; (*also*: **flight of steps**) escalier *m*; **to take** ~ prendre la fuite; **to put to** ~ mettre en fuite

flight attendant N steward *m*, hôtesse *f* de l'air

flight crew N équipage *m*

flight deck N (*Aviat*) poste *m* de pilotage; (*Naut*) pont *m* d'envol

flight path N trajectoire *f* (de vol)

flight recorder N enregistreur *m* de vol

flimsy ['flɪmzɪ] ADJ peu solide; (*clothes*) trop léger(-ère); (*excuse*) pauvre, mince

flinch [flɪntʃ] VI tressaillir; **to** ~ **from** se dérober à, reculer devant

fling [flɪŋ] (*pt, pp* **flung** [flʌŋ]) VT jeter, lancer ▶ N (*love affair*) brève liaison, passade *f*

flint [flɪnt] N silex *m*; (*in lighter*) pierre *f* (à briquet)

flip [flɪp] N chiquenaude *f* ▶ VT (*throw*) donner une chiquenaude à; (*switch*) appuyer sur; (*US*: *pancake*) faire sauter; **to** ~ **sth over** retourner qch ▶ VI: **to** ~ **for sth** (*US*) jouer qch à pile ou face

▶ **flip through** VT FUS feuilleter

flip-flops [flɪpflɔps] NPL (*esp Brit*) tongs *fpl*

flippant ['flɪpənt] ADJ désinvolte, irrévérencieux(-euse)

flipper ['flɪpə**ʳ**] N (*of animal*) nageoire *f*; (*for swimmer*) palme *f*

flip side N (*of record*) deuxième face *f*

flirt [flə:t] VI flirter ▶ N flirteur(-euse)

flirtation [flə:'teɪʃən] N flirt *m*

flit [flɪt] VI voleter

float [fləut] N flotteur *m*; (*in procession*) char *m*; (*sum of money*) réserve *f* ▶ VI flotter; (*bather*) flotter, faire la planche ▶ VT faire flotter; (*loan, business, idea*) lancer

floating ['fləutɪŋ] ADJ flottant(e); ~ **vote** voix flottante; ~ **voter** électeur indécis

flock [flɔk] N (*of sheep*) troupeau *m*; (*of birds*) vol *m*; (*of people*) foule *f*

floe [fləu] N (*also*: **ice floe**) iceberg *m*

flog [flɔg] VT fouetter

flood [flʌd] N inondation *f*; (*of letters, refugees etc*) flot *m* ▶ VT inonder; (*Aut*: *carburettor*) noyer ▶ VI (*place*) être inondé; (*people*): **to** ~ **into** envahir; **to** ~ **the market** (*Comm*) inonder le marché; **in** ~ en crue

flooding ['flʌdɪŋ] N inondation *f*

floodlight ['flʌdlaɪt] N projecteur *m* ▶ VT (*irreg*: *like* **light**) éclairer aux projecteurs, illuminer

floodlit ['flʌdlɪt] PT, PP *of* **floodlight** ▶ ADJ illuminé(e)

flood tide N marée montante

floodwater ['flʌdwɔ:tə**ʳ**] N eau *f* de la crue

floor [flɔːʳ] N sol m; (storey) étage m; (of sea, valley) fond m; (fig: at meeting): **the ~** l'assemblée f, les membres mpl de l'assemblée ▶ VT (knock down) terrasser; (baffle) désorienter; **on the ~** par terre; **ground ~, first ~** (US) rez-de-chaussée m; **first ~, second ~** (US) premier étage; **top ~** dernier étage; **what ~ is it on?** c'est à quel étage?; **to have the ~** (speaker) avoir la parole

floorboard ['flɔːbɔːd] N planche f (du plancher)

flooring ['flɔːrɪŋ] N sol m; (wooden) plancher m; (material to make floor) matériau(x) m(pl) pour planchers; (covering) revêtement m de sol

floor lamp N (US) lampadaire m

floor show N spectacle m de variétés

floorwalker ['flɔːwɔːkəʳ] N (esp US) surveillant m (de grand magasin)

flop [flɔp] N fiasco m ▶ VI (fail) faire fiasco; (fall) s'affaler, s'effondrer

floppy ['flɔpɪ] ADJ lâche, flottant(e) ▶ N (Comput: also: **floppy disk**) disquette f; **~ hat** chapeau m à bords flottants

floppy disk N disquette f, disque m souple

flora ['flɔːrə] N flore f

floral ['flɔːrl] ADJ floral(e); (dress) à fleurs

Florence ['flɔrəns] N Florence

florid ['flɔrɪd] ADJ (complexion) fleuri(e); (style) plein(e) de fioritures

florist ['flɔrɪst] N fleuriste mf

florist's ['flɔrɪsts], **florist's shop** N magasin m or boutique f de fleuriste

flotation [fləu'teɪʃən] N (of shares) émission f; (of company) lancement m (en Bourse)

flounce [flauns] N volant m
  ▶ **flounce out** VI sortir dans un mouvement d'humeur

flounder ['flaundəʳ] N (Zool) flet m ▶ VI patauger

flour ['flauəʳ] N farine f

flourish ['flʌrɪʃ] VI prospérer ▶ VT brandir ▶ N (gesture) moulinet m; (decoration) fioriture f; (of trumpets) fanfare f

flourishing ['flʌrɪʃɪŋ] ADJ prospère, florissant(e)

flout [flaut] VT se moquer de, faire fi de

flow [fləu] N (of water, traffic etc) écoulement m; (tide, influx) flux m; (of orders, letters etc) flot m; (of blood, Elec) circulation f; (of river) courant m ▶ VI couler; (traffic) s'écouler; (robes, hair) flotter

flow chart, flow diagram N organigramme m

flower ['flauəʳ] N fleur f ▶ VI fleurir; **in ~** en fleur

flower bed N plate-bande f

flowerpot ['flauəpɔt] N pot m (à fleurs)

flowery ['flauərɪ] ADJ fleuri(e)

flown [fləun] PP of **fly**

fl. oz. ABBR = **fluid ounce**

flu [fluː] N grippe f

fluctuate ['flʌktjueɪt] VI varier, fluctuer

fluctuation [flʌktju'eɪʃən] N fluctuation f, variation f

flue [fluː] N conduit m

fluency ['fluːənsɪ] N facilité f, aisance f

fluent ['fluːənt] ADJ (speech, style) coulant(e), aisé(e); **he's a ~ speaker/reader** il s'exprime/lit avec aisance or facilité; **he speaks ~ French**, **he's ~ in French** il parle couramment français

fluently ['fluːəntlɪ] ADV couramment; avec aisance or facilité

fluff [flʌf] N duvet m; (on jacket, carpet) peluche f

fluffy ['flʌfɪ] ADJ duveteux(-euse); (jacket, carpet) pelucheux(-euse); (toy) en peluche

fluid ['fluːɪd] N fluide m; (in diet) liquide m ▶ ADJ fluide

fluid ounce N (BRIT) = 0.028 l; 0.05 pints

fluke [fluːk] N coup m de veine

flummox ['flʌməks] VT dérouter, déconcerter

flung [flʌŋ] PT, PP of **fling**

flunky ['flʌŋkɪ] N larbin m

fluorescent [fluə'rɛsnt] ADJ fluorescent(e)

fluoride ['fluəraɪd] N fluor m

fluorine ['fluəriːn] N fluor m

flurry ['flʌrɪ] N (of snow) rafale f, bourrasque f; **a ~ of activity** un affairement soudain; **a ~ of excitement** une excitation soudaine

flush [flʌʃ] N (on face) rougeur f; (fig: of youth etc) éclat m; (of blood) afflux m ▶ VT nettoyer à grande eau; (also: **flush out**) débusquer ▶ VI rougir ▶ ADJ (inf) en fonds; (level): **~ with** au ras de, de niveau avec; **to ~ the toilet** tirer la chasse (d'eau); **hot flushes** (Med) bouffées fpl de chaleur

flushed [flʌʃt] ADJ (tout(e)) rouge

fluster ['flʌstəʳ] N agitation f, trouble m

flustered ['flʌstəd] ADJ énervé(e)

flute [fluːt] N flûte f

flutter ['flʌtəʳ] N (of panic, excitement) agitation f; (of wings) battement m ▶ VI (bird) battre des ailes, voleter; (person) aller et venir dans une grande agitation

flux [flʌks] N: **in a state of ~** fluctuant sans cesse

fly [flaɪ] (pt **flew** [fluː], pp **flown** [fləun]) N (insect) mouche f; (on trousers: also: **flies**) braguette f ▶ VT (plane) piloter; (passengers, cargo) transporter (par avion); (distance) parcourir ▶ VI voler; (passengers) aller en avion; (escape) s'enfuir, fuir; (flag) se déployer; **to ~ open** s'ouvrir brusquement; **to ~ off the handle** s'énerver, s'emporter
  ▶ **fly away, fly off** VI s'envoler
  ▶ **fly in** VI (plane) atterrir; **he flew in yesterday** il est arrivé hier (par avion)
  ▶ **fly out** VI partir (par avion)

fly-drive ['flaɪdraɪv] N formule f avion plus voiture

fly-fishing ['flaɪfɪʃɪŋ] N pêche f à la mouche

flying ['flaɪɪŋ] N (activity) aviation f; (action) vol m ▶ ADJ: **~ visit** visite f éclair inv; **with ~ colours** haut la main; **he doesn't like ~** il n'aime pas voyager en avion

flying buttress N arc-boutant m

flying picket N piquet m de grève volant

flying saucer N soucoupe volante

flying squad N (Police) brigade volante

flying start N: **to get off to a ~** faire un excellent départ

flyleaf ['flaɪliːf] N page f de garde

flyover ['flaɪəuvəʳ] N (BRIT: overpass) pont routier

flypast ['flaɪpɑːst] N défilé aérien

flysheet ['flaɪʃiːt] N (for tent) double toit m

flyweight ['flaɪweɪt] N (*Sport*) poids *m* mouche
flywheel ['flaɪwiːl] N volant *m* (de commande)
FM ABBR (*Brit Mil*) = **field marshal**; (*Radio*: = *frequency modulation*) FM
FMB N ABBR (*US*) = **Federal Maritime Board**
FMCS N ABBR (*US*: = *Federal Mediation and Conciliation Services*) organisme de conciliation en cas de conflits du travail
FO N ABBR (*Brit*) = **Foreign Office**
foal [fəul] N poulain *m*
foam [fəum] N écume *f*; (*on beer*) mousse *f*; (*also*: **foam rubber**) caoutchouc *m* mousse; (*also*: **plastic foam**) mousse cellulaire or de plastique
▶ vi (*liquid*) écumer; (*soapy water*) mousser
foam rubber N caoutchouc *m* mousse
FOB ABBR (= *free on board*) fob
fob [fɔb] N (*also*: **watch fob**) chaîne *f*, ruban *m*
▶ vt: **to ~ sb off with sth** refiler qch à qn
foc ABBR (*Brit*) = **free of charge**
focal ['fəukl] ADJ (*also fig*) focal(e)
focal point N foyer *m*; (*fig*) centre *m* de l'attention, point focal
focus ['fəukəs] N (*pl* **focuses**) foyer *m*; (*of interest*) centre *m* ▶ vt (*field glasses etc*) mettre au point; (*light rays*) faire converger ▶ vi: **to ~ (on)** (*with camera*) régler la mise au point (sur); (*with eyes*) fixer son regard (sur); (*fig: concentrate*) se concentrer (sur); **out of/in ~** (*picture*) flou(e)/net(te); (*camera*) pas au point/au point
fodder ['fɔdə'] N fourrage *m*
FOE N ABBR (= *Friends of the Earth*) AT *mpl* (= *Amis de la Terre*); (*US*: = *Fraternal Order of Eagles*) organisation charitable
foe [fəu] N ennemi *m*
foetus, (*US*) **fetus** ['fiːtəs] N fœtus *m*
fog [fɔg] N brouillard *m*
fogbound ['fɔgbaund] ADJ bloqué(e) par le brouillard
foggy ['fɔgɪ] ADJ: **it's ~** il y a du brouillard
fog lamp, (*US*) **fog light** N (*Aut*) phare *m* anti-brouillard
foible ['fɔɪbl] N faiblesse *f*
foil [fɔɪl] vt déjouer, contrecarrer ▶ N feuille *f* de métal; (*kitchen foil*) papier *m* d'alu(minium); (*Fencing*) fleuret *m*; **to act as a ~ to** (*fig*) servir de repoussoir or de faire-valoir à
foist [fɔɪst] vt: **to ~ sth on sb** imposer qch à qn
fold [fəuld] N (*bend, crease*) pli *m*; (*Agr*) parc *m* à moutons; (*fig*) bercail *m* ▶ vt plier; **to ~ one's arms** croiser les bras
▶ **fold up** vi (*map etc*) se plier, se replier; (*business*) fermer boutique ▶ vt (*map etc*) plier, replier
folder ['fəuldə'] N (*for papers*) chemise *f*; (: *binder*) classeur *m*; (*brochure*) dépliant *m*; (*Comput*) dossier *m*
folding ['fəuldɪŋ] ADJ (*chair, bed*) pliant(e)
foliage ['fəulɪɪdʒ] N feuillage *m*
folk [fəuk] NPL gens *mpl* ▶ CPD folklorique; **folks** NPL (*inf: parents*) famille *f*, parents *mpl*
folklore ['fəuklɔː'] N folklore *m*
folk music N musique *f* folklorique; (*contemporary*) musique folk, folk *m*
folk song N chanson *f* folklorique; (*contemporary*) chanson folk *inv*

follow ['fɔləu] vt suivre ▶ vi suivre; (*result*) s'ensuivre; **to ~ sb's advice** suivre les conseils de qn; **I don't quite ~ you** je ne vous suis plus; **to ~ in sb's footsteps** emboîter le pas à qn; (*fig*) suivre les traces de qn; **it follows that ...** de ce fait, il s'ensuit que ...; **to ~ suit** (*fig*) faire de même
▶ **follow out** vt (*idea, plan*) poursuivre, mener à terme
▶ **follow through** vt = **follow out**
▶ **follow up** vt (*victory*) tirer parti de; (*letter, offer*) donner suite à; (*case*) suivre
follower ['fɔləuə'] N disciple *mf*, partisan(e)
following ['fɔləuɪŋ] ADJ suivant(e) ▶ N partisans *mpl*, disciples *mpl*
follow-up ['fɔləuʌp] N suite *f*; (*on file, case*) suivi *m*
folly ['fɔlɪ] N inconscience *f*; sottise *f*; (*building*) folie *f*
fond [fɔnd] ADJ (*memory, look*) tendre, affectueux(-euse); (*hopes, dreams*) un peu fou (folle); **to be ~ of** aimer beaucoup
fondle ['fɔndl] vt caresser
fondly ['fɔndlɪ] ADV (*lovingly*) tendrement; (*naïvely*) naïvement
fondness ['fɔndnɪs] N (*for things*) attachement *m*; (*for people*) sentiments affectueux; **a special ~ for** une prédilection pour
font [fɔnt] N (*Rel*) fonts baptismaux; (*Typ*) police *f* de caractères
food [fuːd] N nourriture *f*
food chain N chaîne *f* alimentaire
food mixer N mixeur *m*
food poisoning N intoxication *f* alimentaire
food processor N robot *m* de cuisine
food stamp N (*US*) bon *m* de nourriture (*pour indigents*)
foodstuffs ['fuːdstʌfs] NPL denrées *fpl* alimentaires
fool [fuːl] N idiot(e); (*Hist: of king*) bouffon *m*, fou *m*; (*Culin*) mousse *f* de fruits ▶ vt berner, duper
▶ vi (*also*: **fool around**) faire l'idiot or l'imbécile; **to make a ~ of sb** (*ridicule*) ridiculiser qn; (*trick*) avoir or duper qn; **to make a ~ of o.s.** se couvrir de ridicule; **you can't ~ me** vous (ne) me la ferez pas, on (ne) me la fait pas
▶ **fool about, fool around** vi (*pej: waste time*) traînailler, glandouiller; (: *behave foolishly*) faire l'idiot or l'imbécile
foolhardy ['fuːlhɑːdɪ] ADJ téméraire, imprudent(e)
foolish ['fuːlɪʃ] ADJ idiot(e), stupide; (*rash*) imprudent(e)
foolishly ['fuːlɪʃlɪ] ADV stupidement
foolishness ['fuːlɪʃnɪs] N idiotie *f*, stupidité *f*
foolproof ['fuːlpruːf] ADJ (*plan etc*) infaillible
foolscap ['fuːlskæp] N ≈ papier *m* ministre
foot [fut] (*pl* **feet** [fiːt]) N pied *m*; (*of animal*) patte *f*; (*measure*) pied (= 30.48 cm; 12 inches) ▶ vt (*bill*) casquer, payer; **on ~** à pied; **to find one's feet** (*fig*) s'acclimater; **to put one's ~ down** (*Aut*) appuyer sur le champignon; (*say no*) s'imposer
footage ['futɪdʒ] N (*Cine: length*) ≈ métrage *m*; (: *material*) séquences *fpl*

foot-and-mouth [futənd'mauθ], **foot-and-mouth disease** N fièvre aphteuse
football ['futbɔːl] N (ball) ballon m (de football); (sport: BRIT) football m; (: US) football américain
footballer ['futbɔːləʳ] N (BRIT) = **football player**
football ground N terrain m de football
football match N (BRIT) match m de foot(ball)
football player N footballeur(-euse), joueur(-euse) de football; (US) joueur(-euse) de football américain
football pools NPL (US) ≈ loto m sportif, ≈ pronostics mpl (sur les matchs de football)
footbrake ['futbreɪk] N frein m à pédale
footbridge ['futbrɪdʒ] N passerelle f
foothills ['futhɪlz] NPL contreforts mpl
foothold ['futhəuld] N prise f (de pied)
footing ['futɪŋ] N (fig) position f; **to lose one's ~** perdre pied; **on an equal ~** sur pied d'égalité
footlights ['futlaɪts] NPL rampe f
footman ['futmən] N (irreg) laquais m
footnote ['futnəut] N note f (en bas de page)
footpath ['futpɑːθ] N sentier m; (in street) trottoir m
footprint ['futprɪnt] N trace f (de pied)
footrest ['futrɛst] N marchepied m
footsie ['futsɪ] N (inf): **to play ~ with sb** faire du pied à qn
footsore ['futsɔːʳ] ADJ: **to be ~** avoir mal aux pieds
footstep ['futstɛp] N pas m
footwear ['futwɛəʳ] N chaussures fpl
FOR ABBR (= free on rail) franco wagon

(KEYWORD)

for [fɔːʳ] PREP **1** (indicating destination, intention, purpose) pour; **the train for London** le train pour (or à destination de) Londres; **he left for Rome** il est parti pour Rome; **he went for the paper** il est allé chercher le journal; **is this for me?** c'est pour moi?; **it's time for lunch** c'est l'heure du déjeuner; **what's it for?** ça sert à quoi?; **what for?** (why?) pourquoi?; (to what end?) pour quoi faire?, à quoi bon?; **for sale** à vendre; **to pray for peace** prier pour la paix
2 (on behalf of, representing) pour; **the MP for Hove** le député de Hove; **to work for sb/sth** travailler pour qn/qch; **I'll ask him for you** je vais lui demander pour toi; **G for George** G comme Georges
3 (because of) pour; **for this reason** pour cette raison; **for fear of being criticized** de peur d'être critiqué
4 (with regard to) pour; **it's cold for July** il fait froid pour juillet; **a gift for languages** un don pour les langues
5 (in exchange for): **I sold it for £5** je l'ai vendu 5 livres; **to pay 50 pence for a ticket** payer un billet 50 pence
6 (in favour of) pour; **are you for or against us?** êtes-vous pour ou contre nous?; **I'm all for it** je suis tout à fait pour; **vote for X** votez pour X
7 (referring to distance) pendant, sur; **there are roadworks for 5 km** il y a des travaux sur or pendant 5 km; **we walked for miles** nous

avons marché pendant des kilomètres
8 (referring to time) pendant; depuis; pour; **he was away for 2 years** il a été absent pendant 2 ans; **she will be away for a month** elle sera absente (pendant) un mois; **it hasn't rained for 3 weeks** ça fait 3 semaines qu'il ne pleut pas, il ne pleut pas depuis 3 semaines; **I have known her for years** je la connais depuis des années; **can you do it for tomorrow?** est-ce que tu peux le faire pour demain?
9 (with infinitive clauses): **it is not for me to decide** ce n'est pas à moi de décider; **it would be best for you to leave** le mieux serait que vous partiez; **there is still time for you to do it** vous avez encore le temps de le faire; **for this to be possible ...** pour que cela soit possible ...
10 (in spite of): **for all that** malgré cela, néanmoins; **for all his work/efforts** malgré tout son travail/tous ses efforts; **for all his complaints, he's very fond of her** il a beau se plaindre, il l'aime beaucoup
▶ CONJ (since, as: formal) car

forage ['fɔrɪdʒ] N fourrage m ▶ VI fourrager, fouiller
forage cap N calot m
foray ['fɔreɪ] N incursion f
forbad, forbade [fə'bæd] PT of **forbid**
forbearing [fɔː'bɛərɪŋ] ADJ patient(e), tolérant(e)
forbid [fə'bɪd] (pt **forbad** or **forbade** [-'bæd], pp **forbidden** [-'bɪdn]) VT défendre, interdire; **to ~ sb to do** défendre or interdire à qn de faire
forbidden [fə'bɪdn] ADJ défendu(e)
forbidding [fə'bɪdɪŋ] ADJ d'aspect or d'allure sévère ou sombre
force [fɔːs] N force f ▶ VT forcer; (push) pousser (de force); **Forces** NPL: **the Forces** (BRIT Mil) les forces armées; **to ~ o.s. to do** se forcer à faire; **to ~ sb to do sth** forcer qn à faire qch; **in ~** (rule, law, prices) en vigueur; (in large numbers) en force; **to come into ~** entrer en vigueur; **a ~ 5 wind** un vent de force 5; **the sales ~** (Comm) la force de vente; **to join forces** unir ses forces
▶ **force back** VT (crowd, enemy) repousser; (tears) refouler
▶ **force down** VT (food) se forcer à manger
forced [fɔːst] ADJ forcé(e)
force-feed ['fɔːsfiːd] VT nourrir de force
forceful ['fɔːsful] ADJ énergique
forcemeat ['fɔːsmiːt] N (BRIT Culin) farce f
forceps ['fɔːsɛps] NPL forceps m
forcibly ['fɔːsəblɪ] ADV par la force, de force; (vigorously) énergiquement
ford [fɔːd] N gué m ▶ VT passer à gué
fore [fɔːʳ] N: **to the ~** en évidence; **to come to the ~** se faire remarquer
forearm ['fɔːrɑːm] N avant-bras m inv
forebear ['fɔːbɛəʳ] N ancêtre m
foreboding [fɔː'bəudɪŋ] N pressentiment m (néfaste)
forecast ['fɔːkɑːst] N prévision f; (also: **weather forecast**) prévisions fpl météorologiques, météo f ▶ VT (irreg: like **cast**) prévoir

foreclose [fɔː'kləʊz] VT (Law: also: **foreclose on**) saisir

foreclosure [fɔː'kləʊʒər] N saisie f du bien hypothéqué

forecourt ['fɔːkɔːt] N (of garage) devant m

forefathers ['fɔːfɑːðəz] NPL ancêtres mpl

forefinger ['fɔːfɪŋgər] N index m

forefront ['fɔːfrʌnt] N: **in the ~ of** au premier rang or plan de

forego [fɔː'gəʊ] VT (irreg: like **go**) renoncer à

foregoing ['fɔːgəʊɪŋ] ADJ susmentionné(e) ▶ N: **the ~** ce qui précède

foregone ['fɔːgɒn] ADJ: **it's a ~ conclusion** c'est à prévoir, c'est couru d'avance

foreground ['fɔːgraʊnd] N premier plan ▶ CPD (Comput) prioritaire

forehand ['fɔːhænd] N (Tennis) coup droit

forehead ['fɒrɪd] N front m

foreign ['fɒrɪn] ADJ étranger(-ère); (trade) extérieur(e); (travel) à l'étranger

foreign body N corps étranger

foreign currency N devises étrangères

foreigner ['fɒrɪnər] N étranger(-ère)

foreign exchange N (system) change m; (money) devises fpl

foreign exchange market N marché m des devises

foreign exchange rate N cours m des devises

foreign investment N investissement m à l'étranger

Foreign Office N (BRIT) ministère m des Affaires étrangères

Foreign Secretary N (BRIT) ministre m des Affaires étrangères

foreleg ['fɔːlɛg] N patte f de devant, jambe antérieure

foreman ['fɔːmən] N (irreg) (in construction) contremaître m; (Law: of jury) président m (du jury)

foremost ['fɔːməʊst] ADJ le (la) plus en vue, premier(-ière) ▶ ADV: **first and ~** avant tout, tout d'abord

forename ['fɔːneɪm] N prénom m

forensic [fə'rɛnsɪk] ADJ: **~ medicine** médecine légale; **~ expert** expert m de la police, expert légiste

foreplay ['fɔːpleɪ] N stimulation f érotique, prélude m

forerunner ['fɔːrʌnər] N précurseur m

foresee [fɔː'siː] VT (irreg: like **see**) prévoir

foreseeable [fɔː'siːəbl] ADJ prévisible

foreseen [fɔː'siːn] PP of **foresee**

foreshadow [fɔː'ʃædəʊ] VT présager, annoncer, laisser prévoir

foreshorten [fɔː'ʃɔːtn] VT (figure, scene) réduire, faire en raccourci

foresight ['fɔːsaɪt] N prévoyance f

foreskin ['fɔːskɪn] N (Anat) prépuce m

forest ['fɒrɪst] N forêt f

forestall [fɔː'stɔːl] VT devancer

forestry ['fɒrɪstrɪ] N sylviculture f

foretaste ['fɔːteɪst] N avant-goût m

foretell [fɔː'tɛl] VT (irreg: like **tell**) prédire

forethought ['fɔːθɔːt] N prévoyance f

foretold [fɔː'təʊld] PT, PP of **foretell**

forever [fə'rɛvər] ADV pour toujours; (fig: endlessly) continuellement

forewarn [fɔː'wɔːn] VT avertir

forewent [fɔː'wɛnt] PT of **forego**

foreword ['fɔːwəːd] N avant-propos m inv

forfeit ['fɔːfɪt] N prix m, rançon f ▶ VT perdre; (one's life, health) payer de

forgave [fə'geɪv] PT of **forgive**

forge [fɔːdʒ] N forge f ▶ VT (signature) contrefaire; (wrought iron) forger; **to ~ documents/a will** fabriquer de faux papiers/un faux testament; **to ~ money** (BRIT) fabriquer de la fausse monnaie

▶ **forge ahead** VI pousser de l'avant, prendre de l'avance

forged [fɔːdʒd] ADJ faux (fausse)

forger ['fɔːdʒər] N faussaire m

forgery ['fɔːdʒərɪ] N faux m, contrefaçon f

forget [fə'gɛt] (pt **forgot** [-'gɒt], pp **forgotten** [-'gɒtn]) VT, VI oublier; **to ~ to do sth** oublier de faire qch; **to ~ about sth** (accidentally) oublier qch; (on purpose) ne plus penser à qch; **I've forgotten my key/passport** j'ai oublié ma clé/ mon passeport

forgetful [fə'gɛtful] ADJ distrait(e), étourdi(e); **~ of** oublieux(-euse) de

forgetfulness [fə'gɛtfulnɪs] N tendance f aux oublis; (oblivion) oubli m

forget-me-not [fə'gɛtmɪnɒt] N myosotis m

forgive [fə'gɪv] (pt **forgave** [-'geɪv], pp **forgiven** [-'gɪvn]) VT pardonner; **to ~ sb for sth/for doing sth** pardonner qch à qn/à qn de faire qch

forgiveness [fə'gɪvnɪs] N pardon m

forgiving [fə'gɪvɪŋ] ADJ indulgent(e)

forgo [fɔː'gəʊ] (pt **forwent** [-'wɛnt], pp **forgone** [-'gɒn]) VT = **forego**

forgot [fə'gɒt] PT of **forget**

forgotten [fə'gɒtn] PP of **forget**

fork [fɔːk] N (for eating) fourchette f; (for gardening) fourche f; (of roads) bifurcation f; (of railways) embranchement m ▶ VI (road) bifurquer

▶ **fork out** (inf: pay) VT allonger, se fendre de ▶ VI casquer

forked [fɔːkt] ADJ (lightning) en zigzags, ramifié(e)

fork-lift truck ['fɔːklɪft-] N chariot élévateur

forlorn [fə'lɔːn] ADJ (person) délaissé(e); (deserted) abandonné(e); (hope, attempt) désespéré(e)

form [fɔːm] N forme f; (Scol) classe f; (questionnaire) formulaire m ▶ VT former; (habit) contracter; **in the ~ of** sous forme de; **to ~ part of sth** faire partie de qch; **to be on good ~** (Sport: fig) être en forme; **on top ~** en pleine forme

formal ['fɔːməl] ADJ (offer, receipt) en bonne et due forme; (person) cérémonieux(-euse), à cheval sur les convenances; (occasion, dinner) officiel(le); (garden) à la française; (Art, Philosophy) formel(le); (clothes) de soirée

formality [fɔː'mælɪtɪ] N formalité f, cérémonie(s) f(pl)

formalize ['fɔːməlaɪz] VT officialiser

formally ['fɔːməlɪ] ADV officiellement;

formellement; cérémonieusement

format ['fɔːmæt] N format m ▸ VT (Comput) formater

formation [fɔːˈmeɪʃən] N formation f

formative ['fɔːmətɪv] ADJ: ~ **years** années fpl d'apprentissage (fig) or de formation (d'un enfant, d'un adolescent)

former ['fɔːmə'] ADJ ancien(ne); (before n) précédent(e); **the ~ ... the latter** le premier ... le second, celui-là ... celui-ci; **the ~ president** l'ex-président; **the ~ Yugoslavia/Soviet Union** l'ex Yougoslavie/Union Soviétique

formerly ['fɔːməlɪ] ADV autrefois

form feed N (on printer) alimentation f en feuilles

formidable ['fɔːmɪdəbl] ADJ redoutable

formula ['fɔːmjʊlə] N formule f; **F~ One** (Aut) Formule un

formulate ['fɔːmjʊleɪt] VT formuler

fornicate ['fɔːnɪkeɪt] VI forniquer

forsake [fəˈseɪk] (pt **forsook** [-ˈsuk], pp **forsaken** [-ˈseɪkən]) VT abandonner

fort [fɔːt] N fort m; **to hold the ~** (fig) assurer la permanence

forte ['fɔːtɪ] N (point) fort m

forth [fɔːθ] ADV en avant; **to go back and ~** aller et venir; **and so ~** et ainsi de suite

forthcoming [fɔːθˈkʌmɪŋ] ADJ qui va paraître or avoir lieu prochainement; (character) ouvert(e), communicatif(-ive); (available) disponible

forthright ['fɔːθraɪt] ADJ franc (franche), direct(e)

forthwith ['fɔːθˈwɪθ] ADV sur le champ

fortieth ['fɔːtɪɪθ] NUM quarantième

fortification [fɔːtɪfɪˈkeɪʃən] N fortification f

fortified wine ['fɔːtɪfaɪd-] N vin liquoreux or de liqueur

fortify ['fɔːtɪfaɪ] VT (city) fortifier; (person) remonter

fortitude ['fɔːtɪtjuːd] N courage m, force f d'âme

fortnight ['fɔːtnaɪt] N quinzaine f, quinze jours mpl; **it's a ~ since ...** il y a quinze jours que ...

fortnightly ['fɔːtnaɪtlɪ] ADJ bimensuel(le) ▸ ADV tous les quinze jours

FORTRAN ['fɔːtræn] N FORTRAN m

fortress ['fɔːtrɪs] N forteresse f

fortuitous [fɔːˈtjuːɪtəs] ADJ fortuit(e)

fortunate ['fɔːtʃənɪt] ADJ heureux(-euse); (person) chanceux(-euse); **to be ~** avoir de la chance; **it is ~ that** c'est une chance que, il est heureux que

fortunately ['fɔːtʃənɪtlɪ] ADV heureusement, par bonheur

fortune ['fɔːtʃən] N chance f; (wealth) fortune f; **to make a ~** faire fortune

fortune-teller ['fɔːtʃəntɛlə'] N diseuse f de bonne aventure

forty ['fɔːtɪ] NUM quarante

forum ['fɔːrəm] N forum m, tribune f

forward ['fɔːwəd] ADJ (movement, position) en avant, vers l'avant; (not shy) effronté(e); (in time) en avance; (Comm: delivery, sales, exchange) à terme ▸ ADV (also: **forwards**) en avant ▸ N (Sport) avant m ▸ VT (letter) faire suivre; (parcel, goods)

expédier; (fig) promouvoir, favoriser; **to look ~ to sth** attendre qch avec impatience; **to move ~** avancer; **"please ~"** "prière de faire suivre"; **~ planning** planification f à long terme

forwarding address N adresse f de réexpédition

forward slash N barre f oblique

forwent [fɔːˈwɛnt] PT of **forgo**

fossick ['fɔsɪk] VI (AUSTRALIA, NEW ZEALAND inf) chercher; **to ~ around for** fouiner (inf) pour trouver

fossil ['fɔsl] ADJ, N fossile m; **~ fuel** combustible m fossile

foster ['fɔstə'] VT (encourage) encourager, favoriser; (child) élever (sans adopter)

foster brother N frère adoptif; frère de lait

foster child N (irreg) enfant élevé dans une famille d'accueil

foster mother N mère adoptive; mère nourricière

foster parent N parent qui élève un enfant sans l'adopter

foster sister N sœur f de lait

fought [fɔːt] PT, PP of **fight**

foul [faul] ADJ (weather, smell, food) infect(e); (language) ordurier(-ière); (deed) infâme ▸ N (Football) faute f ▸ VT (dirty) salir, encrasser; (football player) commettre une faute sur; (entangle: anchor, propeller) emmêler; **he's got a ~ temper** il a un caractère de chien

foul play N (Sport) jeu déloyal; (Law) acte criminel; **~ is not suspected** la mort (or l'incendie etc) n'a pas de causes suspectes, on écarte l'hypothèse d'un meurtre (or d'un acte criminel)

found [faund] PT, PP of **find** ▸ VT (establish) fonder

foundation [faunˈdeɪʃən] N (act) fondation f; (base) fondement m; (also: **foundation cream**) fond m de teint; **foundations** NPL (of building) fondations fpl; **to lay the foundations** (fig) poser les fondements

foundation stone N première pierre

founder ['faundə'] N fondateur m ▸ VI couler, sombrer

founding ['faundɪŋ] ADJ: **~ fathers** (esp US) pères mpl fondateurs; **~ member** membre m fondateur

foundry ['faundrɪ] N fonderie f

fount [faunt] N source f; (Typ) fonte f

fountain ['fauntɪn] N fontaine f

fountain pen N stylo m (à encre)

four [fɔː'] NUM quatre; **on all fours** à quatre pattes

four-by-four [fɔːbaɪˈfɔː'] N (Aut) 4x4 m

four-letter word ['fɔːlɛtə-] N obscénité f, gros mot

four-poster ['fɔːˈpəustə'] N (also: **four-poster bed**) lit m à baldaquin

foursome ['fɔːsəm] N partie f à quatre; sortie f à quatre

fourteen ['fɔːˈtiːn] NUM quatorze

fourteenth ['fɔːˈtiːnθ] NUM quatorzième

fourth ['fɔːθ] NUM quatrième ▸ N (Aut: also: **fourth gear**) quatrième f

f

four-wheel drive ['fɔ:wi:l-] N (Aut: car) voiture f à quatre roues motrices; **with ~** à quatre roues motrices

fowl [faul] N volaille f

fox [fɔks] N renard m ▸ vt mystifier

fox fur N renard m

foxglove ['fɔksglʌv] N (Bot) digitale f

fox-hunting ['fɔkshʌntɪŋ] N chasse f au renard

foyer ['fɔɪeɪ] N (in hotel) vestibule m; (Theat) foyer m

FP N ABBR (BRIT) = **former pupil**; (US) = **fireplug**

FPA N ABBR (BRIT) = **Family Planning Association**

Fr. ABBR (Rel: = father) P; (= friar) F

fr. ABBR (= franc) F

fracas ['fræka:] N bagarre f

fraction ['frækʃən] N fraction f

fractionally ['frækʃnəlɪ] ADV: **~ smaller** etc un poil plus petit etc

fractious ['frækʃəs] ADJ grincheux(-euse)

fracture ['fræktʃəʳ] N fracture f ▸ vt fracturer

fragile ['frædʒaɪl] ADJ fragile

fragment ['frægmənt] N fragment m

fragmentary ['frægməntərɪ] ADJ fragmentaire

fragrance ['freɪgrəns] N parfum m

fragrant ['freɪgrənt] ADJ parfumé(e), odorant(e)

frail [freɪl] ADJ fragile, délicat(e); (person) frêle

frame [freɪm] N (of building) charpente f; (of human, animal) charpente, ossature f; (of picture) cadre m; (of door, window) encadrement m, chambranle m; (of spectacles: also: **frames**) monture f ▸ vt (picture) encadrer; (theory, plan) construire, élaborer; **to ~ sb** (inf) monter un coup contre qn; **~ of mind** disposition f d'esprit

framework ['freɪmwə:k] N structure f

France [fra:ns] N la France; **in ~** en France

franchise ['fræntʃaɪz] N (Pol) droit m de vote; (Comm) franchise f

franchisee [fræntʃaɪ'zi:] N franchisé m

franchiser ['fræntʃaɪzəʳ] N franchiseur m

frank [fræŋk] ADJ franc (franche) ▸ vt (letter) affranchir

Frankfurt ['fræŋkfə:t] N Francfort

franking machine ['fræŋkɪŋ-] N machine f à affranchir

frankly ['fræŋklɪ] ADV franchement

frankness ['fræŋknɪs] N franchise f

frantic ['fræntɪk] ADJ (hectic) frénétique; (need, desire) effréné(e); (distraught) hors de soi

frantically ['fræntɪklɪ] ADV frénétiquement

fraternal [frə'tə:nl] ADJ fraternel(le)

fraternity [frə'tə:nɪtɪ] N (club) communauté f, confrérie f; (spirit) fraternité f

fraternize ['frætənaɪz] vi fraterniser

fraud [frɔ:d] N supercherie f, fraude f, tromperie f; (person) imposteur m

fraudulent ['frɔ:djulənt] ADJ frauduleux(-euse)

fraught [frɔ:t] ADJ (tense: person) très tendu(e); (: situation) pénible; **~ with** (difficulties etc) chargé(e) de, plein(e) de

fray [freɪ] N bagarre f; (Mil) combat m ▸ vt effilocher ▸ vi s'effilocher; **tempers were frayed** les gens commençaient à s'énerver; **her nerves were frayed** elle était à bout de nerfs

FRB N ABBR (US) = **Federal Reserve Board**

FRCM N ABBR (BRIT) = **Fellow of the Royal College of Music**

FRCO N ABBR (BRIT) = **Fellow of the Royal College of Organists**

FRCP N ABBR (BRIT) = **Fellow of the Royal College of Physicians**

FRCS N ABBR (BRIT) = **Fellow of the Royal College of Surgeons**

freak [fri:k] N (eccentric person) phénomène m; (unusual event) hasard m extraordinaire; (pej: fanatic): **health food ~** fana mf or obsédé(e) de l'alimentation saine ▸ ADJ (storm) exceptionnel(le); (accident) bizarre
▸ **freak out** vi (inf: drop out) se marginaliser; (: on drugs) se défoncer

freakish ['fri:kɪʃ] ADJ insolite, anormal(e)

freckle ['frɛkl] N tache f de rousseur

free [fri:] ADJ libre; (gratis) gratuit(e); (liberal) généreux(-euse), large ▸ vt (prisoner etc) libérer; (jammed object or person) dégager; **is this seat ~?** la place est libre?; **to give sb a ~ hand** donner carte blanche à qn; **~ and easy** sans façon, décontracté(e); **admission ~** entrée libre; **~ (of charge)** gratuitement

freebie ['fri:bɪ] N (inf): **it's a ~** c'est gratuit

freedom ['fri:dəm] N liberté f

freedom fighter N combattant m de la liberté

free enterprise N libre entreprise f

Freefone® ['fri:fəun] N numéro vert

free-for-all ['fri:fərɔ:l] N mêlée générale

free gift N prime f

freehold ['fri:həuld] N propriété foncière libre

free kick N (Sport) coup franc

freelance ['fri:la:ns] ADJ (journalist etc) indépendant(e), free-lance inv; (work) en free-lance ▸ ADV en free-lance

freeloader ['fri:ləudəʳ] N (pej) parasite m

freely ['fri:lɪ] ADV librement; (liberally) libéralement

free-market economy [fri:'ma:kɪt-] N économie f de marché

freemason ['fri:meɪsn] N franc-maçon m

freemasonry ['fri:meɪsnrɪ] N franc-maçonnerie f

Freepost® ['fri:pəust] N (BRIT) port payé

free-range ['fri:'reɪndʒ] ADJ (egg) de ferme; (chicken) fermier

free sample N échantillon gratuit

free speech N liberté f d'expression

free trade N libre-échange m

freeway ['fri:weɪ] N (US) autoroute f

freewheel [fri:'wi:l] vi descendre en roue libre

freewheeling [fri:'wi:lɪŋ] ADJ indépendant(e), libre

free will N libre arbitre m; **of one's own ~** de son plein gré

freeze [fri:z] (pt **froze** [frəuz], pp **frozen** ['frəuzn]) vi geler ▸ vt geler; (food) congeler; (prices, salaries) bloquer, geler ▸ N gel m; (of prices, salaries) blocage m
▸ **freeze over** vi (river) geler; (windscreen) se couvrir de givre or de glace
▸ **freeze up** vi geler

freeze-dried ['fri:zdraɪd] ADJ lyophilisé(e)

freezer ['fri:zə^r] N congélateur m
freezing ['fri:zɪŋ] ADJ: ~ **(cold)** (room etc)
glacial(e); (person, hands) gelé(e), glacé(e) ▶ N: **3
degrees below** ~ 3 degrés au-dessous de zéro;
it's ~ il fait un froid glacial
freezing point N point m de congélation
freight [freɪt] N (goods) fret m, cargaison f;
(money charged) fret, prix m du transport;
~ **forward** port dû; ~ **inward** port payé par le
destinataire
freighter ['freɪtə^r] N (Naut) cargo m
freight forwarder [-fɔ:wədə^r] N transitaire m
freight train N (US) train m de marchandises
French [frɛntʃ] ADJ français(e) ▶ N (Ling) français
m; **the** ~ npl les Français; **what's the** ~ **(word)
for ...?** comment dit-on ... en français?
French bean N (BRIT) haricot vert
French bread N pain m français
French Canadian ADJ canadien(ne) français(e)
▶ N Canadien(ne) français(e)
French dressing N (Culin) vinaigrette f
French fried potatoes, (US) **French fries** NPL
(pommes de terre fpl) frites fpl
French Guiana [-gaɪˈænə] N Guyane française
French horn N (Mus) cor m (d'harmonie)
French kiss N baiser profond
French loaf N ≈ pain m, ≈ parisien m
Frenchman ['frɛntʃmən] N (irreg) Français m
French Riviera N: **the** ~ la Côte d'Azur
French stick N ≈ baguette f
French window N porte-fenêtre f
Frenchwoman ['frɛntʃwumən] N (irreg)
Française f
frenetic [frəˈnɛtɪk] ADJ frénétique
frenzy ['frɛnzɪ] N frénésie f
frequency ['fri:kwənsɪ] N fréquence f
frequency modulation N modulation f de
fréquence
frequent ADJ ['fri:kwənt] fréquent(e) ▶ VT
[frɪˈkwɛnt] fréquenter
frequently ['fri:kwəntlɪ] ADV fréquemment
fresco ['frɛskəu] N fresque f
fresh [frɛʃ] ADJ frais (fraîche); (new) nouveau
(nouvelle); (cheeky) familier(-ière), culotté(e);
to make a ~ **start** prendre un nouveau départ
freshen ['frɛʃən] VI (wind, air) fraîchir
▶ **freshen up** VI faire un brin de toilette
freshener ['frɛʃnə^r] N: **skin** ~ astringent m; **air** ~
désodorisant m
fresher ['frɛʃə^r] N (BRIT University: inf) bizuth m,
étudiant(e) de première année
freshly ['frɛʃlɪ] ADV nouvellement, récemment
freshman ['frɛʃmən] N (irreg) (US) = **fresher**
freshness ['frɛʃnɪs] N fraîcheur f
freshwater ['frɛʃwɔ:tə^r] ADJ (fish) d'eau douce
fret [frɛt] VI s'agiter, se tracasser
fretful ['frɛtful] ADJ (child) grincheux(-euse)
Freudian ['frɔɪdɪən] ADJ freudien(ne); ~ **slip**
lapsus m
FRG N ABBR (= Federal Republic of Germany) RFA f
friar ['fraɪə^r] N moine m, frère m
friction ['frɪkʃən] N friction f, frottement m
friction feed N (on printer) entraînement m par
friction

Friday ['fraɪdɪ] N vendredi m; see also
Tuesday
fridge [frɪdʒ] N (BRIT) frigo m, frigidaire® m
fridge-freezer ['frɪdʒ'fri:zə^r] N réfrigérateur-
congélateur m
fried [fraɪd] PT, PP of **fry** ▶ ADJ frit(e); ~ **egg** œuf
m sur le plat
friend [frɛnd] N ami(e) ▶ VT (Internet) ajouter
comme ami(e); **to make friends with** se lier
(d'amitié) avec
friendliness ['frɛndlɪnɪs] N attitude amicale
friendly ['frɛndlɪ] ADJ amical(e); (kind)
sympathique, gentil(le); (place) accueillant(e);
(Pol: country) ami(e) ▶ N (also: **friendly match**)
match amical; **to be** ~ **with** être ami(e) avec;
to be ~ **to** être bien disposé(e) à l'égard de
friendly fire N: **they were killed by** ~ ils sont
morts sous les tirs de leur propre camp
friendly society N société f mutualiste
friendship ['frɛndʃɪp] N amitié f
fries [fraɪz] (esp US) NPL = **chips**
frieze [fri:z] N frise f, bordure f
frigate ['frɪgɪt] N (Naut: modern) frégate f
fright [fraɪt] N peur f, effroi m; **to give sb a** ~
faire peur à qn; **to take** ~ prendre peur,
s'effrayer; **she looks a** ~ elle a l'air d'un
épouvantail
frighten ['fraɪtn] VT effrayer, faire peur à
▶ **frighten away, frighten off** VT (birds, children
etc) faire fuir, effaroucher
frightened ['fraɪtnd] ADJ: **to be** ~ **(of)** avoir
peur (de)
frightening ['fraɪtnɪŋ] ADJ effrayant(e)
frightful ['fraɪtful] ADJ affreux(-euse)
frightfully ['fraɪtfəlɪ] ADV affreusement
frigid ['frɪdʒɪd] ADJ frigide
frigidity [frɪˈdʒɪdɪtɪ] N frigidité f
frill [frɪl] N (of dress) volant m; (of shirt) jabot m;
without frills (fig) sans manières
frilly ['frɪlɪ] ADJ à fanfreluches
fringe [frɪndʒ] N (BRIT: of hair) frange f;
(edge: of forest etc) bordure f; (: fig): **on the** ~
en marge
fringe benefits NPL avantages sociaux or en
nature
fringe theatre N théâtre m d'avant-garde
Frisbee® ['frɪzbɪ] N Frisbee® m
frisk [frɪsk] VT fouiller
frisky ['frɪskɪ] ADJ vif (vive), sémillant(e)
fritter ['frɪtə^r] N beignet m
▶ **fritter away** VT gaspiller
frivolity [frɪˈvɔlɪtɪ] N frivolité f
frivolous ['frɪvələs] ADJ frivole
frizzy ['frɪzɪ] ADJ crépu(e)
fro [frəu] ADV see **to**
frock [frɔk] N robe f
frog [frɔg] N grenouille f; **to have a** ~ **in one's
throat** avoir un chat dans la gorge
frogman ['frɔgmən] N (irreg) homme-
grenouille m
frogmarch ['frɔgmɑ:tʃ] VT (BRIT): **to** ~ **sb in/out**
faire entrer/sortir qn de force
frolic ['frɔlɪk] N ébats mpl ▶ VI folâtrer,
batifoler

KEYWORD

from [frɔm] PREP **1** (*indicating starting place, origin etc*) de; **where do you come from?**, **where are you from?** d'où venez-vous?; **where has he come from?** d'où arrive-t-il?; **from London to Paris** de Londres à Paris; **to escape from sb/sth** échapper à qn/qch; **a letter/telephone call from my sister** une lettre/un appel de ma sœur; **to drink from the bottle** boire à (même) la bouteille; **tell him from me that …** dites-lui de ma part que …

2 (*indicating time*) (à partir) de; **from one o'clock to** *or* **until** *or* **till two** d'une heure à deux heures; **from January (on)** à partir de janvier **3** (*indicating distance*) de; **the hotel is one kilometre from the beach** l'hôtel est à un kilomètre de la plage

4 (*indicating price, number etc*) de; **prices range from £10 to £50** les prix varient entre 10 livres et 50 livres; **the interest rate was increased from 9% to 10%** le taux d'intérêt est passé de 9% à 10%

5 (*indicating difference*) de; **he can't tell red from green** il ne peut pas distinguer le rouge du vert; **to be different from sb/sth** être différent de qn/qch

6 (*because of, on the basis of*): **from what he says** d'après ce qu'il dit; **weak from hunger** affaibli par la faim

frond [frɔnd] N fronde *f*

front [frʌnt] N (*of house, dress*) devant *m*; (*of coach, train*) avant *m*; (*of book*) couverture *f*; (*promenade: also:* **sea front**) bord *m* de mer; (*Mil, Pol, Meteorology*) front *m*; (*fig: appearances*) contenance *f*, façade *f* ▸ ADJ de devant; (*page, row*) premier(-ière); (*seat, wheel*) avant inv ▸ VI: **to ~ onto sth** donner sur qch; **in ~ (of)** devant

frontage ['frʌntɪdʒ] N façade *f*; (*of shop*) devanture *f*

frontal ['frʌntl] ADJ frontal(e)

front bench N (*Brit Pol*); *voir article*

> Le *front bench* est le banc du gouvernement, placé à la droite du *Speaker*, ou celui du cabinet fantôme, placé à sa gauche. Ils se font face dans l'enceinte de la Chambre des communes. Par extension, *front bench* désigne les dirigeants des groupes parlementaires de la majorité et de l'opposition, qui sont appelés *frontbenchers* par opposition aux autres députés qui sont appelés *backbenchers*.

front desk N (*US: in hotel, at doctor's*) réception *f*
front door N porte *f* d'entrée; (*of car*) portière *f* avant
frontier ['frʌntɪər] N frontière *f*
frontispiece ['frʌntɪspiːs] N frontispice *m*
front page N première page
front room N (*Brit*) pièce *f* de devant, salon *m*
front runner N (*fig*) favori(te)
front-wheel drive ['frʌntwiːl-] N traction *f* avant
frost [frɔst] N gel *m*, gelée *f*; (*also:* **hoarfrost**) givre *m*

frostbite ['frɔstbaɪt] N gelures *fpl*
frosted ['frɔstɪd] ADJ (*glass*) dépoli(e); (*esp US: cake*) glacé(e)
frosting ['frɔstɪŋ] N (*esp US: on cake*) glaçage *m*
frosty ['frɔstɪ] ADJ (*window*) couvert(e) de givre; (*weather, welcome*) glacial(e)
froth [frɔθ] N mousse *f*; écume *f*
frown [fraun] N froncement *m* de sourcils ▸ VI froncer les sourcils
  ▸ **frown on** VT (*fig*) désapprouver
froze [frəuz] PT *of* **freeze**
frozen ['frəuzn] PP *of* **freeze** ▸ ADJ (*food*) congelé(e); (*person, also assets*) gelé(e)
FRS N ABBR (*Brit:* = *Fellow of the Royal Society*) membre de l'Académie des sciences; (*US:* = *Federal Reserve System*) banque centrale américaine
frugal ['fruːgl] ADJ frugal(e)
fruit [fruːt] N (*pl inv*) fruit *m*
fruiterer ['fruːtərə] N fruitier *m*, marchand(e) de fruits; **~'s (shop)** fruiterie *f*
fruit fly N mouche *f* du vinaigre, drosophile *f*
fruitful ['fruːtful] ADJ fructueux(-euse); (*plant, soil*) fécond(e)
fruition [fruːˈɪʃən] N: **to come to ~** se réaliser
fruit juice N jus *m* de fruit
fruitless ['fruːtlɪs] ADJ (*fig*) vain(e), infructueux(-euse)
fruit machine N (*Brit*) machine *f* à sous
fruit salad N salade *f* de fruits
frump [frʌmp] N mocheté *f*
frustrate [frʌsˈtreɪt] VT frustrer; (*plot, plans*) faire échouer
frustrated [frʌsˈtreɪtɪd] ADJ frustré(e)
frustrating [frʌsˈtreɪtɪŋ] ADJ (*job*) frustrant(e); (*day*) démoralisant(e)
frustration [frʌsˈtreɪʃən] N frustration *f*
fry [fraɪ] (*pt, pp* **fried** [-d]) VT (faire) frire ▸ N: **small ~** le menu fretin
frying pan ['fraɪɪŋ-] N poêle *f* (à frire)
FT N ABBR (*Brit:* = *Financial Times*) journal financier
ft. ABBR = **foot**; **feet**
FTC N ABBR (*US*) = **Federal Trade Commission**
FTSE 100 (Share) Index N ABBR (= *Financial Times Stock Exchange 100 (Share) Index*) indice *m* Footsie des cent grandes valeurs
fuchsia ['fjuːʃə] N fuchsia *m*
fuck [fʌk] VT, VI (*inf!*) baiser (!); **~ off!** fous le camp! (!)
fuddled ['fʌdld] ADJ (*muddled*) embrouillé(e), confus(e)
fuddy-duddy ['fʌdɪdʌdɪ] ADJ (*pej*) vieux jeu inv, ringard(e)
fudge [fʌdʒ] N (*Culin*) sorte de confiserie à base de sucre, de beurre et de lait ▸ VT (*issue, problem*) esquiver
fuel [fjuəl] N (*for heating*) combustible *m*; (*for engine*) carburant *m*
fuel oil N mazout *m*
fuel poverty N pauvreté *f* énergétique
fuel pump N (*Aut*) pompe *f* d'alimentation
fuel tank N cuve *f* à mazout, citerne *f*; (*in vehicle*) réservoir *m* de or à carburant
fug [fʌg] N (*Brit*) puanteur *f*, odeur *f* de renfermé
fugitive ['fjuːdʒɪtɪv] N fugitif(-ive)

fulfil, (US) **fulfill** [ful'fɪl] VT (function, condition) remplir; (order) exécuter; (wish, desire) satisfaire, réaliser

fulfilled [ful'fɪld] ADJ (person) comblé(e), épanoui(e)

fulfilment, (US) **fulfillment** [ful'fɪlmənt] N (of wishes) réalisation f

full [ful] ADJ plein(e); (details, hotel, bus) complet(-ète); (price) fort(e), normal(e); (busy: day) chargé(e); (skirt) ample, large ▶ ADV: **to know ~ well that** savoir fort bien que; **~ (up)** (hotel etc) complet(-ète); **I'm ~ (up)** j'ai bien mangé; **~ employment/fare** plein emploi/ tarif; **a ~ two hours** deux bonnes heures; **at ~ speed** à toute vitesse; **in ~** (reproduce, quote, pay) intégralement; (write name etc) en toutes lettres

fullback ['fulbæk] N (Rugby, Football) arrière m

full-blooded ['ful'blʌdɪd] ADJ (vigorous) vigoureux(-euse)

full-cream ['ful'kri:m] ADJ: **~ milk** (BRIT) lait entier

full-grown ['ful'grəun] ADJ arrivé(e) à maturité, adulte

full-length ['ful'lɛŋθ] ADJ (portrait) en pied; (coat) long(ue); **~ film** long métrage

full moon N pleine lune

full-scale ['fulskeɪl] ADJ (model) grandeur nature inv; (search, retreat) complet(-ète), total(e)

full-sized ['ful'saɪzd] ADJ (portrait etc) grandeur nature inv

full stop N point m

full-time ['ful'taɪm] ADJ, ADV (work) à plein temps ▶ N (Sport) fin f du match

fully ['fulɪ] ADV entièrement, complètement; (at least): **~ as big** au moins aussi grand

fully-fledged ['fulɪ'flɛdʒd] ADJ (teacher, barrister) diplômé(e); (citizen, member) à part entière

fulsome ['fulsəm] ADJ (pej: praise) excessif(-ive); (: manner) exagéré(e)

fumble ['fʌmbl] VI fouiller, tâtonner ▶ VT (ball) mal réceptionner, cafouiller
▶ **fumble with** VT FUS tripoter

fume [fju:m] VI (rage) rager

fumes [fju:mz] NPL vapeurs fpl, émanations fpl, gaz mpl

fumigate ['fju:mɪgeɪt] VT désinfecter (par fumigation)

fun [fʌn] N amusement m, divertissement m; **to have ~** s'amuser; **for ~** pour rire; **it's not much ~** ce n'est pas très drôle or amusant; **to make ~ of** se moquer de

function ['fʌŋkʃən] N fonction f; (reception, dinner) cérémonie f, soirée officielle ▶ VI fonctionner; **to ~ as** faire office de

functional ['fʌŋkʃənl] ADJ fonctionnel(le)

function key N (Comput) touche f de fonction

fund [fʌnd] N caisse f, fonds m; (source, store) source f, mine f; **funds** NPL (money) fonds mpl

fundamental [fʌndə'mɛntl] ADJ fondamental(e); **fundamentals** NPL principes mpl de base

fundamentalism [fʌndə'mɛntəlɪzəm] N intégrisme m

fundamentalist [fʌndə'mɛntəlɪst] N intégriste mf

fundamentally [fʌndə'mɛntəlɪ] ADV fondamentalement

funding ['fʌndɪŋ] N financement m

fund-raising ['fʌndreɪzɪŋ] N collecte f de fonds

funeral ['fju:nərəl] N enterrement m, obsèques fpl (more formal occasion)

funeral director N entrepreneur m des pompes funèbres

funeral parlour N (BRIT) dépôt m mortuaire

funeral service N service m funèbre

funereal [fju:'nɪərɪəl] ADJ lugubre, funèbre

funfair ['fʌnfɛər] N (BRIT) fête (foraine)

fungus ['fʌŋgəs] (pl **fungi** [-gaɪ]) N champignon m; (mould) moisissure f

funicular [fju:'nɪkjulər] N (also: **funicular railway**) funiculaire m

funky ['fʌŋkɪ] ADJ (music) funky inv; (inf: excellent) super inv

funnel ['fʌnl] N entonnoir m; (of ship) cheminée f

funnily ['fʌnɪlɪ] ADV drôlement; (strangely) curieusement

funny ['fʌnɪ] ADJ amusant(e), drôle; (strange) curieux(-euse), bizarre

funny bone N endroit sensible du coude

fun run N course f de fond (pour amateurs)

fur [fə:ʳ] N fourrure f; (BRIT: in kettle etc) (dépôt m de) tartre m

fur coat N manteau m de fourrure

furious ['fjuərɪəs] ADJ furieux(-euse); (effort) acharné(e); **to be ~ with sb** être dans une fureur noire contre qn

furiously ['fjuərɪəslɪ] ADV furieusement; avec acharnement

furl [fə:l] VT rouler; (Naut) ferler

furlong ['fə:lɔŋ] N = 201.17 m (terme d'hippisme)

furlough ['fə:ləu] N permission f, congé m

furnace ['fə:nɪs] N fourneau m

furnish ['fə:nɪʃ] VT meubler; (supply) fournir; **furnished flat** or (US) **apartment** meublé m

furnishings ['fə:nɪʃɪŋz] NPL mobilier m, articles mpl d'ameublement

furniture ['fə:nɪtʃəʳ] N meubles mpl, mobilier m; **piece of ~** meuble m

furniture polish N encaustique f

furore [fjuə'rɔ:rɪ] N (protests) protestations fpl

furrier ['fʌrɪəʳ] N fourreur m

furrow ['fʌrəu] N sillon m

furry ['fə:rɪ] ADJ (animal) à fourrure; (toy) en peluche

further ['fə:ðəʳ] ADJ supplémentaire, autre; nouveau (nouvelle) ▶ ADV plus loin; (more) davantage; (moreover) de plus ▶ VT faire avancer or progresser, promouvoir; **how much ~ is it?** quelle distance or combien reste-t-il à parcourir?; **until ~ notice** jusqu'à nouvel ordre or avis; **~ to your letter of …** (Comm) suite à votre lettre du …

further education N enseignement m postscolaire (recyclage, formation professionnelle)

furthermore [fə:ðə'mɔ:ʳ] ADV de plus, en outre

furthermost ['fə:ðəməust] ADJ le (la) plus éloigné(e)

furthest ['fə:ðɪst] SUPERLATIVE of **far**

furtive ['fə:tɪv] ADJ furtif(-ive)

f

fury ['fjʊərɪ] N fureur f
fuse, (US) **fuze** [fju:z] N fusible m; (for bomb etc) amorce f, détonateur m ▸ VT, VI (metal) fondre; (fig) fusionner; (BRIT Elec) **to ~ the lights** faire sauter les fusibles or les plombs; **a ~ has blown** un fusible a sauté
fuse box N boîte f à fusibles
fuselage ['fju:zəlɑ:ʒ] N fuselage m
fuse wire N fusible m
fusillade [fju:zɪ'leɪd] N fusillade f; (fig) feu roulant
fusion ['fju:ʒən] N fusion f
fuss [fʌs] N (anxiety, excitement) chichis mpl, façons fpl; (commotion) tapage m; (complaining, trouble) histoire(s) f(pl) ▸ VI faire des histoires ▸ VT (person) embêter; **to make a ~** faire des façons (or des histoires); **to make a ~ of sb** dorloter qn
▸ **fuss over** VT FUS (person) dorloter
fusspot ['fʌspɒt] N (inf): **don't be such a ~!** ne

fais pas tant d'histoires!
fussy ['fʌsɪ] ADJ (person) tatillon(ne), difficile, chichiteux(-euse); (dress, style) tarabiscoté(e); **I'm not ~** (inf) ça m'est égal
fusty ['fʌstɪ] ADJ (old-fashioned) vieillot(te); (smell) de renfermé or moisi
futile ['fju:taɪl] ADJ futile
futility [fju:'tɪlɪtɪ] N futilité f
futon ['fu:tɒn] N futon m
future ['fju:tʃəʳ] ADJ futur(e) ▸ N avenir m; (Ling) futur m; **futures** NPL (Comm) opérations fpl à terme; **in (the) ~** à l'avenir; **in the near/immediate ~** dans un avenir proche/immédiat
futuristic [fju:tʃə'rɪstɪk] ADJ futuriste
fuze [fju:z] N, VT, VI (US) = **fuse**
fuzzy ['fʌzɪ] ADJ (Phot) flou(e); (hair) crépu(e)
fwd. ABBR = **forward**
fwy ABBR (US) = **freeway**
FY ABBR = **fiscal year**
FYI ABBR = **for your information**

Gg

G¹, g [dʒiː] N (*letter*) G, g m; (*Mus*): **G** sol m; **G for George** G comme Gaston

G² N ABBR (*BRIT Scol*: = *good*) b (= *bien*); (*US Cine*: = *general (audience)*) ≈ tous publics; (*Pol*: = *G8*) G8 m

g. ABBR (= *gram*) g; (= *gravity*) g

G8 N ABBR (*Pol*): **the G8 nations** le G8

G20 N ABBR (*Pol*: = *Group of Twenty*) G20 m

GA ABBR (*US*) = **Georgia**

gab [gæb] N (*inf*): **to have the gift of the ~** avoir la langue bien pendue

gabble ['gæbl] VI bredouiller; jacasser

gaberdine [gæbə'diːn] N gabardine f

gable ['geɪbl] N pignon m

Gabon [gə'bɔn] N Gabon m

gad about ['gædə'baut] VI (*inf*) se balader

gadget ['gædʒɪt] N gadget m

Gaelic ['geɪlɪk] ADJ, N (*Ling*) gaélique (m)

gaffe [gæf] N gaffe f

gaffer ['gæfəʳ] N (*BRIT: foreman*) contremaître m; (*BRIT inf: boss*) patron m

gag [gæg] N (*on mouth*) bâillon m; (*joke*) gag m ▶ VT (*prisoner etc*) bâillonner ▶ VI (*choke*) étouffer

gaga ['gaːgaː] ADJ: **to go ~** devenir gaga *or* gâteux(-euse)

gaiety ['geɪɪtɪ] N gaieté f

gaily ['geɪlɪ] ADV gaiement

gain [geɪn] N (*improvement*) gain m; (*profit*) gain, profit m ▶ VT gagner ▶ VI (*watch*) avancer; **to ~ from/by** gagner de/à; **to ~ on sb** (*catch up*) rattraper qn; **to ~ 3lbs (in weight)** prendre 3 livres; **to ~ ground** gagner du terrain

gainful ['geɪnful] ADJ profitable, lucratif(-ive)

gainfully ['geɪnfəlɪ] ADV: **to be ~ employed** avoir un emploi rémunéré

gainsay [geɪn'seɪ] VT (*irreg: like* **say**) contredire; nier

gait [geɪt] N démarche f

gal. ABBR = **gallon**

gala ['gaːlə] N gala m; **swimming ~** grand concours de natation

Galápagos [gə'læpəgəs] NPL: **the ~ (Islands)** les (îles fpl) Calapagos fpl

galaxy ['gæləksɪ] N galaxie f

gale [geɪl] N coup m de vent; **~ force 10** vent m de force 10

gall [gɔːl] N (*Anat*) bile f; (*fig*) effronterie f ▶ VT ulcérer, irriter

gall. ABBR = **gallon**

gallant ['gælənt] ADJ vaillant(e), brave; (*towards ladies*) empressé(e), galant(e)

gallantry ['gæləntrɪ] N bravoure f, vaillance f; empressement m, galanterie f

gall bladder N vésicule f biliaire

galleon ['gælɪən] N galion m

gallery ['gælərɪ] N galerie f; (*also*: **art gallery**) musée m; (: *private*) galerie; (*for spectators*) tribune f; (: *in theatre*) dernier balcon

galley ['gælɪ] N (*ship's kitchen*) cambuse f; (*ship*) galère f; (*also*: **galley proof**) placard m, galée f

Gallic ['gælɪk] ADJ (*of Gaul*) gaulois(e); (*French*) français(e)

galling ['gɔːlɪŋ] ADJ irritant(e)

gallon ['gæln] N gallon m (*Brit* = 4.543 l; *US* = 3.785 l), = 8 pints

gallop ['gæləp] N galop m ▶ VI galoper; **galloping inflation** inflation galopante

gallows ['gæləuz] N potence f

gallstone ['gɔːlstəun] N calcul m (biliaire)

Gallup Poll ['gæləp-] N sondage m Gallup

galore [gə'lɔːʳ] ADV en abondance, à gogo

galvanize ['gælvənaɪz] VT galvaniser; (*fig*): **to ~ sb into action** galvaniser qn

Gambia ['gæmbɪə] N Gambie f

gambit ['gæmbɪt] N (*fig*): **(opening) ~** manœuvre f stratégique

gamble ['gæmbl] N pari m, risque calculé ▶ VT, VI jouer; **to ~ on the Stock Exchange** jouer en *or* à la Bourse; **to ~ on** (*fig*) miser sur

gambler ['gæmbləʳ] N joueur m

gambling ['gæmblɪŋ] N jeu m

gambol ['gæmbl] VI gambader

game [geɪm] N jeu m; (*event*) match m; (*of tennis, chess, cards*) partie f; (*Hunting*) gibier m ▶ ADJ brave; (*willing*): **to be ~ (for)** être prêt(e) (à *or* pour); **games** NPL (*Scol*) sport m; (*sport event*) jeux; **a ~ of football/tennis** une partie de football/tennis; **big ~** gros gibier

game bird N gibier m à plume

gamekeeper ['geɪmkiːpəʳ] N garde-chasse m

gamely ['geɪmlɪ] ADV vaillamment

gamer ['geɪməʳ] N joueur(-euse) de jeux vidéos

game reserve N réserve animalière

games console ['geɪmz-] N console f de jeux vidéo

game show ['geɪmʃəu] N jeu télévisé

g

gamesmanship ['geɪmzmənʃɪp] N roublardise f
gaming ['geɪmɪŋ] N jeu m, jeux mpl d'argent; (video games) jeux mpl vidéos
gammon ['gæmən] N (bacon) quartier m de lard fumé; (ham) jambon fumé or salé
gamut ['gæmət] N gamme f
gang [gæŋ] N bande f, groupe m; (of workmen) équipe f
  ▶ **gang up** VI: **to ~ up on sb** se liguer contre qn
Ganges ['gændʒi:z] N: **the ~** le Gange
gangland ['gæŋlænd] ADJ: **~ killer** tueur professionnel du milieu; **~ boss** chef m de gang
gangling ['gæŋglɪŋ], **gangly** ['gæŋglɪ] ADJ dégingandé(e)
gangplank ['gæŋplæŋk] N passerelle f
gangrene ['gæŋgri:n] N gangrène f
gangster ['gæŋstəʳ] N gangster m, bandit m
gangway ['gæŋweɪ] N passerelle f; (BRIT: of bus) couloir central
gantry ['gæntrɪ] N portique m; (for rocket) tour f de lancement
GAO N ABBR (US: = General Accounting Office) ≈ Cour f des comptes
gaol [dʒeɪl] N, VT (BRIT) = **jail**
gap [gæp] N trou m; (in time) intervalle m; (fig) lacune f; vide m; (difference): **~ (between)** écart m (entre)
gape [geɪp] VI (person) être or rester bouche bée; (hole, shirt) être ouvert(e)
gaping ['geɪpɪŋ] ADJ (hole) béant(e)
gap year N année que certains étudiants prennent pour voyager ou pour travailler avant d'entrer à l'université
garage ['gærɑːʒ] N garage m
garage sale N vide-grenier m
garb [gɑːb] N tenue f, costume m
garbage ['gɑːbɪdʒ] N (US: rubbish) ordures fpl, détritus mpl; (inf: nonsense) âneries fpl
garbage can N (US) poubelle f, boîte f à ordures
garbage collector N (US) éboueur m
garbage disposal, garbage disposal unit N broyeur m d'ordures
garbage truck N (US) camion m (de ramassage des ordures), benne f à ordures
garbled ['gɑːbld] ADJ déformé(e), faussé(e)
garden ['gɑːdn] N jardin m ▶ VI jardiner; **gardens** NPL (public) jardin public; (private) parc m
garden centre (BRIT) N pépinière f, jardinerie f
garden city N (BRIT) cité-jardin f
gardener ['gɑːdnəʳ] N jardinier m
gardening ['gɑːdnɪŋ] N jardinage m
gargle ['gɑːgl] VI se gargariser ▶ N gargarisme m
gargoyle ['gɑːgɔɪl] N gargouille f
garish ['gɛərɪʃ] ADJ criard(e), voyant(e)
garland ['gɑːlənd] N guirlande f; couronne f
garlic ['gɑːlɪk] N ail m
garment ['gɑːmənt] N vêtement m
garner ['gɑːnəʳ] VT engranger, amasser
garnish ['gɑːnɪʃ] (Culin) VT garnir ▶ N décoration f
garret ['gærɪt] N mansarde f
garrison ['gærɪsn] N garnison f ▶ VT mettre en garnison, stationner

garrulous ['gærjuləs] ADJ volubile, loquace
garter ['gɑːtəʳ] N jarretière f; (US: suspender) jarretelle f
garter belt N (US) porte-jarretelles m inv
gas [gæs] N gaz m; (US: gasoline) essence f ▶ VT asphyxier; (Mil) gazer; **I can smell ~** ça sent le gaz; **to be given ~** (as anaesthetic) se faire endormir
Gascony ['gæskənɪ] N Gascogne f
gas cooker N (BRIT) cuisinière f à gaz
gas cylinder N bouteille f de gaz
gaseous ['gæsɪəs] ADJ gazeux(-euse)
gas fire N (BRIT) radiateur m à gaz
gas-fired ['gæsfaɪəd] ADJ au gaz
gash [gæʃ] N entaille f; (on face) balafre f ▶ VT taillader; balafrer
gasket ['gæskɪt] N (Aut) joint m de culasse
gas mask N masque m à gaz
gas meter N compteur m à gaz
gasoline ['gæsəli:n] N (US) essence f
gasp [gɑːsp] N halètement m; (of shock etc): **she gave a small ~ of pain** la douleur lui coupa le souffle ▶ VI haleter; (fig) avoir le souffle coupé
  ▶ **gasp out** VT (say) dire dans un souffle or d'une voix entrecoupée
gas pedal N (US) accélérateur m
gas ring N brûleur m
gas station N (US) station-service f
gas stove N réchaud m à gaz; (cooker) cuisinière f à gaz
gassy ['gæsɪ] ADJ gazeux(-euse)
gas tank N (US Aut) réservoir m d'essence
gas tap N bouton m (de cuisinière à gaz); (on pipe) robinet m à gaz
gastric ['gæstrɪk] ADJ gastrique
gastric band N (Med) anneau m gastrique
gastric ulcer N ulcère m de l'estomac
gastroenteritis ['gæstrəuentə'raɪtɪs] N gastroentérite f
gastronomy [gæs'trɔnəmɪ] N gastronomie f
gasworks ['gæswə:ks] N, NPL usine f à gaz
gate [geɪt] N (of garden) portail m; (of field, at level crossing) barrière f; (of building, town, at airport) porte f; (of lock) vanne f
gateau ['gætəu] (pl **gateaux** [-z]) N gros gâteau à la crème
gatecrash ['geɪtkræʃ] VT s'introduire sans invitation dans
gatecrasher ['geɪtkræʃəʳ] N intrus(e)
gated community ['geɪtɪd-] N quartier enclos dont l'entrée est gardée; ≈ quartier m sécurisé
gatehouse ['geɪthaus] N loge f
gateway ['geɪtweɪ] N porte f
gather ['gæðəʳ] VT (flowers, fruit) cueillir; (pick up) ramasser; (assemble: objects) rassembler; (: people) réunir; (: information) recueillir; (understand) comprendre; (Sewing) froncer ▶ VI (assemble) se rassembler; (dust) s'amasser; (clouds) s'amonceler; **to ~ (from/that)** conclure or déduire (de/que); **as far as I can ~** d'après ce que je comprends; **to ~ speed** prendre de la vitesse
gathering ['gæðərɪŋ] N rassemblement m
GATT [gæt] N ABBR (= General Agreement on Tariffs and Trade) GATT m

gauche [gəʊʃ] ADJ gauche, maladroit(e)
gaudy ['gɔːdɪ] ADJ voyant(e)
gauge [geɪdʒ] N *(standard measure)* calibre *m*;
  (Rail) écartement *m*; *(instrument)* jauge *f* ▶ VT
  jauger; *(fig: sb's capabilities, character)* juger de; **to
  ~ the right moment** calculer le moment
  propice; **petrol ~**, *(US)* **gas ~** jauge d'essence
Gaul [gɔːl] N *(country)* Gaule *f*; *(person)* Gaulois(e)
gaunt [gɔːnt] ADJ décharné(e); *(grim, desolate)*
  désolé(e)
gauntlet ['gɔːntlɪt] N *(fig)*: **to throw down the ~**
  jeter le gant; **to run the ~ through an angry
  crowd** se frayer un passage à travers une foule
  hostile *or* entre deux haies de manifestants *etc*
  hostiles
gauze [gɔːz] N gaze *f*
gave [geɪv] PT *of* **give**
gawky ['gɔːkɪ] ADJ dégingandé(e), godiche
gawp [gɔːp] VI: **to ~ at** regarder bouche bée
gay [geɪ] ADJ *(homosexual)* homosexuel(le); *(old:
  cheerful)* gai(e), réjoui(e); *(colour)* gai, vif (vive)
gaze [geɪz] N regard *m* fixe ▶ VI: **to ~ at** fixer du
  regard
gazelle [gə'zɛl] N gazelle *f*
gazette [gə'zɛt] N *(newspaper)* gazette *f*; *(official
  publication)* journal officiel
gazetteer [gæzə'tɪə'] N dictionnaire *m*
  géographique
gazump [gə'zʌmp] VI *(Brit)* revenir sur une
  promesse de vente pour accepter un prix plus élevé
GB ABBR = **Great Britain**
GBH N ABBR *(Brit Law: inf)* = **grievous bodily
  harm**
GC N ABBR *(Brit: = George Cross)* distinction
  honorifique
GCE N ABBR *(Brit)* = **General Certificate of
  Education**
GCHQ N ABBR *(Brit: = Government Communications
  Headquarters)* centre d'interception des
  télécommunications étrangères
GCSE N ABBR *(Brit: = General Certificate of Secondary
  Education)* examen passé à l'âge de 16 ans sanctionnant
  les connaissances de l'élève; **she's got eight GCSEs**
  elle a réussi dans huit matières aux épreuves
  du GCSE
Gdns. ABBR = **gardens**
GDP N ABBR = **gross domestic product**
GDR N ABBR *(old: = German Democratic Republic)*
  RDA *f*
gear [gɪə'] N matériel *m*, équipement *m*; *(Tech)*
  engrenage *m*; *(Aut)* vitesse *f* ▶ VT *(fig: adapt)*
  adapter; **top** *or* *(US)* **high/low ~** quatrième *(or*
  cinquième)/première vitesse; **in ~** en prise;
  out of ~ au point mort; **our service is geared
  to meet the needs of people with
  disabilities** notre service répond de façon
  spécifique aux besoins des handicapés
  ▶ **gear up** VI: **to ~ up (to do)** se préparer (à faire)
gear box N boîte *f* de vitesse
gear lever N levier *m* de vitesse
gear shift *(US)* N = **gear lever**
gear stick *(Brit)* N = **gear lever**
GED N ABBR *(US Scol)* = **general educational
  development**

geese [giːs] NPL *of* **goose**
geezer ['giːzə'] N *(Brit inf)* mec *m*
Geiger counter ['gaɪgə-] N compteur *m* Geiger
gel [dʒɛl] N gelée *f*; *(Chem)* colloïde *m*
gelatin, gelatine ['dʒɛləti:n] N gélatine *f*
gelignite ['dʒɛlɪgnaɪt] N plastic *m*
gem [dʒɛm] N pierre précieuse
Gemini ['dʒɛmɪnaɪ] N les Gémeaux *mpl*; **to be ~**
  être des Gémeaux
gen [dʒɛn] N *(Brit inf)*: **to give sb the ~ on sth**
  mettre qn au courant de qch
Gen. ABBR *(Mil: = general)* Gal
gen. ABBR *(= general, generally)* gén
gender ['dʒɛndə'] N genre *m*; *(person's sex)* sexe *m*
gene [dʒiːn] N *(Biol)* gène *m*
genealogy [dʒiːnɪ'ælədʒɪ] N généalogie *f*
general ['dʒɛnərl] N général *m* ▶ ADJ général(e);
  in ~ en général; **the ~ public** le grand public;
  ~ audit *(Comm)* vérification annuelle
general anaesthetic, *(US)* **general
  anesthetic** N anesthésie générale
general delivery N poste restante
general election N élection(s) législative(s)
generalization ['dʒɛnrəlaɪ'zeɪʃən] N
  généralisation *f*
generalize ['dʒɛnrəlaɪz] VI généraliser
general knowledge N connaissances
  générales
generally ['dʒɛnrəlɪ] ADV généralement
general manager N directeur général
general practitioner N généraliste *mf*
general store N épicerie *f*
general strike N grève générale
generate ['dʒɛnəreɪt] VT engendrer; *(electricity)*
  produire
generation [dʒɛnə'reɪʃən] N génération *f*; *(of
  electricity etc)* production *f*
generator ['dʒɛnəreɪtə'] N générateur *m*
generic [dʒɪ'nɛrɪk] ADJ générique
generosity [dʒɛnə'rɔsɪtɪ] N générosité *f*
generous ['dʒɛnərəs] ADJ généreux(-euse);
  (copious) copieux(-euse)
genesis ['dʒɛnɪsɪs] N genèse *f*
genetic [dʒɪ'nɛtɪk] ADJ génétique;
  ~ engineering ingénierie *m* génétique;
  ~ fingerprinting système *m* d'empreinte
  génétique
genetically modified ADJ *(food etc)*
  génétiquement modifié(e)
genetics [dʒɪ'nɛtɪks] N génétique *f*
Geneva [dʒɪ'niːvə] N Genève; **Lake ~** le lac
  Léman
genial ['dʒiːnɪəl] ADJ cordial(e),
  chaleureux(-euse); *(climate)* clément(e)
genitals ['dʒɛnɪtlz] NPL organes génitaux
genitive ['dʒɛnɪtɪv] N génitif *m*
genius ['dʒiːnɪəs] N génie *m*
Genoa ['dʒɛnəuə] N Gênes
genocide ['dʒɛnəusaɪd] N génocide *m*
genome ['dʒiːnəum] N génome *m*
gent [dʒɛnt] N ABBR *(Brit inf)* = **gentleman**
genteel [dʒɛn'tiːl] ADJ de bon ton, distingué(e)
gentle ['dʒɛntl] ADJ doux (douce); *(breeze, touch)*
  léger(-ère)

g

gentleman ['dʒɛntlmən] N (*irreg*) monsieur *m*; (*well-bred man*) gentleman *m*; **~'s agreement** gentleman's agreement *m*

gentlemanly ['dʒɛntlmənlɪ] ADJ bien élevé(e)

gentleness ['dʒɛntlnɪs] N douceur *f*

gently ['dʒɛntlɪ] ADV doucement

gentry ['dʒɛntrɪ] N petite noblesse

gents [dʒɛnts] N W.-C. *mpl* (pour hommes)

genuine ['dʒɛnjuɪn] ADJ véritable, authentique; (*person, emotion*) sincère

genuinely ['dʒɛnjuɪnlɪ] ADV sincèrement, vraiment

geographer [dʒɪ'ɒɡrəfəʳ] N géographe *mf*

geographic [dʒɪə'ɡræfɪk], **geographical** [dʒɪə'ɡræfɪkl] ADJ géographique

geography [dʒɪ'ɒɡrəfɪ] N géographie *f*

geological [dʒɪə'lɒdʒɪkl] ADJ géologique

geologist [dʒɪ'ɒlədʒɪst] N géologue *mf*

geology [dʒɪ'ɒlədʒɪ] N géologie *f*

geometric [dʒɪə'mɛtrɪk], **geometrical** [dʒɪə'mɛtrɪkl] ADJ géométrique

geometry [dʒɪ'ɒmətrɪ] N géométrie *f*

Geordie ['dʒɔːdɪ] N (*inf*) habitant(e) de Tyneside, originaire *mf* de Tyneside.

Georgia ['dʒɔːdʒə] N Géorgie *f*

Georgian ['dʒɔːdʒən] ADJ (*Geo*) géorgien(ne) ▶ N Géorgien(ne); (*Ling*) géorgien *m*

geranium [dʒɪ'reɪnɪəm] N géranium *m*

geriatric [dʒɛrɪ'ætrɪk] ADJ gériatrique ▶ N patient(e) gériatrique

germ [dʒəːm] N (*Med*) microbe *m*; (*Biol: fig*) germe *m*

German ['dʒəːmən] ADJ allemand(e) ▶ N Allemand(e); (*Ling*) allemand *m*

germane [dʒəː'meɪn] ADJ (*formal*): **~ (to)** se rapportant (à)

German measles N rubéole *f*

Germany ['dʒəːmənɪ] N Allemagne *f*

germination [dʒəːmɪ'neɪʃən] N germination *f*

germ warfare N guerre *f* bactériologique

gerrymandering ['dʒɛrɪmændərɪŋ] N tripotage *m* du découpage électoral

gestation [dʒɛs'teɪʃən] N gestation *f*

gesticulate [dʒɛs'tɪkjuleɪt] VI gesticuler

gesture ['dʒɛstjəʳ] N geste *m*; **as a ~ of friendship** en témoignage d'amitié

(KEYWORD)

get [ɡɛt] (*pt, pp* **got** [ɡɒt], *US pp* **gotten** ['ɡɒtn]) VI
1 (*become, be*) devenir; **to get old/tired** devenir vieux/fatigué, vieillir/se fatiguer; **to get drunk** s'enivrer; **to get ready/washed/shaved** *etc* se préparer/laver/raser *etc*; **to get killed** se faire tuer; **to get dirty** se salir; **to get married** se marier; **when do I get paid?** quand est-ce que je serai payé?; **it's getting late** il se fait tard
2 (*go*): **to get to/from** aller à/de; **to get home** rentrer chez soi; **how did you get here?** comment es-tu arrivé ici?; **he got across the bridge/under the fence** il a traversé le pont/ est passé au-dessous de la barrière
3 (*begin*) commencer *or* se mettre à; **to get to know sb** apprendre à connaître qn; **I'm**

getting to like him je commence à l'apprécier; **let's get going** *or* **started** allons-y
4 (*modal aux vb*): **you've got to do it** il faut que vous le fassiez; **I've got to tell the police** je dois le dire à la police
▶ VT **1**: **to get sth done** (*do*) faire qch; (*have done*) faire faire qch; **to get sth/sb ready** préparer qch/qn; **to get one's hair cut** se faire couper les cheveux; **to get the car going** *or* **to go** (faire) démarrer la voiture; **to get sb to do sth** faire faire qch à qn; **to get sb drunk** enivrer qn
2 (*obtain: money, permission, results*) obtenir, avoir; (*buy*) acheter; (*find: job, flat*) trouver; (*fetch: person, doctor, object*) aller chercher; **to get sth for sb** procurer qch à qn; **get me Mr Jones, please** (*on phone*) passez-moi Mr Jones, s'il vous plaît; **can I get you a drink?** est-ce que je peux vous servir à boire?
3 (*receive: present, letter*) recevoir, avoir; (*acquire: reputation*) avoir; (*: prize*) obtenir; **what did you get for your birthday?** qu'est-ce que tu as eu pour ton anniversaire?; **how much did you get for the painting?** combien avez-vous vendu le tableau?
4 (*catch*) prendre, saisir, attraper; (*hit: target etc*) atteindre; **to get sb by the arm/throat** prendre *or* saisir *or* attraper qn par le bras/à la gorge; **get him!** arrête-le!; **the bullet got him in the leg** il a pris la balle dans la jambe; **he really gets me!** il me porte sur les nerfs!
5 (*take, move*): **to get sth to sb** faire parvenir qch à qn; **do you think we'll get it through the door?** on arrivera à le faire passer par la porte?; **I'll get you there somehow** je me débrouillerai pour t'y emmener
6 (*catch, take: plane, bus etc*) prendre; **where do I get the train for Birmingham?** où prend-on le train pour Birmingham?
7 (*understand*) comprendre, saisir; (*hear*) entendre; **I've got it!** j'ai compris!; **I don't get your meaning** je ne vois *or* comprends pas ce que vous voulez dire; **I didn't get your name** je n'ai pas entendu votre nom
8 (*have, possess*): **to have got** avoir; **how many have you got?** vous en avez combien?
9 (*illness*) avoir; **I've got a cold** j'ai le rhume; **she got pneumonia and died** elle a fait une pneumonie et elle en est morte
▶ **get about** VI se déplacer; (*news*) se répandre
▶ **get across** VT: **to get across (to)** (*message, meaning*) faire passer (à) ▶ VI: **to get across (to)** (*speaker*) se faire comprendre (par)
▶ **get along** VI (*agree*) s'entendre; (*depart*) s'en aller; (*manage*) = **get by**
▶ **get at** VT FUS (*attack*) s'en prendre à; (*reach*) attraper, atteindre; **what are you getting at?** à quoi voulez-vous en venir?
▶ **get away** VI partir, s'en aller; (*escape*) s'échapper
▶ **get away with** VT FUS (*punishment*) en être quitte pour; (*crime etc*) se faire pardonner
▶ **get back** VI (*return*) rentrer; **to get back to** (*start again*) retourner *or* revenir à ▶ VT récupérer, recouvrer; (*contact again*) recontacter; **when do**

we get back? quand serons-nous de retour?
▶ **get back at** VT FUS (inf): **to get back at sb** rendre la monnaie de sa pièce à qn
▶ **get by** VI (pass) passer; (manage) se débrouiller; **I can get by in Dutch** je me débrouille en hollandais
▶ **get down** VI, VT FUS descendre ▶ VT descendre; (depress) déprimer
▶ **get down to** VT FUS (work) se mettre à (faire); **to get down to business** passer aux choses sérieuses
▶ **get in** VI entrer; (arrive home) rentrer; (train) arriver ▶ VT (bring in: harvest) rentrer; (: coal) faire rentrer; (: supplies) faire des provisions de
▶ **get into** VT FUS entrer dans; (car, train etc) monter dans; (clothes) mettre, enfiler, endosser; **to get into bed/a rage** se mettre au lit/en colère
▶ **get off** VI (from train etc) descendre; (depart: person, car) s'en aller; (escape) s'en tirer ▶ VT (remove: clothes, stain) enlever; (send off) expédier; (have as leave: day, time): **we got 2 days off** nous avons eu 2 jours de congé ▶ VT FUS (train, bus) descendre de; **where do I get off?** où est-ce que je dois descendre?; **to get off to a good start** (fig) prendre un bon départ
▶ **get on** VI (at exam etc) se débrouiller; (agree): **to get on (with)** s'entendre (avec); **how are you getting on?** comment ça va? ▶ VT FUS monter dans; (horse) monter sur
▶ **get on to** VT FUS (BRIT: deal with: problem) s'occuper de; (: contact: person) contacter
▶ **get out** VI sortir; (of vehicle) descendre; (news etc) s'ébruiter ▶ VT sortir
▶ **get out of** VT FUS sortir de; (duty etc) échapper à, se soustraire à
▶ **get over** VT FUS (illness) se remettre de ▶ VT (communicate: idea etc) communiquer; (finish): **let's get it over (with)** finissons-en
▶ **get round** VI: **to get round to doing sth** se mettre (finalement) à faire qch ▶ VT FUS contourner; (fig: person) entortiller
▶ **get through** VI (Tel) avoir la communication; **to get through to sb** atteindre qn ▶ VT FUS (finish: work, book) finir, terminer
▶ **get together** VI se réunir ▶ VT rassembler
▶ **get up** VI (rise) se lever ▶ VT FUS monter
▶ **get up to** VT FUS (reach) arriver à; (prank etc) faire

getaway ['gɛtəweɪ] N fuite f
getaway car N voiture prévue pour prendre la fuite
get-together ['gɛttəgɛðər] N petite réunion, petite fête
get-up ['gɛtʌp] N (inf: outfit) accoutrement m
get-well card [gɛt'wɛl-] N carte f de vœux de bon rétablissement
geyser ['giːzər] N chauffe-eau m inv; (Geo) geyser m
Ghana ['gɑːnə] N Ghana m
Ghanaian [gɑːˈneɪən] ADJ ghanéen(ne)
▶ N Ghanéen(ne)
ghastly ['gɑːstlɪ] ADJ atroce, horrible; (pale) livide, blême

gherkin ['gəːkɪn] N cornichon m
ghetto ['gɛtəu] N ghetto m
ghetto blaster [-blɑːstər] N (inf) gros radiocassette
ghost [gəust] N fantôme m, revenant m ▶ VT (sb else's book) écrire
ghostly ['gəustlɪ] ADJ fantomatique
ghostwriter ['gəustraɪtər] N nègre m (fig: pej)
ghoul [guːl] N (ghost) vampire m
ghoulish ['guːlɪʃ] ADJ (tastes etc) morbide
GHQ N ABBR (Mil: = general headquarters) GQG m
GI N ABBR (US inf: = government issue) soldat de l'armée américaine, GI m
giant ['dʒaɪənt] N géant(e) ▶ ADJ géant(e), énorme; **~ (size) packet** paquet géant
giant killer N (Sport) équipe inconnue qui remporte un match contre une équipe renommée
gibber ['dʒɪbər] VI émettre des sons inintelligibles
gibberish ['dʒɪbərɪʃ] N charabia m
gibe [dʒaɪb] N sarcasme m ▶ VI: **to ~ at** railler
giblets ['dʒɪblɪts] NPL abats mpl
Gibraltar [dʒɪˈbrɔːltər] N Gibraltar m
giddiness ['gɪdɪnɪs] N vertige m
giddy ['gɪdɪ] ADJ (dizzy): **to be (or feel) ~** avoir le vertige; (height) vertigineux(-euse); (thoughtless) sot(te), étourdi(e)
gift [gɪft] N cadeau m, présent m; (donation, talent) don m; (Comm: also: **free gift**) cadeau(-réclame) m; **to have a ~ for sth** avoir des dons pour or le don de qch
gifted ['gɪftɪd] ADJ doué(e)
gift shop, (US) **gift store** N boutique f de cadeaux
gift token, **gift voucher** N chèque-cadeau m
gig [gɪg] N (inf: concert) concert m
gigabyte ['dʒɪgəbaɪt] N gigaoctet m
gigantic [dʒaɪˈgæntɪk] ADJ gigantesque
giggle ['gɪgl] VI pouffer, ricaner sottement ▶ N petit rire sot, ricanement m
GIGO ['gaɪgəu] ABBR (Comput: inf: = garbage in, garbage out) qualité d'entrée = qualité de sortie
gild [gɪld] VT dorer
gill [dʒɪl] N (measure) = 0.25 pints (Brit = 0.148 l; US = 0.118 l)
gills [gɪlz] NPL (of fish) ouïes fpl, branchies fpl
gilt [gɪlt] N dorure f ▶ ADJ doré(e)
gilt-edged ['gɪltɛdʒd] ADJ (stocks, securities) de premier ordre
gimlet ['gɪmlɪt] N vrille f
gimmick ['gɪmɪk] N truc m; **sales ~** offre promotionnelle
gin [dʒɪn] N gin m
ginger ['dʒɪndʒər] N gingembre m
▶ **ginger up** VT secouer; animer
ginger ale, ginger beer N boisson gazeuse au gingembre
gingerbread ['dʒɪndʒəbrɛd] N pain m d'épices
ginger group N (BRIT) groupe m de pression
ginger-haired ['dʒɪndʒə'hɛəd] ADJ roux (rousse)
gingerly ['dʒɪndʒəlɪ] ADV avec précaution
gingham ['gɪŋəm] N vichy m
ginseng ['dʒɪnsɛŋ] N ginseng m
gipsy ['dʒɪpsɪ] N = **gypsy**

giraffe [dʒɪˈrɑːf] N girafe f
girder [ˈgəːdəʳ] N poutrelle f
girdle [ˈgəːdl] N (corset) gaine f ▶ vt ceindre
girl [gəːl] N fille f, fillette f; (young unmarried woman) jeune fille; (daughter) fille; **an English ~** une jeune Anglaise; **a little English ~** une petite Anglaise
girl band N girls band m
girlfriend [ˈgəːlfrɛnd] N (of girl) amie f; (of boy) petite amie
Girl Guide N (BRIT) éclaireuse f; (Roman Catholic) guide f
girlish [ˈgəːlɪʃ] ADJ de jeune fille
Girl Scout N (US) = **Girl Guide**
Giro [ˈdʒaɪrəu] N: **the National ~** (BRIT) ≈ les comptes chèques postaux
giro [ˈdʒaɪrəu] N (bank giro) virement m bancaire; (post office giro) mandat m
girth [gəːθ] N circonférence f; (of horse) sangle f
gist [dʒɪst] N essentiel m
give [gɪv] (pt **gave** [geɪv], pp **given** [ˈgɪvn]) N (of fabric) élasticité f ▶ vt donner; (stretch: fabric) se prêter; **to ~ sb sth, ~ sth to sb** donner qch à qn; (gift) offrir qch à qn; (message) transmettre qch à qn; **to ~ sb a call/kiss** appeler/embrasser qn; **to ~ a cry/sigh** pousser un cri/un soupir; **how much did you ~ for it?** combien (l')avez-vous payé?; **12 o'clock, ~ or take a few minutes** midi, à quelques minutes près; **to ~ way** céder; (BRIT Aut) donner la priorité
▶ **give away** vt donner; (give free) faire cadeau de; (betray) donner, trahir; (disclose) révéler; (bride) conduire à l'autel
▶ **give back** vt rendre
▶ **give in** vi céder ▶ vt donner
▶ **give off** vt dégager
▶ **give out** vt (food etc) distribuer; (news) annoncer ▶ vi (be exhausted: supplies) s'épuiser; (fail) lâcher
▶ **give up** vi renoncer ▶ vt renoncer à; **to ~ up smoking** arrêter de fumer; **to ~ o.s. up** se rendre
give-and-take [ˈgɪvəndˈteɪk] N concessions mutuelles
giveaway [ˈgɪvəweɪ] N (inf): **her expression was a ~** son expression la trahissait; **the exam was a ~!** cet examen, c'était du gâteau! ▶ CPD: **~ prices** prix sacrifiés
given [ˈgɪvn] PP of **give** ▶ ADJ (fixed: time, amount) donné(e), déterminé(e) ▶ CONJ: **~ the circumstances ...** étant donné les circonstances ..., vu les circonstances ...; **~ that ...** étant donné que ...
glacial [ˈgleɪsɪəl] ADJ (Geo) glaciaire; (wind, weather) glacial(e)
glacier [ˈglæsɪəʳ] N glacier m
glad [glæd] ADJ content(e); **to be ~ about sth/ that** être heureux(-euse) or bien content de qch/que; **I was ~ of his help** j'étais bien content de (pouvoir compter sur) son aide or qu'il m'aide
gladden [ˈglædn] vt réjouir
glade [gleɪd] N clairière f

gladioli [glædɪˈəulaɪ] NPL glaïeuls mpl
gladly [ˈglædlɪ] ADV volontiers
glamorous [ˈglæmərəs] ADJ (person) séduisant(e); (job) prestigieux(-euse)
glamour, (US) **glamor** [ˈglæməʳ] N éclat m, prestige m
glance [glɑːns] N coup m d'œil ▶ vi: **to ~ at** jeter un coup d'œil à
▶ **glance off** vt FUS (bullet) ricocher sur
glancing [ˈglɑːnsɪŋ] ADJ (blow) oblique
gland [glænd] N glande f
glandular [ˈglændjuləʳ] ADJ: **~ fever** (BRIT) mononucléose infectieuse
glare [glɛəʳ] N (of anger) regard furieux; (of light) lumière éblouissante; (of publicity) feux mpl ▶ vi briller d'un éclat aveuglant; **to ~ at** lancer un regard or des regards furieux à
glaring [ˈglɛərɪŋ] ADJ (mistake) criant(e), qui saute aux yeux
glasnost [ˈglæznɔst] N glasnost f
glass [glɑːs] N verre m; (also: **looking glass**) miroir m; **glasses** NPL (spectacles) lunettes fpl
glass-blowing [ˈglɑːsbləuɪŋ] N soufflage m (du verre)
glass ceiling N (fig) plafond dans l'échelle hiérarchique au-dessus duquel les femmes ou les membres d'une minorité ethnique ne semblent pouvoir s'élever
glass fibre N fibre f de verre
glasshouse [ˈglɑːshaus] N serre f
glassware [ˈglɑːswɛəʳ] N verrerie f
glassy [ˈglɑːsɪ] ADJ (eyes) vitreux(-euse)
Glaswegian [glæsˈwiːdʒən] ADJ de Glasgow ▶ N habitant(e) de Glasgow, natif(-ive) de Glasgow
glaze [gleɪz] vt (door) vitrer; (pottery) vernir; (Culin) glacer ▶ N vernis m; (Culin) glaçage m
glazed [gleɪzd] ADJ (eye) vitreux(-euse); (pottery) verni(e); (tiles) vitrifié(e)
glazier [ˈgleɪzɪəʳ] N vitrier m
gleam [gliːm] N lueur f ▶ vi luire, briller; **a ~ of hope** une lueur d'espoir
gleaming [ˈgliːmɪŋ] ADJ luisant(e)
glean [gliːn] vt (information) recueillir
glee [gliː] N joie f
gleeful [ˈgliːful] ADJ joyeux(-euse)
glen [glɛn] N vallée f
glib [glɪb] ADJ qui a du bagou; facile
glide [glaɪd] vi glisser; (Aviat, bird) planer ▶ N glissement m; vol plané
glider [ˈglaɪdəʳ] N (Aviat) planeur m
gliding [ˈglaɪdɪŋ] N (Aviat) vol m à voile
glimmer [ˈglɪməʳ] vi luire ▶ N lueur f
glimpse [glɪmps] N vision passagère, aperçu m ▶ vt entrevoir, apercevoir; **to catch a ~ of** entrevoir
glint [glɪnt] N éclair m ▶ vi étinceler
glisten [ˈglɪsn] vi briller, luire
glitter [ˈglɪtəʳ] vi scintiller, briller ▶ N scintillement m
glitz [glɪts] N (inf) clinquant m
gloat [gləut] vi: **to ~ (over)** jubiler (à propos de)
global [ˈgləubl] ADJ (world-wide) mondial(e); (overall) global(e)
globalization [gləublaɪzˈeɪʃən] N mondialisation f

global warming [-'wɔːmɪŋ] N réchauffement m de la planète

globe [gləub] N globe m

globe-trotter ['gləubtrɔtə'] N globe-trotter m

globule ['glɔbjuːl] N (Anat) globule m; (of water etc) gouttelette f

gloom [gluːm] N obscurité f; (sadness) tristesse f, mélancolie f

gloomy ['gluːmɪ] ADJ (person) morose; (place, outlook) sombre; **to feel ~** avoir or se faire des idées noires

glorification [glɔːrɪfɪ'keɪʃən] N glorification f

glorify ['glɔːrɪfaɪ] VT glorifier

glorious ['glɔːrɪəs] ADJ glorieux(-euse); (beautiful) splendide

glory ['glɔːrɪ] N gloire f; splendeur f ▶ VI: **to ~ in** se glorifier de

glory hole N (inf) capharnaüm m

Glos ABBR (BRIT) = **Gloucestershire**

gloss [glɔs] N (shine) brillant m, vernis m; (also: **gloss paint**) peinture brillante or laquée
▶ **gloss over** VT FUS glisser sur

glossary ['glɔsərɪ] N glossaire m, lexique m

glossy ['glɔsɪ] ADJ brillant(e), luisant(e) ▶ N (also: **glossy magazine**) revue f de luxe

glove [glʌv] N gant m

glove compartment N (Aut) boîte f à gants, vide-poches m inv

glow [gləu] VI rougeoyer; (face) rayonner; (eyes) briller ▶ N rougeoiement m

glower ['glauə'] VI lancer des regards mauvais

glowing ['gləuɪŋ] ADJ (fire) rougeoyant(e); (complexion) éclatant(e); (report, description etc) dithyrambique

glow-worm ['gləuwəːm] N ver luisant

glucose ['gluːkəus] N glucose m

glue [gluː] N colle f ▶ VT coller

glue-sniffing ['gluːsnɪfɪŋ] N inhalation f de colle

glum [glʌm] ADJ maussade, morose

glut [glʌt] N surabondance f ▶ VT rassasier; (market) encombrer

glutinous ['gluːtɪnəs] ADJ visqueux(-euse)

glutton ['glʌtn] N glouton(ne); **a ~ for work** un bourreau de travail

gluttonous ['glʌtənəs] ADJ glouton(ne)

gluttony ['glʌtənɪ] N gloutonnerie f; (sin) gourmandise f

glycerin, glycerine ['glɪsəriːn] N glycérine f

GM ABBR (= genetically modified) génétiquement modifié(e)

gm ABBR (= gram) g

GMAT N ABBR (US: = Graduate Management Admissions Test) examen d'admission dans le 2e cycle de l'enseignement supérieur

GM crop N culture f OGM

GM foods N aliments mpl génétiquement modifiés

GMO N ABBR (= genetically modified organism) OGM m

GMT ABBR (= Greenwich Mean Time) GMT

gnarled [nɑːld] ADJ noueux(-euse)

gnash [næʃ] VT: **to ~ one's teeth** grincer des dents

gnat [næt] N moucheron m

gnaw [nɔː] VT ronger

gnome [nəum] N gnome m, lutin m

GNP N ABBR = **gross national product**

go [gəu] VI (pt **went** [wɛnt], pp **gone** [gɔn]) aller; (depart) partir, s'en aller; (work) marcher; (break) céder; (time) passer; (be sold): **to go for £10** se vendre 10 livres; (become): **to go pale/mouldy** pâlir/moisir ▶ N (pl **goes**): **to have a go (at)** essayer (de faire); **to be on the go** être en mouvement; **whose go is it?** à qui est-ce de jouer?; **to go by car/on foot** aller en voiture/à pied; **he's going to do it** il va le faire, il est sur le point de le faire; **to go for a walk** aller se promener; **to go dancing/shopping** aller danser/faire les courses; **to go looking for sb/ sth** aller or partir à la recherche de qn/qch; **to go to sleep** s'endormir; **to go and see sb, to go see sb** aller voir qn; **how is it going?** comment ça marche?; **how did it go?** comment est-ce que ça s'est passé?; **to go round the back/by the shop** passer par derrière/devant le magasin; **my voice has gone** j'ai une extinction de voix; **the cake is all gone** il n'y a plus de gâteau; **I'll take whatever is going** (BRIT) je prendrai ce qu'il y a (or ce que vous avez); **... to go** (US: food) ... à emporter
▶ **go about** VI (also: **go around**) aller çà et là; (: rumour) se répandre ▶ VT FUS: **how do I go about this?** comment dois-je m'y prendre (pour faire ceci?); **to go about one's business** s'occuper de ses affaires
▶ **go after** VT FUS (pursue) poursuivre, courir après; (job, record etc) essayer d'obtenir
▶ **go against** VT FUS (be unfavourable to) être défavorable à; (be contrary to) être contraire à
▶ **go ahead** VI (make progress) avancer; (take place) avoir lieu; (get going) y aller
▶ **go along** VI aller, avancer ▶ VT FUS longer, parcourir; **as you go along (with your work)** au fur et à mesure (de votre travail); **to go along with** (accompany) accompagner; (agree with: idea) être d'accord sur; (: person) suivre
▶ **go away** VI partir, s'en aller
▶ **go back** VI rentrer; revenir; (go again) retourner
▶ **go back on** VT FUS (promise) revenir sur
▶ **go by** VI (years, time) passer, s'écouler ▶ VT FUS s'en tenir à; (believe) en croire
▶ **go down** VI descendre; (number, price, amount) baisser; (ship) couler; (sun) se coucher ▶ VT FUS descendre; **that should go down well with him** (fig) ça devrait lui plaire
▶ **go for** VT FUS (fetch) aller chercher; (like) aimer; (attack) s'en prendre à; attaquer
▶ **go in** VI entrer
▶ **go in for** VT FUS (competition) se présenter à; (like) aimer
▶ **go into** VT FUS entrer dans; (investigate) étudier, examiner; (embark on) se lancer dans
▶ **go off** VI partir, s'en aller; (food) se gâter; (milk) tourner; (bomb) sauter; (alarm clock) sonner; (alarm) se déclencher; (lights etc) s'éteindre; (event) se dérouler ▶ VT FUS ne plus

g

aimer, ne plus avoir envie de; **the gun went off** le coup est parti; **to go off to sleep** s'endormir; **the party went off well** la fête s'est bien passée or était très réussie

▶ **go on** vi continuer; (*happen*) se passer; (*lights*) s'allumer ▶ vt fus (*be guided by: evidence etc*) se fonder sur; **to go on doing** continuer à faire; **what's going on here?** qu'est-ce qui se passe ici?

▶ **go on at** vt fus (*nag*) tomber sur le dos de

▶ **go on with** vt fus poursuivre, continuer

▶ **go out** vi sortir; (*fire, light*) s'éteindre; (*tide*) descendre; **to go out with sb** sortir avec qn

▶ **go over** vi (*ship*) chavirer ▶ vt fus (*check*) revoir, vérifier; **to go over sth in one's mind** repasser qch dans son esprit

▶ **go past** vt fus: **to go past sth** passer devant qch

▶ **go round** vi (*circulate: news, rumour*) circuler; (*revolve*) tourner; (*suffice*) suffire (pour tout le monde); (*visit*): **to go round to sb's** passer chez qn; aller chez qn; (*make a detour*): **to go round (by)** faire un détour (par)

▶ **go through** vt fus (*town etc*) traverser; (*search through*) fouiller; (*suffer*) subir; (*examine: list, book*) lire or regarder en détail, éplucher; (*perform: lesson*) réciter; (: *formalities*) remplir; (: *programme*) exécuter

▶ **go through with** vt fus (*plan, crime*) aller jusqu'au bout de

▶ **go under** vi (*sink, also fig*) couler; (: *person*) succomber

▶ **go up** vi monter; (*price*) augmenter ▶ vt fus gravir; (*also:* **go up in flames**) flamber, s'enflammer brusquement

▶ **go with** vt fus aller avec

▶ **go without** vt fus se passer de

goad [ɡəud] vt aiguillonner

go-ahead ['ɡəuəhɛd] ADJ dynamique, entreprenant(e) ▶ N feu vert

goal [ɡəul] N but m

goal difference N différence f de buts

goalie ['ɡəulɪ] N (*inf*) goal m

goalkeeper ['ɡəulkiːpəʳ] N gardien m de but

goal-post [ɡəulpəust] N poteau m de but

goat [ɡəut] N chèvre f

gobble ['ɡɔbl] vt (*also:* **gobble down, gobble up**) engloutir

go-between ['ɡəubɪtwiːn] N médiateur m

Gobi Desert ['ɡəubɪ-] N désert m de Gobi

goblet ['ɡɔblɪt] N coupe f

goblin ['ɡɔblɪn] N lutin m

go-cart ['ɡəukɑːt] N kart m ▶ CPD: **~ racing** karting m

god [ɡɔd] N dieu m; **God** Dieu

god-awful [ɡɔd'ɔːfəl] ADJ (*inf*) franchement atroce

godchild ['ɡɔdtʃaɪld] N (*irreg*) filleul(e)

goddamn ['ɡɔddæm], **goddamned** ['ɡɔddæmd] EXCL (*esp US inf*): **~ (it)!** nom de Dieu! ▶ ADJ satané(e), sacré(e) ▶ ADV sacrément

goddaughter ['ɡɔdɔːtəʳ] N filleule f

goddess ['ɡɔdɪs] N déesse f

godfather ['ɡɔdfɑːðəʳ] N parrain m

god-fearing ['ɡɔdfɪərɪŋ] ADJ croyant(e)

god-forsaken ['ɡɔdfəseɪkən] ADJ maudit(e)

godmother ['ɡɔdmʌðəʳ] N marraine f

godparents ['ɡɔdpɛərənts] NPL: **the ~** le parrain et la marraine

godsend ['ɡɔdsɛnd] N aubaine f

godson ['ɡɔdsʌn] N filleul m

goes [ɡəuz] VB *see* **go**

gofer ['ɡəufəʳ] N coursier(-ière)

go-getter ['ɡəuɡɛtəʳ] N arriviste mf

goggle ['ɡɔɡl] vi: **to ~ at** regarder avec des yeux ronds

goggles ['ɡɔɡlz] NPL (*for skiing etc*) lunettes (protectrices); (*for swimming*) lunettes de piscine

going ['ɡəuɪŋ] N (*conditions*) état m du terrain ▶ ADJ: **the ~ rate** le tarif (en vigueur); **a ~ concern** une affaire prospère; **it was slow ~** les progrès étaient lents, ça n'avançait pas vite

going-over [ɡəuɪŋ'əuvəʳ] N (*inf*) vérification f, révision f; (*beating*) passage m à tabac

goings-on ['ɡəuɪŋz'ɔn] NPL (*inf*) manigances fpl

go-kart ['ɡəukɑːt] N = **go-cart**

gold [ɡəuld] N or m ▶ ADJ en or; (*reserves*) d'or

golden ['ɡəuldən] ADJ (*made of gold*) en or; (*gold in colour*) doré(e)

golden age N âge m d'or

golden handshake N (*Brit*) prime f de départ

golden rule N règle f d'or

goldfish ['ɡəuldfɪʃ] N poisson m rouge

gold leaf N or m en feuille

gold medal N (*Sport*) médaille f d'or

goldmine ['ɡəuldmaɪn] N mine f d'or

gold-plated ['ɡəuld'pleɪtɪd] ADJ plaqué(e) or inv

goldsmith ['ɡəuldsmɪθ] N orfèvre m

gold standard N étalon-or m

golf [ɡɔlf] N golf m

golf ball N balle f de golf; (*on typewriter*) boule f

golf club N club m de golf; (*stick*) club m, crosse f de golf

golf course N terrain m de golf

golfer ['ɡɔlfəʳ] N joueur(-euse) de golf

golfing ['ɡɔlfɪŋ] N golf m

gondola ['ɡɔndələ] N gondole f

gondolier [ɡɔndə'lɪəʳ] N gondolier m

gone [ɡɔn] PP *of* **go** ▶ ADJ parti(e)

goner ['ɡɔnəʳ] N (*inf*): **to be a ~** être fichu(e) or foutu(e)

gong [ɡɔŋ] N gong m

good [ɡud] ADJ bon(ne); (*kind*) gentil(le); (*child*) sage; (*weather*) beau (belle) ▶ N bien m; **goods** NPL marchandise f, articles mpl; (*Comm etc*) marchandises f; **~!** bon!, très bien!; **to be ~ at** être bon en; **to be ~ for** être bon pour; **it's ~ for you** c'est bon pour vous; **it's a ~ thing you were there** heureusement que vous étiez là; **she is ~ with children/her hands** elle sait bien s'occuper des enfants/sait se servir de ses mains; **to feel ~** se sentir bien; **it's ~ to see you** ça me fait plaisir de vous voir, je suis content de vous voir; **he's up to no ~** il prépare quelque mauvais coup; **it's no ~ complaining** cela ne sert à rien de se plaindre; **to make ~** (*deficit*) combler; (*losses*) compenser; **for the common ~** dans l'intérêt commun; **for ~ (**for *ever*) pour de bon, une fois pour toutes; **would you be ~ enough to ...?** auriez-vous la bonté *or* l'amabilité de ...?; **that's very ~ of you** c'est très gentil de votre part; **is this any ~?** (*will it do?*) est-ce que ceci fera l'affaire?, est-ce que cela peut vous rendre service?; (*what's it like?*) qu'est-ce que ça vaut?; **goods and chattels** biens *mpl* et effets *mpl*; **a ~ deal (of)** beaucoup (de); **a ~ many** beaucoup (de); **~ morning/afternoon!** bonjour!; **~ evening!** bonsoir!; **~ night!** bonsoir!; (*on going to bed*) bonne nuit!

goodbye [gud'baɪ] EXCL au revoir!; **to say ~ to sb** dire au revoir à qn

good faith N bonne foi

good-for-nothing ['gudfənʌθɪŋ] ADJ bon(ne) *or* propre à rien

Good Friday N Vendredi saint

good-humoured ['gud'hju:məd] ADJ (*person*) jovial(e); (*remark, joke*) sans malice

good-looking ['gud'lukɪŋ] ADJ beau (belle), bien *inv*

good-natured ['gud'neɪtʃəd] ADJ (*person*) qui a un bon naturel; (*discussion*) enjoué(e)

goodness ['gudnɪs] N (*of person*) bonté *f*; **for ~ sake!** je vous en prie!; **~ gracious!** mon Dieu!

goods train N (BRIT) train *m* de marchandises

goodwill [gud'wɪl] N bonne volonté *f*; (*Comm*) réputation *f* (auprès de la clientèle)

goody-goody ['gudɪgudɪ] N (*pej*) petit saint, sainte nitouche

gooey ['gu:ɪ] ADJ (*inf*) gluant(e)

Google® ['gugl] N Google® *m* ▶ VT: **to google** (*word, name*) chercher sur Google

goose [gu:s] (*pl* **geese** [gi:s]) N oie *f*

gooseberry ['guzbərɪ] N groseille *f* à maquereau; **to play ~** (BRIT) tenir la chandelle

goose bumps NPL chair *f* de poule

gooseflesh ['gu:sfleʃ] N, **goose pimples** NPL chair *f* de poule

goose step N (*Mil*) pas *m* de l'oie

GOP N ABBR (*US Pol: inf:* = *Grand Old Party*) parti républicain

gopher ['gəufəʳ] N = **gofer**

gore [gɔ:ʳ] VT encorner ▶ N sang *m*

gorge [gɔ:dʒ] N gorge *f* ▶ VT: **to ~ o.s. (on)** se gorger (de)

gorgeous ['gɔ:dʒəs] ADJ splendide, superbe

gorilla [gə'rɪlə] N gorille *m*

gormless ['gɔ:mlɪs] ADJ (BRIT inf) lourdaud(e)

gorse [gɔ:s] N ajoncs *mpl*

gory ['gɔ:rɪ] ADJ sanglant(e)

gosh [gɔʃ] (*inf*) EXCL mince alors!

go-slow ['gəu'sləu] N (BRIT) grève perlée

gospel ['gɔspl] N évangile *m*

gossamer ['gɔsəməʳ] N (*cobweb*) fils *mpl* de la vierge; (*light fabric*) étoffe très légère

gossip ['gɔsɪp] N (*chat*) bavardages *mpl*; (*malicious*) commérage *m*, cancans *mpl*; (*person*) commère *f* ▶ VI bavarder; cancaner, faire des commérages; **a piece of ~** un ragot, un racontar

gossip column N (*Press*) échos *mpl*

got [gɔt] PT, PP of **get**

Gothic ['gɔθɪk] ADJ gothique

gotten ['gɔtn] (US) PP of **get**

gouge [gaudʒ] VT (*also:* **gouge out**: *hole etc*) évider; (*initials*) tailler; **to ~ sb's eyes out** crever les yeux à qn

gourd [guəd] N calebasse *f*, gourde *f*

gourmet ['guəmeɪ] N gourmet *m*, gastronome *mf*

gout [gaut] N goutte *f*

govern ['gʌvən] VT (*gen: Ling*) gouverner; (*influence*) déterminer

governess ['gʌvənɪs] N gouvernante *f*

governing ['gʌvənɪŋ] ADJ (*Pol*) au pouvoir, au gouvernement; **~ body** conseil *m* d'administration

government ['gʌvnmənt] N gouvernement *m*; (BRIT: *ministers*) ministère *m* ▶ CPD de l'État

governmental [gʌvn'mɛntl] ADJ gouvernemental(e)

government housing N (US) logements sociaux

government stock N titres *mpl* d'État

governor ['gʌvənəʳ] N (*of colony, state, bank*) gouverneur *m*; (*of school, hospital etc*) administrateur(-trice); (BRIT: *of prison*) directeur(-trice)

Govt ABBR (= *government*) gvt

gown [gaun] N robe *f*; (*of teacher, BRIT: of judge*) toge *f*

GP N ABBR (*Med*) = **general practitioner; who's your GP?** qui est votre médecin traitant?

GPMU N ABBR (BRIT) = **Graphical, Paper and Media Union**

GPO N ABBR (BRIT old) = **General Post Office**; (US) = **Government Printing Office**

GPS N ABBR (= *global positioning system*) GPS *m*

gr. ABBR (*Comm*) = **gross**

grab [græb] VT saisir, empoigner; (*property, power*) se saisir de ▶ VI: **to ~ at** essayer de saisir

grace [greɪs] N grâce *f* ▶ VT (*honour*) honorer; (*adorn*) orner; **5 days' ~** un répit de 5 jours; **to say ~** dire le bénédicité; (*after meal*) dire les grâces; **with a good/bad ~** de bonne/mauvaise grâce; **his sense of humour is his saving ~** il se rachète par son sens de l'humour

graceful ['greɪsful] ADJ gracieux(-euse), élégant(e)

gracious ['greɪʃəs] ADJ (*kind*) charmant(e), bienveillant(e); (*elegant*) plein(e) d'élégance, d'une grande élégance; (*formal: pardon etc*) miséricordieux(-euse) ▶ EXCL: **(good) ~!** mon Dieu!

gradation [grə'deɪʃən] N gradation *f*

grade [greɪd] N (*Comm: quality*) qualité *f*; (: *size*) calibre *m*; (: *type*) catégorie *f*; (*in hierarchy*) grade *m*, échelon *m*; (*Scol*) note *f*; (US: *school class*) classe *f*; (: *gradient*) pente *f* ▶ VT classer; (*by size*) calibrer; graduer; **to make the ~** (*fig*) réussir

grade crossing N (US) passage *m* à niveau

grade school N (US) école *f* primaire

gradient ['greɪdɪənt] N inclinaison *f*, pente *f*; (*Geom*) gradient *m*

gradual ['grædjuəl] ADJ graduel(le), progressif(-ive)

gradually ['grædjuəlɪ] ADV peu à peu, graduellement

605

graduate N ['grædjuɪt] diplômé(e) d'université; (US: of high school) diplômé(e) de fin d'études ▸ VI ['grædjueɪt] obtenir un diplôme d'université (or de fin d'études)

graduated pension ['grædjueɪtɪd-] N retraite calculée en fonction des derniers salaires

graduation [grædju'eɪʃən] N cérémonie f de remise des diplômes

graffiti [grə'fi:tɪ] NPL graffiti mpl

graft [grɑ:ft] N (Agr, Med) greffe f; (bribery) corruption f ▸ VT greffer; **hard ~** (BRIT inf) boulot acharné

grain [greɪn] N (single piece) grain m; (no pl: cereals) céréales fpl; (US: corn) blé m; (of wood) fibre f; **it goes against the ~** cela va à l'encontre de sa (or ma etc) nature

gram [græm] N gramme m

grammar ['græmə'] N grammaire f

grammar school N (BRIT) ≈ lycée m

grammatical [grə'mætɪkl] ADJ grammatical(e)

gramme [græm] N = **gram**

gramophone ['græməfəun] N (BRIT) gramophone m

gran [græn] (inf) N (BRIT) mamie f (inf), mémé f (inf); **my ~** (young child speaking) ma mamie or mémé; (older child or adult speaking) ma grand-mère

granary ['grænərɪ] N grenier m

grand [grænd] ADJ magnifique, splendide; (terrific) magnifique, formidable; (gesture etc) noble ▸ N (inf: thousand) mille livres fpl (or dollars mpl)

grandad ['grændæd] N (inf) = **granddad**

grandchild ['græntʃaɪld] (pl **grandchildren** ['græntʃɪldrən]) N petit-fils m, petite-fille f; **grandchildren** NPL petits-enfants

granddad ['grændæd] N (inf) papy m (inf), papi m (inf), pépé m (inf); **my ~** (young child speaking) mon papy or papi or pépé; (older child or adult speaking) mon grand-père

granddaughter ['grændɔ:tə'] N petite-fille f

grandeur ['grændjə'] N magnificence f, splendeur f; (of position etc) éminence f

grandfather ['grændfɑ:ðə'] N grand-père m

grandiose ['grændɪəus] ADJ grandiose; (pej) pompeux(-euse)

grand jury N (US) jury m d'accusation (formé de 12 à 23 jurés)

grandma ['grænmɑ:] N (inf) = **gran**

grandmother ['grænmʌðə'] N grand-mère f

grandpa ['grænpɑ:] N (inf) = **granddad**

grandparents ['grændpɛərənts] NPL grands-parents mpl

grand piano N piano m à queue

Grand Prix ['grɑ̃:'pri:] N (Aut) grand prix automobile

grandson ['grænsʌn] N petit-fils m

grandstand ['grændstænd] N (Sport) tribune f

grand total N total général

granite ['grænɪt] N granit m

granny ['grænɪ] N (inf) = **gran**

grant [grɑ:nt] VT accorder; (a request) accéder à; (admit) concéder ▸ N (Scol) bourse f; (Admin) subside m, subvention f; **to take sth for**

granted considérer qch comme acquis; **to take sb for granted** considérer qn comme faisant partie du décor; **to ~ that** admettre que

granulated ['grænjuleɪtɪd] ADJ: **~ sugar** sucre m en poudre

granule ['grænju:l] N granule m

grape [greɪp] N raisin m; **a bunch of grapes** une grappe de raisin

grapefruit ['greɪpfru:t] N pamplemousse m

grapevine ['greɪpvaɪn] N vigne f; **I heard it on the ~** (fig) je l'ai appris par le téléphone arabe

graph [grɑ:f] N graphique m, courbe f

graphic ['græfɪk] ADJ graphique; (vivid) vivant(e)

graphic designer N graphiste mf

graphic equalizer N égaliseur m graphique

graphics ['græfɪks] N (art) arts mpl graphiques; (process) graphisme m ▸ NPL (drawings) illustrations fpl

graphite ['græfaɪt] N graphite m

graph paper N papier millimétré

grapple ['græpl] VI: **to ~ with** être aux prises avec

grappling iron ['græplɪŋ-] N (Naut) grappin m

grasp [grɑ:sp] VT saisir, empoigner; (understand) saisir, comprendre ▸ N (grip) prise f; (fig) compréhension f, connaissance f; **to have sth within one's ~** avoir qch à sa portée; **to have a good ~ of sth** (fig) bien comprendre qch
▸ **grasp at** VT FUS (rope etc) essayer de saisir; (fig: opportunity) sauter sur

grasping ['grɑ:spɪŋ] ADJ avide

grass [grɑ:s] N herbe f; (lawn) gazon m; (BRIT inf: informer) mouchard(e); (: ex-terrorist) balanceur(-euse)

grasshopper ['grɑ:shɔpə'] N sauterelle f

grassland ['grɑ:slænd] N prairie f

grass roots NPL (fig) base f

grass snake N couleuvre f

grassy ['grɑ:sɪ] ADJ herbeux(-euse)

grate [greɪt] N grille f de cheminée ▸ VI grincer
▸ VT (Culin) râper

grateful ['greɪtful] ADJ reconnaissant(e)

gratefully ['greɪtfəlɪ] ADV avec reconnaissance

grater ['greɪtə'] N râpe f

gratification [grætɪfɪ'keɪʃən] N satisfaction f

gratify ['grætɪfaɪ] VT faire plaisir à; (whim) satisfaire

gratifying ['grætɪfaɪɪŋ] ADJ agréable, satisfaisant(e)

grating ['greɪtɪŋ] N (iron bars) grille f ▸ ADJ (noise) grinçant(e)

gratitude ['grætɪtju:d] N gratitude f

gratuitous [grə'tju:ɪtəs] ADJ gratuit(e)

gratuity [grə'tju:ɪtɪ] N pourboire m

grave [greɪv] N tombe f ▸ ADJ grave, sérieux(-euse)

gravedigger ['greɪvdɪgə'] N fossoyeur m

gravel ['grævl] N gravier m

gravely ['greɪvlɪ] ADV gravement, sérieusement; **~ ill** gravement malade

gravestone ['greɪvstəun] N pierre tombale

graveyard ['greɪvjɑ:d] N cimetière m

gravitate ['grævɪteɪt] VI graviter

gravity ['grævɪtɪ] N (Physics) gravité f; pesanteur f;

(*seriousness*) gravité, sérieux *m*
gravy ['greɪvɪ] N jus *m* (de viande), sauce *f* (au jus de viande)
gravy boat N saucière *f*
gravy train N (*inf*): **to ride the ~** avoir une bonne planque
gray [greɪ] ADJ (*US*) = **grey**
graze [greɪz] VI paître, brouter ▶ VT (*touch lightly*) frôler, effleurer; (*scrape*) écorcher ▶ N écorchure *f*
grazing ['greɪzɪŋ] N (*pasture*) pâturage *m*
grease [gri:s] N (*fat*) graisse *f*; (*lubricant*) lubrifiant *m* ▶ VT graisser; lubrifier; **to ~ the skids** (*US fig*) huiler les rouages
grease gun N graisseur *m*
greasepaint ['gri:speɪnt] N produits *mpl* de maquillage
greaseproof paper ['gri:spru:f-] N (*BRIT*) papier sulfurisé
greasy ['gri:sɪ] ADJ gras(se), graisseux(-euse); (*hands, clothes*) graisseux; (*BRIT: road, surface*) glissant(e)
great [greɪt] ADJ grand(e); (*heat, pain etc*) très fort(e), intense; (*inf*) formidable; **they're ~ friends** ils sont très amis, ce sont de grands amis; **we had a ~ time** nous nous sommes bien amusés; **it was ~!** c'était super or super!; **the ~ thing is that ...** ce qu'il y a de vraiment bien c'est que ...
Great Barrier Reef N: **the ~** la Grande Barrière
Great Britain N Grande-Bretagne *f*
great-grandchild [greɪt'grænt∫aɪld] (*pl* **-children** [-t∫ɪldrən]) N arrière-petit(e)-enfant
great-grandfather [greɪt'grænfɑːðəʳ] N arrière-grand-père *m*
great-grandmother [greɪt'grænmʌðəʳ] N arrière-grand-mère *f*
Great Lakes NPL: **the ~** les Grands Lacs
greatly ['greɪtlɪ] ADV très, grandement; (*with verbs*) beaucoup
greatness ['greɪtnɪs] N grandeur *f*
Grecian ['gri:∫ən] ADJ grec (grecque)
Greece [gri:s] N Grèce *f*
greed [gri:d] N (*also*: **greediness**) avidité *f*; (*for food*) gourmandise *f*
greedily ['gri:dɪlɪ] ADV avidement; avec gourmandise
greedy ['gri:dɪ] ADJ avide; (*for food*) gourmand(e)
Greek [gri:k] ADJ grec (grecque) ▶ N Grec (Grecque); (*Ling*) grec *m*; **ancient/modern ~** grec classique/moderne
green [gri:n] ADJ vert(e); (*inexperienced*) (bien) jeune, naïf(-ïve); (*ecological: product etc*) écologique ▶ N (*colour*) vert *m*; (*on golf course*) green *m*; (*stretch of grass*) pelouse *f*; (*also*: **village green**) = place *f* du village; **greens** NPL (*vegetables*) légumes verts; **to have ~ fingers** or (*US*) **a ~ thumb** (*fig*) avoir le pouce vert; **G~** (*Pol*) écologiste *mf*; **the G~ Party** le parti écologiste
green belt N (*round town*) ceinture verte
green card N (*Aut*) carte verte; (*US: work permit*) permis *m* de travail
greenery ['gri:nərɪ] N verdure *f*
greenfly ['gri:nflaɪ] N (*BRIT*) puceron *m*

greengage ['gri:ngeɪdʒ] N reine-claude *f*
greengrocer ['gri:ngrəusəʳ] N (*BRIT*) marchand *m* de fruits et légumes
greengrocer's ['gri:ngrəusəʳ], **greengrocer's shop** N magasin *m* de fruits et légumes
greenhouse ['gri:nhaus] N serre *f*
greenhouse effect N: **the ~** l'effet *m* de serre
greenhouse gas N gaz *m* contribuant à l'effet de serre
greenish ['gri:nɪ∫] ADJ verdâtre
Greenland ['gri:nlənd] N Groenland *m*
Greenlander ['gri:nləndəʳ] N Groenlandais(e)
green light N: **to give sb/sth the ~** donner le feu vert à qn/qch
green pepper N poivron (vert)
green pound N (*Econ*) livre verte
green salad N salade verte
green tax N écotaxe *f*
greet [gri:t] VT accueillir
greeting ['gri:tɪŋ] N salutation *f*; **Christmas/ birthday greetings** souhaits *mpl* de Noël/de bon anniversaire
greetings card N carte *f* de vœux
gregarious [grə'gεərɪəs] ADJ grégaire; sociable
grenade [grə'neɪd] N (*also*: **hand grenade**) grenade *f*
grew [gru:] PT *of* **grow**
grey, (*US*) **gray** [greɪ] ADJ gris(e); (*dismal*) sombre; **to go ~** (commencer à) grisonner
grey-haired, (*US*) **gray-haired** [greɪ'hεəd] ADJ aux cheveux gris
greyhound ['greɪhaund] N lévrier *m*
grey vote N vote *m* des seniors
grid [grɪd] N grille *f*; (*Elec*) réseau *m*; (*US Aut*) intersection *f* (*matérialisée par des marques au sol*); **off-~** hors-réseau
griddle ['grɪdl] N (*on cooker*) plaque chauffante
gridiron ['grɪdaɪən] N gril *m*
gridlock ['grɪdlɔk] N (*traffic jam*) embouteillage *m*
gridlocked ['grɪdlɔkt] ADJ: **to be ~** (*roads*) être bloqué par un embouteillage; (*talks etc*) être suspendu
grief [gri:f] N chagrin *m*, douleur *f*; **to come to ~** (*plan*) échouer; (*person*) avoir un malheur
grievance ['gri:vəns] N doléance *f*, grief *m*; (*cause for complaint*) grief
grieve [gri:v] VI avoir du chagrin; se désoler ▶ VT faire de la peine à, affliger; **to ~ for sb** pleurer qn; **to ~ at** se désoler de; pleurer
grievous ['gri:vəs] ADJ grave, cruel(le); **~ bodily harm** (*Law*) coups *mpl* et blessures *fpl*
grill [grɪl] N (*on cooker*) gril *m*; (*also*: **mixed grill**) grillade(s) *f(pl)*; (*also*: **grillroom**) rôtisserie *f* ▶ VT (*Culin*) griller; (*inf: question*) interroger longuement, cuisiner
grille [grɪl] N grillage *m*; (*Aut*) calandre *f*
grillroom ['grɪlrum] N rôtisserie *f*
grim [grɪm] ADJ sinistre, lugubre; (*serious, stern*) sévère
grimace [grɪ'meɪs] N grimace *f* ▶ VI grimacer, faire une grimace
grime [graɪm] N crasse *f*
grimy ['graɪmɪ] ADJ crasseux(-euse)
grin [grɪn] N large sourire *m* ▶ VI sourire; **to ~**

g

(at) faire un grand sourire (à)

grind [graɪnd] (pt, pp **ground** [graund]) VT écraser; (coffee, pepper etc) moudre; (US: meat) hacher; (make sharp) aiguiser; (polish: gem, lens) polir ▸ VI (car gears) grincer ▸ N (work) corvée f; **to ~ one's teeth** grincer des dents; **to ~ to a halt** (vehicle) s'arrêter dans un grincement de freins; (fig) s'arrêter, s'immobiliser; **the daily ~** (inf) le train-train quotidien

grinder ['graɪndə'] N (machine: for coffee) moulin m (à café); (: for waste disposal etc) broyeur m

grindstone ['graɪndstəun] N: **to keep one's nose to the ~** travailler sans relâche

grip [grɪp] N (handclasp) poigne f; (control) prise f; (handle) poignée f; (holdall) sac m de voyage ▸ VT saisir, empoigner; (viewer, reader) captiver; **to come to grips with** se colleter avec, en venir aux prises avec; **to ~ the road** (Aut) adhérer à la route; **to lose one's ~** lâcher prise; (fig) perdre les pédales, être dépassé(e)

gripe [graɪp] N (Med) coliques fpl; (inf: complaint) ronchonnement m, rouspétance f ▸ VI (inf) râler

gripping ['grɪpɪŋ] ADJ prenant(e), palpitant(e)

grisly ['grɪzlɪ] ADJ sinistre, macabre

grist [grɪst] N (fig): **it's (all) ~ to his mill** ça l'arrange, ça apporte de l'eau à son moulin

gristle ['grɪsl] N cartilage m (de poulet etc)

grit [grɪt] N gravillon m; (courage) cran m ▸ VT (road) sabler; **to ~ one's teeth** serrer les dents; **to have a piece of ~ in one's eye** avoir une poussière or saleté dans l'œil

grits [grɪts] NPL (US) gruau m de maïs

grizzle ['grɪzl] VI (BRIT) pleurnicher

grizzly ['grɪzlɪ] N (also: **grizzly bear**) grizzli m, ours gris

groan [grəun] N (of pain) gémissement m; (of disapproval, dismay) grognement m ▸ VI gémir; grogner

grocer ['grəusə'] N épicier m

groceries ['grəusərɪz] NPL provisions fpl

grocer's (shop) ['grəusəz-], **grocery** ['grəusərɪ] N épicerie f

grog [grɔg] N grog m

groggy ['grɔgɪ] ADJ groggy inv

groin [grɔɪn] N aine f

groom [gru:m] N (for horses) palefrenier m; (also: **bridegroom**) marié m ▸ VT (horse) panser; (fig): **to ~ sb for** former qn pour

groove [gru:v] N sillon m, rainure f

grope [grəup] VI tâtonner; **to ~ for** chercher à tâtons

gross [grəus] ADJ grossier(-ière); (Comm) brut(e) ▸ N pl inv (twelve dozen) grosse f ▸ VT (Comm): **to ~ £500,000** gagner 500 000 livres avant impôt

gross domestic product N produit brut intérieur

grossly ['grəuslɪ] ADV (greatly) très, grandement

gross national product N produit national brut

grotesque [grə'tɛsk] ADJ grotesque

grotto ['grɔtəu] N grotte f

grotty ['grɔtɪ] ADJ (BRIT inf) minable

grouch [grautʃ] (inf) VI rouspéter ▸ N (person) rouspéteur(-euse)

ground [graund] PT, PP of **grind** ▸ N sol m, terre f; (land) terrain m, terres fpl; (Sport) terrain; (reason: gen pl) raison f; (US: also: **ground wire**) terre f ▸ VT (plane) empêcher de décoller, retenir au sol; (US Elec) équiper d'une prise de terre, mettre à la terre ▸ VI (ship) s'échouer ▸ ADJ (coffee etc) moulu(e); (US: meat) haché(e); **grounds** NPL (gardens etc) parc m, domaine m; (of coffee) marc m; **on the ~, to the ~** par terre; **below ~** sous terre; **to gain/lose ~** gagner/perdre du terrain; **common ~** terrain d'entente; **he covered a lot of ~ in his lecture** sa conférence a traité un grand nombre de questions or la question en profondeur

ground cloth N (US) = **groundsheet**

ground control N (Aviat, Space) centre m de contrôle (au sol)

ground floor N (BRIT) rez-de-chaussée m

grounding ['graundɪŋ] N (in education) connaissances fpl de base

groundless ['graundlɪs] ADJ sans fondement

groundnut ['graundnʌt] N arachide f

ground rent N (BRIT) fermage m

ground rules NPL: **the ~** les principes mpl de base

groundsheet ['graundʃi:t] N (BRIT) tapis m de sol

groundsman ['graundzmən] (irreg), (US) **groundskeeper** ['graundzki:pə'] N (Sport) gardien m de stade

ground staff N équipage m au sol

groundswell ['graundswɛl] N lame f or vague f de fond

ground-to-air ['grauntu'ɛə'] ADJ (Mil) sol-air inv

ground-to-ground ['grauntə'graund] ADJ (Mil) sol-sol inv

groundwork ['graundwə:k] N préparation f

group [gru:p] N groupe m ▸ VT (also: **group together**) grouper ▸ VI (also: **group together**) se grouper

groupie ['gru:pɪ] N groupie f

group therapy N thérapie f de groupe

grouse [graus] N pl inv (bird) grouse f (sorte de coq de bruyère) ▸ VI (complain) rouspéter, râler

grove [grəuv] N bosquet m

grovel ['grɔvl] VI (fig): **to ~ (before)** ramper (devant)

grow [grəu] (pt **grew** [gru:], pp **grown** [grəun]) VI (plant) pousser, croître; (person) grandir; (increase) augmenter, se développer; (become) devenir; **to ~ rich/weak** s'enrichir/s'affaiblir ▸ VT cultiver, faire pousser; (hair, beard) laisser pousser

▸ **grow apart** VI (fig) se détacher (l'un de l'autre)

▸ **grow away from** VT FUS (fig) s'éloigner de

▸ **grow on** VT FUS: **that painting is growing on me** je finirai par aimer ce tableau

▸ **grow out of** VT FUS (clothes) devenir trop grand pour; (habit) perdre (avec le temps); **he'll ~ out of it** ça lui passera

▸ **grow up** VI grandir

grower ['grəuə'] N producteur m; (Agr) cultivateur(-trice)

growing ['grəʊɪŋ] ADJ (fear, amount) croissant(e), grandissant(e); ~ **pains** (Med) fièvre f de croissance; (fig) difficultés fpl de croissance

growl [graʊl] VI grogner

grown [grəʊn] PP of **grow** ▶ ADJ adulte

grown-up [grəʊn'ʌp] N adulte mf, grande personne

growth [grəʊθ] N croissance f, développement m; (what has grown) pousse f; poussée f; (Med) grosseur f, tumeur f

growth rate N taux m de croissance

GRSM N ABBR (BRIT) = **Graduate of the Royal Schools of Music**

grub [grʌb] N larve f; (inf: food) bouffe f

grubby ['grʌbɪ] ADJ crasseux(-euse)

grudge [grʌdʒ] N rancune f ▶ VT: **to ~ sb sth** (in giving) donner qch à qn à contre-cœur; (resent) reprocher qch à qn; **to bear sb a ~ (for)** garder rancune or en vouloir à qn (de); **he grudges spending** il rechigne à dépenser

grudgingly ['grʌdʒɪŋlɪ] ADV à contre-cœur, de mauvaise grâce

gruelling, (US) grueling ['grʊəlɪŋ] ADJ exténuant(e)

gruesome ['gru:səm] ADJ horrible

gruff [grʌf] ADJ bourru(e)

grumble ['grʌmbl] VI rouspéter, ronchonner

grumpy ['grʌmpɪ] ADJ grincheux(-euse)

grunge [grʌndʒ] N (Mus: style) grunge m

grunt [grʌnt] VI grogner ▶ N grognement m

G-string ['dʒi:strɪŋ] N (garment) cache-sexe m inv

GSUSA N ABBR = **Girl Scouts of the United States of America**

GU ABBR (US) = **Guam**

guarantee [gærən'ti:] N garantie f ▶ VT garantir; **he can't ~ (that) he'll come** il n'est pas absolument certain de pouvoir venir

guarantor [gærən'tɔ:ʳ] N garant(e)

guard [gɑ:d] N garde f, surveillance f; (squad: Boxing, Fencing) garde f; (one man) garde m; (BRIT Rail) chef m de train; (safety device: on machine) dispositif m de sûreté; (also: **fireguard**) garde-feu m inv ▶ VT garder, surveiller; (protect): **to ~ sb/sth (against from)** protéger qn/qch (contre); **to be on one's ~** (fig) être sur ses gardes

▶ **guard against** VI: **to ~ against doing sth** se garder de faire qch

guard dog N chien m de garde

guarded ['gɑ:dɪd] ADJ (fig) prudent(e)

guardian ['gɑ:dɪən] N gardien(ne); (of minor) tuteur(-trice)

guard's van ['gɑ:dz-] N (BRIT Rail) fourgon m

Guatemala [gwɑ:tɪ'mɑ:lə] N Guatémala m

Guernsey ['gə:nzɪ] N Guernesey mf

guerrilla [gə'rɪlə] N guérillero m

guerrilla warfare N guérilla f

guess [gɛs] VI deviner ▶ VT deviner; (estimate) évaluer; (US) croire, penser ▶ N supposition f, hypothèse f; **to take or have a ~** essayer de deviner; **to keep sb guessing** laisser qn dans le doute or l'incertitude, tenir qn en haleine

guesstimate ['gɛstɪmɪt] N (inf) estimation f

guesswork ['gɛswə:k] N hypothèse f; **I got the answer by ~** j'ai deviné la réponse

guest [gɛst] N invité(e); (in hotel) client(e); **be my ~** faites comme chez vous

guest house N pension f

guest room N chambre f d'amis

guff [gʌf] N (inf) bêtises fpl

guffaw [gʌ'fɔ:] N gros rire ▶ VI pouffer de rire

guidance ['gaɪdəns] N (advice) conseils mpl; **under the ~ of** conseillé(e) or encadré(e) par, sous la conduite de; **vocational ~** orientation professionnelle; **marriage ~** conseils conjugaux

guide [gaɪd] N (person) guide mf; (book) guide m; (also: **Girl Guide**) éclaireuse f; (: Roman Catholic) guide f ▶ VT guider; **to be guided by sb/sth** se laisser guider par qn/qch; **is there an English-speaking ~?** est-ce que l'un des guides parle anglais?

guidebook ['gaɪdbʊk] N guide m; **do you have a ~ in English?** est-ce que vous avez un guide en anglais?

guided missile ['gaɪdɪd-] N missile téléguidé

guide dog N chien m d'aveugle

guided tour N visite guidée; **what time does the ~ start?** la visite guidée commence à quelle heure?

guidelines ['gaɪdlaɪnz] NPL (advice) instructions générales, conseils mpl

guild [gɪld] N (Hist) corporation f; (sharing interests) cercle m, association f

guildhall ['gɪldhɔ:l] N (BRIT) hôtel m de ville

guile [gaɪl] N astuce f

guileless ['gaɪlɪs] ADJ candide

guillotine ['gɪləti:n] N guillotine f; (for paper) massicot m

guilt [gɪlt] N culpabilité f

guilty ['gɪltɪ] ADJ coupable; **to plead ~/not ~** plaider coupable/non coupable; **to feel ~ about doing sth** avoir mauvaise conscience à faire qch

Guinea ['gɪnɪ] N: **Republic of ~** (République f de) Guinée f

guinea ['gɪnɪ] N (BRIT: formerly) guinée f (= 21 shillings)

guinea pig N cobaye m

guise [gaɪz] N aspect m, apparence f

guitar [gɪ'tɑ:ʳ] N guitare f

guitarist [gɪ'tɑ:rɪst] N guitariste mf

gulch [gʌltʃ] N (US) ravin m

gulf [gʌlf] N golfe m; (abyss) gouffre m; **the (Persian) G~** le golfe Persique

Gulf States NPL: **the ~** (in Middle East) les pays mpl du Golfe

Gulf Stream N: **the ~** le Gulf Stream

gull [gʌl] N mouette f

gullet ['gʌlɪt] N gosier m

gullibility [gʌlɪ'bɪlɪtɪ] N crédulité f

gullible ['gʌlɪbl] ADJ crédule

gully ['gʌlɪ] N ravin m; ravine f; couloir m

gulp [gʌlp] VI avaler sa salive; (from emotion) avoir la gorge serrée, s'étrangler ▶ VT (also: **gulp down**) avaler ▶ N (of drink) gorgée f; **at one ~** d'un seul coup

gum [gʌm] N (Anat) gencive f; (glue) colle f;

(*sweet*) boule *f* de gomme; (*also*: **chewing-gum**) chewing-gum *m* ▸ VT coller

gumboil ['gʌmbɔɪl] N abcès *m* dentaire

gumboots ['gʌmbuːts] NPL (BRIT) bottes *fpl* en caoutchouc

gumption ['gʌmpʃən] N bon sens, jugeote *f*

gun [gʌn] N (*small*) revolver *m*, pistolet *m*; (*rifle*) fusil *m*, carabine *f*; (*cannon*) canon *m* ▸ VT (*also*: **gun down**) abattre; **to stick to one's guns** (*fig*) ne pas en démordre

gunboat ['gʌnbəut] N canonnière *f*

gun dog N chien *m* de chasse

gunfire ['gʌnfaɪə'] N fusillade *f*

gunk [gʌŋk] N (*inf*) saleté *f*

gunman ['gʌnmən] N (*irreg*) bandit armé

gunner ['gʌnə'] N artilleur *m*

gunpoint ['gʌnpɔɪnt] N: **at ~** sous la menace du pistolet (*or* fusil)

gunpowder ['gʌnpaudə'] N poudre *f* à canon

gunrunner ['gʌnrʌnə'] N trafiquant *m* d'armes

gunrunning ['gʌnrʌnɪŋ] N trafic *m* d'armes

gunshot ['gʌnʃɔt] N coup *m* de feu; **within ~** à portée de fusil

gunsmith ['gʌnsmɪθ] N armurier *m*

gurgle ['gəːgl] N gargouillis *m* ▸ VI gargouiller

guru ['guruː] N gourou *m*

gush [gʌʃ] N jaillissement *m*, jet *m* ▸ VI jaillir; (*fig*) se répandre en effusions

gushing ['gʌʃɪŋ] ADJ (*person*) trop exubérant(e) *or* expansif(-ive); (*compliments*) exagéré(e)

gusset ['gʌsɪt] N gousset *m*, soufflet *m*; (*in tights, pants*) entre-jambes *m*

gust [gʌst] N (*of wind*) rafale *f*; (*of smoke*) bouffée *f*

gusto ['gʌstəu] N enthousiasme *m*

gusty ['gʌstɪ] ADJ venteux(-euse); **~ winds** des rafales de vent

gut [gʌt] N intestin *m*, boyau *m*; (*Mus etc*) boyau ▸ VT (*poultry, fish*) vider; (*building*) ne laisser que les murs de; **guts** NPL (*inf: Anat*) boyaux *mpl*; (: *courage*) cran *m*; **to hate sb's guts** ne pas pouvoir voir qn en peinture *or* sentir qn

gut reaction N réaction instinctive

gutsy ['gʌtsɪ] ADJ (*person*) qui a du cran;

(*style*) qui a du punch

gutted ['gʌtɪd] ADJ: **I was ~** (*inf: disappointed*) j'étais carrément dégoûté

gutter ['gʌtə'] N (*of roof*) gouttière *f*; (*in street*) caniveau *m*; (*fig*) ruisseau *m*

gutter press N: **the ~** la presse de bas étage *or* à scandale

guttural ['gʌtərl] ADJ guttural(e)

guy [gaɪ] N (*inf: man*) type *m*; (*also*: **guyrope**) corde *f*; (*figure*) effigie de Guy Fawkes

Guyana [gaɪ'ænə] N Guyane *f*

Guy Fawkes' Night [gaɪ'fɔːks-] N *voir article*

Guy Fawkes' Night, que l'on appelle également *bonfire night*, commémore l'échec du complot (le *Gunpowder Plot*) contre James Ier et son parlement le 5 novembre 1605. L'un des conspirateurs, Guy Fawkes, avait été surpris dans les caves du parlement alors qu'il s'apprêtait à y mettre le feu. Chaque année pour le 5 novembre, les enfants préparent à l'avance une effigie de Guy Fawkes et ils demandent aux passants "un penny pour le Guy" avec lequel ils pourront s'acheter des fusées de feu d'artifice. Beaucoup de gens font encore un feu dans leur jardin sur lequel ils brûlent le *Guy*.

guzzle ['gʌzl] VI s'empiffrer ▸ VT avaler gloutonnement

gym [dʒɪm] N (*also*: **gymnasium**) gymnase *m*; (*also*: **gymnastics**) gym *f*

gymkhana [dʒɪm'kɑːnə] N gymkhana *m*

gymnasium [dʒɪm'neɪzɪəm] N gymnase *m*

gymnast ['dʒɪmnæst] N gymnaste *mf*

gymnastics [dʒɪm'næstɪks] N, NPL gymnastique *f*

gym shoes NPL chaussures *fpl* de gym(nastique)

gynaecologist, (US) **gynecologist** [gaɪnɪ'kɔlədʒɪst] N gynécologue *mf*

gynaecology, (US) **gynecology** [gaɪnə'kɔlədʒɪ] N gynécologie *f*

gypsy ['dʒɪpsɪ] N gitan(e), bohémien(ne) ▸ CPD: **~ caravan** *n* roulotte *f*

gyrate [dʒaɪ'reɪt] VI tournoyer

Hh

H, h [eɪtʃ] N (letter) H, h m; **H for Harry**, (US) **H for How** H comme Henri

habeas corpus ['heɪbɪəs'kɔːpəs] N (Law) habeas corpus m

haberdashery [hæbə'dæʃərɪ] N (BRIT) mercerie f

habit ['hæbɪt] N habitude f; (costume: Rel) habit m; (for riding) tenue f d'équitation; **to get out of/into the ~ of doing sth** perdre/prendre l'habitude de faire qch

habitable ['hæbɪtəbl] ADJ habitable

habitat ['hæbɪtæt] N habitat m

habitation [hæbɪ'teɪʃən] N habitation f

habitual [hə'bɪtjuəl] ADJ habituel(le); (drinker, liar) invétéré(e)

habitually [hə'bɪtjuəlɪ] ADV habituellement, d'habitude

hack [hæk] VT hacher, tailler ▶ N (cut) entaille f; (blow) coup m; (pej: writer) nègre m; (old horse) canasson m

hacker ['hækə'] N (Comput) pirate m (informatique); (: enthusiast) passionné(e) des ordinateurs

hackles ['hæklz] NPL: **to make sb's ~ rise** (fig) mettre qn hors de soi

hackney cab ['hæknɪ-] N fiacre m

hackneyed ['hæknɪd] ADJ usé(e), rebattu(e)

hacksaw ['hæksɔː] N scie f à métaux

had [hæd] PT, PP of **have**

haddock ['hædək] (pl ~ or **haddocks**) N églefin m; **smoked ~** haddock m

hadn't ['hædnt] = **had not**

haematology, (US) **hematology** ['hiːmə'tɔlədʒɪ] N hématologie f

haemoglobin, (US) **hemoglobin** ['hiːmə'gləubɪn] N hémoglobine f

haemophilia, (US) **hemophilia** ['hiːmə'fɪlɪə] N hémophilie f

haemorrhage, (US) **hemorrhage** ['hɛmərɪdʒ] N hémorragie f

haemorrhoids, (US) **hemorrhoids** ['hɛmərɔɪdz] NPL hémorroïdes fpl

hag [hæg] N (ugly) vieille sorcière; (nasty) chameau m, harpie f; (witch) sorcière

haggard ['hægəd] ADJ hagard(e), égaré(e)

haggis ['hægɪs] N haggis m

haggle ['hægl] VI marchander; **to ~ over** chicaner sur

haggling ['hæglɪŋ] N marchandage m

Hague [heɪg] N: **The ~** La Haye

hail [heɪl] N grêle f ▶ VT (call) héler; (greet) acclamer ▶ VI grêler; (originate): **he hails from Scotland** il est originaire d'Écosse

hailstone ['heɪlstəun] N grêlon m

hailstorm ['heɪlstɔːm] N averse f de grêle

hair [hɛə'] N cheveux mpl; (on body) poils mpl, pilosité f; (of animal) pelage m; (single hair: on head) cheveu m; (: on body, of animal) poil m; **to do one's ~** se coiffer

hairband ['hɛəbænd] N (elasticated) bandeau m; (plastic) serre-tête m

hairbrush ['hɛəbrʌʃ] N brosse f à cheveux

haircut ['hɛəkʌt] N coupe f (de cheveux)

hairdo ['hɛəduː] N coiffure f

hairdresser ['hɛədrɛsə'] N coiffeur(-euse)

hairdresser's ['hɛədrɛsə'z] N salon m de coiffure, coiffeur m

hair dryer ['hɛədraɪə'] N sèche-cheveux m, séchoir m

-haired [hɛəd] SUFFIX: **fair/long~** aux cheveux blonds/longs

hair gel N gel m pour cheveux

hairgrip ['hɛəgrɪp] N pince f à cheveux

hairline ['hɛəlaɪn] N naissance f des cheveux

hairline fracture N fêlure f

hairnet ['hɛənɛt] N résille f

hair oil N huile f capillaire

hairpiece ['hɛəpiːs] N postiche m

hairpin ['hɛəpɪn] N épingle f à cheveux

hairpin bend, (US) **hairpin curve** N virage m en épingle à cheveux

hair-raising ['hɛəreɪzɪŋ] ADJ à (vous) faire dresser les cheveux sur la tête

hair remover N dépilateur m

hair removing cream N crème f dépilatoire

hair spray N laque f (pour les cheveux)

hairstyle ['hɛəstaɪl] N coiffure f

hairy ['hɛərɪ] ADJ poilu(e), chevelu(e); (inf: frightening) effrayant(e)

Haiti ['heɪtɪ] N Haïti m

haka ['hɑːkə] N (NEW ZEALAND) haka m

hake [heɪk] (pl ~ or **hakes**) N colin m, merlu m

halcyon ['hælsɪən] ADJ merveilleux(-euse)

hale [heɪl] ADJ: **~ and hearty** robuste, en pleine santé

half [hɑːf] (pl **halves** [hɑːvz]) N moitié f; (of beer: also: **half pint**) ≈ demi m; (Rail, bus: also: **half fare**) demi-tarif m; (*Sport: of match*) mi-temps f; (: *of ground*) moitié (du terrain) ▶ ADJ demi(e) ▶ ADV (à) moitié, à demi; **~ an hour** une demi-heure; **~ a dozen** une demi-douzaine; **~ a pound** une demi-livre, ≈ 250 g; **two and a ~** deux et demi; **a week and a ~** une semaine et demie; **~ (of it)** la moitié; **~ (of)** la moitié de; **~ the amount of** la moitié de; **to cut sth in ~** couper qch en deux; **~ past three** trois heures et demie; **~ empty/ closed** à moitié vide/fermé; **to go halves (with sb)** se mettre la moitié avec qn

half-back ['hɑːfbæk] N (*Sport*) demi m
half-baked ['hɑːf'beɪkt] ADJ (*inf: idea, scheme*) qui ne tient pas debout
half board N (*BRIT: in hotel*) demi-pension f
half-breed ['hɑːfbriːd] N (*offensive*) = **half-caste**
half-brother ['hɑːfbrʌðəʳ] N demi-frère m
half-caste ['hɑːfkɑːst] N (*offensive*) métis(se)
half day N demi-journée f
half fare N demi-tarif m
half-hearted ['hɑːf'hɑːtɪd] ADJ tiède, sans enthousiasme
half-hour [hɑːf'auəʳ] N demi-heure f
half-mast ['hɑːf'mɑːst] N: **at ~** (*flag*) en berne, à mi-mât
halfpenny ['heɪpnɪ] N demi-penny m
half-price ['hɑːf'praɪs] ADJ à moitié prix ▶ ADV (*also*: **at half-price**) à moitié prix
half term N (*BRIT Scol*) vacances fpl (*de demi-trimestre*)
half-time [hɑːf'taɪm] N mi-temps f
halfway ['hɑːf'weɪ] ADV à mi-chemin; **to meet sb ~** (*fig*) parvenir à un compromis avec qn; **~ through sth** au milieu de qch
halfway house N (*hostel*) centre m de réadaptation (*pour anciens prisonniers, malades mentaux etc*); (*fig*): **a ~ (between)** une étape intermédiaire (entre)
half-wit ['hɑːfwɪt] N (*inf*) idiot(e), imbécile mf
half-yearly [hɑːf'jɪəlɪ] ADV deux fois par an ▶ ADJ semestriel(le)
halibut ['hælɪbət] N pl inv flétan m
halitosis [hælɪ'təusɪs] N mauvaise haleine
hall [hɔːl] N salle f; (*entrance way: big*) hall m; (: *small*) entrée f; (*US: corridor*) couloir m; (*mansion*) château m, manoir m
hallmark ['hɔːlmɑːk] N poinçon m; (*fig*) marque f
hallo [hə'ləu] EXCL = **hello**
hall of residence N (*BRIT*) pavillon m or résidence f universitaire
Hallowe'en, Halloween ['hæləu'iːn] N veille f de la Toussaint; *voir article*

> Selon la tradition, *Hallowe'en* est la nuit des fantômes et des sorcières. En Écosse et aux États-Unis surtout (et de plus en plus en Angleterre) les enfants, pour fêter *Hallowe'en*, se déguisent ce soir-là et ils vont ainsi de porte en porte en demandant de petits cadeaux (du chocolat, etc).

hallucination [həluːsɪ'neɪʃən] N hallucination f
hallucinogenic [həluːsɪnəu'dʒenɪk] ADJ hallucinogène
hallway ['hɔːlweɪ] N (*entrance*) vestibule m; (*corridor*) couloir m

halo ['heɪləu] N (*of saint etc*) auréole f; (*of sun*) halo m
halt [hɔːlt] N halte f, arrêt m ▶ VT faire arrêter; (*progress etc*) interrompre ▶ VI faire halte, s'arrêter; **to call a ~ to sth** (*fig*) mettre fin à qch
halter ['hɔːltəʳ] N (*for horse*) licou m
halterneck ['hɔːltənɛk] ADJ (*dress*) (avec) dos nu inv
halve [hɑːv] VT (*apple etc*) partager or diviser en deux; (*reduce by half*) réduire de moitié
halves [hɑːvz] NPL of **half**
ham [hæm] N jambon m; (*inf: also*: **radio ham**) radio-amateur m; (*also*: **ham actor**) cabotin(e)
Hamburg ['hæmbəːg] N Hambourg
hamburger ['hæmbəːgəʳ] N hamburger m
ham-fisted ['hæm'fɪstɪd], (*US*) **ham-handed** ['hæm'hændɪd] ADJ maladroit(e)
hamlet ['hæmlɪt] N hameau m
hammer ['hæməʳ] N marteau m ▶ VT (*nail*) enfoncer; (*fig*) éreinter, démolir ▶ VI (*at door*) frapper à coups redoublés; **to ~ a point home to sb** faire rentrer qch dans la tête de qn
▶ **hammer out** VT (*metal*) étendre au marteau; (*fig: solution*) élaborer
hammock ['hæmək] N hamac m
hamper ['hæmpəʳ] VT gêner ▶ N panier m (d'osier)
hamster ['hæmstəʳ] N hamster m
hamstring ['hæmstrɪŋ] N (*Anat*) tendon m du jarret
hand [hænd] N main f; (*of clock*) aiguille f; (*handwriting*) écriture f; (*at cards*) jeu m; (*measurement: of horse*) paume f; (*worker*) ouvrier(-ière) ▶ VT passer, donner; **to give sb a ~** donner un coup de main à qn; **at ~** à portée de la main; **in ~** (*situation*) en main; (*work*) en cours; **we have the situation in ~** nous avons la situation bien en main; **to be on ~** (*person*) être disponible; (*emergency services*) se tenir prêt(e) (à intervenir); **to ~** (*information etc*) sous la main, à portée de la main; **to force sb's ~** forcer la main à qn; **to have a free ~** avoir carte blanche; **to have sth in one's ~** tenir qch à la main; **on the one ~ ...**, **on the other ~** d'une part ..., d'autre part
▶ **hand down** VT passer; (*tradition, heirloom*) transmettre; (*US: sentence, verdict*) prononcer
▶ **hand in** VT remettre
▶ **hand out** VT distribuer
▶ **hand over** VT remettre; (*powers etc*) transmettre
▶ **hand round** VT (*BRIT: information*) faire circuler; (: *chocolates etc*) faire passer
handbag ['hændbæg] N sac m à main
hand baggage N = **hand luggage**
handball ['hændbɔːl] N handball m
handbasin ['hændbeɪsn] N lavabo m
handbook ['hændbuk] N manuel m
handbrake ['hændbreɪk] N frein m à main
h & c ABBR (*BRIT*) = **hot and cold (water)**
hand cream N crème f pour les mains
handcuffs ['hændkʌfs] NPL menottes fpl
handful ['hændful] N poignée f

hand-held ['hænd'hɛld] ADJ à main
handicap ['hændıkæp] N handicap *m* ▶ VT handicaper
handicraft ['hændıkrɑːft] N travail *m* d'artisanat, technique artisanale
handiwork ['hændıwəːk] N ouvrage *m*; **this looks like his ~** (*pej*) ça a tout l'air d'être son œuvre
handkerchief ['hæŋkətʃıf] N mouchoir *m*
handle ['hændl] N (*of door etc*) poignée *f*; (*of cup etc*) anse *f*; (*of knife etc*) manche *m*; (*of saucepan*) queue *f*; (*for winding*) manivelle *f* ▶ VT toucher, manier; (*deal with*) s'occuper de; (*treat: people*) prendre; **"~ with care"** "fragile"; **to fly off the ~** s'énerver
handlebar ['hændlbɑːʳ] N, **handlebars** ['hændlbɑːz] NPL guidon *m*
handling ['hændlıŋ] N (*Aut*) maniement *m*; (*treatment*): **his ~ of the matter** la façon dont il a traité l'affaire
handling charges NPL frais *mpl* de manutention; (*Banking*) agios *mpl*
hand luggage N bagages *mpl* à main; **one item of ~** un bagage à main
handmade ['hænd'meɪd] ADJ fait(e) à la main
handout ['hændaut] N (*money*) aide *f*, don *m*; (*leaflet*) prospectus *m*; (*press handout*) communiqué *m* de presse; (*at lecture*) polycopié *m*
hand-picked ['hænd'pıkt] ADJ (*produce*) cueilli(e) à la main; (*staff etc*) trié(e) sur le volet
handrail ['hændreıl] N (*on staircase etc*) rampe *f*, main courante
handset ['hændset] N (*Tel*) combiné *m*
hands-free [hændz'frı] ADJ mains libres *inv* ▶ N (*also*: **hands-free kit**) kit *m* mains libres *inv*
handshake ['hændʃeık] N poignée *f* de main; (*Comput*) établissement *m* de la liaison
handsome ['hænsəm] ADJ beau (belle); (*gift*) généreux(-euse); (*profit*) considérable
hands-on [hændz'ɔn] ADJ (*training, experience*) sur le tas; **she has a very ~ approach** sa politique est de mettre la main à la pâte
handstand ['hændstænd] N: **to do a ~** faire l'arbre droit
hand-to-mouth ['hændtə'mauθ] ADJ (*existence*) au jour le jour
handwriting ['hændraıtıŋ] N écriture *f*
handwritten ['hændrıtn] ADJ manuscrit(e), écrit(e) à la main
handy ['hændı] ADJ (*person*) adroit(e); (*close at hand*) sous la main; (*convenient*) pratique; **to come in ~** être (*or* s'avérer) utile
handyman ['hændımæn] N (*irreg*) bricoleur *m*; (*servant*) homme *m* à tout faire
hang [hæŋ] (*pt, pp* **hung** [hʌŋ]) VT accrocher; (*pt, pp* **hanged**: *criminal*) pendre ▶ VI pendre; (*hair, drapery*) tomber ▶ N: **to get the ~ of (doing) sth** (*inf*) attraper le coup pour faire qch
▶ **hang about, hang around** VI flâner, traîner
▶ **hang back** VI (*hesitate*): **to ~ back (from doing)** être réticent(e) (pour faire)
▶ **hang down** VI pendre
▶ **hang on** VI (*wait*) attendre ▶ VT FUS (*depend on*)

dépendre de; **to ~ on to** (*keep hold of*) ne pas lâcher; (*keep*) garder
▶ **hang out** VT (*washing*) étendre (dehors) ▶ VI pendre; (*inf: live*) habiter, percher; (: *spend time*) traîner
▶ **hang round** VI = **hang about**
▶ **hang together** VI (*argument etc*) se tenir, être cohérent(e)
▶ **hang up** VI (*Tel*) raccrocher ▶ VT (*coat, painting etc*) accrocher, suspendre; **to ~ up on sb** (*Tel*) raccrocher au nez de qn
hangar ['hæŋəʳ] N hangar *m*
hangdog ['hæŋdɔg] ADJ (*look, expression*) de chien battu
hanger ['hæŋəʳ] N cintre *m*, portemanteau *m*
hanger-on [hæŋər'ɔn] N parasite *m*
hang-glider ['hæŋglaıdəʳ] N deltaplane *m*
hang-gliding ['hæŋglaıdıŋ] N vol *m* libre or sur aile delta
hanging ['hæŋıŋ] N (*execution*) pendaison *f*
hangman ['hæŋmən] N (*irreg*) bourreau *m*
hangover ['hæŋəuvəʳ] N (*after drinking*) gueule *f* de bois
hang-up ['hæŋʌp] N complexe *m*
hank [hæŋk] N écheveau *m*
hanker ['hæŋkəʳ] VI: **to ~ after** avoir envie de
hankering ['hæŋkərıŋ] N: **to have a ~ for/ to do sth** avoir une grande envie de/de faire qch
hankie, hanky ['hæŋkı] N ABBR = **handkerchief**
Hants ABBR (*BRIT*) = **Hampshire**
haphazard [hæp'hæzəd] ADJ fait(e) au hasard, fait(e) au petit bonheur
hapless ['hæplıs] ADJ malheureux(-euse)
happen ['hæpən] VI arriver, se passer, se produire; **what's happening?** que se passe-t-il?; **she happened to be free** il s'est trouvé (*or* se trouvait) qu'elle était libre; **if anything happened to him** s'il lui arrivait quoi que ce soit; **as it happens** justement
▶ **happen on, happen upon** VT FUS tomber sur
happening ['hæpnıŋ] N événement *m*
happily ['hæpılı] ADV heureusement; (*cheerfully*) joyeusement
happiness ['hæpınıs] N bonheur *m*
happy ['hæpı] ADJ heureux(-euse); **~ with** (*arrangements etc*) satisfait(e) de; **to be ~ to do** faire volontiers; **yes, I'd be ~ to** oui, avec plaisir *or* (*bien*) volontiers; **~ birthday!** bon anniversaire!; **~ Christmas/New Year!** joyeux Noël/bonne année!
happy-go-lucky ['hæpıgəu'lʌkı] ADJ insouciant(e)
happy hour N l'heure *f* de l'apéritif, *heure pendant laquelle les consommations sont à prix réduit*
harangue [hə'ræŋ] VT haranguer
harass ['hærəs] VT accabler, tourmenter
harassed ['hærəst] ADJ tracassé(e)
harassment ['hærəsmənt] N tracasseries *fpl*; **sexual ~** harcèlement sexuel
harbour, (*US*) **harbor** ['hɑːbəʳ] N port *m* ▶ VT héberger, abriter; (*hopes, suspicions*) entretenir; **to ~ a grudge against sb** en vouloir à qn

h

harbour dues, (US) **harbor dues** NPL droits mpl de port

harbour master, (US) **harbor master** N capitaine m du port

hard [hɑːd] ADJ dur(e); (question, problem) difficile; (facts, evidence) concret(-ète) ▶ ADV (work) dur; (think, try) sérieusement; **to look ~ at** regarder fixement; (thing) regarder de près; **to drink ~** boire sec; **~ luck!** pas de veine!; **no ~ feelings!** sans rancune!; **to be ~ of hearing** être dur(e) d'oreille; **to be ~ done by** être traité(e) injustement; **to be ~ on sb** être dur(e) avec qn; **I find it ~ to believe that ...** je n'arrive pas à croire que ...

hard-and-fast ['hɑːdən'fɑːst] ADJ strict(e), absolu(e)

hardback ['hɑːdbæk] N livre relié

hardboard ['hɑːdbɔːd] N Isorel® m

hard-boiled egg ['hɑːd'bɔɪld-] N œuf dur

hard cash N espèces fpl

hard copy N (Comput) sortie f or copie f papier

hard-core ['hɑːd'kɔːʳ] ADJ (pornography) (dit(e)) dur(e); (supporters) inconditionnel(le)

hard court N (Tennis) court m en dur

hard disk N (Comput) disque dur

hard drive N (Comput) disque dur

harden ['hɑːdn] VT durcir; (steel) tremper; (fig) endurcir ▶ VI (substance) durcir

hardened ['hɑːdnd] ADJ (criminal) endurci(e); **to be ~ to sth** s'être endurci(e) à qch, être (devenu(e)) insensible à qch

hard-headed ['hɑːd'hɛdɪd] ADJ réaliste; décidé(e)

hard-hearted ['hɑːd'hɑːtɪd] ADJ dur(e), impitoyable

hard-hitting ['hɑːd'hɪtɪŋ] ADJ (speech, article) sans complaisances

hard labour N travaux forcés

hardliner [hɑːd'laɪnəʳ] N intransigeant(e), dur(e)

hard-luck story [hɑːd'lʌk-] N histoire larmoyante

hardly ['hɑːdlɪ] ADV (scarcely) à peine; (harshly) durement; **it's ~ the case** ce n'est guère le cas; **~ anywhere/ever** presque nulle part/jamais; **I can ~ believe it** j'ai du mal à le croire

hardness ['hɑːdnɪs] N dureté f

hard-nosed ['hɑːd'nəuzd] ADJ impitoyable, dur(e)

hard-pressed ['hɑːd'prɛst] ADJ sous pression

hard sell N vente agressive

hardship ['hɑːdʃɪp] N (difficulties) épreuves fpl; (deprivation) privations fpl

hard shoulder N (BRIT Aut) accotement stabilisé

hard-up [hɑːd'ʌp] ADJ (inf) fauché(e)

hardware ['hɑːdwɛəʳ] N quincaillerie f; (Comput, Mil) matériel m

hardware shop, (US) **hardware store** N quincaillerie f

hard-wearing [hɑːd'wɛərɪŋ] ADJ solide

hard-won ['hɑːd'wʌn] ADJ (si) durement gagné(e)

hard-working [hɑːd'wəːkɪŋ] ADJ travailleur(-euse), consciencieux(-euse)

hardy ['hɑːdɪ] ADJ robuste; (plant) résistant(e) au gel

hare [hɛəʳ] N lièvre m

hare-brained ['hɛəbreɪnd] ADJ farfelu(e), écervelé(e)

harelip ['hɛəlɪp] N (Med) bec-de-lièvre m

harem [hɑːˈriːm] N harem m

hark back [hɑːk-] VI: **to ~ to** (en) revenir toujours à

harm [hɑːm] N mal m; (wrong) tort m ▶ VT (person) faire du mal or du tort à; (thing) endommager; **to mean no ~** ne pas avoir de mauvaises intentions; **there's no ~ in trying** on peut toujours essayer; **out of ~'s way** à l'abri du danger, en lieu sûr

harmful ['hɑːmful] ADJ nuisible

harmless ['hɑːmlɪs] ADJ inoffensif(-ive)

harmonic [hɑːˈmɔnɪk] ADJ harmonique

harmonica [hɑːˈmɔnɪkə] N harmonica m

harmonics [hɑːˈmɔnɪks] NPL harmoniques mpl or fpl

harmonious [hɑːˈməunɪəs] ADJ harmonieux(-euse)

harmonium [hɑːˈməunɪəm] N harmonium m

harmonize ['hɑːmənaɪz] VT harmoniser ▶ VI s'harmoniser

harmony ['hɑːmənɪ] N harmonie f

harness ['hɑːnɪs] N harnais m ▶ VT (horse) harnacher; (resources) exploiter

harp [hɑːp] N harpe f ▶ VI: **to ~ on about** revenir toujours sur

harpist ['hɑːpɪst] N harpiste mf

harpoon [hɑːˈpuːn] N harpon m

harpsichord ['hɑːpsɪkɔːd] N clavecin m

harrowing ['hærəuɪŋ] ADJ déchirant(e)

harsh [hɑːʃ] ADJ (hard) dur(e); (severe) sévère; (rough: surface) rugueux(-euse); (unpleasant: sound) discordant(e); (: light) cru(e); (: taste) âpre

harshly ['hɑːʃlɪ] ADV durement, sévèrement

harshness ['hɑːʃnɪs] N dureté f, sévérité f

harvest ['hɑːvɪst] N (of corn) moisson f; (of fruit) récolte f; (of grapes) vendange f ▶ VI, VT moissonner; récolter; vendanger

harvester ['hɑːvɪstəʳ] N (machine) moissonneuse f; (also: **combine harvester**) moissonneuse-batteuse(-lieuse) f

has [hæz] VB see **have**

has-been ['hæzbiːn] N (inf: person): **he/she's a ~** il/elle a fait son temps or est fini(e)

hash [hæʃ] N (Culin) hachis m; (fig: mess) gâchis m ▶ N ABBR (inf) = **hashish**

hashish ['hæʃɪʃ] N haschisch m

hashtag ['hæʃtæg] N (on Twitter) hashtag m; mot-dièse m

hasn't ['hæznt] = **has not**

hassle ['hæsl] N (inf: fuss) histoire(s) f(pl)

haste [heɪst] N hâte f, précipitation f; **in ~** à la hâte, précipitamment

hasten ['heɪsn] VT hâter, accélérer ▶ VI se hâter, s'empresser; **I ~ to add that ...** je m'empresse d'ajouter que ...

hastily ['heɪstɪlɪ] ADV à la hâte; (leave) précipitamment

hasty ['heɪstɪ] ADJ (decision, action) hâtif(-ive);

(*departure, escape*) précipité(e)
hat [hæt] N chapeau *m*
hatbox ['hætbɔks] N carton *m* à chapeau
hatch [hætʃ] N (*Naut: also:* **hatchway**) écoutille *f*; (*Brit: also:* **service hatch**) passe-plats *m inv* ▶ VI éclore ▶ VT faire éclore; (*fig: scheme*) tramer, ourdir
hatchback ['hætʃbæk] N (*Aut*) modèle *m* avec hayon arrière
hatchet ['hætʃɪt] N hachette *f*
hatchet job N (*inf*) démolissage *m*
hatchet man N (*irreg*) (*inf*) homme *m* de main
hate [heɪt] VT haïr, détester ▶ N haine *f*; **to ~ to do** *or* **doing** détester faire; **I ~ to trouble you, but** ... désolé de vous déranger, mais ...
hateful ['heɪtful] ADJ odieux(-euse), détestable
hater ['heɪtər] N: **cop-~** anti-flic *mf*; **woman-~** misogyne *mf* (haineux(-euse))
hatred ['heɪtrɪd] N haine *f*
hat trick N (*Brit Sport, also fig*): **to get a ~** réussir trois coups (*or* gagner trois matchs *etc*) consécutifs
haughty ['hɔːtɪ] ADJ hautain(e), arrogant(e)
haul [hɔːl] VT traîner, tirer; (*by lorry*) camionner; (*Naut*) haler ▶ N (*of fish*) prise *f*; (*of stolen goods etc*) butin *m*
haulage ['hɔːlɪdʒ] N transport routier
haulage contractor N (*Brit: firm*) entreprise *f* de transport (routier); (*: person*) transporteur routier
haulier ['hɔːlɪər], (*US*) **hauler** ['hɔːlər] N transporteur (routier), camionneur *m*
haunch [hɔːntʃ] N hanche *f*; **~ of venison** cuissot *m* de chevreuil
haunt [hɔːnt] VT (*subj: ghost, fear*) hanter; (*: person*) fréquenter ▶ N repaire *m*
haunted ['hɔːntɪd] ADJ (*castle etc*) hanté(e); (*look*) égaré(e), hagard(e)
haunting ['hɔːntɪŋ] ADJ (*sight, music*) obsédant(e)
Havana [hə'vænə] N La Havane

(KEYWORD)

have [hæv] (*pt, pp* **had**) AUX VB **1** (*gen*) avoir; être; **to have eaten/slept** avoir mangé/dormi; **to have arrived/gone** être arrivé(e)/allé(e); **he has been promoted** il a eu une promotion; **having finished** *or* **when he had finished, he left** quand il a eu fini, il est parti; **we'd already eaten** nous avions déjà mangé

2 (*in tag questions*): **you've done it, haven't you?** vous l'avez fait, n'est-ce pas?

3 (*in short answers and questions*): **no I haven't!/yes we have!** mais non!/mais si!; **so I have!** ah oui!, oui c'est vrai!; **I've been there before, have you?** j'y suis déjà allé, et vous?

▶ MODAL AUX VB (*be obliged*): **to have (got) to do sth** devoir faire qch, être obligé(e) de faire qch; **she has (got) to do it** elle doit le faire, il faut qu'elle le fasse; **you haven't to tell her** vous n'êtes pas obligé de le lui dire; (*must not*) ne le lui dites surtout pas; **do you have to book?** il faut réserver?

▶ VT **1** (*possess*) avoir; **he has (got) blue eyes/dark hair** il a les yeux bleus/les cheveux bruns

2 (*referring to meals etc*): **to have breakfast** prendre le petit déjeuner; **to have dinner/lunch** dîner/déjeuner; **to have a drink** prendre un verre; **to have a cigarette** fumer une cigarette

3 (*receive*) avoir, recevoir; (*obtain*) avoir; **may I have your address?** puis-je avoir votre adresse?; **you can have it for £5** vous pouvez l'avoir pour 5 livres; **I must have it for tomorrow** il me le faut pour demain; **to have a baby** avoir un bébé

4 (*maintain, allow*): **I won't have it!** ça ne se passera pas comme ça!; **we can't have that** nous ne tolérerons pas ça

5 (*by sb else*): **to have sth done** faire faire qch; **to have one's hair cut** se faire couper les cheveux; **to have sb do sth** faire faire qch à qn

6 (*experience, suffer*) avoir; **to have a cold/flu** avoir un rhume/la grippe; **to have an operation** se faire opérer; **she had her bag stolen** elle s'est fait voler son sac

7 (*+noun*): **to have a swim/walk** nager/se promener; **to have a bath/shower** prendre un bain/une douche; **let's have a look** regardons; **to have a meeting** se réunir; **to have a party** organiser une fête; **let me have a try** laissez-moi essayer

8 (*inf: dupe*) avoir; **he's been had** il s'est fait avoir *or* rouler

▶ **have out** VT: **to have it out with sb** (*settle a problem etc*) s'expliquer (franchement) avec qn

haven ['heɪvn] N port *m*; (*fig*) havre *m*
haven't ['hævnt] = **have not**
haversack ['hævəsæk] N sac *m* à dos
haves [hævz] NPL (*inf*): **the ~ and have-nots** les riches et les pauvres
havoc ['hævək] N ravages *mpl*, dégâts *mpl*; **to play ~ with** (*fig*) désorganiser complètement; détraquer
Hawaii [hə'waɪɪ] N (îles *fpl*) Hawaï *m*
Hawaiian [hə'waɪən] ADJ hawaïen(ne) ▶ N Hawaïen(ne); (*Ling*) hawaïen *m*
hawk [hɔːk] N faucon *m* ▶ VT (*goods for sale*) colporter
hawker ['hɔːkər] N colporteur *m*
hawkish ['hɔːkɪʃ] ADJ belliciste
hawthorn ['hɔːθɔːn] N aubépine *f*
hay [heɪ] N foin *m*
hay fever N rhume *m* des foins
haystack ['heɪstæk] N meule *f* de foin
haywire ['heɪwaɪər] ADJ (*inf*): **to go ~** perdre la tête; mal tourner
hazard ['hæzəd] N (*risk*) danger *m*, risque *m*; (*chance*) hasard *m*, chance *f* ▶ VT risquer, hasarder; **to be a health/fire ~** présenter un risque pour la santé/d'incendie; **to ~ a guess** émettre *or* hasarder une hypothèse
hazardous ['hæzədəs] ADJ hasardeux(-euse), risqué(e)
hazard pay N (*US*) prime *f* de risque
hazard warning lights NPL (*Aut*) feux *mpl* de détresse
haze [heɪz] N brume *f*

h

hazel ['heɪzl] N (*tree*) noisetier *m* ▸ ADJ (*eyes*) noisette *inv*

hazelnut ['heɪzlnʌt] N noisette *f*

hazy ['heɪzɪ] ADJ brumeux(-euse); (*idea*) vague; (*photograph*) flou(e)

H-bomb ['eɪtʃbɔm] N bombe *f* H

HD ABBR (= *high definition*) HD (= *haute définition*)

HDTV N ABBR (= *high definition television*) TVHD *f* (= *télévision haute-définition*)

HE ABBR = **high explosive**; (*Rel, Diplomacy*) = **His Excellency; Her Excellency**

he [hi:] PRON il; **it is he who ...** c'est lui qui ...; **here he is** le voici; **he-bear** *etc* ours *etc* mâle

head [hɛd] N tête *f*; (*leader*) chef *m*; (*of school*) directeur(-trice); (*of secondary school*) proviseur *m* ▸ VT (*list*) être en tête de; (*group, company*) être à la tête de; **heads** NPL (*on coin*) (le côté) face; **heads or tails** pile ou face; **~ first** la tête la première; **~ over heels in love** follement *or* éperdument amoureux(-euse); **to ~ the ball** faire une tête; **10 euros a** *or* **per ~** 10 euros par personne; **to sit at the ~ of the table** présider la tablée; **to have a ~ for business** avoir des dispositions pour les affaires; **to have no ~ for heights** être sujet(te) au vertige; **to come to a ~** (*fig: situation etc*) devenir critique
▸ **head for** VT FUS se diriger vers; (*disaster*) aller à
▸ **head off** VT (*threat, danger*) détourner

headache ['hɛdeɪk] N mal *m* de tête; **to have a ~** avoir mal à la tête

headband ['hɛdbænd] N bandeau *m*

headboard ['hɛdbɔ:d] N dosseret *m*

head cold N rhume *m* de cerveau

headdress ['hɛddrɛs] N coiffure *f*

headed notepaper ['hɛdɪd-] N papier *m* à lettres à en-tête

header ['hɛdəʳ] N (*Football*) (coup *m* de) tête *f*; (*inf: fall*) chute *f* (*or* plongeon *m*) la tête la première

head-first ['hɛd'fə:st] ADV (*lit*) la tête la première

headhunt ['hɛdhʌnt] VT: **she was headhunted** elle a été recrutée par un chasseur de têtes

headhunter ['hɛdhʌntəʳ] N chasseur *m* de têtes

heading ['hɛdɪŋ] N titre *m*; (*subject title*) rubrique *f*

headlamp ['hɛdlæmp] (*BRIT*) N = **headlight**

headland ['hɛdlənd] N promontoire *m*, cap *m*

headlight ['hɛdlaɪt] N phare *m*

headline ['hɛdlaɪn] N titre *m*

headlong ['hɛdlɔŋ] ADV (*fall*) la tête la première; (*rush*) tête baissée

headmaster [hɛd'mɑːstəʳ] N directeur *m*, proviseur *m*

headmistress [hɛd'mɪstrɪs] N directrice *f*

head office N siège *m*, bureau *m* central

head-on [hɛd'ɔn] ADJ (*collision*) de plein fouet

headphones ['hɛdfəunz] NPL casque *m* (à écouteurs)

headquarters ['hɛdkwɔ:təz] NPL (*of business*) bureau *or* siège central; (*Mil*) quartier général

headrest ['hɛdrɛst] N appui-tête *m*

headroom ['hɛdrum] N (*in car*) hauteur *f* de plafond; (*under bridge*) hauteur limite; dégagement *m*

headscarf ['hɛdskɑːf] (*pl* **headscarves** [-skɑːvz]) N foulard *m*

headset ['hɛdsɛt] N = **headphones**

headstone ['hɛdstəun] N pierre tombale

headstrong ['hɛdstrɔŋ] ADJ têtu(e), entêté(e)

headteacher [hɛd'tiːtʃəʳ] N directeur(-trice); (*of secondary school*) proviseur *m*

head waiter N maître *m* d'hôtel

headway ['hɛdweɪ] N: **to make ~** avancer, faire des progrès

headwind ['hɛdwɪnd] N vent *m* contraire

heady ['hɛdɪ] ADJ capiteux(-euse), enivrant(e)

heal [hi:l] VT, VI guérir

health [hɛlθ] N santé *f*; **Department of H~** (*BRIT, US*) ≈ ministère *m* de la Santé

health care N services médicaux

health centre N (*BRIT*) centre *m* de santé

health food N aliment(s) naturel(s)

health food shop N magasin *m* diététique

health hazard N risque *m* pour la santé

Health Service N: **the ~** (*BRIT*) ≈ la Sécurité Sociale

healthy ['hɛlθɪ] ADJ (*person*) en bonne santé; (*climate, food, attitude etc*) sain(e)

heap [hi:p] N tas *m*, monceau *m* ▸ VT (*also:* **heap up**) entasser, amonceler; **she heaped her plate with cakes** elle a chargé son assiette de gâteaux; **heaps (of)** (*inf: lots*) des tas (de); **to ~ favours/praise/gifts** *etc* **on sb** combler qn de faveurs/d'éloges/de cadeaux *etc*

hear [hɪəʳ] (*pt, pp* **heard** [hə:d]) VT entendre; (*news*) apprendre; (*lecture*) assister à, écouter
▸ VI entendre; **to ~ about** entendre parler de; (*have news of*) avoir des nouvelles de; **did you ~ about the move?** tu es au courant du déménagement?; **to ~ from sb** recevoir des nouvelles de qn; **I've never heard of that book** je n'ai jamais entendu parler de ce livre
▸ **hear out** VT écouter jusqu'au bout

heard [hə:d] PT, PP *of* **hear**

hearing ['hɪərɪŋ] N (*sense*) ouïe *f*; (*of witnesses*) audition *f*; (*of a case*) audience *f*; (*of committee*) séance *f*; **to give sb a ~** (*BRIT*) écouter ce que qn a à dire

hearing aid N appareil *m* acoustique

hearsay ['hɪəseɪ] N on-dit *mpl*, rumeurs *fpl*; **by ~** *adv* par ouï-dire

hearse [hə:s] N corbillard *m*

heart [hɑːt] N cœur *m*; **hearts** NPL (*Cards*) cœur; **at ~** au fond; **by ~** (*learn, know*) par cœur; **to have a weak ~** avoir le cœur malade, avoir des problèmes de cœur; **to lose/take ~** perdre/ prendre courage; **to set one's ~ on sth/on doing sth** vouloir absolument qch/faire qch; **the ~ of the matter** le fond du problème

heartache ['hɑːteɪk] N chagrin *m*, douleur *f*

heart attack N crise *f* cardiaque

heartbeat ['hɑːtbiːt] N battement *m* de cœur

heartbreak ['hɑːtbreɪk] N immense chagrin *m*

heartbreaking ['hɑːtbreɪkɪŋ] ADJ navrant(e), déchirant(e)

heartbroken ['hɑːtbrəukən] ADJ: **to be ~** avoir beaucoup de chagrin

heartburn ['hɑːtbə:n] N brûlures *fpl* d'estomac

heart disease N maladie f cardiaque

-hearted ['hɑ:tɪd] SUFFIX: **kind~**
généreux(-euse), qui a bon cœur

heartening ['hɑ:tnɪŋ] ADJ encourageant(e),
réconfortant(e)

heart failure N (Med) arrêt m du cœur

heartfelt ['hɑ:tfɛlt] ADJ sincère

hearth [hɑ:θ] N foyer m, cheminée f

heartily ['hɑ:tɪlɪ] ADV chaleureusement; (laugh)
de bon cœur; (eat) de bon appétit; **to agree ~**
être entièrement d'accord; **to be ~ sick of**
(BRIT) en avoir ras le bol de

heartland ['hɑ:tlænd] N centre m, cœur m;
France's heartlands la France profonde

heartless ['hɑ:tlɪs] ADJ (person) sans cœur,
insensible; (treatment) cruel(le)

heartstrings ['hɑ:tstrɪŋz] NPL: **to tug (at) sb's
~** toucher or faire vibrer les cordes sensibles de
qn

heartthrob ['hɑ:tθrɔb] N idole f

heart-to-heart ['hɑ:t'tə'hɑ:t] ADJ, ADV à cœur
ouvert

heart transplant N greffe f du cœur

heartwarming ['hɑ:twɔ:mɪŋ] ADJ
réconfortant(e)

hearty ['hɑ:tɪ] ADJ chaleureux(-euse); (appetite)
solide; (dislike) cordial(e); (meal) copieux(-euse)

heat [hi:t] N chaleur f; (fig) ardeur f; feu m;
(Sport: also: **qualifying heat**) éliminatoire f ▶ VT
chauffer
▶ **heat up** VI (liquid) chauffer; (room) se
réchauffer ▶ VT réchauffer

heated ['hi:tɪd] ADJ chauffé(e); (fig)
passionné(e), échauffé(e), excité(e)

heater ['hi:tər] N appareil m de chauffage;
radiateur m; (in car) chauffage m; (water heater)
chauffe-eau m

heath [hi:θ] N (BRIT) lande f

heathen ['hi:ðn] ADJ, N païen(ne)

heather ['hɛðər] N bruyère f

heating ['hi:tɪŋ] N chauffage m

heat-resistant ['hi:trɪzɪstənt] ADJ résistant(e) à
la chaleur

heat-seeking ['hi:tsi:kɪŋ] ADJ guidé(e) par
infrarouge

heatstroke ['hi:tstrəuk] N coup m de chaleur

heatwave ['hi:tweɪv] N vague f de chaleur

heave [hi:v] VT soulever (avec effort) ▶ VI se
soulever; (retch) avoir des haut-le-cœur ▶ N
(push) poussée f; **to ~ a sigh** pousser un gros
soupir

heaven ['hɛvn] N ciel m, paradis m; (fig) paradis;
~ forbid! surtout pas!; **thank ~!** Dieu merci!;
for ~'s sake! (pleading) je vous en prie!;
(protesting) mince alors!

heavenly ['hɛvnlɪ] ADJ céleste, divin(e)

heavily ['hɛvɪlɪ] ADV lourdement; (drink, smoke)
beaucoup; (sleep, sigh) profondément

heavy ['hɛvɪ] ADJ lourd(e); (work, rain, user, eater)
gros(se); (drinker, smoker) grand(e); (schedule,
week) chargé(e); **it's too ~** c'est trop lourd; **it's ~
going** ça ne va pas tout seul, c'est pénible

heavy cream N (US) crème fraîche épaisse

heavy-duty ['hɛvɪ'dju:tɪ] ADJ à usage intensif

heavy goods vehicle N (BRIT) poids lourd m

heavy-handed ['hɛvɪ'hændɪd] ADJ (fig)
maladroit(e), qui manque de tact

heavy metal N (Mus) heavy metal m

heavy-set ['hɛvɪ'sɛt] ADJ (esp US) costaud(e)

heavyweight ['hɛvɪweɪt] N (Sport) poids lourd

Hebrew ['hi:bru:] ADJ hébraïque ▶ N (Ling)
hébreu m

Hebrides ['hɛbrɪdi:z] NPL: **the ~** les Hébrides fpl

heck [hɛk] N (inf): **why the ~ …?** pourquoi diable
…?; **a ~ of a lot** une sacrée quantité; **he has
done a ~ of a lot for us** il a vraiment beaucoup
fait pour nous

heckle ['hɛkl] VT interpeller (un orateur)

heckler ['hɛklər] N interrupteur m; élément
perturbateur

hectare ['hɛktɑ:r] N (BRIT) hectare m

hectic ['hɛktɪk] ADJ (schedule) très chargé(e);
(day) mouvementé(e); (activity) fiévreux(-euse);
(lifestyle) trépidant(e)

he'd [hi:d] = **he would**; **he had**

hedge [hɛdʒ] N haie f ▶ VI se dérober ▶ VT: **to ~
one's bets** (fig) se couvrir; **as a ~ against
inflation** pour se prémunir contre l'inflation
▶ **hedge in** VT entourer d'une haie

hedgehog ['hɛdʒhɔg] N hérisson m

hedgerow ['hɛdʒrəu] N haie(s) f(pl)

hedonism ['hi:dənɪzəm] N hédonisme m

heed [hi:d] VT (also: **take heed of**) tenir compte
de, prendre garde à

heedless ['hi:dlɪs] ADJ insouciant(e)

heel [hi:l] N talon m ▶ VT (shoe) retalonner; **to
bring to ~** (dog) faire venir à ses pieds; (fig:
person) rappeler à l'ordre; **to take to one's
heels** prendre ses jambes à son cou

hefty ['hɛftɪ] ADJ (person) costaud(e); (parcel)
lourd(e); (piece, price) gros(se)

heifer ['hɛfər] N génisse f

height [haɪt] N (of person) taille f, grandeur f; (of
object) hauteur f; (of plane, mountain) altitude f;
(high ground) hauteur, éminence f; (fig: of glory,
fame, power) sommet m; (: of luxury, stupidity)
comble m; **at the ~ of summer** au cœur de
l'été; **what ~ are you?** combien mesurez-vous?,
quelle est votre taille?; **of average ~** de taille
moyenne; **to be afraid of heights** être
sujet(te) au vertige; **it's the ~ of fashion** c'est
le dernier cri

heighten ['haɪtn] VT hausser, surélever; (fig)
augmenter

heinous ['heɪnəs] ADJ odieux(-euse), atroce

heir [ɛər] N héritier m

heir apparent N héritier présomptif

heiress ['ɛərɛs] N héritière f

heirloom ['ɛəlu:m] N meuble m (or bijou m or
tableau m) de famille

heist [haɪst] N (US inf: hold-up) casse m

held [hɛld] PT, PP of **hold**

helicopter ['hɛlɪkɔptər] N hélicoptère m

heliport ['hɛlɪpɔ:t] N (Aviat) héliport m

helium ['hi:lɪəm] N hélium m

hell [hɛl] N enfer m; **a ~ of a …** (inf) un(e)
sacré(e) …; **oh ~!** (inf) merde!

he'll [hi:l] = **he will**; **he shall**

617

hell-bent [hɛl'bɛnt] ADJ (*inf*): **to be ~ on doing sth** vouloir à tout prix faire qch

hellish ['hɛlɪʃ] ADJ infernal(e)

hello [hə'ləu] EXCL bonjour!; (*to attract attention*) hé!; (*surprise*) tiens!

helm [hɛlm] N (*Naut*) barre f

helmet ['hɛlmɪt] N casque m

helmsman ['hɛlmzmən] N (*irreg*) timonier m

help [hɛlp] N aide f; (*cleaner etc*) femme f de ménage; (*assistant etc*) employé(e) ▶ VT, VI aider; ~! au secours!; ~ **yourself** servez-vous; **can you ~ me?** pouvez-vous m'aider?; **can I ~ you?** (*in shop*) vous désirez?; **with the ~ of** (*person*) avec l'aide de; (*tool etc*) à l'aide de; **to be of ~ to sb** être utile à qn; **to ~ sb (to) do sth** aider qn à faire qch; **I can't ~ saying** je ne peux pas m'empêcher de dire; **he can't ~ it** il n'y peut rien

▶ **help out** VI aider ▶ VT: **to ~ sb out** aider qn

help desk N (*esp Comput*) centre m d'assistance

helper ['hɛlpə'] N aide mf, assistant(e)

helpful ['hɛlpful] ADJ serviable, obligeant(e); (*useful*) utile

helping ['hɛlpɪŋ] N portion f

helping hand N coup m de main; **to give sb a ~** prêter main-forte à qn

helpless ['hɛlplɪs] ADJ impuissant(e); (*baby*) sans défense

helplessly ['hɛlplɪslɪ] ADV (*watch*) sans pouvoir rien faire

helpline ['hɛlplaɪn] N service m d'assistance téléphonique; (*free*) ≈ numéro vert

Helsinki ['hɛlsɪŋkɪ] N Helsinki

helter-skelter ['hɛltə'skɛltə'] N (BRIT: *at amusement park*) toboggan m

hem [hɛm] N ourlet m ▶ VT ourler

▶ **hem in** VT cerner; **to feel hemmed in** (*fig*) avoir l'impression d'étouffer, se sentir oppressé(e) or écrasé(e)

he-man ['hi:mæn] N (*irreg*) (*inf*) macho m

hematology ['hi:mə'tɔlədʒɪ] N (US) = **haematology**

hemisphere ['hɛmɪsfɪə'] N hémisphère m

hemlock ['hɛmlɔk] N ciguë f

hemoglobin ['hi:mə'gləubɪn] N (US) = **haemoglobin**

hemophilia ['hi:mə'fɪlɪə] N (US) = **haemophilia**

hemorrhage ['hɛmərɪdʒ] N (US) = **haemorrhage**

hemorrhoids ['hɛmərɔɪdz] NPL (US) = **haemorrhoids**

hemp [hɛmp] N chanvre m

hen [hɛn] N poule f; (*female bird*) femelle f

hence [hɛns] ADV (*therefore*) d'où, de là; **2 years ~** d'ici 2 ans

henceforth [hɛns'fɔ:θ] ADV dorénavant

henchman ['hɛntʃmən] N (*irreg*) (*pej*) acolyte m, séide m

henna ['hɛnə] N henné m

hen night, hen party N soirée f entre filles (*avant le mariage de l'une d'elles*)

henpecked ['hɛnpɛkt] ADJ dominé par sa femme

hepatitis [hɛpə'taɪtɪs] N hépatite f

her [hə:'] PRON (*direct*) la, l' + *vowel or h mute*; (*indirect*) lui; (*stressed, after prep*) elle ▶ ADJ son (sa), ses pl; **I see ~** je la vois; **give ~ a book** donne-lui un livre; **after ~** après elle; *see also* **me; my**

herald ['hɛrəld] N héraut m ▶ VT annoncer

heraldic [hɛ'rældɪk] ADJ héraldique

heraldry ['hɛrəldrɪ] N héraldique f; (*coat of arms*) blason m

herb [hə:b] N herbe f; **herbs** NPL fines herbes

herbaceous [hə:'beɪʃəs] ADJ herbacé(e)

herbal ['hə:bl] ADJ à base de plantes

herbal tea N tisane f

herbicide ['hə:bɪsaɪd] N herbicide m

herd [hə:d] N troupeau m; (*of wild animals, swine*) troupeau, troupe f ▶ VT (*drive: animals, people*) mener, conduire; (*gather*) rassembler; **herded together** parqués (comme du bétail)

here [hɪə'] ADV ici; (*time*) alors ▶ EXCL tiens!, tenez!; ~! (*present*) présent!; ~ **is**, ~ **are** voici; ~**'s my sister** voici ma sœur; ~ **he/she is** le (la) voici; ~ **she comes** la voici qui vient; **come ~!** viens ici!; ~ **and there** ici et là

hereabouts ['hɪərə'bauts] ADV par ici, dans les parages

hereafter [hɪər'ɑ:ftə'] ADV après, plus tard; ci-après ▶ N: **the ~** l'au-delà m

hereby [hɪə'baɪ] ADV (*in letter*) par la présente

hereditary [hɪ'rɛdɪtrɪ] ADJ héréditaire

heredity [hɪ'rɛdɪtɪ] N hérédité f

heresy ['hɛrəsɪ] N hérésie f

heretic ['hɛrətɪk] N hérétique mf

heretical [hɪ'rɛtɪkl] ADJ hérétique

herewith [hɪə'wɪð] ADV avec ceci, ci-joint

heritage ['hɛrɪtɪdʒ] N héritage m, patrimoine m; **our national ~** notre patrimoine national

hermetically [hə:'mɛtɪklɪ] ADV hermétique

hermit ['hə:mɪt] N ermite m

hernia ['hə:nɪə] N hernie f

hero ['hɪərəu] (*pl* **heroes**) N héros m

heroic [hɪ'rəuɪk] ADJ héroïque

heroin ['hɛrəuɪn] N héroïne f (*drogue*)

heroin addict N héroïnomane mf

heroine ['hɛrəuɪn] N héroïne f (*femme*)

heroism ['hɛrəuɪzəm] N héroïsme m

heron ['hɛrən] N héron m

hero worship N culte m (du héros)

herring ['hɛrɪŋ] N hareng m

hers [hə:z] PRON le (la) sien(ne), les siens (siennes); **a friend of ~** un(e) ami(e) à elle, un(e) de ses ami(e)s; *see also* **mine¹**

herself [hə:'sɛlf] PRON (*reflexive*) se; (*emphatic*) elle-même; (*after prep*) elle; *see also* **oneself**

Herts [hɑ:ts] ABBR (BRIT) = **Hertfordshire**

he's [hi:z] = **he is; he has**

hesitant ['hɛzɪtənt] ADJ hésitant(e), indécis(e); **to be ~ about doing sth** hésiter à faire qch

hesitate ['hɛzɪteɪt] VI: **to ~ (about/to do)** hésiter (sur/à faire)

hesitation [hɛzɪ'teɪʃən] N hésitation f; **I have no ~ in saying (that)** ... je n'hésiterais pas à dire (que) ...

hessian ['hɛsɪən] N (toile f de) jute m

heterogeneous ['hɛtərə'dʒi:nɪəs] ADJ hétérogène

heterosexual ['hɛtərəu'sɛksjuəl] ADJ, N hétérosexuel(le)

het up [hɛt'ʌp] ADJ (inf) agité(e), excité(e)

HEW N ABBR (US: = Department of Health, Education and Welfare) ministère de la santé publique, de l'enseignement et du bien-être

hew [hjuː] VT tailler (à la hache)

hex [hɛks] (US) N sort m ▶ VT jeter un sort sur

hexagon ['hɛksəgən] N hexagone m

hexagonal [hɛk'sægənl] ADJ hexagonal(e)

hey [heɪ] EXCL hé!

heyday ['heɪdeɪ] N: **the ~ of** l'âge m d'or de, les beaux jours de

HF N ABBR (= high frequency) HF f

HGV N ABBR = **heavy goods vehicle**

HI ABBR (US) = **Hawaii**

hi [haɪ] EXCL salut!; (to attract attention) hé!

hiatus [haɪ'eɪtəs] N trou m, lacune f; (Ling) hiatus m

hibernate ['haɪbəneɪt] VI hiberner

hibernation [haɪbə'neɪʃən] N hibernation f

hiccough, hiccup ['hɪkʌp] VI hoqueter ▶ N hoquet m; **to have (the) hiccoughs** avoir le hoquet

hick [hɪk] N (US inf) plouc m, péquenaud(e)

hid [hɪd] PT of **hide**

hidden ['hɪdn] PP of **hide** ▶ ADJ: **there are no ~ extras** absolument tout est compris dans le prix; **~ agenda** intentions non déclarées

hide [haɪd] (pt **hid** [hɪd], pp **hidden** ['hɪdn]) N (skin) peau f ▶ VT cacher; (feelings, truth) dissimuler; **to ~ sth from sb** cacher qch à qn ▶ VI: **to ~ (from sb)** se cacher (de qn)

hide-and-seek ['haɪdən'siːk] N cache-cache m

hideaway ['haɪdəweɪ] N cachette f

hideous ['hɪdɪəs] ADJ hideux(-euse), atroce

hide-out ['haɪdaut] N cachette f

hiding ['haɪdɪŋ] N (beating) correction f, volée f de coups; **to be in ~** (concealed) se tenir caché(e)

hiding place N cachette f

hierarchy ['haɪərɑːkɪ] N hiérarchie f

hieroglyphic [haɪərə'glɪfɪk] ADJ hiéroglyphique; **hieroglyphics** NPL hiéroglyphes mpl

hi-fi ['haɪfaɪ] ADJ, N ABBR (= high fidelity) hi-fi f inv

higgledy-piggledy ['hɪgldɪ'pɪgldɪ] ADV pêle-mêle, dans le plus grand désordre

high [haɪ] ADJ haut(e); (speed, respect, number) grand(e); (price) élevé(e); (wind) fort(e), violent(e); (voice) aigu(ë); (inf: person: on drugs) défoncé(e), fait(e); (: on drink) soûl(e), bourré(e); (BRIT Culin: meat, game) faisandé(e); (: spoilt) avarié(e) ▶ ADV haut, en haut ▶ N (weather) zone f de haute pression; **exports have reached a new ~** les exportations ont atteint un nouveau record; **20 m ~** haut(e) de 20 m; **to pay a ~ price for sth** payer cher pour qch; **~ in the air** haut dans le ciel

highball ['haɪbɔːl] N (US) whisky m à l'eau avec des glaçons

highboy ['haɪbɔɪ] N (US) grande commode

highbrow ['haɪbrau] ADJ, N intellectuel(le)

highchair ['haɪtʃɛəʳ] N (child's) chaise haute

high-class ['haɪ'klɑːs] ADJ (neighbourhood, hotel) chic inv, de grand standing; (performance etc) de haut niveau

High Court N (Law) cour f suprême; voir article

 Dans le système juridique anglais et gallois, la High Court est une cour de droit civil chargée des affaires plus importantes et complexes que celles traitées par les county courts. En Écosse en revanche, la High Court (of Justiciary) est la plus haute cour de justice à laquelle les affaires les plus graves telles que le meurtre et le viol sont soumises et où elles sont jugées devant un jury.

higher ['haɪəʳ] ADJ (form of life, study etc) supérieur(e) ▶ ADV plus haut

higher education N études supérieures

highfalutin [haɪfə'luːtɪn] ADJ (inf) affecté(e)

high finance N la haute finance

high-flier, high-flyer [haɪ'flaɪəʳ] N (ambitious) ambitieux(-euse); (gifted) personne particulièrement douée et promise à un avenir brillant

high-flying [haɪ'flaɪɪŋ] ADJ (fig) ambitieux(-euse), de haut niveau

high-handed [haɪ'hændɪd] ADJ très autoritaire; très cavalier(-ière)

high-heeled [haɪ'hiːld] ADJ à hauts talons

high heels NPL talons hauts, hauts talons

high jump N (Sport) saut m en hauteur

highlands ['haɪləndz] NPL région montagneuse; **the H~** (in Scotland) les Highlands mpl

high-level ['haɪlɛvl] ADJ (talks etc) à un haut niveau; **~ language** (Comput) langage évolué

highlight ['haɪlaɪt] N (fig: of event) point culminant ▶ VT (emphasize) faire ressortir, souligner; **highlights** NPL (in hair) reflets mpl

highlighter ['haɪlaɪtəʳ] N (pen) surligneur (lumineux)

highly ['haɪlɪ] ADV extrêmement, très; (unlikely) fort; (recommended, skilled, qualified) hautement; **~ paid** très bien payé(e); **to speak ~ of** dire beaucoup de bien de

highly strung ADJ nerveux(-euse), toujours tendu(e)

High Mass N grand-messe f

highness ['haɪnɪs] N hauteur f; **His/Her H~** son Altesse f

high-pitched [haɪ'pɪtʃt] ADJ aigu(ë)

high point N: **the ~ (of)** le clou (de), le point culminant (de)

high-powered ['haɪ'pauəd] ADJ (engine) performant(e); (fig: person) dynamique; (: job, businessman) très important(e)

high-pressure ['haɪprɛʃəʳ] ADJ à haute pression

high-rise ['haɪraɪz] N (also: **high-rise block, high-rise building**) tour f (d'habitation)

high school N lycée m; (US) établissement m d'enseignement supérieur; voir article

 Une high school est un établissement d'enseignement secondaire. Aux États-Unis, il y a la Junior High School, qui correspond au collège, et la Senior High School, qui correspond au lycée. En Grande-Bretagne, c'est un nom que l'on donne parfois aux écoles secondaires; voir elementary school.

h

high season N (BRIT) haute saison

high spirits NPL pétulance f; **to be in ~** être plein(e) d'entrain

high street N (BRIT) grand-rue f

high-tech ['haɪ'tɛk] ADJ de pointe

highway ['haɪweɪ] N (BRIT) route f; (US) route nationale; **the information ~** l'autoroute f de l'information

Highway Code N (BRIT) code m de la route

highwayman ['haɪweɪmən] N (irreg) voleur m de grand chemin

hijack ['haɪdʒæk] VT détourner (par la force) ▸ N (also: **hijacking**) détournement m (d'avion)

hijacker ['haɪdʒækəʳ] N auteur m d'un détournement d'avion, pirate m de l'air

hike [haɪk] VI faire des excursions à pied ▸ N excursion f à pied, randonnée f; (inf: in prices etc) augmentation f ▸ VT (inf) augmenter

hiker ['haɪkəʳ] N promeneur(-euse), excursionniste mf

hiking ['haɪkɪŋ] N excursions fpl à pied, randonnée f

hilarious [hɪ'lɛərɪəs] ADJ (behaviour, event) désopilant(e)

hilarity [hɪ'lærɪtɪ] N hilarité f

hill [hɪl] N colline f; (fairly high) montagne f; (on road) côte f

hillbilly ['hɪlbɪlɪ] N (US) montagnard(e) du sud des USA; (pej) péquenaud m

hillock ['hɪlək] N petite colline, butte f

hillside ['hɪlsaɪd] N (flanc m de) coteau m

hill start N (Aut) démarrage m en côte

hill walking N randonnée f de basse montagne

hilly ['hɪlɪ] ADJ vallonné(e), montagneux(-euse); (road) à fortes côtes

hilt [hɪlt] N (of sword) garde f; **to the ~** (fig: support) à fond

him [hɪm] PRON (direct) le, l' + vowel or h mute; (stressed, indirect, after prep) lui; **I see ~** je le vois; **give ~ a book** donne-lui un livre; **after ~** après lui; see also **me**

Himalayas [hɪmə'leɪəz] NPL: **the ~** l'Himalaya m

himself [hɪm'sɛlf] PRON (reflexive) se; (emphatic) lui-même; (after prep) lui; see also **oneself**

hind [haɪnd] ADJ de derrière ▸ N biche f

hinder ['hɪndəʳ] VT gêner; (delay) retarder; (prevent): **to ~ sb from doing** empêcher qn de faire

hindquarters ['haɪnd'kwɔ:təz] NPL (Zool) arrière-train m

hindrance ['hɪndrəns] N gêne f, obstacle m

hindsight ['haɪndsaɪt] N bon sens après coup; **with (the benefit of) ~** avec du recul, rétrospectivement

Hindu ['hɪndu:] N Hindou(e)

Hinduism ['hɪnduɪzəm] N (Rel) hindouisme m

hinge [hɪndʒ] N charnière f ▸ VI (fig): **to ~ on** dépendre de

hint [hɪnt] N allusion f; (advice) conseil m; (clue) indication f ▸ VT: **to ~ that** insinuer que ▸ VI: **to ~ at** faire une allusion à; **to drop a ~** faire une allusion ou insinuation; **give me a ~** (clue) mettez-moi sur la voie, donnez-moi

une indication

hip [hɪp] N hanche f; (Bot) fruit m de l'églantier or du rosier

hip flask N flacon m (pour la poche)

hip hop N hip hop m

hippie, hippy ['hɪpɪ] N hippie mf

hippo ['hɪpəu] (pl **hippos**) N hippopotame m

hippopotamus [hɪpə'pɔtəməs] (pl **hippopotamuses** or **hippopotami** [hɪpə'pɔtəmaɪ]) N hippopotame m

hippy ['hɪpɪ] N = **hippie**

hire ['haɪəʳ] VT (BRIT: car, equipment) louer; (worker) embaucher, engager ▸ N location f; **for ~** à louer; (taxi) libre; **on ~** en location; **I'd like to ~ a car** je voudrais louer une voiture ▸ **hire out** VT louer

hire car, hired car ['haɪəd-] N (BRIT) voiture f de location

hire purchase N (BRIT) achat m (or vente f) à tempérament or crédit; **to buy sth on ~** acheter qch en location-vente

his [hɪz] PRON le (la) sien(ne), les siens (siennes) ▸ ADJ son (sa), ses pl; **this is ~** c'est à lui, c'est le sien; **a friend of ~** un(e) de ses ami(e)s, un(e) ami(e) à lui; see also **mine**[1]; **my**

Hispanic [hɪs'pænɪk] ADJ (in US) hispano-américain(e) ▸ N Hispano-Américain(e)

hiss [hɪs] VI siffler ▸ N sifflement m

histogram ['hɪstəgræm] N histogramme m

historian [hɪ'stɔ:rɪən] N historien(ne)

historic [hɪ'stɔrɪk], **historical** [hɪ'stɔrɪkl] ADJ historique

history ['hɪstərɪ] N histoire f; **medical ~** (of patient) passé médical

histrionics [hɪstrɪ'ɔnɪks] N gestes mpl dramatiques, cinéma m (fig)

hit [hɪt] (pt, pp **~**) VT frapper; (knock against) cogner; (reach: target) atteindre, toucher; (collide with: car) entrer en collision avec, heurter; (fig: affect) toucher; (find) tomber sur ▸ N coup m; (success) coup réussi, succès m; (song) chanson f à succès, tube m; (to website) visite f; (on search engine) résultat m de recherche; **to ~ it off with sb** bien s'entendre avec qn; **to ~ the headlines** être à la une des journaux; **to ~ the road** (inf) se mettre en route

▸ **hit back** VI: **to ~ back at sb** prendre sa revanche sur qn

▸ **hit on** VT FUS (answer) trouver (par hasard); (solution) tomber sur (par hasard)

▸ **hit out at** VT FUS envoyer un coup à; (fig) attaquer

▸ **hit upon** VT FUS = **hit on**

hit-and-miss ['hɪtænd'mɪs] ADJ au petit bonheur (la chance)

hit-and-run driver ['hɪtænd'rʌn-] N chauffard m

hitch [hɪtʃ] VT (fasten) accrocher, attacher; (also: **hitch up**) remonter d'une saccade ▸ VI faire de l'autostop ▸ N (knot) nœud m; (difficulty) anicroche f, contretemps m; **to ~ a lift** faire du stop; **technical ~** incident m technique

▸ **hitch up** VT (horse, cart) atteler; see also **hitch**

hitch-hike ['hɪtʃhaɪk] VI faire de l'auto-stop

hitch-hiker ['hɪtʃhaɪkəʳ] N auto-stoppeur(-euse)
hitch-hiking ['hɪtʃhaɪkɪŋ] N auto-stop m, stop m
(inf)
hi-tech ['haɪ'tɛk] ADJ de pointe ▸ N high-tech m
hitherto [hɪðə'tuː] ADV jusqu'ici, jusqu'à
présent
hit list N liste noire
hitman ['hɪtmæn] N (irreg) (inf) tueur m à gages
hit-or-miss ['hɪtə'mɪs] ADJ au petit bonheur (la
chance); **it's ~ whether ...** il est loin d'être
certain que ... +sub
hit parade N hit parade m
HIV N ABBR (= human immunodeficiency virus) HIV m,
VIH m; **~-negative** séronégatif(-ive);
~-positive séropositif(-ive)
hive [haɪv] N ruche f; **the shop was a ~ of
activity** (fig) le magasin était une véritable
ruche
 ▸ **hive off** VT (inf) mettre à part, séparer
hl ABBR (= hectolitre) hl
HM ABBR (= His (or) Her Majesty) SM
HMG ABBR (BRIT) = **Her Majesty's Government**;
His Majesty's Government
HMI N ABBR (BRIT Scol) = **His Majesty's Inspector**;
Her Majesty's Inspector
HMO N ABBR (US: = health maintenance organization)
organisme médical assurant un forfait entretien de
santé
HMS ABBR (BRIT) = **His Majesty's Ship**; **Her
Majesty's Ship**
HMSO N ABBR (BRIT: = His (or) Her Majesty's
Stationery Office) ≈ Imprimerie nationale
HNC N ABBR (BRIT: = Higher National Certificate)
≈ DUT m
HND N ABBR (BRIT: = Higher National Diploma)
≈ licence f de sciences et techniques
hoard [hɔːd] N (of food) provisions fpl, réserves
fpl; (of money) trésor m ▸ VT amasser
hoarding ['hɔːdɪŋ] N (BRIT) panneau m
d'affichage or publicitaire
hoarfrost ['hɔːfrɒst] N givre m
hoarse [hɔːs] ADJ enroué(e)
hoax [həuks] N canular m
hob [hɒb] N plaque chauffante
hobble ['hɒbl] VI boitiller
hobby ['hɒbɪ] N passe-temps favori
hobby-horse ['hɒbɪhɔːs] N cheval m à bascule;
(fig) dada m
hobnob ['hɒbnɒb] VI: **to ~ with** frayer avec,
fréquenter
hobo ['həubəu] N (US) vagabond m
hock [hɒk] N (BRIT: wine) vin m du Rhin; (of
animal: Culin) jarret m
hockey ['hɒkɪ] N hockey m
hockey stick N crosse f de hockey
hocus-pocus ['həukəs'pəukəs] N (trickery)
supercherie f; (words: of magician) formules fpl
magiques; (: jargon) galimatias m
hod [hɒd] N oiseau m, hotte f
hodgepodge ['hɒdʒpɒdʒ] N = **hotchpotch**
hoe [həu] N houe f, binette f ▸ VT (ground) biner;
(plants etc) sarcler
hog [hɒg] N porc (châtré) ▸ VT (fig) accaparer; **to
go the whole ~** aller jusqu'au bout

Hogmanay [hɒgmə'neɪ] N réveillon m du jour
de l'An, Saint-Sylvestre f; voir article

La Saint-Sylvestre ou New Year's Eve se
nomme Hogmanay en Écosse. En cette
occasion, la famille et les amis se réunissent
pour entendre sonner les douze coups de
minuit et pour fêter le first-footing, une
coutume qui veut qu'on se rende chez ses
amis et voisins en apportant quelque chose
à boire (du whisky en général) et un
morceau de charbon en gage de prospérité
pour la nouvelle année.

hogwash ['hɒgwɒʃ] N (inf) foutaises fpl
hoist [hɔɪst] N palan m ▸ VT hisser
hoity-toity [hɔɪtɪ'tɔɪtɪ] ADJ (inf)
prétentieux(-euse), qui se donne
hold [həuld] (pt, pp held [hɛld]) VT tenir; (contain)
contenir; (meeting) tenir; (keep back) retenir;
(believe) maintenir, considérer; (possess) avoir,
détenir ▸ VI (withstand pressure) tenir (bon); (be
valid) valoir; (on telephone) attendre ▸ N prise f;
(find) influence f; (Naut) cale f; **to catch or get
(a) ~ of** saisir; **to get ~ of** (find) trouver; **to get ~
of o.s.** se contrôler; **~ the line!** (Tel) ne quittez
pas!; **to ~ one's own** (fig) (bien) se défendre; **to
~ office** (Pol) avoir un portefeuille; **to ~ firm** or
fast tenir bon; **he holds the view that ...** il
pense or estime que ..., d'après lui ...; **to ~ sb
responsible for sth** tenir qn pour responsable
de qch
 ▸ **hold back** VT retenir; (secret) cacher; **to ~ sb
back from doing sth** empêcher qn de faire qch
 ▸ **hold down** VT (person) maintenir à terre; (job)
occuper
 ▸ **hold forth** VI pérorer
 ▸ **hold off** VT tenir à distance ▸ VI: **if the rain
holds off** s'il ne pleut pas, s'il ne se met pas à
pleuvoir
 ▸ **hold on** VI tenir bon; (wait) attendre; **~ on!**
(Tel) ne quittez pas!; **to ~ on to sth** (grasp) se
cramponner à qch; (keep) conserver or garder
qch
 ▸ **hold out** VT offrir ▸ VI (resist): **to ~ out
(against)** résister (devant), tenir bon (devant)
 ▸ **hold over** VT (meeting etc) ajourner, reporter
 ▸ **hold up** VT (raise) lever; (support) soutenir;
(delay) retarder; (: traffic) ralentir; (rob) braquer
holdall ['həuldɔːl] N (BRIT) fourre-tout m inv
holder ['həuldəʳ] N (container) support m; (of
ticket, record) détenteur(-trice); (of office, title,
passport etc) titulaire mf
holding ['həuldɪŋ] N (share) intérêts mpl; (farm)
ferme f
holding company N holding m
hold-up ['həuldʌp] N (robbery) hold-up m; (delay)
retard m; (BRIT: in traffic) embouteillage m
hole [həul] N trou m ▸ VT trouer, faire un trou
dans; **~ in the heart** (Med) communication f
interventriculaire; **to pick holes (in)** (fig)
chercher des poux (dans)
 ▸ **hole up** VI se terrer
holiday ['hɒlədɪ] N (BRIT: vacation) vacances fpl;
(day off) jour m de congé; (public) jour férié; **to be
on ~** être en vacances; **I'm here on ~** je suis ici

h

en vacances; **tomorrow is a** ~ demain c'est fête, on a congé demain

holiday camp N (BRIT: *for children*) colonie f de vacances; (*also*: **holiday centre**) camp m de vacances

holiday home N (*rented*) location f de vacances; (*owned*) résidence f secondaire

holiday job N (BRIT) boulot m (*inf*) de vacances

holiday-maker ['hɔlədɪmeɪkəʳ] N (BRIT) vacancier(-ière)

holiday pay N paie f des vacances

holiday resort N centre m de villégiature *or* de vacances

holiday season N période f des vacances

holiness ['həʊlɪnɪs] N sainteté f

holistic [həʊ'lɪstɪk] ADJ holiste, holistique

Holland ['hɔlənd] N Hollande f

holler ['hɔləʳ] VI (*inf*) brailler

hollow ['hɔləʊ] ADJ creux(-euse); (*fig*) faux (fausse) ▶ N creux m; (*in land*) dépression f (de terrain), cuvette f ▶ VT: **to** ~ **out** creuser, évider

holly ['hɔlɪ] N houx m

hollyhock ['hɔlɪhɔk] N rose trémière

Hollywood ['hɔlɪwʊd] N Hollywood m

holocaust ['hɔləkɔːst] N holocauste m

hologram ['hɔləgræm] N hologramme m

hols [hɔlz] NPL (*inf*) vacances f pl

holster ['həʊlstəʳ] N étui m de revolver

holy ['həʊlɪ] ADJ saint(e); (*bread, water*) bénit(e); (*ground*) sacré(e)

Holy Communion N la (sainte) communion

Holy Ghost, Holy Spirit N Saint-Esprit m

Holy Land N: **the** ~ la Terre Sainte

holy orders NPL ordres (majeurs)

homage ['hɔmɪdʒ] N hommage m; **to pay** ~ **to** rendre hommage à

home [həʊm] N foyer m, maison f; (*country*) pays natal, patrie f; (*institution*) maison ▶ ADJ de famille; (*Econ, Pol*) national(e), intérieur(e); (*Sport: team*) qui reçoit; (: *match, win*) sur leur (*or* notre) terrain ▶ ADV chez soi, à la maison; au pays natal; (*right in: nail etc*) à fond; **at** ~ chez soi, à la maison; **to go** (*or* **come**) ~ rentrer (chez soi), rentrer à la maison (*or* au pays); **I'm going** ~ **on Tuesday** je rentre mardi; **make yourself at** ~ faites comme chez vous; **near my** ~ près de chez moi

▶ **home in on** VT FUS (*missile*) se diriger automatiquement vers *or* sur

home address N domicile permanent

home-brew [həʊm'bruː] N vin m (*or* bière f) maison

homecoming ['həʊmkʌmɪŋ] N retour m (au bercail)

home computer N ordinateur m domestique

Home Counties NPL *les comtés autour de Londres*

home economics N économie f domestique

home ground N: **to be on** ~ être sur son terrain

home-grown ['həʊmgrəʊn] ADJ (*not foreign*) du pays; (*from garden*) du jardin

home help N (BRIT) aide-ménagère f

homeland ['həʊmlænd] N patrie f

homeless ['həʊmlɪs] ADJ sans foyer, sans abri; **the homeless** NPL les sans-abri m pl

home loan N prêt m sur hypothèque

homely ['həʊmlɪ] ADJ (*plain*) simple, sans prétention; (*welcoming*) accueillant(e)

home-made [həʊm'meɪd] ADJ fait(e) à la maison

home match N match m à domicile

Home Office N (BRIT) ministère m de l'Intérieur

homeopathy *etc* [həʊmɪ'ɔpəθɪ] (US) N = **homoeopathy**

home owner ['həʊməʊnəʳ] N propriétaire occupant

home page N (*Comput*) page f d'accueil

home rule N autonomie f

Home Secretary N (BRIT) ministre m de l'Intérieur

homesick ['həʊmsɪk] ADJ: **to be** ~ avoir le mal du pays; (*missing one's family*) s'ennuyer de sa famille

homestead ['həʊmstɛd] N propriété f; (*farm*) ferme f

home town N ville natale

home truth N: **to tell sb a few home truths** dire ses quatre vérités à qn

homeward ['həʊmwəd] ADJ (*journey*) du retour ▶ ADV = **homewards**

homewards ['həʊmwədz] ADV vers la maison

homework ['həʊmwəːk] N devoirs m pl

homicidal [hɔmɪ'saɪdl] ADJ homicide

homicide ['hɔmɪsaɪd] N (US) homicide m

homily ['hɔmɪlɪ] N homélie f

homing ['həʊmɪŋ] ADJ (*device, missile*) à tête chercheuse; ~ **pigeon** pigeon voyageur

homoeopath, (US) **homeopath** ['həʊmɪəʊpæθ] N homéopathe m f

homoeopathic, (US) **homeopathic** [həʊmɪəʊ'pæθɪk] ADJ (*medicine*) homéopathique; (*doctor*) homéopathe

homoeopathy, (US) **homeopathy** [həʊmɪ'ɔpəθɪ] N homéopathie f

homogeneous [hɔməʊ'dʒiːnɪəs] ADJ homogène

homogenize [hə'mɔdʒənaɪz] VT homogénéiser

homosexual [hɔməʊ'sɛksjuəl] ADJ, N homosexuel(le)

Hon. ABBR (= *honourable, honorary*) *dans un titre*

Honduras [hɔn'djuərəs] N Honduras m

hone [həʊn] N pierre f à aiguiser ▶ VT affûter, aiguiser

honest ['ɔnɪst] ADJ honnête; (*sincere*) franc (franche); **to be quite** ~ **with you** ... à dire vrai ...

honestly ['ɔnɪstlɪ] ADV honnêtement; franchement

honesty ['ɔnɪstɪ] N honnêteté f

honey ['hʌnɪ] N miel m; (*inf: darling*) chéri(e)

honeycomb ['hʌnɪkəʊm] N rayon m de miel; (*pattern*) nid m d'abeilles, motif alvéolé ▶ VT (*fig*): **to** ~ **with** cribler de

honeymoon ['hʌnɪmuːn] N lune f de miel, voyage m de noces; **we're on** ~ nous sommes en voyage de noces

honeysuckle ['hʌnɪsʌkl] N chèvrefeuille m

Hong Kong ['hɔŋ'kɔŋ] N Hong Kong

honk [hɔŋk] N (*Aut*) coup m de klaxon ▶ VI klaxonner

Honolulu [hɒnə'lu:lu:] N Honolulu
honorary ['ɒnərərɪ] ADJ honoraire; (duty, title) honorifique; ~ **degree** diplôme m honoris causa
honour, (US) **honor** ['ɒnəʳ] VT honorer ▶ N honneur m; **in ~ of** en l'honneur de; **to graduate with honours** obtenir sa licence avec mention
honourable, (US) **honorable** ['ɒnərəbl] ADJ honorable
honour-bound, (US) **honor-bound** ['ɒnə'baund] ADJ: **to be ~ to do** se devoir de faire
honours degree ['ɒnəz-] N (Scol) ≈ licence f avec mention; voir article

> Un honours degree est un diplôme universitaire que l'on reçoit après trois années d'études en Angleterre et quatre années en Écosse. Les mentions qui l'accompagnent sont, par ordre décroissant: first class (très bien/bien), upper second class (assez bien), lower second class (passable), et third class (diplôme sans mention). Le titulaire d'un honours degree a un titre qu'il peut mettre à la suite de son nom, par exemple: Peter Jones BA Hons; voir ordinary degree.

honours list N (BRIT): **the ~** voir article

> L' honours list est la liste des citoyens du Royaume-Uni et du Commonwealth auxquels le souverain confère un titre ou une décoration. Cette liste est préparée par le Premier ministre et paraît deux fois par an, au Nouvel An et lors de l'anniversaire officiel du règne du souverain. Des personnes qui se sont distinguées dans le monde des affaires, des sports et des médias, ainsi que dans les forces armées, mais également des citoyens "ordinaires" qui se consacrent à des œuvres de charité sont ainsi récompensées.

Hons. ABBR (Scol) = **honours degree**
hood [hud] N capuchon m; (of cooker) hotte f; (BRIT Aut) capote f; (US Aut) capot m; (inf) truand m
hoodie ['hudɪ] N (top) sweat m à capuche; (youth) jeune m à capuche
hoodlum ['hu:dləm] N truand m
hoodwink ['hudwɪŋk] VT tromper
hoof [hu:f] (pl **hoofs** or **hooves** [hu:vz]) N sabot m
hook [huk] N crochet m; (on dress) agrafe f; (for fishing) hameçon m ▶ VT accrocher; (dress) agrafer; **off the ~** (Tel) décroché; **~ and eye** agrafe; **by ~ or by crook** de gré ou de force, coûte que coûte; **to be hooked (on)** (inf) être accroché(e) (par); (person) être dingue (de)
▶ **hook up** VT (Radio, TV etc) faire un duplex entre
hooligan ['hu:lɪɡən] N voyou m
hoop [hu:p] N cerceau m; (of barrel) cercle m
hoot [hu:t] VI (BRIT Aut) klaxonner; (siren) mugir; (owl) hululer ▶ VT (jeer at) huer ▶ N huée f; coup m de klaxon; mugissement m; hululement m; **to ~ with laughter** rire aux éclats
hooter ['hu:təʳ] N (BRIT Aut) klaxon m; (Naut, factory) sirène f

Hoover® ['hu:vəʳ] (BRIT) N aspirateur m ▶ VT: **to hoover** (room) passer l'aspirateur dans; (carpet) passer l'aspirateur sur
hooves [hu:vz] NPL of **hoof**
hop [hɒp] VI sauter; (on one foot) sauter à cloche-pied; (bird) sautiller ▶ N saut m
hope [həup] VT, VI espérer ▶ N espoir m; **I ~ so** je l'espère; **I ~ not** j'espère que non
hopeful ['həupful] ADJ (person) plein(e) d'espoir; (situation) prometteur(-euse), encourageant(e); **I'm ~ that she'll manage to come** j'ai bon espoir qu'elle pourra venir
hopefully ['həupfulɪ] ADV (expectantly) avec espoir, avec optimisme; (one hopes) avec un peu de chance; **~, they'll come back** espérons bien qu'ils reviendront
hopeless ['həuplɪs] ADJ désespéré(e), sans espoir; (useless) nul(le)
hopelessly ['həuplɪslɪ] ADV (live etc) sans espoir; **~ confused** etc complètement désorienté etc
hops [hɒps] NPL houblon m
horizon [hə'raɪzn] N horizon m
horizontal [hɒrɪ'zɒntl] ADJ horizontal(e)
hormone ['hɔ:məun] N hormone f
hormone replacement therapy N hormonothérapie substitutive, traitement hormono-supplétif
horn [hɔ:n] N corne f; (Mus) cor m; (Aut) klaxon m
horned [hɔ:nd] ADJ (animal) à cornes
hornet ['hɔ:nɪt] N frelon m
horny ['hɔ:nɪ] ADJ corné(e); (hands) calleux(-euse); (inf: aroused) excité(e)
horoscope ['hɒrəskəup] N horoscope m
horrendous [hə'rɛndəs] ADJ horrible, affreux(-euse)
horrible ['hɒrɪbl] ADJ horrible, affreux(-euse)
horrid ['hɒrɪd] ADJ (person) détestable; (weather, place, smell) épouvantable
horrific [hɒ'rɪfɪk] ADJ horrible
horrify ['hɒrɪfaɪ] VT horrifier
horrifying ['hɒrɪfaɪɪŋ] ADJ horrifiant(e)
horror ['hɒrəʳ] N horreur f
horror film N film m d'épouvante
horror-struck ['hɒrəstrʌk], **horror-stricken** ['hɒrəstrɪkn] ADJ horrifié(e)
hors d'œuvre [ɔ:'də:vrə] N hors d'œuvre m
horse [hɔ:s] N cheval m
horseback ['hɔ:sbæk]: **on ~** adj, adv à cheval
horsebox ['hɔ:sbɒks] N van m
horse chestnut N (nut) marron m (d'Inde); (tree) marronnier m (d'Inde)
horse-drawn ['hɔ:sdrɔ:n] ADJ tiré(e) par des chevaux
horsefly ['hɔ:sflaɪ] N taon m
horseman ['hɔ:smən] N (irreg) cavalier m
horsemanship ['hɔ:smənʃɪp] N talents mpl de cavalier
horseplay ['hɔ:spleɪ] N chahut m (blagues etc)
horsepower ['hɔ:spauəʳ] N puissance f (en chevaux); (unit) cheval-vapeur m (CV)
horse-racing ['hɔ:sreɪsɪŋ] N courses fpl de chevaux

h

horseradish ['hɔːsrædɪʃ] N raifort m
horse riding N (BRIT) équitation f
horseshoe ['hɔːʃuː] N fer m à cheval
horse show N concours m hippique
horse-trading ['hɔːstreɪdɪŋ] N maquignonnage m
horse trials NPL = **horse show**
horsewhip ['hɔːswɪp] VT cravacher
horsewoman ['hɔːswʊmən] N (irreg) cavalière f
horsey ['hɔːsɪ] ADJ (inf) féru(e) d'équitation or de cheval; (appearance) chevalin(e)
horticulture ['hɔːtɪkʌltʃəᵣ] N horticulture f
hose [həʊz] N (also: **hosepipe**) tuyau m; (also: **garden hose**) tuyau d'arrosage
  ▶ **hose down** VT laver au jet
hosepipe ['həʊzpaɪp] N tuyau m; (in garden) tuyau d'arrosage; (for fire) tuyau d'incendie
hosiery ['həʊzɪərɪ] N (rayon m des) bas mpl
hospice ['hɔspɪs] N hospice m
hospitable ['hɔspɪtəbl] ADJ hospitalier(-ière)
hospital ['hɔspɪtl] N hôpital m; **in ~**, (US) **in the ~** à l'hôpital; **where's the nearest ~?** où est l'hôpital le plus proche?
hospitality [hɔspɪ'tælɪtɪ] N hospitalité f
hospitalize ['hɔspɪtəlaɪz] VT hospitaliser
host [həʊst] N hôte m; (in hotel etc) patron m; (TV, Radio) présentateur(-trice), animateur(-trice); (large number): **a ~ of** une foule de; (Rel) hostie f
  ▶ VT (TV programme) présenter, animer
hostage ['hɔstɪdʒ] N otage m
host country N pays m d'accueil, pays-hôte m
hostel ['hɔstl] N foyer m; (also: **youth hostel**) auberge f de jeunesse
hostelling ['hɔstlɪŋ] N: **to go (youth) ~** faire une virée or randonnée en séjournant dans des auberges de jeunesse
hostess ['həʊstɪs] N hôtesse f; (BRIT: also: **air hostess**) hôtesse de l'air; (TV, Radio) présentatrice f; (in nightclub) entraîneuse f
hostile ['hɔstaɪl] ADJ hostile
hostility [hɔ'stɪlɪtɪ] N hostilité f
hot [hɔt] ADJ chaud(e); (as opposed to only warm) très chaud; (spicy) fort(e); (fig: contest) acharné(e); (topic) brûlant(e); (temper) violent(e), passionné(e); **to be ~** (person) avoir chaud; (thing) être (très) chaud; **it's ~** (weather) il fait chaud
  ▶ **hot up** (BRIT inf) VI (situation) devenir tendu(e); (party) s'animer ▶ VT (pace) accélérer, forcer; (engine) gonfler
hot-air balloon [hɔt'ɛə-] N montgolfière f, ballon m
hotbed ['hɔtbɛd] N (fig) foyer m, pépinière f
hotchpotch ['hɔtʃpɔtʃ] N (BRIT) mélange m hétéroclite
hot dog N hot-dog m
hotel [həʊ'tɛl] N hôtel m
hotelier [həʊ'tɛlɪəᵣ] N hôtelier(-ière)
hotel industry N industrie hôtelière
hotel room N chambre f d'hôtel
hot flush N (BRIT) bouffée f de chaleur
hotfoot ['hɔtfut] ADV à toute vitesse
hothead ['hɔthɛd] N (fig) tête brûlée
hotheaded [hɔt'hɛdɪd] ADJ impétueux(-euse)

hothouse ['hɔthaus] N serre chaude
hotline ['hɔtlaɪn] N (Pol) téléphone m rouge, ligne directe
hotly ['hɔtlɪ] ADV passionnément, violemment
hotplate ['hɔtpleɪt] N (on cooker) plaque chauffante
hotpot ['hɔtpɔt] N (BRIT Culin) ragoût m
hot potato N (BRIT inf) sujet brûlant; **to drop sb/sth like a ~** laisser tomber qn/qch brusquement
hot seat N (fig) poste chaud
hotspot ['hɔtspɔt] N (Comput: also: **wireless hotspot**) borne f wifi, hotspot m
hot spot N point chaud
hot spring N source thermale
hot-tempered ['hɔt'tɛmpəd] ADJ emporté(e)
hot-water bottle [hɔt'wɔːtə-] N bouillotte f
hot-wire ['hɔtwaɪəᵣ] VT (inf: car) démarrer en faisant se toucher les fils de contact
hound [haund] VT poursuivre avec acharnement ▶ N chien courant; **the hounds** la meute
hour ['auəᵣ] N heure f; **at 30 miles an ~ ≈** à 50 km à l'heure; **lunch ~** heure du déjeuner; **to pay sb by the ~** payer qn à l'heure
hourly ['auəlɪ] ADJ toutes les heures; (rate) horaire; **~ paid** adj payé(e) à l'heure
house [haus] (pl **houses** ['hauzɪz]) N maison f; (Pol) chambre f; (Theat) salle f; auditoire m ▶ VT [hauz] (person) loger, héberger; **at (or to) my ~** chez moi; **on the ~** (fig) aux frais de la maison; **the H~ of Commons/of Lords** (BRIT) la Chambre des communes/des lords; voir article; **the H~ (of Representatives)** (US) la Chambre des représentants; voir article

Le parlement en Grande-Bretagne est constitué de deux assemblées: la *House of Commons*, présidée par le *Speaker* et composée de plus de 600 députés (les *MPs*) élus au suffrage universel direct. Ceux-ci reçoivent tous un salaire. La Chambre des communes siège environ 175 jours par an. La *House of Lords*, présidée par le *Lord Chancellor* est composée de lords dont le titre est attribué par le souverain à vie; elle peut amender certains projets de loi votés par la *House of Commons*, mais elle n'est pas habilitée à débattre des projets de lois de finances. La *House of Lords* fait également office de juridiction suprême en Angleterre et au pays de Galles.
Aux États-Unis, le parlement, appelé le *Congress*, est constitué du *Senate* et de la *House of Representatives*. Cette dernière comprend 435 membres, le nombre de ses représentants par État étant proportionnel à la densité de population de cet État. Ils sont élus pour deux ans au suffrage universel direct et siègent au *Capitol*, à Washington D.C.

house arrest N assignation f à domicile
houseboat ['hausbəut] N bateau (aménagé en habitation)
housebound ['hausbaund] ADJ confiné(e) chez soi

housebreaking ['hausbreɪkɪŋ] N cambriolage m (avec effraction)
house-broken ['hausbrəukn] ADJ (US) = **house-trained**
housecoat ['hauskəut] N peignoir m
household ['haushəuld] N (Admin etc) ménage m; (people) famille f, maisonnée f; ~ **name** nom connu de tout le monde
householder ['haushəuldər] N propriétaire mf; (head of house) chef m de famille
househunting ['haushʌntɪŋ] N: **to go** ~ se mettre en quête d'une maison (or d'un appartement)
housekeeper ['hauski:pər] N gouvernante f
housekeeping ['hauski:pɪŋ] N (work) ménage m; (also: **housekeeping money**) argent m du ménage; (Comput) gestion f (des disques)
houseman ['hausmən] N (irreg) (BRIT Med) ≈ interne m
house-owner ['hausəunər] N propriétaire mf (de maison ou d'appartement)
house-proud ['hauspraud] ADJ qui tient à avoir une maison impeccable
house-to-house ['haustə'haus] ADJ (enquiries etc) chez tous les habitants (du quartier etc)
house-train ['haustreɪn] VT (pet) apprendre à être propre à
house-trained ['haustreɪnd] ADJ (pet) propre
house-warming ['hauswɔ:mɪŋ] N (also: **house-warming party**) pendaison f de crémaillère
housewife ['hauswaɪf] (irreg) N ménagère f; femme f au foyer
house wine N cuvée f maison or du patron
housework ['hauswə:k] N (travaux mpl du) ménage m
housing ['hauzɪŋ] N logement m ▶ CPD (problem, shortage) de or du logement
housing association N fondation f charitable fournissant des logements
housing benefit N (BRIT) ≈ allocations fpl logement
housing development, (BRIT) **housing estate** N (blocks of flats) cité f; (houses) lotissement m
hovel ['hɔvl] N taudis m
hover ['hɔvər] VI planer; **to** ~ **round sb** rôder or tourner autour de qn
hovercraft ['hɔvəkrɑ:ft] N aéroglisseur m, hovercraft m
hoverport ['hɔvəpɔ:t] N hoverport m
how [hau] ADV comment; ~ **are you?** comment allez-vous?; ~ **do you do?** bonjour; (on being introduced) enchanté(e); ~ **far is it to …?** combien y a-t-il jusqu'à …?; ~ **long have you been here?** depuis combien de temps êtes-vous là?; ~ **lovely/awful!** que or comme c'est joli/affreux!; ~ **many/much?** combien?; ~ **much time/many people?** combien de temps/gens?; ~ **much does it cost?** ça coûte combien?; ~ **old are you?** quel âge avez-vous?; ~ **tall is he?** combien mesure-t-il?; ~ **is school?** ça va à l'école?; ~ **was the film?** comment était le film?; ~**'s life?** (inf) comment ça va?; ~ **about a drink?** si on buvait quelque chose?; ~ **is it**

that …? comment se fait-il que … + sub?
however [hau'evər] CONJ pourtant, cependant ▶ ADV de quelque façon or manière que + sub; (+ adjective) quelque or si … que + sub; (in questions) comment; ~ **I do it** de quelque manière que je m'y prenne; ~ **cold it is** même s'il fait très froid; ~ **did you do it?** comment y êtes-vous donc arrivé?
howitzer ['hauɪtsər] N (Mil) obusier m
howl [haul] N hurlement m ▶ VI hurler; (wind) mugir
howler ['haulər] N gaffe f, bourde f
howling ['haulɪŋ] ADJ: **a** ~ **wind** or **gale** un vent à décorner les bœufs
H.P. N ABBR (BRIT) = **hire purchase**
h.p. ABBR (Aut) = **horsepower**
HQ N ABBR (= headquarters) QG m
HR N ABBR (US) = **House of Representatives**
hr ABBR (= hour) h
HRH ABBR (= His (or Her) Royal Highness) SAR
hrs ABBR (= hours) h
HRT N ABBR = **hormone replacement therapy**
HS N ABBR (US) = **high school**
HST ABBR (US: = Hawaiian Standard Time) heure de Hawaii
HTML N ABBR (= hypertext markup language) HTML m
hub [hʌb] N (of wheel) moyeu m; (fig) centre m, foyer m
hubbub ['hʌbʌb] N brouhaha m
hubcap [hʌbkæp] N (Aut) enjoliveur m
HUD N ABBR (US: = Department of Housing and Urban Development) ministère de l'urbanisme et du logement
huddle ['hʌdl] VI: **to** ~ **together** se blottir les uns contre les autres
hue [hju:] N teinte f, nuance f; ~ **and cry** n tollé (général), clameur f
huff [hʌf] N: **in a** ~ fâché(e); **to take the** ~ prendre la mouche
huffy ['hʌfɪ] ADJ (inf) froissé(e)
hug [hʌg] VT serrer dans ses bras; (shore, kerb) serrer ▶ N étreinte f; **to give sb a** ~ serrer qn dans ses bras
huge [hju:dʒ] ADJ énorme, immense
hulk [hʌlk] N (ship) vieux rafiot; (car, building) carcasse f; (person) mastodonte m, malabar m
hulking ['hʌlkɪŋ] ADJ balourd(e)
hull [hʌl] N (of ship) coque f; (of nuts) coque; (of peas) cosse f
hullabaloo ['hʌləbə'lu:] N (inf: noise) tapage m, raffut m
hullo [hə'ləu] EXCL = **hello**
hum [hʌm] VT (tune) fredonner ▶ VI fredonner; (insect) bourdonner; (plane, tool) vrombir ▶ N fredonnement m; bourdonnement m; vrombissement m
human ['hju:mən] ADJ humain(e) ▶ N (also: **human being**) être humain
humane [hju:'meɪn] ADJ humain(e), humanitaire
humanism ['hju:mənɪzəm] N humanisme m
humanitarian [hju:mænɪ'teərɪən] ADJ humanitaire
humanity [hju:'mænɪtɪ] N humanité f

humanly ['hju:mənlı] ADV humainement
humanoid ['hju:mənɔɪd] ADJ, N humanoïde mf
human rights NPL droits mpl de l'homme
humble ['hʌmbl] ADJ humble, modeste ▸ VT humilier
humbly ['hʌmblɪ] ADV humblement, modestement
humbug ['hʌmbʌg] N fumisterie f; (BRIT: sweet) bonbon m à la menthe
humdrum ['hʌmdrʌm] ADJ monotone, routinier(-ière)
humid ['hju:mɪd] ADJ humide
humidifier [hju:'mɪdɪfaɪər] N humidificateur m
humidity [hju:'mɪdɪtɪ] N humidité f
humiliate [hju:'mɪlɪeɪt] VT humilier
humiliating [hju:'mɪlɪeɪtɪŋ] ADJ humiliant(e)
humiliation [hju:mɪlɪ'eɪʃən] N humiliation f
humility [hju:'mɪlɪtɪ] N humilité f
hummus ['huməs] N houm(m)ous m
humorist ['hju:mərɪst] N humoriste mf
humorous ['hju:mərəs] ADJ humoristique; (person) plein(e) d'humour
humour, (US) **humor** ['hju:mər] N humour m; (mood) humeur f ▸ VT (person) faire plaisir à; se prêter aux caprices de; **sense of ~** sens m de l'humour; **to be in a good/bad ~** être de bonne/mauvaise humeur
humourless, (US) **humorless** ['hu:məlɪs] ADJ dépourvu(e) d'humour
hump [hʌmp] N bosse f
humpback ['hʌmpbæk] N bossu(e); (BRIT: also: **humpback bridge**) dos-d'âne m
humus ['hju:məs] N humus m
hunch [hʌntʃ] N bosse f; (premonition) intuition f; **I have a ~ that** j'ai (comme une vague) idée que
hunchback ['hʌntʃbæk] N bossu(e)
hunched [hʌntʃt] ADJ arrondi(e), voûté(e)
hundred ['hʌndrəd] NUM cent; **about a ~ people** une centaine de personnes; **hundreds of** des centaines de; **I'm a ~ per cent sure** j'en suis absolument certain
hundredth ['hʌndrədɪθ] NUM centième
hundredweight ['hʌndrɪdweɪt] N (BRIT) = 50.8 kg; 112 lb; (US) = 45.3 kg; 100 lb
hung [hʌŋ] PT, PP of **hang**
Hungarian [hʌŋ'gɛərɪən] ADJ hongrois(e) ▸ N Hongrois(e); (Ling) hongrois m
Hungary ['hʌŋgərɪ] N Hongrie f
hunger ['hʌŋgər] N faim f ▸ VI: **to ~ for** avoir faim de, désirer ardemment
hunger strike N grève f de la faim
hungover [hʌŋ'əuvər] ADJ (inf): **to be ~** avoir la gueule de bois
hungrily ['hʌŋgrəlɪ] ADV voracement; (fig) avidement
hungry ['hʌŋgrɪ] ADJ affamé(e); **to be ~** avoir faim; **~ for** (fig) avide de
hung up ADJ (inf) complexé(e), bourré(e) de complexes
hunk [hʌŋk] N gros morceau; (inf: man) beau mec
hunt [hʌnt] VT (seek) chercher; (criminal) pourchasser; (Sport) chasser ▸ VI (search): **to ~ for** chercher (partout); (Sport) chasser

▸ N (Sport) chasse f
▸ **hunt down** VT pourchasser
hunter ['hʌntər] N chasseur m; (BRIT: horse) cheval m de chasse
hunting ['hʌntɪŋ] N chasse f
hurdle ['hə:dl] N (for fences) claie f; (Sport) haie f; (fig) obstacle m
hurl [hə:l] VT lancer (avec violence); (abuse, insults) lancer
hurling ['hə:lɪŋ] N (Sport) genre de hockey joué en Irlande
hurly-burly ['hə:lɪ'bə:lɪ] N tohu-bohu m inv; brouhaha m
hurrah, hurray [hu'ra:, hu'reɪ] EXCL hourra!
hurricane ['hʌrɪkən] N ouragan m
hurried ['hʌrɪd] ADJ pressé(e), précipité(e); (work) fait(e) à la hâte
hurriedly ['hʌrɪdlɪ] ADV précipitamment, à la hâte
hurry ['hʌrɪ] N hâte f, précipitation f ▸ VI se presser, se dépêcher ▸ VT (person) faire presser, faire se dépêcher; (work) presser; **to be in a ~** être pressé(e); **to do sth in a ~** faire qch en vitesse; **to ~ in/out** entrer/sortir précipitamment; **to ~ home** se dépêcher de rentrer
▸ **hurry along** VI marcher d'un pas pressé
▸ **hurry away, hurry off** VI partir précipitamment
▸ **hurry up** VI se dépêcher
hurt [hə:t] (pt, pp **~**) VT (cause pain to) faire mal à; (injure, fig) blesser; (damage: business, interests etc) nuire à; faire du tort à ▸ VI faire mal ▸ ADJ blessé(e); **my arm hurts** j'ai mal au bras; **I ~ my arm** je me suis fait mal au bras; **to ~ o.s.** se faire mal; **where does it ~?** où avez-vous mal?, où est-ce que ça vous fait mal?
hurtful ['hə:tful] ADJ (remark) blessant(e)
hurtle ['hə:tl] VT lancer (de toutes ses forces) ▸ VI: **to ~ past** passer en trombe; **to ~ down** dégringoler
husband ['hʌzbənd] N mari m
hush [hʌʃ] N calme m, silence m ▸ VT faire taire; **~!** chut!
▸ **hush up** VT (fact) étouffer
hush-hush [hʌʃ'hʌʃ] ADJ (inf) ultra-secret(-ète)
husk [hʌsk] N (of wheat) balle f; (of rice, maize) enveloppe f; (of peas) cosse f
husky ['hʌskɪ] ADJ (voice) rauque; (burly) costaud(e) ▸ N chien m esquimau or de traîneau
hustings ['hʌstɪŋz] NPL (BRIT Pol) plate-forme électorale
hustle ['hʌsl] VT pousser, bousculer ▸ N bousculade f; **~ and bustle** n tourbillon m (d'activité)
hut [hʌt] N hutte f; (shed) cabane f
hutch [hʌtʃ] N clapier m
hyacinth ['haɪəsɪnθ] N jacinthe f
hybrid ['haɪbrɪd] ADJ, N hybride (m)
hydrant ['haɪdrənt] N prise f d'eau; (also: **fire hydrant**) bouche f d'incendie
hydraulic [haɪ'drɔ:lɪk] ADJ hydraulique
hydraulics [haɪ'drɔ:lɪks] N hydraulique f

hydrochloric ['haɪdrəu'klɔrɪk] ADJ: ~ **acid** acide *m* chlorhydrique

hydroelectric ['haɪdrəuɪ'lektrɪk] ADJ hydro-électrique

hydrofoil ['haɪdrəfɔɪl] N hydrofoil *m*

hydrogen ['haɪdrədʒən] N hydrogène *m*

hydrogen bomb N bombe *f* à hydrogène

hydrophobia ['haɪdrə'fəubɪə] N hydrophobie *f*

hydroplane ['haɪdrəpleɪn] N (*seaplane*) hydravion *m*; (*jetfoil*) hydroglisseur *m*

hyena [haɪ'iːnə] N hyène *f*

hygiene ['haɪdʒiːn] N hygiène *f*

hygienic [haɪ'dʒiːnɪk] ADJ hygiénique

hymn [hɪm] N hymne *m*; cantique *m*

hype [haɪp] N (*inf*) matraquage *m* publicitaire *or* médiatique

hyperactive ['haɪpər'æktɪv] ADJ hyperactif(-ive)

hyperlink ['haɪpəlɪŋk] N hyperlien *m*

hypermarket ['haɪpəmɑːkɪt] (*BRIT*) N hypermarché *m*

hypertension ['haɪpə'tenʃən] N (*Med*) hypertension *f*

hypertext ['haɪpətekst] N (*Comput*) hypertexte *m*

hyphen ['haɪfn] N trait *m* d'union

hypnosis [hɪp'nəusɪs] N hypnose *f*

hypnotic [hɪp'nɔtɪk] ADJ hypnotique

hypnotism ['hɪpnətɪzəm] N hypnotisme *m*

hypnotist ['hɪpnətɪst] N hypnotiseur(-euse)

hypnotize ['hɪpnətaɪz] VT hypnotiser

hypoallergenic ['haɪpəuæelə'dʒenɪk] ADJ hypoallergénique

hypochondriac [haɪpə'kɔndrɪæk] N hypocondriaque *mf*

hypocrisy [hɪ'pɔkrɪsɪ] N hypocrisie *f*

hypocrite ['hɪpəkrɪt] N hypocrite *mf*

hypocritical [hɪpə'krɪtɪkl] ADJ hypocrite

hypodermic [haɪpə'dəːmɪk] ADJ hypodermique
▶ N (*syringe*) seringue *f* hypodermique

hypotenuse [haɪ'pɔtɪnjuːz] N hypoténuse *f*

hypothermia [haɪpə'θəːmɪə] N hypothermie *f*

hypothesis [haɪ'pɔθɪsɪs] (*pl* **hypotheses** [-siːz]) N hypothèse *f*

hysterectomy [hɪstə'rektəmɪ] N hystérectomie *f*

hysteria [hɪ'stɪərɪə] N hystérie *f*

hysterical [hɪ'sterɪkl] ADJ hystérique; (*funny*) hilarant(e); **to become** ~ avoir une crise de nerfs

hysterics [hɪ'sterɪks] NPL (*violente*) crise de nerfs; (*laughter*) crise de rire; **to be in/have** ~ (*anger, panic*) avoir une crise de nerfs; (*laughter*) attraper un fou rire

Hz ABBR (= *hertz*) Hz

h

I i

I¹, i [aɪ] N (*letter*) I, i *m*; **I for Isaac**, (*US*) **I for Item** I comme Irma

I² [aɪ] PRON je; (*before vowel*) j'; (*stressed*) moi ▶ ABBR (= *island, isle*) I

IA, Ia. ABBR (*US*) = **Iowa**

IAEA N ABBR = **International Atomic Energy Agency**

IBA N ABBR (*BRIT*: = *Independent Broadcasting Authority*) ≈ CNCL *f* (= *Commission nationale de la communication audio-visuelle*)

Iberian [aɪˈbɪərɪən] ADJ ibérique, ibérien(ne)

Iberian Peninsula N: **the ~** la péninsule Ibérique

IBEW N ABBR (*US*: = *International Brotherhood of Electrical Workers*) syndicat international des électriciens

i/c ABBR (*BRIT*) = **in charge**

ICBM N ABBR (= *intercontinental ballistic missile*) ICBM *m*, engin *m* balistique à portée intercontinentale

ICC N ABBR (= *International Chamber of Commerce*) CCI *f*; (*US*) = **Interstate Commerce Commission**

ice [aɪs] N glace *f*; (*on road*) verglas *m* ▶ VT (*cake*) glacer; (*drink*) faire rafraîchir ▶ VI (*also*: **ice over**) geler; (*also*: **ice up**) se givrer; **to put sth on ~** (*fig*) mettre qch en attente

Ice Age N ère *f* glaciaire

ice axe, (*US*) **ice ax** N piolet *m*

iceberg [ˈaɪsbəːg] N iceberg *m*; **the tip of the ~** (*also fig*) la partie émergée de l'iceberg

icebox [ˈaɪsbɔks] N (*US*) réfrigérateur *m*; (*BRIT*) compartiment *m* à glace; (*insulated box*) glacière *f*

icebreaker [ˈaɪsbreɪkəʳ] N brise-glace *m*

ice bucket N seau *m* à glace

ice-cap [ˈaɪskæp] N calotte *f* glaciaire

ice-cold [aɪsˈkəʊld] ADJ glacé(e)

ice cream N glace *f*

ice cube N glaçon *m*

iced [aɪst] ADJ (*drink*) frappé(e); (*coffee, tea, also cake*) glacé(e)

ice hockey N hockey *m* sur glace

Iceland [ˈaɪslənd] N Islande *f*

Icelander [ˈaɪsləndəʳ] N Islandais(e)

Icelandic [aɪsˈlændɪk] ADJ islandais(e) ▶ N (*Ling*) islandais *m*

ice lolly N (*BRIT*) esquimau *m*

ice pick N pic *m* à glace

ice rink N patinoire *f*

ice-skate [ˈaɪsskeɪt] N patin *m* à glace ▶ VI faire du patin à glace

ice skating N patinage *m* (sur glace)

icicle [ˈaɪsɪkl] N glaçon *m* (*naturel*)

icing [ˈaɪsɪŋ] N (*Aviat etc*) givrage *m*; (*Culin*) glaçage *m*

icing sugar N (*BRIT*) sucre *m* glace

ICJ N ABBR = **International Court of Justice**

icon [ˈaɪkɔn] N icône *f*

ICR N ABBR (*US*) = **Institute for Cancer Research**

ICRC N ABBR (= *International Committee of the Red Cross*) CICR *m*

ICT N ABBR (*BRIT Scol*: = *information and communications technology*) TIC *fpl*

ICU N ABBR = **intensive care unit**

icy [ˈaɪsɪ] ADJ glacé(e); (*road*) verglacé(e); (*weather, temperature*) glacial(e)

ID ABBR (*US*) = **Idaho**

I'd [aɪd] = **I would; I had**

Ida. ABBR (*US*) = **Idaho**

ID card N carte *f* d'identité

IDD N ABBR (*BRIT Tel*: = *international direct dialling*) automatique international

idea [aɪˈdɪə] N idée *f*; **good ~!** bonne idée!; **to have an ~ that ...** avoir idée que ...; **I have no ~** je n'ai pas la moindre idée

ideal [aɪˈdɪəl] N idéal *m* ▶ ADJ idéal(e)

idealist [aɪˈdɪəlɪst] N idéaliste *mf*

ideally [aɪˈdɪəlɪ] ADV (*preferably*) dans l'idéal; (*perfectly*): **he is ~ suited to the job** il est parfait pour ce poste; **~ the book should have ...** l'idéal serait que le livre ait ...

identical [aɪˈdentɪkl] ADJ identique

identification [aɪdentɪfɪˈkeɪʃən] N identification *f*; **means of ~** pièce *f* d'identité

identify [aɪˈdentɪfaɪ] VT identifier ▶ VI: **to ~ with** s'identifier à

Identikit® [aɪˈdentɪkɪt] N: **~ (picture)** portrait-robot *m*

identity [aɪˈdentɪtɪ] N identité *f*

identity card N carte *f* d'identité

identity parade N (*BRIT*) parade *f* d'identification

identity theft N usurpation *f* d'identité

ideological [aɪdɪəˈlɔdʒɪkl] ADJ idéologique

ideology [aɪdɪˈɔlədʒɪ] N idéologie *f*

idiocy [ˈɪdɪəsɪ] N idiotie *f*, stupidité *f*

idiom [ˈɪdɪəm] N (*language*) langue *f*, idiome *m*;

(*phrase*) expression *f* idiomatique; (*style*) style *m*

idiomatic [ɪdɪə'mætɪk] ADJ idiomatique

idiosyncrasy [ɪdɪəu'sɪŋkrəsɪ] N particularité *f*, caractéristique *f*

idiot ['ɪdɪət] N idiot(e), imbécile *mf*

idiotic [ɪdɪ'ɔtɪk] ADJ idiot(e), bête, stupide

idle ['aɪdl] ADJ (*doing nothing*) sans occupation, désœuvré(e), (*lazy*) oisif(-ive), paresseux(-euse); (*unemployed*) au chômage; (*machinery*) au repos; (*question, pleasures*) vain(e), futile ▸ vɪ (*engine*) tourner au ralenti; **to lie ~** être arrêté, ne pas fonctionner

▸ **idle away** vt: **to ~ away one's time** passer son temps à ne rien faire

idleness ['aɪdlnɪs] N désœuvrement *m*; oisiveté *f*

idler ['aɪdlə^r] N désœuvré(e), oisif(-ive)

idle time N (*Comm*) temps mort

idol ['aɪdl] N idole *f*

idolize ['aɪdəlaɪz] VT idolâtrer, adorer

idyllic [ɪ'dɪlɪk] ADJ idyllique

i.e. ABBR (= *id est: that is*) c. à d., c'est-à-dire

IED [aiɪ'diː] ABBR (= *Improvised Explosive Device*) EEI *m*

if [ɪf] CONJ si ▸ N: **there are a lot of ifs and buts** il y a beaucoup de si *mpl* et de mais *mpl*; **I'd be pleased if you could do it** je serais très heureux si vous pouviez le faire; **if necessary** si nécessaire, le cas échéant; **if so** si c'est le cas; **if not** sinon; **if only I could!** si seulement je pouvais!; **if only he were here** si seulement il était là; **if only to show him my gratitude** ne serait-ce que pour lui témoigner ma gratitude; *see also* **as**; **even**

iffy ['ɪfɪ] ADJ (*inf*) douteux(-euse)

igloo ['ɪgluː] N igloo *m*

ignite [ɪg'naɪt] VT mettre le feu à, enflammer ▸ vɪ s'enflammer

ignition [ɪg'nɪʃən] N (*Aut*) allumage *m*; **to switch on/off the ~** mettre/couper le contact

ignition key N (*Aut*) clé *f* de contact

ignoble [ɪg'nəubl] ADJ ignoble, indigne

ignominious [ɪgnə'mɪnɪəs] ADJ honteux(-euse), ignominieux(-euse)

ignoramus [ɪgnə'reɪməs] N personne *f* ignare

ignorance ['ɪgnərəns] N ignorance *f*; **to keep sb in ~ of sth** tenir qn dans l'ignorance de qch

ignorant ['ɪgnərənt] ADJ ignorant(e); **to be ~ of** (*subject*) ne rien connaître en; (*events*) ne pas être au courant de

ignore [ɪg'nɔː^r] VT ne tenir aucun compte de; (*mistake*) ne pas relever; (*person: pretend to not see*) faire semblant de ne pas reconnaître; (: *pay no attention to*) ignorer

ikon ['aɪkɔn] N = **icon**

IL ABBR (*US*) = **Illinois**

ILA N ABBR (*US*: = *International Longshoremen's Association*) syndicat international des dockers

ill [ɪl] ADJ (*sick*) malade; (*bad*) mauvais(e) ▸ N mal *m* ▸ ADV: **to speak/think ~ of sb** dire/penser du mal de qn; **to be taken ~** tomber malade

Ill. ABBR (*US*) = **Illinois**

I'll [aɪl] = **I will; I shall**

ill-advised [ɪləd'vaɪzd] ADJ (*decision*) peu

judicieux(-euse); (*person*) malavisé(e)

ill-at-ease [ɪlət'iːz] ADJ mal à l'aise

ill-considered [ɪlkən'sɪdəd] ADJ (*plan*) inconsidéré(e), irréfléchi(e)

ill-disposed [ɪldɪs'pəuzd] ADJ: **to be ~ towards sb/sth** être mal disposé(e) envers qn/qch

illegal [ɪ'liːgl] ADJ illégal(e)

illegally [ɪ'liːgəlɪ] ADV illégalement

illegible [ɪ'lɛdʒɪbl] ADJ illisible

illegitimate [ɪlɪ'dʒɪtɪmət] ADJ illégitime

ill-fated [ɪl'feɪtɪd] ADJ malheureux(-euse); (*day*) néfaste

ill-favoured, (*US*) **ill-favored** [ɪl'feɪvəd] ADJ déplaisant(e)

ill feeling N ressentiment *m*, rancune *f*

ill-gotten ['ɪlgɔtn] ADJ (*gains etc*) mal acquis(e)

ill health N mauvaise santé

illicit [ɪ'lɪsɪt] ADJ illicite

ill-informed [ɪlɪn'fɔːmd] ADJ (*judgment*) erroné(e); (*person*) mal renseigné(e)

illiterate [ɪ'lɪtərət] ADJ illettré(e); (*letter*) plein(e) de fautes

ill-mannered [ɪl'mænəd] ADJ impoli(e), grossier(-ière)

illness ['ɪlnɪs] N maladie *f*

illogical [ɪ'lɔdʒɪkl] ADJ illogique

ill-suited [ɪl'suːtɪd] ADJ (*couple*) mal assorti(e); **he is ~ to the job** il n'est pas vraiment fait pour ce travail

ill-timed [ɪl'taɪmd] ADJ inopportun(e)

ill-treat [ɪl'triːt] VT maltraiter

ill-treatment [ɪl'triːtmənt] N mauvais traitement

illuminate [ɪ'luːmɪneɪt] VT (*room, street*) éclairer; (*for special effect*) illuminer; **illuminated sign** enseigne lumineuse

illuminating [ɪ'luːmɪneɪtɪŋ] ADJ éclairant(e)

illumination [ɪluːmɪ'neɪʃən] N éclairage *m*; illumination *f*

illusion [ɪ'luːʒən] N illusion *f*; **to be under the ~ that** avoir l'illusion que

illusive [ɪ'luːsɪv], **illusory** [ɪ'luːsərɪ] ADJ illusoire

illustrate ['ɪləstreɪt] VT illustrer

illustration [ɪlə'streɪʃən] N illustration *f*

illustrator ['ɪləstreɪtə^r] N illustrateur(-trice)

illustrious [ɪ'lʌstrɪəs] ADJ illustre

ill will N malveillance *f*

ILO N ABBR (= *International Labour Organization*) OIT *f*

ILWU N ABBR (*US*: = *International Longshoremen's and Warehousemen's Union*) syndicat international des dockers et des magasiniers

IM N ABBR (= *instant messaging*) messagerie *f* instantanée ▸ VT envoyer un message instantané à

I'm [aɪm] = **I am**

image ['ɪmɪdʒ] N image *f*; (*public face*) image de marque

imagery ['ɪmɪdʒərɪ] N images *fpl*

imaginable [ɪ'mædʒɪnəbl] ADJ imaginable

imaginary [ɪ'mædʒɪnərɪ] ADJ imaginaire

imagination [ɪmædʒɪ'neɪʃən] N imagination *f*

imaginative [ɪ'mædʒɪnətɪv] ADJ imaginatif(-ive); (*person*) plein(e) d'imagination

imagine [ɪ'mædʒɪn] VT s'imaginer; (*suppose*) imaginer, supposer

imbalance [ɪm'bæləns] N déséquilibre *m*

imbecile ['ɪmbəsi:l] N imbécile *mf*

imbue [ɪm'bju:] VT: **to ~ sth with** imprégner qch de

IMF N ABBR = **International Monetary Fund**

imitate ['ɪmɪteɪt] VT imiter

imitation [ɪmɪ'teɪʃən] N imitation *f*

imitator ['ɪmɪteɪtəʳ] N imitateur(-trice)

immaculate [ɪ'mækjulət] ADJ impeccable; (*Rel*) immaculé(e)

immaterial [ɪmə'tɪərɪəl] ADJ sans importance, insignifiant(e)

immature [ɪmə'tjuəʳ] ADJ (*fruit*) qui n'est pas mûr(e); (*person*) qui manque de maturité

immaturity [ɪmə'tjuərɪtɪ] N immaturité *f*

immeasurable [ɪ'mɛʒrəbl] ADJ incommensurable

immediacy [ɪ'mi:dɪəsɪ] N (*of events etc*) caractère *or* rapport immédiat; (*of needs*) urgence *f*

immediate [ɪ'mi:dɪət] ADJ immédiat(e)

immediately [ɪ'mi:dɪətlɪ] ADV (*at once*) immédiatement; **~ next to** juste à côté de

immense [ɪ'mɛns] ADJ immense, énorme

immensely [ɪ'mɛnslɪ] ADV (+*adj*) extrêmement; (+*vb*) énormément

immensity [ɪ'mɛnsɪtɪ] N immensité *f*

immerse [ɪ'mə:s] VT immerger, plonger; **to ~ sth in** plonger qch dans; **to be immersed in** (*fig*) être plongé dans

immersion heater [ɪ'mə:ʃən-] N (*BRIT*) chauffe-eau *m* électrique

immigrant ['ɪmɪgrənt] N immigrant(e); (*already established*) immigré(e)

immigration [ɪmɪ'greɪʃən] N immigration *f*

immigration authorities NPL service *m* de l'immigration

immigration laws NPL lois *fpl* sur l'immigration

imminent ['ɪmɪnənt] ADJ imminent(e)

immobile [ɪ'məubaɪl] ADJ immobile

immobilize [ɪ'məubɪlaɪz] VT immobiliser

immoderate [ɪ'mɔdərət] ADJ immodéré(e), démesuré(e)

immodest [ɪ'mɔdɪst] ADJ (*indecent*) indécent(e); (*boasting*) pas modeste, présomptueux(-euse)

immoral [ɪ'mɔrl] ADJ immoral(e)

immorality [ɪmɔ'rælɪtɪ] N immoralité *f*

immortal [ɪ'mɔ:tl] ADJ, N immortel(le)

immortalize [ɪ'mɔ:tlaɪz] VT immortaliser

immovable [ɪ'mu:vəbl] ADJ (*object*) fixe; immobilier(-ière); (*person*) inflexible; (*opinion*) immuable

immune [ɪ'mju:n] ADJ: **~ (to)** immunisé(e) (contre)

immune system N système *m* immunitaire

immunity [ɪ'mju:nɪtɪ] N immunité *f*; **diplomatic ~** immunité diplomatique

immunization [ɪmjunaɪ'zeɪʃən] N immunisation *f*

immunize ['ɪmjunaɪz] VT immuniser

imp [ɪmp] N (*small devil*) lutin *m*; (*child*) petit diable

impact ['ɪmpækt] N choc *m*, impact *m*; (*fig*) impact

impair [ɪm'pɛəʳ] VT détériorer, diminuer

impaired [ɪm'pɛəd] ADJ (*organ, vision*) abîmé(e), détérioré(e); **his memory/circulation is ~** il a des problèmes de mémoire/circulation; **visually ~** malvoyant(e); **hearing ~** malentendant(e); **mentally/physically ~** intellectuellement/physiquement diminué(e)

impale [ɪm'peɪl] VT empaler

impart [ɪm'pɑ:t] VT (*make known*) communiquer, transmettre; (*bestow*) conférer, donner

impartial [ɪm'pɑ:ʃl] ADJ impartial(e)

impartiality [ɪmpɑ:ʃɪ'ælɪtɪ] N impartialité *f*

impassable [ɪm'pɑ:səbl] ADJ infranchissable; (*road*) impraticable

impasse [æm'pɑ:s] N (*fig*) impasse *f*

impassioned [ɪm'pæʃənd] ADJ passionné(e)

impassive [ɪm'pæsɪv] ADJ impassible

impatience [ɪm'peɪʃəns] N impatience *f*

impatient [ɪm'peɪʃənt] ADJ impatient(e); **to get** *or* **grow ~** s'impatienter

impatiently [ɪm'peɪʃəntlɪ] ADV avec impatience

impeach [ɪm'pi:tʃ] VT accuser, attaquer; (*public official*) mettre en accusation

impeachment [ɪm'pi:tʃmənt] N (*Law*) (mise *f* en) accusation *f*

impeccable [ɪm'pɛkəbl] ADJ impeccable, parfait(e)

impecunious [ɪmpɪ'kju:nɪəs] ADJ sans ressources

impede [ɪm'pi:d] VT gêner

impediment [ɪm'pɛdɪmənt] N obstacle *m*; (*also:* **speech impediment**) défaut *m* d'élocution

impel [ɪm'pɛl] VT (*force*): **to ~ sb (to do sth)** forcer qn (à faire qch)

impending [ɪm'pɛndɪŋ] ADJ imminent(e)

impenetrable [ɪm'pɛnɪtrəbl] ADJ impénétrable

imperative [ɪm'pɛrətɪv] ADJ nécessaire; (*need*) urgent(e), pressant(e); (*tone*) impérieux(-euse) ▶ N (*Ling*) impératif *m*

imperceptible [ɪmpə'sɛptɪbl] ADJ imperceptible

imperfect [ɪm'pə:fɪkt] ADJ imparfait(e); (*goods etc*) défectueux(-euse) ▶ N (*Ling: also:* **imperfect tense**) imparfait *m*

imperfection [ɪmpə:'fɛkʃən] N imperfection *f*; défectuosité *f*

imperial [ɪm'pɪərɪəl] ADJ impérial(e); (*BRIT: measure*) légal(e)

imperialism [ɪm'pɪərɪəlɪzəm] N impérialisme *m*

imperil [ɪm'pɛrɪl] VT mettre en péril

imperious [ɪm'pɪərɪəs] ADJ impérieux(-euse)

impersonal [ɪm'pə:sənl] ADJ impersonnel(le)

impersonate [ɪm'pə:səneɪt] VT se faire passer pour; (*Theat*) imiter

impersonation [ɪmpə:sə'neɪʃən] N (*Law*) usurpation *f* d'identité; (*Theat*) imitation *f*

impersonator [ɪm'pə:səneɪtəʳ] N imposteur *m*; (*Theat*) imitateur(-trice)

impertinence [ɪm'pə:tɪnəns] N impertinence *f*, insolence *f*

impertinent [ɪm'pə:tɪnənt] ADJ impertinent(e), insolent(e)

imperturbable [ɪmpə'tə:bəbl] ADJ imperturbable

impervious [ɪm'pəːvɪəs] ADJ imperméable; ~ **to** (fig) insensible à; inaccessible à

impetuous [ɪm'pɛtjuəs] ADJ impétueux(-euse), fougueux(-euse)

impetus ['ɪmpətəs] N impulsion f; (of runner) élan m

impinge [ɪm'pɪndʒ]: **to ~ on** vt fus (person) affecter, toucher; (rights) empiéter sur

impish ['ɪmpɪʃ] ADJ espiègle

implacable [ɪm'plækəbl] ADJ implacable

implant [ɪm'plɑːnt] VT (Med) implanter; (fig: idea, principle) inculquer

implausible [ɪm'plɔːzɪbl] ADJ peu plausible

implement N ['ɪmplɪmənt] outil m, instrument m; (for cooking) ustensile m ▶ VT ['ɪmplɪmɛnt] exécuter, mettre à effet

implicate ['ɪmplɪkeɪt] VT impliquer, compromettre

implication [ɪmplɪ'keɪʃən] N implication f; **by ~** indirectement

implicit [ɪm'plɪsɪt] ADJ implicite; (complete) absolu(e), sans réserve

implicitly [ɪm'plɪsɪtlɪ] ADV implicitement; absolument, sans réserve

implore [ɪm'plɔːʳ] VT implorer, supplier

imply [ɪm'plaɪ] VT (hint) suggérer, laisser entendre; (mean) indiquer, supposer

impolite [ɪmpə'laɪt] ADJ impoli(e)

imponderable [ɪm'pɒndərəbl] ADJ impondérable

import VT [ɪm'pɔːt] importer ▶ N ['ɪmpɔːt] (Comm) importation f; (meaning) portée f, signification f ▶ CPD ['ɪmpɔːt] (duty, licence etc) d'importation

importance [ɪm'pɔːtns] N importance f; **to be of great/little ~** avoir beaucoup/peu d'importance

important [ɪm'pɔːtnt] ADJ important(e); **it is ~ that** il importe que, il est important que; **it's not ~** c'est sans importance, ce n'est pas important

importantly [ɪm'pɔːtntlɪ] ADV (with an air of importance) d'un air important; (essentially): **but, more ~** ... mais, (ce qui est) plus important encore ...

importation [ɪmpɔː'teɪʃən] N importation f

imported [ɪm'pɔːtɪd] ADJ importé(e), d'importation

importer [ɪm'pɔːtəʳ] N importateur(-trice)

impose [ɪm'pəuz] VT imposer ▶ VI: **to ~ on sb** abuser de la gentillesse de qn

imposing [ɪm'pəuzɪŋ] ADJ imposant(e), impressionnant(e)

imposition [ɪmpə'zɪʃən] N (of tax etc) imposition f; **to be an ~ on** (person) abuser de la gentillesse ou la bonté de

impossibility [ɪmpɒsə'bɪlɪtɪ] N impossibilité f

impossible [ɪm'pɒsɪbl] ADJ impossible; **it is ~ for me to leave** il m'est impossible de partir

impostor [ɪm'pɒstəʳ] N imposteur m

impotence ['ɪmpətns] N impuissance f

impotent ['ɪmpətnt] ADJ impuissant(e)

impound [ɪm'paund] VT confisquer, saisir

impoverished [ɪm'pɒvərɪʃt] ADJ pauvre, appauvri(e)

impracticable [ɪm'præktɪkəbl] ADJ impraticable

impractical [ɪm'præktɪkl] ADJ pas pratique; (person) qui manque d'esprit pratique

imprecise [ɪmprɪ'saɪs] ADJ imprécis(e)

impregnable [ɪm'prɛgnəbl] ADJ (fortress) imprenable; (fig) inattaquable, irréfutable

impregnate ['ɪmprɛgneɪt] VT imprégner; (fertilize) féconder

impresario [ɪmprɪ'sɑːrɪəu] N impresario m

impress [ɪm'prɛs] VT impressionner, faire impression sur; (mark) imprimer, marquer; **to ~ sth on sb** faire bien comprendre qch à qn

impressed [ɪm'prɛst] ADJ impressionné(e)

impression [ɪm'prɛʃən] N impression f; (of stamp, seal) empreinte f; (imitation) imitation f; **to make a good/bad ~ on sb** faire bonne/mauvaise impression sur qn; **to be under the ~ that** avoir l'impression que

impressionable [ɪm'prɛʃnəbl] ADJ impressionnable, sensible

impressionist [ɪm'prɛʃənɪst] N impressionniste mf

impressive [ɪm'prɛsɪv] ADJ impressionnant(e)

imprint ['ɪmprɪnt] N empreinte f; (Publishing) notice f; (: label) nom m (de collection or d'éditeur)

imprinted [ɪm'prɪntɪd] ADJ: **~ on** imprimé(e) sur; (fig) imprimé(e) or gravé(e) dans

imprison [ɪm'prɪzn] VT emprisonner, mettre en prison

imprisonment [ɪm'prɪznmənt] N emprisonnement m; (period): **to sentence sb to 10 years' ~** condamner qn à 10 ans de prison

improbable [ɪm'prɒbəbl] ADJ improbable; (excuse) peu plausible

impromptu [ɪm'prɒmptjuː] ADJ impromptu(e) ▶ ADV impromptu

improper [ɪm'prɒpəʳ] ADJ (wrong) incorrect(e); (unsuitable) déplacé(e), de mauvais goût; (indecent) indécent(e); (dishonest) malhonnête

impropriety [ɪmprə'praɪətɪ] N inconvenance f; (of expression) impropriété f

improve [ɪm'pruːv] VT améliorer ▶ VI s'améliorer; (pupil etc) faire des progrès ▶ **improve on, improve upon** VT FUS (offer) enchérir sur

improvement [ɪm'pruːvmənt] N amélioration f; (of pupil etc) progrès m; **to make improvements to** apporter des améliorations à

improvisation [ɪmprəvaɪ'zeɪʃən] N improvisation f

improvise ['ɪmprəvaɪz] VT, VI improviser

imprudence [ɪm'pruːdns] N imprudence f

imprudent [ɪm'pruːdnt] ADJ imprudent(e)

impudent ['ɪmpjudnt] ADJ impudent(e)

impugn [ɪm'pjuːn] VT contester, attaquer

impulse ['ɪmpʌls] N impulsion f; **on ~** impulsivement, sur un coup de tête

impulse buy N achat m d'impulsion

impulsive [ɪm'pʌlsɪv] ADJ impulsif(-ive)

impunity [ɪm'pjuːnɪtɪ] N: **with ~** impunément

impure [ɪm'pjuəʳ] ADJ impur(e)

impurity [ɪm'pjʊərɪtɪ] N impureté f
IN ABBR (US) = **Indiana**

(KEYWORD)

in [ɪn] PREP **1** (*indicating place, position*) dans; **in the house/the fridge** dans la maison/le frigo; **in the garden** dans le *or* au jardin; **in town** en ville; **in the country** à la campagne; **in school** à l'école; **in here/there** ici/là
2 (*with place names: of town, region, country*): **in London** à Londres; **in England** en Angleterre; **in Japan** au Japon; **in the United States** aux États-Unis
3 (*indicating time: during*): **in spring** au printemps; **in summer** en été; **in May/2005** en mai/2005; **in the afternoon** (dans) l'après-midi; **at 4 o'clock in the afternoon** à 4 heures de l'après-midi
4 (*indicating time: in the space of*) en; (*: future*) dans; **I did it in 3 hours/days** je l'ai fait en 3 heures/jours; **I'll see you in 2 weeks** *or* **in 2 weeks' time** je te verrai dans 2 semaines; **once in a hundred years** une fois tous les cent ans
5 (*indicating manner etc*) à; **in a loud/soft voice** à voix haute/basse; **in pencil** au crayon; **in writing** par écrit; **in French** en français; **to pay in dollars** payer en dollars; **the boy in the blue shirt** le garçon à *or* avec la chemise bleue
6 (*indicating circumstances*): **in the sun** au soleil; **in the shade** à l'ombre; **in the rain** sous la pluie; **a change in policy** un changement de politique
7 (*indicating mood, state*): **in tears** en larmes; **in anger** sous le coup de la colère; **in despair** au désespoir; **in good condition** en bon état; **to live in luxury** vivre dans le luxe
8 (*with ratios, numbers*): **1 in 10 households, 1 household in 10** 1 ménage sur 10; **20 pence in the pound** 20 pence par livre sterling; **they lined up in twos** ils se mirent en rangs (deux) par deux; **in hundreds** par centaines
9 (*referring to people, works*) chez; **the disease is common in children** c'est une maladie courante chez les enfants; **in (the works of) Dickens** chez Dickens, dans (l'œuvre de) Dickens
10 (*indicating profession etc*) dans; **to be in teaching** être dans l'enseignement
11 (*after superlative*) de; **the best pupil in the class** le meilleur élève de la classe
12 (*with present participle*): **in saying this** en disant ceci
▶ ADV: **to be in** (*person: at home, work*) être là; (*train, ship, plane*) être arrivé(e); (*in fashion*) être à la mode; **to ask sb in** inviter qn à entrer; **to run/limp etc in** entrer en courant/boitant *etc*; **their party is in** leur parti est au pouvoir
▶ N: **the ins and outs (of)** (*of proposal, situation etc*) les tenants et aboutissants (de)

in. ABBR = **inch; inches**
inability [ɪnə'bɪlɪtɪ] N incapacité f; ~ **to pay** incapacité de payer
inaccessible [ɪnək'sɛsɪbl] ADJ inaccessible

inaccuracy [ɪn'ækjʊrəsɪ] N inexactitude f; **manque** m de précision
inaccurate [ɪn'ækjʊrət] ADJ inexact(e); (*person*) qui manque de précision
inaction [ɪn'ækʃən] N inaction f, inactivité f
inactivity [ɪnæk'tɪvɪtɪ] N inactivité f
inadequacy [ɪn'ædɪkwəsɪ] N insuffisance f
inadequate [ɪn'ædɪkwət] ADJ insuffisant(e), inadéquat(e)
inadmissible [ɪnəd'mɪsəbl] ADJ (*behaviour*) inadmissible; (*Law: evidence*) irrecevable
inadvertent [ɪnəd'və:tnt] ADJ (*mistake*) commis(e) par inadvertance
inadvertently [ɪnəd'və:tntlɪ] ADV par mégarde
inadvisable [ɪnəd'vaɪzəbl] ADJ à déconseiller; **it is ~ to** il est déconseillé de
inane [ɪ'neɪn] ADJ inepte, stupide
inanimate [ɪn'ænɪmət] ADJ inanimé(e)
inapplicable [ɪn'æplɪkəbl] ADJ inapplicable
inappropriate [ɪnə'prəʊprɪət] ADJ inopportun(e), mal à propos; (*word, expression*) impropre
inapt [ɪn'æpt] ADJ inapte; peu approprié(e)
inaptitude [ɪn'æptɪtjuːd] N inaptitude f
inarticulate [ɪnɑː'tɪkjʊlət] ADJ (*person*) qui s'exprime mal; (*speech*) indistinct(e)
inasmuch [ɪnəz'mʌtʃ] ADV: ~ **as** vu que, en ce sens que
inattention [ɪnə'tɛnʃən] N manque m d'attention
inattentive [ɪnə'tɛntɪv] ADJ inattentif(-ive), distrait(e); négligent(e)
inaudible [ɪn'ɔːdɪbl] ADJ inaudible
inaugural [ɪ'nɔːgjʊrəl] ADJ inaugural(e)
inaugurate [ɪ'nɔːgjʊreɪt] VT inaugurer; (*president, official*) investir de ses fonctions
inauguration [ɪnɔːgjʊ'reɪʃən] N inauguration f; investiture f
inauspicious [ɪnɔːs'pɪʃəs] ADJ peu propice
in-between [ɪnbɪ'twiːn] ADJ entre les deux
inborn [ɪn'bɔːn] ADJ (*feeling*) inné(e); (*defect*) congénital(e)
inbox ['ɪnbɒks] N (*Comput*) boîte f de réception; (*US: intray*) corbeille f du courrier reçu
inbred [ɪn'brɛd] ADJ inné(e), naturel(le); (*family*) consanguin(e)
inbreeding [ɪn'briːdɪŋ] N croisement m d'animaux de même souche; unions consanguines
Inc. ABBR = **incorporated**
Inca ['ɪŋkə] ADJ (*also:* **Incan**) inca *inv* ▶ N Inca *mf*
incalculable [ɪn'kælkjʊləbl] ADJ incalculable
incapability [ɪnkeɪpə'bɪlɪtɪ] N incapacité f
incapable [ɪn'keɪpəbl] ADJ: ~ **(of)** incapable (de)
incapacitate [ɪnkə'pæsɪteɪt] VT: **to ~ sb from doing** rendre qn incapable de faire
incapacitated [ɪnkə'pæsɪteɪtɪd] ADJ (*Law*) frappé(e) d'incapacité
incapacity [ɪnkə'pæsɪtɪ] N incapacité f
incarcerate [ɪn'kɑːsəreɪt] VT incarcérer
incarnate ADJ [ɪn'kɑːnɪt] incarné(e) ▶ VT ['ɪnkɑːneɪt] incarner
incarnation [ɪnkɑː'neɪʃən] N incarnation f
incendiary [ɪn'sɛndɪərɪ] ADJ incendiaire ▶ N

(bomb) bombe f incendiaire

incense N ['ɪnsɛns] encens m ▸ VT [ɪn'sɛns] *(anger)* mettre en colère

incense burner N encensoir m

incentive [ɪn'sɛntɪv] N encouragement m, raison f de se donner de la peine

incentive scheme N système m de primes d'encouragement

inception [ɪn'sɛpʃən] N commencement m, début m

incessant [ɪn'sɛsnt] ADJ incessant(e)

incessantly [ɪn'sɛsntlɪ] ADV sans cesse, constamment

incest ['ɪnsɛst] N inceste m

inch [ɪntʃ] N pouce m (= 25 mm; 12 in a foot); **within an ~ of** à deux doigts de; **he wouldn't give an ~** *(fig)* il n'a pas voulu céder d'un pouce
▸ **inch forward** VI avancer petit à petit

inch tape N (BRIT) centimètre m (de couturière)

incidence ['ɪnsɪdns] N *(of crime, disease)* fréquence f

incident ['ɪnsɪdnt] N incident m; *(in book)* péripétie f

incidental [ɪnsɪ'dɛntl] ADJ accessoire; *(unplanned)* accidentel(le); **~ to** qui accompagne; **~ expenses** faux frais mpl

incidentally [ɪnsɪ'dɛntəlɪ] ADV *(by the way)* à propos

incidental music N musique f de fond

incident room N *(Police)* salle f d'opérations

incinerate [ɪn'sɪnəreɪt] VT incinérer

incinerator [ɪn'sɪnəreɪtəʳ] N incinérateur m

incipient [ɪn'sɪpɪənt] ADJ naissant(e)

incision [ɪn'sɪʒən] N incision f

incisive [ɪn'saɪsɪv] ADJ incisif(-ive), mordant(e)

incisor [ɪn'saɪzəʳ] N incisive f

incite [ɪn'saɪt] VT inciter, pousser

incl. ABBR = **including; inclusive (of)**

inclement [ɪn'klɛmənt] ADJ inclément(e), rigoureux(-euse)

inclination [ɪnklɪ'neɪʃən] N inclination f; *(desire)* envie f

incline N ['ɪnklaɪn] pente f, plan incliné ▸ VT [ɪn'klaɪn] incliner ▸ VI s'incliner; **to ~ to** avoir tendance à; **to be inclined to do** *(want to)* être enclin(e) à faire; *(have a tendency to do)* avoir tendance à faire; **to be well inclined towards sb** être bien disposé(e) à l'égard de qn

include [ɪn'kluːd] VT inclure, comprendre; **service is/is not included** le service est compris/n'est pas compris

including [ɪn'kluːdɪŋ] PREP y compris; **~ service** service compris

inclusion [ɪn'kluːʒən] N inclusion f

inclusive [ɪn'kluːsɪv] ADJ inclus(e), compris(e); **~ of tax** taxes comprises; **£50 ~ of all surcharges** 50 livres tous frais compris

inclusive terms NPL (BRIT) prix tout compris

incognito [ɪnkɔg'niːtəu] ADV incognito

incoherent [ɪnkəu'hɪərənt] ADJ incohérent(e)

income ['ɪnkʌm] N revenu m; *(from property etc)* rentes fpl; **gross/net ~** revenu brut/net; **~ and expenditure account** compte m de recettes et de dépenses

income support N (BRIT) ≈ revenu m minimum d'insertion, RMI m

income tax N impôt m sur le revenu

income tax inspector N inspecteur m des contributions directes

income tax return N déclaration f des revenus

incoming ['ɪnkʌmɪŋ] ADJ *(passengers, mail)* à l'arrivée; *(government, tenant)* nouveau *(nouvelle)*; **~ tide** marée montante

incommunicado ['ɪnkəmjunɪ'kɑːdəu] ADJ: **to hold sb ~** tenir qn au secret

incomparable [ɪn'kɔmpərəbl] ADJ incomparable

incompatible [ɪnkəm'pætɪbl] ADJ incompatible

incompetence [ɪn'kɔmpɪtns] N incompétence f, incapacité f

incompetent [ɪn'kɔmpɪtnt] ADJ incompétent(e), incapable

incomplete [ɪnkəm'pliːt] ADJ incomplet(-ète)

incomprehensible [ɪnkɔmprɪ'hɛnsɪbl] ADJ incompréhensible

inconceivable [ɪnkən'siːvəbl] ADJ inconcevable

inconclusive [ɪnkən'kluːsɪv] ADJ peu concluant(e); *(argument)* peu convaincant(e)

incongruous [ɪn'kɔŋgruəs] ADJ peu approprié(e); *(remark, act)* incongru(e), déplacé(e)

inconsequential [ɪnkɔnsɪ'kwɛnʃl] ADJ sans importance

inconsiderable [ɪnkən'sɪdərəbl] ADJ: **not ~** non négligeable

inconsiderate [ɪnkən'sɪdərət] ADJ *(action)* inconsidéré(e); *(person)* qui manque d'égards

inconsistency [ɪnkən'sɪstənsɪ] N *(of actions etc)* inconséquence f; *(of work)* irrégularité f; *(of statement etc)* incohérence f

inconsistent [ɪnkən'sɪstnt] ADJ qui manque de constance; *(work)* irrégulier(-ière); *(statement)* peu cohérent(e); **~ with** en contradiction avec

inconsolable [ɪnkən'səuləbl] ADJ inconsolable

inconspicuous [ɪnkən'spɪkjuəs] ADJ qui passe inaperçu(e); *(colour, dress)* discret(-ète); **to make o.s. ~** ne pas se faire remarquer

inconstant [ɪn'kɔnstnt] ADJ inconstant(e), variable

incontinence [ɪn'kɔntɪnəns] N incontinence f

incontinent [ɪn'kɔntɪnənt] ADJ incontinent(e)

incontrovertible [ɪnkɔntrə'vəːtəbl] ADJ irréfutable

inconvenience [ɪnkən'viːnjəns] N inconvénient m; *(trouble)* dérangement m ▸ VT déranger; **don't ~ yourself** ne vous dérangez pas

inconvenient [ɪnkən'viːnjənt] ADJ malcommode; *(time, place)* mal choisi(e), qui ne convient pas; *(visitor)* importun(e); **that time is very ~ for me** c'est un moment qui ne me convient pas du tout

incorporate [ɪn'kɔːpəreɪt] VT incorporer; *(contain)* contenir ▸ VI fusionner; *(two firms)* se constituer en société

incorporated [ɪn'kɔːpəreɪtd] ADJ: **~ company** *(US)* ≈ société f anonyme

incorrect [ɪnkə'rɛkt] ADJ incorrect(e); *(opinion, statement)* inexact(e)

incorrigible [ɪnˈkɔrɪdʒɪbl] ADJ incorrigible
incorruptible [ɪnkəˈrʌptɪbl] ADJ incorruptible
increase N [ˈɪnkriːs] augmentation f ▶ VI, VT [ɪnˈkriːs] augmenter; **an ~ of 5%** une augmentation de 5%; **to be on the ~** être en augmentation
increasing [ɪnˈkriːsɪŋ] ADJ croissant(e)
increasingly [ɪnˈkriːsɪŋlɪ] ADV de plus en plus
incredible [ɪnˈkrɛdɪbl] ADJ incroyable
incredibly [ɪnˈkrɛdɪblɪ] ADV incroyablement
incredulous [ɪnˈkrɛdjuləs] ADJ incrédule
increment [ˈɪnkrɪmənt] N augmentation f
incriminate [ɪnˈkrɪmɪneɪt] VT incriminer, compromettre
incriminating [ɪnˈkrɪmɪneɪtɪŋ] ADJ compromettant(e)
incubate [ˈɪnkjubeɪt] VT (egg) couver, incuber ▶ VI (eggs) couver; (disease) couver
incubation [ɪnkjuˈbeɪʃən] N incubation f
incubation period N période f d'incubation
incubator [ˈɪnkjubeɪtəʳ] N incubateur m; (for babies) couveuse f
inculcate [ˈɪnkʌlkeɪt] VT: **to ~ sth in sb** inculquer qch à qn
incumbent [ɪnˈkʌmbənt] ADJ: **it is ~ on him to … il lui appartient de …** ▶ N titulaire mf
incur [ɪnˈkəːʳ] VT (expenses) encourir; (anger, risk) s'exposer à; (debt) contracter; (loss) subir
incurable [ɪnˈkjuərəbl] ADJ incurable
incursion [ɪnˈkəːʃən] N incursion f
Ind. ABBR (US) = **Indiana**
indebted [ɪnˈdɛtɪd] ADJ: **to be ~ to sb (for)** être redevable à qn (de)
indecency [ɪnˈdiːsnsɪ] N indécence f
indecent [ɪnˈdiːsnt] ADJ indécent(e), inconvenant(e)
indecent assault N (BRIT) attentat m à la pudeur
indecent exposure N outrage m public à la pudeur
indecipherable [ɪndɪˈsaɪfərəbl] ADJ indéchiffrable
indecision [ɪndɪˈsɪʒən] N indécision f
indecisive [ɪndɪˈsaɪsɪv] ADJ indécis(e); (discussion) peu concluant(e)
indeed [ɪnˈdiːd] ADV (confirming, agreeing) en effet, effectivement; (for emphasis) vraiment; (furthermore) d'ailleurs; **yes ~!** certainement!
indefatigable [ɪndɪˈfætɪgəbl] ADJ infatigable
indefensible [ɪndɪˈfɛnsɪbl] ADJ (conduct) indéfendable
indefinable [ɪndɪˈfaɪnəbl] ADJ indéfinissable
indefinite [ɪnˈdɛfɪnɪt] ADJ indéfini(e); (answer) vague; (period, number) indéterminé(e)
indefinitely [ɪnˈdɛfɪnɪtlɪ] ADV (wait) indéfiniment; (speak) vaguement, avec imprécision
indelible [ɪnˈdɛlɪbl] ADJ indélébile
indelicate [ɪnˈdɛlɪkɪt] ADJ (tactless) indélicat(e), grossier(-ière); (not polite) inconvenant(e), malséant(e)
indemnify [ɪnˈdɛmnɪfaɪ] VT indemniser, dédommager
indemnity [ɪnˈdɛmnɪtɪ] N (insurance) assurance f,

garantie f; (compensation) indemnité f
indent [ɪnˈdɛnt] VT (text) commencer en retrait
indentation [ɪndɛnˈteɪʃən] N découpure f; (Typ) alinéa m; (on metal) bosse f
indenture [ɪnˈdɛntʃəʳ] N contrat m d'emploi-formation
independence [ɪndɪˈpɛndns] N indépendance f
Independence Day N (US) fête de l'Indépendance américaine; voir article

> L'Independence Day est la fête nationale aux États-Unis, le 4 juillet. Il commémore l'adoption de la déclaration d'Indépendance, en 1776, écrite par Thomas Jefferson et proclamant la séparation des 13 colonies américaines de la Grande-Bretagne.

independent [ɪndɪˈpɛndnt] ADJ indépendant(e); (radio) libre; **to become ~** s'affranchir
independently [ɪndɪˈpɛndntlɪ] ADV de façon indépendante; **~ of** indépendamment de
independent school N (BRIT) école privée
in-depth [ˈɪndɛpθ] ADJ approfondi(e)
indescribable [ɪndɪˈskraɪbəbl] ADJ indescriptible
indeterminate [ɪndɪˈtəːmɪnɪt] ADJ indéterminé(e)
index [ˈɪndɛks] N (pl **indexes**) (in book) index m; (: in library etc) catalogue m; (pl **indices** [ˈɪndɪsiːz]: ratio, sign) indice m
index card N fiche f
index finger N index m
index-linked [ˈɪndɛksˈlɪŋkt], (US) **indexed** [ˈɪndɛkst] ADJ indexé(e) (sur le coût de la vie etc)
India [ˈɪndɪə] N Inde f
Indian [ˈɪndɪən] ADJ indien(ne) ▶ N Indien(ne); (American) ~ Indien(ne) (d'Amérique)
Indian ink N encre f de Chine
Indian Ocean N: **the ~** l'océan Indien
Indian summer N (fig) été indien, beaux jours en automne
India paper N papier m bible
India rubber N gomme f
indicate [ˈɪndɪkeɪt] VT indiquer ▶ VI (BRIT Aut): **to ~ left/right** mettre son clignotant à gauche/à droite
indication [ɪndɪˈkeɪʃən] N indication f, signe m
indicative [ɪnˈdɪkətɪv] ADJ indicatif(-ive); **to be ~ of sth** être symptomatique de qch ▶ N (Ling) indicatif m
indicator [ˈɪndɪkeɪtəʳ] N (sign) indicateur m; (Aut) clignotant m
indices [ˈɪndɪsiːz] NPL of **index**
indict [ɪnˈdaɪt] VT accuser
indictable [ɪnˈdaɪtəbl] ADJ (person) passible de poursuites; **~ offence** délit m tombant sous le coup de la loi
indictment [ɪnˈdaɪtmənt] N accusation f
indifference [ɪnˈdɪfrəns] N indifférence f
indifferent [ɪnˈdɪfrənt] ADJ indifférent(e); (poor) médiocre, quelconque
indigenous [ɪnˈdɪdʒɪnəs] ADJ indigène
indigestible [ɪndɪˈdʒɛstɪbl] ADJ indigeste
indigestion [ɪndɪˈdʒɛstʃən] N indigestion f, mauvaise digestion

indignant [ɪnˈdɪɡnənt] ADJ: ~ **(at sth/with sb)** indigné(e) (de qch/contre qn)

indignation [ɪndɪɡˈneɪʃən] N indignation f

indignity [ɪnˈdɪɡnɪtɪ] N indignité f, affront m

indigo [ˈɪndɪɡəʊ] ADJ indigo inv ▶ N indigo m

indirect [ɪndɪˈrɛkt] ADJ indirect(e)

indirectly [ɪndɪˈrɛktlɪ] ADV indirectement

indiscreet [ɪndɪˈskriːt] ADJ indiscret(-ète); (rash) imprudent(e)

indiscretion [ɪndɪˈskreʃən] N indiscrétion f; (rashness) imprudence f

indiscriminate [ɪndɪˈskrɪmɪnət] ADJ (person) qui manque de discernement; (admiration) aveugle; (killings) commis(e) au hasard

indispensable [ɪndɪˈspɛnsəbl] ADJ indispensable

indisposed [ɪndɪˈspəʊzd] ADJ (unwell) indisposé(e), souffrant(e)

indisposition [ɪndɪspəˈzɪʃən] N (illness) indisposition f, malaise m

indisputable [ɪndɪˈspjuːtəbl] ADJ incontestable, indiscutable

indistinct [ɪndɪˈstɪŋkt] ADJ indistinct(e); (memory, noise) vague

indistinguishable [ɪndɪˈstɪŋɡwɪʃəbl] ADJ impossible à distinguer

individual [ɪndɪˈvɪdjuəl] N individu m ▶ ADJ individuel(le); (characteristic) particulier(-ière), original(e)

individualist [ɪndɪˈvɪdjuəlɪst] N individualiste mf

individuality [ɪndɪvɪdjuˈælɪtɪ] N individualité f

individually [ɪndɪˈvɪdjuəlɪ] ADV individuellement

indivisible [ɪndɪˈvɪzɪbl] ADJ indivisible; (Math) insécable

Indo-China [ˈɪndəʊˈtʃaɪnə] N Indochine f

indoctrinate [ɪnˈdɒktrɪneɪt] VT endoctriner

indoctrination [ɪndɒktrɪˈneɪʃən] N endoctrinement m

indolent [ˈɪndələnt] ADJ indolent(e), nonchalant(e)

Indonesia [ɪndəˈniːzɪə] N Indonésie f

Indonesian [ɪndəˈniːzɪən] ADJ indonésien(ne) ▶ N Indonésien(ne); (Ling) indonésien m

indoor [ˈɪndɔːʳ] ADJ d'intérieur; (plant) d'appartement; (swimming pool) couvert(e); (sport, games) pratiqué(e) en salle

indoors [ɪnˈdɔːz] ADV à l'intérieur; (at home) à la maison

indubitable [ɪnˈdjuːbɪtəbl] ADJ indubitable, incontestable

induce [ɪnˈdjuːs] VT (persuade) persuader; (bring about) provoquer; (labour) déclencher; **to ~ sb to do sth** inciter or pousser qn à faire qch

inducement [ɪnˈdjuːsmənt] N incitation f; (incentive) but m; (pej: bribe) pot-de-vin m

induct [ɪnˈdʌkt] VT établir dans ses fonctions; (fig) initier

induction [ɪnˈdʌkʃən] N (Med: of birth) accouchement provoqué

induction course N (BRIT) stage m de mise au courant

indulge [ɪnˈdʌldʒ] VT (whim) céder à, satisfaire;

(child) gâter ▶ VI: **to ~ in sth** (luxury) s'offrir qch, se permettre qch; (fantasies etc) se livrer à qch

indulgence [ɪnˈdʌldʒəns] N fantaisie f (que l'on s'offre); (leniency) indulgence f

indulgent [ɪnˈdʌldʒənt] ADJ indulgent(e)

industrial [ɪnˈdʌstrɪəl] ADJ industriel(le); (injury) du travail; (dispute) ouvrier(-ière)

industrial action N action revendicative

industrial estate N (BRIT) zone industrielle

industrialist [ɪnˈdʌstrɪəlɪst] N industriel m

industrialize [ɪnˈdʌstrɪəlaɪz] VT industrialiser

industrial park N (US) zone industrielle

industrial relations NPL relations fpl dans l'entreprise

industrial tribunal N (BRIT) ≈ conseil m de prud'hommes

industrious [ɪnˈdʌstrɪəs] ADJ travailleur(-euse)

industry [ˈɪndəstrɪ] N industrie f; (diligence) zèle m, application f

inebriated [ɪˈniːbrɪeɪtɪd] ADJ ivre

inedible [ɪnˈɛdɪbl] ADJ immangeable; (plant etc) non comestible

ineffective [ɪnɪˈfɛktɪv], **ineffectual** [ɪnɪˈfɛktjuəl] ADJ inefficace; incompétent(e)

inefficiency [ɪnɪˈfɪʃənsɪ] N inefficacité f

inefficient [ɪnɪˈfɪʃənt] ADJ inefficace

inelegant [ɪnˈɛlɪɡənt] ADJ peu élégant(e), inélégant(e)

ineligible [ɪnˈɛlɪdʒɪbl] ADJ (candidate) inéligible; **to be ~ for sth** ne pas avoir droit à qch

inept [ɪˈnɛpt] ADJ inepte

ineptitude [ɪˈnɛptɪtjuːd] N ineptie f

inequality [ɪnɪˈkwɒlɪtɪ] N inégalité f

inequitable [ɪnˈɛkwɪtəbl] ADJ inéquitable, inique

ineradicable [ɪnɪˈrædɪkəbl] ADJ indéracinable, tenace

inert [ɪˈnəːt] ADJ inerte

inertia [ɪˈnəːʃə] N inertie f

inertia-reel seat belt [ɪˈnəːʃəˈriːl-] N ceinture f de sécurité à enrouleur

inescapable [ɪnɪˈskeɪpəbl] ADJ inéluctable, inévitable

inessential [ɪnɪˈsɛnʃl] ADJ superflu(e)

inestimable [ɪnˈɛstɪməbl] ADJ inestimable, incalculable

inevitable [ɪnˈɛvɪtəbl] ADJ inévitable

inevitably [ɪnˈɛvɪtəblɪ] ADV inévitablement, fatalement

inexact [ɪnɪɡˈzækt] ADJ inexact(e)

inexcusable [ɪnɪksˈkjuːzəbl] ADJ inexcusable

inexhaustible [ɪnɪɡˈzɔːstɪbl] ADJ inépuisable

inexorable [ɪnˈɛksərəbl] ADJ inexorable

inexpensive [ɪnɪkˈspɛnsɪv] ADJ bon marché inv

inexperience [ɪnɪkˈspɪərɪəns] N inexpérience f, manque m d'expérience

inexperienced [ɪnɪkˈspɪərɪənst] ADJ inexpérimenté(e); **to be ~ in sth** manquer d'expérience dans qch

inexplicable [ɪnɪkˈsplɪkəbl] ADJ inexplicable

inexpressible [ɪnɪkˈsprɛsɪbl] ADJ inexprimable; indicible

inextricable [ɪnɪkˈstrɪkəbl] ADJ inextricable

infallibility [ɪnfæləˈbɪlɪtɪ] N infaillibilité f

i

infallible [ɪnˈfælɪbl] ADJ infaillible
infamous [ˈɪnfəməs] ADJ infâme, abominable
infamy [ˈɪnfəmɪ] N infamie f
infancy [ˈɪnfənsɪ] N petite enfance, bas âge; (fig) enfance, débuts mpl
infant [ˈɪnfənt] N (baby) nourrisson m; (young child) petit(e) enfant
infantile [ˈɪnfəntaɪl] ADJ infantile
infant mortality N mortalité f infantile
infantry [ˈɪnfəntrɪ] N infanterie f
infantryman [ˈɪnfəntrɪmən] N (irreg) fantassin m
infant school N (BRIT) classes fpl préparatoires (entre 5 et 7 ans)
infatuated [ɪnˈfætjʊeɪtɪd] ADJ: ~ with entiché(e) de; to become ~ (with sb) s'enticher (de qn)
infatuation [ɪnfætjuˈeɪʃən] N toquade f; engouement m
infect [ɪnˈfɛkt] VT (wound) infecter; (person, blood) contaminer; (fig, pej) corrompre; **infected with** (illness) atteint(e) de; **to become infected** (wound) s'infecter
infection [ɪnˈfɛkʃən] N infection f; (contagion) contagion f
infectious [ɪnˈfɛkʃəs] ADJ infectieux(-euse); (also fig) contagieux(-euse)
infer [ɪnˈfəːʳ] VT: **to ~ (from)** conclure (de), déduire (de)
inference [ˈɪnfərəns] N conclusion f, déduction f
inferior [ɪnˈfɪərɪəʳ] ADJ inférieur(e); (goods) de qualité inférieure ▶ N inférieur(e); (in rank) subalterne mf; **to feel ~** avoir un sentiment d'infériorité
inferiority [ɪnfɪərɪˈɔrɪtɪ] N infériorité f
inferiority complex N complexe m d'infériorité
infernal [ɪnˈfəːnl] ADJ infernal(e)
inferno [ɪnˈfəːnəʊ] N enfer m; brasier m
infertile [ɪnˈfəːtaɪl] ADJ stérile
infertility [ɪnfəːˈtɪlɪtɪ] N infertilité f, stérilité f
infested [ɪnˈfɛstɪd] ADJ: ~ **(with)** infesté(e) (de)
infidelity [ɪnfɪˈdɛlɪtɪ] N infidélité f
in-fighting [ˈɪnfaɪtɪŋ] N querelles fpl internes
infiltrate [ˈɪnfɪltreɪt] VT (troops etc) faire s'infiltrer; (enemy line etc) s'infiltrer dans ▶ VI s'infiltrer
infinite [ˈɪnfɪnɪt] ADJ infini(e); (time, money) illimité(e)
infinitely [ˈɪnfɪnɪtlɪ] ADV infiniment
infinitesimal [ɪnfɪnɪˈtɛsɪməl] ADJ infinitésimal(e)
infinitive [ɪnˈfɪnɪtɪv] N infinitif m
infinity [ɪnˈfɪnɪtɪ] N infinité f; (also Math) infini m
infirm [ɪnˈfəːm] ADJ infirme
infirmary [ɪnˈfəːmərɪ] N hôpital m; (in school, factory) infirmerie f
infirmity [ɪnˈfəːmɪtɪ] N infirmité f
inflamed [ɪnˈfleɪmd] ADJ enflammé(e)
inflammable [ɪnˈflæməbl] ADJ (BRIT) inflammable
inflammation [ɪnfləˈmeɪʃən] N inflammation f
inflammatory [ɪnˈflæmətərɪ] ADJ (speech) incendiaire

inflatable [ɪnˈfleɪtəbl] ADJ gonflable
inflate [ɪnˈfleɪt] VT (tyre, balloon) gonfler; (fig: exaggerate) grossir, gonfler; (: increase) gonfler
inflated [ɪnˈfleɪtɪd] ADJ (style) enflé(e); (value) exagéré(e)
inflation [ɪnˈfleɪʃən] N (Econ) inflation f
inflationary [ɪnˈfleɪʃənərɪ] ADJ inflationniste
inflexible [ɪnˈflɛksɪbl] ADJ inflexible, rigide
inflict [ɪnˈflɪkt] VT: **to ~ on** infliger à
infliction [ɪnˈflɪkʃən] N: **without the ~ of pain** sans infliger de douleurs
in-flight [ˈɪnflaɪt] ADJ (refuelling) en vol; (service etc) à bord
inflow [ˈɪnfləʊ] N afflux m
influence [ˈɪnfluəns] N influence f ▶ VT influencer; **under the ~ of** sous l'effet de; **under the ~ of alcohol** en état d'ébriété
influential [ɪnfluˈɛnʃl] ADJ influent(e)
influenza [ɪnfluˈɛnzə] N grippe f
influx [ˈɪnflʌks] N afflux m
info [ˈɪnfəʊ] (inf) N (= information) renseignements mpl
infomercial [ˈɪnfəʊməːʃl] (US) N (for product) publi-information f; (Pol) émission où un candidat présente son programme électoral
inform [ɪnˈfɔːm] VT: **to ~ sb (of)** informer or avertir qn (de) ▶ VI: **to ~ on sb** dénoncer qn, informer contre qn; **to ~ sb about** renseigner qn sur, mettre qn au courant de
informal [ɪnˈfɔːml] ADJ (person, manner, party) simple, sans cérémonie; (visit, discussion) dénué(e) de formalités; (announcement, invitation) non officiel(le); (colloquial) familier(-ère); **"dress ~"** "tenue de ville"
informality [ɪnfɔːˈmælɪtɪ] N simplicité f, absence f de cérémonie; caractère non officiel
informally [ɪnˈfɔːməlɪ] ADV sans cérémonie, en toute simplicité; non officiellement
informant [ɪnˈfɔːmənt] N informateur(-trice)
information [ɪnfəˈmeɪʃən] N information(s) f(pl); renseignements mpl; (knowledge) connaissances fpl; **to get ~ on** se renseigner sur; **a piece of ~** un renseignement; **for your ~** à titre d'information
information bureau N bureau m de renseignements
information desk N accueil m
information office N bureau m de renseignements
information processing N traitement m de l'information
information technology N informatique f
informative [ɪnˈfɔːmətɪv] ADJ instructif(-ive)
informed [ɪnˈfɔːmd] ADJ (bien) informé(e); **an ~ guess** une hypothèse fondée sur la connaissance des faits
informer [ɪnˈfɔːməʳ] N dénonciateur(-trice); (also: **police informer**) indicateur(-trice)
infra dig [ˈɪnfrəˈdɪg] ADJ ABBR (inf: = infra dignitatem) au-dessous de ma (or sa etc) dignité
infra-red [ɪnfrəˈrɛd] ADJ infrarouge
infrastructure [ˈɪnfrəstrʌktʃəʳ] N infrastructure f
infrequent [ɪnˈfriːkwənt] ADJ peu fréquent(e), rare

infringe [ɪn'frɪndʒ] VT enfreindre ▶ VI: **to ~ on** empiéter sur

infringement [ɪn'frɪndʒmənt] N: **~ (of)** infraction f (à)

infuriate [ɪn'fjʊərɪeɪt] VT mettre en fureur

infuriating [ɪn'fjʊərɪeɪtɪŋ] ADJ exaspérant(e)

infuse [ɪn'fjuːz] VT: **to ~ sb with sth** (fig) insuffler qch à qn

infusion [ɪn'fjuːʒən] N (tea etc) infusion f

ingenious [ɪn'dʒiːnjəs] ADJ ingénieux(-euse)

ingenuity [ɪndʒɪ'njuːɪtɪ] N ingéniosité f

ingenuous [ɪn'dʒɛnjuəs] ADJ franc (franche), ouvert(e)

ingot ['ɪŋgət] N lingot m

ingrained [ɪn'greɪnd] ADJ enraciné(e)

ingratiate [ɪn'greɪʃɪeɪt] VT: **to ~ o.s. with** s'insinuer dans les bonnes grâces de, se faire bien voir de

ingratiating [ɪn'greɪʃɪeɪtɪŋ] ADJ (smile, speech) insinuant(e); (person) patelin(e)

ingratitude [ɪn'grætɪtjuːd] N ingratitude f

ingredient [ɪn'griːdɪənt] N ingrédient m; (fig) élément m

ingrowing ['ɪngrəʊɪŋ], **ingrown** ['ɪngrəʊn] ADJ: **~ toenail** ongle incarné

inhabit [ɪn'hæbɪt] VT habiter

inhabitable [ɪn'hæbɪtəbl] ADJ habitable

inhabitant [ɪn'hæbɪtnt] N habitant(e)

inhale [ɪn'heɪl] VT inhaler; (perfume) respirer; (smoke) avaler ▶ VI (breathe in) aspirer; (in smoking) avaler la fumée

inhaler [ɪn'heɪlər] N inhalateur m

inherent [ɪn'hɪərənt] ADJ: **~ (in or to)** inhérent(e) (à)

inherently [ɪn'hɪərəntlɪ] ADV (easy, difficult) en soi; (lazy) fondamentalement

inherit [ɪn'herɪt] VT hériter (de)

inheritance [ɪn'herɪtəns] N héritage m; (fig): **the situation that was his ~ as president** la situation dont il a hérité en tant que président; **law of ~** droit m de la succession

inhibit [ɪn'hɪbɪt] VT (Psych) inhiber; (growth) freiner; **to ~ sb from doing** empêcher or retenir qn de faire

inhibited [ɪn'hɪbɪtɪd] ADJ (person) inhibé(e)

inhibiting [ɪn'hɪbɪtɪŋ] ADJ gênant(e)

inhibition [ɪnhɪ'bɪʃən] N inhibition f

inhospitable [ɪnhɔs'pɪtəbl] ADJ inhospitalier(-ière)

in-house ['ɪn'haus] ADJ (system) interne; (training) effectué(e) sur place or dans le cadre de la compagnie ▶ ADV (train, produce) sur place

inhuman [ɪn'hjuːmən] ADJ inhumain(e)

inhumane [ɪnhjuː'meɪn] ADJ inhumain(e)

inimitable [ɪ'nɪmɪtəbl] ADJ inimitable

iniquity [ɪ'nɪkwɪtɪ] N iniquité f

initial [ɪ'nɪʃl] ADJ initial(e) ▶ N initiale f ▶ VT parafer; **initials** NPL initiales fpl; (as signature) parafe m

initialize [ɪ'nɪʃəlaɪz] VT (Comput) initialiser

initially [ɪ'nɪʃəlɪ] ADV initialement, au début

initiate [ɪ'nɪʃɪeɪt] VT (start) entreprendre; amorcer; (enterprise) lancer; (person) initier; **to ~ sb into a secret** initier qn à un secret; **to ~**

proceedings against sb (Law) intenter une action à qn, engager des poursuites contre qn

initiation [ɪnɪʃɪ'eɪʃən] N (into secret etc) initiation f

initiative [ɪ'nɪʃətɪv] N initiative f; **to take the ~** prendre l'initiative

inject [ɪn'dʒɛkt] VT (liquid, fig: money) injecter; (person): **to ~ sb with sth** faire une piqûre de qch à qn

injection [ɪn'dʒɛkʃən] N injection f, piqûre f; **to have an ~** se faire faire une piqûre

injudicious [ɪndʒu'dɪʃəs] ADJ peu judicieux(-euse)

injunction [ɪn'dʒʌŋkʃən] N (Law) injonction f, ordre m

injure ['ɪndʒər] VT blesser; (wrong) faire du tort à; (damage: reputation etc) compromettre; (: feelings) heurter; **to ~ o.s.** se blesser

injured ['ɪndʒəd] ADJ (person, leg etc) blessé(e); (tone, feelings) offensé(e); **~ party** (Law) partie lésée

injurious [ɪn'dʒuərɪəs] ADJ: **~ (to)** préjudiciable (à)

injury ['ɪndʒərɪ] N blessure f; (wrong) tort m; **to escape without ~** s'en sortir sain et sauf

injury time N (Sport) arrêts mpl de jeu

injustice [ɪn'dʒʌstɪs] N injustice f; **you do me an ~** vous êtes injuste envers moi

ink [ɪŋk] N encre f

ink-jet printer ['ɪŋkdʒɛt-] N imprimante f à jet d'encre

inkling ['ɪŋklɪŋ] N soupçon m, vague idée f

inkpad ['ɪŋkpæd] N tampon m encreur

inky ['ɪŋkɪ] ADJ taché(e) d'encre

inlaid ['ɪnleɪd] ADJ incrusté(e); (table etc) marqueté(e)

inland ADJ ['ɪnlənd] intérieur(e) ▶ ADV [ɪn'lænd] à l'intérieur, dans les terres; **~ waterways** canaux mpl et rivières fpl

Inland Revenue N (BRIT) fisc m

in-laws ['ɪnlɔːz] NPL beaux-parents mpl; belle famille

inlet ['ɪnlɛt] N (Geo) crique f

inlet pipe N (Tech) tuyau m d'arrivée

inmate ['ɪnmeɪt] N (in prison) détenu(e); (in asylum) interné(e)

inmost ['ɪnməust] ADJ le (la) plus profond(e)

inn [ɪn] N auberge f

innards ['ɪnədz] NPL (inf) entrailles fpl

innate [ɪ'neɪt] ADJ inné(e)

inner ['ɪnər] ADJ intérieur(e)

inner city N centre m urbain (souffrant souvent de délabrement, d'embouteillages etc)

inner-city ['ɪnə'sɪtɪ] ADJ (schools, problems) de quartiers déshérités

innermost ['ɪnəməust] ADJ le (la) plus profond(e)

inner tube N (of tyre) chambre f à air

inning ['ɪnɪŋ] N (US Baseball) tour m de batte; **innings** NPL (Cricket) tour de batte; **he has had a good innings** (BRIT fig) il (en) a bien profité

innocence ['ɪnəsns] N innocence f

innocent ['ɪnəsnt] ADJ innocent(e)

innocuous [ɪ'nɔkjuəs] ADJ inoffensif(-ive)

innovation [ˌɪnəʊˈveɪʃən] N innovation f
innovative [ˈɪnəʊˈveɪtɪv] ADJ novateur(-trice);
(*product*) innovant(e)
innuendo [ˌɪnjuˈɛndəʊ] (*pl* **innuendoes**) N
insinuation f, allusion (malveillante)
innumerable [ɪˈnjuːmrəbl] ADJ innombrable
inoculate [ɪˈnɔkjuleɪt] VT: **to ~ sb with sth**
inoculer qch à qn; **to ~ sb against sth** vacciner
qn contre qch
inoculation [ɪnɔkjuˈleɪʃən] N inoculation f
inoffensive [ɪnəˈfɛnsɪv] ADJ inoffensif(-ive)
inopportune [ɪnˈɔpətjuːn] ADJ inopportun(e)
inordinate [ɪˈnɔːdɪnət] ADJ démesuré(e)
inordinately [ɪˈnɔːdɪnətlɪ] ADV démesurément
inorganic [ɪnɔːˈgænɪk] ADJ inorganique
in-patient [ˈɪnpeɪʃənt] N malade hospitalisé(e)
input [ˈɪnput] N (*contribution*) contribution f;
(*resources*) ressources fpl; (*Elec*) énergie f,
puissance f; (*of machine*) consommation f;
(*Comput*) entrée f (de données); (: *data*) données
fpl ▶ VT (*Comput*) introduire, entrer
inquest [ˈɪnkwɛst] N enquête (criminelle);
(*coroner's*) enquête judiciaire
inquire [ɪnˈkwaɪəʳ] VI demander ▶ VT demander,
s'informer de; **to ~ about** s'informer de, se
renseigner sur; **to ~ when/where/whether**
demander quand/où/si
  ▶ **inquire after** VT FUS demander des nouvelles
de
  ▶ **inquire into** VT FUS faire une enquête sur
inquiring [ɪnˈkwaɪərɪŋ] ADJ (*mind*)
curieux(-euse), investigateur(-trice)
inquiry [ɪnˈkwaɪərɪ] N demande f de
renseignements; (*Law*) enquête f, investigation
f; **"inquiries"** "renseignements"; **to hold an ~
into sth** enquêter sur qch
inquiry desk N (*BRIT*) guichet m de
renseignements
inquiry office N (*BRIT*) bureau m de
renseignements
inquisition [ɪnkwɪˈzɪʃən] N enquête f,
investigation f; (*Rel*): **the I~** l'Inquisition f
inquisitive [ɪnˈkwɪzɪtɪv] ADJ curieux(-euse)
inroads [ˈɪnrəʊdz] NPL: **to make ~ into** (*savings,
supplies*) entamer
ins. ABBR = **inches**
insane [ɪnˈseɪn] ADJ fou (folle); (*Med*) aliéné(e)
insanitary [ɪnˈsænɪtərɪ] ADJ insalubre
insanity [ɪnˈsænɪtɪ] N folie f; (*Med*) aliénation
(mentale)
insatiable [ɪnˈseɪʃəbl] ADJ insatiable
inscribe [ɪnˈskraɪb] VT inscrire; (*book etc*): **to ~
(to sb)** dédicacer (à qn)
inscription [ɪnˈskrɪpʃən] N inscription f; (*in
book*) dédicace f
inscrutable [ɪnˈskruːtəbl] ADJ impénétrable
inseam [ˈɪnsiːm] N (*US*): **~ measurement**
hauteur f d'entre-jambe
insect [ˈɪnsɛkt] N insecte m
insect bite N piqûre f d'insecte
insecticide [ɪnˈsɛktɪsaɪd] N insecticide m
insect repellent N crème f anti-insectes
insecure [ɪnsɪˈkjuəʳ] ADJ (*person*) anxieux(-euse);
(*job*) précaire; (*building etc*) peu sûr(e)

insecurity [ɪnsɪˈkjuərɪtɪ] N insécurité f
insensible [ɪnˈsɛnsɪbl] ADJ insensible;
(*unconscious*) sans connaissance
insensitive [ɪnˈsɛnsɪtɪv] ADJ insensible
insensitivity [ɪnsɛnsɪˈtɪvɪtɪ] N insensibilité f
inseparable [ɪnˈsɛprəbl] ADJ inséparable
insert VT [ɪnˈsəːt] insérer ▶ N [ˈɪnsəːt] insertion f
insertion [ɪnˈsəːʃən] N insertion f
in-service [ˈɪnˈsəːvɪs] ADJ (*training*) continu(e);
(*course*) d'initiation; de perfectionnement; de
recyclage
inshore ADJ [ˈɪnʃɔːʳ] côtier(-ière) ▶ ADV [ɪnˈʃɔːʳ]
près de la côte; vers la côte
inside [ˈɪnˈsaɪd] N intérieur m; (*of road:* BRIT) côté
m gauche (*de la route*); (: US, Europe etc) côté droit
(*de la route*) ▶ ADJ intérieur(e) ▶ ADV à l'intérieur,
dedans ▶ PREP à l'intérieur de; (*of time*): **~ 10
minutes** en moins de 10 minutes; **insides**
NPL (*inf*) intestins mpl; **~ information**
renseignements mpl à la source; **~ story** histoire
racontée par un témoin; **to go ~** rentrer
inside forward N (*Sport*) intérieur m
inside lane N (*Aut: in Britain*) voie f de gauche; (: *in
US, Europe*) voie f de droite
inside leg measurement N (*BRIT*) hauteur f
d'entre-jambe
inside out ADV à l'envers; (*know*) à fond; **to turn
sth ~** retourner qch
insider [ɪnˈsaɪdəʳ] N initié(e)
insider dealing, insider trading N (*Stock
Exchange*) délit m d'initiés
insidious [ɪnˈsɪdɪəs] ADJ insidieux(-euse)
insight [ˈɪnsaɪt] N perspicacité f; (*glimpse, idea*)
aperçu m; **to gain (an) ~ into** parvenir à
comprendre
insignia [ɪnˈsɪgnɪə] NPL insignes mpl
insignificant [ɪnsɪgˈnɪfɪknt] ADJ insignifiant(e)
insincere [ɪnsɪnˈsɪəʳ] ADJ hypocrite
insincerity [ɪnsɪnˈsɛrɪtɪ] N manque m de
sincérité, hypocrisie f
insinuate [ɪnˈsɪnjueɪt] VT insinuer
insinuation [ɪnsɪnjuˈeɪʃən] N insinuation f
insipid [ɪnˈsɪpɪd] ADJ insipide, fade
insist [ɪnˈsɪst] VI insister; **to ~ on doing** insister
pour faire; **to ~ on sth** exiger qch; **to ~ that**
insister pour que + *sub*; (*claim*) maintenir *or*
soutenir que
insistence [ɪnˈsɪstəns] N insistance f
insistent [ɪnˈsɪstənt] ADJ insistant(e),
pressant(e); (*noise, action*) ininterrompu(e)
insofar [ɪnsəʊˈfɑːʳ]: **~ as** *conj* dans la mesure où
insole [ˈɪnsəʊl] N semelle intérieure; (*fixed part of
shoe*) première f
insolence [ˈɪnsələns] N insolence f
insolent [ˈɪnsələnt] ADJ insolent(e)
insoluble [ɪnˈsɔljubl] ADJ insoluble
insolvency [ɪnˈsɔlvənsɪ] N insolvabilité f;
faillite f
insolvent [ɪnˈsɔlvənt] ADJ insolvable; (*bankrupt*)
en faillite
insomnia [ɪnˈsɔmnɪə] N insomnie f
insomniac [ɪnˈsɔmnɪæk] N insomniaque mf
inspect [ɪnˈspɛkt] VT inspecter; (*BRIT: ticket*)
contrôler

inspection [ɪn'spɛkʃən] N inspection f; (BRIT: of tickets) contrôle m

inspector [ɪn'spɛktər] N inspecteur(-trice); (BRIT: on buses, trains) contrôleur(-euse)

inspiration [ɪnspə'reɪʃən] N inspiration f

inspire [ɪn'spaɪər] VT inspirer

inspired [ɪn'spaɪəd] ADJ (writer, book etc) inspiré(e); **in an ~ moment** dans un moment d'inspiration

inspiring [ɪn'spaɪərɪŋ] ADJ inspirant(e)

inst. ABBR (BRIT Comm) = **instant**; **of the 16th ~** du 16 courant

instability [ɪnstə'bɪlɪtɪ] N instabilité f

install, (US) **instal** [ɪn'stɔ:l] VT installer

installation [ɪnstə'leɪʃən] N installation f

installment plan N (US) achat m (or vente f) à tempérament or crédit

instalment, (US) **installment** [ɪn'stɔ:lmənt] N (payment) acompte m, versement partiel; (of TV serial etc) épisode m; **in instalments** (pay) à tempérament; (receive) en plusieurs fois

instance ['ɪnstəns] N exemple m; **for ~** par exemple; **in many instances** dans bien des cas; **in that ~** dans ce cas; **in the first ~** tout d'abord, en premier lieu

instant ['ɪnstənt] N instant m ▸ ADJ immédiat(e), urgent(e); (coffee, food) instantané(e), en poudre; **the 10th ~** le 10 courant

instantaneous [ɪnstən'teɪnɪəs] ADJ instantané(e)

instantly ['ɪnstəntlɪ] ADV immédiatement, tout de suite

instant message N message m instantané

instant messaging N messagerie f instantanée

instant replay N (US TV) retour m sur une séquence

instead [ɪn'stɛd] ADV au lieu de cela; **~ of** au lieu de; **~ of sb** à la place de qn

instep ['ɪnstɛp] N cou-de-pied m; (of shoe) cambrure f

instigate ['ɪnstɪgeɪt] VT (rebellion, strike, crime) inciter à; (new ideas etc) susciter

instigation [ɪnstɪ'geɪʃən] N instigation f; **at sb's ~** à l'instigation de qn

instil [ɪn'stɪl] VT: **to ~ (into)** inculquer (à); (courage) insuffler (à)

instinct ['ɪnstɪŋkt] N instinct m

instinctive [ɪn'stɪŋktɪv] ADJ instinctif(-ive)

instinctively [ɪn'stɪŋktɪvlɪ] ADV instinctivement

institute ['ɪnstɪtjuːt] N institut m ▸ VT instituer, établir; (inquiry) ouvrir; (proceedings) entamer

institution [ɪnstɪ'tjuːʃən] N institution f; (school) établissement m (scolaire); (for care) établissement (psychiatrique etc)

institutional [ɪnstɪ'tjuːʃənl] ADJ institutionnel(le); **~ care** soins fournis par un établissement médico-social

instruct [ɪn'strʌkt] VT instruire, former; **to ~ sb in sth** enseigner qch à qn; **to ~ sb to do** charger qn or ordonner à qn de faire

instruction [ɪn'strʌkʃən] N instruction f; **instructions** NPL (orders) directives fpl; **instructions for use** mode m d'emploi

instruction book N manuel m d'instructions

instructive [ɪn'strʌktɪv] ADJ instructif(-ive)

instructor [ɪn'strʌktər] N professeur m; (for skiing, driving) moniteur m

instrument ['ɪnstrumənt] N instrument m

instrumental [ɪnstru'mɛntl] ADJ (Mus) instrumental(e); **to be ~ in sth/in doing sth** contribuer à qch/à faire qch

instrumentalist [ɪnstru'mɛntəlɪst] N instrumentiste mf

instrument panel N tableau m de bord

insubordinate [ɪnsə'bɔ:dənɪt] ADJ insubordonné(e)

insubordination [ɪnsəbɔ:də'neɪʃən] N insubordination f

insufferable [ɪn'sʌfrəbl] ADJ insupportable

insufficient [ɪnsə'fɪʃənt] ADJ insuffisant(e)

insufficiently [ɪnsə'fɪʃəntlɪ] ADV insuffisamment

insular ['ɪnsjulər] ADJ insulaire; (outlook) étroit(e); (person) aux vues étroites

insulate ['ɪnsjuleɪt] VT isoler; (against sound) insonoriser

insulating tape ['ɪnsjuleɪtɪŋ-] N ruban isolant

insulation [ɪnsju'leɪʃən] N isolation f; (against sound) insonorisation f

insulin ['ɪnsjulɪn] N insuline f

insult N ['ɪnsʌlt] insulte f, affront m ▸ VT [ɪn'sʌlt] insulter, faire un affront à

insulting [ɪn'sʌltɪŋ] ADJ insultant(e), injurieux(-euse)

insuperable [ɪn'sjuːprəbl] ADJ insurmontable

insurance [ɪn'ʃuərəns] N assurance f; **fire/life ~** assurance-incendie/-vie; **to take out ~ (against)** s'assurer (contre)

insurance agent N agent m d'assurances

insurance broker N courtier m en assurances

insurance company N compagnie f or société f d'assurances

insurance policy N police f d'assurance

insurance premium N prime f d'assurance

insure [ɪn'ʃuər] VT assurer; **to ~ (o.s.) against** (fig) parer à; **to ~ sb/sb's life** assurer qn/la vie de qn; **to be insured for £5000** être assuré(e) pour 5000 livres

insured [ɪn'ʃuəd] N: **the ~** l'assuré(e)

insurer [ɪn'ʃuərər] N assureur m

insurgent [ɪn'sə:dʒənt] ADJ, N insurgé(e)

insurmountable [ɪnsə'mauntəbl] ADJ insurmontable

insurrection [ɪnsə'rɛkʃən] N insurrection f

intact [ɪn'tækt] ADJ intact(e)

intake ['ɪnteɪk] N (Tech) admission f; (consumption) consommation f; (BRIT Scol): **an ~ of 200 a year** 200 admissions par an

intangible [ɪn'tændʒɪbl] ADJ intangible; (assets) immatériel(le)

integral ['ɪntɪgrəl] ADJ (whole) intégral(e); (part) intégrant(e)

integrate ['ɪntɪgreɪt] VT intégrer ▸ VI s'intégrer

integrated circuit ['ɪntɪgreɪtɪd-] N (Comput) circuit intégré

integration [ɪntɪ'greɪʃən] N intégration f; **racial ~** intégration raciale

integrity [ɪnˈtɛgrɪtɪ] N intégrité f
intellect [ˈɪntəlɛkt] N intelligence f
intellectual [ɪntəˈlɛktjuəl] ADJ, N
  intellectuel(le)
intelligence [ɪnˈtɛlɪdʒəns] N intelligence f;
  (Mil) informations fpl, renseignements mpl
intelligence quotient N quotient intellectuel
Intelligence Service N services mpl de
  renseignements
intelligence test N test m d'intelligence
intelligent [ɪnˈtɛlɪdʒənt] ADJ intelligent(e)
intelligently [ɪnˈtɛlɪdʒəntlɪ] ADV
  intelligemment
intelligible [ɪnˈtɛlɪdʒɪbl] ADJ intelligible
intemperate [ɪnˈtɛmpərət] ADJ immodéré(e);
  (drinking too much) adonné(e) à la boisson
intend [ɪnˈtɛnd] VT (gift etc): **to ~ sth for** destiner
  qch à; **to ~ to do** avoir l'intention de faire
intended [ɪnˈtɛndɪd] ADJ (insult)
  intentionnel(le); (journey) projeté(e); (effect)
  voulu(e)
intense [ɪnˈtɛns] ADJ intense; (person)
  véhément(e)
intensely [ɪnˈtɛnslɪ] ADV intensément; (moving)
  profondément
intensify [ɪnˈtɛnsɪfaɪ] VT intensifier
intensity [ɪnˈtɛnsɪtɪ] N intensité f
intensive [ɪnˈtɛnsɪv] ADJ intensif(-ive)
intensive care N: **to be in ~** être en
  réanimation
intensive care unit N service m de réanimation
intent [ɪnˈtɛnt] N intention f ▶ ADJ
  attentif(-ive), absorbé(e); **to all intents and
  purposes** en fait, pratiquement; **to be ~ on
  doing sth** être (bien) décidé à faire qch
intention [ɪnˈtɛnʃən] N intention f
intentional [ɪnˈtɛnʃənl] ADJ intentionnel(le),
  délibéré(e)
intently [ɪnˈtɛntlɪ] ADV attentivement
inter [ɪnˈtəːʳ] VT enterrer
interact [ɪntərˈækt] VI avoir une action
  réciproque; (people) communiquer
interaction [ɪntərˈækʃən] N interaction f
interactive [ɪntərˈæktɪv] ADJ (group)
  interactif(-ive); (Comput) interactif,
  conversationnel(le)
intercede [ɪntəˈsiːd] VI: **to ~ with sb/on behalf
  of sb** intercéder auprès de qn/en faveur de qn
intercept [ɪntəˈsɛpt] VT intercepter; (person)
  arrêter au passage
interception [ɪntəˈsɛpʃən] N interception f
interchange N [ˈɪntətʃeɪndʒ] (exchange) échange
  m; (on motorway) échangeur m ▶ VT [ɪntəˈtʃeɪndʒ]
  échanger; mettre à la place l'un(e) de l'autre
interchangeable [ɪntəˈtʃeɪndʒəbl] ADJ
  interchangeable
intercity [ɪntəˈsɪtɪ] ADJ: **~ (train)** train m rapide
intercom [ˈɪntəkɔm] N interphone m
interconnect [ɪntəkəˈnɛkt] VI (rooms)
  communiquer
intercontinental [ˈɪntəkɔntɪˈnɛntl] ADJ
  intercontinental(e)
intercourse [ˈɪntəkɔːs] N rapports mpl; **sexual ~**
  rapports sexuels

interdependent [ɪntədɪˈpɛndənt] ADJ
  interdépendant(e)
interest [ˈɪntrɪst] N intérêt m; (Comm: stake,
  share) participation f, intérêts mpl ▶ VT
  intéresser; **compound/simple ~** intérêt
  composé/simple; **British interests in the
  Middle East** les intérêts britanniques au
  Moyen-Orient; **his main ~ is ...** ce qui
  l'intéresse le plus est ...
interested [ˈɪntrɪstɪd] ADJ intéressé(e); **to be ~
  in sth** s'intéresser à qch; **I'm ~ in going** ça
  m'intéresse d'y aller
interest-free [ˈɪntrɪstˈfriː] ADJ sans intérêt
interesting [ˈɪntrɪstɪŋ] ADJ intéressant(e)
interest rate N taux m d'intérêt
interface [ˈɪntəfeɪs] N (Comput) interface f
interfere [ɪntəˈfɪəʳ] VI: **to ~ in** (quarrel)
  s'immiscer dans; (other people's business) se mêler
  de; **to ~ with** (object) tripoter, toucher à; (plans)
  contrecarrer; (duty) être en conflit avec; **don't ~**
  mêlez-vous de vos affaires
interference [ɪntəˈfɪərəns] N (gen) ingérence f;
  (Physics) interférence f; (Radio, TV) parasites mpl
interfering [ɪntəˈfɪərɪŋ] ADJ importun(e)
interim [ˈɪntərɪm] ADJ provisoire; (post)
  intérimaire ▶ N: **in the ~** dans l'intérim
interior [ɪnˈtɪərɪəʳ] N intérieur m ▶ ADJ
  intérieur(e); (minister, department) de l'intérieur
interior decorator, interior designer N
  décorateur(-trice) d'intérieur
interior design N architecture f d'intérieur
interjection [ɪntəˈdʒɛkʃən] N interjection f
interlock [ɪntəˈlɔk] VI s'enclencher ▶ VT
  enclencher
interloper [ˈɪntələupəʳ] N intrus(e)
interlude [ˈɪntəluːd] N intervalle m; (Theat)
  intermède m
intermarry [ɪntəˈmærɪ] VI former des alliances
  entre familles (or tribus); former des unions
  consanguines
intermediary [ɪntəˈmiːdɪərɪ] N intermédiaire
  mf
intermediate [ɪntəˈmiːdɪət] ADJ intermédiaire;
  (Scol: course, level) moyen(ne)
interment [ɪnˈtəːmənt] N inhumation f,
  enterrement m
interminable [ɪnˈtəːmɪnəbl] ADJ sans fin,
  interminable
intermission [ɪntəˈmɪʃən] N pause f; (Theat,
  Cine) entracte m
intermittent [ɪntəˈmɪtnt] ADJ intermittent(e)
intermittently [ɪntəˈmɪtntlɪ] ADV par
  intermittence, par intervalles
intern VT [ɪnˈtəːn] interner ▶ N [ˈɪntəːn] (US)
  interne mf
internal [ɪnˈtəːnl] ADJ interne; (dispute, reform etc)
  intérieur(e); **~ injuries** lésions fpl internes
internally [ɪnˈtəːnəlɪ] ADV intérieurement;
  "not to be taken ~" "pour usage externe"
Internal Revenue Service N (US) fisc m
international [ɪntəˈnæʃənl] ADJ
  international(e) ▶ N (Brit Sport) international m
International Atomic Energy Agency N
  Agence Internationale de l'Énergie Atomique

International Court of Justice N Cour internationale de justice

international date line N ligne f de changement de date

internationally [ɪntə'næʃnəlɪ] ADV dans le monde entier

International Monetary Fund N Fonds monétaire international

international relations NPL relations internationales

internecine [ɪntə'niːsaɪn] ADJ mutuellement destructeur(-trice)

internee [ɪntəː'niː] N interné(e)

Internet [ɪntə'nɛt] N: **the ~** l'Internet m

Internet café N cybercafé m

Internet Service Provider N fournisseur m d'accès à Internet

Internet user N internaute mf

internment [ɪn'təːnmənt] N internement m

interplay ['ɪntəpleɪ] N effet m réciproque, jeu m

Interpol ['ɪntəpɔl] N Interpol m

interpret [ɪn'təːprɪt] VT interpréter ▶ VI servir d'interprète

interpretation [ɪntəːprɪ'teɪʃən] N interprétation f

interpreter [ɪn'təːprɪtər] N interprète mf; **could you act as an ~ for us?** pourriez-vous nous servir d'interprète?

interpreting [ɪn'təːprɪtɪŋ] N (profession) interprétariat m

interrelated [ɪntərɪ'leɪtɪd] ADJ en corrélation, en rapport étroit

interrogate [ɪn'tɛrəʊgeɪt] VT interroger; (suspect etc) soumettre à un interrogatoire

interrogation [ɪntɛrəʊ'geɪʃən] N interrogation f; (by police) interrogatoire m

interrogative [ɪntə'rɔgətɪv] ADJ interrogateur(-trice) ▶ N (Ling) interrogatif m

interrogator [ɪn'tɛrəgeɪtər] N interrogateur(-trice)

interrupt [ɪntə'rʌpt] VT, VI interrompre

interruption [ɪntə'rʌpʃən] N interruption f

intersect [ɪntə'sɛkt] VT couper, croiser; (Math) intersecter ▶ VI se croiser, se couper; s'intersecter

intersection [ɪntə'sɛkʃən] N intersection f; (of roads) croisement m

intersperse [ɪntə'spəːs] VT: **to ~ with** parsemer de

interstate ['ɪntəsteɪt] (US) N autoroute f (qui relie plusieurs États)

intertwine [ɪntə'twaɪn] VT entrelacer ▶ VI s'entrelacer

interval ['ɪntəvl] N intervalle m; (BRIT: Theat) entracte m; (: Sport) mi-temps f; **bright intervals** (in weather) éclaircies fpl; **at intervals** par intervalles

intervene [ɪntə'viːn] VI (time) s'écouler (entre-temps); (event) survenir; (person) intervenir

intervention [ɪntə'vɛnʃən] N intervention f

interview ['ɪntəvjuː] N (Radio, TV) interview f; (for job) entrevue f ▶ VT interviewer, avoir une entrevue avec

interviewee [ɪntəvjuː'iː] N (for job) candidat m (qui passe un entretien); (TV etc) invité(e), personne interviewée

interviewer ['ɪntəvjuər] N (Radio, TV) interviewer m

intestate [ɪn'tɛsteɪt] ADJ intestat f inv

intestinal [ɪn'tɛstɪnl] ADJ intestinal(e)

intestine [ɪn'tɛstɪn] N intestin m; **large ~** gros intestin; **small ~** intestin grêle

intimacy ['ɪntɪməsɪ] N intimité f

intimate ADJ ['ɪntɪmət] intime; (friendship) profond(e); (knowledge) approfondi(e) ▶ VT ['ɪntɪmeɪt] suggérer, laisser entendre; (announce) faire savoir

intimately ['ɪntɪmətlɪ] ADV intimement

intimation [ɪntɪ'meɪʃən] N annonce f

intimidate [ɪn'tɪmɪdeɪt] VT intimider

intimidating [ɪn'tɪmɪdeɪtɪŋ] ADJ intimidant(e)

intimidation [ɪntɪmɪ'deɪʃən] N intimidation f

into ['ɪntu] PREP dans; **~ pieces/French** en morceaux/français; **to change pounds ~ dollars** changer des livres en dollars; **3 ÷ 9 goes 3** 9 divisé par 3 donne 3; **she's ~ opera** c'est une passionnée d'opéra

intolerable [ɪn'tɔlərəbl] ADJ intolérable

intolerance [ɪn'tɔlərns] N intolérance f

intolerant [ɪn'tɔlərnt] ADJ: **~ (of)** intolérant(e) (de); (Med) intolérant(e) (à)

intonation [ɪntəu'neɪʃən] N intonation f

intoxicate [ɪn'tɔksɪkeɪt] VT enivrer

intoxicated [ɪn'tɔksɪkeɪtɪd] ADJ ivre

intoxication [ɪntɔksɪ'keɪʃən] N ivresse f

intractable [ɪn'træktəbl] ADJ (child, temper) indocile, insoumis(e); (problem) insoluble; (illness) incurable

intranet [ɪn'trænet] N intranet m

intransigent [ɪn'trænsɪdʒənt] ADJ intransigeant(e)

intransitive [ɪn'trænsɪtɪv] ADJ intransitif(-ive)

intra-uterine device ['ɪntrə'juːtəraɪn-] N dispositif intra-utérin, stérilet m

intravenous [ɪntrə'viːnəs] ADJ intraveineux(-euse)

in-tray ['ɪntreɪ] N courrier m "arrivée"

intrepid [ɪn'trepɪd] ADJ intrépide

intricacy ['ɪntrɪkəsɪ] N complexité f

intricate ['ɪntrɪkət] ADJ complexe, compliqué(e)

intrigue [ɪn'triːg] N intrigue f ▶ VT intriguer ▶ VI intriguer, comploter

intriguing [ɪn'triːgɪŋ] ADJ fascinant(e)

intrinsic [ɪn'trɪnsɪk] ADJ intrinsèque

introduce [ɪntrə'djuːs] VT introduire; (TV show etc) présenter; **to ~ sb (to sb)** présenter qn (à qn); **to ~ sb to** (pastime, technique) initier qn à; **may I ~ …?** je vous présente …

introduction [ɪntrə'dʌkʃən] N introduction f; (of person) présentation f; (to new experience) initiation f; **a letter of ~** une lettre de recommandation

introductory [ɪntrə'dʌktərɪ] ADJ préliminaire, introductif(-ive); **~ remarks** remarques fpl liminaires; **an ~ offer** une offre de lancement

introspection [ɪntrəu'spɛkʃən] N introspection f

introspective [ɪntrəʊ'spɛktɪv] ADJ introspectif(-ive)

introvert ['ɪntrəʊvəːt] ADJ, N introverti(e)

intrude [ɪn'truːd] VI (person) être importun(e); **to ~ on** or **into** (conversation etc) s'immiscer dans; **am I intruding?** est-ce que je vous dérange?

intruder [ɪn'truːdəʳ] N intrus(e)

intrusion [ɪn'truːʒən] N intrusion f

intrusive [ɪn'truːsɪv] ADJ importun(e), gênant(e)

intuition [ɪntjuː'ɪʃən] N intuition f

intuitive [ɪn'tjuːɪtɪv] ADJ intuitif(-ive)

inundate ['ɪnʌndeɪt] VT: **to ~ with** inonder de

inure [ɪn'juəʳ] VT: **to ~ (to)** habituer (à)

invade [ɪn'veɪd] VT envahir

invader [ɪn'veɪdəʳ] N envahisseur m

invalid N ['ɪnvəlɪd] malade mf; (with disability) invalide mf ▶ ADJ [ɪn'vælɪd] (not valid) invalide, non valide

invalidate [ɪn'vælɪdeɪt] VT invalider, annuler

invalid chair ['ɪnvəlɪd-] N (BRIT) fauteuil m d'infirme

invaluable [ɪn'væljuəbl] ADJ inestimable, inappréciable

invariable [ɪn'vɛərɪəbl] ADJ invariable; (fig) immanquable

invariably [ɪn'vɛərɪəblɪ] ADV invariablement; **she is ~ late** elle est toujours en retard

invasion [ɪn'veɪʒən] N invasion f

invective [ɪn'vɛktɪv] N invective f

inveigle [ɪn'viːgl] VT: **to ~ sb into (doing) sth** amener qn à (faire) qch (par la ruse or la flatterie)

invent [ɪn'vɛnt] VT inventer

invention [ɪn'vɛnʃən] N invention f

inventive [ɪn'vɛntɪv] ADJ inventif(-ive)

inventiveness [ɪn'vɛntɪvnɪs] N esprit inventif or d'invention

inventor [ɪn'vɛntəʳ] N inventeur(-trice)

inventory ['ɪnvəntrɪ] N inventaire m

inventory control N (Comm) contrôle m des stocks

inverse [ɪn'vəːs] ADJ inverse ▶ N inverse m, contraire m; **in ~ proportion (to)** inversement proportionnel(le) (à)

inversely [ɪn'vəːslɪ] ADV inversement

invert [ɪn'vəːt] VT intervertir; (cup, object) retourner

invertebrate [ɪn'vəːtɪbrət] N invertébré m

inverted commas [ɪn'vəːtɪd-] NPL (BRIT) guillemets mpl

invest [ɪn'vɛst] VT investir; (endow): **to ~ sb with sth** conférer qch à qn ▶ VI faire un investissement, investir; **to ~ in** placer de l'argent or investir dans; (fig: acquire) s'offrir, faire l'acquisition de

investigate [ɪn'vɛstɪgeɪt] VT étudier, examiner; (crime) faire une enquête sur

investigation [ɪnvɛstɪ'geɪʃən] N examen m; (of crime) enquête f, investigation f

investigative [ɪn'vɛstɪgeɪtɪv] ADJ: **~ journalism** enquête-reportage f, journalisme m d'enquête

investigator [ɪn'vɛstɪgeɪtəʳ] N investigateur(-trice); **private ~** détective privé

investiture [ɪn'vɛstɪtʃəʳ] N investiture f

investment [ɪn'vɛstmənt] N investissement m, placement m

investment income N revenu m de placement

investment trust N société f d'investissements

investor [ɪn'vɛstəʳ] N épargnant(e); (shareholder) actionnaire mf

inveterate [ɪn'vɛtərət] ADJ invétéré(e)

invidious [ɪn'vɪdɪəs] ADJ injuste; (task) déplaisant(e)

invigilate [ɪn'vɪdʒɪleɪt] (BRIT) VT surveiller ▶ VI être de surveillance

invigilator [ɪn'vɪdʒɪleɪtəʳ] N (BRIT) surveillant m (d'examen)

invigorating [ɪn'vɪgəreɪtɪŋ] ADJ vivifiant(e), stimulant(e)

invincible [ɪn'vɪnsɪbl] ADJ invincible

inviolate [ɪn'vaɪələt] ADJ inviolé(e)

invisible [ɪn'vɪzɪbl] ADJ invisible

invisible assets NPL (BRIT) actif incorporel

invisible ink N encre f sympathique

invisible mending N stoppage m

invitation [ɪnvɪ'teɪʃən] N invitation f; **by ~ only** sur invitation; **at sb's ~** à la demande de qn

invite [ɪn'vaɪt] VT inviter; (opinions etc) demander; (trouble) chercher; **to ~ sb (to do)** inviter qn (à faire); **to ~ sb to dinner** inviter qn à dîner

▶ **invite out** VT inviter (à sortir)

▶ **invite over** VT inviter (chez soi)

inviting [ɪn'vaɪtɪŋ] ADJ engageant(e), attrayant(e); (gesture) encourageant(e)

invoice ['ɪnvɔɪs] N facture f ▶ VT facturer; **to ~ sb for goods** facturer des marchandises à qn

invoke [ɪn'vəʊk] VT invoquer

involuntary [ɪn'vɔləntrɪ] ADJ involontaire

involve [ɪn'vɔlv] VT (entail) impliquer; (concern) concerner; (require) nécessiter; **to ~ sb in** (theft etc) impliquer qn dans; (activity, meeting) faire participer qn à

involved [ɪn'vɔlvd] ADJ (complicated) complexe; **to be ~ in** (take part) participer à; (be engrossed) être plongé(e) dans; **to feel ~** se sentir concerné(e); **to become ~** (in love etc) s'engager

involvement [ɪn'vɔlvmənt] N (personal role) rôle m; (participation) participation f; (enthusiasm) enthousiasme m; (of resources, funds) mise f en jeu

invulnerable [ɪn'vʌlnərəbl] ADJ invulnérable

inward ['ɪnwəd] ADJ (movement) vers l'intérieur; (thought, feeling) profond(e), intime ▶ ADV = **inwards**

inwardly ['ɪnwədlɪ] ADV (feel, think etc) secrètement, en son for intérieur

inwards ['ɪnwədz] ADV vers l'intérieur

I/O ABBR (Comput: = input/output) E/S

IOC N ABBR (= International Olympic Committee) CIO m (= Comité international olympique)

iodine ['aɪəudiːn] N iode m

IOM ABBR = **Isle of Man**

ion ['aɪən] N ion m

Ionian Sea [aɪ'əunɪən-] N: **the ~** la mer Ionienne

ioniser ['aɪənaɪzəʳ] N ioniseur m

iota [aɪˈəʊtə] N (fig) brin m, grain m
IOU N ABBR (= I owe you) reconnaissance f de dette
IOW ABBR (BRIT) = **Isle of Wight**
IPA N ABBR (= International Phonetic Alphabet) API m
iPad® [ˈaɪpæd] N iPad® m
iPhone® [ˈaɪfəʊn] N iPhone® m
iPod® [ˈaɪpɒd] N iPod® m
IQ N ABBR (= intelligence quotient) Q.I. m
IRA N ABBR (= Irish Republican Army) IRA f; (US) = **individual retirement account**
Iran [ɪˈrɑːn] N Iran m
Iranian [ɪˈreɪnɪən] ADJ iranien(ne) ▶ N Iranien(ne); (Ling) iranien m
Iraq [ɪˈrɑːk] N Irak m
Iraqi [ɪˈrɑːkɪ] ADJ irakien(ne) ▶ N Irakien(ne)
irascible [ɪˈræsɪbl] ADJ irascible
irate [aɪˈreɪt] ADJ courroucé(e)
Ireland [ˈaɪələnd] N Irlande f; **Republic of ~** République f d'Irlande
iris, irises [ˈaɪrɪs, -ɪz] N iris m
Irish [ˈaɪrɪʃ] ADJ irlandais(e) ▶ NPL: **the ~** les Irlandais ▶ N (Ling) irlandais m; **the Irish** NPL les Irlandais
Irishman [ˈaɪrɪʃmən] N (irreg) Irlandais m
Irish Sea N: **the ~** la mer d'Irlande
Irishwoman [ˈaɪrɪʃwumən] N (irreg) Irlandaise f
irk [əːk] VT ennuyer
irksome [ˈəːksəm] ADJ ennuyeux(-euse)
IRN N ABBR (= Independent Radio News) agence de presse radiophonique
IRO N ABBR (US) = **International Refugee Organization**
iron [ˈaɪən] N fer m; (for clothes) fer m à repasser ▶ ADJ de or en fer ▶ VT (clothes) repasser; **irons** NPL (chains) fers mpl, chaînes fpl
▶ **iron out** VT (crease) faire disparaître au fer; (fig) aplanir; faire disparaître
Iron Curtain N: **the ~** le rideau de fer
iron foundry N fonderie f de fonte
ironic [aɪˈrɒnɪk], **ironical** [aɪˈrɒnɪkl] ADJ ironique
ironically [aɪˈrɒnɪklɪ] ADV ironiquement
ironing [ˈaɪənɪŋ] N (activity) repassage m; (clothes: ironed) linge repassé; (: to be ironed) linge à repasser
ironing board N planche f à repasser
ironmonger [ˈaɪənmʌŋgəʳ] N (BRIT) quincaillier m; **~'s (shop)** quincaillerie f
iron ore N minerai m de fer
ironworks [ˈaɪənwəːks] N usine f sidérurgique
irony [ˈaɪrənɪ] N ironie f
irrational [ɪˈræʃənl] ADJ irrationnel(le); (person) qui n'est pas rationnel
irreconcilable [ɪrɛkənˈsaɪləbl] ADJ irréconciliable; (opinion): **~ with** inconciliable avec
irredeemable [ɪrɪˈdiːməbl] ADJ (Comm) non remboursable
irrefutable [ɪrɪˈfjuːtəbl] ADJ irréfutable
irregular [ɪˈrɛgjʊləʳ] ADJ irrégulier(-ière); (surface) inégal(e); (action, event) peu orthodoxe
irregularity [ɪrɛgjuˈlærɪtɪ] N irrégularité f
irrelevance [ɪˈrɛləvəns] N manque m de rapport or d'à-propos

irrelevant [ɪˈrɛləvənt] ADJ sans rapport, hors de propos
irreligious [ɪrɪˈlɪdʒəs] ADJ irréligieux(-euse)
irreparable [ɪˈrɛprəbl] ADJ irréparable
irreplaceable [ɪrɪˈpleɪsəbl] ADJ irremplaçable
irrepressible [ɪrɪˈprɛsəbl] ADJ irrépressible
irreproachable [ɪrɪˈprəʊtʃəbl] ADJ irréprochable
irresistible [ɪrɪˈzɪstɪbl] ADJ irrésistible
irresolute [ɪˈrɛzəluːt] ADJ irrésolu(e), indécis(e)
irrespective [ɪrɪˈspɛktɪv]: **~ of** prep sans tenir compte de
irresponsible [ɪrɪˈspɒnsɪbl] ADJ (act) irréfléchi(e); (person) qui n'a pas le sens des responsabilités
irretrievable [ɪrɪˈtriːvəbl] ADJ irréparable, irrémédiable; (object) introuvable
irreverent [ɪˈrɛvərnt] ADJ irrévérencieux(-euse)
irrevocable [ɪˈrɛvəkəbl] ADJ irrévocable
irrigate [ˈɪrɪgeɪt] VT irriguer
irrigation [ɪrɪˈgeɪʃən] N irrigation f
irritable [ˈɪrɪtəbl] ADJ irritable
irritate [ˈɪrɪteɪt] VT irriter
irritating [ˈɪrɪteɪtɪŋ] ADJ irritant(e)
irritation [ɪrɪˈteɪʃən] N irritation f
IRS N ABBR (US) = **Internal Revenue Service**
is [ɪz] VB see **be**
ISA N ABBR (BRIT: = Individual Savings Account) plan m d'épargne défiscalisé
ISBN N ABBR (= International Standard Book Number) ISBN m
ISDN N ABBR (= Integrated Services Digital Network) RNIS m
Islam [ˈɪzlɑːm] N Islam m
Islamic [ɪzˈlɑːmɪk] ADJ islamique; **~ fundamentalists** intégristes mpl musulmans
island [ˈaɪlənd] N île f; (also: **traffic island**) refuge m (pour piétons)
islander [ˈaɪləndəʳ] N habitant(e) d'une île, insulaire mf
isle [aɪl] N île f
isn't [ˈɪznt] = **is not**
isolate [ˈaɪsəleɪt] VT isoler
isolated [ˈaɪsəleɪtɪd] ADJ isolé(e)
isolation [aɪsəˈleɪʃən] N isolement m
ISP N ABBR = **Internet Service Provider**
Israel [ˈɪzreɪl] N Israël m
Israeli [ɪzˈreɪlɪ] ADJ israélien(ne) ▶ N Israélien(ne)
issue [ˈɪʃuː] N question f, problème m; (outcome) résultat m, issue f; (of banknotes) émission f; (of newspaper) numéro m; (of book) publication f, parution f; (offspring) descendance f ▶ VT (rations, equipment) distribuer; (orders) donner; (statement) publier, faire; (certificate, passport) délivrer; (book) faire paraître; publier; (banknotes, cheques, stamps) émettre, mettre en circulation ▶ VI: **to ~ from** provenir de; **at ~** en jeu, en cause; **to avoid the ~** éluder le problème; **to take ~ with sb (over sth)** exprimer son désaccord avec qn (sur qch); **to make an ~ of sth** faire de qch un problème; **to confuse or obscure the ~** embrouiller la question
Istanbul [ɪstænˈbuːl] N Istamboul, Istanbul

i

643

isthmus [ˈɪsməs] N isthme m

IT N ABBR = **information technology**

(KEYWORD)

it [ɪt] PRON **1** (*specific: subject*) il (elle); (*: direct object*) le, la, l'; (*: indirect object*) lui; **it's on the table** c'est *or* il (*or* elle) est sur la table; **I can't find it** je n'arrive pas à le trouver; **give it to me** donne-le-moi

2 (*after prep*): **about/from/of it** en; **I spoke to him about it** je lui en ai parlé; **what did you learn from it?** qu'est-ce que vous en avez retiré?; **I'm proud of it** j'en suis fier; **I've come from it** j'en viens; **in/to it** y; **put the book in it** mettez-y le livre; **it's on it** c'est dessus; **he agreed to it** il y a consenti; **did you go to it?** (*party, concert etc*) est-ce que vous y êtes allé(s)?; **above it**, **over it** (au-)dessus; **below it**, **under it** (en-)dessous; **in front of/behind it** devant/derrière

3 (*impersonal*) il; ce, cela, ça; **it's Friday tomorrow** demain, c'est vendredi *or* nous sommes vendredi; **it's 6 o'clock** il est 6 heures; **how far is it? — it's 10 miles** c'est loin? — c'est à 10 miles; **it's 2 hours by train** c'est à 2 heures de train; **who is it? — it's me** qui est-ce? — c'est moi; **it's raining** il pleut

ITA N ABBR (*Brit*: = *initial teaching alphabet*) alphabet en partie phonétique utilisé pour l'enseignement de la lecture

Italian [ɪˈtæljən] ADJ italien(ne) ▸ N Italien(ne); (*Ling*) italien m

italic [ɪˈtælɪk] ADJ italique

italics [ɪˈtælɪks] NPL italique m

Italy [ˈɪtəlɪ] N Italie f

itch [ɪtʃ] N démangeaison f ▸ VI (*person*) éprouver des démangeaisons; (*part of body*) démanger;

I'm itching to do l'envie me démange de faire

itchy [ˈɪtʃɪ] ADJ qui démange; **my back is ~** j'ai le dos qui me démange

it'd [ˈɪtd] = **it would**; **it had**

item [ˈaɪtəm] N (*gen*) article m; (*on agenda*) question f, point m; (*in programme*) numéro m; (*also*: **news item**) nouvelle f; **items of clothing** articles vestimentaires

itemize [ˈaɪtəmaɪz] VT détailler, spécifier

itemized bill [ˈaɪtəmaɪzd-] N facture détaillée

itinerant [ɪˈtɪnərənt] ADJ itinérant(e); (*musician*) ambulant(e)

itinerary [aɪˈtɪnərərɪ] N itinéraire m

it'll [ˈɪtl] = **it will**; **it shall**

ITN N ABBR (*Brit*: = *Independent Television News*) chaîne de télévision commerciale

its [ɪts] ADJ son (sa), ses pl ▸ PRON le (la) sien(ne), les siens (siennes)

it's [ɪts] = **it is**; **it has**

itself [ɪtˈself] PRON (*reflexive*) se; (*emphatic*) lui-même (elle-même)

ITV N ABBR (*Brit*: = *Independent Television*) chaîne de télévision commerciale

IUD N ABBR = **intra-uterine device**

I've [aɪv] = **I have**

ivory [ˈaɪvərɪ] N ivoire m

Ivory Coast N Côte f d'Ivoire

ivy [ˈaɪvɪ] N lierre m

Ivy League N (*US*); *voir article*

> L'*Ivy League* regroupe les huit universités les plus prestigieuses du nord-est des États-Unis, ainsi surnommées à cause de leurs murs recouverts de lierre. Elles organisent des compétitions sportives entre elles. Ces universités sont: Brown, Columbia, Cornell, Dartmouth College, Harvard, Princeton, l'université de Pennsylvanie et Yale.

J j

J, j [dʒeɪ] N (letter) J, j m; **J for Jack**, (US) **J for Jig** J comme Joseph

JA N ABBR = **judge advocate**

J/A N ABBR = **joint account**

jab [dʒæb] VT: **to ~ sth into** enfoncer or planter qch dans ▶ N coup m; (Med: inf) piqûre f

jabber ['dʒæbə'] VT, VI bredouiller, baragouiner

jack [dʒæk] N (Aut) cric m; (Bowls) cochonnet m; (Cards) valet m
  ▶ **jack in** VT (inf) laisser tomber
  ▶ **jack up** VT soulever (au cric)

jackal ['dʒækl] N chacal m

jackass ['dʒækæs] N (also fig) âne m

jackdaw ['dʒækdɔ:] N choucas m

jacket ['dʒækɪt] N veste f, veston m; (of boiler etc) enveloppe f; (of book) couverture f, jaquette f

jacket potato N pomme f de terre en robe des champs

jack-in-the-box ['dʒækɪnðəbɔks] N diable m à ressort

jackknife ['dʒæknaɪf] N couteau m de poche
  ▶ VI: **the lorry jackknifed** la remorque (du camion) s'est mise en travers

jack-of-all-trades ['dʒækəv'ɔ:ltreɪdz] N bricoleur m

jack plug N (BRIT) jack m

jackpot ['dʒækpɔt] N gros lot

Jacuzzi® [dʒə'ku:zɪ] N jacuzzi® m

jaded ['dʒeɪdɪd] ADJ éreinté(e), fatigué(e)

JAG N ABBR = **Judge Advocate General**

jagged ['dʒægɪd] ADJ dentelé(e)

jaguar ['dʒægjuə'] N jaguar m

jail [dʒeɪl] N prison f ▶ VT emprisonner, mettre en prison

jailbird ['dʒeɪlbə:d] N récidiviste mf

jailbreak ['dʒeɪlbreɪk] N évasion f

jailer ['dʒeɪlə'] N geôlier(-ière)

jail sentence N peine f de prison

jalopy [dʒə'lɔpɪ] N (inf) vieux clou

jam [dʒæm] N confiture f; (of shoppers etc) cohue f; (also: **traffic jam**) embouteillage m ▶ VT (passage etc) encombrer, obstruer; (mechanism, drawer etc) bloquer, coincer; (Radio) brouiller ▶ VI (mechanism, sliding part) se coincer, se bloquer; (gun) s'enrayer; **to be in a ~** (inf) être dans le pétrin; **to get sb out of a ~** (inf) sortir qn du pétrin; **to ~ sth into** (stuff) entasser or comprimer qch dans; (thrust) enfoncer qch

dans; **the telephone lines are jammed** les lignes (téléphoniques) sont encombrées

Jamaica [dʒə'meɪkə] N Jamaïque f

Jamaican [dʒə'meɪkən] ADJ jamaïquain(e)
  ▶ N Jamaïquain(e)

jamb ['dʒæm] N jambage m

jam jar N pot m à confiture

jammed [dʒæmd] ADJ (window etc) coincé(e)

jam-packed [dʒæm'pækt] ADJ: **~ (with)** bourré(e) (de)

jam session N jam session f

jangle ['dʒæŋgl] VI cliqueter

janitor ['dʒænɪtə'] N (caretaker) concierge m

January ['dʒænjuərɪ] N janvier m; see also **July**

Japan [dʒə'pæn] N Japon m

Japanese [dʒæpə'ni:z] ADJ japonais(e) ▶ N pl inv Japonais(e); (Ling) japonais m

jar [dʒɑ:'] N (stone, earthenware) pot m; (glass) bocal m ▶ VI (sound) produire un son grinçant or discordant; (colours etc) détonner, jurer ▶ VT (shake) ébranler, secouer

jargon ['dʒɑ:gən] N jargon m

jarring ['dʒɑ:rɪŋ] ADJ (sound, colour) discordant(e)

Jas. ABBR = **James**

jasmin, jasmine ['dʒæzmɪn] N jasmin m

jaundice ['dʒɔ:ndɪs] N jaunisse f

jaundiced ['dʒɔ:ndɪst] ADJ (fig) envieux(-euse), désapprobateur(-trice)

jaunt [dʒɔ:nt] N balade f

jaunty ['dʒɔ:ntɪ] ADJ enjoué(e), désinvolte

Java ['dʒɑ:və] N Java f

javelin ['dʒævlɪn] N javelot m

jaw [dʒɔ:] N mâchoire f

jawbone ['dʒɔ:bəun] N maxillaire m

jay [dʒeɪ] N geai m

jaywalker ['dʒeɪwɔ:kə'] N piéton indiscipliné

jazz [dʒæz] N jazz m
  ▶ **jazz up** VT animer, égayer

jazz band N orchestre m or groupe m de jazz

jazzy ['dʒæzɪ] ADJ bariolé(e), tapageur(-euse); (beat) de jazz

JCB® N excavatrice f

JCS N ABBR (US) = **Joint Chiefs of Staff**

JD N ABBR (US: = Doctor of Laws) titre universitaire; (= Justice Department) ministère de la Justice

jealous ['dʒɛləs] ADJ jaloux(-ouse)

jealously ['dʒɛləslɪ] ADV jalousement

jealousy ['dʒɛləsɪ] N jalousie f

jeans [dʒiːnz] NPL jean *m*

Jeep® [dʒiːp] N jeep *f*

jeer [dʒɪəʳ] VI: **to ~ (at)** huer; se moquer cruellement (de), railler

jeering [ˈdʒɪərɪŋ] ADJ railleur(-euse), moqueur(-euse) ▶ N huées *fpl*

jeers [ˈdʒɪəz] NPL huées *fpl*; sarcasmes *mpl*

Jehovah's Witness [dʒɪˈhəʊvəz-] N témoin *m* de Jéhovah

Jello® [ˈdʒɛləʊ] (US) N gelée *f*

jelly [ˈdʒɛlɪ] N (*dessert*) gelée *f*; (*US: jam*) confiture *f*

jellyfish [ˈdʒɛlɪfɪʃ] N méduse *f*

jeopardize [ˈdʒɛpədaɪz] VT mettre en danger or péril

jeopardy [ˈdʒɛpədɪ] N: **in ~** en danger or péril

jerk [dʒəːk] N secousse *f*, saccade *f*; (*of muscle*) spasme *m*; (*inf*) pauvre type *m* ▶ VT (*shake*) donner une secousse à; (*pull*) tirer brusquement ▶ VI (*vehicles*) cahoter

jerkin [ˈdʒəːkɪn] N blouson *m*

jerky [ˈdʒəːkɪ] ADJ saccadé(e), cahotant(e)

jerry-built [ˈdʒɛrɪbɪlt] ADJ de mauvaise qualité

jerry can [ˈdʒɛrɪ-] N bidon *m*

Jersey [ˈdʒəːzɪ] N Jersey *f*

jersey [ˈdʒəːzɪ] N tricot *m*; (*fabric*) jersey *m*

Jerusalem [dʒəˈruːsləm] N Jérusalem

jest [dʒɛst] N plaisanterie *f*; **in ~** en plaisantant

jester [ˈdʒɛstəʳ] N (*Hist*) plaisantin *m*

Jesus [ˈdʒiːzəs] N Jésus; **~ Christ** Jésus-Christ

jet [dʒɛt] N (*of gas, liquid*) jet *m*; (*Aut*) gicleur *m*; (*Aviat*) avion *m* à réaction, jet *m*

jet-black [ˈdʒɛtˈblæk] ADJ (d'un noir) de jais

jet engine N moteur *m* à réaction

jet lag N décalage *m* horaire

jetsam [ˈdʒɛtsəm] N objets jetés à la mer (et rejetés sur la côte)

jet-setter [ˈdʒɛtsɛtəʳ] N membre *m* du or de la jet set

jet-ski VI faire du jet-ski or scooter des mers

jettison [ˈdʒɛtɪsn] VT jeter par-dessus bord

jetty [ˈdʒɛtɪ] N jetée *f*, digue *f*

Jew [dʒuː] N Juif *m*

jewel [ˈdʒuːəl] N bijou *m*, joyau *m*; (*in watch*) rubis *m*

jeweller, (*US*) **jeweler** [ˈdʒuːələʳ] N bijoutier(-ière), joaillier *m*

jeweller's, jeweller's shop N (*BRIT*) bijouterie *f*, joaillerie *f*

jewellery, (*US*) **jewelry** [ˈdʒuːəlrɪ] N bijoux *mpl*

Jewess [ˈdʒuːɪs] (*pej*) N Juive *f*

Jewish [ˈdʒuːɪʃ] ADJ juif (juive)

JFK N ABBR (*US*) = **John Fitzgerald Kennedy International Airport**

jib [dʒɪb] N (*Naut*) foc *m*; (*of crane*) flèche *f* ▶ VI (*horse*) regimber; **to ~ at doing sth** rechigner à faire qch

jibe [dʒaɪb] N sarcasme *m*

jiffy [ˈdʒɪfɪ] N (*inf*): **in a ~** en un clin d'œil

jig [dʒɪg] N (*dance, tune*) gigue *m*

jigsaw [ˈdʒɪgsɔ:] N (*also:* **jigsaw puzzle**) puzzle *m*; (*tool*) scie sauteuse

jilt [dʒɪlt] VT laisser tomber, plaquer

jingle [ˈdʒɪŋgl] N (*advertising jingle*) couplet *m* publicitaire ▶ VI cliqueter, tinter

jingoism [ˈdʒɪŋgəʊɪzəm] N chauvinisme *m*

jinx [dʒɪŋks] N (*inf*) (mauvais) sort

jitters [ˈdʒɪtəz] NPL (*inf*): **to get the ~** avoir la trouille or la frousse

jittery [ˈdʒɪtərɪ] ADJ (*inf*) nerveux(-euse); **to be ~** avoir les nerfs en pelote

jiujitsu [dʒuːˈdʒɪtsuː] N jiu-jitsu *m*

job [dʒɔb] N (*chore, task*) travail *m*, tâche *f*; (*employment*) emploi *m*, poste *m*, place *f*; **a part-time/full-time ~** un emploi à temps partiel/à plein temps; **he's only doing his ~** il fait son boulot; **it's a good ~ that …** c'est heureux or c'est une chance que … +*sub*; **just the ~!** (c'est) juste or exactement ce qu'il faut!

jobber [ˈdʒɔbəʳ] N (*BRIT Stock Exchange*) négociant *m* en titres

jobbing [ˈdʒɔbɪŋ] ADJ (*BRIT: workman*) à la tâche, à la journée

job centre [ˈdʒɔbsɛntəʳ] (*BRIT*) N ≈ ANPE *f*, ≈ Agence nationale pour l'emploi

job creation scheme N plan *m* pour la création d'emplois

job description N description *f* du poste

jobless [ˈdʒɔblɪs] ADJ sans travail, au chômage ▶ NPL: **the ~** les sans-emploi *m inv*, les chômeurs *mpl*

job lot N lot *m* (d'articles divers)

job satisfaction N satisfaction professionnelle

job security N sécurité *f* de l'emploi

job specification N caractéristiques *fpl* du poste

Jock [dʒɔk] N (*inf: Scotsman*) Écossais *m*

jockey [ˈdʒɔkɪ] N jockey *m* ▶ VI: **to ~ for position** manœuvrer pour être bien placé

jockey box N (*US Aut*) boîte *f* à gants, vide-poches *m inv*

jockstrap [ˈdʒɔkstræp] N slip *m* de sport

jocular [ˈdʒɔkjuləʳ] ADJ jovial(e), enjoué(e); facétieux(-euse)

jog [dʒɔg] VT secouer ▶ VI (*Sport*) faire du jogging; **to ~ along** cahoter; trotter; **to ~ sb's memory** rafraîchir la mémoire de qn

jogger [ˈdʒɔgəʳ] N jogger *mf*

jogging [ˈdʒɔgɪŋ] N jogging *m*

john [dʒɔn] N (*US inf*): **the ~** (*toilet*) les cabinets *mpl*

join [dʒɔɪn] VT (*put together*) unir, assembler; (*become member of*) s'inscrire à; (*meet*) rejoindre, retrouver; (*queue*) se joindre à ▶ VI (*roads, rivers*) se rejoindre, se rencontrer ▶ N raccord *m*; **will you ~ us for dinner?** vous dînerez bien avec nous?; **I'll ~ you later** je vous rejoindrai plus tard; **to ~ forces (with)** s'associer (à)
▶ **join in** VI se mettre de la partie ▶ VT FUS se mêler à
▶ **join up** VI (*meet*) se rejoindre; (*Mil*) s'engager

joiner [ˈdʒɔɪnəʳ] (*BRIT*) N menuisier *m*

joinery [ˈdʒɔɪnərɪ] N menuiserie *f*

joint [dʒɔɪnt] N (*Tech*) jointure *f*; joint *m*; (*Anat*) articulation *f*, jointure; (*BRIT Culin*) rôti *m*; (*inf: place*) boîte *f*; (*of cannabis*) joint ▶ ADJ commun(e); (*committee*) mixte, paritaire; (*winner*) ex aequo; **~ responsibility** coresponsabilité *f*

joint account N compte joint
jointly ['dʒɔɪntlɪ] ADV ensemble, en commun
joint ownership N copropriété f
joint-stock company ['dʒɔɪntstɔk-] N société f par actions
joint venture N entreprise commune
joist [dʒɔɪst] N solive f
joke [dʒəuk] N plaisanterie f; (also: **practical joke**) farce f ▶ VI plaisanter; **to play a ~ on** jouer un tour à, faire une farce à
joker ['dʒəukəʳ] N plaisantin m, blagueur(-euse); (Cards) joker m
joking ['dʒəukɪŋ] N plaisanterie f
jollity ['dʒɔlɪtɪ] N réjouissances fpl, gaieté f
jolly ['dʒɔlɪ] ADJ gai(e), enjoué(e); (enjoyable) amusant(e), plaisant(e) ▶ ADV (BRIT inf) rudement, drôlement ▶ VT (BRIT): **to ~ sb along** amadouer qn, convaincre or entraîner qn à force d'encouragements; **~ good!** (BRIT) formidable!
jolt [dʒəult] N cahot m, secousse f; (shock) choc m ▶ VT cahoter, secouer
Jordan ['dʒɔːdən] N (country) Jordanie f; (river) Jourdain m
Jordanian [dʒɔː'deɪnɪən] ADJ jordanien(ne) ▶ N Jordanien(ne)
joss stick ['dʒɔs-] N bâton m d'encens
jostle ['dʒɔsl] VT bousculer, pousser ▶ VI jouer des coudes
jot [dʒɔt] N: **not one ~** pas un brin
▶ **jot down** VT inscrire rapidement, noter
jotter ['dʒɔtəʳ] N (BRIT: exercise book) cahier m (de brouillon); (: pad) bloc-notes m
journal ['dʒəːnl] N journal m
journalese [dʒəːnə'liːz] N (pej) style m journalistique
journalism ['dʒəːnəlɪzəm] N journalisme m
journalist ['dʒəːnəlɪst] N journaliste mf
journey ['dʒəːnɪ] N voyage m; (distance covered) trajet m ▶ VI voyager; **the ~ takes two hours** le trajet dure deux heures; **a 5-hour ~** un voyage de 5 heures; **how was your ~?** votre voyage s'est bien passé?
jovial ['dʒəuvɪəl] ADJ jovial(e)
jowl [dʒaul] N mâchoire f (inférieure); bajoue f
joy [dʒɔɪ] N joie f
joyful ['dʒɔɪful], **joyous** ['dʒɔɪəs] ADJ joyeux(-euse)
joyride ['dʒɔɪraɪd] VI: **to go joyriding** faire une virée dans une voiture volée
joyrider ['dʒɔɪraɪdəʳ] N voleur(-euse) de voiture (qui fait une virée dans le véhicule volé)
joy stick N (Aviat) manche m à balai; (Comput) manche à balai, manette f (de jeu)
JP N ABBR = **Justice of the Peace**
Jr ABBR = **junior**
JTPA N ABBR (US: = Job Training Partnership Act) programme gouvernemental de formation
jubilant ['dʒuːbɪlnt] ADJ triomphant(e), réjoui(e)
jubilation [dʒuːbɪ'leɪʃən] N jubilation f
jubilee ['dʒuːbɪliː] N jubilé m; **silver ~** (jubilé du) vingt-cinquième anniversaire
judge [dʒʌdʒ] N juge m ▶ VT juger; (estimate:

weight, size etc) apprécier; (consider) estimer ▶ VI: **judging** or **to ~ by his expression** d'après son expression; **as far as I can ~** autant que je puisse en juger
judge advocate N (Mil) magistrat m militaire
judgment, judgement ['dʒʌdʒmənt] N jugement m; (punishment) châtiment m; **in my ~** à mon avis; **to pass ~ on** (Law) prononcer un jugement (sur)
judicial [dʒuː'dɪʃl] ADJ judiciaire; (fair) impartial(e)
judiciary [dʒuː'dɪʃɪərɪ] N (pouvoir m) judiciaire m
judicious [dʒuː'dɪʃəs] ADJ judicieux(-euse)
judo ['dʒuːdəu] N judo m
jug [dʒʌg] N pot m, cruche f
jugged hare ['dʒʌgd-] N (BRIT) civet m de lièvre
juggernaut ['dʒʌgənɔːt] N (BRIT: huge truck) mastodonte m
juggle ['dʒʌgl] VI jongler
juggler ['dʒʌgləʳ] N jongleur m
Jugoslav ['juːgəu'slɑːv] ADJ, N = **Yugoslav**
jugular ['dʒʌgjulaʳ] ADJ: **~ (vein)** veine f jugulaire
juice [dʒuːs] N jus m; (inf: petrol): **we've run out of ~** c'est la panne sèche
juicy ['dʒuːsɪ] ADJ juteux(-euse)
jukebox ['dʒuːkbɔks] N juke-box m
July [dʒuː'laɪ] N juillet m; **the first of ~** le premier juillet; **(on) the eleventh of ~** le onze juillet; **in the month of ~** au mois de juillet; **at the beginning/end of ~** au début/à la fin (du mois) de juillet, début/fin juillet; **in the middle of ~** au milieu (du mois) de juillet, à la mi-juillet; **during ~** pendant le mois de juillet; **in ~ of next year** en juillet de l'année prochaine; **each** or **every ~** tous les ans or chaque année en juillet; **~ was wet this year** il a beaucoup plu cette année en juillet
jumble ['dʒʌmbl] N fouillis m ▶ VT (also: **jumble up**, **jumble together**) mélanger, brouiller
jumble sale N (BRIT) vente f de charité; voir article

> Les jumble sales ont lieu dans les églises,
> salles des fêtes ou halls d'écoles, et l'on y
> vend des articles de toutes sortes, en général
> bon marché et surtout d'occasion, pour
> collecter des fonds pour une œuvre de
> charité, une école (par exemple, pour
> acheter des ordinateurs), ou encore une
> église (pour réparer un toit etc).

jumbo ['dʒʌmbəu] ADJ (also: **jumbo jet**) (avion) gros porteur (à réaction); **~ size** format maxi or extra-grand
jump [dʒʌmp] VI sauter, bondir; (with fear etc) sursauter; (increase) monter en flèche ▶ VT sauter, franchir ▶ N saut m, bond m; (with fear etc) sursaut m; (fence) obstacle m; **to ~ the queue** (BRIT) passer avant son tour
▶ **jump about** VI sautiller
▶ **jump at** VT FUS (fig) sauter sur; **he jumped at the offer** il s'est empressé d'accepter la proposition
▶ **jump down** VI sauter (pour descendre)
▶ **jump up** VI se lever (d'un bond)

jumped-up [ˈdʒʌmptʌp] ADJ (BRIT pej) parvenu(e)

jumper [ˈdʒʌmpəʳ] N (BRIT: pullover) pull-over m; (US: pinafore dress) robe-chasuble f; (Sport) sauteur(-euse)

jump leads, (US) **jumper cables** NPL câbles mpl de démarrage

jump-start [ˈdʒʌmpstɑːt] VT (car: push) démarrer en poussant; (: with jump leads) démarrer avec des câbles (de démarrage); (fig: project, situation) faire redémarrer promptement

jumpy [ˈdʒʌmpɪ] ADJ nerveux(-euse), agité(e)

Jun. ABBR = **June; junior**

junction [ˈdʒʌŋkʃən] N (BRIT: of roads) carrefour m; (: of rails) embranchement m

juncture [ˈdʒʌŋktʃəʳ] N: **at this ~** à ce moment-là, sur ces entrefaites

June [dʒuːn] N juin m; see also **July**

jungle [ˈdʒʌŋgl] N jungle f

junior [ˈdʒuːnɪəʳ] ADJ, N: **he's ~ to me (by two years), he's my ~ (by two years)** il est mon cadet (de deux ans), il est plus jeune que moi (de deux ans); **he's ~ to me** (seniority) il est en dessous de moi (dans la hiérarchie), j'ai plus d'ancienneté que lui

junior executive N cadre moyen

junior high school N (US) ≈ collège m d'enseignement secondaire; see also **high school**

junior minister N (BRIT) ministre m sous tutelle

junior partner N associé(-adjoint) m

junior school N (BRIT) école f primaire

junior sizes NPL (Comm) tailles fpl fillettes/garçonnets

juniper [ˈdʒuːnɪpəʳ] N: **~ berry** baie f de genièvre

junk [dʒʌŋk] N (rubbish) camelote f; (cheap goods) bric-à-brac m inv; (ship) jonque f ▶ VT (inf) abandonner, mettre au rancart

junk bond N (Comm) obligation hautement spéculative utilisée dans les OPA agressives

junk dealer N brocanteur(-euse)

junket [ˈdʒʌŋkɪt] N (Culin) lait caillé; (BRIT inf): **to go on a ~, go junketing** voyager aux frais de la princesse

junk food N snacks vite prêts (sans valeur nutritive)

junkie [ˈdʒʌŋkɪ] N (inf) junkie m, drogué(e)

junk mail N prospectus mpl; (Comput) messages mpl publicitaires

junk room N (US) débarras m

junk shop N (boutique f de) brocanteur m

Junr ABBR = **junior**

junta [ˈdʒʌntə] N junte f

Jupiter [ˈdʒuːpɪtəʳ] N (planet) Jupiter f

jurisdiction [dʒuərɪsˈdɪkʃən] N juridiction f; **it falls** or **comes within/outside our ~** cela est/n'est pas de notre compétence or ressort

jurisprudence [dʒuərɪsˈpruːdəns] N jurisprudence f

juror [ˈdʒuərəʳ] N juré m

jury [ˈdʒuərɪ] N jury m

jury box N banc m des jurés

juryman [ˈdʒuərɪmən] N (irreg) = **juror**

just [dʒʌst] ADJ juste ▶ ADV: **he's ~ done it/left** il vient de le faire/partir; **~ as I expected** exactement or précisément comme je m'y attendais; **~ right/two o'clock** exactement or juste ce qu'il faut/deux heures; **we were ~ going** nous partions; **I was ~ about to phone** j'allais téléphoner; **~ as he was leaving** au moment or à l'instant précis où il partait; **~ before/enough/here** juste avant/assez/là; **it's ~ me/a mistake** ce n'est que moi/(rien) qu'une erreur; **~ missed/caught** manqué/attrapé de justesse; **~ listen to this!** écoutez un peu ça!; **~ ask someone the way** vous n'avez qu'à demander votre chemin à quelqu'un; **it's ~ as good** c'est (vraiment) aussi bon; **she's ~ as clever as you** elle est tout aussi intelligente que vous; **it's ~ as well that you ...** heureusement que vous ...; **not ~ now** pas tout de suite; **~ a minute!, ~ one moment!** un instant (s'il vous plaît)!

justice [ˈdʒʌstɪs] N justice f; (US: judge) juge m de la Cour suprême; **Lord Chief J~** (BRIT) premier président de la cour d'appel; **this photo doesn't do you ~** cette photo ne vous avantage pas

Justice of the Peace N juge m de paix

justifiable [dʒʌstɪˈfaɪəbl] ADJ justifiable

justifiably [dʒʌstɪˈfaɪəblɪ] ADV légitimement, à juste titre

justification [dʒʌstɪfɪˈkeɪʃən] N justification f

justify [ˈdʒʌstɪfaɪ] VT justifier; **to be justified in doing sth** être en droit de faire qch

justly [ˈdʒʌstlɪ] ADV avec raison, justement

justness [ˈdʒʌstnɪs] N justesse f

jut [dʒʌt] VI (also: **jut out**) dépasser, faire saillie

jute [dʒuːt] N jute m

juvenile [ˈdʒuːvənaɪl] ADJ juvénile; (court, books) pour enfants ▶ N adolescent(e)

juvenile delinquency N délinquance f juvénile

juxtapose [ˈdʒʌkstəpəuz] VT juxtaposer

juxtaposition [dʒʌkstəpəˈzɪʃən] N juxtaposition f

Kk

K, k [keɪ] N (*letter*) K, k *m*; **K for King** K comme Kléber ▶ ABBR (= *one thousand*) K; (BRIT: = *Knight*) *titre honorifique*

kaftan ['kæftæn] N cafetan *m*

Kalahari Desert [kælə'hɑːrɪ-] N désert *m* de Kalahari

kale [keɪl] N chou frisé

kaleidoscope [kə'laɪdəskəup] N kaléidoscope *m*

kamikaze [kæmɪ'kɑːzɪ] ADJ kamikaze

Kampala [kæm'pɑːlə] N Kampala

Kampuchea [kæmpu'tʃɪə] N Kampuchéa *m*

kangaroo [kæŋgə'ruː] N kangourou *m*

Kans. ABBR (*US*) = **Kansas**

kaput [kə'put] ADJ (*inf*) kaput

karaoke [kɑːrə'əukɪ] N karaoké *m*

karate [kə'rɑːtɪ] N karaté *m*

Kashmir [kæʃ'mɪər] N Cachemire *m*

Kazakhstan [kɑːzɑːk'stæn] N Kazakhstan *m*

kB N ABBR (= *kilobyte*) Ko *m*

KC N ABBR (BRIT *Law*: = *King's Counsel*) *titre donné à certains avocats; see also* **QC**

kd ABBR (*US*: = *knocked down*) en pièces détachées

kebab [kə'bæb] N kebab *m*

keel [kiːl] N quille *f*; **on an even ~** (*fig*) à flot ▶ **keel over** VI (*Naut*) chavirer, dessaler; (*person*) tomber dans les pommes

keen [kiːn] ADJ (*eager*) plein(e) d'enthousiasme; (*interest, desire, competition*) vif (vive); (*eye, intelligence*) pénétrant(e); (*edge*) effilé(e); **to be ~ to do** *or* **on doing sth** désirer vivement faire qch, tenir beaucoup à faire qch; **to be ~ on sth/sb** aimer beaucoup qch/qn; **I'm not ~ on going** je ne suis pas chaud pour y aller, je n'ai pas très envie d'y aller

keenly ['kiːnlɪ] ADV (*enthusiastically*) avec enthousiasme; (*feel*) vivement, profondément; (*look*) intensément

keenness ['kiːnnɪs] N (*eagerness*) enthousiasme *m*; **~ to do** vif désir de faire

keep [kiːp] (*pt, pp* **kept** [kɛpt]) VT (*retain, preserve*) garder; (*hold back*) retenir; (*shop, accounts, promise, diary*) tenir; (*support*) entretenir, assurer la subsistance de; (*a promise*) tenir; (*chickens, bees, pigs etc*) élever ▶ VI (*food*) se conserver; (*remain: in a certain state or place*) rester ▶ N (*of castle*) donjon *m*; (*food etc*): **enough for his ~** assez pour (assurer) sa subsistance; **to ~ doing sth**

(*continue*) continuer à faire qch; (*repeatedly*) ne pas arrêter de faire qch; **to ~ sb from doing/ sth from happening** empêcher qn de faire *or* que qn (ne) fasse/que qch (n')arrive; **to ~ sb happy/a place tidy** faire que qn soit content/ qu'un endroit reste propre; **to ~ sb waiting** faire attendre qn; **to ~ an appointment** ne pas manquer un rendez-vous; **to ~ a record of sth** prendre note de qch; **to ~ sth to o.s.** garder qch pour soi, tenir qch secret; **to ~ sth from sb** cacher qch à qn; **to ~ time** (*clock*) être à l'heure, ne pas retarder; **for keeps** (*inf*) pour de bon, pour toujours

▶ **keep away** VT: **to ~ sth/sb away from sb** tenir qch/qn éloigné de qn ▶ VI: **to ~ away (from)** ne pas s'approcher (de)

▶ **keep back** VT (*crowds, tears, money*) retenir; (*conceal: information*): **to ~ sth back from sb** cacher qch à qn ▶ VI rester en arrière

▶ **keep down** VT (*control: prices, spending*) empêcher d'augmenter, limiter; (*retain: food*) garder ▶ VI (*person*) rester assis(e); rester par terre

▶ **keep in** VT (*invalid, child*) garder à la maison; (*Scol*) consigner ▶ VI (*inf*): **to ~ in with sb** rester en bons termes avec qn

▶ **keep off** VT (*dog, person*) éloigner ▶ VI ne pas s'approcher; **if the rain keeps off** s'il ne pleut pas; **~ your hands off!** pas touche! (*inf*); **"~ off the grass"** "pelouse interdite"

▶ **keep on** VI continuer; **to ~ on doing** continuer à faire; **don't ~ on about it!** arrête (d'en parler)!

▶ **keep out** VT empêcher d'entrer ▶ VI (*stay out*) rester en dehors; **"~ out"** "défense d'entrer"

▶ **keep up** VI (*fig: in comprehension*) suivre ▶ VT continuer, maintenir; **to ~ up with sb** (*in work etc*) se maintenir au même niveau que qn; (*in race etc*) aller aussi vite que qn

keeper ['kiːpər] N gardien(ne)

keep-fit [kiːp'fɪt] N gymnastique *f* (d'entretien)

keeping ['kiːpɪŋ] N (*care*) garde *f*; **in ~ with** en harmonie avec

keeps [kiːps] N: **for ~** (*inf*) pour de bon, pour toujours

keepsake ['kiːpseɪk] N souvenir *m*

keg [kɛg] N barrique *f*, tonnelet *m*

Ken. ABBR (*US*) = **Kentucky**

kennel ['kɛnl] N niche f; **kennels** NPL (for boarding) chenil m

Kenya ['kɛnjə] N Kenya m

Kenyan ['kɛnjən] ADJ kényan(ne) ▶ N Kényan(ne)

kept [kɛpt] PT, PP of **keep**

kerb [kəːb] N (BRIT) bordure f du trottoir

kerb crawler [-krɔːləʳ] N personne qui accoste les prostitué(e)s en voiture

kernel ['kəːnl] N amande f; (fig) noyau m

kerosene ['kɛrəsiːn] N kérosène m

ketchup ['kɛtʃəp] N ketchup m

kettle ['kɛtl] N bouilloire f

kettling ['kɛtəlɪŋ] N ≈ tactique f de l'encerclement; tactique policière consistant à encercler des manifestants pour les confiner dans un lieu de façon prolongée

key [kiː] N (gen, Mus) clé f; (of piano, typewriter) touche f; (on map) légende f ▶ ADJ (factor, role, area) clé inv ▶ CPD (-)clé ▶ VT (also: **key in**: text) saisir; **can I have my ~?** je peux avoir ma clé?; **a ~ issue** un problème fondamental

keyboard ['kiːbɔːd] N clavier m ▶ VT (text) saisir

keyboarder ['kiːbɔːdəʳ] N claviste mf

keyed up [kiːd'ʌp] ADJ: **to be (all) ~** être surexcité(e)

keyhole ['kiːhəul] N trou m de la serrure

keyhole surgery N chirurgie très minutieuse où l'incision est minimale

keynote ['kiːnəut] N (Mus) tonique f; (fig) note dominante

keypad ['kiːpæd] N pavé m numérique

keyring ['kiːrɪŋ] N porte-clés m

keystroke ['kiːstrəuk] N frappe f

kg ABBR (= kilogram) K

KGB N ABBR KGB m

khaki ['kɑːkɪ] ADJ, N kaki m

kibbutz [kɪ'buts] N kibboutz m

kick [kɪk] VT donner un coup de pied à ▶ VI (horse) ruer ▶ N coup m de pied; (of rifle) recul m; (inf: thrill): **he does it for kicks** il le fait parce que ça l'excite, il le fait pour le plaisir; **to ~ the habit** (inf) arrêter

▶ **kick around** VI (inf) traîner

▶ **kick off** VI (Sport) donner le coup d'envoi

kick-off ['kɪkɔf] N (Sport) coup m d'envoi

kick-start ['kɪkstɑːt] N (also: **kick-starter**) lanceur m au pied

kid [kɪd] N (inf: child) gamin(e), gosse mf; (animal, leather) chevreau m ▶ VI (inf) plaisanter, blaguer

kid gloves NPL: **to treat sb with ~** traiter qn avec ménagement

kidnap ['kɪdnæp] VT enlever, kidnapper

kidnapper ['kɪdnæpəʳ] N ravisseur(-euse)

kidnapping ['kɪdnæpɪŋ] N enlèvement m

kidney ['kɪdnɪ] N (Anat) rein m; (Culin) rognon m

kidney bean N haricot m rouge

kidney machine N (Med) rein artificiel

Kilimanjaro [kɪlɪmən'dʒɑːrəu] N: **Mount ~** Kilimandjaro m

kill [kɪl] VT tuer; (fig) faire échouer; détruire; supprimer ▶ N mise f à mort; **to ~ time** tuer le temps

▶ **kill off** VT exterminer; (fig) éliminer

killer ['kɪləʳ] N tueur(-euse); (murderer) meurtrier(-ière)

killer instinct N combativité f; **to have the ~** avoir un tempérament de battant

killing ['kɪlɪŋ] N meurtre m; (of group of people) tuerie f, massacre m; (inf): **to make a ~** se remplir les poches, réussir un beau coup ▶ ADJ (inf) tordant(e)

killjoy ['kɪldʒɔɪ] N rabat-joie m inv

kiln [kɪln] N four m

kilo ['kiːləu] N kilo m

kilobyte ['kiːləubaɪt] N (Comput) kilo-octet m

kilogram, kilogramme ['kɪləugræm] N kilogramme m

kilometre, (US) kilometer ['kɪləmiːtəʳ] N kilomètre m

kilowatt ['kɪləuwɔt] N kilowatt m

kilt [kɪlt] N kilt m

kilter ['kɪltəʳ] N: **out of ~** déréglé(e), détraqué(e)

kimono [kɪ'məunəu] N kimono m

kin [kɪn] N see **next-of-kin**; **kith**

kind [kaɪnd] ADJ gentil(le), aimable ▶ N sorte f, espèce f; (species) genre m; **would you be ~ enough to …?, would you be so ~ as to …?** auriez-vous la gentillesse or l'obligeance de …?; **it's very ~ of you (to do)** c'est très aimable à vous (de faire); **to be two of a ~** se ressembler; **in ~** (Comm) en nature; (fig) **to repay sb in ~** rendre la pareille à qn; **~ of** (inf: rather) plutôt; **a ~ of** une sorte de; **what ~ of …?** quelle sorte de …?

kindergarten ['kɪndəgɑːtn] N jardin m d'enfants

kind-hearted [kaɪnd'hɑːtɪd] ADJ bon (bonne)

Kindle® ['kɪndl] N Kindle® m

kindle ['kɪndl] VT allumer, enflammer

kindling ['kɪndlɪŋ] N petit bois

kindly ['kaɪndlɪ] ADJ bienveillant(e), plein(e) de gentillesse ▶ ADV avec bonté; **will you ~ …** auriez-vous la bonté or l'obligeance de …; **he didn't take it ~** il a l'air mal pris

kindness ['kaɪndnɪs] N (quality) bonté f, gentillesse f

kindred ['kɪndrɪd] ADJ apparenté(e); **~ spirit** âme f sœur

kinetic [kɪ'nɛtɪk] ADJ cinétique

king [kɪŋ] N roi m

kingdom ['kɪŋdəm] N royaume m

kingfisher ['kɪŋfɪʃəʳ] N martin-pêcheur m

kingpin ['kɪŋpɪn] N (Tech) pivot m; (fig) cheville ouvrière

king-size ['kɪŋsaɪz], **king-sized** ['kɪŋsaɪzd] ADJ (cigarette) (format) extra-long (longue)

king-size bed, king-sized bed N grand lit (de 1,95 m de large)

kink [kɪŋk] N (of rope) entortillement m; (in hair) ondulation f; (inf: fig) aberration f

kinky ['kɪŋkɪ] ADJ (fig) excentrique; (pej) aux goûts spéciaux

kinship ['kɪnʃɪp] N parenté f

kinsman ['kɪnzmən] N (irreg) parent m

kinswoman ['kɪnzwumən] N (irreg) parente f

kiosk ['kiːɔsk] N kiosque m; (BRIT: also: **telephone kiosk**) cabine f (téléphonique);

(also: **newspaper kiosk**) kiosque à journaux
kipper ['kɪpəʳ] N hareng fumé et salé
Kirghizia [kəː'gɪzɪə] N Kirghizistan m
kiss [kɪs] N baiser m ▶ VT embrasser; **to ~ (each other)** s'embrasser; **to ~ sb goodbye** dire au revoir à qn en l'embrassant
kissagram ['kɪsəgræm] N baiser envoyé à l'occasion d'une célébration par l'intermédiaire d'une personne employée à cet effet
kiss of life N (BRIT) bouche à bouche m
kit [kɪt] N équipement m, matériel m; (set of tools etc) trousse f; (for assembly) kit m; **tool ~** nécessaire m à outils
▶ **kit out** VT (BRIT) équiper
kitbag ['kɪtbæg] N sac m de voyage or de marin
kitchen ['kɪtʃɪn] N cuisine f
kitchen garden N jardin m potager
kitchen sink N évier m
kitchen unit N (BRIT) élément m de cuisine
kitchenware ['kɪtʃɪnwɛəʳ] N vaisselle f; ustensiles mpl de cuisine
kite [kaɪt] N (toy) cerf-volant m; (Zool) milan m
kith [kɪθ] N: **~ and kin** parents et amis mpl
kitten ['kɪtn] N petit chat, chaton m
kitty ['kɪtɪ] N (money) cagnotte f
kiwi ['kiːwiː] N (also: **kiwi fruit**) kiwi m
KKK N ABBR (US) = **Ku Klux Klan**
Kleenex® ['kliːnɛks] N Kleenex® m
kleptomaniac [klɛptəu'meɪnɪæk] N kleptomane mf
km ABBR (= kilometre) km
km/h ABBR (= kilometres per hour) km/h
knack [næk] N: **to have the ~ (of doing)** avoir le coup (pour faire); **there's a ~** il y a un coup à prendre or une combine
knackered ['nækəd] ADJ (inf) crevé(e), nase
knapsack ['næpsæk] N musette f
knave [neɪv] N (Cards) valet m
knead [niːd] VT pétrir
knee [niː] N genou m
kneecap ['niːkæp] N rotule f ▶ VT tirer un coup de feu dans la rotule de
knee-deep ['niː'diːp] ADJ: **the water was ~** l'eau arrivait aux genoux
kneel [niːl] (pt, pp knelt [nɛlt]) VI (also: **kneel down**) s'agenouiller
kneepad ['niːpæd] N genouillère f
knell [nɛl] N glas m
knelt [nɛlt] PT, PP OF **kneel**
knew [njuː] PT OF **know**
knickers ['nɪkəz] NPL (BRIT) culotte f (de femme)
knick-knack ['nɪknæk] N colifichet m
knife [naɪf] (pl **knives** [naɪvz]) N couteau m ▶ VT poignarder, frapper d'un coup de couteau; **~, fork and spoon** couvert m
knife-edge ['naɪfɛdʒ] N: **to be on a ~** être sur le fil du rasoir
knight [naɪt] N chevalier m; (Chess) cavalier m
knighthood ['naɪthud] N chevalerie f; (title): **to get a ~** être fait chevalier
knit [nɪt] VT tricoter; (fig): **to ~ together** unir ▶ VI tricoter; (broken bones) se ressouder; **to ~ one's brows** froncer les sourcils
knitted ['nɪtɪd] ADJ en tricot

knitting ['nɪtɪŋ] N tricot m
knitting machine N machine f à tricoter
knitting needle N aiguille f à tricoter
knitting pattern N modèle m (pour tricot)
knitwear ['nɪtwɛəʳ] N tricots mpl, lainages mpl
knives [naɪvz] NPL OF **knife**
knob [nɔb] N bouton m; (BRIT): **a ~ of butter** une noix de beurre
knobbly ['nɔblɪ], (US) **knobby** ['nɔbɪ] ADJ (wood, surface) noueux(-euse); (knees) noueux
knock [nɔk] VT frapper; (bump into) heurter; (force: nail etc): **to ~ a nail into** enfoncer un clou dans; (inf: fig) dénigrer; (make: hole etc): **to ~ a hole in** faire un trou dans, trouer ▶ VI (engine) cogner; (at door etc): **to ~ at/on** frapper à/sur ▶ N coup m; **he knocked at the door** il frappa à la porte
▶ **knock down** VT renverser; (price) réduire
▶ **knock off** VI (inf: finish) s'arrêter (de travailler) ▶ VT (vase, object) faire tomber; (inf: steal) piquer; (fig: from price etc): **to ~ off £10** faire une remise de 10 livres
▶ **knock out** VT assommer; (Boxing) mettre k.-o.; (in competition) éliminer
▶ **knock over** VT (object) faire tomber; (pedestrian) renverser
knockdown ['nɔkdaun] ADJ (price) sacrifié(e)
knocker ['nɔkəʳ] N (on door) heurtoir m
knocking ['nɔkɪŋ] N coups mpl
knock-kneed [nɔk'niːd] ADJ aux genoux cagneux
knockout ['nɔkaut] N (Boxing) knock-out m, K.-O. m; **~ competition** (BRIT) compétition f avec épreuves éliminatoires
knock-up ['nɔkʌp] N (Tennis): **to have a ~** faire des balles
knot [nɔt] N (gen) nœud m ▶ VT nouer; **to tie a ~** faire un nœud
knotty ['nɔtɪ] ADJ (fig) épineux(-euse)
know [nəu] (pt knew [njuː], pp known [nəun]) VT savoir; (person, place) connaître; **to ~ that** savoir que; **to ~ how to do** savoir faire; **to ~ how to swim** savoir nager; **to ~ about/of sth** (event) être au courant de qch; (subject) connaître qch; **to get to ~ sth** (fact) apprendre qch; (place) apprendre à connaître qch; **I don't ~** je ne sais pas; **I don't ~ him** je ne le connais pas; **do you ~ where I can ...?** savez-vous où je peux ...?; **to ~ right from wrong** savoir distinguer le bon du mauvais; **as far as I ~ ...** à ma connaissance ..., autant que je sache ...
know-all ['nəuɔːl] N (BRIT pej) je-sais-tout mf
know-how ['nəuhau] N savoir-faire m, technique f, compétence f
knowing ['nəuɪŋ] ADJ (look etc) entendu(e)
knowingly ['nəuɪŋlɪ] ADV (on purpose) sciemment; (smile, look) d'un air entendu
know-it-all ['nəuɪtɔːl] N (US) = **know-all**
knowledge ['nɔlɪdʒ] N connaissance f; (learning) connaissances, savoir m; **to have no ~ of** ignorer; **not to my ~** pas à ma connaissance; **without my ~** à mon insu; **to have a working ~ of French** se débrouiller en français; **it is common ~ that ...** chacun sait que ...; **it has come to my ~ that ...** j'ai appris que ...

k

knowledgeable ['nɔlɪdʒəbl] ADJ bien informé(e)

known [nəʊn] PP of **know** ▸ ADJ (*thief, facts*) notoire; (*expert*) célèbre

knuckle ['nʌkl] N articulation *f* (des phalanges), jointure *f*
  ▸ **knuckle down** VI (*inf*) s'y mettre
  ▸ **knuckle under** VI (*inf*) céder

knuckleduster ['nʌkldʌstər] N coup-de-poing américain

KO ABBR = **knock out** ▸ N K.-O. *m* ▸ VT mettre K.-O.

koala [kəʊ'ɑːlə] N (*also*: **koala bear**) koala *m*

kook [kuːk] N (*US inf*) loufoque *mf*

Koran [kɔ'rɑːn] N Coran *m*

Korea [kə'rɪə] N Corée *f*; **North/South** ~ Corée du Nord/Sud

Korean [kə'rɪən] ADJ coréen(ne) ▸ N Coréen(ne)

kosher ['kəʊʃər] ADJ kascher *inv*

Kosovar, Kosovan ['kɔsəvɑːr, 'kɔsəvæn] ADJ kosovar(e)

Kosovo ['kɔsɔvəu] N Kosovo *m*

kowtow ['kau'tau] VI: **to ~ to sb** s'aplatir devant qn

Kremlin ['krɛmlɪn] N: **the ~** le Kremlin

KS ABBR (*US*) = **Kansas**

Kt ABBR (*BRIT*: = *Knight*) titre honorifique

Kuala Lumpur ['kwɑːlə'lumpuər] N Kuala Lumpur

kudos ['kjuːdɔs] N gloire *f*, lauriers *mpl*

Kurd [kəːd] N Kurde *mf*

Kuwait [ku'weɪt] N Koweït *m*

Kuwaiti [ku'weɪtɪ] ADJ koweïtien(ne)
  ▸ N Koweïtien(ne)

kW ABBR (= *kilowatt*) kW

KY, Ky. ABBR (*US*) = **Kentucky**

Ll

L¹, l [εl] N (*letter*) L, l m; **L for Lucy,** (*US*) **L for Love** L comme Louis

L² ABBR (= *lake, large*) L; (BRIT Aut: = *learner*) signale un conducteur débutant; (= *left*) g

l. ABBR (= *litre*) l

LA N ABBR (*US*) = **Los Angeles** ▶ ABBR (*US*) = **Louisiana**

La. ABBR (*US*) = **Louisiana**

lab [læb] N ABBR (= *laboratory*) labo m

Lab. ABBR (CANADA) = **Labrador**

label ['leɪbl] N étiquette f; (*brand: of record*) marque f ▶ VT étiqueter; **to ~ sb a ...** qualifier qn de ...

labor etc ['leɪbəʳ] (*US*) N = **labour**

laboratory [lə'bɔrətərɪ] N laboratoire m

Labor Day N (US, CANADA) fête f du travail (*le premier lundi de septembre*); *voir article*

> Labor Day aux États-Unis et au Canada est fixée au premier lundi de septembre. Instituée par le Congrès en 1894 après avoir été réclamée par les mouvements ouvriers pendant douze ans, elle a perdu une grande partie de son caractère politique pour devenir un jour férié assez ordinaire et l'occasion de partir pour un long week-end avant la rentrée des classes.

laborious [lə'bɔːrɪəs] ADJ laborieux(-euse)

labor union N (*US*) syndicat m

Labour ['leɪbəʳ] N (BRIT Pol: *also*: **the Labour Party**) le parti travailliste, les travaillistes mpl

labour, (*US*) **labor** ['leɪbəʳ] N (*work*) travail m; (*workforce*) main-d'œuvre f; (*Med*) travail, accouchement m ▶ VI: **to ~ (at)** travailler dur (à), peiner (sur) ▶ VT: **to ~ a point** insister sur un point; **in ~** (*Med*) en travail

labour camp, (*US*) **labor camp** N camp m de travaux forcés

labour cost, (*US*) **labor cost** N coût m de la main-d'œuvre; coût de la façon

laboured, (*US*) **labored** ['leɪbəd] ADJ lourd(e), laborieux(-euse); (*breathing*) difficile, pénible; (*style*) lourd, embarrassé(e)

labourer, (*US*) **laborer** ['leɪbərəʳ] N manœuvre m; **farm ~** ouvrier m agricole

labour force, (*US*) **labor force** N main-d'œuvre f

labour-intensive, (*US*) **labor-intensive** [leɪbərɪn'tɛnsɪv] ADJ intensif(-ive) en main-d'œuvre

labour market, (*US*) **labor market** N marché m du travail

labour pains, (*US*) **labor pains** NPL douleurs fpl de l'accouchement

labour relations, (*US*) **labor relations** NPL relations fpl dans l'entreprise

labour-saving, (*US*) **labor-saving** ['leɪbəseɪvɪŋ] ADJ qui simplifie le travail

labour unrest, (*US*) **labor unrest** N agitation sociale

labyrinth ['læbɪrɪnθ] N labyrinthe m, dédale m

lace [leɪs] N dentelle f; (*of shoe etc*) lacet m ▶ VT (*shoe: also*: **lace up**) lacer; (*drink*) arroser, corser

lacemaking ['leɪsmeɪkɪŋ] N fabrication f de dentelle

laceration [læsə'reɪʃən] N lacération f

lace-up ['leɪsʌp] ADJ (*shoes etc*) à lacets

lack [læk] N manque m ▶ VT manquer de; **through** or **for ~ of** faute de, par manque de; **to be lacking** manquer, faire défaut; **to be lacking in** manquer de

lackadaisical [lækə'deɪzɪkl] ADJ nonchalant(e), indolent(e)

lackey ['lækɪ] N (*also fig*) laquais m

lacklustre ['læklʌstəʳ] ADJ terne

laconic [lə'kɔnɪk] ADJ laconique

lacquer ['lækəʳ] N laque f

lacy ['leɪsɪ] ADJ (*made of lace*) en dentelle; (*like lace*) comme de la dentelle, qui ressemble à de la dentelle

lad [læd] N garçon m, gars m; (BRIT: *in stable etc*) lad m

ladder ['lædəʳ] N échelle f; (BRIT: *in tights*) maille filée f ▶ VT, VI (BRIT: *tights*) filer

laden ['leɪdn] ADJ: **~ (with)** chargé(e) (de); **fully ~** (*truck, ship*) en pleine charge

ladle ['leɪdl] N louche f

lady ['leɪdɪ] N dame f; **"ladies and gentlemen ..."** "Mesdames (et) Messieurs ..."; **young ~** jeune fille f; (*married*) jeune femme f; **L~ Smith** lady Smith; **the ladies' (room)** les toilettes fpl des dames; **a ~ doctor** une doctoresse, une femme médecin

ladybird ['leɪdɪbəːd], (*US*) **ladybug** ['leɪdɪbʌg] N coccinelle f

lady-in-waiting ['leɪdɪn'weɪtɪŋ] N dame f d'honneur

lady-killer ['leɪdɪkɪləʳ] N don Juan m

ladylike ['leɪdɪlaɪk] ADJ distingué(e)
ladyship ['leɪdɪʃɪp] N: **your L~** Madame la comtesse (or la baronne etc)
lag [læg] N retard m ▶ VI (also: **lag behind**) rester en arrière, traîner; (: fig) rester à la traîne ▶ VT (pipes) calorifuger
lager ['lɑ:gəʳ] N bière blonde
lager lout N (BRIT inf) jeune voyou m (porté sur la boisson)
lagging ['lægɪŋ] N enveloppe isolante, calorifuge m
lagoon [lə'gu:n] N lagune f
Lagos ['leɪgɔs] N Lagos
laid [leɪd] PT, PP of **lay**
laid back ADJ (inf) relaxe, décontracté(e)
laid up ADJ alité(e)
lain [leɪn] PP of **lie**
lair [lɛəʳ] N tanière f, gîte m
laissez-faire [lɛseɪ'fɛəʳ] N libéralisme m
laity ['leɪətɪ] N laïques mpl
lake [leɪk] N lac m
Lake District N: **the ~** (BRIT) la région des lacs
lamb [læm] N agneau m
lamb chop N côtelette f d'agneau
lambskin ['læmskɪn] N (peau f d')agneau m
lambswool ['læmzwul] N laine f d'agneau
lame [leɪm] ADJ (also fig) boiteux(-euse); **~ duck** (fig) canard boiteux
lamely ['leɪmlɪ] ADV (fig) sans conviction
lament [lə'mɛnt] N lamentation f ▶ VT pleurer, se lamenter sur
lamentable ['læməntəbl] ADJ déplorable, lamentable
laminated ['læmɪneɪtɪd] ADJ laminé(e); (windscreen) (en verre) feuilleté
lamp [læmp] N lampe f
lamplight ['læmplaɪt] N: **by ~** à la lumière de la (or d'une) lampe
lampoon [læm'pu:n] N pamphlet m
lamppost ['læmppəust] N (BRIT) réverbère m
lampshade ['læmpʃeɪd] N abat-jour m inv
lance [lɑ:ns] N lance f ▶ VT (Med) inciser
lance corporal N (BRIT) (soldat m de) première classe m
lancet ['lɑ:nsɪt] N (Med) bistouri m
Lancs [læŋks] ABBR (BRIT) = **Lancashire**
land [lænd] N (as opposed to sea) terre f (ferme); (country) pays m; (soil) terre; (piece of land) terrain m; (estate) terre(s), domaine(s) m(pl) ▶ VI (from ship) débarquer; (Aviat) atterrir; (fig: fall) (re)tomber ▶ VT (passengers, goods) débarquer; (obtain) décrocher; **to go/travel by ~** se déplacer par voie de terre; **to own ~** être propriétaire foncier; **to ~ on one's feet** (also fig) retomber sur ses pieds; **to ~ sb with sth** (inf) coller qch à qn
▶ **land up** VI atterrir, (finir par) se retrouver
landed gentry ['lændɪd-] N (BRIT) propriétaires terriens or fonciers
landfill site ['lændfɪl-] N centre m d'enfouissement des déchets
landing ['lændɪŋ] N (from ship) débarquement m; (Aviat) atterrissage m; (of staircase) palier m
landing card N carte f de débarquement
landing craft N péniche f de débarquement
landing gear N train m d'atterrissage
landing stage N (BRIT) débarcadère m, embarcadère m
landing strip N piste f d'atterrissage
landlady ['lændleɪdɪ] N propriétaire f, logeuse f; (of pub) patronne f
landline ['lændlaɪn] N ligne f fixe
landlocked ['lændlɔkt] ADJ entouré(e) de terre(s), sans accès à la mer
landlord ['lændlɔ:d] N propriétaire m, logeur m; (of pub etc) patron m
landlubber ['lændlʌbəʳ] N terrien(ne)
landmark ['lændmɑ:k] N (point m de) repère m; **to be a ~** (fig) faire date or époque
landowner ['lændəunəʳ] N propriétaire foncier or terrien
landscape ['lænskeɪp] N paysage m
landscape architect, landscape gardener N paysagiste mf
landscape painting N (Art) paysage m
landslide ['lændslaɪd] N (Geo) glissement m (de terrain); (fig: Pol) raz-de-marée (électoral)
lane [leɪn] N (in country) chemin m; (in town) ruelle f; (Aut: of road) voie f; (: line of traffic) file f; (in race) couloir m; **shipping ~** route f maritime or de navigation
language ['læŋgwɪdʒ] N langue f; (way one speaks) langage m; **what languages do you speak?** quelles langues parlez-vous?; **bad ~** grossièretés fpl, langage grossier
language laboratory N laboratoire m de langues
language school N école f de langue
languid ['læŋgwɪd] ADJ languissant(e), langoureux(-euse)
languish ['læŋgwɪʃ] VI languir
lank [læŋk] ADJ (hair) raide et terne
lanky ['læŋkɪ] ADJ grand(e) et maigre, efflanqué(e)
lanolin, lanoline ['lænəlɪn] N lanoline f
lantern ['læntn] N lanterne f
Laos [laus] N Laos m
lap [læp] N (of track) tour m (de piste); (of body): **in** or **on one's ~** sur les genoux ▶ VT (also: **lap up**) laper ▶ VI (waves) clapoter
▶ **lap up** VT (fig) boire comme du petit-lait, se gargariser de; (: lies etc) gober
La Paz [læ'pæz] N La Paz
lapdog ['læpdɔg] N chien m d'appartement
lapel [lə'pɛl] N revers m
Lapland ['læplænd] N Laponie f
lapse [læps] N défaillance f; (in behaviour) écart m (de conduite) ▶ VI (Law) cesser d'être en vigueur; (contract) expirer; (pass) être périmé; (subscription) prendre fin; **to ~ into bad habits** prendre de mauvaises habitudes; **~ of time** laps m de temps, intervalle m; **a ~ of memory** un trou de mémoire
laptop ['læptɔp], **laptop computer** N (ordinateur m) portable m
larceny ['lɑ:sənɪ] N vol m
larch [lɑ:tʃ] N mélèze m
lard [lɑ:d] N saindoux m

larder ['lɑːdəʳ] N garde-manger m inv
large [lɑːdʒ] ADJ grand(e); (person, animal) gros
(grosse); **to make larger** agrandir; **a ~
number of people** beaucoup de gens; **by and ~**
en général; **on a ~ scale** sur une grande
échelle; **at ~** (free) en liberté; (generally) en
général; pour la plupart; see also **by**
largely ['lɑːdʒlɪ] ADV en grande partie;
(principally) surtout
large-scale ['lɑːdʒ'skeɪl] ADJ (map, drawing etc) à
grande échelle; (fig) important(e)
lark [lɑːk] N (bird) alouette f; (joke) blague f,
farce f
▶ **lark about** VI faire l'idiot, rigoler
larrikin ['lærɪkɪn] N (AUSTRALIA, NEW ZEALAND inf)
fripon m (inf)
larva ['lɑːvə] (pl **larvae** [-iː]) N larve f
laryngitis [lærɪn'dʒaɪtɪs] N laryngite f
larynx ['lærɪŋks] N larynx m
lasagne [lə'zænjə] N lasagne f
lascivious [lə'sɪvɪəs] ADJ lascif(-ive)
laser ['leɪzəʳ] N laser m
laser beam N rayon m laser
laser printer N imprimante f laser
lash [læʃ] N coup m de fouet; (also: **eyelash**) cil m
▶ VT fouetter; (tie) attacher
▶ **lash down** VT attacher; amarrer; arrimer ▶ VI
(rain) tomber avec violence
▶ **lash out** VI: **to ~ out (at** or **against sb/sth)**
attaquer violemment (qn/qch); **to ~ out (on
sth)** (inf: spend) se fendre (de qch)
lashing ['læʃɪŋ] N: **lashings of** (BRIT inf: cream etc)
des masses de
lass [læs] (BRIT) N (jeune) fille f
lasso [læ'suː] N lasso m ▶ VT prendre au lasso
last [lɑːst] ADJ dernier(-ière) ▶ ADV en dernier;
(most recently) la dernière fois; (finally)
finalement ▶ VI durer; **~ week** la semaine
dernière; **~ night** (evening) hier soir; (night) la
nuit dernière; **at ~** enfin; **~ but one** avant-
dernier(-ière); **the ~ time** la dernière fois; **it
lasts (for) 2 hours** ça dure 2 heures
last-ditch ['lɑːst'dɪtʃ] ADJ ultime, désespéré(e)
lasting ['lɑːstɪŋ] ADJ durable
lastly ['lɑːstlɪ] ADV en dernier lieu, pour finir
last-minute ['lɑːstmɪnɪt] ADJ de dernière
minute
latch [lætʃ] N loquet m
▶ **latch onto** VT FUS (cling to: person, group)
s'accrocher à; (: idea) se mettre en tête
latchkey ['lætʃkiː] N clé f (de la porte d'entrée)
late [leɪt] ADJ (not on time) en retard; (far on in day
etc) tardif(-ive); (: edition, delivery) dernier(-ière);
(recent) récent(e), dernier; (former) ancien(ne);
(dead) défunt(e) ▶ ADV tard; (behind time, schedule)
en retard; **to be ~** avoir du retard; **to be 10
minutes ~** avoir 10 minutes de retard; **sorry
I'm ~** désolé d'être en retard; **it's too ~** il est
trop tard; **to work ~** travailler tard; **~ in life** sur
le tard, à un âge avancé; **of ~** dernièrement; **in
~ May** vers la fin (du mois) de mai, fin mai; **the
~ Mr X** feu M. X
latecomer ['leɪtkʌməʳ] N retardataire mf
lately ['leɪtlɪ] ADV récemment

lateness ['leɪtnɪs] N (of person) retard m; (of event)
heure tardive
latent ['leɪtnt] ADJ latent(e); **~ defect** vice caché
later ['leɪtəʳ] ADJ (date etc) ultérieur(e); (version etc)
plus récent(e) ▶ ADV plus tard; **~ on today** plus
tard dans la journée
lateral ['lætərl] ADJ latéral(e)
latest ['leɪtɪst] ADJ tout(e) dernier(-ière); **the ~
news** les dernières nouvelles; **at the ~** au plus
tard
latex ['leɪteks] N latex m
lath [læθ] (pl **laths** [læðz]) N latte f
lathe [leɪð] N tour m
lather ['lɑːðəʳ] N mousse f (de savon) ▶ VT
savonner ▶ VI mousser
Latin ['lætɪn] N latin m ▶ ADJ latin(e)
Latin America N Amérique latine
Latin American ADJ latino-américain(e),
d'Amérique latine ▶ N Latino-Américain(e)
latitude ['lætɪtjuːd] N (also fig) latitude f
latrine [lə'triːn] N latrines fpl
latter ['lætəʳ] ADJ deuxième, dernier(-ière) ▶ N:
the ~ ce dernier, celui-ci
latterly ['lætəlɪ] ADV dernièrement, récemment
lattice ['lætɪs] N treillis m; treillage m
lattice window N fenêtre treillissée, fenêtre à
croisillons
Latvia ['lætvɪə] N Lettonie f
Latvian ['lætvɪən] ADJ letton(ne) ▶ N Letton(ne);
(Ling) letton m
laudable ['lɔːdəbl] ADJ louable
laudatory ['lɔːdətrɪ] ADJ élogieux(-euse)
laugh [lɑːf] N rire m ▶ VI rire; **(to do sth) for a ~**
(faire qch) pour rire
▶ **laugh at** VT FUS se moquer de; (joke) rire de
▶ **laugh off** VT écarter or rejeter par une
plaisanterie or par une boutade
laughable ['lɑːfəbl] ADJ risible, ridicule
laughing ['lɑːfɪŋ] ADJ rieur(-euse); **this is no ~
matter** il n'y a pas de quoi rire, ça n'a rien
d'amusant
laughing gas N gaz hilarant
laughing stock N: **the ~ of** la risée de
laughter ['lɑːftəʳ] N rire m; (of several people) rires
mpl
launch [lɔːntʃ] N lancement m; (boat) chaloupe f;
(also: **motor launch**) vedette f ▶ VT (ship, rocket,
plan) lancer
▶ **launch into** VT FUS se lancer dans
▶ **launch out** VI: **to ~ out (into)** se lancer (dans)
launching ['lɔːntʃɪŋ] N lancement m
launder ['lɔːndəʳ] VT laver; (fig: money) blanchir
Launderette® [lɔːn'dret], (US) **Laundromat®**
['lɔːndrəmæt] N laverie f (automatique)
laundry ['lɔːndrɪ] N (clothes) linge m; (business)
blanchisserie f; (room) buanderie f; **to do the ~**
faire la lessive
laureate ['lɔːrɪət] ADJ see **poet laureate**
laurel ['lɔrl] N laurier m; **to rest on one's
laurels** se reposer sur ses lauriers
lava ['lɑːvə] N lave f
lavatory ['lævətərɪ] N toilettes fpl
lavatory paper N (BRIT) papier m hygiénique
lavender ['lævəndəʳ] N lavande f

655

lavish ['lævɪʃ] ADJ (amount) copieux(-euse); (meal) somptueux(-euse); (hospitality) généreux(-euse); (person: giving freely): ~ **with** prodigue de ▸ VT: **to ~ sth on sb** prodiguer qch à qn; (money) dépenser qch sans compter pour qn

lavishly ['lævɪʃlɪ] ADV (give, spend) sans compter; (furnished) luxueusement

law [lɔː] N loi f; (science) droit m; **against the ~** contraire à la loi; **to study ~** faire du droit; **to go to ~** (BRIT) avoir recours à la justice; ~ **and order** n l'ordre public

law-abiding ['lɔːəbaɪdɪŋ] ADJ respectueux(-euse) des lois

lawbreaker ['lɔːbreɪkəʳ] N personne f qui transgresse la loi

law court N tribunal m, cour f de justice

lawful ['lɔːful] ADJ légal(e), permis(e)

lawfully ['lɔːfəlɪ] ADV légalement

lawless ['lɔːlɪs] ADJ (action) illégal(e); (place) sans loi

Law Lord N (BRIT) juge siégant à la Chambre des Lords

lawmaker ['lɔːmeɪkəʳ] N législateur(-trice)

lawn [lɔːn] N pelouse f

lawnmower ['lɔːnməuəʳ] N tondeuse f à gazon

lawn tennis N tennis m

law school N faculté f de droit

law student N étudiant(e) en droit

lawsuit ['lɔːsuːt] N procès m; **to bring a ~ against** engager des poursuites contre

lawyer ['lɔːjəʳ] N (consultant, with company) juriste m; (for sales, wills etc) ≈ notaire m; (partner, in court) ≈ avocat m

lax [læks] ADJ relâché(e)

laxative ['læksətɪv] N laxatif m

laxity ['læksɪtɪ] N relâchement m

lay [leɪ] PT of **lie** ▸ ADJ laïque; (not expert) profane ▸ VT (pt, pp **laid** [leɪd]) poser, mettre; (eggs) pondre; (trap) tendre; (plans) élaborer; **to ~ the table** mettre la table; **to ~ the facts/one's proposals before sb** présenter les faits/ses propositions à qn; **to get laid** (inf!) baiser (!), se faire baiser (!)
  ▸ **lay aside, lay by** VT mettre de côté
  ▸ **lay down** VT poser; (rules etc) établir; **to ~ down the law** (fig) faire la loi
  ▸ **lay in** VT accumuler, s'approvisionner en
  ▸ **lay into** VI (inf: attack) tomber sur; (: scold) passer une engueulade à
  ▸ **lay off** VT (workers) licencier
  ▸ **lay on** VT (water, gas) mettre, installer; (provide: meal etc) fournir; (paint) étaler
  ▸ **lay out** VT (design) dessiner, concevoir; (display) disposer; (spend) dépenser
  ▸ **lay up** VT (store) amasser; (car) remiser; (ship) désarmer; (illness) forcer à s'aliter

layabout ['leɪəbaut] N fainéant(e)

lay-by ['leɪbaɪ] N (BRIT) aire f de stationnement (sur le bas-côté)

lay days NPL (Naut) estarie f

layer ['leɪəʳ] N couche f

layette [leɪ'ɛt] N layette f

layman ['leɪmən] N (irreg) (Rel) laïque m; (non-expert) profane m

lay-off ['leɪɔf] N licenciement m

layout ['leɪaut] N disposition f, plan m, agencement m; (Press) mise f en page

laze [leɪz] VI paresser

laziness ['leɪzɪnɪs] N paresse f

lazy ['leɪzɪ] ADJ paresseux(-euse)

LB ABBR (CANADA) = **Labrador**

lb. ABBR (weight) = **pound**

lbw ABBR (Cricket: = leg before wicket) faute dans laquelle le joueur a la jambe devant le guichet

LC N ABBR (US) = **Library of Congress**

lc ABBR (Typ: = lower case) b.d.c.

L/C ABBR = **letter of credit**

LCD N ABBR = **liquid crystal display**

Ld ABBR (BRIT: = lord) titre honorifique

LDS N ABBR (= Licentiate in Dental Surgery) diplôme universitaire; (= Latter-day Saints) Église de Jésus-Christ du dernier jour

LEA N ABBR (BRIT: = local education authority) services locaux de l'enseignement

lead¹ [liːd] (pt, pp **led** [lɛd]) N (front position) tête f; (distance, time ahead) avance f; (clue) piste f; (to battery) raccord m; (Elec) fil m; (for dog) laisse f; (Theat) rôle principal ▸ VT (guide) mener, conduire; (induce) amener; (be leader of) être à la tête de; (Sport) être en tête de; (orchestra: BRIT) être le premier violon de; (: US) diriger ▸ VI (Sport) mener, être en tête; **to ~ to** (road, pipe) mener à, conduire à; (result in) conduire à; aboutir à; **to ~ sb astray** détourner qn du droit chemin; **to be in the ~** (Sport: in race) mener, être en tête; (: in match) mener (à la marque); **to take the ~** (Sport) passer en tête, prendre la tête; mener; (fig) prendre l'initiative; **to ~ sb to believe that …** amener qn à croire que …; **to ~ sb to do sth** amener qn à faire qch; **to ~ the way** montrer le chemin
  ▸ **lead away** VT emmener
  ▸ **lead back** VT ramener
  ▸ **lead off** VI (in game etc) commencer
  ▸ **lead on** VT (tease) faire marcher; **to ~ sb on to** (induce) amener qn à
  ▸ **lead up to** VT conduire à; (in conversation) en venir à

lead² [lɛd] N (metal) plomb m; (in pencil) mine f

leaded ['lɛdɪd] ADJ (windows) à petits carreaux

leaded petrol N essence f au plomb

leaden ['lɛdn] ADJ de or en plomb

leader ['liːdəʳ] N (of team) chef m; (of party etc) dirigeant(e), leader m; (Sport: in league) leader; (: in race) coureur m de tête; (in newspaper) éditorial m; **they are leaders in their field** (fig) ils sont à la pointe du progrès dans leur domaine; **the L~ of the House** (BRIT) le chef de la majorité ministérielle

leadership ['liːdəʃɪp] N (position) direction f; **under the ~ of …** sous la direction de …; **qualities of ~** qualités fpl de chef or de meneur

lead-free ['lɛdfriː] ADJ sans plomb

leading ['liːdɪŋ] ADJ de premier plan; (main) principal(e); (in race) de tête; **a ~ question** une question tendancieuse; ~ **role** rôle prépondérant or de premier plan

leading lady N (Theat) vedette (féminine)

leading light N (*person*) sommité *f*, personnalité *f* de premier plan

leading man N (*irreg*) (*Theat*) vedette (masculine)

lead pencil [led-] N crayon noir *or* à papier

lead poisoning [lɛd-] N saturnisme *m*

lead singer [li:d-] N (*in pop group*) (chanteur *m*) vedette *f*

lead time [li:d-] N (*Comm*) délai *m* de livraison

lead weight [lɛd-] N plomb *m*

leaf [li:f] (*pl* **leaves** [li:vz]) N feuille *f*; (*of table*) rallonge *f*; **to turn over a new ~** (*fig*) changer de conduite *or* d'existence; **to take a ~ out of sb's book** (*fig*) prendre exemple sur qn
  ▸ **leaf through** VT (*book*) feuilleter

leaflet ['li:flɪt] N prospectus *m*, brochure *f*; (*Pol, Rel*) tract *m*

leafy ['li:fɪ] ADJ feuillu(e)

league [li:g] N ligue *f*; (*Football*) championnat *m*; (*measure*) lieue *f*; **to be in ~ with** avoir partie liée avec, être de mèche avec

league table N classement *m*

leak [li:k] N (*lit, fig*) fuite *f*; (*in*) infiltration *f* ▸ VI (*pipe, liquid etc*) fuir; (*shoes*) prendre l'eau; (*ship*) faire eau ▸ VT (*liquid*) répandre; (*information*) divulguer
  ▸ **leak out** VI fuir; (*information*) être divulgué(e)

leakage ['li:kɪdʒ] N (*also fig*) fuite *f*

leaky ['li:kɪ] ADJ (*pipe, bucket*) qui fuit, percé(e); (*roof*) qui coule; (*shoe*) qui prend l'eau; (*boat*) qui fait eau

lean [li:n] (*pt, pp* **leaned** *or* **leant** [lɛnt]) ADJ maigre ▸ N (*of meat*) maigre *m* ▸ VT: **to ~ sth on** appuyer qch sur ▸ VI (*slope*) pencher; (*rest*): **to ~ against** s'appuyer contre; être appuyé(e) contre; **to ~ on** s'appuyer sur
  ▸ **lean back** VI se pencher en arrière
  ▸ **lean forward** VI se pencher en avant
  ▸ **lean out** VI: **to ~ out (of)** se pencher au dehors (de)
  ▸ **lean over** VI se pencher

leaning ['li:nɪŋ] ADJ penché(e) ▸ N: **~ (towards)** penchant *m* (pour); **the L~ Tower of Pisa** la tour penchée de Pise

leant [lɛnt] PT, PP *of* **lean**

lean-to ['li:ntu:] N appentis *m*

leap [li:p] (*pt, pp* **leaped** *or* **leapt** [lɛpt]) N bond *m*, saut *m* ▸ VI bondir, sauter; **to ~ at an offer** saisir une offre
  ▸ **leap up** VI (*person*) faire un bond; se lever d'un bond

leapfrog ['li:pfrɔg] N jeu *m* de saute-mouton

leapt [lɛpt] PT, PP *of* **leap**

leap year N année *f* bissextile

learn [lə:n] (*pt, pp* **learned** *or* **learnt** [lə:nt]) VT, VI apprendre; **to ~ (how) to do sth** apprendre à faire qch; **we were sorry to ~ that ...** nous avons appris avec regret que ...; **to ~ about sth** (*Scol*) étudier qch; (*hear, read*) apprendre qch

learned ['lə:nɪd] ADJ érudit(e), savant(e)

learner ['lə:nə'] N débutant(e); (*BRIT: also*: **learner driver**) (conducteur(-trice) débutant(e))

learning ['lə:nɪŋ] N savoir *m*

learnt [lə:nt] PP *of* **learn**

lease [li:s] N bail *m* ▸ VT louer à bail; **on ~** en location
  ▸ **lease back** VT vendre en cession-bail

leaseback ['li:sbæk] N cession-bail *f*

leasehold ['li:shəuld] N (*contract*) bail *m* ▸ ADJ loué(e) à bail

leash [li:ʃ] N laisse *f*

least [li:st] ADJ: **the ~** (+*noun*) le (la) plus petit(e), le (la) moindre; (*smallest amount of*) le moins de ▸ PRON: **(the) ~** le moins ▸ ADV (+*verb*) le moins; (+*adj*): **the ~** le (la) moins; **the ~ money** le moins d'argent; **the ~ expensive** le (la) moins cher (chère); **the ~ possible effort** le moins d'effort possible; **at ~** au moins; (*or rather*) du moins; **you could at ~ have written** tu aurais au moins pu écrire; **not in the ~** pas le moins du monde

leather ['lɛðə'] N cuir *m* ▸ CPD en *or* de cuir; **~ goods** maroquinerie *f*

leave [li:v] (*pt, pp* **left** [lɛft]) VT laisser; (*go away from*) quitter; (*forget*) oublier ▸ VI partir, s'en aller ▸ N (*time off*) congé *m*; (*Mil: also*: consent) permission *f*; **what time does the train/bus ~?** le train/le bus part à quelle heure?; **to ~ sth to sb** (*money etc*) laisser qch à qn; **to be left** rester; **there's some milk left over** il reste du lait; **to ~ school** quitter l'école, terminer sa scolarité; **~ it to me!** laissez-moi faire!, je m'en occupe!; **on ~** en permission; **to take one's ~ of** prendre congé de; **~ of absence** *n* congé exceptionnel; (*Mil*) permission spéciale
  ▸ **leave behind** VT (*also fig*) laisser; (*opponent in race*) distancer; (*forget*) laisser, oublier
  ▸ **leave off** VT (*cover, lid, heating*) ne pas (re)mettre; (*light*) ne pas (r)allumer, laisser éteint(e); (*BRIT inf: stop*): **to ~ off (doing sth)** s'arrêter (de faire qch)
  ▸ **leave on** VT (*coat etc*) garder, ne pas enlever; (*lid*) laisser dessus; (*light, fire, cooker*) laisser allumé(e)
  ▸ **leave out** VT oublier, omettre

leaves [li:vz] NPL *of* **leaf**

leavetaking ['li:vteɪkɪŋ] N adieux *mpl*

Lebanese [lɛbə'ni:z] ADJ libanais(e) ▸ N *pl inv* Libanais(e)

Lebanon ['lɛbənən] N Liban *m*

lecherous ['lɛtʃərəs] ADJ lubrique

lectern ['lɛktə:n] N lutrin *m*, pupitre *m*

lecture ['lɛktʃə'] N conférence *f*; (*Scol*) cours (magistral) ▸ VI donner des cours; enseigner ▸ VT (*scold*) sermonner, réprimander; **to ~ on** faire un cours (*or son cours*) sur; **to give a ~ (on)** faire une conférence (sur), faire un cours (sur)

lecture hall N amphithéâtre *m*

lecturer ['lɛktʃərə'] N (*speaker*) conférencier(-ière); (*BRIT: at university*) professeur *m* (d'université), prof *mf* de fac (*inf*); **assistant ~** (*BRIT*) ≈ assistant(e); **senior ~** (*BRIT*) ≈ chargé(e) d'enseignement

lecture theatre N = **lecture hall**

LED N ABBR (= *light-emitting diode*) LED *f*, diode électroluminescente

led [lɛd] PT, PP *of* **lead**[1]

ledge [lɛdʒ] N (*of window, on wall*) rebord *m*; (*of

mountain) saillie *f*, corniche *f*
ledger ['lɛdʒəʳ] N registre *m*, grand livre
lee [li:] N côté *m* sous le vent; **in the ~ of** à l'abri de
leech [li:tʃ] N sangsue *f*
leek [li:k] N poireau *m*
leer [lɪəʳ] VI: **to ~ at sb** regarder qn d'un air mauvais *or* concupiscent, lorgner qn
leeward ['li:wəd] ADJ, ADV sous le vent ▸ N côté *m* sous le vent; **to ~** sous le vent
leeway ['li:weɪ] N *(fig)*: **to make up ~** rattraper son retard; **to have some ~** avoir une certaine liberté d'action
left [lɛft] PT, PP *of* **leave** ▸ ADJ gauche ▸ ADV à gauche ▸ N gauche *f*; **there are two ~** il en reste deux; **on the ~, to the ~** à gauche; **the L~** *(Pol)* la gauche
left-hand ['lɛfthænd] ADJ: **the ~ side** la gauche, le côté gauche
left-hand drive ['lɛfthænd-] N conduite *f* à gauche; *(vehicle)* véhicule *m* avec la conduite à gauche
left-handed [lɛft'hændɪd] ADJ gaucher(-ère); *(scissors etc)* pour gauchers
leftie ['lɛftɪ] N *(inf)* gaucho *mf*, gauchiste *mf*
leftist ['lɛftɪst] ADJ *(Pol)* gauchiste, de gauche
left-luggage [lɛft'lʌgɪdʒ], **left-luggage office** N *(BRIT)* consigne *f*
left-luggage locker [lɛft'lʌgɪd-] N *(BRIT)* (casier *m* à) consigne *f* automatique
left-overs ['lɛftəuvəz] NPL restes *mpl*
left wing N *(Mil, Sport)* aile *f* gauche; *(Pol)* gauche *f*
left-wing ['lɛft'wɪŋ] ADJ *(Pol)* de gauche
left-winger ['lɛft'wɪŋəʳ] N *(Pol)* membre *m* de la gauche; *(Sport)* ailier *m* gauche
lefty ['lɛftɪ] N *(inf)* = **leftie**
leg [lɛg] N jambe *f*; *(of animal)* patte *f*; *(of furniture)* pied *m*; *(Culin: of chicken)* cuisse *f*; *(of journey)* étape *f*; **1st/2nd ~** *(Sport)* match *m* aller/retour; *(of journey)* 1ère/2ème étape; **~ of lamb** *(Culin)* gigot *m* d'agneau; **to stretch one's legs** se dégourdir les jambes
legacy ['lɛgəsɪ] N *(also fig)* héritage *m*, legs *m*
legal ['li:gl] ADJ *(permitted by law)* légal(e); *(relating to law)* juridique; **to take ~ action** *or* **proceedings against sb** poursuivre qn en justice
legal adviser N conseiller(-ère) juridique
legal holiday *(US)* N jour férié
legality [lɪ'gælɪtɪ] N légalité *f*
legalize ['li:gəlaɪz] VT légaliser
legally ['li:gəlɪ] ADV légalement; **~ binding** juridiquement contraignant(e)
legal tender N monnaie légale
legation [lɪ'geɪʃən] N légation *f*
legend ['lɛdʒənd] N légende *f*
legendary ['lɛdʒəndərɪ] ADJ légendaire
-legged ['lɛgɪd] SUFFIX: **two~** à deux pattes *(or* jambes *or* pieds)
leggings ['lɛgɪŋz] NPL caleçon *m*
leggy ['lɛgɪ] ADJ aux longues jambes
legibility [lɛdʒɪ'bɪlɪtɪ] N lisibilité *f*
legible ['lɛdʒəbl] ADJ lisible

legibly ['lɛdʒəblɪ] ADV lisiblement
legion ['li:dʒən] N légion *f*
legionnaire [li:dʒə'nɛəʳ] N légionnaire *m*; **~'s disease** maladie *f* du légionnaire
legislate ['lɛdʒɪsleɪt] VI légiférer
legislation [lɛdʒɪs'leɪʃən] N législation *f*; **a piece of ~** un texte de loi
legislative ['lɛdʒɪslətɪv] ADJ législatif(-ive)
legislator ['lɛdʒɪsleɪtəʳ] N législateur(-trice)
legislature ['lɛdʒɪslətʃəʳ] N corps législatif
legitimacy [lɪ'dʒɪtɪməsɪ] N légitimité *f*
legitimate [lɪ'dʒɪtɪmət] ADJ légitime
legitimize [lɪ'dʒɪtɪmaɪz] VT légitimer
legless ['lɛglɪs] ADJ *(BRIT inf)* bourré(e)
leg-room ['lɛgru:m] N place *f* pour les jambes
Leics ABBR *(BRIT)* = **Leicestershire**
leisure ['lɛʒəʳ] N *(free time)* temps libre, loisirs *mpl*; **at ~** *(tout)* à loisir; **at your ~** *(later)* à tête reposée
leisure centre N *(BRIT)* centre *m* de loisirs
leisurely ['lɛʒəlɪ] ADJ tranquille, fait(e) sans se presser
leisure suit N *(BRIT)* survêtement *m* *(mode)*
lemon ['lɛmən] N citron *m*
lemonade [lɛmə'neɪd] N *(fizzy)* limonade *f*
lemon cheese, **lemon curd** N crème *f* de citron
lemon juice N jus *m* de citron
lemon squeezer [-skwi:zəʳ] N presse-citron *m* inv
lemon tea N thé *m* au citron
lend [lɛnd] *(pt, pp* **lent** [lɛnt]) VT: **to ~ sth (to sb)** prêter qch (à qn); **could you ~ me some money?** pourriez-vous me prêter de l'argent?; **to ~ a hand** donner un coup de main
lender ['lɛndəʳ] N prêteur(-euse)
lending library ['lɛndɪŋ-] N bibliothèque *f* de prêt
length [lɛŋθ] N longueur *f*; *(section: of road, pipe etc)* morceau *m*, bout *m*; **~ of time** durée *f*; **what ~ is it?** quelle longueur fait-il?; **it is 2 metres in ~** cela fait 2 mètres de long; **to fall full ~** tomber de tout son long; **at ~** *(at last)* enfin, à la fin; *(lengthily)* longuement; **to go to any ~(s) to do sth** faire n'importe quoi pour faire qch, ne reculer devant rien pour faire qch
lengthen ['lɛŋθən] VT allonger, prolonger ▸ VI s'allonger
lengthways ['lɛŋθweɪz] ADV dans le sens de la longueur, en long
lengthy ['lɛŋθɪ] ADJ *(très)* long (longue)
leniency ['li:nɪənsɪ] N indulgence *f*, clémence *f*
lenient ['li:nɪənt] ADJ indulgent(e), clément(e)
leniently ['li:nɪəntlɪ] ADV avec indulgence *or* clémence
lens [lɛnz] N lentille *f*; *(of spectacles)* verre *m*; *(of camera)* objectif *m*
Lent [lɛnt] N carême *m*
lent [lɛnt] PT, PP *of* **lend**
lentil ['lɛntl] N lentille *f*
Leo ['li:əu] N le Lion; **to be ~** être du Lion
leopard ['lɛpəd] N léopard *m*
leotard ['li:əta:d] N justaucorps *m*
leper ['lɛpəʳ] N lépreux(-euse)
leper colony N léproserie *f*

leprosy ['lɛprəsɪ] N lèpre f
lesbian ['lɛzbɪən] N lesbienne f ▸ ADJ lesbien(ne)
lesion ['liːʒən] N (*Med*) lésion f
Lesotho [lɪ'suːtuː] N Lesotho m
less [lɛs] ADJ moins de ▸ PRON, ADV moins
  ▸ PREP: ~ **tax/10% discount** avant impôt/moins
  10% de remise; ~ **than that/you** moins que
  cela/vous; ~ **than half** moins de la moitié;
  ~ **than one/a kilo/3 metres** moins de un/d'un
  kilo/de 3 mètres; ~ **than ever** moins que
  jamais; ~ **and** ~ de moins en moins; **the** ~ **he
  works …** moins il travaille …
lessee [lɛ'siː] N locataire mf (à bail),
  preneur(-euse) du bail
lessen ['lɛsn] VI diminuer, s'amoindrir,
  s'atténuer ▸ VT diminuer, réduire, atténuer
lesser ['lɛsə'] ADJ moindre; **to a** ~ **extent** or
  degree à un degré moindre
lesson ['lɛsn] N leçon f; **a maths** ~ une leçon or
  un cours de maths; **to give lessons in** donner
  des cours de; **to teach sb a** ~ (*fig*) donner une
  bonne leçon à qn; **it taught him a** ~ (*fig*) cela
  lui a servi de leçon
lessor ['lɛsɔː', lɛ'sɔː'] N bailleur(-eresse)
lest [lɛst] CONJ de peur de + *infinitive*, de peur que
  + *sub*
let [lɛt] (*pt, pp* ~) VT laisser; (*BRIT: lease*) louer; **to
  ~ sb do sth** laisser qn faire qch; **to ~ sb know
  sth** faire savoir qch à qn, prévenir qn de qch; **he
  ~ me go** il m'a laissé partir; ~ **the water boil
  and …** faites bouillir l'eau et …; **to ~ go** lâcher
  prise; **to ~ go of sth, to ~ sth go** lâcher qch; ~**'s
  go** allons-y; ~ **him come** qu'il vienne; **"to ~"**
  (*BRIT*) "à louer"
  ▸ **let down** VT (*lower*) baisser; (*dress*) rallonger;
  (*hair*) défaire; (*BRIT: tyre*) dégonfler; (*disappoint*)
  décevoir
  ▸ **let go** VI lâcher prise ▸ VT lâcher
  ▸ **let in** VT laisser entrer; (*visitor etc*) faire entrer;
  what have you ~ yourself in for? à quoi t'es-tu
  engagé?
  ▸ **let off** VT (*allow to leave*) laisser partir; (*not
  punish*) ne pas punir; (*taxi driver, bus driver*)
  déposer; (*firework etc*) faire partir; (*bomb*) faire
  exploser; (*smell etc*) dégager; **to ~ off steam** (*fig:
  inf*) se défouler, décharger sa rate or bile
  ▸ **let on** VI (*inf*): **to ~ on that …**. révéler que …,
  dire que …
  ▸ **let out** VT laisser sortir; (*dress*) élargir; (*scream*)
  laisser échapper; (*BRIT: rent out*) louer
  ▸ **let up** VI diminuer, s'arrêter
let-down ['lɛtdaʊn] N (*disappointment*)
  déception f
lethal ['liːθl] ADJ mortel(le), fatal(e); (*weapon*)
  meurtrier(-ère)
lethargic [lɛ'θɑːdʒɪk] ADJ léthargique
lethargy ['lɛθədʒɪ] N léthargie f
letter ['lɛtə'] N lettre f; **letters** NPL (*Literature*)
  lettres; **small/capital** ~ minuscule f/
  majuscule f; ~ **of credit** lettre f de crédit
letter bomb N lettre piégée
letterbox ['lɛtəbɔks] N (*BRIT*) boîte f aux or à
  lettres
letterhead ['lɛtəhɛd] N en-tête m

lettering ['lɛtərɪŋ] N lettres fpl; caractères mpl
letter opener N coupe-papier m
letterpress ['lɛtəprɛs] N (*method*) typographie f
letter quality N qualité f "courrier"
letters patent NPL brevet m d'invention
lettuce ['lɛtɪs] N laitue f, salade f
let-up ['lɛtʌp] N répit m, détente f
leukaemia, (*US*) **leukemia** [luː'kiːmɪə] N
  leucémie f
level ['lɛvl] ADJ (*flat*) plat(e), plan(e), uni(e);
  (*horizontal*) horizontal(e) ▸ N niveau m; (*flat
  place*) terrain plat; (*also*: **spirit level**) niveau à
  bulle ▸ VT niveler, aplanir; (*gun*) pointer,
  braquer; (*accusation*): **to ~ (against)** lancer or
  porter (contre) ▸ VI (*inf*): **to ~ with sb** être franc
  (franche) avec qn; **A levels** npl (*BRIT*)
  ≈ baccalauréat m; **"O" levels** npl (*BRIT: formerly*)
  *examens passés à l'âge de 16 ans sanctionnant les
  connaissances de l'élève*, ≈ brevet m des collèges;
  a ~ spoonful (*Culin*) une cuillerée rase; **to be ~
  with** être au même niveau que; **to draw ~ with**
  (*team*) arriver à égalité de points avec, égaliser
  avec; arriver au même classement que; (*runner,
  car*) arriver à la hauteur de, rattraper; **on the ~**
  à l'horizontale; (*fig: honest*) régulier(-ière)
  ▸ **level off, level out** VI (*prices etc*) se stabiliser
  ▸ VT (*ground*) aplanir, niveler
level crossing N (*BRIT*) passage m à niveau
level-headed [lɛvl'hɛdɪd] ADJ équilibré(e)
levelling, (*US*) **leveling** ['lɛvlɪŋ] ADJ (*process,
  effect*) de nivellement
level playing field N: **to compete on a ~** jouer
  sur un terrain d'égalité
lever ['liːvə'] N levier m ▸ VT: **to ~ up/out**
  soulever/extraire au moyen d'un levier
leverage ['liːvərɪdʒ] N (*influence*): ~ **(on** or **with)**
  prise f (sur)
levity ['lɛvɪtɪ] N manque m de sérieux, légèreté f
levy ['lɛvɪ] N taxe f, impôt m ▸ VT (*tax*) lever; (*fine*)
  infliger
lewd [luːd] ADJ obscène, lubrique
lexicographer [lɛksɪ'kɔgrəfə'] N lexicographe mf
lexicography [lɛksɪ'kɔgrəfɪ] N lexicographie f
LGBT N ABBR LGBT (= *lesbiennes, gays, bisexuels et
  transgenres*)
LGV N ABBR (= *Large Goods Vehicle*) poids lourd
LI ABBR (*US*) = **Long Island**
liabilities [laɪə'bɪlɪtɪz] NPL (*Comm*) obligations
  fpl, engagements mpl; (*on balance sheet*) passif m
liability [laɪə'bɪlɪtɪ] N responsabilité f;
  (*handicap*) handicap m
liable ['laɪəbl] ADJ (*subject*): ~ **to** sujet(te) à,
  passible de; (*responsible*): ~ **(for)** responsable
  (de); (*likely*): ~ **to do** susceptible de faire; **to be ~
  to a fine** être passible d'une amende
liaise [liː'eɪz] VI: **to ~ with** assurer la liaison avec
liaison [liː'eɪzɔn] N liaison f
liar ['laɪə'] N menteur(-euse)
libel ['laɪbl] N diffamation f; (*document*) écrit m
  diffamatoire ▸ VT diffamer
libellous ['laɪbləs] ADJ diffamatoire
liberal ['lɪbərl] ADJ libéral(e); (*generous*): ~ **with**
  prodigue de, généreux(-euse) avec ▸ N: **L~** (*Pol*)
  libéral(e)

659

Liberal Democrat N (*Brit*) libéral(e)-démocrate *m/f*

liberality [lɪbəˈrælɪtɪ] N (*generosity*) générosité *f*, libéralité *f*

liberalize [ˈlɪbərəlaɪz] VT libéraliser

liberal-minded [ˈlɪbərlˈmaɪndɪd] ADJ libéral(e), tolérant(e)

liberate [ˈlɪbəreɪt] VT libérer

liberation [lɪbəˈreɪʃən] N libération *f*

liberation theology N théologie *f* de libération

Liberia [laɪˈbɪərɪə] N Libéria *m*, Liberia *m*

Liberian [laɪˈbɪərɪən] ADJ libérien(ne) ▸ N Libérien(ne)

liberty [ˈlɪbətɪ] N liberté *f*; **to be at ~** (*criminal*) être en liberté; **to do** libre de faire; **to take the ~ of** prendre la liberté de, se permettre de

libido [lɪˈbiːdəu] N libido *f*

Libra [ˈliːbrə] N la Balance; **to be ~** être de la Balance

librarian [laɪˈbrɛərɪən] N bibliothécaire *mf*

library [ˈlaɪbrərɪ] N bibliothèque *f*

library book N livre *m* de bibliothèque

libretto [lɪˈbretəu] N livret *m*

Libya [ˈlɪbɪə] N Libye *f*

Libyan [ˈlɪbɪən] ADJ libyen(ne), de Libye ▸ N Libyen(ne)

lice [laɪs] NPL *of* **louse**

licence, (*US*) **license** [ˈlaɪsns] N autorisation *f*, permis *m*; (*Comm*) licence *f*; (*Radio, TV*) redevance *f*; (*excessive freedom*) licence; **driving ~**, **driver's license** (*US*) permis *m* (de conduire); **import ~** licence d'importation; **produced under ~** fabriqué(e) sous licence

licence number N (*Brit Aut*) numéro *m* d'immatriculation

license [ˈlaɪsns] N (*US*) = **licence** ▸ VT donner une licence à; (*car*) acheter la vignette de; délivrer la vignette de

licensed [ˈlaɪsnst] ADJ (*for alcohol*) patenté(e) pour la vente des spiritueux, qui a une patente de débit de boissons; (*car*) muni(e) de la vignette

licensee [laɪsnˈsiː] N (*Brit: of pub*) patron(ne), gérant(e)

license plate N (*US Aut*) plaque *f* minéralogique

licensing hours (*Brit*) NPL heures *fpl* d'ouvertures (*des pubs*)

licentious [laɪˈsɛnʃəs] ADJ licencieux(-euse)

lichen [ˈlaɪkən] N lichen *m*

lick [lɪk] VT lécher; (*inf: defeat*) écraser, flanquer une piquette or raclée à ▸ N coup *m* de langue; **a ~ of paint** un petit coup de peinture; **to ~ one's lips** (*fig*) se frotter les mains

licorice [ˈlɪkərɪʃ] N = **liquorice**

lid [lɪd] N couvercle *m*; (*eyelid*) paupière *f*; **to take the ~ off sth** (*fig*) exposer or étaler qch au grand jour

lido [ˈlaɪdəu] N piscine *f* en plein air, complexe *m* balnéaire

lie [laɪ] N mensonge *m* ▸ VI (*pt, pp* **lied**: *tell lies*) mentir; (*pt* **lay** [leɪ], *pp* **lain** [leɪn]) (*rest*) être étendu(e) or allongé(e) or couché(e); (*in grave*) être enterré(e), reposer; (*object: be situated*) se trouver, être; **to ~ low** (*fig*) se cacher, rester

caché(e); **to tell lies** mentir

▸ **lie about, lie around** VI (*things*) traîner; (*Brit: person*) traînasser, flemmarder

▸ **lie back** VI se renverser en arrière

▸ **lie down** VI se coucher, s'étendre

▸ **lie up** VI (*hide*) se cacher

Liechtenstein [ˈlɪktənstaɪn] N Liechtenstein *m*

lie detector N détecteur *m* de mensonges

lie-down [ˈlaɪdaun] N (*Brit*): **to have a ~** s'allonger, se reposer

lie-in [ˈlaɪɪn] N (*Brit*): **to have a ~** faire la grasse matinée

lieu [luː]: **in ~ of** prep au lieu de, à la place de

Lieut. ABBR (= *lieutenant*) Lt

lieutenant [lɛfˈtɛnənt, (*US*) luːˈtɛnənt] N lieutenant *m*

lieutenant-colonel [lɛfˈtɛnəntˈkəːnl, (*US*) luːˈtɛnəntˈkəːnl] N lieutenant-colonel *m*

life [laɪf] (*pl* **lives** [laɪvz]) N vie *f*; **to come to ~** (*fig*) s'animer ▸ CPD de vie; de la vie; à vie; **true to ~** réaliste, fidèle à la réalité; **to paint from ~** peindre d'après nature; **to be sent to prison for ~** être condamné(e) (à la réclusion criminelle) à perpétuité; **country/city ~** la vie à la campagne/à la ville

life annuity N pension *f*, rente viagère

life assurance N (*Brit*) = **life insurance**

lifebelt [ˈlaɪfbɛlt] N (*Brit*) bouée *f* de sauvetage

lifeblood [ˈlaɪfblʌd] N (*fig*) élément moteur

lifeboat [ˈlaɪfbəut] N canot *m* or chaloupe *f* de sauvetage

lifebuoy [ˈlaɪfbɔɪ] N bouée *f* de sauvetage

life expectancy N espérance *f* de vie

lifeguard [ˈlaɪfgɑːd] N surveillant *m* de baignade

life imprisonment N prison *f* à vie; (*Law*) réclusion *f* à perpétuité

life insurance N assurance-vie *f*

life jacket N gilet *m* or ceinture *f* de sauvetage

lifeless [ˈlaɪflɪs] ADJ sans vie, inanimé(e); (*dull*) qui manque de vie or de vigueur

lifelike [ˈlaɪflaɪk] ADJ qui semble vrai(e) or vivant(e), ressemblant(e); (*painting*) réaliste

lifeline [ˈlaɪflaɪn] N corde *f* de sauvetage

lifelong [ˈlaɪflɔŋ] ADJ de toute une vie, de toujours

life preserver [-prɪˈzəːvəʳ] N (*US*) gilet *m* or ceinture *f* de sauvetage

lifer [ˈlaɪfəʳ] N (*inf*) condamné(e) à perpète

life-raft [ˈlaɪfrɑːft] N radeau *m* de sauvetage

life-saver [ˈlaɪfseɪvəʳ] N surveillant *m* de baignade

life-saving [ˈlaɪfseɪvɪŋ] N sauvetage *m*

life sentence N condamnation *f* à vie or à perpétuité

life-size [ˈlaɪfsaɪz], **life-sized** [ˈlaɪfsaɪzd] ADJ grandeur nature *inv*

life span N (durée *f* de) vie *f*

lifestyle [ˈlaɪfstaɪl] N style *m* de vie

life-support system [ˈlaɪfsəpɔːt-] N (*Med*) respirateur artificiel

lifetime [ˈlaɪftaɪm] N: **in his ~** de son vivant; **the chance of a ~** la chance de ma (or sa *etc*) vie, une occasion unique

lift [lɪft] vt soulever, lever; (end) supprimer, lever; (steal) prendre, voler ▶ vi (fog) se lever ▶ N (BRIT: elevator) ascenseur m; **to give sb a ~** (BRIT) emmener or prendre qn en voiture; **can you give me a ~ to the station?** pouvez-vous m'emmener à la gare?
▶ **lift off** vi (rocket, helicopter) décoller
▶ **lift out** vt sortir; (troops, evacuees etc) évacuer par avion or hélicoptère
▶ **lift up** vt soulever
lift-off ['lɪftɔf] N décollage m
ligament ['lɪgəmənt] N ligament m
light [laɪt] (pt, pp **lighted** or **lit** [lɪt]) N lumière f; (daylight) lumière, jour m; (lamp) lampe f; (Aut: rear light) feu m; (: headlamp) phare m; (for cigarette etc): **have you got a ~?** avez-vous du feu? ▶ vt (candle, cigarette, fire) allumer; (room) éclairer
▶ ADJ (room, colour) clair(e); (not heavy, also fig) léger(-ère); (not strenuous) peu fatigant(e) ▶ ADV (travel) avec peu de bagages; **lights** NPL (traffic lights) feux mpl; **to turn the ~ on/off** allumer/éteindre; **to cast** or **shed** or **throw ~ on** éclaircir; **to come to ~** être dévoilé(e) or découvert(e); **in the ~ of** à la lumière de; étant donné; **to make ~ of sth** (fig) prendre qch à la légère, faire peu de cas de qch
▶ **light up** vi s'allumer; (face) s'éclairer; (smoke) allumer une cigarette or une pipe etc ▶ vt (illuminate) éclairer, illuminer
light bulb N ampoule f
lighten ['laɪtn] vi s'éclairer ▶ vt (light up) éclairer; (make lighter) éclaircir; (make less heavy) alléger
lighter ['laɪtər] N (also: **cigarette lighter**) briquet m; (: in car) allume-cigare m inv; (boat) péniche f
light-fingered [laɪt'fɪŋgəd] ADJ chapardeur(-euse)
light-headed [laɪt'hedɪd] ADJ étourdi(e), écervelé(e)
light-hearted [laɪt'hɑːtɪd] ADJ gai(e), joyeux(-euse), enjoué(e)
lighthouse ['laɪthaus] N phare m
lighting ['laɪtɪŋ] N éclairage m; (in theatre) éclairages
lighting-up time [laɪtɪŋ'ʌp-] N (BRIT) heure officielle de la tombée du jour
lightly ['laɪtlɪ] ADV légèrement; **to get off ~** s'en tirer à bon compte
light meter N (Phot) photomètre m, cellule f
lightness ['laɪtnɪs] N clarté f; (in weight) légèreté f
lightning ['laɪtnɪŋ] N foudre f; (flash) éclair m
lightning conductor, (US) **lightning rod** N paratonnerre m
lightning strike N (BRIT) grève f surprise
light pen N crayon m optique
lightship ['laɪtʃɪp] N bateau-phare m
lightweight ['laɪtweɪt] ADJ (suit) léger(-ère) ▶ N (Boxing) poids léger
light year ['laɪtjɪər] N année-lumière f
like [laɪk] vt aimer (bien) ▶ PREP comme ▶ ADJ semblable, pareil(le) ▶ N: **the ~** un(e) pareil(le) or semblable; le (la) pareil(le); (pej) (d')autres du même genre or acabit; **his likes and dislikes**

ses goûts mpl or préférences fpl; **I would ~, I'd ~** je voudrais, j'aimerais; **would you ~ a coffee?** voulez-vous du café?; **to be/look ~ sb/sth** ressembler à qn/qch; **what's he ~?** comment est-il?; **what's the weather ~?** quel temps fait-il?; **what does it look ~?** de quoi est-ce que ça a l'air?; **what does it taste ~?** quel goût est-ce que ça a?; **that's just ~ him** c'est bien de lui, ça lui ressemble; **something ~ that** quelque chose comme ça; **do it ~ this** fais-le comme ceci; **I feel ~ a drink** je boirais bien quelque chose; **if you ~** si vous voulez; **it's nothing ~ ...** ce n'est pas du tout comme ...; **there's nothing ~ ...** il n'y a rien de tel que ...
likeable ['laɪkəbl] ADJ sympathique, agréable
likelihood ['laɪklɪhud] N probabilité f; **in all ~** selon toute vraisemblance
likely ['laɪklɪ] ADJ (result, outcome) probable; (excuse) plausible; **he's ~ to leave** il va sûrement partir, il risque fort de partir; **not ~!** (inf) pas de danger!
like-minded ['laɪk'maɪndɪd] ADJ de même opinion
liken ['laɪkən] vt: **to ~ sth to** comparer qch à
likeness ['laɪknɪs] N ressemblance f
likewise ['laɪkwaɪz] ADV de même, pareillement
liking ['laɪkɪŋ] N (for person) affection f; (for thing) penchant m, goût m; **to take a ~ to sb** se prendre d'amitié pour qn; **to be to sb's ~** être au goût de qn, plaire à qn
lilac ['laɪlək] N lilas m ▶ ADJ lilas inv
Lilo® ['laɪləu] N matelas m pneumatique
lilt [lɪlt] N rythme m, cadence f
lilting ['lɪltɪŋ] ADJ aux cadences mélodieuses; chantant(e)
lily ['lɪlɪ] N lis m; **~ of the valley** muguet m
Lima ['liːmə] N Lima
limb [lɪm] N membre m; **to be out on a ~** (fig) être isolé(e)
limber ['lɪmbər]: **to ~ up** vi se dégourdir, se mettre en train
limbo ['lɪmbəu] N: **to be in ~** (fig) être tombé(e) dans l'oubli
lime [laɪm] N (tree) tilleul m; (fruit) citron vert, lime f; (Geo) chaux f
lime juice N jus m de citron vert
limelight ['laɪmlaɪt] N: **in the ~** (fig) en vedette, au premier plan
limerick ['lɪmərɪk] N petit poème humoristique
limestone ['laɪmstəun] N pierre f à chaux; (Geo) calcaire m
limit ['lɪmɪt] N limite f ▶ vt limiter; **weight/speed ~** limite de poids/de vitesse
limitation [lɪmɪ'teɪʃən] N limitation f, restriction f
limited ['lɪmɪtɪd] ADJ limité(e), restreint(e); **~ edition** édition f à tirage limité; **to be ~ to** se limiter à, ne concerner que
limited company, limited liability company N (BRIT) ≈ société f anonyme
limitless ['lɪmɪtlɪs] ADJ illimité(e)
limousine ['lɪməziːn] N limousine f
limp [lɪmp] N: **to have a ~** boiter ▶ vi boiter
▶ ADJ mou (molle)

limpet ['lɪmpɪt] N patelle *f*; **like a ~** *(fig)* comme une ventouse

limpid ['lɪmpɪd] ADJ limpide

linchpin N esse *f*; *(fig)* pivot *m*

Lincs [lɪŋks] ABBR *(BRIT)* = **Lincolnshire**

line [laɪn] N *(gen)* ligne *f*; *(stroke)* trait *m*; *(wrinkle)* ride *f*; *(rope)* corde *f*; *(wire)* fil *m*; *(of poem)* vers *m*; *(row, series)* rangée *f*; *(of people)* file *f*, queue *f*; *(railway track)* voie *f*; *(Comm: series of goods)* article(s) *m(pl)*, ligne de produits; *(work)* métier *m* ▶ VT *(subj: trees, crowd)* border; **to ~ (with)** *(clothes)* doubler (de); *(box)* garnir or tapisser (de); **to stand in ~** *(US)* faire la queue; **to cut in ~** *(US)* passer avant son tour; **in his ~ of business** dans sa partie, dans son rayon; **on the right lines** sur la bonne voie; **a new ~ in cosmetics** une nouvelle ligne de produits de beauté; **hold the ~ please** *(BRIT Tel)* ne quittez pas; **to be in ~ for sth** *(fig)* être en lice pour qch; **in ~ with** en accord avec, en conformité avec; **in a ~** aligné(e); **to bring sth into ~ with sth** aligner qch sur qch; **to draw the ~ at (doing) sth** *(fig)* se refuser à (faire) qch; ne pas tolérer or admettre (qu'on fasse) qch; **to take the ~ that ...** être d'avis or de l'opinion que ...
▶ **line up** VI s'aligner, se mettre en rang(s); *(in queue)* faire la queue ▶ VT aligner; *(event)* prévoir; *(find)* trouver; **to have sb/sth lined up** avoir qn/qch en vue or de prévu(e)

linear ['lɪnɪəʳ] ADJ linéaire

lined [laɪnd] ADJ *(paper)* réglé(e); *(face)* marqué(e), ridé(e); *(clothes)* doublé(e)

lineman ['laɪnmən] N *(irreg)* *(US: Rail)* poseur *m* de rails; *(: Tel)* ouvrier *m* de ligne; *(: Football)* avant *m*

linen ['lɪnɪn] N linge *m* (de corps or de maison); *(cloth)* lin *m*

line printer N imprimante *f* (ligne par) ligne

liner ['laɪnəʳ] N *(ship)* paquebot *m* de ligne; *(for bin)* sac-poubelle *m*

linesman ['laɪnzmən] N *(irreg)* *(Tennis)* juge *m* de ligne; *(Football)* juge de touche

line-up ['laɪnʌp] N *(US: queue)* file *f*; *(also: **police line-up**)* parade *f* d'identification; *(Sport)* (composition *f* de l')équipe *f*

linger ['lɪŋgəʳ] VI s'attarder; traîner; *(smell, tradition)* persister

lingerie ['lænʒəriː] N lingerie *f*

lingering ['lɪŋgərɪŋ] ADJ persistant(e); qui subsiste; *(death)* lent(e)

lingo ['lɪŋgəu] *(pl* **lingoes**) N *(pej)* jargon *m*

linguist ['lɪŋgwɪst] N linguiste *mf*; **to be a good ~** être doué(e) pour les langues

linguistic [lɪŋ'gwɪstɪk] ADJ linguistique

linguistics [lɪŋ'gwɪstɪks] N linguistique *f*

lining ['laɪnɪŋ] N doublure *f*; *(Tech)* revêtement *m*; *(: of brakes)* garniture *f*

link [lɪŋk] N *(connection)* lien *m*, rapport *m*; *(Internet)* lien; *(of a chain)* maillon *m* ▶ VT relier, lier, unir; **links** NPL *(Golf)* (terrain *m* de) golf *m*; **rail ~** liaison *f* ferroviaire
▶ **link up** VT relier ▶ VI *(people)* se rejoindre; *(companies etc)* s'associer

link-up ['lɪŋkʌp] N lien *m*, rapport *m*; *(of roads)* jonction *f*, raccordement *m*; *(of spaceships)* arrimage *m*; *(Radio, TV)* liaison *f*; *(: programme)* duplex *m*

lino ['laɪnəu] N = **linoleum**

linoleum [lɪ'nəuliəm] N linoléum *m*

linseed oil ['lɪnsiːd-] N huile *f* de lin

lint [lɪnt] N tissu ouaté *(pour pansements)*

lintel ['lɪntl] N linteau *m*

lion ['laɪən] N lion *m*

lion cub N lionceau *m*

lioness ['laɪənɪs] N lionne *f*

lip [lɪp] N lèvre *f*; *(of cup etc)* rebord *m*; *(insolence)* insolences *fpl*

liposuction ['lɪpəusʌkʃən] N liposuccion *f*

lip-read ['lɪpriːd] VI *(irreg: like* **read**) lire sur les lèvres

lip salve [-sælv] N pommade *f* pour les lèvres, pommade rosat

lip service N: **to pay ~ to sth** ne reconnaître le mérite de qch que pour la forme or qu'en paroles

lipstick ['lɪpstɪk] N rouge *m* à lèvres

liquefy ['lɪkwɪfaɪ] VT liquéfier ▶ VI se liquéfier

liqueur [lɪ'kjuəʳ] N liqueur *f*

liquid ['lɪkwɪd] N liquide *m* ▶ ADJ liquide

liquid assets NPL liquidités *fpl*, disponibilités *fpl*

liquidate ['lɪkwɪdeɪt] VT liquider

liquidation [lɪkwɪ'deɪʃən] N liquidation *f*; **to go into ~** déposer son bilan

liquidator ['lɪkwɪdeɪtəʳ] N liquidateur *m*

liquid crystal display N affichage *m* à cristaux liquides

liquidize ['lɪkwɪdaɪz] VT *(BRIT Culin)* passer au mixer

liquidizer ['lɪkwɪdaɪzəʳ] N *(BRIT Culin)* mixer *m*

liquor ['lɪkəʳ] N spiritueux *m*, alcool *m*

liquorice ['lɪkərɪʃ] N *(BRIT)* réglisse *m*

liquor store *(US)* N magasin *m* de vins et spiritueux

Lisbon ['lɪzbən] N Lisbonne

lisp [lɪsp] N zézaiement *m* ▶ VI zézayer

lissom ['lɪsəm] ADJ souple, agile

list [lɪst] N liste *f*; *(of ship)* inclinaison *f* ▶ VT *(write down)* inscrire; *(make list of)* faire la liste de; *(enumerate)* énumérer; *(Comput)* lister ▶ VI *(ship)* gîter, donner de la bande; **shopping ~** liste des courses

listed building ['lɪstɪd-] N *(Archit)* monument classé

listed company ['lɪstɪd-] N société cotée en Bourse

listen ['lɪsn] VI écouter; **to ~ to** écouter

listener ['lɪsnəʳ] N auditeur(-trice)

listeria [lɪs'tɪərɪə] N listéria *f*

listing ['lɪstɪŋ] N *(Comput)* listage *m*; *(: hard copy)* liste *f*, listing *m*

listless ['lɪstlɪs] ADJ indolent(e), apathique

listlessly ['lɪstlɪslɪ] ADV avec indolence or apathie

list price N prix *m* de catalogue

lit [lɪt] PT, PP *of* **light**

litany ['lɪtənɪ] N litanie *f*

liter ['liːtəʳ] N *(US)* = **litre**

literacy ['lɪtərəsɪ] N degré *m* d'alphabétisation,

fait *m* de savoir lire et écrire; (*Brit Scol*)
enseignement *m* de la lecture et de l'écriture
literal ['lɪtərl] ADJ littéral(e)
literally ['lɪtrəlɪ] ADV littéralement; (*really*)
réellement
literary ['lɪtərərɪ] ADJ littéraire
literate ['lɪtərət] ADJ qui sait lire et écrire;
(*educated*) instruit(e)
literature ['lɪtrɪtʃəʳ] N littérature *f*; (*brochures etc*)
copie *f* publicitaire, prospectus *mpl*
lithe [laɪð] ADJ agile, souple
lithography [lɪ'θɔgrəfɪ] N lithographie *f*
Lithuania [lɪθju'eɪnɪə] N Lituanie *f*
Lithuanian [lɪθju'eɪnɪən] ADJ lituanien(ne) ▶ N
Lituanien(ne); (*Ling*) lituanien *m*
litigate ['lɪtɪgeɪt] VT mettre en litige ▶ VI plaider
litigation [lɪtɪ'geɪʃən] N litige *m*; contentieux *m*
litmus ['lɪtməs] N: ~ **paper** papier *m* de
tournesol
litre, (*US*) **liter** ['li:təʳ] N litre *m*
litter ['lɪtəʳ] N (*rubbish*) détritus *mpl*; (*dirtier*)
ordures *fpl*; (*young animals*) portée *f* ▶ VT
éparpiller; laisser des détritus dans; **littered
with** jonché(e) de, couvert(e) de
litter bin N (*Brit*) poubelle *f*
litter lout, (*US*) **litterbug** ['lɪtəbʌg] N personne
qui jette des détritus par terre
little ['lɪtl] ADJ (*small*) petit(e); (*not much*): ~ **milk**
peu de lait ▶ ADV peu; **a** ~ un peu (de); **a ~ milk**
un peu de lait; **a ~ bit** un peu; **for a ~ while**
pendant un petit moment; **with ~ difficulty**
sans trop de difficulté; **as ~ as possible** le
moins possible; ~ **by** ~ petit à petit, peu à peu;
to make ~ **of** faire peu de cas de
little finger N auriculaire *m*, petit doigt
little-known ['lɪtl'nəun] ADJ peu connu(e)
liturgy ['lɪtədʒɪ] N liturgie *f*
live¹ [laɪv] ADJ (*animal*) vivant(e), en vie; (*wire*)
sous tension; (*broadcast*) (transmis(e)) en direct;
(*issue*) d'actualité, brûlant(e); (*unexploded*) non
explosé(e); ~ **ammunition** munitions *fpl* de
combat
live² [lɪv] VI vivre; (*reside*) vivre, habiter; **to ~ in
London** habiter (à) Londres; **where do you ~?**
où habitez-vous?
▶ **live down** VT faire oublier (avec le temps)
▶ **live in** VI être logé(e) et nourri(e); être interne
▶ **live off** VT (*land, fish etc*) vivre de; (*pej: parents
etc*) vivre aux crochets de
▶ **live on** VT FUS (*food*) vivre de ▶ VI survivre; **to ~
on £50 a week** vivre avec 50 livres par semaine
▶ **live out** VI (*Brit: students*) être externe ▶ VT: **to
~ out one's days** or **life** passer sa vie
▶ **live together** VI vivre ensemble, cohabiter
▶ **live up** VT: **to ~ it up** (*inf*) faire la fête; mener
la grande vie
▶ **live up to** VT FUS se montrer à la hauteur de
live-in ['lɪvɪn] ADJ (*nanny*) à demeure; ~ **partner**
concubin(e)
livelihood ['laɪvlɪhud] N moyens *mpl*
d'existence
liveliness ['laɪvlɪnəs] N vivacité *f*, entrain *m*
lively ['laɪvlɪ] ADJ vif (vive), plein(e) d'entrain;
(*place, book*) vivant(e)

liven up ['laɪvn-] VT (*room etc*) égayer; (*discussion,
evening*) animer ▶ VI s'animer
liver ['lɪvəʳ] N foie *m*
liverish ['lɪvərɪʃ] ADJ qui a mal au foie; (*fig*)
grincheux(-euse)
Liverpudlian [lɪvə'pʌdlɪən] ADJ de Liverpool ▶ N
habitant(e) de Liverpool, natif(-ive) de
Liverpool
livery ['lɪvərɪ] N livrée *f*
lives [laɪvz] NPL *of* **life**
livestock ['laɪvstɔk] N cheptel *m*, bétail *m*
live wire [laɪv-] N (*inf: fig*): **to be a (real)** ~ péter
le feu
livid ['lɪvɪd] ADJ livide, blafard(e); (*furious*)
furieux(-euse), furibond(e)
living ['lɪvɪŋ] ADJ vivant(e), en vie ▶ N: **to earn** or
make a ~ gagner sa vie; **within ~ memory** de
mémoire d'homme
living conditions NPL conditions *fpl* de vie
living expenses NPL dépenses courantes
living room N salle *f* de séjour
living standards NPL niveau *m* de vie
living wage N salaire *m* permettant de vivre
(décemment)
living will N directives *fpl* anticipées
lizard ['lɪzəd] N lézard *m*
llama ['lɑːmə] N lama *m*
LLB N ABBR (= *Bachelor of Laws*) titre universitaire
LLD N ABBR (= *Doctor of Laws*) titre universitaire
LMT ABBR (*US*: = *Local Mean Time*) heure locale
load [ləud] N (*weight*) poids *m*; (*thing carried*)
chargement *m*, charge *f*; (*Elec, Tech*) charge ▶ VT
charger; (*also*: **load up**): **to ~ (with)** (*lorry, ship*)
charger (de); (*gun, camera*) charger (avec); **a ~ of,
loads of** (*fig*) un or des tas de, des masses de; **to
talk a ~ of rubbish** (*inf*) dire des bêtises
loaded ['ləudɪd] ADJ (*dice*) pipé(e); (*question*)
insidieux(-euse); (*inf: rich*) bourré(e) de fric;
(: *drunk*) bourré
loading bay ['ləudɪŋ-] N aire *f* de chargement
loaf [ləuf] (*pl* **loaves** [ləuvz]) N pain *m*, miche *f*
▶ VI (*also*: **loaf about, loaf around**) fainéanter,
traîner
loam [ləum] N terreau *m*
loan [ləun] N prêt *m* ▶ VT prêter; **on** ~ prêté(e),
en prêt; **public** ~ emprunt public
loan account N compte *m* de prêt
loan capital N capital *m* d'emprunt
loan shark N (*inf, pej*) usurier *m*
loath [ləuθ] ADJ: **to be ~ to do** répugner à faire
loathe [ləuð] VT détester, avoir en horreur
loathing ['ləuðɪŋ] N dégoût *m*, répugnance *f*
loathsome ['ləuðsəm] ADJ répugnant(e),
détestable
loaves [ləuvz] NPL *of* **loaf**
lob [lɔb] VT (*ball*) lober
lobby ['lɔbɪ] N hall *m*, entrée *f*; (*Pol*) groupe *m* de
pression, lobby *m* ▶ VT faire pression sur
lobbyist ['lɔbɪɪst] N membre *mf* d'un groupe de
pression
lobe [ləub] N lobe *m*
lobster ['lɔbstəʳ] N homard *m*
lobster pot N casier *m* à homards
local ['ləukl] ADJ local(e) ▶ N (*Brit*: *pub*) pub *m* or

café *m* du coin; **the locals** NPL les gens *mpl* du pays *or* du coin

local anaesthetic, (US) **local anesthetic** N anesthésie locale

local authority N collectivité locale, municipalité *f*

local call N (*Tel*) communication urbaine

local government N administration locale *or* municipale

locality [ləu'kælɪtɪ] N région *f*, environs *mpl*; (*position*) lieu *m*

localize ['ləukəlaɪz] VT localiser

locally ['ləukəlɪ] ADV localement; dans les environs *or* la région

locate [ləu'keɪt] VT (*find*) trouver, repérer; (*situate*) situer; **to be located in** être situé à *or* en

location [ləu'keɪʃən] N emplacement *m*; **on ~** (*Cine*) en extérieur

loch [lɔx] N lac *m*, loch *m*

lock [lɔk] N (*of door, box*) serrure *f*; (*of canal*) écluse *f*; (*of hair*) mèche *f*, boucle *f* ▶ VT (*with key*) fermer à clé; (*immobilize*) bloquer ▶ VI (*door etc*) fermer à clé; (*wheels*) se bloquer; **~ stock and barrel** (*fig*) en bloc; **on full ~** (BRIT *Aut*) le volant tourné à fond

▶ **lock away** VT (*valuables*) mettre sous clé; (*criminal*) mettre sous les verrous, enfermer

▶ **lock in** VT enfermer

▶ **lock out** VT enfermer dehors; (*on purpose*) mettre à la porte; (*: workers*) lock-outer

▶ **lock up** VT (*person*) enfermer; (*house*) fermer à clé ▶ VI tout fermer (à clé)

locker ['lɔkə'] N casier *m*; (*in station*) consigne *f* automatique

locker-room ['lɔkəru:m] (US) N (*Sport*) vestiaire *m*

locket ['lɔkɪt] N médaillon *m*

lockjaw ['lɔkdʒɔ:] N tétanos *m*

lockout ['lɔkaut] N (*Industry*) lock-out *m*, grève patronale

locksmith ['lɔksmɪθ] N serrurier *m*

lock-up ['lɔkʌp] N (*prison*) prison *f*; (*cell*) cellule *f* provisoire; (*also*: **lock-up garage**) box *m*

locomotive [ləukə'məutɪv] N locomotive *f*

locum ['ləukəm] N (*Med*) suppléant(e) de médecin *etc*

locust ['ləukəst] N locuste *f*, sauterelle *f*

lodge [lɔdʒ] N pavillon *m* (de gardien); (*also*: **hunting lodge**) pavillon de chasse; (*Freemasonry*) loge *f* ▶ VI (*person*): **to ~ with** être logé(e) chez, être en pension chez; (*bullet*) se loger ▶ VT (*appeal etc*) présenter; déposer; **to ~ a complaint** porter plainte; **to ~ (itself) in/between** se loger dans/entre

lodger ['lɔdʒə'] N locataire *mf*; (*with room and meals*) pensionnaire *mf*

lodging ['lɔdʒɪŋ] N logement *m*; *see also* **board**

lodging house N (BRIT) pension *f* de famille

lodgings ['lɔdʒɪŋz] NPL chambre *f*, meublé *m*

loft [lɔft] N grenier *m*; (*apartment*) grenier aménagé (en appartement) (*gén dans ancien entrepôt ou fabrique*)

lofty ['lɔftɪ] ADJ élevé(e); (*haughty*) hautain(e); (*sentiments, aims*) noble

log [lɔg] N (*of wood*) bûche *f*; (*Naut*) livre *m or* journal *m* de bord; (*of car*) ≈ carte grise ▶ N ABBR (= *logarithm*) log *m* ▶ VT enregistrer

▶ **log in, log on** VI (*Comput*) ouvrir une session, entrer dans le système

▶ **log off, log out** VI (*Comput*) clore une session, sortir du système

logarithm ['lɔgərɪðm] N logarithme *m*

logbook ['lɔgbuk] N (*Naut*) livre *m or* journal *m* de bord; (*Aviat*) carnet *m* de vol; (*of lorry driver*) carnet de route; (*of movement of goods etc*) registre *m*; (*of car*) ≈ carte grise

log cabin N cabane *f* en rondins

log fire N feu *m* de bois

logger ['lɔgə'] N bûcheron *m*

loggerheads ['lɔgəhedz] NPL: **at ~ (with)** à couteaux tirés (avec)

logic ['lɔdʒɪk] N logique *f*

logical ['lɔdʒɪkl] ADJ logique

logically ['lɔdʒɪkəlɪ] ADV logiquement

login ['lɔgɪn] N (*Comput*) identifiant *m*

logistics [lɔ'dʒɪstɪks] N logistique *f*

logjam ['lɔgdʒæm] N: **to break the ~** créer une ouverture dans l'impasse

logo ['ləugəu] N logo *m*

loin [lɔɪn] N (*Culin*) filet *m*, longe *f*; **loins** NPL reins *mpl*

loin cloth N pagne *m*

Loire [lwa:] N: **the (River) ~** la Loire

loiter ['lɔɪtə'] VI s'attarder; **to ~ (about)** traîner, musarder; (*pej*) rôder

LOL ABBR (*inf*: = *laugh out loud*) MDR (= *mort de rire*)

lol ABBR (*Internet, Tel*: = *laugh out loud*) MDR (= *mort(e) de rire*)

loll [lɔl] VI (*also*: **loll about**) se prélasser, fainéanter

lollipop ['lɔlɪpɔp] N sucette *f*

lollipop man/lady N (*irreg*) (BRIT) contractuel(le) qui fait traverser la rue aux enfants; *voir article*

> Les *lollipop men/ladies* sont employés pour aider les enfants à traverser la rue à proximité des écoles à l'heure où ils entrent en classe et à la sortie. On les repère facilement à cause de leur long ciré jaune et ils portent une pancarte ronde pour faire signe aux automobilistes de s'arrêter. On les appelle ainsi car la forme circulaire de cette pancarte rappelle une sucette.

lollop ['lɔləp] VI (BRIT) avancer (*or* courir) maladroitement

lolly ['lɔlɪ] N (*inf*: *ice*) esquimau *m*; (*: lollipop*) sucette *f*; (*: money*) fric *m*

Lombardy ['lɔmbədɪ] N Lombardie *f*

London ['lʌndən] N Londres

Londoner ['lʌndənə'] N Londonien(ne)

lone [ləun] ADJ solitaire

loneliness ['ləunlɪnɪs] N solitude *f*, isolement *m*

lonely ['ləunlɪ] ADJ seul(e); (*childhood etc*) solitaire; (*place*) solitaire, isolé(e)

lonely hearts ADJ: **~ ad** petite annonce (personnelle); **~ club** club *m* de rencontres (*pour personnes seules*)

lone parent N parent *m* unique

loner ['ləunə'] N solitaire *mf*

lonesome ['ləʊnsəm] ADJ seul(e), solitaire

long [lɒŋ] ADJ long (longue) ▸ ADV longtemps ▸ N: **the ~ and the short of it is that ...** (fig) le fin mot de l'histoire c'est que ... ▸ VI: **to ~ for sth/to do sth** avoir très envie de qch/de faire qch, attendre qch avec impatience/attendre avec impatience de faire qch; **he had ~ understood that ...** il avait compris depuis longtemps que ...; **how ~ is this river/course?** quelle est la longueur de ce fleuve/la durée de ce cours?; **6 metres ~** (long) de 6 mètres; **6 months ~** qui dure 6 mois, de 6 mois; **all night ~** toute la nuit; **he no longer comes** il ne vient plus; **I can't stand it any longer** je ne peux plus le supporter; **~ before** longtemps avant; **before ~** (+future) avant peu, dans peu de temps; (+past) peu de temps après; **~ ago** il y a longtemps; **don't be ~!** fais vite!, dépêche-toi!; **I shan't be ~** je n'en ai pas pour longtemps; **at ~ last** enfin; **in the ~ run** à la longue; finalement; **so** or **as ~ as** à condition que +sub

long-distance [lɒŋ'dɪstəns] ADJ (race) de fond; (call) interurbain(e)

longer ADV see **long**

long-haired ['lɒŋ'hɛəd] ADJ (person) aux cheveux longs; (animal) aux longs poils

longhand ['lɒŋhænd] N écriture normale or courante

long-haul ['lɒŋhɔːl] ADJ (flight) long-courrier

longing ['lɒŋɪŋ] N désir m, envie f; (nostalgia) nostalgie f ▸ ADJ plein(e) d'envie or de nostalgie

longingly ['lɒŋɪŋlɪ] ADV avec désir or nostalgie

longitude ['lɒŋgɪtjuːd] N longitude f

long johns [-dʒɒnz] NPL caleçons longs

long jump N saut m en longueur

long-life [lɒŋ'laɪf] ADJ (batteries etc) longue durée inv; (milk) longue conservation

long-lost ['lɒŋlɒst] ADJ perdu(e) depuis longtemps

long-playing ['lɒŋpleɪɪŋ] ADJ: **~ record (LP)** (disque m) 33 tours m inv

long-range ['lɒŋ'reɪndʒ] ADJ à longue portée; (weather forecast) à long terme

longshoreman ['lɒŋʃɔːmən] N (irreg) (US) docker m, débardeur m

long-sighted ['lɒŋ'saɪtɪd] ADJ (BRIT) presbyte; (fig) prévoyant(e)

long-standing ['lɒŋ'stændɪŋ] ADJ de longue date

long-suffering [lɒŋ'sʌfərɪŋ] ADJ empreint(e) d'une patience résignée; extrêmement patient(e)

long-term ['lɒŋtəːm] ADJ à long terme

long wave N (Radio) grandes ondes, ondes longues

long-winded [lɒŋ'wɪndɪd] ADJ intarissable, interminable

loo [luː] N (BRIT inf) w.-c. mpl, petit coin

loofah ['luːfə] N sorte d'éponge végétale

look [lʊk] VI regarder; (seem) sembler, paraître, avoir l'air; (building etc): **to ~ south/on to the sea** donner au sud/sur la mer ▸ N regard m; (appearance) air m, allure f, aspect m; **looks** NPL (good looks) physique m, beauté f; **to ~ like**

ressembler à; **it looks like him** on dirait que c'est lui; **it looks about 4 metres long** je dirais que ça fait 4 mètres de long; **it looks all right to me** ça me paraît bien; **to have a ~** regarder; **to have a ~ at sth** jeter un coup d'œil à qch; **to have a ~ for sth** chercher qch; **to ~ ahead** regarder devant soi; (fig) envisager l'avenir; **~ (here)!** (annoyance) écoutez!

▸ **look after** VT FUS s'occuper de, prendre soin de; (luggage etc: watch over) garder, surveiller

▸ **look around** VI regarder autour de soi

▸ **look at** VT FUS regarder; (problem etc) examiner

▸ **look back** VI: **to ~ back at sth/sb** se retourner pour regarder qch/qn; **to ~ back on** (event, period) évoquer, repenser à

▸ **look down on** VT FUS (fig) regarder de haut, dédaigner

▸ **look for** VT FUS chercher; **we're looking for a hotel/restaurant** nous cherchons un hôtel/restaurant

▸ **look forward to** VT FUS attendre avec impatience; **I'm not looking forward to it** cette perspective ne me réjouit guère; **looking forward to hearing from you** (in letter) dans l'attente de vous lire

▸ **look in** VI: **to ~ in on sb** passer voir qn

▸ **look into** VT FUS (matter, possibility) examiner, étudier

▸ **look on** VI regarder (en spectateur)

▸ **look out** VI (beware): **to ~ out (for)** prendre garde (à), faire attention (à); **~ out!** attention!

▸ **look out for** VT FUS (seek) être à la recherche de; (try to spot) guetter

▸ **look over** VT (essay) jeter un coup d'œil à; (town, building) visiter (rapidement); (person) jeter un coup d'œil à; examiner de la tête aux pieds

▸ **look round** VT FUS (house, shop) faire le tour de ▸ VI (turn) regarder derrière soi, se retourner; **to ~ round for sth** chercher qch

▸ **look through** VT FUS (papers, book) examiner; (: briefly) parcourir; (telescope) regarder à travers

▸ **look to** VT FUS veiller à; (rely on) compter sur

▸ **look up** VI lever les yeux; (improve) s'améliorer ▸ VT (word) chercher; (friend) passer voir

▸ **look up to** VT FUS avoir du respect pour

lookout ['lʊkaʊt] N (tower etc) poste m de guet; (person) guetteur m; **to be on the ~ (for)** guetter

look-up table ['lʊkʌp-] N (Comput) table f à consulter

loom [luːm] N métier m à tisser ▸ VI (also: **loom up**) surgir; (: event) paraître imminent(e); (: threaten) menacer

loony ['luːnɪ] ADJ, N (inf) timbré(e), cinglé(e)

loop [luːp] N boucle f; (contraceptive) stérilet m ▸ VT: **to ~ sth round sth** passer qch autour de qch

loophole ['luːphəʊl] N (fig) porte f de sortie; échappatoire f

loose [luːs] ADJ (knot, screw) desserré(e); (stone) branlant(e); (clothes) vague, ample, lâche; (hair) dénoué(e), épars(e); (not firmly fixed) pas solide; (animal) en liberté, échappé(e); (life) dissolu(e); (morals, discipline) relâché(e); (thinking) peu rigoureux(-euse), vague; (*translation*) approximatif(-ive) ▶ N: **to be on the ~** être en liberté ▶ VT (*free: animal*) lâcher; (: *prisoner*) relâcher, libérer; (*slacken*) détendre, relâcher; desserrer; défaire; donner du mou a; donner du ballant à; (*BRIT: arrow*) tirer; **~ connection** (*Elec*) mauvais contact; **to be at a ~ end** *or* (*US*) **at ~ ends** (*fig*) ne pas trop savoir quoi faire; **to tie up ~ ends** (*fig*) mettre au point *or* régler les derniers détails

loose change N petite monnaie

loose chippings [-'tʃɪpɪŋz] NPL (*on road*) gravillons *mpl*

loose-fitting ['luːsfɪtɪŋ] ADJ (*clothes*) ample

loose-leaf ['luːsliːf] ADJ: **~ binder** *or* **folder** classeur *m* à feuilles *or* feuillets mobiles

loose-limbed [luːs'lɪmd] ADJ agile, souple

loosely ['luːslɪ] ADV sans serrer; (*imprecisely*) approximativement

loosely-knit ['luːslɪ'nɪt] ADJ élastique

loosen ['luːsn] VT desserrer, relâcher, défaire ▶ **loosen up** VI (*before game*) s'échauffer; (*inf: relax*) se détendre, se laisser aller

loot [luːt] N butin *m* ▶ VT piller

looter ['luːtə'] N pillard *m*, casseur *m*

looting ['luːtɪŋ] N pillage *m*

lop [lɔp]: **to ~ off** vt couper, trancher

lop-sided ['lɔp'saɪdɪd] ADJ de travers, asymétrique

lord [lɔːd] N seigneur *m*; **L~ Smith** lord Smith; **the L~** (*Rel*) le Seigneur; **my L~** (*to noble*) Monsieur le comte/le baron; (*to judge*) Monsieur le juge; (*to bishop*) Monseigneur; **good L~!** mon Dieu!

lordly ['lɔːdlɪ] ADJ noble, majestueux(-euse); (*arrogant*) hautain(e)

Lords ['lɔːdz] NPL (*BRIT Pol*): **the (House of) ~** la Chambre des Lords

lordship ['lɔːdʃɪp] N (*BRIT*): **your L~** Monsieur le comte (*or* le baron *or* le Juge)

lore [lɔː'] N tradition(s) *f(pl)*

lorry ['lɔrɪ] N (*BRIT*) camion *m*

lorry driver N (*BRIT*) camionneur *m*, routier *m*

lose [luːz] (*pt, pp* **lost** [lɔst]) VT perdre; (*opportunity*) manquer, perdre; (*pursuers*) distancer, semer ▶ VI perdre; **I've lost my wallet/passport** j'ai perdu mon portefeuille/ passeport; **to ~ (time)** (*clock*) retarder; **to ~ no time (in doing sth)** ne pas perdre de temps (à faire qch); **to get lost** vi (*person*) se perdre; **my watch has got lost** ma montre est perdue ▶ **lose out** VI être perdant(e)

loser ['luːzə'] N perdant(e); **to be a good/bad ~** être beau/mauvais joueur

loss [lɔs] N perte *f*; **to cut one's losses** limiter les dégâts; **to make a ~** enregistrer une perte; **to sell sth at a ~** vendre qch à perte; **to be at a ~** être perplexe *or* embarrassé(e); **to be at a ~ to do** se trouver incapable de faire

loss adjuster N (*Insurance*) responsable *mf* de l'évaluation des dommages

loss leader N (*Comm*) article sacrifié

lost [lɔst] PT, PP *of* **lose** ▶ ADJ perdu(e); **to get ~** vi se perdre; **I'm ~** je me suis perdu; **~ in thought** perdu dans ses pensées; **~ and found property** (*US*) objets trouvés; **~ and found** (*US*) (bureau *m* des) objets trouvés

lost property N (*BRIT*) objets trouvés; **~ office** *or* **department** (bureau *m* des) objets trouvés

lot [lɔt] N (*at auctions, set*) lot *m*; (*destiny*) sort *m*, destinée *f*; **the ~** (*everything*) le tout; (*everyone*) tous *mpl*, toutes *fpl*; **a ~** beaucoup; **a ~ of** beaucoup de; **lots of** des tas de; **to draw lots (for sth)** tirer (qch) au sort

lotion ['ləuʃən] N lotion *f*

lottery ['lɔtərɪ] N loterie *f*

loud [laud] ADJ bruyant(e), sonore; (*voice*) fort(e); (*condemnation etc*) vigoureux(-euse); (*gaudy*) voyant(e), tapageur(-euse) ▶ ADV (*speak etc*) fort; **out ~** tout haut

loud-hailer [laud'heɪlə'] N porte-voix *m inv*

loudly ['laudlɪ] ADV fort, bruyamment

loudspeaker [laud'spiːkə'] N haut-parleur *m*

lounge [laundʒ] N salon *m*; (*of airport*) salle *f*; (*BRIT: also:* **lounge bar**) (salle de) café *m or* bar *m* ▶ VI (*also:* **lounge about**, **lounge around**) se prélasser, paresser

lounge bar N (salle *f* de) bar *m*

lounge suit N (*BRIT*) complet *m*; (: *on invitation*) "tenue de ville"

louse [laus] (*pl* **lice** [laɪs]) N pou *m* ▶ **louse up** [lauz-] VT (*inf*) gâcher

lousy ['lauzɪ] (*inf*) ADJ (*bad quality*) infect(e), moche; **I feel ~** je suis mal fichu(e)

lout [laut] N rustre *m*, butor *m*

louvre, (*US*) **louver** ['luːvə'] ADJ (*door, window*) à claire-voie

lovable ['lʌvəbl] ADJ très sympathique; adorable

love [lʌv] N amour *m* ▶ VT aimer; (*caringly, kindly*) aimer beaucoup; **I ~ chocolate** j'adore le chocolat; **to ~ to do** aimer beaucoup *or* adorer faire; **I'd ~ to come** cela me ferait très plaisir (de venir); **"15 ~"** (*Tennis*) "15 à rien *or* zéro"; **to be/fall in ~ with** être/tomber amoureux(-euse) de; **to make ~** faire l'amour; **~ at first sight** le coup de foudre; **to send one's ~ to sb** adresser ses amitiés à qn; **~ from Anne, ~, Anne** affectueusement, Anne; **I ~ you** je t'aime

love affair N liaison (amoureuse)

love child N (*irreg*) enfant *mf* de l'amour

loved ones ['lʌvdwʌnz] NPL proches *mpl* et amis chers

love-hate relationship [lʌv'heɪt-] N rapport ambigu; **they have a ~** ils s'aiment et se détestent à la fois

love life N vie sentimentale

lovely ['lʌvlɪ] ADJ (*pretty*) ravissant(e); (*friend, wife*) charmant(e); (*holiday, surprise*) très agréable, merveilleux(-euse); **we had a ~ time** c'était vraiment très bien, nous avons eu beaucoup de plaisir

lover ['lʌvə'] N amant *m*; (*person in love*) amoureux(-euse); (*amateur*): **a ~ of** un(e) ami(e) de, un(e) amoureux(-euse) de

lovesick ['lʌvsɪk] ADJ qui se languit d'amour

love song ['lʌvsɔŋ] N chanson *f* d'amour

loving ['lʌvɪŋ] ADJ affectueux(-euse), tendre, aimant(e)

low [ləu] ADJ bas (basse); (*quality*) mauvais(e), inférieur(e) ▶ ADV bas ▶ N (*Meteorology*) dépression *f* ▶ VI (*cow*) mugir; **to feel ~** se sentir déprimé(e); **he's very ~** (*ill*) il est bien bas or très affaibli; **to turn (down)** ~ *vt* baisser; **to be ~ on** (*supplies etc*) être à court de; **to reach a new** or **an all-time ~** tomber au niveau le plus bas

low-alcohol [ləu'ælkəhɔl] ADJ à faible teneur en alcool, peu alcoolisé(e)

lowbrow ['ləubrau] ADJ sans prétentions intellectuelles

low-calorie ['ləu'kælərɪ] ADJ hypocalorique

low-carb [ləu'kɑ:b] ADJ (*inf*) pauvre en glucides

low-cut ['ləukʌt] ADJ (*dress*) décolleté(e)

low-down ['ləudaun] N (*inf*): **he gave me the ~ (on it)** il m'a mis au courant ▶ ADJ (*mean*) méprisable

lower ['ləuə^r] ADJ inférieur(e) ▶ VT baisser; (*resistance*) diminuer ▶ VI ['lauə^r] (*person, sky, clouds*) être menaçant; **to ~ at sb** jeter un regard mauvais or noir à qn; **to ~ o.s. to** s'abaisser à

lower sixth (BRIT) N (*Scol*) première *f*

low-fat ['ləu'fæt] ADJ maigre

low-key ['ləu'ki:] ADJ modéré(e), discret(-ète)

lowland N, **lowlands** NPL ['ləulənd(z)] plaine(s) *f(pl)*

low-level ['ləulɛvl] ADJ bas (basse); (*flying*) à basse altitude

low-loader ['ləuləudə^r] N semi-remorque *f* à plate-forme surbaissée

lowly ['ləulɪ] ADJ humble, modeste

low-lying [ləu'laɪɪŋ] ADJ à faible altitude

low-paid [ləu'peɪd] ADJ mal payé(e), aux salaires bas

low-rise ['ləuraɪz] ADJ bas(se), de faible hauteur

low-tech ['ləutɛk] ADJ sommaire

loyal ['lɔɪəl] ADJ loyal(e), fidèle

loyalist ['lɔɪəlɪst] N loyaliste *mf*

loyalty ['lɔɪəltɪ] N loyauté *f*, fidélité *f*

loyalty card N carte *f* de fidélité

lozenge ['lɔzɪndʒ] N (*Med*) pastille *f*; (*Geom*) losange *m*

LP N ABBR = **long-playing record**

LPG N ABBR (= *liquid petroleum gas*) GPL *m*

L-plates ['ɛlpleɪts] NPL (BRIT) plaques *fpl* (obligatoires) d'apprenti conducteur

LPN N ABBR (US: = *Licensed Practical Nurse*) infirmier(-ière) diplômé(e)

LRAM N ABBR (BRIT) = **Licentiate of the Royal Academy of Music**

LSAT N ABBR (US) = **Law School Admissions Test**

LSD N ABBR (= *lysergic acid diethylamide*) LSD *m*; (BRIT: = *pounds, shillings and pence*) système monétaire en usage en GB jusqu'en 1971

LSE N ABBR = **London School of Economics**

LT ABBR (*Elec*: = *low tension*) BT

Lt ABBR (= *lieutenant*) Lt.

Ltd ABBR (*Comm*: = *limited*) ≈ SA

lubricant ['lu:brɪkənt] N lubrifiant *m*

lubricate ['lu:brɪkeɪt] VT lubrifier, graisser

lucid ['lu:sɪd] ADJ lucide

lucidity [lu:'sɪdɪtɪ] N lucidité *f*

luck [lʌk] N chance *f*; **bad ~** malchance *f*, malheur *m*; **to be in ~** avoir de la chance; **to be**

out of ~ ne pas avoir de chance; **good ~!** bonne chance!; **bad** or **hard** or **tough ~!** pas de chance!

luckily ['lʌkɪlɪ] ADV heureusement, par bonheur

luckless ['lʌklɪs] ADJ (*person*) malchanceux(-euse); (*trip*) marqué(e) par la malchance

lucky ['lʌkɪ] ADJ (*person*) qui a de la chance; (*coincidence*) heureux(-euse); (*number etc*) qui porte bonheur

lucrative ['lu:krətɪv] ADJ lucratif(-ive), rentable, qui rapporte

ludicrous ['lu:dɪkrəs] ADJ ridicule, absurde

ludo ['lu:dəu] N jeu *m* des petits chevaux

lug [lʌg] VT traîner, tirer

luggage ['lʌgɪdʒ] N bagages *mpl*; **our ~ hasn't arrived** nos bagages ne sont pas arrivés; **could you send someone to collect our ~?** pourriez-vous envoyer quelqu'un chercher nos bagages?

luggage lockers NPL consigne *f* automatique

luggage rack N (*in train*) porte-bagages *m inv*; (*: made of string*) filet *m* à bagages; (*on car*) galerie *f*

luggage van, (US) **luggage car** N (*Rail*) fourgon *m* (à bagages)

lugubrious [lu'gu:brɪəs] ADJ lugubre

lukewarm ['lu:kwɔ:m] ADJ tiède

lull [lʌl] N accalmie *f*; (*in conversation*) pause *f* ▶ VT: **to ~ sb to sleep** bercer qn pour qu'il s'endorme; **to be lulled into a false sense of security** s'endormir dans une fausse sécurité

lullaby ['lʌləbaɪ] N berceuse *f*

lumbago [lʌm'beɪgəu] N lumbago *m*

lumber ['lʌmbə^r] N (*wood*) bois *m* de charpente; (*junk*) bric-à-brac *m inv* ▶ VT (BRIT *inf*): **to ~ sb with sth/sb** coller or refiler qch/qn à qn ▶ VI (*also*: **lumber about, lumber along**) marcher pesamment

lumberjack ['lʌmbədʒæk] N bûcheron *m*

lumber room N (BRIT) débarras *m*

lumber yard N entrepôt *m* de bois

luminous ['lu:mɪnəs] ADJ lumineux(-euse)

lump [lʌmp] N morceau *m*; (*in sauce*) grumeau *m*; (*swelling*) grosseur *f* ▶ VT (*also*: **lump together**) réunir, mettre en tas

lump sum N somme globale or forfaitaire

lumpy ['lʌmpɪ] ADJ (*sauce*) qui a des grumeaux; (*bed*) défoncé(e), peu confortable

lunacy ['lu:nəsɪ] N démence *f*, folie *f*

lunar ['lu:nə^r] ADJ lunaire

lunatic ['lu:nətɪk] N fou (folle), dément(e) ▶ ADJ fou (folle), dément(e)

lunatic asylum N asile *m* d'aliénés

lunch [lʌntʃ] N déjeuner *m* ▶ VI déjeuner; **it is his ~ hour** c'est l'heure où il déjeune; **to invite sb to** or **for ~** inviter qn à déjeuner

lunch break, lunch hour N pause *f* de midi, heure *f* du déjeuner

luncheon ['lʌntʃən] N déjeuner *m*

luncheon meat N sorte de saucisson

luncheon voucher N chèque-repas *m*, ticket-repas *m*

lunchtime ['lʌntʃtaɪm] N: **it's ~** c'est l'heure du déjeuner

lung [lʌŋ] N poumon *m*

lung cancer N cancer *m* du poumon
lunge [lʌndʒ] VI (*also*: **lunge forward**) faire un
  mouvement brusque en avant; **to ~ at sb**
  envoyer *or* assener un coup à qn
lupin ['luːpɪn] N lupin *m*
lurch [ləːtʃ] VI vaciller, tituber ▶ N écart *m*
  brusque, embardée *f*; **to leave sb in the ~**
  laisser qn se débrouiller *or* se dépêtrer tout(e)
  seul(e)
lure [luəʳ] N (*attraction*) attrait *m*, charme *m*;
  (*in hunting*) appât *m*, leurre *m* ▶ VT attirer *or*
  persuader par la ruse
lurid ['luərɪd] ADJ affreux(-euse), atroce
lurk [ləːk] VI se tapir, se cacher
luscious ['lʌʃəs] ADJ succulent(e), appétissant(e)
lush [lʌʃ] ADJ luxuriant(e)
lust [lʌst] N (*sexual*) désir (sexuel); (*Rel*) luxure *f*;
  (*fig*): **~ for** soif *f* de
  ▶ **lust after** VT FUS convoiter, désirer
luster ['lʌstəʳ] N (*US*) = **lustre**
lustful ['lʌstful] ADJ lascif(-ive)

lustre, (*US*) **luster** ['lʌstəʳ] N lustre *m*, brillant *m*
lusty ['lʌstɪ] ADJ vigoureux(-euse), robuste
lute [luːt] N luth *m*
Luxembourg ['lʌksəmbəːg] N Luxembourg *m*
luxuriant [lʌg'zjuərɪənt] ADJ luxuriant(e)
luxurious [lʌg'zjuərɪəs] ADJ luxueux(-euse)
luxury ['lʌkʃərɪ] N luxe *m* ▶ CPD de luxe
LV N ABBR (*Brit*) = **luncheon voucher**
LW ABBR (*Radio*: = *long wave*) GO
Lycra® ['laɪkrə] N Lycra® *m*
lying ['laɪɪŋ] N mensonge(s) *m(pl)* ▶ ADJ
  (*statement, story*) mensonger(-ère), faux (fausse);
  (*person*) menteur(-euse)
lynch [lɪntʃ] VT lyncher
lynx [lɪŋks] N lynx *m inv*
Lyons ['ljɔ̃] N Lyon
lyre ['laɪəʳ] N lyre *f*
lyric ['lɪrɪk] ADJ lyrique
lyrical ['lɪrɪkl] ADJ lyrique
lyricism ['lɪrɪsɪzəm] N lyrisme *m*
lyrics ['lɪrɪks] NPL (*of song*) paroles *fpl*

Mm

M, m [ɛm] N (letter) M, m m; **M for Mary**, (US) **M for Mike** M comme Marcel

M N ABBR BRIT: = **motorway; the M8** ≈ l'A8 ▶ ABBR (= medium) M

m. ABBR (= metre) m; (= million) M; (= mile) mi

ma [mɑː] (inf) N maman f

M.A. N ABBR (Scol) = **Master of Arts** ▶ ABBR (US) = **military academy; Massachusetts**

mac [mæk] N (BRIT) imper(méable m) m

macabre [məˈkɑːbrə] ADJ macabre

macaroni [mækəˈrəʊnɪ] N macaronis mpl

macaroon [mækəˈruːn] N macaron m

mace [meɪs] N masse f; (spice) macis m

Macedonia [mæsɪˈdəʊnɪə] N Macédoine f

Macedonian [mæsɪˈdəʊnɪən] ADJ macédonien(ne) ▶ N Macédonien(ne); (Ling) macédonien m

machinations [mækɪˈneɪʃənz] NPL machinations fpl, intrigues fpl

machine [məˈʃiːn] N machine f ▶ VT (dress etc) coudre à la machine; (Tech) usiner

machine code N (Comput) code m machine

machine gun N mitrailleuse f

machine language N (Comput) langage m machine

machine-readable [məˈʃiːnriːdəbl] ADJ (Comput) exploitable par une machine

machinery [məˈʃiːnərɪ] N machinerie f, machines fpl; (fig) mécanisme(s) m(pl)

machine shop N atelier m d'usinage

machine tool N machine-outil f

machine washable ADJ (garment) lavable en machine

machinist [məˈʃiːnɪst] N machiniste mf

macho [ˈmætʃəʊ] ADJ macho m inv

mackerel [ˈmækrl] N (pl inv) maquereau m

mackintosh [ˈmækɪntɔʃ] N (BRIT) imperméable m

macro... [ˈmækrəʊ] PREFIX macro...

macro-economics [ˈmækrəʊiːkəˈnɔmɪks] N macro-économie f

mad [mæd] ADJ fou (folle); (foolish) insensé(e); (angry) furieux(-euse); **to go ~** devenir fou; **to be ~ (keen) about** or **on sth** (inf) être follement passionné de qch, être fou de qch

Madagascar [mædəˈgæskəʳ] N Madagascar m

madam [ˈmædəm] N madame f; **yes ~** oui Madame; **M~ Chairman** Madame la Présidente

madcap [ˈmædkæp] ADJ (inf) écervelé(e)

mad cow disease N maladie f des vaches folles

madden [ˈmædn] VT exaspérer

maddening [ˈmædnɪŋ] ADJ exaspérant(e)

made [meɪd] PT, PP of **make**

Madeira [məˈdɪərə] N (Geo) Madère f; (wine) madère m

made-to-measure [ˈmeɪdtəˈmɛʒəʳ] ADJ (BRIT) fait(e) sur mesure

made-up [ˈmeɪdʌp] ADJ (story) inventé(e), fabriqué(e)

madhouse [ˈmædhaʊs] N (also fig) maison f de fous

madly [ˈmædlɪ] ADV follement; **~ in love** éperdument amoureux(-euse)

madman [ˈmædmən] N (irreg) fou m, aliéné m

madness [ˈmædnɪs] N folie f

Madrid [məˈdrɪd] N Madrid

Mafia [ˈmæfɪə] N maf(f)ia f

mag [mæg] N ABBR (BRIT inf: = magazine) magazine m

magazine [mægəˈziːn] N (Press) magazine m, revue f; (Radio, TV) magazine; (Mil: store) dépôt m, arsenal m; (of firearm) magasin m

maggot [ˈmægət] N ver m, asticot m

magic [ˈmædʒɪk] N magie f ▶ ADJ magique

magical [ˈmædʒɪkl] ADJ magique; (experience, evening) merveilleux(-euse)

magician [məˈdʒɪʃən] N magicien(ne)

magistrate [ˈmædʒɪstreɪt] N magistrat m; juge m; **magistrates' court** (BRIT) ≈ tribunal m d'instance

magnanimous [mægˈnænɪməs] ADJ magnanime

magnate [ˈmægneɪt] N magnat m

magnesium [mægˈniːzɪəm] N magnésium m

magnet [ˈmægnɪt] N aimant m

magnetic [mægˈnɛtɪk] ADJ magnétique

magnetic disk N (Comput) disque m magnétique

magnetic tape N bande f magnétique

magnetism [ˈmægnɪtɪzəm] N magnétisme m

magnification [mægnɪfɪˈkeɪʃən] N grossissement m

magnificence [mægˈnɪfɪsns] N magnificence f

magnificent [mægˈnɪfɪsnt] ADJ superbe, magnifique; (splendid: robe, building) somptueux(-euse), magnifique

m

magnify ['mægnɪfaɪ] VT grossir; (sound) amplifier

magnifying glass ['mægnɪfaɪɪŋ-] N loupe f

magnitude ['mægnɪtjuːd] N ampleur f

magnolia [mæg'nəʊlɪə] N magnolia m

magpie ['mægpaɪ] N pie f

mahogany [mə'hɒgənɪ] N acajou m ▶ CPD en (bois d')acajou

maid [meɪd] N bonne f; (in hotel) femme f de chambre; **old ~** (pej) vieille fille

maiden ['meɪdn] N jeune fille f ▶ ADJ (aunt etc) non mariée; (speech, voyage) inaugural(e)

maiden name N nom m de jeune fille

mail [meɪl] N poste f; (letters) courrier m ▶ VT envoyer (par la poste); **by ~** par la poste

mailbag ['meɪlbæg] N (sack) sac postal; (postman's) sacoche f

mailbox ['meɪlbɒks] N (US, also Comput) boîte f aux lettres

mailing list ['meɪlɪŋ-] N liste f d'adresses

mailman ['meɪlmæn] N (irreg) (US) facteur m

mail-order ['meɪlɔːdəʳ] N vente f or achat m par correspondance ▶ CPD: **~ firm** or **house** maison f de vente par correspondance

mailshot ['meɪlʃɒt] N (BRIT) mailing m

mail train N train postal

mail truck N (US Aut) = **mail van**

mail van N (BRIT: Aut) voiture f or fourgonnette f des postes; (: Rail) wagon-poste m

maim [meɪm] VT mutiler

main [meɪn] ADJ principal(e) ▶ N (pipe) conduite principale, canalisation f; **the mains** (Elec) le secteur; **the ~ thing** l'essentiel m; **in the ~** dans l'ensemble

main course N (Culin) plat m principal

mainframe ['meɪnfreɪm] N (also: **mainframe computer**) (gros) ordinateur, unité centrale

mainland ['meɪnlənd] N continent m

mainline ['meɪnlaɪn] ADJ (Rail) de grande ligne ▶ VT (drugs slang) se shooter à ▶ VI (drugs slang) se shooter

main line N (Rail) grande ligne

mainly ['meɪnlɪ] ADV principalement, surtout

main road N grand axe, route nationale

mainstay ['meɪnsteɪ] N (fig) pilier m

mainstream ['meɪnstriːm] N (fig) courant principal

main street N rue f principale

maintain [meɪn'teɪn] VT entretenir; (continue) maintenir, préserver; (affirm) soutenir; **to ~ that …** soutenir que …

maintenance ['meɪntənəns] N entretien m; (Law: alimony) pension f alimentaire

maintenance contract N contrat m d'entretien

maintenance order N (Law) obligation f alimentaire

maisonette [meɪzə'nɛt] N (BRIT) appartement m en duplex

maize [meɪz] N (BRIT) maïs m

Maj. ABBR (Mil) = **major**

majestic [mə'dʒɛstɪk] ADJ majestueux(-euse)

majesty ['mædʒɪstɪ] N majesté f; (title): **Your M~** Votre Majesté

major ['meɪdʒəʳ] N (Mil) commandant m ▶ ADJ (important) important(e); (most important) principal(e); (Mus) majeur(e) ▶ VI (US Scol): **to ~ (in)** se spécialiser (en); **a ~ operation** (Med) une grosse opération

Majorca [mə'jɔːkə] N Majorque f

major general N (Mil) général m de division

majority [mə'dʒɒrɪtɪ] N majorité f ▶ CPD (verdict, holding) majoritaire

make [meɪk] (pt, pp **made** [meɪd]) VT faire; (manufacture) faire, fabriquer; (earn) gagner; (decision) prendre; (friend) se faire; (speech) prononcer; (cause to be): **to ~ sb sad** etc rendre qn triste etc; (force): **to ~ sb do sth** obliger qn à faire qch, faire faire qch à qn; (equal): **2 and 2 ~ 4** 2 et 2 font 4 ▶ N (manufacture) fabrication f; (brand) marque f; **to ~ the bed** faire le lit; **to ~ a fool of sb** (ridicule) ridiculiser qn; (trick) avoir or duper qn; **to ~ a profit** faire un or des bénéfice(s); **to ~ a loss** essuyer une perte; **to ~ it** (in time etc) y arriver; (succeed) réussir; **what time do you ~ it?** quelle heure avez-vous?; **I ~ it £249** d'après mes calculs ça fait 249 livres; **to be made of** être en; **to ~ good** VI (succeed) faire son chemin, réussir; VT (deficit) combler; (losses) compenser; **to ~ do with** se contenter de; se débrouiller avec
  ▶ **make for** VT FUS (place) se diriger vers
  ▶ **make off** VI filer
  ▶ **make out** VT (write out: cheque) faire; (decipher) déchiffrer; (understand) comprendre; (see) distinguer; (claim, imply) prétendre, vouloir faire croire; **to ~ out a case for sth** présenter des arguments solides en faveur de qch
  ▶ **make over** VT (assign): **to ~ over (to)** céder (à), transférer (au nom de)
  ▶ **make up** VT (invent) inventer, imaginer; (constitute) constituer; (parcel, bed) faire ▶ VI se réconcilier; (with cosmetics) se maquiller, se farder; **to be made up of** se composer de
  ▶ **make up for** VT FUS compenser; (lost time) rattraper

make-believe ['meɪkbɪliːv] N: **a world of ~** un monde de chimères or d'illusions; **it's just ~** c'est de la fantaisie; c'est une illusion

makeover ['meɪkəʊvəʳ] N (by beautician) soins mpl de maquillage; (change of image) changement m d'image; **to give sb a ~** relooker qn

maker ['meɪkəʳ] N fabricant m; (of film, programme) réalisateur(-trice)

makeshift ['meɪkʃɪft] ADJ provisoire, improvisé(e)

make-up ['meɪkʌp] N maquillage m

make-up bag N trousse f de maquillage

make-up remover N démaquillant m

making ['meɪkɪŋ] N (fig): **in the ~** en formation or gestation; **to have the makings of** (actor, athlete) avoir l'étoffe de

maladjusted [mælə'dʒʌstɪd] ADJ inadapté(e)

malaise [mæ'leɪz] N malaise m

malaria [mə'lɛərɪə] N malaria f, paludisme m

Malawi [mə'lɑːwɪ] N Malawi m

Malay [mə'leɪ] ADJ malais(e) ▶ N (person) Malais(e); (language) malais m

Malaya [mə'leɪə] N Malaisie f
Malayan [mə'leɪən] ADJ, N = **Malay**
Malaysia [mə'leɪzɪə] N Malaisie f
Malaysian [mə'leɪzɪən] ADJ malaisien(ne) ▶ N Malaisien(ne)
Maldives ['mɔːldaɪvz] NPL: **the ~** les Maldives fpl
male [meɪl] N (Biol, Elec) mâle m ▶ ADJ (sex, attitude) masculin(e); (animal) mâle; (child etc) du sexe masculin; **~ and female students** étudiants et étudiantes
male chauvinist N phallocrate m
male nurse N infirmier m
malevolence [mə'levələns] N malveillance f
malevolent [mə'levələnt] ADJ malveillant(e)
malfunction [mæl'fʌŋkʃən] N fonctionnement défectueux
malice ['mælɪs] N méchanceté f, malveillance f
malicious [mə'lɪʃəs] ADJ méchant(e), malveillant(e); (Law) avec intention criminelle
malign [mə'laɪn] VT diffamer, calomnier
malignant [mə'lɪɡnənt] ADJ (Med) malin(-igne)
malingerer [mə'lɪŋɡərər] N simulateur(-trice)
mall [mɔːl] N (also: **shopping mall**) centre commercial
malleable ['mælɪəbl] ADJ malléable
mallet ['mælɪt] N maillet m
malnutrition [mælnjuː'trɪʃən] N malnutrition f
malpractice [mæl'præktɪs] N faute professionnelle; (négligence f
malt [mɔːlt] N malt m ▶ CPD (whisky) pur malt
Malta ['mɔːltə] N Malte f
Maltese [mɔːl'tiːz] ADJ maltais(e) ▶ N (pl inv) Maltais(e); (Ling) maltais m
maltreat [mæl'triːt] VT maltraiter
malware ['mælwɛər] N (Comput) logiciel m malveillant
mammal ['mæml] N mammifère m
mammoth ['mæməθ] N mammouth m ▶ ADJ géant(e), monstre
man [mæn] (pl **men** [mɛn]) N homme m; (Sport) joueur m; (Chess) pièce f; (Draughts) pion m ▶ VT (Naut: ship) garnir d'hommes; (machine) assurer le fonctionnement de; (Mil: gun) servir; (: post) être de service à; **an old ~** un vieillard; **~ and wife** mari et femme
Man. ABBR (CANADA) = **Manitoba**
manacles ['mænəklz] NPL menottes fpl
manage ['mænɪdʒ] VI se débrouiller; (succeed) y arriver, réussir ▶ VT (business) gérer; (team, operation) diriger; (control: ship) manier, manœuvrer; (: person) savoir s'y prendre avec; (device, things to do, carry etc) arriver à se débrouiller avec, s'en tirer avec; **to ~ to do** se débrouiller pour faire; (succeed) réussir à faire
manageable ['mænɪdʒəbl] ADJ maniable; (task etc) faisable; (number) raisonnable
management ['mænɪdʒmənt] N (running) administration f, direction f; (people in charge: of business, firm) dirigeants mpl, cadres mpl; (: of hotel, shop, theatre) direction; **"under new ~"** "changement de gérant", "changement de propriétaire"
management accounting N comptabilité f de gestion

management consultant N conseiller(-ère) de direction
manager ['mænɪdʒər] N (of business) directeur m; (of institution etc) administrateur m; (of department, unit) responsable mf, chef m; (of hotel etc) gérant m; (Sport) manager m; (of artist) impresario m; **sales ~** responsable or chef des ventes
manageress [mænɪdʒə'rɛs] N directrice f; (of hotel etc) gérante f
managerial [mænɪ'dʒɪərɪəl] ADJ directorial(e); (skills) de cadre, de gestion; **~ staff** cadres mpl
managing director ['mænɪdʒɪŋ-] N directeur général
Mancunian [mæŋ'kjuːnɪən] ADJ de Manchester ▶ N habitant(e) de Manchester; natif(-ive) de Manchester
mandarin ['mændərɪn] N (also: **mandarin orange**) mandarine f; (person) mandarin m
mandate ['mændeɪt] N mandat m
mandatory ['mændətərɪ] ADJ obligatoire; (powers etc) mandataire
mandolin, mandoline ['mændəlɪn] N mandoline f
mane [meɪn] N crinière f
maneuver [mə'nuːvər] (US) N = **manoeuvre**
manfully ['mænfəlɪ] ADV vaillamment
manganese [mæŋɡə'niːz] N manganèse m
mangetout ['mɒnʒ'tuː] N mange-tout m inv
mangle ['mæŋɡl] VT déchiqueter; mutiler ▶ N essoreuse f; calandre f
mango ['mæŋɡəu] (pl **mangoes**) N mangue f
mangrove ['mæŋɡrəuv] N palétuvier m
mangy ['meɪndʒɪ] ADJ galeux(-euse)
manhandle ['mænhændl] VT (mistreat) maltraiter, malmener; (move by hand) manutentionner
manhole ['mænhəul] N trou m d'homme
manhood ['mænhud] N (age) âge m d'homme; (manliness) virilité f
man-hour ['mænauər] N heure-homme f, heure f de main-d'œuvre
manhunt ['mænhʌnt] N chasse f à l'homme
mania ['meɪnɪə] N manie f
maniac ['meɪnɪæk] N maniaque mf; (fig) fou (folle)
manic ['mænɪk] ADJ maniaque
manic-depressive ['mænɪkdɪ'prɛsɪv] ADJ, N (Psych) maniaco-dépressif(-ive)
manicure ['mænɪkjuər] N manucure f ▶ VT (person) faire les mains à
manicure set N trousse f à ongles
manifest ['mænɪfɛst] VT manifester ▶ ADJ manifeste, évident(e) ▶ N (Aviat, Naut) manifeste m
manifestation [mænɪfɛs'teɪʃən] N manifestation f
manifesto [mænɪ'fɛstəu] N (Pol) manifeste m
manifold ['mænɪfəuld] ADJ multiple, varié(e) ▶ N (Aut etc): **exhaust ~** collecteur m d'échappement
Manila [mə'nɪlə] N Manille, Manila
manila [mə'nɪlə] ADJ: **~ paper** papier m bulle
manipulate [mə'nɪpjuleɪt] VT manipuler; (system, situation) exploiter

m

manipulation [mənɪpjuˈleɪʃən] N manipulation f

mankind [mænˈkaɪnd] N humanité f, genre humain

manliness [ˈmænlɪnɪs] N virilité f

manly [ˈmænlɪ] ADJ viril(e)

man-made [ˈmænˈmeɪd] ADJ artificiel(le); (fibre) synthétique

manna [ˈmænə] N manne f

mannequin [ˈmænɪkɪn] N mannequin m

manner [ˈmænəʳ] N manière f, façon f; (behaviour) attitude f, comportement m; **manners** NPL: **(good) manners** (bonnes) manières; **bad manners** mauvaises manières; **all ~ of** toutes sortes de

mannerism [ˈmænərɪzəm] N particularité f de langage (or de comportement), tic m

mannerly [ˈmænəlɪ] ADJ poli(e), courtois(e)

manoeuvrable, (US) **maneuverable** [məˈnuːvrəbl] ADJ facile à manœuvrer

manoeuvre, (US) **maneuver** [məˈnuːvəʳ] VT (move) manœuvrer; (manipulate: person) manipuler; (: situation) exploiter ▸ N manœuvre f; **to ~ sb into doing sth** manipuler qn pour lui faire faire qch

manor [ˈmænəʳ] N (also: **manor house**) manoir m

manpower [ˈmænpaʊəʳ] N main-d'œuvre f

manservant [ˈmænsəːvənt] (pl **menservants** [ˈmɛn-]) N domestique m

mansion [ˈmænʃən] N château m, manoir m

manslaughter [ˈmænslɔːtəʳ] N homicide m involontaire

mantelpiece [ˈmæntlpiːs] N cheminée f

mantle [ˈmæntl] N cape f; (fig) manteau m

man-to-man [ˈmæntəˈmæn] ADJ, ADV d'homme à homme

manual [ˈmænjʊəl] ADJ manuel(le) ▸ N manuel m

manual worker N travailleur manuel

manufacture [mænjuˈfæktʃəʳ] VT fabriquer ▸ N fabrication f

manufactured goods [mænjuˈfæktʃəd-] NPL produits manufacturés

manufacturer [mænjuˈfæktʃərəʳ] N fabricant m

manufacturing industries [mænjuˈfæktʃərɪŋ-] NPL industries fpl de transformation

manure [məˈnjʊəʳ] N fumier m; (artificial) engrais m

manuscript [ˈmænjuskrɪpt] N manuscrit m

many [ˈmɛnɪ] ADJ beaucoup de, de nombreux(-euses) ▸ PRON beaucoup, un grand nombre; **how ~?** combien?; **a great ~** un grand nombre (de); **too ~ difficulties** trop de difficultés; **twice as ~** deux fois plus; **~ a ...** bien des ..., plus d'un(e) ...

Maori [ˈmaʊrɪ] N Maori(e) ▸ ADJ maori(e)

map [mæp] N carte f; (of town) plan m ▸ VT dresser la carte de; **can you show it to me on the ~?** pouvez-vous me l'indiquer sur la carte?
▸ **map out** VT tracer; (fig: task) planifier; (career, holiday) organiser, préparer (à l'avance); (: essay) faire le plan de

maple [ˈmeɪpl] N érable m

mar [mɑːʳ] VT gâcher, gâter

marathon [ˈmærəθən] N marathon m ▸ ADJ: **a ~ session** une séance-marathon

marathon runner N coureur(-euse) de marathon, marathonien(ne)

marauder [məˈrɔːdəʳ] N maraudeur(-euse)

marble [ˈmɑːbl] N marbre m; (toy) bille f; **marbles** NPL (game) billes

March [mɑːtʃ] N mars m; see also **July**

march [mɑːtʃ] VI marcher au pas; (demonstrators) défiler ▸ N marche f; (demonstration) manifestation f; **to ~ out of/into** etc sortir de/ entrer dans etc (de manière décidée ou impulsive)

marcher [ˈmɑːtʃəʳ] N (demonstrator) manifestant(e), marcheur(-euse)

marching [ˈmɑːtʃɪŋ] N: **to give sb his ~ orders** (fig) renvoyer qn; envoyer promener qn

march-past [ˈmɑːtʃpɑːst] N défilé m

mare [mɛəʳ] N jument f

marg. [mɑːdʒ] N ABBR (inf) = **margarine**

margarine [mɑːdʒəˈriːn] N margarine f

margin [ˈmɑːdʒɪn] N marge f

marginal [ˈmɑːdʒɪnl] ADJ marginal(e); **~ seat** (Pol) siège disputé

marginally [ˈmɑːdʒɪnəlɪ] ADV très légèrement, sensiblement

marigold [ˈmærɪɡəʊld] N souci m

marijuana [mærɪˈwɑːnə] N marijuana f

marina [məˈriːnə] N marina f

marinade N [mærɪˈneɪd] marinade f ▸ VT [ˈmærɪneɪd] = **marinate**

marinate [ˈmærɪneɪt] VT (faire) mariner

marine [məˈriːn] ADJ marin(e) ▸ N fusilier marin; (US) marine m

marine insurance N assurance f maritime

marital [ˈmærɪtl] ADJ matrimonial(e)

marital status N situation f de famille

maritime [ˈmærɪtaɪm] ADJ maritime

maritime law N droit m maritime

marjoram [ˈmɑːdʒərəm] N marjolaine f

mark [mɑːk] N marque f; (of skid etc) trace f; (Brit Scol) note f; (Sport) cible f; (currency) mark m; (Brit Tech): **M~ 2/3** 2ème/3ème série f or version f; (oven temperature): **(gas) ~ 4** thermostat m 4 ▸ VT (Sport: player) marquer; (stain) tacher; (Brit Scol) corriger, noter; (also: **punctuation marks**) signes mpl de ponctuation; **to ~ time** marquer le pas; **to be quick off the ~ (in doing)** (fig) ne pas perdre de temps (pour faire); **up to the ~** (in efficiency) à la hauteur
▸ **mark down** VT (prices, goods) démarquer, réduire le prix de
▸ **mark off** VT (tick off) cocher, pointer
▸ **mark out** VT désigner
▸ **mark up** VT (price) majorer

marked [mɑːkt] ADJ (obvious) marqué(e), net(te)

markedly [ˈmɑːkɪdlɪ] ADV visiblement, manifestement

marker [ˈmɑːkəʳ] N (sign) jalon m; (bookmark) signet m

market [ˈmɑːkɪt] N marché m ▸ VT (Comm) commercialiser; **to be on the ~** être sur le marché; **on the open ~** en vente libre; **to play the ~** jouer à la or spéculer en Bourse

marketable ['mɑ:kɪtəbl] ADJ commercialisable

market analysis N analyse f de marché

market day N jour m de marché

market demand N besoins mpl du marché

market economy N économie f de marché

market forces NPL tendances fpl du marché

market garden N (BRIT) jardin maraîcher

marketing ['mɑ:kɪtɪŋ] N marketing m

marketplace ['mɑ:kɪtpleɪs] N place f du marché; (Comm) marché m

market price N prix marchand

market research N étude f de marché

market value N valeur marchande; valeur du marché

marking ['mɑ:kɪŋ] N (on animal) marque f, tache f; (on road) signalisation f

marksman ['mɑ:ksmən] N (irreg) tireur m d'élite

marksmanship ['mɑ:ksmənʃɪp] N adresse f au tir

mark-up ['mɑ:kʌp] N (Comm: margin) marge f (bénéficiaire); (: increase) majoration f

marmalade ['mɑ:məleɪd] N confiture f d'oranges

maroon [mə'ru:n] VT: **to be marooned** être abandonné(e); (fig) être bloqué(e) ▶ ADJ (colour) bordeaux inv

marquee [mɑ:'ki:] N chapiteau m

marquess, marquis ['mɑ:kwɪs] N marquis m

Marrakech, Marrakesh [mærə'keʃ] N Marrakech

marriage ['mærɪdʒ] N mariage m

marriage bureau N agence matrimoniale

marriage certificate N extrait m d'acte de mariage

marriage guidance, (US) marriage counseling N conseils conjugaux

marriage of convenience N mariage m de convenance

married ['mærɪd] ADJ marié(e); (life, love) conjugal(e)

marrow ['mærəu] N (of bone) moelle f; (vegetable) courge f

marry ['mærɪ] VT épouser, se marier avec; (subj: father, priest etc) marier ▶ VI (also: **get married**) se marier

Mars [mɑ:z] N (planet) Mars f

Marseilles [mɑ:'seɪ] N Marseille

marsh [mɑ:ʃ] N marais m, marécage m

marshal ['mɑ:ʃl] N maréchal m; (US: fire, police) ≈ capitaine m; (for demonstration, meeting) membre m du service d'ordre ▶ VT rassembler

marshalling yard ['mɑ:ʃlɪŋ-] N (Rail) gare f de triage

marshmallow [mɑ:ʃ'mæləu] N (Bot) guimauve f; (sweet) (pâte f de) guimauve

marshy ['mɑ:ʃɪ] ADJ marécageux(-euse)

marsupial [mɑ:'su:pɪəl] ADJ marsupial(e) ▶ N marsupial m

martial ['mɑ:ʃl] ADJ martial(e)

martial arts NPL arts martiaux

martial law N loi martiale

Martian ['mɑ:ʃən] N Martien(ne)

martin ['mɑ:tɪn] N (also: **house martin**) martinet m

martyr ['mɑ:təʳ] N martyr(e) ▶ VT martyriser

martyrdom ['mɑ:tədəm] N martyre m

marvel ['mɑ:vl] N merveille f ▶ VI: **to ~ (at)** s'émerveiller (de)

marvellous, (US) marvelous ['mɑ:vləs] ADJ merveilleux(-euse)

Marxism ['mɑ:ksɪzəm] N marxisme m

Marxist ['mɑ:ksɪst] ADJ, N marxiste (mf)

marzipan ['mɑ:zɪpæn] N pâte f d'amandes

mascara [mæs'kɑ:rə] N mascara m

mascot ['mæskət] N mascotte f

masculine ['mæskjulɪn] ADJ masculin(e) ▶ N masculin m

masculinity [mæskju'lɪnɪtɪ] N masculinité f

MASH [mæʃ] N ABBR (US Mil) = **mobile army surgical hospital**

mash [mæʃ] VT (Culin) faire une purée de

mashed potato N, **mashed potatoes** NPL purée f de pommes de terre

mask [mɑ:sk] N masque m ▶ VT masquer

masochism ['mæsəukɪzəm] N masochisme m

masochist ['mæsəukɪst] N masochiste mf

mason ['meɪsn] N (also: **stonemason**) maçon m; (also: **freemason**) franc-maçon m

masonic [mə'sɔnɪk] ADJ maçonnique

masonry ['meɪsnrɪ] N maçonnerie f

masquerade [mæskə'reɪd] N bal masqué; (fig) mascarade f ▶ VI: **to ~ as** se faire passer pour

mass [mæs] N multitude f, masse f; (Physics) masse; (Rel) messe f ▶ CPD (communication) de masse; (unemployment) massif(-ive) ▶ VI se masser; **masses** NPL: **the masses** les masses; **masses of** (inf) des tas de; **to go to ~** aller à la messe

Mass. ABBR (US) = **Massachusetts**

massacre ['mæsəkəʳ] N massacre m ▶ VT massacrer

massage ['mæsɑ:ʒ] N massage m ▶ VT masser

massive ['mæsɪv] ADJ énorme, massif(-ive)

mass market N marché m grand public

mass media NPL mass-media mpl

mass meeting N rassemblement m de masse

mass-produce ['mæsprə'dju:s] VT fabriquer en série

mass production N fabrication f en série

mast [mɑ:st] N mât m; (Radio, TV) pylône m

mastectomy [mæs'tɛktəmɪ] N mastectomie f

master ['mɑ:stəʳ] N maître m; (in secondary school) professeur m; (in primary school) instituteur m; (title for boys): **M~ X** Monsieur X ▶ VT maîtriser; (learn) apprendre à fond; (understand) posséder parfaitement or à fond; **~ of ceremonies (MC)** n maître des cérémonies; **M~ of Arts/Science (MA/MSc)** n ≈ titulaire mf d'une maîtrise (en lettres/science); **M~ of Arts/Science degree (MA/MSc)** n ≈ maîtrise f; **M~'s degree** n ≈ maîtrise; voir article

> Le *Master's degree* est un diplôme que l'on prépare en général après le *Bachelor's degree*, bien que certaines universités décernent un *Master's* au lieu d'un *Bachelor's*. Il consiste soit à suivre des cours, soit à rédiger un mémoire à partir d'une recherche personnelle, soit encore les deux. Les principaux masters

sont le *MA* (*Master of Arts*), et le *MSc* (*Master of Science*), qui comprennent cours et mémoire, et le *MLitt* (*Master of Letters*) et le *MPhil* (*Master of Philosophy*), qui reposent uniquement sur le mémoire; voir *doctorate*.

master disk N (*Comput*) disque original

masterful ['mɑːstəful] ADJ autoritaire, impérieux(-euse)

master key N passe-partout *m inv*

masterly ['mɑːstəli] ADJ magistral(e)

mastermind ['mɑːstəmaɪnd] N esprit supérieur
  ▶ VT diriger, être le cerveau de

masterpiece ['mɑːstəpiːs] N chef-d'œuvre *m*

master plan N stratégie *f* d'ensemble

master stroke N coup *m* de maître

mastery ['mɑːstəri] N maîtrise *f*; connaissance parfaite

mastiff ['mæstɪf] N mastiff *m*

masturbate ['mæstəbeɪt] VI se masturber

masturbation [mæstə'beɪʃən] N masturbation *f*

mat [mæt] N petit tapis; (*also*: **doormat**) paillasson *m*; (*also*: **tablemat**) set *m* de table
  ▶ ADJ = **matt**

match [mætʃ] N allumette *f*; (*game*) match *m*, partie *f*; (*fig*) égal(e); mariage *m*; parti *m* ▶ VT (*also*: **match up**) assortir; (*go well with*) aller bien avec, s'assortir à; (*equal*) égaler, valoir ▶ VI être assorti(e); **to be a good ~** être bien assorti(e)
  ▶ **match up** VT assortir

matchbox ['mætʃbɒks] N boîte *f* d'allumettes

matching ['mætʃɪŋ] ADJ assorti(e)

matchless ['mætʃlɪs] ADJ sans égal

mate [meɪt] N camarade *mf* de travail; (*inf*) copain (copine); (*animal*) partenaire *mf*, mâle (femelle); (*in merchant navy*) second *m* ▶ VI s'accoupler ▶ VT accoupler

material [mə'tɪərɪəl] N (*substance*) matière *f*, matériau *m*; (*cloth*) tissu *m*, étoffe *f*; (*information, data*) données *fpl* ▶ ADJ matériel(le); (*relevant: evidence*) pertinent(e); (*important*) essentiel(le); **materials** NPL (*equipment*) matériaux *mpl*; **reading ~** de quoi lire, de la lecture

materialistic [mətɪərɪə'lɪstɪk] ADJ matérialiste

materialize [mə'tɪərɪəlaɪz] VI se matérialiser, se réaliser

materially [mə'tɪərɪəlɪ] ADV matériellement; essentiellement

maternal [mə'təːnl] ADJ maternel(le)

maternity [mə'təːnɪtɪ] N maternité *f* ▶ CPD de maternité, de grossesse

maternity benefit N prestation *f* de maternité

maternity dress N robe *f* de grossesse

maternity hospital N maternité *f*

maternity leave N congé *m* de maternité

matey ['meɪtɪ] ADJ (*BRIT inf*) copain-copain *inv*

math [mæθ] N (*US*: = *mathematics*) maths *fpl*

mathematical [mæθə'mætɪkl] ADJ mathématique

mathematician [mæθəmə'tɪʃən] N mathématicien(ne)

mathematics [mæθə'mætɪks] N mathématiques *fpl*

maths [mæθs] N ABBR (*BRIT*: = *mathematics*) maths *fpl*

matinée ['mætɪneɪ] N matinée *f*

mating ['meɪtɪŋ] N accouplement *m*

mating call N appel *m* du mâle

mating season N saison *f* des amours

matriarchal [meɪtrɪ'ɑːkl] ADJ matriarcal(e)

matrices ['meɪtrɪsiːz] NPL *of* **matrix**

matriculation [mətrɪkju'leɪʃən] N inscription *f*

matrimonial [mætrɪ'məunɪəl] ADJ matrimonial(e), conjugal(e)

matrimony ['mætrɪmənɪ] N mariage *m*

matrix ['meɪtrɪks] (*pl* **matrices** ['meɪtrɪsiːz]) N matrice *f*

matron ['meɪtrən] N (*in hospital*) infirmière-chef *f*; (*in school*) infirmière *f*

matronly ['meɪtrənlɪ] ADJ de matrone; imposant(e)

matt [mæt] ADJ mat(e)

matted ['mætɪd] ADJ emmêlé(e)

matter ['mætə'] N question *f*; (*Physics*) matière *f*, substance *f*; (*content*) contenu *m*, fond *m*; (*Med: pus*) pus *m* ▶ VI importer; **matters** NPL (*affairs, situation*) la situation; **it doesn't ~** cela n'a pas d'importance; (*I don't mind*) cela ne fait rien; **what's the ~?** qu'est-ce qu'il y a?, qu'est-ce qui ne va pas?; **no ~ what** quoi qu'il arrive; **that's another ~** c'est une autre affaire; **as a ~ of course** tout naturellement; **as a ~ of fact** en fait; **it's a ~ of habit** c'est une question d'habitude; **printed ~** imprimés *mpl*; **reading ~** (*BRIT*) de quoi lire, de la lecture

matter-of-fact ['mætərəv'fækt] ADJ terre à terre, neutre

matting ['mætɪŋ] N natte *f*

mattress ['mætrɪs] N matelas *m*

mature [mə'tjuə'] ADJ mûr(e); (*cheese*) fait(e); (*wine*) arrivé(e) à maturité ▶ VI mûrir; (*cheese, wine*) se faire

mature student N étudiant(e) plus âgé(e) que la moyenne

maturity [mə'tjuərɪtɪ] N maturité *f*

maudlin ['mɔːdlɪn] ADJ larmoyant(e)

maul [mɔːl] VT lacérer

Mauritania [mɔːrɪ'teɪnɪə] N Mauritanie *f*

Mauritius [mə'rɪʃəs] N l'île *f* Maurice

mausoleum [mɔːsə'lɪəm] N mausolée *m*

mauve [məuv] ADJ mauve

maverick ['mævrɪk] N (*fig*) franc-tireur *m*, non-conformiste *mf*

mawkish ['mɔːkɪʃ] ADJ mièvre; fade

max ABBR = **maximum**

maxim ['mæksɪm] N maxime *f*

maxima ['mæksɪmə] NPL *of* **maximum**

maximize ['mæksɪmaɪz] VT (*profits etc, chances*) maximiser

maximum ['mæksɪməm] (*pl* **maxima** [-mə]) ADJ maximum ▶ N maximum *m*

May [meɪ] N mai *m*; *see also* **July**

may [meɪ] (*conditional* **might**) VI (*indicating possibility*): **he ~ come** il se peut qu'il vienne; (*be allowed to*) **~ I smoke?** puis-je fumer?; (*wishes*) **~ God bless you!** (que) Dieu vous bénisse!; **~ I sit here?** vous permettez que je m'assoie ici?;

he might be there il pourrait bien y être, il se pourrait qu'il y soit; **you ~ as well go** vous feriez aussi bien d'y aller; **I might as well go** je ferais aussi bien d'y aller, autant y aller; **you might like to try** vous pourriez (peut-être) essayer

maybe ['meɪbi:] ADV peut-être; **~ he'll ...** peut-être qu'il ...; **~ not** peut-être pas

mayday ['meɪdeɪ] N S.O.S. *m*

May Day N le Premier mai

mayhem ['meɪhɛm] N grabuge *m*

mayonnaise [meɪə'neɪz] N mayonnaise *f*

mayor [mɛə^r] N maire *m*

mayoress ['mɛərɛs] N *(female mayor)* maire *m*; *(wife of mayor)* épouse *f* du maire

maypole ['meɪpəul] N mât enrubanné *(autour duquel on danse)*

maze [meɪz] N labyrinthe *m*, dédale *m*

MB ABBR *(Comput)* = **megabyte**; (CANADA) = **Manitoba**

MBA N ABBR (= *Master of Business Administration*) titre universitaire

MBBS, MBChB N ABBR (BRIT: = *Bachelor of Medicine and Surgery*) titre universitaire

MBE N ABBR (BRIT: = *Member of the Order of the British Empire*) titre honorifique

MBO N ABBR (BRIT) = **management buyout**

MC N ABBR = **master of ceremonies**

MCAT N ABBR (US) = **Medical College Admissions Test**

MD N ABBR (= *Doctor of Medicine*) titre universitaire; *(Comm)* = **managing director** ▶ ABBR (US) = **Maryland**

Md. ABBR (US) = **Maryland**

MDT ABBR (US: = *Mountain Daylight Time*) heure d'été des Montagnes Rocheuses

ME N ABBR (US: = *medical examiner*) médecin légiste *mf*; *(Med: = myalgic encephalomyelitis)* encéphalomyélite *f* myalgique ▶ ABBR (US) = **Maine**

me [mi:] PRON me, m' + *vowel or h mute*; *(stressed, after prep)* moi; **it's me** c'est moi; **he heard me** il m'a entendu; **give me a book** donnez-moi un livre; **it's for me** c'est pour moi

meadow ['mɛdəu] N prairie *f*, pré *m*

meagre, (US) **meager** ['mi:gə^r] ADJ maigre

meal [mi:l] N repas *m*; *(flour)* farine *f*; **to go out for a ~** sortir manger

meals on wheels NPL (BRIT) repas livrés à domicile aux personnes âgées ou handicapées

mealtime ['mi:ltaɪm] N heure *f* du repas

mealy-mouthed ['mi:lɪmauðd] ADJ mielleux(-euse)

mean [mi:n] *(pt, pp* **meant** [mɛnt]) ADJ *(with money)* avare, radin(e); *(unkind)* mesquin(e), méchant(e); *(shabby)* misérable; *(US inf: animal)* méchant, vicieux(-euse); (: *person)* vache; *(average)* moyen(ne) ▶ VT *(signify)* signifier, vouloir dire; *(refer to)* faire allusion à, parler de; *(intend)*: **to ~ to do** avoir l'intention de faire ▶ N moyenne *f*; **means** NPL *(way, money)* moyens *mpl*; **to be meant for** être destiné(e) à; **do you ~ it?** vous êtes sérieux?; **what do you ~?** que voulez-vous dire?; **by means of** *(instrument)* au

moyen de; **by all means** je vous en prie

meander [mɪ'ændə^r] VI faire des méandres; *(fig)* flâner

meaning ['mi:nɪŋ] N signification *f*, sens *m*

meaningful ['mi:nɪŋful] ADJ significatif(-ive); *(relationship)* valable

meaningless ['mi:nɪŋlɪs] ADJ dénué(e) de sens

meanness ['mi:nnɪs] N avarice *f*; mesquinerie *f*

means test N *(Admin)* contrôle *m* des conditions de ressources

meant [mɛnt] PT, PP *of* **mean**

meantime ['mi:ntaɪm] ADV *(also:* **in the meantime**) pendant ce temps

meanwhile ['mi:nwaɪl] ADV = **meantime**

measles ['mi:zlz] N rougeole *f*

measly ['mi:zlɪ] ADJ *(inf)* minable

measurable ['mɛʒərəbl] ADJ mesurable

measure ['mɛʒə^r] VT, VI mesurer ▶ N mesure *f*; *(ruler)* règle (graduée); **a litre ~** un litre; **some ~ of success** un certain succès; **to take measures to do sth** prendre des mesures pour faire qch

▶ **measure up** VI: **to ~ up (to)** être à la hauteur (de)

measured ['mɛʒəd] ADJ mesuré(e)

measurements ['mɛʒəməntz] NPL mesures *fpl*; **chest/hip ~** tour *m* de poitrine/hanches; **to take sb's ~** prendre les mesures de qn

meat [mi:t] N viande *f*; **I don't eat ~** je ne mange pas de viande; **cold meats** (BRIT) viandes froides; **crab ~** crabe *f*

meatball ['mi:tbɔ:l] N boulette *f* de viande

meat pie N pâté *m* en croûte

meaty ['mi:tɪ] ADJ *(flavour)* de viande; *(fig: argument, book)* étoffé(e), substantiel(le)

Mecca ['mɛkə] N la Mecque; *(fig)*: **a ~ (for)** la Mecque (de)

mechanic [mɪ'kænɪk] N mécanicien *m*; **can you send a ~?** pouvez-vous nous envoyer un mécanicien?

mechanical [mɪ'kænɪkl] ADJ mécanique

mechanical engineering N *(science)* mécanique *f*; *(industry)* construction *f* mécanique

mechanics [mə'kænɪks] N mécanique *f* ▶ NPL mécanisme *m*

mechanism ['mɛkənɪzəm] N mécanisme *m*

mechanization [mɛkənaɪ'zeɪʃən] N mécanisation *f*

MEd N ABBR (= *Master of Education*) titre universitaire

medal ['mɛdl] N médaille *f*

medallion [mɪ'dælɪən] N médaillon *m*

medallist, (US) **medalist** ['mɛdlɪst] N *(Sport)* médaillé(e)

meddle ['mɛdl] VI: **to ~ in** se mêler de, s'occuper de; **to ~ with** toucher à

meddlesome ['mɛdlsəm], **meddling** ['mɛdlɪŋ] ADJ indiscret(-ète), qui se mêle de ce qui ne le (or la) regarde pas; touche-à-tout *inv*

media ['mi:dɪə] NPL media *mpl* ▶ NPL *of* **medium**

media circus N *(event)* battage *m* médiatique; *(group of journalists)* cortège *m* médiatique

mediaeval [mɛdɪ'i:vl] ADJ = **medieval**

median ['mi:dɪən] N (US: *also:* **median strip**) bande médiane

media research N étude f de l'audience
mediate ['miːdɪeɪt] VI servir d'intermédiaire
mediation [miːdɪˈeɪʃən] N médiation f
mediator ['miːdɪeɪtəʳ] N médiateur(-trice)
Medicaid ['mɛdɪkeɪd] N (US) assistance médicale aux indigents
medical ['mɛdɪkl] ADJ médical(e) ▶ N (also: **medical examination**) visite médicale; (: private) examen médical
medical certificate N certificat médical
medical student N étudiant(e) en médecine
Medicare ['mɛdɪkɛəʳ] N (US) régime d'assurance maladie
medicated ['mɛdɪkeɪtɪd] ADJ traitant(e), médicamenteux(-euse)
medication [mɛdɪˈkeɪʃən] N (drugs etc) médication f
medicinal [mɛˈdɪsɪnl] ADJ médicinal(e)
medicine ['mɛdsɪn] N médecine f; (drug) médicament m
medicine chest N pharmacie f (murale ou portative)
medicine man N (irreg) sorcier m
medieval [mɛdɪˈiːvl] ADJ médiéval(e)
mediocre [miːdɪˈəukəʳ] ADJ médiocre
mediocrity [miːdɪˈɔkrɪtɪ] N médiocrité f
meditate ['mɛdɪteɪt] VI: **to ~ (on)** méditer (sur)
meditation [mɛdɪˈteɪʃən] N méditation f
Mediterranean [mɛdɪtəˈreɪnɪən] ADJ méditerranéen(ne); **the ~ (Sea)** la (mer) Méditerranée
medium ['miːdɪəm] ADJ moyen(ne) ▶ N (pl **media** ['miːdɪə]) (means) moyen m; (pl **mediums**: person) médium m; **the happy ~** le juste milieu
medium-dry ['miːdɪəm'draɪ] ADJ demi-sec
medium-sized ['miːdɪəm'saɪzd] ADJ de taille moyenne
medium wave N (Radio) ondes moyennes, petites ondes
medley ['mɛdlɪ] N mélange m
meek [miːk] ADJ doux (douce), humble
meet [miːt] (pt, pp met [mɛt]) VT rencontrer; (by arrangement) retrouver, rejoindre; (for the first time) faire la connaissance de; (go and fetch): **I'll ~ you at the station** j'irai te chercher à la gare; (opponent, danger, problem) faire face à; (requirements) satisfaire à, répondre à; (bill, expenses) régler, honorer ▶ VI (friends) se rencontrer; se retrouver; (in session) se réunir; (join: lines, roads) se joindre ▶ N (BRIT Hunting) rendez-vous m de chasse; (US Sport) rencontre f, meeting m; **pleased to ~ you!** enchanté!; **nice meeting you** ravi d'avoir fait votre connaissance
▶ **meet up** VI: **to ~ up with sb** rencontrer qn
▶ **meet with** VT FUS (difficulty) rencontrer; **to ~ with success** être couronné(e) de succès
meeting ['miːtɪŋ] N (of group of people) réunion f; (between individuals) rendez-vous m; (formal) assemblée f; (Sport: rally) rencontre, meeting m; (: interview) entrevue f; **she's at** or **in a ~** (Comm) elle est en réunion; **to call a ~** convoquer une réunion
meeting place N lieu m de (la) réunion; (for appointment) lieu de rendez-vous

mega ['mɛgə] (inf) ADV: **he's ~ rich** il est hyper-riche
megabyte ['mɛgəbaɪt] N (Comput) méga-octet m
megaphone ['mɛgəfəun] N porte-voix m inv
megapixel ['mɛgəpɪksl] N mégapixel m
meh [mɛ] EXCL bof
melancholy ['mɛlənkəlɪ] N mélancolie f ▶ ADJ mélancolique
mellow ['mɛləu] ADJ velouté(e), doux (douce); (colour) riche et profond(e); (fruit) mûr(e) ▶ VI (person) s'adoucir
melodious [mɪˈləudɪəs] ADJ mélodieux(-euse)
melodrama ['mɛləudrɑːmə] N mélodrame m
melodramatic [mɛlədrəˈmætɪk] ADJ mélodramatique
melody ['mɛlədɪ] N mélodie f
melon ['mɛlən] N melon m
melt [mɛlt] VI fondre; (become soft) s'amollir; (fig) s'attendrir ▶ VT faire fondre
▶ **melt away** VI fondre complètement
▶ **melt down** VT fondre
meltdown ['mɛltdaun] N fusion f (du cœur d'un réacteur nucléaire)
melting point ['mɛltɪŋ-] N point m de fusion
melting pot ['mɛltɪŋ-] N (fig) creuset m; **to be in the ~** être encore en discussion
member ['mɛmbəʳ] N membre m; (of club, political party) membre, adhérent(e) ▶ CPD: **~ country/ state** n pays m/état m membre
Member of Parliament N (BRIT) député m
Member of the European Parliament N Eurodéputé m
Member of the House of Representatives N (US) membre m de la Chambre des représentants
Member of the Scottish Parliament N (BRIT) député m au Parlement écossais
membership ['mɛmbəʃɪp] N (becoming a member) adhésion f; admission f; (being a member) qualité f de membre, fait m d'être membre; (members) membres mpl, adhérents mpl; (number of members) nombre m des membres or adhérents
membership card N carte f de membre
membrane ['mɛmbreɪn] N membrane f
memento [məˈmɛntəu] N souvenir m
memo ['mɛməu] N note f (de service)
memoir ['mɛmwɑːʳ] N mémoire m, étude f; **memoirs** NPL mémoires
memo pad N bloc-notes m
memorable ['mɛmərəbl] ADJ mémorable
memorandum ['mɛməˈrændəm] (pl **memoranda** [-də]) N note f (de service); (Diplomacy) mémorandum m
memorial [mɪˈmɔːrɪəl] N mémorial m ▶ ADJ commémoratif(-ive)
Memorial Day N (US); voir article

Memorial Day est un jour férié aux États-Unis, le dernier lundi de mai dans la plupart des États, à la mémoire des soldats américains morts au combat.

memorize ['mɛməraɪz] VT apprendre or retenir par cœur
memory ['mɛmərɪ] N (also Comput) mémoire f;

(*recollection*) souvenir *m*; **to have a good/bad ~** avoir une bonne/mauvaise mémoire; **loss of ~** perte *f* de mémoire; **in ~ of** à la mémoire de

memory card N (*for digital camera*) carte *f* mémoire

memory stick N (*Comput: flash pen*) clé *f* USB; (: *card*) carte *f* mémoire

men [mɛn] NPL *of* **man**

menace ['mɛnɪs] N menace *f*; (*inf: nuisance*) peste *f*, plaie *f* ▶ VT menacer; **a public ~** un danger public

menacing ['mɛnɪsɪŋ] ADJ menaçant(e)

menagerie [mɪ'nædʒərɪ] N ménagerie *f*

mend [mɛnd] VT réparer; (*darn*) raccommoder, repriser ▶ N reprise *f*; **on the ~** en voie de guérison; **to ~ one's ways** s'amender

mending ['mɛndɪŋ] N raccommodages *mpl*

menial ['mi:nɪəl] ADJ de domestique, inférieur(e); subalterne

meningitis [mɛnɪn'dʒaɪtɪs] N méningite *f*

menopause ['mɛnəupɔ:z] N ménopause *f*

menservants ['mɛnsə:vənts] NPL *of* **manservant**

men's room (*US*) N: **the ~** les toilettes *fpl* pour hommes

menstruate ['mɛnstrueɪt] VI avoir ses règles

menstruation [mɛnstru'eɪʃən] N menstruation *f*

menswear ['mɛnzwɛəʳ] N vêtements *mpl* d'hommes

mental ['mɛntl] ADJ mental(e); **~ illness** maladie mentale

mental hospital N (*pej*) hôpital *m* psychiatrique

mentality [mɛn'tælɪtɪ] N mentalité *f*

mentally ['mɛntlɪ] ADV: **she is ~ ill** elle souffre d'une maladie mentale

menthol ['mɛnθɔl] N menthol *m*

mention ['mɛnʃən] N mention *f* ▶ VT mentionner, faire mention de; **don't ~ it!** je vous en prie, il n'y a pas de quoi!; **I need hardly ~ that ...** est-il besoin de rappeler que ...?; **not to ~ ..., without mentioning ...** sans parler de ..., sans compter ...

mentor ['mɛntɔ:ʳ] N mentor *m*

menu ['mɛnju:] N (*set menu, Comput*) menu *m*; (*list of dishes*) carte *f*; **could we see the ~?** est-ce qu'on peut voir la carte?

menu-driven ['mɛnju:drɪvn] ADJ (*Comput*) piloté(e) par menu

MEP N ABBR = **Member of the European Parliament**

mercantile ['mə:kəntaɪl] ADJ marchand(e); (*law*) commercial(e)

mercenary ['mə:sɪnərɪ] ADJ (*person*) intéressé(e), mercenaire ▶ N mercenaire *m*

merchandise ['mə:tʃəndaɪz] N marchandises *fpl* ▶ VT commercialiser

merchandiser ['mə:tʃəndaɪzəʳ] N marchandiseur *m*

merchant ['mə:tʃənt] N négociant *m*, marchand *m*; **timber/wine ~** négociant en bois/vins, marchand de bois/vins

merchant bank N (*Brit*) banque *f* d'affaires

merchantman ['mə:tʃəntmən] N (*irreg*) navire marchand

merchant navy, (*US*) merchant marine N marine marchande

merciful ['mə:sɪful] ADJ miséricordieux(-euse), clément(e)

mercifully ['mə:sɪflɪ] ADV avec clémence; (*fortunately*) par bonheur, Dieu merci

merciless ['mə:sɪlɪs] ADJ impitoyable, sans pitié

mercurial [mə:'kjuərɪəl] ADJ changeant(e); (*lively*) vif (vive)

mercury ['mə:kjurɪ] N mercure *m*

mercy ['mə:sɪ] N pitié *f*, merci *f*; (*Rel*) miséricorde *f*; **to have ~ on sb** avoir pitié de qn; **at the ~ of** à la merci de

mercy killing N euthanasie *f*

mere [mɪəʳ] ADJ simple; (*chance*) pur(e); **a ~ two hours** seulement deux heures

merely ['mɪəlɪ] ADV simplement, purement

merge [mə:dʒ] VT unir; (*Comput*) fusionner, interclasser ▶ VI (*colours, shapes, sounds*) se mêler; (*roads*) se joindre; (*Comm*) fusionner

merger ['mə:dʒəʳ] N (*Comm*) fusion *f*

meridian [mə'rɪdɪən] N méridien *m*

meringue [mə'ræŋ] N meringue *f*

merit ['mɛrɪt] N mérite *m*, valeur *f* ▶ VT mériter

meritocracy [mɛrɪ'tɔkrəsɪ] N méritocratie *f*

mermaid ['mə:meɪd] N sirène *f*

merriment ['mɛrɪmənt] N gaieté *f*

merry ['mɛrɪ] ADJ gai(e); **M~ Christmas!** joyeux Noël!

merry-go-round ['mɛrɪgəuraund] N manège *m*

mesh [mɛʃ] N mailles *fpl* ▶ VI (*gears*) s'engrener; **wire ~** grillage *m* (métallique), treillis *m* (métallique)

mesmerize ['mɛzməraɪz] VT hypnotiser; fasciner

mess [mɛs] N désordre *m*, fouillis *m*, pagaille *f*; (*muddle: of life*) gâchis *m*; (: *of economy*) pagaille *f*; (*dirt*) saleté *f*; (*Mil*) mess *m*, cantine *f*; **to be (in) a ~** être en désordre; **to be/get o.s. in a ~** (*fig*) être/se mettre dans le pétrin

▶ **mess about, mess around** (*inf*) VI perdre son temps

▶ **mess about with, mess around with** VT FUS (*inf*) chambarder, tripoter

▶ **mess up** VT (*inf: dirty*) salir; (*spoil*) gâcher

▶ **mess with** (*inf*) VT FUS (*challenge, confront*) se frotter à; (*interfere with*) toucher à

message ['mɛsɪdʒ] N message *m* ▶ VT envoyer un message (à); **can I leave a ~?** est-ce que je peux laisser un message?; **are there any messages for me?** est-ce que j'ai des messages?; **to get the ~** (*fig: inf*) saisir, piger; **she messaged me on Facebook** elle m'a envoyé un message sur Facebook

message board N (*on Internet*) forum *m*

message switching [-swɪtʃɪŋ] N (*Comput*) commutation *f* de messages

messenger ['mɛsɪndʒəʳ] N messager *m*

Messiah [mɪ'saɪə] N Messie *m*

Messrs, Messrs. ['mɛsəz] ABBR (*on letters*: = *messieurs*) MM

messy ['mɛsɪ] ADJ (*dirty*) sale; (*untidy*) en désordre

Met [mɛt] N ABBR (*US*) = **Metropolitan Opera**

m

met [mɛt] PT, PP of **meet** ▸ ADJ ABBR
(= *meteorological*) météo *inv*

metabolism [mɛˈtæbəlɪzəm] N métabolisme *m*

metal ['mɛtl] N métal *m* ▸ CPD en métal ▸ VT
empierrer

metallic [mɛˈtælɪk] ADJ métallique

metallurgy [mɛˈtælədʒɪ] N métallurgie *f*

metalwork ['mɛtlwəːk] N (*craft*) ferronnerie *f*

metamorphosis [mɛtəˈmɔːfəsɪs] (*pl*
metamorphoses [-siːz]) N métamorphose *f*

metaphor ['mɛtəfəˀ] N métaphore *f*

metaphysics [mɛtəˈfɪzɪks] N métaphysique *f*

mete [miːt]: **to ~ out** *vt fus* infliger

meteor ['miːtɪəˀ] N météore *m*

meteoric [miːtɪˈɔrɪk] ADJ (*fig*) fulgurant(e)

meteorite [miːtɪəraɪt] N météorite *mf*

meteorological [miːtɪərəˈlɔdʒɪkl] ADJ
météorologique

meteorology [miːtɪəˈrɔlədʒɪ] N météorologie *f*

meter ['miːtəˀ] N (*instrument*) compteur *m*; (*also:*
parking meter) parc(o)mètre *m*; (*US: unit*)
= **metre** ▸ VT (*US Post*) affranchir à la machine

methane ['miːθeɪn] N méthane *m*

method ['mɛθəd] N méthode *f*; **~ of payment**
mode *m or* modalité *f* de paiement

methodical [mɪˈθɔdɪkl] ADJ méthodique

Methodist ['mɛθədɪst] ADJ, N méthodiste (*mf*)

methylated spirit ['mɛθɪleɪtɪd-] N (*BRIT*) alcool
m à brûler

meticulous [mɛˈtɪkjuləs] ADJ méticuleux(-euse)

Met Office N (*BRIT*): **the ~** ≈ la Météorologie
nationale

metre, (*US*) **meter** ['miːtəˀ] N mètre *m*

metric ['mɛtrɪk] ADJ métrique; **to go ~** adopter
le système métrique

metrical ['mɛtrɪkl] ADJ métrique

metrication [mɛtrɪˈkeɪʃən] N conversion *f* au
système métrique

metric system N système *m* métrique

metric ton N tonne *f*

metro ['mɛtrəu] N métro *m*

metronome ['mɛtrənəum] N métronome *m*

metropolis [mɪˈtrɔpəlɪs] N métropole *f*

metropolitan [mɛtrəˈpɔlɪtən] ADJ
métropolitain(e); **the M~ Police** (*BRIT*) la
police londonienne

mettle ['mɛtl] N courage *m*

mew [mjuː] VI (*cat*) miauler

mews [mjuːz] N (*BRIT*): **~ cottage** maisonnette
aménagée dans une ancienne écurie ou remise

Mexican ['mɛksɪkən] ADJ mexicain(e) ▸ N
Mexicain(e)

Mexico ['mɛksɪkəu] N Mexique *m*

Mexico City N Mexico

mezzanine ['mɛtsəniːn] N mezzanine *f*;
(*of shops, offices*) entresol *m*

MFA N ABBR (*US: = Master of Fine Arts*) titre
universitaire

mfr ABBR = **manufacture**; **manufacturer**

mg ABBR (= *milligram*) mg

Mgr ABBR (= *Monseigneur, Monsignor*) Mgr;
(= *manager*) dir

MHR N ABBR (*US*) = **Member of the House of
Representatives**

MHz ABBR (= *megahertz*) MHz

MI ABBR (*US*) = **Michigan**

MI5 N ABBR (*BRIT*: = *Military Intelligence 5*) ≈ DST *f*

MI6 N ABBR (*BRIT*: = *Military Intelligence 6*) ≈ DGSE *f*

MIA ABBR (= *missing in action*) disparu(e) au
combat

miaow [miːˈau] VI miauler

mice [maɪs] NPL of **mouse**

Mich. ABBR (*US*) = **Michigan**

micro ['maɪkrəu] N (*also:* **microcomputer**)
micro(-ordinateur *m*) *m*

micro... ['maɪkrəu] PREFIX micro...

microbe ['maɪkrəub] N microbe *m*

microbiology [maɪkrəbaɪˈɔlədʒɪ] N
microbiologie *f*

microblog ['maɪkrəublɔg] N microblog *m*

microchip ['maɪkrəutʃɪp] N (*Elec*) puce *f*

microcomputer ['maɪkrəukəmˈpjuːtəˀ] N
micro-ordinateur *m*

microcosm ['maɪkrəukɔzəm] N microcosme *m*

microeconomics ['maɪkrəuiːkəˈnɔmɪks] N
micro-économie *f*

microfiche ['maɪkrəufiːʃ] N microfiche *f*

microfilm ['maɪkrəufɪlm] N microfilm *m* ▸ VT
microfilmer

microlight ['maɪkrəulaɪt] N ULM *m*

micrometer [maɪˈkrɔmɪtəˀ] N palmer *m*,
micromètre *m*

microphone ['maɪkrəfəun] N microphone *m*

microprocessor ['maɪkrəuˈprəusɛsəˀ] N
microprocesseur *m*

microscope ['maɪkrəskəup] N microscope *m*;
under the ~ au microscope

microscopic [maɪkrəˈskɔpɪk] ADJ
microscopique

mid [mɪd] ADJ: **~ May** la mi-mai; **~ afternoon** le
milieu de l'après-midi; **in ~ air** en plein ciel;
he's in his ~ thirties il a dans les trente-cinq
ans

midday [mɪdˈdeɪ] N midi *m*

middle ['mɪdl] N milieu *m*; (*waist*) ceinture *f*,
taille *f* ▸ ADJ du milieu; (*average*) moyen(ne); **in
the ~ of the night** au milieu de la nuit; **I'm in
the ~ of reading it** je suis (justement) en train
de le lire

middle age N *tranche d'âge aux limites floues, entre la
quarantaine et le début du troisième âge*

middle-aged [mɪdlˈeɪdʒd] ADJ d'un certain âge,
ni vieux ni jeune; (*pej: values, outlook*)
conventionnel(le), rassis(e)

Middle Ages NPL: **the ~** le moyen âge

middle class N, **middle classes** NPL: **the ~(es)**
≈ les classes moyennes

middle-class [mɪdlˈklɑːs] ADJ bourgeois(e)

Middle East N: **the ~** le Proche-Orient, le
Moyen-Orient

middleman ['mɪdlmæn] N (*irreg*)
intermédiaire *m*

middle management N cadres moyens

middle name N second prénom

middle-of-the-road ['mɪdlɔvðəˈrəud] ADJ
(*policy*) modéré(e), du juste milieu; (*music etc*)
plutôt classique, assez traditionnel(le)

middle school N (*US*) *école pour les enfants de 12 à 14* ans, ≈ collège m; (BRIT) école pour les enfants de 8 à 14 ans

middleweight ['mɪdlweɪt] N (Boxing) poids moyen

middling ['mɪdlɪŋ] ADJ moyen(ne)

midge [mɪdʒ] N moucheron m

midget ['mɪdʒɪt] N (pej) nain(e) ▶ ADJ minuscule

midi system ['mɪdɪ-] N chaîne f midi

Midlands ['mɪdləndz] NPL comtés du centre de l'Angleterre

midnight ['mɪdnaɪt] N minuit m; **at ~** à minuit

midriff ['mɪdrɪf] N estomac m, taille f

midst [mɪdst] N: **in the ~ of** au milieu de

midsummer [mɪd'sʌmə^r] N milieu m de l'été

midway [mɪd'weɪ] ADJ, ADV: **~ (between)** à mi-chemin (entre); **~ through ...** au milieu de ..., en plein(e) ...

midweek [mɪd'wiːk] ADJ du milieu de la semaine ▶ ADV au milieu de la semaine, en pleine semaine

midwife ['mɪdwaɪf] (pl **midwives** [-vz]) N sage-femme f

midwifery ['mɪdwɪfərɪ] N obstétrique f

midwinter [mɪd'wɪntə^r] N milieu m de l'hiver

miffed [mɪft] ADJ (inf) fâché(e), vexé(e)

might [maɪt] VB see **may** ▶ N puissance f, force f

mighty ['maɪtɪ] ADJ puissant(e) ▶ ADV (inf) rudement

migraine ['miːgreɪn] N migraine f

migrant ['maɪgrənt] N (bird, animal) migrateur m; (person) migrant(e); nomade mf ▶ ADJ migrateur(-trice); migrant(e); nomade; (worker) saisonnier(-ière)

migrate [maɪ'greɪt] VI migrer

migration [maɪ'greɪʃən] N migration f

mike [maɪk] N ABBR (= microphone) micro m

Milan [mɪ'læn] N Milan

mild [maɪld] ADJ doux (douce); (reproach, infection) léger(-ère); (illness) bénin(-igne); (interest) modéré(e); (taste) peu relevé(e) ▶ N bière légère

mildew ['mɪldjuː] N mildiou m

mildly ['maɪldlɪ] ADV doucement; légèrement; **to put it ~** (inf) c'est le moins qu'on puisse dire

mildness ['maɪldnɪs] N douceur f

mile [maɪl] N mil(l)e m (= 1609 m); **to do 30 miles per gallon** ≈ faire 9, 4 litres aux cent

mileage ['maɪlɪdʒ] N distance f en milles, ≈ kilométrage m

mileage allowance N ≈ indemnité f kilométrique

mileometer [maɪ'lɔmɪtə^r] N compteur m kilométrique

milestone ['maɪlstəun] N borne f; (fig) jalon m

milieu ['miːljəː] N milieu m

militant ['mɪlɪtnt] ADJ, N militant(e)

militarism ['mɪlɪtərɪzəm] N militarisme m

militaristic [mɪlɪtə'rɪstɪk] ADJ militariste

military ['mɪlɪtərɪ] ADJ militaire ▶ N: **the ~** l'armée f, les militaires mpl

military service N service m (militaire or national)

militate ['mɪlɪteɪt] VI: **to ~ against** militer contre

militia [mɪ'lɪʃə] N milice f

milk [mɪlk] N lait m ▶ VT (cow) traire; (fig: person) dépouiller, plumer; (: situation) exploiter à fond

milk chocolate N chocolat m au lait

milk float N (BRIT) voiture f or camionnette f du or de laitier

milking ['mɪlkɪŋ] N traite f

milkman ['mɪlkmən] N (irreg) laitier m

milk shake N milk-shake m

milk tooth N dent f de lait

milk truck N (US) = **milk float**

milky ['mɪlkɪ] ADJ (drink) au lait; (colour) laiteux(-euse)

Milky Way N Voie lactée

mill [mɪl] N moulin m; (factory) usine f, fabrique f; (spinning mill) filature f; (flour mill) minoterie f; (steel mill) aciérie f ▶ VT moudre, broyer ▶ VI (also: **mill about**) grouiller

millennium [mɪ'lɛnɪəm] (pl **millenniums** or **millennia** [-'lɛnɪə]) N millénaire m

millennium bug N bogue m or bug m de l'an 2000

miller ['mɪlə^r] N meunier m

millet ['mɪlɪt] N millet m

milli... ['mɪlɪ] PREFIX milli...

milligram, milligramme ['mɪlɪgræm] N milligramme m

millilitre, (US) milliliter ['mɪlɪliːtə^r] N millilitre m

millimetre, (US) millimeter ['mɪlɪmiːtə^r] N millimètre m

milliner ['mɪlɪnə^r] N modiste f

millinery ['mɪlɪnərɪ] N modes fpl

million ['mɪljən] N million m; **a ~ pounds** un million de livres sterling

millionaire [mɪljə'nɛə^r] N millionnaire m

millionth [mɪljə'nθ] NUM millionième

millipede ['mɪlɪpiːd] N mille-pattes m inv

millstone ['mɪlstəun] N meule f

millwheel ['mɪlwiːl] N roue f de moulin

milometer [maɪ'lɔmɪtə^r] N = **mileometer**

mime [maɪm] N mime m ▶ VT, VI mimer

mimic ['mɪmɪk] N imitateur(-trice) ▶ VT, VI imiter, contrefaire

mimicry ['mɪmɪkrɪ] N imitation f; (Zool) mimétisme m

Min. ABBR (BRIT Pol) = **ministry**

min. ABBR (= minute(s)) mn.; (= minimum) min.

minaret [mɪnə'rɛt] N minaret m

mince [mɪns] VT hacher ▶ VI (in walking) marcher à petits pas maniérés ▶ N (BRIT Culin) viande hachée, hachis m; **he does not ~ (his) words** il ne mâche pas ses mots

mincemeat ['mɪnsmiːt] N hachis de fruits secs utilisés en pâtisserie; (US) viande hachée, hachis m

mince pie N sorte de tarte aux fruits secs

mincer ['mɪnsə^r] N hachoir m

mincing ['mɪnsɪŋ] ADJ affecté(e)

mind [maɪnd] N esprit m ▶ VT (attend to, look after) s'occuper de; (be careful) faire attention à; (object to): **I don't ~ the noise** je ne crains pas le bruit, le bruit ne me dérange pas; **it is on my ~** cela me préoccupe; **to change one's ~** changer d'avis; **to be in two minds about sth** (BRIT) être indécis(e) or irrésolu(e) en ce qui concerne

m

qch; **to my** ~ à mon avis, selon moi; **to be out of one's** ~ ne plus avoir toute sa raison; **to keep sth in** ~ ne pas oublier qch; **to bear sth in** ~ tenir compte de qch; **to have sb/sth in** ~ avoir qn/qch en tête; **to have in** ~ **to do** avoir l'intention de faire; **it went right out of my** ~ ça m'est complètement sorti de la tête; **to bring** *or* **call sth to** ~ se rappeler qch; **to make up one's** ~ se décider; **do you** ~ **if …?** est-ce que cela vous gêne si …?; **I don't** ~ cela ne me dérange pas; (*don't care*) ça m'est égal; ~ **you, …** remarquez, …; **never** ~ peu importe, ça ne fait rien; (*don't worry*) ne vous en faites pas; **"~ the step"** "attention à la marche"

mind-boggling ['maɪndbɔglɪŋ] ADJ (*inf*) époustouflant(e), ahurissant(e)

-minded ['maɪndɪd] ADJ: **fair~** impartial(e); **an industrially~ nation** une nation orientée vers l'industrie

minder ['maɪndə'] N (*child minder*) gardienne *f*; (*bodyguard*) ange gardien (*fig*)

mindful ['maɪndful] ADJ: ~ **of** attentif(-ive) à, soucieux(-euse) de

mindless ['maɪndlɪs] ADJ irréfléchi(e); (*violence, crime*) insensé(e); (*boring: job*) idiot(e)

mine¹ [maɪn] PRON le (la) mien(ne), les miens (miennes); **a friend of** ~ un de mes amis, un ami à moi; **this book is** ~ ce livre est à moi

mine² [maɪn] N mine *f* ▶ VT (*coal*) extraire; (*ship, beach*) miner

mine detector N détecteur *m* de mines

minefield ['maɪnfiːld] N champ *m* de mines

miner ['maɪnə'] N mineur *m*

mineral ['mɪnərəl] ADJ minéral(e) ▶ N minéral *m*; **minerals** NPL (*BRIT: soft drinks*) boissons gazeuses (sucrées)

mineralogy [mɪnə'rælədʒɪ] N minéralogie *f*

mineral water N eau minérale

minesweeper ['maɪnswiːpə'] N dragueur *m* de mines

mingle ['mɪŋgl] VT mêler, mélanger ▶ VI: **to ~ with** se mêler à

mingy ['mɪndʒɪ] ADJ (*inf*) radin(e)

miniature ['mɪnətʃə'] ADJ (en) miniature ▶ N miniature *f*

minibar ['mɪnɪbɑː'] N minibar *m*

minibus ['mɪnɪbʌs] N minibus *m*

minicab ['mɪnɪkæb] N (*BRIT*) taxi *m* indépendant

minicomputer ['mɪnɪkəm'pjuːtə'] N mini-ordinateur *m*

minim ['mɪnɪm] N (*Mus*) blanche *f*

minima ['mɪnɪmə] NPL *of* **minimum**

minimal ['mɪnɪml] ADJ minimal(e)

minimalist ['mɪnɪməlɪst] ADJ, N minimaliste (*mf*)

minimize ['mɪnɪmaɪz] VT (*reduce*) réduire au minimum; (*play down*) minimiser

minimum ['mɪnɪməm] (*pl* **minima** ['mɪnɪmə]) N minimum *m* ▶ ADJ minimum; **to reduce to a** ~ réduire au minimum

minimum lending rate N (*Econ*) taux *m* de crédit minimum

mining ['maɪnɪŋ] N exploitation minière

▶ ADJ minier(-ière); de mineurs

minion ['mɪnjən] N (*pej*) laquais *m*; favori(te)

mini-series ['mɪnɪsɪəriːz] N téléfilm *m* en plusieurs parties

miniskirt ['mɪnɪskəːt] N mini-jupe *f*

minister ['mɪnɪstə'] N (*BRIT Pol*) ministre *m*; (*Rel*) pasteur *m* ▶ VI: **to ~ to sb** donner ses soins à qn; **to ~ to sb's needs** pourvoir aux besoins de qn

ministerial [mɪnɪs'tɪərɪəl] ADJ (*BRIT Pol*) ministériel(le)

ministry ['mɪnɪstrɪ] N (*BRIT Pol*) ministère *m*; (*Rel*): **to go into the** ~ devenir pasteur

mink [mɪŋk] N vison *m*

mink coat N manteau *m* de vison

Minn. ABBR (*US*) = **Minnesota**

minnow ['mɪnəu] N vairon *m*

minor ['maɪnə'] ADJ petit(e), de peu d'importance; (*Mus, poet, problem*) mineur(e) ▶ N (*Law*) mineur(e)

Minorca [mɪ'nɔːkə] N Minorque *f*

minority [maɪ'nɔrɪtɪ] N minorité *f*; **to be in a** ~ être en minorité

minster ['mɪnstə'] N église abbatiale

minstrel ['mɪnstrəl] N trouvère *m*, ménestrel *m*

mint [mɪnt] N (*plant*) menthe *f*; (*sweet*) bonbon *m* à la menthe ▶ VT (*coins*) battre; **the (Royal) M~, the (US) M~** ≈ l'hôtel *m* de la Monnaie; **in ~ condition** à l'état de neuf

mint sauce N sauce *f* à la menthe

minuet [mɪnju'et] N menuet *m*

minus ['maɪnəs] N (*also*: **minus sign**) signe *m* moins ▶ PREP moins; **12 – 6 equals 6** 12 moins 6 égal 6; **– 24°C** moins 24°C

minuscule ['mɪnəskjuːl] ADJ minuscule

minute¹ ['mɪnɪt] N minute *f*; (*official record*) procès-verbal *m*, compte rendu; **minutes** NPL (*of meeting*) procès-verbal *m*, compte rendu; **it is 5 minutes past 3** il est 3 heures 5; **wait a ~!** (attendez) un instant!; **at the last** ~ à la dernière minute; **up to the** ~ (*fashion*) dernier cri; (*news*) de dernière minute; (*machine, technology*) de pointe

minute² [maɪ'njuːt] ADJ minuscule; (*detailed*) minutieux(-euse); **in ~ detail** par le menu

minute book N registre *m* des procès-verbaux

minute hand N aiguille *f* des minutes

minutely [maɪ'njuːtlɪ] ADV (*by a small amount*) de peu, de manière infime; (*in detail*) minutieusement, dans les moindres détails

minutiae [mɪ'njuːʃɪ:] NPL menus détails

miracle ['mɪrəkl] N miracle *m*

miraculous [mɪ'rækjuləs] ADJ miraculeux(-euse)

mirage ['mɪrɑːʒ] N mirage *m*

mire ['maɪə'] N bourbe *f*, boue *f*

mirror ['mɪrə'] N miroir *m*, glace *f*; (*in car*) rétroviseur *m* ▶ VT refléter

mirror image N image inversée

mirth [məːθ] N gaieté *f*

misadventure [mɪsəd'ventʃə'] N mésaventure *f*; **death by** ~ (*BRIT*) décès accidentel

misanthropist [mɪ'zænθrəpɪst] N misanthrope *mf*

misapply [mɪsə'plaɪ] VT mal employer

misapprehension ['mɪsæprɪ'hɛnʃən] N malentendu *m*, méprise *f*

misappropriate [mɪsə'prəuprɪeɪt] VT détourner

misappropriation ['mɪsəprəuprɪ'eɪʃən] N escroquerie *f*, détournement *m*

misbehave [mɪsbɪ'heɪv] VI mal se conduire

misbehaviour, (US) **misbehavior** [mɪsbɪ'heɪvjə^r] N mauvaise conduite

misc. ABBR = **miscellaneous**

miscalculate [mɪs'kælkjuleɪt] VT mal calculer

miscalculation ['mɪskælkju'leɪʃən] N erreur *f* de calcul

miscarriage ['mɪskærɪdʒ] N (*Med*) fausse couche; **~ of justice** erreur *f* judiciaire

miscarry [mɪs'kærɪ] VI (*Med*) faire une fausse couche; (*fail: plans*) échouer, mal tourner

miscellaneous [mɪsɪ'leɪnɪəs] ADJ (*items, expenses*) divers(es); (*selection*) varié(e)

miscellany [mɪ'sɛlənɪ] N recueil *m*

mischance [mɪs'tʃɑːns] N malchance *f*; **by (some) ~** par malheur

mischief ['mɪstʃɪf] N (*naughtiness*) sottises *fpl*; (*fun*) farce *f*; (*playfulness*) espièglerie *f*; (*harm*) mal *m*, dommage *m*; (*maliciousness*) méchanceté *f*

mischievous ['mɪstʃɪvəs] ADJ (*playful, naughty*) coquin(e), espiègle; (*harmful*) méchant(e)

misconception ['mɪskən'sɛpʃən] N idée fausse

misconduct [mɪs'kɔndʌkt] N inconduite *f*; **professional ~** faute professionnelle

misconstrue [mɪskən'struː] VT mal interpréter

miscount [mɪs'kaunt] VT, VI mal compter

misdeed ['mɪs'diːd] N méfait *m*

misdemeanour, (US) **misdemeanor** [mɪsdɪ'miːnə^r] N écart *m* de conduite; infraction *f*

misdirect [mɪsdɪ'rɛkt] VT (*person*) mal renseigner; (*letter*) mal adresser

miser ['maɪzə^r] N avare *mf*

miserable ['mɪzərəbl] ADJ (*person, expression*) malheureux(-euse); (*conditions*) misérable; (*weather*) maussade; (*offer, donation*) minable; (*failure*) pitoyable; **to feel ~** avoir le cafard

miserably ['mɪzərəblɪ] ADV (*smile, answer*) tristement; (*live, pay*) misérablement; (*fail*) lamentablement

miserly ['maɪzəlɪ] ADJ avare

misery ['mɪzərɪ] N (*unhappiness*) tristesse *f*; (*pain*) souffrances *fpl*; (*wretchedness*) misère *f*

misfire [mɪs'faɪə^r] VI rater; (*car engine*) avoir des ratés

misfit ['mɪsfɪt] N (*person*) inadapté(e)

misfortune [mɪs'fɔːtʃən] N malchance *f*, malheur *m*

misgiving [mɪs'gɪvɪŋ] N (*apprehension*) craintes *fpl*; **to have misgivings about sth** avoir des doutes quant à qch

misguided [mɪs'gaɪdɪd] ADJ malavisé(e)

mishandle [mɪs'hændl] VT (*treat roughly*) malmener; (*mismanage*) mal s'y prendre pour faire *or* résoudre *etc*

mishap ['mɪshæp] N mésaventure *f*

mishear [mɪs'hɪə^r] VT, VI (*irreg: like* **hear**) mal entendre

mishmash ['mɪʃmæʃ] N (*inf*) fatras *m*, méli-mélo *m*

misinform [mɪsɪn'fɔːm] VT mal renseigner

misinterpret [mɪsɪn'tə:prɪt] VT mal interpréter

misinterpretation ['mɪsɪntə:prɪ'teɪʃən] N interprétation erronée, contresens *m*

misjudge [mɪs'dʒʌdʒ] VT méjuger, se méprendre sur le compte de

mislay [mɪs'leɪ] VT (*irreg: like* **lay**) égarer

mislead [mɪs'liːd] VT (*irreg: like* **lead**[1]) induire en erreur

misleading [mɪs'liːdɪŋ] ADJ trompeur(-euse)

misled [mɪs'lɛd] PT, PP *of* **mislead**

mismanage [mɪs'mænɪdʒ] VT mal gérer; mal s'y prendre pour faire *or* résoudre *etc*

mismanagement [mɪs'mænɪdʒmənt] N mauvaise gestion

misnomer [mɪs'nəumə^r] N terme *or* qualificatif trompeur *or* peu approprié

misogynist [mɪ'sɔdʒɪnɪst] N misogyne *mf*

misplace [mɪs'pleɪs] VT égarer; **to be misplaced** (*trust etc*) être mal placé(e)

misprint ['mɪsprɪnt] N faute *f* d'impression

mispronounce [mɪsprə'nauns] VT mal prononcer

misquote [mɪs'kwəut] VT citer erronément *or* inexactement

misread [mɪs'riːd] VT (*irreg: like* **read**) mal lire

misrepresent [mɪsrɛprɪ'zɛnt] VT présenter sous un faux jour

Miss [mɪs] N Mademoiselle; **Dear ~ Smith** Chère Mademoiselle Smith

miss [mɪs] VT (*fail to get, attend, see*) manquer, rater; (*appointment, class*) manquer; (*escape, avoid*) échapper à, éviter; (*notice loss of: money etc*) s'apercevoir de l'absence de; (*regret the absence of*): **I ~ him/it** il/cela me manque ▶ VI manquer ▶ N (*shot*) coup manqué; **we missed our train** nous avons raté notre train; **the bus just missed the wall** le bus a évité le mur de justesse; **you're missing the point** vous êtes à côté de la question; **you can't ~ it** vous ne pouvez pas vous tromper

▶ **miss out** VT (BRIT) oublier

▶ **miss out on** VT FUS (*fun, party*) rater, manquer; (*chance, bargain*) laisser passer

Miss. ABBR (US) = **Mississippi**

missal ['mɪsl] N missel *m*

misshapen [mɪs'ʃeɪpən] ADJ difforme

missile ['mɪsaɪl] N (*Aviat*) missile *m*; (*object thrown*) projectile *m*

missile base N base *f* de missiles

missile launcher [-lɔ:ntʃə^r] N lance-missiles *m*

missing ['mɪsɪŋ] ADJ manquant(e); (*after escape, disaster: person*) disparu(e); **to go ~** disparaître; **~ person** personne disparue, disparu(e); **~ in action** (*Mil*) porté(e) disparu(e)

mission ['mɪʃən] N mission *f*; **on a ~ to sb** en mission auprès de qn

missionary ['mɪʃənrɪ] N missionnaire *mf*

mission statement N déclaration *f* d'intention

missive ['mɪsɪv] N missive *f*

misspell ['mɪs'spɛl] VT (*irreg: like* **spell**) mal orthographier

misspent ['mɪs'spɛnt] ADJ: **his ~ youth** sa folle jeunesse

mist [mɪst] N brume f ▶ VI (*also*: **mist over, mist up**) devenir brumeux(-euse); (: BRIT: *windows*) s'embuer

mistake [mɪs'teɪk] N erreur f, faute f ▶ VT (*irreg*: *like* **take**) (*meaning*) mal comprendre; (*intentions*) se méprendre sur; **to ~ for** prendre pour; **by ~** par erreur, par inadvertance; **to make a ~** (*in writing*) faire une faute; (*in calculating etc*) faire une erreur; **there must be some ~** il doit y avoir une erreur, se tromper; **to make a ~ about sb/sth** se tromper sur le compte de qn/sur qch

mistaken [mɪs'teɪkən] PP *of* **mistake** ▶ ADJ (*idea etc*) erroné(e); **to be ~** faire erreur, se tromper

mistaken identity N erreur f d'identité

mistakenly [mɪs'teɪkənlɪ] ADV par erreur, par mégarde

mister ['mɪstə'] N (*inf*) Monsieur m; *see* **Mr**

mistletoe ['mɪsltəu] N gui m

mistook [mɪs'tuk] PT *of* **mistake**

mistranslation [mɪstræns'leɪʃən] N erreur f de traduction, contresens m

mistreat [mɪs'triːt] VT maltraiter

mistress ['mɪstrɪs] N maîtresse f; (BRIT: *in primary school*) institutrice f; (: *in secondary school*) professeur m

mistrust [mɪs'trʌst] VT se méfier de ▶ N: **~ (of)** méfiance f (à l'égard de)

mistrustful [mɪs'trʌstful] ADJ: **~ (of)** méfiant(e) (à l'égard de)

misty ['mɪstɪ] ADJ brumeux(-euse); (*glasses, window*) embué(e)

misty-eyed ['mɪstɪ'aɪd] ADJ les yeux embués de larmes; (*fig*) sentimental(e)

misunderstand [mɪsʌndə'stænd] VT, VI (*irreg*: *like* **understand**) mal comprendre

misunderstanding [mɪsʌndə'stændɪŋ] N méprise f, malentendu m; **there's been a ~** il y a eu un malentendu

misunderstood [mɪsʌndə'stud] PT, PP *of* **misunderstand** ▶ ADJ (*person*) incompris(e)

misuse N [mɪs'juːs] mauvais emploi; (*of power*) abus m ▶ VT [mɪs'juːz] mal employer; abuser de

MIT N ABBR (US) = **Massachusetts Institute of Technology**

mite [maɪt] N (*small quantity*) grain m, miette f; (BRIT: *small child*) petit(e)

mitigate ['mɪtɪgeɪt] VT atténuer; **mitigating circumstances** circonstances atténuantes

mitigation [mɪtɪ'geɪʃən] N atténuation f

mitre, (US) **miter** ['maɪtə'] N mitre f; (*Carpentry*) onglet m

mitt ['mɪt], **mitten** ['mɪtn] N moufle f; (*fingerless*) mitaine f

mix [mɪks] VT mélanger; (*sauce, drink etc*) préparer ▶ VI se mélanger; (*socialize*): **he doesn't ~ well** il est peu sociable ▶ N mélange m; **to ~ sth with sth** mélanger qch à qch; **to ~ business with pleasure** unir l'utile à l'agréable; **cake ~** préparation f pour gâteau
▶ **mix in** VT incorporer, mélanger
▶ **mix up** VT mélanger; (*confuse*) confondre; **to be mixed up in sth** être mêlé(e) à qch or impliqué(e) dans qch

mixed [mɪkst] ADJ (*feelings, reactions*) contradictoire; (*school, marriage*) mixte

mixed-ability ['mɪkstə'bɪlɪtɪ] ADJ (*class etc*) sans groupes de niveaux

mixed bag N: **it's a (bit of a) ~** il y a (un peu) de tout

mixed blessing N: **it's a ~** cela a du bon et du mauvais

mixed doubles NPL (*Sport*) double m mixte

mixed economy N économie f mixte

mixed grill N (BRIT) assortiment m de grillades

mixed marriage N mariage m mixte

mixed salad N salade f de crudités

mixed-up [mɪkst'ʌp] ADJ (*person*) désorienté(e), embrouillé(e)

mixer ['mɪksə'] N (*for food*) batteur m, mixeur m; (*drink*) boisson gazeuse (*servant à couper un alcool*); (*person*): **he is a good ~** il est très sociable

mixer tap N (robinet m) mélangeur m

mixture ['mɪkstʃə'] N assortiment m, mélange m; (*Med*) préparation f

mix-up ['mɪksʌp] N: **there was a ~** il y a eu confusion

MK ABBR (BRIT Tech) = **mark**

mk ABBR = **mark**

mkt ABBR = **market**

ml ABBR (= *millilitre(s)*) ml

MLitt N ABBR (= *Master of Literature, Master of Letters*) titre universitaire

MLR N ABBR (BRIT) = **minimum lending rate**

mm ABBR (= *millimetre*) mm

MN ABBR (BRIT) = **Merchant Navy**; (US) = **Minnesota**

MO N ABBR (*Med*) = **medical officer**; (US inf: = *modus operandi*) méthode f ▶ ABBR (US) = **Missouri**

m.o. ABBR = **money order**

moan [məun] N gémissement m ▶ VI gémir; (*inf: complain*): **to ~ (about)** se plaindre (de)

moaner ['məunə'] N (*inf*) rouspéteur(-euse), râleur(-euse)

moaning ['məunɪŋ] N gémissements mpl

moat [məut] N fossé m, douves fpl

mob [mɔb] N foule f; (*disorderly*) cohue f; (*pej*): **the ~** la populace ▶ VT assaillir

mobile ['məubaɪl] ADJ mobile ▶ N (*Art*) mobile m; (BRIT inf: *phone*) (téléphone m) portable m, mobile m; **applicants must be ~** (BRIT) les candidats devront être prêts à accepter tout déplacement

mobile home N caravane f

mobile phone N (téléphone m) portable m, mobile m

mobile phone mast N (BRIT Tel) antenne-relais f

mobile shop N (BRIT) camion m magasin

mobility [məu'bɪlɪtɪ] N mobilité f

mobilize ['məubɪlaɪz] VT, VI mobiliser

moccasin ['mɔkəsɪn] N mocassin m

mock [mɔk] VT ridiculiser; (*laugh at*) se moquer de ▶ ADJ faux (fausse); **mocks** NPL (BRIT Scol) examens blancs

mockery ['mɔkərɪ] N moquerie f, raillerie f; **to make a ~ of** ridiculiser, tourner en dérision

mocking ['mɔkɪŋ] ADJ moqueur(-euse)

mockingbird ['mɔkɪŋbə:d] N moqueur m
mock-up ['mɔkʌp] N maquette f
MOD N ABBR (BRIT) = **Ministry of Defence**; see
defence
mod [mɔd] ADJ see **convenience**
mod cons ['mɔd'kɔnz] NPL ABBR (BRIT) = **modern conveniences**; see **convenience**
mode [məud] N mode m; (of transport) moyen m
model ['mɔdl] N modèle m; (person: for fashion)
mannequin m; (: for artist) modèle ▸ VT (with clay
etc) modeler ▸ VI travailler comme mannequin
▸ ADJ (railway: toy) modèle réduit inv; (child,
factory) modèle; **to ~ clothes** présenter des
vêtements; **to ~ o.s. on** imiter; **to ~ sb/sth on**
modeler qn/qch sur
modem ['məudem] N modem m
moderate ['mɔdərət] ADJ modéré(e); (amount,
change) peu important(e) ▸ N (Pol) modéré(e)
▸ VI ['mɔdəreɪt] se modérer, se calmer ▸ VT
['mɔdəreɪt] modérer
moderately ['mɔdərətlɪ] ADV (act) avec
modération or mesure; (expensive, difficult)
moyennement; (pleased, happy)
raisonnablement, assez; **~ priced** à un prix
raisonnable
moderation [mɔdə'reɪʃən] N modération f,
mesure f; **in ~** à dose raisonnable, pris(e) or
pratiqué(e) modérément
moderator ['mɔdəreɪtəʳ] N (Rel): **M~** président
m (de l'Assemblée générale de l'Église presbytérienne);
(Pol) modérateur m
modern ['mɔdən] ADJ moderne
modernization [mɔdənaɪ'zeɪʃən] N
modernisation f
modernize ['mɔdənaɪz] VT moderniser
modern languages NPL langues vivantes
modest ['mɔdɪst] ADJ modeste
modesty ['mɔdɪstɪ] N modestie f
modicum ['mɔdɪkəm] N: **a ~ of** un minimum de
modification [mɔdɪfɪ'keɪʃən] N modification f;
to make modifications faire or apporter des
modifications
modify ['mɔdɪfaɪ] VT modifier
modish ['məudɪʃ] ADJ à la mode
Mods [mɔdz] N ABBR (BRIT: = (Honour) Moderations)
premier examen universitaire (à Oxford)
modular ['mɔdjuləʳ] ADJ (filing, unit) modulaire
modulate ['mɔdjuleɪt] VT moduler
modulation [mɔdju'leɪʃən] N modulation f
module ['mɔdju:l] N module m
mogul ['məugl] N (fig) nabab m; (Ski) bosse f
MOH N ABBR (BRIT) = **Medical Officer of Health**
mohair ['məuhɛəʳ] N mohair m
Mohammed [mə'hæmɛd] N Mahomet m
moist [mɔɪst] ADJ humide, moite
moisten ['mɔɪsn] VT humecter, mouiller
légèrement
moisture ['mɔɪstʃəʳ] N humidité f; (on glass)
buée f
moisturize ['mɔɪstʃəraɪz] VT (skin) hydrater
moisturizer ['mɔɪstʃəraɪzəʳ] N crème
hydratante
molar ['məuləʳ] N molaire f
molasses [məu'læsɪz] N mélasse f

mold etc [məuld] (US) N = **mould**
Moldavia [mɔl'deɪvɪə], **Moldova** [mɔl'dəuvə] N
Moldavie f
Moldavian [mɔl'deɪvɪən], **Moldovan**
[mɔl'dəuvən] ADJ moldave
mole [məul] N (animal, spy) taupe f; (spot) grain m
de beauté
molecule ['mɔlɪkju:l] N molécule f
molehill ['məulhɪl] N taupinière f
molest [məu'lɛst] VT (assault sexually) attenter à
la pudeur de; (attack) molester; (harass)
tracasser
mollusc ['mɔləsk] N mollusque m
mollycoddle ['mɔlɪkɔdl] VT chouchouter,
couver
Molotov cocktail ['mɔlətɔf-] N cocktail m
Molotov
molt [məult] VI (US) = **moult**
molten ['məultən] ADJ fondu(e); (rock) en fusion
mom [mɔm] N (US) = **mum**
moment ['məumənt] N moment m, instant m;
(importance) importance f; **at the ~** en ce
moment; **for the ~** pour l'instant; **in a ~** dans
un instant; **"one ~ please"** "ne quittez pas"
momentarily ['məumənt'ərɪlɪ] ADV
momentanément; (US: soon) bientôt
momentary ['məuməntərɪ] ADJ momentané(e),
passager(-ère)
momentous [məu'mɛntəs] ADJ important(e),
capital(e)
momentum [məu'mɛntəm] N élan m, vitesse
acquise; (fig) dynamique f; **to gather ~** prendre
de la vitesse; (fig) gagner du terrain
mommy ['mɔmɪ] N (US: mother) maman f
Monaco ['mɔnəkəu] N Monaco f
monarch ['mɔnək] N monarque m
monarchist ['mɔnəkɪst] N monarchiste mf
monarchy ['mɔnəkɪ] N monarchie f
monastery ['mɔnəstərɪ] N monastère m
monastic [mə'næstɪk] ADJ monastique
Monday ['mʌndɪ] N lundi m; see also **Tuesday**
monetarist ['mʌnɪtərɪst] N monétariste mf
monetary ['mʌnɪtərɪ] ADJ monétaire
money ['mʌnɪ] N argent m; **to make ~** (person)
gagner de l'argent; (business) rapporter; **I've got
no ~ left** je n'ai plus d'argent, je n'ai plus un
sou
money belt N ceinture-portefeuille f
moneyed ['mʌnɪd] ADJ riche
moneylender ['mʌnɪlɛndəʳ] N prêteur(-euse)
moneymaker ['mʌnɪmeɪkəʳ] N (BRIT inf: business)
affaire lucrative
moneymaking ['mʌnɪmeɪkɪŋ] ADJ
lucratif(-ive), qui rapporte (de l'argent)
money market N marché financier
money order N mandat m
money-spinner ['mʌnɪspɪnəʳ] N (inf) mine f
d'or (fig)
money supply N masse f monétaire
Mongol ['mɔŋgəl] N Mongol(e); (Ling) mongol m
mongol ['mɔŋgəl] ADJ, N (Med) mongolien(ne)
Mongolia [mɔŋ'gəulɪə] N Mongolie f
Mongolian [mɔŋ'gəulɪən] ADJ mongol(e) ▸ N
Mongol(e); (Ling) mongol m

m

mongoose ['mɔŋguːs] N mangouste f
mongrel ['mʌŋgrəl] N (dog) bâtard m
monitor ['mɔnɪtəʳ] N (TV, Comput) écran m, moniteur m; (BRIT Scol) chef m de classe; (US Scol) surveillant m (d'examen) ▸ VT contrôler; (foreign station) être à l'écoute de; (progress) suivre de près
monk [mʌŋk] N moine m
monkey ['mʌŋkɪ] N singe m
monkey nut N (BRIT) cacahuète f
monkey wrench N clé f à molette
mono ['mɔnəu] ADJ mono inv
mono... ['mɔnəu] PREFIX mono...
monochrome ['mɔnəkrəum] ADJ monochrome
monocle ['mɔnəkl] N monocle m
monogamous [mɔ'nɔgəməs] ADJ monogame
monogamy [mɔ'nɔgəmɪ] N monogamie f
monogram ['mɔnəgræm] N monogramme m
monolith ['mɔnəlɪθ] N monolithe m
monologue ['mɔnəlɔg] N monologue m
monoplane ['mɔnəpleɪn] N monoplan m
monopolize [mə'nɔpəlaɪz] VT monopoliser
monopoly [mə'nɔpəlɪ] N monopole m;
Monopolies and Mergers Commission (BRIT) commission britannique d'enquête sur les monopoles
monorail ['mɔnəureɪl] N monorail m
monosodium glutamate
[mɔnə'səudɪəm gluː'təmeɪt] N glutamate m de sodium
monosyllabic [mɔnəsɪ'læbɪk] ADJ monosyllabique; (person) laconique
monosyllable ['mɔnəsɪləbl] N monosyllabe m
monotone ['mɔnətəun] N ton m (or voix f) monocorde; **to speak in a ~** parler sur un ton monocorde
monotonous [mə'nɔtənəs] ADJ monotone
monotony [mə'nɔtənɪ] N monotonie f
monoxide [mɔ'nɔksaɪd] N: **carbon ~** oxyde m de carbone
monsoon [mɔn'suːn] N mousson f
monster ['mɔnstəʳ] N monstre m
monstrosity [mɔns'trɔsɪtɪ] N monstruosité f, atrocité f
monstrous ['mɔnstrəs] ADJ (huge) gigantesque; (atrocious) monstrueux(-euse), atroce
Mont. ABBR (US) = **Montana**
montage [mɔn'taːʒ] N montage m
Mont Blanc [mɔ̃blɑ̃] N Mont Blanc m
month [mʌnθ] N mois m; **every ~** tous les mois; **300 dollars a ~** 300 dollars par mois
monthly ['mʌnθlɪ] ADJ mensuel(le) ▸ ADV mensuellement ▸ N (magazine) mensuel m, publication mensuelle; **twice ~** deux fois par mois
Montreal [mɔntrɪ'ɔːl] N Montréal
monument ['mɔnjumənt] N monument m
monumental [mɔnju'mɛntl] ADJ monumental(e)
monumental mason N marbrier m
moo [muː] VI meugler, beugler
mood [muːd] N humeur f, disposition f; **to be in a good/bad ~** être de bonne/mauvaise humeur; **to be in the ~ for** être d'humeur à, avoir envie de

moody ['muːdɪ] ADJ (variable) d'humeur changeante, lunatique; (sullen) morose, maussade
moon [muːn] N lune f
moonbeam ['muːnbiːm] N rayon m de lune
moon landing N alunissage m
moonlight ['muːnlaɪt] N clair m de lune ▸ VI travailler au noir
moonlighting ['muːnlaɪtɪŋ] N travail m au noir
moonlit ['muːnlɪt] ADJ éclairé(e) par la lune; **a ~ night** une nuit de lune
moonshot ['muːnʃɔt] N (Space) tir m lunaire
moonstruck ['muːnstrʌk] ADJ fou (folle), dérangé(e)
moony ['muːnɪ] ADJ: **to have ~ eyes** avoir l'air dans la lune or rêveur
Moor [muəʳ] N Maure (Mauresque)
moor [muəʳ] N lande f ▸ VT (ship) amarrer ▸ VI mouiller
moorings ['muərɪŋz] NPL (chains) amarres fpl; (place) mouillage m
Moorish ['muərɪʃ] ADJ maure, mauresque
moorland ['muələnd] N lande f
moose [muːs] N (pl inv) élan m
moot [muːt] VT soulever ▸ ADJ: **~ point** point m discutable
mop [mɔp] N balai m à laver; (for dishes) lavette f à vaisselle ▸ VT éponger, essuyer; **~ of hair** tignasse f
▸ **mop up** VT éponger
mope [məup] VI avoir le cafard, se morfondre
▸ **mope about, mope around** VI broyer du noir, se morfondre
moped ['məupɛd] N cyclomoteur m
MOR ADJ ABBR (Mus: = middle-of-the-road) tous publics
moral ['mɔrl] ADJ moral(e) ▸ N morale f; **morals** NPL moralité f
morale [mɔ'raːl] N moral m
morality [mə'rælɪtɪ] N moralité f
moralize ['mɔrəlaɪz] VI: **to ~ (about)** moraliser (sur)
morally ['mɔrəlɪ] ADV moralement
moral victory N victoire morale
morass [mə'ræs] N marais m, marécage m
moratorium [mɔrə'tɔːrɪəm] N moratoire m
morbid ['mɔːbɪd] ADJ morbide

(KEYWORD)

more [mɔːʳ] ADJ **1** (greater in number etc) plus (de), davantage (de); **more people/work (than)** plus de gens/de travail (que)
2 (additional) encore (de); **do you want (some) more tea?** voulez-vous encore du thé?; **is there any more wine?** reste-t-il du vin?; **I have no** or **I don't have any more money** je n'ai plus d'argent; **it'll take a few more weeks** ça prendra encore quelques semaines
▸ PRON plus, davantage; **more than 10** plus de 10; **it cost more than we expected** cela a coûté plus que prévu; **I want more** j'en veux plus or davantage; **is there any more?** est-ce qu'il en reste?; **there's no more** il n'y en a plus; **a little more** un peu plus; **many/much**

more beaucoup plus, bien davantage
▶ ADV plus; **more dangerous/easily (than)**
plus dangereux/facilement (que); **more and
more expensive** de plus en plus cher; **more or
less** plus ou moins; **more than ever** plus que
jamais; **once more** encore une fois, une fois de
plus; **and what's more …** et de plus …, et qui
plus est …

moreover [mɔːˈrəuvəʳ] ADV de plus
morgue [mɔːɡ] N morgue f
MORI [ˈmɔːrɪ] N ABBR (BRIT: = Market & Opinion
Research Institute) institut de sondage
moribund [ˈmɔrɪbʌnd] ADJ moribond(e)
morning [ˈmɔːnɪŋ] N matin m; (as duration)
matinée f ▶ CPD matinal(e); (paper) du matin;
in the ~ le matin; **7 o'clock in the ~** 7 heures du
matin; **this ~** ce matin
morning-after pill [ˈmɔːnɪŋˈɑːftə-] N pilule f du
lendemain
morning sickness N nausées matinales
Moroccan [məˈrɔkən] ADJ marocain(e) ▶ N
Marocain(e)
Morocco [məˈrɔkəu] N Maroc m
moron [ˈmɔːrɔn] (offensive) N idiot(e), minus mf
moronic [məˈrɔnɪk] ADJ idiot(e), imbécile
morose [məˈrəus] ADJ morose, maussade
morphine [ˈmɔːfiːn] N morphine f
morris dancing [ˈmɔrɪs-] N (BRIT) danses
folkloriques anglaises; voir article

> Le *morris dancing* est une danse folklorique
> anglaise traditionnellement réservée aux
> hommes. Habillés tout en blanc et portant
> des clochettes, ils exécutent différentes
> figures avec des mouchoirs et de longs
> bâtons. Cette danse est très populaire dans
> les fêtes de village.

Morse [mɔːs] N (also: **Morse code**) morse m
morsel [ˈmɔːsl] N bouchée f
mortal [ˈmɔːtl] ADJ, N mortel(le)
mortality [mɔːˈtælɪtɪ] N mortalité f
mortality rate N (taux m de) mortalité f
mortar [ˈmɔːtəʳ] N mortier m
mortgage [ˈmɔːɡɪdʒ] N hypothèque f; (loan) prêt
m (or crédit m) hypothécaire ▶ VT hypothéquer;
to take out a ~ prendre une hypothèque, faire
un emprunt
mortgage company N (US) société f de crédit
immobilier
mortgagee [mɔːɡəˈdʒiː] N prêteur(-euse) (sur
hypothèque)
mortgagor [ˈmɔːɡədʒəʳ] N emprunteur(-euse)
(sur hypothèque)
mortician [mɔːˈtɪʃən] N (US) entrepreneur m de
pompes funèbres
mortified [ˈmɔːtɪfaɪd] ADJ mort(e) de honte
mortise lock [ˈmɔːtɪs-] N serrure encastrée
mortuary [ˈmɔːtjuərɪ] N morgue f
mosaic [məuˈzeɪɪk] N mosaïque f
Moscow [ˈmɔskəu] N Moscou
Moslem [ˈmɔzləm] ADJ, N = **Muslim**
mosque [mɔsk] N mosquée f
mosquito [mɔsˈkiːtəu] (pl **mosquitoes**) N
moustique m

mosquito net N moustiquaire f
moss [mɔs] N mousse f
mossy [ˈmɔsɪ] ADJ moussu(e)
most [məust] ADJ (majority of) la plupart de;
(greatest amount of) le plus de ▶ PRON la plupart
▶ ADV le plus; (very) très, extrêmement; **the ~** le
plus; **~ fish** la plupart des poissons; **the ~
beautiful woman in the world** la plus belle
femme du monde; **~ of** (with plural) la plupart
de; (with singular) la plus grande partie de; **~ of
them** la plupart d'entre eux; **~ of the time** la
plupart du temps; **I saw ~** (a lot but not all) j'en ai
vu la plupart; (more than anyone else) c'est moi qui
en ai vu le plus; **at the (very) ~** au plus; **to
make the ~ of** profiter au maximum de
mostly [ˈməustlɪ] ADV (chiefly) surtout,
principalement; (usually) généralement
MOT N ABBR BRIT: = **Ministry of Transport**; **the ~
(test)** visite technique (annuelle) obligatoire des
véhicules à moteur
motel [məuˈtel] N motel m
moth [mɔθ] N papillon m de nuit; (in clothes)
mite f
mothball [ˈmɔθbɔːl] N boule f de naphtaline
moth-eaten [ˈmɔθiːtn] ADJ mité(e)
mother [ˈmʌðəʳ] N mère f ▶ VT (pamper, protect)
dorloter
mother board N (Comput) carte-mère f
motherhood [ˈmʌðəhud] N maternité f
mother-in-law [ˈmʌðərɪnlɔː] N belle-mère f
motherly [ˈmʌðəlɪ] ADJ maternel(le)
mother-of-pearl [ˈmʌðərəvˈpəːl] N nacre f
Mother's Day N fête f des Mères
mother's help N aide f or auxiliaire f familiale
mother-to-be [ˈmʌðətəˈbiː] N future maman
mother tongue N langue maternelle
mothproof [ˈmɔθpruːf] ADJ traité(e) à
l'antimite
motif [məuˈtiːf] N motif m
motion [ˈməuʃən] N mouvement m; (gesture)
geste m; (at meeting) motion f; (BRIT: also: **bowel
motion**) selles fpl ▶ VT, VI: **to ~ (to) sb to do** faire
signe à qn de faire; **to be in ~** (vehicle) être en
marche; **to set in ~** mettre en marche; **to go
through the motions of doing sth** (fig) faire
qch machinalement or sans conviction
motionless [ˈməuʃənlɪs] ADJ immobile, sans
mouvement
motion picture N film m
motivate [ˈməutɪveɪt] VT motiver
motivated [ˈməutɪveɪtɪd] ADJ motivé(e)
motivation [məutɪˈveɪʃən] N motivation f
motive [ˈməutɪv] N motif m, mobile m ▶ ADJ
moteur(-trice); **from the best of motives**
avec les meilleures intentions (du monde)
motley [ˈmɔtlɪ] ADJ hétéroclite; bigarré(e),
bariolé(e)
motor [ˈməutəʳ] N moteur m; (BRIT inf: vehicle)
auto f ▶ ADJ moteur(-trice)
motorbike [ˈməutəbaɪk] N moto f
motorboat [ˈməutəbəut] N bateau m à moteur
motorcade [ˈməutəkeɪd] N cortège m
d'automobiles or de voitures
motorcar [ˈməutəkɑː] N (BRIT) automobile f

m

685

motorcoach ['məʊtəkəʊtʃ] N (BRIT) car *m*
motorcycle ['məʊtəsaɪkl] N moto *f*
motorcycle racing N course *f* de motos
motorcyclist ['məʊtəsaɪklɪst] N
  motocycliste *mf*
motoring ['məʊtərɪŋ] (BRIT) N tourisme *m*
  automobile ▶ ADJ (*accident*) de voiture, de la
  route; ~ **holiday** vacances *fpl* en voiture;
  ~ **offence** infraction *f* au code de la route
motorist ['məʊtərɪst] N automobiliste *mf*
motorize ['məʊtəraɪz] VT motoriser
motor mechanic N mécanicien *m* garagiste
motor oil N huile *f* de graissage
motor racing N (BRIT) course *f* automobile
motor scooter N scooter *m*
motor trade N secteur *m* de l'automobile
motor vehicle N véhicule *m* automobile
motorway ['məʊtəweɪ] N (BRIT) autoroute *f*
mottled ['mɒtld] ADJ tacheté(e), marbré(e)
motto ['mɒtəʊ] (*pl* **mottoes**) N devise *f*
mould, (US) **mold** [məʊld] N moule *m*; (*mildew*)
  moisissure *f* ▶ VT mouler, modeler; (*fig*)
  façonner
moulder, (US) **molder** ['məʊldə*ʳ*] VI (*decay*)
  moisir
moulding, (US) **mold** ['məʊldɪŋ] N (*Archit*)
  moulure *f*
mouldy, (US) **moldy** ['məʊldɪ] ADJ moisi(e);
  (*smell*) de moisi
moult, (US) **molt** [məʊlt] VI muer
mound [maʊnd] N monticule *m*, tertre *m*
mount [maʊnt] N (*hill*) mont *m*, montagne *f*;
  (*horse*) monture *f*; (*for picture*) carton *m* de
  montage; (*for jewel etc*) monture ▶ VT monter;
  (*horse*) monter à; (*bike*) monter sur; (*exhibition*)
  organiser, monter; (*picture*) monter sur carton;
  (*stamp*) coller dans un album ▶ VI (*inflation*,
  tension) augmenter
  ▶ **mount up** VI s'élever, monter; (*bills, problems*,
  savings) s'accumuler
mountain ['maʊntɪn] N montagne *f* ▶ CPD de
  (la) montagne; **to make a ~ out of a molehill**
  (*fig*) se faire une montagne d'un rien
mountain bike N VTT *m*, vélo *m* tout terrain
mountaineer [maʊntɪ'nɪə*ʳ*] N alpiniste *mf*
mountaineering [maʊntɪ'nɪərɪŋ] N alpinisme
  m; **to go ~** faire de l'alpinisme
mountainous ['maʊntɪnəs] ADJ
  montagneux(-euse)
mountain range N chaîne *f* de montagnes
mountain rescue team N colonne *f* de secours
mountainside ['maʊntɪnsaɪd] N flanc *m* or
  versant *m* de la montagne
mounted ['maʊntɪd] ADJ monté(e)
Mount Everest N le mont Everest
mourn [mɔːn] VT pleurer ▶ VI: **to ~ for sb**
  pleurer qn; **to ~ for sth** se lamenter sur qch
mourner ['mɔːnə*ʳ*] N parent(e) or ami(e) du
  défunt; personne *f* en deuil or venue rendre
  hommage au défunt
mourning ['mɔːnɪŋ] N deuil *m* ▶ CPD (*dress*) de
  deuil; **in ~** en deuil
mouse [maʊs] (*pl* **mice** [maɪs]) N (*also Comput*)
  souris *f*

mouse mat N (*Comput*) tapis *m* de souris
mousetrap ['maʊstræp] N souricière *f*
moussaka [muː'saːkə] N moussaka *f*
mousse [muːs] N mousse *f*
moustache, (US) **mustache** [məs'taːʃ] N
  moustache(s) *f(pl)*
mousy ['maʊsɪ] ADJ (*person*) effacé(e); (*hair*) d'un
  châtain terne
mouth [maʊθ] (*pl* **mouths** [maʊðz]) N bouche *f*;
  (*of dog, cat*) gueule *f*; (*of river*) embouchure *f*; (*of
  hole, cave*) ouverture *f*; (*of bottle*) goulot *m*;
  (*opening*) orifice *m*
mouthful ['maʊθful] N bouchée *f*
mouth organ N harmonica *m*
mouthpiece ['maʊθpiːs] N (*of musical instrument*)
  bec *m*, embouchure *f*; (*spokesperson*) porte-parole
  m inv
mouth-to-mouth ['maʊθtə'maʊθ] ADJ:
  ~ **resuscitation** bouche à bouche *m*
mouthwash ['maʊθwɒʃ] N eau *f* dentifrice
mouth-watering ['maʊθwɔːtərɪŋ] ADJ qui met
  l'eau à la bouche
movable ['muːvəbl] ADJ mobile
move [muːv] N (*movement*) mouvement *m*; (*in
  game*) coup *m*; (: *turn to play*) tour *m*; (*change of
  house*) déménagement *m*; (*change of job*)
  changement *m* d'emploi ▶ VT déplacer, bouger;
  (*emotionally*) émouvoir; (*Pol: resolution etc*)
  proposer ▶ VI (*gen*) bouger, remuer; (*traffic*)
  circuler; (*also: move house*) déménager; (*in
  game*) jouer; **can you ~ your car, please?**
  pouvez-vous déplacer votre voiture, s'il vous
  plaît?; **to ~ towards** se diriger vers; **to ~ sb to
  do sth** pousser or inciter qn à faire qch; **to get a
  ~ on** se dépêcher, se remuer
  ▶ **move about, move around** VI (*fidget*) remuer;
  (*travel*) voyager, se déplacer
  ▶ **move along** VI se pousser
  ▶ **move away** VI s'en aller, s'éloigner
  ▶ **move back** VI revenir, retourner
  ▶ **move forward** VI avancer ▶ VT avancer;
  (*people*) faire avancer
  ▶ **move in** VI (*to a house*) emménager; (*police*,
  soldiers) intervenir
  ▶ **move off** VI s'éloigner, s'en aller
  ▶ **move on** VI se remettre en route ▶ VT
  (*onlookers*) faire circuler
  ▶ **move out** VI (*of house*) déménager
  ▶ **move over** VI se pousser, se déplacer
  ▶ **move up** VI avancer; (*employee*) avoir de
  l'avancement; (*pupil*) passer dans la classe
  supérieure
moveable [muːvəbl] ADJ = **movable**
movement ['muːvmənt] N mouvement *m*; ~ **(of
  the bowels)** (*Med*) selles *fpl*
mover ['muːvə*ʳ*] N auteur *m* d'une proposition
movie ['muːvɪ] N film *m*; **movies** NPL: **the
  movies** le cinéma
movie camera N caméra *f*
moviegoer ['muːvɪɡəʊə*ʳ*] N (US) cinéphile *mf*
movie theater N (US) cinéma *m*
moving ['muːvɪŋ] ADJ en mouvement; (*touching*)
  émouvant(e) ▶ N (US) déménagement *m*
mow [məʊ] (*pt* **mowed**, *pp* **mowed** or **mown**

[məun]) vᴛ faucher; (*lawn*) tondre
▶ **mow down** vᴛ faucher

mower ['məuə^r] ɴ (*also:* **lawnmower**) tondeuse *f* à gazon

mown [məun] ᴘᴘ *of* **mow**

Mozambique [məuzəm'bi:k] ɴ Mozambique *m*

MP ɴ ᴀʙʙʀ (= *Military Police*) PM; (*BRIT*) = **Member of Parliament**; (*CANADA*) = **Mounted Police**

MP3 ɴ mp3 *m*

MP3 player ɴ baladeur *m* numérique, lecteur *m* mp3

mpg ɴ ᴀʙʙʀ = **miles per gallon** (*30 mpg = 9,4 l. aux 100 km*)

m.p.h. ᴀʙʙʀ = **miles per hour** (*60 mph = 96 km/h*)

MPhil ɴ ᴀʙʙʀ (*US:* = *Master of Philosophy*) titre universitaire

MPS ɴ ᴀʙʙʀ (*BRIT*) = **Member of the Pharmaceutical Society**

Mr, (*US*) **Mr.** ['mɪstə^r] ɴ: **Mr X** Monsieur X, M. X

MRC ɴ ᴀʙʙʀ (*BRIT:* = *Medical Research Council*) conseil de la recherche médicale

MRCP ɴ ᴀʙʙʀ (*BRIT*) = **Member of the Royal College of Physicians**

MRCS ɴ ᴀʙʙʀ (*BRIT*) = **Member of the Royal College of Surgeons**

MRCVS ɴ ᴀʙʙʀ (*BRIT*) = **Member of the Royal College of Veterinary Surgeons**

Mrs, (*US*) **Mrs.** ['mɪsɪz] ɴ: ~ **X** Madame X, Mme X

MS ɴ ᴀʙʙʀ (= *manuscript*) ms; (= *multiple sclerosis*) SEP *f*; (*US:* = *Master of Science*) titre universitaire
▶ ᴀʙʙʀ (*US*) = **Mississippi**

Ms, (*US*) **Ms.** [mɪz] ɴ (*Miss or Mrs*): **Ms X** Madame X, Mme X; *voir article*

> Ms est un titre utilisé à la place de Mrs (Mme) ou de Miss (Mlle) pour éviter la distinction traditionnelle entre femmes mariées et femmes non mariées.

MSA ɴ ᴀʙʙʀ (*US:* = *Master of Science in Agriculture*) titre universitaire

MSc ɴ ᴀʙʙʀ = **Master of Science**

MSG ɴ ᴀʙʙʀ = **monosodium glutamate**

MSP ɴ ᴀʙʙʀ (= *Member of the Scottish Parliament*) député *m* au Parlement écossais

MST ᴀʙʙʀ (*US:* = *Mountain Standard Time*) heure d'hiver des Montagnes Rocheuses

MT ɴ ᴀʙʙʀ (= *machine translation*) TM ▶ ᴀʙʙʀ (*US*) = **Montana**

Mt ᴀʙʙʀ (*Geo:* = *mount*) Mt

mth ᴀʙʙʀ (= *month*) m

MTV ɴ ᴀʙʙʀ = **music television**

much [mʌtʃ] ᴀᴅᴊ beaucoup de ▶ ᴀᴅᴠ, ɴ, ᴘʀᴏɴ beaucoup; ~ **milk** beaucoup de lait; **we don't have ~ time** nous n'avons pas beaucoup de temps; **how ~ is it?** combien est-ce que ça coûte?; **it's not ~** ce n'est pas beaucoup; **too ~** trop (de); **so ~** tant (de); **I like it very/so ~** j'aime beaucoup/tellement ça; **as ~ as** autant de; **thank you very ~** merci beaucoup; **that's ~ better** c'est beaucoup mieux; **~ to my amazement ...** à mon grand étonnement ...

muck [mʌk] ɴ (*mud*) boue *f*; (*dirt*) ordures *fpl*
▶ **muck about** vɪ (*inf*) faire l'imbécile; (: *waste time*) traînasser; (: *tinker*) bricoler; tripoter
▶ **muck in** vɪ (*BRIT inf*) donner un coup de main

▶ **muck out** vᴛ (*stable*) nettoyer
▶ **muck up** vᴛ (*inf: ruin*) gâcher, esquinter; (*dirty*) salir; (*exam, interview*) se planter à

muckraking ['mʌkreɪkɪŋ] ɴ (*fig: inf*) déterrement *m* d'ordures

mucky ['mʌkɪ] ᴀᴅᴊ (*dirty*) boueux(-euse), sale

mucus ['mju:kəs] ɴ mucus *m*

mud [mʌd] ɴ boue *f*

muddle ['mʌdl] ɴ (*mess*) pagaille *f*, fouillis *m*; (*mix-up*) confusion *f* ▶ vᴛ (*also:* **muddle up**) brouiller, embrouiller; **to be in a ~** (*person*) ne plus savoir où l'on en est; **to get in a ~** (*while explaining etc*) s'embrouiller
▶ **muddle along** vɪ aller son chemin tant bien que mal
▶ **muddle through** vɪ se débrouiller

muddle-headed [mʌdl'hɛdɪd] ᴀᴅᴊ (*person*) à l'esprit embrouillé *or* confus, dans le brouillard

muddy ['mʌdɪ] ᴀᴅᴊ boueux(-euse)

mud flats ɴᴘʟ plage *f* de vase

mudguard ['mʌdgɑ:d] ɴ garde-boue *m inv*

mudpack ['mʌdpæk] ɴ masque *m* de beauté

mud-slinging ['mʌdslɪŋɪŋ] ɴ médisance *f*, dénigrement *m*

muesli ['mju:zlɪ] ɴ muesli *m*

muff [mʌf] ɴ manchon *m* ▶ vᴛ (*inf: shot, catch etc*) rater, louper; **to ~ it** rater *or* louper son coup

muffin ['mʌfɪn] ɴ (*roll*) petit pain rond et plat; (*cake*) petit gâteau au chocolat ou aux fruits

muffle ['mʌfl] vᴛ (*sound*) assourdir, étouffer; (*against cold*) emmitoufler

muffled ['mʌfld] ᴀᴅᴊ étouffé(e), voilé(e)

muffler ['mʌflə^r] ɴ (*scarf*) cache-nez *m inv*; (*US Aut*) silencieux *m*

mufti ['mʌftɪ] ɴ: **in ~** en civil

mug [mʌg] ɴ (*cup*) tasse *f* (*sans soucoupe*); (: *for beer*) chope *f*; (*inf: face*) bouille *f*; (: *fool*) poire *f* ▶ vᴛ (*assault*) agresser; **it's a ~'s game** (*BRIT*) c'est bon pour les imbéciles
▶ **mug up** vᴛ (*BRIT inf: also:* **mug up on**) bosser, bûcher

mugger ['mʌgə^r] ɴ agresseur *m*

mugging ['mʌgɪŋ] ɴ agression *f*

muggins ['mʌgɪnz] ɴ (*inf*) ma pomme

muggy ['mʌgɪ] ᴀᴅᴊ lourd(e), moite

mug shot ɴ (*inf: Police*) photo *f* de criminel; (: *gen: photo*) photo d'identité

mulatto [mju:'lætəu] (*pl* **mulattoes**) (*offensive*) ɴ mulâtre(-tresse)

mulberry ['mʌlbrɪ] ɴ (*fruit*) mûre *f*; (*tree*) mûrier *m*

mule [mju:l] ɴ mule *f*

mull [mʌl]: **to ~ over** vᴛ réfléchir à, ruminer

mulled [mʌld] ᴀᴅᴊ: **~ wine** vin chaud

multi... ['mʌltɪ] ᴘʀᴇғɪx multi...

multi-access ['mʌltɪ'ækses] ᴀᴅᴊ (*Comput*) à accès multiple

multicoloured, (*US*) **multicolored** ['mʌltɪkʌləd] ᴀᴅᴊ multicolore

multifarious [mʌltɪ'fɛərɪəs] ᴀᴅᴊ divers(es), varié(e)

multilateral [mʌltɪ'lætərl] ᴀᴅᴊ (*Pol*) multilatéral(e)

multi-level ['mʌltɪlevl] ᴀᴅᴊ (*US*) = **multistorey**

m

687

multimedia ['mʌltɪ'miːdɪə] ADJ multimédia *inv*
multimillionaire [mʌltɪmɪljə'nɛəʳ] N milliardaire *mf*
multinational [mʌltɪ'næʃənl] N multinationale *f* ▸ ADJ multinational(e)
multiple ['mʌltɪpl] ADJ multiple ▸ N multiple *m*; (BRIT: *also*: **multiple store**) magasin *m* à succursales (multiples)
multiple choice (test) N QCM *m*, questionnaire *m* à choix multiple
multiple crash N carambolage *m*
multiple sclerosis [-sklɪ'rəʊsɪs] N sclérose *f* en plaques
multiplex (cinema) ['mʌltɪplɛks-] N (cinéma *m*) multisalles *m*
multiplication [mʌltɪplɪ'keɪʃən] N multiplication *f*
multiplication table N table *f* de multiplication
multiplicity [mʌltɪ'plɪsɪtɪ] N multiplicité *f*
multiply ['mʌltɪplaɪ] VT multiplier ▸ VI se multiplier
multiracial [mʌltɪ'reɪʃl] ADJ multiracial(e)
multistorey ['mʌltɪ'stɔːrɪ] ADJ (BRIT: *building*) à étages; (: *car park*) à étages *or* niveaux multiples
multitude ['mʌltɪtjuːd] N multitude *f*
mum [mʌm] N (BRIT) maman *f* ▸ ADJ: **to keep ~** ne pas souffler mot; **~'s the word!** motus et bouche cousue!
mumble ['mʌmbl] VT, VI marmotter, marmonner
mumbo jumbo ['mʌmbəʊ-] (*inf*) baragouin *m*, charabia *m*
mummify ['mʌmɪfaɪ] VT momifier
mummy ['mʌmɪ] N (BRIT: *mother*) maman *f*; (*embalmed*) momie *f*
mumps [mʌmps] N oreillons *mpl*
munch [mʌntʃ] VT, VI mâcher
mundane [mʌn'deɪn] ADJ banal(e), terre à terre *inv*
municipal [mjuː'nɪsɪpl] ADJ municipal(e)
municipality [mjuːnɪsɪ'pælɪtɪ] N municipalité *f*
munitions [mjuː'nɪʃənz] NPL munitions *fpl*
mural ['mjuərl] N peinture murale
murder ['məːdəʳ] N meurtre *m*, assassinat *m* ▸ VT assassiner; **to commit ~** commettre un meurtre
murderer ['məːdərəʳ] N meurtrier *m*, assassin *m*
murderess ['məːdərɪs] N meurtrière *f*
murderous ['məːdərəs] ADJ meurtrier(-ière)
murk [məːk] N obscurité *f*
murky ['məːkɪ] ADJ sombre, ténébreux(-euse); (*water*) trouble
murmur ['məːməʳ] N murmure *m* ▸ VT, VI murmurer; **heart ~** (*Med*) souffle *m* au cœur
MusB, MusBac N ABBR (= *Bachelor of Music*) titre universitaire
muscle ['mʌsl] N muscle *m*; (*fig*) force *f*
▸ **muscle in** VI s'imposer, s'immiscer
muscular ['mʌskjulə ʳ] ADJ musculaire; (*person*, *arm*) musclé(e)
muscular dystrophy N dystrophie *f* musculaire
MusD, MusDoc N ABBR (= *Doctor of Music*) titre universitaire

muse [mjuːz] VI méditer, songer ▸ N muse *f*
museum [mjuː'zɪəm] N musée *m*
mush [mʌʃ] N bouillie *f*; (*pej*) sentimentalité *f* à l'eau de rose
mushroom ['mʌʃrum] N champignon *m* ▸ VI (*fig*) pousser comme un (*or* des) champignon(s)
mushy ['mʌʃɪ] ADJ (*vegetables*, *fruit*) en bouillie; (*movie etc*) à l'eau de rose
music ['mjuːzɪk] N musique *f*
musical ['mjuːzɪkl] ADJ musical(e); (*person*) musicien(ne) ▸ N (*show*) comédie musicale
musical box N = **music box**
musical chairs NPL chaises musicales; (*fig*): **to play ~** faire des permutations
musical instrument N instrument *m* de musique
music box N boîte *f* à musique
music centre N chaîne compacte
music hall N music-hall *m*
musician [mjuː'zɪʃən] N musicien(ne)
music stand N pupitre *m* à musique
musk [mʌsk] N musc *m*
musket ['mʌskɪt] N mousquet *m*
muskrat ['mʌskræt] N rat musqué
musk rose N (*Bot*) rose *f* muscade
Muslim ['mʌzlɪm] ADJ, N musulman(e)
muslin ['mʌzlɪn] N mousseline *f*
musquash ['mʌskwɔʃ] N loutre *f*; (*fur*) rat *m* d'Amérique, ondatra *m*
mussel ['mʌsl] N moule *f*
must [mʌst] AUX VB (*obligation*): **I ~ do it** je dois le faire, il faut que je le fasse; (*probability*): **he ~ be there by now** il doit y être maintenant, il y est probablement maintenant; (*suggestion*, *invitation*): **you ~ come and see me** il faut que vous veniez me voir ▸ N nécessité *f*, impératif *m*; **it's a ~** c'est indispensable; **I ~ have made a mistake** j'ai dû me tromper
mustache ['mʌstæʃ] N (US) = **moustache**
mustard ['mʌstəd] N moutarde *f*
mustard gas N ypérite *f*, gaz *m* moutarde
muster ['mʌstəʳ] VT rassembler; (*also*: **muster up**: *strength*, *courage*) rassembler
mustiness ['mʌstɪnɪs] N goût *m* de moisi; odeur *f* de moisi or de renfermé
mustn't ['mʌsnt] = **must not**
musty ['mʌstɪ] ADJ qui sent le moisi *or* le renfermé
mutant ['mjuːtənt] ADJ mutant(e) ▸ N mutant *m*
mutate [mjuː'teɪt] VI subir une mutation
mutation [mjuː'teɪʃən] N mutation *f*
mute [mjuːt] ADJ muet(te)
muted ['mjuːtɪd] ADJ (*noise*) sourd(e), assourdi(e); (*criticism*) voilé(e); (*Mus*) en sourdine; (: *trumpet*) bouché(e)
mutilate ['mjuːtɪleɪt] VT mutiler
mutilation [mjuːtɪ'leɪʃən] N mutilation *f*
mutinous ['mjuːtɪnəs] ADJ (*troops*) mutiné(e); (*attitude*) rebelle
mutiny ['mjuːtɪnɪ] N mutinerie *f* ▸ VI se mutiner
mutter ['mʌtəʳ] VT, VI marmonner, marmotter
mutton ['mʌtn] N mouton *m*

mutual ['mju:tʃuəl] ADJ mutuel(le), réciproque; (*benefit, interest*) commun(e)

mutually ['mju:tʃuəlɪ] ADV mutuellement, réciproquement

Muzak® ['mju:zæk] N (*often pej*) musique f d'ambiance

muzzle ['mʌzl] N museau m; (*protective device*) muselière f; (*of gun*) gueule f ▶ VT museler

MVP N ABBR (*US Sport*) = **most valuable player**

MW ABBR (= *medium wave*) PO

my [maɪ] ADJ mon (ma), mes pl; **my house/car/gloves** ma maison/ma voiture/mes gants; **I've washed my hair/cut my finger** je me suis lavé les cheveux/coupé le doigt; **is this my pen or yours?** c'est mon stylo ou c'est le vôtre?

Myanmar ['maɪænmɑːʳ] N Myanmar m

myopic [maɪˈɔpɪk] ADJ myope

myriad ['mɪrɪəd] N myriade f

myself [maɪˈsɛlf] PRON (*reflexive*) me; (*emphatic*) moi-même; (*after prep*) moi; *see also* **oneself**

mysterious [mɪsˈtɪərɪəs] ADJ mystérieux(-euse)

mystery ['mɪstərɪ] N mystère m

mystery story N roman m à suspense

mystic ['mɪstɪk] N mystique mf ▶ ADJ (*mysterious*) ésotérique

mystical ['mɪstɪkl] ADJ mystique

mystify ['mɪstɪfaɪ] VT (*deliberately*) mystifier; (*puzzle*) ébahir

mystique [mɪsˈtiːk] N mystique f

myth [mɪθ] N mythe m

mythical ['mɪθɪkl] ADJ mythique

mythological [mɪθəˈlɔdʒɪkl] ADJ mythologique

mythology [mɪˈθɔlədʒɪ] N mythologie f

m

N n

N, n [ɛn] N (*letter*) N, n *m*; **N for Nellie**, (US) **N for Nan** N comme Nicolas

N ABBR (= *north*) N

NA N ABBR (US: = *Narcotics Anonymous*) association d'aide aux drogués; (US) = **National Academy**

n/a ABBR (= *not applicable*) n.a.; (*Comm etc*) = **no account**

NAACP N ABBR (US) = **National Association for the Advancement of Colored People**

NAAFI ['næfɪ] N ABBR (BRIT: = *Navy, Army & Air Force Institute*) organisme responsable des magasins et cantines de l'armée

nab [næb] VT (*inf*) pincer, attraper

NACU N ABBR (US) = **National Association of Colleges and Universities**

nadir ['neɪdɪə'] N (*Astronomy*) nadir *m*; (*fig*) fond *m*, point *m* extrême

naff [næf] (BRIT *inf*) ADJ nul(le)

nag [næg] VT (*scold*) être toujours après, reprendre sans arrêt ▶ N (*pej: horse*) canasson *m*; (*person*): **she's an awful ~** elle est constamment après lui (*or eux etc*), elle est très casse-pieds

nagging ['nægɪŋ] ADJ (*doubt, pain*) persistant(e) ▶ N remarques continuelles

nail [neɪl] N (*human*) ongle *m*; (*metal*) clou *m* ▶ VT clouer; **to ~ sth to sth** clouer qch à qch; **to ~ sb down to a date/price** contraindre qn à accepter *or* donner une date/un prix; **to pay cash on the ~** (BRIT) payer rubis sur l'ongle

nailbrush ['neɪlbrʌʃ] N brosse *f* à ongles

nailfile ['neɪlfaɪl] N lime *f* à ongles

nail polish N vernis *m* à ongles

nail polish remover N dissolvant *m*

nail scissors NPL ciseaux *mpl* à ongles

nail varnish N (BRIT) = **nail polish**

Nairobi [naɪˈrəʊbɪ] N Nairobi

naïve [naɪˈiːv] ADJ naïf(-ïve)

naïveté [naɪˈiːveɪ], **naivety** [naɪˈiːvɪtɪ] N naïveté *f*

naked ['neɪkɪd] ADJ nu(e); **with the ~ eye** à l'œil nu

nakedness ['neɪkɪdnɪs] N nudité *f*

NAM N ABBR (US) = **National Association of Manufacturers**

name [neɪm] N nom *m*; (*reputation*) réputation *f* ▶ VT nommer; (*identify: accomplice etc*) citer; (*price, date*) fixer, donner; **by ~** par son nom; de nom; **in the ~ of** au nom de; **what's your ~?**

comment vous appelez-vous?, quel est votre nom?; **my ~ is Peter** je m'appelle Peter; **to take sb's ~ and address** relever l'identité de qn *or* les nom et adresse de qn; **to make a ~ for o.s.** se faire un nom; **to get (o.s.) a bad ~** se faire une mauvaise réputation; **to call sb names** traiter qn de tous les noms

name dropping N mention (*pour se faire valoir*) du nom de personnalités qu'on connaît (*ou prétend connaître*)

nameless ['neɪmlɪs] ADJ sans nom; (*witness, contributor*) anonyme

namely ['neɪmlɪ] ADV à savoir

nameplate ['neɪmpleɪt] N (*on door etc*) plaque *f*

namesake ['neɪmseɪk] N homonyme *m*

nan bread [nɑːn-] N nan *m*

nanny ['nænɪ] N bonne *f* d'enfants

nanny goat N chèvre *f*

nap [næp] N (*sleep*) (petit) somme ▶ VI: **to be caught napping** être pris(e) à l'improviste *or* en défaut

NAPA N ABBR (US: = *National Association of Performing Artists*) syndicat des gens du spectacle

napalm ['neɪpɑːm] N napalm *m*

nape [neɪp] N: **~ of the neck** nuque *f*

napkin ['næpkɪn] N serviette *f* (de table)

Naples ['neɪplz] N Naples

Napoleonic [nəpəʊlɪˈɒnɪk] ADJ napoléonien(ne)

nappy ['næpɪ] N (BRIT) couche *f*

nappy liner N (BRIT) protège-couche *m*

nappy rash N: **to have ~** avoir les fesses rouges

narcissistic [nɑːsɪˈsɪstɪk] ADJ narcissique

narcissus [nɑːˈsɪsəs] (*pl* **narcissi** [-saɪ]) N narcisse *m*

narcotic [nɑːˈkɒtɪk] N (*Med*) narcotique *m*

narcotics [nɑːˈkɒtɪkz] NPL (*illegal drugs*) stupéfiants *mpl*

nark [nɑːk] VT (BRIT *inf*) mettre en rogne

narrate [nəˈreɪt] VT raconter, narrer

narration [nəˈreɪʃən] N narration *f*

narrative ['nærətɪv] N récit *m* ▶ ADJ narratif(-ive)

narrator [nəˈreɪtə'] N narrateur(-trice)

narrow ['nærəʊ] ADJ étroit(e); (*fig*) restreint(e), limité(e) ▶ VI (*road*) devenir plus étroit, se rétrécir; (*gap, difference*) se réduire; **to have a ~ escape** l'échapper belle

▶ **narrow down** VT restreindre

narrow gauge ADJ (Rail) à voie étroite
narrowly ['nærəʊlɪ] ADV: **he ~ missed injury/
the tree** il a failli se blesser/rentrer dans
l'arbre; **he only ~ missed the target** il a
manqué la cible de peu or de justesse
narrow-minded [nærəʊ'maɪndɪd] ADJ à l'esprit
étroit, borné(e); (attitude) borné(e)
NAS N ABBR (US) = **National Academy of
Sciences**
NASA ['næsə] N ABBR (US: = National Aeronautics
and Space Administration) NASA f
nasal ['neɪzl] ADJ nasal(e)
Nassau ['næsɔ:] N (in Bahamas) Nassau
nastily ['nɑ:stɪlɪ] ADV (say, act) méchamment
nastiness ['nɑ:stɪnɪs] N (of person, remark)
méchanceté f
nasturtium [nəs'tə:ʃəm] N capucine f
nasty ['nɑ:stɪ] ADJ (person: malicious) méchant(e);
(: rude) très désagréable; (smell) dégoûtant(e);
(wound, situation) mauvais(e), vilain(e); (weather)
affreux(-euse); **to turn ~** (situation) mal
tourner; (weather) se gâter; (person) devenir
méchant; **it's a ~ business** c'est une sale
affaire
NAS/UWT N ABBR (BRIT: = National Association of
Schoolmasters/Union of Women Teachers) syndicat
enseignant
nation ['neɪʃən] N nation f
national ['næʃənl] ADJ national(e) ▶ N (abroad)
ressortissant(e); (when home) national(e)
national anthem N hymne national
National Curriculum N (BRIT) programme scolaire
commun à toutes les écoles publiques en Angleterre et
au Pays de Galles comprenant dix disciplines
national debt N dette f publique
national dress N costume national
National Guard N (US) milice f (de volontaires)
National Health Service N (BRIT) service national
de santé, = Sécurité Sociale
National Insurance N (BRIT) ≈ Sécurité Sociale
nationalism ['næʃnəlɪzəm] N nationalisme m
nationalist ['næʃnəlɪst] ADJ, N nationaliste mf
nationality [næʃə'nælɪtɪ] N nationalité f
nationalization [næʃnəlaɪ'zeɪʃən] N
nationalisation f
nationalize ['næʃnəlaɪz] VT nationaliser
nationally ['næʃnəlɪ] ADV du point de vue
national; dans le pays entier
national park N parc national
national press N presse nationale
National Security Council N (US) conseil
national de sécurité
national service N (Mil) service m militaire
National Trust N (BRIT) ≈ Caisse f nationale des
monuments historiques et des sites; voir article

Le National Trust est un organisme
indépendant, à but non lucratif, dont
la mission est de protéger et de mettre
en valeur les monuments et les sites
britanniques en raison de leur intérêt
historique ou de leur beauté naturelle.

nationwide ['neɪʃənwaɪd] ADJ s'étendant à
l'ensemble du pays; (problem) à l'échelle du pays
entier ▶ ADV à travers or dans tout le pays

native ['neɪtɪv] N habitant(e) du pays,
autochtone mf; (in colonies) indigène mf ▶ ADJ
du pays, indigène; (country) natal(e); (language)
maternel(le); (ability) inné(e); **a ~ of Russia** une
personne originaire de Russie; **a ~ speaker of
French** une personne de langue maternelle
française
Native American N Indien(ne) d'Amérique
▶ ADJ amérindien(ne)
native speaker N locuteur natif; see also **native**
Nativity [nə'tɪvɪtɪ] N (Rel): **the ~** la Nativité
nativity play N mystère m or miracle m de la
Nativité
NATO ['neɪtəʊ] N ABBR (= North Atlantic Treaty
Organization) OTAN f
natter ['nætər] VI (BRIT) bavarder
natural ['nætʃrəl] ADJ naturel(le); **to die of ~
causes** mourir d'une mort naturelle
natural childbirth N accouchement m sans
douleur
natural gas N gaz naturel
natural history N histoire naturelle
naturalist ['nætʃrəlɪst] N naturaliste mf
naturalization ['nætʃrəlaɪ'zeɪʃən] N
naturalisation f; acclimatation f
naturalize ['nætʃrəlaɪz] VT naturaliser; (plant)
acclimater; **to become naturalized** (person) se
faire naturaliser
naturally ['nætʃrəlɪ] ADV naturellement
natural resources NPL ressources naturelles
natural selection N sélection naturelle
natural wastage N (Industry) départs naturels
et volontaires
nature ['neɪtʃər] N nature f; **by ~** par
tempérament, de nature; **documents of a
confidential ~** documents à caractère
confidentiel
-natured ['neɪtʃəd] SUFFIX: **ill~** qui a mauvais
caractère
nature reserve N (BRIT) réserve naturelle
nature trail N sentier de découverte de la nature
naturist ['neɪtʃərɪst] N naturiste mf
naught [nɔ:t] N = **nought**
naughtiness ['nɔ:tɪnɪs] N (of child)
désobéissance f; (of story etc) grivoiserie f
naughty ['nɔ:tɪ] ADJ (child) vilain(e), pas sage;
(story, film) grivois(e)
nausea ['nɔ:sɪə] N nausée f
nauseate ['nɔ:sɪeɪt] VT écœurer, donner la
nausée à
nauseating ['nɔ:sɪeɪtɪŋ] ADJ écœurant(e),
dégoûtant(e)
nauseous ['nɔ:sɪəs] ADJ nauséabond(e),
écœurant(e); (feeling sick): **to be ~** avoir des
nausées
nautical ['nɔ:tɪkl] ADJ nautique
nautical mile N mille marin (= 1853 m)
naval ['neɪvl] ADJ naval(e)
naval officer N officier m de marine
nave [neɪv] N nef f
navel ['neɪvl] N nombril m
navigable ['nævɪgəbl] ADJ navigable
navigate ['nævɪgeɪt] VT (steer) diriger, piloter
▶ VI naviguer; (Aut) indiquer la route à suivre

n

navigation [nævɪ'geɪʃən] N navigation f
navigator ['nævɪgeɪtər] N navigateur m
navvy ['nævɪ] N (BRIT) terrassier m
navy ['neɪvɪ] N marine f; **Department of the N~** (US) ministère m de la Marine
navy-blue ['neɪvɪ'bluː] ADJ bleu marine inv
Nazi ['nɑːtsɪ] ADJ nazi(e) ▶ N Nazi(e)
NB ABBR (= nota bene) NB; (CANADA) = **New Brunswick**
NBA N ABBR (US) = **National Basketball Association; National Boxing Association**
NBC N ABBR (US: = National Broadcasting Company) chaîne de télévision
NBS N ABBR (US: = National Bureau of Standards) office de normalisation
NC ABBR (Comm etc) = **no charge**; (US) = **North Carolina**
NCC N ABBR (BRIT: = Nature Conservancy Council) organisme de protection de la nature; (US) = **National Council of Churches**
NCO N ABBR = **non-commissioned officer**
ND, N. Dak. ABBR (US) = **North Dakota**
NE ABBR (US) = **Nebraska; New England**
NEA N ABBR (US) = **National Education Association**
neap [niːp] N (also: **neap tide**) mortes-eaux fpl
near [nɪər] ADJ proche ▶ ADV près ▶ PREP (also: **near to**) près de ▶ VT approcher de; **~ here/there** près d'ici/non loin de là; **£25,000 or nearest offer** (BRIT) 25 000 livres à débattre; **in the ~ future** dans un proche avenir; **to come ~** s'approcher
nearby [nɪə'baɪ] ADJ proche ▶ ADV tout près, à proximité
Near East N: **the ~** le Proche-Orient
nearer ['nɪərər] ADJ plus proche ▶ ADV plus près
nearly ['nɪəlɪ] ADV presque; **I ~ fell** j'ai failli tomber; **it's not ~ big enough** ce n'est vraiment pas assez grand, c'est loin d'être assez grand
near miss N collision évitée de justesse; (when aiming) coup manqué de peu or de justesse
nearness ['nɪənɪs] N proximité f
nearside ['nɪəsaɪd] (Aut) N (right-hand drive) côté m gauche; (left-hand drive) côté droit ▶ ADJ de gauche; de droite
near-sighted [nɪə'saɪtɪd] ADJ myope
neat [niːt] ADJ (person, work) soigné(e); (room etc) bien tenu(e) or rangé(e); (solution, plan) habile; (spirits) pur(e); **I drink it ~** je le bois sec or sans eau
neatly ['niːtlɪ] ADV avec soin or ordre; (skilfully) habilement
neatness ['niːtnɪs] N (tidiness) netteté f; (skilfulness) habileté f
Nebr. ABBR (US) = **Nebraska**
nebulous ['nɛbjuləs] ADJ nébuleux(-euse)
necessarily ['nɛsɪsərɪlɪ] ADV nécessairement; **not ~** pas nécessairement or forcément
necessary ['nɛsɪsrɪ] ADJ nécessaire; **if ~** si besoin est, le cas échéant
necessitate [nɪ'sɛsɪteɪt] VT nécessiter
necessity [nɪ'sɛsɪtɪ] N nécessité f; chose

nécessaire or essentielle; **in case of ~** en cas d'urgence
neck [nɛk] N cou m; (of horse, garment) encolure f; (of bottle) goulot m ▶ VI (inf) se peloter; **~ and ~** à égalité; **to stick one's ~ out** (inf) se mouiller
necklace ['nɛklɪs] N collier m
neckline ['nɛklaɪn] N encolure f
necktie ['nɛktaɪ] N (esp US) cravate f
nectar ['nɛktər] N nectar m
nectarine ['nɛktərɪn] N brugnon m, nectarine f
née [neɪ] ADJ: **~ Scott** née Scott
need [niːd] N besoin m ▶ VT avoir besoin de; **to ~ to do** devoir faire; avoir besoin de faire; **you don't ~ to go** vous n'avez pas besoin or vous n'êtes pas obligé de partir; **a signature is needed** il faut une signature; **to be in ~ of** or **have ~ of** avoir besoin de; **£10 will meet my immediate needs** 10 livres suffiront pour mes besoins immédiats; **in case of ~** en cas de besoin, au besoin; **there's no ~ to do ....** il n'y a pas lieu de faire ..., il n'est pas nécessaire de faire ...; **there's no ~ for that** ce n'est pas la peine, cela n'est pas nécessaire
needle ['niːdl] N aiguille f; (on record player) saphir m ▶ VT (inf) asticoter, tourmenter
needlecord ['niːdlkɔːd] N (BRIT) velours m milleraies
needless ['niːdlɪs] ADJ inutile; **~ to say, ...** inutile de dire que ...
needlessly ['niːdlɪslɪ] ADV inutilement
needlework ['niːdlwəːk] N (activity) travaux mpl d'aiguille; (object) ouvrage m
needn't ['niːdnt] = **need not**
needy ['niːdɪ] ADJ nécessiteux(-euse)
negation [nɪ'geɪʃən] N négation f
negative ['nɛgətɪv] N (Phot, Elec) négatif m; (Ling) terme m de négation ▶ ADJ négatif(-ive); **to answer in the ~** répondre par la négative
negative equity N situation dans laquelle la valeur d'une maison est inférieure à celle du prêt immobilier contracté pour la payer
neglect [nɪ'glɛkt] VT négliger; (garden) ne pas entretenir; (duty) manquer à ▶ N (of person, duty, garden) le fait de négliger; **(state of) ~** abandon m; **to ~ to do sth** négliger or omettre de faire qch; **to ~ one's appearance** se négliger
neglected [nɪ'glɛktɪd] ADJ négligé(e), à l'abandon
neglectful [nɪ'glɛktful] ADJ (gen) négligent(e); **to be ~ of sb/sth** négliger qn/qch
negligee ['nɛglɪʒeɪ] N déshabillé m
negligence ['nɛglɪdʒəns] N négligence f
negligent ['nɛglɪdʒənt] ADJ négligent(e)
negligently ['nɛglɪdʒəntlɪ] ADV par négligence; (offhandedly) négligemment
negligible ['nɛglɪdʒɪbl] ADJ négligeable
negotiable [nɪ'gəʊʒɪəbl] ADJ négociable; **not ~** (cheque) non négociable
negotiate [nɪ'gəʊʃɪeɪt] VI négocier ▶ VT négocier; (Comm) négocier; (obstacle) franchir, négocier; (bend in road) négocier; **to ~ with sb for sth** négocier avec qn en vue d'obtenir qch
negotiating table [nɪ'gəʊʃɪeɪtɪŋ-] N table f des négociations

negotiation [nɪgəuʃɪ'eɪʃən] N négociation *f*,
pourparlers *mpl*; **to enter into negotiations
with sb** engager des négociations avec qn
negotiator [nɪ'gəuʃɪeɪtəʳ] N négociateur(-trice)
Negress ['niːgrɪs] *(offensive)* N négresse *f*
Negro ['niːgrəu] *(pl* **Negroes)** *(offensive)* ADJ *(gen)*
noir(e); *(music, arts)* nègre, noir ▶ N Noir(e)
neigh [neɪ] VI hennir
neighbour, *(US)* **neighbor** ['neɪbəʳ] N voisin(e)
neighbourhood, *(US)* **neighborhood**
['neɪbəhud] N *(place)* quartier *m*; *(people)*
voisinage *m*
neighbourhood watch N *(BRIT: also:*
neighbourhood watch scheme) *système de
surveillance, assuré par les habitants d'un même
quartier*
neighbouring, *(US)* **neighboring** ['neɪbərɪŋ]
ADJ voisin(e), avoisinant(e)
neighbourly, *(US)* **neighborly** ['neɪbəlɪ] ADJ
obligeant(e); *(relations)* de bon voisinage
neither ['naɪðəʳ] ADJ, PRON aucun(e) (des deux),
ni l'un(e) ni l'autre ▶ CONJ: **~ do I** moi non plus;
I didn't move and ~ did Claude je n'ai pas
bougé, (et) Claude non plus ▶ ADV: **~ good nor
bad** ni bon ni mauvais; **~ did I refuse** (et *or*
mais) je n'ai pas non plus refusé; **~ of them** ni
l'un ni l'autre
neo... ['niːəu] PREFIX néo-
neolithic [niːəu'lɪθɪk] ADJ néolithique
neologism [nɪ'ɔlədʒɪzəm] N néologisme *m*
neon ['niːɔn] N néon *m*
neon light N lampe *f* au néon
neon sign N enseigne (lumineuse) au néon
Nepal [nɪ'pɔːl] N Népal *m*
nephew ['nɛvjuː] N neveu *m*
nepotism ['nɛpətɪzəm] N népotisme *m*
nerd [nəːd] N *(inf)* pauvre mec *m*, ballot *m*
nerve [nəːv] N nerf *m*; *(bravery)* sang-froid *m*,
courage *m*; *(cheek)* aplomb *m*, toupet *m*; **nerves**
NPL *(nervousness)* nervosité *f*; **he gets on my
nerves** il m'énerve; **to have a fit of nerves**
avoir le trac; **to lose one's ~** *(self-confidence)*
perdre son sang-froid
nerve centre N *(Anat)* centre nerveux; *(fig)*
centre névralgique
nerve gas N gaz *m* neuroplégique
nerve-racking ['nəːvrækɪŋ] ADJ angoissant(e)
nervous ['nəːvəs] ADJ nerveux(-euse); *(anxious)*
inquiet(-ète), plein(e) d'appréhension; *(timid)*
intimidé(e)
nervous breakdown N dépression nerveuse
nervously ['nəːvəslɪ] ADV nerveusement
nervousness ['nəːvəsnɪs] N nervosité *f*;
inquiétude *f*, appréhension *f*
nervous wreck N: **to be a ~** être une boule de
nerfs
nervy ['nəːvɪ] ADJ: **he's very ~** il a les nerfs à
fleur de peau *or* à vif
nest [nɛst] N nid *m* ▶ VI (se) nicher, faire son
nid; **~ of tables** table *f* gigogne
nest egg N *(fig)* bas *m* de laine, magot *m*
nestle ['nɛsl] VI se blottir
nestling ['nɛstlɪŋ] N oisillon *m*
Net [nɛt] N *(Comput)*: **the ~** *(Internet)* le Net

net [nɛt] N filet *m*; *(fabric)* tulle *f* ▶ ADJ net(te)
▶ VT *(fish etc)* prendre au filet; *(money: person)*
toucher; *(: deal, sale)* rapporter; **~ of tax** net
d'impôt; **he earns £20,000 ~ per year** il gagne
20 000 livres net par an
netball ['nɛtbɔːl] N netball *m*
net curtains NPL voilages *mpl*
Netherlands ['nɛðələndz] NPL: **the ~** les
Pays-Bas *mpl*
netiquette ['nɛtɪkɛt] N netiquette *f*
net profit N bénéfice net
nett [nɛt] ADJ = **net**
netting ['nɛtɪŋ] N *(for fence etc)* treillis *m*, grillage
m; *(fabric)* voile *m*
nettle ['nɛtl] N ortie *f*
network ['nɛtwəːk] N réseau *m* ▶ VT *(Radio, TV)*
diffuser sur l'ensemble du réseau; *(computers)*
interconnecter; **there's no ~ coverage here**
(Tel) il n'y a pas de réseau ici
neuralgia [njuə'rældʒə] N névralgie *f*
neurological [njuərə'lɔdʒɪkl] ADJ neurologique
neurosis [njuə'rəusɪs] *(pl* **neuroses** [-siːz]) N
névrose *f*
neurotic [njuə'rɔtɪk] ADJ, N névrosé(e)
neuter ['njuːtəʳ] ADJ neutre ▶ N neutre *m* ▶ VT
(cat etc) châtrer, couper
neutral ['njuːtrəl] ADJ neutre ▶ N *(Aut)* point
mort
neutrality [njuː'trælɪtɪ] N neutralité *f*
neutralize ['njuːtrəlaɪz] VT neutraliser
neutron bomb ['njuːtrɔn-] N bombe *f* à
neutrons
Nev. ABBR *(US)* = **Nevada**
never ['nɛvəʳ] ADV (ne ...) jamais; **I ~ went** je n'y
suis pas allé; **I've ~ been to Spain** je ne suis
jamais allé en Espagne; **~ again** plus jamais;
~ in my life jamais de ma vie; *see also* **mind**
never-ending [nɛvər'ɛndɪŋ] ADJ interminable
nevertheless [nɛvəðə'lɛs] ADV néanmoins,
malgré tout
new [njuː] ADJ nouveau (nouvelle); *(brand new)*
neuf (neuve); **as good as ~** comme neuf
New Age N New Age *m*
newbie ['njuːbɪ] N *(beginner)* newbie *mf*; *(on
forum)* nouveau (nouvelle)
newborn ['njuːbɔːn] ADJ nouveau-né(e)
newcomer ['njuːkʌməʳ] N nouveau venu
(nouvelle venue)
new-fangled ['njuːfæŋgld] ADJ *(pej)*
ultramoderne (et farfelu(e))
new-found ['njuːfaund] ADJ de fraîche date;
(friend) nouveau (nouvelle)
Newfoundland ['njuːfənlənd] N Terre-Neuve *f*
New Guinea N Nouvelle-Guinée *f*
newly ['njuːlɪ] ADV nouvellement, récemment
newly-weds ['njuːlɪwɛdz] NPL jeunes mariés
mpl
new moon N nouvelle lune
newness ['njuːnɪs] N nouveauté *f*; *(of fabric,
clothes etc)* état neuf
New Orleans [-'ɔːliːənz] N la Nouvelle-Orléans
news [njuːz] N informations *fpl*, actualités *fpl*; **a piece of ~** une
nouvelle; **good/bad ~** bonne/mauvaise

nouvelle; **financial ~** (*Press, Radio, TV*) page financière

news agency N agence *f* de presse

newsagent ['nju:zeɪdʒənt] N (*BRIT*) marchand *m* de journaux

news bulletin N (*Radio, TV*) bulletin *m* d'informations

newscaster ['nju:zkɑ:stə'] N (*Radio, TV*) présentateur(-trice)

news flash N flash *m* d'information

newsletter ['nju:zlɛtə'] N bulletin *m*

newspaper ['nju:zpeɪpə'] N journal *m*; **daily ~** quotidien *m*; **weekly ~** hebdomadaire *m*

newsprint ['nju:zprɪnt] N papier *m* (de) journal

newsreader ['nju:zri:də'] N = **newscaster**

newsreel ['nju:zri:l] N actualités (filmées)

newsroom ['nju:zru:m] N (*Press*) salle *f* de rédaction; (*Radio, TV*) studio *m*

news stand N kiosque *m* à journaux

newsworthy ['nju:zwə:ðɪ] ADJ: **to be ~** valoir la peine d'être publié

newt [nju:t] N triton *m*

new town N (*BRIT*) ville nouvelle

New Year N Nouvel An; **Happy ~!** Bonne Année!; **to wish sb a happy ~** souhaiter la Bonne Année à qn

New Year's Day N le jour de l'An

New Year's Eve N la Saint-Sylvestre

New York [-'jɔ:k] N New York; (*also*: **New York State**) New York *m*

New Zealand [-'zi:lənd] N Nouvelle-Zélande *f* ▶ ADJ néo-zélandais(e)

New Zealander [-'zi:ləndə'] N Néo-Zélandais(e)

next [nɛkst] ADJ (*in time*) prochain(e); (*seat, room*) voisin(e), d'à côté; (*meeting, bus stop*) suivant(e) ▶ ADV la fois suivante; la prochaine fois; (*afterwards*) ensuite; **~ to** prep à côté de; **~ to nothing** presque rien; **~ time** adv la prochaine fois; **the ~ day** le lendemain, le jour suivant or d'après; **~ week** la semaine prochaine; **the ~ week** la semaine suivante; **~ year** l'année prochaine; **"turn to the ~ page"** "voir page suivante"; **~ please!** (*at doctor's etc*) au suivant!; **who's ~?** c'est à qui?; **the week after ~** dans deux semaines; **when do we meet ~?** quand nous revoyons-nous?

next door ADV à côté ▶ ADJ (*neighbour*) d'à côté

next-of-kin ['nɛkstəv'kɪn] N parent *m* le plus proche

NF N ABBR (*BRIT Pol*: = *National Front*) ≈ FN ▶ ABBR (*CANADA*) = **Newfoundland**

NFL N ABBR (*US*) = **National Football League**

Nfld. ABBR (*CANADA*) = **Newfoundland**

NG ABBR (*US*) = **National Guard**

NGO N ABBR (*US*: = *non-governmental organization*) ONG *f*

NH ABBR (*US*) = **New Hampshire**

NHL N ABBR (*US*) = **National Hockey League**

NHS N ABBR (*BRIT*) = **National Health Service**

NI ABBR = **Northern Ireland**; (*BRIT*) = **National Insurance**

Niagara Falls [naɪ'ægərə-] NPL les chutes *fpl* du Niagara

nib [nɪb] N (*of pen*) (bec *m* de) plume *f*

nibble ['nɪbl] VT grignoter

Nicaragua [nɪkə'rægjuə] N Nicaragua *m*

Nicaraguan [nɪkə'rægjuən] ADJ nicaraguayen(ne) ▶ N Nicaraguayen(ne)

nice [naɪs] ADJ (*holiday, trip, taste*) agréable; (*flat, picture*) joli(e); (*person*) gentil(le); (*distinction, point*) subtil(e)

nice-looking ['naɪslukɪŋ] ADJ joli(e)

nicely ['naɪslɪ] ADV agréablement; joliment; gentiment; subtilement; **that will do ~** ce sera parfait

niceties ['naɪsɪtɪz] NPL subtilités *fpl*

niche [ni:ʃ] N (*Archit*) niche *f*

nick [nɪk] N (*indentation*) encoche *f*; (*wound*) entaille *f*; (*BRIT inf*): **in good ~** en bon état ▶ VT (*cut*): **to ~ o.s.** se couper; (*BRIT inf*: *steal*) faucher, piquer; (: *arrest*) choper, pincer; **in the ~ of time** juste à temps

nickel ['nɪkl] N nickel *m*; (*US*) pièce *f* de 5 cents

nickname ['nɪkneɪm] N surnom *m* ▶ VT surnommer

Nicosia [nɪkə'si:ə] N Nicosie

nicotine ['nɪkəti:n] N nicotine *f*

nicotine patch N timbre *m* anti-tabac, patch *m*

niece [ni:s] N nièce *f*

nifty ['nɪftɪ] ADJ (*inf*: *car, jacket*) qui a du chic or de la classe; (: *gadget, tool*) astucieux(-euse)

Niger ['naɪdʒə'] N (*country, river*) Niger *m*

Nigeria [naɪ'dʒɪərɪə] N Nigéria *mf*

Nigerian [naɪ'dʒɪərɪən] ADJ nigérien(ne) ▶ N Nigérien(ne)

niggardly ['nɪgədlɪ] ADJ (*person*) parcimonieux(-euse), pingre; (*allowance, amount*) misérable

nigger ['nɪgə'] N (!) nègre (négresse)

niggle ['nɪgl] VT tracasser ▶ VI (*find fault*) trouver toujours à redire; (*fuss*) n'être jamais content(e)

niggling ['nɪglɪŋ] ADJ tatillon(ne); (*detail*) insignifiant(e); (*doubt, pain*) persistant(e)

night [naɪt] N nuit *f*; (*evening*) soir *m*; **at ~** la nuit; **by ~** de nuit; **in the ~, during the ~** pendant la nuit; **last ~** (*evening*) hier soir; (*night-time*) la nuit dernière; **the ~ before last** avant-hier soir

night-bird ['naɪtbə:d] N oiseau *m* nocturne; (*fig*) couche-tard *m inv*, noctambule *mf*

nightcap ['naɪtkæp] N boisson prise avant le coucher

night club N boîte *f* de nuit

nightdress ['naɪtdrɛs] N chemise *f* de nuit

nightfall ['naɪtfɔ:l] N tombée *f* de la nuit

nightie ['naɪtɪ] N chemise *f* de nuit

nightingale ['naɪtɪŋgeɪl] N rossignol *m*

nightlife ['naɪtlaɪf] N vie *f* nocturne

nightly ['naɪtlɪ] ADJ (*news*) du soir; (*by night*) nocturne ▶ ADV (*every evening*) tous les soirs; (*every night*) toutes les nuits

nightmare ['naɪtmɛə'] N cauchemar *m*

night porter N gardien *m* de nuit, concierge *m* de service la nuit

night safe N coffre *m* de nuit

night school N cours *mpl* du soir

nightshade ['naɪtʃeɪd] N: **deadly ~** (*Bot*) belladone *f*

night shift ['naɪtʃɪft] N équipe *f* de nuit

night-time ['naɪttaɪm] N nuit f
night watchman N (*irreg*) veilleur m de nuit; poste m de nuit
nihilism ['naɪɪlɪzəm] N nihilisme m
nil [nɪl] N rien m; (*BRIT Sport*) zéro m
Nile [naɪl] N: **the ~** le Nil
nimble ['nɪmbl] ADJ agile
nine [naɪn] NUM neuf
nineteen [naɪn'tiːn] NUM dix-neuf
nineteenth [naɪn'tiːnθ] NUM dix-neuvième
ninetieth ['naɪntɪɪθ] NUM quatre-vingt-dixième
ninety ['naɪntɪ] NUM quatre-vingt-dix
ninth [naɪnθ] NUM neuvième
nip [nɪp] VT pincer ▶ VI (*BRIT inf*): **to ~ out/down/up** sortir/descendre/monter en vitesse ▶ N pincement m; (*drink*) petit verre; **to ~ into a shop** faire un saut dans un magasin
nipple ['nɪpl] N (*Anat*) mamelon m, bout m du sein
nippy ['nɪpɪ] ADJ (*BRIT: person*) alerte, leste; (: *car*) nerveux(-euse)
nit [nɪt] N (*in hair*) lente f; (*inf: idiot*) imbécile mf, crétin(e)
nit-pick ['nɪtpɪk] VI (*inf*) être tatillon(ne)
nitrogen ['naɪtrədʒən] N azote m
nitroglycerin, nitroglycerine ['naɪtrəʊ'glɪsəriːn] N nitroglycérine f
nitty-gritty ['nɪtɪ'grɪtɪ] N (*inf*): **to get down to the ~** en venir au fond du problème
nitwit ['nɪtwɪt] N (*inf*) nigaud(e)
NJ ABBR (*US*) = **New Jersey**
NLF N ABBR (= *National Liberation Front*) FLN m
NLQ ABBR (= *near letter quality*) qualité f courrier
NLRB N ABBR (*US*: = *National Labor Relations Board*) *organisme de protection des travailleurs*
NM, N. Mex. ABBR (*US*) = **New Mexico**

KEYWORD

no [nəʊ] ADV (*opposite of "yes"*) non; **are you coming? — no (I'm not)** est-ce que vous venez? — non; **would you like some more? — no thank you** vous en voulez encore? — non merci ▶ ADJ (*not any*) (ne ...) pas de, (ne ...) aucun(e); **I have no money/books** je n'ai pas d'argent/de livres; **no student would have done it** aucun étudiant ne l'aurait fait; **"no smoking"** "défense de fumer"; **"no dogs"** "les chiens ne sont pas admis" ▶ N (*pl* **noes**) non m; **I won't take no for an answer** il n'est pas question de refuser

no. ABBR (= *number*) nᵒ
nobble ['nɔbl] VT (*BRIT inf: person: bribe*) soudoyer, acheter; (: *to speak to*) mettre le grappin sur; (*Racing: horse, dog*) droguer (*pour l'empêcher de gagner*)
Nobel prize [nəʊ'bɛl-] N prix m Nobel
nobility [nəʊ'bɪlɪtɪ] N noblesse f
noble ['nəʊbl] ADJ noble
nobleman ['nəʊblmən] N (*irreg*) noble m
nobly ['nəʊblɪ] ADV noblement
nobody ['nəʊbədɪ] PRON (ne ...) personne
no-claims bonus ['nəʊkleɪmz-] N bonus m

nocturnal [nɔk'təːnl] ADJ nocturne
nod [nɔd] VI faire un signe de (la) tête (*affirmatif ou amical*); (*sleep*) somnoler ▶ VT: **to ~ one's head** faire un signe de (la) tête; (*in agreement*) faire signe que oui ▶ N signe m de (la) tête; **they nodded their agreement** ils ont acquiescé d'un signe de la tête
▶ **nod off** VI s'assoupir
no-fly zone [nəʊ'flaɪ-] N zone interdite (*aux avions et hélicoptères*)
noise [nɔɪz] N bruit m; **I can't sleep for the ~** je n'arrive pas à dormir à cause du bruit
noiseless ['nɔɪzlɪs] ADJ silencieux(-euse)
noisily ['nɔɪzɪlɪ] ADV bruyamment
noisy ['nɔɪzɪ] ADJ bruyant(e)
nomad ['nəʊmæd] N nomade mf
nomadic [nəʊ'mædɪk] ADJ nomade
no man's land N no man's land m
nominal ['nɔmɪnl] ADJ (*rent, fee*) symbolique; (*value*) nominal(e)
nominate ['nɔmɪneɪt] VT (*propose*) proposer; (*appoint*) nommer
nomination [nɔmɪ'neɪʃən] N nomination f
nominee [nɔmɪ'niː] N candidat agréé; personne nommée
non- [nɔn] PREFIX non-
nonalcoholic [nɔnælkə'hɔlɪk] ADJ non alcoolisé(e)
nonbreakable [nɔn'breɪkəbl] ADJ incassable
nonce word ['nɔns-] N mot créé pour l'occasion
nonchalant ['nɔnʃələnt] ADJ nonchalant(e)
non-commissioned [nɔnkə'mɪʃənd] ADJ: **~ officer** sous-officier m
noncommittal [nɔnkə'mɪtl] ADJ évasif(-ive)
nonconformist [nɔnkən'fɔːmɪst] N non-conformiste mf ▶ ADJ non-conformiste, dissident(e)
noncooperation ['nɔnkəʊəpə'reɪʃən] N refus m de coopérer, non-coopération f
nondescript ['nɔndɪskrɪpt] ADJ quelconque, indéfinissable
none [nʌn] PRON aucun(e); **~ of you** aucun d'entre vous, personne parmi vous; **I have ~** je n'en ai pas; **I have ~ left** je n'en ai plus; **~ at all** (*not one*) aucun(e); **how much milk? — ~ at all** combien de lait? — pas du tout; **he's ~ the worse for it** il ne s'en porte pas plus mal
nonentity [nɔ'nentɪtɪ] N personne insignifiante
nonessential [nɔnɪ'senʃl] ADJ accessoire, superflu(e) ▶ N: **nonessentials** le superflu
nonetheless ['nʌnðə'les] ADV néanmoins
nonevent [nɔnɪ'vent] N événement manqué
nonexecutive [nɔnɪg'zɛkjutɪv] ADJ: **~ director** administrateur(-trice), conseiller(-ère) de direction
nonexistent [nɔnɪg'zɪstənt] ADJ inexistant(e)
non-fiction [nɔn'fɪkʃən] N littérature f non romanesque
nonintervention ['nɔnɪntə'venʃən] N non-intervention f
no-no ['nəʊnəʊ] N (*inf*): **it's a ~** il n'en est pas question
non obst. ABBR (= *non obstante: notwithstanding*) nonobstant

no-nonsense [nəu'nɔnsəns] ADJ (*manner, person*) plein(e) de bon sens

nonpayment [nɔn'peimənt] N non-paiement *m*

nonplussed [nɔn'plʌst] ADJ perplexe

non-profit-making [nɔn'prɔfitmeikiŋ] ADJ à but non lucratif

nonsense ['nɔnsəns] N absurdités *fpl*, idioties *fpl*; ~! ne dites pas d'idioties!; **it is ~ to say that ...** il est absurde de dire que ....

nonsensical [nɔn'sɛnsikl] ADJ absurde, qui n'a pas de sens

non-smoker ['nɔn'sməukə^r] N non-fumeur *m*

non-smoking ['nɔn'sməukiŋ] ADJ non-fumeur

nonstarter [nɔn'stɑ:tə^r] N: **it's a** ~ c'est voué à l'échec

non-stick ['nɔn'stik] ADJ qui n'attache pas

nonstop ['nɔn'stɔp] ADJ direct(e), sans arrêt (*or* escale) ▶ ADV sans arrêt

nontaxable [nɔn'tæksəbl] ADJ: ~ **income** revenu *m* non imposable

non-U ['nɔn'ju:] ADJ ABBR (*BRIT inf: = non-upper class*) qui ne se dit (*or* se fait) pas

nonvolatile [nɔn'vɔlətail] ADJ: ~ **memory** (*Comput*) mémoire rémanente *or* non volatile

nonvoting [nɔn'vəutiŋ] ADJ: ~ **shares** actions *fpl* sans droit de vote

non-white ['nɔn'wait] ADJ de couleur ▶ N personne *f* de couleur

noodles ['nu:dlz] NPL nouilles *fpl*

nook [nuk] N: **nooks and crannies** recoins *mpl*

noon [nu:n] N midi *m*

no-one ['nəuwʌn] PRON = **nobody**

noose [nu:s] N nœud coulant; (*hangman's*) corde *f*

nor [nɔ:^r] CONJ = **neither** ▶ ADV *see* **neither**

norm [nɔ:m] N norme *f*

normal ['nɔ:ml] ADJ normal(e) ▶ N: **to return to ~** redevenir normal(e)

normality [nɔ:'mæliti] N normalité *f*

normally ['nɔ:məli] ADV normalement

Normandy ['nɔ:məndi] N Normandie *f*

north [nɔ:θ] N nord *m* ▶ ADJ nord *inv*; (*wind*) du nord ▶ ADV au *or* vers le nord

North Africa N Afrique *f* du Nord

North African ADJ nord-africain(e), d'Afrique du Nord ▶ N Nord-Africain(e)

North America N Amérique *f* du Nord

North American N Nord-Américain(e) ▶ ADJ nord-américain(e), d'Amérique du Nord

Northants [nɔ:'θænts] ABBR (*BRIT*) = **Northamptonshire**

northbound ['nɔ:θbaund] ADJ (*traffic*) en direction du nord; (*carriageway*) nord *inv*

north-east [nɔ:θ'i:st] N nord-est *m*

northeastern [nɔ:θ'i:stən] ADJ (du) nord-est *inv*

northerly ['nɔ:ðəli] ADJ (*wind, direction*) du nord

northern ['nɔ:ðən] ADJ du nord, septentrional(e)

Northern Ireland N Irlande *f* du Nord

North Korea N Corée *f* du Nord

North Pole N: **the** ~ le pôle Nord

North Sea N: **the** ~ la mer du Nord

North Sea oil N pétrole *m* de la mer du Nord

northward ['nɔ:θwəd], **northwards** ['nɔ:θwədz] ADV vers le nord

north-west [nɔ:θ'wɛst] N nord-ouest *m*

northwestern ['nɔ:θ'wɛstən] ADJ (du) nord-ouest *inv*

Norway ['nɔ:wei] N Norvège *f*

Norwegian [nɔ:'wi:dʒən] ADJ norvégien(ne) ▶ N Norvégien(ne); (*Ling*) norvégien *m*

nos. ABBR (= *numbers*) n^{os}

nose [nəuz] N nez *m*; (*of dog, cat*) museau *m*; (*fig*) flair *m* ▶ VI (*also*: **nose one's way**) avancer précautionneusement; **to pay through the ~ (for sth)** (*inf*) payer un prix excessif (pour qch) ▶ **nose about, nose around** VI fouiner *or* fureter (partout)

nosebleed ['nəuzbli:d] N saignement *m* de nez

nose-dive ['nəuzdaiv] N (descente *f* en) piqué *m*

nose drops NPL gouttes *fpl* pour le nez

nosey ['nəuzi] ADJ (*inf*) curieux(-euse)

nostalgia [nɔs'tældʒiə] N nostalgie *f*

nostalgic [nɔs'tældʒik] ADJ nostalgique

nostril ['nɔstril] N narine *f*; (*of horse*) naseau *m*

nosy ['nəuzi] (*inf*) ADJ = **nosey**

not [nɔt] ADV (ne ...) pas; **he is ~** *or* **isn't here** il n'est pas ici; **you must ~** *or* **mustn't do that** tu ne dois pas faire ça; **I hope ~** j'espère que non; **~ at all** pas du tout; (*after thanks*) de rien; **it's too late, isn't it?** c'est trop tard, n'est-ce pas?; **~ yet/now** pas encore/maintenant; *see also* **only**

notable ['nəutəbl] ADJ notable

notably ['nəutəbli] ADV (*particularly*) en particulier; (*markedly*) spécialement

notary ['nəutəri] N (*also*: **notary public**) notaire *m*

notation [nəu'teiʃən] N notation *f*

notch [nɔtʃ] N encoche *f* ▶ **notch up** VT (*score*) marquer; (*victory*) remporter

note [nəut] N note *f*; (*letter*) mot *m*; (*banknote*) billet *m* ▶ VT (*also*: **note down**) noter; (*notice*) constater; **just a quick ~ to let you know ...** juste un mot pour vous dire ...; **to take notes** prendre des notes; **to compare notes** (*fig*) échanger des (*or* leurs *etc*) impressions; **to take ~** prendre note de; **a person of ~** une personne éminente

notebook ['nəutbuk] N carnet *m*; (*for shorthand etc*) bloc-notes *m*

note-case ['nəutkeis] N (*BRIT*) porte-feuille *m*

noted ['nəutid] ADJ réputé(e)

notepad ['nəutpæd] N bloc-notes *m*

notepaper ['nəutpeipə^r] N papier *m* à lettres

noteworthy ['nəutwə:ði] ADJ remarquable

nothing ['nʌθiŋ] N rien *m*; **he does ~** il ne fait rien; **~ new** rien de nouveau; **for ~** (*free*) pour rien, gratuitement; (*in vain*) pour rien; **~ at all** rien du tout; **~ much** pas grand-chose

notice ['nəutis] N (*announcement, warning*) avis *m*; (*of leaving*) congé *m*; (*BRIT: review: of play etc*) critique *f*, compte rendu *m* ▶ VT remarquer, s'apercevoir de; **without** ~ sans préavis; **advance** ~ préavis *m*; **to give sb** ~ **of sth** notifier qn de qch; **at short** ~ dans un délai très court; **until further** ~ jusqu'à nouvel ordre; **to**

give ~, **hand in one's** ~ (*employee*) donner sa démission, démissionner; **to take** ~ **of** prêter attention à; **to bring sth to sb's** ~ porter qch à la connaissance de qn; **it has come to my** ~ **that** ... on m'a signalé que ...; **to escape** or **avoid** ~ (essayer de) passer inaperçu or ne pas se faire remarquer

noticeable ['nəʊtɪsəbl] ADJ visible

notice board N (*BRIT*) panneau m d'affichage

notification [nəʊtɪfɪ'keɪʃən] N notification f

notify ['nəʊtɪfaɪ] VT: **to** ~ **sth to sb** notifier qch à qn; **to** ~ **sb of sth** avertir qn de qch

notion ['nəʊʃən] N idée f; (*concept*) notion f; **notions** NPL (*US: haberdashery*) mercerie f

notoriety [nəʊtə'raɪətɪ] N notoriété f

notorious [nəʊ'tɔːrɪəs] ADJ notoire (*souvent en mal*)

notoriously [nəʊ'tɔːrɪəslɪ] ADJ notoirement

Notts [nɔts] ABBR (*BRIT*) = **Nottinghamshire**

notwithstanding [nɔtwɪθ'stændɪŋ] ADV néanmoins ▸ PREP en dépit de

nougat ['nuːɡɑː] N nougat m

nought [nɔːt] N zéro m

noun [naun] N nom m

nourish ['nʌrɪʃ] VT nourrir

nourishing ['nʌrɪʃɪŋ] ADJ nourrissant(e)

nourishment ['nʌrɪʃmənt] N nourriture f

Nov. ABBR (= *November*) nov

Nova Scotia ['nəʊvə'skəʊʃə] N Nouvelle-Écosse f

novel ['nɔvl] N roman m ▸ ADJ nouveau (nouvelle), original(e)

novelist ['nɔvəlɪst] N romancier m

novelty ['nɔvəltɪ] N nouveauté f

November [nəʊ'vɛmbəʳ] N novembre m; *see also* **July**

novice ['nɔvɪs] N novice mf

NOW [nau] N ABBR (*US*) = **National Organization for Women**

now [nau] ADV maintenant ▸ CONJ: ~ (**that**) maintenant (que); **right** ~ tout de suite; **by** ~ à l'heure qu'il est; **that's the fashion just** ~ c'est la mode en ce moment or maintenant; **I saw her just** ~ je viens de la voir, je l'ai vue à l'instant; **I'll read it just** ~ je vais le lire à l'instant or dès maintenant; ~ **and then,** ~ **and again** de temps en temps; **from** ~ **on** dorénavant; **in 3 days from** ~ dans or d'ici trois jours; **between** ~ **and Monday** d'ici (à) lundi; **that's all for** ~ c'est tout pour l'instant

nowadays ['nauədeɪz] ADV de nos jours

nowhere ['nəʊwɛəʳ] ADV nulle part; ~ **else** nulle part ailleurs

no-win situation [nəʊ'wɪn-] N impasse f; **we're in a** ~ nous sommes dans l'impasse

noxious ['nɔkʃəs] ADJ toxique

nozzle ['nɔzl] N (*of hose*) jet m, lance f; (*of vacuum cleaner*) suceur m

NP N ABBR = **notary public**

nr ABBR (*BRIT*) = **near**

NS ABBR (*CANADA*) = **Nova Scotia**

NSC N ABBR (*US*) = **National Security Council**

NSF N ABBR (*US*) = **National Science Foundation**

NSPCC N ABBR (*BRIT*) = **National Society for the Prevention of Cruelty to Children**

NSW ABBR (*AUSTRALIA*) = **New South Wales**

NT N ABBR (= *New Testament*) NT m ▸ ABBR (*CANADA*) = **Northwest Territories**

nth [ɛnθ] ADJ: **for the** ~ **time** (*inf*) pour la énième fois

nuance ['njuːɑːns] N nuance f

nubile ['njuːbaɪl] ADJ nubile; (*attractive*) jeune et désirable

nuclear ['njuːklɪəʳ] ADJ nucléaire

nuclear disarmament N désarmement m nucléaire

nuclear family N famille f nucléaire

nuclear-free zone ['njuːklɪə'friː-] N zone f où le nucléaire est interdit

nucleus ['njuːklɪəs] (*pl* **nuclei** ['njuːklɪaɪ]) N noyau m

NUCPS N ABBR (*BRIT*: = *National Union of Civil and Public Servants*) syndicat des fonctionnaires

nude [njuːd] ADJ nu(e) ▸ N (*Art*) nu m; **in the** ~ (tout(e)) nu(e)

nudge [nʌdʒ] VT donner un (petit) coup de coude à

nudist ['njuːdɪst] N nudiste mf

nudist colony N colonie f de nudistes

nudity ['njuːdɪtɪ] N nudité f

nugget ['nʌɡɪt] N pépite f

nuisance ['njuːsns] N: **it's a** ~ c'est (très) ennuyeux or gênant; **he's a** ~ il est assommant or casse-pieds; **what a** ~! quelle barbe!

NUJ N ABBR (*BRIT*: = *National Union of Journalists*) syndicat des journalistes

nuke [njuːk] N (*inf*) bombe f atomique

null [nʌl] ADJ: ~ **and void** nul(le) et non avenu(e)

nullify ['nʌlɪfaɪ] VT invalider

NUM N ABBR (*BRIT*: = *National Union of Mineworkers*) syndicat des mineurs

numb [nʌm] ADJ engourdi(e); (*with fear*) paralysé(e) ▸ VT engourdir; ~ **with cold** engourdi(e) par le froid, transi(e) (de froid); ~ **with fear** transi de peur, paralysé(e) par la peur

number ['nʌmbəʳ] N nombre m; (*numeral*) chiffre m; (*of house, car, telephone, newspaper*) numéro m ▸ VT numéroter; (*amount to*) compter; **a** ~ **of** un certain nombre de; **they were seven in** ~ ils étaient (au nombre de) sept; **to be numbered among** compter parmi; **the staff numbers 20** le nombre d'employés s'élève à or est de 20; **wrong** ~ (*Tel*) mauvais numéro

numbered account ['nʌmbəd-] N (*in bank*) compte numéroté

number plate N (*BRIT Aut*) plaque f minéralogique or d'immatriculation

Number Ten N (*BRIT*: 10 *Downing Street*) résidence du Premier ministre

numbness ['nʌmnɪs] N torpeur f; (*due to cold*) engourdissement m

numbskull ['nʌmskʌl] N (*inf*) gourde f

numeral ['njuːmərəl] N chiffre m

numerate ['njuːmərɪt] ADJ (*BRIT*): **to be** ~ avoir des notions d'arithmétique

numerical [njuː'mɛrɪkl] ADJ numérique

numerous ['njuːmərəs] ADJ nombreux(-euse)

nun [nʌn] N religieuse f, sœur f

n

nunnery ['nʌnərɪ] N couvent m
nuptial ['nʌpʃəl] ADJ nuptial(e)
nurse [nəːs] N infirmière f; (also: **nursemaid**) bonne f d'enfants ▶ VT (patient, cold) soigner; (baby: BRIT) bercer (dans ses bras); (: US) allaiter, nourrir; (hope) nourrir
nursery ['nəːsərɪ] N (room) nursery f; (institution) crèche f, garderie f; (for plants) pépinière f
nursery rhyme N comptine f, chansonnette f pour enfants
nursery school N école maternelle
nursery slope N (BRIT Ski) piste f pour débutants
nursing ['nəːsɪŋ] N (profession) profession f d'infirmière; (care) soins mpl ▶ ADJ (mother) qui allaite
nursing home N clinique f; (for convalescence) maison f de convalescence or de repos; (for old people) maison de retraite
nurture ['nəːtʃər] VT élever
NUS N ABBR (BRIT: = National Union of Students) syndicat des étudiants
NUT N ABBR (BRIT: = National Union of Teachers) syndicat enseignant
nut [nʌt] N (of metal) écrou m; (fruit: walnut) noix f; (: hazelnut) noisette f; (: peanut) cacahuète f (terme générique en anglais) ▶ ADJ (chocolate etc) aux noisettes; **he's nuts** (inf) il est dingue
nutcase ['nʌtkeɪs] N (inf) dingue mf
nutcrackers ['nʌtkrækəz] NPL casse-noix m inv, casse-noisette(s) m

nutmeg ['nʌtmɛg] N (noix f) muscade f
nutrient ['njuːtrɪənt] ADJ nutritif(-ive) ▶ N substance nutritive
nutrition [njuːˈtrɪʃən] N nutrition f, alimentation f
nutritionist [njuːˈtrɪʃənɪst] N nutritionniste mf
nutritious [njuːˈtrɪʃəs] ADJ nutritif(-ive), nourrissant(e)
nuts [nʌts] (inf) ADJ dingue
nutshell ['nʌtʃɛl] N coquille f de noix; **in a ~** en un mot
nutter ['nʌtər] (BRIT inf) N: **he's a complete ~** il est complètement cinglé
nutty ['nʌtɪ] ADJ (flavour) à la noisette; (inf: person) cinglé(e), dingue
nuzzle ['nʌzl] VI: **to ~ up to** fourrer son nez contre
NV ABBR (US) = **Nevada**
NVQ N ABBR (BRIT) = **National Vocational Qualification**
NWT ABBR (CANADA) = **Northwest Territories**
NY ABBR (US) = **New York**
NYC ABBR (US) = **New York City**
nylon ['naɪlɒn] N nylon m ▶ ADJ de or en nylon; **nylons** NPL bas mpl nylon
nymph [nɪmf] N nymphe f
nymphomaniac ['nɪmfəuˈmeɪnɪæk] ADJ, N nymphomane f
NYSE N ABBR (US) = **New York Stock Exchange**
NZ ABBR = **New Zealand**

Oo

O, o [əu] N (*letter*) O, o *m*; (*US Scol:* = *outstanding*) tb (= *très bien*); **O for Oliver**, (*US*) **O for Oboe** O comme Oscar
oaf [əuf] N balourd *m*
oak [əuk] N chêne *m* ▶ CPD de *or* en (bois de) chêne
O&M N ABBR = **organization and method**
O.A.P. N ABBR (*BRIT*) = **old age pensioner**
oar [ɔːʳ] N aviron *m*, rame *f*; **to put** *or* **shove one's ~ in** (*fig: inf*) mettre son grain de sel
oarsman [ˈɔːzmən], **oarswoman** [ˈɔːzwumən] N (*irreg*) rameur(-euse); (*Naut, Sport*) nageur(-euse)
OAS N ABBR (= *Organization of American States*) OEA *f* (= *Organisation des États américains*)
oasis [əuˈeisis] (*pl* **oases** [əuˈeisiːz]) N oasis *f*
oath [əuθ] N serment *m*; (*swear word*) juron *m*; **to take the ~** prêter serment; **on** (*BRIT*) *or* **under ~** sous serment; assermenté(e)
oatmeal [ˈəutmiːl] N flocons *mpl* d'avoine
oats [əuts] N avoine *f*
OAU N ABBR (= *Organization of African Unity*) OUA *f* (= *Organisation de l'unité africaine*)
obdurate [ˈɔbdjurit] ADJ obstiné(e), impénitent(e); intraitable
OBE N ABBR (*BRIT*: = *Order of the British Empire*) *distinction honorifique*
obedience [əˈbiːdiəns] N obéissance *f*; **in ~ to** conformément à
obedient [əˈbiːdiənt] ADJ obéissant(e); **to be ~ to sb/sth** obéir à qn/qch
obelisk [ˈɔbilisk] N obélisque *m*
obese [əuˈbiːs] ADJ obèse
obesity [əuˈbiːsiti] N obésité *f*
obey [əˈbei] VT obéir à; (*instructions, regulations*) se conformer à ▶ VI obéir
obituary [əˈbitjuəri] N nécrologie *f*
object N [ˈɔbdʒikt] objet *m*; (*purpose*) but *m*, objet; (*Ling*) complément *m* d'objet ▶ VI [əbˈdʒɛkt]: **to ~ to** (*attitude*) désapprouver; (*proposal*) protester contre, élever une objection contre; **I ~!** je proteste!; **he objected that ...** il a fait valoir *or* a objecté que ...; **do you ~ to my smoking?** est-ce que cela vous gêne si je fume?; **what's the ~ of doing that?** quel est l'intérêt de faire cela?; **money is no ~** l'argent n'est pas un problème
objection [əbˈdʒɛkʃən] N objection *f*; (*drawback*) inconvénient *m*; **if you have no ~** si vous n'y voyez pas d'inconvénient; **to make** *or* **raise an ~** élever une objection
objectionable [əbˈdʒɛkʃənəbl] ADJ très désagréable; choquant(e)
objective [əbˈdʒɛktiv] N objectif *m* ▶ ADJ objectif(-ive)
objectivity [ɔbdʒik'tiviti] N objectivité *f*
object lesson N (*fig*) (bonne) illustration
objector [əbˈdʒɛktəʳ] N opposant(e)
obligation [ɔbliˈgeiʃən] N obligation *f*, devoir *m*; (*debt*) dette *f* (de reconnaissance); **"without ~"** "sans engagement"
obligatory [əˈbligətəri] ADJ obligatoire
oblige [əˈblaidʒ] VT (*force*): **to ~ sb to do** obliger *or* forcer qn à faire; (*do a favour*) rendre service à, obliger; **to be obliged to sb for sth** être obligé(e) à qn de qch; **anything to ~!** (*inf*) (toujours prêt à rendre) service!
obliging [əˈblaidʒiŋ] ADJ obligeant(e), serviable
oblique [əˈbliːk] ADJ oblique; (*allusion*) indirect(e) ▶ N (*BRIT Typ*): **~ (stroke)** barre *f* oblique
obliterate [əˈblitəreit] VT effacer
oblivion [əˈbliviən] N oubli *m*
oblivious [əˈbliviəs] ADJ: **~ of** oublieux(-euse) de
oblong [ˈɔblɔŋ] ADJ oblong(ue) ▶ N rectangle *m*
obnoxious [əbˈnɔkʃəs] ADJ odieux(-euse); (*smell*) nauséabond(e)
o.b.o. ABBR (*US: in classified ads:* = *or best offer*) ≈ à débattre
oboe [ˈəubəu] N hautbois *m*
obscene [əbˈsiːn] ADJ obscène
obscenity [əbˈsɛniti] N obscénité *f*
obscure [əbˈskjuəʳ] ADJ obscur(e) ▶ VT obscurcir; (*hide: sun*) cacher
obscurity [əbˈskjuəriti] N obscurité *f*
obsequious [əbˈsiːkwiəs] ADJ obséquieux(-euse)
observable [əbˈzəːvəbl] ADJ observable; (*appreciable*) notable
observance [əbˈzəːvns] N observance *f*, observation *f*; **religious observances** observances religieuses
observant [əbˈzəːvnt] ADJ observateur(-trice)
observation [ɔbzəˈveiʃən] N observation *f*; (*by police etc*) surveillance *f*
observation post N (*Mil*) poste *m* d'observation
observatory [əbˈzəːvətri] N observatoire *m*

observe [əb'zə:v] VT observer; (remark) faire observer or remarquer

observer [əb'zə:vəʳ] N observateur(-trice)

obsess [əb'sɛs] VT obséder; **to be obsessed by** or **with sb/sth** être obsédé(e) par qn/qch

obsession [əb'sɛʃən] N obsession f

obsessive [əb'sɛsɪv] ADJ obsédant(e)

obsolescence [ɔbsə'lɛsns] N vieillissement m; obsolescence f; **built-in** or **planned ~** (Comm) désuétude calculée

obsolescent [ɔbsə'lɛsnt] ADJ obsolescent(e), en voie d'être périmé(e)

obsolete ['ɔbsəli:t] ADJ dépassé(e), périmé(e)

obstacle ['ɔbstəkl] N obstacle m

obstacle race N course f d'obstacles

obstetrician [ɔbstə'trɪʃən] N obstétricien(ne)

obstetrics [ɔb'stɛtrɪks] N obstétrique f

obstinacy ['ɔbstɪnəsɪ] N obstination f

obstinate ['ɔbstɪnɪt] ADJ obstiné(e); (pain, cold) persistant(e)

obstreperous [əb'strɛpərəs] ADJ turbulent(e)

obstruct [əb'strʌkt] VT (block) boucher, obstruer; (halt) arrêter; (hinder) entraver

obstruction [əb'strʌkʃən] N obstruction f; (to plan, progress) obstacle m

obstructive [əb'strʌktɪv] ADJ obstructionniste

obtain [əb'teɪn] VT obtenir ▸ VI avoir cours

obtainable [əb'teɪnəbl] ADJ qu'on peut obtenir

obtrusive [əb'tru:sɪv] ADJ (person) importun(e); (smell) pénétrant(e); (building etc) trop en évidence

obtuse [əb'tju:s] ADJ obtus(e)

obverse ['ɔbvə:s] N (of medal, coin) côté m face; (fig) contrepartie f

obviate ['ɔbvɪeɪt] VT parer à, obvier à

obvious ['ɔbvɪəs] ADJ évident(e), manifeste

obviously ['ɔbvɪəslɪ] ADV manifestement; (of course): **~, he ...** or **he ~ ...** il est bien évident qu'il ...; **~!** bien sûr!; **~ not!** évidemment pas!, bien sûr que non!

OCAS N ABBR (= Organization of Central American States) ODEAC f (= Organisation des États d'Amérique centrale)

occasion [ə'keɪʒən] N occasion f; (event) événement m ▸ VT occasionner, causer; **on that ~** à cette occasion; **to rise to the ~** se montrer à la hauteur de la situation

occasional [ə'keɪʒənl] ADJ pris(e) (or fait(e) etc) de temps en temps; (worker, spending) occasionnel(le)

occasionally [ə'keɪʒənəlɪ] ADV de temps en temps, quelquefois; **very ~** (assez) rarement

occasional table N table décorative

occult [ɔ'kʌlt] ADJ occulte ▸ N: **the ~** le surnaturel

occupancy ['ɔkjupənsɪ] N occupation f

occupant ['ɔkjupənt] N occupant m

occupation [ɔkju'peɪʃən] N occupation f; (job) métier m, profession f; **unfit for ~** (house) impropre à l'habitation

occupational [ɔkju'peɪʃənl] ADJ (accident, disease) du travail; (hazard) du métier

occupational guidance N (BRIT) orientation professionnelle

occupational hazard N risque m du métier

occupational pension N retraite professionnelle

occupational therapy N ergothérapie f

occupier ['ɔkjupaɪəʳ] N occupant(e)

occupy ['ɔkjupaɪ] VT occuper; **to ~ o.s. with** or **by doing** s'occuper à faire; **to be occupied with sth** être occupé avec qch

occur [ə'kə:ʳ] VI se produire; (difficulty, opportunity) se présenter; (phenomenon, error) se rencontrer; **to ~ to sb** venir à l'esprit de qn

occurrence [ə'kʌrəns] N (existence) présence f, existence f; (event) cas m, fait m

ocean ['əuʃən] N océan m; **oceans of** (inf) des masses de

ocean bed N fond (sous-)marin

ocean-going ['əuʃəngəuɪŋ] ADJ de haute mer

Oceania [əuʃɪ'eɪnɪə] N Océanie f

ocean liner N paquebot m

ochre ['əukəʳ] ADJ ocre

o'clock [ə'klɔk] ADV: **it is 5 ~** il est 5 heures

OCR N ABBR = **optical character reader; optical character recognition**

Oct. ABBR (= October) oct

octagonal [ɔk'tægənl] ADJ octogonal(e)

octane ['ɔkteɪn] N octane m; **high-~ petrol** or (US) **gas** essence f à indice d'octane élevé

octave ['ɔktɪv] N octave f

October [ɔk'təubəʳ] N octobre m; see also **July**

octogenarian ['ɔktəudʒɪ'nɛərɪən] N octogénaire mf

octopus ['ɔktəpəs] N pieuvre f

odd [ɔd] ADJ (strange) bizarre, curieux(-euse); (number) impair(e); (left over) qui reste, en plus; (not of a set) dépareillé(e); **60-~** 60 et quelques; **at ~ times** de temps en temps; **the ~ one out** l'exception f

oddball ['ɔdbɔ:l] N (inf) excentrique mf

oddity ['ɔdɪtɪ] N bizarrerie f; (person) excentrique mf

odd-job man [ɔd'dʒɔb-] N (irreg) homme m à tout faire

odd jobs NPL petits travaux divers

oddly ['ɔdlɪ] ADV bizarrement, curieusement

oddments ['ɔdmənts] NPL (BRIT Comm) fins fpl de série

odds [ɔdz] NPL (in betting) cote f; **the ~ are against his coming** il y a peu de chances qu'il vienne; **it makes no ~** cela n'a pas d'importance; **to succeed against all the ~** réussir contre toute attente; **~ and ends** de petites choses; **at ~** en désaccord

odds-on [ɔdz'ɔn] ADJ: **the ~ favourite** le grand favori; **it's ~ that he'll come** il y a toutes les chances or gros à parier qu'il vienne

ode [əud] N ode f

odious ['əudɪəs] ADJ odieux(-euse), détestable

odometer [ɔ'dɔmɪtəʳ] N (US) odomètre m

odour, (US) **odor** ['əudəʳ] N odeur f

odourless, (US) **odorless** ['əudəlɪs] ADJ inodore

OECD N ABBR (= Organization for Economic Cooperation and Development) OCDE f (= Organisation de coopération et de développement économique)

oesophagus, (US) **esophagus** [i:'sɔfəgəs] N œsophage m

oestrogen, (US) **estrogen** ['iːstrəʊdʒən] N œstrogène m

[KEYWORD]

of [ɔv, əv] PREP **1** (gen) de; **a friend of ours** un de nos amis; **a boy of 10** un garçon de 10 ans; **that was kind of you** c'était gentil de votre part **2** (expressing quantity, amount, dates etc) de; **a kilo of flour** un kilo de farine; **how much of this do you need?** combien vous en faut-il?; **there were three of them** (people) ils étaient 3; (objects) il y en avait 3; **three of us went** 3 d'entre nous y sont allés (allées); **the 5th of July** le 5 juillet; **a quarter of 4** (US) 4 heures moins le quart **3** (from, out of) en, de; **a statue of marble** une statue de or en marbre; **made of wood** (fait) en bois

Ofcom ['ɔfkɔm] N ABBR (BRIT: = Office of Communications Regulation) organe de régulation de télécommunications

off [ɔf] ADJ, ADV (engine) coupé(e); (light, TV) éteint(e); (tap) fermé(e); (BRIT: food) mauvais(e), avancé(e); (: milk) tourné(e); (absent) absent(e); (cancelled) annulé(e); **the lid was ~** (removed) le couvercle était retiré or n'était pas mis; **to run/drive ~** (away) partir en courant/en voiture ▶ PREP de; **to be ~** (to leave) partir, s'en aller; **I must be ~** il faut que je file; **to be ~ sick** être absent pour cause de maladie; **a day ~** un jour de congé; **to have an ~ day** n'être pas en forme; **he had his coat ~** il avait enlevé son manteau; **the hook is ~** le crochet s'est détaché; le crochet n'est pas mis; **10% ~** (Comm) 10% de rabais; **5 km ~ (the road)** à 5 km (de la route); **~ the coast** au large de la côte; **a house ~ the main road** une maison à l'écart de la grand-route; **it's a long way ~** c'est loin (d'ici); **I'm ~ meat** je ne mange plus de viande; je n'aime plus la viande; **on the ~ chance** à tout hasard; **to be well/badly ~** être bien/mal loti; (financially) être aisé/dans la gêne; **~ and on, on and ~** de temps à autre; **I'm afraid the chicken is ~** (BRIT: not available) je regrette, il n'y a plus de poulet; **that's a bit ~** (fig: inf) c'est un peu fort

offal ['ɔfl] N (Culin) abats mpl
offbeat ['ɔfbiːt] ADJ excentrique
off-centre [ɔfˈsɛntər] ADJ décentré(e), excentré(e)
off-colour ['ɔfˈkʌlər] ADJ (BRIT: ill) malade, mal fichu(e); **to feel ~** être mal fichu
offence, (US) **offense** [əˈfɛns] N (crime) délit m, infraction f; **to give ~ to** blesser, offenser; **to take ~ at** se vexer de, s'offenser de; **to commit an ~** commettre une infraction
offend [əˈfɛnd] VT (person) offenser, blesser ▶ VI: **to ~ against** (law, rule) contrevenir à, enfreindre
offender [əˈfɛndər] N délinquant(e); (against regulations) contrevenant(e)
offending [əˈfɛndɪŋ] ADJ incriminé(e)
offense [əˈfɛns] N (US) = **offence**
offensive [əˈfɛnsɪv] ADJ offensant(e),

choquant(e); (smell etc) très déplaisant(e); (weapon) offensif(-ive) ▶ N (Mil) offensive f
offer ['ɔfər] N offre f, proposition f ▶ VT offrir, proposer; **to make an ~ for sth** faire une offre pour qch; **to ~ sth to sb, ~ sb sth** offrir qch à qn; **to ~ to do sth** proposer de faire qch; **"on ~"** (Comm) "en promotion"
offering ['ɔfərɪŋ] N offrande f
offhand [ɔfˈhænd] ADJ désinvolte ▶ ADV spontanément; **I can't tell you ~** je ne peux pas vous le dire comme ça
office ['ɔfɪs] N (place) bureau m; (position) charge f, fonction f; **doctor's ~** (US) cabinet (médical); **to take ~** entrer en fonctions; **through his good offices** (fig) grâce à ses bons offices; **O~ of Fair Trading** (BRIT) organisme de protection contre les pratiques commerciales abusives
office automation N bureautique f
office bearer N (of club etc) membre m du bureau
office block, (US) **office building** N immeuble m de bureaux
office boy N garçon m de bureau
office hours NPL heures fpl de bureau; (US Med) heures de consultation
office manager N responsable administratif(-ive)
officer ['ɔfɪsər] N (Mil etc) officier m; (also: **police officer**) agent m (de police); (of organization) membre m du bureau directeur
office work N travail m de bureau
office worker N employé(e) de bureau
official [əˈfɪʃl] ADJ (authorized) officiel(le) ▶ N officiel m; (civil servant) fonctionnaire mf; (of railways, post office, town hall) employé(e)
officialdom [əˈfɪʃldəm] N bureaucratie f
officially [əˈfɪʃəlɪ] ADV officiellement
official receiver N administrateur m judiciaire, syndic m de faillite
officiate [əˈfɪʃɪeɪt] VI (Rel) officier; **to ~ as Mayor** exercer les fonctions de maire; **to ~ at a marriage** célébrer un mariage
officious [əˈfɪʃəs] ADJ trop empressé(e)
offing ['ɔfɪŋ] N: **in the ~** (fig) en perspective
off-key [ɔfˈkiː] ADJ faux (fausse) ▶ ADV faux
off-licence ['ɔflaɪsns] N (BRIT: shop) débit m de vins et de spiritueux
off-limits [ɔfˈlɪmɪts] ADJ (esp US) dont l'accès est interdit
off-line [ɔfˈlaɪn] ADJ (Comput) (en mode) autonome; (: switched off) non connecté(e)
off-load ['ɔfləʊd] VT: **to ~ sth (onto)** (goods) décharger qch (sur); (job) se décharger de qch (sur)
off-peak [ɔfˈpiːk] ADJ aux heures creuses; (electricity, ticket) au tarif heures creuses
off-putting ['ɔfpʊtɪŋ] ADJ (BRIT: remark) rébarbatif(-ive); (person) rebutant(e), peu engageant(e)
off-road vehicle ['ɔfrəʊd-] N véhicule m tout-terrain
off-season ['ɔfsiːzn] ADJ, ADV hors-saison inv
offset ['ɔfsɛt] VT (irreg: like **set**) (counteract) contrebalancer, compenser ▶ N (also: **offset printing**) offset m

offshoot ['ɔfʃuːt] N (fig) ramification f, antenne f; (: of discussion etc) conséquence f

offshore [ɔf'ʃɔːʳ] ADJ (breeze) de terre; (island) proche du littoral; (fishing) côtier(-ière); ~ **oilfield** gisement m pétrolifère en mer

offside ['ɔf'saɪd] N (Aut: with right-hand drive) côté droit; (: with left-hand drive) côté gauche ▶ ADJ (Sport) hors jeu; (Aut: in Britain) de droite; (: in US, Europe) de gauche

offspring ['ɔfsprɪŋ] N progéniture f

offstage [ɔf'steɪdʒ] ADV dans les coulisses

off-the-cuff [ɔfðə'kʌf] ADV au pied levé; de chic

off-the-job ['ɔfðə'dʒɔb] ADJ: ~ **training** formation professionnelle extérieure

off-the-peg ['ɔfðə'pɛg], (US) **off-the-rack** ['ɔfðə'ræk] ADV en prêt-à-porter

off-the-record ['ɔfðə'rɛkɔːd] ADJ (remark) confidentiel(le), sans caractère officiel ▶ ADV officieusement

off-white ['ɔfwaɪt] ADJ blanc cassé inv

often ['ɔfn] ADV souvent; **how ~ do you go?** vous y allez tous les combien?; **every so ~** de temps en temps, de temps à autre; **as ~ as not** la plupart du temps

Ofwat ['ɔfwɔt] N ABBR (BRIT: = Office of Water Services) organisme qui surveille les activités des compagnies des eaux

ogle ['əugl] VT lorgner

ogre ['əugəʳ] N ogre m

OH ABBR (US) = Ohio

oh [əu] EXCL ô!, oh!, ah!

OHMS ABBR (BRIT) = On Her/His Majesty's Service

oil [ɔɪl] N huile f; (petroleum) pétrole m; (for central heating) mazout m ▶ VT (machine) graisser

oilcan ['ɔɪlkæn] N burette f de graissage; (for storing) bidon m à huile

oil change N vidange f

oilfield ['ɔɪlfiːld] N gisement m de pétrole

oil filter N (Aut) filtre m à huile

oil-fired ['ɔɪlfaɪəd] ADJ au mazout

oil gauge N jauge f de niveau d'huile

oil industry N industrie pétrolière

oil level N niveau m d'huile

oil painting N peinture f à l'huile

oil refinery N raffinerie f de pétrole

oil rig N derrick m; (at sea) plate-forme pétrolière

oilskins ['ɔɪlskɪnz] NPL ciré m

oil slick N nappe f de mazout

oil tanker N (ship) pétrolier m; (truck) camion-citerne m

oil well N puits m de pétrole

oily ['ɔɪlɪ] ADJ huileux(-euse); (food) gras(se)

ointment ['ɔɪntmənt] N onguent m

OK ABBR (US) = Oklahoma

O.K., okay ['əu'keɪ] (inf) EXCL d'accord! ▶ VT approuver, donner son accord à ▶ N: **to give sth one's O.K.** donner son accord à ▶ ADJ (not bad) pas mal, en règle; en bon état; sain et sauf; acceptable; **is it O.K.?, are you O.K.?** ça va?; **are you O.K. for money?** ça va or ira question argent?; **it's O.K. with** or **by me** ça me va, c'est d'accord en ce qui me concerne

Okla. ABBR (US) = Oklahoma

old [əuld] ADJ vieux (vieille); (person) vieux, âgé(e); (former) ancien(ne), vieux; **how ~ are you?** quel âge avez-vous?; **he's 10 years ~** il a 10 ans, il est âgé de 10 ans; **older brother/sister** frère/sœur aîné(e); **any ~ thing will do** n'importe quoi fera l'affaire

old age N vieillesse f

old-age pensioner ['əuldeɪdʒ-] N (BRIT) retraité(e)

old-fashioned ['əuld'fæʃnd] ADJ démodé(e); (person) vieux jeu inv

old maid N vieille fille

old people's home N (esp BRIT) maison f de retraite

old-style ['əuldstaɪl] ADJ à l'ancienne (mode)

old-time ['əuld'taɪm] ADJ du temps jadis, d'autrefois

old-timer ['əuld'taɪməʳ] N ancien m

old wives' tale N conte m de bonne femme

O-level ['əulɛvl] N (in England and Wales: formerly) examen passé à l'âge de 16 ans sanctionnant les connaissances de l'élève, ≈ brevet m des collèges

olive ['ɔlɪv] N (fruit) olive f; (tree) olivier m ▶ ADJ (also: **olive-green**) (vert) olive inv

olive oil N huile f d'olive

Olympic [əu'lɪmpɪk] ADJ olympique; **the ~ Games, the Olympics** les Jeux mpl olympiques

OM N ABBR (BRIT: = Order of Merit) titre honorifique

Oman [əu'mɑːn] N Oman m

OMB N ABBR (US: = Office of Management and Budget) service conseillant le président en matière budgétaire

omelette, omelet ['ɔmlɪt] N omelette f; **ham/cheese omelet(te)** omelette au jambon/fromage

omen ['əumən] N présage m

OMG ABBR (inf: = Oh My God!) OMD (= Oh Mon Dieu!)

ominous ['ɔmɪnəs] ADJ menaçant(e), inquiétant(e); (event) de mauvais augure

omission [əu'mɪʃən] N omission f

omit [əu'mɪt] VT omettre; **to ~ to do sth** négliger de faire qch

omnivorous [ɔm'nɪvrəs] ADJ omnivore

ON ABBR (CANADA) = Ontario

(KEYWORD)

on [ɔn] PREP **1** (indicating position) sur; **on the table** sur la table; **on the wall** sur le or au mur; **on the left** à gauche; **I haven't any money on me** je n'ai pas d'argent sur moi

2 (indicating means, method, condition etc): **on foot** à pied; **on the train/plane** (be) dans le train/l'avion; (go) en train/avion; **on the telephone/radio/television** au téléphone/à la radio/à la télévision; **to be on drugs** se droguer; **on holiday, (US) on vacation** en vacances; **on the continent** sur le continent

3 (referring to time): **on Friday** vendredi; **on Fridays** le vendredi; **on June 20th** le 20 juin; **a week on Friday** vendredi en huit; **on arrival** à l'arrivée; **on seeing this** en voyant cela

4 (about, concerning) sur, de; **a book on Balzac/physics** un livre sur Balzac/de physique

5 (at the expense of): **this round is on me** c'est ma tournée

▶ ADV **1** (*referring to dress*): **to have one's coat on** avoir (mis) son manteau; **to put one's coat on** mettre son manteau; **what's she got on?** qu'est-ce qu'elle porte?
2 (*referring to covering*): **screw the lid on tightly** vissez bien le couvercle
3 (*further, continuously*): **to walk** *etc* **on** continuer à marcher *etc*; **on and off** de temps à autre; **from that day on** depuis ce jour
▶ ADJ **1** (*in operation: machine*) en marche; (: *radio, TV, light*) allumé(e); (: *tap, gas*) ouvert(e); (: *brakes*) mis(e); **is the meeting still on?** (*not cancelled*) est-ce que la réunion a bien lieu?; **it was well on in the evening** c'était tard dans la soirée; **when is this film on?** quand passe ce film?
2 (*inf*): **that's not on!** (*not acceptable*) cela ne se fait pas!; (*not possible*) pas question!

ONC N ABBR (*BRIT*: = *Ordinary National Certificate*) ≈ BT *m*
once [wʌns] ADV une fois; (*formerly*) autrefois
▶ CONJ une fois que + *sub*; **~ he had left/it was done** une fois qu'il fut parti/ que ce fut terminé; **at ~** tout de suite, immédiatement; (*simultaneously*) à la fois; **all at ~** *adv* tout d'un coup; **~ a week** une fois par semaine; **~ more** encore une fois; **I knew him ~** je l'ai connu autrefois; **~ and for all** une fois pour toutes; **~ upon a time there was …** il y avait une fois …, il était une fois …
oncoming ['ɒnkʌmɪŋ] ADJ (*traffic*) venant en sens inverse
OND N ABBR (*BRIT*: = *Ordinary National Diploma*) ≈ BTS *m*

KEYWORD

one [wʌn] NUM un(e); **one hundred and fifty** cent cinquante; **one by one** un(e) à *or* par un(e); **one day** un jour
▶ ADJ **1** (*sole*) seul(e), unique; **the one book which** l'unique *or* le seul livre qui; **the one man who** le seul (homme) qui
2 (*same*) même; **they came in the one car** ils sont venus dans la même voiture
▶ PRON **1**: **this one** celui-ci (celle-ci); **that one** celui-là (celle-là); **I've already got one/a red one** j'en ai déjà un(e)/un(e) rouge; **which one do you want?** lequel voulez-vous?
2: **one another** l'un(e) l'autre; **to look at one another** se regarder
3 (*impersonal*) on; **one never knows** on ne sait jamais; **to cut one's finger** se couper le doigt; **one needs to eat** il faut manger
4 (*phrases*): **to be one up on sb** avoir l'avantage sur qn; **to be at one (with sb)** être d'accord (avec qn)

one-armed bandit ['wʌnɑːmd-] N machine *f* à sous
one-day excursion ['wʌndeɪ-] N (*US*) billet *m* d'aller-retour (valable pour la journée)
One-hundred share index ['wʌnhʌndrəd-] N indice *m* Footsie des cent grandes valeurs
one-man ['wʌn'mæn] ADJ (*business*) dirigé(e) *etc*

par un seul homme
one-man band N homme-orchestre *m*
one-off [wʌn'ɒf] N (*BRIT inf*) exemplaire *m* unique ▶ ADJ unique
one-parent family ['wʌnpɛərənt-] N famille monoparentale
one-piece ['wʌnpiːs] ADJ: **~ bathing suit** maillot *m* une pièce
onerous ['ɒnərəs] ADJ (*task, duty*) pénible; (*responsibility*) lourd(e)
oneself [wʌn'sɛlf] PRON se; (*after prep, also emphatic*) soi-même; **to hurt ~** se faire mal; **to keep sth for ~** garder qch pour soi; **to talk to ~** se parler à soi-même; **by ~** tout seul
one-shot [wʌn'ʃɒt] (*US*) N = **one-off**
one-sided [wʌn'saɪdɪd] ADJ (*argument, decision*) unilatéral(e); (*judgment, account*) partial(e); (*contest*) inégal(e)
one-time ['wʌntaɪm] ADJ d'autrefois
one-to-one ['wʌntəwʌn] ADJ (*relationship*) univoque
one-upmanship [wʌn'ʌpmənʃɪp] N: **the art of ~** l'art de faire mieux que les autres
one-way ['wʌnweɪ] ADJ (*street, traffic*) à sens unique
ongoing ['ɒngəʊɪŋ] ADJ en cours; (*relationship*) suivi(e)
onion ['ʌnjən] N oignon *m*
on-line ['ɒnlaɪn] ADJ (*Comput*) en ligne; (: *switched on*) connecté(e)
onlooker ['ɒnlʊkə'] N spectateur(-trice)
only ['əʊnlɪ] ADV seulement **~** ▶ ADJ seul(e), unique ▶ CONJ seulement, mais; **an ~ child** un enfant unique; **not ~ … but also** non seulement … mais aussi; **I ~ took one** j'en ai seulement pris un, je n'en ai pris qu'un; **I saw her ~ yesterday** je l'ai vue hier encore; **I'd be ~ too pleased to help** je ne serais que trop content de vous aider; **I would come, ~ I'm very busy** je viendrais bien mais j'ai beaucoup à faire
ono ABBR (*BRIT*: *in classified ads*: = *or nearest offer*) ≈ à débattre
on-screen [ɒn'skriːn] ADJ à l'écran
onset ['ɒnsɛt] N début *m*; (*of winter, old age*) approche *f*
onshore ['ɒnʃɔː'] ADJ (*wind*) du large
onslaught ['ɒnslɔːt] N attaque *f*, assaut *m*
Ont. ABBR (*CANADA*) = **Ontario**
on-the-job ['ɒnðə'dʒɒb] ADJ: **~ training** formation *f* sur place
onto ['ɒntu] PREP sur
onus ['əʊnəs] N responsabilité *f*; **the ~ is upon him to prove it** c'est à lui de le prouver
onward ['ɒnwəd], **onwards** ['ɒnwədz] ADV (*move*) en avant; **from that time onwards** à partir de ce moment
oops [ʊps] EXCL houp!; **~-a-daisy!** houp-là!
ooze [uːz] VI suinter
opacity [əʊ'pæsɪtɪ] N opacité *f*
opal ['əʊpl] N opale *f*
opaque [əʊ'peɪk] ADJ opaque
OPEC ['əʊpɛk] N ABBR (= *Organization of Petroleum-Exporting Countries*) OPEP *f*

O

open ['əupn] ADJ ouvert(e); (*car*) découvert(e); (*road, view*) dégagé(e); (*meeting*) public(-ique); (*admiration*) manifeste; (*question*) non résolu(e); (*enemy*) déclaré(e) ▶ VT ouvrir ▶ VI (*flower, eyes, door, debate*) s'ouvrir; (*shop, bank, museum*) ouvrir; (*book etc: commence*) commencer, débuter; **is it ~ to the public?** est-ce ouvert au public?; **what time do you ~?** à quelle heure ouvrez-vous?; **in the ~ (air)** en plein air; **the ~ sea** le large; **~ ground** (*among trees*) clairière f; (*waste ground*) terrain m vague; **to have an ~ mind (on sth)** avoir l'esprit ouvert (sur qch)
▶ **open on to** VT FUS (*room, door*) donner sur
▶ **open out** VT ouvrir ▶ VI s'ouvrir
▶ **open up** VT ouvrir; (*blocked road*) dégager ▶ VI s'ouvrir

open-air [əupn'ɛəʳ] ADJ en plein air
open-and-shut ['əupnən'ʃʌt] ADJ: **~ case** cas m limpide
open day N journée f portes ouvertes
open-ended [əupn'ɛndɪd] ADJ (*fig*) non limité(e)
opener ['əupnəʳ] N (*also:* **can opener, tin opener**) ouvre-boîtes m
open-heart surgery [əupn'hɑːt-] N chirurgie f à cœur ouvert
opening ['əupnɪŋ] N ouverture f; (*opportunity*) occasion f; (*work*) débouché m; (*job*) poste vacant
opening hours NPL heures fpl d'ouverture
opening night N (*Theat*) première f
open learning N enseignement universitaire à la carte, notamment par correspondance; (*distance learning*) télé-enseignement m
open learning centre N centre ouvert à tous où l'on dispense un enseignement général à temps partiel
openly ['əupnlɪ] ADV ouvertement
open-minded [əupn'maɪndɪd] ADJ à l'esprit ouvert
open-necked ['əupnnɛkt] ADJ à col ouvert
openness ['əupnnɪs] N (*frankness*) franchise f
open-plan ['əupn'plæn] ADJ sans cloisons
open prison N prison ouverte
open sandwich N canapé m
open shop N entreprise qui admet les travailleurs non syndiqués
Open University N (BRIT) cours universitaires par correspondance; *voir article*

L'Open University a été fondée en 1969. L'enseignement comprend des cours (certaines plages horaires sont réservées à cet effet à la télévision et à la radio), des devoirs qui sont envoyés par l'étudiant à son directeur ou sa directrice d'études, et un séjour obligatoire en université d'été. Il faut préparer un certain nombre d'unités de valeur pendant une période de temps déterminée et obtenir la moyenne à un certain nombre d'entre elles pour recevoir le diplôme visé.

opera ['ɔpərə] N opéra m
opera glasses NPL jumelles fpl de théâtre
opera house N opéra m
opera singer N chanteur(-euse) d'opéra
operate ['ɔpəreɪt] VT (*machine*) faire marcher, faire fonctionner; (*system*) pratiquer ▶ VI

fonctionner; (*drug*) faire effet; **to ~ on sb (for)** (*Med*) opérer qn (de)
operatic [ɔpə'rætɪk] ADJ d'opéra
operating ['ɔpəreɪtɪŋ] ADJ (*Comm: costs, profit*) d'exploitation; (*Med*): **~ table** table f d'opération
operating room N (US Med) salle f d'opération
operating system N (*Comput*) système m d'exploitation
operating theatre N (BRIT Med) salle f d'opération
operation [ɔpə'reɪʃən] N opération f; (*of machine*) fonctionnement m; **to have an ~ (for)** se faire opérer (de); **to be in ~** (*machine*) être en service; (*system*) être en vigueur
operational [ɔpə'reɪʃənl] ADJ opérationnel(le); (*ready for use*) en état de marche; **when the service is fully ~** lorsque le service fonctionnera pleinement
operative ['ɔpərətɪv] ADJ (*measure*) en vigueur
▶ N (*in factory*) ouvrier(-ière); **the ~ word** le mot clef
operator ['ɔpəreɪtəʳ] N (*of machine*) opérateur(-trice); (*Tel*) téléphoniste mf
operetta [ɔpə'rɛtə] N opérette f
ophthalmologist [ɔfθæl'mɔlədʒɪst] N ophtalmologiste mf, ophtalmologue mf
opinion [ə'pɪnjən] N opinion f, avis m; **in my ~** à mon avis; **to seek a second ~** demander un deuxième avis
opinionated [ə'pɪnjəneɪtɪd] ADJ aux idées bien arrêtées
opinion poll N sondage m d'opinion
opium ['əupɪəm] N opium m
opponent [ə'pəunənt] N adversaire mf
opportune ['ɔpətjuːn] ADJ opportun(e)
opportunist [ɔpə'tjuːnɪst] N opportuniste mf
opportunity [ɔpə'tjuːnɪtɪ] N occasion f; **to take the ~ to do** *or* **of doing** profiter de l'occasion pour faire
oppose [ə'pəuz] VT s'opposer à; **to be opposed to sth** être opposé(e) à qch; **as opposed to** par opposition à
opposing [ə'pəuzɪŋ] ADJ (*side*) opposé(e)
opposite ['ɔpəzɪt] ADJ opposé(e); (*house etc*) d'en face ▶ ADV en face ▶ PREP en face de ▶ N opposé m, contraire m; (*of word*) contraire; **"see ~ page"** "voir ci-contre"
opposite number N (BRIT) homologue mf
opposite sex N: **the ~** l'autre sexe
opposition [ɔpə'zɪʃən] N opposition f
oppress [ə'prɛs] VT opprimer
oppression [ə'prɛʃən] N oppression f
oppressive [ə'prɛsɪv] ADJ oppressif(-ive)
opprobrium [ə'prəubrɪəm] N (*formal*) opprobre m
opt [ɔpt] VI: **to ~ for** opter pour; **to ~ to do** choisir de faire
▶ **opt out** VI (*school, hospital*) devenir autonome; (*health service*) devenir privé(e); **to ~ out of** choisir de ne pas participer à *or* de ne pas faire
optical ['ɔptɪkl] ADJ optique; (*instrument*) d'optique
optical character reader N lecteur m optique

optical character recognition N lecture f optique
optical fibre N fibre f optique
optician [ɔpˈtɪʃən] N opticien(ne)
optics [ˈɔptɪks] N optique f
optimism [ˈɔptɪmɪzəm] N optimisme m
optimist [ˈɔptɪmɪst] N optimiste mf
optimistic [ɔptɪˈmɪstɪk] ADJ optimiste
optimum [ˈɔptɪməm] ADJ optimum
option [ˈɔpʃən] N choix m, option f; (Scol) matière f à option; (Comm) option; **to keep one's options open** (fig) ne pas s'engager; **I have no ~** je n'ai pas le choix
optional [ˈɔpʃənl] ADJ facultatif(-ive); (Comm) en option; **~ extras** accessoires mpl en option, options fpl
opulence [ˈɔpjʊləns] N opulence f; abondance f
opulent [ˈɔpjʊlənt] ADJ opulent(e), abondant(e)
OR ABBR (US) = **Oregon**
or [ɔːʳ] CONJ ou; (with negative): **he hasn't seen or heard anything** il n'a rien vu ni entendu; **or else** sinon; ou bien
oracle [ˈɔrəkl] N oracle m
oral [ˈɔːrəl] ADJ oral(e) ▸ N oral m
orange [ˈɔrɪndʒ] N (fruit) orange f ▸ ADJ orange inv
orangeade [ɔrɪndʒˈeɪd] N orangeade f
orange juice N jus m d'orange
oration [ɔːˈreɪʃən] N discours solennel
orator [ˈɔrətəʳ] N orateur(-trice)
oratorio [ɔrəˈtɔːrɪəu] N oratorio m
orb [ɔːb] N orbe m
orbit [ˈɔːbɪt] N orbite f ▸ VT graviter autour de; **to be in/go into ~ (round)** être/entrer en orbite (autour de)
orbital [ˈɔːbɪtl] N (also: **orbital motorway**) périphérique f
orchard [ˈɔːtʃəd] N verger m; **apple ~** verger de pommiers
orchestra [ˈɔːkɪstrə] N orchestre m; (US: seating) (fauteuils mpl d')orchestre
orchestral [ɔːˈkɛstrəl] ADJ orchestral(e); (concert) symphonique
orchestrate [ˈɔːkɪstreɪt] VT (Mus, fig) orchestrer
orchid [ˈɔːkɪd] N orchidée f
ordain [ɔːˈdeɪn] VT (Rel) ordonner; (decide) décréter
ordeal [ɔːˈdiːl] N épreuve f
order [ˈɔːdəʳ] N ordre m; (Comm) commande f ▸ VT ordonner; (Comm) commander; **in ~** en ordre; (document) en règle; **out of ~** (not in correct order) en désordre; (machine) hors service; (telephone) en dérangement; **a machine in working ~** une machine en état de marche; **in ~ of size** par ordre de grandeur; **in ~ to do/that** pour faire/que + sub; **to place an ~ for sth with sb** commander qch auprès de qn, passer commande de qch à qn; **could I ~ now, please?** je peux commander, s'il vous plaît?; **to be on ~** être en commande; **made to ~** fait sur commande; **to be under orders to do sth** avoir ordre de faire qch; **a point of ~** un point de procédure; **to the ~ of** (Banking) à l'ordre de; **to ~ sb to do** ordonner à qn de faire

order book N carnet m de commandes
order form N bon m de commande
orderly [ˈɔːdəlɪ] N (Mil) ordonnance f; (Med) garçon m de salle ▸ ADJ (room) en ordre; (mind) méthodique; (person) qui a de l'ordre
order number N (Comm) numéro m de commande
ordinal [ˈɔːdɪnl] ADJ (number) ordinal(e)
ordinary [ˈɔːdnrɪ] ADJ ordinaire, normal(e); (pej) ordinaire, quelconque; **out of the ~** exceptionnel(le)
ordinary degree N (Scol) ≈ licence f libre; voir article

> Un ordinary degree est un diplôme inférieur à l'honours degree que l'on obtient en général après trois années d'études universitaires. Il peut aussi être décerné en cas d'échec à l'honours degree.

ordinary seaman N (irreg) (BRIT) matelot m
ordinary shares NPL actions fpl ordinaires
ordination [ɔːdɪˈneɪʃən] N ordination f
ordnance [ˈɔːdnəns] N (Mil: unit) service m du matériel
Ordnance Survey map N (BRIT) ≈ carte f d'État-major
ore [ɔːʳ] N minerai m
Ore., Oreg. ABBR (US) = **Oregon**
oregano [ɔrɪˈɡɑːnəu] N origan m
organ [ˈɔːɡən] N organe m; (Mus) orgue m, orgues fpl
organic [ɔːˈɡænɪk] ADJ organique; (crops etc) biologique, naturel(le)
organism [ˈɔːɡənɪzəm] N organisme m
organist [ˈɔːɡənɪst] N organiste mf
organization [ɔːɡənaɪˈzeɪʃən] N organisation f
organization chart N organigramme m
organize [ˈɔːɡənaɪz] VT organiser; **to get organized** s'organiser
organized [ˈɔːɡənaɪzd] ADJ (planned) organisé(e); (efficient) bien organisé
organized crime N crime organisé, grand banditisme
organized labour N main-d'œuvre syndiquée
organizer [ˈɔːɡənaɪzəʳ] N organisateur(-trice)
orgasm [ˈɔːɡæzəm] N orgasme m
orgy [ˈɔːdʒɪ] N orgie f
Orient [ˈɔːrɪənt] N: **the ~** l'Orient m
oriental [ɔːrɪˈɛntl] ADJ oriental(e) ▸ N Oriental(e)
orientate [ˈɔːrɪənteɪt] VT orienter
orientation [ɔːrɪənˈteɪʃən] N (attitudes) tendance f; (in job) orientation f; (of building) orientation, exposition f
orifice [ˈɔrɪfɪs] N orifice m
origin [ˈɔrɪdʒɪn] N origine f; **country of ~** pays m d'origine
original [əˈrɪdʒɪnl] ADJ original(e); (earliest) originel(le) ▸ N original m
originality [ərɪdʒɪˈnælɪtɪ] N originalité f
originally [əˈrɪdʒɪnəlɪ] ADV (at first) à l'origine
originate [əˈrɪdʒɪneɪt] VI: **to ~ from** être originaire de; (suggestion) provenir de; **to ~ in** (custom) prendre naissance dans, avoir son origine dans

o

originator [ə'rɪdʒɪneɪtəʳ] N auteur *m*

Orkney ['ɔːkn] N (*also:* **the Orkneys, the Orkney Islands**) les Orcades *fpl*

ornament ['ɔːnəmənt] N ornement *m*; (*trinket*) bibelot *m*

ornamental [ɔːnə'mɛntl] ADJ décoratif(-ive); (*garden*) d'agrément

ornamentation [ɔːnəmɛn'teɪʃən] N ornementation *f*

ornate [ɔː'neɪt] ADJ très orné(e)

ornithologist [ɔːnɪ'θɒlədʒɪst] N ornithologue *mf*

ornithology [ɔːnɪ'θɒlədʒɪ] N ornithologie *f*

orphan ['ɔːfn] N orphelin(e) ▶ VT: **to be orphaned** devenir orphelin

orphanage ['ɔːfənɪdʒ] N orphelinat *m*

orthodox ['ɔːθədɒks] ADJ orthodoxe

orthopaedic, (US) **orthopedic** [ɔːθə'piːdɪk] ADJ orthopédique

OS ABBR (*Brit:* = *Ordnance Survey*) ≈ IGN *m* (= *Institut géographique national*); (*Naut*) = **ordinary seaman**; (*Dress*) = **outsize**

O/S ABBR = **out of stock**

Oscar ['ɒskəʳ] N oscar *m*

oscillate ['ɒsɪleɪt] VI osciller

OSHA N ABBR (*US:* = *Occupational Safety and Health Administration*) office de l'hygiène et de la sécurité au travail

Oslo ['ɒzləu] N Oslo

ostensible [ɒs'tɛnsɪbl] ADJ prétendu(e); apparent(e)

ostensibly [ɒs'tɛnsɪblɪ] ADV en apparence

ostentation [ɒstɛn'teɪʃən] N ostentation *f*

ostentatious [ɒstɛn'teɪʃəs] ADJ prétentieux(-euse); ostentatoire

osteopath ['ɒstɪəpæθ] N ostéopathe *mf*

ostracize ['ɒstrəsaɪz] VT frapper d'ostracisme

ostrich ['ɒstrɪtʃ] N autruche *f*

OT N ABBR (= *Old Testament*) AT *m*

OTB N ABBR (*US:* = *off-track betting*) paris pris en dehors du champ de course

O.T.E. ABBR (= *on-target earnings*) primes *fpl* sur objectifs inclus

other ['ʌðəʳ] ADJ autre ▶ PRON: **the ~ (one)** l'autre; **others** (*other people*) d'autres ▶ ADV: **~ than** autrement que; à part; **some actor or ~** un certain acteur, je ne sais quel acteur; **somebody or ~** quelqu'un; **some ~ people have still to arrive** on attend encore quelques personnes; **the ~ day** l'autre jour; **the car was none ~ than John's** la voiture n'était autre que celle de John

otherwise ['ʌðəwaɪz] ADV, CONJ autrement; **an ~ good piece of work** par ailleurs, un beau travail

OTT ABBR (*inf*) = **over the top**; *see* **top**

Ottawa ['ɒtəwə] N Ottawa

otter ['ɒtəʳ] N loutre *f*

OU N ABBR (*Brit*) = **Open University**

ouch [autʃ] EXCL aïe!

ought [ɔːt] AUX VB: **I ~ to do it** je devrais le faire, il faudrait que je le fasse; **this ~ to have been corrected** cela aurait dû être corrigé; **he ~ to win** (*probability*) il devrait gagner; **you ~ to go**

and see it vous devriez aller le voir

ounce [auns] N once *f* (*28.35g; 16 in a pound*)

our ['auəʳ] ADJ notre, nos *pl*; *see also* **my**

ours [auəz] PRON le (la) nôtre, les nôtres; *see also* **mine¹**

ourselves [auə'sɛlvz] PL PRON (*reflexive, after preposition*) nous; (*emphatic*) nous-mêmes; **we did it (all) by ~** nous avons fait ça tous seuls; *see also* **oneself**

oust [aust] VT évincer

out [aut] ADV dehors; (*published, not at home etc*) sorti(e); (*light, fire*) éteint(e); (*on strike*) en grève ▶ VT: **to ~ sb** révéler l'homosexualité de qn; **~ here** ici; **~ there** là-bas; **he's ~** (*absent*) il est sorti; (*unconscious*) il est sans connaissance; **to be ~ in one's calculations** s'être trompé dans ses calculs; **to run/back** *etc* **~** sortir en courant/ en reculant *etc*; **to be ~ and about** *or* (*US*) **around again** être de nouveau sur pied; **before the week was ~** avant la fin de la semaine; **the journey ~** l'aller *m*; **the boat was 10 km ~** le bateau était à 10 km du rivage; **~ loud** *adv* à haute voix; **~ of** *prep* (*outside*) en dehors de; (*because of: anger etc*) par; (*from among*): **10 ~ of 10** 10 sur 10; (*without*): **~ of petrol** sans essence, à court d'essence; **made ~ of wood** en *or* de bois; **~ of order** (*machine*) en panne; (*Tel: line*) en dérangement; **~ of stock** (*Comm: article*) épuisé(e); (*shop*) en rupture de stock

outage ['autɪdʒ] N (*esp US: power failure*) panne *f* or coupure *f* de courant

out-and-out ['autəndaut] ADJ véritable

outback ['autbæk] N campagne isolée; (*in Australia*) intérieur *m*

outbid [aut'bɪd] VT (*irreg: like* **bid**) surenchérir

outboard ['autbɔːd] N: **~ (motor)** (moteur *m*) hors-bord *m*

outbound ['autbaund] ADJ: **~ (from/for)** en partance (de/pour)

outbox ['autbɒks] N (*Comput*) boîte *f* d'envoi; (*US: out-tray*) corbeille *f* du courrier au départ

outbreak ['autbreɪk] N (*of violence*) éruption *f*, explosion *f*; (*of disease*) de nombreux cas; **the ~ of war south of the border** la guerre qui s'est déclarée au sud de la frontière

outbuilding ['autbɪldɪŋ] N dépendance *f*

outburst ['autbəːst] N explosion *f*, accès *m*

outcast ['autkɑːst] N exilé(e); (*socially*) paria *m*

outclass [aut'klɑːs] VT surclasser

outcome ['autkʌm] N issue *f*, résultat *m*

outcrop ['autkrɒp] N affleurement *m*

outcry ['autkraɪ] N tollé (général)

outdated [aut'deɪtɪd] ADJ démodé(e)

outdistance [aut'dɪstəns] VT distancer

outdo [aut'duː] VT (*irreg: like* **do**) surpasser

outdoor [aut'dɔːʳ] ADJ de *or* en plein air

outdoors [aut'dɔːz] ADV dehors; au grand air

outer ['autəʳ] ADJ extérieur(e); **~ suburbs** grande banlieue

outer space N espace *m* cosmique

outfit ['autfɪt] N équipement *m*; (*clothes*) tenue *f*; (*inf: Comm*) organisation *f*, boîte *f*

outfitter ['autfɪtəʳ] N (*Brit*): **"(gents') ~'s"** "confection pour hommes"

outgoing ['aʊtɡəʊɪŋ] ADJ (*president, tenant*) sortant(e); (*character*) ouvert(e), extraverti(e)

outgoings ['aʊtɡəʊɪŋz] NPL (BRIT: *expenses*) dépenses *fpl*

outgrow [aʊt'ɡrəʊ] VT (*irreg: like* **grow**) (*clothes*) devenir trop grand(e) pour

outhouse ['aʊthaʊs] N appentis *m*, remise *f*

outing ['aʊtɪŋ] N sortie *f*; excursion *f*

outlandish [aʊt'lændɪʃ] ADJ étrange

outlast [aʊt'lɑːst] VT survivre à

outlaw ['aʊtlɔː] N hors-la-loi *m inv* ▸ VT (*person*) mettre hors la loi; (*practice*) proscrire

outlay ['aʊtleɪ] N dépenses *fpl*; (*investment*) mise *f* de fonds

outlet ['aʊtlet] N (*for liquid etc*) issue *f*, sortie *f*; (*for emotion*) exutoire *m*; (*for goods*) débouché *m*; (*also:* **retail outlet**) point *m* de vente; (US *Elec*) prise *f* de courant

outline ['aʊtlaɪn] N (*shape*) contour *m*; (*summary*) esquisse *f*, grandes lignes ▸ VT (*fig: theory, plan*) exposer à grands traits

outlive [aʊt'lɪv] VT survivre à

outlook ['aʊtlʊk] N perspective *f*; (*point of view*) attitude *f*

outlying ['aʊtlaɪɪŋ] ADJ écarté(e)

outmanoeuvre [aʊtmə'nuːvəʳ] VT (*rival etc*) avoir au tournant

outmoded [aʊt'məʊdɪd] ADJ démodé(e); dépassé(e)

outnumber [aʊt'nʌmbəʳ] VT surpasser en nombre

out-of-court [aʊtəv'kɔːt] ADJ, ADV à l'aimable

out-of-date [aʊtəv'deɪt] ADJ (*passport, ticket*) périmé(e); (*theory, idea*) dépassé(e); (*custom*) désuet(-ète); (*clothes*) démodé(e)

out-of-doors ['aʊtəv'dɔːz] ADV = **outdoors**

out-of-the-way ['aʊtəvðə'weɪ] ADJ loin de tout; (*fig*) insolite

out-of-town [aʊtəv'taʊn] ADJ (*shopping centre etc*) en périphérie

outpatient ['aʊtpeɪʃənt] N malade *mf* en consultation externe

outpost ['aʊtpəʊst] N avant-poste *m*

outpouring ['aʊtpɔːrɪŋ] N (*fig*) épanchement(s) *m(pl)*

output ['aʊtput] N rendement *m*, production *f*; (*Comput*) sortie *f* ▸ VT (*Comput*) sortir

outrage ['aʊtreɪdʒ] N (*anger*) indignation *f*; (*violent act*) atrocité *f*, acte *m* de violence; (*scandal*) scandale *m* ▸ VT outrager

outrageous [aʊt'reɪdʒəs] ADJ atroce; (*scandalous*) scandaleux(-euse)

outrider ['aʊtraɪdəʳ] N (*on motorcycle*) motard *m*

outright ADV [aʊt'raɪt] complètement; (*deny, refuse*) catégoriquement; (*ask*) carrément; (*kill*) sur le coup ▸ ADJ ['aʊtraɪt] complet(-ète); catégorique

outrun [aʊt'rʌn] VT (*irreg: like* **run**) dépasser

outset ['aʊtset] N début *m*

outshine [aʊt'ʃaɪn] VT (*irreg: like* **shine**) (*fig*) éclipser

outside [aʊt'saɪd] N extérieur *m* ▸ ADJ extérieur(e); (*remote, unlikely*): **an ~ chance** une (très) faible chance ▸ ADV (au) dehors, à

l'extérieur ▸ PREP hors de, à l'extérieur de; (*in front of*) devant; **at the ~** (*fig*) au plus *or* maximum; **~ left/right** *n* (*Football*) ailier gauche/droit

outside broadcast N (*Radio, TV*) reportage *m*

outside lane N (*Aut: in Britain*) voie *f* de droite; (*: in US, Europe*) voie de gauche

outside line N (*Tel*) ligne extérieure

outsider [aʊt'saɪdəʳ] N (*in race etc*) outsider *m*; (*stranger*) étranger(-ère)

outsize ['aʊtsaɪz] ADJ énorme; (*clothes*) grande taille *inv*

outskirts ['aʊtskəːts] NPL faubourgs *mpl*

outsmart [aʊt'smɑːt] VT se montrer plus malin(-igne) *or* futé(e) que

outspoken [aʊt'spəʊkən] ADJ très franc (franche)

outspread [aʊt'spred] ADJ (*wings*) déployé(e)

outstanding [aʊt'stændɪŋ] ADJ remarquable, exceptionnel(le); (*unfinished: work, business*) en suspens, en souffrance; (*debt*) impayé(e); (*problem*) non réglé(e); **your account is still ~** vous n'avez pas encore tout remboursé

outstay [aʊt'steɪ] VT: **to ~ one's welcome** abuser de l'hospitalité de son hôte

outstretched [aʊt'stretʃt] ADJ (*hand*) tendu(e); (*body*) étendu(e)

outstrip [aʊt'strɪp] VT (*also fig*) dépasser

out-tray ['aʊttreɪ] N courrier *m* ("départ")

outvote [aʊt'vəʊt] VT: **to ~ sb (by)** mettre qn en minorité (par); **to ~ sth (by)** rejeter qch (par)

outward ['aʊtwəd] ADJ (*sign, appearances*) extérieur(e); (*journey*) (d')aller

outwardly ['aʊtwədlɪ] ADV extérieurement; en apparence

outwards ['aʊtwədz] ADV (*esp* BRIT) = **outward**

outweigh [aʊt'weɪ] VT l'emporter sur

outwit [aʊt'wɪt] VT se montrer plus malin que

oval ['əʊvl] ADJ, N ovale *m*

Oval Office N (US *Pol*): *voir article*

> L'*Oval Office* est le bureau personnel du président des États-Unis à la Maison-Blanche, ainsi appelé du fait de sa forme ovale. Par extension, ce terme désigne la présidence elle-même.

ovarian [əʊ'vɛərɪən] ADJ ovarien(ne); (*cancer*) des ovaires

ovary ['əʊvərɪ] N ovaire *m*

ovation [əʊ'veɪʃən] N ovation *f*

oven ['ʌvn] N four *m*

oven glove N gant *m* de cuisine

ovenproof ['ʌvnpruːf] ADJ allant au four

oven-ready ['ʌvnredɪ] ADJ prêt(e) à cuire

ovenware ['ʌvnwɛəʳ] N plats *mpl* allant au four

over ['əʊvəʳ] ADV (par-)dessus; (*excessively*) trop ▸ ADJ (*finished*) fini(e), terminé(e); (*too much*) en plus ▸ PREP sur; par-dessus; (*above*) au-dessus de; (*on the other side of*) de l'autre côté de; (*more than*) plus de; (*during*) pendant; (*about, concerning*): **they fell out ~ money/her** ils se sont brouillés pour des questions d'argent/à cause d'elle; **~ here** ici; **~ there** là-bas; **all ~** (*everywhere*) partout; (*finished*) fini(e); **~ and ~ (again)** à plusieurs reprises; **~ and above** en plus de; **to ask sb ~** inviter qn (à passer); **to go ~ to sb's** passer chez qn; **to fall ~** tomber; **to turn sth ~** retourner qch; **now ~ to our Paris correspondent** nous passons l'antenne à notre correspondant à Paris; **the world ~** dans le monde entier; **she's not ~ intelligent** (BRIT) elle n'est pas particulièrement intelligente

over... ['əuvəʳ] PREFIX: **overabundant** surabondant(e)

overact [əuvər'ækt] VI (Theat) outrer son rôle

overall ['əuvərɔːl] ADJ (length) total(e); (study, impression) d'ensemble ▶ N (BRIT) blouse f ▶ ADV [əuvər'ɔːl] dans l'ensemble, en général; **overalls** NPL (boiler suit) bleus mpl (de travail)

overall majority N majorité absolue

overanxious [əuvər'æŋkʃəs] ADJ trop anxieux(-euse)

overawe [əuvər'ɔː] VT impressionner

overbalance [əuvə'bæləns] VI basculer

overbearing [əuvə'bɛərɪŋ] ADJ impérieux(-euse), autoritaire

overboard ['əuvəbɔːd] ADV (Naut) par-dessus bord; **to go ~ for sth** (fig) s'emballer (pour qch)

overbook [əuvə'buk] VI faire du surbooking

overcame [əuvə'keɪm] PT of **overcome**

overcapitalize [əuvə'kæpɪtəlaɪz] VT surcapitaliser

overcast ['əuvəkɑːst] ADJ couvert(e)

overcharge [əuvə'tʃɑːdʒ] VT: **to ~ sb for sth** faire payer qch trop cher à qn

overcoat ['əuvəkəut] N pardessus m

overcome [əuvə'kʌm] VT (irreg: like **come**) (defeat) triompher de; (difficulty) surmonter ▶ ADJ (emotionally) bouleversé(e); **~ with grief** accablé(e) de douleur

overconfident [əuvə'kɔnfɪdənt] ADJ trop sûr(e) de soi

overcrowded [əuvə'kraudɪd] ADJ bondé(e); (city, country) surpeuplé(e)

overcrowding [əuvə'kraudɪŋ] N surpeuplement m; (in bus) encombrement m

overdo [əuvə'duː] VT (irreg: like **do**) exagérer; (overcook) trop cuire; **to ~ it, to ~ things** (work too hard) en faire trop, se surmener

overdone [əuvə'dʌn] ADJ (vegetables, steak) trop cuit(e)

overdose ['əuvədəus] N dose excessive

overdraft ['əuvədrɑːft] N découvert m

overdrawn [əuvə'drɔːn] ADJ (account) à découvert

overdrive ['əuvədraɪv] N (Aut) (vitesse f) surmultipliée f

overdue [əuvə'djuː] ADJ en retard; (bill) impayé(e); (change) qui tarde; **that change was long ~** ce changement n'avait que trop tardé

overemphasis [əuvər'ɛmfəsɪs] N: **to put an ~ on** accorder trop d'importance à

overestimate [əuvər'ɛstɪmeɪt] VT surestimer

overexcited [əuvərɪk'saɪtɪd] ADJ surexcité(e)

overexertion [əuvərɪg'zəːʃən] N surmenage m (physique)

overexpose [əuvərɪk'spəuz] VT (Phot) surexposer

overflow VI [əuvə'fləu] déborder ▶ N ['əuvəfləu] trop-plein m; (also: **overflow pipe**) tuyau m d'écoulement, trop-plein m

overfly [əuvə'flaɪ] VT (irreg: like **fly**) survoler

overgenerous [əuvə'dʒɛnərəs] ADJ (person) prodigue; (offer) excessif(-ive)

overgrown [əuvə'grəun] ADJ (garden) envahi(e) par la végétation; **he's just an ~ schoolboy** (fig) c'est un écolier attardé

overhang ['əuvə'hæŋ] VT (irreg: like **hang**) surplomber ▶ VI faire saillie

overhaul VT [əuvə'hɔːl] réviser ▶ N ['əuvəhɔːl] révision f

overhead ADV [əuvə'hɛd] au-dessus ▶ ADJ ['əuvəhɛd] aérien(ne); (lighting) vertical(e) ▶ N ['əuvəhɛd] (US) = **overheads**

overhead projector N rétroprojecteur m

overheads ['əuvəhɛdz] NPL (BRIT) frais généraux

overhear [əuvə'hɪəʳ] VT (irreg: like **hear**) entendre (par hasard)

overheat [əuvə'hiːt] VI devenir surchauffé(e); (engine) chauffer

overjoyed [əuvə'dʒɔɪd] ADJ ravi(e), enchanté(e)

overkill ['əuvəkɪl] N (fig): **it would be ~** ce serait de trop

overland ['əuvəlænd] ADJ, ADV par voie de terre

overlap VI [əuvə'læp] se chevaucher ▶ N ['əuvəlæp] chevauchement m

overleaf [əuvə'liːf] ADV au verso

overload [əuvə'ləud] VT surcharger

overlook [əuvə'luk] VT (have view of) donner sur; (miss) oublier, négliger; (forgive) fermer les yeux sur

overlord ['əuvəlɔːd] N chef m suprême

overmanning [əuvə'mænɪŋ] N sureffectif m, main-d'œuvre f pléthorique

overnight ADV [əuvə'naɪt] (happen) durant la nuit; (fig) soudain ▶ ADJ ['əuvənaɪt] d'une (or de) nuit; soudain(e); **to stay ~ (with sb)** passer la nuit (chez qn); **he stayed there ~** il y a passé la nuit; **if you travel ~ ...** si tu fais le voyage de nuit ...; **he'll be away ~** il ne rentrera pas ce soir

overnight bag N nécessaire m de voyage

overpass ['əuvəpɑːs] N (US: for cars) pont autoroutier; (: for pedestrians) passerelle f, pont m

overpay [əuvə'peɪ] VT (irreg: like **pay**): **to ~ sb by £50** donner à qn 50 livres de trop

overplay [əuvə'pleɪ] VT exagérer; **to ~ one's hand** trop présumer de sa situation

overpower [əuvə'pauəʳ] VT vaincre; (fig) accabler

overpowering [əuvə'pauərɪŋ] ADJ irrésistible; (heat, stench) suffocant(e)

overproduction ['əuvəprə'dʌkʃən] N surproduction f

overrate [əuvə'reɪt] VT surestimer

overreact [əuvəri:'ækt] VI réagir de façon excessive

override [əuvə'raɪd] VT (irreg: like **ride**) (order, objection) passer outre à; (decision) annuler

overriding [əuvə'raɪdɪŋ] ADJ prépondérant(e)

overrule [əuvə'ruːl] VT (decision) annuler; (claim) rejeter; (person) rejeter l'avis de

overrun [əuvə'rʌn] VT (irreg: like **run**) (Mil: country etc) occuper; (time limit etc) dépasser ▶ VI dépasser le temps imparti; **the town is ~ with**

tourists la ville est envahie de touristes
overseas [əuvə'si:z] ADV outre-mer; (*abroad*) à l'étranger ▶ ADJ (*trade*) extérieur(e); (*visitor*) étranger(-ère)
oversee [əuvə'si:] VT (*irreg: like* **see**) surveiller
overseer ['əuvəsɪər] N (*in factory*) contremaître *m*
overshadow [əuvə'ʃædəu] VT (*fig*) éclipser
overshoot [əuvə'ʃu:t] VT (*irreg: like* **shoot**) dépasser
oversight ['əuvəsaɪt] N omission *f*, oubli *m*; **due to an ~** par suite d'une inadvertance
oversimplify [əuvə'sɪmplɪfaɪ] VT simplifier à l'excès
oversleep [əuvə'sli:p] VI (*irreg: like* **sleep**) se réveiller (trop) tard
overspend [əuvə'spɛnd] VI (*irreg: like* **spend**) dépenser de trop; **we have overspent by 5,000 dollars** nous avons dépassé notre budget de 5 000 dollars, nous avons dépensé 5 000 dollars de trop
overspill ['əuvəspɪl] N excédent *m* de population
overstaffed [əuvə'stɑ:ft] ADJ: **to be ~** avoir trop de personnel, être en surnombre
overstate [əuvə'steɪt] VT exagérer
overstatement [əuvə'steɪtmənt] N exagération *f*
overstay [əuvə'steɪ] VT: **to ~ one's welcome (at sb's)** abuser de l'hospitalité de qn
overstep [əuvə'stɛp] VT: **to ~ the mark** dépasser la mesure
overstock [əuvə'stɔk] VT stocker en surabondance
overstretched [əuvə'strɛtʃt] ADJ (*person*) débordé(e); **my budget is ~** j'ai atteint les limites de mon budget
overstrike N ['əuvəstraɪk] (*on printer*) superposition *f*, double frappe *f* ▶ VT [əuvə'straɪk] (*irreg: like* **strike**) surimprimer
overt [əu'və:t] ADJ non dissimulé(e)
overtake [əuvə'teɪk] VT (*irreg: like* **take**) dépasser; (*Brit Aut*) dépasser, doubler
overtaking [əuvə'teɪkɪŋ] N (*Aut*) dépassement *m*
overtax [əuvə'tæks] VT (*Econ*) surimposer; (*fig: strength, patience*) abuser de; **to ~ o.s.** se surmener
overthrow [əuvə'θrəu] VT (*irreg: like* **throw**) (*government*) renverser
overtime ['əuvətaɪm] N heures *fpl* supplémentaires; **to do** *or* **work ~** faire des heures supplémentaires
overtime ban N refus *m* de faire des heures supplémentaires
overtone ['əuvətəun] N (*also:* **overtones**) note *f*, sous-entendus *mpl*
overtook [əuvə'tuk] PT *of* **overtake**
overture ['əuvətʃuər] N (*Mus, fig*) ouverture *f*
overturn [əuvə'tə:n] VT renverser; (*decision, plan*) annuler ▶ VI se retourner
overview ['əuvəvju:] N vue *f* d'ensemble
overweight [əuvə'weɪt] ADJ (*person*) trop gros(se); (*luggage*) trop lourd(e)
overwhelm [əuvə'wɛlm] VT (*subj: emotion*) accabler, submerger; (*enemy, opponent*) écraser

overwhelming [əuvə'wɛlmɪŋ] ADJ (*victory, defeat*) écrasant(e); (*desire*) irrésistible; **one's ~ impression is of heat** on a une impression dominante de chaleur
overwhelmingly [əuvə'wɛlmɪŋlɪ] ADV (*vote*) en masse; (*win*) d'une manière écrasante
overwork [əuvə'wə:k] N surmenage *m* ▶ VT surmener ▶ VI se surmener
overwrite [əuvə'raɪt] VT (*irreg: like* **write**) (*Comput*) écraser
overwrought [əuvə'rɔ:t] ADJ excédé(e)
ovulation [ɔvju'leɪʃən] N ovulation *f*
owe [əu] VT devoir; **to ~ sb sth, to ~ sth to sb** devoir qch à qn; **how much do I ~ you?** combien est-ce que je vous dois?
owing to ['əuɪŋ-] PREP à cause de, en raison de
owl [aul] N hibou *m*
own [əun] VT posséder ▶ VI (*Brit*): **to ~ to sth** reconnaître *or* avouer qch; **to ~ to having done sth** avouer avoir fait qch ▶ ADJ propre; **a room of my ~** une chambre à moi, ma propre chambre; **can I have it for my (very) ~?** puis-je l'avoir pour moi (tout) seul?; **to get one's ~ back** prendre sa revanche; **on one's ~** tout(e) seul(e); **to come into one's ~** trouver sa voie, trouver sa justification
▶ **own up** VI avouer
own brand N (*Comm*) marque *f* de distributeur
owner ['əunər] N propriétaire *mf*
owner-occupier ['əunər'ɔkjupaɪər] N propriétaire occupant
ownership ['əunəʃɪp] N possession *f*; **it's under new ~** (*shop etc*) il y a eu un changement de propriétaire
own goal N: **he scored an ~** (*Sport*) il a marqué un but contre son camp; (*fig*) cela s'est retourné contre lui
ox [ɔks] (*pl* **oxen** ['ɔksn]) N bœuf *m*
Oxbridge ['ɔksbrɪdʒ] N (*Brit*) *les universités d'Oxford et de Cambridge; voir article*

> Oxbridge, nom formé à partir des mots Ox(ford) et (Cam)bridge, s'utilise pour parler de ces deux universités comme formant un tout, dans la mesure où elles sont toutes deux les universités britanniques les plus prestigieuses et mondialement connues.

oxen ['ɔksən] NPL *of* **ox**
Oxfam ['ɔksfæm] N ABBR (*Brit:* = Oxford Committee for Famine Relief) *association humanitaire*
oxide ['ɔksaɪd] N oxyde *m*
Oxon. ['ɔksn] ABBR (*Brit: Oxoniensis*) = **of Oxford**
oxtail ['ɔksteɪl] N: **~ soup** soupe *f* à la queue de bœuf
oxygen ['ɔksɪdʒən] N oxygène *m*
oxygen mask N masque *m* à oxygène
oxygen tent N tente *f* à oxygène
oyster ['ɔɪstər] N huître *f*
oz. ABBR = **ounce; ounces**
ozone ['əuzəun] N ozone *m*
ozone friendly ['əuzəunfrɛndlɪ] ADJ qui n'attaque pas *or* qui préserve la couche d'ozone
ozone hole N trou *m* d'ozone
ozone layer N couche *f* d'ozone

Pp

P, p [pi:] N (*letter*) P, p *m*; **P for Peter** P comme Pierre

P ABBR = **president; prince**

p ABBR (= *page*) p; (*BRIT*) = **penny; pence**

pa [pɑ:] N (*inf*) papa *m*

Pa. ABBR (*US*) = **Pennsylvania**

P.A. N ABBR = **personal assistant; public address system** ▸ ABBR (*US*) = **Pennsylvania**

p.a. ABBR = **per annum**

PAC N ABBR (*US*) = **political action committee**

pace [peɪs] N pas *m*; (*speed*) allure *f*; vitesse *f* ▸ VI: **to ~ up and down** faire les cent pas; **to keep ~ with** aller à la même vitesse que; (*events*) se tenir au courant de; **to set the ~** (*running*) donner l'allure; (*fig*) donner le ton; **to put sb through his paces** (*fig*) mettre qn à l'épreuve

pacemaker ['peɪsmeɪkə'] N (*Med*) stimulateur *m* cardiaque; (*Sport: also:* **pacesetter**) meneur(-euse) de train

Pacific [pə'sɪfɪk] N: **the ~ (Ocean)** le Pacifique, l'océan *m* Pacifique

pacific [pə'sɪfɪk] ADJ pacifique

pacification [pæsɪfɪ'keɪʃən] N pacification *f*

pacifier ['pæsɪfaɪə'] N (*US: dummy*) tétine *f*

pacifist ['pæsɪfɪst] N pacifiste *mf*

pacify ['pæsɪfaɪ] VT pacifier; (*soothe*) calmer

pack [pæk] N paquet *m*; (*bundle*) ballot *m*; (*of hounds*) meute *f*; (*of thieves, wolves etc*) bande *f*; (*of cards*) jeu *m*; (*US: of cigarettes*) paquet; (*back pack*) sac *m* à dos ▸ VT (*goods*) empaqueter, emballer; (*in suitcase etc*) emballer; (*box*) remplir; (*cram*) entasser; (*press down*) tasser; damer; (*Comput*) grouper, tasser ▸ VI: **to ~ (one's bags)** faire ses bagages; **to ~ into** (*room, stadium*) s'entasser dans; **to send sb packing** (*inf*) envoyer promener qn
▸ **pack in** (*BRIT inf*) VI (*machine*) tomber en panne
▸ VT (*boyfriend*) plaquer; **~ it in!** laisse tomber!
▸ **pack off** VT: **to ~ sb off to** expédier qn à
▸ **pack up** VI (*BRIT inf: machine*) tomber en panne; (*person*) se tirer ▸ VT (*belongings*) ranger; (*goods, presents*) empaqueter, emballer

package ['pækɪdʒ] N paquet *m*; (*of goods*) emballage *m*, conditionnement *m*; (*also:* **package deal**: *agreement*) marché global; (*purchase*) forfait *m*; (*Comput*) progiciel *m* ▸ VT (*goods*) conditionner

package holiday N (*BRIT*) vacances organisées

package tour N voyage organisé

packaging ['pækɪdʒɪŋ] N (*wrapping materials*) emballage *m*; (*of goods*) conditionnement *m*

packed [pækt] ADJ (*crowded*) bondé(e)

packed lunch (*BRIT*) N repas froid

packer ['pækə'] N (*person*) emballeur(-euse); conditionneur(-euse)

packet ['pækɪt] N paquet *m*

packet switching [-swɪtʃɪŋ] N (*Comput*) commutation *f* de paquets

pack ice ['pækaɪs] N banquise *f*

packing ['pækɪŋ] N emballage *m*

packing case N caisse *f* (d'emballage)

pact [pækt] N pacte *m*, traité *m*

pad [pæd] N bloc(-notes *m*) *m*; (*to prevent friction*) tampon *m*; (*for inking*) tampon *m* encreur; (*inf: flat*) piaule *f* ▸ VT rembourrer ▸ VI: **to ~ in/ about** *etc* entrer/aller et venir *etc* à pas feutrés

padded ['pædɪd] ADJ (*jacket*) matelassé(e); (*bra*) rembourré(e); **~ cell** cellule capitonnée

padding ['pædɪŋ] N rembourrage *m*; (*fig*) délayage *m*

paddle ['pædl] N (*oar*) pagaie *f*; (*US: for table tennis*) raquette *f* de ping-pong ▸ VI (*with feet*) barboter, faire trempette ▸ VT: **to ~ a canoe** *etc* pagayer

paddle steamer N bateau *m* à aubes

paddling pool ['pædlɪŋ-] N petit bassin

paddock ['pædək] N enclos *m*; (*Racing*) paddock *m*

paddy ['pædɪ] N (*also:* **paddy field**) rizière *f*

padlock ['pædlɔk] N cadenas *m* ▸ VT cadenasser

padre ['pɑːdrɪ] N aumônier *m*

paediatrician, (*US*) **pediatrician** [piːdɪə'trɪʃən] N pédiatre *mf*

paediatrics, (*US*) **pediatrics** [piːdɪ'ætrɪks] N pédiatrie *f*

paedophile, (*US*) **pedophile** ['piːdəufaɪl] N pédophile *m*

pagan ['peɪgən] ADJ, N païen(ne)

page [peɪdʒ] N (*of book*) page *f*; (*also:* **page boy**) groom *m*, chasseur *m*; (: *at wedding*) garçon *m* d'honneur ▸ VT (*in hotel etc*) (faire) appeler

pageant ['pædʒənt] N spectacle *m* historique; grande cérémonie

pageantry ['pædʒəntrɪ] N apparat *m*, pompe *f*

page break N fin *f* or saut *m* de page

pager ['peɪdʒə'] N bip *m* (*inf*), Alphapage® *m*

paginate ['pædʒɪneɪt] VT paginer
pagination [pædʒɪ'neɪʃən] N pagination f
pagoda [pə'gəʊdə] N pagode f
paid [peɪd] PT, PP of **pay** ▶ ADJ (work, official)
rémunéré(e); (holiday) payé(e); **to put ~ to**
(BRIT) mettre fin à, mettre par terre
paid-up, ['peɪdʌp], (US) **paid-in** ['peɪdɪn] ADJ
(member) à jour de sa cotisation; (shares)
libéré(e); ~ **capital** capital versé
pail [peɪl] N seau m
pain [peɪn] N douleur f; (inf: nuisance) plaie f; **to
be in ~** souffrir, avoir mal; **to have a ~ in** avoir
mal à or une douleur à or dans; **to take pains to
do** se donner du mal pour faire; **on ~ of death**
sous peine de mort
pained [peɪnd] ADJ peiné(e), chagrin(e)
painful ['peɪnful] ADJ douloureux(-euse);
(difficult) difficile, pénible
painfully ['peɪnfəlɪ] ADV (fig: very) terriblement
painkiller ['peɪnkɪlə'] N calmant m,
analgésique m
painless ['peɪnlɪs] ADJ indolore
painstaking ['peɪnzteɪkɪŋ] ADJ (person)
soigneux(-euse); (work) soigné(e)
paint [peɪnt] N peinture f ▶ VT peindre; (fig)
dépeindre; **to ~ the door blue** peindre la porte
en bleu; **to ~ in oils** faire de la peinture à
l'huile
paintbox ['peɪntbɒks] N boîte f de couleurs
paintbrush ['peɪntbrʌʃ] N pinceau m
painter ['peɪntə'] N peintre m
painting ['peɪntɪŋ] N peinture f; (picture)
tableau m
paint-stripper ['peɪntstrɪpə'] N décapant m
paintwork ['peɪntwə:k] N (BRIT) peintures fpl;
(: of car) peinture f
pair [peə'] N (of shoes, gloves etc) paire f; (of people)
couple m; (twosome) duo m; ~ **of scissors** (paire
de) ciseaux mpl; ~ **of trousers** pantalon m
▶ **pair off** VI se mettre par deux
pajamas [pə'dʒɑ:məz] NPL (US) pyjama m
Pakistan [pɑ:kɪ'stɑ:n] N Pakistan m
Pakistani [pɑ:kɪ'stɑ:nɪ] ADJ pakistanais(e) ▶ N
Pakistanais(e)
PAL [pæl] N ABBR (TV: = phase alternation line)
PAL m
pal [pæl] N (inf) copain (copine)
palace ['pæləs] N palais m
palatable ['pælɪtəbl] ADJ bon (bonne), agréable
au goût
palate ['pælɪt] N palais m (Anat)
palatial [pə'leɪʃəl] ADJ grandiose, magnifique
palaver [pə'lɑ:və'] N palabres fpl or mpl;
histoire(s) f(pl)
pale [peɪl] ADJ pâle ▶ VI pâlir ▶ N: **to be beyond
the ~** être au ban de la société; **to grow** or **turn
~** (person) pâlir; ~ **blue** adj bleu pâle inv; **to ~ into
insignificance (beside)** perdre beaucoup
d'importance (par rapport à)
paleness ['peɪlnɪs] N pâleur f
Palestine ['pælɪstaɪn] N Palestine f
Palestinian [pælɪs'tɪnɪən] ADJ palestinien(ne)
▶ N Palestinien(ne)
palette ['pælɪt] N palette f

paling ['peɪlɪŋ] N (stake) palis m; (fence) palissade f
palisade [pælɪ'seɪd] N palissade f
pall [pɔ:l] N (of smoke) voile m ▶ VI: **to ~ (on)**
devenir lassant (pour)
pallet ['pælɪt] N (for goods) palette f
pallid ['pælɪd] ADJ blême
pallor ['pælə'] N pâleur f
pally ['pælɪ] ADJ (inf) copain (copine)
palm [pɑ:m] N (Anat) paume f; (also: **palm tree**)
palmier m; (leaf, symbol) palme f ▶ VT: **to ~ sth
off on sb** (inf) refiler qch à qn
palmist ['pɑ:mɪst] N chiromancien(ne)
Palm Sunday N le dimanche des Rameaux
palpable ['pælpəbl] ADJ évident(e), manifeste
palpitation [pælpɪ'teɪʃən] N palpitation f
paltry ['pɔ:ltrɪ] ADJ dérisoire; piètre
pamper ['pæmpə'] VT gâter, dorloter
pamphlet ['pæmflət] N brochure f; (political etc)
tract m
pan [pæn] N (also: **saucepan**) casserole f; (also:
frying pan) poêle f; (of lavatory) cuvette f ▶ VI
(Cine) faire un panoramique ▶ VT (inf: book, film)
éreinter; **to ~ for gold** laver du sable aurifère
panacea [pænə'sɪə] N panacée f
Panama ['pænəmɑ:] N Panama m
Panama Canal N canal m de Panama
pancake ['pænkeɪk] N crêpe f
Pancake Day N (BRIT) mardi gras
pancake roll N rouleau m de printemps
pancreas ['pæŋkrɪəs] N pancréas m
panda ['pændə] N panda m
panda car N (BRIT) ≈ voiture f pie inv
pandemic [pæn'demɪk] N pandémie f
pandemonium [pændɪ'məʊnɪəm] N
tohu-bohu m
pander ['pændə'] VI: **to ~ to** flatter bassement;
obéir servilement à
p&h ABBR (US: = postage and handling) frais mpl de
port
P&L ABBR = **profit and loss**
p&p ABBR (BRIT: = postage and packing) frais mpl de
port
pane [peɪn] N carreau m (de fenêtre), vitre f
panel ['pænl] N (of wood, cloth etc) panneau m;
(Radio, TV) panel m, invités mpl; (for interview,
exams) jury m; (official: of experts) table ronde,
comité m
panel game N (BRIT) jeu m (radiophonique/
télévisé)
panelling, (US) **paneling** ['pænəlɪŋ] N boiseries
fpl
panellist, (US) **panelist** ['pænəlɪst] N invité(e)
(d'un panel), membre d'un panel
pang [pæŋ] N: **pangs of remorse** pincements
mpl de remords; **pangs of hunger/conscience**
tiraillements mpl d'estomac/de la conscience
panhandler ['pænhændlə'] N (US inf)
mendiant(e)
panic ['pænɪk] N panique f, affolement m ▶ VI
s'affoler, paniquer
panic buying [-baɪɪŋ] N achats mpl de
précaution
panicky ['pænɪkɪ] ADJ (person) qui panique or
s'affole facilement

P

711

panic-stricken ['pænɪkstrɪkən] ADJ affolé(e)
pannier ['pænɪəʳ] N (on animal) bât m; (on bicycle) sacoche f
panorama [pænə'rɑːmə] N panorama m
panoramic [pænə'ræmɪk] ADJ panoramique
pansy ['pænzɪ] N (Bot) pensée f; (inf) tapette f, pédé m
pant [pænt] VI haleter
pantechnicon [pæn'tɛknɪkən] N (BRIT) (grand) camion de déménagement
panther ['pænθəʳ] N panthère f
panties ['pæntɪz] NPL slip m, culotte f
pantihose ['pæntɪhəuz] N (US) collant m
panto ['pæntəu] N = **pantomime**
pantomime ['pæntəmaɪm] N (BRIT) spectacle m de Noël; *voir article*

> Une *pantomime* (à ne pas confondre avec le mot tel qu'on l'utilise en français), que l'on appelle également *panto*, est un genre de farce où le personnage principal est souvent un jeune garçon et où il y a toujours une *dame*, c'est-à-dire une vieille femme jouée par un homme, et un méchant. La plupart du temps, l'histoire est basée sur un conte de fées comme Cendrillon ou Le Chat botté, et le public est encouragé à participer en prévenant le héros d'un danger imminent. Ce genre de spectacle, qui s'adresse surtout aux enfants, vise également un public d'adultes au travers des nombreuses plaisanteries faisant allusion à des faits d'actualité.

pantry ['pæntrɪ] N garde-manger m inv; (room) office m
pants [pænts] NPL (BRIT: woman's) culotte f, slip m; (: man's) slip m, caleçon m; (US: trousers) pantalon m
pantsuit ['pæntsuːt] N (US) tailleur-pantalon m
pantyhose ['pæntɪhəuz] NPL (US) collant m
papacy ['peɪpəsɪ] N papauté f
papal ['peɪpəl] ADJ papal(e), pontifical(e)
paparazzi [pæpə'rætsiː] NPL paparazzi mpl
paper ['peɪpəʳ] N papier m; (also: **wallpaper**) papier peint; (also: **newspaper**) journal m; (academic essay) article m; (exam) épreuve écrite ▶ ADJ en or de papier ▶ VT tapisser (de papier peint); **papers** NPL (also: **identity papers**) papiers mpl (d'identité); **a piece of ~** (odd bit) un bout de papier; (sheet) une feuille de papier; **to put sth down on ~** mettre qch par écrit
paper advance N (on printer) avance f (du) papier
paperback ['peɪpəbæk] N livre broché or non relié; (small) livre m de poche ▶ ADJ: **~ edition** édition brochée
paper bag N sac m en papier
paperboy ['peɪpəbɔɪ] N (selling) vendeur m de journaux; (delivering) livreur m de journaux
paper clip N trombone m
paper handkerchief, (inf) **paper hankie** N mouchoir m en papier
paper mill N papeterie f
paper money N papier-monnaie m
paper profit N profit m théorique
paper shop N (BRIT) marchand m de journaux

paperweight ['peɪpəweɪt] N presse-papiers m inv
paperwork ['peɪpəwəːk] N papiers mpl; (pej) paperasserie f
papier-mâché ['pæpɪeɪ'mæʃeɪ] N papier mâché
paprika ['pæprɪkə] N paprika m
Pap test, Pap smear ['pæp-] N (Med) frottis m
par [pɑːʳ] N pair m; (Golf) normale f du parcours; **on a ~ with** à égalité avec, au même niveau que; **at ~** au pair; **above/below ~** au-dessus/au-dessous du pair; **to feel below** or **under** or **not up to ~** ne pas se sentir en forme
parable ['pærəbl] N parabole f (Rel)
parabola [pə'ræbələ] N parabole f (Math)
paracetamol [pærə'siːtəmɔl] N (BRIT) paracétamol m
parachute ['pærəʃuːt] N parachute m ▶ VI sauter en parachute
parachute jump N saut m en parachute
parachutist ['pærəʃuːtɪst] N parachutiste mf
parade [pə'reɪd] N défilé m; (inspection) revue f; (street) boulevard m ▶ VT (fig) faire étalage de ▶ VI défiler; **a fashion ~** (BRIT) un défilé de mode
parade ground N terrain m de manœuvre
paradise ['pærədaɪs] N paradis m
paradox ['pærədɔks] N paradoxe m
paradoxical [pærə'dɔksɪkl] ADJ paradoxal(e)
paradoxically [pærə'dɔksɪklɪ] ADV paradoxalement
paraffin ['pærəfɪn] N (BRIT): **~ (oil)** pétrole (lampant); **liquid ~** huile f de paraffine
paraffin heater N (BRIT) poêle m à mazout
paraffin lamp N (BRIT) lampe f à pétrole
paragon ['pærəgən] N parangon m
paragraph ['pærəgrɑːf] N paragraphe m; **to begin a new ~** aller à la ligne
Paraguay ['pærəgwaɪ] N Paraguay m
Paraguayan [pærə'gwaɪən] ADJ paraguayen(ne) ▶ N Paraguayen(ne)
parallel ['pærəlɛl] ADJ: **~ (with or to)** parallèle (à); (fig) analogue (à) ▶ N (line) parallèle f; (fig, Geo) parallèle m
paralysed ['pærəlaɪzd] ADJ paralysé(e)
paralysis [pə'rælɪsɪs] (pl **paralyses** [-siːz]) N paralysie f
paralytic [pærə'lɪtɪk] ADJ paralytique; (BRIT inf: drunk) ivre mort(e)
paralyze ['pærəlaɪz] VT paralyser
paramedic [pærə'mɛdɪk] N auxiliaire m/f médical(e)
parameter [pə'ræmɪtəʳ] N paramètre m
paramilitary [pærə'mɪlɪtərɪ] ADJ paramilitaire
paramount ['pærəmaunt] ADJ: **of ~ importance** de la plus haute or grande importance
paranoia [pærə'nɔɪə] N paranoïa f
paranoid ['pærənɔɪd] ADJ (Psych) paranoïaque; (neurotic) paranoïde
paranormal [pærə'nɔːml] ADJ paranormal(e)
paraphernalia [pærəfə'neɪlɪə] N attirail m, affaires fpl
paraphrase ['pærəfreɪz] VT paraphraser
paraplegic [pærə'pliːdʒɪk] N paraplégique mf

parapsychology [pærəsaɪˈkɔlədʒɪ] N parapsychologie f

parasite [ˈpærəsaɪt] N parasite m

parasol [ˈpærəsɔl] N ombrelle f; (at café etc) parasol m

paratrooper [ˈpærətruːpəʳ] N parachutiste m (soldat)

parcel [ˈpɑːsl] N paquet m, colis m ▸ VT (also: **parcel up**) empaqueter
▸ **parcel out** VT répartir

parcel bomb N (BRIT) colis piégé

parcel post N service m de colis postaux

parch [pɑːtʃ] VT dessécher

parched [pɑːtʃt] ADJ (person) assoiffé(e)

parchment [ˈpɑːtʃmənt] N parchemin m

pardon [ˈpɑːdn] N pardon m; (Law) grâce f ▸ VT pardonner à; (Law) gracier; ~! pardon!; ~ **me!** (after burping etc) excusez-moi!; **I beg your ~!** (I'm sorry) pardon!, je suis désolé!; (**I beg your**) ~?, (US) ~ **me?** (what did you say?) pardon?

pare [pɛəʳ] VT (BRIT: nails) couper; (fruit etc) peler; (fig: costs etc) réduire

parent [ˈpɛərənt] N (father) père m; (mother) mère f; **parents** NPL parents mpl

parentage [ˈpɛərəntɪdʒ] N naissance f; **of unknown ~** de parents inconnus

parental [pəˈrentl] ADJ parental(e), des parents

parent company N société f mère

parenthesis [pəˈrɛnθɪsɪs] (pl **parentheses** [-siːz]) N parenthèse f; **in parentheses** entre parenthèses

parenthood [ˈpɛərənthud] N paternité f or maternité f

parenting [ˈpɛərəntɪŋ] N le métier de parent, le travail d'un parent

Paris [ˈpærɪs] N Paris

parish [ˈpærɪʃ] N paroisse f; (BRIT: civil) ≈ commune f ▸ ADJ paroissial(e)

parish council N (BRIT) ≈ conseil municipal

parishioner [pəˈrɪʃənəʳ] N paroissien(ne)

Parisian [pəˈrɪzɪən] ADJ parisien(ne), de Paris ▸ N Parisien(ne)

parity [ˈpærɪtɪ] N parité f

park [pɑːk] N parc m, jardin public ▸ VT garer ▸ VI se garer; **can I ~ here?** est-ce que je peux me garer ici?

parka [ˈpɑːkə] N parka m

park and ride N parking-relais m

parking [ˈpɑːkɪŋ] N stationnement m; **"no ~"** "stationnement interdit"

parking lights NPL feux mpl de stationnement

parking lot N (US) parking m, parc m de stationnement

parking meter N parc(o)mètre m

parking offence, (US) **parking violation** N infraction f au stationnement

parking place N place f de stationnement

parking ticket N P.-V. m

Parkinson's [ˈpɑːkɪnsənz] N (also: **Parkinson's disease**) maladie f de Parkinson, parkinson m

parkway [ˈpɑːkweɪ] N (US) route f express (en site vert ou aménagé)

parlance [ˈpɑːləns] N: **in common/modern ~** dans le langage courant/actuel

parliament [ˈpɑːləmənt] N parlement m; voir article

Le Parliament est l'assemblée législative britannique; elle est composée de deux chambres: la House of Commons et la House of Lords. Ses bureaux sont les Houses of Parliament au palais de Westminster à Londres. Chaque Parliament est en général élu pour cinq ans. Les débats du Parliament sont maintenant retransmis à la télévision.

parliamentary [pɑːləˈmɛntərɪ] ADJ parlementaire

parlour, (US) **parlor** [ˈpɑːləʳ] N salon m

parlous [ˈpɑːləs] ADJ (formal) précaire

Parmesan [pɑːmɪˈzæn] N (also: **Parmesan cheese**) Parmesan m

parochial [pəˈrəukɪəl] ADJ paroissial(e); (pej) à l'esprit de clocher

parody [ˈpærədɪ] N parodie f

parole [pəˈrəul] N: **on ~** en liberté conditionnelle

paroxysm [ˈpærəksɪzəm] N (Med, of grief) paroxysme m; (of anger) accès m

parquet [ˈpɑːkeɪ] N: **~ floor(ing)** parquet m

parrot [ˈpærət] N perroquet m

parrot fashion ADV comme un perroquet

parry [ˈpærɪ] VT esquiver, parer à

parsimonious [pɑːsɪˈməunɪəs] ADJ parcimonieux(-euse)

parsley [ˈpɑːslɪ] N persil m

parsnip [ˈpɑːsnɪp] N panais m

parson [ˈpɑːsn] N ecclésiastique m; (Church of England) pasteur m

part [pɑːt] N partie f; (of machine) pièce f; (Theat) rôle m; (Mus) voix f; partie; (of serial) épisode m; (US: in hair) raie f ▸ ADJ partiel(le) ▸ ADV = **partly** ▸ VT séparer ▸ VI (people) se séparer; (crowd) s'ouvrir; (roads) se diviser; **to take ~ in** participer à, prendre part à; **to take sb's ~** prendre le parti de qn, prendre parti pour qn; **on his ~** de sa part; **for my ~** en ce qui me concerne; **for the most ~** en grande partie; dans la plupart des cas; **for the better ~ of the day** pendant la plus grande partie de la journée; **to be ~ and parcel of** faire partie de; **in ~** en partie; **to take sth in good/bad ~** prendre qch du bon/mauvais côté
▸ **part with** VT FUS (person) se séparer de; (possessions) se défaire de

partake [pɑːˈteɪk] VI (irreg: like **take**) (formal): **to ~ of sth** prendre part à qch, partager qch

part exchange N (BRIT) **in ~** en reprise

partial [ˈpɑːʃl] ADJ (incomplete) partiel(le); (unjust) partial(e); **to be ~ to** aimer, avoir un faible pour

partially [ˈpɑːʃəlɪ] ADV en partie, partiellement; partialement

participant [pɑːˈtɪsɪpənt] N (in competition, campaign) participant(e)

participate [pɑːˈtɪsɪpeɪt] VI: **to ~ (in)** participer (à), prendre part (à)

participation [pɑːtɪsɪˈpeɪʃən] N participation f

participle [ˈpɑːtɪsɪpl] N participe m

particle [ˈpɑːtɪkl] N particule f; (of dust) grain m

particular [pəˈtɪkjuləʳ] ADJ (specific)

P

particulier(-ière); (*special*) particulier,
spécial(e); (*fussy*) difficile, exigeant(e); (*careful*)
méticuleux(-euse); **in ~** en particulier, surtout
particularly [pə'tɪkjuləlɪ] ADV
particulièrement; (*in particular*) en particulier
particulars [pə'tɪkjuləz] NPL détails *mpl*;
(*information*) renseignements *mpl*
parting ['pɑːtɪŋ] N séparation *f*; (*BRIT: in hair*)
raie *f* ▶ ADJ d'adieu; **his ~ shot was ...** il lança
en partant ....
partisan [pɑːtɪ'zæn] N partisan(e) ▶ ADJ
partisan(e); de parti
partition [pɑː'tɪʃən] N (*Pol*) partition *f*, division
f; (*wall*) cloison *f*
partly ['pɑːtlɪ] ADV en partie, partiellement
partner ['pɑːtnə'] N (*Comm*) associé(e); (*Sport*)
partenaire *mf*; (*spouse*) conjoint(e); (*lover*)
ami(e); (*at dance*) cavalier(-ière) ▶ VT être
l'associé *or* le partenaire *or* le cavalier de
partnership ['pɑːtnəʃɪp] N association *f*; **to go
into ~ (with), form a ~ (with)** s'associer (avec)
part payment N acompte *m*
partridge ['pɑːtrɪdʒ] N perdrix *f*
part-time ['pɑːt'taɪm] ADJ, ADV à mi-temps, à
temps partiel
part-timer [pɑːt'taɪmə'] N (*also:* **part-time
worker**) travailleur(-euse) à temps partiel
party ['pɑːtɪ] N (*Pol*) parti *m*; (*celebration*) fête *f*;
(*: formal*) réception *f*; (*: in evening*) soirée *f*; (*team*)
équipe *f*; (*group*) groupe *m*; (*Law*) partie *f*;
dinner ~ dîner *m*; **to give** *or* **throw a ~** donner
une réception; **we're having a ~ next
Saturday** nous organisons une soirée *or*
réunion entre amis samedi prochain; **it's for
our son's birthday ~** c'est pour la fête (*or* le
goûter*) d'anniversaire de notre garçon; **to be a
~ to a crime** être impliqué(e) dans un crime
party dress N robe habillée
party line N (*Pol*) ligne *f* politique; (*Tel*) ligne
partagée
party piece N numéro habituel
party political broadcast N émission réservée à
un parti politique.
pass [pɑːs] VT (*time, object*) passer; (*place*) passer
devant; (*friend*) croiser; (*exam*) être reçu(e) à,
réussir; (*candidate*) admettre; (*overtake*)
dépasser; (*approve*) approuver, accepter; (*law*)
promulguer ▶ VI passer; (*Scol*) être reçu(e) *or*
admis(e), réussir ▶ N (*permit*) laissez-passer *m
inv*; (*membership card*) carte *f* d'accès *or*
d'abonnement; (*in mountains*) col *m*; (*Sport*)
passe *f*; (*Scol: also:* **pass mark**) être
reçu(e) (sans mention); **to ~ sb sth** passer qch à
qn; **could you ~ the salt/oil, please?**
pouvez-vous me passer le sel/l'huile, s'il vous
plaît?; **she could ~ for 25** on lui donnerait 25
ans; **to ~ sth through a ring** *etc* (faire) passer
qch dans un anneau *etc*; **could you ~ the
vegetables round?** pourriez-vous faire passer
les légumes?; **things have come to a pretty ~**
(*BRIT*) voilà où on en est!; **to make a ~ at sb** (*inf*)
faire des avances à qn
▶ **pass away** VI mourir
▶ **pass by** VI passer ▶ VT (*ignore*) négliger

▶ **pass down** VT (*customs, inheritance*)
transmettre
▶ **pass on** VI (*die*) s'éteindre, décéder ▶ VT (*hand
on*): **to ~ on (to)** transmettre (à) (*illness*) passer
(à); (*price rises*) répercuter (sur)
▶ **pass out** VI s'évanouir; (*BRIT Mil*) sortir (*d'une
école militaire*)
▶ **pass over** VT (*ignore*) passer sous silence
▶ **pass up** VT (*opportunity*) laisser passer
passable ['pɑːsəbl] ADJ (*road*) praticable; (*work*)
acceptable
passage ['pæsɪdʒ] N (*also:* **passageway**) couloir
m; (*gen, in book*) passage *m*; (*by boat*) traversée *f*
passbook ['pɑːsbuk] N livret *m*
passenger ['pæsɪndʒə'] N passager(-ère)
passer-by [pɑːsə'baɪ] N passant(e)
passing ['pɑːsɪŋ] ADJ (*fig*) passager(-ère); **in ~** en
passant
passing place N (*Aut*) aire *f* de croisement
passion ['pæʃən] N passion *f*; **to have a ~ for
sth** avoir la passion de qch
passionate ['pæʃənɪt] ADJ passionné(e)
passion fruit N fruit *m* de la passion
passion play N mystère *m* de la Passion
passive ['pæsɪv] ADJ (*also: Ling*) passif(-ive)
passive smoking N tabagisme passif
passkey ['pɑːskiː] N passe *m*
Passover ['pɑːsəuvə'] N Pâque juive
passport ['pɑːspɔːt] N passeport *m*
passport control N contrôle *m* des passeports
passport office N bureau *m* de délivrance des
passeports
password ['pɑːswəːd] N mot *m* de passe
past [pɑːst] PREP (*in front of*) devant; (*further than*)
au delà de, plus loin que; *après*; (*later than*)
après ▶ ADV: **to run ~** passer en courant ▶ ADJ
passé(e); (*president etc*) ancien(ne) ▶ N passé *m*;
he's ~ forty il a dépassé la quarantaine, il a
plus de *or* passé quarante ans; **ten/quarter-
eight** (*BRIT*) huit heures dix/un *or* et quart; **it's
~ midnight** il est plus de minuit, il est passé
minuit; **he ran ~ me** il m'a dépassé en courant,
il a passé devant moi en courant; **for the ~
few/3 days** depuis quelques/3 jours; ces
derniers/3 derniers jours; **in the ~** (*gen*) dans le
temps, autrefois; (*Ling*) au passé; **I'm ~ caring**
je ne m'en fais plus; **to be ~ it** (*BRIT inf: person*)
avoir passé l'âge
pasta ['pæstə] N pâtes *fpl*
paste [peɪst] N pâte *f*; (*Culin: meat*) pâté *m* (à
tartiner); (*: tomato*) purée *f*, concentré *m*; (*glue*)
colle *f* (de pâte); (*jewellery*) strass *m* ▶ VT coller
pastel ['pæstl] ADJ pastel *inv* ▶ N (*Art: pencil*)
(crayon *m*) pastel *m*; (*: drawing*) (dessin *m* au)
pastel; (*colour*) ton *m* pastel *inv*
pasteurized ['pæstəraɪzd] ADJ pasteurisé(e)
pastille ['pæstl] N pastille *f*
pastime ['pɑːstaɪm] N passe-temps *m inv*,
distraction *f*
past master N (*BRIT*): **to be a ~ at** être expert en
pastor ['pɑːstə'] N pasteur *m*
pastoral ['pɑːstərl] ADJ pastoral(e)
pastry ['peɪstrɪ] N pâte *f*; (*cake*) pâtisserie *f*
pasture ['pɑːstʃə'] N pâturage *m*

pasty¹ ['pæstɪ] N petit pâté (en croûte)

pasty² ['peɪstɪ] ADJ pâteux(-euse); (*complexion*) terreux(-euse)

pat [pæt] VT donner une petite tape à; (*dog*) caresser ▶ N: **a ~ of butter** une noisette de beurre; **to give sb/o.s. a ~ on the back** (*fig*) congratuler qn/se congratuler; **he knows it (off) ~**, (*US*) **he has it down ~** il sait cela sur le bout des doigts

patch [pætʃ] N (*of material*) pièce f; (*eye patch*) cache m; (*spot*) tache f; (*of land*) parcelle f; (*on tyre*) rustine f ▶ VT (*clothes*) rapiécer; **a bad ~** (BRIT) une période difficile
▶ **patch up** VT réparer

patchwork ['pætʃwɜːk] N patchwork m

patchy ['pætʃɪ] ADJ inégal(e); (*incomplete*) fragmentaire

pate [peɪt] N: **a bald ~** un crâne chauve or dégarni

pâté ['pæteɪ] N pâté m, terrine f

patent ['peɪtnt, (*US*) 'pætnt] N brevet m (d'invention) ▶ VT faire breveter ▶ ADJ patent(e), manifeste

patent leather N cuir verni

patently ['peɪtntlɪ] ADV manifestement

patent medicine N spécialité f pharmaceutique

patent office N bureau m des brevets

paternal [pə'tɜːnl] ADJ paternel(le)

paternity [pə'tɜːnɪtɪ] N paternité f

paternity leave N congé m de paternité

paternity suit N (*Law*) action f en recherche de paternité

path [pɑːθ] N chemin m, sentier m; (*in garden*) allée f; (*of planet*) course f; (*of missile*) trajectoire f

pathetic [pə'θɛtɪk] ADJ (*pitiful*) pitoyable; (*very bad*) lamentable, minable; (*moving*) pathétique

pathological [pæθə'lɔdʒɪkl] ADJ pathologique

pathologist [pə'θɔlədʒɪst] N pathologiste mf

pathology [pə'θɔlədʒɪ] N pathologie f

pathos ['peɪθɔs] N pathétique m

pathway ['pɑːθweɪ] N chemin m, sentier m; (*in garden*) allée f

patience ['peɪʃns] N patience f; (BRIT *Cards*) réussite f; **to lose (one's) ~** perdre patience

patient ['peɪʃnt] N malade mf; (*of dentist etc*) patient(e) ▶ ADJ patient(e)

patiently ['peɪʃntlɪ] ADV patiemment

patio ['pætɪəu] N patio m

patriot ['peɪtrɪət] N patriote mf

patriotic [pætrɪ'ɔtɪk] ADJ patriotique; (*person*) patriote

patriotism ['pætrɪətɪzəm] N patriotisme m

patrol [pə'trəul] N patrouille f ▶ VT patrouiller dans; **to be on ~** être de patrouille

patrol boat N patrouilleur m

patrol car N voiture f de police

patrolman [pə'trəulmən] N (*irreg*) (*US*) agent m de police

patron ['peɪtrən] N (*in shop*) client(e); (*of charity*) patron(ne); **~ of the arts** mécène m

patronage ['pætrənɪdʒ] N patronage m, appui m

patronize ['pætrənaɪz] VT être (un) client or un habitué de; (*fig*) traiter avec condescendance

patronizing ['pætrənaɪzɪŋ] ADJ condescendant(e)

patron saint N saint(e) patron(ne)

patter ['pætə'] N crépitement m, tapotement m; (*sales talk*) boniment m ▶ VI crépiter, tapoter

pattern ['pætən] N modèle m; (*Sewing*) patron m; (*design*) motif m; (*sample*) échantillon m; **behaviour ~** mode m de comportement

patterned ['pætənd] ADJ à motifs

paucity ['pɔːsɪtɪ] N pénurie f, carence f

paunch [pɔːntʃ] N gros ventre, bedaine f

pauper ['pɔːpə'] N indigent(e); **~'s grave** fosse commune

pause [pɔːz] N pause f, arrêt m; (*Mus*) silence m ▶ VI faire une pause, s'arrêter; **to ~ for breath** reprendre son souffle; (*fig*) faire une pause

pave [peɪv] VT paver, daller; **to ~ the way for** ouvrir la voie à

pavement ['peɪvmənt] N (BRIT) trottoir m; (*US*) chaussée f

pavilion [pə'vɪlɪən] N pavillon m; tente f; (*Sport*) stand m

paving ['peɪvɪŋ] N (*material*) pavé m, dalle f; (*area*) pavage m, dallage m

paving stone N pavé m

paw [pɔː] N patte f ▶ VT donner un coup de patte à; (*person: pej*) tripoter

pawn [pɔːn] N gage m; (*Chess, also fig*) pion m ▶ VT mettre en gage

pawnbroker ['pɔːnbrəukə'] N prêteur m sur gages

pawnshop ['pɔːnʃɔp] N mont-de-piété m

pay [peɪ] (*pt, pp* **paid** [peɪd]) N salaire m; (*of manual worker*) paie f ▶ VT payer; (*be profitable to, also fig*) rapporter à ▶ VI payer; (*be profitable*) être rentable; **how much did you ~ for it?** combien l'avez-vous payé?, vous l'avez payé combien?; **I paid £5 for that ticket** j'ai payé ce billet 5 livres; **can I ~ by credit card?** est-ce que je peux payer par carte de crédit?; **to ~ one's way** payer sa part; (*company*) couvrir ses frais; **to ~ dividends** (*fig*) porter ses fruits, s'avérer rentable; **it won't ~ you to do that** vous ne gagnerez rien à faire cela; **to ~ attention (to)** prêter attention (à); **to ~ sb a visit** rendre visite à qn; **to ~ one's respects to sb** présenter ses respects à qn
▶ **pay back** VT rembourser
▶ **pay for** VT FUS payer
▶ **pay in** VT verser
▶ **pay off** VT (*debts*) régler, acquitter; (*person*) rembourser; (*workers*) licencier ▶ VI (*scheme, decision*) se révéler payant(e); **to ~ sth off in instalments** payer qch à tempérament
▶ **pay out** VT (*money*) payer, sortir de sa poche; (*rope*) laisser filer
▶ **pay up** VT (*debts*) régler; (*amount*) payer

payable ['peɪəbl] ADJ payable; **to make a cheque ~ to sb** établir un chèque à l'ordre de qn

pay-as-you-go [peɪəzjə'gəu] ADJ (*mobile phone*) à carte prépayée

pay award N augmentation f

payday ['peɪdeɪ] N jour m de paie

PAYE N ABBR (*Brit*: = *pay as you earn*) système de retenue des impôts à la source
payee [peɪ'i:] N bénéficiaire *mf*
pay envelope N (*US*) paie *f*
paying ['peɪɪŋ] ADJ payant(e); **~ guest** hôte payant
payload ['peɪləʊd] N charge *f* utile
payment ['peɪmənt] N paiement *m*; (*of bill*) règlement *m*; (*of deposit, cheque*) versement *m*; **advance ~** (*part sum*) acompte *m*; (*total sum*) paiement anticipé; **deferred ~, ~ by instalments** paiement par versements échelonnés; **monthly ~** mensualité *f*; **in ~ for, in ~ of** en règlement de; **on ~ of £5** pour 5 livres
payout ['peɪaʊt] N (*from insurance*) dédommagement *m*; (*in competition*) prix *m*
pay packet N (*Brit*) paie *f*
pay phone N cabine *f* téléphonique, téléphone public
pay raise N (*US*) = **pay rise**
pay rise N (*Brit*) augmentation *f* (de salaire)
payroll ['peɪrəʊl] N registre *m* du personnel; **to be on a firm's ~** être employé par une entreprise
pay slip N (*Brit*) bulletin *m* de paie, feuille *f* de paie
pay station N (*US*) cabine *f* téléphonique
pay television N chaînes *fpl* payantes
paywall ['peɪwɔ:l] N (*Comput*) mur *m* (payant)
PBS N ABBR (*US*: = *Public Broadcasting Service*) groupement d'aide à la réalisation d'émissions pour la TV publique
PBX N ABBR (*Brit*: = *private branch exchange*) PBX *m*, commutateur *m* privé
PC N ABBR = **personal computer**; (*Brit*) = **police constable** ▶ ADJ ABBR = **politically correct** ▶ ABBR (*Brit*) = **Privy Councillor**
p.c. ABBR = **per cent**; **postcard**
p/c ABBR = **petty cash**
PCB N ABBR = **printed circuit board**
pcm N ABBR (= *per calendar month*) par mois
PD N ABBR (*US*) = **police department**
pd ABBR = **paid**
PDA N ABBR (= *personal digital assistant*) agenda *m* électronique
PDQ N ABBR = **pretty damn quick**
PDSA N ABBR (*Brit*) = **People's Dispensary for Sick Animals**
PDT ABBR (*US*: = *Pacific Daylight Time*) heure d'été du Pacifique
PE N ABBR (= *physical education*) EPS *f*
pea [pi:] N (petit) pois
peace [pi:s] N paix *f*; (*calm*) calme *m*, tranquillité *f*; **to be at ~ with sb/sth** être en paix avec qn/qch; **to keep the ~** (*policeman*) assurer le maintien de l'ordre; (*citizen*) ne pas troubler l'ordre
peaceable ['pi:səbl] ADJ paisible, pacifique
peaceful ['pi:sful] ADJ paisible, calme
peacekeeper ['pi:ski:pəʳ] N (*force*) force *f* gardienne de la paix
peacekeeping ['pi:ski:pɪŋ] N maintien *m* de la paix
peacekeeping force N forces *fpl* qui assurent le maintien de la paix

peace offering N gage *m* de réconciliation; (*humorous*) gage de paix
peach [pi:tʃ] N pêche *f*
peacock ['pi:kɔk] N paon *m*
peak [pi:k] N (*mountain*) pic *m*, cime *f*; (*of cap*) visière *f*; (*fig: highest level*) maximum *m*; (: *of career, fame*) apogée *m*
peak-hour ['pi:kauəʳ] ADJ (*traffic etc*) de pointe
peak hours NPL heures *fpl* d'affluence *or* de pointe
peak period N période *f* de pointe
peak rate N plein tarif
peaky ['pi:kɪ] ADJ (*Brit inf*) fatigué(e)
peal [pi:l] N (*of bells*) carillon *m*; **peals of laughter** éclats *mpl* de rire
peanut ['pi:nʌt] N arachide *f*, cacahuète *f*
peanut butter N beurre *m* de cacahuète
pear [pɛəʳ] N poire *f*
pearl [pə:l] N perle *f*
peasant ['pɛznt] N paysan(ne)
peat [pi:t] N tourbe *f*
pebble ['pɛbl] N galet *m*, caillou *m*
peck [pɛk] VT (*also*: **peck at**) donner un coup de bec à; (: *food*) picorer ▶ N coup *m* de bec; (*kiss*) bécot *m*
pecking order ['pɛkɪŋ-] N ordre *m* hiérarchique
peckish ['pɛkɪʃ] ADJ (*Brit inf*): **I feel ~** je mangerais bien quelque chose, j'ai la dent
peculiar [pɪ'kju:lɪəʳ] ADJ (*odd*) étrange, bizarre, curieux(-euse); (*particular*) particulier(-ière); **~ to** particulier à
peculiarity [pɪkju:lɪ'ærɪtɪ] N bizarrerie *f*; particularité *f*
pecuniary [pɪ'kju:nɪərɪ] ADJ pécuniaire
pedal ['pɛdl] N pédale *f* ▶ VI pédaler
pedal bin N (*Brit*) poubelle *f* à pédale
pedantic [pɪ'dæntɪk] ADJ pédant(e)
peddle ['pɛdl] VT colporter; (*drugs*) faire le trafic de
peddler ['pɛdləʳ] N colporteur *m*; camelot *m*
pedestal ['pɛdəstl] N piédestal *m*
pedestrian [pɪ'dɛstrɪən] N piéton *m* ▶ ADJ piétonnier(-ière); (*fig*) prosaïque, terre à terre *inv*
pedestrian crossing N (*Brit*) passage clouté
pedestrianized [pɪ'dɛstrɪənaɪzd] ADJ: **a ~ street** une rue piétonne
pedestrian precinct, (*US*) pedestrian zone N zone piétonne
pediatrics [pi:dɪ'ætrɪks] N (*US*) = **paediatrics**
pedigree ['pɛdɪgri:] N ascendance *f*; (*of animal*) pedigree *m* ▶ CPD (*animal*) de race
pedlar ['pɛdləʳ] N = **peddler**
pedophile ['pi:dəʊfaɪl] (*US*) N = **paedophile**
pee [pi:] VI (*inf*) faire pipi, pisser
peek [pi:k] VI jeter un coup d'œil (furtif)
peel [pi:l] N pelure *f*, épluchure *f*; (*of orange, lemon*) écorce *f* ▶ VT peler, éplucher ▶ VI (*paint etc*) s'écailler; (*wallpaper*) se décoller; (*skin*) peler ▶ **peel back** VT décoller
peeler ['pi:ləʳ] N (*potato etc peeler*) éplucheur *m*
peelings ['pi:lɪŋz] NPL pelures *fpl*, épluchures *fpl*
peep [pi:p] N (*look*) coup d'œil furtif; (*sound*) pépiement *m* ▶ VI jeter un coup d'œil (furtif)

▶ **peep out** VI se montrer (furtivement)
peephole ['pi:phəʊl] N judas *m*
peer [pɪəʳ] VI: **to ~ at** regarder attentivement, scruter ▶ N (*noble*) pair *m*; (*equal*) pair, égal(e)
peerage ['pɪərɪdʒ] N pairie *f*
peerless ['pɪəlɪs] ADJ incomparable, sans égal
peeved [pi:vd] ADJ irrité(e), ennuyé(e)
peevish ['pi:vɪʃ] ADJ grincheux(-euse), maussade
peg [pɛg] N cheville *f*; (*for coat etc*) patère *f*; (BRIT: *also*: **clothes peg**) pince f à linge ▶ VT (*clothes*) accrocher; (BRIT: *groundsheet*) fixer (avec des piquets); (*fig: prices, wages*) contrôler, stabiliser
PEI ABBR (CANADA) = **Prince Edward Island**
pejorative [pɪ'dʒɔrətɪv] ADJ péjoratif(-ive)
Pekin [pi:'kɪn], **Peking** [pi:'kɪŋ] N Pékin
Pekinese, Pekingese [pi:kɪ'ni:z] N pékinois *m*
pelican ['pɛlɪkən] N pélican *m*
pelican crossing N (BRIT Aut) feu *m* à commande manuelle
pellet ['pɛlɪt] N boulette *f*; (*of lead*) plomb *m*
pell-mell ['pɛl'mɛl] ADV pêle-mêle
pelmet ['pɛlmɪt] N cantonnière *f*; lambrequin *m*
pelt [pɛlt] VT: **to ~ sb (with)** bombarder qn (de)
▶ VI (*rain*) tomber à seaux; (*inf: run*) courir à toutes jambes ▶ N peau *f*
pelvis ['pɛlvɪs] N bassin *m*
pen [pɛn] N (*for writing*) stylo *m*; (*for sheep*) parc *m*; (US inf: *prison*) taule *f*; **to put ~ to paper** prendre la plume
penal ['pi:nl] ADJ pénal(e)
penalize ['pi:nəlaɪz] VT pénaliser; (*fig*) désavantager
penal servitude [-'sə:vɪtju:d] N travaux forcés
penalty ['pɛnltɪ] N pénalité *f*; sanction *f*; (*fine*) amende *f*; (*Sport*) pénalisation *f*; (*also*: **penalty kick**: *Football*) penalty *m*; (: *Rugby*) pénalité *f*; **to pay the ~ for** être pénalisé(e) pour
penalty area N (BRIT Sport) surface *f* de réparation
penalty clause N clause pénale
penalty kick N (*Football*) penalty *m*
penalty shoot-out [-'ʃu:taʊt] N (*Football*) épreuve *f* des penalties
penance ['pɛnəns] N pénitence *f*
pence [pɛns] NPL *of* **penny**
penchant ['pɑ̃:ʃɑ̃:ŋ] N penchant *m*
pencil ['pɛnsl] N crayon *m*
▶ **pencil in** VT noter provisoirement
pencil case N trousse *f* (d'écolier)
pencil sharpener N taille-crayon(s) *m inv*
pendant ['pɛndnt] N pendentif *m*
pending ['pɛndɪŋ] PREP en attendant ▶ ADJ en suspens
pendulum ['pɛndjuləm] N pendule *m*; (*of clock*) balancier *m*
penetrate ['pɛnɪtreɪt] VT pénétrer dans; (*enemy territory*) entrer en; (*sexually*) pénétrer
penetrating ['pɛnɪtreɪtɪŋ] ADJ pénétrant(e)
penetration [pɛnɪ'treɪʃən] N pénétration *f*
pen friend N (BRIT) correspondant(e)
penguin ['pɛŋgwɪn] N pingouin *m*
penicillin [pɛnɪ'sɪlɪn] N pénicilline *f*
peninsula [pə'nɪnsjulə] N péninsule *f*

penis ['pi:nɪs] N pénis *m*, verge *f*
penitence ['pɛnɪtns] N repentir *m*
penitent ['pɛnɪtnt] ADJ repentant(e)
penitentiary [pɛnɪ'tɛnʃərɪ] N (US) prison *f*
penknife ['pɛnnaɪf] N canif *m*
Penn., Penna. ABBR (US) = **Pennsylvania**
pen name N nom *m* de plume, pseudonyme *m*
pennant ['pɛnənt] N flamme *f*, banderole *f*
penniless ['pɛnɪlɪs] ADJ sans le sou
Pennines ['pɛnaɪnz] NPL: **the ~** les Pennines *fpl*
penny ['pɛnɪ] (*pl* **pennies** ['pɛnɪz] *or* **pence** [pɛns]) N (BRIT) penny *m*; (US) cent *m*
pen pal N correspondant(e)
penpusher ['pɛnpʊʃəʳ] N (*pej*) gratte-papier *m inv*
pension ['pɛnʃən] N (*from company*) retraite *f*; (*Mil*) pension *f*
▶ **pension off** VT mettre à la retraite
pensionable ['pɛnʃnəbl] ADJ qui a droit à une retraite
pensioner ['pɛnʃənəʳ] N (BRIT) retraité(e)
pension fund N caisse *f* de retraite
pension plan N plan *m* de retraite
pensive ['pɛnsɪv] ADJ pensif(-ive)
pentagon ['pɛntəgən] N pentagone *m*; **the P~** (US Pol) le Pentagone; *voir article*

Le *Pentagon* est le nom donné aux bureaux du ministère de la Défense américain, situés à Arlington en Virginie, à cause de la forme pentagonale du bâtiment dans lequel ils se trouvent. Par extension, ce terme est également utilisé en parlant du ministère lui-même.

pentathlon [pɛn'tæθlən] N pentathlon *m*
Pentecost ['pɛntɪkɔst] N Pentecôte *f*
penthouse ['pɛnthaʊs] N appartement *m* (de luxe) en attique
pent-up ['pɛntʌp] ADJ (*feelings*) refoulé(e)
penultimate [pɪ'nʌltɪmət] ADJ pénultième, avant-dernier(-ière)
penury ['pɛnjurɪ] N misère *f*
people ['pi:pl] NPL gens *mpl*; personnes *fpl*; (*inhabitants*) population *f*; (*Pol*) peuple *m* ▶ N (*nation, race*) peuple *m* ▶ VT peupler; **I know ~ who ...** je connais des gens qui ...; **the room was full of ~** la salle était pleine de monde *or* de gens; **several ~ came** plusieurs personnes sont venues; **~ say that ...** on dit *or* les gens disent que ...; **old ~** les personnes âgées; **young ~** les jeunes; **a man of the ~** un homme du peuple
PEP [pɛp] N (= *personal equity plan*) ≈ CEA *m* (= *compte d'épargne en actions*)
pep [pɛp] N (*inf*) entrain *m*, dynamisme *m*
▶ **pep up** VT (*inf*) remonter
pepper ['pɛpəʳ] N poivre *m*; (*vegetable*) poivron *m* ▶ VT (*Culin*) poivrer
pepper mill N moulin *m* à poivre
peppermint ['pɛpəmɪnt] N (*plant*) menthe poivrée; (*sweet*) pastille *f* de menthe
pepperoni [pɛpə'rəʊnɪ] N saucisson sec de porc et de bœuf très poivré.
pepperpot ['pɛpəpɔt] N poivrière *f*
pep talk N (*inf*) (petit) discours d'encouragement
per [pəːʳ] PREP par; **~ hour** (*miles etc*) à l'heure;

P

(fee) (de) l'heure; ~ **kilo** *etc* le kilo *etc*; ~ **day/person** par jour/personne; ~ **annum** par an; **as ~ your instructions** conformément à vos instructions

per annum ADV par an

per capita ADJ, ADV par habitant, par personne

perceive [pə'siːv] VT percevoir; *(notice)* remarquer, s'apercevoir de

per cent ADV pour cent; **a 20 ~ discount** une réduction de 20 pour cent

percentage [pə'sɛntɪdʒ] N pourcentage *m*; **on a ~ basis** au pourcentage

percentage point N: **ten percentage points** dix pour cent

perceptible [pə'sɛptɪbl] ADJ perceptible

perception [pə'sɛpʃən] N perception *f*; *(insight)* sensibilité *f*

perceptive [pə'sɛptɪv] ADJ *(remark, person)* perspicace

perch [pəːtʃ] N *(fish)* perche *f*; *(for bird)* perchoir *m* ▶ VI (se) percher

percolate ['pəːkəleɪt] VT, VI passer

percolator ['pəːkəleɪtə'] N percolateur *m*; cafetière *f* électrique

percussion [pə'kʌʃən] N percussion *f*

peremptory [pə'rɛmptərɪ] ADJ péremptoire

perennial [pə'rɛnɪəl] ADJ perpétuel(le); *(Bot)* vivace ▶ N *(Bot)* (plante *f*) vivace *f*, plante pluriannuelle

perfect ['pəːfɪkt] ADJ parfait(e) ▶ N *(also:* **perfect tense)** parfait *m* ▶ VT [pə'fɛkt] *(technique, skill, work of art)* parfaire; *(method, plan)* mettre au point; **he's a ~ stranger to me** il m'est totalement inconnu

perfection [pə'fɛkʃən] N perfection *f*

perfectionist [pə'fɛkʃənɪst] N perfectionniste *mf*

perfectly ['pəːfɪktlɪ] ADV parfaitement; **I'm ~ happy with the situation** cette situation me convient parfaitement; **you know ~ well** vous le savez très bien

perforate ['pəːfəreɪt] VT perforer, percer

perforated ulcer ['pəːfəreɪtɪd-] N *(Med)* ulcère perforé

perforation [pəːfə'reɪʃən] N perforation *f*; *(line of holes)* pointillé *m*

perform [pə'fɔːm] VT *(carry out)* exécuter, remplir; *(concert etc)* jouer, donner ▶ VI *(actor, musician)* jouer; *(machine, car)* marcher, fonctionner; *(company, economy)*: **to ~ well/badly** produire de bons/mauvais résultats

performance [pə'fɔːməns] N représentation *f*, spectacle *m*; *(of an artist)* interprétation *f*; *(Sport: of car, engine)* performance *f*; *(of company, economy)* résultats *mpl*; **the team put up a good ~** l'équipe a bien joué

performer [pə'fɔːmə'] N artiste *mf*

performing [pə'fɔːmɪŋ] ADJ *(animal)* savant(e)

performing arts NPL: **the ~** les arts *mpl* du spectacle

perfume ['pəːfjuːm] N parfum *m* ▶ VT parfumer

perfunctory [pə'fʌŋktərɪ] ADJ négligent(e), pour la forme

perhaps [pə'hæps] ADV peut-être; ~ **he'll ...**

peut-être qu'il ...; ~ **so/not** peut-être que oui/que non

peril ['pɛrɪl] N péril *m*

perilous ['pɛrɪləs] ADJ périlleux(-euse)

perilously ['pɛrɪləslɪ] ADV: **they came ~ close to being caught** ils ont été à deux doigts de se faire prendre

perimeter [pə'rɪmɪtə'] N périmètre *m*

perimeter wall N mur *m* d'enceinte

period ['pɪərɪəd] N période *f*; *(Hist)* époque *f*; *(Scol)* cours *m*; *(full stop)* point *m*; *(Med)* règles *fpl* ▶ ADJ *(costume, furniture)* d'époque; **for a ~ of three weeks** pour (une période de) trois semaines; **the holiday ~** *(Brit)* la période des vacances

periodic [pɪərɪ'ɔdɪk] ADJ périodique

periodical [pɪərɪ'ɔdɪkl] ADJ périodique ▶ N périodique *m*

periodically [pɪərɪ'ɔdɪklɪ] ADV périodiquement

period pains NPL *(Brit)* douleurs menstruelles

peripatetic [pɛrɪpə'tɛtɪk] ADJ *(salesman)* ambulant; *(Brit: teacher)* qui travaille dans plusieurs établissements

peripheral [pə'rɪfərəl] ADJ périphérique ▶ N *(Comput)* périphérique *m*

periphery [pə'rɪfərɪ] N périphérie *f*

periscope ['pɛrɪskəup] N périscope *m*

perish ['pɛrɪʃ] VI périr, mourir; *(decay)* se détériorer

perishable ['pɛrɪʃəbl] ADJ périssable

perishables ['pɛrɪʃəblz] NPL denrées *fpl* périssables

perishing ['pɛrɪʃɪŋ] ADJ *(Brit inf: cold)* glacial(e)

peritonitis [pɛrɪtə'naɪtɪs] N péritonite *f*

perjure ['pəːdʒə'] VT: **to ~ o.s.** se parjurer

perjury ['pəːdʒərɪ] N *(Law: in court)* faux témoignage; *(breach of oath)* parjure *m*

perk [pəːk] N *(inf)* avantage *m*, à-côté *m* ▶ **perk up** VI *(inf: cheer up)* se ragaillardir

perky ['pəːkɪ] ADJ *(cheerful)* guilleret(te), gai(e)

perm [pəːm] N *(for hair)* permanente *f* ▶ VT: **to have one's hair permed** se faire faire une permanente

permanence ['pəːmənəns] N permanence *f*

permanent ['pəːmənənt] ADJ permanent(e); *(job, position)* permanent, fixe; *(dye, ink)* indélébile; **I'm not ~ here** je ne suis pas ici à titre définitif; ~ **address** adresse habituelle

permanently ['pəːmənəntlɪ] ADV de façon permanente; *(move abroad)* définitivement; *(open, closed)* en permanence; *(tired, unhappy)* constamment

permeable ['pəːmɪəbl] ADJ perméable

permeate ['pəːmɪeɪt] VI s'infiltrer ▶ VT s'infiltrer dans; pénétrer

permissible [pə'mɪsɪbl] ADJ permis(e), acceptable

permission [pə'mɪʃən] N permission *f*, autorisation *f*; **to give sb ~ to do sth** donner à qn la permission de faire qch

permissive [pə'mɪsɪv] ADJ tolérant(e); **the ~ society** la société de tolérance

permit N ['pəːmɪt] permis *m*; *(entrance pass)* autorisation *f*, laissez-passer *m*; *(for goods)*

permutation – petrochemical

licence f ▸ VT [pə'mɪt] permettre; **to ~ sb to do**
autoriser qn à faire, permettre à qn de faire;
weather permitting si le temps le permet
permutation [pə:mjuːˈteɪʃən] N permutation f
pernicious [pəːˈnɪʃəs] ADJ pernicieux(-euse),
nocif(-ive)
pernickety [pəˈnɪkɪtɪ] ADJ (inf)
pointilleux(-euse), tatillon(ne); (task)
minutieux(-euse)
perpendicular [pəːpənˈdɪkjuləʳ] ADJ, N
perpendiculaire f
perpetrate [ˈpəːpɪtreɪt] VT perpétrer,
commettre
perpetual [pəˈpɛtjuəl] ADJ perpétuel(le)
perpetuate [pəˈpɛtjueɪt] VT perpétuer
perpetuity [pəːpɪˈtjuːɪtɪ] N: **in ~** à perpétuité
perplex [pəˈplɛks] VT (person) rendre perplexe;
(complicate) embrouiller
perplexing [pəˈplɛksɪŋ] ADJ embarrassant(e)
perquisites [ˈpəːkwɪzɪts] NPL (also: **perks**)
avantages mpl annexes
persecute [ˈpəːsɪkjuːt] VT persécuter
persecution [pəːsɪˈkjuːʃən] N persécution f
perseverance [pəːsɪˈvɪərns] N persévérance f,
ténacité f
persevere [pəːsɪˈvɪəʳ] VI persévérer
Persia [ˈpəːʃə] N Perse f
Persian [ˈpəːʃən] ADJ persan(e) ▸ N (Ling) persan
m; **the ~ Gulf** le golfe Persique
Persian cat N chat persan
persist [pəˈsɪst] VI: **to ~ (in doing)** persister (à
faire), s'obstiner (à faire)
persistence [pəˈsɪstəns] N persistance f,
obstination f; opiniâtreté f
persistent [pəˈsɪstənt] ADJ persistant(e), tenace;
(lateness, rain) persistant(e); **~ offender** (Law)
multirécidiviste mf
persnickety [pəˈsnɪkɪtɪ] ADJ (US inf) = **pernickety**
person [ˈpəːsn] N personne f; **in ~** en personne;
on or **about one's ~** sur soi; **~ to ~ call** (Tel)
appel m avec préavis
personable [ˈpəːsnəbl] ADJ de belle prestance,
au physique attrayant
personal [ˈpəːsnl] ADJ personnel(le);
~ belongings, ~ effects effets personnels;
~ hygiene hygiène f intime; **a ~ interview** un
entretien
personal allowance N (Tax) part f du revenu
non imposable
personal assistant N secrétaire personnel(le)
personal call N (Tel) communication f avec
préavis
personal column N annonces personnelles
personal computer N ordinateur individuel,
PC m
personal details NPL (on form etc) coordonnées
fpl
personal identification number N (Comput,
Banking) numéro m d'identification personnel
personality [pəːsəˈnælɪtɪ] N personnalité f
personally [ˈpəːsnəlɪ] ADV personnellement; **to
take sth ~** se sentir visé(e) par qch
personal organizer N agenda (personnel);
(electronic) agenda électronique

personal property N biens personnels
personal stereo N Walkman® m, baladeur m
personify [pəːˈsɔnɪfaɪ] VT personnifier
personnel [pəːsəˈnɛl] N personnel m
personnel department N service m du
personnel
personnel manager N chef m du personnel
perspective [pəˈspɛktɪv] N perspective f; **to get
sth into ~** ramener qch à sa juste mesure
perspex® [ˈpəːspɛks] N (BRIT) Plexiglas® m
perspicacity [pəːspɪˈkæsɪtɪ] N perspicacité f
perspiration [pəːspɪˈreɪʃən] N transpiration f
perspire [pəˈspaɪəʳ] VI transpirer
persuade [pəˈsweɪd] VT: **to ~ sb to do sth**
persuader qn de faire qch, amener or décider qn
à faire qch; **to ~ sb of sth/that** persuader qn de
qch/que
persuasion [pəˈsweɪʒən] N persuasion f; (creed)
conviction f
persuasive [pəˈsweɪsɪv] ADJ persuasif(-ive)
pert [pəːt] ADJ coquin(e), mutin(e)
pertaining [pəːˈteɪnɪŋ]: **~ to** prep relatif(-ive) à
pertinent [ˈpəːtɪnənt] ADJ pertinent(e)
perturb [pəˈtəːb] VT troubler, inquiéter
perturbing [pəˈtəːbɪŋ] ADJ troublant(e)
Peru [pəˈruː] N Pérou m
perusal [pəˈruːzl] N lecture (attentive)
Peruvian [pəˈruːvjən] ADJ péruvien(ne) ▸ N
Péruvien(ne)
pervade [pəˈveɪd] VT se répandre dans, envahir
pervasive [pəˈveɪsɪv] ADJ (smell) pénétrant(e);
(influence) insidieux(-euse); (gloom, ideas)
diffus(e)
perverse [pəˈvəːs] ADJ pervers(e); (contrary)
entêté(e), contrariant(e)
perversion [pəˈvəːʃən] N perversion f
perversity [pəˈvəːsɪtɪ] N perversité f
pervert N [ˈpəːvəːt] perverti(e) ▸ VT [pəˈvəːt]
pervertir; (words) déformer
pessimism [ˈpɛsɪmɪzəm] N pessimisme m
pessimist [ˈpɛsɪmɪst] N pessimiste mf
pessimistic [pɛsɪˈmɪstɪk] ADJ pessimiste
pest [pɛst] N animal m (or insecte m) nuisible;
(fig) fléau m
pest control N lutte f contre les nuisibles
pester [ˈpɛstəʳ] VT importuner, harceler
pesticide [ˈpɛstɪsaɪd] N pesticide m
pestilence [ˈpɛstɪləns] N peste f
pestle [ˈpɛsl] N pilon m
pet [pɛt] N animal familier; (favourite) chouchou
m ▸ CPD (favourite) favori(e) ▸ VT choyer; (stroke)
caresser, câliner ▸ VI (inf) se peloter; **~ lion** etc
lion etc apprivoisé; **teacher's ~** chouchou m du
professeur; **~ hate** bête noire
petal [ˈpɛtl] N pétale m
peter [ˈpiːtəʳ]: **to ~ out** vi s'épuiser; s'affaiblir
petite [pəˈtiːt] ADJ menu(e)
petition [pəˈtɪʃən] N pétition f ▸ VT adresser une
pétition à ▸ VI: **to ~ for divorce** demander le
divorce
pet name N (BRIT) petit nom
petrified [ˈpɛtrɪfaɪd] ADJ (fig) mort(e) de peur
petrify [ˈpɛtrɪfaɪ] VT pétrifier
petrochemical [pɛtrəˈkɛmɪkl] ADJ pétrochimique

petrodollars ['pɛtrəudɔləz] NPL pétrodollars *mpl*
petrol ['pɛtrəl] N (*BRIT*) essence *f*; **I've run out of ~** je suis en panne d'essence
petrol bomb N cocktail *m* Molotov
petrol can N (*BRIT*) bidon *m* à essence
petrol engine N (*BRIT*) moteur *m* à essence
petroleum [pə'trəuliəm] N pétrole *m*
petroleum jelly N vaseline *f*
petrol pump N (*BRIT: in car, at garage*) pompe *f* à essence
petrol station N (*BRIT*) station-service *f*
petrol tank N (*BRIT*) réservoir *m* d'essence
petticoat ['pɛtɪkəut] N jupon *m*
pettifogging ['pɛtɪfɔgɪŋ] ADJ chicanier(-ière)
pettiness ['pɛtɪnɪs] N mesquinerie *f*
petty ['pɛtɪ] ADJ (*mean*) mesquin(e); (*unimportant*) insignifiant(e), sans importance
petty cash N caisse *f* des dépenses courantes, petite caisse
petty officer N second-maître *m*
petulant ['pɛtjulənt] ADJ irritable
pew [pju:] N banc *m* (d'église)
pewter ['pju:tə^r] N étain *m*
Pfc ABBR (*US Mil*) = **private first class**
PG N ABBR (*Cine: = parental guidance*) *avis des parents recommandé*
PGA N ABBR = **Professional Golfers Association**
PH N ABBR (*US Mil.: = Purple Heart*) *décoration accordée aux blessés de guerre*
PHA N ABBR (*US: = Public Housing Administration*) *organisme d'aide à la construction*
phallic ['fælɪk] ADJ phallique
phantom ['fæntəm] N fantôme *m*; (*vision*) fantasme *m*
Pharaoh ['fɛərəu] N pharaon *m*
pharmaceutical [fɑːməˈsjuːtɪkl] ADJ pharmaceutique ► N: **pharmaceuticals** produits *mpl* pharmaceutiques
pharmacist ['fɑːməsɪst] N pharmacien(ne)
pharmacy ['fɑːməsɪ] N pharmacie *f*
phase [feɪz] N phase *f*, période *f*
► **phase in** VT introduire progressivement
► **phase out** VT supprimer progressivement
Ph.D. ABBR = **Doctor of Philosophy**
pheasant ['fɛznt] N faisan *m*
phenomena [fə'nɔmɪnə] NPL *of* **phenomenon**
phenomenal [fɪ'nɔmɪnl] ADJ phénoménal(e)
phenomenon [fə'nɔmɪnən] (*pl* **phenomena** [-nə]) N phénomène *m*
phew [fju:] EXCL ouf!
phial ['faɪəl] N fiole *f*
philanderer [fɪ'lændərə^r] N don Juan *m*
philanthropic [fɪlən'θrɔpɪk] ADJ philanthropique
philanthropist [fɪ'lænθrəpɪst] N philanthrope *mf*
philatelist [fɪ'lætəlɪst] N philatéliste *mf*
philately [fɪ'lætəlɪ] N philatélie *f*
Philippines ['fɪlɪpiːnz] NPL (*also:* **Philippine Islands**): **the ~** les Philippines *fpl*
philosopher [fɪ'lɔsəfə^r] N philosophe *m*
philosophical [fɪlə'sɔfɪkl] ADJ philosophique
philosophy [fɪ'lɔsəfɪ] N philosophie *f*

phishing ['fɪʃɪŋ] N phishing *m*
phlegm [flɛm] N flegme *m*
phlegmatic [flɛg'mætɪk] ADJ flegmatique
phobia ['fəubjə] N phobie *f*
phone [fəun] N téléphone *m* ► VT téléphoner à ► VI téléphoner; **to be on the ~** avoir le téléphone; (*be calling*) être au téléphone
► **phone back** VT, VI rappeler
► **phone up** VT téléphoner à ► VI téléphoner
phone bill N facture *f* de téléphone
phone book N annuaire *m*
phone box, (*US*) **phone booth** N cabine *f* téléphonique
phone call N coup *m* de fil *or* de téléphone
phonecard ['fəunkɑːd] N télécarte *f*
phone-in ['fəunɪn] N (*BRIT Radio, TV*) programme *m* à ligne ouverte
phone number N numéro *m* de téléphone
phone tapping [-tæpɪŋ] N mise *f* sur écoutes téléphoniques
phonetics [fə'nɛtɪks] N phonétique *f*
phoney ['fəunɪ] ADJ faux (fausse), factice; (*person*) pas franc (franche) ► N (*person*) charlatan *m*; fumiste *mf*
phonograph ['fəunəgrɑːf] N (*US*) électrophone *m*
phony ['fəunɪ] ADJ, N = **phoney**
phosphate ['fɔsfeɪt] N phosphate *m*
phosphorus ['fɔsfərəs] N phosphore *m*
photo ['fəutəu] N photo *f*; **to take a ~ of** prendre en photo
photo... ['fəutəu] PREFIX photo...
photo album N album *m* de photos
photocall ['fəutəukɔːl] N séance *f* de photos pour la presse
photocopier ['fəutəukɔpɪə^r] N copieur *m*
photocopy ['fəutəukɔpɪ] N photocopie *f* ► VT photocopier
photoelectric [fəutəuɪ'lɛktrɪk] ADJ photoélectrique; **~ cell** cellule *f* photoélectrique
Photofit® ['fəutəufɪt] N portrait-robot *m*
photogenic [fəutəu'dʒɛnɪk] ADJ photogénique
photograph ['fəutəgrɑːf] N photographie *f* ► VT photographier; **to take a ~ of sb** prendre qn en photo
photographer [fə'tɔgrəfə^r] N photographe *mf*
photographic [fəutə'græfɪk] ADJ photographique
photography [fə'tɔgrəfɪ] N photographie *f*
photo opportunity N *occasion, souvent arrangée, pour prendre des photos d'une personnalité.*
Photoshop® ['fəutəuʃɔp] N Photoshop® ► VT: **to photoshop a picture** retoucher une image avec Photoshop
Photostat® ['fəutəustæt] N photocopie *f*, photostat *m*
photosynthesis [fəutəu'sɪnθəsɪs] N photosynthèse *f*
phrase [freɪz] N expression *f*; (*Ling*) locution *f* ► VT exprimer; (*letter*) rédiger
phrase book N recueil *m* d'expressions (pour touristes)
physical ['fɪzɪkl] ADJ physique; **~ examination**

examen médical; ~ **exercises** gymnastique f
physical education N éducation f physique
physically ['fɪzɪklɪ] ADV physiquement
physician [fɪ'zɪʃən] N médecin m
physicist ['fɪzɪsɪst] N physicien(ne)
physics ['fɪzɪks] N physique f
physiological [fɪzɪə'lɔdʒɪkl] ADJ physiologique
physiology [fɪzɪ'ɔlədʒɪ] N physiologie f
physiotherapist [fɪzɪəu'θerəpɪst] N kinésithérapeute mf
physiotherapy [fɪzɪəu'θerəpɪ] N kinésithérapie f
physique [fɪ'ziːk] N (appearance) physique m; (health etc) constitution f
pianist ['piːənɪst] N pianiste mf
piano [pɪ'ænəu] N piano m
piano accordion N (BRIT) accordéon m à touches
Picardy ['pɪkədɪ] N Picardie f
piccolo ['pɪkələu] N piccolo m
pick [pɪk] N (tool: also: **pick-axe**) pic m, pioche f
  ▶ VT choisir; (gather) cueillir; (remove) prendre; (lock) forcer; (scab, spot) gratter, écorcher; **take your ~** faites votre choix; **the ~ of** le (la) meilleur(e) de; **to ~ a bone** ronger un os; **to ~ one's nose** se mettre les doigts dans le nez; **to ~ one's teeth** se curer les dents; **to ~ sb's brains** faire appel aux lumières de qn; **to ~ pockets** pratiquer le vol à la tire; **to ~ a quarrel with sb** chercher noise à qn
  ▶ **pick at** VT FUS: **to ~ at one's food** manger du bout des dents, chipoter
  ▶ **pick off** VT (kill) (viser soigneusement et) abattre
  ▶ **pick on** VT FUS (person) harceler
  ▶ **pick out** VT choisir; (distinguish) distinguer
  ▶ **pick up** VI (improve) remonter, s'améliorer ▶ VT ramasser; (telephone) décrocher; (collect) passer prendre; (Aut: give lift to) prendre; (learn) apprendre; (Radio) capter; **to ~ up speed** prendre de la vitesse; **to ~ o.s. up** se relever; **to ~ up where one left off** reprendre là où l'on s'est arrêté
pickaxe, (US) **pickax** ['pɪkæks] N pioche f
picket ['pɪkɪt] N (in strike) gréviste mf participant à un piquet de grève; piquet m de grève ▶ VT mettre un piquet de grève devant
picket line N piquet m de grève
pickings ['pɪkɪŋz] NPL: **there are rich ~ to be had in ...** il y a gros à gagner dans ...
pickle ['pɪkl] N (also: **pickles**: as condiment) pickles mpl ▶ VT conserver dans du vinaigre or dans de la saumure; **in a ~** (fig) dans le pétrin
pick-me-up ['pɪkmiːʌp] N remontant m
pickpocket ['pɪkpɔkɪt] N pickpocket m
pick-up ['pɪkʌp] N (also: **pick-up truck**) pick-up m inv; (BRIT: on record player) bras m pick-up
picnic ['pɪknɪk] N pique-nique m ▶ VI pique-niquer
picnic area N aire f de pique-nique
picnicker ['pɪknɪkə'] N pique-niqueur(-euse)
pictorial [pɪk'tɔːrɪəl] ADJ illustré(e)
picture ['pɪktʃə'] N (also TV) image f; (painting) peinture f, tableau m; (photograph) photo(graphie) f; (drawing) dessin m; (film) film m;

(fig: description) description f ▶ VT (imagine) se représenter; (describe) dépeindre, représenter; **pictures** NPL: **the pictures** (BRIT) le cinéma; **to take a ~ of sb/sth** prendre qn/qch en photo; **would you take a ~ of us, please?** pourriez-vous nous prendre en photo, s'il vous plaît?; **the overall ~** le tableau d'ensemble; **to put sb in the ~** mettre qn au courant
picture book N livre m d'images
picture frame N cadre m
picture messaging N picture messaging m, messagerie f d'images
picturesque [pɪktʃə'resk] ADJ pittoresque
picture window N baie vitrée, fenêtre f panoramique
piddling ['pɪdlɪŋ] ADJ (inf) insignifiant(e)
pie [paɪ] N tourte f; (of fruit) tarte f; (of meat) pâté m en croûte
piebald ['paɪbɔːld] ADJ pie inv
piece [piːs] N morceau m; (of land) parcelle f; (item): **a ~ of furniture/advice** un meuble/conseil; (Draughts) pion m ▶ VT: **to ~ together** rassembler; **in pieces** (broken) en morceaux, en miettes; (not yet assembled) en pièces détachées; **to take to pieces** démonter; **in one** ~ (object) intact(e); **to get back all in one** ~ (person) rentrer sain et sauf; **a 10p** ~ (BRIT) une pièce de 10p; ~ **by** ~ morceau par morceau; **a six-~ band** un orchestre de six musiciens; **to say one's** ~ réciter son morceau
piecemeal ['piːsmiːl] ADV par bouts
piece rate N taux m or tarif m à la pièce
piecework ['piːswəːk] N travail m aux pièces or à la pièce
pie chart N graphique m à secteurs, camembert m
Piedmont ['piːdmɔnt] N Piémont m
pier [pɪə'] N jetée f; (of bridge etc) pile f
pierce [pɪəs] VT percer, transpercer; **to have one's ears pierced** se faire percer les oreilles
pierced [pɪəst] ADJ (ears) percé(e)
piercing ['pɪəsɪŋ] ADJ (cry) perçant(e)
piety ['paɪətɪ] N piété f
piffling ['pɪflɪŋ] ADJ insignifiant(e)
pig [pɪg] N cochon m, porc m; (pej: unkind person) mufle m; (: greedy person) goinfre m
pigeon ['pɪdʒən] N pigeon m
pigeonhole ['pɪdʒənhəul] N casier m
pigeon-toed ['pɪdʒəntəud] ADJ marchant les pieds en dedans
piggy bank ['pɪgɪ-] N tirelire f
pigheaded ['pɪg'hedɪd] ADJ entêté(e), têtu(e)
piglet ['pɪglɪt] N petit cochon, porcelet m
pigment ['pɪgmənt] N pigment m
pigmentation [pɪgmən'teɪʃən] N pigmentation f
pigmy ['pɪgmɪ] N = **pygmy**
pigskin ['pɪgskɪn] N (peau f de) porc m
pigsty ['pɪgstaɪ] N porcherie f
pigtail ['pɪgteɪl] N natte f, tresse f
pike [paɪk] N (spear) pique f; (fish) brochet m
pilchard ['pɪltʃəd] N pilchard m (sorte de sardine)
pile [paɪl] N (pillar, of books) pile f; (heap) tas m; (of carpet) épaisseur f; **in a ~** en tas

P

▸ **pile on** VT: **to ~ it on** (inf) exagérer
▸ **pile up** VI (accumulate) s'entasser, s'accumuler ▸ VT (put in heap) empiler, entasser; (accumulate) accumuler

piles [paɪlz] NPL hémorroïdes fpl

pile-up ['paɪlʌp] N (Aut) télescopage m, collision f en série

pilfer ['pɪlfəʳ] VT chaparder ▸ VI commettre des larcins

pilfering ['pɪlfərɪŋ] N chapardage m

pilgrim ['pɪlgrɪm] N pèlerin m; voir article

> Les Pilgrim Fathers ("Pères pèlerins") sont un groupe de puritains qui quittèrent l'Angleterre en 1620 pour fuir les persécutions religieuses. Ayant traversé l'Atlantique à bord du Mayflower, ils fondèrent New Plymouth en Nouvelle-Angleterre, dans ce qui est aujourd'hui le Massachusetts. Ces Pères pèlerins sont considérés comme les fondateurs des États-Unis, et l'on commémore chaque année, le jour de Thanksgiving, la réussite de leur première récolte.

pilgrimage ['pɪlgrɪmɪdʒ] N pèlerinage m

pill [pɪl] N pilule f; **the ~** la pilule; **to be on the ~** prendre la pilule

pillage ['pɪlɪdʒ] VT piller

pillar ['pɪləʳ] N pilier m

pillar box N (BRIT) boîte f aux lettres (publique)

pillion ['pɪljən] N (of motor cycle) siège m arrière; **to ride ~** être derrière; (on horse) être en croupe

pillory ['pɪlərɪ] N pilori m ▸ VT mettre au pilori

pillow ['pɪləu] N oreiller m

pillowcase ['pɪləukeɪs], **pillowslip** ['pɪləuslɪp] N taie f d'oreiller

pilot ['paɪlət] N pilote m ▸ CPD (scheme etc) pilote, expérimental(e) ▸ VT piloter

pilot boat N bateau-pilote m

pilot light N veilleuse f

pimento [pɪ'mɛntəu] N piment m

pimp [pɪmp] N souteneur m, maquereau m

pimple ['pɪmpl] N bouton m

pimply ['pɪmplɪ] ADJ boutonneux(-euse)

PIN N ABBR (= personal identification number) code m confidentiel

pin [pɪn] N épingle f; (Tech) cheville f; (BRIT: drawing pin) punaise f; (in grenade) goupille f; (BRIT Elec: of plug) broche f ▸ VT épingler; **pins and needles** fourmis fpl; **to ~ sb against/to** clouer qn contre/à; **to ~ sb down** (fig) coincer qn; **to ~ sth on sb** (fig) mettre qch sur le dos de qn
▸ **pin down** VT (fig): **to ~ sb down** obliger qn à répondre; **there's something strange here but I can't quite ~ it down** il y a quelque chose d'étrange ici, mais je n'arrive pas exactement à savoir quoi

pinafore ['pɪnəfɔːʳ] N tablier m

pinafore dress N robe-chasuble f

pinball ['pɪnbɔːl] N flipper m

pincers ['pɪnsəz] NPL tenailles fpl

pinch [pɪntʃ] N pincement m; (of salt etc) pincée f ▸ VT pincer; (inf: steal) piquer, chiper ▸ VI (shoe) serrer; **at a ~** à la rigueur; **to feel the ~** (fig) se ressentir des restrictions (or de la récession etc)

pinched [pɪntʃt] ADJ (drawn) tiré(e); **~ with cold** transi(e) de froid; **~ for** (short of): **~ for money** à court d'argent; **~ for space** à l'étroit

pincushion ['pɪnkuʃən] N pelote f à épingles

pine [paɪn] N (also: **pine tree**) pin m ▸ VI: **to ~ for** aspirer à, désirer ardemment
▸ **pine away** VI dépérir

pineapple ['paɪnæpl] N ananas m

pine cone N pomme f de pin

ping [pɪŋ] N (noise) tintement m

ping-pong® ['pɪŋpɔŋ] N ping-pong® m

pink [pɪŋk] ADJ rose ▸ N (colour) rose m; (Bot) œillet m, mignardise f

pinking shears ['pɪŋkɪŋ-] NPL ciseaux mpl à denteler

pin money N (BRIT) argent m de poche

pinnacle ['pɪnəkl] N pinacle m

pinpoint ['pɪnpɔɪnt] VT indiquer (avec précision)

pinstripe ['pɪnstraɪp] N rayure très fine

pint [paɪnt] N pinte f (Brit = 0,57 l; US = 0,47 l); (BRIT inf) ≈ demi m, ≈ pot m

pinup ['pɪnʌp] N pin-up f inv

pioneer [paɪə'nɪəʳ] N explorateur(-trice); (early settler) pionnier m; (fig) pionnier, précurseur m ▸ VT être un pionnier de

pious ['paɪəs] ADJ pieux(-euse)

pip [pɪp] N (seed) pépin m; **pips** NPL: **the pips** (BRIT: time signal on radio) le top

pipe [paɪp] N tuyau m, conduite f; (for smoking) pipe f; (Mus) pipeau m ▸ VT amener par tuyau; **pipes** NPL (also: **bagpipes**) cornemuse f
▸ **pipe down** VI (inf) se taire

pipe cleaner N cure-pipe m

piped music [paɪpt-] N musique f de fond

pipe dream N chimère f, utopie f

pipeline ['paɪplaɪn] N (for gas) gazoduc m, pipeline m; (for oil) oléoduc m, pipeline; **it is in the ~** (fig) c'est en route, ça va se faire

piper ['paɪpəʳ] N (flautist) joueur(-euse) de pipeau; (of bagpipes) joueur(-euse) de cornemuse

pipe tobacco N tabac m pour la pipe

piping ['paɪpɪŋ] ADV: **~ hot** très chaud(e)

piquant ['piːkənt] ADJ piquant(e)

pique [piːk] N dépit m

piracy ['paɪərəsɪ] N piraterie f

pirate ['paɪərət] N pirate m ▸ VT (CD, video, book) pirater

pirated ['paɪərətɪd] ADJ pirate

pirate radio N (BRIT) radio f pirate

pirouette [pɪru'ɛt] N pirouette f ▸ VI faire une or des pirouette(s)

Pisces ['paɪsiːz] N les Poissons mpl; **to be ~** être des Poissons

piss [pɪs] VI (inf!) pisser (!); **~ off!** tire-toi! (!)

pissed [pɪst] ADJ (inf!: BRIT: drunk) bourré(e); (: US: angry) furieux(-euse)

pistol ['pɪstl] N pistolet m

piston ['pɪstən] N piston m

pit [pɪt] N trou m, fosse f; (also: **coal pit**) puits m de mine; (also: **orchestra pit**) fosse d'orchestre; (US: fruit stone) noyau m ▸ VT: **to ~ sb against sb** opposer qn à qn; **to ~ o.s.** or **one's wits against**

se mesurer à; **pits** NPL (*in motor racing*) aire f de service

pitapat ['pɪtə'pæt] ADV: **to go ~** (*heart*) battre la chamade; (*rain*) tambouriner

pitch [pɪtʃ] N (BRIT *Sport*) terrain m; (*throw*) lancement m; (*Mus*) ton m; (*of voice*) hauteur f; (*fig: degree*) degré m; (*also*: **sales pitch**) baratin m, boniment m; (*Naut*) tangage m; (*tar*) poix f ▶ VT (*throw*) lancer; (*tent*) dresser; (*set: price, message*) adapter, positionner ▶ VI (*Naut*) tanguer; (*fall*): **to ~ into/off** tomber dans/de; **to be pitched forward** être projeté(e) en avant; **at this ~** à ce rythme

pitch-black ['pɪtʃ'blæk] ADJ noir(e) comme poix

pitched battle [pɪtʃt-] N bataille rangée

pitcher ['pɪtʃə'] N cruche f

pitchfork ['pɪtʃfɔːk] N fourche f

piteous ['pɪtɪəs] ADJ pitoyable

pitfall ['pɪtfɔːl] N trappe f, piège m

pith [pɪθ] N (*of plant*) moelle f; (*of orange etc*) intérieur m de l'écorce; (*fig*) essence f; vigueur f

pithead ['pɪthɛd] N (BRIT) bouche f de puits

pithy ['pɪθɪ] ADJ piquant(e); vigoureux(-euse)

pitiable ['pɪtɪəbl] ADJ pitoyable

pitiful ['pɪtɪful] ADJ (*touching*) pitoyable; (*contemptible*) lamentable

pitifully ['pɪtɪfəlɪ] ADV pitoyablement; lamentablement

pitiless ['pɪtɪlɪs] ADJ impitoyable

pittance ['pɪtns] N salaire m de misère

pitted ['pɪtɪd] ADJ: **~ with** (*chickenpox*) grêlé(e) par; (*rust*) piqué(e) de

pity ['pɪtɪ] N pitié f ▶ VT plaindre; **what a ~!** quel dommage!; **it is a ~ that you can't come** c'est dommage que vous ne puissiez venir; **to have** *or* **take ~ on sb** avoir pitié de qn

pitying ['pɪtɪɪŋ] ADJ compatissant(e)

pivot ['pɪvət] N pivot m ▶ VI pivoter

pixel ['pɪksl] N (*Comput*) pixel m

pixie ['pɪksɪ] N lutin m

pizza [ˈpiːtsə] N pizza f

placard ['plækɑːd] N affiche f; (*in march*) pancarte f

placate [pləˈkeɪt] N apaiser, calmer

placatory [pləˈkeɪtərɪ] ADJ d'apaisement, lénifiant(e)

place [pleɪs] N endroit m, lieu m; (*proper position, job, rank, seat*) place f; (*house*) maison f, logement m; (*in street names*): **Laurel P~** = rue des Lauriers; (*home*): **at/to his ~** chez lui ▶ VT (*position*) placer, mettre; (*identify*) situer; reconnaître; **to take ~** avoir lieu; (*occur*) se produire; **to take sb's ~** remplacer qn; **to change places with sb** changer de place avec qn; **from ~ to ~** d'un endroit à l'autre; **all over the ~** partout; **out of ~** (*not suitable*) déplacé(e), inopportun(e); **I feel out of ~ here** je ne me sens pas à ma place ici; **in the first ~** d'abord, en premier; **to put sb in his ~** (*fig*) remettre qn à sa place; **he's going places** (*fig: inf*) il fait son chemin; **it is not my ~ to do it** ce n'est pas à moi de le faire; **to ~ an order with sb (for)** (*Comm*) passer commande à qn (de); **to be placed** (*in race, exam*) se placer; **how are you placed next week?** comment ça

se présente pour la semaine prochaine?

placebo [pləˈsiːbəʊ] N placebo m

place mat N set m de table; (*in linen etc*) napperon m

placement ['pleɪsmənt] N placement m; (*during studies*) stage m

place name N nom m de lieu

placenta [pləˈsɛntə] N placenta m

placid ['plæsɪd] ADJ placide

placidity [pləˈsɪdɪtɪ] N placidité f

plagiarism ['pleɪdʒərɪzəm] N plagiat m

plagiarist ['pleɪdʒərɪst] N plagiaire mf

plagiarize ['pleɪdʒəraɪz] VT plagier

plague [pleɪg] N fléau m; (*Med*) peste f ▶ VT (*fig*) tourmenter; **to ~ sb with questions** harceler qn de questions

plaice [pleɪs] N (*pl inv*) carrelet m

plaid [plæd] N tissu écossais

plain [pleɪn] ADJ (*in one colour*) uni(e); (*clear*) clair(e), évident(e); (*simple*) simple, ordinaire; (*frank*) franc (franche); (*not handsome*) quelconque, ordinaire; (*cigarette*) sans filtre; (*without seasoning etc*) nature inv ▶ ADV franchement, carrément ▶ N plaine f; **in ~ clothes** (*police*) en civil; **to make sth ~ to sb** faire clairement comprendre qch à qn

plain chocolate N chocolat m à croquer

plainly ['pleɪnlɪ] ADV clairement; (*frankly*) carrément, sans détours

plainness ['pleɪnnɪs] N simplicité f

plain speaking N propos mpl sans équivoque; **she has a reputation for ~** elle est bien connue pour son franc parler *or* sa franchise

plaintiff ['pleɪntɪf] N plaignant(e)

plaintive ['pleɪntɪv] ADJ plaintif(-ive)

plait [plæt] N tresse f, natte f ▶ VT tresser, natter

plan [plæn] N plan m; (*scheme*) projet m ▶ VT (*think in advance*) projeter; (*prepare*) organiser ▶ VI faire des projets; **to ~ to do** projeter de faire; **how long do you ~ to stay?** combien de temps comptez-vous rester?

plane [pleɪn] N (*Aviat*) avion m; (*also*: **plane tree**) platane m; (*tool*) rabot m; (*Art, Math etc*) plan m; (*fig*) niveau m, plan ▶ ADJ plan(e); plat(e) ▶ VT (*with tool*) raboter

planet ['plænɪt] N planète f

planetarium [plænɪˈtɛərɪəm] N planétarium m

plank [plæŋk] N planche f; (*Pol*) point m d'un programme

plankton ['plæŋktən] N plancton m

planned economy [plænd-] N économie planifiée

planner ['plænə'] N planificateur(-trice); (*chart*) planning m; **town** *or* (US) **city ~** urbaniste mf

planning ['plænɪŋ] N planification f; **family ~** planning familial

planning permission N (BRIT) permis m de construire

plant [plɑːnt] N plante f; (*machinery*) matériel m; (*factory*) usine f ▶ VT planter; (*bomb*) déposer, poser; (*microphone, evidence*) cacher

plantation [plænˈteɪʃən] N plantation f

plant pot N (BRIT) pot m de fleurs

plaque [plæk] N plaque f

P

plasma ['plæzmə] N plasma m
plaster ['plɑːstəʳ] N plâtre m; (also: **plaster of Paris**) plâtre à mouler; (BRIT: also: **sticking plaster**) pansement adhésif ▶ VT plâtrer; (cover): **to ~ with** couvrir de; **in ~** (BRIT: leg etc) dans le plâtre
plasterboard ['plɑːstəbɔːd] N Placoplâtre® m
plaster cast N (Med) plâtre m; (model, statue) moule m
plastered ['plɑːstəd] ADJ (inf) soûl(e)
plasterer ['plɑːstərəʳ] N plâtrier m
plastic ['plæstɪk] N plastique m ▶ ADJ (made of plastic) en plastique; (flexible) plastique, malléable; (art) plastique
plastic bag N sac m en plastique
plastic bullet N balle f de plastique
plastic explosive N plastic m
plasticine® ['plæstɪsiːn] N pâte f à modeler
plastic surgery N chirurgie f esthétique
plate [pleɪt] N (dish) assiette f; (sheet of metal, on door, Phot) plaque f; (Typ) cliché m; (in book) gravure f; (dental) dentier m; (Aut: number plate) plaque minéralogique; **gold/silver ~** (dishes) vaisselle f d'or/d'argent
plateau ['plætəʊ] (pl **plateaus** or **plateaux** ['plætəʊz]) N plateau m
plateful ['pleɪtful] N assiette f, assiettée f
plate glass N verre m à vitre, vitre f
platen ['plætən] N (on typewriter, printer) rouleau m
plate rack N égouttoir m
platform ['plætfɔːm] N (at meeting) tribune f; (BRIT: of bus) plate-forme f; (stage) estrade f; (Rail) quai m; (Pol) plateforme f; **the train leaves from ~ 7** le train part de la voie 7
platform ticket N (BRIT) billet m de quai
platinum ['plætɪnəm] N platine m
platitude ['plætɪtjuːd] N platitude f, lieu commun
platoon [plə'tuːn] N peloton m
platter ['plætəʳ] N plat m
plaudits ['plɔːdɪts] NPL applaudissements mpl
plausible ['plɔːzɪbl] ADJ plausible; (person) convaincant(e)
play [pleɪ] N jeu m; (Theat) pièce f (de théâtre) ▶ VT (game) jouer à; (team, opponent) jouer contre; (instrument) jouer de; (part, piece of music, note) jouer; (CD etc) passer ▶ VI jouer; **to bring** or **call into ~** faire entrer en jeu; **~ on words** jeu de mots; **to ~ safe** ne prendre aucun risque; **to ~ a trick on sb** jouer un tour à qn; **they're playing at soldiers** ils jouent aux soldats; **to ~ for time** (fig) chercher à gagner du temps; **to ~ into sb's hands** (fig) faire le jeu de qn
▶ **play about, play around** VI (person) s'amuser
▶ **play along** VI (fig): **to ~ along with** (person) entrer dans le jeu de ▶ VT (fig): **to ~ sb along** faire marcher qn
▶ **play back** VT repasser, réécouter
▶ **play down** VT minimiser
▶ **play on** VT FUS (sb's feelings, credulity) jouer sur; **to ~ on sb's nerves** porter sur les nerfs de qn
▶ **play up** VI (cause trouble) faire des siennes
playact ['pleɪækt] VI jouer la comédie

playboy ['pleɪbɔɪ] N playboy m
played-out ['pleɪd'aut] ADJ épuisé(e)
player ['pleɪəʳ] N joueur(-euse); (Theat) acteur(-trice); (Mus) musicien(ne)
playful ['pleɪful] ADJ enjoué(e)
playgoer ['pleɪgəuəʳ] N amateur(-trice) de théâtre, habitué(e) des théâtres
playground ['pleɪgraund] N cour f de récréation; (in park) aire f de jeux
playgroup ['pleɪgruːp] N garderie f
playing card ['pleɪɪŋ-] N carte f à jouer
playing field ['pleɪɪŋ-] N terrain m de sport
playmaker ['pleɪmeɪkəʳ] N (Sport) joueur qui crée des occasions de marquer des buts pour ses coéquipiers.
playmate ['pleɪmeɪt] N camarade mf, copain (copine)
play-off ['pleɪɔf] N (Sport) belle f
playpen ['pleɪpɛn] N parc m (pour bébé)
playroom ['pleɪruːm] N salle f de jeux
playschool ['pleɪskuːl] N = **playgroup**
plaything ['pleɪθɪŋ] N jouet m
playtime ['pleɪtaɪm] N (Scol) récréation f
playwright ['pleɪraɪt] N dramaturge m
plc ABBR (BRIT: = public limited company) ≈ SARL f
plea [pliː] N (request) appel m; (excuse) excuse f; (Law) défense f
plea bargaining N (Law) négociations entre le procureur, l'avocat de la défense et parfois le juge, pour réduire la gravité des charges.
plead [pliːd] VT plaider; (give as excuse) invoquer ▶ VI (Law) plaider; (beg): **to ~ with sb (for sth)** implorer qn (d'accorder qch); **to ~ for sth** implorer qch; **to ~ guilty/not guilty** plaider coupable/non coupable
pleasant ['plɛznt] ADJ agréable
pleasantly ['plɛzntlɪ] ADV agréablement
pleasantry ['plɛzntrɪ] N (joke) plaisanterie f; **pleasantries** NPL (polite remarks) civilités fpl
please [pliːz] EXCL s'il te (or vous) plaît ▶ VT plaire à ▶ VI (think fit): **do as you ~** faites comme il vous plaira; **my bill, ~** l'addition, s'il vous plaît; **~ don't cry!** je t'en prie, ne pleure pas!; **~ yourself!** (inf) faites comme vous voulez!
pleased [pliːzd] ADJ: **~ (with)** content(e) (de); **~ to meet you** enchanté (de faire votre connaissance); **we are ~ to inform you that ...** nous sommes heureux de vous annoncer que ...
pleasing ['pliːzɪŋ] ADJ plaisant(e), qui fait plaisir
pleasurable ['plɛʒərəbl] ADJ très agréable
pleasure ['plɛʒəʳ] N plaisir m; **"it's a ~"** "je vous en prie"; **with ~** avec plaisir; **is this trip for business or ~?** est-ce un voyage d'affaires ou d'agrément?
pleasure cruise N croisière f
pleat [pliːt] N pli m
plebiscite ['plɛbɪsɪt] N plébiscite m
plebs [plɛbz] NPL (pej) bas peuple
plectrum ['plɛktrəm] N plectre m
pledge [plɛdʒ] N gage m; (promise) promesse f ▶ VT engager; promettre; **to ~ support for sb** s'engager à soutenir qn; **to ~ sb to secrecy** faire promettre à qn de garder le secret
plenary ['pliːnərɪ] ADJ: **in ~ session** en séance plénière

plentiful ['plɛntɪful] ADJ abondant(e), copieux(-euse)

plenty ['plɛntɪ] N abondance f; **~ of** beaucoup de; (sufficient) (bien) assez de; **we've got ~ of time** nous avons largement le temps

pleurisy ['pluərɪsɪ] N pleurésie f

pliable ['plaɪəbl] ADJ flexible; (person) malléable

pliers ['plaɪəz] NPL pinces fpl

plight [plaɪt] N situation f critique

plimsolls ['plɪmsəlz] NPL (BRIT) (chaussures fpl) tennis fpl

plinth [plɪnθ] N socle m

PLO N ABBR (= Palestine Liberation Organization) OLP f

plod [plɔd] VI avancer péniblement; (fig) peiner

plodder ['plɔdə'] N bûcheur(-euse)

plodding ['plɔdɪŋ] ADJ pesant(e)

plonk [plɔŋk] (inf) N (BRIT: wine) pinard m, piquette f ▶ VT: **to ~ sth down** poser brusquement qch

plot [plɔt] N complot m, conspiration f; (of story, play) intrigue f; (of land) lot m de terrain, lopin m ▶ VT (mark out) tracer point par point; (Naut) pointer; (make graph of) faire le graphique de; (conspire) comploter ▶ VI comploter; **a vegetable ~** (BRIT) un carré de légumes

plotter ['plɔtə'] N conspirateur(-trice); (Comput) traceur m

plough, (US) **plow** [plau] N charrue f ▶ VT (earth) labourer; **to ~ money into** investir dans
▶ **plough back** VT (Comm) réinvestir
▶ **plough through** VT FUS (snow etc) avancer péniblement dans

ploughing, (US) **plowing** ['plauɪŋ] N labourage m

ploughman, (US) **plowman** ['plaumən] N (irreg) laboureur m

plow [plau] (US) N = **plough**

ploy [plɔɪ] N stratagème m

pls ABBR (= please) SVP

pluck [plʌk] VT (fruit) cueillir; (musical instrument) pincer; (bird) plumer ▶ N courage m, cran m; **to ~ one's eyebrows** s'épiler les sourcils; **to ~ up courage** prendre son courage à deux mains

plucky ['plʌkɪ] ADJ courageux(-euse)

plug [plʌg] N (stopper) bouchon m, bonde f; (Elec) prise f de courant; (Aut: also: **spark(ing) plug**) bougie f ▶ VT (hole) boucher; (inf: advertise) faire du battage pour, matraquer; **to give sb/sth a ~** (inf) faire de la pub pour qn/qch
▶ **plug in** VT (Elec) brancher ▶ VI (Elec) se brancher

plughole ['plʌghəul] N (BRIT) trou m (d'écoulement)

plug-in ['plʌgɪn] N (Comput) greffon m; module m d'extension

plum [plʌm] N (fruit) prune f ▶ ADJ: **~ job** (inf) travail m en or

plumb [plʌm] ADJ vertical(e) ▶ N plomb m ▶ ADV (exactly) en plein ▶ VT sonder
▶ **plumb in** VT (washing machine) faire le raccordement de

plumber ['plʌmə'] N plombier m

plumbing ['plʌmɪŋ] N (trade) plomberie f; (piping) tuyauterie f

plumbline ['plʌmlaɪn] N fil m à plomb

plume [plu:m] N plume f, plumet m

plummet ['plʌmɪt] VI (person, object) plonger; (sales, prices) dégringoler

plump [plʌmp] ADJ rondelet(te), dodu(e), bien en chair ▶ VT: **to ~ sth (down) on** laisser tomber qch lourdement sur
▶ **plump for** VT FUS (inf: choose) se décider pour
▶ **plump up** VT (cushion) battre (pour lui redonner forme)

plunder ['plʌndə'] N pillage m ▶ VT piller

plunge [plʌndʒ] N plongeon m; (fig) chute f ▶ VT plonger ▶ VI (fall) tomber, dégringoler; (dive) plonger; **to take the ~** se jeter à l'eau

plunger ['plʌndʒə'] N piston m; (for blocked sink) (débouchoir m à) ventouse f

plunging ['plʌndʒɪŋ] ADJ (neckline) plongeant(e)

pluperfect [plu:'pə:fɪkt] N (Ling) plus-que-parfait m

plural ['pluərl] ADJ pluriel(le) ▶ N pluriel m

plus [plʌs] N (also: **plus sign**) signe m plus; (advantage) atout m ▶ PREP plus; **ten/twenty ~** plus de dix/vingt; **it's a ~** c'est un atout

plus fours NPL pantalon m (de) golf

plush [plʌʃ] ADJ somptueux(-euse) ▶ N peluche f

plus-one ['plʌs'wʌn] N personne qui accompagne un invité à une réception ou une cérémonie.

ply [plaɪ] N (of wool) fil m; (of wood) feuille f, épaisseur f ▶ VT (tool) manier; (a trade) exercer ▶ VI (ship) faire la navette; **three ~ (wool)** n laine f trois fils; **to ~ sb with drink** donner continuellement à boire à qn

plywood ['plaɪwud] N contreplaqué m

P.M. N ABBR (BRIT) = **prime minister**

p.m. ADV ABBR (= post meridiem) de l'après-midi

PMS N ABBR (= premenstrual syndrome) syndrome prémenstruel

PMT N ABBR (= premenstrual tension) syndrome prémenstruel

pneumatic [nju:'mætɪk] ADJ pneumatique

pneumatic drill N marteau-piqueur m

pneumonia [nju:'məunɪə] N pneumonie f

PO N ABBR (= Post Office) PTT fpl; (Mil) = **petty officer**

po ABBR = **postal order**

POA N ABBR (BRIT) = **Prison Officers' Association**

poach [pəutʃ] VT (cook) pocher; (steal) pêcher (or chasser) sans permis ▶ VI braconner

poached [pəutʃt] ADJ (egg) poché(e)

poacher ['pəutʃə'] N braconnier m

poaching ['pəutʃɪŋ] N braconnage m

P.O. Box N ABBR = **post office box**

pocket ['pɔkɪt] N poche f ▶ VT empocher; **to be (£5) out of ~** (BRIT) en être de sa poche (pour 5 livres)

pocketbook ['pɔkɪtbuk] N (notebook) carnet m; (US: wallet) portefeuille m; (: handbag) sac m à main

pocket knife N canif m

pocket money N argent m de poche

pockmarked ['pɔkmɑːkt] ADJ (face) grêlé(e)

pod [pɔd] N cosse f ▶ VT écosser

podcast ['pɔdkɑːst] N podcast m ▶ VI podcaster

podcasting ['pɔdkɑːstɪŋ] N podcasting m, baladodiffusion f
podgy ['pɔdʒɪ] ADJ rondelet(te)
podiatrist [pɔ'diːətrɪst] N (US) pédicure mf
podiatry [pɔ'diːətrɪ] N (US) pédicurie f
podium ['pəudɪəm] N podium m
POE N ABBR = **port of embarkation; port of entry**
poem ['pəuɪm] N poème m
poet ['pəuɪt] N poète m
poetic [pəu'etɪk] ADJ poétique
poet laureate N poète lauréat; *voir article*
> En Grande-Bretagne, le *poet laureate* est un poète qui reçoit un traitement en tant que poète de la cour et qui est officier de la maison royale à vie. Le premier d'entre eux fut Ben Jonson, en 1616. Jadis, le "poète lauréat" écrivait des poèmes lors des grandes occasions, mais cette tradition n'est plus guère observée.

poetry ['pəuɪtrɪ] N poésie f
poignant ['pɔɪnjənt] ADJ poignant(e); (*sharp*) vif (vive)
point [pɔɪnt] N (*Geom, Scol, Sport, on scale*) point m; (*tip*) pointe f; (*in time*) moment m; (*in space*) endroit m; (*subject, idea*) point, sujet m; (*purpose*) but m; (*also*: **decimal point**): **2 ~ 3 (2.3)** 2 virgule 3 (2,3); (*BRIT Elec: also*: **power point**) prise f (de courant) ▶ VT (*show*) indiquer; (*wall, window*) jointoyer; (*gun etc*) **to ~ sth at** braquer or diriger qch sur ▶ VI: **to ~ at** montrer du doigt; **points** NPL (*Aut*) vis platinées; (*Rail*) aiguillage m; **good points** qualités fpl; **the train stops at Carlisle and all points south** le train dessert Carlisle et toutes les gares vers le sud; **to make a ~** faire une remarque; **to make a ~ of doing sth** ne pas manquer de faire qch; **to make one's ~** se faire comprendre; **to get/miss the ~** comprendre/ne pas comprendre; **to come to the ~** en venir au fait; **when it comes to the ~** le moment venu; **there's no ~ (in doing)** cela ne sert à rien (de faire); **what's the ~?** à quoi ça sert?; **to be on the ~ of doing sth** être sur le point de faire qch; **that's the whole ~!** précisément!; **to be beside the ~** être à côté de la question; **you've got a ~ there!** (c'est) juste!; **in ~ of fact** en fait, en réalité; **~ of departure** (*also fig*) point de départ; **~ of order** point de procédure; **~ of sale** (*Comm*) point de vente; **to ~ to sth** (*fig*) signaler
> **point out** VT (*show*) montrer, indiquer; (*mention*) faire remarquer, souligner

point-blank ['pɔɪnt'blæŋk] ADV (*fig*) catégoriquement; (*also*: **at point-blank range**) à bout portant ▶ ADJ (*fig*) catégorique
point duty N (*BRIT*): **to be on ~** diriger la circulation
pointed ['pɔɪntɪd] ADJ (*shape*) pointu(e); (*remark*) plein(e) de sous-entendus
pointedly ['pɔɪntɪdlɪ] ADV d'une manière significative
pointer ['pɔɪntəʳ] N (*stick*) baguette f; (*needle*) aiguille f; (*dog*) chien m d'arrêt; (*clue*) indication f; (*advice*) tuyau m

pointless ['pɔɪntlɪs] ADJ inutile, vain(e)
point of view N point m de vue
poise [pɔɪz] N (*balance*) équilibre m; (*of head, body*) port m; (*calmness*) calme m ▶ VT placer en équilibre; **to be poised for** (*fig*) être prêt à
poison ['pɔɪzn] N poison m ▶ VT empoisonner
poisoning ['pɔɪznɪŋ] N empoisonnement m
poisonous ['pɔɪznəs] ADJ (*snake*) venimeux(-euse); (*substance, plant*) vénéneux(-euse); (*fumes*) toxique; (*fig*) pernicieux(-euse)
poke [pəuk] VT (*fire*) tisonner; (*jab with finger, stick etc*) piquer; pousser du doigt; (*put*): **to ~ sth in(to)** fourrer or enfoncer qch dans ▶ N (*jab*) (petit) coup; (*to fire*) coup m de tisonnier; **to ~ fun at sb** se moquer de qn
> **poke about** VI fureter
> **poke out** VI (*stick out*) sortir ▶ VT: **to ~ one's head out of the window** passer la tête par la fenêtre

poker ['pəukəʳ] N tisonnier m; (*Cards*) poker m
poker-faced ['pəukə'feɪst] ADJ au visage impassible
poky ['pəukɪ] ADJ exigu(ë)
Poland ['pəulənd] N Pologne f
polar ['pəuləʳ] ADJ polaire
polar bear N ours blanc
polarize ['pəuləraɪz] VT polariser
Pole [pəul] N Polonais(e)
pole [pəul] N (*of wood*) mât m, perche f; (*Elec*) poteau m; (*Geo*) pôle m
poleaxe ['pəulæks] VT (*fig*) terrasser
pole bean N (US) haricot m (à rames)
polecat ['pəulkæt] N putois m
Pol. Econ. ['pɔlɪkɔn] N ABBR = **political economy**
polemic [pɔ'lemɪk] N polémique f
pole star N étoile f polaire
pole vault N saut m à la perche
police [pə'liːs] NPL police f ▶ VT maintenir l'ordre dans; **a large number of ~ were hurt** de nombreux policiers ont été blessés
police car N voiture f de police
police constable N (*BRIT*) agent m de police
police department N (US) services mpl de police
police force N police f, forces fpl de l'ordre
policeman [pə'liːsmən] N (*irreg*) agent m de police, policier m
police officer N agent m de police
police record N casier m judiciaire
police state N état policier
police station N commissariat m de police
policewoman [pə'liːswumən] N (*irreg*) femme-agent f
policy ['pɔlɪsɪ] N politique f; (*also*: **insurance policy**) police f (d'assurance); (*of newspaper, company*) politique générale; **to take out a ~** (*Insurance*) souscrire une police d'assurance
policy holder N assuré(e)
policy-making ['pɔlɪsɪmeɪkɪŋ] N élaboration f de nouvelles lignes d'action
polio ['pəulɪəu] N polio f
Polish ['pəulɪʃ] ADJ polonais(e) ▶ N (*Ling*) polonais m
polish ['pɔlɪʃ] N (*for shoes*) cirage m; (*for floor*) cire f,

encaustique f; (for nails) vernis m; (shine) éclat m, poli m; (fig: refinement) raffinement m ▶ VT (put polish on: shoes, wood) cirer; (make shiny) astiquer, faire briller; (fig: improve) perfectionner
▶ **polish off** VT (work) expédier; (food) liquider
polished ['pɒlɪʃt] ADJ (fig) raffiné(e)
polite [pə'laɪt] ADJ poli(e); **it's not ~ to do that** ça ne se fait pas
politely [pə'laɪtlɪ] ADV poliment
politeness [pə'laɪtnɪs] N politesse f
politic ['pɒlɪtɪk] ADJ diplomatique
political [pə'lɪtɪkl] ADJ politique
political asylum N asile m politique
politically [pə'lɪtɪklɪ] ADV politiquement; **~ correct** politiquement correct(e)
politician [pɒlɪ'tɪʃən] N homme/femme politique, politicien(ne)
politics ['pɒlɪtɪks] N politique f
polka ['pɒlkə] N polka f
polka dot N pois m
poll [pəul] N scrutin m, vote m; (also: **opinion poll**) sondage m (d'opinion) ▶ VT (votes) obtenir; **to go to the polls** (voters) aller aux urnes; (government) tenir des élections
pollen ['pɒlən] N pollen m
pollen count N taux m de pollen
pollination [pɒlɪ'neɪʃən] N pollinisation f
polling ['pəulɪŋ] N (Pol) élections fpl; (Tel) invitation f à émettre
polling booth N (Brit) isoloir m
polling day N (Brit) jour m des élections
polling station N (Brit) bureau m de vote
pollster ['pəulstər] N sondeur m, enquêteur(-euse)
poll tax N (Brit: formerly) ≈ impôts locaux
pollutant [pə'lu:tənt] N polluant m
pollute [pə'lu:t] VT polluer
pollution [pə'lu:ʃən] N pollution f
polo ['pəuləu] N polo m
polo-neck ['pəuləunɛk] ADJ à col roulé ▶ N (sweater) pull m à col roulé
polo shirt N polo m
poly ['pɒlɪ] N ABBR (Brit) = **polytechnic**
poly bag N (Brit inf) sac m en plastique
polyester [pɒlɪ'ɛstər] N polyester m
polygamy [pə'lɪɡəmɪ] N polygamie f
polygraph ['pɒlɪɡrɑːf] N détecteur m de mensonges
Polynesia [pɒlɪ'niːzɪə] N Polynésie f
Polynesian [pɒlɪ'niːzɪən] ADJ polynésien(ne) ▶ N Polynésien(ne)
polyp ['pɒlɪp] N (Med) polype m
polystyrene [pɒlɪ'staɪriːn] N polystyrène m
polytechnic [pɒlɪ'tɛknɪk] N (college) IUT m, Institut m universitaire de technologie
polythene ['pɒlɪθiːn] N (Brit) polyéthylène m
polythene bag N sac m en plastique
polyurethane [pɒlɪ'juərɪθeɪn] N polyuréthane m
pomegranate ['pɒmɪɡrænɪt] N grenade f
pommel ['pɒml] N pommeau m ▶ VT = **pummel**
pomp [pɒmp] N pompe f, faste f, apparat m
pompom ['pɒmpɒm] N pompon m
pompous ['pɒmpəs] ADJ pompeux(-euse)

pond [pɒnd] N étang m; (stagnant) mare f
ponder ['pɒndər] VI réfléchir ▶ VT considérer, peser
ponderous ['pɒndərəs] ADJ pesant(e), lourd(e)
pong [pɒŋ] (Brit inf) N puanteur f ▶ VI schlinguer
pontiff ['pɒntɪf] N pontife m
pontificate [pɒn'tɪfɪkeɪt] VI (fig): **to ~ (about)** pontifier (sur)
pontoon [pɒn'tuːn] N ponton m; (Brit Cards) vingt-et-un m
pony ['pəunɪ] N poney m
ponytail ['pəunɪteɪl] N queue f de cheval
pony trekking [-trɛkɪŋ] N (Brit) randonnée f équestre or à cheval
poodle ['puːdl] N caniche m
pooh-pooh ['puː'puː] VT dédaigner
pool [puːl] N (of rain) flaque f; (pond) mare f; (artificial) bassin m; (also: **swimming pool**) piscine f; (sth shared) fonds commun; (money at cards) cagnotte f; (billiards) poule f; (Comm: consortium) pool m; (US: monopoly trust) trust m ▶ VT mettre en commun; **pools** NPL (football) ≈ loto sportif; **typing ~**, (US) **secretary ~** pool m dactylographique; **to do the (football) pools** (Brit) ≈ jouer au loto sportif; see also **football pools**
poor [puər] ADJ pauvre; (mediocre) médiocre, faible, mauvais(e) ▶ NPL: **the ~** les pauvres mpl
poorly ['puəlɪ] ADV pauvrement; (badly) mal, médiocrement ▶ ADJ souffrant(e), malade
pop [pɒp] N (noise) bruit sec; (Mus) musique f pop; (inf: drink) soda m; (US inf: father) papa m ▶ VT (put) fourrer, mettre (rapidement) ▶ VI éclater; (cork) sauter; **she popped her head out of the window** elle lui passa la tête par la fenêtre
▶ **pop in** VI entrer en passant
▶ **pop out** VI sortir
▶ **pop up** VI apparaître, surgir
pop concert N concert m pop
popcorn ['pɒpkɔːn] N pop-corn m
pope [pəup] N pape m
poplar ['pɒplər] N peuplier m
poplin ['pɒplɪn] N popeline f
popper ['pɒpər] N (Brit) bouton-pression m
poppy ['pɒpɪ] N (wild) coquelicot m; (cultivated) pavot m
poppycock ['pɒpɪkɒk] N (inf) balivernes fpl
Popsicle® ['pɒpsɪkl] N (US) esquimau m (glace)
pop star N pop star f
populace ['pɒpjuləs] N peuple m
popular ['pɒpjulər] ADJ populaire; (fashionable) à la mode; **to be ~ (with)** (person) avoir du succès (auprès de); (decision) être bien accueilli(e) (par)
popularity [pɒpju'lærɪtɪ] N popularité f
popularize ['pɒpjulərauz] VT populariser; (science) vulgariser
populate ['pɒpjuleɪt] VT peupler
population [pɒpju'leɪʃən] N population f
population explosion N explosion f démographique
populous ['pɒpjuləs] ADJ populeux(-euse)
pop-up ['pɒpʌp] ADJ (Comput: menu, window) pop up inv ▶ N pop up m inv, fenêtre f pop up

727

porcelain ['pɔːslɪn] N porcelaine f
porch [pɔːtʃ] N porche m; (US) véranda f
porcupine ['pɔːkjupaɪn] N porc-épic m
pore [pɔːʳ] N pore m ▶ VI: **to ~ over** s'absorber dans, être plongé(e) dans
pork [pɔːk] N porc m
pork chop N côte f de porc
pork pie N pâté m de porc en croûte
porn [pɔːn] ADJ (inf) porno ▶ N (inf) porno m
pornographic [pɔːnə'græfɪk] ADJ pornographique
pornography [pɔː'nɔgrəfɪ] N pornographie f
porous ['pɔːrəs] ADJ poreux(-euse)
porpoise ['pɔːpəs] N marsouin m
porridge ['pɔrɪdʒ] N porridge m
port [pɔːt] N (harbour) port m; (opening in ship) sabord m; (Naut: left side) bâbord m; (wine) porto m; (Comput) port m, accès m ▶ CPD portuaire, du port; **to ~** (Naut) à bâbord; **~ of call** (port d')escale f
portable ['pɔːtəbl] ADJ portatif(-ive)
portal ['pɔːtl] N portail m
portcullis [pɔːt'kʌlɪs] N herse f
portent ['pɔːtɛnt] N présage m
porter ['pɔːtəʳ] N (for luggage) porteur m; (doorkeeper) gardien(ne); portier m
portfolio [pɔːt'fəuliəu] N portefeuille m; (of artist) portfolio m
porthole ['pɔːthəul] N hublot m
portico ['pɔːtɪkəu] N portique m
portion ['pɔːʃən] N portion f, part f
portly ['pɔːtlɪ] ADJ corpulent(e)
portrait ['pɔːtreɪt] N portrait m
portray [pɔː'treɪ] VT faire le portrait de; (in writing) dépeindre, représenter; (subj: actor) jouer
portrayal [pɔː'treɪəl] N portrait m, représentation f
Portugal ['pɔːtjugl] N Portugal m
Portuguese [pɔːtju'giːz] ADJ portugais(e) ▶ N (pl inv) Portugais(e); (Ling) portugais m
Portuguese man-of-war [-mænəv'wɔːʳ] N (jellyfish) galère f
pose [pəuz] N pose f; (pej) affectation f ▶ VI poser; (pretend): **to ~ as** se faire passer pour ▶ VT poser; (problem) créer; **to strike a ~** poser (pour la galerie)
poser ['pəuzəʳ] N question difficile or embarrassante; (person) = **poseur**
poseur [pəu'zəːʳ] N (pej) poseur(-euse)
posh [pɔʃ] ADJ (inf) chic inv; **to talk ~** parler d'une manière affectée
position [pə'zɪʃən] N position f; (job, situation) situation f ▶ VT mettre en place or en position; **to be in a ~ to do sth** être en mesure de faire qch
positive ['pɔzɪtɪv] ADJ positif(-ive); (certain) sûr(e), certain(e); (definite) formel(le), catégorique; (clear) indéniable, réel(le)
positively ['pɔzɪtɪvlɪ] ADV (affirmatively, enthusiastically) de façon positive; (inf: really) carrément; **to think ~** être positif(-ive)
posse ['pɔsɪ] N (US) détachement m
possess [pə'zɛs] VT posséder; **like one possessed** comme un fou; **whatever can have**

possessed you? qu'est-ce qui vous a pris?
possession [pə'zɛʃən] N possession f; **possessions** NPL (belongings) affaires fpl; **to take ~ of sth** prendre possession de qch
possessive [pə'zɛsɪv] ADJ possessif(-ive)
possessiveness [pə'zɛsɪvnɪs] N possessivité f
possessor [pə'zɛsəʳ] N possesseur m
possibility [pɔsɪ'bɪlɪtɪ] N possibilité f; (event) éventualité f; **he's a ~ for the part** c'est un candidat possible pour le rôle
possible ['pɔsɪbl] ADJ possible; (solution) envisageable, éventuel(le); **it is ~ to do it** il est possible de le faire; **as far as ~** dans la mesure du possible, autant que possible; **if ~** si possible; **as big as ~** aussi gros que possible
possibly ['pɔsɪblɪ] ADV (perhaps) peut-être; **if you ~ can** si cela vous est possible; **I cannot ~ come** il m'est impossible de venir
post [pəust] N (Brit: mail) poste f; (: collection) levée f; (: letters, delivery) courrier m; (job, situation) poste m; (pole) poteau m; (trading post) comptoir (commercial); (Internet) billet m, post m ▶ VT (notice) afficher; (Internet) poster; (Brit: send by post, Mil) poster; (: appoint): **to ~ to** affecter à; **by ~** (Brit) par la poste; **by return of ~** (Brit) par retour du courrier; **where can I ~ these cards?** où est-ce que je peux poster ces cartes postales?; **to keep sb posted** tenir qn au courant
post... [pəust] PREFIX post...; **post 1990** adj d'après 1990 ▶ ADV après 1990
postage ['pəustɪdʒ] N tarifs mpl d'affranchissement; **~ paid** port payé; **~ prepaid** (US) franco (de port)
postage stamp N timbre-poste m
postal ['pəustl] ADJ postal(e)
postal order N mandat(-poste m) m
postbag ['pəustbæg] N (Brit) sac postal; (postman's) sacoche f
postbox ['pəustbɔks] N (Brit) boîte f aux lettres (publique)
postcard ['pəustkɑːd] N carte postale
postcode ['pəustkəud] N (Brit) code postal
postdate ['pəust'deɪt] VT (cheque) postdater
poster ['pəustəʳ] N affiche f
poste restante [pəust'rɛstɑ̃ːnt] N (Brit) poste restante
posterior [pɔs'tɪərɪəʳ] N (inf) postérieur m, derrière m
posterity [pɔs'tɛrɪtɪ] N postérité f
poster paint N gouache f
post exchange N (US Mil) magasin m de l'armée
post-free [pəust'friː] ADJ (Brit) franco (de port)
postgraduate ['pəust'grædjuət] N ≈ étudiant(e) de troisième cycle
posthumous ['pɔstjuməs] ADJ posthume
posthumously ['pɔstjuməslɪ] ADV après la mort de l'auteur, à titre posthume
posting ['pəustɪŋ] N (Brit) affectation f
postman ['pəustmən] N (irreg) (Brit) facteur m
postmark ['pəustmɑːk] N cachet m (de la poste)
postmaster ['pəustmɑːstəʳ] N receveur m des postes
Postmaster General N ≈ ministre m des Postes et Télécommunications

postmistress ['pəustmɪstrɪs] N receveuse f des postes
post-mortem [pəust'mɔːtəm] N autopsie f
postnatal ['pəust'neɪtl] ADJ postnatal(e)
post office N (building) poste f; (organization): **the Post Office** les postes fpl
post office box N boîte postale
post-paid ['pəust'peɪd] ADJ (BRIT) port payé
postpone [pəs'pəun] VT remettre (à plus tard), reculer
postponement [pəs'pəunmənt] N ajournement m, renvoi m
postscript ['pəustskrɪpt] N post-scriptum m
postulate ['pɒstjuleɪt] VT postuler
posture ['pɒstʃəʳ] N posture f; (fig) attitude f ▶ VI poser
postwar [pəust'wɔːʳ] ADJ d'après-guerre
postwoman [pəust'wumən] N (irreg) (BRIT) factrice f
posy ['pəuzɪ] N petit bouquet
pot [pɒt] N (for cooking) marmite f; casserole f; (teapot) théière f; (for coffee) cafetière f; (for plants, jam) pot m; (piece of pottery) poterie f; (inf: marijuana) herbe f ▶ VT (plant) mettre en pot; **to go to ~** (inf) aller à vau-l'eau; **pots of** (BRIT inf) beaucoup de, plein de
potash ['pɒtæʃ] N potasse f
potassium [pə'tæsɪəm] N potassium m
potato [pə'teɪtəu] (pl **potatoes**) N pomme f de terre
potato crisps, (US) **potato chips** NPL chips mpl
potato flour N fécule f
potato peeler N épluche-légumes m
potbellied ['pɒtbelɪd] ADJ (from overeating) bedonnant(e); (from malnutrition) au ventre ballonné
potency ['pəutnsɪ] N puissance f, force f; (of drink) degré m d'alcool
potent ['pəutnt] ADJ puissant(e); (drink) fort(e), très alcoolisé(e); (man) viril
potentate ['pəutnteɪt] N potentat m
potential [pə'tenʃl] ADJ potentiel(le) ▶ N potentiel m; **to have ~** être prometteur(-euse); ouvrir des possibilités
potentially [pə'tenʃəlɪ] ADV potentiellement; **it's ~ dangerous** ça pourrait se révéler dangereux, il y a possibilité de danger
pothole ['pɒthəul] N (in road) nid m de poule; (BRIT: underground) gouffre m, caverne f
potholer ['pɒthəuləʳ] N (BRIT) spéléologue mf
potholing ['pɒthəulɪŋ] N (BRIT): **to go ~** faire de la spéléologie
potion ['pəuʃən] N potion f
potluck [pɒt'lʌk] N: **to take ~** tenter sa chance
pot plant N plante f d'appartement
potpourri [pəu'puriː] N pot-pourri m
pot roast N rôti m à la cocotte
pot shot N: **to take pot shots at** canarder
potted ['pɒtɪd] ADJ (food) en conserve; (plant) en pot; (fig: shortened) abrégé(e)
potter ['pɒtəʳ] N potier m ▶ VI (BRIT): **to ~ around** or **about** bricoler; **~'s wheel** tour m de potier
pottery ['pɒtərɪ] N poterie f; **a piece of ~** une poterie

potty ['pɒtɪ] ADJ (BRIT inf: mad) dingue ▶ N (child's) pot m
potty-training ['pɒtɪtreɪnɪŋ] N apprentissage m de la propreté
pouch [pautʃ] N (Zool) poche f; (for tobacco) blague f; (for money) bourse f
pouf, pouffe [puːf] N (stool) pouf m
poultice ['pəultɪs] N cataplasme m
poultry ['pəultrɪ] N volaille f
poultry farm N élevage m de volaille
poultry farmer N aviculteur m
pounce [pauns] VI: **to ~ (on)** bondir (sur), fondre (sur) ▶ N bond m, attaque f
pound [paund] N livre f (weight = 453g, 16 ounces; money = 100 pence); (for dogs, cars) fourrière f ▶ VT (beat) bourrer de coups, marteler; (crush) piler, pulvériser; (with guns) pilonner ▶ VI (heart) battre violemment, taper; **half a ~ (of)** une demi-livre (de); **a five-~ note** un billet de cinq livres
pounding ['paundɪŋ] N: **to take a ~** (fig) prendre une râclée
pound sterling N livre f sterling
pour [pɔːʳ] VT verser ▶ VI couler à flots; (rain) pleuvoir à verse; **to ~ sb a drink** verser or servir à boire à qn; **to come pouring in** (water) entrer à flots; (letters) arriver par milliers; (cars, people) affluer
  ▶ **pour away, pour off** VT vider
  ▶ **pour in** VI (people) affluer, se précipiter; (news, letters) arriver en masse
  ▶ **pour out** VI (people) sortir en masse ▶ VT vider; (fig) déverser; (serve: a drink) verser
pouring ['pɔːrɪŋ] ADJ: **~ rain** pluie torrentielle
pout [paut] N moue f ▶ VI faire la moue
poverty ['pɒvətɪ] N pauvreté f, misère f
poverty line N seuil m de pauvreté
poverty-stricken ['pɒvətɪstrɪkn] ADJ pauvre, déshérité(e)
poverty trap N (BRIT) piège m de la pauvreté
POW N ABBR = **prisoner of war**
powder ['paudəʳ] N poudre f ▶ VT poudrer; **to ~ one's nose** se poudrer; (euphemism) aller à la salle de bain
powder compact N poudrier m
powdered milk ['paudəd-] N lait m en poudre
powder keg N (fig) poudrière f
powder puff N houppette f
powder room N toilettes fpl (pour dames)
powdery ['paudərɪ] ADJ poudreux(-euse)
power ['pauəʳ] N (strength, nation) puissance f, force f; (ability, Pol: of party, leader) pouvoir m; (Math) puissance; (of speech, thought) faculté f; (Elec) courant m ▶ VT faire marcher, actionner; **to do all in one's ~ to help sb** faire tout ce qui est en son pouvoir pour aider qn; **the world powers** les grandes puissances; **to be in ~** être au pouvoir
powerboat ['pauəbəut] N (BRIT) hors-bord m
power cut N (BRIT) coupure f de courant
powered ['pauəd] ADJ: **~ by** actionné(e) par, fonctionnant à; **nuclear-~ submarine** sous-marin m (à propulsion) nucléaire
power failure N panne f de courant

P

powerful ['pauəful] ADJ puissant(e); (*performance etc*) très fort(e)
powerhouse ['pauəhaus] N (*fig: person*) fonceur *m*; **a ~ of ideas** une mine d'idées
powerless ['pauəlɪs] ADJ impuissant(e)
power line N ligne *f* électrique
power of attorney N procuration *f*
power point N (*BRIT*) prise *f* de courant
power station N centrale *f* électrique
power steering N direction assistée
power struggle N lutte *f* pour le pouvoir
powwow ['pauwau] N conciliabule *m*
p.p. ABBR (= *per procurationem: by proxy*) p.p.
PPE N ABBR (*BRIT Scol*) = **philosophy, politics and economics**
PPS N ABBR (= *post postscriptum*) PPS; (*BRIT*: = *parliamentary private secretary*) parlementaire chargé de mission auprès d'un ministre
PQ ABBR (*CANADA*: = *Province of Quebec*) PQ
PR N ABBR = **proportional representation**; **public relations** ▶ ABBR (*US*) = **Puerto Rico**
Pr. ABBR (= *prince*) Pce
practicability [præktɪkə'bɪlɪtɪ] N possibilité *f* de réalisation
practicable ['præktɪkəbl] ADJ (*scheme*) réalisable
practical ['præktɪkl] ADJ pratique
practicality [præktɪ'kælɪtɪ] N (*of plan*) aspect *m* pratique; (*of person*) sens *m* pratique; **practicalities** NPL détails *mpl* pratiques
practical joke N farce *f*
practically ['præktɪklɪ] ADV (*almost*) pratiquement
practice ['præktɪs] N pratique *f*; (*of profession*) exercice *m*; (*at football etc*) entraînement *m*; (*business*) cabinet *m*; clientèle *f* ▶ VT, VI (*US*) = **practise**; **in ~** (*in reality*) en pratique; **out of ~** rouillé(e); **2 hours' piano ~** 2 heures de travail *or* d'exercices au piano; **target ~** exercices de tir; **it's common ~** c'est courant, ça se fait couramment; **to put sth into ~** mettre qch en pratique
practice match N match *m* d'entraînement
practise, (*US*) **practice** ['præktɪs] VT (*work at: piano, backhand etc*) s'exercer à, travailler; (*train for: sport*) s'entraîner à; (*a sport, religion, method*) pratiquer; (*profession*) exercer ▶ VI s'exercer, travailler; (*train*) s'entraîner; (*lawyer, doctor*) exercer; **to ~ for a match** s'entraîner pour un match
practised, (*US*) **practiced** ['præktɪst] ADJ (*person*) expérimenté(e); (*performance*) impeccable; (*liar*) invétéré(e); **with a ~ eye** d'un œil exercé
practising, (*US*) **practicing** ['præktɪsɪŋ] ADJ (*Christian etc*) pratiquant(e); (*lawyer*) en exercice; (*homosexual*) déclaré
practitioner [præk'tɪʃənəʳ] N praticien(ne)
pragmatic [præg'mætɪk] ADJ pragmatique
Prague [prɑːg] N Prague
prairie ['prɛərɪ] N savane *f*; (*US*): **the prairies** la Prairie
praise [preɪz] N éloge(s) *m(pl)*, louange(s) *f(pl)* ▶ VT louer, faire l'éloge de
praiseworthy ['preɪzwəːðɪ] ADJ digne de louanges

pram [præm] N (*BRIT*) landau *m*, voiture *f* d'enfant
prance [prɑːns] VI (*horse*) caracoler
prank [præŋk] N farce *f*
prat [præt] N (*BRIT inf*) imbécile *m*, andouille *f*
prattle ['prætl] VI jacasser
prawn [prɔːn] N crevette *f* (rose)
prawn cocktail N cocktail *m* de crevettes
pray [preɪ] VI prier
prayer [prɛəʳ] N prière *f*
prayer book N livre *m* de prières
pre... ['priː] PREFIX pré...; **pre-1970** *adj* d'avant 1970 ▶ ADV avant 1970
preach [priːtʃ] VT, VI prêcher; **to ~ at sb** faire la morale à qn
preacher ['priːtʃəʳ] N prédicateur *m*; (*US*: *clergyman*) pasteur *m*
preamble [prɪ'æmbl] N préambule *m*
prearranged [priːə'reɪndʒd] ADJ organisé(e) *or* fixé(e) à l'avance
precarious [prɪ'kɛərɪəs] ADJ précaire
precaution [prɪ'kɔːʃən] N précaution *f*
precautionary [prɪ'kɔːʃənrɪ] ADJ (*measure*) de précaution
precede [prɪ'siːd] VT, VI précéder
precedence ['presɪdəns] N préséance *f*
precedent ['presɪdənt] N précédent *m*; **to establish** *or* **set a ~** créer un précédent
preceding [prɪ'siːdɪŋ] ADJ qui précède (*or* précédait)
precept ['priːsept] N précepte *m*
precinct ['priːsɪŋkt] N (*round cathedral*) pourtour *m*, enceinte *f*; (*US: district*) circonscription *f*, arrondissement *m*; **precincts** NPL (*neighbourhood*) alentours *mpl*, environs *mpl*; **pedestrian ~** (*BRIT*) zone piétonnière; **shopping ~** (*BRIT*) centre commercial
precious ['preʃəs] ADJ précieux(-euse) ▶ ADV (*inf*): **~ little** *or* **few** fort peu; **your ~ dog** (*ironic*) ton chien chéri, ton chéri chien
precipice ['presɪpɪs] N précipice *m*
precipitate [prɪ'sɪpɪtɪt] ADJ (*hasty*) précipité(e) ▶ VT [prɪ'sɪpɪteɪt] précipiter
precipitation [prɪsɪpɪ'teɪʃən] N précipitation *f*
precipitous [prɪ'sɪpɪtəs] ADJ (*steep*) abrupt(e), à pic
précis ['preɪsiː] (*pl* ~ [-z]) N résumé *m*
precise [prɪ'saɪs] ADJ précis(e)
precisely [prɪ'saɪslɪ] ADV précisément
precision [prɪ'sɪʒən] N précision *f*
preclude [prɪ'kluːd] VT exclure, empêcher; **to ~ sb from doing** empêcher qn de faire
precocious [prɪ'kəuʃəs] ADJ précoce
preconceived [priːkən'siːvd] ADJ (*idea*) préconçu(e)
preconception [priːkən'sepʃən] N idée préconçue
precondition ['priːkən'dɪʃən] N condition *f* nécessaire
precursor [priː'kɜːsəʳ] N précurseur *m*
predate ['priː'deɪt] VT (*precede*) antidater
predator ['predətəʳ] N prédateur *m*, rapace *m*
predatory ['predətərɪ] ADJ rapace
predecessor ['priːdɪsesəʳ] N prédécesseur *m*

predestination [priːdɛstɪ'neɪʃən] N
prédestination f
predetermine [priːdɪ'tɜːmɪn] VT déterminer à
l'avance
predicament [prɪ'dɪkəmənt] N situation f
difficile
predicate ['predɪkɪt] N (*Ling*) prédicat m
predict [prɪ'dɪkt] VT prédire
predictable [prɪ'dɪktəbl] ADJ prévisible
predictably [prɪ'dɪktəblɪ] ADV (*behave, react*) de
façon prévisible; **~ she didn't arrive** comme
on pouvait s'y attendre, elle n'est pas venue
prediction [prɪ'dɪkʃən] N prédiction f
predispose [priːdɪs'pəuz] VT prédisposer
predominance [prɪ'dɔmɪnəns] N
prédominance f
predominant [prɪ'dɔmɪnənt] ADJ
prédominant(e)
predominantly [prɪ'dɔmɪnəntlɪ] ADV en
majeure partie; (*especially*) surtout
predominate [prɪ'dɔmɪneɪt] VI prédominer
pre-eminent [priː'emɪnənt] ADJ prééminent(e)
pre-empt [priː'emt] VT (*acquire*) acquérir par
droit de préemption; (*fig*) anticiper sur; **to ~
the issue** conclure avant même d'ouvrir les
débats
pre-emptive [prɪ'emtɪv] ADJ: **~ strike** attaque
(*or action*) préventive
preen [priːn] VT: **to ~ itself** (*bird*) se lisser les
plumes; **to ~ o.s.** s'admirer
prefab ['priːfæb] N ABBR (= *prefabricated building*)
bâtiment préfabriqué
prefabricated [priː'fæbrɪkeɪtɪd] ADJ
préfabriqué(e)
preface ['prefəs] N préface f
prefect ['priːfɛkt] N (*BRIT: in school*) élève chargé de
certaines fonctions de discipline; (*in France*) préfet m
prefer [prɪ'fɜːʳ] VT préférer; (*Law*): **to ~ charges**
procéder à une inculpation; **to ~ coffee to tea**
préférer le café au thé; **to ~ doing** *or* **to do sth**
préférer faire qch
preferable ['prefrəbl] ADJ préférable
preferably ['prefrəblɪ] ADV de préférence
preference ['prefrəns] N préférence f; **in ~ to
sth** plutôt que qch, de préférence à qch
preference shares NPL (*BRIT*) actions
privilégiées
preferential [prefə'renʃəl] ADJ préférentiel(le);
~ treatment traitement m de faveur
preferred stock [prɪ'fɜːd-] NPL (*US*) = **preference
shares**
prefix ['priːfɪks] N préfixe m
pregnancy ['pregnənsɪ] N grossesse f
pregnancy test N test m de grossesse
pregnant ['pregnənt] ADJ enceinte; (*animal*)
pleine; **3 months ~** enceinte de 3 mois
prehistoric ['priːhɪs'tɔrɪk] ADJ préhistorique
prehistory [priː'hɪstərɪ] N préhistoire f
prejudge [priː'dʒʌdʒ] VT préjuger de
prejudice ['predʒudɪs] N préjugé m; (*harm*) tort
m, préjudice m ▶ VT porter préjudice à; (*bias*): **to
~ sb in favour of/against** prévenir qn en
faveur de/contre; **racial ~** préjugés raciaux
prejudiced ['predʒudɪst] ADJ (*person*) plein(e) de

préjugés; (*in a matter*) partial(e); (*view*)
préconçu(e), partial(e); **to be ~ against sb/sth**
avoir un parti-pris contre qn/qch; **to be
racially ~** avoir des préjugés raciaux
prelate ['prelət] N prélat m
preliminaries [prɪ'lɪmɪnərɪz] NPL
préliminaires mpl
preliminary [prɪ'lɪmɪnərɪ] ADJ préliminaire
prelude ['preljuːd] N prélude m
premarital ['priː'mærɪtl] ADJ avant le mariage;
~ contract contrat m de mariage
premature ['premətʃuəʳ] ADJ prématuré(e); **to
be ~ (in doing sth)** aller un peu (trop) vite (en
faisant qch)
premeditated [priː'medɪteɪtɪd] ADJ prémédité(e)
premeditation [priːmedɪ'teɪʃən] N
préméditation f
premenstrual [priː'menstruəl] ADJ
prémenstruel(le)
premenstrual tension N irritabilité f avant les
règles
premier ['premɪəʳ] ADJ premier(-ière),
principal(e) ▶ N (*Pol: Prime Minister*) premier
ministre; (*Pol: President*) chef m de l'État
premiere ['premɪeəʳ] N première f
Premier League N première division
premise ['premɪs] N prémisse f
premises ['premɪsɪz] NPL locaux mpl; **on the ~**
sur les lieux; sur place; **business ~** locaux
commerciaux
premium ['priːmɪəm] N prime f; **to be at a ~** (*fig:
housing etc*) être très demandé(e), être rarissime;
to sell at a ~ (*shares*) vendre au-dessus du pair
premium bond N (*BRIT*) obligation f à prime,
bon m à lots
premium deal N (*Comm*) offre spéciale
premium fuel, (*US*) **premium gasoline** N
super m
premonition [premə'nɪʃən] N prémonition f
preoccupation [priːɔkju'peɪʃən] N
préoccupation f
preoccupied [priː'ɔkjupaɪd] ADJ préoccupé(e)
pre-owned [priː'əund] ADJ (*game, car*) d'occasion
prep [prep] ADJ ABBR = **preparatory school** ▶ N
(*Scol: = preparation*) étude f
prepackaged [priː'pækɪdʒd] ADJ
préempaqueté(e)
prepaid [priː'peɪd] ADJ payé(e) d'avance
preparation [prepə'reɪʃən] N préparation f;
preparations NPL (*for trip, war*) préparatifs mpl;
in ~ for en vue de
preparatory [prɪ'pærətərɪ] ADJ préparatoire;
~ to sth/to doing sth en prévision de qch/
avant de faire qch
preparatory school N (*BRIT*) école primaire
privée; (*US*) lycée privé; *voir article*

> En Grande-Bretagne, une *preparatory school*
> – ou, plus familièrement, une *prep school* – est
> une école payante qui prépare les enfants de
> 7 à 13 ans aux *public schools*.

prepare [prɪ'peəʳ] VT préparer ▶ VI: **to ~ for** se
préparer à
prepared [prɪ'peəd] ADJ: **~ for** préparé(e) à; **~ to**
prêt(e) à

preponderance [prɪ'pɔndərɪns] N prépondérance *f*

preposition [prɛpə'zɪʃən] N préposition *f*

prepossessing [pri:pə'zɛsɪŋ] ADJ avenant(e), engageant(e)

preposterous [prɪ'pɔstərəs] ADJ ridicule, absurde

prep school N = **preparatory school**

prerecord ['pri:rɪ'kɔ:d] VT: **prerecorded broadcast** émission *f* en différé; **prerecorded cassette** cassette enregistrée

prerequisite [pri:'rɛkwɪzɪt] N condition *f* préalable

prerogative [prɪ'rɔgətɪv] N prérogative *f*

presbyterian [prɛzbɪ'tɪərɪən] ADJ, N presbytérien(ne)

presbytery ['prɛzbɪtərɪ] N presbytère *m*

preschool ['pri:'sku:l] ADJ préscolaire; (*child*) d'âge préscolaire

prescribe [prɪ'skraɪb] VT prescrire; **prescribed books** (*Brit Scol*) œuvres *fpl* au programme

prescription [prɪ'skrɪpʃən] N prescription *f*; (*Med*) ordonnance *f*; (: *medicine*) médicament *m* (obtenu sur ordonnance); **to make up** or (*US*) **fill a ~** faire une ordonnance; **could you write me a ~?** pouvez-vous me faire une ordonnance?; **"only available on ~"** "uniquement sur ordonnance"

prescription charges NPL (*Brit*) participation *f* fixe au coût de l'ordonnance

prescriptive [prɪ'skrɪptɪv] ADJ normatif(-ive)

presence ['prɛzns] N présence *f*; **in sb's ~** en présence de qn; **~ of mind** présence d'esprit

present ['prɛznt] ADJ présent(e); (*current*) présent, actuel(le) ▶ N cadeau *m*; (*actuality*): **~ tense** présent *m* ▶ VT [prɪ'zɛnt] présenter; (*prize, medal*) remettre; (*give*): **to ~ sb with sth** offrir qch à qn; **to be ~ at** assister à; **those ~** les présents; **at ~** en ce moment; **to give sb a ~** offrir un cadeau à qn; **to ~ sb (to sb)** présenter qn (à qn)

presentable [prɪ'zɛntəbl] ADJ présentable

presentation [prɛzn'teɪʃən] N présentation *f*; (*gift*) cadeau *m*, présent *m*; (*ceremony*) remise *f* du cadeau (*or* de la médaille *etc*); **on ~ of** (*voucher etc*) sur présentation de

present-day ['prɛzntdeɪ] ADJ contemporain(e), actuel(le)

presenter [prɪ'zɛntər] N (*Brit Radio, TV*) présentateur(-trice)

presently ['prɛzntlɪ] ADV (*soon*) tout à l'heure, bientôt; (*with verb in past*) peu après; (*at present*) en ce moment; (*US: now*) maintenant

preservation [prɛzə'veɪʃən] N préservation *f*, conservation *f*

preservative [prɪ'zə:vətɪv] N agent *m* de conservation

preserve [prɪ'zə:v] VT (*keep safe*) préserver, protéger; (*maintain*) conserver, garder; (*food*) mettre en conserve ▶ N (*for game, fish*) réserve *f*; (*often pl: jam*) confiture *f*; (: *fruit*) fruits *mpl* en conserve

preshrunk [pri:'ʃrʌŋk] ADJ irrétrécissable

preside [prɪ'zaɪd] VI présider

presidency ['prɛzɪdənsɪ] N présidence *f*

president ['prɛzɪdənt] N président(e); (*US: of company*) président-directeur général, PDG *m*

presidential [prɛzɪ'dɛnʃl] ADJ présidentiel(le)

press [prɛs] N (*tool, machine, newspapers*) presse *f*; (*for wine*) pressoir *m*; (*crowd*) cohue *f*, foule *f* ▶ VT (*push*) appuyer sur; (*squeeze*) presser, serrer; (*clothes: iron*) repasser; (*pursue*) talonner; (*insist*): **to ~ sth on sb** presser qn d'accepter qch; (*urge, entreat*): **to ~ sb to do** *or* **into doing sth** pousser qn à faire qch ▶ VI appuyer, peser; se presser; **we are pressed for time** le temps nous manque; **to ~ for sth** faire pression pour obtenir qch; **to ~ sb for an answer** presser qn de répondre; **to ~ charges against sb** (*Law*) engager des poursuites contre qn; **to go to ~** (*newspaper*) aller à l'impression; **to be in the ~** (*being printed*) être sous presse; (*in the newspapers*) être dans le journal

▶ **press ahead** VI = **press on**

▶ **press on** VI continuer

press agency N agence *f* de presse

press clipping N coupure *f* de presse

press conference N conférence *f* de presse

press cutting N = **press clipping**

press-gang ['prɛsgæn] VT (*fig*): **to ~ sb into doing sth** faire pression sur qn pour qu'il fasse qch

pressing ['prɛsɪŋ] ADJ urgent(e), pressant(e) ▶ N repassage *m*

press officer N attaché(e) de presse

press release N communiqué *m* de presse

press stud N (*Brit*) bouton-pression *m*

press-up ['prɛsʌp] N (*Brit*) traction *f*

pressure ['prɛʃər] N pression *f*; (*stress*) tension *f* ▶ VT faire pression sur; **to put ~ on sb (to do sth)** faire pression sur qn (pour qu'il fasse qch)

pressure cooker N cocotte-minute® *f*

pressure gauge N manomètre *m*

pressure group N groupe *m* de pression

pressurize ['prɛʃəraɪz] VT pressuriser; (*Brit fig*): **to ~ sb (into doing sth)** faire pression sur qn (pour qu'il fasse qch)

pressurized ['prɛʃəraɪzd] ADJ pressurisé(e)

prestige [prɛs'ti:ʒ] N prestige *m*

prestigious [prɛs'tɪdʒəs] ADJ prestigieux(-euse)

presumably [prɪ'zju:məblɪ] ADV vraisemblablement; **~ he did it** c'est sans doute lui (qui a fait cela)

presume [prɪ'zju:m] VT présumer, supposer; **to ~ to do** (*dare*) se permettre de faire

presumption [prɪ'zʌmpʃən] N supposition *f*, présomption *f*; (*boldness*) audace *f*

presumptuous [prɪ'zʌmpʃəs] ADJ présomptueux(-euse)

presuppose [pri:sə'pəuz] VT présupposer

pre-tax [pri:'tæks] ADJ avant impôt(s)

pretence, (*US*) **pretense** [prɪ'tɛns] N (*claim*) prétention *f*; (*pretext*) prétexte *m*; **she is devoid of all ~** elle n'est pas du tout prétentieuse; **to make a ~ of doing** faire semblant de faire; **on** *or* **under the ~ of doing sth** sous prétexte de faire qch; **under false pretences** sous des prétextes fallacieux

pretend [prɪˈtɛnd] VT (*feign*) feindre, simuler
▶ VI (*feign*) faire semblant; (*claim*): **to ~ to sth**
prétendre à qch; **to ~ to do** faire semblant de
faire
pretense [prɪˈtɛns] N (*US*) = **pretence**
pretension [prɪˈtɛnʃən] N (*claim*) prétention *f*;
to have no pretensions to sth/to being sth
n'avoir aucune prétention à qch/à être qch
pretentious [prɪˈtɛnʃəs] ADJ prétentieux(-euse)
preterite [ˈprɛtərɪt] N prétérit *m*
pretext [ˈpriːtɛkst] N prétexte *m*; **on** or **under
the ~ of doing sth** sous prétexte de faire qch
pretty [ˈprɪtɪ] ADJ joli(e) ▶ ADV assez
prevail [prɪˈveɪl] VI (*win*) l'emporter, prévaloir;
(*be usual*) avoir cours; (*persuade*): **to ~ (up)on sb
to do** persuader qn de faire
prevailing [prɪˈveɪlɪŋ] ADJ (*widespread*)
courant(e), répandu(e); (*wind*) dominant(e)
prevalent [ˈprɛvələnt] ADJ répandu(e),
courant(e); (*fashion*) en vogue
prevarication [prɪværɪˈkeɪʃən] N (usage *m* de)
faux-fuyants *mpl*
prevent [prɪˈvɛnt] VT: **to ~ (from doing)**
empêcher (de faire)
preventable [prɪˈvɛntəbl] ADJ évitable
preventative [prɪˈvɛntətɪv] ADJ préventif(-ive)
prevention [prɪˈvɛnʃən] N prévention *f*
preventive [prɪˈvɛntɪv] ADJ préventif(-ive)
preview [ˈpriːvjuː] N (*of film*) avant-première *f*;
(*fig*) aperçu *m*
previous [ˈpriːvɪəs] ADJ (*last*) précédent(e);
(*earlier*) antérieur(e); (*question, experience*)
préalable; **I have a ~ engagement** je suis déjà
pris(e); **~ to doing** avant de faire
previously [ˈpriːvɪəslɪ] ADV précédemment,
auparavant
prewar [priːˈwɔːr] ADJ d'avant-guerre
prey [preɪ] N proie *f* ▶ VI: **to ~ on** s'attaquer à; **it
was preying on his mind** ça le rongeait or
minait
price [praɪs] N prix *m*; (*Betting: odds*) cote *f* ▶ VT
(*goods*) fixer le prix de; tarifer; **what is the ~ of
…?** combien coûte …?, quel est le prix de …?; **to
go up** or **rise in ~** augmenter; **to put a ~ on sth**
chiffrer qch; **to be priced out of the market**
(*article*) être trop cher pour soutenir la
concurrence; (*producer, nation*) ne pas pouvoir
soutenir la concurrence; **what ~ his promises
now?** (*BRIT*) que valent maintenant toutes ses
promesses?; **he regained his freedom, but at
a ~** il a retrouvé sa liberté, mais cela lui a coûté
cher
price control N contrôle *m* des prix
price-cutting [ˈpraɪskʌtɪŋ] N réductions *fpl* de
prix
priceless [ˈpraɪslɪs] ADJ sans prix, inestimable;
(*inf: amusing*) impayable
price list N tarif *m*
price range N gamme *f* de prix; **it's within my
~** c'est dans mes prix
price tag N étiquette *f*
price war N guerre *f* des prix
pricey [ˈpraɪsɪ] ADJ (*inf*) chérot *inv*
prick [prɪk] N (*sting*) piqûre *f*; (*inf!*) bitte *f* (!);

connard *m* (!) ▶ VT piquer; **to ~ up one's ears**
dresser or tendre l'oreille
prickle [ˈprɪkl] N (*of plant*) épine *f*; (*sensation*)
picotement *m*
prickly [ˈprɪklɪ] ADJ piquant(e), épineux(-euse);
(*fig: person*) irritable
prickly heat N fièvre *f* miliaire
prickly pear N figue *f* de Barbarie
pride [praɪd] N (*feeling proud*) fierté *f*; (*pej*) orgueil
m; (*self-esteem*) amour-propre *m* ▶ VT: **to ~ o.s.
on** se flatter de; s'enorgueillir de; **to take a ~
in** être (très) fier(-ère) de; **to take a ~ in doing**
mettre sa fierté à faire; **to have ~ of place**
(*BRIT*) avoir la place d'honneur
priest [priːst] N prêtre *m*
priestess [ˈpriːstɪs] N prêtresse *f*
priesthood [ˈpriːsthud] N prêtrise *f*, sacerdoce *m*
prig [prɪg] N poseur(-euse), fat *m*
prim [prɪm] ADJ collet monté *inv*, guindé(e)
prima facie [ˈpraɪməˈfeɪʃɪ] ADJ: **to have a ~ case**
(*Law*) avoir une affaire recevable
primal [ˈpraɪməl] ADJ (*first in time*) primitif(-ive);
(*first in importance*) primordial(e)
primarily [ˈpraɪmərɪlɪ] ADV principalement,
essentiellement
primary [ˈpraɪmərɪ] ADJ primaire; (*first in
importance*) premier(-ière), primordial(e) ▶ N
(*US: election*) (élection *f*) primaire *f*; *voir article*

> Aux États-Unis, les *primaries* constituent
> un processus de sélection préliminaire
> des candidats qui seront choisis par les
> principaux partis lors de la campagne
> électorale pour l'élection présidentielle.
> Elles ont lieu dans 35 États, de février à juin,
> l'année de l'élection. Chaque État envoie en
> juillet – août des *delegates* aux conventions
> démocrate et républicaine chargées de
> désigner leur candidat à la présidence.
> Ces *delegates* sont généralement choisis en
> fonction du nombre de voix obtenu par les
> candidats lors des *primaries*.

primary colour N couleur fondamentale
primary school N (*BRIT*) école *f* primaire;
voir article

> Les *primary schools* en Grande-Bretagne
> accueillent les enfants de 5 à 11 ans.
> Elles marquent le début du cycle scolaire
> obligatoire et elles comprennent deux
> sections: la section des petits (*infant school*)
> et la section des grands (*junior school*); voir
> *secondary school*.

primate N (*Rel*) [ˈpraɪmɪt] primat *m*; (*Zool*)
[ˈpraɪmeɪt] primate *m*
prime [praɪm] ADJ primordial(e),
fondamental(e); (*excellent*) excellent(e) ▶ VT
(*gun, pump*) amorcer; (*fig*) mettre au courant
▶ N: **in the ~ of life** dans la fleur de l'âge
Prime Minister N Premier ministre
primer [ˈpraɪmər] N (*book*) premier livre, manuel
m élémentaire; (*paint*) apprêt *m*
prime time N (*Radio, TV*) heure(s) *f(pl)* de grande
écoute
primeval [praɪˈmiːvl] ADJ primitif(-ive)
primitive [ˈprɪmɪtɪv] ADJ primitif(-ive)

primrose ['prɪmrəuz] N primevère f
primus® ['praɪməs], **primus stove**® N (BRIT)
réchaud m de camping
prince [prɪns] N prince m
princess [prɪn'sɛs] N princesse f
principal ['prɪnsɪpl] ADJ principal(e) ▶ N (head
teacher) directeur m, principal m; (in play) rôle
principal; (money) principal m
principality [prɪnsɪ'pælɪtɪ] N principauté f
principally ['prɪnsɪplɪ] ADV principalement
principle ['prɪnsɪpl] N principe m; **in ~** en
principe; **on ~** par principe
print [prɪnt] N (mark) empreinte f; (letters)
caractères mpl; (fabric) imprimé m; (Art) gravure
f, estampe f; (Phot) épreuve f ▶ VT imprimer;
(publish) publier; (write in capitals) écrire en
majuscules; **out of ~** épuisé(e)
▶ **print out** VT (Comput) imprimer
printed circuit board ['prɪntɪd-] N carte f à
circuit imprimé
printed matter ['prɪntɪd-] N imprimés mpl
printer ['prɪntər] N (machine) imprimante f;
(person) imprimeur m
printhead ['prɪnthɛd] N tête f d'impression
printing ['prɪntɪŋ] N impression f
printing press N presse f typographique
printout ['prɪntaut] N (Comput) sortie f
imprimante
print wheel N marguerite f
prior ['praɪər] ADJ antérieur(e), précédent(e);
(more important) prioritaire ▶ N (Rel) prieur m
▶ ADV: **~ to doing** avant de faire; **without ~
notice** sans préavis; **to have a ~ claim to sth**
avoir priorité pour qch
priority [praɪ'ɔrɪtɪ] N priorité f; **to have** or **take
~ over sth/sb** avoir la priorité sur qch/qn
priory ['praɪərɪ] N prieuré m
prise [praɪz] VT: **to ~ open** forcer
prism ['prɪzəm] N prisme m
prison ['prɪzn] N prison f ▶ CPD pénitentiaire
prison camp N camp m de prisonniers
prisoner ['prɪznər] N prisonnier(-ière); **the ~ at
the bar** l'accusé(e); **to take sb ~** faire qn
prisonnier
prisoner of war N prisonnier(-ière) de guerre
prissy ['prɪsɪ] ADJ bégueule
pristine ['prɪstiːn] ADJ virginal(e)
privacy ['prɪvəsɪ] N intimité f, solitude f
private ['praɪvɪt] ADJ (not public) privé(e);
(personal) personnel(le); (house, car, lesson)
particulier(-ière); (quiet: place) tranquille ▶ N
soldat m de deuxième classe; **"~"** (on envelope)
"personnelle"; (on door) "privé"; **in ~** en privé;
in (his) ~ life dans sa vie privée; **he is a very ~
person** il est très secret; **to be in ~ practice**
être médecin (or dentiste etc) non conventionné;
~ hearing (Law) audience f à huis-clos
private detective N détective privé
private enterprise N entreprise privée
private eye N détective privé
private limited company N (BRIT) société f à
participation restreinte (non cotée en Bourse)
privately ['praɪvɪtlɪ] ADV en privé; (within oneself)
intérieurement

private parts NPL parties (génitales)
private property N propriété privée
private school N école privée
privatize ['praɪvɪtaɪz] VT privatiser
privet ['prɪvɪt] N troène m
privilege ['prɪvɪlɪdʒ] N privilège m
privileged ['prɪvɪlɪdʒd] ADJ privilégié(e); **to be ~
to do sth** avoir le privilège de faire qch
privy ['prɪvɪ] ADJ: **to be ~ to** être au courant de
privy council N conseil privé; voir article

> Le privy council existe en Angleterre depuis
> l'avènement des Normands. À l'époque, ses
> membres étaient les conseillers privés du
> roi, mais en 1688 le cabinet les a supplantés.
> Les ministres du cabinet sont aujourd'hui
> automatiquement conseillers du roi, et ce
> titre est également accordé aux personnes
> qui ont occupé de hautes fonctions en
> politique, dans le clergé ou dans les milieux
> juridiques. Les pouvoirs de ces conseillers en
> tant que tels sont maintenant limités.

prize [praɪz] N prix m ▶ ADJ (example, idiot)
parfait(e); (bull, novel) primé(e) ▶ VT priser, faire
grand cas de
prize-fighter ['praɪzfaɪtər] N boxeur
professionnel
prize-giving ['praɪzgɪvɪŋ] N distribution f des
prix
prize money N argent m du prix
prizewinner ['praɪzwɪnər] N gagnant(e)
prizewinning ['praɪzwɪnɪŋ] ADJ gagnant(e);
(novel, essay etc) primé(e)
PRO N ABBR = **public relations officer**
pro [prəu] N (inf: Sport) professionnel(le) ▶ PREP
pro; **pros** NPL: **the pros and cons** le pour et le
contre
pro- [prəu] PREFIX (in favour of) pro-
pro-active [prəu'æktɪv] ADJ dynamique
probability [prɔbə'bɪlɪtɪ] N probabilité f; **in all
~** très probablement
probable ['prɔbəbl] ADJ probable; **it is ~/hardly
~ that ...** il est probable/peu probable que ...
probably ['prɔbəblɪ] ADV probablement
probate ['prəubɪt] N (Law) validation f,
homologation f
probation [prə'beɪʃən] N (in employment) (période
f d')essai m; (Law) liberté surveillée; (Rel)
noviciat m, probation f; **on ~** (employee) à l'essai;
(Law) en liberté surveillée
probationary [prə'beɪʃənrɪ] ADJ (period) d'essai
probe [prəub] N (Med, Space) sonde f; (enquiry)
enquête f, investigation f ▶ VT sonder, explorer
probity ['prəubɪtɪ] N probité f
problem ['prɔbləm] N problème m; **to have
problems with the car** avoir des ennuis avec
la voiture; **what's the ~?** qu'y a-t-il?, quel est le
problème?; **I had no ~ in finding her** je n'ai
pas eu de mal à la trouver; **no ~!** pas de
problème!
problematic [prɔblə'mætɪk] ADJ problématique
problem-solving ['prɔbləmsɔlvɪŋ] N résolution f
de problèmes; **an approach to ~** une approche
en matière de résolution de problèmes
procedure [prə'siːdʒər] N (Admin, Law) procédure f;

(*method*) marche *f* à suivre, façon *f* de procéder
proceed [prə'si:d] vi (*go forward*) avancer; (*act*)
procéder; (*continue*): **to ~ (with)** continuer,
poursuivre; **to ~ to** aller à; passer à; **to ~ to do**
se mettre à faire; **I am not sure how to ~** je ne
sais pas exactement comment m'y prendre; **to
~ against sb** (*Law*) intenter des poursuites
contre qn
proceedings [prə'si:dɪŋz] NPL (*measures*)
mesures *fpl*; (*Law: against sb*) poursuites *fpl*;
(*meeting*) réunion *f*, séance *f*; (*records*) compte
rendu; actes *mpl*
proceeds ['prəusi:dz] NPL produit *m*, recette *f*
process ['prəusɛs] N processus *m*; (*method*)
procédé *m* ▶ vt traiter; (*go in procession*) défiler; **in ~** en cours; **we are in
the ~ of doing** nous sommes en train de faire
processed cheese ['prəusɛst-] N ≈ fromage
fondu
processing ['prəusɛsɪŋ] N traitement *m*
procession [prə'sɛʃən] N défilé *m*, cortège *m*;
funeral ~ (*on foot*) cortège funèbre; (*in cars*)
convoi *m* mortuaire
pro-choice [prəu'tʃɔɪs] ADJ en faveur de
l'avortement
proclaim [prə'kleɪm] vt déclarer, proclamer
proclamation [prɔklə'meɪʃən] N proclamation *f*
proclivity [prə'klɪvɪtɪ] N inclination *f*
procrastinate [prəu'kræstɪneɪt] vi faire traîner
les choses, vouloir tout remettre au lendemain
procrastination [prəukræstɪ'neɪʃən] N
procrastination *f*
procreation [prəukrɪ'eɪʃən] N procréation *f*
Procurator Fiscal ['prɔkjureɪtə-] N (*SCOTTISH*)
≈ procureur *m* (*de la République*)
procure [prə'kjuər] vt (*for o.s.*) se procurer; (*for sb*)
procurer
procurement [prə'kjuəmənt] N achat *m*,
approvisionnement *m*
prod [prɔd] vt pousser ▶ N (*push, jab*) petit coup,
poussée *f*
prodigal ['prɔdɪgl] ADJ prodigue
prodigious [prə'dɪdʒəs] ADJ prodigieux(-euse)
prodigy ['prɔdɪdʒɪ] N prodige *m*
produce N ['prɔdju:s] (*Agr*) produits *mpl* ▶ vt
[prə'dju:s] produire; (*show*) présenter; (*cause*)
provoquer, causer; (*Theat*) monter, mettre en
scène; (*TV: programme*) réaliser; (*: play, film*)
mettre en scène; (*Radio: programme*) réaliser;
(*: play*) mettre en ondes
producer [prə'dju:sər] N (*Theat*) metteur *m* en
scène; (*Agr, Comm, Cine*) producteur *m*; (*TV: of
programme*) réalisateur *m*; (*: of play, film*) metteur
en scène; (*Radio: of programme*) réalisateur; (*: of
play*) metteur en ondes
product ['prɔdʌkt] N produit *m*
production [prə'dʌkʃən] N production *f*;
(*Theat*) mise *f* en scène; **to put into ~** (*goods*)
entreprendre la fabrication de
production agreement N (*US*) accord *m* de
productivité
production line N chaîne *f* (de fabrication)
production manager N directeur(-trice) de la
production

productive [prə'dʌktɪv] ADJ productif(-ive)
productivity [prɔdʌk'tɪvɪtɪ] N productivité *f*
productivity agreement N (*BRIT*) accord *m* de
productivité
productivity bonus N prime *f* de rendement
Prof. [prɔf] ABBR (= *professor*) Prof
profane [prə'feɪn] ADJ sacrilège; (*lay*) profane
profess [prə'fɛs] vt professer; **I do not ~ to be
an expert** je ne prétends pas être spécialiste
professed [prə'fɛst] ADJ (*self-declared*) déclaré(e)
profession [prə'fɛʃən] N profession *f*; **the
professions** les professions libérales
professional [prə'fɛʃənl] N professionnel(le)
▶ ADJ professionnel(le); (*work*) de professionnel;
he's a ~ man il exerce une profession libérale;
to take ~ advice consulter un spécialiste
professionalism [prə'fɛʃnəlɪzəm] N
professionnalisme *m*
professionally [prə'fɛʃnəlɪ] ADV
professionnellement; (*Sport: play*) en
professionnel; **I only know him ~** je n'ai avec
lui que des relations de travail
professor [prə'fɛsər] N professeur *m* (*titulaire
d'une chaire*); (*US: teacher*) professeur *m*
professorship [prə'fɛsəʃɪp] N chaire *f*
proffer ['prɔfər] vt (*hand*) tendre; (*remark*) faire;
(*apologies*) présenter
proficiency [prə'fɪʃənsɪ] N compétence *f*,
aptitude *f*
proficient [prə'fɪʃənt] ADJ compétent(e), capable
profile ['prəufaɪl] N profil *m*; **to keep a high/
low ~** (*fig*) rester or être très en évidence/
discret(-ète)
profit ['prɔfɪt] N (*from trading*) bénéfice *m*;
(*advantage*) profit *m* ▶ vi: **to ~ (by or from)**
profiter (de); **~ and loss account** compte *m* de
profits et pertes; **to make a ~** faire un or des
bénéfice(s); **to sell sth at a ~** vendre qch à
profit
profitability [prɔfɪtə'bɪlɪtɪ] N rentabilité *f*
profitable ['prɔfɪtəbl] ADJ lucratif(-ive),
rentable; (*fig: beneficial*) avantageux(-euse);
(*: meeting*) fructueux(-euse)
profit centre N centre *m* de profit
profiteering [prɔfɪ'tɪərɪŋ] N (*pej*)
mercantilisme *m*
profit-making ['prɔfɪtmeɪkɪŋ] ADJ à but lucratif
profit margin N marge *f* bénéficiaire
profit-sharing ['prɔfɪtʃɛərɪŋ] N intéressement
m aux bénéfices
profits tax N (*BRIT*) impôt *m* sur les bénéfices
profligate ['prɔflɪgɪt] ADJ (*behaviour, act*)
dissolu(e); (*person*) débauché(e); (*extravagant*):
~ (with) prodigue (de)
pro forma ['prəu'fɔ:mə] ADJ: **~ invoice** facture *f*
pro-forma
profound [prə'faund] ADJ profond(e)
profuse [prə'fju:s] ADJ abondant(e)
profusely [prə'fju:slɪ] ADV abondamment;
(*thank etc*) avec effusion
profusion [prə'fju:ʒən] N profusion *f*,
abondance *f*
progeny ['prɔdʒɪnɪ] N progéniture *f*;
descendants *mpl*

P

prognosis [prɔgˈnəusɪs] (*pl* **prognoses** [prɔgˈnəusiːz]) N pronostic *m*
programme, (*US*) **program** [ˈprəugræm] N (*Comput*) programme *m*; (*Radio, TV*) émission *f* ▶ VT programmer
programmer [ˈprəugræməʳ] N programmeur(-euse)
programming, (*US*) **programing** [ˈprəugræmɪŋ] N programmation *f*
programming language, (*US*) **programing language** N langage *m* de programmation
progress N [ˈprəugrɛs] progrès *m(pl)* ▶ VI [prəˈgrɛs] progresser, avancer; **in ~** en cours; **to make ~** progresser, faire des progrès, être en progrès; **as the match progressed** au fur et à mesure que la partie avançait
progression [prəˈgrɛʃən] N progression *f*
progressive [prəˈgrɛsɪv] ADJ progressif(-ive); (*person*) progressiste
progressively [prəˈgrɛsɪvlɪ] ADV progressivement
progress report N (*Med*) bulletin *m* de santé; (*Admin*) rapport *m* d'activité; rapport sur l'état (d'avancement) des travaux
prohibit [prəˈhɪbɪt] VT interdire, défendre; **to ~ sb from doing sth** défendre *or* interdire à qn de faire qch; **"smoking prohibited"** "défense de fumer"
prohibition [prəuɪˈbɪʃən] N prohibition *f*
prohibitive [prəˈhɪbɪtɪv] ADJ (*price etc*) prohibitif(-ive)
project N [ˈprɔdʒɛkt] (*plan*) projet *m*, plan *m*; (*venture*) opération *f*, entreprise *f*; (*Scol: research*) étude *f*, dossier *m* ▶ VT [prəˈdʒɛkt] projeter ▶ VI [prəˈdʒɛkt] (*stick out*) faire saillie, s'avancer
projectile [prəˈdʒɛktaɪl] N projectile *m*
projection [prəˈdʒɛkʃən] N projection *f*; (*overhang*) saillie *f*
projectionist [prəˈdʒɛkʃənɪst] N (*Cine*) projectionniste *mf*
projection room N (*Cine*) cabine *f* de projection
projector [prəˈdʒɛktəʳ] N (*Cine etc*) projecteur *m*
proletarian [prəulɪˈtɛərɪən] ADJ prolétarien(ne) ▶ N prolétaire *mf*
proletariat [prəulɪˈtɛərɪət] N prolétariat *m*
pro-life [prəuˈlaɪf] ADJ contre l'avortement
proliferate [prəˈlɪfəreɪt] VI proliférer
proliferation [prəlɪfəˈreɪʃən] N prolifération *f*
prolific [prəˈlɪfɪk] ADJ prolifique
prologue [ˈprəulɔg] N prologue *m*
prolong [prəˈlɔŋ] VT prolonger
prom [prɔm] N ABBR = **promenade**; **promenade concert**; (*US: ball*) bal *m* d'étudiants; **the Proms** *série de concerts de musique classique*; *voir article*

En Grande-Bretagne, un *promenade concert* ou *prom* est un concert de musique classique, ainsi appelé car, à l'origine, le public restait debout et se promenait au lieu de rester assis. De nos jours, une partie du public reste debout, mais il y a également des places assises (plus chères). Les *Proms* les plus connus sont les Proms londoniens. La dernière séance (*the Last Night of the Proms*)

est un grand événement médiatique où se jouent des airs traditionnels et patriotiques. Aux États-Unis et au Canada, le *prom* ou *promenade* est un bal organisé par le lycée.

promenade [prɔməˈnɑːd] N (*by sea*) esplanade *f*, promenade *f*
promenade concert N concert *m* (de musique classique)
promenade deck N (*Naut*) pont *m* promenade
prominence [ˈprɔmɪnəns] N proéminence *f*; importance *f*
prominent [ˈprɔmɪnənt] ADJ (*standing out*) proéminent(e); (*important*) important(e); **he is ~ in the field of ...** il est très connu dans le domaine de ...
prominently [ˈprɔmɪnəntlɪ] ADV (*display, set*) bien en évidence; **he figured ~ in the case** il a joué un rôle important dans l'affaire
promiscuity [prɔmɪsˈkjuːɪtɪ] N (*sexual*) légèreté *f* de mœurs
promiscuous [prəˈmɪskjuəs] ADJ (*sexually*) de mœurs légères
promise [ˈprɔmɪs] N promesse *f* ▶ VT, VI promettre; **to make sb a ~** faire une promesse à qn; **a young man of ~** un jeune homme plein d'avenir; **to ~ well** il promet
promising [ˈprɔmɪsɪŋ] ADJ prometteur(-euse)
promissory note [ˈprɔmɪsərɪ-] N billet *m* à ordre
promontory [ˈprɔməntrɪ] N promontoire *m*
promote [prəˈməut] VT promouvoir; (*venture, event*) organiser, mettre sur pied; (*new product*) lancer; **the team was promoted to the second division** (*BRIT Football*) l'équipe est montée en 2ᵉ division
promoter [prəˈməutəʳ] N (*of event*) organisateur(-trice)
promotion [prəˈməuʃən] N promotion *f*
prompt [prɔmpt] ADJ rapide ▶ N (*Comput*) message *m* (de guidage) ▶ VT inciter; (*cause*) entraîner, provoquer; (*Theat*) souffler (son rôle *or* ses répliques) à; **they're very ~** (*punctual*) ils sont ponctuels; **at 8 o'clock ~** à 8 heures précises; **he was ~ to accept** il a tout de suite accepté; **to ~ sb to do** inciter *or* pousser qn à faire
prompter [ˈprɔmptəʳ] N (*Theat*) souffleur *m*
promptly [ˈprɔmptlɪ] ADV (*quickly*) rapidement, sans délai; (*on time*) ponctuellement
promptness [ˈprɔmptnɪs] N rapidité *f*; promptitude *f*; ponctualité *f*
prone [prəun] ADJ (*lying*) couché(e) (face contre terre); (*liable*): **~ to** enclin(e) à; **to be ~ to illness** être facilement malade; **to be ~ to an illness** être sujet à une maladie; **she is ~ to burst into tears if ...** elle a tendance à tomber en larmes si ...
prong [prɔŋ] N pointe *f*; (*of fork*) dent *f*
pronoun [ˈprəunaun] N pronom *m*
pronounce [prəˈnauns] VT prononcer ▶ VI: **to ~ (up)on** se prononcer sur; **how do you ~ it?** comment est-ce que ça se prononce?; **they pronounced him unfit to drive** ils l'ont déclaré inapte à la conduite

pronounced [prə'naunst] ADJ (*marked*) prononcé(e)

pronouncement [prə'naunsmənt] N déclaration f

pronunciation [prənʌnsɪ'eɪʃən] N prononciation f

proof [pru:f] N preuve f; (*test, of book, Phot*) épreuve f; (*of alcohol*) degré m ▶ ADJ: **~ against** à l'épreuve de ▶ VT (*BRIT: tent, anorak*) imperméabiliser; **to be 70° ~** = titrer 40 degrés

proofreader ['pru:fri:dəʳ] N correcteur(-trice) (d'épreuves)

prop [prɔp] N support m, étai m; (*fig*) soutien m ▶ VT (*also*: **prop up**) étayer, soutenir; **props** NPL accessoires mpl; **to ~ sth against** (*lean*) appuyer qch contre or à

Prop. ABBR (*Comm*) = **proprietor**

propaganda [prɔpə'gændə] N propagande f

propagation [prɔpə'geɪʃən] N propagation f

propel [prə'pɛl] VT propulser, faire avancer

propeller [prə'pɛləʳ] N hélice f

propelling pencil [prə'pɛlɪŋ-] N (*BRIT*) porte-mine m inv

propensity [prə'pɛnsɪtɪ] N propension f

proper ['prɔpəʳ] ADJ (*suited, right*) approprié(e), bon (bonne); (*seemly*) correct(e), convenable; (*authentic*) vrai(e), véritable; (*inf: real*) fini(e), vrai(e); (*referring to place*): **the village ~** le village proprement dit; **to go through the ~ channels** (*Admin*) passer par la voie officielle

properly ['prɔpəlɪ] ADV correctement, convenablement; (*really*) bel et bien

proper noun N nom m propre

property ['prɔpətɪ] N (*possessions*) biens mpl; (*house etc*) propriété f; (*land*) terres fpl, domaine m; (*Chem etc: quality*) propriété f; **it's their ~** cela leur appartient, c'est leur propriété

property developer N (*BRIT*) promoteur immobilier

property owner N propriétaire m

property tax N impôt foncier

prophecy ['prɔfɪsɪ] N prophétie f

prophesy ['prɔfɪsaɪ] VT prédire ▶ VI prophétiser

prophet ['prɔfɪt] N prophète m

prophetic [prə'fɛtɪk] ADJ prophétique

proportion [prə'pɔ:ʃən] N proportion f; (*share*) part f; partie f ▶ VT proportionner; **proportions** NPL (*size*) dimensions fpl; **to be in/out of ~ to** or **with sth** être à la mesure de/hors de proportion avec qch; **to see sth in ~** (*fig*) ramener qch à de justes proportions

proportional [prə'pɔ:ʃənl], **proportionate** [prə'pɔ:ʃənɪt] ADJ proportionnel(le)

proportional representation N (*Pol*) représentation proportionnelle

proposal [prə'pəuzl] N proposition f, offre f; (*plan*) projet m; (*of marriage*) demande f en mariage

propose [prə'pəuz] VT proposer, suggérer; (*have in mind*): **to ~ sth/to do** or **doing sth** envisager qch/de faire qch ▶ VI faire sa demande en mariage; **to ~ to do** avoir l'intention de faire

proposer [prə'pəuzəʳ] N (*BRIT: of motion etc*) auteur m

proposition [prɔpə'zɪʃən] N proposition f; **to make sb a ~** faire une proposition à qn

propound [prə'paund] VT proposer, soumettre

proprietary [prə'praɪətərɪ] ADJ de marque déposée; **~ article** article m or produit m de marque; **~ brand** marque déposée

proprietor [prə'praɪətəʳ] N propriétaire mf

propriety [prə'praɪətɪ] N (*seemliness*) bienséance f, convenance f

propulsion [prə'pʌlʃən] N propulsion f

pro rata [prəu'rɑ:tə] ADV au prorata

prosaic [prəu'zeɪɪk] ADJ prosaïque

Pros. Atty. ABBR (*US*) = **prosecuting attorney**

proscribe [prə'skraɪb] VT proscrire

prose [prəuz] N prose f; (*Scol: translation*) thème m

prosecute ['prɔsɪkju:t] VT poursuivre

prosecuting attorney ['prɔsɪkju:tɪŋ-] N (*US*) procureur m

prosecution [prɔsɪ'kju:ʃən] N poursuites fpl judiciaires; (*accusing side: in criminal case*) accusation f; (: *in civil case*) la partie plaignante

prosecutor ['prɔsɪkju:təʳ] N (*lawyer*) procureur m; (*also*: **public prosecutor**) ministère public; (*US: plaintiff*) plaignant(e)

prospect N ['prɔspɛkt] perspective f; (*hope*) espoir m, chances fpl ▶ VT, VI [prə'spɛkt] prospecter; **prospects** NPL (*for work etc*) possibilités fpl d'avenir, débouchés mpl; **we are faced with the ~ of leaving** nous risquons de devoir partir; **there is every ~ of an early victory** tout laisse prévoir une victoire rapide

prospecting [prə'spɛktɪŋ] N prospection f

prospective [prə'spɛktɪv] ADJ (*possible*) éventuel(le); (*future*) futur(e)

prospector [prə'spɛktəʳ] N prospecteur m; **gold ~** chercheur m d'or

prospectus [prə'spɛktəs] N prospectus m

prosper ['prɔspəʳ] VI prospérer

prosperity [prɔ'spɛrɪtɪ] N prospérité f

prosperous ['prɔspərəs] ADJ prospère

prostate ['prɔsteɪt] N (*also*: **prostate gland**) prostate f

prostitute ['prɔstɪtju:t] N prostituée f; **male ~** prostitué m

prostitution [prɔstɪ'tju:ʃən] N prostitution f

prostrate ADJ ['prɔstreɪt] prosterné(e); (*fig*) prostré(e) ▶ VT [prɔ'streɪt]: **to ~ o.s. (before sb)** se prosterner (devant qn)

protagonist [prə'tægənɪst] N protagoniste m

protect [prə'tɛkt] VT protéger

protection [prə'tɛkʃən] N protection f; **to be under sb's ~** être sous la protection de qn

protectionism [prə'tɛkʃənɪzəm] N protectionnisme m

protection racket N racket m

protective [prə'tɛktɪv] ADJ protecteur(-trice); (*clothing*) de protection; **~ custody** (*Law*) détention préventive

protector [prə'tɛktəʳ] N protecteur(-trice)

protégé ['prəuteʒeɪ] N protégé m

protégée ['prəuteʒeɪ] N protégée f

protein ['prəuti:n] N protéine f

pro tem [prəu'tɛm] ADV ABBR (= *pro tempore: for the time being*) provisoirement

P

737

protest N ['prəutɛst] protestation *f* ▶ VI [prə'tɛst]: **to ~ against/about** protester contre/à propos de ▶ VT [prə'tɛst] protester de; **to ~ (that)** protester que

Protestant ['prɒtɪstənt] ADJ, N protestant(e)

protester, protestor [prə'tɛstəʳ] N (*in demonstration*) manifestant(e)

protest march N manifestation *f*

protocol ['prəutəkɒl] N protocole *m*

prototype ['prəutətaɪp] N prototype *m*

protracted [prə'træktɪd] ADJ prolongé(e)

protractor [prə'træktəʳ] N (*Geom*) rapporteur *m*

protrude [prə'truːd] VI avancer, dépasser

protuberance [prə'tjuːbərəns] N protubérance *f*

proud [praud] ADJ fier(-ère); (*pej*) orgueilleux(-euse); **to be ~ to do sth** être fier de faire qch; **to do sb ~** (*inf*) faire honneur à qn; **to do o.s. ~** (*inf*) ne se priver de rien

proudly ['praudlɪ] ADV fièrement

prove [pruːv] VT prouver, démontrer ▶ VI: **to ~ correct** *etc* s'avérer juste *etc*; **to ~ o.s.** montrer ce dont on est capable; **to ~ o.s./itself (to be) useful** *etc* se montrer *or* se révéler utile *etc*; **he was proved right in the end** il s'est avéré qu'il avait raison

proverb ['prɒvəːb] N proverbe *m*

proverbial [prə'vəːbɪəl] ADJ proverbial(e)

provide [prə'vaɪd] VT fournir; **to ~ sb with sth** fournir qch à qn; **to be provided with** (*person*) disposer de; (*thing*) être équipé(e) or muni(e) de
▶ **provide for** VT FUS (*person*) subvenir aux besoins de; (*future event*) prévoir

provided [prə'vaɪdɪd] CONJ: **~ (that)** à condition que+*sub*

Providence ['prɒvɪdəns] N la Providence

providing [prə'vaɪdɪŋ] CONJ à condition que+*sub*

province ['prɒvɪns] N province *f*; (*fig*) domaine *m*

provincial [prə'vɪnʃəl] ADJ provincial(e)

provision [prə'vɪʒən] N (*supply*) provision *f*; (*supplying*) fourniture *f*; approvisionnement *m*; (*stipulation*) disposition *f*; **provisions** NPL (*food*) provisions *fpl*; **to make ~ for** (*one's future*) assurer; (*one's family*) assurer l'avenir de; **there's no ~ for this in the contract** le contrat ne prévoit pas cela

provisional [prə'vɪʒənl] ADJ provisoire ▶ N: **P~** (*IRISH Pol*) Provisional *m* (*membre de la tendance activiste de l'IRA*)

provisional licence N (*BRIT Aut*) permis *m* provisoire

provisionally [prə'vɪʒnəlɪ] ADV provisoirement

proviso [prə'vaɪzəu] N condition *f*; **with the ~ that** à la condition (expresse) que

Provo ['prɒvəu] N ABBR (*inf*) = **Provisional**

provocation [prɒvə'keɪʃən] N provocation *f*

provocative [prə'vɒkətɪv] ADJ provocateur(-trice), provocant(e)

provoke [prə'vəuk] VT provoquer; **to ~ sb to sth/to do** or **into doing sth** pousser qn à qch/à faire qch

provoking [prə'vəukɪŋ] ADJ énervant(e), exaspérant(e)

provost ['prɒvəst] N (*BRIT: of university*) principal *m*; (*SCOTTISH*) maire *m*

prow [prau] N proue *f*

prowess ['prauɪs] N prouesse *f*

prowl [praul] VI (*also*: **prowl about, prowl around**) rôder ▶ N: **to be on the ~** rôder

prowler ['prauləʳ] N rôdeur(-euse)

proximity [prɒk'sɪmɪtɪ] N proximité *f*

proxy ['prɒksɪ] N procuration *f*; **by ~** par procuration

PRP N ABBR (= *performance related pay*) salaire *m* au rendement

prude [pruːd] N prude *f*

prudence ['pruːdns] N prudence *f*

prudent ['pruːdnt] ADJ prudent(e)

prudish ['pruːdɪʃ] ADJ prude, pudibond(e)

prune [pruːn] N pruneau *m* ▶ VT élaguer

pry [praɪ] VI: **to ~ into** fourrer son nez dans

PS N ABBR (= *postscript*) PS *m*

psalm [sɑːm] N psaume *m*

PSAT N ABBR (*US*) = **Preliminary Scholastic Aptitude Test**

PSBR N ABBR (*BRIT*: = *public sector borrowing requirement*) besoins *mpl* d'emprunts des pouvoirs publics

pseud [sjuːd] N (*BRIT inf*: *intellectually*) pseudo-intello *m*; (: *socially*) snob *mf*

pseudo- ['sjuːdəu] PREFIX pseudo-

pseudonym ['sjuːdənɪm] N pseudonyme *m*

PSHE N ABBR (*BRIT Scol*: = *personal, social and health education*) cours d'éducation personnelle, sanitaire et sociale préparant à la vie adulte

PST ABBR (*US*: = *Pacific Standard Time*) heure d'hiver du Pacifique

PSV N ABBR (*BRIT*) = **public service vehicle**

psyche ['saɪkɪ] N psychisme *m*

psychiatric [saɪkɪ'ætrɪk] ADJ psychiatrique

psychiatrist [saɪ'kaɪətrɪst] N psychiatre *mf*

psychiatry [saɪ'kaɪətrɪ] N psychiatrie *f*

psychic ['saɪkɪk] ADJ (*also*: **psychical**) (méta)psychique; (*person*) doué(e) de télépathie *or* d'un sixième sens

psycho ['saɪkəu] N (*inf*) psychopathe *mf*

psychoanalysis [saɪkəuə'nælɪsɪs] (*pl* **psychoanalyses** [-siːz]) N psychanalyse *f*

psychoanalyst [saɪkəu'ænəlɪst] N psychanalyste *mf*

psychological [saɪkə'lɒdʒɪkl] ADJ psychologique

psychologist [saɪ'kɒlədʒɪst] N psychologue *mf*

psychology [saɪ'kɒlədʒɪ] N psychologie *f*

psychopath ['saɪkəupæθ] N psychopathe *mf*

psychosis [saɪ'kəusɪs] (*pl* **psychoses** [-siːz]) N psychose *f*

psychosomatic [saɪkəusə'mætɪk] ADJ psychosomatique

psychotherapy [saɪkəu'θɛrəpɪ] N psychothérapie *f*

psychotic [saɪ'kɒtɪk] ADJ, N psychotique *mf*

PT N ABBR (*BRIT*: = *physical training*) EPS *f*

pt ABBR = **pint; pints; point; points**

Pt. ABBR (*in place names*: = *Point*) Pte

PTA N ABBR = **Parent-Teacher Association**

Pte. ABBR (*BRIT Mil*) = **private**

PTO ABBR (= *please turn over*) TSVP

PTV ABBR (*US*) = **pay television**
pub [pʌb] N ABBR (= *public house*) pub *m*
pub crawl N (*BRIT inf*): **to go on a ~** faire la tournée des bars
puberty ['pjuːbətɪ] N puberté *f*
pubic ['pjuːbɪk] ADJ pubien(ne), du pubis
public ['pʌblɪk] ADJ public(-ique) ▶ N public *m*;
in ~ en public; **the general ~** le grand public;
to be ~ knowledge être de notoriété publique;
to go ~ (*Comm*) être coté(e) en Bourse; **to make ~ rendre public**
public address system N (système *m* de) sonorisation *f*, sono *f* (*inf*)
publican ['pʌblɪkən] N patron *m* or gérant *m* de pub
publication [pʌblɪ'keɪʃən] N publication *f*
public company N société *f* anonyme
public convenience N (*BRIT*) toilettes *fpl*
public holiday N (*BRIT*) jour férié
public house N (*BRIT*) pub *m*
publicity [pʌb'lɪsɪtɪ] N publicité *f*
publicize ['pʌblɪsaɪz] VT (*make known*) faire connaître, rendre public; (*advertise*) faire de la publicité pour
public limited company N ≈ société *f* anonyme (SA) (*cotée en Bourse*)
publicly ['pʌblɪklɪ] ADV publiquement, en public
public opinion N opinion publique
public ownership N: **to be taken into ~** être nationalisé(e), devenir propriété de l'État
public prosecutor N ≈ procureur *m* (*de la République*); **~'s office** parquet *m*
public relations N relations publiques (RP)
public relations officer N responsable *mf* des relations publiques
public school N (*BRIT*) école privée; (*US*) école publique; *voir article*

> Une *public school* est un établissement d'enseignement secondaire privé. Bon nombre d'entre elles sont des pensionnats. Beaucoup ont également une école primaire qui leur est rattachée (une *prep* ou *preparatory school*) pour préparer les élèves au cycle secondaire. Ces écoles sont en général prestigieuses, et les frais de scolarité sont très élevés dans les plus connues (Westminster, Eton, Harrow). Beaucoup d'élèves vont ensuite à l'université, et un grand nombre entre à Oxford ou à Cambridge. Les grands industriels, les députés et les hauts fonctionnaires sortent souvent de ces écoles. Aux États-Unis, le terme *public school* désigne tout simplement une école publique gratuite.

public sector N secteur public
public service vehicle N (*BRIT*) véhicule affecté au transport de personnes
public-spirited [pʌblɪk'spɪrɪtɪd] ADJ qui fait preuve de civisme
public transport, (*US*) **public transportation** N transports *mpl* en commun
public utility N service public
public works NPL travaux publics
publish ['pʌblɪʃ] VT publier

publisher ['pʌblɪʃəʳ] N éditeur *m*
publishing ['pʌblɪʃɪŋ] N (*industry*) édition *f*; (*of a book*) publication *f*
publishing company N maison *f* d'édition
pub lunch N repas *m* de bistrot
puce [pjuːs] ADJ puce
puck [pʌk] N lutin *m*; (*Ice Hockey*) palet *m*
pucker ['pʌkəʳ] VT plisser
pudding ['pudɪŋ] N (*BRIT*: *dessert*) dessert *m*, entremets *m*; (*sweet dish*) pudding *m*, gâteau *m*; (*sausage*) boudin *m*; **rice ~** riz *m* au lait; **black ~**, (*US*) **blood ~** boudin (noir)
puddle ['pʌdl] N flaque *f* d'eau
puerile ['pjuəraɪl] ADJ puéril(e)
Puerto Rico ['pwəːtəuˈriːkəu] N Porto Rico *f*
puff [pʌf] N bouffée *f* ▶ VT: **to ~ one's pipe** tirer sur sa pipe; (*also*: **puff out**: *sails, cheeks*) gonfler ▶ VI sortir par bouffées; (*pant*) haleter; **to ~ out smoke** envoyer des bouffées de fumée
puffed [pʌft] ADJ (*inf*: *out of breath*) tout(e) essoufflé(e)
puffin ['pʌfɪn] N macareux *m*
puff pastry, (*US*) **puff paste** N pâte feuilletée
puffy ['pʌfɪ] ADJ bouffi(e), boursouflé(e)
pugnacious [pʌgˈneɪʃəs] ADJ pugnace, batailleur(-euse)
pull [pul] N (*of moon, magnet, the sea etc*) attraction *f*; (*fig*) influence *f*; (*tug*): **to give sth a ~** tirer sur qch ▶ VT tirer; (*trigger*) presser; (*strain*: *muscle, tendon*) se claquer ▶ VI tirer; **to ~ a face** faire une grimace; **to ~ to pieces** mettre en morceaux; **to ~ one's punches** (*also fig*) ménager son adversaire; **to ~ one's weight** y mettre du sien; **to ~ o.s. together** se ressaisir; **to ~ sb's leg** (*fig*) faire marcher qn; **to ~ strings (for sb)** intervenir (en faveur de qn)
▶ **pull about** VT (*BRIT*: *handle roughly*: *object*) maltraiter; (: *person*) malmener
▶ **pull apart** VT séparer; (*break*) mettre en pièces, démantibuler
▶ **pull away** VI (*vehicle*: *move off*) partir; (*draw back*) s'éloigner
▶ **pull back** VT (*lever etc*) tirer sur; (*curtains*) ouvrir ▶ VI (*refrain*) s'abstenir; (*Mil*: *withdraw*) se retirer
▶ **pull down** VT baisser, abaisser; (*house*) démolir; (*tree*) abattre
▶ **pull in** VI (*Aut*) se ranger; (*Rail*) entrer en gare
▶ **pull off** VT enlever, ôter; (*deal etc*) conclure
▶ **pull out** VI démarrer, partir; (*withdraw*) se retirer; (*Aut*: *come out of line*) déboîter ▶ VT (*from bag, pocket*) sortir; (*remove*) arracher; (*withdraw*) retirer
▶ **pull over** VI (*Aut*) se ranger
▶ **pull round** VI (*unconscious person*) revenir à soi; (*sick person*) se rétablir
▶ **pull through** VI s'en sortir
▶ **pull up** VI (*stop*) s'arrêter ▶ VT remonter; (*uproot*) déraciner, arracher; (*stop*) arrêter
pulley ['pulɪ] N poulie *f*
pull-out ['pulaut] N (*of forces etc*) retrait *m* ▶ CPD (*magazine, pages*) détachable
pullover ['puləuvəʳ] N pull-over *m*, tricot *m*
pulp [pʌlp] N (*of fruit*) pulpe *f*; (*for paper*) pâte *f* à papier; (*pej*: *also*: **pulp magazines** *etc*) presse *f* à

sensation or de bas étage; **to reduce sth to (a)**
~ réduire qch en purée
pulpit ['pulpɪt] N chaire f
pulsate [pʌl'seɪt] vi battre, palpiter; (music) vibrer
pulse [pʌls] N (of blood) pouls m; (of heart)
battement m; (of music, engine) vibrations fpl;
pulses NPL (Culin) légumineuses fpl; **to feel** or
take sb's ~ prendre le pouls à qn
pulverize ['pʌlvəraɪz] vt pulvériser
puma ['pju:mə] N puma m
pumice ['pʌmɪs] N (also: **pumice stone**) pierre f
ponce
pummel ['pʌml] vt rouer de coups
pump [pʌmp] N pompe f; (shoe) escarpin m ▶ vt
pomper; (fig: inf) faire parler; **to ~ sb for
information** essayer de soutirer des
renseignements à qn
▶ **pump up** vt gonfler
pumpkin ['pʌmpkɪn] N potiron m, citrouille f
pun [pʌn] N jeu m de mots, calembour m
punch [pʌntʃ] N (blow) coup m de poing; (fig:
force) vivacité f, mordant m; (tool) poinçon m;
(drink) punch m ▶ vt (make a hole in) poinçonner,
perforer; (hit): **to ~ sb/sth** donner un coup de
poing à qn/sur qch; **to ~ a hole (in)** faire un
trou (dans)
▶ **punch in** vi (US) pointer (en arrivant)
▶ **punch out** vi (US) pointer (en partant)
punch card, punched card [pʌntʃt-] N carte
perforée
punch-drunk ['pʌntʃdrʌŋk] ADJ (BRIT) sonné(e)
punch line N (of joke) conclusion f
punch-up ['pʌntʃʌp] N (BRIT inf) bagarre f
punctual ['pʌŋktjuəl] ADJ ponctuel(le)
punctuality [pʌŋktju'ælɪtɪ] N ponctualité f
punctually ['pʌŋktjuəlɪ] ADV ponctuellement;
it will start ~ at 6 cela commencera à 6 heures
précises
punctuate ['pʌŋktjueɪt] vt ponctuer
punctuation [pʌŋktju'eɪʃən] N ponctuation f
punctuation mark N signe m de ponctuation
puncture ['pʌŋktʃəʳ] N (BRIT) crevaison f ▶ vt
crever; **I have a ~** (Aut) j'ai (un pneu) crevé
pundit ['pʌndɪt] N individu m qui pontifie,
pontife m
pungent ['pʌndʒənt] ADJ piquant(e); (fig)
mordant(e), caustique
punish ['pʌnɪʃ] vt punir; **to ~ sb for sth/for
doing sth** punir qn de qch/d'avoir fait qch
punishable ['pʌnɪʃəbl] ADJ punissable
punishing ['pʌnɪʃɪŋ] ADJ (fig: exhausting)
épuisant(e) ▶ N punition f
punishment ['pʌnɪʃmənt] N punition f,
châtiment m; (fig: inf): **to take a lot of** ~ (boxer)
encaisser; (car, person etc) être mis(e) à dure
épreuve
punk [pʌŋk] N (person: also: **punk rocker**) punk
mf; (music: also: **punk rock**) le punk; (US inf:
hoodlum) voyou m
punt [pʌnt] N (boat) bachot m; (IRISH) livre
irlandaise ▶ vi (BRIT: bet) parier
punter ['pʌntəʳ] N (BRIT inf: gambler)
parieur(-euse); Monsieur m tout le monde;
type m

puny ['pju:nɪ] ADJ chétif(-ive)
pup [pʌp] N chiot m
pupil ['pju:pl] N élève mf; (of eye) pupille f
puppet ['pʌpɪt] N marionnette f, pantin m
puppet government N gouvernement m
fantoche
puppy ['pʌpɪ] N chiot m, petit chien
purchase ['pə:tʃɪs] N achat m; (grip) prise f ▶ vt
acheter; **to get a ~ on** trouver appui sur
purchase order N ordre m d'achat
purchase price N prix m d'achat
purchaser ['pə:tʃɪsəʳ] N acheteur(-euse)
purchase tax N (BRIT) taxe f à l'achat
purchasing power ['pə:tʃɪsɪŋ-] N pouvoir m
d'achat
pure [pjuəʳ] ADJ pur(e); **a ~ wool jumper** un pull
en pure laine; ~ **and simple** pur(e) et simple
purebred ['pjuəbred] ADJ de race
purée ['pjuəreɪ] N purée f
purely ['pjuəlɪ] ADV purement
purge [pə:dʒ] N (Med) purge f; (Pol) épuration f,
purge f ▶ vt purger; (fig) épurer, purger
purification [pjuərɪfɪ'keɪʃən] N purification f
purify ['pjuərɪfaɪ] vt purifier, épurer
purist ['pjuərɪst] N puriste mf
puritan ['pjuərɪtən] N puritain(e)
puritanical [pjuərɪ'tænɪkl] ADJ puritain(e)
purity ['pjuərɪtɪ] N pureté f
purl [pə:l] N maille f à l'envers ▶ vt tricoter à
l'envers
purloin [pə:'lɔɪn] vt dérober
purple ['pə:pl] ADJ violet(te); (face) cramoisi(e)
purport [pə:'pɔ:t] vi: **to ~ to be/do** prétendre
être/faire
purpose ['pə:pəs] N intention f, but m; **on ~**
exprès; **for illustrative purposes** à titre
d'illustration; **for teaching purposes** dans un
but pédagogique; **for the purposes of this
meeting** pour cette réunion; **to no ~** en pure
perte
purpose-built ['pə:pəs'bɪlt] ADJ (BRIT) fait(e) sur
mesure
purposeful ['pə:pəsful] ADJ déterminé(e),
résolu(e)
purposely ['pə:pəslɪ] ADV exprès
purr [pə:ʳ] N ronronnement m ▶ vi ronronner
purse [pə:s] N (BRIT: for money) porte-monnaie m
inv, bourse f; (US: handbag) sac m (à main) ▶ vt
serrer, pincer
purser ['pə:səʳ] N (Naut) commissaire m du bord
purse snatcher [-'snætʃəʳ] N (US) voleur m à
l'arraché
pursue [pə'sju:] vt poursuivre; (pleasures)
rechercher; (inquiry, matter) approfondir
pursuer [pə'sju:əʳ] N poursuivant(e)
pursuit [pə'sju:t] N poursuite f; (occupation)
occupation f, activité f; **scientific pursuits**
recherches fpl scientifiques; **in (the) ~ of sth** à
la recherche de qch
purveyor [pə'veɪəʳ] N fournisseur m
pus [pʌs] N pus m
push [puʃ] N poussée f; (effort) gros effort; (drive)
énergie f ▶ vt pousser; (button) appuyer sur;
(thrust): **to ~ sth (into)** enfoncer qch (dans); (fig:

product) mettre en avant, faire de la publicité pour ▸ vɪ pousser; appuyer; **to ~ a door open/ shut** pousser une porte (pour l'ouvrir/pour la fermer); **"~"** (*on door*) "pousser"; (*on bell*) "appuyer"; **to ~ for** (*better pay, conditions*) réclamer; **to be pushed for time/money** être à court de temps/d'argent; **she is pushing fifty** (*inf*) elle frise la cinquantaine; **at a ~** (Brit *inf*) à la limite, à la rigueur

▸ **push aside** vt écarter

▸ **push in** vɪ s'introduire de force

▸ **push off** vɪ (*inf*) filer, ficher le camp

▸ **push on** vɪ (*continue*) continuer

▸ **push over** vt renverser

▸ **push through** vt (*measure*) faire voter ▸ vɪ (*in crowd*) se frayer un chemin

▸ **push up** vt (*total, prices*) faire monter

push-bike ['pʊʃbaɪk] N (Brit) vélo *m*

push-button ['pʊʃbʌtn] N bouton(-poussoir *m*) *m*

pushchair ['pʊʃtʃɛəʳ] N (Brit) poussette *f*

pusher ['pʊʃəʳ] N (*also:* **drug pusher**) revendeur(-euse) (de drogue), ravitailleur(-euse) (en drogue)

pushover ['pʊʃəʊvəʳ] N (*inf*): **it's a ~** c'est un jeu d'enfant

push-up ['pʊʃʌp] N (US) traction *f*

pushy ['pʊʃɪ] ADJ (*pej*) arriviste

pussy ['pʊsɪ], **pussy-cat** ['pʊsɪkæt] N (*inf*) minet *m*

put [pʊt] (*pt, pp ~*) vt mettre; (*place*) poser, placer; (*say*) dire, exprimer; (*a question*) poser; (*case, view*) exposer, présenter; (*estimate*) estimer; **to ~ sb in a good/bad mood** mettre qn de bonne/mauvaise humeur; **to ~ sb to bed** mettre qn au lit, coucher qn; **to ~ sb to a lot of trouble** déranger qn; **how shall I ~ it?** comment dirais-je?, comment dire?; **to ~ a lot of time into sth** passer beaucoup de temps à qch; **to ~ money on a horse** miser sur un cheval; **I ~ it to you that ...** (Brit) je (vous) suggère que ..., je suis d'avis que ...; **to stay ~** ne pas bouger

▸ **put about** vɪ (*Naut*) virer de bord ▸ vt (*rumour*) faire courir

▸ **put across** vt (*ideas etc*) communiquer; faire comprendre

▸ **put aside** vt mettre de côté

▸ **put away** vt (*store*) ranger

▸ **put back** vt (*replace*) remettre, replacer; (*postpone*) remettre; (*delay, watch, clock*) retarder; **this will ~ us back ten years** cela nous ramènera dix ans en arrière

▸ **put by** vt (*money*) mettre de côté, économiser

▸ **put down** vt (*parcel etc*) poser, déposer; (*pay*) verser; (*in writing*) mettre par écrit, inscrire; (*suppress: revolt etc*) réprimer, écraser; (*attribute*) attribuer; (*animal*) abattre; (*cat, dog*) faire piquer

▸ **put forward** vt (*ideas*) avancer, proposer; (*date, watch, clock*) avancer

▸ **put in** vt (*gas, electricity*) installer; (*complaint*) soumettre; (*time, effort*) consacrer

▸ **put in for** vt fus (*job*) poser sa candidature pour; (*promotion*) solliciter

▸ **put off** vt (*light etc*) éteindre; (*postpone*)

remettre à plus tard, ajourner; (*discourage*) dissuader

▸ **put on** vt (*clothes, lipstick, CD*) mettre; (*light etc*) allumer; (*play etc*) monter; (*extra bus, train etc*) mettre en service; (*food, meal: provide*) servir; (: *cook*) mettre à cuire *or* à chauffer; (*weight*) prendre; (*assume: accent, manner*) prendre; (: *airs*) se donner, prendre; (*inf: tease*) faire marcher; (*inform, indicate*): **to ~ sb on to sb/sth** indiquer qn/qch à qn; **to ~ the brakes on** freiner

▸ **put out** vt (*take outside*) mettre dehors; (*one's hand*) tendre; (*news, rumour*) faire courir, répandre; (*light etc*) éteindre; (*person: inconvenience*) déranger, gêner; (Brit: *dislocate*) se démettre ▸ vɪ (*Naut*): **to ~ out to sea** prendre le large; **to ~ out from Plymouth** quitter Plymouth

▸ **put through** vt (Tel: *caller*) mettre en communication; (: *call*) passer; (*plan*) faire accepter; **~ me through to Miss Blair** passez-moi Miss Blair

▸ **put together** vt mettre ensemble; (*assemble: furniture*) monter, assembler; (: *meal*) préparer

▸ **put up** vt (*raise*) lever, relever, remonter; (*pin up*) afficher; (*hang*) accrocher; (*build*) construire, ériger; (*tent*) monter; (*umbrella*) ouvrir; (*increase*) augmenter; (*accommodate*) loger; (*incite*): **to ~ sb up to doing sth** pousser qn à faire qch; **to ~ sth up for sale** mettre qch en vente

▸ **put upon** vt fus: **to be ~ upon** (*imposed on*) se laisser faire

▸ **put up with** vt fus supporter

putrid ['pjuːtrɪd] ADJ putride

putt [pʌt] vt, vɪ putter ▸ N putt *m*

putter ['pʌtəʳ] N (*Golf*) putter *m*

putting green ['pʌtɪŋ-] N green *m*

putty ['pʌtɪ] N mastic *m*

put-up ['pʊtʌp] ADJ: **~ job** coup monté

puzzle ['pʌzl] N énigme *f*, mystère *m*; (*game*) jeu *m*, casse-tête *m*; (*jigsaw*) puzzle *m*; (*also:* **crossword puzzle**) mots croisés ▸ vt intriguer, rendre perplexe ▸ vɪ se creuser la tête; **to ~ over** chercher à comprendre

puzzled ['pʌzld] ADJ perplexe; **to be ~ about sth** être perplexe au sujet de qch

puzzling ['pʌzlɪŋ] ADJ déconcertant(e), inexplicable

PVC N ABBR (= *polyvinyl chloride*) PVC *m*

Pvt. ABBR (US *Mil*) = **private**

pw ABBR (= *per week*) p. sem.

PX N ABBR (US *Mil*) = **post exchange**

pygmy ['pɪgmɪ] N pygmée *mf*

pyjamas [pɪ'dʒɑːməz] NPL (Brit) pyjama *m*; **a pair of ~** un pyjama

pylon ['paɪlən] N pylône *m*

pyramid ['pɪrəmɪd] N pyramide *f*

Pyrenean [pɪrə'niːən] ADJ pyrénéen(ne), des Pyrénées

Pyrenees [pɪrə'niːz] NPL Pyrénées *fpl*

Pyrex® ['paɪrɛks] N Pyrex® *m* ▸ CPD: **~ dish** plat *m* en Pyrex

python ['paɪθən] N python *m*

Qq

Q, q [kjuː] N (*letter*) Q, q m; **Q for Queen** Q comme Quintal

Qatar [kæˈtɑːʳ] N Qatar m, Katar m

QC N ABBR = **Queen's Counsel**; *voir article*

En Angleterre, un *QC* ou *Queen's Counsel* (ou *KC* pour *King's Counsel*, sous le règne d'un roi) est un avocat qui reçoit un poste de haut fonctionnaire sur recommandation du *Lord Chancellor*. Il fait alors souvent suivre son nom des lettres *QC*, et lorsqu'il va au tribunal, il est toujours accompagné par un autre avocat (un *junior barrister*).

QED ABBR (= *quod erat demonstrandum*) CQFD

q.t. N ABBR (*inf*) = **quiet; on the q.t.** discrètement

qty ABBR (= *quantity*) qté

quack [kwæk] N (*of duck*) coin-coin m inv; (*pej: doctor*) charlatan m ▶ VI faire coin-coin

quad [kwɒd] N ABBR = **quadruplet; quadrangle**

quadrangle [ˈkwɒdræŋgl] N (*Math*) quadrilatère m; (*courtyard: abbr: quad*) cour f

quadruped [ˈkwɒdruped] N quadrupède m

quadruple [kwɒˈdruːpl] ADJ, N quadruple m ▶ VT, VI quadrupler

quadruplet [kwɒˈdruːplɪt] N quadruplé(e)

quagmire [ˈkwægmaɪəʳ] N bourbier m

quail [kweɪl] N (*Zool*) caille f ▶ VI: **to ~ at** or **before** reculer devant

quaint [kweɪnt] ADJ bizarre; (*old-fashioned*) désuet(-ète); (*picturesque*) au charme vieillot, pittoresque

quake [kweɪk] VI trembler ▶ N ABBR = **earthquake**

Quaker [ˈkweɪkəʳ] N quaker(esse)

qualification [kwɒlɪfɪˈkeɪʃən] N (*often pl: degree etc*) diplôme m; (*training*) qualification(s) f(pl); (*ability*) compétence(s) f(pl); (*limitation*) réserve f, restriction f; **what are your qualifications?** qu'avez-vous comme diplômes?; quelles sont vos qualifications?

qualified [ˈkwɒlɪfaɪd] ADJ (*trained*) qualifié(e); (*professionally*) diplômé(e); (*fit, competent*) compétent(e), qualifié(e); (*limited*) conditionnel(le); **it was a ~ success** ce fut un succès mitigé; **~ for/to do** qui a les diplômes requis pour/pour faire; qualifié pour/pour faire

qualify [ˈkwɒlɪfaɪ] VT qualifier; (*modify*) atténuer, nuancer; (*limit: statement*) apporter des réserves à ▶ VI: **to ~ (as)** obtenir son diplôme (de); **to ~ (for)** remplir les conditions requises (pour); (*Sport*) se qualifier (pour)

qualifying [ˈkwɒlɪfaɪɪŋ] ADJ: **~ exam** examen m d'entrée; **~ round** éliminatoires fpl

qualitative [ˈkwɒlɪtətɪv] ADJ qualitatif(-ive)

quality [ˈkwɒlɪtɪ] N qualité f ▶ CPD de qualité; **of good/poor ~** de bonne/mauvaise qualité

quality control N contrôle m de qualité

quality press N (BRIT): **the ~** la presse d'information; *voir article*

La *quality press* ou les *quality (news)papers* englobent les journaux sérieux, quotidiens ou hebdomadaires, par opposition aux journaux populaires (*tabloid press*). Ces journaux visent un public qui souhaite des informations détaillées sur un éventail très vaste de sujets et qui est prêt à consacrer beaucoup de temps à leur lecture. Les *quality newspapers* sont en général de grand format.

quality time N moments privilégiés

qualm [kwɑːm] N doute m; scrupule m; **to have qualms about sth** avoir des doutes sur qch; éprouver des scrupules à propos de qch

quandary [ˈkwɒndrɪ] N: **in a ~** devant un dilemme, dans l'embarras

quango [ˈkwæŋgəu] N ABBR (BRIT: = *quasi-autonomous non-governmental organization*) commission nommée par le gouvernement

quantify [ˈkwɒntɪfaɪ] VT quantifier

quantitative [ˈkwɒntɪtətɪv] ADJ quantitatif(-ive)

quantity [ˈkwɒntɪtɪ] N quantité f; **in ~** en grande quantité

quantity surveyor N (BRIT) métreur vérificateur

quantum leap [ˈkwɒntəm-] N (*fig*) bond m en avant

quarantine [ˈkwɒrntiːn] N quarantaine f

quark [kwɑːk] N quark m

quarrel [ˈkwɒrl] N querelle f, dispute f ▶ VI se disputer, se quereller; **to have a ~ with sb** se quereller avec qn; **I've no ~ with him** je n'ai rien contre lui; **I can't ~ with that** je ne vois rien à redire à cela

quarrelsome [ˈkwɒrəlsəm] ADJ querelleur(-euse)

quarry [ˈkwɒrɪ] N (*for stone*) carrière f; (*animal*) proie f, gibier m ▶ VT (*marble etc*) extraire

quart [kwɔːt] N ≈ litre m
quarter ['kwɔːtər] N quart m; (of year) trimestre m; (district) quartier m; (US, CANADA: 25 cents) (pièce f de) vingt-cinq cents mpl ▶ VT partager en quartiers or en quatre; (Mil) caserner, cantonner; **quarters** NPL logement m; (Mil) quartiers mpl, cantonnement m; **a ~ of an hour** un quart d'heure; **it's a ~ to 3**, (US) **it's a ~ of 3** il est 3 heures moins le quart; **it's a ~ past 3**, (US) **it's a ~ after 3** il est 3 heures et quart; **from all quarters** de tous côtés
quarterback ['kwɔːtəbæk] N (US Football) quarterback mf
quarter-deck ['kwɔːtədɛk] N (Naut) plage f arrière
quarter final N quart m de finale
quarterly ['kwɔːtəlɪ] ADJ trimestriel(le) ▶ ADV tous les trois mois ▶ N (Press) revue trimestrielle
quartermaster ['kwɔːtəmɑːstər] N (Mil) intendant m militaire de troisième classe; (Naut) maître m de manœuvre
quartet, quartette [kwɔːˈtɛt] N quatuor m; (jazz players) quartette m
quarto ['kwɔːtəu] ADJ, N in-quarto m inv
quartz [kwɔːts] N quartz m ▶ CPD de or en quartz; (watch, clock) à quartz
quash [kwɔʃ] VT (verdict) annuler, casser
quasi- ['kweɪzaɪ] PREFIX quasi- + noun; quasi, presque + adjective
quaver ['kweɪvər] N (BRIT Mus) croche f ▶ VI trembler
quay [kiː] N (also: **quayside**) quai m
Que. ABBR (CANADA) = **Quebec**
queasy ['kwiːzɪ] ADJ (stomach) délicat(e); **to feel ~** avoir mal au cœur
Quebec [kwɪˈbɛk] N (city) Québec; (province) Québec m
queen [kwiːn] N (gen) reine f; (Cards etc) dame f
queen mother N reine mère f
Queen's speech N (BRIT) discours m de la reine; voir article

> Le Queen's speech (ou King's speech) est le discours lu par le souverain à l'ouverture du Parliament, dans la House of Lords, en présence des lords et des députés. Il contient le programme de politique générale que propose le gouvernement pour la session, et il est préparé par le Premier ministre en consultation avec le cabinet.

queer [kwɪər] ADJ étrange, curieux(-euse); (suspicious) louche; (BRIT: sick): **I feel ~** je ne me sens pas bien ▶ N (!) homosexuel m
quell [kwɛl] VT réprimer, étouffer
quench [kwɛntʃ] VT (flames) éteindre; **to ~ one's thirst** se désaltérer
querulous ['kwɛrʊləs] ADJ (person) récriminateur(-trice); (voice) plaintif(-ive)
query ['kwɪərɪ] N question f; (doubt) doute m; (question mark) point m d'interrogation ▶ VT (disagree with, dispute) mettre en doute, questionner
quest [kwɛst] N recherche f, quête f
question ['kwɛstʃən] N question f ▶ VT (person) interroger; (plan, idea) mettre en question or en

doute; **to ask sb a ~**, **to put a ~ to sb** poser une question à qn; **to bring** or **call sth into ~** remettre qch en question; **the ~ is ...** la question est de savoir ...; **it's a ~ of doing** il s'agit de faire; **there's some ~ of doing** il est question de faire; **beyond ~** sans aucun doute; **out of the ~** hors de question
questionable ['kwɛstʃənəbl] ADJ discutable
questioner ['kwɛstʃənər] N personne f qui pose une question (or qui a posé la question etc)
questioning ['kwɛstʃənɪŋ] ADJ interrogateur(-trice) ▶ N interrogatoire m
question mark N point m d'interrogation
questionnaire [kwɛstʃəˈnɛər] N questionnaire m
queue [kjuː] (BRIT) N queue f, file f ▶ VI (also: **queue up**) faire la queue; **to jump the ~** passer avant son tour
quibble ['kwɪbl] VI ergoter, chicaner
quiche [kiːʃ] N quiche f
quick [kwɪk] ADJ rapide; (reply) prompt(e), rapide; (mind) vif (vive); (agile) agile, vif (vive) ▶ ADV vite, rapidement ▶ N: **cut to the ~** (fig) touché(e) au vif; **be ~!** dépêche-toi!; **to be ~ to act** agir tout de suite
quicken ['kwɪkən] VT accélérer, presser; (rouse) stimuler ▶ VI s'accélérer, devenir plus rapide
quick fix N solution f de fortune
quicklime ['kwɪklaɪm] N chaux vive
quickly ['kwɪklɪ] ADV (fast) vite, rapidement; (immediately) tout de suite
quickness ['kwɪknɪs] N rapidité f, promptitude f; (of mind) vivacité f
quicksand ['kwɪksænd] N sables mouvants
quickstep ['kwɪkstɛp] N fox-trot m
quick-tempered [kwɪkˈtɛmpəd] ADJ emporté(e)
quick-witted [kwɪkˈwɪtɪd] ADJ à l'esprit vif
quid [kwɪd] N pl inv (BRIT inf) livre f
quid pro quo ['kwɪdprəuˈkwəu] N contrepartie f
quiet ['kwaɪət] ADJ tranquille, calme; (not noisy: engine) silencieux(-euse); (reserved) réservé(e); (voice) bas(se); (not busy: day, business) calme; (ceremony, colour) discret(-ète) ▶ N tranquillité f, calme m; (silence) silence m ▶ VT, VI (US) = **quieten**; **keep ~!** tais-toi!; **on the ~** en secret, discrètement; **I'll have a ~ word with him** je lui en parlerai discrètement
quieten ['kwaɪətn], **quieten down** VI se calmer, s'apaiser ▶ VT calmer, apaiser
quietly ['kwaɪətlɪ] ADV tranquillement; (silently) silencieusement; (discreetly) discrètement
quietness ['kwaɪətnɪs] N tranquillité f, calme m; silence m
quill [kwɪl] N plume f (d'oie)
quilt [kwɪlt] N édredon m; (continental quilt) couette f
quin [kwɪn] N ABBR = **quintuplet**
quince [kwɪns] N coing m; (tree) cognassier m
quinine [kwɪˈniːn] N quinine f
quintet, quintette [kwɪnˈtɛt] N quintette m
quintuplet [kwɪnˈtjuːplɪt] N quintuplé(e)
quip [kwɪp] N remarque piquante or spirituelle, pointe f ▶ VT: **... he quipped** ... lança-t-il
quire ['kwaɪər] N ≈ main f (de papier)

q

quirk [kwə:k] N bizarrerie f; **by some ~ of fate** par un caprice du hasard

quirky ['kwɜ:kɪ] ADJ singulier(-ère)

quit [kwɪt] (pt, pp ~ or **quitted**) VT quitter ▶ VI (give up) abandonner, renoncer; (resign) démissionner; **to ~ doing** arrêter de faire; **~ stalling!** (US inf) arrête de te dérober!; **notice to ~** (BRIT) congé m (signifié au locataire)

quite [kwaɪt] ADV (rather) assez, plutôt; (entirely) complètement, tout à fait; **~ new** plutôt neuf; tout à fait neuf; **she's ~ pretty** elle est plutôt jolie; **I ~ understand** je comprends très bien; **~ a few of them** un assez grand nombre d'entre eux; **that's not ~ right** ce n'est pas tout à fait juste; **not ~ as many as last time** pas tout à fait autant que la dernière fois; **~ (so)!** exactement!

Quito ['ki:təu] N Quito

quits [kwɪts] ADJ: **~ (with)** quitte (envers); **let's call it ~** restons-en là

quiver ['kwɪvəʳ] VI trembler, frémir ▶ N (for arrows) carquois m

quiz [kwɪz] N (on TV) jeu-concours m (télévisé); (in magazine etc) test m de connaissances ▶ VT interroger

quizzical ['kwɪzɪkl] ADJ narquois(e)

quoits [kwɔɪts] NPL jeu m du palet

quorum ['kwɔ:rəm] N quorum m

quota ['kwəutə] N quota m

quotation [kwəu'teɪʃən] N citation f; (of shares etc) cote f, cours m; (estimate) devis m

quotation marks NPL guillemets mpl

quote [kwəut] N citation f; (estimate) devis m ▶ VT (sentence, author) citer; (price) donner, soumettre; (shares) coter ▶ VI: **to ~ from** citer; **to ~ for a job** établir un devis pour des travaux; **quotes** NPL (inverted commas) guillemets mpl; **in quotes** entre guillemets; **~ ... unquote** (in dictation) ouvrez les guillemets ... fermez les guillemets

quotient ['kwəuʃənt] N quotient m

qv ABBR (= quod vide: which see) voir

qwerty keyboard ['kwə:tɪ-] N clavier m QWERTY

Rr

R, r [ɑ:ʳ] N (letter) R, r m; **R for Robert**, (US) **R for Roger** R comme Raoul

R ABBR (= right) dr; (US Cine: = restricted) interdit aux moins de 17 ans; (US Pol) = **republican**; (BRIT) Rex, Regina; (= river) riv., fl; (= Réaumur (scale)) R

RA ABBR = **rear admiral** ▶ N ABBR (BRIT) = **Royal Academy; Royal Academician**

RAAF N ABBR = **Royal Australian Air Force**

Rabat [rə'bɑ:t] N Rabat

rabbi ['ræbaɪ] N rabbin m

rabbit ['ræbɪt] N lapin m ▶ VI: **to ~ (on)** (BRIT) parler à n'en plus finir

rabbit hole N terrier m (de lapin)

rabbit hutch N clapier m

rabble ['ræbl] N (pej) populace f

rabid ['ræbɪd] ADJ enragé(e)

rabies ['reɪbi:z] N rage f

RAC N ABBR (BRIT: = Royal Automobile Club) ≈ ACF m

raccoon, racoon [rə'ku:n] N raton m laveur

race [reɪs] N (species) race f; (competition, rush) course f ▶ VT (person) faire la course avec; (horse) faire courir; (engine) emballer ▶ VI (compete) faire la course, courir; (hurry) aller à toute vitesse, courir; (engine) s'emballer; (pulse) battre très vite; **the human ~** la race humaine; **to ~ in/out** etc entrer/sortir etc à toute vitesse

race car N (US) = **racing car**

race car driver N (US) = **racing driver**

racecourse ['reɪskɔ:s] N champ m de courses

racehorse ['reɪshɔ:s] N cheval m de course

racer ['reɪsəʳ] N (bike) vélo m de course

race relations NPL rapports mpl entre les races

racetrack ['reɪstræk] N piste f

racial ['reɪʃl] ADJ racial(e)

racialism ['reɪʃlɪzəm] N racisme m

racialist ['reɪʃlɪst] ADJ, N raciste (mf)

racing ['reɪsɪŋ] N courses fpl

racing car N (BRIT) voiture f de course

racing driver N (BRIT) pilote m de course

racism ['reɪsɪzəm] N racisme m

racist ['reɪsɪst] ADJ, N raciste mf

rack [ræk] N (for guns, tools) râtelier m; (for clothes) portant m; (for bottles) casier m; (also: **luggage rack**) filet m à bagages; (also: **roof rack**) galerie f; (also: **dish rack**) égouttoir m ▶ VT tourmenter; **magazine ~** porte-revues m inv; **shoe ~** étagère f à chaussures; **toast ~** porte-toast m; **to ~ one's brains** se creuser la cervelle; **to go to ~ and**

ruin (building) tomber en ruine; (business) péricliter
▶ **rack up** VT accumuler

racket ['rækɪt] N (for tennis) raquette f; (noise) tapage m, vacarme m; (swindle) escroquerie f; (organized crime) racket m

racketeer [rækɪ'tɪəʳ] N (esp US) racketteur m

racquet ['rækɪt] N raquette f

racy ['reɪsɪ] ADJ plein(e) de verve, osé(e)

RADA [rɑ:də] N ABBR (BRIT) = **Royal Academy of Dramatic Art**

radar ['reɪdɑ:ʳ] N radar m ▶ CPD radar inv

radar trap N (Aut: police) contrôle m radar

radial ['reɪdɪəl] ADJ (also: **radial-ply**) à carcasse radiale

radiance ['reɪdɪəns] N éclat m, rayonnement m

radiant ['reɪdɪənt] ADJ rayonnant(e); (Physics) radiant(e)

radiate ['reɪdɪeɪt] VT (heat) émettre, dégager ▶ VI (lines) rayonner

radiation [reɪdɪ'eɪʃən] N rayonnement m; (radioactive) radiation f

radiation sickness N mal m des rayons

radiator ['reɪdɪeɪtəʳ] N radiateur m

radiator cap N bouchon m de radiateur

radiator grill N (Aut) calandre f

radical ['rædɪkl] ADJ radical(e)

radii ['reɪdɪaɪ] NPL of **radius**

radio ['reɪdɪəu] N radio f ▶ VI: **to ~ to sb** envoyer un message radio à qn ▶ VT (information) transmettre par radio; (one's position) signaler par radio; (person) appeler par radio; **on the ~** à la radio

radioactive ['reɪdɪəu'æktɪv] ADJ radioactif(-ive)

radioactivity ['reɪdɪəuæk'tɪvɪtɪ] N radioactivité f

radio announcer N annonceur m

radio cassette N radiocassette m

radio-controlled ['reɪdɪəukən'trəuld] ADJ radioguidé(e)

radiographer [reɪdɪ'ɔɡrəfəʳ] N radiologue mf (technicien)

radiography [reɪdɪ'ɔɡrəfɪ] N radiographie f

radiologist [reɪdɪ'ɔlədʒɪst] N radiologue mf (médecin)

radiology [reɪdɪ'ɔlədʒɪ] N radiologie f

radio station N station f de radio

radio taxi N radio-taxi m

radiotelephone ['reɪdɪəu'tɛlɪfəun] N radiotéléphone m

radiotherapist ['reɪdɪəu'θɛrəpɪst] N radiothérapeute mf

radiotherapy ['reɪdɪəu'θɛrəpɪ] N radiothérapie f

radish ['rædɪʃ] N radis m

radium ['reɪdɪəm] N radium m

radius ['reɪdɪəs] (pl **radii** [-ɪaɪ]) N rayon m; (Anat) radius m; **within a ~ of 50 miles** dans un rayon de 50 milles

RAF N ABBR (BRIT) = **Royal Air Force**

raffia ['ræfɪə] N raphia m

raffish ['ræfɪʃ] ADJ dissolu(e), canaille

raffle ['ræfl] N tombola f ▸ VT mettre comme lot dans une tombola

raft [rɑːft] N (craft: also: **life raft**) radeau m; (logs) train m de flottage

rafter ['rɑːftə^r] N chevron m

rag [ræg] N chiffon m; (pej: newspaper) feuille f, torchon m; (for charity) attractions organisées par les étudiants au profit d'œuvres de charité ▸ VT (BRIT) chahuter, mettre en boîte; **rags** NPL haillons mpl; **in rags** (person) en haillons; (clothes) en lambeaux

rag-and-bone man [rægən'bəun-] N (irreg) chiffonnier m

ragbag ['rægbæg] N (fig) ramassis m

rag doll N poupée f de chiffon

rage [reɪdʒ] N (fury) rage f, fureur f ▸ VI (person) être fou (folle) de rage; (storm) faire rage, être déchaîné(e); **to fly into a ~** se mettre en rage; **it's all the ~** cela fait fureur

ragged ['rægɪd] ADJ (edge) inégal(e), qui accroche; (clothes) en loques; (cuff) effiloché(e); (appearance) déguenillé(e)

raging ['reɪdʒɪŋ] ADJ (sea, storm) en furie; (fever, pain) violent(e); **~ toothache** rage f de dents; **in a ~ temper** dans une rage folle

rag trade N (inf): **the ~** la confection

raid [reɪd] N (Mil) raid m; (criminal) hold-up m inv; (by police) descente f, rafle f ▸ VT faire un raid sur or un hold-up dans or une descente dans

raider ['reɪdə^r] N malfaiteur m

rail [reɪl] N (on stair) rampe f; (on bridge, balcony) balustrade f; (of ship) bastingage m; (for train) rail m; **rails** NPL rails mpl, voie ferrée; **by ~** en train, par le train

railcard ['reɪlkɑːd] N (BRIT) carte f de chemin de fer; **young person's ~** carte f jeune

railing ['reɪlɪŋ] N, **railings** ['reɪlɪŋz] NPL grille f

railway ['reɪlweɪ], (US) **railroad** ['reɪlrəud] N chemin m de fer; (track) voie f ferrée

railway engine N locomotive f

railway line N (BRIT) ligne f de chemin de fer; (track) voie ferrée

railwayman ['reɪlweɪmən] N (irreg) cheminot m

railway station N (BRIT) gare f

rain [reɪn] N pluie f ▸ VI pleuvoir; **in the ~** sous la pluie; **it's raining** il pleut; **it's raining cats and dogs** il pleut à torrents

rainbow ['reɪnbəu] N arc-en-ciel m

raincoat ['reɪnkəut] N imperméable m

raindrop ['reɪndrɔp] N goutte f de pluie

rainfall ['reɪnfɔːl] N chute f de pluie; (measurement) hauteur f des précipitations

rainforest ['reɪnfɔrɪst] N forêt tropicale

rainproof ['reɪnpruːf] ADJ imperméable

rainstorm ['reɪnstɔːm] N pluie torrentielle

rainwater ['reɪnwɔːtə^r] N eau f de pluie

rainy ['reɪnɪ] ADJ pluvieux(-euse)

raise [reɪz] N augmentation f ▸ VT (lift) lever; hausser; (end: siege, embargo) lever; (build) ériger; (increase) augmenter; (morale) remonter; (standards) améliorer; (a protest, doubt) provoquer, causer; (a question) soulever; (cattle, family) élever; (crop) faire pousser; (army, funds) rassembler; (loan) obtenir; **to ~ one's glass to sb/sth** porter un toast en l'honneur de qn/qch; **to ~ one's voice** élever la voix; **to ~ sb's hopes** donner de l'espoir à qn; **to ~ a laugh/a smile** faire rire/sourire

raisin ['reɪzn] N raisin sec

Raj [rɑːdʒ] N: **the ~** l'empire m (aux Indes)

rajah ['rɑːdʒə] N radja(h) m

rake [reɪk] N (tool) râteau m; (person) débauché m ▸ VT (garden) ratisser; (fire) tisonner; (with machine gun) balayer ▸ VI: **to ~ through** (fig: search) fouiller (dans)

rake-off ['reɪkɔf] N (inf) pourcentage m

rakish ['reɪkɪʃ] ADJ dissolu(e); cavalier(-ière)

rally ['rælɪ] N (Pol etc) meeting m, rassemblement m; (Aut) rallye m; (Tennis) échange m ▸ VT rassembler, rallier; (support) gagner ▸ VI se rallier; (sick person) aller mieux; (Stock Exchange) reprendre

▸ **rally round** VI venir en aide ▸ VT FUS se rallier à; venir en aide à

rallying point ['rælɪɪŋ-] N (Mil) point m de ralliement

RAM [ræm] N ABBR (Comput: = random access memory) mémoire vive

ram [ræm] N (push) enfoncer; (soil) tasser; (crash into: vehicle) emboutir; (: lamppost etc) percuter; (in battle) éperonner

Ramadan [ræmə'dæn] N Ramadan m

ramble ['ræmbl] N randonnée f ▸ VI (walk) se promener, faire une randonnée; (pej: also: **ramble on**) discourir, pérorer

rambler ['ræmblə^r] N promeneur(-euse), randonneur(-euse); (Bot) rosier grimpant

rambling ['ræmblɪŋ] ADJ (speech) décousu(e); (house) plein(e) de coins et de recoins; (Bot) grimpant(e)

RAMC N ABBR (BRIT) = **Royal Army Medical Corps**

ramification [ræmɪfɪ'keɪʃən] N ramification f

ramp [ræmp] N (incline) rampe f; (Aut) dénivellation f; (in garage) pont m; **on/off ~** (US Aut) bretelle f d'accès

rampage ['ræmpeɪdʒ] N: **to be on the ~** se déchaîner ▸ VI [ræm'peɪdʒ]: **they went rampaging through the town** ils ont envahi les rues et ont tout saccagé sur leur passage

rampant ['ræmpənt] ADJ (disease etc) qui sévit

rampart ['ræmpɑːt] N rempart m

ram raiding [-reɪdɪŋ] N pillage d'un magasin en enfonçant la vitrine avec une voiture volée

ramshackle ['ræmʃækl] ADJ (house) délabré(e); (car etc) déglingué(e)

RAN N ABBR = **Royal Australian Navy**
ran [ræn] PT of **run**
ranch [rɑːntʃ] N ranch m
rancher ['rɑːntʃəʳ] N (owner) propriétaire m de ranch; (ranch hand) cow-boy m
rancid ['rænsɪd] ADJ rance
rancour, (US) **rancor** ['ræŋkəʳ] N rancune f, rancœur f
R&B N ABBR = **rhythm and blues**
R&D N ABBR (= research and development) R-D f
random ['rændəm] ADJ fait(e) or établi(e) au hasard; (Comput, Math) aléatoire ▶ N: **at ~** au hasard
random access memory N (Comput) mémoire vive, RAM f
R&R N ABBR (US Mil) = **rest and recreation**
randy ['rændɪ] ADJ (Brit inf) excité(e); lubrique
rang [ræŋ] PT of **ring**
range [reɪndʒ] N (of mountains) chaîne f; (of missile, voice) portée f; (of products) choix m, gamme f; (also: **shooting range**) champ m de tir; (: indoor) stand m de tir; (also: **kitchen range**) fourneau m (de cuisine) ▶ VT (place) mettre en rang, placer; (roam) parcourir ▶ VI: **to ~ over** couvrir; **to ~ from ... to** aller de ... à; **price ~** éventail m des prix; **do you have anything else in this price ~?** avez-vous autre chose dans ces prix?; **within (firing) ~** à portée (de tir); **ranged left/right** (text) justifié à gauche/à droite
ranger ['reɪndʒəʳ] N garde m forestier
Rangoon [ræŋ'guːn] N Rangoon
rank [ræŋk] N rang m; (Mil) grade m; (Brit: also: **taxi rank**) station f de taxis ▶ VI: **to ~ among** compter or se classer parmi ▶ VT: **I ~ him sixth** je le place sixième ▶ ADJ (smell) nauséabond(e); (hypocrisy, injustice etc) flagrant(e); **he's a ~ outsider** il n'est vraiment pas dans la course; **the ranks** (Mil) la troupe; **the ~ and file** (fig) la masse, la base; **to close ranks** (Mil: fig) serrer les rangs
rankle ['ræŋkl] VI (insult) rester sur le cœur
ransack ['rænsæk] VT fouiller (à fond); (plunder) piller
ransom ['rænsəm] N rançon f; **to hold sb to ~** (fig) exercer un chantage sur qn
rant [rænt] VI fulminer
ranting ['ræntɪŋ] N invectives fpl
rap [ræp] N petit coup sec; tape f; (music) rap m ▶ VT (door) frapper sur or à; (table etc) taper sur
rape [reɪp] N viol m; (Bot) colza m ▶ VT violer
rape oil, rapeseed oil ['reɪpsiːd-] N huile f de colza
rapid ['ræpɪd] ADJ rapide
rapidity [rə'pɪdɪtɪ] N rapidité f
rapidly ['ræpɪdlɪ] ADV rapidement
rapids ['ræpɪdz] NPL (Geo) rapides mpl
rapist ['reɪpɪst] N auteur m d'un viol
rapport [ræ'pɔːʳ] N entente f
rapt [ræpt] ADJ (attention) extrême; **to be ~ in contemplation** être perdu(e) dans la contemplation
rapture ['ræptʃəʳ] N extase f, ravissement m; **to go into raptures over** s'extasier sur

rapturous ['ræptʃərəs] ADJ extasié(e); frénétique
rare [rɛəʳ] ADJ rare; (Culin: steak) saignant(e)
rarebit ['rɛəbɪt] N see **Welsh rarebit**
rarefied ['rɛərɪfaɪd] ADJ (air, atmosphere) raréfié(e)
rarely ['rɛəlɪ] ADV rarement
raring ['rɛərɪŋ] ADJ: **to be ~ to go** (inf) être très impatient(e) de commencer
rarity ['rɛərɪtɪ] N rareté f
rascal ['rɑːskl] N vaurien m
rash [ræʃ] ADJ imprudent(e), irréfléchi(e) ▶ N (Med) rougeur f, éruption f; (of events) série f (noire); **to come out in a ~** avoir une éruption
rasher ['ræʃəʳ] N fine tranche (de lard)
rasp [rɑːsp] N (tool) lime f ▶ VT (speak: also: **rasp out**) dire d'une voix grinçante
raspberry ['rɑːzbərɪ] N framboise f
raspberry bush N framboisier m
rasping ['rɑːspɪŋ] ADJ: **~ noise** grincement m
Rastafarian [ræstə'fɛərɪən] ADJ, N rastafari (mf)
rat [ræt] N rat m
ratable ['reɪtəbl] ADJ see **rateable value**
ratchet ['rætʃɪt] N: **~ wheel** roue f à rochet
rate [reɪt] N (ratio) taux m, pourcentage m; (speed) vitesse f, rythme m; (price) tarif m ▶ VT (price) évaluer, estimer; (people) classer; (deserve) mériter; **rates** NPL (Brit: property tax) impôts locaux; **to ~ sb/sth as** considérer qn/qch comme; **to ~ sb/sth among** classer qn/qch parmi; **to ~ sb/sth highly** avoir une haute opinion de qn/qch; **at a ~ of 60 kph** à une vitesse de 60 km/h; **at any ~** en tout cas; **~ of exchange** taux or cours m du change; **~ of flow** débit m; **~ of return** (taux de) rendement m; **pulse ~** fréquence f des pulsations
rateable value ['reɪtəbl-] N (Brit) valeur locative imposable
ratepayer ['reɪtpeɪəʳ] N (Brit) contribuable mf (payant les impôts locaux)
rather ['rɑːðəʳ] ADV (somewhat) assez, plutôt; (to some extent) un peu; **it's ~ expensive** c'est assez cher; (too much) c'est un peu cher; **there's ~ a lot** il y en a beaucoup; **I would** or **I'd ~ go** j'aimerais mieux or je préférerais partir; **I had ~ go** il vaudrait mieux que je parte; **I'd ~ not leave** j'aimerais mieux ne pas partir; **or ~** (more accurately) ou plutôt; **I ~ think he won't come** je crois bien qu'il ne viendra pas
ratification [rætɪfɪ'keɪʃən] N ratification f
ratify ['rætɪfaɪ] VT ratifier
rating ['reɪtɪŋ] N (assessment) évaluation f; (score) classement m; (Finance) cote f; (Naut: category) classe f; (: sailor: Brit) matelot m; **ratings** NPL (Radio) indice(s) m(pl) d'écoute; (TV) Audimat® m
ratio ['reɪʃɪəu] N proportion f; **in the ~ of 100 to 1** dans la proportion de 100 contre 1
ration ['ræʃən] N ration f ▶ VT rationner; **rations** NPL (food) vivres mpl
rational ['ræʃənl] ADJ raisonnable, sensé(e); (solution, reasoning) logique; (Med: person) lucide
rationale [ræʃə'nɑːl] N raisonnement m; justification f
rationalization [ræʃnəlaɪ'zeɪʃən] N rationalisation f

r

rationalize ['ræʃnəlaɪz] vt rationaliser; (*conduct*) essayer d'expliquer *or* de motiver

rationally ['ræʃnəlɪ] ADV raisonnablement; logiquement

rationing ['ræʃnɪŋ] N rationnement *m*

rat pack N (*Brit inf*) journalistes *mpl* de la presse à sensation

rat poison N mort-aux-rats *f inv*

rat race N foire *f* d'empoigne

rattan [ræ'tæn] N rotin *m*

rattle ['rætl] N (*of door, window*) battement *m*; (*of coins, chain*) cliquetis *m*; (*of train, engine*) bruit *m* de ferraille; (*for baby*) hochet *m*; (*of sports fan*) crécelle *f* ▶ vi cliqueter; (*car, bus*): **to ~ along** rouler en faisant un bruit de ferraille ▶ vt agiter (bruyamment); (*inf: disconcert*) décontenancer; (: *annoy*) embêter

rattlesnake ['rætlsneɪk] N serpent *m* à sonnettes

ratty ['rætɪ] ADJ (*inf*) en rogne

raucous ['rɔːkəs] ADJ rauque

raucously ['rɔːkəslɪ] ADV d'une voix rauque

raunchy ['rɔːntʃɪ] ADJ (*inf: voice, image, act*) sexy; (*scenes, film*) lubrique

ravage ['rævɪdʒ] vt ravager

ravages ['rævɪdʒɪz] NPL ravages *mpl*

rave [reɪv] vi (*in anger*) s'emporter; (*with enthusiasm*) s'extasier; (*Med*) délirer ▶ N (*inf: party*) rave *f*, soirée *f* techno ▶ ADJ (*scene, culture, music*) rave, techno ▶ CPD: **~ review** (*inf*) critique *f* dithyrambique

raven ['reɪvən] N grand corbeau

ravenous ['rævənəs] ADJ affamé(e)

ravine [rə'viːn] N ravin *m*

raving ['reɪvɪŋ] ADJ: **he's ~ mad** il est complètement cinglé

ravings ['reɪvɪŋz] NPL divagations *fpl*

ravioli [rævɪ'əʊlɪ] N ravioli *mpl*

ravish ['rævɪʃ] vt ravir

ravishing ['rævɪʃɪŋ] ADJ enchanteur(-eresse)

raw [rɔː] ADJ (*uncooked*) cru(e); (*not processed*) brut(e); (*sore*) à vif, irrité(e); (*inexperienced*) inexpérimenté(e); (*weather, day*) froid(e) et humide; (*inf: bad bargain*) sale coup *m*; **to get a ~ deal** (*inf: unfair treatment*) être traité(e) injustement; **~ materials** matières premières

Rawalpindi [rɔːl'pɪndɪ] N Rawalpindi

raw material N matière première

ray [reɪ] N rayon *m*; **~ of hope** lueur *f* d'espoir

rayon ['reɪɔn] N rayonne *f*

raze [reɪz] vt (*also*: **raze to the ground**) raser

razor ['reɪzəʳ] N rasoir *m*

razor blade N lame *f* de rasoir

razzle ['ræzl], **razzle-dazzle** ['ræzl'dæzl] N (*Brit inf*): **to go on the ~(-dazzle)** faire la bringue

razzmatazz ['ræzmə'tæz] N (*inf*) tralala *m*, tapage *m*

RCAF N ABBR = **Royal Canadian Air Force**

RCMP N ABBR = **Royal Canadian Mounted Police**

RCN N ABBR = **Royal Canadian Navy**

RD ABBR (*US*) = **rural delivery**

Rd ABBR = **road**

RDC N ABBR (*Brit*) = **rural district council**

RE N ABBR (*Brit*: = *religious education*) instruction religieuse; (*Brit Mil*) = **Royal Engineers**

re [riː] PREP concernant

reach [riːtʃ] N portée *f*, atteinte *f*; (*of river etc*) étendue *f* ▶ vt atteindre, arriver à; (*conclusion, decision*) parvenir à ▶ vi s'étendre; (*stretch out hand*): **to ~ up/down** etc (**for sth**) lever/baisser etc le bras (pour prendre qch); **to ~ sb by phone** joindre qn par téléphone; **out of/within ~** (*object*) hors de/à portée; **within easy ~ (of)** (*place*) à proximité (de), proche (de)
▶ **reach out** vt tendre ▶ vi: **to ~ out (for)** allonger le bras (pour prendre)

react [riː'ækt] vi réagir

reaction [riː'ækʃən] N réaction *f*

reactionary [riː'ækʃənrɪ] ADJ, N réactionnaire (*mf*)

reactor [riː'æktəʳ] N réacteur *m*

read [riːd] (*pt, pp* **~** [rɛd]) vi lire ▶ vt lire; (*understand*) comprendre, interpréter; (*study*) étudier; (*meter*) relever; (*subj: instrument etc*) indiquer, marquer; **to take sth as ~** (*fig*) considérer qch comme accepté; **do you ~ me?** (*Tel*) est-ce que vous me recevez?
▶ **read out** vt lire à haute voix
▶ **read over** vt relire
▶ **read through** vt (*quickly*) parcourir; (*thoroughly*) lire jusqu'au bout
▶ **read up, read up on** vt étudier

readable ['riːdəbl] ADJ facile *or* agréable à lire

reader ['riːdəʳ] N lecteur(-trice); (*book*) livre *m* de lecture; (*Brit: at university*) maître *m* de conférences

readership ['riːdəʃɪp] N (*of paper etc*) (nombre *m* de) lecteurs *mpl*

readily ['rɛdɪlɪ] ADV volontiers, avec empressement; (*easily*) facilement

readiness ['rɛdɪnɪs] N empressement *m*; **in ~** (*prepared*) prêt(e)

reading ['riːdɪŋ] N lecture *f*; (*understanding*) interprétation *f*; (*on instrument*) indications *fpl*

reading lamp N lampe *f* de bureau

reading room N salle *f* de lecture

readjust [riːə'dʒʌst] vt rajuster; (*instrument*) régler de nouveau ▶ vi (*person*): **to ~ (to)** se réadapter (à)

ready ['rɛdɪ] ADJ prêt(e); (*willing*) prêt, disposé(e); (*quick*) prompt(e); (*available*) disponible ▶ N: **at the ~** (*Mil*) prêt à faire feu; (*fig*) tout(e) prêt(e); **~ for use** prêt à l'emploi; **to be ~ to do sth** être prêt à faire qch; **when will my photos be ~?** quand est-ce que mes photos seront prêtes?; **to get ~** (*as vi*) se préparer; (*as vt*) préparer

ready cash N (argent *m*) liquide *m*

ready-cooked ['rɛdɪ'kukd] ADJ précuit(e)

ready-made ['rɛdɪ'meɪd] ADJ tout(e) fait(e)

ready-mix ['rɛdɪmɪks] N (*for cakes etc*) préparation *f* en sachet

ready reckoner [-'rɛknəʳ] N (*Brit*) barème *m*

ready-to-wear ['rɛdɪtə'wɛəʳ] ADJ (en) prêt-à-porter

reagent [riː'eɪdʒənt] N réactif *m*

real [rɪəl] ADJ (*world, life*) réel(le); (*genuine*)

véritable; (*proper*) vrai(e) ▸ ADV (*US inf: very*) vraiment; **in ~ life** dans la réalité

real ale N bière traditionnelle

real estate N biens fonciers *or* immobiliers

realism ['rɪəlɪzəm] N réalisme *m*

realist ['rɪəlɪst] N réaliste *mf*

realistic [rɪə'lɪstɪk] ADJ réaliste

reality [ri:'ælɪtɪ] N réalité *f*; **in ~** en réalité, en fait

reality TV N téléréalité *f*

realization [rɪəlaɪ'zeɪʃən] N (*awareness*) prise *f* de conscience; (*fulfilment: also: of asset*) réalisation *f*

realize ['rɪəlaɪz] VT (*understand*) se rendre compte de, prendre conscience de; (*a project, Comm: asset*) réaliser

really ['rɪəlɪ] ADV vraiment; **~?** vraiment?, c'est vrai?

realm [rɛlm] N royaume *m*; (*fig*) domaine *m*

real-time ['ri:ltaɪm] ADJ (*Comput*) en temps réel

realtor ['rɪəltɔːʳ] N (*US*) agent immobilier

ream [ri:m] N rame *f* (*de papier*); **reams** NPL (*inf: fig*) des pages et des pages

reap [ri:p] VT moissonner; (*fig*) récolter

reaper ['ri:pəʳ] N (*machine*) moissonneuse *f*

reappear [ri:ə'pɪəʳ] VI réapparaître, reparaître

reappearance [ri:ə'pɪərəns] N réapparition *f*

reapply [ri:ə'plaɪ] VI: **to ~ for** (*job*) faire une nouvelle demande d'emploi concernant; reposer sa candidature à; (*loan, grant*) faire une nouvelle demande de

reappraisal [ri:ə'preɪzl] N réévaluation *f*

rear [rɪəʳ] ADJ de derrière, arrière *inv*; (*Aut: wheel etc*) arrière ▸ N arrière *m*, derrière *m* ▸ VT (*cattle, family*) élever ▸ VI (*also: rear up: animal*) se cabrer

rear admiral N vice-amiral *m*

rear-engined ['rɪər'ɛndʒɪnd] ADJ (*Aut*) avec moteur à l'arrière

rearguard ['rɪəgɑːd] N arrière-garde *f*

rearmament [ri:'ɑːməmənt] N réarmement *m*

rearrange [ri:ə'reɪndʒ] VT réarranger

rear-view mirror N (*Aut*) rétroviseur *m*

rear-wheel drive N (*Aut*) traction *f* arrière

reason ['ri:zn] N raison *f* ▸ VI: **to ~ with sb** raisonner qn, faire entendre raison à qn; **the ~ for/why** la raison de/pour laquelle; **to have ~ to think** avoir lieu de penser; **it stands to ~ that** il va sans dire que; **she claims with good ~ that …** elle affirme à juste titre que …; **all the more ~ why** raison de plus pour + *infinitive or* pour que + *sub*; **within ~** dans les limites du raisonnable

reasonable ['ri:znəbl] ADJ raisonnable; (*not bad*) acceptable

reasonably ['ri:znəblɪ] ADV (*behave*) raisonnablement; (*fairly*) assez; **one can ~ assume that …** on est fondé à *or* il est permis de supposer que …

reasoned ['ri:znd] ADJ (*argument*) raisonné(e)

reasoning ['ri:znɪŋ] N raisonnement *m*

reassemble [ri:ə'sɛmbl] VT rassembler; (*machine*) remonter

reassert [ri:ə'sə:t] VT réaffirmer

reassurance [ri:ə'ʃuərəns] N (*factual*) assurance *f*, garantie *f*; (*emotional*) réconfort *m*

reassure [ri:ə'ʃuəʳ] VT rassurer; **to ~ sb of** donner à qn l'assurance répétée de

reassuring [ri:ə'ʃuərɪŋ] ADJ rassurant(e)

reawakening [ri:ə'weɪknɪŋ] N réveil *m*

rebate ['ri:beɪt] N (*on product*) rabais *m*; (*on tax etc*) dégrèvement *m*; (*repayment*) remboursement *m*

rebel N ['rɛbl] rebelle *mf* ▸ VI [rɪ'bɛl] se rebeller, se révolter

rebellion [rɪ'bɛljən] N rébellion *f*, révolte *f*

rebellious [rɪ'bɛljəs] ADJ rebelle

rebirth [ri:'bə:θ] N renaissance *f*

rebound VI [rɪ'baund] (*ball*) rebondir ▸ N ['ri:baund] rebond *m*

rebuff [rɪ'bʌf] N rebuffade *f* ▸ VT repousser

rebuild [ri:'bɪld] VT (*irreg: like* **build**) reconstruire

rebuke [rɪ'bju:k] N réprimande *f*, reproche *m* ▸ VT réprimander

rebut [rɪ'bʌt] VT réfuter

rebuttal [rɪ'bʌtl] N réfutation *f*

recalcitrant [rɪ'kælsɪtrənt] ADJ récalcitrant(e)

recall VT [rɪ'kɔ:l] rappeler; (*remember*) se rappeler, se souvenir de ▸ N ['ri:kɔl] rappel *m*; (*ability to remember*) mémoire *f*; **beyond ~** *adj* irrévocable

recant [rɪ'kænt] VI se rétracter; (*Rel*) abjurer

recap [rɪ'kæp] N récapitulation *f* ▸ VT, VI récapituler

recapture [ri:'kæptʃəʳ] VT reprendre; (*atmosphere*) recréer

recede [rɪ'si:d] VI s'éloigner; reculer

receding [rɪ'si:dɪŋ] ADJ (*forehead, chin*) fuyant(e); **~ hairline** front dégarni

receipt [rɪ'si:t] N (*document*) reçu *m*; (*for parcel etc*) accusé *m* de réception; (*act of receiving*) réception *f*; **receipts** NPL (*Comm*) recettes *fpl*; **to acknowledge ~ of** accuser réception de; **we are in ~ of …** nous avons reçu …; **can I have a ~, please?** je peux avoir un reçu, s'il vous plaît?

receivable [rɪ'si:vəbl] ADJ (*Comm*) recevable; (: *owing*) à recevoir

receive [rɪ'si:v] VT recevoir; (*guest*) recevoir, accueillir; **"received with thanks"** (*Comm*) "pour acquit"; **Received Pronunciation** *voir article*

> En Grande-Bretagne, la *Received Pronunciation* ou *RP* est une prononciation de la langue anglaise qui, récemment encore, était surtout associée à l'aristocratie et à la bourgeoisie, mais qui maintenant est en général considérée comme la prononciation correcte.

receiver [rɪ'si:vəʳ] N (*Tel*) récepteur *m*, combiné *m*; (*Radio*) récepteur; (*of stolen goods*) receleur *m*; (*for bankruptcies*) administrateur *m* judiciaire

receivership [rɪ'si:vəʃɪp] N: **to go into ~** être placé sous administration judiciaire

recent ['ri:snt] ADJ récent(e); **in ~ years** au cours de ces dernières années

recently ['ri:sntlɪ] ADV récemment; **as ~ as** pas plus tard que; **until ~** jusqu'à il y a peu de temps encore

receptacle [rɪ'sɛptɪkl] N récipient *m*

reception [rɪ'sɛpʃən] N réception *f*; (*welcome*) accueil *m*, réception

reception centre N (BRIT) centre m d'accueil
reception desk N réception f
receptionist [rɪ'sɛpʃənɪst] N réceptionniste mf
receptive [rɪ'sɛptɪv] ADJ réceptif(-ive)
recess [rɪ'sɛs] N (in room) renfoncement m; (for bed) alcôve f; (secret place) recoin m; (Pol etc: holiday) vacances fpl; (US Law: short break) suspension f d'audience; (Scol: esp US) récréation f
recession [rɪ'sɛʃən] N (Econ) récession f
recessionista [rɪsɛʃə'nɪstə] N recessionista mf
recharge [ri:'tʃɑːdʒ] VT (battery) recharger
rechargeable [ri:'tʃɑːdʒəbl] ADJ rechargeable
recipe ['rɛsɪpɪ] N recette f
recipient [rɪ'sɪpɪənt] N (of payment) bénéficiaire mf; (of letter) destinataire mf
reciprocal [rɪ'sɪprəkl] ADJ réciproque
reciprocate [rɪ'sɪprəkeɪt] VT retourner, offrir en retour ▸ VI en faire autant
recital [rɪ'saɪtl] N récital m
recite [rɪ'saɪt] VT (poem) réciter; (complaints etc) énumérer
reckless ['rɛkləs] ADJ (driver etc) imprudent(e); (spender etc) insouciant(e)
recklessly ['rɛkləslɪ] ADV imprudemment; avec insouciance
reckon ['rɛkən] VT (count) calculer, compter; (consider) considérer, estimer; (think): **I ~ (that)** ... je pense (que) ..., j'estime (que) ... ▸ VI: **he is somebody to be reckoned with** il ne faut pas le sous-estimer; **to ~ without sb/sth** ne pas tenir compte de qn/qch
▸ **reckon on** VT FUS compter sur, s'attendre à
reckoning ['rɛknɪŋ] N compte m, calcul m; estimation f; **the day of ~** le jour du Jugement
reclaim [rɪ'kleɪm] VT (land: from sea) assécher; (: from forest) défricher; (: with fertilizer) amender; (demand back) réclamer (le remboursement or la restitution de); (waste materials) récupérer
reclamation [rɛklə'meɪʃən] N (of land) amendement m; assèchement m; défrichement m
recline [rɪ'klaɪn] VI être allongé(e) or étendu(e)
reclining [rɪ'klaɪnɪŋ] ADJ (seat) à dossier réglable
recluse [rɪ'kluːs] N reclus(e), ermite m
recognition [rɛkəg'nɪʃən] N reconnaissance f; **in ~ of** en reconnaissance de; **to gain ~** être reconnu(e); **transformed beyond ~** méconnaissable
recognizable ['rɛkəgnaɪzəbl] ADJ: **~ (by)** reconnaissable (à)
recognize ['rɛkəgnaɪz] VT: **to ~ (by/as)** reconnaître (à/comme étant)
recoil [rɪ'kɔɪl] VI (person): **to ~ (from)** reculer (devant) ▸ N (of gun) recul m
recollect [rɛkə'lɛkt] VT se rappeler, se souvenir de
recollection [rɛkə'lɛkʃən] N souvenir m; **to the best of my ~** autant que je m'en souvienne
recommend [rɛkə'mɛnd] VT recommander; **can you ~ a good restaurant?** pouvez-vous me conseiller un bon restaurant?; **she has a lot to ~ her** elle a beaucoup de choses en sa faveur
recommendation [rɛkəmɛn'deɪʃən] N recommandation f

recommended retail price [rɛkə'mɛndɪd-] N (BRIT) prix conseillé
recompense ['rɛkəmpɛns] VT récompenser; (compensate) dédommager ▸ N récompense f; dédommagement m
reconcilable ['rɛkənsaɪləbl] ADJ (ideas) conciliable
reconcile ['rɛkənsaɪl] VT (two people) réconcilier; (two facts) concilier, accorder; **to ~ o.s. to** se résigner à
reconciliation [rɛkənsɪlɪ'eɪʃən] N réconciliation f; conciliation f
recondite [rɪ'kɒndaɪt] ADJ abstrus(e), obscur(e)
recondition [riːkən'dɪʃən] VT remettre à neuf; réviser entièrement
reconnaissance [rɪ'kɒnɪsns] N (Mil) reconnaissance f
reconnoitre, (US) reconnoiter [rɛkə'nɔɪtər] (Mil) VT reconnaître ▸ VI faire une reconnaissance
reconsider [riːkən'sɪdər] VT reconsidérer
reconstitute [riː'kɒnstɪtjuːt] VT reconstituer
reconstruct [riːkən'strʌkt] VT (building) reconstruire; (crime, system) reconstituer
reconstruction [riːkən'strʌkʃən] N reconstruction f; reconstitution f
reconvene [riːkən'viːn] VT reconvoquer ▸ VI se réunir or s'assembler de nouveau
record N ['rɛkɔːd] rapport m, récit m; (of meeting etc) procès-verbal m; (register) registre m; (file) dossier m; (Comput) article m; (also: **police record**) casier m judiciaire; (Mus: disc) disque m; (Sport) record m ▸ ADJ ['rɛkɔːd] record inv ▸ VT [rɪ'kɔːd] (set down) noter; (relate) rapporter; (Mus: song etc) enregistrer; **public records** archives fpl; **to keep a ~ of** noter; **to keep the ~ straight** (fig) mettre les choses au point; **he is on ~ as saying that ...** il a déclaré en public que ...; **Italy's excellent ~** les excellents résultats obtenus par l'Italie; **off the ~** adj officieux(-euse); adv officieusement; **in ~ time** dans un temps record
record card N (in file) fiche f
recorded delivery [rɪ'kɔːdɪd-] N (BRIT Post): **to send sth ~** envoyer qch en recommandé
recorded delivery letter [rɪ'kɔːdɪd-] N (BRIT Post) = lettre recommandée
recorder [rɪ'kɔːdər] N (Law) avocat nommé à la fonction de juge; (Mus) flûte f à bec
record holder N (Sport) détenteur(-trice) du record
recording [rɪ'kɔːdɪŋ] N (Mus) enregistrement m
recording studio N studio m d'enregistrement
record library N discothèque f
record player N tourne-disque m
recount [rɪ'kaunt] VT raconter
re-count N ['riːkaunt] (Pol: of votes) nouveau décompte (des suffrages) ▸ VT [riː'kaunt] recompter
recoup [rɪ'kuːp] VT: **to ~ one's losses** récupérer ce qu'on a perdu, se refaire
recourse [rɪ'kɔːs] N recours m; expédient m; **to have ~ to** recourir à, avoir recours à
recover [rɪ'kʌvər] VT récupérer ▸ VI (from illness)

se rétablir; *(from shock)* se remettre; *(country)* se redresser

re-cover [riːˈkʌvəʳ] vt *(chair etc)* recouvrir

recovery [rɪˈkʌvərɪ] n récupération f; rétablissement m; *(Econ)* redressement m

recreate [riːkrɪˈeɪt] vt recréer

recreation [rɛkrɪˈeɪʃən] n *(leisure)* récréation f, détente f

recreational [rɛkrɪˈeɪʃənl] adj pour la détente, récréatif(-ive)

recreational drug n drogue récréative

recreational vehicle n *(US)* camping-car m

recrimination [rɪkrɪmɪˈneɪʃən] n récrimination f

recruit [rɪˈkruːt] n recrue f ▸ vt recruter

recruiting office [rɪˈkruːtɪŋ-] n bureau m de recrutement

recruitment [rɪˈkruːtmənt] n recrutement m

rectangle [ˈrɛktæŋgl] n rectangle m

rectangular [rɛkˈtæŋgjuləʳ] adj rectangulaire

rectify [ˈrɛktɪfaɪ] vt *(error)* rectifier, corriger; *(omission)* réparer

rector [ˈrɛktəʳ] n *(Rel)* pasteur m; *(in Scottish universities)* personnalité élue par les étudiants pour les représenter

rectory [ˈrɛktərɪ] n presbytère m

rectum [ˈrɛktəm] n *(Anat)* rectum m

recuperate [rɪˈkjuːpəreɪt] vi *(from illness)* se rétablir

recur [rɪˈkəːʳ] vi se reproduire; *(idea, opportunity)* se retrouver; *(symptoms)* réapparaître

recurrence [rɪˈkəːrns] n répétition f; réapparition f

recurrent [rɪˈkəːrnt] adj périodique, fréquent(e)

recurring [rɪˈkəːrɪŋ] adj *(problem)* périodique, fréquent(e); *(Math)* périodique

recyclable [riːˈsaɪkləbl] adj recyclable

recycle [riːˈsaɪkl] vt, vi recycler

recycling [riːˈsaɪklɪŋ] n recyclage m

red [rɛd] n rouge m; *(Pol: pej)* rouge mf ▸ adj rouge; *(hair)* roux (rousse); **in the ~** *(account)* à découvert; *(business)* en déficit

red alert n alerte f rouge

red-blooded [rɛdˈblʌdɪd] adj *(inf)* viril(e), vigoureux(-euse)

redbrick university [ˈrɛdbrɪk-] *(Brit)*; *voir article*

> Une *redbrick university*, ainsi nommée à cause du matériau de construction répandu à l'époque (la brique), est une université britannique provinciale construite assez récemment, en particulier fin XIXᵉ-début XXᵉ siècle. Il y en a notamment une à Manchester, une à Liverpool et une à Bristol. Ce terme est utilisé pour établir une distinction avec les universités les plus anciennes et traditionnelles.

red carpet treatment n réception f en grande pompe

Red Cross n Croix-Rouge f

redcurrant [ˈrɛdkʌrənt] n groseille f (rouge)

redden [ˈrɛdn] vt, vi rougir

reddish [ˈrɛdɪʃ] adj rougeâtre; *(hair)* plutôt roux (rousse)

redecorate [riːˈdɛkəreɪt] vt refaire à neuf, repeindre et retapisser

redeem [rɪˈdiːm] vt *(debt)* rembourser; *(sth in pawn)* dégager; *(fig, also Rel)* racheter

redeemable [rɪˈdiːməbl] adj rachetable; remboursable, amortissable

redeeming [rɪˈdiːmɪŋ] adj *(feature)* qui sauve, qui rachète (le reste)

redefine [riːdɪˈfaɪn] vt redéfinir

redemption [rɪˈdɛmʃən] n *(Rel)* rédemption f; **past** *or* **beyond ~** *(situation)* irrémédiable; *(place)* qui ne peut plus être sauvé(e); *(person)* irrécupérable

redeploy [riːdɪˈplɔɪ] vt *(Mil)* redéployer; *(staff, resources)* reconvertir

redeployment [riːdɪˈplɔɪmənt] n redéploiement m; reconversion f

redevelop [riːdɪˈvɛləp] vt rénover

redevelopment [riːdɪˈvɛləpmənt] n rénovation f

red-haired [rɛdˈhɛəd] adj roux (rousse)

red-handed [rɛdˈhændɪd] adj: **to be caught ~** être pris(e) en flagrant délit *or* la main dans le sac

redhead [ˈrɛdhɛd] n roux (rousse)

red herring n *(fig)* diversion f, fausse piste

red-hot [rɛdˈhɔt] adj chauffé(e) au rouge, brûlant(e)

redirect [riːdaɪˈrɛkt] vt *(mail)* faire suivre

redistribute [riːdɪˈstrɪbjuːt] vt redistribuer

red-letter day [ˈrɛdlɛtə-] n grand jour, jour mémorable

red light n: **to go through a ~** *(Aut)* brûler un feu rouge

red-light district [ˈrɛdlaɪt-] n quartier mal famé

red meat n viande f rouge

redness [ˈrɛdnɪs] n rougeur f; *(of hair)* rousseur f

redo [riːˈduː] vt *(irreg: like do)* refaire

redolent [ˈrɛdələnt] adj: **~ of** qui sent; *(fig)* qui évoque

redouble [riːˈdʌbl] vt: **to ~ one's efforts** redoubler d'efforts

redraft [riːˈdrɑːft] vt remanier

redress [rɪˈdrɛs] n réparation f ▸ vt redresser; **to ~ the balance** rétablir l'équilibre

Red Sea n: **the ~** la mer Rouge

redskin [ˈrɛdskɪn] n Peau-Rouge mf

red tape n *(fig)* paperasserie (administrative)

reduce [rɪˈdjuːs] vt réduire; *(lower)* abaisser; **"~ speed now"** *(Aut)* "ralentir"; **to ~ sth by/to** réduire qch de/à; **to ~ sb to tears** faire pleurer qn

reduced [rɪˈdjuːst] adj réduit(e); **"greatly ~ prices"** "gros rabais"; **at a ~ price** *(goods)* au rabais; *(ticket etc)* à prix réduit

reduction [rɪˈdʌkʃən] n réduction f; *(of price)* baisse f; *(discount)* rabais m; réduction; **is there a ~ for children/students?** y a-t-il une réduction pour les enfants/les étudiants?

redundancy [rɪˈdʌndənsɪ] n *(Brit)* licenciement m, mise f au chômage; **compulsory ~** licenciement; **voluntary ~** départ m volontaire

redundancy payment N (BRIT) indemnité f de licenciement

redundant [rɪ'dʌndnt] ADJ (BRIT: worker) licencié(e), mis(e) au chômage; (detail, object) superflu(e); **to be made ~** (worker) être licencié, être mis au chômage

reed [riːd] N (Bot) roseau m; (Mus: of clarinet etc) anche f

re-educate [riː'edjukeɪt] VT rééduquer

reedy ['riːdɪ] ADJ (voice, instrument) ténu(e)

reef [riːf] N (at sea) récif m, écueil m

reek [riːk] VI: **to ~ (of)** puer, empester

reel [riːl] N bobine f; (Tech) dévidoir m; (Fishing) moulinet m; (Cine) bande f; (dance) quadrille écossais ▶ VT (Tech) bobiner; (also: **reel up**) enrouler ▶ VI (sway) chanceler; **my head is reeling** j'ai la tête qui tourne
▶ **reel in** VT (fish, line) ramener
▶ **reel off** VT (say) énumérer, débiter

re-election [riːɪ'lekʃən] N réélection f

re-enter [riː'entər] VT (also Space) rentrer dans

re-entry [riː'entrɪ] N (also Space) rentrée f

re-export ['riːɪks'pɔːt] réexporter ▶ N [riː'ekspɔːt] marchandise réexportée; (act) réexportation f

ref [ref] N ABBR (inf: = referee) arbitre m

ref. ABBR (Comm: = with reference to) réf

refectory [rɪ'fektərɪ] N réfectoire m

refer [rɪ'fəː] VT: **to ~ sth to** (dispute, decision) soumettre qch à; **to ~ sb to** (inquirer, patient) adresser qn à; (reader: to text) renvoyer qn à ▶ VI: **to ~ to** (allude to) parler de, faire allusion à; (consult) se reporter à; (apply to) s'appliquer à; **referring to your letter** (Comm) en réponse à votre lettre; **he referred me to the manager** il m'a dit de m'adresser au directeur

referee [refə'riː] N arbitre m; (Tennis) juge-arbitre m; (BRIT: for job application) répondant(e) ▶ VT arbitrer

reference ['refrəns] N référence f, renvoi m; (mention) allusion f, mention f; (for job application: letter) références; lettre f de recommandation; (person) répondant(e); **with ~ to** en ce qui concerne; (Comm: in letter) me référant à; **"please quote this ~"** (Comm) "prière de rappeler cette référence"

reference book N ouvrage m de référence

reference library N bibliothèque f d'ouvrages à consulter

reference number N (Comm) numéro m de référence

referendum [refə'rendəm] (pl **referenda** [-də]) N référendum m

referral [rɪ'fəːrəl] N soumission f; **she got a ~ to a specialist** elle a été adressée à un spécialiste

refill VT [riː'fɪl] remplir à nouveau; (pen, lighter etc) recharger ▶ N ['riːfɪl] (for pen etc) recharge f

refine [rɪ'faɪn] VT (sugar, oil) raffiner; (taste) affiner; (idea, theory) peaufiner

refined [rɪ'faɪnd] ADJ (person, taste) raffiné(e)

refinement [rɪ'faɪnmənt] N (of person) raffinement m

refinery [rɪ'faɪnərɪ] N raffinerie f

refit (Naut) N ['riːfɪt] remise f en état ▶ VT [riː'fɪt] remettre en état

reflate [riː'fleɪt] VT (economy) relancer

reflation [riː'fleɪʃən] N relance f

reflationary [riː'fleɪʃənrɪ] ADJ de relance

reflect [rɪ'flekt] VT (light, image) réfléchir, refléter; (fig) refléter ▶ VI (think) réfléchir, méditer; **it reflects badly on him** cela le discrédite; **it reflects well on him** c'est tout à son honneur

reflection [rɪ'flekʃən] N réflexion f; (image) reflet m; **~ on** (criticism) critique f de; atteinte f à; **on ~** réflexion faite

reflector [rɪ'flektər] N (also Aut) réflecteur m

reflex ['riːfleks] ADJ, N réflexe (m)

reflexive [rɪ'fleksɪv] ADJ (Ling) réfléchi(e)

reform [rɪ'fɔːm] N réforme f ▶ VT réformer

reformat [riː'fɔːmæt] VT (Comput) reformater

Reformation [refə'meɪʃən] N: **the ~** la Réforme

reformatory [rɪ'fɔːmətərɪ] N (US) centre m d'éducation surveillée

reformed [rɪ'fɔːmd] ADJ amendé(e), assagi(e)

reformer [rɪ'fɔːmər] N réformateur(-trice)

refrain [rɪ'freɪn] VI: **to ~ from doing** s'abstenir de faire ▶ N refrain m

refresh [rɪ'freʃ] VT rafraîchir; (subj: food, sleep etc) redonner des forces à

refresher course [rɪ'freʃə-] N (BRIT) cours m de recyclage

refreshing [rɪ'freʃɪŋ] ADJ (drink) rafraîchissant(e); (sleep) réparateur(-trice); (fact, idea etc) qui réjouit par son originalité or sa rareté

refreshment [rɪ'freʃmənt] N: **for some ~** (eating) pour se restaurer or sustenter; **in need of ~** (resting etc) ayant besoin de refaire ses forces

refreshments [rɪ'freʃmənts] NPL rafraîchissements mpl

refrigeration [rɪfrɪdʒə'reɪʃən] N réfrigération f

refrigerator [rɪ'frɪdʒəreɪtər] N réfrigérateur m, frigidaire m

refuel [riː'fjuəl] VT ravitailler en carburant ▶ VI se ravitailler en carburant

refuge ['refjuːdʒ] N refuge m; **to take ~ in** se réfugier dans

refugee [refju'dʒiː] N réfugié(e)

refugee camp N camp m de réfugiés

refund N ['riːfʌnd] remboursement m ▶ VT [rɪ'fʌnd] rembourser

refurbish [riː'fəːbɪʃ] VT remettre à neuf

refurnish [riː'fəːnɪʃ] VT remeubler

refusal [rɪ'fjuːzəl] N refus m; **to have first ~ on sth** avoir droit de préemption sur qch

refuse¹ ['refjuːs] N ordures fpl, détritus mpl

refuse² [rɪ'fjuːz] VT, VI refuser; **to ~ to do sth** refuser de faire qch

refuse collection N ramassage m d'ordures

refuse disposal N élimination f des ordures

refusenik [rɪ'fjuːznɪk] N refuznik mf

refute [rɪ'fjuːt] VT réfuter

regain [rɪ'geɪn] VT (lost ground) regagner; (strength) retrouver

regal ['riːgl] ADJ royal(e)

regale [rɪ'geɪl] VT: **to ~ sb with sth** régaler qn de qch

regalia [rɪˈgeɪlɪə] N insignes mpl de la royauté
regard [rɪˈgɑːd] N respect m, estime f, considération f ▶ VT considérer; **to give one's regards to** faire ses amitiés à; **"with kindest regards"** "bien amicalement"; **as regards, with ~ to** en ce qui concerne
regarding [rɪˈgɑːdɪŋ] PREP en ce qui concerne
regardless [rɪˈgɑːdlɪs] ADV quand même; **~ of** sans se soucier de
regatta [rɪˈgætə] N régate f
regency [ˈriːdʒənsɪ] N régence f
regenerate [rɪˈdʒɛnəreɪt] VT régénérer ▶ VI se régénérer
regent [ˈriːdʒənt] N régent(e)
reggae [ˈrɛgeɪ] N reggae m
régime [reɪˈʒiːm] N régime m
regiment [ˈrɛdʒɪmənt] N régiment m ▶ VT [ˈrɛdʒɪmɛnt] imposer une discipline trop stricte à
regimental [rɛdʒɪˈmɛntl] ADJ d'un régiment
regimentation [rɛdʒɪmɛnˈteɪʃən] N réglementation excessive
region [ˈriːdʒən] N région f; **in the ~ of** (fig) aux alentours de
regional [ˈriːdʒənl] ADJ régional(e)
regional development N aménagement m du territoire
register [ˈrɛdʒɪstər] N registre m; (also: **electoral register**) liste électorale ▶ VT enregistrer, inscrire; (birth) déclarer; (vehicle) immatriculer; (luggage) enregistrer; (letter) envoyer en recommandé; (subj: instrument) marquer ▶ VI s'inscrire; (at hotel) signer le registre; (make impression) être (bien) compris(e); **to ~ for a course** s'inscrire à un cours; **to ~ a protest** protester
registered [ˈrɛdʒɪstəd] ADJ (design) déposé(e); (BRIT: letter) recommandé(e); (student, voter) inscrit(e)
registered company N société immatriculée
registered nurse N (US) infirmier(-ière) diplômé(e) d'État
registered office N siège social
registered trademark N marque déposée
registrar [ˈrɛdʒɪstrɑːr] N officier m de l'état civil; secrétaire mf général
registration [rɛdʒɪsˈtreɪʃən] N (act) enregistrement m; (of student) inscription f; (BRIT Aut: also: **registration number**) numéro m d'immatriculation
registry [ˈrɛdʒɪstrɪ] N bureau m de l'enregistrement
registry office N (BRIT) bureau m de l'état civil; **to get married in a ~ ~** se marier à la mairie
regret [rɪˈgrɛt] N regret m ▶ VT regretter; **to ~ that** regretter que + sub; **we ~ to inform you that ...** nous sommes au regret de vous informer que ...
regretfully [rɪˈgrɛtfəlɪ] ADV à or avec regret
regrettable [rɪˈgrɛtəbl] ADJ regrettable, fâcheux(-euse)
regrettably [rɪˈgrɛtəblɪ] ADV (drunk, late) fâcheusement; **~, he ...** malheureusement, il ...

regroup [riːˈgruːp] VT regrouper ▶ VI se regrouper
regt ABBR = **regiment**
regular [ˈrɛgjulər] ADJ régulier(-ière); (usual) habituel(le), normal(e); (listener, reader) fidèle; (soldier) de métier; (Comm: size) ordinaire ▶ N (client etc) habitué(e)
regularity [rɛgjuˈlærɪtɪ] N régularité f
regularly [ˈrɛgjuləlɪ] ADV régulièrement
regulate [ˈrɛgjuleɪt] VT régler
regulation [rɛgjuˈleɪʃən] N (rule) règlement m; (adjustment) réglage m ▶ CPD réglementaire
rehabilitate [riːəˈbɪlɪteɪt] VT (criminal) réinsérer; (drug addict) désintoxiquer; (invalid) rééduquer
rehabilitation [ˈriːəbɪlɪˈteɪʃən] N (of offender) réhabilitation f; (of addict) réadaptation f; (of disabled people) rééducation f, réadaptation f
rehash [riːˈhæʃ] VT (inf) remanier
rehearsal [rɪˈhəːsəl] N répétition f; **dress ~** (répétition) générale f
rehearse [rɪˈhəːs] VT répéter
rehouse [riːˈhauz] VT reloger
reign [reɪn] N règne m ▶ VI régner
reigning [ˈreɪnɪŋ] ADJ (monarch) régnant(e); (champion) actuel(le)
reimburse [riːɪmˈbəːs] VT rembourser
rein [reɪn] N (for horse) rêne f; **to give sb free ~** (fig) donner carte blanche à qn
reincarnation [riːɪnkɑːˈneɪʃən] N réincarnation f
reindeer [ˈreɪndɪər] N (pl inv) renne m
reinforce [riːɪnˈfɔːs] VT renforcer
reinforced concrete [riːɪnˈfɔːst-] N béton armé
reinforcement [riːɪnˈfɔːsmənt] N (action) renforcement m
reinforcements [riːɪnˈfɔːsmənts] NPL (Mil) renfort(s) m(pl)
reinstate [riːɪnˈsteɪt] VT rétablir, réintégrer
reinstatement [riːɪnˈsteɪtmənt] N réintégration f
reissue [riːˈɪʃuː] VT (book) rééditer; (film) ressortir
reiterate [riːˈɪtəreɪt] VT réitérer, répéter
reject N [ˈriːdʒɛkt] (Comm) article m de rebut ▶ VT [rɪˈdʒɛkt] refuser; (Comm: goods) mettre au rebut; (idea) rejeter
rejection [rɪˈdʒɛkʃən] N rejet m, refus m
rejoice [rɪˈdʒɔɪs] VI: **to ~ (at or over)** se réjouir (de)
rejoinder [rɪˈdʒɔɪndər] N (retort) réplique f
rejuvenate [rɪˈdʒuːvəneɪt] VT rajeunir
rekindle [riːˈkɪndl] VT rallumer; (fig) raviver
relapse [rɪˈlæps] N (Med) rechute f
relate [rɪˈleɪt] VT (tell) raconter; (connect) établir un rapport entre ▶ VI: **to ~ to** (connect) se rapporter à; **to ~ to sb** (interact) entretenir des rapports avec qn
related [rɪˈleɪtɪd] ADJ apparenté(e); **~ to** (subject) lié(e) à
relating to [rɪˈleɪtɪŋ-] PREP concernant
relation [rɪˈleɪʃən] N (person) parent(e); (link) rapport m, lien m; **relations** NPL (relatives) famille f; **diplomatic/international relations** relations diplomatiques/

r

internationales; **in ~ to** en ce qui concerne; par rapport à; **to bear no ~ to** être sans rapport avec

relationship [rɪ'leɪʃənʃɪp] N rapport m, lien m; (*personal ties*) relations fpl, rapports; (*also:* **family relationship**) lien de parenté; (*affair*) liaison f; **they have a good ~** ils s'entendent bien

relative ['rɛlətɪv] N parent(e) ▶ ADJ relatif(-ive); (*respective*) respectif(-ive); **all her relatives** toute sa famille

relatively ['rɛlətɪvlɪ] ADV relativement

relax [rɪ'læks] VI (*muscle*) se relâcher; (*person: unwind*) se détendre; (*: calm down*) se calmer ▶ VT relâcher; (*mind, person*) détendre

relaxation [riːlæk'seɪʃən] N relâchement m; (*of mind*) détente f; (*recreation*) détente, délassement m; (*entertainment*) distraction f

relaxed [rɪ'lækst] ADJ relâché(e); détendu(e)

relaxing [rɪ'læksɪŋ] ADJ délassant(e)

relay ['riːleɪ] N (*Sport*) course f de relais ▶ VT (*message*) retransmettre, relayer

release [rɪ'liːs] N (*from prison, obligation*) libération f; (*of gas etc*) émission f; (*of film etc*) sortie f; (*new recording*) disque m; (*device*) déclencheur m ▶ VT (*prisoner*) libérer; (*book, film*) sortir; (*report, news*) rendre public, publier; (*gas etc*) émettre, dégager; (*free: from wreckage etc*) dégager; (*Tech: catch, spring etc*) déclencher; (*let go: person, animal*) relâcher; (*: hand, object*) lâcher; (*: grip, brake*) desserrer; **to ~ one's grip** *or* **hold** lâcher prise; **to ~ the clutch** (*Aut*) débrayer

relegate ['rɛləgeɪt] VT reléguer; (*Brit Sport*): **to be relegated** descendre dans une division inférieure

relent [rɪ'lɛnt] VI se laisser fléchir

relentless [rɪ'lɛntlɪs] ADJ implacable; (*non-stop*) continuel(le)

relevance ['rɛləvəns] N pertinence f; **~ of sth to sth** rapport m entre qch et qch

relevant ['rɛləvənt] ADJ (*question*) pertinent(e); (*corresponding*) approprié(e); (*fact*) significatif(-ive); (*information*) utile; **~ to** ayant rapport à, approprié à

reliability [rɪlaɪə'bɪlɪtɪ] N sérieux m; fiabilité f

reliable [rɪ'laɪəbl] ADJ (*person, firm*) sérieux(-euse), fiable; (*method, machine*) fiable; (*news, information*) sûr(e)

reliably [rɪ'laɪəblɪ] ADV: **to be ~ informed** savoir de source sûre

reliance [rɪ'laɪəns] N: **~ (on)** (*trust*) confiance f (en); (*dependence*) besoin m (de), dépendance f (de)

reliant [rɪ'laɪənt] ADJ: **to be ~ on sth/sb** dépendre de qch/qn

relic ['rɛlɪk] N (*Rel*) relique f; (*of the past*) vestige m

relief [rɪ'liːf] N (*from pain, anxiety*) soulagement m; (*help, supplies*) secours m(pl); (*of guard*) relève f; (*Art, Geo*) relief m; **by way of light ~** pour faire diversion

relief map N carte f en relief

relief road N (*Brit*) route f de délestage

relieve [rɪ'liːv] VT (*pain, patient*) soulager; (*fear, worry*) dissiper; (*bring help*) secourir; (*take over from: gen*) relayer; (*: guard*) relever; **to ~ sb of sth**

débarrasser qn de qch; **to ~ sb of his command** (*Mil*) relever qn de ses fonctions; **to ~ o.s.** (*euphemism*) se soulager, faire ses besoins

relieved [rɪ'liːvd] ADJ soulagé(e); **to be ~ that ...** être soulagé que ...; **I'm ~ to hear it** je suis soulagé de l'entendre

religion [rɪ'lɪdʒən] N religion f

religious [rɪ'lɪdʒəs] ADJ religieux(-euse); (*book*) de piété

religious education N instruction religieuse

relinquish [rɪ'lɪŋkwɪʃ] VT abandonner; (*plan, habit*) renoncer à

relish ['rɛlɪʃ] N (*Culin*) condiment m; (*enjoyment*) délectation f ▶ VT (*food etc*) savourer; **to ~ doing** se délecter à faire

relive [riː'lɪv] VT revivre

reload [riː'ləud] VT recharger

relocate [riːləu'keɪt] VT (*business*) transférer ▶ VI se transférer, s'installer *or* s'établir ailleurs; **to ~ in** (déménager et) s'installer *or* s'établir à, se transférer à

reluctance [rɪ'lʌktəns] N répugnance f

reluctant [rɪ'lʌktənt] ADJ peu disposé(e), qui hésite; **to be ~ to do sth** hésiter à faire qch

reluctantly [rɪ'lʌktəntlɪ] ADV à contrecœur, sans enthousiasme

rely on [rɪ'laɪ-] VT FUS (*be dependent on*) dépendre de; (*trust*) compter sur

remain [rɪ'meɪn] VI rester; **to ~ silent** garder le silence; **I ~, yours faithfully** (*Brit: in letters*) je vous prie d'agréer, Monsieur *etc* l'assurance de mes sentiments distingués

remainder [rɪ'meɪndə^r] N reste m; (*Comm*) fin f de série

remaining [rɪ'meɪnɪŋ] ADJ qui reste

remains [rɪ'meɪnz] NPL restes mpl

remake ['riːmeɪk] N (*Cine*) remake m

remand [rɪ'mɑːnd] N: **on ~** en détention préventive ▶ VT: **to be remanded in custody** être placé(e) en détention préventive

remand home N (*Brit*) centre m d'éducation surveillée

remark [rɪ'mɑːk] N remarque f, observation f ▶ VT (faire) remarquer, dire; (*notice*) remarquer; **to ~ on sth** faire une *or* des remarque(s) sur qch

remarkable [rɪ'mɑːkəbl] ADJ remarquable

remarkably [rɪ'mɑːkəblɪ] ADV remarquablement

remarry [riː'mærɪ] VI se remarier

remedial [rɪ'miːdɪəl] ADJ (*tuition, classes*) de rattrapage

remedy ['rɛmədɪ] N: **~ (for)** remède m (contre *or* à) ▶ VT remédier à

remember [rɪ'mɛmbə^r] VT se rappeler, se souvenir de; (*send greetings*): **~ me to him** saluez-le de ma part; **I ~ seeing it, I ~ having seen it** je me rappelle l'avoir vu *or* que je l'ai vu; **she remembered to do it** elle a pensé à le faire; **~ me to your wife** rappelez-moi au bon souvenir de votre femme

remembrance [rɪ'mɛmbrəns] N souvenir m; mémoire f

Remembrance Day N (*Brit*) ≈ (le jour de) l'Armistice m, ≈ le 11 novembre; *voir article*

Remembrance Day ou *Remembrance Sunday* est le dimanche le plus proche du 11 novembre, jour où la Première Guerre mondiale a officiellement pris fin. Il rend hommage aux victimes des deux guerres mondiales. À cette occasion, on observe deux minutes de silence à 11h, heure de la signature de l'armistice avec l'Allemagne en 1918; certaines membres de la famille royale et du gouvernement déposent des gerbes de coquelicots au cénotaphe de Whitehall, et des couronnes sont placées sur les monuments aux morts dans toute la Grande-Bretagne; par ailleurs, les gens portent des coquelicots artificiels fabriqués et vendus par des membres de la légion britannique blessés au combat, au profit des blessés de guerre et de leur famille.

remind [rɪˈmaɪnd] VT: **to ~ sb of sth** rappeler qch à qn; **to ~ sb to do** faire penser à qn à faire, rappeler à qn qu'il doit faire; **that reminds me!** j'y pense!

reminder [rɪˈmaɪndəʳ] N (*Comm: letter*) rappel *m*; (*note etc*) pense-bête *m*; (*souvenir*) souvenir *m*

reminisce [rɛmɪˈnɪs] VI: **to ~ (about)** évoquer ses souvenirs (de)

reminiscences [rɛmɪˈnɪsnsɪz] NPL réminiscences *fpl*, souvenirs *mpl*

reminiscent [rɛmɪˈnɪsnt] ADJ: **~ of** qui rappelle, qui fait penser à

remiss [rɪˈmɪs] ADJ négligent(e); **it was ~ of me** c'était une négligence de ma part

remission [rɪˈmɪʃən] N rémission *f*; (*of debt, sentence*) remise *f*; (*of fee*) exemption *f*

remit [rɪˈmɪt] VT (*send: money*) envoyer

remittance [rɪˈmɪtns] N envoi *m*, paiement *m*

remnant [ˈrɛmnənt] N reste *m*, restant *m*; (*of cloth*) coupon *m*; **remnants** NPL (*Comm*) fins *fpl* de série

remonstrate [ˈrɛmənstreɪt] VI: **to ~ (with sb about sth)** se plaindre (à qn de qch)

remorse [rɪˈmɔːs] N remords *m*

remorseful [rɪˈmɔːsful] ADJ plein(e) de remords

remorseless [rɪˈmɔːslɪs] ADJ (*fig*) impitoyable

remote [rɪˈməut] ADJ éloigné(e), lointain(e); (*person*) distant(e); (*possibility*) vague; **there is a ~ possibility that ...** il est tout juste possible que ...

remote control N télécommande *f*

remote-controlled [rɪˈməutkənˈtrəuld] ADJ téléguidé(e)

remotely [rɪˈməutlɪ] ADV au loin; (*slightly*) très vaguement

remould [ˈriːməuld] N (*BRIT: tyre*) pneu *m* rechapé

removable [rɪˈmuːvəbl] ADJ (*detachable*) amovible

removal [rɪˈmuːvəl] N (*taking away*) enlèvement *m*; suppression *f*; (*BRIT: from house*) déménagement *m*; (*from office: dismissal*) renvoi *m*; (*of stain*) nettoyage *m*; (*Med*) ablation *f*

removal man N (*irreg*) (*BRIT*) déménageur *m*

removal van N (*BRIT*) camion *m* de déménagement

remove [rɪˈmuːv] VT enlever, retirer; (*employee*) renvoyer; (*stain*) faire partir; (*abuse*) supprimer; (*doubt*) chasser; **first cousin once removed** cousin(e) au deuxième degré

remover [rɪˈmuːvəʳ] N (*for paint*) décapant *m*; (*for varnish*) dissolvant *m*; **make-up ~** démaquillant *m*

remunerate [rɪˈmjuːnəreɪt] VT rémunérer

remuneration [rɪmjuːnəˈreɪʃən] N rémunération *f*

Renaissance [rɪˈneɪsɑ̃s] N: **the ~** la Renaissance

rename [riːˈneɪm] VT rebaptiser

rend [rɛnd] (*pt, pp* **rent** [rɛnt]) VT déchirer

render [ˈrɛndəʳ] VT rendre; (*Culin: fat*) clarifier

rendering [ˈrɛndərɪŋ] N (*Mus etc*) interprétation *f*

rendezvous [ˈrɔndɪvuː] N rendez-vous *m inv* ▶ VI opérer une jonction, se rejoindre; **to ~ with sb** rejoindre qn

renegade [ˈrɛnɪgeɪd] N renégat(e)

renew [rɪˈnjuː] VT renouveler; (*negotiations*) reprendre; (*acquaintance*) renouer

renewable [rɪˈnjuːəbl] ADJ (*energy*) renouvelable; **renewables** énergies renouvelables

renewal [rɪˈnjuːəl] N renouvellement *m*; reprise *f*

renounce [rɪˈnauns] VT renoncer à; (*disown*) renier

renovate [ˈrɛnəveɪt] VT rénover; (*work of art*) restaurer

renovation [rɛnəˈveɪʃən] N rénovation *f*; restauration *f*

renown [rɪˈnaun] N renommée *f*

renowned [rɪˈnaund] ADJ renommé(e)

rent [rɛnt] PT, PP *of* **rend** ▶ N loyer *m* ▶ VT louer; (*car, TV*) louer, prendre en location; (*also:* **rent out**: *car, TV*) louer, donner en location

rental [ˈrɛntl] N (*for television, car*) (prix *m* de) location *f*

rent boy N (*BRIT inf*) jeune prostitué

renunciation [rɪnʌnsɪˈeɪʃən] N renonciation *f*; (*self-denial*) renoncement *m*

reopen [riːˈəupən] VT rouvrir

reorder [riːˈɔːdəʳ] VT commander de nouveau; (*rearrange*) réorganiser

reorganize [riːˈɔːgənaɪz] VT réorganiser

rep [rɛp] N ABBR (*Comm*) = **representative**; (*Theat*) = **repertory**

Rep. ABBR (*Pol*) = **representative**; **republican**

repair [rɪˈpɛəʳ] N réparation *f* ▶ VT réparer; **in good/bad ~** en bon/mauvais état; **under ~** en réparation; **where can I get this repaired?** où est-ce que je peux faire réparer ceci?

repair kit N trousse *f* de réparations

repair man N (*irreg*) réparateur *m*

repair shop N (*Aut etc*) atelier *m* de réparations

repartee [rɛpɑːˈtiː] N repartie *f*

repast [rɪˈpɑːst] N (*formal*) repas *m*

repatriate [riːˈpætrɪeɪt] VT rapatrier

repay [riːˈpeɪ] VT (*irreg: like* **pay**) (*money, creditor*) rembourser; (*sb's efforts*) récompenser

repayment [riːˈpeɪmənt] N remboursement *m*; récompense *f*

r

repeal [rɪ'piːl] N (*of law*) abrogation f; (*of sentence*) annulation f ▸ VT abroger; annuler

repeat [rɪ'piːt] N (*Radio, TV*) reprise f ▸ VT répéter; (*pattern*) reproduire; (*promise, attack, also Comm: order*) renouveler; (*Scol: a class*) redoubler ▸ VI répéter; **can you ~ that, please?** pouvez-vous répéter, s'il vous plaît?

repeatedly [rɪ'piːtɪdlɪ] ADV souvent, à plusieurs reprises

repeat prescription N (BRIT): **I'd like a ~** je voudrais renouveler mon ordonnance

repel [rɪ'pɛl] VT repousser

repellent [rɪ'pɛlənt] ADJ repoussant(e) ▸ N: **insect ~** insectifuge m; **moth ~** produit m antimite(s)

repent [rɪ'pɛnt] VI: **to ~ (of)** se repentir (de)

repentance [rɪ'pɛntəns] N repentir m

repercussions [riːpə'kʌʃənz] NPL répercussions fpl

repertoire ['rɛpətwɑːʳ] N répertoire m

repertory ['rɛpətərɪ] N (*also*: **repertory theatre**) théâtre m de répertoire

repertory company N troupe théâtrale permanente

repetition [rɛpɪ'tɪʃən] N répétition f

repetitious [rɛpɪ'tɪʃəs] ADJ (*speech*) plein(e) de redites

repetitive [rɪ'pɛtɪtɪv] ADJ (*movement, work*) répétitif(-ive); (*speech*) plein(e) de redites

replace [rɪ'pleɪs] VT (*put back*) remettre, replacer; (*take the place of*) remplacer; (*Tel*): **"~ the receiver"** "raccrochez"

replacement [rɪ'pleɪsmənt] N replacement m; (*substitution*) remplacement m; (*person*) remplaçant(e)

replacement part N pièce f de rechange

replay ['riːpleɪ] N (*of match*) match rejoué; (*of tape, film*) répétition f

replenish [rɪ'plɛnɪʃ] VT (*glass*) remplir (de nouveau); (*stock etc*) réapprovisionner

replete [rɪ'pliːt] ADJ rempli(e); (*well-fed*): **~ (with)** rassasié(e) (de)

replica ['rɛplɪkə] N réplique f, copie exacte

reply [rɪ'plaɪ] N réponse f ▸ VI répondre; **in ~ (to)** en réponse (à); **there's no ~** (*Tel*) ça ne répond pas

reply coupon N coupon-réponse m

report [rɪ'pɔːt] N rapport m; (*Press etc*) reportage m; (*BRIT: also*: **school report**) bulletin m (scolaire); (*of gun*) détonation f ▸ VT rapporter, faire un compte rendu de; (*Press etc*) faire un reportage sur; (*notify: accident*) signaler; (: *culprit*) dénoncer ▸ VI (*make a report*) faire un rapport; (*for newspaper*) faire un reportage (sur); **I'd like to ~ a theft** je voudrais signaler un vol; **to ~ (to sb)** (*present o.s.*) se présenter (chez qn); **it is reported that** on dit or annonce que; **it is reported from Berlin that** on nous apprend de Berlin que

report card N (US, SCOTTISH) bulletin m (scolaire)

reportedly [rɪ'pɔːtɪdlɪ] ADV: **she is ~ living in Spain** elle habiterait en Espagne; **he ~ told them to ...** il leur aurait dit de ...

reported speech [rɪ'pɔːtɪd-] N (*Ling*) discours indirect

reporter [rɪ'pɔːtəʳ] N reporter m

repose [rɪ'pəuz] N: **in ~** en or au repos

repossess [riːpə'zɛs] VT saisir

repossession order [riːpə'zɛʃən-] N ordre m de reprise de possession

reprehensible [rɛprɪ'hɛnsɪbl] ADJ répréhensible

represent [rɛprɪ'zɛnt] VT représenter; (*view, belief*) présenter, expliquer; (*describe*): **to ~ sth as** présenter or décrire qch comme; **to ~ to sb that** expliquer à qn que

representation [rɛprɪzɛn'teɪʃən] N représentation f; **representations** NPL (*protest*) démarche f

representative [rɛprɪ'zɛntətɪv] N représentant(e); (*Comm*) représentant(e) (de commerce); (*US Pol*) député m ▸ ADJ représentatif(-ive), caractéristique

repress [rɪ'prɛs] VT réprimer

repression [rɪ'prɛʃən] N répression f

repressive [rɪ'prɛsɪv] ADJ répressif(-ive)

reprieve [rɪ'priːv] N (*Law*) grâce f; (*fig*) sursis m, délai m ▸ VT gracier; accorder un sursis or un délai à

reprimand ['rɛprɪmɑːnd] N réprimande f ▸ VT réprimander

reprint N ['riːprɪnt] réimpression f ▸ VT [riː'prɪnt] réimprimer

reprisal [rɪ'praɪzl] N représailles fpl; **to take reprisals** user de représailles

reproach [rɪ'prəutʃ] N reproche m ▸ VT: **to ~ sb with sth** reprocher qch à qn; **beyond ~** irréprochable

reproachful [rɪ'prəutʃful] ADJ de reproche

reproduce [riːprə'djuːs] VT reproduire ▸ VI se reproduire

reproduction [riːprə'dʌkʃən] N reproduction f

reproductive [riːprə'dʌktɪv] ADJ reproducteur(-trice)

reproof [rɪ'pruːf] N reproche m

reprove [rɪ'pruːv] VT (*action*) réprouver; (*person*): **to ~ (for)** blâmer (de)

reproving [rɪ'pruːvɪŋ] ADJ réprobateur(-trice)

reptile ['rɛptaɪl] N reptile m

Repub. ABBR (*US Pol*) = **republican**

republic [rɪ'pʌblɪk] N république f

republican [rɪ'pʌblɪkən] ADJ, N républicain(e)

repudiate [rɪ'pjuːdɪeɪt] VT (*ally, behaviour*) désavouer; (*accusation*) rejeter; (*wife*) répudier

repugnant [rɪ'pʌɡnənt] ADJ répugnant(e)

repulse [rɪ'pʌls] VT repousser

repulsion [rɪ'pʌlʃən] N répulsion f

repulsive [rɪ'pʌlsɪv] ADJ repoussant(e), répulsif(-ive)

reputable ['rɛpjutəbl] ADJ de bonne réputation; (*occupation*) honorable

reputation [rɛpju'teɪʃən] N réputation f; **to have a ~ for** être réputé(e) pour; **he has a ~ for being awkward** il a la réputation de ne pas être commode

repute [rɪ'pjuːt] N (bonne) réputation

reputed [rɪ'pjuːtɪd] ADJ réputé(e); **he is ~ to be**

rich/intelligent *etc* on dit qu'il est riche/intelligent *etc*

reputedly [rɪ'pjuːtɪdlɪ] ADV d'après ce qu'on dit

request [rɪ'kwɛst] N demande *f*; *(formal)* requête *f* ▶ VT: **to ~ (of** *or* **from sb)** demander (à qn); **at the ~ of** à la demande de

request stop N (*BRIT: for bus*) arrêt facultatif

requiem ['rɛkwɪəm] N requiem *m*

require [rɪ'kwaɪəʳ] VT *(need: subj: person)* avoir besoin de; *(: thing, situation)* nécessiter, demander; *(want)* exiger; *(order)*: **to ~ sb to do sth/sth of sb** exiger que qn fasse qch/qch de qn; **if required** s'il le faut; **what qualifications are required?** quelles sont les qualifications requises?; **required by law** requis par la loi

required [rɪ'kwaɪəd] ADJ requis(e), voulu(e)

requirement [rɪ'kwaɪəmənt] N *(need)* exigence *f*; besoin *m*; *(condition)* condition *f* (requise)

requisite ['rɛkwɪzɪt] N chose *f* nécessaire ▶ ADJ requis(e), nécessaire; **toilet requisites** accessoires *mpl* de toilette

requisition [rɛkwɪ'zɪʃən] N: **~ (for)** demande *f* (de) ▶ VT *(Mil)* réquisitionner

reroute [riː'ruːt] VT *(train etc)* dérouter

resale ['riː'seɪl] N revente *f*

resale price maintenance N vente au détail à prix imposé

resat [riː'sæt] PT, PP of **resit**

rescind [rɪ'sɪnd] VT annuler; *(law)* abroger; *(judgment)* rescinder

rescue ['rɛskjuː] N *(from accident)* sauvetage *m*; *(help)* secours *mpl* ▶ VT sauver; **to come to sb's ~** venir au secours de qn

rescue party N équipe *f* de sauvetage

rescuer ['rɛskjuəʳ] N sauveteur *m*

research [rɪ'səːtʃ] N recherche(s) *f(pl)* ▶ VT faire des recherches sur ▶ VI: **to ~ (into sth)** faire des recherches (sur qch); **a piece of ~** un travail de recherche; **~ and development** recherche-développement

researcher [rɪ'səːtʃəʳ] N chercheur(-euse)

research work N recherches *fpl*

resell [riː'sɛl] VT *(irreg: like* **sell**) revendre

resemblance [rɪ'zɛmbləns] N ressemblance *f*; **to bear a strong ~ to** ressembler beaucoup à

resemble [rɪ'zɛmbl] VT ressembler à

resent [rɪ'zɛnt] VT éprouver du ressentiment de, être contrarié(e) par

resentful [rɪ'zɛntful] ADJ irrité(e), plein(e) de ressentiment

resentment [rɪ'zɛntmənt] N ressentiment *m*

reservation [rɛzə'veɪʃən] N *(booking)* réservation *f*; *(doubt, protected area)* réserve *f*; *(BRIT Aut: also:* **central reservation**) bande médiane; **to make a ~ (in an hotel/a restaurant/on a plane)** réserver *or* retenir une chambre/une table/une place; **with reservations** *(doubts)* avec certaines réserves

reservation desk N *(US: in hotel)* réception *f*

reserve [rɪ'zəːv] N réserve *f*; *(Sport)* remplaçant(e) ▶ VT *(seats etc)* réserver, retenir; **reserves** NPL *(Mil)* réservistes *mpl*; **in ~** en réserve

reserve currency N monnaie *f* de réserve

reserved [rɪ'zəːvd] ADJ réservé(e)

reserve price N *(BRIT)* mise *f* à prix, prix *m* de départ

reserve team N *(BRIT Sport)* deuxième équipe *f*

reservist [rɪ'zəːvɪst] N *(Mil)* réserviste *m*

reservoir ['rɛzəvwɑːʳ] N réservoir *m*

reset [riː'sɛt] VT *(irreg: like* **set**) remettre; *(clock, watch)* mettre à l'heure; *(Comput)* remettre à zéro

reshape [riː'ʃeɪp] VT *(policy)* réorganiser

reshuffle [riː'ʃʌfl] N: **Cabinet ~** *(Pol)* remaniement ministériel

reside [rɪ'zaɪd] VI résider

residence ['rɛzɪdəns] N résidence *f*; **to take up ~** s'installer; **in ~** *(queen etc)* en résidence; *(doctor)* résidant(e)

residence permit N *(BRIT)* permis *m* de séjour

resident ['rɛzɪdənt] N *(of country)* résident(e); *(of area, house)* habitant(e); *(in hotel)* pensionnaire ▶ ADJ résidant(e)

residential [rɛzɪ'dɛnʃəl] ADJ de résidence; *(area)* résidentiel(le); *(course)* avec hébergement sur place

residential school N internat *m*

residue ['rɛzɪdjuː] N reste *m*; *(Chem, Physics)* résidu *m*

resign [rɪ'zaɪn] VT *(one's post)* se démettre de ▶ VI démissionner; **to ~ o.s. to** *(endure)* se résigner à

resignation [rɛzɪg'neɪʃən] N *(from post)* démission *f*; *(state of mind)* résignation *f*; **to tender one's ~** donner sa démission

resigned [rɪ'zaɪnd] ADJ résigné(e)

resilience [rɪ'zɪlɪəns] N *(of material)* élasticité *f*; *(of person)* ressort *m*

resilient [rɪ'zɪlɪənt] ADJ *(person)* qui réagit, qui a du ressort

resin ['rɛzɪn] N résine *f*

resist [rɪ'zɪst] VT résister à

resistance [rɪ'zɪstəns] N résistance *f*

resistant [rɪ'zɪstənt] ADJ: **~ (to)** résistant(e) (à)

resit VT [riː'sɪt] *(irreg: like* **sit**) *(BRIT: exam)* repasser ▶ N ['riːsɪt] deuxième session *f* (d'un examen)

resolute ['rɛzəluːt] ADJ résolu(e)

resolution [rɛzə'luːʃən] N résolution *f*; **to make a ~** prendre une résolution

resolve [rɪ'zɔlv] N résolution *f* ▶ VT *(problem)* résoudre; *(decide)*: **to ~ to do** résoudre *or* décider de faire

resolved [rɪ'zɔlvd] ADJ résolu(e)

resonance ['rɛzənəns] N résonance *f*

resonant ['rɛzənənt] ADJ résonnant(e)

resort [rɪ'zɔːt] N *(seaside town)* station *f* balnéaire; *(for skiing)* station de ski; *(recourse)* recours *m* ▶ VI: **to ~ to** avoir recours à; **in the last ~** en dernier ressort

resound [rɪ'zaund] VI: **to ~ (with)** retentir (de)

resounding [rɪ'zaundɪŋ] ADJ retentissant(e)

resource [rɪ'sɔːs] N ressource *f*; **resources** NPL ressources; **natural resources** ressources naturelles; **to leave sb to his** *(or* **her)** **own resources** *(fig)* livrer qn à lui-même *(or* elle-même)

resourceful [rɪ'sɔːsful] ADJ ingénieux(-euse), débrouillard(e)

r

757

resourcefulness [rɪ'sɔ:sfəlnɪs] N ressource f
respect [rɪs'pekt] N respect m; (point, detail): **in some respects** à certains égards ▶ VT respecter; **respects** NPL respects, hommages mpl; **to have** or **show ~ for sb/sth** respecter qn/ qch; **out of ~ for** par respect pour; **with ~ to** en ce qui concerne; **in ~ of** sous le rapport de, quant à; **in this ~** sous ce rapport, à cet égard; **with due ~ I …** malgré le respect que je vous dois, je …
respectability [rɪspektə'bɪlɪtɪ] N respectabilité f
respectable [rɪs'pektəbl] ADJ respectable; (quite good: result etc) honorable; (: player) assez bon (bonne)
respectful [rɪs'pektful] ADJ respectueux(-euse)
respective [rɪs'pektɪv] ADJ respectif(-ive)
respectively [rɪs'pektɪvlɪ] ADV respectivement
respiration [respɪ'reɪʃən] N respiration f
respirator ['respɪreɪtəʳ] N respirateur m
respiratory ['respərətərɪ] ADJ respiratoire
respite ['respaɪt] N répit m
resplendent [rɪs'plendənt] ADJ resplendissant(e)
respond [rɪs'pɔnd] VI répondre; (react) réagir
respondent [rɪs'pɔndənt] N (Law) défendeur(-deresse)
response [rɪs'pɔns] N réponse f; (reaction) réaction f; **in ~ to** en réponse à
responsibility [rɪspɔnsɪ'bɪlɪtɪ] N responsabilité f; **to take ~ for sth/sb** accepter la responsabilité de qch/d'être responsable de qn
responsible [rɪs'pɔnsɪbl] ADJ (liable): **~ (for)** responsable (de); (person) digne de confiance; (job) qui comporte des responsabilités; **to be ~ to sb (for sth)** être responsable devant qn (de qch)
responsibly [rɪs'pɔnsɪblɪ] ADV avec sérieux
responsive [rɪs'pɔnsɪv] ADJ (student, audience) réceptif(-ive); (brakes, steering) sensible
rest [rest] N repos m; (stop) arrêt m, pause f; (Mus) silence m; (support) support m, appui m; (remainder) reste m, restant m ▶ VI se reposer; (be supported): **to ~ on** appuyer or reposer sur; (remain) rester ▶ VT (lean): **to ~ sth on/against** appuyer qch sur/contre; **the ~ of them** les autres; **to set sb's mind at ~** tranquilliser qn; **it rests with him to** c'est à lui de; **~ assured that …** soyez assuré que …
restart [ri:'stɑ:t] VT (engine) remettre en marche; (work) reprendre
restaurant ['restərɔŋ] N restaurant m
restaurant car N (Brit Rail) wagon-restaurant m
rest cure N cure f de repos
restful ['restful] ADJ reposant(e)
rest home N maison f de repos
restitution [restɪ'tju:ʃən] N (act) restitution f; (reparation) réparation f
restive ['restɪv] ADJ agité(e), impatient(e); (horse) rétif(-ive)
restless ['restlɪs] ADJ agité(e); **to get ~** s'impatienter
restlessly ['restlɪslɪ] ADV avec agitation
restock [ri:'stɔk] VT réapprovisionner

restoration [restə'reɪʃən] N (of building) restauration f; (of stolen goods) restitution f
restorative [rɪ'stɔrətɪv] ADJ reconstituant(e) ▶ N reconstituant m
restore [rɪ'stɔ:ʳ] VT (building) restaurer; (sth stolen) restituer; (peace, health) rétablir; **to ~ to** (former state) ramener à
restorer [rɪ'stɔ:rəʳ] N (Art etc) restaurateur(-trice) (d'œuvres d'art)
restrain [rɪs'treɪn] VT (feeling) contenir; (person): **to ~ (from doing)** retenir (de faire)
restrained [rɪs'treɪnd] ADJ (style) sobre; (manner) mesuré(e)
restraint [rɪs'treɪnt] N (restriction) contrainte f; (moderation) retenue f; (of style) sobriété f; **wage ~** limitations salariales
restrict [rɪs'trɪkt] VT restreindre, limiter
restricted area [rɪs'trɪktɪd-] N (Aut) zone f à vitesse limitée
restriction [rɪs'trɪkʃən] N restriction f, limitation f
restrictive [rɪs'trɪktɪv] ADJ restrictif(-ive)
restrictive practices NPL (Industry) pratiques fpl entravant la libre concurrence
rest room N (US) toilettes fpl
restructure [ri:'strʌktʃəʳ] VT restructurer
result [rɪ'zʌlt] N résultat m ▶ VI: **to ~ (from)** résulter (de); **to ~ in** aboutir à, se terminer par; **as a ~ it is too expensive** il en résulte que c'est trop cher; **as a ~ of** à la suite de
resultant [rɪ'zʌltənt] ADJ résultant(e)
resume [rɪ'zju:m] VT (work, journey) reprendre; (sum up) résumer ▶ VI (work etc) reprendre
résumé ['reɪzju:meɪ] N (summary) résumé m; (US: curriculum vitae) curriculum vitae m inv
resumption [rɪ'zʌmpʃən] N reprise f
resurgence [rɪ'sə:dʒəns] N réapparition f
resurrection [rezə'rekʃən] N résurrection f
resuscitate [rɪ'sʌsɪteɪt] VT (Med) réanimer
resuscitation [rɪsʌsɪ'teɪʃən] N réanimation f
retail ['ri:teɪl] N (vente f au) détail m ▶ ADJ de or au détail ▶ ADV au détail ▶ VT vendre au détail ▶ VI: **to ~ at 10 euros** se vendre au détail à 10 euros
retailer ['ri:teɪləʳ] N détaillant(e)
retail outlet N point m de vente
retail price N prix m de détail
retail price index N ≈ indice m des prix
retain [rɪ'teɪn] VT (keep) garder, conserver; (employ) engager
retainer [rɪ'teɪnəʳ] N (servant) serviteur m; (fee) acompte m, provision f
retaliate [rɪ'tælɪeɪt] VI: **to ~ (against)** se venger (de); **to ~ (on sb)** rendre la pareille (à qn)
retaliation [rɪtælɪ'eɪʃən] N représailles fpl, vengeance f; **in ~ for** par représailles pour
retaliatory [rɪ'tælɪətərɪ] ADJ de représailles
retarded [rɪ'tɑ:dɪd] (pej) ADJ retardé(e)
retch [retʃ] VI avoir des haut-le-cœur
retentive [rɪ'tentɪv] ADJ: **~ memory** excellente mémoire
rethink ['ri:'θɪŋk] VT repenser
reticence ['retɪsns] N réticence f
reticent ['retɪsnt] ADJ réticent(e)

retina ['rɛtɪnə] N rétine f
retinue ['rɛtɪnjuː] N suite f, cortège m
retire [rɪ'taɪəʳ] VI (give up work) prendre sa
retraite; (withdraw) se retirer, partir; (go to bed)
(aller) se coucher
retired [rɪ'taɪəd] ADJ (person) retraité(e)
retirement [rɪ'taɪəmənt] N retraite f
retirement age N âge m de la retraite
retiring [rɪ'taɪərɪŋ] ADJ (person) réservé(e);
(chairman etc) sortant(e)
retort [rɪ'tɔːt] N (reply) riposte f; (container)
cornue f ▸ VI riposter
retrace [riː'treɪs] VT reconstituer; **to ~ one's
steps** revenir sur ses pas
retract [rɪ'trækt] VT (statement, claws) rétracter;
(undercarriage, aerial) rentrer, escamoter ▸ VI se
rétracter; rentrer
retractable [rɪ'træktəbl] ADJ escamotable
retrain [riː'treɪn] VT recycler ▸ VI se recycler
retraining [riː'treɪnɪŋ] N recyclage m
retread VT [riː'trɛd] (Aut: tyre) rechaper ▸ N
['riːtrɛd] pneu rechapé
retreat [rɪ'triːt] N retraite f ▸ VI battre en
retraite; (flood) reculer; **to beat a hasty ~** (fig)
partir avec précipitation
retrial [riː'traɪəl] N nouveau procès
retribution [rɛtrɪ'bjuːʃən] N châtiment m
retrieval [rɪ'triːvəl] N récupération f; réparation
f; recherche f et extraction f
retrieve [rɪ'triːv] VT (sth lost) récupérer; (situation,
honour) sauver; (error, loss) réparer; (Comput)
rechercher
retriever [rɪ'triːvəʳ] N chien m d'arrêt
retroactive [rɛtrəʊ'æktɪv] ADJ rétroactif(-ive)
retrograde ['rɛtrəgreɪd] ADJ rétrograde
retrospect ['rɛtrəspɛkt] N: **in ~**
rétrospectivement, après coup
retrospective [rɛtrə'spɛktɪv] ADJ
rétrospectif(-ive); (law) rétroactif(-ive) ▸ N (Art)
rétrospective f
return [rɪ'tɜːn] N (going or coming back) retour m;
(of sth stolen etc) restitution f; (recompense)
récompense f; (Finance: from land, shares) rapport
m; (report) relevé m, rapport ▸ CPD (journey) de
retour; (Brit: ticket) aller et retour; (match)
retour ▸ VI (person etc: come back) revenir; (: go
back) retourner ▸ VT rendre; (bring back)
rapporter; (send back) renvoyer; (put back)
remettre; (Pol: candidate) élire; **returns** NPL
(Comm) recettes fpl; (Finance) bénéfices mpl;
(: returned goods) marchandises renvoyées; **many
happy returns (of the day)!** bon anniversaire!;
by ~ (of post) par retour (du courrier); **in ~ (for)**
en échange (de); **a ~ (ticket) for …** un billet
aller et retour pour …
returnable [rɪ'tɜːnəbl] ADJ (bottle etc) consigné(e)
returner [rɪ'tɜːnəʳ] N femme qui reprend un travail
après avoir élevé ses enfants
returning officer [rɪ'tɜːnɪŋ-] (Brit Pol)
président m de bureau de vote
return key N (Comput) touche f de retour
return ticket N (esp Brit) billet m aller-retour
retweet [riː'twiːt] VT (on Twitter) retweeter ▸ N
retweet m

reunion [riː'juːnɪən] N réunion f
reunite [riːjuː'naɪt] VT réunir
reuse [riː'juːz] VT réutiliser
rev [rɛv] N ABBR (Aut: = revolution) tour m ▸ VT
(also: **rev up**) emballer ▸ VI (also: **rev up**)
s'emballer
Rev. ABBR = **Reverend**
revaluation [riːvæljuˈeɪʃən] N réévaluation f
revamp [riː'væmp] VT (house) retaper; (firm)
réorganiser
rev counter N (Brit) compte-tours m inv
Revd. ABBR = **Reverend**
reveal [rɪ'viːl] VT (make known) révéler; (display)
laisser voir
revealing [rɪ'viːlɪŋ] ADJ révélateur(-trice); (dress)
au décolleté généreux or suggestif
reveille [rɪ'vælɪ] N (Mil) réveil m
revel ['rɛvl] VI: **to ~ in sth/in doing** se délecter
de qch/à faire
revelation [rɛvə'leɪʃən] N révélation f
reveller ['rɛvləʳ] N fêtard m
revelry ['rɛvlrɪ] N festivités fpl
revenge [rɪ'vɛndʒ] N vengeance f; (in game etc)
revanche f ▸ VT venger; **to take ~ (on)** se venger
(sur)
revengeful [rɪ'vɛndʒful] ADJ vengeur(-eresse),
vindicatif(-ive)
revenue ['rɛvənjuː] N revenu m
reverberate [rɪ'vɜːbəreɪt] VI (sound) retentir, se
répercuter; (light) se réverbérer
reverberation [rɪvɜːbə'reɪʃən] N répercussion f;
réverbération f
revere [rɪ'vɪəʳ] VT vénérer, révérer
reverence ['rɛvərəns] N vénération f, révérence f
Reverend ['rɛvərənd] ADJ vénérable; (in titles):
the ~ John Smith (Anglican) le révérend John
Smith; (Catholic) l'abbé (John) Smith;
(Protestant) le pasteur (John) Smith
reverent ['rɛvərənt] ADJ respectueux(-euse)
reverie ['rɛvərɪ] N rêverie f
reversal [rɪ'vɜːsl] N (of opinion) revirement m; (of
order) renversement m; (of direction) changement m
reverse [rɪ'vɜːs] N contraire m, opposé m; (back)
dos m, envers m; (of paper) verso m; (of coin) revers
m; (Aut: also: **reverse gear**) marche f arrière
▸ ADJ (order, direction) opposé(e), inverse ▸ VT
(order, position) changer, inverser; (direction, policy)
changer complètement de; (decision) annuler;
(roles) renverser; (car) faire marche arrière avec;
(Law: judgment) réformer ▸ VI (Brit Aut) faire
marche arrière; **to go into ~** faire marche
arrière; **in ~ order** en ordre inverse
reverse video N vidéo m inverse
reversible [rɪ'vɜːsəbl] ADJ (garment) réversible;
(procedure) révocable
reversing lights [rɪ'vɜːsɪŋ-] NPL (Brit Aut) feux
mpl de marche arrière or de recul
reversion [rɪ'vɜːʃən] N retour m
revert [rɪ'vɜːt] VI: **to ~ to** revenir à, retourner à
review [rɪ'vjuː] N revue f; (of book, film) critique f;
(of situation, policy) examen m, bilan m; (US:
examination) examen ▸ VT passer en revue; faire
la critique de; examiner; **to come under ~** être
révisé(e)

r

reviewer [rɪ'vju:əʳ] N critique *m*
revile [rɪ'vaɪl] VT injurier
revise [rɪ'vaɪz] VT réviser, modifier; (*manuscript*) revoir, corriger ▶ VI (*study*) réviser; **revised edition** édition revue et corrigée
revision [rɪ'vɪʒən] N révision *f*; (*revised version*) version corrigée
revitalize [ri:'vaɪtəlaɪz] VT revitaliser
revival [rɪ'vaɪvəl] N reprise *f*; (*recovery*) rétablissement *m*; (*of faith*) renouveau *m*
revive [rɪ'vaɪv] VT (*person*) ranimer; (*custom*) rétablir; (*economy*) relancer; (*hope, courage*) raviver, faire renaître; (*play, fashion*) reprendre ▶ VI (*person*) reprendre connaissance; (: *from ill health*) se rétablir; (*hope etc*) renaître; (*activity*) reprendre
revoke [rɪ'vəuk] VT révoquer; (*promise, decision*) revenir sur
revolt [rɪ'vəult] N révolte *f* ▶ VI se révolter, se rebeller ▶ VT révolter, dégoûter
revolting [rɪ'vəultɪŋ] ADJ dégoûtant(e)
revolution [rɛvə'lu:ʃən] N révolution *f*; (*of wheel etc*) tour *m*, révolution
revolutionary [rɛvə'lu:ʃənrɪ] ADJ, N révolutionnaire (*mf*)
revolutionize [rɛvə'lu:ʃənaɪz] VT révolutionner
revolve [rɪ'vɔlv] VI tourner
revolver [rɪ'vɔlvəʳ] N revolver *m*
revolving [rɪ'vɔlvɪŋ] ADJ (*chair*) pivotant(e); (*light*) tournant(e)
revolving door N (porte *f* à) tambour *m*
revue [rɪ'vju:] N (*Theat*) revue *f*
revulsion [rɪ'vʌlʃən] N dégoût *m*, répugnance *f*
reward [rɪ'wɔ:d] N récompense *f* ▶ VT: **to ~ (for)** récompenser (de)
rewarding [rɪ'wɔ:dɪŋ] ADJ (*fig*) qui (en) vaut la peine, gratifiant(e); **financially ~** financièrement intéressant(e)
rewind [ri:'waɪnd] VT (*irreg: like* **wind²**) (*watch*) remonter; (*tape*) réembobiner
rewire [ri:'waɪəʳ] VT (*house*) refaire l'installation électrique de
reword [ri:'wə:d] VT formuler *or* exprimer différemment
rewritable [ri:'raɪtəbl] ADJ (*CD, DVD*) réinscriptible
rewrite [ri:'raɪt] VT (*irreg: like* **write**) récrire
Reykjavik ['reɪkjəvi:k] N Reykjavik
RFD ABBR (*US Post*) = **rural free delivery**
Rh ABBR (= *rhesus*) Rh
rhapsody ['ræpsədɪ] N (*Mus*) rhapsodie *f*; (*fig*) éloge délirant
rhesus negative ['ri:səs-] ADJ (*Med*) de rhésus négatif
rhesus positive ['ri:səs-] ADJ (*Med*) de rhésus positif
rhetoric ['rɛtərɪk] N rhétorique *f*
rhetorical [rɪ'tɔrɪkl] ADJ rhétorique
rheumatic [ru:'mætɪk] ADJ rhumatismal(e)
rheumatism ['ru:mətɪzəm] N rhumatisme *m*
rheumatoid arthritis ['ru:mətɔɪd-] N polyarthrite *f* chronique
Rhine [raɪn] N: **the (River) ~** le Rhin
rhinestone ['raɪnstəun] N faux diamant

rhinoceros [raɪ'nɔsərəs] N rhinocéros *m*
Rhodes [rəudz] N Rhodes *f*
Rhodesia [rəu'di:ʒə] N Rhodésie *f*
Rhodesian [rəu'di:ʒən] ADJ rhodésien(ne) ▶ N Rhodésien(ne)
rhododendron [rəudə'dɛndrn] N rhododendron *m*
rhubarb ['ru:bɑ:b] N rhubarbe *f*
rhyme [raɪm] N rime *f*; (*verse*) vers *mpl* ▶ VI: **to ~ (with)** rimer (avec); **without ~ or reason** sans rime ni raison
rhythm ['rɪðm] N rythme *m*
rhythmic ['rɪðmɪk], **rhythmical** ['rɪðmɪkl] ADJ rythmique
rhythmically ['rɪðmɪklɪ] ADV avec rythme
rhythm method N méthode *f* des températures
RI N ABBR (*BRIT*) = **religious instruction** ▶ ABBR (*US*) = **Rhode Island**
rib [rɪb] N (*Anat*) côte *f* ▶ VT (*mock*) taquiner
ribald ['rɪbəld] ADJ paillard(e)
ribbed [rɪbd] ADJ (*knitting*) à côtes; (*shell*) strié(e)
ribbon ['rɪbən] N ruban *m*; **in ribbons** (*torn*) en lambeaux
rice [raɪs] N riz *m*
rice field N rizière *f*
rice pudding N riz *m* au lait
rich [rɪtʃ] ADJ riche; (*gift, clothes*) somptueux(-euse); **the ~** *npl* les riches *mpl*; **riches** NPL richesses *fpl*; **to be ~ in sth** être riche en qch
richly ['rɪtʃlɪ] ADV richement; (*deserved, earned*) largement, grandement
richness ['rɪtʃnɪs] N richesse *f*
rickets ['rɪkɪts] N rachitisme *m*
rickety ['rɪkɪtɪ] ADJ branlant(e)
rickshaw ['rɪkʃɔ:] N pousse(-pousse) *m inv*
ricochet ['rɪkəʃeɪ] N ricochet *m* ▶ VI ricocher
rid [rɪd] (*pt, pp* ~) VT: **to ~ sb of** débarrasser qn de; **to get ~ of** se débarrasser de
riddance ['rɪdns] N: **good ~!** bon débarras!
ridden ['rɪdn] PP *of* **ride**
riddle ['rɪdl] N (*puzzle*) énigme *f* ▶ VT: **to be riddled with** être criblé(e) de; (*fig*) être en proie à
ride [raɪd] (*pt* **rode** [rəud], *pp* **ridden** ['rɪdn]) N promenade *f*, tour *m*; (*distance covered*) trajet *m* ▶ VI (*as sport*) monter (à cheval), faire du cheval; (*go somewhere: on horse, bicycle*) aller (à cheval *or* bicyclette *etc*); (*travel: on bicycle, motor cycle, bus*) rouler ▶ VT (*a horse*) monter; (*distance*) parcourir, faire; **we rode all day/all the way** nous sommes restés toute la journée en selle/avons fait tout le chemin en selle *or* à cheval; **to ~ a horse/bicycle** monter à cheval/à bicyclette; **can you ~ a bike?** est-ce que tu sais monter à bicyclette?; **to ~ at anchor** (*Naut*) être à l'ancre; **horse/car ~** promenade *or* tour à cheval/en voiture; **to go for a ~** faire une promenade (en voiture *or* à bicyclette *etc*); **to take sb for a ~** (*fig*) faire marcher qn; (*cheat*) rouler qn ▶ **ride out** VT: **to ~ out the storm** (*fig*) surmonter les difficultés
rider ['raɪdəʳ] N cavalier(-ière); (*in race*) jockey *m*; (*on bicycle*) cycliste *mf*; (*on motorcycle*)

motocycliste *mf*; (*in document*) annexe *f*, clause additionnelle

ridge [rɪdʒ] N (*of hill*) faîte *m*; (*of roof, mountain*) arête *f*; (*on object*) strie *f*

ridicule ['rɪdɪkjuːl] N ridicule *m*; dérision *f* ▶ VT ridiculiser, tourner en dérision; **to hold sb/sth up to ~** tourner qn/qch en ridicule

ridiculous [rɪ'dɪkjuləs] ADJ ridicule

riding ['raɪdɪŋ] N équitation *f*

riding school N manège *m*, école *f* d'équitation

rife [raɪf] ADJ répandu(e); **~ with** abondant(e) en

riffraff ['rɪfræf] N racaille *f*

rifle ['raɪfl] N fusil *m* (à canon rayé) ▶ VT vider, dévaliser
▶ **rifle through** VT FUS fouiller dans

rifle range N champ *m* de tir; (*indoor*) stand *m* de tir

rift [rɪft] N fente *f*, fissure *f*; (*fig: disagreement*) désaccord *m*

rig [rɪg] N (*also:* **oil rig**: *on land*) derrick *m*; (: *at sea*) plate-forme pétrolière ▶ VT (*election etc*) truquer
▶ **rig out** VT (*BRIT*) habiller; (: *pej*) fringuer, attifer
▶ **rig up** VT arranger, faire avec des moyens de fortune

rigging ['rɪgɪŋ] N (*Naut*) gréement *m*

right [raɪt] ADJ (*true*) juste, exact(e); (*correct*) bon (bonne); (*suitable*) approprié(e), convenable; (*just*) juste, équitable; (*morally good*) bien inv; (*not left*) droit(e) ▶ N (*moral good*) bien *m*; (*title, claim*) droit *m*; (*not left*) droite *f* ▶ ADV (*answer*) correctement; (*treat*) bien, comme il faut; (*not on the left*) à droite ▶ VT redresser ▶ EXCL bon!; **rights** NPL (*Comm*) droits *mpl*; **the ~ time** (*precise*) l'heure exacte; (*not wrong*) la bonne heure; **do you have the ~ time?** avez-vous l'heure juste *or* exacte?; **to be ~** (*person*) avoir raison; (*answer*) être juste *or* correct(e); **to get sth ~** ne pas se tromper sur qch; **let's get it ~ this time!** essayons de ne pas nous tromper cette fois-ci!; **you did the ~ thing** vous avez bien fait; **to put a mistake ~** (*BRIT*) rectifier une erreur; **by rights** en toute justice; **on the ~** à droite; **~ and wrong** le bien et le mal; **to be in the ~** avoir raison; **film rights** droits d'adaptation cinématographique; **~ now** en ce moment même; (*immediately*) tout de suite; **~ before/ after** juste avant/après; **~ against the wall** tout contre le mur; **~ ahead** tout droit; droit devant; **~ in the middle** en plein milieu; **~ away** immédiatement; **to go ~ to the end of sth** aller jusqu'au bout de qch

right angle N (*Math*) angle droit

righteous ['raɪtʃəs] ADJ droit(e), vertueux(-euse); (*anger*) justifié(e)

righteousness ['raɪtʃəsnɪs] N droiture *f*, vertu *f*

rightful ['raɪtful] ADJ (*heir*) légitime

rightfully ['raɪtfəlɪ] ADV à juste titre, légitimement

right-hand ['raɪthænd] ADJ: **the ~ side** la droite

right-hand drive N conduite *f* à droite; (*vehicle*) véhicule *m* avec la conduite à droite

right-handed [raɪt'hændɪd] ADJ (*person*) droitier(-ière)

right-hand man N (*irreg*) bras droit (*fig*)

rightly ['raɪtlɪ] ADV bien, correctement; (*with reason*) à juste titre; **if I remember ~** (*BRIT*) si je me souviens bien

right-minded ['raɪt'maɪndɪd] ADJ sensé(e), sain(e) d'esprit

right of way N (*on path etc*) droit *m* de passage; (*Aut*) priorité *f*

rights issue N (*Stock Exchange*) émission préférentielle *or* de droit de souscription

right wing N (*Mil, Sport*) aile droite; (*Pol*) droite *f*

right-wing [raɪt'wɪŋ] ADJ (*Pol*) de droite

right-winger [raɪt'wɪŋər] N (*Pol*) membre *m* de la droite; (*Sport*) ailier droit

rigid ['rɪdʒɪd] ADJ rigide; (*principle, control*) strict(e)

rigidity [rɪ'dʒɪdɪtɪ] N rigidité *f*

rigidly ['rɪdʒɪdlɪ] ADV rigidement; (*behave*) inflexiblement

rigmarole ['rɪgmərəul] N galimatias *m*, comédie *f*

rigor ['rɪgər] N (*US*) = **rigour**

rigor mortis ['rɪgə'mɔːtɪs] N rigidité *f* cadavérique

rigorous ['rɪgərəs] ADJ rigoureux(-euse)

rigorously ['rɪgərəslɪ] ADV rigoureusement

rigour, (*US*) **rigor** ['rɪgər] N rigueur *f*

rig-out ['rɪgaut] N (*BRIT inf*) tenue *f*

rile [raɪl] VT agacer

rim [rɪm] N bord *m*; (*of spectacles*) monture *f*; (*of wheel*) jante *f*

rimless ['rɪmlɪs] ADJ (*spectacles*) à monture invisible

rind [raɪnd] N (*of bacon*) couenne *f*; (*of lemon etc*) écorce *f*, zeste *m*; (*of cheese*) croûte *f*

ring [rɪŋ] (*pt* **rang** [ræŋ], *pp* **rung** [rʌŋ]) N anneau *m*; (*on finger*) bague *f*; (*also:* **wedding ring**) alliance *f*; (*for napkin*) rond *m*; (*of people, objects*) cercle *m*; (*of spies*) réseau *m*; (*of smoke etc*) rond *m*; (*arena*) piste *f*, arène *f*; (*for boxing*) ring *m*; (*sound of bell*) sonnerie *f*; (*telephone call*) coup *m* de téléphone ▶ VI (*telephone, bell*) sonner; (*person: by telephone*) téléphoner; (*ears*) bourdonner; (*also:* **ring out**: *voice, words*) retentir ▶ VT (*also:* **ring up**) téléphoner à, appeler; **to ~ the bell** sonner; **to give sb a ~** (*Tel*) passer un coup de téléphone *or* de fil à qn; **that has the ~ of truth about it** cela sonne vrai; **the name doesn't ~ a bell (with me)** ce nom ne me dit rien
▶ **ring back** VT, VI (*BRIT Tel*) rappeler
▶ **ring off** VI (*BRIT Tel*) raccrocher
▶ **ring up** VT (*BRIT Tel*) téléphoner à, appeler

ring binder N classeur *m* à anneaux

ring-fence [rɪŋ'fɛns] VT (*allocate*) réserver; allouer; (*protect*) protéger

ring finger N annulaire *m*

ringing ['rɪŋɪŋ] N (*of bell*) tintement *m*; (*louder: of telephone*) sonnerie *f*; (: *in ears*) bourdonnement *m*

ringing tone N (*BRIT Tel*) tonalité *f* d'appel

ringleader ['rɪŋliːdər] N (*of gang*) chef *m*, meneur *m*

ringlets ['rɪŋlɪts] NPL anglaises *fpl*

ring road N (*BRIT*) rocade *f*; (*motorway*) périphérique *m*

r

ringtone ['rɪŋtəun] N (*on mobile*) sonnerie *f* (*de téléphone portable*)

rink [rɪŋk] N (*also:* **ice rink**) patinoire *f*; (*for roller-skating*) skating *m*

rinse [rɪns] N rinçage *m* ▶ VT rincer

Rio ['riːəu], **Rio de Janeiro** ['riːəudədʒə'nɪərəu] N Rio de Janeiro

riot ['raɪət] N émeute *f*, bagarres *fpl* ▶ VI (*demonstrators*) manifester avec violence; (*population*) se soulever, se révolter; **a ~ of colours** une débauche *or* orgie de couleurs; **to run ~** se déchaîner

rioter ['raɪətəʳ] N émeutier(-ière), manifestant(e)

riot gear N: **in ~** casqué et portant un bouclier

riotous ['raɪətəs] ADJ tapageur(-euse); tordant(e)

riotously ['raɪətəslɪ] ADV: **~ funny** tordant(e)

riot police N forces *fpl* de police intervenant en cas d'émeute; **hundreds of ~** des centaines de policiers casqués et armés

RIP ABBR (= *rest in peace*) RIP

rip [rɪp] N déchirure *f* ▶ VT déchirer ▶ VI se déchirer
  ▶ **rip off** VT (*inf: cheat*) arnaquer
  ▶ **rip up** VT déchirer

ripcord ['rɪpkɔːd] N poignée *f* d'ouverture

ripe [raɪp] ADJ (*fruit*) mûr(e); (*cheese*) fait(e)

ripen ['raɪpn] VT mûrir ▶ VI mûrir; se faire

ripeness ['raɪpnɪs] N maturité *f*

rip-off ['rɪpɔf] N (*inf*): **it's a ~!** c'est du vol manifeste!, c'est de l'arnaque!

riposte [rɪ'pɒst] N riposte *f*

ripple ['rɪpl] N ride *f*, ondulation *f*; (*of applause, laughter*) cascade *f* ▶ VI se rider, onduler ▶ VT rider, faire onduler

rise [raɪz] (*pt* **rose** [rəuz], *pp* **risen** [rɪzn]) N (*slope*) côte *f*, pente *f*; (*hill*) élévation *f*; (*increase: in wages:* BRIT) augmentation *f*; (: *in prices, temperature*) hausse *f*, augmentation; (*fig: to power etc*) ascension *f* ▶ VI s'élever, monter; (*prices, numbers*) augmenter, monter; (*waters, river*) monter; (*sun, wind, person: from chair, bed*) se lever; (*also:* **rise up**: *tower, building*) s'élever; (: *rebel*) se révolter, se rebeller; (*in rank*) s'élever; **~ to power** montée *f* au pouvoir; **to give ~ to** donner lieu à; **to ~ to the occasion** se montrer à la hauteur

risen ['rɪzn] PP of **rise**

rising ['raɪzɪŋ] ADJ (*increasing: number, prices*) en hausse; (*tide*) montant(e); (*sun, moon*) levant(e) ▶ N (*uprising*) soulèvement *m*, insurrection *f*

rising damp N humidité *f* (montant des fondations)

rising star N (*also fig*) étoile montante

risk [rɪsk] N risque *m*, danger *m*; (*deliberate*) risque ▶ VT risquer; **to take** *or* **run the ~ of doing** courir le risque de faire; **at ~** en danger; **at one's own ~** à ses risques et périls; **it's a fire/health ~** cela présente un risque d'incendie/pour la santé; **I'll ~ it** je vais risquer le coup

risk capital N capital-risque *m*

risky ['rɪskɪ] ADJ risqué(e)

risqué ['riːskeɪ] ADJ (*joke*) risqué(e)

rissole ['rɪsəul] N croquette *f*

rite [raɪt] N rite *m*; **the last rites** les derniers sacrements

ritual ['rɪtjuəl] ADJ rituel(le) ▶ N rituel *m*

rival ['raɪvl] N rival(e); (*in business*) concurrent(e) ▶ ADJ rival(e); qui fait concurrence ▶ VT (*match*) égaler; (*compete with*) être en concurrence avec; **to ~ sb/sth in** rivaliser avec qn/qch de

rivalry ['raɪvlrɪ] N rivalité *f*; (*in business*) concurrence *f*

river ['rɪvəʳ] N rivière *f*; (*major, also fig*) fleuve *m* ▶ CPD (*port, traffic*) fluvial(e); **up/down ~** en amont/aval

riverbank ['rɪvəbæŋk] N rive *f*, berge *f*

riverbed ['rɪvəbed] N lit *m* (de rivière *or* de fleuve)

riverside ['rɪvəsaɪd] N bord *m* de la rivière *or* du fleuve

rivet ['rɪvɪt] N rivet *m* ▶ VT riveter; (*fig*) river, fixer

riveting ['rɪvɪtɪŋ] ADJ (*fig*) fascinant(e)

Riviera [rɪvɪ'eərə] N: **the (French) ~** la Côte d'Azur; **the Italian ~** la Riviera (italienne)

Riyadh [rɪ'jaːd] N Riyad

RMT N ABBR (= *Rail, Maritime and Transport*) syndicat des transports

RN N ABBR = **registered nurse**; (BRIT) = **Royal Navy**

RNA N ABBR (= *ribonucleic acid*) ARN *m*

RNLI N ABBR (BRIT: = *Royal National Lifeboat Institution*) ≈ SNSM *f*

RNZAF N ABBR = **Royal New Zealand Air Force**

RNZN N ABBR = **Royal New Zealand Navy**

road [rəud] N route *f*; (*in town*) rue *f*; (*fig*) chemin *m*, voie *f* ▶ CPD (*accident*) de la route; **main ~** grande route; **major/minor ~** route principale *or* à priorité/voie secondaire; **it takes four hours by ~** il y a quatre heures de route; **which ~ do I take for …?** quelle route dois-je prendre pour aller à …?; **"~ up"** (BRIT) "attention travaux"

road accident N accident *m* de la circulation

roadblock ['rəudblɔk] N barrage routier

road haulage N transports routiers

roadhog ['rəudhɔg] N chauffard *m*

road map N carte routière

road rage N comportement très agressif de certains usagers de la route

road safety N sécurité routière

roadside ['rəudsaɪd] N bord *m* de la route, bas-côté *m* ▶ CPD (*situé(e) etc*) au bord de la route; **by the ~** au bord de la route

road sign N panneau *m* de signalisation

road sweeper ['rəudswiːpəʳ] N (BRIT: *person*) balayeur(-euse)

road tax N (BRIT Aut) taxe *f* sur les automobiles

road user N usager *m* de la route

roadway ['rəudweɪ] N chaussée *f*

roadworks ['rəudwəːks] NPL travaux *mpl* (de réfection des routes)

roadworthy ['rəudwəːðɪ] ADJ en bon état de marche

roam [rəum] VI errer, vagabonder ▸ VT parcourir, errer par

roar [rɔːʳ] N rugissement m; (of crowd) hurlements mpl; (of vehicle, thunder, storm) grondement m ▸ VI rugir; hurler; gronder; **to ~ with laughter** rire à gorge déployée

roaring ['rɔːrɪŋ] ADJ: **a ~ fire** une belle flambée; **a ~ success** un succès fou; **to do a ~ trade** faire des affaires en or

roast [rəust] N rôti m ▸ VT (meat) (faire) rôtir; (coffee) griller, torréfier

roast beef N rôti m de bœuf, rosbif m

roasting ['rəustɪŋ] N (inf): **to give sb a ~** sonner les cloches à qn

rob [rɔb] VT (person) voler; (bank) dévaliser; **to ~ sb of sth** voler or dérober qch à qn; (fig: deprive) priver qn de qch

robber ['rɔbəʳ] N bandit m, voleur m

robbery ['rɔbərɪ] N vol m

robe [rəub] N (for ceremony etc) robe f; (also: **bathrobe**) peignoir m; (US: rug) couverture f ▸ VT revêtir (d'une robe)

robin ['rɔbɪn] N rouge-gorge m

robot ['rəubɔt] N robot m

robotics [rə'bɔtɪks] N robotique m

robust [rəu'bʌst] ADJ robuste; (material, appetite) solide

rock [rɔk] N (substance) roche f, roc m; (boulder) rocher m, roche; (US: small stone) caillou m; (BRIT: sweet) ≈ sucre m d'orge ▸ VT (swing gently: cradle) balancer; (: child) bercer; (shake) ébranler, secouer ▸ VI se balancer, être ébranlé(e) or secoué(e); **on the rocks** (drink) avec des glaçons; (ship) sur les écueils; (marriage etc) en train de craquer; **to ~ the boat** (fig) jouer les trouble-fête

rock and roll N rock (and roll) m, rock'n'roll m

rock-bottom ['rɔk'bɔtəm] N (fig) niveau le plus bas ▸ ADJ (fig: prices) sacrifié(e); **to reach** or **touch ~** (price, person) tomber au plus bas

rock climber N varappeur(-euse)

rock climbing N varappe f

rockery ['rɔkərɪ] N (jardin m de) rocaille f

rocket ['rɔkɪt] N fusée f; (Mil) fusée, roquette f; (Culin) roquette ▸ VI (prices) monter en flèche

rocket launcher [-lɔːnʃəʳ] N lance-roquettes m inv

rock face N paroi rocheuse

rock fall N chute f de pierres

rocking chair ['rɔkɪŋ-] N fauteuil m à bascule

rocking horse ['rɔkɪŋ-] N cheval m à bascule

rocky ['rɔkɪ] ADJ (hill) rocheux(-euse); (path) rocailleux(-euse); (unsteady: table) branlant(e)

Rocky Mountains NPL: **the ~** les (montagnes fpl) Rocheuses fpl

rod [rɔd] N (metallic) tringle f; (Tech) tige f; (wooden) baguette f; (also: **fishing rod**) canne f à pêche

rode [rəud] PT of **ride**

rodent ['rəudnt] N rongeur m

rodeo ['rəudɪəu] N rodéo m

roe [rəu] N (species: also: **roe deer**) chevreuil m; (of fish: also: **hard roe**) œufs mpl de poisson; **soft ~** laitance f

roe deer N chevreuil m; chevreuil femelle

rogue [rəug] N coquin(e)

roguish ['rəugɪʃ] ADJ coquin(e)

role [rəul] N rôle m

role-model ['rəulmɔdl] N modèle m à émuler

role play, role playing N jeu m de rôle

roll [rəul] N rouleau m; (of banknotes) liasse f; (also: **bread roll**) petit pain; (register) liste f; (sound: of drums etc) roulement m; (movement: of ship) roulis m ▸ VT rouler; (also: **roll up**: string) enrouler; (also: **roll out**: pastry) étendre au rouleau, abaisser ▸ VI rouler; (wheel) tourner; **cheese ~** ≈ sandwich m au fromage (dans un petit pain)

▸ **roll about, roll around** VI rouler çà et là; (person) se rouler par terre

▸ **roll by** VI (time) s'écouler, passer

▸ **roll in** VI (mail, cash) affluer

▸ **roll over** VI se retourner

▸ **roll up** VI (inf: arrive) arriver, s'amener ▸ VT (carpet, cloth, map) rouler; (sleeves) retrousser; **to ~ o.s. up into a ball** se rouler en boule

roll call N appel m

roller ['rəuləʳ] N rouleau m; (wheel) roulette f; (for road) rouleau compresseur; (for hair) bigoudi m

Rollerblades® ['rəuləbleɪdz] NPL patins mpl en ligne

roller blind N (BRIT) store m

roller coaster N montagnes fpl russes

roller skates NPL patins mpl à roulettes

roller-skating ['rəuləskeɪtɪŋ] N patin m à roulettes; **to go ~** faire du patin à roulettes

rollicking ['rɔlɪkɪŋ] ADJ bruyant(e) et joyeux(-euse); (play) bouffon(ne); **to have a ~ time** s'amuser follement

rolling ['rəulɪŋ] ADJ (landscape) onduleux(-euse)

rolling mill N laminoir m

rolling pin N rouleau m à pâtisserie

rolling stock N (Rail) matériel roulant

roll-on-roll-off ['rəulɔn'rəulɔf] ADJ (BRIT: ferry) roulier-ière)

roly-poly ['rəulɪ'pəulɪ] N (BRIT Culin) roulé m à la confiture

ROM [rɔm] N ABBR (Comput: = read-only memory) mémoire morte, ROM f

Roman ['rəumən] ADJ romain(e) ▸ N Romain(e)

Roman Catholic ADJ, N catholique (mf)

romance [rə'mæns] N (love affair) idylle f; (charm) poésie f; (novel) roman m à l'eau de rose

Romanesque [rəumə'nɛsk] ADJ roman(e)

Romania [rəu'meɪnɪə] N = **Rumania**

Romanian [rəu'meɪnɪən] ADJ, N see **Rumanian**

Roman numeral N chiffre romain

romantic [rə'mæntɪk] ADJ romantique; (novel, attachment) sentimental(e)

romanticism [rə'mæntɪsɪzəm] N romantisme m

Romany ['rɔmənɪ] ADJ de bohémien ▸ N bohémien(ne); (Ling) romani m

Rome [rəum] N Rome

romp [rɔmp] N jeux bruyants ▸ VI (also: **romp about**) s'ébattre, jouer bruyamment; **to ~ home** (horse) arriver bon premier

rompers ['rɔmpəz] NPL barboteuse f

763

rondo ['rɔndəu] N (Mus) rondeau m
roof [ru:f] N toit m; (of tunnel, cave) plafond m
▶ VT couvrir (d'un toit); **the ~ of the mouth** la voûte du palais
roof garden N toit-terrasse m
roofing ['ru:fɪŋ] N toiture f
roof rack N (Aut) galerie f
rook [ruk] N (bird) freux m; (Chess) tour f ▶ VT (inf: cheat) rouler, escroquer
rookie ['rukɪ] N (inf: esp Mil) bleu m
room [ru:m] N (in house) pièce f; (also: **bedroom**) chambre f (à coucher); (in school etc) salle f; (space) place f; **rooms** NPL (lodging) meublé m; **"rooms to let"**, (US) **"rooms for rent"** "chambres à louer"; **is there ~ for this?** est-ce qu'il y a de la place pour ceci?; **to make ~ for sb** faire de la place à qn; **there is ~ for improvement** on peut faire mieux
rooming house ['ru:mɪŋ-] N (US) maison f de rapport
roommate ['ru:mmeɪt] N camarade mf de chambre
room service N service m des chambres (dans un hôtel)
room temperature N température ambiante; **"serve at ~"** (wine) "servir chambré"
roomy ['ru:mɪ] ADJ spacieux(-euse); (garment) ample
roost [ru:st] N juchoir m ▶ VI se jucher
rooster ['ru:stəʳ] N coq m
root [ru:t] N (Bot, Math) racine f; (fig: of problem) origine f, fond m ▶ VI (plant) s'enraciner; **to take ~** (plant, idea) prendre racine
▶ **root about** VI (fig) fouiller
▶ **root for** VT FUS (inf) applaudir
▶ **root out** VT extirper
root beer N (US) sorte de limonade à base d'extraits végétaux
rope [rəup] N corde f; (Naut) cordage m ▶ VT (box) corder; (tie up or together) attacher; (climbers: also: **rope together**) encorder; (area: also: **rope off**) interdire l'accès de; (: divide off) séparer; **to ~ sb in** (fig) embringuer qn; **to know the ropes** (fig) être au courant, connaître les ficelles
rope ladder N échelle f de corde
ropey ['rəupɪ] ADJ (inf) pas fameux(-euse) or brillant(e); **I feel a bit ~ today** c'est pas la forme aujourd'hui
rort [rɔ:t] N (AUSTRALIA, NEW ZEALAND inf) arnaque f (inf) ▶ VT escroquer
rosary ['rəuzərɪ] N chapelet m
rose [rəuz] PT of **rise** ▶ N rose f; (also: **rosebush**) rosier m; (on watering can) pomme f ▶ ADJ rose
rosé ['rəuzeɪ] N rosé m
rosebed ['rəuzbɛd] N massif m de rosiers
rosebud ['rəuzbʌd] N bouton m de rose
rosebush ['rəuzbuʃ] N rosier m
rosemary ['rəuzmərɪ] N romarin m
rosette [rəu'zɛt] N rosette f; (larger) cocarde f
ROSPA ['rɔspə] N ABBR (BRIT) = **Royal Society for the Prevention of Accidents**
roster ['rɔstəʳ] N: **duty ~** tableau m de service
rostrum ['rɔstrəm] N tribune f (pour un orateur etc)
rosy ['rəuzɪ] ADJ rose; **a ~ future** un bel avenir

rot [rɔt] N (decay) pourriture f; (fig: pej: nonsense) idioties fpl, balivernes fpl ▶ VT, VI pourrir; **to stop the ~** (BRIT fig) rétablir la situation; **dry ~** pourriture sèche (du bois); **wet ~** pourriture (du bois)
rota ['rəutə] N liste f, tableau m de service; **on a ~ basis** par roulement
rotary ['rəutərɪ] ADJ rotatif(-ive)
rotate [rəu'teɪt] VT (revolve) faire tourner; (change round: crops) alterner; (: jobs) faire à tour de rôle ▶ VI (revolve) tourner
rotating [rəu'teɪtɪŋ] ADJ (movement) tournant(e)
rotation [rəu'teɪʃən] N rotation f; **in ~** à tour de rôle
rote [rəut] N: **by ~** machinalement, par cœur
rotor ['rəutəʳ] N rotor m
rotten ['rɔtn] ADJ (decayed) pourri(e); (dishonest) corrompu(e); (inf: bad) mauvais(e), moche; **to feel ~** (ill) être mal fichu(e)
rotting ['rɔtɪŋ] ADJ pourrissant(e)
rotund [rəu'tʌnd] ADJ rondelet(te); arrondi(e)
rouble, (US) **ruble** ['ru:bl] N rouble m
rouge [ru:ʒ] N rouge m (à joues)
rough [rʌf] ADJ (cloth, skin) rêche, rugueux(-euse); (terrain) accidenté(e); (path) rocailleux(-euse); (voice) rauque, rude; (person, manner: coarse) rude, fruste; (: violent) brutal(e); (district, weather) mauvais(e); (sea) houleux(-euse); (plan) ébauché(e); (guess) approximatif(-ive) ▶ N (Golf) rough m ▶ VT: **to ~ it** vivre à la dure; **the sea is ~ today** la mer est agitée aujourd'hui; **to have a ~ time (of it)** en voir de dures; **~ estimate** approximation f; **to play ~** jouer avec brutalité; **to sleep ~** (BRIT) coucher à la dure; **to feel ~** (BRIT) être mal fichu(e)
▶ **rough out** VT (draft) ébaucher
roughage ['rʌfɪdʒ] N fibres fpl diététiques
rough-and-ready ['rʌfən'rɛdɪ] ADJ (accommodation, method) rudimentaire
rough-and-tumble ['rʌfən'tʌmbl] N agitation f
roughcast ['rʌfkɑ:st] N crépi m
rough copy, rough draft N brouillon m
roughen ['rʌfn] VT (a surface) rendre rude or rugueux(-euse)
rough justice N justice f sommaire
roughly ['rʌflɪ] ADV (handle) rudement, brutalement; (speak) avec brusquerie; (make) grossièrement; (approximately) à peu près, en gros; **~ speaking** en gros
roughness ['rʌfnɪs] N (of cloth, skin) rugosité f; (of person) rudesse f; brutalité f
roughshod ['rʌfʃɔd] ADV: **to ride ~ over** ne tenir aucun compte de
rough work N (at school etc) brouillon m
roulette [ru:'lɛt] N roulette f
Roumania etc [ru:'meɪnɪə] N = **Romania**
round [raund] ADJ rond(e) ▶ N rond m, cercle m; (BRIT: of toast) tranche f; (duty: of policeman, milkman etc) tournée f; (: of doctor) visites fpl; (game: of cards, in competition) partie f; (Boxing) round m; (of talks) série f ▶ VT (corner) tourner; (bend) prendre; (cape) doubler ▶ PREP autour de ▶ ADV: **right ~, all ~** tout autour; **in ~ figures** en

chiffres ronds; **to go the rounds** (*disease, story*) circuler; **the daily ~** (*fig*) la routine quotidienne; **~ of ammunition** cartouche *f*; **~ of applause** applaudissements *mpl*; **~ of drinks** tournée *f*; **~ of sandwiches** (*BRIT*) sandwich *m*; **the long way ~** (par) le chemin le plus long; **all (the) year ~** toute l'année; **it's just ~ the corner** c'est juste après le coin; (*fig*) c'est tout près; **to ask sb ~** inviter qn (chez soi); **I'll be ~ at 6 o'clock** je serai là à 6 heures; **to go ~** faire le tour *or* un détour; **to go ~ to sb's (house)** aller chez qn; **to go ~ an obstacle** contourner un obstacle; **go ~ the back** passez par derrière; **to go ~ a house** visiter une maison, faire le tour d'une maison; **enough to go ~** assez pour tout le monde; **she arrived ~ (about) noon** (*BRIT*) elle est arrivée vers midi; **~ the clock** 24 heures sur 24
▶ **round off** VT (*speech etc*) terminer
▶ **round up** VT rassembler; (*criminals*) effectuer une rafle de; (*prices*) arrondir (au chiffre supérieur)
roundabout ['raʊndəbaʊt] N (*BRIT: Aut*) rond-point *m* (à sens giratoire); (: *at fair*) manège *m* (de chevaux de bois) ▶ ADJ (*route, means*) détourné(e)
rounded ['raʊndɪd] ADJ arrondi(e); (*style*) harmonieux(-euse)
rounders ['raʊndəz] NPL (*game*) ≈ balle *f* au camp
roundly ['raʊndlɪ] ADV (*fig*) tout net, carrément
round-shouldered ['raʊndˈʃəʊldəd] ADJ au dos rond
round trip N (*voyage m*) aller et retour *m*
roundup ['raʊndʌp] N rassemblement *m*; (*of criminals*) rafle *f*; **a ~ of the latest news** un rappel des derniers événements
rouse [raʊz] VT (*wake up*) réveiller; (*stir up*) susciter, provoquer; (*interest*) éveiller; (*suspicions*) susciter, éveiller
rousing ['raʊzɪŋ] ADJ (*welcome*) enthousiaste
rout [raʊt] N (*Mil*) déroute *f* ▶ VT mettre en déroute
route [ruːt] N itinéraire *m*; (*of bus*) parcours *m*; (*of trade, shipping*) route *f*; **"all routes"** (*Aut*) "toutes directions"; **the best ~ to London** le meilleur itinéraire pour aller à Londres
route map N (*for journey*) croquis *m* d'itinéraire; (*for trains etc*) carte *f* du réseau
routine [ruːˈtiːn] ADJ (*work*) ordinaire, courant(e); (*procedure*) d'usage ▶ N (*habits*) habitudes *fpl*; (*pej*) train-train *m*; (*Theat*) numéro *m*; **daily ~** occupations journalières
roving ['rəʊvɪŋ] ADJ (*life*) vagabond(e)
roving reporter N reporter volant
row¹ [rəʊ] N (*line*) rangée *f*; (*of people, seats, Knitting*) rang *m*; (*behind one another: of cars, people*) file *f* ▶ VI (*in boat*) ramer; (*as sport*) faire de l'aviron ▶ VT (*boat*) faire aller à la rame *or* à l'aviron; **in a ~** (*fig*) d'affilée
row² [raʊ] N (*noise*) vacarme *m*; (*dispute*) dispute *f*, querelle *f*; (*scolding*) réprimande *f*, savon *m* ▶ VI (*also*: **to have a row**) se disputer, se quereller
rowboat ['rəʊbəʊt] N (*US*) canot *m* (à rames)
rowdiness ['raʊdɪnɪs] N tapage *m*, chahut *m*;

(*fighting*) bagarre *f*
rowdy ['raʊdɪ] ADJ chahuteur(-euse); bagarreur(-euse) ▶ N voyou *m*
rowdyism ['raʊdɪɪzəm] N tapage *m*, chahut *m*
rowing ['rəʊɪŋ] N canotage *m*; (*as sport*) aviron *m*
rowing boat N (*BRIT*) canot *m* (à rames)
rowlock ['rɒlək] N (*BRIT*) dame *f* de nage, tolet *m*
royal ['rɔɪəl] ADJ royal(e)
Royal Academy, Royal Academy of Arts N (*BRIT*) l'Académie *f* royale des Beaux-Arts; *voir article*

> La *Royal Academy* ou *Royal Academy of Arts*, fondée en 1768 par George III pour encourager la peinture, la sculpture et l'architecture, est située à Burlington House, sur Piccadilly. Une exposition des œuvres d'artistes contemporains a lieu tous les étés. L'Académie dispense également des cours en peinture, sculpture et architecture.

Royal Air Force N (*BRIT*) *armée de l'air britannique*
royal blue ADJ bleu roi *inv*
royalist ['rɔɪəlɪst] ADJ, N royaliste *mf*
Royal Navy N (*BRIT*) *marine de guerre britannique*
royalty ['rɔɪəltɪ] N (*royal persons*) (membres *mpl* de la) famille royale; (*payment: to author*) droits *mpl* d'auteur; (: *to inventor*) royalties *fpl*
RP N ABBR (*BRIT*: = *received pronunciation*) prononciation *f* standard
RPI N ABBR = **retail price index**
rpm ABBR (= *revolutions per minute*) t/mn *mpl* (= *tours/minute*)
RR ABBR (*US*) = **railway**
RRP ABBR = **recommended retail price**
RSA N ABBR (*BRIT*) = **Royal Society of Arts**; **Royal Scottish Academy**
RSI N ABBR (*Med*: = *repetitive strain injury*) microtraumatisme permanent
RSPB N ABBR (*BRIT*: = *Royal Society for the Protection of Birds*) ≈ LPO *f*
RSPCA N ABBR (*BRIT*: = *Royal Society for the Prevention of Cruelty to Animals*) ≈ SPA *f*
R.S.V.P. ABBR (= *répondez s'il vous plaît*) RSVP
RTA N ABBR (= *road traffic accident*) accident *m* de la route
Rt. Hon. ABBR (*BRIT*: = *Right Honourable*) *titre donné aux députés de la Chambre des communes*
Rt Rev. ABBR (= *Right Reverend*) très révérend
rub [rʌb] N (*with cloth*) coup *m* de chiffon *or* de torchon; (*on person*) friction *f*; **to give sth a ~** donner un coup de chiffon *or* de torchon à qch ▶ VT frotter; (*person*) frictionner; (*hands*) se frotter; **to ~ sb up** (*BRIT*) *or* **to ~ sb** (*US*) **the wrong way** prendre qn à rebrousse-poil
▶ **rub down** VT (*body*) frictionner; (*horse*) bouchonner
▶ **rub in** VT (*ointment*) faire pénétrer
▶ **rub off** VI partir; **to ~ off on** déteindre sur
▶ **rub out** VT effacer ▶ VI s'effacer
rubber ['rʌbə^r] N caoutchouc *m*; (*BRIT*: *eraser*) gomme *f* (à effacer)
rubber band N élastique *m*
rubber bullet N balle *f* en caoutchouc
rubber gloves NPL gants *mpl* en caoutchouc
rubber plant N caoutchouc *m* (*plante verte*)

r

rubber ring N (*for swimming*) bouée f (de natation)

rubber stamp N tampon m

rubber-stamp [ˌrʌbəˈstæmp] VT (*fig*) approuver sans discussion

rubbery [ˈrʌbərɪ] ADJ caoutchouteux(-euse)

rubbish [ˈrʌbɪʃ] N (*from household*) ordures fpl; (*fig: pej*) choses fpl sans valeur; camelote f; (*nonsense*) bêtises fpl, idioties fpl ▶ VT (*BRIT inf*) dénigrer, rabaisser; **what you've just said is ~** tu viens de dire une bêtise

rubbish bin N (*BRIT*) boîte f à ordures, poubelle f

rubbish dump N (*BRIT: in town*) décharge publique, dépotoir m

rubbishy [ˈrʌbɪʃɪ] ADJ (*BRIT inf*) qui ne vaut rien, moche

rubble [ˈrʌbl] N décombres mpl; (*smaller*) gravats mpl; (*Constr*) blocage m

ruble [ˈruːbl] N (*US*) = **rouble**

ruby [ˈruːbɪ] N rubis m

RUC N ABBR (*BRIT*) = **Royal Ulster Constabulary**

rucksack [ˈrʌksæk] N sac m à dos

ructions [ˈrʌkʃənz] NPL grabuge m

rudder [ˈrʌdəʳ] N gouvernail m

ruddy [ˈrʌdɪ] ADJ (*face*) coloré(e); (*inf: damned*) sacré(e), fichu(e)

rude [ruːd] ADJ (*impolite: person*) impoli(e); (: *word, manners*) grossier(-ière); (*shocking*) indécent(e), inconvenant(e); **to be ~ to sb** être grossier envers qn

rudely [ˈruːdlɪ] ADV impoliment; grossièrement

rudeness [ˈruːdnɪs] N impolitesse f; grossièreté f

rudiment [ˈruːdɪmənt] N rudiment m

rudimentary [ruːdɪˈmɛntərɪ] ADJ rudimentaire

rue [ruː] VT se repentir de, regretter amèrement

rueful [ˈruːful] ADJ triste

ruff [rʌf] N fraise f, collerette f

ruffian [ˈrʌfɪən] N brute f, voyou m

ruffle [ˈrʌfl] VT (*hair*) ébouriffer; (*clothes*) chiffonner; (*water*) agiter; (*fig: person*) émouvoir, faire perdre son flegme à; **to get ruffled** s'énerver

rug [rʌg] N petit tapis; (*BRIT: blanket*) couverture f

rugby [ˈrʌgbɪ] N (*also:* **rugby football**) rugby m

rugged [ˈrʌgɪd] ADJ (*landscape*) accidenté(e); (*features, character*) rude; (*determination*) farouche

rugger [ˈrʌgəʳ] N (*BRIT inf*) rugby m

ruin [ˈruːɪn] N ruine f ▶ VT ruiner; (*spoil: clothes*) abîmer; (: *event*) gâcher; **ruins** NPL (*of building*) ruine(s); **in ruins** en ruine

ruination [ruːɪˈneɪʃən] N ruine f

ruinous [ˈruːɪnəs] ADJ ruineux(-euse)

rule [ruːl] N règle f; (*regulation*) règlement m; (*government*) autorité f, gouvernement m; (*dominion etc*): **under British ~** sous l'autorité britannique ▶ VT (*country*) gouverner; (*person*) dominer; (*decide*) décider ▶ VI commander; décider; (*Law*): **to ~ against/in favour of/on** statuer contre/en faveur de/sur; **to ~ that** (*umpire, judge etc*) décider que; **it's against the rules** c'est contraire au règlement; **by ~ of thumb** à vue de nez; **as a ~** normalement, en règle générale

▶ **rule out** VT exclure; **murder cannot be ruled out** l'hypothèse d'un meurtre ne peut être exclue

ruled [ruːld] ADJ (*paper*) réglé(e)

ruler [ˈruːləʳ] N (*sovereign*) souverain(e); (*leader*) chef m (d'État); (*for measuring*) règle f

ruling [ˈruːlɪŋ] ADJ (*party*) au pouvoir; (*class*) dirigeant(e) ▶ N (*Law*) décision f

rum [rʌm] N rhum m ▶ ADJ (*BRIT inf*) bizarre

Rumania [ruːˈmeɪnɪə] N Roumanie f

Rumanian [ruːˈmeɪnɪən] ADJ roumain(e) ▶ N Roumain(e); (*Ling*) roumain m

rumble [ˈrʌmbl] N grondement m; (*of stomach, pipe*) gargouillement m ▶ VI gronder; (*stomach, pipe*) gargouiller

rumbustious [rʌmˈbʌstʃəs], **rumbunctious** [rʌmˈbʌŋkʃəs] ADJ (*US: person*) exubérant(e)

rummage [ˈrʌmɪdʒ] VI fouiller

rumour, (*US*) **rumor** [ˈruːməʳ] N rumeur f, bruit m (qui court) ▶ VT: **it is rumoured that** le bruit court que

rump [rʌmp] N (*of animal*) croupe f

rumple [ˈrʌmpl] VT (*hair*) ébouriffer; (*clothes*) chiffonner, friper

rump steak N romsteck m

rumpus [ˈrʌmpəs] N (*inf*) tapage m, chahut m; (*quarrel*) prise f de bec; **to kick up a ~** faire toute une histoire

run [rʌn] (*pt* **ran** [ræn], *pp* **~** [rʌn]) N (*race*) course f; (*outing*) tour m or promenade f (en voiture); (*distance travelled*) parcours m, trajet m; (*series*) suite f, série f; (*Theat*) série de représentations; (*Ski*) piste f; (*Cricket, Baseball*) point m; (*in tights, stockings*) maille filée, échelle f ▶ VT (*business*) diriger; (*competition, course*) organiser; (*hotel, house*) tenir; (*race*) participer à; (*Comput: program*) exécuter; (*force through: rope, pipe*): **to ~ sth through** faire passer qch à travers; (*to pass: hand, finger*): **to ~ sth over** promener or passer qch sur; (*water, bath*) faire couler; (*Press: feature*) publier ▶ VI courir; (*pass: road etc*) passer; (*work: machine, factory*) marcher; (*bus, train*) circuler; (*continue: play*) se jouer, être à l'affiche; (: *contract*) être valide or en vigueur; (*slide: drawer etc*) glisser; (*flow: river, bath, nose*) couler; (*colours, washing*) déteindre; (*in election*) être candidat, se présenter; **at a ~** au pas de course; **to go for a ~** aller courir or faire un peu de course à pied; (*in car*) faire un tour or une promenade (en voiture); **to break into a ~** se mettre à courir; **a ~ of luck** une série de coups de chance; **to have the ~ of sb's house** avoir la maison de qn à sa disposition; **there was a ~ on** (*meat, tickets*) les gens se sont rués sur; **in the long ~** à la longue, à longue échéance; **in the short ~** à brève échéance, à court terme; **on the ~** en fuite; **to make a ~ for it** s'enfuir; **I'll ~ you to the station** je vais vous emmener or conduire à la gare; **to ~ errands** faire des commissions; **the train runs between Gatwick and Victoria** le train assure le service entre Gatwick et Victoria; **the bus runs every 20 minutes** il y a un autobus toutes les 20 minutes; **it's very cheap to ~** (*car, machine*) c'est très économique;

to ~ on petrol or (US) **gas/on diesel/off batteries** marcher à l'essence/au diesel/sur piles; **to ~ for president** être candidat à la présidence; **to ~ a risk** courir un risque; **their losses ran into millions** leurs pertes se sont élevées à plusieurs millions; **to be ~ off one's feet** (BRIT) ne plus savoir où donner de la tête
▸ **run about** VI (children) courir çà et là
▸ **run across** VT FUS (find) trouver par hasard
▸ **run after** VT FUS (to catch up) courir après; (chase) poursuivre
▸ **run around** VI = **run about**
▸ **run away** VI s'enfuir
▸ **run down** VI (clock) s'arrêter (faute d'avoir été remonté) ▸ VT (Aut: knock over) renverser; (BRIT: reduce: production) réduire progressivement; (: factory/shop) réduire progressivement la production/l'activité de; (criticize) critiquer, dénigrer; **to be ~ down** (tired) être fatigué(e) or à plat
▸ **run in** VT (BRIT: car) roder
▸ **run into** VT FUS (meet: person) rencontrer par hasard; (: trouble) se heurter à; (collide with) heurter; **to ~ into debt** contracter des dettes
▸ **run off** VI s'enfuir ▸ VT (water) laisser s'écouler; (copies) tirer
▸ **run out** VI (person) sortir en courant; (liquid) couler; (lease) expirer; (money) être épuisé(e)
▸ **run out of** VT FUS se trouver à court de; **I've ~ out of petrol** or (US) **gas** je suis en panne d'essence
▸ **run over** VT (Aut) écraser ▸ VT FUS (revise) revoir, reprendre
▸ **run through** VT FUS (recap) reprendre, revoir; (play) répéter
▸ **run up** VI: **to ~ up against** (difficulties) se heurter à ▸ VT: **to ~ up a debt** s'endetter
runaround ['rʌnəraund] N (inf): **to give sb the ~** rester très évasif
runaway ['rʌnəweɪ] ADJ (horse) emballé(e); (truck) fou (folle); (person) fugitif(-ive); (child) fugueur(-euse); (inflation) galopant(e)
rundown ['rʌndaun] N (BRIT: of industry etc) réduction progressive
rung [rʌŋ] PP of **ring** ▸ N (of ladder) barreau m
run-in ['rʌnɪn] N (inf) accrochage m, prise f de bec
runner ['rʌnə'] N (in race: person) coureur(-euse); (: horse) partant m; (on sledge) patin m; (for drawer etc) coulisseau m; (carpet: in hall etc) chemin m
runner bean N (BRIT) haricot m (à rames)
runner-up [rʌnər'ʌp] N second(e)
running ['rʌnɪŋ] N (in race etc) course f; (of business, organization) direction f, gestion f; (of event) organisation f; (of machine etc) marche f, fonctionnement m ▸ ADJ (water) courant(e); (commentary) suivi(e); **6 days ~** 6 jours de suite; **to be in/out of the ~ for sth** être/ne pas être sur les rangs pour qch
running commentary N commentaire détaillé

running costs NPL (of business) frais mpl de gestion; (of car): **the ~ are high** elle revient cher
running head N (Typ, Comput) titre courant
running mate N (US Pol) candidat à la vice-présidence
runny ['rʌnɪ] ADJ qui coule
run-off ['rʌnɔf] N (in contest, election) deuxième tour m; (extra race etc) épreuve f supplémentaire
run-of-the-mill ['rʌnəvðə'mɪl] ADJ ordinaire, banal(e)
runt [rʌnt] N avorton m
run-through ['rʌnθruː] N répétition f, essai m
run-up ['rʌnʌp] N (BRIT): **~ to sth** période f précédant qch
runway ['rʌnweɪ] N (Aviat) piste f (d'envol or d'atterrissage)
rupee [ruː'piː] N roupie f
rupture ['rʌptʃə'] N (Med) hernie f ▸ VT: **to ~ o.s.** se donner une hernie
rural ['ruərl] ADJ rural(e)
ruse [ruːz] N ruse f
rush [rʌʃ] N course précipitée; (of crowd, Comm: sudden demand) ruée f; (hurry) hâte f; (of anger, joy) accès m; (current) flot m; (Bot) jonc m; (for chair) paille f ▸ VT (hurry) transporter or envoyer d'urgence; (attack: town etc) prendre d'assaut; (BRIT inf: overcharge) estamper; faire payer ▸ VI se précipiter; **don't ~ me!** laissez-moi le temps de souffler!; **to ~ sth off** (do quickly) faire qch à la hâte; (send) envoyer qch d'urgence; **is there any ~ for this?** est-ce urgent?; **we've had a ~ of orders** nous avons reçu une avalanche de commandes; **I'm in a ~ (to do)** je suis vraiment pressé (de faire); **gold ~** ruée vers l'or
▸ **rush through** VT FUS (work) exécuter à la hâte ▸ VT (Comm: order) exécuter d'urgence
rush hour N heures fpl de pointe or d'affluence
rush job N travail urgent
rush matting N natte f de paille
rusk [rʌsk] N biscotte f
Russia ['rʌʃə] N Russie f
Russian ['rʌʃən] ADJ russe ▸ N Russe mf; (Ling) russe m
rust [rʌst] N rouille f ▸ VI rouiller
rustic ['rʌstɪk] ADJ rustique ▸ N (pej) rustaud(e)
rustle ['rʌsl] VI bruire, produire un bruissement ▸ VT (paper) froisser; (US: cattle) voler
rustproof ['rʌstpruːf] ADJ inoxydable
rustproofing ['rʌstpruːfɪŋ] N traitement m antirouille
rusty ['rʌstɪ] ADJ rouillé(e)
rut [rʌt] N ornière f; (Zool) rut m; **to be in a ~** (fig) suivre l'ornière, s'encroûter
rutabaga [ruːtə'beɪgə] N (US) rutabaga m
ruthless ['ruːθlɪs] ADJ sans pitié, impitoyable
ruthlessness ['ruːθlɪsnɪs] N dureté f, cruauté f
RV ABBR (= revised version) traduction anglaise de la Bible de 1885 ▸ N ABBR (US) = **recreational vehicle**
rye [raɪ] N seigle m
rye bread N pain m de seigle

r

Ss

S, s [ɛs] N (letter) S, s m; (US Scol: satisfactory) ≈ assez bien; **S for Sugar** S comme Suzanne

S ABBR (= south, small) S; (= saint) St

SA N ABBR = **South Africa**; **South America**

Sabbath ['sæbəθ] N (Jewish) sabbat m; (Christian) dimanche m

sabbatical [sə'bætɪkl] ADJ: ~ **year** année f sabbatique

sabotage ['sæbətɑːʒ] N sabotage m ▶ VT saboter

saccharin, saccharine ['sækərɪn] N saccharine f

sachet ['sæʃeɪ] N sachet m

sack [sæk] N (bag) sac m ▶ VT (dismiss) renvoyer, mettre à la porte; (plunder) piller, mettre à sac; **to give sb the ~** renvoyer qn, mettre qn à la porte; **to get the ~** être renvoyé(e) or mis(e) à la porte

sackful ['sækful] N: **a ~ of** un (plein) sac de

sacking ['sækɪŋ] N toile f à sac; (dismissal) renvoi m

sacrament ['sækrəmənt] N sacrement m

sacred ['seɪkrɪd] ADJ sacré(e)

sacred cow N (fig) chose sacro-sainte

sacrifice ['sækrɪfaɪs] N sacrifice m ▶ VT sacrifier; **to make sacrifices (for sb)** se sacrifier or faire des sacrifices (pour qn)

sacrilege ['sækrɪlɪdʒ] N sacrilège m

sacrosanct ['sækrəusæŋkt] ADJ sacro-saint(e)

sad [sæd] ADJ (unhappy) triste; (deplorable) triste, fâcheux(-euse); (inf: pathetic: thing) triste, lamentable; (: person) minable

sadden ['sædn] VT attrister, affliger

saddle ['sædl] N selle f ▶ VT (horse) seller; **to be saddled with sth** (inf) avoir qch sur les bras

saddlebag ['sædlbæg] N sacoche f

sadism ['seɪdɪzəm] N sadisme m

sadist ['seɪdɪst] N sadique mf

sadistic [sə'dɪstɪk] ADJ sadique

sadly ['sædlɪ] ADV tristement; (unfortunately) malheureusement; (seriously) fort

sadness ['sædnɪs] N tristesse f

sado-masochism [seɪdəu'mæsəkɪzəm] N sadomasochisme m

s.a.e. N ABBR (BRIT: = stamped addressed envelope) enveloppe affranchie pour la réponse

safari [sə'fɑːrɪ] N safari m

safari park N réserve f

safe [seɪf] ADJ (out of danger) hors de danger, en sécurité; (not dangerous) sans danger; (cautious) prudent(e); (sure: bet) assuré(e) ▶ N coffre-fort m; ~ **from** à l'abri de; ~ **and sound** sain(e) et sauf (sauve); **(just) to be on the ~ side** pour plus de sûreté, par précaution; **to play ~** ne prendre aucun risque; **it is ~ to say that ...** on peut dire sans crainte que ...; ~ **journey!** bon voyage!

safe bet N: **it was a ~** ça ne comportait pas trop de risques; **it's a ~ that he'll be late** il y a toutes les chances pour qu'il soit en retard

safe-breaker ['seɪfbreɪkəʳ] N (BRIT) perceur m de coffre-fort

safe-conduct [seɪf'kɔndʌkt] N sauf-conduit m

safe-cracker ['seɪfkrækəʳ] N = **safe-breaker**

safe-deposit ['seɪfdɪpɔzɪt] N (vault) dépôt m de coffres-forts; (box) coffre-fort m

safeguard ['seɪfgɑːd] N sauvegarde f, protection f ▶ VT sauvegarder, protéger

safe haven N zone f de sécurité

safekeeping ['seɪf'kiːpɪŋ] N bonne garde

safely ['seɪflɪ] ADV (assume, say) sans risque d'erreur; (drive, arrive) sans accident; **I can ~ say ...** je peux dire à coup sûr ...

safe passage N: **to grant sb ~** accorder un laissez-passer à qn

safe sex N rapports sexuels protégés

safety ['seɪftɪ] N sécurité f; ~ **first!** la sécurité d'abord!

safety belt N ceinture f de sécurité

safety catch N cran m de sûreté or sécurité

safety net N filet m de sécurité

safety pin N épingle f de sûreté or de nourrice

safety valve N soupape f de sûreté

saffron ['sæfrən] N safran m

sag [sæg] VI s'affaisser, fléchir; (hem, breasts) pendre

saga ['sɑːgə] N saga f; (fig) épopée f

sage [seɪdʒ] N (herb) sauge f; (person) sage m

Sagittarius [sædʒɪ'tɛərɪəs] N le Sagittaire; **to be ~** être du Sagittaire

sago ['seɪgəu] N sagou m

Sahara [sə'hɑːrə] N: **the ~ (Desert)** le (désert du) Sahara m

Sahel [sæ'hɛl] N Sahel m

said [sɛd] PT, PP of **say**

Saigon [saɪ'gɔn] N Saigon

sail [seɪl] N (on boat) voile f; (trip): **to go for a ~**

faire un tour en bateau ▶ VT (*boat*) manœuvrer, piloter ▶ VI (*travel: ship*) avancer, naviguer; (: *passenger*) aller or se rendre (en bateau); (*set off*) partir, prendre la mer; (*Sport*) faire de la voile; **they sailed into Le Havre** ils sont entrés dans le port du Havre

▶ **sail through** VI, VT FUS (*fig*) réussir haut la main

sailboat ['seɪlbəʊt] N (*US*) bateau *m* à voiles, voilier *m*

sailing ['seɪlɪŋ] N (*Sport*) voile *f*; **to go** ~ faire de la voile

sailing boat N bateau *m* à voiles, voilier *m*

sailing ship N grand voilier

sailor ['seɪləʳ] N marin *m*, matelot *m*

saint [seɪnt] N saint(e)

saintly ['seɪntlɪ] ADJ saint(e), plein(e) de bonté

sake [seɪk] N: **for the ~ of** (*out of concern for*) pour (l'amour de), dans l'intérêt de; (*out of consideration for*) par égard pour; (*in order to achieve*) pour plus de, par souci de; **arguing for arguing's** ~ discuter pour le plaisir de discuter; **for heaven's** ~! pour l'amour du ciel!; **for the ~ of argument** à titre d'exemple

salad ['sæləd] N salade *f*; **tomato** ~ salade de tomates

salad bowl N saladier *m*

salad cream N (*BRIT*) (sorte *f* de) mayonnaise *f*

salad dressing N vinaigrette *f*

salad oil N huile *f* de table

salami [sə'lɑːmɪ] N salami *m*

salaried ['sælərɪd] ADJ (*staff*) salarié(e), qui touche un traitement

salary ['sælərɪ] N salaire *m*, traitement *m*

salary scale N échelle *f* des traitements

sale [seɪl] N vente *f*; (*at reduced prices*) soldes *mpl*; **sales** NPL (*total amount sold*) chiffre *m* de ventes; **"for ~"** "à vendre"; **on ~** en vente; **on ~ or return** vendu(e) avec faculté de retour; **closing-down** or (*US*) **liquidation ~** liquidation *f* (*avant fermeture*); **~ and lease back** *n* cession-bail *f*

saleroom ['seɪlruːm] N salle *f* des ventes

sales assistant, (*US*) **sales clerk** N vendeur(-euse)

sales conference N réunion *f* de vente

sales drive N campagne commerciale, animation *f* des ventes

sales force N (ensemble *m* du) service des ventes

salesman ['seɪlzmən] N (*irreg*) (*in shop*) vendeur *m*; (*representative*) représentant *m* de commerce

sales manager N directeur commercial

salesmanship ['seɪlzmənʃɪp] N art *m* de la vente

salesperson ['seɪlzpəːsn] N (*in shop*) vendeur(-euse)

sales rep N (*Comm*) représentant(e) *m/f*

sales tax N (*US*) taxe *f* à l'achat

saleswoman ['seɪlzwumən] N (*irreg*) (*in shop*) vendeuse *f*

salient ['seɪlɪənt] ADJ saillant(e)

saline ['seɪlaɪn] ADJ salin(e)

saliva [sə'laɪvə] N salive *f*

sallow ['sæləʊ] ADJ cireux(-euse)

sally forth, **sally out** ['sælɪ-] VI partir plein(e) d'entrain

salmon ['sæmən] N (*pl inv*) saumon *m*

salmon trout N truite saumonée

salon ['sælɒn] N salon *m*

saloon [sə'luːn] N (*US*) bar *m*; (*BRIT Aut*) berline *f*; (*ship's lounge*) salon *m*

SALT [sɔːlt] N ABBR (= *Strategic Arms Limitation Talks/Treaty*) SALT *m*

salt [sɔːlt] N sel *m* ▶ VT saler ▶ CPD de sel; (*Culin*) salé(e); **an old** ~ un vieux loup de mer
▶ **salt away** VT mettre de côté

salt cellar N salière *f*

salt-free ['sɔːlt'friː] ADJ sans sel

saltwater ['sɔːlt'wɔːtəʳ] ADJ (*fish etc*) (d'eau) de mer

salty ['sɔːltɪ] ADJ salé(e)

salubrious [sə'luːbrɪəs] ADJ salubre

salutary ['sæljutərɪ] ADJ salutaire

salute [sə'luːt] N salut *m*; (*of guns*) salve *f* ▶ VT saluer

salvage ['sælvɪdʒ] N (*saving*) sauvetage *m*; (*things saved*) biens sauvés or récupérés ▶ VT sauver, récupérer

salvage vessel N bateau *m* de sauvetage

salvation [sæl'veɪʃən] N salut *m*

Salvation Army N Armée *f* du Salut

salver ['sælvəʳ] N plateau *m* de métal

salvo ['sælvəu] N salve *f*

Samaritan [sə'mærɪtən] N: **the Samaritans** (*organization*) ≈ S.O.S. Amitié

same [seɪm] ADJ même ▶ PRON: **the** ~ le (la) même, les mêmes; **the ~ book as** le même livre que; **on the ~ day** le même jour; **at the ~ time** en même temps; (*yet*) néanmoins; **all** or **just the** ~ tout de même, quand même; **they're one and the** ~ (*person/thing*) c'est une seule et même personne/chose; **to do the** ~ faire de même, en faire autant; **to do the ~ as sb** faire comme qn; **and the** ~ **to you!** et à vous de même!; (*after insult*) toi-même!; ~ **here!** moi aussi!; **the** ~ **again!** (*in bar etc*) la même chose!

sample ['sɑːmpl] N échantillon *m*; (*Med*) prélèvement *m* ▶ VT (*food, wine*) goûter; **to take a** ~ prélever un échantillon; **free** ~ échantillon gratuit

sanatorium [sænə'tɔːrɪəm] (*pl* **sanatoria** [-rɪə]) N sanatorium *m*

sanctify ['sæŋktɪfaɪ] VT sanctifier

sanctimonious [sæŋktɪ'məunɪəs] ADJ moralisateur(-trice)

sanction ['sæŋkʃən] N approbation *f*, sanction *f* ▶ VT cautionner, sanctionner; **sanctions** NPL (*Pol*) sanctions; **to impose economic sanctions on** or **against** prendre des sanctions économiques contre

sanctity ['sæŋktɪtɪ] N sainteté *f*, caractère sacré

sanctuary ['sæŋktjuərɪ] N (*holy place*) sanctuaire *m*; (*refuge*) asile *m*; (*for wildlife*) réserve *f*

sand [sænd] N sable *m* ▶ VT sabler; (*also:* **sand down:** *wood etc*) poncer

sandal ['sændl] N sandale *f*

sandbag ['sændbæg] N sac *m* de sable

sandblast ['sændblɑːst] VT décaper à la sableuse

S

sandbox ['sændbɔks] N (US: for children) tas m de sable
sand castle ['sændkɑ:sl] N château m de sable
sand dune N dune f de sable
sander ['sændəʳ] N ponceuse f
S&M N ABBR (= sadomasochism) sadomasochisme m
sandpaper ['sændpeɪpəʳ] N papier m de verre
sandpit ['sændpɪt] N (BRIT: for children) tas m de sable
sands [sændz] NPL plage f (de sable)
sandstone ['sændstəun] N grès m
sandstorm ['sændstɔ:m] N tempête f de sable
sandwich ['sændwɪtʃ] N sandwich m ▶ VT (also: **sandwich in**) intercaler; **sandwiched between** pris en sandwich entre; **cheese/ham ~** sandwich au fromage/jambon
sandwich board N panneau m publicitaire (porté par un homme-sandwich)
sandwich course N (BRIT) cours m de formation professionnelle
sandy ['sændɪ] ADJ sablonneux(-euse); couvert(e) de sable; (colour) sable inv, blond roux inv
sane [seɪn] ADJ (person) sain(e) d'esprit; (outlook) sensé(e), sain(e)
sang [sæŋ] PT of **sing**
sanguine ['sæŋgwɪn] ADJ optimiste
sanitarium [sænɪ'tɛərɪəm] (pl **sanitaria** [-rɪə]) N (US) = **sanatorium**
sanitary ['sænɪtərɪ] ADJ (system, arrangements) sanitaire; (clean) hygiénique
sanitary towel, (US) **sanitary napkin** N serviette f hygiénique
sanitation [sænɪ'teɪʃən] N (in house) installations fpl sanitaires; (in town) système m sanitaire
sanitation department N (US) service m de voirie
sanity ['sænɪtɪ] N santé mentale; (common sense) bon sens
sank [sæŋk] PT of **sink**
San Marino ['sænmə'ri:nəu] N Saint-Marin m
Santa Claus [sæntə'klɔ:z] N le Père Noël
Santiago [sæntɪ'ɑ:gəu] N (also: **Santiago de Chile**) Santiago (du Chili)
sap [sæp] N (of plants) sève f ▶ VT (strength) saper, miner
sapling ['sæplɪŋ] N jeune arbre m
sapphire ['sæfaɪəʳ] N saphir m
sarcasm ['sɑ:kæzm] N sarcasme m, raillerie f
sarcastic [sɑ:'kæstɪk] ADJ sarcastique
sarcophagus [sɑ:'kɔfəgəs] (pl **sarcophagi** [-gaɪ]) N sarcophage m
sardine [sɑ:'di:n] N sardine f
Sardinia [sɑ:'dɪnɪə] N Sardaigne f
Sardinian [sɑ:'dɪnɪən] ADJ sarde ▶ N Sarde mf; (Ling) sarde m
sardonic [sɑ:'dɔnɪk] ADJ sardonique
sari ['sɑ:rɪ] N sari m
SARS ['sɑ:rz] N ABBR = **severe acute respiratory syndrome**
sartorial [sɑ:'tɔ:rɪəl] ADJ vestimentaire
SAS N ABBR (BRIT Mil: = Special Air Service) ≈ GIGN m

SASE N ABBR (US: = self-addressed stamped envelope) enveloppe affranchie pour la réponse
sash [sæʃ] N écharpe f
sash window N fenêtre f à guillotine
Sask. ABBR (CANADA) = **Saskatchewan**
SAT, SATs N ABBR (US) = **Scholastic Aptitude Test(s)**
sat [sæt] PT, PP of **sit**
Sat. ABBR (= Saturday) sa
Satan ['seɪtn] N Satan m
satanic [sə'tænɪk] ADJ satanique, démoniaque
satchel ['sætʃl] N cartable m
sated ['seɪtɪd] ADJ repu(e); blasé(e)
satellite ['sætəlaɪt] ADJ, N satellite m
satellite dish N antenne f parabolique
satellite navigation system N système m de navigation par satellite
satellite television N télévision f par satellite
satiate ['seɪʃɪeɪt] VT rassasier
satin ['sætɪn] N satin m ▶ ADJ en or de satin, satiné(e); **with a ~ finish** satiné(e)
satire ['sætaɪəʳ] N satire f
satirical [sə'tɪrɪkl] ADJ satirique
satirist ['sætɪrɪst] N (writer) auteur m satirique; (cartoonist) caricaturiste mf
satirize ['sætɪraɪz] VT faire la satire de, satiriser
satisfaction [sætɪs'fækʃən] N satisfaction f
satisfactory [sætɪs'fæktərɪ] ADJ satisfaisant(e)
satisfied ['sætɪsfaɪd] ADJ satisfait(e); **to be ~ with sth** être satisfait de qch
satisfy ['sætɪsfaɪ] VT satisfaire, contenter; (convince) convaincre, persuader; **to ~ the requirements** remplir les conditions; **to ~ sb (that)** convaincre qn (que); **to ~ o.s. of sth** vérifier qch, s'assurer de qch
satisfying ['sætɪsfaɪɪŋ] ADJ satisfaisant(e)
satsuma [sæt'su:mə] N satsuma f
saturate ['sætʃəreɪt] VT: **to ~ (with)** saturer (de)
saturated fat ['sætʃəreɪtɪd-] N graisse saturée
saturation [sætʃə'reɪʃən] N saturation f
Saturday ['sætədɪ] N samedi m; see also **Tuesday**
sauce [sɔ:s] N sauce f
saucepan ['sɔ:spən] N casserole f
saucer ['sɔ:səʳ] N soucoupe f
saucy ['sɔ:sɪ] ADJ impertinent(e)
Saudi ['saudɪ], **Saudi Arabian** ADJ saoudien(ne) ▶ N Saoudien(ne)
Saudi Arabia N Arabie f Saoudite
sauna ['sɔ:nə] N sauna m
saunter ['sɔ:ntəʳ] VI: **to ~ to** aller en flânant or se balader jusqu'à
sausage ['sɔsɪdʒ] N saucisse f; (salami etc) saucisson m
sausage roll N friand m
sauté ['səuteɪ] ADJ (Culin: potatoes) sauté(e); (: onions) revenu(e) ▶ VT faire sauter; faire revenir
sautéed ['səuteɪd] ADJ sauté(e)
savage ['sævɪdʒ] ADJ (cruel, fierce) brutal(e), féroce; (primitive) primitif(-ive), sauvage ▶ N sauvage mf ▶ VT attaquer férocement
savagery ['sævɪdʒrɪ] N sauvagerie f, brutalité f, férocité f
save [seɪv] VT (person, belongings) sauver; (money)

mettre de côté, économiser; (*time*) (faire) gagner; (*keep*) garder; (*Comput*) sauvegarder; (*Sport: stop*) arrêter; (*avoid: trouble*) éviter ▶ VI (*also:* **save up**) mettre de l'argent de côté ▶ N (*Sport*) arrêt *m* (du ballon) ▶ PREP sauf, à l'exception de; **it will ~ me an hour** ça me fera gagner une heure; **to ~ face** sauver la face; **God ~ the Queen!** vive la Reine!

saving ['seɪvɪŋ] N économie *f* ▶ ADJ: **the ~ grace of** ce qui rachète; **savings** NPL économies *fpl*; **to make savings** faire des économies

savings account N compte *m* d'épargne

savings and loan association (*US*) N ≈ société *f* de crédit immobilier

savings bank N caisse *f* d'épargne

saviour, (*US*) **savior** ['seɪvjə'] N sauveur *m*

savour, (*US*) **savor** ['seɪvə'] N saveur *f*, goût *m* ▶ VT savourer

savoury, (*US*) **savory** ['seɪvərɪ] ADJ savoureux(-euse); (*dish: not sweet*) salé(e)

savvy ['sævɪ] N (*inf*) jugeote *f*

saw [sɔ:] PT of **see** ▶ N (*tool*) scie *f* ▶ VT (*pt* **sawed**, *pp* **sawed** or **sawn** [sɔ:n]) scier; **to ~ sth up** débiter qch à la scie

sawdust ['sɔ:dʌst] N sciure *f*

sawmill ['sɔ:mɪl] N scierie *f*

sawn [sɔ:n] PP of **saw**

sawn-off ['sɔ:nɔf], (*US*) **sawed-off** ['sɔ:dɔf] ADJ: **~ shotgun** carabine *f* à canon scié

sax [sæks] (*inf*) N saxo *m*

saxophone ['sæksəfəun] N saxophone *m*

say [seɪ] (*pt, pp* **said** [sɛd]) VT dire ▶ N: **to have one's ~** dire ce qu'on a à dire; **to have a ~** avoir voix au chapitre; **could you ~ that again?** pourriez-vous répéter ce que vous venez de dire?; **to ~ yes/no** dire oui/non; **she said (that) I was to give you this** elle m'a chargé de vous remettre ceci; **my watch says 3 o'clock** ma montre indique 3 heures, il est 3 heures à ma montre; **shall we ~ Tuesday?** disons mardi?; **that doesn't ~ much for him** ce n'est pas vraiment à son honneur; **when all is said and done** en fin de compte, en définitive; **there is something** *or* **a lot to be said for it** cela a des avantages; **that is to ~** c'est-à-dire; **to ~ nothing of** sans compter; **~ that …** mettons *or* disons que …; **that goes without saying** cela va sans dire, cela va de soi

saying ['seɪɪŋ] N dicton *m*, proverbe *m*

SBA N ABBR (*US: = Small Business Administration*) organisme d'aide aux PME

SC N ABBR (*US*) = **supreme court** ▶ ABBR (*US*) = **South Carolina**

s/c ABBR = **self-contained**

scab [skæb] N croûte *f*; (*pej*) jaune *m*

scabby ['skæbɪ] ADJ croûteux(-euse)

scaffold ['skæfəld] N échafaud *m*

scaffolding ['skæfəldɪŋ] N échafaudage *m*

scald [skɔ:ld] N brûlure *f* ▶ VT ébouillanter

scalding ['skɔ:ldɪŋ] ADJ (*also:* **scalding hot**) brûlant(e), bouillant(e)

scale [skeɪl] N (*of fish*) écaille *f*; (*Mus*) gamme *f*; (*of ruler, thermometer etc*) graduation *f*, échelle (graduée); (*of salaries, fees etc*) barème *m*; (*of map,* *also size, extent*) échelle ▶ VT (*mountain*) escalader; (*fish*) écailler; **scales** NPL balance *f*; (*larger*) bascule *f*; (*also:* **bathroom scales**) pèse-personne *m inv*; **pay ~** échelle des salaires; **~ of charges** tableau *m* des tarifs; **on a large ~** sur une grande échelle, en grand; **to draw sth to ~** dessiner qch à l'échelle; **small-~ model** modèle réduit

▶ **scale down** VT réduire

scaled-down [skeɪld'daun] ADJ à échelle réduite

scale drawing N dessin *m* à l'échelle

scale model N modèle *m* à l'échelle

scallion ['skæljən] N oignon *m*; (*US: salad onion*) ciboule *f*; (: *shallot*) échalote *f*; (: *leek*) poireau *m*

scallop ['skɔləp] N coquille *f* Saint-Jacques; (*Sewing*) feston *m*

scalp [skælp] N cuir chevelu ▶ VT scalper

scalpel ['skælpl] N scalpel *m*

scalper ['skælpə'] N (*US inf: of tickets*) revendeur *m* de billets

scam [skæm] N (*inf*) arnaque *f*

scamp [skæmp] VT bâcler

scamper ['skæmpə'] VI: **to ~ away, ~ off** détaler

scampi ['skæmpɪ] NPL langoustines (frites), scampi *mpl*

scan [skæn] VT (*examine*) scruter, examiner; (*glance at quickly*) parcourir; (*poetry*) scander; (*TV, Radar*) balayer ▶ N (*Med*) scanographie *f*

scandal ['skændl] N scandale *m*; (*gossip*) ragots *mpl*

scandalize ['skændəlaɪz] VT scandaliser, indigner

scandalous ['skændələs] ADJ scandaleux(-euse)

Scandinavia [skændɪ'neɪvɪə] N Scandinavie *f*

Scandinavian [skændɪ'neɪvɪən] ADJ scandinave ▶ N Scandinave *mf*

scanner ['skænə'] N (*Radar, Med*) scanner *m*, scanographe *m*; (*Comput*) scanner

scant [skænt] ADJ insuffisant(e)

scantily ['skæntɪlɪ] ADV: **~ clad** or **dressed** vêtu(e) du strict minimum

scanty ['skæntɪ] ADJ peu abondant(e), insuffisant(e), maigre

scapegoat ['skeɪpgəut] N bouc *m* émissaire

scar [skɑ:'] N cicatrice *f* ▶ VT laisser une cicatrice *or* une marque à

scarce [skɛəs] ADJ rare, peu abondant(e); **to make o.s. ~** (*inf*) se sauver

scarcely ['skɛəslɪ] ADV à peine, presque pas; **~ anybody** pratiquement personne; **I can ~ believe it** j'ai du mal à le croire

scarcity ['skɛəsɪtɪ] N rareté *f*, manque *m*, pénurie *f*

scarcity value N valeur *f* de rareté

scare [skɛə'] N peur *f*, panique *f* ▶ VT effrayer, faire peur à; **to ~ sb stiff** faire une peur bleue à qn; **bomb ~** alerte *f* à la bombe

▶ **scare away, scare off** VT faire fuir

scarecrow ['skɛəkrəu] N épouvantail *m*

scared ['skɛəd] ADJ: **to be ~** avoir peur

scaremonger ['skɛəmʌngə'] N alarmiste *mf*

scarf [skɑ:f] (*pl* **scarves** [skɑ:vz]) N (*long*) écharpe *f*; (*square*) foulard *m*

S

scarlet ['skɑːlɪt] ADJ écarlate
scarlet fever N scarlatine f
scarper ['skɑːpəʳ] VI (BRIT inf) ficher le camp
scarves [skɑːvz] NPL of **scarf**
scary ['skɛərɪ] ADJ (inf) effrayant(e); (film) qui fait peur
scathing ['skeɪðɪŋ] ADJ cinglant(e), acerbe; **to be ~ about sth** être très critique vis-à-vis de qch
scatter ['skætəʳ] VT éparpiller, répandre; (crowd) disperser ▸ VI se disperser
scatterbrained ['skætəbreɪnd] ADJ écervelé(e), étourdi(e)
scattered ['skætəd] ADJ épars(e), dispersé(e)
scatty ['skætɪ] ADJ (BRIT inf) loufoque
scavenge ['skævəndʒ] VI (person): **to ~ (for)** faire les poubelles (pour trouver); **to ~ for food** (hyenas etc) se nourrir de charognes
scavenger ['skævəndʒəʳ] N éboueur m
SCE N ABBR = **Scottish Certificate of Education**
scenario [sɪ'nɑːrɪəu] N scénario m
scene [siːn] N (Theat, fig etc) scène f; (of crime, accident) lieu(x) m(pl), endroit m; (sight, view) spectacle m, vue f; **behind the scenes** (also fig) dans les coulisses; **to make a ~** (inf: fuss) faire une scène or toute une histoire; **to appear on the ~** (also fig) faire son apparition, arriver; **the political ~** la situation politique
scenery ['siːnərɪ] N (Theat) décor(s) m(pl); (landscape) paysage m
scenic ['siːnɪk] ADJ scénique; offrant de beaux paysages or panoramas
scent [sɛnt] N parfum m, odeur f; (fig: track) piste f; (sense of smell) odorat m ▸ VT parfumer; (smell: also fig) flairer; **to put** or **throw sb off the ~** mettre qn sur une mauvaise piste
sceptic, (US) **skeptic** ['skɛptɪk] N sceptique mf
sceptical, (US) **skeptical** ['skɛptɪkl] ADJ sceptique
scepticism, (US) **skepticism** ['skɛptɪsɪzəm] N scepticisme m
sceptre, (US) **scepter** ['sɛptəʳ] N sceptre m
schedule ['ʃɛdjuːl, (US) 'skɛdjuːl] N programme m, plan m; (of trains) horaire m; (of prices etc) barème m, tarif m ▸ VT prévoir; **as scheduled** comme prévu; **on ~** à l'heure (prévue); à la date prévue; **to be ahead of/behind ~** avoir de l'avance/du retard; **we are working to a very tight ~** notre programme de travail est très serré or intense; **everything went according to ~** tout s'est passé comme prévu
scheduled ['ʃɛdjuːld, (US) 'skɛdjuːld] ADJ (date, time) prévu(e), indiqué(e); (visit, event) programmé(e), prévu(e); (train, bus, stop, flight) régulier(-ière)
scheduled flight N vol régulier
schematic [skɪ'mætɪk] ADJ schématique
scheme [skiːm] N plan m, projet m; (method) procédé m; (plot) complot m, combine f; (arrangement) arrangement m, classification f; (pension scheme etc) régime m ▸ VT, VI comploter, manigancer; **colour ~** combinaison f de(s) couleurs
scheming ['skiːmɪŋ] ADJ rusé(e), intrigant(e)

▸ N manigances fpl, intrigues fpl
schism ['skɪzəm] N schisme m
schizophrenia [skɪtsə'friːnɪə] N schizophrénie f
schizophrenic [skɪtsə'frɛnɪk] ADJ schizophrène
scholar ['skɔləʳ] N érudit(e); (pupil) boursier(-ère)
scholarly ['skɔlərlɪ] ADJ érudit(e), savant(e)
scholarship ['skɔləʃɪp] N érudition f; (grant) bourse f (d'études)
school [skuːl] N (gen) école f; (secondary school) collège m; lycée m; (in university) faculté f; (US: university) université f; (of fish) banc m ▸ CPD scolaire ▸ VT (animal) dresser
school age N âge m scolaire
schoolbook ['skuːlbuk] N livre m scolaire or de classe
schoolboy ['skuːlbɔɪ] N écolier m; (at secondary school) collégien m; lycéen m
schoolchildren ['skuːltʃɪldrən] NPL écoliers mpl; (at secondary school) collégiens mpl; lycéens mpl
schooldays ['skuːldeɪz] NPL années fpl de scolarité
schoolgirl ['skuːlɡəːl] N écolière f; (at secondary school) collégienne f; lycéenne f
schooling ['skuːlɪŋ] N instruction f, études fpl
school-leaver ['skuːlliːvəʳ] N (BRIT) jeune qui vient de terminer ses études secondaires
schoolmaster ['skuːlmɑːstəʳ] N (primary) instituteur m; (secondary) professeur m
schoolmistress ['skuːlmɪstrɪs] N (primary) institutrice f; (secondary) professeur m
school report N (BRIT) bulletin m (scolaire)
schoolroom ['skuːlruːm] N (salle f de) classe f
schoolteacher ['skuːltiːtʃəʳ] N (primary) instituteur(-trice); (secondary) professeur m
schoolyard ['skuːljɑːd] N (US) cour f de récréation
schooner ['skuːnəʳ] N (ship) schooner m, goélette f; (glass) grand verre (à xérès)
sciatica [saɪ'ætɪkə] N sciatique f
science ['saɪəns] N science f; **the sciences** les sciences; (Scol) les matières fpl scientifiques
science fiction N science-fiction f
scientific [saɪən'tɪfɪk] ADJ scientifique
scientist ['saɪəntɪst] N scientifique mf; (eminent) savant m
sci-fi ['saɪfaɪ] N ABBR (inf: = science fiction) SF f
Scilly Isles ['sɪlɪ'aɪlz], **Scillies** ['sɪlɪz] NPL: **the ~** les Sorlingues fpl, les îles fpl Scilly
scintillating ['sɪntɪleɪtɪŋ] ADJ scintillant(e), étincelant(e); (wit etc) brillant(e)
scissors ['sɪzəz] NPL ciseaux mpl; **a pair of ~** une paire de ciseaux
sclerosis [sklɪ'rəusɪs] N sclérose f
scoff [skɔf] VT (BRIT inf: eat) avaler, bouffer ▸ VI: **to ~ (at)** (mock) se moquer (de)
scold [skəuld] VT gronder, attraper, réprimander
scolding ['skəuldɪŋ] N réprimande f
scone [skɔn] N sorte de petit pain rond au lait
scoop [skuːp] N pelle f (à main); (for ice cream) boule f à glace; (Press) reportage exclusif or à sensation
▸ **scoop out** VT évider, creuser

▶**scoop up** VT ramasser

scooter ['sku:təʳ] N (*motor cycle*) scooter *m*; (*toy*) trottinette *f*

scope [skəup] N (*capacity: of plan, undertaking*) portée *f*, envergure *f*; (: *of person*) compétence *f*, capacités *fpl*; (*opportunity*) possibilités *fpl*; **within the ~ of** dans les limites de; **there is plenty of ~ for improvement** (BRIT) cela pourrait être beaucoup mieux

scorch [skɔ:tʃ] VT (*clothes*) brûler (légèrement), roussir; (*earth, grass*) dessécher, brûler

scorched earth policy ['skɔ:tʃt-] N politique *f* de la terre brûlée

scorcher ['skɔ:tʃəʳ] N (*inf: hot day*) journée *f* torride

scorching ['skɔ:tʃɪŋ] ADJ torride, brûlant(e)

score [skɔ:ʳ] N score *m*, décompte *m* des points; (*Mus*) partition *f* ▶VT (*goal, point*) marquer; (*success*) remporter; (*cut: leather, wood, card*) entailler, inciser ▶VI marquer des points; (*Football*) marquer un but; (*keep score*) compter les points; **on that ~** sur ce chapitre, à cet égard; **to have an old ~ to settle with sb** (*fig*) avoir un (vieux) compte à régler avec qn; **a ~ of** (*twenty*) vingt; **scores of** (*fig*) des tas de; **to ~ 6 out of 10** obtenir 6 sur 10

▶**score out** VT rayer, barrer, biffer

scoreboard ['skɔ:bɔ:d] N tableau *m*

scorecard ['skɔ:ka:d] N (*Sport*) carton *m*, feuille *f* de marque

scoreline ['skɔ:laɪn] N (*Sport*) score *m*

scorer ['skɔ:rəʳ] N (*Football*) auteur *m* du but; buteur *m*; (*keeping score*) marqueur *m*

scorn [skɔ:n] N mépris *m*, dédain *m* ▶VT mépriser, dédaigner

scornful ['skɔ:nful] ADJ méprisant(e), dédaigneux(-euse)

Scorpio ['skɔ:pɪəu] N le Scorpion; **to be ~** être du Scorpion

scorpion ['skɔ:pɪən] N scorpion *m*

Scot [skɔt] N Écossais(e)

Scotch [skɔtʃ] N whisky *m*, scotch *m*

scotch [skɔtʃ] VT faire échouer; enrayer; étouffer

Scotch tape® (*US*) N scotch® *m*, ruban adhésif

scot-free ['skɔt'fri:] ADJ: **to get off ~** s'en tirer sans être puni(e); s'en sortir indemne

Scotland ['skɔtlənd] N Écosse *f*

Scots [skɔts] ADJ écossais(e)

Scotsman ['skɔtsmən] N (*irreg*) Écossais *m*

Scotswoman ['skɔtswumən] N (*irreg*) Écossaise *f*

Scottish ['skɔtɪʃ] ADJ écossais(e); **the ~ National Party** le parti national écossais; **the ~ Parliament** le Parlement écossais

scoundrel ['skaundrl] N vaurien *m*

scour ['skauəʳ] VT (*clean*) récurer; frotter; décaper; (*search*) battre, parcourir

scourer ['skauərəʳ] N tampon abrasif *or* à récurer; (*powder*) poudre *f* à récurer

scourge [skə:dʒ] N fléau *m*

scout [skaut] N (*Mil*) éclaireur *m*; (*also:* **boy scout**) scout *m*; **girl ~** (*US*) guide *f*

▶**scout around** VI chercher

scowl [skaul] VI se renfrogner, avoir l'air maussade; **to ~ at** regarder de travers

scrabble ['skræbl] VI (*claw*): **to ~ (at)** gratter; **to ~ about** *or* **around for sth** chercher qch à tâtons ▶N: **S-®** Scrabble® *m*

scraggy ['skrægɪ] ADJ décharné(e), efflanqué(e), famélique

scram [skræm] VI (*inf*) ficher le camp

scramble ['skræmbl] N (*rush*) bousculade *f*, ruée *f* ▶VI grimper/descendre tant bien que mal; **to ~ for** se bousculer *or* se disputer pour (avoir); **to go scrambling** (*Sport*) faire du trial

scrambled eggs ['skræmbld-] NPL œufs brouillés

scrap [skræp] N bout *m*, morceau *m*; (*fight*) bagarre *f*; (*also:* **scrap iron**) ferraille *f* ▶VT jeter, mettre au rebut; (*fig*) abandonner, laisser tomber ▶VI se bagarrer; **scraps** NPL (*waste*) déchets *mpl*; **to sell sth for ~** vendre qch à la casse *or* à la ferraille

scrapbook ['skræpbuk] N album *m*

scrap dealer N marchand *m* de ferraille

scrape [skreɪp] VT, VI gratter, racler ▶N: **to get into a ~** s'attirer des ennuis

▶**scrape through** VI (*exam etc*) réussir de justesse

▶**scrape together** VT (*money*) racler ses fonds de tiroir pour réunir

scraper ['skreɪpəʳ] N grattoir *m*, racloir *m*

scrap heap N tas *m* de ferraille; (*fig*): **on the ~** au rancart *or* rebut

scrap merchant N (BRIT) marchand *m* de ferraille

scrap metal N ferraille *f*

scrap paper N papier *m* brouillon

scrappy ['skræpɪ] ADJ fragmentaire, décousu(e)

scrap yard N parc *m* à ferrailles; (*for cars*) cimetière *m* de voitures

scratch [skrætʃ] N égratignure *f*, rayure *f*; (*on paint*) éraflure *f*; (*from claw*) coup *m* de griffe ▶ADJ: **~ team** équipe de fortune *or* improvisée ▶VT (*rub*) (se) gratter; (*record*) rayer; (*paint etc*) érafler; (*with claw, nail*) griffer; (*Comput*) effacer ▶VI (se) gratter; **to start from ~** partir de zéro; **to be up to ~** être à la hauteur

scratch card N carte *f* à gratter

scrawl [skrɔ:l] N gribouillage *m* ▶VI gribouiller

scrawny ['skrɔ:nɪ] ADJ décharné(e)

scream [skri:m] N cri perçant, hurlement *m* ▶VI crier, hurler; **to be a ~** (*inf*) être impayable; **to ~ at sb to do sth** crier *or* hurler à qn de faire qch

scree [skri:] N éboulis *m*

screech [skri:tʃ] N cri strident, hurlement *m*; (*of tyres, brakes*) crissement *m*, grincement *m* ▶VI hurler; crisser, grincer

screen [skri:n] N écran *m*; (*in room*) paravent *m*; (*Cine, TV*) écran; (*fig*) écran, rideau *m* ▶VT masquer, cacher; (*from the wind etc*) abriter, protéger; (*film*) projeter; (*candidates etc*) filtrer; (*for illness*): **to ~ sb for sth** faire subir un test de dépistage de qch à qn

screen editing [-'ɛdɪtɪŋ] N (*Comput*) édition *f* or correction *f* sur écran

s

screening ['skri:nɪŋ] N (*of film*) projection *f*; (*Med*) test *m* (*or* tests) de dépistage; (*for security*) filtrage *m*

screen memory N (*Comput*) mémoire *f* écran

screenplay ['skri:npleɪ] N scénario *m*

screen saver N (*Comput*) économiseur *m* d'écran

screenshot ['skri:nʃɔt] N (*Comput*) capture *f* d'écran

screen test N bout *m* d'essai

screw [skru:] N vis *f*; (*propeller*) hélice *f* ▶ VT (*also*: **screw in**) visser; (*inf!*: *woman*) baiser (!); **to ~ sth to the wall** visser qch au mur; **to have one's head screwed on** (*fig*) avoir la tête sur les épaules

▶ **screw up** VT (*paper etc*) froisser; (*inf*: *ruin*) bousiller; **to ~ up one's eyes** se plisser les yeux; **to ~ up one's face** faire la grimace

screwdriver ['skru:draɪvə^r] N tournevis *m*

screwed-up ['skru:d'ʌp] ADJ (*inf*): **to be ~** être paumé(e)

screwy ['skru:ɪ] ADJ (*inf*) dingue, cinglé(e)

scribble ['skrɪbl] N gribouillage *m* ▶ VT gribouiller, griffonner; **to ~ sth down** griffonner qch

scribe [skraɪb] N scribe *m*

script [skrɪpt] N (*Cine etc*) scénario *m*, texte *m*; (*in exam*) copie *f*; (*writing*) écriture *f* script *m*

scripted ['skrɪptɪd] ADJ (*Radio, TV*) préparé(e) à l'avance

Scripture ['skrɪptʃə^r] N Écriture sainte

scriptwriter ['skrɪptraɪtə^r] N scénariste *mf*, dialoguiste *mf*

scroll [skrəul] N rouleau *m* ▶ VT (*Comput*) faire défiler (sur l'écran)

scrotum ['skrəutəm] N scrotum *m*

scrounge [skraundʒ] (*inf*) VT: **to ~ sth (off** or **from sb**) se faire payer qch (par qn), emprunter qch (à qn) ▶ VI: **to ~ on sb** vivre aux crochets de qn

scrounger ['skraundʒə^r] N parasite *m*

scrub [skrʌb] N (*clean*) nettoyage *m* (à la brosse); (*land*) broussailles *fpl* ▶ VT (*floor*) nettoyer à la brosse; (*pan*) récurer; (*washing*) frotter; (*reject*) annuler

scrubbing brush ['skrʌbɪŋ-] N brosse dure

scruff [skrʌf] N: **by the ~ of the neck** par la peau du cou

scruffy ['skrʌfɪ] ADJ débraillé(e)

scrum ['skrʌm], **scrummage** ['skrʌmɪdʒ] N mêlée *f*

scruple ['skru:pl] N scrupule *m*; **to have no scruples about doing sth** n'avoir aucun scrupule à faire qch

scrupulous ['skru:pjuləs] ADJ scrupuleux(-euse)

scrupulously ['skru:pjuləslɪ] ADV scrupuleusement; **to be ~ honest** être d'une honnêteté scrupuleuse

scrutinize ['skru:tɪnaɪz] VT scruter, examiner minutieusement

scrutiny ['skru:tɪnɪ] N examen minutieux; **under the ~ of sb** sous la surveillance de qn

scuba ['sku:bə] N scaphandre *m* (autonome)

scuba diving N plongée sous-marine

scuff [skʌf] VT érafler

scuffle ['skʌfl] N échauffourée *f*, rixe *f*

scullery ['skʌlərɪ] N arrière-cuisine *f*

sculptor ['skʌlptə^r] N sculpteur *m*

sculpture ['skʌlptʃə^r] N sculpture *f*

scum [skʌm] N écume *f*, mousse *f*; (*pej*: *people*) rebut *m*, lie *f*

scupper ['skʌpə^r] VT (*BRIT*) saborder

scurrilous ['skʌrɪləs] ADJ haineux(-euse), virulent(e); calomnieux(-euse)

scurry ['skʌrɪ] VI filer à toute allure; **to ~ off** détaler, se sauver

scurvy ['skə:vɪ] N scorbut *m*

scuttle ['skʌtl] N (*Naut*) écoutille *f*; (*also*: **coal scuttle**) seau *m* (à charbon) ▶ VT (*ship*) saborder

▶ VI (*scamper*): **to ~ away, ~ off** détaler

scythe [saɪð] N faux *f*

SD, S. Dak. ABBR (*US*) = **South Dakota**

SDI N ABBR (= *Strategic Defense Initiative*) IDS *f*

SDLP N ABBR (*BRIT Pol*) = **Social Democratic and Labour Party**

sea [si:] N mer *f* ▶ CPD marin(e), de (la) mer, maritime; **on the ~** (*boat*) en mer; (*town*) au bord de la mer; **by** or **beside the ~** (*holiday, town*) au bord de la mer; **by ~** par mer, en bateau; **out to ~** au large; (**out**) **at ~** en mer; **heavy** or **rough ~(s)** grosse mer, mer agitée; **a ~ of faces** (*fig*) une multitude de visages; **to be all at ~** (*fig*) nager complètement

sea bed N fond *m* de la mer

sea bird N oiseau *m* de mer

seaboard ['si:bɔ:d] N côte *f*

sea breeze N brise *f* de mer

seafarer ['si:fɛərə^r] N marin *m*

seafaring ['si:fɛərɪŋ] ADJ (*life*) de marin; **~ people** les gens *mpl* de mer

seafood ['si:fu:d] N fruits *mpl* de mer

sea front N bord *m* de mer

seagoing ['si:gəuɪŋ] ADJ (*ship*) de haute mer

seagull ['si:gʌl] N mouette *f*

seal [si:l] N (*animal*) phoque *m*; (*stamp*) sceau *m*, cachet *m*; (*impression*) cachet, estampille *f* ▶ VT sceller; (*envelope*) coller; (: *with seal*) cacheter; (*decide*: *sb's fate*) décider (de); (: *bargain*) conclure; **~ of approval** approbation *f*

▶ **seal off** VT (*close*) condamner; (*forbid entry to*) interdire l'accès de

sea level N niveau *m* de la mer

sealing wax ['si:lɪŋ-] N cire *f* à cacheter

sea lion N lion *m* de mer

sealskin ['si:lskɪn] N peau *f* de phoque

seam [si:m] N couture *f*; (*of coal*) veine *f*, filon *m*; **the hall was bursting at the seams** la salle était pleine à craquer

seaman ['si:mən] N (*irreg*) marin *m*

seamanship ['si:mənʃɪp] N qualités *fpl* de marin

seamless ['si:mlɪs] ADJ sans couture(s)

seamy ['si:mɪ] ADJ louche, mal famé(e)

seance ['seɪɔns] N séance *f* de spiritisme

seaplane ['si:pleɪn] N hydravion *m*

seaport ['si:pɔ:t] N port *m* de mer

search [sə:tʃ] N (*for person, thing, Comput*) recherche(s) *f(pl)*; (*of drawer, pockets*) fouille *f*; (*Law*: *at sb's home*) perquisition *f* ▶ VT fouiller; (*examine*) examiner minutieusement; scruter

▶ VI: **to ~ for** chercher; **in ~ of** à la recherche de
▶ **search through** VT FUS fouiller
search engine N (*Comput*) moteur *m* de recherche
searcher ['sə:tʃəʳ] N chercheur(-euse)
searching ['sə:tʃɪŋ] ADJ (*look, question*) pénétrant(e); (*examination*) minutieux(-euse)
searchlight ['sə:tʃlaɪt] N projecteur *m*
search party N expédition *f* de secours
search warrant N mandat *m* de perquisition
searing ['sɪərɪŋ] ADJ (*heat*) brûlant(e); (*pain*) aigu(ë)
seashore ['si:ʃɔːʳ] N rivage *m*, plage *f*, bord *m* de (la) mer; **on the ~** sur le rivage
seasick ['si:sɪk] ADJ: **to be ~** avoir le mal de mer
seaside ['si:saɪd] N bord *m* de mer
seaside resort N station *f* balnéaire
season ['si:zn] N saison *f* ▶ VT assaisonner, relever; **to be in/out of ~** être/ne pas être de saison; **the busy ~** (*for shops*) la période de pointe; (*for hotels etc*) la pleine saison; **the open ~** (*Hunting*) la saison de la chasse
seasonal ['si:znl] ADJ saisonnier(-ière)
seasoned ['si:znd] ADJ (*wood*) séché(e); (*fig: worker, actor, troops*) expérimenté(e); **a ~ campaigner** un vieux militant, un vétéran
seasoning ['si:znɪŋ] N assaisonnement *m*
season ticket N carte *f* d'abonnement
seat [si:t] N siège *m*; (*in bus, train: place*) place *f*; (*Parliament*) siège; (*buttocks*) postérieur *m*; (*of trousers*) fond *m* ▶ VT faire asseoir, placer; (*have room for*) avoir des places assises pour, pouvoir accueillir; **are there any seats left?** est-ce qu'il reste des places?; **to take one's ~** prendre place; **to be seated** être assis; **please be seated** veuillez vous asseoir
seat belt N ceinture *f* de sécurité
seating ['si:tɪŋ] N sièges *fpl*, places assises
seating capacity N nombre *m* de places assises
sea urchin N oursin *m*
sea water N eau *f* de mer
seaweed ['si:wi:d] N algues *fpl*
seaworthy ['si:wə:ðɪ] ADJ en état de naviguer
SEC N ABBR (*US: = Securities and Exchange Commission*) ≈ COB *f* (*= Commission des opérations de Bourse*)
sec. ABBR (*= second*) sec
secateurs [sɛkə'tə:z] NPL sécateur *m*
secede [sɪ'si:d] VI faire sécession
secluded [sɪ'klu:dɪd] ADJ retiré(e), à l'écart
seclusion [sɪ'klu:ʒən] N solitude *f*
second[1] ['sɛkənd] NUM deuxième, second(e) ▶ ADV (*in race etc*) en seconde position ▶ N (*unit of time*) seconde *f*; (*Aut: also:* **second gear**) seconde; (*in series, position*) deuxième *mf*, second(e); (*Comm: imperfect*) article *m* de second choix; (*BRIT Scol*) ≈ licence *f* avec mention ▶ VT (*motion*) appuyer; **seconds** NPL (*inf: food*) rab *m* (*inf*); **Charles the S~** Charles II; **just a ~!** une seconde!, un instant!; (*stopping sb*) pas si vite!; **~ floor** (*BRIT*) deuxième (étage) *m*; (*US*) premier (étage) *m*; **to ask for a ~ opinion** (*Med*) demander l'avis d'un autre médecin
second[2] [sɪ'kɔnd] VT (*employee*) détacher, mettre en détachement

secondary ['sɛkəndərɪ] ADJ secondaire
secondary school N (*age 11 to 15*) collège *m*; (*age 15 to 18*) lycée *m*
second-best [sɛkənd'bɛst] N deuxième choix *m*; **as a ~** faute de mieux
second-class ['sɛkənd'klɑ:s] ADJ de deuxième classe; (*Rail*) de seconde (classe); (*Post*) au tarif réduit; (*pej*) de qualité inférieure ▶ ADV (*Rail*) en seconde; (*Post*) au tarif réduit; **~ citizen** citoyen(ne) de deuxième classe
second cousin N cousin(e) issu(e) de germains
seconder ['sɛkəndəʳ] N personne *f* qui appuie une motion
second-guess ['sɛkənd'gɛs] VT (*predict*) (essayer d')anticiper; **they're still trying to ~ his motives** ils essaient toujours de comprendre ses raisons
secondhand ['sɛkənd'hænd] ADJ d'occasion; (*information*) de seconde main ▶ ADV (*buy*) d'occasion; **to hear sth ~** apprendre qch indirectement
second hand N (*on clock*) trotteuse *f*
second-in-command ['sɛkəndɪnkə'mɑ:nd] N (*Mil*) commandant *m* en second; (*Admin*) adjoint(e), sous-chef *m*
secondly ['sɛkəndlɪ] ADV deuxièmement; **firstly ... ~ ...** d'abord ... ensuite ... *or* de plus ...
secondment [sɪ'kɔndmənt] N (*BRIT*) détachement *m*
second-rate ['sɛkənd'reɪt] ADJ de deuxième ordre, de qualité inférieure
second thoughts NPL: **to have ~** changer d'avis; **on ~** *or* (*US*) **on ~** thought à la réflexion
secrecy ['si:krəsɪ] N secret *m*; **in ~** en secret
secret ['si:krɪt] ADJ secret(-ète) ▶ N secret *m*; **in ~** *adv* en secret, secrètement, en cachette; **to keep sth ~ from sb** cacher qch à qn, ne pas révéler qch à qn; **to make no ~ of sth** ne pas cacher qch; **keep it ~** n'en parle à personne
secret agent N agent secret
secretarial [sɛkrɪ'tɛərɪəl] ADJ de secrétaire, de secrétariat
secretariat [sɛkrɪ'tɛərɪət] N secrétariat *m*
secretary ['sɛkrətrɪ] N secrétaire *mf*; (*Comm*) secrétaire général; **S~ of State** (*US Pol*) ≈ ministre *m* des Affaires étrangères; **S~ of State (for)** (*Pol*) ministre *m* (de)
secretary-general ['sɛkrətrɪ'dʒɛnərl] N secrétaire général
secrete [sɪ'kri:t] VT (*Anat, Biol, Med*) sécréter; (*hide*) cacher
secretion [sɪ'kri:ʃən] N sécrétion *f*
secretive ['si:krətɪv] ADJ réservé(e); (*pej*) cachottier(-ière), dissimulé(e)
secretly ['si:krɪtlɪ] ADV en secret, secrètement, en cachette
secret police N police secrète
secret service N services secrets
sect [sɛkt] N secte *f*
sectarian [sɛk'tɛərɪən] ADJ sectaire
section ['sɛkʃən] N section *f*; (*department*) section; (*Comm*) rayon *m*; (*of document*) section, article *m*, paragraphe *m*; (*cut*) coupe *f* ▶ VT sectionner; **the business** *etc* **~** (*Press*) la page des affaires *etc*

S

sector ['sɛktə^r] N secteur *m*
secular ['sɛkjʊlə^r] ADJ laïque
secure [sɪ'kjʊə^r] ADJ (*free from anxiety*) sans
inquiétude, sécurisé(e); (*firmly fixed*) solide, bien
attaché(e) (*or* fermé(e) *etc*); (*in safe place*) en lieu
sûr, en sûreté ▶ VT (*fix*) fixer, attacher; (*get*)
obtenir, se procurer; (*Comm: loan*) garantir; **to
make sth ~** bien fixer *or* attacher qch; **to ~ sth
for sb** obtenir qch pour qn, procurer qch à qn
secured creditor [sɪ'kjʊəd-] N créancier(-ière),
privilégié(e)
security [sɪ'kjʊərɪtɪ] N sécurité *f*, mesures *fpl* de
sécurité; (*for loan*) caution *f*, garantie *f*;
securities NPL (*Stock Exchange*) valeurs *fpl*, titres
mpl; **to increase** *or* **tighten ~** renforcer les
mesures de sécurité; **~ of tenure** stabilité *f*
d'un emploi, titularisation *f*
Security Council N: **the ~** le Conseil de sécurité
security forces NPL forces *fpl* de sécurité
security guard N garde chargé de la sécurité;
(*transporting money*) convoyeur *m* de fonds
security risk N menace *f* pour la sécurité de
l'état (*or* d'une entreprise *etc*)
sedan [sə'dæn] N (*US Aut*) berline *f*
sedate [sɪ'deɪt] ADJ calme; posé(e) ▶ VT donner
des sédatifs à
sedation [sɪ'deɪʃən] N (*Med*) sédation *f*; **to be
under ~** être sous calmants
sedative ['sɛdɪtɪv] N calmant *m*, sédatif *m*
sedentary ['sɛdntrɪ] ADJ sédentaire
sediment ['sɛdɪmənt] N sédiment *m*, dépôt *m*
sedition [sɪ'dɪʃən] N sédition *f*
seduce [sɪ'dju:s] VT séduire
seduction [sɪ'dʌkʃən] N séduction *f*
seductive [sɪ'dʌktɪv] ADJ séduisant(e); (*smile*)
séducteur(-trice); (*fig: offer*) alléchant(e)
see [si:] (*pt* **saw** [sɔ:], *pp* **seen** [si:n]) VT (*gen*) voir;
(*accompany*): **to ~ sb to the door** reconduire *or*
raccompagner qn jusqu'à la porte ▶ VI voir ▶ N
évêché *m*; **to ~ that** (*ensure*) veiller à ce que + *sub*,
faire en sorte que + *sub*, s'assurer que; **there
was nobody to be seen** il n'y avait pas un chat;
let me ~ (*show me*) fais(-moi) voir; (*let me think*)
voyons (un peu); **to go and ~ sb** aller voir qn;
~ for yourself voyez vous-même; **I don't know
what she sees in him** je ne sais pas ce qu'elle
lui trouve; **as far as I can ~** pour autant que je
puisse en juger; **~ you!** au revoir!, à bientôt!;
~ you soon/later/tomorrow! à bientôt/plus
tard/demain!
▶ **see about** VT FUS (*deal with*) s'occuper de
▶ **see off** VT accompagner (à l'aéroport *etc*)
▶ **see out** VT (*take to door*) raccompagner à la
porte
▶ **see through** VT mener à bonne fin ▶ VT FUS
voir clair dans
▶ **see to** VT FUS s'occuper de, se charger de
seed [si:d] N graine *f*; (*fig*) germe *m*; (*Tennis etc*)
tête *f* de série; **to go to ~** (*plant*) monter en
graine; (*fig*) se laisser aller
seedless ['si:dlɪs] ADJ sans pépins
seedling ['si:dlɪŋ] N jeune plant *m*, semis *m*
seedy ['si:dɪ] ADJ (*shabby*) minable,
miteux(-euse)

seeing ['si:ɪŋ] CONJ: **~ (that)** vu que, étant
donné que
seek [si:k] (*pt, pp* **sought** [sɔ:t]) VT chercher,
rechercher; **to ~ advice/help from sb**
demander conseil/de l'aide à qn
▶ **seek out** VT (*person*) chercher
seem [si:m] VI sembler, paraître; **there seems
to be ...** il semble qu'il y a ..., on dirait qu'il y a
...; **it seems (that) ...** il semble que ...; **what
seems to be the trouble?** qu'est-ce qui ne va
pas?
seemingly ['si:mɪŋlɪ] ADV apparemment
seen [si:n] PP *of* **see**
seep [si:p] VI suinter, filtrer
seer [sɪə^r] N prophète (prophétesse)
voyant(e)
seersucker ['sɪəsʌkə^r] N cloqué *m*, étoffe
cloquée
seesaw ['si:sɔ:] N (jeu *m* de) bascule *f*
seethe [si:ð] VI être en effervescence; **to ~ with
anger** bouillir de colère
see-through ['si:θru:] ADJ transparent(e)
segment ['sɛgmənt] N segment *m*; (*of orange*)
quartier *m*
segregate ['sɛgrɪgeɪt] VT séparer, isoler
segregation [sɛgrɪ'geɪʃən] N ségrégation *f*
Seine [seɪn] N: **the (River) ~** la Seine
seismic ['saɪzmɪk] ADJ sismique
seize [si:z] VT (*grasp*) saisir, attraper; (*take
possession of*) s'emparer de; (*opportunity*) saisir;
(*Law*) saisir
▶ **seize on** VT FUS saisir, sauter sur
▶ **seize up** VI (*Tech*) se gripper
▶ **seize upon** VT FUS = **seize on**
seizure ['si:ʒə^r] N (*Med*) crise *f*, attaque *f*; (*of
power*) prise *f*; (*Law*) saisie *f*
seldom ['sɛldəm] ADV rarement
select [sɪ'lɛkt] ADJ choisi(e), d'élite; (*hotel,
restaurant, club*) chic *inv*, sélect *inv* ▶ VT
sélectionner, choisir; **a ~ few** quelques
privilégiés
selection [sɪ'lɛkʃən] N sélection *f*, choix *m*
selection committee N comité *m* de sélection
selective [sɪ'lɛktɪv] ADJ sélectif(-ive); (*school*) à
recrutement sélectif
selector [sɪ'lɛktə^r] N (*person*)
sélectionneur(-euse); (*Tech*) sélecteur *m*
self [sɛlf] (*pl* **selves** [sɛlvz]) N: **the ~** le moi *inv*
▶ PREFIX auto-
self-addressed ['sɛlfə'drɛst] ADJ: **~ envelope**
enveloppe *f* à mon (*or* votre *etc*) nom
self-adhesive [sɛlfəd'hi:zɪv] ADJ autocollant(e)
self-assertive [sɛlfə'sə:tɪv] ADJ autoritaire
self-assurance [sɛlfə'ʃuərəns] N assurance *f*
self-assured [sɛlfə'ʃuəd] ADJ sûr(e) de soi,
plein(e) d'assurance
self-catering [sɛlf'keɪtərɪŋ] ADJ (*Brit: flat*) avec
cuisine, où l'on peut faire sa cuisine; (*: holiday*)
en appartement (*or* chalet *etc*) loué
self-centred, (*US*) **self-centered** [sɛlf'sɛntəd]
ADJ égocentrique
self-cleaning [sɛlf'kli:nɪŋ] ADJ autonettoyant(e)
self-confessed [sɛlfkən'fɛst] ADJ (*alcoholic etc*)
déclaré(e), qui ne s'en cache pas

self-confidence [sɛlf'kɒnfɪdns] N confiance f en soi

self-confident [sɛlf'kɒnfɪdnt] ADJ sûr(e) de soi, plein(e) d'assurance

self-conscious [sɛlf'kɒnʃəs] ADJ timide, qui manque d'assurance

self-contained [sɛlfkən'teɪnd] ADJ (BRIT: *flat*) avec entrée particulière, indépendant(e)

self-control [sɛlfkən'trəul] N maîtrise f de soi

self-defeating [sɛlfdɪ'fi:tɪŋ] ADJ qui a un effet contraire à l'effet recherché

self-defence, (*US*) **self-defense** [sɛlfdɪ'fɛns] N autodéfense f; (*Law*) légitime défense f

self-discipline [sɛlf'dɪsɪplɪn] N discipline personnelle

self-drive [sɛlf'draɪv] ADJ (BRIT): **~ car** voiture f de location

self-employed [sɛlfɪm'plɔɪd] ADJ qui travaille à son compte

self-esteem [sɛlfɪ'sti:m] N amour-propre m

self-evident [sɛlf'ɛvɪdnt] ADJ évident(e), qui va de soi

self-explanatory [sɛlfɪk'splænətrɪ] ADJ qui se passe d'explication

self-governing [sɛlf'gʌvənɪŋ] ADJ autonome

self-harm [sɛlf'hɑ:m] VI s'automutiler ▶ N automutilation f

self-help ['sɛlf'hɛlp] N initiative personnelle, efforts personnels

self-importance [sɛlfɪm'pɔ:tns] N suffisance f

self-indulgent [sɛlfɪn'dʌldʒənt] ADJ qui ne se refuse rien

self-inflicted [sɛlfɪn'flɪktɪd] ADJ volontaire

self-interest [sɛlf'ɪntrɪst] N intérêt personnel

selfish ['sɛlfɪʃ] ADJ égoïste

selfishness ['sɛlfɪʃnɪs] N égoïsme m

selfless ['sɛlflɪs] ADJ désintéressé(e)

selflessly ['sɛlflɪslɪ] ADV sans penser à soi

self-made man ['sɛlfmeɪd-] N (*irreg*) self-made man m

self-pity [sɛlf'pɪtɪ] N apitoiement m sur soi-même

self-portrait [sɛlf'pɔ:treɪt] N autoportrait m

self-possessed [sɛlfpə'zɛst] ADJ assuré(e)

self-preservation ['sɛlfprɛzə'veɪʃən] N instinct m de conservation

self-raising [sɛlf'reɪzɪŋ], (*US*) **self-rising** [sɛlf'raɪzɪŋ] ADJ: **~ flour** farine f pour gâteaux (*avec levure incorporée*)

self-reliant [sɛlfrɪ'laɪənt] ADJ indépendant(e)

self-respect [sɛlfrɪs'pɛkt] N respect m de soi, amour-propre m

self-respecting [sɛlfrɪs'pɛktɪŋ] ADJ qui se respecte

self-righteous [sɛlf'raɪtʃəs] ADJ satisfait(e) de soi, pharisaïque

self-rising [sɛlf'raɪzɪŋ] ADJ (*US*) = **self-raising**

self-sacrifice [sɛlf'sækrɪfaɪs] N abnégation f

self-same ['sɛlfseɪm] ADJ même

self-satisfied [sɛlf'sætɪsfaɪd] ADJ content(e) de soi, suffisant(e)

self-sealing [sɛlf'si:lɪŋ] ADJ (*envelope*) autocollant(e)

self-service [sɛlf'sə:vɪs] ADJ, N libre-service (*m*), self-service (*m*)

self-styled ['sɛlfstaɪld] ADJ soi-disant *inv*

self-sufficient [sɛlfsə'fɪʃənt] ADJ indépendant(e)

self-supporting [sɛlfsə'pɔ:tɪŋ] ADJ financièrement indépendant(e)

self-tanning ['sɛlf'tænɪŋ] ADJ: **~ cream** *or* **lotion** *etc* autobronzant m

self-taught [sɛlf'tɔ:t] ADJ autodidacte

sell [sɛl] (*pt, pp* **sold** [səuld]) VT vendre ▶ VI se vendre; **to ~ at** *or* **for 10 euros** se vendre 10 euros; **to ~ sb an idea** (*fig*) faire accepter une idée à qn
   ▶ **sell off** VT liquider
   ▶ **sell out** VI: **to ~ out (of sth)** (*use up stock*) vendre tout son stock (de qch); **to ~ out (to)** (*Comm*) vendre son fonds *or* son affaire (à) ▶ VT vendre tout son stock de; **the tickets are all sold out** il ne reste plus de billets
   ▶ **sell up** VI vendre son fonds *or* son affaire

sell-by date ['sɛlbaɪ-] N date f limite de vente

seller ['sɛlə'] N vendeur(-euse), marchand(e); **~'s market** marché m à la hausse

selling price ['sɛlɪŋ-] N prix m de vente

Sellotape® ['sɛləuteɪp] N (BRIT) scotch® m

sellout ['sɛlaut] N trahison f, capitulation f; (*of tickets*): **it was a ~** tous les billets ont été vendus

selves [sɛlvz] NPL *of* **self**

semantic [sɪ'mæntɪk] ADJ sémantique

semantics [sɪ'mæntɪks] N sémantique f

semaphore ['sɛməfɔ:'] N signaux *mpl* à bras; (*Rail*) sémaphore m

semblance ['sɛmblns] N semblant m

semen ['si:mən] N sperme m

semester [sɪ'mɛstə'] N (*esp US*) semestre m

semi... ['sɛmɪ] PREFIX semi-, demi-; à demi, à moitié ▶ N: **semi = semidetached (house)**

semibreve ['sɛmɪbri:v] N (BRIT) ronde f

semicircle ['sɛmɪsə:kl] N demi-cercle m

semicircular ['sɛmɪ'sə:kjulə'] ADJ en demi-cercle, semi-circulaire

semicolon [sɛmɪ'kəulən] N point-virgule m

semiconductor [sɛmɪkən'dʌktə'] N semi-conducteur m

semiconscious [sɛmɪ'kɒnʃəs] ADJ à demi conscient(e)

semidetached (house) [sɛmɪdɪ'tætʃt-] N (BRIT) maison jumelée *or* jumelle

semi-final [sɛmɪ'faɪnl] N demi-finale f

seminar ['sɛmɪnɑ:'] N séminaire m

seminary ['sɛmɪnərɪ] N (*Rel: for priests*) séminaire m

semiprecious [sɛmɪ'prɛʃəs] ADJ semi-précieux(-euse)

semiquaver ['sɛmɪkweɪvə'] N (BRIT) double croche f

semiskilled [sɛmɪ'skɪld] ADJ: **~ worker** ouvrier(-ière) spécialisé(e)

semi-skimmed ['sɛmɪ'skɪmd] ADJ demi-écrémé(e)

semitone ['sɛmɪtəun] N (*Mus*) demi-ton m

semolina [sɛmə'li:nə] N semoule f

SEN N ABBR (BRIT) = **State Enrolled Nurse**

Sen., sen. ABBR = **senator; senior**
senate ['sɛnɪt] N sénat m; (US): **the S~** le Sénat;
voir article

> Le Senate est la chambre haute du Congress,
> le parlement des États-Unis. Il est composé
> de 100 sénateurs, 2 par État, élus au suffrage
> universel direct tous les 6 ans, un tiers
> d'entre eux étant renouvelé tous les 2 ans.

senator ['sɛnɪtər] N sénateur m
send [sɛnd] (pt, pp **sent** [sɛnt]) VT envoyer; **to ~
by post** or (US) **mail** envoyer or expédier par la
poste; **to ~ sb for sth** envoyer qn chercher qch;
to ~ word that ... faire dire que ...; **she sends
(you) her love** elle vous adresse ses amitiés; **to
~ sb to Coventry** (BRIT) mettre qn en
quarantaine; **to ~ sb to sleep** endormir qn; **to
~ sb into fits of laughter** faire rire qn aux
éclats; **to ~ sth flying** envoyer valser qch
▶ **send away** VT (letter, goods) envoyer, expédier
▶ **send away for** VT FUS commander par
correspondance, se faire envoyer
▶ **send back** VT renvoyer
▶ **send for** VT FUS envoyer chercher; faire venir;
(by post) se faire envoyer, commander par
correspondance
▶ **send in** VT (report, application, resignation)
remettre
▶ **send off** VT (goods) envoyer, expédier; (BRIT
Sport: player) expulser or renvoyer du terrain
▶ **send on** VT (BRIT: letter) faire suivre; (luggage
etc: in advance) (faire) expédier à l'avance
▶ **send out** VT (invitation) envoyer (par la poste);
(emit: light, heat, signal) émettre
▶ **send round** VT (letter, document etc) faire
circuler
▶ **send up** VT (person, price) faire monter; (BRIT:
parody) mettre en boîte, parodier
sender ['sɛndər] N expéditeur(-trice)
send-off ['sɛndɔːf] N: **a good ~** des adieux
chaleureux
Senegal [sɛnɪ'gɔːl] N Sénégal m
Senegalese [sɛnɪgə'liːz] ADJ sénégalais(e) ▶ N
(pl inv) Sénégalais(e)
senile ['siːnaɪl] ADJ sénile
senility [sɪ'nɪlɪtɪ] N sénilité f
senior ['siːnɪər] ADJ (older) aîné(e), plus âgé(e);
(high-ranking) de haut niveau; (of higher rank): **to
be ~ to sb** être le supérieur de qn ▶ N (older): **she
is 15 years his ~** elle est son aînée de 15 ans, elle
est plus âgée que lui de 15 ans; (in service)
personne f qui a plus d'ancienneté; **P. Jones ~**
P. Jones père
senior citizen N personne f du troisième âge
senior high school N (US) ≈ lycée m
seniority [siːnɪ'ɔrɪtɪ] N priorité f d'âge,
ancienneté f; (in rank) supériorité f
(hiérarchique)
sensation [sɛn'seɪʃən] N sensation f; **to create
a ~** faire sensation
sensational [sɛn'seɪʃənl] ADJ qui fait sensation;
(marvellous) sensationnel(le)
sense [sɛns] N sens m; (feeling) sentiment m;
(meaning) sens, signification f; (wisdom) bon sens
▶ VT sentir, pressentir; **senses** NPL raison f; **it**

makes ~ c'est logique; **there is no ~ in (doing)
that** cela n'a pas de sens; **to come to one's
senses** (regain consciousness) reprendre
conscience; (become reasonable) revenir à la raison;
to take leave of one's senses perdre la tête
senseless ['sɛnslɪs] ADJ insensé(e), stupide;
(unconscious) sans connaissance
sense of humour, (US) **sense of humor** N sens
m de l'humour
sensibility [sɛnsɪ'bɪlɪtɪ] N sensibilité f;
sensibilities NPL susceptibilité f
sensible ['sɛnsɪbl] ADJ sensé(e), raisonnable;
(shoes etc) pratique
sensitive ['sɛnsɪtɪv] ADJ: **~ (to)** sensible (à); **he is
very ~ about it** c'est un point très sensible
(chez lui)
sensitivity [sɛnsɪ'tɪvɪtɪ] N sensibilité f
sensual ['sɛnsjuəl] ADJ sensuel(le)
sensuous ['sɛnsjuəs] ADJ voluptueux(-euse),
sensuel(le)
sent [sɛnt] PT, PP of **send**
sentence ['sɛntns] N (Ling) phrase f; (Law:
judgment) condamnation f, sentence f;
(: punishment) peine f ▶ VT: **to ~ sb to death/to 5
years** condamner qn à mort/à 5 ans; **to pass ~
on sb** prononcer une peine contre qn
sentiment ['sɛntɪmənt] N sentiment m;
(opinion) opinion f, avis m
sentimental [sɛntɪ'mɛntl] ADJ sentimental(e)
sentimentality [sɛntɪmɛn'tælɪtɪ] N
sentimentalité f, sensiblerie f
sentry ['sɛntrɪ] N sentinelle f, factionnaire m
sentry duty N: **to be on ~** être de faction
Seoul [səul] N Séoul m
separable ['sɛprəbl] ADJ séparable
separate ADJ ['sɛprɪt] séparé(e); (organization)
indépendant(e); (day, occasion, issue) différent(e)
▶ VT ['sɛpəreɪt] séparer; (distinguish) distinguer
▶ VI ['sɛpəreɪt] se séparer; **~ from** distinct(e) de;
under ~ cover (Comm) sous pli séparé; **to ~ into**
diviser en
separately ['sɛprɪtlɪ] ADV séparément
separates ['sɛprɪts] NPL (clothes) coordonnés mpl
separation [sɛpə'reɪʃən] N séparation f
Sept. ABBR (= September) sept
September [sɛp'tɛmbər] N septembre m; see also
July
septic ['sɛptɪk] ADJ septique; (wound) infecté(e);
to go ~ s'infecter
septicaemia [sɛptɪ'siːmɪə] N septicémie f
septic tank N fosse f septique
sequel ['siːkwl] N conséquence f; séquelles fpl;
(of story) suite f
sequence ['siːkwəns] N ordre m, suite f; (in film)
séquence f; (dance) numéro m; **in ~** par ordre,
dans l'ordre, les uns après les autres; **~ of
tenses** concordance f des temps
sequential [sɪ'kwɛnʃəl] ADJ: **~ access** (Comput)
accès séquentiel
sequin ['siːkwɪn] N paillette f
Serb [səːb] ADJ, N = **Serbian**
Serbia ['səːbɪə] N Serbie f
Serbian ['səːbɪən] ADJ serbe ▶ N Serbe mf; (Ling)
serbe m

Serbo-Croat ['sə:bəu'krəuæt] N (*Ling*) serbo-croate *m*

serenade [sɛrə'neɪd] N sérénade *f* ▶ vt donner une sérénade à

serene [sɪ'ri:n] ADJ serein(e), calme, paisible

serenity [sə'rɛnɪtɪ] N sérénité *f*, calme *m*

sergeant ['sɑ:dʒənt] N sergent *m*; (*Police*) brigadier *m*

sergeant major N sergent-major *m*

serial ['sɪərɪəl] N feuilleton *m* ▶ ADJ (*Comput*: *interface, printer*) série inv; (: *access*) séquentiel(le)

serialize ['sɪərɪəlaɪz] vt publier (*or* adapter) en feuilleton

serial killer N meurtrier *m* tuant en série

serial number N numéro *m* de série

series ['sɪərɪz] N série *f*; (*Publishing*) collection *f*

serious ['sɪərɪəs] ADJ sérieux(-euse); (*accident etc*) grave; **are you ~ (about it)?** parlez-vous sérieusement?

seriously ['sɪərɪəslɪ] ADV sérieusement; (*hurt*) gravement; **~ rich/difficult** (*inf: extremely*) drôlement riche/difficile; **to take sth/sb ~** prendre qch/qn au sérieux

seriousness ['sɪərɪəsnɪs] N sérieux *m*, gravité *f*

sermon ['sə:mən] N sermon *m*

serrated [sɪ'reɪtɪd] ADJ en dents de scie

serum ['sɪərəm] N sérum *m*

servant ['sə:vənt] N domestique *mf*; (*fig*) serviteur (servante)

serve [sə:v] vt (*employer etc*) servir, être au service de; (*purpose*) servir à; (*customer, food, meal*) servir; (*subj: train*) desservir; (*apprenticeship*) faire, accomplir; (*prison term*) faire; purger ▶ vi (*Tennis*) servir; (*be useful*): **to ~ as/for/to do** servir de/à/à faire ▶ N (*Tennis*) service *m*; **are you being served?** est-ce qu'on s'occupe de vous?; **to ~ on a committee/jury** faire partie d'un comité/jury; **it serves him right** c'est bien fait pour lui; **it serves my purpose** cela fait mon affaire

▶ **serve out, serve up** vt (*food*) servir

server [sə:və^r] N (*Comput*) serveur *m*

service ['sə:vɪs] N (*gen*) service *m*; (*Aut*) révision *f*; (*Rel*) office *m* ▶ vt (*car etc*) réviser; **services** NPL (*Econ: tertiary sector*) (secteur *m*) tertiaire *m*, secteur des services; (*Brit: on motorway*) station-service *f*; (*Mil*): **the Services** npl les forces armées; **to be of ~ to sb, to do sb a ~** rendre service à qn; **~ included/not included** service compris/non compris; **to put one's car in for ~** donner sa voiture à réviser; **dinner ~** service de table

serviceable ['sə:vɪsəbl] ADJ pratique, commode

service area N (*on motorway*) aire *f* de services

service charge N (*Brit*) service *m*

service industries NPL les industries *fpl* de service, les services *mpl*

serviceman ['sə:vɪsmən] N (*irreg*) militaire *m*

service station N station-service *f*

serviette [sə:vɪ'ɛt] N (*Brit*) serviette *f* (de table)

session ['sɛʃən] N (*sitting*) séance *f*; (*Scol*) année *f* scolaire (*or* universitaire); **to be in ~** siéger, être en session *or* en séance

session musician N musicien(ne) de studio

set [sɛt] (*pt, pp* ~) N série *f*, assortiment *m*; (*of tools etc*) jeu *m*; (*Radio, TV*) poste *m*; (*Tennis*) set *m*; (*group of people*) cercle *m*, milieu *m*; (*Cine*) plateau *m*; (*Theat: stage*) scène *f*; (: *scenery*) décor *m*; (*Math*) ensemble *m*; (*Hairdressing*) mise *f* en plis ▶ ADJ (*fixed*) fixe, déterminé(e); (*ready*) prêt(e) ▶ vt (*place*) mettre, poser, placer; (*fix, establish*) fixer; (: *record*) établir; (*assign: task, homework*) donner; (*exam*) composer; (*adjust*) régler; (*decide: rules etc*) fixer, choisir; (*Typ*) composer ▶ vi (*sun*) se coucher; (*jam, jelly, concrete*) prendre; (*bone*) se ressouder; **to be ~ on doing** être résolu(e) à faire; **to be all ~ to do** être (fin) prêt(e) pour faire; **to be (dead) ~ against** être (totalement) opposé à; **he's ~ in his ways** il n'est pas très souple, il tient à ses habitudes; **to ~ to music** mettre en musique; **to ~ on fire** mettre le feu à; **to ~ free** libérer; **to ~ sth going** déclencher qch; **to ~ the alarm clock for seven o'clock** mettre le réveil à sonner à sept heures; **to ~ sail** partir, prendre la mer; **a ~ phrase** une expression toute faite, une locution; **a ~ of false teeth** un dentier; **a ~ of dining-room furniture** une salle à manger

▶ **set about** vt fus (*task*) entreprendre, se mettre à; **to ~ about doing sth** se mettre à faire qch

▶ **set aside** vt mettre de côté; (*time*) garder

▶ **set back** vt (*in time*): **to ~ back (by)** retarder (de); (*place*): **a house ~ back from the road** une maison située en retrait de la route

▶ **set down** vt (*subj: bus, train*) déposer

▶ **set in** vi (*infection, bad weather*) s'installer; (*complications*) survenir, surgir; **the rain has ~ in for the day** c'est parti pour qu'il pleuve toute la journée

▶ **set off** vi se mettre en route, partir ▶ vt (*bomb*) faire exploser; (*cause to start*) déclencher; (*show up well*) mettre en valeur, faire valoir

▶ **set out** vi: **to ~ out (from)** partir (de) ▶ vt (*arrange*) disposer; (*state*) présenter, exposer; **to ~ out to do** entreprendre de faire; avoir pour but *or* intention de faire

▶ **set up** vt (*organization*) fonder, créer; (*monument*) ériger; **to ~ up shop** (*fig*) s'établir, s'installer

setback ['sɛtbæk] N (*hitch*) revers *m*, contretemps *m*; (*in health*) rechute *f*

set menu N menu *m*

set square N équerre *f*

settee [sɛ'ti:] N canapé *m*

setting ['sɛtɪŋ] N cadre *m*; (*of jewel*) monture *f*; (*position: of controls*) réglage *m*

setting lotion N lotion *f* pour mise en plis

settle ['sɛtl] vt (*argument, matter, account*) régler; (*problem*) résoudre; (*Med: calm*) calmer; (*colonize: land*) coloniser ▶ vi (*bird, dust etc*) se poser; (*sediment*) se déposer; **to ~ to sth** se mettre sérieusement à qch; **to ~ for sth** accepter qch, se contenter de qch; **to ~ on sth** opter *or* se décider pour qch; **that's settled then** alors, c'est d'accord!; **to ~ one's stomach** calmer des maux d'estomac

S

779

▶ **settle down** VI (*get comfortable*) s'installer; (*become calmer*) se calmer; se ranger

▶ **settle in** VI s'installer

▶ **settle up** VI: **to ~ up with sb** régler (ce que l'on doit à) qn

settlement ['sɛtlmənt] N (*payment*) règlement *m*; (*agreement*) accord *m*; (*colony*) colonie *f*; (*village etc*) village *m*, hameau *m*; **in ~ of our account** (*Comm*) en règlement de notre compte

settler ['sɛtləʳ] N colon *m*

setup ['sɛtʌp] N (*arrangement*) manière *f* dont les choses sont organisées; (*situation*) situation *f*, allure *f* des choses

seven ['sɛvn] NUM sept

seventeen [sɛvn'tiːn] NUM dix-sept

seventeenth [sɛvn'tiːnθ] NUM dix-septième

seventh ['sɛvnθ] NUM septième

seventieth ['sɛvntɪɪθ] NUM soixante-dixième

seventy ['sɛvntɪ] NUM soixante-dix

sever ['sɛvəʳ] VT couper, trancher; (*relations*) rompre

several ['sɛvərl] ADJ, PRON plusieurs *pl*; **~ of us** plusieurs d'entre nous; **~ times** plusieurs fois

severance ['sɛvərəns] N (*of relations*) rupture *f*

severance pay N indemnité *f* de licenciement

severe [sɪ'vɪəʳ] ADJ (*stern*) sévère, strict(e); (*serious*) grave, sérieux(-euse); (*hard*) rigoureux(-euse), dur(e); (*plain*) sévère, austère

severely [sɪ'vɪəlɪ] ADV sévèrement; (*wounded, ill*) gravement

severity [sɪ'vɛrɪtɪ] N sévérité *f*; gravité *f*; rigueur *f*

sew [səu] (*pt* **sewed** [səud], *pp* **sewn** [səun]) VT, VI coudre

▶ **sew up** VT (re)coudre; **it is all sewn up** (*fig*) c'est dans le sac *or* dans la poche

sewage ['suːɪdʒ] N vidange(s) *f(pl)*

sewage works N champ *m* d'épandage

sewer ['suːəʳ] N égout *m*

sewing ['səuɪŋ] N couture *f*; (*item(s)*) ouvrage *m*

sewing machine N machine *f* à coudre

sewn [səun] PP *of* **sew**

sex [sɛks] N sexe *m*; **to have ~ with** avoir des rapports (sexuels) avec

sex act N acte sexuel

sex appeal N sex-appeal *m*

sex education N éducation sexuelle

sexism ['sɛksɪzəm] N sexisme *m*

sexist ['sɛksɪst] ADJ sexiste

sex life N vie sexuelle

sex object N femme-objet *f*, objet sexuel

sextet [sɛks'tɛt] N sextuor *m*

sexual ['sɛksjuəl] ADJ sexuel(le); **~ assault** attentat *m* à la pudeur; **~ harassment** harcèlement sexuel

sexual intercourse N rapports sexuels

sexuality [sɛksju'ælɪtɪ] N sexualité *f*

sexy ['sɛksɪ] ADJ sexy *inv*

Seychelles [seɪ'ʃɛl(z)] NPL: **the ~** les Seychelles *fpl*

SF N ABBR (= *science fiction*) SF *f*

SG N ABBR (*US*) = **Surgeon General**

Sgt ABBR (= *sergeant*) Sgt

shabbiness ['ʃæbɪnɪs] N aspect miteux; mesquinerie *f*

shabby ['ʃæbɪ] ADJ miteux(-euse); (*behaviour*) mesquin(e), méprisable

shack [ʃæk] N cabane *f*, hutte *f*

shackles ['ʃæklz] NPL chaînes *fpl*, entraves *fpl*

shade [ʃeɪd] N ombre *f*; (*for lamp*) abat-jour *m inv*; (*of colour*) nuance *f*, ton *m*; (*US: window shade*) store *m*; (*small quantity*): **a ~ of** un soupçon de ▶ VT abriter du soleil, ombrager; **shades** NPL (*US: sunglasses*) lunettes *fpl* de soleil; **in the ~** à l'ombre; **a ~ smaller** un tout petit peu plus petit

shadow ['ʃædəu] N ombre *f* ▶ VT (*follow*) filer; **without** *or* **beyond a ~ of doubt** sans l'ombre d'un doute

shadow cabinet N (*BRIT Pol*) cabinet parallèle formé par le parti qui n'est pas au pouvoir

shadowy ['ʃædəuɪ] ADJ ombragé(e); (*dim*) vague, indistinct(e)

shady ['ʃeɪdɪ] ADJ ombragé(e); (*fig: dishonest*) louche, véreux(-euse)

shaft [ʃɑːft] N (*of arrow, spear*) hampe *f*; (*Aut, Tech*) arbre *m*; (*of mine*) puits *m*; (*of lift*) cage *f*; (*of light*) rayon *m*, trait *m*; **ventilator ~** conduit *m* d'aération *or* de ventilation

shaggy ['ʃægɪ] ADJ hirsute; en broussaille

shake [ʃeɪk] (*pt* **shook** [ʃuk], *pp* **shaken** ['ʃeɪkn]) VT secouer; (*bottle, cocktail*) agiter; (*house, confidence*) ébranler ▶ VI trembler ▶ N secousse *f*; **to ~ one's head** (*in refusal etc*) dire *or* faire non de la tête; (*in dismay*) secouer la tête; **to ~ hands with sb** serrer la main à qn

▶ **shake off** VT secouer; (*pursuer*) se débarrasser de

▶ **shake up** VT secouer

shake-up ['ʃeɪkʌp] N grand remaniement

shakily ['ʃeɪkɪlɪ] ADV (*reply*) d'une voix tremblante; (*walk*) d'un pas mal assuré; (*write*) d'une main tremblante

shaky ['ʃeɪkɪ] ADJ (*hand, voice*) tremblant(e); (*building*) branlant(e), peu solide; (*memory*) chancelant(e); (*knowledge*) incertain(e)

shale [ʃeɪl] N schiste argileux

shall [ʃæl] AUX VB: **I ~ go** j'irai; **~ I open the door?** j'ouvre la porte?; **I'll get the coffee, ~ I?** je vais chercher le café, d'accord?

shallot [ʃə'lɔt] N (*BRIT*) échalote *f*

shallow ['ʃæləu] ADJ peu profond(e); (*fig*) superficiel(le), qui manque de profondeur

sham [ʃæm] N frime *f*; (*jewellery, furniture*) imitation *f* ▶ ADJ feint(e), simulé(e) ▶ VT feindre, simuler

shambles ['ʃæmblz] N confusion *f*, pagaïe *f*, fouillis *m*; **the economy is (in) a complete ~** l'économie est dans la confusion la plus totale

shambolic [ʃæm'bɔlɪk] ADJ (*inf*) bordélique

shame [ʃeɪm] N honte *f* ▶ VT faire honte à; **it is a ~ (that/to do)** c'est dommage (que + *sub*/de faire); **what a ~!** quel dommage!; **to put sb/sth to ~** (*fig*) faire honte à qn/qch

shamefaced ['ʃeɪmfeɪst] ADJ honteux(-euse), penaud(e)

shameful ['ʃeɪmful] ADJ honteux(-euse), scandaleux(-euse)

shameless ['ʃeɪmlɪs] ADJ éhonté(e), effronté(e); (*immodest*) impudique

shampoo [ʃæm'puː] N shampooing m ▶ VT faire un shampooing à; **~ and set** shampooing et mise f en plis

shamrock ['ʃæmrɔk] N trèfle m (emblème national de l'Irlande)

shandy ['ʃændɪ] N bière panachée

shan't [ʃɑːnt]= **shall not**

shantytown ['ʃæntɪtaun] N bidonville m

SHAPE [ʃeɪp] N ABBR (= Supreme Headquarters Allied Powers, Europe) quartier général des forces alliées en Europe

shape [ʃeɪp] N forme f ▶ VT façonner, modeler; (clay, stone) donner forme à; (statement) formuler; (sb's ideas, character) former; (sb's life) déterminer; (course of events) influer sur le cours de ▶ VI (also: **shape up**: events) prendre tournure; (: person) faire des progrès, s'en sortir; **to take ~** prendre forme or tournure; **in the ~ of a heart** en forme de cœur; **I can't bear gardening in any ~ or form** je déteste le jardinage sous quelque forme que ce soit; **to get o.s. into ~** (re)trouver la forme

-shaped [ʃeɪpt] SUFFIX: **heart~** en forme de cœur

shapeless ['ʃeɪplɪs] ADJ informe, sans forme

shapely ['ʃeɪplɪ] ADJ bien proportionné(e), beau (belle)

share [ʃɛəʳ] N (thing received, contribution) part f; (Comm) action f ▶ VT partager; (have in common) avoir en commun; **to ~ out (among** or **between)** partager (entre); **to ~ in** (joy, sorrow) prendre part à; (profits) participer à, avoir part à; (work) partager

share capital N capital social

share certificate N certificat m or titre m d'action

shareholder ['ʃɛəhəuldəʳ] N (BRIT) actionnaire mf

share index N indice m de la Bourse

shark [ʃɑːk] N requin m

sharp [ʃɑːp] ADJ (razor, knife) tranchant(e), bien aiguisé(e); (point, voice) aigu(ë); (nose, chin) pointu(e); (outline, increase) net(te); (curve, bend) brusque; (cold, pain) vif (vive); (taste) piquant(e), âcre; (Mus) dièse; (person: quick-witted) vif (vive), éveillé(e); (: unscrupulous) malhonnête ▶ N (Mus) dièse m ▶ ADV: **at 2 o'clock ~** à 2 heures pile or tapantes; **turn ~ left** tournez immédiatement à gauche; **to be ~ with sb** être brusque avec qn; **look ~!** dépêche-toi!

sharpen ['ʃɑːpn] VT aiguiser; (pencil) tailler; (fig) aviver

sharpener ['ʃɑːpnəʳ] N (also: **pencil sharpener**) taille-crayon(s) m inv; (also: **knife sharpener**) aiguisoir m

sharp-eyed [ʃɑːp'aɪd] ADJ à qui rien n'échappe

sharpish ['ʃɑːpɪʃ] ADV (BRIT inf: quickly) en vitesse

sharply ['ʃɑːplɪ] ADV (turn, stop) brusquement; (stand out) nettement; (criticize, retort) sèchement, vertement

sharp-tempered [ʃɑːp'tempəd] ADJ prompt(e) à se mettre en colère

sharp-witted [ʃɑːp'wɪtɪd] ADJ à l'esprit vif, malin(-igne)

shatter ['ʃætəʳ] VT fracasser, briser, faire voler

en éclats; (fig: upset) bouleverser; (: ruin) briser, ruiner ▶ VI voler en éclats, se briser, se fracasser

shattered ['ʃætəd] ADJ (overwhelmed, grief-stricken) bouleversé(e); (inf: exhausted) éreinté(e)

shatterproof ['ʃætəpruːf] ADJ incassable

shave [ʃeɪv] VT raser ▶ VI se raser ▶ N: **to have a ~** se raser

shaven ['ʃeɪvn] ADJ (head) rasé(e)

shaver ['ʃeɪvəʳ] N (also: **electric shaver**) rasoir m électrique

shaving ['ʃeɪvɪŋ] N (action) rasage m

shaving brush N blaireau m

shaving cream N crème f à raser

shaving foam N mousse f à raser

shavings ['ʃeɪvɪŋz] NPL (of wood etc) copeaux mpl

shaving soap N savon m à barbe

shawl [ʃɔːl] N châle m

she [ʃiː] PRON elle; **there ~ is** la voilà; **~-elephant** etc éléphant m etc femelle

sheaf [ʃiːf] (pl **sheaves** [ʃiːvz]) N gerbe f

shear [ʃɪəʳ] (pt **sheared**, pp **sheared** or **shorn** [ʃɔːn]) VT (sheep) tondre
▶ **shear off** VT tondre; (branch) élaguer

shears [ʃɪəz] NPL (for hedge) cisaille(s) f(pl)

sheath [ʃiːθ] N gaine f, fourreau m, étui m; (contraceptive) préservatif m

sheathe [ʃiːð] VT gainer; (sword) rengainer

sheath knife N couteau m à gaine

sheaves [ʃiːvz] NPL of **sheaf**

shed [ʃed] (pt, pp **~**) N remise f, resserre f; (Industry, Rail) hangar m ▶ VT (leaves, fur etc) perdre; (tears) verser, répandre; (workers) congédier; **to ~ light on** (problem, mystery) faire la lumière sur

she'd [ʃiːd] = **she had**; **she would**

sheen [ʃiːn] N lustre m

sheep [ʃiːp] N (pl inv) mouton m

sheepdog ['ʃiːpdɔg] N chien m de berger

sheep farmer N éleveur m de moutons

sheepish ['ʃiːpɪʃ] ADJ penaud(e), timide

sheepskin ['ʃiːpskɪn] N peau f de mouton

sheepskin jacket N canadienne f

sheer [ʃɪəʳ] ADJ (utter) pur(e), pur et simple; (steep) à pic, abrupt(e); (almost transparent) extrêmement fin(e) ▶ ADV à pic, abruptement; **by ~ chance** par pur hasard

sheet [ʃiːt] N (on bed) drap m; (of paper) feuille f; (of glass, metal etc) feuille f, plaque f

sheet feed N (on printer) alimentation f en papier (feuille à feuille)

sheet lightning N éclair m en nappe(s)

sheet metal N tôle f

sheet music N partition(s) f(pl)

sheik, sheikh [ʃeɪk] N cheik m

shelf [ʃelf] (pl **shelves** [ʃelvz]) N étagère f, rayon m; **set of shelves** rayonnage m

shelf life N (Comm) durée f de conservation (avant la vente)

shell [ʃel] N (on beach) coquillage m; (of egg, nut etc) coquille f; (explosive) obus m; (of building) carcasse f
▶ VT (crab, prawn etc) décortiquer; (peas) écosser; (Mil) bombarder (d'obus)
▶ **shell out** VI (inf): **to ~ out (for)** casquer (pour)

she'll [ʃiːl] = **she will**; **she shall**

shellfish ['ʃɛlfɪʃ] N (pl inv: crab etc) crustacé m;
(: scallop etc) coquillage m ▶ NPL (as food) fruits
mpl de mer

shell suit N survêtement m

shelter ['ʃɛltə^r] N abri m, refuge m ▶ VT abriter,
protéger; (give lodging to) donner asile à ▶ VI
s'abriter, se mettre à l'abri; **to take ~ (from)**
s'abriter (de)

sheltered ['ʃɛltəd] ADJ (life) retiré(e), à l'abri des
soucis; (spot) abrité(e)

sheltered housing N foyers mpl (pour personnes
âgées ou handicapées)

shelve [ʃɛlv] VT (fig) mettre en suspens or en
sommeil

shelves ['ʃɛlvz] NPL of shelf

shelving ['ʃɛlvɪŋ] N (shelves) rayonnage(s) m(pl)

shepherd ['ʃɛpəd] N berger m ▶ VT (guide) guider,
escorter

shepherdess ['ʃɛpədɪs] N bergère f

shepherd's pie ['ʃɛpədz-] N ≈ hachis m
Parmentier

sherbet ['ʃəːbət] N (BRIT: powder) poudre
acidulée; (US: water ice) sorbet m

sheriff ['ʃɛrɪf] (US) N shérif m

sherry ['ʃɛrɪ] N xérès m, sherry m

she's [ʃiːz] = she is; she has

Shetland ['ʃɛtlənd] N (also: the Shetlands, the
Shetland Isles or Islands) les îles fpl Shetland

Shetland pony N poney m des îles Shetland

shield [ʃiːld] N bouclier m; (protection) écran m de
protection ▶ VT: **to ~ (from)** protéger (de or
contre)

shift [ʃɪft] N (change) changement m; (work period)
période f de travail; (of workers) équipe f, poste m
▶ VT déplacer, changer de place; (remove) enlever
▶ VI changer de place, bouger; **the wind has
shifted to the south** le vent a tourné au sud;
a ~ in demand (Comm) un déplacement de la
demande

shift key N (on typewriter) touche f de majuscule

shiftless ['ʃɪftlɪs] ADJ fainéant(e)

shift work N travail m par roulement; **to do ~**
travailler par roulement

shifty ['ʃɪftɪ] ADJ sournois(e); (eyes) fuyant(e)

Shiite ['ʃiːaɪt] N Chiite mf ▶ ADJ chiite

shilling ['ʃɪlɪŋ] N (BRIT) shilling m (= 12 old pence; 20
in a pound)

shilly-shally ['ʃɪlɪʃælɪ] VI tergiverser, atermoyer

shimmer ['ʃɪmə^r] N miroitement m,
chatoiement m ▶ VI miroiter, chatoyer

shin [ʃɪn] N tibia m ▶ VI: **to ~ up/down a tree**
grimper dans un/descendre d'un arbre

shindig ['ʃɪndɪg] N (inf) bamboula f

shine [ʃaɪn] (pt, pp **shone** [ʃɔn]) N éclat m, brillant m
▶ VI briller ▶ VT (pt, pp **shined**) (polish) faire
briller or reluire; **to ~ sth on sth** (torch) braquer
qch sur qch

shingle ['ʃɪŋgl] N (on beach) galets mpl; (on roof)
bardeau m

shingles ['ʃɪŋglz] N (Med) zona m

shining ['ʃaɪnɪŋ] ADJ brillant(e)

shiny ['ʃaɪnɪ] ADJ brillant(e)

ship [ʃɪp] N bateau m; (large) navire m ▶ VT
transporter (par mer); (send) expédier (par mer);
(load) charger, embarquer; **on board ~** à bord

shipbuilder ['ʃɪpbɪldə^r] N constructeur m de
navires

shipbuilding ['ʃɪpbɪldɪŋ] N construction navale

ship chandler [-'tʃɑːndlə^r] N fournisseur m
maritime, shipchandler m

shipment ['ʃɪpmənt] N cargaison f

shipowner ['ʃɪpəunə^r] N armateur m

shipper ['ʃɪpə^r] N affréteur m, expéditeur m

shipping ['ʃɪpɪŋ] N (ships) navires mpl; (traffic)
navigation f; (the industry) industrie navale;
(transport) transport m

shipping agent N agent m maritime

shipping company N compagnie f de
navigation

shipping lane N couloir m de navigation

shipping line N = shipping company

shipshape ['ʃɪpʃeɪp] ADJ en ordre impeccable

shipwreck ['ʃɪprɛk] N épave f; (event) naufrage m
▶ VT: **to be shipwrecked** faire naufrage

shipyard ['ʃɪpjɑːd] N chantier naval

shire ['ʃaɪə^r] N (BRIT) comté m

shirk [ʃəːk] VT esquiver, se dérober à

shirt [ʃəːt] N chemise f; (woman's) chemisier m;
in ~ sleeves en bras de chemise

shirty ['ʃəːtɪ] ADJ (BRIT inf) de mauvais poil

shit [ʃɪt] EXCL (inf!) merde (!)

shiver ['ʃɪvə^r] N frisson m ▶ VI frissonner

shoal [ʃəul] N (of fish) banc m

shock [ʃɔk] N (impact) choc m, heurt m; (Elec)
secousse f, décharge f; (emotional) choc; (Med)
commotion f, choc ▶ VT (scandalize) choquer,
scandaliser; (upset) bouleverser; **suffering
from ~** (Med) commotionné(e); **it gave us a ~** ça
nous a fait un choc; **it came as a ~ to hear
that ...** nous avons appris avec stupeur que ...

shock absorber [-əbzɔːbə^r] N amortisseur m

shocker ['ʃɔkə^r] N (inf): **the news was a real ~ to
him** il a vraiment été choqué par cette nouvelle

shocking ['ʃɔkɪŋ] ADJ (outrageous) choquant(e),
scandaleux(-euse); (awful) épouvantable

shockproof ['ʃɔkpruːf] ADJ anti-choc inv

shock therapy, shock treatment N (Med)
(traitement m par) électrochoc(s) m(pl)

shock wave N (also fig) onde f de choc

shod [ʃɔd] PT, PP of shoe; **well-~** bien chaussé(e)

shoddy ['ʃɔdɪ] ADJ de mauvaise qualité, mal
fait(e)

shoe [ʃuː] (pt, pp **shod** [ʃɔd]) N chaussure f,
soulier m; (also: **horseshoe**) fer m à cheval; (also:
brake shoe) mâchoire f de frein ▶ VT (horse)
ferrer

shoebrush ['ʃuːbrʌʃ] N brosse f à chaussures

shoehorn ['ʃuːhɔːn] N chausse-pied m

shoelace ['ʃuːleɪs] N lacet m (de soulier)

shoemaker ['ʃuːmeɪkə^r] N cordonnier m,
fabricant m de chaussures

shoe polish N cirage m

shoeshop ['ʃuːʃɔp] N magasin m de chaussures

shoestring ['ʃuːstrɪŋ] N: **on a ~** (fig) avec un
budget dérisoire; avec des moyens très
restreints

shoetree ['ʃuːtriː] N embauchoir m

shone [ʃɔn] PT, PP of shine

shonky ['ʃɒŋkɪ] ADJ (AUSTRALIA, NEW ZEALAND inf: untrustworthy) louche

shoo [ʃuː] EXCL allez, ouste! ▶ VT (also: **shoo away, shoo off**) chasser

shook [ʃʊk] PT of **shake**

shoot [ʃuːt] (pt, pp **shot** [ʃɒt]) N (on branch, seedling) pousse f; (shooting party) partie f de chasse ▶ VT (game: hunt) chasser; (: aim at) tirer; (: kill) abattre; (person) blesser/tuer d'un coup de fusil (or de revolver); (execute) fusiller; (arrow) tirer; (gun) tirer un coup de; (Cine) tourner ▶ VI (with gun, bow): **to ~ (at)** tirer (sur); (Football) shooter, tirer; **to ~ past sb** passer en flèche devant qn; **to ~ in/out** entrer/sortir comme une flèche
  ▶ **shoot down** VT (plane) abattre
  ▶ **shoot up** VI (fig: prices etc) monter en flèche

shooting ['ʃuːtɪŋ] N (shots) coups mpl de feu; (attack) fusillade f; (murder) homicide m (à l'aide d'une arme à feu); (Hunting) chasse f; (Cine) tournage m

shooting range N stand m de tir

shooting star N étoile filante

shop [ʃɒp] N magasin m; (workshop) atelier m ▶ VI (also: **go shopping**) faire ses courses or ses achats; **repair ~** atelier de réparations; **to talk ~** (fig) parler boutique
  ▶ **shop around** VI faire le tour des magasins (pour comparer les prix); (fig) se renseigner avant de choisir or décider

shopaholic [ʃɒpə'hɒlɪk] N (inf) personne qui achète sans pouvoir s'arrêter

shop assistant N (BRIT) vendeur(-euse)

shop floor N (BRIT fig) ouvriers mpl

shopkeeper ['ʃɒpkiːpəʳ] N marchand(e), commerçant(e)

shoplift ['ʃɒplɪft] VI voler à l'étalage

shoplifter ['ʃɒplɪftəʳ] N voleur(-euse) à l'étalage

shoplifting ['ʃɒplɪftɪŋ] N vol m à l'étalage

shopper ['ʃɒpəʳ] N personne f qui fait ses courses, acheteur(-euse)

shopping ['ʃɒpɪŋ] N (goods) achats mpl, provisions fpl

shopping bag N sac m (à provisions)

shopping cart N (US Comput) chariot m; Caddie® m; (Internet) panier m (d'achats)

shopping centre, (US) **shopping center** N centre commercial

shopping mall N centre commercial

shopping trolley N (BRIT) Caddie® m

shop-soiled ['ʃɒpsɔɪld] ADJ défraîchi(e), qui a fait la vitrine

shop window N vitrine f

shore [ʃɔːʳ] N (of sea, lake) rivage m, rive f ▶ VT: **to ~ (up)** étayer; **on ~** à terre

shore leave N (Naut) permission f à terre

shorn [ʃɔːn] PP of **shear** ▶ ADJ: **~ of** dépouillé(e) de

short [ʃɔːt] ADJ (not long) court(e); (soon finished) court, bref (brève); (person, step) petit(e); (curt) brusque, sec (sèche); (insufficient) insuffisant(e) ▶ N (also: **short film**) court métrage; (Elec) court-circuit m; **to be ~ of sth** être à court de or manquer de qch; **to be in ~ supply** manquer, être difficile à trouver; **I'm 3 ~** il m'en manque 3;

in ~ bref; en bref; **~ of doing** à moins de faire; **everything ~ of** tout sauf; **it is ~ for** c'est l'abréviation or le diminutif de; **a ~ time ago** il y a peu de temps; **in the ~ term** à court terme; **to cut ~** (speech, visit) abréger, écourter; (person) couper la parole à; **to fall ~ of** ne pas être à la hauteur de; **to run ~ of** arriver à court de, venir à manquer de; **to stop ~** s'arrêter net; **to stop ~ of** ne pas aller jusqu'à

shortage ['ʃɔːtɪdʒ] N manque m, pénurie f

shortbread ['ʃɔːtbrɛd] N ≈ sablé m

short-change [ʃɔːt'tʃeɪndʒ] VT: **to ~ sb** ne pas rendre assez à qn

short-circuit [ʃɔːt'sɜːkɪt] N court-circuit m ▶ VT court-circuiter ▶ VI se mettre en court-circuit

shortcoming ['ʃɔːtkʌmɪŋ] N défaut m

shortcrust pastry ['ʃɔːt(krʌst)-], (US) **short pastry** N pâte brisée

shortcut ['ʃɔːtkʌt] N raccourci m

shorten ['ʃɔːtn] VT raccourcir; (text, visit) abréger

shortening ['ʃɔːtnɪŋ] N (Culin) matière grasse

shortfall ['ʃɔːtfɔːl] N déficit m

shorthand ['ʃɔːthænd] N (BRIT) sténo(graphie) f; **to take sth down in ~** prendre qch en sténo

shorthand notebook N bloc m sténo

shorthand typist N (BRIT) sténodactylo mf

shortlist ['ʃɔːtlɪst] N (BRIT: for job) liste f des candidats sélectionnés

short-lived ['ʃɔːt'lɪvd] ADJ de courte durée

shortly ['ʃɔːtlɪ] ADV bientôt, sous peu

shortness ['ʃɔːtnɪs] N brièveté f

short notice N: **at ~** au dernier moment

shorts [ʃɔːts] NPL: **(a pair of) ~** un short

short-sighted [ʃɔːt'saɪtɪd] ADJ (BRIT) myope; (fig) qui manque de clairvoyance

short-sleeved [ʃɔːt'sliːvd] ADJ à manches courtes

short-staffed [ʃɔːt'stɑːft] ADJ à court de personnel

short-stay [ʃɔːt'steɪ] ADJ (car park) de courte durée

short story N nouvelle f

short-tempered [ʃɔːt'tɛmpəd] ADJ qui s'emporte facilement

short-term ['ʃɔːttəːm] ADJ (effect) à court terme

short time N: **to work ~, to be on ~** (Industry) être en chômage partiel, travailler à horaire réduit

short wave N (Radio) ondes courtes

shot [ʃɒt] PT, PP of **shoot** ▶ N coup m (de feu); (shotgun pellets) plombs mpl; (try) coup, essai m; (injection) piqûre f; (Phot) photo f; **to be a good/poor ~** (person) tirer bien/mal; **to fire a ~ at sb/sth** tirer sur qn/qch; **to have a ~ at (doing) sth** essayer de faire qch; **like a ~** comme une flèche; (very readily) sans hésiter; **to get ~ of sb/sth** (inf) se débarrasser de qn/qch; **a big ~** (inf) un gros bonnet

shotgun ['ʃɒtɡʌn] N fusil m de chasse

should [ʃʊd] AUX VB: **I ~ go now** je devrais partir maintenant; **he ~ be there now** il devrait être arrivé maintenant; **I ~ go if I were you** si j'étais vous j'irais; **I ~ like to** volontiers, j'aimerais bien; **~ he phone …** si jamais il téléphone …

s

shoulder [ˈʃəʊldəʳ] N épaule f; (BRIT: of road) **hard ~** accotement m ▶ VT (fig) endosser, se charger de; **to look over one's ~** regarder derrière soi (en tournant la tête); **to rub shoulders with sb** (fig) côtoyer qn; **to give sb the cold ~** (fig) battre froid à qn

shoulder bag N sac m à bandoulière

shoulder blade N omoplate f

shoulder strap N bretelle f

shouldn't [ˈʃʊdnt]= **should not**

shout [ʃaʊt] N cri m ▶ VT crier ▶ VI crier, pousser des cris; **to give sb a ~** appeler qn
▶ **shout down** VT huer

shouting [ˈʃaʊtɪŋ] N cris mpl

shouting match N (inf) engueulade f, empoignade f

shove [ʃʌv] VT pousser; (inf: put): **to ~ sth in** fourrer or ficher qch dans ▶ N poussée f; **he shoved me out of the way** il m'a écarté en me poussant
▶ **shove off** VI (Naut) pousser au large; (fig: col) ficher le camp

shovel [ˈʃʌvl] N pelle f ▶ VT pelleter, enlever (or enfourner) à la pelle

show [ʃəʊ] (pt **showed**, pp **shown** [ʃəʊn]) N (of emotion) manifestation f, démonstration f; (semblance) semblant m, apparence f; (exhibition) exposition f, salon m; (Theat, TV) spectacle m; (Cine) séance f ▶ VT montrer; (film) passer; (courage etc) faire preuve de, manifester; (exhibit) exposer ▶ VI se voir, être visible; **can you ~ me where it is, please?** pouvez-vous me montrer où c'est?; **to ask for a ~ of hands** demander que l'on vote à main levée; **to be on ~** être exposé(e); **it's just for ~** c'est juste pour l'effet; **who's running the ~ here?** (inf) qui est-ce qui commande ici?; **to ~ sb to his seat/to the door** accompagner qn jusqu'à sa place/la porte; **to ~ a profit/loss** (Comm) indiquer un bénéfice/ une perte; **it just goes to ~ that** … ça prouve bien que …
▶ **show in** VT faire entrer
▶ **show off** VI (pej) crâner ▶ VT (display) faire valoir; (pej) faire étalage de
▶ **show out** VT reconduire à la porte
▶ **show up** VI (stand out) ressortir; (inf: turn up) se montrer ▶ VT démontrer; (unmask) démasquer, dénoncer; (flaw) faire ressortir

showbiz [ˈʃəʊbɪz] N (inf) showbiz m

show business N le monde du spectacle

showcase [ˈʃəʊkeɪs] N vitrine f

showdown [ˈʃəʊdaʊn] N épreuve f de force

shower [ˈʃaʊəʳ] N (for washing) douche f; (rain) averse f; (of stones etc) pluie f; (US: party) réunion organisée pour la remise de cadeaux ▶ VI prendre une douche, se doucher ▶ VT: **to ~ sb with** (gifts etc) combler qn de; (abuse etc) accabler qn de; (missiles) bombarder qn de; **to have** or **take a ~** prendre une douche, se doucher

shower cap N bonnet m de douche

shower gel N gel m douche

showerproof [ˈʃaʊəpruːf] ADJ imperméable

showery [ˈʃaʊərɪ] ADJ (weather) pluvieux(-euse)

showground [ˈʃəʊɡraʊnd] N champ m de foire

showing [ˈʃəʊɪŋ] N (of film) projection f

show jumping [-dʒʌmpɪŋ] N concours m hippique

showman [ˈʃəʊmən] N (irreg) (at fair, circus) forain m; (fig) comédien m

showmanship [ˈʃəʊmənʃɪp] N art m de la mise en scène

shown [ʃəʊn] PP of **show**

show-off [ˈʃəʊɔf] N (inf: person) crâneur(-euse), m'as-tu-vu(e)

showpiece [ˈʃəʊpiːs] N (of exhibition etc) joyau m, clou m; **that hospital is a ~** cet hôpital est un modèle du genre

showroom [ˈʃəʊrum] N magasin m or salle f d'exposition

show trial N grand procès m médiatique (qui fait un exemple)

showy [ˈʃəʊɪ] ADJ tapageur(-euse)

shrank [ʃræŋk] PT of **shrink**

shrapnel [ˈʃræpnl] N éclats mpl d'obus

shred [ʃred] N (gen pl) lambeau m, petit morceau; (fig: of truth, evidence) parcelle f ▶ VT mettre en lambeaux, déchirer; (documents) détruire; (Culin: grate) râper; (: lettuce etc) couper en lanières

shredder [ˈʃredəʳ] N (for vegetables) râpeur m; (for documents, papers) déchiqueteuse f

shrewd [ʃruːd] ADJ astucieux(-euse), perspicace; (business person) habile

shrewdness [ˈʃruːdnɪs] N perspicacité f

shriek [ʃriːk] N cri perçant or aigu, hurlement m ▶ VT, VI hurler, crier

shrift [ʃrɪft] N: **to give sb short ~** expédier qn sans ménagements

shrill [ʃrɪl] ADJ perçant(e), aigu(ë), strident(e)

shrimp [ʃrɪmp] N crevette grise

shrine [ʃraɪn] N châsse f; (place) lieu m de pèlerinage

shrink [ʃrɪŋk] (pt **shrank** [ʃræŋk], pp **shrunk** [ʃrʌŋk]) VI rétrécir; (fig) diminuer; (also: **shrink away**) reculer ▶ VT (wool) (faire) rétrécir ▶ N (inf, pej) psychanalyste mf; **to ~ from (doing) sth** reculer devant (la pensée de faire) qch

shrinkage [ˈʃrɪŋkɪdʒ] N (of clothes) rétrécissement m

shrink-wrap [ˈʃrɪŋkræp] VT emballer sous film plastique

shrivel [ˈʃrɪvl], **shrivel up** VT ratatiner, flétrir
▶ VI se ratatiner, se flétrir

shroud [ʃraʊd] N linceul m ▶ VT: **shrouded in mystery** enveloppé(e) de mystère

Shrove Tuesday [ˈʃrəʊv-] N (le) Mardi gras

shrub [ʃrʌb] N arbuste m

shrubbery [ˈʃrʌbərɪ] N massif m d'arbustes

shrug [ʃrʌɡ] N haussement m d'épaules ▶ VT, VI: **to ~ (one's shoulders)** hausser les épaules
▶ **shrug off** VT faire fi de; (cold, illness) se débarrasser de

shrunk [ʃrʌŋk] PP of **shrink**

shrunken [ˈʃrʌŋkn] ADJ ratatiné(e)

shudder [ˈʃʌdəʳ] N frisson m, frémissement m ▶ VI frissonner, frémir

shuffle [ˈʃʌfl] VT (cards) battre; **to ~ (one's feet)** traîner les pieds

shun [ʃʌn] VT éviter, fuir
shunt [ʃʌnt] VT (Rail: direct) aiguiller; (: divert) détourner ▶ VI: **to ~ (to and fro)** faire la navette
shunting yard [ˈʃʌntɪŋ-] N voies fpl de garage or de triage
shush [ʃuʃ] EXCL chut!
shut [ʃʌt] (pt, pp **~**) VT fermer ▶ VI (se) fermer
  ▶ **shut down** VT fermer définitivement; (machine) arrêter ▶ VI fermer définitivement
  ▶ **shut off** VT couper, arrêter
  ▶ **shut out** VT (person, cold) empêcher d'entrer; (noise) éviter d'entendre; (block: view) boucher; (: memory of sth) chasser de son esprit
  ▶ **shut up** VI (inf: keep quiet) se taire ▶ VT (close) fermer; (silence) faire taire
shutdown [ˈʃʌtdaun] N fermeture f
shutter [ˈʃʌtər] N volet m; (Phot) obturateur m
shuttle [ˈʃʌtl] N navette f; (also: **shuttle service**) (service m de) navette f ▶ VI (vehicle, person) faire la navette ▶ VT (passengers) transporter par un système de navette
shuttlecock [ˈʃʌtlkɔk] N volant m (de badminton)
shuttle diplomacy N navettes fpl diplomatiques
shy [ʃaɪ] ADJ timide; **to fight ~ of** se dérober devant; **to be ~ of doing sth** hésiter à faire qch, ne pas oser faire qch ▶ VI: **to ~ away from doing sth** (fig) craindre de faire qch
shyness [ˈʃaɪnɪs] N timidité f
Siam [saɪˈæm] N Siam m
Siamese [saɪəˈmiːz] ADJ: **~ cat** chat siamois mpl; **~ twins** (frères mpl) siamois mpl, (sœurs fpl) siamoises fpl
Siberia [saɪˈbɪərɪə] N Sibérie f
siblings [ˈsɪblɪŋz] NPL (formal) frères et sœurs mpl (de mêmes parents)
Sicilian [sɪˈsɪlɪən] ADJ sicilien(ne) ▶ N Sicilien(ne)
Sicily [ˈsɪsɪlɪ] N Sicile f
sick [sɪk] ADJ (ill) malade; (BRIT: humour) noir(e), macabre; (vomiting): **to be ~** vomir; **to feel ~** avoir envie de vomir, avoir mal au cœur; **to fall ~** tomber malade; **to be (off) ~** être absent(e) pour cause de maladie; **a ~ person** un(e) malade; **to be ~ of** (fig) en avoir assez de
sick bag N sac m vomitoire
sick bay N infirmerie f
sick building syndrome N maladie dûe à la climatisation, l'éclairage artificiel etc des bureaux
sicken [ˈsɪkn] VT écœurer ▶ VI: **to be sickening for sth** (cold, flu etc) couver qch
sickening [ˈsɪknɪŋ] ADJ (fig) écœurant(e), révoltant(e), répugnant(e)
sickle [ˈsɪkl] N faucille f
sick leave N congé m de maladie
sickle-cell anaemia [ˈsɪklsɛl-] N anémie f à hématies falciformes, drépanocytose f
sickly [ˈsɪklɪ] ADJ maladif(-ive), souffreteux(-euse); (causing nausea) écœurant(e)
sickness [ˈsɪknɪs] N maladie f; (vomiting) vomissement(s) m(pl)
sickness benefit N (prestations fpl de l')assurance-maladie f
sick note N (from parents) mot m d'absence;

(from doctor) certificat médical
sick pay N indemnité f de maladie (versée par l'employeur)
sickroom [ˈsɪkruːm] N infirmerie f
side [saɪd] N côté m; (of animal) flanc m; (of lake, road) bord m; (of mountain) versant m; (fig: aspect) côté, aspect m; (team: Sport) équipe f; (TV: channel) chaîne f ▶ ADJ (door, entrance) latéral(e) ▶ VI: **to ~ with sb** prendre le parti de qn, se ranger du côté de qn; **by the ~ of** au bord de; **~ by ~** côte à côte; **the right/wrong ~** le bon/mauvais côté, l'endroit/l'envers m; **they are on our ~** ils sont avec nous; **from all sides** de tous côtés; **to rock from ~ to ~** se balancer; **to take sides (with)** prendre parti (pour); **a ~ of beef** ≈ un quartier de bœuf
sideboard [ˈsaɪdbɔːd] N buffet m
sideboards [ˈsaɪdbɔːdz], (US) **sideburns** [ˈsaɪdbəːnz] NPL (whiskers) pattes fpl
sidecar [ˈsaɪdkɑːr] N side-car m
side dish N (plat m d')accompagnement m
side drum N (Mus) tambour plat, caisse claire
side effect N effet m secondaire
sidekick [ˈsaɪdkɪk] N (inf) sous-fifre m
sidelight [ˈsaɪdlaɪt] N (Aut) veilleuse f
sideline [ˈsaɪdlaɪn] N (Sport) (ligne f de) touche f; (fig) activité f secondaire
sidelong [ˈsaɪdlɔŋ] ADJ: **to give sb a ~ glance** regarder qn du coin de l'œil
side order N garniture f
side plate N petite assiette
side road N petite route, route transversale
sidesaddle [ˈsaɪdsædl] ADV en amazone
sideshow [ˈsaɪdʃəu] N attraction f
sidestep [ˈsaɪdstɛp] VT (question) éluder; (problem) éviter ▶ VI (Boxing etc) esquiver
side street N rue transversale
sidetrack [ˈsaɪdtræk] VT (fig) faire dévier de son sujet
sidewalk [ˈsaɪdwɔːk] N (US) trottoir m
sideways [ˈsaɪdweɪz] ADV de côté
siding [ˈsaɪdɪŋ] N (Rail) voie f de garage
sidle [ˈsaɪdl] VI: **to ~ up (to)** s'approcher furtivement (de)
SIDS [sɪdz] N ABBR (= sudden infant death syndrome) mort subite du nourrisson, mort f au berceau
siege [siːdʒ] N siège m; **to lay ~ to** assiéger
siege economy N économie f de (temps de) siège
Sierra Leone [sɪˈɛrəlɪˈəun] N Sierra Leone f
sieve [sɪv] N tamis m, passoire f ▶ VT tamiser, passer (au tamis)
sift [sɪft] VT passer au tamis or au crible; (fig) passer au crible ▶ VI (fig): **to ~ through** passer en revue
sigh [saɪ] N soupir m ▶ VI soupirer, pousser un soupir
sight [saɪt] N (faculty) vue f; (spectacle) spectacle m; (on gun) mire f ▶ VT apercevoir; **in ~** visible; (fig) en vue; **out of ~** hors de vue; **at ~** (Comm) à vue; **at first ~** à première vue, au premier abord; **I know her by ~** je la connais de vue; **to catch ~ of sb/sth** apercevoir qn/qch; **to lose ~ of sb/sth** perdre qn/qch de vue; **to set one's sights on sth** jeter son dévolu sur qch

S

sighted ['saɪtɪd] ADJ qui voit; **partially ~** qui a un certain degré de vision

sightseeing ['saɪtsiːɪŋ] N tourisme m; **to go ~** faire du tourisme

sightseer ['saɪtsiːəʳ] N touriste mf

sign [saɪn] N (gen) signe m; (with hand etc) signe, geste m; (notice) panneau m, écriteau m; (also: **road sign**) panneau de signalisation ▸ VT signer; **as a ~ of** en signe de; **it's a good/bad ~** c'est bon/mauvais signe; **plus/minus ~** signe plus/moins; **there's no ~ of a change of mind** rien ne laisse présager un revirement; **he was showing signs of improvement** il commençait visiblement à faire des progrès; **to ~ one's name** signer; **where do I ~?** où dois-je signer?

▸ **sign away** VT (rights etc) renoncer officiellement à

▸ **sign for** VT FUS (item) signer le reçu pour

▸ **sign in** VI signer le registre (en arrivant)

▸ **sign off** VI (Radio, TV) terminer l'émission

▸ **sign on** VI (Mil) s'engager; (Brit: as unemployed) s'inscrire au chômage; (enrol) s'inscrire ▸ VT (Mil) engager; (employee) embaucher; **to ~ on for a course** s'inscrire pour un cours

▸ **sign out** VI signer le registre (en partant)

▸ **sign over** VT: **to ~ sth over to sb** céder qch par écrit à qn

▸ **sign up** VT (Mil) engager ▸ VI (Mil) s'engager; (for course) s'inscrire

signal ['sɪgnl] N signal m ▸ VI (Aut) mettre son clignotant ▸ VT (person) faire signe à; (message) communiquer par signaux; **to ~ a left/right turn** (Aut) indiquer or signaler que l'on tourne à gauche/droite; **to ~ to sb (to do sth)** faire signe à qn (de faire qch)

signal box N (Rail) poste m d'aiguillage

signalman ['sɪgnlmən] N (irreg) (Rail) aiguilleur m

signatory ['sɪgnətərɪ] N signataire mf

signature ['sɪgnətʃəʳ] N signature f

signature tune N indicatif musical

signet ring ['sɪgnət-] N chevalière f

significance [sɪg'nɪfɪkəns] N signification f; importance f; **that is of no ~** ceci n'a pas d'importance

significant [sɪg'nɪfɪkənt] ADJ significatif(-ive); (important) important(e), considérable

significantly [sɪg'nɪfɪkəntlɪ] ADV (improve, increase) sensiblement; (smile) d'un air entendu, éloquemment; **~, ...** fait significatif, ...

signify ['sɪgnɪfaɪ] VT signifier

sign language N langage m par signes

signpost ['saɪnpəust] N poteau indicateur

Sikh [siːk] ADJ, N Sikh mf

silage ['saɪlɪdʒ] N (fodder) fourrage vert; (method) ensilage m

silence ['saɪlns] N silence m ▸ VT faire taire, réduire au silence

silencer ['saɪlənsəʳ] N (Brit: on gun, Aut) silencieux m

silent ['saɪlnt] ADJ silencieux(-euse); (film) muet(te); **to keep** or **remain ~** garder le silence, ne rien dire

silently ['saɪlntlɪ] ADV silencieusement

silent partner N (Comm) bailleur m de fonds, commanditaire m

silhouette [sɪluːˈɛt] N silhouette f ▸ VT: **silhouetted against** se profilant sur, se découpant contre

silicon ['sɪlɪkən] N silicium m

silicon chip N puce f électronique

silicone ['sɪlɪkəun] N silicone f

silk [sɪlk] N soie f ▸ CPD de or en soie

silky ['sɪlkɪ] ADJ soyeux(-euse)

sill [sɪl] N (also: **windowsill**) rebord m (de la fenêtre); (of door) seuil m; (Aut) bas m de marche

silly ['sɪlɪ] ADJ stupide, sot(te), bête; **to do something ~** faire une bêtise

silo ['saɪləu] N silo m

silt [sɪlt] N vase f; limon m

silver ['sɪlvəʳ] N argent m; (money) monnaie f (en pièces d'argent); (also: **silverware**) argenterie f ▸ ADJ (made of silver) d'argent, en argent; (in colour) argenté(e); (car) gris métallisé inv

silver-plated [sɪlvə'pleɪtɪd] ADJ plaqué(e) argent

silversmith ['sɪlvəsmɪθ] N orfèvre mf

silverware ['sɪlvəwɛəʳ] N argenterie f

silver wedding, silver wedding anniversary N noces fpl d'argent

silvery ['sɪlvrɪ] ADJ argenté(e)

SIM card ['sɪm-] ABBR (Tel: = subscriber identity module card) carte f SIM

similar [ˈsɪmɪləʳ] ADJ: **~ (to)** semblable (à)

similarity [sɪmɪˈlærɪtɪ] N ressemblance f, similarité f

similarly ['sɪmɪləlɪ] ADV de la même façon, de même

simile ['sɪmɪlɪ] N comparaison f

simmer ['sɪməʳ] VI cuire à feu doux, mijoter ▸ **simmer down** VI (fig: inf) se calmer

simper ['sɪmpəʳ] VI minauder

simpering ['sɪmprɪŋ] ADJ stupide

simple ['sɪmpl] ADJ simple; **the ~ truth** la vérité pure et simple

simple interest N (Math, Comm) intérêts mpl simples

simple-minded [sɪmpl'maɪndɪd] ADJ simplet(te), simple d'esprit

simpleton ['sɪmpltən] N nigaud(e), niais(e)

simplicity [sɪm'plɪsɪtɪ] N simplicité f

simplification [sɪmplɪfɪ'keɪʃən] N simplification f

simplify ['sɪmplɪfaɪ] VT simplifier

simply ['sɪmplɪ] ADV simplement; (without fuss) avec simplicité; (absolutely) absolument

simulate ['sɪmjuleɪt] VT simuler, feindre

simulation [sɪmju'leɪʃən] N simulation f

simultaneous [sɪməl'teɪnɪəs] ADJ simultané(e)

simultaneously [sɪməl'teɪnɪəslɪ] ADV simultanément

sin [sɪn] N péché m ▸ VI pécher

Sinai ['saɪneɪaɪ] N Sinaï m

since [sɪns] ADV, PREP depuis ▸ CONJ (time) depuis que; (because) puisque, étant donné que, comme; **~ then, ever ~** depuis ce moment-là; **~ Monday** depuis lundi; **(ever) ~ I arrived** depuis mon arrivée, depuis que je suis arrivé

sincere [sɪn'sɪə^r] ADJ sincère
sincerely [sɪn'sɪəlɪ] ADV sincèrement; **yours ~** (at end of letter) veuillez agréer, Monsieur (or Madame) l'expression de mes sentiments distingués or les meilleurs
sincerity [sɪn'sɛrɪtɪ] N sincérité f
sine [saɪn] N (Math) sinus m
sinew ['sɪnjuː] N tendon m; **sinews** NPL muscles mpl
sinful ['sɪnful] ADJ coupable
sing [sɪŋ] (pt **sang** [sæŋ], pp **sung** [sʌŋ]) VT, VI chanter
Singapore [sɪŋgə'pɔː^r] N Singapour m
singe [sɪndʒ] VT brûler légèrement; (clothes) roussir
singer ['sɪŋə^r] N chanteur(-euse)
Singhalese [sɪŋə'liːz] ADJ = **Sinhalese**
singing ['sɪŋɪŋ] N (of person, bird) chant m; façon f de chanter; (of kettle, bullet, in ears) sifflement m
single ['sɪŋgl] ADJ seul(e), unique; (unmarried) célibataire; (not double) simple ▶ N (BRIT: also: **single ticket**) aller m (simple); (record) 45 tours m; **singles** NPL (US Tennis) simple m; (single people) célibataires mf; **not a ~ one was left** il n'en est pas resté un(e), seul(e); **every ~ day** chaque jour sans exception
▶ **single out** VT choisir; (distinguish) distinguer
single bed N lit m d'une personne or à une place
single-breasted ['sɪŋglbrɛstɪd] ADJ droit(e)
Single European Market N: **the ~** le marché unique européen
single file N: **in ~** en file indienne
single-handed ['sɪŋgl'hændɪd] ADV tout(e) seul(e), sans (aucune) aide
single-minded [sɪŋgl'maɪndɪd] ADJ résolu(e), tenace
single parent N parent unique (or célibataire); **single-parent family** famille monoparentale
single room N chambre f à un lit or pour une personne
singles bar N (esp US) bar m de rencontres pour célibataires
single-sex school [sɪŋgl'sɛks-] N école f non mixte
singlet ['sɪŋglɪt] N tricot m de corps
single-track road [sɪŋgl'træk-] N route f à voie unique
singly ['sɪŋglɪ] ADV séparément
singsong ['sɪŋsɔŋ] ADJ (tone) chantant(e) ▶ N (songs): **to have a ~** chanter quelque chose (ensemble)
singular ['sɪŋgjulə^r] ADJ singulier(-ière); (odd) singulier, étrange; (outstanding) remarquable; (Ling) (au) singulier, du singulier ▶ N (Ling) singulier m; **in the feminine ~** au féminin singulier
singularly ['sɪŋgjuləlɪ] ADV singulièrement; étrangement
Sinhalese [sɪnhə'liːz] ADJ cingalais(e)
sinister ['sɪnɪstə^r] ADJ sinistre
sink [sɪŋk] (pt **sank** [sæŋk], pp **sunk** [sʌŋk]) N évier m; (washbasin) lavabo m ▶ VT (ship) (faire) couler, faire sombrer; (foundations) creuser; (piles etc): **to ~ sth into** enfoncer qch dans ▶ VI couler,

sombrer; (ground etc) s'affaisser; **to ~ into sth** (chair) s'enfoncer dans qch; **he sank into a chair/the mud** il s'est enfoncé dans un fauteuil/la boue; **a sinking feeling** un serrement de cœur
▶ **sink in** VI s'enfoncer, pénétrer; (explanation) rentrer (inf), être compris; **it took a long time to ~ in** il a fallu longtemps pour que ça rentre
sinking fund N fonds mpl d'amortissement
sink unit N bloc-évier m
sinner ['sɪnə^r] N pécheur(-eresse)
Sinn Féin [ʃɪn'feɪn] N Sinn Féin m (parti politique irlandais qui soutient l'IRA)
Sino- ['saɪnəu] PREFIX sino-
sinuous ['sɪnjuəs] ADJ sinueux(-euse)
sinus ['saɪnəs] N (Anat) sinus m inv
sip [sɪp] N petite gorgée ▶ VT boire à petites gorgées
siphon ['saɪfən] N siphon m ▶ VT (also: **siphon off**) siphonner; (fig: funds) transférer; (: illegally) détourner
sir [sə^r] N monsieur m; **S~ John Smith** sir John Smith; **yes ~** oui Monsieur; **Dear S~** (in letter) Monsieur
siren ['saɪərn] N sirène f
sirloin ['sə:lɔɪn] N (also: **sirloin steak**) aloyau m
sirloin steak N bifteck m dans l'aloyau
sirocco [sɪ'rɔkəu] N sirocco m
sisal ['saɪsəl] N sisal m
sissy ['sɪsɪ] N (inf: coward) poule mouillée
sister ['sɪstə^r] N sœur f; (nun) religieuse f, (bonne) sœur; (BRIT: nurse) infirmière f en chef
▶ CPD: **~ organization** organisation f sœur; **~ ship** sister(-)ship m
sister-in-law ['sɪstərɪnlɔ:] N belle-sœur f
sit [sɪt] (pt, pp **sat** [sæt]) VI s'asseoir; (be sitting) être assis(e); (assembly) être en séance, siéger; (for painter) poser; (dress etc) tomber ▶ VT (exam) passer, se présenter à; **to ~ tight** ne pas bouger
▶ **sit about, sit around** VI être assis(e) or rester à ne rien faire
▶ **sit back** VI (in seat) bien s'installer, se carrer
▶ **sit down** VI s'asseoir; **to be sitting down** être assis(e)
▶ **sit in** VI: **to ~ in on a discussion** assister à une discussion
▶ **sit on** VT FUS (jury, committee) faire partie de
▶ **sit up** VI s'asseoir; (straight) se redresser; (not go to bed) rester debout, ne pas se coucher
sitcom ['sɪtkɔm] N ABBR (TV: = situation comedy) sitcom f, comédie f de situation
sit-down ['sɪtdaun] ADJ: **a ~ strike** une grève sur le tas; **a ~ meal** un repas assis
site [saɪt] N emplacement m, site m; (also: **building site**) chantier m; (Internet) site m web ▶ VT placer
sit-in ['sɪtɪn] N (demonstration) sit-in m inv, occupation f de locaux
siting ['saɪtɪŋ] N (location) emplacement m
sitter ['sɪtə^r] N (for painter) modèle m; (also: **babysitter**) baby-sitter mf
sitting ['sɪtɪŋ] N (of assembly etc) séance f; (in canteen) service m

s

sitting member N (Pol) parlementaire mf en exercice

sitting room N salon m

sitting tenant N (BRIT) locataire occupant(e)

situate ['sɪtjueɪt] VT situer

situated ['sɪtjueɪtɪd] ADJ situé(e)

situation [sɪtju'eɪʃən] N situation f; **"situations vacant/wanted"** (BRIT) "offres/demandes d'emploi"

situation comedy N (Theat) comédie f de situation

six [sɪks] NUM six

six-pack ['sɪkspæk] N (esp US) pack m de six canettes

sixteen [sɪks'ti:n] NUM seize

sixteenth [sɪks'ti:nθ] NUM seizième

sixth ['sɪksθ] NUM sixième ▶ N: **the upper/lower ~** (BRIT Scol) la terminale/la première

sixth form N (BRIT) ≈ classes fpl de première et de terminale

sixth-form college N lycée n'ayant que des classes de première et de terminale

sixtieth ['sɪkstɪɪθ] NUM soixantième

sixty ['sɪkstɪ] NUM soixante

size [saɪz] N dimensions fpl; (of person) taille f; (of clothing) taille; (of shoes) pointure f; (of estate, area) étendue f; (of problem) ampleur f; (of company) importance f; (glue) colle f; **I take ~ 14** (of dress etc) ≈ je prends du 42 or la taille 42; **the small/large ~** (of soap powder etc) le petit/grand modèle; **it's the ~ of ...** c'est de la taille (or grosseur) de ..., c'est grand (or gros) comme ...; **cut to ~** découpé(e) aux dimensions voulues ▶ **size up** VT juger, jauger

sizeable ['saɪzəbl] ADJ (object, building, estate) assez grand(e); (amount, problem, majority) assez important(e)

sizzle ['sɪzl] VI grésiller

SK ABBR (CANADA) = **Saskatchewan**

skate [skeɪt] N patin m; (fish: pl inv) raie f ▶ VI patiner ▶ **skate over, skate around** VT (problem, issue) éluder

skateboard ['skeɪtbɔ:d] N skateboard m, planche f à roulettes

skateboarding ['skeɪtbɔ:dɪŋ] N skateboard m

skater ['skeɪtə'] N patineur(-euse)

skating ['skeɪtɪŋ] N patinage m

skating rink N patinoire f

skeleton ['skelɪtn] N squelette m; (outline) schéma m

skeleton key N passe-partout m

skeleton staff N effectifs réduits

skeptic ['skeptɪk] (US) N = **sceptic**

skeptical ['skeptɪkl] (US) ADJ = **sceptical**

sketch [sketʃ] N (drawing) croquis m, esquisse f; (outline plan) aperçu m; (Theat) sketch m, saynète f ▶ VT esquisser, faire un croquis or une esquisse de; (plan etc) esquisser

sketch book N carnet m à dessin

sketch pad N bloc m à dessin

sketchy ['sketʃɪ] ADJ incomplet(-ète), fragmentaire

skew [skju:] N (BRIT): **on the ~** de travers, en biais

skewer ['skju:ə'] N brochette f

ski [ski:] N ski m ▶ VI skier, faire du ski

ski boot N chaussure f de ski

skid [skɪd] N dérapage m ▶ VI déraper; **to go into a ~** déraper

skid mark N trace f de dérapage

skier ['ski:ə'] N skieur(-euse)

skiing ['ski:ɪŋ] N ski m; **to go ~** (aller) faire du ski

ski instructor N moniteur(-trice) de ski

ski jump N (ramp) tremplin m; (event) saut m à skis

skilful, (US) **skillful** ['skɪlful] ADJ habile, adroit(e)

skilfully, (US) **skillfully** ['skɪlfəlɪ] ADV habilement, adroitement

ski lift N remonte-pente m inv

skill [skɪl] N (ability) habileté f, adresse f, talent m; (requiring training) compétences fpl

skilled [skɪld] ADJ habile, adroit(e); (worker) qualifié(e)

skillet ['skɪlɪt] N poêlon m

skillful etc ['skɪlful] (US) ADJ = **skilful**

skim [skɪm] VT (milk) écrémer; (soup) écumer; (glide over) raser, effleurer ▶ VI: **to ~ through** (fig) parcourir

skimmed milk [skɪmd-], (US) **skim milk** N lait écrémé

skimp [skɪmp] VT (work) bâcler, faire à la va-vite; (cloth etc) lésiner sur

skimpy ['skɪmpɪ] ADJ étriqué(e); maigre

skin [skɪn] N peau f ▶ VT (fruit etc) éplucher; (animal) écorcher; **wet** or **soaked to the ~** trempé(e) jusqu'aux os

skin cancer N cancer m de la peau

skin-deep ['skɪn'di:p] ADJ superficiel(le)

skin diver N plongeur(-euse) sous-marin(e)

skin diving N plongée sous-marine

skinflint ['skɪnflɪnt] N grippe-sou m

skin graft N greffe f de peau

skinhead ['skɪnhed] N skinhead m

skinny ['skɪnɪ] ADJ maigre, maigrichon(ne)

skin test N cuti-(réaction) f

skintight ['skɪntaɪt] ADJ (dress etc) collant(e), ajusté(e)

skip [skɪp] N petit bond or saut; (BRIT: container) benne f ▶ VI gambader, sautiller; (with rope) sauter à la corde ▶ VT (pass over) sauter; **to ~ school** (esp US) faire l'école buissonnière

ski pants NPL pantalon m de ski

ski pass N forfait-skieur(s) m

ski pole N bâton m de ski

skipper ['skɪpə'] N (Naut, Sport) capitaine m; (in race) skipper m ▶ VT (boat) commander; (team) être le chef de

skipping rope ['skɪpɪŋ-], (US) **skip rope** N corde f à sauter

ski resort N station f de sports d'hiver

skirmish ['skə:mɪʃ] N escarmouche f, accrochage m

skirt [skə:t] N jupe f ▶ VT longer, contourner

skirting board ['skə:tɪŋ-] N (BRIT) plinthe f

ski run N piste f de ski
ski slope N piste f de ski
ski suit N combinaison f de ski
skit [skɪt] N sketch m satirique
ski tow N = **ski lift**
skittle ['skɪtl] N quille f; **skittles** (game) (jeu m de) quilles fpl
skive [skaɪv] VI (BRIT inf) tirer au flanc
skulk [skʌlk] VI rôder furtivement
skull [skʌl] N crâne m
skullcap ['skʌlkæp] N calotte f
skunk [skʌŋk] N mouffette f; (fur) sconse m
sky [skaɪ] N ciel m; **to praise sb to the skies** porter qn aux nues
sky-blue [skaɪ'bluː] ADJ bleu ciel inv
skydiving ['skaɪdaɪvɪŋ] N parachutisme m (en chute libre)
sky-high ['skaɪ'haɪ] ADV très haut ▸ ADJ exorbitant(e); **prices are ~** les prix sont exorbitants
skylark ['skaɪlɑːk] N (bird) alouette f (des champs)
skylight ['skaɪlaɪt] N lucarne f
skyline ['skaɪlaɪn] N (horizon) (ligne f d')horizon m; (of city) ligne des toits
Skype® [skaɪp] (Internet, Tel) N Skype® ▸ VT contacter via Skype®
skyscraper ['skaɪskreɪpəʳ] N gratte-ciel m inv
slab [slæb] N plaque f; (of stone) dalle f; (of wood) bloc m; (of meat, cheese) tranche épaisse
slack [slæk] ADJ (loose) lâche, desserré(e); (slow) stagnant(e); (careless) négligent(e), peu sérieux(-euse) or consciencieux(-euse); (Comm: market) peu actif(-ive); (: demand) faible; (period) creux(-euse) ▸ N (in rope etc) mou m; **business is ~** les affaires vont mal
slacken ['slækn] VI (also: **slacken off**) ralentir, diminuer ▸ VT relâcher
slacks [slæks] NPL pantalon m
slag [slæg] N scories fpl
slag heap N crassier m
slag off (BRIT inf) VT dire du mal de
slain [sleɪn] PP of **slay**
slake [sleɪk] VT (one's thirst) étancher
slalom ['slɑːləm] N slalom m
slam [slæm] VT (door) (faire) claquer; (throw) jeter violemment, flanquer; (inf: criticize) éreinter, démolir ▸ VI claquer
slammer ['slæməʳ] N (inf): **the ~** la taule
slander ['slɑːndəʳ] N calomnie f; (Law) diffamation f ▸ VT calomnier; diffamer
slanderous ['slɑːndrəs] ADJ calomnieux(-euse); diffamatoire
slang [slæŋ] N argot m
slanging match ['slæŋɪŋ-] N (BRIT inf) engueulade f, empoignade f
slant [slɑːnt] N inclinaison f; (fig) angle m, point m de vue
slanted ['slɑːntɪd] ADJ tendancieux(-euse)
slanting ['slɑːntɪŋ] ADJ en pente, incliné(e); couché(e)
slap [slæp] N claque f, gifle f; (on the back) tape f ▸ VT donner une claque or une gifle (or une tape) à ▸ ADV (directly) tout droit, en plein; **to ~ on**

(paint) appliquer rapidement
slapdash ['slæpdæʃ] ADJ (work) fait(e) sans soin or à la va-vite; (person) insouciant(e), négligent(e)
slaphead ['slæphɛd] N (BRIT inf) chauve m
slapstick ['slæpstɪk] N (comedy) grosse farce (style tarte à la crème)
slap-up ['slæpʌp] ADJ (BRIT): **a ~ meal** un repas extra or fameux
slash [slæʃ] VT entailler, taillader; (fig: prices) casser
slat [slæt] N (of wood) latte f, lame f
slate [sleɪt] N ardoise f ▸ VT (fig: criticize) éreinter, démolir
slaughter ['slɔːtəʳ] N carnage m, massacre m; (of animals) abattage m ▸ VT (animal) abattre; (people) massacrer
slaughterhouse ['slɔːtəhaus] N abattoir m
Slav [slɑːv] ADJ slave
slave [sleɪv] N esclave mf ▸ VI (also: **slave away**) trimer, travailler comme un forçat; **to ~ (away) at sth/at doing sth** se tuer à qch/à faire qch
slave driver N (inf, pej) négrier(-ière)
slave labour N travail m d'esclave; **it's just ~** (fig) c'est de l'esclavage
slaver ['slævəʳ] VI (dribble) baver
slavery ['sleɪvərɪ] N esclavage m
Slavic ['slævɪk] ADJ slave
slavish ['sleɪvɪʃ] ADJ servile
slavishly ['sleɪvɪʃlɪ] ADV (copy) servilement
Slavonic [slə'vɔnɪk] ADJ slave
slay [sleɪ] (pt **slew** [sluː], pp **slain** [sleɪn]) VT (literary) tuer
sleazy ['sliːzɪ] ADJ miteux(-euse), minable
sled [slɛd] (US) N = **sledge**
sledge [slɛdʒ] N luge f
sledgehammer ['slɛdʒhæməʳ] N marteau m de forgeron
sleek [sliːk] ADJ (hair, fur) brillant(e), luisant(e); (car, boat) aux lignes pures or élégantes
sleep [sliːp] (pt, pp **slept** [slɛpt]) N sommeil m ▸ VI dormir; (spend night) dormir, coucher ▸ VT: **we can ~ 4** on peut coucher or loger 4 personnes; **to go to ~** s'endormir; **to have a good night's ~** passer une bonne nuit; **to put to ~** (patient) endormir; (animal: euphemism: kill) piquer; **to ~ lightly** avoir le sommeil léger; **to ~ with sb** (have sex) coucher avec qn
▸ **sleep around** VI coucher à droite et à gauche
▸ **sleep in** VI (oversleep) se réveiller trop tard; (on purpose) faire la grasse matinée
▸ **sleep together** VI (have sex) coucher ensemble
sleeper ['sliːpəʳ] N (person) dormeur(-euse); (BRIT Rail: on track) traverse f; (: train) train-couchettes m; (: carriage) wagon-lits m, voiture-lits f; (: berth) couchette f
sleepily ['sliːpɪlɪ] ADV d'un air endormi
sleeping ['sliːpɪŋ] ADJ qui dort, endormi(e)
sleeping bag N sac m de couchage
sleeping car N wagon-lits m, voiture-lits f
sleeping partner N (BRIT Comm) = **silent partner**
sleeping pill N somnifère m
sleeping sickness N maladie f du sommeil
sleepless ['sliːplɪs] ADJ: **a ~ night** une nuit blanche

S

sleeplessness ['sli:plɪsnɪs] N insomnie f

sleepover ['sli:pəʊvəʳ] N nuit f chez un copain or une copine; **we're having a ~ at Jo's** nous allons passer la nuit chez Jo

sleepwalk ['sli:pwɔ:k] VI marcher en dormant

sleepwalker ['sli:pwɔ:kəʳ] N somnambule mf

sleepy ['sli:pɪ] ADJ qui a envie de dormir; (fig) endormi(e); **to be** or **feel ~** avoir sommeil, envie de dormir

sleet [sli:t] N neige fondue

sleeve [sli:v] N manche f; (of record) pochette f

sleeveless ['sli:vlɪs] ADJ (garment) sans manches

sleigh [sleɪ] N traîneau m

sleight [slaɪt] N: **~ of hand** tour m de passe-passe

slender ['slɛndəʳ] ADJ svelte, mince; (fig) faible, ténu(e)

slept [slɛpt] PT, PP of **sleep**

sleuth [slu:θ] N (inf) détective (privé)

slew [slu:] VI (also: **slew round**) virer, pivoter
▶ PT of **slay**

slice [slaɪs] N tranche f; (round) rondelle f; (utensil) spatule f; (also: **fish slice**) pelle f à poisson ▶ VT couper en tranches (or en rondelles); **sliced bread** pain m en tranches

slick [slɪk] ADJ (skilful) bien ficelé(e); (salesperson) qui a du bagout, mielleux(-euse) ▶ N (also: **oil slick**) nappe f de pétrole, marée noire

slid [slɪd] PT, PP of **slide**

slide [slaɪd] (pt, pp **slid** [slɪd]) N (in playground) toboggan m; (Phot) diapositive f; (BRIT: also: **hair slide**) barrette f; (microscope slide) (lame f) porte-objet m; (in prices) chute f, baisse f ▶ VT (faire) glisser ▶ VI glisser; **to let things ~** (fig) laisser les choses aller à la dérive

slide projector N (Phot) projecteur m de diapositives

slide rule N règle f à calcul

slide show N (Comput) diaporama m

sliding ['slaɪdɪŋ] ADJ (door) coulissant(e); **~ roof** (Aut) toit ouvrant

sliding scale N échelle f mobile

slight [slaɪt] ADJ (slim) mince, menu(e); (frail) frêle; (trivial) faible, insignifiant(e); (small) petit(e), léger(-ère) before noun ▶ N offense f, affront m ▶ VT (offend) blesser, offenser; **the slightest** le (or la) moindre; **not in the slightest** pas le moins du monde, pas du tout

slightly ['slaɪtlɪ] ADV légèrement, un peu; **~ built** fluet(te)

slim [slɪm] ADJ mince ▶ VI maigrir; (diet) suivre un régime amaigrissant

slime [slaɪm] N vase f; substance visqueuse

slimming ['slɪmɪŋ] N amaigrissement m ▶ ADJ (diet, pills) amaigrissant(e), pour maigrir; (food) qui ne fait pas grossir

slimy ['slaɪmɪ] ADJ visqueux(-euse), gluant(e); (covered with mud) vaseux(-euse)

sling [slɪŋ] (pt, pp **slung** [slʌŋ]) N (Med) écharpe f; (for baby) porte-bébé m; (weapon) fronde f, lance-pierre m ▶ VT lancer, jeter; **to have one's arm in a ~** avoir le bras en écharpe

slink [slɪŋk] (pt, pp **slunk** [slʌŋk]) VI: **to ~ away** or **off** s'en aller furtivement

slinky ['slɪŋkɪ] ADJ (clothes) moulant(e)

slip [slɪp] N faux pas; (mistake) erreur f, bévue f; (underskirt) combinaison f; (of paper) petite feuille, fiche f ▶ VT (slide) glisser ▶ VI (slide) glisser; (decline) baisser; (move smoothly): **to ~ into/out of** se glisser or se faufiler dans/hors de; **to let a chance ~ by** laisser passer une occasion; **to ~ sth on/off** enfiler/enlever qch; **it slipped from her hand** cela lui a glissé des mains; **to give sb the ~** fausser compagnie à qn; **a ~ of the tongue** un lapsus
▶ **slip away** VI s'esquiver
▶ **slip in** VT glisser
▶ **slip out** VI sortir
▶ **slip up** VI faire une erreur, gaffer

slip-on ['slɪpɔn] ADJ facile à enfiler; **~ shoes** mocassins mpl

slipped disc [slɪpt-] N déplacement m de vertèbre

slipper ['slɪpəʳ] N pantoufle f

slippery ['slɪpərɪ] ADJ glissant(e); (fig: person) insaisissable

slip road N (BRIT: to motorway) bretelle f d'accès

slipshod ['slɪpʃɔd] ADJ négligé(e), peu soigné(e)

slip-up ['slɪpʌp] N bévue f

slipway ['slɪpweɪ] N cale f (de construction or de lancement)

slit [slɪt] (pt, pp **~**) N fente f; (cut) incision f; (tear) déchirure f ▶ VT fendre; couper, inciser; déchirer; **to ~ sb's throat** trancher la gorge à qn

slither ['slɪðəʳ] VI glisser, déraper

sliver ['slɪvəʳ] N (of glass, wood) éclat m; (of cheese, sausage) petit morceau

slob [slɔb] N (inf) rustaud(e)

slog [slɔg] N (BRIT: effort) gros effort; (: work) tâche fastidieuse ▶ VI travailler très dur

slogan ['sləʊgən] N slogan m

slop [slɔp] VI (also: **slop over**); déborder; se renverser ▶ VT répandre; renverser

slope [sləʊp] N pente f, côte f; (side of mountain) versant m; (slant) inclinaison f ▶ VI: **to ~ down** être or descendre en pente; **to ~ up** monter

sloping ['sləʊpɪŋ] ADJ en pente, incliné(e); (handwriting) penché(e)

sloppy ['slɔpɪ] ADJ (work) peu soigné(e), bâclé(e); (appearance) négligé(e), débraillé(e); (film etc) sentimental(e)

slosh [slɔʃ] VI (inf): **to ~ about** or **around** (children) patauger; (liquid) clapoter

sloshed [slɔʃt] ADJ (inf: drunk) bourré(e)

slot [slɔt] N fente f; (fig: in timetable, Radio, TV) créneau m, plage f ▶ VT: **to ~ sth into** encastrer or insérer qch dans ▶ VI: **to ~ into** s'encastrer or s'insérer dans

sloth [sləʊθ] N (vice) paresse f; (Zool) paresseux m

slot machine N (BRIT: vending machine) distributeur m (automatique), machine f à sous; (for gambling) appareil m or machine à sous

slot meter N (BRIT) compteur m à pièces

slouch [slaʊtʃ] VI avoir le dos rond, être voûté(e)
▶ **slouch about**, **slouch around** VI traîner à ne rien faire

Slovak ['sləʊvæk] ADJ slovaque ▶ N Slovaque mf; (Ling) slovaque m; **the ~ Republic** la République slovaque

Slovakia [sləʊ'vækɪə] N Slovaquie f

Slovakian [sləʊ'vækɪən] ADJ, N = **Slovak**

Slovene [sləʊ'viːn] ADJ slovène ▶ N Slovène mf; (Ling) slovène m

Slovenia [sləʊ'viːnɪə] N Slovénie f

Slovenian [sləʊ'viːnɪən] ADJ, N = **Slovene**

slovenly ['slʌvənlɪ] ADJ sale, débraillé(e), négligé(e)

slow [sləʊ] ADJ lent(e); (watch): **to be ~** retarder ▶ ADV lentement ▶ VT, VI ralentir; **"~"** (road sign) "ralentir"; **at a ~ speed** à petite vitesse; **to be ~ to act/decide** être lent à agir/décider; **my watch is 20 minutes ~** ma montre retarde de 20 minutes; **business is ~** les affaires marchent au ralenti; **to go ~** (driver) rouler lentement; (in industrial dispute) faire la grève perlée
  ▶ **slow down** VI ralentir

slow-acting [sləʊ'æktɪŋ] ADJ qui agit lentement, à action lente

slowcoach ['sləʊkəʊtʃ] N (BRIT inf) lambin(e)

slowly ['sləʊlɪ] ADV lentement

slow motion N: **in ~** au ralenti

slowness ['sləʊnɪs] N lenteur f

slowpoke ['sləʊpəʊk] N (US inf) = **slowcoach**

sludge [slʌdʒ] N boue f

slug [slʌg] N limace f; (bullet) balle f

sluggish ['slʌgɪʃ] ADJ (person) mou (molle), lent(e); (stream, engine, trading) lent(e); (business, sales) stagnant(e)

sluice [sluːs] N écluse f; (also: **sluice gate**) vanne f ▶ VT: **to ~ down** or **out** laver à grande eau

slum [slʌm] N (house) taudis m; **slums** NPL (area) quartiers mpl pauvres

slumber ['slʌmbəʳ] N sommeil m

slump [slʌmp] N baisse soudaine, effondrement m; (Econ) crise f ▶ VI s'effondrer, s'affaisser

slung [slʌŋ] PT, PP of **sling**

slunk [slʌŋk] PT, PP of **slink**

slur [sləːʳ] N bredouillement m; (smear): ~ **(on)** atteinte f (à); insinuation f (contre) ▶ VT mal articuler; **to be a ~ on** porter atteinte à

slurp [sləːp] VT, VI boire à grand bruit

slurred [sləːd] ADJ (pronunciation) inarticulé(e), indistinct(e)

slush [slʌʃ] N neige fondue

slush fund N caisse noire, fonds secrets

slushy ['slʌʃɪ] ADJ (snow) fondu(e); (street) couvert(e) de neige fondue; (BRIT fig) à l'eau de rose

slut [slʌt] N souillon f

sly [slaɪ] ADJ (person) rusé(e); (smile, expression, remark) sournois(e); **on the ~** en cachette

smack [smæk] N (slap) tape f; (on face) gifle f ▶ VT donner une tape à; (on face) gifler; (on bottom) donner la fessée à ▶ VI: **to ~ of** avoir des relents de, sentir ▶ ADV (inf): **it fell ~ in the middle** c'est tombé en plein milieu or en plein dedans; **to ~ one's lips** se lécher les babines

smacker ['smækəʳ] N (inf: kiss) bisou m or bise f

sonore; (: BRIT: pound note) livre f; (: US: dollar bill) dollar m

small [smɔːl] ADJ petit(e); (letter) minuscule ▶ N: **the ~ of the back** le creux des reins; **to get** or **grow smaller** diminuer; **to make smaller** (amount, income) diminuer; (object, garment) rapetisser; **a ~ shopkeeper** un petit commerçant

small ads NPL (BRIT) petites annonces

small arms NPL armes individuelles

small business N petit commerce, petite affaire

small change N petite or menue monnaie

smallholder ['smɔːlhəʊldəʳ] N (BRIT) petit cultivateur

smallholding ['smɔːlhəʊldɪŋ] N (BRIT) petite ferme

small hours NPL: **in the ~** au petit matin

smallish ['smɔːlɪʃ] ADJ plutôt or assez petit(e)

small-minded [smɔːl'maɪndɪd] ADJ mesquin(e)

smallpox ['smɔːlpɒks] N variole f

small print N (in contract etc) clause(s) imprimée(s) en petits caractères

small-scale ['smɔːlskeɪl] ADJ (map, model) à échelle réduite, à petite échelle; (business, farming) peu important(e), modeste

small talk N menus propos

small-time ['smɔːltaɪm] ADJ (farmer etc) petit(e); **a ~ thief** un voleur à la petite semaine

small-town ['smɔːltaʊn] ADJ provincial(e)

smarmy ['smɑːmɪ] ADJ (BRIT pej) flagorneur(-euse), lécheur(-euse)

smart [smɑːt] ADJ élégant(e), chic inv; (clever) intelligent(e); (pej) futé(e); (quick) vif (vive), prompt(e) ▶ VI faire mal, brûler; **the ~ set** le beau monde; **to look ~** être élégant(e); **my eyes are smarting** j'ai les yeux irrités or qui me piquent

smart card N carte f à puce

smarten up ['smɑːtn-] VI devenir plus élégant(e), se faire beau (belle) ▶ VT rendre plus élégant(e)

smart phone N smartphone m

smash [smæʃ] N (also: **smash-up**) collision f, accident m; (Mus) succès foudroyant; (sound) fracas m ▶ VT casser, briser, fracasser; (opponent) écraser; (hopes) ruiner, détruire; (Sport: record) pulvériser ▶ VI se briser, se fracasser; s'écraser
  ▶ **smash up** VT (car) bousiller; (room) tout casser dans

smashing ['smæʃɪŋ] ADJ (inf) formidable

smattering ['smætərɪŋ] N: **a ~ of** quelques notions de

smear [smɪəʳ] N (stain) tache f; (mark) trace f; (Med) frottis m; (insult) calomnie f ▶ VT enduire; (make dirty) salir; (fig) porter atteinte à; **his hands were smeared with oil/ink** il avait les mains maculées de cambouis/d'encre

smear campaign N campagne f de dénigrement

smear test N (BRIT Med) frottis m

smell [smɛl] (pt, pp **smelt** [smɛlt] or **smelled** [smɛld]) N odeur f; (sense) odorat m ▶ VT sentir ▶ VI (pej) sentir mauvais; (food etc): **to ~ (of)** sentir; **it smells good** ça sent bon

smelly ['smɛlɪ] ADJ qui sent mauvais, malodorant(e)

smelt [smɛlt] PT, PP of **smell** ▶ VT (ore) fondre

smile [smaɪl] N sourire m ▶ VI sourire

smiling ['smaɪlɪŋ] ADJ souriant(e)

smirk [smə:k] N petit sourire suffisant or affecté

smith [smɪθ] N maréchal-ferrant m; forgeron m

smithy ['smɪðɪ] N forge f

smitten ['smɪtn] ADJ: ~ **with** pris(e) de; frappé(e) de

smock [smɔk] N blouse f, sarrau m

smog [smɔg] N brouillard mêlé de fumée

smoke [sməuk] N fumée f ▶ VT, VI fumer; **to have a ~** fumer une cigarette; **do you ~?** est-ce que vous fumez?; **do you mind if I ~?** ça ne vous dérange pas que je fume?; **to go up in ~** (house etc) brûler; (fig) partir en fumée

smoke alarm N détecteur m de fumée

smoked [sməukt] ADJ (bacon, glass) fumé(e)

smokeless fuel ['sməuklɪs-] N combustible non polluant

smokeless zone ['sməuklɪs-] N (BRIT) zone f où l'usage du charbon est réglementé

smoker ['sməukə'] N (person) fumeur(-euse); (Rail) wagon m fumeurs

smoke screen N rideau m or écran m de fumée; (fig) paravent m

smoke shop N (US) (bureau m de) tabac m

smoking ['sməukɪŋ] N: "**no ~**" (sign) "défense de fumer"; **to give up ~** arrêter de fumer

smoking compartment, (US) **smoking car** N wagon m fumeurs

smoky ['sməukɪ] ADJ enfumé(e); (taste) fumé(e)

smolder ['sməuldə'] VI (US) = **smoulder**

smoochy ['smu:tʃɪ] ADJ (inf) langoureux(-euse)

smooth [smu:ð] ADJ lisse; (sauce) onctueux(-euse); (flavour, whisky) moelleux(-euse); (cigarette) doux (douce); (movement) régulier(-ière), sans à-coups or heurts; (landing, takeoff) en douceur; (flight) sans secousses; (pej: person) doucereux(-euse), mielleux(-euse) ▶ VT (also: **smooth out**) lisser, défroisser; (: creases, difficulties) faire disparaître
▶ **smooth over** VT: **to ~ things over** (fig) arranger les choses

smoothly ['smu:ðlɪ] ADV (easily) facilement, sans difficulté(s); **everything went ~** tout s'est bien passé

smother ['smʌðə'] VT étouffer

smoulder, (US) **smolder** ['sməuldə'] VI couver

SMS N ABBR (= short message service) SMS m

SMS message N (message m) SMS m

smudge [smʌdʒ] N tache f, bavure f ▶ VT salir, maculer

smug [smʌg] ADJ suffisant(e), content(e) de soi

smuggle ['smʌgl] VT passer en contrebande or en fraude; **to ~ in/out** (goods etc) faire entrer/ sortir clandestinement or en fraude

smuggler ['smʌglə'] N contrebandier(-ière)

smuggling ['smʌglɪŋ] N contrebande f

smut [smʌt] N (grain of soot) grain m de suie; (mark) tache f de suie; (in conversation etc) obscénités fpl

smutty ['smʌtɪ] ADJ (fig) grossier(-ière), obscène

snack [snæk] N casse-croûte m inv; **to have a ~** prendre un en-cas, manger quelque chose (de léger)

snack bar N snack(-bar) m

snag [snæg] N inconvénient m, difficulté f

snail [sneɪl] N escargot m

snake [sneɪk] N serpent m

snap [snæp] N (sound) claquement m, bruit sec; (photograph) photo f, instantané m; (game) sorte de jeu de bataille ▶ ADJ subit(e), fait(e) sans réfléchir ▶ VT (fingers) faire claquer; (break) casser net; (photograph) prendre un instantané de ▶ VI se casser net or avec un bruit sec; (fig: person) craquer; (speak sharply) parler d'un ton brusque; **to ~ open/shut** s'ouvrir/se refermer brusquement; **to ~ one's fingers** (fig) se moquer de; **a cold ~** (of weather) un refroidissement soudain de la température
▶ **snap at** VT FUS (subj: dog) essayer de mordre
▶ **snap off** VT (break) casser net
▶ **snap up** VT sauter sur, saisir

snap fastener N bouton-pression m

snappy ['snæpɪ] ADJ prompt(e); (slogan) qui a du punch; **make it ~!** (inf: hurry up) grouille-toi!, magne-toi!

snapshot ['snæpʃɔt] N photo f, instantané m

snare [snɛə'] N piège m ▶ VT attraper, prendre au piège

snarl [sna:l] N grondement m or grognement m féroce ▶ VI gronder ▶ VT: **to get snarled up** (wool, plans) s'emmêler; (traffic) se bloquer

snatch [snætʃ] N (fig) vol m; (small amount): **snatches of** des fragments mpl or bribes fpl de ▶ VT saisir (d'un geste vif); (steal) voler ▶ VI: **don't ~!** doucement!; **to ~ a sandwich** manger or avaler un sandwich à la hâte; **to ~ some sleep** arriver à dormir un peu
▶ **snatch up** VT saisir, s'emparer de

snazzy ['snæzɪ] ADJ (inf: clothes) classe inv, chouette

sneak [sni:k] N (US pt, pp **snuck** [snʌk]) VI: **to ~ in/ out** entrer/sortir furtivement or à la dérobée ▶ VT: **to ~ a look at sth** regarder furtivement qch ▶ N (inf: pej: informer) faux jeton; **to ~ up on sb** s'approcher de qn sans faire de bruit

sneakers ['sni:kəz] NPL tennis mpl, baskets fpl

sneaking ['sni:kɪŋ] ADJ: **to have a ~ feeling** or **suspicion that ...** avoir la vague impression que ...

sneaky ['sni:kɪ] ADJ sournois(e)

sneer [snɪə'] N ricanement m ▶ VI ricaner, sourire d'un air sarcastique; **to ~ at sb/sth** se moquer de qn/qch avec mépris

sneeze [sni:z] N éternuement m ▶ VI éternuer

snide [snaɪd] ADJ sarcastique, narquois(e)

sniff [snɪf] N reniflement m ▶ VI renifler ▶ VT renifler, flairer; (glue, drug) sniffer, respirer
▶ **sniff at** VT FUS: **it's not to be sniffed at** il ne faut pas cracher dessus, ce n'est pas à dédaigner

sniffer dog ['snɪfə-] N (Police) chien dressé pour la recherche d'explosifs et de stupéfiants

snigger ['snɪgə'] N ricanement m; rire moqueur ▶ VI ricaner

snip [snɪp] N (*cut*) entaille *f*; (*piece*) petit bout; (BRIT *inf*: *bargain*) (bonne) occasion *or* affaire ▸ VT couper

sniper ['snaɪpə^r] N (*marksman*) tireur embusqué

snippet ['snɪpɪt] N bribes *fpl*

snivelling ['snɪvlɪŋ] ADJ larmoyant(e), pleurnicheur(-euse)

snob [snɔb] N snob *mf*

snobbery ['snɔbərɪ] N snobisme *m*

snobbish ['snɔbɪʃ] ADJ snob *inv*

snog [snɔg] VI (*inf*) se bécoter

snooker ['snu:kə^r] N sorte de jeu de billard

snoop [snu:p] VI: **to ~ on sb** espionner qn; **to ~ about** fureter

snooper ['snu:pə^r] N fureteur(-euse)

snooty ['snu:tɪ] ADJ snob *inv*, prétentieux(-euse)

snooze [snu:z] N petit somme ▸ VI faire un petit somme

snore [snɔː^r] VI ronfler ▸ N ronflement *m*

snoring ['snɔːrɪŋ] N ronflement(s) *m(pl)*

snorkel ['snɔːkl] N (*of swimmer*) tuba *m*

snort [snɔːt] N grognement *m* ▸ VI grogner; (*horse*) renâcler ▸ VT (*inf*: *drugs*) sniffer

snotty ['snɔtɪ] ADJ morveux(-euse)

snout [snaut] N museau *m*

snow [snəu] N neige *f* ▸ VI neiger ▸ VT: **to be snowed under with work** être débordé(e) de travail

snowball ['snəubɔːl] N boule *f* de neige

snowboarding ['snəubɔːdɪŋ] N snowboard *m*

snowbound ['snəubaund] ADJ enneigé(e), bloqué(e) par la neige

snow-capped ['snəukæpt] ADJ (*peak, mountain*) couvert(e) de neige

snowdrift ['snəudrɪft] N congère *f*

snowdrop ['snəudrɔp] N perce-neige *m*

snowfall ['snəufɔːl] N chute *f* de neige

snowflake ['snəufleɪk] N flocon *m* de neige

snowman ['snəumæn] N (*irreg*) bonhomme *m* de neige

snowplough, (US) **snowplow** ['snəuplau] N chasse-neige *m inv*

snowshoe ['snəuʃuː] N raquette *f* (*pour la neige*)

snowstorm ['snəustɔːm] N tempête *f* de neige

snowy ['snəuɪ] ADJ neigeux(-euse); (*covered with snow*) enneigé(e)

SNP N ABBR (BRIT *Pol*) = **Scottish National Party**

snub [snʌb] VT repousser, snober ▸ N rebuffade *f*

snub-nosed [snʌb'nəuzd] ADJ au nez retroussé

snuck [snʌk] (US) PT, PP of **sneak**

snuff [snʌf] N tabac *m* à priser ▸ VT (*also*: **snuff out**: *candle*) moucher

snuff movie N (*inf*) film pornographique qui se termine par le meurtre réel de l'un des acteurs

snug [snʌg] ADJ douillet(te), confortable; (*person*) bien au chaud; **it's a ~ fit** c'est bien ajusté(e)

snuggle ['snʌgl] VI: **to ~ down in bed/up to sb** se pelotonner dans son lit/contre qn

SO ABBR (*Banking*) = **standing order**

so [səu] ADV **1** (*thus, likewise*) ainsi, de cette façon; **if so** si oui; **so do** *or* **have I** moi aussi; **it's 5 o'clock — so it is!** il est 5 heures — en effet! *or* c'est vrai!; **I hope/think so** je l'espère/le crois; **so far** jusqu'ici, jusqu'à maintenant; (*in past*) jusque-là; **quite so!** exactement!, c'est bien ça!; **even so** quand même, tout de même
2 (*in comparisons etc*: *to such a degree*) si, tellement; **so big (that)** si *or* tellement grand (que); **she's not so clever as her brother** elle n'est pas aussi intelligente que son frère
3: **so much** adj, adv tant (de); **I've got so much work** j'ai tant de travail; **I love you so much** je vous aime tant; **so many** tant (de)
4 (*phrases*): **10 or so** à peu près *or* environ 10; **so long!** (*inf*: *goodbye*) au revoir!, à un de ces jours!; **so to speak** pour ainsi dire; **so (what)?** (*inf*) (bon) et alors?, et après?
▸ CONJ **1** (*expressing purpose*): **so as to do** pour faire, afin de faire; **so (that)** pour que *or* afin que + *sub*
2 (*expressing result*) donc, par conséquent; **so that** si bien que, de (telle) sorte que; **so that's the reason!** c'est donc (pour) ça!; **so you see, I could have gone** alors tu vois, j'aurais pu y aller

soak [səuk] VT faire *or* laisser tremper; (*drench*) tremper ▸ VI tremper; **to be soaked through** être trempé jusqu'aux os
▸ **soak in** VI pénétrer, être absorbé(e)
▸ **soak up** VT absorber

soaking ['səukɪŋ] ADJ (*also*: **soaking wet**) trempé(e)

so-and-so ['səuənsəu] N (*somebody*) un(e) tel(le)

soap [səup] N savon *m*

soapbox ['səupbɔks] N tribune improvisée (en plein air)

soapflakes ['səupfleɪks] NPL paillettes *fpl* de savon

soap opera N feuilleton télévisé (*quotidienneté réaliste ou embellie*)

soap powder N lessive *f*, détergent *m*

soapsuds ['səupsʌdz] NPL mousse *f* de savon

soapy ['səupɪ] ADJ savonneux(-euse)

soar [sɔː^r] VI monter (en flèche), s'élancer; (*building*) s'élancer; **soaring prices** prix qui grimpent

sob [sɔb] N sanglot *m* ▸ VI sangloter

s.o.b. N ABBR (US: *inf!*: = *son of a bitch*) salaud *m* (!)

sober ['səubə^r] ADJ qui n'est pas (*or* plus) ivre; (*serious*) sérieux(-euse), sensé(e); (*moderate*) mesuré(e); (*colour, style*) sobre, discret(-ète)
▸ **sober up** VT dégriser ▸ VI se dégriser

sobriety [sə'braɪətɪ] N (*not being drunk*) sobriété *f*; (*seriousness, sedateness*) sérieux *m*

sob story N (*inf, pej*) histoire larmoyante

Soc. ABBR (= *society*) Soc

so-called ['səu'kɔːld] ADJ soi-disant *inv*

soccer ['sɔkə^r] N football *m*

soccer pitch N terrain *m* de football

soccer player N footballeur *m*

sociable ['səuʃəbl] ADJ sociable

social ['səuʃl] ADJ social(e); (*sociable*) sociable
▸ N (petite) fête

social climber N arriviste *mf*

S

social club N amicale f, foyer m
Social Democrat N social-démocrate mf
social insurance N (US) sécurité sociale
socialism ['səuʃəlɪzəm] N socialisme m
socialist ['səuʃəlɪst] ADJ, N socialiste (mf)
socialite ['səuʃəlaɪt] N personnalité mondaine
socialize ['səuʃəlaɪz] VI voir or rencontrer des gens, se faire des amis; **to ~ with** (meet often) fréquenter; (get to know) lier connaissance or parler avec
social life N vie sociale; **how's your ~?** est-ce que tu sors beaucoup?
socially ['səuʃəlɪ] ADV socialement, en société
social media NPL médias mpl sociaux
social networking [-'nɛtwə:kɪŋ] N réseaux mpl sociaux
social networking site N site m de réseautage
social science N sciences humaines
social security N aide sociale
social services NPL services sociaux
social welfare N sécurité sociale
social work N assistance sociale
social worker N assistant(e) sociale(e)
society [sə'saɪətɪ] N société f; (club) société, association f; (also: **high society**) (haute) société, grand monde ▶ CPD (party) mondain(e)
socio-economic ['səusɪəuɪ:kə'nɒmɪk] ADJ socioéconomique
sociological [səusɪə'lɒdʒɪkl] ADJ sociologique
sociologist [səusɪ'ɒlədʒɪst] N sociologue mf
sociology [səusɪ'ɒlədʒɪ] N sociologie f
sock [sɒk] N chaussette f ▶ VT (inf: hit) flanquer un coup à; **to pull one's socks up** (fig) se secouer (les puces)
socket ['sɒkɪt] N cavité f; (Elec: also: **wall socket**) prise f de courant; (for light bulb) douille f
sod [sɒd] N (of earth) motte f; (BRIT inf!) con m (!), salaud m (!)
▶ **sod off** VI: **~ off!** (BRIT inf!) fous le camp!, va te faire foutre! (!)
soda ['səudə] N (Chem) soude f; (also: **soda water**) eau f de Seltz; (US: also: **soda pop**) soda m
sodden ['sɒdn] ADJ trempé(e), détrempé(e)
sodium ['səudɪəm] N sodium m
sodium chloride N chlorure m de sodium
sofa ['səufə] N sofa m, canapé m
sofa bed N canapé-lit m
Sofia ['səufɪə] N Sofia
soft [sɒft] ADJ (not rough) doux (douce); (not hard) doux, mou (molle); (not loud) doux, léger(-ère); (kind) doux, gentil(le); (weak) indulgent(e); (stupid) stupide, débile
soft-boiled ['sɒftbɔɪld] ADJ (egg) à la coque
soft drink N boisson non alcoolisée
soft drugs NPL drogues douces
soften ['sɒfn] VT (r)amollir; (fig) adoucir ▶ VI se ramollir; (fig) s'adoucir
softener ['sɒfnər] N (water softener) adoucisseur m; (fabric softener) produit assouplissant
soft fruit N (BRIT) baies fpl
soft furnishings NPL tissus mpl d'ameublement
soft-hearted [sɒft'hɑ:tɪd] ADJ au cœur tendre
softly ['sɒftlɪ] ADV doucement; (touch) légèrement; (kiss) tendrement

softness ['sɒftnɪs] N douceur f
soft option N solution f de facilité
soft sell N promotion f de vente discrète
soft target N cible f facile
soft toy N jouet m en peluche
software ['sɒftwɛər] N (Comput) logiciel m, software m
software package N (Comput) progiciel m
soggy ['sɒgɪ] ADJ (clothes) trempé(e); (ground) détrempé(e)
soil [sɔɪl] N (earth) sol m, terre f ▶ VT salir; (fig) souiller
soiled [sɔɪld] ADJ sale; (Comm) défraîchi(e)
sojourn ['sɒdʒə:n] N (formal) séjour m
solace ['sɒlɪs] N consolation f, réconfort m
solar ['səulər] ADJ solaire
solarium [sə'lɛərɪəm] (pl **solaria** [-rɪə]) N solarium m
solar panel N panneau m solaire
solar plexus [-'plɛksəs] N (Anat) plexus m solaire
solar power N énergie f solaire
solar system N système m solaire
sold [səuld] PT, PP of **sell**
solder ['səuldər] VT souder (au fil à souder) ▶ N soudure f
soldier ['səuldʒər] N soldat m, militaire m ▶ VI: **to ~ on** persévérer, s'accrocher; **toy ~** petit soldat
sold out ADJ (Comm) épuisé(e)
sole [səul] N (of foot) plante f; (of shoe) semelle f; (fish: pl inv) sole f ▶ ADJ seul(e), unique; **the ~ reason** la seule et unique raison
solely ['səullɪ] ADV seulement, uniquement; **I will hold you ~ responsible** je vous en tiendrai pour seul responsable
solemn ['sɒləm] ADJ solennel(le); (person) sérieux(-euse), grave
sole trader N (Comm) chef m d'entreprise individuelle
solicit [sə'lɪsɪt] VT (request) solliciter ▶ VI (prostitute) racoler
solicitor [sə'lɪsɪtər] N (BRIT: for wills etc) ≈ notaire m; (: in court) ≈ avocat m
solid ['sɒlɪd] ADJ (strong, sound, reliable, not liquid) solide; (not hollow: mass) compact(e); (: metal, rock, wood) massif(-ive); (meal) consistant(e), substantiel(le); (vote) unanime ▶ N solide m; **to be on ~ ground** être sur la terre ferme; (fig) être en terrain sûr; **we waited two ~ hours** nous avons attendu deux heures entières
solidarity [sɒlɪ'dærɪtɪ] N solidarité f
solid fuel N combustible m solide
solidify [sə'lɪdɪfaɪ] VI se solidifier ▶ VT solidifier
solidity [sə'lɪdɪtɪ] N solidité f
solid-state ['sɒlɪdsteɪt] ADJ (Elec) à circuits intégrés
soliloquy [sə'lɪləkwɪ] N monologue m
solitaire [sɒlɪ'tɛər] N (gem, BRIT: game) solitaire m; (US: card game) réussite f
solitary ['sɒlɪtərɪ] ADJ solitaire
solitary confinement N (Law) isolement m (cellulaire)
solitude ['sɒlɪtju:d] N solitude f
solo ['səuləu] N solo m ▶ ADV (fly) en solitaire

soloist ['səʊləʊɪst] N soliste mf
Solomon Islands ['sɔləmən-] NPL: **the ~** les (îles fpl) Salomon fpl
solstice ['sɔlstɪs] N solstice m
soluble ['sɔljubl] ADJ soluble
solution [sə'lu:ʃən] N solution f
solve [sɔlv] VT résoudre
solvency ['sɔlvənsɪ] N (Comm) solvabilité f
solvent ['sɔlvənt] ADJ (Comm) solvable ▶ N (Chem) (dis)solvant m
solvent abuse N usage m de solvants hallucinogènes
Somali [səʊ'mɑːlɪ] ADJ somali(e), somalien(ne) ▶ N Somali(e), Somalien(ne)
Somalia [səʊ'mɑːlɪə] N (République f de) Somalie f
Somaliland [səʊ'mɑːlɪlænd] N Somaliland m
sombre, (US) **somber** ['sɔmbəʳ] ADJ sombre, morne

KEYWORD

some [sʌm] ADJ **1** (a certain amount or number of): **some tea/water/ice cream** du thé/de l'eau/de la glace; **some children/apples** des enfants/pommes; **I've got some money but not much** j'ai de l'argent mais pas beaucoup
2 (certain: in contrasts): **some people say that …** il y a des gens qui disent que …; **some films were excellent, but most were mediocre** certains films étaient excellents, mais la plupart étaient médiocres
3 (unspecified): **some woman was asking for you** il y avait une dame qui vous demandait; **he was asking for some book (or other)** il demandait un livre quelconque; **some day** un de ces jours; **some day next week** un jour la semaine prochaine; **after some time** après un certain temps; **at some length** assez longuement; **in some form or other** sous une forme ou une autre, sous une forme quelconque
▶ PRON **1** (a certain number) quelques-uns (quelques-unes), certains (certaines); **I've got some** (books etc) j'en ai (quelques-uns); **some (of them) have been sold** certains ont été vendus
2 (a certain amount) un peu; **I've got some** (money, milk) j'en ai (un peu); **would you like some?** est-ce que vous en voulez?, en voulez-vous?; **could I have some of that cheese?** pourrais-je avoir un peu de ce fromage?; **I've read some of the book** j'ai lu une partie du livre
▶ ADV: **some 10 people** quelque 10 personnes, 10 personnes environ

somebody ['sʌmbədɪ] PRON = **someone**
someday ['sʌmdeɪ] ADV un de ces jours, un jour ou l'autre
somehow ['sʌmhaʊ] ADV d'une façon ou d'une autre; (for some reason) pour une raison ou une autre
someone ['sʌmwʌn] PRON quelqu'un; **~ or other** quelqu'un, je ne sais qui
someplace ['sʌmpleɪs] ADV (US) = **somewhere**

somersault ['sʌməsɔ:lt] N culbute f, saut périlleux ▶ VI faire la culbute or un saut périlleux; (car) faire un tonneau
something ['sʌmθɪŋ] PRON quelque chose m; **~ interesting** quelque chose d'intéressant; **~ to do** quelque chose à faire; **he's ~ like me** il est un peu comme moi; **it's ~ of a problem** il y a là un problème
sometime ['sʌmtaɪm] ADV (in future) un de ces jours, un jour ou l'autre; (in past): **~ last month** au cours du mois dernier
sometimes ['sʌmtaɪmz] ADV quelquefois, parfois
somewhat ['sʌmwɔt] ADV quelque peu, un peu
somewhere ['sʌmwɛəʳ] ADV quelque part; **~ else** ailleurs, autre part
son [sʌn] N fils m
sonar ['səʊnɑːʳ] N sonar m
sonata [sə'nɑːtə] N sonate f
song [sɔŋ] N chanson f; (of bird) chant m
songbook ['sɔŋbuk] N chansonnier m
songwriter ['sɔŋraɪtəʳ] N auteur-compositeur m
sonic ['sɔnɪk] ADJ (boom) supersonique
son-in-law ['sʌnɪnlɔ:] N gendre m, beau-fils m
sonnet ['sɔnɪt] N sonnet m
sonny ['sʌnɪ] N (inf) fiston m
soon [su:n] ADV bientôt; (early) tôt; **~ afterwards** peu après; **quite ~** sous peu; **how ~ can you do it?** combien de temps vous faut-il pour le faire, au plus pressé?; **how ~ can you come back?** quand or dans combien de temps pouvez-vous revenir, au plus tôt?; **see you ~!** à bientôt!; see also **as**
sooner ['su:nəʳ] ADV (time) plus tôt; (preference): **I would ~ do that** j'aimerais autant or je préférerais faire ça; **~ or later** tôt ou tard; **no ~ said than done** sitôt dit, sitôt fait; **the ~ the better** le plus tôt sera le mieux; **no ~ had we left than …** à peine étions-nous partis que …
soot [sut] N suie f
soothe [su:ð] VT calmer, apaiser
soothing ['su:ðɪŋ] ADJ (ointment etc) lénitif(-ive), lénifiant(e); (tone, words etc) apaisant(e); (drink, bath) relaxant(e)
SOP N ABBR = **standard operating procedure**
sop [sɔp] N: **that's only a ~** c'est pour nous (or les etc) amadouer
sophisticated [sə'fɪstɪkeɪtɪd] ADJ raffiné(e), sophistiqué(e); (machinery) hautement perfectionné(e), très complexe; (system etc) très perfectionné(e), sophistiqué
sophistication [səfɪstɪ'keɪʃən] N raffinement m, niveau m (de) perfectionnement m
sophomore ['sɔfəmɔːʳ] N (US) étudiant(e) de seconde année
soporific [sɔpə'rɪfɪk] ADJ soporifique ▶ N somnifère m
sopping ['sɔpɪŋ] ADJ (also: **sopping wet**) tout(e) trempé(e)
soppy ['sɔpɪ] ADJ (pej) sentimental(e)
soprano [sə'prɑːnəʊ] N (voice) soprano m; (singer) soprano mf
sorbet ['sɔːbeɪ] N sorbet m

S

795

sorcerer ['sɔːsərəʳ] N sorcier m
sordid ['sɔːdɪd] ADJ sordide
sore [sɔːʳ] ADJ (painful) douloureux(-euse), sensible; (offended) contrarié(e), vexé(e) ▶ N plaie f; **to have a ~ throat** avoir mal à la gorge; **it's a ~ point** (fig) c'est un point délicat
sorely ['sɔːlɪ] ADV (tempted) fortement
sorrel ['sɔrəl] N oseille f
sorrow ['sɔrəu] N peine f, chagrin m
sorrowful ['sɔrəuful] ADJ triste
sorry ['sɔrɪ] ADJ désolé(e); (condition, excuse, tale) triste, déplorable; (sight) désolant(e); **~!** pardon!, excusez-moi!; **~?** pardon?; **to feel ~ for sb** plaindre qn; **I'm ~ to hear that …** je suis désolé(e) or navré(e) d'apprendre que …; **to be ~ about sth** regretter qch
sort [sɔːt] N genre m, espèce f, sorte f; (make: of coffee, car etc) marque f ▶ VT (also: **sort out**: select which to keep) trier; (: classify) classer; (: tidy) ranger; (: letters etc) trier; (: Comput) trier; **what ~ do you want?** quelle sorte or quel genre voulez-vous?; **what ~ of car?** quelle marque de voiture?; **I'll do nothing of the ~!** je ne ferai rien de tel!; **it's ~ of awkward** (inf) c'est plutôt gênant
  ▶ **sort out** VT (problem) résoudre, régler
sortie ['sɔːtɪ] N sortie f
sorting office ['sɔːtɪŋ-] N (Post) bureau m de tri
SOS N SOS m
so-so ['səusəu] ADV comme ci comme ça
soufflé ['suːfleɪ] N soufflé m
sought [sɔːt] PT, PP of **seek**
sought-after ['sɔːtɑːftəʳ] ADJ recherché(e)
soul [səul] N âme f; **the poor ~ had nowhere to sleep** le pauvre n'avait nulle part où dormir; **I didn't see a ~** je n'ai vu (absolument) personne
soul-destroying ['səuldɪstrɔɪɪŋ] ADJ démoralisant(e)
soulful ['səulful] ADJ plein(e) de sentiment
soulless ['səullɪs] ADJ sans cœur, inhumain(e)
soul mate N âme f sœur
soul-searching ['səulsəːtʃɪŋ] N: **after much ~, I decided …** j'ai longuement réfléchi avant de décider …
sound [saund] ADJ (healthy) en bonne santé, sain(e); (safe, not damaged) solide, en bon état; (reliable, not superficial) sérieux(-euse), solide; (sensible) sensé(e) ▶ ADV: **~ asleep** profondément endormi(e) ▶ N (noise, volume) son m; (louder) bruit m; (Geo) détroit m, bras m de mer ▶ VT (alarm) sonner; (also: **sound out**: opinions) sonder ▶ VI sonner, retentir; (fig: seem) sembler (être); **to be of ~ mind** être sain(e) d'esprit; **I don't like the ~ of it** ça ne me dit rien qui vaille; **to ~ one's horn** (Aut) klaxonner, actionner son avertisseur; **to ~ like** ressembler à; **it sounds as if …** il semblerait que …, j'ai l'impression que …
  ▶ **sound off** VI (inf): **to ~ off (about)** la ramener (sur)
sound barrier N mur m du son
sound bite N phrase toute faite (pour être citée dans les médias)
sound effects NPL bruitage m

sound engineer N ingénieur m du son
sounding ['saundɪŋ] N (Naut etc) sondage m
sounding board N (Mus) table f d'harmonie; (fig): **to use sb as a ~ for one's ideas** essayer ses idées sur qn
soundly ['saundlɪ] ADV (sleep) profondément; (beat) complètement, à plate couture
soundproof ['saundpruːf] VT insonoriser ▶ ADJ insonorisé(e)
sound system N sono(risation) f
soundtrack ['saundtræk] N (of film) bande f sonore
sound wave N (Physics) onde f sonore
soup [suːp] N soupe f, potage m; **in the ~** (fig) dans le pétrin
soup course N potage m
soup kitchen N soupe f populaire
soup plate N assiette creuse or à soupe
soupspoon ['suːpspuːn] N cuiller f à soupe
sour ['sauəʳ] ADJ aigre, acide; (milk) tourné(e), aigre; (fig) acerbe, aigre; revêche; **to go** or **turn ~** (milk, wine) tourner; (fig: relationship, plans) mal tourner; **it's ~ grapes** c'est du dépit
source [sɔːs] N source f; **I have it from a reliable ~ that** je sais de source sûre que
south [sauθ] N sud m ▶ ADJ sud inv; (wind) du sud ▶ ADV au sud, vers le sud; **(to the) ~ of** au sud de; **to travel ~** aller en direction du sud
South Africa N Afrique f du Sud
South African ADJ sud-africain(e) ▶ N Sud-Africain(e)
South America N Amérique f du Sud
South American ADJ sud-américain(e) ▶ N Sud-Américain(e)
southbound ['sauθbaund] ADJ en direction du sud; (carriageway) sud inv
south-east [sauθ'iːst] N sud-est m
South-East Asia N le Sud-Est asiatique
southeastern [sauθ'iːstən] ADJ du or au sud-est
southerly ['sʌðəlɪ] ADJ du sud; au sud
southern ['sʌðən] ADJ (du) sud; méridional(e); **with a ~ aspect** orienté(e) or exposé(e) au sud; **the ~ hemisphere** l'hémisphère sud or austral
South Korea N Corée f du Sud
South of France N: **the ~** le Sud de la France, le Midi
South Pole N: **the ~** le pôle Sud
South Sea Islands NPL: **the ~** l'Océanie f
South Seas NPL: **the ~** les mers fpl du Sud
South Vietnam N Viêt-Nam m du Sud
South Wales N sud m du Pays de Galles
southward ['sauθwəd], **southwards** ['sauθwədz] ADV vers le sud
south-west [sauθ'wɛst] N sud-ouest m
southwestern [sauθ'wɛstən] ADJ du or au sud-ouest
souvenir [suːvə'nɪəʳ] N souvenir m (objet)
sovereign ['sɔvrɪn] ADJ, N souverain(e)
sovereignty ['sɔvrɪntɪ] N souveraineté f
soviet ['səuvɪət] ADJ soviétique
Soviet Union N: **the ~** l'Union f soviétique
sow¹ [səu] (pt **sowed** [səud], pp **sown** [səun]) VT semer
sow² [sau] N truie f

soya ['sɔɪə], (US) **soy** [sɔɪ] N: ~ **bean** graine f de soja; ~ **sauce** sauce f au soja

sozzled ['sɔzld] ADJ (BRIT inf) paf inv

spa [spa:] N (town) station thermale; (US: also: **health spa**) établissement m de cure de rajeunissement

space [speɪs] N (gen) espace m; (room) place f; espace; (length of time) laps m de temps ▶ CPD spatial(e) ▶ VT (also: **space out**) espacer; **to clear a ~ for sth** faire de la place pour qch; **in a confined ~** dans un espace réduit or restreint; **in a short ~ of time** dans peu de temps; **(with)in the ~ of an hour** en l'espace d'une heure

space bar N (on typewriter) barre f d'espacement

spacecraft ['speɪskra:ft] N engin or vaisseau spatial

spaceman ['speɪsmæn] N (irreg) astronaute m, cosmonaute m

spaceship ['speɪsʃɪp] N = **spacecraft**

space shuttle N navette spatiale

spacesuit ['speɪssu:t] N combinaison spatiale

spacewoman ['speɪswumən] N (irreg) astronaute f, cosmonaute f

spacing ['speɪsɪŋ] N espacement m; **single/double ~** (Typ etc) interligne m simple/double

spacious ['speɪʃəs] ADJ spacieux(-euse), grand(e)

spade [speɪd] N (tool) bêche f, pelle f; (child's) pelle; **spades** NPL (Cards) pique m

spadework ['speɪdwə:k] N (fig) gros m du travail

spaghetti [spə'gɛtɪ] N spaghetti mpl

Spain [speɪn] N Espagne f

spam [spæm] N (Comput) pourriel m

span [spæn] N (of bird, plane) envergure f; (of arch) portée f; (in time) espace m de temps, durée f ▶ VT enjamber, franchir; (fig) couvrir, embrasser

Spaniard ['spænjəd] N Espagnol(e)

spaniel ['spænjəl] N épagneul m

Spanish ['spænɪʃ] ADJ espagnol(e), d'Espagne ▶ N (Ling) espagnol m; **the ~** npl les Espagnols; **~ omelette** omelette f à l'espagnole

spank [spæŋk] VT donner une fessée à

spanner ['spænə^r] N (BRIT) clé f (de mécanicien)

spar [spa:^{r}] N espar m ▶ VI (Boxing) s'entraîner

spare [spɛə^r] ADJ de réserve, de rechange; (surplus) de or en trop, de reste ▶ N (part) pièce f de rechange, pièce détachée ▶ VT (do without) se passer de; (afford to give) donner, accorder, passer; (not hurt) épargner; (not use) ménager; **to ~** (surplus) en surplus, de trop; **there are 2 going ~** (BRIT) il y en a 2 de disponible; **to ~ no expense** ne pas reculer devant la dépense; **can you ~ the time?** est-ce que vous avez le temps?; **there is no time to ~** il n'y a pas de temps à perdre; **I've a few minutes to ~** je dispose de quelques minutes

spare part N pièce f de rechange, pièce détachée

spare room N chambre f d'ami

spare time N moments mpl de loisir

spare tyre, (US) **spare tire** N (Aut) pneu m de rechange

spare wheel N (Aut) roue f de secours

sparing ['spɛərɪŋ] ADJ: **to be ~ with** ménager

sparingly ['spɛərɪŋlɪ] ADV avec modération

spark [spa:k] N étincelle f; (fig) étincelle, lueur f

sparkle ['spa:kl] N scintillement m, étincellement m, éclat m ▶ VI étinceler, scintiller; (bubble) pétiller

sparkler ['spa:klə^r] N cierge m magique

sparkling ['spa:klɪŋ] ADJ étincelant(e), scintillant(e); (wine) mousseux(-euse), pétillant(e); (water) pétillant(e), gazeux(-euse)

spark plug N bougie f

sparring partner ['spa:rɪŋ-] N sparring-partner m; (fig) vieil(le) ennemi(e)

sparrow ['spærəu] N moineau m

sparse [spa:s] ADJ clairsemé(e)

spartan ['spa:tən] ADJ (fig) spartiate

spasm ['spæzəm] N (Med) spasme m; (fig) accès m

spasmodic [spæz'mɔdɪk] ADJ (fig) intermittent(e)

spastic ['spæstɪk] (old: pej) N handicapé(e) moteur

spat [spæt] PT, PP of **spit** ▶ N (US) prise f de bec

spate [speɪt] N (fig): ~ **of** avalanche f or torrent m de; **in ~** (river) en crue

spatial ['speɪʃl] ADJ spatial(e)

spatter ['spætə^r] N éclaboussure(s) f(pl) ▶ VT éclabousser ▶ VI gicler

spatula ['spætjulə] N spatule f

spawn [spɔ:n] VT pondre; (pej) engendrer ▶ VI frayer ▶ N frai m

SPCA N ABBR (US: = Society for the Prevention of Cruelty to Animals) ≈ SPA f

SPCC N ABBR (US) = **Society for the Prevention of Cruelty to Children**

speak [spi:k] (pt **spoke** [spəuk], pp **spoken** ['spəukn]) VT (language) parler; (truth) dire ▶ VI parler; (make a speech) prendre la parole; **to ~ to sb/of** or **about sth** parler à qn/de qch; **I don't ~ French** je ne parle pas français; **do you ~ English?** parlez-vous anglais?; **can I ~ to ...?** est-ce que je peux parler à ...?; **speaking!** (on telephone) c'est moi-même!; **to ~ one's mind** dire ce que l'on pense; **it speaks for itself** c'est évident; ~ **up!** parle plus fort!; **he has no money to ~ of** il n'a pas d'argent
▶ **speak for** VT FUS: **to ~ for sb** parler pour qn; **that picture is already spoken for** (in shop) ce tableau est déjà réservé

speaker ['spi:kə^r] N (in public) orateur m; (also: **loudspeaker**) haut-parleur m; (: for stereo etc) baffle m, enceinte f; (Pol): **the S~** (BRIT) le président de la Chambre des communes or des représentants; (US) le président de la Chambre; **are you a Welsh ~?** parlez-vous gallois?

speaking ['spi:kɪŋ] ADJ parlant(e); **French-~ people** les francophones; **to be on ~ terms** se parler

spear [spɪə^r] N lance f ▶ VT transpercer

spearhead ['spɪəhɛd] N fer m de lance; (Mil) colonne f d'attaque ▶ VT (attack etc) mener

spearmint ['spɪəmɪnt] N (Bot etc) menthe verte

spec [spɛk] N (BRIT inf): **on** ~ à tout hasard; **to buy on** ~ acheter avec l'espoir de faire une bonne affaire

special ['spɛʃl] ADJ spécial(e) ▶ N (train) train spécial; **take ~ care** soyez particulièrement prudent; **nothing** ~ rien de spécial; **today's** ~ (at restaurant) le plat du jour

special agent N agent secret

special correspondent N envoyé spécial

special delivery N (Post): **by** ~ en express

special effects NPL (Cine) effets spéciaux

specialist ['spɛʃəlɪst] N spécialiste mf; **heart** ~ cardiologue mf

speciality [spɛʃɪ'ælɪtɪ] N (BRIT) spécialité f

specialize ['spɛʃəlaɪz] VI: **to** ~ (**in**) se spécialiser (dans)

specially ['spɛʃlɪ] ADV spécialement, particulièrement

special needs NPL (BRIT) difficultés fpl d'apprentissage scolaire

special offer N (Comm) réclame f

special school N (BRIT) établissement m d'enseignement spécialisé

specialty ['spɛʃəltɪ] N (US) = speciality

species ['spi:ʃi:z] N (pl inv) espèce f

specific [spə'sɪfɪk] ADJ (not vague) précis(e), explicite; (particular) particulier(-ière); (Bot, Chem etc) spécifique; **to be** ~ **to** être particulier à, être le or un caractère (or les caractères) spécifique(s) de

specifically [spə'sɪfɪklɪ] ADV explicitement, précisément; (intend, ask, design) expressément, spécialement; (exclusively) exclusivement, spécifiquement

specification [spɛsɪfɪ'keɪʃən] N spécification f; stipulation f; **specifications** NPL (of car, building etc) spécification f

specify ['spɛsɪfaɪ] VT spécifier, préciser; **unless otherwise specified** sauf indication contraire

specimen ['spɛsɪmən] N spécimen m, échantillon m; (Med: of blood) prélèvement m; (: of urine) échantillon m

specimen copy N spécimen m

specimen signature N spécimen m de signature

speck [spɛk] N petite tache, petit point; (particle) grain m

speckled ['spɛkld] ADJ tacheté(e), moucheté(e)

specs [spɛks] NPL (inf) lunettes fpl

spectacle ['spɛktəkl] N spectacle m; **spectacles** NPL (BRIT) lunettes fpl

spectacle case N (BRIT) étui m à lunettes

spectacular [spɛk'tækjulər] ADJ spectaculaire ▶ N (Cine etc) superproduction f

spectator [spɛk'teɪtər] N spectateur(-trice)

spectator sport N: **football is a great** ~ le football est un sport qui passionne les foules

spectra ['spɛktrə] NPL of spectrum

spectre, (US) **specter** ['spɛktər] N spectre m, fantôme m

spectrum ['spɛktrəm] (pl spectra [-rə]) N spectre m; (fig) gamme f

speculate ['spɛkjuleɪt] VI spéculer; (try to guess): **to** ~ **about** s'interroger sur

speculation [spɛkju'leɪʃən] N spéculation f; conjectures fpl

speculative ['spɛkjulətɪv] ADJ spéculatif(-ive)

speculator ['spɛkjuleɪtər] N spéculateur(-trice)

sped [spɛd] PT, PP of speed

speech [spi:tʃ] N (faculty) parole f; (talk) discours m, allocution f; (manner of speaking) façon f de parler, langage m; (language) langage m; (enunciation) élocution f

speech day N (BRIT Scol) distribution f des prix

speech impediment N défaut m d'élocution

speechless ['spi:tʃlɪs] ADJ muet(te)

speech therapy N orthophonie f

speed [spi:d] N (swiftness) vitesse f; (promptness) rapidité f ▶ VI (Aut: exceed speed limit) faire un excès de vitesse; **to** ~ **along/by** etc aller/passer etc à toute vitesse; **at** ~ (BRIT) rapidement; **at full** or **top** ~ à toute vitesse or allure; **at a** ~ **of 70 km/h** à une vitesse de 70 km/h; **shorthand/typing speeds** nombre m de mots à la minute en sténographie/dactylographie; **a five-~ gearbox** une boîte cinq vitesses

▶ **speed up** (pt, pp **speeded up**) VI aller plus vite, accélérer ▶ VT accélérer

speedboat ['spi:dbəʊt] N vedette f, hors-bord m inv

speed camera N radar m automatique

speedily ['spi:dɪlɪ] ADV rapidement, promptement

speeding ['spi:dɪŋ] N (Aut) excès m de vitesse

speed limit N limitation f de vitesse, vitesse maximale permise

speedometer [spɪ'dɔmɪtər] N compteur m (de vitesse)

speed trap N (Aut) piège m de police pour contrôle de vitesse

speedway ['spi:dweɪ] N (Sport) piste f de vitesse pour motos; (also: **speedway racing**) épreuve(s) f(pl) de vitesse de motos

speedy [spi:dɪ] ADJ rapide, prompt(e)

speleologist [spɛlɪ'ɔlədʒɪst] N spéléologue mf

spell [spɛl] (pt, pp **spelt** [spɛlt] or **spelled** [spɛld]) N (also: **magic spell**) sortilège m, charme m; (period of time) (courte) période ▶ VT (in writing) écrire, orthographier; (aloud) épeler; (fig) signifier; **to cast a** ~ **on sb** jeter un sort à qn; **he can't** ~ il fait des fautes d'orthographe; **how do you** ~ **your name?** comment écrivez-vous votre nom?; **can you** ~ **it for me?** pouvez-vous me l'épeler?

▶ **spell out** VT (explain): **to** ~ **sth out for sb** expliquer qch clairement à qn

spellbound ['spɛlbaund] ADJ envoûté(e), subjugué(e)

spellchecker ['spɛltʃɛkər] N (Comput) correcteur m or vérificateur m orthographique

spelling ['spɛlɪŋ] N orthographe f

spelt [spɛlt] PT, PP of spell

spend [spɛnd] (pt, pp **spent** [spɛnt]) VT (money) dépenser; (time, life) passer; (devote) consacrer; **to** ~ **time/money/effort on sth** consacrer du temps/de l'argent/de l'énergie à qch

spending ['spɛndɪŋ] N dépenses fpl; **government** ~ les dépenses publiques

spending money N argent m de poche

spending power N pouvoir m d'achat

spendthrift ['spɛndθrɪft] N dépensier(-ière)

spent [spɛnt] PT, PP of spend ▶ ADJ (patience)

épuisé(e), à bout; *(cartridge, bullets)* vide;
~ **matches** vieilles allumettes

sperm [spə:m] N spermatozoïde *m*; *(semen)*
sperme *m*

sperm bank N banque *f* du sperme

sperm whale N cachalot *m*

spew [spju:] VT vomir

sphere [sfɪər] N sphère *f*; *(fig)* sphère, domaine *m*

spherical ['sfɛrɪkl] ADJ sphérique

sphinx [sfɪŋks] N sphinx *m*

spice [spaɪs] N épice *f* ▸ VT épicer

spick-and-span ['spɪkən'spæn] ADJ impeccable

spicy ['spaɪsɪ] ADJ épicé(e), relevé(e); *(fig)*
piquant(e)

spider ['spaɪdər] N araignée *f*; ~'s **web** toile *f*
d'araignée

spiel [spi:l] N laïus *m inv*

spike [spaɪk] N pointe *f*; *(Elec)* pointe de tension;
(Bot) épi *m*; **spikes** NPL *(Sport)* chaussures *fpl* à
pointes

spike heel N *(US)* talon *m* aiguille

spiky ['spaɪkɪ] ADJ *(bush, branch)* épineux(-euse);
(animal) plein(e) de piquants

spill [spɪl] *(pt, pp* **spilt** [spɪlt] *or* **spilled** [spɪld]) VT
renverser; répandre ▸ VI se répandre; **to ~ the
beans** *(inf)* vendre la mèche *(confess)* lâcher le
morceau
 ▸ **spill out** VI sortir à flots, se répandre
 ▸ **spill over** VI déborder

spillage ['spɪlɪdʒ] N *(of oil)* déversement *m*
(accidentel)

spilt [spɪlt] PT, PP *of* **spill**

spin [spɪn] *(pt, pp* **spun** [spʌn]) N *(revolution of
wheel)* tour *m*; *(Aviat)* *(chute f* en) vrille *f*; *(trip in
car)* petit tour, balade *f*; *(on ball)* effet *m* ▸ VT
(wool etc) filer; *(wheel)* faire tourner; *(BRIT:
clothes)* essorer ▸ VI *(turn)* tourner, tournoyer; **to
~ a yarn** débiter une longue histoire; **to ~ a
coin** *(BRIT)* jouer à pile ou face
 ▸ **spin out** VT faire durer

spina bifida ['spaɪnə'bɪfɪdə] N spina-bifida *m inv*

spinach ['spɪnɪtʃ] N épinard *m*; *(as food)* épinards
mpl

spinal ['spaɪnl] ADJ vertébral(e), spinal(e)

spinal column N colonne vertébrale

spinal cord N moelle épinière

spindly ['spɪndlɪ] ADJ grêle, filiforme

spin doctor N *(inf)* personne employée pour présenter
un parti politique sous un jour favorable

spin-dry ['spɪn'draɪ] VT essorer

spin-dryer [spɪn'draɪər] N *(BRIT)* essoreuse *f*

spine [spaɪn] N colonne vertébrale; *(thorn)* épine
f, piquant *m*

spine-chilling ['spaɪntʃɪlɪŋ] ADJ terrifiant(e)

spineless ['spaɪnlɪs] ADJ invertébré(e); *(fig)* mou
(molle), sans caractère

spinner ['spɪnər] N *(of thread)* fileur(-euse)

spinning ['spɪnɪŋ] N *(of thread)* filage *m*; *(by
machine)* filature *f*

spinning top N toupie *f*

spinning wheel N rouet *m*

spin-off ['spɪnɔf] N sous-produit *m*; avantage
inattendu

spinster ['spɪnstər] N célibataire *f*; vieille fille

spiral ['spaɪərl] N spirale *f* ▸ ADJ en spirale
 ▸ VI *(fig: prices etc)* monter en flèche; **the
inflationary** ~ la spirale inflationniste

spiral staircase N escalier *m* en colimaçon

spire ['spaɪər] N flèche *f*, aiguille *f*

spirit ['spɪrɪt] N *(soul)* esprit *m*, âme *f*; *(ghost)*
esprit, revenant *m*; *(mood)* esprit, état *m*
d'esprit; *(courage)* courage *m*, énergie *f*; **spirits**
NPL *(drink)* spiritueux *mpl*, alcool *m*; **in good
spirits** de bonne humeur; **in low spirits**
démoralisé(e); **community** ~ solidarité *f*;
public ~ civisme *m*

spirit duplicator N duplicateur *m* à alcool

spirited ['spɪrɪtɪd] ADJ vif (vive),
fougueux(-euse), plein(e) d'allant

spirit level N niveau *m* à bulle

spiritual ['spɪrɪtjuəl] ADJ spirituel(le); *(religious)*
religieux(-euse) ▸ N *(also:* **Negro spiritual**)
spiritual *m*

spiritualism ['spɪrɪtjuəlɪzəm] N spiritisme *m*

spit [spɪt] *(pt, pp* **spat** [spæt]) N *(for roasting)*
broche *f*; *(spittle)* crachat *m*; *(saliva)* salive *f* ▸ VI
cracher; *(sound)* crépiter; *(rain)* crachiner

spite [spaɪt] N rancune *f*, dépit *m* ▸ VT
contrarier, vexer; **in ~ of** en dépit de, malgré

spiteful ['spaɪtful] ADJ malveillant(e),
rancunier(-ière)

spitroast ['spɪt'rəust] VT faire rôtir à la broche

spitting ['spɪtɪŋ] N: "~ **prohibited**" "défense de
cracher" ▸ ADJ: **to be the ~ image of sb** être le
portrait tout craché de qn

spittle ['spɪtl] N salive *f*; bave *f*; crachat *m*

spiv [spɪv] N *(BRIT inf)* chevalier *m* d'industrie,
aigrefin *m*

splash [splæʃ] N *(sound)* plouf *m*; *(of colour)* tache *f*
 ▸ VT éclabousser ▸ VI *(also:* **splash about**)
barboter, patauger
 ▸ **splash out** VI *(BRIT)* faire une folie

splashdown ['splæʃdaun] N amerrissage *m*

splay [spleɪ] ADJ: **splayfooted** marchant les
pieds en dehors

spleen [spli:n] N *(Anat)* rate *f*

splendid ['splendɪd] ADJ splendide, superbe,
magnifique

splendour, *(US)* **splendor** ['splendər] N
splendeur *f*, magnificence *f*

splice [splaɪs] VT épisser

splint [splɪnt] N attelle *f*, éclisse *f*

splinter ['splɪntər] N *(wood)* écharde *f*; *(metal)*
éclat *m* ▸ VI *(wood)* se fendre; *(glass)* se briser

splinter group N groupe dissident

split [splɪt] *(pt, pp* ~) N fente *f*, déchirure *f*; *(fig:
Pol)* scission *f* ▸ VT fendre, déchirer; *(party)*
diviser; *(work, profits)* partager, répartir ▸ VI
(break) se fendre, se briser; *(divide)* se diviser;
let's ~ the difference coupons la poire en
deux; **to do the splits** faire le grand écart
 ▸ **split up** VI *(couple)* se séparer, rompre;
(meeting) se disperser

split-level ['splɪtlevl] ADJ *(house)* à deux *or*
plusieurs niveaux

split peas NPL pois cassés

split personality N double personnalité *f*

split second N fraction *f* de seconde

S

splitting ['splitiŋ] ADJ: **a ~ headache** un mal de tête atroce

splutter ['splʌtər] VI bafouiller; postillonner

spoil [spɔil] (*pt, pp* **spoiled** *or* **spoilt** [spɔilt]) VT (*damage*) abîmer; (*mar*) gâcher; (*child*) gâter; (*ballot paper*) rendre nul ▶ VI: **to be spoiling for a fight** chercher la bagarre

spoils [spɔilz] NPL butin *m*

spoilsport ['spɔilspɔːt] N trouble-fête *mf*, rabat-joie *m inv*

spoilt [spɔilt] PT, PP *of* **spoil** ▶ ADJ (*child*) gâté(e); (*ballot paper*) nul(le)

spoke [spəuk] PT *of* **speak** ▶ N rayon *m*

spoken ['spəukn] PP *of* **speak**

spokesman ['spəuksmən] N (*irreg*) porte-parole *m inv*

spokesperson ['spəukspəːsn] N porte-parole *m inv*

spokeswoman ['spəukswumən] N (*irreg*) porte-parole *m inv*

sponge [spʌndʒ] N éponge *f*; (*Culin: also:* **sponge cake**) ≈ biscuit *m* de Savoie ▶ VT éponger ▶ VI: **to ~ off** *or* **on** vivre aux crochets de

sponge bag N (*BRIT*) trousse *f* de toilette

sponge cake N ≈ biscuit *m* de Savoie

sponger ['spʌndʒər] N (*pej*) parasite *m*

spongy ['spʌndʒi] ADJ spongieux(-euse)

sponsor ['spɔnsər] N (*Radio, TV, Sport*) sponsor *m*; (*for application*) parrain *m*, marraine *f*; (*BRIT: for fund-raising event*) donateur(-trice) ▶ VT (*programme, competition etc*) parrainer, patronner, sponsoriser; (*Pol: bill*) présenter; (*new member*) parrainer; (*fund-raiser*) faire un don à; **I sponsored him at 3p a mile** (*in fund-raising race*) je me suis engagé à lui donner 3p par mile

sponsorship ['spɔnsəʃip] N sponsoring *m*; patronage *m*, parrainage *m*; dons *mpl*

spontaneity [spɔntə'neiiti] N spontanéité *f*

spontaneous [spɔn'teiniəs] ADJ spontané(e)

spoof [spuːf] N (*parody*) parodie *f*; (*trick*) canular *m*

spooky ['spuːki] ADJ (*inf*) qui donne la chair de poule

spool [spuːl] N bobine *f*

spoon [spuːn] N cuiller *f*

spoon-feed ['spuːnfiːd] VT nourrir à la cuiller; (*fig*) mâcher le travail à

spoonful ['spuːnful] N cuillerée *f*

sporadic [spə'rædik] ADJ sporadique

sport [spɔːt] N sport *m*; (*amusement*) divertissement *m*; (*person*) chic type *m*/chic fille *f* ▶ VT (*wear*) arborer; **indoor/outdoor sports** sports en salle/de plein air; **to say sth in ~** dire qch pour rire

sporting ['spɔːtiŋ] ADJ sportif(-ive); **to give sb a ~ chance** donner sa chance à qn

sport jacket N (*US*) = **sports jacket**

sports car N voiture *f* de sport

sports centre (*BRIT*) N centre sportif

sports drink N boisson *f* pour le sport

sports ground N terrain *m* de sport

sports jacket N (*BRIT*) veste *f* de sport

sportsman ['spɔːtsmən] N (*irreg*) sportif *m*

sportsmanship ['spɔːtsmənʃip] N esprit sportif, sportivité *f*

sports page N page *f* des sports

sports utility vehicle N véhicule *m* de loisirs (*de type SUV*)

sportswear ['spɔːtswɛər] N vêtements *mpl* de sport

sportswoman ['spɔːtswumən] N (*irreg*) sportive *f*

sporty ['spɔːti] ADJ sportif(-ive)

spot [spɔt] N tache *f*; (*dot: on pattern*) pois *m*; (*pimple*) bouton *m*; (*place*) endroit *m*, coin *m*; (*also:* **spot advertisement**) message *m* publicitaire ▶ VT (*notice*) apercevoir, repérer; **on the ~** sur place, sur les lieux; (*immediately*) sur le champ; **to put sb on the ~** (*fig*) mettre qn dans l'embarras; **to come out in spots** se couvrir de boutons, avoir une éruption de boutons

spot check N contrôle intermittent

spotless ['spɔtlis] ADJ immaculé(e)

spotlight ['spɔtlait] N projecteur *m*; (*Aut*) phare *m* auxiliaire

spot-on [spɔt'ɔn] ADJ (*BRIT inf*) en plein dans le mille

spot price N prix *m* sur place

spotted ['spɔtid] ADJ tacheté(e), moucheté(e); à pois; **~ with** tacheté(e) de

spotty ['spɔti] ADJ (*face*) boutonneux(-euse)

spouse [spauz] N époux (épouse)

spout [spaut] N (*of jug*) bec *m*; (*of liquid*) jet *m* ▶ VI jaillir

sprain [sprein] N entorse *f*, foulure *f* ▶ VT: **to ~ one's ankle** se fouler *or* se tordre la cheville

sprang [spræŋ] PT *of* **spring**

sprawl [sprɔːl] VI s'étaler ▶ N: **urban ~** expansion urbaine; **to send sb sprawling** envoyer qn rouler par terre

spray [sprei] N jet *m* (en fines gouttelettes); (*from sea*) embruns *mpl*; (*aerosol*) vaporisateur *m*, bombe *f*; (*for garden*) pulvérisateur *m*; (*of flowers*) petit bouquet ▶ VT vaporiser, pulvériser; (*crops*) traiter ▶ CPD (*deodorant etc*) en bombe *or* atomiseur

spread [spred] (*pt, pp* ~) N (*distribution*) répartition *f*; (*Culin*) pâte *f* à tartiner; (*inf: meal*) festin *m*; (*Press, Typ: two pages*) double page *f* ▶ VT (*paste, contents*) étendre, étaler; (*rumour, disease*) répandre, propager; (*repayments*) échelonner, étaler; (*wealth*) répartir ▶ VI s'étendre; se répandre; se propager; (*stain*) s'étaler; **middle-age ~** embonpoint *m* (pris avec l'âge) ▶ **spread out** VI (*people*) se disperser

spread-eagled ['spredi:gld] ADJ: **to be** *or* **lie ~** être étendu(e) bras et jambes écartés

spreadsheet ['spredʃiːt] N (*Comput*) tableur *m*

spree [spriː] N: **to go on a ~** faire la fête

sprig [sprig] N rameau *m*

sprightly ['spraitli] ADJ alerte

spring [spriŋ] (*pt* **sprang** [spræŋ], *pp* **sprung** [sprʌŋ]) N (*season*) printemps *m*; (*leap*) bond *m*, saut *m*; (*coiled metal*) ressort *m*; (*bounciness*) élasticité *f*; (*of water*) source *f* ▶ VI bondir, sauter ▶ VT: **to ~ a leak** (*pipe etc*) se mettre à fuir; **he sprang the news on me** il m'a annoncé la nouvelle de but en blanc; **in ~, in the ~** au printemps; **to ~ from** provenir de; **to ~ into**

action passer à l'action; **to walk with a ~ in one's step** marcher d'un pas souple
▶ **spring up** VI (*problem*) se présenter, surgir; (*plant, buildings*) surgir de terre

springboard ['sprɪŋbɔːd] N tremplin *m*

spring-clean [sprɪŋ'kliːn] N (*also:* **spring-cleaning**) grand nettoyage de printemps

spring onion N (BRIT) ciboule *f*, cive *f*

spring roll N rouleau *m* de printemps

springtime ['sprɪŋtaɪm] N printemps *m*

springy ['sprɪŋɪ] ADJ élastique, souple

sprinkle ['sprɪŋkl] VT (*pour*) répandre; verser; **to ~ water** etc **on, ~ with water** etc asperger d'eau etc; **to ~ sugar** etc **on, ~ with sugar** etc saupoudrer de sucre etc; **sprinkled with** (*fig*) parsemé(e) de

sprinkler ['sprɪŋklə'] N (*for lawn* etc) arroseur *m*; (*to put out fire*) diffuseur *m* d'extincteur automatique d'incendie

sprinkling ['sprɪŋklɪŋ] N (*of water*) quelques gouttes *fpl*; (*of salt*) pincée *f*; (*of sugar*) légère couche

sprint [sprɪnt] N sprint *m* ▶ VI courir à toute vitesse; (*Sport*) sprinter

sprinter ['sprɪntə'] N sprinteur(-euse)

sprite [spraɪt] N lutin *m*

spritzer ['sprɪtsə'] N boisson à base de vin blanc et d'eau de Seltz

sprocket ['sprɔkɪt] N (*on printer* etc) picot *m*

sprout [spraut] VI germer, pousser

sprouts [sprauts] NPL (*also:* **Brussels sprouts**) choux *mpl* de Bruxelles

spruce [spruːs] N épicéa *m* ▶ ADJ net(te), pimpant(e)
▶ **spruce up** VT (*smarten up: room* etc) apprêter; **to ~ o.s. up** se faire beau (belle)

sprung [sprʌŋ] PP *of* **spring**

spry [spraɪ] ADJ alerte, vif (vive)

SPUC N ABBR = **Society for the Protection of Unborn Children**

spud [spʌd] N (*inf: potato*) patate *f*

spun [spʌn] PT, PP *of* **spin**

spur [spəː'] N éperon *m*; (*fig*) aiguillon *m* ▶ VT (*also:* **spur on**) éperonner; aiguillonner; **on the ~ of the moment** sous l'impulsion du moment

spurious ['spjuərɪəs] ADJ faux (fausse)

spurn [spəːn] VT repousser avec mépris

spurt [spəːt] N jet *m*; (*of blood*) jaillissement *m*; (*of energy*) regain *m*, sursaut *m* ▶ VI jaillir, gicler; **to put in** or **on a ~** (*runner*) piquer un sprint; (*fig: in work* etc) donner un coup de collier

sputter ['spʌtə'] VI = **splutter**

spy [spaɪ] N espion(ne) ▶ VI: **to ~ on** espionner, épier ▶ VT (*see*) apercevoir ▶ CPD (*film, story*) d'espionnage

spying ['spaɪɪŋ] N espionnage *m*

spyware ['spaɪwɛə'] N (*Comput*) logiciel *m* espion

Sq. ABBR (*in address*) = **square**

sq. ABBR (*Math* etc) = **square**

squabble ['skwɔbl] N querelle *f*, chamaillerie *f* ▶ VI se chamailler

squad [skwɔd] N (*Mil, Police*) escouade *f*, groupe *m*; (*Football*) contingent *m*; **flying ~** (*Police*) brigade volante

squad car N (BRIT Police) voiture *f* de police

squaddie ['skwɔdɪ] N (*Mil: inf*) troufion *m*, bidasse *m*

squadron ['skwɔdrn] N (*Mil*) escadron *m*; (*Aviat, Naut*) escadrille *f*

squalid ['skwɔlɪd] ADJ sordide, ignoble

squall [skwɔːl] N rafale *f*, bourrasque *f*

squalor ['skwɔlə'] N conditions *fpl* sordides

squander ['skwɔndə'] VT gaspiller, dilapider

square [skwɛə'] N carré *m*; (*in town*) place *f*; (US: *block of houses*) îlot *m*, pâté *m* de maisons; (*instrument*) équerre *f* ▶ ADJ carré(e); (*honest*) honnête, régulier(-ière); (*inf: ideas, tastes*) vieux jeu *inv*, qui retarde ▶ VT (*arrange*) régler; arranger; (*Math*) élever au carré; (*reconcile*) concilier ▶ VI (*agree*) cadrer, s'accorder; **all ~** quitte; à égalité; **a ~ meal** un repas convenable; **2 metres ~** (de) 2 mètres sur 2; **1 ~ metre** 1 mètre carré; **we're back to ~ one** (*fig*) on se retrouve à la case départ
▶ **square up** VI (BRIT: *settle*) régler; **to ~ up with sb** régler ses comptes avec qn

square bracket N (*Typ*) crochet *m*

squarely ['skwɛəlɪ] ADV carrément; (*honestly, fairly*) honnêtement, équitablement

square root N racine carrée

squash [skwɔʃ] N (BRIT Sport) squash *m*; (US: *vegetable*) courge *f*; (*drink*): **lemon/orange ~** citronnade *f*/orangeade *f* ▶ VT écraser

squat [skwɔt] ADJ petit(e) et épais(se), ramassé(e) ▶ VI (*also:* **squat down**) s'accroupir; (*on property*) squatter, squattériser

squatter ['skwɔtə'] N squatter *m*

squawk [skwɔːk] VI pousser un or des gloussement(s)

squeak [skwiːk] N (*of hinge, wheel* etc) grincement *m*; (*of shoes*) craquement *m*; (*of mouse* etc) petit cri aigu ▶ VI (*hinge, wheel*) grincer; (*mouse*) pousser un petit cri

squeaky ['skwiːkɪ] ADJ grinçant(e); **to be ~ clean** (*fig*) être au-dessus de tout soupçon

squeal [skwiːl] VI pousser un or des cri(s) aigu(s) or perçant(s); (*brakes*) grincer

squeamish ['skwiːmɪʃ] ADJ facilement dégoûté(e); facilement scandalisé(e)

squeeze [skwiːz] N pression *f*; (*also:* **credit squeeze**) encadrement *m* du crédit, restrictions *fpl* de crédit ▶ VT presser; (*hand, arm*) serrer ▶ VI: **to ~ past/under sth** se glisser avec (beaucoup de) difficulté devant/sous qch; **a ~ of lemon** quelques gouttes de citron
▶ **squeeze out** VT exprimer; (*fig*) soutirer

squelch [skwɛltʃ] VI faire un bruit de succion; patauger

squib [skwɪb] N pétard *m*

squid [skwɪd] N calmar *m*

squiggle ['skwɪgl] N gribouillis *m*

squint [skwɪnt] VI loucher ▶ N: **he has a ~** il louche, il souffre de strabisme; **to ~ at sth** regarder qch du coin de l'œil; (*quickly*) jeter un coup d'œil à qch

squire ['skwaɪə'] N (BRIT) propriétaire terrien

squirm [skwəːm] VI se tortiller

squirrel ['skwɪrəl] N écureuil *m*

squirt [skwə:t] N jet *m* ▶ VI jaillir, gicler ▶ VT faire gicler

Sr ABBR = **senior**; (*Rel*) = **sister**

SRC N ABBR (*BRIT*: = *Students' Representative Council*) ≈ CROUS *m*

Sri Lanka [srɪ'læŋkə] N Sri Lanka *m*

SRN N ABBR (*BRIT*) = **State Registered Nurse**

SRO ABBR (*US*) = **standing room only**

SS ABBR (= *steamship*) S/S

SSA N ABBR (*US*: = *Social Security Administration*) organisme de sécurité sociale

SST N ABBR (*US*) = **supersonic transport**

ST ABBR (*US*: = *Standard Time*) heure officielle

St ABBR = **saint**; **street**

stab [stæb] N (*with knife etc*) coup *m* (de couteau *etc*); (*of pain*) lancée *f*; (*inf*: try): **to have a ~ at (doing) sth** s'essayer à (faire) qch ▶ VT poignarder; **to ~ sb to death** tuer qn à coups de couteau

stabbing ['stæbɪŋ] N: **there's been a ~** quelqu'un a été attaqué à coups de couteau ▶ ADJ (*pain, ache*) lancinant(e)

stability [stə'bɪlɪtɪ] N stabilité *f*

stabilization [steɪbəlaɪ'zeɪʃən] N stabilisation *f*

stabilize ['steɪbəlaɪz] VT stabiliser ▶ VI se stabiliser

stabilizer ['steɪbəlaɪzə*r*] N stabilisateur *m*

stable ['steɪbl] N écurie *f* ▶ ADJ stable; **riding stables** centre *m* d'équitation

staccato [stə'ka:təu] ADV staccato ▶ ADJ (*Mus*) piqué(e); (*noise, voice*) saccadé(e)

stack [stæk] N tas *m*, pile *f* ▶ VT empiler, entasser; **there's stacks of time** (*BRIT inf*) on a tout le temps

stadium ['steɪdɪəm] N stade *m*

staff [sta:f] N (*work force*) personnel *m*; (*BRIT Scol*: *also*: **teaching staff**) professeurs *mpl*, enseignants *mpl*, personnel enseignant; (*servants*) domestiques *mpl*; (*Mil*) état-major *m*; (*stick*) perche *f*, bâton *m* ▶ VT pourvoir en personnel

staffroom ['sta:fru:m] N salle *f* des professeurs

Staffs ABBR (*BRIT*) = **Staffordshire**

stag [stæg] N cerf *m*; (*BRIT Stock Exchange*) loup *m*

stage [steɪdʒ] N scène *f*; (*platform*) estrade *f*; (*point*) étape *f*, stade *m*; (*profession*): **the ~** le théâtre ▶ VT (*play*) monter, mettre en scène; (*demonstration*) organiser; (*fig: recovery etc*) effectuer; **in stages** par étapes, par degrés; **to go through a difficult ~** traverser une période difficile; **in the early stages** au début; **in the final stages** à la fin

stagecoach ['steɪdʒkəutʃ] N diligence *f*

stage door N entrée *f* des artistes

stage fright N trac *m*

stagehand ['steɪdʒhænd] N machiniste *m*

stage-manage ['steɪdʒmænɪdʒ] VT (*fig*) orchestrer

stage manager N régisseur *m*

stagger ['stægə*r*] VI chanceler, tituber ▶ VT (*person: amaze*) stupéfier; bouleverser; (*hours, holidays*) étaler, échelonner

staggering ['stægərɪŋ] ADJ (*amazing*) stupéfiant(e), renversant(e)

staging post ['steɪdʒɪŋ-] N relais *m*

stagnant ['stægnənt] ADJ stagnant(e)

stagnate [stæg'neɪt] VI stagner, croupir

stagnation [stæg'neɪʃən] N stagnation *f*

stag night, stag party N enterrement *m* de vie de garçon

staid [steɪd] ADJ posé(e), rassis(e)

stain [steɪn] N tache *f*; (*colouring*) colorant *m* ▶ VT tacher; (*wood*) teindre

stained glass [steɪnd-] N (*decorative*) verre coloré; (*in church*) vitraux *mpl*; **~ window** vitrail *m*

stainless ['steɪnlɪs] ADJ (*steel*) inoxydable

stainless steel N inox *m*, acier *m* inoxydable

stain remover N détachant *m*

stair [stɛə*r*] N (*step*) marche *f*

staircase ['stɛəkeɪs] N = **stairway**

stairs [stɛəz] NPL escalier *m*; **on the ~** dans l'escalier

stairway ['stɛəweɪ] N escalier *m*

stairwell ['stɛəwɛl] N cage *f* d'escalier

stake [steɪk] N pieu *m*, poteau *m*; (*Comm: interest*) intérêts *mpl*; (*Betting*) enjeu *m* ▶ VT risquer, jouer; (*also*: **stake out**: *area*) marquer, délimiter; **to be at ~** être en jeu; **to have a ~ in sth** avoir des intérêts (en jeu) dans qch; **to ~ a claim (to sth)** revendiquer (qch)

stakeout ['steɪkaut] N surveillance *f*; **to be on a ~** effectuer une surveillance

stalactite ['stæləktaɪt] N stalactite *f*

stalagmite ['stæləgmaɪt] N stalagmite *f*

stale [steɪl] ADJ (*bread*) rassis(e); (*food*) pas frais (fraîche); (*beer*) éventé(e); (*smell*) de renfermé; (*air*) confiné(e)

stalemate ['steɪlmeɪt] N pat *m*; (*fig*) impasse *f*

stalk [stɔ:k] N tige *f* ▶ VT traquer ▶ VI: **to ~ out/off** sortir/partir d'un air digne

stall [stɔ:l] N (*in street, market etc*) éventaire *m*, étal *m*; (*in stable*) stalle *f* ▶ VT (*Aut*) caler; (*fig: delay*) retarder ▶ VI (*Aut*) caler; (*fig*) essayer de gagner du temps; **stalls** NPL (*BRIT: in cinema, theatre*) orchestre *m*; **a newspaper/flower ~** un kiosque à journaux/de fleuriste

stallholder ['stɔ:lhəuldə*r*] N (*BRIT*) marchand(e) en plein air

stallion ['stæljən] N étalon *m* (*cheval*)

stalwart ['stɔ:lwət] N partisan *m* fidèle

stamen ['steɪmɛn] N étamine *f*

stamina ['stæmɪnə] N vigueur *f*, endurance *f*

stammer ['stæmə*r*] N bégaiement *m* ▶ VI bégayer

stamp [stæmp] N timbre *m*; (*also*: **rubber stamp**) tampon *m*; (*mark, also fig*) empreinte *f*; (*on document*) cachet *m* ▶ VI (*also*: **stamp one's foot**) taper du pied ▶ VT (*letter*) timbrer; (*with rubber stamp*) tamponner

▶ **stamp out** VT (*fire*) piétiner; (*crime*) éradiquer; (*opposition*) éliminer

stamp album N album *m* de timbres(-poste)

stamp collecting [-kəlɛktɪŋ] N philatélie *f*

stamp duty N (*BRIT*) droit *m* de timbre

stamped addressed envelope N (*BRIT*) enveloppe affranchie pour la réponse

stampede [stæm'pi:d] N ruée *f*; (*of cattle*) débandade *f*

stamp machine N distributeur *m* de timbres
stance [stæns] N position *f*
stand [stænd] (*pt, pp* **stood** [stud]) N (*position*)
position *f*; (*for taxis*) station *f* (de taxis); (*Mil*)
résistance *f*; (*structure*) guéridon *m*; support *m*;
(*Comm*) étalage *m*, stand *m*; (*Sport: also:* **stands**)
tribune *f*; (*also:* **music stand**) pupitre *m* ▶ VI être
or se tenir (debout); (*be placed*) se trouver; (*remain: offer etc*)
rester valable ▶ VT (*place*) mettre, poser;
(*tolerate, withstand*) supporter; (*treat, invite*) offrir,
payer; **to make a ~** prendre position; **to take a**
~ on an issue prendre position sur un
problème; **to ~ for parliament** (*BRIT*) se
présenter aux élections (*comme candidat à la*
députation); **to ~ guard** or **watch** (*Mil*) monter la
garde; **it stands to reason** c'est logique; cela
va de soi; **as things ~** dans l'état actuel des
choses; **to ~ sb a drink/meal** payer à boire/à
manger à qn; **I can't ~ him** je ne peux pas le
voir
  ▶ **stand aside** VI s'écarter
  ▶ **stand back** VI (*move back*) reculer, s'écarter
  ▶ **stand by** VI (*be ready*) se tenir prêt(e) ▶ VT FUS
  (*opinion*) s'en tenir à; (*person*) ne pas
  abandonner, soutenir
  ▶ **stand down** VI (*withdraw*) se retirer; (*Law*)
  renoncer à ses droits
  ▶ **stand for** VT FUS (*signify*) représenter,
  signifier; (*tolerate*) supporter, tolérer
  ▶ **stand in for** VT FUS remplacer
  ▶ **stand out** VI (*be prominent*) ressortir
  ▶ **stand up** VI (*rise*) se lever, se mettre debout
  ▶ **stand up for** VT FUS défendre
  ▶ **stand up to** VT FUS tenir tête à, résister à
stand-alone ['stændələun] ADJ (*Comput*)
autonome
standard ['stændəd] N (*norm*) norme *f*, étalon *m*;
(*level*) niveau *m* (voulu); (*criterion*) critère *m*; (*flag*)
étendard *m* ▶ ADJ (*size etc*) ordinaire, normal(e);
(*model, feature*) standard *inv*; (*practice*) courant(e);
(*text*) de base; **standards** NPL (*morals*) morale *f*,
principes *mpl*; **to be** or **come up to ~** être du
niveau voulu or à la hauteur; **to apply a double**
~ avoir or appliquer deux poids deux mesures
standardization [stændədaɪ'zeɪʃən] N
standardisation *f*
standardize ['stændədaɪz] VT standardiser
standard lamp N (*BRIT*) lampadaire *m*
standard of living N niveau *m* de vie
standard time N heure légale
stand-by ['stændbaɪ] N remplaçant(e) ▶ ADJ
(*provisions*) de réserve; **to be on ~** se tenir prêt(e)
(à intervenir); (*doctor*) être de garde
stand-by generator N générateur *m* de secours
stand-by passenger N passager(-ère) en
stand-by or en attente
stand-by ticket N (*Aviat*) billet *m* stand-by
stand-in ['stændɪn] N remplaçant(e); (*Cine*)
doublure *f*
standing ['stændɪŋ] ADJ debout *inv*; (*permanent*)
permanent(e); (*rule*) immuable; (*army*) de
métier; (*grievance*) constant(e), de longue date
  ▶ N réputation *f*, rang *m*, standing *m*; (*duration*):

of 6 months' ~ qui dure depuis 6 mois; **of**
many years' ~ qui dure or existe depuis
longtemps; **he was given a ~ ovation** on s'est
levé pour l'acclamer; **it's a ~ joke** c'est un
vieux sujet de plaisanterie; **a man of some ~**
un homme estimé
standing committee N commission
permanente
standing order N (*BRIT: at bank*) virement *m*
automatique, prélèvement *m* bancaire;
standing orders NPL (*Mil*) règlement *m*
standing room N places *fpl* debout
stand-off ['stændɔf] N (*esp US: stalemate*)
impasse *f*
stand-offish [stænd'ɔfɪʃ] ADJ distant(e), froid(e)
standpat ['stændpæt] ADJ (*US*) inflexible, rigide
standpipe ['stændpaɪp] N colonne *f*
d'alimentation
standpoint ['stændpɔɪnt] N point *m* de vue
standstill ['stændstɪl] N: **at a ~** à l'arrêt; (*fig*) au
point mort; **to come to a ~** s'immobiliser,
s'arrêter
stank [stæŋk] PT *of* **stink**
stanza ['stænzə] N strophe *f*; couplet *m*
staple ['steɪpl] N (*for papers*) agrafe *f*; (*chief product*)
produit *m* de base ▶ ADJ (*food, crop, industry etc*) de
base principal(e) ▶ VT agrafer
stapler ['steɪplər] N agrafeuse *f*
star [staːr] N étoile *f*; (*celebrity*) vedette *f* ▶ VI: **to ~**
(in) être la vedette (de) ▶ VT (*Cine*) avoir pour
vedette; **stars** NPL: **the stars** (*Astrology*)
l'horoscope *m*; **4-~ hotel** hôtel *m* 4 étoiles; **2-~**
petrol (*BRIT*) essence *f* ordinaire; **4-~ petrol**
(*BRIT*) super *m*
star attraction N grande attraction
starboard ['staːbəd] N tribord *m*; **to ~** à tribord
starch [staːtʃ] N amidon *m*; (*in food*) fécule *f*
starched [staːtʃt] ADJ (*collar*) amidonné(e),
empesé(e)
starchy ['staːtʃɪ] ADJ riche en féculents;
(*person*) guindé(e)
stardom ['staːdəm] N célébrité *f*
stare [stɛər] N regard *m* fixe ▶ VI: **to ~ at** regarder
fixement
starfish ['staːfɪʃ] N étoile *f* de mer
stark [staːk] ADJ (*bleak*) désolé(e), morne;
(*simplicity, colour*) austère; (*reality, poverty*) nu(e)
  ▶ ADV: **~ naked** complètement nu(e)
starkers ['staːkəz] ADJ: **to be ~** (*BRIT inf*) être à
poil
starlet ['staːlɪt] N (*Cine*) starlette *f*
starlight ['staːlaɪt] N: **by ~** à la lumière des
étoiles
starling ['staːlɪŋ] N étourneau *m*
starlit ['staːlɪt] ADJ étoilé(e); illuminé(e) par les
étoiles
starry ['staːrɪ] ADJ étoilé(e)
starry-eyed [staːrɪ'aɪd] ADJ (*innocent*) ingénu(e)
Stars and Stripes NPL: **the ~** la bannière étoilée
star sign N signe zodiacal or du zodiaque
star-studded ['staːstʌdɪd] ADJ: **a ~ cast** une
distribution prestigieuse
start [staːt] N commencement *m*, début *m*; (*of*
race) départ *m*; (*sudden movement*) sursaut *m*;

(*advantage*) avance *f*, avantage *m* ▶ vt
commencer; (*cause: fight*) déclencher; (*rumour*)
donner naissance à; (*fashion*) lancer; (*found:
business, newspaper*) lancer, créer; (*engine*) mettre
en marche ▶ vi (*begin*) commencer; (*begin
journey*) partir, se mettre en route; (*jump*)
sursauter; **when does the film ~?** à quelle
heure est-ce que le film commence?; **at the ~**
au début; **for a ~** d'abord, pour commencer; **to
make an early ~** partir *or* commencer de bonne
heure; **to ~ doing** *or* **to do sth** se mettre à faire
qch; **to ~ (off) with …** (*firstly*) d'abord …; (*at the
beginning*) au commencement …
  ▶ **start off** vi commencer; (*leave*) partir
  ▶ **start out** vi (*begin*) commencer; (*set out*) partir
  ▶ **start over** vi (US) recommencer
  ▶ **start up** vi commencer; (*car*) démarrer ▶ vt
  (*fight*) déclencher; (*business*) créer; (*car*) mettre
  en marche
starter ['stɑːtəʳ] N (*Aut*) démarreur *m*; (*Sport:
official*) starter *m*; (: *runner, horse*) partant *m*; (Brit
Culin) entrée *f*
starting handle ['stɑːtɪŋ-] N (Brit) manivelle *f*
starting point ['stɑːtɪŋ-] N point *m* de départ
starting price ['stɑːtɪŋ-] N prix initial
startle ['stɑːtl] vt faire sursauter; donner un
choc à
startling ['stɑːtlɪŋ] ADJ surprenant(e),
saisissant(e)
star turn N (Brit) vedette *f*
starvation [stɑːˈveɪʃən] N faim *f*, famine *f*; **to
die of ~** mourir de faim *or* d'inanition
starve [stɑːv] vi mourir de faim ▶ vt laisser
mourir de faim; **I'm starving** je meurs de faim
stash [stæʃ] vt (*inf*): **to ~ sth away** planquer qch
state [steɪt] N état *m*; (*Pol*) État; (*pomp*): **in ~** en
grande pompe ▶ vt (*declare*) déclarer, affirmer;
(*specify*) indiquer, spécifier; **States** NPL: **the
States** les États-Unis; **to be in a ~** être dans
tous ses états; **~ of emergency** état d'urgence;
~ of mind état d'esprit; **the ~ of the art** l'état
actuel de la technologie (*or* des connaissances)
state control N contrôle *m* de l'État
stated ['steɪtɪd] ADJ fixé(e), prescrit(e)
State Department N (US) Département *m*
d'État, ≈ ministère *m* des Affaires étrangères
state education N (Brit) enseignement public
stateless ['steɪtlɪs] ADJ apatride
stately ['steɪtlɪ] ADJ majestueux(-euse),
imposant(e)
stately home N manoir *m* *or* château *m* (*ouvert au
public*)
statement ['steɪtmənt] N déclaration *f*; (*Law*)
déposition *f*; (*Econ*) relevé *m*; **official ~**
communiqué officiel; **~ of account**, **bank ~**
relevé de compte
state-owned ['steɪtəund] ADJ étatisé(e)
States [steɪts] NPL: **the ~** les États-Unis *mpl*
state school N école publique
statesman ['steɪtsmən] N (*irreg*) homme *m*
d'État
statesmanship ['steɪtsmənʃɪp] N qualités *fpl*
d'homme d'État
static ['stætɪk] N (*Radio*) parasites *mpl*; (*also:*

static electricity) électricité *f* statique ▶ ADJ
statique
station ['steɪʃən] N gare *f*; (*also:* **police station**)
poste *m* *or* commissariat *m* (de police); (*Mil*)
poste *m* (militaire); (*rank*) condition *f*, rang *m*
▶ vt placer, poster; **action stations** postes de
combat; **to be stationed in** (*Mil*) être en
garnison à
stationary ['steɪʃnərɪ] ADJ à l'arrêt, immobile
stationer ['steɪʃənəʳ] N papetier(-ière)
stationer's (shop) N (Brit) papeterie *f*
stationery ['steɪʃnərɪ] N papier *m* à lettres, petit
matériel de bureau
station wagon N (US) break *m*
statistic [stəˈtɪstɪk] N statistique *f*
statistical [stəˈtɪstɪkl] ADJ statistique
statistics [stəˈtɪstɪks] N (*science*) statistique *f*
statue ['stætjuː] N statue *f*
statuesque [stætjuˈɛsk] ADJ sculptural(e)
statuette [stætjuˈɛt] N statuette *f*
stature ['stætʃəʳ] N stature *f*; (*fig*) envergure *f*
status ['steɪtəs] N position *f*, situation *f*;
(*prestige*) prestige *m*; (*Admin, official position*)
statut *m*
status quo [-ˈkwəu] N: **the ~** le statu quo
status symbol N marque *f* de standing, signe
extérieur de richesse
statute ['stætjuːt] N loi *f*; **statutes** NPL (*of club
etc*) statuts *mpl*
statute book N ≈ code *m*, textes *mpl* de loi
statutory ['stætjutrɪ] ADJ statutaire, prévu(e)
par un article de loi; **~ meeting** assemblée
constitutive *or* statutaire
staunch [stɔːntʃ] ADJ sûr(e), loyal(e) ▶ vt
étancher
stave [steɪv] N (*Mus*) portée *f* ▶ vt: **to ~ off**
(*attack*) parer; (*threat*) conjurer
stay [steɪ] N (*period of time*) séjour *m*; (*Law*): **~ of
execution** sursis *m* à statuer ▶ vi rester; (*reside*)
loger; (*spend some time*) séjourner; **to ~ put** ne
pas bouger; **to ~ with friends** loger chez des
amis; **to ~ the night** passer la nuit
  ▶ **stay away** vi (*from person, building*) ne pas
  s'approcher; (*from event*) ne pas venir
  ▶ **stay behind** vi rester en arrière
  ▶ **stay in** vi (*at home*) rester à la maison
  ▶ **stay on** vi rester
  ▶ **stay out** vi (*of house*) ne pas rentrer; (*strikers*)
  rester en grève
  ▶ **stay up** vi (*at night*) ne pas se coucher
staying power ['steɪɪŋ-] N endurance *f*
STD N ABBR (= *sexually transmitted disease*) MST *f*;
(Brit: = *subscriber trunk dialling*) l'automatique *m*
stead [stɛd] N (Brit): **in sb's ~** à la place de qn;
to stand sb in good ~ être très utile *or* servir
beaucoup à qn
steadfast ['stɛdfɑːst] ADJ ferme, résolu(e)
steadily ['stɛdɪlɪ] ADV (*regularly*)
progressivement; (*firmly*) fermement; (*walk*)
d'un pas ferme; (*fixedly: look*) sans détourner les
yeux
steady ['stɛdɪ] ADJ stable, solide, ferme; (*regular*)
constant(e), régulier(-ière); (*person*) calme,
pondéré(e) ▶ vt assurer, stabiliser; (*nerves*)

calmer; (*voice*) assurer; **a ~ boyfriend** un petit ami; **to ~ oneself** reprendre son aplomb

steak [steɪk] N (*meat*) bifteck *m*, steak *m*; (*fish, pork*) tranche *f*

steakhouse ['steɪkhaʊs] N ≈ grill-room *m*

steal [sti:l] (*pt* **stole** [stəʊl], *pp* **stolen** ['stəʊln]) VT, VI voler; (*move*) se faufiler, se déplacer furtivement; **my wallet has been stolen** on m'a volé mon portefeuille
▶ **steal away, steal off** VI s'esquiver

stealth [stɛlθ] N: **by ~** furtivement

stealthy ['stɛlθɪ] ADJ furtif(-ive)

steam [sti:m] N vapeur *f* ▶ VT passer à la vapeur; (*Culin*) cuire à la vapeur ▶ VI fumer; (*ship*): **to ~ along** filer; **under one's own ~** (*fig*) par ses propres moyens; **to run out of ~** (*fig: person*) caler; être à bout; **to let off ~** (*fig: inf*) se défouler
▶ **steam up** VI (*window*) se couvrir de buée; **to get steamed up about sth** (*fig: inf*) s'exciter à propos de qch

steam engine N locomotive *f* à vapeur

steamer ['sti:mə^r] N (bateau *m* à) vapeur *m*; (*Culin*) ≈ couscoussier *m*

steam iron N fer *m* à repasser à vapeur

steamroller ['sti:mrəʊlə^r] N rouleau compresseur

steamship ['sti:mʃɪp] N = **steamer**

steamy ['sti:mɪ] ADJ humide; (*window*) embué(e); (*sexy*) torride

steed [sti:d] N (*literary*) coursier *m*

steel [sti:l] N acier *m* ▶ CPD d'acier

steel band N steel band *m*

steel industry N sidérurgie *f*

steel mill N aciérie *f*, usine *f* sidérurgique

steelworks ['sti:lwə:ks] N aciérie *f*

steely ['sti:lɪ] ADJ (*determination*) inflexible; (*eyes, gaze*) d'acier

steep [sti:p] ADJ raide, escarpé(e); (*price*) très élevé(e), excessif(-ive) ▶ VT (faire) tremper

steeple ['sti:pl] N clocher *m*

steeplechase ['sti:pltʃeɪs] N steeple(-chase) *m*

steeplejack ['sti:pldʒæk] N réparateur *m* de clochers et de hautes cheminées

steeply ['sti:plɪ] ADV en pente raide

steer [stɪə^r] N bœuf *m* ▶ VT diriger; (*boat*) gouverner; (*lead: person*) guider, conduire ▶ VI tenir le gouvernail; **to ~ clear of sb/sth** (*fig*) éviter qn/qch

steering ['stɪərɪŋ] N (*Aut*) conduite *f*

steering column N (*Aut*) colonne *f* de direction

steering committee N comité *m* d'organisation

steering wheel N volant *m*

stellar ['stɛlə^r] ADJ stellaire

stem [stɛm] N (*of plant*) tige *f*; (*of leaf, fruit*) queue *f*; (*of glass*) pied *m* ▶ VT contenir, endiguer; (*attack, spread of disease*) juguler
▶ **stem from** VT FUS provenir de, découler de

stem cell N cellule *f* souche

stench [stɛntʃ] N puanteur *f*

stencil ['stɛnsl] N stencil *m*; pochoir *m* ▶ VT polycopier

stenographer [stɛ'nɔgrəfə^r] N (US) sténographe *mf*

stenography [stɛ'nɔgrəfɪ] N (US) sténo(graphie) *f*

step [stɛp] N pas *m*; (*stair*) marche *f*; (*action*) mesure *f*, disposition *f* ▶ VI: **to ~ forward/back** faire un pas en avant/arrière, avancer/reculer; **steps** NPL (*Brit*) = **stepladder**; **~ by ~** pas à pas; (*fig*) petit à petit; **to be in/out of ~ (with)** (*fig*) aller dans le sens (de)/être déphasé(e) (par rapport à)
▶ **step down** VI (*fig*) se retirer, se désister
▶ **step in** VI (*fig*) intervenir
▶ **step off** VT FUS descendre de
▶ **step over** VT FUS enjamber
▶ **step up** VT (*production, sales*) augmenter; (*campaign, efforts*) intensifier

step aerobics® NPL step® *m*

stepbrother ['stɛpbrʌðə^r] N demi-frère *m*

stepchild ['stɛptʃaɪld] (*pl* **stepchildren** ['stɛptʃɪldrən]) N beau-fils *m*, belle-fille *f*

stepdaughter ['stɛpdɔ:tə^r] N belle-fille *f*

stepfather ['stɛpfɑ:ðə^r] N beau-père *m*

stepladder ['stɛplædə^r] N (*Brit*) escabeau *m*

stepmother ['stɛpmʌðə^r] N belle-mère *f*

stepping stone ['stɛpɪŋ-] N pierre *f* de gué; (*fig*) tremplin *m*

stepsister ['stɛpsɪstə^r] N demi-sœur *f*

stepson ['stɛpsʌn] N beau-fils *m*

stereo ['stɛrɪəʊ] N (*sound*) stéréo *f*; (*hi-fi*) chaîne *f* stéréo ▶ ADJ (*also*: **stereophonic**) stéréo(phonique); **in ~** en stéréo

stereotype ['stɪərɪətaɪp] N stéréotype *m* ▶ VT stéréotyper

sterile ['stɛraɪl] ADJ stérile

sterility [stɛ'rɪlɪtɪ] N stérilité *f*

sterilization [stɛrɪlaɪ'zeɪʃən] N stérilisation *f*

sterilize ['stɛrɪlaɪz] VT stériliser

sterling ['stə:lɪŋ] ADJ sterling *inv*; (*silver*) de bon aloi, fin(e); (*fig*) à toute épreuve, excellent(e) ▶ N (*currency*) livre *f* sterling *inv*; **a pound ~** une livre sterling

sterling area N zone *f* sterling *inv*

stern [stə:n] ADJ sévère ▶ N (*Naut*) arrière *m*, poupe *f*

sternum ['stə:nəm] N sternum *m*

steroid ['stɪərɔɪd] N stéroïde *m*

stethoscope ['stɛθəskəʊp] N stéthoscope *m*

stevedore ['sti:vədɔ:^r] N docker *m*, débardeur *m*

stew [stju:] N ragoût *m* ▶ VT, VI cuire à la casserole; **stewed tea** thé trop infusé; **stewed fruit** fruits cuits *or* en compote

steward ['stju:əd] N (*Aviat, Naut, Rail*) steward *m*; (*in club etc*) intendant *m*; (*also*: **shop steward**) délégué syndical

stewardess ['stju:ədɛs] N hôtesse *f*

stewardship ['stju:ədʃɪp] N intendance *f*

stewing steak ['stju:ɪŋ-], (US) **stew meat** N bœuf *m* à braiser

St. Ex. ABBR = **stock exchange**

stg ABBR = **sterling**

stick [stɪk] (*pt, pp* **stuck** [stʌk]) N bâton *m*; (*for walking*) canne *f*; (*of chalk etc*) morceau *m* ▶ VT (*glue*) coller; (*thrust*): **to ~ sth into** piquer *or* planter *or* enfoncer qch dans; (*inf: put*) mettre, fourrer; (: *tolerate*) supporter ▶ VI (*adhere*) tenir,

805

coller; (*remain*) rester; (*get jammed: door, lift*) se
bloquer; **to get hold of the wrong end of the
~** (BRIT *fig*) comprendre de travers; **to ~ to** (*one's
promise*) s'en tenir à; (*principles*) rester fidèle à
▶ **stick around** VI (*inf*) rester (dans les parages)
▶ **stick out** VI dépasser, sortir ▶ VT: **to ~ it out**
(*inf*) tenir le coup
▶ **stick up** VI dépasser, sortir
▶ **stick up for** VT FUS défendre

sticker ['stɪkəʳ] N auto-collant *m*
sticking plaster ['stɪkɪŋ-] N sparadrap *m*,
pansement adhésif
sticking point ['stɪkɪŋ-] N (*fig*) point *m* de
friction
stick insect N phasme *m*
stickleback ['stɪklbæk] N épinoche *f*
stickler ['stɪkləʳ] N: **to be a ~ for** être
pointilleux(-euse) sur
stick shift N (US Aut) levier *m* de vitesses
stick-up ['stɪkʌp] N (*inf*) braquage *m*, hold-up *m*
sticky ['stɪkɪ] ADJ poisseux(-euse), (*label*)
adhésif(-ive); (*fig: situation*) délicat(e)
stiff [stɪf] ADJ (*gen*) raide, rigide; (*door, brush*)
dur(e), (*difficult*) difficile, ardu(e); (*cold*) froid(e),
distant(e); (*strong, high*) fort(e), élevé(e) ▶ ADV: **to
be bored/scared/frozen ~** s'ennuyer à mourir/
être mort(e) de peur/froid; **to be** *or* **feel ~**
(*person*) avoir des courbatures; **to have a ~ back**
avoir mal au dos; **~ upper lip** (BRIT *fig*) flegme *m*
(*typiquement britannique*)
stiffen ['stɪfn] VT raidir, renforcer ▶ VI se raidir;
se durcir
stiff neck N torticolis *m*
stiffness ['stɪfnɪs] N raideur *f*
stifle ['staɪfl] VT étouffer, réprimer
stifling ['staɪflɪŋ] ADJ (*heat*) suffocant(e)
stigma ['stɪɡmə] (*pl Bot, Med, Rel* **stigmata**
[stɪɡ'mɑːtə], *fig* **stigmas**) N stigmate *m*
stile [staɪl] N échalier *m*
stiletto [stɪ'lɛtəu] N (BRIT: *also:* **stiletto heel**)
talon *m* aiguille
still [stɪl] ADJ (*motionless*) immobile; (*calm*) calme,
tranquille; (BRIT: *mineral water etc*) non
gazeux(-euse) ▶ ADV (*up to this time*) encore,
toujours; (*even*) encore; (*nonetheless*) quand
même, tout de même ▶ N (*Cine*) photo *f*; **to
stand ~** rester immobile, ne pas bouger; **keep
~!** ne bouge pas!; **he ~ hasn't arrived** il n'est
pas encore arrivé, il n'est toujours pas arrivé
stillborn ['stɪlbɔːn] ADJ mort-né(e)
still life N nature morte
stilt [stɪlt] N échasse *f*; (*pile*) pilotis *m*
stilted ['stɪltɪd] ADJ guindé(e), emprunté(e)
stimulant ['stɪmjulənt] N stimulant *m*
stimulate ['stɪmjuleɪt] VT stimuler
stimulating ['stɪmjuleɪtɪŋ] ADJ stimulant(e)
stimulation [stɪmju'leɪʃən] N stimulation *f*
stimulus ['stɪmjuləs] (*pl* **stimuli** ['stɪmjulaɪ]) N
stimulant *m*; (*Biol, Psych*) stimulus *m*
sting [stɪŋ] (*pt, pp* **stung** [stʌŋ]) N piqûre *f*;
(*organ*) dard *m*; (*inf: confidence trick*) arnaque *m*
▶ VT, VI piquer; **my eyes are stinging** j'ai les
yeux qui piquent
stingy ['stɪndʒɪ] ADJ avare, pingre, chiche

stink [stɪŋk] (*pt* **stank** [stæŋk], *pp* **stunk** [stʌŋk])
N puanteur *f* ▶ VI puer, empester
stinker ['stɪŋkəʳ] N (*inf: problem, exam*) vacherie *f*;
(*person*) dégueulasse *mf*
stinking ['stɪŋkɪŋ] ADJ (*fig: inf*) infect(e); **~ rich**
bourré(e) de pognon
stint [stɪnt] N part *f* de travail ▶ VI: **to ~ on**
lésiner sur, être chiche de
stipend ['staɪpɛnd] N (*of vicar etc*) traitement *m*
stipendiary [staɪ'pɛndɪərɪ] ADJ: **~ magistrate**
juge *m* de tribunal d'instance
stipulate ['stɪpjuleɪt] VT stipuler
stipulation [stɪpju'leɪʃən] N stipulation *f*,
condition *f*
stir [stəːʳ] N agitation *f*, sensation *f* ▶ VT remuer
▶ VI remuer, bouger; **to give sth a ~** remuer
qch; **to cause a ~** faire sensation
▶ **stir up** VT exciter; (*trouble*) fomenter,
provoquer
stir-fry ['stəːfraɪ] VT faire sauter ▶ N: **vegetable
~** légumes sautés à la poêle
stirring ['stəːrɪŋ] ADJ excitant(e); émouvant(e)
stirrup ['stɪrəp] N étrier *m*
stitch [stɪtʃ] N (*Sewing*) point *m*; (*Knitting*) maille
f; (*Med*) point de suture; (*pain*) point de côté
▶ VT coudre, piquer; (*Med*) suturer
stoat [stəut] N hermine *f* (*avec son pelage d'été*)
stock [stɔk] N réserve *f*, provision *f*; (*Comm*)
stock *m*; (*Agr*) cheptel *m*, bétail *m*; (*Culin*)
bouillon *m*; (*Finance*) valeurs *fpl*, titres *mpl*; (*Rail:
also:* **rolling stock**) matériel roulant; (*descent,
origin*) souche *f* ▶ ADJ (*fig: reply etc*) courant(e),
classique ▶ VT (*have in stock*) avoir, vendre;
well-stocked bien approvisionné(e) *or*
fourni(e); **in ~** en stock, en magasin; **out of ~**
épuisé(e); **to take ~** (*fig*) faire le point; **stocks
and shares** valeurs (mobilières), titres;
government ~ fonds publics
▶ **stock up** VI: **to ~ up (with)** s'approvisionner
(en)
stockade [stɔ'keɪd] N palissade *f*
stockbroker ['stɔkbrəukəʳ] N agent *m* de
change
stock control N (*Comm*) gestion *f* des stocks
stock cube N (BRIT *Culin*) bouillon-cube *m*
stock exchange N Bourse *f* (des valeurs)
stockholder ['stɔkhəuldəʳ] N (US) actionnaire
mf
Stockholm ['stɔkhəum] N Stockholm
stocking ['stɔkɪŋ] N bas *m*
stock-in-trade ['stɔkɪn'treɪd] N (*fig*): **it's his ~**
c'est sa spécialité
stockist ['stɔkɪst] N (BRIT) stockiste *m*
stock market N Bourse *f*, marché financier
stock phrase N cliché *m*
stockpile ['stɔkpaɪl] N stock *m*, réserve *f* ▶ VT
stocker, accumuler
stockroom ['stɔkruːm] N réserve *f*, magasin *m*
stocktaking ['stɔkteɪkɪŋ] N (BRIT *Comm*)
inventaire *m*
stocky ['stɔkɪ] ADJ trapu(e), râblé(e)
stodgy ['stɔdʒɪ] ADJ bourratif(-ive), lourd(e)
stoic ['stəuɪk] N stoïque *mf*
stoical ['stəuɪkl] ADJ stoïque

stoke [stəuk] VT garnir, entretenir; chauffer
stoker ['stəukə'] N (*Rail, Naut etc*) chauffeur *m*
stole [stəul] PT *of* **steal** ▸ N étole *f*
stolen ['stəuln] PP *of* **steal**
stolid ['stɒlɪd] ADJ impassible, flegmatique
stomach ['stʌmək] N estomac *m*; (*abdomen*)
  ventre *m* ▸ VT supporter, digérer
stomachache ['stʌməkeɪk] N mal *m* à l'estomac
  or au ventre
stomach pump N pompe stomacale
stomach ulcer N ulcère *m* à l'estomac
stomp [stɒmp] VI: **to ~ in/out** entrer/sortir d'un
  pas bruyant
stone [stəun] N pierre *f*; (*pebble*) caillou *m*, galet
  m; (*in fruit*) noyau *m*; (*Med*) calcul *m*; (*BRIT:
  weight*) = 6.348 kg; 14 pounds ▸ CPD de *or* en pierre
  ▸ VT (*person*) lancer des pierres sur, lapider;
  (*fruit*) dénoyauter; **within a ~'s throw of the
  station** à deux pas de la gare
Stone Age N: **the ~** l'âge *m* de pierre
stone-cold ['stəun'kəuld] ADJ complètement
  froid(e)
stoned [stəund] ADJ (*inf: drunk*) bourré(e); (: *on
  drugs*) défoncé(e)
stone-deaf ['stəun'dɛf] ADJ sourd(e) comme un
  pot
stonemason ['stəunmeɪsn] N tailleur *m* de
  pierre(s)
stonewall [stəun'wɔ:l] VI faire de l'obstruction
  ▸ VT faire obstruction à
stonework ['stəunwə:k] N maçonnerie *f*
stony ['stəunɪ] ADJ pierreux(-euse),
  rocailleux(-euse)
stood [stud] PT, PP *of* **stand**
stooge [stu:dʒ] N (*inf*) larbin *m*
stool [stu:l] N tabouret *m*
stoop [stu:p] VI (*also*: **have a stoop**) être
  voûté(e); (*bend: also*: **stoop down**) se baisser, se
  courber; (*fig*): **to ~ to sth/doing sth** s'abaisser
  jusqu'à qch/jusqu'à faire qch
stop [stɒp] N arrêt *m*; (*short stay*) halte *f*; (*in
  punctuation*) point *m* ▸ VT arrêter; (*break off*)
  interrompre; (*also*: **put a stop to**) mettre fin à;
  (*prevent*) empêcher ▸ VI s'arrêter; (*rain, noise etc*)
  cesser, s'arrêter; **could you ~ here/at the
  corner?** arrêtez-vous ici/au coin, s'il vous plaît;
  to ~ doing sth cesser *or* arrêter de faire qch; **to
  ~ sb (from) doing sth** empêcher qn de faire
  qch; **to ~ dead** VI s'arrêter net; **~ it!** arrête!
  ▸ **stop by** VI s'arrêter (au passage)
  ▸ **stop off** VI faire une courte halte
  ▸ **stop up** VT (*hole*) boucher
stopcock ['stɒpkɒk] N robinet *m* d'arrêt
stopgap ['stɒpgæp] N (*person*) bouche-trou *m*;
  (*also*: **stopgap measure**) mesure *f* intérimaire
stoplights ['stɒplaɪts] NPL (*Aut*) signaux *mpl* de
  stop, feux *mpl* arrière
stopover ['stɒpəuvə'] N halte *f*; (*Aviat*) escale *f*
stoppage ['stɒpɪdʒ] N arrêt *m*; (*of pay*) retenue *f*;
  (*strike*) arrêt *m* de travail; (*obstruction*)
  obstruction *f*
stopper ['stɒpə'] N bouchon *m*
stop press N nouvelles *fpl* de dernière heure
stopwatch ['stɒpwɒtʃ] N chronomètre *m*

storage ['stɔ:rɪdʒ] N emmagasinage *m*; (*of
  nuclear waste etc*) stockage *m*; (*in house*)
  rangement *m*; (*Comput*) mise *f* en mémoire *or*
  réserve
storage heater N (*BRIT*) radiateur *m* électrique
  par accumulation
store [stɔ:'] N (*stock*) provision *f*, réserve *f*; (*depot*)
  entrepôt *m*; (*BRIT: large shop*) grand magasin;
  (*US: shop*) magasin *m* ▸ VT emmagasiner;
  (*nuclear waste etc*) stocker; (*information*)
  enregistrer; (*in filing system*) classer, ranger;
  (*Comput*) mettre en mémoire; **stores** NPL (*food*)
  provisions; **who knows what is in ~ for us?**
  qui sait ce que l'avenir nous réserve *or* ce qui
  nous attend?; **to set great/little ~ by sth** faire
  grand cas/peu de cas de qch
  ▸ **store up** VT mettre en réserve, emmagasiner
storehouse ['stɔ:haus] N entrepôt *m*
storekeeper ['stɔ:ki:pə'] N (*US*) commerçant(e)
storeroom ['stɔ:ru:m] N réserve *f*, magasin *m*
storey, (*US*) **story** ['stɔ:rɪ] N étage *m*
stork [stɔ:k] N cigogne *f*
storm [stɔ:m] N tempête *f*; (*thunderstorm*) orage
  m ▸ VI (*fig*) fulminer ▸ VT prendre d'assaut
storm cloud N nuage *m* d'orage
storm door N double-porte (extérieure)
stormy ['stɔ:mɪ] ADJ orageux(-euse)
story ['stɔ:rɪ] N histoire *f*; récit *m*; (*Press: article*)
  article *m*; (: *subject*) affaire *f*; (*US*) = **storey**
storybook ['stɔ:rɪbuk] N livre *m* d'histoires *or* de
  contes
storyteller ['stɔ:rɪtelə'] N conteur(-euse)
stout [staut] ADJ (*strong*) solide; (*brave*) intrépide;
  (*fat*) gros(se), corpulent(e) ▸ N bière brune
stove [stəuv] N (*for cooking*) fourneau *m*; (: *small*)
  réchaud *m*; (*for heating*) poêle *m*; **gas/electric ~**
  (*cooker*) cuisinière *f* à gaz/électrique
stow [stəu] VT ranger; cacher
stowaway ['stəuəweɪ] N passager(-ère)
  clandestin(e)
straddle ['strædl] VT enjamber, être à cheval sur
strafe [strɑ:f] VT mitrailler
straggle ['strægl] VI être (*or* marcher) en
  désordre; **straggled along the coast**
  disséminé(e) tout au long de la côte
straggler ['stræglə'] N traînard(e)
straggling ['stræglɪŋ], **straggly** ['stræglɪ] ADJ
  (*hair*) en désordre
straight [streɪt] ADJ droit(e); (*hair*) raide; (*frank*)
  honnête, franc (franche); (*simple*) simple;
  (*Theat: part, play*) sérieux(-euse); (*inf: heterosexual*)
  hétéro *inv* ▸ ADV (tout) droit; (*drink*) sec, sans eau
  ▸ N: **the ~** (*Sport*) la ligne droite; **to put** *or* **get ~**
  mettre en ordre, mettre de l'ordre dans; (*fig*)
  mettre au clair; **let's get this ~** mettons les
  choses au point; **10 ~ wins** 10 victoires
  d'affilée; **to go ~ home** rentrer directement à
  la maison; **~ away, ~ off** (*at once*) tout de suite;
  ~ off, ~ out sans hésiter
straighten ['streɪtn] VT ajuster; (*bed*) arranger
  ▸ **straighten out** VT (*fig*) débrouiller; **to ~
  things out** arranger les choses
  ▸ **straighten up** VI (*stand up*) se redresser; (*tidy*)
  ranger

S

straighteners ['streɪtnəz] NPL (for hair) lisseur m

straight-faced [streɪt'feɪst] ADJ impassible
▶ ADV en gardant son sérieux

straightforward [streɪt'fɔ:wəd] ADJ simple; (frank) honnête, direct(e)

strain [streɪn] N (Tech) tension f; pression f; (physical) effort m; (mental) tension (nerveuse); (Med) entorse f; (streak, trace) tendance f; élément m; (breed: of plants) variété f; (: of animals) race f; (of virus) souche f ▶ VT (stretch) tendre fortement; (fig: resources etc) mettre à rude épreuve, grever; (hurt: back etc) se faire mal à; (filter) passer, filtrer; (vegetables) égoutter ▶ VI peiner, fournir un gros effort; **strains** NPL (Mus) accords mpl, accents mpl; **he's been under a lot of ~** il a traversé des moments difficiles, il est très éprouvé nerveusement

strained [streɪnd] ADJ (muscle) froissé(e); (laugh etc) forcé(e), contraint(e); (relations) tendu(e)

strainer ['streɪnəʳ] N passoire f

strait [streɪt] N (Geo) détroit m; **straits** NPL: **to be in dire straits** (fig) avoir de sérieux ennuis

straitjacket ['streɪtdʒækɪt] N camisole f de force

strait-laced [streɪt'leɪst] ADJ collet monté inv

strand [strænd] N (of thread) fil m, brin m; (of rope) toron m; (of hair) mèche f ▶ VT (boat) échouer

stranded ['strændɪd] ADJ en rade, en plan

strange [streɪndʒ] ADJ (not known) inconnu(e); (odd) étrange, bizarre

strangely ['streɪndʒlɪ] ADV étrangement, bizarrement; see also **enough**

stranger ['streɪndʒəʳ] N (unknown) inconnu(e); (from somewhere else) étranger(-ère); **I'm a ~ here** je ne suis pas d'ici

strangle ['stræŋgl] VT étrangler

stranglehold ['stræŋglhəʊld] N (fig) emprise totale, mainmise f

strangulation [stræŋgjʊ'leɪʃən] N strangulation f

strap [stræp] N lanière f, courroie f, sangle f; (of slip, dress) bretelle f ▶ VT attacher (avec une courroie etc)

straphanging ['stræphæŋɪŋ] N (fait m de) voyager debout (dans le métro etc)

strapless ['stræplɪs] ADJ (bra, dress) sans bretelles

strapped [stræpt] ADJ: **to be ~ for cash** (inf) être à court d'argent

strapping ['stræpɪŋ] ADJ bien découplé(e), costaud(e)

strappy ['stræpɪ] ADJ (dress) à bretelles; (sandals) à lanières

Strasbourg ['stræzbə:g] N Strasbourg

strata ['strɑ:tə] NPL of **stratum**

stratagem ['strætɪdʒəm] N stratagème m

strategic [strə'ti:dʒɪk] ADJ stratégique

strategist ['strætɪdʒɪst] N stratège m

strategy ['strætɪdʒɪ] N stratégie f

stratosphere ['strætəsfɪəʳ] N stratosphère f

stratum ['strɑ:təm] (pl **strata** ['strɑ:tə]) N strate f, couche f

straw [strɔ:] N paille f; **that's the last ~!** ça c'est le comble!

strawberry ['strɔ:bərɪ] N fraise f; (plant) fraisier m

stray [streɪ] ADJ (animal) perdu(e), errant(e); (scattered) isolé(e) ▶ VI s'égarer; **~ bullet** balle perdue

streak [stri:k] N bande f, filet m; (in hair) raie f; (fig: of madness etc): **a ~ of** une or des tendance(s) à ▶ VT zébrer, strier ▶ VI: **to ~ past** passer à toute allure; **to have streaks in one's hair** s'être fait faire des mèches; **a winning/losing ~** une bonne/mauvaise série or période

streaker ['stri:kəʳ] N streaker(-euse)

streaky ['stri:kɪ] ADJ zébré(e), strié(e)

streaky bacon N (BRIT) ~ lard m (maigre)

stream [stri:m] N (brook) ruisseau m; (current) courant m, flot m; (of people) défilé ininterrompu, flot ▶ VT (Scol) répartir par niveau ▶ VI ruisseler; **to ~ in/out** entrer/sortir à flots; **against the ~** à contre courant; **on ~** (new power plant etc) en service

streamer ['stri:məʳ] N serpentin m, banderole f

stream feed N (on photocopier etc) alimentation f en continu

streamline ['stri:mlaɪn] VT donner un profil aérodynamique à; (fig) rationaliser

streamlined ['stri:mlaɪnd] ADJ (Aviat) fuselé(e), profilé(e); (Aut) aérodynamique; (fig) rationalisé(e)

street [stri:t] N rue f; **the back streets** les quartiers pauvres; **to be on the streets** (homeless) être à la rue or sans abri

streetcar ['stri:tkɑ:ʳ] N (US) tramway m

street cred [-krɛd] N (inf): **to have ~** être branché(e)

street lamp N réverbère m

street light N réverbère m

street lighting N éclairage public

street map, street plan N plan m des rues

street market N marché m à ciel ouvert

streetwise ['stri:twaɪz] ADJ (inf) futé(e), réaliste

strength [strɛŋθ] N force f; (of girder, knot etc) solidité f; (of chemical solution) titre m; (of wine) degré m d'alcool; **on the ~ of** en vertu de; **at full ~** au grand complet; **below ~** à effectifs réduits

strengthen ['strɛŋθn] VT renforcer; (muscle) fortifier; (building, Econ) consolider

strenuous ['strɛnjʊəs] ADJ vigoureux(-euse), énergique; (tiring) ardu(e), fatigant(e)

stress [strɛs] N (force, pressure) pression f; (mental strain) tension (nerveuse), stress m; (accent) accent m; (emphasis) insistance f ▶ VT insister sur, souligner; (syllable) accentuer; **to lay great ~ on sth** insister beaucoup sur qch; **to be under ~** être stressé(e)

stressed [strɛst] ADJ (tense) stressé(e); (syllable) accentué(e)

stressful ['strɛsful] ADJ (job) stressant(e)

stretch [strɛtʃ] N (of sand etc) étendue f; (of time) période f ▶ VI s'étirer; (extend): **to ~ to** or **as far as** s'étendre jusqu'à; (be enough: money, food): **to ~ to** aller pour ▶ VT tendre, étirer; (spread) étendre; (fig) pousser (au maximum); **at a ~** d'affilée; **to ~ a muscle** se distendre un

muscle; **to ~ one's legs** se dégourdir les jambes
▶ **stretch out** vɪ s'étendre ▶ vᴛ (*arm etc*) allonger,
tendre; (*to spread*) étendre; **to ~ out for sth**
allonger la main pour prendre qch
stretcher ['strɛtʃəʳ] ɴ brancard *m*, civière *f*
stretcher-bearer ['strɛtʃəbɛərəʳ] ɴ
brancardier *m*
stretch marks ɴᴘʟ (*on skin*) vergetures *fpl*
stretchy ['strɛtʃɪ] ADJ élastique
strewn [struːn] ADJ: **~ with** jonché(e) de
stricken ['strɪkən] ADJ très éprouvé(e);
dévasté(e); (*ship*) très endommagé(e); **~ with**
frappé(e) *or* atteint(e) de
strict [strɪkt] ADJ strict(e); **in ~ confidence** tout
à fait confidentiellement
strictly ['strɪktlɪ] ADV strictement;
~ confidential strictement confidentiel(le);
~ speaking à strictement parler
stridden ['strɪdn] PP of **stride**
stride [straɪd] (*pt* **strode** [strəud], *pp* **stridden**
['strɪdn]) ɴ grand pas, enjambée *f* ▶ vɪ marcher
à grands pas; **to take in one's ~** (*fig: changes etc*)
accepter sans sourciller
strident ['straɪdnt] ADJ strident(e)
strife [straɪf] ɴ conflit *m*, dissensions *fpl*
strike [straɪk] (*pt, pp* **struck** [strʌk]) ɴ grève *f*; (*of
oil etc*) découverte *f*; (*attack*) raid *m* ▶ vᴛ frapper;
(*oil etc*) trouver, découvrir; (*make: agreement, deal*)
conclure ▶ vɪ faire grève; (*attack*) attaquer;
(*clock*) sonner; **to go on** *or* **come out on ~** se
mettre en grève, faire grève; **to ~ a match**
frotter une allumette; **to ~ a balance** (*fig*)
trouver un juste milieu
▶ **strike back** vɪ (*Mil, fig*) contre-attaquer
▶ **strike down** vᴛ (*fig*) terrasser
▶ **strike off** vᴛ (*from list*) rayer; (: *doctor etc*) radier
▶ **strike out** vᴛ rayer
▶ **strike up** vᴛ (*Mus*) se mettre à jouer; **to ~ up a
friendship with** se lier d'amitié avec
strikebreaker ['straɪkbreɪkəʳ] ɴ briseur *m* de
grève
striker ['straɪkəʳ] ɴ gréviste *mf*; (*Sport*) buteur *m*
striking ['straɪkɪŋ] ADJ frappant(e),
saisissant(e); (*attractive*) éblouissant(e)
strimmer® ['strɪməʳ] ɴ (BRIT) coupe-bordures *m*
string [strɪŋ] (*pt, pp* **strung** [strʌŋ]) ɴ ficelle *f*, fil
m; (*row: of beads*) rang *m*; (: *of onions, excuses*)
chapelet *m*; (: *of people, cars*) file *f*; (*Mus*) corde *f*;
(*Comput*) chaîne *f* ▶ vᴛ: **to ~ out** échelonner; **to
~ together** enchaîner; **the strings** ɴᴘʟ (*Mus*) les
instruments *mpl* à cordes; **to pull strings** (*fig*)
faire jouer le piston; **to get a job by pulling
strings** obtenir un emploi en faisant jouer le
piston; **with no strings attached** (*fig*) sans
conditions
string bean ɴ haricot vert
stringed instrument, string instrument ɴ
(*Mus*) instrument *m* à cordes
stringent ['strɪndʒənt] ADJ rigoureux(-euse);
(*need*) impérieux(-euse)
string quartet ɴ quatuor *m* à cordes
strip [strɪp] ɴ bande *f*; (*Sport*) tenue *f* ▶ vᴛ
(*undress*) déshabiller; (*paint*) décaper; (*fig*)
dégarnir, dépouiller; (*also*: **strip down**: *machine*)

démonter ▶ vɪ se déshabiller; **wearing the
Celtic ~** en tenue du Celtic
▶ **strip off** vᴛ (*paint etc*) décaper ▶ vɪ (*person*) se
déshabiller
strip cartoon ɴ bande dessinée
stripe [straɪp] ɴ raie *f*, rayure *f*; (*Mil*) galon *m*
striped ['straɪpt] ADJ rayé(e), à rayures
strip light ɴ (BRIT) (tube *m* au) néon *m*
stripper ['strɪpəʳ] ɴ strip-teaseuse *f*
strip-search ['strɪpsəːtʃ] ɴ fouille corporelle (*en
faisant se déshabiller la personne*) ▶ vᴛ: **to ~ sb**
fouiller qn (*en le faisant se déshabiller*)
striptease ['strɪptiːz] ɴ strip-tease *m*
stripy ['straɪpɪ] ADJ rayé(e)
strive [straɪv] (*pt* **strove** [strəuv], *pp* **striven**
['strɪvn]) vɪ: **to ~ to do/for sth** s'efforcer de
faire/d'obtenir qch
strobe [strəub] ɴ (*also*: **strobe light**)
stroboscope *m*
strode [strəud] PT of **stride**
stroke [strəuk] ɴ coup *m*; (*Med*) attaque *f*;
(*caress*) caresse *f*; (*Swimming: style*) (sorte *f* de)
nage *f*; (*of piston*) course *f* ▶ vᴛ caresser; **at a ~**
d'un (seul) coup; **on the ~ of 5** à 5 heures
sonnantes; **a ~ of luck** un coup de chance; **a 2-~
engine** un moteur à 2 temps
stroll [strəul] ɴ petite promenade ▶ vɪ flâner, se
promener nonchalamment; **to go for a ~** aller
se promener *or* faire un tour
stroller ['strəuləʳ] ɴ (US: *for child*) poussette *f*
strong [strɔŋ] ADJ (*gen*) fort(e); (*healthy*)
vigoureux(-euse); (*heart, nerves*) solide; (*distaste,
desire*) vif (vive); (*drugs, chemicals*) puissant(e)
▶ ADV: **to be going ~** (*company*) marcher bien;
(*person*) être toujours solide; **they are 50 ~** ils
sont au nombre de 50
strong-arm ['strɔŋɑːm] ADJ (*tactics, methods*)
musclé(e)
strongbox ['strɔŋbɔks] ɴ coffre-fort *m*
stronghold ['strɔŋhəuld] ɴ forteresse *f*, fort *m*;
(*fig*) bastion *m*
strongly ['strɔŋlɪ] ADV fortement, avec force;
vigoureusement; solidement; **I feel ~ about it**
c'est une question qui me tient
particulièrement à cœur; (*negatively*) j'y suis
profondément opposé(e)
strongman ['strɔŋmæn] ɴ (*irreg*) hercule *m*,
colosse *m*; (*fig*) homme *m* à poigne
strongroom ['strɔŋruːm] ɴ chambre forte
stroppy ['strɔpɪ] ADJ (BRIT *inf*) contrariant(e),
difficile
strove [strəuv] PT of **strive**
struck [strʌk] PT, PP of **strike**
structural ['strʌktʃrəl] ADJ structural(e); (*Constr*)
de construction; affectant les parties portantes
structurally ['strʌktʃrəlɪ] ADV du point de vue
de la construction
structure ['strʌktʃəʳ] ɴ structure *f*; (*building*)
construction *f*
struggle ['strʌɡl] ɴ lutte *f* ▶ vɪ lutter, se battre;
to have a ~ to do sth avoir beaucoup de mal à
faire qch
strum [strʌm] vᴛ (*guitar*) gratter de
strung [strʌŋ] PT, PP of **string**

S

strut [strʌt] N étai m, support m ▶ VI se pavaner

strychnine ['strɪkniːn] N strychnine f

stub [stʌb] N (of cigarette) bout m, mégot m; (of ticket etc) talon m ▶ VT: **to ~ one's toe (on sth)** se heurter le doigt de pied (contre qch)
▶ **stub out** VT écraser

stubble ['stʌbl] N chaume m; (on chin) barbe f de plusieurs jours

stubborn ['stʌbən] ADJ têtu(e), obstiné(e), opiniâtre

stubby ['stʌbɪ] ADJ trapu(e); gros(se) et court(e)

stucco ['stʌkəu] N stuc m

stuck [stʌk] PT, PP of **stick** ▶ ADJ (jammed) bloqué(e), coincé(e); **to get ~** se bloquer or coincer

stuck-up [stʌk'ʌp] ADJ prétentieux(-euse)

stud [stʌd] N (on boots etc) clou m; (collar stud) bouton m de col; (earring) petite boucle d'oreille; (of horses: also: **stud farm**) écurie f, haras m; (also: **stud horse**) étalon m ▶ VT (fig): **studded with** parsemé(e) or criblé(e) de

student ['stjuːdənt] N étudiant(e) ▶ ADJ (life) estudiantin(e), étudiant(e), d'étudiant; (residence, restaurant) universitaire; (loan, movement) étudiant, universitaire, d'étudiant; **law/medical ~** étudiant en droit/ médecine

student driver N (US) (conducteur(-trice)) débutant(e)

students' union N (BRIT: association) ≈ union f des étudiants; (: building) ≈ foyer m des étudiants

studied ['stʌdɪd] ADJ étudié(e), calculé(e)

studio ['stjuːdɪəu] N studio m, atelier m; (TV etc) studio

studio flat, (US) **studio apartment** N studio m

studious ['stjuːdɪəs] ADJ studieux(-euse), appliqué(e); (studied) étudié(e)

studiously ['stjuːdɪəslɪ] ADV (carefully) soigneusement

study ['stʌdɪ] N étude f; (room) bureau m ▶ VT étudier; (examine) examiner ▶ VI étudier, faire ses études; **to make a ~ of sth** étudier qch, faire une étude de qch; **to ~ for an exam** préparer un examen

stuff [stʌf] N (gen) chose(s) f(pl), truc m; (belongings) affaires fpl, trucs; (substance) substance f ▶ VT rembourrer; (Culin) farcir; (inf: push) fourrer; (animal: for exhibition) empailler; **my nose is stuffed up** j'ai le nez bouché; **get stuffed!** (inf!) va te faire foutre! (!); **stuffed toy** jouet m en peluche

stuffing ['stʌfɪŋ] N bourre f, rembourrage m; (Culin) farce f

stuffy ['stʌfɪ] ADJ (room) mal ventilé(e) or aéré(e); (ideas) vieux jeu inv

stumble ['stʌmbl] VI trébucher; **to ~ across** or **on** (fig) tomber sur

stumbling block ['stʌmblɪŋ-] N pierre f d'achoppement

stump [stʌmp] N souche f; (of limb) moignon m ▶ VT: **to be stumped** sécher, ne pas savoir que répondre

stun [stʌn] VT (blow) étourdir; (news) abasourdir, stupéfier

stung [stʌŋ] PT, PP of **sting**

stunk [stʌŋk] PP of **stink**

stunned [stʌnd] ADJ assommé(e); (fig) sidéré(e)

stunning ['stʌnɪŋ] ADJ (beautiful) étourdissant(e); (news etc) stupéfiant(e)

stunt [stʌnt] N tour m de force; (in film) cascade f, acrobatie f; (publicity) truc m publicitaire; (Aviat) acrobatie f ▶ VT retarder, arrêter

stunted ['stʌntɪd] ADJ rabougri(e)

stuntman ['stʌntmæn] N (irreg) cascadeur m

stupefaction [stjuːpɪ'fækʃən] N stupéfaction f, stupeur f

stupefy ['stjuːpɪfaɪ] VT étourdir; abrutir; (fig) stupéfier

stupendous [stjuː'pɛndəs] ADJ prodigieux(-euse), fantastique

stupid ['stjuːpɪd] ADJ stupide, bête

stupidity [stjuː'pɪdɪtɪ] N stupidité f, bêtise f

stupidly ['stjuːpɪdlɪ] ADV stupidement, bêtement

stupor ['stjuːpər] N stupeur f

sturdy ['stəːdɪ] ADJ (person, plant) robuste, vigoureux(-euse); (object) solide

sturgeon ['stəːdʒən] N esturgeon m

stutter ['stʌtər] N bégaiement m ▶ VI bégayer

sty [staɪ] N (of pigs) porcherie f

stye [staɪ] N (Med) orgelet m

style [staɪl] N style m; (of dress etc) genre m; (distinction) allure f, cachet m, style; (design) modèle m; **in the latest ~** à la dernière mode; **hair ~** coiffure f

stylish ['staɪlɪʃ] ADJ élégant(e), chic inv

stylist ['staɪlɪst] N (hair stylist) coiffeur(-euse); (literary stylist) styliste mf

stylized ['staɪlaɪzd] ADJ stylisé(e)

stylus ['staɪləs] (pl **styli** [-laɪ] or **styluses**) N (of record player) pointe f de lecture

Styrofoam® ['staɪrəfəum] N (US) polystyrène expansé ▶ ADJ en polystyrène

suave [swɑːv] ADJ doucereux(-euse), onctueux(-euse)

sub [sʌb] N ABBR = **submarine**; **subscription**

sub... [sʌb] PREFIX sub..., sous-

subcommittee ['sʌbkəmɪtɪ] N sous-comité m

subconscious [sʌb'kɔnʃəs] ADJ subconscient(e) ▶ N subconscient m

subcontinent [sʌb'kɔntɪnənt] N: **the (Indian) ~** le sous-continent indien

subcontract N [sʌb'kɔntrækt] contrat m de sous-traitance ▶ VT [sʌbkən'trækt] sous-traiter

subcontractor ['sʌbkən'træktər] N sous-traitant m

subdivide [sʌbdɪ'vaɪd] VT subdiviser

subdivision ['sʌbdɪvɪʒən] N subdivision f

subdue [səb'djuː] VT subjuguer, soumettre

subdued [səb'djuːd] ADJ contenu(e), atténué(e); (light) tamisé(e); (person) qui a perdu de son entrain

sub-editor ['sʌb'ɛdɪtər] N (BRIT) secrétaire mf de (la) rédaction

subject N ['sʌbdʒɪkt] sujet m; (Scol) matière f ▶ VT [səb'dʒɛkt]: **to ~** soumettre à; exposer à; **to be ~ to** (law) être soumis(e) à; (disease) être sujet(te) à; **~ to confirmation in writing** sous réserve de confirmation écrite; **to change**

the ~ changer de conversation

subjection [səb'dʒɛkʃən] N soumission f, sujétion f

subjective [səb'dʒɛktɪv] ADJ subjectif(-ive)

subject matter N sujet m; (content) contenu m

sub judice [sʌb'dju:dɪsɪ] ADJ (Law) devant les tribunaux

subjugate ['sʌbdʒugeɪt] VT subjuguer

subjunctive [səb'dʒʌŋktɪv] ADJ subjonctif(-ive) ▶ N subjonctif m

sublet [sʌb'lɛt] VT sous-louer

sublime [sə'blaɪm] ADJ sublime

subliminal [sʌb'lɪmɪnl] ADJ subliminal(e)

submachine gun ['sʌbmə'ʃi:n-] N mitraillette f

submarine [sʌbmə'ri:n] N sous-marin m

submerge [səb'mə:dʒ] VT submerger; immerger ▶ VI plonger

submersion [səb'mə:ʃən] N submersion f; immersion f

submission [səb'mɪʃən] N soumission f; (to committee etc) présentation f

submissive [səb'mɪsɪv] ADJ soumis(e)

submit [səb'mɪt] VT soumettre ▶ VI se soumettre

subnormal [sʌb'nɔ:ml] ADJ au-dessous de la normale; (person) arriéré(e)

subordinate [sə'bɔ:dɪnət] ADJ (junior) subalterne; (Grammar) subordonné(e) ▶ N subordonné(e)

subpoena [səb'pi:nə] (Law) N citation f, assignation f ▶ VT citer or assigner (à comparaître)

subprime ['sʌbpraɪm] ADJ (Finance: borrower, loan) à haut risque; ~ **mortgage** prêt m hypothécaire à haut risque; **the ~ crisis** la crise des subprimes

subroutine [sʌbru:'ti:n] N (Comput) sous-programme m

subscribe [səb'skraɪb] VI cotiser; **to ~ to** (opinion, fund) souscrire à; (newspaper) s'abonner à; être abonné(e) à

subscriber [səb'skraɪbə^r] N (to periodical, telephone) abonné(e)

subscript ['sʌbskrɪpt] N (Typ) indice inférieur

subscription [səb'skrɪpʃən] N (to fund) souscription f; (to magazine etc) abonnement m; (membership dues) cotisation f; **to take out a ~ to** s'abonner à

subsequent ['sʌbsɪkwənt] ADJ ultérieur(e), suivant(e); ~ **to** prep à la suite de

subsequently ['sʌbsɪkwəntlɪ] ADV par la suite

subservient [səb'sə:vɪənt] ADJ obséquieux(-euse)

subside [səb'saɪd] VI (land) s'affaisser; (flood) baisser; (wind, feelings) tomber

subsidence [səb'saɪdns] N affaissement m

subsidiarity [səbsɪdɪ'ærɪtɪ] N (Pol) subsidiarité f

subsidiary [səb'sɪdɪərɪ] ADJ subsidiaire; accessoire; (Brit Scol: subject) complémentaire ▶ N filiale f

subsidize ['sʌbsɪdaɪz] VT subventionner

subsidy ['sʌbsɪdɪ] N subvention f

subsist [səb'sɪst] VI: **to ~ on sth** (arriver à) vivre avec or subsister avec qch

subsistence [səb'sɪstəns] N existence f, subsistance f

subsistence allowance N indemnité f de séjour

subsistence level N niveau m de vie minimum

substance ['sʌbstəns] N substance f; (fig) essentiel m; **a man of** ~ un homme jouissant d'une certaine fortune; **to lack** ~ être plutôt mince (fig)

substance abuse N abus m de substances toxiques

substandard [sʌb'stændəd] ADJ (goods) de qualité inférieure, qui laisse à désirer; (housing) inférieur(e) aux normes requises

substantial [səb'stænʃl] ADJ substantiel(le); (fig) important(e)

substantially [səb'stænʃəlɪ] ADV considérablement; en grande partie

substantiate [səb'stænʃɪeɪt] VT étayer, fournir des preuves à l'appui de

substitute ['sʌbstɪtju:t] N (person) remplaçant(e); (thing) succédané m ▶ VT: **to ~ sth/sb for** substituer qch/qn à, remplacer par qch/qn

substitute teacher N (US) suppléant(e)

substitution [sʌbstɪ'tju:ʃən] N substitution f

subterfuge ['sʌbtəfju:dʒ] N subterfuge m

subterranean [sʌbtə'reɪnɪən] ADJ souterrain(e)

subtitled ['sʌbtaɪtld] ADJ sous-titré(e)

subtitles ['sʌbtaɪtlz] NPL (Cine) sous-titres mpl

subtle ['sʌtl] ADJ subtil(e)

subtlety ['sʌtltɪ] N subtilité f

subtly ['sʌtlɪ] ADV subtilement

subtotal [sʌb'təutl] N total partiel

subtract [səb'trækt] VT soustraire, retrancher

subtraction [səb'trækʃən] N soustraction f

subtropical [sʌb'trɔpɪkl] ADJ subtropical(e)

suburb ['sʌbə:b] N faubourg m; **the suburbs** la banlieue

suburban [sə'bə:bən] ADJ de banlieue, suburbain(e)

suburbia [sə'bə:bɪə] N la banlieue

subvention [səb'vɛnʃən] N (subsidy) subvention f

subversion [səb'və:ʃən] N subversion f

subversive [səb'və:sɪv] ADJ subversif(-ive)

subway ['sʌbweɪ] N (Brit: underpass) passage souterrain; (US: railway) métro m

sub-zero [sʌb'zɪərəu] ADJ au-dessous de zéro

succeed [sək'si:d] VI réussir ▶ VT succéder à; **to ~ in doing** réussir à faire

succeeding [sək'si:dɪŋ] ADJ suivant(e), qui suit (or suivent or suivront etc)

success [sək'sɛs] N succès m; réussite f

successful [sək'sɛsful] ADJ qui a du succès; (candidate) choisi(e), agréé(e); (business) prospère, qui réussit; (attempt) couronné(e) de succès; **to be ~ (in doing)** réussir (à faire)

successfully [sək'sɛsfəlɪ] ADV avec succès

succession [sək'sɛʃən] N succession f; **in ~** successivement; **3 years in ~** 3 ans de suite

successive [sək'sɛsɪv] ADJ successif(-ive); **on 3 ~ days** 3 jours de suite or consécutifs

successor [sək'sɛsə^r] N successeur m

succinct [sək'sɪŋkt] ADJ succinct(e), bref (brève)

S

succulent ['sʌkjulənt] ADJ succulent(e) ▸ N (*Bot*): **succulents** plantes grasses

succumb [sə'kʌm] VI succomber

such [sʌtʃ] ADJ tel (telle); (*of that kind*): ~ **book** un livre de ce genre or pareil, un tel livre; (*so much*): ~ **courage** un tel courage ▸ ADV si; ~ **books** des livres de ce genre or pareils, de tels livres; ~ **a long trip** un si long voyage; ~ **good books** de si bons livres; ~ **a long trip that** un voyage si or tellement long que; ~ **a lot of** tellement or tant de; **making** ~ **a noise that** faisant un tel bruit que or tellement de bruit que; ~ **a long time ago** il y a si or tellement longtemps; ~ **as** (*like*) tel (telle) que, comme; **a noise** ~ **as** to un bruit de nature à; ~ **books as I have** les quelques livres que j'ai; **as** ~ *adv* en tant que tel (telle), à proprement parler

such-and-such ['sʌtʃənsʌtʃ] ADJ tel ou tel (telle ou telle)

suchlike ['sʌtʃlaɪk] PRON (*inf*): **and** ~ et le reste

suck [sʌk] VT sucer; (*breast, bottle*) téter; (*pump, machine*) aspirer

sucker ['sʌkər] N (*Bot, Zool, Tech*) ventouse f; (*inf*) naïf(-ïve), poire f

suckle ['sʌkl] VT allaiter

sucrose ['suːkrəʊz] N saccharose m

suction ['sʌkʃən] N succion f

suction pump N pompe aspirante

Sudan [su'dɑːn] N Soudan m

Sudanese [suːdə'niːz] ADJ soudanais(e) ▸ N Soudanais(e)

sudden ['sʌdn] ADJ soudain(e), subit(e); **all of a** ~ soudain, tout à coup

sudden-death [sʌdn'dɛθ] N: ~ **play-off** *partie supplémentaire pour départager les adversaires*

suddenly ['sʌdnlɪ] ADV brusquement, tout à coup, soudain

sudoku [su'dəʊkuː] N sudoku m

suds [sʌdz] NPL eau savonneuse

sue [suː] VT poursuivre en justice, intenter un procès à ▸ VI: **to** ~ **(for)** intenter un procès (pour); **to** ~ **for divorce** engager une procédure de divorce; **to** ~ **sb for damages** poursuivre qn en dommages-intérêts

suede [sweɪd] N daim m, cuir suédé ▸ CPD de daim

suet ['suɪt] N graisse f de rognon or de bœuf

Suez Canal ['suːɪz-] N canal m de Suez

suffer ['sʌfər] VT souffrir, subir; (*bear*) tolérer, supporter, subir ▸ VI souffrir; **to** ~ **from** (*illness*) souffrir de, avoir; **to** ~ **from the effects of alcohol/a fall** se ressentir des effets de l'alcool/des conséquences d'une chute

sufferance ['sʌfərns] N: **he was only there on** ~ sa présence était seulement tolérée

sufferer ['sʌfərər] N malade mf; victime mf

suffering ['sʌfərɪŋ] N souffrance(s) f(pl)

suffice [sə'faɪs] VI suffire

sufficient [sə'fɪʃənt] ADJ suffisant(e); ~ **money** suffisamment d'argent

sufficiently [sə'fɪʃəntlɪ] ADV suffisamment, assez

suffix ['sʌfɪks] N suffixe m

suffocate ['sʌfəkeɪt] VI suffoquer; étouffer

suffocation [sʌfə'keɪʃən] N suffocation f; (*Med*) asphyxie f

suffrage ['sʌfrɪdʒ] N suffrage m; droit m de suffrage or de vote

suffuse [sə'fjuːz] VT baigner, imprégner; **the room was suffused with light** la pièce baignait dans la lumière or était imprégnée de lumière

sugar ['ʃʊgər] N sucre m ▸ VT sucrer

sugar beet N betterave sucrière

sugar bowl N sucrier m

sugar cane N canne f à sucre

sugar-coated ['ʃʊgə'kəʊtɪd] ADJ dragéifié(e)

sugar lump N morceau m de sucre

sugar refinery N raffinerie f de sucre

sugary ['ʃʊgərɪ] ADJ sucré(e)

suggest [sə'dʒest] VT suggérer, proposer; (*indicate*) sembler indiquer; **what do you** ~ **I do?** que vous me suggérez de faire?

suggestion [sə'dʒestʃən] N suggestion f

suggestive [sə'dʒestɪv] ADJ suggestif(-ive)

suicidal [suɪ'saɪdl] ADJ suicidaire

suicide ['suɪsaɪd] N suicide m; **to commit** ~ se suicider; ~ **bombing** attentat m suicide; *see also* **commit**

suicide bomber N kamikaze mf

suit [suːt] N (*man's*) costume m, complet m; (*woman's*) tailleur m, ensemble m; (*Cards*) couleur f; (*lawsuit*) procès m ▸ VT (*subj: clothes, hairstyle*) aller à; (*be convenient for*) convenir à; (*adapt*): **to** ~ **sth to** adapter or approprier qch à; **to be suited to sth** (*suitable for*) être adapté(e) or approprié(e) à qch; **well suited** (*couple*) faits l'un pour l'autre, très bien assortis; **to bring a** ~ **against sb** intenter un procès contre qn; **to follow** ~ (*fig*) faire de même

suitable ['suːtəbl] ADJ qui convient; approprié(e), adéquat(e); **would tomorrow be** ~? est-ce que demain vous conviendrait?; **we found somebody** ~ nous avons trouvé la personne qu'il nous faut

suitably ['suːtəblɪ] ADV comme il se doit (or se devait *etc*), convenablement

suitcase ['suːtkeɪs] N valise f

suite [swiːt] N (*of rooms, also Mus*) suite f; (*furniture*): **bedroom/dining room** ~ (ensemble m de) chambre f à coucher/salle f à manger; **a three-piece** ~ un salon (canapé et deux fauteuils)

suitor ['suːtər] N soupirant m, prétendant m

sulfate ['sʌlfeɪt] N (*US*) = **sulphate**

sulfur ['sʌlfər] (*US*) N = **sulphur**

sulk [sʌlk] VI bouder

sulky ['sʌlkɪ] ADJ boudeur(-euse), maussade

sullen ['sʌlən] ADJ renfrogné(e), maussade; morne

sulphate, (*US*) **sulfate** ['sʌlfeɪt] N sulfate m; **copper** ~ sulfate de cuivre

sulphur, (*US*) **sulfur** ['sʌlfər] N soufre m

sulphur dioxide N anhydride sulfureux

sulphuric, (*US*) **sulfuric** [sʌl'fjuərɪk] ADJ: ~ **acid** acide m sulfurique

sultan ['sʌltən] N sultan m

sultana [sʌl'tɑːnə] N (*fruit*) raisin (sec) de Smyrne

sultry ['sʌltrɪ] ADJ étouffant(e)
sum [sʌm] N somme f; (Scol etc) calcul m
▸ **sum up** VT résumer; (evaluate rapidly) récapituler ▸ VI résumer
Sumatra [su'mɑ:trə] N Sumatra
summarize ['sʌməraɪz] VT résumer
summary ['sʌmərɪ] N résumé m ▸ ADJ (justice) sommaire
summer ['sʌmə^r] N été m ▸ CPD d'été, estival(e); **in (the)** ~ en été, pendant l'été
summer camp N (US) colonie f de vacances
summer holidays NPL grandes vacances
summerhouse ['sʌməhaʊs] N (in garden) pavillon m
summertime ['sʌmətaɪm] N (season) été m
summer time N (by clock) heure f d'été
summery ['sʌmərɪ] ADJ estival(e); d'été
summing-up [sʌmɪŋ'ʌp] N résumé m, récapitulation f
summit ['sʌmɪt] N sommet m; (also: **summit conference**) (conférence f au) sommet m
summon ['sʌmən] VT appeler, convoquer; **to ~ a witness** citer or assigner un témoin
▸ **summon up** VT rassembler, faire appel à
summons ['sʌmənz] N citation f, assignation f ▸ VT citer, assigner; **to serve a ~ on sb** remettre une assignation à qn
sumo ['su:məʊ] N: ~ **wrestling** sumo m
sump [sʌmp] N (Brit Aut) carter m
sumptuous ['sʌmptjʊəs] ADJ somptueux(-euse)
sun [sʌn] N soleil m; **in the** ~ au soleil; **to catch the** ~ prendre le soleil; **everything under the** ~ absolument tout
Sun. ABBR (= Sunday) dim
sunbathe ['sʌnbeɪð] VI prendre un bain de soleil
sunbeam ['sʌnbi:m] N rayon m de soleil
sunbed ['sʌnbɛd] N lit pliant; (with sun lamp) lit à ultra-violets
sunblock ['sʌnblɔk] N écran m total
sunburn ['sʌnbə:n] N coup m de soleil
sunburned ['sʌnbə:nd], **sunburnt** ['sʌnbə:nt] ADJ bronzé(e), hâlé(e); (painfully) brûlé(e) par le soleil
sun cream N crème f (anti-)solaire
sundae ['sʌndeɪ] N sundae m, coupe glacée
Sunday ['sʌndɪ] N dimanche m; see also **Tuesday**
Sunday paper N journal m du dimanche; voir article

> Les *Sunday papers* sont une véritable institution en Grande-Bretagne. Il y a des *quality Sunday papers* et des *popular Sunday papers*, et la plupart des quotidiens ont un journal du dimanche qui leur est associé, bien que leurs équipes de rédacteurs soient différentes. Les quality Sunday papers ont plusieurs suppléments et magazines; voir *quality press* et *tabloid press*.

Sunday school N ≈ catéchisme m
sundial ['sʌndaɪəl] N cadran m solaire
sundown ['sʌndaʊn] N coucher m du soleil
sundries ['sʌndrɪz] NPL articles divers
sundry ['sʌndrɪ] ADJ divers(e), différent(e); **all and** ~ tout le monde, n'importe qui

sunflower ['sʌnflaʊə^r] N tournesol m
sung [sʌŋ] PP of **sing**
sunglasses ['sʌnglɑ:sɪz] NPL lunettes fpl de soleil
sunk [sʌŋk] PP of **sink**
sunken ['sʌŋkn] ADJ (rock, ship) submergé(e); (cheeks) creux(-euse); (bath) encastré(e)
sunlamp ['sʌnlæmp] N lampe f à rayons ultra-violets
sunlight ['sʌnlaɪt] N (lumière f du) soleil m
sunlit ['sʌnlɪt] ADJ ensoleillé(e)
sun lounger N chaise longue
sunny ['sʌnɪ] ADJ ensoleillé(e); (fig) épanoui(e), radieux(-euse); **it is** ~ il fait (du) soleil, il y a du soleil
sunrise ['sʌnraɪz] N lever m du soleil
sun roof N (Aut) toit ouvrant
sunscreen ['sʌnskri:n] N crème f solaire
sunset ['sʌnsɛt] N coucher m du soleil
sunshade ['sʌnʃeɪd] N (lady's) ombrelle f; (over table) parasol m
sunshine ['sʌnʃaɪn] N (lumière f du) soleil m
sunspot ['sʌnspɔt] N tache f solaire
sunstroke ['sʌnstrəʊk] N insolation f, coup m de soleil
suntan ['sʌntæn] N bronzage m
suntan lotion N lotion f or lait m solaire
suntanned ['sʌntænd] ADJ bronzé(e)
suntan oil N huile f solaire
suntrap ['sʌntræp] N coin très ensoleillé
super ['su:pə^r] ADJ (inf) formidable
superannuation [su:pərænju'eɪʃən] N cotisations fpl pour la pension
superb [su:'pə:b] ADJ superbe, magnifique
Super Bowl N (US Sport) Super Bowl m
supercilious [su:pə'sɪlɪəs] ADJ hautain(e), dédaigneux(-euse)
superconductor [su:pəkən'dʌktə^r] N supraconducteur m
superficial [su:pə'fɪʃəl] ADJ superficiel(le)
superficially [su:pə'fɪʃəlɪ] ADV superficiellement
superfluous [su'pə:flʊəs] ADJ superflu(e)
superglue ['su:pəglu:] N colle forte
superhighway ['su:pəhaɪweɪ] N (US) voie f express (à plusieurs files); **the information** ~ la super-autoroute de l'information
superhuman [su:pə'hju:mən] ADJ surhumain(e)
superimpose ['su:pərɪm'pəʊz] VT superposer
superintend [su:pərɪn'tɛnd] VT surveiller
superintendent [su:pərɪn'tɛndənt] N directeur(-trice); (Police) ≈ commissaire m
superior [su'pɪərɪə^r] ADJ supérieur(e); (Comm: goods, quality) de qualité supérieure; (smug) condescendant(e), méprisant(e) ▸ N supérieur(e); **Mother S~** (Rel) Mère supérieure
superiority [supɪərɪ'ɔrɪtɪ] N supériorité f
superlative [su'pə:lətɪv] ADJ sans pareil(le), suprême ▸ N (Ling) superlatif m
superman ['su:pəmæn] N (irreg) surhomme m
supermarket ['su:pəmɑ:kɪt] N supermarché m
supermodel ['su:pəmɔdl] N top model m
supernatural [su:pə'nætʃərəl] ADJ

813

surnaturel(le) ▶ N: **the** ~ le surnaturel

supernova [su:pə'nəuvə] N supernova f

superpower ['su:pəpauə^r] N (Pol) superpuissance f

supersede [su:pə'si:d] VT remplacer, supplanter

supersonic ['su:pə'sɒnɪk] ADJ supersonique

superstar ['su:pəstɑ:^r] N (Cine etc) superstar f; (Sport) superchampion(ne) ▶ ADJ (status, lifestyle) de superstar

superstition [su:pə'stɪʃən] N superstition f

superstitious [su:pə'stɪʃəs] ADJ superstitieux(-euse)

superstore ['su:pəstɔ:^r] N (BRIT) hypermarché m, grande surface

supertanker ['su:pətæŋkə^r] N pétrolier géant, superpétrolier m

supertax ['su:pətæks] N tranche supérieure de l'impôt

supervise ['su:pəvaɪz] VT (children etc) surveiller; (organization, work) diriger

supervision [su:pə'vɪʒən] N surveillance f; (monitoring) contrôle m; (management) direction f; **under medical** ~ sous contrôle du médecin

supervisor ['su:pəvaɪzə^r] N surveillant(e); (in shop) chef m de rayon; (Scol) directeur(-trice) de thèse

supervisory ['su:pəvaɪzəri] ADJ de surveillance

supine ['su:paɪn] ADJ couché(e) or étendu(e) sur le dos

supper ['sʌpə^r] N dîner m; (late) souper m; **to have** ~ dîner; souper

supplant [sə'plɑ:nt] VT supplanter

supple ['sʌpl] ADJ souple

supplement N ['sʌplɪmənt] supplément m ▶ VT [sʌplɪ'mɛnt] ajouter à, compléter

supplementary [sʌplɪ'mɛntəri] ADJ supplémentaire

supplementary benefit N (BRIT) allocation f supplémentaire d'aide sociale

supplier [sə'plaɪə^r] N fournisseur m

supply [sə'plaɪ] VT (provide) fournir; (equip): **to ~ (with)** approvisionner or ravitailler (en); fournir (en); (system, machine): **to ~ sth (with sth)** alimenter qch (en qch); (a need) répondre à ▶ N provision f, réserve f; (supplying) approvisionnement m; (Tech) alimentation f; **supplies** NPL (food) vivres mpl; (Mil) subsistances fpl; **office supplies** fournitures fpl de bureau; **to be in short** ~ être rare, manquer; **the electricity/water/gas** ~ l'alimentation f en électricité/eau/gaz; ~ **and demand** l'offre f et la demande; **it comes supplied with an adaptor** il (or elle) est pourvu(e) d'un adaptateur

supply teacher N (BRIT) suppléant(e)

support [sə'pɔ:t] N (moral, financial etc) soutien m, appui m; (Tech) support m, soutien ▶ VT soutenir, supporter; (financially) subvenir aux besoins de; (uphold) être pour, être partisan de, appuyer; (Sport: team) être pour; **to ~ o.s.** (financially) gagner sa vie

supporter [sə'pɔ:tə^r] N (Pol etc) partisan(e); (Sport) supporter m

supporting [sə'pɔ:tɪŋ] ADJ (wall) d'appui

supporting role N second rôle m

supportive [sə'pɔ:tɪv] ADJ: **my family were very** ~ ma famille m'a été d'un grand soutien

suppose [sə'pəuz] VT, VI supposer; imaginer; **to be supposed to do/be** être censé(e) faire/être; **I don't** ~ **she'll come** je suppose qu'elle ne viendra pas, cela m'étonnerait qu'elle vienne

supposedly [sə'pəuzɪdlɪ] ADV soi-disant

supposing [sə'pəuzɪŋ] CONJ si, à supposer que + sub

supposition [sʌpə'zɪʃən] N supposition f, hypothèse f

suppository [sə'pɒzɪtrɪ] N suppositoire m

suppress [sə'prɛs] VT (revolt, feeling) réprimer; (information) faire disparaître; (scandal, yawn) étouffer

suppression [sə'prɛʃən] N suppression f, répression f

suppressor [sə'prɛsə^r] N (Elec etc) dispositif m antiparasite

supremacy [su'prɛməsɪ] N suprématie f

supreme [su'pri:m] ADJ suprême

Supreme Court N (US) Cour f suprême

supremo [su'pri:məu] N grand chef

Supt. ABBR (Police) = **superintendent**

surcharge ['sɜ:tʃɑ:dʒ] N surcharge f; (extra tax) surtaxe f

sure [ʃuə^r] ADJ (gen) sûr(e); (definite, convinced) sûr, certain(e) ▶ ADV (US inf): **that's** ~ **pretty, that's** ~ **pretty** c'est drôlement joli(e); ~! (of course) bien sûr!; ~ **enough** effectivement; **I'm not** ~ **how/why/when** je ne sais pas très bien comment/pourquoi/quand; **to be** ~ **of o.s.** être sûr de soi; **to make** ~ **of sth/that** s'assurer de qch/que, vérifier qch/que

sure-fire ['ʃuəfaɪə^r] ADJ (inf) certain(e), infaillible

sure-footed ['ʃuə'futɪd] ADJ au pied sûr

surely ['ʃuəlɪ] ADV sûrement; certainement; ~ **you don't mean that!** vous ne parlez pas sérieusement!

surety ['ʃuərətɪ] N caution f; **to go** or **stand** ~ **for sb** se porter caution pour qn

surf [sɜ:f] N (waves) ressac m ▶ VT: **to** ~ **the Net** surfer sur Internet, surfer sur le Net

surface ['sɜ:fɪs] N surface f ▶ VT (road) poser un revêtement sur ▶ VI remonter à la surface; (fig) faire surface; **on the** ~ (fig) au premier abord; **by** ~ **mail** par voie de terre; (by sea) par voie maritime

surface area N superficie f, aire f

surface mail N courrier m par voie de terre (or maritime)

surface-to-surface ['sɜ:fɪstə'sɜ:fɪs] ADJ (Mil) sol-sol inv

surfboard ['sɜ:fbɔ:d] N planche f de surf

surfeit ['sɜ:fɪt] N: **a** ~ **of** un excès de; une indigestion de

surfer ['sɜ:fə^r] N (in sea) surfeur(-euse); **web** or **Net** ~ internaute mf

surfing ['sɜ:fɪŋ] N (in sea) surf m

surge [sɜ:dʒ] N (of emotion) vague f; (Elec) pointe f de courant ▶ VI déferler; **to** ~ **forward** se précipiter (en avant)

surgeon ['sə:dʒən] N chirurgien m

Surgeon General N (US) chef m du service fédéral de la santé publique

surgery ['sə:dʒrɪ] N chirurgie f; (BRIT: room) cabinet m (de consultation); (also: **surgery hours**) heures fpl de consultation; (of MP etc) permanence f (où le député etc reçoit les électeurs etc); **to undergo ~** être opéré(e)

surgery hours NPL (BRIT) heures fpl de consultation

surgical ['sə:dʒɪkl] ADJ chirurgical(e)

surgical spirit N (BRIT) alcool m à 90°

surly ['sə:lɪ] ADJ revêche, maussade

surmise [sə:'maɪz] VT présumer, conjecturer

surmount [sə:'maunt] VT surmonter

surname ['sə:neɪm] N nom m de famille

surpass [sə:'pɑ:s] VT surpasser, dépasser

surplus ['sə:pləs] N surplus m, excédent m ▶ ADJ en surplus, de trop; (Comm) excédentaire; **it is ~ to our requirements** cela dépasse nos besoins; **~ stock** surplus m

surprise [sə'praɪz] N (gen) surprise f; (astonishment) étonnement m ▶ VT surprendre, étonner; **to take by ~** (person) prendre au dépourvu; (Mil: town, fort) prendre par surprise

surprised [sə'praɪzd] ADJ (look, smile) surpris(e), étonné(e); **to be ~** être surpris

surprising [sə'praɪzɪŋ] ADJ surprenant(e), étonnant(e)

surprisingly [sə'praɪzɪŋlɪ] ADV (easy, helpful) étonnamment, étrangement; **(somewhat) ~, he agreed** curieusement, il a accepté

surrealism [sə'rɪəlɪzəm] N surréalisme m

surrealist [sə'rɪəlɪst] ADJ, N surréaliste (mf)

surrender [sə'rɛndə'] N reddition f, capitulation f ▶ VI se rendre, capituler ▶ VT (claim, right) renoncer à

surrender value N valeur f de rachat

surreptitious [sʌrəp'tɪʃəs] ADJ subreptice, furtif(-ive)

surrogate ['sʌrəgɪt] N (BRIT: substitute) substitut m ▶ ADJ de substitution, de remplacement; **a ~ food** un succédané alimentaire; **~ coffee** ersatz m or succédané m de café

surrogate mother N mère porteuse or de substitution

surround [sə'raund] VT entourer; (Mil etc) encercler

surrounding [sə'raundɪŋ] ADJ environnant(e)

surroundings [sə'raundɪŋz] NPL environs mpl, alentours mpl

surtax ['sə:tæks] N surtaxe f

surveillance [sə:'veɪləns] N surveillance f

survey N ['sə:veɪ] enquête f, étude f; (in house buying etc) inspection f, (rapport m d')expertise f; (of land) levé m; (comprehensive view: of situation etc) vue f d'ensemble ▶ VT [sə:'veɪ] (situation) passer en revue; (examine carefully) inspecter; (building) expertiser; (land) faire le levé de; (look at) embrasser du regard

surveying [sə'veɪɪŋ] N arpentage m

surveyor [sə'veɪə'] N (of building) expert m; (of land) (arpenteur m) géomètre m

survival [sə'vaɪvl] N survie f; (relic) vestige m ▶ CPD (course, kit) de survie

survive [sə'vaɪv] VI survivre; (custom etc) subsister ▶ VT (accident etc) survivre à, réchapper de; (person) survivre à

survivor [sə'vaɪvə'] N survivant(e)

susceptible [sə'sɛptəbl] ADJ: **~ (to)** sensible (à); (disease) prédisposé(e) (à)

suspect ADJ, N ['sʌspɛkt] suspect(e) ▶ VT [səs'pɛkt] soupçonner, suspecter

suspected [səs'pɛktɪd] ADJ: **a ~ terrorist** une personne soupçonnée de terrorisme; **he had a ~ broken arm** il avait une supposée fracture du bras

suspend [səs'pɛnd] VT suspendre

suspended animation [səs'pɛndɪd-] N: **in a state of ~** en hibernation

suspended sentence [səs'pɛndɪd-] N (Law) condamnation f avec sursis

suspender belt [səs'pɛndə-] N (BRIT) porte-jarretelles m inv

suspenders [səs'pɛndəz] NPL (BRIT) jarretelles fpl; (US) bretelles fpl

suspense [səs'pɛns] N attente f, incertitude f; (in film etc) suspense m; **to keep sb in ~** tenir qn en suspens, laisser qn dans l'incertitude

suspension [səs'pɛnʃən] N (gen, Aut) suspension f; (of driving licence) retrait m provisoire

suspension bridge N pont suspendu

suspicion [səs'pɪʃən] N soupçon(s) m(pl); **to be under ~** être considéré(e) comme suspect(e), être suspecté(e); **arrested on ~ of murder** arrêté sur présomption de meurtre

suspicious [səs'pɪʃəs] ADJ (suspecting) soupçonneux(-euse), méfiant(e); (causing suspicion) suspect(e); **to be ~ of or about sb/sth** avoir des doutes à propos de qn/sur qch, trouver qn/qch suspect(e)

suss out [sʌs-] VT (BRIT inf: discover) supputer; (: understand) piger

sustain [səs'teɪn] VT soutenir; supporter; corroborer; (subj: food) nourrir, donner des forces à; (damage) subir; (injury) recevoir

sustainable [səs'teɪnəbl] ADJ (rate, growth) qui peut être maintenu(e); (development) durable

sustained [səs'teɪnd] ADJ (effort) soutenu(e), prolongé(e)

sustenance ['sʌstɪnəns] N nourriture f; moyens mpl de subsistance

suture ['su:tʃə'] N suture f

SUV N ABBR (esp US: = sports utility vehicle) SUV m, véhicule m de loisirs

SW ABBR (= short wave) OC

swab [swɔb] N (Med) tampon m; prélèvement m ▶ VT (Naut: also: **swab down**) nettoyer

swagger ['swægə'] VI plastronner, parader

swallow ['swɔləu] N (bird) hirondelle f; (of food etc) gorgée f ▶ VT avaler; (fig: story) gober
▶ **swallow up** VT engloutir

swam [swæm] PT of **swim**

swamp [swɔmp] N marais m, marécage m ▶ VT submerger

swampy ['swɔmpɪ] ADJ marécageux(-euse)

swan [swɔn] N cygne m

swank [swæŋk] VI (inf) faire de l'épate

S

815

swan song N (*fig*) chant *m* du cygne
swap [swɒp] N échange *m*, troc *m* ▶ VT: **to ~ (for)** échanger (contre), troquer (contre)
SWAPO ['swɑːpəʊ] N ABBR (= *South-West Africa People's Organization*) SWAPO *f*
swarm [swɔːm] N essaim *m* ▶ VI (*bees*) essaimer; (*people*) grouiller; **to be swarming with** grouiller de
swarthy ['swɔːðɪ] ADJ basané(e), bistré(e)
swashbuckling ['swɒʃbʌklɪŋ] ADJ (*film*) de cape et d'épée
swastika ['swɒstɪkə] N croix gammée
SWAT N ABBR (*US*: = *Special Weapons and Tactics*) ≈ CRS *f*
swat [swɒt] VT écraser ▶ N (*BRIT: also*: **fly swat**) tapette *f*
swathe [sweɪð] VT: **to ~ in** (*bandages, blankets*) emmitoufler de
swatter ['swɒtə'] N (*also*: **fly swatter**) tapette *f*
sway [sweɪ] VI se balancer, osciller; tanguer ▶ VT (*influence*) influencer ▶ N (*rule, power*): **~ (over)** emprise *f* (sur); **to hold ~ over sb** avoir de l'emprise sur qn
Swaziland ['swɑːzɪlænd] N Swaziland *m*
swear [sweə'] (*pt* **swore** [swɔː'], *pp* **sworn** [swɔːn]) VT, VI jurer; **to ~ to sth** jurer de qch; **to ~ an oath** prêter serment ▶ **swear in** VT assermenter
swearword ['sweəwəːd] N gros mot, juron *m*
sweat [swɛt] N sueur *f*, transpiration *f* ▶ VI suer; **in a ~** en sueur
sweatband ['swɛtbænd] N (*Sport*) bandeau *m*
sweater ['swɛtə'] N tricot *m*, pull *m*
sweatshirt ['swɛtʃəːt] N sweat-shirt *m*
sweatshop ['swɛtʃɒp] N atelier *m* où les ouvriers sont exploités
sweaty ['swɛtɪ] ADJ en sueur, moite *or* mouillé(e) de sueur
Swede [swiːd] N Suédois(e)
swede [swiːd] N (*BRIT*) rutabaga *m*
Sweden ['swiːdn] N Suède *f*
Swedish ['swiːdɪʃ] ADJ suédois(e) ▶ N (*Ling*) suédois *m*
sweep [swiːp] (*pt, pp* **swept** [swɛpt]) N coup *m* de balai; (*curve*) grande courbe; (*range*) champ *m*; (*also*: **chimney sweep**) ramoneur *m* ▶ VT balayer; (*subj: current*) emporter; (*subj: fashion, craze*) se répandre dans ▶ VI avancer majestueusement *or* rapidement; s'élancer; s'étendre
▶ **sweep away** VT balayer; entraîner; emporter
▶ **sweep past** VI passer majestueusement *or* rapidement
▶ **sweep up** VT, VI balayer
sweeper ['swiːpə'] N (*person*) balayeur *m*; (*machine*) balayeuse *f*; (*Football*) libéro *m*
sweeping ['swiːpɪŋ] ADJ (*gesture*) large; circulaire; (*changes, reforms*) radical(e); **a ~ statement** une généralisation hâtive
sweepstake ['swiːpsteɪk] N sweepstake *m*
sweet [swiːt] N (*BRIT: pudding*) dessert *m*; (*: candy*) bonbon *m* ▶ ADJ doux (douce); (*not savoury*) sucré(e); (*fresh*) frais (fraîche),

pur(e); (*kind*) gentil(le); (*baby*) mignon(ne)
▶ ADV: **to smell ~** sentir bon; **to taste ~** avoir un goût sucré; **~ and sour** adj aigre-doux (douce)
sweetbread ['swiːtbrɛd] N ris *m* de veau
sweetcorn ['swiːtkɔːn] N maïs doux
sweeten ['swiːtn] VT sucrer; (*fig*) adoucir
sweetener ['swiːtnə'] N (*Culin*) édulcorant *m*
sweetheart ['swiːthɑːt] N amoureux(-euse)
sweetly ['swiːtlɪ] ADV (*smile*) gentiment; (*sing, play*) mélodieusement
sweetness ['swiːtnɪs] N douceur *f*; (*of taste*) goût sucré
sweet pea N pois *m* de senteur
sweet potato N patate douce
sweetshop ['swiːtʃɒp] N (*BRIT*) confiserie *f*
sweet tooth N: **to have a ~** aimer les sucreries
swell [swɛl] (*pt* **swelled**, *pp* **swollen** ['swəʊlən] *or* **swelled**) N (*of sea*) houle *f* ▶ ADJ (*US inf: excellent*) chouette ▶ VT (*increase*) grossir, augmenter ▶ VI (*increase*) grossir, augmenter; (*sound*) s'enfler; (*Med: also*: **swell up**) enfler
swelling ['swɛlɪŋ] N (*Med*) enflure *f*; (*: lump*) grosseur *f*
sweltering ['swɛltərɪŋ] ADJ étouffant(e), oppressant(e)
swept [swɛpt] PT, PP *of* **sweep**
swerve [swəːv] VI (*to avoid obstacle*) faire une embardée *or* un écart; (*off the road*) dévier
swift [swɪft] N (*bird*) martinet *m* ▶ ADJ rapide, prompt(e)
swiftly ['swɪftlɪ] ADV rapidement, vite
swiftness ['swɪftnɪs] N rapidité *f*
swig [swɪg] N (*inf: drink*) lampée *f*
swill [swɪl] N pâtée *f* ▶ VT (*also*: **swill out**, **swill down**) laver à grande eau
swim [swɪm] (*pt* **swam** [swæm], *pp* **swum** [swʌm]) N: **to go for a ~** aller nager *or* se baigner ▶ VI nager; (*Sport*) faire de la natation; (*fig: head, room*) tourner ▶ VT traverser (à la nage); (*distance*) faire (à la nage); **to ~ a length** nager une longueur; **to go swimming** aller nager
swimmer ['swɪmə'] N nageur(-euse)
swimming ['swɪmɪŋ] N nage *f*, natation *f*
swimming baths NPL (*BRIT*) piscine *f*
swimming cap N bonnet *m* de bain
swimming costume N (*BRIT*) maillot *m* (de bain)
swimmingly ['swɪmɪŋlɪ] ADV: **to go ~** (*wonderfully*) se dérouler à merveille
swimming pool N piscine *f*
swimming trunks NPL maillot *m* de bain
swimsuit ['swɪmsuːt] N maillot *m* (de bain)
swindle ['swɪndl] N escroquerie *f* ▶ VT escroquer
swindler ['swɪndlə'] N escroc *m*
swine [swaɪn] N (*pl inv*) pourceau *m*, porc *m*; (*inf!*) salaud *m* (!)
swine flu N grippe *f* A
swing [swɪŋ] (*pt, pp* **swung** [swʌŋ]) N (*in playground*) balançoire *f*; (*movement*) balancement *m*, oscillations *fpl*; (*change in opinion etc*) revirement *m*; (*Mus*) swing *m*; rythme *m* ▶ VT balancer, faire osciller; (*also*:

swing round) tourner, faire virer ▸ vɪ se balancer, osciller; (*also*: **swing round**) virer, tourner; **a ~ to the left** (*Pol*) un revirement en faveur de la gauche; **to be in full ~** battre son plein; **to get into the ~ of things** se mettre dans le bain; **the road swings south** la route prend la direction sud

swing bridge N pont tournant

swing door N (*Brit*) porte battante

swingeing ['swɪndʒɪŋ] ADJ (*Brit*) écrasant(e); considérable

swinging ['swɪŋɪŋ] ADJ rythmé(e); entraînant(e); (*fig*) dans le vent; **~ door** (*US*) porte battante

swipe [swaɪp] N grand coup; gifle *f* ▸ VT (*hit*) frapper à toute volée; gifler; (*inf*: *steal*) piquer; (*credit card etc*) faire passer (dans la machine)

swipe card N carte *f* magnétique

swirl [swə:l] N tourbillon *m* ▸ vɪ tourbillonner, tournoyer

swish [swɪʃ] ADJ (*Brit inf*: *smart*) rupin(e) ▸ vɪ (*whip*) siffler; (*skirt, long grass*) bruire

Swiss [swɪs] ADJ suisse ▸ N (*pl inv*) Suisse(-sesse)

Swiss French ADJ suisse romand(e)

Swiss German ADJ suisse-allemand(e)

Swiss roll N gâteau roulé

switch [swɪtʃ] N (*for light, radio etc*) bouton *m*; (*change*) changement *m*, revirement *m* ▸ VT (*change*) changer; (*exchange*) intervertir; (*invert*): **to ~ (round** *or* **over)** changer de place
▸ **switch off** VT éteindre; (*engine, machine*) arrêter; **could you ~ off the light?** pouvez-vous éteindre la lumière?
▸ **switch on** VT allumer; (*engine, machine*) mettre en marche; (*Brit*: *water supply*) ouvrir

switchback ['swɪtʃbæk] N (*Brit*) montagnes *fpl* russes

switchblade ['swɪtʃbleɪd] N (*also*: **switchblade knife**) couteau *m* à cran d'arrêt

switchboard ['swɪtʃbɔ:d] N (*Tel*) standard *m*

switchboard operator N (*Tel*) standardiste *mf*

Switzerland ['swɪtsələnd] N Suisse *f*

swivel ['swɪvl] vɪ (*also*: **swivel round**) pivoter, tourner

swollen ['swəulən] PP of **swell** ▸ ADJ (*ankle etc*) enflé(e)

swoon [swu:n] vɪ se pâmer

swoop [swu:p] N (*by police etc*) rafle *f*, descente *f*; (*of bird etc*) descente *f* en piqué
▸ vɪ (*bird*: *also*: **swoop down**) descendre en piqué, piquer

swop [swɔp] N, VT = **swap**

sword [sɔ:d] N épée *f*

swordfish ['sɔ:dfɪʃ] N espadon *m*

swore [swɔ:ʳ] PT of **swear**

sworn [swɔ:n] PP of **swear** ▸ ADJ (*statement, evidence*) donné(e) sous serment; (*enemy*) juré(e)

swot [swɔt] VT, VI bûcher, potasser

swum [swʌm] PP of **swim**

swung [swʌŋ] PT, PP of **swing**

sycamore ['sɪkəmɔ:ʳ] N sycomore *m*

sycophant ['sɪkəfænt] N flagorneur(-euse)

sycophantic [sɪkə'fæntɪk] ADJ flagorneur(-euse)

Sydney ['sɪdnɪ] N Sydney

syllable ['sɪləbl] N syllabe *f*

syllabus ['sɪləbəs] N programme *m*; **on the ~** au programme

symbol ['sɪmbl] N symbole *m*

symbolic [sɪm'bɔlɪk], **symbolical** [sɪm'bɔlɪkl] ADJ symbolique

symbolism ['sɪmbəlɪzəm] N symbolisme *m*

symbolize ['sɪmbəlaɪz] VT symboliser

symmetrical [sɪ'metrɪkl] ADJ symétrique

symmetry ['sɪmɪtrɪ] N symétrie *f*

sympathetic [sɪmpə'θetɪk] ADJ (*showing pity*) compatissant(e); (*understanding*) bienveillant(e), compréhensif(-ive); **~ towards** bien disposé(e) envers

sympathetically [sɪmpə'θetɪklɪ] ADV avec compassion (*or* bienveillance)

sympathize ['sɪmpəθaɪz] vɪ: **to ~ with sb** plaindre qn; (*in grief*) s'associer à la douleur de qn; **to ~ with sth** comprendre qch

sympathizer ['sɪmpəθaɪzəʳ] N (*Pol*) sympathisant(e)

sympathy ['sɪmpəθɪ] N (*pity*) compassion *f*; **sympathies** NPL (*support*) soutien *m*; **in ~ with** en accord avec; (*strike*) en *or* par solidarité avec; **with our deepest ~** en vous priant d'accepter nos sincères condoléances

symphonic [sɪm'fɔnɪk] ADJ symphonique

symphony ['sɪmfənɪ] N symphonie *f*

symphony orchestra N orchestre *m* symphonique

symposium [sɪm'pəuzɪəm] N symposium *m*

symptom ['sɪmptəm] N symptôme *m*; indice *m*

symptomatic [sɪmptə'mætɪk] ADJ symptomatique

synagogue ['sɪnəgɔg] N synagogue *f*

sync [sɪŋk] N (*inf*): **in/out of ~** bien/mal synchronisé(e); **they're in ~ with each other** (*fig*) le courant passe bien entre eux

synchromesh [sɪŋkrəu'meʃ] N (*Aut*) synchronisation *f*

synchronize ['sɪŋkrənaɪz] VT synchroniser ▸ vɪ: **to ~ with** se produire en même temps que

synchronized swimming ['sɪŋkrənaɪzd-] N natation synchronisée

syncopated ['sɪŋkəpeɪtɪd] ADJ syncopé(e)

syndicate ['sɪndɪkɪt] N syndicat *m*, coopérative *f*; (*Press*) agence *f* de presse

syndrome ['sɪndrəum] N syndrome *m*

synonym ['sɪnənɪm] N synonyme *m*

synonymous [sɪ'nɔnɪməs] ADJ: **~ (with)** synonyme (de)

synopsis [sɪ'nɔpsɪs] (*pl* **synopses** [-si:z]) N résumé *m*, synopsis *mf*

syntax ['sɪntæks] N syntaxe *f*

synthesis ['sɪnθəsɪs] (*pl* **syntheses** [-si:z]) N synthèse *f*

synthesizer ['sɪnθəsaɪzəʳ] N (*Mus*) synthétiseur *m*

synthetic [sɪn'θetɪk] ADJ synthétique ▸ N matière *f* synthétique; **synthetics** NPL textiles artificiels

syphilis ['sɪfɪlɪs] N syphilis *f*

syphon ['saɪfən] N, VB = **siphon**

S

Syria ['sɪrɪə] N Syrie f
Syrian ['sɪrɪən] ADJ syrien(ne) ▶ N Syrien(ne)
syringe [sɪ'rɪndʒ] N seringue f
syrup ['sɪrəp] N sirop m; (BRIT: also: **golden syrup**) mélasse raffinée
syrupy ['sɪrəpɪ] ADJ sirupeux(-euse)

system ['sɪstəm] N système m; (order) méthode f; (Anat) organisme m
systematic [sɪstə'mætɪk] ADJ systématique; méthodique
system disk N (Comput) disque m système
systems analyst N analyste-programmeur mf

Tt

T, t [tiː] N (letter) T, t m; **T for Tommy** T comme Thérèse

TA N ABBR (BRIT) = **Territorial Army**

ta [tɑː] EXCL (BRIT inf) merci!

tab [tæb] N ABBR = **tabulator** ▶ N (loop on coat etc) attache f; (label) étiquette f; (on drinks can etc) languette f; **to keep tabs on** (fig) surveiller

tabby ['tæbɪ] N (also: **tabby cat**) chat(te) tigré(e)

table ['teɪbl] N table f ▶ VT (BRIT: motion etc) présenter; **to lay** or **set the ~** mettre le couvert or la table; **to clear the ~** débarrasser la table; **league ~** (BRIT Football, Rugby) classement m (du championnat); **~ of contents** table des matières

tablecloth ['teɪblklɔθ] N nappe f

table d'hôte [tɑːbl'dəut] ADJ (meal) à prix fixe

table football N baby-foot m

table lamp N lampe décorative or de table

tablemat ['teɪblmæt] N (for plate) napperon m, set m; (for hot dish) dessous-de-plat m inv

table salt N sel fin or de table

tablespoon ['teɪblspuːn] N cuiller f de service; (also: **tablespoonful**: as measurement) cuillerée f à soupe

tablet ['tæblɪt] N (Med) comprimé m; (: for sucking) pastille f; (of stone) plaque f; **~ of soap** (BRIT) savonnette f

table tennis N ping-pong m, tennis m de table

table wine N vin m de table

tabloid ['tæblɔɪd] N (newspaper) quotidien m populaire; voir article

> Le terme tabloid press désigne les journaux populaires de demi-format où l'on trouve beaucoup de photos et qui adoptent un style très concis. Ce type de journaux vise des lecteurs s'intéressant aux faits divers ayant un parfum de scandale; voir quality press.

taboo [tə'buː] ADJ, N tabou (m)

tabulate ['tæbjuleɪt] VT (data, figures) mettre sous forme de table(s)

tabulator ['tæbjuleɪtə'] N tabulateur m

tachograph ['tækəgrɑːf] N tachygraphe m

tachometer [tæ'kɔmɪtə'] N tachymètre m

tacit ['tæsɪt] ADJ tacite

taciturn ['tæsɪtəːn] ADJ taciturne

tack [tæk] N (nail) petit clou; (stitch) point m de bâti; (Naut) bord m, bordée f; (fig) direction f ▶ VT (nail) clouer; (sew) bâtir ▶ VI (Naut) tirer un

or des bord(s); **to change ~** virer de bord; **on the wrong ~** (fig) sur la mauvaise voie; **to ~ sth on to (the end of) sth** (of letter, book) rajouter qch à la fin de qch

tackle ['tækl] N matériel m, équipement m; (for lifting) appareil m de levage; (Football, Rugby) plaquage m ▶ VT (difficulty, animal, burglar) s'attaquer à; (person: challenge) s'expliquer avec; (Football, Rugby) plaquer

tacky ['tækɪ] ADJ collant(e); (paint) pas sec (sèche); (inf: shabby) moche; (pej: poor-quality) minable; (: showing bad taste) ringard(e)

tact [tækt] N tact m

tactful ['tæktful] ADJ plein(e) de tact

tactfully ['tæktfəlɪ] ADV avec tact

tactical ['tæktɪkl] ADJ tactique; **~ error** erreur f de tactique

tactician [tæk'tɪʃən] N tacticien(ne)

tactics ['tæktɪks] N, NPL tactique f

tactless ['tæktlɪs] ADJ qui manque de tact

tactlessly ['tæktlɪslɪ] ADV sans tact

tadpole ['tædpəul] N têtard m

Tadzhikistan [tædʒɪkɪ'stɑːn] N = **Tajikistan**

taffy ['tæfɪ] N (US) (bonbon m au) caramel m

tag [tæg] N étiquette f; **price/name ~** étiquette (portant le prix/le nom)
▶ **tag along** VI suivre

Tahiti [tɑː'hiːtɪ] N Tahiti m

tail [teɪl] N queue f; (of shirt) pan m ▶ VT (follow) suivre, filer; **tails** NPL (suit) habit m; **to turn ~** se sauver à toutes jambes; see also **head**
▶ **tail away, tail off** VI (in size, quality etc) baisser peu à peu

tailback ['teɪlbæk] N (BRIT) bouchon m

tail coat N habit m

tail end N bout m, fin f

tailgate ['teɪlgeɪt] N (Aut) hayon m arrière

tail light N (Aut) feu m arrière

tailor ['teɪlə'] N tailleur m (artisan) ▶ VT: **to ~ sth (to)** adapter qch exactement (à); **~'s (shop)** (boutique f de) tailleur m

tailoring ['teɪlərɪŋ] N (cut) coupe f

tailor-made ['teɪlə'meɪd] ADJ fait(e) sur mesure; (fig) conçu(e) spécialement

tailwind ['teɪlwɪnd] N vent m arrière inv

taint [teɪnt] VT (meat, food) gâter; (fig: reputation) salir

tainted ['teɪntɪd] ADJ (food) gâté(e); (water, air)

infecté(e); (fig) souillé(e)

Taiwan ['taɪ'wɑːn] N Taïwan (no article)

Taiwanese [taɪwə'niːz] ADJ taïwanais(e) ▶ N INV Taïwanais(e)

Tajikistan [tædʒɪkɪ'stɑːn] N Tadjikistan mf

take [teɪk] (pt **took** [tuk], pp **taken** ['teɪkn]) VT prendre; (gain: prize) remporter; (require: effort, courage) demander; (tolerate) accepter, supporter; (hold: passengers etc) contenir; (accompany) emmener, accompagner; (bring, carry) apporter, emporter; (exam) passer, se présenter à; (conduct: meeting) présider ▶ VI (dye, fire etc) prendre ▶ N (Cine) prise f de vues; **to ~ sth from** (drawer etc) prendre qch dans; (person) prendre qch à; **I ~ it that** je suppose que; **I took him for a doctor** je l'ai pris pour un docteur; **to ~ sb's hand** prendre qn par la main; **to ~ for a walk** (child, dog) emmener promener; **to be taken ill** tomber malade; **to ~ it upon o.s. to do sth** prendre sur soi de faire qch; **~ the first (street) on the left** prenez la première à gauche; **it won't ~ long** ça ne prendra pas longtemps; **I was quite taken with her/it** elle/cela m'a beaucoup plu

▶ **take after** VT FUS ressembler à

▶ **take apart** VT démonter

▶ **take away** VT (carry off) emporter; (remove) enlever; (subtract) soustraire ▶ VI: **to ~ away from** diminuer

▶ **take back** VT (return) rendre, rapporter; (one's words) retirer

▶ **take down** VT (building) démolir; (dismantle: scaffolding) démonter; (letter etc) prendre, écrire

▶ **take in** VT (deceive) tromper, rouler; (understand) comprendre, saisir; (include) couvrir, inclure; (lodger) prendre; (orphan, stray dog) recueillir; (dress, waistband) reprendre

▶ **take off** VT (Aviat) décoller ▶ VT (remove) enlever; (imitate) imiter, pasticher

▶ **take on** VT (work) accepter, se charger de; (employee) prendre, embaucher; (opponent) accepter de se battre contre

▶ **take out** VT sortir; (remove) enlever; (invite) sortir avec; (licence) prendre, se procurer; **to ~ sth out of** enlever qch de; (out of drawer etc) prendre qch dans; **don't ~ it out on me!** ne t'en prends pas à moi!; **to ~ sb out to a restaurant** emmener qn au restaurant

▶ **take over** VT (business) reprendre ▶ VI: **to ~ over from sb** prendre la relève de qn

▶ **take to** VT FUS (person) se prendre d'amitié pour; (activity) prendre goût à; **to ~ to doing sth** prendre l'habitude de faire qch

▶ **take up** VT (one's story) reprendre; (dress) raccourcir; (occupy: time, space) prendre, occuper; (engage in: hobby etc) se mettre à; (accept: offer, challenge) accepter; (absorb: liquids) absorber ▶ VI: **to ~ up with sb** se lier d'amitié avec qn

takeaway ['teɪkəweɪ] (BRIT) ADJ (food) à emporter ▶ N (shop, restaurant) ≈ magasin m qui vend des plats à emporter

take-home pay ['teɪkhəum-] N salaire net

taken ['teɪkən] PP of **take**

takeoff ['teɪkɔf] N (Aviat) décollage m

takeout ['teɪkaut] ADJ, N (US) = **takeaway**

takeover ['teɪkəuvər] N (Comm) rachat m

takeover bid N offre publique d'achat, OPA f

takings ['teɪkɪŋz] NPL (Comm) recette f

talc [tælk] N (also: **talcum powder**) talc m

tale [teɪl] N (story) conte m, histoire f; (account) récit m; (pej) histoire; **to tell tales** (fig) rapporter

talent ['tælnt] N talent m, don m

talented ['tæləntɪd] ADJ doué(e), plein(e) de talent

talent scout N découvreur m de vedettes (or joueurs etc)

talisman ['tælɪzmən] N talisman m

talk [tɔːk] N (a speech) causerie f, exposé m; (conversation) discussion f; (interview) entretien m, propos mpl; (gossip) racontars mpl (pej) ▶ VI parler; (chatter) bavarder; **talks** NPL (Pol etc) entretiens mpl; conférence f; **to give a ~** faire un exposé; **to ~ about** parler de; (converse) s'entretenir or parler de; **talking of films, have you seen …?** à propos de films, as-tu vu …?; **to ~ sb out of/into doing** persuader qn de ne pas faire/de faire; **to ~ shop** parler métier or affaires

▶ **talk over** VT discuter (de)

talkative ['tɔːkətɪv] ADJ bavard(e)

talking point ['tɔːkɪŋ-] N sujet m de conversation

talking-to ['tɔːkɪŋtu] N: **to give sb a good ~** passer un savon à qn

talk show N (TV, Radio) émission-débat f

tall [tɔːl] ADJ (person) grand(e); (building, tree) haut(e); **to be 6 feet ~** = mesurer 1 mètre 80; **how ~ are you?** combien mesurez-vous?

tallboy ['tɔːlbɔɪ] N (BRIT) grande commode

tallness ['tɔːlnɪs] N grande taille; hauteur f

tall story N histoire f invraisemblable

tally ['tælɪ] N compte m ▶ VI: **to ~ (with)** correspondre (à); **to keep a ~ of sth** tenir le compte de qch

talon ['tælən] N griffe f; (of eagle) serre f

tambourine [tæmbə'riːn] N tambourin m

tame [teɪm] ADJ apprivoisé(e); (fig: story, style) insipide

Tamil ['tæmɪl] ADJ tamoul(e) or tamil(e) ▶ N Tamoul(e) or Tamil(e); (Ling) tamoul m or tamil m

tamper ['tæmpər] VI: **to ~ with** toucher à (en cachette ou sans permission)

tampon ['tæmpən] N tampon m hygiénique or périodique

tan [tæn] N (also: **suntan**) bronzage m ▶ VT, VI bronzer, brunir ▶ ADJ (colour) marron clair inv; **to get a ~** bronzer

tandem ['tændəm] N tandem m

tandoori [tæn'duərɪ] ADJ tandouri

tang [tæŋ] N odeur (or saveur) piquante

tangent ['tændʒənt] N (Math) tangente f; **to go off at a ~** (fig) partir dans une digression

tangerine [tændʒə'riːn] N mandarine f

tangible ['tændʒəbl] ADJ tangible; **~ assets** biens réels

Tangier [tæn'dʒɪər] N Tanger

tangle ['tæŋgl] N enchevêtrement m ▶ VT enchevêtrer; **to get in(to) a ~** s'emmêler

tango ['tæŋgəʊ] N tango m

tank [tæŋk] N réservoir m; (for processing) cuve f; (for fish) aquarium m; (Mil) char m d'assaut, tank m

tankard ['tæŋkəd] N chope f

tanker ['tæŋkəʳ] N (ship) pétrolier m, tanker m; (truck) camion-citerne m; (Rail) wagon-citerne m

tankini [tæn'kiːnɪ] N tankini m

tanned [tænd] ADJ bronzé(e)

tannin ['tænɪn] N tanin m

tanning ['tænɪŋ] N (of leather) tannage m

Tannoy® ['tænɔɪ] N (BRIT) haut-parleur m; **over the ~** par haut-parleur

tantalizing ['tæntəlaɪzɪŋ] ADJ (smell) extrêmement appétissant(e); (offer) terriblement tentant(e)

tantamount ['tæntəmaunt] ADJ: **~ to** qui équivaut à

tantrum ['tæntrəm] N accès m de colère; **to throw a ~** piquer une colère

Tanzania [tænzə'nɪə] N Tanzanie f

Tanzanian [tænzə'nɪən] ADJ tanzanien(ne) ▶ N Tanzanien(ne)

tap [tæp] N (on sink etc) robinet m; (gentle blow) petite tape ▶ VT frapper or taper légèrement; (resources) exploiter, utiliser; (telephone) mettre sur écoute; **on ~** (beer) en tonneau; (fig: resources) disponible

tap dancing N claquettes fpl

tape [teɪp] N (for tying) ruban m; (also: **magnetic tape**) bande f (magnétique); (cassette) cassette f; (sticky) Scotch® m ▶ VT (record) enregistrer (au magnétoscope or sur cassette); (stick) coller avec du Scotch®; **on ~** (song etc) enregistré(e)

tape deck N platine f d'enregistrement

tape measure N mètre m à ruban

taper ['teɪpəʳ] N cierge m ▶ VI s'effiler

tape recorder N magnétophone m

tapered ['teɪpəd], **tapering** ['teɪpərɪŋ] ADJ fuselé(e), effilé(e)

tapestry ['tæpɪstrɪ] N tapisserie f

tape-worm ['teɪpwɜːm] N ver m solitaire, ténia m

tapioca [tæpɪ'əʊkə] N tapioca m

tappet ['tæpɪt] N (Aut) poussoir m (de soupape)

tar [tɑː] N goudron m; **low-/middle-~ cigarettes** cigarettes fpl à faible/moyenne teneur en goudron

tarantula [tə'ræntjulə] N tarentule f

tardy ['tɑːdɪ] ADJ tardif(-ive)

target ['tɑːgɪt] N cible f; (fig: objective) objectif m; **to be on ~** (project) progresser comme prévu

target practice N exercices mpl de tir (à la cible)

tariff ['tærɪf] N (Comm) tarif m; (taxes) tarif douanier

tarmac ['tɑːmæk] N (BRIT: on road) macadam m; (Aviat) aire f d'envol ▶ VT (BRIT) goudronner

tarnish ['tɑːnɪʃ] VT ternir

tarot ['tærəʊ] N tarot m

tarpaulin [tɑː'pɔːlɪn] N bâche goudronnée

tarragon ['tærəgən] N estragon m

tart [tɑːt] N (Culin) tarte f; (BRIT inf: pej: prostitute) poule f ▶ ADJ (flavour) âpre, aigrelet(te)
▶ **tart up** VT (inf): **to ~ o.s. up** se faire beau (belle); (pej) s'attifer

tartan ['tɑːtn] N tartan m ▶ ADJ écossais(e)

tartar ['tɑːtəʳ] N (on teeth) tartre m

tartar sauce, tartare sauce ['tɑːtə-] N sauce f tartare

task [tɑːsk] N tâche f; **to take to ~** prendre à partie

task force N (Mil, Police) détachement spécial

taskmaster ['tɑːskmɑːstəʳ] N: **he's a hard ~** il est très exigeant dans le travail

Tasmania [tæz'meɪnɪə] N Tasmanie f

tassel ['tæsl] N gland m; pompon m

taste [teɪst] N goût m; (fig: glimpse, idea) idée f, aperçu m ▶ VT goûter ▶ VI: **to ~ of** (fish etc) avoir le or un goût de; **it tastes like fish** ça a un or le goût de poisson, on dirait du poisson; **what does it ~ like?** quel goût ça a?; **you can ~ the garlic (in it)** on sent bien l'ail; **to have a ~ of sth** goûter (à) qch; **can I have a ~?** je peux goûter?; **to have a ~ for sth** aimer qch, avoir un penchant pour qch; **to be in good/bad** or **poor ~** être de bon/mauvais goût

taste bud N papille f

tasteful ['teɪstful] ADJ de bon goût

tastefully ['teɪstfəlɪ] ADV avec goût

tasteless ['teɪstlɪs] ADJ (food) insipide; (remark) de mauvais goût

tasty ['teɪstɪ] ADJ savoureux(-euse), délicieux(-euse)

tattered ['tætəd] ADJ see **tatters**

tatters ['tætəz] NPL: **in ~** (also: **tattered**) en lambeaux

tattoo [tə'tuː] N tatouage m; (spectacle) parade f militaire ▶ VT tatouer

tatty ['tætɪ] ADJ (BRIT inf) défraîchi(e), en piteux état

taught [tɔːt] PT, PP of **teach**

taunt [tɔːnt] N raillerie f ▶ VT railler

Taurus ['tɔːrəs] N le Taureau; **to be ~** être du Taureau

taut [tɔːt] ADJ tendu(e)

tavern ['tævən] N taverne f

tawdry ['tɔːdrɪ] ADJ (d'un mauvais goût) criard

tawny ['tɔːnɪ] ADJ fauve (couleur)

tax [tæks] N (on goods etc) taxe f; (on income) impôts mpl, contributions fpl ▶ VT taxer; imposer; (fig: patience etc) mettre à l'épreuve; **before/after ~** avant/après l'impôt; **free of ~** exonéré(e) d'impôt

taxable ['tæksəbl] ADJ (income) imposable

tax allowance N part f du revenu non imposable, abattement m à la base

taxation [tæk'seɪʃən] N taxation f; impôts mpl, contributions fpl; **system of ~** système fiscal

tax avoidance N évasion fiscale

tax collector N percepteur m

tax disc N (BRIT Aut) vignette f (automobile)

tax evasion N fraude fiscale

tax exemption N exonération fiscale, exemption f d'impôts

tax exile N personne qui s'expatrie pour raisons fiscales

t

tax-free ['tæksfriː] ADJ exempt(e) d'impôts
tax haven N paradis fiscal
taxi ['tæksɪ] N taxi *m* ▸ VI (*Aviat*) rouler (lentement) au sol
taxidermist ['tæksɪdəːmɪst] N empailleur(-euse) (*d'animaux*)
taxi driver N chauffeur *m* de taxi
tax inspector N (BRIT) percepteur *m*
taxi rank, (US) **taxi stand** N station *f* de taxis
tax payer [-peɪəʳ] N contribuable *mf*
tax rebate N ristourne *f* d'impôt
tax relief N dégrèvement *or* allègement fiscal, réduction *f* d'impôt
tax return N déclaration *f* d'impôts *or* de revenus
tax year N année fiscale
TB N ABBR = **tuberculosis**
tbc ABBR = **to be confirmed**
TD N ABBR (US) = **Treasury Department**; (: *Football*) = **touchdown**
tea [tiː] N thé *m*; (BRIT: *snack: for children*) goûter *m*; **high ~** (BRIT) *collation combinant goûter et dîner*
tea bag N sachet *m* de thé
tea break N (BRIT) pause-thé *f*
teacake ['tiːkeɪk] N (BRIT) ≈ petit pain aux raisins
teach [tiːtʃ] (*pt, pp* **taught** [tɔːt]) VT: **to ~ sb sth**, **to ~ sth to sb** apprendre qch à qn; (*in school etc*) enseigner qch à qn ▸ VI enseigner; **it taught him a lesson** (*fig*) ça lui a servi de leçon
teacher ['tiːtʃəʳ] N (*in secondary school*) professeur *m*; (*in primary school*) instituteur(-trice); **French ~** professeur de français
teacher training college N (*for primary schools*) ≈ école normale d'instituteurs; (*for secondary schools*) collège *m* de formation pédagogique (*pour l'enseignement secondaire*)
teaching ['tiːtʃɪŋ] N enseignement *m*
teaching aids NPL supports *mpl* pédagogiques
teaching assistant N aide-éducateur(-trice)
teaching hospital N (BRIT) C.H.U. *m*, centre *m* hospitalo-universitaire
teaching staff N (BRIT) enseignants *mpl*
tea cosy N couvre-théière *m*
teacup ['tiːkʌp] N tasse *f* à thé
teak [tiːk] N teck *m* ▸ ADJ en *or* de teck
tea leaves NPL feuilles *fpl* de thé
team [tiːm] N équipe *f*; (*of animals*) attelage *m*
▸ **team up** VI: **to ~ up (with)** faire équipe (avec)
team games NPL jeux *mpl* d'équipe
teamwork ['tiːmwəːk] N travail *m* d'équipe
tea party N thé *m* (*réception*)
teapot ['tiːpɔt] N théière *f*
tear¹ ['tɪəʳ] N larme *f*; **in tears** en larmes; **to burst into tears** fondre en larmes
tear² [tɛəʳ] (*pt* **tore** [tɔːʳ], *pp* **torn** [tɔːn]) N déchirure *f* ▸ VT déchirer ▸ VI se déchirer; **to ~ to pieces** *or* **to bits** *or* **to shreds** mettre en pièces; (*fig*) démolir
▸ **tear along** VI (*rush*) aller à toute vitesse
▸ **tear apart** VT (*also fig*) déchirer
▸ **tear away** VT: **to ~ o.s. away (from sth)** (*fig*) s'arracher (de qch)
▸ **tear down** VT (*building, statue*) démolir; (*poster, flag*) arracher

▸ **tear off** VT (*sheet of paper etc*) arracher; (*one's clothes*) enlever à toute vitesse
▸ **tear out** VT (*sheet of paper, cheque*) arracher
▸ **tear up** VT (*sheet of paper etc*) déchirer, mettre en morceaux *or* pièces
tearaway ['tɛərəweɪ] N (*inf*) casse-cou *m inv*
teardrop ['tɪədrɔp] N larme *f*
tearful ['tɪəful] ADJ larmoyant(e)
tear gas ['tɪə-] N gaz *m* lacrymogène
tearoom ['tiːruːm] N salon *m* de thé
tease [tiːz] N taquin(e) ▸ VT taquiner; (*unkindly*) tourmenter
tea set N service *m* à thé
teashop ['tiːʃɔp] N (BRIT) salon *m* de thé
teaspoon ['tiːspuːn] N petite cuiller; (*as measurement: also:* **teaspoonful**) ≈ cuillerée *f* à café
tea strainer N passoire *f* (à thé)
teat [tiːt] N tétine *f*
teatime ['tiːtaɪm] N l'heure *f* du thé
tea towel N (BRIT) torchon *m* (à vaisselle)
tea urn N fontaine *f* à thé
tech [tɛk] N ABBR (*inf*) = **technology**; **technical college**
technical ['tɛknɪkl] ADJ technique
technical college N C.E.T. *m*, collège *m* d'enseignement technique
technicality [tɛknɪ'kælɪtɪ] N technicité *f*; (*detail*) détail *m* technique; **on a legal ~** à cause de (*or* grâce à) l'application à la lettre d'une subtilité juridique; pour vice de forme
technically ['tɛknɪklɪ] ADV techniquement; (*strictly speaking*) en théorie, en principe
technician [tɛk'nɪʃən] N technicien(ne)
technique [tɛk'niːk] N technique *f*
techno ['tɛknəu] N (*Mus*) techno *f*
technocrat ['tɛknəkræt] N technocrate *mf*
technological [tɛknə'lɔdʒɪkl] ADJ technologique
technologist [tɛk'nɔlədʒɪst] N technologue *mf*
technology [tɛk'nɔlədʒɪ] N technologie *f*
teddy ['tɛdɪ], **teddy bear** N ours *m* (en peluche)
tedious ['tiːdɪəs] ADJ fastidieux(-euse)
tedium ['tiːdɪəm] N ennui *m*
tee [tiː] N (*Golf*) tee *m*
teem [tiːm] VI: **to ~ (with)** grouiller (de); **it is teeming (with rain)** il pleut à torrents
teen [tiːn] ADJ = **teenage** ▸ N (US) = **teenager**
teenage ['tiːneɪdʒ] ADJ (*fashions etc*) pour jeunes, pour adolescents; (*child*) qui est adolescent(e)
teenager ['tiːneɪdʒəʳ] N adolescent(e)
teens [tiːnz] NPL: **to be in one's ~** être adolescent(e)
tee-shirt ['tiːʃəːt] N = **T-shirt**
teeter ['tiːtəʳ] VI chanceler, vaciller
teeth [tiːθ] NPL of **tooth**
teethe [tiːð] VI percer ses dents
teething ring ['tiːðɪŋ-] N anneau *m* (*pour bébé qui perce ses dents*)
teething troubles ['tiːðɪŋ-] NPL (*fig*) difficultés initiales
teetotal ['tiː'təutl] ADJ (*person*) qui ne boit jamais d'alcool
teetotaller, (US) **teetotaler** ['tiː'təutləʳ] N

personne f qui ne boit jamais d'alcool

TEFL ['tɛfl] N ABBR = **Teaching of English as a Foreign Language**

Teflon® ['tɛflɒn] N Téflon® m

Teheran [tɛə'rɑːn] N Téhéran

tel. ABBR (= telephone) tél

Tel Aviv ['tɛlə'viːv] N Tel Aviv

telecast ['tɛlɪkɑːst] VT télédiffuser, téléviser

telecommunications ['tɛlɪkəmjuːnɪ'keɪʃənz] N télécommunications fpl

teleconferencing ['tɛlɪ'kɒnfərənsɪŋ] N téléconférence(s) f(pl)

telegram ['tɛlɪɡræm] N télégramme m

telegraph ['tɛlɪɡrɑːf] N télégraphe m

telegraphic [tɛlɪ'ɡræfɪk] ADJ télégraphique

telegraph pole N poteau m télégraphique

telegraph wire N fil m télégraphique

telepathic [tɛlɪ'pæθɪk] ADJ télépathique

telepathy [tə'lɛpəθɪ] N télépathie f

telephone ['tɛlɪfəun] N téléphone m ▶ VT (person) téléphoner à; (message) téléphoner; **to have a ~, to be on the ~** (subscriber) avoir le téléphone; **to be on the ~** (be speaking) être au téléphone

telephone book N = **telephone directory**

telephone booth, (BRIT) **telephone box** N cabine f téléphonique

telephone call N appel m téléphonique

telephone directory N annuaire m (du téléphone)

telephone exchange N central m (téléphonique)

telephone number N numéro m de téléphone

telephone operator N téléphoniste mf, standardiste mf

telephone tapping [-tæpɪŋ] N mise f sur écoute

telephonist [tə'lɛfənɪst] N (BRIT) téléphoniste mf

telephoto ['tɛlɪfəutəu] ADJ: **~ lens** téléobjectif m

teleprinter ['tɛlɪprɪntəʳ] N téléscripteur m

telesales ['tɛlɪseɪlz] NPL télévente f

telescope ['tɛlɪskəup] N télescope m ▶ VI se télescoper ▶ VT télescoper

telescopic [tɛlɪ'skɒpɪk] ADJ télescopique; (umbrella) à manche télescopique

Teletext® ['tɛlɪtɛkst] N télétexte m

telethon ['tɛlɪθɒn] N téléthon m

televise ['tɛlɪvaɪz] VT téléviser

television ['tɛlɪvɪʒən] N télévision f; **on ~** à la télévision

television licence N (BRIT) redevance f (de l'audio-visuel)

television programme N (BRIT) émission f de télévision

television set N poste m de télévision, téléviseur m

telex ['tɛlɛks] N télex m ▶ VT (message) envoyer par télex; (person) envoyer un télex à ▶ VI envoyer un télex

tell [tɛl] (pt, pp told [təuld]) VT dire; (relate: story) raconter; (distinguish): **to ~ sth from** distinguer qch de ▶ VI (talk): **to ~ of** parler de; (have effect) se faire sentir, se voir; **to ~ sb to do** dire à qn de faire; **to ~ sb about sth** (place, object etc) parler de qch à qn; (what happened etc) raconter qch à qn; **to ~ the time** (know how to) savoir lire l'heure; **can you ~ me the time?** pourriez-vous me dire l'heure?; **(I) ~ you what, ...** écoute, ...; **I can't ~ them apart** je n'arrive pas à les distinguer

▶ **tell off** VT réprimander, gronder

▶ **tell on** VT FUS (inform against) dénoncer, rapporter contre

teller ['tɛləʳ] N (in bank) caissier(-ière)

telling ['tɛlɪŋ] ADJ (remark, detail) révélateur(-trice)

telltale ['tɛlteɪl] N rapporteur(-euse) ▶ ADJ (sign) éloquent(e), révélateur(-trice)

telly ['tɛlɪ] N ABBR (BRIT inf: = television) télé f

temerity [tə'mɛrɪtɪ] N témérité f

temp [tɛmp] N (BRIT: = temporary worker) intérimaire mf ▶ VI travailler comme intérimaire

temper ['tɛmpəʳ] N (nature) caractère m; (mood) humeur f; (fit of anger) colère f ▶ VT (moderate) tempérer, adoucir; **to be in a ~** être en colère; **to lose one's ~** se mettre en colère; **to keep one's ~** rester calme

temperament ['tɛmprəmənt] N (nature) tempérament m

temperamental [tɛmprə'mɛntl] ADJ capricieux(-euse)

temperance ['tɛmpərns] N modération f; (in drinking) tempérance f

temperate ['tɛmprət] ADJ modéré(e); (climate) tempéré(e)

temperature ['tɛmprətʃəʳ] N température f; **to have** or **run a ~** avoir de la fièvre

temperature chart N (Med) feuille f de température

tempered ['tɛmpəd] ADJ (steel) trempé(e)

tempest ['tɛmpɪst] N tempête f

tempestuous [tɛm'pɛstjuəs] ADJ (fig) orageux(-euse); (: person) passionné(e)

tempi ['tɛmpiː] NPL of **tempo**

template ['tɛmplɪt] N patron m

temple ['tɛmpl] N (building) temple m; (Anat) tempe f

templet ['tɛmplɪt] N = **template**

tempo ['tɛmpəu] (pl tempos or tempi ['tɛmpiː]) N tempo m; (fig: of life etc) rythme m

temporal ['tɛmpərl] ADJ temporel(le)

temporarily ['tɛmpərərɪlɪ] ADV temporairement; provisoirement

temporary ['tɛmpərərɪ] ADJ temporaire, provisoire; (job, worker) temporaire; **~ secretary** (secrétaire f) intérimaire f; **a ~ teacher** un professeur remplaçant or suppléant

temporize ['tɛmpəraɪz] VI atermoyer; transiger

tempt [tɛmpt] VT tenter; **to ~ sb into doing** induire qn à faire; **to be tempted to do sth** être tenté(e) de faire qch

temptation [tɛmp'teɪʃən] N tentation f

tempting ['tɛmptɪŋ] ADJ tentant(e); (food) appétissant(e)

ten [tɛn] NUM dix ▶ N: **tens of thousands** des dizaines fpl de milliers

t

tenable ['tɛnəbl] ADJ défendable
tenacious [tə'neɪʃəs] ADJ tenace
tenacity [tə'næsɪtɪ] N ténacité f
tenancy ['tɛnənsɪ] N location f; état m de
locataire
tenant ['tɛnənt] N locataire mf
tend [tɛnd] VT s'occuper de; (sick etc) soigner
▶ VI: **to ~ to do** avoir tendance à faire; **to ~ to**
(colour) tirer sur
tendency ['tɛndənsɪ] N tendance f
tender ['tɛndə'] ADJ tendre; (delicate) délicat(e);
(sore) sensible; (affectionate) tendre, doux (douce)
▶ N (Comm: offer) soumission f; (money): **legal ~**
cours légal ▶ VT offrir; **to ~ one's resignation**
donner sa démission; **to put in a ~ (for)** faire
une soumission (pour); **to put work out to ~**
(BRIT) mettre un contrat en adjudication
tenderize ['tɛndəraɪz] VT (Culin) attendrir
tenderly ['tɛndəlɪ] ADV tendrement
tenderness ['tɛndənɪs] N tendresse f; (of meat)
tendreté f
tendon ['tɛndən] N tendon m
tenement ['tɛnəmənt] N immeuble m (de
rapport)
Tenerife [tɛnə'riːf] N Ténérife f
tenet ['tɛnət] N principe m
Tenn. ABBR (US) = **Tennessee**
tenner ['tɛnə'] N (BRIT inf) billet m de dix livres
tennis ['tɛnɪs] N tennis m ▶ CPD (club, match,
racket, player) de tennis
tennis ball N balle f de tennis
tennis court N (court m de) tennis m
tennis elbow N (Med) synovite f du coude
tennis match N match m de tennis
tennis player N joueur(-euse) de tennis
tennis racket N raquette f de tennis
tennis shoes NPL (chaussures fpl de) tennis mpl
tenor ['tɛnə'] N (Mus) ténor m; (of speech etc) sens
général
tenpin bowling ['tɛnpɪn-] N (BRIT) bowling m (à
10 quilles)
tense [tɛns] ADJ tendu(e); (person) tendu,
crispé(e) ▶ N (Ling) temps m ▶ VT (tighten: muscles)
tendre
tenseness ['tɛnsnɪs] N tension f
tension ['tɛnʃən] N tension f
tent [tɛnt] N tente f
tentacle ['tɛntəkl] N tentacule m
tentative ['tɛntətɪv] ADJ timide, hésitant(e);
(conclusion) provisoire
tenterhooks ['tɛntəhuks] NPL: **on ~** sur des
charbons ardents
tenth [tɛnθ] NUM dixième
tent peg N piquet m de tente
tent pole N montant m de tente
tenuous ['tɛnjuəs] ADJ ténu(e)
tenure ['tɛnjuə'] N (of property) bail m; (of job)
période f de jouissance; statut m de titulaire
tepid ['tɛpɪd] ADJ tiède
Ter. ABBR = **terrace**
term [təːm] N (limit) terme m; (word) terme, mot
m; (Scol) trimestre m; (Law) session f ▶ VT
appeler; **terms** NPL (conditions) conditions fpl;
(Comm) tarif m; **~ of imprisonment** peine f de

prison; **his ~ of office** la période où il était en
fonction; **in the short/long ~** à court/long
terme; **"easy terms"** (Comm) "facilités de
paiement"; **to come to terms with** (problem)
faire face à; **to be on good terms with** bien
s'entendre avec, être en bons termes avec
terminal ['təːmɪnl] ADJ terminal(e); (disease)
dans sa phase terminale; (patient) incurable
▶ N (Elec) borne f; (for oil, ore etc, also Comput)
terminal m; (also: **air terminal**) aérogare f;
(BRIT: also: **coach terminal**) gare routière
terminally ['təːmɪnlɪ] ADV: **to be ~ ill** être
condamné(e)
terminate ['təːmɪneɪt] VT mettre fin à;
(pregnancy) interrompre ▶ VI: **to ~ in** finir en or
par
termination [təːmɪ'neɪʃən] N fin f; cessation f;
(of contract) résiliation f; **~ of pregnancy** (Med)
interruption f de grossesse
termini ['təːmɪnaɪ] NPL of **terminus**
terminology [təːmɪ'nɔlədʒɪ] N terminologie f
terminus ['təːmɪnəs] (pl **termini** ['təːmɪnaɪ]) N
terminus m inv
termite ['təːmaɪt] N termite m
term paper N (US University) dissertation
trimestrielle
terrace ['tɛrəs] N terrasse f; (BRIT: row of houses)
rangée f de maisons (attenantes les unes aux autres);
the terraces (BRIT Sport) les gradins mpl
terraced ['tɛrəst] ADJ (garden) en terrasses; (in a
row: house) attenant(e) aux maisons voisines
terracotta ['tɛrə'kɔtə] N terre cuite
terrain [tɛ'reɪn] N terrain m (sol)
terrestrial [tɪ'rɛstrɪəl] ADJ terrestre
terrible ['tɛrɪbl] ADJ terrible, atroce; (weather,
work) affreux(-euse), épouvantable
terribly ['tɛrɪblɪ] ADV terriblement; (very badly)
affreusement mal
terrier ['tɛrɪə'] N terrier m (chien)
terrific [tə'rɪfɪk] ADJ (very great) fantastique,
incroyable, terrible; (wonderful) formidable,
sensationnel(le)
terrified ['tɛrɪfaɪd] ADJ terrifié(e); **to be ~ of sth**
avoir très peur de qch
terrify ['tɛrɪfaɪ] VT terrifier
terrifying ['tɛrɪfaɪɪŋ] ADJ terrifiant(e)
territorial [tɛrɪ'tɔːrɪəl] ADJ territorial(e)
territorial waters NPL eaux territoriales
territory ['tɛrɪtərɪ] N territoire m
terror ['tɛrə'] N terreur f
terrorism ['tɛrərɪzəm] N terrorisme m
terrorist ['tɛrərɪst] N terroriste mf
terrorist attack N attentat m terroriste
terrorize ['tɛrəraɪz] VT terroriser
terse [təːs] ADJ (style) concis(e); (reply) laconique
tertiary ['təːʃərɪ] ADJ tertiaire; **~ education**
(BRIT) enseignement m postscolaire
TESL ['tɛsl] N ABBR = **Teaching of English as a
Second Language**
test [tɛst] N (trial, check) essai m; (: of goods in
factory) contrôle m; (of courage etc) épreuve f;
(Med) examen m; (Chem) analyse f; (exam: of
intelligence etc) test m (d'aptitude); (Scol)
interrogation f de contrôle; (also: **driving test**)

(examen du) permis *m* de conduire ▶ VT
essayer; contrôler; mettre à l'épreuve;
examiner; analyser; tester; faire subir une
interrogation à; **to put sth to the ~** mettre qch
à l'épreuve

testament ['tɛstəmənt] N testament *m*; **the
Old/New T~** l'Ancien/le Nouveau Testament

test ban N (*also*: **nuclear test ban**) interdiction *f*
des essais nucléaires

test case N (*Law*) affaire *f* qui fait jurisprudence

testes ['tɛstiːz] NPL testicules *mpl*

test flight N vol *m* d'essai

testicle ['tɛstɪkl] N testicule *m*

testify ['tɛstɪfaɪ] VI (*Law*) témoigner, déposer; **to
~ to sth** (*Law*) attester qch; (*gen*) témoigner de
qch

testimonial [tɛstɪ'məunɪəl] N (*reference*)
recommandation *f*; (*gift*) témoignage *m*
d'estime

testimony ['tɛstɪmənɪ] N (*Law*) témoignage *m*,
déposition *f*

testing ['tɛstɪŋ] ADJ (*situation, period*) difficile

test match N (*Cricket, Rugby*) match
international

testosterone [tɛs'tɔstərəun] N testostérone *f*

test paper N (*Scol*) interrogation écrite

test pilot N pilote *m* d'essai

test tube N éprouvette *f*

test-tube baby ['tɛsttjuːb-] N bébé-
éprouvette *m*

testy ['tɛstɪ] ADJ irritable

tetanus ['tɛtənəs] N tétanos *m*

tetchy ['tɛtʃɪ] ADJ hargneux(-euse)

tether ['tɛðəʳ] VT attacher ▶ N: **at the end of
one's ~** à bout (de patience)

Tex. ABBR (*US*) = **Texas**

text [tɛkst] N texte *m*; (*on mobile phone*) SMS *m inv*,
texto® *m* ▶ VT (*inf*) envoyer un SMS *or* texto® à

textbook ['tɛkstbuk] N manuel *m*

textile ['tɛkstaɪl] N textile *m*

text message N SMS *m inv*, texto® *m*

text messaging [-'mɛsɪdʒɪŋ] N messagerie
textuelle

textual ['tɛkstjuəl] ADJ textuel(le)

texture ['tɛkstʃəʳ] N texture *f*; (*of skin, paper etc*)
grain *m*

TGIF ABBR (*inf*) = **thank God it's Friday**

TGWU N ABBR (*Brit*: = *Transport and General Workers'
Union*) syndicat de transporteurs

Thai [taɪ] ADJ thaïlandais(e) ▶ N Thaïlandais(e);
(*Ling*) thaï *m*

Thailand ['taɪlænd] N Thaïlande *f*

Thames [tɛmz] N: **the (River) ~** la Tamise

than [ðæn, ðən] CONJ que; (*with numerals*): **more
~ 10/once** plus de 10/d'une fois; **I have more/
less ~ you** j'en ai plus/moins que toi; **she has
more apples ~ pears** elle a plus de pommes
que de poires; **it is better to phone ~ to write**
il vaut mieux téléphoner (plutôt) qu'écrire; **she
is older ~ you think** elle est plus âgée que tu le
crois; **no sooner did he leave ~ the phone
rang** il venait de partir quand le téléphone a
sonné

thank [θæŋk] VT remercier, dire merci à;

thanks NPL remerciements *mpl*; **thanks!**
merci!; **~ you (very much)** merci (beaucoup);
~ heavens, ~ God Dieu merci; **thanks to** prep
grâce à

thankful ['θæŋkful] ADJ: **~ (for)**
reconnaissant(e) (de); **~ for/that** (*relieved*)
soulagé(e) de/que

thankfully ['θæŋkfəlɪ] ADV avec
reconnaissance; avec soulagement;
(*fortunately*) heureusement; **~ there were few
victims** il y eut fort heureusement peu de
victimes

thankless ['θæŋklɪs] ADJ ingrat(e)

Thanksgiving (Day) ['θæŋksgɪvɪŋ-] N jour *m*
d'action de grâce

> *Thanksgiving (Day)* est un jour de congé aux
> États-Unis, le quatrième jeudi du mois de
> novembre, commémorant la bonne récolte
> que les Pèlerins venus de Grande-Bretagne
> ont eue en 1621; traditionnellement, c'était
> un jour où l'on remerciait Dieu et où l'on
> organisait un grand festin. Une fête
> semblable, mais qui n'a aucun rapport avec
> les Pères Pèlerins, a lieu au Canada le
> deuxième lundi d'octobre.

━━━ (KEYWORD)

that [ðæt] ADJ (*pl* **those**: *demonstrative*) ce, cet +
vowel or h mute, cette *f*; **that man/woman/book**
cet homme/cette femme/ce livre; (*not this*) cet
homme-là/cette femme-là/ce livre-là; **that
one** celui-là (celle-là)

▶ PRON **1** (*pl* **those**: *demonstrative*) ce; (*not this one*)
cela, ça; (*that one*) celui (celle); **who's that?** qui
est-ce?; **what's that?** qu'est-ce que c'est?; **is
that you?** c'est toi?; **I prefer this to that** je
préfère ceci à cela *or* ça; **that's what he said**
c'est *or* voilà ce qu'il a dit; **will you eat all that?**
tu vas manger tout ça?; **that is (to say)**
c'est-à-dire, à savoir; **at** *or* **with that, he …**
là-dessus, il …; **do it like that** fais-le
comme ça

2 (*relative*: *subject*) qui; (: *object*) que; (: *after prep*)
lequel (laquelle), lesquels (lesquelles) *pl*; **the
book that I read** le livre que j'ai lu; **the books
that are in the library** les livres qui sont dans
la bibliothèque; **all that I have** tout ce que j'ai;
the box that I put it in la boîte dans laquelle je
l'ai mis; **the people that I spoke to** les gens
auxquels *or* à qui j'ai parlé; **not that I know of**
pas à ma connaissance

3 (*relative*: *of time*) où; **the day that he came** le
jour où il est venu

▶ CONJ que; **he thought that I was ill** il pensait
que j'étais malade

▶ ADV (*demonstrative*): **I don't like it that much**
ça ne me plaît pas tant que ça; **I didn't know it
was that bad** je ne savais pas que c'était si *or*
aussi mauvais; **that high** aussi haut; si haut;
it's about that high c'est à peu près de cette
hauteur

thatched [θætʃt] ADJ (*roof*) de chaume;
~ cottage chaumière *f*

Thatcherism ['θætʃərɪzəm] N thatchérisme *m*
thaw [θɔː] N dégel *m* ▶ VI (*ice*) fondre; (*food*) dégeler ▶ VT (*food*) (faire) dégeler; **it's thawing** (*weather*) il dégèle

(KEYWORD)

the [ðiː, ðə] DEF ART **1** (*gen*) le, la *f*, l' + *vowel or h mute*, les *pl* (NB: *à* + *le*(*s*) = **au(x)**; *de* + *le* = **du**; *de* + *les* = **des**); **the boy/girl/ink** le garçon/la fille/l'encre; **the children** les enfants; **the history of the world** l'histoire du monde; **give it to the postman** donne-le au facteur; **to play the piano/flute** jouer du piano/de la flûte
2 (+ *adj to form n*) le, la *f*, l' + *vowel or h mute*, les *pl*; **the rich and the poor** les riches et les pauvres; **to attempt the impossible** tenter l'impossible
3 (*in titles*): **Elizabeth the First** Elisabeth première; **Peter the Great** Pierre le Grand
4 (*in comparisons*): **the more he works, the more he earns** plus il travaille, plus il gagne de l'argent; **the sooner the better** le plus tôt sera le mieux

theatre, (*US*) **theater** ['θɪətə'] N théâtre *m*; (*also*: **lecture theatre**) amphithéâtre *m*, amphi *m* (*inf*); (*Med: also*: **operating theatre**) salle *f* d'opération
theatre-goer, (*US*) **theater-goer** ['θɪətəgəʊə'] N habitué(e) du théâtre
theatrical [θɪ'ætrɪkl] ADJ théâtral(e); **~ company** troupe *f* de théâtre
theft [θeft] N vol *m* (*larcin*)
their [ðɛə'] ADJ leur, leurs *pl*; *see also* **my**
theirs [ðɛəz] PRON le (la) leur, les leurs; **it is ~** c'est à eux; **a friend of ~** un de leurs amis; *see also* **mine¹**
them [ðem, ðəm] PRON (*direct*) les; (*indirect*) leur; (*stressed, after prep*) eux (elles); **I see ~** je les vois; **give ~ the book** donne-leur le livre; **give me a few of ~** donnez m'en quelques uns (*or* quelques unes); *see also* **me**
theme [θiːm] N thème *m*
theme park N parc *m* à thème
theme song N chanson principale
themselves [ðəm'selvz] PL PRON (*reflexive*) se; (*emphatic, after prep*) eux-mêmes (elles-mêmes); **between ~** entre eux (elles); *see also* **oneself**
then [ðen] ADV (*at that time*) alors, à ce moment-là; (*next*) puis, ensuite; (*and also*) et puis ▶ CONJ (*therefore*) alors, dans ce cas ▶ ADJ: **the ~ president** le président d'alors *or* de l'époque; **by ~** (*past*) à ce moment-là; (*future*) d'ici là; **from ~ on** dès lors; **before ~** avant; **until ~** jusqu'à ce moment-là, jusque-là; **and ~ what?** et puis après?; **what do you want me to do ~?** (*afterwards*) que veux-tu que je fasse ensuite?; (*in that case*) bon alors, qu'est-ce que je fais?
theologian [θɪə'ləudʒən] N théologien(ne)
theological [θɪə'lɒdʒɪkl] ADJ théologique
theology [θɪ'ɒlədʒɪ] N théologie *f*
theorem ['θɪərəm] N théorème *m*

theoretical [θɪə'rɛtɪkl] ADJ théorique
theorize ['θɪəraɪz] VI élaborer une théorie; (*pej*) faire des théories
theory ['θɪərɪ] N théorie *f*
therapeutic [θerə'pjuːtɪk] ADJ thérapeutique
therapist ['θerəpɪst] N thérapeute *mf*
therapy ['θerəpɪ] N thérapie *f*

(KEYWORD)

there [ðɛə'] ADV **1**: **there is, there are** il y a; **there are 3 of them** (*people, things*) il y en a 3; **there is no-one here/no bread left** il n'y a personne/il n'y a plus de pain; **there has been an accident** il y a eu un accident
2 (*referring to place*) là, là-bas; **it's there** c'est là(-bas); **in/on/up/down there** là-dedans/là-dessus/là-haut/en bas; **he went there on Friday** il y est allé vendredi; **to go there and back** faire l'aller-retour; **I want that book there** je veux ce livre-là; **there he is!** le voilà!
3: **there, there!** (*esp to child*) allons, allons!

thereabouts ['ðɛərə'bauts] ADV (*place*) par là, près de là; (*amount*) environ, à peu près
thereafter [ðɛər'ɑːftə'] ADV par la suite
thereby ['ðɛəbaɪ] ADV ainsi
therefore ['ðɛəfɔː'] ADV donc, par conséquent
there's [ðɛəz] = **there is**; **there has**
thereupon [ðɛərə'pɒn] ADV (*at that point*) sur ce; (*formal: on that subject*) à ce sujet
thermal ['θəːml] ADJ thermique; **~ paper/printer** papier *m*/imprimante *f* thermique; **~ underwear** sous-vêtements *mpl* en Thermolactyl®
thermodynamics ['θəːmədaɪ'næmɪks] N thermodynamique *f*
thermometer [θə'mɒmɪtə'] N thermomètre *m*
thermonuclear ['θəːməu'njuːklɪə'] ADJ thermonucléaire
Thermos® ['θəːməs] N (*also*: **Thermos flask**) thermos® *mf*
thermostat ['θəːməustæt] N thermostat *m*
thesaurus [θɪ'sɔːrəs] N dictionnaire *m* synonymique
these [ðiːz] PL PRON ceux-ci (celles-ci) ▶ PL ADJ ces; (*not those*): **~ books** ces livres-ci
thesis ['θiːsɪs] (*pl* **theses** ['θiːsiːz]) N thèse *f*
they [ðeɪ] PL PRON ils (elles); (*stressed*) eux (elles); **~ say that ...** (*it is said that*) on dit que ...
they'd [ðeɪd] = **they had**; **they would**
they'll [ðeɪl] = **they shall**; **they will**
they're [ðɛə'] = **they are**
they've [ðeɪv] = **they have**
thick [θɪk] ADJ épais(se); (*crowd*) dense; (*stupid*) bête, borné(e) ▶ N: **in the ~ of** au beau milieu de, en plein cœur de; **it's 20 cm ~** ça a 20 cm d'épaisseur
thicken ['θɪkn] VI s'épaissir ▶ VT (*sauce etc*) épaissir
thicket ['θɪkɪt] N fourré *m*, hallier *m*
thickly ['θɪklɪ] ADV (*spread*) en couche épaisse; (*cut*) en tranches épaisses; **~ populated** à forte densité de population
thickness ['θɪknɪs] N épaisseur *f*

thickset [θɪk'sɛt] ADJ trapu(e), costaud(e)
thick-skinned [θɪk'skɪnd] ADJ (fig) peu sensible
thief [θiːf] (pl **thieves** [θiːvz]) N voleur(-euse)
thieving ['θiːvɪŋ] N vol m (larcin)
thigh [θaɪ] N cuisse f
thighbone ['θaɪbəʊn] N fémur m
thimble ['θɪmbl] N dé m (à coudre)
thin [θɪn] ADJ mince; (skinny) maigre; (soup) peu épais(se); (hair, crowd) clairsemé(e); (fog) léger(-ère) ▶ VT (hair) éclaircir; (also: **thin down**: sauce, paint) délayer ▶ VI (fog) s'éclaircir; (also: **thin out**: crowd) se disperser; **his hair is thinning** il se dégarnit
thing [θɪŋ] N chose f; (object) objet m; (contraption) truc m; **things** NPL (belongings) affaires fpl; **first ~ (in the morning)** à la première heure, tout de suite (le matin); **last ~ (at night), he …** juste avant de se coucher, il …; **the ~ is …** c'est que …; **for one ~** d'abord; **the best ~ would be to** le mieux serait de; **how are things?** comment ça va?; **to have a ~ about** (be obsessed by) être obsédé(e) par; (hate) détester; **poor ~!** le (or la) pauvre!
think [θɪŋk] (pt, pp **thought** [θɔːt]) VI penser, réfléchir ▶ VT penser, croire; (imagine) s'imaginer; **to ~ of** penser à; **what do you ~ of it?** qu'en pensez-vous?; **what did you ~ of them?** qu'avez-vous pensé d'eux?; **to ~ about sth/sb** penser à qch/qn; **I'll ~ about it** je vais y réfléchir; **to ~ of doing** avoir l'idée de faire; **I ~ so/not** je crois or pense que oui/non; **to ~ well of** avoir une haute opinion de; **~ again!** attention, réfléchis bien!; **to ~ aloud** penser tout haut
▶ **think out** VT (plan) bien réfléchir à; (solution) trouver
▶ **think over** VT bien réfléchir à; **I'd like to ~ things over** (offer, suggestion) j'aimerais bien y réfléchir un peu
▶ **think through** VT étudier dans tous les détails
▶ **think up** VT inventer, trouver
thinking ['θɪŋkɪŋ] N: **to my (way of) ~** selon moi
think tank N groupe m de réflexion
thinly ['θɪnlɪ] ADV (cut) en tranches fines; (spread) en couche mince
thinness ['θɪnnɪs] N minceur f; maigreur f
third [θəːd] NUM troisième ▶ N troisième mf; (fraction) tiers m; (Aut) troisième (vitesse) f; (Brit Scol: degree) ≈ licence f avec mention passable; **a ~ of** le tiers de
third-degree burns ['θəːdˌdɪgriː-] NPL brûlures fpl au troisième degré
thirdly ['θəːdlɪ] ADV troisièmement
third party insurance N (Brit) assurance f au tiers
third-rate ['θəːd'reɪt] ADJ de qualité médiocre
Third World N: **the ~** le Tiers-Monde
thirst [θəːst] N soif f
thirsty ['θəːstɪ] ADJ qui a soif, assoiffé(e); (work) qui donne soif; **to be ~** avoir soif
thirteen [θəː'tiːn] NUM treize
thirteenth [θəː'tiːnθ] NUM treizième
thirtieth ['θəːtɪɪθ] NUM trentième

thirty ['θəːtɪ] NUM trente

KEYWORD

this [ðɪs] ADJ (pl **these**: demonstrative) ce, cet + vowel or h mute, cette f; **this man/woman/book** cet homme/cette femme/ce livre; (not that) cet homme-ci/cette femme-ci/ce livre-ci; **this one** celui-ci (celle-ci); **this time** cette fois-ci; **this time last year** l'année dernière à la même époque; **this way** (in this direction) par ici; (in this fashion) de cette façon, ainsi
▶ PRON (pl **these**: demonstrative) ce; (not that one) celui-ci (celle-ci), ceci; **who's this?** qui est-ce?; **what's this?** qu'est-ce que c'est?; **I prefer this to that** je préfère ceci à cela; **they were talking of this and that** ils parlaient de choses et d'autres; **this is where I live** c'est ici que j'habite; **this is what he said** voici ce qu'il a dit; **this is Mr Brown** (in introductions) je vous présente Mr Brown; (in photo) c'est Mr Brown; (on telephone) ici Mr Brown
▶ ADV (demonstrative): **it was about this big** c'était à peu près de cette grandeur or grand comme ça; **I didn't know it was this bad** je ne savais pas que c'était si or aussi mauvais

thistle ['θɪsl] N chardon m
thong [θɒŋ] N lanière f
thorn [θɔːn] N épine f
thorny ['θɔːnɪ] ADJ épineux(-euse)
thorough ['θʌrə] ADJ (search) minutieux(-euse); (knowledge, research) approfondi(e); (work, person) consciencieux(-euse); (cleaning) à fond
thoroughbred ['θʌrəbrɛd] N (horse) pur-sang m inv
thoroughfare ['θʌrəfɛər] N rue f; **"no ~"** (Brit) "passage interdit"
thoroughgoing ['θʌrəgəʊɪŋ] ADJ (analysis) approfondi(e); (reform) profond(e)
thoroughly ['θʌrəlɪ] ADV (search) minutieusement; (study) en profondeur; (clean) à fond; (very) tout à fait; **he ~ agreed** il était tout à fait d'accord
thoroughness ['θʌrənɪs] N soin (méticuleux)
those [ðəʊz] PL PRON ceux-là (celles-là) ▶ PL ADJ ces; (not these): **~ books** ces livres-là
though [ðəʊ] CONJ bien que + sub, quoique + sub ▶ ADV pourtant; **even ~** quand bien même + cond; **it's not easy, ~** pourtant, ce n'est pas facile
thought [θɔːt] PT, PP of **think** ▶ N pensée f; (idea) idée f; (opinion) avis m; (intention) intention f; **after much ~** après mûre réflexion; **I've just had a ~** je viens de penser à quelque chose; **to give sth some ~** réfléchir à qch
thoughtful ['θɔːtful] ADJ (deep in thought) pensif(-ive); (serious) réfléchi(e); (considerate) prévenant(e)
thoughtfully ['θɔːtfəlɪ] ADV pensivement; avec prévenance
thoughtless ['θɔːtlɪs] ADJ qui manque de considération
thoughtlessly ['θɔːtlɪslɪ] ADV inconsidérément
thought-provoking ['θɔːtprəvəʊkɪŋ] ADJ stimulant(e)

t

thousand ['θauzənd] NUM mille; **one ~** mille; **two ~** deux mille; **thousands of** des milliers de
thousandth ['θauzəntθ] NUM millième
thrash [θræʃ] VT rouer de coups; (inf: defeat) donner une raclée à (inf)
▸ **thrash about** VI se débattre
▸ **thrash out** VT débattre de
thrashing ['θræʃɪŋ] N (inf) raclée f (inf)
thread [θred] N fil m; (of screw) pas m, filetage m
▸ VT (needle) enfiler; **to ~ one's way between** se faufiler entre
threadbare ['θredbɛəʳ] ADJ râpé(e), élimé(e)
threat [θret] N menace f; **to be under ~ of** être menacé(e) de
threaten ['θretn] VI (storm) menacer ▸ VT: **to ~ sb with sth/to do** menacer qn de qch/de faire
threatening ['θretnɪŋ] ADJ menaçant(e)
three [θri:] NUM trois
three-dimensional [θri:dɪ'mɛnʃənl] ADJ à trois dimensions; (film) en relief
threefold ['θri:fəuld] ADV: **to increase ~** tripler
three-piece suit ['θri:pi:s-] N complet m (avec gilet)
three-piece suite [θri:pi:s-] N salon m (canapé et deux fauteuils)
three-ply [θri:'plaɪ] ADJ (wood) à trois épaisseurs; (wool) trois fils inv
three-quarters [θri:'kwɔːtəz] NPL trois-quarts mpl; **~ full** aux trois-quarts plein
three-wheeler [θri:'wiːləʳ] N (car) voiture f à trois roues
thresh [θreʃ] VT (Agr) battre
threshing machine ['θreʃɪŋ-] N batteuse f
threshold ['θreʃhəuld] N seuil m; **to be on the ~ of** (fig) être au seuil de
threshold agreement N (Econ) accord m d'indexation des salaires
threw [θru:] PT of **throw**
thrift [θrɪft] N économie f
thrifty ['θrɪftɪ] ADJ économe
thrill [θrɪl] N (excitement) émotion f, sensation forte; (shudder) frisson m ▸ VI tressaillir, frissonner ▸ VT (audience) électriser
thrilled [θrɪld] ADJ: **~ (with)** ravi(e) de
thriller ['θrɪləʳ] N film m (or roman m or pièce f) à suspense
thrilling ['θrɪlɪŋ] ADJ (book, play etc) saisissant(e); (news, discovery) excitant(e)
thrive [θraɪv] (pt **thrived** or **throve** [θrəuv], pp **thrived** or **thriven** ['θrɪvn]) VI pousser or se développer bien; (business) prospérer; **he thrives on it** cela lui réussit
thriving ['θraɪvɪŋ] ADJ vigoureux(-euse); (business, community) prospère
throat [θrəut] N gorge f; **to have a sore ~** avoir mal à la gorge
throb [θrɔb] N (of heart) pulsation f; (of engine) vibration f; (of pain) élancement m ▸ VI (heart) palpiter; (engine) vibrer; (pain) lanciner; (wound) causer des élancements; **my head is throbbing** j'ai des élancements dans la tête
throes [θrəuz] NPL: **in the ~ of** au beau milieu de; en proie à; **in the ~ of death** à l'agonie
thrombosis [θrɔm'bəusɪs] N thrombose f

throne [θrəun] N trône m
throng ['θrɔŋ] N foule f ▸ VT se presser dans
throttle ['θrɔtl] N (Aut) accélérateur m ▸ VT étrangler
through [θru:] PREP à travers; (time) pendant, durant; (by means of) par, par l'intermédiaire de; (owing to) à cause de ▸ ADJ (ticket, train, passage) direct(e) ▸ ADV à travers; **(from) Monday ~ Friday** (US) de lundi à vendredi; **to let sb ~** laisser passer qn; **to put sb ~ to sb** (Tel) passer qn à qn; **to be ~** (Brit Tel) avoir la communication; (esp US: have finished) avoir fini; **"no - traffic"** (US) "passage interdit"; **"no - road"** (Brit) "impasse"
throughout [θru:'aut] PREP (place) partout dans; (time) durant tout(e) le (la) ▸ ADV partout
throughput ['θru:put] N (of goods, materials) quantité de matières premières utilisée; (Comput) débit m
throve [θrəuv] PT of **thrive**
throw [θrəu] (pt **threw** [θru:], pp **thrown** [θrəun]) N jet m; (Sport) lancer m ▸ VT lancer, jeter; (Sport) lancer; (rider) désarçonner; (fig) déconcertancer; (pottery) tourner; **to ~ a party** donner une réception
▸ **throw about, throw around** VT (litter etc) éparpiller
▸ **throw away** VT jeter; (money) gaspiller
▸ **throw in** VT (Sport: ball) remettre en jeu; (include) ajouter
▸ **throw off** VT se débarrasser de
▸ **throw out** VT jeter; (reject) rejeter; (person) mettre à la porte
▸ **throw together** VT (clothes, meal etc) assembler à la hâte; (essay) bâcler
▸ **throw up** VI vomir
throwaway ['θrəuəweɪ] ADJ à jeter
throwback ['θrəubæk] N: **it's a ~ to** ça nous etc ramène à
throw-in ['θrəuɪn] N (Sport) remise f en jeu
thrown [θrəun] PP of **throw**
thru [θru:] (US) PREP = **through**
thrush [θrʌʃ] N (Zool) grive f; (Med: esp in children) muguet m; (: in women: Brit) muguet vaginal
thrust [θrʌst] (pt, pp **~**) N (Tech) poussée f ▸ VT pousser brusquement; (push in) enfoncer
thrusting ['θrʌstɪŋ] ADJ dynamique; qui se met trop en avant
thud [θʌd] N bruit sourd
thug [θʌg] N voyou m
thumb [θʌm] N (Anat) pouce m ▸ VT (book) feuilleter; **to ~ a lift** faire de l'auto-stop, arrêter une voiture; **to give sb/sth the thumbs up/thumbs down** donner/refuser de donner le feu vert à qn/qch
▸ **thumb through** VT (book) feuilleter
thumb index N répertoire m (à onglets)
thumbnail ['θʌmneɪl] N ongle m du pouce
thumbnail sketch N croquis m
thumbtack ['θʌmtæk] N (US) punaise f (clou)
thump [θʌmp] N grand coup m; (sound) bruit sourd ▸ VT cogner sur ▸ VI cogner, frapper
thunder ['θʌndəʳ] N tonnerre m ▸ VI tonner; (train etc): **to ~ past** passer dans un grondement

or un bruit de tonnerre

thunderbolt ['θʌndəbəʊlt] N foudre f

thunderclap ['θʌndəklæp] N coup m de tonnerre

thunderous ['θʌndrəs] ADJ étourdissant(e)

thunderstorm ['θʌndəstɔːm] N orage m

thunderstruck ['θʌndəstrʌk] ADJ (fig) abasourdi(e)

thundery ['θʌndərɪ] ADJ orageux(-euse)

Thursday ['θəːzdɪ] N jeudi m; see also **Tuesday**

thus [ðʌs] ADV ainsi

thwart [θwɔːt] VT contrecarrer

thyme [taɪm] N thym m

thyroid ['θaɪrɔɪd] N thyroïde f

tiara [tɪ'ɑːrə] N (woman's) diadème m

Tibet [tɪ'bɛt] N Tibet m

Tibetan [tɪ'bɛtən] ADJ tibétain(e) ▶ N Tibétain(e); (Ling) tibétain m

tibia ['tɪbɪə] N tibia m

tic [tɪk] N tic (nerveux)

tick [tɪk] N (sound: of clock) tic-tac m; (mark) coche f; (Zool) tique f ▶ VI faire tic-tac ▶ VT (item on list) cocher; **to put a ~ against sth** cocher qch; **in a ~** (BRIT inf) dans un instant; **to buy sth on ~** (BRIT inf) acheter qch à crédit

▶ **tick off** VT (item on list) cocher; (person) réprimander, attraper

▶ **tick over** VI (BRIT: engine) tourner au ralenti; (: fig) aller or marcher doucettement

ticker tape ['tɪkə-] N bande f de téléscripteur; (US: in celebrations) ≈ serpentin m

ticket ['tɪkɪt] N billet m; (for bus, tube) ticket m; (in shop: on goods) étiquette f; (from cash register) reçu m, ticket; (for library) carte f; (also: **parking ticket**) contravention f, p.-v. m; (US Pol) liste électorale (soutenue par un parti); **to get a (parking) ~** (Aut) attraper une contravention (pour stationnement illégal)

ticket agency N (Theat) agence f de spectacles

ticket barrier N (BRIT Rail) portillon m automatique

ticket collector N contrôleur(-euse)

ticket holder N personne munie d'un billet

ticket inspector N contrôleur(-euse)

ticket machine N billetterie f automatique

ticket office N guichet m, bureau m de vente des billets

tickle ['tɪkl] N chatouillement m ▶ VI chatouiller ▶ VT chatouiller; (fig) plaire à; faire rire

ticklish ['tɪklɪʃ] ADJ (person) chatouilleux(-euse); (which tickles: blanket) qui chatouille; (: cough) qui irrite; (problem) épineux(-euse)

tidal ['taɪdl] ADJ à marée

tidal wave N raz-de-marée m inv

tidbit ['tɪdbɪt] N (esp US) = **titbit**

tiddlywinks ['tɪdlɪwɪŋks] N jeu m de puce

tide [taɪd] N marée f; (fig: of events) cours m ▶ VT: **to ~ sb over** dépanner qn; **high/low ~** marée haute/basse

tidily ['taɪdɪlɪ] ADV avec soin, soigneusement

tidiness ['taɪdɪnɪs] N bon ordre; goût m de l'ordre

tidy ['taɪdɪ] ADJ (room) bien rangé(e); (dress, work) net (nette), soigné(e); (person) ordonné(e), qui a

de l'ordre; (: in character) soigneux(-euse); (mind) méthodique ▶ VT (also: **tidy up**) ranger; **to ~ o.s. up** s'arranger

tie [taɪ] N (string etc) cordon m; (BRIT: also: **necktie**) cravate f; (fig: link) lien m; (Sport: draw) égalité f de points; match nul; (match) rencontre f; (US Rail) traverse f ▶ VT (parcel) attacher; (ribbon) nouer ▶ VI (Sport) faire match nul; finir à égalité de points; **"black/white ~"** "smoking/habit de rigueur"; **family ties** liens de famille; **to ~ sth in a bow** faire un nœud à or avec qch; **to ~ a knot in sth** faire un nœud à qch

▶ **tie down** VT attacher; **to ~ sb down to** (fig) contraindre qn à accepter; **to feel tied down** (by relationship) se sentir coincé(e)

▶ **tie in** VI: **to ~ in (with)** (correspond) correspondre (à)

▶ **tie on** VT (BRIT: label etc) attacher (avec une ficelle)

▶ **tie up** VT (parcel) ficeler; (dog, boat) attacher; (prisoner) ligoter; (arrangements) conclure; **to be tied up** (busy) être pris(e) or occupé(e)

tie-break ['taɪbreɪk], **tie-breaker** ['taɪbreɪkə'] N (Tennis) tie-break m; (in quiz) question f subsidiaire

tie-on ['taɪɔn] ADJ (BRIT: label) qui s'attache

tie-pin ['taɪpɪn] N (BRIT) épingle f de cravate

tier [tɪə'] N gradin m; (of cake) étage m

Tierra del Fuego [tɪ'ɛrədɛl'fweɪgəu] N Terre f de Feu

tie tack N (US) épingle f de cravate

tiff [tɪf] N petite querelle

tiger ['taɪgə'] N tigre m

tight [taɪt] ADJ (rope) tendu(e), raide; (clothes) étroit(e), très juste; (budget, programme, bend) serré(e); (control) strict(e), sévère; (inf: drunk) ivre, rond(e) ▶ ADV (squeeze) très fort; (shut) à bloc, hermétiquement; **to be packed ~** (suitcase) être bourré(e); (people) être serré(e); **hold ~!** accrochez-vous bien!

tighten ['taɪtn] VT (rope) tendre; (screw) resserrer; (control) renforcer ▶ VI se tendre; se resserrer

tightfisted [taɪt'fɪstɪd] ADJ avare

tight-lipped ['taɪt'lɪpt] ADJ: **to be ~ (about sth)** (silent) ne pas desserrer les lèvres or les dents (au sujet de qch); **she was ~ with anger** elle pinçait les lèvres de colère

tightly ['taɪtlɪ] ADV (grasp) bien, très fort

tightrope ['taɪtrəʊp] N corde f raide

tights [taɪts] NPL (BRIT) collant m

tigress ['taɪgrɪs] N tigresse f

tilde ['tɪldə] N tilde m

tile [taɪl] N (on roof) tuile f; (on wall or floor) carreau m ▶ VT (floor, bathroom etc) carreler

tiled [taɪld] ADJ en tuiles; carrelé(e)

till [tɪl] N caisse (enregistreuse) ▶ VT (land) cultiver ▶ PREP, CONJ = **until**

tiller ['tɪlə'] N (Naut) barre f (du gouvernail)

tilt [tɪlt] VT pencher, incliner ▶ VI pencher, être incliné(e) ▶ N (slope) inclinaison f; **to wear one's hat at a ~** porter son chapeau incliné sur le côté; **(at) full ~** à toute vitesse

t

timber ['tɪmbə'] N (*material*) bois m de construction; (*trees*) arbres mpl

time [taɪm] N temps m; (*epoch: often pl*) époque f, temps; (*by clock*) heure f; (*moment*) moment m; (*occasion, also Math*) fois f; (*Mus*) mesure f ▸ VT (*race*) chronométrer; (*programme*) minuter; (*visit*) fixer; (*remark etc*) choisir le moment de; **a long ~** un long moment, longtemps; **four at a ~** quatre à la fois; **for the ~ being** pour le moment; **from ~ to ~** de temps en temps; **~ after ~, ~ and again** bien des fois; **at times** parfois; **in ~** (*soon enough*) à temps; (*after some time*) avec le temps, à la longue; (*Mus*) en mesure; **in a week's ~** dans une semaine; **in no ~** en un rien de temps; **any ~** n'importe quand; **on ~** à l'heure; **to be 30 minutes behind/ahead of ~** avoir 30 minutes de retard/d'avance; **by the ~ he arrived** quand il est arrivé, le temps qu'il arrive + *sub*; **5 times 5** 5 fois 5; **what ~ is it?** quelle heure est-il?; **what ~ do you make it?** quelle heure avez-vous?; **what ~ is the museum/shop open?** à quelle heure ouvre le musée/magasin?; **to have a good ~** bien s'amuser; **we** (*or* **they** *etc*) **had a hard ~** ça a été difficile *or* pénible; **~'s up!** c'est l'heure!; **I've no ~ for it** (*fig*) cela m'agace; **he'll do it in his own (good) ~** (*without being hurried*) il le fera quand il en aura le temps; **he'll do it in** *or* (*US*) **on his own ~** (*out of working hours*) il le fera à ses heures perdues; **to be behind the times** retarder (sur son temps)

time-and-motion study ['taɪmənd'məʊʃən-] N étude f des cadences

time bomb N bombe f à retardement

time clock N horloge pointeuse

time-consuming ['taɪmkənsjuːmɪŋ] ADJ qui prend beaucoup de temps

time difference N décalage m horaire

time frame N délais mpl

time-honoured, (*US*) **time-honored** ['taɪmɔnəd] ADJ consacré(e)

timekeeper ['taɪmkiːpə'] N (*Sport*) chronomètre m

time lag N (*BRIT*) décalage m; (: *in travel*) décalage horaire

timeless ['taɪmlɪs] ADJ éternel(le)

time limit N limite f de temps, délai m

timely ['taɪmlɪ] ADJ opportun(e)

time off N temps m libre

timer ['taɪmə'] N (*in kitchen*) compte-minutes m inv; (*Tech*) minuteur m

time-saving ['taɪmseɪvɪŋ] ADJ qui fait gagner du temps

timescale ['taɪmskeɪl] N délais mpl

time-share ['taɪmʃɛə'] N maison f/appartement m en multipropriété

time-sharing ['taɪmʃɛərɪŋ] N (*Comput*) temps partagé

time sheet N feuille f de présence

time signal N signal m horaire

time switch N (*BRIT*) minuteur m; (: *for lighting*) minuterie f

timetable ['taɪmteɪbl] N (*Rail*) (indicateur m) horaire m; (*Scol*) emploi m du temps; (*programme of events etc*) programme m

time zone N fuseau m horaire

timid ['tɪmɪd] ADJ timide; (*easily scared*) peureux(-euse)

timidity [tɪ'mɪdɪtɪ] N timidité f

timing ['taɪmɪŋ] N minutage m; (*Sport*) chronométrage m; **the ~ of his resignation** le moment choisi pour sa démission

timing device N (*on bomb*) mécanisme m de retardement

timpani ['tɪmpənɪ] NPL timbales fpl

tin [tɪn] N étain m; (*also:* **tin plate**) fer-blanc m; (*BRIT: can*) boîte f (de conserve); (*for baking*) moule m (à gâteau); (*for storage*) boîte f; **a ~ of paint** un pot de peinture

tinfoil ['tɪnfɔɪl] N papier m d'étain *or* d'aluminium

tinge [tɪndʒ] N nuance f ▸ VT: **tinged with** teinté(e) de

tingle ['tɪŋgl] N picotement m; frisson m ▸ VI picoter; (*person*) avoir des picotements

tinker ['tɪŋkə'] N rétameur ambulant; (*Brit pej: gipsy*) romanichel m
▸ **tinker with** VT FUS bricoler, rafistoler

tinkle ['tɪŋkl] VI tinter ▸ N (*inf*): **to give sb a ~** passer un coup de fil à qn

tin mine N mine f d'étain

tinned [tɪnd] ADJ (*BRIT: food*) en boîte, en conserve

tinnitus ['tɪnɪtəs] N (*Med*) acouphène m

tinny ['tɪnɪ] ADJ métallique

tin opener [-'əʊpnə'] N (*BRIT*) ouvre-boîte(s) m

tinsel ['tɪnsl] N guirlandes fpl de Noël (*argentées*)

tint [tɪnt] N teinte f; (*for hair*) shampooing colorant ▸ VT (*hair*) faire un shampooing colorant à

tinted ['tɪntɪd] ADJ (*hair*) teint(e); (*spectacles, glass*) teinté(e)

tiny ['taɪnɪ] ADJ minuscule

tip [tɪp] N (*end*) bout m; (*protective: on umbrella etc*) embout m; (*gratuity*) pourboire m; (*BRIT: for coal*) terril m; (*BRIT: for rubbish*) décharge f; (*advice*) tuyau m ▸ VT (*waiter*) donner un pourboire à; (*tilt*) incliner; (*overturn: also:* **tip over**) renverser; (*empty: also:* **tip out**) déverser; (*predict: winner etc*) pronostiquer; **he tipped out the contents of the box** il a vidé le contenu de la boîte; **how much should I ~?** combien de pourboire est-ce qu'il faut laisser?
▸ **tip off** VT prévenir, avertir

tip-off ['tɪpɔf] N (*hint*) tuyau m

tipped ['tɪpt] ADJ (*BRIT: cigarette*) (à bout) filtre inv; **steel-~** à bout métallique, à embout de métal

Tipp-Ex® ['tɪpɛks] N (*BRIT*) Tipp-Ex® m

tipple ['tɪpl] VI picoler ▸ N: **to have a ~** boire un petit coup

tipster ['tɪpstə'] N (*Racing*) pronostiqueur m

tipsy ['tɪpsɪ] ADJ un peu ivre, éméché(e)

tiptoe ['tɪptəʊ] N: **on ~** sur la pointe des pieds

tiptop ['tɪptɔp] ADJ: **in ~ condition** en excellent état

tirade [taɪ'reɪd] N diatribe f

tire ['taɪə'] N (*US*) = **tyre** ▸ VT fatiguer ▸ VI se fatiguer

▶ **tire out** VT épuiser
tired ['taɪəd] ADJ fatigué(e); **to be/feel/look ~** être/se sentir/avoir l'air fatigué; **to be ~ of** en avoir assez de, être las (lasse) de
tiredness ['taɪədnɪs] N fatigue f
tireless ['taɪəlɪs] ADJ infatigable, inlassable
tire pressure (US) = **tyre pressure**
tiresome ['taɪsəm] ADJ ennuyeux(-euse)
tiring ['taɪərɪŋ] ADJ fatigant(e)
tissue ['tɪʃuː] N tissu m; (paper handkerchief) mouchoir m en papier, kleenex® m
tissue paper N papier m de soie
tit [tɪt] N (bird) mésange f; (inf: breast) nichon m; **to give ~ for tat** rendre coup pour coup
titanium [tɪ'teɪnɪəm] N titane m
titbit ['tɪtbɪt] N (food) friandise f; (before meal) amuse-gueule m inv; (news) potin m
titillate ['tɪtɪleɪt] VT titiller, exciter
titivate ['tɪtɪveɪt] VT pomponner
title ['taɪtl] N titre m; (Law: right): **~ (to)** droit m (à)
title deed N (Law) titre (constitutif) de propriété
title page N page f de titre
title role N rôle principal
titter ['tɪtə'] VI rire (bêtement)
tittle-tattle ['tɪtltætl] N bavardages mpl
titular ['tɪtjulə'] ADJ (in name only) nominal(e)
tizzy ['tɪzɪ] N: **to be in a ~** être dans tous ses états
T-junction ['tiː'dʒʌŋkʃən] N croisement m en T
TM N ABBR = **trademark**; **transcendental meditation**
TN ABBR (US) = **Tennessee**
TNT N ABBR (= trinitrotoluene) TNT m

(KEYWORD)

to [tuː, tə] PREP (with noun/pronoun) **1** (direction) à; (: towards) vers; envers; **to go to France/ Portugal/London/school** aller en France/au Portugal/à Londres/à l'école; **to go to Claude's/the doctor's** aller chez Claude/le docteur; **the road to Edinburgh** la route d'Édimbourg
2 (as far as) (jusqu')à; **to count to 10** compter jusqu'à 10; **from 40 to 50 people** de 40 à 50 personnes
3 (with expressions of time): **a quarter to 5** 5 heures moins le quart; **it's twenty to 3** il est 3 heures moins vingt
4 (for, of) de; **the key to the front door** la clé de la porte d'entrée; **a letter to his wife** une lettre (adressée) à sa femme
5 (expressing indirect object) à; **to give sth to sb** donner qch à qn; **to talk to sb** parler à qn; **it belongs to him** cela lui appartient, c'est à lui; **to be a danger to sb** être dangereux(-euse) pour qn
6 (in relation to) à; **3 goals to 2** 3 (buts) à 2; **30 miles to the gallon** = 9,4 litres aux cent (km)
7 (purpose, result): **to come to sb's aid** venir au secours de qn, porter secours à qn; **to sentence sb to death** condamner qn à mort; **to my surprise** à ma grande surprise
▶ PREP (with vb) **1** (simple infinitive): **to go/eat** aller/manger

2 (following another vb): **to want/try/start to do** vouloir/essayer de/commencer à faire
3 (with vb omitted): **I don't want to** je ne veux pas
4 (purpose, result) pour; **I did it to help you** je l'ai fait pour vous aider
5 (equivalent to relative clause): **I have things to do** j'ai des choses à faire; **the main thing is to try** l'important est d'essayer
6 (after adjective etc): **ready to go** prêt(e) à partir; **too old/young to ...** trop vieux/jeune pour ...
▶ ADV: **push/pull the door to** tirez/poussez la porte; **to go to and fro** aller et venir

toad [təud] N crapaud m
toadstool ['təudstuːl] N champignon (vénéneux)
toady ['təudɪ] VI flatter bassement
toast [təust] N (Culin) pain grillé, toast m; (drink, speech) toast ▶ VT (Culin) faire griller; (drink to) porter un toast à; **a piece or slice of ~** un toast
toaster ['təustə'] N grille-pain m inv
toastmaster ['təustmɑːstə'] N animateur m pour réceptions
toast rack N porte-toast m inv
tobacco [tə'bækəu] N tabac m; **pipe ~** tabac à pipe
tobacconist [tə'bækənɪst] N marchand(e) de tabac; **~'s (shop)** (bureau m de) tabac m
Tobago [tə'beɪgəu] N see **Trinidad and Tobago**
toboggan [tə'bɒgən] N toboggan m; (child's) luge f
today [tə'deɪ] ADV, N (also fig) aujourd'hui (m); **what day is it ~?** quel jour sommes-nous aujourd'hui?; **what date is it ~?** quelle est la date aujourd'hui?; **~ is the 4th of March** aujourd'hui nous sommes le 4 mars; **a week ago ~** il y a huit jours aujourd'hui
toddler ['tɒdlə'] N enfant mf qui commence à marcher, bambin m
toddy ['tɒdɪ] N grog m
to-do [tə'duː] N (fuss) histoire f, affaire f
toe [təu] N doigt m de pied, orteil m; (of shoe) bout m ▶ VT: **to ~ the line** (fig) obéir, se conformer; **big ~** gros orteil; **little ~** petit orteil
TOEFL N ABBR = **Test(ing) of English as a Foreign Language**
toehold ['təuhəuld] N prise f
toenail ['təuneɪl] N ongle m de l'orteil
toffee ['tɒfɪ] N caramel m
toffee apple N (BRIT) pomme caramélisée
tofu ['təufuː] N fromage m de soja
toga ['təugə] N toge f
together [tə'gɛðə'] ADV ensemble; (at same time) en même temps; **~ with** prep avec
togetherness [tə'gɛðənɪs] N camaraderie f; intimité f
toggle switch ['tɒgl-] N (Comput) interrupteur m à bascule
Togo ['təugəu] N Togo m
togs [tɒgz] NPL (inf: clothes) fringues fpl
toil [tɔɪl] N dur travail, labeur m ▶ VI travailler dur; peiner
toilet ['tɔɪlət] N (BRIT: lavatory) toilettes fpl, cabinets mpl ▶ CPD (bag, soap etc) de toilette; **to**

t

go to the ~ aller aux toilettes; **where's the ~?** où sont les toilettes?

toilet bag N (BRIT) nécessaire m de toilette

toilet bowl N cuvette f des W.-C.

toilet paper N papier m hygiénique

toiletries ['tɔɪlətrɪz] NPL articles mpl de toilette

toilet roll N rouleau m de papier hygiénique

toilet water N eau f de toilette

to-ing and fro-ing ['tu:ɪŋən'frəuɪŋ] N (BRIT) allées et venues fpl

token ['təukən] N (sign) marque f, témoignage m; (metal disc) jeton m; (voucher) bon m, coupon m ▶ ADJ (fee, strike) symbolique; **by the same ~** (fig) de même; **book/record ~** (BRIT) chèque-livre/-disque m

tokenism ['təukənɪzəm] N (Pol): **it's just ~** c'est une politique de pure forme

Tokyo ['təukjəu] N Tokyo

told [təuld] PT, PP of **tell**

tolerable ['tɔlərəbl] ADJ (bearable) tolérable; (fairly good) passable

tolerably ['tɔlərəblɪ] ADV: **~ good** tolérable

tolerance ['tɔlərns] N (also Tech) tolérance f

tolerant ['tɔlərnt] ADJ: **~ (of)** tolérant(e) (à l'égard de)

tolerate ['tɔləreɪt] VT supporter; (Med, Tech) tolérer

toleration [tɔlə'reɪʃən] N tolérance f

toll [təul] N (tax, charge) péage m ▶ VI (bell) sonner; **the accident ~ on the roads** le nombre des victimes de la route

tollbridge ['təulbrɪdʒ] N pont m à péage

toll call N (US Tel) appel m (à) longue distance

toll-free ['təul'fri:] (US) gratuit(e) ▶ ADV gratuitement

tomato [tə'mɑ:təu] (pl **tomatoes**) N tomate f

tomato sauce N sauce f tomate

tomb [tu:m] N tombe f

tombola [tɔm'bəulə] N tombola f

tomboy ['tɔmbɔɪ] N garçon manqué

tombstone ['tu:mstəun] N pierre tombale

tomcat ['tɔmkæt] N matou m

tomorrow [tə'mɔrəu] ADV, N (also fig) demain (m); **the day after ~** après-demain; **a week ~** demain en huit; **~ morning** demain matin

ton [tʌn] N tonne f (Brit: = 1016 kg; US = 907 kg; metric = 1000 kg); (Naut: also: **register ton**) tonneau m (= 2.83 cu.m); **tons of** (inf) des tas de

tonal ['təunl] ADJ tonal(e)

tone [təun] N ton m; (of radio, BRIT Tel) tonalité f ▶ VI (also: **tone in**) s'harmoniser
▶ **tone down** VT (colour, criticism) adoucir; (sound) baisser
▶ **tone up** VT (muscles) tonifier

tone-deaf [təun'dɛf] ADJ qui n'a pas d'oreille

toner ['təunə*] N (for photocopier) encre f

Tonga [tɔŋə] N îles fpl Tonga

tongs [tɔŋz] NPL pinces fpl; (for coal) pincettes fpl; (for hair) fer m à friser

tongue [tʌŋ] N langue f; **~ in cheek** adv ironiquement

tongue-tied ['tʌŋtaɪd] ADJ (fig) muet(te)

tonic ['tɔnɪk] N (Med) tonique m; (Mus) tonique f; (also: **tonic water**) Schweppes® m

tonight [tə'naɪt] ADV, N cette nuit; (this evening) ce soir; **(I'll) see you ~!** à ce soir!

tonnage ['tʌnɪdʒ] N (Naut) tonnage m

tonne [tʌn] N (BRIT: metric ton) tonne f

tonsil ['tɔnsl] N amygdale f; **to have one's tonsils out** se faire opérer des amygdales

tonsillitis [tɔnsɪ'laɪtɪs] N amygdalite f; **to have ~** avoir une angine ou une amygdalite

too [tu:] ADV (excessively) trop; (also) aussi; **it's ~ sweet** c'est trop sucré; **I went ~** moi aussi, j'y suis allé; **~ much** (as adv) trop; (as adj) trop de; **~ many** adj trop de; **~ bad!** tant pis!

took [tuk] PT of **take**

tool [tu:l] N outil m; (fig) instrument m ▶ VT travailler, ouvrager

tool box N boîte f à outils

tool kit N trousse f à outils

toot [tu:t] N coup m de sifflet (or de klaxon) ▶ VI siffler; (with car-horn) klaxonner

tooth [tu:θ] (pl **teeth** [ti:θ]) N (Anat, Tech) dent f; **to have a ~ out** or (US) **pulled** se faire arracher une dent; **to brush one's teeth** se laver les dents; **by the skin of one's teeth** (fig) de justesse

toothache ['tu:θeɪk] N mal m de dents; **to have ~** avoir mal aux dents

toothbrush ['tu:θbrʌʃ] N brosse f à dents

toothpaste ['tu:θpeɪst] N (pâte f) dentifrice m

toothpick ['tu:θpɪk] N cure-dent m

tooth powder N poudre f dentifrice

top [tɔp] N (of mountain, head) sommet m; (of page, ladder, queue) commencement m; (of box, cupboard, table) dessus m; (lid: of box, jar) couvercle m; (: of bottle) bouchon m; (toy) toupie f; (Dress: blouse etc) haut m; (: of pyjamas) veste f ▶ ADJ du haut; (in rank) premier(-ière); (best) meilleur(e) ▶ VT (exceed) dépasser; (be first in) être en tête de; **the ~ of the milk** (BRIT) la crème du lait; **at the ~ of the stairs/page/street** en haut de l'escalier/de la page/de la rue; **from ~ to bottom** de fond en comble; **on ~ of** sur; (in addition to) en plus de; **from ~ to toe** (BRIT) de la tête aux pieds; **at the ~ of the list** en tête de liste; **at the ~ of one's voice** à tue-tête; **at ~ speed** à toute vitesse; **over the ~** (inf: behaviour etc) qui dépasse les limites
▶ **top up,** (US) **top off** VT (bottle) remplir; (salary) compléter; **to ~ up one's mobile (phone)** recharger son compte

topaz ['təupæz] N topaze f

top-class ['tɔp'klɑ:s] ADJ de première classe; (Sport) de haute compétition

topcoat ['tɔpkəut] N pardessus m

topflight ['tɔpflaɪt] ADJ excellent(e)

top floor N dernier étage

top hat N haut-de-forme m

top-heavy [tɔp'hɛvɪ] ADJ (object) trop lourd(e) du haut

topic ['tɔpɪk] N sujet m, thème m

topical ['tɔpɪkl] ADJ d'actualité

topless ['tɔplɪs] ADJ (bather etc) aux seins nus; **~ swimsuit** monokini m

top-level ['tɔplɛvl] ADJ (talks) à l'échelon le plus élevé

topmost ['tɔpməʊst] ADJ le (la) plus haut(e)
top-notch ['tɔp'nɔtʃ] ADJ (inf) de premier ordre
topography [tə'pɔgrəfɪ] N topographie f
topping ['tɔpɪŋ] N (Culin) couche de crème, fromage etc qui recouvre un plat
topple ['tɔpl] VT renverser, faire tomber ▶ VI basculer; tomber
top-ranking ['tɔpræŋkɪŋ] ADJ très haut placé(e)
top-secret ['tɔp'siːkrɪt] ADJ ultra-secret(-ète)
top-security ['tɔpsə'kjuərɪtɪ] ADJ (BRIT) de haute sécurité
topsy-turvy ['tɔpsɪ'təːvɪ] ADJ, ADV sens dessus-dessous
top-up ['tɔpʌp] N (for mobile phone) recharge f, minutes fpl; **would you like a ~?** je vous en remets or rajoute?
top-up card N (for mobile phone) recharge f
top-up loan N (BRIT) prêt m complémentaire
torch [tɔːtʃ] N torche f; (BRIT: electric) lampe f de poche
tore [tɔːʳ] PT of **tear²**
torment N ['tɔːmɛnt] tourment m ▶ VT [tɔː'mɛnt] tourmenter; (fig: annoy) agacer
torn [tɔːn] PP of **tear²** ▶ ADJ: **~ between** (fig) tiraillé(e) entre
tornado [tɔː'neɪdəʊ] (pl **tornadoes**) N tornade f
torpedo [tɔː'piːdəʊ] (pl **torpedoes**) N torpille f
torpedo boat N torpilleur m
torpor ['tɔːpəʳ] N torpeur f
torrent ['tɔrnt] N torrent m
torrential [tɔ'rɛnʃl] ADJ torrentiel(le)
torrid ['tɔrɪd] ADJ torride; (fig) ardent(e)
torso ['tɔːsəʊ] N torse m
tortoise ['tɔːtəs] N tortue f
tortoiseshell ['tɔːtəʃɛl] ADJ en écaille
tortuous ['tɔːtjuəs] ADJ tortueux(-euse)
torture ['tɔːtʃəʳ] N torture f ▶ VT torturer
torturer ['tɔːtʃərəʳ] N tortionnaire m
Tory ['tɔːrɪ] ADJ, N (BRIT Pol) tory mf, conservateur(-trice)
toss [tɔs] VT lancer, jeter; (BRIT: pancake) faire sauter; (head) rejeter en arrière ▶ VI: **to ~ up for sth** (BRIT) jouer qch à pile ou face ▶ N (movement: of head etc) mouvement soudain; (: of coin) tirage m à pile ou face; **to ~ a coin** jouer à pile ou face; **to ~ and turn** (in bed) se tourner et se retourner; **to win/lose the ~** gagner/perdre à pile ou face; (Sport) gagner/perdre le tirage au sort
tot [tɔt] N (BRIT: drink) petit verre; (child) bambin m
▶ **tot up** VT (BRIT: figures) additionner
total ['təʊtl] ADJ total(e) ▶ N total m ▶ VT (add up) faire le total de, additionner; (amount to) s'élever à; **in ~** au total
totalitarian [təʊtælɪ'tɛərɪən] ADJ totalitaire
totality [təʊ'tælɪtɪ] N totalité f
totally ['təʊtəlɪ] ADV totalement
tote bag [təʊt-] N fourre-tout m inv
totem pole ['təʊtəm-] N mât m totémique
totter ['tɔtəʳ] VI chanceler; (object, government) être chancelant(e)
touch [tʌtʃ] N contact m, toucher m; (sense, skill: of pianist etc) toucher; (fig: note, also Football) touche f ▶ VT (gen) toucher; (tamper with)

toucher à; **the personal ~** la petite note personnelle; **to put the finishing touches to sth** mettre la dernière main à qch; **a ~ of** (fig) un petit peu de; une touche de; **in ~ with** en contact or rapport avec; **to get in ~ with** prendre contact avec; **I'll be in ~** je resterai en contact; **to lose ~** (friends) se perdre de vue; **to be out of ~ with events** ne pas être au courant de ce qui se passe
▶ **touch down** VI (Aviat) atterrir; (on sea) amerrir
▶ **touch on** VT FUS (topic) effleurer, toucher
▶ **touch up** VT (paint) retoucher
touch-and-go ['tʌtʃən'gəʊ] ADJ incertain(e); **it was ~ whether we did it** nous avons failli ne pas le faire
touchdown ['tʌtʃdaʊn] N (Aviat) atterrissage m; (on sea) amerrissage m; (US Football) essai m
touched [tʌtʃt] ADJ (moved) touché(e); (inf) cinglé(e)
touching ['tʌtʃɪŋ] ADJ touchant(e), attendrissant(e)
touchline ['tʌtʃlaɪn] N (Sport) (ligne f de) touche f
touch screen N (Tech) écran tactile; **~ mobile** (téléphone) portable m à écran tactile; **~ technology** technologie f à écran tactile
touch-sensitive ['tʌtʃsɛnsɪtɪv] ADJ (keypad) à effleurement; (screen) tactile
touch-type ['tʌtʃtaɪp] VI taper au toucher
touchy ['tʌtʃɪ] ADJ (person) susceptible
tough [tʌf] ADJ dur(e); (resistant) résistant(e), solide; (meat) dur, coriace; (firm) inflexible; (journey) pénible; (task, problem, situation) difficile; (rough) dur ▶ N (gangster etc) dur m; **~ luck!** pas de chance!; tant pis!
toughen ['tʌfn] VT rendre plus dur(e) (or plus résistant(e) or plus solide)
toughness ['tʌfnɪs] N dureté f; résistance f; solidité f
toupee ['tuːpeɪ] N postiche m
tour ['tuəʳ] N voyage m; (also: **package tour**) voyage organisé; (of town, museum) tour m, visite f; (by band) tournée f ▶ VT visiter; **to go on a ~ of** (museum, region) visiter; **to go on ~** partir en tournée
tour guide N (person) guide mf
touring ['tuərɪŋ] N voyages mpl touristiques, tourisme m
tourism ['tuərɪzm] N tourisme m
tourist ['tuərɪst] N touriste mf ▶ ADV (travel) en classe touriste ▶ CPD touristique; **the ~ trade** le tourisme
tourist class N (Aviat) classe f touriste
tourist office N syndicat m d'initiative
tournament ['tuənəmənt] N tournoi m
tourniquet ['tuənɪkeɪ] N (Med) garrot m
tour operator N (BRIT) organisateur m de voyages, tour-opérateur m
tousled ['taʊzld] ADJ (hair) ébouriffé(e)
tout [taut] N (BRIT: ticket tout) revendeur m de billets ▶ VI: **to ~ for** essayer de raccrocher, racoler; **to ~ sth (around)** (BRIT) essayer de placer or (re)vendre qch
tow [təʊ] N: **to give sb a ~** (Aut) remorquer qn ▶ VT remorquer; (caravan, trailer) tracter; **"on ~",**

t

(US) **"in ~"** (*Aut*) "véhicule en remorque"
▶ **tow away** VT (*subj: police*) emmener à la fourrière; (: *breakdown service*) remorquer

toward [təˈwɔːd], **towards** [təˈwɔːdz] PREP vers; (*of attitude*) envers, à l'égard de; (*of purpose*) pour; **~(s) noon/the end of the year** vers midi/la fin de l'année; **to feel friendly ~(s) sb** être bien disposé envers qn

towel [ˈtauəl] N serviette *f* (de toilette); (*also:* **tea towel**) torchon *m*; **to throw in the ~** (*fig*) jeter l'éponge

towelling [ˈtauəlɪŋ] N (*fabric*) tissu-éponge *m*

towel rail, (US) **towel rack** N porte-serviettes *m* inv

tower [ˈtauəʳ] N tour *f* ▶ VI (*building, mountain*) se dresser (majestueusement); **to ~ above** *or* **over sb/sth** dominer qn/qch

tower block N (BRIT) tour *f* (d'habitation)

towering [ˈtauərɪŋ] ADJ très haut(e), imposant(e)

towline [ˈtəulaɪn] N (câble *m* de) remorque *f*

town [taun] N ville *f*; **to go to ~** aller en ville; (*fig*) y mettre le paquet; **in the ~** dans la ville, en ville; **to be out of ~** (*person*) être en déplacement

town centre N (BRIT) centre *m* de la ville, centre-ville *m*

town clerk N ≈ secrétaire *mf* de mairie

town council N conseil municipal

town crier [-ˈkraɪəʳ] N (BRIT) crieur public

town hall N ≈ mairie *f*

townie [ˈtauni] N (BRIT inf) citadin(e)

town plan N plan *m* de ville

town planner N urbaniste *mf*

town planning N urbanisme *m*

township [ˈtaunʃɪp] N banlieue noire (*établie sous le régime de l'apartheid*)

townspeople [ˈtaunzpiːpl] NPL citadins *mpl*

towpath [ˈtəupɑːθ] N (chemin *m* de) halage *m*

towrope [ˈtəurəup] N (câble *m* de) remorque *f*

tow truck N (US) dépanneuse *f*

toxic [ˈtɔksɪk] ADJ toxique

toxic asset N (Econ) actif *m* toxique

toxic bank N (Econ) bad bank *f*, banque *f* toxique

toxin [ˈtɔksɪn] N toxine *f*

toy [tɔɪ] N jouet *m*
▶ **toy with** VT FUS jouer avec; (*idea*) caresser

toyshop [ˈtɔɪʃɔp] N magasin *m* de jouets

trace [treɪs] N trace *f* ▶ VT (*draw*) tracer, dessiner; (*follow*) suivre la trace de; (*locate*) retrouver; **without ~** (*disappear*) sans laisser de traces; **there was no ~ of it** il n'y en avait pas trace

trace element N oligo-élément *m*

trachea [trəˈkiːə] N (Anat) trachée *f*

tracing paper [ˈtreɪsɪŋ-] N papier-calque *m*

track [træk] N (*mark*) trace *f*; (*path: gen*) chemin *m*, piste *f*; (: *of bullet etc*) trajectoire *f*; (: *of suspect, animal*) piste; (*Rail*) voie ferrée, rails *mpl*; (*Comput, Sport*) piste; (*on CD*) piste; (*on record*) plage *f* ▶ VT suivre la trace *or* la piste de; **to keep ~ of** suivre; **to be on the right ~** (*fig*) être sur la bonne voie
▶ **track down** VT (*prey*) trouver et capturer; (*sth lost*) finir par retrouver

tracker dog [ˈtrækə-] N (BRIT) chien dressé pour suivre une piste

track events NPL (Sport) épreuves *fpl* sur piste

tracking station [ˈtrækɪŋ-] N (Space) centre *m* d'observation de satellites

track meet N (US) réunion sportive sur piste

track record N: **to have a good ~** (*fig*) avoir fait ses preuves

tracksuit [ˈtræksuːt] N survêtement *m*

tract [trækt] N (Geo) étendue *f*, zone *f*; (*pamphlet*) tract *m*; **respiratory ~** (*Anat*) système *m* respiratoire

traction [ˈtrækʃən] N traction *f*

tractor [ˈtræktəʳ] N tracteur *m*

trade [treɪd] N commerce *m*; (*skill, job*) métier *m* ▶ VI faire du commerce ▶ VT (*exchange*): **to ~ sth (for sth)** échanger qch (contre qch); **to ~ with/in** faire du commerce avec/le commerce de; **foreign ~** commerce extérieur
▶ **trade in** VT (*old car etc*) faire reprendre

trade barrier N barrière commerciale

trade deficit N déficit extérieur

Trade Descriptions Act N (BRIT) loi contre les appellations et la publicité mensongères

trade discount N remise *f* au détaillant

trade fair N foire(-exposition) commerciale

trade-in [ˈtreɪdɪn] N reprise *f*

trade-in price N prix *m* à la reprise

trademark [ˈtreɪdmɑːk] N marque *f* de fabrique

trade mission N mission commerciale

trade name N marque déposée

trade-off [ˈtreɪdɔf] N (*exchange*) échange *f*; (*balancing*) équilibre *m*

trader [ˈtreɪdəʳ] N commerçant(e), négociant(e)

trade secret N secret *m* de fabrication

tradesman [ˈtreɪdzmən] N (*irreg*) (*shopkeeper*) commerçant *m*; (*skilled worker*) ouvrier qualifié

trade union N syndicat *m*

trade unionist [-ˈjuːnjənɪst] N syndicaliste *mf*

trade wind N alizé *m*

trading [ˈtreɪdɪŋ] N affaires *fpl*, commerce *m*

trading estate N (BRIT) zone industrielle

trading stamp N timbre-prime *m*

tradition [trəˈdɪʃən] N tradition *f*; **traditions** NPL coutumes *fpl*, traditions

traditional [trəˈdɪʃənl] ADJ traditionnel(le)

traffic [ˈtræfɪk] N trafic *m*; (*cars*) circulation *f* ▶ VI: **to ~ in** (*pej: liquor, drugs*) faire le trafic de

traffic calming [-ˈkɑːmɪŋ] N ralentissement *m* de la circulation

traffic circle N (US) rond-point *m*

traffic island N refuge *m* (pour piétons)

traffic jam N embouteillage *m*

trafficker [ˈtræfɪkəʳ] N trafiquant(e)

traffic lights NPL feux *mpl* (de signalisation)

traffic offence N (BRIT) infraction *f* au code de la route

traffic sign N panneau *m* de signalisation

traffic violation N (US) = **traffic offence**

traffic warden N contractuel(le)

tragedy [ˈtrædʒədɪ] N tragédie *f*

tragic [ˈtrædʒɪk] ADJ tragique

trail [treɪl] N (*tracks*) trace *f*, piste *f*; (*path*) chemin *m*, piste; (*of smoke etc*) traînée *f* ▶ VT

(drag) traîner, tirer; *(follow)* suivre ▶ vı traîner;
(in game, contest) être en retard; **to be on sb's ~**
être sur la piste de qn
▶ **trail away, trail off** vı *(sound, voice)* s'évanouir;
(interest) disparaître
▶ **trail behind** vı traîner, être à la traîne
trailer ['treɪlə^r] N *(Aut)* remorque f; *(US: caravan)*
caravane f; *(Cine)* bande-annonce f
trailer truck N *(US)* (camion *m*) semi-
remorque *m*
train [treɪn] N train *m*; *(in underground)* rame f; *(of
dress)* traîne f; *(Brit: series):* **~ of events** série f
d'événements ▶ vт *(apprentice, doctor etc)* former;
(Sport) entraîner; *(dog)* dresser; *(memory)*
exercer; *(point: gun etc):* **to ~ sth on** braquer qch
sur ▶ vı recevoir sa formation; *(Sport)*
s'entraîner; **one's ~ of thought** le fil de la
pensée; **to go by ~** voyager par le train *or* en
train; **what time does the ~ from Paris get
in?** à quelle heure arrive le train de Paris?; **is
this the ~ for …?** c'est bien le train pour …?; **to
~ sb to do sth** apprendre à qn à faire qch;
(employee) former qn à faire qch
train attendant N *(US)* employé(e) des
wagons-lits
trained [treɪnd] ADJ qualifié(e), qui a reçu une
formation; dressé(e)
trainee [treɪ'niː] N stagiaire *mf*; *(in trade)*
apprenti(e)
trainer ['treɪnə^r] N *(Sport)* entraîneur(-euse); *(of
dogs etc)* dresseur(-euse); **trainers** NPL *(shoes)*
chaussures *fpl* de sport
training ['treɪnɪŋ] N formation f; *(Sport)*
entraînement *m*; *(of dog etc)* dressage *m*; **in ~**
(Sport) à l'entraînement; *(fit)* en forme
training college N école professionnelle; *(for
teachers)* ≈ école normale
training course N cours *m* de formation
professionnelle
training shoes NPL chaussures *fpl* de sport
train wreck N *(fig)* épave f; **he's a complete ~**
c'est une épave
traipse [treɪps] vı *(se)* traîner, déambuler
trait [treɪt] N trait *m* (de caractère)
traitor ['treɪtə^r] N traître *m*
trajectory [trə'dʒɛktərɪ] N trajectoire f
tram [træm] N *(Brit: also:* **tramcar)** tram(way) *m*
tramline ['træmlaɪn] N ligne f de tram(way)
tramp [træmp] N *(person)* vagabond(e),
clochard(e); *(inf, pej: woman):* **to be a ~** être
coureuse ▶ vı marcher d'un pas lourd ▶ vт *(walk
through: town, streets)* parcourir à pied
trample ['træmpl] vт: **to ~ (underfoot)**
piétiner; *(fig)* bafouer
trampoline ['træmpəliːn] N trampoline *m*
trance [trɑːns] N transe f; *(Med)* catalepsie f; **to
go into a ~** entrer en transe
tranquil ['træŋkwɪl] ADJ tranquille
tranquillity [træŋ'kwɪlɪtɪ] N tranquillité f
tranquillizer, *(US)* **tranquilizer**
['træŋkwɪlaɪzə^r] N *(Med)* tranquillisant *m*
transact [træn'zækt] vт *(business)* traiter
transaction [træn'zækʃən] N transaction f;
transactions NPL *(minutes)* actes *mpl*; **cash ~**

transaction au comptant
transatlantic ['trænzət'læntɪk] ADJ
transatlantique
transcend [træn'sɛnd] vт transcender; *(excel
over)* surpasser
transcendental [trænsɛn'dɛntl] ADJ:
~ meditation méditation transcendantale
transcribe [træn'skraɪb] vт transcrire
transcript ['trænskrɪpt] N transcription f *(texte)*
transcription [træn'skrɪpʃən] N transcription f
transept ['trænsɛpt] N transept *m*
transfer N ['trænsfə^r] *(gen, also Sport)* transfert *m*;
(Pol: of power) passation f; *(of money)* virement *m*;
(picture, design) décalcomanie f; *(: stick-on)*
autocollant *m* ▶ vт [træns'fə^r] transférer;
passer; virer; décalquer; **to ~ the charges** *(Brit
Tel)* téléphoner en P.C.V.; **by bank ~** par
virement bancaire
transferable [træns'fə:rəbl] ADJ transmissible,
transférable; **"not ~"** "personnel"
transfer desk N *(Aviat)* guichet *m* de transit
transfix [træns'fɪks] vт transpercer; *(fig):*
transfixed with fear paralysé(e) par la peur
transform [træns'fɔ:m] vт transformer
transformation [trænsfə'meɪʃən] N
transformation f
transformer [træns'fɔ:mə^r] N *(Elec)*
transformateur *m*
transfusion [træns'fju:ʒən] N transfusion f
transgress [træns'grɛs] vт transgresser
transient ['trænzɪənt] ADJ transitoire,
éphémère
transistor [træn'zɪstə^r] N *(Elec: also:* **transistor
radio)** transistor *m*
transit ['trænzɪt] N: **in ~** en transit
transit camp N camp *m* de transit
transition [træn'zɪʃən] N transition f
transitional [træn'zɪʃənl] ADJ de transition
transitive ['trænzɪtɪv] ADJ *(Ling)* transitif(-ive)
transit lounge N *(Aviat)* salle f de transit
transitory ['trænzɪtərɪ] ADJ transitoire
translate [trænz'leɪt] vт: **to ~ (from/into)**
traduire (du/en); **can you ~ this for me?**
pouvez-vous me traduire ceci?
translation [trænz'leɪʃən] N traduction f; *(Scol:
as opposed to prose)* version f
translator [trænz'leɪtə^r] N traducteur(-trice)
translucent [trænz'lu:snt] ADJ translucide
transmission [trænz'mɪʃən] N transmission f
transmit [trænz'mɪt] vт transmettre; *(Radio,
TV)* émettre
transmitter [trænz'mɪtə^r] N émetteur *m*
transparency [træns'pɛərnsɪ] N *(Brit Phot)*
diapositive f
transparent [træns'pærnt] ADJ transparent(e)
transpire [træns'paɪə^r] vı *(become known):* **it
finally transpired that …** on a finalement
appris que …; *(happen)* arriver
transplant vт [træns'plɑ:nt] transplanter;
(seedlings) repiquer ▶ N ['trænsplɑ:nt] *(Med)*
transplantation f; **to have a heart ~** subir une
greffe du cœur
transport N ['trænspɔ:t] transport *m* ▶ vт
[træns'pɔ:t] transporter; **public ~** transports en

t

commun; **Department of T~** (BRIT) ministère m des Transports

transportation [trænspɔː'teɪʃən] N (moyen m de) transport m; (of prisoners) transportation f; **Department of T~** (US) ministère m des Transports

transport café N (BRIT) ≈ routier m

transpose [træns'pəʊz] VT transposer

transsexual [trænz'sɛksjuəl] ADJ, N transsexuel(le)

transverse ['trænzvəːs] ADJ transversal(e)

transvestite [trænz'vɛstaɪt] N travesti(e)

trap [træp] N (snare, trick) piège m; (carriage) cabriolet m ▸ VT prendre au piège; (immobilize) bloquer; (confine) coincer; **to set** or **lay a ~ (for sb)** tendre un piège (à qn); **to shut one's ~** (inf) la fermer

trap door N trappe f

trapeze [trə'piːz] N trapèze m

trapper ['træpər] N trappeur m

trappings ['træpɪŋz] NPL ornements mpl; attributs mpl

trash [træʃ] N (inf, pej: goods) camelote f; (: nonsense) sottises fpl; (US: rubbish) ordures fpl

trash can N (US) poubelle f

trashy ['træʃɪ] ADJ (inf) de camelote, qui ne vaut rien

trauma ['trɔːmə] N traumatisme m

traumatic [trɔː'mætɪk] ADJ traumatisant(e)

travel ['trævl] N voyage(s) m(pl) ▸ VI voyager; (move) aller, se déplacer; (news, sound) se propager ▸ VT (distance) parcourir; **this wine doesn't ~ well** ce vin voyage mal

travel agency N agence f de voyages

travel agent N agent m de voyages

travel brochure N brochure f touristique

travel insurance N assurance-voyage f

traveller, (US) **traveler** ['trævlər] N voyageur(-euse); (Comm) représentant m de commerce

traveller's cheque, (US) **traveler's check** N chèque m de voyage

travelling, (US) **traveling** ['trævlɪŋ] N voyage(s) m(pl) ▸ ADJ (circus, exhibition) ambulant(e) ▸ CPD (bag, clock) de voyage; (expenses) de déplacement

travelling salesman, (US) **traveling salesman** N (irreg) voyageur m de commerce

travelogue ['trævəlɔɡ] N (book, talk) récit m de voyage; (film) documentaire m de voyage

travel-sick ['trævlsɪk] ADJ: **to get ~** avoir le mal de la route (or de mer or de l'air)

travel sickness N mal m de la route (or de mer or de l'air)

traverse ['trævəs] VT traverser

travesty ['trævəstɪ] N parodie f

trawler ['trɔːlər] N chalutier m

tray [treɪ] N (for carrying) plateau m; (on desk) corbeille f

treacherous ['trɛtʃərəs] ADJ traître(sse); (ground, tide) dont il faut se méfier; **road conditions are ~** l'état des routes est dangereux

treachery ['trɛtʃərɪ] N traîtrise f

treacle ['triːkl] N mélasse f

tread [trɛd] (pt **trod** [trɔd], pp **trodden** ['trɔdn]) N

(step) pas m; (sound) bruit m de pas; (of tyre) chape f, bande f de roulement ▸ VI marcher
▸ **tread on** VT FUS marcher sur

treadle ['trɛdl] N pédale f (de machine)

treas. ABBR = **treasurer**

treason ['triːzn] N trahison f

treasure ['trɛʒər] N trésor m ▸ VT (value) tenir beaucoup à; (store) conserver précieusement

treasure hunt N chasse f au trésor

treasurer ['trɛʒərər] N trésorier(-ière)

treasury ['trɛʒərɪ] N trésorerie f; **the T~, the T~ Department** (US) ≈ le ministère des Finances

treasury bill N bon m du Trésor

treat [triːt] N petit cadeau, petite surprise ▸ VT traiter; **it was a ~** ça m'a (or nous a etc) vraiment fait plaisir; **to ~ sb to sth** offrir qch à qn; **to ~ sth as a joke** prendre qch à la plaisanterie

treatise ['triːtɪz] N traité m (ouvrage)

treatment ['triːtmənt] N traitement m; **to have ~ for sth** suivre un traitement pour qch

treaty ['triːtɪ] N traité m

treble ['trɛbl] ADJ triple ▸ N (Mus) soprano m ▸ VT, VI tripler

treble clef N clé f de sol

tree [triː] N arbre m

tree-lined ['triːlaɪnd] ADJ bordé(e) d'arbres

treetop ['triːtɔp] N cime f d'un arbre

tree trunk N tronc m d'arbre

trek [trɛk] N (long walk) randonnée f; (tiring walk) longue marche, trotte f ▸ VI (as holiday) faire de la randonnée

trellis ['trɛlɪs] N treillis m, treillage m

tremble ['trɛmbl] VI trembler

trembling ['trɛmblɪŋ] N tremblement m ▸ ADJ tremblant(e)

tremendous [trɪ'mɛndəs] ADJ (enormous) énorme; (excellent) formidable, fantastique

tremendously [trɪ'mɛndəslɪ] ADV énormément, extrêmement + adjective; formidablement

tremor ['trɛmər] N tremblement m; (also: **earth tremor**) secousse f sismique

trench [trɛntʃ] N tranchée f

trench coat N trench-coat m

trench warfare N guerre f de tranchées

trend [trɛnd] N (tendency) tendance f; (of events) cours m; (fashion) mode f; **~ towards/away from doing** tendance à faire/à ne pas faire; **to set the ~** donner le ton; **to set a ~** lancer une mode

trendy ['trɛndɪ] ADJ (idea, person) dans le vent; (clothes) dernier cri inv

trepidation [trɛpɪ'deɪʃən] N vive agitation

trespass ['trɛspəs] VI: **to ~ on** s'introduire sans permission dans; (fig) empiéter sur; **"no trespassing"** "propriété privée", "défense d'entrer"

trespasser ['trɛspəsər] N intrus(e); **"trespassers will be prosecuted"** "interdiction d'entrer sous peine de poursuites"

trestle ['trɛsl] N tréteau m

trestle table N table f à tréteaux

trial ['traɪəl] N (Law) procès m, jugement m; (test: of machine etc) essai m; (worry) souci m; **trials** NPL (unpleasant experiences) épreuves fpl; (Sport) épreuves éliminatoires; **horse trials** concours m hippique; ~ **by jury** jugement par jury; **to be sent for** ~ être traduit(e) en justice; **to be on** ~ passer en jugement; **by** ~ **and error** par tâtonnements

trial balance N (Comm) balance f de vérification

trial basis N: **on a** ~ pour une période d'essai

trial period N période f d'essai

trial run N essai m

triangle ['traɪæŋgl] N (Math, Mus) triangle m

triangular [traɪ'æŋgjulə'] ADJ triangulaire

triathlon [traɪ'æθlən] N triathlon m

tribal ['traɪbl] ADJ tribal(e)

tribe [traɪb] N tribu f

tribesman ['traɪbzmən] N (irreg) membre m de la tribu

tribulation [trɪbju'leɪʃən] N tribulation f, malheur m

tribunal [traɪ'bjuːnl] N tribunal m

tributary ['trɪbjutərɪ] N (river) affluent m

tribute ['trɪbjuːt] N tribut m, hommage m; **to pay** ~ **to** rendre hommage à

trice [traɪs] N: **in a** ~ en un clin d'œil

trick [trɪk] N (magic) tour m; (joke, prank) tour, farce f; (skill, knack) astuce f; (Cards) levée f ▶ VT attraper, rouler; **to play a** ~ **on sb** jouer un tour à qn; **to** ~ **sb into doing sth** persuader qn par la ruse de faire qch; **to** ~ **sb out of sth** obtenir qch de qn par la ruse; **it's a** ~ **of the light** c'est une illusion d'optique causée par la lumière; **that should do the** ~ (inf) ça devrait faire l'affaire

trickery ['trɪkərɪ] N ruse f

trickle ['trɪkl] N (of water etc) filet m ▶ VI couler en un filet or goutte à goutte; **to** ~ **in/out** (people) entrer/sortir par petits groupes

trick question N question-piège f

trickster ['trɪkstə'] N arnaqueur(-euse), filou m

tricky ['trɪkɪ] ADJ difficile, délicat(e)

tricycle ['traɪsɪkl] N tricycle m

trifle ['traɪfl] N bagatelle f; (Culin) ≈ diplomate m ▶ ADV: **a** ~ **long** un peu long ▶ VI: **to** ~ **with** traiter à la légère

trifling ['traɪflɪŋ] ADJ insignifiant(e)

trigger ['trɪgə'] N (of gun) gâchette f ▶ **trigger off** VT déclencher

trigonometry [trɪgə'nɔmətrɪ] N trigonométrie f

trilby ['trɪlbɪ] N (BRIT: also: **trilby hat**) chapeau mou, feutre m

trill [trɪl] N (of bird, Mus) trille m

trilogy ['trɪlədʒɪ] N trilogie f

trim [trɪm] ADJ net(te); (house, garden) bien tenu(e); (figure) svelte ▶ N (haircut etc) légère coupe; (embellishment) finitions fpl; (on car) garnitures fpl ▶ VT (cut) couper légèrement; (Naut: a sail) gréer; (decorate): **to** ~ **(with)** décorer (de); **to keep in (good)** ~ maintenir en (bon) état

trimmings ['trɪmɪŋz] NPL décorations fpl; (extras: esp Culin) garniture f

Trinidad and Tobago ['trɪnɪdæd-] N Trinité et Tobago f

Trinity ['trɪnɪtɪ] N: **the** ~ la Trinité

trinket ['trɪŋkɪt] N bibelot m; (piece of jewellery) colifichet m

trio ['triːəu] N trio m

trip [trɪp] N voyage m; (excursion) excursion f; (stumble) faux pas ▶ VI faire un faux pas, trébucher; (go lightly) marcher d'un pas léger; **on a** ~ en voyage ▶ **trip up** VI trébucher ▶ VT faire un croc-en-jambe f

tripartite [traɪ'pɑːtaɪt] ADJ triparti(e)

tripe [traɪp] N (Culin) tripes fpl; (pej: rubbish) idioties fpl

triple ['trɪpl] ADJ triple ▶ ADV: ~ **the distance/the speed** trois fois la distance/la vitesse

triple jump N triple saut m

triplets ['trɪplɪts] NPL triplés(-ées)

triplicate ['trɪplɪkət] N: **in** ~ en trois exemplaires

tripod ['traɪpɔd] N trépied m

Tripoli ['trɪpəlɪ] N Tripoli

tripper ['trɪpə'] N (BRIT) touriste mf; excursionniste mf

tripwire ['trɪpwaɪə'] N fil m de déclenchement

trite [traɪt] ADJ banal(e)

triumph ['traɪʌmf] N triomphe m ▶ VI: **to** ~ **(over)** triompher (de)

triumphal [traɪ'ʌmfl] ADJ triomphal(e)

triumphant [traɪ'ʌmfənt] ADJ triomphant(e)

trivia ['trɪvɪə] NPL futilités fpl

trivial ['trɪvɪəl] ADJ insignifiant(e); (commonplace) banal(e)

triviality [trɪvɪ'ælɪtɪ] N caractère insignifiant; banalité f

trivialize ['trɪvɪəlaɪz] VT rendre banal(e)

trod [trɔd] PT of **tread**

trodden [trɔdn] PP of **tread**

troll [trɔl] N (Comput) troll m

trolley ['trɔlɪ] N chariot m

trolley bus N trolleybus m

trollop ['trɔləp] N prostituée f

trombone [trɔm'bəun] N trombone m

troop [truːp] N bande f, groupe m ▶ VI: **to** ~ **in/out** entrer/sortir en groupe; **troops** NPL (Mil) troupes fpl; (: men) hommes mpl, soldats mpl; **trooping the colour** (BRIT) (ceremony) le salut au drapeau

troop carrier N (plane) avion m de transport de troupes; (Naut: also: **troopship**) transport m (navire)

trooper ['truːpə'] N (Mil) soldat m de cavalerie; (US: policeman) ≈ gendarme m

troopship ['truːpʃɪp] N transport m (navire)

trophy ['trəufɪ] N trophée m

tropic ['trɔpɪk] N tropique m; **in the tropics** sous les tropiques; **T~ of Cancer/Capricorn** tropique du Cancer/Capricorne

tropical ['trɔpɪkl] ADJ tropical(e)

trot [trɔt] N trot m ▶ VI trotter; **on the** ~ (BRIT fig) d'affilée ▶ **trot out** VT (excuse, reason) débiter; (names, facts) réciter les uns après les autres

trouble ['trʌbl] N difficulté(s) f(pl), problème(s) m(pl); (worry) ennuis mpl, soucis mpl; (bother, effort) peine f; (Pol) conflit(s) m(pl), troubles mpl; (Med) stomach etc ~ troubles gastriques etc ▶ VT (disturb) déranger, gêner; (worry) inquiéter ▶ VI: **to ~ to do** prendre la peine de faire; **troubles** NPL (Pol etc) troubles; (personal) ennuis, soucis; **to be in ~** avoir des ennuis; (ship, climber etc) être en difficulté; **to have ~ doing sth** avoir du mal à faire qch; **to go to the ~ of doing** se donner le mal de faire; **it's no ~!** je vous en prie!; **please don't ~ yourself** je vous en prie, ne vous dérangez pas!; **the ~ is ...** le problème, c'est que ...; **what's the ~?** qu'est-ce qui ne va pas?

troubled ['trʌbld] ADJ (person) inquiet(-ète); (times, life) agité(e)

trouble-free ['trʌblfri:] ADJ sans problèmes or ennuis

troublemaker ['trʌblmeɪkəʳ] N élément perturbateur, fauteur m de troubles

troubleshooter ['trʌblʃu:təʳ] N (in conflict) conciliateur m

troublesome ['trʌblsəm] ADJ (child) fatigant(e), difficile; (cough) gênant(e)

trouble spot N point chaud (fig)

troubling ['trʌblɪŋ] ADJ (times, thought) inquiétant(e)

trough [trɔf] N (also: **drinking trough**) abreuvoir m; (also: **feeding trough**) auge f; (depression) creux m; (channel) chenal m; **~ of low pressure** (Meteorology) dépression f

trounce [trauns] VT (defeat) battre à plates coutures

troupe [tru:p] N troupe f

trouser press N presse-pantalon m inv

trousers ['trauzəz] NPL pantalon m; **short ~** (BRIT) culottes courtes

trouser suit N (BRIT) tailleur-pantalon m

trousseau ['tru:səu] (pl **trousseaux** or **trousseaus** [-z]) N trousseau m

trout [traut] N (pl inv) truite f

trowel ['trauəl] N truelle f; (garden tool) déplantoir m

truant ['truənt] N: **to play ~** (BRIT) faire l'école buissonnière

truce [tru:s] N trêve f

truck [trʌk] N camion m; (Rail) wagon m à plate-forme; (for luggage) chariot m (à bagages)

truck driver N camionneur m

trucker ['trʌkəʳ] N (esp US) camionneur m

truck farm N (US) jardin maraîcher

trucking ['trʌkɪŋ] N (esp US) transport routier

trucking company N (US) entreprise f de transport (routier)

truck stop (US) N routier m, restaurant m de routiers

truculent ['trʌkjulənt] ADJ agressif(-ive)

trudge [trʌdʒ] VI marcher lourdement, se traîner

true [tru:] ADJ vrai(e); (accurate) exact(e); (genuine) vrai, véritable; (faithful) fidèle; (wall) d'aplomb; (beam) droit(e); (wheel) dans l'axe; **to come ~** se réaliser; **~ to life** réaliste

truffle ['trʌfl] N truffe f

truly ['tru:lɪ] ADV vraiment, réellement; (truthfully) sans mentir; (faithfully) fidèlement; **yours ~** (in letter) je vous prie d'agréer, Monsieur (or Madame etc), l'expression de mes sentiments respectueux

trump [trʌmp] N atout m; **to turn up trumps** (fig) faire des miracles

trump card N atout m; (fig) carte maîtresse f

trumped-up [trʌmpt'ʌp] ADJ inventé(e) (de toutes pièces)

trumpet ['trʌmpɪt] N trompette f

truncated [trʌŋ'keɪtɪd] ADJ tronqué(e)

truncheon ['trʌntʃən] N bâton m (d'agent de police); matraque f

trundle ['trʌndl] VT, VI: **to ~ along** rouler bruyamment

trunk [trʌŋk] N (of tree, person) tronc m; (of elephant) trompe f; (case) malle f; (US Aut) coffre m; **trunks** NPL (also: **swimming trunks**) maillot m or slip m de bain

trunk call N (BRIT Tel) communication interurbaine

trunk road N (BRIT) ≈ (route f) nationale f

truss [trʌs] N (Med) bandage m herniaire ▶ VT: **to ~ (up)** (Culin) brider

trust [trʌst] N confiance f; (responsibility): **to place sth in sb's ~** confier la responsabilité de qch à qn; (Law) fidéicommis m; (Comm) trust m ▶ VT (rely on) avoir confiance en; (entrust): **to ~ sth to sb** confier qch à qn; (hope): **to ~ (that)** espérer (que); **to take sth on ~** accepter qch les yeux fermés; **in ~** (Law) par fidéicommis

trust company N société f fiduciaire

trusted ['trʌstɪd] ADJ en qui l'on a confiance

trustee [trʌs'ti:] N (Law) fidéicommissaire mf; (of school etc) administrateur(-trice)

trustful ['trʌstful] ADJ confiant(e)

trust fund N fonds m en fidéicommis

trusting ['trʌstɪŋ] ADJ confiant(e)

trustworthy ['trʌstwə:ðɪ] ADJ digne de confiance

trusty ['trʌstɪ] ADJ fidèle

truth [tru:θ] (pl **truths** [tru:ðz]) N vérité f

truthful ['tru:θful] ADJ (person) qui dit la vérité; (answer) sincère; (description) exact(e), vrai(e)

truthfully ['tru:θfəlɪ] ADV sincèrement, sans mentir

truthfulness ['tru:θfəlnɪs] N véracité f

try [traɪ] N essai m, tentative f; (Rugby) essai ▶ VT (attempt) essayer, tenter; (test: sth new: also: **try out**) essayer, tester; (Law: person) juger; (strain) éprouver ▶ VI essayer; **to ~ to do** essayer de faire; (seek) chercher à faire; **to ~ one's (very) best** or **one's (very) hardest** faire de son mieux; **to give sth a ~** essayer qch
▶ **try on** VT (clothes) essayer; **to ~ it on** (fig) tenter le coup, bluffer
▶ **try out** VT essayer, mettre à l'essai

trying ['traɪɪŋ] ADJ pénible

tsar [zɑːʳ] N tsar m

T-shirt ['ti:ʃəːt] N tee-shirt m

T-square ['ti:skwɛəʳ] N équerre f en T

tsunami [tsu'nɑːmɪ] N tsunami m

TT ADJ ABBR (*Brit inf*) = **teetotal** ▶ ABBR (*US*) = **Trust Territory**

tub [tʌb] N cuve *f*; (*for washing clothes*) baquet *m*; (*bath*) baignoire *f*

tuba ['tju:bə] N tuba *m*

tubby ['tʌbɪ] ADJ rondelet(te)

tube [tju:b] N tube *m*; (*Brit: underground*) métro *m*; (*for tyre*) chambre *f* à air; (*inf: television*): **the ~** la télé

tubeless ['tju:blɪs] ADJ (*tyre*) sans chambre à air

tuber ['tju:bə^r] N (*Bot*) tubercule *m*

tuberculosis [tjubə:kju'ləusɪs] N tuberculose *f*

tube station N (*Brit*) station *f* de métro

tubing ['tju:bɪŋ] N tubes *mpl*; **a piece of ~** un tube

tubular ['tju:bjulə^r] ADJ tubulaire

TUC N ABBR (*Brit*: = *Trades Union Congress*) confédération *f* des syndicats britanniques

tuck [tʌk] N (*Sewing*) pli *m*, rempli *m* ▶ VT (*put*) mettre
  ▶**tuck away** VT cacher, ranger; (*money*) mettre de côté; (*building*): **to be tucked away** être caché(e)
  ▶**tuck in** VT rentrer; (*child*) border ▶ VI (*eat*) manger de bon appétit; attaquer le repas
  ▶**tuck up** VT (*child*) border

tucker ['tʌkə^r] N (*Australia, New Zealand inf*) bouffe *f* (*inf*)

tuck shop N (*Brit Scol*) boutique *f* à provisions

Tuesday ['tju:zdɪ] N mardi *m*; (**the date**) **today is ~ 23 March** nous sommes aujourd'hui le mardi 23 mars; **on ~** mardi; **on Tuesdays** le mardi; **every ~** tous les mardis, chaque mardi; **every other ~** un mardi sur deux; **last/next ~** mardi dernier/prochain; **the ~ next** mardi qui vient; **the following ~** le mardi suivant; **a week/fortnight on ~**, **~ week/fortnight** mardi en huit/quinze; **the ~ before last** l'autre mardi; **the ~ after next** mardi en huit; **~ morning/lunchtime/afternoon/evening** mardi matin/midi/après-midi/soir; **~ night** mardi soir; (*overnight*) la nuit de mardi (à mercredi); **~'s newspaper** le journal de mardi

tuft [tʌft] N touffe *f*

tug [tʌg] N (*ship*) remorqueur *m* ▶ VT tirer (sur)

tug-of-love [tʌgəv'lʌv] N lutte acharnée entre parents divorcés pour avoir la garde d'un enfant

tug-of-war [tʌgəv'wɔ:^r] N lutte *f* à la corde

tuition [tju:'ɪʃən] N (*Brit: lessons*) leçons *fpl*; (: *private*) cours particuliers; (*US: fees*) frais *mpl* de scolarité

tulip ['tju:lɪp] N tulipe *f*

tumble ['tʌmbl] N (*fall*) chute *f*, culbute *f* ▶ VI tomber, dégringoler; (*somersault*) faire une or des culbute(s) ▶ VT renverser, faire tomber; **to ~ to sth** (*inf*) réaliser qch

tumbledown ['tʌmbldaun] ADJ délabré(e)

tumble dryer N (*Brit*) séchoir *m* (à linge) à air chaud

tumbler ['tʌmblə^r] N verre (droit), gobelet *m*

tummy ['tʌmɪ] N (*inf*) ventre *m*

tumour, (*US*) **tumor** ['tju:mə^r] N tumeur *f*

tumult ['tju:mʌlt] N tumulte *m*

tumultuous [tju:'mʌltjuəs] ADJ tumultueux(-euse)

tuna ['tju:nə] N (*pl inv: also*: **tuna fish**) thon *m*

tune [tju:n] N (*melody*) air *m* ▶ VT (*Mus*) accorder; (*Radio, TV, Aut*) régler, mettre au point; **to be in/out of ~** (*instrument*) être accordé/désaccordé; (*singer*) chanter juste/faux; **to be in/out of ~ with** (*fig*) être en accord/désaccord avec; **she was robbed to the ~ of £30,000** (*fig*) on lui a volé la jolie somme de 10 000 livres
  ▶ VT **tune in** (*Radio, TV*): **to ~ in (to)** se mettre à l'écoute (de)
  ▶ **tune up** VI (*musician*) accorder son instrument

tuneful ['tju:nful] ADJ mélodieux(-euse)

tuner ['tju:nə^r] N (*radio set*) tuner *m*; **piano ~** accordeur *m* de pianos

tuner amplifier N ampli-tuner *m*

tungsten ['tʌŋstn] N tungstène *m*

tunic ['tju:nɪk] N tunique *f*

tuning ['tju:nɪŋ] N réglage *m*

tuning fork N diapason *m*

Tunis ['tju:nɪs] N Tunis

Tunisia [tju:'nɪzɪə] N Tunisie *f*

Tunisian [tju:'nɪzɪən] ADJ tunisien(ne) ▶ N Tunisien(ne)

tunnel ['tʌnl] N tunnel *m*; (*in mine*) galerie *f* ▶ VI creuser un tunnel (or une galerie)

tunnel vision N (*Med*) rétrécissement *m* du champ visuel; (*fig*) vision étroite des choses

tunny ['tʌnɪ] N thon *m*

turban ['tə:bən] N turban *m*

turbid ['tə:bɪd] ADJ boueux(-euse)

turbine ['tə:baɪn] N turbine *f*

turbo ['tə:bəu] N turbo *m*

turbojet [tə:bəu'dʒɛt] N turboréacteur *m*

turboprop [tə:bəu'prɔp] N (*engine*) turbopropulseur *m*

turbot ['tə:bət] N (*pl inv*) turbot *m*

turbulence ['tə:bjuləns] N (*Aviat*) turbulence *f*

turbulent ['tə:bjulənt] ADJ turbulent(e); (*sea*) agité(e)

tureen [tə'ri:n] N soupière *f*

turf [tə:f] N gazon *m*; (*clod*) motte *f* (de gazon) ▶ VT gazonner; **the T~** le turf, les courses *fpl*
  ▶ **turf out** VT (*inf*) jeter; jeter dehors

turf accountant N (*Brit*) bookmaker *m*

turgid ['tə:dʒɪd] ADJ (*speech*) pompeux(-euse)

Turin [tjuə'rɪn] N Turin

Turk [tə:k] N Turc (Turque)

Turkey ['tə:kɪ] N Turquie *f*

turkey ['tə:kɪ] N dindon *m*, dinde *f*

Turkish ['tə:kɪʃ] ADJ turc (turque) ▶ N (*Ling*) turc *m*

Turkish bath N bain turc

Turkish delight N loukoum *m*

turmeric ['tə:mərɪk] N curcuma *m*

turmoil ['tə:mɔɪl] N trouble *m*, bouleversement *m*

turn [tə:n] N tour *m*; (*in road*) tournant *m*; (*tendency: of mind, events*) tournure *f*; (*performance*) numéro *m*; (*Med*) crise *f*, attaque *f* ▶ VT tourner; (*collar, steak*) retourner; (*age*) atteindre; (*shape: wood, metal*) tourner; (*milk*) faire tourner; (*change*): **to ~ sth into** changer qch en ▶ VI

t

839

(*object, wind, milk*) tourner; (*person: look back*) se (re)tourner; (*reverse direction*) faire demi-tour; (*change*) changer; (*become*) devenir; **to ~ into** se changer en, se transformer en; **a good ~** un service; **a bad ~** un mauvais tour; **it gave me quite a ~** ça m'a fait un coup; **"no left ~"** (*Aut*) "défense de tourner à gauche"; **~ left/right at the next junction** tournez à gauche/droite au prochain carrefour; **it's your ~** c'est (à) votre tour; **in ~** à son tour; à tour de rôle; **to take turns** se relayer; **to take turns at** faire à tour de rôle; **at the ~ of the year/century** à la fin de l'année/du siècle; **to take a ~ for the worse** (*situation, events*) empirer; **his health** *or* **he has taken a ~ for the worse** son état s'est aggravé
▶ **turn about** VI faire demi-tour; faire un demi-tour
▶ **turn around** VI (*person*) se retourner ▶ VT (*object*) tourner
▶ **turn away** VI se détourner, tourner la tête
▶ VT (*reject: person*) renvoyer; (: *business*) refuser
▶ **turn back** VI revenir, faire demi-tour
▶ **turn down** VT (*refuse*) rejeter, refuser; (*reduce*) baisser; (*fold*) rabattre
▶ **turn in** VI (*inf: go to bed*) aller se coucher ▶ VT (*fold*) rentrer
▶ **turn off** VI (*from road*) tourner ▶ VT (*light, radio etc*) éteindre; (*tap*) fermer; (*engine*) arrêter; **I can't ~ the heating off** je n'arrive pas à éteindre le chauffage
▶ **turn on** VT (*light, radio etc*) allumer; (*tap*) ouvrir; (*engine*) mettre en marche; **I can't ~ the heating on** je n'arrive pas à allumer le chauffage
▶ **turn out** VT (*light, gas*) éteindre; (*produce: goods, novel, good pupils*) produire ▶ VI (*voters, troops*) se présenter; **to ~ out to be ...** s'avérer ..., se révéler ...
▶ **turn over** VI (*person*) se retourner ▶ VT (*object*) retourner; (*page*) tourner
▶ **turn round** VI faire demi-tour; (*rotate*) tourner
▶ **turn to** VT FUS: **to ~ to sb** s'adresser à qn
▶ **turn up** VI (*person*) arriver, se pointer (*inf*); (*lost object*) être retrouvé(e) ▶ VT (*collar*) remonter; (*radio, heater*) mettre plus fort
turnabout ['tə:nəbaut], **turnaround** ['tə:nəraund] N volte-face *f inv*
turncoat ['tə:nkəut] N renégat(e)
turned-up ['tə:ndʌp] ADJ (*nose*) retroussé(e)
turning ['tə:nɪŋ] N (*in road*) tournant *m*; **the first ~ on the right** la première (rue *or* route) à droite
turning circle N (*Brit*) rayon *m* de braquage
turning point N (*fig*) tournant *m*, moment décisif
turning radius N (*US*) = **turning circle**
turnip ['tə:nɪp] N navet *m*
turnout ['tə:naut] N (nombre *m* de personnes dans l')assistance *f*; (*of voters*) taux *m* de participation
turnover ['tə:nəuvə^r] N (*Comm: amount of money*) chiffre *m* d'affaires; (: *of goods*) roulement *m*; (*of staff*) renouvellement *m*, changement *m*; (*Culin*)

sorte de chausson; **there is a rapid ~ in staff** le personnel change souvent
turnpike ['tə:npaɪk] N (*US*) autoroute *f* à péage
turnstile ['tə:nstaɪl] N tourniquet *m* (*d'entrée*)
turntable ['tə:nteɪbl] N (*on record player*) platine *f*
turn-up ['tə:nʌp] N (*Brit: on trousers*) revers *m*
turpentine ['tə:pəntaɪn] N (*also:* **turps**) (essence *f* de) térébenthine *f*
turquoise ['tə:kwɔɪz] N (*stone*) turquoise *f* ▶ ADJ turquoise *inv*
turret ['tʌrɪt] N tourelle *f*
turtle ['tə:tl] N tortue marine
turtleneck (sweater) ['tə:tlnɛk-] N pullover *m* à col montant
Tuscany ['tʌskənɪ] N Toscane *f*
tusk [tʌsk] N défense *f* (*d'éléphant*)
tussle ['tʌsl] N bagarre *f*, mêlée *f*
tutor ['tju:tə^r] N (*Brit Scol: in college*) directeur(-trice) d'études; (*private teacher*) précepteur(-trice)
tutorial [tju:'tɔ:rɪəl] N (*Scol*) (séance *f* de) travaux *mpl* pratiques
tuxedo [tʌk'si:dəu] N (*US*) smoking *m*
TV [ti:'vi:] N ABBR (= *television*) télé *f*, TV *f*
TV dinner N plateau-repas surgelé
twaddle ['twɔdl] N balivernes *fpl*
twang [twæŋ] N (*of instrument*) son vibrant; (*of voice*) ton nasillard ▶ VI vibrer ▶ VT (*guitar*) pincer les cordes de
tweak [twi:k] VT (*nose*) tordre; (*ear, hair*) tirer
tweed [twi:d] N tweed *m*
tweet [twi:t] (*on Twitter*) N tweet *m* ▶ VT, VI tweeter
tweezers ['twi:zəz] NPL pince *f* à épiler
twelfth [twɛlfθ] NUM douzième
Twelfth Night N la fête des Rois
twelve [twɛlv] NUM douze; **at ~ (o'clock)** à midi; (*midnight*) à minuit
twentieth ['twɛntɪɪθ] NUM vingtième
twenty ['twɛntɪ] NUM vingt; **in ~ fourteen** en deux mille quatorze
twerp [twə:p] N (*inf*) imbécile *mf*
twice [twaɪs] ADV deux fois; **~ as much** deux fois plus; **~ a week** deux fois par semaine; **she is ~ your age** elle a deux fois ton âge
twiddle ['twɪdl] VT, VI: **to ~ (with) sth** tripoter qch; **to ~ one's thumbs** (*fig*) se tourner les pouces
twig [twɪg] N brindille *f* ▶ VT, VI (*inf*) piger
twilight ['twaɪlaɪt] N crépuscule *m*; (*morning*) aube *f*; **in the ~** dans la pénombre
twill [twɪl] N sergé *m*
twin [twɪn] ADJ, N jumeau (jumelle) ▶ VT jumeler
twin-bedded room ['twɪn'bɛdɪd-] N = **twin room**
twin beds NPL lits *mpl* jumeaux
twin-carburettor ['twɪnkɑ:bju'rɛtə^r] ADJ à double carburateur
twine [twaɪn] N ficelle *f* ▶ VI (*plant*) s'enrouler
twin-engined [twɪn'ɛndʒɪnd] ADJ bimoteur; **~ aircraft** bimoteur *m*
twinge [twɪndʒ] N (*of pain*) élancement *m*; (*of conscience*) remords *m*

twinkle ['twɪŋkl] N scintillement *m*;
pétillement *m* ▶ VI scintiller; (*eyes*) pétiller
twin room N chambre *f* à deux lits
twin town N ville jumelée
twirl [twəːl] N tournoiement *m* ▶ VT faire
tournoyer ▶ VI tournoyer
twist [twɪst] N torsion *f*, tour *m*; (*in wire, flex*)
tortillon *m*; (*bend: in road*) tournant *m*; (*in story*)
coup *m* de théâtre ▶ VT tordre; (*weave*)
entortiller; (*roll around*) enrouler; (*fig*) déformer
▶ VI s'entortiller; s'enrouler; (*road, river*)
serpenter; **to ~ one's ankle/wrist** (*Med*) se
tordre la cheville/le poignet
twisted ['twɪstɪd] ADJ (*wire, rope*) entortillé(e);
(*ankle, wrist*) tordu(e), foulé(e); (*fig: logic, mind*)
tordu
twit [twɪt] N (*inf*) crétin(e)
twitch [twɪtʃ] N (*pull*) coup sec, saccade *f*;
(*nervous*) tic *m* ▶ VI se convulser; avoir un tic
Twitter® ['twɪtə'] N Twitter® ▶ VI twitter
two [tuː] NUM deux; **~ by ~, in twos** par deux;
to put ~ and ~ together (*fig*) faire le
rapprochement
two-bit [tuːˈbɪt] ADJ (*esp US inf, pej*) de pacotille
two-door [tuːˈdɔː'] ADJ (*Aut*) à deux portes
two-faced [tuːˈfeɪst] ADJ (*pej: person*) faux
(fausse)
twofold ['tuːfəʊld] ADJ (*increase*) de cent pour
cent; (*reply*) en deux parties ▶ ADV: **to increase
~ doubler**
two-piece ['tuːˈpiːs] N (*also*: **two-piece suit**)
(costume *m*) deux-pièces *m inv*; (*also*: **two-piece
swimsuit**) (maillot *m* de bain) deux-pièces
two-seater [tuːˈsiːtə'] N (*plane*) (avion *m*)
biplace *m*; (*car*) voiture *f* à deux places
twosome ['tuːsəm] N (*people*) couple *m*
two-stroke ['tuːstrəʊk] N (*also*: **two-stroke
engine**) moteur *m* à deux temps ▶ ADJ à deux
temps
two-tone ['tuːˈtəʊn] ADJ (*in colour*) à deux tons
two-way ['tuːweɪ] ADJ (*traffic*) dans les deux
sens; **~ radio** émetteur-récepteur *m*

TX ABBR (*US*) = **Texas**
tycoon [taɪˈkuːn] N: **(business)** ~ gros homme
d'affaires
type [taɪp] N (*category*) genre *m*, espèce *f*;
(*model*) modèle *m*; (*example*) type *m*; (*Typ*) type,
caractère *m* ▶ VT (*letter etc*) taper (à la machine);
what ~ do you want? quel genre voulez-vous?;
in bold/italic ~ en caractères gras/en
italiques
typecast ['taɪpkɑːst] ADJ condamné(e) à
toujours jouer le même rôle
typeface ['taɪpfeɪs] N police *f* (de caractères)
typescript ['taɪpskrɪpt] N texte dactylographié
typeset ['taɪpsɛt] VT (*irreg: like* **set**) composer (*en
imprimerie*)
typesetter ['taɪpsɛtə'] N compositeur *m*
typewriter ['taɪpraɪtə'] N machine *f* à écrire
typewritten ['taɪprɪtn] ADJ dactylographié(e)
typhoid ['taɪfɔɪd] N typhoïde *f*
typhoon [taɪˈfuːn] N typhon *m*
typhus ['taɪfəs] N typhus *m*
typical ['tɪpɪkl] ADJ typique, caractéristique
typically ['tɪpɪklɪ] ADV (*as usual*) comme
d'habitude; (*characteristically*) typiquement
typify ['tɪpɪfaɪ] VT être caractéristique de
typing ['taɪpɪŋ] N dactylo(graphie) *f*
typing error N faute *f* de frappe
typing pool N pool *m* de dactylos
typist ['taɪpɪst] N dactylo *mf*
typo ['taɪpəʊ] N ABBR (*inf: = typographical error*)
coquille *f*
typography [taɪˈpɒgrəfɪ] N typographie *f*
tyranny ['tɪrənɪ] N tyrannie *f*
tyrant ['taɪrənt] N tyran *m*
tyre, (*US*) **tire** ['taɪə'] N pneu *m*
tyre pressure N (*BRIT*) pression *f* (de gonflage)
Tyrol [tɪˈrəʊl] N Tyrol *m*
Tyrolean [tɪrəˈliːən], **Tyrolese** [tɪrəˈliːz] ADJ
tyrolien(ne) ▶ N Tyrolien(ne)
Tyrrhenian Sea [tɪˈriːnɪən-] N: **the ~** la mer
Tyrrhénienne
tzar [zɑː'] N = **tsar**

t

Uu

U, u [juː] N (*letter*) U, u *m*; **U for Uncle** U comme Ursule

U N ABBR (*BRIT Cine*: = *universal*) ≈ tous publics

UAW N ABBR (*US*: = *United Automobile Workers*) syndicat des ouvriers de l'automobile

UB40 N ABBR (*BRIT*: = *unemployment benefit form 40*) numéro de référence d'un formulaire d'inscription au chômage: par extension, le bénéficiaire

U-bend ['juːbɛnd] N (*BRIT Aut*) coude *m*, virage *m* en épingle à cheveux; (*in pipe*) coude

ubiquitous [juːˈbɪkwɪtəs] ADJ doué(e) d'ubiquité, omniprésent(e)

UCAS ['juːkæs] N ABBR (*BRIT*) = **Universities and Colleges Admissions Service**

UDA N ABBR (*BRIT*) = **Ulster Defence Association**

UDC N ABBR (*BRIT*) = **Urban District Council**

udder ['ʌdəʳ] N pis *m*, mamelle *f*

UDI N ABBR (*BRIT Pol*) = **unilateral declaration of independence**

UDR N ABBR (*BRIT*) = **Ulster Defence Regiment**

UEFA [juːˈeɪfə] N ABBR (= *Union of European Football Associations*) UEFA *f*

UFO ['juːfəʊ] N ABBR (= *unidentified flying object*) ovni *m*

Uganda [juːˈgændə] N Ouganda *m*

Ugandan [juːˈgændən] ADJ ougandais(e) ▶ N Ougandais(e)

UGC N ABBR (*BRIT*: = *University Grants Committee*) commission d'attribution des dotations aux universités

ugh [əːh] EXCL pouah!

ugliness ['ʌglɪnɪs] N laideur *f*

ugly ['ʌglɪ] ADJ laid(e), vilain(e); (*fig*) répugnant(e)

UHF ABBR (= *ultra-high frequency*) UHF

UHT ADJ ABBR (= *ultra-heat treated*): ~ **milk** lait *m* UHT *or* longue conservation

UK N ABBR = **United Kingdom**

Ukraine [juːˈkreɪn] N Ukraine *f*

Ukrainian [juːˈkreɪnɪən] ADJ ukrainien(ne) ▶ N Ukrainien(ne); (*Ling*) ukrainien *m*

ulcer ['ʌlsəʳ] N ulcère *m*; **mouth ~** aphte *f*

Ulster ['ʌlstəʳ] N Ulster *m*

ulterior [ʌlˈtɪərɪəʳ] ADJ ultérieur(e); ~ **motive** arrière-pensée *f*

ultimate ['ʌltɪmət] ADJ ultime, final(e); (*authority*) suprême ▶ N: **the ~ in luxury** le summum du luxe

ultimately ['ʌltɪmətlɪ] ADV (*at last*) en fin de compte; (*fundamentally*) finalement; (*eventually*) par la suite

ultimatum [ʌltɪˈmeɪtəm] (*pl* **ultimatums** *or* **ultimata** [-tə]) N ultimatum *m*

ultrasonic [ʌltrəˈsɔnɪk] ADJ ultrasonique

ultrasound ['ʌltrəsaund] N (*Med*) ultrason *m*

ultraviolet ['ʌltrəˈvaɪəlɪt] ADJ ultraviolet(te)

umbilical [ʌmbɪˈlaɪkl] ADJ: ~ **cord** cordon ombilical

umbrage ['ʌmbrɪdʒ] N: **to take ~** prendre ombrage, se froisser

umbrella [ʌmˈbrɛlə] N parapluie *m*; (*for sun*) parasol *m*; **under the ~ of** (*fig*) sous les auspices de; chapeauté(e) par

umlaut ['umlaut] N tréma *m*

umpire ['ʌmpaɪəʳ] N arbitre *m*; (*Tennis*) juge *m* de chaise ▶ VT arbitrer

umpteen [ʌmpˈtiːn] ADJ je ne sais combien de; **for the umpteenth time** pour la nième fois

UMW N ABBR (= *United Mineworkers of America*) syndicat des mineurs

UN N ABBR = **United Nations**

unabashed [ʌnəˈbæʃt] ADJ nullement intimidé(e)

unabated [ʌnəˈbeɪtɪd] ADJ non diminué(e)

unable [ʌnˈeɪbl] ADJ: **to be ~ to** ne (pas) pouvoir, être dans l'impossibilité de; (*not capable*) être incapable de

unabridged [ʌnəˈbrɪdʒd] ADJ complet(-ète), intégral(e)

unacceptable [ʌnəkˈsɛptəbl] ADJ (*behaviour*) inadmissible; (*price, proposal*) inacceptable

unaccompanied [ʌnəˈkʌmpənɪd] ADJ (*child, lady*) non accompagné(e); (*singing, song*) sans accompagnement

unaccountably [ʌnəˈkauntəblɪ] ADV inexplicablement

unaccounted [ʌnəˈkauntɪd] ADJ: **two passengers are ~ for** on est sans nouvelles de deux passagers

unaccustomed [ʌnəˈkʌstəmd] ADJ inaccoutumé(e), inhabituel(le); **to be ~ to sth** ne pas avoir l'habitude de qch

unacquainted [ʌnəˈkweɪntɪd] ADJ: **to be ~ with** ne pas connaître

unadulterated [ʌnəˈdʌltəreɪtɪd] ADJ pur(e), naturel(le)

unaffected [ʌnəˈfɛktɪd] ADJ (*person, behaviour*)

naturel(le); (*emotionally*): **to be ~ by** ne pas être touché(e) par

unafraid [ʌnə'freɪd] ADJ: **to be ~** ne pas avoir peur

unaided [ʌn'eɪdɪd] ADJ sans aide, tout(e) seul(e)

unanimity [ju:nə'nɪmɪtɪ] N unanimité f

unanimous [ju:'nænɪməs] ADJ unanime

unanimously [ju:'nænɪməslɪ] ADV à l'unanimité

unanswered [ʌn'ɑ:nsəd] ADJ (*question, letter*) sans réponse

unappetizing [ʌn'æpɪtaɪzɪŋ] ADJ peu appétissant(e)

unappreciative [ʌnə'pri:ʃɪətɪv] ADJ indifférent(e)

unarmed [ʌn'ɑ:md] ADJ (*person*) non armé(e); (*combat*) sans armes

unashamed [ʌnə'ʃeɪmd] ADJ sans honte; impudent(e)

unassisted [ʌnə'sɪstɪd] ADJ non assisté(e) ▶ ADV sans aide, tout(e) seul(e)

unassuming [ʌnə'sju:mɪŋ] ADJ modeste, sans prétentions

unattached [ʌnə'tætʃt] ADJ libre, sans attaches

unattended [ʌnə'tendɪd] ADJ (*car, child, luggage*) sans surveillance

unattractive [ʌnə'træktɪv] ADJ peu attrayant(e); (*character*) peu sympathique

unauthorized [ʌn'ɔ:θəraɪzd] ADJ non autorisé(e), sans autorisation

unavailable [ʌnə'veɪləbl] ADJ (*article, room, book*) (qui n'est) pas disponible; (*person*) (qui n'est) pas libre

unavoidable [ʌnə'vɔɪdəbl] ADJ inévitable

unavoidably [ʌnə'vɔɪdəblɪ] ADV inévitablement

unaware [ʌnə'weəʳ] ADJ: **to be ~ of** ignorer, ne pas savoir, être inconscient(e) de

unawares [ʌnə'weəz] ADV à l'improviste, au dépourvu

unbalanced [ʌn'bælənst] ADJ déséquilibré(e)

unbearable [ʌn'beərəbl] ADJ insupportable

unbeatable [ʌn'bi:təbl] ADJ imbattable

unbeaten [ʌn'bi:tn] ADJ invaincu(e); (*record*) non battu(e)

unbecoming [ʌnbɪ'kʌmɪŋ] ADJ (*unseemly: language, behaviour*) malséant(e), inconvenant(e); (*unflattering: garment*) peu seyant(e)

unbeknown [ʌnbɪ'nəun], **unbeknownst** [ʌnbɪ'nəunst] ADV: **~ to** à l'insu de

unbelief [ʌnbɪ'li:f] N incrédulité f

unbelievable [ʌnbɪ'li:vəbl] ADJ incroyable

unbelievingly [ʌnbɪ'li:vɪŋlɪ] ADV avec incrédulité

unbend [ʌn'bend] VI (*irreg: like* **bend**) se détendre ▶ VT (*wire*) redresser, détordre

unbending [ʌn'bendɪŋ] ADJ (*fig*) inflexible

unbiased, unbiassed [ʌn'baɪəst] ADJ impartial(e)

unblemished [ʌn'blemɪʃt] ADJ impeccable

unblock [ʌn'blɔk] VT (*pipe*) déboucher; (*road*) dégager

unborn [ʌn'bɔ:n] ADJ à naître

unbounded [ʌn'baundɪd] ADJ sans bornes, illimité(e)

unbreakable [ʌn'breɪkəbl] ADJ incassable

unbridled [ʌn'braɪdld] ADJ débridé(e), déchaîné(e)

unbroken [ʌn'brəukn] ADJ intact(e); (*line*) continu(e); (*record*) non battu(e)

unbuckle [ʌn'bʌkl] VT déboucler

unburden [ʌn'bə:dn] VT: **to ~ o.s.** s'épancher, se livrer

unbutton [ʌn'bʌtn] VT déboutonner

uncalled-for [ʌn'kɔ:ldfɔ:ʳ] ADJ déplacé(e), injustifié(e)

uncanny [ʌn'kænɪ] ADJ étrange, troublant(e)

unceasing [ʌn'si:sɪŋ] ADJ incessant(e), continu(e)

unceremonious [ʌnserɪ'məunɪəs] ADJ (*abrupt, rude*) brusque

uncertain [ʌn'sə:tn] ADJ incertain(e); (*hesitant*) hésitant(e); **we were ~ whether ...** nous ne savions pas vraiment si ...; **in no ~ terms** sans équivoque possible

uncertainty [ʌn'sə:tntɪ] N incertitude f, doutes mpl

unchallenged [ʌn'tʃælɪndʒd] ADJ (*gen*) incontesté(e); (*information*) non contesté(e); **to go ~** ne pas être contesté

unchanged [ʌn'tʃeɪndʒd] ADJ inchangé(e)

uncharitable [ʌn'tʃærɪtəbl] ADJ peu charitable

uncharted [ʌn'tʃɑ:tɪd] ADJ inexploré(e)

unchecked [ʌn'tʃekt] ADJ non réprimé(e)

uncivilized [ʌn'sɪvɪlaɪzd] ADJ non civilisé(e); (*fig*) barbare

uncle ['ʌŋkl] N oncle m

unclear [ʌn'klɪəʳ] ADJ (qui n'est) pas clair(e) or évident(e); **I'm still ~ about what I'm supposed to do** je ne sais pas encore exactement ce que je dois faire

uncoil [ʌn'kɔɪl] VT dérouler ▶ VI se dérouler

uncomfortable [ʌn'kʌmfətəbl] ADJ inconfortable, peu confortable; (*uneasy*) mal à l'aise, gêné(e); (*situation*) désagréable

uncomfortably [ʌn'kʌmfətəblɪ] ADV inconfortablement; d'un ton *etc* gêné or embarrassé; désagréablement

uncommitted [ʌnkə'mɪtɪd] ADJ (*attitude, country*) non engagé(e)

uncommon [ʌn'kɔmən] ADJ rare, singulier(-ière), peu commun(e)

uncommunicative [ʌnkə'mju:nɪkətɪv] ADJ réservé(e)

uncomplicated [ʌn'kɔmplɪkeɪtɪd] ADJ simple, peu compliqué(e)

uncompromising [ʌn'kɔmprəmaɪzɪŋ] ADJ intransigeant(e), inflexible

unconcerned [ʌnkən'sə:nd] ADJ (*unworried*): **to be ~ (about)** ne pas s'inquiéter (de)

unconditional [ʌnkən'dɪʃənl] ADJ sans conditions

uncongenial [ʌnkən'dʒi:nɪəl] ADJ peu agréable

unconnected [ʌnkə'nektɪd] ADJ (*unrelated*): **~ (with)** sans rapport (avec)

unconscious [ʌn'kɔnʃəs] ADJ sans connaissance, évanoui(e); (*unaware*): **~ (of)** inconscient(e) (de) ▶ N: **the ~** l'inconscient m; **to knock sb ~** assommer qn

u

unconsciously [ʌnˈkɔnʃəslɪ] ADV inconsciemment

unconstitutional [ʌnkɔnstɪˈtjuːʃənl] ADJ anticonstitutionnel(le)

uncontested [ʌnkənˈtɛstɪd] ADJ (champion) incontesté(e); (Pol: seat) non disputé(e)

uncontrollable [ʌnkənˈtrəʊləbl] ADJ (child, dog) indiscipliné(e); (temper, laughter) irrépressible

uncontrolled [ʌnkənˈtrəʊld] ADJ (laughter, price rises) incontrôlé(e)

unconventional [ʌnkənˈvɛnʃənl] ADJ peu conventionnel(le)

unconvinced [ʌnkənˈvɪnst] ADJ: **to be ~** ne pas être convaincu(e)

unconvincing [ʌnkənˈvɪnsɪŋ] ADJ peu convaincant(e)

uncork [ʌnˈkɔːk] VT déboucher

uncorroborated [ʌnkəˈrɔbəreɪtɪd] ADJ non confirmé(e)

uncouth [ʌnˈkuːθ] ADJ grossier(-ière), fruste

uncover [ʌnˈkʌvər] VT découvrir

unctuous [ˈʌŋktjuəs] ADJ onctueux(-euse), mielleux(-euse)

undamaged [ʌnˈdæmɪdʒd] ADJ (goods) intact(e), en bon état; (fig: reputation) intact

undaunted [ʌnˈdɔːntɪd] ADJ non intimidé(e), inébranlable

undecided [ʌndɪˈsaɪdɪd] ADJ indécis(e), irrésolu(e)

undelivered [ʌndɪˈlɪvəd] ADJ non remis(e), non livré(e)

undeniable [ʌndɪˈnaɪəbl] ADJ indéniable, incontestable

under [ˈʌndər] PREP sous; (less than) (de) moins de; au-dessous de; (according to) selon, en vertu de ▶ ADV au-dessous; en dessous; **from ~ sth** de dessous or de sous qch; **~ there** là-dessous; **in ~ 2 hours** en moins de 2 heures; **~ anaesthetic** sous anesthésie; **~ discussion** en discussion; **~ the circumstances** étant donné les circonstances; **~ repair** en (cours de) réparation

under... [ˈʌndər] PREFIX sous-

underage [ʌndərˈeɪdʒ] ADJ qui n'a pas l'âge réglementaire

underarm [ˈʌndərɑːm] ADV par en-dessous ▶ ADJ (throw) par en-dessous; (deodorant) pour les aisselles

undercapitalized [ʌndəˈkæpɪtəlaɪzd] ADJ sous-capitalisé(e)

undercarriage [ˈʌndəkærɪdʒ] N (BRIT Aviat) train m d'atterrissage

undercharge [ʌndəˈtʃɑːdʒ] VT ne pas faire payer assez à

underclass [ˈʌndəklɑːs] N ≈ quart-monde m

underclothes [ˈʌndəkləʊðz] NPL sous-vêtements mpl; (women's only) dessous mpl

undercoat [ˈʌndəkəʊt] N (paint) couche f de fond

undercover [ʌndəˈkʌvər] ADJ secret(-ète), clandestin(e)

undercurrent [ˈʌndəkʌrnt] N courant sous-jacent

undercut [ʌndəˈkʌt] VT (irreg: like cut) vendre moins cher que

underdeveloped [ˈʌndədɪˈvɛləpt] ADJ sous-développé(e)

underdog [ˈʌndədɔg] N opprimé m

underdone [ʌndəˈdʌn] ADJ (Culin) saignant(e); (: pej) pas assez cuit(e)

underestimate [ˈʌndərˈɛstɪmeɪt] VT sous-estimer, mésestimer

underexposed [ˈʌndərɪksˈpəʊzd] ADJ (Phot) sous-exposé(e)

underfed [ʌndəˈfɛd] ADJ sous-alimenté(e)

underfoot [ʌndəˈfut] ADV sous les pieds

under-funded [ˈʌndəˈfʌndɪd] ADJ: **to be ~** (organization) ne pas être doté(e) de fonds suffisants

undergo [ʌndəˈgəʊ] VT (irreg: like go) subir; (treatment) suivre; **the car is undergoing repairs** la voiture est en réparation

undergraduate [ʌndəˈgrædjuɪt] N étudiant(e) (qui prépare la licence) ▶ CPD: **~ courses** cours mpl préparant à la licence

underground [ˈʌndəgraʊnd] ADJ souterrain(e); (fig) clandestin(e) ▶ N (BRIT: railway) métro m; (Pol) clandestinité f

undergrowth [ˈʌndəgrəʊθ] N broussailles fpl, sous-bois m

underhand [ʌndəˈhænd], **underhanded** [ʌndəˈhændɪd] ADJ (fig) sournois(e), en dessous

underinsured [ʌndərɪnˈʃuəd] ADJ sous-assuré(e)

underlie [ʌndəˈlaɪ] VT (irreg: like lie) être à la base de; **the underlying cause** la cause sous-jacente

underline [ʌndəˈlaɪn] VT souligner

underling [ˈʌndəlɪŋ] N (pej) sous-fifre m, subalterne m

undermanning [ʌndəˈmænɪŋ] N pénurie f de main-d'œuvre

undermentioned [ʌndəˈmɛnʃənd] ADJ mentionné(e) ci-dessous

undermine [ʌndəˈmaɪn] VT saper, miner

underneath [ʌndəˈniːθ] ADV (en) dessous ▶ PREP sous, au-dessous de

undernourished [ʌndəˈnʌrɪʃt] ADJ sous-alimenté(e)

underpaid [ʌndəˈpeɪd] ADJ sous-payé(e)

underpants [ˈʌndəpænts] NPL caleçon m, slip m

underpass [ˈʌndəpɑːs] N (BRIT: for pedestrians) passage souterrain; (: for cars) passage inférieur

underpin [ʌndəˈpɪn] VT (argument, case) étayer

underplay [ʌndəˈpleɪ] VT (BRIT) minimiser

underpopulated [ʌndəˈpɔpjuleɪtd] ADJ sous-peuplé(e)

underprice [ʌndəˈpraɪs] VT vendre à un prix trop bas

underprivileged [ʌndəˈprɪvɪlɪdʒd] ADJ défavorisé(e)

underrate [ʌndəˈreɪt] VT sous-estimer, mésestimer

underscore [ʌndəˈskɔːr] VT souligner

underseal [ʌndəˈsiːl] VT (BRIT) traiter contre la rouille

undersecretary [ˈʌndəˈsɛkrətrɪ] N sous-secrétaire m

undersell [ʌndəˈsɛl] VT (irreg: like sell) (competitors) vendre moins cher que

undershirt ['ʌndəʃəːt] N (US) tricot m de corps
undershorts ['ʌndəʃɔːts] NPL (US) caleçon m, slip m
underside ['ʌndəsaɪd] N dessous m
undersigned ['ʌndə'saɪnd] ADJ, N soussigné(e) m/f
underskirt ['ʌndəskəːt] N (BRIT) jupon m
understaffed [ʌndə'staːft] ADJ qui manque de personnel
understand [ʌndə'stænd] VT, VI (irreg: like **stand**) comprendre; **I don't ~** je ne comprends pas; **I ~ that …** je me suis laissé dire que …, je crois comprendre que …; **to make o.s. understood** se faire comprendre
understandable [ʌndə'stændəbl] ADJ compréhensible
understanding [ʌndə'stændɪŋ] ADJ compréhensif(-ive) ▶ N compréhension f; (agreement) accord m; **to come to an ~ with sb** s'entendre avec qn; **on the ~ that …** à condition que …
understate [ʌndə'steɪt] VT minimiser
understatement ['ʌndəsteɪtmənt] N: **that's an ~** c'est (bien) peu dire, le terme est faible
understood [ʌndə'stud] PT, PP of **understand** ▶ ADJ entendu(e); (implied) sous-entendu(e)
understudy ['ʌndəstʌdɪ] N doublure f
undertake [ʌndə'teɪk] VT (irreg: like **take**) (job, task) entreprendre; (duty) se charger de; **to ~ to do sth** s'engager à faire qch
undertaker ['ʌndəteɪkəʳ] N (BRIT) entrepreneur m des pompes funèbres, croque-mort m
undertaking ['ʌndəteɪkɪŋ] N entreprise f; (promise) promesse f
undertone ['ʌndətəun] N (low voice): **in an ~** à mi-voix; (of criticism etc) nuance cachée
undervalue [ʌndə'vælju:] VT sous-estimer
underwater [ʌndə'wɔːtəʳ] ADV sous l'eau ▶ ADJ sous-marin(e)
underway [ʌndə'weɪ] ADJ: **to be ~** (meeting, investigation) être en cours
underwear ['ʌndəwɛəʳ] N sous-vêtements mpl; (women's only) dessous mpl
underweight [ʌndə'weɪt] ADJ d'un poids insuffisant; (person) (trop) maigre
underwent [ʌndə'wɛnt] PT of **undergo**
underworld ['ʌndəwəːld] N (of crime) milieu m, pègre f
underwrite [ʌndə'raɪt] VT (irreg: like **write**) (Finance) garantir; (Insurance) souscrire
underwriter ['ʌndəraɪtəʳ] N (Insurance) souscripteur m
undeserving [ʌndɪ'zəːvɪŋ] ADJ: **to be ~ of** ne pas mériter
undesirable [ʌndɪ'zaɪərəbl] ADJ peu souhaitable; (person, effect) indésirable
undeveloped [ʌndɪ'vɛləpt] ADJ (land, resources) non exploité(e)
undies ['ʌndɪz] NPL (inf) dessous mpl, lingerie f
undiluted ['ʌndaɪ'luːtɪd] ADJ pur(e), non dilué(e)
undiplomatic ['ʌndɪplə'mætɪk] ADJ peu diplomatique, maladroit(e)
undischarged ['ʌndɪs'tʃɑːdʒd] ADJ: **~ bankrupt** failli(e) non réhabilité(e)

undisciplined [ʌn'dɪsɪplɪnd] ADJ indiscipliné(e)
undisguised ['ʌndɪs'gaɪzd] ADJ (dislike, amusement etc) franc (franche)
undisputed ['ʌndɪs'pjuːtɪd] ADJ incontesté(e)
undistinguished ['ʌndɪs'tɪŋgwɪʃt] ADJ médiocre, quelconque
undisturbed [ʌndɪs'təːbd] ADJ (sleep) tranquille, paisible; **to leave ~** ne pas déranger
undivided [ʌndɪ'vaɪdɪd] ADJ: **can I have your ~ attention?** puis-je avoir toute votre attention?
undo [ʌn'duː] VT (irreg: like **do**) défaire
undoing [ʌn'duːɪŋ] N ruine f, perte f
undone [ʌn'dʌn] PP of **undo** ▶ ADJ: **to come ~** se défaire
undoubted [ʌn'dautɪd] ADJ indubitable, certain(e)
undoubtedly [ʌn'dautɪdlɪ] ADV sans aucun doute
undress [ʌn'drɛs] VI se déshabiller ▶ VT déshabiller
undrinkable [ʌn'drɪŋkəbl] ADJ (unpalatable) imbuvable; (poisonous) non potable
undue [ʌn'djuː] ADJ indu(e), excessif(-ive)
undulating ['ʌndjuleɪtɪŋ] ADJ ondoyant(e), onduleux(-euse)
unduly [ʌn'djuːlɪ] ADV trop, excessivement
undying [ʌn'daɪɪŋ] ADJ éternel(le)
unearned [ʌn'əːnd] ADJ (praise, respect) immérité(e); **~ income** rentes fpl
unearth [ʌn'əːθ] VT déterrer; (fig) dénicher
unearthly [ʌn'əːθlɪ] ADJ surnaturel(le); (hour) indu(e), impossible
uneasy [ʌn'iːzɪ] ADJ mal à l'aise, gêné(e); (worried) inquiet(-ète); (feeling) désagréable; (peace, truce) fragile; **to feel ~ about doing sth** se sentir mal à l'aise à l'idée de faire qch
uneconomic ['ʌniːkə'nɔmɪk], **uneconomical** ['ʌniːkə'nɔmɪkl] ADJ peu économique; peu rentable
uneducated [ʌn'ɛdjukeɪtɪd] ADJ sans éducation
unemployed [ʌnɪm'plɔɪd] ADJ sans travail, au chômage ▶ N: **the ~** les chômeurs mpl
unemployment [ʌnɪm'plɔɪmənt] N chômage m
unemployment benefit, (US) **unemployment compensation** N allocation f de chômage
unending [ʌn'ɛndɪŋ] ADJ interminable
unenviable [ʌn'ɛnvɪəbl] ADJ peu enviable
unequal [ʌn'iːkwəl] ADJ inégal(e)
unequalled, (US) **unequaled** [ʌn'iːkwəld] ADJ inégalé(e)
unequivocal [ʌnɪ'kwɪvəkl] ADJ (answer) sans équivoque; (person) catégorique
unerring [ʌn'əːrɪŋ] ADJ infaillible, sûr(e)
UNESCO [juː'nɛskəu] N ABBR (= United Nations Educational, Scientific and Cultural Organization) UNESCO f
unethical [ʌn'ɛθɪkl] ADJ (methods) immoral(e); (doctor's behaviour) qui ne respecte pas l'éthique
uneven [ʌn'iːvn] ADJ inégal(e); (quality, work) irrégulier(-ière)
uneventful [ʌnɪ'vɛntful] ADJ tranquille, sans histoires

u

unexceptional [ʌnɪk'sɛpʃənl] ADJ banal(e), quelconque

unexciting [ʌnɪk'saɪtɪŋ] ADJ pas passionnant(e)

unexpected [ʌnɪk'spɛktɪd] ADJ inattendu(e), imprévu(e)

unexpectedly [ʌnɪk'spɛktɪdlɪ] ADV (succeed) contre toute attente; (arrive) à l'improviste

unexplained [ʌnɪk'spleɪnd] ADJ inexpliqué(e)

unexploded [ʌnɪk'spləʊdɪd] ADJ non explosé(e) or éclaté(e)

unfailing [ʌn'feɪlɪŋ] ADJ inépuisable; infaillible

unfair [ʌn'fɛəʳ] ADJ: ~ (to) injuste (envers); **it's ~ that ...** il n'est pas juste que ...

unfair dismissal N licenciement abusif

unfairly [ʌn'fɛəlɪ] ADV injustement

unfaithful [ʌn'feɪθful] ADJ infidèle

unfamiliar [ʌnfə'mɪlɪəʳ] ADJ étrange, inconnu(e); **to be ~ with sth** mal connaître qch

unfashionable [ʌn'fæʃnəbl] ADJ (clothes) démodé(e); (place) peu chic inv; (district) déshérité(e), pas à la mode

unfasten [ʌn'fɑːsn] VT défaire; (belt, necklace) détacher; (open) ouvrir

unfathomable [ʌn'fæðəməbl] ADJ insondable

unfavourable, (US) unfavorable [ʌn'feɪvrəbl] ADJ défavorable

unfavourably, (US) unfavorably [ʌn'feɪvrəblɪ] ADV: **to look ~ upon** ne pas être favorable à

unfeeling [ʌn'fiːlɪŋ] ADJ insensible, dur(e)

unfinished [ʌn'fɪnɪʃt] ADJ inachevé(e)

unfit [ʌn'fɪt] ADJ (physically: ill) en mauvaise santé; (: out of condition) pas en forme; (incompetent): ~ (for) impropre (à); (work, service) inapte (à)

unflagging [ʌn'flægɪŋ] ADJ infatigable, inlassable

unflappable [ʌn'flæpəbl] ADJ imperturbable

unflattering [ʌn'flætərɪŋ] ADJ (dress, hairstyle) qui n'avantage pas; (remark) peu flatteur(-euse)

unflinching [ʌn'flɪntʃɪŋ] ADJ stoïque

unfold [ʌn'fəʊld] VT déplier; (fig) révéler, exposer ▶ VI se dérouler

unforeseeable [ʌnfɔː'siːəbl] ADJ imprévisible

unforeseen ['ʌnfɔː'siːn] ADJ imprévu(e)

unforgettable [ʌnfə'gɛtəbl] ADJ inoubliable

unforgivable [ʌnfə'gɪvəbl] ADJ impardonnable

unformatted [ʌn'fɔːmætɪd] ADJ (disk, text) non formaté(e)

unfortunate [ʌn'fɔːtʃnət] ADJ malheureux(-euse); (event, remark) malencontreux(-euse)

unfortunately [ʌn'fɔːtʃnətlɪ] ADV malheureusement

unfounded [ʌn'faʊndɪd] ADJ sans fondement

unfriend [ʌn'frɛnd] VT (Internet) supprimer de sa liste d'amis

unfriendly [ʌn'frɛndlɪ] ADJ peu aimable, froid(e), inamical(e)

unfulfilled [ʌnful'fɪld] ADJ (ambition, prophecy) non réalisé(e); (desire) insatisfait(e); (promise) non tenu(e); (terms of contract) non rempli(e); (person) qui n'a pas su se réaliser

unfurl [ʌn'fɜːl] VT déployer

unfurnished [ʌn'fɜːnɪʃt] ADJ non meublé(e)

ungainly [ʌn'geɪnlɪ] ADJ gauche, dégingandé(e)

ungodly [ʌn'gɔdlɪ] ADJ impie; **at an ~ hour** à une heure indue

ungrateful [ʌn'greɪtful] ADJ qui manque de reconnaissance, ingrat(e)

unguarded [ʌn'gɑːdɪd] ADJ: ~ **moment** moment m d'inattention

unhappily [ʌn'hæpɪlɪ] ADV tristement; (unfortunately) malheureusement

unhappiness [ʌn'hæpɪnɪs] N tristesse f, peine f

unhappy [ʌn'hæpɪ] ADJ triste, malheureux(-euse); (unfortunate: remark etc) malheureux(-euse); (not pleased): ~ **with** mécontent(e) de, peu satisfait(e) de

unharmed [ʌn'hɑːmd] ADJ indemne, sain(e) et sauf (sauve)

UNHCR N ABBR (= United Nations High Commission for Refugees) HCR m

unhealthy [ʌn'hɛlθɪ] ADJ (gen) malsain(e); (person) maladif(-ive)

unheard-of [ʌn'hɜːdɔv] ADJ inouï(e), sans précédent

unhelpful [ʌn'hɛlpful] ADJ (person) peu serviable; (advice) peu utile

unhesitating [ʌn'hɛzɪteɪtɪŋ] ADJ (loyalty) spontané(e); (reply, offer) immédiat(e)

unholy [ʌn'həʊlɪ] ADJ: **an ~ alliance** une alliance contre nature; **he got home at an ~ hour** il est rentré à une heure impossible

unhook [ʌn'hʊk] VT décrocher; dégrafer

unhurt [ʌn'hɜːt] ADJ indemne, sain(e) et sauf (sauve)

unhygienic ['ʌnhaɪ'dʒiːnɪk] ADJ antihygiénique

UNICEF ['juːnɪsɛf] N ABBR (= United Nations International Children's Emergency Fund) UNICEF m, FISE m

unicorn ['juːnɪkɔːn] N licorne f

unidentified [ʌnaɪ'dɛntɪfaɪd] ADJ non identifié(e); see also **UFO**

uniform ['juːnɪfɔːm] N uniforme m ▶ ADJ uniforme

uniformity [juːnɪ'fɔːmɪtɪ] N uniformité f

unify ['juːnɪfaɪ] VT unifier

unilateral [juːnɪ'lætərəl] ADJ unilatéral(e)

unimaginable [ʌnɪ'mædʒɪnəbl] ADJ inimaginable, inconcevable

unimaginative [ʌnɪ'mædʒɪnətɪv] ADJ sans imagination

unimpaired [ʌnɪm'pɛəd] ADJ intact(e)

unimportant [ʌnɪm'pɔːtənt] ADJ sans importance

unimpressed [ʌnɪm'prɛst] ADJ pas impressionné(e)

uninhabited [ʌnɪn'hæbɪtɪd] ADJ inhabité(e)

uninhibited [ʌnɪn'hɪbɪtɪd] ADJ sans inhibitions; sans retenue

uninjured [ʌn'ɪndʒəd] ADJ indemne

uninspiring [ʌnɪn'spaɪərɪŋ] ADJ peu inspirant(e)

uninstall ['ʌnɪnstɔːl] VT (Comput) désinstaller

unintelligent [ʌnɪn'tɛlɪdʒənt] ADJ inintelligent(e)

unintentional [ʌnɪn'tɛnʃənəl] ADJ involontaire

unintentionally [ˌʌnɪnˈtɛnʃnəlɪ] ADV sans le vouloir

uninvited [ˌʌnɪnˈvaɪtɪd] ADJ (*guest*) qui n'a pas été invité(e)

uninviting [ˌʌnɪnˈvaɪtɪŋ] ADJ (*place*) peu attirant(e); (*food*) peu appétissant(e)

union [ˈjuːnjən] N union *f*; (*also*: **trade union**) syndicat *m* ▸ CPD du syndicat, syndical(e)

unionize [ˈjuːnjənaɪz] VT syndiquer

Union Jack N drapeau du Royaume-Uni

Union of Soviet Socialist Republics N (*formerly*) Union *f* des républiques socialistes soviétiques

union shop N *entreprise où tous les travailleurs doivent être syndiqués*

unique [juːˈniːk] ADJ unique

unisex [ˈjuːnɪsɛks] ADJ unisexe

Unison [ˈjuːnɪsn] N (*trade union*) *grand syndicat des services publics en Grande-Bretagne*

unison [ˈjuːnɪsn] N: **in ~** à l'unisson, en chœur

unit [ˈjuːnɪt] N unité *f*; (*section: of furniture etc*) élément *m*, bloc *m*; (*team, squad*) groupe *m*, service *m*; **production ~** atelier *m* de fabrication; **kitchen ~** élément de cuisine; **sink ~** bloc-évier *m*

unit cost N coût *m* unitaire

unite [juːˈnaɪt] VT unir ▸ VI s'unir

united [juːˈnaɪtɪd] ADJ uni(e); (*country, party*) unifié(e); (*efforts*) conjugué(e)

United Arab Emirates NPL Émirats Arabes Unis

United Kingdom N Royaume-Uni *m*

United Nations (Organization) N (Organisation *f* des) Nations unies

United States (of America) N États-Unis *mpl*

unit price N prix *m* unitaire

unit trust N (*BRIT Comm*) fonds commun de placement, FCP *m*

unity [ˈjuːnɪtɪ] N unité *f*

Univ. ABBR = **university**

universal [juːnɪˈvɜːsl] ADJ universel(le)

universe [ˈjuːnɪvɜːs] N univers *m*

university [juːnɪˈvɜːsɪtɪ] N université *f* ▸ CPD (*student, professor*) d'université; (*education, year, degree*) universitaire

unjust [ʌnˈdʒʌst] ADJ injuste

unjustifiable [ʌndʒʌstɪˈfaɪəbl] ADJ injustifiable

unjustified [ʌnˈdʒʌstɪfaɪd] ADJ injustifié(e); (*text*) non justifié(e)

unkempt [ʌnˈkɛmpt] ADJ mal tenu(e), débraillé(e); mal peigné(e)

unkind [ʌnˈkaɪnd] ADJ peu gentil(le), méchant(e)

unkindly [ʌnˈkaɪndlɪ] ADV (*treat, speak*) avec méchanceté

unknown [ʌnˈnəun] ADJ inconnu(e); **~ to me** sans que je le sache; **~ quantity** (*Math, fig*) inconnue *f*

unladen [ʌnˈleɪdn] ADJ (*ship, weight*) à vide

unlawful [ʌnˈlɔːful] ADJ illégal(e)

unleaded [ʌnˈlɛdɪd] N (*also*: **unleaded petrol**) essence *f* sans plomb

unleash [ʌnˈliːʃ] VT détacher; (*fig*) déchaîner, déclencher

unleavened [ʌnˈlɛvnd] ADJ sans levain

unless [ʌnˈlɛs] CONJ: **~ he leaves** à moins qu'il (ne) parte; **~ we leave** à moins de partir, à moins que nous (ne) partions; **~ otherwise stated** sauf indication contraire; **~ I am mistaken** si je ne me trompe

unlicensed [ʌnˈlaɪsnst] ADJ (*BRIT*) non patenté(e) pour la vente des spiritueux

unlike [ʌnˈlaɪk] ADJ dissemblable, différent(e) ▸ PREP à la différence de, contrairement à

unlikelihood [ʌnˈlaɪklɪhud] ADJ improbabilité *f*

unlikely [ʌnˈlaɪklɪ] ADJ (*result, event*) improbable; (*explanation*) invraisemblable

unlimited [ʌnˈlɪmɪtɪd] ADJ illimité(e)

unlisted [ˈʌnˈlɪstɪd] ADJ (*US Tel*) sur la liste rouge; (*Stock Exchange*) non coté(e) en Bourse

unlit [ʌnˈlɪt] ADJ (*room*) non éclairé(e)

unload [ʌnˈləud] VT décharger

unlock [ʌnˈlɔk] VT ouvrir

unlucky [ʌnˈlʌkɪ] ADJ (*person*) malchanceux(-euse); (*object, number*) qui porte malheur; **to be ~** (*person*) ne pas avoir de chance

unmanageable [ʌnˈmænɪdʒəbl] ADJ (*unwieldy: tool, vehicle*) peu maniable; (*: situation*) inextricable

unmanned [ʌnˈmænd] ADJ sans équipage

unmannerly [ʌnˈmænəlɪ] ADJ mal élevé(e), impoli(e)

unmarked [ʌnˈmɑːkt] ADJ (*unstained*) sans marque; **~ police car** voiture de police banalisée

unmarried [ʌnˈmærɪd] ADJ célibataire

unmask [ʌnˈmɑːsk] VT démasquer

unmatched [ʌnˈmætʃt] ADJ sans égal(e)

unmentionable [ʌnˈmɛnʃnəbl] ADJ (*topic*) dont on ne parle pas; (*word*) qui ne se dit pas

unmerciful [ʌnˈmɜːsɪful] ADJ sans pitié

unmistakable, unmistakeable [ʌnmɪsˈteɪkəbl] ADJ indubitable; qu'on ne peut pas ne pas reconnaître

unmitigated [ʌnˈmɪtɪgeɪtɪd] ADJ non mitigé(e), absolu(e), pur(e)

unnamed [ʌnˈneɪmd] ADJ (*nameless*) sans nom; (*anonymous*) anonyme

unnatural [ʌnˈnætʃrəl] ADJ non naturel(le); (*perversion*) contre nature

unnecessary [ʌnˈnɛsəsərɪ] ADJ inutile, superflu(e)

unnerve [ʌnˈnɜːv] VT faire perdre son sang-froid à

unnoticed [ʌnˈnəutɪst] ADJ inaperçu(e); **to go ~** passer inaperçu

UNO [ˈjuːnəu] N ABBR = **United Nations Organization**

unobservant [ʌnəbˈzɜːvnt] ADJ pas observateur(-trice)

unobtainable [ʌnəbˈteɪnəbl] ADJ (*Tel*) impossible à obtenir

unobtrusive [ʌnəbˈtruːsɪv] ADJ discret(-ète)

unoccupied [ʌnˈɔkjupaɪd] ADJ (*seat, table, Mil*) libre; (*house*) inoccupé(e)

unofficial [ʌnəˈfɪʃl] ADJ (*news*) officieux(-euse), non officiel(le); (*strike*) ≈ sauvage

unopposed [ʌnəˈpəuzd] ADJ sans opposition

u

unorthodox [ʌn'ɔːθədɔks] ADJ peu orthodoxe
unpack [ʌn'pæk] VI défaire sa valise, déballer ses affaires ▶ VT (suitcase) défaire; (belongings) déballer
unpaid [ʌn'peɪd] ADJ (bill) impayé(e); (holiday) non-payé(e), sans salaire; (work) non rétribué(e); (worker) bénévole
unpalatable [ʌn'pælətəbl] ADJ (truth) désagréable (à entendre)
unparalleled [ʌn'pærəleld] ADJ incomparable, sans égal
unpatriotic ['ʌnpætrɪ'ɔtɪk] ADJ (person) manquant de patriotisme; (speech, attitude) antipatriotique
unplanned [ʌn'plænd] ADJ (visit) imprévu(e); (baby) non prévu(e)
unpleasant [ʌn'pleznt] ADJ déplaisant(e), désagréable
unplug [ʌn'plʌg] VT débrancher
unpolluted [ʌnpə'luːtɪd] ADJ non pollué(e)
unpopular [ʌn'pɔpjulər] ADJ impopulaire; **to make o.s. ~ (with)** se rendre impopulaire (auprès de)
unprecedented [ʌn'presɪdentɪd] ADJ sans précédent
unpredictable [ʌnprɪ'dɪktəbl] ADJ imprévisible
unprejudiced [ʌn'predʒudɪst] ADJ (not biased) impartial(e); (having no prejudices) qui n'a pas de préjugés
unprepared [ʌnprɪ'peəd] ADJ (person) qui n'est pas suffisamment préparé(e); (speech) improvisé(e)
unprepossessing ['ʌnpriːpə'zesɪŋ] ADJ peu avenant(e)
unpretentious [ʌnprɪ'tenʃəs] ADJ sans prétention(s)
unprincipled [ʌn'prɪnsɪpld] ADJ sans principes
unproductive [ʌnprə'dʌktɪv] ADJ improductif(-ive); (discussion) stérile
unprofessional [ʌnprə'feʃənl] ADJ (conduct) contraire à la déontologie
unprofitable [ʌn'prɔfɪtəbl] ADJ non rentable
UNPROFOR [ʌn'prəufɔːr] N ABBR (= United Nations Protection Force) FORPRONU f
unprotected ['ʌnprə'tektɪd] ADJ (sex) non protégé(e)
unprovoked [ʌnprə'vəukt] ADJ (attack) sans provocation
unpunished [ʌn'pʌnɪʃt] ADJ impuni(e); **to go ~** rester impuni
unqualified [ʌn'kwɔlɪfaɪd] ADJ (teacher) non diplômé(e), sans titres; (success) sans réserve, total(e); (disaster) total(e)
unquestionably [ʌn'kwestʃənəblɪ] ADV incontestablement
unquestioning [ʌn'kwestʃənɪŋ] ADJ (obedience, acceptance) inconditionnel(le)
unravel [ʌn'rævl] VT démêler
unreal [ʌn'rɪəl] ADJ irréel(le); (extraordinary) incroyable
unrealistic ['ʌnrɪə'lɪstɪk] ADJ (idea) irréaliste; (estimate) peu réaliste
unreasonable [ʌn'riːznəbl] ADJ qui n'est pas raisonnable; **to make ~ demands on sb** exiger trop de qn
unrecognizable [ʌn'rekəgnaɪzəbl] ADJ pas reconnaissable
unrecognized [ʌn'rekəgnaɪzd] ADJ (talent, genius) méconnu(e); (Pol: régime) non reconnu(e)
unrecorded [ʌnrɪ'kɔːdɪd] ADJ non enregistré(e)
unrefined [ʌnrɪ'faɪnd] ADJ (sugar, petroleum) non raffiné(e)
unrehearsed [ʌnrɪ'həːst] ADJ (Theat etc) qui n'a pas été répété(e); (spontaneous) spontané(e)
unrelated [ʌnrɪ'leɪtɪd] ADJ sans rapport; (people) sans lien de parenté
unrelenting [ʌnrɪ'lentɪŋ] ADJ implacable; acharné(e)
unreliable [ʌnrɪ'laɪəbl] ADJ sur qui (or quoi) on ne peut pas compter, peu fiable
unrelieved [ʌnrɪ'liːvd] ADJ (monotony) constant(e), uniforme
unremitting [ʌnrɪ'mɪtɪŋ] ADJ inlassable, infatigable, acharné(e)
unrepeatable [ʌnrɪ'piːtəbl] ADJ (offer) unique, exceptionnel(le)
unrepentant [ʌnrɪ'pentənt] ADJ impénitent(e)
unrepresentative ['ʌnreprɪ'zentətɪv] ADJ: **~ (of)** peu représentatif(-ive) (de)
unreserved [ʌnrɪ'zəːvd] ADJ (seat) non réservé(e); (approval, admiration) sans réserve
unreservedly [ʌnrɪ'zəːvɪdlɪ] ADV sans réserve
unresponsive [ʌnrɪs'pɔnsɪv] ADJ insensible
unrest [ʌn'rest] N agitation f, troubles mpl
unrestricted [ʌnrɪ'strɪktɪd] ADJ illimité(e); **to have ~ access to** avoir librement accès or accès en tout temps à
unrewarded [ʌnrɪ'wɔːdɪd] ADJ pas récompensé(e)
unripe [ʌn'raɪp] ADJ pas mûr(e)
unrivalled, (US) **unrivaled** [ʌn'raɪvəld] ADJ sans égal, incomparable
unroll [ʌn'rəul] VT dérouler
unruffled [ʌn'rʌfld] ADJ (person) imperturbable; (hair) qui n'est pas ébouriffé(e)
unruly [ʌn'ruːlɪ] ADJ indiscipliné(e)
unsafe [ʌn'seɪf] ADJ (in danger) en danger; (journey, car) dangereux(-euse); (method) hasardeux(-euse); **~ to drink/eat** non potable/comestible
unsaid [ʌn'sed] ADJ: **to leave sth ~** passer qch sous silence
unsaleable, (US) **unsalable** [ʌn'seɪləbl] ADJ invendable
unsatisfactory ['ʌnsætɪs'fæktərɪ] ADJ peu satisfaisant(e), qui laisse à désirer
unsavoury, (US) **unsavory** [ʌn'seɪvərɪ] ADJ (fig) peu recommandable, répugnant(e)
unscathed [ʌn'skeɪðd] ADJ indemne
unscientific ['ʌnsaɪən'tɪfɪk] ADJ non scientifique
unscrew [ʌn'skruː] VT dévisser
unscrupulous [ʌn'skruːpjuləs] ADJ sans scrupules
unseat [ʌn'siːt] VT (rider) désarçonner; (fig: official) faire perdre son siège à
unsecured ['ʌnsɪ'kjuəd] ADJ: **~ creditor**

créancier(-ière) sans garantie

unseeded [ʌn'si:dɪd] ADJ (*Sport*) non classé(e)

unseemly [ʌn'si:mlɪ] ADJ inconvenant(e)

unseen [ʌn'si:n] ADJ (*person*) invisible; (*danger*) imprévu(e)

unselfish [ʌn'sɛlfɪʃ] ADJ désintéressé(e)

unsettled [ʌn'sɛtld] ADJ (*restless*) perturbé(e); (*unpredictable*) instable; incertain(e); (*not finalized*) non résolu(e)

unsettling [ʌn'sɛtlɪŋ] ADJ qui a un effet perturbateur

unshakable, unshakeable [ʌn'ʃeɪkəbl] ADJ inébranlable

unshaven [ʌn'ʃeɪvn] ADJ non or mal rasé(e)

unsightly [ʌn'saɪtlɪ] ADJ disgracieux(-euse), laid(e)

unskilled [ʌn'skɪld] ADJ: ~ **worker** manœuvre *m*

unsociable [ʌn'səuʃəbl] ADJ (*person*) peu sociable; (*behaviour*) qui manque de sociabilité

unsocial [ʌn'səuʃl] ADJ (*hours*) en dehors de l'horaire normal

unsold [ʌn'səuld] ADJ invendu(e), non vendu(e)

unsolicited [ʌnsə'lɪsɪtɪd] ADJ non sollicité(e)

unsophisticated [ʌnsə'fɪstɪkeɪtɪd] ADJ simple, naturel(le)

unsound [ʌn'saund] ADJ (*health*) chancelant(e); (*floor, foundations*) peu solide; (*policy, advice*) peu judicieux(-euse)

unspeakable [ʌn'spi:kəbl] ADJ indicible; (*awful*) innommable

unspoiled ['ʌn'spɔɪld], **unspoilt** [ʌn'spɔɪlt] ADJ (*place*) non dégradé(e)

unspoken [ʌn'spəukn] ADJ (*word*) qui n'est pas prononcé(e); (*agreement, approval*) tacite

unstable [ʌn'steɪbl] ADJ instable

unsteady [ʌn'stɛdɪ] ADJ mal assuré(e), chancelant(e), instable

unstinting [ʌn'stɪntɪŋ] ADJ (*support*) total(e), sans réserve; (*generosity*) sans limites

unstuck [ʌn'stʌk] ADJ: **to come ~** se décoller; (*fig*) faire fiasco

unsubstantiated ['ʌnsəb'stænʃɪeɪtɪd] ADJ (*rumour*) qui n'est pas confirmé(e); (*accusation*) sans preuve

unsuccessful [ʌnsək'sɛsful] ADJ (*attempt*) infructueux(-euse); (*writer, proposal*) qui n'a pas de succès; (*marriage*) malheureux(-euse), qui ne réussit pas; **to be ~** (*in attempting sth*) ne pas réussir; ne pas avoir de succès; (*application*) ne pas être retenu(e)

unsuccessfully [ʌnsək'sɛsfəlɪ] ADV en vain

unsuitable [ʌn'su:təbl] ADJ qui ne convient pas, peu approprié(e); (*time*) inopportun(e)

unsuited [ʌn'su:tɪd] ADJ: **to be ~ for** or **to** être inapte or impropre à

unsung ['ʌnsʌŋ] ADJ: **an ~ hero** un héros méconnu

unsupported [ʌnsə'pɔːtɪd] ADJ (*claim*) non soutenu(e); (*theory*) qui n'est pas corroboré(e)

unsure [ʌn'ʃuəʳ] ADJ pas sûr(e); **to be ~ of o.s.** ne pas être sûr de soi, manquer de confiance en soi

unsuspecting [ʌnsə'spɛktɪŋ] ADJ qui ne se méfie pas

unsweetened [ʌn'swi:tnd] ADJ non sucré(e)

unswerving [ʌn'swə:vɪŋ] ADJ inébranlable

unsympathetic ['ʌnsɪmpə'θɛtɪk] ADJ hostile; (*unpleasant*) antipathique; **~ to** indifférent(e) à

untangle [ʌn'tæŋgl] VT démêler, débrouiller

untapped [ʌn'tæpt] ADJ (*resources*) inexploité(e)

untaxed [ʌn'tækst] ADJ (*goods*) non taxé(e); (*income*) non imposé(e)

unthinkable [ʌn'θɪŋkəbl] ADJ impensable, inconcevable

unthinkingly [ʌn'θɪŋkɪŋlɪ] ADV sans réfléchir

untidy [ʌn'taɪdɪ] ADJ (*room*) en désordre; (*appearance, person*) débraillé(e); (*person: in character*) sans ordre, désordonné; débraillé; (*work*) peu soigné(e)

untie [ʌn'taɪ] VT (*knot, parcel*) défaire; (*prisoner, dog*) détacher

until [ən'tɪl] PREP jusqu'à; (*after negative*) avant
▶ CONJ jusqu'à ce que + *sub*, en attendant que + *sub*; (*in past, after negative*) avant que + *sub*; **~ he comes** jusqu'à ce qu'il vienne, jusqu'à son arrivée; **~ now** jusqu'à présent, jusqu'ici; **~ then** jusque-là; **from morning ~ night** du matin au soir or jusqu'au soir

untimely [ʌn'taɪmlɪ] ADJ inopportun(e); (*death*) prématuré(e)

untold [ʌn'təuld] ADJ incalculable; indescriptible

untouched [ʌn'tʌtʃt] ADJ (*not used etc*) tel(le) quel(le), intact(e); (*safe: person*) indemne; (*unaffected*): **~ by** indifférent(e) à

untoward [ʌntə'wɔːd] ADJ fâcheux(-euse), malencontreux(-euse)

untrained ['ʌn'treɪnd] ADJ (*worker*) sans formation; (*troops*) sans entraînement; **to the ~ eye** à l'œil non exercé

untrammelled [ʌn'træmld] ADJ sans entraves

untranslatable [ʌntrænz'leɪtəbl] ADJ intraduisible

untrue [ʌn'tru:] ADJ (*statement*) faux (fausse)

untrustworthy [ʌn'trʌstwə:ðɪ] ADJ (*person*) pas digne de confiance, peu sûr(e)

unusable [ʌn'ju:zəbl] ADJ inutilisable

unused¹ [ʌn'ju:zd] ADJ (*new*) neuf (neuve)

unused² [ʌn'ju:st] ADJ: **to be ~ to sth/to doing sth** ne pas avoir l'habitude de qch/de faire qch

unusual [ʌn'ju:ʒuəl] ADJ insolite, exceptionnel(le), rare

unusually [ʌn'ju:ʒuəlɪ] ADV exceptionnellement, particulièrement

unveil [ʌn'veɪl] VT dévoiler

unwanted [ʌn'wɒntɪd] ADJ (*child, pregnancy*) non désiré(e); (*clothes etc*) à donner

unwarranted [ʌn'wɒrəntɪd] ADJ injustifié(e)

unwary [ʌn'wɛərɪ] ADJ imprudent(e)

unwavering [ʌn'weɪvərɪŋ] ADJ inébranlable

unwelcome [ʌn'wɛlkəm] ADJ importun(e); **to feel ~** se sentir de trop

unwell [ʌn'wɛl] ADJ indisposé(e), souffrant(e); **to feel ~** ne pas se sentir bien

unwieldy [ʌn'wi:ldɪ] ADJ difficile à manier

unwilling [ʌn'wɪlɪŋ] ADJ: **to be ~ to do** ne pas vouloir faire

unwillingly [ʌn'wɪlɪŋlɪ] ADV à contrecœur, contre son gré

unwind [ʌn'waɪnd] VT (*irreg: like* **wind²**) dérouler
▶ VI (*relax*) se détendre
unwise [ʌn'waɪz] ADJ imprudent(e), peu
judicieux(-euse)
unwitting [ʌn'wɪtɪŋ] ADJ involontaire
unwittingly [ʌn'wɪtɪŋlɪ] ADV involontairement
unworkable [ʌn'wə:kəbl] ADJ (*plan etc*)
inexploitable
unworthy [ʌn'wə:ðɪ] ADJ indigne
unwrap [ʌn'ræp] VT défaire; ouvrir
unwritten [ʌn'rɪtn] ADJ (*agreement*) tacite
unzip [ʌn'zɪp] VT ouvrir (la fermeture éclair de);
(*Comput*) dézipper

(KEYWORD)

up [ʌp] PREP: **he went up the stairs/the hill** il a
monté l'escalier/la colline; **the cat was up a**
tree le chat était dans un arbre; **they live**
further up the street ils habitent plus haut
dans la rue; **go up that road and turn left**
remontez la rue et tournez à gauche
▶ VI (*inf*): **she upped and left** elle a fichu le
camp sans plus attendre
▶ ADV **1** en haut; en l'air; (*upwards, higher*): **up in**
the sky/the mountains (là-haut) dans le ciel/
les montagnes; **put it a bit higher up**
mettez-le un peu plus haut; **to stand up** (*get*
up) se lever, se mettre debout; (*be standing*) être
debout; **up there** là-haut; **up above**
au-dessus; **"this side up"** "haut"
2: **to be up** (*out of bed*) être levé(e); (*prices*) avoir
augmenté *or* monté; (*finished*): **when the year**
was up à la fin de l'année; **time's up** c'est
l'heure
3: **up to** (*as far as*) jusqu'à; **up to now** jusqu'à
présent
4: **to be up to** (*depending on*): **it's up to you** c'est
à vous de décider; (*equal to*): **he's not up to it**
(*job, task etc*) il n'en est pas capable; (*inf: be doing*):
what is he up to? qu'est-ce qu'il peut bien
faire?
5 (*phrases*): **he's well up in** *or* **on ...** (BRIT:
knowledgeable) il s'y connaît en ...; **up with**
Leeds United! vive Leeds United!; **what's up?**
(*inf*) qu'est-ce qui ne va pas?; **what's up with**
him? (*inf*) qu'est-ce qui lui arrive?
▶ N: **ups and downs** hauts et bas *mpl*

up-and-coming [ʌpənd'kʌmɪŋ] ADJ plein(e)
d'avenir *or* de promesses
upbeat ['ʌpbi:t] N (*Mus*) levé m; (*in economy,*
prosperity) amélioration *f* ▶ ADJ (*optimistic*)
optimiste
upbraid [ʌp'breɪd] VT morigéner
upbringing ['ʌpbrɪŋɪŋ] N éducation *f*
upcoming ['ʌpkʌmɪŋ] ADJ tout(e) prochain(e)
update [ʌp'deɪt] VT mettre à jour
upend [ʌp'end] VT mettre debout
upfront [ʌp'frʌnt] ADJ (*open*) franc (franche)
▶ ADV (*pay*) d'avance; **to be ~ about sth** ne rien
cacher de qch
upgrade [ʌp'greɪd] VT (*person*) promouvoir; (*job*)
revaloriser; (*property, equipment*) moderniser
upheaval [ʌp'hi:vl] N bouleversement m; (*in*

room) branle-bas m; (*event*) crise *f*
uphill [ʌp'hɪl] ADJ qui monte; (*fig: task*) difficile,
pénible ▶ ADV (*face, look*) en amont, vers
l'amont; (*go, move*) vers le haut, en haut;
to go ~ monter
uphold [ʌp'həuld] VT (*irreg: like* **hold**) maintenir;
soutenir
upholstery [ʌp'həulstərɪ] N rembourrage m;
(*cover*) tissu m d'ameublement; (*of car*)
garniture *f*
upkeep ['ʌpki:p] N entretien m
upload ['ʌpləud] VT (*Comput*) télécharger
upmarket [ʌp'mɑːkɪt] ADJ (*product*) haut de
gamme *inv*; (*area*) chic *inv*
upon [ə'pɔn] PREP sur
upper ['ʌpəʳ] ADJ supérieur(e); du dessus
▶ N (*of shoe*) empeigne *f*
upper class N: **the ~** ≈ la haute bourgeoisie
upper-class [ʌpə'klɑ:s] ADJ de la haute société,
aristocratique; (*district*) élégant(e), huppé(e);
(*accent, attitude*) caractéristique des classes
supérieures
uppercut ['ʌpəkʌt] N uppercut m
upper hand N: **to have the ~** avoir le dessus
Upper House N: **the ~** (*in Britain*) la Chambre des
Lords, la Chambre haute; (*in France, in the US etc*)
le Sénat
uppermost ['ʌpəməust] ADJ le (la) plus haut(e),
en dessus; **it was ~ in my mind** j'y pensais
avant tout autre chose
upper sixth N terminale *f*
Upper Volta [-'vɔltə] N Haute Volta
upright ['ʌpraɪt] ADJ droit(e); (*fig*) droit, honnête
▶ N montant m
uprising ['ʌpraɪzɪŋ] N soulèvement m,
insurrection *f*
uproar ['ʌprɔ:ʳ] N tumulte m, vacarme m;
(*protests*) protestations *fpl*
uproarious [ʌp'rɔ:rɪəs] ADJ (*event etc*)
désopilant(e); **~ laughter** un brouhaha
de rires
uproot [ʌp'ru:t] VT déraciner
upset N ['ʌpset] dérangement m ▶ VT [ʌp'set]
(*irreg: like* **set**) (*glass etc*) renverser; (*plan*)
déranger; (*person: offend*) contrarier; (: *grieve*)
faire de la peine à; bouleverser ▶ ADJ [ʌp'set]
contrarié(e); peiné(e); (*stomach*) détraqué(e),
dérangé(e); **to get ~** (*sad*) devenir triste;
(*offended*) se vexer; **to have a stomach ~** (BRIT)
avoir une indigestion
upset price N (*US, Scottish*) mise *f* à prix, prix m
de départ
upsetting [ʌp'setɪŋ] ADJ (*offending*) vexant(e);
(*annoying*) ennuyeux(-euse)
upshot ['ʌpʃɔt] N résultat m; **the ~ of it all was**
that ... il a résulté de tout cela que ...
upside down ['ʌpsaɪd-] ADV à l'envers;
to turn sth ~ (*fig: place*) mettre sens dessus
dessous
upstage ['ʌp'steɪdʒ] VT: **to ~ sb** souffler la
vedette à qn
upstairs [ʌp'steəz] ADV en haut ▶ ADJ (*room*)
du dessus, d'en haut ▶ N: **the ~** l'étage m;
there's no ~ il n'y a pas d'étage

upstart ['ʌpstɑːt] N parvenu(e)
upstream [ʌp'striːm] ADV en amont
upsurge ['ʌpsəːdʒ] N (of enthusiasm etc) vague f
uptake ['ʌpteɪk] N: **he is quick/slow on the ~** il comprend vite/est lent à comprendre
uptight [ʌp'taɪt] ADJ (inf) très tendu(e), crispé(e)
up-to-date ['ʌptə'deɪt] ADJ moderne; (information) très récent(e)
upturn ['ʌptəːn] N (in economy) reprise f
upturned ['ʌptəːnd] ADJ (nose) retroussé(e)
upward ['ʌpwəd] ADJ ascendant(e); vers le haut
  ▶ ADV = **upwards**
upwardly-mobile ['ʌpwədlɪ'məubaɪl] ADJ à mobilité sociale ascendante
upwards ['ʌpwədz] ADV vers le haut; (more than): ~ **of** plus de; **and ~** et plus, et au-dessus
URA N ABBR (US) = **Urban Renewal Administration**
Ural Mountains ['juərəl-] NPL (also: **the Urals**): **the ~** les monts mpl Oural, l'Oural m
uranium [juə'reɪnɪəm] N uranium m
Uranus [juə'reɪnəs] N Uranus f
urban ['əːbən] ADJ urbain(e)
urban clearway N rue f à stationnement interdit
urbane [əː'beɪn] ADJ urbain(e), courtois(e)
urbanization [əːbənaɪ'zeɪʃən] N urbanisation f
urchin ['əːtʃɪn] N gosse m, garnement m
Urdu ['uəduː] N ourdou m
urge [əːdʒ] N besoin (impératif), envie (pressante) ▶ VT (caution etc) recommander avec insistance; (person): **to ~ sb to do** exhorter qn à faire, pousser qn à faire, recommander vivement à qn de faire
  ▶ **urge on** VT pousser, presser
urgency ['əːdʒənsɪ] N urgence f; (of tone) insistance f
urgent ['əːdʒənt] ADJ urgent(e); (plea, tone) pressant(e)
urgently ['əːdʒəntlɪ] ADV d'urgence, de toute urgence; (need) sans délai
urinal ['juərɪnl] N (BRIT: place) urinoir m
urinate ['juərɪneɪt] VI uriner
urine ['juərɪn] N urine f
URL ABBR (= uniform resource locator) URL f
urn [əːn] N urne f; (also: **tea urn**) fontaine f à thé
Uruguay ['juərəgwaɪ] N Uruguay m
Uruguayan [juərə'gwaɪən] ADJ uruguayen(ne) ▶ N Uruguayen(ne)
US N ABBR = **United States**
us [ʌs] PRON nous; see also **me**
USA N ABBR = **United States of America**; (Mil) = **United States Army**
usable ['juːzəbl] ADJ utilisable
USAF N ABBR = **United States Air Force**
usage ['juːzɪdʒ] N usage m
USB stick N clé f USB
USCG N ABBR = **United States Coast Guard**
USDA N ABBR = **United States Department of Agriculture**
USDAW ['ʌzdɔː] N ABBR (BRIT: = Union of Shop,

Distributive and Allied Workers) syndicat du commerce de détail et de la distribution
USDI N ABBR = **United States Department of the Interior**
use N [juːs] emploi m, utilisation f; usage m; (usefulness) utilité f ▶ VT [juːz] se servir de, utiliser, employer; **in ~** en usage; **out of ~** hors d'usage; **to be of ~** servir, être utile; **to make ~ of sth** utiliser qch; **ready for ~** prêt à l'emploi; **it's no ~** ça ne sert à rien; **to have the ~ of** avoir l'usage de; **what's this used for?** à quoi est-ce que ça sert?; **she used to do it** elle le faisait (autrefois), elle avait coutume de le faire; **to be used to** avoir l'habitude de, être habitué(e) à; **to get used to** s'habituer à
  ▶ **use up** VT finir, épuiser; (food) consommer
used [juːzd] ADJ (car) d'occasion
useful ['juːsful] ADJ utile; **to come in ~** être utile
usefulness ['juːsfəlnɪs] N utilité f
useless ['juːslɪs] ADJ inutile; (inf: person) nul(le)
user ['juːzəʳ] N utilisateur(-trice), usager m
user-friendly ['juːzə'frɛndlɪ] ADJ convivial(e), facile d'emploi
username ['juːzəneɪm] N nom m d'utilisateur
USES N ABBR = **United States Employment Service**
usher ['ʌʃəʳ] N placeur m ▶ VT: **to ~ sb in** faire entrer qn
usherette [ʌʃə'rɛt] N (in cinema) ouvreuse f
USIA N ABBR = **United States Information Agency**
USM N ABBR = **United States Mail; United States Mint**
USN N ABBR = **United States Navy**
USP N ABBR = **unique selling proposition**
USPHS N ABBR = **United States Public Health Service**
USPO N ABBR = **United States Post Office**
USS ABBR = **United States Ship; United States Steamer**
USSR N ABBR = **Union of Soviet Socialist Republics**
usu. ABBR = **usually**
usual ['juːʒuəl] ADJ habituel(le); **as ~** comme d'habitude
usually ['juːʒuəlɪ] ADV d'habitude, d'ordinaire
usurer ['juːʒərəʳ] N usurier(-ière)
usurp [juː'zəːp] VT usurper
UT ABBR (US) = **Utah**
ute [juːt] N (AUSTRALIA, NEW ZEALAND) pick-up m inv
utensil [juː'tɛnsl] N ustensile m; **kitchen utensils** batterie f de cuisine
uterus ['juːtərəs] N utérus m
utilitarian [juːtɪlɪ'tɛərɪən] ADJ utilitaire
utility [juː'tɪlɪtɪ] N utilité f; (also: **public utility**) service public
utility room N buanderie f
utilization [juːtɪlaɪ'zeɪʃən] N utilisation f
utilize ['juːtɪlaɪz] VT utiliser; (make good use of) exploiter

u

851

utmost ['ʌtməust] ADJ extrême, le (la) plus grand(e) ▶ N: **to do one's ~** faire tout son possible; **of the ~ importance** d'une importance capitale, de la plus haute importance

utter ['ʌtəʳ] ADJ total(e), complet(-ète) ▶ VT prononcer, proférer; (*sounds*) émettre

utterance ['ʌtrns] N paroles *fpl*

utterly ['ʌtəlɪ] ADV complètement, totalement

U-turn ['juː'təːn] N demi-tour *m*; (*fig*) volte-face *f inv*

Uzbekistan [ʌzbɛkɪ'stɑːn] N Ouzbékistan *m*

V v

V, v [viː] N (*letter*) V, v m; **V for Victor** V comme Victor

v. ABBR = **verse**; (= *vide*) v.; (= *versus*) vs; (= *volt*) V

VA, Va. ABBR (*US*) = **Virginia**

vac [væk] N ABBR (*BRIT inf*) = **vacation**

vacancy ['veɪkənsɪ] N (*job*) poste vacant; (*room*) chambre f disponible; **"no vacancies"** "complet"

vacant ['veɪkənt] ADJ (*post*) vacant(e); (*seat etc*) libre, disponible; (*expression*) distrait(e)

vacant lot N terrain inoccupé; (*for sale*) terrain à vendre

vacate [və'keɪt] VT quitter

vacation [və'keɪʃən] N (*esp US*) vacances fpl; **to take a ~** prendre des vacances; **on ~** en vacances

vacation course N cours mpl de vacances

vacationer [və'keɪʃənər], (*US*) **vacationist** [və'keɪʃənɪst] N vacancier(-ière)

vaccinate ['væksɪneɪt] VT vacciner

vaccination [væksɪ'neɪʃən] N vaccination f

vaccine ['væksiːn] N vaccin m

vacuum ['vækjum] N vide m

vacuum bottle N (*US*) = **vacuum flask**

vacuum cleaner N aspirateur m

vacuum flask N (*BRIT*) bouteille f thermos®

vacuum-packed ['vækjumpækt] ADJ emballé(e) sous vide

vagabond ['vægəbɔnd] N vagabond(e); (*tramp*) chemineau m, clochard(e)

vagary ['veɪgərɪ] N caprice m

vagina [və'dʒaɪnə] N vagin m

vagrancy ['veɪgrənsɪ] N vagabondage m

vagrant ['veɪgrənt] N vagabond(e), mendiant(e)

vague [veɪg] ADJ vague, imprécis(e); (*blurred: photo, memory*) flou(e); **I haven't the vaguest idea** je n'en ai pas la moindre idée

vaguely ['veɪglɪ] ADV vaguement

vain [veɪn] ADJ (*useless*) vain(e); (*conceited*) vaniteux(-euse); **in ~** en vain

valance ['væləns] N (*of bed*) tour m de lit

valedictory [vælɪ'dɪktərɪ] ADJ d'adieu

valentine ['væləntaɪn] N (*also*: **valentine card**) carte f de la Saint-Valentin

Valentine's Day ['væləntaɪnz-] N Saint-Valentin f

valet ['væleɪt] N valet m de chambre

valet parking ['væleɪ-] N parcage m par les soins du personnel (de l'hôtel *etc*)

valet service ['væleɪ-] N (*for clothes*) pressing m; (*for car*) nettoyage complet

valiant ['væliənt] ADJ vaillant(e), courageux(-euse)

valid ['vælɪd] ADJ (*document*) valide, valable; (*excuse*) valable

validate ['vælɪdeɪt] VT (*contract, document*) valider; (*argument, claim*) prouver la justesse de, confirmer

validity [və'lɪdɪtɪ] N validité f

valise [və'liːz] N sac m de voyage

valley ['vælɪ] N vallée f

valour, (*US*) **valor** ['vælər] N courage m

valuable ['væljuəbl] ADJ (*jewel*) de grande valeur; (*time, help*) précieux(-euse)

valuables ['væljuəblz] NPL objets mpl de valeur

valuation [vælju'eɪʃən] N évaluation f, expertise f

value ['væljuː] N valeur f ▶ VT (*fix price*) évaluer, expertiser; (*appreciate*) apprécier; (*cherish*) tenir à; **values** NPL (*principles*) valeurs fpl; **you get good ~ (for money) in that shop** vous en avez pour votre argent dans ce magasin; **to lose (in) ~** (*currency*) baisser; (*property*) se déprécier; **to gain (in) ~** (*currency*) monter; (*property*) prendre de la valeur; **to be of great ~ to sb** (*fig*) être très utile à qn

value added tax [-'ædɪd-] N (*BRIT*) taxe f à la valeur ajoutée

valued ['væljuːd] ADJ (*appreciated*) estimé(e)

valuer ['væljuər] N expert m (en estimations)

valve [vælv] N (*in machine*) soupape f; (*on tyre*) valve f; (*in radio*) lampe f; (*Med*) valve, valvule f

vampire ['væmpaɪər] N vampire m

van [væn] N (*Aut*) camionnette f; (*BRIT Rail*) fourgon m

V and A N ABBR (*BRIT*) = **Victoria and Albert Museum**

vandal ['vændl] N vandale mf

vandalism ['vændəlɪzəm] N vandalisme m

vandalize ['vændəlaɪz] VT saccager

vanguard ['vænɡaːd] N avant-garde m

vanilla [və'nɪlə] N vanille f ▶ CPD (*ice cream*) à la vanille

vanish ['vænɪʃ] VI disparaître

vanity ['vænɪtɪ] N vanité f

vanity case N sac m de toilette

V

vantage ['vɑ:ntɪdʒ] N: ~ **point** bonne position
vaporize ['veɪpəraɪz] VT vaporiser ▶ VI se vaporiser
vapour, (US) **vapor** ['veɪpə'] N vapeur f; (on window) buée f
variable ['vɛərɪəbl] ADJ variable; (mood) changeant(e) ▶ N variable f
variance ['vɛərɪəns] N: **to be at ~ (with)** être en désaccord (avec); (facts) être en contradiction (avec)
variant ['vɛərɪənt] N variante f
variation [vɛərɪ'eɪʃən] N variation f; (in opinion) changement m
varicose ['værɪkəus] ADJ: ~ **veins** varices fpl
varied ['vɛərɪd] ADJ varié(e), divers(e)
variety [və'raɪətɪ] N variété f; (quantity) nombre m, quantité f; **a wide ~ of ...** un grand nombre de ...; **for a ~ of reasons** pour diverses raisons
variety show N (spectacle m de) variétés fpl
various ['vɛərɪəs] ADJ divers(e), différent(e); (several) divers, plusieurs; **at ~ times** (different) en diverses occasions; (several) à plusieurs reprises
varnish ['vɑ:nɪʃ] N vernis m; (for nails) vernis (à ongles) ▶ VT vernir; **to ~ one's nails** se vernir les ongles
vary ['vɛərɪ] VT, VI varier, changer; **to ~ with** or **according to** varier selon
varying ['vɛərɪɪŋ] ADJ variable
vase [vɑ:z] N vase m
vasectomy [væ'sɛktəmɪ] N vasectomie f
Vaseline® ['væsɪli:n] N vaseline f
vast [vɑ:st] ADJ vaste, immense; (amount, success) énorme
vastly ['vɑ:stlɪ] ADV infiniment, extrêmement
vastness ['vɑ:stnɪs] N immensité f
VAT [væt] N ABBR (BRIT: = value added tax) TVA f
vat [væt] N cuve f
Vatican ['vætɪkən] N: **the ~** le Vatican
vatman ['vætmæn] N (irreg) (BRIT inf) contrôleur m de la T.V.A.
vault [vɔ:lt] N (of roof) voûte f; (tomb) caveau m; (in bank) salle f des coffres; chambre forte; (jump) saut m ▶ VT (also: **vault over**) sauter (d'un bond)
vaunted ['vɔ:ntɪd] ADJ: **much-~** tant célébré(e)
VC N ABBR = **vice-chairman**; (BRIT: = Victoria Cross) distinction militaire
VCR N ABBR = **video cassette recorder**
VD N ABBR = **venereal disease**
VDU N ABBR = **visual display unit**
veal [vi:l] N veau m
veer [vɪə'] VI tourner; (car, ship) virer
veg. [vɛdʒ] N ABBR (BRIT inf) = **vegetable**; **vegetables**
vegan ['vi:gən] N végétalien(ne)
vegeburger ['vɛdʒɪbə:gə'] N burger végétarien
vegetable ['vɛdʒtəbl] N légume m ▶ ADJ végétal(e)
vegetable garden N (jardin m) potager m
vegetarian [vɛdʒɪ'tɛərɪən] ADJ, N végétarien(ne); **do you have any ~ dishes?** avez-vous des plats végétariens?
vegetate ['vɛdʒɪteɪt] VI végéter

vegetation [vɛdʒɪ'teɪʃən] N végétation f
vegetative ['vɛdʒɪtətɪv] ADJ (lit) végétal(e); (fig) végétatif(-ive)
veggieburger ['vɛdʒɪbə:gə'] N = **vegeburger**
vehemence ['vi:ɪməns] N véhémence f, violence f
vehement ['vi:ɪmənt] ADJ violent(e), impétueux(-euse); (impassioned) ardent(e)
vehicle ['vi:ɪkl] N véhicule m
vehicular [vɪ'hɪkjulə'] ADJ: **"no ~ traffic"** "interdit à tout véhicule"
veil [veɪl] N voile m ▶ VT voiler; **under a ~ of secrecy** (fig) dans le plus grand secret
veiled [veɪld] ADJ voilé(e)
vein [veɪn] N veine f; (on leaf) nervure f; (fig: mood) esprit m
Velcro® ['vɛlkrəu] N velcro® m
vellum ['vɛləm] N (writing paper) vélin m
velocity [vɪ'lɔsɪtɪ] N vitesse f, vélocité f
velour, velours [və'luə'] N velours m
velvet ['vɛlvɪt] N velours m
vending machine ['vɛndɪŋ-] N distributeur m automatique
vendor ['vɛndə'] N vendeur(-euse); **street ~** marchand ambulant
veneer [və'nɪə'] N placage m de bois; (fig) vernis m
venerable ['vɛnərəbl] ADJ vénérable
venereal [vɪ'nɪərɪəl] ADJ: ~ **disease** maladie vénérienne
Venetian blind [vɪ'ni:ʃən-] N store vénitien
Venezuela [vɛnɛ'zweɪlə] N Venezuela m
Venezuelan [vɛnɛ'zweɪlən] ADJ vénézuélien(ne) ▶ N Vénézuélien(ne)
vengeance ['vɛndʒəns] N vengeance f; **with a ~** (fig) vraiment, pour de bon
vengeful ['vɛndʒful] ADJ vengeur(-geresse)
Venice ['vɛnɪs] N Venise f
venison ['vɛnɪsn] N venaison f
venom ['vɛnəm] N venin m
venomous ['vɛnəməs] ADJ venimeux(-euse)
vent [vɛnt] N conduit m d'aération; (in dress, jacket) fente f ▶ VT (fig: one's feelings) donner libre cours à
ventilate ['vɛntɪleɪt] VT (room) ventiler, aérer
ventilation [vɛntɪ'leɪʃən] N ventilation f, aération f
ventilation shaft N conduit m de ventilation or d'aération
ventilator ['vɛntɪleɪtə'] N ventilateur m
ventriloquist [vɛn'trɪləkwɪst] N ventriloque mf
venture ['vɛntʃə'] N entreprise f ▶ VT risquer, hasarder ▶ VI s'aventurer, se risquer; **a business ~** une entreprise commerciale; **to ~ to do sth** se risquer à faire qch
venture capital N capital-risque m
venue ['vɛnju:] N lieu m; (of conference etc) lieu de la réunion (or manifestation etc); (of match) lieu de la rencontre
Venus ['vi:nəs] N (planet) Vénus f
veracity [və'ræsɪtɪ] N véracité f
veranda, verandah [və'rændə] N véranda f
verb [və:b] N verbe m
verbal ['və:bl] ADJ verbal(e); (translation) littéral(e)

verbally ['və:bəlɪ] ADV verbalement
verbatim [və:'beɪtɪm] ADJ, ADV mot pour mot
verbose [və:'bəus] ADJ verbeux(-euse)
verdict ['və:dɪkt] N verdict *m*; **~ of guilty/not guilty** verdict de culpabilité/de non-culpabilité
verge [və:dʒ] N bord *m*; **"soft verges"** (BRIT) "accotements non stabilisés"; **on the ~ of doing** sur le point de faire
▶ **verge on** VT FUS approcher de
verger ['və:dʒə'] N (Rel) bedeau *m*
verification [vɛrɪfɪ'keɪʃən] N vérification *f*
verify ['vɛrɪfaɪ] VT vérifier
veritable ['vɛrɪtəbl] ADJ véritable
vermin ['və:mɪn] NPL animaux *mpl* nuisibles; (insects) vermine *f*
vermouth ['və:məθ] N vermouth *m*
vernacular [və'nækjulə'] N langue *f* vernaculaire, dialecte *m*
versatile ['və:sətaɪl] ADJ polyvalent(e)
verse [və:s] N vers *mpl*; (stanza) strophe *f*; (in Bible) verset *m*; **in ~** en vers
versed [və:st] ADJ: **(well-)~ in** versé(e) dans
version ['və:ʃən] N version *f*
versus ['və:səs] PREP contre
vertebra ['və:tɪbrə] (pl **vertebrae** [-bri:]) N vertèbre *f*
vertebrate ['və:tɪbrɪt] N vertébré *m*
vertical ['və:tɪkl] ADJ vertical(e) ▶ N verticale *f*
vertically ['və:tɪklɪ] ADV verticalement
vertigo ['və:tɪgəu] N vertige *m*; **to suffer from ~** avoir des vertiges
verve [və:v] N brio *m*; enthousiasme *m*
very ['vɛrɪ] ADV très ▶ ADJ: **the ~ book which** le livre même que; **the ~ thought (of it) ...** rien que d'y penser ...; **at the ~ end** tout à la fin; **the ~ last** le tout dernier; **at the ~ least** au moins; **~ well** très bien; **~ little** très peu; **~ much** beaucoup
vespers ['vɛspəz] NPL vêpres *fpl*
vessel ['vɛsl] N (Anat, Naut) vaisseau *m*; (container) récipient *m*; see also **blood vessel**
vest [vɛst] N (BRIT: underwear) tricot *m* de corps; (US: waistcoat) gilet *m* ▶ VT: **to ~ sb with sth, to ~ sth in sb** investir qn de qch
vested interest N: **to have a ~ in doing** avoir tout intérêt à faire; **vested interests** NPL (Comm) droits acquis
vestibule ['vɛstɪbju:l] N vestibule *m*
vestige ['vɛstɪdʒ] N vestige *m*
vestry ['vɛstrɪ] N sacristie *f*
Vesuvius [vɪ'su:vɪəs] N Vésuve *m*
vet [vɛt] N ABBR (BRIT: = veterinary surgeon) vétérinaire *mf*; (US: = veteran) ancien(ne) combattant(e) ▶ VT examiner minutieusement; (text) revoir; (candidate) se renseigner soigneusement sur, soumettre à une enquête approfondie
veteran ['vɛtərn] N vétéran *m*; (also: **war veteran**) ancien combattant ▶ ADJ: **she's a ~ campaigner for ...** cela fait très longtemps qu'elle lutte pour ...
veteran car N voiture *f* d'époque
veterinarian [vɛtrɪ'nɛərɪən] N (US) = **veterinary surgeon**

veterinary ['vɛtrɪnərɪ] ADJ vétérinaire
veterinary surgeon (BRIT) N vétérinaire *mf*
veto ['vi:təu] (pl **vetoes**) N veto *m* ▶ VT opposer son veto à; **to put a ~ on** mettre (or opposer) son veto à
vetting ['vɛtɪŋ] N: **positive ~** enquête *f* de sécurité
vex [vɛks] VT fâcher, contrarier
vexed [vɛkst] ADJ (question) controversé(e)
VFD N ABBR (US) = **voluntary fire department**
VG N ABBR (BRIT Scol etc: = very good) tb (= très bien)
VHF ABBR (= very high frequency) VHF
VI ABBR (US) = **Virgin Islands**
via ['vaɪə] PREP par, via
viability [vaɪə'bɪlɪtɪ] N viabilité *f*
viable ['vaɪəbl] ADJ viable
viaduct ['vaɪədʌkt] N viaduc *m*
vial ['vaɪəl] N fiole *f*
vibes [vaɪbz] NPL (inf): **I get good/bad ~ about it** je le sens bien/ne le sens pas; **there are good/bad ~ between us** entre nous le courant passe bien/ne passe pas
vibrant ['vaɪbrnt] ADJ (sound, colour) vibrant(e)
vibraphone ['vaɪbrəfəun] N vibraphone *m*
vibrate [vaɪ'breɪt] VI: **to ~ (with)** vibrer (de); (resound) retentir (de)
vibration [vaɪ'breɪʃən] N vibration *f*
vibrator [vaɪ'breɪtə'] N vibromasseur *m*
vicar ['vɪkə'] N pasteur *m* (de l'Église anglicane)
vicarage ['vɪkərɪdʒ] N presbytère *m*
vicarious [vɪ'kɛərɪəs] ADJ (pleasure, experience) indirect(e)
vice [vaɪs] N (evil) vice *m*; (Tech) étau *m*
vice- [vaɪs-] PREFIX vice-
vice-chairman [vaɪs'tʃɛəmən] N (irreg) vice-président(e)
vice-chancellor [vaɪs'tʃɑ:nsələ'] N (BRIT) ≈ président(e) d'université
vice-president [vaɪs'prɛzɪdənt] N vice-président(e)
viceroy ['vaɪsrɔɪ] N vice-roi *m*
vice squad N ≈ brigade mondaine
vice versa ['vaɪsɪ'və:sə] ADV vice versa
vicinity [vɪ'sɪnɪtɪ] N environs *mpl*, alentours *mpl*
vicious ['vɪʃəs] ADJ (remark) cruel(le), méchant(e); (blow) brutal(e); (dog) méchant(e), dangereux(-euse); **a ~ circle** un cercle vicieux
viciousness ['vɪʃəsnɪs] N méchanceté *f*, cruauté *f*; brutalité *f*
vicissitudes [vɪ'sɪsɪtju:dz] NPL vicissitudes *fpl*
victim ['vɪktɪm] N victime *f*; **to be the ~ of** être victime de
victimization [vɪktɪmaɪ'zeɪʃən] N brimades *fpl*; représailles *fpl*
victimize ['vɪktɪmaɪz] VT brimer; exercer des représailles sur
victor ['vɪktə'] N vainqueur *m*
Victorian [vɪk'tɔ:rɪən] ADJ victorien(ne)
victorious [vɪk'tɔ:rɪəs] ADJ victorieux(-euse)
victory ['vɪktərɪ] N victoire *f*; **to win a ~ over sb** remporter une victoire sur qn
video ['vɪdɪəu] N (video film) vidéo *f*; (also: **video cassette**) vidéocassette *f*; (also: **video cassette recorder**) magnétoscope *m* ▶ VT (with recorder)

V

855

enregistrer; (with camera) filmer ▶ CPD vidéo inv

video camera N caméra f vidéo inv

video cassette N vidéocassette f

video cassette recorder N = **video recorder**

videodisc ['vɪdɪəʊdɪsk] N vidéodisque m

video game N jeu m vidéo inv

video nasty N vidéo à caractère violent ou pornographique

videophone ['vɪdɪəʊfəʊn] N vidéophone m, visiophone m

video recorder N magnétoscope m

video recording N enregistrement m (en) vidéo inv

video shop N vidéoclub m

video tape N bande f vidéo inv; (cassette) vidéocassette f

video wall N mur m d'images vidéo

vie [vaɪ] VI: **to ~ with** lutter avec, rivaliser avec

Vienna [vɪ'ɛnə] N Vienne

Vietnam, Viet Nam ['vjɛt'næm] N Viêt-nam or Vietnam m

Vietnamese [vjɛtnə'miːz] ADJ vietnamien(ne) ▶ N (pl inv) Vietnamien(ne); (Ling) vietnamien m

view [vjuː] N vue f; (opinion) avis m, vue ▶ VT voir, regarder; (situation) considérer; (house) visiter; **on ~** (in museum etc) exposé(e); **in full ~ of sb** sous les yeux de qn; **to be within ~ (of sth)** être à portée de vue (de qch); **an overall ~ of the situation** une vue d'ensemble de la situation; **in my ~** à mon avis; **in ~ of the fact that** étant donné que; **with a ~ to doing sth** dans l'intention de faire qch

viewdata ['vjuːdeɪtə] N (BRIT) télétexte m (version téléphonique)

viewer ['vjuːəʳ] N (viewfinder) viseur m; (small projector) visionneuse f; (TV) téléspectateur(-trice)

viewfinder ['vjuːfaɪndəʳ] N viseur m

viewpoint ['vjuːpɔɪnt] N point m de vue

vigil ['vɪdʒɪl] N veille f; **to keep ~** veiller

vigilance ['vɪdʒɪləns] N vigilance f

vigilant ['vɪdʒɪlənt] ADJ vigilant(e)

vigilante [vɪdʒɪ'læntɪ] N justicier ou membre d'un groupe d'autodéfense

vigorous ['vɪɡərəs] ADJ vigoureux(-euse)

vigour, (US) **vigor** ['vɪɡəʳ] N vigueur f

vile [vaɪl] ADJ (action) vil(e); (smell, food) abominable; (temper) massacrant(e)

vilify ['vɪlɪfaɪ] VT calomnier, vilipender

villa ['vɪlə] N villa f

village ['vɪlɪdʒ] N village m

villager ['vɪlɪdʒəʳ] N villageois(e)

villain ['vɪlən] N (scoundrel) scélérat m; (BRIT: criminal) bandit m; (in novel etc) traître m

VIN N ABBR (US) = **vehicle identification number**

vinaigrette [vɪneɪ'ɡrɛt] N vinaigrette f

vindicate ['vɪndɪkeɪt] VT défendre avec succès; justifier

vindication [vɪndɪ'keɪʃən] N: **in ~ of** pour justifier

vindictive [vɪn'dɪktɪv] ADJ vindicatif(-ive), rancunier(-ière)

vine [vaɪn] N vigne f; (climbing plant) plante grimpante

vinegar ['vɪnɪɡəʳ] N vinaigre m

vine grower N viticulteur m

vine-growing ['vaɪnɡrəʊɪŋ] ADJ viticole ▶ N viticulture f

vineyard ['vɪnjɑːd] N vignoble m

vintage ['vɪntɪdʒ] N (year) année f, millésime m ▶ CPD (car) d'époque; (wine) de grand cru; **the 1970 ~** le millésime 1970

vinyl ['vaɪnl] N vinyle m

viola [vɪ'əʊlə] N alto m

violate ['vaɪəleɪt] VT violer

violation [vaɪə'leɪʃən] N violation f; **in ~ of** (rule, law) en infraction à, en violation de

violence ['vaɪələns] N violence f; (Pol etc) incidents violents

violent ['vaɪələnt] ADJ violent(e); **a ~ dislike of sb/sth** une aversion profonde pour qn/qch

violently ['vaɪələntlɪ] ADV violemment; (ill, angry) terriblement

violet ['vaɪələt] ADJ (colour) violet(te) ▶ N (plant) violette f

violin [vaɪə'lɪn] N violon m

violinist [vaɪə'lɪnɪst] N violoniste mf

VIP N ABBR (= very important person) VIP mf

viper ['vaɪpəʳ] N vipère f

viral ['vaɪərəl] ADJ viral(e)

virgin ['vəːdʒɪn] N vierge f ▶ ADJ vierge; **she is a ~** elle est vierge; **the Blessed V~** la Sainte Vierge

virginity [vəː'dʒɪnɪtɪ] N virginité f

Virgo ['vəːɡəʊ] N la Vierge; **to be ~** être de la Vierge

virile ['vɪraɪl] ADJ viril(e)

virility [vɪ'rɪlɪtɪ] N virilité f

virtual ['vəːtjuəl] ADJ (Comput, Physics) virtuel(le); (in effect): **it's a ~ impossibility** c'est quasiment impossible; **the ~ leader** le chef dans la pratique

virtually ['vəːtjuəlɪ] ADV (almost) pratiquement; **it is ~ impossible** c'est quasiment impossible

virtual reality N (Comput) réalité virtuelle

virtue ['vəːtjuː] N vertu f; (advantage) mérite m, avantage m; **by ~ of** en vertu or raison de

virtuosity [vəːtju'ɔsɪtɪ] N virtuosité f

virtuoso [vəːtju'əʊzəu] N virtuose mf

virtuous ['vəːtjuəs] ADJ vertueux(-euse)

virulent ['vɪrulənt] ADJ virulent(e)

virus ['vaɪərəs] N (Med, Comput) virus m

visa ['viːzə] N visa m

vis-à-vis [viːzə'viː] PREP vis-à-vis de

viscount ['vaɪkaunt] N vicomte m

viscous ['vɪskəs] ADJ visqueux(-euse), gluant(e)

vise [vaɪs] N (US Tech) = **vice**

visibility [vɪzɪ'bɪlɪtɪ] N visibilité f

visible ['vɪzəbl] ADJ visible; **~ exports/imports** exportations/importations fpl visibles

visibly ['vɪzəblɪ] ADV visiblement

vision ['vɪʒən] N (sight) vue f, vision f; (foresight, in dream) vision

visionary ['vɪʒənrɪ] N visionnaire mf

visit ['vɪzɪt] N visite f; (stay) séjour m ▶ VT (person: US: also: **visit with**) rendre visite à; (place) visiter; **on a private/official ~** en visite privée/officielle

visiting ['vɪzɪtə] ADJ (*speaker, team*) invité(e), de l'extérieur

visiting card N carte *f* de visite

visiting hours NPL heures *fpl* de visite

visitor ['vɪzɪtə'] N visiteur(-euse); (*to one's house*) invité(e); (*in hotel*) client(e)

visitor centre, (US) **visitor center** N hall *m* or centre *m* d'accueil

visitors' book N livre *m* d'or; (*in hotel*) registre *m*

visor ['vaɪzə'] N visière *f*

VISTA ['vɪstə] N ABBR (= *Volunteers in Service to America*) *programme d'assistance bénévole aux régions pauvres*

vista ['vɪstə] N vue *f*, perspective *f*

visual ['vɪzjuəl] ADJ visuel(le)

visual aid N support visuel (pour l'enseignement)

visual arts NPL arts *mpl* plastiques

visual display unit N console *f* de visualisation, visuel *m*

visualize ['vɪzjuəlaɪz] VT se représenter; (*foresee*) prévoir

visually ['vɪzjuəlɪ] ADV visuellement

visually-impaired ['vɪzjuəliːm'peəd] ADJ malvoyant(e)

vital ['vaɪtl] ADJ vital(e); **of ~ importance (to sb/sth)** d'une importance capitale (pour qn/qch)

vitality [vaɪ'tælɪtɪ] N vitalité *f*

vitally ['vaɪtəlɪ] ADV extrêmement

vital statistics NPL (*of population*) statistiques *fpl* démographiques; (*inf: woman's*) mensurations *fpl*

vitamin ['vɪtəmɪn] N vitamine *f*

vitiate ['vɪʃɪeɪt] VT vicier

vitreous ['vɪtrɪəs] ADJ (*china*) vitreux(-euse); (*enamel*) vitrifié(e)

vitriolic [vɪtrɪ'ɔlɪk] ADJ (*fig*) venimeux(-euse)

viva ['vaɪvə] N (*also:* **viva voce**) (examen) oral

vivacious [vɪ'veɪʃəs] ADJ animé(e), qui a de la vivacité

vivacity [vɪ'væsɪtɪ] N vivacité *f*

vivid ['vɪvɪd] ADJ (*account*) frappant(e), vivant(e); (*light, imagination*) vif (vive)

vividly ['vɪvɪdlɪ] ADV (*describe*) d'une manière vivante; (*remember*) de façon précise

vivisection [vɪvɪ'sekʃən] N vivisection *f*

vixen ['vɪksn] N renarde *f*; (*pej: woman*) mégère *f*

viz [vɪz] ABBR (= *vide licet: namely*) à savoir, c. à d.

VLF ABBR = **very low frequency**

V-neck ['viːnek] N décolleté *m* en V

VOA N ABBR (= *Voice of America*) voix *f* de l'Amérique (*émissions de radio à destination de l'étranger*)

vocabulary [vəu'kæbjuləri] N vocabulaire *m*

vocal ['vəukl] ADJ vocal(e); (*articulate*) qui n'hésite pas à s'exprimer, qui sait faire entendre ses opinions; **vocals** NPL voix *fpl*

vocal cords NPL cordes vocales

vocalist ['vəukəlɪst] N chanteur(-euse)

vocation [vəu'keɪʃən] N vocation *f*

vocational [vəu'keɪʃənl] ADJ professionnel(le); **~ guidance/training** orientation/formation professionnelle

vociferous [və'sɪfərəs] ADJ bruyant(e)

vodka ['vɔdkə] N vodka *f*

vogue [vəug] N mode *f*; (*popularity*) vogue *f*; **to be in ~** être en vogue or à la mode

voice [vɔɪs] N voix *f*; (*opinion*) avis *m* ▶ VT (*opinion*) exprimer, formuler; **in a loud/soft ~** à voix haute/basse; **to give ~ to** exprimer

voice mail N (*system*) messagerie *f* vocale, boîte *f* vocale; (*device*) répondeur *m*

voice-over ['vɔɪsəuvə'] N voix off *f*

void [vɔɪd] N vide *m* ▶ ADJ (*invalid*) nul(le); (*empty*): **~ of** vide de, dépourvu(e) de

voile [vɔɪl] N voile *m* (*tissu*)

vol. ABBR (= *volume*) vol

volatile ['vɔlətaɪl] ADJ volatil(e); (*fig: person*) versatile; (*: situation*) explosif(-ive)

volcanic [vɔl'kænɪk] ADJ volcanique

volcano [vɔl'keɪnəu] (*pl* **volcanoes**) N volcan *m*

volition [və'lɪʃən] N: **of one's own ~** de son propre gré

volley ['vɔlɪ] N (*of gunfire*) salve *f*; (*of stones etc*) pluie *f*, volée *f*; (*Tennis etc*) volée

volleyball ['vɔlɪbɔːl] N volley(-ball) *m*

volt [vəult] N volt *m*

voltage ['vəultɪdʒ] N tension *f*, voltage *m*; **high/low ~** haute/basse tension

voluble ['vɔljubl] ADJ volubile

volume ['vɔljuːm] N volume *m*; (*of tank*) capacité *f*; **~ one/two** (*of book*) tome un/deux; **his expression spoke volumes** son expression en disait long

volume control N (*Radio, TV*) bouton *m* de réglage du volume

volume discount N (*Comm*) remise *f* sur la quantité

voluminous [və'luːmɪnəs] ADJ volumineux(-euse)

voluntarily ['vɔləntrɪlɪ] ADV volontairement; bénévolement

voluntary ['vɔləntərɪ] ADJ volontaire; (*unpaid*) bénévole

voluntary liquidation N (*Comm*) dépôt *m* de bilan

voluntary redundancy N (BRIT) départ *m* volontaire (*en cas de licenciements*)

volunteer [vɔlən'tɪə'] N volontaire *mf* ▶ VT (*information*) donner spontanément ▶ VI (*Mil*) s'engager comme volontaire; **to ~ to do** se proposer pour faire

voluptuous [və'lʌptjuəs] ADJ voluptueux(-euse)

vomit ['vɔmɪt] N vomissure *f* ▶ VT, VI vomir

voracious [və'reɪʃəs] ADJ vorace; (*reader*) avide

vote [vəut] N vote *m*, suffrage *m*; (*votes cast*) voix *f*, vote; (*franchise*) droit *m* de vote ▶ VT (*bill*) voter; (*chairman*) élire; (*propose*): **to ~ that** proposer que +*sub* ▶ VI voter; **to put sth to the ~, to take a ~ on sth** mettre qch aux voix, procéder à un vote sur qch; **~ for** or **in favour of/against** vote pour/contre; **to ~ to do sth** voter en faveur de faire qch; **~ of censure** motion *f* de censure; **~ of thanks** discours *m* de remerciement

voter ['vəutə'] N électeur(-trice)

voting ['vəutɪŋ] N scrutin *m*, vote *m*

voting paper N (BRIT) bulletin *m* de vote

V

voting right N droit *m* de vote
vouch [vautʃ]: **to ~ for** *vt fus* se porter garant de
voucher ['vautʃə^r] N (*for meal, petrol, gift*) bon *m*;
  (*receipt*) reçu *m*; **travel ~** bon *m* de transport
vow [vau] N vœu *m*, serment *m* ▶ vi jurer;
  to take *or* **make a ~ to do sth** faire le vœu de
  faire qch
vowel ['vauəl] N voyelle *f*
voyage ['vɔɪɪdʒ] N voyage *m* par mer, traversée *f*;
  (*by spacecraft*) voyage
voyeur [vwɑːjəː^r] N voyeur *m*

VP N ABBR = **vice-president**
vs ABBR (= *versus*) vs
VSO N ABBR (BRIT: = *Voluntary Service Overseas*)
  ≈ coopération civile
VT, Vt. ABBR (US) = **Vermont**
vulgar ['vʌlgə^r] ADJ vulgaire
vulgarity [vʌl'gærɪtɪ] N vulgarité *f*
vulnerability [vʌlnərə'bɪlɪtɪ] N
  vulnérabilité *f*
vulnerable ['vʌlnərəbl] ADJ vulnérable
vulture ['vʌltʃə^r] N vautour *m*

Ww

W, w ['dʌblju:] N (letter) W, w m; **W for William** W comme William

W ABBR (= west) O; (Elec: = watt) W

WA ABBR (US) = **Washington**

wad [wɔd] N (of cotton wool, paper) tampon m; (of banknotes etc) liasse f

wadding ['wɔdɪŋ] N rembourrage m

waddle ['wɔdl] VI se dandiner

wade [weɪd] VI: **to ~ through** marcher dans, patauger dans; (fig: book) venir à bout de ▶ VT passer à gué

wafer ['weɪfə'] N (Culin) gaufrette f; (Rel) pain m d'hostie; (Comput) tranche f (de silicium)

wafer-thin ['weɪfə'θɪn] ADJ ultra-mince, mince comme du papier à cigarette

waffle ['wɔfl] N (Culin) gaufre f; (inf) rabâchage m; remplissage m ▶ VI parler pour ne rien dire; faire du remplissage

waffle iron N gaufrier m

waft [wɔft] VT porter ▶ VI flotter

wag [wæg] VT agiter, remuer ▶ VI remuer; **the dog wagged its tail** le chien a remué la queue

wage [weɪdʒ] N (also: **wages**) salaire m, paye f ▶ VT: **to ~ war** faire la guerre; **a day's wages** un jour de salaire

wage claim N demande f d'augmentation de salaire

wage differential N éventail m des salaires

wage earner [-ə:nə'] N salarié(e); (breadwinner) soutien m de famille

wage freeze N blocage m des salaires

wage packet N (BRIT) (enveloppe f de) paye f

wager ['weɪdʒə'] N pari m ▶ VT parier

waggle ['wægl] VT, VI remuer

wagon, waggon ['wægən] N (horse-drawn) chariot m; (BRIT Rail) wagon m (de marchandises)

wail [weɪl] N gémissement m; (of siren) hurlement m ▶ VI gémir; (siren) hurler

waist [weɪst] N taille f, ceinture f

waistcoat ['weɪskəut] N (BRIT) gilet m

waistline ['weɪstlaɪn] N (tour m de) taille f

wait [weɪt] N attente f ▶ VI attendre; **to ~ for sb/ sth** attendre qn/qch; **to keep sb waiting** faire attendre qn; **~ for me, please** attendez-moi, s'il vous plaît; **~ a minute!** un instant!; **"repairs while you ~"** "réparations minute"; **I can't ~ to ...** (fig) je meurs d'envie de ...;

to lie in ~ for guetter

▶ **wait behind** VI rester (à attendre)

▶ **wait on** VT FUS servir

▶ **wait up** VI attendre, ne pas se coucher; **don't ~ up for me** ne m'attendez pas pour aller vous coucher

waiter ['weɪtə'] N garçon m (de café), serveur m

waiting ['weɪtɪŋ] N: **"no ~"** (BRIT Aut) "stationnement interdit"

waiting list N liste f d'attente

waiting room N salle f d'attente

waitress ['weɪtrɪs] N serveuse f

waive [weɪv] VT renoncer à, abandonner

waiver ['weɪvə'] N dispense f

wake [weɪk] (pt woke [wəuk] or **waked**, pp **woken** ['wəukn] or **waked**) VT (also: **wake up**) réveiller ▶ VI (also: **wake up**) se réveiller ▶ N (for dead person) veillée f mortuaire; (Naut) sillage m; **to ~ up to sth** (fig) se rendre compte de qch; **in the ~ of** (fig) à la suite de; **to follow in sb's ~** (fig) marcher sur les traces de qn

waken ['weɪkn] VT, VI = **wake**

Wales [weɪlz] N pays m de Galles; **the Prince of ~** le prince de Galles

walk [wɔːk] N promenade f; (short) petit tour; (gait) démarche f; (path) chemin m; (in park etc) allée f; (pace): **at a quick ~** d'un pas rapide ▶ VI marcher; (for pleasure, exercise) se promener ▶ VT (distance) faire à pied; (dog) promener; **10 minutes' ~ from** à 10 minutes de marche de; **to go for a ~** se promener; faire un tour; **from all walks of life** de toutes conditions sociales; **I'll ~ you home** je vais vous raccompagner chez vous

▶ **walk out** VI (go out) sortir; (as protest) partir (en signe de protestation); (strike) se mettre en grève; **to ~ out on sb** quitter qn

walkabout ['wɔːkəbaut] N: **to go (on a) ~** (VIP) prendre un bain de foule

walker ['wɔːkə'] N (person) marcheur(-euse)

walkie-talkie ['wɔːkɪ'tɔːkɪ] N talkie-walkie m

walking ['wɔːkɪŋ] N marche f à pied; **it's within ~ distance** on peut y aller à pied

walking holiday N vacances passées à faire de la randonnée

walking shoes NPL chaussures fpl de marche

walking stick N canne f

Walkman® ['wɔːkmən] N Walkman® m

walk-on [ˈwɔːkɔn] ADJ (*Theat: part*) de figurant(e)
walkout [ˈwɔːkaut] N (*of workers*) grève-surprise *f*
walkover [ˈwɔːkəuvəʳ] N (*inf*) victoire *f* or examen *m etc* facile
walkway [ˈwɔːkweɪ] N promenade *f*, cheminement piéton
wall [wɔːl] N mur *m*; (*of tunnel, cave*) paroi *f*; **to go to the ~** (*fig: firm etc*) faire faillite
▸ **wall in** VT (*garden etc*) entourer d'un mur
wall cupboard N placard mural
walled [wɔːld] ADJ (*city*) fortifié(e)
wallet [ˈwɔlɪt] N portefeuille *m*; **I can't find my ~** je ne retrouve plus mon portefeuille
wallflower [ˈwɔːlflauəʳ] N giroflée *f*; **to be a ~** (*fig*) faire tapisserie
wall hanging N tenture (murale), tapisserie *f*
wallop [ˈwɔləp] VT (*BRIT inf*) taper sur, cogner
wallow [ˈwɔləu] VI se vautrer; **to ~ in one's grief** se complaire à sa douleur
wallpaper [ˈwɔːlpeɪpəʳ] N papier peint ▸ VT tapisser
wall-to-wall [ˈwɔːltəˈwɔːl] ADJ: **~ carpeting** moquette *f*
walnut [ˈwɔːlnʌt] N noix *f*; (*tree, wood*) noyer *m*
walrus [ˈwɔːlrəs] (*pl* **~** or **walruses**) N morse *m*
waltz [wɔːlts] N valse *f* ▸ VI valser
wan [wɔn] ADJ pâle; triste
wand [wɔnd] N (*also:* **magic wand**) baguette *f* (magique)
wander [ˈwɔndəʳ] VI (*person*) errer, aller sans but; (*thoughts*) vagabonder; (*river*) serpenter ▸ VT errer dans
wanderer [ˈwɔndərəʳ] N vagabond(e)
wandering [ˈwɔndrɪŋ] ADJ (*tribe*) nomade; (*minstrel, actor*) ambulant(e)
wane [weɪn] VI (*moon*) décroître; (*reputation*) décliner
wangle [ˈwæŋgl] (*BRIT inf*) VT se débrouiller pour avoir; carotter ▸ N combine *f*, magouille *f*
wanker [ˈwæŋkəʳ] N (*inf!*) branleur *m* (!)
want [wɔnt] VT vouloir; (*need*) avoir besoin de; (*lack*) manquer de ▸ N (*poverty*) pauvreté *f*, besoin *m*; **wants** NPL (*needs*) besoins *mpl*; **for ~ of** par manque de, faute de; **to ~ to do** vouloir faire; **to ~ sb to do** vouloir que qn fasse; **you're wanted on the phone** on vous demande au téléphone; **"cook wanted"** "on demande un cuisinier"
want ads NPL (*US*) petites annonces
wanted [ˈwɔntɪd] ADJ (*criminal*) recherché(e) par la police
wanting [ˈwɔntɪŋ] ADJ: **to be ~ (in)** manquer (de); **to be found ~** ne pas être à la hauteur
wanton [ˈwɔntn] ADJ capricieux(-euse), dévergondé(e)
war [wɔːʳ] N guerre *f*; **to go to ~** se mettre en guerre; **to make ~ (on)** faire la guerre (à)
warble [ˈwɔːbl] N (*of bird*) gazouillis *m* ▸ VI gazouiller
war cry N cri *m* de guerre
ward [wɔːd] N (*in hospital*) salle *f*; (*Pol*) section électorale; (*Law: child: also:* **ward of court**) pupille *mf*
▸ **ward off** VT parer, éviter

warden [ˈwɔːdn] N (*BRIT: of institution*) directeur(-trice); (*of park, game reserve*) gardien(ne); (*BRIT: also:* **traffic warden**) contractuel(le); (*of youth hostel*) responsable *mf*
warder [ˈwɔːdəʳ] N (*BRIT*) gardien *m* de prison
wardrobe [ˈwɔːdrəub] N (*cupboard*) armoire *f*; (*clothes*) garde-robe *f*; (*Theat*) costumes *mpl*
warehouse [ˈwɛəhaus] N entrepôt *m*
wares [wɛəz] NPL marchandises *fpl*
warfare [ˈwɔːfɛəʳ] N guerre *f*
war game N jeu *m* de stratégie militaire
warhead [ˈwɔːhed] N (*Mil*) ogive *f*
warily [ˈwɛərɪlɪ] ADV avec prudence, avec précaution
warlike [ˈwɔːlaɪk] ADJ guerrier(-ière)
warm [wɔːm] ADJ chaud(e); (*person, thanks, welcome, applause*) chaleureux(-euse); (*supporter*) ardent(e), enthousiaste; **it's ~** il fait chaud; **I'm ~** j'ai chaud; **to keep sth ~** tenir qch au chaud; **with my warmest thanks/ congratulations** avec mes remerciements/ mes félicitations les plus sincères
▸ **warm up** VI (*person, room*) se réchauffer; (*water*) chauffer; (*athlete, discussion*) s'échauffer ▸ VT (*food*) (faire) réchauffer; (*water*) (faire) chauffer; (*engine*) faire chauffer
warm-blooded [ˈwɔːmˈblʌdɪd] ADJ (*Zool*) à sang chaud
war memorial N monument *m* aux morts
warm-hearted [wɔːmˈhɑːtɪd] ADJ affectueux(-euse)
warmly [ˈwɔːmlɪ] ADV (*dress*) chaudement; (*thank, welcome*) chaleureusement
warmonger [ˈwɔːmʌŋgəʳ] N belliciste *mf*
warmongering [ˈwɔːmʌŋgrɪŋ] N propagande *f* belliciste, bellicisme *m*
warmth [wɔːmθ] N chaleur *f*
warm-up [ˈwɔːmʌp] N (*Sport*) période *f* d'échauffement
warn [wɔːn] VT avertir, prévenir; **to ~ sb (not) to do** conseiller à qn de (ne pas) faire
warning [ˈwɔːnɪŋ] N avertissement *m*; (*notice*) avis *m*; (*signal*) avertisseur *m*; **without (any)** (*suddenly*) inopinément; (*without notifying*) sans prévenir; **gale ~** (*Meteorology*) avis de grand vent
warning light N avertisseur lumineux
warning triangle N (*Aut*) triangle *m* de présignalisation
warp [wɔːp] N (*Textiles*) chaîne *f* ▸ VI (*wood*) travailler, se voiler or gauchir ▸ VT voiler; (*fig*) pervertir
warpath [ˈwɔːpɑːθ] N: **to be on the ~** (*fig*) être sur le sentier de la guerre
warped [wɔːpt] ADJ (*wood*) gauchi(e); (*fig*) perverti(e)
warrant [ˈwɔrnt] N (*guarantee*) garantie *f*; (*Law: to arrest*) mandat *m* d'arrêt; (*: to search*) mandat de perquisition ▸ VT (*justify, merit*) justifier
warrant officer N (*Mil*) adjudant *m*; (*Naut*) premier-maître *m*
warranty [ˈwɔrəntɪ] N garantie *f*; **under ~** (*Comm*) sous garantie
warren [ˈwɔrən] N (*of rabbits*) terriers *mpl*, garenne *f*

warring ['wɔːrɪŋ] ADJ (*nations*) en guerre; (*interests etc*) contradictoire, opposé(e)

warrior ['wɔrɪəʳ] N guerrier(-ière)

Warsaw ['wɔːsɔː] N Varsovie

warship ['wɔːʃɪp] N navire m de guerre

wart [wɔːt] N verrue f

wartime ['wɔːtaɪm] N: **in ~** en temps de guerre

wary ['wɛərɪ] ADJ prudent(e); **to be ~ about** or **of doing sth** hésiter beaucoup à faire qch

was [wɔz] PT of **be**

wash [wɔʃ] VT laver; (*sweep, carry: sea etc*) emporter, entraîner; (: *ashore*) rejeter ▶ VI se laver; (*sea*): **to ~ over/against sth** inonder/ baigner qch ▶ N (*paint*) badigeon m; (*clothes*) lessive f; (*washing programme*) lavage m; (*of ship*) sillage m; **to give sth a ~** laver qch; **to have a ~** se laver, faire sa toilette; **he was washed overboard** il a été emporté par une vague
  ▶ **wash away** VT (*stain*) enlever au lavage; (*subj: river etc*) emporter
  ▶ **wash down** VT laver; laver à grande eau
  ▶ **wash off** VI partir au lavage
  ▶ **wash up** VI (BRIT) faire la vaisselle; (US: *have a wash*) se débarbouiller

Wash. ABBR (US) = **Washington**

washable ['wɔʃəbl] ADJ lavable

washbasin ['wɔʃbeɪsn] N lavabo m

washer ['wɔʃəʳ] N (*Tech*) rondelle f, joint m

washing ['wɔʃɪŋ] N (BRIT: *linen etc: dirty*) linge m; (: *clean*) lessive f

washing line N (BRIT) corde f à linge

washing machine N machine f à laver

washing powder N (BRIT) lessive f (en poudre)

Washington ['wɔʃɪŋtən] N (*city, state*) Washington m

washing-up [wɔʃɪŋˈʌp] N (BRIT) vaisselle f

washing-up liquid N (BRIT) produit m pour la vaisselle

wash-out ['wɔʃaut] N (*inf*) désastre m

washroom ['wɔʃrum] N (US) toilettes fpl

wasn't ['wɔznt] = **was not**

WASP, Wasp [wɔsp] N ABBR (US *inf*: = *White Anglo-Saxon Protestant*) surnom, souvent péjoratif, donné à l'américain de souche anglo-saxonne, aisé et de tendance conservatrice

wasp [wɔsp] N guêpe f

waspish ['wɔspɪʃ] ADJ irritable

wastage ['weɪstɪdʒ] N gaspillage m; (*in manufacturing, transport etc*) déchet m

waste [weɪst] N gaspillage m; (*of time*) perte f; (*rubbish*) déchets mpl; (*also*: **household waste**) ordures fpl ▶ ADJ (*energy, heat*) perdu(e); (*food*) inutilisé(e); (*land, ground: in city*) à l'abandon; (: *in country*) inculte, en friche; (*leftover*): **~ material** déchets ▶ VT gaspiller; (*time, opportunity*) perdre; **wastes** NPL étendue f désertique; **it's a ~ of money** c'est de l'argent jeté en l'air; **to go to ~** être gaspillé(e); **to lay ~** (*destroy*) dévaster
  ▶ **waste away** VI dépérir

wastebasket ['weɪstbɑːskɪt] N = **wastepaper basket**

waste disposal, waste disposal unit N (BRIT) broyeur m d'ordures

wasteful ['weɪstful] ADJ gaspilleur(-euse);

(*process*) peu économique

waste ground N (BRIT) terrain m vague

wasteland ['weɪstlənd] N terres fpl à l'abandon; (*in town*) terrain(s) m(pl) vague(s)

wastepaper basket ['weɪstpeɪpə-] N corbeille f à papier

waste pipe N (tuyau m de) vidange f

waste products NPL (*Industry*) déchets mpl (de fabrication)

waster ['weɪstəʳ] N (*inf*) bon(ne) à rien

watch [wɔtʃ] N montre f; (*act of watching*) surveillance f; (*guard: Mil*) sentinelle f; (: *Naut*) homme m de quart; (*Naut: spell of duty*) quart m ▶ VT (*look at*) observer; (: *match, programme*) regarder; (*spy on, guard*) surveiller; (*be careful of*) faire attention à ▶ VI regarder; (*keep guard*) monter la garde; **to keep a close ~ on sb/sth** surveiller qn/qch de près; **to keep ~** faire le guet; **~ what you're doing** fais attention à ce que tu fais
  ▶ **watch out** VI faire attention

watchband ['wɔtʃbænd] N (US) bracelet m de montre

watchdog ['wɔtʃdɔg] N chien m de garde; (*fig*) gardien(ne)

watchful ['wɔtʃful] ADJ attentif(-ive), vigilant(e)

watchmaker ['wɔtʃmeɪkəʳ] N horloger(-ère)

watchman ['wɔtʃmən] N (*irreg*) gardien m; (*also*: **night watchman**) veilleur m de nuit

watch stem N (US) remontoir m

watch strap ['wɔtʃstræp] N bracelet m de montre

watchword ['wɔtʃwəːd] N mot m de passe

water ['wɔːtəʳ] N eau f ▶ VT (*plant, garden*) arroser ▶ VI (*eyes*) larmoyer; **a drink of ~** un verre d'eau; **in British waters** dans les eaux territoriales Britanniques; **to pass ~** uriner; **to make sb's mouth ~** mettre l'eau à la bouche de qn
  ▶ **water down** VT (*milk etc*) couper avec de l'eau; (*fig: story*) édulcorer

water closet N (BRIT) w.-c. mpl, waters mpl

watercolour N, (US) **watercolor** NPL ['wɔːtəkʌləʳ] aquarelle f; **watercolours** NPL couleurs fpl pour aquarelle

water-cooled ['wɔːtəkuːld] ADJ à refroidissement par eau

watercress ['wɔːtəkrɛs] N cresson m (de fontaine)

waterfall ['wɔːtəfɔːl] N chute f d'eau

waterfront ['wɔːtəfrʌnt] N (*seafront*) front m de mer; (*at docks*) quais mpl

water heater N chauffe-eau m

water hole N mare f

water ice N (BRIT) sorbet m

watering can ['wɔːtərɪŋ-] N arrosoir m

water level N niveau m de l'eau; (*of flood*) niveau des eaux

water lily N nénuphar m

waterline ['wɔːtəlaɪn] N (*Naut*) ligne f de flottaison

waterlogged ['wɔːtəlɔgd] ADJ détrempé(e); imbibé(e) d'eau

water main N canalisation f d'eau

watermark ['wɔːtəmɑːk] N (*on paper*) filigrane m

W

watermelon ['wɔːtəmɛlən] N pastèque f
water polo N water-polo m
waterproof ['wɔːtəpruːf] ADJ imperméable
water-repellent ['wɔːtərɪˈpɛlnt] ADJ hydrofuge
watershed ['wɔːtəʃɛd] N (Geo) ligne f de partage des eaux; (fig) moment m critique, point décisif
water-skiing ['wɔːtəskiːɪŋ] N ski m nautique
water softener N adoucisseur m d'eau
water tank N réservoir m d'eau
watertight ['wɔːtətaɪt] ADJ étanche
water vapour N vapeur f d'eau
waterway ['wɔːtəweɪ] N cours m d'eau navigable
waterworks ['wɔːtəwəːks] NPL station f hydraulique
watery ['wɔːtərɪ] ADJ (colour) délavé(e); (coffee) trop faible
watt [wɔt] N watt m
wattage ['wɔtɪdʒ] N puissance f or consommation f en watts
wattle ['wɔtl] N clayonnage m
wave [weɪv] N vague f; (of hand) geste m, signe m; (Radio) onde f; (in hair) ondulation f; (fig: of enthusiasm, strikes etc) vague ▶ VI faire signe de la main; (flag) flotter au vent; (grass) ondoyer ▶ VT (handkerchief) agiter; (stick) brandir; (hair) onduler; **short/medium ~** (Radio) ondes courtes/moyennes; **long ~** (Radio) grandes ondes; **the new ~** (Cine, Mus) la nouvelle vague; **to ~ goodbye to sb** dire au revoir de la main à qn
▶ **wave aside, wave away** VT (fig: suggestion, objection) rejeter, repousser; (: doubts) chasser; (person): **to ~ sb aside** faire signe à qn de s'écarter
waveband ['weɪvbænd] N bande f de fréquences
wavelength ['weɪvlɛŋθ] N longueur f d'ondes
waver ['weɪvə'] VI vaciller; (voice) trembler; (person) hésiter
wavy ['weɪvɪ] ADJ (hair, surface) ondulé(e); (line) onduleux(-euse)
wax [wæks] N cire f; (for skis) fart m ▶ VT cirer; (car) lustrer; (skis) farter ▶ VI (moon) croître
waxworks ['wækswɔːks] NPL personnages mpl de cire; musée m de cire
way [weɪ] N chemin m, voie f; (path, access) passage m; (distance) distance f; (direction) chemin, direction f; (manner) façon f, manière f; (habit) habitude f, façon; (condition) état m; **which ~? — this ~/that ~** par où or de quel côté? — par ici/par là; **to crawl one's ~ to ...** ramper jusqu'à ...; **to lie one's ~ out of it** s'en sortir par un mensonge; **to lose one's ~** perdre son chemin; **on the ~ (to)** en route (pour); **to be on one's ~** être en route; **to be in the ~** bloquer le passage; (fig) gêner; **to keep out of sb's ~** éviter qn; **it's a long ~ away** c'est loin d'ici; **the village is rather out of the ~** le village est plutôt à l'écart or isolé; **to go out of one's ~ to do** (fig) se donner beaucoup de mal pour faire; **to be under ~** (work, project) être en cours; **to make ~ (for sb/sth)** faire place (à qn/qch), s'écarter pour laisser passer (qn/qch); **to get**

one's own ~ arriver à ses fins; **put it the right ~ up** (BRIT) mettez-le dans le bon sens; **to be the wrong ~ round** être à l'envers, ne pas être dans le bon sens; **he's in a bad ~** il va mal; **in a ~** dans un sens; **by the ~** à propos; **in some ways** à certains égards; d'un côté; **in the ~ of** en fait de, comme; **by ~ of** (through) en passant par, via; (as a sort of) en guise de; **"~ in"** (BRIT) "entrée"; **"~ out"** (BRIT) "sortie"; **the ~ back** le chemin du retour; **this ~ and that** par-ci par-là; **"give ~"** (BRIT Aut) "cédez la priorité"; **no ~!** (inf) pas question!
waybill ['weɪbɪl] N (Comm) récépissé m
waylay [weɪˈleɪ] VT (irreg: like **lay**) attaquer; (fig): **I got waylaid** quelqu'un m'a accroché
wayside ['weɪsaɪd] N bord m de la route; **to fall by the ~** (fig) abandonner; (morally) quitter le droit chemin
way station N (US: Rail) petite gare; (: fig) étape f
wayward ['weɪwəd] ADJ capricieux(-euse), entêté(e)
W.C. N ABBR (BRIT: = water closet) w.-c. mpl, waters mpl
WCC N ABBR (= World Council of Churches) COE m (Conseil œcuménique des Églises)
we [wiː] PL PRON nous
weak [wiːk] ADJ faible; (health) fragile; (beam etc) peu solide; (tea, coffee) léger(-ère); **to grow ~(er)** s'affaiblir, faiblir
weaken ['wiːkn] VI faiblir ▶ VT affaiblir
weak-kneed ['wiːk'niːd] ADJ (fig) lâche, faible
weakling ['wiːklɪŋ] N gringalet m; faible mf
weakly ['wiːklɪ] ADJ chétif(-ive) ▶ ADV faiblement
weakness ['wiːknɪs] N faiblesse f; (fault) point m faible
wealth [wɛlθ] N (money, resources) richesse(s) f(pl); (of details) profusion f
wealth tax N impôt m sur la fortune
wealthy ['wɛlθɪ] ADJ riche
wean [wiːn] VT sevrer
weapon ['wɛpən] N arme f; **weapons of mass destruction** armes fpl de destruction massive
wear [wɛə'] (pt **wore** [wɔː'], pp **worn** [wɔːn]) N (use) usage m; (deterioration through use) usure f ▶ VT (clothes) porter; (put on) mettre; (beard etc) avoir; (damage: through use) user ▶ VI (last) faire de l'usage; (rub etc through) s'user; **sports/ babywear** vêtements mpl de sport/pour bébés; **evening ~** tenue f de soirée; **~ and tear** usure f; **to ~ a hole in sth** faire (à la longue) un trou dans qch
▶ **wear away** VT user, ronger ▶ VI s'user, être rongé(e)
▶ **wear down** VT user; (strength) épuiser
▶ **wear off** VI disparaître
▶ **wear on** VI se poursuivre; passer
▶ **wear out** VT user; (person, strength) épuiser
wearable ['wɛərəbl] ADJ mettable
wearily ['wɪərɪlɪ] ADV avec lassitude
weariness ['wɪərɪnɪs] N épuisement m, lassitude f
wearisome ['wɪərɪsəm] ADJ (tiring) fatigant(e); (boring) ennuyeux(-euse)

weary ['wɪərɪ] ADJ (*tired*) épuisé(e); (*dispirited*) las (lasse); abattu(e) ▶ VT lasser ▶ VI: **to ~ of** se lasser de

weasel ['wi:zl] N (*Zool*) belette *f*

weather ['wɛðəʳ] N temps *m* ▶ VT (*wood*) faire mûrir; (*storm: lit, fig*) essuyer; (*crisis*) survivre à; **what's the ~ like?** quel temps fait-il?; **under the ~** (*fig: ill*) mal fichu(e)

weather-beaten ['wɛðəbi:tn] ADJ (*person*) hâlé(e); (*building*) dégradé(e) par les intempéries

weather forecast N prévisions *fpl* météorologiques, météo *f*

weatherman ['wɛðəmæn] N (*irreg*) météorologue *m*

weatherproof ['wɛðəpru:f] ADJ (*garment*) imperméable; (*building*) étanche

weather report N bulletin *m* météo, météo *f*

weather vane [-veɪn] N girouette *f*

weave [wi:v] (*pt* **wove** [wəuv], *pp* **woven** ['wəuvn]) VT (*cloth*) tisser; (*basket*) tresser ▶ VI (*pt, pp* **weaved**) (*fig: move in and out*) se faufiler

weaver ['wi:vəʳ] N tisserand(e)

weaving ['wi:vɪŋ] N tissage *m*

web [wɛb] N (*of spider*) toile *f*; (*on duck's foot*) palmure *f*; (*fig*) tissu *m*; (*Comput*): **the (World-Wide) W~** le Web

web address N adresse *f* Web

webbed ['wɛbd] ADJ (*foot*) palmé(e)

webbing ['wɛbɪŋ] N (*on chair*) sangles *fpl*

webcam ['wɛbkæm] N webcam *f*

webinar ['wɛbɪnɑ:ʳ] N (*Comput*) conférence *f* en ligne; webinaire *m*

weblog ['wɛblɔg] N blog *m*, blogue *m*

webmail ['wɛbmeɪl] N (*Comput*) webmail *m*

web page N (*Comput*) page *f* Web

website ['wɛbsaɪt] N (*Comput*) site *m* Web

wed [wɛd] (*pt, pp* **wedded**) VT épouser ▶ VI se marier ▶ N: **the newly-weds** les jeunes mariés

we'd [wi:d] = **we had; we would**

wedded ['wɛdɪd] PT, PP *of* **wed**

wedding ['wɛdɪŋ] N mariage *m*

wedding anniversary N anniversaire *m* de mariage; **silver/golden ~** noces *fpl* d'argent/d'or

wedding day N jour *m* du mariage

wedding dress N robe *f* de mariée

wedding present N cadeau *m* de mariage

wedding ring N alliance *f*

wedge [wɛdʒ] N (*of wood etc*) coin *m*; (*under door etc*) cale *f*; (*of cake*) part *f* ▶ VT (*fix*) caler; (*push*) enfoncer, coincer

wedge-heeled shoes ['wɛdʒhi:ld-] NPL chaussures *fpl* à semelles compensées

wedlock ['wɛdlɔk] N (*union f du*) mariage *m*

Wednesday ['wɛdnzdɪ] N mercredi *m*; *see also* **Tuesday**

wee [wi:] ADJ (*SCOTTISH*) petit(e); tout(e) petit(e)

weed [wi:d] N mauvaise herbe *f* ▶ VT désherber ▶ **weed out** VT éliminer

weedkiller ['wi:dkɪləʳ] N désherbant *m*

weedy ['wi:dɪ] ADJ (*man*) gringalet

week [wi:k] N semaine *f*; **once/twice a ~** une fois/deux fois par semaine; **in two weeks' time** dans quinze jours; **a ~ today/on Tuesday**

aujourd'hui/mardi en huit

weekday ['wi:kdeɪ] N jour *m* de semaine; (*Comm*) jour ouvrable; **on weekdays** en semaine

weekend [wi:k'ɛnd] N week-end *m*

weekend case N sac *m* de voyage

weekly ['wi:klɪ] ADV une fois par semaine, chaque semaine ▶ ADJ, N hebdomadaire (*m*)

weep [wi:p] (*pt, pp* **wept** [wɛpt]) VI (*person*) pleurer; (*Med: wound etc*) suinter

weeping willow ['wi:pɪŋ-] N saule pleureur

weepy ['wi:pɪ] N (*inf: film*) mélo *m*

weft [wɛft] N (*Textiles*) trame *f*

weigh [weɪ] VT, VI peser; **to ~ anchor** lever l'ancre; **to ~ the pros and cons** peser le pour et le contre
▶ **weigh down** VT (*branch*) faire plier; (*fig: with worry*) accabler
▶ **weigh out** VT (*goods*) peser
▶ **weigh up** VT examiner

weighbridge ['weɪbrɪdʒ] N pont-bascule *m*

weighing machine ['weɪɪŋ-] N balance *f*, bascule *f*

weight [weɪt] N poids *m* ▶ VT alourdir; (*fig: factor*) pondérer; **sold by ~** vendu au poids; **to put on/lose ~** grossir/maigrir; **weights and measures** poids et mesures

weighting ['weɪtɪŋ] N: **~ allowance** indemnité *f* de résidence

weightlessness ['weɪtlɪsnɪs] N apesanteur *f*

weightlifter ['weɪtlɪftəʳ] N haltérophile *m*

weightlifting ['weɪtlɪftɪŋ] N haltérophilie *f*

weight training N musculation *f*

weighty ['weɪtɪ] ADJ lourd(e)

weir [wɪəʳ] N barrage *m*

weird [wɪəd] ADJ bizarre; (*eerie*) surnaturel(le)

weirdo ['wɪədəu] N (*inf*) type *m* bizarre

welcome ['wɛlkəm] ADJ bienvenu(e) ▶ N accueil *m* ▶ VT accueillir; (*also:* **bid welcome**) souhaiter la bienvenue à; (*be glad of*) se réjouir de; **to be ~** être le (la) bienvenu(e); **to make sb ~** faire bon accueil à qn; **you're ~ to try** vous pouvez essayer si vous voulez; **you're ~!** (*after thanks*) de rien, il n'y a pas de quoi

welcoming ['wɛlkəmɪŋ] ADJ accueillant(e); (*speech*) d'accueil

weld [wɛld] N soudure *f* ▶ VT souder

welder ['wɛldəʳ] N (*person*) soudeur *m*

welding ['wɛldɪŋ] N soudure *f* (autogène)

welfare ['wɛlfɛəʳ] N (*wellbeing*) bien-être *m*; (*social aid*) assistance sociale

welfare state N État-providence *m*

welfare work N travail social

well [wɛl] N puits *m* ▶ ADV bien ▶ ADJ: **to be ~** aller bien ▶ EXCL eh bien!; (*relief also*) bon!; (*resignation*) enfin!; **~ done!** bravo!; **I don't feel ~** je ne me sens pas bien; **get ~ soon!** remets-toi vite!; **to do ~** bien réussir; (*business*) prospérer; **to think ~ of sb** penser du bien de qn; **as ~** (*in addition*) aussi, également; **you might as ~ tell me** tu ferais aussi bien de me le dire; **as ~ as** aussi bien que *or* de; en plus de; **~, as I was saying …** donc, comme je disais …
▶ **well up** VI (*tears, emotions*) monter

W

863

we'll [wiːl] = **we will; we shall**

well-behaved ['wɛlbɪ'heɪvd] ADJ sage, obéissant(e)

well-being ['wɛl'biːɪŋ] N bien-être m

well-bred ['wɛl'brɛd] ADJ bien élevé(e)

well-built ['wɛl'bɪlt] ADJ (house) bien construit(e); (person) bien bâti(e)

well-chosen ['wɛl'tʃəuzn] ADJ (remarks, words) bien choisi(e), pertinent(e)

well-deserved ['wɛldɪ'zəːvd] ADJ (bien) mérité(e)

well-developed ['wɛldɪ'vɛləpt] ADJ (girl) bien fait(e)

well-disposed ['wɛldɪs'pəuzd] ADJ: ~ **to(wards)** bien disposé(e) envers

well-dressed ['wɛl'drɛst] ADJ bien habillé(e), bien vêtu(e)

well-earned ['wɛl'əːnd] ADJ (rest) bien mérité(e)

well-groomed ['wɛl'gruːmd] ADJ très soigné(e)

well-heeled ['wɛl'hiːld] ADJ (inf: wealthy) fortuné(e), riche

wellies ['wɛlɪz] NPL (BRIT inf) = **wellingtons**

well-informed ['wɛlɪn'fɔːmd] ADJ (having knowledge of sth) bien renseigné(e); (having general knowledge) cultivé(e)

Wellington ['wɛlɪŋtən] N Wellington

wellingtons ['wɛlɪŋtənz] NPL (also: **wellington boots**) bottes fpl en caoutchouc

well-kept ['wɛl'kɛpt] ADJ (house, grounds) bien tenu(e), bien entretenu(e); (secret) bien gardé(e); (hair, hands) soigné(e)

well-known ['wɛl'nəun] ADJ (person) bien connu(e)

well-mannered ['wɛl'mænəd] ADJ bien élevé(e)

well-meaning ['wɛl'miːnɪŋ] ADJ bien intentionné(e)

well-nigh ['wɛl'naɪ] ADV: ~ **impossible** pratiquement impossible

well-off ['wɛl'ɔf] ADJ aisé(e), assez riche

well-paid ['wɛl'peɪd] ADJ bien payé(e)

well-read ['wɛl'rɛd] ADJ cultivé(e)

well-spoken ['wɛl'spəukn] ADJ (person) qui parle bien; (words) bien choisi(e)

well-stocked ['wɛl'stɔkt] ADJ bien approvisionné(e)

well-timed ['wɛl'taɪmd] ADJ opportun(e)

well-to-do ['wɛltə'duː] ADJ aisé(e), assez riche

well-wisher ['wɛlwɪʃəʳ] N ami(e), admirateur(-trice); **scores of well-wishers had gathered** de nombreux amis et admirateurs s'étaient rassemblés; **letters from well-wishers** des lettres d'encouragement

well-woman clinic ['wɛlwumən-] N centre prophylactique et thérapeutique pour femmes

Welsh [wɛlʃ] ADJ gallois(e) ► N (Ling) gallois m; **the Welsh** NPL (people) les Gallois

Welsh Assembly N Parlement gallois

Welshman ['wɛlʃmən] N (irreg) Gallois m

Welsh rarebit N croûte f au fromage

Welshwoman ['wɛlʃwumən] N (irreg) Galloise f

welter ['wɛltəʳ] N fatras m

went [wɛnt] PT of **go**

wept [wɛpt] PT, PP of **weep**

were [wəːʳ] PT of **be**

we're [wɪəʳ] = **we are**

weren't [wəːnt] = **were not**

werewolf ['wɪəwulf] (pl **werewolves** [-wulvz]) N loup-garou m

west [wɛst] N ouest m ► ADJ (wind) d'ouest; (side) ouest inv ► ADV à or vers l'ouest; **the W~** l'Occident m, l'Ouest

westbound ['wɛstbaund] ADJ en direction de l'ouest; (carriageway) ouest inv

West Country N: **the ~** le sud-ouest de l'Angleterre

westerly ['wɛstəlɪ] ADJ (situation) à l'ouest; (wind) d'ouest

western ['wɛstən] ADJ occidental(e), de or à l'ouest ► N (Cine) western m

westerner ['wɛstənəʳ] N occidental(e)

westernized ['wɛstənaɪzd] ADJ occidentalisé(e)

West German (formerly) ADJ ouest-allemand(e) ► N Allemand(e) de l'Ouest

West Germany N (formerly) Allemagne f de l'Ouest

West Indian ADJ antillais(e) ► N Antillais(e)

West Indies [-'ɪndɪz] NPL Antilles fpl

Westminster ['wɛstmɪnstəʳ] N (BRIT Parliament) Westminster m

westward ['wɛstwəd], **westwards** ['wɛstwədz] ADV vers l'ouest

wet [wɛt] ADJ mouillé(e); (damp) humide; (soaked: also: **wet through**) trempé(e); (rainy) pluvieux(-euse) ► VT: **to ~ one's pants** or **o.s.** mouiller sa culotte, faire pipi dans sa culotte; **to get ~** se mouiller; **"~ paint"** "attention peinture fraîche"

wet blanket N (fig) rabat-joie m inv

wetness ['wɛtnɪs] N humidité f

wetsuit ['wɛtsuːt] N combinaison f de plongée

we've [wiːv] = **we have**

whack [wæk] VT donner un grand coup à

whacked [wækt] ADJ (BRIT inf: tired) crevé(e)

whale [weɪl] N (Zool) baleine f

whaler ['weɪləʳ] N (ship) baleinier m

whaling ['weɪlɪŋ] N pêche f à la baleine

wharf [wɔːf] (pl **wharves** [wɔːvz]) N quai m

(KEYWORD)

what [wɔt] ADJ **1** (in questions) quel(le); **what size is he?** quelle taille fait-il?; **what colour is it?** de quelle couleur est-ce?; **what books do you need?** quels livres vous faut-il?

2 (in exclamations): **what a mess!** quel désordre!; **what a fool I am!** que je suis bête!

► PRON **1** (interrogative) que; de/à/en etc quoi; **what are you doing?** que faites-vous?, qu'est-ce que vous faites?; **what is happening?** qu'est-ce qui se passe?, que se passe-t-il?; **what are you talking about?** de quoi parlez-vous?; **what are you thinking about?** à quoi pensez-vous?; **what is it called?** comment est-ce que ça s'appelle?; **what about me?** et moi?; **what about doing ...?** et si on faisait ...?

2 (relative: subject) ce qui; (: direct object) ce que; (: indirect object) ce à quoi, ce dont; **I saw what you did/was on the table** j'ai vu ce que vous

avez fait/ce qui était sur la table; **tell me what you remember** dites-moi ce dont vous vous souvenez; **what I want is a cup of tea** ce que je veux, c'est une tasse de thé
▶ EXCL *(disbelieving)* quoi!, comment!

whatever [wɔt'ɛvə^r] ADJ **take ~ book you prefer** prenez le livre que vous préférez, peu importe lequel; **~ book you take** quel que soit le livre que vous preniez ▶ PRON: **do ~ is necessary** faites (tout) ce qui est nécessaire; **~ happens** quoi qu'il arrive; **no reason ~** *or* **whatsoever** pas la moindre raison; **nothing ~** *or* **whatsoever** rien du tout

whatsoever [wɔtsəu'ɛvə^r] ADJ *see* **whatever**
wheat [wi:t] N blé *m*, froment *m*
wheatgerm ['wi:tdʒə:m] N germe *m* de blé
wheatmeal ['wi:tmi:l] N farine bise
wheedle ['wi:dl] VT: **to ~ sb into doing sth** cajoler *or* enjôler qn pour qu'il fasse qch; **to ~ sth out of sb** obtenir qch de qn par des cajoleries
wheel [wi:l] N roue *f*; *(Aut: also:* **steering wheel**) volant *m*; *(Naut)* gouvernail *m* ▶ VT *(pram etc)* pousser, rouler ▶ VI *(birds)* tournoyer; *(also:* **wheel round**: *person)* se retourner, faire volte-face
wheelbarrow ['wi:lbærəu] N brouette *f*
wheelbase ['wi:lbeis] N empattement *m*
wheelchair ['wi:ltʃɛə^r] N fauteuil roulant
wheel clamp N *(Aut)* sabot *m* (de Denver)
wheeler-dealer ['wi:lə'di:lə^r] N *(pej)* combinard(e), affairiste *mf*
wheelie-bin ['wi:libin] N *(BRIT)* poubelle *f* à roulettes
wheeling ['wi:liŋ] N: **~ and dealing** *(pej)* manigances *fpl*, magouilles *fpl*
wheeze [wi:z] N respiration bruyante *(d'asthmatique)* ▶ VI respirer bruyamment
wheezy ['wi:zi] ADJ sifflant(e)

when [wen] ADV quand; **when did he go?** quand est-ce qu'il est parti?
▶ CONJ **1** *(at, during, after the time that)* quand, lorsque; **she was reading when I came in** elle lisait quand *or* lorsque je suis entré
2 *(on, at which)*: **on the day when I met him** le jour où je l'ai rencontré
3 *(whereas)* alors que; **I thought I was wrong when in fact I was right** j'ai cru que j'avais tort alors qu'en fait j'avais raison

whenever [wɛn'ɛvə^r] ADV quand donc ▶ CONJ quand; *(every time that)* chaque fois que; **I go – I can** j'y vais quand *or* chaque fois que je le peux
where [wɛə^r] ADV, CONJ où; **this is ~** c'est là que; **~ are you from?** d'où venez vous?
whereabouts ['wɛərə'bauts] ADV où donc ▶ N: **nobody knows his ~** personne ne sait où il se trouve
whereas [wɛər'æz] CONJ alors que
whereby [wɛə'bai] ADV *(formal)* par lequel *(or* laquelle *etc)*

whereupon [wɛərə'pɔn] ADV sur quoi, et sur ce
wherever [wɛər'ɛvə^r] ADV où donc ▶ CONJ où que +*sub*; **sit ~ you like** asseyez-vous (là) où vous voulez
wherewithal ['wɛəwiðɔ:l] N: **the ~ (to do sth)** les moyens *mpl* (de faire qch)
whet [wet] VT aiguiser
whether ['wɛðə^r] CONJ si; **I don't know ~ to accept or not** je ne sais pas si je dois accepter ou non; **it's doubtful ~** il est peu probable que +*sub*; **~ you go or not** que vous y alliez ou non
whey ['wei] N petit-lait *m*

which [witʃ] ADJ **1** *(interrogative: direct, indirect)* quel(le); **which picture do you want?** quel tableau voulez-vous?; **which one?** lequel (laquelle)?
2: **in which case** auquel cas; **we got there at 8pm, by which time the cinema was full** quand nous sommes arrivés à 20h, le cinéma était complet
▶ PRON **1** *(interrogative)* lequel (laquelle), lesquels (lesquelles) *pl*; **I don't mind which** peu importe lequel; **which (of these) are yours?** lesquels sont à vous?; **tell me which you want** dites-moi lesquels *or* ceux que vous voulez
2 *(relative: subject)* qui; *(: object)* que; sur/vers *etc* lequel (laquelle) (NB: *à* + *lequel* = **auquel**; *de* + *lequel* = **duquel**); **the apple which you ate/which is on the table** la pomme que vous avez mangée/ qui est sur la table; **the chair on which you are sitting** la chaise sur laquelle vous êtes assis; **the book of which you spoke** le livre dont vous avez parlé; **he said he knew, which is true/I was afraid of** il a dit qu'il le savait, ce qui est vrai/ce que je craignais; **after which** après quoi

whichever [witʃ'ɛvə^r] ADJ: **take ~ book you prefer** prenez le livre que vous préférez, peu importe lequel; **~ book you take** quel que soit le livre que vous preniez; **~ way you** de quelque façon que vous +*sub*
whiff [wif] N bouffée *f*; **to catch a ~ of sth** sentir l'odeur de qch
while [wail] N moment *m* ▶ CONJ pendant que; *(as long as)* tant que; *(as, whereas)* alors que; *(though)* bien que +*sub*, quoique +*sub*; **for a ~** pendant quelque temps; **in a ~** dans un moment; **all the ~** pendant tout ce temps-là; **we'll make it worth your ~** nous vous récompenserons de votre peine
▶ **while away** VT *(time)* (faire) passer
whilst [wailst] CONJ = **while**
whim [wim] N caprice *m*
whimper ['wimpə^r] N geignement *m* ▶ VI geindre
whimsical ['wimzikl] ADJ *(person)* capricieux(-euse); *(look)* étrange
whine [wain] N gémissement *m*; *(of engine, siren)* plainte stridente ▶ VI gémir, geindre, pleurnicher; *(dog, engine, siren)* gémir
whip [wip] N fouet *m*; *(for riding)* cravache *f*; *(Pol:*

W

person) chef m de file (*assurant la discipline dans son groupe parlementaire*) ▶ VT fouetter; (*snatch*) enlever (*or* sortir) brusquement

▶ **whip up** VT (*cream*) fouetter; (*inf: meal*) préparer en vitesse; (*stir up: support*) stimuler; (: *feeling*) attiser, aviver; *voir article*

> Un *whip* est un député dont le rôle est, entre autres, de s'assurer que les membres de son parti sont régulièrement présents à la *House of Commons*, surtout lorsque les votes ont lieu. Les convocations que les *whips* envoient se distinguent, selon leur degré d'importance, par le fait qu'elles sont soulignées 1, 2 ou 3 fois (les 1-, 2-, ou 3-*line whips*).

whiplash ['wɪplæʃ] N (*Med: also:* **whiplash injury**) coup m du lapin

whipped cream [wɪpt-] N crème fouettée

whipping boy ['wɪpɪŋ-] N (*fig*) bouc m émissaire

whip-round ['wɪpraund] N (*BRIT*) collecte f

whirl [wəːl] N tourbillon m ▶ VI tourbillonner; (*dancers*) tournoyer ▶ VT faire tourbillonner; faire tournoyer

whirlpool ['wəːlpuːl] N tourbillon m

whirlwind ['wəːlwɪnd] N tornade f

whirr [wəːʳ] VI bruire; ronronner; vrombir

whisk [wɪsk] N (*Culin*) fouet m ▶ VT (*eggs*) fouetter, battre; **to ~ sb away** *or* **off** emmener qn rapidement

whiskers ['wɪskəz] NPL (*of animal*) moustaches fpl; (*of man*) favoris mpl

whisky, (*IRISH, US*) **whiskey** ['wɪskɪ] N whisky m

whisper ['wɪspəʳ] N chuchotement m; (*fig: of leaves*) bruissement m; (*rumour*) rumeur f ▶ VT, VI chuchoter

whispering ['wɪspərɪŋ] N chuchotement(s) m(pl)

whist [wɪst] N (*BRIT*) whist m

whistle ['wɪsl] N (*sound*) sifflement m; (*object*) sifflet m ▶ VI siffler ▶ VT siffler, siffloter

whistle-stop ['wɪslstɔp] ADJ: **to make a ~ tour of** (*Pol*) faire la tournée électorale des petits patelins de

Whit [wɪt] N la Pentecôte

white [waɪt] ADJ blanc (blanche); (*with fear*) blême ▶ N blanc m; (*person*) blanc (blanche); **to turn** *or* **go ~** (*person*) pâlir, blêmir; (*hair*) blanchir; **the whites** (*washing*) le linge blanc; **tennis whites** tenue f de tennis

whitebait ['waɪtbeɪt] N blanchaille f

whiteboard ['waɪtbɔːd] N tableau m blanc; **interactive ~** tableau m (blanc) interactif

white coffee N (*BRIT*) café m au lait, (*café*) crème m

white-collar worker ['waɪtkɔlə-] N employé(e) de bureau

white elephant N (*fig*) objet dispendieux et superflu

white goods NPL (*appliances*) (gros) électroménager m; (*linen etc*) linge m de maison

white-hot [waɪt'hɔt] ADJ (*metal*) incandescent(e)

White House N (*US*): **the ~** la Maison-Blanche; *voir article*

> La *White House* est un grand bâtiment blanc situé à Washington D.C. où réside le Président des États-Unis. Par extension, ce terme désigne l'exécutif américain.

white lie N pieux mensonge

whiteness ['waɪtnɪs] N blancheur f

white noise N son m blanc

whiteout ['waɪtaut] N jour blanc

white paper N (*Pol*) livre blanc

whitewash ['waɪtwɔʃ] N (*paint*) lait m de chaux ▶ VT blanchir à la chaux; (*fig*) blanchir

whiting ['waɪtɪŋ] N (*pl inv: fish*) merlan m

Whit Monday N le lundi de Pentecôte

Whitsun ['wɪtsn] N la Pentecôte

whittle ['wɪtl] VT: **to ~ away**, **to ~ down** (*costs*) réduire, rogner

whizz [wɪz] VI aller (*or* passer) à toute vitesse

whizz kid N (*inf*) petit prodige

WHO N ABBR (= *World Health Organization*) OMS f (*Organisation mondiale de la Santé*)

who [huː] PRON qui

whodunit [huːˈdʌnɪt] N (*inf*) roman policier

whoever [huːˈɛvəʳ] PRON: **~ finds it** celui (celle) qui le trouve(, qui que ce soit), quiconque le trouve; **ask ~ you like** demandez à qui vous voulez; **~ he marries** qui que ce soit *or* quelle que soit la personne qu'il épouse; **~ told you that?** qui a bien pu vous dire ça?, qui donc vous a dit ça?

whole [həul] ADJ (*complete*) entier(-ière), tout(e); (*not broken*) intact(e), complet(-ète) ▶ N (*entire unit*) tout m; (*all*): **the ~ of** la totalité de, tout(e) le (la); **the ~ lot (of it)** tout; **the ~ lot (of them)** tous (sans exception); **the ~ of the time** tout le temps; **the ~ of the town** la ville tout entière; **on the ~**, **as a ~** dans l'ensemble

wholefood ['həulfuːd] N, **wholefoods** ['həulfuːdz] NPL aliments complets

wholehearted [həul'hɑːtɪd] ADJ sans réserve(s), sincère

wholeheartedly [həul'hɑːtɪdlɪ] ADV sans réserve; **to agree ~** être entièrement d'accord

wholemeal ['həulmiːl] ADJ (*BRIT: flour, bread*) complet(-ète)

whole note N (*US*) ronde f

wholesale ['həulseɪl] N (*vente f en*) gros m ▶ ADJ (*price*) de gros; (*destruction*) systématique

wholesaler ['həulseɪləʳ] N grossiste mf

wholesome ['həulsəm] ADJ sain(e); (*advice*) salutaire

wholewheat ['həulwiːt] ADJ = **wholemeal**

wholly ['həulɪ] ADV entièrement, tout à fait

(KEYWORD)

whom [huːm] PRON **1** (*interrogative*) qui; **whom did you see?** qui avez-vous vu?; **to whom did you give it?** à qui l'avez-vous donné?
2 (*relative*) que; à/de *etc* qui; **the man whom I saw/to whom I spoke** l'homme que j'ai vu/à qui j'ai parlé

whooping cough ['huːpɪŋ-] N coqueluche f

whoops [wuːps] EXCL (*also:* **whoops-a-daisy**) oups!, houp-là!

whoosh [wuʃ] VI: **the skiers whooshed past** les skieurs passèrent dans un glissement rapide

whopper ['wɔpəʳ] N (inf: lie) gros bobard; (: large thing) monstre m, phénomène m

whopping ['wɔpɪŋ] ADJ (inf: big) énorme

whore [hɔːʳ] N (inf, pej) putain f

(KEYWORD)

whose [huːz] ADJ **1** (possessive: interrogative): **whose book is this?, whose is this book?** à qui est ce livre?; **whose pencil have you taken?** à qui est le crayon que vous avez pris?, c'est le crayon de qui que vous avez pris?; **whose daughter are you?** de qui êtes-vous la fille?

2 (possessive: relative): **the man whose son I rescued** l'homme dont or de qui vous avez sauvé le fils; **the girl whose sister you were speaking to** la fille à la sœur de qui or de laquelle vous parliez; **the woman whose car was stolen** la femme dont la voiture a été volée ▸ PRON à qui; **whose is this?** à qui est ceci?; **I know whose it is** je sais à qui c'est

Who's Who ['huːz'huː] N ≈ Bottin Mondain

(KEYWORD)

why [waɪ] ADV pourquoi; **why is he late?** pourquoi est-il en retard?; **why not?** pourquoi pas?

▸ CONJ: **I wonder why he said that** je me demande pourquoi il a dit ça; **that's not why I'm here** ce n'est pas pour ça que je suis là; **the reason why** la raison pour laquelle

▸ EXCL eh bien!, tiens!; **why, it's you!** tiens, c'est vous!; **why, that's impossible!** voyons, c'est impossible!

whyever [waɪ'ɛvəʳ] ADV pourquoi donc, mais pourquoi

WI N ABBR (BRIT: = Women's Institute) amicale de femmes au foyer ▸ ABBR (Geo) = **West Indies**; (US) = **Wisconsin**

wick [wɪk] N mèche f (de bougie)

wicked ['wɪkɪd] ADJ méchant(e); (mischievous: grin, look) espiègle, malicieux(-euse); (crime) pervers(e); (terrible: prices, weather) épouvantable; (inf: very good) génial(e) (inf)

wicker ['wɪkəʳ] N osier m; (also: **wickerwork**) vannerie f

wicket ['wɪkɪt] N (Cricket: stumps) guichet m; (: grass area) espace compris entre les deux guichets

wicket keeper N (Cricket) gardien m de guichet

wide [waɪd] ADJ large; (area, knowledge) vaste, très étendu(e); (choice) grand(e) ▸ ADV: **to open** ~ ouvrir tout grand; **to shoot** ~ tirer à côté; **it is 3 metres** ~ cela fait 3 mètres de large

wide-angle lens ['waɪdæŋgl-] N objectif m grand-angulaire

wide-awake [waɪdə'weɪk] ADJ bien éveillé(e)

wide-eyed [waɪd'aɪd] ADJ aux yeux écarquillés; (fig) naïf(-ïve), crédule

widely ['waɪdlɪ] ADV (different) radicalement; (spaced) sur une grande étendue; (believed) généralement; (travel) beaucoup; **to be** ~ **read** (author) être beaucoup lu(e); (reader) avoir beaucoup lu, être cultivé(e)

widen ['waɪdn] VT élargir ▸ VI s'élargir

wideness ['waɪdnɪs] N largeur f

wide open ADJ grand(e) ouvert(e)

wide-ranging [waɪd'reɪndʒɪŋ] ADJ (survey, report) vaste; (interests) divers(e)

widespread ['waɪdsprɛd] ADJ (belief etc) très répandu(e)

widget ['wɪdʒɪt] N (Comput) widget m

widow ['wɪdəu] N veuve f

widowed ['wɪdəud] ADJ (qui est devenu(e)) veuf (veuve)

widower ['wɪdəuəʳ] N veuf m

width [wɪdθ] N largeur f; **it's 7 metres in** ~ cela fait 7 mètres de large

widthways ['wɪdθweɪz] ADV en largeur

wield [wiːld] VT (sword) manier; (power) exercer

wife [waɪf] (pl **wives** [waɪvz]) N femme f, épouse f

Wi-Fi ['waɪfaɪ] N wifi m ▸ N ABBR (= wireless fidelity) WiFi m ▸ ADJ (hot spot, network) WiFi inv

wig [wɪg] N perruque f

wigging ['wɪgɪŋ] N (BRIT inf) savon m, engueulade f

wiggle ['wɪgl] VT agiter, remuer ▸ VI (loose screw etc) branler; (worm) se tortiller

wiggly ['wɪglɪ] ADJ (line) ondulé(e)

wiki ['wɪkɪ] N (Internet) wiki m

wild [waɪld] ADJ sauvage; (sea) déchaîné(e); (idea, life) fou (folle); (behaviour) déchaîné(e), extravagant(e); (inf: angry) hors de soi, furieux(-euse); (: enthusiastic): **to be** ~ **about** être fou (folle) or dingue de ▸ N: **the** ~ la nature; **wilds** NPL régions fpl sauvages

wild card N (Comput) caractère m de remplacement

wildcat ['waɪldkæt] N chat m sauvage

wildcat strike N grève f sauvage

wilderness ['wɪldənɪs] N désert m, région f sauvage

wildfire ['waɪldfaɪəʳ] N: **to spread like** ~ se répandre comme une traînée de poudre

wild-goose chase [waɪld'guːs-] N (fig) fausse piste

wildlife ['waɪldlaɪf] N faune f (et flore f)

wildly ['waɪldlɪ] ADV (behave) de manière déchaînée; (applaud) frénétiquement; (hit, guess) au hasard; (happy) follement

wiles [waɪlz] NPL ruses fpl, artifices mpl

wilful, (US) **willful** ['wɪlful] ADJ (person) obstiné(e); (action) délibéré(e); (crime) prémédité(e)

(KEYWORD)

will [wɪl] AUX VB **1** (forming future tense): **I will finish it tomorrow** je le finirai demain; **I will have finished it by tomorrow** je l'aurai fini d'ici demain; **will you do it?** — **yes I will/no I won't** le ferez-vous? — oui/non; **you won't lose it, will you?** vous ne le perdrez pas, n'est-ce pas?

2 (*in conjectures, predictions*): **he will** or **he'll be there by now** il doit être arrivé à l'heure qu'il est; **that will be the postman** ça doit être le facteur

3 (*in commands, requests, offers*): **will you be quiet!** voulez-vous bien vous taire!; **will you help me?** est-ce que vous pouvez m'aider?; **will you have a cup of tea?** voulez-vous une tasse de thé?; **I won't put up with it!** je ne le tolérerai pas!

▸ VT (*pt, pp* **willed**): **to will sb to do** souhaiter ardemment que qn fasse; **he willed himself to go on** par un suprême effort de volonté, il continua

▸ N **1** volonté *f*; **to do sth of one's own free will** faire qch de son propre gré; **against one's will** à contre-cœur

2 (*document*) testament *m*

willful ['wɪlful] ADJ (*US*) = **wilful**
willing ['wɪlɪŋ] ADJ de bonne volonté, serviable
▸ N: **to show ~** faire preuve de bonne volonté; **he's ~ to do it** il est disposé à le faire, il veut bien le faire
willingly ['wɪlɪŋlɪ] ADV volontiers
willingness ['wɪlɪŋnɪs] N bonne volonté
will-o'-the-wisp ['wɪləðə'wɪsp] N (*also fig*) feu follet *m*
willow ['wɪləu] N saule *m*
willpower ['wɪl'pauər] N volonté *f*
willy-nilly ['wɪlɪ'nɪlɪ] ADV bon gré mal gré
wilt [wɪlt] VI dépérir
Wilts [wɪlts] ABBR (*BRIT*) = **Wiltshire**
wily ['waɪlɪ] ADJ rusé(e)
wimp [wɪmp] N (*inf*) mauviette *f*
win [wɪn] (*pt, pp* **won** [wʌn]) N (*in sports etc*) victoire *f* ▸ VT (*battle, money*) gagner; (*prize, contract*) remporter; (*popularity*) acquérir ▸ VI gagner
▸ **win over** VT convaincre
▸ **win round** VT gagner, se concilier
wince [wɪns] N tressaillement *m* ▸ VI tressaillir
winch [wɪntʃ] N treuil *m*
Winchester disk ['wɪntʃɪstə-] N (*Comput*) disque *m* Winchester
wind¹ [wɪnd] N (*also Med*) vent *m*; (*breath*) souffle *m* ▸ VT (*take breath away*) couper le souffle à; **the ~(s)** (*Mus*) les instruments *mpl* à vent; **into** or **against the ~** contre le vent; **to get ~ of sth** (*fig*) avoir vent de qch; **to break ~** avoir des gaz
wind² [waɪnd] (*pt, pp* **wound** [waund]) VT enrouler; (*wrap*) envelopper; (*clock, toy*) remonter ▸ VI (*road, river*) serpenter
▸ **wind down** VT (*car window*) baisser; (*fig: production, business*) réduire progressivement
▸ **wind up** VT (*clock*) remonter; (*debate*) terminer, clôturer
windbreak ['wɪndbreɪk] N brise-vent *m inv*
windcheater ['wɪndtʃi:tər], (*US*) **windbreaker** ['wɪndbreɪkər] N anorak *m*
winder ['waɪndər] N (*BRIT: on watch*) remontoir *m*
windfall ['wɪndfɔ:l] N coup *m* de chance
wind farm N ferme *f* éolienne
winding ['waɪndɪŋ] ADJ (*road*) sinueux(-euse);

(*staircase*) tournant(e)
wind instrument N (*Mus*) instrument *m* à vent
windmill ['wɪndmɪl] N moulin *m* à vent
window ['wɪndəu] N fenêtre *f*; (*in car, train: also*: **windowpane**) vitre *f*; (*in shop etc*) vitrine *f*
window box N jardinière *f*
window cleaner N (*person*) laveur(-euse) de vitres
window dressing N arrangement *m* de la vitrine
window envelope N enveloppe *f* à fenêtre
window frame N châssis *m* de fenêtre
window ledge N rebord *m* de la fenêtre
window pane N vitre *f*, carreau *m*
window seat N (*on plane*) place *f* côté hublot
window-shopping ['wɪndəuʃɔpɪŋ] N: **to go ~** faire du lèche-vitrines
windowsill ['wɪndəusɪl] N (*inside*) appui *m* de la fenêtre; (*outside*) rebord *m* de la fenêtre
windpipe ['wɪndpaɪp] N gosier *m*
wind power N énergie éolienne
windscreen ['wɪndskri:n] N pare-brise *m inv*
windscreen washer N lave-glace *m inv*
windscreen wiper, (*US*) **windshield wiper** [-waɪpər] N essuie-glace *m inv*
windshield ['wɪndʃi:ld] N (*US*) = **windscreen**
windsurfing ['wɪndsə:fɪŋ] N planche *f* à voile
windswept ['wɪndswɛpt] ADJ balayé(e) par le vent
wind tunnel N soufflerie *f*
wind turbine N éolienne *f*
windy ['wɪndɪ] ADJ (*day*) de vent, venteux(-euse); (*place, weather*) venteux; **it's ~** il y a du vent
wine [waɪn] N ▸ VT: **to ~ and dine sb** offrir un dîner bien arrosé à qn
wine bar N bar *m* à vin
wine cellar N cave *f* à vins
wine glass N verre *m* à vin
wine list N carte *f* des vins
wine merchant N marchand(e) de vins
wine tasting [-teɪstɪŋ] N dégustation *f* (de vins)
wine waiter N sommelier *m*
wing [wɪŋ] N aile *f*; (*in air force*) groupe *m* d'escadrilles; **wings** NPL (*Theat*) coulisses *fpl*
winger ['wɪŋər] N (*Sport*) ailier *m*
wing mirror N (*BRIT*) rétroviseur latéral
wing nut N papillon *m*, écrou *m* à ailettes
wingspan ['wɪŋspæn], **wingspread** ['wɪŋspred] N envergure *f*
wink [wɪŋk] N clin *m* d'œil ▸ VI faire un clin d'œil; (*blink*) cligner des yeux
winkle ['wɪŋkl] N bigorneau *m*
winner ['wɪnər] N gagnant(e)
winning ['wɪnɪŋ] ADJ (*team*) gagnant(e); (*goal*) décisif(-ive); (*charming*) charmeur(-euse)
winning post N poteau *m* d'arrivée
winnings ['wɪnɪŋz] NPL gains *mpl*
winsome ['wɪnsəm] ADJ avenant(e), engageant(e)
winter ['wɪntər] N hiver *m* ▸ VI hiverner; **in ~** en hiver
winter sports NPL sports *mpl* d'hiver
wintertime ['wɪntətaɪm] N hiver *m*
wintry ['wɪntrɪ] ADJ hivernal(e)

wipe [waɪp] N coup *m* de torchon (*or* de chiffon *or* d'éponge); **to give sth a ~** donner un coup de torchon/de chiffon/d'éponge à qch ▶ VT essuyer; (*erase: tape*) effacer; **to ~ one's nose** se moucher
▶ **wipe off** VT essuyer
▶ **wipe out** VT (*debt*) éteindre, amortir; (*memory*) effacer; (*destroy*) anéantir
▶ **wipe up** VT essuyer

wire ['waɪəʳ] N fil *m* (de fer); (*Elec*) fil électrique; (*Tel*) télégramme *m* ▶ VT (*fence*) grillager; (*house*) faire l'installation électrique de; (*also*: **wire up**) brancher; (*person: send telegram to*) télégraphier à

wire brush N brosse *f* métallique

wire cutters [-kʌtəz] NPL cisaille *f*

wireless ['waɪəlɪs] N (BRIT) télégraphie *f* sans fil; (*set*) T.S.F. *f* ▶ ADJ sans fil

wireless technology N technologie *f* sans fil

wire netting N treillis *m* métallique, grillage *m*

wire service N (US) revue *f* de presse (*par téléscripteur*)

wire-tapping ['waɪə'tæpɪŋ] N écoute *f* téléphonique

wiring ['waɪərɪŋ] N (*Elec*) installation *f* électrique

wiry ['waɪərɪ] ADJ noueux(-euse), nerveux(-euse)

Wis. ABBR (US) = **Wisconsin**

wisdom ['wɪzdəm] N sagesse *f*; (*of action*) prudence *f*

wisdom tooth N dent *f* de sagesse

wise [waɪz] ADJ sage, prudent(e); (*remark*) judicieux(-euse); **I'm none the wiser** je ne suis pas plus avancé(e) pour autant
▶ **wise up** VI (*inf*) **to ~ up to** commencer à se rendre compte de

...wise [waɪz] SUFFIX: **timewise** en ce qui concerne le temps, question temps

wisecrack ['waɪzkræk] N sarcasme *m*

wish [wɪʃ] N (*desire*) désir *m*; (*specific desire*) souhait *m*, vœu *m* ▶ VT souhaiter, désirer, vouloir; **best wishes** (*on birthday etc*) meilleurs vœux; **with best wishes** (*in letter*) bien amicalement; **give her my best wishes** faites-lui mes amitiés; **to ~ sb goodbye** dire au revoir à qn; **he wished me well** il m'a souhaité bonne chance; **to ~ to do/sb to do** désirer *or* vouloir faire/que qn fasse; **to ~ for** souhaiter; **to ~ sth on sb** souhaiter qch à qn

wishbone ['wɪʃbəun] N fourchette *f*

wishful ['wɪʃful] ADJ: **it's ~ thinking** c'est prendre ses désirs pour des réalités

wishy-washy ['wɪʃɪ'wɔʃɪ] ADJ (*inf: person*) qui manque de caractère falot(e); (: *ideas, thinking*) faiblard(e)

wisp [wɪsp] N fine mèche (*de cheveux*); (*of smoke*) mince volute *f*; **a ~ of straw** un fétu de paille

wistful ['wɪstful] ADJ mélancolique

wit [wɪt] N (*also*: **wits**: *intelligence*) intelligence *f*, esprit *m*; (*presence of mind*) présence *f* d'esprit; (*wittiness*) esprit; (*person*) homme/femme d'esprit; **to be at one's wits' end** (*fig*) ne plus savoir que faire; **to have one's wits about one** avoir toute sa présence d'esprit, ne pas perdre la tête; **to ~** adv à savoir

witch [wɪtʃ] N sorcière *f*

witchcraft ['wɪtʃkrɑːft] N sorcellerie *f*

witch doctor N sorcier *m*

witch-hunt ['wɪtʃhʌnt] N chasse *f* aux sorcières

(KEYWORD)

with [wɪð, wɪθ] PREP **1** (*in the company of*) avec; (*at the home of*) chez; **we stayed with friends** nous avons logé chez des amis; **I'll be with you in a minute** je suis à vous dans un instant
2 (*descriptive*): **a room with a view** une chambre avec vue; **the man with the grey hair/blue eyes** l'homme au chapeau gris/aux yeux bleus
3 (*indicating manner, means, cause*): **with tears in her eyes** les larmes aux yeux; **to walk with a stick** marcher avec une canne; **red with anger** rouge de colère; **to shake with fear** trembler de peur; **to fill sth with water** remplir qch d'eau
4 (*in phrases*): **I'm with you** (*I understand*) je vous suis; **to be with it** (*inf: up-to-date*) être dans le vent

withdraw [wɪθ'drɔː] VT (*irreg: like draw*) retirer
▶ VI se retirer; (*go back on promise*) se rétracter; **to ~ into o.s.** se replier sur soi-même

withdrawal [wɪθ'drɔːəl] N retrait *m*; (*Med*) état *m* de manque

withdrawal symptoms NPL: **to have ~** être en état de manque, présenter les symptômes *mpl* de sevrage

withdrawn [wɪθ'drɔːn] PP *of* **withdraw** ▶ ADJ (*person*) renfermé(e)

withdrew [wɪθ'druː] PT *of* **withdraw**

wither ['wɪðəʳ] VI se faner

withered ['wɪðəd] ADJ fané(e), flétri(e); (*limb*) atrophié(e)

withhold [wɪθ'həuld] VT (*irreg: like hold*) (*money*) retenir; (*decision*) remettre; **to ~ (from)** (*permission*) refuser (à); (*information*) cacher (à)

within [wɪð'ɪn] PREP à l'intérieur de ▶ ADV à l'intérieur; **~ his reach** à sa portée; **~ sight of** en vue de; **~ a mile of** à moins d'un mille de; **~ the week** avant la fin de la semaine; **~ an hour from now** d'ici une heure; **to be ~ the law** être légal(e) *or* dans les limites de la légalité

without [wɪð'aut] PREP sans; **~ a coat** sans manteau; **~ speaking** sans parler; **~ anybody knowing** sans que personne ne sache; **to go** *or* **do ~ sth** se passer de qch

withstand [wɪθ'stænd] VT (*irreg: like stand*) résister à

witness ['wɪtnɪs] N (*person*) témoin *m*; (*evidence*) témoignage *m* ▶ VT (*event*) être témoin de; (*document*) attester l'authenticité de; **to bear ~ to sth** témoigner de qch; **~ for the prosecution/defence** témoin à charge/à décharge; **to ~ to sth/having seen sth** témoigner de qch/d'avoir vu qch

witness box, (US) **witness stand** N barre *f* des témoins

witticism ['wɪtɪsɪzəm] N mot *m* d'esprit

witty ['wɪtɪ] ADJ spirituel(le), plein(e) d'esprit

W

wives [waɪvz] NPL *of* **wife**

wizard ['wɪzəd] N magicien *m*

wizened ['wɪznd] ADJ ratatiné(e)

wk ABBR = **week**

Wm. ABBR = **William**

WMD. ABBR = **weapons of mass destruction**

WO N ABBR = **warrant officer**

wobble ['wɔbl] VI trembler; (*chair*) branler

wobbly ['wɔblɪ] ADJ tremblant(e), branlant(e)

woe [wəu] N malheur *m*

woeful ['wəuful] ADJ (*sad*) malheureux(-euse); (*terrible*) affligeant(e)

wok [wɔk] N wok *m*

woke [wəuk] PT *of* **wake**

woken ['wəukn] PP *of* **wake**

wolf [wulf] (*pl* **wolves** [wulvz]) N loup *m*

woman ['wumən] (*pl* **women** ['wɪmɪn]) N femme *f* ▶ CPD: **~ doctor** femme *f* médecin; **~ friend** amie *f*; **~ teacher** professeur *m* femme; **young ~** jeune femme; **women's page** (*Press*) page *f* des lectrices

womanize ['wumənaɪz] VI jouer les séducteurs

womanly ['wumənlɪ] ADJ féminin(e)

womb [wu:m] N (*Anat*) utérus *m*

women ['wɪmɪn] NPL *of* **woman**

won [wʌn] PT, PP *of* **win**

wonder ['wʌndə'] N merveille *f*, miracle *m*; (*feeling*) émerveillement *m* ▶ VI: **to ~ whether/why** se demander si/pourquoi; **to ~ at** (*surprise*) s'étonner de; (*admiration*) s'émerveiller de; **to ~ about** songer à; **it's no ~ that** il n'est pas étonnant que + *sub*

wonderful ['wʌndəful] ADJ merveilleux(-euse)

wonderfully ['wʌndəfəlɪ] ADV (+ *adj*) merveilleusement; (+ *vb*) à merveille

wonky ['wɔŋkɪ] ADJ (BRIT *inf*) qui ne va *or* ne marche pas très bien

wont [wəunt] N: **as is his/her ~** comme de coutume

won't [wəunt] = **will not**

woo [wu:] VT (*woman*) faire la cour à

wood [wud] N (*timber, forest*) bois *m* ▶ CPD de bois, en bois

wood carving N sculpture *f* en *or* sur bois

wooded ['wudɪd] ADJ boisé(e)

wooden ['wudn] ADJ en bois; (*fig: actor*) raide; (: *performance*) qui manque de naturel

woodland ['wudlənd] N forêt *f*, région boisée

woodpecker ['wudpɛkə'] N pic *m* (*oiseau*)

wood pigeon N ramier *m*

woodwind ['wudwɪnd] N (*Mus*) bois *m*; **the ~** les bois *mpl*

woodwork ['wudwə:k] N menuiserie *f*

woodworm ['wudwə:m] N ver *m* du bois; **the table has got ~** la table est piquée des vers

woof [wuf] N (*of dog*) aboiement *m* ▶ VI aboyer; **~, ~!** oua, oua!

wool [wul] N laine *f*; **to pull the ~ over sb's eyes** (*fig*) en faire accroire à qn

woollen, (US) **woolen** ['wulən] ADJ de *or* en laine; (*industry*) lainier(-ière) ▶ N: **woollens** lainages *mpl*

woolly, (US) **wooly** ['wulɪ] ADJ laineux(-euse); (*fig: ideas*) confus(e)

woozy ['wu:zɪ] ADJ (*inf*) dans les vapes

word [wə:d] N mot *m*; (*spoken*) mot, parole *f*; (*promise*) parole; (*news*) nouvelles *fpl* ▶ VT rédiger, formuler; **~ for ~** (*repeat*) mot pour mot; (*translate*) mot à mot; **what's the ~ for "pen" in French?** comment dit-on "pen" en français?; **to put sth into words** exprimer qch; **in other words** en d'autres termes; **to have a ~ with sb** toucher un mot à qn; **to have words with sb** (*quarrel with*) avoir des mots avec qn; **to break/keep one's ~** manquer à sa parole/tenir (sa) parole; **I'll take your ~ for it** je vous crois sur parole; **to send ~ of** prévenir de; **to leave ~ (with sb/for sb) that ...** laisser un mot (à qn/pour qn) disant que ...

wording ['wə:dɪŋ] N termes *mpl*, langage *m*; (*of document*) libellé *m*

word of mouth N: **by** *or* **through ~** de bouche à oreille

word-perfect ['wə:d'pə:fɪkt] ADJ: **he was ~ (in his speech** *etc*), **his speech** *etc* **was ~** il savait son discours *etc* sur le bout du doigt

word processing N traitement *m* de texte

word processor [-prəusɛsə'] N machine *f* de traitement de texte

wordwrap ['wə:dræp] N (*Comput*) retour *m* (automatique) à la ligne

wordy ['wə:dɪ] ADJ verbeux(-euse)

wore [wɔ:'] PT *of* **wear**

work [wə:k] N travail *m*; (*Art, Literature*) œuvre *f* ▶ VI travailler; (*mechanism*) marcher, fonctionner; (*plan etc*) marcher; (*medicine*) agir ▶ VT (*clay, wood etc*) travailler; (*mine etc*) exploiter; (*machine*) faire marcher *or* fonctioner; (*miracles etc*) faire; **works** *n* (BRIT: *factory*) usine *f*; NPL (*of clock, machine*) mécanisme *m*; **how does this ~?** comment est-ce que ça marche?; **the TV isn't working** la télévision est en panne *or* ne marche pas; **to go to ~** aller travailler; **to set to ~**, **to start ~** se mettre à l'œuvre; **to be at ~ (on sth)** travailler (sur qch); **to be out of ~** être au chômage *or* sans emploi; **to ~ hard** travailler dur; **to ~ loose** se défaire, se desserrer; **road works** travaux *mpl* (d'entretien des routes)

▶ **work on** VT FUS travailler à; (*principle*) se baser sur

▶ **work out** VI (*plans etc*) marcher; (*Sport*) s'entraîner ▶ VT (*problem*) résoudre; (*plan*) élaborer; **it works out at £100** ça fait 100 livres

▶ **work up** VT: **to get worked up** se mettre dans tous ses états

workable ['wə:kəbl] ADJ (*solution*) réalisable

workaholic [wə:kə'hɔlɪk] N bourreau *m* de travail

workbench ['wə:kbɛntʃ] N établi *m*

worked up ['wə:kt-] ADJ: **to get ~** se mettre dans tous ses états

worker ['wə:kə'] N travailleur(-euse), ouvrier(-ière); **office ~** employé(e) de bureau

work experience N stage *m*

workforce ['wə:kfɔ:s] N main-d'œuvre *f*

work-in ['wə:kɪn] N (BRIT) occupation *f* d'usine *etc* (*sans arrêt de la production*)

working ['wə:kɪŋ] ADJ (*day, tools etc, conditions*) de

travail; (wife) qui travaille; (partner, population) actif(-ive); **in ~ order** en état de marche; **a ~ knowledge of English** une connaissance toute pratique de l'anglais

working capital N (Comm) fonds mpl de roulement

working class N classe ouvrière ▸ ADJ: **working-class** ouvrier(-ière), de la classe ouvrière

working man N (irreg) travailleur m

working party N (BRIT) groupe m de travail

working week N semaine f de travail

work-in-progress ['wəːkɪnˈprəugres] N (Comm) en-cours m inv; (: value) valeur f des en-cours

workload ['wəːkləud] N charge f de travail

workman ['wəːkmən] N (irreg) ouvrier m

workmanship ['wəːkmənʃɪp] N métier m, habileté f; facture f

workmate ['wəːkmeɪt] N collègue mf

work of art N œuvre f d'art

workout ['wəːkaut] N (Sport) séance f d'entraînement

work permit N permis m de travail

workplace ['wəːkpleɪs] N lieu m de travail

works council N comité m d'entreprise

worksheet ['wəːkʃiːt] N (Scol) feuille f d'exercices; (Comput) feuille f de programmation

workshop ['wəːkʃɔp] N atelier m

work station N poste m de travail

work study N étude f du travail

work surface N plan m de travail

worktop ['wəːktɔp] N plan m de travail

work-to-rule ['wəːktəˈruːl] N (BRIT) grève f du zèle

world [wəːld] N monde m ▸ CPD (champion) du monde; (power, war) mondial(e); **all over the ~** dans le monde entier, partout dans le monde; **to think the ~ of sb** (fig) ne jurer que par qn; **what in the ~ is he doing?** qu'est-ce qu'il peut bien être en train de faire?; **to do sb a ~ of good** faire le plus grand bien à qn; **W~ War One/ Two, the First/Second W~ War** la Première/ Deuxième Guerre mondiale; **out of this ~** adj extraordinaire

World Cup N: **the ~** (Football) la Coupe du monde

world-famous [wəːldˈfeɪməs] ADJ de renommée mondiale

worldly ['wəːldlɪ] ADJ de ce monde

world music N world music f

World Series N: **the ~** (US: Baseball) le championnat national de baseball

world-wide ['wəːld'waɪd] ADJ universel(le) ▸ ADV dans le monde entier

World-Wide Web N: **the ~** le Web

worm [wəːm] N (also: **earthworm**) ver m

worn [wɔːn] PP of **wear** ▸ ADJ usé(e)

worn-out ['wɔːnaut] ADJ (object) complètement usé(e); (person) épuisé(e)

worried ['wʌrɪd] ADJ inquiet(-ète); **to be ~ about sth** être inquiet au sujet de qch

worrier ['wʌrɪəʳ] N inquiet(-ète)

worrisome ['wʌrɪsəm] ADJ inquiétant(e)

worry ['wʌrɪ] N souci m ▸ VT inquiéter ▸ VI

s'inquiéter, se faire du souci; **to ~ about** or **over sth/sb** se faire du souci pour or à propos de qch/ qn

worrying ['wʌrɪɪŋ] ADJ inquiétant(e)

worse [wəːs] ADJ pire, plus mauvais(e) ▸ ADV plus mal ▸ N pire m; **to get ~** (condition, situation) empirer, se dégrader; **a change for the ~** une détérioration; **he is none the ~ for it** il ne s'en porte pas plus mal; **so much the ~ for you!** tant pis pour vous!

worsen ['wəːsn] VT, VI empirer

worse off ADJ moins à l'aise financièrement; (fig): **you'll be ~ this way** ça ira moins bien de cette façon; **he is now ~ than before** il se retrouve dans une situation pire qu'auparavant

worship ['wəːʃɪp] N culte m ▸ VT (God) rendre un culte à; (person) adorer; **Your W~** (BRIT: to mayor) Monsieur le Maire (: to judge) Monsieur le Juge

worshipper ['wəːʃɪpəʳ] N adorateur(-trice); (in church) fidèle mf

worst [wəːst] ADJ le (la) pire, le plus mauvais(e) ▸ ADV le plus mal ▸ N pire m; **at ~** au pis aller; **if the ~ comes to the ~** si le pire doit arriver

worst-case ['wəːstkeɪs] ADJ: **the ~ scenario** le pire scénario or cas de figure

worsted ['wustɪd] N: (wool) **~** laine peignée

worth [wəːθ] N valeur f ▸ ADJ: **to be ~** valoir; **how much is it ~?** ça vaut combien?; **it's ~ it** cela en vaut la peine, ça vaut la peine; **it is ~ one's while (to do)** ça vaut le coup (inf) (de faire); **50 pence ~ of apples** (pour) 50 pence de pommes

worthless ['wəːθlɪs] ADJ qui ne vaut rien

worthwhile ['wəːθ'waɪl] ADJ (activity) qui en vaut la peine; (cause) louable; **a ~ book** un livre qui vaut la peine d'être lu

worthy ['wəːðɪ] ADJ (person) digne; (motive) louable; **~ of** digne de

(KEYWORD)

would [wud] AUX VB **1** (conditional tense): **if you asked him he would do it** si vous le lui demandiez, il le ferait; **if you had asked him he would have done it** si vous le lui aviez demandé, il l'aurait fait

2 (in offers, invitations, requests): **would you like a biscuit?** voulez-vous un biscuit?; **would you close the door please?** voulez-vous fermer la porte, s'il vous plaît?

3 (in indirect speech): **I said I would do it** j'ai dit que je le ferais

4 (emphatic): **it WOULD have to snow today!** naturellement il neige aujourd'hui!, il fallait qu'il neige aujourd'hui!

5 (insistence): **she wouldn't do it** elle n'a pas voulu or elle a refusé de le faire

6 (conjecture): **it would have been midnight** il devait être minuit; **it would seem so** on dirait bien

7 (indicating habit): **he would go there on Mondays** il y allait le lundi

would-be ['wudbiː] ADJ (pej) soi-disant

W

wouldn't ['wudnt] = **would not**
wound¹ [wu:nd] N blessure f ▶ VT blesser;
  wounded in the leg blessé à la jambe
wound² [waund] PT, PP of **wind²**
wove [wəuv] PT of **weave**
woven ['wəuvn] PP of **weave**
WP N ABBR = **word processing**; **word processor**
  ▶ ABBR (BRIT inf) = **weather permitting**
WPC N ABBR (BRIT) = **woman police constable**
wpm ABBR (= words per minute) mots/minute
WRAC N ABBR (BRIT: = Women's Royal Army Corps)
  auxiliaires féminines de l'armée de terre
WRAF N ABBR (BRIT: = Women's Royal Air Force)
  auxiliaires féminines de l'armée de l'air
wrangle ['ræŋgl] N dispute f ▶ VI se disputer
wrap [ræp] N (stole) écharpe f; (cape) pèlerine f
  ▶ VT (also: **wrap up**) envelopper; (: parcel)
  emballer; (wind) enrouler; **under wraps** (fig:
  plan, scheme) secret(-ète)
wrapper ['ræpə^r] N (on chocolate etc) papier m;
  (BRIT: of book) couverture f
wrapping ['ræpɪŋ] N (of sweet, chocolate) papier m;
  (of parcel) emballage m
wrapping paper N papier m d'emballage; (for
  gift) papier cadeau
wrath [rɔθ] N courroux m
wreak [ri:k] VT (destruction) entraîner; **to ~
  havoc** faire des ravages; **to ~ vengeance on**
  se venger de, exercer sa vengeance sur
wreath [ri:θ] N couronne f
wreck [rɛk] N (sea disaster) naufrage m; (ship)
  épave f; (vehicle) véhicule accidenté; (pej: person)
  loque (humaine) ▶ VT démolir; (ship) provoquer
  le naufrage de; (fig) briser, ruiner
wreckage ['rɛkɪdʒ] N débris mpl; (of building)
  décombres mpl; (of ship) naufrage m
wrecker ['rɛkə^r] N (US: breakdown van)
  dépanneuse f
WREN [rɛn] N ABBR (BRIT) membre du WRNS
wren [rɛn] N (Zool) troglodyte m
wrench [rɛntʃ] N (Tech) clé f (à écrous);
  (tug) violent mouvement de torsion; (fig)
  déchirement m ▶ VT tirer violemment sur,
  tordre; **to ~ sth from** arracher qch
  (violemment) à or de
wrest [rɛst] VT: **to ~ sth from sb** arracher or
  ravir qch à qn
wrestle ['rɛsl] VI: **to ~ (with sb)** lutter (avec qn);
  to ~ with (fig) se débattre avec, lutter contre
wrestler ['rɛslə^r] N lutteur(-euse)
wrestling ['rɛslɪŋ] N lutte f; (BRIT: also: **all-in
  wrestling**) catch m
wrestling match N rencontre f de lutte (or de
  catch)
wretch [rɛtʃ] N pauvre malheureux(-euse);
  little ~! (often humorous) petit(e) misérable!
wretched ['rɛtʃɪd] ADJ misérable; (inf)
  maudit(e)
wriggle ['rɪgl] N tortillement m ▶ VI (also:
  wriggle about) se tortiller
wring [rɪŋ] (pt, pp **wrung** [rʌŋ]) VT tordre; (wet
  clothes) essorer; (fig): **to ~ sth out of** arracher
  qch à
wringer ['rɪŋə^r] N essoreuse f

wringing ['rɪŋɪŋ] ADJ (also: **wringing wet**) tout
  mouillé(e), trempé(e)
wrinkle ['rɪŋkl] N (on skin) ride f; (on paper etc) pli
  m ▶ VT rider, plisser ▶ VI se plisser
wrinkled ['rɪŋkld], **wrinkly** ['rɪŋklɪ] ADJ (fabric,
  paper) froissé(e), plissé(e); (surface) plissé; (skin)
  ridé(e), plissé
wrist [rɪst] N poignet m
wristband ['rɪstbænd] N (BRIT: of shirt) poignet
  m; (: of watch) bracelet m
wrist watch N montre-bracelet f
writ [rɪt] N acte m judiciaire; **to issue a ~
  against sb, to serve a ~ on sb** assigner qn en
  justice
writable ['raɪtəbl] ADJ (CD, DVD) inscriptible
write [raɪt] (pt **wrote** [rəut], pp **written** ['rɪtn])
  VT, VI écrire; (prescription) rédiger; **to ~ sb a
  letter** écrire une lettre à qn
  ▶ **write away** VI: **to ~ away for** (information)
  (écrire pour) demander; (goods) (écrire pour)
  commander
  ▶ **write down** VT noter; (put in writing) mettre
  par écrit
  ▶ **write off** VT (debt) passer aux profits et pertes;
  (project) mettre une croix sur; (depreciate)
  amortir; (smash up: car etc) démolir
  complètement
  ▶ **write out** VT écrire; (copy) recopier
  ▶ **write up** VT rédiger
write-off ['raɪtɔf] N perte totale; **the car is a ~**
  la voiture est bonne pour la casse
write-protect ['raɪtprə'tɛkt] VT (Comput)
  protéger contre l'écriture
writer ['raɪtə^r] N auteur m, écrivain m
write-up ['raɪtʌp] N (review) critique f
writhe [raɪð] VI se tordre
writing ['raɪtɪŋ] N écriture f; (of author) œuvres
  fpl; **in ~** par écrit; **in my own ~** écrit(e) de ma
  main
writing case N nécessaire m de correspondance
writing desk N secrétaire m
writing paper N papier m à lettres
written ['rɪtn] PP of **write**
WRNS N ABBR (BRIT: = Women's Royal Naval Service)
  auxiliaires féminines de la marine
wrong [rɔŋ] ADJ (incorrect) faux (fausse);
  (incorrectly chosen: number, road etc) mauvais(e);
  (not suitable) qui ne convient pas; (wicked) mal;
  (unfair) injuste ▶ ADV mal ▶ N tort m ▶ VT faire
  du tort à, léser; **to be ~** (answer) être faux
  (fausse); (in doing/saying) avoir tort (de dire/
  faire); **you are ~ to do it** tu as tort de le faire;
  it's ~ to steal, stealing is ~ c'est mal de voler;
  you are ~ about that, you've got it ~ tu te
  trompes; **to be in the ~** avoir tort; **what's ~?**
  qu'est-ce qui ne va pas?; **there's nothing ~**
  tout va bien; **what's ~ with the car?** qu'est-ce
  qu'elle a, la voiture?; **to go ~** (person) se tromper;
  (plan) mal tourner; (machine) se détraquer; **I
  took a ~ turning** je me suis trompé de route
wrongdoer ['rɔŋduːə^r] N malfaiteur m
wrong-foot [rɔŋ'fut] VT (Sport) prendre à
  contre-pied; (fig) prendre au dépourvu
wrongful ['rɔŋful] ADJ injustifié(e); **~ dismissal**

(*Industry*) licenciement abusif

wrongly ['rɒŋlɪ] ADV à tort; (*answer, do, count*) mal, incorrectement; (*treat*) injustement

wrong number N (*Tel*): **you have the ~** vous vous êtes trompé de numéro

wrong side N (*of cloth*) envers *m*

wrote [rəut] PT *of* **write**

wrought [rɔːt] ADJ: **~ iron** fer forgé

wrung [rʌŋ] PT, PP *of* **wring**

WRVS N ABBR (*BRIT*: = *Women's Royal Voluntary Service*) auxiliaires féminines bénévoles au service de la collectivité

wry [raɪ] ADJ désabusé(e)

wt. ABBR (= *weight*) pds.

WV, W.Va. ABBR (*US*) = **West Virginia**

WWW N ABBR = **World-Wide Web**

WY, Wyo. ABBR (*US*) = **Wyoming**

WYSIWYG ['wɪzɪwɪg] ABBR (*Comput*: = *what you see is what you get*) ce que vous voyez est ce que vous aurez

W

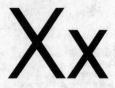
Xx

X, x [ɛks] N (*letter*) X, x *m*; (*Brit Cine: formerly*) film interdit aux moins de 18 ans; **X for Xmas** X comme Xavier
Xerox® ['zɪərɔks] N (*also:* **Xerox machine**) photocopieuse *f*; (*photocopy*) photocopie *f* ▸ vT photocopier
XL ABBR (= *extra large*) XL

Xmas ['ɛksməs] N ABBR = **Christmas**
X-rated ['ɛks'reɪtɪd] ADJ (*US: film*) interdit(e) aux moins de 18 ans
X-ray ['ɛksreɪ] N (*ray*) rayon *m* X; (*photograph*) radio(graphie) *f* ▸ vT radiographier
xylophone ['zaɪləfəun] N xylophone *m*

Y y

Y, y [waɪ] N (*letter*) Y, y m; **Y for Yellow**, (US) **Y for Yoke** Y comme Yvonne

yacht [jɒt] N voilier m; (*motor, luxury yacht*) yacht m

yachting ['jɒtɪŋ] N yachting m, navigation f de plaisance

yachtsman ['jɒtsmən] N (*irreg*) yacht(s)man m

yam [jæm] N igname f

Yank [jæŋk], **Yankee** ['jæŋkɪ] N (*pej*) Amerloque mf, Ricain(e)

yank [jæŋk] VT tirer d'un coup sec

yap [jæp] VI (*dog*) japper

yard [jɑːd] N (*of house etc*) cour f; (US: *garden*) jardin m; (*measure*) yard m (= 914 mm; 3 feet); **builder's ~** chantier m

yard sale N (US) brocante f (dans son propre jardin)

yardstick ['jɑːdstɪk] N (*fig*) mesure f, critère m

yarn [jɑːn] N fil m; (*tale*) longue histoire

yawn [jɔːn] N bâillement m ▶ VI bâiller

yawning ['jɔːnɪŋ] ADJ (*gap*) béant(e)

yd. ABBR = **yard**; **yards**

yeah [jɛə] ADV (*inf*) ouais

year [jɪəʳ] N an m, année f; (*Scol etc*) année f; **every ~** tous les ans, chaque année; **this ~** cette année; **a** or **per ~** par an; **~ in, ~ out** année après année; **to be 8 years old** avoir 8 ans; **an eight-~-old child** un enfant de huit ans

yearbook ['jɪəbuk] N annuaire m

yearly ['jɪəlɪ] ADJ annuel(le) ▶ ADV annuellement; **twice ~** deux fois par an

yearn [jəːn] VI: **to ~ for sth/to do** aspirer à qch/à faire

yearning ['jəːnɪŋ] N désir ardent, envie f

yeast [jiːst] N levure f

yell [jɛl] N hurlement m, cri m ▶ VI hurler

yellow ['jɛləu] ADJ jaune ▶ N jaune (m)

yellow fever N fièvre f jaune

yellowish ['jɛləuɪʃ] ADJ qui tire sur le jaune, jaunâtre (*pej*)

Yellow Pages® NPL (*Tel*) pages fpl jaunes

Yellow Sea N: **the ~** la mer Jaune

yelp [jɛlp] N jappement m; glapissement m ▶ VI japper; glapir

Yemen ['jɛmən] N Yémen m

yen [jɛn] N (*currency*) yen m; (*craving*): **~ for/to do** grande envie de/de faire

yeoman ['jəumən] N (*irreg*): **Y~ of the Guard** hallebardier m de la garde royale

yes [jɛs] ADV oui; (*answering negative question*) si ▶ N oui m; **to say ~ (to)** dire oui (à)

yesterday ['jɛstədɪ] ADV, N hier (m); **~ morning/evening** hier matin/soir; **the day before ~** avant-hier; **all day ~** toute la journée d'hier

yet [jɛt] ADV encore; (*in questions*) déjà ▶ CONJ pourtant, néanmoins; **it is not finished ~** ce n'est pas encore fini or toujours pas fini; **must you go just ~?** dois-tu déjà partir?; **have you eaten ~?** vous avez déjà mangé?; **the best ~** le meilleur jusqu'ici or jusque-là; **as ~** jusqu'ici, encore; **a few days ~** encore quelques jours; **~ again** une fois de plus

yew [juː] N if m

Y-fronts® ['waɪfrʌnts] NPL (BRIT) slip m kangourou

YHA N ABBR (BRIT) = **Youth Hostels Association**

Yiddish ['jɪdɪʃ] N yiddish m

yield [jiːld] N production f, rendement m; (*Finance*) rapport m ▶ VT produire, rendre, rapporter; (*surrender*) céder ▶ VI céder; (US *Aut*) céder la priorité; **a ~ of 5%** un rendement de 5%

YMCA N ABBR (= *Young Men's Christian Association*) ≈ union chrétienne de jeunes gens (UCJG)

yob ['jɒb], **yobbo** ['jɒbəu] N (BRIT *inf*) loubar(d) m

yodel ['jəudl] VI faire des tyroliennes, jodler

yoga ['jəugə] N yoga m

yoghurt, yogurt ['jɒgət] N yaourt m

yoke [jəuk] N joug m ▶ VT (*also*: **yoke together**: *oxen*) accoupler

yolk [jəuk] N jaune m (d'œuf)

yonder ['jɒndəʳ] ADV là(-bas)

yonks [jɒŋks] (*inf*): **for ~** très longtemps; **we've been here for ~** ça fait une éternité qu'on est ici; **we were there for ~** on est resté là pendant des lustres

Yorks [jɔːks] ABBR (BRIT) = **Yorkshire**

KEYWORD

you [juː] PRON **1** (*subject*) tu; (: *polite form*) vous; (: *plural*) vous; **you are very kind** vous êtes très gentil; **you French enjoy your food** vous autres Français, vous aimez bien manger; **you and I will go** toi et moi or vous et moi, nous irons; **there you are!** vous voilà!
2 (*object*: *direct, indirect*) te, t' + *vowel*; vous; **I know**

y

you je te *or* vous connais; **I gave it to you** je te l'ai donné, je vous l'ai donné
3 (*stressed*) toi; vous; **I told you to do it** c'est à toi *or* vous que j'ai dit de le faire
4 (*after prep, in comparisons*) toi; vous; **it's for you** c'est pour toi *or* vous; **she's younger than you** elle est plus jeune que toi *or* vous
5 (*impersonal: one*) on; **fresh air does you good** l'air frais fait du bien; **you never know** on ne sait jamais; **you can't do that!** ça ne se fait pas!

you'd [ju:d] = **you had**; **you would**
you'll [ju:l] = **you will**; **you shall**
young [jʌŋ] ADJ jeune ▶ NPL (*of animal*) petits *mpl*; **the ~** (*people*) les jeunes, la jeunesse; **a ~ man** un jeune homme; **a ~ lady** (*unmarried*) une jeune fille, une demoiselle; (*married*) une jeune femme *or* dame; **my younger brother** mon frère cadet; **the younger generation** la jeune génération
younger [jʌŋgəʳ] ADJ (*brother etc*) cadet(te)
youngish ['jʌŋɪʃ] ADJ assez jeune
youngster ['jʌŋstəʳ] N jeune *mf*; (*child*) enfant *mf*
your [jɔːʳ] ADJ ton (ta), tes *pl*; (*polite form, pl*) votre, vos *pl*; *see also* **my**
you're [juəʳ] = **you are**
yours [jɔːz] PRON le (la) tien(ne), les tiens (tiennes); (*polite form, pl*) le (la) vôtre, les vôtres; **is it ~?** c'est à toi (*or* à vous)?; **a friend of ~** un(e) de tes (*or* de vos) amis; *see also* **faithfully**; **mine**[1]; **sincerely**
yourself [jɔː'sɛlf] PRON (*reflexive*) te; (: *polite form*) vous; (*after prep*) toi; vous; (*emphatic*) toi-même; vous-même; **you ~ told me** c'est vous qui me l'avez dit, vous me l'avez dit vous-même; *see also* **oneself**
yourselves [jɔː'sɛlvz] PL PRON vous; (*emphatic*) vous-mêmes; *see also* **oneself**
youth [ju:θ] N jeunesse *f*; (*pl* **youths** [ju:ðz]: *young man*) jeune homme *m*; **in my ~** dans ma jeunesse, quand j'étais jeune
youth club N centre *m* de jeunes
youthful ['ju:θful] ADJ jeune; (*enthusiasm etc*) juvénile; (*misdemeanour*) de jeunesse
youthfulness ['ju:θfəlnɪs] N jeunesse *f*
youth hostel N auberge *f* de jeunesse
youth movement N mouvement *m* de jeunes
you've [ju:v] = **you have**
yowl [jaul] N hurlement *m*; miaulement *m* ▶ VI hurler; miauler
YT ABBR (CANADA) = **Yukon Territory**
Yugoslav ['ju:gəuslɑːv] ADJ (*Hist*) yougoslave ▶ N Yougoslave *mf*
Yugoslavia [ju:gəu'slɑːvɪə] N (*Hist*) Yougoslavie *f*
Yugoslavian [ju:gəu'slɑːvɪən] ADJ (*Hist*) yougoslave
yuppie ['jʌpɪ] N yuppie *mf*
YWCA N ABBR (= *Young Women's Christian Association*) union chrétienne féminine

Zz

Z, z [zɛd, (US) ziː] N (letter) Z, z m; **Z for Zebra** Z comme Zoé
Zaïre [zɑːˈiːəʳ] N Zaïre m
Zambia [ˈzæmbɪə] N Zambie f
Zambian [ˈzæmbɪən] ADJ zambien(ne) ▶ N Zambien(ne)
zany [ˈzeɪnɪ] ADJ farfelu(e), loufoque
zap [zæp] VT (Comput) effacer
zeal [ziːl] N (revolutionary etc) ferveur f; (keenness) ardeur f, zèle m
zealot [ˈzɛlət] N fanatique mf
zealous [ˈzɛləs] ADJ fervent(e); ardent(e), zélé(e)
zebra [ˈziːbrə] N zèbre m
zebra crossing N (Brit) passage clouté or pour piétons
zenith [ˈzɛnɪθ] N (Astronomy) zénith m; (fig) zénith, apogée m
zero [ˈzɪərəu] N zéro m ▶ VI: **to ~ in on** (target) se diriger droit sur; **5° below ~** 5 degrés au-dessous de zéro
zero hour N l'heure f H
zero option N (Pol): **the ~** l'option f zéro
zero-rated [ˈziːrəureɪtɪd] ADJ (Brit) exonéré(e) de TVA
zest [zɛst] N entrain m, élan m; (of lemon etc) zeste m
zigzag [ˈzɪgzæg] N zigzag m ▶ VI zigzaguer, faire des zigzags
Zimbabwe [zɪmˈbɑːbwɪ] N Zimbabwe m

Zimbabwean [zɪmˈbɑːbwɪən] ADJ zimbabwéen(ne) ▶ N Zimbabwéen(ne)
Zimmer® [ˈzɪməʳ] N (also: **Zimmer frame**) déambulateur m
zinc [zɪŋk] N zinc m
Zionism [ˈzaɪənɪzəm] N sionisme m
Zionist [ˈzaɪənɪst] ADJ sioniste ▶ N Sioniste mf
zip [zɪp] N (also: **zip fastener**) fermeture f éclair® or à glissière; (energy) entrain m ▶ VT (file) zipper; (also: **zip up**) fermer (avec une fermeture éclair®)
zip code N (US) code postal
zip file N (Comput) fichier m zip inv
zipper [ˈzɪpəʳ] N (US) = **zip**
zit [zɪt] (inf) N bouton m
zither [ˈzɪðəʳ] N cithare f
zodiac [ˈzəudɪæk] N zodiaque m
zombie [ˈzɒmbɪ] N (fig): **like a ~** avec l'air d'un zombie, comme un automate
zone [zəun] N zone f
zoo [zuː] N zoo m
zoological [zuəˈlɒdʒɪkl] ADJ zoologique
zoologist [zuˈɒlədʒɪst] N zoologiste mf
zoology [zuːˈɒlədʒɪ] N zoologie f
zoom [zuːm] VI: **to ~ past** passer en trombe; **to ~ in (on sb/sth)** (Phot, Cine) zoomer (sur qn/qch)
zoom lens N zoom m, objectif m à focale variable
zucchini [zuːˈkiːnɪ] N (US) courgette f
Zulu [ˈzuːluː] ADJ zoulou ▶ N Zoulou mf
Zürich [ˈzjuərɪk] N Zurich

Grammar
Grammaire

Using the grammar

The Grammar section deals systematically and comprehensively with all the information you will need in order to communicate accurately in French. The user-friendly layout explains the grammar point on a left-hand page, leaving the facing page free for illustrative examples. The numbers, → ❶ etc, direct you to the relevant example in every case.

The Grammar section also provides invaluable guidance on the danger of translating English structures by identical structures in French. Use of Numbers and Punctuation are important areas covered towards the end of the section. Finally, the index lists the main words and grammatical terms in both English and French.

Abbreviations

fem.	*feminine*
infin.	*infinitive*
masc.	*masculine*
perf.	*perfect*
plur.	*plural*
qch	quelque chose
qn	quelqu'un
sb	somebody
sing.	*singular*
sth	something

Irregular Verbs

Contents

Verbs

Simple Tenses: formation

In French the simple tenses are:

        Present → **①**
        Imperfect → **②**
        Future → **③**
        Conditional → **④**
        Past Historic → **⑤**
        Present Subjunctive → **⑥**
        Imperfect Subjunctive → **⑦**

They are formed by adding endings to a verb stem. The endings show the number and person of the subject of the verb → **⑧**

The stem and endings of regular verbs are totally predictable. The following sections show all the patterns for regular verbs. For irregular verbs see page 74 onwards.

Regular Verbs

There are three regular verb patterns (called conjugations), each identifiable by the ending of the infinitive:

        First conjugation verbs end in **-er** e.g. **donner** to give

        Second conjugation verbs end in **-ir** e.g. **finir** to finish

        Third conjugation verbs end in **-re** e.g. **vendre** to sell

These three conjugations are treated in order on the following pages.

1. je donne

   I give
   I am giving
   I do give

2. je donnais

   I gave
   I was giving
   I used to give

3. je donnerai

   I shall give
   I shall be giving

4. je donnerais

   I should/would give
   I should/would be giving

5. je donnai

   I gave

6. (que) je donne

   (that) I give/gave

7. (que) je donnasse

   (that) I gave

8. je donne
   nous donnons
   je donnerais
   nous donnerions

   I give
   we give
   I would give
   we would give

Verbs

Simple Tenses: First Conjugation

The stem is formed as follows:

TENSE	FORMATION	EXAMPLE
Present Imperfect Past Historic Present Subjunctive Imperfect Subjunctive	infinitive minus -er	**donn-**
Future Conditional	infinitive	**donner-**

To the appropriate stem add the following endings:

		① PRESENT	② IMPERFECT	③ PAST HISTORIC
	1ˢᵗ person	-e	-ais	-ai
sing.	2ⁿᵈ person	-es	-ais	-as
	3ʳᵈ person	-e	-ait	-a
	1ˢᵗ person	-ons	-ions	-âmes
plur.	2ⁿᵈ person	-ez	-iez	-âtes
	3ʳᵈ person	-ent	-aient	-èrent

		④ PRESENT SUBJUNCTIVE	⑤ IMPERFECT SUBJUNCTIVE
	1ˢᵗ person	-e	-asse
sing.	2ⁿᵈ person	-es	-asses
	3ʳᵈ person	-e	-ât
	1ˢᵗ person	-ions	-assions
plur.	2ⁿᵈ person	-iez	-assiez
	3ʳᵈ person	-ent	-assent

		⑥ FUTURE	⑦ CONDITIONAL
	1ˢᵗ person	-ai	-ais
sing.	2ⁿᵈ person	-as	-ais
	3ʳᵈ person	-a	-ait
	1ˢᵗ person	-ons	-ions
plur.	2ⁿᵈ person	-ez	-iez
	3ʳᵈ person	-ont	-aient

1 PRESENT
je donne
tu donnes
il donne
elle donne
nous donnons
vous donnez
ils donnent
elles donnent

2 IMPERFECT
je donnais
tu donnais
il donnait
elle donnait
nous donnions
vous donniez
ils donnaient
elles donnaient

3 PAST HISTORIC
je donnai
tu donnas
il donna
elle donna
nous donnâmes
vous donnâtes
ils donnèrent
elles donnèrent

4 PRESENT SUBJUNCTIVE
je donne
tu donnes
il donne
elle donne
nous donnions
vous donniez
ils donnent
elles donnent

5 IMPERFECT SUBJUNCTIVE
je donnasse
tu donnasses
il donnât
elle donnât
nous donnassions
vous donnassiez
ils donnassent
elles donnassent

6 FUTURE
je donnerai
tu donneras
il donnera
elle donnera
nous donnerons
vous donnerez
ils donneront
elles donneront

7 CONDITIONAL
je donnerais
tu donnerais
il donnerait
elle donnerait
nous donnerions
vous donneriez
ils donneraient
elles donneraient

Verbs

Simple Tenses: Second Conjugation

The stem is formed as follows:

TENSE	FORMATION	EXAMPLE
Present Imperfect Past Historic Present Subjunctive Imperfect Subjunctive	infinitive minus -ir	**fin-**
Future Conditional	infinitive	**finir-**

To the appropriate stem add the following endings:

		❶ PRESENT	**❷ IMPERFECT**	**❸ PAST HISTORIC**
	1st person	**-is**	**-issais**	**-is**
sing.	2nd person	**-is**	**-issais**	**-is**
	3rd person	**-it**	**-issait**	**-it**
	1st person	**-issons**	**-issions**	**-îmes**
plur.	2nd person	**-issez**	**-issiez**	**-îtes**
	3rd person	**-issent**	**-issaient**	**-irent**

		❹ PRESENT SUBJUNCTIVE	**❺ IMPERFECT SUBJUNCTIVE**
	1st person	**-isse**	**-isse**
sing.	2nd person	**-isses**	**-isses**
	3rd person	**-isse**	**-ît**
	1st person	**-issions**	**-issions**
plur.	2nd person	**-issiez**	**-issiez**
	3rd person	**-issent**	**-issent**

		❻ FUTURE	**❼ CONDITIONAL**
	1st person	**-ai**	**-ais**
sing.	2nd person	**-as**	**-ais**
	3rd person	**-a**	**-ait**
	1st person	**-ons**	**-ions**
plur.	2nd person	**-ez**	**-iez**
	3rd person	**-ont**	**-aient**

1 PRESENT

je finis
tu finis
il finit
elle finit
nous finissons
vous finissez
ils finissent
elles finissent

2 IMPERFECT

je finissais
tu finissais
il finissait
elle finissait
nous finissions
vous finissiez
ils finissaient
elles finissaient

3 PAST HISTORIC

je finis
tu finis
il finit
elle finit
nous finîmes
vous finîtes
ils finirent
elles finirent

4 PRESENT SUBJUNCTIVE

je finisse
tu finisses
il finisse
elle finisse
nous finissions
vous finissiez
ils finissent
elles finissent

5 IMPERFECT SUBJUNCTIVE

je finisse
tu finisses
il finît
elle finît
nous finissions
vous finissiez
ils finissent
elles finissent

6 FUTURE

je finirai
tu finiras
il finira
elle finira
nous finirons
vous finirez
ils finiront
elles finiront

7 CONDITIONAL

je finirais
tu finirais
il finirait
elle finirait
nous finirions
vous finiriez
ils finiraient
elles finiraient

Verbs

Simple Tenses: Third Conjugation

The stem is formed as follows:

TENSE	FORMATION	EXAMPLE
Present		
Imperfect		
Past Historic	infinitive minus -re	vend-
Present Subjunctive		
Imperfect Subjunctive		
Future	infinitive minus -e	vendr-
Conditional		

To the appropriate stem add the following endings:

		① PRESENT	② IMPERFECT	③ PAST HISTORIC
sing.	1st person	-s	-ais	-is
	2nd person	-s	-ais	-is
	3rd person	–	-ait	-it
plur.	1st person	-ons	-ions	-îmes
	2nd person	-ez	-iez	-îtes
	3rd person	-ent	-aient	-irent

		④ PRESENT SUBJUNCTIVE	⑤ IMPERFECT SUBJUNCTIVE
sing.	1st person	-e	-isse
	2nd person	-es	-isses
	3rd person	-e	-ît
plur.	1st person	-ions	-issions
	2nd person	-iez	-issiez
	3rd person	-ent	-issent

		⑥ FUTURE	⑦ CONDITIONAL
sing.	1st person	-ai	-ais
	2nd person	-as	-ais
	3rd person	-a	-ait
plur.	1st person	-ons	-ions
	2nd person	-ez	-iez
	3rd person	-ont	-aient

1 PRESENT

je vends
tu vends
il vend
elle vend
nous vendons
vous vendez
ils vendent
elles vendent

2 IMPERFECT

je vendais
tu vendais
il vendait
elle vendait
nous vendions
vous vendiez
ils vendaient
elles vendaient

3 PAST HISTORIC

je vendis
tu vendis
il vendit
elle vendit
nous vendîmes
vous vendîtes
ils vendirent
elles vendirent

4 PRESENT SUBJUNCTIVE

je vende
tu vendes
il vende
elle vende
nous vendions
vous vendiez
ils vendent
elles vendent

5 IMPERFECT SUBJUNCTIVE

je vendisse
tu vendisses
il vendît
elle vendît
nous vendissions
vous vendissiez
ils vendissent
elles vendissent

6 FUTURE

je vendrai
tu vendras
il vendra
elle vendra
nous vendrons
vous vendrez
ils vendront
elles vendront

7 CONDITIONAL

je vendrais
tu vendrais
il vendrait
elle vendrait
nous vendrions
vous vendriez
ils vendraient
elles vendraient

Verbs

First Conjugation Spelling Irregularities

Before certain endings, the stems of some '-er' verbs may change slightly.

Below, and on subsequent pages, the verb types are identified, and the changes described are illustrated by means of a representative verb.

Verbs ending: **-cer**
Change: **c** becomes **ç** before **a** or **o**
Tenses affected: Present, Imperfect, Past Historic, Imperfect
                   Subjunctive, Present Participle
Model: **lancer** to throw → ❶

Why the change occurs: A cedilla is added to the **c** to retain its soft [s]
                         pronunciation before the vowels **a** and **o**.

Verbs ending: **-ger**
Change: **g** becomes **ge** before **a** or **o**
Tenses affected: Present, Imperfect, Past Historic, Imperfect
                   Subjunctive, Present Participle
Model: **manger** to eat → ❷

Why the change occurs: An **e** is added after the **g** to retain its soft [ʒ]
                         pronunciation before the vowels **a** and **o**.

① INFINITIVE
lancer

PRESENT PARTICIPLE
lançant

PRESENT
je lance
tu lances
il/elle lance
nous **lançons**
vous lancez
ils/elles lancent

IMPERFECT
je **lançais**
tu **lançais**
il/elle **lançait**
nous lancions
vous lanciez
ils/elles **lançaient**

PAST HISTORIC
je **lançai**
tu **lanças**
il/elle **lança**
nous **lançâmes**
vous **lançâtes**
ils/elles lancèrent

IMPERFECT SUBJUNCTIVE
je **lançasse**
tu **lançasses**
il/elle **lançât**
nous **lançassions**
vous **lançassiez**
ils/elles **lançassent**

② INFINITIVE
manger

PRESENT PARTICIPLE
mangeant

PRESENT
je mange
tu manges
il/elle mange
nous **mangeons**
vous mangez
ils/elles mangent

IMPERFECT
je **mangeais**
tu **mangeais**
il/elle **mangeait**
nous mangions
vous mangiez
ils/elles **mangeaient**

PAST HISTORIC
je **mangeai**
tu mangeas
il/elle **mangea**
nous **mangeâmes**
vous **mangeâtes**
ils/elles mangèrent

IMPERFECT SUBJUNCTIVE
je **mangeasse**
tu **mangeasses**
il/elle **mangeât**
nous **mangeassions**
vous **mangeassiez**
ils/elles **mangeassent**

Verbs

First Conjugation Spelling Irregularities *continued*

Verbs ending	**-eler**
Change:	**-l** doubles before **-e, -es, -ent** and throughout the Future and Conditional tenses
Tenses affected:	Present, Present Subjunctive, Future, Conditional
Model:	**appeler** to call → ❶
EXCEPTIONS:	**geler** to freeze; **peler** to peel → like **mener** (page 18)

Verbs ending	**-eter**
Change:	**-t** doubles before **-e, -es, -ent** and throughout the Future and Conditional tenses
Tenses affected:	Present, Present Subjunctive, Future, Conditional
Model:	**jeter** to throw → ❷
EXCEPTIONS:	**acheter** to buy; **haleter** to pant → like **mener** (page 18)

Verbs ending	**-yer**
Change:	**y** changes to **i** before **-e, -es, -ent** and throughout the Future and Conditional tenses
Tenses affected:	Present, Present Subjunctive, Future, Conditional
Model:	**essuyer** to wipe → ❸

The change described is optional for verbs ending in **-ayer**
e.g. **payer** to pay; **essayer** to try.

① PRESENT (+ SUBJUNCTIVE)

j'appelle
tu appelles
il/elle appelle
nous appelons
(appelions)
vous appelez
(appeliez)
ils/elles appellent

FUTURE

j'appellerai
tu appelleras
il appellera *etc*

CONDITIONAL

j'appellerais
tu appellerais
il appellerait *etc*

② PRESENT (+ SUBJUNCTIVE)

je jette
tu jettes
il/elle jette
nous jetons
(jetions)
vous jetez
(jetiez)
ils/elles jettent

FUTURE

je jetterai
tu jetteras
il jettera *etc*

CONDITIONAL

je jetterais
tu jetterais
il jetterait *etc*

③ PRESENT (+ SUBJUNCTIVE)

j'essuie
tu essuies
il/elle essuie
nous essuyons
(essuyions)
vous essuyez
(essuyiez)
ils/elles essuient

FUTURE

j'essuierai
tu essuieras
il essuiera *etc*

CONDITIONAL

j'essuierais
tu essuierais
il essuierait *etc*

Verbs

First Conjugation Spelling Irregularities *continued*

Verbs ending	**mener, peser, lever** *etc*
Change:	**e** changes to **è**, before -e, -es, -ent and throughout the Future and Conditional tenses
Tenses affected:	Present, Present Subjunctive, Future, Conditional
Model:	**mener** to lead → ❶

Verbs like:	**céder, régler, espérer** *etc*
Change:	**é** changes to **è** before -e, -es, -ent
Tenses affected:	Present, Present Subjunctive
Model:	**céder** to yield → ❷

1 PRESENT (+ SUBJUNCTIVE)
je **mène**
tu **mènes**
il/elle **mène**
nous menons
    (menions)
vous menez
    (meniez)
ils/elles **mènent**

2 PRESENT (+ SUBJUNCTIVE)
je **cède**
tu **cèdes**
il/elle **cède**
nous cédons
    (cédions)
vous cédez
    (cédiez)
ils/elles **cèdent**

FUTURE
je **mènerai**
tu **mèneras**
il **mènera** *etc*

CONDITIONAL
je **mènerais**
tu **mènerais**
il **mènerait** *etc*

Verbs

The Imperative

The imperative is the form of the verb used to give commands or orders. It can be used politely, as in English 'Shut the door, please'.

The imperative is the same as the present tense **tu**, **nous** and **vous** forms without the subject pronouns:

> **donne*** give   **finis** finish   **vends** sell
>
> * The final 's' of the present tense of first conjugation verbs is dropped, except before **y** and **en** → **①**
>
> **donnons** let's give   **finissons** let's finish   **vendons** let's sell
>
> **donnez** give   **finissez** finish   **vendez** sell

The imperative of irregular verbs is given in the verb tables, page 74 onwards.

Position of object pronouns with the imperative:
- in *positive* commands: they follow the verb and are attached to it by hyphens → **②**
- in *negative* commands: they precede the verb and are not attached to it → **③**

For the order of object pronouns, see page 170.

For reflexive verbs – e.g. **se lever** to get up – the object pronoun is the reflexive pronoun → **④**

1 Compare:
Tu donnes de l'argent à Paul   You give (some) money to Paul
and:
Donne de l'argent à Paul   Give (some) money to Paul

2 Excusez-moi   Excuse me
Envoyons-les-leur   Let's send them to them
Crois-nous   Believe us
Expliquez-le-moi   Explain it to me
Attendons-la   Let's wait for her/it
Rends-la-lui   Give it back to him/her

3 Ne me dérange pas   Don't disturb me
Ne leur en parlons pas   Let's not speak to them about it
Ne les appelons pas   Let's not call them
N'y pense plus   Don't think about it any more
Ne leur répondez pas   Don't answer them
Ne la lui rends pas   Don't give it back to him/her

4 Lève-toi   Get up
Ne te lève pas   Don't get up
Dépêchons-nous   Let's hurry
Ne nous affolons pas   Let's not panic
Levez-vous   Get up
Ne vous levez pas   Don't get up

Verbs

Compound Tenses: formation

In French the compound tenses are:

      Perfect → ❶
      Pluperfect → ❷
      Future Perfect → ❸
      Conditional Perfect → ❹
      Past Anterior → ❺
      Perfect Subjunctive → ❻
      Pluperfect Subjunctive → ❼

They consist of the past participle of the verb together with an auxiliary verb. Most verbs take the auxiliary **avoir**, but some take **être** (see page 28).

Compound tenses are formed in exactly the same way for both regular and irregular verbs, the only difference being that irregular verbs may have an irregular past participle.

The Past Participle

For all compound tenses you need to know how to form the past participle of the verb. For regular verbs this is as follows:

      First conjugation: replace the **-er** of the infinitive by **-é** → ❽

      Second conjugation: replace the **-ir** of the infinitive by **-i** → ❾

      Third conjugation: replace the **-re** of the infinitive by **-u** → ❿

      See page 50 for agreement of past participles.

with **avoir**	with **être**
1 j'ai donné I gave, have given	je suis tombé I fell, have fallen
2 j'avais donné I had given	j'étais tombé I had fallen
3 j'aurai donné I shall have given	je serai tombé I shall have fallen
4 j'aurais donné I should/would have given	je serais tombé I should/would have fallen
5 j'eus donné I had given	je fus tombé I had fallen
6 (que) j'aie donné (that) I gave, have given	(que) je sois tombé (that) I fell, have fallen
7 (que) j'eusse donné (that) I had given	(que) je fusse tombé (that) I had fallen

8 **donner** to give → **donné** given

9 **finir** to finish → **fini** finished

10 **vendre** to sell → **vendu** sold

Verbs

Compound Tenses: formation *continued*

Verbs taking the auxiliary avoir

PERFECT TENSE
The present tense of **avoir** plus the past participle → ❶

PLUPERFECT TENSE
The imperfect tense of **avoir** plus the past participle → ❷

FUTURE PERFECT
The future tense of **avoir** plus the past participle → ❸

CONDITIONAL PERFECT
The conditional of **avoir** plus the past participle → ❹

PAST ANTERIOR
The past historic of **avoir** plus the past participle → ❺

PERFECT SUBJUNCTIVE
The present subjunctive of **avoir** plus the past participle → ❻

PLUPERFECT SUBJUNCTIVE
The imperfect subjunctive of **avoir** plus the past participle → ❼

For how to form the past participle of regular verbs see page 22. The past participle of irregular verbs is given for each verb in the verb tables, page 74 onwards.

The past participle must agree in number and in gender with any preceding direct object (see page 50).

1 PERFECT

j'ai donné	nous avons donné
tu as donné	vous avez donné
il/elle a donné	ils/elles ont donné

2 PLUPERFECT

j'avais donné	nous avions donné
tu avais donné	vous aviez donné
il/elle avait donné	ils/elles avaient donné

3 FUTURE PERFECT

j'aurai donné	nous aurons donné
tu auras donné	vous aurez donné
il/elle aura donné	ils/elles auront donné

4 CONDITIONAL PERFECT

j'aurais donné	nous aurions donné
tu aurais donné	vous auriez donné
il/elle aurait donné	ils/elles auraient donné

5 PAST ANTERIOR

j'eus donné	nous eûmes donné
tu eus donné	vous eûtes donné
il/elle eut donné	ils/elles eurent donné

6 PERFECT SUBJUNCTIVE

j'aie donné	nous ayons donné
tu aies donné	vous ayez donné
il/elle ait donné	ils/elles aient donné

7 PLUPERFECT SUBJUNCTIVE

j'eusse donné	nous eussions donné
tu eusses donné	vous eussiez donné
il/elle eût donné	ils/elles eussent donné

Verbs

Compound Tenses: formation *continued*

Verbs taking the auxiliary être

PERFECT TENSE
The present tense of **être** plus the past participle → ❶

PLUPERFECT TENSE
The imperfect tense of **être** plus the past participle → ❷

FUTURE PERFECT
The future tense of **être** plus the past participle → ❸

CONDITIONAL PERFECT
The conditional of **être** plus the past participle → ❹

PAST ANTERIOR
The past historic of **être** plus the past participle → ❺

PERFECT SUBJUNCTIVE
The present subjunctive of **être** plus the past participle → ❻

PLUPERFECT SUBJUNCTIVE
The imperfect subjunctive of **être** plus the past participle → ❼

For how to form the past participle of regular verbs see page 22. The past participle of irregular verbs is given for each verb in the verb tables, page 74 onwards.

For agreement of past participles, see page 50.

For a list of verbs and verb types that take the auxiliary **être**, see page 28.

① PERFECT

je suis tombé(e)   nous sommes tombé(e)s
tu es tombé(e)   vous êtes tombé(e)(s)
il est tombé   ils sont tombés
elle est tombée   elles sont tombées

② PLUPERFECT

j'étais tombé(e)   nous étions tombé(e)s
tu étais tombé(e)   vous étiez tombé(e)(s)
il était tombé   ils étaient tombés
elle était tombée   elles étaient tombées

③ FUTURE PERFECT

je serai tombé(e)   nous serons tombé(e)s
tu seras tombé(e)   vous serez tombé(e)(s)
il sera tombé   ils seront tombés
elle sera tombée   elles seront tombées

④ CONDITIONAL PERFECT

je serais tombé(e)   nous serions tombé(e)s
tu serais tombé(e)   vous seriez tombé(e)(s)
il serait tombé   ils seraient tombés
elle serait tombée   elles seraient tombées

⑤ PAST ANTERIOR

je fus tombé(e)   nous fûmes tombé(e)s
tu fus tombé(e)   vous fûtes tombé(e)(s)
il fut tombé   ils furent tombés
elle fut tombée   elles furent tombées

⑥ PERFECT SUBJUNCTIVE

je sois tombé(e)   nous soyons tombé(e)s
tu sois tombé(e)   vous soyez tombé(e)(s)
il soit tombé   ils soient tombés
elle soit tombée   elles soient tombées

⑦ PLUPERFECT SUBJUNCTIVE

je fusse tombé(e)   nous fussions tombé(e)s
tu fusses tombé(e)   vous fussiez tombé(e)(s)
il fût tombé   ils fussent tombés
elle fût tombée   elles fussent tombées

Verbs

Compound Tenses *continued*

The following verbs take the auxiliary être

Reflexive verbs (see page 30) → ❶

The following intransitive verbs (i.e. verbs which cannot take a direct object), largely expressing motion or a change of state:

aller to go → ❷	**passer** to pass
arriver to arrive; to happen	**rentrer** to go back/in
descendre to go/come down	**rester** to stay → ❺
devenir to become	**retourner** to go back
entrer to go/come in	**revenir** to come back
monter to go/come up	**sortir** to go/come out
mourir to die → ❸	**tomber** to fall
naître to be born	**venir** to come → ❻
partir to leave → ❹	

Of these, the following are conjugated with **avoir** when used transitively (i.e. with a direct object):

descendre to bring/take down
entrer to bring/take in
monter to bring/take up → ❼
passer to pass; to spend → ❽
rentrer to bring/take in
retourner to turn over
sortir to bring/take out → ❾

ⓘ Note that the past participle must show an agreement in number and gender whenever the auxiliary is **être** except for reflexive verbs where the reflexive pronoun is the indirect object (see page 50).

❶	je me suis arrêté(e)	I stopped
	elle s'est trompée	she made a mistake
	tu t'es levé(e)	you got up
	ils s'étaient battus	they had fought (one another)
❷	elle est allée	she went
❸	ils sont morts	they died
❹	vous êtes partie	you left (*addressing a female person*)
	vous êtes parties	you left (*addressing more than one female person*)
❺	nous sommes resté(e)s	we stayed
❻	elles étaient venues	they (*female*) had come
❼	Il a monté les valises	He's taken up the cases
❽	Nous avons passé trois semaines chez elle	We spent three weeks at her place
❾	Avez-vous sorti la voiture?	Have you taken the car out?

Verbs

Reflexive Verbs

A reflexive verb is one accompanied by a reflexive pronoun,
e.g. **se lever** to get up; **se laver** to wash (oneself).
The reflexive pronouns are:

	SINGULAR	PLURAL
1st person	me (m')	nous
2nd person	te (t')	vous
3rd person	se (s')	se (s')

The forms shown in brackets are used before a vowel, an **h** 'mute', or the pronoun **y** → ❶

> In positive commands, **te** changes to **toi** → ❷
>
> The reflexive pronoun 'reflects back' to the subject, but it is not always translated in English → ❸
>
> The plural pronouns are sometimes translated as 'one another', 'each other' (the *reciprocal* meaning) → ❹
>
> The reciprocal meaning may be emphasized by **l'un(e) l'autre (les un(e)s les autres)** → ❺

Simple tenses of reflexive verbs are conjugated in exactly the same way as those of non-reflexive verbs except that the reflexive pronoun is always used. Compound tenses are formed with the auxiliary **être**. A sample reflexive verb is conjugated in full on pages 34 and 35.

For agreement of past participles, see page 32.

Position of Reflexive Pronouns

In constructions other than the imperative affirmative the pronoun comes before the verb → ❻

In the imperative affirmative, the pronoun follows the verb and is attached to it by a hyphen → ❼

1	Je m'ennuie	I'm bored
	Elle s'habille	She's getting dressed
	Ils s'y intéressent	They are interested in it
2	Assieds-toi	Sit down
	Tais-toi	Be quiet
3	Je me prépare	I'm getting (myself) ready
	Nous nous lavons	We're washing (ourselves)
	Elle se lève	She gets up
4	Nous nous parlons	We speak to each other
	Ils se ressemblent	They resemble one another
5	Ils se regardent l'un l'autre	They are looking at each other
6	Je me couche tôt	I go to bed early
	Comment vous appelez-vous?	What is your name?
	Il ne s'est pas rasé	He hasn't shaved
	Ne te dérange pas pour nous	Don't put yourself out on our account
7	Dépêche-toi	Hurry (up)
	Renseignons-nous	Let's find out
	Asseyez-vous	Sit down

Verbs

Reflexive Verbs *continued*

Past Participle Agreement

In most reflexive verbs the reflexive pronoun is a *direct* object pronoun → **❶**

When a direct object accompanies the reflexive verb the pronoun is then the *indirect* object → **❷**

The past participle of a reflexive verb agrees in number and gender with a direct object which *precedes* the verb (usually, but not always, the reflexive pronoun) → **❸**

The past participle does not change if the direct object follows the verb → **❹**

Here are some common reflexive verbs:

s'en aller to go away	**se hâter** to hurry
s'amuser to enjoy oneself	**se laver** to wash (oneself)
s'appeler to be called	**se lever** to get up
s'arrêter to stop	**se passer** to happen
s'asseoir to sit (down)	**se promener** to go for a walk
se baigner to go swimming	**se rappeler** to remember
se blesser to hurt oneself	**se ressembler** to resemble each other
se coucher to go to bed	**se retourner** to turn round
se demander to wonder	**se réveiller** to wake up
se dépêcher to hurry	**se sauver** to run away
se diriger to make one's way	**se souvenir de** to remember
s'endormir to fall asleep	**se taire** to be quiet
s'ennuyer to be/get bored	**se tromper** to be mistaken
se fâcher to get angry	**se trouver** to be (situated)
s'habiller to dress (oneself)	

① Je m'appelle   I'm called (*literally*: I call myself)
Asseyez-vous   Sit down (*literally*: Seat yourself)
Ils se lavent   They wash (themselves)

② Elle se lave les mains   She's washing her hands
         (*literally*: She's washing to
         herself the hands)

Je me brosse les dents   I brush my teeth
Nous nous envoyons des   We send presents to each
   cadeaux à Noël   other at Christmas

③ 'Je me suis endormi' s'est-il excusé   'I fell asleep', he apologized
Pauline s'est dirigée vers la sortie   Pauline made her way towards
     the exit

Ils se sont levés vers dix heures   They got up around ten o'clock
Elles se sont excusées de leur   They apologized for their
   erreur   mistake
Est-ce que tu t'es blessée, Cécile?   Have you hurt yourself, Cécile?

④ Elle s'est lavé les cheveux   She (has) washed her hair
Nous nous sommes serré la main   We shook hands
Christine s'est cassé la jambe   Christine has broken her leg

Verbs

Reflexive Verbs *continued*

Conjugation of: **se laver** to wash (oneself)

1 SIMPLE TENSES

PRESENT

je me lave	nous nous lavons
tu te laves	vous vous lavez
il/elle se lave	ils/elles se lavent

IMPERFECT

je me lavais	nous nous lavions
tu te lavais	vous vous laviez
il/elle se lavait	ils/elles se lavaient

FUTURE

je me laverai	nous nous laverons
tu te laveras	vous vous laverez
il/elle se lavera	ils/elles se laveront

CONDITIONAL

je me laverais	nous nous laverions
tu te laverais	vous vous laveriez
il/elle se laverait	ils/elles se laveraient

PAST HISTORIC

je me lavai	nous nous lavâmes
tu te lavas	vous vous lavâtes
il/elle se lava	ils/elles se lavèrent

PRESENT SUBJUNCTIVE

je me lave	nous nous lavions
tu te laves	vous vous laviez
il/elle se lave	ils/elles se lavent

IMPERFECT SUBJUNCTIVE

je me lavasse	nous nous lavassions
tu te lavasses	vous vous lavassiez
il/elle se lavât	ils/elles se lavassent

Verbs

Reflexive Verbs *continued*

Conjugation of: se laver to wash (oneself)

2 COMPOUND TENSES

PERFECT

je me suis lavé(e)
tu t'es lavé(e)
il/elle s'est lavé(e)

nous nous sommes lavé(e)s
vous vous êtes lavé(e)(s)
ils/elles se sont lavé(e)s

PLUPERFECT

je m'étais lavé(e)
tu t'étais lavé(e)
il/elle s'était lavé(e)

nous nous étions lavé(e)s
vous vous étiez lavé(e)(s)
ils/elles s'étaient lavé(e)s

FUTURE PERFECT

je me serai lavé(e)
tu te seras lavé(e)
il/elle se sera lavé(e)

nous nous serons lavé(e)s
vous vous serez lavé(e)(s)
ils/elles se seront lavé(e)s

CONDITIONAL PERFECT

je me serais lavé(e)
tu te serais lavé(e)
il/elle se serait lavé(e)

nous nous serions lavé(e)s
vous vous seriez lavé(e)(s)
ils/elles se seraient lavé(e)s

PAST ANTERIOR

je me fus lavé(e)
tu te fus lavé(e)
il/elle se fut lavé(e)

nous nous fûmes lavé(e)s
vous vous fûtes lavé(e)(s)
ils/elles se furent lavé(e)s

PERFECT SUBJUNCTIVE

je me sois lavé(e)
tu te sois lavé(e)
il/elle se soit lavé(e)

nous nous soyons lavé(e)s
vous vous soyez lavé(e)(s)
ils/elles se soient lavé(e)s

PLUPERFECT SUBJUNCTIVE

je me fusse lavé(e)
tu te fusses lavé(e)
il/elle se fût lavé(e)

nous nous fussions lavé(e)s
vous vous fussiez lavé(e)(s)
ils/elles se fussent lavé(e)s

Verbs

The Passive

In the passive, the subject *receives* the action (e.g. I was hit) as opposed to *performing* it (e.g. I hit him). In English the verb 'to be' is used with the past participle. In French the passive is formed in exactly the same way, i.e.:

a tense of **être** + *past participle*.

The past participle agrees in number and gender with the subject → ❶

A sample verb is conjugated in the passive voice on pages 38 and 39.

The indirect object in French cannot become the subject in the passive: in quelqu'un m'a donné un livre the indirect object **m'** cannot become the subject of a passive verb (unlike English: someone gave me a book → I was given a book).

The passive meaning is often expressed in French by:
- **on** plus a verb in the active voice → ❷
- a reflexive verb (see page 30) → ❸

❶	Philippe a été récompensé	Philippe has been rewarded
	Son travail est très admiré	His work is greatly admired
	Ils le feront pourvu qu'ils soient payés	They'll do it provided they're paid
	Les enfants seront punis	The children will be punished
	Cette mesure aurait été critiquée si ...	This measure would have been criticized if ...
	Les portes avaient été fermées	The doors had been closed
❷	On leur a envoyé une lettre	They were sent a letter
	On nous a montré le jardin	We were shown the garden
	On m'a dit que ...	I was told that ...
❸	Ils se vendent 3 euros (la) pièce	They are sold for 3 euros each
	Ce mot ne s'emploie plus	This word is no longer used

Verbs

The Passive *continued*

Conjugation of: **être aimé** to be liked

PRESENT

je suis aimé(e)	nous sommes aimé(e)s
tu es aimé(e)	vous êtes aimé(e)(s)
il/elle est aimé(e)	ils/elles sont aimé(e)s

IMPERFECT

j'étais aimé(e)	nous étions aimé(e)s
tu étais aimé(e)	vous étiez aimé(e)(s)
il/elle était aimé(e)	ils/elles étaient aimé(e)s

FUTURE

je serai aimé(e)	nous serons aimé(e)s
tu seras aimé(e)	vous serez aimé(e)(s)
il/elle sera aimé(e)	ils/elles seront aimé(e)s

CONDITIONAL

je serais aimé(e)	nous serions aimé(e)s
tu serais aimé(e)	vous seriez aimé(e)(s)
il/elle serait aimé(e)	ils/elles seraient aimé(e)s

PAST HISTORIC

je fus aimé(e)	nous fûmes aimé(e)s
tu fus aimé(e)	vous fûtes aimé(e)(s)
il/elle fut aimé(e)	ils/elles furent aimé(e)s

PRESENT SUBJUNCTIVE

je sois aimé(e)	nous soyons aimé(e)s
tu sois aimé(e)	vous soyez aimé(e)(s)
il/elle soit aimé(e)	ils/elles soient aimé(e)s

IMPERFECT SUBJUNCTIVE

je fusse aimé(e)	nous fussions aimé(e)s
tu fusses aimé(e)	vous fussiez aimé(e)(s)
il/elle fût aimé(e)	ils/elles fussent aimé(e)s

Verbs

The Passive *continued*

Conjugation of: **être aimé** to be liked

PERFECT
j'ai été aimé(e)

tu as été aimé(e)

il/elle a été aimé(e)

nous avons été aimé(e)s

vous avez été aimé(e)(s)

ils/elles ont été aimé(e)s

PLUPERFECT
j'avais été aimé(e)

tu avais été aimé(e)

il/elle avait été aimé(e)

nous avions été aimé(e)s

vous aviez été aimé(e)(s)

ils/elles avaient été aimé(e)s

FUTURE PERFECT
j'aurai été aimé(e)

tu auras été aimé(e)

il/elle aura été aimé(e)

nous aurons été aimé(e)s

vous aurez été aimé(e)(s)

ils/elles auront été aimé(e)s

CONDITIONAL PERFECT
j'aurais été aimé(e)

tu aurais été aimé(e)

il/elle aurait été aimé(e)

nous aurions été aimé(e)s

vous auriez été aimé(e)(s)

ils/elles auraient été aimé(e)s

PAST ANTERIOR
j'eus été aimé(e)

tu eus été aimé(e)

il/elle eut été aimé(e)

nous eûmes été aimé(e)s

vous eûtes été aimé(e)(s)

ils/elles eurent été aimé(e)s

PERFECT SUBJUNCTIVE
j'aie été aimé(e)

tu aies été aimé(e)

il/elle ait été aimé(e)

nous ayons été aimé(e)s

vous ayez été aimé(e)(s)

ils/elles aient été aimé(e)s

PLUPERFECT SUBJUNCTIVE
j'eusse été aimé(e)

tu eusses été aimé(e)

il/elle eût été aimé(e)

nous eussions été aimé(e)s

vous eussiez été aimé(e)(s)

ils/elles eussent été aimé(e)s

Verbs

Impersonal Verbs

Impersonal verbs are used only in the infinitive and in the third person singular with the subject pronoun **il**, generally translated as 'it'.

e.g. il pleut it's raining
      il est facile de dire que ... it's easy to say that ...

The most common impersonal verbs are:

INFINITIVE	CONSTRUCTIONS
s'agir	il s'agit de + *noun* → ❶
	it's a question/matter of something, it's about something
	il s'agit de + *infinitive* → ❷
	it's a question/matter of doing; somebody must do
falloir	il faut + *noun object* (+ *indirect object*) → ❸
	(somebody) needs something, something is necessary (to somebody)
	il faut + *infinitive* (+ *indirect object*) → ❹
	it is necessary to do
	il faut que + *subjunctive* → ❺
	it is necessary to do, somebody must do
grêler	il grêle it's hailing
neiger	il neige it's snowing
pleuvoir	il pleut it's raining
tonner	il tonne it's thundering
	→ ❻
valoir mieux	il vaut mieux + *infinitive* → ❼
	it's better to do
	il vaut mieux que + *subjunctive* → ❽
	it's better to do/that somebody does

① Il ne s'agit pas d'argent — It isn't a question/matter of money

De quoi s'agit-il? — What is it about?

Il s'agit de la vie d'une famille au début du siècle — It's about the life of a family at the turn of the century

② Il s'agit de faire vite — We must act quickly

③ Il faut du courage pour faire ça — One needs courage to do that

Il me faut une chaise de plus — I need an extra chair

④ Il faut partir — It is necessary to leave / We/I/You must leave*

Il me fallait prendre une décision — I had to make a decision

⑤ Il faut que vous partiez — You must leave

Il faudrait que je fasse mes valises — I ought to pack my cases

⑥ Il pleuvait à verse — It was pouring with rain

⑦ Il vaut mieux refuser — It's better to refuse / You/He/I had better refuse*

Il vaudrait mieux rester — You/We/She had better stay*

⑧ Il vaudrait mieux que nous ne venions pas — It would be better if we didn't come / We'd better not come

---

* The translation here obviously depends on context

Verbs

Impersonal Verbs

The following verbs are also commonly used in impersonal constructions:

INFINITIVE	CONSTRUCTIONS
avoir	**il y a** + *noun* → ①
	there is/are
être	**il est** + *noun* → ②
	it is, there are (*very literary style*)
	il est + *adjective* + **de** + *infinitive* → ③
	it is
faire	**il fait** + *adjective of weather* → ④
	it is
	il fait + *noun depicting weather/dark/light etc* → ⑤
	it is
manquer	**il manque** + *noun* (+ *indirect object*) → ⑥
	there is/are … missing, something is missing
paraître	**il paraît que** + *subjunctive* → ⑦
	it seems/appears that
	il paraît + *indirect object* + **que** + *indicative* → ⑧
	it seems/appears to somebody that
rester	**il reste** + *noun* (+ *indirect object*) → ⑨
	there is/are … left, (somebody) has something left
sembler	**il semble que** + *subjunctive* → ⑩
	it seems/appears that
	il semble + *indirect object* + **que** + *indicative* → ⑪
	it seems/appears to somebody that
suffire	**il suffit de** + *infinitive* → ⑫
	it is enough to do
	il suffit de + *noun* → ⑬
	something is enough, it only takes something

①	Il y a du pain (qui reste)	There is some bread (left)
	Il n'y avait pas de iettres ce matin	There were no letters this morning
②	Il est dix heures	It's ten o'clock
	Il est des gens qui ...	There are (some) people who ...
③	Il était inutile de protester	It was useless to protest
	Il est facile de critiquer	Criticizing is easy
④	Il fait beau/mauvais	It's lovely/horrible weather
⑤	Il faisait du soleil/du vent	It was sunny/windy
	Il fait jour/nuit	It's light/dark
⑥	Il manque deux tasses	There are two cups missing
		Two cups are missing
	Il manquait un bouton à sa chemise	His shirt had a button missing
⑦	Il paraît qu'ils partent demain	It appears they are leaving tomorrow
⑧	Il nous paraît certain qu'il aura du succès	It seems certain to us that he'll be successful
⑨	Il reste deux miches de pain	There are two loaves left
	Il lui restait cinquante euros	He/She had fifty euros left
⑩	Il semble que vous ayez raison	It seems that you are right
⑪	Il me semblait qu'il conduisait trop vite	It seemed to me (that) he was driving too fast
⑫	Il suffit de téléphoner pour réserver une place	It is enough to reserve a seat by phone
⑬	Il suffit d'une seule erreur pour tout gâcher	One single error is enough to ruin everything

Verbs

The Infinitive

The infinitive is the form of the verb found in dictionary entries meaning 'to … ', e.g. **donner** to give; **vivre** to live.

There are three main types of verbal construction involving the infinitive:
- with no linking preposition → ❶
- with the linking preposition **à** (see also page 64) → ❷
- with the linking preposition **de** (see also page 64) → ❸

Verbs followed by an infinitive with no linking preposition

devoir, **pouvoir**, **savoir**, **vouloir** and **falloir** (i.e. modal auxiliary verbs: page 52 → ❶).

valoir mieux: see Impersonal Verbs, page 40.

verbs of seeing or hearing e.g. **voir** to see; **entendre** to hear → ❹

intransitive verbs of motion e.g. **aller** to go; **descendre** to come/go down → ❺

envoyer to send → ❻

faillir → ❼

faire → ❽

laisser to let, allow → ❾

The following common verbs:

adorer to love	**espérer** to hope → ⓮
aimer to like, love → ❿	**oser** to dare → ⓯
aimer mieux to prefer → ⓫	**préférer** to prefer
compter to expect	**sembler** to seem → ⓰
désirer to wish, want → ⓬	**souhaiter** to wish
détester to hate → ⓭	

1	Voulez-vous attendre?	Would you like to wait?
2	J'apprends à nager	I'm learning to swim
3	Essayez de venir	Try to come
4	Il nous a vus arriver	He saw us arriving
	On les entend chanter	You can hear them singing
5	Allez voir Nicolas	Go and see Nicholas
	Descends leur demander	Go down and ask them
6	Je l'ai envoyé les voir	I sent him to see them
7	J'ai failli tomber	I almost fell
8	Ne me faites pas rire!	Don't make me laugh!
	J'ai fait réparer ma voiture	I've had my car repaired
9	Laissez-moi passer	Let me pass
10	Il aime nous accompagner	He likes to come with us
11	J'aimerais mieux le choisir moi-même	I'd rather choose it myself
12	Elle ne désire pas venir	She doesn't wish to come
13	Je déteste me lever le matin	I hate getting up in the morning
14	Espérez-vous partir en vacances?	Are you hoping to go on holiday?
15	Nous n'avons pas osé y retourner	We haven't dared go back
16	Vous semblez être inquiet	You seem to be worried

Verbs

The Infinitive: Set Expressions

The following are set in French with the meaning shown:

> **aller chercher** to go for, to go and get → ①
> **envoyer chercher** to send for → ②
> **entendre dire que** to hear it said that → ③
> **entendre parler de** to hear of/about → ④
> **faire entrer** to show in → ⑤
> **faire sortir** to let out → ⑥
> **faire venir** to send for → ⑦
> **laisser tomber** to drop → ⑧
> **vouloir dire** to mean → ⑨

The Perfect Infinitive

The perfect infinitive is formed using the auxiliary verb **avoir** or **être** as appropriate with the past participle of the verb → ⑩

The perfect infinitive is found:
- following the preposition **après** after → ⑪
- following certain verbal constructions → ⑫

1. Va chercher tes photos — Go and get your photos
   Il est allé chercher Alexandre — He's gone to get Alexander

2. J'ai envoyé chercher un médecin — I've sent for a doctor

3. J'ai entendu dire qu'il est malade — I've heard it said that he's ill

4. Je n'ai plus entendu parler de lui — I didn't hear anything more (said) of him

5. Fais entrer nos invités — Show our guests in

6. J'ai fait sortir le chat — I've let the cat out

7. Je vous ai fait venir parce que … — I sent for you because …

8. Il a laissé tomber le vase — He dropped the vase

9. Qu'est-ce que cela veut dire? — What does that mean?

10. avoir fini — to have finished
    être allé — to have gone
    s'être levé — to have got up

11. Après avoir pris cette décision, il nous a appelés — After making/having made that decision, he called us
    Après être sorties, elles se sont dirigées vers le parking — After leaving/having left, they headed for the car park
    Après nous être levé(e)s, nous avons lu les journaux — After getting up/having got up, we read the papers

12. pardonner à qn d'avoir fait — to forgive sb for doing/having done
    remercier qn d'avoir fait — to thank sb for doing/having done
    regretter d'avoir fait — to be sorry for doing/having done

Verbs

The Present Participle

Formation

First conjugation:
Replace the **-er** of the infinitive by **-ant** → ❶
- Verbs ending in **-cer**: **c** changes to **ç** → ❷
- Verbs ending in **-ger**: **g** changes to **ge** → ❸

Second conjugation:
Replace the **-ir** of the infinitive by **-issant** → ❹

Third conjugation:
Replace the **-re** of the infinitive by **-ant** → ❺

For irregular present participles, see irregular verbs, page 74 onwards.

Uses

The present participle has a more restricted use in French than in English.

Used as a verbal form, the present participle is invariable. It is found:
- on its own, where it corresponds to the English present participle → ❻
- following the preposition **en** → ❼
- ⓘ Note, in particular, the construction:
  verb + **en** + *present participle*
  which is often translated by an English phrasal verb, i.e. one followed by a preposition like 'to run down', 'to bring up' → ❽

Used as an adjective, the present participle agrees in number and gender with the noun or pronoun → ❾
- ⓘ Note, in particular, the use of **ayant** and **étant** – the present participles of the auxiliary verbs **avoir** and **être** – with a past participle → ❿

1. donner to give → donnant giving

2. lancer to throw → lançant throwing

3. manger to eat → mangeant eating

4. finir to finish → finissant finishing

5. vendre to sell → vendant selling

6. David, habitant près de Paris, a la possibilité de ...
David, living near Paris, has the opportunity of ...
Elle, pensant que je serais fâché, a dit ...
She, thinking that I would be angry, said ...
Ils m'ont suivi, criant à tue-tête
They followed me, shouting at the top of their voices

7. En attendant sa sœur, Richard s'est endormi
While waiting for his sister, Richard fell asleep
Téléphone-nous en arrivant chez toi
Phone us when you get home
En appuyant sur ce bouton, on peut ...
By pressing this button, you can ...
Il s'est blessé en essayant de sauver un chat
He hurt himself trying to rescue a cat

8. sortir en courant
to run out (*literally*: to go out running)
avancer en boitant
to limp along (*literally*: to go forward limping)

9. le soleil couchant
the setting sun
une lumière éblouissante
a dazzling light
ils sont dégoûtants
they are disgusting
elles étaient étonnantes
they were surprising

10. Ayant mangé plus tôt, il a pu ...
Having eaten earlier, he was able to ...
Étant arrivée en retard, elle a dû ...
Having arrived late, she had to ...

Verbs

Past Participle Agreement

Like adjectives, a past participle must sometimes agree in number and gender with a noun or pronoun. For the rules of agreement, see below. Example: **donné**

	MASCULINE	FEMININE
SING.	donné	donnée
PLUR.	donné**s**	donnée**s**

When the masculine singular form already ends in **-s**, no further **s** is added in the masculine plural, e.g. **pris** taken.

Rules of Agreement in Compound Tenses

When the auxiliary verb is **avoir**:

> The past participle remains in the masculine singular form, unless a direct object precedes the verb. The past participle then agrees in number and gender with the preceding direct object → ❶

When the auxiliary verb is **être**:

> The past participle of a non-reflexive verb agrees in number and gender with the subject → ❷
> The past participle of a reflexive verb agrees in number and gender with the reflexive pronoun, if the pronoun is a direct object → ❸
> No agreement is made if the reflexive pronoun is an indirect object → ❹

The Past Participle as an adjective

The past participle agrees in number and gender with the noun or pronoun → ❺

① Voici le livre que vous avez demandé	Here's the book you asked for
Laquelle avaient-elles choisie?	Which one had they chosen?
Ces amis? Je les ai rencontrés à Édimbourg	Those friends? I met them in Edinburgh
Il a gardé toutes les lettres qu'elle a écrites	He has kept all the letters she wrote
② Est-ce que ton frère est allé à l'étranger?	Did your brother go abroad?
Elle était restée chez elle	She had stayed at home
Ils sont partis dans la matinée	They left in the morning
Mes cousines sont revenues hier	My cousins came back yesterday
③ Tu t'es rappelé d'acheter du pain, Georges?	Did you remember to buy bread, Georges?
Martine s'est demandée pourquoi il l'appelait	Martine wondered why he was calling her
'Lui et moi nous nous sommes cachés' a-t-elle dit	'He and I hid,' she said
Les vendeuses se sont mises en grève	The shop assistants have gone on strike
Vous vous êtes brouillés?	Have you fallen out with each other?
Les enfants s'étaient entraidés	The children had helped one another
④ Elle s'est lavé les mains	She washed her hands
Ils se sont parlé pendant des heures	They talked to each other for hours
⑤ à un moment donné	at a given time
la porte ouverte	the open door
ils sont bien connus	they are well-known
elles semblent fatiguées	they seem tired

Verbs

Modal Auxiliary Verbs

In French, the modal auxiliary verbs are: **devoir**, **pouvoir**, **savoir**, **vouloir** and **falloir**.

They are followed by a verb in the infinitive and have the following meanings:

devoir   to have to, must → **1**
               to be due to → **2**
               in the conditional/conditional perfect:
               should/should have, ought/ought to have → **3**

pouvoir to be able to, can → **4**
               to be allowed to, can, may → **5**
               indicating possibility: may/might/could → **6**

savoir   to know how to, can → **7**

vouloir   to want/wish to → **8**
               to be willing to, will → **9**
               in polite phrases → **10**

falloir   to be necessary: see Impersonal Verbs, page 40.

1. | Je dois leur rendre visite | I must visit them |
   | Elle a dû partir | She (has) had to leave |
   | Il a dû regretter d'avoir parlé | He must have been sorry he spoke |

2. | Vous devez revenir demain | You're due (to come) back tomorrow |
   | Je devais attraper le train de neuf heures mais ... | I was (supposed) to catch the nine o'clock train but ... |

3. | Je devrais le faire | I ought to do it |
   | J'aurais dû m'excuser | I ought to have apologized |

4. | Il ne peut pas lever le bras | He can't raise his arm |
   | Pouvez-vous réparer cette montre? | Can you mend this watch? |

5. | Puis-je les accompagner? | May I go with them? |

6. | Il peut encore changer d'avis | He may change his mind yet |
   | Cela pourrait être vrai | It could/might be true |

7. | Savez-vous conduire? | Can you drive? |
   | Je ne sais pas faire une omelette | I don't know how to make an omelette |

8. | Elle veut rester encore un jour | She wants to stay another day |

9. | Ils ne voulaient pas le faire | They wouldn't do it |
   | | They weren't willing to do it |
   | Ma voiture ne veut pas démarrer | My car won't start |

10. | Voulez-vous boire quelque chose? | Would you like something to drink? |

Verbs

Use of Tenses

The Present

Unlike English, French does not distinguish between the simple present (e.g. I smoke, he reads, we live) and the continuous present (e.g. I am smoking, he is reading, we are living) → **①**

To emphasize continuity, the following constructions may be used:
être en train de faire, être à faire to be doing → **②**

French uses the present tense where English uses the perfect in the following cases:
- with certain prepositions of time – notably **depuis** for/since – when an action begun in the past is continued in the present → **③**
  Note, however, that the perfect is used as in English when the verb is negative or the action has been completed → **④**
- in the construction **venir de faire** to have just done → **⑤**

The Future

The future is generally used as in English, but note the following:

Immediate future time is often expressed by means of the present tense of **aller** plus an infinitive → **⑥**

In time clauses expressing future action, French uses the future where English uses the present → **⑦**

The Future Perfect

Used as in English to mean 'shall/will have done' → **⑧**

In time clauses expressing future action, where English uses the perfect tense → **⑨**

1 Je fume — I smoke *or* I am smoking
Il lit — He reads *or* He is reading
Nous habitons — We live *or* We are living

2 Il est en train de travailler — He's (busy) working

3 Paul apprend à nager depuis six mois — Paul's been learning to swim for six months (and still is)
Je suis debout depuis sept heures — I've been up since seven
Il y a longtemps que vous attendez? — Have you been waiting long?
Voilà deux semaines que nous sommes ici — That's two weeks we've been here (now)

4 Ils ne se sont pas vus depuis des mois — They haven't seen each other for months
Elle est revenue il y a un an — She came back a year ago

5 Elisabeth vient de partir — Elizabeth has just left

6 Tu vas tomber si tu ne fais pas attention — You'll fall if you're not careful
Il va manquer le train — He's going to miss the train
Ça va prendre une demi-heure — It'll take half an hour

7 Quand il viendra vous serez en vacances — When he comes you'll be on holiday
Faites-nous savoir aussitôt qu'elle arrivera — Let us know as soon as she arrives

8 J'aurai fini dans une heure — I shall have finished in an hour

9 Quand tu auras lu ce roman, rends-le-moi — When you've read the novel, give it back to me
Je partirai dès que j'aurai fini — I'll leave as soon as I've finished

Verbs

Use of Tenses *continued*

The Imperfect

The imperfect describes:
- an action (or state) in the past without definite limits in time → ①
- habitual action(s) in the past (often translated by means of 'would' or 'used to') → ②

French uses the imperfect tense where English uses the pluperfect in the following cases:
- with certain prepositions of time – notably **depuis** for/since – when an action begun in the remoter past was continued in the more recent past → ③

  Note, however, that the pluperfect is used as in English, when the verb is negative or the action has been completed → ④
  - in the construction **venir de faire** to have just done → ⑤

The Perfect

The perfect is used to recount a completed action or event in the past. Note that this corresponds to a perfect tense or a simple past tense in English → ⑥

The Past Historic

Only ever used in *written, literary* French, the past historic recounts a completed action in the past, corresponding to a simple past tense in English → ⑦

The Past Anterior

This tense is used instead of the pluperfect when a verb in another part of the sentence is in the past historic. That is:
- in time clauses, after conjunctions like: **quand, lorsque** when; **dès que, aussitôt que** as soon as; **après que** after → ⑧
- after **à peine** hardly, scarcely → ⑨

The Subjunctive

In spoken French, the present subjunctive generally replaces the imperfect subjunctive. See also page 58 onwards.

1	Elle regardait par la fenêtre	She was looking out of the window
	Il pleuvait quand je suis sorti de chez moi	It was raining when I left the house
	Nos chambres donnaient sur la plage	Our rooms overlooked the beach
2	Quand il était étudiant, il se levait à l'aube	When he was a student he got up at dawn
	Nous causions des heures entières	We would talk for hours on end
	Elle te taquinait, n'est-ce pas?	She used to tease you, didn't she?
3	Nous habitions à Londres depuis deux ans	We had been living in London for two years (and still were)
	Il était malade depuis 2012	He had been ill since 2012
	Il y avait assez longtemps qu'il le faisait	He had been doing it for quite a long time
4	Voilà un an que je ne l'avais pas vu	I hadn't seen him for a year
	Il y avait une heure qu'elle était arrivée	She had arrived one hour before
5	Je venais de les rencontrer	I had just met them
6	Nous sommes allés au bord de la mer	We went/have been to the seaside
	Il a refusé de nous aider	He (has) refused to help us
	La voiture ne s'est pas arrêtée	The car didn't stop/hasn't stopped
7	Le roi mourut en 1592	The king died in 1592
8	Quand il eut fini, il se leva	When he had finished, he got up
9	À peine eut-il fini de parler qu'on frappa à la porte	He had scarcely finished speaking when there was a knock at the door

Verbs

The Subjunctive: when to use it

For how to form the subjunctive see page 6 onwards.

The subjunctive is used :

After certain conjunctions:

quoique ⎤ bien que ⎦	although → ❶
pour que ⎤ afin que ⎦	so that → ❷
pourvu que	provided that → ❸
jusqu'à ce que	until → ❹
avant que (... ne)	before → ❺
à moins que (... ne)	unless → ❻
de peur que (... ne) ⎤ de crainte que (... ne) ⎦	for fear that, lest → ❼

ⓘ Note that the **ne** following the conjunctions in examples ❺ to ❼ has no translation value. It is often omitted in spoken informal French.

After the conjunctions:

de sorte que ⎤ de façon que ⎥ de manière que ⎦	so that (*indicating a purpose*) → ❽

When these conjunctions introduce a result and not a purpose, the subjunctive is not used → ❾

After impersonal constructions which express necessity, possibility etc:

il faut que ⎤ il est nécessaire que ⎦	it is necessary that → ❿
il est possible que	it is possible that → ⓫
il semble que	it seems that, it appears that → ⓬
il vaut mieux que	it is better that → ⓭
il est dommage que	it's a pity that, it's a shame that → ⓮

①	Bien qu'il fasse beaucoup d'efforts, il est peu récompensé	Although he makes a lot of effort, he isn't rewarded for it
②	Demandez un reçu afin que vous puissiez être remboursé	Ask for a receipt so that you can get a refund
③	Nous partirons ensemble pourvu que Sylvie soit d'accord	We'll leave together provided Sylvie agrees
④	Reste ici jusqu'à ce que nous revenions	Stay here until we come back
⑤	Je le ferai avant que tu ne partes	I'll do it before you leave
⑥	Ce doit être Paul, à moins que je ne me trompe	That must be Paul, unless I'm mistaken
⑦	Parlez bas de peur qu'on ne vous entende	Speak softly for fear that someone hears you
⑧	Retournez-vous de sorte que je vous voie	Turn round so that I can see you
⑨	Il refuse de le faire de sorte que je dois le faire moi-même	He refuses to do it so that I have to do it myself
⑩	Il faut que je vous parle immédiatement	I must speak to you right away It is necessary that I speak to you right away
⑪	Il est possible qu'ils aient raison	They may be right It's possible that they are right
⑫	Il semble qu'elle ne soit pas venue	It appears that she hasn't come
⑬	Il vaut mieux que vous restiez chez vous	It's better that you stay at home
⑭	Il est dommage qu'elle ait perdu cette adresse	It's a shame/a pity that she's lost the address

Verbs

The Subjunctive: when to use it *continued*

After verbs of:
- wishing
  vouloir que
  désirer que   to wish that, want → ❶
  souhaiter que

- fearing
  craindre que
  avoir peur que   to be afraid that → ❷

ⓘ Note that **ne** in the first phrase of example ❷ has no translation value. It is often omitted in spoken informal French.

- ordering, forbidding, allowing
  ordonner que   to order that → ❸
  défendre que   to forbid that → ❹
  permettre que   to allow that → ❺

- opinion, expressing uncertainty
  croire que
  penser que   to think that → ❻
  douter que   to doubt that → ❼

- emotion (e.g. regret, shame, pleasure)
  regretter que   to be sorry that → ❽
  être content/surpris *etc* **que** to be pleased/surprised *etc* that → ❾

After a superlative → ❿

After certain adjectives expressing some sort of 'uniqueness' → ⓫
  dernier ... qui/que   last ... who/that
  premier ... qui/que   first ... who/that
  meilleur ... qui/que   best ... who/that
  seul ... qui/que
  unique ... qui/que   only ... who/that

1. Nous voulons qu'elle soit contente — We want her to be happy (*literally*: We want that she is happy)
   Désirez-vous que je le fasse? — Do you want me to do it?

2. Il craint qu'il ne soit trop tard — He's afraid it may be too late
   Avez-vous peur qu'il ne revienne pas? — Are you afraid that he won't come back?

3. Il a ordonné qu'ils soient désormais à l'heure — He has ordered that they be on time from now on

4. Elle défend que vous disiez cela — She forbids you to say that

5. Permettez que nous vous aidions — Allow us to help you

6. Je ne pense pas qu'ils soient venus — I don't think they came

7. Nous doutons qu'il ait dit la vérité — We doubt that he told the truth

8. Je regrette que vous ne puissiez pas venir — I'm sorry that you cannot come

9. Je suis content que vous les aimiez — I'm pleased that you like them

10. la personne la plus sympathique que je connaisse — the nicest person I know
    l'article le moins cher que j'aie jamais acheté — the cheapest item I have ever bought

11. Voici la dernière lettre qu'elle m'ait écrite — This is the last letter she wrote to me
    David est la seule personne qui puisse me conseiller — David is the only person who can advise me

Verbs

The Subjunctive: when to use it *continued*

After:
>   **si (...) que** however → ❶
>   **qui que** whoever → ❷
>   **quoi que** whatever → ❸

After **que** in the following:
> - to form the 3rd person imperative or to express a wish → ❹
> - when **que** has the meaning 'if', replacing **si** in a clause → ❺
> - when **que** has the meaning 'whether' → ❻

In relative clauses following certain types of indefinite and negative construction → ❼/❽

In set expressions → ❾

❶	si courageux qu'il soit	however brave he may be
	si peu que ce soit	however little it is
❷	Qui que vous soyez, allez-vous-en!	Whoever you are, go away!
❸	Quoi que nous fassions, ...	Whatever we do, ...
❹	Qu'il entre!	Let him come in!
	Que cela vous serve de leçon!	Let that be a lesson to you!
❺	S'il fait beau et que tu te sentes mieux, nous irons ...	If it's nice and you're feeling better, we'll go ...
❻	Que tu viennes ou non, je ...	Whether you come or not, I ...
❼	Il cherche une maison qui ait une piscine	He's looking for a house which has a swimming pool (*subjunctive used since such a house may or may not exist*)
	J'ai besoin d'un livre qui décrive l'art du mime	I need a book which describes the art of mime (*subjunctive used since such a book may or may not exist*)
❽	Je n'ai rencontré personne qui la connaisse	I haven't met anyone who knows her
	Il n'y a rien qui puisse vous empêcher de ...	There's nothing that can prevent you from ...
❾	Vive le roi!	Long live the king!
	Que Dieu vous bénisse!	God bless you!

Verbs

Verbs governing à and de

The following lists (pages 64 to 72) contain common verbal constructions using the prepositions **à** and **de**

Note the following abbreviations:
infin.	*infinitive*
perf. infin.	*perfect infinitive**
qch	quelque chose
qn	quelqu'un
sb	somebody
sth	something

accuser qn de qch/de + *perf. infin.*	to accuse sb of sth/of doing, having done → ❶
accoutumer qn à qch/à + *infin.*	to accustom sb to sth/to doing
acheter qch à qn	to buy sth from sb/for sb → ❷
achever de + *infin.*	to end up doing
aider qn à + *infin.*	to help sb to do → ❸
s'amuser à + *infin.*	to have fun doing
s'apercevoir de qch	to notice sth → ❹
apprendre qch à qn	to teach sb sth
apprendre à + *infin.*	to learn to do → ❺
apprendre à qn à + *infin.*	to teach sb to do → ❻
s'approcher de qn/qch	to approach sb/sth → ❼
arracher qch à qn	to snatch sth from sb → ❽
(s')arrêter de + *infin.*	to stop doing → ❾
arriver à + *infin.*	to manage to do → ❿
assister à qch	to attend sth, be at sth
s'attendre à + *infin.*	to expect to do → ⓫
blâmer qn de qch/de + *perf. infin.*	to blame sb for sth/for having done → ⓬
cacher qch à qn	to hide sth from sb → ⓭
cesser de + *infin.*	to stop doing → ⓮

* For formation see page 46

1. Il m'a accusé d'avoir menti — He accused me of lying

2. Marie-Christine leur a acheté deux billets — Marie-Christine bought two tickets from/for them

3. Aidez-moi à porter ces valises — Help me to carry these cases

4. Il ne s'est pas aperçu de son erreur — He didn't notice his mistake

5. Elle apprend à lire — She's learning to read

6. Je lui apprends à nager — I'm teaching him/her to swim

7. Elle s'est approchée de moi, en disant … — She approached me, saying …

8. Le voleur lui a arraché l'argent — The thief snatched the money from him/her

9. Arrêtez de faire du bruit! — Stop making so much noise!

10. Le professeur n'arrive pas à se faire obéir de sa classe — The teacher couldn't manage to control the class

11. Est-ce qu'elle s'attendait à le voir? — Was she expecting to see him?

12. Je ne la blâme pas de l'avoir fait — I don't blame her for doing it

13. Cache-les-leur! — Hide them from them!

14. Est-ce qu'il a cessé de pleuvoir? — Has it stopped raining?

Verbs

Verbs governing à and de *continued*

changer de qch	to change sth → ❶
se charger de qch/de + *infin.*	to see to sth/undertake to do
chercher à + *infin.*	to try to do
commander à qn de + *infin.*	to order sb to do → ❷
commencer à/de + *infin.*	to begin to do, to start to do → ❸
conseiller à qn de + *infin.*	to advise sb to do → ❹
consentir à qch/à + *infin.*	to agree to sth/to do → ❺
continuer à/de + *infin.*	to continue to do
craindre de + *infin.*	to be afraid to do/of doing
décider de + *infin.*	to decide to → ❻
se décider à + *infin.*	to make up one's mind to do
défendre à qn de + *infin.*	to forbid sb to do → ❼
demander qch à qn	to ask sb sth/for sth → ❽
demander à qn de + *infin.*	to ask sb to do → ❾
se dépêcher de + *infin.*	to hurry to do
dépendre de qn/qch	to depend on sb/sth
déplaire à qn	to displease sb → ❿
désobéir à qn	to disobey sb → ⓫
dire à qn de + *infin.*	to tell sb to do → ⓬
dissuader qn de + *infin.*	to dissuade sb from doing
douter de qch	to doubt sth
se douter de qch	to suspect sth
s'efforcer de + *infin.*	to strive to do
empêcher qn de + *infin.*	to prevent sb from doing → ⓭
emprunter qch à qn	to borrow sth from sb → ⓮
encourager qn à + *infin.*	to encourage sb to do → ⓯
enlever qch à qn	to take sth away from sb
enseigner qch à qn	to teach sb sth
enseigner à qn à + *infin.*	to teach sb to do
entreprendre de + *infin.*	to undertake to do
essayer de + *infin.*	to try to do → ⓰
éviter de + *infin.*	to avoid doing → ⓱

1. J'ai changé d'avis/de robe — I changed my mind/my dress
   Il faut changer de train à Toulouse — You have to change trains at Toulouse

2. Il leur a commandé de tirer — He ordered them to shoot

3. Il commence à neiger — It's starting to snow

4. Il leur a conseillé d'attendre — He advised them to wait

5. Je n'ai pas consenti à l'aider — I haven't agreed to help him/her

6. Qu'est-ce que vous avez décidé de faire? — What have you decided to do?

7. Je leur ai défendu de sortir — I've forbidden them to go out

8. Je lui ai demandé l'heure — I asked him/her the time
   Il lui a demandé un livre — He asked him/her for a book

9. Demande à Alain de le faire — Ask Alan to do it

10. Leur attitude lui déplaît — He/She doesn't like their attitude

11. Ils lui désobéissent souvent — They often disobey him/her

12. Dites-leur de se taire — Tell them to be quiet

13. Le bruit m'empêche de travailler — The noise is preventing me from working

14. Puis-je vous emprunter ce stylo? — May I borrow this pen from you?

15. Elle encourage ses enfants à être indépendants — She encourages her children to be independent

16. Essayez d'arriver à l'heure — Try to arrive on time

17. Il évite de lui parler — He avoids speaking to him/her

Verbs

Verbs governing à and de *continued*

s'excuser de qch/de + *(perf.) infin.* to apologize for sth/for doing, having done → ❶

exceller à + *infin.* to excel at doing

se fâcher de qch to be annoyed at sth

feindre de + *infin.* to pretend to do → ❷

féliciter qn de qch/de + *(perf.) infin.* to congratulate sb on sth/on doing, having done → ❸

se fier à qn to trust sb → ❹

finir de + *infin.* to finish doing → ❺

forcer qn à + *infin.* to force sb to do

habituer qn à + *infin.* to accustom sb to doing

s'habituer à + *infin.* to get/be used to doing → ❻

se hâter de + *infin.* to hurry to do

hésiter à + *infin.* to hesitate to do

interdire à qn de + *infin.* to forbid sb to do → ❼

s'intéresser à qn/qch/à + *infin.* to be interested in sb/sth/in doing → ❽

inviter qn à + *infin.* to invite sb to do → ❾

jouer à (+ *sports, games*) to play → ❿

jouer de (+ *musical instruments*) to play → ⓫

jouir de qch to enjoy sth → ⓬

jurer de + *infin.* to swear to do

louer qn de qch to praise sb for sth

manquer à qn to be missed by sb → ⓭

manquer de qch to lack sth

manquer de + *infin.* to fail to do → ⓮

se marier à qn to marry sb

se méfier de qn to distrust sb

menacer de + *infin.* to threaten to do → ⓯

mériter de + *infin.* to deserve to do → ⓰

se mettre à + *infin.* to begin to do

se moquer de qn/qch to make fun of sb/sth

négliger de + *infin.* to fail to do

❶	Je m'excuse d'être (arrivé) en retard	I apologize for being/arriving late
❷	Elle feint de dormir	She's pretending to be asleep
❸	Je l'ai félicitée d'avoir gagné	I congratulated her on winning
❹	Je ne me fie pas à ces gens-là	I don't trust those people
❺	Avez-vous fini de lire ce journal?	Have you finished reading this newspaper?
❻	Il s'est habitué à boire moins de café	He got used to drinking less coffee
❼	Il a interdit aux enfants de jouer avec des allumettes	He's forbidden the children to play with matches
❽	Elle s'intéresse beaucoup au sport	She's very interested in sport
❾	Il m'a invitée à dîner	He invited me for dinner
❿	Elle joue au tennis et au hockey	She plays tennis and hockey
⑪	Il joue du piano et de la guitare	He plays the piano and the guitar
⑫	Il jouit d'une santé solide	He enjoys good health
⑬	Tu manques à tes parents	Your parents miss you
⑭	Je ne manquerai pas de le lui dire	I'll be sure to tell him/her about it
⑮	Elle a menacé de démissionner tout de suite	She threatened to resign straight away
⑯	Ils méritent d'être promus	They deserve to be promoted

Verbs

Verbs governing à and de *continued*

nuire à qch	to harm sth, to do damage to sth → ①
obéir à qn	to obey sb
obliger qn à + *infin.*	to oblige/force sb to do → ②
s'occuper de qch/qn	to look after sth/sb → ③
offrir de + *infin.*	to offer to do → ④
omettre de + *infin.*	to fail to do
ordonner à qn de + *infin.*	to order sb to do → ⑤
ôter qch à qn	to take sth away from sb
oublier de + *infin.*	to forget to do
pardonner qch à qn	to forgive sb for sth
pardonner à qn de + *perf. infin.*	to forgive sb for having done → ⑥
parvenir à + *infin.*	to manage to do
se passer de qch	to do/go without sth → ⑦
penser à qn/qch	to think about sb/sth → ⑧
permettre qch à qn	to allow sb sth
permettre à qn de + *infin.*	to allow sb to do → ⑨
persister à + *infin.*	to persist in doing
persuader qn de + *infin.*	to persuade sb to do → ⑩
se plaindre de qch	to complain about sth
plaire à qn	to please sb → ⑪
pousser qn à + *infin.*	to urge sb to do
prendre qch à qn	to take sth from sb → ⑫
préparer qn à + *infin.*	to prepare sb to do
se préparer à + *infin.*	to get ready to do
prier qn de + *infin.*	to beg sb to do
profiter de qch/de + *infin.*	to take advantage of sth/of doing
promettre à qn de + *infin.*	to promise sb to do → ⑬
proposer de + *infin.*	to suggest doing → ⑭
punir qn de qch	to punish sb for sth → ⑮
récompenser qn de qch	to reward sb for sth
réfléchir à qch	to think about sth
refuser de + *infin.*	to refuse to do → ⑯

❶	Ce mode de vie va nuire à sa santé	This lifestyle will damage her health
❷	Il les a obligés à faire la vaisselle	He forced them to do the washing-up
❸	Je m'occupe de ma nièce	I'm looking after my niece
❹	Stuart a offert de nous accompagner	Stuart has offered to go with us
❺	Les soldats leur ont ordonné de se rendre	The soldiers ordered them to give themselves up
❻	Est-ce que tu as pardonné à Charles de t'avoir menti?	Have you forgiven Charles for lying to you?
❼	Je me suis passé d'électricité pendant plusieurs jours	I did without electricity for several days
❽	Je pense souvent à toi	I often think about you
❾	Permettez-moi de continuer, s'il vous plaît	Allow me to go on, please
❿	Elle nous a persuadés de rester	She persuaded us to stay
⓫	Ce genre de film lui plaît	He/she likes this kind of film
⓬	Je lui ai pris son mobile	I took his mobile phone from him
⓭	Ils ont promis à Pascale de venir	They promised Pascale that they would come
⓮	J'ai proposé de les inviter	I suggested inviting them
⓯	Il a été puni de sa malhonnêteté	He has been punished for his dishonesty
⓰	Il a refusé de coopérer	He has refused to cooperate

Verbs

Verbs governing à and de *continued*

regretter de + *perf. infin.*	to regret doing, having done → ❶
remercier qn de qch/de + *perf. infin.*	to thank sb for sth/for doing, having done → ❷
renoncer à qch/à + *infin.*	to give sth up/give up doing
reprocher qch à qn	to reproach sb with/for sth → ❸
résister à qch	to resist sth → ❹
résoudre de + *infin.*	to resolve to do
ressembler à qn/qch	to look/be like sb/sth → ❺
réussir à + *infin.*	to manage to do → ❻
rire de qn/qch	to laugh at sb/sth
risquer de + *infin.*	to risk doing → ❼
servir à qch/à + *infin.*	to be used for sth/for doing → ❽
se servir de qch	to use sth; to help oneself to sth → ❾
songer à + *infin.*	to think of doing
se souvenir de qn/qch/de + *perf. infin.*	to remember sb/sth/doing, having done → ❿
succéder à qn	to succeed sb
survivre à qn	to outlive sb → ⓫
tâcher de + *infin.*	to try to do → ⓬
tarder à + *infin.*	to delay doing → ⓭
tendre à + *infin.*	to tend to do
tenir à + *infin.*	to be keen to do → ⓮
tenter de + *infin.*	to try to do → ⓯
se tromper de qch	to be wrong about sth → ⓰
venir de* + *infin.*	to have just done → ⓱
vivre de qch	to live on sth
voler qch à qn	to steal sth from sb

* See also Use of Tenses, pages 54 and 56

①	Je regrette de ne pas l'avoir vue plus souvent quand elle était ici	I regret not having seen her more while she was here
②	Nous les avons remerciés de leur gentillesse	We thanked them for their kindness
③	On lui reproche son manque d'enthousiasme	They're reproaching him for his lack of enthusiasm
④	Comment résistez-vous à la tentation?	How do you resist temptation?
⑤	Elles ressemblent beaucoup à leur mère	They look very like their mother
⑥	Vous avez réussi à me convaincre	You've managed to convince me
⑦	Vous risquez de tomber en faisant cela	You risk falling doing that
⑧	Ce bouton sert à régler le volume	This knob is (used) for adjusting the volume
⑨	Il s'est servi d'un tournevis pour l'ouvrir	He used a screwdriver to open it
⑩	Vous vous souvenez de Lucienne? Il ne se souvient pas de l'avoir perdu	Do you remember Lucienne? He doesn't remember losing it
⑪	Elle a survécu à son mari	She outlived her husband
⑫	Tâchez de ne pas être en retard!	Try not to be late!
⑬	Il n'a pas tardé à prendre une décision	He was not long in taking a decision
⑭	Elle tient à le faire elle-même	She's keen to do it herself
⑮	J'ai tenté de la comprendre	I've tried to understand her
⑯	Je me suis trompé de route	I took the wrong road
⑰	Mon père vient de téléphoner Nous venions d'arriver	My father's just phoned We had just arrived

Irregular Verbs

Irregular Verbs

The verbs listed opposite and conjugated on pages 76 to 131 provide the main patterns for irregular verbs. The verbs are grouped opposite according to their infinitive ending (except **avoir** and **être**), and are shown in the following tables in alphabetical order.

In the tables, the most important irregular verbs are given in their most common simple tenses, together with the imperative and the present participle.

The auxiliary (**avoir** or **être**) is also shown for each verb, together with the past participle, to enable you to form all the compound tenses, as on pages 24 and 26.

For a fuller list of irregular verbs, the reader is referred to Collins Easy Learning French Verbs, which shows you how to conjugate some 2000 French verbs.

Irregular Verbs

avoir
être

'-er': aller
envoyer

'-ir': acquérir
bouillir
courir
cueillir
dormir
fuir
haïr
mourir
ouvrir
partir
sentir
servir
sortir
tenir
venir
vêtir

'-oir': s'asseoir
devoir
falloir
pleuvoir
pouvoir
recevoir
savoir
valoir
voir
vouloir

'-re': battre
boire
connaître
coudre
craindre
croire
croître
cuire
dire
écrire
faire
lire
mettre
moudre
naître
paraître
plaire
prendre
résoudre
rire
rompre
suffire
suivre
se taire
vaincre
vivre

acquérir (to acquire)

	PRESENT		IMPERFECT
	j'acquiers		j'acquérais
tu	acquiers	tu	acquérais
il	acquiert	il	acquérait
nous	acquérons	nous	acquérions
vous	acquérez	vous	acquériez
ils	acquièrent	ils	acquéraient

	FUTURE		CONDITIONAL
	j'acquerrai		j'acquerrais
tu	acquerras	tu	acquerrais
il	acquerra	il	acquerrait
nous	acquerrons	nous	acquerrions
vous	acquerrez	vous	acquerriez
ils	acquerront	ils	acquerraient

	PRESENT SUBJUNCTIVE		PAST HISTORIC
	j'acquière		j'acquis
tu	acquières	tu	acquis
il	acquière	il	acquit
nous	acquérions	nous	acquîmes
vous	acquériez	vous	acquîtes
ils	acquièrent	ils	acquirent

PAST PARTICIPLE
acquis

IMPERATIVE
acquiers
acquérons
acquérez

PRESENT PARTICIPLE
acquérant

AUXILIARY
avoir

Irregular Verbs

aller (to go)

	PRESENT		IMPERFECT
je	vais		j'allais
tu	vas	tu	allais
il	va	il	allait
nous	allons	nous	allions
vous	allez	vous	alliez
ils	vont	ils	allaient

	FUTURE		CONDITIONAL
	j'irai		j'irais
tu	iras	tu	irais
il	ira	il	irait
nous	irons	nous	irions
vous	irez	vous	iriez
ils	iront	ils	iraient

	PRESENT SUBJUNCTIVE		PAST HISTORIC
	j'aille		j'allai
tu	ailles	tu	allas
il	aille	il	alla
nous	allions	nous	allâmes
vous	alliez	vous	allâtes
ils	aillent	ils	allèrent

PAST PARTICIPLE	IMPERATIVE
allé	va
	allons
	allez

PRESENT PARTICIPLE	AUXILIARY
allant	être

s'asseoir (to sit down)

	PRESENT		IMPERFECT
je	m'assieds *or* assois	je	m'asseyais
tu	t'assieds *or* assois	tu	t'asseyais
il	s'assied *or* assoit	il	s'asseyait
nous	nous asseyons *or* assoyons	nous	nous asseyions
vous	vous asseyez *or* assoyez	vous	vous asseyiez
ils	s'asseyent *or* assoient	ils	s'asseyaient

	FUTURE		CONDITIONAL
je	m'assiérai	je	m'assiérais
tu	t'assiéras	tu	t'assiérais
il	s'assiéra	il	s'assiérait
nous	nous assiérons	nous	nous assiérions
vous	vous assiérez	vous	vous assiériez
ils	s'assiéront	ils	s'assiéraient

	PRESENT SUBJUNCTIVE		PAST HISTORIC
je	m'asseye	je	m'assis
tu	t'asseyes	tu	t'assis
il	s'asseye	il	s'assit
nous	nous asseyions	nous	nous assîmes
vous	vous asseyiez	vous	vous assîtes
ils	s'asseyent	ils	s'assirent

PAST PARTICIPLE
assis

IMPERATIVE
assieds-toi
asseyons-nous
asseyez-vous

PRESENT PARTICIPLE
s'asseyant

AUXILIARY
être

Irregular Verbs

avoir (to have)

	PRESENT		IMPERFECT
	j'ai		j'avais
tu	as	tu	avais
il	a	il	avait
nous	avons	nous	avions
vous	avez	vous	aviez
ils	ont	ils	avaient

	FUTURE		CONDITIONAL
	j'aurai		j'aurais
tu	auras	tu	aurais
il	aura	il	aurait
nous	aurons	nous	aurions
vous	aurez	vous	auriez
ils	auront	ils	auraient

	PRESENT SUBJUNCTIVE		PAST HISTORIC
	j'aie		j'eus
tu	aies	tu	eus
il	ait	il	eut
nous	ayons	nous	eûmes
vous	ayez	vous	eûtes
ils	aient	ils	eurent

PAST PARTICIPLE
eu

IMPERATIVE
aie
ayons
ayez

PRESENT PARTICIPLE
ayant

AUXILIARY
avoir

battre (to beat)

	PRESENT		IMPERFECT
je	**bats**	je	battais
tu	**bats**	tu	battais
il	**bat**	il	battait
nous	battons	nous	battions
vous	battez	vous	battiez
ils	battent	ils	battaient

	FUTURE		CONDITIONAL
je	battrai	je	battrais
tu	battras	tu	battrais
il	battra	il	battrait
nous	battrons	nous	battrions
vous	battrez	vous	battriez
ils	battront	ils	battraient

	PRESENT SUBJUNCTIVE		PAST HISTORIC
je	batte	je	battis
tu	battes	tu	battis
il	batte	il	battit
nous	battions	nous	battîmes
vous	battiez	vous	battîtes
ils	battent	ils	battirent

PAST PARTICIPLE	IMPERATIVE
battu	**bats**
	battons
	battez

PRESENT PARTICIPLE	AUXILIARY
battant	**avoir**

Irregular Verbs

boire (to drink)

	PRESENT		IMPERFECT
je	bois	je	buvais
tu	bois	tu	buvais
il	boit	il	buvait
nous	buvons	nous	buvions
vous	buvez	vous	buviez
ils	boivent	ils	buvaient

	FUTURE		CONDITIONAL
je	boirai	je	boirais
tu	boiras	tu	boirais
il	boira	il	boirait
nous	boirons	nous	boirions
vous	boirez	vous	boiriez
ils	boiront	ils	boiraient

	PRESENT SUBJUNCTIVE		PAST HISTORIC
je	boive	je	bus
tu	boives	tu	bus
il	boive	il	but
nous	buvions	nous	bûmes
vous	buviez	vous	bûtes
ils	boivent	ils	burent

PAST PARTICIPLE
bu

IMPERATIVE
bois
buvons
buvez

PRESENT PARTICIPLE
buvant

AUXILIARY
avoir

bouillir (to boil)

	PRESENT			IMPERFECT
je	bous		je	bouillais
tu	bous		tu	bouillais
il	bout		il	bouillait
nous	bouillons		nous	bouillions
vous	bouillez		vous	bouilliez
ils	bouillent		ils	bouillaient

	FUTURE			CONDITIONAL
je	bouillirai		je	bouillirais
tu	bouilliras		tu	bouillirais
il	bouillira		il	bouillirait
nous	bouillirons		nous	bouillirions
vous	bouillirez		vous	bouilliriez
ils	bouilliront		ils	bouilliraient

	PRESENT SUBJUNCTIVE			PAST HISTORIC
je	bouille		je	bouillis
tu	bouilles		tu	bouillis
il	bouille		il	bouillit
nous	bouillions		nous	bouillîmes
vous	bouilliez		vous	bouillîtes
ils	bouillent		ils	bouillirent

PAST PARTICIPLE	IMPERATIVE
bouilli	bous
	bouillons
	bouillez

PRESENT PARTICIPLE	AUXILIARY
bouillant	avoir

connaître (to know)

	PRESENT		IMPERFECT
je	connais	je	connaissais
tu	connais	tu	connaissais
il	connaît	il	connaissait
nous	connaissons	nous	connaissions
vous	connaissez	vous	connaissiez
ils	connaissent	ils	connaissaient

	FUTURE		CONDITIONAL
je	connaîtrai	je	connaîtrais
tu	connaîtras	tu	connaîtrais
il	connaîtra	il	connaîtrait
nous	connaîtrons	nous	connaîtrions
vous	connaîtrez	vous	connaîtriez
ils	connaîtront	ils	connaîtraient

	PRESENT SUBJUNCTIVE		PAST HISTORIC
je	connaisse	je	connus
tu	connaisses	tu	connus
il	connaisse	il	connut
nous	connaissions	nous	connûmes
vous	connaissiez	vous	connûtes
ils	connaissent	ils	connurent

PAST PARTICIPLE
connu

IMPERATIVE
connais
connaissons
connaissez

PRESENT PARTICIPLE
connaissant

AUXILIARY
avoir

Irregular Verbs

coudre (to sew)

	PRESENT		IMPERFECT
je	couds	je	cousais
tu	couds	tu	cousais
il	coud	il	cousait
nous	cousons	nous	cousions
vous	cousez	vous	cousiez
ils	cousent	ils	cousaient

	FUTURE		CONDITIONAL
je	coudrai	je	coudrais
tu	coudras	tu	coudrais
il	coudra	il	coudrait
nous	coudrons	nous	coudrions
vous	coudrez	vous	coudriez
ils	coudront	ils	coudraient

	PRESENT SUBJUNCTIVE		PAST HISTORIC
je	couse	je	cousis
tu	couses	tu	cousis
il	couse	il	cousit
nous	cousions	nous	cousîmes
vous	cousiez	vous	cousîtes
ils	cousent	ils	cousirent

PAST PARTICIPLE
cousu

IMPERATIVE
couds
cousons
cousez

PRESENT PARTICIPLE
cousant

AUXILIARY
avoir

Irregular Verbs

courir (to run)

	PRESENT		IMPERFECT
je	cours	je	courais
tu	cours	tu	courais
il	court	il	courait
nous	courons	nous	courions
vous	courez	vous	couriez
ils	courent	ils	couraient

	FUTURE		CONDITIONAL
je	courrai	je	courrais
tu	courras	tu	courrais
il	courra	il	courrait
nous	courrons	nous	courrions
vous	courrez	vous	courriez
ils	courront	ils	courraient

	PRESENT SUBJUNCTIVE		PAST HISTORIC
je	coure	je	courus
tu	coures	tu	courus
il	coure	il	courut
nous	courions	nous	courûmes
vous	couriez	vous	courûtes
ils	courent	ils	coururent

PAST PARTICIPLE	IMPERATIVE
couru	cours
	courons
	courez

PRESENT PARTICIPLE	AUXILIARY
courant	avoir

Irregular Verbs

craindre (to fear)

	PRESENT		IMPERFECT
je	crains	je	craignais
tu	crains	tu	craignais
il	craint	il	craignait
nous	craignons	nous	craignions
vous	craignez	vous	craigniez
ils	craignent	ils	craignaient

	FUTURE		CONDITIONAL
je	craindrai	je	craindrais
tu	craindras	tu	craindrais
il	craindra	il	craindrait
nous	craindrons	nous	craindrions
vous	craindrez	vous	craindriez
ils	craindront	ils	craindraient

	PRESENT SUBJUNCTIVE		PAST HISTORIC
je	craigne	je	craignis
tu	craignes	tu	craignis
il	craigne	il	craignit
nous	craignions	nous	craignîmes
vous	craigniez	vous	craignîtes
ils	craignent	ils	craignirent

PAST PARTICIPLE	IMPERATIVE
craint	crains
	craignons
	craignez

PRESENT PARTICIPLE	AUXILIARY
craignant	avoir

Note that verbs ending in **-eindre** and **-oindre** are conjugated similarly

Irregular Verbs

croire (to believe)

	PRESENT		IMPERFECT
je	crois	je	croyais
tu	crois	tu	croyais
il	croit	il	croyait
nous	croyons	nous	croyions
vous	croyez	vous	croyiez
ils	croient	ils	croyaient

	FUTURE		CONDITIONAL
je	croirai	je	croirais
tu	croiras	tu	croirais
il	croira	il	croirait
nous	croirons	nous	croirions
vous	croirez	vous	croiriez
ils	croiront	ils	croiraient

	PRESENT SUBJUNCTIVE		PAST HISTORIC
je	croie	je	crus
tu	croies	tu	crus
il	croie	il	crut
nous	croyions	nous	crûmes
vous	croyiez	vous	crûtes
ils	croient	ils	crurent

PAST PARTICIPLE
cru

IMPERATIVE
crois
croyons
croyez

PRESENT PARTICIPLE
croyant

AUXILIARY
avoir

croître (to grow)

	PRESENT			IMPERFECT
je	croîs		je	croissais
tu	croîs		tu	croissais
il	croît		il	croissait
nous	croissons		nous	croissions
vous	croissez		vous	croissiez
ils	croissent		ils	croissaient

	FUTURE			CONDITIONAL
je	croîtrai		je	croîtrais
tu	croîtras		tu	croîtrais
il	croîtra		il	croîtrait
nous	croîtrons		nous	croîtrions
vous	croîtrez		vous	croîtriez
ils	croîtront		ils	croîtraient

	PRESENT SUBJUNCTIVE			PAST HISTORIC
je	croisse		je	crûs
tu	croisses		tu	crûs
il	croisse		il	crût
nous	croissions		nous	crûmes
vous	croissiez		vous	crûtes
ils	croissent		ils	crûrent

PAST PARTICIPLE	IMPERATIVE
crû	croîs
	croissons
	croissez

PRESENT PARTICIPLE	AUXILIARY
croissant	avoir

Irregular Verbs

cueillir (to pick)

	PRESENT		IMPERFECT
je	cueille	je	cueillais
tu	cueilles	tu	cueillais
il	cueille	il	cueillait
nous	cueillons	nous	cueillions
vous	cueillez	vous	cueilliez
ils	cueillent	ils	cueillaient

	FUTURE		CONDITIONAL
je	cueillerai	je	cueillerais
tu	cueilleras	tu	cueillerais
il	cueillera	il	cueillerait
nous	cueillerons	nous	cueillerions
vous	cueillerez	vous	cueilleriez
ils	cueilleront	ils	cueilleraient

	PRESENT SUBJUNCTIVE		PAST HISTORIC
je	cueille	je	cueillis
tu	cueilles	tu	cueillis
il	cueille	il	cueillit
nous	cueillions	nous	cueillîmes
vous	cueilliez	vous	cueillîtes
ils	cueillent	ils	cueillirent

PAST PARTICIPLE	IMPERATIVE
cueilli	cueille
	cueillons
	cueillez

PRESENT PARTICIPLE	AUXILIARY
cueillant	avoir

Irregular Verbs

cuire (to cook)

	PRESENT		IMPERFECT
je	cuis	je	cuisais
tu	cuis	tu	cuisais
il	cuit	il	cuisait
nous	cuisons	nous	cuisions
vous	cuisez	vous	cuisiez
ils	cuisent	ils	cuisaient

	FUTURE		CONDITIONAL
je	cuirai	je	cuirais
tu	cuiras	tu	cuirais
il	cuira	il	cuirait
nous	cuirons	nous	cuirions
vous	cuirez	vous	cuiriez
ils	cuiront	ils	cuiraient

	PRESENT SUBJUNCTIVE		PAST HISTORIC
je	cuise	je	cuisis
tu	cuises	tu	cuisis
il	cuise	il	cuisit
nous	cuisions	nous	cuisîmes
vous	cuisiez	vous	cuisîtes
ils	cuisent	ils	cuisirent

PAST PARTICIPLE	IMPERATIVE
cuit	cuis
	cuisons
	cuisez

PRESENT PARTICIPLE	AUXILIARY
cuisant	avoir

Note that **nuire** (to harm) is conjugated similarly, but past participle is **nui**

Irregular Verbs

devoir (to have to, to owe)

	PRESENT			IMPERFECT
je	dois		je	devais
tu	dois		tu	devais
il	doit		il	devait
nous	devons		nous	devions
vous	devez		vous	deviez
ils	doivent		ils	devaient

	FUTURE			CONDITIONAL
je	devrai		je	devrais
tu	devras		tu	devrais
il	devra		il	devrait
nous	devrons		nous	devrions
vous	devrez		vous	devriez
ils	devront		ils	devraient

	PRESENT SUBJUNCTIVE			PAST HISTORIC
je	doive		je	dus
tu	doives		tu	dus
il	doive		il	dut
nous	devions		nous	dûmes
vous	deviez		vous	dûtes
ils	doivent		ils	durent

PAST PARTICIPLE
dû

IMPERATIVE
dois
devons
devez

PRESENT PARTICIPLE
devant

AUXILIARY
avoir

dire (to say, to tell)

	PRESENT			IMPERFECT
je	dis		je	disais
tu	dis		tu	disais
il	dit		il	disait
nous	disons		nous	disions
vous	dites		vous	disiez
ils	disent		ils	disaient

	FUTURE			CONDITIONAL
je	dirai		je	dirais
tu	diras		tu	dirais
il	dira		il	dirait
nous	dirons		nous	dirions
vous	direz		vous	diriez
ils	diront		ils	diraient

	PRESENT SUBJUNCTIVE			PAST HISTORIC
je	dise		je	dis
tu	dises		tu	dis
il	dise		il	dit
nous	disions		nous	dîmes
vous	disiez		vous	dîtes
ils	disent		ils	dirent

PAST PARTICIPLE	IMPERATIVE
dit	dis
	disons
	dites

PRESENT PARTICIPLE	AUXILIARY
disant	avoir

Note that **interdire** (to forbid) is conjugated similarly, but the second person plural of the present tense is **vous interdisez**

Irregular Verbs

dormir (to sleep)

	PRESENT		IMPERFECT
je	dors	je	dormais
tu	dors	tu	dormais
il	dort	il	dormait
nous	dormons	nous	dormions
vous	dormez	vous	dormiez
ils	dorment	ils	dormaient

	FUTURE		CONDITIONAL
je	dormirai	je	dormirais
tu	dormiras	tu	dormirais
il	dormira	il	dormirait
nous	dormirons	nous	dormirions
vous	dormirez	vous	dormiriez
ils	dormiront	ils	dormiraient

	PRESENT SUBJUNCTIVE		PAST HISTORIC
je	dorme	je	dormis
tu	dormes	tu	dormis
il	dorme	il	dormit
nous	dormions	nous	dormîmes
vous	dormiez	vous	dormîtes
ils	dorment	ils	dormirent

PAST PARTICIPLE
dormi

IMPERATIVE
dors
dormons
dormez

PRESENT PARTICIPLE
dormant

AUXILIARY
avoir

Irregular Verbs

écrire (to write)

	PRESENT			IMPERFECT
	j'écris			j'écrivais
tu	écris		tu	écrivais
il	écrit		il	écrivait
nous	écrivons		nous	écrivions
vous	écrivez		vous	écriviez
ils	écrivent		ils	écrivaient

	FUTURE			CONDITIONAL
	j'écrirai			j'écrirais
tu	écriras		tu	écrirais
il	écrira		il	écrirait
nous	écrirons		nous	écririons
vous	écrirez		vous	écririez
ils	écriront		ils	écriraient

	PRESENT SUBJUNCTIVE			PAST HISTORIC
	j'écrive			j'écrivis
tu	écrives		tu	écrivis
il	écrive		il	écrivit
nous	écrivions		nous	écrivîmes
vous	écriviez		vous	écrivîtes
ils	écrivent		ils	écrivirent

PAST PARTICIPLE	IMPERATIVE
écrit	écris
	écrivons
	écrivez

PRESENT PARTICIPLE	AUXILIARY
écrivant	avoir

Irregular Verbs

envoyer (to send)

	PRESENT		IMPERFECT
	j'envoie		j'envoyais
tu	envoies	tu	envoyais
il	envoie	il	envoyait
nous	envoyons	nous	envoyions
vous	envoyez	vous	envoyiez
ils	envoient	ils	envoyaient

	FUTURE		CONDITIONAL
	j'enverrai		j'enverrais
tu	enverras	tu	enverrais
il	enverra	il	enverrait
nous	enverrons	nous	enverrions
vous	enverrez	vous	enverriez
ils	enverront	ils	enverraient

	PRESENT SUBJUNCTIVE		PAST HISTORIC
	j'envoie		j'envoyai
tu	envoies	tu	envoyas
il	envoie	il	envoya
nous	envoyions	nous	envoyâmes
vous	envoyiez	vous	envoyâtes
ils	envoient	ils	envoyèrent

PAST PARTICIPLE
envoyé

IMPERATIVE
envoie
envoyons
envoyez

PRESENT PARTICIPLE
envoyant

AUXILIARY
avoir

Irregular Verbs

être (to be)

	PRESENT		IMPERFECT
je	suis		j'étais
tu	es	tu	étais
il	est	il	était
nous	sommes	nous	étions
vous	êtes	vous	étiez
ils	sont	ils	étaient

	FUTURE		CONDITIONAL
je	serai	je	serais
tu	seras	tu	serais
il	sera	il	serait
nous	serons	nous	serions
vous	serez	vous	seriez
ils	seront	ils	seraient

	PRESENT SUBJUNCTIVE		PAST HISTORIC
je	sois	je	fus
tu	sois	tu	fus
il	soit	il	fut
nous	soyons	nous	fûmes
vous	soyez	vous	fûtes
ils	soient	ils	furent

PAST PARTICIPLE	IMPERATIVE
été	sois
	soyons
	soyez

PRESENT PARTICIPLE	AUXILIARY
étant	avoir

Irregular Verbs

faire (to do, to make)

	PRESENT		IMPERFECT
je	fais	je	faisais
tu	fais	tu	faisais
il	fait	il	faisait
nous	faisons	nous	faisions
vous	faites	vous	faisiez
ils	font	ils	faisaient

	FUTURE		CONDITIONAL
je	ferai	je	ferais
tu	feras	tu	ferais
il	fera	il	ferait
nous	ferons	nous	ferions
vous	ferez	vous	feriez
ils	feront	ils	feraient

	PRESENT SUBJUNCTIVE		PAST HISTORIC
je	fasse	je	fis
tu	fasses	tu	fis
il	fasse	il	fit
nous	fassions	nous	fîmes
vous	fassiez	vous	fîtes
ils	fassent	ils	firent

PAST PARTICIPLE	IMPERATIVE
fait	fais
	faisons
	faites

PRESENT PARTICIPLE	AUXILIARY
faisant	avoir

Irregular Verbs

falloir (to be necessary)

	PRESENT		IMPERFECT
il	faut	il	fallait

	FUTURE		CONDITIONAL
il	faudra	il	faudrait

	PRESENT SUBJUNCTIVE		PAST HISTORIC
il	faille	il	fallut

PAST PARTICIPLE	IMPERATIVE
fallu	*not used*

PRESENT PARTICIPLE	AUXILIARY
not used	avoir

Irregular Verbs

fuir (to flee)

	PRESENT			IMPERFECT
je	fuis		je	**fuyais**
tu	fuis		tu	**fuyais**
il	fuit		il	**fuyait**
nous	**fuyons**		nous	**fuyions**
vous	**fuyez**		vous	**fuyiez**
ils	**fuient**		ils	**fuyaient**

	FUTURE			CONDITIONAL
je	fuirai		je	fuirais
tu	fuiras		tu	fuirais
il	fuira		il	fuirait
nous	fuirons		nous	fuirions
vous	fuirez		vous	fuiriez
ils	fuiront		ils	fuiraient

	PRESENT SUBJUNCTIVE			PAST HISTORIC
je	**fuie**		je	fuis
tu	**fuies**		tu	fuis
il	**fuie**		il	fuit
nous	**fuyions**		nous	fuîmes
vous	**fuyiez**		vous	fuîtes
ils	**fuient**		ils	fuirent

PAST PARTICIPLE	IMPERATIVE
fui	fuis
	fuyons
	fuyez

PRESENT PARTICIPLE	AUXILIARY
fuyant	**avoir**

Irregular Verbs

haïr (to hate)

	PRESENT		IMPERFECT
je	hais	je	haïssais
tu	hais	tu	haïssais
il	hait	il	haïssait
nous	haïssons	nous	haïssions
vous	haïssez	vous	haïssiez
ils	haïssent	ils	haïssaient

	FUTURE		CONDITIONAL
je	haïrai	je	haïrais
tu	haïras	tu	haïrais
il	haïra	il	haïrait
nous	haïrons	nous	haïrions
vous	haïrez	vous	haïriez
ils	haïront	ils	haïraient

	PRESENT SUBJUNCTIVE		PAST HISTORIC
je	haïsse	je	haïs
tu	haïsses	tu	haïs
il	haïsse	il	haït
nous	haïssions	nous	haïmes
vous	haïssiez	vous	haïtes
ils	haïssent	ils	haïrent

PAST PARTICIPLE
haï

IMPERATIVE
hais
haïssons
haïssez

PRESENT PARTICIPLE
haïssant

AUXILIARY
avoir

Irregular Verbs

lire (to read)

	PRESENT			IMPERFECT
je	lis		je	lisais
tu	lis		tu	lisais
il	lit		il	lisait
nous	lisons		nous	lisions
vous	lisez		vous	lisiez
ils	lisent		ils	lisaient

	FUTURE			CONDITIONAL
je	lirai		je	lirais
tu	liras		tu	lirais
il	lira		il	lirait
nous	lirons		nous	lirions
vous	lirez		vous	liriez
ils	liront		ils	liraient

	PRESENT SUBJUNCTIVE			PAST HISTORIC
je	lise		je	lus
tu	lises		tu	lus
il	lise		il	lut
nous	lisions		nous	lûmes
vous	lisiez		vous	lûtes
ils	lisent		ils	lurent

PAST PARTICIPLE
lu

IMPERATIVE
lis
lisons
lisez

PRESENT PARTICIPLE
lisant

AUXILIARY
avoir

Irregular Verbs

mettre (to put)

	PRESENT			IMPERFECT
je	mets		je	mettais
tu	mets		tu	mettais
il	met		il	mettait
nous	mettons		nous	mettions
vous	mettez		vous	mettiez
ils	mettent		ils	mettaient

	FUTURE			CONDITIONAL
je	mettrai		je	mettrais
tu	mettras		tu	mettrais
il	mettra		il	mettrait
nous	mettrons		nous	mettrions
vous	mettrez		vous	mettriez
ils	mettront		ils	mettraient

	PRESENT SUBJUNCTIVE			PAST HISTORIC
je	mette		je	mis
tu	mettes		tu	mis
il	mette		il	mit
nous	mettions		nous	mîmes
vous	mettiez		vous	mîtes
ils	mettent		ils	mirent

PAST PARTICIPLE	IMPERATIVE
mis	mets
	mettons
	mettez

PRESENT PARTICIPLE	AUXILIARY
mettant	avoir

moudre (to grind)

	PRESENT		IMPERFECT
je	mouds	je	moulais
tu	mouds	tu	moulais
il	moud	il	moulait
nous	moulons	nous	moulions
vous	moulez	vous	mouliez
ils	moulent	ils	moulaient

	FUTURE		CONDITIONAL
je	moudrai	je	moudrais
tu	moudras	tu	moudrais
il	moudra	il	moudrait
nous	moudrons	nous	moudrions
vous	moudrez	vous	moudriez
ils	moudront	ils	moudraient

	PRESENT SUBJUNCTIVE		PAST HISTORIC
je	moule	je	moulus
tu	moules	tu	moulus
il	moule	il	moulut
nous	moulions	nous	moulûmes
vous	mouliez	vous	moulûtes
ils	moulent	ils	moulurent

PAST PARTICIPLE
moulu

IMPERATIVE
mouds
moulons
moulez

PRESENT PARTICIPLE
moulant

AUXILIARY
avoir

Irregular Verbs

mourir (to die)

	PRESENT		IMPERFECT
je	meurs	je	mourais
tu	meurs	tu	mourais
il	meurt	il	mourait
nous	mourons	nous	mourions
vous	mourez	vous	mouriez
ils	meurent	ils	mouraient

	FUTURE		CONDITIONAL
je	mourrai	je	mourrais
tu	mourras	tu	mourrais
il	mourra	il	mourrait
nous	mourrons	nous	mourrions
vous	mourrez	vous	mourriez
ils	mourront	ils	mourraient

	PRESENT SUBJUNCTIVE		PAST HISTORIC
je	meure	je	mourus
tu	meures	tu	mourus
il	meure	il	mourut
nous	mourions	nous	mourûmes
vous	mouriez	vous	mourûtes
ils	meurent	ils	moururent

PAST PARTICIPLE	IMPERATIVE
mort	meurs
	mourons
	mourez

PRESENT PARTICIPLE	AUXILIARY
mourant	être

Irregular Verbs

naître (to be born)

	PRESENT		IMPERFECT
je	nais	je	naissais
tu	nais	tu	naissais
il	naît	il	naissait
nous	naissons	nous	naissions
vous	naissez	vous	naissiez
ils	naissent	ils	naissaient

	FUTURE		CONDITIONAL
je	naîtrai	je	naîtrais
tu	naîtras	tu	naîtrais
il	naîtra	il	naîtrait
nous	naîtrons	nous	naîtrions
vous	naîtrez	vous	naîtriez
ils	naîtront	ils	naîtraient

	PRESENT SUBJUNCTIVE		PAST HISTORIC
je	naisse	je	naquis
tu	naisses	tu	naquis
il	naisse	il	naquit
nous	naissions	nous	naquîmes
vous	naissiez	vous	naquîtes
ils	naissent	ils	naquirent

PAST PARTICIPLE	IMPERATIVE
né	nais
	naissons
	naissez

PRESENT PARTICIPLE	AUXILIARY
naissant	être

ouvrir (to open)

	PRESENT		IMPERFECT
	j'ouvre		j'ouvrais
tu	ouvres	tu	ouvrais
il	ouvre	il	ouvrait
nous	ouvrons	nous	ouvrions
vous	ouvrez	vous	ouvriez
ils	ouvrent	ils	ouvraient

	FUTURE		CONDITIONAL
	j'ouvrirai		j'ouvrirais
tu	ouvriras	tu	ouvrirais
il	ouvrira	il	ouvrirait
nous	ouvrirons	nous	ouvririons
vous	ouvrirez	vous	ouvririez
ils	ouvriront	ils	ouvriraient

	PRESENT SUBJUNCTIVE		PAST HISTORIC
	j'ouvre		j'ouvris
tu	ouvres	tu	ouvris
il	ouvre	il	ouvrit
nous	ouvrions	nous	ouvrîmes
vous	ouvriez	vous	ouvrîtes
ils	ouvrent	ils	ouvrirent

PAST PARTICIPLE	IMPERATIVE
ouvert	ouvre
	ouvrons
	ouvrez

PRESENT PARTICIPLE	AUXILIARY
ouvrant	avoir

Note that **offrir** (to offer) and **souffrir** (to suffer) are conjugated similarly

Irregular Verbs

paraître (to appear)

	PRESENT			IMPERFECT
je	parais		je	paraissais
tu	parais		tu	paraissais
il	paraît		il	paraissait
nous	paraissons		nous	paraissions
vous	paraissez		vous	paraissiez
ils	paraissent		ils	paraissaient

	FUTURE			CONDITIONAL
je	paraîtrai		je	paraîtrais
tu	paraîtras		tu	paraîtrais
il	paraîtra		il	paraîtrait
nous	paraîtrons		nous	paraîtrions
vous	paraîtrez		vous	paraîtriez
ils	paraîtront		ils	paraîtraient

	PRESENT SUBJUNCTIVE			PAST HISTORIC
je	paraisse		je	parus
tu	paraisses		tu	parus
il	paraisse		il	parut
nous	paraissions		nous	parûmes
vous	paraissiez		vous	parûtes
ils	paraissent		ils	parurent

PAST PARTICIPLE
paru

IMPERATIVE
parais
paraissons
paraissez

PRESENT PARTICIPLE
paraissant

AUXILIARY
avoir

Irregular Verbs

partir (to leave)

	PRESENT		IMPERFECT
je	pars	je	partais
tu	pars	tu	partais
il	part	il	partait
nous	partons	nous	partions
vous	partez	vous	partiez
ils	partent	ils	partaient

	FUTURE		CONDITIONAL
je	partirai	je	partirais
tu	partiras	tu	partirais
il	partira	il	partirait
nous	partirons	nous	partirions
vous	partirez	vous	partiriez
ils	partiront	ils	partiraient

	PRESENT SUBJUNCTIVE		PAST HISTORIC
je	parte	je	partis
tu	partes	tu	partis
il	parte	il	partit
nous	partions	nous	partîmes
vous	partiez	vous	partîtes
ils	partent	ils	partirent

PAST PARTICIPLE	IMPERATIVE
parti	pars
	partons
	partez

PRESENT PARTICIPLE	AUXILIARY
partant	être

Irregular Verbs

plaire (to please)

	PRESENT			IMPERFECT
je	plais		je	plaisais
tu	plais		tu	plaisais
il	plaît		il	plaisait
nous	plaisons		nous	plaisions
vous	plaisez		vous	plaisiez
ils	plaisent		ils	plaisaient

	FUTURE			CONDITIONAL
je	plairai		je	plairais
tu	plairas		tu	plairais
il	plaira		il	plairait
nous	plairons		nous	plairions
vous	plairez		vous	plairiez
ils	plairont		ils	plairaient

	PRESENT SUBJUNCTIVE			PAST HISTORIC
je	plaise		je	plus
tu	plaises		tu	plus
il	plaise		il	plut
nous	plaisions		nous	plûmes
vous	plaisiez		vous	plûtes
ils	plaisent		ils	plurent

PAST PARTICIPLE	IMPERATIVE
plu	plais
	plaisons
	plaisez

PRESENT PARTICIPLE	AUXILIARY
plaisant	avoir

pleuvoir (to rain)

PRESENT	IMPERFECT
il **pleut**	il **pleuvait**

FUTURE	CONDITIONAL
il **pleuvra**	il **pleuvrait**

PRESENT SUBJUNCTIVE	PAST HISTORIC
il **pleuve**	il **plut**

PAST PARTICIPLE	IMPERATIVE
plu	*not used*

PRESENT PARTICIPLE	AUXILIARY
pleuvant	**avoir**

Irregular Verbs

pouvoir (to be able to)

	PRESENT			IMPERFECT
je	peux*		je	pouvais
tu	peux		tu	pouvais
il	peut		il	pouvait
nous	pouvons		nous	pouvions
vous	pouvez		vous	pouviez
ils	peuvent		ils	pouvaient

	FUTURE			CONDITIONAL
je	pourrai		je	pourrais
tu	pourras		tu	pourrais
il	pourra		il	pourrait
nous	pourrons		nous	pourrions
vous	pourrez		vous	pourriez
ils	pourront		ils	pourraient

	PRESENT SUBJUNCTIVE			PAST HISTORIC
je	puisse		je	pus
tu	puisses		tu	pus
il	puisse		il	put
nous	puissions		nous	pûmes
vous	puissiez		vous	pûtes
ils	puissent		ils	purent

PAST PARTICIPLE	IMPERATIVE
pu	*not used*

PRESENT PARTICIPLE	AUXILIARY
pouvant	avoir

* In questions **puis-je?** is used

prendre (to take)

	PRESENT			IMPERFECT
je	prends		je	prenais
tu	prends		tu	prenais
il	prend		il	prenait
nous	prenons		nous	prenions
vous	prenez		vous	preniez
ils	prennent		ils	prenaient

	FUTURE			CONDITIONAL
je	prendrai		je	prendrais
tu	prendras		tu	prendrais
il	prendra		il	prendrait
nous	prendrons		nous	prendrions
vous	prendrez		vous	prendriez
ils	prendront		ils	prendraient

	PRESENT SUBJUNCTIVE			PAST HISTORIC
je	prenne		je	pris
tu	prennes		tu	pris
il	prenne		il	prit
nous	prenions		nous	prîmes
vous	preniez		vous	prîtes
ils	prennent		ils	prirent

PAST PARTICIPLE	IMPERATIVE
pris	prends
	prenons
	prenez

PRESENT PARTICIPLE	AUXILIARY
prenant	avoir

Irregular Verbs

recevoir (to receive)

	PRESENT			IMPERFECT
je	reçois		je	recevais
tu	reçois		tu	recevais
il	reçoit		il	recevait
nous	recevons		nous	recevions
vous	recevez		vous	receviez
ils	reçoivent		ils	recevaient

	FUTURE			CONDITIONAL
je	recevrai		je	recevrais
tu	recevras		tu	recevrais
il	recevra		il	recevrait
nous	recevrons		nous	recevrions
vous	recevrez		vous	recevriez
ils	recevront		ils	recevraient

	PRESENT SUBJUNCTIVE			PAST HISTORIC
je	reçoive		je	reçus
tu	reçoives		tu	reçus
il	reçoive		il	reçut
nous	recevions		nous	reçûmes
vous	receviez		vous	reçûtes
ils	reçoivent		ils	reçurent

PAST PARTICIPLE
reçu

IMPERATIVE
reçois
recevons
recevez

PRESENT PARTICIPLE
recevant

AUXILIARY
avoir

résoudre (to solve)

	PRESENT			IMPERFECT
je	résous		je	résolvais
tu	résous		tu	résolvais
il	résout		il	résolvait
nous	résolvons		nous	résolvions
vous	résolvez		vous	résolviez
ils	résolvent		ils	résolvaient

	FUTURE			CONDITIONAL
je	résoudrai		je	résoudrais
tu	résoudras		tu	résoudrais
il	résoudra		il	résoudrait
nous	résoudrons		nous	résoudrions
vous	résoudrez		vous	résoudriez
ils	résoudront		ils	résoudraient

	PRESENT SUBJUNCTIVE			PAST HISTORIC
je	résolve		je	résolus
tu	résolves		tu	résolus
il	résolve		il	résolut
nous	résolvions		nous	résolûmes
vous	résolviez		vous	résolûtes
ils	résolvent		ils	résolurent

PAST PARTICIPLE	IMPERATIVE
résolu	résous
	résolvons
	résolvez

PRESENT PARTICIPLE	AUXILIARY
résolvant	avoir

Irregular Verbs

rire (to laugh)

	PRESENT			IMPERFECT
je	ris		je	riais
tu	ris		tu	riais
il	**rit**		il	riait
nous	rions		nous	riions
vous	riez		vous	riiez
ils	rient		ils	riaient

	FUTURE			CONDITIONAL
je	rirai		je	rirais
tu	riras		tu	rirais
il	rira		il	rirait
nous	rirons		nous	ririons
vous	rirez		vous	ririez
ils	riront		ils	riraient

	PRESENT SUBJUNCTIVE			PAST HISTORIC
je	rie		je	**ris**
tu	ries		tu	**ris**
il	rie		il	**rit**
nous	riions		nous	**rîmes**
vous	riiez		vous	**rîtes**
ils	rient		ils	**rirent**

PAST PARTICIPLE
ri

IMPERATIVE
ris
rions
riez

PRESENT PARTICIPLE
riant

AUXILIARY
avoir

rompre (to break)

	PRESENT			IMPERFECT
je	romps		je	rompais
tu	romps		tu	rompais
il	**rompt**		il	rompait
nous	rompons		nous	rompions
vous	rompez		vous	rompiez
ils	rompent		ils	rompaient

	FUTURE			CONDITIONAL
je	romprai		je	romprais
tu	rompras		tu	romprais
il	rompra		il	romprait
nous	romprons		nous	romprions
vous	romprez		vous	rompriez
ils	rompront		ils	rompraient

	PRESENT SUBJUNCTIVE			PAST HISTORIC
je	rompe		je	rompis
tu	rompes		tu	rompis
il	rompe		il	rompit
nous	rompions		nous	rompîmes
vous	rompiez		vous	rompîtes
ils	rompent		ils	rompirent

PAST PARTICIPLE	IMPERATIVE
rompu	romps
	rompons
	rompez

PRESENT PARTICIPLE	AUXILIARY
rompant	**avoir**

Irregular Verbs

savoir (to know)

	PRESENT			IMPERFECT
je	sais		je	savais
tu	sais		tu	savais
il	sait		il	savait
nous	savons		nous	savions
vous	savez		vous	saviez
ils	savent		ils	savaient

	FUTURE			CONDITIONAL
je	saurai		je	saurais
tu	sauras		tu	saurais
il	saura		il	saurait
nous	saurons		nous	saurions
vous	saurez		vous	sauriez
ils	sauront		ils	sauraient

	PRESENT SUBJUNCTIVE			PAST HISTORIC
je	sache		je	sus
tu	saches		tu	sus
il	sache		il	sut
nous	sachions		nous	sûmes
vous	sachiez		vous	sûtes
ils	sachent		ils	surent

PAST PARTICIPLE	IMPERATIVE
su	sache
	sachons
	sachez

PRESENT PARTICIPLE	AUXILIARY
sachant	avoir

sentir (to feel, to smell)

	PRESENT		IMPERFECT
je	sens	je	sentais
tu	sens	tu	sentais
il	sent	il	sentait
nous	sentons	nous	sentions
vous	sentez	vous	sentiez
ils	sentent	ils	sentaient

	FUTURE		CONDITIONAL
je	sentirai	je	sentirais
tu	sentiras	tu	sentirais
il	sentira	il	sentirait
nous	sentirons	nous	sentirions
vous	sentirez	vous	sentiriez
ils	sentiront	ils	sentiraient

	PRESENT SUBJUNCTIVE		PAST HISTORIC
je	sente	je	sentis
tu	sentes	tu	sentis
il	sente	il	sentit
nous	sentions	nous	sentîmes
vous	sentiez	vous	sentîtes
ils	sentent	ils	sentirent

PAST PARTICIPLE	IMPERATIVE
senti	sens
	sentons
	sentez

PRESENT PARTICIPLE	AUXILIARY
sentant	avoir

Irregular Verbs

servir (to serve)

	PRESENT		IMPERFECT
je	sers	je	servais
tu	sers	tu	servais
il	sert	il	servait
nous	servons	nous	servions
vous	servez	vous	serviez
ils	servent	ils	servaient

	FUTURE		CONDITIONAL
je	servirai	je	servirais
tu	serviras	tu	servirais
il	servira	il	servirait
nous	servirons	nous	servirions
vous	servirez	vous	serviriez
ils	serviront	ils	serviraient

	PRESENT SUBJUNCTIVE		PAST HISTORIC
je	serve	je	servis
tu	serves	tu	servis
il	serve	il	servit
nous	servions	nous	servîmes
vous	serviez	vous	servîtes
ils	servent	ils	servirent

PAST PARTICIPLE	IMPERATIVE
servi	sers
	servons
	servez

PRESENT PARTICIPLE	AUXILIARY
servant	avoir

Irregular Verbs

sortir (to go, to come out)

	PRESENT		IMPERFECT
je	sors	je	sortais
tu	sors	tu	sortais
il	sort	il	sortait
nous	sortons	nous	sortions
vous	sortez	vous	sortiez
ils	sortent	ils	sortaient

	FUTURE		CONDITIONAL
je	sortirai	je	sortirais
tu	sortiras	tu	sortirais
il	sortira	il	sortirait
nous	sortirons	nous	sortirions
vous	sortirez	vous	sortiriez
ils	sortiront	ils	sortiraient

	PRESENT SUBJUNCTIVE		PAST HISTORIC
je	sorte	je	sortis
tu	sortes	tu	sortis
il	sorte	il	sortit
nous	sortions	nous	sortîmes
vous	sortiez	vous	sortîtes
ils	sortent	ils	sortirent

PAST PARTICIPLE
sorti

IMPERATIVE
sors
sortons
sortez

PRESENT PARTICIPLE
sortant

AUXILIARY
être

Irregular Verbs

suffire (to be enough)

	PRESENT			IMPERFECT
je	suffis		je	suffisais
tu	suffis		tu	suffisais
il	suffit		il	suffisait
nous	suffisons		nous	suffisions
vous	suffisez		vous	suffisiez
ils	suffisent		ils	suffisaient

	FUTURE			CONDITIONAL
je	suffirai		je	suffirais
tu	suffiras		tu	suffirais
il	suffira		il	suffirait
nous	suffirons		nous	suffirions
vous	suffirez		vous	suffiriez
ils	suffiront		ils	suffiraient

	PRESENT SUBJUNCTIVE			PAST HISTORIC
je	suffise		je	suffis
tu	suffises		tu	suffis
il	suffise		il	suffit
nous	suffisions		nous	suffîmes
vous	suffisiez		vous	suffîtes
ils	suffisent		ils	suffirent

PAST PARTICIPLE
suffi

IMPERATIVE
suffis
suffisons
suffisez

PRESENT PARTICIPLE
suffisant

AUXILIARY
avoir

Irregular Verbs

suivre (to follow)

	PRESENT		IMPERFECT
je	**suis**	je	suivais
tu	**suis**	tu	suivais
il	**suit**	il	suivait
nous	suivons	nous	suivions
vous	suivez	vous	suiviez
ils	suivent	ils	suivaient

	FUTURE		CONDITIONAL
je	suivrai	je	suivrais
tu	suivras	tu	suivrais
il	suivra	il	suivrait
nous	suivrons	nous	suivrions
vous	suivrez	vous	suivriez
ils	suivront	ils	suivraient

	PRESENT SUBJUNCTIVE		PAST HISTORIC
je	suive	je	suivis
tu	suives	tu	suivis
il	suive	il	suivit
nous	suivions	nous	suivîmes
vous	suiviez	vous	suivîtes
ils	suivent	ils	suivirent

PAST PARTICIPLE	IMPERATIVE
suivi	**suis**
	suivons
	suivez

PRESENT PARTICIPLE	AUXILIARY
suivant	**avoir**

Irregular Verbs

se taire (to stop talking)

	PRESENT			IMPERFECT
je	me tais		je	me taisais
tu	te tais		tu	te taisais
il	se tait		il	se taisait
nous	nous taisons		nous	nous taisions
vous	vous taisez		vous	vous taisiez
ils	se taisent		ils	se taisaient

	FUTURE			CONDITIONAL
je	me tairai		je	me tairais
tu	te tairas		tu	te tairais
il	se taira		il	se tairait
nous	nous tairons		nous	nous tairions
vous	vous tairez		vous	vous tairiez
ils	se tairont		ils	se tairaient

	PRESENT SUBJUNCTIVE			PAST HISTORIC
je	me taise		je	me tus
tu	te taises		tu	te tus
il	se taise		il	se tut
nous	nous taisions		nous	nous tûmes
vous	vous taisiez		vous	vous tûtes
ils	se taisent		ils	se turent

PAST PARTICIPLE
tu

IMPERATIVE
tais-toi
taisons-nous
taisez-vous

PRESENT PARTICIPLE
se taisant

AUXILIARY
être

Irregular Verbs

tenir (to hold)

	PRESENT			IMPERFECT
je	tiens		je	tenais
tu	tiens		tu	tenais
il	tient		il	tenait
nous	tenons		nous	tenions
vous	tenez		vous	teniez
ils	tiennent		ils	tenaient

	FUTURE			CONDITIONAL
je	tiendrai		je	tiendrais
tu	tiendras		tu	tiendrais
il	tiendra		il	tiendrait
nous	tiendrons		nous	tiendrions
vous	tiendrez		vous	tiendriez
ils	tiendront		ils	tiendraient

	PRESENT SUBJUNCTIVE			PAST HISTORIC
je	tienne		je	tins
tu	tiennes		tu	tins
il	tienne		il	tint
nous	tenions		nous	tînmes
vous	teniez		vous	tîntes
ils	tiennent		ils	tinrent

PAST PARTICIPLE
tenu

IMPERATIVE
tiens
tenons
tenez

PRESENT PARTICIPLE
tenant

AUXILIARY
avoir

Irregular Verbs

vaincre (to defeat)

	PRESENT		IMPERFECT
je	vaincs	je	vainquais
tu	vaincs	tu	vainquais
il	vainc	il	vainquait
nous	vainquons	nous	vainquions
vous	vainquez	vous	vainquiez
ils	vainquent	ils	vainquaient

	FUTURE		CONDITIONAL
je	vaincrai	je	vaincrais
tu	vaincras	tu	vaincrais
il	vaincra	il	vaincrait
nous	vaincrons	nous	vaincrions
vous	vaincrez	vous	vaincriez
ils	vaincront	ils	vaincraient

	PRESENT SUBJUNCTIVE		PAST HISTORIC
je	vainque	je	vainquis
tu	vainques	tu	vainquis
il	vainque	il	vainquit
nous	vainquions	nous	vainquîmes
vous	vainquiez	vous	vainquîtes
ils	vainquent	ils	vainquirent

PAST PARTICIPLE
vaincu

IMPERATIVE
vaincs
vainquons
vainquez

PRESENT PARTICIPLE
vainquant

AUXILIARY
avoir

Irregular Verbs

valoir (to be worth)

	PRESENT		IMPERFECT
je	vaux	je	valais
tu	vaux	tu	valais
il	vaut	il	valait
nous	valons	nous	valions
vous	valez	vous	valiez
ils	valent	ils	valaient

	FUTURE		CONDITIONAL
je	vaudrai	je	vaudrais
tu	vaudras	tu	vaudrais
il	vaudra	il	vaudrait
nous	vaudrons	nous	vaudrions
vous	vaudrez	vous	vaudriez
ils	vaudront	ils	vaudraient

	PRESENT SUBJUNCTIVE		PAST HISTORIC
je	vaille	je	valus
tu	vailles	tu	valus
il	vaille	il	valut
nous	valions	nous	valûmes
vous	valiez	vous	valûtes
ils	vaillent	ils	valurent

PAST PARTICIPLE
valu

IMPERATIVE
vaux
valons
valez

PRESENT PARTICIPLE
valant

AUXILIARY
avoir

Irregular Verbs

venir (to come)

	PRESENT			IMPERFECT
je	viens		je	venais
tu	viens		tu	venais
il	vient		il	venait
nous	venons		nous	venions
vous	venez		vous	veniez
ils	viennent		ils	venaient

	FUTURE			CONDITIONAL
je	viendrai		je	viendrais
tu	viendras		tu	viendrais
il	viendra		il	viendrait
nous	viendrons		nous	viendrions
vous	viendrez		vous	viendriez
ils	viendront		ils	viendraient

	PRESENT SUBJUNCTIVE			PAST HISTORIC
je	vienne		je	vins
tu	viennes		tu	vins
il	vienne		il	vint
nous	venions		nous	vînmes
vous	veniez		vous	vîntes
ils	viennent		ils	vinrent

PAST PARTICIPLE
venu

IMPERATIVE
viens
venons
venez

PRESENT PARTICIPLE
venant

AUXILIARY
être

Irregular Verbs

vêtir (to dress)

	PRESENT			IMPERFECT
je	vêts		je	vêtais
tu	vêts		tu	vêtais
il	vêt		il	vêtait
nous	vêtons		nous	vêtions
vous	vêtez		vous	vêtiez
ils	vêtent		ils	vêtaient

	FUTURE			CONDITIONAL
je	vêtirai		je	vêtirais
tu	vêtiras		tu	vêtirais
il	vêtira		il	vêtirait
nous	vêtirons		nous	vêtirions
vous	vêtirez		vous	vêtiriez
ils	vêtiront		ils	vêtiraient

	PRESENT SUBJUNCTIVE			PAST HISTORIC
je	vête		je	vêtis
tu	vêtes		tu	vêtis
il	vête		il	vêtit
nous	vêtions		nous	vêtîmes
vous	vêtiez		vous	vêtîtes
ils	vêtent		ils	vêtirent

PAST PARTICIPLE
vêtu

IMPERATIVE
vêts
vêtons
vêtez

PRESENT PARTICIPLE
vêtant

AUXILIARY
avoir

Irregular Verbs

vivre (to live)

	PRESENT			IMPERFECT
je	**vis**		je	vivais
tu	**vis**		tu	vivais
il	**vit**		il	vivait
nous	vivons		nous	vivions
vous	vivez		vous	viviez
ils	vivent		ils	vivaient

	FUTURE			CONDITIONAL
je	vivrai		je	vivrais
tu	vivras		tu	vivrais
il	vivra		il	vivrait
nous	vivrons		nous	vivrions
vous	vivrez		vous	vivriez
ils	vivront		ils	vivraient

	PRESENT SUBJUNCTIVE			PAST HISTORIC
je	vive		je	**vécus**
tu	vives		tu	**vécus**
il	vive		il	**vécut**
nous	vivions		nous	**vécûmes**
vous	viviez		vous	**vécûtes**
ils	vivent		ils	**vécurent**

PAST PARTICIPLE
vécu

IMPERATIVE
vis
vivons
vivez

PRESENT PARTICIPLE
vivant

AUXILIARY
avoir

Irregular Verbs

voir (to see)

	PRESENT		IMPERFECT
je	vois	je	voyais
tu	vois	tu	voyais
il	voit	il	voyait
nous	voyons	nous	voyions
vous	voyez	vous	voyiez
ils	voient	ils	voyaient

	FUTURE		CONDITIONAL
je	verrai	je	verrais
tu	verras	tu	verrais
il	verra	il	verrait
nous	verrons	nous	verrions
vous	verrez	vous	verriez
ils	verront	ils	verraient

	PRESENT SUBJUNCTIVE		PAST HISTORIC
je	voie	je	vis
tu	voies	tu	vis
il	voie	il	vit
nous	voyions	nous	vîmes
vous	voyiez	vous	vîtes
ils	voient	ils	virent

PAST PARTICIPLE
vu

IMPERATIVE
vois
voyons
voyez

PRESENT PARTICIPLE
voyant

AUXILIARY
avoir

vouloir (to wish, to want)

	PRESENT		IMPERFECT
je	veux	je	voulais
tu	veux	tu	voulais
il	veut	il	voulait
nous	voulons	nous	voulions
vous	voulez	vous	vouliez
ils	veulent	ils	voulaient

	FUTURE		CONDITIONAL
je	voudrai	je	voudrais
tu	voudras	tu	voudrais
il	voudra	il	voudrait
nous	voudrons	nous	voudrions
vous	voudrez	vous	voudriez
ils	voudront	ils	voudraient

	PRESENT SUBJUNCTIVE		PAST HISTORIC
je	veuille	je	voulus
tu	veuilles	tu	voulus
il	veuille	il	voulut
nous	voulions	nous	voulûmes
vous	vouliez	vous	voulûtes
ils	veuillent	ils	voulurent

PAST PARTICIPLE
voulu

IMPERATIVE
veuille
veuillons
veuillez

PRESENT PARTICIPLE
voulant

AUXILIARY
avoir

Nouns

The Gender of Nouns

In French, all nouns are either masculine or feminine, whether denoting people, animals or things. Unlike English, there is no neuter gender for inanimate objects and abstract nouns.

Gender is largely unpredictable and has to be learnt for each noun. However, the following guidelines will help you determine the gender for certain types of nouns:

Nouns denoting male people and animals are usually – but not always – masculine, e.g.

un homme a man
un taureau a bull
un infirmier a (*male*) nurse
un cheval a horse

Nouns denoting female people and animals are usually – but not always – feminine, e.g.

une fille a girl
une vache a cow
une infirmière a nurse
une brebis a ewe

Some nouns are masculine *or* feminine depending on the sex of the person to whom they refer, e.g.

un camarade a (*male*) friend
une camarade a (*female*) friend
un Belge a Belgian (*man*)
une Belge a Belgian (*woman*)

Other nouns referring to either men or women have only one gender which applies to both, e.g.

un professeur a teacher
une personne a person
une sentinelle a sentry
un témoin a witness
une victime a victim
une recrue a recruit

Nouns

Sometimes the ending of the noun indicates its gender. Shown below are some of the most important to guide you:

Masculine endings

-age	**le courage** courage; **le rinçage** rinsing EXCEPTIONS: **une cage** a cage; **une image** a picture; **la nage** swimming; **une page** a page; **une plage** a beach; **une rage** a rage
-ment	**le commencement** the beginning EXCEPTION: **une jument** a mare
-oir	**un couloir** a corridor; **un miroir** a mirror
-sme	**le pessimisme** pessimism; **l'enthousiasme** enthusiasm

Feminine endings

-ance, -anse	**la confiance** confidence; **la danse** dancing
-ence, -ense	**la prudence** caution; **la défense** defence EXCEPTION: **le silence** silence
-ion	**une région** a region; **une addition** a bill EXCEPTIONS: **un pion** a pawn; **un espion** a spy
-oire	**une baignoire** a bath(tub)
-té, -tié	**la beauté** beauty; **la moitié** half

Suffixes which differentiate between male and female are shown on pages 134 and 136.

The following words have different meanings depending on gender:

le crêpe crêpe	**la crêpe** pancake
le livre book	**la livre** pound
le manche handle	**la manche** sleeve
le mode method	**la mode** fashion
le moule mould	**la moule** mussel
le page page(boy)	**la page** page (*in book*)
le physique physique	**la physique** physics
le poêle stove	**la poêle** frying pan
le somme nap	**la somme** sum
le tour turn	**la tour** tower
le voile veil	**la voile** sail

Nouns

Gender: the Formation of Feminines

As in English, male and female are sometimes differentiated by the use of two quite separate words, e.g.

> **mon oncle** my uncle
> **ma tante** my aunt
> **un taureau** a bull
> **une vache** a cow

There are, however, some words in French which show this distinction by the form of their ending:

> Some nouns add an **e** to the masculine singular form to form the feminine → **1**

> If the masculine singular form already ends in **-e**, no further **e** is added in the feminine → **2**

> Some nouns undergo a further change when **e** is added. These changes occur regularly and are shown on page 136.

Feminine forms to note

MASCULINE	FEMININE	
un âne	une ânesse	donkey
le comte	la comtesse	count/countess
le duc	la duchesse	duke/duchess
un Esquimau	une Esquimaude	Eskimo
le fou	la folle	madman/madwoman
le Grec	la Grecque	Greek
un hôte	une hôtesse	host/hostess
le jumeau	la jumelle	twin
le maître	la maîtresse	master/mistress
le prince	la princesse	prince/princess
le tigre	la tigresse	tiger/tigress
le traître	la traîtresse	traitor
le Turc	la Turque	Turk
le vieux	la vieille	old man/old woman

1 un ami   a (*male*) friend
une amie   a (*female*) friend
un employé   a (*male*) employee
une employée   a (*female*) employee
un Français   a Frenchman
une Française   a Frenchwoman

2 un élève   a (*male*) pupil
une élève   a (*female*) pupil
un collègue   a (*male*) colleague
une collègue   a (*female*) colleague
un camarade   a (*male*) friend
une camarade   a (*female*) friend

Nouns

Regular feminine endings

The following are regular feminine endings:

MASC. SING.	FEM. SING.
-f	-ve → ①
-x	-se → ②
-eur	-euse → ③
-teur	-teuse → ④
	-trice → ⑤

Some nouns double the final consonant before adding **e**:

MASC. SING.	FEM. SING.
-an	-anne → ⑥
-en	-enne → ⑦
-on	-onne → ⑧
-et	-ette → ⑨
-el	-elle → ⑩

Some nouns add an accent to the final syllable before adding **e**:

MASC. SING.	FEM. SING.
-er	-ère → ⑪

Pronunciation and feminine endings

This is dealt with on page 244.

1. un sportif a sportsman   une sportive a sportswoman
   un veuf a widower   une veuve a widow

2. un époux a husband   une épouse a wife
   un amoureux a man in love   une amoureuse a woman in love

3. un danseur a dancer   une danseuse a dancer
   un voleur a thief   une voleuse a thief

4. un menteur a liar   une menteuse a liar
   un chanteur a singer   une chanteuse a singer

5. un acteur an actor   une actrice an actress
   un conducteur a driver   une conductrice a driver

6. un paysan a countryman   une paysanne a countrywoman

7. un Parisien a Parisian (*man*)   une Parisienne a Parisian (*woman*)

8. un baron a baron   une baronne a baroness

9. le cadet the youngest (child)   la cadette the youngest (child)

10. un intellectuel an intellectual   une intellectuelle an intellectual

11. un étranger a foreigner   une étrangère a foreigner
    le dernier the last (one)   la dernière the last (one)

Nouns

The Formation of Plurals

Most nouns add **s** to the singular form → **①**

When the singular form already ends in **-s**, **-x** or **-z**, no further **s** is added → **②**

For nouns ending in **-au**, **-eau** or **-eu**, the plural ends in **-aux**, **-eaux** or **-eux** → **③**

EXCEPTIONS: **pneu** tyre   (*plural*: **pneus**)
bleu bruise   (*plural*: **bleus**)

For nouns ending in **-al** or **-ail**, the plural ends in **-aux** → **④**

EXCEPTIONS: **bal** ball   (*plural*: **bals**)
festival festival   (*plural*: **festivals**)
chandail sweater   (*plural*: **chandails**)
détail detail   (*plural*: **détails**)

Forming the plural of compound nouns is complicated and you are advised to check each one individually in a dictionary.

Irregular plural forms

Some masculine nouns ending in **-ou** add **x** in the plural. These are:

bijou jewel   **genou** knee   **joujou** toy
caillou pebble   **hibou** owl   **pou** louse
chou cabbage

Some other nouns are totally unpredictable. The most important of these are:

SINGULAR		PLURAL
œil	eye	**yeux**
ciel	sky	**cieux**
Monsieur	Mr	**Messieurs**
Madame	Mrs	**Mesdames**
Mademoiselle	Miss	**Mesdemoiselles**

Pronunciation of plural forms

This is dealt with on page 244.

1

le jardin	the garden
les jardins	the gardens
une voiture	a car
des voitures	(some) cars
l'hôtel	the hotel
les hôtels	the hotels

2

un bois	a wood
des bois	(some) woods
une voix	a voice
des voix	(some) voices
le gaz	the gas
les gaz	the gases

3

un tuyau	a pipe
des tuyaux	(some) pipes
le chapeau	the hat
les chapeaux	the hats
le feu	the fire
les feux	the fires

4

le journal	the newspaper
les journaux	the newspapers
un travail	a job
des travaux	(some) jobs

Articles

The Definite Article

le (l')/la (l'), les

	WITH MASC. NOUN	WITH FEM. NOUN	
SING.	**le (l')**	**la (l')**	the
PLUR.	**les**	**les**	the

The gender and number of the noun determines the form of the article → ❶

le and **la** change to **l'** before a vowel or an **h** 'mute' → ❷

For uses of the definite article see page 142.

à + le/la (l'), à + les

	WITH MASC. NOUN	WITH FEM. NOUN
SING.	**au (à l')**	**à la (à l')**
PLUR.	**aux**	**aux**

The definite article combines with the preposition **à**, as shown above. You should pay particular attention to the masculine singular form **au**, and both plural forms **aux**, since these are not visually the sum of their parts → ❸

de + le/la (l'), de + les

	WITH MASC. NOUN	WITH FEM. NOUN
SING.	**du (de l')**	**de la (de l')**
PLUR.	**des**	**des**

The definite article combines with the preposition **de**, as shown above. You should pay particular attention to the masculine singular form **du**, and both plural forms **des**, since these are not visually the sum of their parts → ❹

MASCULINE	FEMININE
1 le train the train	la gare the station
le garçon the boy	la fille the girl
les hôtels the hotels	les écoles the schools
les professeurs the teachers	les femmes the women
2 l'acteur the actor	l'actrice the actress
l'effet the effect	l'eau the water
l'ingrédient the ingredient	l'idée the idea
l'objet the object	l'ombre the shadow
l'univers the universe	l'usine the factory
l'hôpital the hospital	l'heure the time
3 au cinéma at/to the cinema	à la bibliothèque at/to the library
à l'employé to the employee	à l'infirmière to the nurse
à l'hôpital at/to the hospital	à l'hôtesse to the hostess
aux étudiants to the students	aux maisons to the houses
4 du bureau from/of the office	de la réunion from/of the meeting
de l'auteur from/of the author	de l'Italienne from/of the Italian woman
de l'hôte from/of the host	de l'horloge of the clock
des États-Unis from/of the United States	des vendeuses from/of the saleswomen

Articles

Uses of the Definite Article

While the definite article is used in much the same way in French as it is in English, its use is more widespread in French. Unlike English the definite article is also used:

with abstract nouns, except when following certain prepositions → ①

in generalizations, especially with plural or uncountable* nouns → ②

with names of countries → ③
EXCEPTIONS: no article with countries following **en** to/in → ④

with parts of the body → ⑤
'Ownership' is often indicated by an indirect object pronoun or a reflexive pronoun → ⑥

in expressions of quantity/rate/price → ⑦

with titles/ranks/professions followed by a proper name → ⑧

The definite article is *not* used with nouns in apposition → ⑨

---

* An uncountable noun is one which cannot be used in the plural or with an indefinite article, e.g. **l'acier** steel; **le lait** milk.

1. Les prix montent — Prices are rising
   L'amour rayonne dans ses yeux — Love shines in his eyes
   BUT:
   avec plaisir — with pleasure
   sans espoir — without hope

2. Je n'aime pas le café — I don't like coffee
   Les enfants ont besoin d'être aimés — Children need to be loved

3. le Japon — Japan
   la France — France
   l'Italie — Italy
   les Pays-Bas — The Netherlands

4. aller en Écosse — to go to Scotland
   Il travaille en Allemagne — He works in Germany

5. Tournez la tête à gauche — Turn your head to the left
   J'ai mal à la gorge — My throat is sore, I have a sore throat

6. La tête me tourne — My head is spinning
   Elle s'est brossé les dents — She brushed her teeth

7. 4 euros le mètre/le kilo/la douzaine/la pièce — 4 euros a metre/a kilo/a dozen/each
   rouler à 80 km à l'heure — to go at 50 mph
   payé à l'heure/au jour/au mois — paid by the hour/by the day/by the month

8. le roi Georges III — King George III
   le capitaine Darbeau — Captain Darbeau
   le docteur Rousseau — Dr Rousseau
   Monsieur le président — Mr Chairman/President

9. Victor Hugo, grand écrivain du dix-neuvième siècle — Victor Hugo, a great author of the nineteenth century
   Joseph Leblanc, inventeur et entrepreneur, a été le premier ... — Joseph Leblanc, an inventor and entrepreneur, was the first ...

Articles

The Partitive Article

The partitive article has the sense of 'some' or 'any', although the French is not always translated in English.

Forms of the partitive

du (de l')/de la (de l'), des

	WITH MASC. NOUN	WITH FEM. NOUN	
SING.	du (de l')	de la (de l')	some, any
PLUR.	des	des	some, any

The gender and number of the noun determines the form of the partitive → ❶

The forms shown in brackets (**de l'**) are used before a vowel or an **h** 'mute' → ❷

des becomes **de** (**d'** + *vowel*) before an adjective → ❸
EXCEPTION: if the adjective and noun are seen as forming one unit → ❹

In negative sentences **de** (**d'** + *vowel*) is used for both genders, singular and plural → ❺
EXCEPTION: after **ne ... que** 'only', the positive forms above are used → ❻

1. Avez-vous du sucre? — Have you any sugar?
   J'ai acheté de la farine et de la margarine — I bought (some) flour and margarine
   Il a mangé des gâteaux — He ate some cakes
   Est-ce qu'il y a des lettres pour moi? — Are there (any) letters for me?

2. Il me doit de l'argent — He owes me (some) money
   C'est de l'histoire ancienne — That's ancient history

3. Il a fait de gros efforts pour nous aider — He made a great effort to help us
   Cette région a de belles églises — This region has some beautiful churches

4. des grandes vacances — summer holidays
   des jeunes gens — young people

5. Je n'ai pas de nourriture/d'argent — I don't have any food/money
   Vous n'avez pas de timbres/d'œufs? — Have you no stamps/eggs?
   Je ne mange jamais de viande/d'omelettes — I never eat meat/omelettes
   Il ne veut plus de visiteurs/d'eau — He doesn't want any more visitors/water

6. Il ne boit que du thé/de la bière/de l'eau — He only drinks tea/beer/water
   Je n'ai que des problèmes avec cette machine — I have nothing but trouble with this machine

Articles

The Indefinite Article

un/une, des

	WITH MASC. NOUN	WITH FEM. NOUN	
SING.	**un**	**une**	a
PLUR.	**des**	**des**	some

> **des** is also the plural of the partitive article (see page 144).
>
> In negative sentences, **de** (**d'** + *vowel*) is used for both singular and plural → ❶
>
> The indefinite article is used in French largely as it is in English *except*:
>
> > there is no article when a person's profession is being stated → ❷
> > EXCEPTION: the article *is* present following **ce** (**c'** + *vowel*) → ❸
> >
> > the English article is not translated by **un/une** in constructions like 'what a surprise', 'what an idiot' → ❹
> >
> > in structures of the type given in example ❺ the article **un/une** is used in French and not translated in English → ❺

1. Je n'ai pas de livre/d'enfants — I don't have a book/(any) children

2. Il est professeur — He's a teacher
   Ma mère est infirmière — My mother's a nurse

3. C'est un médecin — He's/She's a doctor
   Ce sont des acteurs — They're actors

4. Quelle surprise! — What a surprise!
   Quel dommage! — What a shame!

5. avec une grande sagesse/un courage admirable — with great wisdom /admirable courage
   Il a fait preuve d'un sang-froid incroyable — He showed incredible calmness
   un produit d'une qualité incomparable — a product of incomparable quality

Adjectives

Adjectives

Most adjectives agree in number and in gender with the noun or pronoun.

The formation of feminines

Most adjectives add an **e** to the masculine singular form → **❶**

If the masculine singular form already ends in **-e**, no further **e** is added → **❷**

Some adjectives undergo a further change when **e** is added. These changes occur regularly and are shown on page 150.

Irregular feminine forms are shown on page 152.

The formation of plurals

The plural of both regular and irregular adjectives is formed by adding an **s** to the masculine or feminine singular form, as appropriate → **❸**

When the masculine singular form already ends in **-s** or **-x**, no further **s** is added → **❹**

For masculine singulars ending in **-au** and **-eau**, the masculine plural is **-aux** and **-eaux** → **❺**

For masculine singulars ending in **-al**, the masculine plural is **-aux** → **❻**
EXCEPTIONS: **final**   (*masculine plural* **finals**)
                    fatal   (*masculine plural* **fatals**)
                    naval   (*masculine plural* **navals**)

Pronunciation of feminine and plural adjectives

This is dealt with on page 244.

1. mon frère aîné — my elder brother
ma sœur aînée — my elder sister
le petit garçon — the little boy
la petite fille — the little girl
un sac gris — a grey bag
une chemise grise — a grey shirt
un bruit fort — a loud noise
une voix forte — a loud voice

2. un jeune homme — a young man
une jeune femme — a young woman
l'autre verre — the other glass
l'autre assiette — the other plate

3. le dernier train — the last train
les derniers trains — the last trains
une vieille maison — an old house
de vieilles maisons — old houses
un long voyage — a long journey
de longs voyages — long journeys
la rue étroite — the narrow street
les rues étroites — the narrow streets

4. un diplomate français — a French diplomat
des diplomates français — French diplomats
un homme dangereux — a dangerous man
des hommes dangereux — dangerous men

5. le nouveau professeur — the new teacher
les nouveaux professeurs — the new teachers
un chien esquimau — a husky (*literally*: an Eskimo dog)
des chiens esquimaux — huskies (*literally*: Eskimo dogs)

6. un ami loyal — a loyal friend
des amis loyaux — loyal friends
un geste amical — a friendly gesture
des gestes amicaux — friendly gestures

Adjectives

Regular feminine endings

MASC SING.	FEM. SING.	EXAMPLES
-f	-ve	neuf, vif → ❶
-x	-se	heureux, jaloux → ❷
-eur	-euse	travailleur, flâneur → ❸
-teur	-teuse	flatteur, menteur → ❹
	-trice	destructeur, séducteur → ❺

EXCEPTIONS: **bref**: see page 152
doux, faux, roux, vieux: see page 152
extérieur, inférieur, intérieur, meilleur, supérieur:
all add **e** to the masculine
enchanteur: *fem.* = **enchanteresse**

MASC SING.	FEM. SING.	EXAMPLES
-an	-anne	paysan → ❻
-en	-enne	ancien, parisien → ❼
-on	-onne	bon, breton → ❽
-as	-asse	bas, las → ❾
-et*	-ette	muet, violet → ❿
-el	-elle	annuel, mortel → ⓫
-eil	-eille	pareil, vermeil → ⓬

EXCEPTION: **ras**: *fem.* = **rase**

MASC SING.	FEM. SING.	EXAMPLES
-et*	-ète	secret, complet → ⓭
-er	-ète	étranger, fier → ⓮

* Note that there are two feminine endings for masculine adjectives
ending in **-et**.

1. un résultat positif — a positive result
   une attitude positive — a positive attitude

2. d'un ton sérieux — in a serious tone (of voice)
   une voix sérieuse — a serious voice

3. un enfant trompeur — a deceitful child
   une déclaration trompeuse — a misleading statement

4. un tableau flatteur — a flattering picture
   une comparaison flatteuse — a flattering comparison

5. un geste protecteur — a protective gesture
   une couche protectrice — a protective layer

6. un problème paysan — a farming problem
   la vie paysanne — country life

7. un avion égyptien — an Egyptian plane
   une statue égyptienne — an Egyptian statue

8. un bon repas — a good meal
   de bonne humeur — in a good mood

9. un plafond bas — a low ceiling
   à voix basse — in a low voice

10. un travail net — a clean piece of work
    une explication nette — a clear explanation

11. un homme cruel — a cruel man
    une remarque cruelle — a cruel remark

12. un livre pareil — such a book
    en pareille occasion — on such an occasion

13. un regard inquiet — an anxious look
    une attente inquiète — an anxious wait

14. un goût amer — a bitter taste
    une amère déception — a bitter disappointment

Adjectives

Adjectives with irregular feminine forms

MASC SING.	FEM. SING.	
aigu	aiguë	sharp; high-pitched → ❶
ambigu	ambiguë	ambiguous
beau (bel*)	belle	beautiful
bénin	bénigne	benign
blanc	blanche	white
bref	brève	brief, short → ❷
doux	douce	soft; sweet
épais	épaisse	thick
esquimau	esquimaude	Eskimo
faux	fausse	wrong
favori	favorite	favourite → ❸
fou (fol*)	folle	mad
frais	fraîche	fresh → ❹
franc	franche	frank
gentil	gentille	kind
grec	grecque	Greek
gros	grosse	big
jumeau	jumelle	twin → ❺
long	longue	long
malin	maligne	malignant
mou (mol*)	molle	soft
nouveau (nouvel*)	nouvelle	new
nul	nulle	no
public	publique	public → ❻
roux	rousse	red-haired
sec	sèche	dry
sot	sotte	foolish
turc	turque	Turkish
vieux (vieil*)	vieille	old

* This form is used when the following word begins with a vowel or an **h** 'mute' → ❼

1. un son aigu — a high-pitched sound
   une douleur aiguë — a sharp pain

2. un bref discours — a short speech
   une brève rencontre — a short meeting

3. mon sport favori — my favourite sport
   ma chanson favorite — my favourite song

4. du pain frais — fresh bread
   de la crème fraîche — fresh cream

5. mon frère jumeau — my twin brother
   ma sœur jumelle — my twin sister

6. un jardin public — a (public) park
   l'opinion publique — public opinion

7. un bel appartement — a beautiful flat
   le nouvel ordinateur — the new computer
   un vieil arbre — an old tree
   un bel habit — a beautiful outfit
   un nouvel harmonica — a new harmonica
   un vieil hôtel — an old hotel

Adjectives

Comparatives and Superlatives

Comparatives

These are formed using the following constructions:

        plus ... (que) more ... (than) → ❶
        moins ... (que) less ... (than) → ❷
        aussi ... que as ... as → ❸
        si ... que* as ... as → ❹

* used mainly after a negative

Superlatives

These are formed using the following constructions:

        le/la/les plus ... (que) the most ... (that) → ❺
        le/la/les moins ... (que) the least ... (that) → ❻

When the possessive adjective is present, two constructions are possible → ❼

After a superlative the preposition **de** is often translated as 'in' → ❽

If a clause follows a superlative, the verb is in the subjunctive → ❾

Adjectives with irregular comparatives/superlatives

ADJECTIVE	COMPARATIVE	SUPERLATIVE
bon	**meilleur**	**le meilleur**
good	better	the best
mauvais	**pire** *or* **plus mauvais**	**le pire** *or* **le plus mauvais**
bad	worse	the worst
petit	**moindre*** *or* **plus petit**	**le moindre*** *or* **le plus petit**
small	smaller; lesser	the smallest; the least

* used only with abstract nouns

Comparative and superlative adjectives agree in number and in gender with the noun, just like any other adjective → ❿

1. une raison plus grave — a more serious reason
   Elle est plus petite que moi — She is smaller than me

2. un film moins connu — a less well-known film
   C'est moins cher qu'il ne pense — It's cheaper than he thinks

3. Robert était aussi inquiet que moi — Robert was as worried as I was
   Cette ville n'est pas aussi grande que Bordeaux — This town isn't as big as Bordeaux

4. Ils ne sont pas si contents que ça — They aren't as happy as all that

5. le guide le plus utile — the most useful guidebook
   la voiture la plus petite — the smallest car
   les plus grandes maisons — the biggest houses

6. le mois le moins agréable — the least pleasant month
   la fille la moins forte — the weakest girl
   les peintures les moins chères — the least expensive paintings

7. Mon désir le plus cher est de voyager — My dearest wish is to travel
   Mon plus cher désir est de voyager

8. la plus grande gare de Londres — the biggest station in London
   l'habitant le plus âgé du village/ de la région — the oldest inhabitant in the village/in the area

9. la personne la plus gentille que je connaisse — the nicest person I know

10. les moindres difficultés — the least difficulties
    la meilleure qualité — the best quality

Adjectives

Demonstrative Adjectives

ce (cet)/cette, ces

	MASCULINE	FEMININE	
SING.	ce (cet)	cette	this; that
PLUR.	ces	ces	these; those

Demonstrative adjectives agree in number and gender with the noun → ❶

cet is used when the following word begins with a vowel or an **h** 'mute' → ❷

For emphasis or in order to distinguish between people or objects, **-ci** or **-là** is added to the noun: **-ci** indicates proximity (usually translated 'this') and **là** distance 'that' → ❸

1 Ce stylo ne marche pas — This/That pen isn't working

Comment s'appelle cette entreprise? — What's this/that company called?

Ces livres sont les miens — These/Those books are mine

Ces couleurs sont plus jolies — These/Those colours are nicer

2 cet oiseau — this/that bird

cet article — this/that article

cet homme — this/that man

3 Combien coûte ce manteau-ci? — How much is this coat?

Je voudrais cinq de ces pommes-là — I'd like five of those apples

Est-ce que tu reconnais cette personne-là? — Do you recognize that person?

Mettez ces vêtements-ci dans cette valise-là — Put these clothes in that case

Ce garçon-là appartient à ce groupe-ci — That boy belongs to this group

Adjectives

Interrogative Adjectives

quel/quelle, quels/quelles?

	MASCULINE	FEMININE	
SING.	**quel?**	**quelle?**	what?; which?
PLUR.	**quels?**	**quelles?**	what?; which?

Interrogative adjectives agree in number and gender with the noun → ❶

The forms shown above are also used in indirect questions → ❷

Exclamatory Adjectives

quel/quelle, quels/quelles!

	MASCULINE	FEMININE	
SING.	**quel!**	**quelle!**	what (a)!
PLUR.	**quels!**	**quelles!**	what!

Exclamatory adjectives agree in number and gender with the noun → ❸

For other exclamations, see page 214.

1. Quel genre d'homme est-ce? — What type of man is he?
Quelle est leur décision? — What is their decision?
Vous jouez de quels instruments? — What instruments do you play?
Quelles offres avez-vous reçues? — What offers have you received?
Quel vin recommandez-vous? — Which wine do you recommend?
Quelles couleurs préférez-vous? — Which colours do you prefer?

2. Je ne sais pas à quelle heure il est arrivé — I don't know what time he arrived
Dites-moi quels sont les livres les plus chers — Tell me which books are the most expensive

3. Quel dommage! — What a pity!
Quelle idée! — What an idea!
Quels livres intéressants vous avez! — What interesting books you have!
Quelles jolies fleurs! — What nice flowers!

Adjectives

Possessive Adjectives

| WITH SING. NOUN | | WITH PLUR. NOUN | |
MASC.	FEM.	MASC./FEM.	
mon	ma (mon)	mes	my
ton	ta (ton)	tes	your
son	sa (son)	ses	his; her; its
notre	notre	nos	our
votre	votre	vos	your
leur	leur	leurs	their

Possessive adjectives agree in number and gender with the noun, not with the owner → ❶

The forms shown in brackets are used when the following word begins with a vowel or an **h** 'mute' → ❷

son, **sa**, **ses** have the additional meaning of 'one's' → ❸

1. Catherine a oublié son parapluie — Catherine has left her umbrella
   Paul cherche sa montre — Paul's looking for his watch
   Mon frère et ma sœur habitent à Glasgow — My brother and sister live in Glasgow
   Est-ce que tes voisins ont vendu leur voiture? — Did your neighbours sell their car?
   Rangez vos affaires — Put your things away

2. mon appareil-photo — my camera
   ton histoire — your story
   son erreur — his/her mistake
   mon autre sœur — my other sister

3. perdre son équilibre — to lose one's balance
   présenter ses excuses — to offer one's apologies

Adjectives

Position of Adjectives

French adjectives usually follow the noun → ❶

Adjectives of colour or nationality *always* follow the noun → ❷

As in English, demonstrative, possessive, numerical and interrogative adjectives precede the noun → ❸

The adjectives **autre** (other) and **chaque** (each, every) precede the noun → ❹

The following common adjectives can precede the noun:

beau beautiful	**jeune** young
bon good	**joli** pretty
court short	**long** long
dernier last	**mauvais** bad
grand great	**petit** small
gros big	**tel** such (a)
haut high	**vieux** old

The meaning of the following adjectives varies according to their position:

	BEFORE NOUN	AFTER NOUN
ancien	former	old, ancient → ❺
brave	good	brave → ❻
cher	dear (*beloved*)	expensive → ❼
grand	great	tall → ❽
même	same	very → ❾
pauvre	poor (*wretched*)	poor (*not rich*) → ❿
propre	own	clean → ⓫
seul	single, sole	on one's own → ⓬
simple	mere, simple	simple, easy → ⓭
vrai	real	true → ⓮

Adjectives following the noun are linked by **et** → ⓯

①	le chapitre suivant	the following chapter
	l'heure exacte	the right time
②	une cravate rouge	a red tie
	un mot français	a French word
③	ce dictionnaire	this dictionary
	mon père	my father
	le premier étage	the first floor
	deux exemples	two examples
	quel homme?	which man?
④	une autre fois	another time
	chaque jour	every day
⑤	un ancien collègue	a former colleague
	l'histoire ancienne	ancient history
⑥	un brave homme	a good man
	un homme brave	a brave man
⑦	mes chers amis	my dear friends
	une robe chère	an expensive dress
⑧	un grand peintre	a great painter
	un homme grand	a tall man
⑨	la même réponse	the same answer
	vos paroles mêmes	your very words
⑩	cette pauvre femme	that poor woman
	une nation pauvre	a poor nation
⑪	ma propre vie	my own life
	une chemise propre	a clean shirt
⑫	une seule réponse	a single reply
	une femme seule	a woman on her own
⑬	un simple regard	a mere look
	un problème simple	a simple problem
⑭	la vraie raison	the real reason
	les faits vrais	the true facts
⑮	un acte lâche et trompeur	a cowardly, deceitful act
	un acte lâche, trompeur et ignoble	a cowardly, deceitful and ignoble act

Pronouns

Personal Pronouns

	SUBJECT PRONOUNS	
	SINGULAR	PLURAL
1st person	**je (j')** I	**nous** we
2nd person	**tu** you	**vous** you
3rd person (*masc.*)	**il** he; it	**ils** they
(*fem.*)	**elle** she; it	**elles** they

je changes to **j'** before a vowel, an **h** 'mute', or the pronoun **y** → **①**

tu/vous
Vous, as well as being the second person plural, is also used when addressing one person. As a general rule, use **tu** only when addressing a friend, a child, a relative, someone you know very well, or when invited to do so. In all other cases use **vous**. For singular and plural uses of **vous**, see example **②**

il/elle; ils/elles
The form of the 3rd person pronouns reflects the number and gender of the noun(s) they replace, referring to animals and things as well as to people. **Ils** also replaces a combination of masculine and feminine nouns → **③**

Sometimes stressed pronouns replace the subject pronouns, see page 172.

1 J'arrive!   I'm just coming!
J'en ai trois   I've got three of them
J'hésite à le déranger   I hesitate to disturb him
J'y pense souvent   I often think about it

2 Compare:
Vous êtes certain, Monsieur   Are you sure, Mr Leclerc?
  Leclerc?
and:
Vous êtes certains, les enfants?   Are you sure, children?
Compare:
Vous êtes partie quand, Estelle?   When did you leave, Estelle?
and:
Estelle et Sophie – vous êtes   Estelle and Sophie – when did
  parties quand?   you leave?

3 Où logent ton père et ta mère   Where do your father and mother
  quand ils vont à Rome?   stay when they go to Rome?
Donne-moi le journal et les   Give me the newspaper and the
  lettres quand ils arriveront   letters when they arrive

Pronouns

Personal Pronouns *continued*

	DIRECT OBJECT PRONOUNS	
	SINGULAR	PLURAL
1st person	**me (m')** me	**nous** us
2nd person	**te (t')** you	**vous** you
3rd person (*masc.*)	**le (l')** him; it	**ils** them
(*fem.*)	**la (l')** her; it	**elles** them

The forms shown in brackets are used before a vowel, an **h** 'mute', or the pronoun **y** → ❶

In positive commands **me** and **te** change to **moi** and **toi** except before **en** or **y** → ❷

le sometimes functions as a 'neuter' pronoun, referring to an idea or information contained in a previous statement or question. It is often not translated → ❸

Position of direct object pronouns

In constructions other than the imperative affirmative, the pronoun comes before the verb → ❹

The same applies when the verb is in the infinitive → ❺

In the imperative affirmative, the pronoun follows the verb and is attached to it by a hyphen → ❻

For further information, see Order of Object Pronouns, page 170.

Reflexive Pronouns

These are dealt with under reflexive verbs, page 30.

1. Il m'a vu — He saw me
   Je ne t'oublierai jamais — I'll never forget you
   Ça l'habitue à travailler seul — That gets him/her used to working on his/her own

   Je veux l'y accoutumer — I want to accustom him/her to it

2. Avertis-moi de ta décision — Inform me of your decision
   Avertis-m'en — Inform me of it

3. Il n'est pas là. — Je le sais bien. — He isn't there. — I know that.
   Aidez-moi si vous le pouvez — Help me if you can
   Elle viendra demain. — Je l'espère bien. — She'll come tomorrow. — I hope so.

4. Je t'aime — I love you
   Les voyez-vous? — Can you see them?
   Elle ne nous connaît pas — She doesn't know us
   Est-ce que tu ne les aimes pas? — Don't you like them?
   Ne me faites pas rire — Don't make me laugh

5. Puis-je vous aider? — May I help you?

6. Aidez-moi — Help me
   Suivez-nous — Follow us

Pronouns

Personal Pronouns *continued*

	INDIRECT OBJECT PRONOUNS	
	SINGULAR	PLURAL
1st person	me (m')	nous
2nd person	te (t')	vous
3rd person (*masc.*)	lui	leur
(*fem.*)	lui	leur

me and **te** change to **m'** and **t'** before a vowel or an **h** 'mute' → ❶

In positive commands, **me** and **te** change to **moi** and **toi** except before **en** → ❷

The pronouns shown in the above table replace the preposition **à** + *noun*, where the noun is a person or an animal → ❸

The verbal construction affects the translation of the pronoun → ❹

Position of indirect object pronouns

In constructions other than the imperative affirmative, the pronoun comes before the verb → ❺

The same applies when the verb is in the infinitive → ❻

In the imperative affirmative, the pronoun follows the verb and is attached to it by a hyphen → ❼

For further information, see Order of Object Pronouns, page 170.

Reflexive Pronouns

These are dealt with under reflexive verbs, page 30.

1 Tu m'as donné ce livre — You gave me this book
Ils t'ont caché les faits — They hid the facts from you

2 Donnez-moi du sucre — Give me some sugar
Donnez-m'en — Give me some
Garde-toi assez d'argent — Keep enough money for yourself
Garde-t'en assez — Keep enough for yourself

3 J'écris à Suzanne — I'm writing to Suzanne
Je lui écris — I'm writing to her
Donne du lait au chat — Give the cat some milk
Donne-lui du lait — Give it some milk

4 arracher qch à qn: — to snatch sth from sb:
  Un voleur m'a arraché mon porte-monnaie — A thief snatched my purse from me
promettre qch à qn: — to promise sb sth:
  Il leur a promis un cadeau — He promised them a present
demander à qn de faire: — to ask sb to do:
  Elle nous avait demandé de revenir — She had asked us to come back

5 Elle vous a écrit — She's written to you
Vous a-t-elle écrit? — Has she written to you?
Il ne nous parle pas — He doesn't speak to us
Est-ce que cela ne vous intéresse pas? — Doesn't it interest you?
Ne leur répondez pas — Don't answer them

6 Voulez-vous leur envoyer l'adresse? — Do you want to send them the address?

7 Répondez-moi — Answer me
Donnez-nous la réponse — Tell us the answer

Pronouns

Personal Pronouns *continued*

Order of object pronouns

When two object pronouns of different persons come before the verb, the order is: indirect before direct, i.e.

me			
te		**le**	
nous	before	**la**	→ ❶
vous		**les**	

When two 3rd person object pronouns come before the verb, the order is: direct before indirect, i.e.

le			
la	before	**lui**	→ ❷
les		**leur**	

When two object pronouns come after the verb (i.e. in the imperative affirmative), the order is: direct before indirect, i.e.

		moi	
		toi	
le		**lui**	
la	before	**nous**	→ ❸
les		**vous**	
		leur	

The pronouns **y** and **en** (see pages 176 and 174) always come last → ❹

① Dominique vous l'envoie demain — Dominique's sending it to you tomorrow

Est-ce qu'il te les a montrés? — Has he shown them to you?

Ne me le dis pas — Don't tell me (it)

Il ne veut pas nous la prêter — He won't lend it to us

② Elle le leur a emprunté — She borrowed it from them

Je les lui ai lus — I read them to him/her

Ne la leur donne pas — Don't give it to them

Je voudrais les lui rendre — I'd like to give them back to him/ her

③ Rends-les-moi — Give them back to me

Donnez-le-nous — Give it to us

Apportons-les-leur — Let's take them to them

④ Donnez-leur-en — Give them some

Je l'y ai déposé — I dropped him there

Ne nous en parlez plus — Don't speak to us about it any more

Pronouns

Personal Pronouns *continued*

	STRESSED OR DISJUNCTIVE PRONOUNS	
	SINGULAR	PLURAL
1st person	**moi** me	**nous** us
2nd person	**toi** you	**vous** you
3rd person (*masc.*)	**lui** him; it	**eux** them
(*fem.*)	**elle** her; it	**elles** them
(*reflexive*)	**soi** oneself	

These pronouns are used:
- after prepositions → ①
- on their own → ②
- following **c'est, ce sont** it is → ③
- for emphasis, especially where contrast is involved → ④
- when the subject consists of two or more pronouns → ⑤
- when the subject consists of a pronoun and a noun → ⑥
- in comparisons → ⑦
- before relative pronouns → ⑧

For particular emphasis **-même** (*singular*) or **-mêmes** (*plural*) is added to the pronoun → ⑨

moi-même myself   **nous-mêmes** ourselves
toi-même yourself   **vous-même** yourself
lui-même himself; itself   **vous-mêmes** yourselves
elle-même herself; itself   **eux-mêmes** themselves
soi-même oneself   **elles-mêmes** themselves

① Je pense à toi	I think about you
Partez sans eux	Leave without them
C'est pour elle	This is for her
Assieds-toi à côté de lui	Sit beside him
Venez avec moi	Come with me
Il a besoin de nous	He needs us
② Qui a fait cela? — Lui.	Who did that? — He did.
Qui est-ce qui gagne? — Moi.	Who's winning? — Me.
③ C'est toi, Simon? — Non, c'est moi, David.	Is that you, Simon? — No, it's me, David.
Qui est-ce? — Ce sont eux.	Who is it? — It's them.
④ Ils voyagent séparément: lui par le train, elle en autobus	They travel separately: he by train and she by bus
Toi, tu ressembles à ton père, eux pas	You look like your father, they don't
Il n'a pas l'air de s'ennuyer, lui!	He doesn't look bored!
⑤ Lui et moi partons demain	He and I are leaving tomorrow
Ni vous ni elles ne pouvez rester	Neither you nor they can stay
⑥ Mon père et elle ne s'entendent pas	My father and she don't get on
⑦ plus jeune que moi	younger than me
Il est moins grand que toi	He's smaller than you (are)
⑧ Moi, qui étais malade, je n'ai pas pu les accompagner	I, who was ill, couldn't go with them
Ce sont eux qui font du bruit, pas nous	They're the ones making the noise, not us
⑨ Je l'ai fait moi-même	I did it myself

Pronouns

The pronoun en

en replaces the preposition **de** + *noun* → ①

The verbal construction can affect the translation → ②

en also replaces the partitive article (English = some, any) + *noun* → ③

In expressions of quantity en represents the noun → ④

Position: **en** comes before the verb, except in positive commands when it follows and is attached to the verb by a hyphen → ⑤

en follows other object pronouns → ⑥

① Il est fier de son succès — He's proud of his success
Il en est fier — He's proud of it
Elle est sortie du cinéma — She came out of the cinema
Elle en est sortie — She came out (of it)
Je suis couvert de peinture — I'm covered in paint
J'en suis couvert — I'm covered in it
Il a beaucoup d'amis — He has lots of friends
Il en a beaucoup — He has lots (of them)

② avoir besoin de qch: — to need sth:
J'en ai besoin — I need it/them
avoir peur de qch: — to be afraid of sth:
J'en ai peur — I'm afraid of it/them

③ Avez-vous de l'argent? — Do you have any money?
En avez-vous? — Do you have any?
Je veux acheter des timbres — I want to buy some stamps
Je veux en acheter — I want to buy some

④ J'ai deux crayons — I've two pencils
J'en ai deux — I've two (of them)
Combien de sœurs as-tu? — J'en ai trois. — How many sisters do you have? — I have three.

⑤ Elle en a discuté avec moi — She discussed it with me
En êtes-vous content? — Are you pleased with it/them?
Je veux en garder trois — I want to keep three of them
N'en parlez plus — Don't talk about it any more
Prenez-en — Take some
Soyez-en fier — Be proud of it/them

⑥ Donnez-leur-en — Give them some
Il m'en a parlé — He spoke to me about it

Pronouns

The pronoun y

y replaces the preposition **à** + *noun* → **①**

The verbal construction can affect the translation → **②**

y also replaces the prepositions **dans** and **sur** + *noun* → **③**

y can also mean 'there' → **④**

Position: **y** comes before the verb, except in positive commands when it follows and is attached to the verb by a hyphen → **⑤**

y follows other object pronouns → **⑥**

1 Ne touchez pas à ce bouton — Don't touch this switch
N'y touchez pas — Don't touch it
Il participe aux concerts — He takes part in the concerts
Il y participe — He takes part (in them)

2 penser à qch: — to think about sth:
J'y pense souvent — I often think about it
consentir à qch: — to agree to sth:
Tu y as consenti? — Have you agreed to it?

3 Mettez-les dans la boîte — Put them in the box
Mettez-les-y — Put them in it
Il les a mis sur les étagères — He put them on the shelves
Il les y a mis — He put them on them
J'ai placé de l'argent sur ce compte — I've put money into this account
J'y ai placé de l'argent — I've put money into it

4 Elle y passe tout l'été — She spends the whole summer there

5 Il y a ajouté du sucre — He added sugar to it
Elle n'y a pas écrit son nom — She hasn't written her name on it
Comment fait-on pour y aller? — How do you get there?
N'y pense plus! — Don't give it another thought!
Restez-y — Stay there
Réfléchissez-y — Think it over

6 Elle m'y a conduit — She drove me there
Menez-nous-y — Take us there

Pronouns

Indefinite Pronouns

The following are indefinite pronouns:

aucun(e) none, not any → ❶
certain(e)s some, certain → ❷
chacun(e) each (one); everybody → ❸
on one, you; somebody; they, people; we (*informal use*) → ❹
personne nobody → ❺
plusieurs several → ❻
quelque chose something; anything → ❼
quelques-un(e)s some, a few → ❽
quelqu'un somebody; anybody → ❾
rien nothing → ❿
tout all; everything → ⓫
tous (toutes) all → ⓬
l'un(e) ... l'autre (the) one ... the other
les un(e)s ... les autres some ... others → ⓭

aucun(e), personne, rien
When used as subject or object of the verb, these require the word **ne**
placed immediately before the verb. Note that **aucun** further needs the
pronoun **en** when used as an object → ⓮

quelque chose, rien
When qualified by an adjective, these pronouns require the preposition
de before the adjective → ⓯

①	Combien en avez-vous? — Aucun.	How many have you got? — None.
②	Certains pensent que ...	Some (people) think that ...
③	Chacune de ces boîtes est pleine	Each of these boxes is full
	Chacun son tour!	Everybody in turn!
④	On voit l'église de cette fenêtre	You can see the church from this window
	En semaine on se couche tôt	During the week they/we go to bed early
	Est-ce qu'on lui a permis de rester?	Was he/she allowed to stay?
⑤	Qui voyez-vous? — Personne.	Who can you see? — Nobody.
⑥	Ils sont plusieurs	There are several of them
⑦	Mange donc quelque chose!	Eat something!
	Tu as vu quelque chose?	Did you see anything?
⑧	Je connais quelques-uns de ses amis	I know some of his/her friends
⑨	Quelqu'un a appelé	Somebody called (out)
	Tu as vu quelqu'un?	Did you see anybody?
⑩	Qu'est-ce que tu as dans la main? — Rien.	What have you got in your hand? — Nothing.
⑪	Il a tout gâché	He has spoiled everything
	Tout va bien	All's well
⑫	Tu les as tous?	Do you have all of them?
	Elles sont toutes venues	They all came
⑬	Les uns sont satisfaits, les autres pas	Some are satisfied, (the) others aren't
⑭	Je ne vois personne	I can't see anyone
	Rien ne lui plaît	Nothing pleases him/her
	Aucune des entreprises ne veut ...	None of the companies wants ...
	Il n'en a aucun	He hasn't any (of them)
⑮	quelque chose de grand	something big
	rien d'intéressant	nothing interesting

Pronouns

Relative Pronouns

qui who; which
que who(m); which
These are subject and direct object pronouns that introduce a clause and refer to people or things.

	PEOPLE	THINGS
SUBJECT	**qui**	**qui**
	who, that → ❶	which, that → ❸
DIRECT OBJECT	**que (qu')**	**que (qu')**
	who(m), that → ❷	which, that → ❹

que changes to **qu'** before a vowel → ❷/❹

You cannot omit the object relative pronoun in French as you can in English → ❷/❹

After a preposition:
When referring to people, use **qui** → ❺
EXCEPTIONS: after **parmi** 'among' and **entre** 'between' use **lesquels/ lesquelles**; see below → ❻

When referring to things, use forms of **lequel**:

	MASCULINE	FEMININE	
SING.	**lequel**	**laquelle**	which
PLUR.	**lesquels**	**lesquelles**	which

The pronoun agrees in number and gender with the noun → ❼

After the prepositions **à** and **de**, **lequel** and **lesquel(le)s** contract as follows:
à + lequel → auquel
à + lesquels → auxquels → ❽
à + lesquelles → auxquelles

de + lequel → duquel
de + lesquels → desquels → ❾
de + lesquelles → desquelles

1. Mon frère, qui a vingt ans, est à l'université — My brother, who's twenty, is at university

2. Les amis que je vois le plus sont ... — The friends (that) I see most are ...
   Lucienne, qu'il connaît depuis longtemps, est ... — Lucienne, whom he has known for a long time, is ...

3. Il y a un escalier qui mène au toit — There's a staircase which leads to the roof

4. La maison que nous avons achetée a ... — The house (which) we've bought has ...
   Voici le cadeau qu'elle m'a envoyé — This is the present (that) she sent me

5. la personne à qui il parle — the person he's talking to
   la personne avec qui je voyage — the person with whom I travel
   les enfants pour qui je l'ai acheté — the children for whom I bought it

6. Il y avait des jeunes, parmi lesquels Robert — There were some young people, Robert among them
   les filles entre lesquelles j'étais assis — the girls between whom I was sitting

7. le torchon avec lequel il l'essuie — the cloth with which he's wiping it
   la table sur laquelle je l'ai mis — the table on which I put it
   les moyens par lesquels il l'accomplit — the means by which he achieves it
   les pièces pour lesquelles elle est connue — the plays for which she is famous

8. le magasin auquel il livre ces marchandises — the shop to which he delivers these goods

9. les injustices desquelles il se plaint — the injustices about which he's complaining

Pronouns

Relative Pronouns *continued*

quoi which, what

> When the relative pronoun does not refer to a specific noun, **quoi** is used after a preposition → ❶

dont whose, of whom, of which

> **dont** often (but not always) replaces **de qui, duquel, de laquelle,** and **desquel(le)s** → ❷

> It cannot replace **de qui, duquel** *etc* in the construction *preposition + noun +* **de qui/duquel** → ❸

1. C'est en quoi vous vous trompez · That's where you're wrong
   À quoi, j'ai répondu … · To which I replied, …

2. la femme dont (= *de qui*) la voiture est garée en face · the woman whose car is parked opposite
   un prix dont (= *de qui*) je suis fier · an award I am proud of
   un ami dont (= *de qui*) je connais le frère · a friend whose brother I know
   les enfants dont (= *de qui*) vous vous occupez · the children you look after
   le film dont (= *duquel*) il a parlé · the film of which he spoke
   la fenêtre dont (= *de laquelle*) les rideaux sont tirés · the window the curtains of which are drawn
   des garçons dont (= *desquels*) j'ai oublié les noms · boys whose names I've forgotten
   les maladies dont (= *desquelles*) il souffre · the illnesses he suffers from

3. une personne sur l'aide de qui on peut compter · a person whose help one can rely on
   les enfants aux parents de qui j'écris · the children to whose parents I'm writing
   la maison dans le jardin de laquelle il y a … · the house in whose garden there is …

Pronouns

Relative Pronouns *continued*

ce qui, ce que that which, what

These are used when the relative pronoun does not refer to a specific noun, and they are often translated as 'what' (*literally*: that which):

> **ce qui** is used as the subject → **1**

> **ce que*** is used as the direct object → **2**

> * **que** changes to **qu'** before a vowel → **2**

> Note the construction:
> **tout ce qui**
> **tout ce que** everything/all that → **3**

> **de + ce que** → **ce dont** → **4**

> *preposition* + **ce que** → **ce** + *preposition* + **quoi** → **5**

> When **ce qui, ce que** etc, refers to a previous clause the translation is 'which' → **6**

1. Ce qui m'intéresse ne l'intéresse pas forcément
   What interests me doesn't necessarily interest him
   Je n'ai pas vu ce qui s'est passé
   I didn't see what happened

2. Ce que j'aime c'est la musique classique
   What I like is classical music
   Montrez-moi ce qu'il vous a donné
   Show me what he gave you

3. Tout ce qui reste c'est ...
   All that's left is ...
   Donnez-moi tout ce que vous avez
   Give me everything you have

4. Il risque de perdre ce dont il est si fier
   He risks losing what he's so proud of
   Voilà ce dont il s'agit
   That's what it's about

5. Ce n'est pas ce à quoi je m'attendais
   It's not what I was expecting
   Ce à quoi je m'intéresse particulièrement c'est ...
   What I'm particularly interested in is ...

6. Il est d'accord, ce qui m'étonne
   He agrees, which surprises me
   Il a dit qu'elle ne venait pas, ce que nous savions déjà
   He said she wasn't coming, which we already knew

Pronouns

Interrogative Pronouns

These pronouns are used in direct questions:

qui? who; whom?
que? what?
quoi? what?

The form of the pronoun depends on:
- whether it refers to people or to things
- whether it is the subject or object of the verb, or if it comes after a preposition

Qui and **que** have longer forms, as shown in the tables below.

Referring to people:

SUBJECT	qui?	who? → ❶
	qui est-ce qui?	
OBJECT	qui?	who(m)? → ❷
	qui est-ce que*?	
AFTER PREPOSITIONS	qui?	who(m)? → ❸

Referring to things:

SUBJECT	qu'est-ce qui?	what? → ❹
OBJECT	que*?	what? → ❺
	qu'est-ce que*?	
AFTER PREPOSITIONS	quoi?	what? → ❻

* **que** changes to **qu'** before a vowel → ❷/❺

1. Qui vient? — Who's coming?
   Qui est-ce qui vient?

2. Qui vois-tu? — Who(m) can you see?
   Qui est-ce que tu vois?
   Qui a-t-elle rencontré? — Who(m) did she meet?
   Qui est-ce qu'elle a rencontré?

3. De qui parle-t-il? — Who's he talking about?
   Pour qui est ce livre? — Who's this book for?
   À qui avez-vous écrit? — To whom did you write?

4. Qu'est-ce qui se passe? — What's happening?
   Qu'est-ce qui a vexé Paul? — What upset Paul?

5. Que faites-vous? — What are you doing?
   Qu'est-ce que vous faites?
   Qu'a-t-il dit? — What did he say?
   Qu'est-ce qu'il a dit?

6. À quoi cela sert-il? — What's that used for?
   De quoi a-t-on parlé? — What was the discussion about?
   Sur quoi vous basez-vous? — What do you base it on?

Pronouns

Interrogative Pronouns *continued*

These pronouns are used in indirect questions:

qui who; whom
ce qui what
ce que what
quoi what

The form of the pronoun depends on:
- whether it refers to people or to things
- whether it is the subject or object of the verb, or if it comes after a preposition

Referring to people: use **qui** in all instances → **1**

Referring to things:

SUBJECT	**ce qui**	what → **2**
OBJECT	**ce que**＊	what → **3**
AFTER PREPOSITIONS	**quoi?**	what → **4**

＊ **que** changes to **qu'** before a vowel → **3**

1. Demande-lui qui est venu | Ask him who came
   Je me demande qui ils ont vu | I wonder who they saw
   Dites-moi qui vous préférez | Tell me who you prefer
   Elle ne sait pas à qui s'adresser | She doesn't know who to apply to
   Demandez-leur pour qui elles travaillent | Ask them who they work for

2. Il se demande ce qui se passe | He's wondering what's happening

   Je ne sais pas ce qui vous fait croire que ... | I don't know what makes you think that ...

3. Raconte-nous ce que tu as fait | Tell us what you did
   Je me demande ce qu'elle pense | I wonder what she's thinking

4. On ne sait pas de quoi vivent ces animaux | We don't know what these animals live on
   Je vais lui demander à quoi il fait allusion | I'm going to ask him what he's hinting at

Pronouns

Interrogative Pronouns *continued*

lequel/laquelle, lesquels/lesquelles?

	MASCULINE	FEMININE	
SING.	**lequel?**	**laquelle?**	which (one)?
PLUR.	**lesquels?**	**lesquelles?**	which (ones)?

The pronoun agrees in number and gender with the noun it refers to → ❶

The same forms are used in indirect questions → ❷

After the prepositions à and **de**, **lequel** and **lesquel(le)s** contract as follows:

      à + lequel? → auquel?
      à + lesquels? → auxquels?
      à + lesquelles? → auxquelles?

      de + lequel? → duquel?
      de + lesquels? → desquels?
      de + lesquelles? → desquelles?

1 J'ai choisi un livre. — Lequel?

Laquelle de ces valises est la vôtre?

Amenez quelques amis. — Lesquels?

Lesquelles de vos sœurs sont mariées?

2 Je me demande laquelle des maisons est la leur

Dites-moi lesquels d'entre eux étaient là

I've chosen a book. —Which one?

Which of these cases is yours?

Bring some friends. — Which ones?

Which of your sisters are married?

I wonder which is their house

Tell me which of them were there

Pronouns

Possessive Pronouns

Singular:

MASCULINE	FEMININE	
le mien	la mienne	mine
le tien	la tienne	yours
le sien	la sienne	his; hers; its
le nôtre	la nôtre	ours
le vôtre	la vôtre	yours
le leur	la leur	theirs

Plural:

MASCULINE	FEMININE	
les miens	les miennes	mine
les tiens	les tiennes	yours
les siens	les siennes	his; hers; its
les nôtres	les nôtres	ours
les vôtres	les vôtres	yours
les leurs	les leurs	theirs

The pronoun agrees in number and gender with the noun it replaces, not with the owner → **1**

Alternative translations are 'my own', 'your own' etc; **le sien, la sienne** *etc* may also mean 'one's own' → **2**

After the prepositions **à** and **de** the articles **le** and **les** are contracted in the normal way (see page 140):

      à + le mien → au mien
      à + les miens → aux miens → **3**
      à + les miennes → aux miennes

      de + le mien → du mien
      de + les miens → des miens → **4**
      de + les miennes → des miennes

1. Demandez à Carole si ce stylo est le sien — Ask Carole if this pen is hers

Quelle équipe a gagné – la leur ou la nôtre? — Which team won – theirs or ours?

Mon portable est plus rapide que le tien — My laptop is faster than yours

Richard a pris mes affaires pour les siennes — Richard mistook my belongings for his

Si tu n'as pas de DVD, emprunte les miens — If you don't have any DVDs, borrow mine

Nos maisons sont moins grandes que les vôtres — Our houses are smaller than yours

2. Est-ce que leur entreprise est aussi grande que la vôtre? — Is their company as big as your own?

Leurs prix sont moins élevés que les nôtres — Their prices are lower than our own

Le bonheur des autres importe plus que le sien — Other people's happiness matters more than one's own

3. Pourquoi préfères-tu ce manteau au mien? — Why do you prefer this coat to mine?

Quelles maisons ressemblent aux leurs? — Which houses resemble theirs?

4. Leur voiture est garée à côté de la tienne — Their car is parked next to yours

Vos livres sont au-dessus des miens — Your books are on top of mine

Pronouns

Demonstrative Pronouns

celui/celle, ceux/celles

	MASCULINE	FEMININE	
SING.	celui	celle	the one
PLUR.	ceux	celles	the ones

The pronoun agrees in number and gender with the noun it replaces → ①

Uses:
- preceding a relative pronoun, meaning 'the one(s) who/which' → ①
- preceding the preposition **de**, meaning 'the one(s) belonging to', 'the one(s) of' → ②
- with **-ci** and **-là**, for emphasis or to distinguish between two things:

	MASCULINE	FEMININE		
SING.	celui-ci	celle-ci	this (one)	→ ③
PLUR.	ceux-ci	celles-ci	these (ones)	

	MASCULINE	FEMININE		
SING.	celui-là	celle-là	that (one)	→ ③
PLUR.	ceux-là	celles-là	those (ones)	

- an additional meaning of **celui-ci/celui-là** *etc* is 'the former/the latter'.

❶ Lequel? — Celui qui parle à Anne.

Which man? — The one who's talking to Anne.

Quelle robe désirez-vous? — Celle qui est en vitrine.

Which dress do you want? — The one which is in the window.

Est-ce que ces livres sont ceux qu'il t'a donnés?

Are these the books that he gave you?

Quelles filles? — Celles que nous avons vues hier.

Which girls? — The ones we saw yesterday.

Cet article n'est pas celui dont vous m'avez parlé

This article isn't the one you spoke to me about

❷ Ce jardin est plus grand que celui de mes parents

This garden is bigger than my parents' (garden)

Est-ce que ta fille est plus âgée que celle de Gabrielle?

Is your daughter older than Gabrielle's (daughter)?

Je préfère les chiens de Paul à ceux de Roger

I prefer Paul's dogs to Roger's (dogs)

Comparez vos réponses à celles de votre voisin

Compare your answers with your neighbour's (answers)

les montagnes d'Écosse et celles du pays de Galles

the mountains of Scotland and those of Wales

❸ Quel tailleur préférez-vous: celui-ci ou celui-là?

Which suit do you prefer: this one or that one?

Cette chemise a deux poches mais celle-là n'en a pas

This shirt has two pockets but that one has none

Quels œufs choisirais-tu: ceux-ci ou ceux-là?

Which eggs would you choose: these (ones) or those (ones)?

De toutes mes jupes, celle-ci me va le mieux

Of all my skirts, this one fits me best

Pronouns

Demonstrative Pronouns *continued*

ce (c') it, that

> Usually used with **être**, in the expressions **c'est**, **c'était**, **ce sont** *etc* → ❶

> Note the spelling **ç**, when followed by the letter **a** → ❷

> Uses:
> - to identify a person or object → ❸
> - for emphasis → ❹
> - as a neuter pronoun, referring to a statement, idea *etc* → ❺

ce qui, **ce que**, **ce dont** *etc*: see Relative Pronouns (page 184), and Interrogative Pronouns (page 188).

cela, **ça** it, that

> **cela** and **ça** are used as 'neuter' pronouns, referring to a statement, an idea, an object → ❻

> In everyday spoken language **ça** is used in preference to **cela**.

ceci this → ❼

> **ceci** is not used as often as 'this' in English; **cela**, **ça** are often used where we use 'this'.

1 C'est ...　　　　　　　　　　　　It's/That's ...
　　C'était moi　　　　　　　　　　It was me

2 Ç'a été la cause de ...　　　　　It has been cause of ...

3 Qui est-ce?　　　　　　　　　Who is it?; Who's this/that?;
　　　　　　　　　　　　　　　　　Who's he/she?

　　C'est lui/mon frère/nous　　　It's/That's him/my brother/us
　　Ce sont eux　　　　　　　　　It's them
　　C'est une infirmière*　　　　　She's a nurse
　　Ce sont des professeurs*　　　They're teachers
　　Qu'est-ce que c'est?　　　　　What's this/that?
　　Qu'est-ce que c'est que ça?　　What's that?
　　C'est une agrafeuse　　　　　It's a stapler
　　Ce sont des trombones　　　　They're paper clips

4 C'est moi qui ai téléphoné　　　It was me who phoned
　　Ce sont les enfants qui importent　It's the children who matter
　　　le plus　　　　　　　　　　　most

5 C'est très intéressant　　　　　That's/It's very interesting
　　Ce serait dangereux　　　　　That/It would be dangerous

6 Ça ne fait rien　　　　　　　　It doesn't matter
　　À quoi bon faire ça?　　　　　What's the use of doing that?
　　Cela ne compte pas　　　　　That doesn't count
　　Cela demande du temps　　　　It/That takes time

7 À qui est ceci?　　　　　　　　Whose is this?
　　Ouvrez-le comme ceci　　　　Open it like this

* See pages 146 and 147 for the use of the article when stating a person's profession

Adverbs

Adverbs

Formation

Most adverbs are formed by adding **-ment** to the feminine form of the adjective → ①

-ment is added to the *masculine* form when the masculine form ends in -é, -i or -u → ②
EXCEPTION: **gai** → ③

Occasionally the **u** changes to **û** before **-ment** is added → ④

If the adjective ends in **-ant** or **-ent**, the adverb ends in **-amment** or **-emment** → ⑤
EXCEPTIONS: **lent, présent** → ⑥

Irregular Adverbs

ADJECTIVE	ADVERB
aveugle blind	**aveuglément** blindly
bon good	**bien** well → ⑦
bref brief	**brièvement** briefly
énorme enormous	**énormément** enormously
exprès express	**expressément** expressly → ⑧
gentil kind	**gentiment** kindly
mauvais bad	**mal** badly → ⑨
meilleur better	**mieux** better
pire worse	**pis** worse
précis precise	**précisément** precisely
profond deep	**profondément** deeply → ⑩
traître treacherous	**traîtreusement** treacherously

Adjectives used as adverbs

Certain adjectives are used adverbially. These include: **bas, bon, cher, clair, court, doux, droit, dur, faux, ferme, fort, haut, mauvais** and **net** → ⑪

1 MASC./FEM. ADJECTIVE   ADVERB
heureux/heureuse fortunate   heureusement fortunately
franc/franche frank   franchement frankly
extrême/extrême extreme   extrêmement extremely

2 MASC. ADJECTIVE   ADVERB
désespéré desperate   désespérément desperately
vrai true   vraiment truly
résolu resolute   résolument resolutely

3 gai cheerful   gaiement or gaîment cheerfully

4 continu continuous   continûment continuously

5 constant constant   constamment constantly
courant fluent   couramment fluently
évident obvious   évidemment obviously
fréquent frequent   fréquemment frequently

6 lent slow   lentement slowly
présent present   présentement presently

7 Elle travaille bien   She works well

8 Il a expressément défendu qu'on parte   He has expressly forbidden us to leave

9 un emploi mal payé   a badly paid job

10 J'ai été profondément ému   I was deeply moved

11 parler bas/haut   to speak softly/loudly
coûter cher   to be expensive
voir clair   to see clearly
travailler dur   to work hard
chanter faux   to sing off key
sentir bon/mauvais   to smell nice/horrible

Adverbs

Position of Adverbs

When the adverb accompanies a verb in a simple tense, it generally follows the verb → ❶

When the adverb accompanies a verb in a compound tense, it generally comes between the auxiliary verb and the past participle → ❷

Some adverbs, however, follow the past participle → ❸

When the adverb accompanies an adjective or another adverb it generally precedes the adjective/adverb → ❹

Comparatives of Adverbs

These are formed using the following constructions:

plus ... (que) more ... (than) → ❺
moins ... (que) less ... (than) → ❻
aussi ... que as ... as → ❼
si ... que* as ... as → ❽

* used mainly after a negative

Superlatives of Adverbs

These are formed using the following constructions:

le plus ... (que) the most ... (that) → ❾
le moins ... (que) the least ... (that) → ❿

Adverbs with irregular comparatives/superlatives

ADVERB	COMPARATIVE	SUPERLATIVE
beaucoup a lot	**plus** more	**le plus** (the) most
bien well	**mieux** better	**le mieux** (the) best
mal badly	**pis/plus mal** worse	**le pis/plus mal** (the) worst
peu little	**moins** less	**le moins** (the) least

❶	Il dort encore	He's still asleep
	Je pense souvent à toi	I often think about you
❷	Ils sont déjà partis	They've already gone
	J'ai toujours cru que …	I've always thought that …
	J'ai presque fini	I'm almost finished
	Il a trop mangé	He's eaten too much
❸	On les a vus partout	We saw them everywhere
	Elle est revenue hier	She came back yesterday
❹	un très beau chemisier	a very nice blouse
	une femme bien habillée	a well-dressed woman
	beaucoup plus vite	much faster
	peu souvent	not very often
❺	plus vite	more quickly
	plus régulièrement	more regularly
	Elle chante plus fort que moi	She sings louder than I do
❻	moins facilement	less easily
	moins souvent	less often
	Nous nous voyons moins	We see each other less
	fréquemment qu'auparavant	frequently than before
❼	Faites-le aussi vite que possible	Do it as quickly as possible
	Il en sait aussi long que nous	He knows as much about it as we do
❽	Ce n'est pas si loin que je pensais	It's not as far as I thought
❾	Marianne court le plus vite	Marianne runs fastest
❿	Le plus tôt que je puisse venir c'est samedi	The earliest that I can come is Saturday
⓫	C'est l'auteur que je connais le moins bien	He's the writer I'm least familiar with

Adverbs

Common adverbs and their usage

Some common adverbs:

assez enough; quite → ① *See also below*
aussi also, too; as → ②
autant as much → ③ *See also below*
beaucoup a lot; much → ④ *See also below*
bien well; very; very much; 'indeed' → ⑤ *See also below*
combien how much; how many → ⑥ *See also below*
comme how; what → ⑦
déjà already; before → ⑧
encore still; yet; more; even → ⑨
moins less → ⑩ *See also below*
peu little, not much; not very → ⑪ *See also below*
plus more → ⑫ *See also below*
si so; such → ⑬
tant so much → ⑭ *See also below*
toujours always; still → ⑮
trop too much; too → ⑯ *See also below*

assez, autant, beaucoup, combien *etc* are used in the construction
adverb + **de** + *noun* with the following meanings:

assez de enough → ⑰
autant de as much; as many; so much; so many
beaucoup de a lot of
combien de how much; how many
moins de less; fewer → ⑰
peu de little, not much; few, not many
plus de more
tant de so much; so many
trop de too much; too many

bien can be followed by a partitive article (see page 144) plus a noun to
mean *a lot of*; *a good many* → ⑱

1. Avez-vous assez chaud? — Are you warm enough?
   Il est assez tard — It's quite late

2. Je préfère ça aussi — I prefer it too
   Elle est aussi grande que moi — She is as tall as I am

3. Je voyage autant que lui — I travel as much as him

4. Tu lis beaucoup? — Do you read a lot?
   C'est beaucoup plus loin? — Is it much further?

5. Bien joué! — Well played!
   Je suis bien content que … — I'm very pleased that …
   Il s'est bien amusé — He enjoyed himself very much
   Je l'ai bien fait — I DID do it

6. Combien coûte ce livre? — How much is this book?
   Vous êtes combien? — How many of you are there?

7. Comme tu es jolie! — How pretty you look!
   Comme il fait beau! — What lovely weather!

8. Je l'ai déjà fait — I've already done it
   Êtes-vous déjà allé en France? — Have you been to France before?

9. J'en ai encore deux — I've still got two
   Elle n'est pas encore là — She isn't there yet
   Encore du café, Alain? — More coffee, Alan?
   Encore mieux! — Even better!

10. Travaillez moins! — Work less!
    Je suis moins étonné que toi — I'm less surprised than you are

11. Elle mange peu — She doesn't eat very much
    C'est peu important — It's not very important

12. Il se détend plus — He relaxes more
    Elle est plus timide que Sophie — She is shyer than Sophie

13. Simon est si charmant — Simon is so charming
    une si belle vue — such a lovely view

14. Elle l'aime tant — She loves him so much

15. Il dit toujours ça! — He always says that!
    Tu le vois toujours? — Do you still see him?

16. J'ai trop mangé — I've eaten too much
    C'est trop cher — It's too expensive

17. assez d'argent/de livres — enough money/books
    moins de temps/d'amis — less time/fewer friends

18. bien du mal/des gens — a lot of harm/a good many people

Prepositions

On the following pages you will find some of the most frequent uses of prepositions in French. Particular attention is paid to cases where usage differs markedly from English. It is often difficult to give an English equivalent for French prepositions, since usage does vary so much between the two languages.

In the list below, the broad meaning of the preposition is given on the left, with examples of usage following.

Prepositions are dealt with in alphabetical order, except **à**, **de** and **en** which are shown first.

à

at	**lancer qch à qn** to throw sth at sb
	il habite à St Pierre he lives at St Pierre
	à 2 euros (la) pièce (at) 2 euros each
	à 100 km à l'heure at 100 km per hour
in	**à la campagne** in the country
	à Londres in London
	au lit in bed (*also* to bed)
	un livre à la main with a book in his/her hand
on	**un tableau au mur** a picture on the wall
to	**aller au cinéma** to go to the cinema
	donner qch à qn to give sth to sb
	le premier/dernier à faire the first/last to do
	demander qch à qn to ask sb sth
from	**arracher qch à qn** to snatch sth from sb
	acheter qch à qn to buy sth from sb
	cacher qch à qn to hide sth from sb
	emprunter qch à qn to borrow sth from sb
	prendre qch à qn to take sth from sb
	voler qch à qn to steal sth from sb

Prepositions

descriptive	**la femme au chapeau vert** the woman with the green hat
	un garçon aux yeux bleus a boy with blue eyes
manner, means	**à l'ancienne** in the old-fashioned way
	fait à la main handmade
	à bicyclette/cheval by bicycle/on horseback
	*(but note other forms of transport used with **en** and **par**)*
	à pied on foot
	chauffer au gaz to heat with/by gas
	à pas lents with slow steps
	cuisiner au beurre to cook with butter
time, date: at, in	**à minuit** at midnight
	à trois heures cinq at five past three
	au XXe siècle in the 20th century
	à Noël/Pâques at Christmas/Easter
distance	**à 6 km d'ici** (at a distance of) 6 km from here
	à deux pas de chez moi just a step from my place
destined for	**une tasse à thé** a teacup
	*(compare **une tasse de thé**)*
	un service à café a coffee service
after certain adjectives	**son écriture est difficile à lire** his writing is difficult to read
	*(compare the usage with **de**, page 206)*
	prêt à tout ready for anything
after certain verbs	see page 64

Prepositions

de

from	**venir de Londres** to come from London
	du matin au soir from morning till night
	du 21 juin au 5 juillet from 21st June till 5th July
	de 10 à 15 from 10 to 15

| belonging to, of | **un ami de la famille** a friend of the family |
| | **les vents d'automne** the autumn winds |

contents, composition, material	**une boîte d'allumettes** a box of matches
	une tasse de thé a cup of tea
	(*compare* **une tasse à thé**)
	une robe de soie a silk dress

| *manner* | **d'une façon irrégulière** in an irregular way |
| | **d'un seul coup** at one go |

| *quality* | **la société de consommation** the consumer society |
| | **des objets de valeur** valuable items |

| *comparative + a number* | **Il y avait plus/moins de cent personnes** There were more/fewer than a hundred people |

| in (*after superlatives*) | **la plus/moins belle ville du monde** the most/least beautiful city in the world |

after certain adjectives	**surpris de voir** surprised to see
	Il est difficile d'y accéder Access is difficult
	(*compare the usage with* **à**, *page 205*)

| *after certain verbs* | **see page 64** |

Prepositions

en

to, in, on (*place*)	**en ville** in/to town
	en pleine mer on the open sea
	en France in/to France
	(*note that masculine countries use* **à**)
in (*dates, months*)	**en 2013** in 2013
	en janvier in January
transport	**en voiture** by car
	en avion by plane
	(*but note usage of* **à** *and* **par** *in other expressions*)
language	**en français** in French
duration	**Je le ferai en trois jours** I'll do it in three days
	(i.e. I'll take 3 days to do it: *compare* **dans trois jours**)
material	**un bracelet en or** a bracelet made of gold
	(*note that the use of* **en** *stresses the material more than the use of* **de**)
	consister en to consist of
in the manner of, like a	**parler en vrai connaisseur** to speak like a real connoisseur
	déguisé en cow-boy dressed up as a cowboy
+ *present participle*	**il l'a vu en passant devant la porte** he saw it as he came past the door

Prepositions

avant

before	**Il est arrivé avant toi** He arrived before you
+ *infinitive (add* **de**)	**Je vais finir ça avant de manger** I'm going to finish this before eating
preference	**la santé avant tout** health above everything

chez

at the home of	**chez lui/moi** at his/my house **être chez soi** to be at home **venez chez nous** come round to our place
at/to (a shop)	**chez le boucher** at/to the butcher's
in (*a person, among a group of people or animals*)	**Ce que je n'aime pas chez lui c'est son ...** What I don't like in him is his ... **chez les fourmis** among ants

dans

position	**dans une boîte** in(to) a box
circumstance	**dans son enfance** in his childhood
future time	**dans trois jours** in three days' time (*compare* **en trois jours**, *page 207*)

depuis

since (*time/place*)	**depuis mardi** since Tuesday **Il pleut depuis Paris** It's been raining since Paris
for	**Il habite cette maison depuis 3 ans** He's been living in this house for 3 years (*note tense*)

Prepositions

dès

past time	**dès mon enfance** since my childhood
future time	**Je le ferai dès mon retour** I'll do it as soon as I get back

entre

between	**entre 8 et 10** between 8 and 10
among	**Jean et Pierre, entre autres** Jean and Pierre, among others
reciprocal	**s'aider entre eux** to help each other (out)

d'entre

of, among	**trois d'entre eux** three of them

par

by (*agent of passive*)	**renversé par une voiture** knocked down by a car **tué par la foudre** killed by lightning
weather conditions	**par un beau jour d'été** on a lovely summer's day
by (means of)	**par un couloir/sentier** by a corridor/path **par le train** by train (*but see also* **à** *and* **en**) **par l'intermédiaire de M. Duval** through Mr Duval
distribution	**deux par deux** two by two **par groupes de dix** in groups of ten **deux fois par jour** twice a day

Prepositions

pour

for	**C'est pour vous** It's for you
	C'est pour demain It's for tomorrow
	une chambre pour 2 nuits a room for 2 nights
	Pour un enfant, il se débrouille bien
	For a child he manages very well
	Il part pour l'Espagne He's leaving for Spain
	Il l'a fait pour vous He did it for you
	Il lui a donné 5 euros pour ce livre
	He gave him 5 euros for this book
	Je ne suis pas pour cette idée I'm not for that idea
	Pour qui me prends-tu? Who do you take me for?
	Il passe pour un idiot He's taken for a fool

+ *infinitive*: (in order) to	**Elle se pencha pour le ramasser**
	She bent down to pick it up
	C'est trop fragile pour servir de siège
	It's too fragile to be used as a seat

to(wards)	**être bon/gentil pour qn** to be kind to sb

with prices, time	**pour 30 euros d'essence** 30 euros' worth of petrol
	J'en ai encore pour une heure
	I'll be another hour (at it) yet

sans

without	**sans eau** without water
	sans ma femme without my wife

+ *infinitive*	**sans compter les autres** without counting the others

Prepositions

sauf

except (for)
    tous sauf lui all except him
    sauf quand il pleut except when it's raining

barring
    sauf imprévu barring the unexpected
    sauf avis contraire unless you hear to the
                        contrary

sur

on
    sur le siège on the seat
    sur l'armoire on top of the wardrobe
    sur le mur on (top of) the wall
    (*if the meaning is* 'hanging on the wall' *use* **à**, *page 204*)
    sur votre gauche on your left
    être sur le point de faire to be on the point of
                        doing

on (to)
    mettez-le sur la table put it on the table

out of, by (*proportion*)
    8 sur 10 8 out of 10
    un automobiliste sur 5 one motorist in 5
    la pièce fait 2 mètres sur 3 the room measures 2
                        metres by 3

Conjunctions

Conjunctions

There are conjunctions which introduce a main clause, such as **et** (and), **mais** (but), **si** (if), **ou** (or) and so on, and those which introduce subordinate clauses like **parce que** (because), **pendant que** (while), **après que** (after) and so on. They are all used in much the same way as in English, but the following points are of note:

Some conjunctions in French require a following subjunctive, see page 58

Some conjunctions are 'split' in French like 'both ... and', 'either ... or' in English:

et ... et both ... and → **①**
ni ... ni ... ne neither ... nor → **②**
ou (bien) ... ou (bien) either ... or (else) → **③**
soit ... soit either ... or → **④**

si + il(s) → **s'il(s)** → **⑤**

que
- meaning *that* → **⑥**
- replacing another conjunction → **⑦**
- replacing **si**, see page 62
- in comparisons, meaning 'as', 'than' → **⑧**
- followed by the subjunctive, see page 62

aussi (so, therefore): the subject and verb are inverted if the subject is a pronoun → **⑨**

1. Ces fleurs poussent et en été et en hiver

   These flowers grow in both summer and winter

2. Ni lui ni elle ne sont venus

   Neither he nor she came

   Ils n'ont ni argent ni nourriture

   They have neither money nor food

3. Elle doit être ou naïve ou stupide

   She must be either naïve or stupide

   Ou bien il m'évite ou bien il ne me reconnaît pas

   Either he's avoiding me or else he doesn't recognize me

4. Il faut choisir soit l'un soit l'autre

   You have to choose either one or the other

5. Je ne sais pas s'il vient/s'ils viennent

   I don't know if he's coming/if they're coming

   Dis-moi s'il y a des erreurs

   Tell me if there are any mistakes

   Votre passeport, s'il vous plaît

   Your passeport, please

6. Il dit qu'il t'a vu

   He says (that) he saw you

   Est-ce qu'elle sait que vous êtes là?

   Does she know that you're here?

7. Quand tu seras plus grand et que tu auras une maison à toi, ...

   When you're older and you have a house of your own, ...

   Comme il pleuvait et que je n'avais pas de parapluie, ...

   As it was raining and I didn't have an umbrella, ...

8. Ils n'y vont pas aussi souvent que nous

   They don't go there as often as we do

   Il les aime plus que jamais

   He likes them more than ever

   L'argent est moins lourd que le plomb

   Silver is lighter than lead

9. Ceux-ci sont plus rares, aussi coûtent-ils cher

   These ones are rarer, so they're expensive

Sentence structure

Word Order

Word order in French is largely the same as in English, except for the following points. Most of these have already been dealt with under the appropriate part of speech, but are summarized here along with other instances not covered elsewhere.

Object pronouns nearly always come before the verb → ❶
For details, see pages 166 to 170

Certain adjectives come after the noun → ❷
For details, see page 162

Adverbs accompanying a verb in a simple tense usually follow the verb → ❸
For details, see page 200

After **aussi** (so, therefore), **à peine** (hardly), **peut-être** (perhaps), the verb and subject are inverted → ❹

After the relative pronoun **dont** (whose), word order can affect the meaning → ❺
For details, see page 182

In exclamations, **que** and **comme** do not affect the normal word order → ❻

Following direct speech:
- the *verb + subject* order is inverted to become *subject + verb* → ❼
- with a pronoun subject, the verb and pronoun are linked by a hyphen → ❽
- when the verb ends in a vowel in the 3rd person singular, **-t-** is inserted between the pronoun and the verb → ❾

For word order in negative sentences, see page 216.

For word order in interrogative sentences, see pages 220 and 222.

1. Je les vois!   I can see them!
   Il me l'a donné   He gave it to me

2. une ville française   a French town
   du vin rouge   some red wine

3. Il pleut encore   It's still raining
   Elle m'aide quelquefois   She sometimes helps me

4. Il vit tout seul, aussi fait-il ce qu'il veut   He lives alone, so he does what he likes
   À peine la pendule avait-elle sonné trois heures que ...   Hardly had the clock struck three when ...
   Peut-être avez-vous raison   Perhaps you're right

5. Compare:
   un homme dont je connais la fille   a man whose daughter I know
   and:
   un homme dont la fille me connaît   a man whose daughter knows me
   If the person (or object) 'owned' is the object of the verb, the order is:
   dont + *verb* + *noun* (*first sentence*)
   If the person (or object) 'owned' is the subject of the verb, the order is:
   dont + *noun* + *verb* (*second sentence*)
   Note also:
   l'homme dont elle est la fille   the man whose daughter she is

6. Qu'il fait chaud!   How warm it is!
   Que je suis content de vous voir!   How pleased I am to see you!
   Comme c'est cher   How expensive it is!
   Que tes voisins sont gentils!   How kind your neighbours are!

7. «Je pense que oui» a dit Luc   ' I think so,' said Luke
   «Ça ne fait rien» répondit Julie   'It doesn't matter,' Julie replied

8. «Quelle horreur!» me suis-je exclamé   'How awful!' I exclaimed

9. «Pourquoi pas?» a-t-elle demandé   'Why not?' she asked
   «Si c'est vrai», continua-t-il ...   'If it's true', he went on ...

Sentence structure

Negatives

The following are the most common negative pairs:

ne ... pas not
ne ... point (*literary*) not
ne ... rien nothing
ne ... personne nobody
ne ... plus no longer, no more
ne ... jamais never
ne ... que only
ne ... aucun(e) no
ne ... nul(le) no
ne ... nulle part nowhere
ne ... ni neither ... nor
ne ... ni ... ni neither ... nor

Word order

In simple tenses and the imperative:
- **ne** precedes the verb (and any object pronouns) and the second element follows the verb → **①**

In compound tenses:
- **ne ... pas, ne ... point, ne ... rien, ne ... plus, ne ... jamais, ne ... guère** follow the pattern:
  ne + *auxiliary verb* + **pas** + *past participle* → **②**
- **ne ... personne, ne ... que, ne ... aucun(e), ne ... nul(le), ne ... nulle part, ne ... ni (... ni)** follow the pattern:
  ne + *auxiliary verb* + *past participle* + **personne** → **③**

With a verb in the infinitive:
- **ne ... pas, ne ... point** (*etc*, see above) come together → **④**

For use of **rien**, **personne** and **aucun** as pronouns, see page 178.

① Je ne fume pas — I don't smoke
Ne changez rien — Don't change anything
Je ne vois personne — I can't see anybody
Nous ne nous verrons plus — We won't see each other any more

Il n'arrive jamais à l'heure — He never arrives on time
Il n'avait qu'une valise — He only had one suitcase
Je n'ai reçu aucune réponse — I have received no reply
Il ne boit ni ne fume — He neither drinks nor smokes
Ni mon fils ni ma fille ne les connaissaient — Neither my son nor my daughter knew them

② Elle n'a pas fait ses devoirs — She hasn't done her homework
Ne vous a-t-il rien dit? — Didn't he say anything to you?
Ils n'avaient jamais vu une si belle maison — They had never seen such a beautiful house

③ Tu n'as guère changé — You've hardly changed

Je n'ai parlé à personne — I haven't spoken to anybody
Il n'avait mangé que la moitié du repas — He had only eaten half the meal
Elle ne les a trouvés nulle part — She couldn't find them anywhere
Il ne l'avait ni vu ni entendu — He had neither seen nor heard him

④ Il essayait de ne pas rire — He was trying not to laugh

Sentence structure

Negatives *continued*

These are the most common combinations of negative particles:

> ne ... plus jamais → ❶
> ne ... plus personne → ❷
> ne ... plus rien → ❸
> ne ... plus ni ... ni ... → ❹
> ne ... jamais personne → ❺
> ne ... jamais rien → ❻
> ne ... jamais que → ❼
> ne ... jamais ni ... ni ... → ❽
> (ne ... pas) non plus → ❾

non and pas

non (no) is the usual negative response to a question → ❿
It is often translated as 'not' → ⓫

pas is generally used when a distinction is being made, or for emphasis → ⓬
It is often translated as 'not' → ⓭

❶	Je ne le ferai plus jamais	I'll never do it again
❷	Je ne connais plus personne à Rouen	I don't know anybody in Rouen any more
❸	Ces marchandises ne valaient plus rien	Those goods were no longer worth anything
❹	Ils n'ont plus ni chats ni chiens	They no longer have either cats or dogs
❺	On n'y voit jamais personne	You never see anybody there
❻	Ils ne font jamais rien d'intéressant	They never do anything interesting
❼	Je n'ai jamais parlé qu'à sa femme	I've only ever spoken to his wife
❽	Il ne m'a jamais ni écrit ni téléphoné	He has never either written to me or phoned me
❾	Ils n'ont pas d'enfants et nous non plus	They don't have any children and neither do we
	Je ne les aime pas. — Moi non plus.	I don't like them. — Neither do I / I don't either.
❿	Vous voulez nous accompagner? — Non.	Do you want to come with us? — No (I don't).
⓫	Tu viens ou non?	Are you coming or not?
	J'espère que non	I hope not
⓬	Ma sœur aime le ski, moi pas	My sister likes skiing, I don't
⓭	Qui a fait ça? — Pas moi!	Who did that? — Not me!
	Est-il de retour? — Pas encore.	Is he back? — Not yet.
	Tu as froid? — Pas du tout.	Are you cold? — Not at all.

Sentence structure

Question forms: direct

There are four ways of forming direct questions in French:

> by inverting the normal word order so that *pronoun subject + verb* becomes *verb + pronoun subject*. A hyphen links the verb and pronoun → **①**
>
> - When the subject is a noun, a pronoun is inserted after the verb and linked to it by a hyphen → **②**
> - When the verb ends in a vowel in the third person singular, **-t-** is inserted before the pronoun → **③**
>
> by maintaining the word order *subject + verb*, but by using a rising intonation at the end of the sentence → **④**
>
> by inserting **est-ce que** before the construction *subject + verb* → **⑤**
>
> by using an interrogative word at the beginning of the sentence, together with inversion or the **est-ce que** form above → **⑥**

1. Aimez-vous la France? — Do you like France?
   Avez-vous fini? — Have you finished?
   Est-ce possible? — Is it possible?
   Est-elle restée? — Did she stay?
   Part-on tout de suite? — Are we leaving right away?

2. Tes parents sont-ils en vacances? — Are your parents on holiday?
   Jean-Benoît est-il parti? — Has Jean-Benoît left?

3. A-t-elle de l'argent? — Has she any money?
   La pièce dure-t-elle longtemps? — Does the play last long?
   Mon père a-t-il téléphoné? — Has my father phoned?

4. Il l'a fini — He's finished it
   Il l'a fini? — Has he finished it?
   Robert va venir — Robert's coming
   Robert va venir? — Is Robert coming?

5. Est-ce que tu la connais? — Do you know her?
   Est-ce que tes parents sont revenus d'Italie? — Have your parents come back from Italy?

6. Quel train prends-tu? ⎤
   Quel train est-ce que tu prends? ⎦ What train are you getting?
   Lequel est-ce que ta sœur préfère? ⎤
   Lequel ta sœur préfère-t-elle? ⎦ Which one does your sister prefer?
   Quand êtes-vous arrivé? ⎤
   Quand est-ce que vous êtes arrivé? ⎦ When did you arrive?
   Pourquoi ne sont-ils pas venus? ⎤
   Pourquoi est-ce qu'ils ne sont pas venus? ⎦ Why haven't they come?

Sentence structure

Question forms: indirect

An indirect question is one that is 'reported', e.g. 'he asked me what the time was'; 'tell me which way to go'. Word order in indirect questions is as follows:

>   *interrogative word + subject + verb* → **❶**

>   when the subject is a noun, and not a pronoun, the subject and verb are often inverted → **❷**

n'est-ce pas

This is used wherever English would use 'isn't it?', 'don't they?', 'weren't we?', 'is it?' and so on tagged on to the end of a sentence → **❸**

oui and si

Oui is the word for 'yes' in answer to a question put in the affirmative → **❹**

Si is the word for 'yes' in answer to a question put in the negative or to contradict a negative statement → **❺**

❶ Je me demande s'il viendra — I wonder if he'll come

Je ne sais pas à quoi ça sert — I don't know what it's for

Dites-moi quel autobus va à la gare — Tell me which bus goes to the station

Il m'a demandé combien d'argent j'avais — He asked me how much money I had

❷ Elle ne sait pas à quelle heure commence le film — She doesn't know what time the film starts

Je me demande où sont mes clés — I wonder where my keys are

Elle nous a demandé comment allait notre père — She asked us how our father was

Je ne sais pas ce que veulent dire ces mots — I don't know what these words mean

❸ Il fait chaud, n'est-ce pas? — It's warm, isn't it?

Vous n'oublierez pas, n'est-ce pas? — You won't forget, will you?

❹ Tu l'as fait? — Oui. — Have you done it? — Yes (I have).

❺ Tu ne l'as pas fait? — Si. — Haven't you done it? — Yes (I have).

Numbers

Cardinal (one, two etc)		Ordinal (first, second etc)	
zéro	0		
un (une)	1	premier (première)	1er, 1ère
deux	2	deuxième, second(e)	2ème
trois	3	troisième	3ème
quatre	4	quatrième	4ème
cinq	5	cinquième	5ème
six	6	sixième	6ème
sept	7	septième	7ème
huit	8	huitième	8ème
neuf	9	neuvième	9ème
dix	10	dixième	10ème
onze	11	onzième	11ème
douze	12	douzième	12ème
treize	13	treizième	13ème
quatorze	14	quatorzième	14ème
quinze	15	quinzième	15ème
seize	16	seizième	16ème
dix-sept	17	dix-septième	17ème
dix-huit	18	dix-huitième	18ème
dix-neuf	19	dix-neuvième	19ème
vingt	20	vingtième	20ème
vingt et un (une)	21	vingt et unième	21ème
vingt-deux	22	vingt-deuxième	22ème
vingt-trois	23	vingt-troisième	23ème
trente	30	trentième	30ème
quarante	40	quarantième	40ème
cinquante	50	cinquantième	50ème
soixante	60	soixantième	60ème
soixante-dix	70	soixante-dixième	70ème
soixante et onze	71	soixante et onzième	71ème
soixante-douze	72	soixante-douzième	72ème
quatre-vingts	80	quatre-vingtième	80ème
quatre-vingt-un (une)	81	quatre-vingt-unième	81ème
quatre-vingt-dix	90	quatre-vingt-dixième	90ème
quatre-vingt-onze	91	quatre-vingt-onzième	91ème

Numbers

Cardinal

cent	100
cent un (une)	101
cent deux	102
cent dix	110
cent quarante-deux	142
deux cents	200
deux cent un (une)	201
deux cent deux	202
trois cents	300
quatre cents	400
cinq cents	500
six cents	600
sept cents	700
huit cents	800
neuf cents	900
mille	1000
mille un (une)	1001
mille deux	1002
deux mille	2000
cent mille	100.000
un million	1.000.000
deux millions	2.000.000

Ordinal

centième	100^e
cent unième	101^e
cent deuxième	102^e
cent dixième	110^e
cent quarante-deuxième	142^e
deux centième	200^e
deux cent unième	201^e
deux cent deuxième	202^e
trois centième	300^e
quatre centième	400^e
cinq centième	500^e
six centième	600^e
sept centième	700^e
huit centième	800^e
neuf centième	900^e
millième	1000^e
mille unième	1001^e
mille deuxième	1002^e
deux millième	2000^e
cent millième	100.000^e
millionième	$1.000.000^e$
deux millionième	$2.000.000^e$

Fractions

un demi, une demie	a half
un tiers	a third
deux tiers	two thirds
un quart	a quarter
trois quarts	three quarters
un cinquième	one fifth
cinq et trois quarts	five and three quarters

Others

zéro virgule cinq (0,5)	0.5
un virgule trois (1,3)	1.3
dix pour cent	10%
deux plus deux	2 + 2
deux moins deux	2 − 2
deux fois deux	2 × 2
deux divisé par deux	2 ÷ 2

ⓘ Note that while points are sometimes used with large numbers, commas are always used with fractions, i.e. the opposite of English usage.

Numbers

Other Uses

-aine denoting approximate numbers:
> une douzaine (de pommes) about a dozen (apples)
> une quinzaine (d'hommes) about fifteen (men)
> des centaines de personnes hundreds of people
> BUT: un millier (de voitures) about a thousand (cars)

measurements:
> vingt mètres carrés 20 square metres
> vingt mètres cubes 20 cubic metres
> un pont long de quarante mètres a bridge 40 metres long
> avoir trois mètres de large/de haut to be 3 metres wide/ high

miscellaneous:
> Il habite au dix He lives at number 10
> C'est au chapitre sept It's in chapter 7
> (C'est) à la page 17 (It's) on page 17
> (Il habite) au septième étage (He lives) on the 7th floor
> Il est arrivé le septième He came in 7th
> échelle au vingt-cinq millième scale 1:25,000

Telephone numbers

Je voudrais Édimbourg trois cent trente, vingt-deux, dix
  I would like Edinburgh 330 22 10
Je voudrais le soixante-cinq, treize, vingt-deux, zéro deux
  Could you get me 65 13 22 02
Poste trois cent trente-cinq Extension number 335
Poste vingt-deux, trente-trois Extension number 22 33

ⓘ In French, telephone numbers are broken down into groups of two
  or three numbers (never four), and are not spoken separately as in
  English. They are also written in groups of two or three numbers.

Calendar

Dates

Quelle est la date d'aujourd'hui?	What's the date today?
Quel jour sommes-nous?	

C'est ...

Nous sommes ...   It's the ...

 ... le premier février ... 1st of February

 ... le deux février   ... 2nd of February

 ... le vingt-huit février ... 28th of February

Il vient le sept mars   He's coming on the 7th of March

(i) Use cardinal numbers except for the first of the month.

Years

Elle est née en 1930   She was born in 1930

le douze février mille neuf cent trente

le douze février mil neuf cent trente (on) 12th February 1930

(i) There are two ways of expressing the year (see last example). Note the spelling of **mil** (one thousand) in dates.

Other expressions

dans les années cinquante	during the fifties
au vingtième siècle	in the twentieth century
en mai	in May
lundi (quinze)	on Monday (the 15th)
le lundi	on Mondays
dans dix jours	in 10 days' time
il y a dix jours	10 days ago

Time

Quelle heure est-il? Il est ...	What time is it? It's ...

00.00	minuit	midnight, twelve o'clock
00.10	minuit dix, zéro heure dix	
00.15	minuit et quart, zéro heure quinze	
00.30	minuit et demi, zéro heure trente	
00.45	une heure moins (le) quart, zéro heure quarante-cinq	
01.00	une heure du matin	one a.m., one o'clock in the morning
01.10	une heure dix (du matin)	
01.15	une heure et quart, une heure quinze	
01.30	une heure et demie, une heure trente	
01.45	deux heures moins (le) quart, une heure quarante-cinq	
01.50	deux heures moins dix, une heure cinquante	
01.59	deux heures moins une, une heure cinquante-neuf	
12.00	midi, douze heures	noon, twelve o'clock
12.30	midi et demi, douze heures trente	
13.00	une heure de l'après-midi, treize heures	one p.m., one o'clock in the afternoon
01.30	une heure et demie (de l'après-midi), treize heures trente	
19.00	sept heures du soir, dix-neuf heures	seven p.m., seven o'clock in the evening
19.30	sept heures et demie (du soir), dix-neuf heures trente	

À quelle heure venez-vous? — À sept heures.	What time are you coming? — At seven o'clock.
Les bureaux sont fermés de midi à quatorze heures	The offices are closed from twelve until two
à deux heures du matin/de l'après-midi	at two o'clock in the morning/ afternoon; at two a.m./p.m.
à sept heures du soir	at seven o'clock in the evening; at seven p.m.
à cinq heures précises *or* pile	at five o'clock sharp
vers neuf heures	about nine o'clock
peu avant/après midi	shortly before/after noon
entre huit et neuf heures	between eight and nine o'clock
Il est plus de trois heures et demie	It's after half past three
Il faut y être à dix heures au plus tard/au plus tôt	You have to be there by ten o'clock at the latest/earliest
Ne venez pas plus tard que onze heures moins le quart	Come no later than a quarter to eleven
Il en a pour une demi-heure	He'll be half an hour (at it)
Elle est restée sans connaissance pendant un quart d'heure	She was unconscious for (a) quarter of an hour
Je les attends depuis une heure	I've been waiting for them for an hour/since one o'clock
Ils sont partis il y a quelques minutes	They left a few minutes ago
Je l'ai fait en vingt minutes	I did it in twenty minutes
Le train arrive dans une heure	The train arrives in an hour('s time)
Combien de temps dure ce film?	How long does this film last?

Translation problems

Beware of translating word for word. While on occasion this is quite possible, quite often it is not. The need for caution is illustrated by the following:

> English phrasal verbs (i.e. verbs followed by a preposition) e.g. 'to run away', 'to fall down' are often translated by one word in French → ❶
>
> English verbal constructions often contain a preposition where none exists in French, or vice versa → ❷
>
> Two or more prepositions in English may have a single rendering in French → ❸
>
> A word which is singular in English may be plural in French, or vice versa → ❹
>
> French has no equivalent of the possessive construction denoted by -'s/-s' → ❺

See also at/in/to, page 234.

The following pages look at some specific problems.

-ing

This is translated in a variety of ways in French:

> 'to be …-ing' is translated by a simple verb → ❻
> EXCEPTION: when a physical position is denoted, a past participle is used → ❼
>
> in the construction 'to see/hear sb …-ing', use an infinitive or **qui** + *verb* → ❽

'-ing' can also be translated by:
- an infinitive, see page 44 → ❾
- a perfect infinitive, see page 46 → ❿
- a present participle, see page 48 → ⓫
- a noun → ⓬

①	s'enfuir	to run away
	tomber	to fall down
	céder	to give in
②	payer	to pay for
	regarder	to look at
	écouter	to listen to
	obéir à	to obey
	nuire à	to harm
	manquer de	to lack
③	s'étonner de	to be surprised at
	satisfait de	satisfied with
	voler qch à	to steal sth from
	apte à	capable of; fit for
④	les bagages	the luggage
	ses cheveux	his/her hair
	le bétail	the cattle
	mon pantalon	my trousers
⑤	la voiture de mon frère	my brother's car (*literally*: ... of my brother)
	la chambre des enfants	the children's bedroom (*literally*: ... of the children)
⑥	Il part demain	He's leaving tomorrow
	Je lisais un roman	I was reading a novel
⑦	Elle est assise là-bas	She's sitting over there
	Il était couché par terre	He was lying on the ground
⑧	Je les vois venir	I can see them coming
	Je les vois qui viennent	
	Je l'ai entendue chanter	I heard her singing
	Je l'ai entendue qui chantait	
⑨	J'aime aller au cinéma	I like going to the cinema
	Arrêtez de parler!	Stop talking!
	Au lieu de répondre	Instead of answering
	Avant de partir	Before leaving
⑩	Après avoir ouvert la boîte, il ...	After opening the box, he ...
⑪	Étant plus timide que moi, elle ...	Being shyer than me, she ...
⑫	Le ski me maintient en forme	Skiing keeps me fit

Translation problems

to be

'to be' is generally translated by **être** → ❶

When physical location is implied, **se trouver** may be used → ❷

In set expressions, describing physical and emotional conditions, **avoir** is used:
    avoir chaud/froid to be warm/cold
    avoir faim/soif to be hungry/thirsty
    avoir peur/honte to be afraid/ashamed
    avoir tort/raison to be wrong/right

Describing the weather, e.g. what's the weather like?, it's windy/sunny, use **faire** → ❸

For ages, e.g. he is 6, use **avoir** → ❹

For state of health, e.g. he's unwell, how are you?, use **aller** → ❺

it is, it's

'It is' and 'it's' are usually translated by **il/elle est**, when referring to a noun → ❻

For expressions of time, also use **il est** → ❼

To describe the weather, e.g. it's windy, see above.

In the construction: it is difficult/easy to do sth, use **il est** → ❽

In all other constructions, use **c'est** → ❾

can, be able

Physical ability is expressed by **pouvoir** → ❿

If the meaning is 'to know how to', use **savoir** → ⓫

'can' + a 'verb of hearing or seeing etc' in English is not translated in French → ⓬

1. Il est tard — It's late
   C'est peu probable — It's not very likely

2. Où se trouve la gare? — Where's the station?
   Quel temps fait-il? — What's the weather like?

3. Il fait beau/mauvais/du vent — It's lovely/miserable/windy

4. Quel âge avez-vous? — How old are you?
   J'ai quinze ans — I'm fifteen

5. Comment allez-vous? — How are you?
   Je vais très bien — I'm very well
   Où est mon parapluie? — Il est là, dans le coin. — Where's my umbrella? — It's there, in the corner.

6. Descends la valise si elle n'est pas trop lourde — Bring down the case if it isn't too heavy

7. Quelle heure est-il? — Il est sept heures et demie. — What's the time? — It's half past seven.

8. Il est difficile de répondre à cette question — It's difficult to reply to this question

9. C'est moi qui ne l'aime pas — It's me who doesn't like him
   C'est Charles/ma mère qui l'a dit — It's Charles/my mother who said so
   C'est ici que je les ai achetés — It's here that I bought them
   C'est parce que la poste est fermée que … — It's because the post office is closed that …

10. Pouvez-vous atteindre cette étagère? — Can you reach up to that shelf?

11. Elle ne sait pas nager — She can't swim
    Je ne vois rien — I can't see anything

12. Il les entendait — He could hear them

Translation problems

to (*see also below*)

'to' is generally translated by **à**, see page 204 → ❶

In time expressions, e.g. 10 to 6, use **moins** → ❷

When the meaning is 'in order to', use **pour** → ❸

Following a verb, as in 'to try to do', 'to like to do', see pages 44 and 64

'easy/difficult/impossible' etc to do: the preposition used depends on whether a specific noun is referred to → ❹ or not → ❺

at/in/to

With feminine countries, use **en** → ❻

With masculine countries, use **au** (**aux** with plural countries) → ❼

With towns, use **à** → ❽

'at/to the butcher's/grocer's' etc: use **à** + *noun* designating the shop, or **chez** + *noun* designating the shopkeeper → ❾

'at/to the dentist's/doctor's' etc: use **chez** → ❿

'at/to -'s/-s' house': use **chez** → ⓫

there is/there are

Both are translated by **il y a** → ⓬

1. Donne le livre à Patrick — Give the book to Patrick

2. dix heures moins cinq — five to ten
   à sept heures moins le quart — at a quarter to seven

3. Je l'ai fait pour vous aider — I did it to help you
   Il se pencha pour nouer son lacet — He bent down to tie his shoelace

4. Ce livre est difficile à lire — This book is difficult to read

5. Il est difficile de comprendre leurs raisons — It's difficult to understand their reasons

6. Il est allé en France/en Suisse — He has gone to France/to Switzerland
   un village en Norvège/en Belgique — a village in Norway/in Belgium

7. Êtes-vous allé au Canada/au Danemark/aux États-Unis? — Have you been to Canada/to Denmark/to the United States?
   une ville au Japon/au Brésil — a town in Japan/in Brazil

8. Il est allé à Vienne/à Bruxelles — He has gone to Vienna/to Brussels
   Il habite à Londres/à Genève — He lives in London/in Geneva
   Ils logent dans un hôtel à St Pierre — They're staying in a hotel at St Pierre

9. Je l'ai acheté à l'épicerie — I bought it at the grocer's
   Je l'ai acheté chez l'épicier
   Elle est allée à la boulangerie — She's gone to the baker's
   Elle est allée chez le boulanger

10. J'ai un rendez-vous chez le dentiste — I've an appointment at the dentist's
    Il est allé chez le médecin — He has gone to the doctor's

11. chez Christian — at/to Christian's house
    chez les Pagot — at/to the Pagots' house

12. Il y a quelqu'un à la porte — There's somebody at the door
    Il y a cinq livres sur la table — There are five books on the table

Pronunciation

General Points

Activity of the lips

The lips play a very important part in French. When a vowel is described as having 'rounded' lips, the lips are slightly drawn together and pursed, as when an English speaker expresses exaggerated surprise with the vowel 'ooh!' Equally, if the lips are said to be 'spread', the corners are pulled firmly back towards the cheeks, tending to reveal the front teeth.

In English, lip position is not important, and vowel sounds tend to merge because of this. In French, the activity of the lips means that every vowel sound is clearly distinct from every other.

No diphthongs

A diphthong is a glide between two vowel sounds in the same syllable. In English, there are few 'pure' vowel sounds, but largely diphthongs instead. Although speakers of English may think they produce one vowel sound in the word 'day', in fact they use a diphthong, which in this instance is a glide between the vowels [e] and [ɪ]: [deɪ]. In French the tension maintained in the lips, tongue and the mouth in general prevents diphthongs occurring, as the vowel sound is kept constant throughout. Hence the French word corresponding to the above example, 'dé', is pronounced with no final [ɪ] sound, but is phonetically represented thus: [de].

Consonants

In English, consonants are often pronounced with a degree of laxness that can result in their practically disappearing altogether although not strictly 'silent'. In a relaxed pronunciation of a word such as 'hat', the 't' is often scarcely heard, or is replaced by a 'glottal stop' (a sort of jerk in the throat). This never occurs in French, where consonants are always given their full value.

Pronunciation

Pronunciation of Consonants

Some consonants are pronounced almost exactly as in English:
[b, p, f, v, g, k, m, w].

Most others are similar to English, but slight differences should be noted.

	EXAMPLES	HINTS ON PRONUNCIATION
[d]	**d**in**d**e	The tip of the tongue touches the upper
[t]	**t**en**t**e	front teeth and not the roof of the mouth
[n]	**n**o**nn**e	as in English
[l]	**L**i**ll**e	
[s]	tou**s** **ç**a	The tip of the tongue is down behind the
[z]	**z**éro ro**s**e	bottom front teeth, lower than in English
[ʃ]	**ch**ose ta**ch**e	Like the 'sh' of English 'shout'
[ʒ]	**j**e **g**ilet bei**g**e	Like the 's' of English 'measure'
[j]	**y**eux pai**ll**e	Like the 'y' of English 'yes'

Three consonants are not heard in English:

[ʀ]	**r**are veni**r**	'r' is often silent in English, e.g. farm. In French the [ʀ] is never silent, unless it follows an **e** at the end of a word e.g. cherch**er**. To pronounce it, try to make a short sound like gargling. Similar, too, to the Scottish pronunciation of 'loch'
[ɲ]	vi**gn**e a**gn**eau	Similar to the 'ni' of the English word 'Spaniard'
[ɥ]	**h**uile lueur	Like a very rapid [y] (see page 239) followed immediately by the next vowel of the word

Pronunciation

Pronunciation of Vowels

EXAMPLES	HINTS ON PRONUNCIATION
[a] patte plat amour	Similar to the vowel in English 'pat'
[ɑ] bas pâte	Longer than the sound above, it resembles the English exclamation of surprise 'ah!' Similar, too, to the English vowel in 'car' without the final 'r' sound
[ɛ] lait jouet merci	Similar to the English vowel in 'pet'. Beware of using the English diphthong [eɪ] as in 'pay'
[e] été jouer	A pure vowel, again quite different from the diphthong in English 'pay'
[ə] le premier	Similar to the English sound in 'butter' when the 'r' is not pronounced
[i] ici vie lycée	The lips are well spread towards the cheeks while uttering this sound. Shorter than the English vowel in 'see'
[ɔ] mort homme	The lips are well rounded while producing a sound similar to the 'o' of English 'cot'
[o] mot dôme eau	A pure vowel with strongly rounded lips quite different from the diphthong in the English words 'bone', 'low'

Pronunciation

EXAMPLES	HINTS ON PRONUNCIATION
[u] gen**ou** r**ou**e	A pure vowel with strongly rounded lips. Similar to the English 'ooh!' of surprise
[y] r**ue** vêt**u**	Often the most difficult for English speakers to produce: round your lips and try to pronounce [i] (see page 238). There is no [j] sound (see page 237) as there is in English 'pure'
[œ] s**œu**r b**eu**rre	Similar to the vowel in English 'fir' or 'murmur', but without the 'r' sound and with the lips more strongly rounded
[ø] p**eu** d**eux**	To pronounce this, try to say [e] (see page 238) with the lips strongly rounded

Nasal Vowels

These are spelt with a vowel followed by a 'nasal' consonant – **n** or **m**. The production of nasal vowels really requires the help of a teacher or a recording of the sound. However, to help you, the vowel is pronounced by allowing the air from the lungs to come partly down the nose and partly through the mouth, and the **n** or **m** is not pronounced at all.

[ɑ̃] l**en**t s**an**g d**an**s	In each case, the vowel shown in the
[ɛ̃] mat**in** pl**ein**	phonetic symbol is pronounced as
[ɔ̃] n**on** p**on**t	described above, but air is allowed to come
[œ̃] br**un** **un** parf**um**	through the nose as well as the mouth

Pronunciation

From Spelling to Sounds

Although it may not seem so at first sight, there are some fairly precise 'rules' which can help you to know how to pronounce French words from their spelling.

Vowels

SPELLING	PRONOUNCED	EXAMPLES
a, à	[a]	chatte table à
a, â	[ɑ]	pâte pas
er, é	[e]	été marcher
e, è, ê	[ɛ]	fenêtre fermer chère
e	[ə]	double fenêtre
i, î, y	[i]	lit abîmer lycée
o, ô	[o]	pot trop dôme
o	[ɔ]	sotte orange
u, û	[y]	battu fût pur

Vowel Groups

There are several groups of vowels in French spelling which are regularly pronounced in the same way:

SPELLING	PRONOUNCED	EXAMPLES
ai	[ɛ] or [e]	maison marchai faire
ail	[aj]	portail
ain, aim, (e)in, im	[ɛ̃]	pain faim frein impair
au	[o]	auberge landau
an, am, en, em	[ɑ̃]	plan ample entrer temps
eau	[o]	bateau eau
eu	[œ] or [ø]	feu peur
euil(le), ueil	[œj]	feuille recueil
oi, oy	[wa]	voir voyage
on, om	[ɔ̃]	ton compter
ou	[u]	hibou outil
œu	[œ]	sœur cœur
ue	[y]	rue
un, um	[œ̃]	brun parfum

Pronunciation

Added to these are the many groups of letters occurring at the end of words, where their pronunciation is predictable, bearing in mind the tendency (see page 242) of final consonants to remain silent.

Pronunciation

From Spelling to Sounds *continued*

Consonants

Final consonants are usually silent → ①

n or **m** at the end of a syllable or word are silent, but they have the effect of 'nasalizing' the preceding vowel(s) (see page 239 on Nasal Vowels).

The letter **h** is either 'silent' ('mute') or 'aspirate' when it begins a word. When silent, the word behaves as though it started with a vowel and takes a liaison with the preceding word where appropriate.

When the **h** is aspirate, no liaison is made → ②

There is no way of predicting which words start with which sort of **h** – this simply has to be learnt with each word

The following consonants in spelling have predictable pronunciations: b, d, f, k, l, p, r, t, v, w, x, y, z.

Others vary:

SPELLING	PRONOUNCED	ENGLISH EXAMPLES
c + a, o, u	[k]	can cot cut → ③
+ l, r		class cram
c + e, i, y	[s]	ceiling ice → ④
ç + a, o, u	[s]	ceiling ice → ⑤
ch	[ʃ]	shop lash → ⑥
g + a, o, u	[g]	gate got gun → ⑦
+ l, r		glass gramme
g + e, i, y	[ʒ]	leisure → ⑧
gn	[ɲ]	companion onion → ⑨
j	[ʒ]	measure → ⑩
q, qu	[k]	quay kit → ⑪
s (*between vowels*)	[z]	rose → ⑫
s (*elsewhere*)	[s]	sit
th	[t]	Thomas → ⑬
t in **-tion**	[s]	sit → ⑭

❶ éclat [ekla] **nez** [ne]
chaud [ʃo] **aider** [ɛde]

❷ silent h: **aspirate h:**
des hôtels [de zotɛl] **des haricots** [de aʀiko]

❸ café [kafe] **côte** [kot] **culture** [kyltyʀ]
classe [klas] **croûte** [kʀut]

❹ ceci [səsi] **cil** [sil] **cycliste** [siklist]

❺ ça [sa] **garçon** [gaʀsɔ̃] **déçu** [desy]

❻ chat [ʃa] **riche** [ʀiʃ]

❼ gare [gaʀ] **gourde** [guʀd] **aigu** [ɛgy]
glaise [glɛz] **gramme** [gʀam]

❽ gemme [ʒem] **gilet** [ʒilɛ] **gymnaste** [ʒimnast]

❾ vigne [viɲ] **oignon** [ɔɲɔ̃]

❿ joli [ʒɔli] **Jules** [ʒyl]

⓫ quiche [kiʃ] **quitter** [kite]

⓬ sable [sablə] **maison** [mɛzɔ̃]

⓭ théâtre [teɑtʀ] **Thomas** [tɔma]

⓮ nation [nasjɔ̃] **action** [aksjɔ̃]

Pronunciation

Feminine Forms and Pronunciation

For adjectives and nouns ending in a vowel in the masculine, the addition of an **e** to form the feminine does not alter the pronunciation → **①**

If the masculine ends with a silent consonant, generally **-d**, **-s**, **-r** or **-t**, the consonant is sounded in the feminine → **②**
This also applies when the final consonant is doubled before the addition of the feminine **e** → **③**

If the masculine ends in a nasal vowel and a silent **n**, e.g. **-an**, **-on**, **-in**, the vowel is no longer nasalized and the **-n** is pronounced in the feminine → **④**
This also applies when the final **-n** is doubled before the addition of the feminine **e** → **⑤**

Where the masculine and feminine forms have totally different endings (see pages 136 and 150), the pronunciation of course varies accordingly → **⑥**

Plural Forms and Pronunciation

The addition of **s** or **x** to form regular plurals generally does not affect pronunciation → **⑦**

Where liaison has to be made, the final **-s** or **-x** of the plural form is pronounced → **⑧**

Where the masculine singular and plural forms have totally different endings (see pages 138 and 148), the pronunciation of course varies accordingly → **⑨**

Note the change in pronunciation in the following nouns:

SINGULAR	PLURAL
bœuf [bœf] ox	**bœufs** [bø] oxen
œuf [œf] egg	**œufs** [ø] eggs
os [ɔs] bone	**os** [o] bones

ADJECTIVES	NOUNS
① **joli** [ʒɔli] → **jolie** [ʒɔli]	**un ami** [ami] → **une amie** [ami]
déçu [desy] → **déçue** [desy]	**un employé** [ãplwaje] →
	une employée [ãplwaje]
② **chaud** [ʃo] → **chaude** [ʃod]	**un étudiant** [etydjã] →
	une étudiante [etydjãt]
français [fʀãsɛ] →	**un Anglais** [ãglɛ] →
française [fʀãsɛz]	**une Anglaise** [ãglɛz]
inquiet [ɛ̃kjɛ] →	**un étranger** [etʀãʒe] →
inquiète [ɛ̃kjɛt]	**une étrangère** [etʀãʒeʀ]
③ **violet** [vjɔlɛ] → **violette** [vjɔlɛt]	**le cadet** [kadɛ] →
	la cadette [kadɛt]
gras [gʀɑ] → **grasse** [gʀɑs]	
④ **plein** [plɛ̃] → **pleine** [plɛn]	**le souverain** [suvʀɛ̃] →
	la souveraine [suvʀɛn]
fin [fɛ̃] → **fine** [fin]	**Le Persan** [pɛʀsã] →
	la Persane [pɛʀsan]
brun [bʀœ̃] → **brune** [bʀyn]	**le voisin** [vwazɛ̃] →
	la voisine [vwazin]
⑤ **canadien** [kanadjɛ̃] →	**le paysan** [peizã] →
canadienne [kanadjɛn]	**la paysanne** [peizan]
breton [bʀətɔ̃] →	**le baron** [baʀɔ̃] →
bretonne [bʀətɔn]	**la baronne** [baʀɔn]
⑥ **vif** [vif] → **vive** [viv]	**le veuf** [vœf] → **la veuve** [vœv]
traître [tʀɛtʀə] →	**le maître** [mɛtʀə] →
traîtresse [tʀɛtʀɛs]	**la maîtresse** [mɛtʀɛs]
⑦ **beau** [bo] → **beaux** [bo]	**la maison** [mɛzɔ̃] →
	les maisons [mɛzɔ̃]
⑧ **des anciens élèves**	**de beaux arbres**
[de zãsjɛ̃ zelɛv]	[də bo zaʀbʀ(ə)]
⑨ **amical** [amikal] →	**un journal** [ʒuʀnal] →
amicaux [amiko]	**des journaux** [ʒuʀno]

The alphabet

The Alphabet

A, a [ɑ]	**J, j** [ʒi]	**S, s** [ɛs]
B, b [be]	**K, k** [ka]	**T, t** [te]
C, c [se]	**L, l** [ɛl]	**U, u** [y]
D, d [de]	**M, m** [ɛm]	**V, v** [ve]
E, e [ə]	**N, n** [ɛn]	**W, w** [dubləve]
F, f [ɛf]	**O, o** [o]	**X, x** [iks]
G, g [ʒe]	**P, p** [pe]	**Y, y** [igʀɛk]
H, h [aʃ]	**Q, q** [ky]	**Z, z** [zɛd]
I, i [i]	**R, r** [ɛʀ]	

Capital letters are used as in English except for the following:

adjectives of nationality
e.g. une ville espagnole a Spanish town
un auteur français a French author

languages
e.g. Parlez-vous anglais? Do you speak English?
Il parle français et allemand He speaks French and German

days of the week:
lundi Monday
mardi Tuesday
mercredi Wednesday
jeudi Thursday
vendredi Friday
samedi Saturday
dimanche Sunday

months of the year:

janvier January	**juillet** July
février February	**août** August
mars March	**septembre** September
avril April	**octobre** October
mai May	**novembre** November
juin June	**décembre** December

Index

The following index lists comprehensively both grammatical terms and key words in French and English contained in this book.

Index

Index

Index

Index

Index

Index

Index